HOW TO USE THE
THESAURUS OF ERIC® DESCRIPTORS
FOR AN EFFECTIVE ERIC SEARCH

FIRST....

1. Identify your specific topic, in your own terms.

2. "Translate" your topic into ERIC Descriptors (subject index terms). The Rotated Descriptor Display in the back of the *Thesaurus* may help you.

3. List the best Descriptors and locate them in the Alphabetical Descriptor Display (the main part of the *Thesaurus*).

   a. Read the Scope Notes (SN) for information on how ERIC uses the terms.

   b. Check the Broader Terms (BTs), Narrower Terms (NTs), and Related Terms (RTs) under your Descriptors and identify possible other Descriptors relevant to your topic.

   c. Make a list of other Descriptors that you might also use.

   d. Look up those Descriptors and repeat steps 3a-c.

4. Make a final list of the Descriptors most likely to have been used to represent your topic.

THEN....

FOR A MANUAL SEARCH: Look under your Descriptors in the Subject Index of *Resources in Education* (RIE) and *Current Index to Journals in Education* (CIJE) monthly and cumulative issues to find titles relevant to your search.

FOR A COMPUTER SEARCH: Follow the directions of your particular library or information retrieval system for a search of the ERIC database (all or any group of years).

> NOTE: The Introduction to the *Thesaurus* contains information helpful to searchers on ERIC indexing rules, deleted and invalid Descriptors, and useful parts of the Descriptor entry, such as the date the term was added to the *Thesaurus* and the number of times it has been used.

Thesaurus of ERIC® Descriptors

11th Edition—1987

James E. Houston
Editor/Lexicographer
ERIC Processing and Reference Facility
ORI, Inc.

Introduction by

Lynn Barnett
Assistant Director
ERIC Clearinghouse on Higher Education
The George Washington University

ORYX PRESS
2214 North Central at Encanto
Phoenix, Arizona 85004-1483

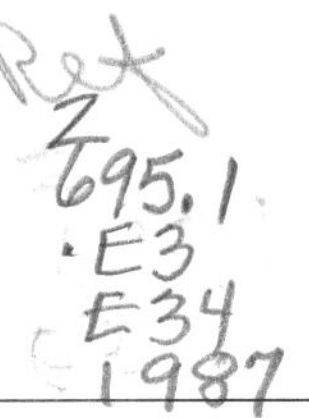

The rare Arabian Oryx is believed to have inspired the myth of the unicorn. This desert antelope became virtually extinct in the early 1960s. At that time several groups of international conservationists arranged to have 9 animals sent to the Phoenix Zoo to be the nucleus of a captive breeding herd. Today the Oryx population is over 400 and herds have been returned to reserves in Israel, Jordan, and Oman.

2214 North Central at Encanto
Phoenix, Arizona 85004-1483

The material contained herein was generated under contracts with the Office of Educational Research and Improvement, Department of Education. However, the contents do not necessarily reflect the position or policy of that Agency and no U.S. Government endorsement is to be inferred.

Published simultaneously in Canada

Printed and Bound in the United States of America

Library of Congress Cataloging in Publication Data

Educational Resources Information Center (U.S.).

Thesaurus of ERIC descriptors.

1. Subject headings—Education. I. Houston, James E. II. Title.
Z695.1.E3E34 1987 025.4'937 86-42555
ISBN 0-89774-159-5

CONTENTS

PREFACE

The *Thesaurus of ERIC Descriptors*—1987 edition, has been developed under the auspices of the Educational Resources Information Center (ERIC) of the Office of Educational Research and Improvement (OERI), U.S. Department of Education. Its content reflects ERIC's 20 years of monitoring the educational literature. This 11th edition is the result of ERIC's continued efforts to maintain quality in its controlled vocabulary and to respond to the changing nature of education. As in previous editions, the *Thesaurus* reflects ERIC's response to the needs of the educational user community. ERIC remains committed to maintaining a *Thesaurus* that represents the definitive vocabulary for education.

The 1987 edition contains 9,459 vocabulary terms, of which 5,296 are main-entry Descriptors and 4,163 are non-indexable Use references and "dead" terms. New terms not appearing in previous editions include 224 Descriptors and 190 Use references. This edition also reflects several hundred Scope Note and cross-reference modifications to earlier Descriptor displays.

Again as in the past, the *Thesaurus* revision has been made possible by the joint efforts and sound judgments of personnel throughout the entire ERIC system responding to both the literature and the users in the field. ERIC vocabulary coordinators, who, as members of the system-wide "Vocabulary Review Group," oversee this effort, are listed below:

ERIC VOCABULARY REVIEW GROUP

ERIC Clearinghouse Vocabulary Coordinators

Lynn Barnett, ERIC Clearinghouse on Higher Education at The George Washington University

Nancy Beekman, ERIC Clearinghouse on Counseling and Personnel Services at the University of Michigan

Anita Colby, ERIC Clearinghouse for Junior Colleges at the University of California—Los Angeles

Judi Conrad, ERIC Clearinghouse on Handicapped and Gifted Children at the Council for Exceptional Children

Mary Lou Finne, ERIC Clearinghouse on Educational Management at the University of Oregon

Stanley Helgeson, ERIC Clearinghouse for Science, Mathematics, and Environmental Education at Ohio State University

Jane Henson, ERIC Clearinghouse for Social Studies/Social Science Education at Indiana University

Jim Houston, ERIC Processing and Reference Facility at ORI, Inc.

Norma Howard, ERIC Clearinghouse on Elementary and Early Childhood Education at the University of Illinois

Sandra Kerka, ERIC Clearinghouse on Adult, Career, and Vocational Education at Ohio State University

Jane McClellan, ERIC Clearinghouse on Reading and Communication Skills at the National Council of Teachers of English

Barbara Minor, ERIC Clearinghouse on Information Resources at Syracuse University

Manuela Quezada-Aragon, ERIC Clearinghouse on Rural Education and Small Schools at New Mexico State University

Jeanne Rennie, ERIC Clearinghouse on Languages and Linguistics at the Center for Applied Linguistics

Wendy Schwartz, ERIC Clearinghouse on Urban Education at Teachers College, Columbia University

Betsy Smith, ERIC Clearinghouse on Tests, Measurement, and Evaluation at the Educational Testing Service

Mary Tregillus, ERIC Clearinghouse on Teacher Education at the American Association of Colleges for Teacher Education

Carolyn Weller, ERIC Processing and Reference Facility at ORI, Inc.

ERIC Vocabulary Coordinators in the User Community

Jo Ann Davison, Gilman School, Baltimore, Maryland

Sara Lake, San Mateo Educational Resources Center, Redwood City, California

Suzanne Wise, Belk Library, Appalachian State University, Boone, North Carolina

Users are invited to direct comments on the *Thesaurus* or the ERIC System as a whole to Alan Moorehead, Director, ERIC, Department of Education, Washington, DC 20208.

Anita Colby
Chair, Vocabulary Review Group
ERIC Clearinghouse for Junior Colleges
University of California, Los Angeles

Jim Houston
Lexicographer
ERIC Processing and Reference Facility
ORI, Inc.

Pat Coulter
Project Monitor
Central ERIC/Office of Educational Research and Improvement
U.S. Department of Education

NEW DESCRIPTORS

These Descriptors have been added to the *Thesaurus* since October 1983 and do not appear in previous editions.

Access to Information
Adaptive Testing
Adjunct Faculty
Aerobics
Aging in Academia
Air Traffic Control
Alternative Energy Sources
Andragogy
Anger
Appropriate Technology
Aquatic Sports
Assistive Devices (for Disabled)
Audiodisks
Auditing (Coursework)
Audits (Verification)

Badminton
Behaviorism
Bibliographic Utilities
Bibliometrics
Bioethics
Blue Ribbon Commissions
Bowling
Brain Hemisphere Functions
Brainstorming
Breastfeeding
British Infant Schools
Bulimia

Cardiopulmonary Resuscitation
Citation Analysis
Client Characteristics (Human Services)
Cognitive Dissonance
Cognitive Psychology
College Athletics
Communication Audits
Community Psychology
Comparable Worth
Compliance (Psychology)
Computer Networks
Computer Software
Computer Software Reviews
Computer Uses in Education
Concurrent Validity
Conflict of Interest
Conservatism
Construct Validity
Content Validity
Corporate Education
Corporate Support
Course Selection (Students)
Courseware

Data Interpretation
Database Management Systems
Database Producers
Deception
Dislocated Workers
Diving

Early Retirement
Editors
Electronic Mail
Electronic Publishing
Elitism
Employee Assistance Programs
Endangered Species
Energy Audits
Energy Education
Energy Management
English for Academic Purposes
English for Science and Technology
Epidemiology
Estuaries
Evaluation Problems
Expert Systems
Eye Contact

Facial Expressions
Faculty Publishing
Failure to Thrive
Family History
Family Violence
Fencing (Sport)
Financial Audits
Formal Operations
Freedom of Information
Freshman Composition

Genealogy
Geothermal Energy
Gestalt Therapy

Habituation
Handball
Handicap Discrimination
Hazardous Materials
Holidays
Homeless People
Hospices (Terminal Care)

Ice Hockey
Ideology
In School Suspension
Industrial Psychology
Inferences
Information Technology
Information Transfer
Institutional Mission
Institutional Survival
Instructional Effectiveness
Instructional Leadership
Instructional Material Evaluation
Interactive Video

Intergenerational Programs

Keyboarding (Data Entry)

Language Skill Attrition
Latchkey Children
Law Related Education
Legal Education (Professions)
Liberalism
Library Collection Development
Library Statistics
Licensing Examinations (Professions)
Local Area Networks
Logarithms
Lying

Machine Readable Cataloging
Marijuana
Maritime Education
Marxian Analysis
Marxism
Mathematics Tests
Media Adaptation
Menu Driven Software
Merit Scholarships
Mineralogy
Minerals
Misconceptions
Mission Statements
Monte Carlo Methods
Montessori Method
Multitrait Multimethod Techniques

Naturalistic Observation
No Need Scholarships
No Shows
Nontenured Faculty

Obedience
Online Catalogs
Online Searching
Online Vendors
Optical Data Disks
Optical Disks

Outcomes of Treatment
Outlining (Discourse)
Ownership

Parenting Skills
Participant Observation
Peer Institutions
Phenomenology
Photojournalism
Piagetian Theory
Place Value
Plate Tectonics
Political Campaigns
Political Candidates
Polymers
Popularity
Prepositions
Presidential Campaigns (United States)
Presidents of the United States
Program Termination
Protocol Analysis
Public Colleges
Public Service
Publish or Perish Issue

Qualitative Research
Quality Circles
Quality of Working Life

Racquet Sports
Racquetball
Reader Text Relationship
Reading Writing Relationship
Reality Therapy
Religious Holidays
Research Administration
Research Papers (Students)
Research Universities
Respiratory Therapy
Restraints (Vehicle Safety)
Resumes (Personal)
Rhetorical Invention
Robotics
Role of Education

Sailing
Science and Society
Scientific and Technical Information
Search Committees (Personnel)
Self Destructive Behavior
Sexual Identity
Shared Library Resources
Shared Resources and Services
Small Engine Mechanics
Social Desirability
Songs
Statistical Inference
Stopouts
Story Grammar
Structural Unemployment
Student Teacher Attitudes
Student Teacher Evaluation
Suggestopedia
Surfing

Table Tennis
Teacher Student Ratio
Teacher Student Relationship
Team Handball
Team Sports
Terrorism
Theory Practice Relationship
Toddlers
Trust (Psychology)

Underwater Diving
Undocumented Immigrants
User Needs (Information)
Users (Information)

Videodisks
Vocational English (Second Language)

Waiters and Waitresses
Water Polo
Word Problems (Mathematics)
Writing Laboratories

TRANSFERRED DESCRIPTORS

These former Descriptors have been downgraded to USE references. Postings for such terms are transferred to other "preferred" terms. Their entries in the Alphabetical Descriptor Display identify the receiving Descriptors. Postings transfers of approximately 840 Descriptors before December 1980 (when the last reload of the ERIC file occurred) are reflected in the ERIC database, and these Descriptors no longer need to be considered in online or other computer searching. Transfers after December 1980, however, have *not* been fully implemented in the ERIC file, and both old and new versions of a term must be used in retrospective searching. *All* "transferred" ERIC Descriptors that are still searchable are listed below:

Acceleration
After School Day Care
Agricultural Research Projects
Appliance Repairers
Appliance Repairing
Audiodisc Recordings

Bricklayers

Carpenters
Cerebral Dominance
Clinic Personnel (School)
Computer Programs
Cosmetologists
Craftsmen

Data Bases
Delinquent Behavior
Diffusion
Drafters

Food Service Industry
Food Service Occupations
Food Service Workers
Foster Homes

Geographic Mobility

Handwriting Instruction
Handwriting Materials
Handwriting Readiness
Handwriting Skills

Illegal Immigrants
Inhalation Therapists
Interest

Marihuana

Practical Nurses

Quantitative Tests

Research Apprenticeships
Retention Studies
Roofers

Rural Dropouts

Shared Services
Sheet Metal Workers
Solar Radiation
Spatial Perception
Stenographers
Student Teacher Ratio
Student Teacher Relationship

Trainable Mentally Handicapped
Transitional Classes
Typists

Urban Dropouts

Videodisc Recordings

Welders
Wheel Chairs
Women Teachers

INVALID ("DEAD") DESCRIPTORS

These Descriptors are no longer used in indexing (see p. xxiii). They may be used for searching database entries prior to September 1980 (see *, **, *** for the exceptions). More recent literature on topics represented by these terms is searchable using related Descriptors. For further reference, see entries for the terms in the Alphabetical Descriptor Display.

Academically Handicapped
Administrative Agencies
Advanced Programs
American Culture
American History
Analytical Criticism
Ancillary Services
Architectural Barriers
Aristotelian Criticism
Assistant Superintendent Role

Basic Reading
Black Housing

Career Opportunities
Caricatures
Child Care
Class Attitudes
Class Average
Classroom Guidance Programs
College Language Programs
Conceptual Schemes
Conference Reports
Congruence
Continuation Education
Controlled Environment
Counseling Instructional Programs
Creative Reading

Developmental Reading
Direction Writing

Educational Problems
Educational Programs
Educational Retardation
Educational Specifications

Elective Reading
English Education
English Neoclassic Literary Period
Episode Teaching
Ethnic Grouping
Exceptional Child Education
Exceptional Child Services
Exercise (Physiology)

Factual Reading
Flexible Schedules
Formal Criticism
Former Teachers

Grade Charts
Group Norms
Group Reading
Growth Patterns

Handicapped Children
Handicapped Students
Health Occupations Centers
Historical Criticism
Human Development
Human Living

Impressionistic Criticism
Individual Reading
Inequalities
Instructional Programs
Interpretive Reading

Laboratory Techniques
Language Ability
Language Aids
Language and Area Centers
Language Guides
Language Instruction
Language Learning Levels
Language Programs

*Legal Education
Literary Discrimination
Literary Influences
Literary Mood
Literary Perspective
Literature Guides
Literature Programs
Low Ability Students

Mathematical Experience
Maturation
Measurement Instruments
Moral Criticism
Mythic Criticism

**Negro Housing
Northern Schools

Performance Criteria
Performance Specifications
Plant Science
Platonic Criticism
Preschool Learning
Pressure
Programing Problems
Project Applications
Projects
Publicize

Racial Characteristics
Racism
Reading Development
Reading Difficulty
Reading Level
Recognition
Research Criteria
Research Reviews (Publications)

School Planning
***Security

Self Directed Classrooms
Self Evaluation
Sex (Characteristics)
Social Relations
Social Welfare
Sound Tracks
Southern Citizens
Southern Community
Southern Schools
Space Orientation
Spatial Relationship
Speech Education
Stimulus Devices
Structural Analysis
Student Distribution
Studio Floor Plans
Supreme Court Litigation
Supreme Courts
Systems Concepts

Talent Utilization
Task Performance
Teaching
Teaching Assignment
Teaching Programs
TENL
Textbook Publications
Textual Criticism
Theoretical Criticism
Tracking
Training Laboratories
Transfers

Unit Plan
Unwritten Language

Weight
Welfare

*Invalid only since August 1986.
**Not used after 1977—see also "Black Housing."
***All postings are earlier than May 1978.

DELETED DESCRIPTORS

This designation refers to former Descriptors that no longer appear in the *Thesaurus,* even as USE references. Two terms from the preceding edition of the *Thesaurus* fall into this category.

Chiluba

Kinyaruanda

INDEXING AND RETRIEVAL IN ERIC: THE 20TH YEAR

by Lynn Barnett
Assistant Director
ERIC Clearinghouse on Higher Education
The George Washington University

INTRODUCTION

This 11th edition of the *Thesaurus of ERIC Descriptors* is significant because it coincides with the twentieth anniversary of the ERIC database. Both ERIC and the *Thesaurus* have come a long way since 1966, from a fledgling project within the federal government to an information system known and accessed worldwide. ERIC has grown from a database of 3,000 items to one of 600,000 references. Its *Thesaurus,* which began with 2,300 core terms (compiled by "free indexing" 1,700 documents on teaching the disadvantaged), is now recognized as the definitive vocabulary of education and a model for other databases.

THE ERIC SYSTEM

The Educational Resources Information Center (ERIC) is a national information system established in 1966 by the federal government to provide ready access to educational literature by and for educational practitioners and scholars.[1] It is funded today by the Office of Educational Research and Improvement (OERI) of the U.S. Department of Education. ERIC collects and disseminates virtually all types of print materials, mostly unpublished, that deal with education—for example, program descriptions and evaluations, research reports and surveys, curriculum and teaching guides, instructional materials, and resource materials.

Central ERIC at OERI establishes policy and oversees the operation of the ERIC system. Centers of educational expertise at universities and professional associations operate the 16 decentralized ERIC Clearinghouses.[2] These Clearinghouses identify, acquire, and process educational information in specific subject areas such as elementary, secondary, and higher education, educational management, social studies, languages and linguistics, and rural and urban education. Support organizations perform other technical services for the ERIC system. Among these services are maintenance of central computer tape files, reproduction of noncopyrighted literature, and development of specialized publications, such as this *Thesaurus.*

ERIC acquires and announces the availability of educational literature (e.g., journal articles, research reports, conference papers, bibliographies, innovative practice reports). The literature is cataloged, abstracted, and then indexed using key words from the controlled vocabulary—the *Thesaurus of ERIC Descriptors.* Abstracted citations for nonjournal literature appear each month in a bibliographic journal, *Resources in Education (RIE).* Annotated references to journal articles are found in the companion monthly publication *Current Index to Journals in Education (CIJE).* With the help of the *Thesaurus,* all materials processed by ERIC can be identified by manual searches of the printed indexes in *RIE* and *CIJE* or by computer searches of the ERIC tapes. ERIC provides convenient access to the actual text of nearly 270,000 documents at over 700 libraries and resource centers that subscribe to and maintain ERIC microfiche collections of most documents cited in *RIE* (see footnote 5, p. xii).

Important components of ERIC are its subject-area Clearinghouses. Responsible for locating, acquiring, and selecting literature in its respective area of education, each Clearinghouse indexes that material using the terms from the *Thesaurus.* Thus each Clearinghouse has a stake in the content of the *Thesaurus* and contributes regularly to updating of the ERIC vocabulary.

[1]See Delmer J. Trester's *ERIC—The First 15 Years. A History of the Educational Resources Information Center* (ERIC Document Reproduction Service No. ED 195 289).

[2]Note the "scope of interest" statements on the inside back cover of this publication to see the diversity of the ERIC system and to identify individual Clearinghouses' areas of expertise.

VOCABULARY MAINTENANCE

The Vocabulary Improvement Project

After years of collecting, indexing, and disseminating educational literature, ERIC found that the thesaural constructions and terminology developed in 1966 (when the database was established) were not sufficient for the needs of the 1980s. The vocabulary, allowed to develop slowly over the years, needed some major revisions to bring it up-to-date. Many Descriptors entered in ERIC's early years had become obsolete. Others originally entered without definitions needed some clarification in order to be understood and used consistently. The hierarchical relationships needed some rearranging in order to reflect current thinking in education. As a result, in 1977 Central ERIC made a major commitment to upgrade the quality and usefulness of the controlled vocabulary by revising the *Thesaurus* totally—an unprecedented effort for an established, ongoing information system. The Vocabulary Improvement Project (VIP) was undertaken to implement this unusual and major revision. All 16 ERIC Clearinghouses, the ERIC Processing and Reference Facility, and users of the ERIC system were asked to participate in the project.

The project was conducted in two phases, labeled "Thesaurus Review" and "Production." Phase I took place between March and August 1978, during which time Clearinghouse vocabulary coordinators, users, and database searchers critically evaluated the *Thesaurus*. By August, over 60,000 Descriptor assessments had been completed, about 10,000 by non-ERIC personnel. The objectives of this phase were to verify the utility of *Thesaurus* terms, identify problems requiring action, and recommend solutions.

An interim period, September and October 1978, followed Phase I. Clearinghouse vocabulary coordinators were assigned groups of Descriptors, for which they collated and assessed Phase I evaluations. Having decided that efficient retrieval was the overriding VIP objective, the axiom "Usage determines meaning" was adopted for Phase II.

During Phase II (November 1978 through September 1979) VIP personnel wrote new Scope Notes and modified old ones, merged synonymous terms, updated terminology, and revised cross-references. Over 10,000 separate transactions were prepared over the 11-month period. All transactions were keyed into an interim "*Play Thesaurus*" (as distinguished from the "real" *Thesaurus*). Because of the absence of an electronic mail system or online revision procedures, the *Play Thesaurus* was used to coordinate across geographic distances all recommendations of the Clearinghouses and the Facility. The *Play Thesaurus* was updated 12 times during the project. All suggested adds, deletes, and changes were included in the *Play Thesaurus*, identified by originating Clearinghouse, and coded (approved/disapproved) by the Facility lexicographers. In this way, all VIP staff were informed of each action taken on specific terms. When they had objections or suggestions, they could respond in a special "Comment" field that was incorporated within the Descriptor display for inter-Clearinghouse messages.

After the distribution of the last edition of the *Play Thesaurus,* Clearinghouse vocabulary coordinators and the Facility lexicographic staff spent several weeks reviewing the final recommendations and resolving unforeseen conflicts. The working copies of the "new" *Thesaurus* were ready by March 1980 for use in ERIC indexing. The master *Thesaurus* computer tapes—as well as the *RIE* and *CIJE* resume files—were then updated to reflect the VIP changes.

By the time the VIP project was completed, extensive revisions had taken place. The 1980 *Thesaurus of ERIC Descriptors—Completely Revised* (the 8th edition) reflected the following: over 600 new Descriptors, over 1,000 deleted Descriptors, and over 1,400 new or modified Scope Notes. This edition of the *Thesaurus* also reflected deliberate changes in sexist terminology.

The Vocabulary Improvement Project was a massive undertaking—an unprecedented effort by a large information system to systematically evaluate its indexing authority, to cross-check it against the database, and to let usage determine meaning and outcome of each term.[3] Although such a *thorough* revision will not be repeated in the near future, ERIC remains committed to maintaining a current and accurate vocabulary.

The Vocabulary Review Group

As a result of the success of the Vocabulary Improvement Project, some of the procedures established for it have been adapted for general ERIC implementation. Three features in particular remain: a specific vocabulary coordinator from each Clearinghouse to monitor the language of its own scope area (see p. v); user participation in vocabulary review; and a regular interactive process for vocabulary maintenance.

The Clearinghouse vocabulary coordinators, the ERIC lexicographic staff, a Central ERIC representative, and members from the user community now comprise the ERIC Vocabulary Review Group. The following user groups are represented: school librarians, university librarians, practitioners, and online search facilities. The Review Group both initiates and evaluates new terminology or modifications to existing vocabulary.

The interactive nature of the evaluation process allows all points of view to be heard before decisions are made in *Thesaurus* revisions. Effective retrieval remains the objective.

ERIC continues actively to serve the educational community. Users are encouraged to submit comments on this edition and suggestions for future editions of the

[3]See Barbara Booth's "A 'New' ERIC Thesaurus, Fine-Tuned for Searching." *Online* v3 n3 July 1979. pp. 20–29.

Thesaurus to Alan Moorehead, Director, ERIC, Department of Education, Washington, DC 20208.

INFORMATION RETRIEVAL METHODS AND TOOLS

Retrieval takes two forms: manual and computer (batch or online). For manual or batch searching, ERIC provides several printed reference tools; for online searching, a computer terminal provides immediate access to the same information cumulated from those reference tools.

Manual Searching

Manual searching makes use primarily of the monthly printed versions of *Resources in Education (RIE)* and *Current Index to Journals in Education (CIJE)*. Users locate titles in these publications through various indexes. *RIE* provides a Subject Index (made up of Major Descriptors and Major Identifiers—see pp. xiv and xvi), an Author Index,[4] an Institution Index (showing institutions responsible for a document and/or the agency sponsoring it), and a Publication Type Index (see p. xvii). In *CIJE*, there are the Subject Index, Author Index (see footnote 4), and Journal Contents Index (indicating titles of articles listed by journal names). Semiannual or annual cumulations of both publications, including their indexes, are provided.[5]

Computer Searching

Computer searching permits a review of part or all of the ERIC database (*RIE* and *CIJE*) in a single effort, eliminating the difficulty of scanning separate monthly or even annual publications. Computerized retrieval makes possible searches, not only of Major and Minor Descriptors and Identifiers, authors, institutions, specific journals, and Publication Types, but also of words or phrases not found in any of the printed indexes. In short, computer searching gives users the option to search every word of the document resume (i.e., bibliographic information, Descriptors, Identifiers, and abstracts or annotations) as published in *RIE* and *CIJE*. It should be noted that full-text searching in ERIC refers to searching individual words of the document *resume* and not of the document itself.

An exception to this traditional guideline is ERIC's new "ERIC Digests Online" (EDO) file, made available on The Source's ED-Line in April 1986. This new database consists of approximately 200 short reports ("digests") on current issues in education prepared by all 16 of the ERIC Clearinghouses. The full text of each digest is online, and each digest can be accessed by menu, key words (Descriptors from the ERIC *Thesaurus*), or fast command. Each digest also has its own "Notespace" for user comments. The EDO file will be expanded gradually. Most of the digests in EDO are announced in *RIE* and therefore can be identified in computer searches of ERIC via DIALOG, BRS, or SDC; however, the full text of each digest is currently available online only via The Source.

> NOTE: Procedures for searching the ERIC database vary with each of the major online vendors, DIALOG, BRS, and SDC's Orbit. See p. xiii for the comparative chart, "ERIC's Searchable Fields and Vendors' Field Access Labels," or consult the vendor training materials for specific online commands.

A review of the procedures outlined in the "ERIC's Indexing" section of this Introduction (see p. xiii) is useful in determining whether manual or online searching is most appropriate. The relevant strategy then can be devised using the *Thesaurus* and possibly the *Identifier Authority List* (see p. xvi).

---

[4]For documents/articles listing three or more authors, only the first author is indexed in ERIC. For collected works or proceedings containing works by three or more authors and not listing an editor or compiler of the whole, *no* authors are indexed; however, individual author names appearing in such collections are usually included within the text of the ERIC abstract/annotation and can be retrieved by full-text computer searching.

[5]*RIE,* covering education documents, is issued monthly by the Superintendent of Documents, U.S. Government Printing Office (GPO), Washington, DC 20402. GPO also issues semiannual *RIE* indexes.

CIJE, covering education journal articles, is published monthly by The Oryx Press, 2214 North Central at Encanto, Phoenix, AZ 85004-1483. Oryx Press also publishes the following:

—*CIJE Semiannual Cumulations*

One-volume cumulations of all main entries (descriptions of journal articles) and all indexes for a 6-month period. Prior to 1979, these were published by Macmillan Information, 866 Third Avenue, New York, NY 10022.

—*RIE Annual Cumulations*

Each in three volumes, two of cumulated main entries (abstracts) and one of cumulated indexes. Similar cumulations prior to 1979 were published under the title *Educational Documents Abstracts/Index* by Macmillan Information.

—*Microfiche Cumulations*

RIE Main Entry 1966–1980 and Annual Updates; *CIJE* Main Entry 1969–1980 and Annual Updates; Combined *RIE/CIJE* Subject and Fiche Index 1966–1980 and Annual Updates; Complete *RIE/CIJE* Cumulation 1966–1980 and Annual Updates.

Most *RIE* documents, identified by "ED" numbers in the ERIC database, can be ordered (microfiche or paper) from the ERIC Document Reproduction Service (EDRS), 3900 Wheeler Avenue, Alexandria, VA 22304-5110. EDRS delivers monthly *RIE* microfiche sets to over 700 standing-order subscribers. Cumulated *RIE* indexes on microfiche (1966-present) by subject, author, and institution, as well as by *RIE* title, are also available from EDRS.

ERIC's Searchable Fields and Vendors' Field Access Labels*

Searchable Field ERIC	BRS	DIALOG II	SDC
1. Descriptor—			
a. Multiword Descriptor	*-hyphen*	*no label necessary*	*no label necessary*
b. Descriptor Word(s)—word(s) within descriptor	.DE.	/DE	/IW
c Single-Word Descriptor	.MJ,MN.	/DF	/IT
d. Major Subject Descriptor	.MJ.	/MAJ	*
e. Minor Subject Descriptor	.MN.	/MIN	
2. Identifier—describes subject fields with terms not found in ERIC thesaurus			
a. Multiword Identifier	.ID. (*free text*)	*no label necessary*	*no label necessary*
b. Identifier Word(s)—word(s) within identifier	.ID. (*free text*)	/ID	/IW
c. Single-Word Identifier		/IF	/IT
d. Major Subject Identifier		/MAJ	*
e. Minor Subject Identifier		/MIN	
3. Title	.TI.	/TI	/TI
4. Abstract/ Annotation	.AB.	/AB	/AB
5. Personal Author	.AU.	AU=	/AU
6. ERIC Accession Number—document number as found in RIE or CIJE	.AN.	*Type ED# or EJ#*	/AN
7. Clearinghouse Accession Number—number assigned to document by an ERIC Clearinghouse	.CH.	AN=	/CHAN
• Clearinghouse Code—two-letter prefix to Clearinghouse Accession Number	.CH.	CH=	/CC
8. Publication Year	.YR.	PY=	/SO
9. Update	.AN.	UD=	/UP
10. Geographic Source of Document (field added 1979)	.GS.	CP=	/LO
11. Institution—corporate author	.IN.	CS=	/OS
12. Sponsoring Agency—funding agency	.SN.	SP=	/SPO
13. Journal Citation	.SO.	JN=	/SO
14. File Segment—RIE or CIJE (derived from ERIC Accession Number field)	ED.AN. EJ.AN.	/ED /EJ	RIE/FS CIJE/FS
15. Availability			
a. ERIC availability (from EDRS)		AV=	/AV
b. Alternate availability	.AV.		/AV
16. Governmental Status of Document (field added 1979)—federal, state, local	.GV.	GL=	/LO
17. Report Number	.NO.	RN=	/NU
18. Grant, Contract Number	.NO.	CN=	/NU
19. Publication Type	.PT.	DT=	/DT
20. Language of Document (field added 1979)—language of text	.LG.	LA=	/LA
21. Target Audience (field added 1984)	.ID.	TA=	/TG
22. Descriptive Note—extends description of publication, e.g., "Paper presented at Vocational Education Association National Conference"	.NT.	/NT	/NO

*Adapted from "Searchable Fields in ERIC—A Computer User's Guide via BRS, DIALOG, ORBIT," a brochure prepared by the ERIC Clearinghouse on Rural Education and Small Schools (1986).

ERIC'S INDEXING

General Guidelines

Knowing how something is stored obviously makes finding it easier. Understanding the methods by which literature is prepared for input into a computerized database facilitates retrieval of that literature. Just as an indexer must consider the user's needs, so must the user/searcher be aware of the rules and guidelines followed during the indexing process.

ERIC's indexing aims to provide subject access to the documents and articles contained in the database and announced in *RIE* and *CIJE*. To this end, two fundamental rules outweigh all others:

- Index only what is in the document.
- Index at the level of specificity of the document.

These rules mean that implied statements are not indexed, and that very general Descriptors (e.g., SCHOOLS, rather than HIGH SCHOOLS or PRIVATE SCHOOLS or MEDICAL SCHOOLS) are not used unless that subject is treated extremely broadly in the document. These two guidelines should be kept in mind by users for effective retrieval.

Indexing rules are set forth in the *ERIC Processing Manual*,[6] the system's official guide. Additional instructions, suggestions, and specific examples are detailed in the 400-page training-oriented *ERIC Abstractor/Indexer Workbook*.[7]

Major points relevant to retrieval are:

1. "Indexable" concepts, or key words, of a document are translated into Descriptors from the *Thesaurus*. Using the *Thesaurus* helps maintain consistency and avoids proliferation or scattering of concepts in the subject indexes.
2. Precoordinated (i.e., multiple-word) Descriptors are used whenever possible, rather than two or more Descriptors representing their component concepts. Thus SCIENCE CURRICULUM would be used rather than SCIENCE plus CURRICULUM.
3. Descriptors are assigned to identify subject content, educational level, age level, validation status of a program, research methodology employed, tests utilized, form or type of document, etc. (See pp. xv, xvi, xvii for lists of Mandatory Educational Level Descriptors, optional Age Level Descriptors, and Publication Types.)
4. Up to six "Major" Descriptors are assigned to a single document. They cover the main focus of the document. Major Descriptors appear in the *RIE* and *CIJE* printed Subject Indexes. In the document resume section of *RIE* and the main entry section of *CIJE*, Major Descriptors are identified by an asterisk.
5. Additional Descriptors, called "Minor" Descriptors, are also assigned to a document or journal article. They appear in the printed resumes (without an asterisk) but *do not* appear in the printed Subject Indexes of *RIE* or *CIJE*. (See examples that follow.)
6. Major Descriptors cover the main focus or *subject* of a document. Minor Descriptors indicate less important aspects within the document, as well as such nonsubject features as methodology, form, or educational level.

> NOTE: Major Descriptors appear in the Subject Indexes of *RIE* and *CIJE* and therefore can be searched manually. Minor Descriptors do not appear in the Subject Indexes but are searchable by computer.

SAMPLE *RIE* ENTRY

ED 253 865 CS 007 985
Anderson, Richard C. And Others
Becoming a Nation of Readers: The Report of the Commission on Reading.
Illinois Univ., Urbana. Center for the Study of Reading.; National Academy of Education, Washington, D.C.
Spons Agency—National Inst. of Education (ED), Washington, DC.
Pub Date—85
Contract—400-83-0057
Note—155p.
Available from—University of Illinois, Becoming a Nation of Readers, P.O. Box 2774, Station A, Champaign, IL 61820-8774 ($4.50 ea., including postage; overseas orders, add $1.00).
Pub Type—Books (010)—Reports-Descriptive (141)
EDRS Price - MF01/PC07 Plus Postage.
Descriptors—Classroom Environment, Classroom Techniques, Elementary Secondary Education, *Literacy, *Literacy Education, Professional Development, *Reading Improvement, *Reading Instruction, *Reading Processes, *Reading Tests, Teacher Education, Teacher Effectiveness

Fulfilling a need for careful and thorough synthesis of an extensive body of findings on reading, this report presents leading experts' interpretations of both current knowledge of reading and the state of the art and practice of teaching reading. The introduction contains two claims: (1) the knowledge is now available to make worthwhile improvements in reading throughout the United States, and (2) if the practices seen in the classrooms of the best teachers in the best schools could be introduced everywhere, improvement in reading would be dramatic. . . .

DESCRIPTORS

SAMPLE *CIJE* ENTRY

EJ 330 620 SP 515 489
The University and the Community: Partnerships for Excellence in Teacher Education. Roth, Robert A.; And Others *Action in Teacher Education;* v7 n4 p29-34 Win 1985-86 (Reprint: UMI)
Descriptors: *Preservice Teacher Education; *Educational Cooperation; *Cooperative Programs; Higher Education; *Program Development
Identifiers: Sun Coast Area Teacher Training Program; Florida
The Sun Coast Area Teacher Training Program is an honors program at the University of South Florida which complements the teacher education program. It maintains partnerships with local school districts, organizations, and educational agencies as well as the legislature, business community, and the University of South Florida Medical School. (MT)

---

[6]The *ERIC Processing Manual* (1980-82 revision) is available for $40.00 from the ERIC Processing and Reference Facility, 4833 Rugby Avenue, Suite 301, Bethesda, MD 20814. Sections relevant to retrieval, *Section 6: Abstracting/Annotating* (Sep80) and *Section 7: Indexing* (Oct80), may be purchased for $3.75 each from the ERIC Facility. The manual also appears in the ERIC Microfiche Collection (entire manual, ED 219 082; Abstracting Section, ED 219 087; Indexing Section, ED 219 088) and is available from the ERIC Document Reproduction Service.

[7]Revised edition, 1981, in ERIC Microfiche Collection (ED 207 614) and available from the ERIC Document Reproduction Service.

Educational/Age Level Descriptors

Since ERIC indexes educational literature from all levels—preschool through postdoctoral, infant through adult—it is important, where appropriate, to "tag" documents with "leveling" terms. These leveling terms are Descriptors from the *Thesaurus* that are included in the Descriptor Field of the *RIE* and *CIJE* resumes. They refer to either the educational level or age level of the population discussed in the document. Sometimes both educational *and* age level Descriptors may be assigned.

Assignment of at least one of the "Educational Level" Descriptors is mandatory for every document and journal article, unless it is entirely inappropriate (such as an essay on "the role of education in society"). Since a variety of *Thesaurus* terms could conceivably be used to tag these levels, ERIC has developed lists of preferred leveling Descriptors. The Mandatory Educational Level Descriptors procedure was implemented in February 1975.

This required assignment of Educational Level Descriptors has a practical implication for the searcher. For example, a computer search of the Descriptor READING SKILLS would pull out all the references in ERIC to reading skills, regardless of educational level. Adding the Descriptor SECONDARY EDUCATION would limit the output to those references dealing with grades 7 through 12; adding HIGH SCHOOLS instead would limit the output to reading skills in the upper secondary grades. Similarly, the Descriptor TWO YEAR COLLEGES would focus a search more discretely than would the term POSTSECONDARY EDUCATION. Thus the same guideline holds here in searching as in subject indexing: use the most specific Descriptor available for a specific search.

On the other hand, a document indexed at a narrow educational level would, in most instances, not also be "indexed up" to a broader level, and exhaustive searches of broader levelers require that each of their respective narrower levelers also be used. For example, one would need to search SECONDARY EDUCATION, JUNIOR HIGH SCHOOLS, HIGH SCHOOLS, and HIGH SCHOOL EQUIVALENCY PROGRAMS to achieve an exhaustive search at the SECONDARY EDUCATION level.

> NOTE: Use the most specific Educational Level Descriptor possible. Use broader *and* narrower Educational Level Descriptors to retrieve at broader levels.

Age Level Descriptors were mandatory from 1980 until mid-1982, when the requirement was abolished. Eleven Age Level Descriptors still are used to index age level, however. Each covers an approximate age range, and one or more are used when a document or journal article is *concerned strictly with age-level groups or populations.* It should be noted that the use of specific other terms such as ADOPTED CHILDREN and ADULT DROPOUTS would eliminate the need also to index such generic terms as CHILDREN and ADULTS.

The Mandatory Educational Level Descriptors and the Age Level Descriptors appear with their Scope Notes in the following charts:

MANDATORY "EDUCATIONAL LEVEL" DESCRIPTORS
(Procedure Implemented February 1975)

- EARLY CHILDHOOD EDUCATION
  Scope Note: Activities and/or experiences that are intended to effect developmental changes in children, from birth through the primary units of elementary school (grades K–3).
  - •• PRESCHOOL EDUCATION
    Scope Note: Activities and/or experiences that are intended to effect developmental changes in children, from birth to entrance in kindergarten (or grade 1 when kindergarten is not attended).
  - •• PRIMARY EDUCATION
    Scope Note: Education provided in kindergarten through grade 3.
- ELEMENTARY SECONDARY EDUCATION
  Scope Note: Formal education provided in kindergarten or grade 1 through grade 12.
  - •• ELEMENTARY EDUCATION
    Scope Note: Education provided in kindergarten or grade 1 through grade 6, 7, or 8.
    - ••• ADULT BASIC EDUCATION
      Scope Note: Education provided for adults at the elementary level (through grade 8), usually with emphasis on communicative, computational, and social skills.
    - ••• PRIMARY EDUCATION
      Scope Note: (See above.)
    - ••• INTERMEDIATE GRADES
      Scope Note: Includes the middle and/or upper elementary grades, but usually 4, 5, and 6.
  - •• SECONDARY EDUCATION
    Scope Note: Education provided in grade 7, 8, or 9 through grade 12.
    - ••• JUNIOR HIGH SCHOOLS
      Scope Note: Providing formal education in grades 7, 8, and 9—less commonly 7 and 8, or 8 and 9.
    - ••• HIGH SCHOOLS (Changed from "Senior High Schools" in March 1980.)
      Scope Note: Providing formal education in grades 9 or 10 through 12.
    - ••• HIGH SCHOOL EQUIVALENCY PROGRAMS
      Scope Note: Adult educational activities concerned with the preparation for and the taking of tests which lead to a high school equivalency certificate, e.g., General Educational Development program.
- POSTSECONDARY EDUCATION
  Scope Note: All education beyond the secondary level—includes learning activities and experiences beyond the compulsory school attendance age, with the exception of adult basic education and high school equivalency programs. (Before Apr75, restricted to "education beyond grade 12 and less than the baccalaureate level.")
  - •• HIGHER EDUCATION
    Scope Note: All education beyond the secondary level leading to a formal degree.
  - •• TWO YEAR COLLEGES (Changed from "Junior Colleges" in March 1980.)
    Scope Note: Public or private postsecondary institutions providing at least 2, but less than 4, years of academic and/or occupational education.

OPTIONAL "AGE LEVEL" DESCRIPTORS

INFANTS
Scope Note: Aged birth to approximately 24 months.

YOUNG CHILDREN
Scope Note: Aged birth through approximately 8 years.

CHILDREN
Scope Note: Aged birth through approximately 12 years.

TODDLERS
Scope Note: Approximately 1-3 years of age.

PRESCHOOL CHILDREN
Scope Note: Approximately 2-5 years of age.

PREADOLESCENTS
Scope Note: Approximately 9-12 years of age.

ADOLESCENTS
Scope Note: Approximately 13-17 years of age.

YOUNG ADULTS
Scope Note: Approximately 18-30 years of age.

ADULTS
Scope Note: Approximately 18+ years of age.

MIDDLE AGED ADULTS
Scope Note: Approximately 45-64 years of age.

OLDER ADULTS
Scope Note: Approximately 65+ years of age.

The Mandatory Educational Level Descriptors are flagged within the body of the *Thesaurus* with a special instruction in the Scope Note:

SECONDARY EDUCATION
SN Education provided in grade 7, 8, or 9 through grade 12 (note: also appears in the list of mandatory educational level descriptors)

NOTE: As mandatory terms, Educational Level Descriptors always have precedence over the Age Level terms. Educational Level terms are *never* Major Descriptors unless they are the *subject* of the document.

Identifiers

"Identifiers" are key words or "indexable" concepts intended to add a depth to subject indexing that is not always possible with Descriptors alone. Identifiers are not found in the *Thesaurus,* since they are generally: (1) proper names, or (2) concepts not yet represented by approved Descriptors. In the resume sections of *RIE* and *CIJE* they appear in a separate field below the Descriptors. They may be "majored" with an asterisk just as Descriptors are. Major Identifiers, like Major Descriptors, appear in the printed Subject Indexes of *RIE* and *CIJE*.

EJ 330 014 HE 520 347
Summaries of Changes in Regulations Approved by the NCAA Convention. *Chronicle of Higher Education;* v31 n19 p34-35 Jan 22 1986 (Reprint: UMI)
Descriptors: Higher Education; Intercollegiate Cooperation; *Student Financial Aid; *Student Recruitment; Group Membership; *Eligibility; Governance; *Standards; Scheduling; Personnel Policy; Competition; Drug Abuse; Screening Tests; Program Administration; Athletic Coaches; *College Athletics
IDENTIFIERS ——► *Identifiers:* *National Collegiate Athletic Association; Amateurism
The National Collegiate Athletic Association's regulation changes concerning student financial aid, program administration, recruiting, association membership, eligibility, association governance, coach employment policy, playing and practice seasons, and amateurism are summarized. (MSE)

Identifiers are used to index geographic locations, personal names, test or program names, specific legislation, etc., as well as concepts not found in the *Thesaurus.* In the latter case, the Identifier Field provides a "tryout" for candidate Descriptors. Identifiers are examined regularly for their suitability as Descriptors. Since ERIC is a literature-based information system, every Descriptor must be supported by a document or article in the database; Identifiers often provide that evidence and serve as the justification for Clearinghouse proposals for new *Thesaurus* terms.

Recent examples of former Identifiers that now appear in the *Thesaurus* as Descriptors are COMPUTER NETWORKS, CONFLICT OF INTEREST, FACULTY PUBLISHING, BEHAVIORISM, ACCESS TO INFORMATION, CORPORATE EDUCATION, ANGER, SCIENCE AND SOCIETY, and COGNITIVE DISSONANCE. New Descriptors are announced in the monthly issues of *RIE* and *CIJE*. Identifiers that are proper names (person, place, program, organization, etc.) rarely become Descriptors.

As of mid-1980, all terms in the Identifier Field must conform in format to terms in the *ERIC Identifier Authority List* [8] *(IAL)* or to the rules and guidelines for creating new Identifiers.[9] Items are purged from the *IAL* as they are upgraded to Descriptor status and shifted to the *Thesaurus.*

As Identifiers are elevated to the *Thesaurus,* their index postings are transferred to the Descriptor field. All such Identifier-to-Descriptor conversions occurring before December 1980 are fully reflected in the ERIC file. December 1980 was the last time a general reload of the ERIC backfile was performed. Conversions since that time, therefore, are *not* fully reflected in the database, and posting counts for Descriptors added after December 1980 may represent combined Descriptor/Identifier usages. (See related discussion under "Transferred Descriptors," p. viii.)

[8]The *IAL* is available for purchase from the ERIC Processing and Reference Facility: *Alphabetical Display* ($20.00, approx. 300 pp.); *Category Display* ($20.00, approx. 200 pp.). The main *Alphabetical Display* lists all approved Identifiers in the ERIC files, alphabetically A to Z, together with postings data for each; some cross-references and Scope Notes are provided. The *Category Display* serves as a companion volume to the main display, listing Identifiers alphabetically within 20 broad categories (e.g., Geographic Locations, Project/Programs, Tests/Testing).

[9]Guidelines are detailed in the *ERIC Processing Manual, Section 8: Vocabulary Development and Maintenance (Part 2)—Identifiers* (Apr81), available for $3.75 from the ERIC Facility or as ED 219 090 from the ERIC Document Reproduction Service.

NOTE:

1. Like Major Descriptors, Major Identifiers appear in the Subject Indexes of *RIE* and *CIJE*.
2. Major and Minor Identifiers can be searched online similarly to the way Descriptors can. See "ERIC's Searchable Fields" on p. xiii for variations among vendors.
3. To be safe, searches of Descriptors with add dates after December 1980 (when the last general ERIC reload occurred) should consider usages (postings) not only in the Descriptor field, but in the Identifier field as well.

Publication Types

PUBTYPE Codes

All documents are categorized by their "form" of publication (i.e., Publication Type or PUBTYPE) as well as by their subject. A special section of the document resume identifies the PUBTYPE by means of a three-digit code. PUBTYPEs are assigned to *every* document and journal article (beginning September 1974 for *RIE,* August 1979 for *CIJE*). They appear in the monthly printed issues of *RIE* along with the bibliographic information.

ED 265 521 CS 008 298
All Our Kids Can Learn to Read: Guide to Parent and Citizen Action, Chicago SCHOOLWATCH.
Designs for Change, Chicago, Ill.
Pub Date—85
Note—178p.
Available from—Designs for Change, 220 South State St., Suite 1616, Chicago, IL 60604 ($3.50, including postage).
PUBTYPE ——➤ Pub Type—Guides - Non-Classroom (055)
EDRS Price - MF01 Plus Postage. PC Not Available from EDRS.
Descriptors—Community Involvement, *Educational Improvement, *Evaluation Criteria, *Parent Participation, Reading Achievement, *Reading Improvement, *Reading Instruction, Reading Skills, *School Community Programs, School Organization, Test Interpretation
Identifiers—Illinois (Chicago), Schoolwatch IL
Intended for parents and all citizens concerned about improving Chicago's 592 public schools, this handbook explains how important reading is to a decent education and future. . . .

Printed issues of *CIJE* do not include PUBTYPE designations. However, all assigned PUBTYPEs for both *RIE* and *CIJE* are on the ERIC tapes and are searchable by computer.

In *RIE,* they are also searchable manually in the Publication Type Index (first published in July 1979). This index is organized numerically by PUBTYPE code and provides reference to title and accession (ED) number for each document having that code:

PUBTYPE INDEX

(055) Guides - Non-Classroom

——➤ All Our Kids Can Learn to Read: Guide to Parent and Citizen Action, Chicago SCHOOLWATCH.
ED 265 521

Alternative Education Programs for Disruptive Students.
ED 265 655

Asbestos in Our Schools. Taming the Silent Killer. A Handbook for Association Leaders Produced by NEA.
ED 265 665

Codes and category names for the 36 PUBTYPES are:

CODE	PUBLICATION/DOCUMENT TYPES
010	BOOKS
	COLLECTED WORKS
020	—General
021	—Conference Proceedings (See also 150)
022	—Serials
030	CREATIVE WORKS (Literature, Drama, Fine Arts)
	DISSERTATIONS/THESES
040	—Undetermined
041	—Doctoral Dissertations
042	—Masters Theses
043	—Practicum Papers
	GUIDES
050	—General
	—Classroom Use
051	—For *Learner* (Instructional Materials)
052	—For *Teacher* (Teaching Guides)
055	—Non-Classroom Use (For *Administrative and Support Staff, Teachers, Parents, Clergy, Researchers*)
060	HISTORICAL MATERIALS
070	INFORMATION ANALYSES (Literature Reviews, State-of-the-Art Papers)
071	—ERIC Information Analysis Products
080	JOURNAL ARTICLES
090	LEGAL/LEGISLATIVE/REGULATORY MATERIALS
100	AUDIOVISUAL MATERIALS/NON-PRINT MATERIALS
**101	—Computer Programs
110	STATISTICAL DATA (Numerical/Quantitative)
120	VIEWPOINTS (Opinion Papers, Position Papers, Essays, etc.)
	REFERENCE MATERIALS
130	—General
131	—Bibliographies
132	—Directories/Catalogs
133	—Geographic Materials
134	—Vocabularies/Classifications/Dictionaries/ Glossaries
	REPORTS
140	—General
141	—Descriptive (Program/Project Descriptions)
142	—Evaluative/Feasibility
143	—Research/Technical
150	SPEECHES, CONFERENCE PAPERS (Individual) (See also 021)
160	TESTS, EVALUATION INSTRUMENTS
170	TRANSLATIONS
*171	—Multilingual/Bilingual Materials
999	OTHER/MISCELLANEOUS (Not Classifiable Elsewhere) (Avoid use of this category, if at all possible)

*Added April 1983.
**Added July 1984.

GUIDE FOR ASSIGNING PUBTYPE CODES (A CROSS-REFERENCE FROM SPECIFIC KINDS OF DOCUMENTS TO MOST APPLICABLE PUBLICATION TYPE CODE)

(Bracketed terms are not Descriptors)

PUBLICATION TYPE	PUBTYPE CODE MOST APPLICABLE
Abstracts	131
Administrator Guides	055
Annotated Bibliographies	131
Annual Reports	141
Answer Keys	160
Answer Sheets	160
Anthologies	020
[Archival Documents]	060
Atlases	133
Audiodisks	100
Audiotape Recordings	100
*Audiovisual Aids	100
Autobiographies	060
*Bibliographies	131
[Bilingual Materials]	171
Biographical Inventories	060 (132)
Biographies	060
[Booklists]	131
*Books	010
Book Reviews	070
Bulletins	022
[Bylaws]	090
Cartoons	100 (030)
Case Records [or] Case Studies	141 or 143 or 140
Catalogs	132
Charts	100
Check Lists	130 or 160
[Childrens Books]	010 and 030
Childrens Literature	030 (010)
Chronicles	060 (020)
Citation Indexes	131
[Class Newspapers]	022
[Classroom Games]	051 (100)
[Classroom Materials]	051 or 052
Codes of Ethics	090
Comics (Publications)	030
Computer Output Microfilm	100
*Computer Software	101
Computer Software Reviews	142 or 070
[Concordances]	134
*Conference Papers	150
*Conference Proceedings	021
[Conference Summaries]	021
Contracts	090
Course Descriptions	052 or 050 or 051
[Courtroom Transcripts]	090
[Creative Works]	030
Curriculum Guides	052 or 050 or 051
[Data Sheets]	110 or 130
Diagrams	100
Diaries	120 (060 or 030)
*Dictionaries	134
[Dictionary Catalogs]	131
*Directories	132
[Discipline Codes]	090
Discographies	131
*Doctoral Dissertations	041
Documentaries	100 (141)
Drama	030
Editorials	120
Encyclopedias	130
[ERIC IAPs]	071
Essays	120 or 030
[Evaluation Studies]	142
Facility Guidelines	055
Faculty Handbooks	055
Feasibility Studies	142

PUBLICATION TYPE	PUBTYPE CODE MOST APPLICABLE
Filmographies	131
Films	100
Filmstrips	100
Flow Charts	100
Foreign Language Books	010 (170)
Foreign Language Films	100 (170)
Foreign Language Periodicals	022 (170)
Games	999 or 051
Glossaries	134
Graphs	100
Guidelines	050 or 052 or 055
*Guides	050 or 051 or 052 or 055
Hearings	090
[Historical Reviews]	060
Illustrations	100
Indexes	130 or 131
[Information Analyses]	070 or 071
Instructional Materials	051
Interviews	120 or 160
Item Banks	160
[Journal Articles]	080
[Journals]	022
[Judicial Materials]	090
Kinescope Recordings	100
Laboratory Manuals	051
[Language Guides]	051 or 030 (170)
Large Type Materials	051
Leaders Guides	052
[Lecture]	150 (051)
[Legal Analysis]	090
Legislation	090
Lesson Plans	052
Letters (Correspondence)	030
[Literature Guides]	131
Literature Reviews	131 (070)
[Lobbying Papers]	090 and 120
Magnetic Tape Cassettes	100
Magnetic Tapes	100
[Manuals]	050 or 051 or 052 or 055
Maps	133
Master Plans	090
[Master Tapes (Audio)]	100
*Masters Theses	042
Matrices	100
Microforms	100
Models	100 or 143
*Multilingual Materials	171
[Musical Materials]	030
Negotiation Agreements	090
Newsletters	022
Newspapers	022
Nonprint Media	100
Opinions	120
[Oral History Transcripts]	060
Pamphlets	Document Dependent
[Parent Guides]	055
Patents	090
Periodicals	022
Permuted Indexes	130 or 131

PUBLICATION TYPE	PUBTYPE CODE MOST APPLICABLE
[Phonograph Records]	100
Photographs	100
Poetry	030
Position Papers	120
*Practicum Papers	043
Program Descriptions	141
Program Evaluation	142
Program Guides	141
Program Proposals	141
[Programed Texts]	010 and 051
Puzzles	999
Questionnaires	160
Rating Scales	160
[Recommendations]	120
Records (Forms)	100 or 110 or 050 group
*Reference Materials	130 (010)
[Regulations]	090
*Reports	140
[Research Methodology Guides]	055
Research Proposals	143
*Research Reports	143
[Research Reviews (Publications)]	070
Resource Materials	050 or 051 or 052 or 055
Scholarly Journals	022
School Newspapers	022
School Publications	Document Dependent
Scripts	030
*Serials	022
Short Stories	030
Slides	100
Specifications	090
*Speeches	150
Standards	090
State of the Art Reviews	070
*Statistical Data	110
Student Publications	Document Dependent
Study Guides	051
Surveys	160 or 143
Tables (Data)	110
Talking Books	100
Tape Recordings	100
[Taxonomy]	134
Teaching Guides	052
[Technical Reports]	143
Test Reviews	142
*Tests	160
Textbooks	010 and 051
Thesauri	134
*Theses	040
[Transcripts (Interview)]	120
[Transcripts (Legal)]	090
[Transcripts (Oral History)]	060
Videodisks	100
Videotape Recordings	100
*Vocabulary	134
Word Lists	134
Workbooks	051
Worksheets	051
Yearbooks	141 (022)

FOOTNOTES: 1. All terms not in brackets have been selected from the ERIC *Thesaurus.*

2. Conventions A or B = one or the other category is appropriate, depending on item.
A and B = two categories are appropriate.
A (B) = a second category might be appropriate, depending on item.
* = category and term are synonymous. Term should be used in descriptor field only when it denotes subject matter.

3. These terms, like all other Descriptors identifying the form or type of a document, should be used as major Descriptors only when they represent the subject of the document in hand.

To determine the proper PUBTYPE code for a document, an ERIC indexer examines the item and then checks the "Descriptor-to-Publication Type Table" (see p. xviii). For example, if the document in hand is a feasibility study, the table readily identifies it as a "code 142" item.

Similarly, this cross-reference chart is useful in the retrieval process. For example, if a user wanted samples of facility guidelines, the PUBTYPE code 055 could be searched; or an examination of the PUBTYPE code 060 could be used to help find autobiographies.

> NOTE: To allow flexibility in classification, up to three PUBTYPE code assignments are permitted for a single document or article. All may be searched online. All cataloged for *RIE* appear in the Publication Type Index of that journal.

Publication Type Descriptors

Labeling of publication type or document characteristics is also done by the use of Descriptors. For example, a document that includes the complete survey instrument (e.g., a questionnaire) used in a research study would be PUBTYPE-coded 143 (Research/Technical Reports) and 160 (Tests, Evaluation Instruments). But it would also carry the Minor Descriptor QUESTIONNAIRES (Minor, because "questionnaire" is not the *subject* of the document). The use of specific form terms is not unusual in the Descriptor Field. However, as of March 1980, certain very broad form terms that coincide exactly with names of PUBTYPE Categories are *not* used for indexing document form in the Descriptor Field. These 22 form terms and their corresponding PUBTYPE codes are:

DESCRIPTORS CORRESPONDING TO PUBLICATION TYPE CATEGORIES

DESCRIPTOR	PUBTYPE CODE
AUDIOVISUAL AIDS	100
BIBLIOGRAPHIES	131
BOOKS	010
COMPUTER SOFTWARE	101
CONFERENCE PAPERS	150
CONFERENCE PROCEEDINGS	021
DICTIONARIES	134
DIRECTORIES	132
DOCTORAL DISSERTATIONS	041
GUIDES	050
MASTERS THESES	042
MULTILINGUAL MATERIALS	171
PRACTICUM PAPERS	043
REFERENCE MATERIALS	130
REPORTS	140
RESEARCH REPORTS	143
SERIALS	022
SPEECHES	150
STATISTICAL DATA	110
TESTS	160
THESES	040
VOCABULARY	134

These very broad terms may be used as Descriptors (Major or Minor) *if* they apply to the *subject* of the document, as noted in the *Thesaurus:*

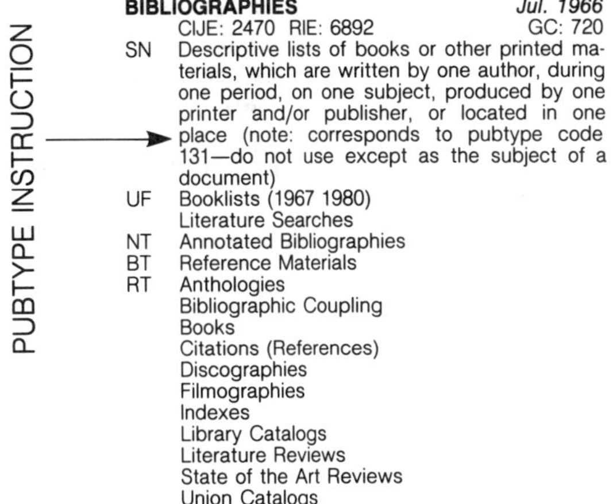
PUBTYPE INSTRUCTION

BIBLIOGRAPHIES *Jul. 1966*
CIJE: 2470 RIE: 6892 GC: 720
SN Descriptive lists of books or other printed materials, which are written by one author, during one period, on one subject, produced by one printer and/or publisher, or located in one place (note: corresponds to pubtype code 131—do not use except as the subject of a document)
UF Booklists (1967 1980)
Literature Searches
NT Annotated Bibliographies
BT Reference Materials
RT Anthologies
Bibliographic Coupling
Books
Citations (References)
Discographies
Filmographies
Indexes
Library Catalogs
Literature Reviews
State of the Art Reviews
Union Catalogs

Thus if a document were a bibliography about how to compile bibliographies, it would have the PUBTYPE 131 (Bibliographies) and *also* the Major Descriptor BIBLIOGRAPHIES (major, because it is the subject of the document).

> NOTE: "Document type" Descriptors (see table on p. xviii) should *not be Major* Descriptors unless they are the *subject* of the document.

FURTHER HINTS FOR RELEVANT RETRIEVAL

Non-Subject Access

One usually looks for information in ERIC by subject area, using Descriptors, Identifiers, and/or free-text phrases. Publication Type offers an additional refinement of the search process. There are other elements of ERIC's cataloging that are separate from the indexing process, however, that help limit a computer search even more precisely. They include a document's language, geographic origin (country, or country and state/province), and Target Audience.[10] All three of these data elements are searchable *only* by computer. Language appears on both *RIE* and *CIJE* citations as of January 1979. Geographic origin is used only for *RIE,* effective January 1979.

[10]Further details on the Language, Geographic Origin, and Target Audience fields are given in the *ERIC Processing Manual, Section 5: Cataloging,* available for $3.75 from the ERIC Facility. An earlier version of this document (without the Target Audience description) is available as ED 219 086 from the ERIC Document Reproduction Service.

Target Audience

Educational documents and journal articles are sometimes written for particular audiences. ERIC currently identifies these audiences in a special "Target Audience" field. *The field is used when an author clearly specifies an intended audience; otherwise, it is left blank.*

For consistency, eleven distinct audiences have been defined by ERIC, as follows:

- Policymakers
- Researchers
- Practitioners
  - Administrators
  - Teachers
  - Counselors
  - Media Staff
  - Support Staff
- Students
- Parents
- Community

> NOTE: The ERIC computer system automatically adds the generic audience "Practitioners" to records cataloged by any of the five "practitioner" sub-categories.

The Target Audience field may be used to limit a computer search more narrowly. For example, adding Target Audience-Practitioners to a search of the Descriptor DROPOUT PREVENTION would focus the search on literature on dropout prevention written specifically for practitioners.

Target Audience is an optional cataloging element. Not all documents identify an audience; some identify more than one. There are no restrictions on the number of audiences that may be cataloged as long as the above authority list is adhered to; however, if the number of practitioner groups involved is three or more (out of the five available), only the generic term "Practitioners" is cataloged.

The Target Audience field has been a fully defined cataloging element for *RIE* since January 1984, and for *CIJE* since September 1984. The terms "Practitioners" and/or "Students" have been added retrospectively to selected *RIE* citations announced during the period May 1975 through December 1983. No citations prior to May 1975 contain the Target Audience field.

Each of the major online retrieval vendors provides computer access to ERIC's Target Audience data in a different way and has a different segment of records containing Target Audience data on its file. These differences are summarized below:

DIALOG

Access:	Via the prefix "TA = ," e.g., S TA = PRACTITIONERS
File Segment:	RIE from Jan84; CIJE from Sep84. Retrospective RIE postings (May75–Dec83, "Practitioners" and "Students" only).

BRS

Access:	"Target Audience" data merged with Identifier data, e.g.: IDENTIFIERS: Great Britain, West Indians, Caribbean. TARGET AUDIENCE: Policymakers. Searching must be done with this in mind, e.g.: POLICYMAKERS.ID. AND (TARGET ADJ AUDIENCE).ID.
File Segment:	RIE from Jan84; CIJE from Sep84. Retrospective RIE postings (Nov83–Dec83, "Practitioners" and "Students" only).

SDC

Access:	Via the suffix "/TG," e.g., PRACTITIONERS/TG
File Segment:	RIE from Aug85; CIJE from Aug85.

> NOTE:
>
> 1. Target Audience was added as a new data element to *RIE* in January 1984 and to *CIJE* in September 1984. There are some retrospective *RIE* postings of "Practitioners" and "Students."
> 2. Target Audience is not captured for all documents and journal articles, but only for those approximately 25% explicitly claiming a target audience.
> 3. Target Audience does not appear in the printed *RIE* and *CIJE* abstract journals.
> 4. Online access to Target Audience varies from one vendor to another.

CONCLUSION

This brief review of the ERIC system has been intended to make users more aware of the system as a whole, of how the educational literature is indexed for the database, and of how the *Thesaurus* fits into the overall information dissemination process.

Throughout this process, ERIC is committed to high quality performance standards while serving the entire spectrum of the educational community. Close contact and interaction with users in the field is of prime importance to ERIC. In this sense, ERIC is more than a database (or a thesaurus); it is an active network of dedicated professionals, responding to and anticipating the information needs of both the scholar and the practitioner in the broad field of education.

THESAURUS CONSTRUCTION AND FORMAT

The *Thesaurus of ERIC Descriptors,* 1987 edition, contains an alphabetical listing of terms used for indexing and searching in the ERIC system. It actually consists of four parts—the main Alphabetical Display, the Rotated Display, the Hierarchical Display, and the Descriptor Group Display.

ALPHABETICAL DESCRIPTOR DISPLAY

The main, word-by-word Alphabetical Display is probably the most familiar since it provides a variety of information (a "display") for each Descriptor. This includes a Scope Note (SN), Add Date, Descriptor Group Code, Posting Notes, Used For (UF) and Use (USE) references, Narrower Terms (NT), Broader Terms (BT), and Related Terms (RT). Each of these segments of the *Thesaurus* display is explained in detail below.

SN (Scope Note)

A Scope Note is a brief statement of the intended usage of a Descriptor. It may be used to clarify an ambiguous term or to restrict the usage of a term. Special indexing notes are often included.

TESTS
SN Devices, procedures, or sets of items that are used to measure ability, skill, understanding, knowledge, or achievement (note: use a more specific term if possible—this broad term corresponds to pubtype code 160 and should not be used except as the subject of a document)

Recommends use of a Narrower Term and directs indexers and searchers to PUBTYPE category

ORAL INTERPRETATION
SN The oral interpretation and presentation of a work of literature to an audience (note: prior to mar80, the instruction "oral interpretation, use interpretive reading" was carried in the thesaurus)

Alerts users and searchers to an earlier *Thesaurus* instruction

NONFORMAL EDUCATION
SN Organized education without formal schooling or institutionalization in which knowledge, skills, and values are taught by relatives, peers, or other community members (note: do not confuse with "nonschool educational programs" or the identifier "informal education")

Suggests another Descriptor or an Identifier that may be more appropriate

UF (Used For)

The "UF" reference is employed generally to solve problems of synonymy occurring in natural language. Terms following the UF notation are *not to be used in indexing.* They most often represent either (1) synonymous or variant forms of the main term, or (2) specific terms that, for purposes of storage and retrieval, are indexed under a more general term. The examples below illustrate both types of UFs:

MAINSTREAMING
UF Desegregation (Disabled Students)
Integration (Disabled Students)
Least Restrictive Environment (Disabled)
Regular Class Placement (1968 1978)

LIFELONG LEARNING
UF Continuous Learning (1967 1980)
Education Permanente
Lifelong Education
Life Span Education
Permanent Education
Recurrent Education

LABOR FORCE DEVELOPMENT
UF Human Resources Development (Labor)
Manpower Development (1966 1980)

PHYSICAL DISABILITIES
UF Crippled Children (1968 1980)
Orthopedically Handicapped (1968 1980)
Physical Handicaps (1966 1980)

A former Descriptor that has been downgraded to the status of a UF term is accompanied by a "life span" notation in parentheses: e.g., (1966 1980). This indicates the time period during which the term was used in indexing. It provides useful information for searching older printed indexes, or computer files that have not been updated.

> NOTE: The present status of "downgraded" Descriptors in the ERIC database is discussed under "Transferred Descriptors," p. viii, accompanied by a list of all such terms still searchable on the file.

Sometimes a UF needs more than one Descriptor to represent it adequately. In such cases a pound sign (#) following the UF term signifies that two or more main terms are to be used in coordination. The term's main entry in the Alphabetical Display shows the appropriate coordination. A footnote to this effect appears at the bottom of those pages where the pound sign appears. Sample "multiple UFs" follow:

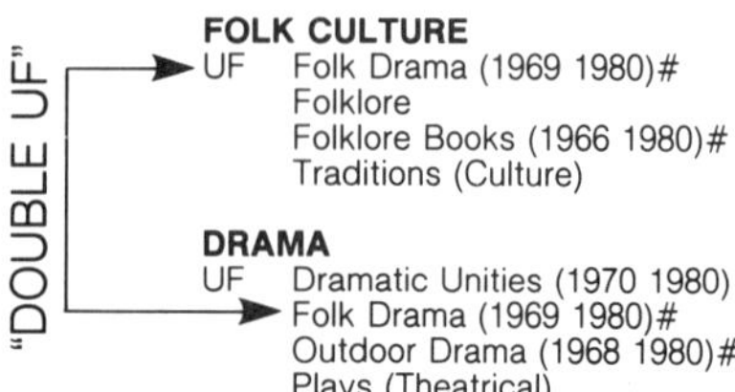

USE

The USE reference, the mandatory reciprocal of the UF, refers an indexer or searcher from a nonusable (nonindexable) term to the preferred indexable term or terms.

In the examples below, there is only one USE term for each entry. This means that there is a direct, one-to-one correlation in the ERIC system from the UF to the USE term.

Regular Class Placement (1968 1978)
USE MAINSTREAMING

Continuous Learning (1967 1980)
USE LIFELONG LEARNING

Orthopedically Handicapped (1968 1980)
USE PHYSICAL DISABILITIES

Manpower
USE LABOR FORCE

A coordinate or multiple USE reference (the reciprocal of the "double UF" above) looks a little different. The following example illustrates the use of two main terms together to represent a single concept, both for indexing and searching:

Folk Drama (1969 1980)
USE DRAMA; FOLK CULTURE

BT (Broader Term) and NT (Narrower Term)

The BT/NT notations are used to indicate the existence of a hierarchical relationship between a class and its subclasses. Narrower terms (terms following the NT notation) are included in the broader class represented by the main entry.

LIBRARIES
NT Academic Libraries
Branch Libraries
Depository Libraries
Public Libraries
Research Libraries
School Libraries
Special Libraries

MODELS
NT Mathematical Models
Role Models
Student Writing Models
Teaching Models

The Broader Term (BT) is the mandatory reciprocal of the NT. Broader Terms (terms following the BT symbol) include as a subclass the concept represented by the main (narrower) term.

SCHOOL LIBRARIES
BT Libraries

MATHEMATICAL MODELS
BT Models

Sometimes a term may have more than one Broader Term:

REMEDIAL READING
BT Reading
Reading Instruction
Remedial Instruction

> NOTE: In ERIC, computer searching of a Broad Term will *not* automatically retrieve documents representing the concepts of its Narrower Terms, *unless those NTs have also been assigned to the documents in indexing* (e.g., searching LIBRARIES will not *automatically* also retrieve literature on SCHOOL LIBRARIES or any of the other NTs to LIBRARIES).

RT (Related Term)

The terms following the RT notation have a close conceptual relationship to the main term, but not the direct class/subclass relationship described by BTs/NTs. Part-whole relationships, near-synonyms, and other conceptually related terms, which might be helpful to the user, appear as RTs.

HIGH SCHOOL SENIORS
RT College Bound Students
Grade 12
High School Freshmen
High School Graduates
Noncollege Bound Students

MINIMUM COMPETENCY TESTING
RT Academic Achievement
Academic Standards
Basic Skills
Competence
Competency Based Education
Mastery Tests
Minimum Competencies
National Competency Tests
Student Certification

SECOND LANGUAGE PROGRAMS
RT Bilingual Education Programs
Conversational Language Courses
English (Second Language)
Fles
Intensive Language Courses
Language Enrollment
Language Laboratories
Modern Language Curriculum
Multilevel Classes (Second Language Instruction)
Native Speakers
Notional Functional Syllabi
Second Language Instruction
Second Language Learning
Second Languages

TWO YEAR COLLEGES
RT Associate Degrees
Multicampus Colleges
Multicampus Districts
Postsecondary Education
State Colleges
Technical Education
Trade and Industrial Education
Two Year College Students
Undergraduate Study
Upper Division Colleges

Parenthetical Qualifiers

A Parenthetical Qualifier is used to identify a particular indexable meaning of a homograph. In other words, it discriminates between terms (either Descriptors or USE references) that might otherwise be confused with each other. Examples include LETTERS (ALPHABET) and LETTERS (CORRESPONDENCE); SELF EVALUATION (INDIVIDUALS) and SELF EVALUATION (GROUPS).

> NOTE: The Qualifier is considered an integral part of the Descriptor, and must be used with the Descriptor in indexing *and* searching.

Add Dates

An Add (entry into the *Thesaurus* and thus the computer tapes) Date is printed to the right of each Descriptor or main term. The earliest "real" Add Date is Aug. 1968. Month and year of entry are given for each Descriptor added from Aug. 1968 to the present. All earlier Descriptors have been given the arbitrary Add Date of Jul. 1966, the appropriate point in time at which ERIC indexing (*RIE* only at that point) began. Add Dates are intended to help users in the preparation of search strategies. They represent calendar dates, not *RIE* or *CIJE* issue dates. Rigid interpretation of Add Dates should be avoided.

It should also be noted that new Scope Notes are occasionally added to older Descriptors, i.e., terms with earlier Add Dates. In cases where that may affect searching, an instructional statement is included in the new Scope Note:

FOUNDATION PROGRAMS *Jul. 1966*
SN Systems whereby state funds are used to supplement local or intermediate school district funds for elementary and secondary education—a "minimum foundation" of financial support is usually guaranteed regardless of the local district's ability to support education (note: prior to mar80, this term was not scoped and was sometimes used to index "philanthropic foundations")

Descriptor Group Codes

Descriptor Group Codes are also provided for each term at its main alphabetical entry point. The three-digit number indicates the broad category to which that term belongs. The codes are useful for identifying other Descriptors that are conceptually related to the term, but that do not necessarily appear in the term's main display. (See p. xxv for a complete list of the categories, and the Descriptor Group Display for lists of all Descriptors assigned within each category and having the same Group Code number.)

In the example below, the number 540 near the term's Add Date shows that SEX FAIRNESS is in the Descriptor Group 540, "Bias and Equity."

SEX FAIRNESS *Aug. 1978*
CIJE: 257 RIE: 970 GC: 540
SN The correction of sex bias or discrimination (note: use for descriptions of materials, procedures, activities, or programs that treat the sexes equitably)

Postings Notes

As an additional aid to users, a Postings Note is provided for each Descriptor at its main alphabetical entry point. This notation appears above the Scope Note and indicates the number of times—as of July 1986—that the term was used as a Major or Minor Descriptor or Identifier in *RIE* and *CIJE*.

EQUAL EDUCATION *Jul. 1966*
CIJE: 2,290 RIE: 3,174 GC: 540

Examination of the counts for a Descriptor may lead the user to check a term's NTs or RTs before the search strategy is formulated completely. For example, a term with 3,000 postings will not be searched easily manually, but one or more of its NTs could be. On the other hand, a term with only 15 postings might suggest that the searcher also consider including the term's RTs or even its BTs in the search strategy.

> NOTE: All terms in the ERIC *Thesaurus* have actually been used in indexing (either in their present form or a close variant form). Terms showing zero postings are generally very new terms replacing earlier obsolete terms, e.g., VIDEODISKS (0 postings) was added in August 1986 to replace the earlier VIDEODISC RECORDINGS (300+ postings). Even though ERIC provides posting transfers from old to new in such situations, such transfers are not reflected in the ERIC database until general reloads are performed. The last such general reload was in December 1980. (See discussion under "Transferred Descriptors," p. viii. All Descriptors like VIDEODISC RECORDINGS, that have been removed from the *Thesaurus* since December 1980 and that must still be considered in retrospective searching, are listed there.)
>
> Postings counts for any Descriptor added to the *Thesaurus* after December 1980 may include the usage that term had as an earlier Identifier. For example, GENEALOGY, added as a Descriptor in January 1985, was earlier an Identifier and its postings count reflects its usage in both the Descriptor and Identifier fields. Identifier-to-Descriptor conversions are provided by ERIC, but, as with Descriptor transfers, are not actually reflected in the database until the next general reload. (See also discussion on p. xvi.)

Invalid Descriptors

Occasionally, Descriptors have been added to the *Thesaurus* that, because of inherent ambiguity or subsequent indexing practices, have been used with such little consistency that their usefulness in retrieval has been diminished. Such Descriptors, when discovered, are generally deleted as usable terms in the *Thesaurus*. They are reentered as invalid or "dead" terms. Each Invalid Descriptor has two characteristics: a "life span" notation indicating the span of time that the term was actually used in indexing, and a Scope Note intended to indicate how the term was used and to lead indexers and searchers to more precise or meaningful terminology.

LANGUAGE INSTRUCTION (1966 1980)
Mar. 1980
SN Invalid descriptor—used for both foreign and native language instruction—see "second language instruction," "english instruction," or "native language instruction"

STRUCTURAL ANALYSIS (1966 1980)
Mar. 1980
SN Invalid descriptor—originally intended as a linguistics term but used indiscriminately—see "structural analysis (linguistics)" and "structural analysis (science)"— see also such descriptors as "cognitive structures," "chemical analysis," "literary criticism," and "group structure," or such identifiers as "musical analysis," "structure of knowledge," and "structural learning"

> NOTE: Postings for all Invalid Descriptors are still accessible online, and Invalid Descriptors must often be coordinated with other Descriptors to achieve comprehensive searching. A list of ERIC's Invalid Descriptors is provided on p. viii.

ROTATED DESCRIPTOR DISPLAY

The Rotated Display (see p. 269) provides an alphabetical index to all words found in Descriptors or their USE references in the *Thesaurus*. A single-word term will file in only one location, a two-word term will file in two locations, etc. Examples for the Descriptors LIFELONG LEARNING and CROSS CULTURAL STUDIES will illustrate:

LIFELONG LEARNING

LEARNING LABORATORIES
LANGUAGE LEARNING LEVELS (1967 1980)
———► LIFELONG LEARNING
MASTERY LEARNING

URBAN LIFE Use URBAN CULTURE
———► LIFELONG EDUCATION Use LIFELONG LEARNING
———► LIFELONG LEARNING
LIFETIME SPORTS

CROSS CULTURAL STUDIES

CROSS AGE TEACHING
CROSS CULTURAL COMMUNICATION Use INTERCULTURAL COMMUNICATION
———► CROSS CULTURAL STUDIES
CROSS CULTRUAL TESTS Use CULTURE FAIR TESTS
CROSS CULTURAL TRAINING
CROSS EYES Use STRABISMUS

CULTURAL OPPORTUNITIES
CULTURAL PLURALISM
———► CROSS CULTURAL STUDIES
CROSS CULTURAL TESTS Use CULTURE FAIR TESTS
CROSS CULTURAL TRAINING

BLACK STUDIES
CASE STUDIES
CORRELATION STUDIES Use CORRELATION
———► CROSS CULTURAL STUDIES
CROSS SECTIONAL STUDIES
UNIFIED STUDIES CURRICULUM

The Rotated Descriptor Display is useful in determining all usages of a particular word in the *Thesaurus,* without respect to its position in a multiword Descriptor or USE reference. This Display tends to group related terms when they often may be separated in the main Alphabetical Display. This grouping aids indexers in more thoroughly examining the *Thesaurus* for the most specific Descriptors, helps searchers translate inquiries into the language of the system, and also helps Clearinghouse staff and lexicographers in structuring new Descriptors.

> NOTE: Indexers and searchers are cautioned not to restrict their examination of the *Thesaurus* to the Rotated Display, since a special meaning of a term is not always obvious without reading the Scope Note.

HIERARCHICAL DISPLAY

The Hierarchical Display (see p. 459) provides so-called "generic trees" for each Descriptor. That is, a Descriptor may have both Broader and Narrower Terms. The Hierarchical Display, therefore, depicts entire families of Descriptors related by class membership, providing complete two-way visibility of the broader-narrower relationships of all main (indexable) terms in the *Thesaurus*. Each generic tree is carried to its farthest extreme in both directions.

A sample generic tree for the term LANGUAGE SKILLS is shown below.

::ABILITY
:SKILLS
LANGUAGE SKILLS
.AUDIOLINGUAL SKILLS
..LISTENING SKILLS
..SPEECH SKILLS
.COMMUNICATIVE COMPETENCE (LANGUAGES)
..THRESHOLD LEVEL (LANGUAGES)
.READING SKILLS
..READING COMPREHENSION
..READING RATE
.VOCABULARY SKILLS
.WRITING SKILLS

The Broader Term (BT) SKILLS is identified by a colon; multiple colons indicate successively higher levels of BTs (ABILITY). Narrower Terms (NTs) are identified by periods—AUDIOLINGUAL SKILLS, COMMUNICATIVE COMPETENCE (LANGUAGES), READING SKILLS, VOCABULARY SKILLS, and WRITING SKILLS. Multiple periods indicate successively lower levels of NTs. Thus, for example, LISTENING SKILLS and SPEECH SKILLS are NTs to AUDIOLINGUAL SKILLS.

The Hierarchical Display serves as a valuable tool for indexers in their attempts to index documents to the most appropriate level of specificity and for searchers in developing comprehensive search strategies.

NOTE: The Hierarchical Display is filed letter-by-letter, e.g., LANGUAGES files before LANGUAGE SKILLS. The main Alphabetical Display is filed word-by-word.

Computer searching a broader term (BT) will not automatically retrieve citations posted by a narrower term (NT); searches requiring postings of both a BT and an NT would need to include both terms.

DESCRIPTOR GROUPS

The *Thesaurus of ERIC Descriptors*—like many similar vocabulary authorities—incorporates a system of broad categories into which all Descriptors are grouped. The purpose of these Descriptor Groups is to provide an easy access point, especially for users unfamiliar with the terms included in the *Thesaurus*. The Descriptor Groups, in a sense, offer a "table of contents" to the vocabulary. The Descriptor Group Code appears within the main entry of each term in the Alphabetical Display of the *Thesaurus* (see p. xxiii).

As part of the system-wide Vocabulary Improvement Project (1977 to 1980), the Descriptor Group categories and the term assignments were revised. The current Descriptor Groups and their codes are listed below:

Groups Related to LEARNING AND DEVELOPMENT
110 LEARNING AND PERCEPTION
120 INDIVIDUAL DEVELOPMENT AND CHARACTERISTICS

Groups Related to PHYSICAL AND MENTAL CONDITIONS
210 HEALTH AND SAFETY
220 DISABILITIES
230 MENTAL HEALTH
240 COUNSELING

Groups Related to EDUCATIONAL PROCESSES AND STRUCTURES
310 THE EDUCATIONAL PROCESS: CLASSROOM PERSPECTIVES
320 THE EDUCATIONAL PROCESS: SCHOOL PERSPECTIVES
330 THE EDUCATIONAL PROCESS: SOCIETAL PERSPECTIVES
340 EDUCATIONAL LEVELS, DEGREES, AND ORGANIZATIONS
350 CURRICULUM ORGANIZATION
360 STUDENTS, TEACHERS, SCHOOL PERSONNEL

Groups Related to CURRICULUM AREAS
400 SUBJECTS OF INSTRUCTION
410 AGRICULTURE AND NATURAL RESOURCES
420 ARTS
430 HUMANITIES
440 LANGUAGES
450 LANGUAGE AND SPEECH
460 READING
470 PHYSICAL EDUCATION AND RECREATION
480 MATHEMATICS
490 SCIENCE AND TECHNOLOGY

Groups Related to HUMAN SOCIETY
510 THE INDIVIDUAL IN SOCIAL CONTEXT
520 SOCIAL PROCESSES AND STRUCTURES
530 SOCIAL PROBLEMS
540 BIAS AND EQUITY
550 HUMAN GEOGRAPHY
560 PEOPLES AND CULTURES

Groups Related to SOCIAL/ECONOMIC ENTERPRISE
610 GOVERNMENT AND POLITICS
620 ECONOMICS AND FINANCE
630 LABOR AND EMPLOYMENT
640 OCCUPATIONS
650 BUSINESS, COMMERCE, AND INDUSTRY

Groups Related to INFORMATION AND COMMUNICATIONS
710 INFORMATION/COMMUNICATIONS SYSTEMS
720 COMMUNICATIONS MEDIA
730 PUBLICATION/DOCUMENT TYPES

Groups Related to RESEARCH AND MEASUREMENT
810 RESEARCH AND THEORY
820 MEASUREMENT
830 TESTS AND SCALES

Groups Related to FACILITIES AND EQUIPMENT
910 EQUIPMENT
920 FACILITIES

The Descriptors assigned to each of these groups are listed alphabetically within each group in the Descriptor Group Display (see p. 570).

Each term in the *Thesaurus* is assigned to one Descriptor Group and to only one. This principle of single-group assignment reflects guidelines established to determine the placement of Descriptors which, because of the breadth of their scope, *could* be assigned to more than one group. Terms are assigned to groups based upon (1) the broadest application of the term in indexing or (2) the way the term has been used most frequently in indexing. Thus terms that have been scoped to include subject areas outside of the field of education may be assigned to the "Groups Related to EDUCATIONAL PROCESSES AND STRUCTURES" because, in the ERIC database, the terms are used most frequently in this manner. These two guidelines also reflect the assignment of terms that were not entirely appropriate to any existing Descriptor Group.

ALPHABETICAL DESCRIPTOR DISPLAY

The Alphabetical Descriptor Display is the primary arrangement of the *Thesaurus.* It is the only display containing the complete records of all *Thesaurus* terms. All valid Descriptors (main terms), invalid Descriptors ("dead" terms), and USE references appear in this display interfiled alphabetically word-by-word.

ABBREVIATIONS *Jan. 1969*
CIJE: 39 RIE: 49 GC: 710
UF Acronyms
RT Mnemonics
Orthographic Symbols
Shorthand
Written Language

ABILITY *Jul. 1966*
CIJE: 340 RIE: 315 GC: 120
SN The degree of actual power present in an organism or system to perform a given physical or mental act (note: use a more specific term if possible)
NT Academic Ability
Cognitive Ability
Competence
Language Proficiency
Leadership
Nonverbal Ability
Skills
Spatial Ability
Verbal Ability
RT Ability Grouping
Ability Identification
Achievement
Aptitude
Aspiration
Difficulty Level
Disabilities
Gifted
Performance
Productivity
Qualifications
Readiness
Talent

ABILITY GROUPING *Jul. 1966*
CIJE: 298 RIE: 329 GC: 310
SN Selection or classification of students for schools, classes, or other educational programs based on differences in ability or achievement
BT Homogeneous Grouping
RT Ability
Ability Identification
Academic Ability
Academic Achievement
Advanced Placement
Flexible Progression
Instructional Program Divisions
Nongraded Instructional Grouping
Track System (Education)

ABILITY IDENTIFICATION *Jul. 1966*
CIJE: 247 RIE: 326 GC: 110
SN Identification of an individual's actual power to perform various acts (note: do not confuse with "talent identification," which frequently refers to innate aptitudes or abilities, especially of the gifted)
BT Identification
RT Ability
Ability Grouping
Aptitude Tests
Critical Incidents Method
Factor Analysis
Handicap Identification
Intelligence Tests
Probationary Period
Skill Analysis
Talent Identification

Able Students (1966 1978)
USE ACADEMICALLY GIFTED

Abnormal Psychology
USE PSYCHOPATHOLOGY

ABORTIONS *Sep. 1970*
CIJE: 137 RIE: 97 GC: 210
RT Contraception
Family Planning
Gynecology
Medical Services
Obstetrics
Pregnancy
Surgery

Abreaction
USE CATHARSIS

Absence (Students)
USE ATTENDANCE

Absence (Teachers)
USE TEACHER ATTENDANCE

Absolute Humidity
USE HUMIDITY

Absolute Pressure
USE PRESSURE (PHYSICS)

Abstract Bibliographies
USE ANNOTATED BIBLIOGRAPHIES

ABSTRACT REASONING *Jul. 1966*
CIJE: 713 RIE: 576 GC: 110
SN Process of reaching conclusions through the use of symbols or generalizations rather than on concrete factual information
UF Abstraction Levels (1968 1980)
Intellectualization (1970 1980)
NT Generalization
BT Cognitive Processes
RT Comprehension
Concept Formation
Deduction
Formal Operations
Language Processing
Logical Thinking

ABSTRACTING *Jul. 1966*
CIJE: 67 RIE: 105 GC: 710
BT Documentation
Writing (Composition)
RT Abstracts
Annotated Bibliographies
Indexing
Information Retrieval
Library Technical Processes
Technical Writing

Abstraction Levels (1968 1980)
USE ABSTRACT REASONING

Abstraction Tests (1967 1980)
USE COGNITIVE TESTS

ABSTRACTS *Jul. 1966*
CIJE: 177 RIE: 1778 GC: 730
UF Annotations
BT Reference Materials
RT Abstracting
Annotated Bibliographies
Indexes

Abused Children
USE CHILD ABUSE

Abused Elderly
USE ELDER ABUSE

Abused Women
USE BATTERED WOMEN

ACADEMIC ABILITY *Jul. 1966*
CIJE: 802 RIE: 895 GC: 120
SN The degree of actual competence to perform in scholastic or educational activities (note: for potential competence, use "academic aptitude" -- for measured achievement, use "academic achievement")
UF Scholastic Ability
Student Ability (1966 1980)
BT Ability
RT Ability Grouping
Academic Achievement
Academically Gifted
Academic Aptitude
Academic Aspiration
Aptitude Treatment Interaction
Cognitive Ability
College Entrance Examinations
High Risk Students
Intelligence
Scholarship
Spatial Ability
Student Characteristics
Verbal Ability

ACADEMIC ACHIEVEMENT *Jul. 1966*
CIJE: 7975 RIE: 10596 GC: 310
UF Academic Performance (1966 1974)
Academic Progress
Academic Success
Educational Achievement
Educational Level
Scholastic Achievement
Student Achievement
NT Educational Attainment
Student Promotion
BT Achievement
RT Ability Grouping
Academic Ability
Academically Gifted
Academic Aptitude
Academic Aspiration
Academic Failure
Academic Probation
Academic Records
Academic Standards
Achievement Gains
Achievement Rating
Advanced Placement
Class Rank
College Entrance Examinations
Degree Requirements
Educationally Disadvantaged
Educational Mobility
Grades (Scholastic)
Grading
Graduation Requirements
Instructional Effectiveness
Intelligence
Knowledge Level
Learning Plateaus
Learning Problems
Mastery Learning
Mastery Tests
Mathematics Achievement
Minimum Competency Testing
Performance
Performance Contracts
Reading Achievement
Report Cards
Scholarship
School Effectiveness
Student Characteristics
Student Evaluation
Student Improvement
Teacher Effectiveness
Teacher Influence

ACADEMIC ADVISING *Nov. 1981*
CIJE: 163 RIE: 211 GC: 240
SN A decision-making process in which a student and academic adviser use the resources of a postsecondary education institution to analyze and coordinate learning experiences consistent with the student's needs, abilities, interests, values, and goals (note: use "educational counseling" for academic advising at the secondary school level)
BT Educational Counseling
RT College Credits
College Curriculum
Faculty Advisers
Higher Education
Postsecondary Education

ACADEMIC APTITUDE *Jul. 1966*
CIJE: 380 RIE: 435 GC: 120
SN An individual's potential ability to perform in scholastic or educational activities (note: for actual academic competence, use "academic ability" -- for measured achievement, use "academic achievement")
UF Scholastic Potential
Student Aptitude
BT Aptitude
RT Academic Ability
Academic Achievement
Academically Gifted
Academic Aspiration
Aptitude Treatment Interaction
High Risk Students
Intelligence
Student Characteristics
Vocational Aptitude

ACADEMIC ASPIRATION *Jul. 1966*
CIJE: 290 RIE: 721 GC: 120
SN Desire to reach a level of academic achievement
BT Aspiration
RT Academic Ability
Academic Achievement
Academic Aptitude
College Bound Students
College Choice
Educational Mobility
Learning Motivation
Noncollege Bound Students
Student Motivation
Teacher Motivation

Academic Calendars
USE SCHOOL SCHEDULES

Academic Curriculum
USE ACADEMIC EDUCATION

ACADEMIC DEANS *Mar. 1980*
CIJE: 59 RIE: 71 GC: 360
SN Administrative officials in a college or other school who are responsible for the instructional program
UF Chief Academic Officers
Deans Of Faculty
Deans Of Instruction
BT Deans
RT Academic Education
College Administration
College Curriculum
Deans Of Students
Instructional Leadership

Academic Departments
USE DEPARTMENTS

Academic Disciplines
USE INTELLECTUAL DISCIPLINES

ACADEMIC EDUCATION *Jul. 1966*
CIJE: 301 RIE: 426 GC: 400
SN Relating to college preparatory studies or liberal and classical studies in higher education, as contrasted with technical or vocational studies
UF Academic Curriculum
Academic Subjects
BT Education
RT Academic Deans
College Preparation
English For Academic Purposes
General Education
Humanities Instruction
Intellectual Disciplines
Liberal Arts

Academic Enrichment (1966 1980)
USE ENRICHMENT

Academic Environment
USE EDUCATIONAL ENVIRONMENT

ACADEMIC FAILURE *Jul. 1966*
CIJE: 243 RIE: 291 GC: 310
UF Scholastic Failure
NT Reading Failure
BT Failure
RT Academic Achievement
Academic Probation
Dropouts
Expulsion
Grade Repetition
High Risk Students
Learning Disabilities
Learning Problems
Low Achievement
Student Promotion
Suspension
Underachievement

ACADEMIC FREEDOM *Jul. 1966*
CIJE: 769 RIE: 533 GC: 330
SN Right of teacher or student to be free from external or institutional coercion, censorship, or other forms of restrictive interference in academic matters
UF Teaching Freedom
RT Censorship
Civil Liberties
College Environment
Educational Environment
Faculty College Relationship
Freedom Of Information
Freedom Of Speech
Institutional Autonomy
Intellectual Freedom
Personal Autonomy
Professional Autonomy
Student Rights
Teacher Rights
Teacher Welfare
Teaching Conditions

Academic Games
USE EDUCATIONAL GAMES

Academic Learning Time
USE TIME ON TASK

ACADEMIC LIBRARIES *Jan. 1979*
CIJE: 632 RIE: 687 GC: 710
SN Libraries forming part of, or associated with, institutions of higher education
NT College Libraries
BT Libraries
RT Archives
Depository Libraries
Learning Resources Centers
Research Libraries
Special Libraries

Academic Malpractice
USE EDUCATIONAL MALPRACTICE

Academic Performance (1966 1974)
USE ACADEMIC ACHIEVEMENT

ACADEMIC PERSISTENCE *Mar. 1980*
CIJE: 150 RIE: 477 GC: 310
SN Continuance of a student in school or college enrollment
BT Persistence
RT Attendance
Dropout Research
Dropouts
School Holding Power
Stopouts
Student Attrition
Withdrawal (Education)

Academic Planning
USE EDUCATIONAL PLANNING

ACADEMIC PROBATION *Jul. 1966*
CIJE: 20 RIE: 69 GC: 320
SN Trial period in which the student must improve academic achievement to avoid being dismissed
UF Scholastic Probation
BT Probationary Period
RT Academic Achievement
Academic Failure
Academic Standards
Expulsion
Grades (Scholastic)
Student School Relationship
Suspension

Academic Progress
USE ACADEMIC ACHIEVEMENT

Academic Promotion
USE STUDENT PROMOTION

ACADEMIC RANK (PROFESSIONAL) *Jul. 1966*
CIJE: 204 RIE: 258 GC: 320
SN Professional position or standing among faculty members of an educational institution, usually expressed by official titles (professor, lecturer, instructor, etc.)
UF Faculty Rank
Professorial Rank
BT Employment Level
RT Adjunct Faculty
College Faculty
Degrees (Academic)
Faculty
Faculty Promotion
Nontenured Faculty
Professors
Seniority
Teacher Employment Benefits
Teacher Promotion
Tenure
Tenured Faculty

ACADEMIC RECORDS *Jul. 1966*
CIJE: 97 RIE: 183 GC: 320
UF Transcripts (Academic)
BT Student Records
RT Academic Achievement
College Credits
Credits
Grades (Scholastic)
Profiles
Registrars (School)
Report Cards
Student Evaluation

Academic Senates
USE COLLEGE GOVERNING COUNCILS

ACADEMIC STANDARDS *Jul. 1966*
CIJE: 1111 RIE: 1051 GC: 320
SN Criteria established by an educational institution to determine levels of student achievement
NT Graduation Requirements
BT Standards
RT Academic Achievement
Academic Probation
Accreditation (Institutions)
Accrediting Agencies
Admission (School)
Admission Criteria
Back To Basics
Competency Based Education
Competency Based Teacher Education
Degree Requirements
Educational Malpractice
Grade Inflation
Grade Point Average
Mastery Learning
Mastery Tests
Minimum Competency Testing
Open Enrollment
Pass Fail Grading
Scholarly Journals
Selective Admission
Selective Colleges

Academic Subjects
USE ACADEMIC EDUCATION

Academic Success
USE ACADEMIC ACHIEVEMENT

Academically Disadvantaged
USE EDUCATIONALLY DISADVANTAGED

ACADEMICALLY GIFTED *Jan. 1978*
CIJE: 443 RIE: 564 GC: 360
SN Persons with superior ability or aptitude for academic learning
UF Able Students (1966 1978)
Gifted Students
Superior Students (1966 1978)
BT Gifted
RT Academic Ability
Academic Achievement
Academic Aptitude
Acceleration (Education)
Advanced Placement
Advanced Placement Programs
Advanced Students
Honors Curriculum
Mainstreaming

ACADEMICALLY HANDICAPPED (1966 1980) *Mar. 1980*
CIJE: 70 RIE: 101 GC: 220
SN Invalid descriptor -- used inconsistently in indexing -- see such descriptors as "academic ability," "academic aptitude," "learning disabilities," "learning problems," "slow learners," "educationally disadvantaged," etc.

Accelerated Courses (1966 1980)
USE ACCELERATION (EDUCATION)

Accelerated Programs (1966 1980)
USE ACCELERATION (EDUCATION)

ACCELERATION (EDUCATION) *Nov. 1982*
CIJE: 47 RIE: 29 GC: 310
SN The process of progressing through an educational program at a rate faster than that of the average student
UF Accelerated Courses (1966 1980)
Accelerated Programs (1966 1980)
Acceleration (1966 1982) (Education)
Three Year Bachelors Degrees #
Time Shortened Degree Programs
BT Flexible Progression
RT Academically Gifted
Advanced Courses
Advanced Placement
Advanced Placement Programs
Advanced Students
Age Grade Placement
Early Admission
Honors Curriculum
Student Placement
Transitional Programs

ACCELERATION (PHYSICS) *Aug. 1982*
CIJE: 67 RIE: 2 GC: 490
SN Change in velocity of an object with respect to time
UF Acceleration (1966 1982) (Physics)
Deceleration
BT Motion
RT Fluid Mechanics
Force
Gravity (Physics)
Kinetic Molecular Theory
Kinetics
Mechanics (Physics)
Physics
Quantum Mechanics
Weight (Mass)

Acceleration (1966 1982) (Education)
USE ACCELERATION (EDUCATION)

Acceleration (1966 1982) (Physics)
USE ACCELERATION (PHYSICS)

ACCESS TO EDUCATION *Sep. 1977*
CIJE: 784 RIE: 1470 GC: 330
SN Accessibility of an education to a student, including access to appropriate educational institutions, materials, and personnel (note: do not confuse with "accessibility (for disabled)")
UF Educational Access
BT Educational Opportunities
RT Admission (School)
Admission Criteria
Attendance
College Admission
College Attendance
Compulsory Education
Distance Education
Education
Educational Demand
Educational Discrimination
Educational Finance
Educational Supply
Enrollment
Equal Education
Extension Education
External Degree Programs
Free Education
Geographic Location
Higher Education
Intellectual Freedom
Noncampus Colleges
Nondiscriminatory Education
Nontraditional Education
Open Enrollment
Open Universities
Prior Learning
School Location
Special Education
Student Costs
Student Financial Aid

Access To Ideas
USE INTELLECTUAL FREEDOM

ACCESS TO INFORMATION *Aug. 1986*
CIJE: 159 RIE: 58 GC: 710
SN Means, processes, or rights related to obtaining or providing information -- also, the degree of information availability
NT Freedom Of Information
RT Information Needs
Information Retrieval
Information Seeking
Information Services
Information Sources
Information Transfer
Information Utilization
Users (Information)

ACCESSIBILITY (FOR DISABLED) *Mar. 1980*
CIJE: 142 RIE: 268 GC: 220
SN Characteristics of facilities, programs, and services that allow them to be entered or used by individuals despite visual, hearing, mobility, or other impairments (note: for physical access, coordinate with "physical mobility" or "visually handicapped mobility" -- prior to jun80, see also "architectural barriers")
UF Barrier Free Environment (For Disabled)
RT Architecture
Deaf Interpreting
Design Requirements
Disabilities
Older Adults
Physical Mobility
Sensory Aids
Structural Elements (Construction)

ACCIDENT PREVENTION *Jul. 1966*
CIJE: 307 RIE: 376 GC: 210
BT Prevention
RT Accidents
Alarm Systems
Safety
Safety Education
Safety Equipment

ACCIDENTS *Jul. 1966*
CIJE: 98 RIE: 140 GC: 210
NT School Accidents
Traffic Accidents
RT Accident Prevention
Emergency Medical Technicians
Emergency Squad Personnel
Injuries
Rescue
Safety
Safety Education

ACCOUNTABILITY *Apr. 1974*
CIJE: 2265 RIE: 2424 GC: 330
SN Being held responsible and answerable for specified results or outcomes of an activity (over which one has authority)
UF Educational Accountability (1970 1980)
BT Responsibility
RT Audits (Verification)
Codes Of Ethics
Competence
Competency Based Education
Competency Based Teacher Education
Consumer Protection
Contracts
Cost Effectiveness
Educational Malpractice
Evaluation Criteria
Evaluation Utilization
Legal Responsibility
Malpractice
Management By Objectives
Organizational Objectives
Outcomes Of Education
Performance
Productivity
Program Effectiveness
Program Validation
Quality Control
Relevance (Education)
School Effectiveness
Validated Programs

ACCOUNTANTS *Jul. 1966*
CIJE: 34 RIE: 21 GC: 640
NT Certified Public Accountants
BT Professional Personnel
RT Accounting
Farm Accounts
Financial Services

ACCOUNTING *Jul. 1966*
CIJE: 352 RIE: 405 GC: 620
NT Property Accounting
School Accounting
BT Technology
RT Accountants
Bookkeeping
Budgeting
Business Education
Business Skills
Certified Public Accountants
Farm Accounts
Financial Audits
Financial Services
Office Occupations Education

ACCREDITATION (INSTITUTIONS) *Jul. 1966*
CIJE: 681 RIE: 903 GC: 330
BT Certification
RT Academic Standards
Accrediting Agencies
Eligibility
Institutional Evaluation
Quality Control
Standards
State Standards

= Two or more Descriptors are used to represent this term.
The term's main entry shows the appropriate coordination.

ACCREDITING AGENCIES *Mar. 1980*
CIJE: 158 RIE: 149 GC: 330
SN Agencies that establish operating standards for educational or professional institutions and programs, determine the extent to which the standards are met, and publicly announce their findings
UF Accrediting Associations
BT Agencies
RT Academic Standards
Accreditation (Institutions)
Agency Role
Educational Quality
Institutional Evaluation
State Licensing Boards
State Standards

Accrediting Associations
USE ACCREDITING AGENCIES

ACCULTURATION *Jul. 1966*
CIJE: 532 RIE: 871 GC: 560
SN Absorption into any group of certain features of the culture
UF Assimilation (Cultural)
RT Biculturalism
Cultural Pluralism
Culture
Immigrants
Refugees
Social Integration
Subcultures

Acetylene Welding
USE WELDING

ACHIEVEMENT *Jul. 1966*
CIJE: 1017 RIE: 1434 GC: 120
SN Level of attainment or proficiency in relation to a standard measure of performance, or, of success in bringing about a desired end (note: use a more specific term if possible)
UF Achievement Level
Achievement Prediction #
NT Academic Achievement
Black Achievement
Graduation
High Achievement
Knowledge Level
Low Achievement
Mathematics Achievement
Overachievement
Reading Achievement
Scholarship
Underachievement
RT Ability
Achievement Gains
Achievement Need
Achievement Rating
Achievement Tests
Aptitude
Aspiration
Competence
Evaluation
Expectation
Failure
Fear Of Success
Gifted
Improvement
Learning Plateaus
Mastery Learning
Mastery Tests
Motivation
National Competency Tests
Performance
Performance Factors
Prerequisites
Productivity
Qualifications
Recognition (Achievement)
Standards
Success
Talent

Achievement Comparison
USE ACHIEVEMENT RATING

ACHIEVEMENT GAINS *Jul. 1966*
CIJE: 294 RIE: 1160 GC: 310
SN Progress towards attaining a specified level of proficiency or bringing about a desired end
UF Achievement Losses
BT Improvement
RT Academic Achievement
Achievement
Achievement Rating
Achievement Tests
Knowledge Level
Mathematics Achievement
Reading Achievement
Success

Achievement Incentives
USE INCENTIVES

Achievement Level
USE ACHIEVEMENT

Achievement Losses
USE ACHIEVEMENT GAINS

Achievement Motivation
USE ACHIEVEMENT NEED

ACHIEVEMENT NEED *Jul. 1966*
CIJE: 331 RIE: 221 GC: 120
SN Forces that drive an individual to improve, succeed, or excel in things considered both difficult and important (note: prior to mar80, the instruction "achievement motivation, use motivation" was carried in the thesaurus)
UF Achievement Motivation
BT Motivation
Psychological Needs
RT Achievement
Affiliation Need
Aspiration
Competition
Failure
Goal Orientation
Status Need
Success

Achievement Prediction
USE ACHIEVEMENT; PREDICTION

ACHIEVEMENT RATING *Jul. 1966*
CIJE: 301 RIE: 437 GC: 820
SN Judging individuals' or groups' levels of attainment or accomplishment and assigning quantitative or qualitative values to them according to specified standards or procedures
UF Achievement Comparison
NT Grading
BT Measurement
RT Academic Achievement
Achievement
Achievement Gains
Achievement Tests
Awards
Merit Rating
Merit Scholarships
Rating Scales
Report Cards
Student Evaluation

ACHIEVEMENT TESTS *Jul. 1966*
CIJE: 1104 RIE: 2270 GC: 830
SN Tests used to measure knowledge, abilities, understanding, or skills acquired from academic work (note: prior to mar80, the instruction "achievement prediction, use achievement tests" was carried in the thesaurus)
NT Equivalency Tests
Mastery Tests
National Competency Tests
BT Tests
RT Achievement
Achievement Gains
Achievement Rating
Aptitude Tests
College Entrance Examinations
Criterion Referenced Tests
Educational Testing
Essay Tests
Language Tests
Listening Comprehension Tests
Mathematics Tests
Norm Referenced Tests
Open Book Tests
Performance Tests
Reading Tests
Science Tests

Acoustic Barriers
USE ACOUSTIC INSULATION

ACOUSTIC INSULATION *Nov. 1969*
CIJE: 31 RIE: 17 GC: 920
UF Acoustic Barriers
Anechoic Materials
Sound Barriers
Sound Insulation
Soundproofing
BT Structural Elements (Construction)
RT Acoustical Environment
Acoustics
Construction (Process)
Construction Materials
Noise (Sound)

ACOUSTIC PHONETICS *Jul. 1966*
CIJE: 148 RIE: 107 GC: 450
SN Study of the physical properties of speech sounds during transmission and as they are heard by the listener (note: prior to mar80, the use of this term was not restricted by a scope note)
BT Phonetics
RT Acoustics
Artificial Speech
Auditory Perception
Consonants
Distinctive Features (Language)
Sound Spectrographs
Speech

ACOUSTICAL ENVIRONMENT *Jul. 1966*
CIJE: 112 RIE: 121 GC: 920
UF Sonic Environment
NT Noise (Sound)
BT Physical Environment
RT Acoustic Insulation
Acoustics
Building Design
Design Requirements
Environmental Influences
Human Factors Engineering
Interior Design
Music Facilities
Theaters

ACOUSTICS *Jul. 1966*
CIJE: 281 RIE: 151 GC: 490
SN Science of sound -- includes the study of the transmission of sound through various media or in various enclosures
UF Sound
Sound Transmission
Sound Waves
NT Psychoacoustics
BT Sciences
RT Acoustical Environment
Acoustic Insulation
Acoustic Phonetics
Architecture
Audio Equipment
Auditory Stimuli
Noise (Sound)
Physics
Sound Effects

Acronyms
USE ABBREVIATIONS

ACTING *Jul. 1966*
CIJE: 192 RIE: 185 GC: 420
BT Theater Arts
RT Characterization
Creative Dramatics
Drama
Dramatics
Film Industry
Film Production
Film Study
Opera
Pantomime
Readers Theater

Action Learning
USE EXPERIENTIAL LEARNING

Action Programs (Community) (1966 1980)
USE COMMUNITY ACTION

ACTION RESEARCH *Jul. 1966*
CIJE: 140 RIE: 219 GC: 810
SN Research designed to yield practical results that are immediately applicable to a specific situation or problem (note: as of oct81, use as a minor descriptor for examples of this kind of research -- use as a major descriptor only as the subject of a document)
BT Research
RT Community Action
Evaluation Methods
Methods Research
Operations Research
Program Improvement
Social Action
Theory Practice Relationship

Activated Sludge
USE SLUDGE

ACTIVISM *Jan. 1969*
CIJE: 1436 RIE: 698 GC: 610
SN Movements and procedures designed to force changes in rules and practices or to hasten social change
UF Militancy
Political Protest
Student Protest
BT Social Behavior
RT Alienation
Citizen Participation
Civil Disobedience
Demonstrations (Civil)
Dissent
Lobbying
Participation
Political Attitudes
Revolution
School Boycotts
Social Action
Social Attitudes
Student Alienation
Student College Relationship
Student Rights
Student Subcultures
Terrorism

ACTIVITIES *Jul. 1966*
CIJE: 250 RIE: 472 GC: 120
SN Pursuits or experiences, usually requiring active participation, engaged in because they are of intrinsic interest or lead to some goal sought by the participant (note: use a more specific term if possible)
NT Art Activities
Creative Activities
Cultural Activities
Enrichment Activities
Games
Group Activities
Health Activities
Individual Activities
Integrated Activities
Learning Activities
Lobbying
Music Activities
Outdoor Activities
Physical Activities
Play
Recreational Activities
Review (Reexamination)
School Activities
Science Activities
Television Viewing
Travel
RT Activity Units
Experience
Interests
Participation

Activity Learning (1968 1978)
USE EXPERIENTIAL LEARNING

Activity Level (Motor Behavior)
USE PHYSICAL ACTIVITY LEVEL

ACTIVITY UNITS *Jul. 1966*
CIJE: 116 RIE: 440 GC: 350
SN Units of study in which students participate actively, usually in informal groups
UF Experience Units
BT Units Of Study
RT Activities
Discovery Learning
Experiential Learning
Learning Activities
Resource Units

Ad Valorem Tax
USE PROPERTY TAXES

Adages
USE PROVERBS

= Two or more Descriptors are used to represent this term.
The term's main entry shows the appropriate coordination.

Adaptability (Personality)
USE ADJUSTMENT (TO ENVIRONMENT); PERSONALITY TRAITS

ADAPTATION LEVEL THEORY *Jul. 1966*
CIJE: 55 RIE: 34 GC: 810
SN Theory that individuals judge the magnitude of any stimuli (e.g., loudness, size, wieght) by establishing subjective scales against which the stimuli are measured
BT Behavior Theories
RT Arousal Patterns
Attention
Cognitive Processes
Individual Psychology
Novelty (Stimulus Dimension)
Perception

ADAPTED PHYSICAL EDUCATION *Mar. 1974*
CIJE: 92 RIE: 204 GC: 220
SN Adaptation of regular physical education programs to meet the needs of disabled individuals
BT Physical Education
Special Education
RT Disabilities
Individualized Instruction
Physical Activities

Adaptive Behavior
USE ADJUSTMENT (TO ENVIRONMENT)

ADAPTIVE BEHAVIOR (OF DISABLED) *Apr. 1982*
CIJE: 65 RIE: 44 GC: 220
SN Ways in which disabled individuals meet the personal and social standards of their age or cultural groups
BT Adjustment (To Environment)
RT Coping
Daily Living Skills
Disabilities
Emotional Adjustment
Mental Disorders
Mental Retardation
Normalization (Handicapped)
Self Care Skills
Social Adjustment

Adaptive Equipment (Disabled)
USE ASSISTIVE DEVICES (FOR DISABLED)

ADAPTIVE TESTING *Feb. 1984*
CIJE: 14 RIE: 75 GC: 820
SN Testing that involves selecting test items according to the examinee's ability as shown by responses to earlier test items
UF Computerized Adaptive Testing #
Computerized Tailored Testing #
Flexilevel Testing
Response Contingent Testing
Stradaptive Testing
Tailored Testing
BT Testing
RT Bayesian Statistics
Computer Assisted Testing
Individual Testing
Item Banks
Latent Trait Theory
Response Style (Tests)
Sequential Approach
Test Items

ADDITION *Oct. 1968*
CIJE: 217 RIE: 201 GC: 480
BT Arithmetic
RT Division
Multiplication
Subtraction

Additional Aid
USE EQUALIZATION AID

Addresses
USE SPEECHES

ADHESIVES *Jul. 1969*
CIJE: 7 RIE: 10 GC: 910
UF Cements (Adhesives)
Glues
Pastes (Adhesives)
Sealants
Stickers
BT Supplies
RT Art Materials
Construction Materials
Finishing

ADJECTIVES *Jul. 1966*
CIJE: 253 RIE: 142 GC: 450
BT Form Classes (Languages)
RT Adverbs
Morphology (Languages)
Semantic Differential
Sentence Structure
Syntax
Vocabulary

ADJUNCT FACULTY *Aug. 1986*
CIJE: 7 RIE: 4 GC: 360
SN Temporary, part-time, or other auxiliary faculty of a school or college, usually with limited duties and benefits and often primarily employed outside of academia
UF Adjunct Professors
BT Faculty
RT Academic Rank (Professional)
College Faculty
Multiple Employment
Nontenured Faculty
Part Time Faculty
Specialists
Teachers

Adjunct Professors
USE ADJUNCT FACULTY

ADJUSTMENT (TO ENVIRONMENT) *Jul. 1966*
CIJE: 2344 RIE: 1788 GC: 230
SN A condition of harmonious relation to the environment, in which internal needs are satisfied and external demands are met (note: for specificity on this aspect, use "well being") -- also, the process of altering internal or external factors to attain this harmonious condition
UF Adaptability (Personality) #
Adaptive Behavior
Adjustment Problems (1966 1980)
Group Adjustment
Individual Adjustment
Maladjustment (1966 1980)
Personal Adjustment (1966 1980)
NT Adaptive Behavior (Of Disabled)
Coping
Emotional Adjustment
Social Adjustment
Student Adjustment
Vocational Adjustment
BT Behavior
RT Adjustment Counselors
Attitude Change
Behavior Problems
Counseling
Ecology
Environment
Health
Individual Development
Intelligence
Maturity (Individuals)
Mental Health
Orientation
Personality Problems
Psychoeducational Methods
Rehabilitation
Rehabilitation Counseling
Stress Management
Therapy
Well Being

ADJUSTMENT COUNSELORS *Jul. 1966*
CIJE: 32 RIE: 15 GC: 240
BT Counselors
RT Adjustment (To Environment)
School Counseling
School Social Workers

Adjustment Problems (1966 1980)
USE ADJUSTMENT (TO ENVIRONMENT)

ADMINISTRATION *Jul. 1966*
CIJE: 1655 RIE: 2450 GC: 320
SN Planning, organizing, directing, and controlling human or material resources to accomplish predetermined goals (note: use a more specific term if possible)
UF Management (1966 1980)
NT Building Operation
Business Administration
Construction Management
Educational Administration
Energy Management
Farm Management
Home Management
Institutional Administration
Management By Objectives
Middle Management
Money Management
Office Management
Personnel Management
Program Administration
Public Administration
Research Administration
Supervision
Time Management
BT Governance
RT Administrative Change
Administrative Organization
Administrative Policy
Administrative Principles
Administrative Problems
Administrator Responsibility
Administrator Role
Administrators
Budgeting
Committees
Coordination
Governing Boards
Management Information Systems
Management Systems
Management Teams
Managerial Occupations
Organization
Organizational Effectiveness
Participative Decision Making
Planning
Policy Formation
Quality Circles
Resource Allocation
Staff Utilization

ADMINISTRATIVE AGENCIES (1966 1980) *Mar. 1980*
CIJE: 111 RIE: 219 GC: 610
SN Invalid descriptor -- used inconsistently in indexing -- see "agencies" or "public agencies"

ADMINISTRATIVE CHANGE *Jul. 1966*
CIJE: 204 RIE: 276 GC: 320
SN Change in administrative personnel (reassignment, dismissal, etc.) or in the structure of an organization's administration
BT Change
RT Administration
Administrators
Change Strategies
Organizational Change
Organizational Development

Administrative Occupations
USE MANAGERIAL OCCUPATIONS

ADMINISTRATIVE ORGANIZATION *Jul. 1966*
CIJE: 1183 RIE: 1919 GC: 320
SN The manner in which the authority, duties, and responsibilities of administrators, managers, or supervisors are structured -- also, the structuring of an organization so that these duties, etc. can be carried out
NT Centralization
Decentralization
Departments
Management Teams
Participative Decision Making
BT Organization
RT Administration
Bureaucracy
Governance
Governing Boards
Informal Organization
Management Systems
Middle Management
Power Structure
School Organization

Administrative Personnel (1966 1980)
USE ADMINISTRATORS

Administrative Planning
USE PLANNING

ADMINISTRATIVE POLICY *Jul. 1966*
CIJE: 962 RIE: 1537 GC: 320
SN Statement of an administrative body outlining the principles and practices to be followed with respect to specific matters -- also, the fixed procedures and practices of administration
NT Board Of Education Policy
BT Policy
RT Administration
Administrative Principles
Administrator Guides
Administrator Responsibility
Interdistrict Policies
Professional Autonomy

ADMINISTRATIVE PRINCIPLES *Aug. 1968*
CIJE: 262 RIE: 365 GC: 320
SN The assumptions, beliefs, values, or accepted practices that underlie administrative policy and activity (note: prior to mar80, the use of this term was not restricted by a scope note)
BT Standards
RT Administration
Administrative Policy
Administrator Guides
Administrator Responsibility
Business Administration
Educational Principles
Supervisory Methods

ADMINISTRATIVE PROBLEMS *Jul. 1966*
CIJE: 698 RIE: 692 GC: 320
SN (Note: use a more precise term if possible)
BT Problems
RT Administration

Administrative Secretaries
USE SECRETARIES

Administrative Teams
USE MANAGEMENT TEAMS

Administrator Appraisal
USE ADMINISTRATOR EVALUATION

ADMINISTRATOR ATTITUDES *Jul. 1966*
CIJE: 1505 RIE: 2165 GC: 320
SN Attitudes, opinions, or views held by administrators
UF Administrator Opinions
BT Attitudes
RT Administrator Characteristics
Administrator Evaluation
Administrators
Employers

Administrator Background (1967 1980)
USE ADMINISTRATOR CHARACTERISTICS

ADMINISTRATOR CHARACTERISTICS *Jul. 1966*
CIJE: 601 RIE: 600 GC: 320
SN Background and personal qualities of administrators (note: do not confuse with "administrator qualifications")
UF Administrator Background (1967 1980)
RT Administrator Attitudes
Administrator Evaluation
Administrator Qualifications
Administrators
Administrator Selection
Individual Characteristics

ADMINISTRATOR EDUCATION *Nov. 1971*
CIJE: 981 RIE: 1368 GC: 400
SN Preservice programs, usually offered by colleges or universities, designed to prepare individuals for administrative or managerial positions (note: prior to mar80, this term was not restricted to preservice programs -- see also "management development")
UF Administrator Preparation
Management Education (1967 1980)
BT Professional Education
RT Administrator Qualifications
Business Administration Education
Management Development
Public Administration Education
Specialist In Education Degrees
Supervisor Qualifications

ADMINISTRATOR EVALUATION *Jul. 1966*
CIJE: 381 RIE: 455 GC: 320
SN The evaluation or appraisal of administrators or managers (note: prior to mar80, the use of this term was not restricted by a scope note)
UF Administrator Appraisal
BT Personnel Evaluation
RT Administrator Attitudes
Administrator Characteristics
Administrator Qualifications
Administrators
Administrator Selection
Assessment Centers (Personnel)
Faculty Evaluation

ADMINISTRATOR GUIDES *Jul. 1966*
CIJE: 431 RIE: 1506 GC: 730
BT Guides
RT Administrative Policy
Administrative Principles
Administrator Responsibility
Administrator Role
Administrators
Board Administrator Relationship
Faculty Handbooks
Guidelines
Program Guides
Teacher Administrator Relationship

Administrator Opinions
USE ADMINISTRATOR ATTITUDES

Administrator Preparation
USE ADMINISTRATOR EDUCATION

ADMINISTRATOR QUALIFICATIONS *Jul. 1966*
CIJE: 315 RIE: 381 GC: 320
SN The education, experience, and physical, social, and mental characteristics that determine an individual's fitness for an administrative position
BT Qualifications
RT Administrator Characteristics
Administrator Education
Administrator Evaluation
Administrators
Administrator Selection
Employment Qualifications
Leadership Qualities
Supervisor Qualifications

ADMINISTRATOR RESPONSIBILITY *Jul. 1966*
CIJE: 1059 RIE: 1107 GC: 320
BT Responsibility
RT Administration
Administrative Policy
Administrative Principles
Administrator Guides
Administrator Role
Administrators
Educational Responsibility
Faculty Handbooks
Faculty Workload
Leadership Responsibility
Teacher Responsibility

ADMINISTRATOR ROLE *Jul. 1966*
CIJE: 2758 RIE: 2756 GC: 320
SN Functions and behaviors expected of or performed by persons in administrative positions
RT Administration
Administrator Guides
Administrator Responsibility
Administrators
Faculty Handbooks

ADMINISTRATOR SELECTION *Jul. 1966*
CIJE: 282 RIE: 263 GC: 320
SN Process of assessing and choosing candidates for administrative positions
BT Personnel Selection
RT Administrator Characteristics
Administrator Evaluation
Administrator Qualifications
Administrators
Assessment Centers (Personnel)
Faculty Recruitment
Search Committees (Personnel)

Administrator Teacher Relationship
USE TEACHER ADMINISTRATOR RELATIONSHIP

Administrator Training
USE MANAGEMENT DEVELOPMENT

ADMINISTRATORS *Mar. 1980*
CIJE: 2366 RIE: 3364 GC: 360
SN Persons involved in planning, organizing, directing, and controlling human or material resources to accomplish predetermined goals
UF Administrative Personnel (1966 1980)
Business Officials (Industry)
Chief Administrators (1967 1980)
Community School Directors (1967 1980) #
Management Personnel
Managers
School Administrators
NT Admissions Officers
Assistant Principals
Coordinators
Deans
Department Heads
Medical Record Administrators
Personnel Directors
Presidents
Principals
Registrars (School)
Research Directors
School Business Officials
Student Financial Aid Officers
Superintendents
Supervisors
Trustees
Vocational Directors
BT Personnel
RT Administration
Administrative Change
Administrator Attitudes
Administrator Characteristics
Administrator Evaluation
Administrator Guides
Administrator Qualifications
Administrator Responsibility
Administrator Role
Administrator Selection
Board Administrator Relationship
Educational Administration
Faculty
Middle Management
Professional Personnel
Teacher Administrator Relationship

ADMISSION (SCHOOL) *Jul. 1966*
CIJE: 404 RIE: 398 GC: 320
UF Matriculation
School Admission
NT College Admission
Early Admission
Open Enrollment
Selective Admission
RT Academic Standards
Access To Education
Admission Criteria
Admissions Counseling
Admissions Officers
Competitive Selection
Educational Supply
Eligibility
Enrollment
Late Registration
Placement
Portfolios (Background Materials)
School Catalogs
School Choice
School Registration
Schools
Student Placement
Student Recruitment
Transitional Programs

ADMISSION CRITERIA *Jul. 1966*
CIJE: 1256 RIE: 1419 GC: 320
UF Student Selection
BT Criteria
RT Academic Standards
Access To Education
Admission (School)
Admissions Officers
College Applicants
College Entrance Examinations
Competitive Selection
Early Admission
Enrollment Influences
Open Enrollment
Prerequisites
Prior Learning
Residence Requirements
School Catalogs
Selective Admission
Student Recruitment
Transfer Policy

Admission Tests (Higher Education)
USE COLLEGE ENTRANCE EXAMINATIONS

Admission Tests (Occupational)
USE OCCUPATIONAL TESTS

ADMISSIONS COUNSELING *Mar. 1980*
CIJE: 147 RIE: 53 GC: 240
UF Admissions Counselors (1973 1980)
BT Educational Counseling
RT Admission (School)
Admissions Officers
College Admission
College Bound Students
College Day
College Preparation
College School Cooperation
Post High School Guidance
Referral
Student Placement

Admissions Counselors (1973 1980)
USE ADMISSIONS COUNSELING

ADMISSIONS OFFICERS *Mar. 1980*
CIJE: 86 RIE: 28 GC: 360
SN Administrative officials, usually at postsecondary institutions, with principal responsibility for the recruitment, selection, and admission of students
BT Administrators
School Personnel
RT Admission (School)
Admission Criteria
Admissions Counseling
College Administration
College Admission
College Preparation
Enrollment Projections
Middle Management
Registrars (School)
School Administration
Student Personnel Workers
Student Recruitment

Adolescence (1966 1980)
USE ADOLESCENTS

ADOLESCENT DEVELOPMENT *Mar. 1980*
CIJE: 276 RIE: 156 GC: 120
BT Individual Development
RT Adolescents
Developmental Stages
Developmental Tasks
Youth

ADOLESCENT LITERATURE *Oct. 1973*
CIJE: 565 RIE: 278 GC: 430
SN Any reading material written primarily for, or read widely by, youth of secondary school age
BT Literature
RT Adolescents
Childrens Literature
Reading Materials

Adolescent Parents
USE EARLY PARENTHOOD

ADOLESCENTS *Jul. 1966*
CIJE: 5454 RIE: 3451 GC: 120
SN Approximately 13-17 years of age
UF Adolescence (1966 1980)
Teenagers (1966 1980)
BT Age Groups
RT Adolescent Development
Adolescent Literature
Children
Early Parenthood
Preadolescents
Secondary School Students
Youth

ADOPTED CHILDREN *Jul. 1966*
CIJE: 107 RIE: 59 GC: 510
BT Children
RT Adoption
Biological Parents
Child Welfare
Foster Children
Foster Family

ADOPTION *Jul. 1966*
CIJE: 158 RIE: 191 GC: 520
RT Adopted Children
Biological Parents
Child Welfare
Foster Care
Foster Family
Kinship
Placement

ADOPTION (IDEAS) *Jul. 1966*
CIJE: 401 RIE: 673 GC: 520
SN Process of accepting new ideas or practices
RT Attitude Change
Change Strategies
Diffusion (Communication)
Discovery Processes
Evaluation Utilization
Information Utilization
Innovation
Linking Agents
Pilot Projects
Research Utilization
Theory Practice Relationship

ADULT BASIC EDUCATION *Jul. 1966*
CIJE: 619 RIE: 2137 GC: 340
SN Education provided for adults at the elementary level (through grade 8), usually with emphasis on communicative, computational, and social skills (note: also appears in the list of mandatory educational level descriptors)
UF Fundamental Education (Adults)
BT Adult Education
Elementary Education
RT Adult Literacy
Adult Reading Programs
Basic Skills
Functional Literacy
High School Equivalency Programs
Literacy Education
Migrant Adult Education
Primary Education
Public School Adult Education

Adult Characteristics (1967 1980)
USE ADULTS; INDIVIDUAL CHARACTERISTICS

ADULT COUNSELING *Jul. 1966*
CIJE: 191 RIE: 304 GC: 240
BT Counseling
RT Adult Dropouts
Adult Programs
Adults
Career Counseling
Counselors

ADULT DAY CARE *Mar. 1978*
CIJE: 23 RIE: 33 GC: 220
SN Care of disabled adults (handicapped, elderly, and those who are ill) during the day, in which health and social services are offered by professional and paraprofessional staff
BT Social Services
RT Adult Programs
Adults
Attendants
Day Care
Home Health Aides
Older Adults
Visiting Homemakers

ADULT DEVELOPMENT *Jul. 1966*
CIJE: 453 RIE: 489 GC: 120
SN Physiological, psychological, and sociological growth or maturation occurring throughout an adult's lifetime
BT Individual Development
RT Adult Education
Adult Learning
Adults
Aging (Individuals)
Developmental Stages
Developmental Tasks
Educational Gerontology
Gerontology
Midlife Transitions

ADULT DROPOUTS *Jul. 1966*
CIJE: 34 RIE: 115 GC: 510
SN Adults who withdraw from an activity before its completion
BT Adults
Dropouts

= Two or more Descriptors are used to represent this term.
The term's main entry shows the appropriate coordination.

RT Adult Counseling
Adult Education

ADULT EDUCATION *Jul. 1966*
CIJE: 4434 RIE: 7655 GC: 340
SN Providing or coordinating purposeful learning activities for adults
UF Adult Education Programs (1966 1980) #
Further Education
NT Adult Basic Education
Adult Vocational Education
Continuing Education
Labor Education
Migrant Adult Education
Parent Education
Preretirement Education
Public School Adult Education
Veterans Education
BT Education
RT Adult Development
Adult Dropouts
Adult Learning
Adult Programs
Adult Reading Programs
Adults
Adult Students
Andragogy
Community Education
Continuing Education Centers
Continuing Education Units
Correctional Education
Educational Gerontology
Extension Education
High School Equivalency Programs
Lifelong Learning
Noncredit Courses
Nonschool Educational Programs
Postsecondary Education
Professional Continuing Education
Professional Education
Refresher Courses
Retraining
Special Degree Programs
Training Allowances
Womens Education

Adult Education Programs (1966 1980)
USE ADULT EDUCATION; ADULT PROGRAMS

ADULT EDUCATORS *Jul. 1966*
CIJE: 351 RIE: 566 GC: 360
SN Teachers who specialize in adult education
BT Teachers
RT Extension Agents
Instructor Coordinators
Trainers

ADULT FARMER EDUCATION *Jul. 1966*
CIJE: 115 RIE: 150 GC: 410
SN Vocational education in agriculture for adults aged 25 or over engaged in production agriculture (note: for younger adults, use "young farmer education")
BT Adult Vocational Education
Agricultural Education
RT Farmers
Farm Visits
Rural Education
Rural Extension
Young Farmer Education

ADULT FOSTER CARE *Aug. 1982*
CIJE: 2 RIE: 2 GC: 220
SN Care of disabled adults (handicapped, elderly, and those who are ill) in private homes -- caretakers are usually not close relatives and are paid an established fee for their services (note: do not confuse with "residential care")
UF Foster Homes (1970 1982) (Adults)
BT Social Services
RT Adult Programs
Adults
Attendants
Boarding Homes
Deinstitutionalization (Of Disabled)
Foster Care
Foster Family
Group Homes
Home Health Aides
Older Adults
Visiting Homemakers

Adult Leaders (1967 1980)
USE LEADERS

ADULT LEARNING *Jul. 1966*
CIJE: 585 RIE: 855 GC: 110
BT Learning
RT Adult Development
Adult Education
Adult Programs
Adults
Adult Students
Andragogy
Lifelong Learning

ADULT LITERACY *Jul. 1970*
CIJE: 461 RIE: 726 GC: 460
UF Illiterate Adults (1966 1980) #
BT Literacy
RT Adult Basic Education
Adult Reading Programs
Adults
Functional Literacy
Functional Reading
Illiteracy
Literacy Education
Reading Skills
Writing Skills

ADULT PROGRAMS *Jul. 1966*
CIJE: 757 RIE: 1628 GC: 340
SN Programs for adults (note: when appropriate, coordinate with an age-leveler, i.e., "young adults," "middle aged adults," "older adults," or with a mandatory educational level descriptor)
UF Adult Education Programs (1966 1980) #
NT Adult Reading Programs
High School Equivalency Programs
BT Programs
RT Adult Counseling
Adult Day Care
Adult Education
Adult Foster Care
Adult Learning
Adults
Alumni Education
Evening Programs

ADULT READING PROGRAMS *Jul. 1966*
CIJE: 113 RIE: 316 GC: 460
BT Adult Programs
Reading Programs
RT Adult Basic Education
Adult Education
Adult Literacy
Correctional Education
Functional Literacy
Functional Reading
High School Equivalency Programs
Literacy Education
Reading Instruction
Speed Reading

Adult Runaways
USE RUNAWAYS

ADULT STUDENTS *Jul. 1966*
CIJE: 990 RIE: 1498 GC: 360
BT Adults
Students
RT Adult Education
Adult Learning
Andragogy
Continuing Education
Evening Students
Married Students
Nontraditional Students
Reentry Students
Self Supporting Students
Single Students
Special Degree Programs
Stopouts

ADULT VOCATIONAL EDUCATION *Jul. 1966*
CIJE: 255 RIE: 1167 GC: 400
SN Education for adults or out-of-school youth aged 16 or over engaged in or preparing to enter an occupation
NT Adult Farmer Education
Young Farmer Education
BT Adult Education
Vocational Education
RT Career Ladders
Cooperative Education
Industrial Training
Job Training
Public School Adult Education
Retraining
Trade And Industrial Education
Vocational Rehabilitation

ADULTS *Jul. 1966*
CIJE: 3444 RIE: 3265 GC: 120
SN Approximately 18+ years of age
UF Adult Characteristics (1967 1980) #
NT Adult Dropouts
Adult Students
Middle Aged Adults
Older Adults
Young Adults
BT Age Groups
RT Adult Counseling
Adult Day Care
Adult Development
Adult Education
Adult Foster Care
Adult Learning
Adult Literacy
Adult Programs
Parents

ADVANCE ORGANIZERS *Mar. 1977*
CIJE: 159 RIE: 190 GC: 310
SN Preview questions and comments used to increase learners' comprehension and recall
BT Instructional Materials
RT Comprehension
Directed Reading Activity
Intentional Learning
Learning
Learning Activities
Reading
Reading Improvement
Recall (Psychology)
Retention (Psychology)
Study Guides
Study Skills
Teaching Methods
Verbal Learning

ADVANCED COURSES *Mar. 1980*
CIJE: 86 RIE: 61 GC: 350
SN Courses beyond the introductory or basic level
BT Courses
RT Acceleration (Education)
Advanced Placement
Advanced Placement Programs
Advanced Students
Elective Courses
Introductory Courses
Majors (Students)
Required Courses

Advanced Credit Examinations
USE EQUIVALENCY TESTS

Advanced Education
USE HIGHER EDUCATION

Advanced Nations
USE DEVELOPED NATIONS

ADVANCED PLACEMENT *Jul. 1966*
CIJE: 88 RIE: 143 GC: 320
SN Permitting students with academic credit or test scores beyond minimum requirements to bypass coursework (note: prior to mar80, this term was not restricted by a scope note -- do not confuse with the more specific "advanced placement programs")
BT Placement
RT Ability Grouping
Academic Achievement
Academically Gifted
Acceleration (Education)
Advanced Courses
Advanced Placement Programs
Advanced Students
College Entrance Examinations
Equivalency Tests
Honors Curriculum
Prior Learning
Student Placement

ADVANCED PLACEMENT PROGRAMS *Jul. 1966*
CIJE: 90 RIE: 124 GC: 320
SN Programs adopted in u.s. in 1956 under which high school students can take college entrance examination board (ceeb) tests, receive college credit for acceptable scores, and be placed into sophomore-level college classes (note: prior to mar80, the use of this term was not restricted by a scope note)
BT Programs
RT Academically Gifted
Acceleration (Education)
Advanced Courses
Advanced Placement
Advanced Students
Articulation (Education)
College Bound Students
College Entrance Examinations
College School Cooperation
Educational Attainment
Equivalency Tests

ADVANCED PROGRAMS (1966 1980) *Mar. 1980*
CIJE: 38 RIE: 60 GC: 320
SN Invalid descriptor -- used inconsistently in indexing -- see such descriptors as "acceleration (education)," "advanced courses," "advanced placement programs," etc.

Advanced Standing Examinations
USE EQUIVALENCY TESTS

ADVANCED STUDENTS *Jul. 1966*
CIJE: 111 RIE: 95 GC: 360
SN Students studying a particular subject at an advanced level (note: do not confuse with "academically gifted")
BT Students
RT Academically Gifted
Acceleration (Education)
Advanced Courses
Advanced Placement
Advanced Placement Programs

Advancement
USE PROMOTION (OCCUPATIONAL)

ADVANTAGED *Mar. 1980*
CIJE: 44 RIE: 56 GC: 510
SN Individuals or groups who have high status in a particular society for reasons of race, sex, ethnicity, economics, language, geographic location, environment, education, etc.
UF Culturally Advantaged (1967 1980)
Economically Advantaged
Socially Advantaged
BT Groups
RT Affluent Youth
Cultural Differences
Disadvantaged
Living Standards
Middle Class
Quality Of Life
Social Status
Upper Class

ADVENTITIOUS IMPAIRMENTS *Mar. 1980*
CIJE: 23 RIE: 7 GC: 220
SN Conditions resulting from illness or injury during the developmental or adult years
UF Adventitiously Handicapped (1975 1980)
BT Disabilities
RT Congenital Impairments
Diseases
Exceptional Persons
Injuries

Adventitiously Handicapped (1975 1980)
USE ADVENTITIOUS IMPAIRMENTS

ADVENTURE EDUCATION *Mar. 1980*
CIJE: 78 RIE: 131 GC: 400
SN Type of outdoor education that attempts to teach environmental awareness and build self-confidence through activities that involve risk or stress, such as rock climbing, survival training, etc.
UF Adventure Learning
BT Outdoor Education
RT Camping
Discovery Learning
Environmental Education
Experiential Learning
Field Experience Programs
Field Trips
Interdisciplinary Approach
Outdoor Activities
Risk

Self Concept
Stress Management
Trails

Adventure Learning
USE ADVENTURE EDUCATION

Adverbials
USE ADVERBS

ADVERBS *Jul. 1966*
CIJE: 116 RIE: 70 GC: 450
UF Adverbials
BT Form Classes (Languages)
RT Adjectives
Morphology (Languages)
Sentence Structure
Syntax
Verbs
Vocabulary

ADVERTISING *Mar. 1980*
CIJE: 571 RIE: 680 GC: 720
SN Persuasive presentation or promotion of ideas, goods, or services by means of mass communication
NT Television Commercials
BT Publicity
RT Commercial Art
Consumer Protection
Mass Media
Merchandising
Persuasive Discourse
Political Campaigns
Propaganda
Salesmanship

Advertising Art
USE COMMERCIAL ART

Advisory Boards
USE ADVISORY COMMITTEES

ADVISORY COMMITTEES *Jul. 1966*
CIJE: 569 RIE: 1444 GC: 320
UF Advisory Boards
BT Committees
RT Blue Ribbon Commissions
Consultants
Governing Boards
Needs Assessment
Participative Decision Making
Planning Commissions
Policy Formation
Research Committees
Search Committees (Personnel)
Specialists

ADVOCACY *Nov. 1981*
CIJE: 126 RIE: 147 GC: 520
SN Full and active support for and representation of an individual, group, cause, or idea
UF Citizen Advocacy
NT Child Advocacy
RT Citizen Participation
Legal Aid
Needs
Services
Social Action
Social Behavior

Advocates (Law)
USE LAWYERS

Aerobic Dance
USE AEROBICS; DANCE

AEROBICS *Jun. 1984*
CIJE: 41 RIE: 19 GC: 470
SN Method of achieving physical conditioning and fitness by stimulating heart (pulse rate) and lung (oxygen intake) activity through successively longer periods of vigorous exercise, thereby gradually expanding the capacity of the cardiovascular and respiratory systems
UF Aerobic Dance #
BT Exercise
RT Cardiovascular System
Heart Rate
Physical Fitness

AEROSPACE EDUCATION *Apr. 1972*
CIJE: 339 RIE: 182 GC: 490
UF Aerospace Science Education
BT Education
RT Aerospace Technology
Air Transportation
Astronomy
Aviation Technology
Aviation Vocabulary
Engineering Education
Science Education
Space Sciences
Technical Education

AEROSPACE INDUSTRY *Jul. 1966*
CIJE: 37 RIE: 97 GC: 650
BT Manufacturing Industry
RT Aerospace Technology
Air Transportation
Aviation Mechanics
Aviation Technology
Aviation Vocabulary
Electromechanical Technology

Aerospace Science Education
USE AEROSPACE EDUCATION

Aerospace Sciences
USE AEROSPACE TECHNOLOGY

AEROSPACE TECHNOLOGY *Jul. 1966*
CIJE: 225 RIE: 230 GC: 490
UF Aerospace Sciences
NT Aviation Technology
BT Technology
RT Aerospace Education
Aerospace Industry
Aircraft Pilots
Air Traffic Control
Air Transportation
Astronomy
Engineering
Engineering Technology
Lunar Research
Physical Sciences
Satellites (Aerospace)
Space Exploration
Space Sciences

AESTHETIC EDUCATION *Mar. 1972*
CIJE: 628 RIE: 319 GC: 420
NT Art Appreciation
Film Study
Music Appreciation
BT Education
RT Aesthetic Values
Art Education
Cultural Enrichment
Dance Education
Music Education
Visual Literacy

Aesthetic Judgment
USE AESTHETIC VALUES; VALUE JUDGMENT

AESTHETIC VALUES *Oct. 1982*
CIJE: 62 RIE: 25 GC: 520
SN Objective or subjective principles and standards related to human preferences among, or assessments of, artistic forms and qualities (in music, literature, visual arts, etc.)
UF Aesthetic Judgment #
BT Values
RT Aesthetic Education
Art
Art Expression
Cultural Context
Design Preferences
Perception
Sensory Experience
Social Values

AFFECTION *Jul. 1966*
CIJE: 65 RIE: 47 GC: 120
BT Psychological Needs
RT Affiliation Need
Emotional Experience
Interpersonal Attraction

AFFECTIVE BEHAVIOR *Feb. 1969*
CIJE: 1202 RIE: 1190 GC: 120
SN Behavior that involves or expresses emotions, feelings, or sentiments
UF Emotional Behavior
BT Behavior
RT Affective Measures
Affective Objectives
Attachment Behavior
Attitudes
Desensitization
Emotional Development
Emotional Response
Interests
Prosocial Behavior
Psychological Patterns

Affective Education
USE HUMANISTIC EDUCATION

AFFECTIVE MEASURES *Mar. 1980*
CIJE: 256 RIE: 294 GC: 830
SN Procedures or devices used to obtain quantified descriptions of an individual's feelings, emotional states, or dispositions
UF Affective Tests (1971 1980)
BT Measures (Individuals)
RT Affective Behavior
Affective Objectives
Association Measures
Attitude Measures
Emotional Adjustment
Emotional Development
Emotional Response
Forced Choice Technique
Interest Inventories
Personality Measures
Projective Measures
Self Concept Measures

AFFECTIVE OBJECTIVES *Jul. 1969*
CIJE: 439 RIE: 775 GC: 310
SN Behavioral objectives which emphasize changes in interest, attitudes, and values, or a degree of adjustment, acceptance, or rejection
BT Behavioral Objectives
RT Affective Behavior
Affective Measures
Cognitive Objectives
Emotional Development
Humanistic Education
Psychomotor Objectives

Affective Tests (1971 1980)
USE AFFECTIVE MEASURES

AFFILIATED SCHOOLS *Jul. 1966*
CIJE: 15 RIE: 43 GC: 340
SN Schools providing experiences for student teachers or teacher interns, although not integral parts of teacher education institutions
UF Cooperating Schools
BT Schools
RT College School Cooperation
Cooperating Teachers
Cooperative Education
Educational Cooperation
Elementary Schools
Field Experience Programs
Laboratory Schools
Preservice Teacher Education
Secondary Schools
Student Teaching
Teacher Education
Teaching Experience

AFFILIATION NEED *Jul. 1966*
CIJE: 98 RIE: 47 GC: 120
SN Psychological drive for association with others
NT Peer Acceptance
BT Psychological Needs
RT Achievement Need
Affection
Status Need

AFFIRMATIVE ACTION *Nov. 1975*
CIJE: 670 RIE: 973 GC: 540
SN Positive action taken to overcome underrepresentation of women and minority groups in employment (including career advancement programs) and in the makeup of post-secondary student bodies, as compared to the composition of the area population
RT College Admission
College Desegregation
Desegregation Methods
Desegregation Plans
Disadvantaged
Educational Discrimination
Educational Opportunities
Employed Women
Employment Practices
Employment Services
Equal Education
Equal Opportunities (Jobs)
Ethnic Distribution
Faculty Integration
Handicap Discrimination
Minority Groups
Nondiscriminatory Education
Nontraditional Occupations
Personnel Integration
Personnel Policy
Personnel Selection
Quotas
Racial Balance
Racial Bias
Racial Composition
Racial Discrimination
Racial Integration
Racially Balanced Schools
Recruitment
Religious Discrimination
Reverse Discrimination
School Demography
Selective Admission
Sex Bias
Sex Discrimination
Sex Fairness
Teacher Integration
Tokenism

AFFLUENT YOUTH *Jul. 1966*
CIJE: 22 RIE: 18 GC: 510
BT Youth
RT Advantaged
Socioeconomic Status
Upper Class

African American Studies (1969 1977)
USE BLACK STUDIES

African Americans
USE BLACKS

AFRICAN CULTURE *Jul. 1966*
CIJE: 346 RIE: 375 GC: 560
BT Culture
RT African History
African Literature
Black Culture
Middle Eastern History
Middle Eastern Studies
Non Western Civilization
Tribes

AFRICAN HISTORY *Jul. 1969*
CIJE: 151 RIE: 191 GC: 430
BT History
RT African Culture
African Literature
Black Culture
Black History
Black Literature
Black Studies
Middle Eastern History
Middle Eastern Studies
Non Western Civilization
Slavery
Tribes

AFRICAN LANGUAGES *Jul. 1966*
CIJE: 75 RIE: 201 GC: 440
NT Akan
Bantu Languages
Basaa
Bini
Dyula
Ewe
Fulani
Ga
Gbaya
Ibo
Igbo
Luo
Mandingo
Mende
Mossi
Nembe
Sango
Sara
Susu
Wolof
Yoruba
BT Languages
RT African Literature
Language Classification

= Two or more Descriptors are used to represent this term.
The term's main entry shows the appropriate coordination.

AFRICAN LITERATURE *May. 1970*
CIJE: 59 RIE: 71 GC: 430
BT Literature
RT African Culture
African History
African Languages
Black Literature

AFRIKAANS *May. 1970*
CIJE: 4 RIE: 18 GC: 440
BT Indo European Languages
RT Dutch

Afro Americans
USE BLACKS

AFRO ASIATIC LANGUAGES *Jul. 1966*
CIJE: 7 RIE: 16 GC: 440
NT Berber Languages
Chad Languages
Semitic Languages
Somali
BT Languages

After School Activities (1967 1980)
USE AFTER SCHOOL PROGRAMS

AFTER SCHOOL CENTERS *Jul. 1966*
CIJE: 4 RIE: 16 GC: 920
BT Educational Facilities
RT After School Education
After School Programs
Study Centers

After School Day Care (1978 1983)
USE AFTER SCHOOL PROGRAMS; SCHOOL AGE DAY CARE

AFTER SCHOOL EDUCATION *Jul. 1966*
CIJE: 14 RIE: 46 GC: 350
UF After School Tutoring (1966 1980) #
BT Education
RT After School Centers
After School Programs
Compensatory Education
Extended School Day
Supplementary Education

AFTER SCHOOL PROGRAMS *Jul. 1966*
CIJE: 79 RIE: 155 GC: 350
UF After School Activities (1967 1980)
After School Day Care (1978 1983) #
BT Programs
RT After School Centers
After School Education
Enrichment Activities
Extended School Day
Extracurricular Activities
School Activities
School Age Day Care
School Recreational Programs

After School Tutoring (1966 1980)
USE AFTER SCHOOL EDUCATION; TUTORING

AGE *Jul. 1966*
CIJE: 809 RIE: 1169 GC: 120
UF Age Level
NT Chronological Age
Mental Age
School Entrance Age
BT Individual Characteristics
RT Age Differences
Age Grade Placement
Age Groups
Aging (Individuals)
Aging In Academia
Developmental Stages
Maturity (Individuals)

AGE DIFFERENCES *Jul. 1966*
CIJE: 4082 RIE: 2423 GC: 120
BT Individual Differences
RT Age
Age Groups
Aging Education
Andragogy
Developmental Stages
Generation Gap
Intergenerational Programs

AGE DISCRIMINATION *Mar. 1980*
CIJE: 176 RIE: 145 GC: 540
SN Discriminatory attitudes or practices on account of an individual's age
BT Social Discrimination
RT Aging (Individuals)
Educational Discrimination
Equal Education
Equal Opportunities (Jobs)
Handicap Discrimination
Middle Aged Adults
Older Adults
Racial Discrimination
Retirement
Reverse Discrimination
Sex Discrimination
Social Bias

AGE GRADE PLACEMENT *Jul. 1966*
CIJE: 42 RIE: 72 GC: 320
SN Use of a student's age as the basis for assignment to a grade level or for school entrance -- also, the relationship between age and grade level
UF Age Grade Status
BT Placement
RT Acceleration (Education)
Age
Homogeneous Grouping
Instructional Program Divisions
Nongraded Instructional Grouping
School Entrance Age
School Readiness
Student Placement
Student Promotion

Age Grade Status
USE AGE GRADE PLACEMENT

AGE GROUPS *Jul. 1966*
CIJE: 152 RIE: 360 GC: 120
SN (Note: see also list of age leveling descriptors)
NT Adolescents
Adults
Children
BT Groups
RT Age
Age Differences
Chronological Age
Developmental Stages
Intergenerational Programs
Peer Groups
Youth

Age Level
USE AGE

Aged
USE OLDER ADULTS

AGENCIES *Jul. 1966*
CIJE: 162 RIE: 450 GC: 610
SN Organizations serving the public -- also, administrative units of government (note: use a more specific term if possible)
NT Accrediting Agencies
Private Agencies
Public Agencies
Social Agencies
Urban Renewal Agencies
Voluntary Agencies
Youth Agencies
BT Organizations (Groups)
RT Agency Cooperation
Agency Role
Government (Administrative Body)
Nonprofit Organizations

AGENCY COOPERATION *Mar. 1980*
CIJE: 546 RIE: 1791 GC: 610
SN Cooperation of agencies with each other or with other organizations, groups, etc.
UF Interagency Cooperation (1967 1980)
Interagency Coordination (1967 1980) #
Interagency Planning (1966 1980) #
BT Cooperation
RT Agencies
Cooperative Planning
Educational Cooperation
Institutional Cooperation
Interdistrict Policies
Regional Cooperation
Research Coordinating Units
Shared Resources And Services

Agency Function
USE AGENCY ROLE

AGENCY ROLE *Jul. 1966*
CIJE: 520 RIE: 1185 GC: 610
UF Agency Function
BT Institutional Role
RT Accrediting Agencies
Agencies
Private Agencies
Public Agencies
Social Agencies
State Agencies
Urban Renewal Agencies
Voluntary Agencies
Welfare Agencies
Youth Agencies

AGGRESSION *Jul. 1966*
CIJE: 756 RIE: 492 GC: 230
SN Hostile actions or behavior (note: for forceful behavior that is not hostile, see "assertiveness")
BT Antisocial Behavior
RT Animal Behavior
Assertiveness
Catharsis
Competition
Crime
Hostility
Rape
Terrorism
Violence

AGING (INDIVIDUALS) *Jul. 1980*
CIJE: 453 RIE: 479 GC: 120
SN The physiological and psychological process of growing old
NT Aging In Academia
BT Individual Development
RT Adult Development
Age
Age Discrimination
Aging Education
Developmental Stages
Educational Gerontology
Elder Abuse
Geriatrics
Gerontology
Middle Aged Adults
Midlife Transitions
Older Adults

AGING EDUCATION *Apr. 1982*
CIJE: 42 RIE: 47 GC: 400
SN Educational programs at all levels aimed at helping students gain a personal understanding of the process and problems of growing old (note: use "educational gerontology" for aging education as a professional field of study)
BT Education
RT Age Differences
Aging (Individuals)
Educational Gerontology

AGING IN ACADEMIA *Aug. 1986*
CIJE: RIE: GC: 330
SN The gradual aging of a particular academic staff or the general academic community due to demographics and work-life extensions, with implications for hiring, tenure, salary costs, etc.
UF Aging Professoriate
Graying Of Faculty
BT Aging (Individuals)
RT Age
College Faculty
Faculty
Retirement
Seniority
Teacher Persistence
Teacher Retirement
Teachers
Tenure

Aging Professoriate
USE AGING IN ACADEMIA

Agreements (Formal)
USE CONTRACTS

AGRIBUSINESS *Jul. 1971*
CIJE: 144 RIE: 272 GC: 410
SN All activities pertaining to manufacturing, processing, servicing, and distributing agricultural supplies and products
BT Business
RT Agricultural Education
Agricultural Engineering
Agricultural Machinery
Agricultural Occupations
Agricultural Production
Agricultural Supplies
Agricultural Trends
Agriculture
Distributive Education
Feed Industry
Field Crops
Meat Packing Industry
Off Farm Agricultural Occupations
Producer Services

Agricultural Agents
USE EXTENSION AGENTS

AGRICULTURAL CHEMICAL OCCUPATIONS *Jul. 1966*
CIJE: 17 RIE: 66 GC: 410
BT Off Farm Agricultural Occupations
RT Agriculture
Chemical Engineering
Chemical Industry
Chemistry
Fertilizers
Herbicides
Insecticides
Pesticides

AGRICULTURAL COLLEGES *Jul. 1966*
CIJE: 24 RIE: 84 GC: 340
BT Colleges
RT Agricultural Education
Agricultural Engineering
Agriculture
Experiment Stations
Land Grant Universities
State Colleges

AGRICULTURAL EDUCATION *Jul. 1966*
CIJE: 1795 RIE: 1905 GC: 410
SN Formal preparation, at any level, for an agricultural occupation (note: prior to mar80, this term was a narrower term of "vocational education")
UF Agricultural Education (Vocational) #
Vocational Agriculture (1967 1980) #
Vocational Agriculture Teachers (1967 1980) #
NT Adult Farmer Education
Supervised Farm Practice
Young Farmer Education
BT Education
RT Agribusiness
Agricultural Colleges
Agricultural Engineering
Agricultural Occupations
Agricultural Personnel
Agricultural Production
Agricultural Skills
Agriculture
Extension Agents
Farm Management
Land Grant Universities
Natural Resources
Rural Extension
Technical Education
Vocational Education

Agricultural Education (Vocational)
USE AGRICULTURAL EDUCATION; VOCATIONAL EDUCATION

AGRICULTURAL ENGINEERING *Jul. 1966*
CIJE: 102 RIE: 180 GC: 410
SN Application of engineering principles to agriculture, including soil and water management, rural electrification, processing of agricultural products, and design and use of agricultural machinery
UF Agricultural Mechanics (Subject)
Farm Mechanics (Subject)
BT Engineering
RT Agribusiness
Agricultural Colleges
Agricultural Education
Agricultural Machinery
Agricultural Machinery Occupations
Agriculture
Assembly (Manufacturing)
Farm Management

Agricultural Extension
USE RURAL EXTENSION

Agricultural Labor Disputes (1966 1980)
USE LABOR DEMANDS

AGRICULTURAL LABORERS *Jul. 1966*
CIJE: 88 RIE: 332 GC: 410
SN Unskilled manual workers employed by farms, ranches, or other agricultural operations -- may be regular, seasonal, local, migrant, full-time, or part-time
UF Agricultural Workers
NT Migrant Workers
Seasonal Laborers
BT Agricultural Personnel
Laborers
RT Agriculture
Braceros
Crew Leaders
Farm Labor
Sharecroppers

AGRICULTURAL MACHINERY *Jul. 1966*
CIJE: 57 RIE: 115 GC: 410
BT Equipment
RT Agribusiness
Agricultural Engineering
Agricultural Machinery Occupations
Agriculture
Assembly (Manufacturing)
Diesel Engines
Engines
Fuels
Hydraulics
Machinery Industry
Tractors

AGRICULTURAL MACHINERY OCCUPATIONS *Jul. 1966*
CIJE: 19 RIE: 78 GC: 410
UF Farm Mechanics (Occupation) (1967 1980)
BT Off Farm Agricultural Occupations
RT Agricultural Engineering
Agricultural Machinery
Agriculture
Machinery Industry
Mechanics (Process)

Agricultural Mechanics (Subject)
USE AGRICULTURAL ENGINEERING

Agricultural Migrant Workers
USE MIGRANT WORKERS

Agricultural Migrants
USE MIGRANTS

AGRICULTURAL OCCUPATIONS *Jul. 1966*
CIJE: 90 RIE: 258 GC: 410
NT Farm Occupations
Off Farm Agricultural Occupations
BT Occupations
RT Agribusiness
Agricultural Education
Agricultural Personnel
Agriculture
Farmers
Farm Management
Technical Occupations

AGRICULTURAL PERSONNEL *Jul. 1966*
CIJE: 15 RIE: 46 GC: 410
NT Agricultural Laborers
Agricultural Technicians
Farmers
BT Personnel
RT Agricultural Education
Agricultural Occupations
Agriculture
Animal Caretakers
Extension Agents
Farm Labor

AGRICULTURAL PRODUCTION *Jul. 1966*
CIJE: 211 RIE: 457 GC: 410
SN The provision of plant and animal commodities
UF Crop Production
Livestock Production
RT Agribusiness
Agricultural Education
Agricultural Supplies
Agricultural Trends
Agriculture
Agronomy
Crop Processing Occupations
Farmers
Farm Management
Field Crops
Harvesting
Pesticides
Pests
Plant Growth

Agricultural Research Projects (1966 1981)
USE RESEARCH PROJECTS

AGRICULTURAL SAFETY *Jul. 1966*
CIJE: 16 RIE: 32 GC: 410
BT Safety
RT Agriculture
Safety Education

AGRICULTURAL SKILLS *Jul. 1966*
CIJE: 36 RIE: 155 GC: 410
BT Skills
RT Agricultural Education
Agriculture
Practical Arts

AGRICULTURAL SUPPLIES *Jul. 1966*
CIJE: 5 RIE: 49 GC: 410
UF Farm Supplies
BT Supplies
RT Agribusiness
Agricultural Production
Agricultural Supply Occupations
Agriculture
Feed Industry
Feed Stores
Fertilizers
Herbicides
Insecticides
Pesticides

AGRICULTURAL SUPPLY OCCUPATIONS *Jul. 1966*
CIJE: 10 RIE: 48 GC: 410
BT Off Farm Agricultural Occupations
RT Agricultural Supplies
Agriculture
Feed Industry
Sales Occupations
Sales Workers
Service Occupations

AGRICULTURAL TECHNICIANS *Jul. 1966*
CIJE: 39 RIE: 52 GC: 410
SN Personnel who work in supporting or supplemental capacities with agricultural scientists, engineers, and other professionals, in agricultural production, processing, and distribution
BT Agricultural Personnel
Paraprofessional Personnel
RT Agriculture

AGRICULTURAL TRENDS *Jul. 1966*
CIJE: 52 RIE: 95 GC: 410
RT Agribusiness
Agricultural Production
Agriculture
Trend Analysis

Agricultural Workers
USE AGRICULTURAL LABORERS

AGRICULTURE *Jul. 1966*
CIJE: 334 RIE: 773 GC: 410
NT Agronomy
Animal Husbandry
Harvesting
Horticulture
BT Technology
RT Agribusiness
Agricultural Chemical Occupations
Agricultural Colleges
Agricultural Education
Agricultural Engineering
Agricultural Laborers
Agricultural Machinery
Agricultural Machinery Occupations
Agricultural Occupations
Agricultural Personnel
Agricultural Production
Agricultural Safety
Agricultural Skills
Agricultural Supplies
Agricultural Supply Occupations
Agricultural Technicians
Agricultural Trends
Botany
Dairy Farmers
Entomology
Experiment Stations
Farmers
Farm Management
Farm Occupations
Farm Visits
Feed Industry
Fisheries
Food
Forestry
Genetics
Land Use
Natural Resources
Off Farm Agricultural Occupations
Ornithology
Part Time Farmers
Seasonal Employment
Sharecroppers
Supervised Farm Practice
Tractors
Veterinary Medicine

AGRONOMY *Sep. 1968*
CIJE: 24 RIE: 95 GC: 410
SN Branch of agriculture that deals with field crop production and soil management
UF Crop Planting
BT Agriculture
RT Agricultural Production
Crop Processing Occupations
Fertilizers
Field Crops
Grains (Food)
Harvesting
Herbicides
Insecticides
Land Use
Pesticides
Plant Growth
Plant Pathology
Soil Conservation
Soil Science
Trees
Weeds

Air Bags
USE RESTRAINTS (VEHICLE SAFETY)

Air Bases
USE MILITARY AIR FACILITIES

AIR CONDITIONING *Jul. 1966*
CIJE: 64 RIE: 223 GC: 920
BT Climate Control
RT Air Conditioning Equipment
Air Flow
Building Trades
Fuel Consumption
Heating
Heat Recovery
Humidity
Refrigeration
Temperature
Thermal Environment
Ventilation
Windowless Rooms

AIR CONDITIONING EQUIPMENT *Jul. 1966*
CIJE: 29 RIE: 59 GC: 910
BT Equipment
RT Air Conditioning
Climate Control
Fuel Consumption
Heating
Refrigeration Mechanics
Sheet Metal Work
Temperature
Thermal Environment
Ventilation

Air Conditioning Mechanics
USE REFRIGERATION MECHANICS

AIR FLOW *Oct. 1969*
CIJE: 19 RIE: 26 GC: 490
SN Movement of air in or around a structure, e.g., a building or vehicle (note: do not confuse with "wind (meteorology)")
RT Air Conditioning
Building Design
Chimneys
Heating
Motion
Refrigeration
Temperature
Ventilation

Air Force Bases
USE MILITARY AIR FACILITIES

Air Inflated Structures (1972 1980)
USE AIR STRUCTURES

AIR POLLUTION *Mar. 1980*
CIJE: 511 RIE: 407 GC: 410
UF Air Pollution Control (1967 1980)
Atmospheric Pollution
Smog
BT Pollution
RT Asbestos
Chimneys
Climate
Climate Control
Conservation (Environment)
Ecology
Environmental Education
Environmental Standards
Urban Environment
Ventilation
Waste Disposal
Wind (Meteorology)

Air Pollution Control (1967 1980)
USE AIR POLLUTION

Air Raid Shelters
USE FALLOUT SHELTERS

AIR STRUCTURES *Sep. 1968*
CIJE: 47 RIE: 17 GC: 920
SN Buildings or shelters that are pneumatically inflated or that use inflated structural elements
UF Air Inflated Structures (1972 1980)
Air Supported Structures (1972 1980)
Hybrid Air Structures (1972 1980)
Inflatable Structures
NT Pneumatic Forms
BT Facilities
RT Buildings
Encapsulated Facilities
Prefabrication
Relocatable Facilities

Air Supported Structures (1972 1980)
USE AIR STRUCTURES

AIR TRAFFIC CONTROL *Jan. 1985*
CIJE: 3 RIE: 4 GC: 490
SN Scheduling and monitoring the flow of air traffic at airports, during approaches, and en route
BT Traffic Control
RT Aerospace Technology
Airports
Air Transportation
Aviation Technology
Aviation Vocabulary
Electronic Equipment
Military Air Facilities
Radar

AIR TRANSPORTATION *Oct. 1980*
CIJE: 8 RIE: 28 GC: 650
BT Transportation
RT Aerospace Education
Aerospace Industry
Aerospace Technology
Aircraft Pilots
Airports
Air Traffic Control
Aviation Technology

Airborne Field Trips (1968 1980)
USE FIELD TRIPS

Airborne Television (1966 1980)
USE TELEVISION

Aircraft Mechanics
USE AVIATION MECHANICS

AIRCRAFT PILOTS *Oct. 1968*
CIJE: 27 RIE: 115 GC: 640
UF Airline Pilots
Airplane Pilots
Commercial Pilots
Copilots
Helicopter Pilots
BT Personnel
RT Aerospace Technology
Air Transportation
Aviation Technology
Aviation Vocabulary

Airline Pilots
USE AIRCRAFT PILOTS

Airplane Pilots
USE AIRCRAFT PILOTS

AIRPORTS *Feb. 1971*
CIJE: 7 RIE: 23 GC: 920
BT Facilities
RT Air Traffic Control
Air Transportation
Aviation Technology
Military Air Facilities

AKAN *Jul. 1966*
CIJE: 3 RIE: 9 GC: 440
UF Twi
BT African Languages

ALARM SYSTEMS *Mar. 1978*
CIJE: 51 RIE: 47 GC: 910
SN Methods and materials employed to sound or signal emergencies or impending dangers
UF Burglar Alarms
Intrusion Detectors
Security Systems (Alarms)
Smoke Alarms
RT Accident Prevention
Civil Defense
Closed Circuit Television
Crime
Crime Prevention
Electrical Systems
Electronic Equipment
Emergency Programs
Emergency Squad Personnel
Fire Fighters
Fire Protection
Police
Police Action
Rescue
Safety
School Safety
School Security
Security Personnel

ALASKA NATIVES *Mar. 1976*
CIJE: 72 RIE: 464 GC: 560
SN Peoples indigenous to alaska (alaska's american indians, aleuts, and eskimos)
BT Ethnic Groups
North Americans
RT American Indians
Athapascan Languages
Canada Natives
Eskimo Aleut Languages
Eskimos
Minority Groups
Nonreservation American Indians
Tribes

ALBANIAN *Jul. 1966*
CIJE: 3 RIE: 36 GC: 440
BT Indo European Languages

ALCOHOL EDUCATION *Jul. 1966*
CIJE: 298 RIE: 323 GC: 400
BT Education
RT Alcoholic Beverages
Alcoholism
Drinking
Drug Education
Health Education

ALCOHOLIC BEVERAGES *Feb. 1974*
CIJE: 167 RIE: 111 GC: 210
RT Alcohol Education
Alcoholism
Drinking
Drug Use

ALCOHOLISM *May. 1974*
CIJE: 611 RIE: 520 GC: 530
BT Diseases
RT Alcohol Education
Alcoholic Beverages
Antisocial Behavior
Behavior Disorders
Drinking
Drug Abuse
Drug Addiction
Physical Health
Special Health Problems

Aleut
USE ESKIMO ALEUT LANGUAGES

ALGEBRA *Jul. 1966*
CIJE: 892 RIE: 656 GC: 480
NT Matrices
Vectors (Mathematics)
BT Mathematics
RT Analytic Geometry
Equations (Mathematics)
Topology
Transformations (Mathematics)

Algorisms
USE ALGORITHMS

ALGORITHMS *Jul. 1966*
CIJE: 639 RIE: 360 GC: 480
UF Algorisms
BT Mathematical Applications
Mathematical Logic
Methods
RT Computation
Mathematics
Programing

Alien Culture
USE FOREIGN CULTURE

Alien Illegality
USE UNDOCUMENTED IMMIGRANTS

ALIENATION *Mar. 1980*
CIJE: 125 RIE: 78 GC: 230
SN Estrangement from others, especially those from whom a relationship was expected, or from the prevalent values, goals, or trends of society (note: use a more specific term if possible)
NT Student Alienation
Teacher Alienation
BT Psychological Patterns
RT Activism
Anger
Apathy
Cultural Isolation
Dropout Attitudes
Emotional Adjustment
Identification (Psychology)
Interpersonal Relationship
Loneliness
Rejection (Psychology)
Resentment
Role Conflict
Social Adjustment
Social Attitudes
Social Isolation
Withdrawal (Psychology)

ALLEGORY *Jun. 1969*
CIJE: 56 RIE: 10 GC: 430
BT Figurative Language
RT Epics
Fables
Metaphors

ALLERGY *Jul. 1966*
CIJE: 41 RIE: 20 GC: 210
UF Hypersensitivity
BT Diseases
RT Asthma
Physical Health
Physiology
Special Health Problems
Toxicology

Allied Health Education
USE ALLIED HEALTH OCCUPATIONS EDUCATION

ALLIED HEALTH OCCUPATIONS *Mar. 1980*
CIJE: 175 RIE: 465 GC: 210
SN Professional, technical, and supportive occupations in patient services, administration, teaching, and research that support, complement, or supplement the functions of physicians, dentists, and registered nurses or other independent practitioners -- also includes environmental health occupations
UF Allied Health Professions
Allied Medical Occupations
Health Related Professions
Paramedical Occupations (1967 1980)
BT Health Occupations
RT Allied Health Occupations Education
Allied Health Personnel
Educational Gerontology
Health
Health Services
Optometry
Physical Therapy
Practical Nursing
Professional Occupations
Respiratory Therapy
Technical Occupations
Therapeutic Recreation
Therapy

ALLIED HEALTH OCCUPATIONS EDUCATION *Mar. 1980*
CIJE: 622 RIE: 1768 GC: 210
SN Formal preparation for occupations in allied health at all levels (note: before mar80, "health occupations education" was displayed as a narrower term under "vocational education")
UF Allied Health Education
Health Occupations Education (1967 1980)
Health Occupations Education (Vocational) #
BT Education
RT Allied Health Occupations
Allied Health Personnel
Clinical Experience
Clinical Teaching (Health Professions)
Health Education
Medical Education
Medicine
Professional Education
Teaching Hospitals
Technical Education
Vocational Education

ALLIED HEALTH PERSONNEL *Mar. 1980*
CIJE: 102 RIE: 104 GC: 210
UF Audiologists (1968 1980) #
Audiometrists (1967 1980) #
Clinic Personnel (School) (1966 1980) #
Paramedics
NT Dental Assistants
Dental Hygienists
Dental Technicians
Dietitians
Emergency Medical Technicians
Environmental Technicians
Home Health Aides
Medical Assistants
Medical Record Administrators
Medical Record Technicians
Medical Technologists
Nurses Aides
Occupational Therapy Assistants
Optometrists
Physical Therapy Aides
Physicians Assistants
Psychiatric Aides
Radiologic Technologists
Surgical Technicians
Therapists
Veterinary Assistants
BT Health Personnel
RT Allied Health Occupations
Allied Health Occupations Education
Attendants
Paraprofessional Personnel
Professional Personnel
Scientific Personnel
Visiting Homemakers

Allied Health Professions
USE ALLIED HEALTH OCCUPATIONS

Allied Medical Occupations
USE ALLIED HEALTH OCCUPATIONS

Allocation Of Resources
USE RESOURCE ALLOCATION

Allomorphs (1967 1980)
USE MORPHEMES

Alphabetic Filing
USE FILING

ALPHABETIZING SKILLS *Jul. 1966*
CIJE: 6 RIE: 26 GC: 400
BT Basic Skills
RT Dictionaries
Filing
Spelling
Word Study Skills

ALPHABETS *Jul. 1966*
CIJE: 88 RIE: 111 GC: 450
NT Cyrillic Alphabet
Initial Teaching Alphabet
Phonemic Alphabets
RT Letters (Alphabet)
Phonetic Transcription
Romanization
Written Language

Altaic Languages
USE URALIC ALTAIC LANGUAGES

Alternative Education
USE NONTRADITIONAL EDUCATION

ALTERNATIVE ENERGY SOURCES *Oct. 1984*
CIJE: 29 RIE: 96 GC: 490
SN Sources of energy other than conventional fossil fuels (petroleum, coal, natural gas) or nuclear fission/fusion (note: see also related identifiers such as "renewable resources" and "synthetic fuels")
RT Electricity
Energy
Energy Conservation
Energy Education
Energy Management
Energy Occupations
Geothermal Energy
Heat Recovery
Natural Resources
Power Technology
Solar Energy
Wind Energy

Alternative Futures
USE FUTURES (OF SOCIETY)

Alternative Life Styles
USE LIFE STYLE

Alternative Schools (1972 1980)
USE NONTRADITIONAL EDUCATION

ALTRUISM *Apr. 1973*
CIJE: 175 RIE: 117 GC: 120
SN Consideration for the welfare of others, sometimes in accordance with an ethical system
UF Humaneness
Kindness
RT Cooperation
Ethics
Humanitarianism
Interpersonal Relationship
Prosocial Behavior
Psychological Patterns
Social Attitudes
Social Exchange Theory
Values

ALUMNI *Jan. 1970*
CIJE: 262 RIE: 179 GC: 360
SN Graduates or former students of a school, college, university, or educational program
NT Graduates
BT Groups
RT Alumni Associations
Alumni Education
Graduate Surveys

ALUMNI ASSOCIATIONS *Mar. 1980*
CIJE: 42 RIE: 19 GC: 520
BT Organizations (Groups)
RT Alumni
College Graduates
Graduates
Nonprofit Organizations

Alumni Colleges
USE ALUMNI EDUCATION

ALUMNI EDUCATION *Nov. 1968*
CIJE: 14 RIE: 9 GC: 320
SN Educational activities carried on by a college or university for the benefit of its graduates and former students -- includes special seminars, courses, educational trips, postcollegiate professional instruction, etc.
UF Alumni Colleges
BT Education

= Two or more Descriptors are used to represent this term.
The term's main entry shows the appropriate coordination.

RT Adult Programs
Alumni
College Graduates
College Programs
Minicourses
Professional Continuing Education
Summer Programs
Vacation Programs

Ambient Pressure
USE PRESSURE (PHYSICS)

AMBIGUITY *Apr. 1970*
CIJE: 162 RIE: 86 GC: 430
BT Figurative Language

Ambition
USE ASPIRATION

Ambulance Attendants
USE EMERGENCY MEDICAL TECHNICIANS

Amerasians
USE ASIAN AMERICANS

AMERICAN CULTURE (1966 1980) *Mar. 1980*
CIJE: 456 RIE: 362 GC: 560
SN Invalid descriptor -- used for north, south, central american culture -- see "north american culture" or "latin american culture"

American English (1968 1980)
USE NORTH AMERICAN ENGLISH

American Government (Course) (1966 1980)
USE UNITED STATES GOVERNMENT (COURSE)

AMERICAN HISTORY (1966 1980) *Mar. 1980*
CIJE: 414 RIE: 456 GC: 430
SN Invalid descriptor -- although scope note referred to north, south, and central america, term used frequently for u.s. history -- see "north american history," "latin american history," or "united states history"

AMERICAN INDIAN CULTURE *May. 1969*
CIJE: 410 RIE: 715 GC: 560
BT Culture
RT American Indian History
American Indian Languages
American Indian Literature
American Indians
American Indian Studies
Latin American Culture
North American Culture
Tribes

AMERICAN INDIAN EDUCATION *Oct. 1979*
CIJE: 227 RIE: 907 GC: 330
SN Formal and nonformal process of educating american indians to their own and to the broader society (note: prior to oct79, this concept was indexed under "american indians")
BT Education
RT American Indian Languages
American Indians
American Indian Studies
Federal Indian Relationship
Trust Responsibility (Government)

AMERICAN INDIAN HISTORY *Jun. 1983*
CIJE: 61 RIE: 180 GC: 430
BT History
RT American Indian Culture
American Indian Literature
American Indian Reservations
American Indians
American Indian Studies
Federal Indian Relationship
Latin American History
North American History
Oral History
Relocation
Tribal Sovereignty
Tribes

AMERICAN INDIAN LANGUAGES *Jul. 1966*
CIJE: 198 RIE: 392 GC: 440
NT Athapascan Languages
Aymara
Cakchiquel
Cherokee
Choctaw
Cree
Guarani
Mayan Languages
Ojibwa
Pomo
Quechua
Salish
Tzeltal
Tzotzil
Uto Aztecan Languages
BT Languages
RT American Indian Culture
American Indian Education
American Indians
American Indian Studies
Eskimo Aleut Languages
Language Classification
Native Speakers

AMERICAN INDIAN LITERATURE *Oct. 1979*
CIJE: 67 RIE: 142 GC: 430
BT Literature
RT American Indian Culture
American Indian History
American Indians
American Indian Studies
Latin American Literature
Legends
Mythology
North American Literature

AMERICAN INDIAN RESERVATIONS *Mar. 1980*
CIJE: 204 RIE: 672 GC: 610
SN Tracts of land, set aside by agreements between governments and indian tribes, that are reserved for the exclusive use and occupancy of those tribes
UF Reservations (Indian) (1971 1980)
BT Political Divisions (Geographic)
RT American Indian History
American Indians
Federal Indian Relationship
Land Settlement
Nonreservation American Indians
Reservation American Indians
Treaties
Tribal Sovereignty
Tribes
Trust Responsibility (Government)

AMERICAN INDIAN STUDIES *Oct. 1979*
CIJE: 35 RIE: 99 GC: 400
SN Curriculum or subject area encompassing the culture, history, achievements, and contemporary concerns of american indians
BT Ethnic Studies
RT American Indian Culture
American Indian Education
American Indian History
American Indian Languages
American Indian Literature
American Indians
American Studies
Cultural Background
Cultural Education
Cultural Images
Cultural Traits

AMERICAN INDIANS *Jul. 1966*
CIJE: 1953 RIE: 4344 GC: 560
SN Both north and south american indians
NT Nonreservation American Indians
Reservation American Indians
BT Ethnic Groups
RT Alaska Natives
American Indian Culture
American Indian Education
American Indian History
American Indian Languages
American Indian Literature
American Indian Reservations
American Indian Studies
Canada Natives
Federal Indian Relationship
Latin Americans
Mexicans
Minority Groups
North Americans
Relocation
Tribal Sovereignty
Tribes
Trust Responsibility (Government)

American Jews
USE JEWS

American Literature (1966 1980) (Latin America)
USE LATIN AMERICAN LITERATURE

American Literature (1966 1980) (United States)
USE UNITED STATES LITERATURE

American Negroes
USE BLACKS

American Orientals
USE ASIAN AMERICANS

American Revolutionary War
USE REVOLUTIONARY WAR (UNITED STATES)

American Samoans
USE SAMOAN AMERICANS

AMERICAN SIGN LANGUAGE *Sep. 1982*
CIJE: 90 RIE: 23 GC: 220
SN Visual/gestural language used by the deaf community in the united states and parts of canada -- distinct from signed english, asl has its own highly articulated linguistic system that makes use of the eyes, face, head, and body posture as well as the signer's hands
UF Ameslan
BT Languages
Sign Language

AMERICAN STUDIES *Apr. 1973*
CIJE: 56 RIE: 135 GC: 400
SN Interdisciplinary studies of the united states (note: prior to mar80, this term was scoped to include studies of all of north america above mexico)
BT Area Studies
RT American Indian Studies
Black Studies
North American Culture
United States Government (Course)
United States History
United States Literature

Ameslan
USE AMERICAN SIGN LANGUAGE

AMETROPIA *Jul. 1966*
CIJE: 3 RIE: 1 GC: 220
UF Error Of Refraction
Ocular Refractive Errors
Refractive Errors
NT Hyperopia
Myopia
BT Visual Impairments
RT Vision
Visual Acuity

AMHARIC *Jul. 1966*
CIJE: 4 RIE: 22 GC: 440
BT Semitic Languages

AMISH *Jul. 1966*
CIJE: 20 RIE: 22 GC: 560
BT Protestants

AMPUTATIONS *Mar. 1980*
CIJE: 13 RIE: 19 GC: 220
SN Loss of limbs or digits from the body
UF Amputees (1967 1980)
BT Physical Disabilities
RT Physical Therapy
Prostheses
Surgery

Amputees (1967 1980)
USE AMPUTATIONS

ANALOG COMPUTERS *Jul. 1966*
CIJE: 27 RIE: 45 GC: 910
SN Computers that translate physical conditions (flow, temperature, pressure, etc.) into related mechanical or electrical quantities (length, voltage, current, etc.) -- unlike digital computers, which count discrete quantities, analog computers measure continuous variables
BT Computers
RT Digital Computers

Analysis
USE EVALUATION METHODS

ANALYSIS OF COVARIANCE *Dec. 1970*
CIJE: 233 RIE: 216 GC: 820
SN Statistical technique used to compare two or more groups with reference to one variable when differences on some other correlated variable may affect the comparison
UF Ancova
BT Statistical Analysis
RT Analysis Of Variance
Correlation
Hypothesis Testing
Predictor Variables
Statistical Significance

ANALYSIS OF VARIANCE *Jul. 1966*
CIJE: 1048 RIE: 911 GC: 820
SN Statistical technique for determining if differences among the means of different groups of observations exceed what may be expected by chance
UF Anova
BT Statistical Analysis
RT Analysis Of Covariance
Generalizability Theory
Hypothesis Testing
Predictor Variables
Statistical Significance

ANALYTIC GEOMETRY *Jul. 1966*
CIJE: 95 RIE: 62 GC: 480
UF Coordinate Geometry
BT Geometry
RT Algebra
Calculus
Plane Geometry
Solid Geometry

ANALYTICAL CRITICISM (1969 1980) *Mar. 1980*
CIJE: 552 RIE: 131 GC: 430
SN Invalid descriptor -- used indiscriminately for all types of analysis -- see various "analysis" and "evaluation" descriptors -- for discussions of analytical criticism in a literary sense, use "literary criticism"

ANATOMY *Jul. 1966*
CIJE: 159 RIE: 161 GC: 490
BT Biological Sciences
RT Biology
Cardiovascular System
Ears
Embryology
Evolution
Eyes
Human Body
Medicine
Neurology
Pathology
Physiology
Scientific Research
Surgery
Zoology

Ancestral Lineage
USE GENEALOGY

ANCIENT HISTORY *Jul. 1966*
CIJE: 166 RIE: 105 GC: 430
BT History
RT Archaeology
Biblical Literature
Classical Literature
Greek Civilization
Greek Literature
Latin Literature

ANCILLARY SCHOOL SERVICES *Mar. 1980*
CIJE: 210 RIE: 731 GC: 320
SN Noninstructional services offered by schools or educational programs (note: prior to mar80, this concept was indexed under "ancillary services")
UF Auxiliary School Services
School Services (1966 1980)

NT Mobile Educational Services
Pupil Personnel Services
School Health Services
Student Personnel Services
BT Social Services
RT Counseling Services
Day Care
Education Service Centers
Guidance Programs
Library Services
Lunch Programs
Psychological Services
School Age Day Care
School Business Officials
School Recreational Programs
Schools
Student Development
Student Transportation

ANCILLARY SERVICES (1967 1980) *Jun. 1980*
CIJE: 103 RIE: 530 GC: 520
SN Invalid descriptor -- see more precise descriptors such as "ancillary school services," "community services," "social services," etc.

Ancova
USE ANALYSIS OF COVARIANCE

ANDRAGOGY *Mar. 1984*
CIJE: 56 RIE: 55 GC: 310
SN The art and science of the facilitation of adult learning, distinguished from child-oriented "pedagogy" in terms of learner self-direction, application of knowledge and experience, learning readiness, orientation to the present, and problem-centeredness
UF Androgogy
RT Adult Education
Adult Learning
Adult Students
Age Differences
Educational Theories
Learning Strategies

Androgogy
USE ANDRAGOGY

ANDROGYNY *Mar. 1977*
CIJE: 209 RIE: 187 GC: 120
SN Integration of male and female characteristics (roles, behaviors, personality traits, biological traits, etc.)
RT Individual Psychology
Sex Differences
Sex Role
Sexual Identity

Anechoic Materials
USE ACOUSTIC INSULATION

ANEMIA *Apr. 1973*
CIJE: 28 RIE: 30 GC: 210
UF Iron Deficiency Anemia
NT Sickle Cell Anemia
BT Diseases
RT Lead Poisoning
Nutrition
Physical Health
Prenatal Influences
Special Health Problems

ANESTHESIOLOGY *Jul. 1966*
CIJE: 24 RIE: 11 GC: 210
BT Medicine
RT Medical Services
Surgery

ANGER *Aug. 1986*
CIJE: 39 RIE: 15 GC: 230
SN Strong displeasure
NT Hostility
BT Psychological Patterns
RT Alienation
Anxiety
Catharsis
Depression (Psychology)
Emotional Problems
Helplessness
Jealousy
Loneliness
Rejection (Psychology)
Resentment

ANGLO AMERICANS *Jul. 1966*
CIJE: 237 RIE: 487 GC: 560
SN Permanent residents of the americas who are of english descent -- commonly used in the u.s. as a label for the white and/or english-speaking majority, especially in comparisons with minority ethnic groups (note: for specificity, coordinate with such identifiers as "english americans" and "british americans" -- use "whites" or "white students" for comparisons of whites with other groups)
UF Anglos
BT Ethnic Groups
North Americans
RT Whites

Anglo Saxon
USE OLD ENGLISH

Anglos
USE ANGLO AMERICANS

ANIMAL BEHAVIOR *May. 1969*
CIJE: 401 RIE: 108 GC: 120
BT Behavior
RT Aggression
Animal Facilities
Animals
Behavior Development
Veterinary Medicine
Zoology

Animal Biology
USE ZOOLOGY

ANIMAL CARETAKERS *Jan. 1969*
CIJE: 29 RIE: 24 GC: 640
UF Animal Keepers
BT Semiskilled Workers
RT Agricultural Personnel
Animal Facilities
Animal Husbandry
Animals
Off Farm Agricultural Occupations
Veterinary Assistants
Veterinary Medicine

ANIMAL FACILITIES *Sep. 1969*
CIJE: 72 RIE: 29 GC: 920
NT Zoos
BT Facilities
RT Animal Behavior
Animal Caretakers
Animal Husbandry
Animals
Laboratory Animals
Laboratory Equipment
Wildlife Management

ANIMAL HUSBANDRY *Mar. 1980*
CIJE: 167 RIE: 163 GC: 410
SN Branch of agriculture concerned with the production and care of domestic animals
UF Animal Science (1967 1980)
Livestock Technology
BT Agriculture
RT Animal Caretakers
Animal Facilities
Animals
Dairy Farmers
Farm Occupations
Horses
Laboratory Animals
Livestock
Meat Packing Industry
Ornithology
Veterinarians
Veterinary Assistants
Veterinary Medical Education
Veterinary Medicine
Zoology

Animal Keepers
USE ANIMAL CARETAKERS

Animal Life
USE ANIMALS

Animal Science (1967 1980)
USE ANIMAL HUSBANDRY

ANIMALS *Aug. 1980*
CIJE: 319 RIE: 186 GC: 490
SN (Note: use a more specific term if possible -- prior to aug80, the instruction "animal life, use zoology" was carried in the thesaurus)
UF Animal Life
NT Horses
Laboratory Animals
Livestock
Rats
RT Animal Behavior
Animal Caretakers
Animal Facilities
Animal Husbandry
Endangered Species
Pests
Veterinary Medicine
Wildlife
Zoology

ANIMATION *May. 1971*
CIJE: 72 RIE: 60 GC: 720
SN Film or video techniques that bring movement to inanimate objects or drawings
BT Special Effects
RT Cartoons
Characterization
Film Industry
Film Production

ANNOTATED BIBLIOGRAPHIES *Jul. 1966*
CIJE: 1511 RIE: 6524 GC: 730
UF Abstract Bibliographies
BT Bibliographies
RT Abstracting
Abstracts

Annotations
USE ABSTRACTS

ANNUAL REPORTS *Jul. 1966*
CIJE: 185 RIE: 1824 GC: 730
SN Includes data on progress, finance, material, personnel, instruction, etc.
BT Reports
Serials
RT Yearbooks

Annuals
USE YEARBOOKS

Anomalies (1967 1980)
USE CONGENITAL IMPAIRMENTS

ANOREXIA NERVOSA *Oct. 1983*
CIJE: 35 RIE: 18 GC: 210
SN Disorder characterized by prolonged refusal to eat, attended by serious psychological problems (e.g., intense fear of gaining weight) and leading to emaciation and nutritional deficiencies -- most often seen in adolescent females
BT Diseases
RT Body Weight
Bulimia
Eating Habits
Emotional Disturbances
Nutrition
Physical Health

Anova
USE ANALYSIS OF VARIANCE

Answer Booklets
USE ANSWER SHEETS

Answer Cards
USE ANSWER SHEETS

ANSWER KEYS *Jul. 1966*
CIJE: 18 RIE: 273 GC: 730
SN Devices that display correct answers for particular tests
UF Scoring Keys
RT Answer Sheets
Objective Tests
Scoring
Test Construction
Test Manuals
Tests
Test Scoring Machines

ANSWER SHEETS *Sep. 1974*
CIJE: 16 RIE: 39 GC: 730
SN Separate forms, sheets, or cards on which examinees record their responses to tests or questionnaires
UF Answer Booklets
Answer Cards
RT Answer Keys
Questionnaires
Scoring
Test Construction
Test Manuals
Tests
Test Scoring Machines

ANTHOLOGIES *Jul. 1966*
CIJE: 70 RIE: 338 GC: 730
SN Collections of selected writings or other materials, usually in one form, from one period, or on one subject
UF Collected Readings
Readings (Collections)
BT Reference Materials
RT Bibliographies
Conference Proceedings
Literature Reviews

Anthracite
USE COAL

ANTHROPOLOGICAL LINGUISTICS *Oct. 1977*
CIJE: 40 RIE: 41 GC: 450
SN Application of anthropological and linguistic techniques to the study of speech communities, particularly those with no writing system -- attention is given to specific interrelationships in the concurrent and systematic development of culture and language
UF Linguistic Anthropology
BT Anthropology
Linguistics
RT Cultural Context
Diachronic Linguistics
Ethnography
Ethnology
Language Research
Linguistic Theory
Sociolinguistics
Unwritten Languages

ANTHROPOLOGY *Jul. 1966*
CIJE: 455 RIE: 726 GC: 400
NT Anthropological Linguistics
Archaeology
Educational Anthropology
Ethnography
Ethnology
BT Social Sciences
RT Area Studies
Componential Analysis
Cross Cultural Studies
Cultural Pluralism
Folk Culture
Human Geography
Museums
Primatology
Race
Social Science Research
Social Scientists
Social Studies
Zoology

Anti Discrimination Legislation
USE CIVIL RIGHTS LEGISLATION

ANTI INTELLECTUALISM *Jul. 1966*
CIJE: 41 RIE: 5 GC: 540
BT Attitudes
RT Fascism
Negative Attitudes

Anti Poverty Programs
USE POVERTY PROGRAMS

Anti Segregation Programs (1967 1980)
USE RACIAL INTEGRATION

ANTI SEMITISM *Jul. 1966*
CIJE: 60 RIE: 39 GC: 540
RT Ethnic Bias
Ethnic Discrimination
Ghettos
Jews
Nazism
Religious Discrimination

Anti Social Behavior (1966 1980)
USE ANTISOCIAL BEHAVIOR

ANTISOCIAL BEHAVIOR *Mar. 1980*
CIJE: 661 RIE: 600 GC: 530
SN Behavior that violates the normative rules, standards, understandings, or expectations of society
UF Anti Social Behavior (1966 1980)
Socially Deviant Behavior (1966 1980)
NT Aggression
Cheating
Child Abuse
Child Neglect
Crime
Elder Abuse
Incest
Sexual Abuse
Sexual Harassment
Stealing
Terrorism
Vandalism
Violence
BT Social Behavior
RT Alcoholism
Behavior Disorders
Behavior Problems
Conflict
Drug Abuse
Drug Addiction
Illegal Drug Use
Lying
Obscenity
Prosocial Behavior
Recidivism
Self Destructive Behavior

ANTITHESIS *May. 1969*
CIJE: 6 RIE: 1 GC: 430
BT Figurative Language
RT Philosophy
Poetry

ANXIETY *Jul. 1966*
CIJE: 1864 RIE: 865 GC: 230
NT Communication Apprehension
Mathematics Anxiety
Separation Anxiety
Test Anxiety
Writing Apprehension
BT Psychological Patterns
RT Anger
Catharsis
Depression (Psychology)
Desensitization
Emotional Disturbances
Emotional Problems
Fear
Inhibition
Jealousy
Personality Traits
Relaxation Training
School Phobia

APACHE *Apr. 1969*
CIJE: 2 RIE: 9 GC: 440
SN Athapascan language spoken by six culturally related tribes of the north american southwest (the jicarilla, mescalero, san carlos, white mountain, chiricahua, and kiowa apache)
BT Athapascan Languages

APATHY *Aug. 1978*
CIJE: 32 RIE: 19 GC: 120
SN Lack of feeling about, or interest in, things generally found stimulating or interesting
UF Indifference
BT Psychological Patterns
RT Alienation
Aspiration
Emotional Problems
Personality Problems

APHASIA *Jul. 1966*
CIJE: 173 RIE: 94 GC: 220
SN Impairment of the ability to comprehend or produce the symbols of spoken or written language due to brain dysfunction, not to mental or intellectual deficiency
BT Language Handicaps
Neurological Impairments
RT Communication Disorders
Dyslexia
Echolalia
Expressive Language
Learning Disabilities
Minimal Brain Dysfunction
Perceptual Handicaps
Receptive Language
Speech Handicaps

Apparel Industry
USE FASHION INDUSTRY

APPLIANCE REPAIR *Sep. 1981*
CIJE: 5 RIE: 14 GC: 640
SN Concerned with installation and maintenance of appliances, as well as their repair
UF Appliance Repairers (1980 1981)
Appliance Repairing (1968 1981)
Appliance Service Technicians (1967 1980)
Electrical Appliance Servicemen (1968 1980)
Home Appliance Repair
BT Repair
RT Electrical Appliances
Electrical Occupations
Electricians
Skilled Occupations

Appliance Repairers (1980 1981)
USE APPLIANCE REPAIR

Appliance Repairing (1968 1981)
USE APPLIANCE REPAIR

Appliance Service Technicians (1967 1980)
USE APPLIANCE REPAIR

Appliances
USE EQUIPMENT

APPLIED LINGUISTICS *Jul. 1966*
CIJE: 475 RIE: 594 GC: 450
SN Application of the findings of linguistic science to practical language problems, such as language teaching, lexicography, translation, speech therapy, etc.
BT Linguistics
RT English (Second Language)
Nonstandard Dialects
Second Language Instruction
Structural Linguistics
Substitution Drills
Unwritten Languages

APPLIED MUSIC *Jul. 1966*
CIJE: 85 RIE: 42 GC: 420
SN Musical performance, or instruction in vocal or instrumental music
UF Practical Music
BT Music
RT Bands (Music)
Music Activities
Music Education
Orchestras
Singing
Vocal Music

Applied Reading (1966 1980)
USE READING

Applied Research
USE RESEARCH

Applied Sciences
USE TECHNOLOGY

Appraisal
USE EVALUATION

APPRENTICESHIPS *Jul. 1966*
CIJE: 223 RIE: 543 GC: 630
BT On The Job Training
RT Experiential Learning
Field Experience Programs
Industrial Training
Inplant Programs
Skilled Occupations
Skilled Workers
Trade And Industrial Education
Trainees
Vocational Education
Work Experience Programs

APPROPRIATE TECHNOLOGY *Aug. 1986*
CIJE: 12 RIE: 26 GC: 550
SN Technology suited to the psychosocial and biophysical needs in a particular place and time
BT Technology
RT Development
Environment
Futures (Of Society)
Needs
Quality Of Life
Science And Society
Technical Assistance
Technological Advancement
Technological Literacy
Technology Transfer
World Affairs

Approved Programs (Validated)
USE VALIDATED PROGRAMS

Approximation (Mathematics)
USE ESTIMATION (MATHEMATICS)

Approximative Systems (Language Learning)
USE INTERLANGUAGE

APTITUDE *Jul. 1966*
CIJE: 131 RIE: 225 GC: 120
SN The potential ability of an individual to perform an as yet unlearned task, skill, or act
NT Academic Aptitude
Language Aptitude
Vocational Aptitude
RT Ability
Achievement
Aptitude Tests
Aspiration
Cognitive Ability
Expectation
Gifted
Learning
Performance
Qualifications
Talent

APTITUDE TESTS *Jul. 1966*
CIJE: 431 RIE: 1355 GC: 830
SN Tests that are used to predict future performance, as well as tests that measure those abilities which are not readily developed by formal training
UF Talent Tests
NT Reading Readiness Tests
School Readiness Tests
BT Tests
RT Ability Identification
Achievement Tests
Aptitude
College Entrance Examinations
Intelligence Tests
Interest Inventories
Mathematics Tests
Occupational Tests
Performance Tests
Predictive Measurement
Screening Tests
Talent Identification

APTITUDE TREATMENT INTERACTION *Apr. 1980*
CIJE: 208 RIE: 179 GC: 310
SN Relationship between learner characteristics or traits and the characteristics of the learning task, learning situation, teacher, or teaching methods and materials
UF Trait Treatment Interaction
BT Interaction
RT Academic Ability
Academic Aptitude
Classroom Environment
Cognitive Style
Learning Processes
Student Characteristics
Student School Relationship
Teacher Characteristics
Teacher Student Relationship

AQUATIC SPORTS *Jan. 1985*
CIJE: 4 RIE: 1 GC: 470
UF Water Sports
NT Diving
Sailing
Surfing
Swimming
Water Polo
Waterskiing
BT Athletics
RT Swimming Pools
Underwater Diving
Water

Arab Americans
USE ARABS; NORTH AMERICANS

ARABIC *Jul. 1966*
CIJE: 84 RIE: 266 GC: 440
BT Semitic Languages
RT Arabs

ARABS *Jan. 1970*
CIJE: 88 RIE: 91 GC: 560
UF Arab Americans #
BT Groups
RT Arabic
Ethnic Groups
Middle Eastern Studies
Non Western Civilization

ARBITRATION *Mar. 1969*
CIJE: 271 RIE: 304 GC: 630
SN The process by which the parties to a dispute submit their differences to the judgment of an impartial party appointed by mutual consent or statutory provision
UF Mediation (Labor)
RT Board Of Education Policy
Collective Bargaining
Employer Employee Relationship
Employment Problems
Faculty College Relationship
Grievance Procedures
Labor Demands
Labor Economics
Labor Legislation
Labor Problems
Negotiation Agreements
Negotiation Impasses
Sanctions
Strikes
Teacher Militancy
Teacher Strikes
Unions

Arc Welding
USE WELDING

ARCHAEOLOGY *Jul. 1966*
CIJE: 162 RIE: 104 GC: 400
BT Anthropology
RT Ancient History
Ethnology
Paleontology

ARCHERY *Nov. 1973*
CIJE: 9 RIE: 22 GC: 470
BT Athletics
RT Lifetime Sports

ARCHITECTS *Jul. 1966*
CIJE: 162 RIE: 105 GC: 420
BT Professional Personnel
RT Architectural Education
Architecture
Building Design
Construction Industry

ARCHITECTURAL BARRIERS (1970 1980) *Jun. 1980*
CIJE: 111 RIE: 125 GC: 220
SN Invalid descriptor -- coordinate other architecture/facility terms with "physical mobility" or "visually handicapped mobility" -- also use "accessibility (for disabled)" if appropriate

Architectural Changes
USE BUILDING DESIGN

ARCHITECTURAL CHARACTER *Jul. 1966*
CIJE: 293 RIE: 87 GC: 920
SN Stylistic expression of verticality, scale, richness, variety and unity inherent to architectural tradition
UF Architectural Style
Architectural Tradition

= Two or more Descriptors are used to represent this term.
The term's main entry shows the appropriate coordination.

RT Architecture
Building Design
Campus Planning
Educational Facilities Design
Structural Elements (Construction)

Architectural Design
USE BUILDING DESIGN

ARCHITECTURAL DRAFTING *Sep. 1969*
CIJE: 25 RIE: 46 GC: 640
SN The art or practice of drawing architectural and structural features of any class of buildings and like structures -- includes delineating design and details, and confirming compliance with building codes
BT Drafting
RT Architectural Education
Architectural Programing
Architecture
Building Plans
Engineering Drawing

ARCHITECTURAL EDUCATION *Aug. 1968*
CIJE: 150 RIE: 39 GC: 400
BT Professional Education
RT Architects
Architectural Drafting
Architectural Research
Architecture
Art Education
Technical Education

Architectural Elements (1968 1980)
USE STRUCTURAL ELEMENTS (CONSTRUCTION)

ARCHITECTURAL PROGRAMING *Aug. 1968*
CIJE: 143 RIE: 149 GC: 920
SN The process of identification and systematic organization of the functional, architectural, structural, mechanical, and esthetic criteria which influence decision making for the design of a functional space, building, or facility
RT Architectural Drafting
Architectural Research
Architecture
Building Design
Building Innovation
Decision Making
Design
Design Requirements
Educational Facilities Planning
Facility Planning
Systems Analysis

ARCHITECTURAL RESEARCH *Feb. 1970*
CIJE: 75 RIE: 55 GC: 810
SN Basic, applied, and developmental research focusing on architectural theory, design, or education (note: as of oct81, use as a minor descriptor for examples of this kind of research -- use as a major descriptor only as the subject of a document)
BT Research
RT Architectural Education
Architectural Programing
Architecture
Behavioral Science Research
Construction Materials
Environmental Research
Mechanical Equipment
Physical Environment

Architectural Style
USE ARCHITECTURAL CHARACTER

Architectural Tradition
USE ARCHITECTURAL CHARACTER

ARCHITECTURE *Jul. 1966*
CIJE: 233 RIE: 229 GC: 420
BT Visual Arts
RT Accessibility (For Disabled)
Acoustics
Architects
Architectural Character
Architectural Drafting
Architectural Education
Architectural Programing
Architectural Research
Art
Building Design
Design
Design Requirements
Interior Design
Lighting Design
Neoclassicism
Physical Mobility
Spatial Relationship (Facilities)
Structural Elements (Construction)

ARCHIVES *Jul. 1966*
CIJE: 254 RIE: 271 GC: 710
SN Repositories for public records or documents of historical importance concerning the activities of a nation, community, corporation, family, or historical figure -- also includes the material preserved
BT Information Sources
RT Academic Libraries
Government Libraries
Libraries
Library Collections
National Libraries
Public Libraries
Records (Forms)
State Libraries

AREA *Oct. 1983*
CIJE: 46 RIE: 14 GC: 480
SN Two-dimensional space
UF Planar Area
Surface Area
BT Geometric Concepts
Space
RT Plane Geometry
Volume (Mathematics)

AREA STUDIES *Jul. 1966*
CIJE: 400 RIE: 851 GC: 400
SN Study of political or geographical area including history, geography, language and general culture
NT American Studies
Asian Studies
Middle Eastern Studies
BT Curriculum
RT Anthropology
Cross Cultural Studies
Cultural Awareness
Developed Nations
Developing Nations
Ecology
Economics
Ethnic Studies
Field Studies
Geographic Regions
Geography
Greek Civilization
History
Human Geography
Interdisciplinary Approach
International Studies
Middle Eastern History
Non Western Civilization
Political Science
Regional Characteristics
Regional Dialects
Relocation
Research
Social Science Research
Social Sciences
Sociology
Urban Studies
Western Civilization

Area Vocational Schools (1966 1980)
USE REGIONAL SCHOOLS; VOCATIONAL SCHOOLS

Areas (Geographic)
USE GEOGRAPHIC REGIONS

Argumentation
USE PERSUASIVE DISCOURSE

ARISTOTELIAN CRITICISM (1969 1980) *Mar. 1980*
CIJE: 19 RIE: 17 GC: 430
SN Invalid descriptor -- originally intended as a literary term, but used indiscriminately in indexing -- for literary documents, see "literary criticism" and the identifier "aristotle"

ARITHMETIC *Jul. 1966*
CIJE: 594 RIE: 842 GC: 480
UF Arithmetic Curriculum (1966 1980) #
Arithmetic Tests #
Number Operations
Remedial Arithmetic (1966 1980) #
NT Addition
Division
Multiplication
Subtraction
BT Mathematics
RT Computation
Fractions
Integers
Mathematical Enrichment
Number Concepts
Numbers
Percentage
Place Value
Set Theory

Arithmetic Curriculum (1966 1980)
USE ARITHMETIC; MATHEMATICS CURRICULUM

Arithmetic Systems
USE NUMBER SYSTEMS

Arithmetic Tests
USE ARITHMETIC; MATHEMATICS TESTS

ARMED FORCES *Sep. 1968*
CIJE: 124 RIE: 467 GC: 610
UF Federal Troops (1966 1980)
BT Military Organizations
RT Disarmament
Foreign Countries
Military Personnel
Military Service
National Defense
War

ARMENIAN *Jul. 1966*
CIJE: 1 RIE: 14 GC: 440
BT Indo European Languages

Arms Control
USE DISARMAMENT

Army Air Bases
USE MILITARY AIR FACILITIES

AROUSAL PATTERNS *Jul. 1966*
CIJE: 217 RIE: 113 GC: 110
BT Behavior Patterns
RT Adaptation Level Theory
Attention
Emotional Response
Habituation
Novelty (Stimulus Dimension)
Perception
Stimulation

ART *Jul. 1966*
CIJE: 841 RIE: 623 GC: 420
SN Broad term for the processes and results of aesthetic expression (note: see also the more precise descriptors "art products," "visual arts," "fine arts," "painting (visual arts)," etc.
NT Art Products
Commercial Art
Creative Art
RT Aesthetic Values
Architecture
Art Activities
Art Appreciation
Art Education
Art Expression
Art History
Artists
Art Materials
Arts Centers
Art Teachers
Art Therapy
Color
Dance
Design
Drama
Dramatics
Fine Arts
Literature
Music
Popular Culture
Symmetry
Theater Arts
Visual Arts

ART ACTIVITIES *Jul. 1966*
CIJE: 1098 RIE: 595 GC: 420
SN Productive or appreciative participation in aesthetic experiences, including the use of such experiences generally in the school curriculum
BT Activities
RT Art
Art Appreciation
Art Education
Art Materials
Art Products
Arts Centers
Art Therapy
Childrens Art
Creative Activities
Creative Art
Cultural Activities
Enrichment Activities
Extracurricular Activities
Fine Arts
Handicrafts
Recreational Activities
Visual Arts

ART APPRECIATION *Jul. 1966*
CIJE: 392 RIE: 241 GC: 420
BT Aesthetic Education
RT Art
Art Activities
Art History
Childrens Art
Fine Arts
Visual Literacy

ART EDUCATION *Jul. 1966*
CIJE: 2587 RIE: 999 GC: 420
SN Education concerned with one or more of the fine or applied arts, including studies and creative experiences
BT Education
RT Aesthetic Education
Architectural Education
Art
Art Activities
Art History
Art Materials
Art Teachers
Childrens Art
Commercial Art
Fine Arts
Visual Arts

ART EXPRESSION *Jul. 1966*
CIJE: 458 RIE: 199 GC: 420
SN Process of communicating thoughts or feelings aesthetically, as in painting, sculpture, music, etc.
RT Aesthetic Values
Art
Art Products
Art Therapy
Creativity
Expressionism
Impressionism
Literary Styles
Modernism
Naturalism
Neoclassicism
Realism
Romanticism
Self Expression
Surrealism
Symbolism

Art Galleries
USE ARTS CENTERS

ART HISTORY *Mar. 1980*
CIJE: 131 RIE: 67 GC: 420
SN Study of art expression through the ages, including specific periods, artists, or schools of art
BT Intellectual History
RT Art
Art Appreciation
Art Education
Artists
Fine Arts
Visual Arts

ART MATERIALS *Jul. 1966*
CIJE: 577 RIE: 115 GC: 420
RT Adhesives
Art
Art Activities
Art Education
Ceramics

= Two or more Descriptors are used to represent this term.
The term's main entry shows the appropriate coordination.

Childrens Art
Glass
Instructional Materials
Leather
Paper (Material)
Plastics
Supplies
Visual Arts

ART PRODUCTS *Jul. 1966*
CIJE: 628 RIE: 66 GC: 420
SN The final products of the creative process involving the use of an art medium or performance
BT Art
RT Art Activities
Art Expression
Art Therapy
Childrens Art
Handicrafts
Musical Composition
Painting (Visual Arts)
Photographs
Sculpture

ART SONG *Jul. 1966*
CIJE: 20 RIE: 4 GC: 420
SN A song of serious artistic intent for one voice written by a trained composer -- as opposed to a folk song
BT Songs
RT Singing

ART TEACHERS *Sep. 1969*
CIJE: 400 RIE: 53 GC: 360
BT Teachers
RT Art
Art Education
Artists
Fine Arts
Visual Arts

ART THERAPY *Jun. 1977*
CIJE: 46 RIE: 36 GC: 230
SN The therapeutic use of art forms (painting, sculpturing, drawing, etc.) in achieving self-expression and emotional release, usually in a context of remediation or rehabilitation
BT Therapy
RT Art
Art Activities
Art Expression
Art Products
Creative Art
Educational Therapy
Music Therapy
Play Therapy
Psychotherapy
Self Expression
Therapeutic Recreation
Visual Arts

Articles (Grammar)
USE DETERMINERS (LANGUAGES)

ARTICULATION (EDUCATION) *Mar. 1980*
CIJE: 400 RIE: 1251 GC: 330
SN Systematic coordination of course and/or program content within and between educational institutions to facilitate the continuous and efficient progress of students from grade to grade, school to school, and from school to the working world
UF Articulation (Program) (1967 1980)
RT Advanced Placement Programs
College School Cooperation
College Transfer Students
Curriculum Development
Developmental Continuity
Education
Educational Mobility
Educational Planning
Institutional Cooperation
Intercollegiate Cooperation
Program Content
Transfer Policy
Transfer Programs
Unified Studies Curriculum
Upper Division Colleges

Articulation (Program) (1967 1980)
USE ARTICULATION (EDUCATION)

ARTICULATION (SPEECH) *Jul. 1966*
CIJE: 577 RIE: 355 GC: 450
UF Enunciation Improvement (1966 1980) #
BT Speech
RT Articulation Impairments
Diction
Language Rhythm
Phonetics
Speech Improvement
Speech Tests
Syllables
Vowels

ARTICULATION IMPAIRMENTS *Mar. 1980*
CIJE: 74 RIE: 21 GC: 220
SN Disorders involving the substitution, omission, distortion, and addition of speech sounds that are uncharacteristic of particular age groups (note: prior to mar80, this concept was indexed under "articulation (speech)")
BT Speech Handicaps
RT Articulation (Speech)
Cleft Palate
Speech
Speech Habits
Speech Improvement
Speech Tests
Speech Therapy
Stuttering
Visible Speech

Articulation Tests
USE SPEECH TESTS

ARTIFICIAL INTELLIGENCE *Feb. 1971*
CIJE: 180 RIE: 251 GC: 710
SN Capability of a device to perform functions normally associated with human intelligence
NT Expert Systems
RT Bionics
Cognitive Processes
Cognitive Psychology
Computers
Computer Science
Cybernetics
Heuristics
Intelligence
Logical Thinking
Robotics

ARTIFICIAL LANGUAGES *Jul. 1973*
CIJE: 38 RIE: 27 GC: 440
SN Languages created for international communication, e.g., esperanto and interlingua
UF Constructed Languages
BT Language
RT International Trade Vocabulary
Language Universals
Programing Languages

Artificial Satellites
USE SATELLITES (AEROSPACE)

ARTIFICIAL SPEECH *Aug. 1968*
CIJE: 30 RIE: 40 GC: 450
UF Simulated Speech
Synthetic Speech
BT Speech
RT Acoustic Phonetics
Distinctive Features (Language)
Language
Phonology
Sound Spectrographs

Artisans
USE CRAFT WORKERS

Artistic Talent
USE TALENT

ARTISTS *Jul. 1966*
CIJE: 492 RIE: 127 GC: 420
NT Musicians
BT Groups
RT Art
Art History
Art Teachers
Fine Arts
Painting (Visual Arts)

ARTS CENTERS *Jul. 1966*
CIJE: 120 RIE: 100 GC: 920
UF Art Galleries
Fine Arts Centers
BT Resource Centers
RT Art
Art Activities
Auditoriums
Cultural Centers
Drama Workshops
Educational Facilities
Fine Arts
Museums
Stages (Facilities)
Theaters

ASBESTOS *Nov. 1982*
CIJE: 40 RIE: 30 GC: 410
SN A variety of fibrous silicate minerals suitable for use where incombustible, nonconductive, or chemically resistant material is required
BT Minerals
RT Air Pollution
Construction Materials
Fire Protection
Geology
Hazardous Materials
Mining
Natural Resources
Physical Health

ASIAN AMERICANS *Aug. 1974*
CIJE: 208 RIE: 725 GC: 560
SN Citizens or permanent residents of the united states who are descendants of the indigenous peoples of east asia (china, japan, korea, mongolia) and southeast asia (note: prior to mar80, descendants of pacific islanders were included in this scope note)
UF Amerasians
American Orientals
Cambodian Americans #
Indochinese Americans #
Laotian Americans #
Oriental Americans
Vietnamese Americans #
NT Chinese Americans
Filipino Americans
Japanese Americans
Korean Americans
BT North Americans
RT Cambodians
Ethnic Groups
Indochinese
Laotians
Minority Groups
Pacific Americans
Vietnamese People

ASIAN HISTORY *Jul. 1966*
CIJE: 69 RIE: 177 GC: 430
BT History
RT Asian Studies
Middle Eastern History
Middle Eastern Studies
Non Western Civilization

Asian Music
USE ORIENTAL MUSIC

ASIAN STUDIES *Mar. 1973*
CIJE: 86 RIE: 272 GC: 400
SN Studies, usually interdisciplinary in approach, of such geographic areas as asiatic u.s.s.r., bangladesh, bhutan, china, india, indonesia, japan, korea, maldive islands, mongolia, nepal, pakistan, the philippines, sri lanka, and the southeast asian subcontinent
BT Area Studies
RT Asian History
Burmese Culture
Chinese Culture
Foreign Culture
Indians
Islamic Culture
Korean Culture
Middle Eastern Studies
Non Western Civilization

ASPHALTS *Jan. 1969*
CIJE: 5 RIE: 11 GC: 920
BT Construction Materials
RT Flooring
Road Construction
Roofing

ASPIRATION *Jul. 1966*
CIJE: 275 RIE: 570 GC: 120
SN Desire for the realization of ambitions, ideals, or accomplishments
UF Ambition
Aspiration Level
Low Level Aspiration (1966 1980)
NT Academic Aspiration
Occupational Aspiration
Parent Aspiration
RT Ability
Achievement
Achievement Need
Apathy
Aptitude
Goal Orientation
Motivation
Objectives
Performance
Self Concept
Student Educational Objectives

Aspiration Level
USE ASPIRATION

ASSEMBLY (MANUFACTURING) *Jul. 1966*
CIJE: 17 RIE: 80 GC: 650
BT Manufacturing
RT Agricultural Engineering
Agricultural Machinery
Equipment
Manufacturing Industry
Mass Production
Metal Working
Production Technicians
Sheet Metal Work

ASSEMBLY PROGRAMS *Jul. 1966*
CIJE: 24 RIE: 21 GC: 350
BT Programs
RT Group Activities
Group Instruction
Meetings
School Activities
Student Participation

Assertive Training
USE ASSERTIVENESS

ASSERTIVENESS *Mar. 1977*
CIJE: 325 RIE: 199 GC: 120
SN Bold, forceful expression of opinions or defense of one's interests
UF Assertiveness Training
Assertive Training
BT Behavior
RT Aggression
Counseling Techniques
Individual Psychology
Inhibition
Interpersonal Communication
Personality Traits
Psychological Patterns
Self Esteem
Self Expression
Social Behavior
Socialization

Assertiveness Training
USE ASSERTIVENESS

ASSESSED VALUATION *Jul. 1966*
CIJE: 45 RIE: 107 GC: 620
BT Property Appraisal
RT Building Obsolescence
Buildings
Estate Planning
Property Taxes
School Taxes
Taxes

ASSESSMENT CENTERS (PERSONNEL) *Oct. 1983*
CIJE: 39 RIE: 18 GC: 820
SN Personnel evaluation centers using multiple assessment techniques for staff selection, promotion, or development -- typically included are simulated work experiences and the use of multiple observers to appraise job-related behaviors
BT Facilities
RT Administrator Evaluation
Administrator Selection
Evaluation Methods
Job Performance
Job Placement
Management Development

= Two or more Descriptors are used to represent this term.
The term's main entry shows the appropriate coordination.

Observation
Occupational Tests
Personnel Evaluation
Personnel Selection
Professional Development
Promotion (Occupational)
Simulation
Situational Tests

ASSIGNMENTS *Jul. 1966*
CIJE: 337 RIE: 214 GC: 310
SN Learning tasks that are allotted to students or groups of students (note: prior to mar80, the use of this term was not restricted by a scope note)
UF Student Assignments
Textbook Assignments (1966 1980)
NT Homework
Reading Assignments
Research Papers (Students)
BT Instruction

Assimilation (Cultural)
USE ACCULTURATION

ASSISTANT PRINCIPALS *Jul. 1974*
CIJE: 72 RIE: 61 GC: 360
UF Vice Principals
BT Administrators
School Personnel
RT Principals
School Administration

ASSISTANT SUPERINTENDENT ROLE (1966 1980) *Jun. 1980*
CIJE: 9 RIE: 6 GC: 360
SN Invalid descriptor -- use "superintendents" (note: occasionally used indiscriminately in the past for "assistant principal role" -- see "assistant principals" for that concept)

Assistant Superintendents
USE SUPERINTENDENTS

ASSISTANTSHIPS *Oct. 1980*
CIJE: 2 RIE: 14 GC: 620
SN Financial aid in which college students, usually at the graduate level, are awarded assistant staff positions carrying stipends and, frequently, exemptions from fees
BT Student Financial Aid
RT Awards
Educational Finance
Eligibility
Fellowships
Grants
Internship Programs
Merit Scholarships
Professional Education
Research Assistants
Resident Assistants
Scholarship Funds
Student Costs
Student Employment
Teaching Assistants
Work Study Programs

ASSISTIVE DEVICES (FOR DISABLED) *Apr. 1986*
CIJE: RIE: GC: 220
SN Devices to aid the disabled to perform normal living or vocational tasks
UF Adaptive Equipment (Disabled)
Self Help Devices (Disabled)
NT Mobility Aids
Prostheses
BT Equipment
RT Biomedical Equipment
Communication Aids (For Disabled)
Disabilities
Normalization (Handicapped)
Sensory Aids

ASSOCIATE DEGREES *Jul. 1966*
CIJE: 183 RIE: 589 GC: 340
SN Degrees granted upon completion of an educational program of at least 2 but less than 4 academic years of college work, generally for completion of a curriculum of a 2-year institution -- includes associate in arts, associate in science, and associate in applied science degrees
UF Two Year College Degrees
BT Degrees (Academic)
RT Bachelors Degrees
Community Colleges
Degree Requirements
Technical Institutes
Two Year Colleges
Undergraduate Study

Association (Psychological) (1968 1980)
USE ASSOCIATION (PSYCHOLOGY)

ASSOCIATION (PSYCHOLOGY) *Mar. 1980*
CIJE: 230 RIE: 182 GC: 120
SN Process or state of establishing functional relationships between new and previously known stimuli and/or responses, so that the presence of one tends to evoke the other(s)
UF Association (Psychological) (1968 1980)
BT Cognitive Processes
RT Association Measures
Associative Learning
Behavior Chaining
Connected Discourse
Generalization
Learning Processes
Paired Associate Learning
Recognition (Psychology)
Serial Learning

ASSOCIATION MEASURES *Mar. 1980*
CIJE: 50 RIE: 51 GC: 830
SN Procedures or devices used to evaluate an individual's feelings, motives, or attitudes by requiring responses (usually spontaneous) to a set of verbal or pictorial stimuli (note: do not use for tests measuring paired associate learning)
UF Association Tests (1968 1980)
BT Projective Measures
RT Affective Measures
Association (Psychology)
Associative Learning
Attitude Measures
Patterned Responses
Personality Assessment
Personality Measures
Psychological Evaluation
Verbal Stimuli
Visual Stimuli

Association Tests (1968 1980)
USE ASSOCIATION MEASURES

Associations (Groups)
USE ORGANIZATIONS (GROUPS)

ASSOCIATIVE LEARNING *Jul. 1966*
CIJE: 399 RIE: 279 GC: 110
SN Learning that occurs through the establishment of functional relationships between new and previously known stimuli and/or responses
UF Word Associations (Reading)
NT Paired Associate Learning
BT Learning
RT Association (Psychology)
Association Measures
Aural Learning
Behavior Chaining
Learning Strategies
Nonverbal Learning
Serial Learning
Symbolic Learning
Visual Learning
Word Recognition

ASTHMA *Sep. 1968*
CIJE: 31 RIE: 14 GC: 210
BT Diseases
RT Allergy
Physical Health
Physiology
Special Health Problems

ASTRONOMY *Jul. 1966*
CIJE: 717 RIE: 275 GC: 490
BT Physical Sciences
RT Aerospace Education
Aerospace Technology
Earth Science
Evolution
Lunar Research
Navigation
Planetariums
Scientific Research
Space Exploration
Space Sciences
Spectroscopy

At Risk (Persons)
USE HIGH RISK PERSONS

Athabascan Languages
USE ATHAPASCAN LANGUAGES

ATHAPASCAN LANGUAGES *Sep. 1975*
CIJE: 5 RIE: 97 GC: 440
UF Athabascan Languages
NT Apache
Navajo
BT American Indian Languages
RT Alaska Natives

ATHLETES *Dec. 1969*
CIJE: 394 RIE: 242 GC: 470
BT Groups
RT Athletics
Eligibility
Sport Psychology

Athletic Activities (1966 1974)
USE ATHLETICS

ATHLETIC COACHES *Mar. 1971*
CIJE: 280 RIE: 199 GC: 470
BT Professional Personnel
RT Athletics
Physical Education
Physical Education Teachers
School Personnel
Sport Psychology

ATHLETIC EQUIPMENT *Jul. 1966*
CIJE: 96 RIE: 138 GC: 910
BT Equipment
RT Athletics
Educational Equipment
Gymnasiums
Physical Education
Physical Education Facilities
Physical Fitness
Physical Recreation Programs

ATHLETIC FIELDS *Jul. 1966*
CIJE: 42 RIE: 23 GC: 470
BT Facilities
RT Athletics
Field Houses
Gymnasiums
Parks
Physical Education
Physical Education Facilities
Physical Recreation Programs
Playgrounds
Recreational Activities
Recreational Facilities

Athletic Programs (1966 1980)
USE ATHLETICS

ATHLETICS *Jul. 1966*
CIJE: 1539 RIE: 1179 GC: 470
SN Sports, games, or physical contests often engaged in competitively
UF Athletic Activities (1966 1974)
Athletic Programs (1966 1980)
Sports
Sports News #
Sports Reporting #
NT Aquatic Sports
Archery
Bowling
College Athletics
Extramural Athletics
Fencing (Sport)
Golf
Gymnastics
Handball
Ice Skating
Intramural Athletics
Lifetime Sports
Orienteering
Racquet Sports
Roller Skating
Skiing
Table Tennis
Team Sports
Track And Field
Weightlifting
Womens Athletics
Wrestling
BT Physical Activities
RT Athletes
Athletic Coaches
Athletic Equipment
Athletic Fields
Bicycling
Eligibility
Exercise
Extracurricular Activities
Field Houses
Games
Gymnasiums
Horseback Riding
Jogging
Locker Rooms
News Reporting
Outdoor Activities
Physical Education
Physical Education Facilities
Physical Education Teachers
Physical Fitness
Physical Recreation Programs
Playground Activities
Recreational Activities
Running
Sport Psychology

ATLASES *Jul. 1966*
CIJE: 30 RIE: 40 GC: 730
BT Reference Materials
RT Cartography
Charts
Geography
Maps

Atmosphere (Social)
USE SOCIAL ENVIRONMENT

Atmospheric Pollution
USE AIR POLLUTION

Atomic Energy
USE NUCLEAR ENERGY

Atomic Physics
USE NUCLEAR PHYSICS

ATOMIC STRUCTURE *Jul. 1966*
CIJE: 269 RIE: 35 GC: 490
RT Atomic Theory
Chemistry
Crystallography
Force
Inorganic Chemistry
Matter
Molecular Structure
Nuclear Physics
Organic Chemistry
Physical Sciences
Physics
Radiation Biology
Radioisotopes
Space
Spectroscopy
Structural Analysis (Science)

ATOMIC THEORY *Jul. 1966*
CIJE: 216 RIE: 45 GC: 490
BT Theories
RT Atomic Structure
Force
Matter
Nuclear Energy
Nuclear Physics
Nuclear Warfare
Physics
Radiation Biology
Radioisotopes
Space

Atomic Warfare
USE NUCLEAR WARFARE

ATTACHMENT BEHAVIOR *Feb. 1975*
CIJE: 242 RIE: 172 GC: 120
SN Behavior exhibited by an individual attracted (maintaining proximity) to and dependent on a specific person or object for emotional satisfaction
UF Bonding (Behavior)
BT Behavior
RT Affective Behavior
Behavior Development
Emotional Development
Emotional Response
Exploratory Behavior
Identification (Psychology)
Infant Behavior
Interpersonal Relationship
Parent Child Relationship
Separation Anxiety

= Two or more Descriptors are used to represent this term.
The term's main entry shows the appropriate coordination.

ATTENDANCE *Jul. 1966*
CIJE: 327 RIE: 700 GC: 320
UF Absence (Students)
Attendance Services (1968 1980) #
Class Attendance (1966 1980)
School Attendance
NT Average Daily Attendance
College Attendance
Teacher Attendance
RT Academic Persistence
Access To Education
Attendance Officers
Attendance Patterns
Attendance Records
Auditing (Coursework)
Dropouts
Enrollment
Expulsion
Leaves Of Absence
No Shows
Out Of School Youth
Participation
Reentry Students
School Attendance Legislation
School Holding Power
School Registration
School Size
Stopouts
Students
Suspension
Transfer Policy
Transfer Students
Truancy
Withdrawal (Education)

ATTENDANCE OFFICERS *Jul. 1966*
CIJE: 8 RIE: 15 GC: 360
BT Pupil Personnel Workers
RT Attendance
Attendance Patterns
Attendance Records

ATTENDANCE PATTERNS *Jul. 1966*
CIJE: 153 RIE: 296 GC: 320
RT Attendance
Attendance Officers
Attendance Records
Average Daily Attendance
College Attendance
Truancy

ATTENDANCE RECORDS *Jul. 1966*
CIJE: 29 RIE: 82 GC: 320
BT Records (Forms)
RT Attendance
Attendance Officers
Attendance Patterns
Average Daily Attendance

Attendance Services (1968 1980)
USE ATTENDANCE; PUPIL PERSONNEL SERVICES

Attendant Training (1968 1980)
USE ATTENDANTS; JOB TRAINING

ATTENDANTS *Jul. 1966*
CIJE: 52 RIE: 60 GC: 640
SN Individuals who attend or accompany others to give service
UF Attendant Training (1968 1980) #
Companions (Occupation) (1968 1980)
BT Service Workers
RT Adult Day Care
Adult Foster Care
Allied Health Personnel
Home Health Aides
Household Workers
Nurses Aides
Occupational Home Economics
Resident Advisers
Residential Care

ATTENTION *Jul. 1966*
CIJE: 618 RIE: 327 GC: 110
RT Adaptation Level Theory
Arousal Patterns
Attention Control
Attention Deficit Disorders
Attention Span
Behavior
Curiosity
Habituation
Listening
Novelty (Stimulus Dimension)
Perception
Redundancy
Time On Task

ATTENTION CONTROL *Jul. 1966*
CIJE: 195 RIE: 124 GC: 110
RT Attention
Meditation
Motivation

ATTENTION DEFICIT DISORDERS *Jun. 1983*
CIJE: 34 RIE: 18 GC: 220
SN Developmentally inappropriate inattention and impulsivity
BT Disabilities
RT Attention
Attention Span
Behavior Disorders
Emotional Disturbances
Exceptional Persons
Hyperactivity
Learning Disabilities
Neurological Impairments

ATTENTION SPAN *Jul. 1966*
CIJE: 296 RIE: 142 GC: 120
BT Psychological Characteristics
RT Attention
Attention Deficit Disorders
Conceptual Tempo
Hyperactivity
Motivation
Shift Studies

ATTITUDE CHANGE *Mar. 1980*
CIJE: 2932 RIE: 2722 GC: 120
UF Changing Attitudes (1966 1980)
BT Change
RT Adjustment (To Environment)
Adoption (Ideas)
Attitudes
Behavior Change
Change Agents
Change Strategies
Cognitive Restructuring
Personality Change

ATTITUDE MEASURES *Mar. 1980*
CIJE: 942 RIE: 1509 GC: 830
SN Procedures or devices used to obtain quantified descriptions of an individual's predispositions to react to certain people, objects, situations, ideas, etc.
UF Attitude Tests (1966 1980)
Opinion Scales
NT Semantic Differential
BT Measures (Individuals)
RT Affective Measures
Association Measures
Attitudes
Beliefs
Forced Choice Technique
Interest Inventories
Opinions
Personality Measures
Questionnaires
Social Desirability
Surveys
Values

Attitude Tests (1966 1980)
USE ATTITUDE MEASURES

ATTITUDES *Jul. 1966*
CIJE: 3709 RIE: 3070 GC: 120
SN Predispositions to react to certain persons, objects, situations, ideas, etc. in a particular manner -- not always consciously held (as are beliefs) nor readily verbalized (as are opinions), they are characterized as either affective or valuative (note: use a more specific term if possible)
NT Administrator Attitudes
Anti Intellectualism
Beliefs
Black Attitudes
Childhood Attitudes
Community Attitudes
Counselor Attitudes
Design Preferences
Dropout Attitudes
Educational Attitudes
Employee Attitudes
Employer Attitudes
Family Attitudes
Language Attitudes
Life Satisfaction
Majority Attitudes
Marital Satisfaction
Negative Attitudes
Opinions
Parent Attitudes
Participant Satisfaction
Political Attitudes
Program Attitudes
Racial Attitudes
Reading Attitudes
Regional Attitudes
School Attitudes
Scientific Attitudes
Social Attitudes
Sportsmanship
Stereotypes
Student Attitudes
Student Teacher Attitudes
Teacher Attitudes
Trust (Psychology)
User Satisfaction (Information)
Work Attitudes
RT Affective Behavior
Attitude Change
Attitude Measures
Behavior
Bias
Cognitive Dissonance
Cognitive Structures
Expectation
Human Dignity
Humanization
Interests
Psychological Patterns
Reputation
Response Style (Tests)
Semantic Differential

Attorneys
USE LAWYERS

Attractiveness (Between Persons)
USE INTERPERSONAL ATTRACTION

ATTRIBUTION THEORY *Oct. 1976*
CIJE: 645 RIE: 478 GC: 810
SN Theory focusing on perceived causes of behavior
UF Causal Attributions
BT Behavior Theories
RT Etiology
Locus Of Control
Personality
Psychological Characteristics
Self Concept
Social Cognition

ATTRITION (RESEARCH STUDIES) *Jun. 1977*
CIJE: 25 RIE: 71 GC: 810
SN Reduction in size of the population sample during the period of time covered by a longitudinal study (note: do not confuse with "student attrition")
UF Mortality (Research Studies)
RT Control Groups
Dropouts
Experimental Groups
Longitudinal Studies
Matched Groups
Research
Research Design
Research Methodology
Research Problems
Sample Size
Sampling
Statistical Bias

Attrition (Students)
USE STUDENT ATTRITION

AUDIENCE ANALYSIS *Oct. 1983*
CIJE: 72 RIE: 119 GC: 810
SN Gathering and interpreting information about the recipients of oral, written, or visual communication
BT Evaluation Methods
RT Audience Participation
Audiences
Communication Research
Mass Media Effects
Media Research
Public Speaking
Writing (Composition)

AUDIENCE PARTICIPATION *Jul. 1966*
CIJE: 49 RIE: 48 GC: 720
BT Participation
RT Audience Analysis
Audiences

AUDIENCES *Aug. 1968*
CIJE: 578 RIE: 564 GC: 720
UF Spectators
BT Groups
RT Audience Analysis
Audience Participation
Communication (Thought Transfer)
Drama
Listening Groups
Mass Instruction
Mass Media
Mass Media Effects
Radio
Television Viewing
Theater Arts

Audio Active Compare Laboratories (1967 1980)
USE LANGUAGE LABORATORIES

Audio Active Laboratories (1967 1980)
USE LANGUAGE LABORATORIES

AUDIO EQUIPMENT *Jul. 1966*
CIJE: 209 RIE: 200 GC: 910
UF Central Sound Systems (1966 1980)
Sound Equipment
Sound Systems
NT Audiotape Recorders
Hearing Aids
Microphones
Sound Spectrographs
BT Equipment
RT Acoustics
Audiodisks
Audiotape Cassettes
Audiotape Recordings
Audiovisual Aids
Broadcast Reception Equipment
Language Laboratories
Noise (Sound)
Photographic Equipment
Projection Equipment
Radio
Sound Effects
Special Effects
Telephone Communications Systems
Video Equipment

Audio Passive Laboratories (1968 1980)
USE LANGUAGE LABORATORIES

Audio Video Laboratories (1967 1980)
USE AUDIOVISUAL CENTERS

Audiodisc Recordings (1980 1986)
USE AUDIODISKS

AUDIODISKS *Aug. 1986*
CIJE: RIE: GC: 720
UF Audiodisc Recordings (1980 1986)
Language Records (Phonograph) (1966 1980)
Phonograph Records (1966 1980)
BT Nonprint Media
RT Audio Equipment
Audiotape Recordings
Audiovisual Aids
Discographies
Optical Disks
Oral History
Programing (Broadcast)
Radio
Talking Books
Videodisks

Audiolingual Approaches
USE AUDIOLINGUAL METHODS

AUDIOLINGUAL METHODS *Jul. 1966*
CIJE: 361 RIE: 859 GC: 450
SN Foreign language teaching methods, based on behaviorist theory, that emphasize the development of oral skills through habit formation, fostered via repetition and reinforcement
UF Audiolingual Approaches
BT Teaching Methods
RT Audiolingual Skills
Aural Learning
Conversational Language Courses
Grammar Translation Method
Interference (Language)
Second Language Instruction
Second Language Learning

= Two or more Descriptors are used to represent this term.
The term's main entry shows the appropriate coordination.

AUDIOLINGUAL SKILLS *Jul. 1966*
CIJE: 143 RIE: 401 GC: 450
UF Aural Oral Skills
NT Listening Skills
Speech Skills
BT Language Skills
RT Audiolingual Methods
Basic Skills
Communication Skills
Conversational Language Courses
Language Fluency

Audiologists (1968 1980)
USE ALLIED HEALTH PERSONNEL; AUDIOLOGY

AUDIOLOGY *Jul. 1966*
CIJE: 107 RIE: 79 GC: 210
SN Study of hearing and hearing impairments -- includes assessment, therapy, and rehabilitation of hearing-impaired individuals
UF Audiologists (1968 1980) #
Audiometrists (1967 1980) #
BT Medicine
RT Auditory Evaluation
Auditory Tests
Ears
Hearing (Physiology)
Hearing Aids
Hearing Conservation
Hearing Impairments
Hearing Therapy
Speech And Hearing Clinics

AUDIOMETRIC TESTS *Jul. 1966*
CIJE: 72 RIE: 34 GC: 830
SN Tests assessing hearing acuity and range using an audiometer
BT Auditory Tests
RT Auditory Evaluation
Hearing (Physiology)
Hearing Impairments

Audiometrists (1967 1980)
USE ALLIED HEALTH PERSONNEL; AUDIOLOGY

Audiotape Cartridges
USE AUDIOTAPE CASSETTES

Audiotape Cassette Recorders
USE AUDIOTAPE CASSETTES; AUDIOTAPE RECORDERS

AUDIOTAPE CASSETTES *Mar. 1980*
CIJE: 32 RIE: 42 GC: 720
UF Audiotape Cartridges
Audiotape Cassette Recorders #
BT Magnetic Tape Cassettes
RT Audio Equipment
Audiotape Recorders
Audiotape Recordings
Videotape Cassettes
Videotape Recordings

AUDIOTAPE RECORDERS *Mar. 1980*
CIJE: 1 RIE: 12 GC: 910
UF Audiotape Cassette Recorders #
BT Audio Equipment
Tape Recorders
RT Audiotape Cassettes
Audiotape Recordings
Audiovisual Aids
Videotape Recorders

AUDIOTAPE RECORDINGS *Jan. 1979*
CIJE: 314 RIE: 397 GC: 720
SN Magnetic tapes on which electric signals are recorded and can be reproduced mechanically or electronically as sound -- stored on open reels, cassettes, or cartridges
UF Language Tapes
Master Tapes (Audio) (1968 1980)
Phonotape Recordings (1966 1978)
Sound Tape Recordings
BT Tape Recordings
RT Audiodisks
Audio Equipment
Audiotape Cassettes
Audiotape Recorders
Audiovisual Aids
Oral History
Programing (Broadcast)
Radio
Sound Effects
Talking Books
Videotape Recordings

AUDIOVISUAL AIDS *Jul. 1966*
CIJE: 2854 RIE: 3543 GC: 720
SN Nonprint instructional materials and the equipment required for their display (note: prior to mar80, the instruction "nonprint media, use audiovisual aids" was carried in the thesaurus -- corresponds to pubtype code 100 -- do not use except as the subject of a document)
UF Audiovisual Equipment
Audiovisual Materials
Audiovisual Media
NT Instructional Films
Protocol Materials
BT Educational Media
RT Audiodisks
Audio Equipment
Audiotape Recorders
Audiotape Recordings
Audiovisual Centers
Audiovisual Communications
Audiovisual Coordinators
Audiovisual Instruction
Autoinstructional Aids
Bulletin Boards
Cartoons
Chalkboards
Courseware
Display Aids
Documentaries
Educational Equipment
Educational Technology
Electromechanical Aids
Electronic Equipment
Filmstrips
Instructional Materials
Learning Resources Centers
Mass Media
Microphones
Nonprint Media
Optical Disks
Photographic Equipment
Photographs
Programed Instructional Materials
Projection Equipment
Screens (Displays)
Sensory Aids
Slides
Talking Books
Three Dimensional Aids
Transparencies
Videodisks
Video Equipment
Videotape Recorders
Videotape Recordings
Visual Aids

AUDIOVISUAL CENTERS *Jul. 1966*
CIJE: 172 RIE: 236 GC: 920
SN Instructional areas with equipment for the storage and use of audiovisual aids
UF Audio Video Laboratories (1967 1980)
BT Educational Facilities
Resource Centers
RT Audiovisual Aids
Audiovisual Communications
Audiovisual Coordinators
Learning Laboratories
Learning Resources Centers

Audiovisual Communication (1967 1980)
USE AUDIOVISUAL COMMUNICATIONS

AUDIOVISUAL COMMUNICATIONS *Mar. 1980*
CIJE: 201 RIE: 261 GC: 720
SN Transmission of instructional information by audio and/or visual systems (note: prior to mar80, "audiovisual communication" was not scoped and was occasionally used in noninstructional settings)
UF Audiovisual Communication (1967 1980)
NT Dial Access Information Systems
Educational Radio
Educational Television
Loop Induction Systems
BT Communications
RT Audiovisual Aids
Audiovisual Centers
Audiovisual Instruction
Educational Technology
Media Selection

AUDIOVISUAL COORDINATORS *Feb. 1969*
CIJE: 38 RIE: 39 GC: 360
SN Individuals at the school unit or district level who have responsibility for audiovisual materials and equipment
UF Audiovisual Directors (1969 1980)
BT Coordinators
Media Specialists
School Personnel
RT Audiovisual Aids
Audiovisual Centers
Audiovisual Instruction

Audiovisual Directors (1969 1980)
USE AUDIOVISUAL COORDINATORS

Audiovisual Education
USE AUDIOVISUAL INSTRUCTION

Audiovisual Equipment
USE AUDIOVISUAL AIDS

AUDIOVISUAL INSTRUCTION *Jul. 1966*
CIJE: 879 RIE: 1001 GC: 310
SN Production, selection, and utilization of audiovisual aids in instruction
UF Audiovisual Education
Audiovisual Programs (1966 1980)
BT Multimedia Instruction
RT Audiovisual Aids
Audiovisual Communications
Audiovisual Coordinators
Educational Radio
Educational Television
Instructional Films
Intermode Differences
Listening Groups
Protocol Materials
Repetitive Film Showings
Telecourses

Audiovisual Materials
USE AUDIOVISUAL AIDS

Audiovisual Media
USE AUDIOVISUAL AIDS

Audiovisual Programs (1966 1980)
USE AUDIOVISUAL INSTRUCTION

AUDITING (COURSEWORK) *Aug. 1986*
CIJE: RIE: GC: 320
SN Attendance in classes or courses without receiving academic credit
RT Attendance
Continuing Education
Continuing Education Units
Courses
Credits
Enrollment
Remedial Programs
Student Interests

Audition (Physiology) (1967 1980)
USE HEARING (PHYSIOLOGY)

AUDITORIUMS *Jul. 1966*
CIJE: 35 RIE: 52 GC: 920
BT Facilities
RT Arts Centers
Dramatics
Educational Facilities
Music Facilities
Recreational Facilities
Stages (Facilities)
Theaters
Windowless Rooms

Auditory Comprehension
USE LISTENING COMPREHENSION

AUDITORY DISCRIMINATION *Jul. 1966*
CIJE: 346 RIE: 378 GC: 110
SN Ability to distinguish sounds of varying frequencies, intensities, and patterns
BT Auditory Perception
RT Auditory Stimuli
Auditory Tests
Auditory Training
Aural Learning
Discrimination Learning
Psychoacoustics

AUDITORY EVALUATION *Jul. 1966*
CIJE: 83 RIE: 86 GC: 820
SN Determination of an individual's ability to hear and of any needed treatment
BT Medical Evaluation
RT Audiology
Audiometric Tests
Auditory Tests
Hearing (Physiology)
Hearing Impairments
Hearing Therapy
Speech And Hearing Clinics

AUDITORY PERCEPTION *Jul. 1966*
CIJE: 821 RIE: 520 GC: 110
SN Ability to identify and assign meaning to sounds
NT Auditory Discrimination
BT Perception
RT Acoustic Phonetics
Auditory Tests
Auditory Training
Aural Learning
Echolocation
Figural Aftereffects
Hearing (Physiology)
Language Processing
Listening Comprehension
Perception Tests
Perceptual Handicaps
Psychoacoustics
Sensory Experience

AUDITORY STIMULI *Mar. 1980*
CIJE: 474 RIE: 200 GC: 110
UF Aural Stimuli (1966 1980)
BT Stimuli
RT Acoustics
Auditory Discrimination
Echolocation
Electrical Stimuli
Hearing (Physiology)
Listening
Noise (Sound)
Psychoacoustics
Verbal Stimuli
Visual Stimuli

AUDITORY TESTS *Jul. 1966*
CIJE: 191 RIE: 122 GC: 830
SN Tests designed to assess hearing ability
UF Auditory Visual Tests (1966 1980) #
Hearing Tests
Otological Tests
NT Audiometric Tests
BT Tests
RT Audiology
Auditory Discrimination
Auditory Evaluation
Auditory Perception
Diagnostic Tests
Ears
Hearing (Physiology)
Hearing Impairments
Perception Tests
Physical Examinations
Screening Tests

AUDITORY TRAINING *Jul. 1966*
CIJE: 119 RIE: 154 GC: 400
SN Training in the recognition and interpretation of common sounds, such as musical sounds or speech (note: use "hearing therapy" for auditory training of the hearing-impaired -- prior to mar80, the use of this term was not restricted by a scope note)
BT Sensory Training
RT Auditory Discrimination
Auditory Perception
Aural Learning
Hearing Therapy
Language Acquisition
Listening Comprehension
Perceptual Handicaps
Sensory Integration

Auditory Visual Tests (1966 1980)
USE AUDITORY TESTS; VISION TESTS

= Two or more Descriptors are used to represent this term.
The term's main entry shows the appropriate coordination.

AUDITS (VERIFICATION) *Aug. 1986*
CIJE: RIE: GC: 820
SN Verifications of legality, fidelity, efficiency, or feasibility of procedures, operations, transactions, or expenditures, often by an independent person or agency
NT Communication Audits
Energy Audits
Financial Audits
RT Accountability
Compliance (Legal)
Evaluation Methods
Inspection
Measurement Techniques
Program Administration
Program Effectiveness
Quality Control
Recordkeeping
Standards

Aural Comprehension
USE LISTENING COMPREHENSION

Aural Language Learning
USE AURAL LEARNING; LANGUAGE ACQUISITION

AURAL LEARNING *Jul. 1966*
CIJE: 213 RIE: 211 GC: 110
SN Learning through listening (note: do not confuse with "auditory training")
UF Aural Language Learning #
BT Learning
RT Associative Learning
Audiolingual Methods
Auditory Discrimination
Auditory Perception
Auditory Training
Learning Modalities
Listening Comprehension
Multisensory Learning
Phonics

Aural Oral Skills
USE AUDIOLINGUAL SKILLS

Aural Stimuli (1966 1980)
USE AUDITORY STIMULI

Aurally Handicapped (1966 1980)
USE HEARING IMPAIRMENTS

AUSTRALIAN ABORIGINAL LANGUAGES *Jul. 1966*
CIJE: 10 RIE: 20 GC: 440
BT Languages
RT Australian Literature

AUSTRALIAN LITERATURE *Jun. 1970*
CIJE: 10 RIE: 11 GC: 430
BT Literature
RT Australian Aboriginal Languages

AUSTRO ASIATIC LANGUAGES *Jul. 1966*
CIJE: 3 RIE: 13 GC: 440
NT Cambodian
BT Languages
RT Sino Tibetan Languages

Austronesian Languages
USE MALAYO POLYNESIAN LANGUAGES

AUTEURISM *May. 1976*
CIJE: 16 RIE: 18 GC: 430
SN The consideration of films as embodiments of the personalities of film directors
UF Film Auteurism
RT Creativity
Film Production
Film Production Specialists
Films
Film Study

AUTHORING AIDS (PROGRAMING) *Oct. 1983*
CIJE: 48 RIE: 23 GC: 730
SN Guidelines and instructions to assist in designing, writing, and editing of computer software -- such aids may themselves be software
UF Authoring Languages #
Authoring Systems
RT Computer Assisted Instruction
Computer Oriented Programs
Computer Software
Guidelines
Programing
Programing Languages

Authoring Languages
USE AUTHORING AIDS (PROGRAMING); PROGRAMING LANGUAGES

Authoring Systems
USE AUTHORING AIDS (PROGRAMING)

AUTHORITARIANISM *Dec. 1969*
CIJE: 221 RIE: 124 GC: 120
RT Dogmatism
Imperialism
Personal Autonomy
Political Attitudes
Political Science
Sociology
Totalitarianism

Authority Structure
USE POWER STRUCTURE

AUTHORS *Sep. 1969*
CIJE: 1027 RIE: 414 GC: 430
UF Writers
NT Poets
BT Groups
RT Editors
Faculty Publishing
Literature
Publications
Writing For Publication

AUTISM *Jul. 1966*
CIJE: 633 RIE: 244 GC: 220
BT Psychosis
RT Behavior Disorders
Developmental Disabilities
Emotional Disturbances
Interpersonal Relationship
Personality Problems
Schizophrenia
Withdrawal (Psychology)

AUTO BODY REPAIRERS *Mar. 1980*
CIJE: 2 RIE: 83 GC: 640
UF Auto Body Repairmen (1966 1980)
Body And Fender Repairers
BT Skilled Workers
RT Auto Mechanics
Motor Vehicles
Painting (Industrial Arts)
Repair

Auto Body Repairmen (1966 1980)
USE AUTO BODY REPAIRERS

AUTO MECHANICS *Jul. 1966*
CIJE: 94 RIE: 523 GC: 640
UF Auto Mechanics (Occupation) (1968 1980)
Automobile Mechanics
Diesel Mechanics
Truck Mechanics
BT Mechanics (Process)
RT Auto Body Repairers
Diesel Engines
Engines
Industrial Arts
Motor Vehicles
Power Technology
Skilled Occupations
Small Engine Mechanics

Auto Mechanics (Occupation) (1968 1980)
USE AUTO MECHANICS

AUTO PARTS CLERKS *Mar. 1980*
CIJE: RIE: 20 GC: 640
UF Auto Parts Men (1968 1980)
BT Sales Workers
RT Motor Vehicles
Sales Occupations

Auto Parts Men (1968 1980)
USE AUTO PARTS CLERKS

AUTOBIOGRAPHIES *Jul. 1966*
CIJE: 194 RIE: 98 GC: 730
SN Accounts people write of their own lives
BT Biographies
RT Diaries
Personal Narratives

AUTOINSTRUCTIONAL AIDS *Jul. 1966*
CIJE: 373 RIE: 1038 GC: 730
SN Instructional materials, equipment, or systems used, without the aid of a teacher, in individual or individualized instruction to present information and inform learners of their progress
UF Self Instruction Aids
NT Teaching Machines
BT Educational Media
RT Audiovisual Aids
Computer Assisted Instruction
Courseware
Educational Equipment
Electromechanical Aids
Electronic Classrooms
Independent Study
Individual Instruction
Individualized Instruction
Instructional Materials
Learning Laboratories
Programed Instruction
Programed Instructional Materials

Autoinstructional Laboratories (1967 1980)
USE LEARNING LABORATORIES

Autoinstructional Methods (1966 1980)
USE PROGRAMED INSTRUCTION

Autoinstructional Programs (1966 1980)
USE PROGRAMED INSTRUCTION

Automatic Data Processing
USE DATA PROCESSING

AUTOMATIC INDEXING *Oct. 1970*
CIJE: 125 RIE: 87 GC: 710
SN Selection of keywords from a document and construction of index entries using a machine
UF Computer Assisted Indexing
Machine Aided Indexing
BT Indexing
RT Automation
Computational Linguistics
Indexes
Machine Translation
Permuted Indexes

AUTOMATION *Jul. 1966*
CIJE: 451 RIE: 734 GC: 490
SN Investigation, design, development, and application of methods of rendering processes automatic, self-moving, or self-controlling
UF Mechanization
NT Library Automation
Robotics
BT Technology
RT Automatic Indexing
Computers
Computer Science
Cybernetics
Data Processing
Electromechanical Technology
Electronic Control
Instrumentation
Job Simplification
Machine Translation
Man Machine Systems
Numerical Control
Obsolescence
Technological Advancement
Test Scoring Machines
Word Processing

Automobile Mechanics
USE AUTO MECHANICS

AUXILIARY LABORERS *Jul. 1966*
CIJE: RIE: 7 GC: 630
UF Auxiliary Workers
BT Laborers

Auxiliary School Services
USE ANCILLARY SCHOOL SERVICES

Auxiliary Workers
USE AUXILIARY LABORERS

AVERAGE DAILY ATTENDANCE *Jul. 1966*
CIJE: 16 RIE: 113 GC: 320
SN Average of the number of students present at (as opposed to enrolled in) a school during the time it is in session
BT Attendance
Incidence
RT Attendance Patterns
Attendance Records
Average Daily Membership
School Attendance Legislation

Average Daily Enrollment (1968 1980)
USE AVERAGE DAILY MEMBERSHIP

AVERAGE DAILY MEMBERSHIP *Mar. 1980*
CIJE: 5 RIE: 49 GC: 320
SN Average of the number of students registered or enrolled (as opposed to in attendance) in a school during the time it is in session
UF Average Daily Enrollment (1968 1980)
BT Enrollment Rate
RT Average Daily Attendance
Declining Enrollment
Enrollment
Enrollment Influences
Enrollment Projections
Enrollment Trends
School Demography

Average Students (1967 1980)
USE STUDENTS

AVIATION MECHANICS *Jul. 1966*
CIJE: 11 RIE: 95 GC: 640
UF Aircraft Mechanics
BT Aviation Technology
Mechanics (Process)
RT Aerospace Industry
Aviation Vocabulary
Engines
Power Technology
Skilled Occupations

AVIATION TECHNOLOGY *Jul. 1966*
CIJE: 104 RIE: 185 GC: 490
NT Aviation Mechanics
BT Aerospace Technology
RT Aerospace Education
Aerospace Industry
Aircraft Pilots
Airports
Air Traffic Control
Air Transportation
Aviation Vocabulary
Navigation
Technical Education

AVIATION VOCABULARY *Jul. 1966*
CIJE: 4 RIE: 25 GC: 450
BT Vocabulary
RT Aerospace Education
Aerospace Industry
Aircraft Pilots
Air Traffic Control
Aviation Mechanics
Aviation Technology

AWARDS *Jun. 1975*
CIJE: 291 RIE: 165 GC: 520
SN Verbal or material commendations, calling attention to activities, performances, or qualities
BT Recognition (Achievement)
RT Achievement Rating
Assistantships
Fellowships
Grants
Honor Societies
Incentives
Performance
Prestige
Professional Recognition
Rewards
Sanctions
Scholarships

Awareness
USE PERCEPTION

Away From The Job Training
USE OFF THE JOB TRAINING

= Two or more Descriptors are used to represent this term.
The term's main entry shows the appropriate coordination.

AYMARA *Sep. 1968*
CIJE: 2 RIE: 10 GC: 440
SN Language of the south american indians living in the southern part of the titicaca plateau of the central andes (a geographic area roughly corresponding to bolivia and peru)
BT American Indian Languages

AZERBAIJANI *Jul. 1966*
CIJE: RIE: 7 GC: 440
BT Turkic Languages

Baccalaureate Degrees
USE BACHELORS DEGREES

Bachelor Of Arts Degrees
USE BACHELORS DEGREES

Bachelor Of Science Degrees
USE BACHELORS DEGREES

BACHELORS DEGREES *Jul. 1966*
CIJE: 334 RIE: 524 GC: 340
UF Baccalaureate Degrees
Bachelor Of Arts Degrees
Bachelor Of Science Degrees
Three Year Bachelors Degrees #
BT Degrees (Academic)
RT Associate Degrees
College Graduates
Degree Requirements
Doctoral Degrees
External Degree Programs
Masters Degrees
Specialist In Education Degrees
Undergraduate Study

BACK TO BASICS *Sep. 1982*
CIJE: 80 RIE: 50 GC: 330
SN Educational movement stressing basic skills, achievement, and accountability -- begun in the early 1970s as a protest against school permissiveness and declining student performance
BT Education
RT Academic Standards
Basic Skills
Competency Based Education
Conventional Instruction
Educational Quality
Minimum Competencies
Traditional Schools

BACKGROUND *Jul. 1966*
CIJE: 195 RIE: 213 GC: 120
SN Sum of the regular and persistent influences (experiences, conditions, circumstances, events, etc.) contributing to the present development or characteristics of an individual, group, or organization (note: use a more specific term if possible -- do not confuse with "history")
NT Cultural Background
Educational Background
Experience
Parent Background
Socioeconomic Background
Teacher Background
RT Biographical Inventories
Credentials
Environment
History
Individual Characteristics
Individual Development
Individual Differences
Influences
Opportunities
Prerequisites
Profiles
Qualifications
Reputation

BADMINTON *Jun. 1984*
CIJE: 6 RIE: 13 GC: 470
BT Racquet Sports

Bahasa Indonesia
USE INDONESIAN

Bakeries
USE BAKERY INDUSTRY

BAKERY INDUSTRY *Jun. 1977*
CIJE: 2 RIE: 15 GC: 650
SN Concerned with producing and marketing baked goods (e.g., breads, cakes)
UF Bakeries
BT Industry
RT Food
Food Processing Occupations
Food Service
Occupational Home Economics

BALLADS *Jan. 1970*
CIJE: 21 RIE: 9 GC: 430
BT Literary Genres
Lyric Poetry
Songs
RT Epics
Odes
Sonnets

Ballet (1966 1980)
USE DANCE

BALTIC LANGUAGES *Nov. 1970*
CIJE: 7 RIE: 7 GC: 440
NT Latvian
Lithuanian
BT Indo European Languages
RT Estonian

BALUCHI *Jul. 1966*
CIJE: RIE: 4 GC: 440
BT Indo European Languages

BANDS (MUSIC) *Jul. 1966*
CIJE: 129 RIE: 53 GC: 420
UF Marching Bands
RT Applied Music
Jazz
Music
Music Activities
Musical Instruments
Musicians
Music Techniques
Orchestras

BANKING *Jul. 1966*
CIJE: 116 RIE: 226 GC: 620
UF Banking Industry
BT Industry
RT Banking Vocabulary
Business Education
Capital
Economics
Finance Occupations
Financial Services
Investment
Monetary Systems
Money Management
Student Loan Programs

Banking Industry
USE BANKING

BANKING VOCABULARY *Jul. 1966*
CIJE: 3 RIE: 12 GC: 450
BT Vocabulary
RT Banking

BANTU LANGUAGES *Apr. 1970*
CIJE: 14 RIE: 43 GC: 440
NT Bemba
Chinyanja
Ganda
Kirundi
Kituba
Lingala
Shona
Siswati
Swahili
BT African Languages

BARBERS *Jul. 1966*
CIJE: 1 RIE: 24 GC: 640
BT Service Workers

Barbiturates
USE SEDATIVES

Bards
USE POETS

BAROQUE LITERATURE *May. 1970*
CIJE: 11 RIE: 2 GC: 430
SN Literature of the late sixteenth to early eighteenth centuries characterized by elaborate, sometimes grotesque, ornamentation and complexity
BT Literature
RT Eighteenth Century Literature
Seventeenth Century Literature
Sixteenth Century Literature
World Literature

Barrier Free Environment (For Disabled)
USE ACCESSIBILITY (FOR DISABLED)

Barristers
USE LAWYERS

BASAA *Jun. 1971*
CIJE: RIE: 3 GC: 440
BT African Languages

BASAL READING *Mar. 1980*
CIJE: 201 RIE: 195 GC: 460
SN Instruction that develops reading skills through the use of a series of reading materials which are designed in sequential steps for successive levels of achievement (note: do not confuse with "beginning reading")
BT Reading
Reading Instruction
RT Basic Vocabulary
Beginning Reading
Phonics
Reading Materials
Reading Programs
Sight Method
Sight Vocabulary

BASEBALL *Jun. 1975*
CIJE: 43 RIE: 35 GC: 470
BT Team Sports
RT Softball

BASHKIR *Jul. 1966*
CIJE: RIE: 3 GC: 440
BT Turkic Languages

BASIC BUSINESS EDUCATION *Jun. 1983*
CIJE: 5 RIE: 8 GC: 400
SN Instruction or study in personal business affairs -- areas of concentration include legal knowledge, recordkeeping, buying, and money management
UF General Business Education
BT Education
RT Business Skills
Citizenship Education
Consumer Education
Daily Living Skills
Economics Education
Home Management
Money Management

Basic Language Patterns
USE LANGUAGE PATTERNS

BASIC READING (1967 1980) *Mar. 1980*
CIJE: 168 RIE: 385 GC: 460
SN Invalid descriptor -- used indiscriminately in indexing -- see such descriptors as "basal reading," "beginning reading," "functional reading," "reading readiness," etc.

Basic Research
USE RESEARCH

BASIC SKILLS *Jul. 1966*
CIJE: 1487 RIE: 2955 GC: 400
SN Fundamental skills that are the basis of later learning and achievement (note: coordinate with subject-matter descriptors -- do not confuse with "minimum competencies")
UF Fundamental Skills (School)
NT Alphabetizing Skills
BT Skills
RT Adult Basic Education
Audiolingual Skills
Back To Basics
Basic Vocabulary
Beginning Reading
Communication Skills
Developmental Studies Programs
Functional Literacy
Language Skills
Literacy
Literacy Education
Mathematics Skills
Minimum Competencies
Minimum Competency Testing
Reading Skills
Skill Development
Spatial Ability
Study Skills
Verbal Ability
Vocabulary Skills
Writing Skills

BASIC VOCABULARY *Jul. 1966*
CIJE: 40 RIE: 111 GC: 450
SN Fundamental vocabulary considered essential to effective comprehension and expression (common to all fields and subjects)
BT Vocabulary
RT Basal Reading
Basic Skills
Reading Comprehension
Reading Readiness
Sight Vocabulary
Vocabulary Skills
Word Lists

Basic Word Lists
USE WORD LISTS

BASKETBALL *Feb. 1978*
CIJE: 54 RIE: 42 GC: 470
BT Team Sports

BASQUE *Jul. 1966*
CIJE: 12 RIE: 5 GC: 440
BT Languages

BATTERED WOMEN *Mar. 1980*
CIJE: 61 RIE: 78 GC: 530
SN Women who are victims of persistent physical or emotional abuse by their mates
UF Abused Women
BT Females
RT Child Abuse
Elder Abuse
Family Problems
Family Violence
Marital Instability
Rape
Sexual Abuse
Victims Of Crime
Violence

Batteries (Electric)
USE ELECTRIC BATTERIES

BAYESIAN STATISTICS *Aug. 1971*
CIJE: 107 RIE: 120 GC: 480
SN Procedures that combine data from new observations with prior observations or estimates to derive new and more precise estimates
BT Statistical Analysis
Statistics
RT Adaptive Testing
Expectancy Tables
Hypothesis Testing
Nonparametric Statistics
Predictive Measurement
Probability
Statistical Inference
Statistical Significance

Beauticians
USE COSMETOLOGY

Beauty Culture
USE COSMETOLOGY

Beauty Operators
USE COSMETOLOGY

Beginning Farmer Education
USE YOUNG FARMER EDUCATION

BEGINNING READING *Jul. 1966*
CIJE: 895 RIE: 1347 GC: 460
SN Initial activities, processes, or behaviors involved in learning to read
BT Reading
RT Basal Reading
Basic Skills
Decoding (Reading)

= Two or more Descriptors are used to represent this term.
The term's main entry shows the appropriate coordination.

Early Reading
Initial Teaching Alphabet
Language Experience Approach
Phonics
Prereading Experience
Reading Readiness
Sight Method
Sight Vocabulary

BEGINNING TEACHERS *Jul. 1966*
CIJE: 388 RIE: 518 GC: 360
SN Certified teachers entering their first teaching position
UF First Year Teachers
BT Teachers
RT Master Teachers
Probationary Period
Teacher Certification
Teacher Employment
Teacher Orientation
Teaching Experience

Beginning Workers
USE ENTRY WORKERS

BEHAVIOR *Jul. 1966*
CIJE: 974 RIE: 827 GC: 120
SN The aggregate of observable responses of an organism to internal and external stimuli (note: use a more specific term if possible)
UF Conduct (1966 1980)
NT Adjustment (To Environment)
Affective Behavior
Animal Behavior
Assertiveness
Attachment Behavior
Competition
Cooperation
Drinking
Drug Use
Exploratory Behavior
Group Behavior
Hyperactivity
Imitation
Infant Behavior
Leadership Styles
Life Style
Modeling (Psychology)
Paranoid Behavior
Participation
Performance
Persistence
Physical Activity Level
Responses
Response Style (Tests)
Self Control
Self Destructive Behavior
Smoking
Social Behavior
Spontaneous Behavior
Student Behavior
Teacher Behavior
RT Attention
Attitudes
Behavioral Objectives
Behavioral Sciences
Behavior Chaining
Behavior Change
Behavior Development
Behavior Disorders
Behaviorism
Behavior Modification
Behavior Patterns
Behavior Problems
Behavior Rating Scales
Behavior Standards
Behavior Theories
Counseling Theories
Ethology
Feedback
Human Dignity
Individual Power
Leadership
Motivation
Play
Protocol Materials
Psychology
Psychomotor Skills
Psychopathology
Self Congruence
Sleep
Sociology
Sportsmanship

BEHAVIOR CHAINING *Sep. 1970*
CIJE: 28 RIE: 16 GC: 110
SN Process of learning a conditioned sequence of behaviors so that, when learned, the completion of one behavior provides a semiautomatic cue for the next, e.g., reciting a memorized poem (note: prior to mar80, the scope note referred to "learning a behavior change")
UF Chain Reflexes (Behavior)
BT Learning Processes
RT Association (Psychology)
Associative Learning
Behavior
Behavior Modification
Contingency Management
Paired Associate Learning
Serial Learning

BEHAVIOR CHANGE *Jul. 1966*
CIJE: 3762 RIE: 2568 GC: 120
SN Complete or partial alteration in the observable activities or responses of an organism (note: prior to mar80, the scope note was restricted to changes "learned" by "persons")
BT Change
RT Attitude Change
Behavior
Behavioral Objectives
Behavior Development
Behavior Modification
Behavior Patterns
Change Strategies
Conditioning
Contingency Management
Habit Formation
Midlife Transitions
Modeling (Psychology)
Negative Practice
Nondirective Counseling
Personality Change

BEHAVIOR DEVELOPMENT *Jul. 1966*
CIJE: 424 RIE: 461 GC: 120
NT Habit Formation
BT Individual Development
RT Animal Behavior
Attachment Behavior
Behavior
Behavior Change
Behaviorism
Bibliotherapy
Developmental Psychology
Developmental Stages
Ethology
Exploratory Behavior
Nature Nurture Controversy
Object Manipulation
Pretend Play
Probationary Period
Self Actualization
Social Behavior

BEHAVIOR DISORDERS *Jun. 1983*
CIJE: 137 RIE: 98 GC: 230
SN Chronic or severe disorders of conduct, i.e., generally aberrant and unacceptable behaviors with or without serious underlying psychopathology (note: do not confuse with "behavior problems" -- prior to jun83, "behavior problems" was not scoped and was frequently used for this concept)
BT Disabilities
RT Alcoholism
Antisocial Behavior
Attention Deficit Disorders
Autism
Behavior
Behavior Patterns
Behavior Problems
Clinical Psychology
Drug Addiction
Emotional Disturbances
Learning Problems
Mental Disorders
Neurological Impairments
Personality Problems
Problem Children
Psychiatry
Psychopathology
Recidivism
Self Destructive Behavior
Self Mutilation
Suicide
Withdrawal (Psychology)

BEHAVIOR MODIFICATION *Mar. 1980*
CIJE: 1176 RIE: 507 GC: 110
SN Alteration of behavior by the use of conditioning techniques (note: prior to mar80, the instruction "behavior modification, use behavior change" was carried in the thesaurus)
UF Behavioral Counseling (1967 1980)
Behavior Therapy
Cognitive Behavior Modification #
NT Contingency Management
Desensitization
BT Conditioning
RT Behavior
Behavior Chaining
Behavior Change
Biofeedback
Classical Conditioning
Cognitive Restructuring
Counseling
Intervention
Operant Conditioning
Psychotherapy
Rational Emotive Therapy
Reality Therapy
Rehabilitation
Reinforcement
Self Control
Self Help Programs
Social Reinforcement
Special Education
Timeout
Token Economy
Transcendental Meditation

BEHAVIOR PATTERNS *Jul. 1966*
CIJE: 4129 RIE: 2571 GC: 120
SN Complex acts made up of distinguishable lesser acts
UF Patterned Behavior
NT Arousal Patterns
Reading Habits
Recidivism
Speech Habits
Study Habits
RT Behavior
Behavioral Objectives
Behavior Change
Behavior Disorders
Behavior Problems
Behavior Rating Scales
Coping
Deception
Ethology
Identification (Psychology)
Imitation
Pretend Play
Psychological Patterns
Sociobiology
Sportsmanship
Writing Processes

BEHAVIOR PROBLEMS *Jul. 1966*
CIJE: 2057 RIE: 1152 GC: 120
SN Transient or mild problems in conduct (note: do not confuse with "behavior disorders" -- prior to jun83, the use of this term was not restricted by a scope note)
UF Misbehavior (1966 1980)
BT Problems
RT Adjustment (To Environment)
Antisocial Behavior
Behavior
Behavior Disorders
Behavior Patterns
Discipline
Emotional Problems
Hyperactivity
Mental Disorders
Minimal Brain Dysfunction
Obedience
Paranoid Behavior
Personality Problems
Problem Children
Psychological Patterns
Psychopathology
Self Control
Self Destructive Behavior
Student Problems
Withdrawal (Psychology)

BEHAVIOR RATING SCALES *Jul. 1966*
CIJE: 701 RIE: 727 GC: 830
SN Devices used to observe and record the occurrence of specific behaviors (note: do not confuse with "check lists")
BT Rating Scales
RT Behavior
Behavior Patterns
Classroom Observation Techniques
Personality Assessment
Personality Measures
Precision Teaching
Student Evaluation

BEHAVIOR STANDARDS *Jul. 1966*
CIJE: 224 RIE: 177 GC: 520
UF Normative Behavior
Social Norms #
NT Codes Of Ethics
BT Standards
RT Behavior
Discipline Policy
Ideology
Loyalty Oaths
Probationary Period
Social Control

BEHAVIOR THEORIES *Jul. 1966*
CIJE: 805 RIE: 532 GC: 810
NT Adaptation Level Theory
Attribution Theory
Mediation Theory
BT Theories
RT Behavior
Counseling Theories
Personality Theories
Social Theories

Behavior Therapy
USE BEHAVIOR MODIFICATION

Behavioral Analysis
USE BEHAVIORAL SCIENCE RESEARCH

Behavioral Contracts
USE PERFORMANCE CONTRACTS

Behavioral Counseling (1967 1980)
USE BEHAVIOR MODIFICATION

BEHAVIORAL OBJECTIVES *Jul. 1966*
CIJE: 1706 RIE: 6477 GC: 310
SN Aims of instruction or any learning activity stated as actual performance criteria or as observable descriptions of measurable behavior
UF Learning Objectives
Performance Objectives
NT Affective Objectives
Cognitive Objectives
Psychomotor Objectives
BT Objectives
RT Behavior
Behavior Change
Behaviorism
Behavior Patterns
Competency Based Education
Competency Based Teacher Education
Contingency Management
Continuous Progress Plan
Counseling Objectives
Course Objectives
Guidance Objectives
Learning Modules
Learning Strategies
Mastery Learning
Mastery Tests
Performance Contracts
Process Education
Protocol Materials
Student Behavior
Student Centered Curriculum
Training Objectives

BEHAVIORAL SCIENCE RESEARCH *Jul. 1966*
CIJE: 2791 RIE: 1737 GC: 810
SN Basic, applied, and developmental research conducted to advance knowledge in the behavioral sciences (note: as of oct81, use as a minor descriptor for examples of this kind of research -- use as a major descriptor only as the subject of a document)
UF Behavioral Analysis
NT Integration Studies
Psychological Studies
BT Research
RT Architectural Research
Behavioral Sciences
Communication Research
Educational Research
Exceptional Child Research
Interaction Process Analysis

= Two or more Descriptors are used to represent this term.
The term's main entry shows the appropriate coordination.

Language Universals
Naturalistic Observation
Organizational Development
Social Science Research

BEHAVIORAL SCIENCES *Jul. 1966*
CIJE: 396 RIE: 367 GC: 400
UF Behavioral Technology
NT Ethology
Psychology
Sociobiology
Sociology
BT Sciences
RT Behavior
Behavioral Science Research
Social Sciences

Behavioral Situation Films
USE PROTOCOL MATERIALS

Behavioral Technology
USE BEHAVIORAL SCIENCES

BEHAVIORISM *Aug. 1986*
CIJE: 39 RIE: 20 GC: 120
SN School of psychological thought, founded by j.b. watson in 1913, concerned with the observable, tangible, objective facts of behavior, rather than with subjective phenomena such as thoughts, emotions, or impulses -- contemporary behaviorism also emphasizes the study of mental states such as feelings and fantasies to the extent that they can be directly observed and measured
UF Behaviorist Psychology
BT Psychology
RT Behavior
Behavioral Objectives
Behavior Development
Cognitive Psychology
Conditioning
Developmental Psychology
Experimental Psychology
Learning Theories
Psychometrics
Reinforcement
Social Psychology

Behaviorist Psychology
USE BEHAVIORISM

BELIEFS *Jul. 1966*
CIJE: 592 RIE: 415 GC: 120
SN Ideas, doctrines, tenets, etc. that are accepted as true on grounds which are not immediately susceptible to rigorous proof
UF Faith
BT Attitudes
RT Attitude Measures
Credibility
Dissent
Dogmatism
Ideology
Opinions
Religion
Trust (Psychology)
Values

Believability
USE CREDIBILITY

Belorussian
USE BIELORUSSIAN

BEMBA *Aug. 1969*
CIJE: 1 RIE: 5 GC: 440
UF Chibemba
Icibemba
BT Bantu Languages

Benefit Cost Analysis
USE COST EFFECTIVENESS

BENGALI *Jul. 1966*
CIJE: 2 RIE: 23 GC: 440
BT Indo European Languages

BERBER LANGUAGES *Aug. 1968*
CIJE: 1 RIE: 11 GC: 440
NT Kabyle
Riff
BT Afro Asiatic Languages

BIAS *Dec. 1969*
CIJE: 860 RIE: 648 GC: 540
SN An inclination, or a lack of balance (note: use a more specific term if possible)
UF Prejudice
NT Social Bias
Statistical Bias
Test Bias
Textbook Bias
RT Attitudes
Egocentrism
Mental Rigidity

Bibles
USE BIBLICAL LITERATURE

BIBLICAL LITERATURE *Jul. 1966*
CIJE: 108 RIE: 68 GC: 430
UF Bibles
BT Literature
RT Ancient History
Christianity
Classical Literature
Judaism
Religion

Bibliocounseling
USE BIBLIOTHERAPY

Bibliographic Citations (1969 1980)
USE CITATIONS (REFERENCES)

Bibliographic Control
USE CATALOGING

BIBLIOGRAPHIC COUPLING *Aug. 1968*
CIJE: 22 RIE: 26 GC: 710
SN Application of citation analysis in which documents are related by virtue of common bibliographic citations
BT Citation Analysis
RT Bibliographies
Citation Indexes
Citations (References)
Relevance (Information Retrieval)

Bibliographic References
USE CITATIONS (REFERENCES)

BIBLIOGRAPHIC UTILITIES *Apr. 1986*
CIJE: 37 RIE: 9 GC: 710
SN Online library networking organizations with large bibliographic databases that are shared by participating libraries for a variety of technical purposes, including cataloging, interlibrary loans, acquisitions, and authority file control (note: see also such identifiers as "oclc," "research libraries information network," "washington library network," and "university of toronto library automation systems")
BT Library Networks
Organizations (Groups)
RT Library Automation
Library Technical Processes
Online Systems
Online Vendors

BIBLIOGRAPHIES *Jul. 1966*
CIJE: 2470 RIE: 6892 GC: 720
SN Descriptive lists of books or other printed materials, which are written by one author, during one period, on one subject, produced by one printer and/or publisher, or located in one place (note: corresponds to pubtype code 131 -- do not use except as the subject of a document)
UF Booklists (1967 1980)
Literature Searches
NT Annotated Bibliographies
BT Reference Materials
RT Anthologies
Bibliographic Coupling
Books
Citation Analysis
Citations (References)
Discographies
Filmographies
Indexes
Library Catalogs
Literature Reviews
State Of The Art Reviews
Union Catalogs

BIBLIOMETRICS *Aug. 1986*
CIJE: 47 RIE: 19 GC: 820
SN The application of mathematical and statistical methods in the study of bodies of writings to reveal the historical development of subject fields and patterns of authorship, publication, and use
UF Statistical Bibliography
NT Citation Analysis
BT Documentation
RT Books
Cataloging
Classification
Cluster Grouping
Indexing
Information Sources
Information Utilization
Library Collection Development
Literature Reviews
Periodicals
Statistical Analysis

BIBLIOTHERAPY *Jul. 1966*
CIJE: 134 RIE: 134 GC: 230
SN Use of selected reading and related materials for therapeutic purposes in physical medicine, mental health, and education
UF Bibliocounseling
Reading Therapy
BT Therapy
RT Behavior Development
Psychotherapy
Reading

Bicultural Education
USE MULTICULTURAL EDUCATION

Bicultural Training
USE CROSS CULTURAL TRAINING

BICULTURALISM *Jul. 1969*
CIJE: 314 RIE: 914 GC: 560
BT Cultural Pluralism
RT Acculturation
Bidialectalism
Bilingualism
Cross Cultural Studies
Cross Cultural Training
Cultural Awareness
Cultural Background
Cultural Context
Cultural Differences
Cultural Influences
Cultural Interrelationships
Culture
Culture Conflict
Culture Contact
Ethnic Groups
Intercultural Communication
Intercultural Programs
Minority Groups
Multicultural Education
Sociocultural Patterns
Spanish Speaking

BICYCLING *Feb. 1978*
CIJE: 28 RIE: 39 GC: 470
BT Physical Activities
RT Athletics
Outdoor Activities
Recreational Activities

BIDIALECTALISM *Oct. 1983*
CIJE: 26 RIE: 27 GC: 450
SN Familiarity with and use of two dialects of the same language
RT Biculturalism
Bilingualism
Black Dialects
Code Switching (Language)
Cross Cultural Studies
Dialects
Dialect Studies
Diglossia
Intercultural Communication
Interference (Language)
Language Usage
Language Variation
Minority Groups
Mutual Intelligibility
Native Language Instruction
Native Speakers
Nonstandard Dialects
Psycholinguistics
Regional Dialects
Social Dialects
Sociolinguistics

BIDS *Feb. 1970*
CIJE: 99 RIE: 63 GC: 620
UF Competitive Bidding
Construction Bidding
RT Contracts
Educational Economics
Educational Finance
Expenditures
Grantsmanship
Program Proposals
Proposal Writing
Purchasing
School Construction

BIELORUSSIAN *Jul. 1966*
CIJE: RIE: 8 GC: 440
UF Belorussian
Byelorussian
BT Slavic Languages

Bigotry
USE SOCIAL DISCRIMINATION

BIKOL *Sep. 1968*
CIJE: RIE: 6 GC: 440
BT Indonesian Languages

BILINGUAL EDUCATION *Oct. 1968*
CIJE: 1178 RIE: 4083 GC: 330
SN Encouragement of bilingualism through the teaching of regular school courses in both the national language and a second language (note: use a more precise term if possible)
BT Education
RT Bilingual Education Programs
Bilingual Instructional Materials
Bilingualism
Bilingual Schools
Bilingual Students
Bilingual Teacher Aides
Bilingual Teachers
Educational Policy
English (Second Language)
Immersion Programs
Intercultural Programs
Language Dominance
Language Enrichment
Language Maintenance
Language Of Instruction
Language Planning
Limited English Speaking
Mexican American Education
Migrant Adult Education
Migrant Education
Multicultural Education
Multicultural Textbooks
Multilingualism
Non English Speaking
Official Languages
Second Language Instruction
Second Language Learning
Second Languages

BILINGUAL EDUCATION PROGRAMS *Aug. 1982*
CIJE: 60 RIE: 348 GC: 450
SN Activities that offer content area instruction in two languages -- appreciation of participants' cultural heritage is emphasized, and native speakers of both languages may be present -- attention is given to developing the academic skills of minority students while they learn the language of the majority culture (note: do not confuse with "second language programs")
BT Programs
RT Bilingual Education
Bilingual Instructional Materials
Bilingualism
Bilingual Schools
Bilingual Teacher Aides
Bilingual Teachers
English (Second Language)
Intercultural Programs
Language Maintenance
Language Of Instruction
Limited English Speaking
Native Language Instruction
Native Speakers
Non English Speaking
Second Language Instruction
Second Language Programs

= Two or more Descriptors are used to represent this term.
The term's main entry shows the appropriate coordination.

BILINGUAL INSTRUCTIONAL MATERIALS *Aug. 1982*
CIJE: 5 RIE: 148 GC: 730
SN Print and/or nonprint educational materials developed specifically for use with students who need proficiency in two languages
BT Instructional Materials
Multilingual Materials
RT Bilingual Education
Bilingual Education Programs
Bilingualism
Bilingual Schools
Language Maintenance
Language Of Instruction
Multicultural Textbooks
Native Language Instruction
Second Language Instruction
Second Language Learning
Second Languages

Bilingual Materials
USE MULTILINGUAL MATERIALS

BILINGUAL SCHOOLS *Jul. 1966*
CIJE: 82 RIE: 181 GC: 340
BT Schools
RT Bilingual Education
Bilingual Education Programs
Bilingual Instructional Materials
Bilingualism
Bilingual Teacher Aides
Bilingual Teachers

BILINGUAL STUDENTS *Jul. 1966*
CIJE: 385 RIE: 1074 GC: 360
SN Students who can communicate effectively in more than one language (note: do not confuse with "limited english speaking" or "non english speaking")
BT Students
RT Bilingual Education
Bilingualism
Bilingual Teacher Aides
Bilingual Teachers
Code Switching (Language)
Immersion Programs
Language Dominance
Native Speakers
Spanish Speaking

BILINGUAL TEACHER AIDES *Jul. 1966*
CIJE: 17 RIE: 84 GC: 360
SN Teacher aides who can communicate effectively in more than one language
BT Teacher Aides
RT Bilingual Education
Bilingual Education Programs
Bilingualism
Bilingual Schools
Bilingual Students
Bilingual Teachers
English (Second Language)
Language Dominance
Limited English Speaking
Native Speakers
Non English Speaking
School Aides
Second Languages

BILINGUAL TEACHERS *Jul. 1966*
CIJE: 100 RIE: 352 GC: 360
SN Teachers who can communicate effectively in more than one language
BT Teachers
RT Bilingual Education
Bilingual Education Programs
Bilingualism
Bilingual Schools
Bilingual Students
Bilingual Teacher Aides
English (Second Language)
Language Dominance
Limited English Speaking
Native Speakers
Non English Speaking
Second Languages

BILINGUALISM *Jul. 1966*
CIJE: 870 RIE: 1677 GC: 450
RT Biculturalism
Bidialectalism
Bilingual Education
Bilingual Education Programs
Bilingual Instructional Materials
Bilingual Schools
Bilingual Students
Bilingual Teacher Aides
Bilingual Teachers
Child Language
Code Switching (Language)
Cross Cultural Studies
Cultural Pluralism
Diglossia
English (Second Language)
Immersion Programs
Intercultural Communication
Interference (Language)
Language Dominance
Language Maintenance
Language Planning
Language Proficiency
Language Research
Languages
Language Skill Attrition
Limited English Speaking
Minority Groups
Modern Languages
Monolingualism
Multicultural Education
Multilingualism
Multilingual Materials
Native Speakers
Psycholinguistics
Second Language Learning
Second Languages
Sociolinguistics
Spanish Speaking

BINI *Jul. 1966*
CIJE: 1 RIE: 5 GC: 440
BT African Languages

Biochemical Effects
USE BIOCHEMISTRY

Biochemical Tests
USE BIOCHEMISTRY

BIOCHEMISTRY *Aug. 1968*
CIJE: 765 RIE: 106 GC: 490
UF Biochemical Effects
Biochemical Tests
Physiological Chemistry
BT Biological Sciences
Chemistry
RT Biology
Biomedicine
Chromatography
Cytology
Enzymes
Genetic Engineering
Human Body
Medicine
Metabolism
Nucleic Acids
Organic Chemistry
Physical Sciences
Physiology
Plant Growth
Rh Factors
Toxicology

BIOETHICS *Jan. 1985*
CIJE: 29 RIE: 10 GC: 430
SN Discipline dealing with the moral and social implications of practices and developments in the biological sciences and medicine
BT Ethics
RT Biological Sciences
Medicine
Moral Values
Social Biology

BIOFEEDBACK *Aug. 1982*
CIJE: 95 RIE: 45 GC: 490
SN Auditory, visual, or other sensory feedback on physiological processes or states (e.g., heart rate, muscle tension, brain waves, skin temperature) in order to facilitate control of these normally involuntary functions
BT Biological Sciences
Feedback
RT Behavior Modification
Biology
Biomechanics
Bionics
Cardiovascular System
Conditioning
Electroencephalography
Health
Human Body
Metabolism
Physiology
Psychophysiology
Reinforcement
Relaxation Training
Self Control
Self Help Programs
Stimulation
Transcendental Meditation

BIOGRAPHICAL INVENTORIES *May. 1971*
CIJE: 215 RIE: 124 GC: 830
SN Sets of questions used to gather information on an individual's background
UF Biographical Profiles
BT Measures (Individuals)
RT Background
Biographies
Case Records
Individual Characteristics
Interest Inventories
Profiles
Questionnaires
Surveys

Biographical Profiles
USE BIOGRAPHICAL INVENTORIES

BIOGRAPHIES *Jul. 1966*
CIJE: 764 RIE: 521 GC: 730
SN Written histories of people's lives (note: prior to mar80, the instruction "life histories, use biographical inventories" was carried in the thesaurus)
UF Hagiographies (1971 1980)
Life Histories
NT Autobiographies
BT Literary Genres
Nonfiction
RT Biographical Inventories
Personal Narratives

BIOLOGICAL INFLUENCES *Jul. 1966*
CIJE: 309 RIE: 192 GC: 120
NT Rh Factors
BT Influences
RT Biology
Environmental Influences
Evolution
Genetic Engineering
Medicine
Nature Nurture Controversy
Perinatal Influences
Prenatal Influences
Sexual Identity

BIOLOGICAL PARENTS *Oct. 1983*
CIJE: 12 RIE: 5 GC: 510
SN The genetic parents of a child, in contrast to adoptive, foster, and psychological parents or stepparents
UF Birth Parents
Natural Parents
BT Parents
RT Adopted Children
Adoption
Biology
Foster Children
Foster Family
Genetics
Stepfamily

BIOLOGICAL SCIENCES *Jul. 1966*
CIJE: 782 RIE: 529 GC: 490
UF Life Sciences
NT Anatomy
Biochemistry
Biofeedback
Biology
Biomedicine
Biophysics
Botany
Cytology
Ecology
Embryology
Ethology
Genetics
Physiology
Sociobiology
Zoology
BT Natural Sciences
RT Bioethics
Conservation Education
Environmental Education
Human Body
Wildlife

BIOLOGY *Jul. 1966*
CIJE: 3440 RIE: 1605 GC: 490
UF Biology Instruction (1966 1980) #
Human Biology
NT Marine Biology
Microbiology
Radiation Biology
Social Biology
BT Biological Sciences
RT Anatomy
Biochemistry
Biofeedback
Biological Influences
Biological Parents
Biomechanics
Biomedicine
Biophysics
Botany
Chromatography
Cytology
Ecology
Embryology
Enzymes
Evolution
Genetic Engineering
Genetics
Heredity
Human Body
Metabolism
Nucleic Acids
Physiology
Pregnancy
Race
Radioisotopes
Rh Factors
Scientific Research
Sex
Soil Science
Zoology

Biology Instruction (1966 1980)
USE BIOLOGY; SCIENCE INSTRUCTION

BIOMECHANICS *Mar. 1978*
CIJE: 53 RIE: 47 GC: 490
SN Science of the action of forces, internal and external, on living things
BT Biophysics
RT Biofeedback
Biology
Bionics
Exercise Physiology
Force
Human Body
Human Factors Engineering
Kinesthetic Perception
Kinetics
Motor Development
Motor Reactions
Movement Education
Physical Activity Level
Physiology

BIOMEDICAL EQUIPMENT *Jul. 1966*
CIJE: 44 RIE: 47 GC: 910
BT Equipment
RT Assistive Devices (For Disabled)
Electroencephalography
Laboratory Equipment
Measurement Equipment
Medical Laboratory Assistants
Medicine
Surgery
Wheelchairs

Biomedical Equipment Technicians
USE MEDICAL LABORATORY ASSISTANTS

Biomedical Research
USE BIOMEDICINE

BIOMEDICINE *Mar. 1980*
CIJE: 63 RIE: 34 GC: 210
SN Branch of science concerned with the capacity of human beings to survive and function in specific environments
UF Biomedical Research
BT Biological Sciences
Medicine
RT Biochemistry
Biology
Biophysics
Human Factors Engineering

= Two or more Descriptors are used to represent this term.
The term's main entry shows the appropriate coordination.

BIONICS *Aug. 1971*
CIJE: 8 RIE: 10 GC: 490
SN Science which deals with the transformation of the functions of living systems into electronic, mechanical, or other analogs
UF Intellectronics
NT Robotics
BT Biophysics
RT Artificial Intelligence
Biofeedback
Biomechanics
Cybernetics
Human Factors Engineering
Man Machine Systems

BIOPHYSICS *Aug. 1968*
CIJE: 66 RIE: 15 GC: 490
SN Application of physical methods and principles to biological problems
NT Biomechanics
Bionics
BT Biological Sciences
Physics
RT Biology
Biomedicine
Diffusion (Physics)
Human Body
Physical Sciences
Physiology
Radiation Biology

BIRACIAL COMMITTEES *Jul. 1966*
CIJE: 3 RIE: 7 GC: 540
BT Committees
RT Community Cooperation
Racial Integration
Racial Relations

Biracial Elementary Schools (1966 1980)
USE SCHOOL DESEGREGATION

Biracial Schools (1966 1980)
USE SCHOOL DESEGREGATION

Biracial Secondary Schools (1966 1980)
USE SCHOOL DESEGREGATION

Bird Studies
USE ORNITHOLOGY

BIRTH *Oct. 1977*
CIJE: 75 RIE: 104 GC: 120
UF Childbirth
Labor (Childbirth)
Parturition
RT Birth Order
Birth Rate
Birth Weight
Illegitimate Births
Obstetrics
Perinatal Influences
Physiology
Pregnancy
Reproduction (Biology)
Sex Education

Birth Control
USE CONTRACEPTION

Birth Defects
USE CONGENITAL IMPAIRMENTS

BIRTH ORDER *May. 1969*
CIJE: 219 RIE: 94 GC: 120
BT Family Structure
RT Birth
Family (Sociological Unit)
Siblings

Birth Parents
USE BIOLOGICAL PARENTS

BIRTH RATE *Jul. 1974*
CIJE: 180 RIE: 334 GC: 550
SN Ratio between the number of births and the number of individuals in a specified population
UF Fertility Rate
Natality
BT Demography
Incidence
RT Birth
Contraception
Family Planning
Family Size
Overpopulation
Population Distribution
Population Growth
Population Trends
Pregnancy
Reproduction (Biology)

BIRTH WEIGHT *Oct. 1983*
CIJE: 21 RIE: 25 GC: 120
SN Body weight at time of birth
BT Body Weight
RT Birth
Neonates
Perinatal Influences
Premature Infants
Prenatal Influences

Bituminous Coal
USE COAL

BLACK ACHIEVEMENT *Jul. 1977*
CIJE: 176 RIE: 202 GC: 330
SN Accomplishments by blacks in the areas of education, politics, social life, etc.
UF Negro Achievement (1966 1977)
BT Achievement
RT Black Education
Black Employment
Black History
Black Institutions
Black Leadership
Black Power
Blacks
Black Studies
Educational Mobility
Occupational Mobility
Racial Factors
Racial Integration
Social Mobility

Black Americans
USE BLACKS

Black And White Films
USE FILMS

BLACK ATTITUDES *Jul. 1977*
CIJE: 538 RIE: 357 GC: 520
UF Negro Attitudes (1966 1977)
BT Attitudes
RT Black Community
Black Culture
Black Power
Blacks
Racial Attitudes
Racial Identification

BLACK BUSINESSES *Jul. 1977*
CIJE: 36 RIE: 36 GC: 650
UF Negro Businesses (1967 1977)
BT Business
RT Black Employment
Blacks

Black Children
USE BLACK YOUTH

BLACK COLLEGES *Jul. 1977*
CIJE: 373 RIE: 517 GC: 340
SN Colleges whose enrollments are, or have traditionally been, predominantly black
UF Historically Black Colleges
Negro Colleges (1968 1977)
BT Black Institutions
Colleges
RT Black Education
Blacks
Black Students
Black Teachers
College Segregation
Developing Institutions

BLACK COMMUNITY *Aug. 1968*
CIJE: 529 RIE: 403 GC: 520
UF Negro Community
BT Community
RT Black Attitudes
Black Culture
Black Institutions
Black Power
Blacks
Black Studies
Community Influence
Ethnic Groups
Socioeconomic Influences

BLACK CULTURE *Jul. 1977*
CIJE: 562 RIE: 491 GC: 560
UF Black Subculture
Negro Culture (1966 1977)
BT Culture
RT African Culture
African History
Black Attitudes
Black Community
Black Dialects
Black Family
Black History
Black Influences
Black Institutions
Black Literature
Blacks
Black Studies
Latin American Culture
North American Culture
Slavery

BLACK DIALECTS *Jul. 1977*
CIJE: 394 RIE: 529 GC: 450
UF Black English
Ebonics
Negro Dialects (1966 1977)
BT Dialects
RT Bidialectalism
Black Culture
Blacks
Nonstandard Dialects
Regional Dialects
Social Dialects
Urban Language

BLACK EDUCATION *Jul. 1977*
CIJE: 618 RIE: 582 GC: 330
SN Education of black people (note: do not confuse with "black studies")
UF Negro Education (1966 1977)
BT Education
RT Black Achievement
Black Colleges
Black Institutions
Blacks
Black Students
Black Studies
Black Teachers
Racially Balanced Schools
School Desegregation
School Segregation

BLACK EMPLOYMENT *Jul. 1977*
CIJE: 171 RIE: 262 GC: 630
UF Negro Employment (1966 1977)
BT Employment
RT Black Achievement
Black Businesses
Blacks

Black English
USE BLACK DIALECTS

BLACK FAMILY *Oct. 1983*
CIJE: 22 RIE: 34 GC: 520
BT Family (Sociological Unit)
RT Black Culture
Black Mothers
Blacks
Black Studies
Extended Family
Family Life
Family Structure
Kinship
Slavery

BLACK HISTORY *Jul. 1977*
CIJE: 597 RIE: 492 GC: 430
UF Negro History (1966 1977)
BT History
RT African History
Black Achievement
Black Culture
Black Influences
Black Literature
Blacks
Black Studies
Latin American History
North American History
Racial Relations
Racial Segregation
Slavery
United States History

BLACK HOUSING (1977 1980) *Mar. 1980*
CIJE: 7 RIE: 52 GC: 550
SN Invalid descriptor -- used inconsistently in indexing -- see "housing discrimination," "residential patterns," or "homeowners," in coordination with appropriate "black" term(s)

BLACK INFLUENCES *Mar. 1980*
CIJE: 273 RIE: 197 GC: 520
SN Influences of blacks on society (note: the uses of "negro role" and "black role" were not restricted by scope notes)
UF Black Role (1977 1980)
Negro Role (1966 1977)
BT Influences
RT Black Culture
Black History
Black Leadership
Black Organizations
Black Power
Blacks
Black Studies
Minority Group Influences

BLACK INSTITUTIONS *Jul. 1977*
CIJE: 57 RIE: 81 GC: 520
SN Institutions whose ownership, leadership, and membership is primarily black (note: prior to mar80, the use of this term was not restricted by a scope note)
UF Negro Institutions (1966 1977)
NT Black Colleges
BT Institutions
RT Black Achievement
Black Community
Black Culture
Black Education
Black Organizations
Blacks
Black Studies

BLACK LEADERSHIP *Jul. 1977*
CIJE: 265 RIE: 166 GC: 540
UF Negro Leadership (1966 1977)
BT Leadership
RT Black Achievement
Black Influences
Black Organizations
Black Power
Blacks
Civil Rights
Leadership Training

BLACK LITERATURE *Jul. 1977*
CIJE: 464 RIE: 310 GC: 430
UF Negro Literature (1968 1977)
BT Literature
RT African History
African Literature
Black Culture
Black History
Blacks
Black Studies
Latin American Literature
United States Literature

BLACK MOTHERS *Jul. 1977*
CIJE: 60 RIE: 122 GC: 510
UF Negro Mothers (1966 1977)
BT Blacks
Mothers
RT Black Family

Black Nationalism
USE BLACK POWER

BLACK ORGANIZATIONS *Jul. 1977*
CIJE: 96 RIE: 73 GC: 520
UF Negro Organizations (1966 1977)
BT Organizations (Groups)
RT Black Influences
Black Institutions
Black Leadership
Black Power
Blacks
Civil Rights

BLACK POPULATION TRENDS *Jul. 1977*
CIJE: 49 RIE: 62 GC: 550
UF Negro Population Trends (1966 1977)
BT Population Trends
RT Blacks
Ethnic Distribution
Racial Distribution

= Two or more Descriptors are used to represent this term.
The term's main entry shows the appropriate coordination.

BLACK POWER *Aug. 1968*
CIJE: 320 RIE: 159 GC: 540
UF Black Nationalism
RT Black Achievement
Black Attitudes
Black Community
Black Influences
Black Leadership
Black Organizations
Blacks
Black Studies
Civil Rights
Ethnicity
Group Unity
Nationalism
Political Power
Power Structure
Racial Identification
Racial Relations
Segregationist Organizations
Self Determination

Black Role (1977 1980)
USE BLACK INFLUENCES

BLACK STEREOTYPES *Jul. 1977*
CIJE: 156 RIE: 118 GC: 540
SN Unreflective, oversimplified, or unfounded beliefs based on the premise that all blacks are typified by, or conform to, an unvarying pattern of character, characteristics, etc. (note: prior to mar80, this term was not restricted by a scope note)
UF Negro Stereotypes (1966 1977)
BT Ethnic Stereotypes
RT Blacks
Racial Attitudes
Racial Bias
Racial Differences
Racial Identification

BLACK STUDENTS *Jul. 1977*
CIJE: 1576 RIE: 2239 GC: 360
UF Negro Students (1966 1977)
BT Blacks
Students
RT Black Colleges
Black Education
Black Youth

BLACK STUDIES *Jul. 1977*
CIJE: 557 RIE: 434 GC: 400
SN Curriculum or subject area encompassing the history and contemporary social, political, and cultural situation of blacks
UF African American Studies (1969 1977)
Negro Studies
BT Ethnic Studies
RT African History
American Studies
Black Achievement
Black Community
Black Culture
Black Education
Black Family
Black History
Black Influences
Black Institutions
Black Literature
Black Power
Blacks
Cultural Background
Cultural Education
Cultural Images
Cultural Traits
Multicultural Education
Racial Identification
Slavery
United States History

Black Subculture
USE BLACK CULTURE

BLACK TEACHERS *Jul. 1977*
CIJE: 145 RIE: 154 GC: 360
UF Negro Teachers (1966 1977)
BT Blacks
Teachers
RT Black Colleges
Black Education
Minority Group Teachers

Black White Relations
USE RACIAL RELATIONS

BLACK YOUTH *Jul. 1977*
CIJE: 543 RIE: 563 GC: 510
UF Black Children
Negro Youth (1966 1977)
BT Blacks
Youth
RT Black Students
Minority Group Children

Blackboards
USE CHALKBOARDS

BLACKS *Jul. 1977*
CIJE: 2556 RIE: 3084 GC: 560
UF African Americans
Afro Americans
American Negroes
Black Americans
Negroes (1966 1977)
NT Black Mothers
Black Students
Black Teachers
Black Youth
BT Groups
RT Black Achievement
Black Attitudes
Black Businesses
Black Colleges
Black Community
Black Culture
Black Dialects
Black Education
Black Employment
Black Family
Black History
Black Influences
Black Institutions
Black Leadership
Black Literature
Black Organizations
Black Population Trends
Black Power
Black Stereotypes
Black Studies
Ethnic Groups
Minority Groups
Race
Racial Relations

Blind (1966 1980)
USE BLINDNESS

Blind Children (1966 1980)
USE BLINDNESS

BLINDNESS *Mar. 1980*
CIJE: 775 RIE: 535 GC: 220
SN Having no sight or such limited vision that hearing and touch are the chief means of perception and learning -- legal blindness is usually defined as having central visual acuity of 20/200 or less in the better eye with correction or having a visual field no greater than 20 degrees
UF Blind (1966 1980)
Blind Children (1966 1980)
BT Visual Impairments
RT Braille
Deaf Blind
Echolocation
Low Vision Aids
Partial Vision
Raised Line Drawings
Tactile Adaptation
Talking Books
Vision
Visual Acuity

BLOCK GRANTS *Sep. 1982*
CIJE: 59 RIE: 120 GC: 620
SN Financial assistance for broad ranges of activities and services, of which specific dispensations of allocated funds are made at the discretion of the grantee within the bounds of a statutory formula
BT Grants
RT Educational Finance
Federal Aid
Federal State Relationship
Government School Relationship
Institutional Autonomy
Revenue Sharing
School District Autonomy
State Aid

Block Time Teaching
USE TIME BLOCKS

BLOOD CIRCULATION *Jun. 1969*
CIJE: 56 RIE: 14 GC: 210
UF Hemodynamics
BT Metabolism
RT Cardiovascular System
Heart Rate
Human Body
Hypertension
Physiology
Sickle Cell Anemia

Blood Donors
USE TISSUE DONORS

BLUE COLLAR OCCUPATIONS *Jul. 1966*
CIJE: 86 RIE: 127 GC: 640
SN Occupations that require manual labor -- includes skilled, semiskilled, and unskilled occupations (note: use to distinguish from "white collar occupations")
BT Occupations
RT Building Trades
Semiskilled Occupations
Skilled Occupations
Trade And Industrial Education
Unskilled Occupations
White Collar Occupations
Working Class

BLUE RIBBON COMMISSIONS *Aug. 1986*
CIJE: 8 RIE: 44 GC: 610
SN Panels of knowledgeable public leaders and informed private citizens appointed by government executives or legislative bodies for fixed durations to study and make recommendations on specific problems or topics
BT Organizations (Groups)
RT Advisory Committees
Change Agents
Consultants
Needs Assessment
Planning Commissions
Policy Formation
Political Issues
Statewide Planning

BLUEPRINTS *Jul. 1966*
CIJE: 7 RIE: 72 GC: 920
BT Building Plans
RT Building Design
Drafting
Engineering Drawing
Orthographic Projection

BOARD ADMINISTRATOR RELATIONSHIP *Jul. 1966*
CIJE: 294 RIE: 337 GC: 330
BT Interpersonal Relationship
RT Administrator Guides
Administrators
Federal State Relationship
Governing Boards
Interprofessional Relationship
Politics Of Education
School Administration
Student School Relationship
Teacher Administrator Relationship

BOARD CANDIDATES *Jul. 1966*
CIJE: 59 RIE: 48 GC: 610
BT Groups
RT Boards Of Education
Political Candidates
Trustees

Board Of Education Members
USE BOARDS OF EDUCATION

BOARD OF EDUCATION POLICY *Jul. 1966*
CIJE: 561 RIE: 828 GC: 330
UF School Board Policy
School District Policy
BT Administrative Policy
RT Arbitration
Boards Of Education
Dress Codes
Educational Policy
Interdistrict Policies
Married Students
Negotiation Agreements
Negotiation Impasses
Politics Of Education
Pregnant Students
School Closing
School District Autonomy
School Policy
Superintendents
Teacher Welfare

BOARD OF EDUCATION ROLE *Jul. 1966*
CIJE: 402 RIE: 653 GC: 330
UF School Board Role
RT Boards Of Education
Role Of Education
School District Autonomy

Board Of Regents
USE GOVERNING BOARDS

Board Of Trustees
USE GOVERNING BOARDS

BOARDING HOMES *Jul. 1966*
CIJE: 11 RIE: 31 GC: 920
BT Housing
RT Adult Foster Care
Boarding Schools
College Housing
Foster Care
Rehabilitation Centers
Residential Institutions

BOARDING SCHOOLS *Apr. 1970*
CIJE: 87 RIE: 195 GC: 340
SN Educational institutions at the elementary-secondary level in which students are in residence while enrolled in an instructional program (note: see "residential schools" for boarding schools for disabled children)
NT Residential Schools
BT Residential Institutions
Schools
RT Boarding Homes
Folk Schools
Regional Schools
Resident Advisers
Residential Programs

BOARDS OF EDUCATION *Jul. 1966*
CIJE: 1067 RIE: 1129 GC: 330
UF Board Of Education Members
School Board Members
School Boards
NT State Boards Of Education
BT Governing Boards
RT Board Candidates
Board Of Education Policy
Board Of Education Role
County School Districts
Intermediate Administrative Units
Loyalty Oaths
Public School Teachers
School Administration
School District Autonomy
School Districts
Schools
Superintendents
Trustees

BOAT OPERATORS *Mar. 1980*
CIJE: 10 RIE: 27 GC: 640
SN (Note: may be used in a recreational as well as an occupational context)
UF Boatmen (1967 1980)
Motorboat Operators
BT Semiskilled Workers
RT Maritime Education
Navigation
Sailing
Seafarers

Boatmen (1967 1980)
USE BOAT OPERATORS

Body And Fender Repairers
USE AUTO BODY REPAIRERS

Body Attitude
USE HUMAN POSTURE

Body Care
USE HYGIENE

BODY HEIGHT *Jun. 1969*
CIJE: 59 RIE: 37 GC: 120
BT Physical Characteristics
RT Human Body
Physical Development

BODY IMAGE *Jun. 1969*
CIJE: 204 RIE: 132 GC: 120
SN Conceptual representation of one's own body derived from internal and external sensations, emotions, and fantasies related to orientation, movement, and behavior
UF Body Schema
BT Self Concept
RT Human Body
Interpersonal Attraction
Kinesthetic Perception
Movement Education
Personal Space

BODY LANGUAGE *Jan. 1973*
CIJE: 188 RIE: 183 GC: 120
UF Gestures (Nonverbal Communication)
Kinesics
BT Nonverbal Communication
RT Eye Contact
Eye Movements
Facial Expressions
Human Posture
Interaction Process Analysis
Movement Education
Paralinguistics

Body Schema
USE BODY IMAGE

BODY WEIGHT *Jun. 1969*
CIJE: 251 RIE: 141 GC: 120
NT Birth Weight
Obesity
BT Physical Characteristics
RT Anorexia Nervosa
Bulimia
Eating Habits
Failure To Thrive
Human Body
Physical Development

Bomb Shelters
USE FALLOUT SHELTERS

BOND ISSUES *Jul. 1966*
CIJE: 94 RIE: 124 GC: 620
RT Educational Finance
Local Issues
Political Issues
Voting

Bonding (Behavior)
USE ATTACHMENT BEHAVIOR

Book Buying
USE LIBRARY ACQUISITION

BOOK CATALOGS *Aug. 1968*
CIJE: 29 RIE: 79 GC: 710
SN Literary catalogs in book form -- individual catalog entries are photocopied or printed page by page
BT Library Catalogs

Book Industry
USE PUBLISHING INDUSTRY

Book Lending
USE LIBRARY CIRCULATION

BOOK REVIEWS *Jul. 1966*
CIJE: 969 RIE: 318 GC: 730
BT Publications
RT Books
Literary Criticism
Literature Reviews
Textbook Evaluation

Book Thefts (1969 1980)
USE BOOKS; STEALING

BOOKKEEPING *Jul. 1966*
CIJE: 142 RIE: 151 GC: 620
BT Business Skills
RT Accounting
Clerical Occupations
Financial Audits
Financial Services
Office Occupations
Office Occupations Education
Recordkeeping

Booklists (1967 1980)
USE BIBLIOGRAPHIES

BOOKMOBILES *Jan. 1970*
CIJE: 35 RIE: 58 GC: 910
SN Large motor vehicles, specially equipped to carry books and other library materials, that serve as traveling libraries
UF Mobile Libraries
BT Library Equipment
Service Vehicles
RT Branch Libraries
Library Extension
Library Services
Mobile Educational Services
Outreach Programs

BOOKS *Jul. 1966*
CIJE: 2101 RIE: 2052 GC: 720
SN (Note: corresponds to pubtype code 010 -- do not use except as the subject of a document)
UF Book Thefts (1969 1980) #
Childrens Books (1966 1980) #
Folklore Books (1966 1980) #
Health Books (1966 1980) #
NT Foreign Language Books
High Interest Low Vocabulary Books
Paperback Books
Picture Books
Textbooks
Yearbooks
BT Publications
RT Bibliographies
Bibliometrics
Book Reviews
Literature
Novels
Reading Materials
Serials
Short Stories
Talking Books

Border Patrol Officers
USE IMMIGRATION INSPECTORS

Borderline Mental Retardation
USE SLOW LEARNERS

BOTANY *Jul. 1966*
CIJE: 459 RIE: 192 GC: 490
UF Plant Biology
BT Biological Sciences
RT Agriculture
Biology
Culturing Techniques
Ecology
Embryology
Evolution
Field Crops
Floriculture
Forestry
Genetics
Herbicides
Horticulture
Insecticides
Landscaping
Microbiology
Photosynthesis
Plant Growth
Plant Identification
Plant Pathology
Plant Propagation
Soil Science
Trees
Weeds
Wildlife

BOWLING *Apr. 1985*
CIJE: 11 RIE: 9 GC: 470
SN (Note: do not confuse with the identifiers "lawn bowling" and "cricket (sport)")
UF Tenpins
BT Athletics
RT Lifetime Sports

Boys
USE MALES

Bracero Programs (1966 1980)
USE BRACEROS

BRACEROS *Jul. 1966*
CIJE: 7 RIE: 31 GC: 410
SN Mexican laborers permitted to enter the united states under immigration treaties to work for limited periods of time in agriculture or industry
UF Bracero Programs (1966 1980)
BT Foreign Workers
Mexicans
RT Agricultural Laborers
Migrant Employment
Migrants
Migrant Workers
Seasonal Employment
Seasonal Laborers

Brahmins (1967 1980)
USE CASTE

BRAILLE *Jul. 1966*
CIJE: 133 RIE: 153 GC: 220
BT Written Language
RT Blindness
Raised Line Drawings
Reading
Reading Instruction
Sensory Aids
Tactile Adaptation

Brain Damage
USE NEUROLOGICAL IMPAIRMENTS

BRAIN HEMISPHERE FUNCTIONS *Aug. 1986*
CIJE: RIE: 1 GC: 120
SN Specialized roles of the right and left halves of the brain
UF Cerebral Dominance (1967 1986)
Hemispheric Specialization (Brain)
BT Neurological Organization
RT Lateral Dominance
Neurology
Perceptual Development

BRAINSTORMING *Dec. 1985*
CIJE: 30 RIE: 20 GC: 520
SN Activity or technique to encourage the creative generation of ideas -- usually a group process, in which group members contribute suggestions in a spontaneous, noncritical manner
BT Creative Activities
RT Divergent Thinking
Group Discussion
Group Dynamics
Problem Solving
Spontaneous Behavior

BRANCH LIBRARIES *Nov. 1969*
CIJE: 35 RIE: 40 GC: 710
SN Libraries other than the main or central one in a system
UF Satellite Libraries
BT Libraries
RT Bookmobiles
County Libraries
Library Networks
Public Libraries
Satellite Facilities
Special Libraries

BRANCHING *Jul. 1966*
CIJE: 35 RIE: 132 GC: 710
SN An operation, frequently used in computer programing or programed instruction, in which a choice is automatically made between two or more courses of action based on the result of some preceding operation, such as the answer to a question
UF Optional Branching (1966 1980)
BT Methods
RT Computer Oriented Programs
Fixed Sequence
Menu Driven Software
Programed Instruction
Programing

Breadwinners
USE HEADS OF HOUSEHOLDS

BREAKFAST PROGRAMS *Jul. 1966*
CIJE: 40 RIE: 137 GC: 210
BT Health Programs
RT Dining Facilities
Food Handling Facilities
Food Standards
Hunger
Lunch Programs
Nutrition
School Health Services

BREASTFEEDING *Apr. 1986*
CIJE: 13 RIE: 35 GC: 210
BT Nutrition
RT Infants

BRICK INDUSTRY *Aug. 1970*
CIJE: RIE: 5 GC: 650
BT Industry
RT Construction Industry
Manufacturing Industry

Brick Masonry
USE BRICKLAYING

Bricklayers (1968 1981)
USE BRICKLAYING

BRICKLAYING *Jul. 1966*
CIJE: 1 RIE: 34 GC: 640
UF Bricklayers (1968 1981)
Brick Masonry
BT Masonry
RT Building Trades
Skilled Occupations

BRITISH INFANT SCHOOLS *Dec. 1985*
CIJE: RIE: GC: 340
SN Lower-division schools of the british primary system for children aged 5 to 7 or 8, often associated with an informal, open approach to teaching and student-selected learning activities (note: coordinate non-u.s., including british, applications with geographic identifiers)
UF Infant Schools (British Primary System)
BT Schools
RT Elementary Schools
Open Education
Primary Education

Broadcast Communications
USE TELECOMMUNICATIONS

BROADCAST INDUSTRY *Jul. 1966*
CIJE: 416 RIE: 740 GC: 650
BT Industry
RT Broadcast Television
Commercial Television
Copyrights
Film Industry
Mass Media
News Reporting
News Writing
Programing (Broadcast)
Radio
Television
Television Curriculum

BROADCAST RECEPTION EQUIPMENT *Jul. 1966*
CIJE: 25 RIE: 64 GC: 910
BT Electronic Equipment
RT Audio Equipment
Broadcast Television
Radio
Television
Television Studios
Video Equipment

Broadcast Scheduling
USE PROGRAMING (BROADCAST)

BROADCAST TELEVISION *Jul. 1966*
CIJE: 196 RIE: 345 GC: 720
SN System whereby television signals are transmitted through the air at preassigned frequencies and received by a general and geographically scattered audience simultaneously
UF Open Circuit Television (1966 1980)
BT Television
RT Broadcast Industry
Broadcast Reception Equipment

Brochures
USE PAMPHLETS

Brothers
USE SIBLINGS

Bucolic Literature
USE PASTORAL LITERATURE

= Two or more Descriptors are used to represent this term.
The term's main entry shows the appropriate coordination.

BUDDHISM *Mar. 1983*
CIJE: 9 RIE: 19 GC: 430
SN Religion based on the teachings of gautama buddha (india, 5th century b.c.)
BT Religion
RT Non Western Civilization
Philosophy
Religious Cultural Groups

Budget Allocations
USE BUDGETING

Budget Cuts
USE BUDGETING; RETRENCHMENT

BUDGETING *Jul. 1966*
CIJE: 769 RIE: 1385 GC: 620
SN The process of determining estimates of proposed expenditures for a given period or purpose and the proposed means of financing them (note: prior to mar80, this term was not restricted by a scope note and may have been confused with "budgets," which are the actual estimates and means)
UF Budget Allocations
Budget Cuts #
NT Program Budgeting
BT Planning
RT Accounting
Administration
Budgets
Cost Estimates
Educational Finance
Expenditures
Financial Audits
Money Management
Resource Allocation
Retrenchment
School Based Management

BUDGETS *Jul. 1966*
CIJE: 404 RIE: 818 GC: 620
SN Estimates of proposed expenditures for a given period or purpose and the proposed means of financing them (note: prior to mar80, this term was not restricted by a scope note and may have been confused with "budgeting," which is the process of creating budgets)
RT Budgeting
Educational Finance
Expenditures
Income
Operating Expenses
Program Budgeting
Resource Allocation
School Budget Elections

BUILDING CONVERSION *Jul. 1966*
CIJE: 158 RIE: 94 GC: 920
SN Modifying a building to make it suitable for a new use or purpose
BT Change
RT Building Innovation
Building Obsolescence
Buildings
Construction (Process)
Construction Costs
Construction Needs
Facility Expansion
Facility Guidelines
Facility Improvement
Facility Requirements
Facility Utilization Research
Found Spaces
School Expansion
Space Utilization

BUILDING DESIGN *Jul. 1966*
CIJE: 864 RIE: 717 GC: 920
SN Conceiving and selecting the structure, elements, arrangement, materials, etc. for a building -- also, the plan or layout that results
UF Architectural Changes
Architectural Design
NT Modular Building Design
BT Design
RT Acoustical Environment
Air Flow
Architects
Architectural Character
Architectural Programing
Architecture
Blueprints
Building Innovation
Building Plans
Buildings
Color Planning
Construction (Process)
Construction Materials
Design Build Approach
Design Requirements
Educational Facilities Design
Facilities
Facility Case Studies
Facility Guidelines
Facility Requirements
Facility Utilization Research
Fire Protection
Flexible Lighting Design
Interior Design
Interior Space
Life Cycle Costing
Lighting Design
Physical Mobility
Space Utilization
Spatial Relationship (Facilities)
Structural Elements (Construction)
Thermal Environment
Visual Environment

Building Equipment (1966 1980)
USE EQUIPMENT

Building Improvement (1966 1980)
USE FACILITY IMPROVEMENT

BUILDING INNOVATION *Jul. 1966*
CIJE: 224 RIE: 97 GC: 920
SN Introduction of innovative approaches in the design and construction of new buildings
BT Innovation
RT Architectural Programing
Building Conversion
Building Design
Buildings
Construction Materials
Design Build Approach
Encapsulated Facilities
Facility Guidelines
Facility Requirements
Flexible Facilities
Relocatable Facilities
Systems Building
Underground Facilities

Building Materials (1968 1980)
USE CONSTRUCTION MATERIALS

BUILDING OBSOLESCENCE *Jul. 1966*
CIJE: 29 RIE: 31 GC: 920
SN Decline of functional utility due to changes in style, practice, and technology, not including physical deterioration
BT Obsolescence
RT Assessed Valuation
Building Conversion
Buildings
Facility Improvement
Facility Utilization Research
Property Appraisal
Space Utilization

BUILDING OPERATION *Jul. 1966*
CIJE: 136 RIE: 149 GC: 920
BT Administration
RT Buildings
Building Trades
Climate Control
Energy Management
Life Cycle Costing
Operating Expenses
School Maintenance

BUILDING PLANS *Dec. 1969*
CIJE: 64 RIE: 135 GC: 920
NT Blueprints
RT Architectural Drafting
Building Design
Buildings
Design
Design Build Approach
Educational Facilities Design
Educational Facilities Planning
Facility Case Studies
Facility Planning
Facility Requirements
Facility Utilization Research
House Plan
Life Cycle Costing
Master Plans
Planning
Space Classification
Space Utilization
Spatial Relationship (Facilities)
Specifications
Systems Building

Building Programs
USE CONSTRUCTION PROGRAMS

Building Renovation
USE FACILITY IMPROVEMENT

BUILDING SYSTEMS *Dec. 1976*
CIJE: 77 RIE: 142 GC: 920
SN Assemblies of building subsystems and components (structural and mechanical), with instructions for putting them together -- normally these components are mass-produced and used for specific generic projects in building construction
UF Component Building Systems (1968 1976)
Component Systems
NT Structural Building Systems
BT Structural Elements (Construction)
RT Buildings
Construction (Process)
Construction Programs
Life Cycle Costing
Modular Building Design
Prefabrication
Systems Building

BUILDING TRADES *Jul. 1966*
CIJE: 61 RIE: 365 GC: 640
UF Construction Occupations
Structural Work Occupations
BT Occupations
RT Air Conditioning
Blue Collar Occupations
Bricklaying
Building Operation
Buildings
Cabinetmaking
Carpentry
Construction (Process)
Construction Industry
Craft Workers
Electricians
Flooring
Industrial Arts
Masonry
Operating Engineering
Painting (Industrial Arts)
Plumbing
Roofing
Semiskilled Occupations
Skilled Occupations
Trade And Industrial Education
Woodworking

BUILDINGS *Jul. 1966*
CIJE: 62 RIE: 106 GC: 920
NT School Buildings
BT Facilities
RT Air Structures
Assessed Valuation
Building Conversion
Building Design
Building Innovation
Building Obsolescence
Building Operation
Building Plans
Building Systems
Building Trades
Ceilings
Construction Costs
Construction Industry
Construction Materials
Encapsulated Facilities
Facility Improvement
Facility Utilization Research
Flooring
Hotels
Maintenance
Prefabrication
Real Estate Occupations
Repair
Roofing
Space Utilization
Structural Building Systems
Structural Elements (Construction)
Systems Building
Underground Facilities
Visual Arts

BULGARIAN *Jul. 1966*
CIJE: 5 RIE: 17 GC: 440
BT Slavic Languages

Bulimarexia
USE BULIMIA

BULIMIA *Apr. 1986*
CIJE: 39 RIE: 19 GC: 210
SN Disorder characterized by recurrent binge eating, usually followed by self-induced purging -- attended by depressed moods and self-deprecating thoughts
UF Bulimarexia
BT Diseases
RT Anorexia Nervosa
Body Weight
Eating Habits
Emotional Disturbances
Nutrition
Physical Health

BULLETIN BOARDS *Jul. 1966*
CIJE: 73 RIE: 64 GC: 910
UF Tackboards
BT Visual Aids
RT Audiovisual Aids
Chalkboards
Educational Equipment

BULLETINS *Apr. 1969*
CIJE: 11 RIE: 256 GC: 730
BT Serials
RT Newsletters
Newspapers
Periodicals
Program Descriptions
Reports

BUREAUCRACY *Jul. 1966*
CIJE: 385 RIE: 246 GC: 520
BT Organization
RT Administrative Organization
Governmental Structure

Burglar Alarms
USE ALARM SYSTEMS

BURIAT *Jul. 1966*
CIJE: RIE: 2 GC: 440
BT Mongolian Languages

BURMESE *Jul. 1966*
CIJE: 6 RIE: 14 GC: 440
BT Sino Tibetan Languages
RT Burmese Culture

BURMESE CULTURE *Jul. 1966*
CIJE: 4 RIE: 14 GC: 560
BT Culture
RT Asian Studies
Burmese
Non Western Civilization

BURNOUT *Sep. 1981*
CIJE: 102 RIE: 49 GC: 230
SN Negative feelings and/or behaviors resulting from unsuccessful attempts to cope with stress conditions -- characterized by physical and emotional exhaustion, chronic negative attitudes, very low productivity, etc. (note: if possible, use the more specific term "teacher burnout")
NT Teacher Burnout
BT Responses
RT Coping
Emotional Response
Job Satisfaction
Morale
Motivation
Negative Attitudes
Organizational Climate
Persistence
Psychological Patterns
Stress Variables

BURUSHASKI *Jul. 1966*
CIJE: RIE: 1 GC: 440
BT Languages

= Two or more Descriptors are used to represent this term.
The term's main entry shows the appropriate coordination.

BUS TRANSPORTATION *Jul. 1966*
CIJE: 358 RIE: 389 GC: 320
BT Transportation
RT Busing
Feeder Patterns
School Buses
Student Transportation

Buses
USE SERVICE VEHICLES

BUSINESS *Jul. 1966*
CIJE: 732 RIE: 1071 GC: 650
SN Activities concerned with the production or exchange of goods or the rendering of financial or other services to the public for profit
UF Commercial Enterprises
NT Agribusiness
Black Businesses
Industry
Small Businesses
RT Business Administration
Business Administration Education
Business Communication
Business Correspondence
Business Cycles
Business Education
Business Responsibility
Cooperatives
Corporate Education
Corporate Support
Economics
Entrepreneurship
Exports
Insurance Companies
International Trade
Marketing
Merchants
Mergers
Office Machines
Office Occupations
Organization Size (Groups)
Ownership
Producer Services
School Business Relationship

BUSINESS ADMINISTRATION *Sep. 1969*
CIJE: 281 RIE: 526 GC: 650
SN The organization and management of commercial enterprises (note: prior to mar80, this term was scoped to mean the "subject" or "curriculum" of business administration -- see also "business administration education")
UF Small Business Management #
BT Administration
RT Administrative Principles
Business
Business Administration Education
Entrepreneurship
Managerial Occupations
Public Administration

BUSINESS ADMINISTRATION EDUCATION *Mar. 1980*
CIJE: 153 RIE: 148 GC: 400
SN Professional study of the organization and management of commercial enterprises, usually at the baccalaureate level and above (note: do not confuse with "business education")
BT Professional Education
RT Administrator Education
Business
Business Administration
Business Education
Management Development
Professional Training
Public Administration Education

BUSINESS COMMUNICATION *Dec. 1974*
CIJE: 549 RIE: 310 GC: 650
SN Interchange of verbal and nonverbal messages in commercial or mercantile environments
UF Commercial Communication
Industrial Communication
NT Business Correspondence
BT Organizational Communication
RT Business
Business Education
Business English
Labor Relations

BUSINESS CORRESPONDENCE *Jul. 1966*
CIJE: 161 RIE: 113 GC: 650
SN Written communication between people or organizations engaged in business
UF Business Letters
BT Business Communication
Verbal Communication
RT Business
Business English
Dictation
Letters (Correspondence)
Office Occupations Education

BUSINESS CYCLES *Jul. 1966*
CIJE: 114 RIE: 95 GC: 620
UF Business Fluctuations
Economic Cycles
Economic Fluctuations
RT Business
Economic Climate
Economic Factors
Economic Progress
Economics
Inflation (Economics)
Labor Economics
Monetary Systems

BUSINESS EDUCATION *Jul. 1966*
CIJE: 2385 RIE: 1758 GC: 400
SN Formal preparation for occupations in business below the baccalaureate degree (note: do not confuse with "basic business education" or "business administration education" -- if appropriate, use the more specific term "office occupations education" -- before mar80, the use of this term was not restricted by a scope note)
UF Business Subjects (1967 1980)
Commercial Education
Vocational Business Education
NT Office Occupations Education
BT Vocational Education
RT Accounting
Banking
Business
Business Administration Education
Business Communication
Business Education Facilities
Business Education Teachers
Business Skills
Clerical Occupations
Data Processing Occupations
Distributive Education
Economics Education
Marketing
Office Occupations

BUSINESS EDUCATION FACILITIES *Apr. 1970*
CIJE: 26 RIE: 22 GC: 920
BT Educational Facilities
RT Business Education
Classrooms
Office Occupations Education

BUSINESS EDUCATION TEACHERS *Sep. 1968*
CIJE: 277 RIE: 68 GC: 360
UF Business Teachers
BT Vocational Education Teachers
RT Business Education
Office Occupations Education

BUSINESS ENGLISH *Jul. 1966*
CIJE: 78 RIE: 115 GC: 400
BT English
RT Business Communication
Business Correspondence
Language Usage
Office Occupations Education
Technical Writing

Business Fluctuations
USE BUSINESS CYCLES

Business Games
USE MANAGEMENT GAMES

Business Letters
USE BUSINESS CORRESPONDENCE

Business Machines
USE OFFICE MACHINES

Business Officials (Industry)
USE ADMINISTRATORS

Business Officials (School)
USE SCHOOL BUSINESS OFFICIALS

BUSINESS RESPONSIBILITY *Jul. 1966*
CIJE: 155 RIE: 263 GC: 650
SN Obligations of the commercial business community
BT Responsibility
RT Business
Corporate Support
Leadership Responsibility

Business School Relationship
USE SCHOOL BUSINESS RELATIONSHIP

BUSINESS SKILLS *Jul. 1966*
CIJE: 296 RIE: 591 GC: 400
NT Bookkeeping
Keyboarding (Data Entry)
Recordkeeping
Typewriting
BT Skills
RT Accounting
Basic Business Education
Business Education
Dictation
Employment Qualifications
Filing
Job Skills
Office Practice
Practical Arts
Shorthand

Business Subjects (1967 1980)
USE BUSINESS EDUCATION

Business Teachers
USE BUSINESS EDUCATION TEACHERS

BUSING *Mar. 1980*
CIJE: 104 RIE: 112 GC: 540
SN Transporting students for the purpose of school desegregation (note: prior to mar80, the instruction "busing, use bus transportation" was carried in the thesaurus)
BT Desegregation Methods
RT Bus Transportation
Desegregation Plans
Feeder Patterns
Magnet Schools
Racial Composition
Racial Integration
Racially Balanced Schools
School Buses
School Desegregation

Byelorussian
USE BIELORUSSIAN

Cabinetmakers
USE CABINETMAKING

CABINETMAKING *Jul. 1966*
CIJE: 3 RIE: 21 GC: 640
SN Cutting, shaping, assembling, and repairing prepared parts of complex wood products such as store fixtures, office equipment, and home furniture
UF Cabinetmakers
Millwork
BT Construction (Process)
Woodworking
RT Building Trades
Carpentry
Industrial Arts
Skilled Occupations

CABLE TELEVISION *Jan. 1970*
CIJE: 325 RIE: 640 GC: 720
SN System whereby distant television signals are brought to subscribers in a community via coaxial cable rather than being broadcast
UF Catv
Community Antennas (1966 1980)
BT Television
RT Closed Circuit Television

Cafeterias
USE DINING FACILITIES

Cai
USE COMPUTER ASSISTED INSTRUCTION

CAKCHIQUEL *Jul. 1966*
CIJE: 1 RIE: 2 GC: 440
SN A mayan language spoken by the indian people of highland guatemala
BT American Indian Languages

Calculation (1966 1980)
USE COMPUTATION

CALCULATORS *Mar. 1980*
CIJE: 448 RIE: 224 GC: 910
SN Electronic or mechanical devices for performing mathematical or arithmetic operations
UF Electronic Calculators
Hand Calculators
Pocket Calculators
BT Equipment
RT Computation
Computers
Data Processing
Electromechanical Aids
Electronic Equipment
Instrumentation
Keyboarding (Data Entry)
Mathematics
Mechanical Equipment
Office Machines
Semiconductor Devices

CALCULUS *Jul. 1966*
CIJE: 355 RIE: 159 GC: 480
BT Mathematics
RT Analytic Geometry
Functions (Mathematics)
Trigonometry
Vectors (Mathematics)

CALISTHENICS *Jul. 1966*
CIJE: 12 RIE: 14 GC: 470
BT Exercise
RT Gymnastics
Muscular Strength
Physical Fitness

Calligraphy
USE MANUSCRIPT WRITING (HANDLETTERING)

CALORIMETERS *Jan. 1970*
CIJE: 17 RIE: 1 GC: 910
SN Instruments that measure heat quantities generated or emitted by such processes as chemical reactions, changes of state, or formation of solutions
UF Microcalorimeters
BT Measurement Equipment
RT Heat
Thermodynamics

CAMBODIAN *Aug. 1968*
CIJE: RIE: 57 GC: 440
UF Khmer (Language)
BT Austro Asiatic Languages

Cambodian Americans
USE ASIAN AMERICANS; CAMBODIANS

CAMBODIANS *Mar. 1980*
CIJE: 6 RIE: 48 GC: 560
UF Cambodian Americans #
Khmer (People)
BT Indochinese
RT Asian Americans
Laotians
Vietnamese People

Cameras
USE PHOTOGRAPHIC EQUIPMENT

Camp Counselors (1968 1980)
USE CAMPING

CAMPING *Jul. 1966*
CIJE: 219 RIE: 353 GC: 470
UF Camp Counselors (1968 1980)
BT Recreational Activities
RT Adventure Education
Day Camp Programs
Outdoor Activities
Resident Camp Programs
Tourism
Trails

= Two or more Descriptors are used to represent this term.
The term's main entry shows the appropriate coordination.

CAMPUS PLANNING *Jul. 1966*
CIJE: 224 RIE: 349 GC: 920
SN Grounds and facilities planning, usually at postsecondary institutions (note: prior to mar80, this term was not scoped and was often confused with "college planning")
BT Educational Facilities Planning
RT Architectural Character
Campuses
College Buildings
College Environment
College Planning
Educational Facilities
Educational Facilities Design
Parking Facilities
Physical Mobility
School Buildings
School Location
Space Utilization

Campus Schools
USE LABORATORY SCHOOLS

Campus Security
USE SCHOOL SECURITY

CAMPUSES *Jul. 1966*
CIJE: 97 RIE: 65 GC: 920
BT Educational Complexes
RT Campus Planning
College Buildings
Colleges
Educational Parks
Multicampus Colleges
Multicampus Districts
School Buildings
School Security

CANADA NATIVES *Aug. 1977*
CIJE: 142 RIE: 190 GC: 560
SN Peoples indigenous to canada (canada's american indians, eskimos, or peoples whose ancestry is mixed with these groups)
BT Ethnic Groups
North Americans
RT Alaska Natives
American Indians
Canadian Literature
Eskimos
Minority Groups
Tribes

CANADIAN LITERATURE *Jul. 1975*
CIJE: 47 RIE: 38 GC: 430
UF French Canadian Literature
BT North American Literature
RT Canada Natives

CANCER *Oct. 1979*
CIJE: 182 RIE: 88 GC: 210
SN Malignant and invasive growth or tumor
UF Carcinogens
Carcinoma
Malignant Neoplasms
Sarcoma
Tumors (Malignant)
BT Diseases
RT Occupational Diseases
Oncology
Physical Health
Radiologic Technologists
Radiology
Smoking
Special Health Problems
Surgery

Cannabis
USE MARIJUANA

Canonical Correlation
USE MULTIVARIATE ANALYSIS

CANTONESE *Jul. 1966*
CIJE: 29 RIE: 62 GC: 440
BT Chinese

CAPITAL *Jul. 1966*
CIJE: 31 RIE: 97 GC: 620
BT Financial Support
RT Banking
Capital Outlay (For Fixed Assets)
Educational Finance
Endowment Funds
Estate Planning
Fund Raising
Money Management
Ownership
Private Financial Support
Resource Allocation
Scholarship Funds
School Funds
Trusts (Financial)

CAPITAL OUTLAY (FOR FIXED ASSETS) *Jul. 1966*
CIJE: 76 RIE: 247 GC: 620
SN Expenditure that results in acquisition of fixed assets or additions to fixed assets such as expenditure for land or existing buildings, improvement of grounds, construction or modification of buildings, or initial or additional equipment -- includes installment or lease payments on such property
BT Expenditures
RT Capital
Construction Costs
Educational Finance
Facility Improvement
Facility Planning
Land Acquisition

CAPITALISM *Oct. 1974*
CIJE: 184 RIE: 121 GC: 610
BT Social Systems
RT Communism
Democracy
Economics
Entrepreneurship
Fascism
Government (Administrative Body)
Imperialism
Marxism
Political Science
Socialism
United States History

CAPITALIZATION (ALPHABETIC) *Jul. 1966*
CIJE: 16 RIE: 54 GC: 450
RT Punctuation
Sentence Structure
Spelling
Writing Skills
Written Language

CAPTIONS *Dec. 1974*
CIJE: 80 RIE: 22 GC: 720
SN Explanatory comments accompanying photographs or illustrations
UF Cutlines
RT Cartoons
Films
Illustrations
Journalism
Layout (Publications)
Newspapers
Photographs
Photojournalism

Carcinogens
USE CANCER

Carcinoma
USE CANCER

CARD CATALOGS *Apr. 1980*
CIJE: 24 RIE: 46 GC: 710
SN Library catalogs made up of cards, with each card usually bearing a single entry
BT Library Catalogs

Cardiac (Person) (1968 1980)
USE HEART DISORDERS

CARDIOPULMONARY RESUSCITATION *Apr. 1986*
CIJE: 23 RIE: 8 GC: 210
SN Procedure to restore normal breathing and heartbeat following cardiac arrest -- may include mouth-to-mouth ventilation, external chest compression, and use of drugs
UF Cpr (Medicine)
BT First Aid
RT Cardiovascular System
Heart Disorders

CARDIOVASCULAR SYSTEM *Jun. 1969*
CIJE: 279 RIE: 135 GC: 210
UF Circulatory System
Vascular System
RT Aerobics
Anatomy
Biofeedback
Blood Circulation
Cardiopulmonary Resuscitation
Exercise Physiology
Heart Disorders
Heart Rate
Human Body
Hypertension
Physiology
Zoology

CAREER AWARENESS *Feb. 1975*
CIJE: 462 RIE: 1802 GC: 400
SN Appreciation for and understanding of the variety of types of careers -- often refers to the initial phase of career education appropriate to the elementary school
UF Occupational Awareness
Vocational Awareness
BT Career Development
RT Career Choice
Career Education
Career Guidance
Career Planning
Careers
Occupations
School Guidance

CAREER CHANGE *Jan. 1969*
CIJE: 363 RIE: 383 GC: 120
UF Employment Change
Job Change
Midcareer Change #
Vocational Change
Work Change
BT Change
RT Career Choice
Career Development
Career Planning
Careers
Dislocated Workers
Early Retirement
Education Work Relationship
Emerging Occupations
Employment Opportunities
Job Satisfaction
Job Search Methods
Labor Turnover
Midlife Transitions
Occupational Mobility
Persistence
Professional Development
Promotion (Occupational)
Vocational Adjustment

CAREER CHOICE *Jul. 1966*
CIJE: 2302 RIE: 2724 GC: 120
UF Career Objectives
Occupational Choice (1966 1980)
Vocational Choice
BT Selection
RT Career Awareness
Career Change
Career Development
Career Education
Career Exploration
Career Guidance
Career Planning
Careers
Decision Making
Education Work Relationship
Eligibility
Employment Opportunities
Interest Inventories
Nontraditional Occupations
Occupational Aspiration
Occupations
Prevocational Education
Reentry Workers
Vocational Aptitude
Vocational Interests
Vocational Maturity

CAREER COUNSELING *Mar. 1980*
CIJE: 1568 RIE: 1949 GC: 240
SN Counseling activities to assist clients in selecting appropriate career options
UF Occupational Counseling
Vocational Counseling (1966 1980)
BT Career Guidance
Counseling
RT Adult Counseling
Career Development
Career Planning
Careers
Employment Counselors
Job Placement
Occupational Tests
Occupations
Outplacement Services (Employment)
Prevocational Education
Rehabilitation Counseling
Vocational Adjustment
Vocational Education
Vocational Interests
Vocational Training Centers

CAREER DEVELOPMENT *Jan. 1979*
CIJE: 1655 RIE: 2825 GC: 120
SN The continuous process of making career decisions based on the individual's experiences and interactions (e.g., the child's first impression of the working world, the adolescent's consideration of vocational alternatives, or the adult's decision to change careers)
UF Vocational Development (1967 1978)
NT Career Awareness
Career Exploration
BT Individual Development
RT Career Change
Career Choice
Career Counseling
Career Education
Career Guidance
Career Planning
Careers
Education Work Relationship
Occupational Aspiration
Occupational Information
Occupations
Promotion (Occupational)
Vocational Interests
Vocational Maturity

CAREER EDUCATION *Oct. 1971*
CIJE: 2310 RIE: 6844 GC: 400
SN A comprehensive educational program that focuses on individual career development, beginning with grade 1 or earlier and continuing through the adult years
BT Education
RT Career Awareness
Career Choice
Career Development
Career Exploration
Career Guidance
Career Planning
Careers
Cooperative Education
Education Work Relationship
Occupations
Prevocational Education
Relevance (Education)
School Business Relationship
Vocational Education
Work Experience Programs

CAREER EXPLORATION *Sep. 1975*
CIJE: 430 RIE: 1427 GC: 400
SN Investigating occupational interest areas often through real or simulated job experience -- frequently found in career education programs for grades 6 through 10
UF Occupational Exploration
BT Career Development
RT Career Choice
Career Education
Career Guidance
Career Planning
Careers
Occupations
Prevocational Education
School Guidance
Vocational Interests
Vocational Maturity
Work Experience
Work Experience Programs

CAREER GUIDANCE *Mar. 1980*
CIJE: 966 RIE: 2549 GC: 240
SN Spectrum of activities and programs designed to help people plan, choose, and succeed in their careers (note: if applicable, use the more specific term "career counseling")

= Two or more Descriptors are used to represent this term.
The term's main entry shows the appropriate coordination.

UF Occupational Guidance (1966 1980)
Vocational Guidance
NT Career Counseling
BT Guidance
RT Career Awareness
Career Choice
Career Development
Career Education
Career Exploration
Career Planning
Careers
Employment Potential
Job Placement
Occupations
Outplacement Services (Employment)
Post High School Guidance
School Guidance
Vocational Interests

CAREER LADDERS *May. 1971*
CIJE: 272 RIE: 453 GC: 630
SN Hierarchy of occupational progression, with training, from entry level position to higher levels in the same occupation
UF Job Ladders
BT Occupational Mobility
RT Adult Vocational Education
Careers
Employment Level
Entry Workers
Inservice Education
Labor Force Development
Promotion (Occupational)
Training

Career Maturity
USE VOCATIONAL MATURITY

Career Objectives
USE CAREER CHOICE

CAREER OPPORTUNITIES (1966 1980) *Mar. 1980*
CIJE: 624 RIE: 953 GC: 630
SN Invalid descriptor -- used inconsistently in indexing -- use "careers," and, if appropriate, "employment opportunities"

Career Orientation
USE CAREER PLANNING

CAREER PLANNING *Jul. 1966*
CIJE: 1392 RIE: 2298 GC: 240
UF Career Orientation
BT Planning
RT Career Awareness
Career Change
Career Choice
Career Counseling
Career Development
Career Education
Career Exploration
Career Guidance
Careers
Demand Occupations
Education Work Relationship
Goal Orientation
Job Search Methods
Prevocational Education
Vocational Aptitude

CAREERS *Jul. 1966*
CIJE: 378 RIE: 548 GC: 630
SN The progressively developing sequences of related occupational roles or work experiences through which individuals move during their working lives, often with increasing prestige and rewards -- also, the intended sequence of such roles established by individuals as part of their life plans (note: prior to mar80, the use of this term was not restricted by a scope note)
NT Science Careers
RT Career Awareness
Career Change
Career Choice
Career Counseling
Career Development
Career Education
Career Exploration
Career Guidance
Career Ladders
Career Planning
Dual Career Family
Education Work Relationship
Employment
Entrepreneurship
Occupational Mobility
Occupations
Quality Of Working Life
Self Actualization
Work Experience
Work Life Expectancy

CARICATURES (1966 1980) *Mar. 1980*
CIJE: 11 RIE: 6 GC: 420
SN Invalid descriptor -- see the more precise terms "cartoons" and "characterization"

Carpenters (1969 1981)
USE CARPENTRY

CARPENTRY *Sep. 1981*
CIJE: 15 RIE: 75 GC: 640
SN Building or repairing structures and fixtures made from wood or materials that can be worked like wood, e.g., plastic, fiber glass
UF Carpenters (1969 1981)
BT Construction (Process)
Woodworking
RT Building Trades
Cabinetmaking
Industrial Arts
Skilled Occupations

Carpet Layers
USE FLOOR LAYERS

CARPETING *Aug. 1968*
CIJE: 62 RIE: 47 GC: 920
UF Carpets
BT Flooring
RT Construction Materials
Floor Layers

Carpets
USE CARPETING

CARRELS *Jul. 1966*
CIJE: 33 RIE: 37 GC: 910
UF Study Carrels
BT Study Facilities
RT Library Equipment

CARTOGRAPHY *Aug. 1977*
CIJE: 60 RIE: 57 GC: 400
SN Science or art of making maps
UF Mapping
BT Graphic Arts
RT Atlases
Civil Engineering
Earth Science
Geographic Location
Geography
Locational Skills (Social Studies)
Maps
Map Skills
Topography

CARTOONS *Jul. 1966*
CIJE: 173 RIE: 126 GC: 720
BT Visual Aids
RT Animation
Audiovisual Aids
Captions
Childrens Television
Comics (Publications)
Films
Film Study
Freehand Drawing
Illustrations
Instructional Materials
Nonprint Media

CASE (GRAMMAR) *May. 1969*
CIJE: 169 RIE: 101 GC: 450
BT Linguistic Theory
RT Form Classes (Languages)
Grammar
Language Patterns
Language Universals
Syntax

CASE RECORDS *Jul. 1966*
CIJE: 102 RIE: 110 GC: 320
NT Medical Case Histories
BT Records (Forms)
RT Biographical Inventories
Case Studies
Caseworker Approach
Confidential Records
Disclosure
Profiles
Recordkeeping
Student Records

CASE STUDIES *Apr. 1970*
CIJE: 3346 RIE: 4223 GC: 810
SN Detailed analyses, usually focusing on a particular problem of an individual, group, or organization (note: do not confuse with "medical case histories" -- as of oct81, use as a minor descriptor for examples of this kind of research -- use as a major descriptor only as the subject of a document)
UF Case Studies (Education) (1966 1980)
NT Cross Sectional Studies
Facility Case Studies
Longitudinal Studies
BT Evaluation Methods
Research
RT Case Records
Counseling
Qualitative Research

Case Studies (Education) (1966 1980)
USE CASE STUDIES

CASEWORKER APPROACH *Jul. 1966*
CIJE: 137 RIE: 72 GC: 240
SN Techniques, strategies, and procedures used by caseworkers, counselors, social workers, etc. for working with individuals or groups -- includes determining and solving problems, recordkeeping, and followup activities
BT Methods
RT Case Records
Caseworkers
Counseling Techniques
Field Interviews
Rehabilitation Counseling
Social Work

CASEWORKERS *Jul. 1966*
CIJE: 62 RIE: 52 GC: 240
SN Social service personnel responsible for solving or mitigating the specific problems of individuals, families, etc.
NT Parole Officers
Probation Officers
Social Workers
BT Personnel
RT Caseworker Approach
Counselors
Guidance Personnel
Rehabilitation
School Social Workers
Social Work

Cassettes (Tape)
USE MAGNETIC TAPE CASSETTES

CASTE *Nov. 1972*
CIJE: 17 RIE: 17 GC: 540
SN A closed social stratum based on heredity that determines its members' prestige, occupation, place of residence, and social relationships
UF Brahmins (1967 1980)
BT Social Class
RT Religious Cultural Groups
Social Discrimination
Social Stratification

CATALOGING *Jul. 1966*
CIJE: 849 RIE: 775 GC: 710
UF Bibliographic Control
Library Cataloging
NT Machine Readable Cataloging
BT Documentation
RT Bibliometrics
Classification
Filing
Indexing
Library Catalogs
Library Technical Processes
Subject Index Terms

CATALOGS *Jul. 1966*
CIJE: 189 RIE: 733 GC: 710
SN (Note: use a more specific term if possible -- see also "reference materials" hierarchy for more precise terminology)
NT Library Catalogs
Online Catalogs
School Catalogs
BT Publications

CATEGORICAL AID *Sep. 1982*
CIJE: 23 RIE: 57 GC: 620
SN Financial assistance for specific, limited programs or services prescribed by law or administrative regulations
BT Financial Support
RT Educational Finance
Equalization Aid
Federal Aid
Grants
Legal Responsibility
Resource Allocation
State Aid
Tax Allocation

Categorization
USE CLASSIFICATION

CATHARSIS *Apr. 1969*
CIJE: 37 RIE: 22 GC: 230
SN Relaxation of emotional tension by expressive reaction
UF Abreaction
Psychocatharsis
BT Emotional Experience
RT Aggression
Anger
Anxiety
Emotional Development
Hostility
Psychological Patterns
Psychotherapy
Self Expression
Stress Management

CATHOLIC EDUCATORS *Jul. 1966*
CIJE: 161 RIE: 48 GC: 360
SN Teachers in catholic schools or in diocesan educational programs (note: prior to mar80, the use of this term was not restricted by a scope note)
BT Teachers
RT Catholics
Catholic Schools
Church Related Colleges
Church Workers
Religious Education

Catholic Elementary Schools (1967 1980)
USE CATHOLIC SCHOOLS

Catholic High Schools (1967 1980)
USE CATHOLIC SCHOOLS

Catholic Parents (1966 1980)
USE CATHOLICS; PARENTS

CATHOLIC SCHOOLS *Jul. 1966*
CIJE: 568 RIE: 287 GC: 340
UF Catholic Elementary Schools (1967 1980)
Catholic High Schools (1967 1980)
BT Parochial Schools
RT Catholic Educators
Church Related Colleges
Lay Teachers
Private Education
Private School Aid
Religious Education

CATHOLICS *Jul. 1966*
CIJE: 225 RIE: 98 GC: 560
UF Catholic Parents (1966 1980) #
BT Religious Cultural Groups
RT Catholic Educators
Christianity
Nuns
Priests

Catv
USE CABLE TELEVISION

CAUCASIAN LANGUAGES *Jul. 1966*
CIJE: 2 RIE: 8 GC: 440
SN Languages spoken in the area of the caucasus mountain range which do not belong to the indo-european, semitic, or uralic-altaic families
UF Circassian
Darghi
Georgian
BT Languages

Caucasian Race (1967 1980)
USE WHITES

= Two or more Descriptors are used to represent this term.
The term's main entry shows the appropriate coordination.

Caucasian Students (1967 1980)
USE WHITE STUDENTS

Caucasians (1967 1980)
USE WHITES

Causal Attributions
USE ATTRIBUTION THEORY

Causal Factors
USE INFLUENCES

Cctv
USE CLOSED CIRCUIT TELEVISION

Cd Recordings
USE OPTICAL DISKS

Cd Rom
USE OPTICAL DATA DISKS

CEBUANO *Jul. 1966*
CIJE: RIE: 8 GC: 440
BT Visayan
RT Dialects

CEILINGS *Jul. 1966*
CIJE: 9 RIE: 30 GC: 920
BT Structural Elements (Construction)
RT Buildings
Construction (Process)

Cell Theory (1966 1980)
USE CYTOLOGY

CEMENT INDUSTRY *Jul. 1966*
CIJE: 3 RIE: 33 GC: 650
UF Concrete Industry
BT Manufacturing Industry
RT Chemical Engineering
Construction Industry
Construction Materials
Prestressed Concrete

Cements (Adhesives)
USE ADHESIVES

CENSORSHIP *Jul. 1966*
CIJE: 695 RIE: 469 GC: 520
RT Academic Freedom
Freedom Of Information
Freedom Of Speech
Intellectual Freedom
Moral Issues
Moral Values
Sanctions

CENSUS FIGURES *Jul. 1966*
CIJE: 199 RIE: 717 GC: 730
BT Statistical Data
RT Cohort Analysis
Community Size
Demography
Incidence
Profiles
Statistical Analysis

Centers Of Interest (1966 1980)
USE LEARNING CENTERS (CLASSROOM)

Central American History
USE LATIN AMERICAN HISTORY

Central American Literature
USE LATIN AMERICAN LITERATURE

Central Americans
USE LATIN AMERICANS

Central Sound Systems (1966 1980)
USE AUDIO EQUIPMENT

CENTRALIZATION *Jul. 1966*
CIJE: 297 RIE: 299 GC: 520
BT Administrative Organization
RT Decentralization
Mergers
Organizational Change
School Organization

Centralized Schools
USE CONSOLIDATED SCHOOLS

Centroid Method Of Factor Analysis
USE FACTOR ANALYSIS

CERAMICS *Sep. 1968*
CIJE: 101 RIE: 68 GC: 420
UF Pottery
BT Handicrafts
RT Art Materials
Childrens Art
Design Crafts
Glass
Industrial Arts
Visual Arts

Cerebral Dominance (1967 1986)
USE BRAIN HEMISPHERE FUNCTIONS

CEREBRAL PALSY *Jul. 1966*
CIJE: 154 RIE: 161 GC: 220
BT Congenital Impairments
Neurological Impairments
RT Developmental Disabilities
Mental Retardation
Multiple Disabilities
Speech Handicaps

CERTIFICATION *Jul. 1966*
CIJE: 584 RIE: 1054 GC: 330
UF Licensing
NT Accreditation (Institutions)
Counselor Certification
Student Certification
Teacher Certification
RT Credentials
Credits
Educational Certificates
Eligibility
Equivalency Tests
Experiential Learning
High School Equivalency Programs
Licensing Examinations (Professions)
Portfolios (Background Materials)
Prior Learning
Proprietary Schools
Qualifications
Quality Control
Special Degree Programs
Standards
State Licensing Boards

Certified Nurses
USE NURSES

CERTIFIED PUBLIC ACCOUNTANTS *Jul. 1966*
CIJE: 13 RIE: 10 GC: 640
BT Accountants
RT Accounting
Financial Services

Ceu
USE CONTINUING EDUCATION UNITS

CHAD LANGUAGES *Jul. 1966*
CIJE: 2 RIE: 7 GC: 440
NT Hausa
BT Afro Asiatic Languages
RT Language Classification

Chain Reflexes (Behavior)
USE BEHAVIOR CHAINING

CHALKBOARDS *Jul. 1966*
CIJE: 41 RIE: 23 GC: 910
UF Blackboards
BT Visual Aids
RT Audiovisual Aids
Bulletin Boards
Educational Equipment

CHAMORRO *Feb. 1975*
CIJE: 3 RIE: 68 GC: 440
SN Native language of guam and the other mariana islands
BT Malayo Polynesian Languages

Chancellors (Education)
USE COLLEGE PRESIDENTS

Chancroid
USE VENEREAL DISEASES

CHANGE *Mar. 1980*
CIJE: 234 RIE: 139 GC: 520
SN Act or process of altering, modifying, transforming, substituting, or otherwise making or becoming different -- includes deviation from established character, condition, sequence, or direction (note: do not confuse with "development," which refers to sequential, progressive changes -- use a more specific term if possible)
NT Administrative Change
Attitude Change
Behavior Change
Building Conversion
Career Change
Community Change
Economic Change
Educational Change
Media Adaptation
Midlife Transitions
Organizational Change
Personality Change
Social Change
RT Change Agents
Change Strategies
Development
History
Influences
Innovation
Inventions
Revolution

CHANGE AGENTS *Jul. 1966*
CIJE: 1203 RIE: 1675 GC: 330
SN Individuals or groups who attempt change, aid in its accomplishment, or help to cope with it (note: use a more specific term if possible)
NT Extension Agents
Linking Agents
BT Groups
RT Attitude Change
Blue Ribbon Commissions
Change
Change Strategies
Community Change
Community Leaders
Consultants
Educational Change
Social Change

CHANGE STRATEGIES *May. 1974*
CIJE: 1951 RIE: 2958 GC: 330
SN Methods used by those who would alter the practice of some organization, institution, or other group to incorporate new knowledge, products, procedures, or values toward improved service or results
BT Methods
RT Administrative Change
Adoption (Ideas)
Attitude Change
Behavior Change
Change
Change Agents
Community Change
Economic Change
Educational Change
Educational Strategies
Finance Reform
Improvement
Incentives
Organizational Change
Social Change

Changing Attitudes (1966 1980)
USE ATTITUDE CHANGE

Character
USE PERSONALITY

Character Portrayal
USE CHARACTERIZATION

CHARACTER RECOGNITION *Oct. 1969*
CIJE: 32 RIE: 22 GC: 710
SN Technology of using a machine to sense and encode written or printed characters into a machine language (note: prior to mar80, the use of this term was not restricted by a scope note)
UF Magnetic Ink Character Recognition
Ocr #
Optical Character Recognition #
BT Pattern Recognition
RT Information Processing
Optical Scanners

CHARACTERIZATION *Jul. 1977*
CIJE: 831 RIE: 265 GC: 430
SN The creation and convincing representation of human characters or personalities as in fiction or drama
UF Characterization (Literature) (1969 1977)
Character Portrayal
BT Literary Devices
RT Acting
Animation
Literary Styles

Characterization (Literature) (1969 1977)
USE CHARACTERIZATION

Charitable Trusts
USE TRUSTS (FINANCIAL)

CHARTS *Jul. 1966*
CIJE: 660 RIE: 386 GC: 720
NT Experience Charts
Flow Charts
BT Visual Aids
RT Atlases
Diagrams
Graphs
Illustrations
Instructional Materials
Nonprint Media
Precision Teaching
Profiles
Records (Forms)
Tables (Data)

CHEATING *Jul. 1966*
CIJE: 138 RIE: 64 GC: 530
BT Antisocial Behavior
RT Codes Of Ethics
Discipline Problems
Lying
Plagiarism

CHECK LISTS *Jul. 1966*
CIJE: 527 RIE: 1277 GC: 730
SN Lists from which items can be compared, scheduled, verified, or identified
BT Records (Forms)
RT Guidelines
Indexes
Informal Assessment
Rating Scales

Chefs
USE COOKS

CHEMICAL ANALYSIS *Jan. 1970*
CIJE: 841 RIE: 102 GC: 490
UF Chemical Determination
Composition Measurement
Determination (Chemical)
BT Evaluation Methods
RT Chemical Engineering
Chemical Reactions
Chemistry
Chromatography
Metallurgy
Mineralogy
Spectroscopy
Structural Analysis (Science)
Water Treatment

CHEMICAL BONDING *Jul. 1966*
CIJE: 267 RIE: 17 GC: 490
BT Chemical Reactions
RT Chemistry
Crystallography
Inorganic Chemistry
Molecular Structure
Organic Chemistry
Physical Sciences
Structural Analysis (Science)

Chemical Dependency (Drugs)
USE DRUG ADDICTION

Chemical Determination
USE CHEMICAL ANALYSIS

CHEMICAL ENGINEERING *Aug. 1982*
CIJE: 253 RIE: 10 GC: 490
SN Branch of engineering concerned with industrial chemical processes involved in converting raw materials into products, and the design/operation of plants/equipment to accomplish this work

= Two or more Descriptors are used to represent this term.
The term's main entry shows the appropriate coordination.

BT Engineering
RT Agricultural Chemical Occupations
Cement Industry
Chemical Analysis
Chemical Industry
Chemistry
Kinetics
Manufacturing Industry
Mass Production
Petroleum Industry
Polymers
Power Technology
Water Treatment

CHEMICAL EQUILIBRIUM *Jan. 1970*
CIJE: 207 RIE: 20 GC: 490
SN Condition in which a chemical reaction is occurring at equal rates in its forward and reverse directions, so that concentrations of the reacting substances do not change with time
UF Equilibrium Constants
RT Chemical Reactions
Chemistry
Thermodynamics

CHEMICAL INDUSTRY *Aug. 1969*
CIJE: 277 RIE: 38 GC: 650
BT Manufacturing Industry
RT Agricultural Chemical Occupations
Chemical Engineering
Chemical Technicians
Chemistry
Petroleum Industry

CHEMICAL NOMENCLATURE *Oct. 1972*
CIJE: 83 RIE: 15 GC: 490
BT Vocabulary
RT Chemistry
Classification

CHEMICAL REACTIONS *Jan. 1970*
CIJE: 1040 RIE: 69 GC: 490
UF Chemical Synthesis
NT Chemical Bonding
Oxidation
Photochemical Reactions
RT Chemical Analysis
Chemical Equilibrium
Chemistry
Diffusion (Physics)
Enzymes
Inorganic Chemistry
Molecular Structure
Nucleic Acids
Organic Chemistry
Polymers

Chemical Synthesis
USE CHEMICAL REACTIONS

CHEMICAL TECHNICIANS *Jul. 1966*
CIJE: 25 RIE: 29 GC: 640
BT Paraprofessional Personnel
RT Chemical Industry
Chemistry
Environmental Technicians
Metallurgical Technicians
Nuclear Power Plant Technicians
Scientific Personnel

CHEMISTRY *Jul. 1966*
CIJE: 6456 RIE: 1076 GC: 490
UF Chemistry Instruction (1967 1980) #
Chemistry Teachers (1967 1980) #
NT Biochemistry
Inorganic Chemistry
Organic Chemistry
BT Physical Sciences
RT Agricultural Chemical Occupations
Atomic Structure
Chemical Analysis
Chemical Bonding
Chemical Engineering
Chemical Equilibrium
Chemical Industry
Chemical Nomenclature
Chemical Reactions
Chemical Technicians
Chromatography
Coordination Compounds
Crystallography
Earth Science
Metallurgy
Mineralogy
Molecular Structure
Oxidation
Photochemical Reactions
Polymers
Radiation Biology
Radioisotopes
Scientific Research
Soil Science
Spectroscopy
Water

Chemistry Instruction (1967 1980)
USE CHEMISTRY; SCIENCE INSTRUCTION

Chemistry Teachers (1967 1980)
USE CHEMISTRY; SCIENCE TEACHERS

Chemotherapy
USE DRUG THERAPY

CHEREMIS *Jul. 1966*
CIJE: RIE: 2 GC: 440
BT Finno Ugric Languages

CHEROKEE *Apr. 1970*
CIJE: 5 RIE: 8 GC: 440
BT American Indian Languages

Chibemba
USE BEMBA

Chief Academic Officers
USE ACADEMIC DEANS

Chief Administrators (1967 1980)
USE ADMINISTRATORS

CHILD ABUSE *Jul. 1966*
CIJE: 680 RIE: 669 GC: 530
UF Abused Children
Child Sexual Abuse #
BT Antisocial Behavior
RT Battered Women
Child Neglect
Children
Child Welfare
Family Problems
Family Violence
Parent Child Relationship
Sexual Abuse
Victims Of Crime
Violence

CHILD ADVOCACY *Mar. 1974*
CIJE: 305 RIE: 424 GC: 520
SN Active mobilization of social, economic, and legal resources for the purpose of ensuring the individual child's basic rights and developmental needs (including those related to home, community, and school)
BT Advocacy
RT Childhood Needs
Children
Childrens Rights
Child Welfare
Helping Relationship
Individual Power
Legal Aid

CHILD CARE (1966 1980) *Mar. 1980*
CIJE: 348 RIE: 547 GC: 520
SN Invalid descriptor -- see "child rearing" or "day care"

Child Care Centers (1967 1980)
USE DAY CARE CENTERS

CHILD CARE OCCUPATIONS *Jul. 1966*
CIJE: 39 RIE: 136 GC: 640
BT Service Occupations
RT Child Caregivers
Child Development Specialists
Day Care
Day Care Centers
Foster Care
Home Economics Skills
Occupational Home Economics
Parenting Skills

Child Care Workers (1967 1980)
USE CHILD CAREGIVERS

CHILD CAREGIVERS *Apr. 1980*
CIJE: 281 RIE: 714 GC: 640
SN Persons who take care of children -- includes professionals, nonprofessionals, parents, and others (note: for documents/articles involving parents, use a more precise term such as "parents," "mothers," "fathers," or other "parent" term)
UF Child Care Workers (1967 1980)
BT Groups
RT Child Care Occupations
Child Rearing
Day Care
Day Care Centers
Foster Care
Parents
Preschool Teachers
Social Workers

Child Centered Curriculum
USE STUDENT CENTERED CURRICULUM

CHILD CUSTODY *Oct. 1983*
CIJE: 60 RIE: 42 GC: 520
SN Court-authorized arrangement for the primary care of children
RT Child Rearing
Children
Child Welfare
Divorce
Family Problems
One Parent Family
Parent Child Relationship

CHILD DEVELOPMENT *Jul. 1966*
CIJE: 2562 RIE: 2813 GC: 120
BT Individual Development
RT Child Development Centers
Child Development Specialists
Child Language
Child Psychology
Child Rearing
Children
Child Responsibility
Delayed Speech
Developmental Stages
Developmental Tasks
Failure To Thrive
Family Environment
Parenthood Education
Piagetian Theory

CHILD DEVELOPMENT CENTERS *Jul. 1966*
CIJE: 62 RIE: 114 GC: 920
SN Educational facilities for preschool children, which also provide health and family services -- originally used in connection with project head start for centers in which cooperation of family, community, and professional staff contribute to the total development of the child
BT Educational Facilities
RT Child Development
Child Development Specialists
Day Care Centers
Early Childhood Education
Nursery Schools
Preschool Children
Preschool Education

CHILD DEVELOPMENT SPECIALISTS *Jul. 1966*
CIJE: 35 RIE: 44 GC: 360
SN Persons whose professional training has prepared them to understand and work with the changes that take place in children as they develop from birth to maturity -- these specialists may work with other professionals, paraprofessionals, or parents, as well as with children
BT Specialists
RT Child Care Occupations
Child Development
Child Development Centers
Child Psychology
Children

CHILD LABOR *Jul. 1966*
CIJE: 52 RIE: 73 GC: 630
UF Child Labor Laws (1966 1974) #
Child Labor Legislation (1966 1980) #
BT Labor
RT Children
Child Welfare

Child Labor Laws (1966 1974)
USE CHILD LABOR; LABOR LEGISLATION

Child Labor Legislation (1966 1980)
USE CHILD LABOR; LABOR LEGISLATION

CHILD LANGUAGE *Nov. 1968*
CIJE: 1153 RIE: 1420 GC: 450
BT Language
RT Bilingualism
Child Development
Children
Egocentrism
Immersion Programs
Language Acquisition
Language Arts
Language Experience Approach
Language Handicaps
Language Patterns
Language Research
Monolingualism
Oral Language
Pronunciation
Psycholinguistics
Speech Habits
Verbal Development

CHILD NEGLECT *Mar. 1980*
CIJE: 190 RIE: 342 GC: 530
SN Failure of parents or caretakers to provide to children the care essential for normal development
UF Neglected Children (1977 1980)
BT Antisocial Behavior
RT Child Abuse
Child Rearing
Children
Child Welfare
Failure To Thrive
Family Problems
Parent Child Relationship
Victims Of Crime

Child Parent Relationship
USE PARENT CHILD RELATIONSHIP

CHILD PSYCHOLOGY *Jul. 1966*
CIJE: 296 RIE: 189 GC: 230
BT Psychology
RT Child Development
Child Development Specialists
Children
Developmental Psychology
Individual Psychology

CHILD REARING *Jul. 1966*
CIJE: 781 RIE: 902 GC: 520
SN Care of children by parents, guardians, or other primary caregivers (note: see also "day care" -- prior to mar80, "child care" was also a valid descriptor)
UF Parenting
RT Child Caregivers
Child Custody
Child Development
Child Neglect
Children
Family Relationship
Parent Child Relationship
Parenthood Education
Parenting Skills

CHILD RESPONSIBILITY *Jul. 1966*
CIJE: 72 RIE: 68 GC: 510
SN Responsibility of, not for, a child (note: prior to mar80, the use of this term was not restricted by a scope note)
BT Responsibility
RT Child Development
Childhood Needs
Children
Childrens Rights
Child Role
Parent Responsibility
Student Responsibility
Teacher Responsibility

Child Restraints (Vehicle Safety)
USE RESTRAINTS (VEHICLE SAFETY)

CHILD ROLE *Jul. 1966*
CIJE: 62 RIE: 51 GC: 510
RT Children
Child Responsibility
Family Role

Child Sexual Abuse
USE CHILD ABUSE; SEXUAL ABUSE

= Two or more Descriptors are used to represent this term.
The term's main entry shows the appropriate coordination.

CHILD WELFARE *Jul. 1966*
CIJE: 525 RIE: 600 GC: 520
BT Well Being
RT Adopted Children
Adoption
Child Abuse
Child Advocacy
Child Custody
Childhood Needs
Child Labor
Child Neglect
Children
Childrens Rights
Early Parenthood
Foster Care
Foster Children
Foster Family
Latchkey Children
Runaways
Student Welfare

Childbirth
USE BIRTH

Childhood (1966 1980)
USE CHILDREN

CHILDHOOD ATTITUDES *Jul. 1966*
CIJE: 756 RIE: 526 GC: 120
SN Attitudes of, not toward, children (note: prior to mar80, the use of this term was not restricted by a scope note)
UF Childrens Attitudes
BT Attitudes
RT Childhood Interests
Children
Student Attitudes

Childhood Friendship (1966 1980)
USE FRIENDSHIP

CHILDHOOD INTERESTS *Jul. 1966*
CIJE: 223 RIE: 152 GC: 120
SN Objects, activities, persons, etc. that engage the attention of children
UF Childrens Interests
BT Interests
RT Childhood Attitudes
Children
Student Interests

CHILDHOOD NEEDS *Jul. 1966*
CIJE: 386 RIE: 417 GC: 120
SN Those experiences, attentions, etc. which are necessary for the physical, biological, intellectual, personal, and social development of children
UF Childrens Needs
BT Individual Needs
RT Child Advocacy
Children
Childrens Rights
Child Responsibility
Child Welfare
Psychological Needs
Student Needs

CHILDREN *Jul. 1966*
CIJE: 5353 RIE: 3230 GC: 120
SN Aged birth through approximately 12 years
UF Childhood (1966 1980)
NT Adopted Children
Foster Children
Grandchildren
Hospitalized Children
Latchkey Children
Migrant Children
Minority Group Children
Preadolescents
Problem Children
Transient Children
Young Children
BT Age Groups
RT Adolescents
Child Abuse
Child Advocacy
Child Custody
Child Development
Child Development Specialists
Childhood Attitudes
Childhood Interests
Childhood Needs
Child Labor
Child Language
Child Neglect
Child Psychology
Child Rearing
Childrens Art
Childrens Games
Childrens Literature
Childrens Rights
Childrens Television
Child Responsibility
Child Role
Child Welfare
Dependents
Elementary School Students
Family (Sociological Unit)
Family Life
Family Problems
Juvenile Courts
Parent Child Relationship
Parenting Skills
Play
Youth

CHILDRENS ART *Jun. 1977*
CIJE: 180 RIE: 55 GC: 420
SN The process and/or the results of children's production of art objects or artifacts
BT Visual Arts
RT Art Activities
Art Appreciation
Art Education
Art Materials
Art Products
Ceramics
Children
Creative Art
Freehand Drawing
Handicrafts
Painting (Visual Arts)

Childrens Attitudes
USE CHILDHOOD ATTITUDES

Childrens Books (1966 1980)
USE BOOKS; CHILDRENS LITERATURE

Childrens Courts
USE JUVENILE COURTS

CHILDRENS GAMES *Jul. 1966*
CIJE: 124 RIE: 171 GC: 470
BT Games
RT Children
Play
Playground Activities
Toys

Childrens Interests
USE CHILDHOOD INTERESTS

CHILDRENS LITERATURE *May. 1974*
CIJE: 2115 RIE: 1615 GC: 430
SN Any reading material written primarily for, or read widely by, children from their early years to adolescence
UF Childrens Books (1966 1980) #
BT Literature
RT Adolescent Literature
Children
Comics (Publications)
Didacticism
Picture Books
Reading Materials

Childrens Needs
USE CHILDHOOD NEEDS

Childrens Play
USE PLAY

CHILDRENS RIGHTS *Mar. 1983*
CIJE: 94 RIE: 46 GC: 520
SN Legal and human rights of children, pertaining to physical and psychological welfare in such areas as guardianship, custody, child abuse, and juvenile court proceedings
BT Civil Liberties
RT Child Advocacy
Childhood Needs
Children
Child Responsibility
Child Welfare
Civil Rights
Due Process
Parent Rights
Student Rights

CHILDRENS TELEVISION *Dec. 1976*
CIJE: 150 RIE: 210 GC: 720
SN Television programing designed for or aimed at children's interests
BT Television
RT Cartoons
Children

Childrens Theater
USE THEATER ARTS

CHIMNEYS *Oct. 1969*
CIJE: 4 RIE: 7 GC: 920
UF Exhaust Stacks
Smokestacks
BT Structural Elements (Construction)
RT Air Flow
Air Pollution
Heat
Heating
Pollution
Ventilation

CHINESE *Jul. 1966*
CIJE: 370 RIE: 389 GC: 440
NT Cantonese
Foochow
Mandarin Chinese
BT Sino Tibetan Languages
RT Chinese Americans
Chinese Culture
Ideography

CHINESE AMERICANS *Jul. 1966*
CIJE: 108 RIE: 329 GC: 560
BT Asian Americans
Ethnic Groups
RT Chinese

CHINESE CULTURE *Jul. 1966*
CIJE: 234 RIE: 262 GC: 560
BT Culture
RT Asian Studies
Chinese
Non Western Civilization

CHINYANJA *Jul. 1966*
CIJE: RIE: 5 GC: 440
UF Cinyanja
Nyanja
BT Bantu Languages

Chippewa
USE OJIBWA

Chlorination (Water)
USE WATER TREATMENT

CHOCTAW *Apr. 1970*
CIJE: 3 RIE: 16 GC: 440
BT American Indian Languages

Choirs
USE SINGING

CHORAL MUSIC *Oct. 1968*
CIJE: 62 RIE: 32 GC: 420
SN Music intended for group singing
BT Vocal Music
RT Hymns
Music Activities
Musical Composition
Music Education
Music Techniques
Singing

CHORAL SPEAKING *Jul. 1966*
CIJE: 32 RIE: 35 GC: 420
SN Ensemble speaking often using various voice combinations and contrasts to bring out the meaning or tonal beauty of a passage of poetry or prose
BT Theater Arts
RT Literature
Literature Appreciation
Oral Interpretation
Poetry
Speech

Choreography
USE DANCE

Choruses (1968 1980)
USE SINGING

CHRISTIANITY *May. 1969*
CIJE: 216 RIE: 96 GC: 430
BT Religion
RT Biblical Literature
Catholics
Judaism
Philosophy
Protestants
Religious Cultural Groups
Western Civilization

CHROMATOGRAPHY *Jul. 1969*
CIJE: 254 RIE: 8 GC: 490
SN Method of separating and analyzing mixtures of chemical substances
UF Electrochromatography
BT Laboratory Procedures
RT Biochemistry
Biology
Chemical Analysis
Chemistry

Chronic Illnesses
USE DISEASES

CHRONICLES *Sep. 1969*
CIJE: 49 RIE: 25 GC: 430
SN Historical, chronological accounts of events
BT Literary Genres
Nonfiction
RT History
Medieval Literature
Poetry
Renaissance Literature

CHRONOLOGICAL AGE *Apr. 1980*
CIJE: 34 RIE: 29 GC: 120
SN Actual physical age of the individual expressed in terms of years and months
BT Age
RT Age Groups
Physical Characteristics
Physical Development

Church Action
USE CHURCH ROLE

Church Migrant Projects (1966 1980)
USE CHURCH PROGRAMS; MIGRANT PROGRAMS

CHURCH PROGRAMS *Jul. 1966*
CIJE: 65 RIE: 129 GC: 520
UF Church Migrant Projects (1966 1980) #
Church Projects
BT Programs
RT Churches
Church Related Colleges
Church Role
Church Workers
Migrant Programs
Nonprofit Organizations
Religion
Religious Education

Church Projects
USE CHURCH PROGRAMS

CHURCH RELATED COLLEGES *Jul. 1966*
CIJE: 227 RIE: 359 GC: 340
UF Denominational Colleges
Sectarian Colleges
Seminaries #
BT Colleges
RT Catholic Educators
Catholic Schools
Church Programs
Parochial Schools
Private Colleges
Private Education
Private School Aid
Religious Education
Religious Organizations
Single Sex Colleges
Small Colleges
Theological Education

CHURCH RESPONSIBILITY *Jul. 1966*
CIJE: 22 RIE: 55 GC: 520
BT Responsibility
RT Churches
Leadership Responsibility

= Two or more Descriptors are used to represent this term.
The term's main entry shows the appropriate coordination.

CHURCH ROLE *Jul. 1966*
CIJE: 176 RIE: 246 GC: 520
UF Church Action
BT Institutional Role
RT Churches
Church Programs
Religion
State Church Separation

Church State Separation
USE STATE CHURCH SEPARATION

CHURCH WORKERS *Nov. 1969*
CIJE: 25 RIE: 28 GC: 520
UF Parish Workers
BT Personnel
RT Catholic Educators
Churches
Church Programs
Clergy
Lay People
Lay Teachers
Nuns
Priests
Religion
Religious Education

CHURCHES *Jul. 1966*
CIJE: 48 RIE: 75 GC: 920
BT Institutions
RT Church Programs
Church Responsibility
Church Role
Church Workers
Mergers
Nonprofit Organizations
Priests
Religion
Religious Organizations
State Church Separation
Theological Education

CHUVASH *Jul. 1966*
CIJE: RIE: 3 GC: 440
BT Turkic Languages

Cigarette Smoking
USE SMOKING

Cinema
USE FILMS

Cinema Study
USE FILM STUDY

Cinyanja
USE CHINYANJA

Circassian
USE CAUCASIAN LANGUAGES

Circuit Teachers
USE ITINERANT TEACHERS

Circuits (Electronic)
USE ELECTRIC CIRCUITS

Circulatory System
USE CARDIOVASCULAR SYSTEM

CITATION ANALYSIS *Aug. 1986*
CIJE: 55 RIE: 3 GC: 810
SN Bibliometric application in which a body of literature is separated and classified through interconnections of bibliographic citations
NT Bibliographic Coupling
BT Bibliometrics
RT Bibliographies
Citation Indexes
Citations (References)
Classification

CITATION INDEXES *Jul. 1966*
CIJE: 59 RIE: 84 GC: 710
SN Indexing system for identifying later writings that refer to (cite) earlier works
BT Indexes
RT Bibliographic Coupling
Citation Analysis
Citations (References)
Indexing

Citations (Legal)
USE LAW ENFORCEMENT

CITATIONS (REFERENCES) *Mar. 1980*
CIJE: 431 RIE: 573 GC: 730
SN References that identify works which have been used as authorities or from which passages have been quoted
UF Bibliographic Citations (1969 1980)
Bibliographic References
Footnotes (Bibliographic)
BT Reference Materials
RT Bibliographic Coupling
Bibliographies
Citation Analysis
Citation Indexes

Cities
USE MUNICIPALITIES

Citizen Advocacy
USE ADVOCACY

Citizen Involvement
USE CITIZEN PARTICIPATION

CITIZEN PARTICIPATION *Jul. 1966*
CIJE: 720 RIE: 1251 GC: 610
SN Political or social involvement in the community, government, or school in order to improve or maintain the status quo or to have impact on policy formation and decision making
UF Citizen Involvement
Civic Involvement
Public Participation
BT Participation
RT Activism
Advocacy
Citizens Councils
Citizenship
Citizenship Education
Citizenship Responsibility
Civil Disobedience
Community Action
Community Change
Community Control
Community Cooperation
Community Development
Community Involvement
Community Organizations
Community Role
Community Support
Participative Decision Making
Political Campaigns
Public Affairs Education
Public Service
Social Action
Social Responsibility
Student Projects
Voting

Citizen Responsibility
USE CITIZENSHIP RESPONSIBILITY

CITIZEN ROLE *Jul. 1966*
CIJE: 93 RIE: 131 GC: 610
RT Citizenship
Citizenship Education

CITIZENS COUNCILS *Jul. 1966*
CIJE: 57 RIE: 97 GC: 610
BT Community Organizations
RT Citizen Participation

CITIZENSHIP *Jul. 1966*
CIJE: 229 RIE: 559 GC: 610
SN Status of being a member of a political community with the attendant rights, responsibilities, and privileges
UF Good Citizenship
BT Status
RT Citizen Participation
Citizen Role
Citizenship Education
Citizenship Responsibility
Civics
Community Attitudes
Foreign Nationals
Political Attitudes
Student Rights

CITIZENSHIP EDUCATION *Mar. 1980*
CIJE: 328 RIE: 409 GC: 400
SN Learning activities, curriculum, and/or educational programs, at any educational level, concerned with rights and responsibilities of citizenship -- the purpose is to promote knowledge, skills, and attitudes conducive to effective participation in civic life
BT Education
RT Basic Business Education
Citizen Participation
Citizen Role
Citizenship
Citizenship Responsibility
Civics
Critical Thinking
Current Events
Ethical Instruction
Global Approach
Law Related Education
Public Affairs Education
Values Education

CITIZENSHIP RESPONSIBILITY *Jul. 1966*
CIJE: 223 RIE: 352 GC: 610
UF Citizen Responsibility
Civic Responsibility
BT Social Responsibility
RT Citizen Participation
Citizenship
Citizenship Education
Community Responsibility
Humanitarianism
Leadership Responsibility
Patriotism
Public Affairs Education
Voting

City Demography (1966 1980)
USE URBAN DEMOGRAPHY

CITY GOVERNMENT *Jul. 1966*
CIJE: 148 RIE: 248 GC: 610
UF Municipal Government
BT Local Government
RT City Officials
Community
Government Employees
Government School Relationship
Public Agencies
School District Autonomy
Urban Improvement
Urban Planning
Urban Programs

City Improvement (1966 1980)
USE URBAN IMPROVEMENT

CITY OFFICIALS *Jul. 1966*
CIJE: 37 RIE: 68 GC: 610
UF Elected City Officials
BT Public Officials
RT City Government
County Officials
Legislators

City Planning (1966 1980)
USE URBAN PLANNING

City Problems (1966 1980)
USE URBAN PROBLEMS

City Schools
USE URBAN SCHOOLS

City Wide Commissions (1966 1980)
USE PLANNING COMMISSIONS; URBAN PLANNING

City Wide Programs (1967 1980)
USE URBAN PROGRAMS

Civic Belief (1966 1980)
USE POLITICAL ATTITUDES

Civic Groups
USE COMMUNITY ORGANIZATIONS

Civic Involvement
USE CITIZEN PARTICIPATION

Civic Organizations
USE COMMUNITY ORGANIZATIONS

Civic Programs
USE COMMUNITY PROGRAMS

Civic Relations
USE COMMUNITY RELATIONS

Civic Responsibility
USE CITIZENSHIP RESPONSIBILITY

CIVICS *Jul. 1966*
CIJE: 172 RIE: 352 GC: 400
SN The part of social studies dealing with the fundamental philosophical, political, social, economic, and historical aspects of government and citizenship
BT Social Studies
RT Citizenship
Citizenship Education
Government (Administrative Body)
United States Government (Course)

CIVIL DEFENSE *Jul. 1966*
CIJE: 17 RIE: 81 GC: 610
RT Alarm Systems
Community Programs
Emergency Programs
Fallout Shelters
Military Science
National Defense
Natural Disasters
Nuclear Warfare

CIVIL DISOBEDIENCE *Nov. 1969*
CIJE: 53 RIE: 48 GC: 610
RT Activism
Citizen Participation
Civil Rights
Civil Rights Legislation
Demonstrations (Civil)
Segregationist Organizations
Torts

CIVIL ENGINEERING *Jul. 1966*
CIJE: 39 RIE: 61 GC: 490
UF Highway Engineering
BT Engineering
RT Cartography
Engineering Drawing
Engineering Graphics
Highway Engineering Aides
Road Construction
Structural Building Systems
Water Treatment

CIVIL LIBERTIES *Nov. 1969*
CIJE: 886 RIE: 788 GC: 610
SN Freedom from arbitrary governmental, social, or personal interference with person, property, or opinion (note: prior to mar80, the use of this term was not restricted by a scope note)
UF Human Rights
Individual Rights
Personal Liberty
NT Childrens Rights
Civil Rights
Due Process
Freedom Of Speech
Parent Rights
Student Rights
Teacher Rights
RT Academic Freedom
Constitutional Law
Democracy
Freedom Of Information
Home Schooling
Intellectual Freedom
International Crimes
Justice
Laws
Privacy
Search And Seizure
Slavery

CIVIL RIGHTS *Jul. 1966*
CIJE: 1157 RIE: 1316 GC: 540
SN Rights of all individuals to equality under the law, sometimes denied because of personal characteristics (e.g., race, sex, ethnic background)
UF Minority Rights
NT Equal Education
Equal Opportunities (Jobs)
Equal Protection
Voting Rights
BT Civil Liberties
RT Black Leadership
Black Organizations
Black Power
Childrens Rights
Civil Disobedience
Civil Rights Legislation
Constitutional Law
Democracy

= Two or more Descriptors are used to represent this term.
The term's main entry shows the appropriate coordination.

Demonstrations (Civil)
Due Process
Equal Facilities
Feminism
Freedom Of Speech
Freedom Schools
Justice
Minority Groups
Parent Rights
Racial Integration
Racial Segregation
Search And Seizure
Segregationist Organizations
Sex Discrimination
Slavery
Social Discrimination
Student Rights
Teacher Rights
Torts

CIVIL RIGHTS LEGISLATION *Jul. 1966*
CIJE: 254 RIE: 324 GC: 610
SN Legislation that aims to protect the constitutional rights of citizens, especially to rectify past discriminatory actions toward minority groups
UF Anti Discrimination Legislation
BT Legislation
RT Civil Disobedience
Civil Rights
Constitutional Law
Discriminatory Legislation
Equal Education
Equal Facilities
Equal Opportunities (Jobs)
Equal Protection
Laws
Minority Groups
Racial Integration
Social Discrimination

Civil Service Employees
USE GOVERNMENT EMPLOYEES

Civil War
USE WAR

CIVIL WAR (UNITED STATES) *Jul. 1966*
CIJE: 45 RIE: 80 GC: 430
BT United States History
RT Reconstruction Era
Slavery

CLASS ACTIVITIES *Jul. 1966*
CIJE: 1987 RIE: 2140 GC: 310
SN (Note: when possible, coordinate with terms that identify the activities)
UF Class Newspapers (1967 1980) #
Class Projects
Classroom Activities
Classroom Games (1966 1980) #
Classroom Participation (1966 1980) #
BT School Activities
RT Classes (Groups Of Students)
Classroom Techniques
Dramatic Play
Field Trips
Learning Activities
Play

Class Attendance (1966 1980)
USE ATTENDANCE

CLASS ATTITUDES (1966 1980) *Mar. 1980*
CIJE: 39 RIE: 36 GC: 520
SN Invalid descriptor -- used for both social class attitudes and classroom attitudes -- see more precise attitude terms -- refer to "attitudes" in the hierarchical display

CLASS AVERAGE (1966 1980) *Mar. 1980*
CIJE: 17 RIE: 11 GC: 310
SN Invalid descriptor -- for related concepts, see "grade point average" or "class rank"

Class Desegregation
USE CLASSROOM DESEGREGATION

Class Discussion
USE DISCUSSION (TEACHING TECHNIQUE)

Class Management (1966 1980)
USE CLASSROOM TECHNIQUES

Class Newspapers (1967 1980)
USE CLASS ACTIVITIES; STUDENT PUBLICATIONS

CLASS ORGANIZATION *Jul. 1966*
CIJE: 311 RIE: 356 GC: 310
SN The way in which a class or group of students is structured to facilitate instruction (includes student grouping, scheduling of classes and classroom activities, classroom and materials arrangement)
BT Organization
RT Classes (Groups Of Students)
Classroom Design
Classroom Environment
Classroom Techniques
Cluster Grouping
Course Organization
Grouping (Instructional Purposes)
Open Plan Schools
School Organization
School Schedules
Self Contained Classrooms
Teaching Methods

Class Projects
USE CLASS ACTIVITIES

CLASS RANK *Mar. 1980*
CIJE: 42 RIE: 38 GC: 310
SN Academic standing within a class (note: prior to mar80, this concept may have been indexed under "class average")
UF Rank In Class
RT Academic Achievement
Classes (Groups Of Students)
Competition
Grade Point Average
Grades (Scholastic)

CLASS SIZE *Jul. 1966*
CIJE: 261 RIE: 427 GC: 310
RT Classes (Groups Of Students)
Classroom Environment
Crowding
Flexible Scheduling
Small Classes
Teacher Student Ratio

Class Status
USE SOCIAL STATUS

CLASSES (GROUPS OF STUDENTS) *Jul. 1966*
CIJE: 76 RIE: 140 GC: 310
NT Multigraded Classes
Multilevel Classes (Second Language Instruction)
Nonauthoritarian Classes
Small Classes
Special Classes
BT Groups
RT Class Activities
Class Organization
Class Rank
Classroom Communication
Classroom Desegregation
Classroom Environment
Classroom Observation Techniques
Classroom Techniques
Class Size
Grouping (Instructional Purposes)

CLASSICAL CONDITIONING *Dec. 1970*
CIJE: 42 RIE: 19 GC: 110
SN A form of conditioning in which an arbitrary or neutral stimulus (e.g., the bell in pavlov's experiment) comes to elicit a response (e.g., salivation) after it is repeatedly paired with reinforcement (e.g., food)
BT Conditioning
RT Behavior Modification
Operant Conditioning

Classical Greek
USE GREEK

CLASSICAL LANGUAGES *Jul. 1966*
CIJE: 238 RIE: 195 GC: 440
NT Latin
Sanskrit
BT Languages
RT Classical Literature
College Second Language Programs
Greek
Latin Literature

CLASSICAL LITERATURE *Jul. 1966*
CIJE: 300 RIE: 150 GC: 430
SN Literature of ancient greece and rome
NT Latin Literature
BT Literature
RT Ancient History
Biblical Literature
Classical Languages
Epics
Greek Civilization
Greek Literature
Latin
Legends
Literary History
Mythology
Platonism
World Literature

Classical Mechanics
USE MECHANICS (PHYSICS)

CLASSIFICATION *Jul. 1966*
CIJE: 2538 RIE: 2236 GC: 710
SN Ordering of related phenomena into categories, groups, families, or systems according to characteristics or attributes
UF Categorization
Grouping Procedures (1966 1980)
Sorting Procedures (1966 1980)
Taxonomy (1967 1980)
Typology (1967 1980)
NT Cluster Grouping
Codification
Grouping (Instructional Purposes)
Labeling (Of Persons)
Language Classification
Space Classification
BT Organization
RT Bibliometrics
Cataloging
Chemical Nomenclature
Citation Analysis
Cluster Analysis
Content Analysis
Data Analysis
Documentation
Groups
Identification
Indexing
Library Technical Processes
Relationship
Statistical Distributions

Classification Clerks
USE FILE CLERKS

Classroom Activities
USE CLASS ACTIVITIES

Classroom Arrangement (1966 1980)
USE CLASSROOM DESIGN

CLASSROOM COMMUNICATION *Jul. 1966*
CIJE: 800 RIE: 842 GC: 310
BT Communication (Thought Transfer)
RT Classes (Groups Of Students)
Classroom Environment
Classroom Observation Techniques
Classroom Techniques
Nonverbal Communication
Student Behavior
Teacher Behavior
Teacher Student Relationship
Verbal Communication

CLASSROOM DESEGREGATION *Mar. 1980*
CIJE: 77 RIE: 103 GC: 540
SN Process of bringing students of different ethnic or racial groups into the same classroom
UF Class Desegregation
Classroom Integration (1967 1980)
Desegregated Classes
Integrated Classes
BT Social Integration
RT Classes (Groups Of Students)
Heterogeneous Grouping
Racial Integration
School Desegregation

CLASSROOM DESIGN *Jul. 1966*
CIJE: 298 RIE: 346 GC: 920
SN Conceiving and selecting the structure, elements, arrangement, and materials that make up or are enclosed by a classroom -- also, the plan or layout that results
UF Classroom Arrangement (1966 1980)
BT Design
RT Class Organization
Classroom Environment
Classroom Furniture
Classroom Research
Classrooms
Design Requirements
Educational Facilities Design
Flexible Facilities
Flexible Lighting Design
Glass Walls
Interior Design
Interior Space
Multipurpose Classrooms
Open Plan Schools
Space Dividers
Space Utilization

Classroom Discipline
USE CLASSROOM TECHNIQUES; DISCIPLINE

CLASSROOM ENVIRONMENT *Jul. 1966*
CIJE: 1871 RIE: 1848 GC: 310
SN Intellectual, social, physical, etc., conditions within or exogenous to a classroom that influence the learning situation
UF Classroom Situation
BT Educational Environment
RT Aptitude Treatment Interaction
Classes (Groups Of Students)
Class Organization
Classroom Communication
Classroom Design
Classroom Observation Techniques
Classrooms
Classroom Techniques
Class Size
College Environment
Student Attitudes
Teacher Attitudes
Teacher Student Relationship
Teaching Conditions

Classroom Equipment
USE EDUCATIONAL EQUIPMENT

CLASSROOM FURNITURE *Jul. 1966*
CIJE: 69 RIE: 65 GC: 910
UF Furniture (Classroom)
BT Educational Equipment
Furniture
RT Classroom Design
Classrooms
Furniture Arrangement
Furniture Design

Classroom Games (1966 1980)
USE CLASS ACTIVITIES; EDUCATIONAL GAMES

CLASSROOM GUIDANCE PROGRAMS (1968 1980) *Mar. 1980*
CIJE: 44 RIE: 58 GC: 240
SN Invalid descriptor -- used inconsistently in indexing -- see more precise terms "counselor teacher cooperation," "group guidance," "career guidance," etc.

Classroom Integration (1967 1980)
USE CLASSROOM DESEGREGATION

Classroom Libraries (1966 1980)
USE INSTRUCTIONAL MATERIALS

Classroom Materials (1966 1980)
USE INSTRUCTIONAL MATERIALS

Classroom Methods
USE CLASSROOM TECHNIQUES

CLASSROOM OBSERVATION TECHNIQUES *Mar. 1969*
CIJE: 779 RIE: 1411 GC: 820
SN Procedures used to obtain quantified descriptions of teacher and student behavior and interaction in a classroom setting
BT Measurement Techniques

= Two or more Descriptors are used to represent this term.
The term's main entry shows the appropriate coordination.

RT Behavior Rating Scales
Classes (Groups Of Students)
Classroom Communication
Classroom Environment
Classroom Research
Content Analysis
Interaction Process Analysis
Lesson Observation Criteria
Naturalistic Observation
Observation
Participant Observation
Student Behavior
Student Evaluation
Teacher Behavior
Teacher Evaluation

Classroom Participation (1966 1980)
USE CLASS ACTIVITIES; STUDENT PARTICIPATION

CLASSROOM RESEARCH *Jul. 1966*
CIJE: 521 RIE: 794 GC: 810
SN Systematic investigations conducted in or about a classroom setting -- includes studies of instructors, students, and facilities (note: as of oct81, use as a minor descriptor for examples of this kind of research -- use as a major descriptor only as the subject of a document)
BT Educational Research
RT Classroom Design
Classroom Observation Techniques
Classrooms

Classroom Situation
USE CLASSROOM ENVIRONMENT

CLASSROOM TECHNIQUES *Jul. 1966*
CIJE: 2251 RIE: 2916 GC: 310
SN Techniques used in the classroom by those in authority (e.g., teachers, aides, administrators) -- may either be directly educational or facilitate educational processes
UF Class Management (1966 1980)
Classroom Discipline #
Classroom Methods
BT Educational Methods
RT Class Activities
Classes (Groups Of Students)
Class Organization
Classroom Communication
Classroom Environment
Classrooms
Discipline
Educational Diagnosis
Educational Therapy
Learning Strategies
Proctoring
Teaching Methods

CLASSROOMS *Jul. 1966*
CIJE: 136 RIE: 210 GC: 920
SN Spaces designed or adapted for group instruction -- includes general and special classrooms but excludes such large assembly rooms as auditoriums, lunch rooms, and gymnasiums
UF Flexible Classrooms (1968 1980) #
NT Electronic Classrooms
Mobile Classrooms
Multipurpose Classrooms
Self Contained Classrooms
BT Educational Facilities
RT Business Education Facilities
Classroom Design
Classroom Environment
Classroom Furniture
Classroom Research
Classroom Techniques
Laboratories
Music Facilities
School Shops
School Space
Science Facilities

Clean Water
USE WATER QUALITY

CLEANING *Mar. 1969*
CIJE: 67 RIE: 65 GC: 210
NT Dishwashing
BT Sanitation
RT Disease Control
Equipment Maintenance
Housekeepers
Hygiene
Maintenance
Preservation
School Maintenance

CLEARINGHOUSES *Jul. 1966*
CIJE: 125 RIE: 325 GC: 710
SN Organizations that collect, process, maintain, and disseminate material, usually derived from current research, on a particular topic
BT Information Centers

Cleft Lip (1967 1980)
USE CLEFT PALATE

CLEFT PALATE *Jul. 1966*
CIJE: 32 RIE: 20 GC: 220
UF Cleft Lip (1967 1980)
BT Congenital Impairments
Physical Disabilities
Speech Handicaps
RT Articulation Impairments
Speech Therapy

CLERGY *Mar. 1980*
CIJE: 128 RIE: 125 GC: 640
UF Clergymen (1968 1980)
Ministers
Parsons
Preachers
NT Priests
BT Personnel
RT Church Workers
Lay People
Nuns
Religion
Religious Cultural Groups
Religious Education
Religious Organizations
Theological Education

Clergymen (1968 1980)
USE CLERGY

CLERICAL OCCUPATIONS *Jul. 1966*
CIJE: 67 RIE: 286 GC: 640
SN Occupations concerned with preparing, transcribing, systematizing, and preserving written communications and records, distributing information, or collecting accounts
BT Occupations
RT Bookkeeping
Business Education
Clerical Workers
Data Processing Occupations
Keyboarding (Data Entry)
Office Occupations
Office Occupations Education
Office Practice
Recordkeeping
Shorthand
Typewriting
White Collar Occupations
Word Processing

CLERICAL WORKERS *Jul. 1966*
CIJE: 79 RIE: 164 GC: 640
NT Court Reporters
Examiners
File Clerks
Receptionists
Secretaries
BT Nonprofessional Personnel
RT Clerical Occupations
Employees

Clerk Stenographers
USE SHORTHAND

Clerk Typists
USE TYPEWRITING

Clerkships (Medicine)
USE CLINICAL EXPERIENCE

CLICHES *Sep. 1970*
CIJE: 18 RIE: 5 GC: 430
SN Trite phrases or expressions
RT Language Styles

Client Background (Human Services)
USE CLIENT CHARACTERISTICS (HUMAN SERVICES)

Client Caseworkers (1966 1980)
USE SOCIAL WORKERS

Client Centered Counseling
USE NONDIRECTIVE COUNSELING

CLIENT CHARACTERISTICS (HUMAN SERVICES) *Oct. 1984*
CIJE: 32 RIE: 35 GC: 120
SN Distinguishing traits or qualities of persons who engage the assistance of human service workers (counselors, psychologists, physicians, nurses, social workers, etc.)
UF Client Background (Human Services)
RT Counselor Client Relationship
Human Services
Individual Characteristics
Participant Characteristics
Patients

Client Counselor Ratio
USE COUNSELOR CLIENT RATIO

Client Counselor Relationship
USE COUNSELOR CLIENT RELATIONSHIP

CLIMATE *Mar. 1980*
CIJE: 167 RIE: 166 GC: 490
SN The prevailing conditions of the physical environment, indoor or outdoor
UF Climatic Factors (1969 1980)
BT Physical Environment
RT Air Pollution
Climate Control
Diffusion (Physics)
Earth Science
Ecology
Environment
Environmental Influences
Geographic Location
Heat
Humidity
Light
Meteorology
Oceanography
Pollution
Solar Energy
Temperature
Thermal Environment
Water
Weather
Wind (Meteorology)

CLIMATE CONTROL *Jul. 1966*
CIJE: 130 RIE: 162 GC: 490
UF Hvac
NT Air Conditioning
Heating
Heat Recovery
Refrigeration
Ventilation
RT Air Conditioning Equipment
Air Pollution
Building Operation
Climate
Design Requirements
Electrical Systems
Energy Conservation
Energy Management
Environmental Influences
Humidity
Lighting
Physical Environment
Solar Energy
Temperature
Thermal Environment
Weather
Windowless Rooms
Windows

Climatic Factors (1969 1980)
USE CLIMATE

Clinic Personnel (School) (1966 1980)
USE ALLIED HEALTH PERSONNEL; SCHOOL HEALTH SERVICES

CLINICAL DIAGNOSIS *Jul. 1966*
CIJE: 1027 RIE: 500 GC: 210
SN Identification of diseases or disorders and the prescription of treatment
UF Diagnosis (Clinical)
BT Identification
RT Clinical Psychology
Diagnostic Tests
Educational Diagnosis
Etiology
Handicap Identification
Internal Medicine
Medical Case Histories
Medical Evaluation
Physical Examinations

CLINICAL EXPERIENCE *Sep. 1968*
CIJE: 863 RIE: 331 GC: 210
SN Practical experience in medical and health-related services that occurs as part of an educational program (note: if possible, use the more precise term "clinical teaching (health professions)")
UF Clerkships (Medicine)
Clinical Learning Experience
Externships (Medicine)
Preceptorships (Medicine)
BT Learning Experience
RT Allied Health Occupations Education
Clinical Teaching (Health Professions)
Clinics
Experiential Learning
Field Experience Programs
Graduate Medical Education
Internship Programs
Medical Education
Medical School Faculty
Pharmaceutical Education
Practicums
Practicum Supervision
Student Experience
Teaching Hospitals
Work Experience Programs

Clinical Judgment (Medicine)
USE MEDICAL EVALUATION

Clinical Judgment (Psychology)
USE PSYCHOLOGICAL EVALUATION

Clinical Learning Experience
USE CLINICAL EXPERIENCE

Clinical Professors (1967 1980) (Education)
USE STUDENT TEACHER SUPERVISORS

Clinical Professors (1967 1980) (Medicine)
USE MEDICAL SCHOOL FACULTY

CLINICAL PSYCHOLOGY *Oct. 1977*
CIJE: 215 RIE: 65 GC: 230
SN Branch of psychology devoted to psychological methods of diagnosing and treating mental and emotional disorders, as well as research into the causes of these disorders and the effects of therapy
BT Psychology
RT Behavior Disorders
Clinical Diagnosis
Community Psychology
Emotional Disturbances
Experimental Psychology
Mental Disorders
Personality Problems
Psychiatry
Psychological Evaluation
Psychological Studies
Psychological Testing
Psychometrics
Psychopathology
Psychophysiology
Psychotherapy
Social Psychology

Clinical Services
USE CLINICS

CLINICAL TEACHING (HEALTH PROFESSIONS) *Sep. 1981*
CIJE: 72 RIE: 43 GC: 210
SN Instruction in the clinical setting where actual symptoms are studied and treatment is given
BT Teaching Methods
RT Allied Health Occupations Education
Clinical Experience
Medical Education
Medical School Faculty
Practicums
Practicum Supervision
Teaching Hospitals

Clinical Teaching (Individualized Instruction)
USE INDIVIDUALIZED INSTRUCTION

CLINICS *Jul. 1966*
CIJE: 268 RIE: 190 GC: 920
UF Clinical Services
Preschool Clinics (1966 1980) #
Rural Clinics (1966 1980) #
Treatment Centers
NT Dental Clinics
Mental Health Clinics
Mobile Clinics
Psychoeducational Clinics
Speech And Hearing Clinics
RT Clinical Experience
Facilities
Health
Health Facilities
Hospitals
Medical Services
Meetings
Services

Clockmakers
USE WATCHMAKERS

CLOSED CIRCUIT TELEVISION *Jul. 1966*
CIJE: 259 RIE: 327 GC: 720
SN System whereby the transmission of television signals is limited to those audiences directly connected to the origination point by coaxial cable or microwave link -- usually limited to a building, campus, etc.
UF Cctv
BT Television
RT Alarm Systems
Cable Television
Educational Television

Closed Schools
USE SCHOOL CLOSING

CLOTHING *Jul. 1966*
CIJE: 122 RIE: 225 GC: 210
UF Fashions (Clothing)
RT Clothing Design
Clothing Instruction
Fashion Industry
Laundry Drycleaning Occupations
Needle Trades
Self Care Skills
Sewing Instruction
Sewing Machine Operators
Textiles Instruction

CLOTHING DESIGN *Jul. 1966*
CIJE: 49 RIE: 58 GC: 420
UF Costume Design
Dress Design
BT Design
RT Clothing
Clothing Instruction
Design Crafts
Fashion Industry
Needle Trades
Patternmaking

Clothing Industry
USE FASHION INDUSTRY

CLOTHING INSTRUCTION *Jul. 1966*
CIJE: 25 RIE: 158 GC: 400
BT Instruction
RT Clothing
Clothing Design
Consumer Science
Fashion Industry
Home Economics
Laundry Drycleaning Occupations
Needle Trades
Sewing Instruction
Sewing Machine Operators
Textiles Instruction

CLOZE PROCEDURE *Jul. 1966*
CIJE: 391 RIE: 487 GC: 460
SN Completion exercises requiring the reader to insert missing words with the aid of surrounding context
UF Cloze Techniques
BT Methods
RT Context Clues
Informal Reading Inventories
Language Skills
Language Tests
Readability
Reading
Reading Comprehension
Reading Skills
Reading Tests
Substitution Drills
Teaching Methods

Cloze Techniques
USE CLOZE PROCEDURE

CLUBS *Jul. 1966*
CIJE: 78 RIE: 91 GC: 520
UF Homemakers Clubs (1966 1980) #
NT Science Clubs
Youth Clubs
BT Groups
RT Extracurricular Activities

Clues
USE CUES

CLUSTER ANALYSIS *Mar. 1971*
CIJE: 243 RIE: 162 GC: 820
SN Systematic method of grouping measures or variables together according to their degree of similarity in a correlation matrix or table
BT Multivariate Analysis
RT Classification
Cluster Grouping
Correlation
Factor Analysis
Multidimensional Scaling

CLUSTER COLLEGES *Feb. 1971*
CIJE: 20 RIE: 47 GC: 340
SN Colleges, in close physical proximity, that constitute a single institution, share facilities and services, and usually have a centralized administration -- generally each college in the cluster focuses on one area of study (note: do not confuse with "consortia" -- prior to mar80, this term was not restricted by a scope note)
BT Colleges
RT Consortia
Educational Complexes
Experimental Colleges
House Plan
Shared Facilities

CLUSTER GROUPING *Jul. 1966*
CIJE: 268 RIE: 242 GC: 820
SN Classifying or selecting the items within a collection (of people, ideas, objects, etc.) on the basis of specified similarities (note: use a more precise term if possible)
BT Classification
RT Bibliometrics
Class Organization
Cluster Analysis
Group Structure
Homogeneous Grouping
Judgment Analysis Technique
Occupational Clusters
Peer Institutions

Cmi
USE COMPUTER MANAGED INSTRUCTION

Co Op Programs
USE COOPERATIVE PROGRAMS

Co Ops
USE COOPERATIVES

Coaching Teachers (1966 1974)
USE TUTORS

COAL *Aug. 1982*
CIJE: 39 RIE: 56 GC: 410
SN Combustible solid of organic origin used as a fuel (note: use also for coal by-products such as coal gas, coal tar, cokeite, etc.)
UF Anthracite
Bituminous Coal
Coal Mining #
Coal Resources
Lignite
BT Fuels
Natural Resources
RT Geology
Mining
Soil Science

Coal Mining
USE COAL; MINING

Coal Resources
USE COAL

Coast Guard Air Stations
USE MILITARY AIR FACILITIES

COCOUNSELING *May. 1970*
CIJE: 56 RIE: 18 GC: 240
SN Two or more counselors working as a team with a single client or group of clients, usually at the same time but sometimes consecutively
UF Conjoint Counseling
Team Counseling
BT Counseling
RT Teamwork

Cocurricular Activities (1966 1980)
USE EXTRACURRICULAR ACTIVITIES

CODE SWITCHING (LANGUAGE) *Aug. 1978*
CIJE: 72 RIE: 125 GC: 450
SN The alternating use of languages, dialects, or language styles in the speech of an individual (e.g., the bilingual's use of two languages in speech) -- may occur at the word, phrase, clause, or sentence level
UF Switching (Language)
RT Bidialectalism
Bilingualism
Bilingual Students
Interference (Language)
Language
Language Patterns
Language Usage
Language Variation
Linguistic Borrowing
Linguistic Performance
Morphology (Languages)
Multilingualism
Phonology
Sociolinguistics
Syntax
Vocabulary

CODES OF ETHICS *Jan. 1978*
CIJE: 174 RIE: 134 GC: 520
SN Standards of ethical conduct, violation of which may subject individuals to disciplinary action
UF Honor Codes
BT Behavior Standards
RT Accountability
Cheating
Codification
Conflict Of Interest
Discipline
Discipline Policy
Ethics
Faculty College Relationship
Loyalty Oaths
Lying
Malpractice
Moral Development
Moral Values
Plagiarism
Stealing
Student College Relationship

CODIFICATION *Jul. 1966*
CIJE: 111 RIE: 185 GC: 710
SN Process of collecting and arranging laws and standards according to a system
BT Classification
RT Codes Of Ethics
Documentation
Laws
Standards

COEDUCATION *May. 1969*
CIJE: 151 RIE: 99 GC: 330
BT Education
RT Heterogeneous Grouping
Single Sex Colleges
Single Sex Schools
Womens Education

COGNITIVE ABILITY *Jul. 1966*
CIJE: 1053 RIE: 822 GC: 120
SN (Note: prior to apr80, the instruction "mental ability, use intelligence" was carried in the thesaurus)
UF Mental Ability
BT Ability
RT Academic Ability
Aptitude
Cognitive Development
Cognitive Measurement
Cognitive Psychology
Cognitive Structures
Cognitive Tests
Encoding (Psychology)
Epistemology
Formal Operations
Habituation
Heuristics
Intelligence
Intuition
Metacognition
Productive Thinking
Schemata (Cognition)
Social Cognition
Spatial Ability

Cognitive Behavior Modification
USE BEHAVIOR MODIFICATION; COGNITIVE RESTRUCTURING

COGNITIVE DEVELOPMENT *Jul. 1966*
CIJE: 4310 RIE: 4048 GC: 120
SN Increasing complexity of awareness, including perceiving, conceiving, reasoning, and judging, through adaptation to the environment and assimilation of information (note: prior to mar80, this term was not restricted by a scope note)
UF Mental Development (1966 1980)
NT Intellectual Development
Perceptual Development
Verbal Development
BT Individual Development
RT Cognitive Ability
Cognitive Measurement
Cognitive Objectives
Cognitive Processes
Cognitive Psychology
Cognitive Structures
Cognitive Style
Cognitive Tests
Concept Formation
Developmental Disabilities
Developmental Psychology
Developmental Stages
Epistemology
Learning Readiness
Learning Strategies
Piagetian Theory
Schemata (Cognition)
School Readiness

COGNITIVE DISSONANCE *Aug. 1986*
CIJE: 23 RIE: 19 GC: 120
SN Psychological conflict resulting from incongruous attitudes or beliefs held simultaneously, or from inconsistency between attitudes and behavior
BT Psychological Patterns
RT Attitudes
Cognitive Processes
Cognitive Structures
Congruence (Psychology)
Motivation
Socialization

COGNITIVE MAPPING *Oct. 1983*
CIJE: 46 RIE: 45 GC: 110
SN Patterning by an individual of experiences and expectations to form perceptions of cause-effect or means-ends relationships
BT Learning Processes
RT Cognitive Structures
Cognitive Style
Expectation
Learning Modalities
Perception
Schemata (Cognition)
Spatial Ability

COGNITIVE MEASUREMENT *Jul. 1966*
CIJE: 518 RIE: 560 GC: 820
SN The use of systematic procedures to obtain indications of individuals' cognitive ability, style, development, or other mental processes that are primarily cognitive rather than affective or psychomotor
BT Measurement
RT Cognitive Ability
Cognitive Development
Cognitive Objectives
Cognitive Processes
Cognitive Psychology
Cognitive Structures

= Two or more Descriptors are used to represent this term.
The term's main entry shows the appropriate coordination.

Cognitive Style
Cognitive Tests
Intelligence Tests
Psychometrics

Cognitive Modification
USE COGNITIVE RESTRUCTURING

COGNITIVE OBJECTIVES *Jul. 1969*
CIJE: 334 RIE: 663 GC: 310
SN Behavioral objectives that emphasize remembering or reproducing something which has presumably been learned, or that involve the solving of some intellectual task
BT Behavioral Objectives
RT Affective Objectives
Cognitive Development
Cognitive Measurement
Psychomotor Objectives

COGNITIVE PROCESSES *Jul. 1966*
CIJE: 6646 RIE: 5153 GC: 110
SN Processes based on perception, introspection, or memory through which an individual obtains knowledge or conceptual understanding, e.g., perceiving, judging, abstracting, reasoning, imagining, remembering, and anticipating (note: use a more specific term if possible -- see displays of the narrower terms)
UF Information Processes (Psychological)
Thinking Processes
Thought Processes (1966 1980)
NT Abstract Reasoning
Association (Psychology)
Conflict Resolution
Convergent Thinking
Creative Thinking
Critical Thinking
Decision Making
Encoding (Psychology)
Intuition
Language Processing
Learning Processes
Logical Thinking
Memory
Metacognition
Perception
Problem Solving
Role Perception
Serial Ordering
Social Cognition
Visualization
RT Adaptation Level Theory
Artificial Intelligence
Cognitive Development
Cognitive Dissonance
Cognitive Measurement
Cognitive Psychology
Cognitive Structures
Cognitive Style
Cognitive Tests
Compensation (Concept)
Comprehension
Conceptual Tempo
Conservation (Concept)
Epistemology
Field Dependence Independence
Formal Operations
Intelligence
Learning
Learning Disabilities
Learning Strategies
Learning Theories
Mediation Theory
Object Permanence
Piagetian Theory
Protocol Analysis
Sensory Deprivation
Synthesis
Task Analysis

COGNITIVE PSYCHOLOGY *Dec. 1985*
CIJE: 26 RIE: 20 GC: 110
SN Branch of psychology concerned with the nature and structure of complex "knowledge processes" (e.g., recognizing, conceiving, judging, and reasoning) and their effects on, or interactions with, behavior -- particularly identified with "information processing" models of human cognition, usually simulated on computers
BT Psychology
RT Artificial Intelligence
Behaviorism
Cognitive Ability
Cognitive Development
Cognitive Measurement
Cognitive Processes
Cognitive Structures
Cognitive Style
Epistemology
Experimental Psychology
Intelligence
Piagetian Theory
Protocol Analysis
Psychological Studies
Psychometrics
Psychophysiology
Schemata (Cognition)

COGNITIVE RESTRUCTURING *Oct. 1983*
CIJE: 92 RIE: 33 GC: 110
SN Use of counseling, therapy, or self-monitoring techniques to alter attitudes, concepts, and/or expectations
UF Cognitive Behavior Modification #
Cognitive Modification
Cognitive Therapy
RT Attitude Change
Behavior Modification
Cognitive Structures
Counseling
Intervention
Learning Disabilities
Learning Theories
Psychoeducational Methods
Psychotherapy
Rational Emotive Therapy
Rehabilitation
Self Control

COGNITIVE STRUCTURES *Oct. 1983*
CIJE: 77 RIE: 65 GC: 110
SN Frameworks or forms of thinking that can change with age and experience
UF Knowledge Structures
RT Attitudes
Cognitive Ability
Cognitive Development
Cognitive Dissonance
Cognitive Mapping
Cognitive Measurement
Cognitive Processes
Cognitive Psychology
Cognitive Restructuring
Cognitive Style
Cognitive Tests
Concept Formation
Epistemology
Expectation
Ideology
Interests
Learning Processes
Misconceptions
Schemata (Cognition)

COGNITIVE STYLE *Oct. 1976*
CIJE: 1283 RIE: 1031 GC: 110
SN Information processing habits which represent the learner's typical modes of perceiving, thinking, remembering, and problem solving
UF Learning Style
Perceptual Style
NT Conceptual Tempo
Field Dependence Independence
BT Psychological Characteristics
RT Aptitude Treatment Interaction
Cognitive Development
Cognitive Mapping
Cognitive Measurement
Cognitive Processes
Cognitive Psychology
Cognitive Structures
Cognitive Tests
Encoding (Psychology)
Intuition
Learning Modalities
Learning Strategies
Personality Traits
Phenomenology
Schemata (Cognition)

COGNITIVE TESTS *Jul. 1966*
CIJE: 313 RIE: 464 GC: 830
SN Tests used to obtain indications of an individual's cognitive style, development, or other characteristics of cognitive functioning (note: use a more specific term if possible)
UF Abstraction Tests (1967 1980)
NT Intelligence Tests
Perception Tests
BT Tests
RT Cognitive Ability
Cognitive Development
Cognitive Measurement
Cognitive Processes
Cognitive Structures
Cognitive Style

Cognitive Theory
USE EPISTEMOLOGY

Cognitive Therapy
USE COGNITIVE RESTRUCTURING

COHERENCE *Nov. 1981*
CIJE: 79 RIE: 72 GC: 450
SN The presentation of thoughts or statements so that the meaning is clear and intelligible
BT Rhetoric
RT Cohesion (Written Composition)
Comprehension
Discourse Analysis
Language Processing
Outlining (Discourse)
Paragraphs
Semantics
Speech
Story Grammar
Verbal Communication
Writing (Composition)
Writing Evaluation

COHESION (WRITTEN COMPOSITION) *Nov. 1981*
CIJE: 82 RIE: 107 GC: 450
SN The combination of language usage and stylistic choices to hold the parts of a written discourse together as a unit
BT Connected Discourse
RT Coherence
Comprehension
Discourse Analysis
Language Usage
Paragraph Composition
Sentence Structure
Story Grammar
Syntax
Writing (Composition)
Writing Evaluation
Writing Skills

COHORT ANALYSIS *Dec. 1976*
CIJE: 178 RIE: 172 GC: 820
SN Group by group analytic treatment of individuals having a statistical factor in common to each group -- group members share a particular characteristic (e.g., born, married, etc. within a given year) or a common experience (e.g., entering a particular training phase at a given time) (note: as of oct81, use as a major desc. only for document subject)
BT Research
RT Census Figures
Community Study
Cross Sectional Studies
Demography
Population Trends

Collaboration
USE COOPERATION

Collaborative Decision Making
USE PARTICIPATIVE DECISION MAKING

Collected Readings
USE ANTHOLOGIES

Collection Development (Libraries)
USE LIBRARY COLLECTION DEVELOPMENT

COLLECTIVE BARGAINING *Jul. 1966*
CIJE: 1570 RIE: 1606 GC: 630
SN Negotiation on wages, hours, and other conditions of employment between an organization and its employees as represented by a union or an employee association
UF Collective Negotiation (1967 1977)
Professional Negotiation
NT Scope Of Bargaining
RT Arbitration
Employer Employee Relationship
Employment Problems
Faculty College Relationship
Grievance Procedures
Labor Demands
Labor Legislation
Labor Problems
Labor Relations
Negotiation Agreements
Negotiation Impasses
Sanctions
Strikes
Teacher Discipline
Teacher Militancy
Teacher Rights
Teacher Strikes
Teacher Welfare
Unions

Collective Behavior
USE GROUP BEHAVIOR

Collective Decision Making
USE PARTICIPATIVE DECISION MAKING

Collective Negotiation (1967 1977)
USE COLLECTIVE BARGAINING

COLLECTIVE SETTLEMENTS *Jul. 1966*
CIJE: 48 RIE: 45 GC: 550
SN Communities practicing common ownership and cooperative living
UF Communal Living #
Communistic Settlements
BT Community
RT Communism
Cooperatives
Municipalities
Neighborhoods
Rural Areas
Settlement Houses
Socialism

COLLEGE ADMINISTRATION *Jul. 1966*
CIJE: 2073 RIE: 1739 GC: 320
UF University Administration (1967 1980)
BT School Administration
RT Academic Deans
Admissions Officers
College Governing Councils
College Planning
College Presidents
Colleges
Deans
Governing Boards
Registrars (School)

COLLEGE ADMISSION *Jul. 1966*
CIJE: 992 RIE: 996 GC: 320
BT Admission (School)
RT Access To Education
Admissions Counseling
Admissions Officers
Affirmative Action
College Applicants
College Attendance
College Bound Students
College Choice
College Entrance Examinations
College Freshmen
Colleges
College School Cooperation
Higher Education
Selective Admission
Selective Colleges

COLLEGE APPLICANTS *Mar. 1980*
CIJE: 261 RIE: 238 GC: 360
SN Individuals applying for admission to institutions of higher education -- includes those accepted who do not attend as well as those not accepted
UF Law School Applicants #
Medical School Applicants #
Student Application (1966 1980)
BT Groups
RT Admission Criteria
College Admission
College Bound Students
College Choice
College Freshmen
Eligibility
Financial Aid Applicants
No Shows
Portfolios (Background Materials)

= Two or more Descriptors are used to represent this term.
The term's main entry shows the appropriate coordination.

COLLEGE ATHLETICS *Aug. 1986*
CIJE: 61 RIE: 15 GC: 470
UF Intercollegiate Athletics #
BT Athletics
RT College Curriculum
Colleges
Extramural Athletics
Intramural Athletics
Physical Education

COLLEGE ATTENDANCE *Jul. 1966*
CIJE: 165 RIE: 457 GC: 330
SN Past or present attendance by students in an institution of higher education (note: use "attendance" for the concept of college students' class attendance -- prior to mar80, this term was not restricted by a scope note)
BT Attendance
RT Access To Education
Attendance Patterns
College Admission
College Bound Students
Colleges
College Transfer Students
Enrollment
Expulsion
Higher Education
School Holding Power
School Registration
Student Attrition
Suspension
Withdrawal (Education)

College Bookstores
USE COLLEGE STORES

COLLEGE BOUND STUDENTS *Jul. 1966*
CIJE: 480 RIE: 676 GC: 360
SN High school students planning to attend a degree-granting postsecondary institution (note: see also "reentry students" and "nontraditional students")
BT High School Students
RT Academic Aspiration
Admissions Counseling
Advanced Placement Programs
College Admission
College Applicants
College Attendance
College Choice
College Day
College Freshmen
College Preparation
College School Cooperation
College Students
Higher Education
High School Graduates
High School Seniors
Noncollege Bound Students

COLLEGE BUILDINGS *Jul. 1966*
CIJE: 193 RIE: 228 GC: 920
BT School Buildings
RT Campuses
Campus Planning
College Housing
Colleges
Dormitories
Educational Equipment
Educational Facilities Design
Facility Utilization Research
Living Learning Centers
Space Utilization

College Catalogs
USE SCHOOL CATALOGS

College Characteristics
USE INSTITUTIONAL CHARACTERISTICS

COLLEGE CHOICE *Aug. 1968*
CIJE: 269 RIE: 561 GC: 330
BT School Choice
RT Academic Aspiration
College Admission
College Applicants
College Bound Students
College Day
College Freshmen
College Preparation
Colleges
Consumer Protection
Decision Making
Eligibility

College Closing
USE SCHOOL CLOSING

College Community Relationship
USE SCHOOL COMMUNITY RELATIONSHIP

College Cooperation (1966 1980)
USE INTERCOLLEGIATE COOPERATION

College Costs (Incurred By Students)
USE STUDENT COSTS

College Counselors
USE SCHOOL COUNSELORS

COLLEGE CREDITS *Jul. 1966*
CIJE: 288 RIE: 579 GC: 340
SN Units for expressing quantitatively the work completed by a student in a college course, in a program accepted by the college, or for prior learning accepted by the college
BT Credits
RT Academic Advising
Academic Records
College Curriculum
Colleges
Credit Courses
Credit No Credit Grading
Degree Requirements
Experiential Learning
Grades (Scholastic)
Pass Fail Grading
Prior Learning
Special Degree Programs
Transfer Policy
Transfer Programs

COLLEGE CURRICULUM *Jul. 1966*
CIJE: 1155 RIE: 1235 GC: 350
NT College English
College Mathematics
College Science
College Second Language Programs
Education Courses
Freshman Composition
Postsecondary Education As A Field Of Study
Teacher Education Curriculum
BT Curriculum
RT Academic Advising
Academic Deans
College Athletics
College Credits
College Instruction
Colleges
Higher Education

COLLEGE DAY *Jul. 1966*
CIJE: 14 RIE: 4 GC: 330
SN Event or program of activities during which high school students and their parents can meet with representatives of colleges and universities to learn about programs or services offered
UF College Night
BT Programs
RT Admissions Counseling
College Bound Students
College Choice
Colleges
College School Cooperation

College Deans (1968 1980)
USE DEANS; HIGHER EDUCATION

COLLEGE DESEGREGATION *Mar. 1980*
CIJE: 90 RIE: 172 GC: 540
SN Process of bringing ethnically or racially mixed students into the same colleges or universities
UF College Integration (1966 1980)
Desegregated Colleges
Integrated Colleges
BT School Desegregation
RT Affirmative Action
Colleges
Racial Integration

College Dropouts
USE DROPOUTS

COLLEGE ENGLISH *Mar. 1980*
CIJE: 471 RIE: 219 GC: 400
SN English curriculum at the college level (note: for english as a second language at the college level, use "college second language programs" and "english (second language)")
BT College Curriculum
English Curriculum
RT English
English Departments
English Instruction
Freshman Composition

College Enrollment
USE ENROLLMENT

COLLEGE ENTRANCE EXAMINATIONS *Jul. 1966*
CIJE: 437 RIE: 614 GC: 830
SN Aptitude, achievement, or other measures used in connection with admissions programs for colleges, universities, or graduate or professional schools
UF Admission Tests (Higher Education)
BT Tests
RT Academic Ability
Academic Achievement
Achievement Tests
Admission Criteria
Advanced Placement
Advanced Placement Programs
Aptitude Tests
College Admission
Colleges
Graduate Study
Predictive Measurement
Professional Education
Screening Tests
Standardized Tests

COLLEGE ENVIRONMENT *Jul. 1966*
CIJE: 615 RIE: 691 GC: 320
SN Conditions, forces, or factors that affect institutions of higher education and/or the people associated with them
BT Educational Environment
Institutional Environment
RT Academic Freedom
Campus Planning
Classroom Environment
Colleges
Deans Of Students
Faculty College Relationship
Institutional Characteristics
Residential Colleges
Student College Relationship

COLLEGE FACULTY *Jul. 1966*
CIJE: 3845 RIE: 4511 GC: 360
SN Academic staff members engaged in instruction, research, administration, or related educational activities in a college or university
UF College Teachers (1967 1980)
NT College Presidents
Counselor Educators
Graduate School Faculty
Professors
Student Teacher Supervisors
Teacher Educators
Teaching Assistants
BT Faculty
RT Academic Rank (Professional)
Adjunct Faculty
Aging In Academia
College Governing Councils
College Instruction
Colleges
Doctor Of Arts Degrees
Faculty College Relationship
Faculty Development
Faculty Handbooks
Faculty Organizations
Higher Education
Nontenured Faculty
Postsecondary Education As A Field Of Study
Student Personnel Workers
Teachers
Tenured Faculty
Universities

COLLEGE FRESHMEN *Jul. 1966*
CIJE: 1334 RIE: 1640 GC: 360
SN First-year students at higher education, generally four-year, institutions (note: prior to mar80, "freshmen" was also a valid descriptor)
UF Freshmen (1967 1980) (First Year College Students)
BT College Students
RT College Admission
College Applicants
College Bound Students
College Choice
Colleges
College Seniors
Freshman Composition
Undergraduate Students

COLLEGE GOVERNING COUNCILS *Dec. 1976*
CIJE: 43 RIE: 65 GC: 320
SN Organizations of faculty representatives, sometimes including administrators and students, that consider administrative, academic, or operational policies of the institution
UF Academic Senates
Faculty Senates
University Senates
BT Organizations (Groups)
RT College Administration
College Faculty
College Planning
Faculty College Relationship
Faculty Organizations
Governance
Institutional Autonomy
Participative Decision Making
Policy Formation

COLLEGE GRADUATES *Jul. 1966*
CIJE: 559 RIE: 938 GC: 360
SN Individuals who have completed the requirements of a college or university program and have been awarded a degree
BT Graduates
RT Alumni Associations
Alumni Education
Bachelors Degrees
Colleges
College Seniors
College Students
Commencement Ceremonies
Degrees (Academic)
Graduate Students
Graduate Study
Graduation
Undergraduate Students

College High School Cooperation (1967 1980)
USE COLLEGE SCHOOL COOPERATION

COLLEGE HOUSING *Jul. 1966*
CIJE: 300 RIE: 239 GC: 920
SN Living quarters (e.g., dormitories, apartments) for college or university students or staff, usually but not necessarily on campus
UF Student Housing (College)
BT Housing
RT Boarding Homes
College Buildings
Colleges
College Students
Dormitories
Living Learning Centers
On Campus Students
Resident Advisers
Resident Assistants
Residential Colleges

COLLEGE INSTRUCTION *Jul. 1966*
CIJE: 978 RIE: 897 GC: 320
UF College Teaching
BT Instruction
RT College Curriculum
College Faculty
Colleges
Higher Education

College Integration (1966 1980)
USE COLLEGE DESEGREGATION

COLLEGE LANGUAGE PROGRAMS (1967 1980) *Mar. 1980*
CIJE: 548 RIE: 445 GC: 450
SN Invalid descriptor -- used for both native and foreign language programs -- see such descriptors as "college second language programs," "college english," "native language instruction," and "english teacher education"

= Two or more Descriptors are used to represent this term.
The term's main entry shows the appropriate coordination.

COLLEGE LIBRARIES *Jul. 1966*
CIJE: 1244 RIE: 1625 GC: 710
SN Libraries established, maintained, and administered by institutions of higher education to meet the needs of their students and faculty
UF Junior College Libraries (1966 1980) #
University Libraries (1968 1980)
BT Academic Libraries
RT Colleges

College Majors (1968 1980)
USE MAJORS (STUDENTS)

COLLEGE MATHEMATICS *Jul. 1966*
CIJE: 1346 RIE: 594 GC: 480
BT College Curriculum
Mathematics Curriculum
RT Elementary School Mathematics
Mathematics
Mathematics Education
Mathematics Instruction
Secondary School Mathematics

College Night
USE COLLEGE DAY

College Placement (1966 1980)
USE STUDENT PLACEMENT

COLLEGE PLANNING *Jul. 1966*
CIJE: 680 RIE: 1317 GC: 320
SN Administrative planning at higher education institutions (note: prior to mar80, this term was not scoped and was often confused with "campus planning")
BT Educational Planning
RT Campus Planning
College Administration
College Governing Councils
College Role
Colleges
Institutional Research
Intercollegiate Cooperation
Mission Statements

COLLEGE PREPARATION *Jul. 1966*
CIJE: 277 RIE: 434 GC: 330
BT Secondary Education
RT Academic Education
Admissions Counseling
Admissions Officers
College Bound Students
College Choice
Colleges
Developmental Studies Programs
Educational Counseling
Higher Education
Post High School Guidance
Transitional Programs

COLLEGE PRESIDENTS *Mar. 1980*
CIJE: 294 RIE: 203 GC: 360
SN Principal administrative officers responsible for the direction of all affairs and operations of a higher education institution (note: prior to mar80, "presidents" was used for both college presidents and nonacademic presidents)
UF Chancellors (Education)
BT College Faculty
Presidents
RT College Administration
Deans

COLLEGE PROGRAMS *Jul. 1966*
CIJE: 789 RIE: 1353 GC: 320
SN Programs offered by institutions of higher education (note: use a more specific term if possible)
NT Doctoral Programs
External Degree Programs
Masters Programs
BT Programs
RT Alumni Education
Colleges
Higher Education
Special Degree Programs
Student Personnel Workers

College Registrars
USE REGISTRARS (SCHOOL)

College Registration
USE SCHOOL REGISTRATION

COLLEGE ROLE *Jul. 1966*
CIJE: 1471 RIE: 1577 GC: 330
SN Functions expected of or carried out by the college in society
BT School Role
RT College Planning
Colleges
Educational Responsibility
Living Learning Centers
Role Of Education

COLLEGE SCHOOL COOPERATION *Jul. 1966*
CIJE: 678 RIE: 1010 GC: 330
SN Cooperation between colleges, universities, or professional schools and other kinds of schools (e.g., elementary, secondary, vocational, technical, special education...) (note: use "intercollegiate cooperation" for cooperation between two or more colleges, etc.)
UF College High School Cooperation (1967 1980)
High School College Cooperation
School College Cooperation
BT Educational Cooperation
Institutional Cooperation
RT Admissions Counseling
Advanced Placement Programs
Affiliated Schools
Articulation (Education)
College Admission
College Bound Students
College Day
Colleges
Intercollegiate Cooperation
Laboratory Schools
Schools
Student Teachers

COLLEGE SCIENCE *Jul. 1966*
CIJE: 10307 RIE: 1540 GC: 490
BT College Curriculum
Science Curriculum
RT Elementary School Science
Science Departments
Science Education
Science Instruction
Secondary School Science

COLLEGE SECOND LANGUAGE PROGRAMS *Mar. 1980*
CIJE: 169 RIE: 190 GC: 450
SN (Note: prior to mar80, this concept was indexed under "college language programs")
BT College Curriculum
Second Language Programs
RT Classical Languages
Modern Language Curriculum
Second Language Instruction
Second Language Learning

COLLEGE SEGREGATION *Jul. 1966*
CIJE: 13 RIE: 12 GC: 540
SN Exclusion on the basis of race or ethnic status from admission to, or full participation in, a college or university (note: prior to mar80, the use of this term was not restricted by a scope note)
BT School Segregation
RT Black Colleges
Colleges
Racial Segregation

COLLEGE SENIORS *Mar. 1980*
CIJE: 62 RIE: 80 GC: 360
SN Students in their last year of a baccalaureate program (note: prior to mar80, this concept was indexed under "seniors," which also referred to high school seniors)
UF Seniors (1966 1980) (Last Year Undergraduates)
BT College Students
RT College Freshmen
College Graduates
Colleges

COLLEGE STORES *Apr. 1975*
CIJE: 118 RIE: 12 GC: 920
SN Higher educational facilities that sell books and other merchandise for student needs
UF College Bookstores
BT Facilities
RT Colleges
Educational Facilities
Merchandising
Retailing
Student Unions

College Student Relationship
USE STUDENT COLLEGE RELATIONSHIP

COLLEGE STUDENTS *Jul. 1966*
CIJE: 11026 RIE: 7527 GC: 360
SN Students attending an institution of higher education -- includes all levels, 1st-year through postgraduate (note: coordinate with the appropriate mandatory educational level descriptor -- if possible, use a more specific term)
UF Middle Class College Students (1966 1980) #
University Students
NT College Freshmen
College Seniors
College Transfer Students
Graduate Students
In State Students
On Campus Students
Out Of State Students
Resident Assistants
Student Teachers
Two Year College Students
Undergraduate Students
BT Students
RT College Bound Students
College Graduates
College Housing
Colleges
Degree Requirements
Nontraditional Students
Reentry Students
Self Supporting Students
Stopouts
Student College Relationship
Universities
Young Adults

College Supervisors (1967 1980)
USE STUDENT TEACHER SUPERVISORS

College Teachers (1967 1980)
USE COLLEGE FACULTY

College Teaching
USE COLLEGE INSTRUCTION

COLLEGE TRANSFER STUDENTS *Mar. 1980*
CIJE: 71 RIE: 450 GC: 360
SN Students who have transferred or intend to transfer from one higher education institution or program to another to achieve more advanced or different educational goals
BT College Students
Transfer Students
RT Articulation (Education)
College Attendance
Educational Mobility
Enrollment
Student Mobility

College Unions
USE STUDENT UNIONS

College Work Study Programs
USE WORK STUDY PROGRAMS

COLLEGES *Jul. 1966*
CIJE: 937 RIE: 1373 GC: 340
SN Degree granting institutions of higher education (note: use a more specific term if possible -- for specific aspects of colleges, use "school" terms if corresponding "college" terms are not available)
UF Higher Education Institutions
NT Agricultural Colleges
Black Colleges
Church Related Colleges
Cluster Colleges
Commuter Colleges
Dental Schools
Developing Institutions
Experimental Colleges
Law Schools
Library Schools
Medical Schools
Multicampus Colleges
Noncampus Colleges
Private Colleges
Public Colleges
Residential Colleges
Selective Colleges
Single Sex Colleges
Small Colleges
Two Year Colleges
Universities
Upper Division Colleges
BT Schools
RT Campuses
College Administration
College Admission
College Athletics
College Attendance
College Buildings
College Choice
College Credits
College Curriculum
College Day
College Desegregation
College Entrance Examinations
College Environment
College Faculty
College Freshmen
College Graduates
College Housing
College Instruction
College Libraries
College Planning
College Preparation
College Programs
College Role
College School Cooperation
College Segregation
College Seniors
College Stores
College Students
Extension Education
Faculty College Relationship
Faculty Handbooks
Higher Education
Intercollegiate Cooperation
Living Learning Centers
Nonprofit Organizations
Postsecondary Education
School Counseling
School Counselors
School Guidance
Student College Relationship
Undergraduate Study

Colleges Of Education
USE SCHOOLS OF EDUCATION

Colloquial Standard Usage
USE STANDARD SPOKEN USAGE

Colloquiums (Meetings)
USE MEETINGS

COLONIAL HISTORY (UNITED STATES) *Jul. 1966*
CIJE: 133 RIE: 197 GC: 430
BT United States History
RT Colonialism
Puritans
Revolutionary War (United States)
Slavery

COLONIALISM *Sep. 1968*
CIJE: 188 RIE: 109 GC: 610
BT Imperialism
RT Colonial History (United States)
International Relations
Nationalism
Political Attitudes
Political Divisions (Geographic)
Revolutionary War (United States)

Colonization
USE LAND SETTLEMENT

COLOR *Oct. 1969*
CIJE: 461 RIE: 181 GC: 490
UF Color Presentation (1969 1980)
Color Television (1969 1980) #
Hue
RT Art
Color Planning
Contrast
Dimensional Preference
Light
Painting (Visual Arts)
Visual Environment
Visual Perception

Color Films
USE FILMS

COLOR PLANNING *Oct. 1968*
CIJE: 45 RIE: 23 GC: 420
BT Planning
RT Building Design
Color
Interior Design
Painting (Industrial Arts)
Visual Arts
Visual Environment

Color Presentation (1969 1980)
USE COLOR

Color Television (1969 1980)
USE COLOR; TELEVISION

Com
USE COMPUTER OUTPUT MICROFILM

COMEDY *Jul. 1966*
CIJE: 67 RIE: 51 GC: 430
UF Comedy Of Manners
NT Skits
BT Drama
RT Humor
Literary Devices
Literary Genres
Scripts
Tragedy

Comedy Of Manners
USE COMEDY

COMICS (PUBLICATIONS) *Jun. 1975*
CIJE: 90 RIE: 53 GC: 720
SN Narrative series of drawings or pictures, usually accompanied by balloons giving conversation, which present humorous incidents or dramatic adventures -- includes comic strips and comic books
BT Publications
RT Cartoons
Childrens Literature
Fiction
Humor
Instructional Materials
Newspapers
Parody
Satire
Serials
Visual Aids

COMMENCEMENT CEREMONIES *Mar. 1980*
CIJE: 14 RIE: 7 GC: 320
SN Occasions at which formal recognition is given for a student's completion of a program of study, usually in the form of a certificate, degree, or diploma
UF Graduate Ceremonies
BT Recognition (Achievement)
RT College Graduates
Degrees (Academic)
Graduation

COMMERCIAL ART *Oct. 1968*
CIJE: 40 RIE: 93 GC: 420
UF Advertising Art
BT Art
RT Advertising
Art Education
Graphic Arts
Merchandising
Television Commercials
Visual Arts

Commercial Communication
USE BUSINESS COMMUNICATION

Commercial Correspondence Schools
USE CORRESPONDENCE SCHOOLS

Commercial Education
USE BUSINESS EDUCATION

Commercial Enterprises
USE BUSINESS

Commercial Pilots
USE AIRCRAFT PILOTS

Commercial Search Services (Online)
USE ONLINE VENDORS

COMMERCIAL TELEVISION *Jul. 1966*
CIJE: 361 RIE: 428 GC: 720
SN Television system operating for profit and accepting paid advertising
BT Television
RT Broadcast Industry
Public Television
Television Commercials

COMMITTEES *Jul. 1966*
CIJE: 392 RIE: 438 GC: 520
NT Advisory Committees
Biracial Committees
Research Committees
Search Committees (Personnel)
RT Administration
Governing Boards
Organizations (Groups)
Planning

Common Fractions (1966 1980)
USE FRACTIONS

Communal Living
USE COLLECTIVE SETTLEMENTS; GROUP EXPERIENCE

COMMUNICABLE DISEASES *Jul. 1966*
CIJE: 115 RIE: 84 GC: 210
UF Contagious Diseases
Infectious Diseases (1966 1974)
NT Rubella
Venereal Diseases
BT Diseases
RT Disease Control
Immunization Programs
Physical Health
Public Health

COMMUNICATION (THOUGHT TRANSFER) *Jul. 1966*
CIJE: 3515 RIE: 4205 GC: 520
SN Transmission and reception of signals or meanings through a system of symbols (codes, gestures, language, etc.) common to sender and receiver (note: use a more specific term if possible -- prior to mar80, the instruction "communication theory, use information theory" was carried in the thesaurus)
UF Communication Theory
Intercommunication (1966 1980)
NT Classroom Communication
Diffusion (Communication)
Discussion
Intercultural Communication
Interpersonal Communication
Manual Communication
Nonverbal Communication
Organizational Communication
Propaganda
Publicity
Speech Communication
Total Communication
Verbal Communication
RT Audiences
Communication Aids (For Disabled)
Communication Apprehension
Communication Disorders
Communication Problems
Communication Research
Communication Skills
Content Analysis
Credibility
Cybernetics
Deaf Interpreting
Deception
Disclosure
Expressive Language
Feedback
Inferences
Information Dissemination
Information Networks
Information Seeking
Information Theory
Information Transfer
Interaction
Intergroup Relations
Interpreters
Language Arts
Mutual Intelligibility
Network Analysis
Networks
Persuasive Discourse
Receptive Language
Social Networks

COMMUNICATION AIDS (FOR DISABLED) *Nov. 1981*
CIJE: 47 RIE: 32 GC: 220
SN Devices and materials that enable persons with communication disorders to communicate more normally
RT Assistive Devices (For Disabled)
Communication (Thought Transfer)
Communication Disorders
Hearing Aids
Sensory Aids
Total Communication

COMMUNICATION APPREHENSION *Aug. 1982*
CIJE: 90 RIE: 128 GC: 120
SN Fear or anxiety experienced by an individual in anticipation of and/or during the course of communication--usually oral--with another person or group (note: do not confuse with "writing apprehension")
BT Anxiety
RT Communication (Thought Transfer)
Communication Problems
Speech Communication

COMMUNICATION AUDITS *Aug. 1986*
CIJE: 6 RIE: 9 GC: 520
SN Assessments of communication effectiveness within organizations, or between organizations and external groups or the public
BT Audits (Verification)
RT Institutional Advancement
Network Analysis
Organizational Communication
Public Relations

COMMUNICATION DISORDERS *Mar. 1980*
CIJE: 116 RIE: 87 GC: 220
SN Impairments of an individual's ability to communicate due to disorders of hearing, speech, language, etc. (note: use a more precise term if possible, and do not confuse with "communication problems," which are not the result of impairments)
BT Disabilities
RT Aphasia
Communication (Thought Transfer)
Communication Aids (For Disabled)
Communication Problems
Developmental Disabilities
Exceptional Persons
Hearing Impairments
Language Handicaps
Learning Disabilities
Speech Handicaps

COMMUNICATION PROBLEMS *Jul. 1966*
CIJE: 921 RIE: 974 GC: 120
BT Problems
RT Communication (Thought Transfer)
Communication Apprehension
Communication Disorders
Intercultural Communication
Nonverbal Communication

COMMUNICATION RESEARCH *Sep. 1980*
CIJE: 695 RIE: 1431 GC: 810
SN Investigation into the nature and function of human communication, both verbal and nonverbal, in one-to-one or group settings (note: do not confuse with "language research")
UF Speech Communication Research #
BT Research
RT Audience Analysis
Behavioral Science Research
Communication (Thought Transfer)
Discourse Analysis
Interaction Process Analysis
Language Research
Network Analysis
Reading Research
Social Science Research
Writing Research

Communication Satellites (1967 1980)
USE COMMUNICATIONS SATELLITES

COMMUNICATION SKILLS *Jul. 1966*
CIJE: 2650 RIE: 3349 GC: 400
UF Conference Skills (Communication)
NT Communicative Competence (Languages)
BT Skills
RT Audiolingual Skills
Basic Skills
Communication (Thought Transfer)
Credibility
Daily Living Skills
Deaf Interpreting
Expressive Language
Inferences
Language Skills
Manual Communication
Metacognition
Nonverbal Communication
Oral Communication Method
Receptive Language
Social Cognition
Teaching Skills
Telephone Usage Instruction
Total Communication
Transactional Analysis
Verbal Ability
Verbal Communication

Communication Theory
USE COMMUNICATION (THOUGHT TRANSFER)

COMMUNICATIONS *Jul. 1966*
CIJE: 1077 RIE: 1492 GC: 710
SN Science and technology of the transmission and reception of information (note: prior to mar80, the thesaurus carried the instructions, "communication networks, services, or systems, use telecommunication")
UF Communications Networks
Communications Services
Communications Systems
Mass Media Technology #
Media Technology (1968 1980)
NT Audiovisual Communications
Telecommunications
BT Technology
RT Cybernetics
Delivery Systems
Distributive Education
Information Networks
Information Processing
Information Technology
Information Theory
Information Transfer
Interactive Video
Mass Media
Network Analysis
Networks
Nonprint Media
Propaganda
Publications
Publicity
Social Networks

Communications Media
USE MASS MEDIA

Communications Networks
USE COMMUNICATIONS

COMMUNICATIONS SATELLITES *Mar. 1980*
CIJE: 238 RIE: 496 GC: 710
UF Communication Satellites (1967 1980)
BT Satellites (Aerospace)
Telecommunications
RT Distance Education
Information Networks

Communications Services
USE COMMUNICATIONS

Communications Systems
USE COMMUNICATIONS

Communications Theory
USE INFORMATION THEORY

COMMUNICATIVE COMPETENCE (LANGUAGES) *Aug. 1976*
CIJE: 640 RIE: 833 GC: 450
SN The ability to converse or correspond with a native speaker of the target language in a real-life situation, with emphasis on communication of ideas rather than on correctness of language form
NT Threshold Level (Languages)
BT Communication Skills
Language Skills
RT Conversational Language Courses
Dialogs (Language)
Language Fluency

= Two or more Descriptors are used to represent this term.
The term's main entry shows the appropriate coordination.

Language Proficiency
Linguistic Competence
Linguistic Performance
Notional Functional Syllabi
Second Language Learning
Speech Communication
Verbal Communication

COMMUNISM *Jul. 1966*
CIJE: 388 RIE: 177 GC: 610
BT Social Systems
RT Capitalism
Collective Settlements
Democracy
Economics
Fascism
Government (Administrative Body)
Imperialism
Marxism
Political Science
Socialism
Totalitarianism

Communistic Settlements
USE COLLECTIVE SETTLEMENTS

COMMUNITY *Jul. 1966*
CIJE: 148 RIE: 211 GC: 520
SN A social group linked by common interests through residence in a specific locality, or, whether or not in physical proximity, whose members perceive themselves as sharing a common ideology, interest, or other characteristic
NT Black Community
Collective Settlements
Municipalities
Neighborhoods
Planned Communities
RT City Government
Community Action
Community Attitudes
Community Benefits
Community Centers
Community Change
Community Characteristics
Community Colleges
Community Control
Community Cooperation
Community Coordination
Community Development
Community Education
Community Health Services
Community Influence
Community Involvement
Community Leaders
Community Organizations
Community Planning
Community Problems
Community Programs
Community Psychology
Community Relations
Community Resources
Community Responsibility
Community Role
Community Satisfaction
Community Schools
Community Services
Community Study
Community Support
Community Surveys
Community Zoning
Ethnic Distribution
Group Unity
Local Government
Local Issues
Place Of Residence
Police Community Relationship
School Community Programs
School Community Relationship
Suburbs

COMMUNITY ACTION *Jul. 1966*
CIJE: 287 RIE: 718 GC: 520
SN Grass roots mobilization of local resources to meet community needs
UF Action Programs (Community) (1966 1980)
Community Effort
BT Social Action
RT Action Research
Citizen Participation
Community
Community Change
Community Control
Community Cooperation
Community Development
Community Involvement
Community Organizations
Community Problems
Community Responsibility
Community Role
Community Services
Community Support
Local Issues
Self Help Programs
Social Responsibility

Community Agencies (Public) (1966 1980)
USE PUBLIC AGENCIES

Community Analysis
USE COMMUNITY STUDY

Community Antennas (1966 1980)
USE CABLE TELEVISION

COMMUNITY ATTITUDES *Jul. 1966*
CIJE: 492 RIE: 1019 GC: 520
NT Community Satisfaction
BT Attitudes
RT Citizenship
Community
Community Characteristics
Community Cooperation
Community Involvement
Community Relations
Community Role
Community Support
Local Issues
Political Attitudes
Social Attitudes

COMMUNITY BENEFITS *Jul. 1966*
CIJE: 77 RIE: 136 GC: 330
SN Advantages derived by communities from their association with institutions, industries, programs, etc. (note: for advantages provided by communities, use such descriptors as "community services," "community programs," "community resources," etc. -- prior to mar80, the use of this term was not restricted by a scope note)
RT Community
Community Cooperation
Community Coordination
Community Development
Community Relations

COMMUNITY CENTERS *Mar. 1980*
CIJE: 105 RIE: 170 GC: 920
SN Facilities at which social, educational, recreational, and other activities are held for the benefit of the community (note: use of the original term, "neighborhood centers," was not restricted by a scope note)
UF Community Rooms (1967 1980)
Neighborhood Centers (1966 1980)
BT Facilities
RT Community
Community Education
Community Organizations
Community Programs
Community Recreation Programs
Community Resources
Community Services

COMMUNITY CHANGE *Jul. 1966*
CIJE: 99 RIE: 279 GC: 550
SN Change in or of a community -- may be either planned or unplanned, initiated in the community or by outside forces, toward or away from improvement
BT Change
RT Change Agents
Change Strategies
Citizen Participation
Community
Community Action
Community Development
Community Involvement
Community Leaders
Community Planning
Culture Lag
Economic Change
Local Issues
Social Change
Urban Renewal

COMMUNITY CHARACTERISTICS *Jul. 1966*
CIJE: 250 RIE: 753 GC: 520
UF Community Traits
NT Community Size
RT Community
Community Attitudes
Community Cooperation
Community Development
Community Resources
Local History
Local Issues
Neighborhoods
Place Of Residence
Regional Characteristics
Urban Environment

COMMUNITY COLLEGES *Jul. 1966*
CIJE: 3728 RIE: 7982 GC: 340
SN Public, postsecondary institutions commonly organized into 2-year programs and offering instruction adapted in content, level, and schedule to the needs of the community in which they are located -- usually offer a comprehensive curriculum with transfer, occupational, general education, and adult education components
BT Public Colleges
Two Year Colleges
RT Associate Degrees
Community
Community Education
Community Services
Multicampus Colleges
Multicampus Districts
Postsecondary Education
Public Education
School Community Relationship
State Colleges
Technical Institutes
Two Year College Students
Undergraduate Study

Community Committees
USE COMMUNITY ORGANIZATIONS

Community Compliance
USE COMMUNITY COOPERATION

Community Consultant Programs (1966 1980)
USE CONSULTATION PROGRAMS

Community Consultants (1966 1980)
USE CONSULTANTS

COMMUNITY CONTROL *Aug. 1969*
CIJE: 322 RIE: 364 GC: 330
SN Control of community programs, institutions, agencies, etc. by recognized groups within the community (e.g., minority controlled schools, elitist versus pluralistic control, etc.)
BT Governance
RT Citizen Participation
Community
Community Action
Community Involvement
Community Schools
Decentralization
Ethnic Relations
Government School Relationship
Majority Attitudes
Minority Group Influences
Participative Decision Making
Policy Formation
Politics
School Community Relationship
School District Autonomy
Self Determination

COMMUNITY COOPERATION *Jul. 1966*
CIJE: 189 RIE: 360 GC: 520
SN Cooperation of a community as a whole (i.e., local government and constituents) in any activity or endeavor (note: do not confuse with "community coordination" -- prior to mar80, this term was not restricted by a scope note)
UF Community Compliance
BT Cooperation
RT Biracial Committees
Citizen Participation
Community
Community Action
Community Attitudes
Community Benefits
Community Characteristics
Community Coordination
Community Involvement
Community Organizations
Community Programs
Community Psychology
Community Relations
Community Role
Community Services
Community Support
Cooperative Planning
Institutional Cooperation
Police Community Relationship
School Community Relationship

COMMUNITY COORDINATION *Jul. 1966*
CIJE: 65 RIE: 156 GC: 520
SN Process of bringing together the diverse elements of a community (people, groups, agencies, organizations) into a working whole (note: do not confuse with "community cooperation" -- prior to mar80, this term was not restricted by a scope note)
UF Community Coordinators (1966 1980) #
BT Coordination
RT Community
Community Benefits
Community Cooperation
Community Development
Community Education
Community Organizations
Community Planning
Community Problems
Community Programs
Community Psychology
Community Services
Local Issues
Police Community Relationship
School Community Relationship

Community Coordinators (1966 1980)
USE COMMUNITY COORDINATION; COORDINATORS

COMMUNITY DEVELOPMENT *Jul. 1966*
CIJE: 523 RIE: 1092 GC: 550
SN Process by which communities and outside agencies plan, organize, or implement general improvements of community resources, facilities, economic conditions, etc.
BT Development
RT Citizen Participation
Community
Community Action
Community Benefits
Community Change
Community Characteristics
Community Coordination
Community Education
Community Planning
Community Resources
Community Responsibility
Developing Nations
Economic Development
Living Standards
Modernization
Neighborhood Improvement
Quality Of Life
Rural Development
Technical Assistance
Urban Improvement

COMMUNITY EDUCATION *Jul. 1966*
CIJE: 626 RIE: 888 GC: 340
SN Extending existing educational resources and programs (primarily those offered by public schools and community colleges) into the community to serve all age groups, and special target groups not adequately served by regular school programs
BT Education
RT Adult Education
Community
Community Centers
Community Colleges
Community Coordination
Community Development
Community Resources
Community Schools
Community Services
Continuing Education
Extension Education
Lifelong Learning
Nonschool Educational Programs
Outreach Programs

Community Effort
USE COMMUNITY ACTION

Community Enterprises
USE COMMUNITY PROGRAMS

Community Experience
USE EXPERIENTIAL LEARNING

Community Health (1966 1980)
USE PUBLIC HEALTH

COMMUNITY HEALTH SERVICES *Jul. 1966*
CIJE: 381 RIE: 304 GC: 210
UF Community Health Workers #
BT Community Services
Health Services
RT Community
Community Psychology
Home Health Aides
Home Visits
Immunization Programs
Medical Care Evaluation
Public Health

Community Health Workers
USE COMMUNITY HEALTH SERVICES; HEALTH PERSONNEL

Community History
USE LOCAL HISTORY

COMMUNITY INFLUENCE *Jul. 1966*
CIJE: 176 RIE: 243 GC: 520
SN The influence exerted by a community (note: prior to mar80, the use of this term was not restricted by a scope note)
BT Influences
RT Black Community
Community
Community Involvement
Community Leaders
Community Role
Community Support

Community Information Centers
USE COMMUNITY INFORMATION SERVICES

COMMUNITY INFORMATION SERVICES *Feb. 1975*
CIJE: 120 RIE: 171 GC: 710
SN Those services of local libraries or other community groups that provide direct access or referral to nontraditional information (e.g., unpublished materials, government agency information on public services, broadcast information on current topics, data for use in emergencies, etc.)
UF Community Information Centers
Information Services (Community)
Local Information Services
Referral Services (Community) #
NT Hotlines (Public)
BT Community Services
Information Services
RT Information Centers
Public Libraries
Reference Services
Referral
Social Services

COMMUNITY INVOLVEMENT *Jul. 1966*
CIJE: 1671 RIE: 3189 GC: 330
SN Involvement of a community in activities or programs (note: do not confuse with "citizen participation" -- prior to mar80, the use of this term was not restricted by a scope note)
UF Community Participation
BT Participation
RT Citizen Participation
Community
Community Action
Community Attitudes
Community Change
Community Control
Community Cooperation
Community Influence
Community Role
Community Services
Community Support
Outreach Programs
Public Service

COMMUNITY LEADERS *Jul. 1966*
CIJE: 129 RIE: 340 GC: 520
BT Groups
Leaders
RT Change Agents
Community
Community Change
Community Influence
Leadership
Political Candidates
Public Officials

Community Legislation
USE LOCAL LEGISLATION

Community Migrant Projects (1966 1980)
USE COMMUNITY PROGRAMS; MIGRANT PROGRAMS

COMMUNITY ORGANIZATIONS *Jul. 1966*
CIJE: 371 RIE: 867 GC: 520
UF Civic Groups
Civic Organizations
Community Committees
Community Workers
NT Citizens Councils
BT Organizations (Groups)
RT Citizen Participation
Community
Community Action
Community Centers
Community Cooperation
Community Coordination
Community Programs
Community Services
Cooperatives
National Organizations
Public Affairs Education
Social Organizations

Community Outreach
USE OUTREACH PROGRAMS

Community Participation
USE COMMUNITY INVOLVEMENT

COMMUNITY PLANNING *Jul. 1966*
CIJE: 114 RIE: 310 GC: 550
BT Planning
RT Community
Community Change
Community Coordination
Community Development
Community Programs
Community Zoning
Facility Planning
Land Use
Planning Commissions
Urban Planning

Community Police Relationship
USE POLICE COMMUNITY RELATIONSHIP

COMMUNITY PROBLEMS *Jul. 1966*
CIJE: 133 RIE: 276 GC: 530
UF Community Tensions
BT Problems
RT Community
Community Action
Community Coordination
Local Issues
Urban Problems

COMMUNITY PROGRAMS *Jul. 1966*
CIJE: 595 RIE: 1191 GC: 520
UF Civic Programs
Community Enterprises
Community Migrant Projects (1966 1980) #
Community Projects
Local Community Programs
NT Community Recreation Programs
School Community Programs
BT Programs
RT Civil Defense
Community
Community Centers
Community Cooperation
Community Coordination
Community Organizations
Community Planning
Community Resources
Community Responsibility
County Programs
Crime Prevention
Deinstitutionalization (Of Disabled)
Group Homes
Intergenerational Programs
Migrant Programs
Public Agencies
Public Service
Settlement Houses
Social Responsibility
Youth Programs

Community Projects
USE COMMUNITY PROGRAMS

COMMUNITY PSYCHOLOGY *Apr. 1986*
CIJE: 5 RIE: 14 GC: 230
SN The application of psychological methods (in collaboration with psychiatry, sociology, social work, etc.) to problems arising in a community and soluble only through a community-wide approach -- attention is given to problems of mental health, social welfare, group relationships, education, social action, etc., involving the well-being of all community members
BT Psychology
RT Clinical Psychology
Community
Community Cooperation
Community Coordination
Community Health Services
Community Relations
Community Role
Community Services
Psychopathology
Social Psychology

Community Recreation Legislation (1966 1978)
USE LOCAL LEGISLATION; RECREATION LEGISLATION

COMMUNITY RECREATION PROGRAMS *Jul. 1966*
CIJE: 96 RIE: 58 GC: 470
BT Community Programs
Recreational Programs
RT Community Centers
Community Resources
Community Services
Lifetime Sports
Recreational Facilities

COMMUNITY RELATIONS *Jul. 1966*
CIJE: 156 RIE: 279 GC: 520
UF Civic Relations
BT Relationship
RT Community
Community Attitudes
Community Benefits
Community Cooperation
Community Psychology

COMMUNITY RESOURCES *Jul. 1966*
CIJE: 540 RIE: 1319 GC: 520
SN The financial, material, and/or human assets of a community
BT Resources
RT Community
Community Centers
Community Characteristics
Community Development
Community Education
Community Programs
Community Recreation Programs
Community Satisfaction
Community Services
Financial Support
Human Resources
Information Sources
Museums
Natural Resources
Parks
Public Libraries
Recreational Facilities

COMMUNITY RESPONSIBILITY *Jul. 1966*
CIJE: 86 RIE: 130 GC: 520
SN Obligations, duties, or trusts given to or assumed by a community (note: do not confuse with "community role" -- prior to mar80, this term was not restricted by a scope note)
BT Responsibility
RT Citizenship Responsibility
Community
Community Action
Community Development
Community Programs
Community Role
Community Services
Humanitarianism
Neighborhood Improvement
Social Responsibility
Urban Improvement

COMMUNITY ROLE *Jul. 1966*
CIJE: 258 RIE: 494 GC: 520
SN Functions expected of or performed by a community
RT Citizen Participation
Community
Community Action
Community Attitudes
Community Cooperation
Community Influence
Community Involvement
Community Psychology
Community Responsibility
Community Services
Community Support
Institutional Role

Community Rooms (1967 1980)
USE COMMUNITY CENTERS

COMMUNITY SATISFACTION *Jun. 1978*
CIJE: 36 RIE: 71 GC: 520
SN The extent to which individuals or groups are content with the quality of life in their immediate locale
BT Community Attitudes
RT Community
Community Resources
Need Gratification
Quality Of Life

Community School Directors (1967 1980)
USE ADMINISTRATORS; COMMUNITY SCHOOLS

Community School Programs
USE SCHOOL COMMUNITY PROGRAMS

Community School Relationship
USE SCHOOL COMMUNITY RELATIONSHIP

COMMUNITY SCHOOLS *Jul. 1966*
CIJE: 255 RIE: 345 GC: 340
SN Schools which are closely connected with the life of the community in which they are located and in which instruction and other activities are intended to be relevant to most or all segments of that community's population
UF Community School Directors (1967 1980) #
BT Schools
RT Community
Community Control
Community Education
Folk Schools
Neighborhood Schools
Nontraditional Education
Outreach Programs
Public School Adult Education
School Community Relationship
Shared Facilities

Community Service Programs (1966 1980)
USE COMMUNITY SERVICES

COMMUNITY SERVICES *Jul. 1966*
CIJE: 870 RIE: 1608 GC: 520
SN Includes educational, recreational, cultural, and social welfare services, and/or the provision of facilities for such activities, offered for the benefit of the general public by community groups or agencies, often as an adjunct to their primary functions
UF Community Service Programs (1966 1980)
NT Community Health Services
Community Information Services
BT Services
RT Community
Community Action
Community Centers
Community Colleges
Community Cooperation
Community Coordination
Community Education
Community Involvement
Community Organizations
Community Psychology
Community Recreation Programs

= Two or more Descriptors are used to represent this term.
The term's main entry shows the appropriate coordination.

Community Resources
Community Responsibility
Community Role
Community Support
Continuing Education
Eligibility
Local Government
Outreach Programs
Social Services

COMMUNITY SIZE *Nov. 1968*
CIJE: 58 RIE: 85 GC: 550
BT Community Characteristics
RT Census Figures
Demography
Geographic Distribution
Overpopulation
Population Distribution
Population Growth
Population Trends
Urban Demography
Urban Population

COMMUNITY STUDY *Jul. 1966*
CIJE: 204 RIE: 563 GC: 810
SN Analysis of the work, amusements, reading, beliefs, and customs of a whole community in an effort to understand community life and problems (note: as of oct81, use as a minor descriptor for examples of this kind of research -- use as a major descriptor only as the subject of a document)
UF Community Analysis
BT Research
RT Cohort Analysis
Community
Local History

COMMUNITY SUPPORT *Jul. 1966*
CIJE: 274 RIE: 423 GC: 330
SN Support by the community of something (issue, program, policy, etc.)
RT Citizen Participation
Community
Community Action
Community Attitudes
Community Cooperation
Community Influence
Community Involvement
Community Role
Community Services
Local Issues
Public Support
School Support

COMMUNITY SURVEYS *Jul. 1966*
CIJE: 161 RIE: 650 GC: 810
SN Investigations of social conditions and resources, community attitudes, uses of community agencies, institutional practices, etc., as they exist at a given time in a given community (note: as of oct81, use as a minor descriptor for examples of this kind of survey -- use as a major descriptor only as the subject of a document)
BT Surveys
RT Community
Occupational Surveys

Community Tensions
USE COMMUNITY PROBLEMS

Community Traits
USE COMMUNITY CHARACTERISTICS

Community Workers
USE COMMUNITY ORGANIZATIONS

COMMUNITY ZONING *Jul. 1966*
CIJE: 8 RIE: 14 GC: 550
BT Zoning
RT Community
Community Planning

COMMUTER COLLEGES *Mar. 1980*
CIJE: 20 RIE: 44 GC: 340
SN Institutions of higher education that primarily serve commuting students
UF Nonresidential Schools (1967 1980)
BT Colleges
RT Commuting Students
Residential Colleges
School Location
Student Transportation

COMMUTING STUDENTS *Jul. 1966*
CIJE: 60 RIE: 137 GC: 360
SN Students living off campus who travel to an institution for classes, study, and other activities
BT Students
RT Commuter Colleges
On Campus Students
Student Transportation

Compact Disks
USE OPTICAL DISKS

Companions (Occupation) (1968 1980)
USE ATTENDANTS

Company Size (Industry)
USE ORGANIZATION SIZE (GROUPS)

Comparable Institutions
USE PEER INSTITUTIONS

COMPARABLE WORTH *Jan. 1986*
CIJE: 34 RIE: 19 GC: 540
SN Principle of equal pay for work of comparable value, i.e., equal pay for jobs that may have different duties but that require similar levels of skill, effort, and responsibility under similar working conditions -- frequently advocated to redress sex-based pay inequities, i.e., between comparable female- and male-dominated jobs (some analyses consider race/ethnicity among job types as well)
UF Pay Equity
RT Employed Women
Employment Practices
Equal Opportunities (Jobs)
Nontraditional Occupations
Personnel Policy
Salary Wage Differentials

COMPARATIVE ANALYSIS *Jul. 1966*
CIJE: 7407 RIE: 8888 GC: 820
SN (Note: as of oct81, use as a minor descriptor to convey the use of this technique in a document -- use as a major descriptor only as the subject of a document)
UF Comparative Evaluation
Comparative Statistics (1966 1980) #
Comparative Study
NT Educational Status Comparison
Error Analysis (Language)
BT Evaluation Methods
RT Comparative Testing
Correlation
Cross Cultural Studies
Differences
Etymology
Glottochronology
International Studies
Language Classification
Lexicology
Meta Analysis
Multiple Regression Analysis
Multitrait Multimethod Techniques
Multivariate Analysis
National Norms
Peer Institutions
Surveys
Synthesis
Trend Analysis

COMPARATIVE EDUCATION *Jul. 1966*
CIJE: 3619 RIE: 1750 GC: 400
SN Field of study dealing with the comparison of educational theory and practice in different countries
BT Education
RT Cross Cultural Studies
Educational Anthropology
Foreign Culture
Foundations Of Education
International Education
International Educational Exchange
Nonformal Education

Comparative Evaluation
USE COMPARATIVE ANALYSIS

Comparative Linguistics
USE CONTRASTIVE LINGUISTICS

Comparative Statistics (1966 1980)
USE COMPARATIVE ANALYSIS; STATISTICAL ANALYSIS

Comparative Study
USE COMPARATIVE ANALYSIS

COMPARATIVE TESTING *Jul. 1966*
CIJE: 422 RIE: 288 GC: 820
SN Testing in which two or more individuals, groups, or tests are compared
BT Testing
RT Comparative Analysis
Concurrent Validity
Differences
National Norms
Norm Referenced Tests
Test Format
Test Norms
Test Reviews

COMPENSATION (CONCEPT) *Jan. 1973*
CIJE: 17 RIE: 9 GC: 110
SN The principle that material undergoing a transformation in one dimension is accompanied by a reciprocal change in another dimension -- in developmental psychology, the recognition or understanding of this principle
BT Fundamental Concepts
RT Cognitive Processes
Concept Formation
Conservation (Concept)
Developmental Stages

COMPENSATION (REMUNERATION) *Oct. 1979*
CIJE: 175 RIE: 159 GC: 630
SN Total payment awarded, including wage or salary, fringe benefits, and perquisites
UF Remuneration
BT Expenditures
RT Costs
Fringe Benefits
Income
Professional Recognition
Recognition (Achievement)
Retirement Benefits
Rewards
Salaries
Wages

Compensatory Development
USE COMPENSATORY EDUCATION

COMPENSATORY EDUCATION *Jul. 1966*
CIJE: 570 RIE: 2777 GC: 330
SN Education that seeks to compensate for environmental and experiential deficits in relation to such areas as schooling, housing, employment, poverty, racism, and other social and cultural factors
UF Compensatory Development
Compensatory Education Programs (1966 1980)
Compensatory Opportunity
BT Education
RT After School Education
Cultural Enrichment
Developmental Studies Programs
Educationally Disadvantaged
Extended School Day
High Risk Students
Rehabilitation Programs
Remedial Instruction
Remedial Programs
Study Centers
Supplementary Education
Transitional Programs

Compensatory Education Programs (1966 1980)
USE COMPENSATORY EDUCATION

Compensatory Opportunity
USE COMPENSATORY EDUCATION

COMPETENCE *Oct. 1979*
CIJE: 617 RIE: 902 GC: 120
SN The individual's demonstrated capacity to perform, i.e., the possession of knowledge, skills, and personal characteristics needed to satisfy the special demands or requirements of a particular situation (note: prior to oct79, the instruction "competencies, use skills" was carried in the thesaurus)
UF Competency
NT Interpersonal Competence
Minimum Competencies
BT Ability
RT Accountability
Achievement
Competency Based Education
Competency Based Teacher Education
Job Performance
Minimum Competency Testing
Performance
Personnel Evaluation
Skills
Student Evaluation
Vocational Evaluation

Competency
USE COMPETENCE

COMPETENCY BASED EDUCATION *Mar. 1980*
CIJE: 884 RIE: 2881 GC: 330
SN Educational system that emphasizes the specification, learning, and demonstration of those competencies (knowledge, skills, behaviors) that are of central importance to a given task, activity, or career
UF Consequence Based Education
Criterion Referenced Education
Output Oriented Education
Performance Based Education (1974 1980)
Proficiency Based Education
NT Competency Based Teacher Education
BT Education
RT Academic Standards
Accountability
Back To Basics
Behavioral Objectives
Competence
Individualized Instruction
Minimum Competencies
Minimum Competency Testing
Performance
Student Certification

COMPETENCY BASED TEACHER EDUCATION *Mar. 1980*
CIJE: 629 RIE: 1971 GC: 400
SN Educational system that stresses the explicit demonstration of specified performance as evidence of what a teacher should know and be able to do
UF Consequence Based Teacher Education
Criterion Referenced Teacher Education
Output Oriented Teacher Education
Performance Based Teacher Education (1972 1980)
Proficiency Based Teacher Education
BT Competency Based Education
Teacher Education
RT Academic Standards
Accountability
Behavioral Objectives
Competence
Individualized Instruction
Performance

COMPETITION *Mar. 1978*
CIJE: 620 RIE: 334 GC: 520
SN Rivalry between individuals or groups seeking the same object or goal
NT Competitive Selection
BT Behavior
RT Achievement Need
Aggression
Class Rank
Cooperation
Goal Orientation
Group Activities
Intergroup Relations
Interpersonal Relationship
Performance
Social Behavior
Social Exchange Theory

Competitive Bidding
USE BIDS

= Two or more Descriptors are used to represent this term.
The term's main entry shows the appropriate coordination.

COMPETITIVE SELECTION *Jul. 1966*
CIJE: 239 RIE: 180 GC: 330
BT Competition
Selection
RT Admission (School)
Admission Criteria
Educational Opportunities
Educational Supply
Employment Opportunities
Open Enrollment
Personnel Selection
Screening Tests
Selective Admission

Complexity Level (1968 1979)
USE DIFFICULTY LEVEL

COMPLIANCE (LEGAL) *Oct. 1979*
CIJE: 340 RIE: 866 GC: 610
SN Conforming to laws or legal directives
BT Compliance (Psychology)
RT Audits (Verification)
Court Judges
Court Litigation
Federal Regulation
Law Enforcement
Laws
Legal Problems
Legal Responsibility
Legislation

COMPLIANCE (PSYCHOLOGY) *Aug. 1986*
CIJE: RIE: GC: 120
SN Yielding to desires, requests, dictates, instructions, regulations, standards, etc. (note: use a more specific term if possible)
UF Noncompliance (Psychology)
NT Compliance (Legal)
Obedience
BT Cooperation
RT Conformity
Personality Traits
Self Control
Social Behavior
Social Control
Socialization
Social Psychology

Component Building Systems (1968 1976)
USE BUILDING SYSTEMS

Component Systems
USE BUILDING SYSTEMS

COMPONENTIAL ANALYSIS *May. 1969*
CIJE: 112 RIE: 116 GC: 450
SN Methodological procedure in linguistics and cognitive anthropology used to explain, distinguish, or study the meaning of sounds, words, and sentences (including the concepts behind terminological choices of particular cultures) by specifying common components, features, or relationships (note: prior to jun81, the use of this term was not restricted by a scope note)
BT Evaluation Methods
RT Anthropology
Distinctive Features (Language)
Lexicology
Linguistic Theory
Phonology
Scientific Methodology
Semantics
Sound Spectrographs
Structural Analysis (Linguistics)

Composition (Literary) (1966 1980)
USE WRITING (COMPOSITION)

Composition (Music)
USE MUSICAL COMPOSITION

Composition Measurement
USE CHEMICAL ANALYSIS

Composition Processes (Literary)
USE WRITING PROCESSES

Composition Skills (Literary) (1966 1980)
USE WRITING SKILLS

COMPREHENSION *Jul. 1966*
CIJE: 997 RIE: 914 GC: 110
UF Comprehension Development (1966 1980)
NT Listening Comprehension
Reading Comprehension
BT Intelligence
RT Abstract Reasoning
Advance Organizers
Cognitive Processes
Coherence
Cohesion (Written Composition)
Concept Formation
Difficulty Level
Encoding (Psychology)
Inferences
Intuition
Knowledge Level
Language Arts
Language Processing
Linguistic Competence
Metacognition
Misconceptions
Outlining (Discourse)
Perception
Schemata (Cognition)
Scientific Literacy
Technological Literacy

Comprehension Development (1966 1980)
USE COMPREHENSION

Comprehensive Districts (1967 1980)
USE SCHOOL DISTRICTS

Comprehensive High Schools (1967 1980)
USE HIGH SCHOOLS

COMPREHENSIVE PROGRAMS *Jul. 1966*
CIJE: 133 RIE: 213 GC: 320
SN A full set of curricula including college preparatory, commercial, and vocational courses, usually implemented at the secondary level (note: prior to mar80, the use of this term was not restricted by a scope note)
BT Programs
RT Secondary Education

Compressed Work Week
USE FLEXIBLE WORKING HOURS

Compulsory Attendance
USE COMPULSORY EDUCATION

COMPULSORY EDUCATION *Mar. 1980*
CIJE: 104 RIE: 72 GC: 330
SN Education that is legally required to be available to, and attended by, the school-age population
UF Compulsory Attendance
Mandatory Education
NT Home Schooling
BT Education
RT Access To Education
Educationally Disadvantaged
Educational Opportunities
Educational Supply
Elementary Secondary Education
Free Education
Government School Relationship
Public Education
School Attendance Legislation
Special Education

COMPUTATION *Mar. 1980*
CIJE: 641 RIE: 402 GC: 480
SN The act or method of calculating or estimating through the use of number operations and/or other mathematical processes
UF Calculation (1966 1980)
Counting
NT Estimation (Mathematics)
BT Mathematical Applications
RT Algorithms
Arithmetic
Calculators
Mathematical Formulas
Mathematics
Mathematics Tests
Measurement
Numbers
Ratios (Mathematics)

COMPUTATIONAL LINGUISTICS *Jul. 1966*
CIJE: 109 RIE: 333 GC: 450
SN Branch of linguistics concerned with the use of computers for the analysis and synthesis of language data -- for example, in machine translation, word frequency counts, and speech recognition and synthesis
NT Machine Translation
BT Linguistics
RT Automatic Indexing
Computer Science
Language Processing
Linguistic Theory
Mathematical Linguistics
Mathematical Logic
Programing Languages
Semantics
Statistics
Structural Analysis (Linguistics)
Word Frequency

Computer Aided Instruction
USE COMPUTER ASSISTED INSTRUCTION

Computer Aided Instructional Management
USE COMPUTER MANAGED INSTRUCTION

Computer Applications
USE COMPUTER ORIENTED PROGRAMS

Computer Assisted Indexing
USE AUTOMATIC INDEXING

COMPUTER ASSISTED INSTRUCTION *Jul. 1966*
CIJE: 3789 RIE: 4298 GC: 310
SN Interactive instructional technique in which a computer is used to present instructional material, monitor learning, and select additional instructional material in accordance with individual learner needs
UF Cai
Computer Aided Instruction
Computer Assisted Learning
Computer Based Instruction
Computer Based Laboratories (1967 1980) #
BT Computer Uses In Education
Programed Instruction
RT Authoring Aids (Programing)
Autoinstructional Aids
Computer Managed Instruction
Computers
Computer Simulation
Courseware
Educational Media
Feedback
Individualized Instruction
Interactive Video
Intermode Differences
Man Machine Systems
Programed Instructional Materials
Programed Tutoring
Teaching Machines

Computer Assisted Learning
USE COMPUTER ASSISTED INSTRUCTION

COMPUTER ASSISTED TESTING *Mar. 1980*
CIJE: 222 RIE: 240 GC: 820
SN Use of computers in test administration or construction
UF Computerized Adaptive Testing #
Computerized Tailored Testing #
BT Computer Uses In Education
Testing
RT Adaptive Testing
Computers
Computer Science
Item Banks
Test Construction
Test Items
Tests

Computer Based Instruction
USE COMPUTER ASSISTED INSTRUCTION

Computer Based Instructional Management
USE COMPUTER MANAGED INSTRUCTION

Computer Based Laboratories (1967 1980)
USE COMPUTER ASSISTED INSTRUCTION; LABORATORIES

Computer Based Message Systems
USE ELECTRONIC MAIL

Computer Based Reference Services
USE ONLINE SYSTEMS; REFERENCE SERVICES

Computer Conferencing
USE TELECONFERENCING

COMPUTER GRAPHICS *Feb. 1970*
CIJE: 453 RIE: 367 GC: 710
SN Techniques for graphic or pictorial representation of information in a computer -- representations may be in hardcopy or on display screens
UF Drawing (Computerized)
BT Graphic Arts
RT Computers
Computer Simulation
Display Systems
Engineering Graphics
Input Output Devices
Photocomposition

Computer Languages
USE PROGRAMING LANGUAGES

COMPUTER LITERACY *Apr. 1982*
CIJE: 662 RIE: 613 GC: 330
SN Awareness of or knowledge about computers (their capabilities, applications, and limitations) -- may include the ability to interact with computers to solve problems
BT Technological Literacy
RT Computer Oriented Programs
Computers
Computer Science Education
Computer Uses In Education
Mathematical Logic
Online Searching
Programing
Scientific Literacy
Search Strategies

COMPUTER MANAGED INSTRUCTION *Jan. 1979*
CIJE: 309 RIE: 455 GC: 310
SN Use of a computer to maintain and analyze data on learner performance and instructional progress as an aid to teachers in selecting learning activities
UF Cmi
Computer Aided Instructional Management
Computer Based Instructional Management
BT Computer Uses In Education
Information Systems
RT Computer Assisted Instruction
Computers
Educational Media
Management Information Systems

COMPUTER NETWORKS *Aug. 1986*
CIJE: 42 RIE: 26 GC: 710
SN Interconnected computers and peripherals, linked for resource sharing
NT Local Area Networks
BT Networks
RT Computer Oriented Programs
Computers
Computer Science
Computer Uses In Education
Data Processing
Information Networks
Man Machine Systems

COMPUTER ORIENTED PROGRAMS *Jul. 1966*
CIJE: 2632 RIE: 2644 GC: 320
SN The application of computer technology to such tasks as instruction, documentation, research, administration, etc. (note: use a more precise term if possible)
UF Computer Applications
BT Programs
RT Authoring Aids (Programing)
Branching
Computer Literacy
Computer Networks
Computers
Computer Simulation
Computer Uses In Education
Dial Access Information Systems
Educational Technology

= Two or more Descriptors are used to represent this term.
The term's main entry shows the appropriate coordination.

Electronic Mail
Flow Charts
Information Technology
Keyboarding (Data Entry)
Machine Readable Cataloging
Management Information Systems
Man Machine Systems
Programed Instruction
Programing
Selective Dissemination Of Information
Word Processing

COMPUTER OUTPUT MICROFILM *Feb. 1970*
CIJE: 78 RIE: 61 GC: 720
SN Microfilm produced as direct computer output, without printout as intermediary
UF Com
BT Microfilm
RT Computers
Input Output Devices

Computer Program Documentation
USE COMPUTER SOFTWARE

Computer Program Reviews
USE COMPUTER SOFTWARE REVIEWS

Computer Programing
USE PROGRAMING

Computer Programs (1966 1984)
USE COMPUTER SOFTWARE

COMPUTER SCIENCE *Jul. 1966*
CIJE: 1023 RIE: 787 GC: 710
SN Study of the theory, design, analysis, and applications of computers and computer-based systems
NT Programing
BT Information Science
RT Artificial Intelligence
Automation
Computational Linguistics
Computer Assisted Testing
Computer Networks
Computers
Computer Science Education
Cybernetics
Data Processing
Electromechanical Technology
Information Systems
Information Theory
Systems Analysis

COMPUTER SCIENCE EDUCATION *Jul. 1966*
CIJE: 676 RIE: 626 GC: 400
BT Education
RT Computer Literacy
Computers
Computer Science
Computer Uses In Education
Data Processing Occupations
Programing
Technical Education
Technical Occupations

COMPUTER SIMULATION *Oct. 1983*
CIJE: 282 RIE: 148 GC: 310
SN Computer-based representation of real situations or systems
BT Simulation
RT Computer Assisted Instruction
Computer Graphics
Computer Oriented Programs
Computers
Models
Monte Carlo Methods
Role Playing
Teaching Methods

COMPUTER SOFTWARE *Jun. 1984*
CIJE: 1108 RIE: 585 GC: 720
SN Logical sequences of instructions used to direct the actions of a computer system, and accompanying documentation (note: corresponds to pubtype code 101 and should not be used except as the subject of a document -- this restriction was not carried prior to jun84 under the former term "computer programs" -- if appropriate, use a more specific term)
UF Computer Program Documentation
Computer Programs (1966 1984)
Software (Computers)
NT Courseware
Database Management Systems
Menu Driven Software
BT Specifications
RT Authoring Aids (Programing)
Computers
Computer Software Reviews
Computer Uses In Education
Data Processing
Information Technology
Numerical Control
Programing
Programing Languages

COMPUTER SOFTWARE REVIEWS *Aug. 1986*
CIJE: RIE: GC: 730
UF Computer Program Reviews
Courseware Reviews #
Software Reviews (Computers)
BT Publications
RT Computers
Computer Software
Courseware

COMPUTER STORAGE DEVICES *Jul. 1966*
CIJE: 145 RIE: 169 GC: 910
UF Computer Tapes #
Memory Devices (Computers)
BT Computers
RT Data Processing
Information Storage
Input Output Devices
Magnetic Tapes
Optical Disks

Computer Tapes
USE COMPUTER STORAGE DEVICES; MAGNETIC TAPES

Computer Technology
USE COMPUTERS

Computer Terminals
USE INPUT OUTPUT DEVICES

COMPUTER USES IN EDUCATION *Aug. 1986*
CIJE: 209 RIE: 305 GC: 330
SN The use of computers for instruction, testing, student/pupil personnel services, school administrative support services, and other educational purposes (note: use a more specific term if possible -- prior to aug86, this concept was frequently indexed by "computer oriented programs")
UF Educational Computing
NT Computer Assisted Instruction
Computer Assisted Testing
Computer Managed Instruction
RT Computer Literacy
Computer Networks
Computer Oriented Programs
Computers
Computer Science Education
Computer Software
Educational Technology

Computerized Adaptive Testing
USE ADAPTIVE TESTING; COMPUTER ASSISTED TESTING

Computerized Tailored Testing
USE ADAPTIVE TESTING; COMPUTER ASSISTED TESTING

COMPUTERS *Jul. 1966*
CIJE: 2690 RIE: 2492 GC: 910
SN Devices that solve problems by accepting information, performing prescribed operations on it, and supplying the results obtained -- usually consist of units for input, output, storage, control, and arithmetic or logical operations (note: use a more specific term if possible)
UF Computer Technology
NT Analog Computers
Computer Storage Devices
Digital Computers
Display Systems
Input Output Devices
Microcomputers
Minicomputers
Online Systems
BT Electronic Equipment
RT Artificial Intelligence
Automation
Calculators
Computer Assisted Instruction
Computer Assisted Testing
Computer Graphics
Computer Literacy
Computer Managed Instruction
Computer Networks
Computer Oriented Programs
Computer Output Microfilm
Computer Science
Computer Science Education
Computer Simulation
Computer Software
Computer Software Reviews
Computer Uses In Education
Cybernetics
Databases
Data Processing
Electromechanical Aids
Electronic Publishing
Expert Systems
Information Systems
Information Technology
Input Output
Instrumentation
Man Machine Systems
Online Vendors
Optical Data Disks
Optical Disks
Programing
Programing Languages
Technological Advancement
Telecommunications
Time Sharing
Videotex

Concept Development
USE CONCEPT FORMATION

CONCEPT FORMATION *Jul. 1966*
CIJE: 3094 RIE: 2253 GC: 110
UF Concept Development
Conceptual Distinctions
BT Learning Processes
RT Abstract Reasoning
Cognitive Development
Cognitive Structures
Compensation (Concept)
Comprehension
Concept Teaching
Conservation (Concept)
Creative Thinking
Creativity
Developmental Stages
Discrimination Learning
Encoding (Psychology)
Epistemology
Fundamental Concepts
Generalization
Misconceptions
Object Permanence
Piagetian Theory

CONCEPT TEACHING *Jul. 1966*
CIJE: 644 RIE: 1106 GC: 400
BT Instruction
RT Concept Formation
Fundamental Concepts
Generalization
Geographic Concepts

Conceptual Distinctions
USE CONCEPT FORMATION

CONCEPTUAL SCHEMES (1967 1980) *Mar. 1980*
CIJE: 801 RIE: 851 GC: 110
SN Invalid descriptor -- used indiscriminately for the organization of individuals' understanding as well as the logical structure of theories -- see such descriptors as "models," "schemata (cognition)," "concept formation," "cognitive style," etc.

CONCEPTUAL TEMPO *Jul. 1972*
CIJE: 239 RIE: 134 GC: 110
SN An index of time spent in problem solving sequences used to characterize the reflective/impulsive dimension of cognitive style
UF Impulsivity
Reflectivity
BT Cognitive Style
RT Attention Span
Cognitive Processes
Reaction Time
Time Factors (Learning)

CONCERTS *Jul. 1966*
CIJE: 53 RIE: 28 GC: 420
BT Music Activities
RT Jazz
Music
Musicians
Orchestras
Singing

Concordances (1967 1980)
USE INDEXES

Concrete Industry
USE CEMENT INDUSTRY

CONCURRENT VALIDITY *Aug. 1986*
CIJE: 1 RIE: GC: 820
SN The extent to which a measure or some other factor approximates the results of another criterion available at the same time, e.g., the degree of correlation between a new short-form test and a longer, more established measure of the same construct
UF Criterion Validity (Concurrent)
BT Validity
RT Comparative Testing
Predictive Validity
Scores
Testing
Test Validity

Conditioned Response (1967 1980)
USE RESPONSES

Conditioned Stimulus (1966 1980)
USE STIMULI

CONDITIONING *Dec. 1970*
CIJE: 333 RIE: 216 GC: 110
SN Experimental procedures that attempt systematically to modify or control natural behavior
UF Psychological Conditioning
NT Behavior Modification
Classical Conditioning
Operant Conditioning
RT Behavior Change
Behaviorism
Biofeedback
Counseling Techniques
Ethology
Extinction (Psychology)
Learning Processes
Learning Theories
Meditation
Psychology
Reinforcement
Responses
Stimulation
Stimuli

Conduct (1966 1980)
USE BEHAVIOR

CONFERENCE PAPERS *Mar. 1980*
CIJE: 36 RIE: 46 GC: 720
SN Individual papers presented at conferences (note: the previous term "conference reports" was not scoped and was frequently used for this concept -- do not confuse with "conference proceedings" -- corresponds to pubtype code 150 -- do not use except as the subject of a document)
BT Reports
RT Conferences
Institutes (Training Programs)
Meetings
Speeches
Workshops

CONFERENCE PROCEEDINGS *Mar. 1980*
CIJE: 30 RIE: 68 GC: 720
SN Collections of papers presented at conferences (note: the previous term "conference reports" was not scoped and was frequently used for this concept -- do not confuse with "conference papers" -- corresponds to pubtype code 021 -- do not use except as the subject of a document)

= Two or more Descriptors are used to represent this term.
The term's main entry shows the appropriate coordination.

BT Serials
RT Anthologies
Conferences
Institutes (Training Programs)
Meetings
Workshops

CONFERENCE REPORTS (1967 1980) *Mar. 1980*
CIJE: 918 RIE: 3906 GC: 730
SN Invalid descriptor -- used for both "conference proceedings" and "conference papers" -- see the more precise terms

Conference Skills (Communication)
USE COMMUNICATION SKILLS

CONFERENCES *Jul. 1966*
CIJE: 1332 RIE: 1898 GC: 710
UF Symposia (1967 1980)
NT Parent Conferences
Parent Teacher Conferences
RT Conference Papers
Conference Proceedings
Continuing Education
Institutes (Training Programs)
Meetings
Organizations (Groups)
Teleconferencing
Workshops

CONFIDENCE TESTING *Feb. 1972*
CIJE: 47 RIE: 45 GC: 820
SN Testing technique that determines examinees' knowledge in objective or multiple choice tests by requiring them to indicate the degree of confidence they have in their answer (note: do not use for "confidence limits" or other statistical measures -- prior to mar80, the use of this term was not restricted by a scope note)
BT Testing
RT Guessing (Tests)
Knowledge Level
Multiple Choice Tests
Objective Tests
Response Style (Tests)
Scoring Formulas
Testing Problems
Test Interpretation
Test Reliability
Test Validity

Confidential Information
USE CONFIDENTIALITY

CONFIDENTIAL RECORDS *Jul. 1966*
CIJE: 167 RIE: 140 GC: 320
BT Records (Forms)
RT Case Records
Confidentiality
Disclosure
Freedom Of Information
Privacy
Student Records

CONFIDENTIALITY *Feb. 1971*
CIJE: 262 RIE: 239 GC: 520
SN Protection of privileged information
UF Confidential Information
Private Information
Privileged Communication
BT Privacy
RT Confidential Records
Counselor Role
Disclosure
Ethics
Interpersonal Communication

CONFLICT *Jul. 1966*
CIJE: 690 RIE: 665 GC: 530
NT Conflict Of Interest
Culture Conflict
Religious Conflict
Revolution
Role Conflict
War
RT Antisocial Behavior
Conflict Resolution
Controversial Issues (Course Content)
Disarmament
Dissent
International Relations
Social Problems

CONFLICT OF INTEREST *Aug. 1986*
CIJE: 27 RIE: 21 GC: 520
SN Incompatibility or opposition among needs and responsibilities, especially between private or personal interests and public or professional obligations
BT Conflict
RT Codes Of Ethics
Ethics
Legal Responsibility
Multiple Employment
Personnel Policy
Role Conflict

CONFLICT RESOLUTION *Jul. 1966*
CIJE: 1020 RIE: 1022 GC: 520
BT Cognitive Processes
RT Conflict
Decision Making
International Law
Interpersonal Communication
Peace
Problem Solving
Revolution
Social Cognition
Social Control

Confluent Education
USE HUMANISTIC EDUCATION

CONFORMITY *Jul. 1966*
CIJE: 293 RIE: 125 GC: 520
BT Social Behavior
RT Compliance (Psychology)
Congruence (Psychology)
Identification (Psychology)
Peer Groups
Peer Influence
Personality Traits
Social Adjustment

CONFUCIANISM *Mar. 1983*
CIJE: 8 RIE: 5 GC: 430
SN Religion based on the teachings of confucius (china, 5th century b.c.)
BT Religion
RT Non Western Civilization
Philosophy
Religious Cultural Groups

CONGENITAL IMPAIRMENTS *Mar. 1980*
CIJE: 203 RIE: 78 GC: 220
SN Impairments present or originating at birth
UF Anomalies (1967 1980)
Birth Defects
Congenitally Handicapped (1975 1980)
NT Cerebral Palsy
Cleft Palate
Downs Syndrome
BT Disabilities
RT Adventitious Impairments
Exceptional Persons
Genetics
Heredity
Perinatal Influences
Prenatal Influences

Congenitally Handicapped (1975 1980)
USE CONGENITAL IMPAIRMENTS

Congress Role
USE GOVERNMENT ROLE

Congressmen
USE LEGISLATORS

Congresswomen
USE LEGISLATORS

CONGRUENCE (MATHEMATICS) *Mar. 1980*
CIJE: 6 RIE: 1 GC: 480
SN Property of geometric figures that can be made to coincide by a rigid transformation
BT Geometric Concepts
RT Geometry
Symmetry
Transformations (Mathematics)

CONGRUENCE (PSYCHOLOGY) *Mar. 1980*
CIJE: 133 RIE: 95 GC: 230
SN In accord or agreement with others or oneself
NT Self Congruence
BT Psychological Patterns
RT Cognitive Dissonance
Conformity
Egocentrism
Empathy
Identification (Psychology)
Interpersonal Attraction
Locus Of Control
Personality Traits

CONGRUENCE (1970 1980) *Mar. 1980*
CIJE: 31 RIE: 12 GC: 820
SN Invalid descriptor -- used for both mathematical and psychological congruence

Conjoint Counseling
USE COCOUNSELING

CONNECTED DISCOURSE *Aug. 1968*
CIJE: 115 RIE: 170 GC: 450
NT Cohesion (Written Composition)
RT Association (Psychology)
Dialogs (Language)
Discourse Analysis
Language Patterns
Paragraphs
Prose
Psycholinguistics
Semantics
Syntax
Word Frequency

Consequence Based Education
USE COMPETENCY BASED EDUCATION

Consequence Based Teacher Education
USE COMPETENCY BASED TEACHER EDUCATION

CONSERVATION (CONCEPT) *Sep. 1968*
CIJE: 576 RIE: 302 GC: 110
SN The principle that mass, number, and volume do not vary despite transformations in their form or embodiment (e.g., a pound of clay is a pound of clay whether in the form of a ball or a sausage) -- in developmental psychology, the recognition or understanding of this phenomena
BT Fundamental Concepts
RT Cognitive Processes
Compensation (Concept)
Concept Formation
Learning Processes
Mathematical Concepts
Scientific Concepts
Serial Ordering

CONSERVATION (ENVIRONMENT) *Jul. 1974*
CIJE: 430 RIE: 458 GC: 410
SN Preservation of the environment, including natural resources, from loss, waste, or harm
NT Energy Conservation
Soil Conservation
RT Air Pollution
Conservation Education
Depleted Resources
Ecological Factors
Ecology
Endangered Species
Environment
Environmental Education
Forestry
Fuel Consumption
Mining
Natural Resources
Physical Environment
Recycling
Wastes
Water Pollution
Water Quality
Water Resources
Wildlife Management
World Problems

CONSERVATION EDUCATION *Jul. 1966*
CIJE: 511 RIE: 1167 GC: 410
BT Environmental Education
RT Biological Sciences
Conservation (Environment)
Energy Conservation
Energy Education
Fire Science Education
Forestry
Geography
Natural Resources
Outdoor Education
Physical Sciences
Soil Conservation
Trails

CONSERVATISM *Jan. 1985*
CIJE: 64 RIE: 28 GC: 520
SN Philosophy or disposition that generally supports the preservation or reinstatement of traditional values and statuses in social or political affairs
RT Government Role
Liberalism
Political Attitudes
Political Socialization
Social Values
Traditionalism

Consistency
USE RELIABILITY

CONSOLIDATED SCHOOLS *Aug. 1969*
CIJE: 65 RIE: 123 GC: 340
UF Centralized Schools
School Consolidation
BT Schools
RT Mergers
Regional Schools
Rural Schools
School Closing
School District Reorganization
School Districts
School Zoning

CONSONANTS *Jul. 1966*
CIJE: 347 RIE: 309 GC: 450
BT Phonemes
RT Acoustic Phonetics
Distinctive Features (Language)
Phonemic Alphabets
Phonetics
Syllables
Vowels

CONSORTIA *Jan. 1970*
CIJE: 304 RIE: 593 GC: 330
SN Associations of institutions (usually higher education or libraries) that share resources and/or students to strengthen programs or services and reduce costs (note: do not confuse with "cluster colleges")
UF Consortiums
BT Organizations (Groups)
RT Cluster Colleges
Cooperative Planning
Cooperative Programs
Coordination
Dual Enrollment
Educational Cooperation
Institutional Cooperation
Intercollegiate Cooperation
Library Cooperation
Library Networks
Shared Resources And Services

Consortiums
USE CONSORTIA

Constituent Structure
USE PHRASE STRUCTURE

CONSTITUTIONAL HISTORY *Jul. 1966*
CIJE: 77 RIE: 118 GC: 430
BT History
RT Constitutional Law
Government (Administrative Body)
Governmental Structure
Government Role
Political Science
United States Government (Course)
United States History
World History

CONSTITUTIONAL LAW *Dec. 1974*
CIJE: 579 RIE: 374 GC: 610
BT Laws
RT Civil Liberties
Civil Rights
Civil Rights Legislation
Constitutional History
Discriminatory Legislation
Government (Administrative Body)
Governmental Structure
Government Role
Government School Relationship
Justice
Law Related Education

Legal Education (Professions)
Political Science
Privacy
Search And Seizure
Torts
United States Government (Course)

CONSTRUCT VALIDITY *Aug. 1986*
CIJE: 10 RIE: 1 GC: 820
SN The extent to which a test measures a hypothetical construct or trait (e.g., creativity, analytical ability, persistence, mechanical competence, achievement motivation) that is the basis for test performance
BT Test Validity
RT Content Validity
Factor Structure
Testing

Constructed Languages
USE ARTIFICIAL LANGUAGES

CONSTRUCTED RESPONSE *Jul. 1966*
CIJE: 20 RIE: 39 GC: 110
SN Response that is created rather than selected from a set of alternative answers (note: prior to mar80, the use of this term was not restricted by a scope note)
BT Responses
RT Essay Tests

CONSTRUCTION (PROCESS) *Jul. 1966*
CIJE: 262 RIE: 329 GC: 920
SN Act of putting parts together to form a physical structure or facility (note: before mar80, the scope note read "act of putting parts together")
NT Cabinetmaking
Carpentry
Masonry
Prefabrication
Road Construction
School Construction
RT Acoustic Insulation
Building Conversion
Building Design
Building Systems
Building Trades
Ceilings
Construction Costs
Construction Industry
Construction Management
Construction Materials
Construction Needs
Construction Programs
Design Build Approach
Facility Expansion
Flooring
Industrial Arts
Roofing
Site Development
Structural Building Systems
Structural Elements (Construction)
Systems Building
Welding

Construction Bidding
USE BIDS

CONSTRUCTION COSTS *Jul. 1966*
CIJE: 242 RIE: 276 GC: 620
BT Costs
RT Building Conversion
Buildings
Capital Outlay (For Fixed Assets)
Construction (Process)
Construction Management
Construction Materials
Construction Needs
Construction Programs
Design Build Approach
Facility Planning
Life Cycle Costing

CONSTRUCTION INDUSTRY *Jul. 1966*
CIJE: 89 RIE: 189 GC: 650
NT Housing Industry
BT Industry
RT Architects
Brick Industry
Buildings
Building Trades
Cement Industry
Construction (Process)

CONSTRUCTION MANAGEMENT *Dec. 1972*
CIJE: 67 RIE: 51 GC: 920
BT Administration
RT Construction (Process)
Construction Costs
Construction Programs
Critical Path Method
Design Build Approach
Facility Planning
Fast Track Scheduling
Systems Building

CONSTRUCTION MATERIALS *Mar. 1980*
CIJE: 137 RIE: 255 GC: 920
UF Building Materials (1968 1980)
NT Asphalts
Prestressed Concrete
RT Acoustic Insulation
Adhesives
Architectural Research
Asbestos
Building Design
Building Innovation
Buildings
Carpeting
Cement Industry
Construction (Process)
Construction Costs
Construction Needs
Doors
Encapsulated Facilities
Facilities
Flooring
Masonry
Prefabrication
Roofing
School Buildings
Structural Elements (Construction)
Supplies

CONSTRUCTION NEEDS *Jul. 1966*
CIJE: 26 RIE: 118 GC: 920
BT Needs
RT Building Conversion
Construction (Process)
Construction Costs
Construction Materials
Construction Programs
Facility Guidelines
Facility Planning
Facility Requirements
Structural Elements (Construction)

Construction Occupations
USE BUILDING TRADES

CONSTRUCTION PROGRAMS *Jul. 1966*
CIJE: 115 RIE: 219 GC: 920
UF Building Programs
BT Programs
RT Building Systems
Construction (Process)
Construction Costs
Construction Management
Construction Needs
Design Build Approach
Educational Facilities Planning
Facility Expansion
Facility Inventory
Facility Planning
Facility Utilization Research
Fast Track Scheduling
Structural Building Systems
Systems Building

CONSULTANTS *Jul. 1966*
CIJE: 804 RIE: 893 GC: 240
UF Community Consultants (1966 1980)
NT Medical Consultants
Reading Consultants
Science Consultants
BT Personnel
RT Advisory Committees
Blue Ribbon Commissions
Change Agents
Consultation Programs
Counselors
Faculty
Guidance Personnel
Human Resources
Professional Services
Referral
Resource Staff
Resource Teachers
School Psychologists
Specialists
Supervisors
Technical Assistance

CONSULTATION PROGRAMS *Jul. 1966*
CIJE: 453 RIE: 449 GC: 240
SN Formal procedures whereby consulting services are provided by specialists (e.g., health workers, extension agents, counselors) to individuals or groups (e.g., teachers, students, administrators, parents, communities)
UF Community Consultant Programs (1966 1980)
BT Programs
RT Consultants
Counseling
Counselor Teacher Cooperation
Guidance
Intermediate Administrative Units
Intervention
Professional Services
Referral
Technical Assistance

Consumer Behavior
USE CONSUMER ECONOMICS

CONSUMER ECONOMICS *Jul. 1966*
CIJE: 339 RIE: 655 GC: 620
SN Economic principles and forces that affect the consumer and the interpretation of economic theories in terms of consumer interest as distinguished from producer interest
UF Consumer Behavior
Consumer Expenditures
Family Economics
BT Economics
RT Consumer Education
Consumer Protection
Consumer Science
Educational Economics
Home Economics
Home Management
Merchandise Information
Purchasing

CONSUMER EDUCATION *Aug. 1968*
CIJE: 631 RIE: 1393 GC: 400
SN Study of intelligent and effective methods of buying and using goods and services, competent money management, and relationship of consumer to the economic system
NT Consumer Science
BT Education
RT Basic Business Education
Consumer Economics
Consumer Protection
Consumer Science
Economics Education
Energy Education
Family Life Education
Health Education
Home Economics
Home Economics Education
Home Management
Money Management
Practical Arts
Purchasing

Consumer Expenditures
USE CONSUMER ECONOMICS

CONSUMER PROTECTION *Dec. 1975*
CIJE: 206 RIE: 411 GC: 520
SN Methods or processes intended to prevent the sale of unsafe or deceptively presented goods or services, or to assist the consumer to make informed decisions regarding purchase of goods or services
UF Consumerism
RT Accountability
Advertising
College Choice
Consumer Economics
Consumer Education
Deception
Educational Quality
Marketing
Merchandise Information
Purchasing
Responsibility
Safety

CONSUMER SCIENCE *Jul. 1966*
CIJE: 37 RIE: 61 GC: 400
SN Those phases of science needed by or useful to the consumer including operation and repair of simple household equipment, effects of cleaning and other products, and preservation and care of food and clothing
UF Household Science
BT Consumer Education
Technology
RT Clothing Instruction
Consumer Economics
Consumer Education
Foods Instruction
Home Economics
Maintenance
Repair

Consumerism
USE CONSUMER PROTECTION

Contagious Diseases
USE COMMUNICABLE DISEASES

Contemporary History
USE MODERN HISTORY

CONTENT ANALYSIS *Aug. 1968*
CIJE: 1538 RIE: 1402 GC: 810
SN Systematic, objective, and quantitative description of the manifest or latent content of print or nonprint communications
BT Evaluation Methods
RT Classification
Classroom Observation Techniques
Communication (Thought Transfer)
Course Content
Curriculum Research
Data Analysis
Difficulty Level
Film Criticism
Item Analysis
Literary Criticism
Readability Formulas
Research Methodology
Skill Analysis
Task Analysis
Textbook Content

CONTENT AREA READING *Mar. 1980*
CIJE: 718 RIE: 1069 GC: 460
SN Instruction concerned with reading assignments -- also, instructional material in such subject areas as social studies, mathematics, science, and english
UF Content Reading (1967 1980)
Reading In Content Areas
BT Reading
Reading Instruction
RT Critical Reading
Directed Reading Activity
Functional Reading
Readability
Reading Assignments
Reading Comprehension
Reading Skills
Study Skills

CONTENT AREA WRITING *Jun. 1983*
CIJE: 113 RIE: 126 GC: 400
SN Written composition or writing instruction for specific academic or vocational subject areas
BT Writing (Composition)
Writing Instruction
RT Literary Devices
News Writing
Research Papers (Students)
Technical Writing
Writing Exercises
Writing Skills

Content Reading (1967 1980)
USE CONTENT AREA READING

CONTENT VALIDITY *Aug. 1986*
CIJE: 19 RIE: 29 GC: 820
SN The extent to which a test adequately represents the subject-matter content or behavior to be measured -- commonly used in evaluating achievement or proficiency tests
BT Test Validity

RT Construct Validity
Item Analysis
Testing
Test Items

CONTEXT CLUES *Jul. 1966*
CIJE: 482 RIE: 389 GC: 460
SN Indications of the meaning of a word gained from the surrounding words, phrases, or sentences as well as the accompanying pictures
BT Cues
RT Cloze Procedure
Decoding (Reading)
Inferences
Miscue Analysis
Reading
Reading Comprehension
Structural Analysis (Linguistics)
Vocabulary Development
Vocabulary Skills
Word Recognition

CONTEXT FREE GRAMMAR *Jul. 1966*
CIJE: 4 RIE: 19 GC: 450
BT Transformational Generative Grammar
RT Grammar
Machine Translation
Phrase Structure

Contingency Contracts
USE CONTINGENCY MANAGEMENT

CONTINGENCY MANAGEMENT *Feb. 1975*
CIJE: 367 RIE: 234 GC: 110
SN Systematic arrangement of reinforcing events in order to strengthen or weaken specific behavior
UF Contingency Contracts
BT Behavior Modification
RT Behavioral Objectives
Behavior Chaining
Behavior Change
Extinction (Psychology)
Learning Processes
Motivation Techniques
Operant Conditioning
Performance Contracts
Reinforcement
Teaching Methods
Timeout
Token Economy

CONTINUATION EDUCATION (1968 1980) *Jun. 1980*
CIJE: 71 RIE: 55 GC: 330
SN Invalid descriptor -- scoped to refer to instruction for potential learners who have rejected conventional schooling, but used indiscriminately for "continuing education" -- see "continuation students"

Continuation High Schools (1968 1980)
USE CONTINUATION STUDENTS

CONTINUATION STUDENTS *Jul. 1966*
CIJE: 31 RIE: 58 GC: 360
SN Students enrolled in special continuation education programs -- continuation education enables youth and adults who have previously dropped out of or otherwise rejected conventional schooling to complete their formal education (note: prior to jun80, "continuation education" was also used to index this concept)
UF Continuation High Schools (1968 1980)
BT Students
RT Delinquent Rehabilitation
Dropout Prevention
Dropout Programs
Dropouts
High School Equivalency Programs
High Schools
Late Registration
Nontraditional Education
Reentry Students
Rehabilitation Programs
Remedial Programs
Secondary Education
Special Education
Student Adjustment
Terminal Students
Transfer Students
Truancy
Vocational Education

CONTINUING EDUCATION *Apr. 1980*
CIJE: 582 RIE: 724 GC: 340
SN Educational programs and services, usually on the postsecondary level, designed to serve adults who seek particular learning experiences on a part-time or short term basis for personal, academic, or occupational development
NT Professional Continuing Education
BT Adult Education
RT Adult Students
Auditing (Coursework)
Community Education
Community Services
Conferences
Continuing Education Centers
Continuing Education Units
Corporate Education
Correspondence Study
Distance Education
Evening Programs
Extension Education
Lifelong Learning
Noncredit Courses
Nontraditional Education
Outreach Programs
Postsecondary Education
Special Degree Programs
Staff Development
Womens Education

CONTINUING EDUCATION CENTERS *Jul. 1966*
CIJE: 134 RIE: 154 GC: 920
BT Educational Facilities
RT Adult Education
Continuing Education
Extension Education
Living Learning Centers

CONTINUING EDUCATION UNITS *Feb. 1976*
CIJE: 48 RIE: 85 GC: 340
SN Uniform units of measurement reflecting participation in organized continuing (noncredit) education programs under responsible sponsorship -- designed to provide a national standard for recognition of adult participation in post-degree and non-degree education programs (one unit equals ten contact hours)
UF Ceu
BT Credits
RT Adult Education
Auditing (Coursework)
Continuing Education
Credentials
Lifelong Learning
Noncredit Courses
Professional Continuing Education
Retraining
Student Certification
Units Of Study

Continuity Of Education
USE DEVELOPMENTAL CONTINUITY

Continuous Guidance (1966 1980)
USE GUIDANCE

Continuous Learning (1967 1980)
USE LIFELONG LEARNING

CONTINUOUS PROGRESS PLAN *Jul. 1966*
CIJE: 68 RIE: 139 GC: 350
SN Curriculum organized so that students can progress at their own rates through a sequence of increasingly difficult courses
BT Curriculum
RT Behavioral Objectives
Flexible Progression
Flexible Scheduling
Nongraded Instructional Grouping

CONTRACEPTION *Apr. 1969*
CIJE: 292 RIE: 339 GC: 210
UF Birth Control
RT Abortions
Birth Rate
Family Planning
Gynecology
Illegitimate Births
Overpopulation
Pregnancy
Reproduction (Biology)
Sex Education

Contract Grading
USE GRADING; PERFORMANCE CONTRACTS

CONTRACT SALARIES *Jul. 1966*
CIJE: 27 RIE: 58 GC: 620
SN Salaries stipulated by a formal agreement limited by an expiration date
BT Salaries
RT Contracts
Teacher Salaries
Tenure

Contractor Vehicles
USE SERVICE VEHICLES

CONTRACTS *Jul. 1966*
CIJE: 723 RIE: 912 GC: 620
SN Formal agreements between two or more parties in which, for a benefit or to avoid a penalty, one or more of the parties agrees to do a certain thing
UF Agreements (Formal)
NT Performance Contracts
RT Accountability
Bids
Contract Salaries
Faculty Workload
Grantsmanship
Labor Demands
Laws
Legal Responsibility
Negotiation Agreements
Ownership
Personnel Policy
Probationary Period
Specifications
Teacher Dismissal
Teaching Load
Tenure

CONTRAST *Apr. 1970*
CIJE: 20 RIE: 11 GC: 420
SN The perceived diversity of adjacent elements in the visual field
UF Contrast Ratios
RT Color
Light
Lighting
Lighting Design
Visual Discrimination

Contrast Ratios
USE CONTRAST

Contrastive Language Analysis
USE CONTRASTIVE LINGUISTICS

CONTRASTIVE LINGUISTICS *Jul. 1966*
CIJE: 483 RIE: 684 GC: 450
SN Study of the similarities and differences between languages or dialects or between different periods in the historical development of one language
UF Comparative Linguistics
Contrastive Language Analysis
BT Linguistics
RT Cross Cultural Studies
Diachronic Linguistics
Error Analysis (Language)
Interference (Language)
Language Classification
Language Typology
Language Variation
Lexicology
Machine Translation
Mutual Intelligibility
Phoneme Grapheme Correspondence
Phonemics
Second Language Learning

CONTROL GROUPS *Jul. 1966*
CIJE: 155 RIE: 374 GC: 820
SN Groups that match experimental groups except that they are not exposed to the experimental variables being studied -- differences arising between the groups are then attributed to these variables (note: use only for discussions of the identification, selection, or treatment of control groups)
BT Groups
RT Attrition (Research Studies)
Effect Size
Experimental Groups
Matched Groups
Participant Characteristics
Quasiexperimental Design
Research Design
Research Methodology
Sample Size
Sampling

CONTROLLED ENVIRONMENT (1966 1980) *Mar. 1980*
CIJE: 108 RIE: 154 GC: 920
SN Invalid descriptor -- primarily used for control of the physical environment, but also used for manipulation of social or psychological environments -- use such descriptors as "climate control," "physical environment," "social environment," "behavior change," "milieu therapy," "behavior modification," etc.

CONTROVERSIAL ISSUES (COURSE CONTENT) *Oct. 1980*
CIJE: 213 RIE: 196 GC: 330
SN Matters of public concern and controversy that are taught, often through discussion, in social studies, current events, science, and other classes (note: for the issues themselves as opposed to teaching about them, use more precise terms)
RT Conflict
Course Content
Critical Thinking
Current Events
Curriculum
Dissent
Moral Issues
Political Issues
Public Affairs Education
Social Change
Social Problems
Social Sciences
Social Studies
Values
World Problems

Convalescent Homes
USE NURSING HOMES

CONVENTIONAL INSTRUCTION *Jul. 1966*
CIJE: 323 RIE: 454 GC: 310
UF Traditional Instruction
BT Teaching Methods
RT Back To Basics
Experimental Teaching
Lecture Method
Self Contained Classrooms
Traditional Schools

Conventional Warfare
USE WAR

CONVERGENT THINKING *Nov. 1968*
CIJE: 68 RIE: 64 GC: 110
SN Thought processes involved in searching for the one right, best, or conventional answer to a problem
BT Cognitive Processes
RT Critical Thinking
Divergent Thinking
Logical Thinking
Problem Solving
Productive Thinking

CONVERSATIONAL LANGUAGE COURSES *Jul. 1966*
CIJE: 177 RIE: 346 GC: 450
SN Courses that develop conversational skills in a foreign language (note: prior to mar80, this term was not scoped and was often misused to index "conversation")
BT Courses
Modern Language Curriculum
RT Audiolingual Methods
Audiolingual Skills
Communicative Competence (Languages)
Language Fluency
Language Proficiency
Languages
Second Language Instruction
Second Language Learning
Second Language Programs
Speech Communication
Standard Spoken Usage

Convicts
USE CRIMINALS

COOKING INSTRUCTION *Jul. 1966*
CIJE: 60 RIE: 170 GC: 400
BT Instruction
RT Cooks
Foods Instruction
Home Economics
Nutrition Instruction

COOKS *Jul. 1966*
CIJE: 9 RIE: 66 GC: 640
UF Chefs
BT Service Workers
RT Cooking Instruction
Dietitians
Dining Facilities
Food
Food Service
Foods Instruction
Home Economics Skills
Nutrition Instruction
Occupational Home Economics

Cooperating Schools
USE AFFILIATED SCHOOLS

COOPERATING TEACHERS *Jul. 1966*
CIJE: 304 RIE: 462 GC: 360
SN Experienced elementary or secondary teachers employed to supervise student teachers or teacher interns in affiliated schools (note: do not confuse with the more general concept "master teachers" or with "student teacher supervisors")
UF Supervising Teachers
BT Teachers
RT Affiliated Schools
Master Teachers
Practicum Supervision
Preservice Teacher Education
Student Teachers
Student Teacher Supervisors
Student Teaching
Teacher Education
Teacher Educator Education
Teacher Educators
Teacher Interns
Teacher Supervision

COOPERATION *Mar. 1978*
CIJE: 602 RIE: 486 GC: 520
SN Act of working together toward a common goal (note: use a more specific term if possible)
UF Collaboration
NT Agency Cooperation
Community Cooperation
Compliance (Psychology)
Educational Cooperation
Institutional Cooperation
International Cooperation
Regional Cooperation
BT Behavior
RT Altruism
Competition
Cooperative Planning
Cooperative Programs
Coordination
Group Activities
Group Unity
Intergroup Relations
Interpersonal Relationship
Networks
Prosocial Behavior
Shared Resources And Services
Social Behavior
Social Exchange Theory
Social Reinforcement
Social Support Groups
Teamwork
Trust (Psychology)

Cooperative Activities
USE GROUP ACTIVITIES

COOPERATIVE EDUCATION *Jul. 1966*
CIJE: 562 RIE: 1010 GC: 400
SN Work and school experiences under the direction of a teacher coordinator, arranged between school and employer to complement each other toward an occupational goal -- often more formally structured and supervised than other work experience programs
UF Cooperative Training
Vocational Work Experience
BT Vocational Education
RT Adult Vocational Education
Affiliated Schools
Career Education
Cooperative Programs
Distributive Education
Educational Cooperation
Experiential Learning
Field Experience Programs
Instructor Coordinators
Practicums
School Business Relationship
Supervised Farm Practice
Work Experience
Work Experience Programs

Cooperative Extension
USE EXTENSION EDUCATION

COOPERATIVE PLANNING *Jul. 1966*
CIJE: 649 RIE: 1317 GC: 520
SN Process by which individuals or groups determine mutual objectives and the means for attaining them
UF Interagency Planning (1966 1980) #
BT Planning
RT Agency Cooperation
Community Cooperation
Consortia
Cooperation
Counselor Teacher Cooperation
Delphi Technique
Educational Cooperation
Institutional Cooperation
Parent Teacher Cooperation
Regional Cooperation
School Community Relationship
Shared Resources And Services
Team Teaching
Teamwork

COOPERATIVE PROGRAMS *Jul. 1966*
CIJE: 1235 RIE: 2371 GC: 330
SN Programs conducted between or among independent institutions or organizations (note: prior to mar80, the use of this term was not restricted by a scope note)
UF Co Op Programs
Program Coordination (1966 1980) #
BT Programs
RT Consortia
Cooperation
Cooperative Education
Coordination
Dual Enrollment
Educational Cooperation
Experiential Learning
Institutional Cooperation
Off The Job Training
School Business Relationship
School Community Relationship
Shared Resources And Services
Work Experience Programs
Work Study Programs

Cooperative Teaching (1966 1980)
USE TEAM TEACHING

Cooperative Training
USE COOPERATIVE EDUCATION

COOPERATIVES *Jul. 1966*
CIJE: 53 RIE: 104 GC: 650
SN Economic enterprises wholly owned by their users
UF Co Ops
BT Organizations (Groups)
RT Business
Collective Settlements
Community Organizations
Economic Opportunities
Industrial Structure
Industry
Marketing
Ownership
Participative Decision Making
Purchasing

Coordinate Geometry
USE ANALYTIC GEOMETRY

COORDINATE INDEXES *Jan. 1969*
CIJE: 21 RIE: 44 GC: 730
UF Post Coordinate Indexes
Uniterm Indexes
BT Indexes
RT Indexing
Permuted Indexes
Thesauri

COORDINATION *Jul. 1966*
CIJE: 852 RIE: 2294 GC: 520
SN Process of bringing about or organizing cooperative actions
UF Educational Coordination (1967 1980) #
Interagency Coordination (1967 1980) #
Program Coordination (1966 1980) #
NT Community Coordination
RT Administration
Consortia
Cooperation
Cooperative Programs
Coordinators
Managerial Occupations
Networks
Organization
Planning
Relationship
Research Coordinating Units
Scheduling
Statewide Planning

Coordination (Psychomotor)
USE PSYCHOMOTOR SKILLS

COORDINATION COMPOUNDS *Jan. 1970*
CIJE: 48 RIE: GC: 490
SN Compounds with central atoms or ions and groups of ions or molecules surrounding them
RT Chemistry
Inorganic Chemistry
Molecular Structure
Organic Chemistry

Coordinator Trainers
USE INSTRUCTOR COORDINATORS

COORDINATORS *Jul. 1966*
CIJE: 92 RIE: 204 GC: 360
SN Liaison agents between groups of people or organizations
UF Community Coordinators (1966 1980) #
NT Audiovisual Coordinators
Instructor Coordinators
BT Administrators
RT Coordination

Copilots
USE AIRCRAFT PILOTS

COPING *Jan. 1979*
CIJE: 826 RIE: 615 GC: 230
SN Contending with difficulties without altering purposes or goals
BT Adjustment (To Environment)
RT Adaptive Behavior (Of Disabled)
Behavior Patterns
Burnout
Daily Living Skills
Decision Making
Goal Orientation
Individual Power
Mental Health
Persistence
Problem Solving
Psychological Patterns
Stress Management
Well Being

Copyediting
USE EDITING

Copyeditors
USE EDITORS

Copying (Reproduction)
USE REPROGRAPHY

COPYRIGHTS *Jul. 1966*
CIJE: 412 RIE: 332 GC: 710
SN Exclusive privileges to publish, sell, or otherwise control works that can be reproduced, granted by governments to authors, composers, artists, publishers, etc. for a specified number of years
BT Intellectual Property
RT Broadcast Industry
Federal Regulation
Film Industry
Films
Government Role
Legal Responsibility
National Libraries
Plagiarism
Programing (Broadcast)
Publications
Publishing Industry
Reprography

Core Courses (1966 1980)
USE CORE CURRICULUM

CORE CURRICULUM *Jul. 1966*
CIJE: 476 RIE: 720 GC: 350
SN Studies, activities, or courses that meet the common needs of students
UF Core Courses (1966 1980)
Teaching Core
BT Curriculum
RT General Science
Interdisciplinary Approach
Introductory Courses
Minimum Competencies
Nonmajors
Relevance (Education)
Required Courses

Corn (Field Crop) (1968 1980)
USE GRAINS (FOOD)

CORPORAL PUNISHMENT *Jul. 1974*
CIJE: 136 RIE: 140 GC: 330
SN Disciplinary action involving infliction of physical pain upon one person by another
BT Punishment
RT Discipline
Discipline Policy
Negative Reinforcement

Corporate Colleges
USE CORPORATE EDUCATION

CORPORATE EDUCATION *Aug. 1986*
CIJE: 12 RIE: 11 GC: 330
SN Broad array of courses, curricula, and educational services offered by business and industry -- may be completely inhouse or offered cooperatively with an educational institution (note: do not confuse with "industrial training")
UF Corporate Colleges
BT Education
RT Business
Continuing Education
Education Work Relationship
Industrial Training
Industry
Inplant Programs
Labor Force Development
Nonschool Educational Programs
Nontraditional Education
Postsecondary Education
Private Education
Professional Continuing Education
School Business Relationship

Corporate Giving
USE CORPORATE SUPPORT

CORPORATE SUPPORT *Aug. 1986*
CIJE: 31 RIE: 39 GC: 620
SN Aid provided by business and industry (e.g., money, equipment, materials, technical assistance)
UF Corporate Giving
RT Business
Business Responsibility
Donors
Educational Finance
Industry
Private Financial Support
School Business Relationship
School Support

= Two or more Descriptors are used to represent this term.
The term's main entry shows the appropriate coordination.

Corporate Training
USE INDUSTRIAL TRAINING

CORRECTIONAL EDUCATION *Jul. 1966*
CIJE: 283 RIE: 459 GC: 330
SN Educational programs provided for adults or youth in correctional institutions (note: prior to mar80, the use of this term was not restricted by a scope note)
UF Prison Education
BT Education
RT Adult Education
Adult Reading Programs
Correctional Institutions
Correctional Rehabilitation
Criminals
Delinquent Rehabilitation
Human Services
Institutionalized Persons
Prisoners
Prison Libraries
Rehabilitation Programs
Released Time
Therapeutic Recreation
Vocational Rehabilitation

CORRECTIONAL INSTITUTIONS *Mar. 1980*
CIJE: 345 RIE: 497 GC: 920
UF Corrective Institutions (1966 1980)
Prisons
Training Schools (Juvenile Offenders)
BT Residential Institutions
RT Correctional Education
Correctional Rehabilitation
Crime
Criminals
Criminology
Delinquent Rehabilitation
Institutionalized Persons
Institutional Personnel
Prisoners
Prison Libraries
Sentencing

CORRECTIONAL REHABILITATION *Nov. 1969*
CIJE: 337 RIE: 365 GC: 520
SN Activities designed to help prisoners and other offenders to lead useful lives
UF Corrections (Criminal Justice)
NT Delinquent Rehabilitation
BT Rehabilitation
RT Correctional Education
Correctional Institutions
Crime
Crime Prevention
Criminals
Criminology
Human Services
Parole Officers
Prisoners
Probationary Period
Probation Officers
Recidivism
Vocational Rehabilitation

Corrections (Criminal Justice)
USE CORRECTIONAL REHABILITATION

Corrective Institutions (1966 1980)
USE CORRECTIONAL INSTITUTIONS

CORRECTIVE READING *Jul. 1966*
CIJE: 13 RIE: 68 GC: 460
SN Reading instruction within a regular class for students with reading problems (note: do not confuse with "remedial reading")
BT Reading
Reading Instruction
RT Reading Difficulties
Remedial Reading

CORRELATION *Jul. 1966*
CIJE: 1823 RIE: 1422 GC: 820
SN Description of the degree of association or concomitant variation between two independently measured traits
UF Correlation Studies
Multiple Correlation
Part Correlation
Partial Correlation
Statistical Association Methods
BT Statistical Analysis
RT Analysis Of Covariance
Cluster Analysis
Comparative Analysis
Factor Analysis
Input Output Analysis
Least Squares Statistics
Meta Analysis
Multidimensional Scaling
Multiple Regression Analysis
Multitrait Multimethod Techniques
Multivariate Analysis
Nonparametric Statistics
Oblique Rotation
Orthogonal Rotation
Path Analysis
Predictor Variables
Regression (Statistics)
Reliability
Scores
Statistical Inference
Statistics
Transformations (Mathematics)
Validity

Correlation Studies
USE CORRELATION

Correspondence (Letters)
USE LETTERS (CORRESPONDENCE)

Correspondence Courses (1966 1980)
USE CORRESPONDENCE STUDY

CORRESPONDENCE SCHOOLS *Jul. 1966*
CIJE: 41 RIE: 70 GC: 340
UF Commercial Correspondence Schools
BT Schools
RT Correspondence Study
Distance Education
Extension Education
Part Time Students
Private Schools
Proprietary Schools

CORRESPONDENCE STUDY *Jul. 1966*
CIJE: 264 RIE: 569 GC: 350
SN Method of instruction with teacher student interaction by mail
UF Correspondence Courses (1966 1980)
BT Distance Education
RT Continuing Education
Correspondence Schools
Home Study
Independent Study
Lifelong Learning
Nontraditional Education

CORRIDORS *Jul. 1966*
CIJE: 6 RIE: 16 GC: 920
UF Hallways
BT Facilities
RT School Space
Windowless Rooms

Cosmetic Prostheses (1967 1980)
USE PROSTHESES

Cosmetics Inspectors
USE FOOD AND DRUG INSPECTORS

Cosmetologists (1969 1981)
USE COSMETOLOGY

COSMETOLOGY *Jan. 1969*
CIJE: 6 RIE: 86 GC: 640
UF Beauticians
Beauty Culture
Beauty Operators
Cosmetologists (1969 1981)
BT Technology
RT Service Occupations

Cost Analysis
USE COST EFFECTIVENESS

Cost Benefit Analysis
USE COST EFFECTIVENESS

COST EFFECTIVENESS *Jul. 1966*
CIJE: 2501 RIE: 3380 GC: 620
SN Evaluation of the monetary gains and losses associated with various decisions, outcomes, or actions
UF Benefit Cost Analysis
Cost Analysis
Cost Benefit Analysis
Cost Effectiveness Analysis
Cost Utility Analysis
BT Evaluation Methods
RT Accountability
Cost Estimates
Costs
Efficiency
Expenditures
Input Output Analysis
Job Simplification
Life Cycle Costing
Operations Research
Organizational Effectiveness
Program Effectiveness
Resource Allocation
Retrenchment
Risk
School Effectiveness
Systems Analysis

Cost Effectiveness Analysis
USE COST EFFECTIVENESS

COST ESTIMATES *Mar. 1980*
CIJE: 139 RIE: 416 GC: 620
UF Estimated Costs (1966 1980)
BT Costs
RT Budgeting
Cost Effectiveness
Program Costs
Unit Costs

COST INDEXES *Jul. 1974*
CIJE: 87 RIE: 145 GC: 620
SN Measures of the difference in cost or price (prices of consumer goods, school costs, etc.) from that which existed during a designated base period
UF Index Numbers (Costs)
Price Indexes
RT Costs
Economic Change
Economics
Expenditures
Inflation (Economics)

Cost Utility Analysis
USE COST EFFECTIVENESS

COSTS *Jul. 1966*
CIJE: 1375 RIE: 1790 GC: 620
SN Amount charged, but not necessarily paid, for something (note: do not confuse with "expenditures" -- prior to mar80, the use of this term was not restricted by a scope note)
UF Police Costs (1966 1980) #
NT Construction Costs
Cost Estimates
Fees
Interest (Finance)
Legal Costs
Program Costs
Student Costs
Unit Costs
RT Compensation (Remuneration)
Cost Effectiveness
Cost Indexes
Educational Finance
Expenditure Per Student
Expenditures
Inflation (Economics)
Library Expenditures
Loan Repayment
Operating Expenses
Ownership
Private Financial Support
Retrenchment
Salaries
School District Spending

Costume Design
USE CLOTHING DESIGN

Cottage Parents
USE RESIDENT ADVISERS

COUNSELING *Jul. 1966*
CIJE: 1844 RIE: 1372 GC: 240
SN Process of helping individuals and groups understand and cope with adjustment problems -- involves giving advice, information, or encouragement, engaging in therapeutic discussions, or administering and interpreting tests (note: "counseling" is one aspect of the total process of "guidance")
UF Counseling Process
NT Adult Counseling
Career Counseling
Cocounseling
Educational Counseling
Family Counseling
Group Counseling
Individual Counseling
Marriage Counseling
Nondirective Counseling
Parent Counseling
Peer Counseling
Rehabilitation Counseling
School Counseling
BT Guidance
RT Adjustment (To Environment)
Behavior Modification
Case Studies
Cognitive Restructuring
Consultation Programs
Counseling Effectiveness
Counseling Objectives
Counseling Services
Counseling Techniques
Counseling Theories
Counselor Client Relationship
Counselors
Crisis Intervention
Guidance Centers
Helping Relationship
Microcounseling
Ombudsmen
Outcomes Of Treatment
Psychotherapy
Rehabilitation
Social Support Groups
Social Work
Termination Of Treatment
Therapeutic Environment

Counseling Centers (1966 1977)
USE GUIDANCE CENTERS

COUNSELING EFFECTIVENESS *Jul. 1966*
CIJE: 1789 RIE: 715 GC: 240
RT Counseling
Counseling Objectives
Counseling Techniques
Counselor Performance
Counselor Role
Outcomes Of Treatment

Counseling Goals (1966 1980)
USE COUNSELING OBJECTIVES

COUNSELING INSTRUCTIONAL PROGRAMS (1967 1980) *Mar. 1980*
CIJE: 27 RIE: 67 GC: 240
SN Invalid descriptor -- used for both counseling-instructional programs for students and counselor training -- see such descriptors as "counselor teacher cooperation" and "counselor training"

Counseling Methods
USE COUNSELING TECHNIQUES

COUNSELING OBJECTIVES *Mar. 1980*
CIJE: 452 RIE: 266 GC: 240
SN Aims or ends toward which the counseling process (one aspect of the total process of "guidance") is directed
UF Counseling Goals (1966 1980)
BT Guidance Objectives
RT Behavioral Objectives
Counseling
Counseling Effectiveness

Counseling Process
USE COUNSELING

Counseling Programs (1966 1980)
USE COUNSELING SERVICES

COUNSELING SERVICES *Jul. 1966*
CIJE: 1514 RIE: 1594 GC: 240
SN Organized activities designed to help individuals or groups understand and cope with adjustment problems
UF Counseling Programs (1966 1980)
Evening Counseling Programs (1966 1980) #
BT Human Services
RT Ancillary School Services
Counseling
Counselor Characteristics
Counselors
Employee Assistance Programs
Guidance Centers
Hotlines (Public)
Individualized Programs

= Two or more Descriptors are used to represent this term.
The term's main entry shows the appropriate coordination.

Outplacement Services (Employment)
Outreach Programs
Psychiatric Services
Pupil Personnel Services
Pupil Personnel Workers
Student Personnel Services
Student Personnel Workers

COUNSELING TECHNIQUES *Mar. 1980*
CIJE: 1546 RIE: 550 GC: 240
SN Methods, procedures, and approaches used by counselors in working with clients (note: prior to mar80, the instruction "counseling techniques, use counseling" was carried in the thesaurus)
UF Counseling Methods
BT Methods
RT Assertiveness
Caseworker Approach
Conditioning
Counseling
Counseling Effectiveness
Counseling Theories
Counselor Client Relationship
Counselor Role
Desensitization
Empathy
Gestalt Therapy
Interviews
Laboratory Training
Microcounseling
Modeling (Psychology)
Rapport
Reality Therapy
Role Playing
Self Disclosure (Individuals)
Sensitivity Training
Simulation
Stress Management
Transactional Analysis

COUNSELING THEORIES *Jul. 1966*
CIJE: 555 RIE: 183 GC: 240
BT Theories
RT Behavior
Behavior Theories
Counseling
Counseling Techniques
Nondirective Counseling

Counselor Acceptance (1968 1980)
USE COUNSELOR CLIENT RELATIONSHIP

COUNSELOR ATTITUDES *Sep. 1968*
CIJE: 681 RIE: 342 GC: 240
SN Attitudes of, not toward, counselors
UF Counselor Opinion
Counselor Reaction
BT Attitudes
RT Counselor Characteristics
Counselor Client Relationship
Counselor Evaluation
Counselor Performance
Counselors

Counselor Background
USE COUNSELOR CHARACTERISTICS

COUNSELOR CERTIFICATION *Jul. 1966*
CIJE: 93 RIE: 64 GC: 240
UF Counselor Licensing
BT Certification
RT Counselor Evaluation
Counselor Qualifications
Counselors

COUNSELOR CHARACTERISTICS *Jul. 1966*
CIJE: 611 RIE: 196 GC: 240
SN Physical and psychological characteristics of counselors, e.g., personality traits, values, experience, age, race, sex (note: do not confuse with "counselor qualifications")
UF Counselor Background
RT Counseling Services
Counselor Attitudes
Counselor Client Relationship
Counselor Evaluation
Counselor Performance
Counselor Qualifications
Counselor Role
Counselors
Counselor Selection
Individual Characteristics

COUNSELOR CLIENT RATIO *Jul. 1966*
CIJE: 19 RIE: 14 GC: 240
UF Client Counselor Ratio
BT Ratios (Mathematics)
RT Counselors

COUNSELOR CLIENT RELATIONSHIP *Mar. 1980*
CIJE: 713 RIE: 254 GC: 240
UF Client Counselor Relationship
Counselor Acceptance (1968 1980)
BT Interpersonal Relationship
RT Client Characteristics (Human Services)
Counseling
Counseling Techniques
Counselor Attitudes
Counselor Characteristics
Counselor Role
Counselors
Helping Relationship
Physician Patient Relationship
Therapeutic Environment

Counselor Education
USE COUNSELOR TRAINING

COUNSELOR EDUCATORS *Jul. 1966*
CIJE: 277 RIE: 108 GC: 360
SN Members of a college or university faculty who are primarily concerned with the preparation of counselors
BT College Faculty
RT Counselor Evaluation
Counselor Training
Practicum Supervision
Professors

COUNSELOR EVALUATION *Jul. 1966*
CIJE: 330 RIE: 226 GC: 240
SN Process of judging counselor performance as related to established criteria
BT Personnel Evaluation
RT Counselor Attitudes
Counselor Certification
Counselor Characteristics
Counselor Educators
Counselor Performance
Counselor Qualifications
Counselors
Counselor Selection

Counselor Functions (1967 1977)
USE COUNSELOR ROLE

Counselor Licensing
USE COUNSELOR CERTIFICATION

Counselor Opinion
USE COUNSELOR ATTITUDES

COUNSELOR PERFORMANCE *Jul. 1966*
CIJE: 486 RIE: 201 GC: 240
BT Performance
RT Counseling Effectiveness
Counselor Attitudes
Counselor Characteristics
Counselor Evaluation
Counselor Qualifications
Counselor Role
Counselors

Counselor Preparation
USE COUNSELOR TRAINING

COUNSELOR QUALIFICATIONS *Jul. 1966*
CIJE: 169 RIE: 85 GC: 240
SN Abilities, aptitudes, or achievements that suit counselors for professional practice or employment, especially including the legal and educational requirements for counseling positions (note: do not confuse with "counselor characteristics")
BT Qualifications
RT Counselor Certification
Counselor Characteristics
Counselor Evaluation
Counselor Performance
Counselors
Counselor Selection
Employment Qualifications

Counselor Reaction
USE COUNSELOR ATTITUDES

COUNSELOR ROLE *Jul. 1966*
CIJE: 2881 RIE: 1136 GC: 240
UF Counselor Functions (1967 1977)
RT Confidentiality
Counseling Effectiveness
Counseling Techniques
Counselor Characteristics
Counselor Client Relationship
Counselor Performance
Counselors
Staff Role

COUNSELOR SELECTION *Nov. 1969*
CIJE: 70 RIE: 29 GC: 240
SN Selection of counselors for employment (note: prior to mar80, this term was not scoped and was occasionally used for counselor selection of clients)
BT Personnel Selection
RT Counselor Characteristics
Counselor Evaluation
Counselor Qualifications
Counselors
Counselor Training

COUNSELOR TEACHER COOPERATION *Mar. 1980*
CIJE: 107 RIE: 43 GC: 240
UF Teacher Counselor Cooperation
BT Educational Cooperation
RT Consultation Programs
Cooperative Planning
Diagnostic Teaching
Educational Diagnosis
Psychoeducational Methods
School Counseling
School Counselors
School Guidance
Teacher Guidance
Teachers

COUNSELOR TRAINING *Jul. 1966*
CIJE: 1694 RIE: 998 GC: 240
SN Any formal or informal program that develops counseling skills of professionals or nonprofessionals
UF Counselor Education
Counselor Preparation
BT Training
RT Counselor Educators
Counselors
Counselor Selection
Microcounseling
Practicums

COUNSELORS *Jul. 1966*
CIJE: 1525 RIE: 786 GC: 240
UF Special Counselors (1966 1980) #
NT Adjustment Counselors
Employment Counselors
School Counselors
BT Guidance Personnel
RT Adult Counseling
Caseworkers
Consultants
Counseling
Counseling Services
Counselor Attitudes
Counselor Certification
Counselor Characteristics
Counselor Client Ratio
Counselor Client Relationship
Counselor Evaluation
Counselor Performance
Counselor Qualifications
Counselor Role
Counselor Selection
Counselor Training
Parole Officers
Probation Officers
Psychologists
Social Workers
Specialists

Counting
USE COMPUTATION

County Extension Agents
USE EXTENSION AGENTS

County Government
USE LOCAL GOVERNMENT

County History
USE LOCAL HISTORY

COUNTY LIBRARIES *Mar. 1969*
CIJE: 7 RIE: 80 GC: 710
BT Public Libraries
RT Branch Libraries
Regional Libraries

County Norms
USE LOCAL NORMS

COUNTY OFFICIALS *Jul. 1966*
CIJE: 16 RIE: 45 GC: 610
BT Public Officials
RT City Officials
Extension Agents
Legislators
Local Government
State Officials

COUNTY PROGRAMS *Jul. 1970*
CIJE: 43 RIE: 134 GC: 610
BT Programs
RT Community Programs
Federal Programs
Regional Programs
State Programs

COUNTY SCHOOL DISTRICTS *Mar. 1980*
CIJE: 27 RIE: 166 GC: 340
SN School systems that encompass the public schools (sometimes with specific exceptions) within a county
UF County School Systems (1967 1980)
BT School Districts
RT Boards Of Education
Rural Schools

County School Systems (1967 1980)
USE COUNTY SCHOOL DISTRICTS

COURSE CONTENT *Jul. 1966*
CIJE: 2565 RIE: 3684 GC: 310
SN Subject matter or activities of a course of study
BT Course Organization
RT Content Analysis
Controversial Issues (Course Content)
Course Descriptions
Course Objectives
Curriculum
Curriculum Development
Curriculum Guides
Elective Courses
Program Content
Program Validation
Textbook Content
Validated Programs

COURSE DESCRIPTIONS *Jul. 1966*
CIJE: 3908 RIE: 2852 GC: 730
SN (Note: prior to mar80, the thesaurus carried the instructions, "'course outlines' or 'syllabus,' use 'curriculum guides'")
UF Course Outlines
Syllabi
RT Course Content
Course Objectives
Course Organization
Courses
Curriculum Guides
Profiles
School Catalogs

Course Enrichment
USE CURRICULUM ENRICHMENT

COURSE EVALUATION *Jul. 1966*
CIJE: 1167 RIE: 1162 GC: 310
BT Evaluation
RT Course Objectives
Course Organization
Courses
Course Selection (Students)
Curriculum Evaluation
Instructional Effectiveness
Instructional Material Evaluation
Program Evaluation
Program Validation
Student Evaluation
Student Evaluation Of Teacher Performance
Summative Evaluation
Teacher Evaluation
Validated Programs

= Two or more Descriptors are used to represent this term.
The term's main entry shows the appropriate coordination.

COURSE OBJECTIVES *Jul. 1966*
CIJE: 886 RIE: 1695 GC: 310
BT Objectives
RT Behavioral Objectives
Course Content
Course Descriptions
Course Evaluation
Courses

Course Of Instruction
USE COURSE ORGANIZATION

COURSE ORGANIZATION *Jul. 1966*
CIJE: 669 RIE: 802 GC: 310
SN General plan of instruction prepared by the teacher for use with particular groups of students for a specific period of time (note: use a more specific term if possible)
UF Course Of Instruction
NT Course Content
BT Organization
RT Class Organization
Course Descriptions
Course Evaluation
Courses
Study Guides
Teaching Methods

Course Outlines
USE COURSE DESCRIPTIONS

COURSE SELECTION (STUDENTS) *Aug. 1986*
CIJE: RIE: GC: 320
SN Student choice of an instructional class or course, or of a class/course cluster
BT Selection
RT Course Evaluation
Courses
Curriculum Design
Decision Making
Elective Courses
Enrollment Influences
Majors (Students)
Nonmajors
Relevance (Education)
Required Courses
Student Educational Objectives
Student Interests
Student Needs

Course Withdrawal
USE WITHDRAWAL (EDUCATION)

COURSES *Jul. 1966*
CIJE: 483 RIE: 582 GC: 350
SN Educational units within the curriculum dealing systematically with a particular subject or discipline for a given period of time (note: use a more specific term if possible)
NT Advanced Courses
Conversational Language Courses
Credit Courses
Education Courses
Elective Courses
Intensive Language Courses
Introductory Courses
Methods Courses
Minicourses
Noncredit Courses
Practicums
Refresher Courses
Required Courses
Telecourses
United States Government (Course)
Units Of Study
BT Curriculum
RT Auditing (Coursework)
Course Descriptions
Course Evaluation
Course Objectives
Course Organization
Course Selection (Students)
Courseware
Intellectual Disciplines

COURSEWARE *Jun. 1984*
CIJE: 161 RIE: 171 GC: 720
SN Computer software and accompanying documentation written for instructional applications (note: prior to jun84, this concept was indexed by "computer programs," postings of which have since been merged to "computer software")
UF Courseware Reviews #
Instructional Software
BT Computer Software
Instructional Materials
RT Audiovisual Aids
Autoinstructional Aids
Computer Assisted Instruction
Computer Software Reviews
Courses
Programed Instructional Materials
Teaching Machines

Courseware Reviews
USE COMPUTER SOFTWARE REVIEWS; COURSEWARE

Court Action
USE COURT LITIGATION

Court Cases (1966 1980)
USE COURT LITIGATION

Court Decisions
USE COURT LITIGATION

COURT DOCTRINE *Jul. 1966*
CIJE: 112 RIE: 81 GC: 610
BT Standards
RT Courts
Public Policy

COURT JUDGES *Aug. 1980*
CIJE: 42 RIE: 40 GC: 610
SN Public officials authorized to hear and decide cases in courts of law
UF Magistrates
BT Judges
Public Officials
RT Compliance (Legal)
Court Litigation
Courts
Hearings
Justice
Lawyers
Legal Responsibility
Legislators
Sentencing

COURT LITIGATION *Jul. 1966*
CIJE: 3708 RIE: 2575 GC: 610
SN Legal action or process in a court
UF Court Action
Court Cases (1966 1980)
Court Decisions
Federal Court Litigation (1966 1980) #
Judicial Action
Legal Decisions
Legal Judgment
Litigation
State Court Litigation #
NT Desegregation Litigation
RT Compliance (Legal)
Court Judges
Court Reporters
Courts
Educational Malpractice
Federal Courts
Juvenile Courts
Laws
Lawyers
Legal Problems
Legal Responsibility
Malpractice
State Courts
Torts

COURT REPORTERS *Jul. 1966*
CIJE: 6 RIE: 13 GC: 640
SN Workers involved in the recording (by stenotype) and transcription of legal proceedings
BT Clerical Workers
RT Court Litigation
Courts
Shorthand
Typewriting

COURT ROLE *Jul. 1966*
CIJE: 262 RIE: 252 GC: 610
UF Judicial Role
BT Institutional Role
RT Courts
Government Role

COURTS *Jul. 1966*
CIJE: 87 RIE: 178 GC: 610
NT Federal Courts
Juvenile Courts
State Courts
BT Institutions
RT Court Doctrine
Court Judges
Court Litigation
Court Reporters
Court Role
Equal Protection
Hearings
Justice
Laws
Sentencing

COVERT RESPONSE *Jul. 1966*
CIJE: 23 RIE: 38 GC: 110
BT Responses
RT Overt Response

Cpr (Medicine)
USE CARDIOPULMONARY RESUSCITATION

CRAFT WORKERS *Apr. 1981*
CIJE: 31 RIE: 21 GC: 640
UF Artisans
Craftsmen (1970 1981)
BT Skilled Workers
RT Building Trades
Design Crafts
Handicrafts
Industrial Arts
Needle Trades

Crafts
USE HANDICRAFTS

Crafts Rooms (1966 1980)
USE EDUCATIONAL FACILITIES; HANDICRAFTS

Craftsmen (1970 1981)
USE CRAFT WORKERS

CREATIONISM *May. 1981*
CIJE: 175 RIE: 50 GC: 430
SN Theory or belief that the universe and various forms of life were created by a transcendent god out of nothing -- also, the theological doctrine that god creates a new human soul for each individual born
UF Scientific Creationism
Special Creation Theory
RT Evolution
Religion
Religious Factors

Creative Ability (1968 1980)
USE CREATIVITY

CREATIVE ACTIVITIES *Jul. 1966*
CIJE: 520 RIE: 342 GC: 310
NT Brainstorming
Creative Art
Creative Expression
Creative Writing
BT Activities
RT Art Activities
Creative Development
Creativity
Enrichment Activities
Handicrafts

CREATIVE ART *Jul. 1966*
CIJE: 275 RIE: 127 GC: 420
SN Art involving original thought, imagination, structural ogranization, and personal expression or interpretation -- also includes programs encouraging creative art
NT Creative Dramatics
BT Art
Creative Activities
RT Art Activities
Art Therapy
Childrens Art
Freehand Drawing
Surrealism

CREATIVE DEVELOPMENT *Jul. 1966*
CIJE: 549 RIE: 320 GC: 120
SN Development of creative skills and aptitudes
BT Individual Development
RT Creative Activities
Creativity
Creativity Tests
Intellectual Development
Talent Development

CREATIVE DRAMATICS *Jul. 1966*
CIJE: 272 RIE: 234 GC: 420
SN Activities where participants create informal, nonscripted plays using their own words and movements
BT Creative Art
Dramatics
RT Acting
Dramatic Play
Pantomime
Readers Theater
Skits

CREATIVE EXPRESSION *Jul. 1966*
CIJE: 495 RIE: 292 GC: 420
BT Creative Activities
RT Creativity
Creativity Tests
Self Expression

CREATIVE READING (1966 1980) *Mar. 1980*
CIJE: 49 RIE: 57 GC: 460
SN Invalid descriptor -- used inconsistently in indexing -- see such descriptors as "oral interpretation," "critical reading," "creative thinking," etc.

CREATIVE TEACHING *Jul. 1966*
CIJE: 266 RIE: 166 GC: 310
SN Development and use of novel, original, or inventive teaching methods (note: refers to teaching that results from the teacher's creativity, not to teaching that is intended to develop the learner's creativity)
BT Teaching Methods
RT Creativity
Instructional Innovation

CREATIVE THINKING *Jul. 1966*
CIJE: 683 RIE: 449 GC: 110
NT Divergent Thinking
Productive Thinking
BT Cognitive Processes
RT Concept Formation
Creativity
Creativity Tests
Discovery Processes
Heuristics
Imagination
Intuition
Inventions
Problem Solving
Transcendental Meditation
Visualization

Creative Thinking Tests
USE CREATIVITY TESTS

CREATIVE WRITING *Jul. 1966*
CIJE: 1007 RIE: 741 GC: 400
SN Writing characterized by originality, imaginativeness, and expressiveness
BT Creative Activities
Writing (Composition)
RT Descriptive Writing
Expository Writing
Heuristics
Literary Devices
Playwriting
Poetry
Prose
Rhetorical Invention
Student Writing Models

CREATIVITY *Jul. 1966*
CIJE: 2059 RIE: 1098 GC: 120
SN The attribute of constructive originality, often manifested in the ability to discover new solutions to problems or find new modes of artistic expression
UF Creative Ability (1968 1980)
Originality (1966 1980)
NT Imagination
BT Psychological Characteristics

= Two or more Descriptors are used to represent this term.
The term's main entry shows the appropriate coordination.

RT Art Expression
Auteurism
Concept Formation
Creative Activities
Creative Development
Creative Expression
Creative Teaching
Creative Thinking
Creativity Research
Creativity Tests
Discovery Processes
Individualism
Intelligence
Inventions
Personality Traits
Rhetorical Invention
Self Expression
Talent

Creativity Measures
USE CREATIVITY TESTS

CREATIVITY RESEARCH *Jul. 1966*
CIJE: 209 RIE: 215 GC: 810
SN Basic, applied, and developmental research conducted to advance knowledge about constructive originality (note: as of oct81, use as a minor descriptor for examples of this kind of research -- use as a major descriptor only as the subject of a document)
BT Research
RT Creativity
Creativity Tests

CREATIVITY TESTS *Mar. 1971*
CIJE: 173 RIE: 121 GC: 830
SN Tests used to indicate an individual's originality, inventiveness, or imagination
UF Creative Thinking Tests
Creativity Measures
BT Tests
RT Creative Development
Creative Expression
Creative Thinking
Creativity
Creativity Research
Intelligence Tests
Projective Measures
Talent Identification

CREDENTIALS *Jul. 1966*
CIJE: 176 RIE: 221 GC: 340
NT Educational Certificates
Portfolios (Background Materials)
Resumes (Personal)
BT Records (Forms)
RT Background
Certification
Continuing Education Units
Degrees (Academic)
Equivalency Tests
Evaluation
Experience
Prerequisites
Qualifications
Reputation
Selection
Special Degree Programs
Standards

CREDIBILITY *Dec. 1974*
CIJE: 332 RIE: 271 GC: 520
SN Compatibility of a statement or situation with what is generally perceived as true or possible
UF Believability
Source Credibility
Trustworthiness
BT Relationship
RT Beliefs
Communication (Thought Transfer)
Communication Skills
Deception
Ethics
Integrity
Interpersonal Relationship
Opinions
Persuasive Discourse
Political Attitudes
Psychological Patterns
Public Opinion
Reputation
Trust (Psychology)
Values

CREDIT (FINANCE) *Aug. 1968*
CIJE: 79 RIE: 288 GC: 620
RT Economics
Eligibility
Financial Aid Applicants
Financial Needs
Financial Services
Financial Support
Interest (Finance)
Investment
Loan Repayment
Merchandising
Money Management
Ownership
Student Loan Programs

Credit By Examination
USE EQUIVALENCY TESTS

CREDIT COURSES *Jul. 1966*
CIJE: 118 RIE: 287 GC: 350
BT Courses
RT College Credits
Credits
Grades (Scholastic)
Noncredit Courses

CREDIT NO CREDIT GRADING *Sep. 1971*
CIJE: 20 RIE: 39 GC: 320
SN Grading system in which a student's failure either is not recorded or is recorded as "no credit," which does not affect his or her grade point average, and students who pass are given regular grades
UF Pass No Credit Grading
Pass No Record Grading
BT Grading
RT College Credits
Credits
Cutting Scores
Grades (Scholastic)
Nongraded Student Evaluation
Pass Fail Grading

CREDITS *Jul. 1966*
CIJE: 94 RIE: 224 GC: 340
SN Units for expressing quantitatively the work completed by a student (note: for postsecondary students, use "college credits")
UF Student Credit Hours
NT College Credits
Continuing Education Units
RT Academic Records
Auditing (Coursework)
Certification
Credit Courses
Credit No Credit Grading
Educational Certificates
Experiential Learning
Grades (Scholastic)
Graduation Requirements
Pass Fail Grading
Prerequisites
Prior Learning
Required Courses
Transfer Policy
Transfer Programs

CREE *Apr. 1969*
CIJE: 9 RIE: 17 GC: 440
BT American Indian Languages

CREOLES *Jul. 1966*
CIJE: 83 RIE: 103 GC: 440
SN Mixed natural languages--composed of elements of different languages in areas of intensive language contact--that develop from pidgins and have native speakers
NT Gullah
Haitian Creole
Mauritian Creole
Sierra Leone Creole
BT Languages
Language Variation
RT Linguistic Borrowing
Pidgins

CREW LEADERS *Jul. 1966*
CIJE: 3 RIE: 16 GC: 410
UF Farm Foremen
BT Supervisors
RT Agricultural Laborers
Migrant Workers

CRIME *Jul. 1966*
CIJE: 449 RIE: 547 GC: 530
NT Delinquency
International Crimes
BT Antisocial Behavior
RT Aggression
Alarm Systems
Correctional Institutions
Correctional Rehabilitation
Crime Prevention
Criminal Law
Criminals
Criminology
Drug Addiction
Family Violence
Fines (Penalties)
Illegal Drug Use
Incest
Juvenile Courts
Law Enforcement
Malpractice
Parole Officers
Police
Police Action
Polygraphs
Probation Officers
Rape
School Security
Search And Seizure
Security Personnel
Sentencing
Stealing
Terrorism
Vandalism
Victims Of Crime
Violence

CRIME PREVENTION *Mar. 1982*
CIJE: 51 RIE: 76 GC: 520
SN Measures taken to forestall a delinquent or criminal act
NT Delinquency Prevention
BT Prevention
RT Alarm Systems
Community Programs
Correctional Rehabilitation
Crime
Criminal Law
Criminals
Law Enforcement
Police
Police Action
Police Community Relationship
Police School Relationship
School Security
Security Personnel

CRIMINAL LAW *Dec. 1974*
CIJE: 85 RIE: 181 GC: 610
SN Branch of jurisprudence that relates to crimes and their punishments
BT Laws
RT Crime
Crime Prevention
Criminals
Criminology
Law Enforcement
Law Related Education
Legal Education (Professions)
Police
Police Education
Sentencing

CRIMINALS *Jul. 1966*
CIJE: 255 RIE: 185 GC: 530
UF Convicts
BT Groups
RT Correctional Education
Correctional Institutions
Correctional Rehabilitation
Crime
Crime Prevention
Criminal Law
Delinquency
Prisoners
Recidivism
Sentencing

CRIMINOLOGY *May. 1969*
CIJE: 80 RIE: 78 GC: 400
BT Sociology
RT Correctional Institutions
Correctional Rehabilitation
Crime
Criminal Law
Prisoners
Social Psychology

Crippled Children (1968 1980)
USE PHYSICAL DISABILITIES

CRISIS INTERVENTION *Mar. 1980*
CIJE: 266 RIE: 189 GC: 230
UF Crisis Therapy (1969 1980)
BT Intervention
RT Counseling
Hotlines (Public)
Psychiatric Services
Psychotherapy

Crisis Therapy (1969 1980)
USE CRISIS INTERVENTION

CRITERIA *Jul. 1966*
CIJE: 329 RIE: 399 GC: 520
SN Objective things, specifications, or requirements by reference to which judgments are made or confirmed
NT Admission Criteria
Evaluation Criteria
Lesson Observation Criteria
BT Standards
RT Predictor Variables
Prerequisites
Quotas
Specifications

Criterion Referenced Education
USE COMPETENCY BASED EDUCATION

Criterion Referenced Teacher Education
USE COMPETENCY BASED TEACHER EDUCATION

CRITERION REFERENCED TESTS *Sep. 1970*
CIJE: 531 RIE: 1382 GC: 830
SN Tests in which the items are linked to explicitly stated objectives and where the scores are interpreted in terms of these objectives rather than a group norm
UF Objective Referenced Tests
NT Mastery Tests
BT Tests
RT Achievement Tests
Cutting Scores
Diagnostic Tests
Informal Reading Inventories
Item Banks
Measurement Techniques
Norm Referenced Tests
Performance Tests
Standardized Tests
Test Construction
Test Interpretation

Criterion Validity (Concurrent)
USE CONCURRENT VALIDITY

Criterion Validity (Predictive)
USE PREDICTIVE VALIDITY

CRITICAL INCIDENTS METHOD *Jul. 1966*
CIJE: 49 RIE: 103 GC: 820
SN Procedure used to gather examples of effective or ineffective behavior with respect to a designated activity to determine the requirements for its success
BT Methods
RT Ability Identification
Evaluation Methods
Job Analysis
Observation
Problem Solving
Research Methodology
Simulation
Skill Analysis
Task Analysis

CRITICAL PATH METHOD *Jul. 1966*
CIJE: 64 RIE: 108 GC: 320
SN Technique used to coordinate and schedule the sequential activities of a project to complete it as efficiently and quickly as possible (note: see also the identifier "program evaluation and review technique" -- prior to mar80, the instruction "path analysis, use critical path method" was carried in the thesaurus)
BT Methods
RT Construction Management
Fast Track Scheduling
Flow Charts
Graphs

Management Systems
Operations Research
Planning
Scheduling
Sequential Approach
Systems Analysis

CRITICAL READING *Jul. 1966*
CIJE: 473 RIE: 461 GC: 460
SN Reading carefully to thoroughly comprehend and evaluate what is read
BT Reading
RT Content Area Reading
Inferences
Literary Criticism
Reading Comprehension

Critical Scores
USE CUTTING SCORES

CRITICAL THINKING *Jul. 1966*
CIJE: 1449 RIE: 863 GC: 110
NT Evaluative Thinking
BT Cognitive Processes
RT Citizenship Education
Controversial Issues (Course Content)
Convergent Thinking
Decision Making
Formal Operations
Heuristics
Inferences
Logical Thinking
Problem Solving
Productive Thinking

Crop Harvesting
USE HARVESTING

Crop Planting
USE AGRONOMY; HORTICULTURE

CROP PROCESSING OCCUPATIONS *Jan. 1969*
CIJE: 4 RIE: 15 GC: 410
UF Grain Elevator Occupations
BT Off Farm Agricultural Occupations
RT Agricultural Production
Agronomy
Field Crops
Harvesting

Crop Production
USE AGRICULTURAL PRODUCTION

Cross Age Helping
USE CROSS AGE TEACHING

CROSS AGE TEACHING *Oct. 1968*
CIJE: 176 RIE: 210 GC: 310
SN Utilization of older students from higher grade levels to provide increased help and attention for younger students at lower grade levels
UF Cross Age Helping
BT Teaching Methods
RT Interpersonal Relationship
Peer Teaching
Remedial Instruction
Social Experience
Socialization
Tutorial Programs
Tutoring

Cross Cultural Communication
USE INTERCULTURAL COMMUNICATION

CROSS CULTURAL STUDIES *Aug. 1969*
CIJE: 1653 RIE: 1783 GC: 400
SN Systematic efforts to compare sociological, psychological, anthropological...aspects of two or more cultural groups, either within the same country or in different countries
UF Cultural Comparisons
BT Research
RT Anthropology
Area Studies
Biculturalism
Bidialectalism
Bilingualism
Comparative Analysis
Comparative Education
Contrastive Linguistics
Cultural Background
Cultural Context
Cultural Differences
Cultural Education
Cultural Exchange
Cultural Influences
Cultural Interrelationships
Cultural Pluralism
Cultural Traits
Culture
Culture Conflict
Culture Contact
Culture Fair Tests
Ethnic Groups
Ethnicity
Ethnic Relations
Ethnic Studies
Ethnology
Folk Culture
Foreign Culture
Human Geography
Intercultural Programs
Intergroup Relations
International Education
International Studies
Migrants
Minority Groups
Multicultural Education
Multicultural Textbooks
Multilingualism
Sociocultural Patterns
Sociology
Subcultures
Urban Culture

Cross Cultural Tests
USE CULTURE FAIR TESTS

CROSS CULTURAL TRAINING *Jul. 1966*
CIJE: 343 RIE: 687 GC: 400
SN Training in communicative, behavioral, and attitudinal skills required for successful interaction with individuals of other cultures -- often used with personnel about to undertake overseas assignments (note: prior to jan79, "cross cultural training" was frequently used for "multicultural education")
UF Bicultural Training
Multicultural Training
Multiethnic Training
BT Training
RT Biculturalism
Cultural Awareness
Cultural Background
Cultural Differences
Cultural Education
Cultural Interrelationships
Cultural Pluralism
Culture
Culture Contact
Ethnic Relations
Exchange Programs
Foreign Culture
Indigenous Personnel
Intercultural Communication
Intercultural Programs
Interdisciplinary Approach
Intergroup Relations
International Educational Exchange
International Relations
Multicultural Education
Social Integration
Sociocultural Patterns

Cross Eyes
USE STRABISMUS

CROSS SECTIONAL STUDIES *Apr. 1970*
CIJE: 95 RIE: 102 GC: 810
SN Studies that establish norms by assessing large groups of people, practices, or programs at a given time, as differentiated from longitudinal studies of groups, etc. at various times (note: as of oct81, use as a minor descriptor for examples of this kind of research -- use as a major descriptor only as the subject of a document)
BT Case Studies
RT Cohort Analysis
Longitudinal Studies
Norms
Sampling

CROWDING *Mar. 1982*
CIJE: 35 RIE: 22 GC: 520
SN Excessive number of individuals or entities in relation to available space
RT Class Size
Ecological Factors
Environmental Influences
Environmental Standards
Overpopulation
Personal Space
Physical Environment
Physical Mobility
Proximity
Social Behavior
Space Utilization
Stress Variables
Urban Environment

Crude Scores
USE RAW SCORES

CRYSTALLOGRAPHY *Aug. 1982*
CIJE: 31 RIE: 10 GC: 490
SN The science of crystal structure and phenomena
BT Physical Sciences
RT Atomic Structure
Chemical Bonding
Chemistry
Earth Science
Electronics
Geology
Matter
Metallurgy
Mineralogy
Molecular Structure
Optics
Physics
Radiology
Semiconductor Devices
Spectroscopy
Structural Analysis (Science)

Cuban Americans
USE CUBANS; HISPANIC AMERICANS

CUBANS *Jun. 1973*
CIJE: 72 RIE: 165 GC: 560
UF Cuban Americans #
BT Latin Americans
RT Ethnic Groups
Hispanic Americans
Spanish Speaking

Cubic Measure
USE VOLUME (MATHEMATICS)

Cue Cards
USE CUES

CUED SPEECH *Apr. 1969*
CIJE: 14 RIE: 11 GC: 220
SN Method of language learning for the deaf utilizing manual configurations as a supplement to lipreading
BT Manual Communication
RT Deaf Interpreting
Finger Spelling
Lipreading
Oral Communication Method
Speech
Visual Learning

CUES *Oct. 1968*
CIJE: 876 RIE: 306 GC: 110
UF Clues
Cue Cards
Prompts
NT Context Clues
BT Stimuli
RT Dimensional Preference
Memory
Miscue Analysis
Mnemonics
Notetaking
Prompting
Recall (Psychology)
Retention (Psychology)

Cuing
USE PROMPTING

CULTURAL ACTIVITIES *Jul. 1966*
CIJE: 237 RIE: 444 GC: 560
SN Experiences, events, ceremonies, etc., that increase individuals' knowledge or enjoyment of their own or another group's cultural, social, intellectual, or artistic heritage
UF Cultural Events (1966 1980)
BT Activities
RT Art Activities
Cultural Awareness
Cultural Background
Cultural Education
Cultural Enrichment
Cultural Interrelationships
Cultural Opportunities
Culture
Dance
Enrichment Activities
Fine Arts
Holidays
Multicultural Education
Music Activities
Religion
Theater Arts
Visual Arts

CULTURAL AWARENESS *Jul. 1966*
CIJE: 1558 RIE: 2339 GC: 560
UF Cultural Understanding
RT Area Studies
Biculturalism
Cross Cultural Training
Cultural Activities
Cultural Background
Cultural Images
Cultural Influences
Cultural Opportunities
Cultural Pluralism
Culture
Culture Conflict
Culture Contact
Ethnicity
Freedom Schools
Global Approach
Intercultural Communication
Intercultural Programs
Multicultural Education
Nationalism
Second Language Learning
Student Exchange Programs

CULTURAL BACKGROUND *Jul. 1966*
CIJE: 852 RIE: 1784 GC: 560
SN Collection of mores, folkways, and institutions that constitutes the social heritage of an individual or group
UF Cultural Heritage
Ethnic Heritage
BT Background
RT American Indian Studies
Biculturalism
Black Studies
Cross Cultural Studies
Cross Cultural Training
Cultural Activities
Cultural Awareness
Cultural Education
Cultural Pluralism
Cultural Traits
Culture
Ethnic Groups
Ethnic Origins
Ethnic Studies
Ethnology
Indigenous Populations
Multicultural Education
Non Western Civilization
Western Civilization

CULTURAL CENTERS *Jul. 1966*
CIJE: 48 RIE: 77 GC: 920
BT Resource Centers
RT Arts Centers
Cultural Enrichment
Culture
Museums

Cultural Characteristics
USE CULTURAL TRAITS

Cultural Comparisons
USE CROSS CULTURAL STUDIES

CULTURAL CONTEXT *Jul. 1966*
CIJE: 1020 RIE: 1066 GC: 560
UF Cultural Environment (1966 1980)
BT Environment
RT Aesthetic Values
Anthropological Linguistics
Biculturalism
Cross Cultural Studies
Cultural Influences
Cultural Isolation
Cultural Traits
Culture
Culture Contact
Educational Anthropology
Ethnography
Ethnology

= Two or more Descriptors are used to represent this term.
The term's main entry shows the appropriate coordination.

Holidays
Multicultural Education
Non Western Civilization
Proverbs
Social Characteristics
Social Environment
Social History
Social Structure
Social Values
Sociocultural Patterns
Western Civilization

CULTURAL DIFFERENCES *Jul. 1966*
CIJE: 1824 RIE: 2148 GC: 560
SN (Note: use a more precise term if possible)
UF Cultural Diversity
BT Differences
RT Advantaged
Biculturalism
Cross Cultural Studies
Cross Cultural Training
Cultural Interrelationships
Cultural Pluralism
Cultural Traits
Culture
Ethnic Groups
Ethnicity
Ethnic Relations
Ethnocentrism
Individual Differences
Intercultural Communication
Intermarriage
Minority Groups
Multicultural Education
Nature Nurture Controversy
Racial Attitudes
Racial Differences
Racial Relations
Rural Urban Differences
Social Bias
Social Differences
Subcultures

Cultural Disadvantagement (1966 1980)
USE DISADVANTAGED

Cultural Diversity
USE CULTURAL DIFFERENCES

CULTURAL EDUCATION *Jul. 1966*
CIJE: 740 RIE: 1767 GC: 400
SN Education concerned with a group's cultural, social, intellectual, or artistic heritage
BT Education
RT American Indian Studies
Black Studies
Cross Cultural Studies
Cross Cultural Training
Cultural Activities
Cultural Background
Cultural Enrichment
Culture
Ethnic Groups
Ethnic Studies
Folk Culture
Folk Schools
Freedom Schools
Intercultural Programs
Multicultural Textbooks
Social Studies

CULTURAL ENRICHMENT *Jul. 1966*
CIJE: 403 RIE: 548 GC: 310
BT Enrichment
RT Aesthetic Education
Compensatory Education
Cultural Activities
Cultural Centers
Cultural Education
Cultural Exchange
Culture
Fine Arts
Freedom Schools
Intercultural Programs

Cultural Environment (1966 1980)
USE CULTURAL CONTEXT

Cultural Events (1966 1980)
USE CULTURAL ACTIVITIES

CULTURAL EXCHANGE *Jul. 1966*
CIJE: 226 RIE: 259 GC: 560
UF Cultural Interaction
RT Cross Cultural Studies
Cultural Enrichment
Cultural Influences
Culture
Culture Contact
Exchange Programs
Intercultural Communication
Intercultural Programs
International Educational Exchange

Cultural Factors (1966 1980)
USE CULTURAL INFLUENCES

Cultural Geography
USE HUMAN GEOGRAPHY

Cultural Heritage
USE CULTURAL BACKGROUND

CULTURAL IMAGES *Jul. 1966*
CIJE: 278 RIE: 238 GC: 540
RT American Indian Studies
Black Studies
Cultural Awareness
Cultural Traits
Culture
Ethnic Groups
Ethnicity
Ethnocentrism
Stereotypes

CULTURAL INFLUENCES *Mar. 1980*
CIJE: 2021 RIE: 2226 GC: 520
UF Cultural Factors (1966 1980)
BT Influences
RT Biculturalism
Cross Cultural Studies
Cultural Awareness
Cultural Context
Cultural Exchange
Cultural Interrelationships
Cultural Pluralism
Cultural Traits
Culture
Culture Contact
Culture Lag
Ethnic Studies
Intercultural Programs
Language Role
Life Style
Minority Group Influences
Modernization
Nature Nurture Controversy
Racial Factors
Religious Factors
Social Influences
Sociocultural Patterns
Subcultures
Traditionalism

Cultural Interaction
USE CULTURAL EXCHANGE

CULTURAL INTERRELATIONSHIPS *Jul. 1966*
CIJE: 273 RIE: 424 GC: 560
BT Relationship
RT Biculturalism
Cross Cultural Studies
Cross Cultural Training
Cultural Activities
Cultural Differences
Cultural Influences
Cultural Pluralism
Cultural Traits
Culture
Ethnic Relations
Ethnology
Intercultural Communication
Intercultural Programs
Multicultural Education
Racial Relations
Social Influences
Social Integration
Sociocultural Patterns

CULTURAL ISOLATION *Jul. 1966*
CIJE: 71 RIE: 90 GC: 560
SN A subculture's relative lack of participation in, or communication with, the larger cultural system -- can be internally or externally imposed
RT Alienation
Cultural Context
Culture
Culture Conflict
Culture Contact
Culture Lag
Disadvantaged Environment
Social Isolation
Subcultures

Cultural Lag
USE CULTURE LAG

CULTURAL OPPORTUNITIES *Jul. 1966*
CIJE: 27 RIE: 53 GC: 540
SN Circumstances or conditions that enable individuals or groups to attend or participate in cultural activities
BT Opportunities
RT Cultural Activities
Cultural Awareness
Culture

CULTURAL PLURALISM *Jul. 1966*
CIJE: 770 RIE: 961 GC: 520
UF Multiculturalism
NT Biculturalism
RT Acculturation
Anthropology
Bilingualism
Cross Cultural Studies
Cross Cultural Training
Cultural Awareness
Cultural Background
Cultural Differences
Cultural Influences
Cultural Interrelationships
Culture
Culture Conflict
Culture Contact
Ethnicity
Ethnic Relations
Ethnology
Intercultural Communication
Intercultural Programs
Minority Groups
Multicultural Education
Multilingualism
Racial Relations
Sociocultural Patterns
United States History

CULTURAL TRAITS *Jul. 1966*
CIJE: 289 RIE: 398 GC: 560
UF Cultural Characteristics
RT American Indian Studies
Black Studies
Cross Cultural Studies
Cultural Background
Cultural Context
Cultural Differences
Cultural Images
Cultural Influences
Cultural Interrelationships
Culture
Ethnicity
Ideology
Personal Space
Place Of Residence
Racial Identification
Regional Characteristics
Social Characteristics
Student Subcultures
Subcultures

Cultural Understanding
USE CULTURAL AWARENESS

Culturally Advantaged (1967 1980)
USE ADVANTAGED

Culturally Disadvantaged (1966 1980)
USE DISADVANTAGED

CULTURE *Jul. 1966*
CIJE: 335 RIE: 501 GC: 560
SN Set of patterns, of and for behavior, that regulate interaction and enable mutual communication among a plurality of people, establishing them into a particular and distinct human group -- occasionally used in the more limited sense of the intellectual and aesthetic products of culture (note: use a more specific term if possible)
UF Customs (Culture)
NT African Culture
American Indian Culture
Black Culture
Burmese Culture
Chinese Culture
Dutch Culture
Folk Culture
Foreign Culture
Islamic Culture
Korean Culture
Latin American Culture
Middle Class Culture
Non Western Civilization
North American Culture
Popular Culture
Spanish Culture
Subcultures
Urban Culture
Western Civilization
RT Acculturation
Biculturalism
Cross Cultural Studies
Cross Cultural Training
Cultural Activities
Cultural Awareness
Cultural Background
Cultural Centers
Cultural Context
Cultural Differences
Cultural Education
Cultural Enrichment
Cultural Exchange
Cultural Images
Cultural Influences
Cultural Interrelationships
Cultural Isolation
Cultural Opportunities
Cultural Pluralism
Cultural Traits
Culture Conflict
Culture Contact
Culture Lag
Educational Anthropology
Ethnic Groups
Humanities
Intellectual History
Intercultural Communication
Intercultural Programs
Minority Groups
Multicultural Education
Nonformal Education
Race
Religious Cultural Groups
Social History
Sociocultural Patterns

CULTURE CONFLICT *Jul. 1966*
CIJE: 514 RIE: 705 GC: 520
UF Culture Shock
BT Conflict
RT Biculturalism
Cross Cultural Studies
Cultural Awareness
Cultural Isolation
Cultural Pluralism
Culture
Ethnicity
Ethnocentrism
Family School Relationship
Religious Conflict
Revolution
Social Differences
Social Environment
Values

CULTURE CONTACT *Jul. 1966*
CIJE: 174 RIE: 274 GC: 560
RT Biculturalism
Cross Cultural Studies
Cross Cultural Training
Cultural Awareness
Cultural Context
Cultural Exchange
Cultural Influences
Cultural Isolation
Cultural Pluralism
Culture
Intercultural Communication
Intercultural Programs
Multicultural Education

CULTURE FAIR TESTS *Mar. 1980*
CIJE: 153 RIE: 208 GC: 540
SN Tests designed to minimize the effects of the differing cultures or experiences of national, ethnic, sexual, or socioeconomic groups
UF Cross Cultural Tests
Culture Free Tests (1967 1980)
BT Tests
RT Cross Cultural Studies
Ethnic Groups
Multicultural Education

= Two or more Descriptors are used to represent this term.
The term's main entry shows the appropriate coordination.

Nonverbal Tests
Test Bias
Test Construction
Testing Problems

Culture Free Tests (1967 1980)
USE CULTURE FAIR TESTS

CULTURE LAG *Jul. 1966*
CIJE: 18 RIE: 24 GC: 560
SN Delay that occurs when one part of a culture changes more slowly than another part -- also refers to the strain that results from this discrepancy
UF Cultural Lag
RT Community Change
Cultural Influences
Cultural Isolation
Culture
Developing Nations
Economic Change
Futures (Of Society)
Industrialization
Modernization
Social Change
Sociocultural Patterns
Technological Advancement
Urbanization

Culture Shock
USE CULTURE CONFLICT

CULTURING TECHNIQUES *May. 1969*
CIJE: 97 RIE: 9 GC: 490
SN Cultivation of living cells or micro-organisms in a controlled artificial environment
BT Laboratory Procedures
RT Botany
Cytology
Genetic Engineering
Microbiology
Physiology
Zoology

CURIOSITY *Jul. 1966*
CIJE: 139 RIE: 84 GC: 120
BT Personality Traits
RT Attention
Exploratory Behavior
Interests
Motivation

Current Awareness Services
USE SELECTIVE DISSEMINATION OF INFORMATION

CURRENT EVENTS *Jul. 1966*
CIJE: 216 RIE: 148 GC: 400
RT Citizenship Education
Controversial Issues (Course Content)
Political Science
Social Studies
World Affairs

CURRICULUM *Jul. 1966*
CIJE: 4372 RIE: 5043 GC: 350
SN Plan incorporating a structured series of intended learning outcomes and associated learning experiences -- generally organized as a related combination or series of courses (note: use a more specific term if possible)
UF Curriculum Content
Teaching Areas
NT Area Studies
College Curriculum
Continuous Progress Plan
Core Curriculum
Courses
Elementary School Curriculum
English Curriculum
Ethnic Studies
Experimental Curriculum
Fused Curriculum
Home Economics
Honors Curriculum
Integrated Curriculum
Mathematics Curriculum
Military Science
Modern Language Curriculum
Preschool Curriculum
Science Curriculum
Secondary School Curriculum
Shop Curriculum
Social Studies
Speech Curriculum
Spiral Curriculum
Student Centered Curriculum
Television Curriculum
Unified Studies Curriculum
Urban Studies
Womens Studies
RT Controversial Issues (Course Content)
Course Content
Curriculum Design
Curriculum Development
Curriculum Enrichment
Curriculum Evaluation
Curriculum Guides
Curriculum Problems
Curriculum Research
Education
English (Second Language)
Extracurricular Activities
Hidden Curriculum
Immersion Programs
Instruction
Intellectual Disciplines
Language Of Instruction
Pretechnology Programs
School Activities
Specialization
State Curriculum Guides

Curriculum Adaptation
USE CURRICULUM DEVELOPMENT

Curriculum Content
USE CURRICULUM

CURRICULUM DESIGN *Jul. 1966*
CIJE: 2203 RIE: 2255 GC: 320
SN Arrangement of the component parts of a curriculum (note: prior to mar80, the use of this term was not restricted by a scope note)
BT Design
RT Course Selection (Students)
Curriculum
Curriculum Development
Curriculum Research
Educational Strategies
Flexible Progression
Horizontal Organization
Instructional Design
Instructional Development
Interdisciplinary Approach
Sequential Approach
Student Centered Curriculum
Thematic Approach
Vertical Organization

CURRICULUM DEVELOPMENT *Jul. 1966*
CIJE: 10819 RIE: 13713 GC: 320
SN Activities such as conceptualizing, planning, implementing, field testing, and researching that are intended to produce new curricula or improve existing ones (note: prior to mar80, the use of this term was not restricted by a scope note)
UF Curriculum Adaptation
Curriculum Improvement
Curriculum Planning (1966 1980)
Curriculum Reform
Curriculum Reorganization
Curriculum Revisions
BT Educational Development
RT Articulation (Education)
Course Content
Curriculum
Curriculum Design
Curriculum Enrichment
Curriculum Evaluation
Curriculum Guides
Curriculum Problems
Curriculum Research
Curriculum Study Centers
Formative Evaluation
Instructional Development
Instructional Leadership
Instructional Materials
Material Development
Media Adaptation
Relevance (Education)
School Supervision

CURRICULUM ENRICHMENT *Jul. 1966*
CIJE: 551 RIE: 576 GC: 310
SN Process of selectively modifying a curriculum by adding educational content or new learning opportunities (e.g., out of school visits, special learning activities for gifted or deprived students, audiovisual presentations, etc.)
UF Course Enrichment
BT Enrichment
RT Curriculum
Curriculum Development

CURRICULUM EVALUATION *Jul. 1966*
CIJE: 1380 RIE: 2409 GC: 320
SN Determining the efficacy, value, etc. of a specific curriculum in terms of the validity of objectives, relevancy and sequence of content, and achievement of specified goals (note: as of oct81, use as a minor descriptor for examples of this kind of evaluation -- use as a major descriptor only as the subject of a document)
UF Curriculum Reevaluation
BT Evaluation
RT Course Evaluation
Curriculum
Curriculum Development
Curriculum Research
Educational Quality
Instructional Development
Instructional Effectiveness
Instructional Material Evaluation
Program Evaluation
Program Validation
Relevance (Education)
Summative Evaluation
Validated Programs

CURRICULUM GUIDES *Jul. 1966*
CIJE: 568 RIE: 7927 GC: 730
SN (Note: prior to mar80, the thesaurus carried the instructions, "'course outlines' or 'syllabus,' use 'curriculum guides'")
UF Fles Guides (1967 1980) #
NT State Curriculum Guides
BT Guides
RT Course Content
Course Descriptions
Curriculum
Curriculum Development
Curriculum Problems
Learning Modules
Lesson Plans
Teaching Guides

Curriculum Improvement
USE CURRICULUM DEVELOPMENT

Curriculum Laboratories
USE CURRICULUM STUDY CENTERS

Curriculum Materials
USE INSTRUCTIONAL MATERIALS

Curriculum Planning (1966 1980)
USE CURRICULUM DEVELOPMENT

CURRICULUM PROBLEMS *Jul. 1966*
CIJE: 365 RIE: 330 GC: 320
BT Problems
RT Curriculum
Curriculum Development
Curriculum Guides

Curriculum Reevaluation
USE CURRICULUM EVALUATION

Curriculum Reform
USE CURRICULUM DEVELOPMENT

Curriculum Relevance
USE RELEVANCE (EDUCATION)

Curriculum Reorganization
USE CURRICULUM DEVELOPMENT

CURRICULUM RESEARCH *Jul. 1966*
CIJE: 346 RIE: 904 GC: 810
SN Systematic investigation, collection, and analysis of information about a structured series of learning outcomes and associated experiences (note: as of oct81, use as a minor descriptor for examples of this kind of research -- use as a major descriptor only as the subject of a document)
BT Educational Research
RT Content Analysis
Curriculum
Curriculum Design
Curriculum Development
Curriculum Evaluation
Curriculum Study Centers
Institutional Research

Curriculum Resources
USE EDUCATIONAL RESOURCES

Curriculum Revisions
USE CURRICULUM DEVELOPMENT

CURRICULUM STUDY CENTERS *Jul. 1966*
CIJE: 31 RIE: 93 GC: 920
SN Facilities where assistance (e.g., curriculum materials, audiovisual aids, curriculum research and development) is provided to educators in planning and preparing for instruction -- may range from regional centers to units within schools
UF Curriculum Laboratories
BT Educational Facilities
Resource Centers
RT Curriculum Development
Curriculum Research
Demonstration Centers
Education Service Centers
Research And Development Centers
Research And Instruction Units
Resource Units

Curriculum Vitae
USE RESUMES (PERSONAL)

CURSIVE WRITING *Jul. 1966*
CIJE: 47 RIE: 32 GC: 400
SN Handwriting characterized by running or flowing lines, with strokes joined within the word
BT Handwriting
RT Manuscript Writing (Handlettering)

Custodial Mentally Handicapped (1968 1980)
USE SEVERE MENTAL RETARDATION

CUSTODIAN TRAINING *Jul. 1966*
CIJE: 23 RIE: 44 GC: 400
BT Job Training
RT School Maintenance

Customs (Culture)
USE CULTURE

Cutaneous Sense (1968 1980)
USE TACTUAL PERCEPTION

Cutlines
USE CAPTIONS

CUTTING SCORES *May. 1972*
CIJE: 91 RIE: 613 GC: 820
SN A selected point on a score scale which divides individuals earning scores above and below it into two groups for some purpose
UF Critical Scores
BT Scores
RT Credit No Credit Grading
Criterion Referenced Tests
Equated Scores
Mastery Tests
Pass Fail Grading
Raw Scores
Scoring Formulas
True Scores

CYBERNETICS *Jul. 1966*
CIJE: 106 RIE: 177 GC: 710
SN Comparative study of control and communication processes of organisms and machines
BT Technology
RT Artificial Intelligence
Automation
Bionics
Communication (Thought Transfer)
Communications
Computers
Computer Science
Educational Technology
Electronic Control
Feedback
Game Theory
Human Factors Engineering
Information Processing
Information Science
Information Technology
Information Theory
Input Output

= Two or more Descriptors are used to represent this term.
The term's main entry shows the appropriate coordination.

Instrumentation
Man Machine Systems
Numerical Control
Pattern Recognition
Robotics
Systems Approach
Technological Advancement

Cyesis
USE PREGNANCY

CYRILLIC ALPHABET *Jul. 1966*
CIJE: 10 RIE: 47 GC: 450
BT Alphabets
RT Slavic Languages

CYTOLOGY *Sep. 1968*
CIJE: 131 RIE: 27 GC: 490
UF Cell Theory (1966 1980)
BT Biological Sciences
RT Biochemistry
Biology
Culturing Techniques
Embryology
Enzymes
Evolution
Genetic Engineering
Molecular Structure
Nucleic Acids
Physiology
Rh Factors

CZECH *Jul. 1966*
CIJE: 15 RIE: 38 GC: 440
BT Slavic Languages
RT Czech Literature

CZECH LITERATURE *Dec. 1969*
CIJE: 3 RIE: 1 GC: 430
BT Literature
RT Czech

Dactylology
USE FINGER SPELLING

DAGUR *Jul. 1966*
CIJE: RIE: 2 GC: 440
BT Mongolian Languages

DAILY LIVING SKILLS *Mar. 1974*
CIJE: 376 RIE: 768 GC: 220
SN Personal management and social skills which are necessary for adequate functioning on an independent basis (note: if applicable, use the more specific term "self care skills")
UF Fundamental Skills (Daily Living)
Life Skills
Survival Skills (Daily Living)
NT Self Care Skills
BT Skills
RT Adaptive Behavior (Of Disabled)
Basic Business Education
Communication Skills
Coping
Decision Making Skills
Health
Home Economics Skills
Homemaking Skills
Interpersonal Competence
Job Skills
Language Skills
Normalization (Handicapped)
Practical Arts
Psychomotor Skills
Rehabilitation
Safety
Special Education
Telephone Usage Instruction
Travel Training
Visually Handicapped Mobility

DAIRY FARMERS *Mar. 1980*
CIJE: 8 RIE: 48 GC: 410
UF Dairymen (1966 1980)
BT Farmers
RT Agriculture
Animal Husbandry
Farm Occupations

Dairy Product Inspectors
USE FOOD AND DRUG INSPECTORS

Dairymen (1966 1980)
USE DAIRY FARMERS

DANCE *Jul. 1966*
CIJE: 312 RIE: 382 GC: 420
UF Aerobic Dance #
Ballet (1966 1980)
Choreography
BT Fine Arts
Physical Activities
RT Art
Cultural Activities
Dance Education
Dance Therapy
Dramatics
Folk Culture
Movement Education
Music
Pantomime
Theater Arts

DANCE EDUCATION *Mar. 1983*
CIJE: 33 RIE: 20 GC: 420
SN Any learning activities involving dance -- may be integral to physical education or offered as a separate program of study
BT Education
RT Aesthetic Education
Dance
Fine Arts
Movement Education
Music Education
Physical Education

DANCE THERAPY *Feb. 1978*
CIJE: 16 RIE: 16 GC: 230
SN The therapeutic use of rhythmical motor activity (folk dancing, ballroom dancing, exercising to music, etc.) as a bridge to mental or physical well-being
BT Therapy
RT Dance
Movement Education
Music Therapy
Physical Therapy
Play Therapy
Psychotherapy
Self Expression
Therapeutic Recreation

Dangerous Materials
USE HAZARDOUS MATERIALS

Darghi
USE CAUCASIAN LANGUAGES

DATA *Jul. 1966*
CIJE: 101 RIE: 285 GC: 710
SN Information, often numerical and especially in a form suitable for processing by a computer or for other analysis
NT Databases
Personnel Data
Profiles
Scores
Statistical Data
RT Data Analysis
Data Processing
Diagrams
Measurement
Tables (Data)

Data Accumulation
USE DATA COLLECTION

DATA ANALYSIS *Jul. 1966*
CIJE: 2800 RIE: 2773 GC: 820
SN Preparation of factual information items for dissemination or further treatment (includes compiling, verifying, ordering, classifying, and interpreting)
NT Data Collection
Data Interpretation
Statistical Analysis
Trend Analysis
BT Evaluation Methods
RT Classification
Content Analysis
Data
Data Processing
Hypothesis Testing
Research
Research Methodology

Data Banks
USE DATABASES

Data Bases (1969 1981)
USE DATABASES

DATA COLLECTION *Jul. 1966*
CIJE: 1309 RIE: 2863 GC: 810
SN Generating or bringing together information that has been systematically observed, recorded, organized, categorized, or defined in such a way that logical processing and inferences may occur
UF Data Accumulation
NT Sampling
BT Data Analysis
Information Processing
RT Data Processing
Demography
Generalizability Theory
Observation
Questionnaires
Recordkeeping
Research
Research Methodology
Surveys
Testing
Worksheets

Data Dissemination
USE INFORMATION DISSEMINATION

DATA INTERPRETATION *Jan. 1985*
CIJE: 63 RIE: 54 GC: 820
SN Explanation of the meaning, implications, or limitations of factual information
NT Statistical Inference
Test Interpretation
BT Data Analysis
RT Evaluation
Evaluative Thinking
Experiments
Generalizability Theory
Hypothesis Testing
Inferences
Information Utilization
Interpretive Skills
Research
Research Methodology
Statistical Analysis
Validity

Data Needs
USE INFORMATION NEEDS

DATA PROCESSING *Jul. 1966*
CIJE: 1042 RIE: 1724 GC: 710
SN Systematic handling, manipulation, and computation of information by machines
UF Automatic Data Processing
Data Tabulation
Electronic Data Processing (1967 1980)
NT Input Output
Time Sharing
BT Information Processing
RT Automation
Calculators
Computer Networks
Computers
Computer Science
Computer Software
Computer Storage Devices
Data
Data Analysis
Database Management Systems
Databases
Data Collection
Data Processing Occupations
Electromechanical Technology
Electronic Equipment
Expert Systems
Information Systems
Information Technology
Input Output Devices
Instrumentation
Machine Readable Cataloging
Machine Translation
Management Information Systems
Mechanical Equipment
Online Systems
Optical Data Disks
Optical Scanners
Programing
Programing Languages
Worksheets

DATA PROCESSING OCCUPATIONS *Jul. 1966*
CIJE: 35 RIE: 85 GC: 640
BT Occupations
RT Business Education
Clerical Occupations
Computer Science Education
Data Processing
Electronic Technicians
Keyboarding (Data Entry)
Office Occupations
Semiskilled Occupations
Skilled Occupations
Trade And Industrial Education
White Collar Occupations

Data Sheets (1966 1980)
USE WORKSHEETS

Data Tabulation
USE DATA PROCESSING

Database Hosts
USE ONLINE VENDORS

DATABASE MANAGEMENT SYSTEMS *Apr. 1986*
CIJE: 62 RIE: 27 GC: 710
SN Software used to create, organize, secure, access, and update databases
UF Dbms
File Management Systems
BT Computer Software
Management Systems
RT Databases
Data Processing
Information Retrieval
Information Storage
Management Information Systems

DATABASE PRODUCERS *Apr. 1986*
CIJE: 14 RIE: 10 GC: 710
SN Publishers, businesses, government agencies, or other organizations that create computer-readable information files, often for public access
BT Organizations (Groups)
RT Databases
Online Vendors
Publishing Industry

Database Vendors
USE ONLINE VENDORS

DATABASES *Apr. 1981*
CIJE: 1513 RIE: 1605 GC: 710
SN Collections of information items that are organized and stored in machine-readable records and which are accessible and manipulable by computer through designated elements in the records
UF Data Banks
Data Bases (1969 1981)
NT Online Catalogs
BT Data
Information Sources
RT Computers
Database Management Systems
Database Producers
Data Processing
Electronic Publishing
Information Retrieval
Information Storage
Library Collections
Online Vendors
Research Tools
Search Strategies

DATING (SOCIAL) *Jul. 1966*
CIJE: 147 RIE: 75 GC: 510
BT Interpersonal Relationship
RT Friendship
Interpersonal Attraction
Mate Selection
Recreational Activities
Social Life

DAUGHTERS *Sep. 1981*
CIJE: 44 RIE: 35 GC: 510
BT Females
RT Family (Sociological Unit)
Family Environment
Family Life
Kinship
Parent Child Relationship
Parents
Sons

= Two or more Descriptors are used to represent this term.
The term's main entry shows the appropriate coordination.

DAY CAMP PROGRAMS *Jul. 1966*
CIJE: 36 RIE: 53 GC: 470
UF Day Camps
BT Recreational Programs
RT Camping
Resident Camp Programs
Summer Programs

Day Camps
USE DAY CAMP PROGRAMS

DAY CARE *Mar. 1980*
CIJE: 636 RIE: 1661 GC: 520
SN Care of children by persons other than their parents or guardians on a partial or full day basis (note: see also "child rearing" -- prior to mar80, "child care" was also a valid descriptor)
UF Day Care Programs (1966 1980)
Day Care Services (1967 1980)
NT Employer Supported Day Care
Family Day Care
School Age Day Care
BT Social Services
RT Adult Day Care
Ancillary School Services
Child Caregivers
Child Care Occupations
Day Care Centers
Employed Parents
Home Economics Education
Occupational Home Economics

DAY CARE CENTERS *Mar. 1980*
CIJE: 230 RIE: 564 GC: 920
SN Professionally run facilities that care for groups of children on a partial or full day basis (note: prior to mar80, the instruction "day care centers, use day care services" was carried in the thesaurus)
UF Child Care Centers (1967 1980)
Migrant Child Care Centers (1966 1980) #
BT Facilities
RT Child Caregivers
Child Care Occupations
Child Development Centers
Day Care
Early Childhood Education
Employer Supported Day Care
Nursery Schools
Preschool Education
School Age Day Care

Day Care Programs (1966 1980)
USE DAY CARE

Day Care Services (1967 1980)
USE DAY CARE

Day Classes
USE DAY PROGRAMS

DAY PROGRAMS *Jul. 1966*
CIJE: 34 RIE: 43 GC: 350
SN Programs conducted during the daytime hours
UF Day Classes
Daytime Programs (1967 1980)
BT Programs
RT Day Schools
Day Students
Evening Programs
Full Time Students

Day Release
USE RELEASED TIME

DAY SCHOOLS *Jul. 1966*
CIJE: 34 RIE: 82 GC: 340
SN Schools attended by students during part of the day, as distinguished from schools where students are boarded and lodged
BT Schools
RT Day Programs
Day Students

DAY STUDENTS *Jul. 1966*
CIJE: 6 RIE: 77 GC: 360
BT Students
RT Day Programs
Day Schools
Evening Students
Full Time Students

Daylight (1970 1980)
USE LIGHT

Daytime Programs (1967 1980)
USE DAY PROGRAMS

Dbms
USE DATABASE MANAGEMENT SYSTEMS

DE FACTO SEGREGATION *Mar. 1980*
CIJE: 57 RIE: 151 GC: 540
UF Defacto Segregation (1966 1980)
BT Racial Segregation
RT School Resegregation
Tokenism

DE JURE SEGREGATION *Apr. 1980*
CIJE: 28 RIE: 43 GC: 540
SN Racial separation directly guaranteed by law
UF Dejure Segregation (1966 1980)
Legal Segregation (1966 1980)
BT Racial Segregation

Deaf (1966 1980)
USE DEAFNESS

DEAF BLIND *Jul. 1966*
CIJE: 136 RIE: 196 GC: 220
BT Multiple Disabilities
RT Blindness
Deafness
Severe Disabilities

Deaf Children (1966 1980)
USE DEAFNESS

Deaf Education (1968 1980)
USE DEAFNESS

DEAF INTERPRETING *Jul. 1966*
CIJE: 68 RIE: 48 GC: 220
SN Process of acting as interpreter to facilitate communications between deaf and hearing persons
UF Interpreting For The Deaf
BT Translation
RT Accessibility (For Disabled)
Communication (Thought Transfer)
Communication Skills
Cued Speech
Deafness
Finger Spelling
Interpreters
Interpretive Skills
Lipreading
Manual Communication
Sign Language

Deaf Research (1968 1980)
USE DEAFNESS

DEAFNESS *Mar. 1980*
CIJE: 1453 RIE: 855 GC: 220
SN Deprivation of the functional use of the sense of hearing -- usually a loss of more than 75 decibels
UF Deaf (1966 1980)
Deaf Children (1966 1980)
Deaf Education (1968 1980)
Deaf Research (1968 1980)
BT Hearing Impairments
RT Deaf Blind
Deaf Interpreting
Hearing (Physiology)
Manual Communication
Oral Communication Method
Partial Hearing
Total Communication

DEANS *Mar. 1980*
CIJE: 215 RIE: 164 GC: 360
SN Administrative officials in a college or other school who are responsible for the academic program, student life, student services, etc. (note: use a more specific term if possible)
UF College Deans (1968 1980) #
NT Academic Deans
Deans Of Students
BT Administrators
Faculty
RT College Administration
College Presidents
Middle Management
School Administration

Deans Of Faculty
USE ACADEMIC DEANS

Deans Of Instruction
USE ACADEMIC DEANS

Deans Of Men
USE DEANS OF STUDENTS

DEANS OF STUDENTS *Mar. 1980*
CIJE: 24 RIE: 13 GC: 360
SN Administrative officials in a college or other school who are responsible for all phases of student life, including student activities, personnel services, housing, employment, etc.
UF Deans Of Men
Deans Of Women
BT Deans
RT Academic Deans
College Environment
Pupil Personnel Workers
Student Development
Student Personnel Workers
Student School Relationship
Student Welfare

Deans Of Women
USE DEANS OF STUDENTS

DEATH *Mar. 1969*
CIJE: 929 RIE: 343 GC: 120
UF Death Education
Thanatology
NT Infant Mortality
Suicide
RT Grief
Hospices (Terminal Care)
Pathology
Physiology
Widowed

Death Education
USE DEATH

DEBATE *Jul. 1966*
CIJE: 317 RIE: 322 GC: 400
UF Presidential Debates (United States) #
BT Language Arts
RT Persuasive Discourse
Political Campaigns
Political Candidates
Public Speaking
Social Problems
Verbal Communication

Debate Judges
USE JUDGES

Deceleration
USE ACCELERATION (PHYSICS)

DECENTRALIZATION *Jul. 1966*
CIJE: 502 RIE: 589 GC: 520
SN The dispersion or distribution of functions and powers from a central authority to a local, community, or individual office unit authority
UF Decentralized Library Systems (1968 1980) #
Decentralized School Design (1966 1980) #
BT Administrative Organization
RT Centralization
Community Control
Institutional Autonomy
Networks
Organizational Change
School Based Management
School Organization

Decentralized Library Systems (1968 1980)
USE DECENTRALIZATION; LIBRARY NETWORKS

Decentralized School Design (1966 1980)
USE DECENTRALIZATION; EDUCATIONAL FACILITIES DESIGN

DECEPTION *Aug. 1986*
CIJE: 32 RIE: 18 GC: 520
SN Intentional or unintentional misrepresentation or delusion
NT Lying
RT Behavior Patterns
Communication (Thought Transfer)
Consumer Protection
Credibility
Propaganda

DECIMAL FRACTIONS *Jan. 1969*
CIJE: 113 RIE: 113 GC: 480
UF Decimals
BT Fractions

Decimals
USE DECIMAL FRACTIONS

DECISION MAKING *Jul. 1966*
CIJE: 5172 RIE: 6040 GC: 110
NT Participative Decision Making
BT Cognitive Processes
RT Architectural Programing
Career Choice
College Choice
Conflict Resolution
Coping
Course Selection (Students)
Critical Thinking
Decision Making Skills
Delphi Technique
Discussion
Evaluation Utilization
Evaluative Thinking
Expert Systems
Futures (Of Society)
Game Theory
Heuristics
Holistic Approach
Individual Power
Information Utilization
Judgment Analysis Technique
Management Games
Management Information Systems
Management Systems
Personal Autonomy
Policy Formation
Problem Solving
Professional Autonomy
Psychology
Risk
School Based Management
School Choice
Systems Analysis
Systems Approach
Vocational Maturity

DECISION MAKING SKILLS *Jul. 1966*
CIJE: 599 RIE: 912 GC: 110
BT Skills
RT Daily Living Skills
Decision Making
Problem Solving

DECLINING ENROLLMENT *Dec. 1976*
CIJE: 519 RIE: 650 GC: 330
SN Diminishing numbers of students in educational institutions
BT Enrollment Rate
RT Average Daily Membership
Educational Demand
Educational Supply
Enrollment
Enrollment Influences
Enrollment Projections
Enrollment Trends
School Closing
School Demography

DECODING (READING) *Dec. 1972*
CIJE: 292 RIE: 371 GC: 460
SN Acquisition of meaning from written language by trial and error process of graphophonic, semantic, and syntactic analyses
BT Reading Processes
RT Beginning Reading
Context Clues
Miscue Analysis
Oral Reading
Phoneme Grapheme Correspondence
Phonics
Reading
Reading Comprehension
Reading Skills
Semantics
Structural Analysis (Linguistics)
Word Recognition

DEDUCTION *Mar. 1980*
CIJE: 260 RIE: 165 GC: 110
SN Logical thought process that attempts to reach conclusions by reasoning from general rules, principles, laws, or conditions to specific instances or cases
UF Deductive Methods (1967 1980)
BT Logical Thinking
RT Abstract Reasoning
Experiments
Induction
Learning Processes
Research Methodology
Scientific Methodology
Validity

Deductive Methods (1967 1980)
USE DEDUCTION

Deep Sea Diving
USE UNDERWATER DIVING

DEEP STRUCTURE *Jul. 1966*
CIJE: 397 RIE: 323 GC: 450
SN Concept in transformational grammar referring to the abstract underlying form of a sentence that determines its meaning but is not necessarily represented in its oral or written expression
BT Transformational Generative Grammar
RT Grammar
Linguistics
Linguistic Theory
Phrase Structure
Semantics
Sentence Diagraming
Sentence Structure
Surface Structure
Syntax

Defacto Segregation (1966 1980)
USE DE FACTO SEGREGATION

Defaulting On Loans
USE LOAN REPAYMENT

Deferred Tuition
USE INCOME CONTINGENT LOANS

DEFINITIONS *Dec. 1969*
CIJE: 2138 RIE: 1875 GC: 710
RT Dictionaries
Etymology
Glossaries
Lexicography
Lexicology
Semantics
Vocabulary

DEGREE REQUIREMENTS *Jul. 1966*
CIJE: 641 RIE: 566 GC: 320
SN Specifications of minimum courses, course distribution, and grades required for a higher education degree in a particular field of study (note: use "graduation requirements" for high school diploma requirements or general specifications for college graduation -- prior to mar80, the use of this term was not restricted by a scope note)
BT Graduation Requirements
RT Academic Achievement
Academic Standards
Associate Degrees
Bachelors Degrees
College Credits
College Students
Degrees (Academic)
Doctoral Degrees
Doctoral Programs
Doctor Of Arts Degrees
External Degree Programs
Graduate Study
Majors (Students)
Masters Degrees
Masters Programs
Nonmajors
Nontraditional Education
Required Courses
School Catalogs
Special Degree Programs
Specialist In Education Degrees
Undergraduate Study

DEGREES (ACADEMIC) *Mar. 1980*
CIJE: 364 RIE: 980 GC: 340
UF Degrees (Titles) (1966 1980)
First Professional Degrees #
NT Associate Degrees
Bachelors Degrees
Doctoral Degrees
Masters Degrees
Specialist In Education Degrees
RT Academic Rank (Professional)
College Graduates
Commencement Ceremonies
Credentials
Degree Requirements
Doctoral Dissertations
External Degree Programs
Higher Education
Majors (Students)
Qualifications
Special Degree Programs

Degrees (Titles) (1966 1980)
USE DEGREES (ACADEMIC)

Dehumanization
USE HUMANIZATION

DEINSTITUTIONALIZATION (OF DISABLED) *Aug. 1980*
CIJE: 130 RIE: 118 GC: 220
SN Processes and services that enable disabled persons to live outside of the confines of asylums, nursing homes, and other residential institutions
BT Normalization (Handicapped)
RT Adult Foster Care
Community Programs
Disabilities
Group Homes
Institutionalized Persons
Rehabilitation
Residential Programs

Dejure Segregation (1966 1980)
USE DE JURE SEGREGATION

DELAY OF GRATIFICATION *Oct. 1976*
CIJE: 54 RIE: 22 GC: 120
SN The self-imposed delay of reinforcement or voluntary deferment of reward
BT Self Control
RT Discipline
Goal Orientation
Locus Of Control
Motivation
Need Gratification
Psychological Needs
Reinforcement
Rewards
Self Concept
Self Reward

DELAYED SPEECH *Mar. 1980*
CIJE: 78 RIE: 64 GC: 120
SN Speech skill development that is below age level standards
UF Retarded Speech Development (1968 1980)
BT Speech Handicaps
RT Child Development
Language Acquisition
Speech Habits
Speech Skills
Speech Therapy

DELINQUENCY *Jul. 1966*
CIJE: 836 RIE: 953 GC: 530
UF Delinquent Behavior (1966 1983)
Delinquent Identification (1966 1980) #
Delinquent Role (1966 1980)
Delinquents (1966 1980)
Juvenile Delinquency
BT Crime
RT Criminals
Delinquency Causes
Delinquency Prevention
Delinquent Rehabilitation
Group Homes
Juvenile Courts
Juvenile Gangs
Law Enforcement
Police School Relationship
Recidivism
Runaways
Social Psychology
Stealing
Vandalism
Violence
Youth Problems

DELINQUENCY CAUSES *Jul. 1966*
CIJE: 110 RIE: 122 GC: 530
RT Delinquency
Etiology

DELINQUENCY PREVENTION *Jul. 1966*
CIJE: 154 RIE: 314 GC: 520
BT Crime Prevention
RT Delinquency
Delinquent Rehabilitation
Law Enforcement

Delinquent Behavior (1966 1983)
USE DELINQUENCY

Delinquent Identification (1966 1980)
USE DELINQUENCY; IDENTIFICATION

DELINQUENT REHABILITATION *Jul. 1966*
CIJE: 197 RIE: 383 GC: 240
BT Correctional Rehabilitation
RT Continuation Students
Correctional Education
Correctional Institutions
Delinquency
Delinquency Prevention
Juvenile Courts
Probationary Period
Probation Officers
Recidivism

Delinquent Role (1966 1980)
USE DELINQUENCY

Delinquents (1966 1980)
USE DELINQUENCY

DELIVERY SYSTEMS *May. 1974*
CIJE: 1068 RIE: 2631 GC: 520
SN Organizational and administrative aspects of the provision of services
BT Services
RT Communications
Information Dissemination
Needs Assessment
Outreach Programs
Resource Allocation

DELPHI TECHNIQUE *Apr. 1982*
CIJE: 119 RIE: 158 GC: 820
SN Method of synthesizing diverse opinions into a consensus (most frequently, among experts) -- usually carried out by a series of questionnaires, the technique is characterized by minimal influence from social pressures through anonymity, repeated rounds of controlled feedback, and weighted responses
BT Methods
RT Cooperative Planning
Decision Making
Feedback
Futures (Of Society)
Long Range Planning
Maximum Likelihood Statistics
Operations Research
Opinions
Planning
Policy Formation
Prediction

Demand For Education
USE EDUCATIONAL DEMAND

DEMAND OCCUPATIONS *Apr. 1969*
CIJE: 70 RIE: 172 GC: 640
SN Occupations for which personnel are needed, at the present or in the projected future
NT Emerging Occupations
BT Occupations
RT Career Planning
Educational Demand
Employment Opportunities
Employment Patterns
Employment Potential
Employment Projections
Labor Market
Labor Needs
Occupational Information

Dementia Praecox
USE SCHIZOPHRENIA

DEMOCRACY *Jul. 1966*
CIJE: 256 RIE: 236 GC: 610
RT Capitalism
Civil Liberties
Civil Rights
Communism
Democratic Values
Freedom Of Information
Freedom Of Speech
Intellectual Freedom
Personal Autonomy
Self Determination
Totalitarianism

Democratic Management
USE PARTICIPATIVE DECISION MAKING

DEMOCRATIC VALUES *Jul. 1966*
CIJE: 460 RIE: 427 GC: 610
BT Values
RT Democracy
Political Attitudes
Social Values

DEMOGRAPHY *Jul. 1966*
CIJE: 1180 RIE: 3100 GC: 550
UF National Demography (1966 1980)
Population Research
NT Birth Rate
Employment Patterns
Geographic Distribution
Population Distribution
Population Growth
Population Trends
Racial Composition
Residential Patterns
School Demography
Social Distribution
Urban Demography
BT Social Sciences
RT Census Figures
Cohort Analysis
Community Size
Data Collection
Employment Projections
Human Geography
Incidence
Industrialization
Land Settlement
Migration
Migration Patterns
Overpopulation
Place Of Residence
Population Education
Rural Population
Social Science Research
Social Scientists
Sociocultural Patterns
Sociology
Topography
Urbanization

DEMONSTRATION CENTERS *Jul. 1966*
CIJE: 28 RIE: 95 GC: 920
SN Areas of educational facilities set up to solve specified educational problems through research and experimentation (note: prior to mar80, the use of this term was not restricted by a scope note)
BT Educational Facilities
RT Curriculum Study Centers
Demonstration Programs
Demonstrations (Educational)
Educational Experiments
Educational Research
Education Service Centers
Laboratories

DEMONSTRATION PROGRAMS *Jul. 1966*
CIJE: 499 RIE: 2917 GC: 330
UF Demonstration Projects (1966 1980)
Exemplary Programs
Model Programs
BT Programs
RT Demonstration Centers
Experimental Programs
Field Tests
Innovation
Program Validation
Validated Programs

Demonstration Projects (1966 1980)
USE DEMONSTRATION PROGRAMS

= Two or more Descriptors are used to represent this term.
The term's main entry shows the appropriate coordination.

DEMONSTRATIONS (CIVIL) *Jul. 1966*
CIJE: 148 RIE: 100 GC: 610
UF Public Demonstrations
RT Activism
Civil Disobedience
Civil Rights
School Boycotts
Student Rights
Violence

DEMONSTRATIONS (EDUCATIONAL) *Jul. 1966*
CIJE: 1041 RIE: 216 GC: 310
SN Teaching method in which explanations are given by example or experiment
BT Teaching Methods
RT Demonstration Centers
Educational Experiments
Laboratories
Laboratory Procedures

Denominational Colleges
USE CHURCH RELATED COLLEGES

Dental Assessment
USE DENTAL EVALUATION

DENTAL ASSISTANTS *Jul. 1966*
CIJE: 15 RIE: 123 GC: 210
SN Personnel who assist dentists at chairside in dental operatory, perform reception and clerical functions, and carry out dental radiography and selected dental laboratory work
BT Allied Health Personnel
RT Dental Clinics
Dental Evaluation
Dental Hygienists
Dental Technicians
Dentistry

Dental Associations (1966 1980)
USE DENTISTRY; PROFESSIONAL ASSOCIATIONS

DENTAL CLINICS *Jul. 1966*
CIJE: 19 RIE: 23 GC: 210
BT Clinics
RT Dental Assistants
Dental Evaluation
Dental Health
Dental Hygienists
Dental Schools
Dental Technicians
Dentistry
Dentists

DENTAL EVALUATION *Jul. 1966*
CIJE: 24 RIE: 40 GC: 210
SN Determination of an individual's dental health and of any needed treatment -- also, the appraisal of dental procedures, programs, equipment, etc. according to professional standards
UF Dental Assessment
BT Medical Evaluation
RT Dental Assistants
Dental Clinics
Dental Health
Dental Hygienists
Dental Technicians
Dentistry
Dentists

DENTAL HEALTH *Jul. 1966*
CIJE: 184 RIE: 197 GC: 210
BT Physical Health
RT Dental Clinics
Dental Evaluation
Dental Hygienists
Dentistry
Fluoridation
Hygiene

DENTAL HYGIENISTS *Aug. 1968*
CIJE: 36 RIE: 72 GC: 210
SN Licensed oral health clinicians and educators who help the public develop and maintain optimum oral health -- they may perform preventive, restorative, and therapeutic services under the supervision of dentists
UF Oral Hygienists
Prophylacticians
BT Allied Health Personnel
RT Dental Assistants
Dental Clinics
Dental Evaluation
Dental Health
Dental Technicians
Dentistry
Hygiene

Dental Laboratory Technicians
USE DENTAL TECHNICIANS

Dental School Faculty
USE DENTAL SCHOOLS; MEDICAL SCHOOL FACULTY

DENTAL SCHOOLS *Jul. 1966*
CIJE: 238 RIE: 125 GC: 340
UF Dental School Faculty #
Schools Of Dentistry
BT Colleges
RT Dental Clinics
Dental Students
Dentistry
Dentists
Medical Education
Medical School Faculty
Medical Schools
Professional Education

Dental Sciences
USE DENTISTRY

DENTAL STUDENTS *Oct. 1982*
CIJE: 71 RIE: 18 GC: 360
SN Students enrolled in dental schools (note: excludes undergraduate students preparing for dental school)
BT Graduate Students
RT Dental Schools
Dentistry
Medical Students
Professional Education

Dental Surgeons
USE DENTISTS

DENTAL TECHNICIANS *Jul. 1966*
CIJE: 11 RIE: 48 GC: 210
SN Personnel who construct complete and partial dentures, make orthodontic appliances, fix bridgework, crowns, and other dental restorations and appliances, as authorized by dentists
UF Dental Laboratory Technicians
Orthodontic Technicians
BT Allied Health Personnel
RT Dental Assistants
Dental Clinics
Dental Evaluation
Dental Hygienists
Dentistry
Laboratory Technology

DENTISTRY *Jul. 1966*
CIJE: 192 RIE: 132 GC: 210
UF Dental Associations (1966 1980) #
Dental Sciences
Orthodontics
BT Medicine
RT Dental Assistants
Dental Clinics
Dental Evaluation
Dental Health
Dental Hygienists
Dental Schools
Dental Students
Dental Technicians
Dentists
Health
Medical Services

DENTISTS *Aug. 1968*
CIJE: 64 RIE: 107 GC: 210
UF Dental Surgeons
Orthodontists
BT Health Personnel
Professional Personnel
RT Dental Clinics
Dental Evaluation
Dental Schools
Dentistry
Medical Services

Deoxyribonucleic Acid
USE DNA

Department Chairpersons
USE DEPARTMENT HEADS

Department Directors (School) (1966 1980)
USE DEPARTMENT HEADS

DEPARTMENT HEADS *Mar. 1980*
CIJE: 282 RIE: 230 GC: 360
SN Faculty members responsible for the coordination or administration of an academic area of study (note: prior to apr76, the instruction "department chairmen, use administrative personnel" was carried in the thesaurus)
UF Department Chairpersons
Department Directors (School) (1966 1980)
BT Administrators
Faculty
RT Departments
Instructional Leadership
Middle Management
School Administration
Teachers

Departmental Majors
USE MAJORS (STUDENTS)

Departmental Teaching Plans (1968 1980)
USE DEPARTMENTS

Departmentalization
USE DEPARTMENTS

DEPARTMENTS *Sep. 1969*
CIJE: 549 RIE: 578 GC: 350
UF Academic Departments
Departmentalization
Departmental Teaching Plans (1968 1980)
NT English Departments
Science Departments
State Departments Of Education
BT Administrative Organization
RT Department Heads
Intellectual Disciplines
School Organization

Dependability
USE RELIABILITY

DEPENDENTS *Jul. 1966*
CIJE: 28 RIE: 92 GC: 510
BT Groups
RT Children
Family Size
Family Structure
Older Adults

DEPLETED RESOURCES *Jul. 1966*
CIJE: 134 RIE: 125 GC: 410
BT Resources
RT Conservation (Environment)
Energy Conservation
Fuel Consumption
Natural Resources
Physical Environment
Recycling
Soil Conservation
Water Resources

DEPOSITORY LIBRARIES *Nov. 1968*
CIJE: 56 RIE: 84 GC: 710
SN Libraries that receive public documents from national, provincial, or local governmental units with the provision that they will provide public access to the collections
BT Libraries
RT Academic Libraries
Government (Administrative Body)
Government Libraries
Government Publications
Law Libraries
Public Libraries
Research Libraries
Special Libraries

Depressed Areas (Geographic) (1966 1980)
USE POVERTY AREAS

DEPRESSION (PSYCHOLOGY) *Aug. 1978*
CIJE: 482 RIE: 223 GC: 230
SN Emotional state of dejection and sadness, ranging from mild discouragement to utter despair
UF Despair
Despondency
Dysthymia
Melancholia
BT Psychological Patterns
RT Anger
Anxiety
Emotional Disturbances
Emotional Problems
Fear
Grief
Helplessness
Loneliness
Personality Problems
Psychopathology

Deprivation
USE DISADVANTAGED ENVIRONMENT

Deprived
USE DISADVANTAGED

Deprived Children
USE DISADVANTAGED YOUTH

Deprived Environment
USE DISADVANTAGED ENVIRONMENT

DEPTH PERCEPTION *Mar. 1980*
CIJE: 55 RIE: 14 GC: 110
UF Stereopsis (1968 1980)
BT Visual Perception
RT Vision

Dermal Sense
USE TACTUAL PERCEPTION

DESCRIPTIVE LINGUISTICS *Jul. 1966*
CIJE: 698 RIE: 578 GC: 450
SN Approach to linguistics that is concerned with the observation and description of a language at one point in time -- describes language as it is actually used rather than prescribing how it should be used (note: prior to mar80, the use of this term was not restricted by a scope note)
UF Synchronic Linguistics (1967 1980)
NT Grammar
Semantics
BT Linguistics
RT Error Analysis (Language)
Language Typology
Linguistic Borrowing
Phonemics
Phonology
Structural Analysis (Linguistics)
Structural Grammar
Tone Languages

DESCRIPTIVE WRITING *Jul. 1966*
CIJE: 117 RIE: 183 GC: 400
BT Writing (Composition)
RT Creative Writing
Expository Writing
Literary Devices
Poetry
Prose
Student Writing Models

Descriptors
USE SUBJECT INDEX TERMS

Desegregated Classes
USE CLASSROOM DESEGREGATION

Desegregated Colleges
USE COLLEGE DESEGREGATION

Desegregated Schools
USE SCHOOL DESEGREGATION

Desegregation (Disabled Students)
USE MAINSTREAMING

= Two or more Descriptors are used to represent this term.
The term's main entry shows the appropriate coordination.

DESEGREGATION EFFECTS *Mar. 1980*
CIJE: 402 RIE: 722 GC: 540
UF Desegregation Impact
Integration Effects (1966 1980)
Integration Impact
RT Integration Studies
Racial Integration
School Desegregation
Social Integration

Desegregation Impact
USE DESEGREGATION EFFECTS

DESEGREGATION LITIGATION *Mar. 1980*
CIJE: 210 RIE: 313 GC: 540
UF Integration Litigation (1966 1980)
BT Court Litigation
RT Racial Integration
School Desegregation

DESEGREGATION METHODS *Mar. 1980*
CIJE: 301 RIE: 595 GC: 540
UF Integration Methods (1966 1980)
NT Busing
BT Methods
RT Affirmative Action
Desegregation Plans
Open Enrollment
Racial Integration
School Desegregation
Selective Admission
Social Integration

DESEGREGATION PLANS *Mar. 1980*
CIJE: 160 RIE: 351 GC: 540
UF Integration Plans (1966 1980)
BT Planning
RT Affirmative Action
Busing
Desegregation Methods
Integration Readiness
Racial Integration
School Desegregation
Social Integration
Voluntary Desegregation

Desegregation Readiness
USE INTEGRATION READINESS

DESENSITIZATION *Dec. 1971*
CIJE: 188 RIE: 60 GC: 230
SN Planned exposure to anxiety producing stimuli in order to reduce illogical fears
UF Systematic Desensitization
BT Behavior Modification
RT Affective Behavior
Anxiety
Counseling Techniques
Gestalt Therapy
Relaxation Training
Stimuli

DESIGN *Jul. 1966*
CIJE: 490 RIE: 353 GC: 420
SN The process of conceiving and selecting the structure, elements, arrangement, materials, steps, or procedures of some activity or thing -- also, the plan, layout, or mental scheme that results (note: use a more specific term if possible)
NT Building Design
Classroom Design
Clothing Design
Curriculum Design
Educational Facilities Design
Furniture Design
Instructional Design
Interior Design
Lighting Design
Park Design
Program Design
Research Design
RT Architectural Programing
Architecture
Art
Building Plans
Design Crafts
Designers
Design Preferences
Design Requirements
Development
Guidelines
Mechanical Design Technicians
Organization
Planning
Specifications

DESIGN BUILD APPROACH *Sep. 1974*
CIJE: 20 RIE: 6 GC: 920
SN Entering into a single contract for design services and construction services
UF Design Construct Method
Turnkey Building
BT Systems Building
RT Building Design
Building Innovation
Building Plans
Construction (Process)
Construction Costs
Construction Management
Construction Programs
Facility Planning
Fast Track Scheduling

Design Construct Method
USE DESIGN BUILD APPROACH

DESIGN CRAFTS *Jul. 1966*
CIJE: 100 RIE: 55 GC: 420
SN The artistic creation or decoration of a structure or material, either by hand or by machine
BT Visual Arts
RT Ceramics
Clothing Design
Craft Workers
Design
Furniture Design
Handicrafts
Industrial Arts
Skilled Occupations

Design Needs (1968 1980)
USE DESIGN REQUIREMENTS

DESIGN PREFERENCES *Jul. 1966*
CIJE: 109 RIE: 90 GC: 420
BT Attitudes
RT Aesthetic Values
Design
Design Requirements
Individual Needs
Values

DESIGN REQUIREMENTS *Mar. 1980*
CIJE: 553 RIE: 828 GC: 920
SN Specifications that must be met for the designs of facilities or objects in order to satisfy the physical or psychological needs of users
UF Design Needs (1968 1980)
Physical Design Needs (1968 1980)
Psychological Design Needs (1968 1980)
BT Specifications
RT Accessibility (For Disabled)
Acoustical Environment
Architectural Programing
Architecture
Building Design
Classroom Design
Climate Control
Design
Design Preferences
Educational Facilities Design
Educational Facilities Planning
Facility Planning
Facility Requirements
Facility Utilization Research
Flexible Facilities
Furniture Design
Human Factors Engineering
Humanization
Individual Needs
Interior Design
Interior Space
Lighting Design
Physical Environment
Physical Mobility
Privacy
Psychological Needs
Safety
Sanitation
Space Utilization
Spatial Relationship (Facilities)
Storage
Thermal Environment
Visual Environment

DESIGNERS *Jan. 1969*
CIJE: 35 RIE: 19 GC: 640
BT Personnel
RT Design
Drafting

Desktop Computers
USE MICROCOMPUTERS

Desoxyribonucleic Acid
USE DNA

Despair
USE DEPRESSION (PSYCHOLOGY)

Despondency
USE DEPRESSION (PSYCHOLOGY)

Destiny Control
USE SELF DETERMINATION

Determination (Chemical)
USE CHEMICAL ANALYSIS

DETERMINERS (LANGUAGES) *Jul. 1966*
CIJE: 86 RIE: 51 GC: 450
UF Articles (Grammar)
BT Form Classes (Languages)
RT Function Words
Morphology (Languages)
Syntax

DEVELOPED NATIONS *Jan. 1969*
CIJE: 471 RIE: 616 GC: 610
UF Advanced Nations
Economically Advanced Nations
Industrial Nations
BT Geographic Regions
RT Area Studies
Developing Nations
Development
Economic Development
Human Resources
Industrialization
Industrial Personnel
Industrial Structure
International Programs
International Relations
International Trade
Labor Economics
Labor Force
Living Standards
Modernization
National Programs
Productivity
Quality Of Life
Technical Assistance
Technological Advancement
Technology
World Affairs

DEVELOPING INSTITUTIONS *Mar. 1980*
CIJE: 19 RIE: 73 GC: 340
SN Smaller colleges and universities that, for reasons beyond their control, are not realizing their full potential, are struggling for survival, and are isolated from the mainstream of academic life -- specifically, institutions affected by title iii of the higher education act of 1965
BT Colleges
RT Black Colleges
Equalization Aid
Federal Aid
Government School Relationship
Higher Education
Institutional Survival
Small Colleges

DEVELOPING NATIONS *Jul. 1966*
CIJE: 3186 RIE: 3454 GC: 610
UF Emerging Nations
Third World Countries
Underdeveloped Nations
BT Geographic Regions
RT Area Studies
Community Development
Culture Lag
Developed Nations
Development
Economic Development
Foreign Nationals
Human Resources
Industrialization
International Programs
International Relations
International Trade
Labor Economics
Living Standards
Modernization
Nationalism
National Programs
Nonformal Education
Productivity
Quality Of Life
Revolution
Technical Assistance
Technological Advancement
World Affairs
World Problems

DEVELOPMENT *Jul. 1966*
CIJE: 410 RIE: 438 GC: 520
SN Progression from earlier to later stages of growth or organization -- includes gradual realization of potential, usually accompanied by advances in size, complexity, efficiency, etc. (note: do not confuse with "change," which refers to alterations, modifications, etc., that are not sequential and progressive -- use a more specific term if possible)
NT Community Development
Economic Development
Educational Development
Evolution
Facility Expansion
Individual Development
Industrialization
Job Development
Labor Force Development
Library Collection Development
Material Development
Modernization
Organizational Development
Plant Growth
Population Growth
Program Development
Rural Development
Site Development
Student Development
Systems Development
Technological Advancement
Urbanization
Vocabulary Development
RT Appropriate Technology
Change
Design
Developed Nations
Developing Nations
Developmental Continuity
Developmental Disabilities
Developmental Programs
Developmental Stages
Developmental Tasks
History
Improvement
Influences
Innovation
Planning
Research And Development
Research And Development Centers
Technology

DEVELOPMENTAL CONTINUITY *Oct. 1983*
CIJE: 21 RIE: 61 GC: 520
SN Transitional continuity in human learning and development, e.g., between different elements and levels of schooling
UF Continuity Of Education
BT Relationship
RT Articulation (Education)
Development
Developmental Psychology
Developmental Stages
Epistemology
Experience
Humanization
Individual Development

DEVELOPMENTAL DISABILITIES *Jun. 1977*
CIJE: 301 RIE: 445 GC: 220
SN Category in federal legislation referring to disabilities resulting from mental retardation, cerebral palsy, epilepsy, autism, or other neurological conditions closely related to mental retardation that originate before age 18 and are considered substantial handicaps to normal functioning
BT Disabilities
RT Autism
Cerebral Palsy
Cognitive Development
Communication Disorders
Development
Epilepsy
Exceptional Persons
Learning Disabilities
Mental Retardation
Neurological Impairments

Developmental Guidance (1967 1980)
USE GUIDANCE

DEVELOPMENTAL PROGRAMS *Jul. 1966*
CIJE: 365 RIE: 802 GC: 520
SN Programs promoting gradual growth of persons or systems through progressive advances in size, complexity, capacity, or efficiency (note: coordinate with appropriate "development" term if possible)
NT Developmental Studies Programs
BT Programs
RT Development
Economic Development
Educational Development
Individual Development
Labor Force Development

DEVELOPMENTAL PSYCHOLOGY *Jul. 1966*
CIJE: 695 RIE: 460 GC: 230
BT Psychology
RT Behavior Development
Behaviorism
Child Psychology
Cognitive Development
Developmental Continuity
Developmental Stages
Developmental Tasks
Emotional Development
Individual Development
Individual Psychology
Nature Nurture Controversy
Personality Development
Piagetian Theory
Sexual Identity

DEVELOPMENTAL READING (1966 1980) *Mar. 1980*
CIJE: 115 RIE: 351 GC: 460
SN Invalid descriptor -- used for the development of average or above average readers' skills in elementary and secondary education and for the development of below average readers' skills in higher education -- see "reading instruction" for the former concept and "remedial reading" for the latter

DEVELOPMENTAL STAGES *Oct. 1976*
CIJE: 1368 RIE: 1078 GC: 120
SN Natural or common divisions of the human developmental process, characterized by types of behavior (as in the oral stage), by biological properties or manifestations (as in the embryonic stage), or by mental processes (as in piaget's "concrete operations" stage)
UF Stages Of Development
Stage Theory
RT Adolescent Development
Adult Development
Age
Age Differences
Age Groups
Aging (Individuals)
Behavior Development
Child Development
Cognitive Development
Compensation (Concept)
Concept Formation
Development
Developmental Continuity
Developmental Psychology
Developmental Tasks
Emotional Development
Epistemology
Formal Operations
Individual Development
Infant Behavior
Object Permanence
Physical Development
Piagetian Theory

DEVELOPMENTAL STUDIES PROGRAMS *Mar. 1980*
CIJE: 125 RIE: 238 GC: 310
SN Comprehensive programs with both cognitive and affective components designed to develop the learning and academic skills and the attitudes toward self and others needed to enter and succeed at postsecondary institutions (note: do not confuse with "developmental programs," which prior to mar80, was frequently used for "developmental studies programs")
BT Developmental Programs
RT Basic Skills
College Preparation
Compensatory Education
Educationally Disadvantaged
High Risk Students
Individual Development
Remedial Programs
Skill Development
Transitional Programs

DEVELOPMENTAL TASKS *Jul. 1966*
CIJE: 213 RIE: 254 GC: 120
SN Tasks that arise during different stages of individual development, and whose successful completion is regarded by a society or culture as appropriate and necessary for acceptable functioning and subsequent development
RT Adolescent Development
Adult Development
Child Development
Development
Developmental Psychology
Developmental Stages
Readiness

DIABETES *Apr. 1969*
CIJE: 62 RIE: 42 GC: 210
BT Diseases
RT Physical Health
Physiology
Special Health Problems

DIACHRONIC LINGUISTICS *Jul. 1966*
CIJE: 425 RIE: 380 GC: 450
SN Study of languages or linguistic features through the course of their historical development
UF Historical Linguistics
History Of Language
Language History
NT Etymology
Glottochronology
BT Linguistics
RT Anthropological Linguistics
Contrastive Linguistics
Language Classification
Language Research
Language Universals
Language Variation
Lexicology
Linguistic Borrowing
Middle English
Morphology (Languages)
Old English
Onomastics
Phonemics
Phonology
Structural Analysis (Linguistics)
Structural Linguistics

DIACRITICAL MARKING *Jul. 1966*
CIJE: 27 RIE: 17 GC: 450
BT Orthographic Symbols
RT Graphemes
Phonetics
Phonetic Transcription
Pronunciation
Reading
Spelling

Diagnosis
USE IDENTIFICATION

Diagnosis (Clinical)
USE CLINICAL DIAGNOSIS

Diagnosis (Educational)
USE EDUCATIONAL DIAGNOSIS

DIAGNOSTIC TEACHING *Jul. 1966*
CIJE: 398 RIE: 781 GC: 310
SN Process of diagnosing student abilities, needs, and objectives and prescribing requisite learning activities
UF Prescriptive Teaching
BT Teaching Methods
RT Counselor Teacher Cooperation
Diagnostic Tests
Educational Diagnosis
Educational Therapy
Individualized Education Programs
Individualized Instruction
Informal Assessment
Learning Problems
Miscue Analysis
Psychoeducational Methods
Remedial Instruction
Special Education

DIAGNOSTIC TESTS *Jul. 1966*
CIJE: 624 RIE: 807 GC: 830
SN Tests used to identify the nature and source of an individual's educational, psychological, or medical difficulties or disabilities in order to facilitate correction or remediation
BT Tests
RT Auditory Tests
Clinical Diagnosis
Criterion Referenced Tests
Diagnostic Teaching
Educational Diagnosis
Handicap Identification
Identification
Informal Reading Inventories
Medical Evaluation
Personality Measures
Physical Examinations
Preschool Tests
Prognostic Tests
Projective Measures
Psychological Evaluation
Psychological Testing
Reading Readiness Tests
School Readiness Tests
Screening Tests
Vision Tests
Vocational Evaluation
Work Sample Tests

DIAGRAMS *Dec. 1969*
CIJE: 886 RIE: 176 GC: 720
BT Visual Aids
RT Charts
Data
Geometric Constructions
Graphic Arts
Illustrations
Instructional Materials
Mathematical Models
Nonprint Media
Records (Forms)
Sentence Diagraming

DIAL ACCESS INFORMATION SYSTEMS *Aug. 1968*
CIJE: 74 RIE: 89 GC: 710
SN Telecommunication systems in which users select (using a dial similar to a telephone dial) stored audio and/or video programs from remote locations
BT Audiovisual Communications
Information Systems
RT Computer Oriented Programs
Information Networks
Language Laboratories
Learning Laboratories
Online Systems
Telephone Communications Systems

Dialect Interference
USE DIALECTS; INTERFERENCE (LANGUAGE)

DIALECT STUDIES *Jul. 1966*
CIJE: 254 RIE: 417 GC: 810
SN Studies of the different ways in which the same language is spoken in different geographic regions or among different social classes (note: as of oct81, use as a minor descriptor for examples of this kind of research -- use as a major descriptor only as the subject of a document)
BT Language Research
Sociolinguistics
RT Bidialectalism
Dialects
Diglossia
Etymology
Language Variation

Dialectical Materialism
USE MARXISM

DIALECTS *Jul. 1966*
CIJE: 312 RIE: 469 GC: 450
SN Special varieties within a language distinguished by differences in vocabulary, pronunciation, and grammar but not sufficiently different to be regarded as separate languages
UF Dialect Interference #
NT Black Dialects
Nonstandard Dialects
Regional Dialects
Social Dialects
BT Languages
Language Variation
RT Bidialectalism
Cebuano
Dialect Studies
Diglossia
Foochow
Grammatical Acceptability
Idioms
Language
Language Classification
Language Standardization
Language Usage
Linguistics
Mutual Intelligibility
Native Speakers
North American English
Sociolinguistics

DIALOGS (LANGUAGE) *Apr. 1980*
CIJE: 118 RIE: 207 GC: 450
RT Communicative Competence (Languages)
Connected Discourse
Interpersonal Communication
Language Fluency
Language Patterns
Language Proficiency
Pattern Drills (Language)
Second Language Instruction
Speech Acts
Speech Communication

DIALOGS (LITERARY) *Apr. 1980*
CIJE: 208 RIE: 88 GC: 430
UF Dialogue (1969 1980)
BT Literary Devices
RT Drama

Dialogue (1969 1980)
USE DIALOGS (LITERARY)

DIARIES *Aug. 1968*
CIJE: 93 RIE: 85 GC: 430
SN Records, written daily or at frequent intervals, of the experiences, observations, attitudes, etc., of their authors (note: prior to mar80, this term was not scoped and carried the instruction "minutes (records), use diaries")
BT Literary Genres
Nonfiction
RT Autobiographies
Literature
Personal Narratives

DICTATION *Jun. 1983*
CIJE: 67 RIE: 38 GC: 720
SN Saying or reading aloud for transcription or machine recording -- also, the resulting transcribed or recorded text
UF Machine Dictation
BT Verbal Communication
RT Business Correspondence
Business Skills
Language Skills
Second Language Learning
Secretaries
Shorthand

Dictatorship
USE TOTALITARIANISM

DICTION *Jul. 1966*
CIJE: 21 RIE: 28 GC: 450
RT Articulation (Speech)
Language Fluency
Language Patterns
Pronunciation
Speech
Speech Tests

DICTIONARIES *Jul. 1966*
CIJE: 338 RIE: 568 GC: 720
SN (Note: corresponds to pubtype code 134 -- do not use except as the subject of a document)
UF Lexicons
NT Glossaries
BT Reference Materials
RT Alphabetizing Skills
Definitions
Lexicography

= Two or more Descriptors are used to represent this term.
The term's main entry shows the appropriate coordination.

Lexicology
Thesauri
Word Lists

Dictionary Catalogs (1968 1980)
USE LIBRARY CATALOGS

DIDACTICISM *Apr. 1970*
CIJE: 39 RIE: 12 GC: 430
SN Instructive qualities in literature, especially concerning moral, ethical, or religious matters
RT Childrens Literature
Epics
Fables
Legends
Literary Criticism

DIESEL ENGINES *Jul. 1966*
CIJE: 7 RIE: 93 GC: 910
BT Engines
RT Agricultural Machinery
Auto Mechanics
Locomotive Engineers
Motor Vehicles
Small Engine Mechanics

Diesel Fuel
USE FUELS

Diesel Mechanics
USE AUTO MECHANICS

DIETETICS *Sep. 1968*
CIJE: 306 RIE: 228 GC: 210
UF Diets
BT Medicine
RT Dietitians
Eating Habits
Food
Food Standards
Nutrition
Obesity

DIETITIANS *Jul. 1966*
CIJE: 12 RIE: 45 GC: 210
BT Allied Health Personnel
RT Cooks
Dietetics
Food
Food Service
Foods Instruction
Food Standards
Home Economics Skills
Nutrition
Occupational Home Economics

Diets
USE DIETETICS

DIFFERENCES *Jan. 1978*
CIJE: 185 RIE: 181 GC: 520
SN Distinguishing elements or factors which differentiate one entity from another (note: use a more specific term if possible)
UF Institutional Differences #
Regional Differences #
NT Cultural Differences
Individual Differences
Intermode Differences
Racial Differences
Religious Differences
Rural Urban Differences
Salary Wage Differentials
Social Differences
RT Comparative Analysis
Comparative Testing
Evaluation
Specialization

Differential Psychology
USE INDIVIDUAL PSYCHOLOGY

DIFFERENTIATED STAFFS *May. 1969*
CIJE: 143 RIE: 288 GC: 360
SN Staffs utilizing various levels of professional and semiprofessional personnel
BT Personnel
RT Master Teachers
Merit Pay
Paraprofessional School Personnel
Staff Utilization
Teacher Interns
Teachers

DIFFICULTY LEVEL *Mar. 1980*
CIJE: 696 RIE: 648 GC: 810
UF Complexity Level (1968 1979)
Intricacy Level
Item Difficulty #
Task Difficulty
RT Ability
Comprehension
Content Analysis
Item Analysis
Performance
Problems
Readability Formulas
Skill Analysis
Skills
Task Analysis

DIFFUSION (COMMUNICATION) *Sep. 1982*
CIJE: 36 RIE: 74 GC: 710
SN Process by which an idea gets from its source or origin to its place of ultimate use
UF Diffusion (1967 1982) (Communication)
BT Communication (Thought Transfer)
RT Adoption (Ideas)
Information Dissemination
Information Transfer
Information Utilization
Linking Agents
Networks
Research Utilization
Technology Transfer
Theory Practice Relationship
Transfer Of Training

DIFFUSION (PHYSICS) *Sep. 1982*
CIJE: 7 RIE: 4 GC: 490
SN Spontaneous movement and scattering of particles (atoms, molecules, electrons, etc.)
UF Diffusion (1967 1982) (Physics)
BT Kinetics
RT Biophysics
Chemical Reactions
Climate
Electronics
Energy
Kinetic Molecular Theory
Matter
Motion
Optics
Physics
Thermodynamics

Diffusion (1967 1982) (Communication)
USE DIFFUSION (COMMUNICATION)

Diffusion (1967 1982) (Physics)
USE DIFFUSION (PHYSICS)

Diffusion (1967 1982) (Populations)
USE POPULATION DISTRIBUTION

DIGITAL COMPUTERS *Jul. 1966*
CIJE: 59 RIE: 135 GC: 910
SN Computers that process discrete or discontinuous data, performing sequences of arithmetic and logical operations
BT Computers
RT Analog Computers

Digital Optical Data Disks
USE OPTICAL DATA DISKS

DIGLOSSIA *Jul. 1966*
CIJE: 68 RIE: 66 GC: 450
SN Situation in which two (or more) languages or language varieties are used for differing functions (e.g., vernacular and literary, colloquial and formal) within a single speech community
RT Bidialectalism
Bilingualism
Dialects
Dialect Studies
Language Classification
Language Standardization
Language Variation
Multilingualism
Mutual Intelligibility
Nonstandard Dialects
Social Dialects
Sociolinguistics

DIMENSIONAL PREFERENCE *Jul. 1972*
CIJE: 132 RIE: 38 GC: 110
SN Cue response to color, form or size
BT Responses
RT Color
Cues
Learning Modalities
Novelty (Stimulus Dimension)
Patterned Responses
Stimuli
Tactual Perception
Visual Perception

DINING FACILITIES *Jul. 1966*
CIJE: 70 RIE: 98 GC: 920
UF Cafeterias
Restaurants
Snack Bars
BT Facilities
RT Breakfast Programs
Cooks
Dishwashing
Food Handling Facilities
Food Service
Hospitality Occupations
Lunch Programs
Waiters And Waitresses

Diploma Requirements
USE GRADUATION REQUIREMENTS

Diplomacy
USE INTERNATIONAL RELATIONS

DIPLOMATIC HISTORY *Jun. 1973*
CIJE: 23 RIE: 19 GC: 610
SN History of negotiations among nations, including the study of international alliances, treaties, and other agreements
BT History
RT Foreign Diplomats
Foreign Policy
International Education
International Relations
Political Science
World Affairs
World History

Diplomatic Policy
USE FOREIGN POLICY

DIRECTED READING ACTIVITY *Jul. 1966*
CIJE: 126 RIE: 171 GC: 460
SN Teacher-guided reading activity -- usually includes the following steps: readiness, concept development, silent reading, discussion, and reinforcement of new skills and concepts (note: prior to mar80, the use of this term was not restricted by a scope note)
BT Reading
Reading Instruction
RT Advance Organizers
Content Area Reading
Learning Activities
Reading Assignments
Reading Comprehension

DIRECTION WRITING (1966 1980) *Mar. 1980*
CIJE: 13 RIE: 12 GC: 400
SN Invalid descriptor -- used inconsistently in indexing

DIRECTORIES *Jul. 1966*
CIJE: 325 RIE: 1681 GC: 720
SN Systematically arranged lists of persons or organizations, usually including locational information (note: corresponds to pubtype code 132 -- do not use except as the subject of a document)
BT Reference Materials
RT Guides
Indexes

Directors Of Research
USE RESEARCH DIRECTORS

DISABILITIES *Mar. 1980*
CIJE: 3334 RIE: 4188 GC: 220
SN Physical, mental, or sensory impairments that render major life activities more difficult (note: use a more specific term if possible)
UF Disabled
Handicapped (1966 1980)
Handicaps
NT Adventitious Impairments
Attention Deficit Disorders
Behavior Disorders
Communication Disorders
Congenital Impairments
Developmental Disabilities
Diseases
Hearing Impairments
Injuries
Language Handicaps
Learning Disabilities
Mental Disorders
Mental Retardation
Mild Disabilities
Multiple Disabilities
Perceptual Handicaps
Physical Disabilities
Severe Disabilities
Special Health Problems
Speech Handicaps
Visual Impairments
RT Ability
Accessibility (For Disabled)
Adapted Physical Education
Adaptive Behavior (Of Disabled)
Assistive Devices (For Disabled)
Deinstitutionalization (Of Disabled)
Exceptional Child Research
Exceptional Persons
Gifted Disabled
Group Homes
Handicap Discrimination
Handicap Identification
Health
High Risk Persons
Mainstreaming
Normalization (Handicapped)
Patients
Rehabilitation
Residential Care
Respite Care
Self Care Skills
Sheltered Workshops
Special Education
Special Education Teachers
Therapy

Disabled
USE DISABILITIES

DISADVANTAGED *Mar. 1980*
CIJE: 1312 RIE: 3351 GC: 540
SN Individuals or groups who have low status in a particular society for reasons of race, sex, ethnicity, economics, language, geographic location, environment, education, disabilities, etc. (note: use a more specific term if possible)
UF Cultural Disadvantagement (1966 1980)
Culturally Disadvantaged (1966 1980)
Deprived
Disadvantaged Groups (1966 1980)
Social Disadvantagement (1966 1980)
Socially Disadvantaged (1966 1980)
Underprivileged
NT Disadvantaged Youth
Economically Disadvantaged
Educationally Disadvantaged
Gifted Disadvantaged
BT Groups
RT Advantaged
Affirmative Action
Disadvantaged Environment
Living Standards
Lower Class
Quality Of Life
Rehabilitation
Social Status

Disadvantaged Children
USE DISADVANTAGED YOUTH

DISADVANTAGED ENVIRONMENT *Jul. 1966*
CIJE: 124 RIE: 204 GC: 550
SN An environment characterized by neglect, poverty, or social, cultural, racial, or linguistic isolation
UF Deprivation
Deprived Environment
Disadvantagement
BT Environment
RT Cultural Isolation
Disadvantaged
Disadvantaged Schools

= Two or more Descriptors are used to represent this term.
The term's main entry shows the appropriate coordination.

Educationally Disadvantaged
Poverty
Poverty Areas
Slum Environment
Social Isolation

Disadvantaged Groups (1966 1980)
USE DISADVANTAGED

DISADVANTAGED SCHOOLS *Jul. 1966*
CIJE: 32 RIE: 88 GC: 340
SN Schools whose programs, facilities, or resources do not meet the basic educational needs of their students (note: prior to mar80, the use of this term was not restricted by a scope note)
BT Schools
RT Disadvantaged Environment
Educationally Disadvantaged
Equalization Aid
Slum Schools

DISADVANTAGED YOUTH *Jul. 1966*
CIJE: 2049 RIE: 4789 GC: 540
UF Deprived Children
Disadvantaged Children
Slum Children
BT Disadvantaged
Youth
RT Lower Class Students

Disadvantagement
USE DISADVANTAGED ENVIRONMENT

DISARMAMENT *Apr. 1972*
CIJE: 124 RIE: 144 GC: 610
UF Arms Control
Multilateral Disarmament
Nuclear Control
Unilateral Disarmament
RT Armed Forces
Conflict
International Relations
Military Science
National Defense
Nuclear Warfare
Peace
War
World Problems

Disaster Readiness
USE EMERGENCY PROGRAMS

Disbursements (Money)
USE EXPENDITURES

Disciplinary Action
USE DISCIPLINE

DISCIPLINE *Jul. 1966*
CIJE: 1012 RIE: 1007 GC: 330
UF Classroom Discipline #
Disciplinary Action
NT Dismissal (Personnel)
Expulsion
Suspension
Teacher Discipline
RT Behavior Problems
Classroom Techniques
Codes Of Ethics
Corporal Punishment
Delay Of Gratification
Discipline Policy
Discipline Problems
Obedience
Proctoring
Punishment
Reality Therapy
Sanctions
Self Control

DISCIPLINE POLICY *Jul. 1966*
CIJE: 560 RIE: 510 GC: 330
BT Policy
RT Behavior Standards
Codes Of Ethics
Corporal Punishment
Discipline
Dress Codes
In School Suspension
School Policy
Student Rights

DISCIPLINE PROBLEMS *Jul. 1966*
CIJE: 402 RIE: 326 GC: 530
BT Problems
RT Cheating
Discipline
Lying
Plagiarism
Stealing
Vandalism

DISCLOSURE *Mar. 1978*
CIJE: 211 RIE: 167 GC: 710
SN Communication of personal, organizational, or institutional information and records
UF Public Disclosure
NT Self Disclosure (Individuals)
RT Case Records
Communication (Thought Transfer)
Confidentiality
Confidential Records
Freedom Of Information
Information Dissemination
Intellectual Freedom
Privacy
Student Records
Student Rights

DISCOGRAPHIES *Feb. 1976*
CIJE: 30 RIE: 23 GC: 730
SN Organized lists of phonograph records
UF Phonograph Record Lists
BT Reference Materials
RT Audiodisks
Bibliographies
Filmographies
Indexes
Library Catalogs
Music
Oral History

DISCOURSE ANALYSIS *Aug. 1968*
CIJE: 870 RIE: 924 GC: 450
BT Structural Analysis (Linguistics)
RT Coherence
Cohesion (Written Composition)
Communication Research
Connected Discourse
Grammar
Language Research
Morphology (Languages)
Narration
Paragraph Composition
Pragmatics
Semantics
Sentences
Speech Acts
Story Grammar
Syntax

Discovery
USE DISCOVERY PROCESSES

DISCOVERY LEARNING *Jul. 1966*
CIJE: 843 RIE: 471 GC: 110
SN Learning situation in which the principal content of what is to be learned is not given but must be independently discovered by the learner
UF Exploratory Learning
BT Learning
RT Activity Units
Adventure Education
Discovery Processes
Experiential Learning
Heuristics
Independent Study
Inquiry
Learning Activities
Learning Centers (Classroom)
Learning Strategies
Montessori Method
Observational Learning
Open Education
Questioning Techniques

DISCOVERY PROCESSES *Jul. 1966*
CIJE: 215 RIE: 168 GC: 110
SN Behaviors (e.g., inquiry, exploration, experimentation, etc.) used by persons in ascertaining things not hitherto known, or known by them (note: compare "inventions" -- do not confuse with "exploratory behavior")
UF Discovery
BT Learning Processes
RT Adoption (Ideas)
Creative Thinking
Creativity
Discovery Learning
Experience
Experiments
Innovation
Intellectual Property
Inventions
Perception
Productive Thinking
Research

DISCRIMINANT ANALYSIS *Jul. 1966*
CIJE: 245 RIE: 214 GC: 820
SN Statistical method for combining a set of measures, or score profiles, to obtain the maximum difference or discrimination between two or more groups
UF Discriminant Function Analysis
Discriminatory Analysis
Multiple Discriminant Analysis
BT Multivariate Analysis
RT Factor Analysis
Item Analysis
Mathematical Models
Multidimensional Scaling
Multitrait Multimethod Techniques

Discriminant Function Analysis
USE DISCRIMINANT ANALYSIS

Discrimination (Social)
USE SOCIAL DISCRIMINATION

DISCRIMINATION LEARNING *Jul. 1966*
CIJE: 896 RIE: 328 GC: 110
SN Learning to detect and respond to differences among stimuli
BT Learning
RT Auditory Discrimination
Concept Formation
Perception
Sensory Training
Shift Studies
Visual Discrimination

Discrimination Transfer
USE SHIFT STUDIES

Discriminatory Analysis
USE DISCRIMINANT ANALYSIS

Discriminatory Attitudes (Social) (1966 1980)
USE SOCIAL BIAS

DISCRIMINATORY LEGISLATION *Jul. 1966*
CIJE: 125 RIE: 135 GC: 540
SN Legislation that is biased against a particular group
UF Legislative Discrimination
BT Legislation
RT Civil Rights Legislation
Constitutional Law
Laws
Legal Problems
Majority Attitudes
Social Bias
Social Discrimination

DISCUSSION *Mar. 1980*
CIJE: 145 RIE: 153 GC: 720
SN Oral, and sometimes written, exchange of opinions -- usually to analyze, clarify, or reach conclusions about issues, questions, or problems
UF Discussion Experience (1966 1980)
Discussion Programs (1966 1980)
NT Group Discussion
BT Communication (Thought Transfer)
RT Decision Making
Discussion (Teaching Technique)
Discussion Groups
Interpersonal Communication
Interviews
Participation
Problem Solving
Speech Communication

DISCUSSION (TEACHING TECHNIQUE) *Jul. 1966*
CIJE: 498 RIE: 511 GC: 310
UF Class Discussion
Discussion Guides #
BT Teaching Methods
RT Discussion
Discussion Groups
Lecture Method
Questioning Techniques

Discussion Experience (1966 1980)
USE DISCUSSION

DISCUSSION GROUPS *Jul. 1966*
CIJE: 263 RIE: 256 GC: 310
SN Groups that meet to discuss subjects of mutual interest (note: do not confuse with "group discussion")
NT Listening Groups
BT Groups
RT Discussion
Discussion (Teaching Technique)
Group Discussion

Discussion Guides
USE DISCUSSION (TEACHING TECHNIQUE); TEACHING GUIDES

Discussion Programs (1966 1980)
USE DISCUSSION

DISEASE CONTROL *Jul. 1966*
CIJE: 253 RIE: 261 GC: 210
NT Fluoridation
RT Cleaning
Communicable Diseases
Disease Incidence
Diseases
Dishwashing
Drinking Water
Epidemiology
Health
Health Education
Hygiene
Immunization Programs
Pesticides
Pests
Pollution
Preventive Medicine
Public Health
Sanitation
Water Treatment

DISEASE INCIDENCE *Mar. 1980*
CIJE: 64 RIE: 45 GC: 210
UF Disease Rate (1967 1980)
BT Incidence
RT Disease Control
Diseases
Epidemiology
Public Health

Disease Rate (1967 1980)
USE DISEASE INCIDENCE

DISEASES *Jul. 1966*
CIJE: 519 RIE: 281 GC: 210
SN (Note: use "special health problems" for discussions of the effects (or potential effects) of particular diseases on individual learning and development -- prior to mar80, this term did not carry a scope note)
UF Chronic Illnesses
Illnesses
Sicknesses
NT Alcoholism
Allergy
Anemia
Anorexia Nervosa
Asthma
Bulimia
Cancer
Communicable Diseases
Diabetes
Drug Addiction
Failure To Thrive
Hypertension
Obesity
Occupational Diseases
Poisoning
Seizures
BT Disabilities
RT Adventitious Impairments
Disease Control
Disease Incidence
Epidemiology
Exceptional Persons
Gynecology
Health
Heart Disorders
Hygiene
Internal Medicine

= Two or more Descriptors are used to represent this term.
The term's main entry shows the appropriate coordination.

Pathology
Patient Education
Perinatal Influences
Pests
Physical Health
Pollution
Prenatal Influences
Radiation Effects
Rehabilitation
Stress Variables
Surgery

Disemployment
USE DISLOCATED WORKERS

DISHWASHING *Mar. 1969*
CIJE: 9 RIE: 20 GC: 210
BT Cleaning
RT Dining Facilities
Disease Control
Food Handling Facilities
Food Service
Hygiene
Sanitary Facilities

DISLOCATED WORKERS *Mar. 1984*
CIJE: 25 RIE: 81 GC: 630
SN Workers who have lost their jobs because of economic and technological changes in a business or industry, e.g., plant closings or relocation, increased competition, automation, or market fluctuations
UF Disemployment
Displaced Workers
BT Personnel
RT Career Change
Dismissal (Personnel)
Employees
Employment
Employment Patterns
Employment Practices
Job Applicants
Job Layoff
Job Search Methods
Job Skills
Labor Economics
Labor Force
Labor Market
Labor Turnover
Outplacement Services (Employment)
Reduction In Force
Retraining
Skill Obsolescence
Structural Unemployment
Technological Advancement
Unemployment

DISMISSAL (PERSONNEL) *Mar. 1980*
CIJE: 85 RIE: 57 GC: 630
SN Termination of employment when initiated by the employer (note: if applicable, use the more specific term "teacher dismissal" -- prior to mar80, the instruction "dismissal, use disqualification" was carried in the thesaurus)
UF Personnel Discharge
Personnel Dismissal
NT Teacher Dismissal
BT Discipline
RT Dislocated Workers
Disqualification
Employment Practices
Job Layoff
Outplacement Services (Employment)
Personnel Evaluation
Personnel Policy
Reduction In Force

DISPLACED HOMEMAKERS *Mar. 1980*
CIJE: 15 RIE: 125 GC: 510
SN Women over age 35 who have become responsible for their own support due to divorce, separation, or the death of their husbands and who have been outside the work force for an extended period of time -- they may face earning a living with minimal skills and experience
BT Females
RT Divorce
Fatherless Family
Heads Of Households
Homemakers
Job Applicants
Labor Market
Marital Instability
Mothers
Reentry Workers
Widowed

Displaced Workers
USE DISLOCATED WORKERS

DISPLAY AIDS *Mar. 1980*
CIJE: 41 RIE: 74 GC: 720
SN Materials and/or equipment used for visual displays
UF Display Panels (1968 1980)
BT Visual Aids
RT Audiovisual Aids
Educational Equipment
Exhibits
Merchandising
Nonprint Media
Screens (Displays)
Three Dimensional Aids

Display Panels (1968 1980)
USE DISPLAY AIDS

DISPLAY SYSTEMS *Jul. 1966*
CIJE: 189 RIE: 184 GC: 710
SN Combination hardware and software systems that present information visually on console screens or similar devices connected to computers (note: prior to mar80, this term was not scoped and was sometimes used for audiovisual displays)
BT Computers
RT Computer Graphics
Information Retrieval
Information Systems
Input Output Devices
Interactive Video
Man Machine Systems

DISQUALIFICATION *Jul. 1966*
CIJE: 28 RIE: 28 GC: 520
SN The act of making ineligible
UF Ineligibility
RT Dismissal (Personnel)
Eligibility
Expulsion
Qualifications
Suspension
Teacher Dismissal
Withdrawal (Education)

DISSENT *Apr. 1972*
CIJE: 201 RIE: 128 GC: 610
BT Social Behavior
RT Activism
Beliefs
Conflict
Controversial Issues (Course Content)
Opinions
Political Attitudes
Revolution
Social Action
Social Attitudes
Values

DISTANCE *Aug. 1968*
CIJE: 138 RIE: 109 GC: 480
UF Range (Distance)
RT Geographic Location
Height
Intervals
Proximity
Relationship
School Location
Scientific Concepts
Space
Time
Topology
Transportation

DISTANCE EDUCATION *Oct. 1983*
CIJE: 213 RIE: 290 GC: 330
SN Education via the communications media (correspondence, radio, television, and others) with little or no classroom or other face-to-face contact between students and teachers
NT Correspondence Study
BT Education
RT Access To Education
Communications Satellites
Continuing Education
Correspondence Schools
Educational Radio
Educational Television
Extension Education
External Degree Programs
Home Study
Independent Study
Lifelong Learning
Mass Instruction
Nontraditional Education
Open Universities
Outreach Programs
Part Time Students
Telecommunications
Telecourses

DISTINCTIVE FEATURES (LANGUAGE) *Mar. 1980*
CIJE: 262 RIE: 199 GC: 450
SN Features that distinguish linguistic units from one another -- most commonly used in phonology, where phonemes may be defined in terms of such distinctive features as voicing, point of articulation, and manner of articulation
UF Distinctive Features (1967 1980)
BT Linguistics
RT Acoustic Phonetics
Artificial Speech
Componential Analysis
Consonants
Language Universals
Phonemes
Phonetics
Phonology

Distinctive Features (1967 1980)
USE DISTINCTIVE FEATURES (LANGUAGE)

Distribution (Economics)
USE MARKETING

Distribution Free Statistics
USE NONPARAMETRIC STATISTICS

Distributions (Statistics)
USE STATISTICAL DISTRIBUTIONS

DISTRIBUTIVE EDUCATION *Jul. 1966*
CIJE: 282 RIE: 743 GC: 400
SN Formal preparation for occupations in the field of distribution and marketing covering such activities as selling, buying, transporting, storing, promoting, financing, marketing research, and management
UF Retail Training
BT Vocational Education
RT Agribusiness
Business Education
Communications
Cooperative Education
Distributive Education Teachers
Food Service
Insurance Occupations
Manufacturing
Marketing
Merchandising
Office Occupations
Real Estate Occupations
Retailing
Salesmanship
Sales Occupations
Transportation
Utilities
Wholesaling

DISTRIBUTIVE EDUCATION TEACHERS *Sep. 1968*
CIJE: 20 RIE: 35 GC: 360
BT Vocational Education Teachers
RT Distributive Education

District Libraries
USE REGIONAL LIBRARIES

District Norms
USE LOCAL NORMS

DIVERGENT THINKING *Nov. 1968*
CIJE: 246 RIE: 142 GC: 110
SN Creative, imaginative, and flexible thinking that results in a variety and abundance of ideas or answers to a problem
BT Creative Thinking
RT Brainstorming
Convergent Thinking
Problem Solving
Productive Thinking

Divided Catalogs (1968 1980)
USE LIBRARY CATALOGS

DIVING *Jan. 1985*
CIJE: 10 RIE: 8 GC: 470
SN Plunging into water in a prescribed manner (note: do not confuse with "underwater diving")
UF Platform Diving
Springboard Diving
Tower Diving
BT Aquatic Sports
RT Swimming
Swimming Pools

DIVISION *Jul. 1966*
CIJE: 167 RIE: 91 GC: 480
BT Arithmetic
RT Addition
Multiplication
Subtraction

DIVORCE *Feb. 1976*
CIJE: 603 RIE: 292 GC: 520
SN The legal dissolution of a marriage
UF Divorced Persons
RT Child Custody
Displaced Homemakers
Family Problems
Fatherless Family
Marital Instability
Marital Status
Marriage
Marriage Counseling
Motherless Family
One Parent Family
Remarriage
Spouses

Divorced Persons
USE DIVORCE

DNA *Oct. 1982*
CIJE: 44 RIE: 10 GC: 490
SN Any of the class of nucleic acids that contains deoxyribose, found chiefly in cell nuclei and associated with the transmission of genetic information
UF Deoxyribonucleic Acid
Desoxyribonucleic Acid
Recombinant Dna #
BT Nucleic Acids
RT Genetic Engineering
Genetics

DOCTOR OF ARTS DEGREES *Mar. 1976*
CIJE: 24 RIE: 20 GC: 340
SN Degrees emphasizing broad subject-matter competence and teaching skills and designed for students entering careers as college teachers
BT Doctoral Degrees
RT College Faculty
Degree Requirements
Doctoral Programs
Graduate Study

Doctor Patient Relationship
USE PHYSICIAN PATIENT RELATIONSHIP

DOCTORAL DEGREES *Jul. 1966*
CIJE: 422 RIE: 630 GC: 340
NT Doctor Of Arts Degrees
BT Degrees (Academic)
RT Bachelors Degrees
Degree Requirements
Doctoral Dissertations
Doctoral Programs
Graduate Study
Masters Degrees
Specialist In Education Degrees
Teacher Educator Education

DOCTORAL DISSERTATIONS *Mar. 1980*
CIJE: 294 RIE: 4305 GC: 720
SN Theses submitted in partial fulfillment of doctoral degree requirements (note: corresponds to pubtype code 041 -- do not use except as the subject of a document)
UF Doctoral Theses (1967 1980)
BT Theses
RT Degrees (Academic)
Doctoral Degrees
Doctoral Programs
Graduate Study
Practicum Papers

= Two or more Descriptors are used to represent this term.
The term's main entry shows the appropriate coordination.

DOCTORAL PROGRAMS *Jul. 1966*
CIJE: 459 RIE: 474 GC: 340
SN Formal graduate programs in higher education institutions that culminate in the award of a doctoral degree, such as a ph d or ed d
BT College Programs
RT Degree Requirements
Doctoral Degrees
Doctoral Dissertations
Doctor Of Arts Degrees
Graduate School Faculty
Graduate Students
Graduate Study
Higher Education
Masters Programs
Postdoctoral Education
Teacher Educator Education

Doctoral Theses (1967 1980)
USE DOCTORAL DISSERTATIONS

Document Readers
USE OPTICAL SCANNERS

DOCUMENTARIES *Sep. 1971*
CIJE: 88 RIE: 108 GC: 720
SN Factual film, videotape, or audio recordings of some real event or historic subject
BT Nonprint Media
RT Audiovisual Aids
Educational Radio
Educational Television
Film Industry
Films
Film Study
Instructional Films
Tape Recordings

DOCUMENTATION *Jul. 1966*
CIJE: 272 RIE: 583 GC: 710
SN Techniques used to collect, process, organize, store, and retrieve documents (note: use "computer software" for computer program documentation)
NT Abstracting
Bibliometrics
Cataloging
Filing
Indexing
BT Information Processing
RT Classification
Codification
Information Dissemination
Information Retrieval
Information Storage
Information Systems
Special Libraries
Technical Writing

DOGMATISM *Jul. 1966*
CIJE: 196 RIE: 94 GC: 120
RT Authoritarianism
Beliefs
Ideology
Opinions
Personality Traits
Totalitarianism

Domestic Violence (Family)
USE FAMILY VIOLENCE

Domestics (1970 1980)
USE HOUSEHOLD WORKERS

Dominican Americans
USE DOMINICANS; HISPANIC AMERICANS

DOMINICANS *Sep. 1975*
CIJE: 6 RIE: 10 GC: 560
SN Citizens of, or those who identify themselves as bearers of the culture of, the dominican republic
UF Dominican Americans #
BT Latin Americans
RT Ethnic Groups
Hispanic Americans
Spanish Speaking

DONORS *Oct. 1982*
CIJE: 100 RIE: 59 GC: 620
SN Individuals or organizations who donate money, land, or material goods to a cause, fund, or institution (note: for donors of body organs, blood, etc., use "tissue donors")
UF Financial Donors
BT Groups
RT Corporate Support
Endowment Funds
Fund Raising
Philanthropic Foundations
Private Financial Support
Social Support Groups
Trusts (Financial)

DOORS *Jul. 1969*
CIJE: 11 RIE: 8 GC: 920
BT Structural Elements (Construction)
RT Construction Materials

DORMITORIES *Jul. 1966*
CIJE: 355 RIE: 240 GC: 920
UF Dormitory Living #
Residence Halls
BT Housing
RT College Buildings
College Housing
Educational Facilities
House Plan
Living Learning Centers
On Campus Students
Resident Advisers
Resident Assistants
Residential Colleges

Dormitory Living
USE DORMITORIES; GROUP EXPERIENCE

Double Employment
USE MULTIPLE EMPLOYMENT

DOUBLE SESSIONS *Dec. 1969*
CIJE: 6 RIE: 10 GC: 350
SN School days consisting of separate sessions for two groups of students in the same instructional space, e.g., one room used by one fourth-grade class in the morning and by another fourth-grade class in the afternoon
UF Split Sessions
BT School Schedules
RT School Organization
Space Utilization

Downs Anomaly
USE DOWNS SYNDROME

DOWNS SYNDROME *Jan. 1978*
CIJE: 320 RIE: 103 GC: 220
UF Downs Anomaly
Mongolism (1968 1978)
BT Congenital Impairments
Mental Retardation
RT Genetics
Mild Mental Retardation
Moderate Mental Retardation
Neurological Impairments
Physical Characteristics

Drafters (1980 1981)
USE DRAFTING

DRAFTING *Jul. 1966*
CIJE: 301 RIE: 210 GC: 640
SN Communication of ideas through drawings, sketches, charts, graphs, and maps according to mathematical rules of projection -- also, the use of drafting instruments in lettering, sketching, geometric construction, orthographic and pictorial drawings, working drawings, etc.
UF Drafters (1980 1981)
Draftsmen (1968 1980)
Drawing (Precision Draft)
NT Architectural Drafting
Engineering Drawing
Technical Illustration
BT Visual Arts
RT Blueprints
Designers
Graphic Arts
Industrial Arts
Orthographic Projection
Technical Occupations

Draftsmen (1968 1980)
USE DRAFTING

DRAMA *Jul. 1966*
CIJE: 935 RIE: 865 GC: 430
UF Dramatic Unities (1970 1980)
Folk Drama (1969 1980) #
Outdoor Drama (1968 1980) #
Plays (Theatrical)
NT Comedy
Scripts
Tragedy
BT Literature
Theater Arts
RT Acting
Art
Audiences
Dialogs (Literary)
Dramatics
Fiction
Folk Culture
Literary Devices
Literary Genres
Literary Styles
Monologs
Oral Interpretation
Poetry
Prose

DRAMA WORKSHOPS *Jul. 1966*
CIJE: 23 RIE: 27 GC: 420
BT Workshops
RT Arts Centers
Dramatics
Theaters

Dramatic Arts
USE DRAMATICS

DRAMATIC PLAY *Jul. 1966*
CIJE: 197 RIE: 177 GC: 420
BT Role Playing
RT Class Activities
Creative Dramatics
Play
Pretend Play
Self Expression
Teaching Methods

Dramatic Unities (1970 1980)
USE DRAMA

DRAMATICS *Jul. 1966*
CIJE: 391 RIE: 389 GC: 420
SN Activities in the creation, preparation, and production of plays
UF Dramatic Arts
NT Creative Dramatics
BT Theater Arts
RT Acting
Art
Auditoriums
Dance
Drama
Drama Workshops
Language Arts
Pantomime
Playwriting
Prompting
Skits
Theaters

DRAVIDIAN LANGUAGES *Jul. 1966*
CIJE: 6 RIE: 22 GC: 440
NT Kannada
Malayalam
Tamil
Telugu
BT Languages
RT Language Classification
Native Speakers

Drawing (Computerized)
USE COMPUTER GRAPHICS

Drawing (Freehand)
USE FREEHAND DRAWING

Drawing (Precision Draft)
USE DRAFTING

DRESS CODES *Oct. 1971*
CIJE: 50 RIE: 73 GC: 320
SN Regulations governing personal dress and appearance including clothing, beards, hair, and cleanliness
BT Standards
RT Board Of Education Policy
Discipline Policy
Due Process
Employment Practices
Personnel Policy
Student Behavior
Student Rights
Student School Relationship

Dress Design
USE CLOTHING DESIGN

Drill Press Operators
USE MACHINE TOOL OPERATORS

Drill Presses
USE MACHINE TOOLS

DRILLS (PRACTICE) *Mar. 1980*
CIJE: 195 RIE: 136 GC: 310
SN Repetition of tasks or procedures
NT Pattern Drills (Language)
BT Teaching Methods
RT Memorization
Rote Learning
Study

DRINKING *May. 1974*
CIJE: 362 RIE: 304 GC: 210
SN Consumption of alcoholic beverages
UF Social Drinking
BT Behavior
RT Alcohol Education
Alcoholic Beverages
Alcoholism
Drug Use
Health Education
Recreational Activities

DRINKING WATER *Nov. 1982*
CIJE: 7 RIE: 19 GC: 410
UF Potable Water
BT Water
RT Disease Control
Fluoridation
Physical Health
Public Health
Utilities
Water Quality
Water Treatment

DRIVER EDUCATION *Jul. 1966*
CIJE: 90 RIE: 333 GC: 400
UF Driver Training
BT Education
RT Traffic Safety

Driver Training
USE DRIVER EDUCATION

DRIVEWAYS *Jan. 1969*
CIJE: RIE: 8 GC: 920
BT Facilities
RT Parking Facilities
Traffic Circulation
Vehicular Traffic

DROPOUT ATTITUDES *Jul. 1966*
CIJE: 68 RIE: 194 GC: 330
SN Attitudes of, not toward, dropouts (note: prior to mar80, the use of this term was not restricted by a scope note)
BT Attitudes
RT Alienation
Dropout Characteristics
Dropouts
Student Alienation

DROPOUT CHARACTERISTICS *Jul. 1966*
CIJE: 210 RIE: 557 GC: 330
UF Dropout Identification (1966 1980)
RT Dropout Attitudes
Dropout Prevention
Dropouts
Individual Characteristics
Participant Characteristics
Potential Dropouts

Dropout Employment
USE DROPOUT PROGRAMS

Dropout Identification (1966 1980)
USE DROPOUT CHARACTERISTICS

DROPOUT PREVENTION *Jul. 1966*
CIJE: 265 RIE: 717 GC: 320
BT Prevention
RT Continuation Students
Dropout Characteristics
Dropout Programs

= Two or more Descriptors are used to represent this term.
The term's main entry shows the appropriate coordination.

Dropout Research
Dropouts
Potential Dropouts

Dropout Problems (1966 1980)
USE DROPOUTS

DROPOUT PROGRAMS *Jul. 1966*
CIJE: 137 RIE: 326 GC: 320
UF Dropout Employment
Dropout Rehabilitation (1966 1980)
Dropout Teaching (1966 1980)
BT Rehabilitation Programs
RT Continuation Students
Dropout Prevention
Dropouts
High School Equivalency Programs

DROPOUT RATE *Jul. 1966*
CIJE: 128 RIE: 416 GC: 330
BT Incidence
RT Dropout Research
Dropouts
Student Attrition

Dropout Rehabilitation (1966 1980)
USE DROPOUT PROGRAMS

DROPOUT RESEARCH *Jul. 1966*
CIJE: 208 RIE: 565 GC: 810
SN Systematic investigations focusing on the characteristics, motives, etc. of individuals who withdraw from an activity before its completion (note: as of oct81, use as a minor descriptor for examples of this kind of research -- use as a major descriptor only as the subject of a document)
BT Research
RT Academic Persistence
Dropout Prevention
Dropout Rate
Dropouts
Persistence
School Holding Power
Student Attrition
Withdrawal (Education)

Dropout Role (1966 1980)
USE DROPOUTS

Dropout Teaching (1966 1980)
USE DROPOUT PROGRAMS

DROPOUTS *Jul. 1966*
CIJE: 784 RIE: 1319 GC: 510
SN Individuals who withdraw from an activity (e.g., educational program) before its completion
UF College Dropouts
Dropout Problems (1966 1980)
Dropout Role (1966 1980)
Early School Leavers
High School Dropouts
Rural Dropouts (1966 1981)
School Dropouts
Urban Dropouts (1966 1981)
NT Adult Dropouts
BT Groups
RT Academic Failure
Academic Persistence
Attendance
Attrition (Research Studies)
Continuation Students
Dropout Attitudes
Dropout Characteristics
Dropout Prevention
Dropout Programs
Dropout Rate
Dropout Research
Enrollment
Expulsion
High School Equivalency Programs
No Shows
Out Of School Youth
Persistence
Potential Dropouts
Reentry Students
Reentry Workers
Rehabilitation
Retraining
Runaways
School Holding Power
Stopouts
Student Attrition
Truancy
Withdrawal (Education)

Drowsiness
USE SLEEP

DRUG ABUSE *Jul. 1966*
CIJE: 1278 RIE: 1110 GC: 530
SN Excessive use or misuse of drugs, causing physical, emotional, mental, or sensory injury or impairment (note: if applicable, use the more specific term "drug addiction")
NT Drug Addiction
BT Drug Use
RT Alcoholism
Antisocial Behavior
Drug Education
Drug Legislation
Drug Rehabilitation
Illegal Drug Use
Lysergic Acid Diethylamide
Narcotics
Pharmacology
Prenatal Influences
Sedatives
Self Destructive Behavior
Smoking
Stimulants
Tobacco

DRUG ADDICTION *Jul. 1966*
CIJE: 333 RIE: 269 GC: 530
UF Chemical Dependency (Drugs)
Narcotics Addiction
BT Diseases
Drug Abuse
RT Alcoholism
Antisocial Behavior
Behavior Disorders
Crime
Drug Education
Drug Legislation
Drug Rehabilitation
Illegal Drug Use
Lysergic Acid Diethylamide
Marijuana
Narcotics
Pharmacology
Special Health Problems

DRUG EDUCATION *Jan. 1972*
CIJE: 609 RIE: 561 GC: 400
SN Study of the varied aspects of drugs, their source, abuse, chemical composition, and physical, personal, and social effects
BT Education
RT Alcohol Education
Drug Abuse
Drug Addiction
Drug Rehabilitation
Drug Use
Health Education
Narcotics
Pharmaceutical Education

Drug Inspectors
USE FOOD AND DRUG INSPECTORS

DRUG LEGISLATION *Jul. 1966*
CIJE: 77 RIE: 94 GC: 610
BT Public Health Legislation
RT Drug Abuse
Drug Addiction
Illegal Drug Use
Laws
Marijuana
Narcotics
Pharmacy

DRUG REHABILITATION *Mar. 1980*
CIJE: 90 RIE: 89 GC: 210
SN Process of restoring drug addicts or abusers to the best possible level of physical, mental, emotional, social, or vocational functioning (note: do not confuse with "drug therapy")
UF Drug Withdrawal
Withdrawal (Drugs)
BT Rehabilitation
RT Drug Abuse
Drug Addiction
Drug Education
Narcotics
Sedatives
Stimulants

DRUG THERAPY *May. 1969*
CIJE: 561 RIE: 203 GC: 210
SN Treatment or prevention of diseases and other disorders by the administration of drugs (note: prior to mar80, this term was not restricted by a scope note and was sometimes confused with "drug rehabilitation")
UF Chemotherapy
BT Therapy
RT Drug Use
Genetic Engineering
Medical Services
Pharmaceutical Education
Pharmacy

DRUG USE *Mar. 1980*
CIJE: 270 RIE: 211 GC: 210
SN Medicinal or nonmedicinal use of drugs
NT Drug Abuse
Illegal Drug Use
BT Behavior
RT Alcoholic Beverages
Drinking
Drug Education
Drug Therapy
Lysergic Acid Diethylamide
Marijuana
Narcotics
Pharmacology
Sedatives
Smoking
Stimulants
Tobacco

Drug Withdrawal
USE DRUG REHABILITATION

Druggists
USE PHARMACISTS

Drycleaning Laundry Occupations
USE LAUNDRY DRYCLEANING OCCUPATIONS

DUAL CAREER FAMILY *Oct. 1982*
CIJE: 70 RIE: 59 GC: 510
SN Family in which both partners or spouses pursue careers (i.e., long-term and developmentally sequential occupational activities outside of family life) (note: do not confuse with "employed parents")
BT Family (Sociological Unit)
RT Careers
Employed Parents
Employed Women
Family Structure

Dual Earner Parents
USE EMPLOYED PARENTS

DUAL ENROLLMENT *Aug. 1968*
CIJE: 18 RIE: 44 GC: 330
SN Enrollment of students in two schools at the same time
UF Shared Time (Education)
Split Time
BT Enrollment
RT Consortia
Cooperative Programs
Institutional Cooperation
Shared Resources And Services

DUE PROCESS *Oct. 1971*
CIJE: 670 RIE: 729 GC: 610
SN A course of proceedings established in the law for the enforcement and protection of private rights
UF Procedural Due Process
BT Civil Liberties
RT Childrens Rights
Civil Rights
Dress Codes
Equal Protection
Freedom Of Speech
Justice
Laws
Parent Rights
Search And Seizure
Student Behavior
Student Rights
Student School Relationship
Teacher Discipline
Teacher Dismissal
Teacher Rights

Dues
USE FEES

Duplicating
USE REPROGRAPHY

DUSUN *Jul. 1966*
CIJE: RIE: 1 GC: 440
BT Indonesian Languages

DUTCH *Jul. 1966*
CIJE: 59 RIE: 48 GC: 440
BT Indo European Languages
RT Afrikaans

DUTCH CULTURE *Jul. 1966*
CIJE: 5 RIE: 7 GC: 560
BT Culture

Dwellings
USE HOUSING

Dyadic Communication
USE INTERPERSONAL COMMUNICATION

DYSLEXIA *Jul. 1966*
CIJE: 336 RIE: 186 GC: 220
SN Impairment in the ability to read despite adequate intelligence and proper instruction
BT Language Handicaps
RT Aphasia
Learning Disabilities
Minimal Brain Dysfunction
Neurological Impairments
Perceptual Handicaps
Reading Difficulties
Reading Failure
Remedial Reading

Dysphonia
USE VOICE DISORDERS

Dysthymia
USE DEPRESSION (PSYCHOLOGY)

DYULA *Jul. 1966*
CIJE: RIE: 3 GC: 440
BT African Languages

EARLY ADMISSION *Jul. 1966*
CIJE: 49 RIE: 71 GC: 320
BT Admission (School)
RT Acceleration (Education)
Admission Criteria
School Entrance Age
School Readiness

Early Childhood (1966 1980)
USE YOUNG CHILDREN

EARLY CHILDHOOD EDUCATION *Jul. 1966*
CIJE: 3249 RIE: 4869 GC: 340
SN Activities and/or experiences that are intended to effect developmental changes in children, from birth through the primary units of elementary school (grades k-3) (note: also appears in the list of mandatory educational level descriptors)
NT Preschool Education
Primary Education
BT Education
RT Child Development Centers
Day Care Centers
Elementary Education
Kindergarten
Montessori Method
Nursery Schools
Young Children

Early Detection
USE IDENTIFICATION

EARLY EXPERIENCE *Jul. 1966*
CIJE: 273 RIE: 399 GC: 120
SN Experiences in infancy or early childhood that influence subsequent development
UF Preschool Experience
BT Experience
RT Prereading Experience
Young Children

EARLY PARENTHOOD *Nov. 1982*
CIJE: 65 RIE: 96 GC: 520
SN Parenthood assumed before age 20
UF Adolescent Parents
RT Adolescents
Child Welfare
Family Planning
Family Problems
Family Relationship
Parent Child Relationship
Parents
Pregnancy
Youth Problems

EARLY READING *Jul. 1966*
CIJE: 158 RIE: 229 GC: 460
SN Reading by children before they reach school age
BT Reading
RT Beginning Reading
Prereading Experience
Reading Readiness

EARLY RETIREMENT *Mar. 1984*
CIJE: 43 RIE: 39 GC: 630
SN Withdrawal from one's occupation or career at an earlier age or time than is mandatory or customary
BT Retirement
RT Career Change
Employment Practices
Fringe Benefits
Middle Aged Adults
Midlife Transitions
Personnel Policy
Reduction In Force
Teacher Retirement
Work Life Expectancy

Early School Leavers
USE DROPOUTS

EARS *Jul. 1966*
CIJE: 13 RIE: 17 GC: 210
RT Anatomy
Audiology
Auditory Tests
Hearing (Physiology)
Hearing Impairments
Human Body

EARTH SCIENCE *Jul. 1966*
CIJE: 1173 RIE: 716 GC: 490
UF Geoscience
NT Geology
Geophysics
Meteorology
Oceanography
Physical Geography
Seismology
Soil Science
BT Physical Sciences
RT Astronomy
Cartography
Chemistry
Climate
Crystallography
Physical Environment
Physics
Planetariums
Plate Tectonics
Satellites (Aerospace)
Space Sciences
Topography
Water
Wind (Meteorology)

EARTHQUAKES *Oct. 1983*
CIJE: 21 RIE: 23 GC: 490
RT Motion
Natural Disasters
Plate Tectonics
Seismology

Eastern Civilization
USE NON WESTERN CIVILIZATION

EATING HABITS *Jul. 1966*
CIJE: 427 RIE: 306 GC: 210
RT Anorexia Nervosa
Body Weight
Bulimia
Dietetics
Nutrition
Obesity
Physical Health
Self Care Skills

Ebonics
USE BLACK DIALECTS

ECHOLALIA *Sep. 1968*
CIJE: 29 RIE: 9 GC: 230
SN Involuntary and senseless repetition of words heard spoken by another person
UF Echophasia
BT Psychosis
RT Aphasia
Language Handicaps
Language Patterns
Schizophrenia

ECHOLOCATION *Oct. 1968*
CIJE: 6 RIE: 4 GC: 220
SN Ability of organisms to locate objects or to spatially orient themselves by means of reflected sound waves
RT Auditory Perception
Auditory Stimuli
Blindness
Psychoacoustics
Spatial Ability
Travel Training
Visually Handicapped Mobility

Echophasia
USE ECHOLALIA

ECOLOGICAL FACTORS *Jul. 1966*
CIJE: 337 RIE: 232 GC: 410
BT Influences
RT Conservation (Environment)
Crowding
Ecology
Energy Conservation
Poisons
Pollution
Radiation Effects

ECOLOGY *Jul. 1966*
CIJE: 1590 RIE: 1342 GC: 490
SN Study of the interrelationships between organisms and their environment
UF Ecosystems
BT Biological Sciences
RT Adjustment (To Environment)
Air Pollution
Area Studies
Biology
Botany
Climate
Conservation (Environment)
Ecological Factors
Energy Conservation
Environment
Environmental Education
Environmental Standards
Estuaries
Ethology
Evolution
Human Geography
Marine Biology
Noise (Sound)
Ocean Engineering
Pests
Photosynthesis
Quality Of Life
Radiation Biology
Recycling
Scientific Research
Social Biology
Soil Conservation
Waste Disposal
Wastes
Water
Water Pollution
Water Quality
Weather
Wind (Meteorology)
Zoology

Economic Analysis
USE ECONOMIC RESEARCH

ECONOMIC CHANGE *Jun. 1969*
CIJE: 296 RIE: 413 GC: 620
BT Change
RT Change Strategies
Community Change
Cost Indexes
Culture Lag
Economic Climate
Economic Development
Economic Factors
Economic Progress
Economics
Economic Status
Finance Reform
Institutional Survival
Revolution
Social Change
Structural Unemployment

ECONOMIC CLIMATE *Jul. 1966*
CIJE: 280 RIE: 329 GC: 620
NT Inflation (Economics)
BT Environment
RT Business Cycles
Economic Change
Economic Opportunities
Economics
Quality Of Life

Economic Cycles
USE BUSINESS CYCLES

ECONOMIC DEVELOPMENT *Jul. 1966*
CIJE: 784 RIE: 1686 GC: 620
NT Economic Progress
BT Development
RT Community Development
Developed Nations
Developing Nations
Developmental Programs
Economic Change
Economics
Educational Economics
Labor Force Development

Economic Disadvantagement (1966 1980)
USE POVERTY

Economic Education (1971 1980)
USE ECONOMICS EDUCATION

ECONOMIC FACTORS *Jul. 1966*
CIJE: 1577 RIE: 2189 GC: 620
UF Poverty Factors #
BT Influences
RT Business Cycles
Economic Change
Educational Demand
Employment
Employment Patterns
Fiscal Capacity
Inflation (Economics)
Labor Utilization
Living Standards
Marxian Analysis
Ownership
Productivity
Socioeconomic Influences

Economic Fluctuations
USE BUSINESS CYCLES

Economic Geography
USE HUMAN GEOGRAPHY

Economic Insecurity
USE POVERTY

ECONOMIC OPPORTUNITIES *Jul. 1966*
CIJE: 140 RIE: 207 GC: 540
SN Circumstances or conditions that enable individuals or groups to improve their financial status
BT Opportunities
RT Cooperatives
Economic Climate
Economic Progress
Economics
Economic Status
Employment Opportunities
Entrepreneurship
Ownership
Socioeconomic Influences

Economic Plight
USE POVERTY

ECONOMIC PROGRESS *Jul. 1966*
CIJE: 118 RIE: 181 GC: 620
BT Economic Development
RT Business Cycles
Economic Change
Economic Opportunities
Economics
Modernization
Technology Transfer

ECONOMIC RESEARCH *Jul. 1966*
CIJE: 273 RIE: 563 GC: 810
SN Basic, applied, and developmental research conducted to advance knowledge in economics (note: as of oct81, use as a minor descriptor for examples of this kind of research -- use as a major descriptor only as the subject of a document)
UF Economic Analysis
BT Social Science Research
RT Economics
Input Output Analysis
Labor Economics
Linear Programing

ECONOMIC STATUS *Jul. 1966*
CIJE: 226 RIE: 371 GC: 510
NT Poverty
BT Status
RT Economic Change
Economic Opportunities
Economics
Income
Inflation (Economics)
Ownership
Quality Of Life
Socioeconomic Status

Economic Support
USE FINANCIAL SUPPORT

Economically Advanced Nations
USE DEVELOPED NATIONS

Economically Advantaged
USE ADVANTAGED

Economically Depressed Areas
USE POVERTY AREAS

Economically Deprived
USE ECONOMICALLY DISADVANTAGED

ECONOMICALLY DISADVANTAGED *Jul. 1966*
CIJE: 633 RIE: 1703 GC: 540
UF Economically Deprived
Poor
Poverty Stricken
BT Disadvantaged
RT Group Homes
Homeless People
Low Income Groups
Poverty
Welfare Recipients

ECONOMICS *Jul. 1966*
CIJE: 996 RIE: 1384 GC: 620
UF Economy
NT Consumer Economics
Educational Economics
Labor Economics
Rural Economics
BT Social Sciences
RT Area Studies
Banking
Business
Business Cycles
Capitalism
Communism
Cost Indexes
Credit (Finance)
Economic Change
Economic Climate
Economic Development
Economic Opportunities
Economic Progress
Economic Research
Economics Education
Economic Status
Efficiency
Entrepreneurship
Exports
Fascism
Finance Occupations
Human Capital
Inflation (Economics)
Interest (Finance)
International Studies
International Trade
International Trade Vocabulary
Investment
Marxism
Monetary Systems
Ownership
Productivity
Retrenchment

= Two or more Descriptors are used to represent this term.
The term's main entry shows the appropriate coordination.

Social History
Socialism
Social Science Research
Social Scientists
Social Studies
Socioeconomic Background
Socioeconomic Influences
Socioeconomic Status
Urban Studies

Economics Curriculum
USE ECONOMICS EDUCATION

ECONOMICS EDUCATION *Mar. 1980*
CIJE: 819 RIE: 858 GC: 400
UF Economic Education (1971 1980)
Economics Curriculum
Economics Instruction
BT Education
RT Basic Business Education
Business Education
Consumer Education
Economics

Economics Instruction
USE ECONOMICS EDUCATION

Economics Of Education
USE EDUCATIONAL ECONOMICS

Economy
USE ECONOMICS

Ecosystems
USE ECOLOGY

EDITING *Jul. 1973*
CIJE: 359 RIE: 273 GC: 720
SN To make suitable for publication or for public presentation by selecting, emending, revising, and compiling
UF Copyediting
RT Editors
Film Production
Film Study
Journalism
Language Arts
Language Styles
News Media
News Writing
Publications
Quality Control
Technical Writing
Word Processing

EDITORIALS *Oct. 1972*
CIJE: 356 RIE: 74 GC: 720
BT News Media
RT Editors
Journalism
Newspapers
Opinions
Periodicals
Persuasive Discourse
Press Opinion
Publications

EDITORS *Aug. 1986*
CIJE: 48 RIE: 30 GC: 710
SN Persons who prepare materials, usually works of others, for publication or public presentation
UF Copyeditors
BT Personnel
RT Authors
Editing
Editorials
Layout (Publications)
Mass Media
News Media
Periodicals
Publications
Publishing Industry
Scholarly Journals
School Publications
Student Publications
Writing For Publication

Educable Mentally Handicapped (1966 1980)
USE MILD MENTAL RETARDATION

EDUCATION *Jul. 1966*
CIJE: 1009 RIE: 1848 GC: 330
SN Process of imparting or obtaining knowledge, attitudes, skills, or socially valued qualities of character or behavior -- includes the philosophy, purposes, programs, methods, organizational patterns, etc., of the entire educational process as most broadly conceived (note: the most general term -- use a more specific term if possible)
NT Academic Education
Adult Education
Aerospace Education
Aesthetic Education
After School Education
Aging Education
Agricultural Education
Alcohol Education
Allied Health Occupations Education
Alumni Education
American Indian Education
Art Education
Back To Basics
Basic Business Education
Bilingual Education
Black Education
Career Education
Citizenship Education
Coeducation
Community Education
Comparative Education
Compensatory Education
Competency Based Education
Compulsory Education
Computer Science Education
Consumer Education
Corporate Education
Correctional Education
Cultural Education
Dance Education
Distance Education
Driver Education
Drug Education
Early Childhood Education
Economics Education
Elementary Secondary Education
Energy Education
Environmental Education
Equal Education
Extension Education
Family Life Education
Free Education
General Education
Health Education
Humanistic Education
Industrial Education
Inservice Education
Intergroup Education
International Education
Journalism Education
Law Related Education
Leisure Education
Literacy Education
Marine Education
Mathematics Education
Mexican American Education
Migrant Education
Music Education
Nondiscriminatory Education
Nonformal Education
Nontraditional Education
Open Education
Outdoor Education
Patient Education
Physical Education
Police Education
Population Education
Postsecondary Education
Private Education
Process Education
Professional Education
Progressive Education
Public Affairs Education
Public Education
Religious Education
Rural Education
Safety Education
Science Education
Special Education
Study Abroad
Supplementary Education
Terminal Education
Urban Education
Values Education
Vocational Education
Womens Education
RT Access To Education
Articulation (Education)
Curriculum
Educational Attitudes
Educational Background
Educational Benefits
Educational Certificates
Educational Change
Educational Complexes
Educational Counseling
Educational Demand
Educational Development
Educational Discrimination
Educational Environment
Educational Equipment
Educational Experience
Educational Experiments
Educational Facilities
Educational Finance
Educational Improvement
Educational Innovation
Educational Legislation
Educationally Disadvantaged
Educational Malpractice
Educational Media
Educational Methods
Educational Mobility
Educational Needs
Educational Objectives
Educational Opportunities
Educational Planning
Educational Policy
Educational Practices
Educational Principles
Educational Quality
Educational Research
Educational Resources
Educational Responsibility
Educational Status Comparison
Educational Strategies
Educational Supply
Educational Technology
Educational Testing
Educational Theories
Educational Therapy
Educational Trends
Education Courses
Education Majors
Education Service Centers
Education Work Relationship
Foundations Of Education
Instruction
Learning
Outcomes Of Education
Politics Of Education
Role Of Education
Schools
Training

Education And Work
USE EDUCATION WORK RELATIONSHIP

EDUCATION COURSES *Feb. 1969*
CIJE: 161 RIE: 210 GC: 400
BT College Curriculum
Courses
RT Education
Education Majors
Methods Courses
Postsecondary Education As A Field Of Study
Schools Of Education
Teacher Education
Teacher Education Curriculum
Teacher Education Programs

Education Departments (School)
USE SCHOOLS OF EDUCATION

EDUCATION MAJORS *Jul. 1966*
CIJE: 383 RIE: 491 GC: 360
BT Majors (Students)
RT Education
Education Courses
Postsecondary Education As A Field Of Study
Schools Of Education
Specialist In Education Degrees
Student Teachers
Teacher Education
Teacher Education Curriculum
Teacher Education Programs

Education Permanente
USE LIFELONG LEARNING

Education Role
USE ROLE OF EDUCATION

EDUCATION SERVICE CENTERS *Jul. 1966*
CIJE: 120 RIE: 266 GC: 920
SN Multipurpose educational facilities that provide cooperative services to school districts within a region -- typical services include research, curriculum development, instructional materials, inservice training, data processing, legal and financial advice, psychological programs, and direct services to students
UF Educational Service Centers
Supplementary Educational Centers (1966 1980) #
BT Educational Facilities
Resource Centers
RT Ancillary School Services
Curriculum Study Centers
Demonstration Centers
Education
Information Centers
Nature Centers
Regional Programs
Science Teaching Centers
Shared Resources And Services
Teacher Centers

Education Vouchers (1971 1980)
USE EDUCATIONAL VOUCHERS

EDUCATION WORK RELATIONSHIP *Oct. 1979*
CIJE: 992 RIE: 1550 GC: 330
SN Relationship between educational programs or courses of study and status or opportunities (social, financial, etc.) in the work force (note: do not confuse with "work study programs" or "school business relationship")
UF Education And Work
School To Work Transition
Work And Education
Work Education Relationship
BT Relationship
RT Career Change
Career Choice
Career Development
Career Education
Career Planning
Careers
Corporate Education
Education
Educational Benefits
Educational Demand
Educational Objectives
Educational Philosophy
Educational Status Comparison
Employment
Employment Opportunities
Employment Patterns
Employment Potential
Entrepreneurship
Liberal Arts
Occupations
Opportunities
Promotion (Occupational)
Relevance (Education)
School Business Relationship
Student Educational Objectives
Technology
Vocational Followup

Educational Access
USE ACCESS TO EDUCATION

Educational Accountability (1970 1980)
USE ACCOUNTABILITY

Educational Achievement
USE ACADEMIC ACHIEVEMENT

EDUCATIONAL ADMINISTRATION *Jul. 1966*
CIJE: 2239 RIE: 3325 GC: 320
SN Planning, organizing, directing, and controlling human or material resources in an educational setting, and the study of this process (note: use a more specific term if possible)
UF Educational Management
NT School Administration
BT Administration
RT Administrators
Educational Finance
Educational Planning
Educational Policy
Politics Of Education
Retrenchment
Trustees

Educational Advantages
USE EDUCATIONAL OPPORTUNITIES

Educational Alternatives (1974 1980)
USE NONTRADITIONAL EDUCATION

= Two or more Descriptors are used to represent this term.
The term's main entry shows the appropriate coordination.

EDUCATIONAL ANTHROPOLOGY *Jun. 1973*
CIJE: 157 RIE: 193 GC: 400
SN Application of anthropological concepts and methods to the study of educational institutions and processes
BT Anthropology
Foundations Of Education
RT Comparative Education
Cultural Context
Culture
Educational History
Educational Principles
Educational Psychology
Educational Sociology
Educational Theories
Ethnography
Ethnology
Nonformal Education
Sociocultural Patterns

EDUCATIONAL ASSESSMENT *Jan. 1974*
CIJE: 1738 RIE: 3588 GC: 810
SN Determining and interpreting the attainment of educational objectives (nationwide, statewide, or locally) for use in educational planning, development, policy formation, and resource allocation (note: do not confuse with "educational diagnosis" or "testing")
UF Educational Quality Assessment #
BT Evaluation
RT Educational Needs
Educational Objectives
Educational Planning
Educational Policy
Evaluation Methods
Formative Evaluation
Input Output Analysis
National Programs
National Surveys
Needs Assessment
Outcomes Of Education
Program Effectiveness
Program Evaluation
Program Validation
Public Policy
Resource Allocation
Role Of Education
School Effectiveness
State Programs
State Surveys
Summative Evaluation
Surveys
Validated Programs

EDUCATIONAL ATTAINMENT *Mar. 1980*
CIJE: 257 RIE: 431 GC: 510
SN Years of successfully completed schooling or the equivalent according to some accreditation standard (note: prior to mar80, the instruction "educational attainment, use academic achievement" was carried in the thesaurus)
BT Academic Achievement
RT Advanced Placement Programs
Educational Experience
Educational Status Comparison
External Degree Programs
Graduation
High School Equivalency Programs
Student Educational Objectives

EDUCATIONAL ATTITUDES *Jul. 1966*
CIJE: 910 RIE: 768 GC: 330
SN Attitudes toward or about education
BT Attitudes
RT Education
Reading Attitudes

EDUCATIONAL BACKGROUND *Jul. 1966*
CIJE: 590 RIE: 1207 GC: 510
NT Educational Experience
BT Background
RT Education
Educational Mobility
Educational Opportunities
Educational Status Comparison
Employment Potential
Knowledge Level
Participant Characteristics

EDUCATIONAL BENEFITS *Jul. 1966*
CIJE: 541 RIE: 683 GC: 330
SN Individual benefits obtained from acquisition of education (note: prior to mar80, the use of this term was restricted to benefits from advanced education)
BT Outcomes Of Education
RT Education
Educational Mobility
Educational Status Comparison
Education Work Relationship
Employment Potential
Higher Education
Professional Recognition
Rewards
Socioeconomic Status
Student Educational Objectives

EDUCATIONAL CERTIFICATES *Jul. 1966*
CIJE: 71 RIE: 236 GC: 340
BT Credentials
RT Certification
Credits
Education
Equivalency Tests
High School Equivalency Programs
Student Certification
Teacher Certification

EDUCATIONAL CHANGE *Jul. 1966*
CIJE: 6888 RIE: 5159 GC: 330
SN Alterations in the scope of the total educational endeavor -- includes modification of curriculum, teaching methods, enrollment patterns, etc. (note: prior to mar80, the use of this term was not restricted by a scope note)
UF Educational Reform
BT Change
RT Change Agents
Change Strategies
Education
Educational Development
Educational Environment
Educational Improvement
Educational Innovation
Educational Trends
Transitional Schools

Educational Choice
USE SCHOOL CHOICE

EDUCATIONAL COMPLEXES *Jul. 1966*
CIJE: 24 RIE: 55 GC: 920
SN Large aggregations of educational facilities (note: use a more specific term if possible)
NT Campuses
Educational Parks
BT Educational Facilities
RT Cluster Colleges
Education
Educational Facilities Planning
Facility Utilization Research
House Plan
School Buildings
Site Analysis
Site Development
Space Utilization

Educational Computing
USE COMPUTER USES IN EDUCATION

EDUCATIONAL COOPERATION *Mar. 1980*
CIJE: 546 RIE: 1160 GC: 330
SN Cooperation of educators or educational organizations, agencies, or institutions among themselves or with outside persons, organizations, agencies, or institutions (note: use a more specific term if possible)
UF Educational Coordination (1967 1980) #
NT College School Cooperation
Counselor Teacher Cooperation
Intercollegiate Cooperation
Parent Teacher Cooperation
BT Cooperation
RT Affiliated Schools
Agency Cooperation
Consortia
Cooperative Education
Cooperative Planning
Cooperative Programs
Educational Planning
Institutional Cooperation
Interschool Communication
Teacher Centers
Team Teaching

Educational Coordination (1967 1980)
USE COORDINATION; EDUCATIONAL COOPERATION

EDUCATIONAL COUNSELING *Jul. 1966*
CIJE: 389 RIE: 582 GC: 240
SN Assisting individuals to select a program of studies suited to their abilities, interests, future plans, and general circumstances
UF Educational Guidance (1966 1977)
NT Academic Advising
Admissions Counseling
BT Counseling
RT College Preparation
Education
Educational Psychology
Educational Therapy
Faculty Advisers
Faculty Workload
Post High School Guidance
School Counseling
School Orientation
Student Educational Objectives
Student Placement

EDUCATIONAL DEMAND *Jul. 1966*
CIJE: 454 RIE: 580 GC: 330
SN Consumer demand for education
UF Demand For Education
RT Access To Education
Declining Enrollment
Demand Occupations
Economic Factors
Education
Educational Economics
Educational Needs
Educational Opportunities
Educational Supply
Educational Trends
Education Work Relationship
Enrollment
Enrollment Influences
Equal Education
Teacher Supply And Demand

EDUCATIONAL DEVELOPMENT *Dec. 1969*
CIJE: 2500 RIE: 2364 GC: 330
SN Growth, differentiation, or evolution of educational systems (note: do not confuse with "student development" or "faculty development")
NT Curriculum Development
Instructional Development
BT Development
RT Developmental Programs
Education
Educational Change
Educational Improvement
Educational Innovation
Educational Mobility
Educational Planning
Educational Research
Educational Technology
Formative Evaluation
Nontraditional Education
Program Development
Research And Development
Research And Development Centers
Systems Development

EDUCATIONAL DIAGNOSIS *Jul. 1966*
CIJE: 814 RIE: 1088 GC: 310
SN Identification of the nature and cause of learning disabilities, problems, or other conditions that may impede or promote school performance
UF Diagnosis (Educational)
NT Reading Diagnosis
BT Identification
RT Classroom Techniques
Clinical Diagnosis
Counselor Teacher Cooperation
Diagnostic Teaching
Diagnostic Tests
Educational Testing
Educational Therapy
Etiology
Learning Disabilities
Learning Problems
Psychoeducational Clinics
Psychoeducational Methods
Student Evaluation
Testing Programs
Writing Evaluation

Educational Disadvantagement (1966 1980)
USE EDUCATIONALLY DISADVANTAGED

EDUCATIONAL DISCRIMINATION *Jul. 1966*
CIJE: 217 RIE: 249 GC: 540
NT School Segregation
BT Social Discrimination
RT Access To Education
Affirmative Action
Age Discrimination
Education
Educational Opportunities
Equal Education
Handicap Discrimination
Nondiscriminatory Education
Racial Discrimination
Reverse Discrimination
Selective Admission
Sex Discrimination

EDUCATIONAL ECONOMICS *Feb. 1969*
CIJE: 785 RIE: 977 GC: 620
UF Economics Of Education
NT Educational Finance
BT Economics
Foundations Of Education
RT Bids
Consumer Economics
Economic Development
Educational Demand
Educational Supply
Educational Vouchers
Efficiency
Financial Policy
Financial Support
Fiscal Capacity
Human Capital
Institutional Survival
Instructional Student Costs
Investment
Productivity
Resource Allocation
School Support
Student Costs

Educational Endowments
USE ENDOWMENT FUNDS

EDUCATIONAL ENVIRONMENT *Jul. 1966*
CIJE: 2222 RIE: 2124 GC: 320
SN Conditions, forces, or factors within or exogenous to an educational setting capable of influencing the setting or those within it (note: use a more specific term if possible)
UF Academic Environment
School Climate
School Conditions (1966 1980)
School Environment (1966 1980)
NT Classroom Environment
College Environment
Teaching Conditions
BT Environment
RT Academic Freedom
Education
Educational Change
Educational Facilities
Educational Facilities Design
Educational Innovation
Educational Objectives
Educational Philosophy
Hidden Curriculum
Institutional Environment
Instruction
Learning
Organizational Climate
Role Of Education
School Organization
School Role
Schools
Student Rights
Student School Relationship
Student Subcultures

Educational Equality (1966 1976)
USE EQUAL EDUCATION

EDUCATIONAL EQUIPMENT *Jul. 1966*
CIJE: 420 RIE: 514 GC: 910
SN Furnishings, machines, or other manufactured accessories that are used in educational settings
UF Classroom Equipment
NT Classroom Furniture
BT Equipment
RT Athletic Equipment
Audiovisual Aids
Autoinstructional Aids
Bulletin Boards
Chalkboards
College Buildings

= Two or more Descriptors are used to represent this term.
The term's main entry shows the appropriate coordination.

Display Aids
Education
Educational Facilities
Educational Media
Educational Resources
Educational Technology
Library Equipment
Projection Equipment
School Buildings
Science Equipment

EDUCATIONAL EQUITY (FINANCE) *Nov. 1982*
CIJE: 107 RIE: 131 GC: 620
SN Equal distribution of financial inputs and costs of education, including revenues, expenditures, resources, services, tax burdens, and tax effort, based on student needs and taxpayers' ability to pay
UF Equity (Educational Finance)
Fiscal Equity (Education)
School Finance Equity
Tax Equity (Education)
RT Educational Finance
Equalization Aid
Expenditure Per Student
Finance Reform
Financial Needs
Financial Policy
Financial Problems
Financial Support
Fiscal Capacity
Foundation Programs
Nondiscriminatory Education
Resource Allocation
School District Spending
School Support
School Taxes
Student Costs
Tax Allocation
Tax Effort
Tax Rates

Educational Equity (Opportunities)
USE EQUAL EDUCATION

EDUCATIONAL EXPERIENCE *Jul. 1966*
CIJE: 396 RIE: 470 GC: 510
UF School Experience
BT Educational Background
Experience
RT Education
Educational Attainment
Educational Status Comparison
Prior Learning
Resumes (Personal)

EDUCATIONAL EXPERIMENTS *Jul. 1966*
CIJE: 453 RIE: 553 GC: 810
BT Experiments
RT Demonstration Centers
Demonstrations (Educational)
Education

EDUCATIONAL FACILITIES *Jul. 1966*
CIJE: 1105 RIE: 1974 GC: 920
UF Crafts Rooms (1966 1980) #
School Facilities
School Plants
Teaching Facilities
NT After School Centers
Audiovisual Centers
Business Education Facilities
Child Development Centers
Classrooms
Continuing Education Centers
Curriculum Study Centers
Demonstration Centers
Educational Complexes
Education Service Centers
Found Spaces
Guidance Centers
Learning Centers (Classroom)
Learning Laboratories
Learning Resources Centers
Living Learning Centers
Off Campus Facilities
Physical Education Facilities
Reading Centers
School Buildings
School Shops
School Space
Science Teaching Centers
Skill Centers
Student Unions
Study Facilities
Vocational Training Centers
Writing Laboratories
BT Facilities
RT Arts Centers
Auditoriums
Campus Planning
College Stores
Dormitories
Education
Educational Environment
Educational Equipment
Educational Facilities Design
Educational Facilities Planning
Educational Resources
Facility Guidelines
Facility Inventory
Facility Requirements
Facility Utilization Research
Museums
Music Facilities
Noncampus Colleges
Parks
Planetariums
School Construction
School Expansion
Schools
Structural Elements (Construction)
Teaching Hospitals
Theaters
Zoos

EDUCATIONAL FACILITIES DESIGN *Mar. 1980*
CIJE: 642 RIE: 570 GC: 920
SN Conceiving and selecting the structure, elements, arrangement, materials, etc. for a school building or facility -- also, the plan or layout that results
UF Decentralized School Design (1966 1980) #
High School Design (1966 1980)
School Architecture (1966 1980)
School Design (1966 1980)
BT Design
RT Architectural Character
Building Design
Building Plans
Campus Planning
Classroom Design
College Buildings
Design Requirements
Educational Environment
Educational Facilities
Educational Facilities Planning
Flexible Facilities
Life Cycle Costing
Mobile Classrooms
Modular Building Design
Open Plan Schools
Physical Mobility
School Buildings
School Construction
Schools
School Size
School Space
Site Development
Site Selection
Structural Elements (Construction)

EDUCATIONAL FACILITIES IMPROVEMENT *Mar. 1980*
CIJE: 331 RIE: 316 GC: 920
UF School Improvement (1966 1980)
School Renovation
BT Facility Improvement
RT Educational Facilities Planning
School Buildings
School Expansion
School Maintenance
Schools
School Safety

EDUCATIONAL FACILITIES PLANNING *Mar. 1980*
CIJE: 111 RIE: 126 GC: 920
SN Planning the facilities and grounds of educational institutions (note: prior to mar80, this concept was indexed under "school planning")
NT Campus Planning
BT Educational Planning
Facility Planning
RT Architectural Programing
Building Plans
Construction Programs
Design Requirements
Educational Complexes
Educational Facilities
Educational Facilities Design
Educational Facilities Improvement
Facility Guidelines
Facility Requirements
Facility Utilization Research
Flexible Facilities
Land Use
Life Cycle Costing
Physical Mobility
School Buildings
School Business Officials
School Construction
School Expansion
Schools
School Safety
School Size
School Space
Site Analysis
Site Development
Site Selection
Space Utilization
Spatial Relationship (Facilities)
Systems Building

EDUCATIONAL FINANCE *Jul. 1966*
CIJE: 3721 RIE: 7054 GC: 620
SN Any aspect of raising and spending revenue for educational purposes (note: use a more precise term if possible)
UF Educational Support
School Aid
School Finance
BT Educational Economics
RT Access To Education
Assistantships
Bids
Block Grants
Bond Issues
Budgeting
Budgets
Capital
Capital Outlay (For Fixed Assets)
Categorical Aid
Corporate Support
Costs
Education
Educational Administration
Educational Equity (Finance)
Educational Planning
Educational Vouchers
Endowment Funds
Equalization Aid
Expenditure Per Student
Expenditures
Federal Aid
Fellowships
Finance Reform
Financial Needs
Financial Policy
Financial Problems
Financial Services
Financial Support
Fiscal Capacity
Foundation Programs
Full State Funding
Fund Raising
Grants
Incentive Grants
Inflation (Economics)
Instructional Student Costs
Loan Repayment
Noninstructional Student Costs
Politics Of Education
Private Financial Support
Private School Aid
Property Taxes
Proprietary Schools
Purchasing
Retrenchment
Revenue Sharing
Salary Wage Differentials
Scholarship Funds
Scholarships
School Accounting
School Budget Elections
School Business Officials
School District Spending
School Funds
School Support
School Taxes
State Aid
State Federal Aid
State School District Relationship
Student Costs
Student Financial Aid
Student Financial Aid Officers
Student Loan Programs
Tax Allocation
Tax Effort
Training Allowances

Educational Foundations
USE PHILANTHROPIC FOUNDATIONS

Educational Futures
USE EDUCATIONAL TRENDS; FUTURES (OF SOCIETY)

EDUCATIONAL GAMES *Jul. 1966*
CIJE: 1566 RIE: 1183 GC: 720
SN Individual or group games that have cognitive, social, behavioral, and/or emotional, etc., dimensions which are related to educational objectives (note: prior to mar80, this term was not restricted by a scope note)
UF Academic Games
Classroom Games (1966 1980) #
Heuristic Games
NT Reading Games
BT Games
RT Instructional Materials
Learning Activities
Puzzles
Simulation

EDUCATIONAL GERONTOLOGY *Aug. 1976*
CIJE: 215 RIE: 118 GC: 400
SN Study and practice of educational endeavors for the aged and aging, and preparation of persons to work with these groups (note: do not confuse with "aging education")
BT Gerontology
RT Adult Development
Adult Education
Aging (Individuals)
Aging Education
Allied Health Occupations
Geriatrics
Older Adults
Preretirement Education
Professional Education
Retirement

Educational Goals
USE EDUCATIONAL OBJECTIVES

Educational Goals Of Students
USE STUDENT EDUCATIONAL OBJECTIVES

Educational Guidance (1966 1977)
USE EDUCATIONAL COUNSELING

EDUCATIONAL HISTORY *Jul. 1966*
CIJE: 3646 RIE: 2394 GC: 330
UF History Of Education
NT Science Education History
BT Foundations Of Education
History
RT Educational Anthropology
Educational Practices
Educational Theories
Educational Trends

EDUCATIONAL IMPROVEMENT *Jul. 1966*
CIJE: 2331 RIE: 3015 GC: 330
SN Enhancing the value or quality of education (note: use a more specific term if possible)
NT Instructional Improvement
BT Improvement
RT Education
Educational Change
Educational Development
Educational Innovation
Educational Needs
Educational Quality
Formative Evaluation
Relevance (Education)
Research And Instruction Units

Educational Inequality
USE EQUAL EDUCATION

EDUCATIONAL INNOVATION *Jul. 1966*
CIJE: 3587 RIE: 4107 GC: 330
SN Introduction of new ideas or practices into educational programs, systems, or structures (note: prior to mar80, the use of this term was not restricted by a scope note -- do not confuse with "instructional innovation")
NT Instructional Innovation
BT Innovation
RT Education
Educational Change
Educational Development

Educational Environment
Educational Improvement
Educational Research
Educational Technology
Experimental Colleges
Experimental Curriculum
Experimental Schools
Experimental Teaching
Nontraditional Education
Research And Development
Theory Practice Relationship

Educational Institutions
USE SCHOOLS

Educational Interest (1967 1980)
USE STUDENT EDUCATIONAL OBJECTIVES

EDUCATIONAL LEGISLATION *Jul. 1966*
CIJE: 1258 RIE: 2365 GC: 330
NT School Attendance Legislation
BT Legislation
RT Education
Government School Relationship
Laws
Politics Of Education
School Law

Educational Level
USE ACADEMIC ACHIEVEMENT

EDUCATIONAL MALPRACTICE *Oct. 1980*
CIJE: 44 RIE: 56 GC: 330
SN Wrongful or negligent acts on the part of teachers or schools that result (or may result) in student detriments, especially including the failure of students to learn
UF Academic Malpractice
BT Malpractice
RT Academic Standards
Accountability
Court Litigation
Education
Educational Responsibility
Laws
Legal Problems
Legal Responsibility
Torts

Educational Management
USE EDUCATIONAL ADMINISTRATION

Educational Materials
USE INSTRUCTIONAL MATERIALS

EDUCATIONAL MEDIA *Mar. 1980*
CIJE: 3141 RIE: 3034 GC: 720
SN Equipment and materials used for communication in instruction (note: use a more specific term if possible)
UF Instructional Aids (1966 1980)
Instructional Media (1967 1980)
Mechanical Teaching Aids (1966 1980)
NT Audiovisual Aids
Autoinstructional Aids
Instructional Materials
RT Computer Assisted Instruction
Computer Managed Instruction
Education
Educational Equipment
Educational Resources
Educational Technology
Electronic Classrooms
Intermode Differences
Learning Laboratories
Learning Resources Centers
Mass Media
Media Adaptation
Media Research
Media Selection
Media Specialists
Multimedia Instruction
Nonprint Media
Production Techniques
Programed Instruction
Telephone Instruction
Visual Aids

Educational Media Adaptation
USE MEDIA ADAPTATION

Educational Media Selection
USE MEDIA SELECTION

EDUCATIONAL METHODS *Jul. 1966*
CIJE: 474 RIE: 622 GC: 310
SN (Note: use a more specific term if instruction or training is the primary emphasis)
NT Classroom Techniques
Educational Strategies
Psychoeducational Methods
Teaching Methods
BT Methods
RT Education
Educational Practices
Educational Technology
Methods Research
Nontraditional Education

EDUCATIONAL MOBILITY *Jul. 1966*
CIJE: 62 RIE: 90 GC: 330
SN Changes in an individual's or group's level of formal education, often resulting in improved social and economic status (note: use "student mobility" or "faculty mobility" for the geographic mobility of those groups -- prior to mar80, this term was not restricted by a scope note)
BT Mobility
RT Academic Achievement
Academic Aspiration
Articulation (Education)
Black Achievement
College Transfer Students
Education
Educational Background
Educational Benefits
Educational Development
Educational Opportunities
Educational Status Comparison
Social Mobility
Transfer Students

EDUCATIONAL NEEDS *Jul. 1966*
CIJE: 5189 RIE: 6931 GC: 330
SN Necessary knowledge, skills, or attitudes that may be obtained through learning experiences -- also, the needs of educational systems (note: use a more precise term if possible)
BT Needs
RT Education
Educational Assessment
Educational Demand
Educational Improvement
Educationally Disadvantaged
Educational Objectives
Educational Planning
Educational Responsibility
Nontraditional Education
Relevance (Education)
Special Education

EDUCATIONAL OBJECTIVES *Jul. 1966*
CIJE: 9609 RIE: 10573 GC: 330
SN Objectives relating to the outcomes or organization of the educational process -- includes goals proposed or established by educational authorities at all levels (note: prior to mar80, this term was not scoped and was used for institutional and and personal goals relating to education -- for these concepts, see other, more precise, "objectives" descriptors)
UF Educational Goals
Educational Purposes
BT Objectives
RT Education
Educational Assessment
Educational Environment
Educational Needs
Educational Philosophy
Educational Planning
Educational Principles
Educational Quality
Educational Theories
Education Work Relationship
Outcomes Of Education
Relevance (Education)
Role Of Education
School Role

Educational Objectives Of Students
USE STUDENT EDUCATIONAL OBJECTIVES

EDUCATIONAL OPPORTUNITIES *Jul. 1966*
CIJE: 1163 RIE: 1841 GC: 330
SN Circumstances or conditions that enable individuals or groups to improve their educational status
UF Educational Advantages
Training Opportunities
NT Access To Education
BT Opportunities
RT Affirmative Action
Competitive Selection
Compulsory Education
Education
Educational Background
Educational Demand
Educational Discrimination
Educationally Disadvantaged
Educational Mobility
Equal Education
Nondiscriminatory Education
Nontraditional Education
Open Enrollment

Educational Outcomes
USE OUTCOMES OF EDUCATION

EDUCATIONAL PARKS *Jul. 1966*
CIJE: 13 RIE: 75 GC: 540
SN Complex of schools, usually ranging from kindergarten through high school or the two-year college, that draws students from a metropolitan area and is intended to minimize the effects of segregation (note: prior to mar80, the use of this term was not restricted by a scope note)
BT Educational Complexes
RT Campuses
Magnet Schools
Neighborhood Schools
Racial Integration
School Desegregation

EDUCATIONAL PHILOSOPHY *Jul. 1966*
CIJE: 4439 RIE: 2756 GC: 330
UF School Philosophy
BT Foundations Of Education
Philosophy
RT Educational Environment
Educational Objectives
Educational Principles
Educational Theories
Education Work Relationship
Traditional Schools
Transitional Schools

EDUCATIONAL PLANNING *Jul. 1966*
CIJE: 2667 RIE: 5360 GC: 330
SN Process of determining the objectives of education, educational institutions, or educational programs and the means (activities, procedures, resources, etc.) for attaining them (note: use a more specific term if possible)
UF Academic Planning
Educational Plans
NT College Planning
Educational Facilities Planning
BT Planning
RT Articulation (Education)
Education
Educational Administration
Educational Assessment
Educational Cooperation
Educational Development
Educational Finance
Educational Needs
Educational Objectives
Educational Strategies
Formative Evaluation
Resource Allocation

Educational Plans
USE EDUCATIONAL PLANNING

EDUCATIONAL POLICY *Jul. 1966*
CIJE: 3353 RIE: 4134 GC: 330
BT Policy
RT Bilingual Education
Board Of Education Policy
Education
Educational Administration
Educational Assessment
Educational Principles
Language Of Instruction
Language Planning
Official Languages
Politics Of Education
School District Autonomy
School Policy
Self Determination

Educational Politics
USE POLITICS OF EDUCATION

Educational Practice (1967 1980)
USE EDUCATIONAL PRACTICES

EDUCATIONAL PRACTICES *Mar. 1980*
CIJE: 2076 RIE: 1721 GC: 330
SN Customary operations in education, from the educational system as a whole to the individual classroom or teacher (note: use a more precise term if possible)
UF Educational Practice (1967 1980)
RT Education
Educational History
Educational Methods
Educational Principles
Educational Research
Educational Trends
Progressive Education
Theory Practice Relationship

EDUCATIONAL PRINCIPLES *Jul. 1966*
CIJE: 602 RIE: 367 GC: 330
SN Values or assumptions that guide decisions concerning educational methods or objectives
BT Foundations Of Education
Standards
RT Administrative Principles
Education
Educational Anthropology
Educational Objectives
Educational Philosophy
Educational Policy
Educational Practices
Educational Psychology
Educational Research
Educational Theories
Nontraditional Education
Values

EDUCATIONAL PROBLEMS (1966 1980) *Mar. 1980*
CIJE: 2210 RIE: 1673 GC: 330
SN Invalid descriptor -- used inconsistently in indexing -- see more precise descriptors relating to the particular problem

Educational Processes
USE LEARNING PROCESSES

Educational Production Functions
USE PRODUCTIVITY

EDUCATIONAL PROGRAMS (1966 1980) *Mar. 1980*
CIJE: 3151 RIE: 5172 GC: 320
SN Invalid descriptor -- used inconsistently in indexing -- coordinate more specific descriptors

EDUCATIONAL PSYCHOLOGY *Jul. 1966*
CIJE: 752 RIE: 530 GC: 400
BT Foundations Of Education
Psychology
RT Educational Anthropology
Educational Counseling
Educational Principles
Educational Sociology
Educational Theories
Intervention
Social Psychology

Educational Purposes
USE EDUCATIONAL OBJECTIVES

EDUCATIONAL QUALITY *Jul. 1966*
CIJE: 2043 RIE: 2104 GC: 330
SN Degrees of excellence in meeting educational objectives (note: use a more precise term if possible)
UF Educational Quality Assessment #
Quality Education
RT Accrediting Agencies
Back To Basics
Consumer Protection
Curriculum Evaluation
Education
Educational Improvement
Educational Objectives
Equal Education

= Two or more Descriptors are used to represent this term.
The term's main entry shows the appropriate coordination.

Instructional Effectiveness
Program Effectiveness
Quality Of Life
School Effectiveness
Teacher Effectiveness

Educational Quality Assessment
USE EDUCATIONAL ASSESSMENT; EDUCATIONAL QUALITY

EDUCATIONAL RADIO *Jul. 1966*
CIJE: 388 RIE: 550 GC: 720
UF Instructional Radio
BT Audiovisual Communications
Radio
RT Audiovisual Instruction
Distance Education
Documentaries
Educational Television
Listening Groups
Mass Instruction

Educational Reform
USE EDUCATIONAL CHANGE

Educational Relevance
USE RELEVANCE (EDUCATION)

EDUCATIONAL RESEARCH *Jul. 1966*
CIJE: 10987 RIE: 13011 GC: 810
SN Basic, applied, and developmental research conducted to advance knowledge in the field of education or bearing on educational problems (note: use a more specific term if possible -- as of oct81, use as a minor descriptor for examples of educational research -- use as a major descriptor only as the subject of a document)
NT Classroom Research
Curriculum Research
Reading Research
Writing Research
BT Research
RT Behavioral Science Research
Demonstration Centers
Education
Educational Development
Educational Innovation
Educational Practices
Educational Principles
Educational Researchers
Educational Status Comparison
Educational Testing
Exceptional Child Research
Experimental Curriculum
Experimental Teaching
Field Studies
Graduate Surveys
Institutional Research
Laboratory Schools
Program Effectiveness
Research And Development
Research And Instruction Units
Research Committees
Research Coordinating Units
School Statistics
School Surveys
Social Science Research
Theory Practice Relationship

EDUCATIONAL RESEARCHERS *Jul. 1966*
CIJE: 243 RIE: 439 GC: 360
UF Research Specialists (Education)
BT Researchers
RT Educational Research
Evaluators
Research Directors

EDUCATIONAL RESOURCES *Jul. 1966*
CIJE: 1090 RIE: 2822 GC: 330
SN The equipment, facilities, materials, and personnel available for education (note: use a more precise term if possible)
UF Curriculum Resources
Learning Resources
Teaching Resources
NT Educational Supply
BT Resources
RT Education
Educational Equipment
Educational Facilities
Educational Media
Educational Technology
Faculty
Information Sources
Instructional Materials

EDUCATIONAL RESPONSIBILITY *Jul. 1966*
CIJE: 1135 RIE: 686 GC: 330
SN Obligations or duties to meet educational needs (note: use a more precise term if possible -- prior to mar80, the use of this term was not restricted by a scope note)
BT Responsibility
RT Administrator Responsibility
College Role
Education
Educational Malpractice
Educational Needs
Noninstructional Responsibility
Parent Responsibility
Relevance (Education)
Role Of Education
School Responsibility
School Role
Social Responsibility
Student Responsibility
Teacher Responsibility

EDUCATIONAL RETARDATION (1966 1980) *Mar. 1980*
CIJE: 9 RIE: 43 GC: 220
SN Invalid descriptor -- used inconsistently in indexing -- see such descriptors as "slow learners," "educationally disadvantaged," "learning disabilities," "learning problems," "academic ability," etc.

Educational Service Centers
USE EDUCATION SERVICE CENTERS

EDUCATIONAL SOCIOLOGY *Jul. 1966*
CIJE: 543 RIE: 297 GC: 400
BT Foundations Of Education
Sociology
RT Educational Anthropology
Educational Psychology
School Community Relationship
Social Psychology

EDUCATIONAL SPECIFICATIONS (1967 1980) *Mar. 1980*
CIJE: 95 RIE: 360 GC: 320
SN Invalid descriptor -- used inconsistently in indexing -- see such descriptors as "educational facilities design," "facility guidelines," "curriculum development," etc.

EDUCATIONAL STATUS COMPARISON *Jul. 1966*
CIJE: 162 RIE: 304 GC: 510
SN Comparison of the level of education achieved by individuals or groups and their socioeconomic status
BT Comparative Analysis
RT Education
Educational Attainment
Educational Background
Educational Benefits
Educational Experience
Educationally Disadvantaged
Educational Mobility
Educational Research
Education Work Relationship
Social Mobility
Socioeconomic Status

EDUCATIONAL STRATEGIES *Jul. 1966*
CIJE: 1449 RIE: 1594 GC: 310
SN Overall plans for implementing instructional goals, methods or techniques
BT Educational Methods
RT Change Strategies
Curriculum Design
Education
Educational Planning
Instructional Design
Instructional Development
Learning Strategies
Motivation Techniques
Teaching Methods

EDUCATIONAL SUPPLY *Aug. 1968*
CIJE: 207 RIE: 273 GC: 330
SN Education provided to meet consumer demand
UF Supply Of Education
BT Educational Resources
RT Access To Education
Admission (School)
Competitive Selection
Compulsory Education
Declining Enrollment
Education
Educational Demand
Educational Economics
Educational Trends
Enrollment
Enrollment Influences

Educational Support
USE EDUCATIONAL FINANCE

Educational Surveys
USE SCHOOL SURVEYS

EDUCATIONAL TECHNOLOGY *Jul. 1969*
CIJE: 2561 RIE: 2602 GC: 330
SN Systematic identification, development, organization, or utilization of educational resources and/or the management of these processes -- occasionally used in a more limited sense to describe the use of equipment-oriented techniques or audiovisual aids in educational settings
UF Instructional Technology (1966 1978)
NT Instructional Systems
BT Technology
RT Audiovisual Aids
Audiovisual Communications
Computer Oriented Programs
Computer Uses In Education
Cybernetics
Education
Educational Development
Educational Equipment
Educational Innovation
Educational Media
Educational Methods
Educational Resources
Information Technology
Instruction
Instructional Design
Instructional Development
Instructional Improvement
Instructional Innovation
Instructional Materials
Multimedia Instruction
Programed Instruction

EDUCATIONAL TELEVISION *Jul. 1966*
CIJE: 2121 RIE: 2735 GC: 720
SN Transmission of educational or informational programs or material by television (note: use a more specific term if possible -- see also "telecourses")
UF Etv
Fixed Service Television (1969 1980)
Instructional Television (1966 1974)
Instructor Centered Television (1966 1980)
Itfs
Itv
Televised Instruction (1966 1974)
BT Audiovisual Communications
Television
RT Audiovisual Instruction
Closed Circuit Television
Distance Education
Documentaries
Educational Radio
Home Programs
Instructional Films
Listening Groups
Mass Instruction
Public Television
Telecourses
Television Teachers

EDUCATIONAL TESTING *Jul. 1966*
CIJE: 741 RIE: 1222 GC: 820
SN Use of tests to assess the effect of educational programs and activities on students (note: prior to mar80, the use of this term was not restricted by a scope note)
UF Student Testing (1966 1980)
BT Testing
RT Achievement Tests
Education
Educational Diagnosis
Educational Research
Grading
Precision Teaching
Prognostic Tests
Student Evaluation
Student Placement

EDUCATIONAL THEORIES *Jul. 1966*
CIJE: 2297 RIE: 1292 GC: 810
BT Foundations Of Education
Theories
RT Andragogy
Education
Educational Anthropology
Educational History
Educational Objectives
Educational Philosophy
Educational Principles
Educational Psychology
Hidden Curriculum
Nontraditional Education
Progressive Education

EDUCATIONAL THERAPY *Jul. 1966*
CIJE: 90 RIE: 70 GC: 310
SN Educational practices that contribute to the treatment of students' organic or functional disorders (e.g., remedial reading instruction that improves self-esteem)
BT Therapy
RT Art Therapy
Classroom Techniques
Diagnostic Teaching
Education
Educational Counseling
Educational Diagnosis
Intervention
Music Therapy
Psychoeducational Clinics
Psychoeducational Methods
Reality Therapy
Rehabilitation
Remedial Programs
School Counseling
Therapeutic Environment

EDUCATIONAL TRENDS *Jul. 1966*
CIJE: 3446 RIE: 3018 GC: 330
UF Educational Futures #
RT Education
Educational Change
Educational Demand
Educational History
Educational Practices
Educational Supply
Enrollment Trends
Reentry Students
School Statistics
Trend Analysis

EDUCATIONAL VOUCHERS *Mar. 1980*
CIJE: 187 RIE: 206 GC: 620
SN Allocations of public funds to parents to pay the costs of their children's education in the public or private school of their choice
UF Education Vouchers (1971 1980)
Voucher Plans
BT Grants
RT Educational Economics
Educational Finance
Fellowships
Private School Aid
Scholarships
School Choice
Student Costs
Student Financial Aid
Tuition Grants

Educationally Deprived
USE EDUCATIONALLY DISADVANTAGED

EDUCATIONALLY DISADVANTAGED *Jul. 1966*
CIJE: 845 RIE: 2181 GC: 540
SN Individuals or groups whose schooling is judged to be qualitatively or quantitatively inferior as compared with what is considered necessary for achievement in a particular society
UF Academically Disadvantaged
Educational Disadvantagement (1966 1980)
Educationally Deprived
Progressive Retardation (1966 1980) (In School)
BT Disadvantaged
RT Academic Achievement
Compensatory Education
Compulsory Education
Developmental Studies Programs
Disadvantaged Environment
Disadvantaged Schools
Education

Educational Needs
Educational Opportunities
Educational Status Comparison
Equal Education
High Risk Students
Illiteracy
Individualized Education Programs
Learning Problems
Nontraditional Students
Open Enrollment
Remedial Programs
Slow Learners
Supplementary Education
Transitional Programs

Eeg
USE ELECTROENCEPHALOGRAPHY

EFFECT SIZE *Oct. 1983*
CIJE: 54 RIE: 36 GC: 820
SN Statistical calculation of the magnitude of a measurable effect, e.g., the mean difference on a variable between experimental and control groups divided by the standard deviation on that variable of the pooled groups or of the control group alone
UF Magnitude Of Effect
BT Statistical Analysis
RT Control Groups
Experimental Groups
Experiments
Matched Groups
Mathematical Models
Meta Analysis
Predictor Variables
Research Design
Research Methodology
Sample Size
Statistical Significance
Statistics

Effective Schooling
USE SCHOOL EFFECTIVENESS

Effective Teaching (1966 1980)
USE TEACHER EFFECTIVENESS

EFFICIENCY *Jan. 1974*
CIJE: 442 RIE: 388 GC: 620
SN Capacity to produce desired results with a minimum expenditure of energy, time, money, or materials
RT Cost Effectiveness
Economics
Educational Economics
Evaluation Criteria
Job Simplification
Organizational Effectiveness
Performance
Productivity
Program Effectiveness
Resource Allocation
Time Management

Efl
USE ENGLISH (SECOND LANGUAGE)

Egg Inspectors
USE FOOD AND DRUG INSPECTORS

Ego
USE SELF CONCEPT

EGOCENTRISM *Feb. 1975*
CIJE: 148 RIE: 79 GC: 120
SN State of mind characterized by preoccupation with the self -- often refers to the piagetian stage in mental development when the child sees things only from his own limited point of view
UF Egotism
Self Bias
BT Psychological Patterns
RT Bias
Child Language
Congruence (Psychology)
Interpersonal Relationship
Personality Traits
Perspective Taking
Self Concept
Social Attitudes
Social Cognition
Social Development
Values

Egotism
USE EGOCENTRISM

EIDETIC IMAGERY *Mar. 1980*
CIJE: 30 RIE: 21 GC: 110
SN Vividly clear, detailed imagery of something (usually visual) that has been previously perceived
UF Eidetic Images (1967 1980)
Photographic Memory
BT Memory
RT Visualization

Eidetic Images (1967 1980)
USE EIDETIC IMAGERY

Eight Millimeter Projectors (1970 1980)
USE PROJECTION EQUIPMENT

EIGHTEENTH CENTURY LITERATURE *Jun. 1969*
CIJE: 92 RIE: 35 GC: 430
BT Literature
RT Baroque Literature
Literary History
Neoclassicism
Romanticism

ELDER ABUSE *Jun. 1983*
CIJE: 8 RIE: 21 GC: 530
SN Physical, psychological, financial, and/or legal abuse of older persons by their relatives or caretakers
UF Abused Elderly
BT Antisocial Behavior
RT Aging (Individuals)
Battered Women
Family Problems
Family Violence
Middle Aged Adults
Older Adults
Parent Child Relationship
Victims Of Crime
Violence

Elderly
USE OLDER ADULTS

Elected City Officials
USE CITY OFFICIALS

Election Campaigns
USE POLITICAL CAMPAIGNS

ELECTIONS *Jul. 1966*
CIJE: 295 RIE: 303 GC: 610
UF Presidential Elections (United States) #
NT School Budget Elections
BT Selection
RT Local Issues
Political Campaigns
Political Candidates
Political Issues
Political Science
Politics
Voter Registration
Voting
Voting Rights

ELECTIVE COURSES *Jun. 1977*
CIJE: 308 RIE: 332 GC: 350
SN Courses from which students may select on the basis of personal preference
UF Elective Subjects (1966 1977)
Optional Courses
BT Courses
RT Advanced Courses
Course Content
Course Selection (Students)
Majors (Students)
Minicourses
Noncredit Courses
Required Courses
Student Interests

ELECTIVE READING (1966 1980) *Mar. 1980*
CIJE: 12 RIE: 28 GC: 460
SN Invalid descriptor -- used inconsistently in indexing -- see "independent reading," "recreational reading," etc.

Elective Subjects (1966 1977)
USE ELECTIVE COURSES

ELECTRIC BATTERIES *Sep. 1968*
CIJE: 34 RIE: 40 GC: 910
UF Batteries (Electric)
Storage Batteries
BT Supplies
RT Electric Circuits
Electricity
Electronics

ELECTRIC CIRCUITS *Sep. 1968*
CIJE: 219 RIE: 175 GC: 910
UF Circuits (Electronic)
Electronic Circuits
BT Equipment
RT Electric Batteries
Electricity
Electronics
Potentiometers (Instruments)

ELECTRIC MOTORS *Jul. 1966*
CIJE: 22 RIE: 50 GC: 910
BT Engines
RT Electrical Appliances
Electricity
Motor Vehicles

Electric Systems
USE ELECTRICAL SYSTEMS

Electric Utilities
USE UTILITIES

Electrical Appliance Servicemen (1968 1980)
USE APPLIANCE REPAIR

ELECTRICAL APPLIANCES *Jul. 1966*
CIJE: 24 RIE: 71 GC: 910
BT Equipment
RT Appliance Repair
Electricity
Electric Motors
Home Furnishings

Electrical Controls
USE ELECTRONIC CONTROL

ELECTRICAL OCCUPATIONS *Jul. 1966*
CIJE: 16 RIE: 199 GC: 640
UF Electromechanical Occupations #
BT Occupations
RT Appliance Repair
Electricians
Electricity
Electromechanical Technology
Electronics
Electronic Technicians
Energy Occupations
Equipment Maintenance
Semiskilled Occupations
Skilled Occupations
Trade And Industrial Education

ELECTRICAL STIMULI *Sep. 1968*
CIJE: 42 RIE: 12 GC: 110
BT Stimuli
RT Auditory Stimuli
Electricity
Pictorial Stimuli
Verbal Stimuli
Visual Stimuli

ELECTRICAL SYSTEMS *Aug. 1968*
CIJE: 127 RIE: 177 GC: 920
UF Electric Systems
RT Alarm Systems
Climate Control
Electricians
Electricity
Electronic Control
Electronics
Lighting
Utilities

Electrical Technicians
USE ELECTRONIC TECHNICIANS

ELECTRICIANS *Aug. 1968*
CIJE: 4 RIE: 80 GC: 640
BT Skilled Workers
RT Appliance Repair
Building Trades
Electrical Occupations
Electrical Systems
Electricity
Electronics
Electronic Technicians

ELECTRICITY *Jul. 1966*
CIJE: 602 RIE: 577 GC: 490
RT Alternative Energy Sources
Electrical Appliances
Electrical Occupations
Electrical Stimuli
Electrical Systems
Electric Batteries
Electric Circuits
Electricians
Electric Motors
Electromechanical Aids
Electromechanical Technology
Electronics
Electronic Technicians
Force
Geothermal Energy
Magnets
Physics
Potentiometers (Instruments)
Power Technology
Solar Energy
Superconductors
Transistors
Wind Energy

Electrochromatography
USE CHROMATOGRAPHY

ELECTROENCEPHALOGRAPHY *Jul. 1966*
CIJE: 82 RIE: 48 GC: 210
UF Eeg
BT Medicine
RT Biofeedback
Biomedical Equipment
Laboratory Technology
Medical Evaluation
Medical Services
Neurology

ELECTROMECHANICAL AIDS *Jul. 1966*
CIJE: 129 RIE: 201 GC: 910
BT Equipment
RT Audiovisual Aids
Autoinstructional Aids
Calculators
Computers
Electricity
Electromechanical Technology
Electronic Classrooms
Electronic Equipment
Low Vision Aids
Mobility Aids
Prostheses
Sensory Aids

Electromechanical Occupations
USE ELECTRICAL OCCUPATIONS; ELECTROMECHANICAL TECHNOLOGY

ELECTROMECHANICAL TECHNOLOGY *Jul. 1966*
CIJE: 66 RIE: 130 GC: 490
SN Technology of mechanical devices, systems, or processes which are electrostatically or electromagnetically actuated or controlled
UF Electromechanical Occupations #
BT Technology
RT Aerospace Industry
Automation
Computer Science
Data Processing
Electrical Occupations
Electricity
Electromechanical Aids
Electronic Control
Electronics
Electronics Industry
Engineering
Engineering Technology
Horology
Mechanical Design Technicians
Robotics
Technical Education

Electronic Aids
USE ELECTRONIC EQUIPMENT

Electronic Bulletin Boards
USE ELECTRONIC MAIL

Electronic Calculators
USE CALCULATORS

Electronic Circuits
USE ELECTRIC CIRCUITS

= Two or more Descriptors are used to represent this term.
The term's main entry shows the appropriate coordination.

Electronic Classroom Use (1966 1980)
USE ELECTRONIC CLASSROOMS

ELECTRONIC CLASSROOMS *Jul. 1966*
CIJE: 28 RIE: 39 GC: 920
SN Classrooms equipped with electromechanical aids, such as those used in language instruction
UF Electronic Classroom Use (1966 1980)
BT Classrooms
RT Autoinstructional Aids
Educational Media
Electromechanical Aids
Electronic Equipment
Language Laboratories
Learning Laboratories
Programed Instruction

Electronic Communications Systems
USE TELECOMMUNICATIONS

ELECTRONIC CONTROL *Jan. 1969*
CIJE: 54 RIE: 39 GC: 490
SN Control of a machine or process by circuits using electron tubes, transistors, magnetic amplifiers, or other devices having comparable functions
UF Electrical Controls
Magnetic Amplifiers
Static Controls
RT Automation
Cybernetics
Electrical Systems
Electromechanical Technology
Electronic Equipment
Electronics
Instrumentation
Numerical Control
Robotics

Electronic Data Processing (1967 1980)
USE DATA PROCESSING

ELECTRONIC EQUIPMENT *Jul. 1966*
CIJE: 763 RIE: 461 GC: 910
UF Electronic Aids
NT Broadcast Reception Equipment
Computers
Microphones
Polygraphs
Radar
Semiconductor Devices
Sound Spectrographs
Tape Recorders
Video Equipment
BT Equipment
RT Air Traffic Control
Alarm Systems
Audiovisual Aids
Calculators
Data Processing
Electromechanical Aids
Electronic Classrooms
Electronic Control
Electronic Mail
Electronic Publishing
Electronics
Electronics Industry
Facsimile Transmission
Instrumentation
Loop Induction Systems
Radio
Telecommunications
Teleconferencing
Television
Word Processing

Electronic Information Exchange
USE INFORMATION NETWORKS; TELECOMMUNICATIONS

ELECTRONIC MAIL *Apr. 1986*
CIJE: 44 RIE: 50 GC: 710
SN The processing and delivery of printed messages (text or graphics) via telecommunications terminals
UF Computer Based Message Systems
Electronic Bulletin Boards
BT Telecommunications
RT Computer Oriented Programs
Electronic Equipment
Facsimile Transmission
Information Dissemination
Information Networks
Input Output Devices
Online Systems

ELECTRONIC PUBLISHING *Apr. 1986*
CIJE: 53 RIE: 25 GC: 710
SN Use of computers, instead of traditional print media, to produce and distribute information
BT Production Techniques
Telecommunications
RT Computers
Databases
Electronic Equipment
Information Dissemination
Information Networks
Publishing Industry
Videotex

ELECTRONIC TECHNICIANS *Jul. 1966*
CIJE: 34 RIE: 154 GC: 640
UF Electrical Technicians
BT Paraprofessional Personnel
RT Data Processing Occupations
Electrical Occupations
Electricians
Electricity
Electronics
Engineering Technicians
Instrumentation Technicians
Medical Laboratory Assistants
Nuclear Power Plant Technicians

ELECTRONICS *Jul. 1966*
CIJE: 439 RIE: 513 GC: 490
BT Physics
RT Crystallography
Diffusion (Physics)
Electrical Occupations
Electrical Systems
Electric Batteries
Electric Circuits
Electricians
Electricity
Electromechanical Technology
Electronic Control
Electronic Equipment
Electronics Industry
Electronic Technicians
Industrial Arts
Instrumentation Technicians
Lasers
Magnets
Optics
Radar
Robotics
Transistors

ELECTRONICS INDUSTRY *Jul. 1966*
CIJE: 35 RIE: 41 GC: 650
BT Manufacturing Industry
RT Electromechanical Technology
Electronic Equipment
Electronics
Semiconductor Devices

Electrooptics (1968 1980)
USE OPTICS

ELEMENTARY EDUCATION *Jul. 1966*
CIJE: 17523 RIE: 15655 GC: 340
SN Education provided in kindergarten or grade 1 through grade 6, 7, or 8 (note: also appears in the list of mandatory educational level descriptors)
UF Elementary Grades (1966 1980)
NT Adult Basic Education
Primary Education
BT Elementary Secondary Education
RT Early Childhood Education
Elementary School Curriculum
Elementary Schools
Elementary School Students
Elementary School Teachers
Grade 1
Grade 2
Grade 3
Grade 4
Grade 5
Grade 6
Grade 7
Grade 8
Intermediate Grades
Kindergarten

Elementary Grades (1966 1980)
USE ELEMENTARY EDUCATION

Elementary School Children
USE ELEMENTARY SCHOOL STUDENTS

Elementary School Counseling (1967 1980)
USE SCHOOL COUNSELING

Elementary School Counselors (1967 1980)
USE SCHOOL COUNSELORS

ELEMENTARY SCHOOL CURRICULUM *Aug. 1968*
CIJE: 370 RIE: 603 GC: 350
NT Elementary School Mathematics
Elementary School Science
Fles
BT Curriculum
RT Elementary Education
Elementary Schools
Preschool Curriculum

Elementary School Guidance (1967 1980)
USE SCHOOL GUIDANCE

Elementary School Libraries (1966 1980)
USE SCHOOL LIBRARIES

ELEMENTARY SCHOOL MATHEMATICS *Jul. 1966*
CIJE: 2914 RIE: 2273 GC: 480
SN Mathematics curriculum or instruction provided in kindergarten or grade 1 through grade 6, 7, or 8
BT Elementary School Curriculum
Mathematics Curriculum
RT College Mathematics
Mathematics
Mathematics Education
Mathematics Instruction
Modern Mathematics
Secondary School Mathematics

Elementary School Role (1966 1980)
USE SCHOOL ROLE

ELEMENTARY SCHOOL SCIENCE *Jul. 1966*
CIJE: 2894 RIE: 2189 GC: 490
UF Elementary Science (1966 1980)
BT Elementary School Curriculum
Science Curriculum
RT College Science
Science Departments
Science Education
Science Instruction
Secondary School Science

ELEMENTARY SCHOOL STUDENTS *Jul. 1966*
CIJE: 5528 RIE: 3706 GC: 360
SN (Note: coordinate with the appropriate mandatory educational level descriptor)
UF Elementary School Children
BT Students
RT Children
Elementary Education
Elementary Schools

Elementary School Supervisors (1966 1980)
USE SCHOOL SUPERVISION

ELEMENTARY SCHOOL TEACHERS *Jul. 1966*
CIJE: 1365 RIE: 1821 GC: 360
BT Teachers
RT Elementary Education
Elementary Schools
Public School Teachers

ELEMENTARY SCHOOLS *Jul. 1966*
CIJE: 995 RIE: 1728 GC: 340
BT Schools
RT Affiliated Schools
British Infant Schools
Elementary Education
Elementary School Curriculum
Elementary School Students
Elementary School Teachers
Laboratory Schools
Multiunit Schools

Elementary Science (1966 1980)
USE ELEMENTARY SCHOOL SCIENCE

ELEMENTARY SECONDARY EDUCATION *Feb. 1975*
CIJE: 28948 RIE: 29184 GC: 340
SN Formal education provided in kindergarten or grade 1 through grade 12 (note: also appears in the list of mandatory educational level descriptors)
NT Elementary Education
Secondary Education
BT Education
RT Compulsory Education

ELIGIBILITY *Aug. 1978*
CIJE: 147 RIE: 600 GC: 520
SN Qualifying for certain benefits or services (e.g., student eligibility for financial aid, institutional eligibility for accreditation, family eligibility for welfare assistance, employee eligibility for retirement)
UF Institutional Eligibility
Student Eligibility
RT Accreditation (Institutions)
Admission (School)
Assistantships
Athletes
Athletics
Career Choice
Certification
College Applicants
College Choice
Community Services
Credit (Finance)
Disqualification
Federal Aid
Fellowships
Financial Aid Applicants
Financial Services
Financial Support
Grants
Health Services
Insurance
Legal Aid
Need Analysis (Student Financial Aid)
Personnel Selection
Prerequisites
Scholarships
School Choice
Services
Social Services
Standards
State Aid
Status
Student Financial Aid
Student Loan Programs
Welfare Recipients
Welfare Services

Elite Colleges
USE SELECTIVE COLLEGES

ELITISM *Aug. 1986*
CIJE: 38 RIE: 15 GC: 520
SN Rule or participation by a select subgroup
RT Ideology
Intergroup Relations
Political Science
Selective Colleges
Social Stratification
Sociology
Values

Emancipated Students (1975 1980)
USE SELF SUPPORTING STUDENTS

EMBRYOLOGY *May. 1969*
CIJE: 45 RIE: 8 GC: 490
BT Biological Sciences
RT Anatomy
Biology
Botany
Cytology
Evolution
Genetic Engineering
Genetics
Heredity
Medicine
Nucleic Acids
Pathology
Physiology
Plant Growth
Rh Factors
Zoology

EMERGENCY MEDICAL TECHNICIANS *Nov. 1982*
CIJE: 4 RIE: 32 GC: 210
SN Personnel trained to respond to medical emergencies, evaluate the nature of the emergency, provide aid or treatment according to a physician's orders, and transport victim(s) to medical facilities
UF Ambulance Attendants

BT Allied Health Personnel
Emergency Squad Personnel
RT Accidents
First Aid
Medical Assistants
Medical Services
Rescue

EMERGENCY PROGRAMS *Jul. 1966*
CIJE: 122 RIE: 188 GC: 320
UF Disaster Readiness
BT Programs
RT Alarm Systems
Civil Defense
Natural Disasters
Rescue
Safety
School Safety
Terrorism

EMERGENCY SQUAD PERSONNEL *Jul. 1966*
CIJE: 19 RIE: 79 GC: 640
UF Rescue Squad Personnel
NT Emergency Medical Technicians
BT Service Workers
RT Accidents
Alarm Systems
Fire Fighters
Police
Rescue

Emerging Nations
USE DEVELOPING NATIONS

EMERGING OCCUPATIONS *Oct. 1983*
CIJE: 36 RIE: 58 GC: 640
SN Occupations that are new or that consist of new combinations of existing skills and knowledge, and for which considerable demand exists or is projected
BT Demand Occupations
RT Career Change
Futures (Of Society)
Industrialization
Job Development
Labor Force Development
Technological Advancement

EMOTIONAL ADJUSTMENT *Jul. 1966*
CIJE: 837 RIE: 428 GC: 230
UF Emotional Maladjustment (1966 1980)
BT Adjustment (To Environment)
RT Adaptive Behavior (Of Disabled)
Affective Measures
Alienation
Emotional Disturbances
Emotional Problems
Morale
Psychiatry
Psychopathology
Psychotherapy

Emotional Behavior
USE AFFECTIVE BEHAVIOR

EMOTIONAL DEVELOPMENT *Jul. 1966*
CIJE: 509 RIE: 656 GC: 120
BT Individual Development
RT Affective Behavior
Affective Measures
Affective Objectives
Attachment Behavior
Catharsis
Developmental Psychology
Developmental Stages
Empathy
Identification (Psychology)
Learning Readiness
Personality Development
Perspective Taking
Psychological Patterns
School Readiness

EMOTIONAL DISTURBANCES *Mar. 1980*
CIJE: 1872 RIE: 1481 GC: 230
SN Persistent, serious emotional disorders and resulting behavior problems (note: for lesser, transient emotional difficulties, see "emotional problems")
UF Emotionally Disturbed (1966 1980)
Emotionally Disturbed Children (1967 1980)
NT Psychosomatic Disorders
BT Mental Disorders
RT Anorexia Nervosa
Anxiety
Attention Deficit Disorders
Autism
Behavior Disorders
Bulimia
Clinical Psychology
Depression (Psychology)
Emotional Adjustment
Emotional Problems
Exceptional Persons
Helplessness
Hyperactivity
Mental Health
Neurosis
Personality Problems
Psychiatry
Psychopathology
Psychosis
Psychotherapy
Rehabilitation
Schizophrenia
Self Mutilation

EMOTIONAL EXPERIENCE *Jul. 1966*
CIJE: 303 RIE: 153 GC: 120
NT Catharsis
BT Experience
RT Affection
Emotional Response
Psychological Patterns
Security (Psychology)

Emotional Health
USE MENTAL HEALTH

Emotional Maladjustment (1966 1980)
USE EMOTIONAL ADJUSTMENT

Emotional Needs
USE PSYCHOLOGICAL NEEDS

Emotional Patterns
USE PSYCHOLOGICAL PATTERNS

EMOTIONAL PROBLEMS *Jul. 1966*
CIJE: 610 RIE: 290 GC: 120
SN Transient emotional difficulties, usually the result of a specific event or situation
BT Problems
RT Anger
Anxiety
Apathy
Behavior Problems
Depression (Psychology)
Emotional Adjustment
Emotional Disturbances
Fear
Grief
Helplessness
Jealousy
Learning Disabilities
Loneliness
Paranoid Behavior
Personality Problems
Psychological Patterns
Psychopathology

EMOTIONAL RESPONSE *Dec. 1970*
CIJE: 827 RIE: 498 GC: 120
BT Responses
RT Affective Behavior
Affective Measures
Arousal Patterns
Attachment Behavior
Burnout
Emotional Experience
Interpersonal Attraction
Prosocial Behavior
Psychological Patterns
Separation Anxiety
Spontaneous Behavior
Stranger Reactions
Violence

Emotional Security
USE SECURITY (PSYCHOLOGY)

Emotionally Disturbed (1966 1980)
USE EMOTIONAL DISTURBANCES

Emotionally Disturbed Children (1967 1980)
USE EMOTIONAL DISTURBANCES

EMPATHY *Jul. 1966*
CIJE: 583 RIE: 273 GC: 120
BT Psychological Patterns
RT Congruence (Psychology)
Counseling Techniques
Emotional Development
Identification (Psychology)
Interpersonal Relationship
Nondirective Counseling
Perspective Taking
Social Cognition

Employability
USE EMPLOYMENT POTENTIAL

Employable Skills
USE EMPLOYMENT POTENTIAL; JOB SKILLS

Employed Mothers
USE EMPLOYED PARENTS; MOTHERS

EMPLOYED PARENTS *Mar. 1980*
CIJE: 156 RIE: 225 GC: 510
SN Parents engaged in remunerative work, usually away from the family household (note: if appropriate, use the more precise term "dual career family")
UF Dual Earner Parents
Employed Mothers #
Working Parents (1966 1980)
BT Parents
RT Day Care
Dual Career Family
Employed Women
Employment
Fathers
Flexible Working Hours
Labor Force
Latchkey Children
Mothers
Personnel
Reentry Workers

EMPLOYED WOMEN *Mar. 1980*
CIJE: 1483 RIE: 1563 GC: 630
UF Women Workers
Working Women (1968 1980)
NT Women Faculty
BT Females
RT Affirmative Action
Comparable Worth
Dual Career Family
Employed Parents
Employment
Flexible Working Hours
Labor Force
Nontraditional Occupations
Personnel
Reentry Workers
Sex Discrimination

EMPLOYEE ASSISTANCE PROGRAMS *Aug. 1986*
CIJE: 24 RIE: 8 GC: 630
SN Programs sponsored by employers to help employees remedy personal problems affecting job performance (e.g., alcohol rehabilitation, mental health assistance, financial counseling)
BT Programs
RT Counseling Services
Employees
Employer Employee Relationship
Fringe Benefits
Guidance Programs
Mental Health Programs
Personnel Policy
Quality Of Working Life

EMPLOYEE ATTITUDES *Jul. 1966*
CIJE: 592 RIE: 598 GC: 630
SN Attitudes of, not toward, employees
UF Employee Opinions
Employee Work Attitudes #
BT Attitudes
RT Employees
Employer Employee Relationship
Job Enrichment
Vocational Maturity
Work Attitudes

Employee Employer Relationship
USE EMPLOYER EMPLOYEE RELATIONSHIP

Employee Evaluation
USE PERSONNEL EVALUATION

Employee Fringe Benefits
USE FRINGE BENEFITS

Employee Opinions
USE EMPLOYEE ATTITUDES

Employee Performance
USE JOB PERFORMANCE

Employee Relations
USE LABOR RELATIONS

EMPLOYEE RESPONSIBILITY *Jul. 1966*
CIJE: 87 RIE: 77 GC: 630
SN Responsibility assumed by, not for, employees (note: prior to mar80, this term was not scoped)
BT Responsibility
RT Employees
Employer Employee Relationship
Indemnity Bonds
Probationary Period

Employee Work Attitudes
USE EMPLOYEE ATTITUDES; WORK ATTITUDES

EMPLOYEES *Jul. 1966*
CIJE: 360 RIE: 258 GC: 630
NT Entry Workers
BT Personnel
RT Clerical Workers
Dislocated Workers
Employee Assistance Programs
Employee Attitudes
Employee Responsibility
Employer Attitudes
Employer Employee Relationship
Employers
Employment
Employment Interviews
Fringe Benefits
Industrial Personnel
Labor
Laborers
Paraprofessional Personnel
Personnel Needs
Professional Personnel
Reentry Workers
Sales Workers
Semiskilled Workers
Seniority
Service Workers
Skilled Workers
Teachers
Tenure
Unskilled Workers
Working Class

EMPLOYER ATTITUDES *Jul. 1966*
CIJE: 419 RIE: 1004 GC: 630
SN Attitudes of, not toward, employers
UF Employer Opinions
BT Attitudes
RT Employees
Employer Employee Relationship
Employers

EMPLOYER EMPLOYEE RELATIONSHIP *Jul. 1966*
CIJE: 1023 RIE: 869 GC: 630
UF Employee Employer Relationship
BT Interpersonal Relationship
RT Arbitration
Collective Bargaining
Employee Assistance Programs
Employee Attitudes
Employee Responsibility
Employees
Employer Attitudes
Employers
Employment
Faculty College Relationship
Faculty Handbooks
Faculty Workload
Fringe Benefits
Grievance Procedures
Job Enrichment
Job Satisfaction
Labor Legislation
Labor Relations
Management By Objectives
Organizational Development
Participative Decision Making
Personnel Management
Probationary Period
Quality Circles
Quality Of Working Life

= Two or more Descriptors are used to represent this term.
The term's main entry shows the appropriate coordination.

Released Time
Seniority
Teacher Administrator Relationship
Tenure
Unions
Vocational Adjustment
Work Environment

Employer Opinions
USE EMPLOYER ATTITUDES

Employer Sponsored Day Care
USE EMPLOYER SUPPORTED DAY CARE

EMPLOYER SUPPORTED DAY CARE *Aug. 1982*
CIJE: 12 RIE: 47 GC: 630
SN Child care services that are partially or fully financed and/or organized by employers as a benefit to their employees -- includes work-site centers, cooperative arrangements with the community, etc.
UF Employer Sponsored Day Care
BT Day Care
RT Day Care Centers
Family Day Care
Fringe Benefits
School Age Day Care

EMPLOYERS *Jul. 1966*
CIJE: 125 RIE: 241 GC: 630
BT Groups
RT Administrator Attitudes
Employees
Employer Attitudes
Employer Employee Relationship
Employment
Employment Interviews
Industrial Personnel

EMPLOYMENT *Jul. 1966*
CIJE: 861 RIE: 1754 GC: 630
SN State or condition of engaging in remunerative work (note: use a more specific term if possible)
UF Jobs (1966 1980)
Work
NT Black Employment
Migrant Employment
Multiple Employment
Overseas Employment
Part Time Employment
Seasonal Employment
Student Employment
Teacher Employment
Underemployment
Youth Employment
RT Careers
Dislocated Workers
Economic Factors
Education Work Relationship
Employed Parents
Employed Women
Employees
Employer Employee Relationship
Employers
Employment Experience
Employment Interviews
Employment Level
Employment Opportunities
Employment Patterns
Employment Potential
Employment Practices
Employment Problems
Employment Programs
Employment Projections
Employment Qualifications
Employment Services
Employment Statistics
Fringe Benefits
Job Applicants
Job Application
Job Development
Job Layoff
Job Performance
Job Placement
Job Search Methods
Job Training
Labor
Labor Economics
Labor Force
Labor Force Nonparticipants
Labor Market
Labor Utilization
Occupational Information
Occupational Safety And Health
Occupational Surveys
Occupations
Personnel
Probationary Period
Quality Of Working Life
Reentry Workers
Seniority
Tenure
Work Attitudes
Work Environment
Working Hours

Employment Adjustment
USE VOCATIONAL ADJUSTMENT

Employment Change
USE CAREER CHANGE

EMPLOYMENT COUNSELORS *Nov. 1969*
CIJE: 203 RIE: 76 GC: 630
BT Counselors
RT Career Counseling
Employment Opportunities
Employment Services
Outplacement Services (Employment)

Employment Discrimination
USE EQUAL OPPORTUNITIES (JOBS)

EMPLOYMENT EXPERIENCE *Jul. 1966*
CIJE: 184 RIE: 434 GC: 630
SN Experience gained through participation in remunerative work (note: prior to mar80, the instruction "job experience, use work experience" was carried in the thesaurus)
UF Job Experience
BT Work Experience
RT Employment
Employment Potential
Employment Qualifications
Entry Workers
Experiential Learning
Job Performance
Job Skills
Labor Market
Occupational Mobility
Personnel Data
Prior Learning
Resumes (Personal)
Seniority
Tenure

Employment Forecasts
USE EMPLOYMENT PROJECTIONS

EMPLOYMENT INTERVIEWS *Jul. 1966*
CIJE: 423 RIE: 398 GC: 630
UF Job Interviews
BT Interviews
RT Employees
Employers
Employment
Employment Qualifications
Employment Services
Job Applicants
Job Application
Job Search Methods
Personnel Selection
Resumes (Personal)

EMPLOYMENT LEVEL *Jul. 1966*
CIJE: 363 RIE: 612 GC: 630
SN Employment rank, position, or status achieved by an individual or group (note: for the labor force as a whole, use "employment patterns" -- prior to mar80, the use of this term was not restricted by a scope note)
UF Employment Status
Occupational Level
NT Academic Rank (Professional)
Tenure
BT Status
RT Career Ladders
Employment
Employment Patterns
Entry Workers
Equal Opportunities (Jobs)
Full Time Equivalency
Full Time Faculty
Income
Job Skills
Part Time Faculty
Professional Recognition
Promotion (Occupational)
Reentry Workers
Seniority
Socioeconomic Status

Employment Market
USE LABOR MARKET

EMPLOYMENT OPPORTUNITIES *Jul. 1966*
CIJE: 2068 RIE: 3042 GC: 630
SN Available remunerative work, as well as the outlook or trend in particular occupations or industries at a given time
UF Job Opportunities
Job Vacancies
NT Equal Opportunities (Jobs)
BT Opportunities
RT Career Change
Career Choice
Competitive Selection
Demand Occupations
Economic Opportunities
Education Work Relationship
Employment
Employment Counselors
Employment Patterns
Employment Programs
Employment Projections
Employment Services
Job Applicants
Job Application
Job Development
Job Search Methods
Job Skills
Labor Market
Labor Needs
Nontraditional Occupations
Occupational Mobility
Occupational Surveys
Occupations
Promotion (Occupational)
Recruitment
Reentry Workers
Youth Opportunities

EMPLOYMENT PATTERNS *Jul. 1966*
CIJE: 1197 RIE: 2373 GC: 630
UF Employment Trends (1966 1980)
Job Holding Patterns
BT Demography
RT Demand Occupations
Dislocated Workers
Economic Factors
Education Work Relationship
Employment
Employment Level
Employment Opportunities
Employment Projections
Employment Statistics
Labor Economics
Labor Market
Labor Turnover
Migration Patterns
Nontraditional Occupations
Occupational Surveys
Quality Of Working Life
Teacher Supply And Demand
Trend Analysis
Underemployment
Unemployment
Vocational Followup

EMPLOYMENT POTENTIAL *Jul. 1966*
CIJE: 353 RIE: 834 GC: 630
UF Employability
Employable Skills #
Marketable Skills #
RT Career Guidance
Demand Occupations
Educational Background
Educational Benefits
Education Work Relationship
Employment
Employment Experience
Employment Qualifications
Job Skills
Skill Obsolescence
Structural Unemployment

EMPLOYMENT PRACTICES *Jul. 1966*
CIJE: 643 RIE: 1067 GC: 630
RT Affirmative Action
Comparable Worth
Dislocated Workers
Dismissal (Personnel)
Dress Codes
Early Retirement
Employment
Job Layoff
Job Sharing
Labor Legislation
Loyalty Oaths
Midlife Transitions
Outplacement Services (Employment)
Personnel Integration
Personnel Management
Personnel Policy
Reduction In Force
Salary Wage Differentials
Scope Of Bargaining
Seniority
Tenure

Employment Preparation
USE JOB TRAINING

EMPLOYMENT PROBLEMS *Jul. 1966*
CIJE: 416 RIE: 671 GC: 630
BT Problems
RT Arbitration
Collective Bargaining
Employment
Job Development
Labor Problems
Negotiation Impasses
Underemployment
Unemployment

EMPLOYMENT PROGRAMS *Jul. 1966*
CIJE: 331 RIE: 1105 GC: 630
BT Programs
RT Employment
Employment Opportunities
Employment Services

EMPLOYMENT PROJECTIONS *Jul. 1966*
CIJE: 287 RIE: 777 GC: 730
UF Employment Forecasts
BT Prediction
RT Demand Occupations
Demography
Employment
Employment Opportunities
Employment Patterns
Labor Market
Labor Needs

EMPLOYMENT QUALIFICATIONS *Jul. 1966*
CIJE: 682 RIE: 1194 GC: 630
BT Qualifications
RT Administrator Qualifications
Business Skills
Counselor Qualifications
Employment
Employment Experience
Employment Interviews
Employment Potential
Entry Workers
Home Economics Skills
Job Analysis
Job Applicants
Job Application
Job Search Methods
Job Skills
Loyalty Oaths
Mechanical Skills
Occupational Information
Occupational Tests
Office Occupations
Personnel Data
Personnel Evaluation
Promotion (Occupational)
Reentry Workers
Resumes (Personal)
Skill Obsolescence
Supervisor Qualifications
Teacher Qualifications
Tenure
Vocational Aptitude
Work Experience

Employment Referral Services
USE EMPLOYMENT SERVICES

Employment Satisfaction
USE JOB SATISFACTION

EMPLOYMENT SERVICES *Jul. 1966*
CIJE: 279 RIE: 577 GC: 630
UF Employment Referral Services
NT Outplacement Services (Employment)
BT Human Services
RT Affirmative Action
Employment
Employment Counselors
Employment Interviews
Employment Opportunities
Employment Programs
Job Applicants

= Two or more Descriptors are used to represent this term.
The term's main entry shows the appropriate coordination.

Job Application
Job Placement
Job Search Methods

EMPLOYMENT STATISTICS *Jul. 1966*
CIJE: 285 RIE: 746 GC: 730
NT Worker Days
BT Statistical Data
RT Employment
Employment Patterns
Labor Market
Statistical Analysis

Employment Status
USE EMPLOYMENT LEVEL

Employment Surveys
USE OCCUPATIONAL SURVEYS

Employment Tests
USE OCCUPATIONAL TESTS

Employment Trends (1966 1980)
USE EMPLOYMENT PATTERNS

ENCAPSULATED FACILITIES *Sep. 1974*
CIJE: 10 RIE: 4 GC: 920
SN Environmentally controlled enclosures made of lightweight material to provide high mobility and flexibility--usually built at less cost than traditional structures
BT Facilities
RT Air Structures
Building Innovation
Buildings
Construction Materials
Flexible Facilities
Prefabrication
Relocatable Facilities

ENCODING (PSYCHOLOGY) *Oct. 1983*
CIJE: 51 RIE: 36 GC: 110
SN The mental conversion of signals or information into stored nerve impulses -- also, the psychological transformation of one message or image into another, e.g., writing into oral language, ideas into words
UF Information Storage (Psychology)
Recoding (Psychology)
BT Cognitive Processes
RT Cognitive Ability
Cognitive Style
Comprehension
Concept Formation
Epistemology
Language Processing
Learning Processes
Learning Strategies
Memory
Perception
Reaction Time
Recall (Psychology)
Recognition (Psychology)
Responses
Retention (Psychology)

ENCYCLOPEDIAS *Jul. 1966*
CIJE: 55 RIE: 71 GC: 730
BT Reference Materials

End Users (Information)
USE USERS (INFORMATION)

ENDANGERED SPECIES *Oct. 1984*
CIJE: 29 RIE: 26 GC: 410
SN Plants or animals in danger of extinction
BT Wildlife
RT Animals
Conservation (Environment)
Natural Resources
Physical Environment
Plant Pathology
Wildlife Management

Endowed Scholarships
USE SCHOLARSHIPS

ENDOWMENT FUNDS *Sep. 1977*
CIJE: 78 RIE: 89 GC: 620
SN Capital sums set aside as sources of income -- the principal of each sum is usually left intact and invested, while the income may be expended
UF Educational Endowments
BT Financial Support
RT Capital
Donors
Educational Finance
Fund Raising
Income
Investment
Money Management
Philanthropic Foundations
School Funds
Trustees
Trusts (Financial)

ENERGY *Sep. 1968*
CIJE: 1357 RIE: 1509 GC: 490
NT Geothermal Energy
Heat
Radiation
Wind Energy
BT Scientific Concepts
RT Alternative Energy Sources
Diffusion (Physics)
Energy Audits
Energy Conservation
Energy Education
Energy Management
Energy Occupations
Fatigue (Biology)
Force
Fuels
Kinetics
Lasers
Mechanics (Physics)
Motion
Optics
Physics
Power Technology
Quantum Mechanics
Relativity

ENERGY AUDITS *Aug. 1986*
CIJE: 9 RIE: 26 GC: 410
SN Verifications of energy efficiency of a structure, production process, or piece of equipment
BT Audits (Verification)
RT Energy
Energy Conservation
Energy Management
Environmental Standards
Fuel Consumption

ENERGY CONSERVATION *Apr. 1974*
CIJE: 941 RIE: 1120 GC: 410
SN Preventing loss or waste of energy
NT Heat Recovery
BT Conservation (Environment)
RT Alternative Energy Sources
Climate Control
Conservation Education
Depleted Resources
Ecological Factors
Ecology
Energy
Energy Audits
Energy Education
Energy Management
Energy Occupations
Environmental Education
Fuel Consumption
Fuels
Life Cycle Costing
Motor Vehicles
Natural Resources
Underground Facilities
Water Resources

ENERGY EDUCATION *Jan. 1985*
CIJE: 96 RIE: 387 GC: 400
SN Learning/teaching activities, often interdisciplinary in nature, that focus on such topics as energy resources, conversions, conservation, forms, uses, and issues -- includes both general and technical educational programs
BT Education
RT Alternative Energy Sources
Conservation Education
Consumer Education
Energy
Energy Conservation
Energy Occupations
Environmental Education
Fuels
Science Education
Utilities

ENERGY MANAGEMENT *Jan. 1986*
CIJE: 37 RIE: 29 GC: 410
SN Planning, operating, and maintaining facilities and equipment for maximum energy efficiency -- includes conserving energy and procuring more economical fuels
BT Administration
RT Alternative Energy Sources
Building Operation
Climate Control
Energy
Energy Audits
Energy Conservation
Environmental Standards
Fuel Consumption
Life Cycle Costing
Utilities

ENERGY OCCUPATIONS *Nov. 1982*
CIJE: 1 RIE: 45 GC: 640
SN Occupations related to the production, transfer, or use of energy
UF Nuclear Energy Occupations #
BT Occupations
RT Alternative Energy Sources
Electrical Occupations
Energy
Energy Conservation
Energy Education
Engineering Technology
Fuels
Nuclear Power Plant Technicians
Petroleum Industry
Power Technology
Technical Occupations
Utilities

Energy Technology
USE POWER TECHNOLOGY

Engaged Time (Learning)
USE TIME ON TASK

Engine Development Technicians
USE MECHANICAL DESIGN TECHNICIANS

ENGINEERING *Jul. 1966*
CIJE: 910 RIE: 764 GC: 490
NT Agricultural Engineering
Chemical Engineering
Civil Engineering
Ocean Engineering
Operating Engineering
BT Technology
RT Aerospace Technology
Electromechanical Technology
Engineering Education
Engineering Technicians
Engineering Technology
Engineers
Highway Engineering Aides
Manufacturing
Mining
Nuclear Technology
Sciences
Site Development

Engineering Aides
USE ENGINEERING TECHNICIANS

ENGINEERING DRAWING *Jul. 1966*
CIJE: 20 RIE: 61 GC: 490
SN Preparation of clear, complete, and accurate working plans and detail drawings from rough or detailed sketches or notes for engineering or manufacturing purposes, according to specified dimensions (note: prior to sep81, the use of this term was not restricted by a scope note)
UF Mechanical Drawing
BT Drafting
Engineering Graphics
RT Architectural Drafting
Blueprints
Civil Engineering
Technical Illustration

ENGINEERING EDUCATION *Jul. 1966*
CIJE: 2142 RIE: 890 GC: 490
BT Professional Education
RT Aerospace Education
Engineering
Engineering Technology
Engineers
Land Grant Universities
Science Education
Technical Education

ENGINEERING GRAPHICS *Jul. 1966*
CIJE: 17 RIE: 35 GC: 490
SN Technical functions including engineering drawing, problem solving or analytical graphics, and descriptive geometry -- also, the illustrations resulting from these functions
NT Engineering Drawing
BT Graphic Arts
RT Civil Engineering
Computer Graphics
Orthographic Projection
Signs

ENGINEERING TECHNICIANS *Jul. 1966*
CIJE: 43 RIE: 95 GC: 640
UF Engineering Aides
NT Highway Engineering Aides
BT Paraprofessional Personnel
RT Electronic Technicians
Engineering
Engineering Technology
Mechanical Design Technicians
Metallurgical Technicians
Nuclear Power Plant Technicians
Production Technicians

ENGINEERING TECHNOLOGY *Jun. 1969*
CIJE: 207 RIE: 154 GC: 490
BT Technology
RT Aerospace Technology
Electromechanical Technology
Energy Occupations
Engineering
Engineering Education
Engineering Technicians
Engineers
Nuclear Technology
Physical Sciences
Power Technology
Technical Education

ENGINEERS *Jul. 1966*
CIJE: 424 RIE: 464 GC: 640
BT Professional Personnel
RT Engineering
Engineering Education
Engineering Technology
Mathematicians
Scientific Personnel
Scientists

ENGINES *Jul. 1966*
CIJE: 42 RIE: 206 GC: 910
NT Diesel Engines
Electric Motors
BT Equipment
RT Agricultural Machinery
Auto Mechanics
Aviation Mechanics
Fuels
Hydraulics
Kinetics
Locomotive Engineers
Lubricants
Power Technology
Small Engine Mechanics

ENGLISH *Jul. 1966*
CIJE: 1431 RIE: 2109 GC: 440
NT Business English
English (Second Language)
Middle English
North American English
Old English
Oral English
BT Indo European Languages
RT College English
English Curriculum
English Instruction
English Literature
English Teacher Education
Linguistics
Welsh

ENGLISH (SECOND LANGUAGE) *Jul. 1966*
CIJE: 3334 RIE: 4891 GC: 440
SN English as a foreign or non-native language (i.e., english for non-english speakers)
UF Efl
Esl
Esol
Tefl

= Two or more Descriptors are used to represent this term.
The term's main entry shows the appropriate coordination.

Tenes
Tesl
Tesol
NT English For Special Purposes
BT English
Second Languages
RT Applied Linguistics
Bilingual Education
Bilingual Education Programs
Bilingualism
Bilingual Teacher Aides
Bilingual Teachers
Curriculum
Immersion Programs
Language Dominance
Language Of Instruction
Language Skills
Limited English Speaking
Linguistics
Mexican American Education
Migrant Adult Education
Migrant Education
Multilingualism
Non English Speaking
Second Language Instruction
Second Language Learning
Second Language Programs
Spanish Speaking

ENGLISH CURRICULUM *Jul. 1966*
CIJE: 1097 RIE: 1577 GC: 400
UF English Programs (1966 1980)
NT College English
World Literature
BT Curriculum
RT English
English Instruction
Language Arts

ENGLISH DEPARTMENTS *Jun. 1969*
CIJE: 339 RIE: 125 GC: 350
BT Departments
RT College English
Science Departments

ENGLISH EDUCATION (1967 1980) *Mar. 1980*
CIJE: 538 RIE: 385 GC: 400
SN Invalid descriptor -- see the more precise terms "english teacher education," "english instruction," and "english curriculum"

ENGLISH FOR ACADEMIC PURPOSES *Dec. 1985*
CIJE: 16 RIE: 8 GC: 440
SN English for non-english speakers who require specialized skills in the language in order to pursue studies at the college or college-preparatory level
BT English For Special Purposes
RT Academic Education

ENGLISH FOR SCIENCE AND TECHNOLOGY *Dec. 1985*
CIJE: 13 RIE: 14 GC: 440
SN Specialized english for non-english speakers who are studying or working in scientific and technological fields
BT English For Special Purposes
RT Natural Sciences
Sciences
Technology

ENGLISH FOR SPECIAL PURPOSES *Oct. 1974*
CIJE: 164 RIE: 228 GC: 440
SN English for non-english speakers who need a certain specialized knowledge of the language in their studies, profession, or trade
NT English For Academic Purposes
English For Science And Technology
Vocational English (Second Language)
BT English (Second Language)
Languages For Special Purposes
RT Second Language Instruction
Second Language Learning

ENGLISH INSTRUCTION *Jul. 1966*
CIJE: 3816 RIE: 3938 GC: 400
SN (Note: for instruction in english as a second language, coordinate "second language instruction" and "english (second language)")
BT Native Language Instruction
RT College English
English
English Curriculum
English Teacher Education
Language Teachers
Student Writing Models

ENGLISH LITERATURE *Jul. 1966*
CIJE: 324 RIE: 262 GC: 430
NT Old English Literature
BT Literature
RT English
United States Literature

ENGLISH NEOCLASSIC LITERARY PERIOD (1968 1980) *Mar. 1980*
CIJE: 4 RIE: 3 GC: 430
SN Invalid descriptor -- see such descriptors as "english literature," "neoclassicism," "seventeenth century literature," "eighteenth century literature," etc.

English Programs (1966 1980)
USE ENGLISH CURRICULUM

ENGLISH TEACHER EDUCATION *Mar. 1980*
CIJE: 194 RIE: 76 GC: 400
SN Teacher education in the field of english language arts (note: before mar80, this concept was indexed by the term "english education," usually in coordination with "teacher education" or one of its narrower terms)
BT Teacher Education
RT English
English Instruction

Enlargement Methods
USE MAGNIFICATION METHODS

Enlisted Men (1967 1976)
USE ENLISTED PERSONNEL

ENLISTED PERSONNEL *May. 1976*
CIJE: 40 RIE: 281 GC: 640
UF Enlisted Men (1967 1976)
Enlisted Women
BT Military Personnel
RT Military Science
Military Service
Military Training
Veterans

Enlisted Women
USE ENLISTED PERSONNEL

ENRICHMENT *Jul. 1966*
CIJE: 295 RIE: 334 GC: 310
UF Academic Enrichment (1966 1980)
Enrichment Experience (1966 1980)
NT Cultural Enrichment
Curriculum Enrichment
Job Enrichment
Language Enrichment
Mathematical Enrichment
RT Enrichment Activities

ENRICHMENT ACTIVITIES *Jul. 1966*
CIJE: 427 RIE: 773 GC: 310
SN Supplementary or compensatory activities and programs
UF Enrichment Programs (1966 1980)
BT Activities
RT After School Programs
Art Activities
Creative Activities
Cultural Activities
Enrichment
Exchange Programs
Extracurricular Activities
Improvement Programs
Music Activities
Supplementary Education
Weekend Programs

Enrichment Experience (1966 1980)
USE ENRICHMENT

Enrichment Programs (1966 1980)
USE ENRICHMENT ACTIVITIES

ENROLLMENT *Jul. 1966*
CIJE: 816 RIE: 2508 GC: 320
SN The total number of individuals registered as participants in a program or activity (note: for the act or process of enrolling in school, see "school registration")
UF College Enrollment
School Enrollment
Student Enrollment (1966 1977)
NT Dual Enrollment
Language Enrollment
Student Attrition
RT Access To Education
Admission (School)
Attendance
Auditing (Coursework)
Average Daily Membership
College Attendance
College Transfer Students
Declining Enrollment
Dropouts
Educational Demand
Educational Supply
Enrollment Influences
Enrollment Projections
Enrollment Rate
Enrollment Trends
Full Time Equivalency
Full Time Students
Group Membership
No Shows
Participation
Part Time Students
Registrars (School)
School District Size
School Entrance Age
School Registration
School Schedules
School Size
Stopouts
Student Recruitment
Students
Transfer Policy
Transfer Students

ENROLLMENT INFLUENCES *Jul. 1966*
CIJE: 385 RIE: 758 GC: 320
SN Factors affecting enrollment
BT Influences
RT Admission Criteria
Average Daily Membership
Course Selection (Students)
Declining Enrollment
Educational Demand
Educational Supply
Enrollment
Enrollment Rate
Enrollment Trends

ENROLLMENT PROJECTIONS *Jul. 1966*
CIJE: 264 RIE: 874 GC: 730
BT Prediction
RT Admissions Officers
Average Daily Membership
Declining Enrollment
Enrollment
Enrollment Rate
Enrollment Trends
School Demography
School Statistics

ENROLLMENT RATE *Jul. 1966*
CIJE: 235 RIE: 535 GC: 330
NT Average Daily Membership
Declining Enrollment
BT Incidence
RT Enrollment
Enrollment Influences
Enrollment Projections
Enrollment Trends
Full Time Equivalency
Language Enrollment

ENROLLMENT TRENDS *Jul. 1966*
CIJE: 901 RIE: 2494 GC: 330
RT Average Daily Membership
Declining Enrollment
Educational Trends
Enrollment
Enrollment Influences
Enrollment Projections
Enrollment Rate
Feeder Patterns
Language Enrollment
School Demography
Trend Analysis

Enterprisers
USE ENTREPRENEURSHIP

ENTOMOLOGY *Jul. 1966*
CIJE: 178 RIE: 152 GC: 490
UF Insect Studies
BT Zoology
RT Agriculture
Horticulture
Insecticides
Pests

Entrepreneurs
USE ENTREPRENEURSHIP

ENTREPRENEURSHIP *Oct. 1982*
CIJE: 96 RIE: 280 GC: 650
SN Initiation, organization, promotion, and/or management of a business or enterprise with assumption of the risk of loss or failure
UF Enterprisers
Entrepreneurs
RT Business
Business Administration
Capitalism
Careers
Economic Opportunities
Economics
Education Work Relationship
Financial Support
Merchants
Occupations
Risk
Small Businesses

ENTRY WORKERS *Feb. 1969*
CIJE: 121 RIE: 260 GC: 630
UF Beginning Workers
BT Employees
RT Career Ladders
Employment Experience
Employment Level
Employment Qualifications

Enunciation Improvement (1966 1980)
USE ARTICULATION (SPEECH); SPEECH IMPROVEMENT

ENVIRONMENT *Jul. 1966*
CIJE: 1626 RIE: 1594 GC: 410
SN Surrounding conditions, forces, or factors potentially capable of influencing, modifying, or interacting with an organism, material, or other entity (note: use a more specific term if possible)
NT Cultural Context
Disadvantaged Environment
Economic Climate
Educational Environment
Family Environment
Institutional Environment
Organizational Climate
Permissive Environment
Physical Environment
Rural Environment
Simulated Environment
Slum Environment
Social Environment
Suburban Environment
Therapeutic Environment
Urban Environment
Work Environment
RT Adjustment (To Environment)
Appropriate Technology
Background
Climate
Conservation (Environment)
Ecology
Environmental Education
Environmental Influences
Environmental Research
Humanization
Influences
Nature Nurture Controversy
Place Of Residence
Regional Characteristics
Resources
Well Being

Environment Heredity Controversy
USE NATURE NURTURE CONTROVERSY

Environmental Criteria (1967 1980)
USE ENVIRONMENTAL STANDARDS

ENVIRONMENTAL EDUCATION *Oct. 1969*
CIJE: 3540 RIE: 4118 GC: 400
NT Conservation Education
BT Education
RT Adventure Education
Air Pollution
Biological Sciences
Conservation (Environment)
Ecology
Energy Conservation
Energy Education
Environment
Forestry
Marine Education
Mining
Natural Resources
Outdoor Education
Pollution
Population Education
Science And Society
Social Biology
Soil Conservation
Water Pollution

Environmental Factors
USE ENVIRONMENTAL INFLUENCES

ENVIRONMENTAL INFLUENCES *Jul. 1966*
CIJE: 2460 RIE: 2284 GC: 120
SN Influences of the physical environment (note: prior to mar80, this term was not scoped and was also used for influences of social, educational, cultural, etc. environments -- see also such descriptors as "biological influences," "nature nurture controversy," "cultural context," "family environment," "social influences," "educational environment," etc.
UF Environmental Factors
BT Influences
RT Acoustical Environment
Biological Influences
Climate
Climate Control
Crowding
Environment
Environmental Research
Hazardous Materials
Nature Nurture Controversy
Physical Environment
Pollution
Radiation Effects
Sanitation
Thermal Environment
Visual Environment
Weather

ENVIRONMENTAL RESEARCH *Jul. 1966*
CIJE: 420 RIE: 340 GC: 810
SN Study of the physical environment (note: prior to mar80, the use of this term was restricted to research on the physical environment's relationship to humans -- as of oct81, use as a minor descriptor for examples of this kind of research -- use as a major descriptor only as the subject of a document -- see also "environmental influences" and "social science research")
BT Research
RT Architectural Research
Environment
Environmental Influences
Physical Environment
Scientific Research
Use Studies

ENVIRONMENTAL STANDARDS *Mar. 1980*
CIJE: 252 RIE: 298 GC: 610
SN Laws, rules, or regulations relating to the quality of the physical environment
UF Environmental Criteria (1967 1980)
BT Standards
RT Air Pollution
Crowding
Ecology
Energy Audits
Energy Management
Hazardous Materials
Labor Standards
Living Standards
Motor Vehicles
Noise (Sound)
Occupational Safety And Health
Pests
Physical Environment
Poisons
Pollution
Public Health
Quality Of Life
Waste Disposal
Water Pollution
Water Quality

ENVIRONMENTAL TECHNICIANS *Mar. 1969*
CIJE: 109 RIE: 168 GC: 640
UF Sanitary Inspectors
Sanitary Technicians
BT Allied Health Personnel
Paraprofessional Personnel
RT Chemical Technicians
Sanitation
Water Treatment

Environmental Therapy
USE MILIEU THERAPY

Envy
USE JEALOUSY

ENZYMES *Oct. 1982*
CIJE: 74 RIE: 2 GC: 490
SN Group of catalytic proteins produced by living cells that mediate and promote the chemical processes of life without themselves being changed
RT Biochemistry
Biology
Chemical Reactions
Cytology
Genetics
Medicine
Metabolism
Nucleic Acids
Physiology

Epee Fencing
USE FENCING (SPORT)

EPICS *Jul. 1966*
CIJE: 64 RIE: 38 GC: 430
SN Narrative poems about events, settings, or (especially) characters of heroic proportions, frequently treating the early history of a tribe or nation
BT Literary Genres
Poetry
RT Allegory
Ballads
Classical Literature
Didacticism
Legends
Lyric Poetry
Medieval Literature
Mythology
Poets
World Literature

Epidemic Roseola
USE RUBELLA

EPIDEMIOLOGY *Aug. 1986*
CIJE: 28 RIE: 24 GC: 210
SN Science of the incidence, distribution, control, and contributing factors of epidemic illness or disease
BT Medicine
RT Disease Control
Disease Incidence
Diseases
Etiology
Health
Health Conditions
Immunization Programs
Medical Services
Pathology
Preventive Medicine
Public Health

EPILEPSY *Jul. 1966*
CIJE: 84 RIE: 82 GC: 220
BT Neurological Impairments
RT Developmental Disabilities
Minimal Brain Dysfunction
Seizures

EPISODE TEACHING (1967 1980) *Mar. 1980*
CIJE: 3 RIE: 6 GC: 310
SN Invalid descriptor -- previously used to index a method of introducing student teachers to teaching, as well as a technique for presenting material in social studies instruction

EPISTEMOLOGY *Oct. 1980*
CIJE: 293 RIE: 185 GC: 110
SN The study of how knowledge is acquired
UF Cognitive Theory
BT Philosophy
RT Cognitive Ability
Cognitive Development
Cognitive Processes
Cognitive Psychology
Cognitive Structures
Concept Formation
Developmental Continuity
Developmental Stages
Encoding (Psychology)
Knowledge Level
Learning
Phenomenology
Piagetian Theory

Epistles (1970 1980)
USE LETTERS (CORRESPONDENCE)

EQUAL EDUCATION *Jul. 1966*
CIJE: 2290 RIE: 3174 GC: 540
SN System of education extending comparable opportunities to all individuals regardless of race, color, creed, age, sex, socioeconomic class, or ability
UF Educational Equality (1966 1976)
Educational Equity (Opportunities)
Educational Inequality
Equal Educational Opportunities
Equality Of Education
Equity (Educational Opportunities)
Universal Education (1968 1976)
BT Civil Rights
Education
RT Access To Education
Affirmative Action
Age Discrimination
Civil Rights Legislation
Educational Demand
Educational Discrimination
Educationally Disadvantaged
Educational Opportunities
Educational Quality
Equal Facilities
Handicap Discrimination
Individualized Education Programs
Nondiscriminatory Education
Open Enrollment
Racial Discrimination
Reverse Discrimination
Selective Admission
Sex Discrimination
Tokenism

Equal Educational Opportunities
USE EQUAL EDUCATION

Equal Employment
USE EQUAL OPPORTUNITIES (JOBS)

EQUAL FACILITIES *Jul. 1966*
CIJE: 17 RIE: 63 GC: 540
SN Facilities that are qualitatively equal without regard to the characteristics (e.g., sex, ethnicity, social class) of the groups that use or benefit from them (note: do not confuse with "accessiblity (for disabled)")
UF Equalized Facilities
BT Facilities
RT Civil Rights
Civil Rights Legislation
Equal Education
Public Facilities
Racial Discrimination
Sex Discrimination
Sex Fairness
Social Discrimination

EQUAL OPPORTUNITIES (JOBS) *Jul. 1966*
CIJE: 1317 RIE: 1482 GC: 540
UF Employment Discrimination
Equal Employment
Job Discrimination
BT Civil Rights
Employment Opportunities
RT Affirmative Action
Age Discrimination
Civil Rights Legislation
Comparable Worth
Employment Level
Equal Protection
Faculty Integration
Handicap Discrimination
Job Development
Nontraditional Occupations
Personnel Integration
Racial Discrimination
Reverse Discrimination
Salary Wage Differentials
Sex Discrimination
Sex Fairness
Teacher Integration
Tokenism

Equal Pay
USE SALARY WAGE DIFFERENTIALS

EQUAL PROTECTION *Jul. 1966*
CIJE: 386 RIE: 322 GC: 540
BT Civil Rights
RT Civil Rights Legislation
Courts
Due Process
Equal Opportunities (Jobs)
Justice
Laws
Married Students
Pregnant Students
Sex Fairness
Student Rights

Equality Of Education
USE EQUAL EDUCATION

EQUALIZATION AID *Jan. 1969*
CIJE: 263 RIE: 523 GC: 620
SN State and/or federal monies that are given in inverse proportion to local resources
UF Additional Aid
BT Financial Support
RT Categorical Aid
Developing Institutions
Disadvantaged Schools
Educational Equity (Finance)
Educational Finance
Expenditure Per Student
Federal Aid
Finance Reform
Fiscal Capacity
Foundation Programs
Full State Funding
Grants
Resource Allocation
Revenue Sharing
State Aid
State Federal Aid
Tax Effort

Equalized Facilities
USE EQUAL FACILITIES

EQUATED SCORES *Jul. 1966*
CIJE: 56 RIE: 216 GC: 820
SN Scores from different forms of the same test, or from different tests measuring the same trait, that are converted to a common score scale so that they can be treated as equivalent and directly compared
BT Scores
RT Cutting Scores
Grade Equivalent Scores
Latent Trait Theory
Raw Scores
Scaling
Statistical Analysis
Test Theory
True Scores
Weighted Scores

EQUATIONS (MATHEMATICS) *Apr. 1982*
CIJE: 95 RIE: 48 GC: 480
SN Statements of equality among mathematical entities
BT Mathematical Formulas
RT Algebra
Functions (Mathematics)
Mathematical Concepts
Relationship

Equilibrium Constants
USE CHEMICAL EQUILIBRIUM

EQUIPMENT *Jul. 1966*
CIJE: 676 RIE: 894 GC: 910
SN Any instrument, machine, apparatus, or set of articles used in an operation or activity without losing its original shape or appearance (note: use a more specific term if possible)

UF Appliances
Building Equipment (1966 1980)
NT Agricultural Machinery
Air Conditioning Equipment
Assistive Devices (For Disabled)
Athletic Equipment
Audio Equipment
Biomedical Equipment
Calculators
Educational Equipment
Electrical Appliances
Electric Circuits
Electromechanical Aids
Electronic Equipment
Engines
Furniture
Hand Tools
Home Furnishings
Laboratory Equipment
Library Equipment
Machine Tools
Measurement Equipment
Mechanical Equipment
Motor Vehicles
Musical Instruments
Office Machines
Photographic Equipment
Projection Equipment
Safety Equipment
Science Equipment
Space Dividers
Test Scoring Machines
Vending Machines
RT Assembly (Manufacturing)
Equipment Evaluation
Equipment Maintenance
Equipment Manufacturers
Equipment Standards
Equipment Storage
Equipment Utilization
Facilities
Facility Inventory
Machinery Industry
Maintenance
Resources
Sanitary Facilities
School Buses
Supplies

EQUIPMENT EVALUATION *Jul. 1966*
CIJE: 390 RIE: 253 GC: 910
SN Judging apparatus, furnishings, instruments, machinery, tools, or other devices in terms of established standards
UF Field Check (1967 1980)
BT Evaluation
RT Equipment
Equipment Standards
Field Tests
Inspection
Life Cycle Costing

Equipment Inventory
USE FACILITY INVENTORY

EQUIPMENT MAINTENANCE *Jul. 1966*
CIJE: 246 RIE: 664 GC: 910
UF Equipment Repair
Equipment Upkeep
BT Maintenance
RT Cleaning
Electrical Occupations
Equipment
Equipment Storage
Machine Repairers
Repair
School Maintenance
Skilled Occupations

EQUIPMENT MANUFACTURERS *Jul. 1966*
CIJE: 196 RIE: 68 GC: 650
BT Personnel
RT Equipment
Equipment Standards
Industry
Manufacturing
Manufacturing Industry

Equipment Purchasing
USE PURCHASING

Equipment Repair
USE EQUIPMENT MAINTENANCE

EQUIPMENT STANDARDS *Jul. 1966*
CIJE: 186 RIE: 224 GC: 910
SN Specifications, requirements, and criteria for evaluating the construction and performance of apparatus, furnishings, instruments, machinery, tools, and other devices
BT Standards
RT Equipment
Equipment Evaluation
Equipment Manufacturers
Purchasing

EQUIPMENT STORAGE *Jul. 1966*
CIJE: 28 RIE: 48 GC: 910
BT Storage
RT Equipment
Equipment Maintenance
Facility Utilization Research
Furniture
Furniture Design
Locker Rooms
Space Utilization
Warehouses

Equipment Upkeep
USE EQUIPMENT MAINTENANCE

EQUIPMENT UTILIZATION *Jul. 1966*
CIJE: 490 RIE: 614 GC: 910
RT Equipment
Facility Inventory
Operating Engineering

Equity (Educational Finance)
USE EDUCATIONAL EQUITY (FINANCE)

Equity (Educational Opportunities)
USE EQUAL EDUCATION

Equity (Impartiality)
USE JUSTICE

EQUIVALENCY TESTS *Aug. 1968*
CIJE: 134 RIE: 342 GC: 830
SN Tests to measure the extent to which previous schooling, knowledge, or experience satisfies course or job requirements (note: see also the identifier "general educational development tests" -- prior to sep77 and mar80 respectively, the instructions "ged tests, use equivalency tests" and "proficiency examinations, use equivalency tests" were carried in the thesaurus)
UF Advanced Credit Examinations
Advanced Standing Examinations
Credit By Examination
BT Achievement Tests
RT Advanced Placement
Advanced Placement Programs
Certification
Credentials
Educational Certificates
Experiential Learning
Grade Equivalent Scores
High School Equivalency Programs
Job Skills
Licensing Examinations (Professions)
Prior Learning
Special Degree Programs
Student Placement

Ergonomics
USE HUMAN FACTORS ENGINEERING

ERROR ANALYSIS (LANGUAGE) *Mar. 1977*
CIJE: 383 RIE: 359 GC: 450
SN In language teaching and testing, a technique of measuring progress and of devising teaching methods by recording and classifying the mistakes made by students -- in linguistics, the observation of errors in the speech process as a means of understanding the phonological and semantic components of language, interactional processes, and speakers' discourse strategies
BT Comparative Analysis
RT Contrastive Linguistics
Descriptive Linguistics
Error Patterns
Interference (Language)
Interlanguage
Language Patterns
Language Skills
Language Usage
Linguistic Difficulty (Inherent)
Phonetic Analysis
Phonology
Second Language Instruction
Second Language Learning
Semantics
Structural Analysis (Linguistics)
Syntax

ERROR OF MEASUREMENT *Mar. 1980*
CIJE: 230 RIE: 211 GC: 820
SN Difference between observed and true scores due to random errors introduced by the measuring instrument or administering person, i.e., that portion of a score variance that can not be accounted for systematically (note: do not use for test bias errors)
UF Error Variance
Measurement Error
Standard Error Of Estimate
Standard Error Of Measurement (1970 1980)
BT Statistical Analysis
RT Generalizability Theory
Interrater Reliability
Least Squares Statistics
Meta Analysis
Multitrait Multimethod Techniques
Predictor Variables
Raw Scores
Reliability
Sampling
Scores
Scoring
Statistical Bias
Testing Problems
Test Interpretation
Test Norms
Test Reliability
True Scores

Error Of Refraction
USE AMETROPIA

ERROR PATTERNS *May. 1970*
CIJE: 652 RIE: 440 GC: 820
SN Systematically recurring errors
RT Error Analysis (Language)
Evaluation Methods
Item Analysis
Redundancy
Reliability
Research
Statistical Bias
Test Bias
Testing

Error Variance
USE ERROR OF MEASUREMENT

Escapees
USE REFUGEES

ESKIMO ALEUT LANGUAGES *Sep. 1975*
CIJE: 5 RIE: 106 GC: 440
UF Aleut
BT Languages
RT Alaska Natives
American Indian Languages
Eskimos

ESKIMOS *Jul. 1966*
CIJE: 111 RIE: 397 GC: 560
UF Inuit
BT Groups
RT Alaska Natives
Canada Natives
Eskimo Aleut Languages
Ethnic Groups
Minority Groups
North Americans
Trust Responsibility (Government)

Esl
USE ENGLISH (SECOND LANGUAGE)

Esol
USE ENGLISH (SECOND LANGUAGE)

ESSAY TESTS *Jul. 1966*
CIJE: 178 RIE: 160 GC: 830
SN Tests in which respondents are asked to compose written statements, discussions, summaries, or descriptions that are to be used as measures of knowledge, understanding, or writing proficiency
BT Verbal Tests
RT Achievement Tests
Constructed Response
Essays
Objective Tests
Writing Evaluation
Writing Skills

ESSAYS *Jul. 1966*
CIJE: 542 RIE: 491 GC: 430
SN Short analytic, interpretative, or critical literary compositions, usually in prose
BT Literary Genres
Nonfiction
RT Essay Tests
Expository Writing
Opinion Papers
Theses

ESTATE PLANNING *Sep. 1969*
CIJE: 32 RIE: 34 GC: 620
BT Planning
RT Assessed Valuation
Capital
Finance Occupations
Financial Services
Investment
Money Management
Ownership
Property Accounting
Property Appraisal
Taxes
Trustees
Trusts (Financial)
Wills

Estimated Costs (1966 1980)
USE COST ESTIMATES

ESTIMATION (MATHEMATICS) *Apr. 1982*
CIJE: 184 RIE: 186 GC: 480
SN Process of determining an approximate solution for numerical or measurement problems
UF Approximation (Mathematics)
BT Computation
RT Mathematical Models
Mathematics
Measurement
Monte Carlo Methods
Prediction
Predictive Measurement
Probability
Statistical Inference
Statistics

ESTONIAN *Jul. 1966*
CIJE: 2 RIE: 15 GC: 440
BT Finno Ugric Languages
RT Baltic Languages

ESTUARIES *Apr. 1985*
CIJE: 5 RIE: 26 GC: 410
SN Mouths of rivers, and other semi-enclosed bodies of water, that are open to the sea and within which fresh and salt water are mixed by runoff and tides
RT Ecology
Fisheries
Marine Biology
Marine Education
Oceanography
Water
Water Resources

ETHICAL INSTRUCTION *Nov. 1969*
CIJE: 651 RIE: 325 GC: 400
SN Instruction having to do with morality and good conduct
UF Moral Instruction
BT Instruction
RT Citizenship Education
Ethics
Moral Values
Religious Education
Sex Education
Values Education

Ethical Values (1966 1980)
USE MORAL VALUES

ETHICS *Nov. 1969*
CIJE: 1271 RIE: 668 GC: 430
UF Morals
NT Bioethics
BT Philosophy
RT Altruism
Codes Of Ethics
Confidentiality
Conflict Of Interest
Credibility
Ethical Instruction
Integrity
Intellectual Freedom
Moral Development
Moral Values
Plagiarism
Privacy
Religious Education
Sex Education

ETHNIC BIAS *Mar. 1980*
CIJE: 63 RIE: 95 GC: 540
SN Prejudicial opinions about particular groups because of their ethnic origins (note: do not confuse with "ethnic discrimination," which refers to actions based on those attitudes)
BT Social Bias
RT Anti Semitism
Ethnic Discrimination
Ethnic Groups
Ethnicity
Ethnic Relations
Ethnic Stereotypes
Ethnocentrism
Racial Bias

Ethnic Community
USE ETHNIC GROUPS

Ethnic Consciousness
USE ETHNICITY

Ethnic Cultural Groups
USE ETHNIC GROUPS

ETHNIC DISCRIMINATION *Mar. 1980*
CIJE: 70 RIE: 106 GC: 540
SN Restriction or denial of rights, privileges, and choice because of ethnic origins (note: do not confuse with "ethnic bias")
BT Social Discrimination
RT Anti Semitism
Ethnic Bias
Ethnic Distribution
Ethnic Groups
Ethnic Relations
Ethnic Stereotypes
Ethnocentrism
Racial Discrimination
Religious Discrimination

ETHNIC DISTRIBUTION *Jul. 1966*
CIJE: 61 RIE: 252 GC: 550
BT Population Distribution
RT Affirmative Action
Black Population Trends
Community
Ethnic Discrimination
Ethnic Groups
Ethnic Origins
Geographic Distribution
Incidence
Neighborhood Integration
Racial Distribution

Ethnic Group Studies
USE ETHNIC STUDIES

ETHNIC GROUPING (1966 1980) *Mar. 1980*
CIJE: 23 RIE: 44 GC: 550
SN Invalid descriptor -- used inconsistently in indexing -- see such descriptors as "ethnicity," "ethnic groups," "ethnic distribution," "demography," "classification," etc.

ETHNIC GROUPS *Jul. 1966*
CIJE: 1533 RIE: 2597 GC: 560
SN Subgroups within a larger cultural or social order that are distinguished from the majority and each other by their national, religious, linguistic, cultural, and sometimes racial background (note: do not confuse with "minority groups," which has the connotation of being the object of prejudice or discrimination -- use a more specific term if possible)
UF Ethnic Community
Ethnic Cultural Groups
Racial Cultural Groups
NT Alaska Natives
American Indians
Anglo Americans
Canada Natives
Chinese Americans
Filipino Americans
Greek Americans
Hawaiians
Italian Americans
Japanese Americans
Korean Americans
Mexican Americans
Polish Americans
Portuguese Americans
Samoan Americans
Spanish Americans
BT Groups
RT Arabs
Asian Americans
Biculturalism
Black Community
Blacks
Cross Cultural Studies
Cubans
Cultural Background
Cultural Differences
Cultural Education
Cultural Images
Culture
Culture Fair Tests
Dominicans
Eskimos
Ethnic Bias
Ethnic Discrimination
Ethnic Distribution
Ethnicity
Ethnic Origins
Ethnic Status
Ethnic Stereotypes
Ethnic Studies
Ethnography
Ethnology
Foreign Culture
Ghettos
Haitians
Hispanic Americans
Indians
Indigenous Populations
Indochinese
Intercultural Programs
Jews
Limited English Speaking
Mexicans
Minority Groups
Multicultural Education
Nationalism
Native Language Instruction
Native Speakers
Non English Speaking
North Americans
Pacific Americans
Puerto Ricans
Race
Religious Cultural Groups
Self Determination
Social Integration
Subcultures
Tribes

Ethnic Heritage
USE CULTURAL BACKGROUND

Ethnic Identification
USE ETHNICITY

Ethnic Integration
USE SOCIAL INTEGRATION

ETHNIC ORIGINS *Jul. 1966*
CIJE: 99 RIE: 162 GC: 560
RT Cultural Background
Ethnic Distribution
Ethnic Groups
Ethnicity
Ethnic Studies
Ethnology
Genealogy
Regional Dialects

ETHNIC RELATIONS *Jul. 1966*
CIJE: 199 RIE: 240 GC: 540
SN Contact and interaction between or among ethnic groups
BT Intergroup Relations
RT Community Control
Cross Cultural Studies
Cross Cultural Training
Cultural Differences
Cultural Interrelationships
Cultural Pluralism
Ethnic Bias
Ethnic Discrimination
Ethnicity
Ethnic Status
Ethnocentrism
Intercultural Communication
Interfaith Relations
Multicultural Education
Racial Relations
Religious Cultural Groups
Social Integration

ETHNIC STATUS *Jul. 1966*
CIJE: 82 RIE: 111 GC: 510
BT Status
RT Ethnic Groups
Ethnicity
Ethnic Relations

ETHNIC STEREOTYPES *Jul. 1966*
CIJE: 284 RIE: 331 GC: 540
UF Jewish Stereotypes (1966 1980) #
NT Black Stereotypes
BT Stereotypes
RT Ethnic Bias
Ethnic Discrimination
Ethnic Groups
Ethnicity
Ethnic Studies
Racial Attitudes
Racial Differences
Racial Identification

ETHNIC STUDIES *Aug. 1969*
CIJE: 398 RIE: 955 GC: 400
UF Ethnic Group Studies
NT American Indian Studies
Black Studies
BT Curriculum
RT Area Studies
Cross Cultural Studies
Cultural Background
Cultural Education
Cultural Influences
Ethnic Groups
Ethnicity
Ethnic Origins
Ethnic Stereotypes
History
Integration Studies
Interdisciplinary Approach
Minority Groups
Social Science Research
Social Sciences
Urban Studies

Ethnic Unity
USE GROUP UNITY

ETHNICITY *Oct. 1977*
CIJE: 516 RIE: 530 GC: 120
SN Identification with a specific kind of ethnic character, quality, or peculiarity -- awareness of the ethnic character of oneself or others
UF Ethnic Consciousness
Ethnic Identification
BT Sociocultural Patterns
RT Black Power
Cross Cultural Studies
Cultural Awareness
Cultural Differences
Cultural Images
Cultural Pluralism
Cultural Traits
Culture Conflict
Ethnic Bias
Ethnic Groups
Ethnic Origins
Ethnic Relations
Ethnic Status
Ethnic Stereotypes
Ethnic Studies
Ethnocentrism
Group Unity
Identification (Psychology)
Minority Groups
Multicultural Education
Nationalism
Psychological Patterns
Race
Racial Attitudes
Racial Identification
Religious Conflict
Self Concept
Socialization
Traditionalism

ETHNOCENTRISM *Sep. 1973*
CIJE: 150 RIE: 140 GC: 540
SN Habitual disposition to judge foreign peoples or groups by the standards and practices of one's own culture or ethnic group
RT Cultural Differences
Cultural Images
Culture Conflict
Ethnic Bias
Ethnic Discrimination
Ethnicity
Ethnic Relations
Foreign Culture
Intergroup Relations
International Relations
Multicultural Education
Psychological Patterns
Racial Differences
Sociocultural Patterns
Stereotypes
Values

ETHNOGRAPHY *Jan. 1979*
CIJE: 238 RIE: 408 GC: 400
SN Descriptive study (i.e., observation and reporting) of human culture and societies
BT Anthropology
RT Anthropological Linguistics
Cultural Context
Educational Anthropology
Ethnic Groups
Ethnology
Folk Culture
Kinship
Naturalistic Observation
Participant Observation
Qualitative Research
Social Science Research
Social Scientists
Sociocultural Patterns
Sociology

ETHNOLOGY *Aug. 1968*
CIJE: 114 RIE: 213 GC: 400
SN Historical, analytic, or comparative study of human culture and societies
BT Anthropology
RT Anthropological Linguistics
Archaeology
Cross Cultural Studies
Cultural Background
Cultural Context
Cultural Interrelationships
Cultural Pluralism
Educational Anthropology
Ethnic Groups
Ethnic Origins
Ethnography
Folk Culture
Human Geography
Kinship
Social Science Research
Social Scientists
Sociocultural Patterns
Sociology

ETHOLOGY *Mar. 1983*
CIJE: 34 RIE: 17 GC: 490
SN Study of the behavior of humans and other animals under natural conditions from both evolutionary/genetic and ecological/experiential perspectives
BT Behavioral Sciences
Biological Sciences
RT Behavior
Behavior Development
Behavior Patterns
Conditioning
Ecology
Evolution
Naturalistic Observation
Sociobiology
Zoology

= Two or more Descriptors are used to represent this term.
The term's main entry shows the appropriate coordination.

ETIOLOGY *Jul. 1966*
CIJE: 546 RIE: 361 GC: 210
SN Study of causes, origins, or reasons
BT Technology
RT Attribution Theory
Clinical Diagnosis
Delinquency Causes
Educational Diagnosis
Epidemiology
Handicap Identification
Identification
Pathology

Etv
USE EDUCATIONAL TELEVISION

ETYMOLOGY *Jul. 1966*
CIJE: 192 RIE: 100 GC: 450
NT Onomastics
BT Diachronic Linguistics
RT Comparative Analysis
Definitions
Dialect Studies
Glottochronology
Language Classification
Language Research
Languages
Language Typology
Lexicography
Lexicology
North American English
Semantics

EUROPEAN HISTORY *Jul. 1966*
CIJE: 249 RIE: 165 GC: 430
BT History
RT Western Civilization

EVALUATION *Jul. 1966*
CIJE: 3918 RIE: 5016 GC: 820
SN Appraising or judging persons, organizations, or things in relation to stated objectives, standards, or criteria (note: use a more specific term if possible -- see also "testing" and "measurement")
UF Appraisal
NT Course Evaluation
Curriculum Evaluation
Educational Assessment
Equipment Evaluation
Formative Evaluation
Holistic Evaluation
Informal Assessment
Institutional Evaluation
Instructional Material Evaluation
Medical Care Evaluation
Medical Evaluation
Needs Assessment
Peer Evaluation
Personnel Evaluation
Preschool Evaluation
Program Evaluation
Property Appraisal
Psychological Evaluation
Recognition (Achievement)
Self Evaluation (Groups)
Self Evaluation (Individuals)
Student Evaluation
Student Teacher Evaluation
Summative Evaluation
Vocational Evaluation
Writing Evaluation
RT Achievement
Credentials
Data Interpretation
Differences
Evaluation Criteria
Evaluation Methods
Evaluation Needs
Evaluation Problems
Evaluation Utilization
Evaluative Thinking
Evaluators
Expectation
Failure
Inspection
Judgment Analysis Technique
Literary Criticism
Measurement
Measures (Individuals)
Objectives
Observation
Participant Satisfaction
Performance Factors
Prerequisites
Quality Of Life
Research
Research And Development
Specifications
Standards
Success
Testing
Tests
User Satisfaction (Information)
Validity

EVALUATION CRITERIA *Jul. 1966*
CIJE: 3462 RIE: 4916 GC: 820
SN Specifications or standards that may be used to judge or appraise individuals, organizations, or things
NT Reliability
Validity
BT Criteria
RT Accountability
Efficiency
Evaluation
Evaluation Methods
Evaluation Needs
Evaluation Problems
Minimum Competencies
Performance
Performance Factors
Productivity
Selection
Specifications
Values

Evaluation Designs
USE EVALUATION METHODS

EVALUATION METHODS *Jul. 1966*
CIJE: 6037 RIE: 8775 GC: 820
SN Objective or subjective procedures used to obtain and organize information for appraisal in relation to stated objectives, standards, or criteria (note: prior to mar80, this term was not restricted by a scope note)
UF Analysis
Evaluation Designs
Evaluation Procedures
Evaluation Techniques (1966 1974)
NT Audience Analysis
Case Studies
Chemical Analysis
Comparative Analysis
Componential Analysis
Content Analysis
Cost Effectiveness
Data Analysis
Hypothesis Testing
Input Output Analysis
Inspection
Interviews
Job Analysis
Life Cycle Costing
Need Analysis (Student Financial Aid)
Phonetic Analysis
Pretesting
Quality Control
Readability Formulas
Site Analysis
Skill Analysis
Structural Analysis (Linguistics)
Structural Analysis (Science)
Surveys
Synthesis
Task Analysis
BT Methods
RT Action Research
Assessment Centers (Personnel)
Audits (Verification)
Critical Incidents Method
Educational Assessment
Error Patterns
Evaluation
Evaluation Criteria
Evaluation Needs
Evaluation Problems
Evaluation Utilization
Informal Assessment
Interrater Reliability
Investigations
Measurement Techniques
Measures (Individuals)
Methods Research
Needs Assessment
Participant Observation
Portfolios (Background Materials)
Precision Teaching
Qualitative Research
Questionnaires
Relevance (Information Retrieval)
Research
Research Methodology
Sample Size
Sampling
Supervisory Methods
Use Studies

EVALUATION NEEDS *Jul. 1966*
CIJE: 431 RIE: 676 GC: 820
SN Questions or problems that require evaluation (note: prior to mar80, the use of this term was not restricted by a scope note)
BT Needs
RT Evaluation
Evaluation Criteria
Evaluation Methods
Evaluation Problems
Evaluation Utilization
Information Needs
Measurement Objectives
Research Needs

EVALUATION PROBLEMS *Jan. 1986*
CIJE: 125 RIE: 102 GC: 820
SN Difficulties associated with the methodology, interpretation, or use of appraisals of persons, organizations, or things (note: do not confuse with "testing problems" and "research problems")
BT Problems
RT Evaluation
Evaluation Criteria
Evaluation Methods
Evaluation Needs
Evaluation Utilization
Research Problems
Testing Problems

Evaluation Procedures
USE EVALUATION METHODS

Evaluation Specialists
USE EVALUATORS

Evaluation Techniques (1966 1974)
USE EVALUATION METHODS

EVALUATION UTILIZATION *Mar. 1983*
CIJE: 131 RIE: 192 GC: 820
SN The use of evaluative information in communication, learning, motivation, accountability, program improvement, decision making, or other processes
BT Information Utilization
RT Accountability
Adoption (Ideas)
Decision Making
Evaluation
Evaluation Methods
Evaluation Needs
Evaluation Problems
Formative Evaluation
Research Utilization
Summative Evaluation
Test Use

EVALUATIVE THINKING *Nov. 1968*
CIJE: 424 RIE: 234 GC: 110
SN Process of determining or judging the appropriateness, efficacy, or value of something with respect to specified objectives or standards
UF Judgmental Processes
NT Value Judgment
BT Critical Thinking
RT Data Interpretation
Decision Making
Evaluation
Judgment Analysis Technique
Problem Solving
Productive Thinking

EVALUATORS *Sep. 1977*
CIJE: 260 RIE: 312 GC: 360
SN Individuals who collect information according to a design and use such information as a basis for judging either the absolute or relative value of programs, products, or personnel
UF Evaluation Specialists
BT Personnel
RT Educational Researchers
Evaluation
Interrater Reliability
Researchers

Evening Classes (1967 1980)
USE EVENING PROGRAMS

Evening Colleges (1967 1980)
USE EVENING PROGRAMS

Evening Counseling Programs (1966 1980)
USE COUNSELING SERVICES; EVENING PROGRAMS

EVENING PROGRAMS *Jul. 1966*
CIJE: 111 RIE: 261 GC: 350
SN Programs, usually educational, offered by institutions, businesses, or communities during the evening
UF Evening Classes (1967 1980)
Evening Colleges (1967 1980)
Evening Counseling Programs (1966 1980) #
Night Schools (1966 1980)
BT Programs
RT Adult Programs
Continuing Education
Day Programs
Evening Students
Extension Education
High School Equivalency Programs
Part Time Students

EVENING STUDENTS *Jul. 1966*
CIJE: 30 RIE: 125 GC: 360
BT Students
RT Adult Students
Day Students
Evening Programs
Extension Education
External Degree Programs
Part Time Students

EVOLUTION *Sep. 1968*
CIJE: 574 RIE: 141 GC: 490
NT Heredity
BT Development
RT Anatomy
Astronomy
Biological Influences
Biology
Botany
Creationism
Cytology
Ecology
Embryology
Ethology
Genetics
Paleontology
Physiology
Sociobiology
Zoology

EWE *Jul. 1966*
CIJE: 1 RIE: 6 GC: 440
BT African Languages

Examinations
USE TESTS

Examiner Characteristics
USE EXAMINERS; EXPERIMENTER CHARACTERISTICS

EXAMINERS *Jan. 1970*
CIJE: 121 RIE: 79 GC: 640
SN Individuals who administer tests
UF Examiner Characteristics #
Test Administrators
BT Clerical Workers
RT Experimenter Characteristics
Interrater Reliability
Psychometrics
Testing
Tests

Exceptional (Atypical) (1966 1978)
USE EXCEPTIONAL PERSONS

EXCEPTIONAL CHILD EDUCATION (1968 1980) *Mar. 1980*
CIJE: 2714 RIE: 3122 GC: 220
SN Invalid descriptor -- used inconsistently in indexing -- see "special education"

EXCEPTIONAL CHILD RESEARCH *Jul. 1966*
CIJE: 5603 RIE: 2482 GC: 810
BT Research
RT Behavioral Science Research
Disabilities
Educational Research
Gifted

= Two or more Descriptors are used to represent this term.
The term's main entry shows the appropriate coordination.

Medical Research
Personality Studies
Psychological Studies

EXCEPTIONAL CHILD SERVICES (1968 1980) *Mar. 1980*
CIJE: 703 RIE: 745 GC: 220
SN Invalid descriptor -- used inconsistently in indexing -- coordinate more specific descriptors

Exceptional Children (1966 1978)
USE EXCEPTIONAL PERSONS

EXCEPTIONAL PERSONS *Jan. 1978*
CIJE: 380 RIE: 421 GC: 120
SN Persons atypical due to disabilities and/ or giftedness (note: this term refers to both disabilities and giftedness -- use a more precise term for documents dealing with either of the two conditions)
UF Exceptional (Atypical) (1966 1978)
Exceptional Children (1966 1978)
Exceptional Students (1966 1978)
NT Gifted
BT Groups
RT Adventitious Impairments
Attention Deficit Disorders
Communication Disorders
Congenital Impairments
Developmental Disabilities
Disabilities
Diseases
Emotional Disturbances
Hearing Impairments
Individualized Education Programs
Injuries
Language Handicaps
Learning Disabilities
Mental Disorders
Mental Retardation
Mild Disabilities
Multiple Disabilities
Neurological Impairments
Perceptual Handicaps
Physical Disabilities
Severe Disabilities
Special Education
Special Education Teachers
Special Health Problems
Speech Handicaps
Visual Impairments

Exceptional Students (1966 1978)
USE EXCEPTIONAL PERSONS

EXCHANGE PROGRAMS *Jul. 1966*
CIJE: 172 RIE: 173 GC: 330
NT Student Exchange Programs
Teacher Exchange Programs
BT Programs
RT Cross Cultural Training
Cultural Exchange
Enrichment Activities
Institutional Cooperation
Intercultural Programs
International Cooperation
International Educational Exchange

Excursions (Instruction)
USE FIELD TRIPS

Executive Development
USE MANAGEMENT DEVELOPMENT

Executive Secretaries
USE SECRETARIES

Exemplary Programs
USE DEMONSTRATION PROGRAMS

EXERCISE *Mar. 1980*
CIJE: 143 RIE: 114 GC: 470
SN Bodily exertion to develop and maintain physical strength, skills, or fitness
UF Muscular Exercise
Physical Exercise
NT Aerobics
Calisthenics
BT Physical Activities
RT Athletics
Exercise Physiology
Human Body
Lifetime Sports
Muscular Strength
Physical Fitness
Psychomotor Skills

EXERCISE (PHYSIOLOGY) (1969 1980) *Mar. 1980*
CIJE: 289 RIE: 232 GC: 470
SN Invalid descriptor -- see the more precise terms "exercise" and "exercise physiology"

EXERCISE PHYSIOLOGY *Mar. 1980*
CIJE: 91 RIE: 76 GC: 210
SN Study of the physiological effects of bodily exertion
BT Physiology
RT Biomechanics
Cardiovascular System
Exercise
Fatigue (Biology)
Medical Research
Metabolism
Motor Reactions
Physical Activity Level
Physical Education
Physical Health
Stress Variables

Exhaust Stacks
USE CHIMNEYS

Exhausting (1969 1980)
USE VENTILATION

Exhaustion
USE FATIGUE (BIOLOGY)

EXHIBITS *Jul. 1966*
CIJE: 307 RIE: 152 GC: 720
SN Thematic displays or shows for the public, as well as the collection of objects that is presented
UF Expositions (1971 1980)
Fairs
NT Science Fairs
BT Nonprint Media
RT Display Aids
Instructional Materials
Museums
Realia
Screens (Displays)
Three Dimensional Aids

Exiles
USE REFUGEES

EXISTENTIALISM *May. 1969*
CIJE: 164 RIE: 75 GC: 430
BT Philosophy
RT Individualism
Phenomenology
Twentieth Century Literature

Exogamous Marriage
USE INTERMARRIAGE

Expectancy
USE EXPECTATION

EXPECTANCY TABLES *Jul. 1966*
CIJE: 49 RIE: 40 GC: 480
BT Tables (Data)
RT Bayesian Statistics
Expectation
Predictive Measurement
Predictive Validity
Predictor Variables
Probability
Statistical Analysis
Statistical Distributions
Statistical Inference
Statistics

EXPECTATION *Dec. 1969*
CIJE: 1262 RIE: 957 GC: 120
SN Anticipation of future events, conditions, or trends, and the effects of that anticipation
UF Expectancy
NT Work Life Expectancy
RT Achievement
Aptitude
Attitudes
Cognitive Mapping
Cognitive Structures
Evaluation
Expectancy Tables
Failure
Intuition
Opinions
Performance
Prediction
Predictive Validity
Probability
Reliability
Stereotypes
Success

EXPENDITURE PER STUDENT *Sep. 1968*
CIJE: 335 RIE: 768 GC: 620
SN Average amount of expenses incurred per student by an institution for a designated service for a given period of time (note: do not confuse with "student costs" -- prior to mar80, this term was not restricted by a scope note)
BT Expenditures
RT Costs
Educational Equity (Finance)
Educational Finance
Equalization Aid
Full State Funding
Program Costs
School District Spending
School Statistics
Student Costs

EXPENDITURES *Jul. 1966*
CIJE: 341 RIE: 1274 GC: 620
SN Actual payments, or commitments to make future payments, for something received (note: do not confuse with "costs" -- prior to mar80, the use of this term was not restricted by a scope note)
UF Disbursements (Money)
Expenses
Initial Expenses (1966 1980)
Minimum Initial Expenses
NT Capital Outlay (For Fixed Assets)
Compensation (Remuneration)
Expenditure Per Student
Library Expenditures
Merit Pay
Operating Expenses
Premium Pay
Salaries
School District Spending
Wages
RT Bids
Budgeting
Budgets
Cost Effectiveness
Cost Indexes
Costs
Educational Finance
Financial Audits
Resource Allocation
Retrenchment
Tax Rates

Expenses
USE EXPENDITURES

EXPERIENCE *Jul. 1966*
CIJE: 246 RIE: 171 GC: 120
SN The process of observing, encountering, or undergoing a set of circumstances or events from which knowledge, understanding, skills, or attitudes are derived -- also, the cumulative result of this process (note: use a more specific term if possible)
NT Early Experience
Educational Experience
Emotional Experience
Group Experience
Intellectual Experience
Learning Experience
Prereading Experience
Sensory Experience
Social Experience
Student Experience
Teaching Experience
Work Experience
BT Background
RT Activities
Credentials
Developmental Continuity
Discovery Processes
Experiential Learning
Lifelong Learning
Participation
Prior Learning
Transfer Programs

Experience Based Education
USE EXPERIENTIAL LEARNING

EXPERIENCE CHARTS *Jul. 1966*
CIJE: 8 RIE: 14 GC: 310
SN Charts prepared by the teacher and based upon some experience in which the students participate -- often used in reading instruction and instruction of the disabled
BT Charts
Instructional Materials
RT Experiential Learning
Precision Teaching
Reading Instruction
Student Developed Materials
Student Experience
Student Participation
Teacher Developed Materials

Experience Units
USE ACTIVITY UNITS

Experienced Laborers (1966 1980)
USE LABORERS

EXPERIENTIAL LEARNING *Jun. 1978*
CIJE: 1825 RIE: 1795 GC: 310
SN Learning by doing -- includes knowledge and skills acquired outside of book/lecture learning situations through work, play, and other life experiences (note: do not confuse with "learning experience")
UF Action Learning
Activity Learning (1968 1978)
Community Experience
Experience Based Education
Home Experience
Prior Experiential Learning #
NT Field Experience Programs
Internship Programs
BT Learning
RT Activity Units
Adventure Education
Apprenticeships
Certification
Clinical Experience
College Credits
Cooperative Education
Cooperative Programs
Credits
Discovery Learning
Employment Experience
Equivalency Tests
Experience
Experience Charts
Farm Visits
Field Instruction
Field Trips
High School Equivalency Programs
Informal Assessment
Laboratory Procedures
Laboratory Schools
Learning Activities
Learning Centers (Classroom)
Learning Experience
Learning Strategies
Lifelong Learning
Living Learning Centers
Manipulative Materials
On The Job Training
Outdoor Education
Physical Education
Portfolios (Background Materials)
Practical Arts
Practicums
Prior Learning
Professional Education
Sensory Experience
Simulation
Social Experience
Special Degree Programs
Student Experience
Student Projects
Teaching Experience
Vocational Education
Volunteer Training
Work Experience
Work Experience Programs

EXPERIMENT STATIONS *Sep. 1968*
CIJE: 4 RIE: 9 GC: 410
SN Field stations at which experiments are conducted -- usually maintained by a university and concerned with experiments in agriculture or other applied sciences
UF Field Experiment Stations
BT Facilities

= Two or more Descriptors are used to represent this term.
The term's main entry shows the appropriate coordination.

RT Agricultural Colleges
Agriculture
Experiments
Extension Agents
Research And Development Centers
Research Projects
Scientific Research

EXPERIMENTAL COLLEGES *Nov. 1969*
CIJE: 135 RIE: 101 GC: 340
SN Higher education institutions characterized by innovative curricula, learning experiences, teaching methods, etc. -- also refers to institutions or programs set up by dissident students and faculty, especially in the u.s. during the 1960's
UF Free Universities
BT Colleges
Experimental Schools
RT Cluster Colleges
Educational Innovation
Experimental Curriculum
Experimental Programs
Experimental Teaching
Instructional Innovation
Nontraditional Education
Open Universities
Relevance (Education)
Student College Relationship
Student Interests
Student Participation

EXPERIMENTAL CURRICULUM *Jul. 1966*
CIJE: 193 RIE: 436 GC: 350
SN Curriculum marked by new or innovative ideas, methods, or organization of subject matter -- often used in comparison with a standard curriculum to assess the relative effectiveness of each
BT Curriculum
RT Educational Innovation
Educational Research
Experimental Colleges
Experimental Programs
Experimental Schools
Experimental Teaching
Fused Curriculum
Instructional Innovation
Nontraditional Education
Spiral Curriculum

Experimental Design
USE RESEARCH DESIGN

Experimental Extinction
USE EXTINCTION (PSYCHOLOGY)

EXPERIMENTAL GROUPS *Jul. 1966*
CIJE: 149 RIE: 393 GC: 820
SN Subjects who are exposed to an experimental treatment or condition, and whose subsequent performance may be attributed to that treatment or condition (note: use only for discussions of the identification, selection, or treatment of experimental groups)
BT Groups
RT Attrition (Research Studies)
Control Groups
Effect Size
Matched Groups
Participant Characteristics
Quasiexperimental Design
Research Design
Research Methodology
Sample Size
Sampling

Experimental Procedures
USE RESEARCH METHODOLOGY

EXPERIMENTAL PROGRAMS *Jul. 1966*
CIJE: 684 RIE: 1383 GC: 320
BT Programs
RT Demonstration Programs
Experimental Colleges
Experimental Curriculum
Experimental Schools
Experimental Teaching
Experiments
Feasibility Studies
Institutional Research
Pilot Projects
Research Projects

EXPERIMENTAL PSYCHOLOGY *Jul. 1966*
CIJE: 901 RIE: 113 GC: 230
BT Psychology
RT Behaviorism
Clinical Psychology
Cognitive Psychology
Experiments
Laboratory Experiments
Psychological Studies
Research

EXPERIMENTAL SCHOOLS *Jul. 1966*
CIJE: 188 RIE: 264 GC: 340
SN Schools in which new teaching methods, new organizations of subject matter, personnel practices, and advanced educational theories and hypotheses are tested
UF Project Schools
NT Experimental Colleges
BT Schools
RT Educational Innovation
Experimental Curriculum
Experimental Programs
Experimental Teaching
Free Schools
Instructional Innovation
Laboratory Schools
Nontraditional Education
Open Education
Relevance (Education)
Student Interests
Student Participation
Teaching Experience
Transitional Schools

EXPERIMENTAL TEACHING *Jul. 1966*
CIJE: 208 RIE: 223 GC: 310
SN Teaching that uses new or innovative ideas, methods, or devices (note: prior to mar80, this term was a narrower term of "educational research")
BT Teaching Methods
RT Conventional Instruction
Educational Innovation
Educational Research
Experimental Colleges
Experimental Curriculum
Experimental Programs
Experimental Schools
Instructional Innovation

Experimentation
USE EXPERIMENTS

Experimenter Bias
USE EXPERIMENTER CHARACTERISTICS

EXPERIMENTER CHARACTERISTICS *May. 1976*
CIJE: 117 RIE: 66 GC: 810
SN Distinguishing traits or qualities of an experimenter which may influence experimental results
UF Examiner Characteristics #
Experimenter Bias
Researcher Characteristics #
RT Examiners
Experiments
Individual Characteristics
Interrater Reliability
Researchers
Research Methodology
Research Problems
Scientists
Social Scientists
Testing Problems

EXPERIMENTS *Jul. 1966*
CIJE: 969 RIE: 312 GC: 810
UF Experimentation
NT Educational Experiments
Laboratory Experiments
Science Experiments
RT Data Interpretation
Deduction
Discovery Processes
Effect Size
Experimental Programs
Experimental Psychology
Experimenter Characteristics
Experiment Stations
Generalization
Induction
Innovation
Inventions
Investigations
Observation
Research
Research Needs

EXPERT SYSTEMS *Aug. 1986*
CIJE: 35 RIE: 13 GC: 710
SN Computer systems capable of matching a database of factual information with a knowledge base of judgmental rules to answer questions, make decisions, or teach a skill
UF Knowledge Based Systems
BT Artificial Intelligence
RT Computers
Data Processing
Decision Making
Information Systems
Man Machine Systems
Problem Solving

EXPLORATORY BEHAVIOR *Mar. 1983*
CIJE: 42 RIE: 15 GC: 120
SN Movements made by organisms to acquaint themselves with their surroundings -- commonly refers to infant/child behavior (note: do not confuse with "discovery processes")
BT Behavior
RT Attachment Behavior
Behavior Development
Curiosity
Novelty (Stimulus Dimension)
Perceptual Motor Coordination
Spontaneous Behavior

Exploratory Learning
USE DISCOVERY LEARNING

Export Trade
USE EXPORTS

EXPORTS *Jul. 1966*
CIJE: 62 RIE: 52 GC: 650
UF Export Trade
RT Business
Economics
International Relations
International Trade
International Trade Vocabulary

Exposition (Literary)
USE EXPOSITORY WRITING

Expositions (1971 1980)
USE EXHIBITS

EXPOSITORY WRITING *Nov. 1968*
CIJE: 287 RIE: 429 GC: 400
SN Form of written prose that deals with definitions, processes, generalizations, and the clarification of ideas and principles, with the intent of presenting meanings in readily communicable and unemotive language
UF Exposition (Literary)
BT Writing (Composition)
RT Creative Writing
Descriptive Writing
Essays
Journalism
Journalism Education
News Reporting
News Writing
Prose
Research Papers (Students)
Rhetoric
Student Writing Models
Technical Writing
Theses

EXPRESSIONISM *Jun. 1969*
CIJE: 39 RIE: 6 GC: 430
SN Early 20th century movement in the creative arts that depicts the subjective emotions and responses of the artist/author to objects or events, often using distortion, exaggeration, or symbolism
RT Art Expression
Intellectual History
Literary Styles
Music
Twentieth Century Literature

EXPRESSIVE LANGUAGE *Jul. 1966*
CIJE: 347 RIE: 240 GC: 450
SN The cognitive processing involved in the transmission of oral, symbolic, or written language (note: prior to mar80, the use of this term was not restricted by a scope note)
BT Language Processing
RT Aphasia
Communication (Thought Transfer)
Communication Skills
Language Acquisition
Language Fluency
Language Handicaps
Language Skills
Language Styles
Oral Language
Psycholinguistics
Receptive Language

EXPULSION *Jul. 1966*
CIJE: 91 RIE: 120 GC: 330
SN Forced withdrawal from school
BT Discipline
RT Academic Failure
Academic Probation
Attendance
College Attendance
Disqualification
Dropouts
Out Of School Youth
School Attendance Legislation
Student Attrition
Suspension
Withdrawal (Education)

EXTENDED FAMILY *Jun. 1977*
CIJE: 108 RIE: 81 GC: 520
SN A form of family organization consisting of blood relatives and their several nuclear family units
BT Family (Sociological Unit)
RT Black Family
Family Life
Family Relationship
Family Size
Family Structure
Genealogy
Kinship
Nuclear Family
One Parent Family
Stepfamily

EXTENDED SCHOOL DAY *Jul. 1966*
CIJE: 28 RIE: 75 GC: 350
SN Plan that extends the time a school is open during the day, either before or after normal school hours -- may be for academic, recreational, day care, or other purposes
UF Staggered Sessions
BT School Schedules
RT After School Education
After School Programs
Compensatory Education
Extracurricular Activities
Flexible Scheduling
School Age Day Care
School Recreational Programs
Time Factors (Learning)

EXTENDED SCHOOL YEAR *Oct. 1968*
CIJE: 93 RIE: 182 GC: 350
SN Plan that mandates an increase in the number of days students must attend school (note: prior to mar80, this term was not scoped and was often confused with "year round schools")
BT School Schedules
RT Flexible Scheduling
Quarter System
Summer Schools
Time Factors (Learning)
Trimester System
Year Round Schools

Extended Universities
USE OPEN UNIVERSITIES

EXTENSION AGENTS *Jul. 1966*
CIJE: 148 RIE: 393 GC: 410
UF Agricultural Agents
County Extension Agents
Farm Agents
Four H Club Agents
Home Demonstration Agents
Village Extension Agents

= Two or more Descriptors are used to represent this term.
The term's main entry shows the appropriate coordination.

BT Change Agents
Government Employees
RT Adult Educators
Agricultural Education
Agricultural Personnel
County Officials
Experiment Stations
Home Economics Education
Home Economics Teachers
State Officials

EXTENSION EDUCATION *Jul. 1966*
CIJE: 863 RIE: 1349 GC: 350
SN Instructional activities offered beyond the confines of regular classes in school or on campus in order to serve a wider clientele -- may include evening classes, short courses, exhibits, telecourses, correspondence courses, seminars, and institutes
UF Cooperative Extension
Extension Services
Extramural Departments
Off Campus Education
University Extension (1967 1980)
NT External Degree Programs
Library Extension
Rural Extension
Urban Extension
BT Education
RT Access To Education
Adult Education
Colleges
Community Education
Continuing Education
Continuing Education Centers
Correspondence Schools
Distance Education
Evening Programs
Evening Students
Higher Education
Home Study
Industrial Training
Mobile Educational Services
Noncampus Colleges
Nontraditional Education
Off Campus Facilities
Open Universities
Outreach Programs
Part Time Students
Professional Continuing Education
Satellite Facilities
Universities

Extension Services
USE EXTENSION EDUCATION

EXTERNAL DEGREE PROGRAMS *Aug. 1972*
CIJE: 401 RIE: 448 GC: 350
SN Higher education programs offering validated degrees to students who have studied outside the institution -- e.g., programs offered by nova university or university without walls
BT College Programs
Extension Education
RT Access To Education
Bachelors Degrees
Degree Requirements
Degrees (Academic)
Distance Education
Educational Attainment
Evening Students
High School Equivalency Programs
Independent Study
Noncampus Colleges
Nontraditional Education
Open Universities
Part Time Students
Special Degree Programs

Externships (Medicine)
USE CLINICAL EXPERIENCE

EXTINCTION (PSYCHOLOGY) *Jul. 1969*
CIJE: 105 RIE: 30 GC: 110
SN Progressive reduction in conditioned response after prolonged repetition of the eliciting stimulus without reinforcement
UF Experimental Extinction
BT Learning Processes
RT Conditioning
Contingency Management
Negative Reinforcement
Retention (Psychology)
Timeout

EXTRACURRICULAR ACTIVITIES *Mar. 1980*
CIJE: 547 RIE: 690 GC: 470
SN Activities, under the sponsorship or direction of a school, of the type for which participation generally is not required and credit generally is not awarded
UF Cocurricular Activities (1966 1980)
School Related Activities
Student Activities (Extraclass)
BT School Activities
RT After School Programs
Art Activities
Athletics
Clubs
Curriculum
Enrichment Activities
Extended School Day
Music Activities
Recreational Activities
School Newspapers
School Recreational Programs
Science Fairs
Student Interests
Student Organizations
Student Projects
Students
Student Unions
Student Volunteers
Supplementary Education

Extradimensional Shift
USE SHIFT STUDIES

Extrainstructional Duties
USE NONINSTRUCTIONAL RESPONSIBILITY

Extramural Athletic Programs (1966 1980)
USE EXTRAMURAL ATHLETICS

EXTRAMURAL ATHLETICS *Mar. 1980*
CIJE: 45 RIE: 31 GC: 470
UF Extramural Athletic Programs (1966 1980)
Extramural Sports
Interscholastic Athletics
BT Athletics
RT College Athletics
Intramural Athletics
School Recreational Programs

Extramural Departments
USE EXTENSION EDUCATION

Extramural Sports
USE EXTRAMURAL ATHLETICS

Extrateaching Duties
USE NONINSTRUCTIONAL RESPONSIBILITY

Extraterrestrial Exploration
USE SPACE EXPLORATION

EYE CONTACT *Apr. 1985*
CIJE: 30 RIE: 9 GC: 120
SN Direct eye-to-eye contact between individuals
BT Nonverbal Communication
RT Body Language
Eye Fixations
Eyes
Facial Expressions
Interaction Process Analysis
Interpersonal Communication

EYE FIXATIONS *Jul. 1966*
CIJE: 158 RIE: 79 GC: 110
SN Directing and focusing of the eye(s) toward an object or point so that the image falls on the retina(s)
BT Eye Movements
RT Eye Contact
Reading Processes
Strabismus
Visual Perception

EYE HAND COORDINATION *Jul. 1966*
CIJE: 74 RIE: 87 GC: 120
BT Perceptual Motor Coordination
RT Eye Movements
Lateral Dominance
Motor Development
Object Manipulation
Tactual Visual Tests

EYE MOVEMENTS *Jul. 1966*
CIJE: 213 RIE: 163 GC: 110
UF Eye Regressions (1966 1980)
NT Eye Fixations
BT Motor Reactions
RT Body Language
Eye Hand Coordination
Eyes
Eye Voice Span
Facial Expressions
Pupillary Dilation
Visual Impairments

Eye Regressions (1966 1980)
USE EYE MOVEMENTS

EYE VOICE SPAN *Jul. 1966*
CIJE: 5 RIE: 17 GC: 460
SN During oral reading, the distance (measured in letters) between the word being spoken and the word on which the eyes are focused
BT Perceptual Motor Coordination
RT Eye Movements
Oral Reading
Reading Skills
Speech Skills
Visual Perception

EYES *Aug. 1968*
CIJE: 89 RIE: 48 GC: 210
RT Anatomy
Eye Contact
Eye Movements
Human Body
Ophthalmology
Optometrists
Optometry
Pupillary Dilation
Vision
Vision Tests
Visual Impairments

FABLES *Jul. 1966*
CIJE: 63 RIE: 73 GC: 430
SN Short fictional tales about supernatural or unusual incidents, usually told to teach a moral and frequently having animals or inanimate objects as characters
BT Tales
RT Allegory
Didacticism
Fantasy
Fiction
Mythology

Fabrication
USE MANUFACTURING

FACIAL EXPRESSIONS *Apr. 1986*
CIJE: 41 RIE: 25 GC: 120
BT Nonverbal Communication
RT Body Language
Eye Contact
Eye Movements

FACILITIES *Jul. 1966*
CIJE: 378 RIE: 918 GC: 920
SN Any physical structures or spaces constructed, installed, or established to perform particular functions or to serve particular ends (note: use a more specific term if possible)
UF Institutional Facilities (1967 1980)
Physical Facilities (1966 1980)
NT Airports
Air Structures
Animal Facilities
Assessment Centers (Personnel)
Athletic Fields
Auditoriums
Buildings
College Stores
Community Centers
Corridors
Day Care Centers
Dining Facilities
Driveways
Educational Facilities
Encapsulated Facilities
Equal Facilities
Experiment Stations
Fallout Shelters
Feed Stores
Field Houses
Fisheries
Flexible Facilities
Food Handling Facilities
Food Stores
Foundries
Greenhouses
Gymnasiums
Health Facilities
Housing
Interior Space
Laboratories
Library Facilities
Locker Rooms
Military Air Facilities
Museums
Music Facilities
Nuclear Power Plants
Nurseries (Horticulture)
Offices (Facilities)
Parking Facilities
Parks
Planetariums
Public Facilities
Recreational Facilities
Rehabilitation Centers
Relocatable Facilities
Research And Development Centers
Resource Centers
Sanitary Facilities
Satellite Facilities
Science Facilities
Settlement Houses
Shared Facilities
Swimming Pools
Television Studios
Theaters
Trails
Underground Facilities
Warehouses
Windowless Rooms
RT Building Design
Clinics
Construction Materials
Equipment
Facility Expansion
Facility Guidelines
Facility Improvement
Facility Inventory
Facility Planning
Facility Requirements
Facility Utilization Research
Maintenance
Resources
Space Utilization
Structural Elements (Construction)

FACILITY CASE STUDIES *Jul. 1966*
CIJE: 25 RIE: 195 GC: 810
SN Gathering and organizing of all relevant material to enable analysis and explication of facilities (note: as of oct81, use as a minor descriptor for examples of this kind of research -- use as a major descriptor only as the subject of a document)
BT Case Studies
RT Building Design
Building Plans
Facility Guidelines
Facility Inventory
Facility Planning
Facility Requirements
Facility Utilization Research
Site Analysis
Space Utilization

Facility Design
USE FACILITY GUIDELINES

FACILITY EXPANSION *Jul. 1966*
CIJE: 104 RIE: 188 GC: 920
SN Adding to a facility or altering it to accommodate additional people, equipment, etc.
NT School Expansion
BT Development
RT Building Conversion
Construction (Process)
Construction Programs
Facilities
Facility Guidelines
Facility Improvement
Facility Planning
Facility Requirements
Facility Utilization Research
Found Spaces
Relocatable Facilities
Site Analysis
Site Development
Space Utilization

FACILITY GUIDELINES *Jul. 1966*
CIJE: 229 RIE: 747 GC: 920
SN Written guidelines, specifications, standards, or criteria used in assessing physical facility requirements
UF Facility Design
Facility Specifications
Facility Standards
BT Guidelines
RT Building Conversion
Building Design
Building Innovation
Construction Needs
Educational Facilities
Educational Facilities Planning
Facilities
Facility Case Studies
Facility Expansion
Facility Improvement
Facility Inventory
Facility Planning
Facility Requirements
Facility Utilization Research
Life Cycle Costing
Master Plans
Site Analysis
Space Utilization

FACILITY IMPROVEMENT *Jul. 1966*
CIJE: 313 RIE: 263 GC: 920
SN Remedying deficiencies in existing facilities or bringing facilities up to higher standards
UF Building Improvement (1966 1980)
Building Renovation
NT Educational Facilities Improvement
BT Improvement
RT Building Conversion
Building Obsolescence
Buildings
Capital Outlay (For Fixed Assets)
Facilities
Facility Expansion
Facility Guidelines
Facility Requirements

FACILITY INVENTORY *Jul. 1966*
CIJE: 113 RIE: 239 GC: 920
UF Equipment Inventory
Materials Inventory
Property Inventory
RT Construction Programs
Educational Facilities
Equipment
Equipment Utilization
Facilities
Facility Case Studies
Facility Guidelines
Facility Requirements
Facility Utilization Research
Property Accounting
Resources
Space Classification
Supplies

Facility Needs
USE FACILITY REQUIREMENTS

FACILITY PLANNING *May. 1974*
CIJE: 481 RIE: 532 GC: 920
SN Process of determining the purposes of facilities and the means (activities, procedures, resources, etc.) for attaining them
NT Educational Facilities Planning
BT Planning
RT Architectural Programing
Building Plans
Capital Outlay (For Fixed Assets)
Community Planning
Construction Costs
Construction Management
Construction Needs
Construction Programs
Design Build Approach
Design Requirements
Facilities
Facility Case Studies
Facility Expansion
Facility Guidelines
Facility Requirements
Facility Utilization Research
Fast Track Scheduling
Found Spaces
Land Use
Life Cycle Costing
Master Plans
Relocatable Facilities
Shared Facilities
Site Analysis
Site Development
Site Selection
Space Utilization
Spatial Relationship (Facilities)
Systems Building
Underground Facilities
Urban Planning

FACILITY REQUIREMENTS *Aug. 1968*
CIJE: 291 RIE: 732 GC: 920
SN Any aspect of the physical plant determined necessary to accommodate various functions
UF Facility Needs
BT Specifications
RT Building Conversion
Building Design
Building Innovation
Building Plans
Construction Needs
Design Requirements
Educational Facilities
Educational Facilities Planning
Facilities
Facility Case Studies
Facility Expansion
Facility Guidelines
Facility Improvement
Facility Inventory
Facility Planning
Facility Utilization Research
Master Plans
Space Utilization
Storage

Facility Specifications
USE FACILITY GUIDELINES

Facility Standards
USE FACILITY GUIDELINES

FACILITY UTILIZATION RESEARCH *Jul. 1966*
CIJE: 156 RIE: 374 GC: 810
BT Use Studies
RT Building Conversion
Building Design
Building Obsolescence
Building Plans
Buildings
College Buildings
Construction Programs
Design Requirements
Educational Complexes
Educational Facilities
Educational Facilities Planning
Equipment Storage
Facilities
Facility Case Studies
Facility Expansion
Facility Guidelines
Facility Inventory
Facility Planning
Facility Requirements
School Buildings
School Expansion
School Space
Space Classification
Space Utilization
Spatial Relationship (Facilities)
Storage

Facsimile Communication Systems (1968 1980)
USE FACSIMILE TRANSMISSION

FACSIMILE TRANSMISSION *Jul. 1966*
CIJE: 31 RIE: 60 GC: 710
UF Facsimile Communication Systems (1968 1980)
Fax
Telefacsimile
Telefax
BT Telecommunications
RT Electronic Equipment
Electronic Mail
Information Networks
Information Transfer
Input Output Devices
Reprography
Telephone Communications Systems

FACTOR ANALYSIS *Jul. 1966*
CIJE: 1772 RIE: 1319 GC: 820
SN Mathematical methods used to explain the relationships observed among a large number of descriptive variables in terms of a smaller number of underlying or inferred factors
UF Centroid Method Of Factor Analysis
Maximum Likelihood Factor Analysis #
Principal Components Analysis
NT Oblique Rotation
Orthogonal Rotation
BT Multivariate Analysis
RT Ability Identification
Cluster Analysis
Correlation
Discriminant Analysis
Factor Structure
Goodness Of Fit
Item Analysis
Least Squares Statistics
Maximum Likelihood Statistics
Multidimensional Scaling
Multitrait Multimethod Techniques
Path Analysis
Personality Assessment
Q Methodology
Research Methodology
Test Construction
Testing
Test Validity
Transformations (Mathematics)
Trend Analysis

FACTOR STRUCTURE *Jul. 1966*
CIJE: 567 RIE: 369 GC: 820
SN The end product of factor analysis when the interrelationships and relative positions of the underlying factors used in the analysis have been established
RT Construct Validity
Factor Analysis
Item Analysis
Oblique Rotation
Orthogonal Rotation
Test Interpretation
Test Validity

FACTUAL READING (1966 1980) *Mar. 1980*
CIJE: 19 RIE: 36 GC: 460
SN Invalid descriptor -- used inconsistently in indexing -- see "functional reading" and "reading comprehension"

FACULTY *Jul. 1966*
CIJE: 709 RIE: 652 GC: 360
SN Academic staff members engaged in instruction, research, administration, or related educational activities in a school, college, or university (note: use a more specific term if possible)
NT Adjunct Faculty
College Faculty
Deans
Department Heads
Faculty Advisers
Full Time Faculty
Nontenured Faculty
Part Time Faculty
Tenured Faculty
Women Faculty
BT Professional Personnel
School Personnel
RT Academic Rank (Professional)
Administrators
Aging In Academia
Consultants
Educational Resources
Faculty Development
Faculty Evaluation
Faculty Fellowships
Faculty Handbooks
Faculty Integration
Faculty Mobility
Faculty Organizations
Faculty Promotion
Faculty Publishing
Faculty Recruitment
Faculty Workload
Ombudsmen
Teachers

Faculty Advancement
USE FACULTY PROMOTION

FACULTY ADVISERS *Mar. 1980*
CIJE: 385 RIE: 242 GC: 240
SN Academic staff members assigned to counsel students in academic and sometimes nonacademic matters
UF Faculty Advisors (1967 1980)
Faculty Counselors
BT Faculty
RT Academic Advising
Educational Counseling
Faculty Workload
Foreign Student Advisers
Pupil Personnel Workers
School Counseling
School Counselors
Student Adjustment
Student College Relationship
Student Personnel Workers
Student School Relationship

Faculty Advisors (1967 1980)
USE FACULTY ADVISERS

FACULTY COLLEGE RELATIONSHIP *Oct. 1979*
CIJE: 299 RIE: 322 GC: 320
SN The relationship between a college or university and its faculty
UF Teacher College Relationship
BT Relationship
RT Academic Freedom
Arbitration
Codes Of Ethics
Collective Bargaining
College Environment
College Faculty
College Governing Councils
Colleges
Employer Employee Relationship
Faculty Handbooks
Faculty Workload
Negotiation Agreements
Participative Decision Making
Student College Relationship
Teacher Administrator Relationship
Teacher Discipline
Teacher Rights
Teacher Welfare
Unions

Faculty Counselors
USE FACULTY ADVISERS

Faculty Desegregation
USE FACULTY INTEGRATION

FACULTY DEVELOPMENT *Oct. 1977*
CIJE: 773 RIE: 1092 GC: 320
SN Activities to encourage and enhance faculty professional growth
UF Faculty Growth
Faculty Improvement
BT Professional Development
Staff Development
RT College Faculty
Faculty
Faculty Evaluation
Faculty Fellowships
Faculty Handbooks
Faculty Promotion
Faculty Publishing
Individual Development
Inservice Education
Inservice Teacher Education
Organizational Development
Professional Continuing Education
Professional Training
Sabbatical Leaves
Teacher Evaluation
Teacher Exchange Programs
Teacher Improvement
Teacher Promotion

FACULTY EVALUATION *Jul. 1966*
CIJE: 447 RIE: 599 GC: 320
SN Judging the value or competence of administrative, instructional, or other academic staff in schools, colleges, or universities based on established criteria (note: for documents/articles only involving instructional staff or administrators, use "teacher evaluation" or "administrator evaluation" -- before mar80, this term did not carry a scope note)
BT Personnel Evaluation

= Two or more Descriptors are used to represent this term.
The term's main entry shows the appropriate coordination.

RT Administrator Evaluation
Faculty
Faculty Development
Faculty Promotion
Faculty Workload
Teacher Evaluation

FACULTY FELLOWSHIPS *Jul. 1966*
CIJE: 16 RIE: 22 GC: 620
BT Fellowships
RT Faculty
Faculty Development
Sabbatical Leaves

Faculty Growth
USE FACULTY DEVELOPMENT

FACULTY HANDBOOKS *Aug. 1978*
CIJE: 9 RIE: 237 GC: 730
SN Guidelines developed and published by a school, college, or university that outline the duties of faculty members, their roles within the institution, procedures, and/or organizational information
BT Guides
School Publications
RT Administrator Guides
Administrator Responsibility
Administrator Role
College Faculty
Colleges
Employer Employee Relationship
Faculty
Faculty College Relationship
Faculty Development
Faculty Workload
Schools
Staff Orientation
Staff Role
Teacher Administrator Relationship
Teacher Orientation
Teacher Responsibility
Teacher Role
Teacher Student Relationship
Teaching Conditions
Universities

Faculty Improvement
USE FACULTY DEVELOPMENT

FACULTY INTEGRATION *Jul. 1966*
CIJE: 75 RIE: 94 GC: 540
SN Process of balancing the racial, ethnic, or sexual composition of the instructional, administrative, or other academic staff of schools, colleges, or universities (note: for documents/articles involving only instructional staff, use "teacher integration" -- prior to mar80, this differentiation was not made)
UF Faculty Desegregation
Integrated Faculty
BT Personnel Integration
RT Affirmative Action
Equal Opportunities (Jobs)
Faculty
Teacher Integration

Faculty Load
USE FACULTY WORKLOAD

FACULTY MOBILITY *Jul. 1966*
CIJE: 150 RIE: 200 GC: 330
SN (Note: if possible, use the more precise term "teacher transfer")
UF Teacher Attrition
Teacher Mobility
Teacher Turnover
BT Occupational Mobility
RT Faculty
Teacher Persistence
Teacher Placement
Teacher Transfer
Teaching (Occupation)

Faculty Offices
USE OFFICES (FACILITIES)

FACULTY ORGANIZATIONS *Jul. 1966*
CIJE: 123 RIE: 188 GC: 320
SN Associations or groups composed of instructional, administrative, and other academic staff, usually at the college or university level (note: see also "teacher associations" -- prior to mar80, this term was not restricted by a scope note)
BT Organizations (Groups)
RT College Faculty
College Governing Councils
Faculty
Faculty Workload
Professional Associations
Teacher Associations
Unions

FACULTY PROMOTION *Jul. 1966*
CIJE: 231 RIE: 335 GC: 320
SN Advancement in position or rank of administrative, instructional, or other academic staff in schools, colleges, or universities (note: for documents/articles relating to the advancement of instructional staff only, use "teacher promotion" -- prior to mar80, this differentiation was not made)
UF Faculty Advancement
BT Promotion (Occupational)
RT Academic Rank (Professional)
Faculty
Faculty Development
Faculty Evaluation
Faculty Publishing
Faculty Workload
Teacher Promotion
Tenure

FACULTY PUBLISHING *Aug. 1986*
CIJE: 48 RIE: 29 GC: 720
SN The production and issuance of scholarly writings by academia
RT Authors
Faculty
Faculty Development
Faculty Promotion
Faculty Workload
Productivity
Publications
Publish Or Perish Issue
Research
Scholarly Journals
Writing For Publication

Faculty Rank
USE ACADEMIC RANK (PROFESSIONAL)

FACULTY RECRUITMENT *Jul. 1966*
CIJE: 154 RIE: 157 GC: 320
SN Process of attracting qualified academic staff members to vacant positions (note: for recuritment of instructional staff only, use "teacher recruitment" -- prior to mar80, this differentiation was not made)
BT Recruitment
RT Administrator Selection
Faculty
Teacher Recruitment

Faculty Senates
USE COLLEGE GOVERNING COUNCILS

FACULTY WORKLOAD *Oct. 1976*
CIJE: 162 RIE: 326 GC: 320
SN The sum of all activities that take the time of the teacher or other faculty member and that are related either directly or indirectly to professional duties, responsibilities, and interests (note: prior to oct76, the instruction "faculty load, use teaching load" was carried in the thesaurus)
UF Faculty Load
NT Teaching Load
RT Administrator Responsibility
Contracts
Educational Counseling
Employer Employee Relationship
Faculty
Faculty Advisers
Faculty College Relationship
Faculty Evaluation
Faculty Handbooks
Faculty Organizations
Faculty Promotion
Faculty Publishing
Full Time Faculty
Noninstructional Responsibility
Parent Teacher Conferences
Part Time Faculty
Sabbatical Leaves
School Counseling
Staff Meetings
Staff Utilization
State Standards
Teacher Administrator Relationship
Teacher Evaluation
Teacher Promotion
Teacher Responsibility
Teaching Conditions
Working Hours

FAILURE *Mar. 1980*
CIJE: 659 RIE: 543 GC: 820
SN Achievements or accomplishments that do not meet stated expectations, requirements, or standards
UF Failure Factors (1966 1980)
NT Academic Failure
BT Performance
RT Achievement
Achievement Need
Evaluation
Expectation
Fear Of Success
Goal Orientation
Helplessness
Low Achievement
Motivation
Objectives
Outcomes Of Education
Standards
Success
Underachievement

Failure Factors (1966 1980)
USE FAILURE

FAILURE TO THRIVE *Apr. 1986*
CIJE: 4 RIE: 1 GC: 120
SN Growth disorder of infants and children associated with nutritional and/or emotional deprivation -- characterized by low weight gain and psychosocial retardation
UF Nonorganic Failure To Thrive
BT Diseases
RT Body Weight
Child Development
Child Neglect
Infant Behavior
Nutrition
Parent Child Relationship
Physical Health
Psychosomatic Disorders

Fairs
USE EXHIBITS

Faith
USE BELIEFS

FALLOUT SHELTERS *Jul. 1966*
CIJE: 2 RIE: 32 GC: 920
UF Air Raid Shelters
Bomb Shelters
BT Facilities
RT Civil Defense
Radiation
Radiation Effects
Safety
Underground Facilities
Windowless Rooms

Fame
USE REPUTATION

FAMILY (SOCIOLOGICAL UNIT) *Jul. 1966*
CIJE: 1044 RIE: 931 GC: 520
SN Group of individuals related by blood, marriage, adoption, or cohabitation (note: use a more specific term if possible)
UF Households
NT Black Family
Dual Career Family
Extended Family
Foster Family
Nuclear Family
One Parent Family
Rural Family
Stepfamily
BT Groups
RT Birth Order
Children
Daughters
Family Attitudes
Family Characteristics
Family Environment
Family Financial Resources
Family Health
Family History
Family Income
Family Influence
Family Involvement
Family Life
Family Mobility
Family Planning
Family Problems
Family Programs
Family Relationship
Family Role
Family School Relationship
Family Size
Family Status
Family Structure
Family Violence
Genealogy
Grandparents
Heads Of Households
Homemakers
Home Management
Kinship
Marriage
Parents
Siblings
Sons
Spouses
Twins

FAMILY ATTITUDES *Jul. 1966*
CIJE: 233 RIE: 226 GC: 510
BT Attitudes
RT Family (Sociological Unit)
Family Counseling
Parent Attitudes

Family Background (1966 1980)
USE FAMILY CHARACTERISTICS

Family Breadwinners
USE HEADS OF HOUSEHOLDS

FAMILY CHARACTERISTICS *Jul. 1966*
CIJE: 749 RIE: 1269 GC: 510
SN Family attributes such as size, structure, socioeconomic status, health, ethnicity, etc.
UF Family Background (1966 1980)
RT Family (Sociological Unit)
Family Financial Resources
Family History
Family Income
Family Relationship
Family Size
Family Status
Family Structure
Parent Background

Family Choice (Education)
USE SCHOOL CHOICE

FAMILY COUNSELING *Jul. 1966*
CIJE: 862 RIE: 314 GC: 240
BT Counseling
RT Family Attitudes
Family Influence
Family Problems
Family Relationship
Group Counseling
Group Dynamics
Group Therapy
Hospices (Terminal Care)
Marriage Counseling
Milieu Therapy
Parent Counseling

Family Culture
USE FAMILY LIFE

FAMILY DAY CARE *Feb. 1975*
CIJE: 58 RIE: 272 GC: 520
SN Care of children, by persons other than their parents or guardians, in private homes
UF Home Day Care
BT Day Care
RT Employer Supported Day Care
Family Environment
School Age Day Care

Family Economics
USE CONSUMER ECONOMICS

FAMILY ENVIRONMENT *Jul. 1966*
CIJE: 656 RIE: 797 GC: 510
UF Home
Home Conditions
Home Environment
BT Environment

RT Child Development
Daughters
Family (Sociological Unit)
Family Day Care
Family Influence
Family Relationship
Grandparents
Home Furnishings
Home Management
Housing
Parents
Permissive Environment
Sons

FAMILY FINANCIAL RESOURCES *Mar. 1980*
CIJE: 85 RIE: 130 GC: 620
SN A family's immediate and/or possible sources of revenue
UF Family Resources (1966 1980)
BT Resources
RT Family (Sociological Unit)
Family Characteristics
Family Income
Family Status
Parent Financial Contribution

FAMILY HEALTH *Jul. 1966*
CIJE: 119 RIE: 134 GC: 210
BT Health
RT Family (Sociological Unit)
Family Practice (Medicine)
Hygiene
Primary Health Care

FAMILY HISTORY *Jan. 1985*
CIJE: 20 RIE: 18 GC: 430
SN History that identifies or traces the structure, size, membership, customs, ethnicity, migration, socioeconomic status, biological characteristics, or lineal descent of a family or families
NT Genealogy
BT History
RT Family (Sociological Unit)
Family Characteristics
Family Life
Family Relationship
Kinship
Local History
Oral History
Social History

FAMILY INCOME *Jul. 1966*
CIJE: 240 RIE: 688 GC: 620
BT Income
RT Family (Sociological Unit)
Family Characteristics
Family Financial Resources
Family Status
Parent Financial Contribution

FAMILY INFLUENCE *Jul. 1966*
CIJE: 759 RIE: 853 GC: 510
UF Home Influence
BT Influences
RT Family (Sociological Unit)
Family Counseling
Family Environment
Family Involvement
Family Role
Family Status
Parent Influence

FAMILY INVOLVEMENT *Jul. 1966*
CIJE: 232 RIE: 288 GC: 510
UF Family Participation
BT Participation
RT Family (Sociological Unit)
Family Influence
Family Life Education
Family Role
Parent Participation

FAMILY LIFE *Jul. 1966*
CIJE: 749 RIE: 972 GC: 510
UF Family Culture
Family Living
Home Life
RT Black Family
Children
Daughters
Extended Family
Family (Sociological Unit)
Family History
Family Life Education
Family Programs
Grandparents
Group Experience
Homemakers
Homemaking Skills
Marital Instability
Marital Satisfaction
Marriage
Marriage Counseling
Nuclear Family
Parenthood Education
Parents
Siblings
Sons
Spouses
Stepfamily

FAMILY LIFE EDUCATION *Jul. 1966*
CIJE: 377 RIE: 500 GC: 400
UF Home And Family Life Education
NT Parenthood Education
Sex Education
BT Education
RT Consumer Education
Family Involvement
Family Life
Family Relationship
Home Management

Family Living
USE FAMILY LIFE

Family Management (1966 1980)
USE HOME MANAGEMENT

FAMILY MOBILITY *Jul. 1966*
CIJE: 46 RIE: 68 GC: 550
SN Geographic movement of families (note: for family social mobility, coordinate "social mobility" and appropriate "family" descriptors -- prior to mar80, this term was not restricted by a scope note)
BT Migration
RT Family (Sociological Unit)
Place Of Residence
Relocation
Residential Patterns
Student Mobility

Family Participation
USE FAMILY INVOLVEMENT

FAMILY PLANNING *Jul. 1966*
CIJE: 284 RIE: 583 GC: 210
SN Voluntary regulation of the spacing and/or number of births in a family -- includes programs or counseling to assist individuals or couples with such planning
BT Planning
RT Abortions
Birth Rate
Contraception
Early Parenthood
Family (Sociological Unit)
Family Size
Overpopulation
Population Education
Population Growth
Population Trends
Pregnancy
Reproduction (Biology)

FAMILY PRACTICE (MEDICINE) *Mar. 1980*
CIJE: 157 RIE: 26 GC: 210
UF General Practice (Medicine)
BT Medicine
RT Family Health
Gynecology
Internal Medicine
Medical Services
Obstetrics
Pediatrics
Primary Health Care

FAMILY PROBLEMS *Jul. 1966*
CIJE: 911 RIE: 755 GC: 530
BT Problems
RT Battered Women
Child Abuse
Child Custody
Child Neglect
Children
Divorce
Early Parenthood
Elder Abuse
Family (Sociological Unit)
Family Counseling
Family Violence
Group Homes
Hospices (Terminal Care)
Marital Instability
Marriage Counseling
Parents
Problem Children
Respite Care
Runaways
Visiting Homemakers

FAMILY PROGRAMS *Jul. 1966*
CIJE: 137 RIE: 422 GC: 520
SN Plans or courses of action developed and/or implemented by governmental units or other organizations to provide supporting services and resources to families (note: prior to sep81, the use of this term was not restricted by a scope note)
UF Family Projects (1966 1980)
Family Services Policy #
BT Programs
RT Family (Sociological Unit)
Family Life

Family Projects (1966 1980)
USE FAMILY PROGRAMS

FAMILY RELATIONSHIP *Jul. 1966*
CIJE: 1230 RIE: 899 GC: 510
NT Parent Child Relationship
BT Interpersonal Relationship
RT Child Rearing
Early Parenthood
Extended Family
Family (Sociological Unit)
Family Characteristics
Family Counseling
Family Environment
Family History
Family Life Education
Family Size
Family Status
Family Structure
Kinship
Midlife Transitions
Nuclear Family
Parenthood Education
Parenting Skills
Significant Others
Stepfamily

Family Resources (1966 1980)
USE FAMILY FINANCIAL RESOURCES

FAMILY ROLE *Jul. 1966*
CIJE: 488 RIE: 418 GC: 510
RT Child Role
Family (Sociological Unit)
Family Influence
Family Involvement
Parent Role

FAMILY SCHOOL RELATIONSHIP *Jul. 1966*
CIJE: 243 RIE: 422 GC: 330
UF Home School Relationship
School Family Relationship
School Home Relationship
NT Parent School Relationship
BT Relationship
RT Culture Conflict
Family (Sociological Unit)
Politics Of Education
School Attitudes
School Community Relationship
School Involvement
School Role
Schools
Student School Relationship

Family Services Policy
USE FAMILY PROGRAMS; PUBLIC POLICY

FAMILY SIZE *Jun. 1983*
CIJE: 61 RIE: 65 GC: 520
RT Birth Rate
Dependents
Extended Family
Family (Sociological Unit)
Family Characteristics
Family Planning
Family Relationship
Family Structure
Housing
Nuclear Family
One Parent Family
Population Growth
Population Trends
Siblings

FAMILY STATUS *Jul. 1966*
CIJE: 51 RIE: 155 GC: 510
BT Group Status
RT Family (Sociological Unit)
Family Characteristics
Family Financial Resources
Family income
Family Influence
Family Relationship

FAMILY STRUCTURE *Jul. 1966*
CIJE: 606 RIE: 492 GC: 520
SN Organizational framework that determines family membership, and the functions and hierarchical position of family members
NT Birth Order
BT Group Structure
RT Black Family
Dependents
Dual Career Family
Extended Family
Family (Sociological Unit)
Family Characteristics
Family Relationship
Family Size
Homemakers
Kinship
Nuclear Family
One Parent Family
Siblings
Social Structure
Stepfamily
Unwed Mothers

Family Trees
USE GENEALOGY

Family Unity
USE GROUP UNITY

FAMILY VIOLENCE *Oct. 1984*
CIJE: 43 RIE: 44 GC: 530
SN Injurious or abusive physical force among members of a family or household
UF Domestic Violence (Family)
BT Violence
RT Battered Women
Child Abuse
Crime
Elder Abuse
Family (Sociological Unit)
Family Problems
Marital Instability
Victims Of Crime

FANTASY *Jul. 1966*
CIJE: 360 RIE: 168 GC: 120
RT Fables
Fiction
Imagination
Pretend Play
Science Fiction

Fantasy Play
USE PRETEND PLAY

FARM ACCOUNTS *Jul. 1966*
CIJE: 17 RIE: 45 GC: 410
BT Records (Forms)
RT Accountants
Accounting
Farm Management

Farm Agents
USE EXTENSION AGENTS

Farm Foremen
USE CREW LEADERS

FARM LABOR *Jul. 1966*
CIJE: 41 RIE: 172 GC: 410
SN All labor involved in farm operations (note: for unskilled farm labor, coordinate this term with "agricultural laborers" -- prior to mar80, the thesaurus carried the instruction "farm laborers or farm workers, use agricultural laborers")
UF Farm Labor Legislation (1966 1980) #
Farm Labor Problems (1966 1980) #
Farm Labor Supply (1966 1980) #
BT Labor

= Two or more Descriptors are used to represent this term.
The term's main entry shows the appropriate coordination.

RT Agricultural Laborers
Agricultural Personnel
Farmers
Farm Occupations

Farm Labor Legislation (1966 1980)
USE FARM LABOR; LABOR LEGISLATION

Farm Labor Problems (1966 1980)
USE FARM LABOR; LABOR PROBLEMS

Farm Labor Supply (1966 1980)
USE FARM LABOR; LABOR SUPPLY

FARM MANAGEMENT *Jul. 1966*
CIJE: 87 RIE: 247 GC: 410
BT Administration
RT Agricultural Education
Agricultural Engineering
Agricultural Occupations
Agricultural Production
Agriculture
Farm Accounts
Farmers
Farm Visits

Farm Mechanics (Occupation) (1967 1980)
USE AGRICULTURAL MACHINERY OCCUPATIONS

Farm Mechanics (Subject)
USE AGRICULTURAL ENGINEERING

FARM OCCUPATIONS *Jul. 1966*
CIJE: 35 RIE: 116 GC: 410
BT Agricultural Occupations
RT Agriculture
Animal Husbandry
Dairy Farmers
Farmers
Farm Labor
Off Farm Agricultural Occupations
Part Time Farmers
Sharecroppers
Supervised Farm Practice

Farm Operators
USE FARMERS

Farm Related Occupations
USE OFF FARM AGRICULTURAL OCCUPATIONS

Farm Supplies
USE AGRICULTURAL SUPPLIES

FARM VISITS *Aug. 1968*
CIJE: 19 RIE: 23 GC: 410
BT Field Trips
RT Adult Farmer Education
Agriculture
Experiential Learning
Farmers
Farm Management
Supervised Farm Practice
Young Farmer Education

Farm Youth
USE RURAL YOUTH

FARMERS *Jul. 1966*
CIJE: 150 RIE: 350 GC: 410
UF Farm Operators
NT Dairy Farmers
Part Time Farmers
Sharecroppers
BT Agricultural Personnel
RT Adult Farmer Education
Agricultural Occupations
Agricultural Production
Agriculture
Farm Labor
Farm Management
Farm Occupations
Farm Visits
Rural Farm Residents
Young Farmer Education

Farsi (Language)
USE PERSIAN

Farsightedness
USE HYPEROPIA

FASCISM *Mar. 1982*
CIJE: 10 RIE: 4 GC: 610
SN A political philosophy or movement that exalts nation and stands for a centralized autocratic government, economic and social regimentation, and suppression of opposition
NT Nazism
BT Social Systems
RT Anti Intellectualism
Capitalism
Communism
Economics
Government (Administrative Body)
Imperialism
Nationalism
Political Science
Socialism
Totalitarianism

FASHION INDUSTRY *Jun. 1977*
CIJE: 21 RIE: 67 GC: 650
SN Concerned with the design, production, and marketing of clothing
UF Apparel Industry
Clothing Industry
Garment Industry
BT Industry
RT Clothing
Clothing Design
Clothing Instruction
Needle Trades
Occupational Home Economics
Service Occupations
Sewing Instruction
Sewing Machine Operators
Textiles Instruction

Fashions (Clothing)
USE CLOTHING

FAST TRACK SCHEDULING *Dec. 1972*
CIJE: 39 RIE: 11 GC: 920
SN A construction management technique in which design and construction process activities are scheduled to overlap rather than scheduled sequentially
BT Scheduling
RT Construction Management
Construction Programs
Critical Path Method
Design Build Approach
Facility Planning
Systems Building

Father Absence
USE FATHERLESS FAMILY

FATHER ATTITUDES *Aug. 1982*
CIJE: 13 RIE: 9 GC: 510
SN Attitudes of, not toward, fathers
BT Parent Attitudes
RT Fathers
Mother Attitudes

Father Role
USE FATHERS; PARENT ROLE

FATHERLESS FAMILY *Jul. 1966*
CIJE: 135 RIE: 113 GC: 510
UF Father Absence
BT One Parent Family
RT Displaced Homemakers
Divorce
Heads Of Households
Illegitimate Births
Motherless Family
Mothers
Unwed Mothers
Widowed

FATHERS *Jul. 1966*
CIJE: 415 RIE: 300 GC: 510
UF Father Role #
Middle Class Fathers (1966 1980) #
BT Males
Parents
RT Employed Parents
Father Attitudes
Heads Of Households
Motherless Family
One Parent Family
Parent Associations
Parent Child Relationship
Parent Influence
Parent Role

FATIGUE (BIOLOGY) *Apr. 1969*
CIJE: 78 RIE: 30 GC: 210
UF Exhaustion
Weariness
RT Energy
Exercise Physiology
Health
Physical Fitness
Sensory Deprivation
Sleep

Fax
USE FACSIMILE TRANSMISSION

FEAR *Jul. 1966*
CIJE: 388 RIE: 155 GC: 230
NT Fear Of Success
School Phobia
BT Psychological Patterns
RT Anxiety
Depression (Psychology)
Emotional Problems
Helplessness
Neurosis
Paranoid Behavior
Withdrawal (Psychology)

FEAR OF SUCCESS *Aug. 1978*
CIJE: 68 RIE: 49 GC: 230
SN Need to refrain from maximally utilizing one's abilities in achievement situations because of expected negative consequences
UF Success Avoidance
BT Fear
RT Achievement
Failure
Goal Orientation
Inhibition
Low Achievement
Motivation
Sex Role
Success
Underachievement

FEASIBILITY STUDIES *Jul. 1966*
CIJE: 114 RIE: 870 GC: 810
SN Investigations or surveys to determine the practicability of instituting a program, course, larger study, or other proposed activity (note: as of oct81, use as a minor descriptor for examples of this kind of research -- use as a major descriptor only as the subject of a document)
BT Research
RT Experimental Programs
Pilot Projects
Surveys

FEDERAL AID *Jul. 1966*
CIJE: 2341 RIE: 4458 GC: 620
UF Federal Grants
NT Revenue Sharing
State Federal Aid
RT Block Grants
Categorical Aid
Developing Institutions
Educational Finance
Eligibility
Equalization Aid
Federal Government
Federal Indian Relationship
Federal Programs
Federal Regulation
Finance Reform
Financial Support
Foundation Programs
Government School Relationship
Grantsmanship
Incentive Grants
Land Grant Universities
Private School Aid
Public Support
School Funds
School Support
Technical Assistance
Training Allowances
Veterans Education

Federal Control
USE FEDERAL REGULATION

Federal Court Litigation (1966 1980)
USE COURT LITIGATION; FEDERAL COURTS

FEDERAL COURTS *Jul. 1966*
CIJE: 312 RIE: 321 GC: 610
UF Federal Court Litigation (1966 1980) #
BT Courts
RT Court Litigation
Federal Government
Federal Legislation
State Courts

FEDERAL GOVERNMENT *Jul. 1966*
CIJE: 1462 RIE: 2087 GC: 610
UF Federal Libraries #
BT Government (Administrative Body)
RT Federal Aid
Federal Courts
Federal Indian Relationship
Federal Legislation
Federal Programs
Federal Regulation
Federal State Relationship
Government Employees
Government School Relationship
Military Organizations
National Security
Presidential Campaigns (United States)
Presidents Of The United States
Public Agencies
State Church Separation
Treaties
Tribal Sovereignty
Trust Responsibility (Government)

Federal Grants
USE FEDERAL AID

FEDERAL INDIAN RELATIONSHIP *Oct. 1979*
CIJE: 98 RIE: 265 GC: 610
SN Relationship between the united states government and the american indians, including legal obligations to protect and enhance indian trust resources and tribal self-government while providing economic and social programs necessary to a level comparable to non-indian society
BT Relationship
RT American Indian Education
American Indian History
American Indian Reservations
American Indians
Federal Aid
Federal Government
Federal Programs
Treaties
Tribal Sovereignty
Tribes
Trust Responsibility (Government)

Federal Laws (1966 1974)
USE FEDERAL LEGISLATION

FEDERAL LEGISLATION *Jul. 1966*
CIJE: 2831 RIE: 5143 GC: 610
UF Federal Laws (1966 1974)
Federal Recreation Legislation (1966 1978) #
BT Legislation
RT Federal Courts
Federal Government
Federal Regulation
Laws
Legislators
Local Legislation
Revenue Sharing
State Legislation
Treaties
Tribal Sovereignty

Federal Libraries
USE FEDERAL GOVERNMENT; GOVERNMENT LIBRARIES

FEDERAL PROGRAMS *Jul. 1966*
CIJE: 1808 RIE: 5717 GC: 610
SN Programs sponsored by the federal government (note: do not confuse with "national programs" -- prior to mar80, the use of this term was not restricted by a scope note)
BT Programs
RT County Programs
Federal Aid
Federal Government
Federal Indian Relationship
Federal State Relationship
Individualized Education Programs
National Programs

= Two or more Descriptors are used to represent this term.
The term's main entry shows the appropriate coordination.

Public Agencies
Public Policy
State Programs
Student Loan Programs

Federal Recreation Legislation (1966 1978)
USE FEDERAL LEGISLATION; RECREATION LEGISLATION

FEDERAL REGULATION *Sep. 1977*
CIJE: 742 RIE: 1013 GC: 610
SN Federal government control or influence based on legislation
UF Federal Control
BT Governance
RT Compliance (Legal)
Copyrights
Federal Aid
Federal Government
Federal Legislation
Federal State Relationship
Government Role
Government School Relationship
Institutional Autonomy
Patents

Federal State Aid
USE STATE FEDERAL AID

FEDERAL STATE RELATIONSHIP *Jul. 1966*
CIJE: 341 RIE: 842 GC: 610
UF State Federal Relationship
BT Relationship
RT Block Grants
Board Administrator Relationship
Federal Government
Federal Programs
Federal Regulation
Government School Relationship
Revenue Sharing
State Government
States Powers
Statewide Planning

Federal Troops (1966 1980)
USE ARMED FORCES

FEED INDUSTRY *Jul. 1966*
CIJE: 1 RIE: 16 GC: 410
BT Industry
RT Agribusiness
Agricultural Supplies
Agricultural Supply Occupations
Agriculture
Feed Stores
Food
Food Processing Occupations
Grains (Food)
Off Farm Agricultural Occupations

FEED STORES *Jul. 1966*
CIJE: RIE: 3 GC: 410
UF Livestock Feed Stores
BT Facilities
RT Agricultural Supplies
Feed Industry
Merchandising

FEEDBACK *Jul. 1966*
CIJE: 1861 RIE: 1570 GC: 710
SN A response within a system that returns to the input a part of the output, thus influencing the continued activity or productivity of that system
UF Knowledge Of Results
NT Biofeedback
BT Interaction
RT Behavior
Communication (Thought Transfer)
Computer Assisted Instruction
Cybernetics
Delphi Technique
Information Processing
Learning Processes
Man Machine Systems
Motivation
Performance
Programed Instruction
Reinforcement
Teacher Response

FEEDER PATTERNS *Jul. 1966*
CIJE: 5 RIE: 21 GC: 330
SN Routes or plans by which students are brought into a school jurisdiction
UF Feeder Programs (1966 1980)
RT Busing
Bus Transportation
Enrollment Trends
Magnet Schools
School Demography
School District Reorganization

Feeder Programs (1966 1980)
USE FEEDER PATTERNS

FEES *Sep. 1969*
CIJE: 222 RIE: 307 GC: 620
UF Dues
NT Fines (Penalties)
Tuition
BT Costs
RT Financial Support
Student Costs

Fellows (Medical)
USE GRADUATE MEDICAL STUDENTS

FELLOWSHIPS *Jul. 1966*
CIJE: 111 RIE: 260 GC: 620
SN Awards, usually in graduate education, given to assist students with the cost of study -- may or may not require teaching or other special duties
NT Faculty Fellowships
BT Student Financial Aid
RT Assistantships
Awards
Educational Finance
Educational Vouchers
Eligibility
Grants
Instructional Student Costs
Noninstructional Student Costs
Research Assistants
Scholarship Funds
Scholarships
Student Costs
Teaching Assistants

Female Homosexuality
USE LESBIANISM

Female Role
USE FEMALES; SEX ROLE

FEMALES *Jul. 1966*
CIJE: 6443 RIE: 6685 GC: 120
UF Female Role #
Girls
Women
NT Battered Women
Daughters
Displaced Homemakers
Employed Women
Mothers
Nuns
Pregnant Students
BT Groups
RT Feminism
Gynecology
Lesbianism
Obstetrics
Sex
Sex Differences
Sex Role
Sex Stereotypes
Single Sex Colleges
Single Sex Schools
Sororities
Spouses
Womens Athletics
Womens Education
Womens Studies

FEMINISM *Nov. 1970*
CIJE: 1152 RIE: 912 GC: 540
UF Womens Liberation
Womens Rights
RT Civil Rights
Females
Life Style
Sex Discrimination
Sex Fairness
Womens Studies

FENCING (SPORT) *Jun. 1984*
CIJE: RIE: GC: 470
UF Epee Fencing
BT Athletics

Fenestration
USE WINDOWS

Fenno Ugric Languages
USE FINNO UGRIC LANGUAGES

Fertility Rate
USE BIRTH RATE

FERTILIZERS *Jul. 1966*
CIJE: 11 RIE: 53 GC: 410
RT Agricultural Chemical Occupations
Agricultural Supplies
Agronomy
Plant Growth
Soil Science

FICTION *Jul. 1966*
CIJE: 762 RIE: 555 GC: 430
NT Novels
Science Fiction
Short Stories
BT Prose
RT Comics (Publications)
Drama
Fables
Fantasy
Humor
Imagination
Legends
Literary Devices
Literary Genres
Nonfiction
Poetry
Tales

Field Check (1967 1980)
USE EQUIPMENT EVALUATION

FIELD CROPS *Sep. 1968*
CIJE: 35 RIE: 106 GC: 410
NT Grains (Food)
Tobacco
RT Agribusiness
Agricultural Production
Agronomy
Botany
Crop Processing Occupations
Harvesting
Horticulture

Field Dependence
USE FIELD DEPENDENCE INDEPENDENCE

FIELD DEPENDENCE INDEPENDENCE *Oct. 1983*
CIJE: 136 RIE: 108 GC: 110
SN Cognitive style or aspect of personality seen in the psychological perception of objects in a background field -- field dependence refers to a tendency to experience events globally, while field independence refers to a tendency to approach the environment in analytical terms
UF Field Dependence
Field Independence
BT Cognitive Style
RT Cognitive Processes
Locus Of Control
Perception Tests
Personality Measures
Visual Perception

FIELD EXPERIENCE PROGRAMS *Jul. 1966*
CIJE: 893 RIE: 1070 GC: 350
SN Practical experiential learning activities under institutional or organizational sponsorship, usually away from the classroom or campus -- associated most often with grades 10-16, and characterized as less formal and concentrated than professional internship programs (note: before jun78, the use of this term was not restricted by a scope note)
UF Field Laboratory Experience
NT Supervised Farm Practice
BT Experiential Learning
Programs
RT Adventure Education
Affiliated Schools
Apprenticeships
Clinical Experience
Cooperative Education
Field Instruction
Field Trips
Internship Programs
Nontraditional Education
On The Job Training
Practicums
Practicum Supervision
Student Experience
Student Teaching
Teacher Centers
Teaching Experience
Work Experience Programs

Field Experiment Stations
USE EXPERIMENT STATIONS

FIELD HOCKEY *Dec. 1975*
CIJE: 1 RIE: 12 GC: 470
BT Team Sports

FIELD HOUSES *Jul. 1966*
CIJE: 14 RIE: 14 GC: 920
BT Facilities
RT Athletic Fields
Athletics
Gymnasiums
Physical Education Facilities
Physical Recreation Programs
Recreational Facilities

Field Independence
USE FIELD DEPENDENCE INDEPENDENCE

FIELD INSTRUCTION *Jul. 1966*
CIJE: 206 RIE: 167 GC: 350
SN Instruction that takes place outside the school and enables students to learn about something by taking an active part in it
UF Field Teaching
BT Instruction
RT Experiential Learning
Field Experience Programs
Field Trips

FIELD INTERVIEWS *Jul. 1966*
CIJE: 59 RIE: 242 GC: 810
BT Interviews
RT Caseworker Approach

Field Laboratory Experience
USE FIELD EXPERIENCE PROGRAMS

FIELD STUDIES *Jul. 1966*
CIJE: 459 RIE: 767 GC: 810
SN Academic or other investigative studies undertaken in a natural setting, rather than in laboratories, classrooms, or other structured environments (note: as of oct81, use as a minor descriptor for examples of this kind of research -- use as a major descriptor only as the subject of a document)
BT Research
RT Area Studies
Educational Research
Naturalistic Observation
Qualitative Research
Research Methodology

Field Teaching
USE FIELD INSTRUCTION

FIELD TESTS *Mar. 1980*
CIJE: 63 RIE: 188 GC: 830
SN On site evaluation of equipment, programs, personnel, etc.
UF On Site Tests
BT Tests
RT Demonstration Programs
Equipment Evaluation
Inspection
Program Evaluation

FIELD TRIPS *Jul. 1966*
CIJE: 755 RIE: 665 GC: 350
UF Airborne Field Trips (1968 1980)
Excursions (Instruction)
Instructional Trips (1966 1980)
Study Trips
NT Farm Visits

RT Adventure Education
Class Activities
Experiential Learning
Field Experience Programs
Field Instruction
Outdoor Education
Travel

FIFTEENTH CENTURY LITERATURE *May. 1969*
CIJE: 10 RIE: 2 GC: 430
BT Literature
RT Literary History
Medieval Literature
Renaissance Literature

FIGURAL AFTEREFFECTS *Jun. 1969*
CIJE: 26 RIE: 9 GC: 110
BT Sensory Experience
RT Auditory Perception
Kinesthetic Perception
Perception
Psychophysiology
Tactual Perception
Visual Perception

FIGURATIVE LANGUAGE *Jul. 1966*
CIJE: 203 RIE: 178 GC: 430
UF Figures Of Speech
NT Allegory
Ambiguity
Antithesis
Imagery
Irony
Metaphors
Puns
Symbols (Literary)
BT Language
Literary Devices
RT Literature
Parody
Satire

Figures Of Speech
USE FIGURATIVE LANGUAGE

FILE CLERKS *Aug. 1968*
CIJE: 3 RIE: 12 GC: 640
UF Classification Clerks
Record Clerks
BT Clerical Workers
RT Filing
Medical Record Technicians

File Management Systems
USE DATABASE MANAGEMENT SYSTEMS

FILING *Jul. 1969*
CIJE: 64 RIE: 122 GC: 710
SN Process of arranging materials in a useful order
UF Alphabetic Filing
Numeric Filing
BT Documentation
RT Alphabetizing Skills
Business Skills
Cataloging
File Clerks
Indexing
Information Storage
Medical Record Technicians

Filing Systems
USE INFORMATION STORAGE

FILIPINO AMERICANS *Sep. 1968*
CIJE: 18 RIE: 121 GC: 560
BT Asian Americans
Ethnic Groups

Film (Cameras)
USE PHOTOGRAPHIC EQUIPMENT

Film Auteurism
USE AUTEURISM

Film Clips
USE FILMSTRIPS

FILM CRITICISM *May. 1976*
CIJE: 97 RIE: 69 GC: 430
SN Act and art of analyzing and judging the quality of films
RT Content Analysis
Films
Imagery
Motifs
Rhetorical Criticism

FILM INDUSTRY *Jun. 1977*
CIJE: 40 RIE: 42 GC: 650
BT Industry
RT Acting
Animation
Broadcast Industry
Copyrights
Documentaries
Film Production
Film Production Specialists
Films
Mass Media
Theater Arts
Videotape Recordings

FILM LIBRARIES *Jan. 1971*
CIJE: 67 RIE: 124 GC: 710
UF Videotape Libraries
BT Special Libraries
RT Filmographies
Films
Filmstrips
Kinescope Recordings
Videotape Recordings

Film Lists
USE FILMOGRAPHIES

Film Loops
USE FILMSTRIPS

FILM PRODUCTION *Jul. 1966*
CIJE: 423 RIE: 403 GC: 720
UF Filmmaking
BT Production Techniques
Visual Arts
RT Acting
Animation
Auteurism
Editing
Film Industry
Film Production Specialists
Films
Filmstrips
Film Study
Photographic Equipment
Photography
Special Effects
Theater Arts
Videotape Recordings

FILM PRODUCTION SPECIALISTS *Jul. 1966*
CIJE: 35 RIE: 71 GC: 720
UF Filmmakers
BT Specialists
RT Auteurism
Film Industry
Film Production

Film Projectors
USE PROJECTION EQUIPMENT

FILM STUDY *Nov. 1968*
CIJE: 464 RIE: 428 GC: 400
SN Study of film (as an art form) and filmmaking (note: for the use of film in teaching, see "instructional films" -- prior to mar80, this term was not restricted by a scope note)
UF Cinema Study
Screen Education
BT Aesthetic Education
RT Acting
Auteurism
Cartoons
Documentaries
Editing
Filmographies
Film Production
Films
Filmstrips
Photography
Repetitive Film Showings
Special Effects
Theater Arts
Visual Literacy

Filmmakers
USE FILM PRODUCTION SPECIALISTS

Filmmaking
USE FILM PRODUCTION

FILMOGRAPHIES *May. 1976*
CIJE: 88 RIE: 189 GC: 730
SN Lists of films, sometimes including other media and/or commentary
UF Film Lists
BT Reference Materials
RT Bibliographies
Discographies
Film Libraries
Films
Film Study
Indexes
Library Catalogs

FILMS *Jul. 1966*
CIJE: 1426 RIE: 1904 GC: 720
UF Black And White Films
Cinema
Color Films
Motion Pictures
Silent Films
Sound Films (1966 1980)
NT Foreign Language Films
Instructional Films
Kinescope Recordings
Single Concept Films
BT Mass Media
Nonprint Media
Visual Aids
RT Auteurism
Captions
Cartoons
Copyrights
Documentaries
Film Criticism
Film Industry
Film Libraries
Filmographies
Film Production
Filmstrips
Film Study
Literary Styles
Photographs
Popular Culture
Repetitive Film Showings
Theater Arts
Transparencies
Videotape Recordings

FILMSTRIP PROJECTORS *Jul. 1966*
CIJE: 12 RIE: 19 GC: 910
BT Projection Equipment
RT Filmstrips

FILMSTRIPS *Jul. 1966*
CIJE: 212 RIE: 537 GC: 720
UF Film Clips
Film Loops
BT Nonprint Media
Visual Aids
RT Audiovisual Aids
Film Libraries
Film Production
Films
Filmstrip Projectors
Film Study
Microfilm
Single Concept Films
Slides

FINANCE OCCUPATIONS *Sep. 1968*
CIJE: 16 RIE: 53 GC: 640
BT Occupations
RT Banking
Economics
Estate Planning
Financial Services
Fund Raising
Investment
Money Management
Office Occupations
Trusts (Financial)

FINANCE REFORM *Dec. 1974*
CIJE: 335 RIE: 550 GC: 620
SN A change in income/revenue sources or in money management methods, designed to remove inequities or other faults in existing systems
UF Tax Reform
BT Improvement
RT Change Strategies
Economic Change
Educational Equity (Finance)
Educational Finance
Equalization Aid
Federal Aid
Financial Policy
Financial Problems
Financial Support
Fiscal Capacity
Money Management
State Aid
Tax Effort
Taxes

FINANCIAL AID APPLICANTS *Mar. 1980*
CIJE: 54 RIE: 162 GC: 360
SN Individuals requesting financial support
UF Loan Applicants
BT Groups
RT College Applicants
Credit (Finance)
Eligibility
Financial Needs
Financial Problems
Financial Services
Financial Support
Grants
Loan Repayment
Student Financial Aid

FINANCIAL AUDITS *Aug. 1986*
CIJE: 3 RIE: 8 GC: 620
SN Verifications of the stated financial assets and liabilities of an individual or group
BT Audits (Verification)
RT Accounting
Bookkeeping
Budgeting
Expenditures
Financial Policy
Financial Services
Financial Support
Fiscal Capacity
Income
Money Management

Financial Barriers
USE FINANCIAL PROBLEMS

Financial Donors
USE DONORS

Financial Management
USE MONEY MANAGEMENT

FINANCIAL NEEDS *Jul. 1966*
CIJE: 322 RIE: 785 GC: 620
BT Needs
RT Credit (Finance)
Educational Equity (Finance)
Educational Finance
Financial Aid Applicants
Financial Support
Fund Raising
Income
Loan Repayment
Need Analysis (Student Financial Aid)
Purchasing
Resource Allocation
Self Supporting Students
Student Loan Programs
Tax Allocation

FINANCIAL POLICY *Jul. 1966*
CIJE: 540 RIE: 1200 GC: 620
UF Fiscal Policy
BT Policy
RT Educational Economics
Educational Equity (Finance)
Educational Finance
Finance Reform
Financial Audits
Financial Support
Fiscal Capacity
Money Management

FINANCIAL PROBLEMS *Jul. 1966*
CIJE: 916 RIE: 993 GC: 620
UF Financial Barriers
Fiscal Strain
BT Problems
RT Educational Equity (Finance)
Educational Finance
Finance Reform
Financial Aid Applicants
Fund Raising

Income
Inflation (Economics)
Institutional Survival
Loan Repayment
Retrenchment

FINANCIAL SERVICES *Jul. 1966*
CIJE: 80 RIE: 199 GC: 620
SN Programs that offer aid with money management (note: use a more precise term if possible)
BT Services
RT Accountants
Accounting
Banking
Bookkeeping
Certified Public Accountants
Credit (Finance)
Educational Finance
Eligibility
Estate Planning
Finance Occupations
Financial Aid Applicants
Financial Audits
Financial Support
Fund Raising
Insurance
Loan Repayment
Money Management
Ownership
Student Loan Programs
Trusts (Financial)

FINANCIAL SUPPORT *Jul. 1966*
CIJE: 2872 RIE: 5389 GC: 620
UF Economic Support
Financing
Funding
NT Capital
Categorical Aid
Endowment Funds
Equalization Aid
Full State Funding
Grants
Private Financial Support
Private School Aid
Recreation Finances
Revenue Sharing
Scholarship Funds
School Funds
Student Financial Aid
Tax Allocation
Training Allowances
Unemployment Insurance
Workers Compensation
RT Community Resources
Credit (Finance)
Educational Economics
Educational Equity (Finance)
Educational Finance
Eligibility
Entrepreneurship
Federal Aid
Fees
Finance Reform
Financial Aid Applicants
Financial Audits
Financial Needs
Financial Policy
Financial Services
Foundation Programs
Fund Raising
Grantsmanship
Income
Insurance
Investment
Loan Repayment
Need Analysis (Student Financial Aid)
Program Proposals
Proposal Writing
Public Support
Research Opportunities
Resources
School Support
State Aid
State Federal Aid
Student Financial Aid Officers
Student Loan Programs
Technical Assistance
Trusts (Financial)
Wills
Work Study Programs

Financing
USE FINANCIAL SUPPORT

FINE ARTS *Jul. 1966*
CIJE: 408 RIE: 613 GC: 420
SN Any of the arts for which aesthetic purposes are primary or uppermost
NT Dance
Music
Theater Arts
Visual Arts
BT Humanities
RT Art
Art Activities
Art Appreciation
Art Education
Art History
Artists
Arts Centers
Art Teachers
Cultural Activities
Cultural Enrichment
Dance Education
Music Activities
Music Appreciation
Music Education
Musicians
Music Teachers

Fine Arts Centers
USE ARTS CENTERS

FINES (PENALTIES) *Feb. 1970*
CIJE: 13 RIE: 18 GC: 620
UF Library Fines
BT Fees
RT Crime
Incentives
Law Enforcement
Legal Responsibility
Library Administration
Library Circulation
Sanctions

FINGER SPELLING *Jul. 1966*
CIJE: 64 RIE: 34 GC: 220
SN Spelling by finger movements
UF Dactylology
BT Manual Communication
Spelling
RT Cued Speech
Deaf Interpreting
Sign Language
Total Communication

FINISHING *Mar. 1969*
CIJE: 10 RIE: 55 GC: 640
UF Metal Finishing
Surface Finishing
Textile Finishing
Wood Finishing
RT Adhesives
Metal Working
Welding
Woodworking

FINNISH *Jul. 1966*
CIJE: 26 RIE: 53 GC: 440
BT Finno Ugric Languages

FINNO UGRIC LANGUAGES *Jul. 1966*
CIJE: 4 RIE: 12 GC: 440
UF Fenno Ugric Languages
NT Cheremis
Estonian
Finnish
Hungarian
Ostyak
Vogul
BT Uralic Altaic Languages

FIRE FIGHTERS *Jul. 1966*
CIJE: 22 RIE: 100 GC: 640
UF Firemen
BT Service Workers
RT Alarm Systems
Emergency Squad Personnel
Fire Science Education

FIRE INSURANCE *Sep. 1968*
CIJE: 12 RIE: 14 GC: 620
BT Insurance
RT Fire Protection
Insurance Occupations

Fire Prevention
USE FIRE PROTECTION

FIRE PROTECTION *Jul. 1966*
CIJE: 113 RIE: 240 GC: 210
UF Fire Prevention
BT Safety
RT Alarm Systems
Asbestos
Building Design
Fire Insurance
Fire Science Education
Preservation
Prevention
Safety Education
School Safety

FIRE SCIENCE EDUCATION *Jul. 1966*
CIJE: 22 RIE: 102 GC: 400
BT Technical Education
RT Conservation Education
Fire Fighters
Fire Protection
Safety Education

Firemen
USE FIRE FIGHTERS

FIRST AID *Jul. 1966*
CIJE: 70 RIE: 256 GC: 210
NT Cardiopulmonary Resuscitation
BT Medical Services
RT Emergency Medical Technicians
Health Education
Health Facilities
Injuries
Rescue

First Professional Degrees
USE DEGREES (ACADEMIC); PROFESSIONAL EDUCATION

First Year Teachers
USE BEGINNING TEACHERS

FISCAL CAPACITY *Jul. 1966*
CIJE: 90 RIE: 255 GC: 620
SN Wealth of a government, institution, organization, or individual -- also, the relative ability to obtain revenue
RT Economic Factors
Educational Economics
Educational Equity (Finance)
Educational Finance
Equalization Aid
Finance Reform
Financial Audits
Financial Policy
Inflation (Economics)
Ownership
Property Taxes
Resource Allocation
Tax Effort

Fiscal Equity (Education)
USE EDUCATIONAL EQUITY (FINANCE)

Fiscal Policy
USE FINANCIAL POLICY

Fiscal Strain
USE FINANCIAL PROBLEMS

Fish Inspectors
USE FOOD AND DRUG INSPECTORS

Fish Studies
USE ICHTHYOLOGY

FISHERIES *Jul. 1966*
CIJE: 40 RIE: 92 GC: 410
BT Facilities
RT Agriculture
Estuaries
Ichthyology
Marine Biology
Oceanography

FIXED SEQUENCE *Jul. 1966*
CIJE: 5 RIE: 16 GC: 350
BT Methods
RT Branching
Pacing
Programed Instruction
Sequential Approach

Fixed Service Television (1969 1980)
USE EDUCATIONAL TELEVISION

FLES *Jul. 1966*
CIJE: 217 RIE: 456 GC: 450
UF Fles Guides (1967 1980) #
Fles Materials (1967 1980) #
Fles Programs (1967 1980) #
Fles Teachers (1967 1980) #
Foreign Languages In The Elementary School
BT Elementary School Curriculum
Modern Language Curriculum
RT Immersion Programs
Languages
Second Language Instruction
Second Language Learning
Second Language Programs
Second Languages

Fles Guides (1967 1980)
USE CURRICULUM GUIDES; FLES

Fles Materials (1967 1980)
USE FLES; INSTRUCTIONAL MATERIALS

Fles Programs (1967 1980)
USE FLES; SECOND LANGUAGE PROGRAMS

Fles Teachers (1967 1980)
USE FLES; LANGUAGE TEACHERS

Flexible Classrooms (1968 1980)
USE CLASSROOMS; FLEXIBLE FACILITIES

FLEXIBLE FACILITIES *Jul. 1966*
CIJE: 333 RIE: 286 GC: 920
SN Facilities designed to be adaptable for more than one purpose or use
UF Flexible Classrooms (1968 1980) #
BT Facilities
RT Building Innovation
Classroom Design
Design Requirements
Educational Facilities Design
Educational Facilities Planning
Encapsulated Facilities
Flexible Lighting Design
Furniture Arrangement
Interior Space
Mobile Classrooms
Movable Partitions
Multipurpose Classrooms
Open Plan Schools
Relocatable Facilities
School Space
Shared Facilities
Space Dividers
Space Utilization
Spatial Relationship (Facilities)
Structural Elements (Construction)

FLEXIBLE LIGHTING DESIGN *Jul. 1966*
CIJE: 22 RIE: 7 GC: 920
SN Lighting unit arrangement as well as lighting fixture design that allows for flexible lighting requirements
BT Lighting Design
RT Building Design
Classroom Design
Flexible Facilities
Lighting

FLEXIBLE PROGRESSION *Jul. 1966*
CIJE: 48 RIE: 77 GC: 350
SN Advancement of students through an educational program at different rates, depending on their abilities, preferences, or other factors (note: prior to mar80, the use of this term was not restricted by a scope note, and the instruction "track system, use flexible progression" was carried in the thesaurus)
NT Acceleration (Education)
RT Ability Grouping
Continuous Progress Plan
Curriculum Design
Nongraded Instructional Grouping
Student Promotion

FLEXIBLE SCHEDULES (1967 1980) *Jun. 1980*
CIJE: 70 RIE: 80 GC: 320
SN Invalid descriptor -- used inconsistently in indexing for both school and job schedules -- see "flexible scheduling" and "flexible working hours" respectively for those concepts

FLEXIBLE SCHEDULING *Jul. 1966*
CIJE: 284 RIE: 347 GC: 320
SN Responsive instructional scheduling that provides for team teaching, variations in student groupings within and among courses, and changes in the frequency and length of time courses meet (note: prior to mar80, the use of this term was not restricted by a scope note)
UF Modular Scheduling
Schedule Modules (1968 1980)
BT School Schedules
RT Class Size
Continuous Progress Plan
Extended School Day
Extended School Year
Grouping (Instructional Purposes)
Instructional Development
Instructional Innovation
Team Teaching
Time Blocks

FLEXIBLE WORKING HOURS *Mar. 1980*
CIJE: 69 RIE: 58 GC: 630
SN Scheduling method by which the time of arrival and departure from work, the number of hours worked per day, or the number of days worked per week may be varied, provided that a full complement of hours is worked
UF Compressed Work Week
Flextime
Four Day Work Week
BT Working Hours
RT Employed Parents
Employed Women
Job Satisfaction
Job Sharing
Partnership Teachers
Part Time Employment
Released Time
Work Environment

Flexilevel Testing
USE ADAPTIVE TESTING

Flextime
USE FLEXIBLE WORKING HOURS

FLIGHT TRAINING *Jul. 1966*
CIJE: 44 RIE: 239 GC: 400
SN Training of military or civilian aircraft personnel
UF Pilot Training
BT Training
RT Job Training
Military Training

Floor Covering
USE FLOORING

Floor Installation
USE FLOORING

FLOOR LAYERS *Jul. 1966*
CIJE: 1 RIE: 14 GC: 640
UF Carpet Layers
BT Skilled Workers
RT Carpeting
Flooring

FLOORING *Jul. 1966*
CIJE: 32 RIE: 75 GC: 920
UF Floor Covering
Floor Installation
Floors
Resilient Floor Covering
NT Carpeting
BT Structural Elements (Construction)
RT Asphalts
Buildings
Building Trades
Construction (Process)
Construction Materials
Floor Layers

Floors
USE FLOORING

FLORICULTURE *Jul. 1966*
CIJE: 9 RIE: 42 GC: 410
BT Ornamental Horticulture
RT Botany
Landscaping
Plant Identification
Plant Pathology
Plant Propagation

FLOW CHARTS *Dec. 1970*
CIJE: 571 RIE: 373 GC: 720
SN Diagrammatic representation of sequenced events or processes
BT Charts
RT Computer Oriented Programs
Critical Path Method
Graphs
Planning
Records (Forms)

FLUID MECHANICS *Mar. 1980*
CIJE: 50 RIE: 40 GC: 490
SN Science that deals with fluids, either at rest or in motion, and with pressures, velocities, and accelerations in fluids
UF Fluid Power Education (1967 1980)
BT Mechanics (Physics)
RT Acceleration (Physics)
Force
Hydraulics
Kinetics
Motion
Power Technology
Pressure (Physics)

Fluid Power Education (1967 1980)
USE FLUID MECHANICS

Fluid Pressure
USE PRESSURE (PHYSICS)

FLUORIDATION *Aug. 1982*
CIJE: 14 RIE: 6 GC: 210
SN Treatment of water and teeth with fluorides in order to reduce tooth decay
BT Disease Control
RT Dental Health
Drinking Water
Health Services
Preventive Medicine
Public Health
Water Treatment

Folding Partitions
USE MOVABLE PARTITIONS

FOLK CULTURE *Jul. 1966*
CIJE: 464 RIE: 786 GC: 560
SN Traditional modes of behavior and expression that are transmitted from generation to generation (by firsthand interaction) among a group or people
UF Folk Drama (1969 1980) #
Folklore
Folklore Books (1966 1980) #
Traditions (Culture)
BT Culture
RT Anthropology
Cross Cultural Studies
Cultural Education
Dance
Drama
Ethnography
Ethnology
Legends
Literature
Music
Mythology
Nonformal Education
Poetry
Proverbs

Folk Drama (1969 1980)
USE DRAMA; FOLK CULTURE

FOLK SCHOOLS *Jul. 1966*
CIJE: 33 RIE: 41 GC: 340
SN Schools, often residential, that are established with voluntary funds and concerned with the culture and lives of the people in the surrounding community (note: coordinate with geographic identifiers when possible -- prior to mar80, the use of this term was not restricted by a scope note)
BT Schools
RT Boarding Schools
Community Schools
Cultural Education
Nontraditional Education

Folklore
USE FOLK CULTURE

Folklore Books (1966 1980)
USE BOOKS; FOLK CULTURE

Followup Programs
USE FOLLOWUP STUDIES

FOLLOWUP STUDIES *Jul. 1966*
CIJE: 1086 RIE: 2045 GC: 810
SN Studies that focus on the activities, progress, attitudes, etc. of individuals or groups after some treatment or following their participation in a program, course of study, guidance process, etc. (note: as of oct81, use as a minor descriptor for examples of this kind of study -- use as a major descriptor only as the subject of a document)
UF Followup Programs
NT Graduate Surveys
Vocational Followup
BT Longitudinal Studies
RT Outcomes Of Education

FOOCHOW *Jul. 1966*
CIJE: RIE: 6 GC: 440
BT Chinese
RT Dialects

FOOD *Jul. 1966*
CIJE: 550 RIE: 687 GC: 210
UF Seafood (1968 1980)
NT Grains (Food)
Meat
RT Agriculture
Bakery Industry
Cooks
Dietetics
Dietitians
Feed Industry
Food And Drug Inspectors
Food Handling Facilities
Food Processing Occupations
Food Service
Foods Instruction
Food Standards
Food Stores
Hunger
Meat Packing Industry
Nutrition
Vending Machines

FOOD AND DRUG INSPECTORS *Jan. 1969*
CIJE: 10 RIE: 15 GC: 640
UF Cosmetics Inspectors
Dairy Product Inspectors
Drug Inspectors
Egg Inspectors
Fish Inspectors
Food Inspectors
Fruit And Vegetable Inspectors
Meat Inspectors
Peanut Inspectors
Processed Foods Inspectors
BT Government Employees
RT Food
Food Processing Occupations
Food Service
Food Standards
Meat Packing Industry

FOOD HANDLING FACILITIES *Jul. 1966*
CIJE: 82 RIE: 83 GC: 920
SN Equipment and space for storing, preparing, and serving food
BT Facilities
RT Breakfast Programs
Dining Facilities
Dishwashing
Food
Food Service
Lunch Programs
Vending Machines

Food Inspectors
USE FOOD AND DRUG INSPECTORS

Food Markets
USE FOOD STORES

FOOD PROCESSING OCCUPATIONS *Aug. 1968*
CIJE: 21 RIE: 76 GC: 640
BT Off Farm Agricultural Occupations
RT Bakery Industry
Feed Industry
Food
Food And Drug Inspectors
Meat Packing Industry

FOOD SERVICE *Jul. 1966*
CIJE: 272 RIE: 484 GC: 210
UF Food Service Industry (1967 1981)
Food Service Occupations (1968 1981)
Food Service Workers (1968 1981)
BT Human Services
RT Bakery Industry
Cooks
Dietitians
Dining Facilities
Dishwashing
Distributive Education
Food
Food And Drug Inspectors
Food Handling Facilities
Foods Instruction
Food Standards
Food Stores
Home Economics Skills
Hospitality Occupations
Hygiene
Occupational Home Economics
Vending Machines
Waiters And Waitresses

Food Service Industry (1967 1981)
USE FOOD SERVICE

Food Service Occupations (1968 1981)
USE FOOD SERVICE

Food Service Workers (1968 1981)
USE FOOD SERVICE

FOOD STANDARDS *Jul. 1966*
CIJE: 100 RIE: 165 GC: 210
BT Standards
RT Breakfast Programs
Dietetics
Dietitians
Food
Food And Drug Inspectors
Food Service
Foods Instruction
Lunch Programs
Meat Packing Industry
Nutrition

FOOD STORES *Aug. 1968*
CIJE: 25 RIE: 50 GC: 920
SN Retail markets selling foodstuffs
UF Food Markets
Grocery Stores
Supermarkets
BT Facilities
RT Food
Food Service
Meat
Merchandising
Retailing

FOODS INSTRUCTION *Jul. 1966*
CIJE: 106 RIE: 322 GC: 400
BT Instruction
RT Consumer Science
Cooking Instruction
Cooks
Dietitians
Food
Food Service
Food Standards
Home Economics
Nutrition Instruction

FOOTBALL *Dec. 1975*
CIJE: 91 RIE: 54 GC: 470
BT Team Sports

Footnotes (Bibliographic)
USE CITATIONS (REFERENCES)

FORCE *Oct. 1968*
CIJE: 253 RIE: 58 GC: 490
UF Force (Physical)
BT Scientific Concepts
RT Acceleration (Physics)
Atomic Structure
Atomic Theory
Biomechanics
Electricity
Energy
Fluid Mechanics
Gravity (Physics)
Kinetic Molecular Theory
Kinetics
Mechanics (Physics)
Motion

= Two or more Descriptors are used to represent this term.
The term's main entry shows the appropriate coordination.

Nuclear Physics
Physics
Pressure (Physics)
Quantum Mechanics
Vectors (Mathematics)
Weight (Mass)
Wind Energy

Force (Physical)
USE FORCE

FORCE FIELD ANALYSIS *Jul. 1966*
CIJE: 16 RIE: 32 GC: 820
SN Method of distinguishing factors in the psychological environment of individuals or groups, based on lewins theory
BT Psychological Studies
RT Interdisciplinary Approach
Research Methodology

FORCED CHOICE TECHNIQUE *Jul. 1966*
CIJE: 63 RIE: 42 GC: 820
SN Procedure in which individuals are required to choose among options that have equal acceptability but unequal validity -- used to minimize the ability of individuals to give overly favorable responses
BT Measurement Techniques
RT Affective Measures
Attitude Measures
Interest Inventories
Personality Measures
Q Methodology
Rating Scales
Response Style (Tests)
Social Desirability
Testing
Tests

Forecast
USE PREDICTION

FOREIGN COUNTRIES *Jul. 1966*
CIJE: 11424 RIE: 9607 GC: 610
SN Countries other than the u.s. (note: coordinate with geographic identifiers to indicate document subject -- prior to mar80, the use of this term was not restricted by a scope note)
BT Geographic Regions
RT Armed Forces
Foreign Diplomats
Foreign Policy
International Relations
International Studies
Overseas Employment

FOREIGN CULTURE *Jul. 1966*
CIJE: 322 RIE: 419 GC: 560
SN Culture regarded as foreign from the perspective of the document or journal article (note: use major geographic identifiers to identify the foreign culture, and minor geographic identifiers to identify the native culture -- prior to mar80, this term was not restricted by a scope note and carried no special instruction)
UF Alien Culture
BT Culture
RT Asian Studies
Comparative Education
Cross Cultural Studies
Cross Cultural Training
Ethnic Groups
Ethnocentrism
Intercultural Communication
International Education
International Educational Exchange
Middle Eastern Studies
Multicultural Education
Native Speakers

FOREIGN DIPLOMATS *Jul. 1966*
CIJE: 12 RIE: 10 GC: 610
BT Government Employees
RT Diplomatic History
Foreign Countries
Foreign Policy
Foreign Workers
International Relations

FOREIGN LANGUAGE BOOKS *Jul. 1966*
CIJE: 47 RIE: 88 GC: 730
UF Second Language Books
BT Books
RT Foreign Language Films
Foreign Language Periodicals
Languages
Second Language Learning

Foreign Language Enrollment
USE LANGUAGE ENROLLMENT

FOREIGN LANGUAGE FILMS *Jul. 1966*
CIJE: 56 RIE: 75 GC: 720
UF Second Language Films
BT Films
RT Foreign Language Books
Foreign Language Periodicals
Languages
Second Language Learning

Foreign Language Instruction
USE SECOND LANGUAGE INSTRUCTION

Foreign Language Learning
USE SECOND LANGUAGE LEARNING

FOREIGN LANGUAGE PERIODICALS *Jul. 1966*
CIJE: 72 RIE: 66 GC: 730
UF Second Language Periodicals
BT Periodicals
RT Foreign Language Books
Foreign Language Films
Languages
Second Language Learning

Foreign Language Programs
USE SECOND LANGUAGE PROGRAMS

Foreign Language Teachers
USE LANGUAGE TEACHERS

Foreign Languages
USE SECOND LANGUAGES

Foreign Languages In The Elementary School
USE FLES

FOREIGN MEDICAL GRADUATES *Oct. 1979*
CIJE: 33 RIE: 31 GC: 360
SN Medical students or physicians, either u.s. or foreign nationals, who have graduated from non-u.s. medical schools (note: includes foreign graduate medical students transferring from non-u.s. to u.s. medical schools)
UF Foreign Trained Physicians
BT Graduates
Physicians
RT Foreign Students
Graduate Medical Education
Graduate Medical Students
International Educational Exchange
Medical Schools
Medical Students
Study Abroad

FOREIGN NATIONALS *Sep. 1970*
CIJE: 76 RIE: 86 GC: 520
SN Citizens of countries other than those in which they reside
RT Citizenship
Developing Nations
Foreign Students
Foreign Workers
Immigrants
Indigenous Populations
International Programs
Migrants
Refugees

FOREIGN POLICY *Aug. 1968*
CIJE: 272 RIE: 342 GC: 610
UF Diplomatic Policy
International Policy
NT Imperialism
BT Policy
RT Diplomatic History
Foreign Countries
Foreign Diplomats
International Education
International Law
International Programs
International Relations
International Studies
International Trade
Nationalism
Peace
Political Science
Self Determination
World Affairs

Foreign Relations (1966 1976)
USE INTERNATIONAL RELATIONS

FOREIGN STUDENT ADVISERS *Dec. 1969*
CIJE: 29 RIE: 34 GC: 360
SN Faculty or staff members who coordinate services provided to foreign students and counsel them in academic and personal matters, including problems with government regulations such as visas, work permits, etc.
BT School Personnel
RT Faculty Advisers
Foreign Students
Student Adjustment
Student College Relationship
Student Exchange Programs
Student Personnel Workers

FOREIGN STUDENTS *Jul. 1966*
CIJE: 529 RIE: 723 GC: 360
UF International Students
Nonresident Students (1967 1980) (Foreign)
BT Students
RT Foreign Medical Graduates
Foreign Nationals
Foreign Student Advisers
International Educational Exchange
Student Exchange Programs

Foreign Trained Physicians
USE FOREIGN MEDICAL GRADUATES

FOREIGN WORKERS *Jul. 1966*
CIJE: 48 RIE: 59 GC: 630
SN Personnel working in other than their native countries
UF Undocumented Workers #
NT Braceros
BT Personnel
RT Foreign Diplomats
Foreign Nationals
Migrant Workers
Refugees

Foremen
USE SUPERVISORS

Forensics
USE PERSUASIVE DISCOURSE

Forester Aides
USE FORESTRY AIDES

FORESTRY *Jul. 1966*
CIJE: 101 RIE: 248 GC: 410
BT Technology
RT Agriculture
Botany
Conservation (Environment)
Conservation Education
Environmental Education
Forestry Aides
Forestry Occupations
Land Use
Lumber Industry
Natural Resources
Nurseries (Horticulture)
Soil Conservation
Soil Science
Trees
Wildlife Management

FORESTRY AIDES *Jul. 1966*
CIJE: 2 RIE: 12 GC: 410
UF Forester Aides
BT Paraprofessional Personnel
RT Forestry
Forestry Occupations

FORESTRY OCCUPATIONS *May. 1969*
CIJE: 22 RIE: 56 GC: 410
BT Occupations
RT Forestry
Forestry Aides
Lumber Industry
Off Farm Agricultural Occupations

Forgetting
USE MEMORY

FORM CLASSES (LANGUAGES) *Jul. 1966*
CIJE: 465 RIE: 366 GC: 450
UF Parts Of Speech
NT Adjectives
Adverbs
Determiners (Languages)
Function Words
Nouns
Prepositions
Pronouns
Verbs
BT Syntax
RT Case (Grammar)
Language Patterns
Morphology (Languages)
Phrase Structure
Plurals
Structural Grammar
Suffixes
Tenses (Grammar)
Traditional Grammar

FORMAL CRITICISM (1969 1980) *Mar. 1980*
CIJE: 245 RIE: 25 GC: 430
SN Invalid descriptor -- originally intended as a literary term, but used indiscriminately in indexing

FORMAL OPERATIONS *Aug. 1986*
CIJE: 50 RIE: 24 GC: 110
SN Fourth and final stage in piaget's theory of intellectual development, beginning at approximately 12 years, in which abstraction and suppositional capacities are acquired
BT Intelligence
RT Abstract Reasoning
Cognitive Ability
Cognitive Processes
Critical Thinking
Developmental Stages
Intellectual Development
Logical Thinking
Piagetian Theory

Formal Organizations
USE ORGANIZATIONS (GROUPS)

Format (Publications)
USE LAYOUT (PUBLICATIONS)

FORMATIVE EVALUATION *Jun. 1971*
CIJE: 496 RIE: 1117 GC: 310
SN Evaluation that is used to modify or improve products, programs, or activities and is based on feedback obtained during their planning and development
UF Process Evaluation
BT Evaluation
RT Curriculum Development
Educational Assessment
Educational Development
Educational Improvement
Educational Planning
Evaluation Utilization
Material Development
Pretesting
Program Development
Program Improvement
Self Evaluation (Groups)
Summative Evaluation
Systems Development

FORMER TEACHERS (1967 1980) *Mar. 1980*
CIJE: 2 RIE: 8 GC: 360
SN Invalid descriptor -- see such descriptors as "teacher retirement," "career change," etc.

Fossils
USE PALEONTOLOGY

FOSTER CARE *Aug. 1982*
CIJE: 37 RIE: 58 GC: 520
SN Care and rearing of children in private homes by persons other than the natural parents, with or without adoption
UF Foster Homes (1970 1982) (Children)
BT Social Services
RT Adoption
Adult Foster Care
Boarding Homes

= Two or more Descriptors are used to represent this term.
The term's main entry shows the appropriate coordination.

Child Caregivers
Child Care Occupations
Child Welfare
Foster Children
Foster Family
Group Homes

FOSTER CHILDREN *Nov. 1969*
CIJE: 150 RIE: 123 GC: 510
BT Children
RT Adopted Children
Biological Parents
Child Welfare
Foster Care
Foster Family

FOSTER FAMILY *Jul. 1966*
CIJE: 132 RIE: 131 GC: 510
UF Foster Parents
BT Family (Sociological Unit)
RT Adopted Children
Adoption
Adult Foster Care
Biological Parents
Child Welfare
Foster Care
Foster Children
Placement

Foster Homes (1970 1982) (Adults)
USE ADULT FOSTER CARE

Foster Homes (1970 1982) (Children)
USE FOSTER CARE

Foster Parents
USE FOSTER FAMILY

FOUND SPACES *Dec. 1972*
CIJE: 31 RIE: 32 GC: 920
SN Spaces which do not resemble traditional school facilities but can easily be converted, e.g. hotels, supermarkets, residences, and enclosed or semi-enclosed outdoor areas adjacent to new or existing facilities
BT Educational Facilities
RT Building Conversion
Facility Expansion
Facility Planning
Site Development
Space Utilization

Foundation Courses (Introductory)
USE INTRODUCTORY COURSES

Foundation Courses (Required)
USE REQUIRED COURSES

FOUNDATION PROGRAMS *Jul. 1966*
CIJE: 148 RIE: 259 GC: 620
SN Systems whereby state funds are used to supplement local or intermediate school district funds for elementary and secondary education -- a "minimum foundation" of financial support is usually guaranteed regardless of the local district's ability to support education (note: prior to mar80, this term was not scoped and was sometimes used to index "philanthropic foundations")
BT Programs
State Aid
RT Educational Equity (Finance)
Educational Finance
Equalization Aid
Federal Aid
Financial Support
Incentive Grants
School Funds
School Support

Foundations (Institutions)
USE PHILANTHROPIC FOUNDATIONS

FOUNDATIONS OF EDUCATION *May. 1971*
CIJE: 232 RIE: 160 GC: 400
SN The philosophy, social forces, institutions, and human relations upon which the formal educational system is based
NT Educational Anthropology
Educational Economics
Educational History
Educational Philosophy
Educational Principles
Educational Psychology
Educational Sociology
Educational Theories
RT Comparative Education
Education
Teacher Education Curriculum

FOUNDRIES *Jun. 1969*
CIJE: 19 RIE: 16 GC: 920
UF Iron Foundries
Steel Foundries
BT Facilities
RT Industrial Arts
Metal Industry
Metal Working

Four Day Work Week
USE FLEXIBLE WORKING HOURS

Four H Club Agents
USE EXTENSION AGENTS

FRACTIONS *Jul. 1966*
CIJE: 282 RIE: 226 GC: 480
UF Common Fractions (1966 1980)
NT Decimal Fractions
BT Numbers
RT Arithmetic
Reciprocals (Mathematics)

FRATERNITIES *Jul. 1966*
CIJE: 54 RIE: 20 GC: 520
BT Organizations (Groups)
RT Honor Societies
National Organizations
Professional Associations
Social Organizations
Sororities
Student Organizations

FREE CHOICE TRANSFER PROGRAMS *Jul. 1966*
CIJE: 15 RIE: 59 GC: 330
SN Transfer programs that allow students to attend the school of their choice
BT Transfer Programs
RT Open Enrollment
School Choice
Transfer Policy
Transfer Students

FREE EDUCATION *Oct. 1980*
CIJE: 14 RIE: 7 GC: 330
SN Education that does not require the payment of tuition (note: do not confuse with "free schools")
BT Education
RT Access To Education
Compulsory Education
Open Universities
Private Education
Public Education
Tuition

Free Play
USE PLAY

FREE SCHOOLS *Mar. 1980*
CIJE: 21 RIE: 26 GC: 340
SN Alternative schools offering a completely voluntaristic framework, including an unstructured curriculum and a spontaneous learning environment -- students are free to select what to learn, with whom, when, and how -- grades, competition, and comparisons between individuals are discarded (note: do not confuse with "free education" or "freedom schools")
BT Schools
RT Experimental Schools
Humanistic Education
Nongraded Student Evaluation
Nontraditional Education
Open Education
Progressive Education
Relevance (Education)
Student Interests
Student Rights

Free Translation
USE TRANSLATION

Free Universities
USE EXPERIMENTAL COLLEGES

FREEDOM OF INFORMATION *Aug. 1986*
CIJE: 19 RIE: 43 GC: 610
SN Freedom from interference with the flow of information, especially unrestricted public access to government records and documents without compromising rights of privacy or endangering government security
UF Right To Know
BT Access To Information
RT Academic Freedom
Censorship
Civil Liberties
Confidential Records
Democracy
Disclosure
Freedom Of Speech
Government Publications
Information Dissemination
Intellectual Freedom
Journalism
Laws
News Media
Privacy

FREEDOM OF SPEECH *Jul. 1966*
CIJE: 702 RIE: 667 GC: 610
UF Freedom Of The Press
BT Civil Liberties
RT Academic Freedom
Censorship
Civil Rights
Democracy
Due Process
Freedom Of Information
Intellectual Freedom
Journalism
News Media
Press Opinion
Student Rights
Teacher Rights

Freedom Of The Press
USE FREEDOM OF SPEECH

Freedom Of Thought
USE INTELLECTUAL FREEDOM

FREEDOM SCHOOLS *Jul. 1966*
CIJE: 18 RIE: 11 GC: 340
SN Schools or classes outside the regular school system, organized to teach minority group children about their cultural heritage or, on occasion, when strikes or other problems prevent these children from attending the public schools (note: do not confuse with "free schools")
BT Schools
RT Civil Rights
Cultural Awareness
Cultural Education
Cultural Enrichment
Nontraditional Education

Freedom To Read
USE INTELLECTUAL FREEDOM

FREEHAND DRAWING *Aug. 1968*
CIJE: 359 RIE: 115 GC: 420
UF Drawing (Freehand)
BT Visual Arts
RT Cartoons
Childrens Art
Creative Art
Painting (Visual Arts)

FRENCH *Jul. 1966*
CIJE: 2828 RIE: 1569 GC: 440
BT Romance Languages
RT French Literature

French Canadian Literature
USE CANADIAN LITERATURE

FRENCH LITERATURE *Apr. 1969*
CIJE: 354 RIE: 52 GC: 430
BT Literature
RT French

Frequency Distributions
USE STATISTICAL DISTRIBUTIONS

FRESHMAN COMPOSITION *Aug. 1986*
CIJE: 72 RIE: 75 GC: 400
SN Writing instruction intended for first-year college students
BT College Curriculum
Writing (Composition)
Writing Instruction
RT College English
College Freshmen

Freshmen (1967 1980) (First Year College Students)
USE COLLEGE FRESHMEN

Freshmen (1967 1980) (Grade 9)
USE HIGH SCHOOL FRESHMEN

FRIENDSHIP *Jul. 1966*
CIJE: 329 RIE: 247 GC: 510
UF Childhood Friendship (1966 1980)
BT Interpersonal Relationship
RT Dating (Social)
Peer Relationship
Popularity
Prosocial Behavior
Significant Others
Social Development
Social Life

FRINGE BENEFITS *Jul. 1966*
CIJE: 279 RIE: 623 GC: 630
UF Employee Fringe Benefits
Perquisites (Employment)
RT Compensation (Remuneration)
Early Retirement
Employee Assistance Programs
Employees
Employer Employee Relationship
Employer Supported Day Care
Employment
Health Insurance
Labor Relations
Leaves Of Absence
Personnel Policy
Preretirement Education
Retirement Benefits
Salaries
Scope Of Bargaining
Teacher Employment Benefits
Unemployment Insurance
Vacations
Wages

Fruit And Vegetable Inspectors
USE FOOD AND DRUG INSPECTORS

Fte
USE FULL TIME EQUIVALENCY

FUEL CONSUMPTION *Sep. 1968*
CIJE: 249 RIE: 264 GC: 410
RT Air Conditioning
Air Conditioning Equipment
Conservation (Environment)
Depleted Resources
Energy Audits
Energy Conservation
Energy Management
Fuels
Heating
Heat Recovery
Temperature
Thermal Environment
Ventilation

Fuel Oil
USE FUELS

FUELS *Jul. 1966*
CIJE: 316 RIE: 299 GC: 410
UF Diesel Fuel
Fuel Oil
Gasoline
Heating Oils
Natural Gases
NT Coal
RT Agricultural Machinery
Energy
Energy Conservation
Energy Education
Energy Occupations
Engines
Fuel Consumption
Heat
Heating
Kinetics
Minerals

Mining
Motor Vehicles
Natural Resources
Petroleum Industry
Power Technology
Utilities

Ful
USE FULANI

Fula
USE FULANI

FULANI *Jul. 1966*
CIJE: RIE: 4 GC: 440
UF Ful
Fula
Fulfulde
Peul
Pheul
BT African Languages

Fulfulde
USE FULANI

FULL STATE FUNDING *Jan. 1973*
CIJE: 43 RIE: 130 GC: 620
SN Financial support provided wholly by a state government
BT Financial Support
State Aid
RT Educational Finance
Equalization Aid
Expenditure Per Student
Government School Relationship
Institutional Autonomy
School District Autonomy
School District Spending
School Support
School Taxes
State Federal Aid
Tax Allocation

FULL TIME EQUIVALENCY *Mar. 1980*
CIJE: 7 RIE: 113 GC: 320
SN Part-time status (as of students, personnel, etc.) expressed as a percentage of corresponding full-time status
UF Fte
BT Status
RT Employment Level
Enrollment
Enrollment Rate
Full Time Faculty
Full Time Students
Measurement
Part Time Employment
Part Time Faculty
Part Time Students

FULL TIME FACULTY *Oct. 1979*
CIJE: 49 RIE: 186 GC: 360
SN Faculty members considered by the institution to be carrying a full workload
UF Full Time Teachers
BT Faculty
RT Employment Level
Faculty Workload
Full Time Equivalency
Part Time Faculty
Teacher Employment
Teachers
Teaching Load
Tenured Faculty
Working Hours

FULL TIME STUDENTS *Oct. 1979*
CIJE: 34 RIE: 342 GC: 360
SN Students carrying a full credit load as defined by the institution
BT Students
RT Day Programs
Day Students
Enrollment
Full Time Equivalency
On Campus Students
Part Time Students

Full Time Teachers
USE FULL TIME FACULTY

FUNCTION WORDS *Jul. 1966*
CIJE: 116 RIE: 81 GC: 450
UF Functors
BT Form Classes (Languages)
RT Determiners (Languages)
Morphology (Languages)
Prepositions
Sentence Structure
Structural Grammar
Surface Structure
Syntax
Tagmemic Analysis

Functional Illiteracy (1968 1980)
USE FUNCTIONAL LITERACY

FUNCTIONAL LITERACY *Mar. 1980*
CIJE: 230 RIE: 352 GC: 460
SN Ability to read and write at the level necessary to participate effectively in society
UF Functional Illiteracy (1968 1980)
Survival Literacy
NT Functional Reading
BT Literacy
RT Adult Basic Education
Adult Literacy
Adult Reading Programs
Basic Skills
Literacy Education
Minimum Competencies
Reading Skills
Writing Skills

Functional Notional Syllabi
USE NOTIONAL FUNCTIONAL SYLLABI

FUNCTIONAL READING *Jul. 1966*
CIJE: 71 RIE: 126 GC: 460
SN Ability to read nonacademic, nonfiction materials such as bus schedules, tax forms, recipes, street signs, insurance forms, and job-related items
UF Survival Reading Skills
BT Functional Literacy
Reading
RT Adult Literacy
Adult Reading Programs
Content Area Reading
Literacy Education
Reading Skills

Functional Systems Theory
USE SYSTEMS ANALYSIS

FUNCTIONS (MATHEMATICS) *Apr. 1982*
CIJE: 128 RIE: 59 GC: 480
SN Mathematical associations in which a variable is so related to another that for each value assumed by one there is a value determined for the other
UF Mappings (Mathematics)
BT Mathematical Formulas
RT Calculus
Equations (Mathematics)
Logarithms
Mathematical Concepts
Statistical Distributions
Transformations (Mathematics)
Vectors (Mathematics)

Functors
USE FUNCTION WORDS

FUND RAISING *Feb. 1978*
CIJE: 478 RIE: 268 GC: 620
SN Identifying, soliciting, acquiring, and cultivating financial resources (note: prior to feb78, the instruction "fund raising, use financial support" was carried in the thesaurus)
NT Grantsmanship
RT Capital
Donors
Educational Finance
Endowment Funds
Finance Occupations
Financial Needs
Financial Problems
Financial Services
Financial Support
Income
Institutional Advancement
Investment
Political Campaigns
Private Financial Support
Program Proposals
Proposal Writing
Scholarship Funds
School Funds
Trusts (Financial)

FUNDAMENTAL CONCEPTS *Jul. 1966*
CIJE: 359 RIE: 456 GC: 110
SN Elementary or essential ideas and constructs
NT Compensation (Concept)
Conservation (Concept)
Object Permanence
RT Concept Formation
Concept Teaching
Geographic Concepts
Mathematical Concepts
Scientific Concepts

Fundamental Education (Adults)
USE ADULT BASIC EDUCATION

Fundamental Skills (Daily Living)
USE DAILY LIVING SKILLS

Fundamental Skills (School)
USE BASIC SKILLS

Funding
USE FINANCIAL SUPPORT

FURNITURE *Jul. 1966*
CIJE: 32 RIE: 64 GC: 910
NT Classroom Furniture
BT Equipment
RT Equipment Storage
Furniture Arrangement
Furniture Design
Furniture Industry
Home Furnishings

Furniture (Classroom)
USE CLASSROOM FURNITURE

FURNITURE ARRANGEMENT *Jul. 1966*
CIJE: 56 RIE: 47 GC: 920
BT Organization
RT Classroom Furniture
Flexible Facilities
Furniture
Furniture Design
Home Furnishings
Interior Design
Interior Space
Space Utilization

FURNITURE DESIGN *Jul. 1966*
CIJE: 41 RIE: 47 GC: 420
BT Design
RT Classroom Furniture
Design Crafts
Design Requirements
Equipment Storage
Furniture
Furniture Arrangement
Furniture Industry
Lumber Industry

FURNITURE INDUSTRY *Aug. 1969*
CIJE: 5 RIE: 6 GC: 650
BT Manufacturing Industry
RT Furniture
Furniture Design
Home Furnishings
Lumber Industry
Woodworking

Further Education
USE ADULT EDUCATION

FUSED CURRICULUM *Jul. 1966*
CIJE: 40 RIE: 379 GC: 350
SN Curriculum that combines two or more subjects and studies their interrelationship (e.g., a high school course that combines the study of literature and history)
BT Curriculum
RT Experimental Curriculum
Integrated Curriculum
Interdisciplinary Approach
Unified Studies Curriculum

Future Studies
USE FUTURES (OF SOCIETY)

FUTURES (OF SOCIETY) *Jun. 1973*
CIJE: 4425 RIE: 3330 GC: 520
UF Alternative Futures
Educational Futures #
Future Studies
Futurism
Futuristics
Futurology
RT Appropriate Technology
Culture Lag
Decision Making
Delphi Technique
Emerging Occupations
Long Range Planning
Planning
Prediction
Public Policy
Relevance (Education)
Revolution
Science And Society
Social Change
Social Indicators
Technological Advancement
Trend Analysis
Values
World Affairs

Futures Planning
USE LONG RANGE PLANNING

Futurism
USE FUTURES (OF SOCIETY)

Futuristics
USE FUTURES (OF SOCIETY)

Futurology
USE FUTURES (OF SOCIETY)

G Scores
USE GRADE EQUIVALENT SCORES

GA *Jul. 1966*
CIJE: 1 RIE: 4 GC: 440
BT African Languages

GAME THEORY *Jul. 1966*
CIJE: 269 RIE: 191 GC: 810
BT Operations Research
Theories
RT Cybernetics
Decision Making
Heuristics
Management Games
Mathematical Logic
Mathematical Models
Monte Carlo Methods
Probability
Problem Solving
Risk
Simulation
Statistics

Gamekeeping
USE WILDLIFE MANAGEMENT

GAMES *Jul. 1966*
CIJE: 920 RIE: 706 GC: 470
NT Childrens Games
Educational Games
Management Games
Puzzles
BT Activities
RT Athletics
Play
Recreational Activities
Toys

GANDA *Jul. 1966*
CIJE: RIE: 8 GC: 440
UF Luganda
BT Bantu Languages

Garbage
USE SOLID WASTES

Gardeners
USE GROUNDS KEEPERS

Garment Industry
USE FASHION INDUSTRY

Gas Utilities
USE UTILITIES

Gas Welding
USE WELDING

= Two or more Descriptors are used to represent this term.
The term's main entry shows the appropriate coordination.

Gasoline
USE FUELS

Gauges
USE MEASUREMENT EQUIPMENT

GBAYA *Jul. 1966*
CIJE: RIE: 2 GC: 440
UF Gbeya
BT African Languages

Gbeya
USE GBAYA

Ged Programs
USE HIGH SCHOOL EQUIVALENCY PROGRAMS

Gender (Sex)
USE SEX

Gender Differences (Sex)
USE SEX DIFFERENCES

Gender Identity (Sex)
USE SEXUAL IDENTITY

GENEALOGY *Jan. 1985*
CIJE: 27 RIE: 23 GC: 430
SN History or account of lineal descent from an ancestor or ancestors
UF Ancestral Lineage
Family Trees
BT Family History
RT Ethnic Origins
Extended Family
Family (Sociological Unit)
Information Sources
Kinship

General Business Education
USE BASIC BUSINESS EDUCATION

GENERAL EDUCATION *Jul. 1966*
CIJE: 1280 RIE: 1043 GC: 400
SN Integrated learning experiences structured across subject disciplines to provide the set of skills and knowledge needed to function in society
UF General High Schools (1966 1980)
Liberal Education
BT Education
RT Academic Education
Liberal Arts

General Educational Development Programs
USE HIGH SCHOOL EQUIVALENCY PROGRAMS

General High Schools (1966 1980)
USE GENERAL EDUCATION

General Mechanics
USE MECHANICS (PROCESS)

General Methods Courses
USE METHODS COURSES

General Practice (Medicine)
USE FAMILY PRACTICE (MEDICINE)

GENERAL SCIENCE *Jul. 1966*
CIJE: 255 RIE: 233 GC: 490
SN Science courses, frequently introductory, that include such components as physical, biological, space, and earth sciences
BT Science Curriculum
RT Core Curriculum
Science Education
Science Instruction

General Semantics
USE SEMANTICS

General Shop
USE SHOP CURRICULUM

GENERALIZABILITY THEORY *Oct. 1983*
CIJE: 50 RIE: 46 GC: 810
SN Statistical model for interpreting variance components associated with a specified universe of conditions
BT Theories
RT Analysis Of Variance
Data Collection
Data Interpretation
Error Of Measurement
Interrater Reliability
Mathematical Models
Measurement
Multivariate Analysis
Reliability
Research Design
Sample Size
Sampling
Scores
Statistical Analysis
Statistical Data
Statistical Distributions
Statistical Inference
Test Interpretation
Test Reliability
Test Theory
True Scores

GENERALIZATION *Jun. 1969*
CIJE: 495 RIE: 225 GC: 110
SN Process of drawing inferences or forming general conclusions from a number of specific instances -- also, the tendency to make the same response to new but similar stimuli
NT Stimulus Generalization
BT Abstract Reasoning
Learning Processes
RT Association (Psychology)
Concept Formation
Concept Teaching
Experiments
Induction
Inferences
Learning Theories
Mediation Theory
Patterned Responses
Research Methodology
Scientific Methodology
Theories
Transfer Of Training
Validity

GENERATION GAP *Apr. 1970*
CIJE: 219 RIE: 71 GC: 530
RT Age Differences
Intergenerational Programs
Parent Child Relationship
Student Alienation
Youth Problems

GENERATIVE GRAMMAR *Oct. 1968*
CIJE: 189 RIE: 139 GC: 450
SN A grammar, or system of rules, designed to generate (i.e., produce or predict) all of and only the well-formed (i.e., "grammatical") sentences of a language
NT Transformational Generative Grammar
BT Linguistic Theory
RT Generative Phonology
Grammar
Sentence Structure
Syntax

GENERATIVE PHONOLOGY *Sep. 1974*
CIJE: 47 RIE: 46 GC: 450
SN Theory or system of rules which describes or predicts well-formed phonological outputs, and is used to express the ability of speakers to produce the sounds of their native language
BT Linguistic Theory
Phonology
RT Generative Grammar
Phonemics
Phonetics

Generative Transformational Grammar
USE TRANSFORMATIONAL GENERATIVE GRAMMAR

GENETIC ENGINEERING *Oct. 1982*
CIJE: 63 RIE: 22 GC: 490
SN Human manipulation of genetic material to effect biological change
UF Recombinant Dna #
BT Genetics
Technology
RT Biochemistry
Biological Influences
Biology
Culturing Techniques
Cytology
Dna
Drug Therapy
Embryology
Medicine
Microbiology
Nucleic Acids
Radiation Biology
Radiology
Reproduction (Biology)
Scientific Research

GENETICS *Jul. 1966*
CIJE: 806 RIE: 274 GC: 490
SN Biological science which deals with the phenomena of heredity and the variation between parents and offspring
NT Genetic Engineering
BT Biological Sciences
RT Agriculture
Biological Parents
Biology
Botany
Congenital Impairments
Dna
Downs Syndrome
Embryology
Enzymes
Evolution
Heredity
Medicine
Microbiology
Nature Nurture Controversy
Nucleic Acids
Prenatal Influences
Radiation Biology
Radioisotopes
Reproduction (Biology)
Rh Factors
Sickle Cell Anemia
Sociobiology
Zoology

GEOGRAPHIC CONCEPTS *Jul. 1966*
CIJE: 191 RIE: 193 GC: 400
SN Abstract ideas related to geography that are usually emphasized in instruction (i.e., mobility, population distribution, demographic variation, spatial distribution, microclimate, energy flow, etc.)
RT Concept Teaching
Fundamental Concepts
Geography
Geography Instruction

Geographic Dialects
USE REGIONAL DIALECTS

GEOGRAPHIC DISTRIBUTION *Jul. 1966*
CIJE: 162 RIE: 452 GC: 550
BT Demography
RT Community Size
Ethnic Distribution
Geography
Human Geography
Incidence
Physical Geography
Population Distribution
Racial Distribution
School District Size
Teacher Distribution

GEOGRAPHIC LOCATION *Jul. 1966*
CIJE: 159 RIE: 324 GC: 550
RT Access To Education
Cartography
Climate
Distance
Geography
Physical Geography
Place Of Residence
Proximity
Relocation
School Location
Site Analysis
Topography

Geographic Mobility (1980)
USE MIGRATION

GEOGRAPHIC REGIONS *Jul. 1966*
CIJE: 189 RIE: 598 GC: 550
UF Areas (Geographic)
NT Developed Nations
Developing Nations
Foreign Countries
Low Income Counties
Low Income States
Metropolitan Areas
Physical Divisions (Geographic)
Political Divisions (Geographic)
Poverty Areas
Rural Areas
Urban Areas
RT Area Studies
Geography
Physical Geography
Place Of Residence
Regional Attitudes
Regional Characteristics
Regional Dialects
Regional Schools
School Districts

GEOGRAPHY *Jul. 1966*
CIJE: 480 RIE: 693 GC: 400
NT Human Geography
Physical Geography
World Geography
BT Social Sciences
RT Area Studies
Atlases
Cartography
Conservation Education
Geographic Concepts
Geographic Distribution
Geographic Location
Geographic Regions
Geography Instruction
Maps
Map Skills
Oceanography
Physical Divisions (Geographic)
Political Divisions (Geographic)
Social Science Research
Social Scientists
Social Studies
Topography

GEOGRAPHY INSTRUCTION *Jul. 1966*
CIJE: 818 RIE: 544 GC: 400
BT Instruction
RT Geographic Concepts
Geography

GEOLOGY *Jul. 1966*
CIJE: 946 RIE: 339 GC: 490
NT Mineralogy
Paleontology
BT Earth Science
RT Asbestos
Coal
Crystallography
Geophysics
Geothermal Energy
Minerals
Mining
Oceanography
Physical Geography
Plate Tectonics
Scientific Research
Seismology
Soil Science

GEOMETRIC CONCEPTS *Jul. 1966*
CIJE: 1047 RIE: 397 GC: 480
NT Area
Congruence (Mathematics)
Orthographic Projection
Vectors (Mathematics)
Volume (Mathematics)
BT Mathematical Concepts
RT Geometric Constructions
Geometry
Patternmaking
Symmetry

GEOMETRIC CONSTRUCTIONS *Apr. 1982*
CIJE: 97 RIE: 21 GC: 480
SN Diagrams and other forms that illustrate geometric relationships, figures, or patterns
BT Visual Aids
RT Diagrams
Geometric Concepts
Geometry
Mathematics Materials

Geometrical Optics
USE OPTICS

Geometrodynamics
USE RELATIVITY

= Two or more Descriptors are used to represent this term.
The term's main entry shows the appropriate coordination.

GEOMETRY *Jul. 1966*
CIJE: 861 RIE: 549 GC: 480
NT Analytic Geometry
Plane Geometry
Solid Geometry
Topology
BT Mathematics
RT Congruence (Mathematics)
Geometric Concepts
Geometric Constructions
Symmetry
Transformations (Mathematics)
Vectors (Mathematics)

GEOPHYSICS *Dec. 1969*
CIJE: 90 RIE: 25 GC: 490
NT Plate Tectonics
BT Earth Science
RT Geology
Geothermal Energy
Gravity (Physics)
Mineralogy
Mining
Physics
Seismology
Wind Energy

Georgian
USE CAUCASIAN LANGUAGES

Geoscience
USE EARTH SCIENCE

GEOTHERMAL ENERGY *Oct. 1984*
CIJE: 7 RIE: 13 GC: 490
SN Power derived from the earth's heat
BT Energy
RT Alternative Energy Sources
Electricity
Geology
Geophysics
Heat
Power Technology
Water Resources

GERIATRICS *Aug. 1968*
CIJE: 324 RIE: 138 GC: 210
SN Branch of medicine dealing with the physiology and pathology of old age
BT Medicine
RT Aging (Individuals)
Educational Gerontology
Gerontology
Medical Services
Older Adults

GERMAN *Jul. 1966*
CIJE: 1231 RIE: 804 GC: 440
NT Yiddish
BT Indo European Languages
RT German Literature

GERMAN LITERATURE *Apr. 1969*
CIJE: 259 RIE: 42 GC: 430
BT Literature
RT German

German Measles
USE RUBELLA

GERONTOLOGY *Aug. 1976*
CIJE: 836 RIE: 446 GC: 400
SN Scientific study of aging and problems of the aged
NT Educational Gerontology
BT Social Sciences
RT Adult Development
Aging (Individuals)
Geriatrics
Older Adults
Retirement
Social Science Research
Social Scientists

GESTALT THERAPY *Jan. 1985*
CIJE: 41 RIE: 14 GC: 230
SN Form of psychotherapy focusing on the totality of the individual's current functioning and relationships rather than on past experiences or developmental history -- individual or group techniques are designed to elicit spontaneous feelings and self-awareness
BT Holistic Approach
Psychotherapy
RT Counseling Techniques
Desensitization
Laboratory Training
Phenomenology
Self Actualization
Self Concept

Gestation
USE PREGNANCY

Gestures (Deaf Communication)
USE SIGN LANGUAGE

Gestures (Nonverbal Communication)
USE BODY LANGUAGE

GHETTOS *Jul. 1966*
CIJE: 193 RIE: 169 GC: 550
SN Residential areas, usually within cities, in which members of a particular racial or cultural group live, primarily because of social, economic, or legal factors (note: prior to mar80, this term was not scoped and was often used synonymously with "slums")
RT Anti Semitism
Ethnic Groups
Housing Discrimination
Inner City
Jews
Racial Discrimination
Racial Segregation
Slums
Social Discrimination
Subcultures
Urban Population

GIFTED *Jul. 1966*
CIJE: 2174 RIE: 1704 GC: 120
UF Gifted Children
Gifted Teachers
Gifted Youth
Mentally Advanced Children
NT Academically Gifted
Gifted Disabled
Gifted Disadvantaged
BT Exceptional Persons
RT Ability
Achievement
Aptitude
Exceptional Child Research
Special Education
Special Education Teachers
Talent

Gifted Children
USE GIFTED

GIFTED DISABLED *Oct. 1983*
CIJE: 3 RIE: 4 GC: 220
SN Persons of superior ability or potential who also have physical, sensory, emotional, or behavioral disabilities
UF Gifted Handicapped
BT Gifted
RT Disabilities
Gifted Disadvantaged

GIFTED DISADVANTAGED *Oct. 1983*
CIJE: 10 RIE: 22 GC: 540
SN Persons of superior ability or potential who are also economically, educationally, or socially disadvantaged
BT Disadvantaged
Gifted
RT Gifted Disabled

Gifted Handicapped
USE GIFTED DISABLED

Gifted Students
USE ACADEMICALLY GIFTED

Gifted Teachers
USE GIFTED

Gifted Youth
USE GIFTED

Girls
USE FEMALES

Girls Clubs (1966 1980)
USE YOUTH CLUBS

GLARE *Apr. 1969*
CIJE: 12 RIE: 19 GC: 920
RT Light
Lighting
Lighting Design
Luminescence
Visual Environment
Windows

GLASS *Jul. 1966*
CIJE: 20 RIE: 24 GC: 910
RT Art Materials
Ceramics
Glaziers
Industrial Arts

Glass Installers
USE GLAZIERS

GLASS WALLS *Jul. 1966*
CIJE: 12 RIE: 10 GC: 920
SN Walls consisting largely of windows
UF Window Walls
BT Structural Elements (Construction)
RT Classroom Design
Windows

GLAZIERS *Jul. 1966*
CIJE: RIE: 10 GC: 640
UF Glass Installers
BT Skilled Workers
RT Glass

Glee Clubs
USE SINGING

GLOBAL APPROACH *Oct. 1974*
CIJE: 1004 RIE: 1216 GC: 310
SN Approach to social, cultural, scientific, and humanistic questions involving an orientation to the world as a single interacting system
UF International Approach
Worldmindedness
Worldwide Approach
BT Holistic Approach
RT Citizenship Education
Cultural Awareness
Group Unity
Intercultural Programs
Interdisciplinary Approach
International Cooperation
International Relations
Social Sciences
World Affairs
World Problems

GLOSSARIES *Jul. 1966*
CIJE: 128 RIE: 790 GC: 730
SN Dictionaries of special or technical terms with limited subject scope
BT Dictionaries
RT Definitions
Lexicography
Thesauri
Vocabulary

GLOTTOCHRONOLOGY *Jul. 1966*
CIJE: 5 RIE: 5 GC: 450
SN A technique for estimating by statistical comparison of vocabulary samples the time during which two or more languages have evolved separately from a common source
BT Diachronic Linguistics
RT Comparative Analysis
Etymology
Language Classification
Language Research
Languages
Lexicography
Lexicology
Linguistics
Vocabulary

Glues
USE ADHESIVES

Goal Attainment
USE SUCCESS

GOAL ORIENTATION *Jul. 1966*
CIJE: 607 RIE: 778 GC: 120
SN Psychological disposition toward achieving ones objectives
BT Orientation
RT Achievement Need
Aspiration
Career Planning
Competition
Coping
Delay Of Gratification
Failure
Fear Of Success
Motivation
Need Gratification
Objectives
Personality Assessment
Psychological Characteristics
Psychological Needs
Student Educational Objectives
Success
Values Clarification

Goals
USE OBJECTIVES

GOLF *Jun. 1975*
CIJE: 22 RIE: 18 GC: 470
BT Athletics
RT Lifetime Sports

Gonorrhea
USE VENEREAL DISEASES

Good Citizenship
USE CITIZENSHIP

GOODNESS OF FIT *Nov. 1970*
CIJE: 186 RIE: 194 GC: 820
SN Statistical estimate of the extent to which a score distribution, or other numerical series of observations, differs significantly from the numerical values predicted by a mathematical model (i.e., an estimation of how well the theory fits the data)
BT Statistical Analysis
RT Factor Analysis
Mathematical Models
Maximum Likelihood Statistics
Statistical Significance
Statistics

GOVERNANCE *Jul. 1966*
CIJE: 1074 RIE: 1962 GC: 330
SN The policy-making, objective-setting, and exercise of authority in an organization, institution, or agency -- includes administrative or management functions to the extent that they relate to the execution of policy and authority
NT Administration
Community Control
Federal Regulation
RT Administrative Organization
College Governing Councils
Governing Boards
Government (Administrative Body)
Government School Relationship
Institutional Autonomy
Policy Formation
Politics
Professional Autonomy
School District Autonomy
Tribal Sovereignty
Trustees

GOVERNING BOARDS *Jul. 1966*
CIJE: 511 RIE: 645 GC: 330
SN Group charged with the responsibility for some degree of control over managing the affairs of public or private institutions
UF Board Of Regents
Board Of Trustees
NT Boards Of Education
BT Organizations (Groups)
RT Administration
Administrative Organization
Advisory Committees
Board Administrator Relationship
College Administration
Committees
Governance
Institutional Administration
Policy Formation

School Administration
State Departments Of Education
Trustees

GOVERNMENT (ADMINISTRATIVE BODY) *Jul. 1966*
CIJE: 216 RIE: 434 GC: 610
NT Federal Government
Local Government
State Government
Student Government
BT Organizations (Groups)
RT Agencies
Capitalism
Civics
Communism
Constitutional History
Constitutional Law
Depository Libraries
Fascism
Governance
Governmental Structure
Government Employees
Government Libraries
Government Publications
Government Role
Government School Relationship
Hearings
Legislation
Loyalty Oaths
Nonprofit Organizations
Police
Political Affiliation
Political Campaigns
Political Candidates
Politics
Producer Services
Public Administration
Public Administration Education
Public Agencies
Public Service Occupations
Socialism
Totalitarianism
United States Government (Course)

Government Agencies
USE PUBLIC AGENCIES

Government Documents
USE GOVERNMENT PUBLICATIONS

GOVERNMENT EMPLOYEES *Jul. 1966*
CIJE: 456 RIE: 587 GC: 610
UF Civil Service Employees
Public Employees
NT Extension Agents
Food And Drug Inspectors
Foreign Diplomats
Immigration Inspectors
Military Personnel
Police
Public Officials
Public School Teachers
BT Personnel
RT City Government
Federal Government
Government (Administrative Body)
Governmental Structure
Local Government
Public Service Occupations
Service Workers
State Government

Government Functions
USE GOVERNMENT ROLE

GOVERNMENT LIBRARIES *Jul. 1966*
CIJE: 50 RIE: 120 GC: 710
SN Special libraries maintained out of government funds (note: use a more specific term if possible)
UF Federal Libraries #
NT National Libraries
State Libraries
BT Special Libraries
RT Archives
Depository Libraries
Government (Administrative Body)
Law Libraries

GOVERNMENT PUBLICATIONS *Nov. 1968*
CIJE: 249 RIE: 675 GC: 730
SN Publications that are funded, prepared, and/or distributed by national, state, or local government units
UF Government Documents
Public Documents
BT Publications
RT Depository Libraries
Freedom Of Information
Government (Administrative Body)

GOVERNMENT ROLE *Jul. 1966*
CIJE: 3054 RIE: 4188 GC: 610
UF Congress Role
Government Functions
RT Conservatism
Constitutional History
Constitutional Law
Copyrights
Court Role
Federal Regulation
Government (Administrative Body)
Government School Relationship
Institutional Autonomy
Institutional Role
Liberalism
National Security
Patents
Public Agencies
Public Policy
Revenue Sharing
School District Autonomy
State Action
Tribal Sovereignty
Trust Responsibility (Government)

GOVERNMENT SCHOOL RELATIONSHIP *Sep. 1977*
CIJE: 1061 RIE: 1573 GC: 330
SN Any interaction of an educational institution or school district with a local, provincial, or central government
UF School Government Relationship
NT State School District Relationship
BT Relationship
RT Block Grants
City Government
Community Control
Compulsory Education
Constitutional Law
Developing Institutions
Educational Legislation
Federal Aid
Federal Government
Federal Regulation
Federal State Relationship
Full State Funding
Governance
Government (Administrative Body)
Government Role
Institutional Autonomy
Local Government
National Competency Tests
Politics Of Education
Private School Aid
Public Policy
Public Service
School Administration
School Attitudes
School District Autonomy
School Involvement
School Role
Schools
State Aid
State Government
Student Records

Government Structure
USE GOVERNMENTAL STRUCTURE

GOVERNMENTAL STRUCTURE *Jul. 1966*
CIJE: 121 RIE: 243 GC: 610
UF Government Structure
BT Group Structure
RT Bureaucracy
Constitutional History
Constitutional Law
Government (Administrative Body)
Government Employees
Public Administration Education
Social Structure

Grade A Year Integration (1966 1980)
USE SCHOOL DESEGREGATION

Grade Average
USE GRADE POINT AVERAGE

Grade Cards
USE REPORT CARDS

GRADE CHARTS (1966 1980) *Mar. 1980*
CIJE: 1 RIE: 5 GC: 310
SN Invalid descriptor -- used for curriculum charts that are organized by instructional program "grades," or for student skill charts that either record scholastic "grades" or student progression through several instructional program "grades"

Grade Equivalent Scales (1967 1980)
USE GRADE EQUIVALENT SCORES

GRADE EQUIVALENT SCORES *Nov. 1970*
CIJE: 46 RIE: 87 GC: 820
SN Ability or achievement scores that have been converted to the grade level norm -- usually expressed in years and tenths, e.g., 6.4 means sixth grade, fourth month (note: do not use for readability level of written material)
UF Grade Equivalent Scales (1967 1980)
Grade Scores
G Scores
BT Scores
RT Equated Scores
Equivalency Tests
High School Equivalency Programs
Measurement
Measurement Techniques
Norm Referenced Tests
Raw Scores
Student Certification
Testing
Test Norms
Weighted Scores

GRADE INFLATION *Oct. 1979*
CIJE: 54 RIE: 51 GC: 320
SN A continuous rise in the proportion of higher scholastic grades awarded, often associated with a perceived laxity in academic standards
UF Inflated Grades
BT Grades (Scholastic)
RT Academic Standards
Grade Point Average
Grading
Scoring

Grade Levels
USE INSTRUCTIONAL PROGRAM DIVISIONS

Grade Organization (1966 1980)
USE INSTRUCTIONAL PROGRAM DIVISIONS

GRADE POINT AVERAGE *Jul. 1966*
CIJE: 574 RIE: 920 GC: 820
SN A measure of scholastic achievement in several subjects or courses obtained by dividing the sum of the total grade points by the total number of hours of course work (note: prior to mar80, the instruction "grade average, use class average" was carried in the thesaurus)
UF Grade Average
Quality Point Ratio
BT Grades (Scholastic)
RT Academic Standards
Class Rank
Grade Inflation
Grade Prediction

GRADE PREDICTION *Jul. 1966*
CIJE: 184 RIE: 225 GC: 820
SN Estimation of future achievement, expressed in scholastic grades or marks, on the basis of past and current information
BT Prediction
RT Grade Point Average
Grades (Scholastic)
Grading
Predictive Measurement

GRADE REPETITION *Jul. 1966*
CIJE: 58 RIE: 105 GC: 320
RT Academic Failure
Low Achievement
Student Promotion
Underachievement

Grade Scores
USE GRADE EQUIVALENT SCORES

GRADE 1 *Jul. 1966*
CIJE: 841 RIE: 1577 GC: 340
BT Instructional Program Divisions
RT Elementary Education
Primary Education

GRADE 2 *Jul. 1966*
CIJE: 441 RIE: 1102 GC: 340
BT Instructional Program Divisions
RT Elementary Education
Primary Education

GRADE 3 *Jul. 1966*
CIJE: 497 RIE: 1188 GC: 340
BT Instructional Program Divisions
RT Elementary Education
Primary Education

GRADE 4 *Jul. 1966*
CIJE: 551 RIE: 1348 GC: 340
BT Instructional Program Divisions
RT Elementary Education
Intermediate Grades

GRADE 5 *Jul. 1966*
CIJE: 627 RIE: 1438 GC: 340
BT Instructional Program Divisions
RT Elementary Education
Intermediate Grades

GRADE 6 *Jul. 1966*
CIJE: 684 RIE: 1505 GC: 340
BT Instructional Program Divisions
RT Elementary Education
Intermediate Grades

GRADE 7 *Jul. 1966*
CIJE: 408 RIE: 1132 GC: 340
BT Instructional Program Divisions
RT Elementary Education
Junior High Schools
Secondary Education

GRADE 8 *Jul. 1966*
CIJE: 386 RIE: 1156 GC: 340
BT Instructional Program Divisions
RT Elementary Education
Junior High Schools
Secondary Education

GRADE 9 *Jul. 1966*
CIJE: 330 RIE: 1080 GC: 340
BT Instructional Program Divisions
RT High School Freshmen
High Schools
Junior High Schools
Secondary Education

GRADE 10 *Jul. 1966*
CIJE: 187 RIE: 751 GC: 340
BT Instructional Program Divisions
RT High Schools
Secondary Education

GRADE 11 *Jul. 1966*
CIJE: 141 RIE: 712 GC: 340
BT Instructional Program Divisions
RT High Schools
Secondary Education

GRADE 12 *Jul. 1966*
CIJE: 151 RIE: 816 GC: 340
BT Instructional Program Divisions
RT High Schools
High School Seniors
Secondary Education

Grade 13 (1970 1980)
USE POSTSECONDARY EDUCATION

Grade 14 (1970 1980)
USE POSTSECONDARY EDUCATION

Grades (Program Divisions)
USE INSTRUCTIONAL PROGRAM DIVISIONS

GRADES (SCHOLASTIC) *Jul. 1966*
CIJE: 667 RIE: 684 GC: 310
UF Marks (Scholastic)
NT Grade Inflation
Grade Point Average
RT Academic Achievement
Academic Probation
Academic Records
Class Rank
College Credits
Credit Courses

= Two or more Descriptors are used to represent this term.
The term's main entry shows the appropriate coordination.

Credit No Credit Grading
Credits
Grade Prediction
Grading
Graduation Requirements
Pass Fail Grading
Report Cards
Scores
Student Evaluation

GRADING *Jul. 1966*
CIJE: 1019 RIE: 727 GC: 310
SN Process of rating an individual's or group's performance, achievement, or less frequently, behavior, using specifically established scales of values
UF Contract Grading #
Marking (Scholastic)
NT Credit No Credit Grading
Pass Fail Grading
BT Achievement Rating
RT Academic Achievement
Educational Testing
Grade Inflation
Grade Prediction
Grades (Scholastic)
Holistic Evaluation
Informal Assessment
Report Cards
Scoring
Student Evaluation
Summative Evaluation
Teacher Student Relationship
Writing Evaluation

Graduate Ceremonies
USE COMMENCEMENT CEREMONIES

Graduate Education
USE GRADUATE STUDY

GRADUATE MEDICAL EDUCATION *Aug. 1976*
CIJE: 351 RIE: 81 GC: 210
SN Medical education beyond the undergraduate medical school and the attainment of the professional degree, leading to eligibility for certification in a specialty
UF Internships (Medical)
Residency Programs (Medical)
BT Graduate Study
Medical Education
RT Clinical Experience
Foreign Medical Graduates
Graduate Medical Students
Medical School Faculty
Medical Schools
Medicine
Physicians
Teaching Hospitals

GRADUATE MEDICAL STUDENTS *Aug. 1976*
CIJE: 274 RIE: 32 GC: 360
SN Medical school graduates preparing for professional certification as specialists, usually in teaching hospitals
UF Fellows (Medical)
Interns (Medical)
Physicians In Training
Residents (Medical)
BT Medical Students
RT Foreign Medical Graduates
Graduate Medical Education
Hospital Personnel
Medical Schools
Physicians

Graduate Professors (1966 1980)
USE GRADUATE SCHOOL FACULTY

GRADUATE SCHOOL FACULTY *Mar. 1980*
CIJE: 88 RIE: 56 GC: 360
SN Academic staff members engaged in instruction, research, administration, or related educational activities in a graduate school of a college or university (note: do not confuse with "teaching assistants")
UF Graduate Professors (1966 1980)
NT Medical School Faculty
BT College Faculty
RT Doctoral Programs
Graduate Study
Masters Programs

GRADUATE STUDENTS *Jul. 1966*
CIJE: 1230 RIE: 1147 GC: 360
NT Dental Students
Law Students
Medical Students
BT College Students
RT College Graduates
Doctoral Programs
Graduates
Graduate Study
Higher Education
Masters Programs
Research Assistants
Teaching Assistants

GRADUATE STUDY *Jul. 1966*
CIJE: 2016 RIE: 2336 GC: 340
UF Graduate Education
Graduate Training
NT Graduate Medical Education
Postsecondary Education As A Field Of Study
BT Higher Education
RT College Entrance Examinations
College Graduates
Degree Requirements
Doctoral Degrees
Doctoral Dissertations
Doctoral Programs
Doctor Of Arts Degrees
Graduate School Faculty
Graduate Students
Masters Degrees
Masters Programs
Masters Theses
Postdoctoral Education
Professional Education
Undergraduate Study
Universities
Upper Division Colleges

GRADUATE SURVEYS *Jul. 1966*
CIJE: 415 RIE: 1242 GC: 810
SN Followup studies of students who have graduated (note: as of oct81, use as a minor descriptor for examples of this kind of study -- use as a major descriptor only as the subject of a document)
BT Followup Studies
Surveys
RT Alumni
Educational Research
Graduates
School Surveys
Vocational Followup

Graduate Training
USE GRADUATE STUDY

GRADUATES *Jul. 1966*
CIJE: 94 RIE: 177 GC: 360
SN Individuals who have satisfactorily completed the requirements of an educational program and have been awarded a certificate, diploma, or degree
NT College Graduates
Foreign Medical Graduates
High School Graduates
BT Alumni
RT Alumni Associations
Graduate Students
Graduate Surveys

GRADUATION *Jul. 1966*
CIJE: 45 RIE: 81 GC: 320
SN The process of receiving a diploma or degree for completing a phase of formal education (note: do not confuse with "commencement ceremonies" -- use a more precise term if possible)
BT Achievement
RT College Graduates
Commencement Ceremonies
Educational Attainment
Graduation Requirements
High School Graduates
Recognition (Achievement)

GRADUATION REQUIREMENTS *Jul. 1966*
CIJE: 283 RIE: 490 GC: 320
SN Educational and other specifications or minimum competencies of a program, school, college, or university that a student must satisfactorily complete to graduate (often stated in terms of semester hours, credits, residence requirements, or minimum grades)
UF Diploma Requirements
NT Degree Requirements
BT Academic Standards
RT Academic Achievement
Credits
Grades (Scholastic)
Graduation
Required Courses
Residence Requirements
School Catalogs

Grain Elevator Occupations
USE CROP PROCESSING OCCUPATIONS

Grain Marketing
USE GRAINS (FOOD)

Grain Processing
USE GRAINS (FOOD)

Grain Production
USE GRAINS (FOOD)

GRAINS (FOOD) *Feb. 1970*
CIJE: 33 RIE: 48 GC: 410
UF Corn (Field Crop) (1968 1980)
Grain Marketing
Grain Processing
Grain Production
BT Field Crops
Food
RT Agronomy
Feed Industry

GRAMMAR *Jul. 1966*
CIJE: 2334 RIE: 2548 GC: 450
NT Morphology (Languages)
Syntax
BT Descriptive Linguistics
RT Case (Grammar)
Context Free Grammar
Deep Structure
Discourse Analysis
Generative Grammar
Grammar Translation Method
Grammatical Acceptability
Idioms
Kernel Sentences
Sentence Diagraming
Sentences
Sentence Structure
Structural Grammar
Surface Structure
Tagmemic Analysis
Traditional Grammar
Writing Skills

GRAMMAR TRANSLATION METHOD *Jul. 1966*
CIJE: 85 RIE: 55 GC: 450
SN Traditional foreign language teaching method that emphasizes grammatical rules and their application to translation -- emphasis is on reading and writing rather than oral communication
BT Teaching Methods
RT Audiolingual Methods
Grammar
Second Language Instruction
Translation

GRAMMATICAL ACCEPTABILITY *Apr. 1980*
CIJE: 30 RIE: 14 GC: 450
SN The judgment of a speaker of a language concerning the acceptability or grammatical "correctness" of a given utterance or structure in that language
BT Language Attitudes
RT Dialects
Grammar
Language Usage
Language Variation
Psycholinguistics
Sociolinguistics

GRANDCHILDREN *Dec. 1970*
CIJE: 13 RIE: 12 GC: 510
UF Granddaughters
Grandsons
BT Children

Granddaughters
USE GRANDCHILDREN

Grandfathers
USE GRANDPARENTS

Grandmothers
USE GRANDPARENTS

GRANDPARENTS *Dec. 1970*
CIJE: 73 RIE: 57 GC: 510
UF Grandfathers
Grandmothers
BT Parents
RT Family (Sociological Unit)
Family Environment
Family Life
Older Adults

Grandsons
USE GRANDCHILDREN

Grant Proposals
USE GRANTS; PROGRAM PROPOSALS

GRANTS *Jul. 1966*
CIJE: 526 RIE: 1072 GC: 620
SN Funds given by a foundation, government, institution, or other organization, usually for a specific purpose (note: prior to mar80, this term was not restricted to pecuniary bestowments)
UF Grant Proposals #
Subsidies
NT Block Grants
Educational Vouchers
Incentive Grants
Tuition Grants
BT Financial Support
RT Assistantships
Awards
Categorical Aid
Educational Finance
Eligibility
Equalization Aid
Fellowships
Financial Aid Applicants
Grantsmanship
Philanthropic Foundations
Revenue Sharing
Scholarships
Student Costs
Student Financial Aid
Training Allowances

GRANTSMANSHIP *Mar. 1980*
CIJE: 77 RIE: 106 GC: 620
SN Skills and procedures for applying for external funding
BT Fund Raising
RT Bids
Contracts
Federal Aid
Financial Support
Grants
Private Financial Support
Program Proposals
Proposal Writing
Research Opportunities
State Aid

Grapheme Phoneme Correspondence
USE PHONEME GRAPHEME CORRESPONDENCE

GRAPHEMES *Jul. 1966*
CIJE: 88 RIE: 96 GC: 450
BT Written Language
RT Diacritical Marking
Letters (Alphabet)
Orthographic Symbols
Phoneme Grapheme Correspondence
Phonemes
Phonetics
Romanization
Spelling
Structural Analysis (Linguistics)

GRAPHIC ARTS *Jul. 1966*
CIJE: 333 RIE: 371 GC: 420
NT Cartography
Computer Graphics
Engineering Graphics
Layout (Publications)
Printing
BT Visual Arts
RT Commercial Art
Diagrams
Drafting
Industrial Arts
Orthographic Projection
Photocomposition

= Two or more Descriptors are used to represent this term.
The term's main entry shows the appropriate coordination.

Sign Painters
Signs
Technical Illustration

GRAPHS *Jul. 1966*
CIJE: 596 RIE: 569 GC: 720
BT Visual Aids
RT Charts
Critical Path Method
Flow Charts
Illustrations
Instructional Materials
Nonprint Media
Records (Forms)
Tables (Data)
Topology

Gravitation
USE GRAVITY (PHYSICS)

GRAVITY (PHYSICS) *Oct. 1982*
CIJE: 34 RIE: 8 GC: 490
SN Mutual attraction among all bodies in the universe, dependent on their respective masses, distance apart, and speed of motion relative to each other
UF Gravitation
BT Scientific Concepts
RT Acceleration (Physics)
Force
Geophysics
Kinetic Molecular Theory
Kinetics
Mechanics (Physics)
Motion
Physical Environment
Physics
Pressure (Physics)
Relativity
Space
Weight (Mass)

Graying Of Faculty
USE AGING IN ACADEMIA

Grease
USE LUBRICANTS

GREEK *Jul. 1966*
CIJE: 150 RIE: 128 GC: 440
UF Classical Greek
Modern Greek
BT Indo European Languages
RT Classical Languages
Greek Civilization
Greek Literature

GREEK AMERICANS *Oct. 1980*
CIJE: 7 RIE: 33 GC: 560
BT Ethnic Groups
North Americans
RT Minority Groups

GREEK CIVILIZATION *Jul. 1966*
CIJE: 55 RIE: 49 GC: 430
SN Studies of modern or ancient greece
RT Ancient History
Area Studies
Classical Literature
Greek
Greek Literature
Western Civilization
World History

GREEK LITERATURE *Jul. 1970*
CIJE: 68 RIE: 35 GC: 430
SN Classical and modern greek literature
BT Literature
RT Ancient History
Classical Literature
Greek
Greek Civilization

Greenhouse Workers
USE NURSERY WORKERS (HORTICULTURE)

GREENHOUSES *Jul. 1966*
CIJE: 18 RIE: 44 GC: 410
UF Hothouses
BT Facilities
RT Nurseries (Horticulture)
Ornamental Horticulture
Plant Growth

Gregariousness
USE INTERPERSONAL COMPETENCE

GRIEF *Sep. 1977*
CIJE: 227 RIE: 80 GC: 230
SN Emotional state of intense sadness associated with external loss or deprivation
UF Mourning
BT Psychological Patterns
RT Death
Depression (Psychology)
Emotional Problems

GRIEVANCE PROCEDURES *Jul. 1966*
CIJE: 290 RIE: 555 GC: 630
BT Methods
RT Arbitration
Collective Bargaining
Employer Employee Relationship
Interpersonal Communication
Labor Demands
Negotiation Agreements
Negotiation Impasses
Ombudsmen

Grinding Machines
USE MACHINE TOOLS

Grocery Stores
USE FOOD STORES

Gross Scores
USE RAW SCORES

Grounds Caretakers
USE GROUNDS KEEPERS

GROUNDS KEEPERS *Jul. 1966*
CIJE: 13 RIE: 37 GC: 410
UF Gardeners
Grounds Caretakers
Yard Workers (Horticulture)
BT Semiskilled Workers
RT Landscaping
Ornamental Horticulture Occupations
Plant Propagation
Turf Management

GROUP ACTIVITIES *Jul. 1966*
CIJE: 463 RIE: 584 GC: 310
UF Cooperative Activities
BT Activities
RT Assembly Programs
Competition
Cooperation
Group Experience
Groups
Participation
Self Directed Groups

Group Adjustment
USE ADJUSTMENT (TO ENVIRONMENT)

GROUP BEHAVIOR *Jul. 1966*
CIJE: 513 RIE: 465 GC: 520
SN Behavior of a group as a whole, as well as the behavior of an individual as influenced by his or her membership in a group
UF Collective Behavior
NT Teamwork
BT Behavior
RT Group Dynamics
Group Membership
Groups
Social Behavior
Sociometric Techniques

Group Cohesiveness
USE GROUP UNITY

GROUP COUNSELING *Jul. 1966*
CIJE: 952 RIE: 403 GC: 240
SN Using the dynamics of a group in a counselor-structured situation to increase counselees' self-understanding and adjustment
BT Counseling
Group Guidance
RT Family Counseling
Group Discussion
Group Dynamics
Groups
Group Therapy
Individual Counseling

GROUP DISCUSSION *Jul. 1966*
CIJE: 577 RIE: 537 GC: 310
SN Discussion in groups
BT Discussion
RT Brainstorming
Discussion Groups
Group Counseling
Group Dynamics
Group Guidance
Groups
Interpersonal Communication
Peer Groups

GROUP DYNAMICS *Jul. 1966*
CIJE: 1982 RIE: 1680 GC: 520
SN Formation and functioning of human groups -- includes both the interaction within and among groups
UF Group Interaction
Group Pressures
Group Processes
Group Relations (1966 1980)
BT Interaction
RT Brainstorming
Family Counseling
Group Behavior
Group Counseling
Group Discussion
Group Experience
Group Guidance
Group Instruction
Group Membership
Groups
Group Structure
Humanistic Education
Informal Leadership
Interaction Process Analysis
Interpersonal Communication
Organizational Communication
Peer Influence
Role Playing
Self Directed Groups
Sensitivity Training
Social Psychology
Sociometric Techniques
Speech Communication
Transactional Analysis

GROUP EXPERIENCE *Jul. 1966*
CIJE: 459 RIE: 305 GC: 520
SN Experience of a group as a whole, as well as the experience of an individual resulting from his or her membership in a group
UF Communal Living #
Dormitory Living #
Group Living (1966 1977)
BT Experience
RT Family Life
Group Activities
Group Dynamics
Group Homes
Group Membership
Groups
Human Relations
Living Learning Centers
Normalization (Handicapped)
Residential Programs
Self Directed Groups

GROUP GUIDANCE *Jul. 1966*
CIJE: 162 RIE: 130 GC: 240
SN Guidance carried on in groups to assist members to develop realistic and satisfying goals, plans, and activities
NT Group Counseling
BT Guidance
RT Group Discussion
Group Dynamics
Group Instruction
Groups
Group Therapy

GROUP HOMES *Aug. 1980*
CIJE: 110 RIE: 59 GC: 220
SN Nonconfining residential facilities providing professional supervision in a group living arrangement for either adults or juveniles, usually those who are unable to function independently -- intended to reproduce as closely as possible the circumstances of family life, and at minimum providing access to community activities and resources (note: do not confuse with "personal care homes")
UF Halfway Houses #
BT Housing
RT Adult Foster Care
Community Programs
Deinstitutionalization (Of Disabled)
Delinquency
Disabilities
Economically Disadvantaged
Family Problems
Foster Care
Group Experience
Groups
Normalization (Handicapped)
Personal Care Homes
Rehabilitation Centers
Resident Advisers
Social Services

GROUP INSTRUCTION *Jul. 1966*
CIJE: 259 RIE: 382 GC: 310
NT Large Group Instruction
Small Group Instruction
BT Instruction
RT Assembly Programs
Group Dynamics
Group Guidance
Grouping (Instructional Purposes)
Groups
Individual Instruction
Individualized Instruction
Listening Groups

Group Intelligence Testing (1966 1980)
USE GROUP TESTING; INTELLIGENCE TESTS

Group Intelligence Tests (1966 1980)
USE GROUP TESTING; INTELLIGENCE TESTS

Group Interaction
USE GROUP DYNAMICS

Group Interests
USE INTERESTS

Group Living (1966 1977)
USE GROUP EXPERIENCE

GROUP MEMBERSHIP *Jul. 1966*
CIJE: 272 RIE: 214 GC: 510
NT Political Affiliation
RT Enrollment
Group Behavior
Group Dynamics
Group Experience
Groups
Participant Characteristics
Social Stratification

GROUP NORMS (1968 1980) *Mar. 1980*
CIJE: 164 RIE: 179 GC: 520
SN Invalid descriptor -- used inconsistently in indexing -- see such descriptors as "norms," "standards," or "behavior standards"

Group Pacing
USE PACING

Group Pressures
USE GROUP DYNAMICS

Group Processes
USE GROUP DYNAMICS

GROUP READING (1966 1980) *Mar. 1980*
CIJE: 20 RIE: 32 GC: 460
SN Invalid descriptor -- used indiscriminately in indexing -- see such descriptors as "reading," "choral speaking," and "grouping (instructional purposes)"

Group Relations (1966 1980)
USE GROUP DYNAMICS

GROUP STATUS *Jul. 1966*
CIJE: 97 RIE: 96 GC: 520
SN Status of a group (note: prior to mar80, this term was not scoped and was used to index both the status of a group and the status of individuals within a group)
NT Family Status
BT Status
RT Groups
Group Structure
Group Unity
Reference Groups
Social Stratification

= Two or more Descriptors are used to represent this term.
The term's main entry shows the appropriate coordination.

GROUP STRUCTURE *Jul. 1966*
CIJE: 252 RIE: 262 GC: 520
NT Family Structure
Governmental Structure
BT Organization
RT Cluster Grouping
Group Dynamics
Groups
Group Status
Interaction Process Analysis
Power Structure
Social Structure
Social Systems
Sociometric Techniques

GROUP TESTING *Mar. 1980*
CIJE: 117 RIE: 202 GC: 820
SN Process of administering tests to groups
UF Group Intelligence Testing (1966 1980) #
Group Intelligence Tests (1966 1980) #
Group Tests (1966 1980)
BT Testing
RT Groups
Individual Testing

Group Tests (1966 1980)
USE GROUP TESTING

GROUP THERAPY *Jul. 1966*
CIJE: 569 RIE: 200 GC: 230
BT Therapy
RT Family Counseling
Group Counseling
Group Guidance
Groups
Milieu Therapy
Psychotherapy
Sensitivity Training
Transactional Analysis

GROUP UNITY *Aug. 1968*
CIJE: 304 RIE: 212 GC: 520
SN Cohesiveness of groups of people, families, tribes and nations
UF Ethnic Unity
Family Unity
Group Cohesiveness
Unification
BT Interpersonal Relationship
RT Black Power
Community
Cooperation
Ethnicity
Global Approach
Groups
Group Status
Ideology
Morale
Nationalism
Patriotism
Trust (Psychology)

Group Values
USE SOCIAL VALUES

GROUPING (INSTRUCTIONAL PURPOSES) *Jul. 1966*
CIJE: 584 RIE: 724 GC: 310
SN Organization or classification of students according to specified criteria for instructional purposes
UF Student Grouping (1966 1980)
NT Heterogeneous Grouping
Homogeneous Grouping
Nongraded Instructional Grouping
BT Classification
RT Classes (Groups Of Students)
Class Organization
Flexible Scheduling
Group Instruction
Groups
Instructional Program Divisions
Labeling (Of Persons)
Special Education
Student Placement
Transitional Programs
Tutorial Programs

Grouping Procedures (1966 1980)
USE CLASSIFICATION

GROUPS *Jul. 1966*
CIJE: 213 RIE: 182 GC: 520
NT Advantaged
Age Groups
Alumni
Arabs
Artists
Athletes
Audiences
Authors
Blacks
Board Candidates
Change Agents
Child Caregivers
Classes (Groups Of Students)
Clubs
College Applicants
Community Leaders
Control Groups
Criminals
Dependents
Disadvantaged
Discussion Groups
Donors
Dropouts
Employers
Eskimos
Ethnic Groups
Exceptional Persons
Experimental Groups
Family (Sociological Unit)
Females
Financial Aid Applicants
Heads Of Households
High Risk Persons
Homeless People
Homemakers
Homeowners
Indians
Indigenous Populations
Indochinese
Institutionalized Persons
Job Applicants
Judges
Juvenile Gangs
Labor Force Nonparticipants
Landlords
Latin Americans
Lay People
Leaders
Left Handed Writer
Limited English Speaking
Low Income Groups
Males
Matched Groups
Migrants
Minority Groups
Native Speakers
Non English Speaking
North Americans
No Shows
Organizations (Groups)
Parents
Patients
Peer Groups
Personnel
Political Candidates
Potential Dropouts
Quality Circles
Recreationists
Reference Groups
Religious Cultural Groups
Research And Instruction Units
Role Models
Runaways
Rural Population
Seafarers
Self Directed Groups
Siblings
Slow Learners
Social Class
Social Support Groups
Spouses
Stopouts
Students
Tissue Donors
Trainees
Tribes
Union Members
Urban Population
Users (Information)
Veterans
Victims Of Crime
Volunteers
Welfare Recipients
Whites
Widowed
Youth
Youth Leaders
RT Classification
Group Activities
Group Behavior
Group Counseling
Group Discussion
Group Dynamics
Group Experience
Group Guidance
Group Homes
Grouping (Instructional Purposes)
Group Instruction
Group Membership
Group Status
Group Structure
Group Testing
Group Therapy
Group Unity
Interaction Process Analysis
Labeling (Of Persons)
Social Psychology
Sociometric Techniques

Growth Motivation
USE SELF ACTUALIZATION

GROWTH PATTERNS (1966 1980) *Mar. 1980*
CIJE: 190 RIE: 181 GC: 520
SN Invalid descriptor -- used inconsistently in indexing -- see the displays and hierarchies of "development" and "change," as well as more precise descriptors such as "employment patterns," "population growth," "trend analysis," etc.

GUARANI *Mar. 1971*
CIJE: 5 RIE: 7 GC: 440
SN Native language spoken by the tupi guaranian indians of bolivia, paraguay, and southern brazil
BT American Indian Languages

GUARANTEED INCOME *Aug. 1968*
CIJE: 30 RIE: 52 GC: 620
UF Negative Income Tax
BT Income
RT Minimum Wage
Salaries
Wages

Guards (Border Patrol)
USE IMMIGRATION INSPECTORS

Guards (Security)
USE SECURITY PERSONNEL

Guerrilla Warfare
USE WAR

GUESSING (TESTS) *Nov. 1970*
CIJE: 145 RIE: 127 GC: 820
SN Responding to test items without certainty of the correct answers
BT Response Style (Tests)
RT Confidence Testing
Multiple Choice Tests
Objective Tests
Raw Scores
Scoring Formulas
Test Coaching
Testing
Testing Problems
Test Interpretation
Test Reliability
Tests
Test Wiseness
True Scores

GUIDANCE *Jul. 1966*
CIJE: 266 RIE: 566 GC: 240
SN Process of assisting individuals and groups to develop realistic and satisfying goals, plans, and activities (note: "counseling" is one aspect of the total process of "guidance")
UF Continuous Guidance (1966 1980)
Developmental Guidance (1967 1980)
NT Career Guidance
Counseling
Group Guidance
Post High School Guidance
School Guidance
Teacher Guidance
RT Consultation Programs
Guidance Centers
Guidance Objectives
Guidance Personnel
Guidance Programs

GUIDANCE CENTERS *Jul. 1966*
CIJE: 253 RIE: 175 GC: 240
UF Counseling Centers (1966 1977)
Guidance Facilities (1967 1977)
BT Educational Facilities
RT Counseling
Counseling Services
Guidance
Guidance Programs

Guidance Counseling (1966 1980)
USE SCHOOL COUNSELING

Guidance Counselors
USE SCHOOL COUNSELORS

Guidance Facilities (1967 1977)
USE GUIDANCE CENTERS

Guidance Functions (1968 1980)
USE GUIDANCE OBJECTIVES

Guidance Goals
USE GUIDANCE OBJECTIVES

GUIDANCE OBJECTIVES *Jul. 1966*
CIJE: 203 RIE: 314 GC: 240
SN Aims or ends toward which the guidance process is directed (note: if appropriate, use the more specific term "counseling objectives")
UF Guidance Functions (1968 1980)
Guidance Goals
NT Counseling Objectives
BT Objectives
RT Behavioral Objectives
Guidance
Guidance Programs

GUIDANCE PERSONNEL *Jul. 1966*
CIJE: 140 RIE: 267 GC: 240
SN Professionals engaged in assisting individuals and groups to develop realistic and satisfying plans, goals, and activities (note: prior to mar80, the instruction "guidance workers, use counselors" was carried in the thesaurus)
UF Guidance Specialists #
NT Counselors
BT Personnel
RT Caseworkers
Consultants
Guidance
Guidance Programs
Instructor Coordinators
Parole Officers
Probation Officers
Pupil Personnel Workers
School Psychologists
School Social Workers
Social Workers
Student Personnel Workers

GUIDANCE PROGRAMS *Jul. 1966*
CIJE: 554 RIE: 1173 GC: 240
SN Ongoing activities designed to assist individuals and groups develop realistic and satisfying goals, plans, and activities
UF Guidance Services (1966 1980)
BT Programs
RT Ancillary School Services
Employee Assistance Programs
Guidance
Guidance Centers
Guidance Objectives
Guidance Personnel
Individualized Programs
Outreach Programs
Pupil Personnel Services
Rehabilitation Programs
Student Personnel Services

Guidance Services (1966 1980)
USE GUIDANCE PROGRAMS

Guidance Specialists
USE GUIDANCE PERSONNEL; SPECIALISTS

Guidebooks
USE GUIDES

= Two or more Descriptors are used to represent this term.
The term's main entry shows the appropriate coordination.

GUIDELINES *Jul. 1966*
CIJE: 3902 RIE: 6232 GC: 730
NT Facility Guidelines
RT Administrator Guides
Authoring Aids (Programing)
Check Lists
Design
Guides
Objectives
Planning
Specifications

GUIDES *Jul. 1966*
CIJE: 570 RIE: 4776 GC: 720
SN (Note: corresponds to pubtype code 050-- do not use except as the subject of a document)
UF Guidebooks
Handbooks
Health Activities Handbooks (1966 1980) #
Health Guides (1966 1980) #
Manuals (1966 1980)
NT Administrator Guides
Curriculum Guides
Faculty Handbooks
Laboratory Manuals
Leaders Guides
Library Guides
Program Guides
Study Guides
Teaching Guides
Test Manuals
BT Reference Materials
RT Directories
Guidelines
Orientation Materials
Parent Materials

GUJARATI *Jul. 1966*
CIJE: RIE: 6 GC: 440
UF Gujerati
BT Indo European Languages

Gujerati
USE GUJARATI

GULLAH *Feb. 1970*
CIJE: 5 RIE: 11 GC: 440
BT Creoles

GYMNASIUMS *Jul. 1966*
CIJE: 65 RIE: 33 GC: 920
BT Facilities
RT Athletic Equipment
Athletic Fields
Athletics
Field Houses
Physical Education Facilities
Physical Recreation Programs
Recreational Facilities

GYMNASTICS *Feb. 1978*
CIJE: 45 RIE: 52 GC: 470
NT Tumbling
BT Athletics
RT Calisthenics

GYNECOLOGY *Oct. 1977*
CIJE: 63 RIE: 21 GC: 210
SN Branch of medicine dealing with the diseases, hygiene, and reproduction function of females
BT Medicine
RT Abortions
Contraception
Diseases
Family Practice (Medicine)
Females
Medical Services
Obstetrics
Pregnancy
Reproduction (Biology)

HABIT FORMATION *Jul. 1966*
CIJE: 142 RIE: 91 GC: 110
BT Behavior Development
RT Behavior Change
Listening Habits
Personality
Reading Habits
Self Care Skills
Speech Habits

HABITUATION *Oct. 1984*
CIJE: 47 RIE: 14 GC: 110
SN Progressive decrease in responsiveness to repetitive stimuli (note: for drug habituation, use "drug abuse" or "drug addiction")
BT Learning Processes
RT Arousal Patterns
Attention
Cognitive Ability
Novelty (Stimulus Dimension)
Perception
Redundancy
Retention (Psychology)
Sensory Experience

Hagiographies (1971 1980)
USE BIOGRAPHIES

HAIKU *Apr. 1970*
CIJE: 34 RIE: 16 GC: 430
UF Hokku
BT Literary Genres
Poetry
RT Imagery

HAITIAN CREOLE *Jul. 1966*
CIJE: 10 RIE: 41 GC: 440
BT Creoles

HAITIANS *Oct. 1980*
CIJE: 22 RIE: 77 GC: 560
SN Peoples of haiti or haitian descent
BT Latin Americans
RT Ethnic Groups

Half Reversal Shift
USE SHIFT STUDIES

Halfway Houses
USE GROUP HOMES; REHABILITATION CENTERS

Hallways
USE CORRIDORS

Hand Calculators
USE CALCULATORS

HAND TOOLS *Jul. 1966*
CIJE: 19 RIE: 225 GC: 910
BT Equipment
RT Machine Tools
Metal Working
Shop Curriculum
Woodworking

HANDBALL *Apr. 1985*
CIJE: 1 RIE: 1 GC: 470
SN Singles or doubles game played by striking a small rubber ball against a wall or walls with the hands (note: do not confuse with "team handball")
BT Athletics
RT Racquetball

Handbooks
USE GUIDES

Handicap Detection (1966 1980)
USE HANDICAP IDENTIFICATION

HANDICAP DISCRIMINATION *Jun. 1984*
CIJE: 9 RIE: 11 GC: 540
SN Restriction or denial of rights, privileges, and choice because of physical, mental, or sensory impairment
BT Social Discrimination
RT Affirmative Action
Age Discrimination
Disabilities
Educational Discrimination
Equal Education
Equal Opportunities (Jobs)
Normalization (Handicapped)
Reverse Discrimination
Social Bias

HANDICAP IDENTIFICATION *Mar. 1980*
CIJE: 367 RIE: 435 GC: 220
UF Handicap Detection (1966 1980)
BT Identification
RT Ability Identification
Clinical Diagnosis
Diagnostic Tests
Disabilities
Etiology
High Risk Persons
Medical Evaluation
Screening Tests

Handicapped (1966 1980)
USE DISABILITIES

HANDICAPPED CHILDREN (1966 1980) *Mar. 1980*
CIJE: 2623 RIE: 3350 GC: 220
SN Invalid descriptor -- coordinate specific descriptors from the "disabilities" display with appropriate age-level or mandatory educational level descriptors (note: in mar80, the postings of "blind, crippled, deaf, homebound, neurotic, psychotic, and retarded children" were transferred here, as well as to the appropriate "disabilities" terms)

HANDICAPPED STUDENTS (1967 1980) *Mar. 1980*
CIJE: 527 RIE: 697 GC: 220
SN Invalid descriptor -- coordinate specific descriptors from the "disabilities" display with appropriate "student," age-level, or mandatory educational level descriptors

Handicaps
USE DISABILITIES

HANDICRAFTS *Jul. 1966*
CIJE: 217 RIE: 279 GC: 420
SN Creative activities of making articles by hand, often with the aid of simple tools or machines -- also, the handiworks resulting from such activities
UF Crafts
Crafts Rooms (1966 1980) #
NT Ceramics
BT Visual Arts
RT Art Activities
Art Products
Childrens Art
Craft Workers
Creative Activities
Design Crafts
Leather
Metal Working
Plastics
School Shops
Skilled Occupations
Woodworking

HANDWRITING *Jul. 1966*
CIJE: 168 RIE: 165 GC: 400
UF Handwriting Development (1966 1980) #
Handwriting Instruction (1966 1983) #
Handwriting Materials (1966 1983) #
Handwriting Readiness (1966 1983) #
Handwriting Skills (1966 1983) #
NT Cursive Writing
Manuscript Writing (Handlettering)
BT Language Arts
RT Left Handed Writer
Writing (Composition)
Writing Difficulties
Writing Exercises
Writing Improvement
Writing Instruction
Writing Readiness
Writing Research
Writing Skills

Handwriting Development (1966 1980)
USE HANDWRITING; WRITING SKILLS

Handwriting Instruction (1966 1983)
USE HANDWRITING; WRITING INSTRUCTION

Handwriting Materials (1966 1983)
USE HANDWRITING; INSTRUCTIONAL MATERIALS

Handwriting Readiness (1966 1983)
USE HANDWRITING; WRITING READINESS

Handwriting Skills (1966 1983)
USE HANDWRITING; WRITING SKILLS

Hangul
USE KOREAN

Hanja
USE KOREAN

Hankul
USE KOREAN

Haptic Perception (1967 1980)
USE TACTUAL PERCEPTION

Hard Of Hearing (1967 1980)
USE PARTIAL HEARING

HARVESTING *Jul. 1966*
CIJE: 8 RIE: 40 GC: 410
UF Crop Harvesting
BT Agriculture
RT Agricultural Production
Agronomy
Crop Processing Occupations
Field Crops
Horticulture

Hashish
USE MARIJUANA

HAUSA *Jul. 1966*
CIJE: 6 RIE: 23 GC: 440
BT Chad Languages

HAWAIIAN *Aug. 1969*
CIJE: 6 RIE: 25 GC: 440
BT Malayo Polynesian Languages
RT Hawaiians

HAWAIIANS *Mar. 1976*
CIJE: 18 RIE: 119 GC: 560
SN Polynesian or part-polynesian people indigenous to the hawaiian islands
BT Ethnic Groups
Pacific Americans
RT Hawaiian

HAZARDOUS MATERIALS *Oct. 1984*
CIJE: 52 RIE: 75 GC: 210
SN Ignitable, corrosive, infectious, reactive, or toxic materials that pose a present or potential threat to living things
UF Dangerous Materials
Hazardous Wastes #
NT Poisons
RT Asbestos
Environmental Influences
Environmental Standards
Laboratory Safety
Occupational Safety And Health
Physical Environment
Physical Health
Pollution
Public Health
Radiation
Safety
Sanitation
School Safety
Wastes

Hazardous Wastes
USE HAZARDOUS MATERIALS; WASTES

Head Banging
USE SELF MUTILATION

HEADLINES *Dec. 1974*
CIJE: 45 RIE: 26 GC: 720
SN Titles of news articles or newscasts
RT Journalism
Layout (Publications)
News Media
Newspapers
News Reporting
News Writing

HEADS OF HOUSEHOLDS *Nov. 1969*
CIJE: 61 RIE: 165 GC: 510
UF Breadwinners
Family Breadwinners
Household Heads
BT Groups
RT Displaced Homemakers
Family (Sociological Unit)
Fatherless Family
Fathers
Motherless Family
Mothers
One Parent Family
Parents

= Two or more Descriptors are used to represent this term.
The term's main entry shows the appropriate coordination.

HEALTH *Jul. 1966*
CIJE: 812 RIE: 1289 GC: 210
NT Family Health
Mental Health
Occupational Safety And Health
Physical Health
Public Health
RT Adjustment (To Environment)
Allied Health Occupations
Biofeedback
Clinics
Daily Living Skills
Dentistry
Disabilities
Disease Control
Diseases
Epidemiology
Fatigue (Biology)
Health Activities
Health Conditions
Health Education
Health Facilities
Health Insurance
Health Materials
Health Needs
Health Occupations
Health Personnel
Health Programs
Health Services
Human Body
Hygiene
Injuries
Medical Evaluation
Medicine
Nutrition
Patient Education
Perinatal Influences
Pests
Pollution
Prenatal Influences
Primary Health Care
Radiation Effects
Safety
Sanitation
Self Care Skills
Sleep
Special Health Problems
Stress Variables
Ventilation
Water Quality
Water Treatment

HEALTH ACTIVITIES *Jul. 1966*
CIJE: 103 RIE: 103 GC: 210
BT Activities
RT Health
Health Education
Health Materials
Physical Activities

Health Activities Handbooks (1966 1980)
USE GUIDES; HEALTH MATERIALS

Health Books (1966 1980)
USE BOOKS; HEALTH MATERIALS

Health Care Evaluation
USE MEDICAL CARE EVALUATION

HEALTH CONDITIONS *Jul. 1966*
CIJE: 143 RIE: 167 GC: 210
RT Epidemiology
Health
Sanitary Facilities

HEALTH EDUCATION *Jul. 1966*
CIJE: 2419 RIE: 2205 GC: 400
SN Educational activities that promote understanding, attitudes, and practices consistent with individual, family, and community health needs (note: for study and training in the health/health-related occupations, use "medical education" or "allied health occupations education")
BT Education
RT Alcohol Education
Allied Health Occupations Education
Consumer Education
Disease Control
Drinking
Drug Education
First Aid
Health
Health Activities
Health Materials
Health Programs
Human Body
Hygiene
Nutrition Instruction
Patient Education
Smoking
Stress Management
Tobacco
Venereal Diseases

HEALTH FACILITIES *Jul. 1966*
CIJE: 163 RIE: 236 GC: 210
UF Infirmaries
NT Nursing Homes
BT Facilities
RT Clinics
First Aid
Health
Health Needs
Health Services
Hospices (Terminal Care)
Hospitals
Medical Care Evaluation
Medical Services
Public Facilities
Sanitary Facilities

Health Guides (1966 1980)
USE GUIDES; HEALTH MATERIALS

HEALTH INSURANCE *Jul. 1966*
CIJE: 123 RIE: 189 GC: 210
BT Insurance
RT Fringe Benefits
Health
Health Services
Insurance Occupations
Teacher Employment Benefits
Unemployment Insurance
Workers Compensation

HEALTH MATERIALS *Mar. 1980*
CIJE: 59 RIE: 168 GC: 730
UF Health Activities Handbooks (1966 1980) #
Health Books (1966 1980) #
Health Guides (1966 1980) #
RT Health
Health Activities
Health Education
Instructional Materials
Resource Materials
Science Materials

HEALTH NEEDS *Jul. 1966*
CIJE: 407 RIE: 656 GC: 210
BT Needs
RT Health
Health Facilities
Health Services

HEALTH OCCUPATIONS *Jul. 1966*
CIJE: 217 RIE: 614 GC: 210
NT Allied Health Occupations
BT Occupations
RT Health
Health Personnel
Health Services
Medical Associations
Medical Education
Medicine
Professional Occupations
Technical Occupations

HEALTH OCCUPATIONS CENTERS (1968 1980) *Mar. 1980*
CIJE: 17 RIE: 21 GC: 210
SN Invalid descriptor -- used inconsistently in indexing -- for "health education centers," coordinate "allied health occupations education," "medical education," etc. with appropriate facilities descriptors

Health Occupations Education (Vocational)
USE ALLIED HEALTH OCCUPATIONS EDUCATION; VOCATIONAL EDUCATION

Health Occupations Education (1967 1980)
USE ALLIED HEALTH OCCUPATIONS EDUCATION

Health Occupations Personnel
USE HEALTH PERSONNEL

HEALTH PERSONNEL *Jul. 1966*
CIJE: 556 RIE: 850 GC: 210
UF Community Health Workers #
Health Occupations Personnel
Health Service Personnel
Health Service Workers
Health Workers
NT Allied Health Personnel
Dentists
Hospital Personnel
Medical Consultants
Nurses
Pharmacists
Physicians
Psychologists
Veterinarians
BT Personnel
RT Health
Health Occupations
Health Services
Medical Education
Medical Evaluation
Medical Libraries
Paraprofessional Personnel
Professional Personnel
Pupil Personnel Workers
Scientific Personnel
Student Personnel Workers

HEALTH PROGRAMS *Jul. 1966*
CIJE: 595 RIE: 576 GC: 210
NT Breakfast Programs
Immunization Programs
Lunch Programs
Mental Health Programs
BT Programs
RT Health
Health Education
Health Services
Outreach Programs

Health Related Professions
USE ALLIED HEALTH OCCUPATIONS

Health Sciences Libraries
USE MEDICAL LIBRARIES

Health Service Personnel
USE HEALTH PERSONNEL

Health Service Workers
USE HEALTH PERSONNEL

HEALTH SERVICES *Jul. 1966*
CIJE: 972 RIE: 1650 GC: 210
NT Community Health Services
Hospices (Terminal Care)
Medical Services
Migrant Health Services
School Health Services
BT Human Services
RT Allied Health Occupations
Eligibility
Fluoridation
Health
Health Facilities
Health Insurance
Health Needs
Health Occupations
Health Personnel
Health Programs
Hospitals
Medical Care Evaluation
Medical Libraries
Optometry

Health Workers
USE HEALTH PERSONNEL

HEARING (PHYSIOLOGY) *Mar. 1980*
CIJE: 79 RIE: 92 GC: 110
SN Sense or act of hearing
UF Audition (Physiology) (1967 1980)
RT Audiology
Audiometric Tests
Auditory Evaluation
Auditory Perception
Auditory Stimuli
Auditory Tests
Deafness
Ears
Hearing Aids
Hearing Impairments
Hearing Therapy
Partial Hearing
Psychoacoustics

HEARING AIDS *Jul. 1966*
CIJE: 110 RIE: 54 GC: 220
BT Audio Equipment
Sensory Aids
RT Audiology
Communication Aids (For Disabled)
Hearing (Physiology)
Hearing Impairments
Hearing Therapy
Loop Induction Systems
Partial Hearing
Total Communication

Hearing Clinics (1968 1980)
USE SPEECH AND HEARING CLINICS

HEARING CONSERVATION *Jul. 1966*
CIJE: 15 RIE: 19 GC: 210
SN Activities (such as the wearing of ear protectors in loud industrial settings) designed to prevent hearing loss
BT Prevention
RT Audiology
Hearing Impairments
Noise (Sound)
Occupational Diseases

HEARING IMPAIRMENTS *Mar. 1980*
CIJE: 2168 RIE: 1310 GC: 220
SN Mild to total hearing losses
UF Aurally Handicapped (1966 1980)
Hearing Loss (1967 1980)
NT Deafness
Partial Hearing
BT Disabilities
RT Audiology
Audiometric Tests
Auditory Evaluation
Auditory Tests
Communication Disorders
Ears
Exceptional Persons
Hearing (Physiology)
Hearing Aids
Hearing Conservation
Hearing Therapy
Language Handicaps
Learning Problems
Loop Induction Systems
Manual Communication
Oral Communication Method
Sensory Aids
Speech And Hearing Clinics
Speech Handicaps
Total Communication
Visible Speech

Hearing Loss (1967 1980)
USE HEARING IMPAIRMENTS

Hearing Rehabilitation
USE HEARING THERAPY

Hearing Tests
USE AUDITORY TESTS

Hearing Therapists (1967 1980)
USE HEARING THERAPY; THERAPISTS

HEARING THERAPY *Jul. 1966*
CIJE: 29 RIE: 46 GC: 220
SN Treatment of the hearing impaired to improve hearing skills and make maximum use of residual hearing (note: do not confuse with "auditory training" -- prior to mar80, the use of this term was not restricted by a scope note)
UF Hearing Rehabilitation
Hearing Therapists (1967 1980) #
BT Therapy
RT Audiology
Auditory Evaluation
Auditory Training
Hearing (Physiology)
Hearing Aids
Hearing Impairments
Lipreading
Manual Communication
Oral Communication Method
Speech And Hearing Clinics
Total Communication

= Two or more Descriptors are used to represent this term.
The term's main entry shows the appropriate coordination.

HEARINGS *Sep. 1977*
CIJE: 90 RIE: 928 GC: 610
SN Sessions in which witnesses are heard and testimony is recorded (note: for u.s. congressional hearings, coordinate "hearings" with such identifiers as "congress," "congress 95th," etc.)
UF Public Hearings
RT Court Judges
Courts
Government (Administrative Body)
Laws
Legislation
Meetings

HEART DISORDERS *Mar. 1980*
CIJE: 127 RIE: 58 GC: 210
UF Cardiac (Person) (1968 1980)
BT Physical Disabilities
RT Cardiopulmonary Resuscitation
Cardiovascular System
Diseases
Heart Rate
Physical Health
Special Health Problems

HEART RATE *Jun. 1969*
CIJE: 222 RIE: 77 GC: 210
UF Pulse Rate
BT Metabolism
RT Aerobics
Blood Circulation
Cardiovascular System
Heart Disorders
Human Body
Hypertension
Physical Fitness
Physical Health
Physiology

HEAT *Jul. 1966*
CIJE: 209 RIE: 98 GC: 490
BT Energy
RT Calorimeters
Chimneys
Climate
Fuels
Geothermal Energy
Kinetic Molecular Theory
Kinetics
Solar Energy
Temperature
Thermodynamics

Heat Equations
USE THERMODYNAMICS

HEAT RECOVERY *Oct. 1976*
CIJE: 70 RIE: 43 GC: 910
SN Transfer of excess heat generated by people, lighting, equipment, and other sources into either heating or cooling systems as required
BT Climate Control
Energy Conservation
RT Air Conditioning
Alternative Energy Sources
Fuel Consumption
Heating
Refrigeration
Thermal Environment
Ventilation

HEATING *Jul. 1966*
CIJE: 194 RIE: 362 GC: 920
UF Solar Heating #
BT Climate Control
RT Air Conditioning
Air Conditioning Equipment
Air Flow
Chimneys
Fuel Consumption
Fuels
Heat Recovery
Humidity
Temperature
Thermal Environment
Utilities
Ventilation

Heating Oils
USE FUELS

HEBREW *Jul. 1966*
CIJE: 82 RIE: 138 GC: 440
BT Semitic Languages

HEIGHT *Jun. 1969*
CIJE: 11 RIE: 8 GC: 490
SN (Note: for living organisms, use "body height")
BT Scientific Concepts
RT Distance
Mathematics
Proximity

Helicopter Pilots
USE AIRCRAFT PILOTS

HELPING RELATIONSHIP *Nov. 1970*
CIJE: 1394 RIE: 596 GC: 240
SN Relationship characterized by the provision of assistance -- helping behavior may be one-sided or reciprocal
BT Interpersonal Relationship
RT Child Advocacy
Counseling
Counselor Client Relationship
Individual Counseling
Intervention
Outcomes Of Treatment
Peer Counseling
Physician Patient Relationship
Social Support Groups
Termination Of Treatment
Therapy

HELPLESSNESS *Sep. 1981*
CIJE: 87 RIE: 47 GC: 230
SN Being or feeling powerless to control or cope with events
UF Learned Helplessness
RT Anger
Depression (Psychology)
Emotional Disturbances
Emotional Problems
Failure
Fear
Inhibition
Paranoid Behavior
Psychological Patterns

Hemispheric Specialization (Brain)
USE BRAIN HEMISPHERE FUNCTIONS

Hemodynamics
USE BLOOD CIRCULATION

HERBICIDES *Jul. 1966*
CIJE: 20 RIE: 74 GC: 410
BT Pesticides
RT Agricultural Chemical Occupations
Agricultural Supplies
Agronomy
Botany
Horticulture
Insecticides
Plant Growth
Plant Pathology
Weeds

HEREDITY *Jul. 1966*
CIJE: 299 RIE: 162 GC: 490
SN The transmission of developmental potentialities from one generation of living things to the next and following generations through the natural process of reproduction
BT Evolution
RT Biology
Congenital Impairments
Embryology
Genetics
Nature Nurture Controversy
Nucleic Acids
Prenatal Influences
Reproduction (Biology)

Heredity Environment Controversy
USE NATURE NURTURE CONTROVERSY

HETEROGENEOUS GROUPING *Jul. 1966*
CIJE: 142 RIE: 130 GC: 310
SN Organization or classification of students according to specified criteria for the purpose of forming instructional groups with a high degree of dissimilarity
BT Grouping (Instructional Purposes)
RT Classroom Desegregation
Coeducation
Homogeneous Grouping
Mainstreaming
Multicultural Education
Multigraded Classes
Multilevel Classes (Second Language Instruction)

Heterophoria (1968 1974)
USE STRABISMUS

Heterotropia (1968 1974)
USE STRABISMUS

Heuristic Games
USE EDUCATIONAL GAMES

HEURISTICS *Oct. 1983*
CIJE: 120 RIE: 90 GC: 810
SN Learning or problem-solving processes, neither wholly rule-governed nor trial and error, in which one tries each of several plausible approaches and evaluates progress toward a satisfactory conclusion after each attempt
BT Methods
RT Artificial Intelligence
Cognitive Ability
Creative Thinking
Creative Writing
Critical Thinking
Decision Making
Discovery Learning
Game Theory
Inquiry
Learning Processes
Learning Strategies
Logical Thinking
Mathematical Models
Problem Solving
Simulation

HIDDEN CURRICULUM *Jun. 1983*
CIJE: 58 RIE: 25 GC: 330
SN Unstated norms, values, and beliefs that are transmitted to students through the underlying educational structure
RT Curriculum
Educational Environment
Educational Theories
Incidental Learning
Socialization
Student Development
Student School Relationship
Values

Hierarchy
USE VERTICAL ORGANIZATION

HIGH ACHIEVEMENT *Mar. 1980*
CIJE: 204 RIE: 288 GC: 120
UF High Achievers (1966 1980)
BT Achievement
RT Low Achievement
Overachievement
Success

High Achievers (1966 1980)
USE HIGH ACHIEVEMENT

High Blood Pressure
USE HYPERTENSION

HIGH INTEREST LOW VOCABULARY BOOKS *Jul. 1966*
CIJE: 40 RIE: 115 GC: 720
SN Books designed to interest learners whose reading abilities are below age or grade level
BT Books
RT Instructional Materials
Readability
Reading Materials
Remedial Reading
Supplementary Reading Materials

HIGH RISK PERSONS *Apr. 1982*
CIJE: 188 RIE: 185 GC: 120
SN Individuals or groups identified as possibly having or potentially developing a problem (physical, mental, educational, etc.) requiring further evaluation and/or intervention (note: if possible, use the more specific term "high risk students")
UF At Risk (Persons)
NT High Risk Students
BT Groups
RT Disabilities
Handicap Identification
Incidence

HIGH RISK STUDENTS *Mar. 1980*
CIJE: 117 RIE: 271 GC: 360
SN Students, with normal intelligence, whose academic background or prior performance may cause them to be perceived as candidates for future academic failure or early withdrawal (note: prior to mar80, this concept was occasionally indexed under "educationally disadvantaged")
BT High Risk Persons
Students
RT Academic Ability
Academic Aptitude
Academic Failure
Compensatory Education
Developmental Studies Programs
Educationally Disadvantaged
Nontraditional Students
Open Enrollment
Potential Dropouts
Remedial Programs
Transitional Programs

High School College Cooperation
USE COLLEGE SCHOOL COOPERATION

High School Curriculum (1967 1980)
USE SECONDARY SCHOOL CURRICULUM

High School Design (1966 1980)
USE EDUCATIONAL FACILITIES DESIGN

High School Dropouts
USE DROPOUTS

HIGH SCHOOL EQUIVALENCY PROGRAMS *Feb. 1975*
CIJE: 71 RIE: 320 GC: 340
SN Adult educational activities concerned with the preparation for and the taking of tests which lead to a high school equivalency certificate, e.g., general educational development programs (note: also appears in the list of mandatory educational level descriptors)
UF Ged Programs
General Educational Development Programs
BT Adult Programs
RT Adult Basic Education
Adult Education
Adult Reading Programs
Certification
Continuation Students
Dropout Programs
Dropouts
Educational Attainment
Educational Certificates
Equivalency Tests
Evening Programs
Experiential Learning
External Degree Programs
Grade Equivalent Scores
High School Graduates
Nontraditional Education
Public School Adult Education
Secondary Education
Student Certification

HIGH SCHOOL FRESHMEN *Mar. 1980*
CIJE: 19 RIE: 15 GC: 360
SN Students in their first year of high school (note: prior to mar80, "freshmen" was also a valid descriptor -- for curriculum or classroom-based materials, use "grade 9" or "grade 10")
UF Freshmen (1967 1980) (Grade 9)
BT High School Students
RT Grade 9
High Schools
High School Seniors

HIGH SCHOOL GRADUATES *Jul. 1966*
CIJE: 196 RIE: 758 GC: 360
BT Graduates
RT College Bound Students
Graduation
High School Equivalency Programs
High Schools
High School Seniors
High School Students
Post High School Guidance

High School Libraries
USE SCHOOL LIBRARIES

= Two or more Descriptors are used to represent this term.
The term's main entry shows the appropriate coordination.

High School Organization (1966 1980)
USE SCHOOL ORGANIZATION

High School Role (1966 1980)
USE SCHOOL ROLE

HIGH SCHOOL SENIORS *Mar. 1980*
CIJE: 207 RIE: 372 GC: 360
SN Students in their last year of high school (note: prior to mar80, "seniors" was also a valid descriptor -- for curriculum or classroom-based materials, use "grade 12")
UF Seniors (1966 1980) (Grade 12)
BT High School Students
RT College Bound Students
Grade 12
High School Freshmen
High School Graduates
Noncollege Bound Students

HIGH SCHOOL STUDENTS *Jul. 1966*
CIJE: 2645 RIE: 2915 GC: 360
SN Students in grade 9 or 10 through grade 12 (note: coordinate with the appropriate mandatory educational level descriptor)
UF Senior High School Students
NT College Bound Students
High School Freshmen
High School Seniors
Noncollege Bound Students
BT Secondary School Students
RT High School Graduates
High Schools
Junior High School Students
Reentry Students

High School Supervisors (1966 1980)
USE SCHOOL SUPERVISION

High School Teachers
USE SECONDARY SCHOOL TEACHERS

HIGH SCHOOLS *Jul. 1966*
CIJE: 3986 RIE: 4621 GC: 340
SN Providing formal education in grades 9 or 10 through 12 (note: also appears in the list of mandatory educational level descriptors)
UF Comprehensive High Schools (1967 1980)
Precollege Level
Senior High Schools (1966 1980)
NT Vocational High Schools
BT Secondary Schools
RT Continuation Students
Grade 9
Grade 10
Grade 11
Grade 12
High School Freshmen
High School Graduates
High School Students
Junior High Schools
Middle Schools
Post High School Guidance
Secondary Education
Secondary School Curriculum

High Technology
USE TECHNOLOGICAL ADVANCEMENT

HIGHER EDUCATION *Jul. 1966*
CIJE: 58648 RIE: 39429 GC: 340
SN All education beyond the secondary level leading to a formal degree (note: also appears in the list of mandatory educational level descriptors)
UF Advanced Education
College Deans (1968 1980) #
Private Higher Education #
Public Higher Education #
NT Graduate Study
Postdoctoral Education
Undergraduate Study
BT Postsecondary Education
RT Academic Advising
Access To Education
College Admission
College Attendance
College Bound Students
College Curriculum
College Instruction
College Preparation
College Programs
Colleges
Degrees (Academic)
Developing Institutions
Doctoral Programs
Educational Benefits
Extension Education
Graduate Students
Masters Programs
Nontraditional Students
Postsecondary Education As A Field Of Study
Undergraduate Students
Universities

Higher Education As A Field Of Study
USE POSTSECONDARY EDUCATION AS A FIELD OF STUDY

Higher Education Institutions
USE COLLEGES

Highway Construction
USE ROAD CONSTRUCTION

Highway Engineering
USE CIVIL ENGINEERING

HIGHWAY ENGINEERING AIDES *Jul. 1966*
CIJE: RIE: 9 GC: 640
BT Engineering Technicians
RT Civil Engineering
Engineering
Road Construction

HINDI *Jul. 1966*
CIJE: 23 RIE: 78 GC: 440
BT Indo European Languages
RT Urdu

HISPANIC AMERICAN CULTURE *Mar. 1980*
CIJE: 41 RIE: 88 GC: 560
SN Culture of the residents or citizens of the united states who are of hispanic heritage
UF Mexican American Culture #
BT North American Culture
RT Hispanic American Literature
Hispanic Americans
Latin American Culture
Mexican Americans
Portuguese Americans
Spanish Americans
Spanish Culture

HISPANIC AMERICAN LITERATURE *Mar. 1980*
CIJE: 299 RIE: 64 GC: 430
SN Literature of spanish- or portuguese-speaking people in the united states (note: for hispanic literature outside the united states, see "spanish literature" or "latin american literature")
UF Spanish American Literature (1969 1980)
NT Mexican American Literature
BT United States Literature
RT Hispanic American Culture
Hispanic Americans
Latin American Literature
Spanish Americans
Spanish Speaking

HISPANIC AMERICANS *Mar. 1980*
CIJE: 376 RIE: 1100 GC: 560
SN Residents or citizens of the united states who are of hispanic heritage (note: use a more specific term if possible)
UF Cuban Americans #
Dominican Americans #
NT Mexican Americans
Portuguese Americans
Spanish Americans
BT North Americans
RT Cubans
Dominicans
Ethnic Groups
Hispanic American Culture
Hispanic American Literature
Latin American History
Latin Americans
Minority Groups
Puerto Ricans
Spanish Speaking

HISTORICAL CRITICISM (1969 1980) *Mar. 1980*
CIJE: 203 RIE: 47 GC: 430
SN Invalid descriptor -- originally intended as a literary term, but used indiscriminately in indexing -- see "literary criticism" and appropriate "history" term(s) for this concept -- see also "literary history" or "historiography"

Historical Geography
USE HUMAN GEOGRAPHY

Historical Linguistics
USE DIACHRONIC LINGUISTICS

Historical Reviews (1966 1980)
USE HISTORY

Historically Black Colleges
USE BLACK COLLEGES

HISTORIOGRAPHY *Apr. 1974*
CIJE: 352 RIE: 118 GC: 430
SN Study of the principles and methodology of historical writing, including study of the trends in historical interpretation
BT History
RT History Instruction
Intellectual History
Oral History
Primary Sources
Social History
Social Science Research

HISTORY *Jul. 1966*
CIJE: 3365 RIE: 2771 GC: 430
SN The most general term for the study of the past -- also used for historical reviews or discussions of various topics (note: use a more specific term if possible -- prior to mar80, this term did not carry a scope note)
UF Historical Reviews (1966 1980)
NT African History
American Indian History
Ancient History
Asian History
Black History
Constitutional History
Diplomatic History
Educational History
European History
Family History
Historiography
Intellectual History
Latin American History
Local History
Medieval History
Middle Eastern History
Modern History
North American History
Oral History
Science History
Social History
World History
BT Humanities
Social Sciences
RT Area Studies
Background
Change
Chronicles
Development
Ethnic Studies
History Instruction
History Textbooks
Literature
Museums
Non Western Civilization
Peace
Primary Sources
Revolution
Social Science Research
Social Scientists
Social Studies
War
Western Civilization

History Curriculum
USE HISTORY INSTRUCTION

History Education
USE HISTORY INSTRUCTION

HISTORY INSTRUCTION *Jul. 1966*
CIJE: 1183 RIE: 617 GC: 430
UF History Curriculum
History Education
BT Humanities Instruction
RT Historiography
History
History Textbooks

History Of Education
USE EDUCATIONAL HISTORY

History Of Language
USE DIACHRONIC LINGUISTICS

HISTORY TEXTBOOKS *Jul. 1966*
CIJE: 101 RIE: 77 GC: 730
BT Textbooks
RT History
History Instruction

HOBBIES *Jul. 1966*
CIJE: 46 RIE: 42 GC: 470
BT Recreational Activities
RT Individual Activities
Interests

Hokku
USE HAIKU

Holding Power (Of Schools)
USE SCHOOL HOLDING POWER

HOLIDAYS *Oct. 1984*
CIJE: 25 RIE: 64 GC: 520
SN Days set aside for commemorating historical, cultural, religious, or other special events -- often marked by cessation of ordinary work or school activity (note: if appropriate, use the more specific term "religious holidays")
NT Religious Holidays
RT Cultural Activities
Cultural Context
Leaves Of Absence
Leisure Time
Social History
Vacations

HOLISTIC APPROACH *Apr. 1982*
CIJE: 202 RIE: 138 GC: 810
SN Techniques and/or philosophies that consider an entity or phenomenon in totality, rather than as an aggregate of constituent parts
UF Whole Person Approach
Wholistic Approach
NT Gestalt Therapy
Global Approach
Systems Approach
BT Methods
RT Decision Making
Holistic Evaluation
Humanization
Integrated Activities
Interdisciplinary Approach
Philosophy
Planning
Research Methodology
Scientific Methodology

HOLISTIC EVALUATION *Jun. 1981*
CIJE: 50 RIE: 113 GC: 820
SN Determination of the overall quality of a piece of work or an endeavor by considering various aspects or components of the work without marking or tallying them
BT Evaluation
RT Grading
Holistic Approach
Program Evaluation
Scaling
Scoring
Student Evaluation
Writing Evaluation

HOLOGRAPHY *Nov. 1971*
CIJE: 48 RIE: 16 GC: 720
SN A technique for producing three dimensional images by wavefront reconstruction
BT Photography
RT Lasers
Three Dimensional Aids

Holy Days
USE RELIGIOUS HOLIDAYS

Home
USE FAMILY ENVIRONMENT

Home And Family Life Education
USE FAMILY LIFE EDUCATION

Home Appliance Repair
USE APPLIANCE REPAIR

Home Attendants
USE HOME HEALTH AIDES

Home Conditions
USE FAMILY ENVIRONMENT

Home Day Care
USE FAMILY DAY CARE

Home Demonstration Agents
USE EXTENSION AGENTS

HOME ECONOMICS *Jul. 1966*
CIJE: 340 RIE: 833 GC: 400
SN Study, below the postsecondary level, of home management -- includes budgeting, child care, nutrition, cooking, sewing, etc. (note: do not confuse with "home economics education)
UF Homemaking Education (1967 1980)
BT Curriculum
RT Clothing Instruction
Consumer Economics
Consumer Education
Consumer Science
Cooking Instruction
Foods Instruction
Home Economics Education
Home Economics Skills
Home Economics Teachers
Homemakers
Homemaking Skills
Home Management
Nutrition Instruction
Occupational Home Economics
Sewing Instruction
Textiles Instruction

HOME ECONOMICS EDUCATION *Jul. 1966*
CIJE: 413 RIE: 660 GC: 400
SN Instruction offered at the college or graduate-school level for professional careers requiring home economics knowledge and skills (note: prior to mar80, this term was not scoped and was often used for elementary, secondary, or vocational courses -- for these concepts, see "home economics" or "occupational home economics")
BT Professional Education
RT Consumer Education
Day Care
Extension Agents
Home Economics
Home Economics Skills
Home Economics Teachers
Homemaking Skills
Occupational Home Economics

HOME ECONOMICS SKILLS *Jul. 1966*
CIJE: 18 RIE: 133 GC: 400
SN Abilities in such areas as clothing, nutrition, household work, food service, etc. (note: do not confuse with "homemaking skills")
BT Skills
RT Child Care Occupations
Cooks
Daily Living Skills
Dietitians
Employment Qualifications
Food Service
Home Economics
Home Economics Education
Homemaking Skills
Household Workers
Housekeepers
Housing Management Aides
Job Skills
Laundry Drycleaning Occupations
Needle Trades
Occupational Home Economics
Visiting Homemakers

HOME ECONOMICS TEACHERS *Jul. 1966*
CIJE: 134 RIE: 97 GC: 360
BT Teachers
RT Extension Agents
Home Economics
Home Economics Education
Occupational Home Economics
Vocational Education Teachers

Home Environment
USE FAMILY ENVIRONMENT

Home Experience
USE EXPERIENTIAL LEARNING

HOME FURNISHINGS *Jul. 1966*
CIJE: 9 RIE: 85 GC: 910
BT Equipment
RT Electrical Appliances
Family Environment
Furniture
Furniture Arrangement
Furniture Industry
Housing

HOME HEALTH AIDES *May. 1971*
CIJE: 22 RIE: 60 GC: 210
SN Workers who, under professional supervision, provide routine health/personal care and housekeeping services in homes of disabled, ill, or elderly clients
UF Home Attendants
BT Allied Health Personnel
Household Workers
RT Adult Day Care
Adult Foster Care
Attendants
Community Health Services
Home Programs
Hospices (Terminal Care)
Nurses Aides
Public Health
Visiting Homemakers

Home Influence
USE FAMILY INFLUENCE

HOME INSTRUCTION *Jul. 1966*
CIJE: 95 RIE: 221 GC: 350
SN Instruction provided in the home, by educational personnel, for children with special needs (usually homebound or preschool) or their parents (note: do not confuse with "home schooling" or "home study")
BT Instruction
RT Homebound
Home Programs
Home Visits
Individual Instruction
Itinerant Teachers
Preschool Education
Telephone Instruction

Home Life
USE FAMILY LIFE

HOME MANAGEMENT *Jul. 1966*
CIJE: 148 RIE: 333 GC: 400
SN Utilization of human and physical resources to maximize individual and familial development within the home
UF Family Management (1966 1980)
BT Administration
RT Basic Business Education
Consumer Economics
Consumer Education
Family (Sociological Unit)
Family Environment
Family Life Education
Home Economics
Homemakers
Homemaking Skills
Housing
Money Management
Visiting Homemakers

HOME PROGRAMS *Jul. 1966*
CIJE: 173 RIE: 413 GC: 330
SN Planned activities or procedures (e.g., educational, health, counseling) that take place in the home
BT Programs
RT Educational Television
Homebound
Home Health Aides
Home Instruction
Home Schooling
Home Study
Home Visits
Hospices (Terminal Care)
Videotex
Visiting Homemakers

Home School Relationship
USE FAMILY SCHOOL RELATIONSHIP

HOME SCHOOLING *Oct. 1982*
CIJE: 16 RIE: 18 GC: 330
SN Provision of compulsory education in the home as an alternative to traditional public/private schooling -- often motivated by parental desire to exclude their children from the traditional school environment (note: do not confuse with "home instruction" or "home study")
BT Compulsory Education
RT Civil Liberties
Home Programs
Nontraditional Education
Parents
Parent Student Relationship
Private Education
School Attendance Legislation

HOME STUDY *Jul. 1966*
CIJE: 86 RIE: 182 GC: 310
SN Studying done at home outside school hours, including work on school assignments, community projects, or individual problems (note: do not confuse with "home instruction" or "home schooling")
NT Homework
BT Study
RT Correspondence Study
Distance Education
Extension Education
Home Programs
Independent Study
Nontraditional Education

HOME VISITS *Jul. 1966*
CIJE: 120 RIE: 390 GC: 330
BT Methods
RT Community Health Services
Home Instruction
Home Programs
Parents
Parent Teacher Cooperation
Students
Teachers
Visiting Homemakers

HOMEBOUND *Jul. 1966*
CIJE: 43 RIE: 87 GC: 220
SN Individuals who are confined to their homes due to illness or disability
UF Homebound Children (1966 1980)
RT Home Instruction
Home Programs
Itinerant Teachers
Special Education
Telephone Instruction

Homebound Children (1966 1980)
USE HOMEBOUND

Homebound Teachers (1966 1980)
USE ITINERANT TEACHERS

HOMELESS PEOPLE *Jan. 1986*
CIJE: 12 RIE: 9 GC: 530
SN Individuals or families without permanent or fixed residences, typically living in abandoned buildings, public places, or the streets and, at times, seeking temporary shelter with public or private charities
UF Homelessness
Street People
BT Groups
RT Economically Disadvantaged
Housing Needs
Poverty
Runaways

Homelessness
USE HOMELESS PEOPLE

HOMEMAKERS *Mar. 1980*
CIJE: 141 RIE: 153 GC: 640
SN Men or women who carry major responsibilities for household or family management
UF Househusbands
Housewives (1968 1980)
BT Groups
RT Displaced Homemakers
Family (Sociological Unit)
Family Life
Family Structure
Home Economics
Homemaking Skills
Home Management
Spouses

Homemakers Clubs (1966 1980)
USE CLUBS; HOMEMAKING SKILLS

Homemaking Education (1967 1980)
USE HOME ECONOMICS

HOMEMAKING SKILLS *Jul. 1966*
CIJE: 62 RIE: 216 GC: 400
SN Ability to create, manage, and maintain a home environment (note: do not confuse with "home economics skills")
UF Homemakers Clubs (1966 1980)#
BT Skills
RT Daily Living Skills
Family Life
Home Economics
Home Economics Education
Home Economics Skills
Homemakers
Home Management
Practical Arts

HOMEOWNERS *Mar. 1980*
CIJE: 20 RIE: 14 GC: 510
SN People who own houses and, generally, live in them
BT Groups
RT Housing
Landlords
Ownership

Homes For The Aged
USE PERSONAL CARE HOMES

HOMEWORK *Jul. 1966*
CIJE: 179 RIE: 138 GC: 310
BT Assignments
Home Study

HOMOGENEOUS GROUPING *Jul. 1966*
CIJE: 89 RIE: 104 GC: 310
SN Organization or classification of students according to specified criteria for the purpose of forming instructional groups with a high degree of similarity
NT Ability Grouping
BT Grouping (Instructional Purposes)
RT Age Grade Placement
Cluster Grouping
Heterogeneous Grouping
Single Sex Colleges
Single Sex Schools

HOMOSEXUALITY *Jan. 1974*
CIJE: 251 RIE: 86 GC: 120
SN Sexual attraction and/or intercourse between members of the same sex (note: use a more specific term if possible)
NT Lesbianism
BT Sexuality

Honor Codes
USE CODES OF ETHICS

HONOR SOCIETIES *Jul. 1966*
CIJE: 20 RIE: 18 GC: 330
BT Organizations (Groups)
RT Awards
Fraternities
Honors Curriculum
National Organizations
Sororities

Honors Classes (1966 1980)
USE HONORS CURRICULUM

Honors Courses
USE HONORS CURRICULUM

= Two or more Descriptors are used to represent this term.
The term's main entry shows the appropriate coordination.

HONORS CURRICULUM *Jul. 1966*
CIJE: 95 RIE: 122 GC: 310
UF Honors Classes (1966 1980)
Honors Courses
BT Curriculum
RT Academically Gifted
Acceleration (Education)
Advanced Placement
Honor Societies
Independent Study

HOPI *Mar. 1971*
CIJE: 6 RIE: 12 GC: 440
SN A shoshonean language spoken by some pueblo indians and the hopi tribe of american indians residing in northeastern arizona
BT Uto Aztecan Languages

HORIZONTAL ORGANIZATION *Jul. 1966*
CIJE: 21 RIE: 28 GC: 520
BT Organization
RT Curriculum Design
Pyramid Organization
Vertical Organization

Horologists
USE WATCHMAKERS

HOROLOGY *Jan. 1969*
CIJE: 5 RIE: 1 GC: 490
BT Technology
RT Electromechanical Technology
Instrumentation
Motion
Skilled Occupations
Technical Education
Time
Watchmakers

HORSEBACK RIDING *Feb. 1978*
CIJE: 7 RIE: 10 GC: 470
BT Physical Activities
RT Athletics
Horses
Outdoor Activities
Recreational Activities

HORSES *Jul. 1966*
CIJE: 11 RIE: 17 GC: 410
BT Animals
RT Animal Husbandry
Horseback Riding
Livestock

HORTICULTURE *Jul. 1966*
CIJE: 112 RIE: 175 GC: 410
UF Crop Planting
Planting (1966 1980)
Transplanting (1968 1980)
NT Ornamental Horticulture
BT Agriculture
RT Botany
Entomology
Field Crops
Harvesting
Herbicides
Nurseries (Horticulture)
Ornithology
Plant Growth
Plant Identification
Plant Propagation

HOSPICES (TERMINAL CARE) *Aug. 1986*
CIJE: RIE: GC: 210
SN Multidisciplinary programs or facilities offering care and comfort to dying patients and their families
BT Health Services
RT Death
Family Counseling
Family Problems
Health Facilities
Home Health Aides
Home Programs
Hospitals
Medical Services
Nursing Homes
Social Services
Visiting Homemakers

Hospital Attendants
USE NURSES AIDES

HOSPITAL LIBRARIES *Apr. 1980*
CIJE: 8 RIE: 12 GC: 710
SN Libraries provided for use by hospital patients and sometimes the staff
BT Institutional Libraries
RT Hospitals
Psychiatric Hospitals

HOSPITAL PERSONNEL *Jul. 1966*
CIJE: 132 RIE: 139 GC: 210
BT Health Personnel
RT Graduate Medical Students
Institutional Personnel
Medical Services
Nurses
Physicians
Psychiatrists

Hospital Record Administrators
USE MEDICAL RECORD ADMINISTRATORS

Hospital Record Technicians
USE MEDICAL RECORD TECHNICIANS

HOSPITAL SCHOOLS *Jul. 1966*
CIJE: 19 RIE: 18 GC: 340
SN Schools in hospitals for formal instruction of hospitalized children (note: do not confuse with "teaching hospitals" or "patient education" -- prior to oct79, this term was not scoped)
BT Institutional Schools
RT Hospitalized Children
Hospitals
Itinerant Teachers

HOSPITALITY OCCUPATIONS *Nov. 1982*
CIJE: 5 RIE: 54 GC: 640
SN Customer/guest service occupations in restaurants, hotels, motels, amusement and recreation facilities, and the tourism industry
BT Service Occupations
RT Dining Facilities
Food Service
Hotels
Parks
Recreation
Recreational Facilities
Tourism

HOSPITALIZED CHILDREN *Jul. 1966*
CIJE: 110 RIE: 102 GC: 210
BT Children
Patients
RT Hospital Schools
Itinerant Teachers

HOSPITALS *Jul. 1966*
CIJE: 407 RIE: 331 GC: 210
UF Sanatoriums
NT Psychiatric Hospitals
Teaching Hospitals
BT Institutions
RT Clinics
Health Facilities
Health Services
Hospices (Terminal Care)
Hospital Libraries
Hospital Schools
Medical Services
Nonprofit Organizations
Nursing Homes
Patients
Surgery

HOSTILITY *Jul. 1966*
CIJE: 159 RIE: 73 GC: 230
SN Enmity or animosity, frequently marked by aggressiveness
BT Anger
RT Aggression
Catharsis
Paranoid Behavior
Resentment

HOTELS *Jul. 1966*
CIJE: 19 RIE: 64 GC: 920
UF Inns
Motels
Tourist Courts
BT Housing
RT Buildings
Hospitality Occupations
Tourism

Hothouses
USE GREENHOUSES

HOTLINES (PUBLIC) *Mar. 1980*
CIJE: 45 RIE: 24 GC: 240
SN Telephone services that provide information, assistance, or crisis counseling (note: prior to mar80, the instruction "hot lines (public), use community information services" was carried in the thesaurus)
UF Telephone Crisis Services
BT Community Information Services
RT Counseling Services
Crisis Intervention
Information Needs
Information Sources
Outreach Programs

Hours Of Work
USE WORKING HOURS

HOUSE PLAN *Jul. 1966*
CIJE: 21 RIE: 43 GC: 350
SN The organization of a secondary school or college into smaller units or communities, each having its own program, services, or facilities
UF Schools Within A School Plan
BT School Organization
RT Building Plans
Cluster Colleges
Dormitories
Educational Complexes

Household Heads
USE HEADS OF HOUSEHOLDS

Household Occupations
USE HOUSEHOLD WORKERS; SERVICE OCCUPATIONS

Household Science
USE CONSUMER SCIENCE

HOUSEHOLD WORKERS *Mar. 1980*
CIJE: 11 RIE: 64 GC: 640
SN Employees working in private homes
UF Domestics (1970 1980)
Household Occupations #
Maids (1968 1980)
NT Home Health Aides
BT Service Workers
RT Attendants
Home Economics Skills
Housekeepers

Households
USE FAMILY (SOCIOLOGICAL UNIT)

Househusbands
USE HOMEMAKERS

HOUSEKEEPERS *Mar. 1980*
CIJE: 5 RIE: 39 GC: 640
SN Workers who perform or supervise activities to maintain cleanliness and orderliness in private homes, hotels, restaurants, hospitals, or other institutions
UF Housekeeping Aides
BT Service Workers
RT Cleaning
Home Economics Skills
Household Workers
Occupational Home Economics
Visiting Homemakers

Housekeeping Aides
USE HOUSEKEEPERS

Houseparents
USE RESIDENT ADVISERS

Housewives (1968 1980)
USE HOMEMAKERS

HOUSING *Jul. 1966*
CIJE: 261 RIE: 950 GC: 920
SN Buildings or other shelters in which people live -- also, the provision of such shelters (note: use a more specific term if possible)
UF Dwellings
Living Quarters
Local Housing Authorities (1966 1980)
NT Boarding Homes
College Housing
Dormitories
Group Homes
Hotels
Low Rent Housing
Middle Income Housing
Migrant Housing
Suburban Housing
Teacher Housing
BT Facilities
RT Family Environment
Family Size
Home Furnishings
Home Management
Homeowners
Housing Deficiencies
Housing Discrimination
Housing Industry
Housing Management Aides
Housing Needs
Housing Opportunities
Human Services
Landlords
Place Of Residence
Planned Communities
Real Estate Occupations
Rehabilitation Centers
Residential Institutions
Residential Patterns
Residential Programs

HOUSING DEFICIENCIES *Jul. 1966*
CIJE: 42 RIE: 77 GC: 530
RT Housing
Housing Needs
Neighborhood Improvement
Urban Renewal

HOUSING DISCRIMINATION *Jul. 1966*
CIJE: 97 RIE: 111 GC: 540
BT Social Discrimination
RT Ghettos
Housing
Housing Opportunities
Neighborhood Integration
Racial Segregation
Reverse Discrimination

HOUSING INDUSTRY *Jul. 1966*
CIJE: 22 RIE: 31 GC: 650
BT Construction Industry
RT Housing
Housing Opportunities
Real Estate Occupations

HOUSING MANAGEMENT AIDES *Aug. 1968*
CIJE: 1 RIE: 6 GC: 640
SN Persons who aid public or private housing residents concerning regulations, relocations, etc. in addition to providing records for owners or managers
BT Paraprofessional Personnel
Service Workers
RT Home Economics Skills
Housing
Occupational Home Economics
Public Housing
Real Estate Occupations
Welfare Services

HOUSING NEEDS *Jul. 1966*
CIJE: 143 RIE: 201 GC: 920
BT Needs
RT Homeless People
Housing
Housing Deficiencies
Neighborhood Improvement

HOUSING OPPORTUNITIES *Jul. 1966*
CIJE: 57 RIE: 85 GC: 540
BT Opportunities
RT Housing
Housing Discrimination
Housing Industry
Neighborhood Integration

Housing Patterns (1966 1980)
USE RESIDENTIAL PATTERNS

Hue
USE COLOR

Human Biology
USE BIOLOGY

= Two or more Descriptors are used to represent this term.
The term's main entry shows the appropriate coordination.

HUMAN BODY *Jul. 1966*
CIJE: 407 RIE: 298 GC: 210
RT Anatomy
Biochemistry
Biofeedback
Biological Sciences
Biology
Biomechanics
Biophysics
Blood Circulation
Body Height
Body Image
Body Weight
Cardiovascular System
Ears
Exercise
Eyes
Health
Health Education
Heart Rate
Human Posture
Hygiene
Medicine
Metabolism
Movement Education
Physical Activity Level
Physiology

HUMAN CAPITAL *Jul. 1966*
CIJE: 157 RIE: 183 GC: 620
SN Investment in the education and skills of a nation's population (note: do not confuse with "human resources")
BT Investment
RT Economics
Educational Economics
Human Resources
Labor Force
Labor Supply
Population Education
Productivity

HUMAN DEVELOPMENT (1966 1980) *Mar. 1980*
CIJE: 661 RIE: 481 GC: 520
SN Invalid descriptor -- used inconsistently in indexing -- use more specific descriptors, i.e., nt's of "individual development," "evolution," "history," etc.

HUMAN DIGNITY *Jul. 1966*
CIJE: 185 RIE: 158 GC: 540
UF Individual Dignity
RT Attitudes
Behavior
Humanism
Humanitarianism
Humanization
Individualism
Individual Needs
Self Esteem

Human Engineering (1967 1980)
USE HUMAN FACTORS ENGINEERING

HUMAN FACTORS ENGINEERING *Mar. 1980*
CIJE: 172 RIE: 218 GC: 490
SN Area of knowledge dealing with the capabilities and limitations of human performance in relation to the design or modification of machines, jobs, and other aspects of a person's environment
UF Ergonomics
Human Engineering (1967 1980)
RT Acoustical Environment
Biomechanics
Biomedicine
Bionics
Cybernetics
Design Requirements
Lighting
Man Machine Systems
Physical Environment
Quality Of Life
Quality Of Working Life
Thermal Environment
Work Environment

HUMAN GEOGRAPHY *Aug. 1971*
CIJE: 287 RIE: 355 GC: 550
SN Study of the distribution of human groups and the interaction of these groups with their physical environment
UF Cultural Geography
Economic Geography
Historical Geography
Political Geography
Social Geography
Urban Geography
BT Geography
RT Anthropology
Area Studies
Cross Cultural Studies
Demography
Ecology
Ethnology
Geographic Distribution
Political Science
Population Distribution
Population Trends
Racial Distribution
Social Systems
Urban Studies

HUMAN LIVING (1966 1980) *Mar. 1980*
CIJE: 105 RIE: 82 GC: 520
SN Invalid descriptor -- used inconsistently in indexing -- see such descriptors as "life style," "quality of life," "living standards," "ecology," etc.

HUMAN POSTURE *Jul. 1966*
CIJE: 42 RIE: 42 GC: 210
UF Body Attitude
Posture Development
Posture Patterns
RT Body Language
Human Body

HUMAN RELATIONS *Jul. 1966*
CIJE: 808 RIE: 1142 GC: 520
SN Patterns of interaction between and among people that persist over time and cause common expectations and influences
UF Human Relations Units (1966 1980) #
NT Intergroup Relations
Peace
Slavery
BT Relationship
RT Group Experience
Humanistic Education
Humanization
Human Relations Programs
Interaction
Intergroup Education
Interpersonal Relationship
Laboratory Training
Rapport
Social Integration
Sociocultural Patterns

Human Relations Organizations (1966 1980)
USE HUMAN RELATIONS PROGRAMS

HUMAN RELATIONS PROGRAMS *Jul. 1966*
CIJE: 97 RIE: 153 GC: 540
UF Human Relations Organizations (1966 1980)
BT Programs
RT Human Relations

Human Relations Training
USE SENSITIVITY TRAINING

Human Relations Units (1966 1980)
USE HUMAN RELATIONS; UNITS OF STUDY

HUMAN RESOURCES *Jul. 1966*
CIJE: 491 RIE: 887 GC: 520
SN People who can be drawn upon for their knowledge, skills, or productive capacities (note: do not confuse with "human capital")
NT Labor Force
Labor Supply
BT Resources
RT Community Resources
Consultants
Developed Nations
Developing Nations
Human Capital
Information Sources
Labor
Personnel
Technical Assistance

Human Resources Development (Labor)
USE LABOR FORCE DEVELOPMENT

Human Rights
USE CIVIL LIBERTIES

HUMAN SERVICES *Mar. 1969*
CIJE: 445 RIE: 930 GC: 520
SN Fields of public service in which human interaction is part of the provision of the services
NT Counseling Services
Employment Services
Food Service
Health Services
Psychological Services
Social Services
BT Services
RT Client Characteristics (Human Services)
Correctional Education
Correctional Rehabilitation
Housing
Law Enforcement
Public Relations
Rehabilitation Programs
Residential Programs
Social Support Groups

Human Sexuality
USE SEXUALITY

Humaneness
USE ALTRUISM

HUMANISM *Jul. 1969*
CIJE: 710 RIE: 327 GC: 430
SN A philosophy that asserts the dignity and worth of man
BT Philosophy
RT Human Dignity
Humanistic Education
Individualism
Literature
Poetry
Renaissance Literature

HUMANISTIC EDUCATION *Nov. 1974*
CIJE: 1209 RIE: 926 GC: 400
SN Educational system designed to achieve affective outcomes or psychological growth -- learning activities in math, social studies, english, and so on, are oriented toward improving self-awareness and mutual understanding among people
UF Affective Education
Confluent Education
Psychological Education
BT Education
RT Affective Objectives
Free Schools
Group Dynamics
Humanism
Humanization
Human Relations
Individualized Instruction
Interpersonal Competence
Laboratory Training
Learning Centers (Classroom)
Liberalism
Multicultural Education
Open Education
Progressive Education
Psychoeducational Methods
Self Actualization
Self Concept
Sensitivity Training
Values
Values Education

HUMANITARIANISM *Mar. 1980*
CIJE: 17 RIE: 21 GC: 520
SN Theory or actual promotion of human welfare and social reform, often by philanthropic or charitable means
BT Sociocultural Patterns
RT Altruism
Citizenship Responsibility
Community Responsibility
Human Dignity
Political Attitudes
Social Action
Social Responsibility
Social Services
Social Support Groups
Social Values
Welfare Services

HUMANITIES *Jul. 1966*
CIJE: 855 RIE: 880 GC: 430
NT Fine Arts
History
Literature
Philosophy
BT Liberal Arts
RT Culture
Humanities Instruction
Religion

HUMANITIES INSTRUCTION *Jul. 1966*
CIJE: 346 RIE: 483 GC: 430
NT History Instruction
Native Language Instruction
Second Language Instruction
BT Instruction
RT Academic Education
Humanities

HUMANIZATION *Dec. 1972*
CIJE: 424 RIE: 311 GC: 520
SN The process of changing the environment (attitudes, structures, relationships) to be more humane and better adapted to human needs
UF Dehumanization
RT Attitudes
Design Requirements
Developmental Continuity
Environment
Holistic Approach
Human Dignity
Humanistic Education
Human Relations
Liberalism
Life Style
Milieu Therapy
Open Education
Psychological Needs
Quality Of Life

Humid Areas
USE HUMIDITY

HUMIDITY *Apr. 1970*
CIJE: 17 RIE: 14 GC: 490
UF Absolute Humidity
Humid Areas
Relative Humidity
RT Air Conditioning
Climate
Climate Control
Heating
Meteorology
Temperature
Thermal Environment
Water

HUMOR *Nov. 1969*
CIJE: 449 RIE: 154 GC: 430
RT Comedy
Comics (Publications)
Fiction
Literary Devices
Literary Genres
Literature
Personality Traits

HUNGARIAN *Jul. 1966*
CIJE: 17 RIE: 48 GC: 440
BT Finno Ugric Languages

HUNGER *Nov. 1969*
CIJE: 124 RIE: 147 GC: 210
RT Breakfast Programs
Food
Lunch Programs
Nutrition
Poverty
World Problems

Husbands
USE SPOUSES

Hvac
USE CLIMATE CONTROL

Hybrid Air Structures (1972 1980)
USE AIR STRUCTURES

HYDRAULICS *Jul. 1966*
CIJE: 27 RIE: 59 GC: 490
BT Technology
RT Agricultural Machinery
Engines
Fluid Mechanics
Kinetics
Water

= Two or more Descriptors are used to represent this term.
The term's main entry shows the appropriate coordination.

HYGIENE *Jul. 1966*
CIJE: 154 RIE: 337 GC: 210
UF Body Care
Personal Grooming
Personal Health
RT Cleaning
Dental Health
Dental Hygienists
Disease Control
Diseases
Dishwashing
Family Health
Food Service
Health
Health Education
Human Body
Medicine
Mental Health
Occupational Safety And Health
Physical Health
Physiology
Preventive Medicine
Public Health
Sanitary Facilities
Sanitation
Self Care Skills
Special Health Problems

HYMNS *Jul. 1970*
CIJE: 9 RIE: GC: 420
BT Literary Genres
Lyric Poetry
Songs
RT Choral Music
Religion
Singing

HYPERACTIVITY *Jul. 1966*
CIJE: 593 RIE: 190 GC: 220
SN Behavior characterized by overactivity, restlessness, distractibility, and short attention span
UF Hyperkinesis
BT Behavior
RT Attention Deficit Disorders
Attention Span
Behavior Problems
Emotional Disturbances
Learning Disabilities
Minimal Brain Dysfunction
Neurological Impairments
Perceptual Handicaps
Physical Activity Level

Hyperkinesis
USE HYPERACTIVITY

HYPEROPIA *Jul. 1966*
CIJE: RIE: 1 GC: 220
UF Farsightedness
BT Ametropia
RT Myopia
Vision
Visual Acuity

Hypersensitivity
USE ALLERGY

HYPERTENSION *Nov. 1975*
CIJE: 69 RIE: 44 GC: 210
UF High Blood Pressure
BT Diseases
RT Blood Circulation
Cardiovascular System
Heart Rate
Physical Health
Relaxation Training
Special Health Problems
Stress Variables

HYPNOSIS *Jul. 1966*
CIJE: 89 RIE: 57 GC: 230
RT Meditation
Psychotherapy
Relaxation Training
Suggestopedia

Hypnotics
USE SEDATIVES

HYPOTHESIS TESTING *Jul. 1966*
CIJE: 1383 RIE: 665 GC: 820
SN Processes by which hypotheses are accepted or rejected (note: prior to mar80, the use of this term was not restricted by a scope note)
BT Evaluation Methods
RT Analysis Of Covariance
Analysis Of Variance
Bayesian Statistics
Data Analysis
Data Interpretation
Mathematical Models
Meta Analysis
Monte Carlo Methods
Research Design
Scientific Methodology
Statistical Analysis
Statistical Inference
Statistical Significance
Theories

IBO *Jul. 1966*
CIJE: 3 RIE: 3 GC: 440
BT African Languages

ICE HOCKEY *Apr. 1985*
CIJE: 6 RIE: 11 GC: 470
BT Team Sports

ICE SKATING *Feb. 1978*
CIJE: 9 RIE: 4 GC: 470
BT Athletics

ICHTHYOLOGY *Aug. 1982*
CIJE: 10 RIE: 19 GC: 490
UF Fish Studies
BT Zoology
RT Fisheries
Marine Biology
Oceanography

Icibemba
USE BEMBA

IDENTIFICATION *Jul. 1966*
CIJE: 906 RIE: 1259 GC: 820
SN Recognition of the attributes by which an individual, condition, thing, etc. can be classified
UF Delinquent Identification (1966 1980) #
Diagnosis
Early Detection
NT Ability Identification
Clinical Diagnosis
Educational Diagnosis
Handicap Identification
Plant Identification
Racial Identification
Talent Identification
RT Classification
Diagnostic Tests
Etiology
Labeling (Of Persons)
Recognition (Psychology)
Screening Tests

Identification (Psychological) (1968 1980)
USE IDENTIFICATION (PSYCHOLOGY)

IDENTIFICATION (PSYCHOLOGY) *Mar. 1980*
CIJE: 982 RIE: 553 GC: 120
SN Process or state of imitating or merging emotionally with someone or something
UF Identification (Psychological) (1968 1980)
Introjection
BT Psychological Patterns
RT Alienation
Attachment Behavior
Behavior Patterns
Conformity
Congruence (Psychology)
Emotional Development
Empathy
Ethnicity
Imitation
Modeling (Psychology)
Observational Learning
Perspective Taking
Reference Groups
Role Models
Role Perception
Role Theory
Self Actualization
Self Concept
Self Concept Measures
Sexual Identity
Significant Others

Identification Tests (1966 1980)
USE TESTS

IDEOGRAPHY *Aug. 1973*
CIJE: 48 RIE: 62 GC: 450
SN System of writing using pictures or symbolic characters instead of letters or syllable signs
BT Written Language
RT Chinese
Language Patterns
Symbolic Language

IDEOLOGY *Aug. 1986*
CIJE: 99 RIE: 46 GC: 520
SN The body of ideas reflecting the social needs and aspirations of an individual, group, class, or culture
RT Behavior Standards
Beliefs
Cognitive Structures
Cultural Traits
Dogmatism
Elitism
Group Unity
Political Attitudes
Public Opinion
Social Action
Social Attitudes
Socialization
Social Systems
Social Theories
Social Values
Sociocultural Patterns
Sociology
Values

Idiomatic Expressions
USE IDIOMS

IDIOMS *Jul. 1966*
CIJE: 164 RIE: 112 GC: 450
UF Idiomatic Expressions
BT Language Patterns
RT Dialects
Grammar
Languages
North American English
Proverbs
Regional Dialects
Structural Analysis (Linguistics)

IGBO *Jul. 1966*
CIJE: 4 RIE: 11 GC: 440
BT African Languages

Illegal Aliens
USE UNDOCUMENTED IMMIGRANTS

ILLEGAL DRUG USE *Mar. 1980*
CIJE: 42 RIE: 65 GC: 530
BT Drug Use
RT Antisocial Behavior
Crime
Drug Abuse
Drug Addiction
Drug Legislation
Lysergic Acid Diethylamide
Marijuana
Narcotics

Illegal Immigrants (1976 1984)
USE UNDOCUMENTED IMMIGRANTS

Illegitimacy
USE ILLEGITIMATE BIRTHS

ILLEGITIMATE BIRTHS *Jul. 1966*
CIJE: 67 RIE: 67 GC: 530
UF Illegitimacy
RT Birth
Contraception
Fatherless Family
Marital Instability
One Parent Family
Pregnancy
Unwed Mothers

ILLITERACY *Jul. 1966*
CIJE: 333 RIE: 403 GC: 460
UF Illiterate Adults (1966 1980) #
RT Adult Literacy
Educationally Disadvantaged
Literacy

Illiterate Adults (1966 1980)
USE ADULT LITERACY; ILLITERACY

Illnesses
USE DISEASES

Illocutionary Acts
USE SPEECH ACTS

Illumination Levels (1968 1980)
USE LIGHTING

ILLUSTRATIONS *Jul. 1966*
CIJE: 1009 RIE: 506 GC: 720
BT Visual Aids
RT Captions
Cartoons
Charts
Diagrams
Graphs
Instructional Materials
Maps
Nonprint Media
Photographs
Photojournalism
Picture Books
Raised Line Drawings
Technical Illustration

IMAGERY *Jun. 1969*
CIJE: 640 RIE: 222 GC: 430
BT Figurative Language
RT Film Criticism
Haiku
Metaphors
Sonnets
Symbols (Literary)

IMAGINATION *Jul. 1966*
CIJE: 458 RIE: 224 GC: 120
SN The ability to form a mental image of qualities, objects, situations, relationships, etc., that are not apparent to the senses (note: prior to mar80, the use of this term was not restricted by a scope note)
BT Creativity
RT Creative Thinking
Fantasy
Fiction
Intuition
Pretend Play
Surrealism

IMITATION *Jul. 1966*
CIJE: 492 RIE: 205 GC: 110
SN Copying, whether consciously or not, the appearance, mannerisms, speech, behavior, or actions of others
BT Behavior
RT Behavior Patterns
Identification (Psychology)
Modeling (Psychology)
Observational Learning
Pretend Play
Role Models
Socialization

Imitative Learning
USE OBSERVATIONAL LEARNING

Immaturity (1966 1980)
USE MATURITY (INDIVIDUALS)

IMMERSION PROGRAMS *Aug. 1977*
CIJE: 196 RIE: 246 GC: 450
SN Educational programs in which all curriculum materials are taught in a second language, generally at the elementary level and almost always within the context of a first language school
BT Second Language Programs
RT Bilingual Education
Bilingualism
Bilingual Students
Child Language
Curriculum
English (Second Language)
Fles
Language Of Instruction
Language Planning
Modern Languages
Native Speakers
Second Language Instruction
Second Language Learning
Second Languages
Sociolinguistics

Immigrant Illegality
USE UNDOCUMENTED IMMIGRANTS

= Two or more Descriptors are used to represent this term.
The term's main entry shows the appropriate coordination.

IMMIGRANTS *Jul. 1966*
CIJE: 890 RIE: 1171 GC: 510
NT Undocumented Immigrants
BT Migrants
RT Acculturation
Foreign Nationals
Migration
Refugees
Transient Children

IMMIGRATION INSPECTORS *Jul. 1969*
CIJE: 5 RIE: 7 GC: 640
UF Border Patrol Officers
Guards (Border Patrol)
BT Government Employees
RT Law Enforcement
Migrants
Police
Undocumented Immigrants

IMMUNIZATION PROGRAMS *Jul. 1966*
CIJE: 48 RIE: 48 GC: 210
BT Health Programs
RT Communicable Diseases
Community Health Services
Disease Control
Epidemiology
Internal Medicine
Preventive Medicine

Impasse Resolution
USE NEGOTIATION IMPASSES

Imperative Mood
USE VERBS

IMPERIALISM *Nov. 1969*
CIJE: 33 RIE: 28 GC: 610
NT Colonialism
BT Foreign Policy
RT Authoritarianism
Capitalism
Communism
Fascism
Nationalism
Political Attitudes
Political Divisions (Geographic)
Political Power
Socialism
World Problems

IMPRESSIONISM *Jul. 1970*
CIJE: 14 RIE: 2 GC: 430
SN Artistic style of the late 19th and early 20th centuries associated primarily with painting that seeks to capture the effects of light on canvas with short brush strokes -- extended to literature and music, it seeks to evoke moods and impressions rather than to convey precise details of reality
RT Art Expression
Intellectual History
Literary Styles
Music
Nineteenth Century Literature
Twentieth Century Literature

IMPRESSIONISTIC CRITICISM (1969 1980) *Mar. 1980*
CIJE: 188 RIE: 11 GC: 430
SN Invalid descriptor -- originally intended as a literary term, but used indiscriminately in indexing -- see "literary criticism" and "reader response"

IMPROVEMENT *Jul. 1966*
CIJE: 155 RIE: 134 GC: 520
SN Remedying deficiencies in existing conditions or bringing satisfactory conditions to a higher level of excellence (note: use a more specific term if possible)
UF Renovation
Upgrading
NT Achievement Gains
Educational Improvement
Facility Improvement
Finance Reform
Neighborhood Improvement
Program Improvement
Reading Improvement
Speech Improvement
Student Improvement
Teacher Improvement
Urban Improvement
Writing Improvement
RT Achievement
Change Strategies
Development
Improvement Programs
Innovation
Pretests Posttests
Success

IMPROVEMENT PROGRAMS *Jul. 1966*
CIJE: 220 RIE: 480 GC: 320
SN Systematic plans to upgrade and increase effectiveness of skills, conditions, methods, curricula, facilities, persons, etc.
NT Self Help Programs
BT Programs
RT Enrichment Activities
Improvement
Inservice Education
Professional Training
Refresher Courses

Impulse Control
USE SELF CONTROL

Impulsivity
USE CONCEPTUAL TEMPO

IN SCHOOL SUSPENSION *Aug. 1986*
CIJE: 17 RIE: 17 GC: 320
SN Practice in which a student who has been temporarily removed from classes for disciplinary reasons is required to participate in a special program within the school, which stresses behavior change and may incorporate instructional and counseling activities as well
BT Suspension
RT Discipline Policy
Intervention
Special Classes
Study Centers

IN STATE STUDENTS *Mar. 1980*
CIJE: 40 RIE: 202 GC: 360
SN College students who are legal residents of the state or province in which they attend school
UF Resident Students (1967 1980) (In State)
BT College Students
RT Place Of Residence
Residence Requirements
Tuition

Inadequate Employment
USE UNDEREMPLOYMENT

INCENTIVE GRANTS *Jul. 1966*
CIJE: 29 RIE: 104 GC: 620
SN Grants intended to encourage recipients to perform or produce in a specified way or according to a specified schedule
BT Grants
RT Educational Finance
Federal Aid
Foundation Programs
State Aid

Incentive Systems (1967 1980)
USE INCENTIVES

INCENTIVES *Mar. 1980*
CIJE: 359 RIE: 342 GC: 520
SN Factors motivating or inciting to action or effort (note: prior to mar80, the instruction "incentives, use motivation" was carried in the thesaurus)
UF Achievement Incentives
Incentive Systems (1967 1980)
RT Awards
Change Strategies
Fines (Penalties)
Merit Pay
Motivation
Motivation Techniques
Positive Reinforcement
Recognition (Achievement)
Rewards
Sanctions
Token Economy

INCEST *Jun. 1983*
CIJE: 37 RIE: 29 GC: 530
SN Sexual activity between persons of closer kinship than law or social custom allows
UF Incest Taboo
BT Antisocial Behavior
RT Crime
Rape
Sexual Abuse
Sexuality
Victims Of Crime

Incest Taboo
USE INCEST

INCIDENCE *Jul. 1966*
CIJE: 360 RIE: 349 GC: 480
SN Frequency with which a condition or event occurs within a given time and population
UF Prevalence
NT Average Daily Attendance
Birth Rate
Disease Incidence
Dropout Rate
Enrollment Rate
RT Census Figures
Demography
Ethnic Distribution
Geographic Distribution
High Risk Persons
Infant Mortality
Longitudinal Studies
Population Distribution
Probability
Racial Distribution
Ratios (Mathematics)
Social Distribution
Teacher Distribution

INCIDENTAL LEARNING *Jul. 1966*
CIJE: 143 RIE: 81 GC: 110
BT Learning
RT Hidden Curriculum
Intentional Learning
Observational Learning
Test Wiseness

INCOME *Jul. 1966*
CIJE: 809 RIE: 1883 GC: 620
UF Income Patterns
Revenue
NT Family Income
Guaranteed Income
Interest (Finance)
Low Income
Merit Pay
Premium Pay
Salaries
Wages
RT Budgets
Compensation (Remuneration)
Economic Status
Employment Level
Endowment Funds
Financial Audits
Financial Needs
Financial Problems
Financial Support
Fund Raising
Income Contingent Loans
Inflation (Economics)
Middle Income Housing
Money Management
Overtime
Retirement Benefits
Social Class
Socioeconomic Status
Trusts (Financial)

INCOME CONTINGENT LOANS *Aug. 1976*
CIJE: 11 RIE: 15 GC: 620
SN Loans for which repayment is based on a percentage of future annual income
UF Deferred Tuition
Tuition Postponement
BT Student Financial Aid
RT Income
Loan Repayment
Student Loan Programs

Income Patterns
USE INCOME

INDEMNITY BONDS *Sep. 1968*
CIJE: 4 RIE: 8 GC: 620
RT Employee Responsibility
Insurance
Legal Responsibility

Independent Colleges
USE PRIVATE COLLEGES

Independent Learning
USE INDEPENDENT STUDY

INDEPENDENT READING *Jul. 1966*
CIJE: 65 RIE: 157 GC: 460
SN Reading that a student does without assistance from a teacher, usually at his or her own option
BT Reading
RT Independent Study
Individualized Reading
Intellectual Freedom
Reading Interests
Recreational Reading
Supplementary Reading Materials

Independent Schools
USE PRIVATE SCHOOLS

Independent Students (Self Supporting)
USE SELF SUPPORTING STUDENTS

INDEPENDENT STUDY *Jul. 1966*
CIJE: 1100 RIE: 1468 GC: 310
SN Individual study, usually self-initiated, that may be directed or assisted by instructional staff through periodic consultations (note: do not confuse with "individual instruction")
UF Independent Learning
Individual Study (1966 1980)
Self Directed Learning
Self Instruction
Self Teaching
BT Study
RT Autoinstructional Aids
Correspondence Study
Discovery Learning
Distance Education
External Degree Programs
Home Study
Honors Curriculum
Independent Reading
Individual Instruction
Intellectual Freedom
Learning Laboratories
Learning Modules
Lifelong Learning
Open Education
Pacing
Personal Autonomy
Student Projects
Student Research
Study Guides

Independent Variables
USE PREDICTOR VARIABLES

Index Numbers (Costs)
USE COST INDEXES

Index Terms
USE SUBJECT INDEX TERMS

INDEXES *Mar. 1980*
CIJE: 452 RIE: 1266 GC: 730
SN Systematic guides to information, consisting of lists of logically arranged items with references that show where the items are located (note: do not use for "cost indexes")
UF Concordances (1967 1980)
Indexes (Locaters) (1967 1980)
NT Citation Indexes
Coordinate Indexes
Permuted Indexes
BT Reference Materials
RT Abstracts
Automatic Indexing
Bibliographies
Check Lists
Directories
Discographies
Filmographies
Indexing
Information Retrieval
Information Utilization

Library Catalogs
Subject Index Terms
Thesauri

Indexes (Locaters) (1967 1980)
USE INDEXES

INDEXING *Jul. 1966*
CIJE: 354 RIE: 458 GC: 710
SN Assignment of index terms to documents or objects in order to later retrieve or locate these documents or objects according to the selected concepts designated by the index terms (note: do not use for "cost indexes")
UF Subject Access
NT Automatic Indexing
BT Documentation
RT Abstracting
Bibliometrics
Cataloging
Citation Indexes
Classification
Coordinate Indexes
Filing
Indexes
Information Retrieval
Library Technical Processes
Permuted Indexes
Search Strategies
Subject Index Terms
Thesauri

INDIANS *Jul. 1966*
CIJE: 108 RIE: 119 GC: 560
SN Natives of india or of the east indies
BT Groups
RT Asian Studies
Ethnic Groups

Indicative Mood
USE VERBS

Indifference
USE APATHY

INDIGENOUS PERSONNEL *Jul. 1966*
CIJE: 24 RIE: 114 GC: 630
SN Workers who share a common background or culture with the people they represent or serve
BT Personnel
RT Cross Cultural Training
Outreach Programs

INDIGENOUS POPULATIONS *Mar. 1980*
CIJE: 34 RIE: 29 GC: 550
SN People born in a specific region, country, etc., or whose ancestry is connected therewith
UF Natives
BT Groups
RT Cultural Background
Ethnic Groups
Foreign Nationals
Race

INDIVIDUAL ACTIVITIES *Jul. 1966*
CIJE: 69 RIE: 123 GC: 310
BT Activities
RT Hobbies
Lifetime Sports

Individual Adjustment
USE ADJUSTMENT (TO ENVIRONMENT)

Individual Autonomy
USE PERSONAL AUTONOMY

INDIVIDUAL CHARACTERISTICS *Jul. 1966*
CIJE: 2506 RIE: 2327 GC: 120
SN Physical and psychological characteristics of a single individual, or a single group of individuals, within any species (note: prior to mar80, the use of this term was restricted to humans, and the instruction "personality traits, use individual characteristics" was carried in the thesaurus)
UF Adult Characteristics (1967 1980) #
NT Age
Maturity (Individuals)
Physical Characteristics
Psychological Characteristics
RT Administrator Characteristics
Background
Biographical Inventories
Client Characteristics (Human Services)
Counselor Characteristics
Dropout Characteristics
Experimenter Characteristics
Individual Development
Individual Differences
Participant Characteristics
Reputation
Social Characteristics
Student Characteristics
Teacher Characteristics

INDIVIDUAL COUNSELING *Jul. 1966*
CIJE: 193 RIE: 167 GC: 240
SN Counseling that is direct, active, personal, and focused on increasing the individual client's self-understanding and adjustment (note: do not confuse with "nondirective counseling")
BT Counseling
RT Group Counseling
Helping Relationship
Parent Counseling

INDIVIDUAL DEVELOPMENT *Jul. 1966*
CIJE: 2339 RIE: 2128 GC: 120
SN Growth or maturation in the individuals of a species due to aging, learning, or experience (note: prior to mar80, the use of this term was not restricted by a scope note -- use a more specific term if possible)
UF Personal Development
Personal Growth (1967 1980)
Self Growth
NT Adolescent Development
Adult Development
Aging (Individuals)
Behavior Development
Career Development
Child Development
Cognitive Development
Creative Development
Emotional Development
Moral Development
Personality Development
Physical Development
Skill Development
Social Development
Talent Development
BT Development
RT Adjustment (To Environment)
Background
Developmental Continuity
Developmental Programs
Developmental Psychology
Developmental Stages
Developmental Studies Programs
Faculty Development
Individual Characteristics
Individual Differences
Individual Psychology
Learning
Maturity (Individuals)
Maturity Tests
Nature Nurture Controversy
Professional Development
Readiness
Self Actualization
Self Help Programs
Student Development

INDIVIDUAL DIFFERENCES *Jul. 1966*
CIJE: 2110 RIE: 1469 GC: 120
SN Differences in personality, attitudes, physiology, learning or perceptual processes, etc., that account for variation in performance or behavior
NT Age Differences
Intelligence Differences
Sex Differences
BT Differences
RT Background
Cultural Differences
Individual Characteristics
Individual Development
Nature Nurture Controversy
Racial Differences
Religious Differences
Social Differences

Individual Dignity
USE HUMAN DIGNITY

INDIVIDUAL INSTRUCTION *Jul. 1966*
CIJE: 355 RIE: 849 GC: 310
SN Instruction of individuals (i.e., not group instruction) (note: do not confuse with "independent study" or "individualized instruction")
NT Tutoring
BT Instruction
RT Autoinstructional Aids
Group Instruction
Home Instruction
Independent Study
Individualized Instruction
Individual Needs
Itinerant Teachers
Teaching Methods
Telephone Instruction
Tutorial Programs

INDIVIDUAL NEEDS *Jul. 1966*
CIJE: 873 RIE: 981 GC: 120
UF Special Needs (Individuals)
NT Childhood Needs
Psychological Needs
BT Needs
RT Design Preferences
Design Requirements
Human Dignity
Individual Instruction
Individualized Education Programs
Individualized Instruction
Individualized Programs
Need Gratification
Special Education
Special Programs
Student Needs
Well Being

INDIVIDUAL POWER *Jul. 1966*
CIJE: 509 RIE: 487 GC: 120
SN Feeling of power to effect changes in ones social and physical surroundings by decision making
UF Individual Volition
Volition
RT Behavior
Child Advocacy
Coping
Decision Making
Individualism
Life Satisfaction
Locus Of Control
Mental Health
Personal Autonomy
Psychological Patterns
Self Actualization
Self Concept
Self Control
Self Determination
Self Expression

INDIVIDUAL PSYCHOLOGY *Jul. 1966*
CIJE: 244 RIE: 272 GC: 230
SN Branch of psychology whose theory and practice stress the unique wholeness of the individual and regard the purposive striving of the psyche as the motive force of human development -- also sometimes used to refer to the study of individual differences
UF Differential Psychology
BT Psychology
RT Adaptation Level Theory
Androgyny
Assertiveness
Child Psychology
Developmental Psychology
Individual Development
Life Style
Personal Autonomy
Personality
Psychological Characteristics
Psychological Needs
Psychotherapy
Self Actualization

INDIVIDUAL READING (1966 1980) *Mar. 1980*
CIJE: 19 RIE: 49 GC: 460
SN Invalid descriptor -- used inconsistently in indexing -- see such descriptors as "individualized reading," "independent reading," and "recreational reading"

Individual Rights
USE CIVIL LIBERTIES

Individual Study (1966 1980)
USE INDEPENDENT STUDY

INDIVIDUAL TESTING *Mar. 1980*
CIJE: 106 RIE: 145 GC: 820
SN Process of administering tests to individuals (i.e., not in a group setting)
UF Individual Tests (1966 1980)
BT Testing
RT Adaptive Testing
Group Testing

Individual Tests (1966 1980)
USE INDIVIDUAL TESTING

Individual Volition
USE INDIVIDUAL POWER

INDIVIDUALISM *Oct. 1969*
CIJE: 264 RIE: 107 GC: 430
SN A theory or policy having primary regard for the liberty, rights, or independent actions of individuals
RT Creativity
Existentialism
Human Dignity
Humanism
Individual Power
Intellectual Freedom
Personal Autonomy
Phenomenology
Philosophy
Self Actualization
Self Determination
Self Expression
Social Development
Social Values

Individualized Curriculum (1966 1980)
USE INDIVIDUALIZED INSTRUCTION

Individualized Education
USE INDIVIDUALIZED INSTRUCTION

INDIVIDUALIZED EDUCATION PROGRAMS *Oct. 1980*
CIJE: 262 RIE: 514 GC: 330
SN Educational programs for individual students, each geared to the particular student's needs and conducted in accordance with a written plan agreed on between the student (and/or parents) and school officials -- iep's were originally conceived for use in educating handicapped children and were gradually expanded to include all special needs groups
BT Special Programs
RT Diagnostic Teaching
Educationally Disadvantaged
Equal Education
Exceptional Persons
Federal Programs
Individualized Instruction
Individual Needs
Mainstreaming
Nontraditional Education
Resource Room Programs
Special Education

INDIVIDUALIZED INSTRUCTION *Jan. 1969*
CIJE: 3916 RIE: 5545 GC: 310
SN Adapting instruction to individual needs within the group (note: do not confuse with "independent study" or "individual instruction")
UF Clinical Teaching (Individualized Instruction)
Individualized Curriculum (1966 1980)
Individualized Education
Personalized Instruction
Self Paced Instruction #
BT Teaching Methods
RT Adapted Physical Education
Autoinstructional Aids
Competency Based Education
Competency Based Teacher Education
Computer Assisted Instruction
Diagnostic Teaching
Group Instruction
Humanistic Education
Individual Instruction
Individualized Education Programs
Individualized Programs
Individualized Reading
Individual Needs
Learning Centers (Classroom)
Learning Laboratories

Learning Modules
Mass Instruction
Montessori Method
Multilevel Classes (Second Language Instruction)
Pacing
Programed Instruction
Small Group Instruction
Special Education

INDIVIDUALIZED PROGRAMS *Jul. 1966*
CIJE: 695 RIE: 1281 GC: 310
SN Noneducational programs (e.g., therapeutic, work-related, medicinal) adapted to meet individualized needs within a group (note: prior to mar80, the use of this term was not restricted to noneducational programs -- see also "individualized instruction," "individualized reading," and "individualized education programs")
BT Programs
RT Counseling Services
Guidance Programs
Individualized Instruction
Individualized Reading
Individual Needs
Rehabilitation Programs
Sheltered Workshops
Special Programs

INDIVIDUALIZED READING *Jul. 1966*
CIJE: 152 RIE: 389 GC: 460
SN Type of reading instruction that emphasizes self-pacing and student selection of reading materials
BT Reading
Reading Instruction
RT Independent Reading
Individualized Instruction
Individualized Programs
Pacing
Reading Assignments
Reading Centers
Reading Interests
Reading Programs

INDO EUROPEAN LANGUAGES *Jul. 1966*
CIJE: 57 RIE: 112 GC: 440
NT Afrikaans
Albanian
Armenian
Baltic Languages
Baluchi
Bengali
Dutch
English
German
Greek
Gujarati
Hindi
Kashmiri
Kurdish
Marathi
Nepali
Norwegian
Ossetic
Panjabi
Pashto
Persian
Romance Languages
Singhalese
Slavic Languages
Swedish
Tajik
Urdu
Welsh
BT Languages
RT Language Classification
Middle English
Native Speakers
Old English

INDOCHINESE *Mar. 1976*
CIJE: 74 RIE: 290 GC: 560
UF Indochinese Americans #
NT Cambodians
Laotians
Vietnamese People
BT Groups
RT Asian Americans
Ethnic Groups

Indochinese Americans
USE ASIAN AMERICANS; INDOCHINESE

INDONESIAN *Jul. 1966*
CIJE: 20 RIE: 46 GC: 440
UF Bahasa Indonesia
BT Indonesian Languages

INDONESIAN LANGUAGES *Jul. 1966*
CIJE: 8 RIE: 42 GC: 440
NT Bikol
Dusun
Indonesian
Javanese
Malagasy
Malay
Maranao
Tagalog
Visayan
BT Malayo Polynesian Languages

INDUCTION *Mar. 1980*
CIJE: 328 RIE: 338 GC: 110
SN Logical thought process that attempts to reach conclusions by reasoning from specific instances or cases to general rules, principles, laws, or conditions
UF Inductive Methods (1967 1980)
BT Logical Thinking
RT Deduction
Experiments
Generalization
Learning Processes
Research Methodology
Scientific Methodology
Validity

Inductive Methods (1967 1980)
USE INDUCTION

Industrial And Organizational Psychology
USE INDUSTRIAL PSYCHOLOGY

INDUSTRIAL ARTS *Jul. 1966*
CIJE: 1068 RIE: 1010 GC: 400
UF Industrial Crafts
NT Painting (Industrial Arts)
RT Auto Mechanics
Building Trades
Cabinetmaking
Carpentry
Ceramics
Construction (Process)
Craft Workers
Design Crafts
Drafting
Electronics
Foundries
Glass
Graphic Arts
Industrial Arts Teachers
Industrial Education
Industry
Laboratory Technology
Leather
Manufacturing
Metal Working
Needle Trades
Patternmaking
Plastics
Power Technology
Practical Arts
Printing
Robotics
School Shops
Shop Curriculum
Small Engine Mechanics
Trade And Industrial Education
Vocational Education
Woodworking

Industrial Arts Shops
USE SCHOOL SHOPS

INDUSTRIAL ARTS TEACHERS *Jul. 1966*
CIJE: 140 RIE: 93 GC: 360
BT Teachers
RT Industrial Arts
Industrial Education
Trade And Industrial Teachers
Vocational Education Teachers

Industrial Communication
USE BUSINESS COMMUNICATION

Industrial Crafts
USE INDUSTRIAL ARTS

INDUSTRIAL EDUCATION *Jul. 1966*
CIJE: 624 RIE: 602 GC: 400
SN All types of education related to industry including industrial arts and education for occupations in industry at all levels (note: use a more precise term if possible)
BT Education
RT Industrial Arts
Industrial Arts Teachers
Industrial Training
Industry
Labor Education
Technical Education
Trade And Industrial Education
Trade And Industrial Teachers
Vocational Education

Industrial Nations
USE DEVELOPED NATIONS

INDUSTRIAL PERSONNEL *Jul. 1966*
CIJE: 170 RIE: 175 GC: 640
BT Personnel
RT Developed Nations
Employees
Employers
Industry
Laborers
Trade And Industrial Education

INDUSTRIAL PSYCHOLOGY *Aug. 1986*
CIJE: 8 RIE: 6 GC: 230
SN Application of psychological knowledge and methods to the study of human behavior in the workplace, often with the goals of increasing organizational efficiency and enhancing the quality of working life
UF Industrial And Organizational Psychology
Occupational Psychology
Organizational Psychology (Work Environment)
BT Psychology
RT Job Satisfaction
Labor Relations
Occupations
Organizational Climate
Organizational Development
Personnel
Personnel Management
Quality Of Working Life
Social Psychology
Vocational Adjustment
Work Environment

Industrial Relations (1969 1980)
USE LABOR RELATIONS

Industrial Robotics
USE ROBOTICS

INDUSTRIAL STRUCTURE *Jul. 1966*
CIJE: 71 RIE: 101 GC: 650
BT Organization
RT Cooperatives
Developed Nations
Industrialization
Industry
Mergers
Middle Management
Organizational Development
Organization Size (Groups)
Ownership
Social Structure
Structural Unemployment
Vertical Organization

Industrial Technology (1969 1980)
USE INDUSTRY; TECHNOLOGY

INDUSTRIAL TRAINING *Jul. 1966*
CIJE: 576 RIE: 514 GC: 400
SN Technical and skills training conducted by industrial organizations for their employees (note: do not confuse with "corporate education")
UF Corporate Training
BT Training
RT Adult Vocational Education
Apprenticeships
Corporate Education
Extension Education
Industrial Education
Inplant Programs
Inservice Education
Job Training
Labor Education
Labor Force Development
Management Development
Off The Job Training
On The Job Training
Professional Development
Professional Training
Released Time
Staff Development
Trade And Industrial Education
Trainees
Trainers
Training Allowances

Industrial X Ray Operators
USE RADIOGRAPHERS

INDUSTRIALIZATION *Jul. 1966*
CIJE: 300 RIE: 438 GC: 650
BT Development
RT Culture Lag
Demography
Developed Nations
Developing Nations
Emerging Occupations
Industrial Structure
Industry
Modernization
Revolution
Socioeconomic Influences
Technological Advancement
Technological Literacy
Technology
Technology Transfer
Urbanization

INDUSTRY *Jul. 1966*
CIJE: 1402 RIE: 1706 GC: 650
SN Productive enterprises, especially manufacturing or certain service enterprises such as transportation and communications, which employ relatively large amounts of capital and labor
UF Industrial Technology (1969 1980) #
NT Bakery Industry
Banking
Brick Industry
Broadcast Industry
Construction Industry
Fashion Industry
Feed Industry
Film Industry
Insurance Companies
Lumber Industry
Manufacturing Industry
Meat Packing Industry
Petroleum Industry
Publishing Industry
Telephone Communications Industry
Tourism
BT Business
RT Cooperatives
Corporate Education
Corporate Support
Equipment Manufacturers
Industrial Arts
Industrial Education
Industrialization
Industrial Personnel
Industrial Structure
Mergers
Office Machines
Organizations (Groups)
Organization Size (Groups)
Producer Services
Production Techniques
School Business Relationship
Technology

Industry School Relationship
USE SCHOOL BUSINESS RELATIONSHIP

Ineligibility
USE DISQUALIFICATION

INEQUALITIES (1970 1980) *Jun. 1980*
CIJE: 51 RIE: 30 GC: 540
SN Invalid descriptor -- used inconsistently in indexing -- for mathematical inequalities, use "inequality (mathematics)" -- for educational inequalities, use "equal education" -- for social or economic inequalities, see "disadvantaged" or descriptors relating to social, race, sex, or ethnic bias or discrimination

= Two or more Descriptors are used to represent this term.
The term's main entry shows the appropriate coordination.

INEQUALITY (MATHEMATICS) *Mar. 1980*
CIJE: 2 RIE: 3 GC: 480
SN Mathematical expression or proposition concerning the difference in size between two quantities (note: for educational or socioeconomic inequality, refer to scope note of "inequalities (1970 1980)")
BT Mathematical Concepts

Infancy (1966 1980)
USE INFANTS

INFANT BEHAVIOR *Jul. 1966*
CIJE: 656 RIE: 422 GC: 120
BT Behavior
RT Attachment Behavior
Developmental Stages
Failure To Thrive
Infants
Neonates
Separation Anxiety
Stranger Reactions

Infant Death Rate
USE INFANT MORTALITY

INFANT MORTALITY *Aug. 1970*
CIJE: 66 RIE: 107 GC: 210
UF Infant Death Rate
BT Death
RT Incidence
Infants
Neonates
Premature Infants

Infant Schools (British Primary System)
USE BRITISH INFANT SCHOOLS

INFANTS *Jul. 1966*
CIJE: 2072 RIE: 1532 GC: 120
SN Aged birth to approximately 24 months
UF Infancy (1966 1980)
NT Neonates
Premature Infants
BT Young Children
RT Breastfeeding
Infant Behavior
Infant Mortality
Pediatrics
Toddlers

Infectious Diseases (1966 1974)
USE COMMUNICABLE DISEASES

INFERENCES *Jan. 1985*
CIJE: 48 RIE: 36 GC: 110
SN Judgments or conclusions derived from premises or evidence (note: see also such identifiers as "causal inferences," "transitive inferences," and "social inferences")
NT Statistical Inference
RT Communication (Thought Transfer)
Communication Skills
Comprehension
Context Clues
Critical Reading
Critical Thinking
Data Interpretation
Generalization
Language Skills
Learning Strategies
Logical Thinking
Perception
Reading Skills

Inferential Statistics
USE STATISTICAL INFERENCE; STATISTICS

Infirmaries
USE HEALTH FACILITIES

Inflatable Structures
USE AIR STRUCTURES

Inflated Grades
USE GRADE INFLATION

INFLATION (ECONOMICS) *Jul. 1977*
CIJE: 172 RIE: 202 GC: 620
SN Disproportionate increase in the quantity of money or credit, or both, relative to goods and services available for purchase
BT Economic Climate
RT Business Cycles
Cost Indexes
Costs
Economic Factors
Economics
Economic Status
Educational Finance
Financial Problems
Fiscal Capacity
Income
Interest (Finance)
Monetary Systems
Money Management
Poverty
Productivity

INFLUENCES *Mar. 1980*
CIJE: 448 RIE: 426 GC: 520
SN Factors directly or indirectly affecting the condition (behavior, development, etc.) of an organism or entity, that alter some situation, or determine some result (note: use a more specific term if possible)
UF Causal Factors
NT Biological Influences
Black Influences
Community Influence
Cultural Influences
Ecological Factors
Economic Factors
Enrollment Influences
Environmental Influences
Family Influence
Minority Group Influences
Parent Influence
Peer Influence
Performance Factors
Perinatal Influences
Political Influences
Prenatal Influences
Racial Factors
Religious Factors
Social Influences
Socioeconomic Influences
Teacher Influence
Time Factors (Learning)
RT Background
Change
Development
Environment
Opportunities
Relationship

INFORMAL ASSESSMENT *Jun. 1977*
CIJE: 163 RIE: 276 GC: 820
SN Appraisal of an individual's or group's status or growth by means other than standardized instruments
BT Evaluation
RT Check Lists
Diagnostic Teaching
Evaluation Methods
Experiential Learning
Grading
Informal Reading Inventories
Nongraded Student Evaluation
Personnel Evaluation
Portfolios (Background Materials)
Rating Scales
Student Evaluation
Testing

Informal Conversational Usage
USE STANDARD SPOKEN USAGE

INFORMAL LEADERSHIP *Jul. 1966*
CIJE: 14 RIE: 34 GC: 520
SN Guidance or direction provided by individuals or groups whose authority is not officially derived
BT Leadership
RT Group Dynamics
Informal Organization
Instructional Leadership
Interpersonal Relationship
Peer Influence

INFORMAL ORGANIZATION *Jul. 1966*
CIJE: 68 RIE: 74 GC: 520
SN An informal network of communication and interaction among groups (e.g., employees, supervisors, members, etc.) within a formal organization (note: prior to mar80, the use of this term was not restricted by a scope note)
BT Organization
RT Administrative Organization
Informal Leadership
Organizational Climate
Organizations (Groups)
Power Structure
Social Exchange Theory

INFORMAL READING INVENTORIES *Mar. 1980*
CIJE: 117 RIE: 168 GC: 830
SN Use of observation or informal procedures to diagnose or evaluate reading proficiency or reading problems
UF Informal Reading Inventory (1968 1980)
BT Reading Tests
RT Cloze Procedure
Criterion Referenced Tests
Diagnostic Tests
Informal Assessment
Reading
Reading Comprehension
Reading Diagnosis

Informal Reading Inventory (1968 1980)
USE INFORMAL READING INVENTORIES

Informatics
USE INFORMATION SCIENCE

Information And Referral Services
USE INFORMATION SERVICES; REFERRAL

Information Brokers
USE INFORMATION SCIENTISTS

INFORMATION CENTERS *Jul. 1966*
CIJE: 407 RIE: 795 GC: 710
SN Facilities or programs that provide a variety of information services
NT Clearinghouses
BT Information Sources
Resource Centers
RT Community Information Services
Education Service Centers
Information Dissemination
Information Networks
Information Services
Library Services

INFORMATION DISSEMINATION *Jul. 1966*
CIJE: 1845 RIE: 4355 GC: 710
SN Distribution of information from a storage point to users
UF Data Dissemination
NT Propaganda
Publicity
Referral
Selective Dissemination Of Information
BT Information Services
RT Communication (Thought Transfer)
Delivery Systems
Diffusion (Communication)
Disclosure
Documentation
Electronic Mail
Electronic Publishing
Freedom Of Information
Information Centers
Information Networks
Information Processing
Information Storage
Information Systems
Information Technology
Information Theory
Information Transfer
Information Utilization
Library Circulation
Library Extension
Linking Agents
Mass Media
Publishing Industry
Reference Services
Technology Transfer

Information Flow
USE INFORMATION TRANSFER

INFORMATION NEEDS *Jul. 1966*
CIJE: 995 RIE: 1867 GC: 710
UF Data Needs
BT Needs
RT Access To Information
Evaluation Needs
Hotlines (Public)
Information Networks
Information Seeking
Information Services
Information Sources
Information Systems
Information Utilization
Online Searching
Research Needs
Search Strategies
Selective Dissemination Of Information
User Needs (Information)

INFORMATION NETWORKS *Feb. 1969*
CIJE: 697 RIE: 1363 GC: 710
SN Interconnected or interrelated communication channels, linked for the transmission or exchange of information
UF Electronic Information Exchange #
NT Library Networks
BT Networks
RT Communication (Thought Transfer)
Communications
Communications Satellites
Computer Networks
Dial Access Information Systems
Electronic Mail
Electronic Publishing
Facsimile Transmission
Information Centers
Information Dissemination
Information Needs
Information Services
Information Systems
Information Technology
Information Theory
Information Transfer
Social Networks
Telecommunications
Teleconferencing
Videotex

Information Processes (Psychological)
USE COGNITIVE PROCESSES

INFORMATION PROCESSING *Jul. 1966*
CIJE: 1113 RIE: 1415 GC: 710
SN Acquisition, storage, and manipulation of information so that it appears in a useful form (note: prior to mar80, this term was not scoped and was sometimes used instead of "cognitive processes" or "data processing" for psychological or machine processing of information -- use a more specific term if possible)
NT Data Collection
Data Processing
Documentation
Information Retrieval
Information Storage
Word Processing
BT Information Services
RT Character Recognition
Communications
Cybernetics
Feedback
Information Dissemination
Information Science
Information Systems
Information Technology
Information Theory
Information Transfer
Library Technical Processes
Pattern Recognition

INFORMATION RETRIEVAL *Jul. 1966*
CIJE: 1835 RIE: 1942 GC: 710
SN Techniques used to recover specific information from large quantities of stored data
NT Online Searching
BT Information Processing
RT Abstracting
Access To Information
Database Management Systems
Databases
Display Systems
Documentation
Indexes
Indexing
Information Science
Information Seeking
Information Systems
Information Theory
Relevance (Information Retrieval)
Search Strategies
Selective Dissemination Of Information
Thesauri
User Needs (Information)
User Satisfaction (Information)

= Two or more Descriptors are used to represent this term.
The term's main entry shows the appropriate coordination.

INFORMATION SCIENCE *Jul. 1966*
CIJE: 533 RIE: 793 GC: 710
SN Study of the properties of information, i.e., its generation, transformation, communication, transfer, storage, and use
UF Informatics
NT Computer Science
Library Science
BT Sciences
RT Cybernetics
Information Processing
Information Retrieval
Information Scientists
Information Services
Information Systems
Information Technology
Information Theory
Information Utilization
Library Associations
Library Education
Library Schools

INFORMATION SCIENTISTS *Jul. 1971*
CIJE: 128 RIE: 140 GC: 710
SN Individuals who observe, measure, and describe the behavior of information, as well as those who organize information and provide services for its use
UF Information Brokers
Information Specialists
NT Librarians
BT Professional Personnel
RT Information Science
Library Associations

INFORMATION SEEKING *Aug. 1968*
CIJE: 417 RIE: 565 GC: 110
NT Search Strategies
RT Access To Information
Communication (Thought Transfer)
Information Needs
Information Retrieval
Information Services
Information Sources
Information Systems
Information Utilization
Inquiry
Library Instruction
Problem Solving
User Needs (Information)
Users (Information)

INFORMATION SERVICES *Jul. 1966*
CIJE: 1057 RIE: 1670 GC: 710
SN The activities (e.g., information selection, collection, organization, and dissemination), programs, and facilities by which information is made available for use
UF Information And Referral Services #
NT Community Information Services
Information Dissemination
Information Processing
Library Services
Reference Services
Videotex
BT Services
RT Access To Information
Information Centers
Information Needs
Information Networks
Information Science
Information Seeking
Information Sources
Information Systems
Information Utilization
Libraries
Online Vendors
Scientific And Technical Information
User Needs (Information)
Users (Information)
User Satisfaction (Information)

Information Services (Community)
USE COMMUNITY INFORMATION SERVICES

INFORMATION SOURCES *Jul. 1966*
CIJE: 1270 RIE: 2180 GC: 710
SN Persons, places, or things from which information is derived
NT Archives
Databases
Information Centers
Libraries
Primary Sources
RT Access To Information
Bibliometrics
Community Resources
Educational Resources
Genealogy
Hotlines (Public)
Human Resources
Information Needs
Information Seeking
Information Services
Information Transfer
Information Utilization
Journalism
Mass Media
Online Systems
Research Tools
Scientific And Technical Information
Use Studies

Information Specialists
USE INFORMATION SCIENTISTS

INFORMATION STORAGE *Jul. 1966*
CIJE: 535 RIE: 862 GC: 710
UF Filing Systems
BT Information Processing
Storage
RT Computer Storage Devices
Database Management Systems
Databases
Documentation
Filing
Information Dissemination
Information Systems
Magnetic Tapes
Microfiche
Microfilm
Microforms
Optical Disks
Recordkeeping
Records (Forms)
Search Strategies

Information Storage (Psychology)
USE ENCODING (PSYCHOLOGY)

INFORMATION SYSTEMS *Jul. 1966*
CIJE: 1444 RIE: 2688 GC: 710
SN Procedures, operations, and functions devoted to processing information within an organization (note: use a more specific term if possible)
NT Computer Managed Instruction
Dial Access Information Systems
Management Information Systems
RT Computers
Computer Science
Data Processing
Display Systems
Documentation
Expert Systems
Information Dissemination
Information Needs
Information Networks
Information Processing
Information Retrieval
Information Science
Information Seeking
Information Services
Information Storage
Information Technology
Information Theory
Information Utilization
Keyboarding (Data Entry)
Management Systems
Online Systems
Optical Data Disks
Organizational Communication
Search Strategies
Users (Information)
Word Processing

INFORMATION TECHNOLOGY *Aug. 1986*
CIJE: 47 RIE: 48 GC: 710
SN The application of modern communication and computing technologies to the creation, management, and use of information
BT Technology
RT Communications
Computer Oriented Programs
Computers
Computer Software
Cybernetics
Data Processing
Educational Technology
Information Dissemination
Information Networks
Information Processing
Information Science
Information Systems
Library Automation
Library Technical Processes
Reprography
Telecommunications

INFORMATION THEORY *Jul. 1966*
CIJE: 352 RIE: 598 GC: 810
SN Mathematical theory concerned with the rate and accuracy of information transmission within a system as affected by the number and width of channels, distortion, noise, etc. (note: prior to mar80, the instruction "communication theory, use information theory" was carried in the thesaurus)
UF Communications Theory
BT Theories
RT Communication (Thought Transfer)
Communications
Computer Science
Cybernetics
Information Dissemination
Information Networks
Information Processing
Information Retrieval
Information Science
Information Systems
Information Transfer
Input Output
Mathematical Models
Operations Research
Systems Analysis
Systems Approach

INFORMATION TRANSFER *Aug. 1986*
CIJE: 54 RIE: 62 GC: 710
SN The process or result of moving information from one point to another
UF Information Flow
RT Access To Information
Communication (Thought Transfer)
Communications
Diffusion (Communication)
Facsimile Transmission
Information Dissemination
Information Networks
Information Processing
Information Sources
Information Theory
Information Utilization
Linking Agents
Reprography
Technology Transfer

Information User Needs
USE USER NEEDS (INFORMATION)

Information User Satisfaction
USE USER SATISFACTION (INFORMATION)

Information Users
USE USERS (INFORMATION)

Information Utilities (Online)
USE ONLINE VENDORS

INFORMATION UTILIZATION *Jul. 1966*
CIJE: 726 RIE: 1408 GC: 710
NT Evaluation Utilization
Research Utilization
RT Access To Information
Adoption (Ideas)
Bibliometrics
Data Interpretation
Decision Making
Diffusion (Communication)
Indexes
Information Dissemination
Information Needs
Information Science
Information Seeking
Information Services
Information Sources
Information Systems
Information Transfer
Linking Agents
Problem Solving
Search Strategies
Surveys
Technology Transfer
Users (Information)
Use Studies

Inhalation Therapists (1969 1985)
USE RESPIRATORY THERAPY; THERAPISTS

INHIBITION *Jul. 1966*
CIJE: 238 RIE: 58 GC: 120
SN Condition in which action or mental function is arrested or blocked, either by internal or external influences
UF Proactive Inhibition
Reactive Inhibition
Retroactive Inhibition
RT Anxiety
Assertiveness
Fear Of Success
Helplessness
Psychological Patterns
Self Control
Socialization

Initial Expenses (1966 1980)
USE EXPENDITURES

INITIAL TEACHING ALPHABET *Jul. 1966*
CIJE: 93 RIE: 155 GC: 460
SN A 44-character orthography used in beginning reading instruction in which each character represents one english phoneme
UF Ita
BT Alphabets
RT Beginning Reading
Orthographic Symbols
Phonics
Reading
Reading Instruction

INJURIES *Jul. 1966*
CIJE: 209 RIE: 245 GC: 210
BT Disabilities
RT Accidents
Adventitious Impairments
Exceptional Persons
First Aid
Health
Medical Services
Rehabilitation
Safety
Special Health Problems

Inmates
USE PRISONERS

INNER CITY *Jul. 1966*
CIJE: 460 RIE: 621 GC: 550
SN Central section of a city which is usually older and more densely populated
BT Urban Areas
RT Ghettos
Slums
Urban Demography

Inner City Education
USE URBAN EDUCATION

INNER SPEECH (SUBVOCAL) *Jul. 1966*
CIJE: 44 RIE: 26 GC: 450
BT Speech
RT Reading
Silent Reading

INNOVATION *Jul. 1966*
CIJE: 746 RIE: 906 GC: 520
SN The introduction of new ideas, methods, devices, etc. (note: use a more specific term if possible)
NT Building Innovation
Educational Innovation
RT Adoption (Ideas)
Change
Demonstration Programs
Development
Discovery Processes
Experiments
Improvement
Inventions
Linking Agents
Modernization
Research
Research And Development
Technological Literacy
Technology Transfer
Theory Practice Relationship

Inns
USE HOTELS

= Two or more Descriptors are used to represent this term.
The term's main entry shows the appropriate coordination.

INORGANIC CHEMISTRY *Aug. 1982*
CIJE: 66 RIE: 4 GC: 490
SN Study of chemical reactions and properties of all elements and their compounds other than hydrocarbons
BT Chemistry
RT Atomic Structure
Chemical Bonding
Chemical Reactions
Coordination Compounds
Metallurgy
Mineralogy
Molecular Structure
Radioisotopes

INPLANT PROGRAMS *Jul. 1966*
CIJE: 126 RIE: 150 GC: 630
SN Educational or training programs carried on within business or industrial establishments
BT Programs
RT Apprenticeships
Corporate Education
Industrial Training
Inservice Education
Labor Education
Nonschool Educational Programs
Off The Job Training
On The Job Training
Staff Development

Input Devices
USE INPUT OUTPUT DEVICES

Input Evaluation
USE INPUT OUTPUT ANALYSIS

INPUT OUTPUT *Jul. 1966*
CIJE: 64 RIE: 167 GC: 710
SN Process of transmitting information from an external source to the computer or from the computer to an external source
NT Keyboarding (Data Entry)
BT Data Processing
RT Computers
Cybernetics
Information Theory
Input Output Devices
Time Sharing

INPUT OUTPUT ANALYSIS *Jul. 1966*
CIJE: 130 RIE: 261 GC: 620
SN Detailed analysis of the relationship between the products of an economy, system, or program and the resources required to produce them (note: prior to mar80, the use of this term was not restricted by a scope note)
UF Input Evaluation
BT Evaluation Methods
RT Correlation
Cost Effectiveness
Economic Research
Educational Assessment
Program Evaluation
Resource Allocation
Systems Analysis

INPUT OUTPUT DEVICES *Sep. 1968*
CIJE: 293 RIE: 340 GC: 910
SN Equipment used to communicate with a computer, i.e., those units designed to accept data and produce the results in forms readable by humans or other processing units
UF Computer Terminals
Input Devices
Output Devices
NT Optical Scanners
BT Computers
RT Computer Graphics
Computer Output Microfilm
Computer Storage Devices
Data Processing
Display Systems
Electronic Mail
Facsimile Transmission
Input Output
Keyboarding (Data Entry)
Magnetic Tapes
Online Systems
Optical Disks
Telecommunications
Word Processing

INQUIRY *Mar. 1980*
CIJE: 783 RIE: 815 GC: 810
SN Method or process of seeking knowledge, understanding, or information (note: prior to mar80, the instruction "inquiry, use questioning techniques" was carried in the thesaurus)
UF Inquiry Training (1967 1980)
BT Methods
RT Discovery Learning
Heuristics
Information Seeking
Interviews
Learning Processes
Learning Strategies
Questioning Techniques
Research Methodology
Scientific Attitudes
Surveys

Inquiry Training (1967 1980)
USE INQUIRY

Insect Studies
USE ENTOMOLOGY

INSECTICIDES *Jul. 1966*
CIJE: 44 RIE: 53 GC: 410
BT Pesticides
RT Agricultural Chemical Occupations
Agricultural Supplies
Agronomy
Botany
Entomology
Herbicides
Plant Growth

Insecurity (1966 1980)
USE SECURITY (PSYCHOLOGY)

Inservice Courses (1966 1980)
USE INSERVICE EDUCATION

INSERVICE EDUCATION *Jul. 1966*
CIJE: 1373 RIE: 3133 GC: 630
SN Courses or programs designed to provide employee/staff growth in job-related competencies or skills, often sponsored by employers, usually at the professional level (note: if applicable, use the more specific term "inservice teacher education")
UF Inservice Courses (1966 1980)
Inservice Education Programs
Inservice Programs (1966 1980)
Inservice Teaching (1966 1980) #
NT Inservice Teacher Education
BT Education
RT Career Ladders
Faculty Development
Improvement Programs
Industrial Training
Inplant Programs
Institutes (Training Programs)
Management Development
Minicourses
Off The Job Training
On The Job Training
Professional Continuing Education
Professional Development
Professional Training
Refresher Courses
Retraining
Staff Development

Inservice Education Programs
USE INSERVICE EDUCATION

Inservice Programs (1966 1980)
USE INSERVICE EDUCATION

INSERVICE TEACHER EDUCATION *Jul. 1966*
CIJE: 3173 RIE: 6551 GC: 320
UF Inservice Teacher Training
BT Inservice Education
Teacher Education
RT Faculty Development
Institutes (Training Programs)
Internship Programs
Preservice Teacher Education
Professional Training
School Visitation
Teacher Centers
Teacher Educator Education
Teacher Improvement
Teacher Interns
Teacher Workshops

Inservice Teacher Training
USE INSERVICE TEACHER EDUCATION

Inservice Teaching (1966 1980)
USE INSERVICE EDUCATION; TEACHING (OCCUPATION)

Inservice Teaching Experience
USE TEACHING EXPERIENCE

INSPECTION *Jul. 1966*
CIJE: 42 RIE: 153 GC: 650
SN Official examination or review
BT Evaluation Methods
RT Audits (Verification)
Equipment Evaluation
Evaluation
Field Tests
Observation
Quality Control
Standards

Institute Type Courses (1966 1980)
USE INSTITUTES (TRAINING PROGRAMS)

INSTITUTES (TRAINING PROGRAMS) *Jul. 1966*
CIJE: 444 RIE: 1313 GC: 350
SN Programs of training designed to provide advanced study in a subject field, usually more intensive than conventions or conferences but less elaborate than workshops
UF Institute Type Courses (1966 1980)
Science Institutes (1967 1980) #
Summer Institutes (1967 1980) #
BT Programs
RT Conference Papers
Conference Proceedings
Conferences
Inservice Education
Inservice Teacher Education
Meetings
Minicourses
Off The Job Training
Professional Continuing Education
Professional Training
Seminars
Teacher Centers
Teacher Education
Training Methods
Workshops

Institution Libraries (1969 1980)
USE INSTITUTIONAL LIBRARIES

INSTITUTIONAL ADMINISTRATION *Jul. 1966*
CIJE: 166 RIE: 260 GC: 320
SN Planning, organizing, directing, and controlling human or material resources in public service organizations, e.g., schools, churches, hospitals, prisons, etc.
NT Library Administration
School Administration
BT Administration
RT Governing Boards
Institutional Autonomy
Institutional Mission
Institutions
Retrenchment

INSTITUTIONAL ADVANCEMENT *Oct. 1982*
CIJE: 226 RIE: 74 GC: 720
SN Interpretation and promotion of an institution to its various constituencies -- includes fund raising, internal and external communications, government relations, and public relations
BT Publicity
RT Communication Audits
Fund Raising
Institutions
Lobbying
Marketing
Mission Statements
Organizational Communication
Public Relations

Institutional Assessment
USE INSTITUTIONAL EVALUATION

INSTITUTIONAL AUTONOMY *Sep. 1977*
CIJE: 279 RIE: 230 GC: 330
SN Freedom of an institution to act without external control
NT School Based Management
RT Academic Freedom
Block Grants
College Governing Councils
Decentralization
Federal Regulation
Full State Funding
Governance
Government Role
Government School Relationship
Institutional Administration
Institutions
Intellectual Freedom
Professional Autonomy
School District Autonomy
Self Determination

INSTITUTIONAL CHARACTERISTICS *Jun. 1978*
CIJE: 584 RIE: 1204 GC: 320
SN Descriptive features of an institution, such as funding, size, demographics, and governance
UF College Characteristics
Institutional Differences #
School Characteristics
University Characteristics
NT School Size
RT College Environment
Institutional Environment
Institutional Evaluation
Institutions
Organization Size (Groups)
Peer Institutions
Reputation
School Demography
School Organization
Schools

INSTITUTIONAL COOPERATION *Mar. 1980*
CIJE: 717 RIE: 1288 GC: 330
SN Cooperation of institutions with each other or with other organizations, groups, etc.
UF Interinstitutional Cooperation (1968 1980)
NT College School Cooperation
Intercollegiate Cooperation
Library Cooperation
BT Cooperation
RT Agency Cooperation
Articulation (Education)
Community Cooperation
Consortia
Cooperative Planning
Cooperative Programs
Dual Enrollment
Educational Cooperation
Exchange Programs
Institutional Survival
Institutions
Interdistrict Policies
International Cooperation
Interschool Communication
Peer Institutions
Regional Cooperation
Research Coordinating Units
Shared Facilities
Shared Resources And Services
Statewide Planning
Teacher Centers

Institutional Differences
USE DIFFERENCES; INSTITUTIONAL CHARACTERISTICS

Institutional Eligibility
USE ELIGIBILITY

INSTITUTIONAL ENVIRONMENT *Jul. 1966*
CIJE: 219 RIE: 251 GC: 320
SN Conditions, forces, or factors that affect institutions (note: use a more specific term if possible)
NT College Environment
BT Environment
RT Educational Environment
Institutional Characteristics
Institutional Mission
Institutions
Organizational Climate

= Two or more Descriptors are used to represent this term.
The term's main entry shows the appropriate coordination.

INSTITUTIONAL EVALUATION *Oct. 1979*
CIJE: 167 RIE: 395 GC: 320
SN Formal or informal assessment of an institution from without, often for accreditation purposes (note: do not confuse with "institutional research" or "self evaluation (groups)")
UF Institutional Assessment
BT Evaluation
RT Accreditation (Institutions)
Accrediting Agencies
Institutional Characteristics
Institutional Research
Institutions
Program Evaluation
Self Evaluation (Groups)
Summative Evaluation

Institutional Facilities (1967 1980)
USE FACILITIES

Institutional Function
USE INSTITUTIONAL ROLE

Institutional Goals
USE ORGANIZATIONAL OBJECTIVES

INSTITUTIONAL LIBRARIES *Apr. 1980*
CIJE: 58 RIE: 116 GC: 710
SN (Note: coordinate with another term to identify type of institution)
UF Institution Libraries (1969 1980)
NT Hospital Libraries
Prison Libraries
BT Special Libraries
RT Institutions

INSTITUTIONAL MISSION *Aug. 1986*
CIJE: 55 RIE: 40 GC: 320
SN The purpose(s) for which a particular institution is established and around which policies of the institution evolve (note: prior to aug86, the thesaurus carried the instruction "institutional mission, use institutional role")
BT Organizational Objectives
RT Institutional Administration
Institutional Environment
Institutional Role
Institutions
Mission Statements
Public Policy
School Policy

Institutional Objectives
USE ORGANIZATIONAL OBJECTIVES

INSTITUTIONAL PERSONNEL *Jul. 1966*
CIJE: 83 RIE: 71 GC: 520
BT Personnel
RT Correctional Institutions
Hospital Personnel
Institutions

INSTITUTIONAL RESEARCH *Jul. 1966*
CIJE: 497 RIE: 2057 GC: 810
SN Research on an institution, usually to provide greater understanding of its operations (note: as of oct81, use as a minor descriptor for examples of this kind of research -- use as a major descriptor only as the subject of a document)
BT Research
RT College Planning
Curriculum Research
Educational Research
Experimental Programs
Institutional Evaluation
Institutions
Media Research
Peer Institutions
Research Directors
Self Evaluation (Groups)
Use Studies

INSTITUTIONAL ROLE *May. 1969*
CIJE: 786 RIE: 785 GC: 330
SN Function performed by or expected of an institution
UF Institutional Function
NT Agency Role
Church Role
Court Role
Library Role
School Role
RT Community Role
Government Role
Institutional Mission
Institutional Survival
Institutions
Leadership
Research
Responsibility
Services

INSTITUTIONAL SCHOOLS *Jul. 1966*
CIJE: 21 RIE: 43 GC: 340
SN Schools that are part of larger residential institutions such as hospitals or correctional institutions (note: prior to mar80, the use of this term was not restricted by a scope note)
NT Hospital Schools
BT Special Schools
RT Institutions
Residential Schools

Institutional Self Study
USE SELF EVALUATION (GROUPS)

INSTITUTIONAL SURVIVAL *Aug. 1986*
CIJE: 38 RIE: 22 GC: 330
SN Continuance of an institution as a viable entity, as opposed to closure or merger
RT Developing Institutions
Economic Change
Educational Economics
Financial Problems
Institutional Cooperation
Institutional Role
Institutions
Retrenchment
School Closing
School Support
Small Schools
Social Change

Institutionalized (Persons) (1967 1976)
USE INSTITUTIONALIZED PERSONS

INSTITUTIONALIZED PERSONS *May. 1976*
CIJE: 1068 RIE: 506 GC: 220
UF Institutionalized (Persons) (1967 1976)
NT Prisoners
BT Groups
RT Correctional Education
Correctional Institutions
Deinstitutionalization (Of Disabled)
Mental Disorders
Patients
Residential Programs
Severe Disabilities

INSTITUTIONS *Jul. 1966*
CIJE: 214 RIE: 301 GC: 520
SN Established organizations, usually of a public nature, that are dedicated to an educational, economic, political, religious, charitable, or other social purpose -- includes foundations, societies, corporations, etc. (note: use a more specific term if possible)
UF Social Institutions (Organizations)
NT Black Institutions
Churches
Courts
Hospitals
Libraries
Peer Institutions
Philanthropic Foundations
Residential Institutions
Schools
RT Institutional Administration
Institutional Advancement
Institutional Autonomy
Institutional Characteristics
Institutional Cooperation
Institutional Environment
Institutional Evaluation
Institutional Libraries
Institutional Mission
Institutional Personnel
Institutional Research
Institutional Role
Institutional Schools
Institutional Survival
Nonprofit Organizations
Organizational Objectives
Organizations (Groups)
Rehabilitation Centers
Religious Organizations
Resources

INSTRUCTION *Jul. 1966*
CIJE: 8269 RIE: 3317 GC: 310
SN Process by which knowledge, attitudes, or skills are deliberately conveyed -- includes the total instructional process, from planning and implementation through evaluation and feedback (note: use a more specific term if possible -- for standard approaches, see "teaching methods")
UF Pedagogy
Teaching (Process)
NT Assignments
Clothing Instruction
College Instruction
Concept Teaching
Cooking Instruction
Ethical Instruction
Field Instruction
Foods Instruction
Geography Instruction
Group Instruction
Home Instruction
Humanities Instruction
Individual Instruction
Library Instruction
Mass Instruction
Mathematics Instruction
Nutrition Instruction
Reading Instruction
Remedial Instruction
Science Instruction
Sewing Instruction
Speech Instruction
Spelling Instruction
Telephone Usage Instruction
Test Coaching
Textiles Instruction
Writing Instruction
RT Curriculum
Education
Educational Environment
Educational Technology
Instructional Design
Instructional Development
Instructional Effectiveness
Instructional Improvement
Instructional Innovation
Instructional Leadership
Instructional Materials
Instructional Systems
Laboratory Procedures
Language Of Instruction
Learning
School Supervision
Teaching Methods
Teaching Models

Instructional Aids (1966 1980)
USE EDUCATIONAL MEDIA

Instructional Alternatives
USE NONTRADITIONAL EDUCATION

INSTRUCTIONAL DESIGN *Jul. 1966*
CIJE: 1326 RIE: 1389 GC: 310
SN Analysis and prescription of optimal instructional methods (note: prior to apr80, the use of this term was not restricted by a scope note)
BT Design
RT Curriculum Design
Educational Strategies
Educational Technology
Instruction
Instructional Development
Instructional Improvement
Instructional Innovation

INSTRUCTIONAL DEVELOPMENT *Mar. 1980*
CIJE: 425 RIE: 538 GC: 310
SN Systematic approach to design, production, evaluation, and utilization of instructional systems and programs, including the management of these components
UF Instructional Planning
BT Educational Development
RT Curriculum Design
Curriculum Development
Curriculum Evaluation
Educational Strategies
Educational Technology
Flexible Scheduling
Instruction
Instructional Design
Instructional Improvement
Instructional Innovation
Instructional Leadership
Instructional Material Evaluation
Instructional Systems

INSTRUCTIONAL EFFECTIVENESS *Aug. 1986*
CIJE: 97 RIE: 61 GC: 310
SN Degree to which instructional materials or programs are successful in accomplishing their objectives
RT Academic Achievement
Course Evaluation
Curriculum Evaluation
Educational Quality
Instruction
Instructional Improvement
Instructional Innovation
Instructional Leadership
Instructional Material Evaluation
Instructional Materials
Outcomes Of Education
Program Effectiveness
School Effectiveness
Teacher Effectiveness
Teaching Methods

INSTRUCTIONAL FILMS *Jul. 1966*
CIJE: 357 RIE: 728 GC: 720
BT Audiovisual Aids
Films
Instructional Materials
RT Audiovisual Instruction
Documentaries
Educational Television
Programed Instructional Materials
Protocol Materials
Single Concept Films
Teaching Methods

INSTRUCTIONAL IMPROVEMENT *Jul. 1966*
CIJE: 1627 RIE: 1970 GC: 310
SN Enhancing the value or quality of instruction
BT Educational Improvement
RT Educational Technology
Instruction
Instructional Design
Instructional Development
Instructional Effectiveness
Instructional Innovation
Instructional Leadership
Research And Instruction Units
School Supervision
Student Evaluation Of Teacher Performance
Teacher Effectiveness
Teacher Improvement

INSTRUCTIONAL INNOVATION *Jul. 1966*
CIJE: 1439 RIE: 1705 GC: 310
SN Introduction of new teaching ideas, methods, or devices (note: do not confuse with "educational innovation")
UF Teaching Innovations
BT Educational Innovation
RT Creative Teaching
Educational Technology
Experimental Colleges
Experimental Curriculum
Experimental Schools
Experimental Teaching
Flexible Scheduling
Instruction
Instructional Design
Instructional Development
Instructional Effectiveness
Instructional Improvement
Instructional Leadership
Multiunit Schools
Nontraditional Education
Spiral Curriculum
Teacher Effectiveness

Instructional Language
USE LANGUAGE OF INSTRUCTION

INSTRUCTIONAL LEADERSHIP *Aug. 1986*
CIJE: 20 RIE: 26 GC: 320
SN Providing direction, coordination, and resources for the improvement of curriculum and instruction
BT Leadership
RT Academic Deans
Curriculum Development
Department Heads
Informal Leadership
Instruction
Instructional Development

= Two or more Descriptors are used to represent this term.
The term's main entry shows the appropriate coordination.

Instructional Effectiveness
Instructional Improvement
Instructional Innovation
Leadership Responsibility
Leadership Training
Principals
School Administration
School Supervision
Superintendents
Teacher Administrator Relationship
Teaching Methods

Instructional Material Adaptation
USE MEDIA ADAPTATION

Instructional Material Development
USE MATERIAL DEVELOPMENT

INSTRUCTIONAL MATERIAL EVALUATION *Jun. 1984*
CIJE: 47 RIE: 112 GC: 310
SN Determining the efficacy, value, etc. of any type of instructional material with respect to stated objectives, standards, or criteria (note: use as a minor descriptor for examples of this kind of evaluation -- use as a major descriptor only as the subject of a document)
NT Textbook Evaluation
BT Evaluation
RT Course Evaluation
Curriculum Evaluation
Instructional Development
Instructional Effectiveness
Instructional Materials
Material Development
Media Adaptation
Media Selection
Program Evaluation

Instructional Material Selection
USE MEDIA SELECTION

INSTRUCTIONAL MATERIALS *Jul. 1966*
CIJE: 9290 RIE: 18872 GC: 730
SN Print and/or nonprint materials used in instruction
UF Classroom Libraries (1966 1980)
Classroom Materials (1966 1980)
Curriculum Materials
Educational Materials
Fles Materials (1967 1980) #
Handwriting Materials (1966 1983) #
Teaching Materials
NT Advance Organizers
Bilingual Instructional Materials
Courseware
Experience Charts
Instructional Films
Laboratory Manuals
Learning Modules
Manipulative Materials
Problem Sets
Programed Instructional Materials
Protocol Materials
Student Developed Materials
Study Guides
Teacher Developed Materials
Textbooks
Workbooks
BT Educational Media
RT Art Materials
Audiovisual Aids
Autoinstructional Aids
Cartoons
Charts
Comics (Publications)
Curriculum Development
Diagrams
Educational Games
Educational Resources
Educational Technology
Exhibits
Graphs
Health Materials
High Interest Low Vocabulary Books
Illustrations
Instruction
Instructional Effectiveness
Instructional Material Evaluation
Large Type Materials
Learning Resources Centers
Library Materials
Maps
Material Development
Mathematics Materials
Microforms
Orientation Materials
Publications
Reading Materials
Realia
Reference Materials
Resource Materials
Science Course Improvement Projects
Science Materials
Signs
Supplementary Reading Materials
Teaching Guides
Telegraphic Materials
Tests
Toys
Visual Aids

Instructional Materials Centers (1966 1980)
USE LEARNING RESOURCES CENTERS

Instructional Media (1967 1980)
USE EDUCATIONAL MEDIA

Instructional Methods
USE TEACHING METHODS

Instructional Outcomes
USE OUTCOMES OF EDUCATION

Instructional Planning
USE INSTRUCTIONAL DEVELOPMENT

INSTRUCTIONAL PROGRAM DIVISIONS *Jul. 1966*
CIJE: 174 RIE: 617 GC: 340
SN Divisions marked by the use of grade levels or other groupings to structure the formal educational process
UF Grade Levels
Grade Organization (1966 1980)
Grades (Program Divisions)
Six Three Three Organization
NT Grade 1
Grade 2
Grade 3
Grade 4
Grade 5
Grade 6
Grade 7
Grade 8
Grade 9
Grade 10
Grade 11
Grade 12
Intermediate Grades
Kindergarten
RT Ability Grouping
Age Grade Placement
Grouping (Instructional Purposes)
Multigraded Classes
Nongraded Instructional Grouping
School Organization
Student Promotion

INSTRUCTIONAL PROGRAMS (1966 1980) *Mar. 1980*
CIJE: 509 RIE: 1084 GC: 310
SN Invalid descriptor -- used inconsistently in indexing -- coordinate more specific descriptors

Instructional Radio
USE EDUCATIONAL RADIO

Instructional Software
USE COURSEWARE

Instructional Staff (1966 1980)
USE TEACHERS

INSTRUCTIONAL STUDENT COSTS *Dec. 1975*
CIJE: 22 RIE: 75 GC: 620
SN Costs incurred by students specifically for instruction, e.g., tuition, laboratory fees (note: use "noninstructional student costs" for student costs not directly related to instruction, such as transportation expenses and room and board)
NT Tuition
BT Student Costs
RT Educational Economics
Educational Finance
Fellowships
Noninstructional Student Costs
Operating Expenses
Program Costs
Scholarships
Student Financial Aid
Student Loan Programs
Tuition Grants

INSTRUCTIONAL SYSTEMS *Mar. 1971*
CIJE: 413 RIE: 600 GC: 310
SN Combination, arrangement, and management of instructional components to solve problems or achieve other educational objectives
BT Educational Technology
RT Instruction
Instructional Development
Systems Analysis
Systems Approach

Instructional Teams
USE TEAM TEACHING

Instructional Technology (1966 1978)
USE EDUCATIONAL TECHNOLOGY

Instructional Television (1966 1974)
USE EDUCATIONAL TELEVISION

Instructional Trips (1966 1980)
USE FIELD TRIPS

Instructionally Effective Schools
USE SCHOOL EFFECTIVENESS

Instructor Centered Television (1966 1980)
USE EDUCATIONAL TELEVISION

INSTRUCTOR COORDINATORS *Jul. 1966*
CIJE: 68 RIE: 183 GC: 360
SN Teachers responsible for coordinating students' education and on-the-job activities
UF Coordinator Trainers
Teacher Coordinators
BT Coordinators
Teachers
RT Adult Educators
Cooperative Education
Guidance Personnel
School Guidance
Vocational Education Teachers

Instructor Manuals
USE TEACHING GUIDES

Instructors
USE TEACHERS

Instrumental Conditioning
USE OPERANT CONDITIONING

INSTRUMENTATION *Jul. 1966*
CIJE: 502 RIE: 221 GC: 910
SN Use of physical instruments or instrument systems for detection, observation, measurement, communication, control, etc.
NT Visible Speech
RT Automation
Calculators
Computers
Cybernetics
Data Processing
Electronic Control
Electronic Equipment
Horology
Instrumentation Technicians
Measurement Equipment
Polygraphs
Sound Spectrographs
Test Scoring Machines
Transistors

INSTRUMENTATION TECHNICIANS *Jul. 1966*
CIJE: 8 RIE: 28 GC: 640
BT Paraprofessional Personnel
RT Electronics
Electronic Technicians
Instrumentation

INSURANCE *Mar. 1980*
CIJE: 178 RIE: 299 GC: 620
SN Method of pooling or shifting probable losses among a group to reduce economic risk
UF Insurance Programs (1968 1980)
NT Fire Insurance
Health Insurance
Unemployment Insurance
Workers Compensation
BT Methods
RT Eligibility
Financial Services
Financial Support
Indemnity Bonds
Insurance Companies
Insurance Occupations
Ownership
Property Appraisal
Retirement Benefits
Risk

INSURANCE COMPANIES *Jul. 1966*
CIJE: 42 RIE: 62 GC: 650
UF Insurance Industry
BT Industry
RT Business
Insurance
Insurance Occupations

Insurance Industry
USE INSURANCE COMPANIES

INSURANCE OCCUPATIONS *Sep. 1968*
CIJE: 19 RIE: 27 GC: 640
BT Occupations
RT Distributive Education
Fire Insurance
Health Insurance
Insurance
Insurance Companies
Sales Occupations
Unemployment Insurance

Insurance Programs (1968 1980)
USE INSURANCE

INTEGERS *Feb. 1970*
CIJE: 79 RIE: 37 GC: 480
NT Prime Numbers
BT Rational Numbers
RT Arithmetic

INTEGRATED ACTIVITIES *Jul. 1966*
CIJE: 391 RIE: 463 GC: 310
SN Systematic organization of units into a meaningful pattern (note: use a more specific term if possible -- prior to mar80, the instruction "integrated learning, use integrated curriculum" was carried in the thesaurus)
UF Integrated Learning #
Integrated Teaching Method #
NT Integrated Curriculum
BT Activities
RT Holistic Approach
Interdisciplinary Approach
Living Learning Centers
Systems Analysis
Teaching Methods

Integrated Classes
USE CLASSROOM DESEGREGATION

Integrated Colleges
USE COLLEGE DESEGREGATION

INTEGRATED CURRICULUM *Jul. 1966*
CIJE: 656 RIE: 968 GC: 350
SN Systematic organization of curriculum content and parts into a meaningful pattern
UF Integrated Education
BT Curriculum
Integrated Activities
RT Fused Curriculum
Unified Studies Curriculum

Integrated Education
USE INTEGRATED CURRICULUM

Integrated Faculty
USE FACULTY INTEGRATION

Integrated Learning
USE INTEGRATED ACTIVITIES; LEARNING ACTIVITIES

Integrated Neighborhoods
USE NEIGHBORHOOD INTEGRATION

= Two or more Descriptors are used to represent this term.
The term's main entry shows the appropriate coordination.

Integrated Public Facilities (1966 1980)
USE PUBLIC FACILITIES; RACIAL INTEGRATION

Integrated Schools
USE SCHOOL DESEGREGATION

Integrated Teaching Method
USE INTEGRATED ACTIVITIES; TEACHING METHODS

Integration (Disabled Students)
USE MAINSTREAMING

Integration (Racial)
USE RACIAL INTEGRATION

Integration (Social)
USE SOCIAL INTEGRATION

Integration Effects (1966 1980)
USE DESEGREGATION EFFECTS

Integration Impact
USE DESEGREGATION EFFECTS

Integration Litigation (1966 1980)
USE DESEGREGATION LITIGATION

Integration Methods (1966 1980)
USE DESEGREGATION METHODS

Integration Plans (1966 1980)
USE DESEGREGATION PLANS

INTEGRATION READINESS *Jul. 1966*
CIJE: 31 RIE: 78 GC: 540
SN Preparedness of individuals or groups to accept their own desegregation/integration with other ethnic or racial groups
UF Desegregation Readiness
BT Readiness
RT Desegregation Plans
Integration Studies
Neighborhood Integration
Racial Attitudes
Racial Integration
School Desegregation
Social Integration

INTEGRATION STUDIES *Jul. 1966*
CIJE: 74 RIE: 221 GC: 810
BT Behavioral Science Research
RT Desegregation Effects
Ethnic Studies
Integration Readiness
Racial Integration

Integrative Analysis
USE META ANALYSIS

INTEGRITY *Jul. 1966*
CIJE: 96 RIE: 37 GC: 120
RT Credibility
Ethics
Moral Development
Moral Values
Reputation

Intellectronics
USE BIONICS

INTELLECTUAL DEVELOPMENT *Jul. 1966*
CIJE: 1035 RIE: 924 GC: 120
SN Increasing complexity or growth of reasoning and thought processes (note: prior to mar80, the use of this term was not restricted by a scope note)
BT Cognitive Development
RT Creative Development
Formal Operations
Intellectual Experience
Intellectual Freedom
Intelligence
Intelligence Differences
Intelligence Tests
Mental Age
Mental Rigidity
Piagetian Theory

INTELLECTUAL DISCIPLINES *Jul. 1966*
CIJE: 714 RIE: 538 GC: 350
SN Areas of knowledge or instruction
UF Academic Disciplines
Subject Disciplines
RT Academic Education
Courses
Curriculum
Departments
Majors (Students)

INTELLECTUAL EXPERIENCE *Jul. 1966*
CIJE: 73 RIE: 53 GC: 110
BT Experience
RT Intellectual Development
Intelligence

INTELLECTUAL FREEDOM *Oct. 1983*
CIJE: 111 RIE: 30 GC: 330
SN The absence of external coercion, censorship, or other forms of restrictive interference on the exercise of thought
UF Access To Ideas
Freedom Of Thought
Freedom To Read
RT Academic Freedom
Access To Education
Censorship
Civil Liberties
Democracy
Disclosure
Ethics
Freedom Of Information
Freedom Of Speech
Independent Reading
Independent Study
Individualism
Institutional Autonomy
Intellectual Development
Personal Autonomy
Privacy
Professional Autonomy
Public Libraries
State Church Separation

INTELLECTUAL HISTORY *Aug. 1977*
CIJE: 100 RIE: 109 GC: 430
SN Branch of history that deals with the evolution of ideas, how these ideas were influenced by various factors, and what happens to these ideas or thoughts among people in a given society
NT Art History
Literary History
BT History
RT Culture
Expressionism
Historiography
Impressionism
Social History

INTELLECTUAL PROPERTY *Mar. 1980*
CIJE: 41 RIE: 27 GC: 710
SN Expressions or results of mental activity (especially such things as literary, artistic, or scholarly creations, research designs, etc.) for which one has a legal right to own, use, reproduce, or sell
UF Ownership Of Ideas
NT Copyrights
Patents
BT Ownership
RT Discovery Processes
Inventions
Legal Responsibility
Plagiarism
Research Utilization

Intellectualization (1970 1980)
USE ABSTRACT REASONING

INTELLIGENCE *Jul. 1966*
CIJE: 1459 RIE: 1022 GC: 120
UF Intelligence Factors (1966 1980)
Intelligence Level (1966 1980)
National Intelligence Norm (1966 1980) #
NT Comprehension
Formal Operations
Mental Age
BT Psychological Characteristics
RT Academic Ability
Academic Achievement
Academic Aptitude
Adjustment (To Environment)
Artificial Intelligence
Cognitive Ability
Cognitive Processes
Cognitive Psychology
Creativity
Intellectual Development
Intellectual Experience
Intelligence Differences
Intelligence Quotient
Intelligence Tests
Mental Retardation
Nature Nurture Controversy

Intelligence Age
USE MENTAL AGE

INTELLIGENCE DIFFERENCES *Jul. 1966*
CIJE: 483 RIE: 313 GC: 120
BT Individual Differences
RT Intellectual Development
Intelligence
Intelligence Quotient
Intelligence Tests
Mental Age
Nature Nurture Controversy

Intelligence Factors (1966 1980)
USE INTELLIGENCE

Intelligence Level (1966 1980)
USE INTELLIGENCE

Intelligence Measures
USE INTELLIGENCE TESTS

INTELLIGENCE QUOTIENT *Jul. 1966*
CIJE: 834 RIE: 469 GC: 820
UF Iq
BT Ratios (Mathematics)
RT Intelligence
Intelligence Differences
Intelligence Tests
Mental Age
Talent Identification

INTELLIGENCE TESTS *Jul. 1966*
CIJE: 1616 RIE: 839 GC: 830
SN Measures used to indicate an individual's cognitive ability to adjust to the environment, i.e., the ability to learn, deal with new situations, or solve problems
UF Group Intelligence Testing (1966 1980) #
Group Intelligence Tests (1966 1980) #
Intelligence Measures
BT Cognitive Tests
RT Ability Identification
Aptitude Tests
Cognitive Measurement
Creativity Tests
Intellectual Development
Intelligence
Intelligence Differences
Intelligence Quotient
Mental Age
Psychological Testing
Talent Identification

Intelligent Video
USE INTERACTIVE VIDEO

INTENSIVE LANGUAGE COURSES *Jul. 1966*
CIJE: 112 RIE: 422 GC: 450
SN Foreign language courses that involve more contact hours per day than conventional courses offer -- the work of two or more conventional courses is completed within one intensive course
BT Courses
Modern Language Curriculum
RT Language Proficiency
Languages
Second Language Instruction
Second Language Learning
Second Language Programs

INTENTIONAL LEARNING *Oct. 1970*
CIJE: 62 RIE: 41 GC: 110
SN Purposive learning according to a predetermined pattern
BT Learning
RT Advance Organizers
Incidental Learning
Learning Motivation
Learning Processes
Learning Strategies
Observational Learning
Test Wiseness

INTERACTION *Jul. 1966*
CIJE: 1728 RIE: 1683 GC: 510
SN Mutual or reciprocal action and response between two or more persons, systems, or other entities (note: use a more specific term if possible -- prior to mar80, the instruction "interaction analysis, use interaction process analysis" was carried in the thesaurus)
UF Interaction Analysis
NT Aptitude Treatment Interaction
Feedback
Group Dynamics
BT Relationship
RT Communication (Thought Transfer)
Human Relations
Interaction Process Analysis
Intergroup Relations
Interpersonal Relationship
Man Machine Systems
Participation
Statistical Analysis

Interaction Analysis
USE INTERACTION

INTERACTION PROCESS ANALYSIS *Jul. 1966*
CIJE: 2008 RIE: 1848 GC: 820
SN Method of studying social groups wherein all explicit interactions in small face-to-face groups are carefully recorded according to a systematic classification and analyzed (note: prior to mar80, the use of this term was not restricted by a scope note)
BT Research Methodology
RT Behavioral Science Research
Body Language
Classroom Observation Techniques
Communication Research
Eye Contact
Group Dynamics
Groups
Group Structure
Interaction
Interpersonal Relationship
Naturalistic Observation
Paralinguistics
Self Directed Groups
Social Behavior
Social Integration
Sociometric Techniques

Interactive Searching (Online)
USE ONLINE SEARCHING

Interactive Systems (Online)
USE ONLINE SYSTEMS

INTERACTIVE VIDEO *Apr. 1986*
CIJE: 57 RIE: 32 GC: 710
SN Online video computing systems capable of rapid, accept-and-react communications with human operators
UF Intelligent Video
BT Online Systems
RT Communications
Computer Assisted Instruction
Display Systems
Menu Driven Software
Optical Data Disks
Optical Disks
Videodisks
Video Equipment
Videotape Cassettes
Videotape Recordings

Interagency Cooperation (1967 1980)
USE AGENCY COOPERATION

Interagency Coordination (1967 1980)
USE AGENCY COOPERATION; COORDINATION

Interagency Planning (1966 1980)
USE AGENCY COOPERATION; COOPERATIVE PLANNING

Intercollegiate Athletics
USE COLLEGE ATHLETICS; INTERCOLLEGIATE COOPERATION

= Two or more Descriptors are used to represent this term.
The term's main entry shows the appropriate coordination.

INTERCOLLEGIATE COOPERATION *Mar. 1980*
CIJE: 305 RIE: 374 GC: 330
SN Cooperation between or among colleges, universities, or professional schools
UF College Cooperation (1966 1980)
Intercollegiate Athletics #
Intercollegiate Programs (1967 1980)
BT Educational Cooperation
Institutional Cooperation
RT Articulation (Education)
College Planning
Colleges
College School Cooperation
Consortia

Intercollegiate Programs (1967 1980)
USE INTERCOLLEGIATE COOPERATION

Intercommunication (1966 1980)
USE COMMUNICATION (THOUGHT TRANSFER)

INTERCULTURAL COMMUNICATION *Aug. 1982*
CIJE: 121 RIE: 234 GC: 330
SN Verbal and nonverbal communication among people of different cultures
UF Cross Cultural Communication
BT Communication (Thought Transfer)
RT Biculturalism
Bidialectalism
Bilingualism
Communication Problems
Cross Cultural Training
Cultural Awareness
Cultural Differences
Cultural Exchange
Cultural Interrelationships
Cultural Pluralism
Culture
Culture Contact
Ethnic Relations
Foreign Culture
Intercultural Programs
International Relations
Multicultural Education
Multilingualism
Multilingual Materials
Speech Communication

Intercultural Education
USE MULTICULTURAL EDUCATION

INTERCULTURAL PROGRAMS *Jul. 1966*
CIJE: 178 RIE: 329 GC: 560
BT Programs
RT Biculturalism
Bilingual Education
Bilingual Education Programs
Cross Cultural Studies
Cross Cultural Training
Cultural Awareness
Cultural Education
Cultural Enrichment
Cultural Exchange
Cultural Influences
Cultural Interrelationships
Cultural Pluralism
Culture
Culture Contact
Ethnic Groups
Exchange Programs
Global Approach
Intercultural Communication
Interdisciplinary Approach
Intergroup Education
International Programs
International Studies
Multicultural Education

Interdimensional Shift
USE SHIFT STUDIES

INTERDISCIPLINARY APPROACH *Jul. 1966*
CIJE: 3637 RIE: 3960 GC: 310
SN Participation or cooperation of two or more disciplines
BT Methods
RT Adventure Education
Area Studies
Core Curriculum
Cross Cultural Training
Curriculum Design
Ethnic Studies
Force Field Analysis
Fused Curriculum
Global Approach
Holistic Approach
Integrated Activities
Intercultural Programs
International Studies
Multicultural Education
Nonmajors
Outdoor Education
Science And Society
Thematic Approach
Unified Studies Curriculum
Urban Studies

INTERDISTRICT POLICIES *Jul. 1966*
CIJE: 12 RIE: 41 GC: 330
SN Policies that have been cooperatively determined by two or more school districts
BT Policy
RT Administrative Policy
Agency Cooperation
Board Of Education Policy
Institutional Cooperation
School Districts
School Policy

INTEREST (FINANCE) *Nov. 1981*
CIJE: 16 RIE: 22 GC: 620
SN The price paid for the use of money over time
UF Interest (1967 1981)
BT Costs
Income
RT Credit (Finance)
Economics
Inflation (Economics)
Investment
Loan Repayment
Monetary Systems

Interest (1967 1981)
USE INTEREST (FINANCE)

Interest Centers (Classroom)
USE LEARNING CENTERS (CLASSROOM)

INTEREST INVENTORIES *Mar. 1980*
CIJE: 503 RIE: 397 GC: 830
SN Measures designed to reveal the objects and activities that are of interest to, preferred, liked, or disliked by an individual (note: do not confuse with "attitude measures")
UF Interest Scales (1966 1980)
Interest Tests (1966 1980)
BT Measures (Individuals)
RT Affective Measures
Aptitude Tests
Attitude Measures
Biographical Inventories
Career Choice
Forced Choice Technique
Interest Research
Interests
Occupational Tests
Opinions
Personality Measures
Predictive Measurement
Predictive Validity
Predictor Variables
Profiles
Prognostic Tests

INTEREST RESEARCH *Jul. 1966*
CIJE: 98 RIE: 101 GC: 810
SN Systematic investigation of those activities, avocations, objects, etc. that have special worth or significance to individuals or groups (note: as of oct81, use as a minor descriptor for examples of this kind of research -- use as a major descriptor only as the subject of a document)
BT Psychological Studies
RT Interest Inventories
Interests

Interest Scales (1966 1980)
USE INTEREST INVENTORIES

Interest Tests (1966 1980)
USE INTEREST INVENTORIES

INTERESTS *Jul. 1966*
CIJE: 339 RIE: 298 GC: 120
SN Activities, avocations, objects, etc. that have special worth or significance for individuals or groups and are given special attention (note: use a more specific term if possible)
UF Group Interests
Personal Interests (1966 1980)
NT Childhood Interests
Reading Interests
Science Interests
Student Interests
Vocational Interests
RT Activities
Affective Behavior
Attitudes
Cognitive Structures
Curiosity
Hobbies
Interest Inventories
Interest Research
Participation

INTERFAITH RELATIONS *Jul. 1966*
CIJE: 6 RIE: 11 GC: 520
BT Intergroup Relations
RT Ethnic Relations
Religion
Religious Conflict
Religious Cultural Groups
Religious Differences
Religious Discrimination
Social Integration

Interference (Language Learning) (1968 1980)
USE INTERFERENCE (LANGUAGE)

INTERFERENCE (LANGUAGE) *Mar. 1980*
CIJE: 395 RIE: 440 GC: 450
SN The negative effect of carrying over features of pronunciation, grammar, or vocabulary from one language or dialect to another
UF Dialect Interference #
Interference (Language Learning) (1968 1980)
Linguistic Difficulty (Contrastive)
BT Language Processing
RT Audiolingual Methods
Bidialectalism
Bilingualism
Code Switching (Language)
Contrastive Linguistics
Error Analysis (Language)
Interlanguage
Language Dominance
Learning Processes
Multilingualism
Psycholinguistics
Second Language Learning

INTERGENERATIONAL PROGRAMS *Apr. 1986*
CIJE: 16 RIE: 45 GC: 520
SN Programs that provide interaction among generational age groups, usually between older adults and younger persons
BT Programs
RT Age Differences
Age Groups
Community Programs
Generation Gap
Older Adults

Intergovernmental Organizations
USE INTERNATIONAL ORGANIZATIONS

INTERGROUP EDUCATION *Jul. 1966*
CIJE: 46 RIE: 124 GC: 330
SN Learning activities, curriculum, and/or educational programs, at any educational level, concerned with improving human relations and increasing intercultural and intergroup understanding
NT Multicultural Education
BT Education
RT Human Relations
Intercultural Programs
Intergroup Relations
Multicultural Textbooks
Social Integration

INTERGROUP RELATIONS *Jul. 1966*
CIJE: 372 RIE: 448 GC: 520
NT Ethnic Relations
Interfaith Relations
Racial Relations
BT Human Relations
RT Communication (Thought Transfer)
Competition
Cooperation
Cross Cultural Studies
Cross Cultural Training
Elitism
Ethnocentrism
Interaction
Intergroup Education
Intermarriage
Multicultural Education
Social Bias
Social Discrimination
Social Integration
Social Mobility
Social Networks
Sociometric Techniques

Interinstitutional Cooperation (1968 1980)
USE INSTITUTIONAL COOPERATION

Interior Decoration
USE INTERIOR DESIGN

INTERIOR DESIGN *Jan. 1970*
CIJE: 152 RIE: 100 GC: 420
UF Interior Decoration
BT Design
RT Acoustical Environment
Architecture
Building Design
Classroom Design
Color Planning
Design Requirements
Furniture Arrangement
Interior Space
Lighting Design
Offices (Facilities)
Painting (Industrial Arts)
Physical Environment
Space Classification
Spatial Relationship (Facilities)
Thermal Environment

Interior Monologues
USE MONOLOGS

INTERIOR SPACE *Jul. 1966*
CIJE: 77 RIE: 127 GC: 920
SN Area available within a building
BT Facilities
RT Building Design
Classroom Design
Design Requirements
Flexible Facilities
Furniture Arrangement
Interior Design
Offices (Facilities)
Open Plan Schools
Physical Environment
School Space
Space Classification
Space Utilization
Storage

Interjudge Agreement
USE INTERRATER RELIABILITY

INTERLANGUAGE *Jul. 1980*
CIJE: 84 RIE: 89 GC: 450
SN A learner's systematic, internally structured, and autonomous version of a target language -- this system evolves, is governed by rules, and defines the developing linguistic competence of the learner
UF Approximative Systems (Language Learning)
BT Language
RT Error Analysis (Language)
Interference (Language)
Learning Processes
Linguistic Competence
Linguistic Performance
Psycholinguistics
Second Language Learning

INTERLIBRARY LOANS *Jul. 1966*
CIJE: 199 RIE: 470 GC: 710
BT Library Circulation
RT Library Cooperation
Library Networks
Shared Library Resources
Union Catalogs

INTERMARRIAGE *Jul. 1966*
CIJE: 45 RIE: 27 GC: 520
SN Marriage between members of different racial, social, or religious groups
UF Exogamous Marriage
BT Marriage
RT Cultural Differences
Intergroup Relations
Mate Selection
Racial Differences
Religious Differences
Social Differences

INTERMEDIATE ADMINISTRATIVE UNITS *Jul. 1966*
CIJE: 35 RIE: 165 GC: 340
SN Administrative units smaller than the state that exist to provide consulting, advisory, administrative, or statistical services to local school districts, and/or to exercise regulatory functions over local districts
UF Intermediate School Districts
Intermediate Service Districts
RT Boards Of Education
Consultation Programs
Professional Services
Regional Cooperation
School District Reorganization
School Districts
State School District Relationship

INTERMEDIATE GRADES *Jul. 1966*
CIJE: 1559 RIE: 2184 GC: 340
SN Includes the middle and/or upper elementary grades, but usually 4, 5, and 6 (note: also appears in the list of mandatory educational level descriptors)
BT Instructional Program Divisions
RT Elementary Education
Grade 4
Grade 5
Grade 6
Middle Schools
Preadolescents

Intermediate School Districts
USE INTERMEDIATE ADMINISTRATIVE UNITS

Intermediate Service Districts
USE INTERMEDIATE ADMINISTRATIVE UNITS

INTERMODE DIFFERENCES *Jul. 1966*
CIJE: 142 RIE: 289 GC: 310
SN Variations among instructional materials or modes of presentation
BT Differences
RT Audiovisual Instruction
Computer Assisted Instruction
Educational Media
Learning Modalities
Media Adaptation
Multimedia Instruction
Programed Instruction
Teaching Methods

Intern Teachers
USE TEACHER INTERNS

Internal External Locus Of Control
USE LOCUS OF CONTROL

Internal Immigrants
USE MIGRANTS

INTERNAL MEDICINE *Oct. 1979*
CIJE: 90 RIE: 5 GC: 210
SN Branch of medicine dealing with the diagnosis and nonsurgical treatment of diseases
BT Medicine
RT Clinical Diagnosis
Diseases
Family Practice (Medicine)
Immunization Programs
Medical Services
Oncology
Primary Health Care

Internal Review (Organizations)
USE SELF EVALUATION (GROUPS)

Internal Scaling (1966 1980)
USE SCALING

Internation Behavior
USE INTERNATIONAL RELATIONS

International Approach
USE GLOBAL APPROACH

INTERNATIONAL COOPERATION *Jun. 1983*
CIJE: 126 RIE: 161 GC: 520
SN Cooperation between or among nations or international bodies
BT Cooperation
RT Exchange Programs
Global Approach
Institutional Cooperation
International Education
International Educational Exchange
International Law
International Organizations
International Programs
International Relations
International Trade
International Trade Vocabulary
World Affairs
World Problems

INTERNATIONAL CRIMES *Apr. 1972*
CIJE: 16 RIE: 17 GC: 530
SN Crimes such as piracy, illicit trade in narcotics, or slave trading that are in violation of international law
UF War Crimes
BT Crime
RT Civil Liberties
International Law
Laws
Nazism
Slavery
Terrorism
War

INTERNATIONAL EDUCATION *Jul. 1966*
CIJE: 1310 RIE: 1379 GC: 400
SN Study of educational, social, political, economic, and environmental forces of international relations, with special emphasis on the role and potentialities of educational forces
BT Education
RT Comparative Education
Cross Cultural Studies
Diplomatic History
Foreign Culture
Foreign Policy
International Cooperation
International Educational Exchange
International Law
International Organizations
International Programs
International Relations
International Studies
International Trade
International Trade Vocabulary
Peace

INTERNATIONAL EDUCATIONAL EXCHANGE *Aug. 1976*
CIJE: 277 RIE: 446 GC: 330
SN Exchange among nations of instructional materials, techniques, students, teachers, and technicians for purposes of sharing knowledge and furthering international understanding
RT Comparative Education
Cross Cultural Training
Cultural Exchange
Exchange Programs
Foreign Culture
Foreign Medical Graduates
Foreign Students
International Cooperation
International Education
International Organizations
International Programs
International Relations
International Trade
Student Exchange Programs
Study Abroad
Teacher Exchange Programs
Technical Assistance

INTERNATIONAL LAW *Apr. 1972*
CIJE: 59 RIE: 96 GC: 610
UF International Legal Analysis
International Torts
Law Of Nations
BT Laws
RT Conflict Resolution
Foreign Policy
International Cooperation
International Crimes
International Education
International Organizations
International Relations
International Studies
Law Related Education
Legal Education (Professions)
Political Science
Treaties
War
World Affairs

International Legal Analysis
USE INTERNATIONAL LAW

INTERNATIONAL ORGANIZATIONS *Jul. 1966*
CIJE: 624 RIE: 965 GC: 610
UF Intergovernmental Organizations
BT Organizations (Groups)
RT International Cooperation
International Education
International Educational Exchange
International Law
International Programs
International Relations
International Studies
National Organizations
Peace
Professional Associations

International Peace
USE PEACE

International Policy
USE FOREIGN POLICY

International Politics
USE INTERNATIONAL RELATIONS

INTERNATIONAL PROGRAMS *Jul. 1966*
CIJE: 851 RIE: 1125 GC: 610
SN Programs sponsored by governments, institutions, or private organizations that involve more than one country
UF International Technical Assistance #
BT Programs
RT Developed Nations
Developing Nations
Foreign Nationals
Foreign Policy
Intercultural Programs
International Cooperation
International Education
International Educational Exchange
International Organizations
International Relations
International Trade
Technical Assistance

INTERNATIONAL RELATIONS *Aug. 1976*
CIJE: 773 RIE: 984 GC: 610
SN Relations among political units of national rank -- also, a field of study (often considered as a branch of political science) dealing primarily with foreign policies, the organization and function of governmental agencies concerned with foreign policy, and the factors (as geography and economics) underlying foreign policy
UF Diplomacy
Foreign Relations (1966 1976)
International Politics
Internation Behavior
BT Relationship
RT Colonialism
Conflict
Cross Cultural Training
Developed Nations
Developing Nations
Diplomatic History
Disarmament
Ethnocentrism
Exports
Foreign Countries
Foreign Diplomats
Foreign Policy
Global Approach
Intercultural Communication
International Cooperation
International Education
International Educational Exchange
International Law
International Organizations
International Programs
International Studies
International Trade
Nationalism
National Security
Peace
Political Science
Treaties
War
World Affairs

International Students
USE FOREIGN STUDENTS

INTERNATIONAL STUDIES *Aug. 1976*
CIJE: 181 RIE: 245 GC: 400
SN Multidisciplinary field of inquiry concerned with analyzing social phenomena that occur within, between, and transcending nationally organized politics -- commonly identified subfields are "international politics," "foreign policy," "international law," "international organization," "international economics," and "comparative area studies"
BT Social Sciences
RT Area Studies
Comparative Analysis
Cross Cultural Studies
Economics
Foreign Countries
Foreign Policy
Intercultural Programs
Interdisciplinary Approach
International Education
International Law
International Organizations
International Relations
Multilingual Materials
Political Science
Politics
Social Science Research
Social Scientists

International Technical Assistance
USE INTERNATIONAL PROGRAMS; TECHNICAL ASSISTANCE

International Torts
USE INTERNATIONAL LAW

INTERNATIONAL TRADE *Jun. 1983*
CIJE: 50 RIE: 90 GC: 650
SN Exchange of goods and services among nations
RT Business
Developed Nations
Developing Nations
Economics
Exports
Foreign Policy
International Cooperation
International Education
International Educational Exchange
International Programs
International Relations
International Trade Vocabulary
Marketing
Monetary Systems
Structural Unemployment
World Affairs

INTERNATIONAL TRADE VOCABULARY *Jul. 1966*
CIJE: 15 RIE: 24 GC: 450
SN Words and terms used frequently in international trade -- more specifically, the vocabulary needed for participation in the multilingual environment of international trade
BT Vocabulary
RT Artificial Languages
Economics
Exports
International Cooperation
International Education
International Trade
Professional Training

= Two or more Descriptors are used to represent this term.
The term's main entry shows the appropriate coordination.

International War
USE WAR

Interns (Medical)
USE GRADUATE MEDICAL STUDENTS

INTERNSHIP PROGRAMS *Jul. 1966*
CIJE: 644 RIE: 761 GC: 350
SN Programs offering supervised practical experience for advanced students or recent graduates in professional fields (note: use "graduate medical education" for graduate medical internship or residency programs)
BT Experiential Learning Programs
RT Assistantships
Clinical Experience
Field Experience Programs
Inservice Teacher Education
On The Job Training
Practicums
Practicum Supervision
Professional Education
Student Experience
Teacher Interns
Teaching Experience

Internships (Medical)
USE GRADUATE MEDICAL EDUCATION

Interobserver Reliability
USE INTERRATER RELIABILITY

INTERPERSONAL ATTRACTION *Aug. 1978*
CIJE: 200 RIE: 148 GC: 510
SN Perceived personal qualities (physical, mental, emotional, and social) drawing persons to one another
UF Attractiveness (Between Persons)
BT Interpersonal Relationship
RT Affection
Body Image
Congruence (Psychology)
Dating (Social)
Emotional Response
Interpersonal Communication
Physical Characteristics
Psychological Characteristics
Rapport
Social Life

INTERPERSONAL COMMUNICATION *Nov. 1982*
CIJE: 423 RIE: 561 GC: 510
SN The interpersonal sharing of opinions, interests, and feelings -- includes verbal and nonverbal exchanges between two or more persons, in which participants are actively involved as both senders and receivers
UF Dyadic Communication
BT Communication (Thought Transfer)
RT Assertiveness
Confidentiality
Conflict Resolution
Dialogs (Language)
Discussion
Eye Contact
Grievance Procedures
Group Discussion
Group Dynamics
Interpersonal Attraction
Interpersonal Competence
Interpersonal Relationship
Interviews
Letters (Correspondence)
Rapport
Self Disclosure (Individuals)
Self Expression
Social Cognition
Speech Communication
Standard Spoken Usage

INTERPERSONAL COMPETENCE *Jul. 1966*
CIJE: 2023 RIE: 2078 GC: 120
UF Gregariousness
Interpersonal Skills
Perceptiveness (Between Persons) #
Sociability
Social Awareness
Social Competence
Social Skills
BT Competence
RT Daily Living Skills
Humanistic Education
Interpersonal Communication
Interpersonal Relationship
Laboratory Training
Maturity (Individuals)
Personality Traits
Popularity
Prosocial Behavior
Reality Therapy
Sensitivity Training
Skills
Social Adjustment
Social Attitudes
Social Behavior
Social Characteristics
Social Cognition
Social Development
Social Experience
Socialization
Teamwork
Transactional Analysis

Interpersonal Perception
USE SOCIAL COGNITION

Interpersonal Problems (1966 1980)
USE INTERPERSONAL RELATIONSHIP

INTERPERSONAL RELATIONSHIP *Jul. 1966*
CIJE: 3877 RIE: 2678 GC: 510
UF Interpersonal Problems (1966 1980)
Personal Relationship (1966 1974)
Social Interaction
NT Board Administrator Relationship
Counselor Client Relationship
Dating (Social)
Employer Employee Relationship
Family Relationship
Friendship
Group Unity
Helping Relationship
Interpersonal Attraction
Interprofessional Relationship
Kinship
Marriage
Peer Relationship
Physician Patient Relationship
Rapport
Significant Others
Teacher Administrator Relationship
Teacher Student Relationship
BT Relationship
RT Alienation
Altruism
Attachment Behavior
Autism
Competition
Cooperation
Credibility
Cross Age Teaching
Egocentrism
Empathy
Human Relations
Informal Leadership
Interaction
Interaction Process Analysis
Interpersonal Communication
Interpersonal Competence
Jealousy
Mentors
Personal Autonomy
Perspective Taking
Privacy
Professional Autonomy
Reference Groups
Rejection (Psychology)
Sexual Identity
Social Cognition
Social Exchange Theory
Social Integration
Social Life
Social Mobility
Social Networks
Sociometric Techniques
Teamwork
Trust (Psychology)

Interpersonal Skills
USE INTERPERSONAL COMPETENCE

INTERPRETERS *Jul. 1966*
CIJE: 125 RIE: 67 GC: 640
UF Translators
BT Personnel
RT Communication (Thought Transfer)
Deaf Interpreting
Language Skills
Speech Communication
Speech Skills
Translation

Interpreting For The Deaf
USE DEAF INTERPRETING

INTERPRETIVE READING (1966 1980) *Mar. 1980*
CIJE: 143 RIE: 148 GC: 460
SN Invalid descriptor -- used to index items on reading comprehension, oral reading, and listening comprehension -- see such descriptors as "comprehension," "oral interpretation," and "critical reading"

INTERPRETIVE SKILLS *Jul. 1966*
CIJE: 135 RIE: 95 GC: 450
BT Skills
RT Data Interpretation
Deaf Interpreting
Language Skills
Translation

INTERPROFESSIONAL RELATIONSHIP *Jul. 1966*
CIJE: 431 RIE: 420 GC: 520
BT Interpersonal Relationship
RT Board Administrator Relationship
Mentors
Peer Evaluation
Professional Autonomy
Professional Services
Teacher Administrator Relationship
Teamwork

Interracial Relations
USE RACIAL RELATIONS

INTERRATER RELIABILITY *Mar. 1983*
CIJE: 108 RIE: 102 GC: 820
SN The degree of agreement among raters or observers in evaluating subjects' behavior/performance or other specific entity/event
UF Interjudge Agreement
Interobserver Reliability
Interscorer Reliability
BT Reliability
RT Error Of Measurement
Evaluation Methods
Evaluators
Examiners
Experimenter Characteristics
Generalizability Theory
Judges
Measurement Techniques
Observation
Rating Scales
Scores
Scoring
Testing Problems
Test Reliability
True Scores

Interscholastic Athletics
USE EXTRAMURAL ATHLETICS

INTERSCHOOL COMMUNICATION *Jul. 1966*
CIJE: 41 RIE: 80 GC: 330
BT Organizational Communication
RT Educational Cooperation
Institutional Cooperation
Schools

Interschool Visits
USE SCHOOL VISITATION

Interscorer Reliability
USE INTERRATER RELIABILITY

Intersensory Integration
USE SENSORY INTEGRATION

Intersession School Programs
USE VACATION PROGRAMS

INTERSTATE PROGRAMS *Jul. 1966*
CIJE: 24 RIE: 138 GC: 610
BT Programs
RT State Programs

Interstate Workers (1966 1980) (Migrants)
USE MIGRANT WORKERS

Interval Pacing (1967 1980)
USE PACING

INTERVALS *Jul. 1969*
CIJE: 47 RIE: 20 GC: 490
RT Distance
Proximity
Scheduling
Scientific Concepts
Space
Time

INTERVENTION *Aug. 1968*
CIJE: 2051 RIE: 2196 GC: 240
SN Action performed to direct or influence behavior (note: if possible, use "crisis intervention" or other, more precise terminology)
NT Crisis Intervention
RT Behavior Modification
Cognitive Restructuring
Consultation Programs
Educational Psychology
Educational Therapy
Helping Relationship
In School Suspension
Medical Services
Outreach Programs
Prognostic Tests
Psychoeducational Methods
Psychology
Rehabilitation
Resource Room Programs
Special Education

Interviewing
USE INTERVIEWS

INTERVIEWS *Jul. 1966*
CIJE: 2403 RIE: 2723 GC: 810
UF Interviewing
Question Answer Interviews (1966 1980)
NT Employment Interviews
Field Interviews
BT Evaluation Methods
RT Counseling Techniques
Discussion
Inquiry
Interpersonal Communication
Measures (Individuals)
Oral History
Personal Narratives
Qualitative Research
Questioning Techniques
Speech Communication
Surveys

INTONATION *Jul. 1966*
CIJE: 277 RIE: 255 GC: 450
SN Melodic pattern produced by the variation in pitch of the voice during speech
UF Intonation Contours
Suprasegmental Morphemes
BT Suprasegmentals
RT Morphology (Languages)
Paralinguistics
Phonemes
Phonology
Sentences
Stress (Phonology)
Structural Analysis (Linguistics)
Syllables
Tone Languages

Intonation Contours
USE INTONATION

Intramural Athletic Programs (1966 1980)
USE INTRAMURAL ATHLETICS

INTRAMURAL ATHLETICS *Mar. 1980*
CIJE: 92 RIE: 73 GC: 470
UF Intramural Athletic Programs (1966 1980)
Intramural Sports
BT Athletics
RT College Athletics
Extramural Athletics
School Recreational Programs

Intramural Sports
USE INTRAMURAL ATHLETICS

Intricacy Level
USE DIFFICULTY LEVEL

= Two or more Descriptors are used to represent this term.
The term's main entry shows the appropriate coordination.

INTRODUCTORY COURSES *Mar. 1980*
CIJE: 266 RIE: 188 GC: 350
SN Preliminary or basic courses that are frequently intended to provide an overview of a topic or to lay the foundation for advanced courses in the same subject
UF Foundation Courses (Introductory)
Survey Courses
BT Courses
RT Advanced Courses
Core Curriculum
Minicourses
Nonmajors
Required Courses

Introjection
USE IDENTIFICATION (PSYCHOLOGY)

Intrusion Detectors
USE ALARM SYSTEMS

INTUITION *Oct. 1983*
CIJE: 47 RIE: 33 GC: 110
SN Knowing or understanding without conscious use of reasoning
BT Cognitive Processes
RT Cognitive Ability
Cognitive Style
Comprehension
Creative Thinking
Expectation
Imagination
Learning Processes
Mathematical Applications
Perception
Problem Solving
Spontaneous Behavior

Inuit
USE ESKIMOS

Invalids
USE PATIENTS

INVENTIONS *Mar. 1978*
CIJE: 46 RIE: 30 GC: 490
SN Original products or processes (things not previously existing) developed by creative thought or experimentation -- (note: for "discoveries," see the descriptor "discovery processes")
RT Change
Creative Thinking
Creativity
Discovery Processes
Experiments
Innovation
Intellectual Property
Patents
Problem Solving
Productive Thinking
Research
Technological Advancement
Technology
Technology Transfer

Inventories (Measurement)
USE MEASURES (INDIVIDUALS)

INVESTIGATIONS *Jul. 1966*
CIJE: 99 RIE: 425 GC: 810
BT Research
RT Evaluation Methods
Experiments
Surveys

INVESTMENT *Jul. 1966*
CIJE: 231 RIE: 271 GC: 620
NT Human Capital
RT Banking
Credit (Finance)
Economics
Educational Economics
Endowment Funds
Estate Planning
Finance Occupations
Financial Support
Fund Raising
Interest (Finance)
Ownership
Productivity
Trusts (Financial)

Iq
USE INTELLIGENCE QUOTIENT

Iris Reflex
USE PUPILLARY DILATION

Iron Deficiency Anemia
USE ANEMIA

Iron Foundries
USE FOUNDRIES

IRONY *Jul. 1969*
CIJE: 51 RIE: 15 GC: 430
UF Sarcasm
BT Figurative Language
RT Literary Styles

Isiswati
USE SISWATI

ISLAMIC CULTURE *Aug. 1968*
CIJE: 58 RIE: 66 GC: 560
BT Culture
RT Asian Studies
Middle Eastern Studies
Religion

Isolation (Perceptual)
USE SENSORY DEPRIVATION

Ita
USE INITIAL TEACHING ALPHABET

ITALIAN *Jul. 1966*
CIJE: 176 RIE: 203 GC: 440
BT Romance Languages
RT Italian Literature

ITALIAN AMERICANS *Jul. 1966*
CIJE: 37 RIE: 119 GC: 560
BT Ethnic Groups
North Americans
RT Minority Groups

ITALIAN LITERATURE *Jun. 1969*
CIJE: 104 RIE: 15 GC: 430
BT Literature
RT Italian

ITEM ANALYSIS *Jul. 1966*
CIJE: 729 RIE: 982 GC: 820
SN Determining the difficulty, discriminability, internal consistency, reliability, and validity of items in a test, questionnaire, or rating scale
BT Statistical Analysis
RT Content Analysis
Content Validity
Difficulty Level
Discriminant Analysis
Error Patterns
Factor Analysis
Factor Structure
Latent Trait Theory
Multitrait Multimethod Techniques
Q Methodology
Standardized Tests
Test Construction
Testing
Test Items
Test Reliability
Tests
Test Theory
Test Validity
Weighted Scores

ITEM BANKS *Oct. 1972*
CIJE: 96 RIE: 294 GC: 830
SN Collection of test items classified according to objectives, subtests, difficulty, grade level, content, etc., which may be used to construct tests to meet the user's specifications
UF Item Pools
RT Adaptive Testing
Computer Assisted Testing
Criterion Referenced Tests
Item Sampling
Problem Sets
Test Construction
Testing
Test Items
Test Manuals
Tests

Item Characteristic Curve Theory
USE LATENT TRAIT THEORY

Item Difficulty
USE DIFFICULTY LEVEL; TEST ITEMS

Item Pools
USE ITEM BANKS

Item Response Theory
USE LATENT TRAIT THEORY

ITEM SAMPLING *Oct. 1970*
CIJE: 91 RIE: 118 GC: 820
SN Estimation of total test score statistics (mean and variance) by administering random subsets of test items to randomly selected students
UF Matrix Sampling
Multiple Matrix Sampling
BT Sampling
RT Item Banks
Measurement Techniques
National Norms
Statistical Analysis
Test Construction
Test Items
Test Norms

Item Types
USE TEST FORMAT

Itfs
USE EDUCATIONAL TELEVISION

Itinerant Clinics (1966 1980)
USE MOBILE CLINICS

ITINERANT TEACHERS *Jul. 1966*
CIJE: 44 RIE: 81 GC: 360
SN Teachers who travel from school to school, or to homes and hospitals, to teach students with special needs (note: prior to mar80, the thesaurus carried the instruction "visiting teachers, use school social workers")
UF Circuit Teachers
Homebound Teachers (1966 1980)
Traveling Teachers
Visiting Teachers
BT Teachers
RT Homebound
Home Instruction
Hospitalized Children
Hospital Schools
Individual Instruction
Mainstreaming
Mobile Clinics
Mobile Educational Services
Resource Room Programs
Resource Teachers
Special Education
Special Education Teachers
Specialists

Itv
USE EDUCATIONAL TELEVISION

Jail Inmates
USE PRISONERS

Jan Technique
USE JUDGMENT ANALYSIS TECHNIQUE

JAPANESE *Jul. 1966*
CIJE: 211 RIE: 300 GC: 440
NT Okinawan
BT Languages

JAPANESE AMERICAN CULTURE *Jul. 1966*
CIJE: 24 RIE: 44 GC: 560
BT North American Culture
RT Japanese Americans

JAPANESE AMERICANS *Sep. 1968*
CIJE: 93 RIE: 202 GC: 560
BT Asian Americans
Ethnic Groups
RT Japanese American Culture

JAVANESE *Jul. 1966*
CIJE: 1 RIE: 5 GC: 440
BT Indonesian Languages

JAZZ *Apr. 1969*
CIJE: 84 RIE: 15 GC: 420
UF Ragtime Music
Swing Music
BT Music
RT Bands (Music)
Concerts
Musical Composition
Music Techniques
North American Culture

JEALOUSY *Mar. 1982*
CIJE: 4 RIE: 8 GC: 230
SN Intolerance or wariness of rivalry or faithlessness
UF Envy
BT Psychological Patterns
RT Anger
Anxiety
Emotional Problems
Interpersonal Relationship
Negative Attitudes
Personality Traits
Resentment

Jewish Stereotypes (1966 1980)
USE ETHNIC STEREOTYPES; JEWS

JEWS *Jul. 1966*
CIJE: 252 RIE: 261 GC: 560
UF American Jews
Jewish Stereotypes (1966 1980) #
BT Religious Cultural Groups
RT Anti Semitism
Ethnic Groups
Ghettos
Judaism
Middle Eastern Studies
Minority Groups

Job Adjustment
USE VOCATIONAL ADJUSTMENT

JOB ANALYSIS *Jul. 1966*
CIJE: 455 RIE: 1260 GC: 630
SN Process of determining the aspects of a particular job or the tasks performed within an occupational area (note: for the product of such an analysis, use "occupational information" -- do not confuse with "task analysis," this term's former nt -- before mar80, the use of this term was not restricted by a scope note)
UF Job Content Analysis
Occupational Analysis
BT Evaluation Methods
RT Critical Incidents Method
Employment Qualifications
Job Development
Job Enrichment
Job Performance
Job Simplification
Job Skills
Occupational Clusters
Occupational Information
Skill Analysis
Task Analysis

JOB APPLICANTS *Jul. 1966*
CIJE: 356 RIE: 689 GC: 630
UF Job Seekers
BT Groups
RT Dislocated Workers
Displaced Homemakers
Employment
Employment Interviews
Employment Opportunities
Employment Qualifications
Employment Services
Job Application
Job Placement
Job Search Methods
Portfolios (Background Materials)
Resumes (Personal)

JOB APPLICATION *Jul. 1966*
CIJE: 193 RIE: 401 GC: 630
RT Employment
Employment Interviews
Employment Opportunities
Employment Qualifications
Employment Services
Job Applicants
Job Placement
Job Search Methods

= Two or more Descriptors are used to represent this term.
The term's main entry shows the appropriate coordination.

Portfolios (Background Materials)
Reentry Workers
Resumes (Personal)

Job Behaviors
USE JOB SKILLS

Job Change
USE CAREER CHANGE

Job Clusters
USE OCCUPATIONAL CLUSTERS

Job Conditions
USE WORK ENVIRONMENT

Job Content
USE OCCUPATIONAL INFORMATION

Job Content Analysis
USE JOB ANALYSIS

Job Creation
USE JOB DEVELOPMENT

Job Descriptions
USE OCCUPATIONAL INFORMATION

Job Design
USE JOB DEVELOPMENT

JOB DEVELOPMENT *Jan. 1969*
CIJE: 273 RIE: 544 GC: 630
SN (Note: prior to mar80, the instruction "job redesign, use work simplification" was carried in the thesaurus)
UF Job Creation
Job Design
Job Redesign
Job Restructuring
NT Job Enrichment
Job Simplification
BT Development
RT Emerging Occupations
Employment
Employment Opportunities
Employment Problems
Equal Opportunities (Jobs)
Job Analysis
Labor Force Development
Occupational Information
Organizational Development
Promotion (Occupational)
Scope Of Bargaining

Job Discrimination
USE EQUAL OPPORTUNITIES (JOBS)

Job Elimination
USE JOB LAYOFF

JOB ENRICHMENT *Feb. 1976*
CIJE: 80 RIE: 60 GC: 630
SN Redesign of a job to provide more meaningful job content, thus increasing employee/staff responsibility, satisfaction, and motivation
UF Work Enrichment
BT Enrichment
Job Development
RT Employee Attitudes
Employer Employee Relationship
Job Analysis
Job Satisfaction
Organizational Development
Quality Of Working Life
Vocational Adjustment
Work Attitudes
Work Environment

Job Experience
USE EMPLOYMENT EXPERIENCE

Job Families
USE OCCUPATIONAL CLUSTERS

Job Holding Patterns
USE EMPLOYMENT PATTERNS

Job Interviews
USE EMPLOYMENT INTERVIEWS

Job Ladders
USE CAREER LADDERS

JOB LAYOFF *Jul. 1966*
CIJE: 150 RIE: 145 GC: 630
SN Temporary or indefinite ending of jobs by employers
UF Job Elimination
BT Reduction In Force
RT Dislocated Workers
Dismissal (Personnel)
Employment
Employment Practices
Labor Market
Labor Turnover
Outplacement Services (Employment)
Personnel Policy
Seniority
Structural Unemployment
Tenure
Unemployment

Job Loss Services
USE OUTPLACEMENT SERVICES (EMPLOYMENT)

Job Market (1966 1980)
USE LABOR MARKET

Job Mobility
USE OCCUPATIONAL MOBILITY

Job Opportunities
USE EMPLOYMENT OPPORTUNITIES

JOB PERFORMANCE *Mar. 1980*
CIJE: 413 RIE: 430 GC: 630
SN Accomplishment of work-related tasks or skills by an employee or trainee -- may refer to specific skills or to overall performance -- also use for factors associated with success or failure in job situations (note: prior to mar80, the instruction "job performance, use task performance" was carried in the thesaurus)
UF Employee Performance
BT Performance
RT Assessment Centers (Personnel)
Competence
Employment
Employment Experience
Job Analysis
Job Skills
Occupational Tests
Personnel Evaluation
Promotion (Occupational)
Vocational Evaluation
Work Sample Tests

JOB PLACEMENT *Jul. 1966*
CIJE: 862 RIE: 1539 GC: 630
UF Student Job Placement #
Vocational Placement
NT Teacher Placement
BT Placement
RT Assessment Centers (Personnel)
Career Counseling
Career Guidance
Employment
Employment Services
Job Applicants
Job Application
Job Search Methods
Outplacement Services (Employment)
Personnel Evaluation
Prior Learning
Reentry Workers
Student Employment
Transfer Programs
Vocational Education

Job Redesign
USE JOB DEVELOPMENT

Job Restructuring
USE JOB DEVELOPMENT

Job Safety
USE OCCUPATIONAL SAFETY AND HEALTH

Job Sample Tests
USE WORK SAMPLE TESTS

Job Samples
USE WORK SAMPLE TESTS

JOB SATISFACTION *Jul. 1966*
CIJE: 1590 RIE: 1400 GC: 630
UF Employment Satisfaction
Occupational Satisfaction
Vocational Satisfaction
Work Satisfaction
BT Work Attitudes
RT Burnout
Career Change
Employer Employee Relationship
Flexible Working Hours
Industrial Psychology
Job Enrichment
Life Satisfaction
Need Gratification
Organizational Climate
Organizational Development
Quality Of Working Life
Self Actualization
Vocational Adjustment
Work Environment

JOB SEARCH METHODS *Dec. 1976*
CIJE: 302 RIE: 546 GC: 630
SN Procedures preceding job application whereby employment opportunities are determined
BT Methods
RT Career Change
Career Planning
Dislocated Workers
Employment
Employment Interviews
Employment Opportunities
Employment Qualifications
Employment Services
Job Applicants
Job Application
Job Placement
Labor Market
Occupational Surveys
Reentry Workers
Resumes (Personal)
Unemployment

Job Seekers
USE JOB APPLICANTS

JOB SHARING *Nov. 1982*
CIJE: 28 RIE: 33 GC: 630
SN Division of available work or work hours among eligible employees, providing part-time employment options -- sometimes used as an alternative to layoffs
UF Work Sharing
BT Part Time Employment
RT Employment Practices
Flexible Working Hours
Labor Market
Labor Utilization
Partnership Teachers
Personnel Policy
Underemployment

JOB SIMPLIFICATION *Mar. 1980*
CIJE: 40 RIE: 53 GC: 630
SN Redesign of a job to improve production and efficiency
UF Work Simplification (1968 1980)
BT Job Development
RT Automation
Cost Effectiveness
Efficiency
Job Analysis
Labor Utilization
Productivity

JOB SKILLS *Jul. 1966*
CIJE: 1282 RIE: 4458 GC: 630
UF Employable Skills #
Job Behaviors
Marketable Skills #
Vocational Skills
BT Skills
RT Business Skills
Daily Living Skills
Dislocated Workers
Employment Experience
Employment Level
Employment Opportunities
Employment Potential
Employment Qualifications
Equivalency Tests
Home Economics Skills
Job Analysis
Job Performance
Job Training
Lifting
Mechanical Skills
Merit Rating
Minimum Competencies
Occupational Tests
Personnel Evaluation
Professional Training
Promotion (Occupational)
Reentry Workers
Salesmanship
Skilled Occupations
Skilled Workers
Skill Obsolescence
Structural Unemployment
Teaching Skills
Vocational Education
Vocational English (Second Language)
Vocational Evaluation
Work Sample Tests

Job Specifications
USE OCCUPATIONAL INFORMATION

Job Tenure (1967 1978)
USE TENURE

JOB TRAINING *Jul. 1966*
CIJE: 1155 RIE: 3003 GC: 630
SN (Note: prior to mar80, the instruction "occupational training, use vocational education" was carried in the thesaurus)
UF Attendant Training (1968 1980) #
Employment Preparation
Occupational Training
NT Custodian Training
Off The Job Training
On The Job Training
BT Training
RT Adult Vocational Education
Employment
Flight Training
Industrial Training
Job Skills
Labor Force Development
Occupations
Office Occupations
Retraining
Scope Of Bargaining
Sheltered Workshops
Supervisory Training
Trainees
Training Allowances
Vocational Education
Vocational Training Centers
Work Experience Programs

Job Vacancies
USE EMPLOYMENT OPPORTUNITIES

Job Vacancy Surveys
USE OCCUPATIONAL SURVEYS

Jobs (1966 1980)
USE EMPLOYMENT

JOGGING *Feb. 1978*
CIJE: 32 RIE: 11 GC: 470
SN The exercise of running at a slow, regular pace, often alternately with walking
BT Running
RT Athletics

Joint Occupancy
USE SHARED FACILITIES

JOURNALISM *Jul. 1966*
CIJE: 1922 RIE: 1300 GC: 720
SN Preparation and dissemination of information on current affairs
NT New Journalism
News Reporting
News Writing
Photojournalism
BT Technology
RT Captions
Editing
Editorials
Expository Writing
Freedom Of Information
Freedom Of Speech
Headlines
Information Sources
Journalism Education
Layout (Publications)
Literature
Mass Media
News Media
Newspapers

Periodicals
Photography
Press Opinion
Publications
Radio
Serials
Television
Writing For Publication

JOURNALISM EDUCATION *Mar. 1977*
CIJE: 998 RIE: 228 GC: 400
SN Preparing students to pursue careers or work in journalism as writers, reporters, broadcasters, technicians, and teachers
BT Education
RT Expository Writing
Journalism
Language Arts
Mass Media
News Media
Newspapers
Periodicals
Publications
Radio
School Publications
Serials
Student Publications
Television
Television Curriculum
Writing Instruction

Journals
USE PERIODICALS

Journey Workers
USE SKILLED WORKERS

JUDAISM *May. 1969*
CIJE: 59 RIE: 54 GC: 430
BT Religion
RT Biblical Literature
Christianity
Jews
Philosophy
Religious Cultural Groups
Western Civilization

JUDGES *Mar. 1980*
CIJE: 48 RIE: 52 GC: 640
SN Persons selected or appointed to decide in competitions or contests (note: if possible, use the more specific term "court judges")
UF Debate Judges
NT Court Judges
BT Groups
RT Interrater Reliability
Justice
Professional Personnel

JUDGMENT ANALYSIS TECHNIQUE *Oct. 1982*
CIJE: 7 RIE: 1 GC: 820
SN A statistical process combining a multiple regression approach with a hierarchical grouping procedure to identify and describe evaluation policies and strategies within groups of decision makers
UF Jan Technique
BT Statistical Analysis
RT Cluster Grouping
Decision Making
Evaluation
Evaluative Thinking
Multiple Regression Analysis
Operations Research
Policy Formation
Sociometric Techniques

Judgmental Processes
USE EVALUATIVE THINKING

Judicial Action
USE COURT LITIGATION

Judicial Role
USE COURT ROLE

Junior College Libraries (1966 1980)
USE COLLEGE LIBRARIES; TWO YEAR COLLEGES

Junior College Students (1969 1980)
USE TWO YEAR COLLEGE STUDENTS

Junior Colleges (1966 1980)
USE TWO YEAR COLLEGES

Junior High School Role (1966 1980)
USE SCHOOL ROLE

JUNIOR HIGH SCHOOL STUDENTS *Jul. 1966*
CIJE: 1038 RIE: 1217 GC: 360
SN (Note: coordinate with the appropriate mandatory educational level descriptor)
BT Secondary School Students
RT High School Students
Junior High Schools

Junior High School Teachers
USE SECONDARY SCHOOL TEACHERS

JUNIOR HIGH SCHOOLS *Jul. 1966*
CIJE: 2068 RIE: 3393 GC: 340
SN Providing formal education in grades 7, 8, and 9 -- less commonly 7 and 8, or 8 and 9 (note: also appears in the list of mandatory educational level descriptors)
BT Secondary Schools
RT Grade 7
Grade 8
Grade 9
High Schools
Junior High School Students
Middle Schools
Secondary Education

JUSTICE *Dec. 1974*
CIJE: 334 RIE: 405 GC: 610
SN Fair and equitable treatment -- includes the maintenance or administration of what is just
UF Equity (Impartiality)
RT Civil Liberties
Civil Rights
Constitutional Law
Court Judges
Courts
Due Process
Equal Protection
Judges
Laws
Sex Fairness
Social Attitudes
Social Problems
Social Values
Torts
Values

JUVENILE COURTS *Aug. 1968*
CIJE: 130 RIE: 260 GC: 610
UF Childrens Courts
BT Courts
RT Children
Court Litigation
Crime
Delinquency
Delinquent Rehabilitation
Youth Problems

Juvenile Delinquency
USE DELINQUENCY

JUVENILE GANGS *Jul. 1966*
CIJE: 38 RIE: 31 GC: 530
BT Groups
RT Delinquency
Peer Groups
Youth Clubs

Juvenile Runaways
USE RUNAWAYS

KABYLE *Jul. 1966*
CIJE: RIE: 3 GC: 440
BT Berber Languages

KANNADA *Jul. 1966*
CIJE: 1 RIE: 17 GC: 440
BT Dravidian Languages

KASHMIRI *Jul. 1966*
CIJE: RIE: 6 GC: 440
BT Indo European Languages

Kechua
USE QUECHUA

KERNEL SENTENCES *Jul. 1966*
CIJE: 35 RIE: 56 GC: 450
BT Sentences
Transformational Generative Grammar
RT Grammar
Phonology
Phrase Structure
Sentence Combining
Sentence Structure
Syntax

Key Word In Context
USE PERMUTED INDEXES

KEYBOARDING (DATA ENTRY) *Aug. 1986*
CIJE: RIE: GC: 710
SN Act of using an alphanumeric keyboard to prepare computer-readable data or to communicate directly with a computer
UF Keypunching
BT Business Skills
Input Output
RT Calculators
Clerical Occupations
Computer Oriented Programs
Data Processing Occupations
Information Systems
Input Output Devices
Office Machines
Office Occupations
Office Occupations Education
Typewriting
Word Processing

Keypunching
USE KEYBOARDING (DATA ENTRY)

Khalkha
USE MONGOLIAN

Khmer (Language)
USE CAMBODIAN

Khmer (People)
USE CAMBODIANS

Kikongo Ya Leta
USE KITUBA

KINDERGARTEN *Jul. 1966*
CIJE: 541 RIE: 1425 GC: 340
BT Instructional Program Divisions
RT Early Childhood Education
Elementary Education
Kindergarten Children
Preschool Education
Primary Education

KINDERGARTEN CHILDREN *Jul. 1966*
CIJE: 931 RIE: 1032 GC: 120
BT Young Children
RT Kindergarten
Preschool Children

Kindergarten Teachers
USE PRESCHOOL TEACHERS

Kindness
USE ALTRUISM

KINESCOPE RECORDINGS *Jul. 1966*
CIJE: 2 RIE: 28 GC: 720
UF Kinescopes
BT Films
RT Film Libraries
Television
Videotape Recordings

Kinescopes
USE KINESCOPE RECORDINGS

Kinesics
USE BODY LANGUAGE

Kinesthesia
USE KINESTHETIC PERCEPTION

Kinesthesis
USE KINESTHETIC PERCEPTION

Kinesthetic Memory
USE KINESTHETIC PERCEPTION

KINESTHETIC METHODS *Jul. 1966*
CIJE: 55 RIE: 55 GC: 110
BT Teaching Methods
RT Kinesthetic Perception
Paralinguistics
Reading Instruction
Speech Instruction

KINESTHETIC PERCEPTION *Aug. 1968*
CIJE: 147 RIE: 105 GC: 110
SN Sense perception of movement, weight, resistance, and position
UF Kinesthesia
Kinesthesis
Kinesthetic Memory
Muscle Sense
BT Perception
RT Biomechanics
Body Image
Figural Aftereffects
Kinesthetic Methods
Learning Modalities
Manipulative Materials
Perception Tests
Perceptual Motor Learning
Personal Space
Tactual Perception

KINETIC MOLECULAR THEORY *Jul. 1966*
CIJE: 97 RIE: 23 GC: 490
BT Theories
RT Acceleration (Physics)
Diffusion (Physics)
Force
Gravity (Physics)
Heat
Kinetics
Mechanics (Physics)
Molecular Structure
Motion
Physics

KINETICS *Jul. 1966*
CIJE: 411 RIE: 70 GC: 490
SN Branch of science that deals with the effects of forces upon the motions of material bodies or with changes in physical or chemical systems
UF Power Transfer Systems
NT Diffusion (Physics)
BT Mechanics (Physics)
RT Acceleration (Physics)
Biomechanics
Chemical Engineering
Energy
Engines
Fluid Mechanics
Force
Fuels
Gravity (Physics)
Heat
Hydraulics
Kinetic Molecular Theory
Motion
Relativity
Wind Energy

KINSHIP *Oct. 1983*
CIJE: 30 RIE: 13 GC: 520
SN Socially recognized relationship based on real or supposed common descent, or such rituals as marriage and adoption
UF Kinship Role
BT Interpersonal Relationship
RT Adoption
Black Family
Daughters
Ethnography
Ethnology
Extended Family
Family (Sociological Unit)
Family History
Family Relationship
Family Structure
Genealogy
Kinship Terminology
Marriage
Nuclear Family
Parents
Remarriage
Siblings
Sociocultural Patterns
Sons
Spouses
Stepfamily

Kinship Role
USE KINSHIP

KINSHIP TERMINOLOGY *Oct. 1983*
CIJE: RIE: 2 GC: 450
SN Vocabulary representing kinship ties, e.g., "husband‰/‰wife‰/‰spouse," "father‰/‰mother‰/‰parent," "father-in-law‰/‰mother-in-law," "uncle‰/‰aunt," "cousin"
BT Vocabulary
RT Kinship
Language Patterns
Sociolinguistics

KIRGHIZ *Aug. 1968*
CIJE: RIE: 3 GC: 440
UF Kirgiz
BT Turkic Languages

Kirgiz
USE KIRGHIZ

KIRUNDI *Jul. 1966*
CIJE: RIE: 2 GC: 440
BT Bantu Languages

KITUBA *Jul. 1966*
CIJE: RIE: 4 GC: 440
UF Kikongo Ya Leta
Munukutaba
BT Bantu Languages

Knowledge Based Systems
USE EXPERT SYSTEMS

KNOWLEDGE LEVEL *Jul. 1966*
CIJE: 972 RIE: 915 GC: 120
SN Extent of knowledge attained
BT Achievement
RT Academic Achievement
Achievement Gains
Comprehension
Confidence Testing
Educational Background
Epistemology
Learning
Learning Plateaus
Performance
Scholarship

Knowledge Of Results
USE FEEDBACK

Knowledge Structures
USE COGNITIVE STRUCTURES

KOREAN *Jul. 1966*
CIJE: 21 RIE: 91 GC: 440
UF Hangul
Hanja
Hankul
BT Languages

KOREAN AMERICANS *Sep. 1968*
CIJE: 23 RIE: 121 GC: 560
BT Asian Americans
Ethnic Groups
RT Korean Culture

KOREAN CULTURE *Jul. 1966*
CIJE: 13 RIE: 48 GC: 560
BT Culture
RT Asian Studies
Korean Americans
Non Western Civilization

Krio
USE SIERRA LEONE CREOLE

KURDISH *Jul. 1966*
CIJE: RIE: 12 GC: 440
BT Indo European Languages

Kwic Indexes
USE PERMUTED INDEXES

Kwoc Indexes
USE PERMUTED INDEXES

LABELING (OF PERSONS) *Sep. 1975*
CIJE: 443 RIE: 224 GC: 540
SN Designating a special or complex condition of an individual or group by a simplistic word or phrase which may connote status, and perhaps, stigma
BT Classification
RT Grouping (Instructional Purposes)
Groups
Identification
Normalization (Handicapped)
Social Bias
Special Education
Stereotypes

LABOR *Jul. 1966*
CIJE: 63 RIE: 68 GC: 630
SN Human activity that provides the goods and services in an economy -- also, the services performed by workers for wages as distinguished from those rendered by entrepreneurs for profits (note: use for general works and theory -- use a more specific term if possible)
NT Child Labor
Farm Labor
RT Employees
Employment
Human Resources
Labor Conditions
Labor Demands
Labor Economics
Laborers
Labor Force
Labor Legislation
Labor Market
Labor Needs
Labor Problems
Labor Relations
Labor Standards
Labor Supply
Labor Utilization

Labor (Childbirth)
USE BIRTH

Labor Camps (1966 1980) (Migrants)
USE MIGRANT HOUSING

LABOR CONDITIONS *Jul. 1966*
CIJE: 73 RIE: 118 GC: 630
RT Labor
Labor Demands
Labor Economics
Laborers
Labor Legislation
Labor Needs
Labor Problems
Labor Relations
Labor Standards
Quality Of Working Life
Work Environment

LABOR DEMANDS *Jul. 1966*
CIJE: 101 RIE: 105 GC: 630
SN Demands of labor (note: do not confuse with "labor needs")
UF Agricultural Labor Disputes (1966 1980)
RT Arbitration
Collective Bargaining
Contracts
Grievance Procedures
Labor
Labor Conditions
Labor Economics
Labor Legislation
Labor Problems
Labor Standards
Negotiation Impasses
Sanctions
Strikes
Unions

LABOR ECONOMICS *Jul. 1966*
CIJE: 219 RIE: 294 GC: 620
BT Economics
RT Arbitration
Business Cycles
Developed Nations
Developing Nations
Dislocated Workers
Economic Research
Employment
Employment Patterns
Labor
Labor Conditions
Labor Demands
Labor Force
Labor Force Development
Labor Market
Labor Needs
Labor Relations
Labor Supply
Labor Utilization
Marxism
Negotiation Impasses
Structural Unemployment
Unemployment

LABOR EDUCATION *Jul. 1966*
CIJE: 281 RIE: 193 GC: 630
SN Education and training of workers often sponsored by labor unions and sometimes in cooperation with educational institutions
UF Workers Education
BT Adult Education
RT Industrial Education
Industrial Training
Inplant Programs
Labor Force
Nonschool Educational Programs
Off The Job Training
Unions

LABOR FORCE *Jul. 1966*
CIJE: 523 RIE: 953 GC: 630
SN (Note: prior to mar80, the instruction "work force, use laborers" was carried in the thesaurus)
UF Manpower
Work Force
BT Human Resources
RT Developed Nations
Dislocated Workers
Employed Parents
Employed Women
Employment
Human Capital
Labor
Labor Economics
Labor Education
Laborers
Labor Force Nonparticipants
Labor Market
Labor Needs
Labor Supply
Labor Turnover
Labor Utilization
Occupational Surveys
Organization Size (Groups)
Reentry Workers
Strikes
Unions
Working Class

LABOR FORCE DEVELOPMENT *Mar. 1980*
CIJE: 884 RIE: 1971 GC: 630
UF Human Resources Development (Labor)
Manpower Development (1966 1980)
NT Management Development
Professional Development
Staff Development
BT Development
RT Career Ladders
Corporate Education
Developmental Programs
Economic Development
Emerging Occupations
Industrial Training
Job Development
Job Training
Labor Economics
Labor Needs
Labor Utilization
Retraining
Technical Assistance
Training Allowances
Vocational Education
Work Experience Programs

LABOR FORCE NONPARTICIPANTS *Jul. 1966*
CIJE: 94 RIE: 127 GC: 630
SN Persons neither employed nor looking for employment
BT Groups
RT Employment
Labor Force
Labor Supply
Labor Utilization
Retirement
Unemployment
Work Attitudes

Labor Force Surveys
USE OCCUPATIONAL SURVEYS

Labor Laws (1966 1974)
USE LABOR LEGISLATION

LABOR LEGISLATION *Jul. 1966*
CIJE: 276 RIE: 395 GC: 610
UF Child Labor Laws (1966 1974) #
Child Labor Legislation (1966 1980) #
Farm Labor Legislation (1966 1980) #
Labor Laws (1966 1974)
BT Legislation
RT Arbitration
Collective Bargaining
Employer Employee Relationship
Employment Practices
Labor
Labor Conditions
Labor Demands
Laborers
Labor Standards
Laws
Negotiation Impasses
Unions

LABOR MARKET *Jul. 1966*
CIJE: 1072 RIE: 1510 GC: 630
UF Employment Market
Job Market (1966 1980)
NT Teacher Supply And Demand
RT Demand Occupations
Dislocated Workers
Displaced Homemakers
Employment
Employment Experience
Employment Opportunities
Employment Patterns
Employment Projections
Employment Statistics
Job Layoff
Job Search Methods
Job Sharing
Labor
Labor Economics
Laborers
Labor Force
Labor Needs
Labor Supply
Labor Turnover
Occupational Surveys
Personnel Selection
Reduction In Force
Reentry Workers
Structural Unemployment
Teacher Employment
Underemployment
Unemployment

Labor Mobility
USE OCCUPATIONAL MOBILITY

LABOR NEEDS *Mar. 1980*
CIJE: 777 RIE: 1872 GC: 630
SN Demands for labor in the economy as a whole or in particular sectors or industries (note: do not confuse with "labor demands")
UF Manpower Needs (1968 1980)
NT Personnel Needs
BT Needs
RT Demand Occupations
Employment Opportunities
Employment Projections
Labor
Labor Conditions
Labor Economics
Labor Force
Labor Force Development
Labor Market
Labor Utilization
Promotion (Occupational)

LABOR PROBLEMS *Jul. 1966*
CIJE: 167 RIE: 201 GC: 630
UF Farm Labor Problems (1966 1980) #
BT Problems
RT Arbitration
Collective Bargaining
Employment Problems
Labor
Labor Conditions
Labor Demands
Laborers
Labor Turnover
Negotiation Impasses
Relocation
Seniority
Strikes
Teacher Strikes
Tenure

= Two or more Descriptors are used to represent this term.
The term's main entry shows the appropriate coordination.

LABOR RELATIONS *Mar. 1980*
CIJE: 467 RIE: 387 GC: 630
SN All of the relationships that grow out of the fact of employment
UF Employee Relations
Industrial Relations (1969 1980)
BT Relationship
RT Business Communication
Collective Bargaining
Employer Employee Relationship
Fringe Benefits
Industrial Psychology
Labor
Labor Conditions
Labor Economics
Personnel
Public Relations
Quality Of Working Life
Unions

LABOR STANDARDS *Jul. 1966*
CIJE: 31 RIE: 78 GC: 630
SN Standards for acceptable employment conditions, e.g., working hours, wage rates, safety and health conditions (note: prior to mar80, the use of this term was not restricted by a scope note)
UF Occupational Safety And Health Standards #
BT Standards
RT Environmental Standards
Labor
Labor Conditions
Labor Demands
Laborers
Labor Legislation

LABOR SUPPLY *Sep. 1968*
CIJE: 226 RIE: 495 GC: 630
UF Farm Labor Supply (1966 1980) #
Supply Of Labor
BT Human Resources
RT Human Capital
Labor
Labor Economics
Labor Force
Labor Force Nonparticipants
Labor Market
Labor Turnover
Labor Utilization
Occupational Surveys
Working Class

LABOR TURNOVER *Jul. 1966*
CIJE: 172 RIE: 164 GC: 630
UF Retention (Of Employees)
RT Career Change
Dislocated Workers
Employment Patterns
Job Layoff
Labor Force
Labor Market
Labor Problems
Labor Supply
Occupational Mobility
Reduction In Force
Relocation
Stopouts
Teacher Persistence
Tenure

Labor Unions (1966 1980)
USE UNIONS

LABOR UTILIZATION *Mar. 1980*
CIJE: 405 RIE: 1257 GC: 630
UF Manpower Utilization (1966 1980)
NT Staff Utilization
RT Economic Factors
Employment
Job Sharing
Job Simplification
Labor
Labor Economics
Labor Force
Labor Force Development
Labor Force Nonparticipants
Labor Needs
Labor Supply
Reduction In Force
Relocation
Underemployment
Unemployment
Use Studies
Worker Days

LABORATORIES *Jul. 1966*
CIJE: 334 RIE: 334 GC: 920
SN Facilities specifically designed and equipped for experimentation, demonstration, observation, practice, or research in a field of study (note: use a more specific term if possible)
UF Computer Based Laboratories (1967 1980) #
NT Learning Laboratories
Mobile Laboratories
Regional Laboratories
Science Laboratories
Writing Laboratories
BT Facilities
RT Classrooms
Demonstration Centers
Demonstrations (Educational)
Laboratory Animals
Laboratory Equipment
Laboratory Experiments
Laboratory Manuals
Laboratory Procedures
Laboratory Safety
Laboratory Technology

LABORATORY ANIMALS *Aug. 1980*
CIJE: 46 RIE: 14 GC: 490
BT Animals
RT Animal Facilities
Animal Husbandry
Laboratories
Laboratory Experiments
Laboratory Procedures
Medical Research
Rats
Zoology

LABORATORY EQUIPMENT *Jul. 1966*
CIJE: 1122 RIE: 299 GC: 910
UF Language Laboratory Equipment (1966 1980) #
NT Microscopes
BT Equipment
RT Animal Facilities
Biomedical Equipment
Laboratories
Laboratory Procedures
Measurement Equipment
Science Equipment

LABORATORY EXPERIMENTS *Jul. 1966*
CIJE: 1881 RIE: 235 GC: 490
BT Experiments
RT Experimental Psychology
Laboratories
Laboratory Animals
Laboratory Procedures
Science Experiments

LABORATORY MANUALS *Jul. 1966*
CIJE: 26 RIE: 201 GC: 730
BT Guides
Instructional Materials
RT Laboratories
Laboratory Procedures
Laboratory Safety
Textbooks
Workbooks

LABORATORY PROCEDURES *Jul. 1966*
CIJE: 1799 RIE: 406 GC: 490
SN Procedures used in the laboratory
NT Chromatography
Culturing Techniques
BT Methods
RT Demonstrations (Educational)
Experiential Learning
Instruction
Laboratories
Laboratory Animals
Laboratory Equipment
Laboratory Experiments
Laboratory Manuals
Laboratory Safety
Laboratory Technology
Science Activities
Science Experiments
Science Projects
Simulation
Teaching Methods

LABORATORY SAFETY *Jul. 1966*
CIJE: 342 RIE: 121 GC: 210
BT Safety
RT Hazardous Materials
Laboratories
Laboratory Manuals
Laboratory Procedures
Laboratory Technology
Radiation
Radiation Effects
Safety Education
School Safety

LABORATORY SCHOOLS *Jul. 1966*
CIJE: 80 RIE: 109 GC: 340
SN Schools of elementary and secondary grades attached to universities or colleges for purposes of research and teacher training
UF Campus Schools
University Schools
BT Schools
RT Affiliated Schools
College School Cooperation
Educational Research
Elementary Schools
Experiential Learning
Experimental Schools
Laboratory Training
Schools Of Education
Secondary Schools
Teacher Education
Teaching Experience

LABORATORY TECHNIQUES (1967 1980) *Jun. 1980*
CIJE: 799 RIE: 148 GC: 490
SN Invalid descriptor -- used inconsistently in indexing -- use "laboratory training" for human relations laboratory techniques -- otherwise, use "laboratory procedures"

LABORATORY TECHNOLOGY *Jul. 1966*
CIJE: 43 RIE: 54 GC: 490
BT Technology
RT Dental Technicians
Electroencephalography
Industrial Arts
Laboratories
Laboratory Procedures
Laboratory Safety
Medical Laboratory Assistants

LABORATORY TRAINING *Jul. 1966*
CIJE: 233 RIE: 236 GC: 240
SN Method of training designed to facilitate self insight, process awareness, interpersonal competence, and dynamics of change
BT Training
RT Counseling Techniques
Gestalt Therapy
Humanistic Education
Human Relations
Interpersonal Competence
Laboratory Schools
Microteaching
Practicums
Practicum Supervision
Protocol Materials
Sensitivity Training
Simulation
Teacher Centers
Teacher Education
Teaching Experience
Trainers
Transactional Analysis

LABORERS *Jul. 1966*
CIJE: 70 RIE: 87 GC: 630
UF Experienced Laborers (1966 1980)
NT Agricultural Laborers
Auxiliary Laborers
BT Unskilled Workers
RT Employees
Industrial Personnel
Labor
Labor Conditions
Labor Force
Labor Legislation
Labor Market
Labor Problems
Labor Standards

LACROSSE *Feb. 1978*
CIJE: 4 RIE: 11 GC: 470
BT Team Sports

LAND ACQUISITION *Jan. 1972*
CIJE: 74 RIE: 69 GC: 920
RT Capital Outlay (For Fixed Assets)
Land Settlement
Land Use
Ownership
Site Development
Site Selection

Land Colonization
USE LAND SETTLEMENT

Land Grant Colleges
USE LAND GRANT UNIVERSITIES

LAND GRANT UNIVERSITIES *Jul. 1966*
CIJE: 73 RIE: 205 GC: 340
SN Universities that have received grants of land from the federal government, especially those made in accordance with the morrill act of 1862, originally to promote study in practical subjects like engineering and agriculture but now usually expanded to include a wide range of disciplines
UF Land Grant Colleges
BT Universities
RT Agricultural Colleges
Agricultural Education
Engineering Education
Federal Aid
Rural Extension
State Colleges
State Universities

LAND SETTLEMENT *Jan. 1970*
CIJE: 96 RIE: 200 GC: 550
UF Colonization
Land Colonization
Resettlement
Settlement Patterns
NT Rural Resettlement
BT Land Use
RT American Indian Reservations
Demography
Land Acquisition
Nomads
Place Of Residence
Population Trends
Refugees
Relocation

LAND USE *Jul. 1966*
CIJE: 383 RIE: 718 GC: 550
NT Land Settlement
Soil Conservation
RT Agriculture
Agronomy
Community Planning
Educational Facilities Planning
Facility Planning
Forestry
Land Acquisition
Landlords
Mining
Real Estate
Road Construction
Soil Science
Turf Management
Underground Facilities
Urban Planning
Use Studies
Zoning

Landladies
USE LANDLORDS

LANDLORDS *Sep. 1968*
CIJE: 9 RIE: 23 GC: 640
UF Landladies
BT Groups
RT Homeowners
Housing
Land Use
Real Estate
Real Estate Occupations

LANDSCAPING *Jul. 1966*
CIJE: 51 RIE: 119 GC: 410
BT Ornamental Horticulture
RT Botany
Floriculture
Grounds Keepers
Plant Identification
Site Development
Trails
Turf Management

= Two or more Descriptors are used to represent this term.
The term's main entry shows the appropriate coordination.

LANGUAGE *Jul. 1966*
CIJE: 584 RIE: 787 GC: 450
SN Systematic means of communicating ideas and feelings through the use of signs, gestures, words, and/or auditory symbols (note: for natural languages and language families, see "languages")
NT Artificial Languages
Child Language
Figurative Language
Interlanguage
Language Of Instruction
Languages For Special Purposes
Language Universals
Official Languages
Oral Language
Programing Languages
Second Languages
Sign Language
Symbolic Language
Tone Languages
Uncommonly Taught Languages
Unwritten Languages
Urban Language
Written Language
RT Artificial Speech
Code Switching (Language)
Dialects
Language Acquisition
Language Arts
Language Attitudes
Language Enrichment
Language Handicaps
Language Patterns
Language Planning
Language Processing
Language Proficiency
Language Research
Language Rhythm
Language Role
Languages
Language Skill Attrition
Language Skills
Language Styles
Language Tests
Language Universals
Language Usage
Language Variation
Linguistics
Onomastics
Semiotics
Social Dialects
Speech
Speech Communication
Verbal Communication
Word Frequency

LANGUAGE ABILITY (1966 1980) *Mar. 1980*
CIJE: 374 RIE: 393 GC: 450
SN Invalid descriptor -- used inconsistently in indexing -- see such descriptors as "language aptitude," "language proficiency," "language skills," etc.

LANGUAGE ACQUISITION *Mar. 1980*
CIJE: 3233 RIE: 3707 GC: 120
SN Development in the individual of his/her native language (note: do not use for "second language learning" -- prior to mar80, the thesaurus carried the instruction "language acquisition, use language development" -- "language development" did not carry a scope note)
UF Aural Language Learning #
Language Development (1966 1980)
Visual Language Learning #
BT Verbal Development
RT Auditory Training
Child Language
Delayed Speech
Expressive Language
Language
Language Aptitude
Language Enrichment
Language Fluency
Language Handicaps
Language Processing
Language Skill Attrition
Language Skills
Language Universals
Linguistic Competence
Linguistic Difficulty (Inherent)
Linguistic Performance
Oral Language
Psycholinguistics
Receptive Language
Verbal Learning
Written Language

LANGUAGE AIDS (1966 1980) *Jun. 1980*
CIJE: 49 RIE: 63 GC: 450
SN Invalid descriptor -- used for both "native language instruction" and "second language instruction" -- see those descriptors as well as "educational media"

LANGUAGE AND AREA CENTERS (1968 1980) *Mar. 1980*
CIJE: 7 RIE: 35 GC: 920
SN Invalid descriptor -- see such descriptors as "area studies," "resource centers," "second language programs," "second language instruction," etc.

LANGUAGE APTITUDE *Mar. 1980*
CIJE: 29 RIE: 26 GC: 450
BT Aptitude
RT Language Acquisition
Language Fluency
Language Proficiency
Language Skills
Second Language Learning
Verbal Ability

LANGUAGE ARTS *Jul. 1966*
CIJE: 1603 RIE: 3487 GC: 450
NT Debate
Handwriting
Listening
Outlining (Discourse)
Reading
Rhetoric
Speech
Spelling
Story Telling
Writing (Composition)
RT Child Language
Communication (Thought Transfer)
Comprehension
Dramatics
Editing
English Curriculum
Journalism Education
Language
Language Experience Approach
Language Skills
Lexicology
Literature
Reading Writing Relationship
Self Expression
Speech Communication
Speech Curriculum
Translation
Verbal Ability
Verbal Communication
Vocabulary

LANGUAGE ATTITUDES *Mar. 1976*
CIJE: 498 RIE: 482 GC: 450
SN Reactions, beliefs, or values about language and language use
NT Grammatical Acceptability
BT Attitudes
RT Language
Language Planning
Language Role
Language Usage
Psycholinguistics
Social Attitudes
Sociolinguistics

Language Attrition (Skills)
USE LANGUAGE SKILL ATTRITION

LANGUAGE CLASSIFICATION *Jul. 1966*
CIJE: 103 RIE: 158 GC: 450
SN Arrangement of languages into groups on the basis of historical development, structural features (see "language typology"), or geographic location
NT Language Typology
BT Classification
RT African Languages
American Indian Languages
Chad Languages
Comparative Analysis
Contrastive Linguistics
Diachronic Linguistics
Dialects
Diglossia
Dravidian Languages
Etymology
Glottochronology
Indo European Languages
Language Research
Languages
Language Styles
Malayo Polynesian Languages
Mutual Intelligibility
North American English
Regional Dialects
Sino Tibetan Languages
Slavic Languages
Urban Language

Language Development (1966 1980)
USE LANGUAGE ACQUISITION

Language Disabilities
USE LANGUAGE HANDICAPS

LANGUAGE DOMINANCE *Aug. 1978*
CIJE: 51 RIE: 134 GC: 450
SN The bilingual or multilingual individual's greater command of one of the languages in his/her repertoire
RT Bilingual Education
Bilingualism
Bilingual Students
Bilingual Teacher Aides
Bilingual Teachers
English (Second Language)
Interference (Language)
Language Of Instruction
Language Proficiency
Languages
Language Skills
Language Tests
Language Usage
Limited English Speaking
Multilingualism
Non English Speaking
Second Languages

LANGUAGE ENRICHMENT *Jul. 1966*
CIJE: 144 RIE: 246 GC: 450
UF Language Experience
BT Enrichment
RT Bilingual Education
Language
Language Acquisition
Languages
Second Language Instruction
Second Language Learning

LANGUAGE ENROLLMENT *Jul. 1966*
CIJE: 212 RIE: 173 GC: 320
SN Enrollment of students in foreign or second language courses or programs (prior to mar80, the use of this term was not restricted by a scope note)
UF Foreign Language Enrollment
Second Language Enrollment
BT Enrollment
RT Enrollment Rate
Enrollment Trends
Languages
Second Language Instruction
Second Language Programs

Language Experience
USE LANGUAGE ENRICHMENT

LANGUAGE EXPERIENCE APPROACH *Jul. 1966*
CIJE: 291 RIE: 381 GC: 450
SN An approach to teaching reading and language arts that uses words and stories from the student's own language and experience
BT Teaching Methods
RT Beginning Reading
Child Language
Language Arts
Narration
Reading Comprehension
Reading Instruction
Reading Programs
Student Developed Materials

LANGUAGE FLUENCY *Jul. 1966*
CIJE: 211 RIE: 246 GC: 450
SN Ability to speak a language easily, smoothly, and readily (note: prior to mar80, the use of this term was not restricted by a scope note)
BT Language Proficiency
RT Audiolingual Skills
Communicative Competence (Languages)
Conversational Language Courses
Dialogs (Language)
Diction
Expressive Language
Language Acquisition
Language Aptitude
Languages
Language Skills
Second Language Learning
Speech Skills

LANGUAGE GUIDES (1966 1980) *Jun. 1980*
CIJE: 8 RIE: 146 GC: 730
SN Invalid descriptor -- used for both "native language instruction" and "second language instruction" -- see those descriptors as well as "curriculum guides," "dictionaries," etc.

Language Handicapped (1967 1980)
USE LANGUAGE HANDICAPS

LANGUAGE HANDICAPS *Jul. 1966*
CIJE: 830 RIE: 687 GC: 220
SN Receptive or expressive language disabilities (note: use "learning disabilities" if the disability is being considered in an educational setting -- use "speech handicaps" for impairments of the peripheral speech mechanisms)
UF Language Disabilities
Language Handicapped (1967 1980)
NT Aphasia
Dyslexia
BT Disabilities
RT Child Language
Communication Disorders
Echolalia
Exceptional Persons
Expressive Language
Hearing Impairments
Language
Language Acquisition
Learning Disabilities
Neurolinguistics
Neurological Impairments
Perceptual Handicaps
Reading Difficulties
Receptive Language
Speech Handicaps
Writing Difficulties

Language History
USE DIACHRONIC LINGUISTICS

LANGUAGE INSTRUCTION (1966 1980) *Mar. 1980*
CIJE: 6639 RIE: 5908 GC: 450
SN Invalid descriptor -- used for both foreign and native language instruction -- see "second language instruction," "english instruction," or "native language instruction"

LANGUAGE LABORATORIES *Jul. 1966*
CIJE: 514 RIE: 533 GC: 920
UF Audio Active Compare Laboratories (1967 1980)
Audio Active Laboratories (1967 1980)
Audio Passive Laboratories (1968 1980)
Language Laboratory Equipment (1966 1980) #
Language Laboratory Use (1966 1980)
BT Learning Laboratories
RT Audio Equipment
Dial Access Information Systems
Electronic Classrooms
Languages
Programed Instruction
Second Language Instruction
Second Language Programs
Writing Laboratories

Language Laboratory Equipment (1966 1980)
USE LABORATORY EQUIPMENT; LANGUAGE LABORATORIES

Language Laboratory Use (1966 1980)
USE LANGUAGE LABORATORIES

Language Learning (Foreign)
USE SECOND LANGUAGE LEARNING

= Two or more Descriptors are used to represent this term.
The term's main entry shows the appropriate coordination.

LANGUAGE LEARNING LEVELS (1967 1980) *Mar. 1980*
CIJE: 261 RIE: 398 GC: 450
SN Invalid descriptor -- used for levels of achievement in both native and foreign language -- see "second language learning" or "language acquisition"

Language Loss (Skills)
USE LANGUAGE SKILL ATTRITION

LANGUAGE MAINTENANCE *Oct. 1977*
CIJE: 133 RIE: 168 GC: 450
SN The maintenance of a given language rather than its displacement by another language (includes maintaining the languages of cultural minority groups through family practices, rituals, concerted educational endeavors with society at large, etc.)
RT Bilingual Education
Bilingual Education Programs
Bilingual Instructional Materials
Bilingualism
Language Of Instruction
Language Planning
Language Role
Languages
Language Skill Attrition
Language Usage
Multilingualism
Sociolinguistics

LANGUAGE OF INSTRUCTION *Mar. 1976*
CIJE: 197 RIE: 335 GC: 450
SN Language in which curriculum subjects are presented
UF Instructional Language
Medium Of Instruction (Language)
Teaching Language
BT Language
RT Bilingual Education
Bilingual Education Programs
Bilingual Instructional Materials
Curriculum
Educational Policy
English (Second Language)
Immersion Programs
Instruction
Language Dominance
Language Maintenance
Language Planning
Languages
Language Usage
Native Speakers
Official Languages
Second Language Instruction
Second Language Learning
Second Languages
Sociolinguistics

LANGUAGE PATTERNS *Jul. 1966*
CIJE: 1473 RIE: 1540 GC: 450
UF Basic Language Patterns
Linguistic Patterns (1966 1980)
NT Idioms
Language Rhythm
Paragraphs
Phoneme Grapheme Correspondence
RT Case (Grammar)
Child Language
Code Switching (Language)
Connected Discourse
Dialogs (Language)
Diction
Echolalia
Error Analysis (Language)
Form Classes (Languages)
Ideography
Kinship Terminology
Language
Languages
Language Styles
Language Typology
Language Universals
Language Usage
Lexicology
Linguistic Borrowing
Linguistics
Morphology (Languages)
Native Speakers
North American English
Phonemics
Pragmatics
Pronouns
Semantics
Semiotics
Sentence Combining
Sentence Diagraming
Speech Acts
Speech Communication
Speech Habits
Speech Skills
Standard Spoken Usage
Syntax
Tagmemic Analysis
Urban Language
Verbal Communication

LANGUAGE PLANNING *Aug. 1969*
CIJE: 166 RIE: 287 GC: 450
SN Planned language change directed toward improving the utility of a language or increasing its use in a given country or region
NT Language Standardization
BT Planning
Sociolinguistics
RT Bilingual Education
Bilingualism
Educational Policy
Immersion Programs
Language
Language Attitudes
Language Maintenance
Language Of Instruction
Languages
Language Usage
Multilingualism
National Norms
National Programs
Official Languages
Second Languages
Sociolinguistics

LANGUAGE PROCESSING *Aug. 1978*
CIJE: 586 RIE: 640 GC: 450
SN The cognitive processing of spoken or written language, ranging from the construction of spoken or written messages to the abstraction of meaning from language -- includes the computerized simulation of these processes
NT Expressive Language
Interference (Language)
Reading Processes
Receptive Language
BT Cognitive Processes
RT Abstract Reasoning
Auditory Perception
Coherence
Comprehension
Computational Linguistics
Encoding (Psychology)
Language
Language Acquisition
Language Research
Language Skills
Language Usage
Learning Processes
Learning Strategies
Linguistic Difficulty (Inherent)
Linguistic Performance
Linguistics
Linguistic Theory
Listening
Neurolinguistics
Psycholinguistics
Reading
Speech Communication
Structural Analysis (Linguistics)
Verbal Communication
Verbal Stimuli
Visual Perception
Writing (Composition)
Writing Processes

LANGUAGE PROFICIENCY *Jul. 1966*
CIJE: 785 RIE: 1093 GC: 450
SN Degree or level of accuracy and fluency of language use for communication
NT Language Fluency
Threshold Level (Languages)
BT Ability
RT Bilingualism
Communicative Competence (Languages)
Conversational Language Courses
Dialogs (Language)
Intensive Language Courses
Language
Language Aptitude
Language Dominance
Languages
Language Skill Attrition
Language Skills
Language Tests
Limited English Speaking
Linguistic Competence
Linguistic Performance
Multilevel Classes (Second Language Instruction)
Second Language Instruction
Second Language Learning

LANGUAGE PROGRAMS (1966 1980) *Mar. 1980*
CIJE: 606 RIE: 1199 GC: 450
SN Invalid descriptor -- used for both native and foreign language programs -- see such descriptors as "second language programs," "english instruction," and "native language instruction"

Language Records (Phonograph) (1966 1980)
USE AUDIODISKS

LANGUAGE RESEARCH *Jul. 1966*
CIJE: 2792 RIE: 3262 GC: 810
SN Study of either the acquisition of spoken/written language or the elements of language as defined by linguistics, e.g., phonology, morphology, syntax, lexicon (note: do not confuse with "communication research" -- as of oct81, use as a minor descriptor for examples of this kind of research -- use as a major descriptor only as the subject of a document)
UF Linguistic Research
NT Dialect Studies
BT Research
RT Anthropological Linguistics
Bilingualism
Child Language
Communication Research
Diachronic Linguistics
Discourse Analysis
Etymology
Glottochronology
Language
Language Classification
Language Processing
Language Role
Languages
Language Universals
Linguistics
Onomastics
Phonetic Analysis
Sociolinguistics
Speech Compression
Structural Analysis (Linguistics)
Tagmemic Analysis
Unwritten Languages
Urban Language

LANGUAGE RHYTHM *Sep. 1968*
CIJE: 183 RIE: 88 GC: 450
SN Regular or intermittent pattern in the flow of spoken or written language
BT Language Patterns
RT Articulation (Speech)
Language
Language Styles
Oral Language
Poetry
Prose
Speech Communication
Speech Habits
Speech Skills
Written Language

LANGUAGE ROLE *Jul. 1966*
CIJE: 626 RIE: 669 GC: 450
RT Cultural Influences
Language
Language Attitudes
Language Maintenance
Language Research
Social Dialects
Social Influences
Sociolinguistics

LANGUAGE SKILL ATTRITION *Jan. 1985*
CIJE: 4 RIE: 1 GC: 450
SN The loss of native or second language skills due to discontinued use (note: do not confuse with "language handicaps")
UF Language Attrition (Skills)
Language Loss (Skills)
RT Bilingualism
Language
Language Acquisition
Language Maintenance
Language Proficiency
Language Skills
Language Usage
Multilingualism
Psycholinguistics
Retention (Psychology)
Second Language Learning
Sociolinguistics

LANGUAGE SKILLS *Jul. 1966*
CIJE: 1978 RIE: 2957 GC: 450
NT Audiolingual Skills
Communicative Competence (Languages)
Reading Skills
Vocabulary Skills
Writing Skills
BT Skills
RT Basic Skills
Cloze Procedure
Communication Skills
Daily Living Skills
Dictation
English (Second Language)
Error Analysis (Language)
Expressive Language
Inferences
Interpreters
Interpretive Skills
Language
Language Acquisition
Language Aptitude
Language Arts
Language Dominance
Language Fluency
Language Processing
Language Proficiency
Languages
Language Skill Attrition
Language Tests
Linguistic Competence
Linguistic Performance
Listening Comprehension
Monolingualism
Psycholinguistics
Receptive Language
Second Language Learning
Sentence Combining
Translation
Verbal Ability
Word Study Skills

LANGUAGE STANDARDIZATION *Jul. 1966*
CIJE: 154 RIE: 167 GC: 450
SN The official acceptance by at least some groups within a speech community of certain general patterns of pronunciation, grammar, orthography, and/or vocabulary
BT Language Planning
RT Dialects
Diglossia
Languages
National Norms
National Programs
Native Language Instruction
Official Languages
Romanization
Sociolinguistics
Standard Spoken Usage

LANGUAGE STYLES *Jul. 1966*
CIJE: 721 RIE: 719 GC: 450
SN Optional variants in sounds, structures, and vocabulary of a language which are characteristic of different users, situations, or literary types
UF Linguistic Styles
BT Language Usage
Language Variation
RT Cliches
Editing
Expressive Language
Language
Language Classification
Language Patterns
Language Rhythm
Literary Devices
Native Speakers
Speech Skills
Standard Spoken Usage
Writing Skills

Language Tapes
USE AUDIOTAPE RECORDINGS

LANGUAGE TEACHERS *Jul. 1966*
CIJE: 668 RIE: 772 GC: 360
UF Fles Teachers (1967 1980) #
Foreign Language Teachers
Second Language Teachers
BT Teachers
RT English Instruction
Languages
Native Language Instruction
Second Language Instruction

LANGUAGE TESTS *Jul. 1966*
CIJE: 890 RIE: 1170 GC: 830
SN Tests to measure proficiency, diagnose strengths and weaknesses, or predict future performance in a native or foreign language (note: for foreign language tests, coordinate this term with "second language learning," and, when appropriate, the language)
BT Verbal Tests
RT Achievement Tests
Cloze Procedure
Language
Language Dominance
Language Proficiency
Languages
Language Skills
Listening Comprehension Tests
Reading Tests
Second Language Learning
Speech Tests
Writing Evaluation
Writing Skills

LANGUAGE TYPOLOGY *Jul. 1966*
CIJE: 65 RIE: 100 GC: 450
SN Classification of languages on the basis of similarities and differences in their structural features--phonology, grammar, and vocabulary, including semantic meaning in specific contexts
BT Language Classification
RT Contrastive Linguistics
Descriptive Linguistics
Etymology
Language Patterns
Language Universals
Morphology (Languages)
Phonemes
Phonology
Syntax
Tone Languages

LANGUAGE UNIVERSALS *Aug. 1968*
CIJE: 220 RIE: 247 GC: 450
SN Characteristics assumed to be common to all languages
UF Linguistic Universals
BT Language
RT Artificial Languages
Behavioral Science Research
Case (Grammar)
Diachronic Linguistics
Distinctive Features (Language)
Language
Language Acquisition
Language Patterns
Language Research
Languages
Language Typology
Linguistic Difficulty (Inherent)
Linguistic Theory
Negative Forms (Language)
Structural Analysis (Linguistics)

LANGUAGE USAGE *Jul. 1966*
CIJE: 2386 RIE: 2112 GC: 450
UF Sexist Language #
NT Language Styles
Standard Spoken Usage
RT Bidialectalism
Business English
Code Switching (Language)
Cohesion (Written Composition)
Dialects
Error Analysis (Language)
Grammatical Acceptability
Language
Language Attitudes
Language Dominance
Language Maintenance
Language Of Instruction
Language Patterns
Language Planning
Language Processing
Languages
Language Skill Attrition
Language Variation
Linguistic Borrowing
Linguistics
Miscue Analysis
Native Language Instruction
Native Speakers
North American English
Obscenity
Oral Language
Pragmatics
Sociolinguistics
Speech Habits
Urban Language
Written Language

LANGUAGE VARIATION *Jun. 1975*
CIJE: 443 RIE: 506 GC: 450
SN Differences in systems of a language that result from historical, geographic, social, or functional changes
NT Creoles
Dialects
Language Styles
Linguistic Borrowing
Pidgins
BT Sociolinguistics
RT Bidialectalism
Code Switching (Language)
Contrastive Linguistics
Diachronic Linguistics
Dialect Studies
Diglossia
Grammatical Acceptability
Language
Language Usage
Urban Language

LANGUAGES *Jul. 1966*
CIJE: 119 RIE: 294 GC: 440
SN (Note: use a more specific term if possible)
NT African Languages
Afro Asiatic Languages
American Indian Languages
American Sign Language
Australian Aboriginal Languages
Austro Asiatic Languages
Basque
Burushaski
Caucasian Languages
Classical Languages
Creoles
Dialects
Dravidian Languages
Eskimo Aleut Languages
Indo European Languages
Japanese
Korean
Malayo Polynesian Languages
Modern Languages
Pidgins
Sino Tibetan Languages
Uralic Altaic Languages
Vietnamese
RT Bilingualism
Conversational Language Courses
Etymology
Fles
Foreign Language Books
Foreign Language Films
Foreign Language Periodicals
Glottochronology
Idioms
Intensive Language Courses
Language
Language Classification
Language Dominance
Language Enrichment
Language Enrollment
Language Fluency
Language Laboratories
Language Maintenance
Language Of Instruction
Language Patterns
Language Planning
Language Proficiency
Language Research
Languages For Special Purposes
Language Skills
Language Standardization
Language Teachers
Language Tests
Language Universals
Language Usage
Middle English
Monolingualism
Multilevel Classes (Second Language Instruction)
Multilingualism
Multilingual Materials
Mutual Intelligibility
Notional Functional Syllabi
Old English
Second Language Instruction
Word Frequency

LANGUAGES FOR SPECIAL PURPOSES *Apr. 1975*
CIJE: 157 RIE: 192 GC: 440
SN Languages taught to or learned by nonnative speakers who need a certain specialized foreign language capability in their studies, profession, or trade
NT English For Special Purposes
BT Language
RT Languages
Second Language Instruction
Second Language Learning

LAO *Jul. 1966*
CIJE: RIE: 37 GC: 440
UF Laotian
BT Sino Tibetan Languages

Laotian
USE LAO

Laotian Americans
USE ASIAN AMERICANS; LAOTIANS

LAOTIANS *Mar. 1980*
CIJE: 4 RIE: 51 GC: 560
UF Laotian Americans #
BT Indochinese
RT Asian Americans
Cambodians
Vietnamese People

Lap Belts
USE RESTRAINTS (VEHICLE SAFETY)

Laps
USE LEARNING MODULES

Large Cities
USE URBAN AREAS

LARGE GROUP INSTRUCTION *Jul. 1966*
CIJE: 93 RIE: 101 GC: 310
SN Teaching of students in large classroom situations (note: do not confuse with "mass instruction")
BT Group Instruction
RT Mass Instruction
Small Group Instruction
Teaching Methods

Large Scale Production
USE MASS PRODUCTION

Large Type Books
USE LARGE TYPE MATERIALS

LARGE TYPE MATERIALS *Jul. 1966*
CIJE: 30 RIE: 44 GC: 220
UF Large Type Books
BT Reading Materials
RT Instructional Materials
Low Vision Aids
Magnification Methods
Partial Vision
Reading Instruction
Sensory Aids

Laser Disks
USE OPTICAL DISKS

Laser Oscillators
USE LASERS

LASERS *Dec. 1969*
CIJE: 205 RIE: 31 GC: 490
UF Laser Oscillators
Light Amplifiers (Lasers)
Optical Masers
RT Electronics
Energy
Holography
Light
Optical Data Disks
Optical Disks
Optics
Physics
Radiation
Science Equipment
Semiconductor Devices
Spectroscopy

LATCHKEY CHILDREN *Apr. 1986*
CIJE: 22 RIE: 36 GC: 510
SN Children left alone or unsupervised before or after the school day
BT Children
RT Child Welfare
Employed Parents
School Age Day Care

LATE REGISTRATION *Aug. 1980*
CIJE: 2 RIE: 12 GC: 320
SN Enrolling after the school semester, quarter, etc. has begun (note: for the age of students when they enter school, see "school entrance age")
BT School Registration
RT Admission (School)
Continuation Students

LATENT TRAIT THEORY *Apr. 1980*
CIJE: 164 RIE: 345 GC: 810
SN The study of test and item scores based on assumptions concerning the mathematical relationship between abilities (or other hypothesized traits) and item responses (note: "latent trait theory" includes both the "rasch model" and the "birnbaum models" -- see those identifiers)
UF Item Characteristic Curve Theory
Item Response Theory
BT Test Theory
RT Adaptive Testing
Equated Scores
Item Analysis
Mathematical Models
Psychometrics
Scores
Scoring
Test Construction
Testing
Test Interpretation
Test Items
Test Reliability
Tests
Test Validity

LATERAL DOMINANCE *Jul. 1966*
CIJE: 231 RIE: 107 GC: 120
SN Consistent preference for the use of the muscles and limbs on one side of the body, generally thought to be the result of the dominance of one hemisphere of the brain over the other
BT Physical Characteristics
RT Brain Hemisphere Functions
Eye Hand Coordination
Left Handed Writer
Motor Development
Neurological Organization
Physical Development
Psychomotor Skills

Lathes
USE MACHINE TOOLS

LATIN *Jul. 1966*
CIJE: 357 RIE: 319 GC: 440
BT Classical Languages
Romance Languages
RT Classical Literature
Latin Literature

LATIN AMERICAN CULTURE *Jul. 1966*
CIJE: 196 RIE: 300 GC: 560
SN Culture of the caribbean islands, mexico, central and south america, including the culture of non-hispanic peoples in that area -- e.g., jamaicans, haitians, guyanese, etc.
NT Luso Brazilian Culture
Puerto Rican Culture
BT Culture
RT American Indian Culture
Black Culture
Hispanic American Culture
Latin American History
Latin American Literature
Latin Americans
Spanish Culture
Western Civilization

= Two or more Descriptors are used to represent this term.
The term's main entry shows the appropriate coordination.

LATIN AMERICAN HISTORY *Mar. 1980*
CIJE: 46 RIE: 58 GC: 430
SN History of the caribbean islands, mexico, central and south america, including the history of non-hispanic peoples in that area -- e.g., jamaicans, haitians, guyanese, etc.
UF Central American History
South American History
BT History
RT American Indian History
Black History
Hispanic Americans
Latin American Culture
Latin American Literature
Latin Americans
Western Civilization

LATIN AMERICAN LITERATURE *Mar. 1980*
CIJE: 25 RIE: 20 GC: 430
SN Literature of mexico, central and south america, and the caribbean countries (note: see also the identifier "mexican literature" -- prior to mar80, the instruction "mexican literature, use spanish american literature" was carried in the thesaurus)
UF American Literature (1966 1980) (Latin America)
Central American Literature
South American Literature
BT Literature
RT American Indian Literature
Black Literature
Hispanic American Literature
Latin American Culture
Latin American History
Latin Americans
Mexican American Literature

LATIN AMERICANS *Mar. 1980*
CIJE: 32 RIE: 62 GC: 560
SN Indigenous peoples, permanent residents, or citizens of the caribbean islands, mexico, central and south america, including non-hispanic peoples in that area -- e.g., jamaicans, haitians, guyanese, etc.
UF Central Americans
South Americans
NT Cubans
Dominicans
Haitians
Mexicans
Puerto Ricans
BT Groups
RT American Indians
Hispanic Americans
Latin American Culture
Latin American History
Latin American Literature

LATIN LITERATURE *Jul. 1970*
CIJE: 71 RIE: 45 GC: 430
UF Roman Literature
BT Classical Literature
RT Ancient History
Classical Languages
Latin

LATVIAN *Nov. 1970*
CIJE: 2 RIE: 6 GC: 440
BT Baltic Languages

LAUNDRY DRYCLEANING OCCUPATIONS *Mar. 1980*
CIJE: 3 RIE: 20 GC: 640
UF Drycleaning Laundry Occupations
BT Service Occupations
RT Clothing
Clothing Instruction
Home Economics Skills
Needle Trades
Occupational Home Economics
Semiskilled Occupations
Textiles Instruction

LAW ENFORCEMENT *Jul. 1966*
CIJE: 290 RIE: 620 GC: 610
UF Citations (Legal)
NT Police Action
Sentencing
RT Compliance (Legal)
Crime
Crime Prevention
Criminal Law
Delinquency
Delinquency Prevention
Fines (Penalties)
Human Services
Immigration Inspectors
Laws
National Security
Police
School Security
Security Personnel
Social Control

Law Enforcement Officers
USE POLICE

LAW LIBRARIES *Jul. 1966*
CIJE: 44 RIE: 70 GC: 710
SN Libraries consisting of law-related materials and providing services to those interested in legal practices
UF Legislative Reference Libraries (1968 1980)
BT Special Libraries
RT Depository Libraries
Government Libraries
Laws
Law Schools
Research Libraries

Law Of Nations
USE INTERNATIONAL LAW

Law Of Primacy
USE PRIMACY EFFECT

LAW RELATED EDUCATION *Aug. 1986*
CIJE: RIE: 67 GC: 400
SN Learning activities, often at grades k-12 but sometimes at postsecondary levels, concerned with law and legal systems (note: do not confuse with "legal education (professions)" -- prior to aug86, this concept was indexed by "legal education")
BT Education
RT Citizenship Education
Constitutional Law
Criminal Law
International Law
Laws
Police Education
Social Studies

Law School Applicants
USE COLLEGE APPLICANTS; LAW SCHOOLS

Law School Education
USE LEGAL EDUCATION (PROFESSIONS)

LAW SCHOOLS *Jul. 1966*
CIJE: 383 RIE: 113 GC: 340
SN Schools or colleges, usually affiliated with universities, that prepare students who have completed baccalaureate programs to be attorneys -- typical degrees granted include doctor of jurisprudence, doctor of law, and master of law
UF Law School Applicants #
BT Colleges
RT Law Libraries
Law Students
Lawyers
Legal Education (Professions)
Professional Education

LAW STUDENTS *Mar. 1980*
CIJE: 105 RIE: 40 GC: 360
SN Students enrolled in law schools and pursuing a professional education for preparation as attorneys
BT Graduate Students
RT Law Schools
Lawyers
Legal Education (Professions)
Professional Education

Lawmakers
USE LEGISLATORS

Lawn Maintenance
USE TURF MANAGEMENT

LAWS *Jul. 1966*
CIJE: 788 RIE: 886 GC: 610
SN Rules of conduct or action established by authority, society, or custom
NT Constitutional Law
Criminal Law
International Law
School Law
BT Standards
RT Civil Liberties
Civil Rights Legislation
Codification
Compliance (Legal)
Contracts
Court Litigation
Courts
Discriminatory Legislation
Drug Legislation
Due Process
Educational Legislation
Educational Malpractice
Equal Protection
Federal Legislation
Freedom Of Information
Hearings
International Crimes
Justice
Labor Legislation
Law Enforcement
Law Libraries
Law Related Education
Lawyers
Legal Education (Professions)
Legal Responsibility
Legislation
Local Legislation
Malpractice
Minimum Wage Legislation
Ownership
Privacy
Public Health Legislation
Recreation Legislation
Sanctions
School Attendance Legislation
State Legislation
Torts

LAWYERS *Jan. 1969*
CIJE: 372 RIE: 226 GC: 640
UF Advocates (Law)
Attorneys
Barristers
Solicitors (Law)
BT Professional Personnel
RT Court Judges
Court Litigation
Laws
Law Schools
Law Students
Legal Aid
Legal Assistants
Legal Education (Professions)
Legal Problems

LAY PEOPLE *Mar. 1980*
CIJE: 45 RIE: 48 GC: 520
SN People lacking special training or knowledge in a given field -- also refers to members of the laity as opposed to the clergy
UF Laymen (1966 1980)
Nonspecialists
NT Lay Teachers
BT Groups
RT Church Workers
Clergy
Professional Personnel

LAY TEACHERS *Jul. 1966*
CIJE: 19 RIE: 26 GC: 360
BT Lay People
Teachers
RT Catholic Schools
Church Workers
Parochial Schools
Religious Education

Laymen (1966 1980)
USE LAY PEOPLE

LAYOUT (PUBLICATIONS) *Jul. 1973*
CIJE: 353 RIE: 211 GC: 720
UF Format (Publications)
BT Graphic Arts
RT Captions
Editors
Headlines
Journalism
Newspapers
Photography
Photojournalism
Printing
Publications

Lea
USE SCHOOL DISTRICTS

Lead Lecture Plan (1966 1980)
USE LECTURE METHOD

LEAD POISONING *Apr. 1973*
CIJE: 52 RIE: 36 GC: 210
BT Poisoning
RT Anemia
Neurological Impairments
Occupational Diseases
Physical Health
Pollution
Special Health Problems

Leader Participation (1966 1980)
USE LEADERSHIP

Leaderless Groups
USE SELF DIRECTED GROUPS

LEADERS *Mar. 1980*
CIJE: 135 RIE: 234 GC: 510
UF Adult Leaders (1967 1980)
Team Leader (Teaching) (1966 1980) #
NT Community Leaders
Youth Leaders
BT Groups
RT Leaders Guides
Leadership
Leadership Qualities
Leadership Responsibility
Leadership Styles
Leadership Training
Supervisors

LEADERS GUIDES *Jul. 1966*
CIJE: 15 RIE: 335 GC: 730
BT Guides
RT Leaders
Leadership
Leadership Training

LEADERSHIP *Jul. 1966*
CIJE: 1256 RIE: 1322 GC: 520
UF Leader Participation (1966 1980)
NT Black Leadership
Informal Leadership
Instructional Leadership
Student Leadership
BT Ability
RT Behavior
Community Leaders
Institutional Role
Leaders
Leaders Guides
Leadership Qualities
Leadership Responsibility
Leadership Training
Middle Management
Nonauthoritarian Classes
Supervision

LEADERSHIP QUALITIES *Jul. 1966*
CIJE: 565 RIE: 524 GC: 520
RT Administrator Qualifications
Leaders
Leadership
Leadership Responsibility
Leadership Training
Prestige

LEADERSHIP RESPONSIBILITY *Jul. 1966*
CIJE: 583 RIE: 569 GC: 520
BT Responsibility
RT Administrator Responsibility
Business Responsibility
Church Responsibility
Citizenship Responsibility
Instructional Leadership
Leaders
Leadership
Leadership Qualities
School Responsibility
Social Responsibility
Teacher Responsibility

= Two or more Descriptors are used to represent this term.
The term's main entry shows the appropriate coordination.

LEADERSHIP STYLES *Jul. 1966*
CIJE: 558 RIE: 557 GC: 520
BT Behavior
RT Leaders
Supervisory Methods
Teaching Styles

LEADERSHIP TRAINING *Jul. 1966*
CIJE: 590 RIE: 1349 GC: 400
BT Training
RT Black Leadership
Instructional Leadership
Leaders
Leaders Guides
Leadership
Leadership Qualities
Management Development
Student Leadership
Supervisory Training
Trainers
Youth Leaders

Leaflets
USE PAMPHLETS

Learned Helplessness
USE HELPLESSNESS

Learner Autonomy
USE PERSONAL AUTONOMY

Learner Outcomes
USE OUTCOMES OF EDUCATION

LEARNING *Jul. 1966*
CIJE: 2094 RIE: 2249 GC: 110
SN Process of acquiring knowledge, attitudes, or skills from study, instruction, or experience (note: use a more specific term if possible)
UF Learning Characteristics (1968 1980)
NT Adult Learning
Associative Learning
Aural Learning
Discovery Learning
Discrimination Learning
Experiential Learning
Incidental Learning
Intentional Learning
Lifelong Learning
Mastery Learning
Multisensory Learning
Nonverbal Learning
Observational Learning
Prior Learning
Rote Learning
Second Language Learning
Sequential Learning
Serial Learning
Symbolic Learning
Transfer Of Training
Verbal Learning
Visual Learning
RT Advance Organizers
Aptitude
Cognitive Processes
Education
Educational Environment
Epistemology
Individual Development
Instruction
Knowledge Level
Learning Activities
Learning Experience
Learning Modalities
Learning Modules
Learning Motivation
Learning Plateaus
Learning Problems
Learning Processes
Learning Readiness
Learning Strategies
Learning Theories
Mnemonics
Nature Nurture Controversy
Recall (Psychology)
Schemata (Cognition)
Scholarship
Time Factors (Learning)

LEARNING ACTIVITIES *Jul. 1966*
CIJE: 4899 RIE: 11231 GC: 310
SN Activities engaged in by the learner for the purpose of acquiring certain skills, concepts, or knowledge, whether guided by an instructor or not (note: do not confuse with mental process terms, e.g., "cognitive processes" or "learning processes")
UF Integrated Learning #
NT Study
BT Activities
RT Activity Units
Advance Organizers
Class Activities
Directed Reading Activity
Discovery Learning
Educational Games
Experiential Learning
Learning
Learning Experience
Learning Modules
Learning Strategies
Negative Practice
Observational Learning
Problem Sets
School Activities
Time On Task

Learning Activity Packages
USE LEARNING MODULES

Learning Activity Packets
USE LEARNING MODULES

LEARNING CENTERS (CLASSROOM) *Mar. 1980*
CIJE: 117 RIE: 129 GC: 310
SN Areas arranged by teachers (usually within the classroom) in which materials are provided so that individuals or very small groups can explore a topic without direct instruction from the teacher (note: prior to mar80, the instruction "learning centers, use learning laboratories" was carried in the thesaurus)
UF Centers Of Interest (1966 1980)
Interest Centers (Classroom)
Learning Stations (Classroom)
BT Educational Facilities
Resource Centers
RT Discovery Learning
Experiential Learning
Humanistic Education
Individualized Instruction
Open Education
Writing Laboratories

Learning Characteristics (1968 1980)
USE LEARNING

Learning Contracts
USE PERFORMANCE CONTRACTS

Learning Cycles
USE LEARNING PROCESSES

Learning Difficulties (1966 1980)
USE LEARNING PROBLEMS

LEARNING DISABILITIES *Jul. 1966*
CIJE: 4003 RIE: 2463 GC: 220
SN Category in federal legislation referring to disorders involved in understanding or using language, manifested in imperfect ability to listen, think, speak, read, write, spell, or do mathematical calculations (note: use "language handicaps" if the disability is being considered in a non-educational setting -- do not confuse with "learning problems")
UF Specific Learning Disabilities
BT Disabilities
RT Academic Failure
Aphasia
Attention Deficit Disorders
Cognitive Processes
Cognitive Restructuring
Communication Disorders
Developmental Disabilities
Dyslexia
Educational Diagnosis
Emotional Problems
Exceptional Persons
Hyperactivity
Language Handicaps
Learning Problems
Minimal Brain Dysfunction
Neurological Impairments
Perceptual Handicaps
Reading Difficulties
Recall (Psychology)
Recognition (Psychology)
Remedial Reading
Writing Difficulties

LEARNING EXPERIENCE *Jul. 1966*
CIJE: 1048 RIE: 802 GC: 110
SN Any experience that results in learning (note: prior to jun78, this term was frequently used for "experiential learning")
NT Clinical Experience
BT Experience
RT Experiential Learning
Learning
Learning Activities
Learning Readiness
Mnemonics
Prior Learning

Learning Kits
USE LEARNING MODULES

LEARNING LABORATORIES *Jul. 1966*
CIJE: 454 RIE: 608 GC: 920
SN Facilities with programed or autoinstructional materials and the equipment required for their display -- used primarily for independent study or individualized instruction (note: prior to mar80, the instruction "learning centers, use learning laboratories" was carried in the thesaurus)
UF Autoinstructional Laboratories (1967 1980)
NT Language Laboratories
BT Educational Facilities
Laboratories
RT Audiovisual Centers
Autoinstructional Aids
Dial Access Information Systems
Educational Media
Electronic Classrooms
Independent Study
Individualized Instruction
Learning Resources Centers
Programed Instruction
Reading Centers
Skill Centers
Writing Laboratories

Learning Maturation Controversy
USE NATURE NURTURE CONTROVERSY

LEARNING MODALITIES *Oct. 1971*
CIJE: 337 RIE: 284 GC: 110
SN The sense modalities used in learning -- for example, information may be processed visually, aurally, or tactually
RT Aural Learning
Cognitive Mapping
Cognitive Style
Dimensional Preference
Intermode Differences
Kinesthetic Perception
Learning
Learning Processes
Learning Strategies
Multisensory Learning
Nonverbal Learning
Perceptual Development
Perceptual Motor Learning
Sensory Experience
Tactual Perception
Teaching Methods
Verbal Learning
Visual Learning

LEARNING MODULES *Oct. 1976*
CIJE: 387 RIE: 3550 GC: 730
SN Packets of subject-related teaching materials containing objectives, directions for use, and test items
UF Laps
Learning Activity Packages
Learning Activity Packets
Learning Kits
Learning Packages
Modular Learning
BT Instructional Materials
RT Behavioral Objectives
Curriculum Guides
Independent Study
Individualized Instruction
Learning
Learning Activities
Learning Strategies
Minicourses
Programed Instructional Materials
Resource Units
Teaching Guides
Teaching Methods
Units Of Study

LEARNING MOTIVATION *Jul. 1966*
CIJE: 815 RIE: 748 GC: 110
BT Motivation
RT Academic Aspiration
Intentional Learning
Learning
Learning Readiness
Learning Strategies
Student Motivation

Learning Objectives
USE BEHAVIORAL OBJECTIVES

Learning Packages
USE LEARNING MODULES

LEARNING PLATEAUS *Jul. 1966*
CIJE: 32 RIE: 21 GC: 110
SN Time periods during which there is no evidence of learning progress (note: prior to mar80, the use of this term was not restricted by a scope note)
RT Academic Achievement
Achievement
Knowledge Level
Learning
Learning Processes
Learning Theories
Psychological Characteristics
Skill Development
Student Improvement

LEARNING PROBLEMS *Mar. 1980*
CIJE: 649 RIE: 641 GC: 110
SN Category in federal legislation referring to problems encountered in the process of learning -- may be the result of visual, hearing, or motor impairments, mental retardation, behavioral disorders, or health impairments, or of cultural, environmental, or economic disadvantage (note: do not confuse with "learning disabilities")
UF Learning Difficulties (1966 1980)
BT Problems
RT Academic Achievement
Academic Failure
Behavior Disorders
Diagnostic Teaching
Educational Diagnosis
Educationally Disadvantaged
Hearing Impairments
Learning
Learning Disabilities
Learning Readiness
Low Achievement
Mental Retardation
Motor Development
Reading Difficulties
Remedial Instruction
Remedial Reading
Slow Learners
Special Health Problems
Student Problems
Underachievement
Visual Impairments
Writing Difficulties

LEARNING PROCESSES *Jul. 1966*
CIJE: 4483 RIE: 3519 GC: 110
UF Educational Processes
Learning Cycles
NT Behavior Chaining
Cognitive Mapping
Concept Formation
Discovery Processes
Extinction (Psychology)
Generalization
Habituation
Memorization
Primacy Effect
BT Cognitive Processes
RT Aptitude Treatment Interaction
Association (Psychology)
Cognitive Structures
Conditioning
Conservation (Concept)
Contingency Management
Deduction
Encoding (Psychology)
Feedback
Heuristics
Induction

= Two or more Descriptors are used to represent this term.
The term's main entry shows the appropriate coordination.

Inquiry
Intentional Learning
Interference (Language)
Interlanguage
Intuition
Language Processing
Learning
Learning Modalities
Learning Plateaus
Learning Readiness
Learning Strategies
Learning Theories
Mediation Theory
Memory
Metacognition
Misconceptions
Mnemonics
Observational Learning
Psychoeducational Methods
Questioning Techniques
Recall (Psychology)
Recognition (Psychology)
Shift Studies

LEARNING READINESS *Jul. 1966*
CIJE: 224 RIE: 302 GC: 120
SN State or condition of an individual that makes it possible for him or her to engage profitably in a given learning activity -- learning readiness depends on such factors as past experiences, cognitive development, affective factors, and motivation as well as on the instructional methods and materials to be used
BT Readiness
RT Cognitive Development
Emotional Development
Learning
Learning Experience
Learning Motivation
Learning Problems
Learning Processes
Mastery Learning
Reading Readiness
School Entrance Age
School Readiness
Writing Readiness

Learning Reinforcement
USE REINFORCEMENT

Learning Resources
USE EDUCATIONAL RESOURCES

LEARNING RESOURCES CENTERS *Mar. 1980*
CIJE: 872 RIE: 1054 GC: 710
SN Areas within schools that provide services and equipment for the use of an integrated collection of print and nonprint materials (note: do not confuse with "learning laboratories" or "learning centers (classroom)")
UF Instructional Materials Centers (1966 1980)
Lrc
School Media Centers
BT Educational Facilities
Resource Centers
RT Academic Libraries
Audiovisual Aids
Audiovisual Centers
Educational Media
Instructional Materials
Learning Laboratories
Media Specialists
Resource Materials
School Libraries

Learning Specialists (1966 1980)
USE SPECIALISTS

Learning Stations (Classroom)
USE LEARNING CENTERS (CLASSROOM)

LEARNING STRATEGIES *Oct. 1983*
CIJE: 443 RIE: 403 GC: 110
SN Rules, principles, and procedures used to facilitate learning, frequently applicable to a variety of specific learning tasks (note: for self-discovered, self-selected learning strategies, coordinate with "cognitive style")
UF Learning To Learn
NT Reading Strategies
BT Methods
RT Andragogy
Associative Learning
Behavioral Objectives
Classroom Techniques
Cognitive Development
Cognitive Processes
Cognitive Style
Discovery Learning
Educational Strategies
Encoding (Psychology)
Experiential Learning
Heuristics
Inferences
Inquiry
Intentional Learning
Language Processing
Learning
Learning Activities
Learning Modalities
Learning Modules
Learning Motivation
Learning Processes
Mastery Learning
Memory
Metacognition
Mnemonics
Observational Learning
Pacing
Problem Solving
Prompting
Psychoeducational Methods
Sequential Learning
Simulation
Skill Development
Study Skills
Task Analysis
Teaching Methods
Transfer Of Training

Learning Style
USE COGNITIVE STYLE

LEARNING THEORIES *Jul. 1966*
CIJE: 2966 RIE: 2392 GC: 810
BT Theories
RT Behaviorism
Cognitive Processes
Cognitive Restructuring
Conditioning
Generalization
Learning
Learning Plateaus
Learning Processes
Mnemonics
Paired Associate Learning
Piagetian Theory
Primacy Effect
Rote Learning
Schemata (Cognition)
Serial Learning

Learning To Learn
USE LEARNING STRATEGIES

Least Restrictive Environment (Disabled)
USE MAINSTREAMING

LEAST SQUARES STATISTICS *Oct. 1980*
CIJE: 69 RIE: 27 GC: 820
SN Statistics that are designed to provide estimates that minimize the probability of large errors by minimizing the sum of squared errors (the "least squares method" fits a curve to a given set of data such that the sum of the squares of the distances from each point of the data to the fitted curve is a minimum)
BT Statistical Analysis
Statistics
RT Correlation
Error Of Measurement
Factor Analysis
Predictive Measurement
Probability
Regression (Statistics)
Statistical Significance

LEATHER *Mar. 1980*
CIJE: 4 RIE: 12 GC: 910
SN (Note: prior to mar80, the instruction "leather crafts, use handicrafts" was carried in the thesaurus)
UF Leather Crafts
RT Art Materials
Handicrafts
Industrial Arts
Patternmaking

Leather Crafts
USE LEATHER

Leave Of Absence (1968 1980)
USE LEAVES OF ABSENCE

LEAVES OF ABSENCE *Mar. 1980*
CIJE: 76 RIE: 317 GC: 630
SN Authorized absences from duty or employment
UF Leave Of Absence (1968 1980)
NT Sabbatical Leaves
RT Attendance
Fringe Benefits
Holidays
Personnel Policy
Reentry Workers
Released Time
Scope Of Bargaining
Stopouts
Teacher Employment Benefits
Vacations

Lecture (1966 1980)
USE LECTURE METHOD

LECTURE METHOD *Mar. 1980*
CIJE: 546 RIE: 426 GC: 310
SN Teaching method in which information is presented orally to a class with a minimal amount of class participation
UF Lead Lecture Plan (1966 1980)
Lecture (1966 1980)
BT Teaching Methods
RT Conventional Instruction
Discussion (Teaching Technique)
Speeches

LEFT HANDED WRITER *Jul. 1966*
CIJE: 52 RIE: 12 GC: 120
BT Groups
RT Handwriting
Lateral Dominance

LEGAL AID *Jul. 1966*
CIJE: 106 RIE: 201 GC: 520
UF Legal Aid Projects (1966 1980)
Legal Services
RT Advocacy
Child Advocacy
Eligibility
Lawyers
Legal Assistants
Legal Costs
Legal Problems

Legal Aid Projects (1966 1980)
USE LEGAL AID

LEGAL ASSISTANTS *Dec. 1976*
CIJE: 13 RIE: 41 GC: 640
SN Trained paraprofessionals who, under a lawyer's supervision or on legal authorization, perform certain legal activities traditionally carried out only by lawyers
UF Paralegal Education #
Paralegals
BT Paraprofessional Personnel
RT Lawyers
Legal Aid
Legal Education (Professions)
Legal Problems

LEGAL COSTS *Jul. 1966*
CIJE: 14 RIE: 21 GC: 620
BT Costs
RT Legal Aid

Legal Decisions
USE COURT LITIGATION

LEGAL EDUCATION (PROFESSIONS) *Aug. 1986*
CIJE: 5 RIE: 1 GC: 400
SN Programs of academic study within a law school or other postsecondary institution that prepare students to enter the legal profession as attorneys or paralegals (note: do not confuse with "law related education" -- prior to aug86, this concept was indexed by "legal education" and "professional education")
UF Law School Education
Paralegal Education #
BT Professional Education
RT Constitutional Law
Criminal Law
International Law
Laws
Law Schools
Law Students
Lawyers
Legal Assistants

LEGAL EDUCATION (1977 1986) *Aug. 1986*
CIJE: 908 RIE: 657 GC: 400
SN Invalid descriptor -- see "law related education" and "legal education (professions)" -- (note: includes the former postings of "law instruction," merged here in jun77)

Legal Judgment
USE COURT LITIGATION

LEGAL PROBLEMS *Jul. 1966*
CIJE: 1171 RIE: 1087 GC: 610
BT Problems
RT Compliance (Legal)
Court Litigation
Discriminatory Legislation
Educational Malpractice
Lawyers
Legal Aid
Legal Assistants
Legal Responsibility
Malpractice
Torts

LEGAL RESPONSIBILITY *Jul. 1966*
CIJE: 1275 RIE: 1226 GC: 610
UF Liability (Responsibility)
NT Trust Responsibility (Government)
BT Responsibility
RT Accountability
Categorical Aid
Compliance (Legal)
Conflict Of Interest
Contracts
Copyrights
Court Judges
Court Litigation
Educational Malpractice
Fines (Penalties)
Indemnity Bonds
Intellectual Property
Laws
Legal Problems
Licensing Examinations (Professions)
Loan Repayment
Malpractice
Ownership
Patents
Torts
Treaties

Legal Secretaries
USE SECRETARIES

Legal Segregation (1966 1980)
USE DE JURE SEGREGATION

Legal Services
USE LEGAL AID

LEGENDS *Jul. 1966*
CIJE: 123 RIE: 274 GC: 430
BT Literary Genres
Literature
RT American Indian Literature
Classical Literature
Didacticism
Epics
Fiction
Folk Culture
Medieval Literature
Metaphors
Mythology

LEGISLATION *Jul. 1966*
CIJE: 694 RIE: 1146 GC: 610
SN The enactments of, or matters under consideration by, a legislative body (note: use a more specific term if possible)
NT Civil Rights Legislation
Discriminatory Legislation
Educational Legislation
Federal Legislation
Labor Legislation
Local Legislation
Minimum Wage Legislation

= Two or more Descriptors are used to represent this term.
The term's main entry shows the appropriate coordination.

Public Health Legislation
Recreation Legislation
State Legislation
RT Compliance (Legal)
Government (Administrative Body)
Hearings
Laws
Legislators
Lobbying
Policy Formation
Political Issues
Politics
Public Policy

Legislative Discrimination
USE DISCRIMINATORY LEGISLATION

Legislative Reference Libraries (1968 1980)
USE LAW LIBRARIES

LEGISLATORS *Jul. 1969*
CIJE: 206 RIE: 253 GC: 610
UF Congressmen
Congresswomen
Lawmakers
Representatives
Senators
BT Public Officials
RT City Officials
County Officials
Court Judges
Federal Legislation
Legislation
Lobbying
Local Legislation
State Legislation
State Officials

Leisure
USE LEISURE TIME

Leisure Counseling
USE LEISURE EDUCATION

LEISURE EDUCATION *Oct. 1983*
CIJE: 26 RIE: 20 GC: 400
SN Organized activities intended to help individuals or groups use non-work time in a manner conducive to physical and mental well-being
UF Leisure Counseling
BT Education
RT Leisure Time
Recreation
Recreationists

LEISURE TIME *Jul. 1966*
CIJE: 731 RIE: 617 GC: 470
UF Leisure
RT Holidays
Leisure Education
Recreation
Recreational Activities
Recreationists
Vacations

Leisure Time Reading
USE RECREATIONAL READING

Leitmotifs
USE MOTIFS

Leitmotivs
USE MOTIFS

LESBIANISM *Mar. 1980*
CIJE: 39 RIE: 28 GC: 120
UF Female Homosexuality
BT Homosexuality
RT Females

Less Commonly Taught Languages
USE UNCOMMONLY TAUGHT LANGUAGES

Lesson Notes
USE LESSON PLANS

LESSON OBSERVATION CRITERIA *Jul. 1966*
CIJE: 48 RIE: 112 GC: 820
SN Rules or standards used by observers to evaluate teachers' lessons and classroom performances
BT Criteria
RT Classroom Observation Techniques
Lesson Plans
Observation
Student Teaching
Teacher Evaluation

LESSON PLANS *Jul. 1966*
CIJE: 577 RIE: 2348 GC: 730
UF Lesson Notes
RT Curriculum Guides
Lesson Observation Criteria
Planning
Units Of Study

Lesson Units
USE UNITS OF STUDY

Letter Sound Correspondence
USE PHONEME GRAPHEME CORRESPONDENCE

LETTERS (ALPHABET) *Mar. 1971*
CIJE: 247 RIE: 122 GC: 450
BT Orthographic Symbols
RT Alphabets
Graphemes
Literacy
Phonemes

LETTERS (CORRESPONDENCE) *Aug. 1968*
CIJE: 286 RIE: 178 GC: 720
UF Correspondence (Letters)
Epistles (1970 1980)
BT Verbal Communication
RT Business Correspondence
Interpersonal Communication
Literature
Writing (Composition)

LEXICOGRAPHY *Jul. 1966*
CIJE: 180 RIE: 143 GC: 710
SN The writing or compilation of dictionaries or thesauri (note: do not confuse with "lexicology")
BT Technology
RT Definitions
Dictionaries
Etymology
Glossaries
Glottochronology
Lexicology
Thesauri
Vocabulary Development

LEXICOLOGY *Jul. 1966*
CIJE: 353 RIE: 154 GC: 710
SN Study of the vocabulary or words of a language (note: do not confuse with "lexicography")
BT Semantics
RT Comparative Analysis
Componential Analysis
Contrastive Linguistics
Definitions
Diachronic Linguistics
Dictionaries
Etymology
Glottochronology
Language Arts
Language Patterns
Lexicography
Linguistic Borrowing
Morphology (Languages)
Onomastics
Vocabulary

Lexicons
USE DICTIONARIES

Liability (Responsibility)
USE LEGAL RESPONSIBILITY

LIBERAL ARTS *Jul. 1966*
CIJE: 1160 RIE: 856 GC: 400
UF Liberal Arts Majors (1967 1980) #
NT Humanities
Mathematics
Sciences
RT Academic Education
Education Work Relationship
General Education
Technology

Liberal Arts Majors (1967 1980)
USE LIBERAL ARTS; MAJORS (STUDENTS)

Liberal Education
USE GENERAL EDUCATION

LIBERALISM *Jan. 1985*
CIJE: 55 RIE: 17 GC: 520
SN Philosophy or disposition that seeks to use social and political institutions to foster human development and well-being -- originally advocated freedom from government encroachment, but currently endorses government intervention when necessary to ensure individual welfare
RT Conservatism
Government Role
Humanistic Education
Humanization
Political Attitudes
Political Socialization
Social Values

LIBRARIANS *Jul. 1966*
CIJE: 1722 RIE: 1191 GC: 710
UF Library Specialists
BT Information Scientists
Library Personnel
RT Libraries
Library Associations
Library Education
Library Schools
Library Science
Library Technicians
Media Specialists

Librarianship
USE LIBRARY SCIENCE

LIBRARIES *Jul. 1966*
CIJE: 1203 RIE: 1283 GC: 710
SN Institutions housing collections of systematically acquired and organized information resources, and usually providing assistance to users (note: use a more specific term if possible)
NT Academic Libraries
Branch Libraries
Depository Libraries
Public Libraries
Research Libraries
School Libraries
Special Libraries
BT Information Sources
Institutions
RT Archives
Information Services
Librarians
Library Administration
Library Automation
Library Catalogs
Library Collection Development
Library Collections
Library Cooperation
Library Equipment
Library Expenditures
Library Extension
Library Facilities
Library Guides
Library Instruction
Library Materials
Library Networks
Library Personnel
Library Planning
Library Research
Library Role
Library Science
Library Services
Library Skills
Library Standards
Library Statistics
Library Surveys
Library Technical Processes
Library Technicians
Resource Centers
Shared Library Resources
Users (Information)

LIBRARY ACQUISITION *Jul. 1966*
CIJE: 513 RIE: 575 GC: 710
SN Process of acquiring library materials by purchase, gift, or exchange, as well as the development and maintenance of essential records of these acquisitions
UF Book Buying
NT Library Material Selection
BT Library Technical Processes
RT Library Collection Development
Library Materials
Nonprint Media
Publications
Purchasing

LIBRARY ADMINISTRATION *Sep. 1975*
CIJE: 499 RIE: 561 GC: 710
UF Library Administrators
Library Management
BT Institutional Administration
RT Fines (Penalties)
Libraries
Library Collection Development
Library Expenditures
Library Planning
Library Role
Library Services
Library Standards
Library Technical Processes

Library Administrators
USE LIBRARY ADMINISTRATION

Library Aides
USE LIBRARY TECHNICIANS

Library Aids
USE LIBRARY EQUIPMENT

LIBRARY ASSOCIATIONS *Jul. 1966*
CIJE: 459 RIE: 360 GC: 520
SN Groups of librarians organized on a local, district, state, national, or international basis for consideration of and action on professional matters
UF Library Organizations
BT Professional Associations
RT Information Science
Information Scientists
Librarians
Library Science

LIBRARY AUTOMATION *Aug. 1971*
CIJE: 822 RIE: 707 GC: 710
SN Application of computers and related equipment to the processing of data in libraries
UF Library Mechanization
BT Automation
RT Bibliographic Utilities
Information Technology
Libraries
Library Equipment
Library Technical Processes

Library Cataloging
USE CATALOGING

LIBRARY CATALOGS *Mar. 1980*
CIJE: 340 RIE: 265 GC: 710
SN Lists of library materials arranged in some definite order, which record, describe, and index the resources of collections, libraries, or groups of libraries (note: prior to mar80, "catalogs" was used to index this concept)
UF Dictionary Catalogs (1968 1980)
Divided Catalogs (1968 1980)
NT Book Catalogs
Card Catalogs
Union Catalogs
BT Catalogs
Reference Materials
RT Bibliographies
Cataloging
Discographies
Filmographies
Indexes
Libraries
Library Materials
Online Catalogs
Subject Index Terms

LIBRARY CIRCULATION *Jul. 1966*
CIJE: 355 RIE: 401 GC: 710
UF Book Lending
Library Loans
NT Interlibrary Loans
BT Library Services
RT Fines (Penalties)
Information Dissemination
Library Materials

Library Clerks
USE LIBRARY TECHNICIANS

= Two or more Descriptors are used to represent this term.
The term's main entry shows the appropriate coordination.

Library Clients
USE USERS (INFORMATION)

LIBRARY COLLECTION DEVELOPMENT *Apr. 1985*
CIJE: 37 RIE: 37 GC: 710
SN Activities related to building, maintaining, evaluating, and expanding library collections -- includes user needs assessment, budget management, selection policy formation, resource sharing, and weeding (note: prior to apr85, the instruction "collection development (libraries), use library acquisition" was carried in the thesaurus)
UF Collection Development (Libraries)
BT Development
RT Bibliometrics
Libraries
Library Acquisition
Library Administration
Library Collections
Library Expenditures
Library Materials
Library Material Selection
Library Planning
Library Research
Library Standards
User Needs (Information)

LIBRARY COLLECTIONS *Jul. 1966*
CIJE: 1113 RIE: 1425 GC: 710
SN Libraries' organized holdings on particular subjects
UF Library Holdings
BT Library Materials
RT Archives
Databases
Libraries
Library Collection Development
Nonprint Media
Publications

LIBRARY COOPERATION *Jul. 1966*
CIJE: 527 RIE: 1017 GC: 710
BT Institutional Cooperation
RT Consortia
Interlibrary Loans
Libraries
Library Networks
Library Services
Shared Library Resources
Union Catalogs

LIBRARY EDUCATION *Jul. 1966*
CIJE: 842 RIE: 738 GC: 400
SN Postsecondary education or training of library personnel, including professionals and paraprofessionals (note: do not confuse with "library instruction")
BT Postsecondary Education
RT Information Science
Librarians
Library Personnel
Library Schools
Library Science
Library Technicians
Professional Education
Vocational Education

Library Employees
USE LIBRARY PERSONNEL

LIBRARY EQUIPMENT *Jul. 1966*
CIJE: 139 RIE: 188 GC: 910
SN (Note: prior to mar80, the instruction "library aids, use library facilities" was carried in the thesaurus)
UF Library Aids
NT Bookmobiles
BT Equipment
RT Carrels
Educational Equipment
Libraries
Library Automation
Library Expenditures
Library Facilities
Library Materials

LIBRARY EXPENDITURES *Jul. 1966*
CIJE: 185 RIE: 437 GC: 620
BT Expenditures
RT Costs
Libraries
Library Administration
Library Collection Development
Library Equipment
Library Facilities
Library Materials
Library Services
Library Technical Processes
Operating Expenses

LIBRARY EXTENSION *Jul. 1966*
CIJE: 47 RIE: 116 GC: 710
SN Provision of special activities within and/or outside libraries to draw attention to and promote their services
BT Extension Education
Library Services
RT Bookmobiles
Information Dissemination
Libraries
Publicity
Public Relations

LIBRARY FACILITIES *Jul. 1966*
CIJE: 355 RIE: 598 GC: 920
SN Structures or spaces that are constructed, installed, or established to serve specified library functions
BT Facilities
RT Libraries
Library Equipment
Library Expenditures
Library Guides
Library Planning
Study Facilities

Library Fines
USE FINES (PENALTIES)

LIBRARY GUIDES *Jul. 1966*
CIJE: 28 RIE: 238 GC: 730
SN Handbooks designed to acquaint users with the functions, resources, and facilities of particular libraries
UF Library Handbooks
BT Guides
RT Libraries
Library Facilities
Library Instruction
Library Materials
Library Role
Library Services

Library Handbooks
USE LIBRARY GUIDES

Library Holdings
USE LIBRARY COLLECTIONS

LIBRARY INSTRUCTION *Jul. 1966*
CIJE: 439 RIE: 540 GC: 400
SN Training of patrons in the workings and use of the library (note: do not confuse with "library education" -- prior to mar80, the use of this term was not restricted by a scope note)
UF Library Orientation
BT Instruction
RT Information Seeking
Libraries
Library Guides
Library Skills
Orientation Materials
Users (Information)

Library Loans
USE LIBRARY CIRCULATION

Library Management
USE LIBRARY ADMINISTRATION

LIBRARY MATERIAL SELECTION *Jul. 1966*
CIJE: 517 RIE: 409 GC: 710
SN Professional choice of library materials from a number of alternatives on the basis of specified criteria
BT Library Acquisition
Media Selection
RT Library Collection Development
Library Materials
Nonprint Media
Publications
Reading Material Selection

LIBRARY MATERIALS *Jul. 1966*
CIJE: 622 RIE: 935 GC: 710
SN Books, periodicals, pamphlets, reports, microforms, maps, records, tapes, and other materials that are acquired by libraries (note: use a more specific term if possible)
UF Library Reference Materials #
NT Library Collections
RT Instructional Materials
Libraries
Library Acquisition
Library Catalogs
Library Circulation
Library Collection Development
Library Equipment
Library Expenditures
Library Guides
Library Material Selection
Library Planning
Library Services
Library Technical Processes
Nonprint Media
Publications
Reference Materials
Research Tools
Resource Materials
User Needs (Information)
User Satisfaction (Information)

Library Mechanization
USE LIBRARY AUTOMATION

LIBRARY NETWORKS *Jan. 1969*
CIJE: 603 RIE: 1114 GC: 710
SN Formal associations of two or more libraries, established to increase resources, improve services, and reduce costs
UF Decentralized Library Systems (1968 1980) #
Library Systems
NT Bibliographic Utilities
BT Information Networks
RT Branch Libraries
Consortia
Interlibrary Loans
Libraries
Library Cooperation
Library Planning
Library Services
Public Libraries
Shared Library Resources
Union Catalogs

Library Organizations
USE LIBRARY ASSOCIATIONS

Library Orientation
USE LIBRARY INSTRUCTION

Library Patrons
USE USERS (INFORMATION)

LIBRARY PERSONNEL *Mar. 1980*
CIJE: 188 RIE: 320 GC: 710
SN Professional, paraprofessional, and nonprofessional library employees (note: use a more specific term if possible)
UF Library Employees
NT Librarians
Library Technicians
BT Personnel
RT Libraries
Library Education
Library Services
Library Standards

LIBRARY PLANNING *Feb. 1969*
CIJE: 556 RIE: 1139 GC: 710
SN Formulation of plans for achieving library objectives
BT Planning
RT Libraries
Library Administration
Library Collection Development
Library Facilities
Library Materials
Library Networks
Library Research
Library Role
Library Science
Library Services
Library Standards
Mission Statements

Library Programs (1966 1980)
USE LIBRARY SERVICES

Library Reference Materials
USE LIBRARY MATERIALS; REFERENCE MATERIALS

Library Reference Services (1968 1980)
USE LIBRARY SERVICES; REFERENCE SERVICES

LIBRARY RESEARCH *Jul. 1966*
CIJE: 391 RIE: 625 GC: 810
SN Research about libraries (note: for research in libraries, coordinate "information seeking" with "libraries" or a more specific "library" term -- prior to mar80, this term was not restricted by a scope note -- as of oct81, use as a minor descriptor for examples of this kind of research -- use as a major descriptor only as the subject of a document)
BT Research
RT Libraries
Library Collection Development
Library Planning
Library Science
Library Statistics
Library Surveys
Use Studies

LIBRARY ROLE *Feb. 1975*
CIJE: 571 RIE: 499 GC: 710
SN Functions expected of or carried out by libraries
BT Institutional Role
RT Libraries
Library Administration
Library Guides
Library Planning
Library Services
Library Standards

LIBRARY SCHOOLS *Jul. 1966*
CIJE: 460 RIE: 188 GC: 340
SN Professional schools, departments, or divisions organized and maintained by an institution of higher education for the preparation of students in professional librarianship
BT Colleges
RT Information Science
Librarians
Library Education
Library Science
Professional Education

LIBRARY SCIENCE *Jul. 1966*
CIJE: 590 RIE: 504 GC: 710
SN Study and profession of the administration of libraries and their contents -- includes the procedures by which libraries recognize, acquire, organize, disseminate, and utilize information
UF Librarianship
BT Information Science
RT Librarians
Libraries
Library Associations
Library Education
Library Planning
Library Research
Library Schools
Library Services

LIBRARY SERVICES *Jul. 1966*
CIJE: 2631 RIE: 3228 GC: 710
SN Acquiring, selecting, evaluating, organizing, and disseminating information in libraries
UF Library Programs (1966 1980)
Library Reference Services (1968 1980) #
NT Library Circulation
Library Extension
Library Technical Processes
BT Information Services
RT Ancillary School Services
Bookmobiles
Information Centers
Libraries
Library Administration
Library Cooperation
Library Expenditures
Library Guides
Library Materials
Library Networks
Library Personnel
Library Planning
Library Role
Library Science
Library Standards
Library Surveys
Outreach Programs

= Two or more Descriptors are used to represent this term.
The term's main entry shows the appropriate coordination.

Reference Services
Selective Dissemination Of Information
User Needs (Information)
Users (Information)
User Satisfaction (Information)

LIBRARY SKILLS *Jul. 1966*
CIJE: 256 RIE: 421 GC: 710
SN Competency in the use of a library
BT Skills
RT Libraries
Library Instruction
Research Skills
Users (Information)

Library Specialists
USE LIBRARIANS

LIBRARY STANDARDS *Jul. 1966*
CIJE: 210 RIE: 414 GC: 710
SN Criteria by which the quality of library services, operations, personnel, facilities, equipment, etc. are judged
BT Standards
RT Libraries
Library Administration
Library Collection Development
Library Personnel
Library Planning
Library Role
Library Services
Library Statistics
Library Surveys

LIBRARY STATISTICS *Apr. 1985*
CIJE: 41 RIE: 178 GC: 730
BT Statistical Data
RT Libraries
Library Research
Library Standards
Library Surveys
Statistical Analysis

LIBRARY SURVEYS *Jul. 1966*
CIJE: 493 RIE: 990 GC: 810
BT Surveys
RT Libraries
Library Research
Library Services
Library Standards
Library Statistics
User Needs (Information)
User Satisfaction (Information)
Use Studies

Library Systems
USE LIBRARY NETWORKS

Library Technical Assistants
USE LIBRARY TECHNICIANS

LIBRARY TECHNICAL PROCESSES *Jul. 1966*
CIJE: 673 RIE: 764 GC: 710
SN Acquisition, preparation, and organization of library materials for use
UF Technical Processes (Libraries)
Technical Services (Libraries)
NT Library Acquisition
BT Library Services
RT Abstracting
Bibliographic Utilities
Cataloging
Classification
Indexing
Information Processing
Information Technology
Libraries
Library Administration
Library Automation
Library Expenditures
Library Materials

LIBRARY TECHNICIANS *Jul. 1966*
CIJE: 78 RIE: 178 GC: 710
SN Paraprofessional or nonprofessional library and information personnel, proficient in one or more functional areas, who provide support to professional librarians
UF Library Aides
Library Clerks
Library Technical Assistants
NT Medical Record Technicians
BT Library Personnel
RT Librarians
Libraries
Library Education
Paraprofessional Personnel

Library User Needs
USE USER NEEDS (INFORMATION)

Library User Satisfaction
USE USER SATISFACTION (INFORMATION)

Library Users
USE USERS (INFORMATION)

Licensed Nurses
USE NURSES

Licensing
USE CERTIFICATION

LICENSING EXAMINATIONS (PROFESSIONS) *Aug. 1986*
CIJE: RIE: GC: 830
SN Legally required qualifying examinations (as from a state) that individuals must pass before obtaining a license to practice a profession
BT Tests
RT Certification
Equivalency Tests
Legal Responsibility
Mastery Tests
Occupational Tests
Predictive Measurement
Professional Education
Standardized Tests
State Licensing Boards

Lie Detectors
USE POLYGRAPHS

Life Costs (Facilities And Equipment)
USE LIFE CYCLE COSTING

LIFE CYCLE COSTING *Oct. 1976*
CIJE: 38 RIE: 46 GC: 620
SN Calculation of initial facility or equipment costs, plus operation and maintenance expenses (including energy and replacement costs) for life expectancy of the facility or equipment
UF Life Costs (Facilities And Equipment)
BT Evaluation Methods
RT Building Design
Building Operation
Building Plans
Building Systems
Construction Costs
Cost Effectiveness
Educational Facilities Design
Educational Facilities Planning
Energy Conservation
Energy Management
Equipment Evaluation
Facility Guidelines
Facility Planning
Maintenance
Operating Expenses
School Construction

Life Histories
USE BIOGRAPHIES

Life Quality
USE QUALITY OF LIFE

LIFE SATISFACTION *Mar. 1982*
CIJE: 195 RIE: 137 GC: 230
SN Contentment with life, particularly in regard to the fulfillment of one's needs and expectations
BT Attitudes
RT Individual Power
Job Satisfaction
Marital Satisfaction
Mental Health
Need Gratification
Quality Of Life
Quality Of Working Life
Self Actualization
Social Indicators
Values
Well Being

Life Sciences
USE BIOLOGICAL SCIENCES

Life Skills
USE DAILY LIVING SKILLS

Life Span Education
USE LIFELONG LEARNING

LIFE STYLE *Oct. 1973*
CIJE: 792 RIE: 813 GC: 520
SN Manner of living chosen as a personal response to the social and cultural milieu
UF Alternative Life Styles
BT Behavior
RT Cultural Influences
Feminism
Humanization
Individual Psychology
Personal Autonomy
Role Theory
Social History
Sociocultural Patterns

Lifelong Education
USE LIFELONG LEARNING

LIFELONG LEARNING *Mar. 1980*
CIJE: 902 RIE: 1042 GC: 340
SN Process by which individuals consciously acquire formal or informal education throughout their life spans for personal development or career advancement
UF Continuous Learning (1967 1980)
Education Permanente
Lifelong Education
Life Span Education
Permanent Education
Recurrent Education
BT Learning
RT Adult Education
Adult Learning
Community Education
Continuing Education
Continuing Education Units
Correspondence Study
Distance Education
Experience
Experiential Learning
Independent Study
Nonformal Education
Professional Continuing Education
Self Help Programs
Student Educational Objectives

LIFETIME SPORTS *Dec. 1975*
CIJE: 72 RIE: 78 GC: 470
SN Sports where participation can be carried on throughout one's lifetime -- generally includes (but is not necessarily limited to) a variety of individual and dual sports for which facilities are widely available, and body contact is limited or unnecessary
BT Athletics
RT Archery
Bowling
Community Recreation Programs
Exercise
Golf
Individual Activities
Recreational Activities
Swimming
Tennis
Track And Field

LIFTING *Jul. 1966*
CIJE: 5 RIE: 17 GC: 630
SN Act of raising or elevating a weighted object
NT Weightlifting
BT Physical Activities
RT Job Skills

LIGHT *Sep. 1968*
CIJE: 421 RIE: 74 GC: 490
SN (Note: use "lighting" for the illumination of facilities or the process of creating artificial light -- prior to apr80, this differentiation was not made)
UF Daylight (1970 1980)
Light Radiation
Optical Spectrum
Visible Radiation
Visible Spectrum
BT Radiation
RT Climate
Color
Contrast
Glare
Lasers
Lighting
Luminescence
Optics
Photosynthesis
Physics
Relativity
Solar Energy
Spectroscopy
Visual Environment

Light Amplifiers (Lasers)
USE LASERS

Light Radiation
USE LIGHT

Lighted Playgrounds (1966 1980)
USE PLAYGROUNDS

LIGHTING *Jul. 1966*
CIJE: 218 RIE: 293 GC: 920
UF Illumination Levels (1968 1980)
Lights (1966 1980)
Outdoor Lighting (1971 1980)
NT Television Lighting
RT Climate Control
Contrast
Electrical Systems
Flexible Lighting Design
Glare
Human Factors Engineering
Light
Lighting Design
Luminescence
Optics
Utilities
Visual Environment
Windowless Rooms
Windows

LIGHTING DESIGN *Apr. 1970*
CIJE: 106 RIE: 45 GC: 920
NT Flexible Lighting Design
BT Design
RT Architecture
Building Design
Contrast
Design Requirements
Glare
Interior Design
Lighting
Windowless Rooms

Lights (1966 1980)
USE LIGHTING

Lignite
USE COAL

LIMITED ENGLISH SPEAKING *Aug. 1982*
CIJE: 104 RIE: 706 GC: 450
SN Individuals who know english as a foreign language but without sufficient proficiency to participate fully in an english-speaking society
BT Groups
RT Bilingual Education
Bilingual Education Programs
Bilingualism
Bilingual Teacher Aides
Bilingual Teachers
English (Second Language)
Ethnic Groups
Language Dominance
Language Proficiency
Minority Groups
Native Speakers
Non English Speaking
Second Language Learning
Spanish Speaking

LINEAR PROGRAMING *Jul. 1966*
CIJE: 63 RIE: 145 GC: 480
SN Technique, often used in operations research or business and economic planning, to solve problems involving many variables where a best value or set of values is to be found (e.g., determining the blend of gasoline that yields the highest octane at the minimum cost)
BT Mathematical Applications
RT Economic Research
Management Systems
Mathematical Models
Monte Carlo Methods
Operations Research

Linear Regression
USE REGRESSION (STATISTICS)

LINGALA *Jul. 1966*
CIJE: RIE: 4 GC: 440
UF Mangala
BT Bantu Languages

Linguistic Anthropology
USE ANTHROPOLOGICAL LINGUISTICS

LINGUISTIC BORROWING *Oct. 1976*
CIJE: 98 RIE: 96 GC: 450
SN Process whereby one language absorbs words and expressions, and possibly sounds and grammatical forms, from another language and adapts them to its own use
UF Loan Words
Phonological Borrowing
Syntactic Borrowing
Word Borrowing
BT Language Variation
RT Code Switching (Language)
Creoles
Descriptive Linguistics
Diachronic Linguistics
Language Patterns
Language Usage
Lexicology
Linguistics
Morphology (Languages)
Phonology
Pidgins
Sociolinguistics
Syntax
Vocabulary

LINGUISTIC COMPETENCE *Mar. 1969*
CIJE: 441 RIE: 441 GC: 450
SN Concept in chomskyan theory referring to the intuitive knowledge of the rules of a language that enables native speaker-hearers to understand and produce sentences they have never heard or uttered before (note: prior to mar80, the use of this term was not restricted by a scope note)
BT Linguistic Theory
RT Communicative Competence (Languages)
Comprehension
Interlanguage
Language Acquisition
Language Proficiency
Language Skills
Linguistic Performance
Linguistics
Psycholinguistics
Verbal Ability

Linguistic Difficulty (Contrastive)
USE INTERFERENCE (LANGUAGE)

LINGUISTIC DIFFICULTY (INHERENT) *Sep. 1974*
CIJE: 38 RIE: 26 GC: 450
SN Universal difficulty (or ease) in articulating, auditing, or processing particular linguistic units and unit sequences
RT Error Analysis (Language)
Language Acquisition
Language Processing
Language Universals
Linguistics
Linguistic Theory
Native Speakers
Psycholinguistics

Linguistic Patterns (1966 1980)
USE LANGUAGE PATTERNS

LINGUISTIC PERFORMANCE *Mar. 1969*
CIJE: 292 RIE: 347 GC: 450
SN Concept in chomskyan theory referring to the actual production and comprehension of oral or written language -- reflects linguistic competence but is also affected by situational variables such as fatigue and distraction (note: prior to mar80, the use of this term was not restricted by a scope note)
BT Linguistic Theory
RT Code Switching (Language)
Communicative Competence (Languages)
Interlanguage
Language Acquisition
Language Processing
Language Proficiency
Language Skills
Linguistic Competence
Linguistics
Psycholinguistics
Verbal Ability

Linguistic Research
USE LANGUAGE RESEARCH

Linguistic Styles
USE LANGUAGE STYLES

LINGUISTIC THEORY *Jul. 1966*
CIJE: 1506 RIE: 1360 GC: 450
UF Transformation Theory (Language) (1967 1980) #
NT Case (Grammar)
Generative Grammar
Generative Phonology
Linguistic Competence
Linguistic Performance
Semiotics
Structural Grammar
Traditional Grammar
BT Theories
RT Anthropological Linguistics
Componential Analysis
Computational Linguistics
Deep Structure
Language Processing
Language Universals
Linguistic Difficulty (Inherent)
Linguistics
Neurolinguistics
Psycholinguistics
Sociolinguistics
Surface Structure

Linguistic Universals
USE LANGUAGE UNIVERSALS

LINGUISTICS *Jul. 1966*
CIJE: 1052 RIE: 1498 GC: 450
SN The study of language -- this term is used primarily for material dealing with the field of linguistics as a whole (note: use a more specific term if possible -- prior to mar80, the use of this term was not restricted by a scope note)
UF Philology
NT Anthropological Linguistics
Applied Linguistics
Computational Linguistics
Contrastive Linguistics
Descriptive Linguistics
Diachronic Linguistics
Distinctive Features (Language)
Mathematical Linguistics
Neurolinguistics
Paralinguistics
Phonology
Psycholinguistics
Sociolinguistics
Structural Linguistics
RT Deep Structure
Dialects
English
English (Second Language)
Glottochronology
Language
Language Patterns
Language Processing
Language Research
Language Usage
Linguistic Borrowing
Linguistic Competence
Linguistic Difficulty (Inherent)
Linguistic Performance
Linguistic Theory
Middle English
Miscue Analysis
North American English
Old English
Onomastics
Phoneme Grapheme Correspondence
Phonemics
Semiotics
Sentence Diagraming
Social Dialects
Speech
Speech Communication
Structural Analysis (Linguistics)
Surface Structure
Traditional Grammar
Verbal Communication

LINKING AGENTS *Oct. 1980*
CIJE: 43 RIE: 398 GC: 330
SN Individuals or groups who attempt change by connecting knowledge and related resources to practitioners -- the linker's role often includes providing necessary support for adoption/adaptation of new ideas or developments
BT Change Agents
RT Adoption (Ideas)
Diffusion (Communication)
Information Dissemination
Information Transfer
Information Utilization
Innovation
Networks
Outreach Programs
Research And Development
Research And Development Centers
Research Utilization
Resource Allocation
Technical Assistance
Technology Transfer
Theory Practice Relationship

LIPREADING *Jul. 1966*
CIJE: 106 RIE: 49 GC: 220
UF Speech Reading
BT Oral Communication Method
RT Cued Speech
Deaf Interpreting
Hearing Therapy
Total Communication

LISTENING *Jul. 1966*
CIJE: 242 RIE: 383 GC: 310
BT Language Arts
RT Attention
Auditory Stimuli
Language Processing
Listening Comprehension
Listening Habits
Listening Skills
Speech Communication

LISTENING COMPREHENSION *Jul. 1966*
CIJE: 866 RIE: 968 GC: 110
UF Auditory Comprehension
Aural Comprehension
BT Comprehension
RT Auditory Perception
Auditory Training
Aural Learning
Language Skills
Listening
Listening Comprehension Tests
Listening Habits
Listening Skills
Oral Interpretation
Receptive Language

LISTENING COMPREHENSION TESTS *Mar. 1980*
CIJE: 77 RIE: 93 GC: 830
SN Tests of aural comprehension either in native or foreign language
UF Listening Tests (1970 1980)
BT Verbal Tests
RT Achievement Tests
Language Tests
Listening Comprehension
Listening Skills

LISTENING GROUPS *Jul. 1966*
CIJE: 26 RIE: 36 GC: 310
SN Organized groups that meet to hear radio or television programs and discuss the subjects presented
BT Discussion Groups
RT Audiences
Audiovisual Instruction
Educational Radio
Educational Television
Group Instruction
Mass Instruction

LISTENING HABITS *Jul. 1966*
CIJE: 71 RIE: 80 GC: 120
RT Habit Formation
Listening
Listening Comprehension
Listening Skills

LISTENING SKILLS *Jul. 1966*
CIJE: 598 RIE: 1001 GC: 120
SN Skills involved in literal, evaluative, and critical listening
BT Audiolingual Skills
RT Listening
Listening Comprehension
Listening Comprehension Tests
Listening Habits

Listening Tests (1970 1980)
USE LISTENING COMPREHENSION TESTS

LITERACY *Jul. 1966*
CIJE: 676 RIE: 700 GC: 460
SN Ability to read and write -- also, communication with written or printed symbols (i.e., reading and writing)
UF Literacy Skills
NT Adult Literacy
Functional Literacy
Reading
Scientific Literacy
Writing (Composition)
RT Basic Skills
Illiteracy
Letters (Alphabet)
Literacy Education
Reading Skills
Reading Writing Relationship
Writing Skills

Literacy Classes (1966 1980)
USE LITERACY EDUCATION

LITERACY EDUCATION *Jul. 1966*
CIJE: 549 RIE: 834 GC: 460
SN Teaching of reading, writing and social skills to prepare persons to function at the fifth grade level
UF Literacy Classes (1966 1980)
BT Education
RT Adult Basic Education
Adult Literacy
Adult Reading Programs
Basic Skills
Functional Literacy
Functional Reading
Literacy
Minimum Competencies
Reading Instruction
Reading Skills
Writing Skills

Literacy Skills
USE LITERACY

Literary Analysis (1968 1980)
USE LITERARY CRITICISM

Literary Conventions (1968 1980)
USE LITERARY DEVICES

LITERARY CRITICISM *Jul. 1966*
CIJE: 2171 RIE: 1171 GC: 430
SN Analysis, interpretation, or evaluation of literature -- often includes the examination of literary contexts, types, themes, trends, history, or principles (note: do not confuse with "writing evaluation" -- prior to mar80, the use of this term was not restricted by a scope note)
UF Literary Analysis (1968 1980)
NT Rhetorical Criticism
RT Book Reviews
Content Analysis
Critical Reading
Didacticism
Evaluation
Literary Devices
Literary Genres
Literary History
Literary Styles
Literature
Reader Response

LITERARY DEVICES *Mar. 1980*
CIJE: 321 RIE: 249 GC: 430
SN Modes or techniques of expression, usually, but not always, literary
UF Literary Conventions (1968 1980)
NT Characterization
Dialogs (Literary)
Figurative Language
Monologs
Motifs
Narration

= Two or more Descriptors are used to represent this term.
The term's main entry shows the appropriate coordination.

RT Comedy
Content Area Writing
Creative Writing
Descriptive Writing
Drama
Fiction
Humor
Language Styles
Literary Criticism
Literary Genres
Literary Styles
Literature
Nonfiction
Parallelism (Literary)
Playwriting
Rhetoric
Symbols (Literary)
Tragedy
Writing (Composition)

LITERARY DISCRIMINATION (1966 1980) *Mar. 1980*
CIJE: 58 RIE: 73 GC: 430
SN Invalid descriptor -- use "literary criticism," "reading comprehension," "critical reading," etc.

LITERARY GENRES *Jul. 1966*
CIJE: 189 RIE: 216 GC: 430
SN Divisions of literature into categories or classes that group works by form or type, such as biographies, essays, or poetry, rather than by movements such as naturalism, realism, or romanticism
NT Ballads
Biographies
Chronicles
Diaries
Epics
Essays
Haiku
Hymns
Legends
Novels
Odes
Parody
Satire
Scripts
Short Stories
Skits
Sonnets
Tales
RT Comedy
Drama
Fiction
Humor
Literary Criticism
Literary Devices
Literary History
Literary Styles
Literature
Nonfiction
Poetry
Prose
Tragedy
World Literature

LITERARY HISTORY *Jul. 1966*
CIJE: 285 RIE: 236 GC: 430
SN Study of literary trends and movements, as well as the development of various branches or genres of literature (e.g., australian literary history, history of the polish novel, etc.)
BT Intellectual History
RT Classical Literature
Eighteenth Century Literature
Fifteenth Century Literature
Literary Criticism
Literary Genres
Literary Styles
Literature
Nineteenth Century Literature
Old English Literature
Seventeenth Century Literature
Sixteenth Century Literature
Twentieth Century Literature
World Literature

LITERARY INFLUENCES (1969 1980) *Mar. 1980*
CIJE: 301 RIE: 73 GC: 430
SN Invalid descriptor -- used inconsistently in indexing -- see such descriptors as "literature," "literary styles," "figurative language," "literary criticism," "literary history," etc.

LITERARY MOOD (1970 1980) *Mar. 1980*
CIJE: 24 RIE: 20 GC: 430
SN Invalid descriptor -- used inconsistently in indexing -- see such descriptors as "literature," "literary criticism," "literary devices," "figurative language," etc.

LITERARY PERSPECTIVE (1969 1980) *Mar. 1980*
CIJE: 254 RIE: 65 GC: 430
SN Invalid descriptor -- see such descriptors as "literature," "literary devices," "literary criticism," "literary styles," "figurative language," etc.

LITERARY STYLES *Jul. 1969*
CIJE: 775 RIE: 199 GC: 430
SN Aspects of written language that distinguish and characterize individual writers, literary movements, or literary periods
RT Art Expression
Characterization
Drama
Expressionism
Films
Impressionism
Irony
Literary Criticism
Literary Devices
Literary Genres
Literary History
Literature
Modernism
Music
Mysticism
Naturalism
Neoclassicism
Nonfiction
Parody
Poetry
Prose
Realism
Romanticism
Satire
Surrealism
Symbolism
Writing (Composition)

LITERATURE *Jul. 1966*
CIJE: 1736 RIE: 1945 GC: 430
NT Adolescent Literature
African Literature
American Indian Literature
Australian Literature
Baroque Literature
Biblical Literature
Black Literature
Childrens Literature
Classical Literature
Czech Literature
Drama
Eighteenth Century Literature
English Literature
Fifteenth Century Literature
French Literature
German Literature
Greek Literature
Italian Literature
Latin American Literature
Legends
Medieval Literature
Nineteenth Century Literature
North American Literature
Pastoral Literature
Poetry
Polish Literature
Prose
Renaissance Literature
Russian Literature
Seventeenth Century Literature
Sixteenth Century Literature
Spanish Literature
Twentieth Century Literature
Victorian Literature
BT Humanities
RT Art
Authors
Books
Choral Speaking
Diaries
Figurative Language
Folk Culture
History
Humanism
Humor
Journalism
Language Arts
Letters (Correspondence)
Literary Criticism
Literary Devices
Literary Genres
Literary History
Literary Styles
Literature Appreciation
Literature Reviews
Local Color Writing
Mythology
Philosophy
Poets
Popular Culture
Rhetorical Criticism
Symbols (Literary)
World Literature

LITERATURE APPRECIATION *Jul. 1966*
CIJE: 1717 RIE: 1395 GC: 400
UF Reading Enjoyment
RT Choral Speaking
Literature
Oral Interpretation
Reader Response
Recreational Reading

LITERATURE GUIDES (1966 1980) *Mar. 1980*
CIJE: 28 RIE: 159 GC: 730
SN Invalid descriptor -- used indiscriminately in indexing -- see such descriptors as "bibliographies," "literature reviews," etc.

LITERATURE PROGRAMS (1966 1980) *Mar. 1980*
CIJE: 138 RIE: 190 GC: 400
SN Invalid descriptor -- coordinate "literature" or its narrower terms with such descriptors as "english curriculum," "reading programs," "second language programs," etc.

LITERATURE REVIEWS *Jul. 1966*
CIJE: 4698 RIE: 5354 GC: 730
SN Surveys of the materials published on a topic (note: prior to mar80, "research reviews (publications)" was also a valid descriptor)
UF Literature Surveys
Reviews Of The Literature
BT Publications
RT Anthologies
Bibliographies
Bibliometrics
Book Reviews
Literature
Meta Analysis
Research
Research Methodology
Research Tools
State Of The Art Reviews
Surveys

Literature Searches
USE BIBLIOGRAPHIES

Literature Surveys
USE LITERATURE REVIEWS

LITHUANIAN *Nov. 1970*
CIJE: 3 RIE: 8 GC: 440
BT Baltic Languages

Litigation
USE COURT LITIGATION

Litter
USE SOLID WASTES

LIVESTOCK *Aug. 1969*
CIJE: 33 RIE: 98 GC: 410
BT Animals
RT Animal Husbandry
Horses
Veterinary Medicine

Livestock Feed Stores
USE FEED STORES

Livestock Production
USE AGRICULTURAL PRODUCTION

Livestock Technology
USE ANIMAL HUSBANDRY

LIVING LEARNING CENTERS *Mar. 1980*
CIJE: 21 RIE: 14 GC: 920
SN Residential facilities of a higher education institution designed to enhance students' educational experiences by enabling them to integrate their academic activities with their ordinary living activities (note: prior to mar80, this concept may have been indexed under "residential colleges")
BT Educational Facilities
RT College Buildings
College Housing
College Role
Colleges
Continuing Education Centers
Dormitories
Experiential Learning
Group Experience
Integrated Activities
On Campus Students
Peer Relationship
Relevance (Education)
Residential Colleges

Living Quarters
USE HOUSING

LIVING STANDARDS *Jul. 1966*
CIJE: 109 RIE: 284 GC: 520
BT Standards
RT Advantaged
Community Development
Developed Nations
Developing Nations
Disadvantaged
Economic Factors
Environmental Standards
Quality Of Life
Social Indicators

Loan Applicants
USE FINANCIAL AID APPLICANTS

LOAN REPAYMENT *Feb. 1978*
CIJE: 48 RIE: 133 GC: 620
SN Repayment of financial debts or credits
UF Defaulting On Loans
RT Costs
Credit (Finance)
Educational Finance
Financial Aid Applicants
Financial Needs
Financial Problems
Financial Services
Financial Support
Income Contingent Loans
Interest (Finance)
Legal Responsibility
Money Management
Student Financial Aid
Student Loan Programs
Student Responsibility

Loan Words
USE LINGUISTIC BORROWING

LOBBYING *Mar. 1980*
CIJE: 158 RIE: 100 GC: 610
SN Conducting activities to influence public officials, especially members of a legislative body, on legislation
UF Political Advocacy
BT Activities
RT Activism
Institutional Advancement
Legislation
Legislators
Political Influences
Political Issues
Political Power
Politics
Position Papers
Public Officials

LOCAL AREA NETWORKS *Aug. 1986*
CIJE: 6 RIE: 4 GC: 710
SN Interconnected computer equipment and peripherals contained within a small geographic area, typically a single building or plant
BT Computer Networks
RT Microcomputers
Minicomputers
Office Machines
Office Management

Local Autonomy (Of Schools)
USE SCHOOL DISTRICT AUTONOMY

LOCAL COLOR WRITING *May. 1969*
CIJE: 38 RIE: 25 GC: 430
SN Composition that emphasizes the speech, dress, mannerisms, habits, or peculiarities of particular places or regions
BT Writing (Composition)
RT Literature
Poetry

Local Community Programs
USE COMMUNITY PROGRAMS

Local Control (Of Schools)
USE SCHOOL DISTRICT AUTONOMY

Local Education Agencies
USE SCHOOL DISTRICTS

Local Education Authorities
USE SCHOOL DISTRICTS

LOCAL GOVERNMENT *Sep. 1971*
CIJE: 252 RIE: 617 GC: 610
UF County Government
NT City Government
BT Government (Administrative Body)
RT Community
Community Services
County Officials
Government Employees
Government School Relationship
Local Legislation
Public Agencies
Revenue Sharing
School District Autonomy
School Districts
Tribal Sovereignty

LOCAL HISTORY *Nov. 1974*
CIJE: 215 RIE: 346 GC: 430
SN History associated with a neighborhood, town, county, or other specific subdivision of a larger geopolitical region
UF Community History
County History
BT History
RT Community Characteristics
Community Study
Family History
Local Issues
Oral History
Social History
State History

Local Housing Authorities (1966 1980)
USE HOUSING

Local Information Services
USE COMMUNITY INFORMATION SERVICES

LOCAL ISSUES *Jul. 1966*
CIJE: 155 RIE: 245 GC: 610
SN Matters of concern to a particular community, neighborhood, or locality
RT Bond Issues
Community
Community Action
Community Attitudes
Community Change
Community Characteristics
Community Coordination
Community Problems
Community Support
Elections
Local History
Local Legislation
Political Issues
Voting

LOCAL LEGISLATION *Jan. 1979*
CIJE: 11 RIE: 34 GC: 610
SN Ordinances and regulations relating to a particular locality within a state or province
UF Community Legislation
Community Recreation Legislation (1966 1978) #
Local Recreation Legislation (1966 1978) #
BT Legislation
RT Federal Legislation
Laws
Legislators
Local Government
Local Issues
State Legislation

LOCAL NORMS *Mar. 1980*
CIJE: 11 RIE: 61 GC: 820
SN Statistical description of the typical performance, behavior, achievement, function, etc. of a particular locality (e.g., school, school district, community, corporation, etc.) (note: use only for numerical data and not for subjectively described standards)
UF County Norms
District Norms
School District Norms
BT Norms
RT National Norms
State Norms

Local Recreation Legislation (1966 1978)
USE LOCAL LEGISLATION; RECREATION LEGISLATION

Local Unions (1966 1980)
USE UNIONS

LOCATIONAL SKILLS (SOCIAL STUDIES) *Jul. 1966*
CIJE: 48 RIE: 64 GC: 400
SN Ability to locate physical features and political or cultural boundaries of the earth
BT Skills
RT Cartography
Maps
Map Skills
Social Studies
Study Skills

LOCKER ROOMS *Jul. 1966*
CIJE: 2 RIE: 12 GC: 920
BT Facilities
RT Athletics
Equipment Storage
Physical Education Facilities
Sanitary Facilities

LOCOMOTIVE ENGINEERS *Jul. 1966*
CIJE: RIE: 4 GC: 640
BT Skilled Workers
RT Diesel Engines
Engines
Mechanics (Process)

LOCUS OF CONTROL *Jan. 1973*
CIJE: 1080 RIE: 682 GC: 120
SN Personality construct referring to an individuals perception of the locus of events as determined internally by his own behavior vs. fate, luck, or external forces
UF Internal External Locus Of Control
BT Personality Traits
RT Attribution Theory
Congruence (Psychology)
Delay Of Gratification
Field Dependence Independence
Individual Power
Personal Autonomy
Self Concept

LOGARITHMS *Oct. 1984*
CIJE: 38 RIE: 12 GC: 480
SN Exponents that indicate the power to which base numbers are raised to produce given numbers
BT Numbers
RT Functions (Mathematics)

LOGIC *Jul. 1966*
CIJE: 453 RIE: 338 GC: 400
NT Mathematical Logic
BT Philosophy
RT Logical Thinking
Paradox
Validity

LOGICAL THINKING *Jul. 1966*
CIJE: 796 RIE: 621 GC: 110
SN Process of reasoning from premise to conclusion
NT Deduction
Induction
BT Cognitive Processes
RT Abstract Reasoning
Artificial Intelligence
Convergent Thinking
Critical Thinking
Formal Operations
Heuristics
Inferences
Logic
Piagetian Theory
Problem Solving

LONELINESS *Aug. 1980*
CIJE: 73 RIE: 45 GC: 230
SN Unhappiness caused by a lack of friends or companions
BT Psychological Patterns
RT Alienation
Anger
Depression (Psychology)
Emotional Problems
Social Isolation

LONG RANGE PLANNING *Oct. 1979*
CIJE: 399 RIE: 589 GC: 330
SN Systematic planning based on assumptions about situations and needs beyond a 1-year period
UF Futures Planning
Long Term Planning
BT Planning
RT Delphi Technique
Futures (Of Society)
Management Systems
Master Plans
Operations Research
Planning Commissions
Prediction
Trend Analysis

LONG TERM MEMORY *Nov. 1981*
CIJE: 50 RIE: 29 GC: 110
SN Process of recalling information or performing appropriately a long time after instruction or presentation of material -- characterized by slow decay and a large volume of remembered material (in contrast to "short term memory")
BT Memory
RT Short Term Memory

Long Term Planning
USE LONG RANGE PLANNING

LONGITUDINAL STUDIES *Jul. 1966*
CIJE: 1566 RIE: 2553 GC: 810
NT Followup Studies
BT Case Studies
RT Attrition (Research Studies)
Cross Sectional Studies
Incidence
Outcomes Of Education
Sampling
Trend Analysis

Look Guess Method
USE SIGHT METHOD

Look Say Method
USE SIGHT METHOD

LOOP INDUCTION SYSTEMS *May. 1969*
CIJE: 10 RIE: 2 GC: 220
SN Electronic system consisting of microphone, amplifier, and a loop of wire circling the room. sound is transmitted to students through coils in their hearing aids
BT Audiovisual Communications
RT Electronic Equipment
Hearing Aids
Hearing Impairments
Sensory Aids

LOW ABILITY STUDENTS (1967 1980) *Mar. 1980*
CIJE: 147 RIE: 293 GC: 360
SN Invalid descriptor -- see "academic ability," "slow learners," "learning problems," "low achievement," "educationally disadvantaged," etc.

LOW ACHIEVEMENT *Mar. 1980*
CIJE: 462 RIE: 851 GC: 120
UF Low Achievement Factors (1966 1980)
Low Achievers (1966 1980)
BT Achievement
RT Academic Failure
Failure
Fear Of Success
Grade Repetition
High Achievement
Learning Problems
Underachievement

Low Achievement Factors (1966 1980)
USE LOW ACHIEVEMENT

Low Achievers (1966 1980)
USE LOW ACHIEVEMENT

LOW INCOME *Jul. 1966*
CIJE: 80 RIE: 281 GC: 620
BT Income
RT Lower Class
Low Income Counties
Low Income Groups
Low Income States
Poverty
Poverty Programs
Underemployment

LOW INCOME COUNTIES *Jul. 1966*
CIJE: 6 RIE: 51 GC: 550
BT Geographic Regions
RT Low Income
Low Income Groups
Low Income States
Poverty Areas

LOW INCOME GROUPS *Jul. 1966*
CIJE: 449 RIE: 1162 GC: 520
BT Groups
RT Economically Disadvantaged
Lower Class
Low Income
Low Income Counties
Low Income States
Poverty
Welfare Recipients

LOW INCOME STATES *Jul. 1966*
CIJE: 2 RIE: 10 GC: 550
BT Geographic Regions
RT Low Income
Low Income Counties
Low Income Groups
Poverty Areas

Low Level Aspiration (1966 1980)
USE ASPIRATION

Low Motivation (1966 1980)
USE MOTIVATION

LOW RENT HOUSING *Jul. 1966*
CIJE: 31 RIE: 40 GC: 550
NT Public Housing
BT Housing

LOW VISION AIDS *Jun. 1977*
CIJE: 27 RIE: 23 GC: 220
SN Lenses or devices other than conventional eyeglasses used to improve visual functioning in the partially sighted
BT Sensory Aids
RT Blindness
Electromechanical Aids
Large Type Materials
Magnification Methods
Mobility Aids
Partial Vision
Vision
Visual Impairments

LOWER CLASS *Jul. 1966*
CIJE: 209 RIE: 283 GC: 520
UF Lower Class Males (1966 1980) #
BT Social Class
RT Disadvantaged
Lower Class Parents
Lower Class Students
Lower Middle Class
Low Income
Low Income Groups
Middle Class
Poverty
Upper Class
Working Class

= Two or more Descriptors are used to represent this term.
The term's main entry shows the appropriate coordination.

Lower Class Males (1966 1980)
USE LOWER CLASS; MALES

LOWER CLASS PARENTS *Jul. 1966*
CIJE: 28 RIE: 43 GC: 510
BT Parents
RT Lower Class

LOWER CLASS STUDENTS *Jul. 1966*
CIJE: 144 RIE: 148 GC: 360
BT Students
RT Disadvantaged Youth
Lower Class
Middle Class Students

LOWER MIDDLE CLASS *Jul. 1966*
CIJE: 25 RIE: 27 GC: 520
BT Social Class
RT Lower Class
Middle Class
Upper Class
Working Class

LOYALTY OATHS *Apr. 1969*
CIJE: 18 RIE: 8 GC: 630
RT Behavior Standards
Boards Of Education
Codes Of Ethics
Employment Practices
Employment Qualifications
Government (Administrative Body)
Patriotism
Personnel Policy

Lozanov Method
USE SUGGESTOPEDIA

Lrc
USE LEARNING RESOURCES CENTERS

Lsd
USE LYSERGIC ACID DIETHYLAMIDE

LUBRICANTS *Jul. 1966*
CIJE: 2 RIE: 24 GC: 910
UF Grease
Motor Oils
RT Engines
Petroleum Industry

Luganda
USE GANDA

LUMBER INDUSTRY *Jul. 1966*
CIJE: 25 RIE: 73 GC: 410
UF Lumbering
Timber Based Industry
BT Industry
RT Forestry
Forestry Occupations
Furniture Design
Furniture Industry
Woodworking

Lumbering
USE LUMBER INDUSTRY

LUMINESCENCE *Jan. 1970*
CIJE: 37 RIE: 6 GC: 490
UF Photometric Brightness
RT Glare
Light
Lighting
Physics
Radiation

Lunar Exploration
USE LUNAR RESEARCH

LUNAR RESEARCH *Apr. 1972*
CIJE: 52 RIE: 20 GC: 810
SN Scientific activities designed to provide information about the origin, structure, and properties of the moon
UF Lunar Exploration
BT Space Exploration
RT Aerospace Technology
Astronomy
Planetariums
Satellites (Aerospace)
Space Sciences

LUNCH PROGRAMS *Jul. 1966*
CIJE: 221 RIE: 290 GC: 210
BT Health Programs
RT Ancillary School Services
Breakfast Programs
Dining Facilities
Food Handling Facilities
Food Standards
Hunger
Nutrition
School Health Services

LUO *Jul. 1970*
CIJE: 2 RIE: 5 GC: 440
BT African Languages

LUSO BRAZILIAN CULTURE *Jul. 1966*
CIJE: 4 RIE: 19 GC: 560
SN Aspects of portuguese influence reflected in brazilian culture
BT Latin American Culture

LYING *Aug. 1986*
CIJE: 15 RIE: 5 GC: 530
SN The deliberate conveyance of falsehood
BT Deception
Social Behavior
RT Antisocial Behavior
Cheating
Codes Of Ethics
Discipline Problems
Polygraphs

LYRIC POETRY *Jun. 1969*
CIJE: 129 RIE: 26 GC: 430
NT Ballads
Hymns
Odes
Sonnets
BT Poetry
RT Epics
Poets
Songs

Lyric Poets
USE POETS

LYSERGIC ACID DIETHYLAMIDE *Jul. 1966*
CIJE: 41 RIE: 69 GC: 210
UF Lsd
RT Drug Abuse
Drug Addiction
Drug Use
Illegal Drug Use

Machine Aided Indexing
USE AUTOMATIC INDEXING

Machine Dictation
USE DICTATION

MACHINE READABLE CATALOGING *Aug. 1986*
CIJE: 46 RIE: 89 GC: 710
SN (Note: for the library of congress format and program, see identifiers "marc" and "marc ii")
BT Cataloging
RT Computer Oriented Programs
Data Processing
Online Catalogs

MACHINE REPAIRERS *Mar. 1980*
CIJE: 9 RIE: 72 GC: 640
UF Machine Repairmen (1968 1980)
Machinery Maintenance Workers
Maintenance Machinists
Shop Mechanics
BT Machinists
RT Equipment Maintenance
Mechanics (Process)
Repair
Service Workers

Machine Repairmen (1968 1980)
USE MACHINE REPAIRERS

MACHINE TOOL OPERATORS *Jul. 1966*
CIJE: 15 RIE: 122 GC: 640
SN Workers who operate power-driven tools used for shaping, cutting, turning, boring, drilling, grinding, or polishing (note: prior to sep81, the use of this term was not restricted by a scope note)
UF Drill Press Operators
Production Machine Operators
Punch Press Operators
Sheet Metal Machine Operators #
BT Machinists
RT Machine Tools
Manufacturing Industry
Sheet Metal Work
Tool And Die Makers

MACHINE TOOLS *Aug. 1968*
CIJE: 31 RIE: 187 GC: 910
UF Drill Presses
Grinding Machines
Lathes
Milling Machines
Punch Presses
Shapers
BT Equipment
RT Hand Tools
Machinery Industry
Machine Tool Operators
Machinists
Manufacturing Industry
Mechanics (Process)
Metal Working
Numerical Control
Tool And Die Makers

MACHINE TRANSLATION *Jul. 1966*
CIJE: 61 RIE: 107 GC: 710
SN Translation of text from one language to another by computer
UF Mechanical Translation
BT Computational Linguistics
Translation
RT Automatic Indexing
Automation
Context Free Grammar
Contrastive Linguistics
Data Processing
Structural Analysis (Linguistics)
Word Processing

MACHINERY INDUSTRY *Jul. 1966*
CIJE: 5 RIE: 23 GC: 650
SN Manufacturers of machinery and equipment other than electrical or transportation eqipment
UF Machinery Manufacturing Industry
BT Manufacturing Industry
RT Agricultural Machinery
Agricultural Machinery Occupations
Equipment
Machine Tools
Machinists
Mechanical Equipment
Tool And Die Makers

Machinery Maintenance Workers
USE MACHINE REPAIRERS

Machinery Manufacturing Industry
USE MACHINERY INDUSTRY

MACHINISTS *Aug. 1968*
CIJE: 17 RIE: 108 GC: 640
SN Workers who make, operate, or repair machines
NT Machine Repairers
Machine Tool Operators
Tool And Die Makers
BT Skilled Workers
RT Machinery Industry
Machine Tools
Mechanics (Process)
Metal Working

Magazines
USE PERIODICALS

Magistrates
USE COURT JUDGES

Magnet Centers
USE MAGNET SCHOOLS

MAGNET SCHOOLS *Oct. 1979*
CIJE: 99 RIE: 172 GC: 340
SN Schools offering special courses not available in the regular school curriculum and designed to attract students on a voluntary basis from all parts of a school district without reference to the usual attendance zone rules -- often used to aid in school desegregation
UF Magnet Centers
BT Schools
RT Busing
Educational Parks
Feeder Patterns
Nontraditional Education
School Desegregation
Urban Schools
Voluntary Desegregation

Magnetic Amplifiers
USE ELECTRONIC CONTROL

Magnetic Ink Character Recognition
USE CHARACTER RECOGNITION

Magnetic Tape Cartridges
USE MAGNETIC TAPE CASSETTES

Magnetic Tape Cassette Recorders (1970 1980)
USE MAGNETIC TAPE CASSETTES; TAPE RECORDERS

MAGNETIC TAPE CASSETTES *Sep. 1970*
CIJE: 129 RIE: 102 GC: 720
UF Cassettes (Tape)
Magnetic Tape Cartridges
Magnetic Tape Cassette Recorders (1970 1980) #
NT Audiotape Cassettes
Videotape Cassettes
BT Magnetic Tapes
RT Tape Recorders
Tape Recordings

MAGNETIC TAPES *Jan. 1969*
CIJE: 44 RIE: 69 GC: 720
SN Tapes coated on one side with a magnetic oxide, on which data is stored by the selective polarization of portions of the surface -- used for recording video, audio, or computer data (note: use a more specific term if possible)
UF Computer Tapes #
NT Magnetic Tape Cassettes
BT Supplies
RT Computer Storage Devices
Information Storage
Input Output Devices
Tape Recorders
Tape Recordings

MAGNETS *Sep. 1968*
CIJE: 130 RIE: 44 GC: 490
UF Permanent Magnets
RT Electricity
Electronics
Physics

MAGNIFICATION METHODS *Jul. 1966*
CIJE: 16 RIE: 7 GC: 720
UF Enlargement Methods
BT Methods
RT Large Type Materials
Low Vision Aids
Microform Readers
Microscopes
Photography
Projection Equipment
Reprography
Sensory Aids
Tactile Adaptation

Magnitude Of Effect
USE EFFECT SIZE

Maids (1968 1980)
USE HOUSEHOLD WORKERS

MAINSTREAMING *Jun. 1978*
CIJE: 1905 RIE: 1895 GC: 220
SN Progressively including and maintaining exceptional students (disabled or gifted) in classes and schools with regular or normal students, with steps taken to see that special needs are satisfied within this arrangement
UF Desegregation (Disabled Students)
Integration (Disabled Students)
Least Restrictive Environment (Disabled)
Regular Class Placement (1968 1978)
BT Placement
RT Academically Gifted
Disabilities
Heterogeneous Grouping
Individualized Education Programs
Itinerant Teachers

= Two or more Descriptors are used to represent this term.
The term's main entry shows the appropriate coordination.

Normalization (Handicapped)
Resource Room Programs
Resource Teachers
Special Education
Student Placement
Transitional Programs

MAINTENANCE *Jul. 1966*
CIJE: 134 RIE: 333 GC: 920
SN Preservation or continuance of a condition
NT Equipment Maintenance
Preservation
Repair
School Maintenance
RT Buildings
Cleaning
Consumer Science
Equipment
Facilities
Life Cycle Costing
Obsolescence
Supplies

Maintenance Machinists
USE MACHINE REPAIRERS

Maintenance Vehicles
USE SERVICE VEHICLES

MAJORITY ATTITUDES *Jul. 1966*
CIJE: 145 RIE: 146 GC: 520
BT Attitudes
RT Community Control
Discriminatory Legislation
Minority Groups
Public Opinion
Public Support
Reputation

Majority Culture
USE MIDDLE CLASS CULTURE

MAJORS (STUDENTS) *Mar. 1980*
CIJE: 669 RIE: 1167 GC: 320
UF College Majors (1968 1980)
Departmental Majors
Liberal Arts Majors (1967 1980) #
NT Education Majors
BT Students
RT Advanced Courses
Course Selection (Students)
Degree Requirements
Degrees (Academic)
Elective Courses
Intellectual Disciplines
Nonmajors
Required Courses
Specialization

Make Believe Play
USE PRETEND PLAY

Maladjusted Students
USE STUDENT ADJUSTMENT

Maladjustment (1966 1980)
USE ADJUSTMENT (TO ENVIRONMENT)

MALAGASY *Jul. 1966*
CIJE: 3 RIE: 4 GC: 440
BT Indonesian Languages

MALAY *Jul. 1966*
CIJE: 14 RIE: 25 GC: 440
BT Indonesian Languages

MALAYALAM *Sep. 1969*
CIJE: RIE: 6 GC: 440
BT Dravidian Languages

MALAYO POLYNESIAN LANGUAGES *Jul. 1966*
CIJE: 26 RIE: 98 GC: 440
UF Austronesian Languages
NT Chamorro
Hawaiian
Indonesian Languages
Melanesian Languages
Samoan
BT Languages
RT Language Classification
Native Speakers

Male Role
USE MALES; SEX ROLE

MALES *Jul. 1966*
CIJE: 3392 RIE: 3122 GC: 120
UF Boys
Lower Class Males (1966 1980) #
Male Role #
Men
NT Fathers
Sons
BT Groups
RT Sex
Sex Differences
Sex Role
Sex Stereotypes
Single Sex Colleges
Single Sex Schools
Spouses

Malignant Neoplasms
USE CANCER

Malnutrition
USE NUTRITION

MALPRACTICE *Oct. 1980*
CIJE: 24 RIE: 4 GC: 530
SN Wrongful or negligent treatment of clients by professional personnel that results (or may result) in damage, injury, or loss (note: coordinate with such descriptors as "medical services," "psychological services," etc. as appropriate, or use the more specific descriptor "educational malpractice" -- for malpractice of lawyers, court judges, etc., use the identifier "legal malpractice")
NT Educational Malpractice
RT Accountability
Codes Of Ethics
Court Litigation
Crime
Laws
Legal Problems
Legal Responsibility
Professional Services
Torts
Victims Of Crime

Man Days (1968 1980)
USE WORKER DAYS

Man Machine Dialogs
USE MAN MACHINE SYSTEMS

Man Machine Interface
USE MAN MACHINE SYSTEMS

MAN MACHINE SYSTEMS *Aug. 1968*
CIJE: 360 RIE: 531 GC: 710
SN Interactive organizations of individuals and machines (usually computers) that regulate and control events as single systems
UF Man Machine Dialogs
Man Machine Interface
RT Automation
Bionics
Computer Assisted Instruction
Computer Networks
Computer Oriented Programs
Computers
Cybernetics
Display Systems
Expert Systems
Feedback
Human Factors Engineering
Interaction
Management Information Systems
Online Systems
Robotics

Management (1966 1980)
USE ADMINISTRATION

MANAGEMENT BY OBJECTIVES *Jul. 1974*
CIJE: 284 RIE: 334 GC: 320
SN Method of combining performance appraisal with the process of developing and refining organizational goals -- involves mutual goal setting between manager and subordinate, during which specific performance or measurement criteria are spelled out and agreed upon
BT Administration
Management Systems
RT Accountability
Employer Employee Relationship
Objectives
Organizational Development
Organizational Objectives
Performance
Performance Contracts
Personnel Evaluation

MANAGEMENT DEVELOPMENT *Jul. 1966*
CIJE: 1001 RIE: 1030 GC: 320
SN Inservice programs designed to increase the supervisory and managerial skills of administrators, managers, and management trainees (note: use "administrator education" for formal preservice education programs -- prior to mar80, this term was not restricted to inservice programs)
UF Administrator Training
Executive Development
Management Training
BT Labor Force Development
RT Administrator Education
Assessment Centers (Personnel)
Business Administration Education
Industrial Training
Inservice Education
Leadership Training
Off The Job Training
Professional Continuing Education
Professional Development
Professional Training
Public Administration Education
Staff Development
Supervisory Training

Management Education (1967 1980)
USE ADMINISTRATOR EDUCATION

MANAGEMENT GAMES *Jul. 1966*
CIJE: 152 RIE: 192 GC: 310
UF Business Games
BT Games
Training Methods
RT Decision Making
Game Theory
Management Systems
Problem Solving
Simulated Environment
Simulation

MANAGEMENT INFORMATION SYSTEMS *Jul. 1971*
CIJE: 581 RIE: 976 GC: 710
SN Communications systems that are designed to furnish management and supervisory personnel with information needed for decision making
UF Mis
BT Information Systems
Management Systems
RT Administration
Computer Managed Instruction
Computer Oriented Programs
Database Management Systems
Data Processing
Decision Making
Man Machine Systems

Management Personnel
USE ADMINISTRATORS

MANAGEMENT SYSTEMS *Oct. 1969*
CIJE: 722 RIE: 1165 GC: 320
SN A general term indicating that a systems approach has been used in dealing with management concerns (note: use a more specific term if possible -- prior to mar80, the use of this term was not restricted by a scope note)
NT Database Management Systems
Management By Objectives
Management Information Systems
RT Administration
Administrative Organization
Critical Path Method
Decision Making
Information Systems
Linear Programing
Long Range Planning
Management Games
Operations Research
Organizational Communication
Problem Solving
Simulation
Systems Analysis
Systems Approach
Systems Development

MANAGEMENT TEAMS *Mar. 1980*
CIJE: 134 RIE: 136 GC: 320
UF Administrative Teams
Team Administration (1967 1980)
Team Management
BT Administrative Organization
RT Administration
Organizational Development
Participative Decision Making
Power Structure
Quality Circles
Teamwork

Management Training
USE MANAGEMENT DEVELOPMENT

MANAGERIAL OCCUPATIONS *Jul. 1966*
CIJE: 181 RIE: 220 GC: 640
UF Administrative Occupations
BT Occupations
RT Administration
Business Administration
Coordination
Professional Occupations
White Collar Occupations

Managers
USE ADMINISTRATORS

MANCHU *Mar. 1971*
CIJE: RIE: 2 GC: 440
BT Uralic Altaic Languages

MANDARIN CHINESE *Jul. 1966*
CIJE: 58 RIE: 137 GC: 440
BT Chinese

Mandatory Courses
USE REQUIRED COURSES

Mandatory Education
USE COMPULSORY EDUCATION

MANDINGO *Jul. 1966*
CIJE: 1 RIE: 12 GC: 440
BT African Languages

Mangala
USE LINGALA

MANIPULATIVE MATERIALS *Jul. 1966*
CIJE: 496 RIE: 232 GC: 720
SN Instructional materials that are designed to be touched or handled by students and which develop their muscles, perceptual skills, psychomotor skills, etc.
UF Tactile Materials
BT Instructional Materials
RT Experiential Learning
Kinesthetic Perception
Montessori Method
Object Manipulation
Perceptual Motor Learning
Psychomotor Skills
Sensory Aids
Tactual Perception

Manpower
USE LABOR FORCE

Manpower Development (1966 1980)
USE LABOR FORCE DEVELOPMENT

Manpower Needs (1968 1980)
USE LABOR NEEDS

Manpower Utilization (1966 1980)
USE LABOR UTILIZATION

MANUAL COMMUNICATION *Jul. 1966*
CIJE: 200 RIE: 97 GC: 220
SN A form of communication with and among the deaf in which sign language and finger spelling are substituted for speech
UF Signed English
NT Cued Speech
Finger Spelling
Sign Language
BT Communication (Thought Transfer)
RT Communication Skills
Deaf Interpreting
Deafness
Hearing Impairments
Hearing Therapy
Oral Communication Method
Total Communication

= Two or more Descriptors are used to represent this term. The term's main entry shows the appropriate coordination.

Manuals (1966 1980)
USE GUIDES

MANUFACTURING *Jul. 1966*
CIJE: 97 RIE: 181 GC: 650
UF Fabrication
Manufacturing Methods
Manufacturing Techniques
NT Assembly (Manufacturing)
Mass Production
BT Technology
RT Distributive Education
Engineering
Equipment Manufacturers
Industrial Arts
Manufacturing Industry
Production Technicians

MANUFACTURING INDUSTRY *Jul. 1966*
CIJE: 145 RIE: 164 GC: 650
NT Aerospace Industry
Cement Industry
Chemical Industry
Electronics Industry
Furniture Industry
Machinery Industry
Metal Industry
BT Industry
RT Assembly (Manufacturing)
Brick Industry
Chemical Engineering
Equipment Manufacturers
Machine Tool Operators
Machine Tools
Manufacturing
Mechanical Design Technicians
Production Technicians

Manufacturing Methods
USE MANUFACTURING

Manufacturing Techniques
USE MANUFACTURING

MANUSCRIPT WRITING (HANDLETTERING) *Jul. 1966*
CIJE: 43 RIE: 57 GC: 420
SN Handwriting based on adaptations of the printed letter forms
UF Calligraphy
Printscript
Uncial Script
BT Handwriting
RT Cursive Writing

Map Reading Skills
USE MAP SKILLS

MAP SKILLS *Jul. 1966*
CIJE: 264 RIE: 292 GC: 400
UF Map Reading Skills
BT Skills
RT Cartography
Geography
Locational Skills (Social Studies)
Maps

Mapping
USE CARTOGRAPHY

Mappings (Mathematics)
USE FUNCTIONS (MATHEMATICS)

MAPS *Jul. 1966*
CIJE: 323 RIE: 380 GC: 720
BT Visual Aids
RT Atlases
Cartography
Geography
Illustrations
Instructional Materials
Locational Skills (Social Studies)
Map Skills
Nonprint Media
Topography

MARANAO *Jul. 1966*
CIJE: RIE: 2 GC: 440
BT Indonesian Languages

MARATHI *Jul. 1966*
CIJE: 4 RIE: 19 GC: 440
BT Indo European Languages

Marching Bands
USE BANDS (MUSIC)

Marihuana (1969 1986)
USE MARIJUANA

MARIJUANA *Aug. 1986*
CIJE: RIE: GC: 210
UF Cannabis
Hashish
Marihuana (1969 1986)
BT Narcotics
RT Drug Addiction
Drug Legislation
Drug Use
Illegal Drug Use

MARINE BIOLOGY *Jul. 1966*
CIJE: 262 RIE: 310 GC: 490
BT Biology
RT Ecology
Estuaries
Fisheries
Ichthyology
Marine Education
Marine Technicians
Ocean Engineering
Oceanography
Radiation Biology

Marine Corps Air Stations
USE MILITARY AIR FACILITIES

MARINE EDUCATION *Oct. 1983*
CIJE: 92 RIE: 104 GC: 400
SN Interdisciplinary group of learning/teaching activities concerning the earth's waters and seas (note: use a more precise term if possible)
UF Marine Science Education
NT Maritime Education
BT Education
RT Environmental Education
Estuaries
Marine Biology
Oceanography
Science Education
Underwater Diving
Water

Marine Science Education
USE MARINE EDUCATION

MARINE TECHNICIANS *Jul. 1966*
CIJE: 26 RIE: 53 GC: 640
BT Paraprofessional Personnel
RT Marine Biology
Oceanography
Scientific Personnel
Seafarers
Underwater Diving

Mariners
USE SEAFARERS

Marital Counseling
USE MARRIAGE COUNSELING

MARITAL INSTABILITY *Jul. 1966*
CIJE: 458 RIE: 159 GC: 530
RT Battered Women
Displaced Homemakers
Divorce
Family Life
Family Problems
Family Violence
Illegitimate Births
Marriage
Marriage Counseling
One Parent Family

MARITAL SATISFACTION *Oct. 1983*
CIJE: 162 RIE: 53 GC: 510
SN Level of contentment with one's married life
BT Attitudes
RT Family Life
Life Satisfaction
Marriage
Marriage Counseling
Need Gratification
Self Actualization

MARITAL STATUS *Aug. 1974*
CIJE: 359 RIE: 491 GC: 510
BT Status
RT Divorce
Marriage
Married Students
Single Students
Spouses
Widowed

MARITIME EDUCATION *Feb. 1984*
CIJE: 3 RIE: 6 GC: 490
SN Learning/teaching activities concerned with building, operating, and navigating boats, ships, and other floating structures, as well as related harbor and dock technology
BT Marine Education
RT Boat Operators
Oceanography
Sailing
Seafarers
Water

Marketable Skills
USE EMPLOYMENT POTENTIAL; JOB SKILLS

MARKETING *Jul. 1966*
CIJE: 787 RIE: 952 GC: 650
SN An aggregate of functions involved in the transfer of goods from producer to consumer
UF Distribution (Economics)
NT Merchandising
Retailing
Salesmanship
Wholesaling
BT Technology
RT Business
Business Education
Consumer Protection
Cooperatives
Distributive Education
Institutional Advancement
International Trade
Merchandise Information
Merchants
Rail Transportation
Technology Transfer

Marking (Scholastic)
USE GRADING

Marks (Scholastic)
USE GRADES (SCHOLASTIC)

MARKSMANSHIP *Jul. 1966*
CIJE: 4 RIE: 12 GC: 400
BT Psychomotor Skills
RT Military Science

MARRIAGE *Jul. 1966*
CIJE: 778 RIE: 475 GC: 520
NT Intermarriage
Remarriage
BT Interpersonal Relationship
RT Divorce
Family (Sociological Unit)
Family Life
Kinship
Marital Instability
Marital Satisfaction
Marital Status
Marriage Counseling
Married Students
Mate Selection
Spouses

MARRIAGE COUNSELING *Apr. 1970*
CIJE: 468 RIE: 94 GC: 240
UF Marital Counseling
BT Counseling
RT Divorce
Family Counseling
Family Life
Family Problems
Marital Instability
Marital Satisfaction
Marriage

Married Persons
USE SPOUSES

MARRIED STUDENTS *Aug. 1974*
CIJE: 55 RIE: 74 GC: 360
BT Students
RT Adult Students
Board Of Education Policy
Equal Protection
Marital Status
Marriage
Self Supporting Students
Single Students
Spouses
Student Rights

MARXIAN ANALYSIS *Mar. 1984*
CIJE: 35 RIE: 15 GC: 810
SN Application of marxist concepts, principles, and models in any field (e.g., educational or historical or literary criticism)
UF Marxist Criticism
BT Methods
RT Economic Factors
Marxism
Social Change
Social Science Research
Social Stratification
Sociology

MARXISM *Mar. 1984*
CIJE: 89 RIE: 47 GC: 610
SN Body of social, economic, and political thought originating with karl marx and friedrich engels -- distinguished by the labor theory of value, the principles of dialectical materialism and economic determinism, and the doctrine of revolutionary change leading to a classless society
UF Dialectical Materialism
BT Philosophy
RT Capitalism
Communism
Economics
Labor Economics
Marxian Analysis
Political Attitudes
Political Power
Political Science
Revolution
Social Class
Socialism
Sociology
Twentieth Century Literature
Working Class

Marxist Criticism
USE MARXIAN ANALYSIS

MASONRY *Sep. 1969*
CIJE: 5 RIE: 68 GC: 920
SN Building or working with stone or brick
UF Masons (Trade)
NT Bricklaying
BT Construction (Process)
Technology
RT Building Trades
Construction Materials
Prefabrication
Prestressed Concrete
Skilled Occupations
Structural Building Systems

Masons (Trade)
USE MASONRY

Mass Communications
USE MASS MEDIA

Mass Culture
USE POPULAR CULTURE

MASS INSTRUCTION *Jul. 1966*
CIJE: 88 RIE: 78 GC: 350
SN Large-scale activities aimed at disseminating information to or influencing the opinion of the general public (note: prior to mar80, the use of this term was not restricted by a scope note)
BT Instruction
RT Audiences
Distance Education
Educational Radio
Educational Television
Individualized Instruction
Large Group Instruction
Listening Groups
Mass Media
Public Opinion
Teaching Methods

MASS MEDIA *Jul. 1966*
CIJE: 1969 RIE: 2479 GC: 720
SN Systems or instruments of communication intended to reach general and geographically dispersed audiences simultaneously

UF Communications Media
Mass Communications
Mass Media Technology #
NT Films
News Media
Radio
Television
RT Advertising
Audiences
Audiovisual Aids
Broadcast Industry
Communications
Editors
Educational Media
Film Industry
Information Dissemination
Information Sources
Journalism
Journalism Education
Mass Instruction
Mass Media Effects
Media Research
Nonprint Media
Political Campaigns
Popular Culture
Press Opinion
Propaganda
Publications
Publicity
Publishing Industry
Television Commercials

MASS MEDIA EFFECTS *Aug. 1982*
CIJE: 237 RIE: 273 GC: 520
SN The impact or consequences of mass media on social structures, laws, and/or human behavior
RT Audience Analysis
Audiences
Mass Media
Media Research
Public Opinion

Mass Media Technology
USE COMMUNICATIONS; MASS MEDIA

MASS PRODUCTION *Sep. 1969*
CIJE: 32 RIE: 21 GC: 650
UF Large Scale Production
BT Manufacturing
RT Assembly (Manufacturing)
Chemical Engineering
Production Technicians
Production Techniques

Massed Negative Reinforcement
USE NEGATIVE REINFORCEMENT

Master Of Arts Degrees
USE MASTERS DEGREES

Master Of Arts In College Teaching
USE MASTERS DEGREES

Master Of Arts In Teaching
USE MASTERS DEGREES

Master Of Science Degrees
USE MASTERS DEGREES

Master Of Science In Teaching
USE MASTERS DEGREES

MASTER PLANS *Jul. 1966*
CIJE: 109 RIE: 651 GC: 730
RT Building Plans
Facility Guidelines
Facility Planning
Facility Requirements
Long Range Planning
Mission Statements
Planning
Planning Commissions
Policy Formation
Specifications
Statewide Planning

Master Tapes (Audio) (1968 1980)
USE AUDIOTAPE RECORDINGS

MASTER TEACHERS *Jul. 1966*
CIJE: 106 RIE: 125 GC: 360
SN Elementary or secondary school teachers who, because of advance professional preparation and teaching experience, are qualified to assist in the preparation of student teachers or teacher interns, to give guidance to inexperienced teachers, or to coordinate and lead teams of teachers (note: do not confuse with the more precise term "cooperating teachers")
UF Senior Teacher Role (1966 1980) #
BT Teachers
RT Beginning Teachers
Cooperating Teachers
Differentiated Staffs
Merit Pay
Student Teachers
Student Teaching
Teacher Education
Teacher Educator Education
Teacher Educators
Teacher Interns
Team Teaching

MASTERS DEGREES *Jul. 1966*
CIJE: 286 RIE: 557 GC: 340
UF Master Of Arts Degrees
Master Of Arts In College Teaching
Master Of Arts In Teaching
Master Of Science Degrees
Master Of Science In Teaching
BT Degrees (Academic)
RT Bachelors Degrees
Degree Requirements
Doctoral Degrees
Graduate Study
Masters Programs
Masters Theses
Specialist In Education Degrees
Teacher Educator Education

MASTERS PROGRAMS *Mar. 1980*
CIJE: 158 RIE: 129 GC: 340
SN Formal graduate programs in higher education institutions that culminate in the award of a master's degree
BT College Programs
RT Degree Requirements
Doctoral Programs
Graduate School Faculty
Graduate Students
Graduate Study
Higher Education
Masters Degrees
Masters Theses

MASTERS THESES *Jul. 1966*
CIJE: 78 RIE: 693 GC: 720
SN Written reports of some extensiveness submitted in partial fulfillment of master's degree requirements (note: corresponds to pubtype code 042 -- do not use except as the subject of a document)
BT Theses
RT Graduate Study
Masters Degrees
Masters Programs
Practicum Papers

MASTERY LEARNING *Dec. 1976*
CIJE: 307 RIE: 384 GC: 310
SN Strategy characterized by: the definition of learning objectives and expected achievement level, a design that permits as many students as possible to achieve objectives to specified level, and the assignment of grades based on achievement of objectives at specified level
BT Learning
RT Academic Achievement
Academic Standards
Achievement
Behavioral Objectives
Learning Readiness
Learning Strategies
Mastery Tests
Minimum Competencies
Objectives
Pacing
Performance
Skill Development
Skills

MASTERY TESTS *Dec. 1976*
CIJE: 110 RIE: 197 GC: 830
SN Tests used to place individuals into two distinct groups: those who have clearly reached a predetermined standard of competency and those who have not
BT Achievement Tests
Criterion Referenced Tests
RT Academic Achievement
Academic Standards
Achievement
Behavioral Objectives
Cutting Scores
Licensing Examinations (Professions)
Mastery Learning
Minimum Competency Testing
National Competency Tests
Performance
Skill Development
Skills

MATCHED GROUPS *Jul. 1966*
CIJE: 31 RIE: 52 GC: 820
SN Groups, used in experiments, who are equivalent in all necessary respects so that any differences arising among them can be attributed to experimental treatments
BT Groups
RT Attrition (Research Studies)
Control Groups
Effect Size
Experimental Groups
Participant Characteristics
Quasiexperimental Design
Research Design
Research Methodology
Sampling
Statistical Bias

Matching Tests
USE OBJECTIVE TESTS

MATE SELECTION *Mar. 1977*
CIJE: 57 RIE: 23 GC: 510
SN Process of choosing a partner for marriage or cohabitation
BT Selection
RT Dating (Social)
Intermarriage
Marriage
Social Development

Material Adaptation
USE MEDIA ADAPTATION

MATERIAL DEVELOPMENT *Jul. 1966*
CIJE: 1066 RIE: 1783 GC: 310
UF Instructional Material Development
Material Research
NT Test Construction
BT Development
RT Curriculum Development
Formative Evaluation
Instructional Material Evaluation
Instructional Materials
Media Adaptation
Pretesting
Programing (Broadcast)
Student Developed Materials
Teacher Developed Materials

Material Research
USE MATERIAL DEVELOPMENT

Material Selection
USE MEDIA SELECTION

Material Sources
USE RESOURCE MATERIALS

Materials Inventory
USE FACILITY INVENTORY

MATHEMATICAL APPLICATIONS *Jul. 1966*
CIJE: 1182 RIE: 675 GC: 480
UF Practical Mathematics (1966 1980)
NT Algorithms
Computation
Linear Programing
Mathematical Formulas
Word Problems (Mathematics)
RT Intuition
Mathematical Models
Mathematics
Mathematics Skills
Problem Sets
Problem Solving

MATHEMATICAL CONCEPTS *Jul. 1966*
CIJE: 1053 RIE: 619 GC: 480
NT Geometric Concepts
Inequality (Mathematics)
Number Concepts
RT Conservation (Concept)
Equations (Mathematics)
Functions (Mathematics)
Fundamental Concepts
Mathematical Models
Mathematics
Mathematics Skills
Mathematics Tests
Misconceptions
Nonparametric Statistics
Percentage
Probability
Proof (Mathematics)
Quotas
Ratios (Mathematics)
Reciprocals (Mathematics)
Transformations (Mathematics)
Trigonometry

MATHEMATICAL ENRICHMENT *Jul. 1966*
CIJE: 680 RIE: 175 GC: 480
SN Experiences which replace, supplement, or extend normally offered mathematics instruction
BT Enrichment
RT Arithmetic
Mathematics
Mathematics Instruction
Mathematics Materials
Trigonometry

MATHEMATICAL EXPERIENCE (1966 1980) *Mar. 1980*
CIJE: 71 RIE: 36 GC: 480
SN Invalid descriptor -- used inconsistently in indexing -- see more precise "mathematics" descriptors

Mathematical Expressions
USE MATHEMATICAL FORMULAS

MATHEMATICAL FORMULAS *Aug. 1978*
CIJE: 268 RIE: 151 GC: 480
SN Equations or rules relating mathematical objects or quantities
UF Mathematical Expressions
Mathematical Sentences
NT Equations (Mathematics)
Functions (Mathematics)
BT Mathematical Applications
Mathematical Logic
RT Computation
Mathematical Models
Mathematics
Symbols (Mathematics)

MATHEMATICAL LINGUISTICS *Jul. 1966*
CIJE: 54 RIE: 49 GC: 450
UF Statistical Linguistics
BT Linguistics
RT Computational Linguistics
Mathematics
Word Frequency

MATHEMATICAL LOGIC *Jul. 1966*
CIJE: 164 RIE: 103 GC: 480
UF Symbolic Logic
NT Algorithms
Mathematical Formulas
Proof (Mathematics)
Set Theory
BT Logic
RT Computational Linguistics
Computer Literacy
Game Theory
Mathematics
Mathematics Skills
Matrices
Statistics

MATHEMATICAL MODELS *Jul. 1966*
CIJE: 1600 RIE: 1377 GC: 730
BT Models
RT Diagrams
Discriminant Analysis
Effect Size
Estimation (Mathematics)
Game Theory
Generalizability Theory
Goodness Of Fit
Heuristics
Hypothesis Testing
Information Theory

= Two or more Descriptors are used to represent this term.
The term's main entry shows the appropriate coordination.

Latent Trait Theory
Linear Programing
Mathematical Applications
Mathematical Concepts
Mathematical Formulas
Mathematics
Measurement
Monte Carlo Methods
Multitrait Multimethod Techniques
Multivariate Analysis
Operations Research
Proof (Mathematics)
Scaling
Statistics
Test Theory

Mathematical Sentences
USE MATHEMATICAL FORMULAS

Mathematical Statistics
USE STATISTICS

MATHEMATICAL VOCABULARY *Jul. 1966*
CIJE: 117 RIE: 94 GC: 480
BT Vocabulary
RT Mathematics
Trigonometry

MATHEMATICIANS *Sep. 1968*
CIJE: 148 RIE: 44 GC: 640
BT Professional Personnel
Scientific Personnel
RT Engineers
Mathematics
Mathematics Teachers
Systems Analysts

MATHEMATICS *Jul. 1966*
CIJE: 2272 RIE: 2597 GC: 480
NT Algebra
Arithmetic
Calculus
Geometry
Probability
Statistics
Technical Mathematics
Trigonometry
BT Liberal Arts
RT Algorithms
Calculators
College Mathematics
Computation
Elementary School Mathematics
Estimation (Mathematics)
Height
Mathematical Applications
Mathematical Concepts
Mathematical Enrichment
Mathematical Formulas
Mathematical Linguistics
Mathematical Logic
Mathematical Models
Mathematical Vocabulary
Mathematicians
Mathematics Achievement
Mathematics Anxiety
Mathematics Curriculum
Mathematics Education
Mathematics Instruction
Mathematics Materials
Mathematics Skills
Mathematics Teachers
Mathematics Tests
Numbers
Number Systems
Proof (Mathematics)
Quantum Mechanics
Remedial Mathematics
Sciences
Secondary School Mathematics
Symbols (Mathematics)
Word Problems (Mathematics)

MATHEMATICS ACHIEVEMENT *Sep. 1981*
CIJE: 304 RIE: 513 GC: 480
SN Level of attainment in any or all mathematical skills, usually estimated by performance on a test
BT Achievement
RT Academic Achievement
Achievement Gains
Mathematics
Mathematics Skills
Mathematics Tests

MATHEMATICS ANXIETY *Mar. 1980*
CIJE: 119 RIE: 138 GC: 480
UF Mathematics Avoidance
Mathophobia
BT Anxiety
RT Mathematics
School Phobia

Mathematics Avoidance
USE MATHEMATICS ANXIETY

MATHEMATICS CURRICULUM *Jul. 1966*
CIJE: 806 RIE: 1047 GC: 480
UF Arithmetic Curriculum (1966 1980) #
NT College Mathematics
Elementary School Mathematics
Modern Mathematics
Secondary School Mathematics
BT Curriculum
RT Mathematics
Mathematics Instruction

MATHEMATICS EDUCATION *Jul. 1966*
CIJE: 5191 RIE: 3592 GC: 480
BT Education
RT College Mathematics
Elementary School Mathematics
Mathematics
Mathematics Instruction
Secondary School Mathematics

MATHEMATICS INSTRUCTION *Jul. 1966*
CIJE: 2951 RIE: 2642 GC: 480
NT Remedial Mathematics
BT Instruction
RT College Mathematics
Elementary School Mathematics
Mathematical Enrichment
Mathematics
Mathematics Curriculum
Mathematics Education
Mathematics Materials
Mathematics Teachers
Secondary School Mathematics

MATHEMATICS MATERIALS *Jul. 1966*
CIJE: 279 RIE: 346 GC: 730
RT Geometric Constructions
Instructional Materials
Mathematical Enrichment
Mathematics
Mathematics Instruction

MATHEMATICS SKILLS *Mar. 1983*
CIJE: 82 RIE: 317 GC: 480
SN Complex behaviors developed through practice in order to complete mathematical tasks (note: use for documents whose specific focus is on the acquisition and/or use of mathematics skills -- do not use as an automatic adjunct to "mathematics curriculum," "mathematics education," etc.)
BT Skills
RT Basic Skills
Mathematical Applications
Mathematical Concepts
Mathematical Logic
Mathematics
Mathematics Achievement
Mathematics Tests
Measurement
Minimum Competencies
Numbers

MATHEMATICS TEACHERS *Jul. 1966*
CIJE: 292 RIE: 247 GC: 360
BT Teachers
RT Mathematicians
Mathematics
Mathematics Instruction

MATHEMATICS TESTS *Dec. 1985*
CIJE: 7 RIE: 11 GC: 830
SN Tests of ability, achievement, or aptitude in arithmetic or other aspects of mathematics
UF Arithmetic Tests #
Number Skills Tests
Quantitative Tests (1980 1985) (Mathematics)
BT Tests
RT Achievement Tests
Aptitude Tests
Computation
Mathematical Concepts
Mathematics
Mathematics Achievement
Mathematics Skills
Number Concepts
Numbers
Verbal Tests
Word Problems (Mathematics)

Mathophobia
USE MATHEMATICS ANXIETY

MATRICES *Jun. 1973*
CIJE: 377 RIE: 224 GC: 480
BT Algebra
RT Mathematical Logic
Multitrait Multimethod Techniques
Oblique Rotation
Orthogonal Rotation
Statistical Analysis
Vectors (Mathematics)

Matriculation
USE ADMISSION (SCHOOL)

Matrix Sampling
USE ITEM SAMPLING

MATTER *Jul. 1966*
CIJE: 105 RIE: 58 GC: 490
NT Minerals
Polymers
Sludge
Wastes
Water
RT Atomic Structure
Atomic Theory
Crystallography
Diffusion (Physics)
Nuclear Physics
Physics
Quantum Mechanics
Radioisotopes
Relativity
Weight (Mass)

MATURATION (1967 1980) *Mar. 1980*
CIJE: 307 RIE: 276 GC: 120
SN Invalid descriptor -- see "development," "individual development," and "maturity (individuals)"

Maturation Learning Controversy
USE NATURE NURTURE CONTROVERSY

MATURITY (INDIVIDUALS) *Mar. 1980*
CIJE: 189 RIE: 190 GC: 120
SN Full growth or development of the individual (note: prior to mar80, "maturation" was a valid descriptor -- see "individual development" or other "development" terms for the process of maturing)
UF Immaturity (1966 1980)
Social Immaturity (1966 1980)
Social Maturity (1966 1980)
NT Vocational Maturity
BT Individual Characteristics
RT Adjustment (To Environment)
Age
Individual Development
Interpersonal Competence
Maturity Tests
Personality Traits
Physical Characteristics
Psychological Characteristics
Self Care Skills
Self Control

MATURITY TESTS *Jul. 1966*
CIJE: 44 RIE: 62 GC: 830
SN Measures of social, emotional, behavioral, or physiological development of individuals from infancy through adulthood
BT Tests
RT Individual Development
Maturity (Individuals)
Occupational Tests
Personality Measures
Preschool Tests
School Readiness Tests
Vocational Maturity

MAURITIAN CREOLE *Jun. 1971*
CIJE: RIE: 4 GC: 440
BT Creoles

Maximum Likelihood Factor Analysis
USE FACTOR ANALYSIS; MAXIMUM LIKELIHOOD STATISTICS

MAXIMUM LIKELIHOOD STATISTICS *Oct. 1980*
CIJE: 79 RIE: 79 GC: 820
SN Statistics that are designed to provide estimates that maximize the probability of zero, or negligible, error (that is, estimates most likely to be correct)
UF Maximum Likelihood Factor Analysis #
BT Statistical Analysis
Statistics
RT Delphi Technique
Factor Analysis
Goodness Of Fit
Predictive Measurement
Probability
Sampling
Statistical Significance

MAYAN LANGUAGES *Dec. 1970*
CIJE: 13 RIE: 14 GC: 440
NT Quiche
Yucatec
BT American Indian Languages

MEASUREMENT *Jul. 1966*
CIJE: 1630 RIE: 1308 GC: 820
SN Process of obtaining a numerical description of the extent to which persons, organizations, or things possess specified characteristics (note: see also "testing" and "evaluation")
NT Achievement Rating
Cognitive Measurement
Merit Rating
Predictive Measurement
Scoring
RT Computation
Data
Estimation (Mathematics)
Evaluation
Full Time Equivalency
Generalizability Theory
Grade Equivalent Scores
Mathematical Models
Mathematics Skills
Measurement Objectives
Measurement Techniques
Measures (Individuals)
Metric System
Norms
Observation
Proof (Mathematics)
Scores
Standards
Statistical Analysis
Statistical Data
Testing
Tests

MEASUREMENT EQUIPMENT *Mar. 1980*
CIJE: 150 RIE: 69 GC: 910
UF Gauges
Meters
NT Calorimeters
Polygraphs
Potentiometers (Instruments)
Sound Spectrographs
BT Equipment
RT Biomedical Equipment
Instrumentation
Laboratory Equipment
Science Equipment

Measurement Error
USE ERROR OF MEASUREMENT

Measurement Goals (1966 1980)
USE MEASUREMENT OBJECTIVES

MEASUREMENT INSTRUMENTS (1966 1980) *Mar. 1980*
CIJE: 1566 RIE: 1840 GC: 910
SN Invalid descriptor -- used for equipment as well as mental measures -- see the displays of "measurement equipment" and "measures (individuals)" or "measurement techniques" respectively for these concepts

= Two or more Descriptors are used to represent this term.
The term's main entry shows the appropriate coordination.

MEASUREMENT OBJECTIVES *Mar. 1980*
CIJE: 183 RIE: 276 GC: 820
SN Aims or ends toward which measurement efforts are directed, including desired improvements in the technology of quantification
UF Measurement Goals (1966 1980)
BT Objectives
RT Evaluation Needs
Measurement
Research Needs
Testing

MEASUREMENT TECHNIQUES *Jul. 1966*
CIJE: 2405 RIE: 2593 GC: 820
SN Procedures used to systematically obtain quantified descriptions of the extent to which persons, organizations, or things possess specific characteristics (note: prior to mar80, the use of this term was not restricted by a scope note)
NT Classroom Observation Techniques
Forced Choice Technique
Q Methodology
Scaling
Scoring Formulas
Sociometric Techniques
Testing
BT Methods
RT Audits (Verification)
Criterion Referenced Tests
Evaluation Methods
Grade Equivalent Scores
Interrater Reliability
Item Sampling
Measurement
Measures (Individuals)
Monte Carlo Methods
Multitrait Multimethod Techniques
Rating Scales
Readability Formulas
Research Methodology
Sample Size
Sampling
Scientific Methodology

MEASURES (INDIVIDUALS) *Mar. 1980*
CIJE: 476 RIE: 350 GC: 830
SN Procedures, devices, or sets of items that are used to estimate or rate the characteristics of individuals, e.g., their abilities, attitudes, opinions, or mental traits (note: use a more specific term if possible)
UF Inventories (Measurement)
Scales
NT Affective Measures
Attitude Measures
Biographical Inventories
Interest Inventories
Personality Measures
Projective Measures
Questionnaires
Rating Scales
Tests
RT Evaluation
Evaluation Methods
Interviews
Measurement
Measurement Techniques
Surveys

MEAT *Feb. 1970*
CIJE: 17 RIE: 23 GC: 410
BT Food
RT Food Stores
Meat Packing Industry

Meat Inspectors
USE FOOD AND DRUG INSPECTORS

MEAT PACKING INDUSTRY *Jul. 1966*
CIJE: 13 RIE: 25 GC: 650
BT Industry
RT Agribusiness
Animal Husbandry
Food
Food And Drug Inspectors
Food Processing Occupations
Food Standards
Meat

MECHANICAL DESIGN TECHNICIANS *Aug. 1968*
CIJE: 3 RIE: 17 GC: 640
UF Engine Development Technicians
Mechanical Engineering Assistants
Propulsion Development Technicians
BT Paraprofessional Personnel
RT Design
Electromechanical Technology
Engineering Technicians
Manufacturing Industry
Mechanics (Process)

Mechanical Devices
USE MECHANICAL EQUIPMENT

Mechanical Drawing
USE ENGINEERING DRAWING

Mechanical Engineering Assistants
USE MECHANICAL DESIGN TECHNICIANS

MECHANICAL EQUIPMENT *Nov. 1968*
CIJE: 91 RIE: 137 GC: 910
SN Machinery or tools which automatically perform operations in controlling or producing a physical change in environment or in accomplishment of a given task
UF Mechanical Devices
BT Equipment
RT Architectural Research
Calculators
Data Processing
Machinery Industry
Mechanical Skills
Word Processing

MECHANICAL SKILLS *Jul. 1966*
CIJE: 28 RIE: 106 GC: 400
BT Skills
RT Employment Qualifications
Job Skills
Mechanical Equipment
Mechanics (Process)
Trade And Industrial Education

Mechanical Teaching Aids (1966 1980)
USE EDUCATIONAL MEDIA

Mechanical Translation
USE MACHINE TRANSLATION

MECHANICS (PHYSICS) *Mar. 1973*
CIJE: 558 RIE: 108 GC: 490
SN The science that deals with the effects of energy and force on the equilibrium, deformation, or motion of solid, liquid, and gaseous bodies -- includes both classical (newtonian) and modern (atomic-level) mechanics
UF Classical Mechanics
NT Fluid Mechanics
Kinetics
Quantum Mechanics
BT Physics
RT Acceleration (Physics)
Energy
Force
Gravity (Physics)
Kinetic Molecular Theory
Motion
Pressure (Physics)
Relativity

MECHANICS (PROCESS) *Jul. 1966*
CIJE: 30 RIE: 134 GC: 640
SN Assembly, operation, and repair of machines (note: prior to mar80, the use of this term was not restricted by a scope note)
UF General Mechanics
NT Auto Mechanics
Aviation Mechanics
Refrigeration Mechanics
Small Engine Mechanics
BT Technology
RT Agricultural Machinery Occupations
Locomotive Engineers
Machine Repairers
Machine Tools
Machinists
Mechanical Design Technicians
Mechanical Skills
Nuclear Power Plant Technicians

Mechanization
USE AUTOMATION

MEDIA ADAPTATION *Jan. 1985*
CIJE: 4 RIE: 9 GC: 720
SN Modification of existing information and materials to meet alternative needs
UF Educational Media Adaptation
Instructional Material Adaptation
Material Adaptation
NT Tactile Adaptation
BT Change
RT Curriculum Development
Educational Media
Instructional Material Evaluation
Intermode Differences
Material Development
Media Selection
Media Specialists

MEDIA RESEARCH *Jul. 1966*
CIJE: 1288 RIE: 1496 GC: 810
SN Systematic investigations of the use, characteristics, and effects of print and nonprint media (note: as of oct81, use as a minor descriptor for examples of this kind of research -- use as a major descriptor only as the subject of a document)
NT Television Research
Textbook Research
BT Research
RT Audience Analysis
Educational Media
Institutional Research
Mass Media
Mass Media Effects
Media Specialists
Use Studies

MEDIA SELECTION *Aug. 1971*
CIJE: 576 RIE: 882 GC: 720
SN Choice of the most appropriate material or channel of communication
UF Educational Media Selection
Instructional Material Selection
Material Selection
NT Library Material Selection
Reading Material Selection
Textbook Selection
BT Selection
RT Audiovisual Communications
Educational Media
Instructional Material Evaluation
Media Adaptation
Media Specialists
Multimedia Instruction
Nonprint Media

MEDIA SPECIALISTS *Jul. 1966*
CIJE: 462 RIE: 492 GC: 720
SN Persons who specialize in the development, organization, and application of various types of educational media
NT Audiovisual Coordinators
BT Specialists
RT Educational Media
Learning Resources Centers
Librarians
Media Adaptation
Media Research
Media Selection
Multimedia Instruction
School Libraries

Media Technology (1968 1980)
USE COMMUNICATIONS

Mediation (Labor)
USE ARBITRATION

MEDIATION THEORY *Jul. 1966*
CIJE: 213 RIE: 138 GC: 810
SN Theory that stimuli do not directly initiate behavior but rather activate intervening processes that initiate the behavior
BT Behavior Theories
RT Cognitive Processes
Generalization
Learning Processes
Recall (Psychology)
Retention (Psychology)
Shift Studies
Stimulus Generalization
Verbal Learning

Medical Assistance
USE MEDICAL SERVICES

MEDICAL ASSISTANTS *Jul. 1969*
CIJE: 14 RIE: 115 GC: 210
NT Medical Laboratory Assistants
BT Allied Health Personnel
RT Emergency Medical Technicians
Medical Services
Nurses Aides
Secretaries

MEDICAL ASSOCIATIONS *Jul. 1966*
CIJE: 25 RIE: 20 GC: 520
BT Professional Associations
RT Health Occupations
Medicine
Nurses
Pharmacists
Physicians
Psychiatrists

Medical Audit
USE MEDICAL CARE EVALUATION

Medical Care
USE MEDICAL SERVICES

MEDICAL CARE EVALUATION *Dec. 1976*
CIJE: 144 RIE: 126 GC: 210
SN Judgment of the amount, quality, and appropriateness of the services and facilities provided for sick and injured persons, and also of the quality of preventive medical care
UF Health Care Evaluation
Medical Audit
Patient Care Evaluation
BT Evaluation
RT Community Health Services
Health Facilities
Health Services
Medical Evaluation
Medical Services
Medicine
Outcomes Of Treatment
Physician Patient Relationship
Primary Health Care

MEDICAL CASE HISTORIES *Jul. 1966*
CIJE: 320 RIE: 64 GC: 210
BT Case Records
RT Clinical Diagnosis
Medical Evaluation
Medical Record Administrators
Medical Record Technicians
Medical Research
Medical Services
Medicine
Patients
Profiles

MEDICAL CONSULTANTS *Jul. 1966*
CIJE: 31 RIE: 19 GC: 210
BT Consultants
Health Personnel
RT Medical Services
Physicians
Psychiatrists

Medical Doctors
USE PHYSICIANS

MEDICAL EDUCATION *Aug. 1969*
CIJE: 2966 RIE: 1018 GC: 210
SN Professional education and training concerned with the health of individuals or the care and treatment of patients -- presented by or under the supervision of physicians, dentists, nurses, etc. (note: do not confuse with "health education")
NT Graduate Medical Education
Nursing Education
Pharmaceutical Education
Veterinary Medical Education
BT Professional Education
RT Allied Health Occupations Education
Clinical Experience
Clinical Teaching (Health Professions)
Dental Schools
Health Occupations
Health Personnel
Medical School Faculty
Medical Schools
Medical Students

Medicine
Premedical Students
Teaching Hospitals

MEDICAL EVALUATION *Jul. 1966*
CIJE: 358 RIE: 231 GC: 210
SN Determination of an individual's health and of any needed treatment -- also, the judgment of the efficacy of a program, procedure, etc. from a medical or pharmacological perspective
UF Clinical Judgment (Medicine)
NT Auditory Evaluation
Dental Evaluation
Physical Examinations
Speech Evaluation
BT Evaluation
RT Clinical Diagnosis
Diagnostic Tests
Electroencephalography
Handicap Identification
Health
Health Personnel
Medical Care Evaluation
Medical Case Histories
Medical Services
Medicine
Patients
Physician Patient Relationship

MEDICAL LABORATORY ASSISTANTS *Jul. 1966*
CIJE: 15 RIE: 86 GC: 210
UF Biomedical Equipment Technicians
Medical Technicians
BT Medical Assistants
RT Biomedical Equipment
Electronic Technicians
Laboratory Technology
Medical Technologists

Medical Laboratory Technologists
USE MEDICAL TECHNOLOGISTS

MEDICAL LIBRARIES *Jul. 1966*
CIJE: 132 RIE: 208 GC: 710
SN Libraries devoted to information and related services in the science and practice of medicine
UF Health Sciences Libraries
BT Special Libraries
RT Health Personnel
Health Services
Medical Research
Medical Schools
Medicine
Research Libraries

MEDICAL RECORD ADMINISTRATORS *Mar. 1980*
CIJE: 5 RIE: 15 GC: 210
SN Individuals who plan, develop, and administer medical record systems for hospitals, clinics, health centers, etc. (note: for librarians in medical libraries, coordinate "librarians" and "medical libraries" -- for librarians who are directly involved in patient care, use the identifier "clinical medical librarians")
UF Hospital Record Administrators
Medical Record Librarians (1969 1980)
BT Administrators
Allied Health Personnel
RT Medical Case Histories
Medical Record Technicians

Medical Record Clerks
USE MEDICAL RECORD TECHNICIANS

Medical Record Librarians (1969 1980)
USE MEDICAL RECORD ADMINISTRATORS

MEDICAL RECORD TECHNICIANS *Aug. 1968*
CIJE: 4 RIE: 38 GC: 210
SN Individuals who compile and maintain medical records of hospital, clinic, or health center patients
UF Hospital Record Technicians
Medical Record Clerks
BT Allied Health Personnel
Library Technicians
RT File Clerks
Filing
Medical Case Histories
Medical Record Administrators
Recordkeeping

MEDICAL RESEARCH *Jul. 1966*
CIJE: 532 RIE: 238 GC: 810
SN Basic, applied, and developmental research conducted to advance knowledge in medicine (note: as of oct81, use as a minor descriptor for examples of this kind of research -- use as a major descriptor only as the subject of a document)
BT Research
RT Exceptional Child Research
Exercise Physiology
Laboratory Animals
Medical Case Histories
Medical Libraries
Medical Services
Medicine
Scientific Research

Medical School Applicants
USE COLLEGE APPLICANTS; MEDICAL SCHOOLS

MEDICAL SCHOOL FACULTY *Mar. 1980*
CIJE: 235 RIE: 74 GC: 360
SN Persons instructing in medical or dental programs, including field supervisors of related clinical experience programs (e.g., externships or preceptorships)
UF Clinical Professors (1967 1980) (Medicine)
Dental School Faculty #
BT Graduate School Faculty
RT Clinical Experience
Clinical Teaching (Health Professions)
Dental Schools
Graduate Medical Education
Medical Education
Medical Schools
Practicum Supervision

MEDICAL SCHOOLS *Jul. 1966*
CIJE: 798 RIE: 428 GC: 340
SN Schools or colleges of medicine, usually professional schools of universities, that prepare students who have completed baccalaureate programs to be physicians and award doctor of medicine (m.d.) degrees
UF Medical School Applicants #
Schools Of Medicine
BT Colleges
RT Dental Schools
Foreign Medical Graduates
Graduate Medical Education
Graduate Medical Students
Medical Education
Medical Libraries
Medical School Faculty
Medical Students
Medicine
Professional Education
Teaching Hospitals

Medical Sciences
USE MEDICINE

Medical Secretaries
USE SECRETARIES

MEDICAL SERVICES *Jul. 1966*
CIJE: 1403 RIE: 1258 GC: 210
UF Medical Assistance
Medical Care
Medical Treatment (1967 1980)
NT First Aid
Psychiatric Services
BT Health Services
RT Abortions
Anesthesiology
Clinics
Dentistry
Dentists
Drug Therapy
Electroencephalography
Emergency Medical Technicians
Epidemiology
Family Practice (Medicine)
Geriatrics
Gynecology
Health Facilities
Hospices (Terminal Care)
Hospital Personnel
Hospitals
Injuries
Internal Medicine
Intervention
Medical Assistants
Medical Care Evaluation
Medical Case Histories
Medical Consultants
Medical Evaluation
Medical Research
Medical Technologists
Medicine
Nurses
Nursing
Nursing Homes
Obstetrics
Occupational Therapy
Oncology
Ophthalmology
Osteopathy
Outcomes Of Treatment
Patients
Pediatrics
Pharmacists
Pharmacy
Physical Therapy
Physician Patient Relationship
Physicians
Physicians Assistants
Podiatry
Preventive Medicine
Primary Health Care
Professional Services
Prognostic Tests
Psychiatrists
Psychiatry
Rehabilitation
Respiratory Therapy
Speech Therapy
Surgery
Surgical Technicians
Termination Of Treatment
Therapy
Tissue Donors
Toxicology
Veterinary Medicine

MEDICAL STUDENTS *Jul. 1966*
CIJE: 1158 RIE: 280 GC: 360
SN Students enrolled in medical schools (note: for undergraduates preparing for medical school, use "premedical students" -- prior to oct81, the use of this term was not restricted by a scope note)
NT Graduate Medical Students
BT Graduate Students
RT Dental Students
Foreign Medical Graduates
Medical Education
Medical Schools
Premedical Students
Professional Education

Medical Technicians
USE MEDICAL LABORATORY ASSISTANTS

MEDICAL TECHNOLOGISTS *May. 1969*
CIJE: 29 RIE: 102 GC: 210
SN Personnel responsible for performing chemical, microscopic, serologic, hematologic, immunohematologic, parasitic, and bacteriologic tests to provide data for use in treatment and diagnosis of disease -- may supervise medical laboratory technicians/assistants
UF Medical Laboratory Technologists
BT Allied Health Personnel
RT Medical Laboratory Assistants
Medical Services

Medical Treatment (1967 1980)
USE MEDICAL SERVICES

MEDICAL VOCABULARY *Jul. 1966*
CIJE: 25 RIE: 92 GC: 210
BT Vocabulary
RT Medicine
Physicians
Professional Training

MEDICINE *Aug. 1969*
CIJE: 653 RIE: 313 GC: 210
UF Medical Sciences
Paramedical Sciences
NT Anesthesiology
Audiology
Biomedicine
Dentistry
Dietetics
Electroencephalography
Epidemiology
Family Practice (Medicine)
Geriatrics
Gynecology
Internal Medicine
Neurology
Nursing
Obstetrics
Oncology
Ophthalmology
Osteopathy
Pathology
Pediatrics
Pharmacology
Pharmacy
Podiatry
Preventive Medicine
Primary Health Care
Psychiatry
Surgery
Toxicology
Veterinary Medicine
BT Technology
RT Allied Health Occupations Education
Anatomy
Biochemistry
Bioethics
Biological Influences
Biomedical Equipment
Embryology
Enzymes
Genetic Engineering
Genetics
Graduate Medical Education
Health
Health Occupations
Human Body
Hygiene
Medical Associations
Medical Care Evaluation
Medical Case Histories
Medical Education
Medical Evaluation
Medical Libraries
Medical Research
Medical Schools
Medical Services
Medical Vocabulary
Microbiology
Nurse Practitioners
Physical Health
Physicians
Physiology
Radiation Biology
Radiology
Therapy

MEDIEVAL HISTORY *Jul. 1966*
CIJE: 59 RIE: 55 GC: 430
BT History
RT Medieval Literature

MEDIEVAL LITERATURE *Jun. 1969*
CIJE: 104 RIE: 37 GC: 430
SN Literature of the middle ages (about 500 to 1500 ad)
UF Medieval Romance (1969 1980)
BT Literature
RT Chronicles
Epics
Fifteenth Century Literature
Legends
Medieval History
Middle English
Mythology
World Literature

Medieval Romance (1969 1980)
USE MEDIEVAL LITERATURE

MEDITATION *Oct. 1982*
CIJE: 45 RIE: 12 GC: 110
SN Integration of ideas, feelings, and attitudes through focused concentration or sustained reflection, often as a devotional act
NT Transcendental Meditation
BT Metacognition
RT Attention Control
Conditioning
Hypnosis
Psychophysiology
Psychotherapy
Religion
Self Congruence
Sensory Experience
Suggestopedia

Medium Of Instruction (Language)
USE LANGUAGE OF INSTRUCTION

= Two or more Descriptors are used to represent this term.
The term's main entry shows the appropriate coordination.

MEETINGS *Jul. 1966*
CIJE: 367 RIE: 383 GC: 520
UF Colloquiums (Meetings)
Planning Meetings (1966 1980)
NT Seminars
Staff Meetings
RT Assembly Programs
Clinics
Conference Papers
Conference Proceedings
Conferences
Hearings
Institutes (Training Programs)
Workshops

Melancholia
USE DEPRESSION (PSYCHOLOGY)

MELANESIAN LANGUAGES *Jan. 1970*
CIJE: 1 RIE: 2 GC: 440
BT Malayo Polynesian Languages

MEMORIZATION *Mar. 1980*
CIJE: 218 RIE: 135 GC: 110
SN Process of committing to memory
UF Memorizing (1967 1980)
BT Learning Processes
RT Drills (Practice)
Memory
Mnemonics
Primacy Effect
Recall (Psychology)
Retention (Psychology)
Rote Learning
Serial Learning
Verbal Learning
Visualization

Memorizing (1967 1980)
USE MEMORIZATION

MEMORY *Jul. 1966*
CIJE: 2966 RIE: 1283 GC: 110
UF Forgetting
Remembering
NT Eidetic Imagery
Long Term Memory
Recall (Psychology)
Recognition (Psychology)
Retention (Psychology)
Short Term Memory
BT Cognitive Processes
RT Cues
Encoding (Psychology)
Learning Processes
Learning Strategies
Memorization
Metacognition
Mnemonics
Visualization

Memory Devices (Computers)
USE COMPUTER STORAGE DEVICES

Men
USE MALES

MENDE *Jul. 1966*
CIJE: 1 RIE: 8 GC: 440
BT African Languages

Mental Ability
USE COGNITIVE ABILITY

MENTAL AGE *Apr. 1980*
CIJE: 37 RIE: 11 GC: 120
SN The individual's intelligence level expressed as equivalent to the chronological age at which the average person attains that level
UF Intelligence Age
BT Age
Intelligence
RT Intellectual Development
Intelligence Differences
Intelligence Quotient
Intelligence Tests

Mental Development (1966 1980)
USE COGNITIVE DEVELOPMENT

MENTAL DISORDERS *Mar. 1980*
CIJE: 524 RIE: 277 GC: 230
SN General term for any emotional or organic mental impairments (note: do not confuse with "mental retardation," and, use a more specific term if possible)
UF Mental Illness (1966 1980)
NT Emotional Disturbances
Neurosis
Psychosis
BT Disabilities
RT Adaptive Behavior (Of Disabled)
Behavior Disorders
Behavior Problems
Clinical Psychology
Exceptional Persons
Institutionalized Persons
Mental Health
Neurological Impairments
Personality Problems
Physical Disabilities
Psychiatric Hospitals
Psychiatric Services
Psychiatry
Psychopathology
Psychotherapy
Self Destructive Behavior

MENTAL HEALTH *Jul. 1966*
CIJE: 1157 RIE: 1074 GC: 230
SN Relatively enduring state of adjustment in which people have feelings of well-being, are realizing their abilities, and coping with everyday demands without excessive stress -- also includes efforts to maintain and promote this state to prevent mental disorders
UF Emotional Health
Mental Hygiene
BT Health
RT Adjustment (To Environment)
Coping
Emotional Disturbances
Hygiene
Individual Power
Life Satisfaction
Mental Disorders
Mental Health Clinics
Mental Health Programs
Morale
Neurology
Neurosis
Psychiatric Services
Psychiatry
Psychological Services
Psychosis
Psychotherapy
Public Health
Self Actualization

MENTAL HEALTH CLINICS *Jul. 1966*
CIJE: 186 RIE: 171 GC: 230
BT Clinics
RT Mental Health
Psychiatric Hospitals
Psychoeducational Clinics
Rehabilitation Centers
Therapeutic Environment

MENTAL HEALTH PROGRAMS *Jul. 1966*
CIJE: 584 RIE: 578 GC: 230
UF Mental Health Resources
BT Health Programs
RT Employee Assistance Programs
Mental Health
Psychiatric Services
Rehabilitation Programs
Residential Programs

Mental Health Resources
USE MENTAL HEALTH PROGRAMS

Mental Hygiene
USE MENTAL HEALTH

Mental Illness (1966 1980)
USE MENTAL DISORDERS

MENTAL RETARDATION *Jul. 1966*
CIJE: 4733 RIE: 3104 GC: 220
SN Intellectual functioning that is two or more standard deviations below the mean (usually below 70 iq range), concurrent with deficits in adaptive behavior, and manifested during the developmental period (note: use a more specific term if possible)
UF Mentally Handicapped (1966 1980)
Retardation (1966 1980)
Retarded Children (1966 1980)
NT Downs Syndrome
Mild Mental Retardation
Moderate Mental Retardation
Severe Mental Retardation
BT Disabilities
RT Adaptive Behavior (Of Disabled)
Cerebral Palsy
Developmental Disabilities
Exceptional Persons
Intelligence
Learning Problems
Neurological Impairments
Special Health Problems

MENTAL RIGIDITY *Jul. 1966*
CIJE: 35 RIE: 21 GC: 120
BT Personality Traits
RT Bias
Intellectual Development

Mental Tests (1966 1980)
USE PSYCHOLOGICAL TESTING

Mentally Advanced Children
USE GIFTED

Mentally Handicapped (1966 1980)
USE MENTAL RETARDATION

MENTORS *Mar. 1980*
CIJE: 177 RIE: 138 GC: 520
SN Trusted and experienced supervisors or advisers who have personal and direct interest in the development and/or education of younger or less experienced individuals, usually in professional education or professional occupations
BT Role Models
RT Interpersonal Relationship
Interprofessional Relationship
Modeling (Psychology)
Professional Development
Significant Others
Teacher Student Relationship

MENU DRIVEN SOFTWARE *Apr. 1986*
CIJE: 1 RIE: GC: 720
SN User-friendly software that presents lists of options at various stages of a program sequence -- from each list, a selection is made to initiate subsequent actions
BT Computer Software
RT Branching
Interactive Video
Online Systems
Users (Information)
Videotex
Word Processing

MERCHANDISE INFORMATION *Jul. 1966*
CIJE: 362 RIE: 181 GC: 650
SN Literature or labels identifying product value, regulation, service, and care for the consumer and the trade
UF Product Information
Product Labels
RT Consumer Economics
Consumer Protection
Marketing
Merchandising
Salesmanship

MERCHANDISING *Jul. 1966*
CIJE: 188 RIE: 265 GC: 650
SN Sales promotion as a comprehensive function including market research, advertising, and selling
UF Sales Promotion
BT Marketing
RT Advertising
College Stores
Commercial Art
Credit (Finance)
Display Aids
Distributive Education
Feed Stores
Food Stores
Merchandise Information
Merchants
Retailing
Salesmanship
Sales Occupations
Television Commercials

MERCHANTS *Apr. 1969*
CIJE: 37 RIE: 14 GC: 640
BT Personnel
RT Business
Entrepreneurship
Marketing
Merchandising
Retailing
Sales Occupations
Sales Workers
Wholesaling

MERGERS *Jul. 1969*
CIJE: 72 RIE: 73 GC: 520
SN Combination of two or more organizations or institutions
BT Organizational Change
RT Business
Centralization
Churches
Consolidated Schools
Industrial Structure
Industry
Organization
Organizations (Groups)
Organization Size (Groups)
School Closing

MERIT PAY *Oct. 1972*
CIJE: 165 RIE: 128 GC: 630
BT Expenditures
Income
RT Differentiated Staffs
Incentives
Master Teachers
Merit Rating
Personnel Policy
Premium Pay
Recognition (Achievement)
Salaries
Salary Wage Differentials
Teacher Employment
Wages

MERIT RATING *Mar. 1980*
CIJE: 61 RIE: 63 GC: 320
SN Periodic evaluation of individual efficiency as a basis for compensation and/or promotion
UF Merit Rating Programs (1967 1980)
BT Measurement
RT Achievement Rating
Job Skills
Merit Pay
Peer Evaluation
Personnel Evaluation
Recognition (Achievement)
Rewards

Merit Rating Programs (1967 1980)
USE MERIT RATING

MERIT SCHOLARSHIPS *Aug. 1986*
CIJE: 2 RIE: 2 GC: 620
SN Financial aid awards given to students in recognition of academic, athletic, or artistic achievement (note: see also identifiers "national merit scholarship program" and "national merit scholars")
NT No Need Scholarships
BT Scholarships
RT Achievement Rating
Assistantships
Recognition (Achievement)
Scholarship Funds
Tuition Grants

META ANALYSIS *Oct. 1983*
CIJE: 167 RIE: 133 GC: 820
SN Statistical analysis of the summary findings of many empirical studies
UF Integrative Analysis
BT Statistical Analysis
RT Comparative Analysis
Correlation
Effect Size
Error Of Measurement
Hypothesis Testing
Literature Reviews
Research
Research Methodology
Statistical Data
Synthesis

Meta Knowledge
USE METACOGNITION

METABOLISM *Nov. 1969*
CIJE: 149 RIE: 32 GC: 210
NT Blood Circulation
Heart Rate
RT Biochemistry
Biofeedback
Biology

= Two or more Descriptors are used to represent this term.
The term's main entry shows the appropriate coordination.

Enzymes
Exercise Physiology
Human Body
Photosynthesis
Physiology

METACOGNITION *Oct. 1980*
CIJE: 171 RIE: 178 GC: 110
SN Knowledge or beliefs about factors affecting one's own cognitive activities -- also, reflection on or monitoring of one's own cognitive processes, such as memory or comprehension
UF Meta Knowledge
Metamemory
NT Meditation
BT Cognitive Processes
RT Cognitive Ability
Communication Skills
Comprehension
Learning Processes
Learning Strategies
Memory
Self Control
Self Evaluation (Individuals)
Social Cognition
Study Skills

Metal Finishing
USE FINISHING

Metal Forming Occupations
USE METAL WORKING

METAL INDUSTRY *Dec. 1969*
CIJE: 40 RIE: 62 GC: 650
UF Steel Industry (1967 1980)
BT Manufacturing Industry
RT Foundries
Metallurgical Technicians
Metallurgy
Metals
Metal Working

Metal Trades
USE METAL WORKING

METAL WORKING *Mar. 1980*
CIJE: 28 RIE: 217 GC: 640
UF Metal Forming Occupations
Metal Trades
Metal Working Occupations (1968 1980)
NT Sheet Metal Work
BT Technology
RT Assembly (Manufacturing)
Finishing
Foundries
Handicrafts
Hand Tools
Industrial Arts
Machine Tools
Machinists
Metal Industry
Metals
Patternmaking
Semiskilled Occupations
Shop Curriculum
Skilled Occupations
Tool And Die Makers
Visual Arts
Welding

Metal Working Occupations (1968 1980)
USE METAL WORKING

METALLURGICAL TECHNICIANS *Jul. 1966*
CIJE: 3 RIE: 7 GC: 640
BT Paraprofessional Personnel
RT Chemical Technicians
Engineering Technicians
Metal Industry
Metallurgy
Physics
Radiographers
Scientific Personnel

METALLURGY *May. 1969*
CIJE: 51 RIE: 42 GC: 490
BT Technology
RT Chemical Analysis
Chemistry
Crystallography
Inorganic Chemistry
Metal Industry
Metallurgical Technicians
Metals
Mineralogy
Physics

METALS *Sep. 1969*
CIJE: 198 RIE: 96 GC: 490
RT Metal Industry
Metallurgy
Metal Working
Minerals
Mining

Metamemory
USE METACOGNITION

METAPHORS *May. 1969*
CIJE: 326 RIE: 173 GC: 430
BT Figurative Language
RT Allegory
Imagery
Legends
Sonnets
Symbols (Literary)

METEOROLOGY *Jul. 1966*
CIJE: 197 RIE: 137 GC: 490
BT Earth Science
RT Climate
Humidity
Physics
Solar Energy
Temperature
Thermal Environment
Water
Weather
Wind (Meteorology)

Meters
USE MEASUREMENT EQUIPMENT

Methodology (1966 1974)
USE METHODS

METHODS *Jul. 1966*
CIJE: 1086 RIE: 957 GC: 810
SN Systematic approaches to the conduct of an operation or process -- includes steps of procedure, application of techniques, systems of reasoning or analysis, and the modes of inquiry employed by a science or discipline (note: use a more specific term if possible)
UF Methodology (1966 1974)
Procedures
Techniques (1966 1974)
NT Algorithms
Branching
Caseworker Approach
Change Strategies
Cloze Procedure
Counseling Techniques
Critical Incidents Method
Critical Path Method
Delphi Technique
Desegregation Methods
Educational Methods
Evaluation Methods
Fixed Sequence
Grievance Procedures
Heuristics
Holistic Approach
Home Visits
Inquiry
Insurance
Interdisciplinary Approach
Job Search Methods
Laboratory Procedures
Learning Strategies
Magnification Methods
Marxian Analysis
Measurement Techniques
Motivation Techniques
Music Techniques
Network Analysis
Pacing
Production Techniques
Prompting
Questioning Techniques
Research Methodology
Sequential Approach
Simulation
Supervisory Methods
Systems Analysis
RT Methods Courses
Methods Research
Methods Teachers

METHODS COURSES *Jul. 1966*
CIJE: 452 RIE: 417 GC: 400
SN Courses in standard classroom procedures that may be used in teaching any subject
UF General Methods Courses
Special Methods Courses
BT Courses
Teacher Education Curriculum
RT Education Courses
Methods
Methods Research
Methods Teachers
Student Teaching
Teacher Education
Teacher Education Programs

METHODS RESEARCH *Jul. 1966*
CIJE: 220 RIE: 312 GC: 810
SN Systematic investigation of the procedures, materials, tools, and/or equipment used to perform a task (note: as of oct81, use as a minor descriptor for examples of this kind of research -- use as a major descriptor only as the subject of a document)
BT Research
RT Action Research
Educational Methods
Evaluation Methods
Methods
Methods Courses
Program Effectiveness
Research Methodology
Teaching Methods
Theory Practice Relationship

METHODS TEACHERS *Jul. 1966*
CIJE: 20 RIE: 35 GC: 360
SN Teacher educators who provide instruction in how to teach a particular subject or general classroom procedures that may be used in teaching any subject
BT Teacher Educators
RT Methods
Methods Courses
Teacher Education

METRIC SYSTEM *Oct. 1971*
CIJE: 528 RIE: 453 GC: 480
UF Metrication
Si Units
BT Standards
RT Measurement

Metrication
USE METRIC SYSTEM

METROPOLITAN AREAS *Jul. 1966*
CIJE: 220 RIE: 436 GC: 550
SN Geographic areas consisting of a large population nucleus (i.e., a city), as well as the surrounding areas that are linked to the center by social, economic, or political considerations
NT Suburbs
BT Geographic Regions
RT Municipalities
Neighborhoods
Urban Areas
Urban Demography

Mexican American Culture
USE HISPANIC AMERICAN CULTURE; MEXICAN AMERICANS

MEXICAN AMERICAN EDUCATION *Mar. 1980*
CIJE: 29 RIE: 202 GC: 330
SN Education for mexican americans (note: prior to mar80, this concept was indexed under "mexican americans")
BT Education
RT Bilingual Education
English (Second Language)
Mexican Americans
Multicultural Education

MEXICAN AMERICAN HISTORY *Jul. 1966*
CIJE: 54 RIE: 162 GC: 430
SN History of the mexican american people and of the united states' relations with mexico (note: do not use to index "mexican history")
BT United States History
RT Mexican American Literature
Mexican Americans
Mexicans
Modern History

MEXICAN AMERICAN LITERATURE *Mar. 1980*
CIJE: 12 RIE: 34 GC: 430
BT Hispanic American Literature
RT Latin American Literature
Mexican American History
Mexican Americans
Spanish Speaking

MEXICAN AMERICANS *Jul. 1966*
CIJE: 1220 RIE: 2708 GC: 560
UF Mexican American Culture #
BT Ethnic Groups
Hispanic Americans
RT Hispanic American Culture
Mexican American Education
Mexican American History
Mexican American Literature
Mexicans
Spanish Americans
Spanish Speaking

MEXICANS *Jul. 1972*
CIJE: 124 RIE: 151 GC: 560
SN Citizens of mexico
NT Braceros
BT Latin Americans
RT American Indians
Ethnic Groups
Mexican American History
Mexican Americans
Spanish Speaking

MICROBIOLOGY *Aug. 1968*
CIJE: 274 RIE: 107 GC: 490
BT Biology
RT Botany
Culturing Techniques
Genetic Engineering
Genetics
Medicine
Pests
Physiology
Zoology

Microcalorimeters
USE CALORIMETERS

MICROCOMPUTERS *Mar. 1980*
CIJE: 2872 RIE: 1430 GC: 910
SN Physically the smallest computer and distinguished from other computers by size rather than capacity -- often incorporated into other devices, e.g., electronic calculators, videodisc recorders, to perform specific logical and control functions -- component parts are usually contained on a single circuit board composed of lsi (large-scale integration) semiconductor chips
UF Desktop Computers
Microprocessors
Personal Computers
Pocket Computers
Portable Computers
BT Computers
RT Local Area Networks
Minicomputers
Online Systems

MICROCOUNSELING *Nov. 1968*
CIJE: 67 RIE: 37 GC: 240
SN Method of counselor training in which simulated counseling sessions (often videotaped) are used to analyze trainees' specific counseling skills and behaviors
BT Training Methods
RT Counseling
Counseling Techniques
Counselor Training
Microteaching
Practicums
Videotape Recordings

MICROFICHE *Jul. 1966*
CIJE: 152 RIE: 249 GC: 720
SN Sheet of photographic negative film that contains microimages of pages, drawings, etc. in an array of frames, and, at the top, a catalog entry or title that is readable with the naked eye
UF Ultramicrofiche

= Two or more Descriptors are used to represent this term.
The term's main entry shows the appropriate coordination.

BT Microforms
RT Information Storage
Microfilm

MICROFILM *Jul. 1966*
CIJE: 99 RIE: 130 GC: 720
NT Computer Output Microfilm
BT Microforms
RT Filmstrips
Information Storage
Microfiche

Microfilming
USE MICROREPRODUCTION

Microform Reader Printers (1971 1980)
USE MICROFORM READERS

MICROFORM READERS *Jan. 1971*
CIJE: 46 RIE: 56 GC: 910
UF Microform Reader Printers (1971 1980)
BT Projection Equipment
RT Magnification Methods
Microforms
Microreproduction

MICROFORMS *Sep. 1969*
CIJE: 211 RIE: 208 GC: 720
UF Microimages
Microtexts
NT Microfiche
Microfilm
BT Visual Aids
RT Information Storage
Instructional Materials
Microform Readers
Microreproduction
Reprography

Micrographics
USE MICROREPRODUCTION

Microimages
USE MICROFORMS

MICROPHONES *Jul. 1966*
CIJE: 12 RIE: 16 GC: 910
BT Audio Equipment
Electronic Equipment
RT Audiovisual Aids

Microphotography
USE MICROREPRODUCTION

Microprocessors
USE MICROCOMPUTERS

MICROREPRODUCTION *Sep. 1971*
CIJE: 94 RIE: 46 GC: 720
SN Production of copy by photographic or other means in sizes too small to be read without magnification
UF Microfilming
Micrographics
Microphotography
BT Reprography
RT Microform Readers
Microforms

MICROSCOPES *Jul. 1966*
CIJE: 82 RIE: 19 GC: 910
BT Laboratory Equipment
RT Magnification Methods

MICROTEACHING *Jul. 1966*
CIJE: 316 RIE: 445 GC: 310
SN Method of teacher training in which simulated teaching sessions (often videotaped) are used to develop and analyze trainees' specific teaching skills and behaviors
BT Training Methods
RT Laboratory Training
Microcounseling
Protocol Materials
Student Teachers
Student Teaching
Teacher Education
Teaching Experience
Teaching Skills
Videotape Recordings

Microtexts
USE MICROFORMS

Microwave Relay Systems (1971 1980)
USE TELECOMMUNICATIONS

Midcareer Change
USE CAREER CHANGE; MIDLIFE TRANSITIONS

Middle Aged (1966 1980)
USE MIDDLE AGED ADULTS

MIDDLE AGED ADULTS *Mar. 1980*
CIJE: 319 RIE: 329 GC: 120
SN Approximately 45-64 years of age
UF Middle Aged (1966 1980)
Midlife
BT Adults
RT Age Discrimination
Aging (Individuals)
Early Retirement
Elder Abuse
Midlife Transitions
Older Adults
Preretirement Education
Young Adults

MIDDLE CLASS *Jul. 1966*
CIJE: 273 RIE: 332 GC: 520
BT Social Class
RT Advantaged
Lower Class
Lower Middle Class
Middle Class Culture
Middle Class Parents
Middle Class Standards
Middle Class Students
Upper Class
Working Class

Middle Class College Students (1966 1980)
USE COLLEGE STUDENTS; MIDDLE CLASS STUDENTS

MIDDLE CLASS CULTURE *Jul. 1966*
CIJE: 72 RIE: 54 GC: 560
UF Majority Culture
BT Culture
RT Middle Class
Middle Class Standards

Middle Class Fathers (1966 1980)
USE FATHERS; MIDDLE CLASS PARENTS

Middle Class Mothers (1966 1980)
USE MIDDLE CLASS PARENTS; MOTHERS

Middle Class Norm (1966 1980)
USE MIDDLE CLASS STANDARDS

MIDDLE CLASS PARENTS *Jul. 1966*
CIJE: 40 RIE: 57 GC: 510
UF Middle Class Fathers (1966 1980) #
Middle Class Mothers (1966 1980) #
BT Parents
RT Middle Class

MIDDLE CLASS STANDARDS *Mar. 1980*
CIJE: 128 RIE: 128 GC: 520
UF Middle Class Norm (1966 1980)
Middle Class Values (1966 1980)
BT Standards
RT Middle Class
Middle Class Culture

MIDDLE CLASS STUDENTS *Mar. 1980*
CIJE: 29 RIE: 47 GC: 360
UF Middle Class College Students (1966 1980) #
BT Students
RT Lower Class Students
Middle Class

Middle Class Values (1966 1980)
USE MIDDLE CLASS STANDARDS

MIDDLE EASTERN HISTORY *Jun. 1969*
CIJE: 27 RIE: 36 GC: 430
SN History of all or part of the geographic area that includes afghanistan, cyprus, egypt, iran, iraq, israel, jordan, lebanon, libya, sudan, syria, turkey, and the arabian peninsula
UF Near Eastern History
BT History
RT African Culture
African History
Area Studies
Asian History
Middle Eastern Studies
Non Western Civilization

MIDDLE EASTERN STUDIES *Jun. 1973*
CIJE: 63 RIE: 58 GC: 400
SN Studies, usually interdisciplinary in approach, of all or part of the geographic area that includes afghanistan, cyprus, egypt, iran, iraq, israel, jordan, lebanon, libya, sudan, syria, turkey, and the arabian peninsula
BT Area Studies
RT African Culture
African History
Arabs
Asian History
Asian Studies
Foreign Culture
Islamic Culture
Jews
Middle Eastern History
Non Western Civilization

MIDDLE ENGLISH *May. 1969*
CIJE: 10 RIE: 8 GC: 440
BT English
RT Diachronic Linguistics
Indo European Languages
Languages
Linguistics
Medieval Literature
Welsh

MIDDLE INCOME HOUSING *Jul. 1966*
CIJE: 10 RIE: 4 GC: 550
BT Housing
RT Income

Middle Level Management
USE MIDDLE MANAGEMENT

MIDDLE MANAGEMENT *Jun. 1978*
CIJE: 56 RIE: 68 GC: 630
SN The intermediate level of management, excluding top-level management on the one hand and first-level supervision on the other
UF Middle Level Management
Midmanagement
BT Administration
RT Administrative Organization
Administrators
Admissions Officers
Deans
Department Heads
Industrial Structure
Leadership
Power Structure
School Business Officials
Student Financial Aid Officers

MIDDLE SCHOOLS *Jul. 1966*
CIJE: 914 RIE: 1006 GC: 340
BT Schools
RT High Schools
Intermediate Grades
Junior High Schools

Midlife
USE MIDDLE AGED ADULTS

MIDLIFE TRANSITIONS *Jun. 1981*
CIJE: 84 RIE: 72 GC: 120
SN Physical, occupational, social, or psychological changes occurring among middle aged adults
UF Midcareer Change #
BT Change
RT Adult Development
Aging (Individuals)
Behavior Change
Career Change
Early Retirement
Employment Practices
Family Relationship
Middle Aged Adults
Physical Health
Preretirement Education
Psychological Characteristics
Self Actualization
Social Development

Midmanagement
USE MIDDLE MANAGEMENT

Midtwentieth Century Literature
USE TWENTIETH CENTURY LITERATURE

Midwifery
USE OBSTETRICS

MIGRANT ADULT EDUCATION *Jul. 1966*
CIJE: 12 RIE: 56 GC: 330
SN Learning activities and experiences provided by a school district, etc. to migratory workers and/or their families -- includes postsecondary, adult, and vocational education
BT Adult Education
RT Adult Basic Education
Bilingual Education
English (Second Language)
Migrant Education
Migrant Problems
Migrant Programs
Migrants
Migrant Workers
Migrant Youth

Migrant Adults
USE MIGRANTS

Migrant Child Care Centers (1966 1980)
USE DAY CARE CENTERS; MIGRANT CHILDREN

Migrant Child Education (1967 1980)
USE MIGRANT EDUCATION

MIGRANT CHILDREN *Jul. 1966*
CIJE: 87 RIE: 416 GC: 510
SN Children who travel with their families from one temporary residence to another so that one or more family members might secure temporary or seasonal employment (note: do not confuse with "transient children")
UF Migrant Child Care Centers (1966 1980) #
Migratory Children
BT Children
Migrants
RT Migrant Education
Migrant Youth
Student Mobility
Transfer Students

MIGRANT EDUCATION *Jul. 1966*
CIJE: 116 RIE: 1182 GC: 330
SN Formal supplementary learning activities and experiences provided by a school district, etc. to the children of migratory workers from early childhood through grade 12
UF Migrant Child Education (1967 1980)
Migrant Schools (1966 1980)
BT Education
RT Bilingual Education
English (Second Language)
Migrant Adult Education
Migrant Children
Migrant Problems
Migrant Programs
Migrant Youth
Migration
Mobile Educational Services
Multicultural Education
Student Mobility
Supplementary Education

MIGRANT EMPLOYMENT *Jul. 1966*
CIJE: 24 RIE: 63 GC: 630
BT Employment
RT Braceros
Migrant Problems
Migrant Programs
Migrants
Seasonal Employment
Seasonal Laborers

MIGRANT HEALTH SERVICES *Jul. 1966*
CIJE: 18 RIE: 171 GC: 210
BT Health Services
RT Migrant Problems
Migrant Programs
Migrants

MIGRANT HOUSING *Jul. 1966*
CIJE: 8 RIE: 96 GC: 920
SN Dwellings for migratory workers and their families -- includes the immediate surroundings, and related services or facilities
UF Labor Camps (1966 1980) (Migrants)
BT Housing
RT Migrant Problems
Migrant Programs
Migrants

= Two or more Descriptors are used to represent this term.
The term's main entry shows the appropriate coordination.

Migrant Population
USE MIGRANTS

MIGRANT PROBLEMS *Jul. 1966*
CIJE: 56 RIE: 150 GC: 530
SN Problems of migrants
BT Problems
RT Migrant Adult Education
Migrant Education
Migrant Employment
Migrant Health Services
Migrant Housing
Migrant Programs
Migrants
Migrant Welfare Services
Migrant Workers

MIGRANT PROGRAMS *Mar. 1980*
CIJE: 30 RIE: 192 GC: 520
SN Projects or programs for or by migrant workers and their families designed to further their social or economic progress -- often include educational, medical, or occupational assistance
UF Church Migrant Projects (1966 1980) #
Community Migrant Projects (1966 1980) #
Migrant Projects
Migrant Worker Projects (1966 1980) #
BT Programs
RT Church Programs
Community Programs
Migrant Adult Education
Migrant Education
Migrant Employment
Migrant Health Services
Migrant Housing
Migrant Problems
Migrants
Migrant Welfare Services
Outreach Programs

Migrant Projects
USE MIGRANT PROGRAMS

Migrant Schools (1966 1980)
USE MIGRANT EDUCATION

Migrant Transportation (1966 1980)
USE MIGRANTS; TRANSPORTATION

MIGRANT WELFARE SERVICES *Jul. 1966*
CIJE: 4 RIE: 76 GC: 520
BT Welfare Services
RT Migrant Problems
Migrant Programs
Migrants

Migrant Worker Projects (1966 1980)
USE MIGRANT PROGRAMS; MIGRANT WORKERS

MIGRANT WORKERS *Jul. 1966*
CIJE: 108 RIE: 407 GC: 630
UF Agricultural Migrant Workers
Interstate Workers (1966 1980) (Migrants)
Migrant Worker Projects (1966 1980) #
Migratory Agricultural Workers
BT Agricultural Laborers
Migrants
RT Braceros
Crew Leaders
Foreign Workers
Migrant Adult Education
Migrant Problems
Migrant Youth
Seasonal Employment
Seasonal Laborers

MIGRANT YOUTH *Jul. 1966*
CIJE: 41 RIE: 126 GC: 510
SN Young persons, approximately 12 to 21 years of age, who travel alone or with their families from one temporary residence to another so that they, or other family members, might secure temporary or seasonal employment
BT Migrants
Youth
RT Migrant Adult Education
Migrant Children
Migrant Education
Migrant Workers
Rural Youth
Student Mobility
Transfer Students

MIGRANTS *Jul. 1966*
CIJE: 130 RIE: 371 GC: 510
SN Persons who move from place to place
UF Agricultural Migrants
Internal Immigrants
Migrant Adults
Migrant Population
Migrant Transportation (1966 1980) #
Native Migrants
NT Immigrants
Migrant Children
Migrant Workers
Migrant Youth
Nomads
Refugees
Transient Children
BT Groups
RT Braceros
Cross Cultural Studies
Foreign Nationals
Immigration Inspectors
Migrant Adult Education
Migrant Employment
Migrant Health Services
Migrant Housing
Migrant Problems
Migrant Programs
Migrant Welfare Services
Migration
Migration Patterns
Occupational Mobility
Relocation

MIGRATION *Jul. 1966*
CIJE: 180 RIE: 424 GC: 550
SN Demographic movements of individuals or groups
UF Geographic Mobility (1980)
Northward Movement
Population Movements
Population Shifts
White Flight #
NT Family Mobility
Migration Patterns
Relocation
Rural To Urban Migration
Student Mobility
Urban To Rural Migration
Urban To Suburban Migration
BT Mobility
RT Demography
Immigrants
Migrant Education
Migrants
Nomads
Occupational Mobility
Place Of Residence
Population Distribution
Population Trends
Refugees
Relocation
Residential Patterns
Transient Children
Undocumented Immigrants

MIGRATION PATTERNS *Jul. 1966*
CIJE: 225 RIE: 497 GC: 550
SN Specific migration which constitutes an identifiable or even predictable movement of people
UF Migration Trends
BT Migration
RT Demography
Employment Patterns
Migrants
Population Distribution
Population Trends
Relocation
Residential Patterns
Rural To Urban Migration
Trend Analysis
Urban To Rural Migration
Urban To Suburban Migration

Migration Trends
USE MIGRATION PATTERNS

Migratory Agricultural Workers
USE MIGRANT WORKERS

Migratory Children
USE MIGRANT CHILDREN

MILD DISABILITIES *Mar. 1980*
CIJE: 137 RIE: 103 GC: 220
SN Impairments that are sufficiently mild so that generally normal functioning is possible when appropriate medical, educational, or other special services are provided
NT Mild Mental Retardation
Minimal Brain Dysfunction
BT Disabilities
RT Exceptional Persons
Partial Hearing
Severe Disabilities

MILD MENTAL RETARDATION *Mar. 1980*
CIJE: 1413 RIE: 1231 GC: 220
SN Intellectual functioning that ranges two to three standard deviations below the mean (usually 55-69 iq range), concurrent with adaptive deficiencies -- mildly or educable retarded individuals are able to acquire functional academic skills through special education and adults can usually maintain themselves at least semi-independently in a community
UF Educable Mentally Handicapped (1966 1980)
BT Mental Retardation
Mild Disabilities
RT Downs Syndrome
Moderate Mental Retardation
Residential Schools
Severe Mental Retardation
Slow Learners

MILIEU THERAPY *Jul. 1966*
CIJE: 50 RIE: 26 GC: 230
SN Treatment that modifies a person's life circumstances or immediate environment (note: mental institutions or rehabilitation centers that use milieu therapy are often called therapeutic communities, and, prior to mar80, this concept was usually indexed under "therapeutic environment")
UF Environmental Therapy
Situational Therapy
Therapeutic Communities
BT Psychotherapy
RT Family Counseling
Group Therapy
Humanization
Psychiatric Hospitals
Rehabilitation Centers
Therapeutic Environment

Militancy
USE ACTIVISM

MILITARY AIR FACILITIES *Aug. 1969*
CIJE: 9 RIE: 43 GC: 920
UF Air Bases
Air Force Bases
Army Air Bases
Coast Guard Air Stations
Marine Corps Air Stations
Naval Air Stations
BT Facilities
RT Airports
Air Traffic Control
Military Science
Military Service
Military Training

MILITARY ORGANIZATIONS *Mar. 1969*
CIJE: 54 RIE: 129 GC: 610
NT Armed Forces
BT Organizations (Groups)
RT Federal Government
Military Personnel
National Defense

MILITARY PERSONNEL *Jul. 1966*
CIJE: 275 RIE: 998 GC: 640
NT Enlisted Personnel
Officer Personnel
BT Government Employees
RT Armed Forces
Military Organizations
Military Science
Military Service
Military Training
National Defense
Seafarers
Veterans
Veterans Education

MILITARY SCHOOLS *Jan. 1969*
CIJE: 38 RIE: 129 GC: 340
BT Schools
RT Military Science
Military Training

MILITARY SCIENCE *Jul. 1966*
CIJE: 38 RIE: 145 GC: 400
BT Curriculum
RT Civil Defense
Disarmament
Enlisted Personnel
Marksmanship
Military Air Facilities
Military Personnel
Military Schools
Military Service
Military Training
National Defense
Nuclear Warfare
Officer Personnel
Political Science
War

MILITARY SERVICE *Jul. 1966*
CIJE: 118 RIE: 267 GC: 640
RT Armed Forces
Enlisted Personnel
Military Air Facilities
Military Personnel
Military Science
Military Training
Officer Personnel
Veterans

MILITARY TRAINING *Jul. 1966*
CIJE: 183 RIE: 1466 GC: 400
BT Training
RT Enlisted Personnel
Flight Training
Military Air Facilities
Military Personnel
Military Schools
Military Science
Military Service
National Defense
Officer Personnel

Milling Machines
USE MACHINE TOOLS

Millwork
USE CABINETMAKING

Mime
USE PANTOMIME

MINERALOGY *Oct. 1984*
CIJE: 25 RIE: 3 GC: 490
SN Science dealing with minerals, including their distribution, identification, and properties
BT Geology
RT Chemical Analysis
Chemistry
Crystallography
Geophysics
Inorganic Chemistry
Metallurgy
Minerals
Physical Geography
Soil Science

MINERALS *Oct. 1984*
CIJE: 27 RIE: 21 GC: 410
SN Solid homogeneous chemical elements or compounds, usually with characteristic crystalline properties, that result from inorganic processes of nature
NT Asbestos
BT Matter
RT Fuels
Geology
Metals
Mineralogy
Mining
Natural Resources

MINICOMPUTERS *Mar. 1980*
CIJE: 84 RIE: 96 GC: 910
SN Compact, low cost (relative to mainframes), general purpose computers capable of either stand-alone operation or attachment to other computers
BT Computers

RT Local Area Networks
Microcomputers
Online Systems

MINICOURSES *Mar. 1980*
CIJE: 248 RIE: 363 GC: 350
SN Courses at any educational level that are of relatively short duration (e.g., shorter than a school's regular academic term or session) and intended to achieve certain limited objectives
UF Short Courses (1970 1980)
BT Courses
RT Alumni Education
Elective Courses
Inservice Education
Institutes (Training Programs)
Introductory Courses
Learning Modules
Noncredit Courses
Professional Continuing Education
Refresher Courses
Seminars
Summer Programs
Supplementary Education
Workshops

MINIMAL BRAIN DYSFUNCTION *Mar. 1980*
CIJE: 216 RIE: 149 GC: 220
SN Mild neurological abnormality that causes learning and/or motor difficulties
UF Minimally Brain Injured (1966 1980)
BT Mild Disabilities
Neurological Impairments
RT Aphasia
Behavior Problems
Dyslexia
Epilepsy
Hyperactivity
Learning Disabilities

Minimal Competencies
USE MINIMUM COMPETENCIES

Minimal Competency Testing
USE MINIMUM COMPETENCY TESTING

Minimally Brain Injured (1966 1980)
USE MINIMAL BRAIN DYSFUNCTION

MINIMUM COMPETENCIES *Mar. 1980*
CIJE: 190 RIE: 418 GC: 330
SN Skills that are deemed essential for a given age, grade, or performance level
UF Minimal Competencies
BT Competence
Skills
RT Back To Basics
Basic Skills
Competency Based Education
Core Curriculum
Evaluation Criteria
Functional Literacy
Job Skills
Literacy Education
Mastery Learning
Mathematics Skills
Minimum Competency Testing
National Competency Tests
Performance
Reading Skills
Writing Skills

MINIMUM COMPETENCY TESTING *Jan. 1979*
CIJE: 426 RIE: 666 GC: 820
SN Measurement of the attainment of skills deemed essential for a particular level of education
UF Minimal Competency Testing
BT Testing
RT Academic Achievement
Academic Standards
Basic Skills
Competence
Competency Based Education
Mastery Tests
Minimum Competencies
National Competency Tests
Student Certification

Minimum Initial Expenses
USE EXPENDITURES

Minimum Operating Expenses
USE OPERATING EXPENSES

MINIMUM WAGE *Jul. 1966*
CIJE: 23 RIE: 42 GC: 630
BT Wages
RT Guaranteed Income
Minimum Wage Legislation

Minimum Wage Laws (1966 1974)
USE MINIMUM WAGE LEGISLATION

MINIMUM WAGE LEGISLATION *Jul. 1966*
CIJE: 20 RIE: 39 GC: 610
UF Minimum Wage Laws (1966 1974)
BT Legislation
RT Laws
Minimum Wage
Wages

MINING *Sep. 1982*
CIJE: 38 RIE: 71 GC: 410
SN Process or business involved in extracting ore, coal, precious stones, etc. from the earth
UF Coal Mining #
BT Technology
RT Asbestos
Coal
Conservation (Environment)
Engineering
Environmental Education
Fuels
Geology
Geophysics
Land Use
Metals
Minerals
Natural Resources
Ventilation

Ministers
USE CLERGY

Minnesingers
USE POETS

Minority Culture
USE MINORITY GROUPS

MINORITY GROUP CHILDREN *Jul. 1966*
CIJE: 467 RIE: 815 GC: 510
BT Children
RT Black Youth
Minority Groups

MINORITY GROUP INFLUENCES *Mar. 1980*
CIJE: 95 RIE: 127 GC: 520
SN Influences of minority groups on other groups or society as a whole
UF Minority Role (1966 1980)
BT Influences
RT Black Influences
Community Control
Cultural Influences
Minority Groups
Racial Factors
Social Influences
Sociocultural Patterns

MINORITY GROUP TEACHERS *Jul. 1966*
CIJE: 76 RIE: 130 GC: 360
SN Teachers who are members of minority groups
BT Teachers
RT Black Teachers
Minority Groups

MINORITY GROUPS *Jul. 1966*
CIJE: 2839 RIE: 4812 GC: 520
SN Subgroups within a larger society that are distinguished from the majority and each other by race, national heritage, or sometimes by religious or cultural affiliation (note: unlike "ethnic groups," "minority groups" also have the connotation of being objects of prejudice or discrimination)
UF Minority Culture
Population Minorities
BT Groups
RT Affirmative Action
Alaska Natives
American Indians
Asian Americans
Biculturalism
Bidialectalism
Bilingualism
Blacks
Canada Natives
Civil Rights
Civil Rights Legislation
Cross Cultural Studies
Cultural Differences
Cultural Pluralism
Culture
Eskimos
Ethnic Groups
Ethnicity
Ethnic Studies
Greek Americans
Hispanic Americans
Italian Americans
Jews
Limited English Speaking
Majority Attitudes
Minority Group Children
Minority Group Influences
Minority Group Teachers
Multicultural Education
Non English Speaking
Pacific Americans
Polish Americans
Race
Religious Cultural Groups
Self Determination
Slavery
Social Bias
Social Discrimination
Spanish Americans
Subcultures

Minority Rights
USE CIVIL RIGHTS

Minority Role (1966 1980)
USE MINORITY GROUP INFLUENCES

Miosis
USE MYOPIA

Mis
USE MANAGEMENT INFORMATION SYSTEMS

Misbehavior (1966 1980)
USE BEHAVIOR PROBLEMS

MISCONCEPTIONS *Aug. 1986*
CIJE: 70 RIE: 48 GC: 110
SN Ideas or interpretations that are inaccurate or that contradict scientific knowledge
UF Mistaken Conceptions
RT Cognitive Structures
Comprehension
Concept Formation
Learning Processes
Mathematical Concepts
Scientific Concepts

MISCUE ANALYSIS *Feb. 1974*
CIJE: 137 RIE: 198 GC: 460
SN Examination and interpretation of observed responses in oral reading which do not match expected responses, as a technique for measuring the learner's control of the reading process
UF Miscue Taxonomy
BT Reading Diagnosis
RT Context Clues
Cues
Decoding (Reading)
Diagnostic Teaching
Language Usage
Linguistics
Oral Reading
Phoneme Grapheme Correspondence
Phonetic Analysis
Reading
Reading Instruction
Reading Processes
Structural Analysis (Linguistics)

Miscue Taxonomy
USE MISCUE ANALYSIS

MISSION STATEMENTS *Aug. 1986*
CIJE: 25 RIE: 24 GC: 730
SN Written statements of institutional purpose -- each statement reflects the official purpose(s) of a particular institution as developed or approved by the founders or governing body
BT Position Papers
RT College Planning
Institutional Advancement
Institutional Mission
Library Planning
Master Plans
Policy Formation

Mistaken Conceptions
USE MISCONCEPTIONS

MNEMONICS *Jul. 1966*
CIJE: 198 RIE: 120 GC: 110
SN Techniques for improving memory
RT Abbreviations
Cues
Learning
Learning Experience
Learning Processes
Learning Strategies
Learning Theories
Memorization
Memory
Notetaking
Recall (Psychology)
Retention (Psychology)
Suggestopedia

MOBILE CLASSROOMS *Aug. 1968*
CIJE: 56 RIE: 89 GC: 920
SN Readily movable vehicles, or attachments to vehicles, that are used as classrooms
BT Classrooms
RT Educational Facilities Design
Flexible Facilities
Mobile Educational Services
Relocatable Facilities
School Expansion
Transportation

MOBILE CLINICS *Mar. 1980*
CIJE: 5 RIE: 4 GC: 920
UF Itinerant Clinics (1966 1980)
BT Clinics
RT Itinerant Teachers
Mobile Laboratories
Outreach Programs
Relocatable Facilities

MOBILE EDUCATIONAL SERVICES *Jul. 1966*
CIJE: 77 RIE: 158 GC: 330
BT Ancillary School Services
RT Bookmobiles
Extension Education
Itinerant Teachers
Migrant Education
Mobile Classrooms
Outreach Programs
Special Education

MOBILE LABORATORIES *Jul. 1966*
CIJE: 27 RIE: 36 GC: 920
BT Laboratories
RT Mobile Clinics
Relocatable Facilities

Mobile Libraries
USE BOOKMOBILES

MOBILITY *Jul. 1966*
CIJE: 112 RIE: 176 GC: 550
SN Geographic, physical, or social movement of people (note: use a more specific term if possible -- prior to mar80, this term was not restricted by a scope note)
NT Educational Mobility
Migration
Occupational Mobility
Physical Mobility
Social Mobility

MOBILITY AIDS *Jul. 1966*
CIJE: 72 RIE: 72 GC: 220
SN Devices which assist handicapped persons to move freely within their environment
NT Wheelchairs
BT Assistive Devices (For Disabled)
RT Electromechanical Aids
Low Vision Aids
Physical Disabilities
Physical Mobility
Prostheses

= Two or more Descriptors are used to represent this term.
The term's main entry shows the appropriate coordination.

Travel Training
Visual Impairments
Visually Handicapped Mobility

Model Programs
USE DEMONSTRATION PROGRAMS

Modeling (Psychological) (1977 1980)
USE MODELING (PSYCHOLOGY)

MODELING (PSYCHOLOGY) *Mar. 1980*
CIJE: 381 RIE: 178 GC: 120
SN Process in which salient characteristics of an agent or model are acquired by an observer
UF Modeling (Psychological) (1977 1980)
BT Behavior
RT Behavior Change
Counseling Techniques
Identification (Psychology)
Imitation
Mentors
Observational Learning
Role Models
Significant Others
Socialization

MODELS *Jul. 1966*
CIJE: 10602 RIE: 11201 GC: 730
SN Representations of objects, principles, processes, or ideas -- often used for imitation or emulation
UF Paradigms
Theoretical Models
NT Mathematical Models
Role Models
Student Writing Models
Teaching Models
BT Simulation
RT Computer Simulation
Network Analysis
Operations Research
Research Design
Research Methodology
Research Tools
Schematic Studies
Standards
Systems Analysis
Systems Approach
Theories
Theory Practice Relationship
Three Dimensional Aids

MODERATE MENTAL RETARDATION *Mar. 1980*
CIJE: 672 RIE: 93 GC: 220
SN Intellectual functioning that ranges three to four standard deviations below the mean (usually 40-54 iq range), concurrent with adaptive deficiencies -- moderately or trainable retarded individuals can learn self-help, communication, social, or simple vocational skills but only limited academic skills
UF Trainable Mentally Handicapped (1967 1980)
BT Mental Retardation
RT Downs Syndrome
Mild Mental Retardation
Residential Schools
Severe Mental Retardation

Modern Greek
USE GREEK

MODERN HISTORY *Jul. 1966*
CIJE: 114 RIE: 135 GC: 430
SN History of recent centuries -- usually thought of as beginning with the renaissance and extending to the present
UF Contemporary History
BT History
RT Mexican American History
Nuclear Warfare
Oral History
United States History

MODERN LANGUAGE CURRICULUM *Jul. 1966*
CIJE: 428 RIE: 328 GC: 450
NT Conversational Language Courses
Fles
Intensive Language Courses
Notional Functional Syllabi
BT Curriculum
RT College Second Language Programs
Modern Languages
Multilevel Classes (Second Language Instruction)
Second Language Learning
Second Language Programs

MODERN LANGUAGES *Jul. 1966*
CIJE: 752 RIE: 1322 GC: 440
BT Languages
RT Bilingualism
Immersion Programs
Modern Language Curriculum
Multilingualism
Multilingual Materials
Second Language Learning

MODERN MATHEMATICS *Jul. 1966*
CIJE: 191 RIE: 98 GC: 480
SN Curricular innovations in precollege mathematics
UF New Mathematics
BT Mathematics Curriculum
RT Elementary School Mathematics
Secondary School Mathematics

Modern Science (1966 1980)
USE SCIENCES

MODERNISM *May. 1969*
CIJE: 69 RIE: 26 GC: 430
SN Reflection, in religion and the creative arts, of a deliberate break with the past and a search for new forms of expression
RT Art Expression
Literary Styles
Music
Nineteenth Century Literature
Philosophy
Religion
Twentieth Century Literature

MODERNIZATION *Mar. 1982*
CIJE: 54 RIE: 65 GC: 520
SN Process of change in a society or social institution in which the most recent ways, ideas, or styles are adapted or acquired
BT Development
Social Change
RT Community Development
Cultural Influences
Culture Lag
Developed Nations
Developing Nations
Economic Progress
Industrialization
Innovation
Rural Development
Socioeconomic Influences
Technological Advancement
Technology Transfer
Traditionalism
Urbanization

MODULAR BUILDING DESIGN *Jul. 1966*
CIJE: 85 RIE: 44 GC: 920
SN Orderly planning so arranged as to make logical and extensive use of a repetitive module or dimension of one foot or more
UF Modular Drafting
BT Building Design
RT Building Systems
Educational Facilities Design
School Construction
Systems Building

Modular Drafting
USE MODULAR BUILDING DESIGN

Modular Learning
USE LEARNING MODULES

Modular Scheduling
USE FLEXIBLE SCHEDULING

Mole
USE MOSSI

MOLECULAR STRUCTURE *Oct. 1972*
CIJE: 344 RIE: 5 GC: 490
RT Atomic Structure
Chemical Bonding
Chemical Reactions
Chemistry
Coordination Compounds
Crystallography
Cytology
Inorganic Chemistry
Kinetic Molecular Theory
Organic Chemistry
Physical Sciences
Physics
Polymers
Spectroscopy
Structural Analysis (Science)

MONETARY SYSTEMS *Mar. 1980*
CIJE: 50 RIE: 89 GC: 620
SN Policies and practices affecting the money of nations
UF Money Systems (1966 1980)
RT Banking
Business Cycles
Economics
Inflation (Economics)
Interest (Finance)
International Trade

MONEY MANAGEMENT *Jul. 1966*
CIJE: 413 RIE: 1028 GC: 620
UF Financial Management
BT Administration
RT Banking
Basic Business Education
Budgeting
Capital
Consumer Education
Credit (Finance)
Endowment Funds
Estate Planning
Finance Occupations
Finance Reform
Financial Audits
Financial Policy
Financial Services
Home Management
Income
Inflation (Economics)
Loan Repayment
School Funds
Tax Rates
Trusts (Financial)

Money Systems (1966 1980)
USE MONETARY SYSTEMS

Mongol
USE MONGOLIAN

MONGOLIAN *Jul. 1966*
CIJE: RIE: 11 GC: 440
UF Khalkha
Mongol
BT Mongolian Languages

MONGOLIAN LANGUAGES *Jul. 1966*
CIJE: 1 RIE: 5 GC: 440
NT Buriat
Dagur
Mongolian
BT Uralic Altaic Languages

Mongolism (1968 1978)
USE DOWNS SYNDROME

MONOLINGUALISM *Jan. 1973*
CIJE: 53 RIE: 77 GC: 450
RT Bilingualism
Child Language
Languages
Language Skills
Multilingualism
Native Speakers
Sociolinguistics

MONOLOGS *Oct. 1980*
CIJE: 11 RIE: 10 GC: 430
UF Interior Monologues
Monologues (1970 1980)
Soliloquies
BT Literary Devices
RT Drama
Personal Narratives
Poetry
Speech

Monologues (1970 1980)
USE MONOLOGS

MONTE CARLO METHODS *Mar. 1984*
CIJE: 75 RIE: 64 GC: 820
SN Statistical simulation techniques using random numbers to derive probabilistic approximations to the solutions of problems -- used especially for complex problems with many variables or interrelationships
BT Simulation
RT Computer Simulation
Estimation (Mathematics)
Game Theory
Hypothesis Testing
Linear Programing
Mathematical Models
Measurement Techniques
Operations Research
Predictor Variables
Probability
Problem Solving
Research Methodology
Sampling
Statistical Analysis
Statistical Distributions
Statistical Studies
Statistics

MONTESSORI METHOD *Dec. 1985*
CIJE: 40 RIE: 61 GC: 310
SN Child-centered approach to teaching, developed by maria montessori and most often used in the early childhood years, that features a wide range of graded, self-motivational techniques and materials specially designed to provide sensorimotor pathways to higher learning
BT Teaching Methods
RT Discovery Learning
Early Childhood Education
Individualized Instruction
Manipulative Materials
Sensory Experience
Student Centered Curriculum

Moonlighting
USE MULTIPLE EMPLOYMENT

MORAL CRITICISM (1969 1980) *Mar. 1980*
CIJE: 169 RIE: 19 GC: 430
SN Invalid descriptor -- originally intended as a literary term, but used indiscriminately in indexing -- see "literary criticism," and "moral issues" or "moral values"

MORAL DEVELOPMENT *Nov. 1972*
CIJE: 1165 RIE: 574 GC: 120
SN Developmental processes in the formation of moral reasoning and judgments
BT Individual Development
RT Codes Of Ethics
Ethics
Integrity
Moral Values
Personality Development
Social Cognition
Values

Moral Instruction
USE ETHICAL INSTRUCTION

MORAL ISSUES *Jul. 1966*
CIJE: 448 RIE: 307 GC: 520
RT Censorship
Controversial Issues (Course Content)
Moral Values
Obscenity
Plagiarism

Moral Judgment
USE MORAL VALUES; VALUE JUDGMENT

MORAL VALUES *Jul. 1966*
CIJE: 1764 RIE: 878 GC: 520
SN Principles and standards which determine the extent to which human action or conduct is right or wrong
UF Ethical Values (1966 1980)
Moral Judgment #
BT Values
RT Bioethics
Censorship
Codes Of Ethics
Ethical Instruction
Ethics
Integrity

= Two or more Descriptors are used to represent this term.
The term's main entry shows the appropriate coordination.

Moral Development
Moral Issues
Social Values

MORALE *Jul. 1966*
CIJE: 206 RIE: 145 GC: 230
NT Teacher Morale
BT Psychological Patterns
RT Burnout
Emotional Adjustment
Group Unity
Mental Health
Motivation
Need Gratification
Organizational Climate
Peer Acceptance
Recognition (Achievement)
Self Actualization
Self Concept
Sportsmanship
Teamwork

Morals
USE ETHICS

More
USE MOSSI

MORPHEMES *Jul. 1966*
CIJE: 168 RIE: 144 GC: 450
SN Smallest units of meaning in a language (e.g., a word is composed of one or more morphemes)
UF Allomorphs (1967 1980)
NT Negative Forms (Language)
Plurals
Suffixes
Tenses (Grammar)
BT Morphology (Languages)
RT Morphophonemics
Phonemes
Syntax

Morphemics
USE MORPHOLOGY (LANGUAGES)

MORPHOLOGY (LANGUAGES) *Jul. 1966*
CIJE: 800 RIE: 731 GC: 450
SN Study of the forms and formation of words
UF Morphemics
NT Morphemes
Morphophonemics
BT Grammar
RT Adjectives
Adverbs
Code Switching (Language)
Determiners (Languages)
Diachronic Linguistics
Discourse Analysis
Form Classes (Languages)
Function Words
Intonation
Language Patterns
Language Typology
Lexicology
Linguistic Borrowing
Nouns
Phonology
Prepositions
Pronouns
Suprasegmentals
Surface Structure
Syntax
Traditional Grammar
Verbs

MORPHOPHONEMICS *Jul. 1966*
CIJE: 98 RIE: 108 GC: 450
SN Study of the phonemic aspects of morphemes
BT Morphology (Languages)
RT Morphemes
Negative Forms (Language)
Phonemes
Phonemics
Phonetics
Phonology
Stress (Phonology)
Suffixes
Suprasegmentals
Surface Structure
Tone Languages

Mortality (Research Studies)
USE ATTRITION (RESEARCH STUDIES)

MOSSI *Jul. 1966*
CIJE: RIE: 4 GC: 440
UF Mole
More
BT African Languages

Motels
USE HOTELS

Mother Absence
USE MOTHERLESS FAMILY

MOTHER ATTITUDES *Jul. 1966*
CIJE: 250 RIE: 251 GC: 510
SN Attitudes of, not toward, mothers
BT Parent Attitudes
RT Father Attitudes
Mothers

Mother Role
USE MOTHERS; PARENT ROLE

Motherhood
USE MOTHERS

MOTHERLESS FAMILY *Mar. 1980*
CIJE: 10 RIE: 4 GC: 510
UF Mother Absence
BT One Parent Family
RT Divorce
Fatherless Family
Fathers
Heads Of Households
Widowed

MOTHERS *Jul. 1966*
CIJE: 1380 RIE: 1152 GC: 510
UF Employed Mothers #
Middle Class Mothers (1966 1980) #
Motherhood
Mother Role #
NT Black Mothers
Unwed Mothers
BT Females
Parents
RT Displaced Homemakers
Employed Parents
Fatherless Family
Heads Of Households
Mother Attitudes
One Parent Family
Parent Associations
Parent Child Relationship
Parent Influence
Parent Role

MOTIFS *May. 1969*
CIJE: 254 RIE: 26 GC: 430
UF Leitmotifs
Leitmotivs
BT Literary Devices
RT Film Criticism
Symbols (Literary)

MOTION *Sep. 1968*
CIJE: 606 RIE: 166 GC: 490
UF Movement
NT Acceleration (Physics)
BT Scientific Concepts
RT Air Flow
Diffusion (Physics)
Earthquakes
Energy
Fluid Mechanics
Force
Gravity (Physics)
Horology
Kinetic Molecular Theory
Kinetics
Mechanics (Physics)
Physics
Quantum Mechanics
Relativity
Vectors (Mathematics)
Wind (Meteorology)

Motion Pictures
USE FILMS

MOTIVATION *Jul. 1966*
CIJE: 2462 RIE: 2172 GC: 120
SN Forces that initiate, direct, and sustain individual or group behavior in order to satisfy a need or attain a goal
UF Low Motivation (1966 1980)
NT Achievement Need
Learning Motivation
Student Motivation
Teacher Motivation
RT Achievement
Aspiration
Attention Control
Attention Span
Behavior
Burnout
Cognitive Dissonance
Curiosity
Delay Of Gratification
Failure
Fear Of Success
Feedback
Goal Orientation
Incentives
Morale
Motivation Techniques
Needs
Pacing
Performance
Professional Recognition
Readiness
Reinforcement
Rewards
Self Actualization
Self Reward
Sportsmanship
Stimulation
Stimuli
Success

MOTIVATION TECHNIQUES *Jul. 1966*
CIJE: 913 RIE: 774 GC: 310
SN Techniques used to prompt an individual or group to act in a specified way
BT Methods
RT Contingency Management
Educational Strategies
Incentives
Motivation
Performance Contracts
Persuasive Discourse
Prewriting
Self Directed Groups

Motor Ability
USE PSYCHOMOTOR SKILLS

MOTOR DEVELOPMENT *Aug. 1968*
CIJE: 566 RIE: 777 GC: 120
BT Physical Development
RT Biomechanics
Eye Hand Coordination
Lateral Dominance
Learning Problems
Motor Reactions
Movement Education
Neurological Impairments
Neurological Organization
Object Manipulation
Perceptual Motor Coordination
Perceptual Motor Learning
Physical Activity Level
Psychomotor Objectives
Psychomotor Skills
Skill Development

Motor Oils
USE LUBRICANTS

MOTOR REACTIONS *Jul. 1969*
CIJE: 291 RIE: 129 GC: 120
UF Muscular Activities
Muscular Extensions
Muscular Flexions
NT Eye Movements
Pupillary Dilation
BT Responses
RT Biomechanics
Exercise Physiology
Motor Development
Muscular Strength
Osteopathy
Physical Activity Level
Physiology
Psychomotor Skills
Reaction Time

Motor Skills
USE PSYCHOMOTOR SKILLS

MOTOR VEHICLES *Jul. 1966*
CIJE: 85 RIE: 369 GC: 910
NT Service Vehicles
Tractors
BT Equipment
RT Auto Body Repairers
Auto Mechanics
Auto Parts Clerks
Diesel Engines
Electric Motors
Energy Conservation
Environmental Standards
Fuels
Parking Controls
Parking Facilities
Traffic Circulation
Traffic Control
Traffic Safety
Transportation
Travel
Vehicular Traffic

Motorboat Operators
USE BOAT OPERATORS

Mourning
USE GRIEF

MOVABLE PARTITIONS *Jul. 1966*
CIJE: 28 RIE: 33 GC: 920
SN Interior walls that can be readily moved
UF Folding Partitions
BT Space Dividers
RT Flexible Facilities
Prefabrication

Movement
USE MOTION

MOVEMENT EDUCATION *Feb. 1978*
CIJE: 186 RIE: 224 GC: 470
SN Developing and applying coordinated and rhythmical body movements in learning situations
BT Physical Education
RT Biomechanics
Body Image
Body Language
Dance
Dance Education
Dance Therapy
Human Body
Motor Development
Pantomime
Perceptual Motor Coordination
Perceptual Motor Learning
Physical Activities
Psychomotor Objectives
Psychomotor Skills
Self Expression

Mtmm Methodology
USE MULTITRAIT MULTIMETHOD TECHNIQUES

MULTICAMPUS COLLEGES *Feb. 1978*
CIJE: 61 RIE: 127 GC: 340
SN Higher education institutions, including universities, which have multiple (two or more) locations
BT Colleges
RT Campuses
Community Colleges
Multicampus Districts
State Colleges
State Universities
Two Year Colleges
Universities

MULTICAMPUS DISTRICTS *Jul. 1966*
CIJE: 22 RIE: 191 GC: 340
SN Community or junior college districts that contain more than one campus (note: prior to mar80, the use of this term was not restricted by a scope note)
BT School Districts
RT Campuses
Community Colleges
Multicampus Colleges
School Location
Two Year Colleges
Zoning

Multichannel Programing (1966 1980)
USE PROGRAMING (BROADCAST)

= Two or more Descriptors are used to represent this term.
The term's main entry shows the appropriate coordination.

MULTICULTURAL EDUCATION *Jan. 1979*
CIJE: 513 RIE: 1105 GC: 540
SN Education involving two or more ethnic groups and designed to help participants clarify their own ethnic identity and appreciate that of others, reduce prejudice and stereotyping, and promote cultural pluralism and equal participation (note: do not confuse with "cross cultural training," which, prior to jan79, was frequently used for "multicultural education")
UF Bicultural Education
Intercultural Education
Multiethnic Education
BT Intergroup Education
RT Biculturalism
Bilingual Education
Bilingualism
Black Studies
Cross Cultural Studies
Cross Cultural Training
Cultural Activities
Cultural Awareness
Cultural Background
Cultural Context
Cultural Differences
Cultural Interrelationships
Cultural Pluralism
Culture
Culture Contact
Culture Fair Tests
Ethnic Groups
Ethnicity
Ethnic Relations
Ethnocentrism
Foreign Culture
Heterogeneous Grouping
Humanistic Education
Intercultural Communication
Intercultural Programs
Interdisciplinary Approach
Intergroup Relations
Mexican American Education
Migrant Education
Minority Groups
Multicultural Textbooks
Multilingualism
Social Integration

MULTICULTURAL TEXTBOOKS *Aug. 1968*
CIJE: 44 RIE: 77 GC: 540
BT Textbooks
RT Bilingual Education
Bilingual Instructional Materials
Cross Cultural Studies
Cultural Education
Intergroup Education
Multicultural Education
Textbook Bias
Textbook Content

Multicultural Training
USE CROSS CULTURAL TRAINING

Multiculturalism
USE CULTURAL PLURALISM

MULTIDIMENSIONAL SCALING *Aug. 1972*
CIJE: 264 RIE: 113 GC: 820
SN Procedures used to analyze judgments, usually about the similarities and differences among a set of items, to determine the number of independent factors which underlie the judgments
BT Multivariate Analysis
Scaling
RT Cluster Analysis
Correlation
Discriminant Analysis
Factor Analysis
Semantic Differential
Sociometric Techniques

Multiethnic Education
USE MULTICULTURAL EDUCATION

Multiethnic Training
USE CROSS CULTURAL TRAINING

MULTIGRADED CLASSES *Jul. 1966*
CIJE: 25 RIE: 48 GC: 310
SN Classes composed of students in two or more grades (note: do not confuse with "nongraded instructional grouping")
BT Classes (Groups Of Students)
RT Heterogeneous Grouping
Instructional Program Divisions
Multilevel Classes (Second Language Instruction)
Nongraded Instructional Grouping

Multilateral Disarmament
USE DISARMAMENT

MULTILEVEL CLASSES (SECOND LANGUAGE INSTRUCTION) *Oct. 1983*
CIJE: 4 RIE: GC: 450
SN Second language classes composed of students with a wide range of proficiency in the language being taught
BT Classes (Groups Of Students)
RT Heterogeneous Grouping
Individualized Instruction
Language Proficiency
Languages
Modern Language Curriculum
Multigraded Classes
Second Language Instruction
Second Language Learning
Second Language Programs

MULTILINGUAL MATERIALS *Nov. 1982*
CIJE: 3 RIE: 15 GC: 720
SN Print and/or nonprint materials whose contents include equivalent or near-equivalent information in two or more languages (note: corresponds to pubtype 171 -- do not use except as the subject of a document)
UF Bilingual Materials
NT Bilingual Instructional Materials
RT Bilingualism
Intercultural Communication
International Studies
Languages
Modern Languages
Multilingualism
Reference Materials
Resource Materials
Second Language Learning
Vocabulary

MULTILINGUALISM *Jul. 1966*
CIJE: 160 RIE: 204 GC: 450
UF Plurilingualism
RT Bilingual Education
Bilingualism
Code Switching (Language)
Cross Cultural Studies
Cultural Pluralism
Diglossia
English (Second Language)
Intercultural Communication
Interference (Language)
Language Dominance
Language Maintenance
Language Planning
Languages
Language Skill Attrition
Modern Languages
Monolingualism
Multicultural Education
Multilingual Materials
Psycholinguistics
Sociolinguistics

Multilithing
USE REPROGRAPHY

MULTIMEDIA INSTRUCTION *Jul. 1966*
CIJE: 696 RIE: 914 GC: 310
SN The integration of more than one medium in a presentation or module of instruction
NT Audiovisual Instruction
BT Teaching Methods
RT Educational Media
Educational Technology
Intermode Differences
Media Selection
Media Specialists

MULTIPLE CHOICE TESTS *Jul. 1966*
CIJE: 512 RIE: 597 GC: 830
SN Tests in which two or more answers are offered as alternative responses for each item
BT Objective Tests
RT Confidence Testing
Guessing (Tests)
Scoring Formulas

Multiple Correlation
USE CORRELATION

MULTIPLE DISABILITIES *Mar. 1980*
CIJE: 603 RIE: 553 GC: 220
SN Concomitant impairments, the combination of which causes adjustment and educational problems
UF Multiply Handicapped (1967 1980)
NT Deaf Blind
BT Disabilities
RT Cerebral Palsy
Exceptional Persons
Severe Disabilities

Multiple Discriminant Analysis
USE DISCRIMINANT ANALYSIS

MULTIPLE EMPLOYMENT *Jan. 1969*
CIJE: 23 RIE: 39 GC: 630
UF Double Employment
Moonlighting
Multiple Jobholding
Secondary Employment
BT Employment
RT Adjunct Faculty
Conflict Of Interest
Part Time Employment
Seasonal Employment

Multiple Jobholding
USE MULTIPLE EMPLOYMENT

Multiple Matrix Sampling
USE ITEM SAMPLING

MULTIPLE REGRESSION ANALYSIS *Oct. 1970*
CIJE: 649 RIE: 615 GC: 820
SN Prediction of a criterion score, or dependent variable, from a weighted combination of scores for two or more independent variables
BT Regression (Statistics)
RT Comparative Analysis
Correlation
Judgment Analysis Technique
Path Analysis
Predictive Measurement
Predictor Variables
Statistics
Suppressor Variables
Validity
Weighted Scores

MULTIPLICATION *Oct. 1968*
CIJE: 239 RIE: 113 GC: 480
BT Arithmetic
RT Addition
Division
Subtraction

Multiply Handicapped (1967 1980)
USE MULTIPLE DISABILITIES

MULTIPURPOSE CLASSROOMS *Jul. 1966*
CIJE: 21 RIE: 27 GC: 920
SN Classrooms designed for more than one use, such as for a discussion area and laboratory
BT Classrooms
RT Classroom Design
Flexible Facilities
Open Plan Schools
School Space
Stages (Facilities)

MULTISENSORY LEARNING *Jul. 1966*
CIJE: 145 RIE: 139 GC: 110
SN Learning that involves the processing of stimuli through two or more senses (e.g., through hearing as well as seeing)
BT Learning
RT Aural Learning
Learning Modalities
Perceptual Motor Learning
Sensory Integration
Sensory Training
Visual Learning

MULTITRAIT MULTIMETHOD TECHNIQUES *Apr. 1985*
CIJE: 39 RIE: 23 GC: 820
SN Experimental validation designs requiring the assessment of two or more traits, each by two or more methods -- the purpose is to provide a dual approach in which different methods of measuring the same trait should have high correlations (convergent validity), and different traits measured with the same method should have low correlations with the trait of interest (discriminant validity)
UF Mtmm Methodology
BT Research Methodology
RT Comparative Analysis
Correlation
Discriminant Analysis
Error Of Measurement
Factor Analysis
Item Analysis
Mathematical Models
Matrices
Measurement Techniques
Rating Scales
Testing
Test Validity

MULTIUNIT SCHOOLS *Sep. 1971*
CIJE: 33 RIE: 81 GC: 340
SN Schools featuring nongraded (rather than age-graded) classroom units for instruction and research, building-level committees for instructional improvement, and system-wide committees for policy making (note: do not confuse with "multicampus colleges" -- see also the identifier "individually guided education")
BT Schools
RT Elementary Schools
Instructional Innovation
Nongraded Instructional Grouping
Research And Instruction Units
School Organization
Team Teaching

MULTIVARIATE ANALYSIS *Mar. 1980*
CIJE: 229 RIE: 118 GC: 820
SN Study of the relationships among three or more variables that are either dependent or neither dependent nor independent (note: do not confuse with "multiple regression analysis" -- prior to mar80, the instruction "multivariate analysis, use statistical analysis" was carried in the thesaurus)
UF Canonical Correlation
Multivariate Analysis Of Variance
Multivariate Statistics
NT Cluster Analysis
Discriminant Analysis
Factor Analysis
Multidimensional Scaling
Path Analysis
BT Statistical Analysis
RT Comparative Analysis
Correlation
Generalizability Theory
Mathematical Models
Sampling

Multivariate Analysis Of Variance
USE MULTIVARIATE ANALYSIS

Multivariate Statistics
USE MULTIVARIATE ANALYSIS

Municipal Government
USE CITY GOVERNMENT

MUNICIPALITIES *Jul. 1966*
CIJE: 87 RIE: 133 GC: 550
SN Towns, cities, or other districts having powers of local self-government provided by specific charter or state statute
UF Cities
Towns
BT Community
Urban Areas
RT Collective Settlements
Metropolitan Areas
Suburbs

Munukutaba
USE KITUBA

Muscle Sense
USE KINESTHETIC PERCEPTION

Muscular Activities
USE MOTOR REACTIONS

Muscular Exercise
USE EXERCISE

Muscular Extensions
USE MOTOR REACTIONS

Muscular Flexions
USE MOTOR REACTIONS

MUSCULAR STRENGTH *Jun. 1969*
CIJE: 169 RIE: 135 GC: 120
UF Physical Strength
Strength (Biology)
BT Physical Characteristics
RT Calisthenics
Exercise
Motor Reactions
Physical Development
Physical Education
Physical Fitness
Weightlifting

MUSEUMS *Jul. 1966*
CIJE: 428 RIE: 319 GC: 920
BT Facilities
RT Anthropology
Arts Centers
Community Resources
Cultural Centers
Educational Facilities
Exhibits
History
Realia
Recreational Facilities
Resource Centers
Science Teaching Centers

MUSIC *Jul. 1966*
CIJE: 949 RIE: 859 GC: 420
NT Applied Music
Jazz
Oriental Music
Vocal Music
BT Fine Arts
RT Art
Bands (Music)
Concerts
Dance
Discographies
Expressionism
Folk Culture
Impressionism
Literary Styles
Modernism
Music Activities
Musical Composition
Musical Instruments
Music Appreciation
Music Education
Music Facilities
Musicians
Music Reading
Music Teachers
Music Techniques
Music Theory
Music Therapy
Neoclassicism
Opera
Orchestras
Popular Culture
Romanticism
Suggestopedia

MUSIC ACTIVITIES *Jul. 1966*
CIJE: 434 RIE: 353 GC: 420
NT Concerts
Singing
BT Activities
RT Applied Music
Bands (Music)
Choral Music
Cultural Activities
Enrichment Activities
Extracurricular Activities
Fine Arts
Music
Musical Composition
Music Appreciation
Music Education
Music Facilities
Music Techniques
Music Therapy
Orchestras
Recreational Activities
Songs
Vocal Music

MUSIC APPRECIATION *Jun. 1969*
CIJE: 255 RIE: 150 GC: 420
BT Aesthetic Education
RT Fine Arts
Music
Music Activities
Music Education

MUSIC EDUCATION *Jul. 1966*
CIJE: 1611 RIE: 749 GC: 420
BT Education
RT Aesthetic Education
Applied Music
Choral Music
Dance Education
Fine Arts
Music
Music Activities
Music Appreciation
Musicians
Music Teachers
Music Techniques
Orchestras
Songs
Vocal Music

MUSIC FACILITIES *Oct. 1968*
CIJE: 36 RIE: 29 GC: 920
BT Facilities
RT Acoustical Environment
Auditoriums
Classrooms
Educational Facilities
Music
Music Activities
Stages (Facilities)
Theaters

MUSIC READING *Jul. 1966*
CIJE: 60 RIE: 60 GC: 420
UF Score Reading
Sight Playing
Sight Singing
BT Reading
RT Music

MUSIC TEACHERS *Apr. 1970*
CIJE: 279 RIE: 49 GC: 360
BT Teachers
RT Fine Arts
Music
Music Education

MUSIC TECHNIQUES *Jul. 1966*
CIJE: 210 RIE: 106 GC: 420
SN Technical skills used to produce musical results, either vocally or on instruments
BT Methods
RT Bands (Music)
Choral Music
Jazz
Music
Music Activities
Musical Composition
Musical Instruments
Music Education
Musicians
Orchestras
Songs
Vocal Music

MUSIC THEORY *Jul. 1966*
CIJE: 107 RIE: 63 GC: 420
BT Theories
RT Music
Musical Composition

MUSIC THERAPY *Jun. 1977*
CIJE: 36 RIE: 31 GC: 230
SN The therapeutic use of musical forms (concerts, music appreciation sessions, group singing, individual performance, etc.) in achieving self-awareness, self-esteem, and emotional release, usually in a context of remediation or rehabilitation
BT Therapy
RT Art Therapy
Dance Therapy
Educational Therapy
Music
Music Activities
Play Therapy
Psychotherapy
Self Expression
Therapeutic Recreation

MUSICAL COMPOSITION *Oct. 1969*
CIJE: 299 RIE: 69 GC: 420
SN A written piece of music, or the act of creating a musical composition
UF Composition (Music)
RT Art Products
Choral Music
Jazz
Music
Music Activities
Music Techniques
Music Theory
Opera
Oriental Music
Songs
Vocal Music

MUSICAL INSTRUMENTS *Oct. 1969*
CIJE: 254 RIE: 133 GC: 420
BT Equipment
RT Bands (Music)
Music
Musicians
Music Techniques
Orchestras

MUSICIANS *Jul. 1969*
CIJE: 232 RIE: 37 GC: 420
BT Artists
RT Bands (Music)
Concerts
Fine Arts
Music
Musical Instruments
Music Education
Music Techniques
Orchestras

MUTUAL INTELLIGIBILITY *Jul. 1966*
CIJE: 45 RIE: 61 GC: 450
RT Bidialectalism
Communication (Thought Transfer)
Contrastive Linguistics
Dialects
Diglossia
Language Classification
Languages
Sociolinguistics
Speech Acts
Verbal Communication

MYOPIA *Jul. 1966*
CIJE: 2 RIE: 1 GC: 220
UF Miosis
Myosis
Nearsightedness
BT Ametropia
RT Hyperopia
Vision
Visual Acuity

Myosis
USE MYOPIA

MYSTICISM *Jul. 1970*
CIJE: 44 RIE: 12 GC: 430
SN Theory of knowing or communing with god or the ultimate reality using a human faculty that transcends intellect
RT Literary Styles
Philosophy
Religion

MYTHIC CRITICISM (1969 1980) *Mar. 1980*
CIJE: 64 RIE: 11 GC: 430
SN Invalid descriptor -- originally intended as a literary term, but used indiscriminately in indexing -- see "literary criticism" and the identifiers "frye (northrop)" or "archetypes" -- see also "mythology"

MYTHOLOGY *Jul. 1966*
CIJE: 317 RIE: 256 GC: 430
UF Myths
RT American Indian Literature
Classical Literature
Epics
Fables
Folk Culture
Legends
Literature
Medieval Literature
Symbols (Literary)

Myths
USE MYTHOLOGY

N C Systems
USE NUMERICAL CONTROL

NARCOTICS *Jul. 1966*
CIJE: 152 RIE: 177 GC: 210
NT Marijuana
Sedatives
RT Drug Abuse
Drug Addiction
Drug Education
Drug Legislation
Drug Rehabilitation
Drug Use
Illegal Drug Use
Stimulants

Narcotics Addiction
USE DRUG ADDICTION

NARRATION *Apr. 1970*
CIJE: 265 RIE: 182 GC: 430
BT Literary Devices
RT Discourse Analysis
Language Experience Approach
Personal Narratives
Story Grammar
Story Telling
Writing (Composition)

Natality
USE BIRTH RATE

NATIONAL COMPETENCY TESTS *Jul. 1966*
CIJE: 147 RIE: 177 GC: 830
SN Tests used to establish national norms and/or standards for achievement
BT Achievement Tests
RT Achievement
Government School Relationship
Mastery Tests
Minimum Competencies
Minimum Competency Testing
National Norms
National Surveys
Norm Referenced Tests
Skills

NATIONAL DEFENSE *Sep. 1968*
CIJE: 121 RIE: 181 GC: 610
SN Mobilization of a nation's military/civilian forces and other resources to deter war, to provide protection from aggression or enemy attack, and to wage war
BT National Security
RT Armed Forces
Civil Defense
Disarmament
Military Organizations
Military Personnel
Military Science
Military Training
Peace
War

National Demography (1966 1980)
USE DEMOGRAPHY

National Intelligence Norm (1966 1980)
USE INTELLIGENCE; NATIONAL NORMS

National Languages
USE OFFICIAL LANGUAGES

NATIONAL LIBRARIES *Mar. 1969*
CIJE: 174 RIE: 247 GC: 710
SN Libraries, maintained out of government funds, that serve the nation as a whole -- functions may include collecting and preserving the country's publications, compiling union catalogs and national bibliographies, or acting as a national bibliographic center
BT Government Libraries
RT Archives
Copyrights
Union Catalogs

NATIONAL NORMS *Jul. 1966*
CIJE: 124 RIE: 360 GC: 820
SN Statistical description of the typical performance, behavior, form, function, etc. of a nation (note: use only for numerical data and not for subjectively described standards -- prior to mar80, the use of this term was not restricted by a scope note)

= Two or more Descriptors are used to represent this term.
The term's main entry shows the appropriate coordination.

UF National Intelligence Norm (1966 1980) #
BT Norms
RT Comparative Analysis
Comparative Testing
Item Sampling
Language Planning
Language Standardization
Local Norms
National Competency Tests
National Surveys
Norm Referenced Tests
State Norms

NATIONAL ORGANIZATIONS *Jul. 1966*
CIJE: 564 RIE: 426 GC: 520
BT Organizations (Groups)
RT Community Organizations
Fraternities
Honor Societies
International Organizations
National Programs
Professional Associations
Sororities

NATIONAL PROGRAMS *Jul. 1966*
CIJE: 972 RIE: 1530 GC: 610
SN Privately or publicly sponsored nationwide programs (note: do not confuse with "federal programs" -- prior to mar80, the use of this term was not restricted by a scope note)
BT Programs
RT Developed Nations
Developing Nations
Educational Assessment
Federal Programs
Language Planning
Language Standardization
Nationalism
National Organizations
National Security
National Surveys
Public Policy

NATIONAL SECURITY *Oct. 1983*
CIJE: 25 RIE: 37 GC: 610
SN Policies and programs undertaken by a nation to protect itself (i.e., its people, institutions, resources, communications, interests, etc.) -- encompasses economic, scientific, and military aspects of security
NT National Defense
RT Federal Government
Government Role
International Relations
Law Enforcement
National Programs
Safety

National Socialism
USE NAZISM

NATIONAL SURVEYS *Jul. 1966*
CIJE: 1955 RIE: 3942 GC: 810
SN Nationwide investigations of a field to determine current practices, trends, and/or norms (note: as of oct81, use as a minor descriptor for examples of this kind of survey -- use as a major descriptor only as the subject of a document)
BT Surveys
RT Educational Assessment
National Competency Tests
National Norms
National Programs
State Surveys

NATIONALISM *Jul. 1966*
CIJE: 268 RIE: 202 GC: 610
NT Patriotism
RT Black Power
Colonialism
Cultural Awareness
Developing Nations
Ethnic Groups
Ethnicity
Fascism
Foreign Policy
Group Unity
Imperialism
International Relations
National Programs
Political Attitudes
Political Divisions (Geographic)
Self Determination

Native Informants
USE NATIVE SPEAKERS

NATIVE LANGUAGE INSTRUCTION *Mar. 1980*
CIJE: 93 RIE: 270 GC: 450
SN Teaching languages to native speakers of those languages (note: for english, use "english instruction" except when emphasis is explicitly on teaching standard english to speakers of nonstandard english dialects -- in those cases, coordinate "native language instruction" and "english instruction")
NT English Instruction
BT Humanities Instruction
RT Bidialectalism
Bilingual Education Programs
Bilingual Instructional Materials
Ethnic Groups
Language Standardization
Language Teachers
Language Usage
Native Speakers
Nonstandard Dialects
Spanish Speaking

Native Migrants
USE MIGRANTS

NATIVE SPEAKERS *Jul. 1969*
CIJE: 240 RIE: 282 GC: 450
SN (Note: used primarily to index material involving the use of native informants in linguistic studies and the use of native speakers in the teaching of a foreign language)
UF Native Informants
NT Spanish Speaking
BT Groups
RT American Indian Languages
Bidialectalism
Bilingual Education Programs
Bilingualism
Bilingual Students
Bilingual Teacher Aides
Bilingual Teachers
Dialects
Dravidian Languages
Ethnic Groups
Foreign Culture
Immersion Programs
Indo European Languages
Language Of Instruction
Language Patterns
Language Styles
Language Usage
Limited English Speaking
Linguistic Difficulty (Inherent)
Malayo Polynesian Languages
Monolingualism
Native Language Instruction
Non English Speaking
Official Languages
Regional Dialects
Second Language Instruction
Second Language Programs
Second Languages
Sino Tibetan Languages
Slavic Languages
Sociolinguistics
Speech Habits

Natives
USE INDIGENOUS POPULATIONS

NATURAL DISASTERS *Jun. 1983*
CIJE: 30 RIE: 28 GC: 210
SN Calamitous occurrences produced by natural forces, often widespread and generally resulting in distress, loss, or material damage (e.g., floods, tornados, earthquakes, droughts)
RT Civil Defense
Earthquakes
Emergency Programs
Safety
Weather

Natural Gases
USE FUELS

Natural Parents
USE BIOLOGICAL PARENTS

NATURAL RESOURCES *Jul. 1966*
CIJE: 1328 RIE: 1981 GC: 410
NT Coal
Water Resources
BT Resources
RT Agricultural Education
Agriculture
Alternative Energy Sources
Asbestos
Community Resources
Conservation (Environment)
Conservation Education
Depleted Resources
Endangered Species
Energy Conservation
Environmental Education
Forestry
Fuels
Minerals
Mining
Parks
Physical Environment
Recycling
Soil Conservation
Wildlife

NATURAL SCIENCES *Jul. 1966*
CIJE: 249 RIE: 322 GC: 490
NT Biological Sciences
Physical Sciences
BT Sciences
RT English For Science And Technology
Nature Centers
Scientific And Technical Information
Scientific Enterprise

NATURALISM *May. 1969*
CIJE: 59 RIE: 12 GC: 430
SN In philosophy and theology, the notion that the human mind is part of the material world, including the doctrine that moral values can be empirically discovered and verified -- in literature and the arts, the environmental and evolutionary view of life that finds expression in attempts to make art reflect (by accurate representation, depiction, etc.) the objective reality of nature
RT Art Expression
Literary Styles
Nineteenth Century Literature
Philosophy
Religion
Twentieth Century Literature

NATURALISTIC OBSERVATION *Oct. 1984*
CIJE: 32 RIE: 50 GC: 820
SN Observation of behaviors and events in natural settings without experimental manipulation or other interference
BT Observation
RT Behavioral Science Research
Classroom Observation Techniques
Ethnography
Ethology
Field Studies
Interaction Process Analysis
Participant Observation
Qualitative Research
Research Methodology
Scientific Methodology
Sociometric Techniques

NATURE CENTERS *Jul. 1966*
CIJE: 98 RIE: 107 GC: 920
BT Resource Centers
RT Education Service Centers
Natural Sciences
Science Teaching Centers

NATURE NURTURE CONTROVERSY *May. 1974*
CIJE: 258 RIE: 125 GC: 120
SN Argument concerning the relative influences of hereditary and environmental factors in determining behavior patterns
UF Environment Heredity Controversy
Heredity Environment Controversy
Learning Maturation Controversy
Maturation Learning Controversy
RT Behavior Development
Biological Influences
Cultural Differences
Cultural Influences
Developmental Psychology
Environment
Environmental Influences
Genetics
Heredity
Individual Development
Individual Differences
Intelligence
Intelligence Differences
Learning
Prenatal Influences
Race
Racial Differences
Social Bias
Sociobiology

Nature Trails
USE TRAILS

Navaho (1967 1978)
USE NAVAJO

NAVAJO *Jun. 1978*
CIJE: 73 RIE: 198 GC: 440
SN Athapascan language spoken by the dine or navajo indians of arizona, utah, and northern new mexico
UF Navaho (1967 1978)
BT Athapascan Languages

Naval Air Stations
USE MILITARY AIR FACILITIES

NAVIGATION *Jul. 1966*
CIJE: 30 RIE: 78 GC: 490
BT Technology
RT Astronomy
Aviation Technology
Boat Operators
Radar
Seafarers
Space Sciences
Vectors (Mathematics)

NAZISM *Mar. 1982*
CIJE: 46 RIE: 28 GC: 610
SN The body of fascist political and economic doctrines based on principles of totalitarian government, state control of industry, and racist nationalism -- first brought to power in 1933 in the third german reich
UF National Socialism
Neo Nazism
BT Fascism
Totalitarianism
RT Anti Semitism
International Crimes
Segregationist Organizations

Near Eastern History
USE MIDDLE EASTERN HISTORY

Nearsightedness
USE MYOPIA

NEED ANALYSIS (STUDENT FINANCIAL AID) *Oct. 1979*
CIJE: 34 RIE: 147 GC: 620
SN Process of evaluating the resources of a student to determine his/her need or eligibility for financial aid
BT Evaluation Methods
RT Eligibility
Financial Needs
Financial Support
Needs Assessment
No Need Scholarships
Parent Financial Contribution
Self Supporting Students
Student Costs
Student Financial Aid
Student Loan Programs
Student Needs

NEED GRATIFICATION *Jul. 1966*
CIJE: 182 RIE: 181 GC: 120
SN Satisfaction of basic needs
UF Need Reduction
RT Community Satisfaction
Delay Of Gratification
Goal Orientation
Individual Needs
Job Satisfaction
Life Satisfaction
Marital Satisfaction
Morale
Needs
Psychological Needs
Self Actualization

= Two or more Descriptors are used to represent this term.
The term's main entry shows the appropriate coordination.

Need Reduction
USE NEED GRATIFICATION

NEEDLE TRADES *Jul. 1966*
CIJE: 7 RIE: 94 GC: 640
UF Seamstresses (1968 1980)
Tailors
BT Occupations
RT Clothing
Clothing Design
Clothing Instruction
Craft Workers
Fashion Industry
Home Economics Skills
Industrial Arts
Laundry Drycleaning Occupations
Occupational Home Economics
Patternmaking
Semiskilled Occupations
Sewing Instruction
Sewing Machine Operators

NEEDS *Jul. 1966*
CIJE: 253 RIE: 428 GC: 520
SN Conditions or factors necessary for optimal function, development, or well-being, the lack of which may impair efficiency or trigger action toward fulfillment (note: use a more specific term if possible)
NT Construction Needs
Educational Needs
Evaluation Needs
Financial Needs
Health Needs
Housing Needs
Individual Needs
Information Needs
Labor Needs
Research Needs
Student Needs
User Needs (Information)
RT Advocacy
Appropriate Technology
Motivation
Need Gratification
Needs Assessment
Objectives
Resources

NEEDS ASSESSMENT *Feb. 1976*
CIJE: 1870 RIE: 4752 GC: 810
SN Identifying needs and deciding on priorities among them
UF Priority Determination
BT Evaluation
RT Advisory Committees
Blue Ribbon Commissions
Delivery Systems
Educational Assessment
Evaluation Methods
Need Analysis (Student Financial Aid)
Needs
Objectives
Planning
Policy Formation
Position Papers
Resource Allocation
Self Evaluation (Groups)
Surveys
Systems Analysis
Testing

NEGATIVE ATTITUDES *Jul. 1966*
CIJE: 499 RIE: 359 GC: 540
BT Attitudes
RT Anti Intellectualism
Burnout
Jealousy
Resentment
Social Bias

NEGATIVE FORMS (LANGUAGE) *Aug. 1968*
CIJE: 93 RIE: 78 GC: 450
SN The structures of a language that signify negation
BT Morphemes
RT Language Universals
Morphophonemics
Semantics
Tagmemic Analysis

Negative Income Tax
USE GUARANTEED INCOME

NEGATIVE PRACTICE *Jul. 1966*
CIJE: 5 RIE: 5 GC: 310
SN Systematic repetition of erroneous responses to emphasize differences between appropriate and inappropriate performance
BT Teaching Methods
RT Behavior Change
Learning Activities
Negative Reinforcement

NEGATIVE REINFORCEMENT *Jul. 1966*
CIJE: 146 RIE: 102 GC: 110
SN Conditioning technique whereby the removal of an aversive stimulus increases the probability that a specified behavior will occur (note: do not confuse with "punishment" or "extinction (psychology)"
UF Massed Negative Reinforcement
Spaced Negative Reinforcement
BT Reinforcement
RT Corporal Punishment
Extinction (Psychology)
Negative Practice
Positive Reinforcement
Punishment
Social Reinforcement

Neglected Children (1977 1980)
USE CHILD NEGLECT

Neglected Languages
USE UNCOMMONLY TAUGHT LANGUAGES

NEGOTIATION AGREEMENTS *Nov. 1968*
CIJE: 221 RIE: 385 GC: 630
SN Documents containing a clause which recognizes one or more organizations as representative of employees on employment issues
RT Arbitration
Board Of Education Policy
Collective Bargaining
Contracts
Faculty College Relationship
Grievance Procedures
Negotiation Impasses
Public School Teachers
Teacher Strikes
Unions

NEGOTIATION IMPASSES *Apr. 1969*
CIJE: 126 RIE: 137 GC: 630
UF Impasse Resolution
RT Arbitration
Board Of Education Policy
Collective Bargaining
Employment Problems
Grievance Procedures
Labor Demands
Labor Economics
Labor Legislation
Labor Problems
Negotiation Agreements
Sanctions
Strikes
Teacher Militancy
Teacher Strikes
Unions

Negro Achievement (1966 1977)
USE BLACK ACHIEVEMENT

Negro Attitudes (1966 1977)
USE BLACK ATTITUDES

Negro Businesses (1967 1977)
USE BLACK BUSINESSES

Negro Colleges (1968 1977)
USE BLACK COLLEGES

Negro Community
USE BLACK COMMUNITY

Negro Culture (1966 1977)
USE BLACK CULTURE

Negro Dialects (1966 1977)
USE BLACK DIALECTS

Negro Education (1966 1977)
USE BLACK EDUCATION

Negro Employment (1966 1977)
USE BLACK EMPLOYMENT

Negro History (1966 1977)
USE BLACK HISTORY

NEGRO HOUSING (1966 1977) *Mar. 1980*
CIJE: 19 RIE: GC: 550
SN Invalid descriptor -- postings transferred to "black housing," which was invalidated mar80 -- see "housing discrimination," "residential patterns," or "homeowners" in coordination with appropriate "black" descriptor(s)

Negro Institutions (1966 1977)
USE BLACK INSTITUTIONS

Negro Leadership (1966 1977)
USE BLACK LEADERSHIP

Negro Literature (1968 1977)
USE BLACK LITERATURE

Negro Mothers (1966 1977)
USE BLACK MOTHERS

Negro Organizations (1966 1977)
USE BLACK ORGANIZATIONS

Negro Population Trends (1966 1977)
USE BLACK POPULATION TRENDS

Negro Role (1966 1977)
USE BLACK INFLUENCES

Negro Stereotypes (1966 1977)
USE BLACK STEREOTYPES

Negro Students (1966 1977)
USE BLACK STUDENTS

Negro Studies
USE BLACK STUDIES

Negro Teachers (1966 1977)
USE BLACK TEACHERS

Negro Youth (1966 1977)
USE BLACK YOUTH

Negroes (1966 1977)
USE BLACKS

Neighborhood (1966 1980)
USE NEIGHBORHOODS

Neighborhood Centers (1966 1980)
USE COMMUNITY CENTERS

NEIGHBORHOOD IMPROVEMENT *Jul. 1966*
CIJE: 51 RIE: 77 GC: 550
BT Improvement
RT Community Development
Community Responsibility
Housing Deficiencies
Housing Needs
Neighborhoods
Social Responsibility
Urban Improvement
Urban Renewal

NEIGHBORHOOD INTEGRATION *Jul. 1966*
CIJE: 76 RIE: 64 GC: 540
UF Integrated Neighborhoods
Residential Desegregation
BT Social Integration
RT Ethnic Distribution
Housing Discrimination
Housing Opportunities
Integration Readiness
Neighborhoods
Racial Composition
Racial Distribution
Racial Integration
Residential Patterns
Tokenism

Neighborhood School Policy (1966 1980)
USE NEIGHBORHOOD SCHOOLS; SCHOOL POLICY

NEIGHBORHOOD SCHOOLS *Jul. 1966*
CIJE: 69 RIE: 91 GC: 340
SN Schools in which most or all of the student population comes from the immediate geographic area in which the school is located
UF Neighborhood School Policy (1966 1980) #
BT Schools
RT Community Schools
Educational Parks
Neighborhoods
School Desegregation

Neighborhood Settlements
USE SETTLEMENT HOUSES

NEIGHBORHOODS *Mar. 1980*
CIJE: 113 RIE: 169 GC: 550
SN Small sections or districts within larger communities, usually marked by distinctive physical or human features (e.g., age, architecture, or social characteristics of the residents) that provide a sense of local identity
UF Neighborhood (1966 1980)
BT Community
RT Collective Settlements
Community Characteristics
Metropolitan Areas
Neighborhood Improvement
Neighborhood Integration
Neighborhood Schools
Place Of Residence
Residential Patterns
Suburbs

NEMBE *Feb. 1970*
CIJE: RIE: 3 GC: 440
BT African Languages

Neo Nazism
USE NAZISM

NEOCLASSICISM *Jul. 1971*
CIJE: 5 RIE: 2 GC: 430
SN A style of artistic expression based on or felt to be based on the classical style
RT Architecture
Art Expression
Eighteenth Century Literature
Literary Styles
Music
Seventeenth Century Literature

NEONATES *Jun. 1977*
CIJE: 181 RIE: 104 GC: 120
SN Aged birth to 1 month
UF Newborn Infants
BT Infants
RT Birth Weight
Infant Behavior
Infant Mortality
Pediatrics
Premature Infants

Neopsychoanalysis
USE PSYCHIATRY

NEPALI *Jul. 1966*
CIJE: RIE: 17 GC: 440
BT Indo European Languages

NETWORK ANALYSIS *Nov. 1982*
CIJE: 22 RIE: 41 GC: 820
SN Examination of the interactive communication patterns among individuals, groups, and/or organizations (note: do not confuse with "systems analysis" or "critical path method")
BT Methods
RT Communication (Thought Transfer)
Communication Audits
Communication Research
Communications
Models
Networks
Research Methodology
Systems Analysis

NETWORKS *Jul. 1966*
CIJE: 364 RIE: 504 GC: 710
SN Series of points interconnected by communication channels (note: use more specific term if possible)
NT Computer Networks
Information Networks
Social Networks
RT Communication (Thought Transfer)
Communications
Cooperation
Coordination

Decentralization
Diffusion (Communication)
Linking Agents
Network Analysis
Radio
Telecommunications
Television

NEUROLINGUISTICS *Jun. 1972*
CIJE: 125 RIE: 108 GC: 450
SN Study of the biological foundations of language and the brain mechanisms underlying its acquisition and use
BT Linguistics
RT Language Handicaps
Language Processing
Linguistic Theory
Neurological Impairments
Neurological Organization
Neurology
Psycholinguistics

Neurological Defects (1966 1980)
USE NEUROLOGICAL IMPAIRMENTS

NEUROLOGICAL IMPAIRMENTS *Mar. 1980*
CIJE: 555 RIE: 306 GC: 220
SN Organic disorders of the brain or nervous system
UF Brain Damage
Neurological Defects (1966 1980)
Neurologically Handicapped (1966 1980)
Paraplegia
Quadriplegia (1969 1980)
Tetraplegia
NT Aphasia
Cerebral Palsy
Epilepsy
Minimal Brain Dysfunction
BT Physical Disabilities
RT Attention Deficit Disorders
Behavior Disorders
Developmental Disabilities
Downs Syndrome
Dyslexia
Exceptional Persons
Hyperactivity
Language Handicaps
Lead Poisoning
Learning Disabilities
Mental Disorders
Mental Retardation
Motor Development
Neurolinguistics
Neurological Organization
Neurology
Perceptual Handicaps
Psychomotor Skills
Seizures

NEUROLOGICAL ORGANIZATION *Jul. 1966*
CIJE: 382 RIE: 221 GC: 210
NT Brain Hemisphere Functions
BT Physical Characteristics
RT Lateral Dominance
Motor Development
Neurolinguistics
Neurological Impairments
Neurology
Perception
Perceptual Development
Physical Development
Physiology
Psychomotor Skills
Stimulation

Neurologically Handicapped (1966 1980)
USE NEUROLOGICAL IMPAIRMENTS

NEUROLOGY *Jul. 1966*
CIJE: 324 RIE: 132 GC: 210
BT Medicine
RT Anatomy
Brain Hemisphere Functions
Electroencephalography
Mental Health
Neurolinguistics
Neurological Impairments
Neurological Organization
Pathology
Physiology

NEUROSIS *Jul. 1966*
CIJE: 164 RIE: 55 GC: 230
UF Neurotic Children (1966 1980)
BT Mental Disorders
RT Emotional Disturbances
Fear
Mental Health
Personality Problems
Psychosomatic Disorders
School Phobia

Neurotic Children (1966 1980)
USE NEUROSIS

NEW JOURNALISM *Dec. 1974*
CIJE: 27 RIE: 25 GC: 430
SN Reporting which combines traditional journalism techniques with such devices of fiction writing as: scene by scene reconstruction of settings, recording of dialogue, use of third person point-of-view, and extensive recording of external characteristics of individual characters -- emphasis is on capturing the "concrete reality" or "immediacy" of cultural phenomena
BT Journalism
RT News Media
Newspapers
News Writing
Nonfiction
Publications

New Mathematics
USE MODERN MATHEMATICS

Newborn Infants
USE NEONATES

NEWS MEDIA *Jul. 1966*
CIJE: 747 RIE: 958 GC: 720
UF Press
Sports News #
NT Editorials
Newspapers
BT Mass Media
RT Editing
Editors
Freedom Of Information
Freedom Of Speech
Headlines
Journalism
Journalism Education
New Journalism
News Reporting
News Writing
Photojournalism
Press Opinion
Radio
Television

NEWS REPORTING *Jan. 1974*
CIJE: 1253 RIE: 747 GC: 720
UF Sports Reporting #
BT Journalism
RT Athletics
Broadcast Industry
Expository Writing
Headlines
News Media
News Writing
Photojournalism
Reports

NEWS WRITING *Jul. 1977*
CIJE: 289 RIE: 160 GC: 720
SN Writing about events and activities for dissemination through newspapers, news broadcasts, or the news services
BT Journalism
Writing (Composition)
RT Broadcast Industry
Content Area Writing
Editing
Expository Writing
Headlines
New Journalism
News Media
News Reporting
Writing For Publication

NEWSLETTERS *Jul. 1966*
CIJE: 103 RIE: 669 GC: 730
BT Newspapers
RT Bulletins

NEWSPAPERS *Jul. 1966*
CIJE: 1207 RIE: 1176 GC: 720
NT Newsletters
School Newspapers
BT News Media
Serials
RT Bulletins
Captions
Comics (Publications)
Editorials
Headlines
Journalism
Journalism Education
Layout (Publications)
New Journalism
Photojournalism
Reading Materials

Night Schools (1966 1980)
USE EVENING PROGRAMS

NINETEENTH CENTURY LITERATURE *May. 1969*
CIJE: 334 RIE: 101 GC: 430
BT Literature
RT Impressionism
Literary History
Modernism
Naturalism
Romanticism
Symbolism
Victorian Literature

NO NEED SCHOLARSHIPS *Aug. 1986*
CIJE: 2 RIE: 5 GC: 620
SN Scholarship awards based on merit regardless of financial need
BT Merit Scholarships
RT Need Analysis (Student Financial Aid)
Scholarship Funds

NO SHOWS *Aug. 1986*
CIJE: 1 RIE: 13 GC: 520
SN Individuals who arrange to be somewhere (e.g., attending a meeting, beginning a course of study, enrolling in college) but who fail to appear
BT Groups
RT Attendance
College Applicants
Dropouts
Enrollment

NOISE (SOUND) *Oct. 1982*
CIJE: 44 RIE: 104 GC: 490
UF Noise Control
Noise Levels
Noise Pollution
Noise Testing
Volume (Sound)
BT Acoustical Environment
RT Acoustic Insulation
Acoustics
Audio Equipment
Auditory Stimuli
Ecology
Environmental Standards
Hearing Conservation
Pollution
Psychoacoustics
Sound Effects

Noise Control
USE NOISE (SOUND)

Noise Levels
USE NOISE (SOUND)

Noise Pollution
USE NOISE (SOUND)

Noise Testing
USE NOISE (SOUND)

NOMADS *Jan. 1970*
CIJE: 12 RIE: 17 GC: 560
UF Pastoral Peoples
Transhumance
BT Migrants
RT Land Settlement
Migration
Transient Children
Tribes

Nominals (1967 1980)
USE NOUNS

Non Discursive Measures
USE VISUAL MEASURES

NON ENGLISH SPEAKING *Jul. 1966*
CIJE: 134 RIE: 518 GC: 450
BT Groups
RT Bilingual Education
Bilingual Education Programs
Bilingual Teacher Aides
Bilingual Teachers
English (Second Language)
Ethnic Groups
Language Dominance
Limited English Speaking
Minority Groups
Native Speakers
Spanish Speaking

NON WESTERN CIVILIZATION *Sep. 1968*
CIJE: 208 RIE: 349 GC: 560
SN Includes asia and africa
UF Eastern Civilization
Oriental Civilization
South Asian Civilization
BT Culture
RT African Culture
African History
Arabs
Area Studies
Asian History
Asian Studies
Buddhism
Burmese Culture
Chinese Culture
Confucianism
Cultural Background
Cultural Context
History
Korean Culture
Middle Eastern History
Middle Eastern Studies
Sociocultural Patterns
Taoism
World History

NONAUTHORITARIAN CLASSES *Jul. 1966*
CIJE: 10 RIE: 16 GC: 310
BT Classes (Groups Of Students)
RT Leadership
Permissive Environment

Nonbook Materials
USE NONPRINT MEDIA

NONCAMPUS COLLEGES *Oct. 1977*
CIJE: 20 RIE: 34 GC: 340
SN Postsecondary institutions which dispense with the fixed campus in favor of rented, borrowed, or mobile facilities in many locations
BT Colleges
RT Access To Education
Educational Facilities
Extension Education
External Degree Programs
Nontraditional Education
Outreach Programs
Postsecondary Education

NONCOLLEGE BOUND STUDENTS *Mar. 1980*
CIJE: 62 RIE: 103 GC: 360
SN Students not planning on attending an institution of higher education
UF Noncollege Preparatory Students (1967 1980)
BT High School Students
RT Academic Aspiration
College Bound Students
High School Seniors
Vocational Education

Noncollege Preparatory Students (1967 1980)
USE NONCOLLEGE BOUND STUDENTS

Noncompliance (Psychology)
USE COMPLIANCE (PSYCHOLOGY)

NONCREDIT COURSES *Jul. 1966*
CIJE: 84 RIE: 292 GC: 350
BT Courses
RT Adult Education
Continuing Education
Continuing Education Units
Credit Courses

= Two or more Descriptors are used to represent this term.
The term's main entry shows the appropriate coordination.

Elective Courses
Minicourses
Student Interests

NONDIRECTIVE COUNSELING *Jul. 1966*
CIJE: 96 RIE: 46 GC: 240
SN Counseling procedure in which the counselor is empathetic and does not evaluate or direct (but may clarify) clients' remarks, thus assisting them to accept responsibility for their own problem-solving
UF Client Centered Counseling
BT Counseling
RT Behavior Change
Counseling Theories
Empathy

NONDISCRIMINATORY EDUCATION *Jul. 1966*
CIJE: 126 RIE: 277 GC: 540
BT Education
RT Access To Education
Affirmative Action
Educational Discrimination
Educational Equity (Finance)
Educational Opportunities
Equal Education
Sex Fairness

Nonfarm Agricultural Occupations
USE OFF FARM AGRICULTURAL OCCUPATIONS

NONFICTION *Sep. 1974*
CIJE: 187 RIE: 113 GC: 430
NT Biographies
Chronicles
Diaries
Essays
BT Prose
RT Fiction
Literary Devices
Literary Genres
Literary Styles
New Journalism

NONFORMAL EDUCATION *Jul. 1973*
CIJE: 307 RIE: 576 GC: 330
SN Organized education without formal schooling or institutionalization in which knowledge, skills, and values are taught by relatives, peers, or other community members (note: do not confuse with "nonschool educational programs" or the identifier "informal education")
BT Education
RT Comparative Education
Culture
Developing Nations
Educational Anthropology
Folk Culture
Lifelong Learning
Nontraditional Education
Socialization
Tribes

Nongraded Classes (1966 1980)
USE NONGRADED INSTRUCTIONAL GROUPING

NONGRADED INSTRUCTIONAL GROUPING *Mar. 1980*
CIJE: 192 RIE: 366 GC: 350
SN Grouping students according to such characteristics as academic achievement, mental and physical ability, or emotional development rather than by age or grade level (note: some of the former "nongraded/ungraded" descriptors merged with this term were occasionally used to index "nongraded student evaluation")
UF Nongraded Classes (1966 1980)
Nongraded Primary System (1966 1980)
Nongraded System (1966 1980)
Ungraded Classes (1966 1980)
Ungraded Curriculum (1966 1980)
Ungraded Elementary Programs (1966 1980)
Ungraded Primary Programs (1966 1980)
Ungraded Programs (1966 1980)
Ungraded Schools (1966 1980)
BT Grouping (Instructional Purposes)
RT Ability Grouping
Age Grade Placement
Continuous Progress Plan
Flexible Progression
Instructional Program Divisions
Multigraded Classes
Multiunit Schools
Open Education

Nongraded Primary System (1966 1980)
USE NONGRADED INSTRUCTIONAL GROUPING

NONGRADED STUDENT EVALUATION *Mar. 1980*
CIJE: 17 RIE: 12 GC: 320
SN Evaluation of student progress or achievement without the use of letter grades or other summary ratings -- provides feedback about a student's specific strengths and weaknesses rather than summarizing his or her overall performance (note: some of the former "nongraded/ungraded" descriptors merged with "nongraded instructional grouping" were occasionally used to index this concept)
BT Student Evaluation
RT Credit No Credit Grading
Free Schools
Informal Assessment
Pass Fail Grading

Nongraded System (1966 1980)
USE NONGRADED INSTRUCTIONAL GROUPING

NONINSTRUCTIONAL RESPONSIBILITY *Jul. 1966*
CIJE: 163 RIE: 181 GC: 320
SN Duties assumed by, or assigned to, teachers that are outside of their regular teaching responsibilities (e.g., lunchroom duty, advising, community involvement)
UF Extrainstructional Duties
Extrateaching Duties
Nonteaching Duties
BT Teacher Responsibility
RT Educational Responsibility
Faculty Workload
School Responsibility
Teacher Role
Teachers

NONINSTRUCTIONAL STUDENT COSTS *Dec. 1975*
CIJE: 8 RIE: 53 GC: 620
SN Costs met by students that are not instructional costs (tuition, etc.) but are necessary in the pursuit of an education -- includes room and board, transportation expenses, book costs, personal expenses, forgone income, etc.
BT Student Costs
RT Educational Finance
Fellowships
Instructional Student Costs
Scholarships
Student Financial Aid
Student Loan Programs

NONMAJORS *Mar. 1980*
CIJE: 85 RIE: 63 GC: 360
BT Students
RT Core Curriculum
Course Selection (Students)
Degree Requirements
Interdisciplinary Approach
Introductory Courses
Majors (Students)

Nonorganic Failure To Thrive
USE FAILURE TO THRIVE

NONPARAMETRIC STATISTICS *Nov. 1970*
CIJE: 160 RIE: 52 GC: 480
SN Forms of descriptive or sampling statistics applied to data when no assumptions can be made about the distributions involved
UF Distribution Free Statistics
BT Statistics
RT Bayesian Statistics
Correlation
Mathematical Concepts
Statistical Analysis
Statistical Studies

NONPRINT MEDIA *Mar. 1980*
CIJE: 108 RIE: 178 GC: 720
SN Materials used in communication that are not in the print medium nor textual or book-like in nature (note: use "audiovisual aids" for instructional nonprint media -- prior to mar80, this concept was indexed under "audiovisual aids")
UF Nonbook Materials
NT Audiodisks
Documentaries
Exhibits
Films
Filmstrips
Optical Disks
Realia
Tape Recordings
Transparencies
Videodisks
RT Audiovisual Aids
Cartoons
Charts
Communications
Diagrams
Display Aids
Educational Media
Graphs
Illustrations
Library Acquisition
Library Collections
Library Materials
Library Material Selection
Maps
Mass Media
Media Selection
Photographs
Publications
Resource Materials
Talking Books
Visual Aids

NONPROFESSIONAL PERSONNEL *Jul. 1966*
CIJE: 250 RIE: 463 GC: 630
NT Clerical Workers
Sales Workers
Semiskilled Workers
Service Workers
Skilled Workers
Unskilled Workers
BT Personnel
RT Paraprofessional Personnel
Professional Personnel

NONPROFIT ORGANIZATIONS *Jan. 1978*
CIJE: 137 RIE: 146 GC: 520
SN Organizations not designed primarily to pay dividends on invested capital (note: prior to dec77, the instruction "nonprofit organizations, use voluntary agencies" was carried in the thesaurus)
BT Organizations (Groups)
RT Agencies
Alumni Associations
Churches
Church Programs
Colleges
Government (Administrative Body)
Hospitals
Institutions
Philanthropic Foundations
Religious Organizations
Schools
Settlement Houses
Universities

Nonpublic Agencies
USE PRIVATE AGENCIES

Nonpublic Education
USE PRIVATE EDUCATION

Nonpublic School Aid (1972 1980)
USE PRIVATE SCHOOL AID

Nonpublic Schools
USE PRIVATE SCHOOLS

NONRESERVATION AMERICAN INDIANS *Oct. 1972*
CIJE: 24 RIE: 135 GC: 560
SN American indians living off reservations who remain on the tribal census roll or who maintain their indian identity
UF Off Reservation American Indians
NT Rural American Indians
Urban American Indians
BT American Indians
RT Alaska Natives
American Indian Reservations
Relocation
Reservation American Indians

Nonresident Farmers
USE PART TIME FARMERS

Nonresident Students (1967 1980) (Foreign)
USE FOREIGN STUDENTS

Nonresident Students (1967 1980) (Out Of District)
USE RESIDENCE REQUIREMENTS

Nonresident Students (1967 1980) (Out Of State)
USE OUT OF STATE STUDENTS

Nonresidential Schools (1967 1980)
USE COMMUTER COLLEGES

Nonreversal Shift
USE SHIFT STUDIES

NONSCHOOL EDUCATIONAL PROGRAMS *Mar. 1980*
CIJE: 70 RIE: 104 GC: 330
SN Programs with formal educational intent offered by institutions or organizations other than schools, e.g., businesses, churches, community agencies, etc. (note: do not confuse with "home schooling" or "nonformal education")
BT Programs
RT Adult Education
Community Education
Corporate Education
Inplant Programs
Labor Education

Nonspecialists
USE LAY PEOPLE

NONSTANDARD DIALECTS *Jul. 1966*
CIJE: 399 RIE: 638 GC: 450
SN Varieties of a language that differ in pronunciation, grammar, or vocabulary from recognized standards
BT Dialects
RT Applied Linguistics
Bidialectalism
Black Dialects
Diglossia
Native Language Instruction
Oral Language
Regional Dialects
Social Dialects
Sociolinguistics
Standard Spoken Usage
Urban Language

Nonteaching Duties
USE NONINSTRUCTIONAL RESPONSIBILITY

NONTENURED FACULTY *Feb. 1984*
CIJE: 18 RIE: 10 GC: 360
SN Academic staff who have not received tenure (permanence of position) at their school or institution -- includes those awaiting tenured appointments and those who are ineligible for tenure
UF Nontenured Teachers
Untenured Faculty
BT Faculty
RT Academic Rank (Professional)
Adjunct Faculty
College Faculty
Part Time Faculty
Probationary Period
Teachers
Tenure
Tenured Faculty

Nontenured Teachers
USE NONTENURED FACULTY

Nontraditional Careers
USE NONTRADITIONAL OCCUPATIONS

NONTRADITIONAL EDUCATION *Mar. 1980*
CIJE: 1644 RIE: 2032 GC: 330
SN Educational programs that are offered as alternatives within or without the formal educational system and provide innovative and flexible instruction, curriculum, grading systems, or degree requirements
UF Alternative Education
Alternative Schools (1972 1980)
Educational Alternatives (1974 1980)
Instructional Alternatives
Teaching Alternatives
Training Alternatives
BT Education
RT Access To Education
Community Schools
Continuation Students
Continuing Education
Corporate Education
Correspondence Study
Degree Requirements
Distance Education
Educational Development
Educational Innovation
Educational Methods
Educational Needs
Educational Opportunities
Educational Principles
Educational Theories
Experimental Colleges
Experimental Curriculum
Experimental Schools
Extension Education
External Degree Programs
Field Experience Programs
Folk Schools
Freedom Schools
Free Schools
High School Equivalency Programs
Home Schooling
Home Study
Individualized Education Programs
Instructional Innovation
Magnet Schools
Noncampus Colleges
Nonformal Education
Nontraditional Students
Open Education
Open Universities
Prior Learning
Reentry Students
Relevance (Education)
School Choice
Special Degree Programs
Traditional Schools
Transitional Schools

NONTRADITIONAL OCCUPATIONS *Oct. 1979*
CIJE: 196 RIE: 423 GC: 540
SN Occupations in which, historically, certain groups have been underrepresented -- usually applies to the sexes (e.g., men in nursing, women in auto mechanics)
UF Nontraditional Careers
BT Occupations
RT Affirmative Action
Career Choice
Comparable Worth
Employed Women
Employment Opportunities
Employment Patterns
Equal Opportunities (Jobs)
Occupational Aspiration
Personnel Integration
Sex Fairness
Work Attitudes

NONTRADITIONAL STUDENTS *Jun. 1977*
CIJE: 411 RIE: 660 GC: 360
SN Adults beyond traditional school age (beyond the mid-twenties), ethnic minorities, women with dependent children, underprepared students, and other special groups who have historically been underrepresented in postsecondary education
BT Students
RT Adult Students
College Students
Educationally Disadvantaged
Higher Education
High Risk Students
Nontraditional Education
Open Enrollment
Postsecondary Education
Prior Learning
Reentry Students
Special Degree Programs

NONVERBAL ABILITY *Jul. 1966*
CIJE: 88 RIE: 63 GC: 120
SN Ability in such nonlanguage areas as music, psychomotor skills, mathematics, and spatial relations (note: use "nonverbal communication" for nonverbal communicative skills -- prior to mar80, the use of this term was not restricted by a scope note)
BT Ability
RT Nonverbal Communication
Nonverbal Learning
Nonverbal Tests
Verbal Ability

NONVERBAL COMMUNICATION *Mar. 1969*
CIJE: 954 RIE: 905 GC: 120
SN Communication through nonverbal symbols, i.e., facial expression, body movement, spatial relationships, and nonverbal vocal cues
NT Body Language
Eye Contact
Facial Expressions
BT Communication (Thought Transfer)
RT Classroom Communication
Communication Problems
Communication Skills
Nonverbal Ability
Nonverbal Learning
Paralinguistics
Personal Space
Speech Communication
Verbal Communication
Visual Literacy

NONVERBAL LEARNING *Jul. 1966*
CIJE: 78 RIE: 103 GC: 110
SN Learning that does not involve the use of language
NT Perceptual Motor Learning
BT Learning
RT Associative Learning
Learning Modalities
Nonverbal Ability
Nonverbal Communication
Nonverbal Tests
Psychomotor Skills
Verbal Learning
Visual Learning

NONVERBAL TESTS *Jan. 1969*
CIJE: 115 RIE: 93 GC: 830
SN Tests which minimize or do not require the use of speech or language by examiner or subject -- items may consist of symbols, figures, numbers, or pictures, but not words
NT Visual Measures
BT Tests
RT Culture Fair Tests
Nonverbal Ability
Nonverbal Learning
Performance Tests
Preschool Tests
Verbal Tests

Norm Referenced Measures
USE NORM REFERENCED TESTS

NORM REFERENCED TESTS *Sep. 1970*
CIJE: 204 RIE: 418 GC: 830
SN Tests used to describe an individual's performance in relation to the performance of others on the same test (note: do not confuse with "standardized tests" or "objective tests," which are often norm-referenced)
UF Norm Referenced Measures
BT Tests
RT Achievement Tests
Comparative Testing
Criterion Referenced Tests
Grade Equivalent Scores
National Competency Tests
National Norms
Standardized Tests
Test Interpretation
Test Norms

NORMALIZATION (HANDICAPPED) *Mar. 1974*
CIJE: 286 RIE: 328 GC: 220
SN Use of culturally normative means (patterns and conditions of everyday life) to facilitate adjustment and functioning by the handicapped
NT Deinstitutionalization (Of Disabled)
RT Adaptive Behavior (Of Disabled)
Assistive Devices (For Disabled)
Daily Living Skills
Disabilities
Group Experience
Group Homes
Handicap Discrimination
Labeling (Of Persons)
Mainstreaming
Rehabilitation
Special Education

Normative Behavior
USE BEHAVIOR STANDARDS

NORMS *Oct. 1970*
CIJE: 139 RIE: 760 GC: 820
SN Statistical description of the typical performance, behavior, form, function, etc. of a given population (note: use only for numerical data and not for subjectively described standards)
NT Local Norms
National Norms
State Norms
Test Norms
BT Statistical Data
RT Cross Sectional Studies
Measurement
Participant Characteristics
Sampling
Scaling
Standards
Statistical Analysis
Statistical Distributions
Values

NORTH AMERICAN CULTURE *Mar. 1980*
CIJE: 62 RIE: 48 GC: 560
SN Culture of the united states and canada
NT Hispanic American Culture
Japanese American Culture
BT Culture
RT American Indian Culture
American Studies
Black Culture
Jazz
North American History
North American Literature
North Americans
Western Civilization

NORTH AMERICAN ENGLISH *Mar. 1980*
CIJE: 164 RIE: 296 GC: 450
SN English as used in the united states and canada -- differs from british or other varieties of english principally in certain features of vocabulary, pronunciation, grammar, and spelling
UF American English (1968 1980)
BT English
RT Dialects
Etymology
Idioms
Language Classification
Language Patterns
Language Usage
Linguistics
North American Literature
Regional Dialects
Speech Habits
Standard Spoken Usage

NORTH AMERICAN HISTORY *Mar. 1980*
CIJE: 31 RIE: 75 GC: 430
SN History of the geographic area that includes the united states and canada
NT United States History
BT History
RT American Indian History
Black History
North American Culture
North American Literature
North Americans
Western Civilization

NORTH AMERICAN LITERATURE *Mar. 1980*
CIJE: 13 RIE: 5 GC: 430
SN Literature of the united states and canada
NT Canadian Literature
United States Literature
BT Literature
RT American Indian Literature
North American Culture
North American English
North American History
North Americans

NORTH AMERICANS *Mar. 1980*
CIJE: 20 RIE: 34 GC: 560
SN Indigenous peoples, permanent residents, or citizens of the united states and canada
UF Arab Americans #
NT Alaska Natives
Anglo Americans
Asian Americans
Canada Natives
Greek Americans
Hispanic Americans
Italian Americans
Pacific Americans
Polish Americans
BT Groups
RT American Indians
Eskimos
Ethnic Groups
North American Culture
North American History
North American Literature

Northern Attitudes (1968 1980)
USE REGIONAL ATTITUDES

NORTHERN SCHOOLS (1966 1980) *Mar. 1980*
CIJE: 36 RIE: 51 GC: 340
SN Invalid descriptor -- coordinate appropriate "school" or "education" descriptors with the identifier "united states (north)"

Northward Movement
USE MIGRATION

NORWEGIAN *Jul. 1966*
CIJE: 14 RIE: 23 GC: 440
BT Indo European Languages

NOTETAKING *Oct. 1982*
CIJE: 112 RIE: 76 GC: 310
SN Making a brief written record to aid the memory
BT Writing (Composition)
RT Cues
Mnemonics
Outlining (Discourse)
Prewriting
Study Skills
Writing Skills

NOTIONAL FUNCTIONAL SYLLABI *Oct. 1980*
CIJE: 76 RIE: 57 GC: 450
SN Foreign language course curricula based upon the learner's communicative needs and organized according to the content of what is to be communicated rather than the grammatical form of the language or specific situational requirements
UF Functional Notional Syllabi
BT Modern Language Curriculum
RT Communicative Competence (Languages)
Languages
Second Language Instruction
Second Language Learning
Second Language Programs

NOUNS *Apr. 1980*
CIJE: 403 RIE: 346 GC: 450
SN Words that name a subject of discourse
UF Nominals (1967 1980)
BT Form Classes (Languages)
RT Morphology (Languages)
Phrase Structure
Sentence Structure
Syntax
Vocabulary

= Two or more Descriptors are used to represent this term.
The term's main entry shows the appropriate coordination.

Novella
USE NOVELS

NOVELS *Jul. 1966*
CIJE: 1006 RIE: 428 GC: 430
UF Novella
Sociological Novels (1969 1980)
BT Fiction
Literary Genres
RT Books

NOVELTY (STIMULUS DIMENSION) *Mar. 1978*
CIJE: 68 RIE: 22 GC: 110
SN A stimulus dimension which reflects the quality or state of being new or unfamiliar to an individual
RT Adaptation Level Theory
Arousal Patterns
Attention
Dimensional Preference
Exploratory Behavior
Habituation
Perception
Redundancy
Sensory Experience
Stimuli

Nuclear Control
USE DISARMAMENT

NUCLEAR ENERGY *Oct. 1980*
CIJE: 81 RIE: 184 GC: 490
SN Power derived from the fission (splitting) of the nuclei of heavy elements such as uranium, or the fusion of light elements such as the hydrogen isotopes deuterium and tritium
UF Atomic Energy
Nuclear Energy Occupations #
BT Radiation
RT Atomic Theory
Nuclear Physics
Nuclear Power Plants
Nuclear Power Plant Technicians
Nuclear Technology
Nuclear Warfare
Radiation Biology
Radiation Effects
Radioisotopes

Nuclear Energy Occupations
USE ENERGY OCCUPATIONS; NUCLEAR ENERGY

NUCLEAR FAMILY *Jun. 1977*
CIJE: 78 RIE: 49 GC: 520
SN A family group consisting of father, mother, and children
UF Traditional Family Unit
Two Parent Family
BT Family (Sociological Unit)
RT Extended Family
Family Life
Family Relationship
Family Size
Family Structure
Kinship
One Parent Family
Stepfamily

Nuclear Medicine
USE RADIOLOGY

Nuclear Medicine Technologists
USE RADIOLOGIC TECHNOLOGISTS

NUCLEAR PHYSICS *Jul. 1966*
CIJE: 388 RIE: 191 GC: 490
UF Atomic Physics
BT Physics
RT Atomic Structure
Atomic Theory
Force
Matter
Nuclear Energy
Nuclear Power Plants
Nuclear Power Plant Technicians
Nuclear Technology
Nuclear Warfare
Quantum Mechanics
Radiation
Radiation Biology
Radiation Effects
Radioisotopes
Scientific Research
Thermodynamics

NUCLEAR POWER PLANT TECHNICIANS *Aug. 1982*
CIJE: 3 RIE: 59 GC: 640
BT Paraprofessional Personnel
RT Chemical Technicians
Electronic Technicians
Energy Occupations
Engineering Technicians
Mechanics (Process)
Nuclear Energy
Nuclear Physics
Nuclear Power Plants
Nuclear Technology
Scientific Personnel

NUCLEAR POWER PLANTS *Aug. 1982*
CIJE: 22 RIE: 75 GC: 920
SN Facilities in which nuclear energy is converted into heat to provide electric power
BT Facilities
RT Nuclear Energy
Nuclear Physics
Nuclear Power Plant Technicians
Nuclear Technology
Utilities

NUCLEAR TECHNOLOGY *Oct. 1982*
CIJE: 27 RIE: 124 GC: 490
SN Application and use of nuclear fission or fusion processes
BT Power Technology
RT Engineering
Engineering Technology
Nuclear Energy
Nuclear Physics
Nuclear Power Plants
Nuclear Power Plant Technicians
Nuclear Warfare
Physical Sciences
Radiation
Radiation Biology
Radiation Effects
Radiographers
Radioisotopes
Radiologic Technologists
Radiology
Technical Education

NUCLEAR WARFARE *Nov. 1969*
CIJE: 211 RIE: 160 GC: 610
UF Atomic Warfare
BT War
RT Atomic Theory
Civil Defense
Disarmament
Military Science
Modern History
Nuclear Energy
Nuclear Physics
Nuclear Technology
Radiation Effects
World Problems

NUCLEIC ACIDS *Oct. 1982*
CIJE: 15 RIE: GC: 490
SN Large chainlike molecules containing nitrogen, sugar, and phosphoric acid that are found in all living organisms and in viruses -- they are important in the transference of genetic characteristics and in synthesizing protein
NT Dna
Rna
RT Biochemistry
Biology
Chemical Reactions
Cytology
Embryology
Enzymes
Genetic Engineering
Genetics
Heredity
Physiology
Polymers
Reproduction (Biology)

NUMBER CONCEPTS *Jul. 1966*
CIJE: 1443 RIE: 733 GC: 480
NT Place Value
BT Mathematical Concepts
RT Arithmetic
Mathematics Tests
Numbers

Number Operations
USE ARITHMETIC

Number Skills Tests
USE MATHEMATICS TESTS

NUMBER SYSTEMS *Jul. 1966*
CIJE: 177 RIE: 149 GC: 480
UF Arithmetic Systems
BT Numbers
RT Mathematics

Number Use
USE NUMBERS

NUMBERS *Jul. 1966*
CIJE: 289 RIE: 139 GC: 480
UF Number Use
NT Fractions
Logarithms
Number Systems
Rational Numbers
Reciprocals (Mathematics)
Whole Numbers
BT Symbols (Mathematics)
RT Arithmetic
Computation
Mathematics
Mathematics Skills
Mathematics Tests
Number Concepts
Place Value
Statistics

Numeric Filing
USE FILING

NUMERICAL CONTROL *Jul. 1966*
CIJE: 16 RIE: 32 GC: 710
SN Technique involving coded, numerical instructions for the automatic control and performance of a machine tool
UF N C Systems
RT Automation
Computer Software
Cybernetics
Electronic Control
Machine Tools

Nun Teachers (1966 1980)
USE NUNS

NUNS *Jul. 1966*
CIJE: 25 RIE: 11 GC: 640
UF Nun Teachers (1966 1980)
BT Females
RT Catholics
Church Workers
Clergy
Religion
Religious Cultural Groups
Theological Education

NURSE PRACTITIONERS *Nov. 1982*
CIJE: 56 RIE: 23 GC: 210
SN Registered nurses who have additional training and certification in a specialized field and who perform highly independent roles in clinical care and teaching of patients
UF School Nurse Practitioners #
BT Nurses
RT Medicine
Patient Education
Physicians Assistants

NURSERIES (HORTICULTURE) *Sep. 1968*
CIJE: 8 RIE: 38 GC: 410
BT Facilities
RT Forestry
Greenhouses
Horticulture
Nursery Workers (Horticulture)
Ornamental Horticulture

NURSERY SCHOOLS *Jul. 1966*
CIJE: 212 RIE: 260 GC: 340
SN Schools for preschool children, usually 2 1/2 to 5 1/2 years of age -- nursery school programs are either part-day or part-week and may be operated as a service by public schools, or for profit by other agencies or individuals
BT Schools
RT Child Development Centers
Day Care Centers
Early Childhood Education
Preschool Education

NURSERY WORKERS (HORTICULTURE) *Jul. 1966*
CIJE: 2 RIE: 34 GC: 410
UF Greenhouse Workers
BT Semiskilled Workers
RT Nurseries (Horticulture)
Ornamental Horticulture Occupations
Plant Propagation

NURSES *Jul. 1966*
CIJE: 655 RIE: 531 GC: 210
SN (Note: if applicable, use the more specific terms "school nurses" and/or "nurse practitioners")
UF Certified Nurses
Licensed Nurses
Practical Nurses (1967 1981) #
Professional Nurses
Registered Nurses
Teacher Nurses (1966 1980)
NT Nurse Practitioners
School Nurses
BT Health Personnel
Professional Personnel
RT Hospital Personnel
Medical Associations
Medical Services
Nurses Aides
Nursing
Nursing Education

NURSES AIDES *Jul. 1966*
CIJE: 24 RIE: 148 GC: 210
UF Hospital Attendants
Nursing Aides
Nursing Assistants
Rest Home Aides
BT Allied Health Personnel
RT Attendants
Home Health Aides
Medical Assistants
Nurses
Nursing
Psychiatric Aides

NURSING *Jul. 1966*
CIJE: 552 RIE: 577 GC: 210
NT Practical Nursing
BT Medicine
RT Medical Services
Nurses
Nurses Aides
Nursing Education
Nursing Homes

Nursing Aides
USE NURSES AIDES

Nursing Assistants
USE NURSES AIDES

NURSING EDUCATION *Mar. 1980*
CIJE: 595 RIE: 659 GC: 210
SN Formal instruction in nursing offered by a school, college, or university, often affiliated with a hospital -- includes 2-year, 3-year, 4-year, and graduate programs (note: prior to mar80, this concept was frequently indexed under "nursing")
BT Medical Education
RT Nurses
Nursing
Pharmaceutical Education
Teaching Hospitals

NURSING HOMES *Jul. 1966*
CIJE: 156 RIE: 158 GC: 920
SN Resident facilities providing skilled nursing care as their primary and predominant function
UF Convalescent Homes
BT Health Facilities
Residential Institutions
RT Hospices (Terminal Care)
Hospitals
Medical Services
Nursing
Personal Care Homes
Practical Nursing
Residential Care

= Two or more Descriptors are used to represent this term.
The term's main entry shows the appropriate coordination.

NUTRITION *Jul. 1966*
CIJE: 949 RIE: 1384 GC: 210
UF Malnutrition
NT Breastfeeding
RT Anemia
Anorexia Nervosa
Breakfast Programs
Bulimia
Dietetics
Dietitians
Eating Habits
Failure To Thrive
Food
Food Standards
Health
Hunger
Lunch Programs
Nutrition Instruction
Obesity
Physical Health
Physiology
Vending Machines

NUTRITION INSTRUCTION *Jul. 1966*
CIJE: 465 RIE: 581 GC: 400
BT Instruction
RT Cooking Instruction
Cooks
Foods Instruction
Health Education
Home Economics
Nutrition

Nyanja
USE CHINYANJA

OBEDIENCE *Aug. 1986*
CIJE: 11 RIE: 3 GC: 110
SN Compliance with the demands or requests of persons in authority
BT Compliance (Psychology)
Social Behavior
RT Behavior Problems
Discipline
Problem Children

OBESITY *Oct. 1980*
CIJE: 128 RIE: 68 GC: 210
SN Body condition characterized by a disfiguring excess of weight or fat
UF Overweight (Excessive Body Fat)
BT Body Weight
Diseases
RT Dietetics
Eating Habits
Nutrition
Physical Health

Object Concept
USE OBJECT PERMANENCE

OBJECT MANIPULATION *Jul. 1966*
CIJE: 84 RIE: 48 GC: 310
BT Psychomotor Skills
RT Behavior Development
Eye Hand Coordination
Manipulative Materials
Motor Development
Perceptual Motor Coordination
Skill Analysis
Tactual Perception

OBJECT PERMANENCE *Oct. 1980*
CIJE: 37 RIE: 14 GC: 110
SN The knowledge that objects continue to exist even when one is not perceiving them
UF Object Concept
BT Fundamental Concepts
RT Cognitive Processes
Concept Formation
Developmental Stages

Objective Referenced Tests
USE CRITERION REFERENCED TESTS

OBJECTIVE TESTS *Jul. 1966*
CIJE: 242 RIE: 259 GC: 830
SN Tests that have predetermined lists of correct answers so that subjective opinions or judgments are eliminated in scoring (note: do not confuse with "standardized tests")
UF Matching Tests
Objectively Scored Tests
True False Tests
NT Multiple Choice Tests
BT Tests
RT Answer Keys
Confidence Testing
Essay Tests
Guessing (Tests)
Projective Measures
Scoring
Scoring Formulas
Standardized Tests
Test Bias

Objectively Scored Tests
USE OBJECTIVE TESTS

OBJECTIVES *Jul. 1966*
CIJE: 1289 RIE: 2321 GC: 520
SN Aims or ends toward which effort is directed (note: use a more specific term if possible)
UF Goals
NT Behavioral Objectives
Course Objectives
Educational Objectives
Guidance Objectives
Measurement Objectives
Organizational Objectives
Student Educational Objectives
Training Objectives
RT Aspiration
Evaluation
Failure
Goal Orientation
Guidelines
Management By Objectives
Mastery Learning
Needs
Needs Assessment
Performance
Quotas
Standards
Success
Task Analysis

OBLIQUE ROTATION *Nov. 1970*
CIJE: 73 RIE: 21 GC: 820
SN Method for transforming the results of a factor analysis that permits the factors to be correlated
BT Factor Analysis
RT Correlation
Factor Structure
Matrices
Orthogonal Rotation
Transformations (Mathematics)

OBSCENITY *Oct. 1983*
CIJE: 23 RIE: 29 GC: 530
SN Character or quality of any act, expression, idea, etc. that offends one's sensibility
RT Antisocial Behavior
Language Usage
Moral Issues
Pornography

OBSERVATION *Jul. 1966*
CIJE: 922 RIE: 1115 GC: 820
SN Directed or intentional examination of persons, situations, or things to obtain information -- includes the quantified values by which observed facts are represented
NT Naturalistic Observation
Participant Observation
School Visitation
RT Assessment Centers (Personnel)
Classroom Observation Techniques
Critical Incidents Method
Data Collection
Evaluation
Experiments
Inspection
Interrater Reliability
Lesson Observation Criteria
Measurement
Observational Learning
Performance
Research
Research Methodology

OBSERVATIONAL LEARNING *Nov. 1972*
CIJE: 308 RIE: 154 GC: 110
SN Learning resulting from the observation of a model or event
UF Imitative Learning
BT Learning
RT Discovery Learning
Identification (Psychology)
Imitation
Incidental Learning
Intentional Learning
Learning Activities
Learning Processes
Learning Strategies
Modeling (Psychology)
Observation
Role Models

OBSOLESCENCE *Jan. 1969*
CIJE: 59 RIE: 35 GC: 490
SN Condition of being no longer useful or in fashion, usually because of outmoded design or hard wear
NT Building Obsolescence
Skill Obsolescence
RT Automation
Maintenance
Preservation
Repair
Technological Advancement
Time

OBSTETRICS *Oct. 1979*
CIJE: 33 RIE: 28 GC: 210
SN Branch of medicine concerned with pregnancy and childbirth
UF Midwifery
BT Medicine
RT Abortions
Birth
Family Practice (Medicine)
Females
Gynecology
Medical Services
Perinatal Influences
Pregnancy
Prenatal Influences
Reproduction (Biology)
Rh Factors

Obtained Scores
USE RAW SCORES

Occidental Civilization
USE WESTERN CIVILIZATION

Occupational Adjustment
USE VOCATIONAL ADJUSTMENT

Occupational Analysis
USE JOB ANALYSIS

OCCUPATIONAL ASPIRATION *Sep. 1968*
CIJE: 768 RIE: 1080 GC: 120
SN Desire for, or expectation of, personal occupational accomplishment
UF Occupational Aspiration Level
Vocational Aspiration
BT Aspiration
RT Career Choice
Career Development
Nontraditional Occupations
Occupations
Promotion (Occupational)
Vocational Interests
Vocational Maturity
Work Attitudes

Occupational Aspiration Level
USE OCCUPATIONAL ASPIRATION

Occupational Awareness
USE CAREER AWARENESS

Occupational Choice (1966 1980)
USE CAREER CHOICE

OCCUPATIONAL CLUSTERS *Jul. 1966*
CIJE: 188 RIE: 999 GC: 640
SN Occupations grouped together on the basis of similar job requirements or worker characteristics
UF Job Clusters
Job Families
Occupational Families
RT Cluster Grouping
Job Analysis
Occupations

Occupational Counseling
USE CAREER COUNSELING

OCCUPATIONAL DISEASES *Jul. 1966*
CIJE: 36 RIE: 29 GC: 210
BT Diseases
RT Cancer
Hearing Conservation
Lead Poisoning
Occupational Safety And Health
Occupations
Physical Health

Occupational Exploration
USE CAREER EXPLORATION

Occupational Families
USE OCCUPATIONAL CLUSTERS

Occupational Followup
USE VOCATIONAL FOLLOWUP

Occupational Guidance (1966 1980)
USE CAREER GUIDANCE

Occupational Health
USE OCCUPATIONAL SAFETY AND HEALTH

OCCUPATIONAL HOME ECONOMICS *Jul. 1966*
CIJE: 82 RIE: 535 GC: 400
SN Formal preparation for occupations using home economics knowledge and skills -- below the baccalaureate level (note: for the baccalaureate level and above, use "home economics education")
BT Vocational Education
RT Attendants
Bakery Industry
Child Care Occupations
Cooks
Day Care
Dietitians
Fashion Industry
Food Service
Home Economics
Home Economics Education
Home Economics Skills
Home Economics Teachers
Housekeepers
Housing Management Aides
Laundry Drycleaning Occupations
Needle Trades
Sewing Machine Operators
Visiting Homemakers

OCCUPATIONAL INFORMATION *Jul. 1966*
CIJE: 1206 RIE: 3492 GC: 630
SN Descriptive information about the functions and characteristics of specific occupations -- may include duties, working conditions, requirements, methods of entry and advancement, rewards, and/or supply and demand
UF Job Content
Job Descriptions
Job Specifications
RT Career Development
Demand Occupations
Employment
Employment Qualifications
Job Analysis
Job Development
Occupations

Occupational Level
USE EMPLOYMENT LEVEL

OCCUPATIONAL MOBILITY *Jul. 1966*
CIJE: 446 RIE: 731 GC: 630
UF Job Mobility
Labor Mobility
Occupational Succession
NT Career Ladders
Faculty Mobility
Teacher Transfer
BT Mobility
RT Black Achievement
Career Change
Careers
Employment Experience
Employment Opportunities
Labor Turnover
Migrants
Migration
Overseas Employment
Persistence
Population Trends
Promotion (Occupational)

Relocation
Social Mobility
Tenure
Vocational Adjustment

Occupational Psychology
USE INDUSTRIAL PSYCHOLOGY

OCCUPATIONAL SAFETY AND HEALTH *Aug. 1982*
CIJE: 70 RIE: 142 GC: 210
SN Area of activities concerned with promoting comfortable, safe employment conditions, including the prevention of workplace accidents and diseases
UF Job Safety
Occupational Health
Occupational Safety And Health Standards #
BT Health
Safety
RT Employment
Environmental Standards
Hazardous Materials
Hygiene
Occupational Diseases
Occupations
Public Health
Safety Education
Work Environment

Occupational Safety And Health Standards
USE LABOR STANDARDS; OCCUPATIONAL SAFETY AND HEALTH

Occupational Satisfaction
USE JOB SATISFACTION

Occupational Succession
USE OCCUPATIONAL MOBILITY

OCCUPATIONAL SURVEYS *Jul. 1966*
CIJE: 568 RIE: 1253 GC: 810
SN Investigations to gather pertinent information about industries or occupations in an area, about occupational opportunities or trends on regional or national levels, or about the need for training in an occupational area (note: as of oct81, use as a minor descriptor for examples of this kind of survey -- use as a major descriptor only as the subject of a document)
UF Employment Surveys
Job Vacancy Surveys
Labor Force Surveys
BT Surveys
RT Community Surveys
Employment
Employment Opportunities
Employment Patterns
Job Search Methods
Labor Force
Labor Market
Labor Supply
Occupations

OCCUPATIONAL TESTS *Jul. 1966*
CIJE: 157 RIE: 354 GC: 830
SN Tests designed to predict job performance by recording specific abilities and interests that correspond with those of persons successfully engaging in the particular field of work (note: for occupational interest inventories, use "interest inventories")
UF Admission Tests (Occupational)
Employment Tests
Personnel Tests
Vocational Tests
NT Work Sample Tests
BT Tests
RT Aptitude Tests
Assessment Centers (Personnel)
Career Counseling
Employment Qualifications
Interest Inventories
Job Performance
Job Skills
Licensing Examinations (Professions)
Maturity Tests
Performance Tests
Personnel Evaluation
Predictive Measurement
Vocational Aptitude
Vocational Evaluation
Vocational Interests

OCCUPATIONAL THERAPISTS *Jul. 1966*
CIJE: 64 RIE: 41 GC: 230
BT Therapists
RT Occupational Therapy
Occupational Therapy Assistants

OCCUPATIONAL THERAPY *Jul. 1966*
CIJE: 148 RIE: 69 GC: 230
SN Purposeful, often medically prescribed, work-related activities using manual, creative, or industrial arts to treat physical and psychiatric disorders or disabilities, and frequently serving to promote vocational skills
BT Therapy
RT Medical Services
Occupational Therapists
Occupational Therapy Assistants
Physical Therapy
Psychotherapy
Rehabilitation
Therapeutic Recreation

OCCUPATIONAL THERAPY ASSISTANTS *Jul. 1969*
CIJE: 3 RIE: 18 GC: 230
BT Allied Health Personnel
RT Occupational Therapists
Occupational Therapy

Occupational Training
USE JOB TRAINING

OCCUPATIONS *Jul. 1966*
CIJE: 393 RIE: 912 GC: 640
SN General categories of job or work specializations, as characterized by duties, skill levels, status, pay, responsibility levels, or other distinguishing factors (note: use a more specific term if possible)
UF Vocations
NT Agricultural Occupations
Blue Collar Occupations
Building Trades
Clerical Occupations
Data Processing Occupations
Demand Occupations
Electrical Occupations
Energy Occupations
Finance Occupations
Forestry Occupations
Health Occupations
Insurance Occupations
Managerial Occupations
Needle Trades
Nontraditional Occupations
Office Occupations
Professional Occupations
Public Service Occupations
Real Estate Occupations
Sales Occupations
Semiskilled Occupations
Service Occupations
Skilled Occupations
Technical Occupations
Unskilled Occupations
White Collar Occupations
RT Career Awareness
Career Choice
Career Counseling
Career Development
Career Education
Career Exploration
Career Guidance
Careers
Education Work Relationship
Employment
Employment Opportunities
Entrepreneurship
Industrial Psychology
Job Training
Occupational Aspiration
Occupational Clusters
Occupational Diseases
Occupational Information
Occupational Safety And Health
Occupational Surveys
Quality Of Working Life
Retraining
Specialization
Vocational Education
Work Environment
Work Life Expectancy

OCEAN ENGINEERING *Feb. 1970*
CIJE: 46 RIE: 45 GC: 490
SN Application of engineering technology to problems in oceans, seas, and large bodies of fresh water
BT Engineering
RT Ecology
Marine Biology
Oceanography
Water

OCEANOGRAPHY *Mar. 1980*
CIJE: 381 RIE: 478 GC: 490
SN Science that deals with the oceans and other large bodies of water, including their exploration, preservation, use, and interactions with air, dry land, and all life forms
UF Oceanology (1966 1980)
BT Earth Science
RT Climate
Estuaries
Fisheries
Geography
Geology
Ichthyology
Marine Biology
Marine Education
Marine Technicians
Maritime Education
Ocean Engineering
Physical Geography
Plate Tectonics
Seafarers
Underwater Diving
Water

Oceanology (1966 1980)
USE OCEANOGRAPHY

Ocr
USE CHARACTER RECOGNITION; OPTICAL SCANNERS

Ocular Refractive Errors
USE AMETROPIA

ODES *Sep. 1969*
CIJE: 3 RIE: 1 GC: 430
BT Literary Genres
Lyric Poetry
RT Ballads
Pastoral Literature
Sonnets

Off Campus Education
USE EXTENSION EDUCATION

OFF CAMPUS FACILITIES *Jul. 1966*
CIJE: 66 RIE: 120 GC: 920
SN Those facilities located some distance away from the educational institutions to which they are related
BT Educational Facilities
RT Extension Education
Outreach Programs
Satellite Facilities
Shared Facilities

Off Campus Student Teaching
USE STUDENT TEACHING

OFF FARM AGRICULTURAL OCCUPATIONS *Jul. 1966*
CIJE: 68 RIE: 208 GC: 410
UF Farm Related Occupations
Nonfarm Agricultural Occupations
NT Agricultural Chemical Occupations
Agricultural Machinery Occupations
Agricultural Supply Occupations
Crop Processing Occupations
Food Processing Occupations
Ornamental Horticulture Occupations
BT Agricultural Occupations
RT Agribusiness
Agriculture
Animal Caretakers
Farm Occupations
Feed Industry
Forestry Occupations

Off Reservation American Indians
USE NONRESERVATION AMERICAN INDIANS

Off Site Training
USE OFF THE JOB TRAINING

OFF THE JOB TRAINING *Jul. 1966*
CIJE: 46 RIE: 99 GC: 630
SN Conducted in a company school or arranged with technical schools, universities, or professional agencies
UF Away From The Job Training
Off Site Training
BT Job Training
RT Cooperative Programs
Industrial Training
Inplant Programs
Inservice Education
Institutes (Training Programs)
Labor Education
Management Development
On The Job Training
Released Time
Skill Centers
Staff Development
Vocational Training Centers

Office Communication
USE ORGANIZATIONAL COMMUNICATION

Office Education
USE OFFICE OCCUPATIONS EDUCATION

OFFICE MACHINES *Jul. 1966*
CIJE: 158 RIE: 169 GC: 910
UF Business Machines
BT Equipment
RT Business
Calculators
Industry
Keyboarding (Data Entry)
Local Area Networks
Office Management
Office Practice
Typewriting
Word Processing

OFFICE MANAGEMENT *Jul. 1966*
CIJE: 146 RIE: 111 GC: 650
BT Administration
RT Local Area Networks
Office Machines
Office Occupations
Office Occupations Education
Office Practice
Personnel
Personnel Management
Records (Forms)

OFFICE OCCUPATIONS *Jul. 1966*
CIJE: 114 RIE: 214 GC: 640
SN Occupations associated with the management and operation of offices
BT Occupations
RT Bookkeeping
Business
Business Education
Clerical Occupations
Data Processing Occupations
Distributive Education
Employment Qualifications
Finance Occupations
Job Training
Keyboarding (Data Entry)
Office Management
Office Occupations Education
Office Practice
Recordkeeping
Shorthand
Typewriting
White Collar Occupations
Word Processing

OFFICE OCCUPATIONS EDUCATION *Jul. 1966*
CIJE: 479 RIE: 823 GC: 400
SN Formal preparation for occupations related to the facilitating functions of the office -- such functions include a variety of activities such as recording and retrieval of data, supervision and coordination of office activities, internal and external communication, and the reporting of information (note: before mar80, the use of this term was not restricted by a scope note)
UF Office Education
BT Business Education
RT Accounting
Bookkeeping
Business Correspondence
Business Education Facilities
Business Education Teachers
Business English

= Two or more Descriptors are used to represent this term.
The term's main entry shows the appropriate coordination.

Clerical Occupations
Keyboarding (Data Entry)
Office Management
Office Occupations
Office Practice
Recordkeeping
Shorthand
Typewriting
Word Processing

OFFICE PRACTICE *Jul. 1966*
CIJE: 180 RIE: 145 GC: 400
BT Practicums
RT Business Skills
Clerical Occupations
Office Machines
Office Management
Office Occupations
Office Occupations Education
Simulation

Office Supplies
USE SUPPLIES

OFFICER PERSONNEL *Jul. 1966*
CIJE: 25 RIE: 193 GC: 640
BT Military Personnel
RT Military Science
Military Service
Military Training
Veterans

OFFICES (FACILITIES) *Oct. 1968*
CIJE: 60 RIE: 48 GC: 920
UF Faculty Offices
Staff Offices
BT Facilities
RT Interior Design
Interior Space
School Space
Space Classification

OFFICIAL LANGUAGES *Jul. 1966*
CIJE: 137 RIE: 222 GC: 450
SN Languages authorized or prescribed by law -- usually for official or public purposes such as government activity, business, and education
UF National Languages
BT Language
RT Bilingual Education
Educational Policy
Language Of Instruction
Language Planning
Language Standardization
Native Speakers
Sociolinguistics

OJIBWA *Jan. 1971*
CIJE: 6 RIE: 13 GC: 440
UF Chippewa
BT American Indian Languages

OKINAWAN *Jul. 1966*
CIJE: 1 RIE: 1 GC: 440
BT Japanese

Old Age
USE OLDER ADULTS

OLD ENGLISH *May. 1969*
CIJE: 17 RIE: 14 GC: 440
UF Anglo Saxon
BT English
RT Diachronic Linguistics
Indo European Languages
Languages
Linguistics
Old English Literature
Welsh

OLD ENGLISH LITERATURE *Apr. 1970*
CIJE: 8 RIE: 11 GC: 430
BT English Literature
RT Literary History
Old English

OLDER ADULTS *Jul. 1966*
CIJE: 3029 RIE: 2308 GC: 120
SN Approximately 65+ years of age
UF Aged
Elderly
Old Age
Senior Citizens (1967 1980)
BT Adults
RT Accessibility (For Disabled)
Adult Day Care
Adult Foster Care
Age Discrimination
Aging (Individuals)
Dependents
Educational Gerontology
Elder Abuse
Geriatrics
Gerontology
Grandparents
Intergenerational Programs
Middle Aged Adults
Personal Care Homes
Physical Mobility
Preretirement Education
Retirement

OMBUDSMEN *Nov. 1969*
CIJE: 63 RIE: 43 GC: 360
SN Officials designated to hear and investigate complaints by single parties against institutions or organizations
BT Personnel
RT Counseling
Faculty
Grievance Procedures
Pupil Personnel Workers
Student College Relationship
Student Personnel Workers
Student Rights
Student School Relationship
Student Welfare

ON CAMPUS STUDENTS *Mar. 1980*
CIJE: 23 RIE: 63 GC: 360
SN College students living on campus (note: prior to mar80, this concept was sometimes indexed under "resident students," which did not carry a scope note)
BT College Students
RT College Housing
Commuting Students
Dormitories
Full Time Students
Living Learning Centers
Resident Assistants
Residential Colleges

On Line Systems (1971 1980)
USE ONLINE SYSTEMS

On Site Tests
USE FIELD TESTS

ON THE JOB TRAINING *Jul. 1966*
CIJE: 396 RIE: 759 GC: 630
NT Apprenticeships
BT Job Training
RT Experiential Learning
Field Experience Programs
Industrial Training
Inplant Programs
Inservice Education
Internship Programs
Off The Job Training
Staff Development
Trade And Industrial Education
Work Experience Programs

ONCOLOGY *Oct. 1979*
CIJE: 21 RIE: 9 GC: 210
SN Branch of medicine dealing with tumors
BT Medicine
RT Cancer
Internal Medicine
Medical Services
Pathology
Surgery

ONE PARENT FAMILY *Jul. 1966*
CIJE: 311 RIE: 342 GC: 510
SN (Note: use a more specific term if possible)
UF Parent Absence
Single Parent Family
NT Fatherless Family
Motherless Family
BT Family (Sociological Unit)
RT Child Custody
Divorce
Extended Family
Family Size
Family Structure
Fathers
Heads Of Households
Illegitimate Births
Marital Instability
Mothers
Nuclear Family
Parents
Runaways
Widowed

One Room Schools
USE ONE TEACHER SCHOOLS

ONE TEACHER SCHOOLS *Jul. 1966*
CIJE: 19 RIE: 70 GC: 340
UF One Room Schools
BT Small Schools
RT Rural Schools
Teachers

ONLINE CATALOGS *Aug. 1986*
CIJE: 30 RIE: 58 GC: 710
SN Machine-readable catalogs that can be accessed through interactive communications terminals
UF Online Public Access Catalogs
BT Catalogs
Databases
Online Systems
RT Library Catalogs
Machine Readable Cataloging

Online Information Retrieval
USE ONLINE SEARCHING

Online Public Access Catalogs
USE ONLINE CATALOGS

Online Reference Services
USE ONLINE SYSTEMS; REFERENCE SERVICES

ONLINE SEARCHING *Apr. 1985*
CIJE: 114 RIE: 35 GC: 710
SN Use of an interactive communications terminal to access and retrieve information stored in a computer (note: prior to apr85, this concept was indexed under "online systems" and "information retrieval")
UF Interactive Searching (Online)
Online Information Retrieval
BT Information Retrieval
RT Computer Literacy
Information Needs
Online Systems
Online Vendors
Reference Services
Relevance (Information Retrieval)
Search Strategies
Selective Dissemination Of Information
User Needs (Information)

ONLINE SYSTEMS *Mar. 1980*
CIJE: 1732 RIE: 1200 GC: 710
SN Computer systems in which peripheral devices, which may include remote terminals, are in direct and continuing communication with the central processor
UF Computer Based Reference Services #
Interactive Systems (Online)
Online Reference Services #
On Line Systems (1971 1980)
NT Interactive Video
Online Catalogs
BT Computers
RT Bibliographic Utilities
Data Processing
Dial Access Information Systems
Electronic Mail
Information Sources
Information Systems
Input Output Devices
Man Machine Systems
Menu Driven Software
Microcomputers
Minicomputers
Online Searching
Online Vendors
Teleconferencing
Time Sharing
Videotex
Word Processing

ONLINE VENDORS *Apr. 1986*
CIJE: RIE: 1 GC: 710
SN Organizations that maintain databases and related software on their computer systems and sell online retrieval time to clients at multiple remote locations (note: see also such identifiers as "dialog," "bibliographic retrieval services," and "system development corporation")
UF Commercial Search Services (Online)
Database Hosts
Database Vendors
Information Utilities (Online)
BT Organizations (Groups)
RT Bibliographic Utilities
Computers
Database Producers
Databases
Information Services
Online Searching
Online Systems

ONOMASTICS *Aug. 1968*
CIJE: 22 RIE: 12 GC: 450
UF Onomatology
BT Etymology
RT Diachronic Linguistics
Language
Language Research
Lexicology
Linguistics

Onomatology
USE ONOMASTICS

OPAQUE PROJECTORS *Jul. 1966*
CIJE: 2 RIE: 14 GC: 910
BT Projection Equipment

Open Admission
USE OPEN ENROLLMENT

Open Area Schools
USE OPEN PLAN SCHOOLS

OPEN BOOK TESTS *Jul. 1974*
CIJE: 10 RIE: 2 GC: 830
SN Examinations during which individuals may consult textbooks, reference books, or notes, the purpose being to emphasize command of knowledge as distinguished from recall of factual information
BT Tests
RT Achievement Tests

Open Circuit Television (1966 1980)
USE BROADCAST TELEVISION

OPEN EDUCATION *Jan. 1972*
CIJE: 824 RIE: 777 GC: 350
SN An approach to teaching and learning emphasizing the student's right to make decisions and that views the teacher as facilitator of learning rather than as transmitter of knowledge -- it may include such characteristics as vertical grouping, cross-age teaching, independent study, individualized rates of progression, open plan schools, and unstructured time and curriculum
UF Open Schools
BT Education
RT British Infant Schools
Discovery Learning
Experimental Schools
Free Schools
Humanistic Education
Humanization
Independent Study
Learning Centers (Classroom)
Nongraded Instructional Grouping
Nontraditional Education
Open Plan Schools
Personal Autonomy
Progressive Education
Self Contained Classrooms
Self Directed Groups
Student Centered Curriculum
Transitional Schools

= Two or more Descriptors are used to represent this term.
The term's main entry shows the appropriate coordination.

OPEN ENROLLMENT *Jul. 1966*
CIJE: 292 RIE: 326 GC: 330
SN Admissions policy (usually at college level) of accepting candidates regardless of their grade point average and sometimes (usually at elementary or secondary level) regardless of their place of residence
UF Open Admission
BT Admission (School)
RT Academic Standards
Access To Education
Admission Criteria
Competitive Selection
Desegregation Methods
Educationally Disadvantaged
Educational Opportunities
Equal Education
Free Choice Transfer Programs
High Risk Students
Nontraditional Students
Open Universities
Selective Admission

OPEN PLAN SCHOOLS *Feb. 1970*
CIJE: 391 RIE: 278 GC: 920
SN Schools without interior walls
UF Open Area Schools
BT Schools
RT Class Organization
Classroom Design
Educational Facilities Design
Flexible Facilities
Interior Space
Multipurpose Classrooms
Open Education
School Buildings
School Space
Team Teaching

Open Schools
USE OPEN EDUCATION

OPEN UNIVERSITIES *Mar. 1980*
CIJE: 243 RIE: 136 GC: 340
SN Higher education institutions with liberal admission policies that feature external degree programs and often use nontraditional delivery systems (telecourses, etc.) -- e.g., open university of the united kingdom, university of mid-america (note: before mar80, the thesaurus carried the instruction "open university, use external degree programs")
UF Extended Universities
Universities Without Walls
BT Universities
RT Access To Education
Distance Education
Experimental Colleges
Extension Education
External Degree Programs
Free Education
Nontraditional Education
Open Enrollment
Outreach Programs

OPERA *Jul. 1966*
CIJE: 52 RIE: 34 GC: 420
BT Theater Arts
RT Acting
Music
Musical Composition
Vocal Music

OPERANT CONDITIONING *Jul. 1966*
CIJE: 662 RIE: 377 GC: 110
SN Form of conditioning in which reinforcement (e.g., food) is contingent upon the occurrence of the response (e.g., a hungry animal pressing a lever)
UF Instrumental Conditioning
NT Verbal Operant Conditioning
BT Conditioning
RT Behavior Modification
Classical Conditioning
Contingency Management
Reinforcement
Timeout
Token Economy

OPERATING ENGINEERING *Jul. 1966*
CIJE: 2 RIE: 32 GC: 640
SN Onsite operation of power construction equipment to excavate and grade earth, erect structural and reinforcing steel, pour concrete, etc.
BT Engineering
RT Building Trades
Equipment Utilization
Technical Occupations

OPERATING EXPENSES *Jul. 1966*
CIJE: 190 RIE: 518 GC: 620
UF Minimum Operating Expenses
BT Expenditures
RT Budgets
Building Operation
Costs
Instructional Student Costs
Library Expenditures
Life Cycle Costing
Resource Allocation
Salaries

Operating Room Technicians
USE SURGICAL TECHNICIANS

Operations (Surgery)
USE SURGERY

Operations Analysis
USE OPERATIONS RESEARCH

OPERATIONS RESEARCH *Jul. 1966*
CIJE: 160 RIE: 391 GC: 810
SN The application of scientific and especially mathematical methods to the analysis of operating procedures in an organization or system (note: as of oct81, use as a minor descriptor for examples of this kind of research -- use as a major descriptor only as the subject of a document)
UF Operations Analysis
NT Game Theory
BT Research
RT Action Research
Cost Effectiveness
Critical Path Method
Delphi Technique
Information Theory
Judgment Analysis Technique
Linear Programing
Long Range Planning
Management Systems
Mathematical Models
Models
Monte Carlo Methods
Planning
Quality Control
Search Strategies

OPHTHALMOLOGY *Jul. 1966*
CIJE: 46 RIE: 23 GC: 210
BT Medicine
RT Eyes
Medical Services
Optometry
Vision
Vision Tests
Visual Acuity
Visual Impairments

OPINION PAPERS *Mar. 1980*
CIJE: 131 RIE: 78 GC: 730
SN Statements of personal viewpoints
BT Reports
RT Essays
Opinions
Personal Narratives
Position Papers

Opinion Scales
USE ATTITUDE MEASURES

OPINIONS *Jul. 1966*
CIJE: 1890 RIE: 735 GC: 120
SN Judgments or conclusions based on evidence that is insufficient to produce certainty
NT Press Opinion
Public Opinion
BT Attitudes
RT Attitude Measures
Beliefs
Credibility
Delphi Technique
Dissent
Dogmatism
Editorials
Expectation
Interest Inventories
Opinion Papers
Questionnaires
Reputation
Surveys

OPPORTUNITIES *Jul. 1966*
CIJE: 38 RIE: 58 GC: 540
SN Circumstances or conditions that make possible any actions leading to betterment -- includes the absence of barriers that prevent such possibilities (note: use a more specific term if possible)
NT Cultural Opportunities
Economic Opportunities
Educational Opportunities
Employment Opportunities
Housing Opportunities
Research Opportunities
Youth Opportunities
RT Background
Education Work Relationship
Influences

Opportunity Classes (1966 1980)
USE SPECIAL CLASSES

Optical Character Recognition
USE CHARACTER RECOGNITION; OPTICAL SCANNERS

OPTICAL DATA DISKS *Aug. 1986*
CIJE: RIE: GC: 720
SN Optical disks formatted for storage and retrieval of text, i.e., computer-readable alphanumeric data (with or without accompanying graphics and/or sound)
UF Cd Rom
Digital Optical Data Disks
BT Optical Disks
RT Computers
Data Processing
Information Systems
Interactive Video
Lasers

OPTICAL DISKS *Aug. 1986*
CIJE: 14 RIE: 3 GC: 720
SN Information storage devices, typically made of plastic, on which high-density audio and/or video images are recorded and read by laser beams
UF Cd Recordings
Compact Disks
Laser Disks
Optical Videodisks #
NT Optical Data Disks
BT Nonprint Media
RT Audiodisks
Audiovisual Aids
Computers
Computer Storage Devices
Information Storage
Input Output Devices
Interactive Video
Lasers
Optics
Programing (Broadcast)
Videodisks

Optical Masers
USE LASERS

OPTICAL SCANNERS *Sep. 1968*
CIJE: 26 RIE: 44 GC: 910
UF Document Readers
Ocr #
Optical Character Recognition #
Page Readers
Visual Scanners
BT Input Output Devices
RT Character Recognition
Data Processing
Optics
Test Scoring Machines

Optical Spectrum
USE LIGHT

Optical Videodisks
USE OPTICAL DISKS; VIDEODISKS

OPTICS *Dec. 1969*
CIJE: 480 RIE: 63 GC: 490
UF Electrooptics (1968 1980)
Geometrical Optics
Physical Optics
BT Physics
RT Crystallography
Diffusion (Physics)
Electronics
Energy
Lasers
Light
Lighting
Optical Disks
Optical Scanners
Radiation
Relativity
Spectroscopy

Optional Branching (1966 1980)
USE BRANCHING

Optional Courses
USE ELECTIVE COURSES

OPTOMETRISTS *Jul. 1966*
CIJE: 26 RIE: 49 GC: 210
BT Allied Health Personnel
Professional Personnel
RT Eyes
Optometry
Vision
Vision Tests

OPTOMETRY *Oct. 1979*
CIJE: 99 RIE: 31 GC: 210
SN The practice or profession of testing the eyes for defects in vision in order to prescribe corrective lenses
BT Technology
RT Allied Health Occupations
Eyes
Health Services
Ophthalmology
Optometrists
Vision
Vision Tests
Visual Acuity
Visual Impairments

Oral Communication (1966 1977)
USE SPEECH COMMUNICATION

ORAL COMMUNICATION METHOD *Jul. 1977*
CIJE: 51 RIE: 41 GC: 220
SN The use of vocal communication (lipreading and talking), as opposed to manual communication (sign language or finger spelling), in teaching the hearing impaired
NT Lipreading
BT Teaching Methods
RT Communication Skills
Cued Speech
Deafness
Hearing Impairments
Hearing Therapy
Manual Communication
Partial Hearing
Speech Communication
Total Communication
Verbal Communication

ORAL ENGLISH *Jul. 1966*
CIJE: 87 RIE: 177 GC: 450
BT English
RT Speech Communication
Standard Spoken Usage

Oral Expression (1966 1977)
USE SPEECH COMMUNICATION

Oral Facility
USE SPEECH SKILLS

ORAL HISTORY *Feb. 1976*
CIJE: 191 RIE: 211 GC: 430
SN History via recordings and transcripts of speech
BT History
RT American Indian History
Audiodisks
Audiotape Recordings
Discographies
Family History
Historiography
Interviews
Local History
Modern History
Primary Sources
Social History
Speech Communication

= Two or more Descriptors are used to represent this term.
The term's main entry shows the appropriate coordination.

Oral Hygienists
USE DENTAL HYGIENISTS

ORAL INTERPRETATION *Mar. 1980*
CIJE: 111 RIE: 161 GC: 420
SN The oral interpretation and presentation of a work of literature to an audience (note: prior to mar80, the instruction "oral interpretation, use interpretive reading" was carried in the thesaurus)
BT Speech Communication
RT Choral Speaking
Drama
Listening Comprehension
Literature Appreciation
Oral Reading
Readers Theater
Reading Aloud To Others
Reading Comprehension
Speech Instruction

ORAL LANGUAGE *Apr. 1980*
CIJE: 306 RIE: 402 GC: 450
SN Spoken aspect of language that can be heard, interpreted, and understood (note: do not confuse with the behavioral concept of "speech communication")
BT Language
RT Child Language
Expressive Language
Language Acquisition
Language Rhythm
Language Usage
Nonstandard Dialects
Second Language Learning
Speech
Speech Communication
Standard Spoken Usage
Verbal Communication
Written Language

ORAL READING *Jul. 1966*
CIJE: 550 RIE: 526 GC: 460
SN The act of reading aloud, often used to develop or test reading skills (note: use "reading aloud to others" when the purpose of oral reading is to inform or entertain a listener or group of listeners)
BT Reading
RT Decoding (Reading)
Eye Voice Span
Miscue Analysis
Oral Interpretation
Reading Aloud To Others
Reading Instruction
Silent Reading

Oral Skills
USE SPEECH SKILLS

Orbiting Satellites
USE SATELLITES (AEROSPACE)

ORCHESTRAS *Aug. 1968*
CIJE: 46 RIE: 41 GC: 420
UF Repertory Orchestras
Symphony Orchestras
RT Applied Music
Bands (Music)
Concerts
Music
Music Activities
Musical Instruments
Music Education
Musicians
Music Techniques
Theater Arts

Organ Donors
USE TISSUE DONORS

ORGANIC CHEMISTRY *Oct. 1968*
CIJE: 833 RIE: 66 GC: 490
SN Study of chemical reactions and properties of the organic compounds (hydrocarbons)
BT Chemistry
RT Atomic Structure
Biochemistry
Chemical Bonding
Chemical Reactions
Coordination Compounds
Molecular Structure
Polymers
Radiation Biology

Organic Curriculum
USE STUDENT CENTERED CURRICULUM

ORGANIZATION *Jul. 1966*
CIJE: 1100 RIE: 1584 GC: 520
SN The structure or framework of formal and functional relations that unites the parts of a system into a coherent whole -- also, the process by which such a structure is identified and established (note: use a more specific term if possible)
UF Structural Arrangement
NT Administrative Organization
Bureaucracy
Classification
Class Organization
Course Organization
Furniture Arrangement
Group Structure
Horizontal Organization
Industrial Structure
Informal Organization
Power Structure
Pyramid Organization
School District Reorganization
School Organization
Social Structure
Vertical Organization
RT Administration
Coordination
Design
Mergers
Organizational Theories
Organizations (Groups)
Planning

ORGANIZATION SIZE (GROUPS) *Jul. 1966*
CIJE: 93 RIE: 106 GC: 320
SN Size of an organization as measured by the dimensions of its physical plant or by the number of employees or members
UF Company Size (Industry)
NT School District Size
RT Business
Industrial Structure
Industry
Institutional Characteristics
Labor Force
Mergers
Organizations (Groups)
Small Businesses

ORGANIZATIONAL CHANGE *Jul. 1966*
CIJE: 1052 RIE: 1125 GC: 320
SN Any alteration in the form, nature, content, future course, etc. of an organization (note: use a more precise term if possible)
NT Mergers
BT Change
RT Administrative Change
Centralization
Change Strategies
Decentralization
Organizational Development
Organizations (Groups)

ORGANIZATIONAL CLIMATE *Jul. 1966*
CIJE: 955 RIE: 847 GC: 320
SN Properties, procedures, conditions, etc. of an organization that influence or interact with its members
BT Environment
RT Burnout
Educational Environment
Industrial Psychology
Informal Organization
Institutional Environment
Job Satisfaction
Morale
Organizational Development
Organizations (Groups)
Power Structure
Quality Of Working Life
Work Environment

ORGANIZATIONAL COMMUNICATION *Dec. 1974*
CIJE: 593 RIE: 962 GC: 320
SN Exchange of thoughts, messages, etc., within and between organizations (groups of people) -- includes exchanges between specific organizations and the general public
UF Office Communication
NT Business Communication
Interschool Communication
BT Communication (Thought Transfer)
RT Communication Audits
Group Dynamics
Information Systems
Institutional Advancement
Management Systems
Organizations (Groups)
Public Relations

ORGANIZATIONAL DEVELOPMENT *Apr. 1973*
CIJE: 796 RIE: 730 GC: 320
SN The application of behavioral technology to organizations by attempting to integrate individual needs for growth and development with organizational goals and objectives
BT Development
RT Administrative Change
Behavioral Science Research
Employer Employee Relationship
Faculty Development
Industrial Psychology
Industrial Structure
Job Development
Job Enrichment
Job Satisfaction
Management By Objectives
Management Teams
Organizational Change
Organizational Climate
Organizational Objectives
Organizations (Groups)
Participative Decision Making
Power Structure
Program Administration
Quality Circles
Quality Of Working Life
Social Exchange Theory
Staff Development
Systems Development
Teamwork
Work Environment

ORGANIZATIONAL EFFECTIVENESS *Jul. 1974*
CIJE: 633 RIE: 782 GC: 320
SN Degree to which organizations (groups of people) are successful in satisfying their objectives or functions
NT School Effectiveness
RT Administration
Cost Effectiveness
Efficiency
Organizational Theories
Organizations (Groups)
Productivity
Program Effectiveness
Self Evaluation (Groups)
Success
Systems Analysis

Organizational Goals
USE ORGANIZATIONAL OBJECTIVES

ORGANIZATIONAL OBJECTIVES *Mar. 1980*
CIJE: 376 RIE: 387 GC: 320
SN Short- or long-term goals of organizations or institutions for management, operations, functional outcomes, etc. (note: prior to mar80, the term "educational objectives" was frequently used for the objectives of educational institutions)
UF Institutional Goals
Institutional Objectives
Organizational Goals
NT Institutional Mission
BT Objectives
RT Accountability
Institutions
Management By Objectives
Organizational Development
Organizations (Groups)
Planning

Organizational Plans
USE PLANNING

Organizational Psychology (Work Environment)
USE INDUSTRIAL PSYCHOLOGY

Organizational Self Study
USE SELF EVALUATION (GROUPS)

ORGANIZATIONAL THEORIES *Jul. 1974*
CIJE: 486 RIE: 553 GC: 810
SN Ideas or hypotheses relating to the form and structure of organizations (groups of people), describing how such organizations do operate or should operate
BT Social Theories
RT Organization
Organizational Effectiveness
Organizations (Groups)
Social Exchange Theory

ORGANIZATIONS (GROUPS) *Jul. 1966*
CIJE: 1100 RIE: 1314 GC: 520
UF Associations (Groups)
Formal Organizations
NT Agencies
Alumni Associations
Bibliographic Utilities
Black Organizations
Blue Ribbon Commissions
College Governing Councils
Community Organizations
Consortia
Cooperatives
Database Producers
Faculty Organizations
Fraternities
Governing Boards
Government (Administrative Body)
Honor Societies
International Organizations
Military Organizations
National Organizations
Nonprofit Organizations
Online Vendors
Parent Associations
Professional Associations
Religious Organizations
Research Coordinating Units
School Districts
Segregationist Organizations
Social Organizations
Sororities
Student Organizations
Unions
BT Groups
RT Committees
Conferences
Industry
Informal Organization
Institutions
Mergers
Organization
Organizational Change
Organizational Climate
Organizational Communication
Organizational Development
Organizational Effectiveness
Organizational Objectives
Organizational Theories
Organization Size (Groups)
Resources
Social Exchange Theory

Oriental Americans
USE ASIAN AMERICANS

Oriental Civilization
USE NON WESTERN CIVILIZATION

ORIENTAL MUSIC *Jul. 1966*
CIJE: 6 RIE: 13 GC: 420
SN Music of china, japan, indochina, polynesia, india, arabia, and north africa
UF Asian Music
BT Music
RT Musical Composition

ORIENTATION *Jul. 1966*
CIJE: 266 RIE: 340 GC: 120
SN Awareness or the process of becoming aware of one's position or direction in relation to persons, situations, expectations, or the physical environment (note: use a more specific term if possible)
NT Goal Orientation
School Orientation
Staff Orientation
Teacher Orientation
RT Adjustment (To Environment)
Orientation Materials

ORIENTATION MATERIALS *Jul. 1966*
CIJE: 47 RIE: 218 GC: 730
RT Guides
Instructional Materials
Library Instruction
Orientation
Resource Materials

ORIENTEERING *Feb. 1978*
CIJE: 9 RIE: 14 GC: 470
SN The act or sport of cross-country navigation using a map and compass as guides -- emphasis is on determining, then taking, the shortest and quickest way to a specified destination
BT Athletics
RT Trails

Original Scores
USE RAW SCORES

Original Sources
USE PRIMARY SOURCES

Originality (1966 1980)
USE CREATIVITY

ORNAMENTAL HORTICULTURE *Jul. 1966*
CIJE: 55 RIE: 128 GC: 410
NT Floriculture
Landscaping
Turf Management
BT Horticulture
RT Greenhouses
Nurseries (Horticulture)
Ornamental Horticulture Occupations
Plant Growth
Plant Identification
Plant Propagation
Trees

Ornamental Horticulture Occupation (1967 1976)
USE ORNAMENTAL HORTICULTURE OCCUPATIONS

ORNAMENTAL HORTICULTURE OCCUPATIONS *May. 1976*
CIJE: 6 RIE: 72 GC: 410
UF Ornamental Horticulture Occupation (1967 1976)
BT Off Farm Agricultural Occupations
RT Grounds Keepers
Nursery Workers (Horticulture)
Ornamental Horticulture

ORNITHOLOGY *Mar. 1982*
CIJE: 45 RIE: 11 GC: 490
UF Bird Studies
BT Zoology
RT Agriculture
Animal Husbandry
Horticulture

Orthodontic Technicians
USE DENTAL TECHNICIANS

Orthodontics
USE DENTISTRY

Orthodontists
USE DENTISTS

Orthogonal Projection (1967 1980)
USE ORTHOGRAPHIC PROJECTION

ORTHOGONAL ROTATION *Nov. 1970*
CIJE: 94 RIE: 44 GC: 820
SN Method for processing the results of a factor analysis so that the factors will not be correlated
BT Factor Analysis
RT Correlation
Factor Structure
Matrices
Oblique Rotation
Transformations (Mathematics)

ORTHOGRAPHIC PROJECTION *Mar. 1980*
CIJE: 21 RIE: 25 GC: 480
SN Projection in which the projecting lines are perpendicular to the plane of projection
UF Orthogonal Projection (1967 1980)
BT Geometric Concepts
RT Blueprints
Drafting
Engineering Graphics
Graphic Arts
Technical Illustration

ORTHOGRAPHIC SYMBOLS *Jul. 1966*
CIJE: 184 RIE: 233 GC: 450
NT Diacritical Marking
Letters (Alphabet)
Phonetic Transcription
BT Written Language
RT Abbreviations
Graphemes
Initial Teaching Alphabet
Romanization
Spelling

Orthopedically Handicapped (1968 1980)
USE PHYSICAL DISABILITIES

OSSETIC *Jul. 1966*
CIJE: RIE: 3 GC: 440
BT Indo European Languages

OSTEOPATHY *Oct. 1979*
CIJE: 10 RIE: 26 GC: 210
SN Medical study or practice of restoring or preserving health chiefly by manipulation of the skeleton and muscles
BT Medicine
RT Medical Services
Motor Reactions
Physical Therapy

OSTYAK *Jul. 1966*
CIJE: RIE: 3 GC: 440
BT Finno Ugric Languages

Otological Tests
USE AUDITORY TESTS

OUT OF SCHOOL YOUTH *Jul. 1966*
CIJE: 51 RIE: 239 GC: 510
SN Children of compulsory school age who have been excused from attending school, or adolescents over 16 years of age who are out of school legally
BT Youth
RT Attendance
Dropouts
Expulsion
Suspension
Withdrawal (Education)

OUT OF STATE STUDENTS *Mar. 1980*
CIJE: 37 RIE: 171 GC: 360
SN College students who are legal residents of a state or province other than the one in which they attend school
UF Nonresident Students (1967 1980) (Out Of State)
BT College Students
RT Place Of Residence
Residence Requirements
Tuition

OUTCOMES OF EDUCATION *Mar. 1980*
CIJE: 916 RIE: 1301 GC: 330
SN Results or consequences of education (note: use only for materials indicating actual results attained -- for discussions of desired results, use "educational objectives," "student educational objectives," etc.)
UF Educational Outcomes
Instructional Outcomes
Learner Outcomes
Results Of Education
Student Outcomes
NT Educational Benefits
RT Accountability
Education
Educational Assessment
Educational Objectives
Failure
Followup Studies
Instructional Effectiveness
Longitudinal Studies
Program Effectiveness
Program Evaluation
Role Of Education
School Effectiveness
Student Development
Student Educational Objectives
Success

OUTCOMES OF TREATMENT *Aug. 1986*
CIJE: RIE: GC: 210
SN Results or consequences of personal health treatment (medical, psychological, etc.)
RT Counseling
Counseling Effectiveness
Helping Relationship
Medical Care Evaluation
Medical Services
Termination Of Treatment
Therapy

OUTDOOR ACTIVITIES *Mar. 1980*
CIJE: 185 RIE: 206 GC: 470
SN Activities taking place in the open air (note: if applicable, use the more precise term "outdoor education")
UF Outdoor Drama (1968 1980) #
Outdoor Theaters (1968 1980) #
BT Activities
RT Adventure Education
Athletics
Bicycling
Camping
Horseback Riding
Outdoor Education
Playground Activities
Recreational Activities
Tourism
Travel

Outdoor Drama (1968 1980)
USE DRAMA; OUTDOOR ACTIVITIES

OUTDOOR EDUCATION *Jul. 1966*
CIJE: 1012 RIE: 1507 GC: 400
SN Utilization of the outdoor environment to promote experiential learning and enrich the curriculum
NT Adventure Education
BT Education
RT Conservation Education
Environmental Education
Experiential Learning
Field Trips
Interdisciplinary Approach
Outdoor Activities
Rural Education
Summer Programs
Trails

Outdoor Lighting (1971 1980)
USE LIGHTING

Outdoor Theaters (1968 1980)
USE OUTDOOR ACTIVITIES; THEATERS

Outer Space Research
USE SPACE EXPLORATION

OUTLINING (DISCOURSE) *Jan. 1985*
CIJE: 2 RIE: 3 GC: 310
SN The sequential enumeration in condensed form of the main ideas and supporting details of written or spoken material
BT Language Arts
RT Coherence
Comprehension
Notetaking
Prewriting
Speech Communication
Study Skills
Writing (Composition)
Writing Skills

OUTPLACEMENT SERVICES (EMPLOYMENT) *Oct. 1983*
CIJE: 8 RIE: 10 GC: 630
SN Services designed to help terminated employees deal with the stress of job loss, engage in job/career planning, and secure re-employment
UF Job Loss Services
BT Employment Services
RT Career Counseling
Career Guidance
Counseling Services
Dislocated Workers
Dismissal (Personnel)
Employment Counselors
Employment Practices
Job Layoff
Job Placement
Personnel Policy
Reduction In Force

Output Devices
USE INPUT OUTPUT DEVICES

Output Oriented Education
USE COMPETENCY BASED EDUCATION

Output Oriented Teacher Education
USE COMPETENCY BASED TEACHER EDUCATION

Outreach Counseling
USE OUTREACH PROGRAMS

OUTREACH PROGRAMS *May. 1974*
CIJE: 421 RIE: 747 GC: 330
SN Efforts to increase the availability and utilization of services, especially through direct intervention and interaction with the target population
UF Community Outreach
Outreach Counseling
BT Programs
RT Bookmobiles
Community Education
Community Involvement
Community Schools
Community Services
Continuing Education
Counseling Services
Delivery Systems
Distance Education
Extension Education
Guidance Programs
Health Programs
Hotlines (Public)
Indigenous Personnel
Intervention
Library Services
Linking Agents
Migrant Programs
Mobile Clinics
Mobile Educational Services
Noncampus Colleges
Off Campus Facilities
Open Universities
Recreational Programs
Rehabilitation Programs
School Community Programs
Use Studies

OVERACHIEVEMENT *Mar. 1980*
CIJE: 17 RIE: 32 GC: 120
SN Achievement beyond expectations
UF Overachievers (1966 1980)
BT Achievement
RT High Achievement
Success
Underachievement

Overachievers (1966 1980)
USE OVERACHIEVEMENT

OVERHEAD PROJECTORS *Jul. 1966*
CIJE: 181 RIE: 62 GC: 910
UF Overhead Transparency Projectors
Transparency Projectors
BT Projection Equipment

Overhead Television (1966 1980)
USE TELEVISION

Overhead Transparencies
USE TRANSPARENCIES

Overhead Transparency Projectors
USE OVERHEAD PROJECTORS

OVERPOPULATION *Jul. 1966*
CIJE: 116 RIE: 110 GC: 550
RT Birth Rate
Community Size
Contraception
Crowding
Demography
Family Planning
Population Distribution
Population Growth
Population Trends

OVERSEAS EMPLOYMENT *Aug. 1968*
CIJE: 76 RIE: 70 GC: 630
UF Working Abroad
Working Overseas
BT Employment
RT Foreign Countries
Occupational Mobility

= Two or more Descriptors are used to represent this term.
The term's main entry shows the appropriate coordination.

OVERT RESPONSE *Jul. 1966*
CIJE: 53 RIE: 62 GC: 110
BT Responses
RT Covert Response

OVERTIME *Jul. 1966*
CIJE: 7 RIE: 28 GC: 630
RT Income
Payroll Records
Personnel Policy
Premium Pay
Salary Wage Differentials
Scope Of Bargaining
Wages
Working Hours

Overweight (Excessive Body Fat)
USE OBESITY

OWNERSHIP *Aug. 1986*
CIJE: 34 RIE: 41 GC: 620
SN Legal possession of material or intellectual property
NT Intellectual Property
Real Estate
RT Business
Capital
Contracts
Cooperatives
Costs
Credit (Finance)
Economic Factors
Economic Opportunities
Economics
Economic Status
Estate Planning
Financial Services
Fiscal Capacity
Homeowners
Industrial Structure
Insurance
Investment
Land Acquisition
Laws
Legal Responsibility
Productivity
Property Appraisal
Purchasing
Resources
Socioeconomic Status
Stealing
Taxes
Trusts (Financial)

Ownership Of Ideas
USE INTELLECTUAL PROPERTY

OXIDATION *Jan. 1970*
CIJE: 95 RIE: 6 GC: 490
BT Chemical Reactions
RT Chemistry

Oxygen Inhalation Therapy
USE RESPIRATORY THERAPY

PACIFIC AMERICANS *Sep. 1982*
CIJE: 6 RIE: 73 GC: 560
SN Citizens or permanent residents of the united states who are descendants of the indigenous peoples of micronesia, polynesia, and melanesia
NT Hawaiians
Samoan Americans
BT North Americans
RT Asian Americans
Ethnic Groups
Minority Groups

PACING *Jul. 1966*
CIJE: 210 RIE: 347 GC: 310
SN Act of directing the performance of individuals or groups by indicating the speed to be achieved
UF Group Pacing
Interval Pacing (1967 1980)
Self Paced Instruction #
Self Pacing
BT Methods
RT Fixed Sequence
Independent Study
Individualized Instruction
Individualized Reading
Learning Strategies
Mastery Learning
Motivation
Programed Instruction
Sequential Approach
Sequential Learning
Teaching Machines
Teaching Methods
Time Factors (Learning)
Time Management

Page Readers
USE OPTICAL SCANNERS

PAINTING (INDUSTRIAL ARTS) *Mar. 1980*
CIJE: 7 RIE: 44 GC: 640
SN Act of or training for automotive painting, construction and maintenance painting, or interior decoration painting (note: prior to mar80, this concept was indexed under "painting")
UF Painting (1966 1980) (Industrial)
BT Industrial Arts
RT Auto Body Repairers
Building Trades
Color Planning
Interior Design
Sign Painters
Skilled Occupations

PAINTING (VISUAL ARTS) *Mar. 1980*
CIJE: 324 RIE: 94 GC: 420
SN Act or result of producing two-dimensional works in a variety of media such as oils, water color, tempera, casein, synthetics, or mixed media (note: prior to mar80, this concept was indexed under "painting")
UF Painting (1966 1980) (Artistic)
BT Visual Arts
RT Artists
Art Products
Childrens Art
Color
Freehand Drawing

Painting (1966 1980) (Artistic)
USE PAINTING (VISUAL ARTS)

Painting (1966 1980) (Industrial)
USE PAINTING (INDUSTRIAL ARTS)

PAIRED ASSOCIATE LEARNING *Jul. 1966*
CIJE: 551 RIE: 256 GC: 110
SN Learning in which items (words, designs, etc.) are presented in pairs -- learning and retention are then measured by presenting the first element and asking the subject to respond with the second
BT Associative Learning
RT Association (Psychology)
Behavior Chaining
Learning Theories
Patterned Responses
Perception
Recall (Psychology)
Serial Learning

Palaeontology
USE PALEONTOLOGY

PALEONTOLOGY *Jul. 1966*
CIJE: 141 RIE: 38 GC: 490
UF Fossils
Palaeontology
BT Geology
RT Archaeology
Evolution
Zoology

PAMPHLETS *Jul. 1969*
CIJE: 63 RIE: 243 GC: 730
UF Brochures
Leaflets
BT Publications

PANJABI *Jul. 1966*
CIJE: 2 RIE: 21 GC: 440
UF Punjabi
BT Indo European Languages

PANTOMIME *Jun. 1970*
CIJE: 41 RIE: 41 GC: 420
UF Mime
BT Theater Arts
RT Acting
Creative Dramatics
Dance
Dramatics
Movement Education
Skits

PAPAGO *Jul. 1966*
CIJE: 4 RIE: 17 GC: 440
BT Uto Aztecan Languages

PAPER (MATERIAL) *Sep. 1968*
CIJE: 77 RIE: 52 GC: 910
RT Art Materials
Printing
Supplies

PAPERBACK BOOKS *Jul. 1966*
CIJE: 156 RIE: 131 GC: 720
UF Soft Cover Books
BT Books

Paradigms
USE MODELS

PARADOX *May. 1971*
CIJE: 48 RIE: 10 GC: 430
RT Logic
Philosophy

PARAGRAPH COMPOSITION *Jul. 1966*
CIJE: 104 RIE: 157 GC: 400
BT Writing (Composition)
RT Cohesion (Written Composition)
Discourse Analysis
Paragraphs
Writing Skills

PARAGRAPHS *Nov. 1968*
CIJE: 64 RIE: 69 GC: 450
NT Sentences
BT Language Patterns
RT Coherence
Connected Discourse
Paragraph Composition
Parallelism (Literary)
Traditional Grammar
Writing (Composition)

Paralanguage
USE PARALINGUISTICS

Paralegal Education
USE LEGAL ASSISTANTS; LEGAL EDUCATION (PROFESSIONS)

Paralegals
USE LEGAL ASSISTANTS

PARALINGUISTICS *Jul. 1966*
CIJE: 102 RIE: 106 GC: 450
SN Study of those aspects of speech communication that do not pertain to linguistic structure or content, e.g., vocal qualifiers, intonation, and body language
UF Paralanguage
BT Linguistics
RT Body Language
Interaction Process Analysis
Intonation
Kinesthetic Methods
Nonverbal Communication
Speech Communication
Speech Habits
Stress (Phonology)
Suprasegmentals

PARALLELISM (LITERARY) *Apr. 1970*
CIJE: 7 RIE: 10 GC: 430
SN Similarity of meaning or of structural arrangement in parts of a sentence, sentences, paragraphs, or larger units of writing
BT Writing (Composition)
RT Literary Devices
Paragraphs
Poetry
Sentence Structure
Writing Skills

Paramedical Occupations (1967 1980)
USE ALLIED HEALTH OCCUPATIONS

Paramedical Sciences
USE MEDICINE

Paramedics
USE ALLIED HEALTH PERSONNEL

PARANOID BEHAVIOR *Nov. 1972*
CIJE: 23 RIE: 6 GC: 230
SN Behavior characterized by suspiciousness or delusions of persecution or grandeur
BT Behavior
RT Behavior Problems
Emotional Problems
Fear
Helplessness
Hostility
Personality Problems
Psychological Patterns
Psychosis
Schizophrenia

Paraplegia
USE NEUROLOGICAL IMPAIRMENTS

PARAPROFESSIONAL PERSONNEL *Feb. 1976*
CIJE: 331 RIE: 851 GC: 630
SN Persons engaged to work with professionals in secondary or supplementary capacities
UF Subprofessionals (1967 1977)
Technicians
NT Agricultural Technicians
Chemical Technicians
Electronic Technicians
Engineering Technicians
Environmental Technicians
Forestry Aides
Housing Management Aides
Instrumentation Technicians
Legal Assistants
Marine Technicians
Mechanical Design Technicians
Metallurgical Technicians
Nuclear Power Plant Technicians
Paraprofessional School Personnel
Production Technicians
Radiographers
Veterinary Assistants
Visiting Homemakers
BT Personnel
RT Allied Health Personnel
Employees
Health Personnel
Library Technicians
Nonprofessional Personnel
Professional Personnel
Research Assistants
Technical Education
Technical Occupations
Vocational Education

PARAPROFESSIONAL SCHOOL PERSONNEL *Jan. 1969*
CIJE: 288 RIE: 774 GC: 360
SN Persons engaged to work with school professional staffs in secondary or supplemental capacities (note: use a more specific term if possible)
NT School Aides
Teacher Aides
BT Paraprofessional Personnel
School Personnel
RT Differentiated Staffs
Student Teachers
Teacher Interns
Volunteers

Parent Absence
USE ONE PARENT FAMILY

PARENT ASPIRATION *Mar. 1980*
CIJE: 81 RIE: 111 GC: 510
SN Level of achievement or quality of performance that parents desire for their children (note: the use of "parental aspiration" was not restricted by a scope note)
UF Parental Aspiration (1966 1980)
BT Aspiration
RT Parent Attitudes
Parent Child Relationship
Parent Influence
Parent Role
Parents

= Two or more Descriptors are used to represent this term.
The term's main entry shows the appropriate coordination.

PARENT ASSOCIATIONS *Sep. 1968*
CIJE: 92 RIE: 151 GC: 330
BT Organizations (Groups)
RT Fathers
Mothers
Parent Participation
Parent Responsibility
Parents

PARENT ATTITUDES *Jul. 1966*
CIJE: 1683 RIE: 2399 GC: 510
SN Attitudes of, not toward, parents (note: prior to apr80, the use of this term was not restricted by a scope note)
UF Parent Opinions
Parent Reaction (1966 1980)
NT Father Attitudes
Mother Attitudes
BT Attitudes
RT Family Attitudes
Parent Aspiration
Parent Background
Parent Counseling
Parent Grievances
Parents

PARENT BACKGROUND *Mar. 1980*
CIJE: 160 RIE: 307 GC: 510
UF Parental Background (1966 1980)
BT Background
RT Family Characteristics
Parent Attitudes
Parent Child Relationship
Parents
Parent School Relationship

Parent Behavior
USE PARENT CHILD RELATIONSHIP

Parent Child Interaction
USE PARENT CHILD RELATIONSHIP

PARENT CHILD RELATIONSHIP *Jul. 1966*
CIJE: 3289 RIE: 2490 GC: 510
SN (Note: if appropriate, use the more specific term "parent student relationship")
UF Child Parent Relationship
Parent Behavior
Parent Child Interaction
NT Parent Student Relationship
BT Family Relationship
RT Attachment Behavior
Child Abuse
Child Custody
Child Neglect
Child Rearing
Children
Daughters
Early Parenthood
Elder Abuse
Failure To Thrive
Fathers
Generation Gap
Mothers
Parent Aspiration
Parent Background
Parent Counseling
Parent Education
Parenthood Education
Parent Influence
Parenting Skills
Parent Role
Parents
Sons

PARENT CONFERENCES *Jul. 1966*
CIJE: 43 RIE: 57 GC: 330
UF Parent Forums
Parent Study Groups
BT Conferences
RT Parent Education
Parent Participation
Parent Responsibility
Parents
Parent Workshops

PARENT COUNSELING *Jul. 1966*
CIJE: 311 RIE: 268 GC: 240
SN Counseling of parents
BT Counseling
RT Family Counseling
Individual Counseling
Parent Attitudes
Parent Child Relationship
Parent Participation
Parents
Parent School Relationship
Parent Teacher Conferences
Parent Teacher Cooperation

PARENT EDUCATION *Jul. 1966*
CIJE: 773 RIE: 1556 GC: 330
SN Instruction or information directed toward parents on effective parenting (note: do not confuse with "parenthood education" -- prior to mar80, the use of this term was not restricted by a scope note)
BT Adult Education
RT Parent Child Relationship
Parent Conferences
Parenting Skills
Parent Materials
Parent Role
Parents
Parent School Relationship
Parent Teacher Conferences
Parent Teacher Cooperation
Parent Workshops

PARENT FINANCIAL CONTRIBUTION *Mar. 1980*
CIJE: 32 RIE: 107 GC: 620
SN Partial or complete financial support of a student's educational expenses by a parent
UF Parental Financial Contribution (1978 1980)
BT Student Financial Aid
RT Family Financial Resources
Family Income
Need Analysis (Student Financial Aid)
Parent Responsibility
Parents
Self Supporting Students
Student Costs
Student Loan Programs
Tax Credits

Parent Forums
USE PARENT CONFERENCES

PARENT GRIEVANCES *Mar. 1980*
CIJE: 41 RIE: 37 GC: 330
UF Parental Grievances (1967 1980)
RT Parent Attitudes
Parents
Parent School Relationship

PARENT INFLUENCE *Jul. 1966*
CIJE: 831 RIE: 798 GC: 510
BT Influences
RT Family Influence
Fathers
Mothers
Parent Aspiration
Parent Child Relationship
Parent Participation
Parent Role
Parents

Parent Involvement
USE PARENT PARTICIPATION

PARENT MATERIALS *Oct. 1982*
CIJE: 44 RIE: 165 GC: 730
SN Print and/or nonprint materials intended primarily for parents (or prospective parents)
UF Parenting Materials
RT Guides
Parent Education
Parenthood Education
Parenting Skills
Parents
Resource Materials

Parent Opinions
USE PARENT ATTITUDES

PARENT PARTICIPATION *Jul. 1966*
CIJE: 1682 RIE: 3546 GC: 330
UF Parent Involvement
BT Participation
RT Family Involvement
Parent Associations
Parent Conferences
Parent Counseling
Parent Influence
Parent Role
Parents
Parent School Relationship
Parent Teacher Conferences

Parent Reaction (1966 1980)
USE PARENT ATTITUDES

PARENT RESPONSIBILITY *Jul. 1966*
CIJE: 292 RIE: 342 GC: 510
UF Parental Obligations
BT Responsibility
RT Child Responsibility
Educational Responsibility
Parent Associations
Parent Conferences
Parent Financial Contribution
Parent Rights
Parents

PARENT RIGHTS *Oct. 1983*
CIJE: 28 RIE: 43 GC: 520
SN Rights of parents, either legal or granted by custom, in areas involving their children
BT Civil Liberties
RT Childrens Rights
Civil Rights
Due Process
Parent Responsibility
Parents

PARENT ROLE *Jul. 1966*
CIJE: 1619 RIE: 1699 GC: 510
UF Father Role #
Mother Role #
RT Family Role
Fathers
Mothers
Parent Aspiration
Parent Child Relationship
Parent Education
Parenthood Education
Parent Influence
Parenting Skills
Parent Participation
Parents
Student Role

PARENT SCHOOL RELATIONSHIP *Jul. 1966*
CIJE: 1103 RIE: 1378 GC: 330
UF School Parent Relationship
BT Family School Relationship
RT Parent Background
Parent Counseling
Parent Education
Parent Grievances
Parent Participation
Parents
Parent Student Relationship
Parent Teacher Conferences
Parent Teacher Cooperation
Politics Of Education
School Attitudes
School Community Relationship
School Involvement
School Role
Schools
Student School Relationship

Parent Skills
USE PARENTING SKILLS

Parent Student Conferences (1967 1980)
USE PARENT TEACHER CONFERENCES

PARENT STUDENT RELATIONSHIP *Jul. 1966*
CIJE: 298 RIE: 224 GC: 330
SN Relationship between parent and child that focuses on the child's role as student (note: prior to mar80, the use of this term was not restricted by a scope note)
UF Student Parent Relationship
BT Parent Child Relationship
RT Home Schooling
Parents
Parent School Relationship
Parent Teacher Conferences
Self Supporting Students
Students
Student School Relationship

Parent Study Groups
USE PARENT CONFERENCES

PARENT TEACHER CONFERENCES *Jul. 1966*
CIJE: 171 RIE: 160 GC: 330
UF Parent Student Conferences (1967 1980)
Teacher Parent Conferences
BT Conferences
RT Faculty Workload
Parent Counseling
Parent Education
Parent Participation
Parents
Parent School Relationship
Parent Student Relationship
Parent Teacher Cooperation
Teachers

PARENT TEACHER COOPERATION *Jul. 1966*
CIJE: 508 RIE: 532 GC: 330
UF Teacher Parent Cooperation
BT Educational Cooperation
RT Cooperative Planning
Home Visits
Parent Counseling
Parent Education
Parents
Parent School Relationship
Parent Teacher Conferences
Teachers

PARENT WORKSHOPS *Jul. 1966*
CIJE: 73 RIE: 155 GC: 330
BT Workshops
RT Parent Conferences
Parent Education
Parents

Parental Aspiration (1966 1980)
USE PARENT ASPIRATION

Parental Background (1966 1980)
USE PARENT BACKGROUND

Parental Financial Contribution (1978 1980)
USE PARENT FINANCIAL CONTRIBUTION

Parental Grievances (1967 1980)
USE PARENT GRIEVANCES

Parental Obligations
USE PARENT RESPONSIBILITY

PARENTHOOD EDUCATION *Jul. 1973*
CIJE: 158 RIE: 266 GC: 400
SN Programs designed to help children and adolescents prepare for effective parenthood by learning about child development and the role of parents, and by working closely with young children
BT Family Life Education
RT Child Development
Child Rearing
Family Life
Family Relationship
Parent Child Relationship
Parenting Skills
Parent Materials
Parent Role
Parents

Parenting
USE CHILD REARING

Parenting Materials
USE PARENT MATERIALS

PARENTING SKILLS *Oct. 1984*
CIJE: 42 RIE: 40 GC: 120
SN Child rearing skills used by parents or other primary caregivers
UF Parent Skills
BT Skills
RT Child Care Occupations
Child Rearing
Children
Family Relationship
Parent Child Relationship
Parent Education
Parenthood Education
Parent Materials
Parent Role
Parents

= Two or more Descriptors are used to represent this term.
The term's main entry shows the appropriate coordination.

PARENTS *Jul. 1966*
CIJE: 761 RIE: 726 GC: 510
UF Catholic Parents (1966 1980) #
NT Biological Parents
Employed Parents
Fathers
Grandparents
Lower Class Parents
Middle Class Parents
Mothers
BT Groups
RT Adults
Child Caregivers
Daughters
Early Parenthood
Family (Sociological Unit)
Family Environment
Family Life
Family Problems
Heads Of Households
Home Schooling
Home Visits
Kinship
One Parent Family
Parent Aspiration
Parent Associations
Parent Attitudes
Parent Background
Parent Child Relationship
Parent Conferences
Parent Counseling
Parent Education
Parent Financial Contribution
Parent Grievances
Parenthood Education
Parent Influence
Parenting Skills
Parent Materials
Parent Participation
Parent Responsibility
Parent Rights
Parent Role
Parent School Relationship
Parent Student Relationship
Parent Teacher Conferences
Parent Teacher Cooperation
Parent Workshops
Sons
Spouses

Parish Workers
USE CHURCH WORKERS

PARK DESIGN *Jul. 1966*
CIJE: 55 RIE: 19 GC: 920
BT Design
RT Parks
Recreational Facilities
Trails

Parking Areas (1966 1980)
USE PARKING FACILITIES

PARKING CONTROLS *Oct. 1968*
CIJE: 4 RIE: 15 GC: 920
UF Parking Meters (1968 1980)
Parking Permits
Parking Regulations
RT Motor Vehicles
Parking Facilities
Traffic Circulation
Traffic Control
Vehicular Traffic

PARKING FACILITIES *Oct. 1968*
CIJE: 26 RIE: 63 GC: 920
SN On and off street surface areas, and above and/or below ground structures for storage of vehicles
UF Parking Areas (1966 1980)
Parking Garages
Parking Lots
Parking Ramps
Street Parking Areas
BT Facilities
RT Campus Planning
Driveways
Motor Vehicles
Parking Controls
Traffic Circulation
Traffic Control
Vehicular Traffic

Parking Garages
USE PARKING FACILITIES

Parking Lots
USE PARKING FACILITIES

Parking Meters (1968 1980)
USE PARKING CONTROLS

Parking Permits
USE PARKING CONTROLS

Parking Ramps
USE PARKING FACILITIES

Parking Regulations
USE PARKING CONTROLS

PARKS *Jul. 1966*
CIJE: 308 RIE: 142 GC: 920
BT Facilities
RT Athletic Fields
Community Resources
Educational Facilities
Hospitality Occupations
Natural Resources
Park Design
Physical Education Facilities
Recreational Facilities
Trails
Zoos

PARLIAMENTARY PROCEDURES *Jul. 1971*
CIJE: 21 RIE: 52 GC: 610
SN The rules, precedents, or agreed upon conventions governing the proceedings of deliberative assemblies and other organizations
BT Standards

Parochial School Aid (1972 1980)
USE PAROCHIAL SCHOOLS; PRIVATE SCHOOL AID

PAROCHIAL SCHOOLS *Jul. 1966*
CIJE: 253 RIE: 334 GC: 340
UF Parochial School Aid (1972 1980) #
NT Catholic Schools
BT Private Schools
RT Church Related Colleges
Lay Teachers
Private Education
Private School Aid
Religious Education

PARODY *Jun. 1969*
CIJE: 52 RIE: 14 GC: 430
BT Literary Genres
RT Comics (Publications)
Figurative Language
Literary Styles
Satire

PAROLE OFFICERS *Jul. 1966*
CIJE: 9 RIE: 34 GC: 640
BT Caseworkers
RT Correctional Rehabilitation
Counselors
Crime
Guidance Personnel
Police
Probation Officers
Social Workers

Parsons
USE CLERGY

Part Correlation
USE CORRELATION

PART TIME EMPLOYMENT *Mar. 1980*
CIJE: 158 RIE: 228 GC: 630
UF Part Time Jobs (1966 1980)
Part Time Work
NT Job Sharing
BT Employment
RT Flexible Working Hours
Full Time Equivalency
Multiple Employment
Part Time Faculty
Part Time Farmers
Student Employment
Underemployment
Working Hours
Work Study Programs
Youth Employment

PART TIME FACULTY *Mar. 1980*
CIJE: 210 RIE: 372 GC: 360
UF Part Time Teachers (1967 1980)
Part Time Teaching (1967 1980)
NT Partnership Teachers
BT Faculty
RT Adjunct Faculty
Employment Level
Faculty Workload
Full Time Equivalency
Full Time Faculty
Nontenured Faculty
Part Time Employment
Substitute Teachers
Teacher Employment
Teachers
Teaching Load
Working Hours

PART TIME FARMERS *Jul. 1966*
CIJE: 1 RIE: 19 GC: 410
UF Nonresident Farmers
BT Farmers
RT Agriculture
Farm Occupations
Part Time Employment

Part Time Jobs (1966 1980)
USE PART TIME EMPLOYMENT

PART TIME STUDENTS *Jul. 1966*
CIJE: 213 RIE: 620 GC: 360
BT Students
RT Correspondence Schools
Distance Education
Enrollment
Evening Programs
Evening Students
Extension Education
External Degree Programs
Full Time Equivalency
Full Time Students

Part Time Teachers (1967 1980)
USE PART TIME FACULTY

Part Time Teaching (1967 1980)
USE PART TIME FACULTY

Part Time Work
USE PART TIME EMPLOYMENT

Partial Correlation
USE CORRELATION

PARTIAL HEARING *Mar. 1980*
CIJE: 106 RIE: 132 GC: 220
SN Mild to moderate hearing impairment -- usually a loss of less than 75 decibels
UF Hard Of Hearing (1967 1980)
BT Hearing Impairments
RT Deafness
Hearing (Physiology)
Hearing Aids
Mild Disabilities
Oral Communication Method
Total Communication

PARTIAL VISION *Mar. 1980*
CIJE: 149 RIE: 123 GC: 220
SN Severe visual impairment requiring special aid for perception of printed material and/or mobility -- legally defined as having central visual acuity between 20/200 and 20/70 in the better eye with correction
UF Partially Sighted (1967 1980)
BT Visual Impairments
RT Blindness
Large Type Materials
Low Vision Aids
Special Education
Talking Books
Vision
Visual Acuity

Partially Sighted (1967 1980)
USE PARTIAL VISION

PARTICIPANT CHARACTERISTICS *Jul. 1966*
CIJE: 292 RIE: 1026 GC: 330
RT Client Characteristics (Human Services)
Control Groups
Dropout Characteristics
Educational Background
Experimental Groups
Group Membership
Individual Characteristics
Matched Groups
Norms
Participation
Research Design
Sampling

Participant Involvement (1967 1980)
USE PARTICIPATION

PARTICIPANT OBSERVATION *Oct. 1984*
CIJE: 36 RIE: 46 GC: 820
SN Observation in which the investigator participates in the situation being studied
BT Observation
RT Classroom Observation Techniques
Ethnography
Evaluation Methods
Naturalistic Observation
Participation
Qualitative Research
Research Methodology
Social Science Research

PARTICIPANT SATISFACTION *Jul. 1966*
CIJE: 645 RIE: 1337 GC: 310
SN An individual's assessment of the degree to which an experience meets his or her needs or expectations
BT Attitudes
RT Evaluation
Participation
Summative Evaluation

PARTICIPATION *Jul. 1966*
CIJE: 833 RIE: 1006 GC: 120
SN Sharing or taking part in an activity (note: use a more specific term if possible)
UF Participant Involvement (1967 1980)
NT Audience Participation
Citizen Participation
Community Involvement
Family Involvement
Parent Participation
School Involvement
Student Participation
Teacher Participation
BT Behavior
RT Activism
Activities
Attendance
Discussion
Enrollment
Experience
Group Activities
Interaction
Interests
Participant Characteristics
Participant Observation
Participant Satisfaction
Participative Decision Making
Performance

PARTICIPATIVE DECISION MAKING *Aug. 1982*
CIJE: 261 RIE: 293 GC: 320
SN Formal involvement of people besides administrators (e.g., staff, students, workers, or community members) in the governance, management, or policy-making processes of an institution or organization of which they are a part -- the extent of participation can vary from advising to power-sharing
UF Collaborative Decision Making
Collective Decision Making
Democratic Management
Participative Management
Participative Problem Solving #
BT Administrative Organization
Decision Making
RT Administration
Advisory Committees
Citizen Participation
College Governing Councils
Community Control
Cooperatives
Employer Employee Relationship
Faculty College Relationship
Management Teams
Organizational Development
Participation
Policy Formation
Power Structure
Quality Circles
School Based Management
School Community Relationship
Student Participation
Student School Relationship

= Two or more Descriptors are used to represent this term.
The term's main entry shows the appropriate coordination.

Teacher Administrator Relationship
Teacher Participation
Teamwork

Participative Management
USE PARTICIPATIVE DECISION MAKING

Participative Problem Solving
USE PARTICIPATIVE DECISION MAKING; PROBLEM SOLVING

PARTNERSHIP TEACHERS *Jul. 1966*
CIJE: 5 RIE: 9 GC: 360
SN Two part-time teachers hired as one full-time teacher
BT Part Time Faculty
RT Flexible Working Hours
Job Sharing

Parts Of Speech
USE FORM CLASSES (LANGUAGES)

Parturition
USE BIRTH

PASHTO *Jul. 1966*
CIJE: RIE: 13 GC: 440
UF Pashtu
Pushto
Pushtu
BT Indo European Languages

Pashtu
USE PASHTO

PASS FAIL GRADING *Jul. 1966*
CIJE: 116 RIE: 92 GC: 320
SN Grading system in which students receive marks of "pass" or "fail" rather than the more conventional letter grades
BT Grading
RT Academic Standards
College Credits
Credit No Credit Grading
Credits
Cutting Scores
Grades (Scholastic)
Nongraded Student Evaluation
Scoring

Pass No Credit Grading
USE CREDIT NO CREDIT GRADING

Pass No Record Grading
USE CREDIT NO CREDIT GRADING

Pastes (Adhesives)
USE ADHESIVES

PASTORAL LITERATURE *Jul. 1969*
CIJE: 10 RIE: 1 GC: 430
UF Bucolic Literature
BT Literature
RT Odes
Poetry

Pastoral Peoples
USE NOMADS

PATENTS *Aug. 1968*
CIJE: 72 RIE: 59 GC: 610
SN Government grants that give people or companies sole rights to make, use, or sell new inventions for a specified number of years
BT Intellectual Property
RT Federal Regulation
Government Role
Inventions
Legal Responsibility
Technology Transfer

PATH ANALYSIS *Mar. 1980*
CIJE: 137 RIE: 109 GC: 820
SN Method of multivariate analysis used to evaluate hypothesized causal relationships among the traits represented in a study (note: prior to mar80, the instruction "path analysis, use critical path method" was carried in the thesaurus)
UF Structural Equations
BT Multivariate Analysis
RT Correlation
Factor Analysis
Multiple Regression Analysis
Predictor Variables
Suppressor Variables
Validity

Pathogenesis
USE PATHOLOGY

PATHOLOGY *Jul. 1966*
CIJE: 113 RIE: 58 GC: 210
UF Pathogenesis
NT Plant Pathology
Psychopathology
Speech Pathology
BT Medicine
RT Anatomy
Death
Diseases
Embryology
Epidemiology
Etiology
Neurology
Oncology
Physiology
Psychophysiology
Toxicology
Zoology

Pathways
USE TRAILS

Patient Care Evaluation
USE MEDICAL CARE EVALUATION

PATIENT EDUCATION *Mar. 1980*
CIJE: 92 RIE: 65 GC: 210
SN Teaching patients about disease management, health care, physician services, etc. (note: do not confuse with the more general descriptor "health education")
BT Education
RT Diseases
Health
Health Education
Nurse Practitioners
Patients
Physician Patient Relationship
Preventive Medicine
Primary Health Care

Patient Physician Relationship
USE PHYSICIAN PATIENT RELATIONSHIP

PATIENTS *Mar. 1980*
CIJE: 1086 RIE: 308 GC: 210
SN Persons who are ill or ailing, usually awaiting or undergoing medical treatment
UF Invalids
Patients (Persons) (1968 1980)
NT Hospitalized Children
BT Groups
RT Client Characteristics (Human Services)
Disabilities
Hospitals
Institutionalized Persons
Medical Case Histories
Medical Evaluation
Medical Services
Patient Education
Physician Patient Relationship
Rehabilitation
Surgery

Patients (Persons) (1968 1980)
USE PATIENTS

PATRIOTISM *Mar. 1982*
CIJE: 19 RIE: 21 GC: 610
SN Love for or devotion to one's country
BT Nationalism
RT Citizenship Responsibility
Group Unity
Loyalty Oaths
Political Socialization

PATTERN DRILLS (LANGUAGE) *Jul. 1966*
CIJE: 348 RIE: 665 GC: 450
NT Substitution Drills
BT Drills (Practice)
RT Dialogs (Language)
Patterned Responses
Second Language Instruction

PATTERN RECOGNITION *Oct. 1969*
CIJE: 360 RIE: 124 GC: 710
NT Character Recognition
BT Recognition (Psychology)
RT Cybernetics
Information Processing
Perception
Reading
Serial Ordering

Patterned Behavior
USE BEHAVIOR PATTERNS

PATTERNED RESPONSES *Jul. 1966*
CIJE: 97 RIE: 90 GC: 110
SN Using various organizations of stimuli to cue desired responses
UF Stimulus Synthesis
BT Responses
RT Association Measures
Dimensional Preference
Generalization
Paired Associate Learning
Pattern Drills (Language)
Perception
Stimulus Generalization

PATTERNMAKING *Jul. 1966*
CIJE: 24 RIE: 20 GC: 640
SN (Note: do not use for the study of numerical patterns -- see the identifier "number sequences" for that concept)
RT Clothing Design
Geometric Concepts
Industrial Arts
Leather
Metal Working
Needle Trades
Plastics
Skilled Occupations
Visual Arts
Woodworking

Pay Equity
USE COMPARABLE WORTH

PAYROLL RECORDS *Jul. 1966*
CIJE: 11 RIE: 45 GC: 630
UF Wage Statements (1966 1980)
BT Records (Forms)
RT Overtime
Premium Pay
Salaries
Wages

PEACE *Apr. 1972*
CIJE: 236 RIE: 331 GC: 610
UF International Peace
World Peace
BT Human Relations
RT Conflict Resolution
Disarmament
Foreign Policy
History
International Education
International Organizations
International Relations
National Defense
Prosocial Behavior
Treaties
War
World Affairs

Peanut Inspectors
USE FOOD AND DRUG INSPECTORS

Pedagogy
USE INSTRUCTION

Pedestrian Circulation
USE PEDESTRIAN TRAFFIC

PEDESTRIAN TRAFFIC *Oct. 1968*
CIJE: 21 RIE: 50 GC: 920
UF Pedestrian Circulation
RT Traffic Circulation
Traffic Control
Vehicular Traffic

PEDIATRICS *Mar. 1980*
CIJE: 190 RIE: 69 GC: 210
SN Branch of medicine dealing with the development, care, and diseases of children
UF Pediatrics Training (1966 1980)
BT Medicine
RT Family Practice (Medicine)
Infants
Medical Services
Neonates
Primary Health Care

Pediatrics Training (1966 1980)
USE PEDIATRICS

PEER ACCEPTANCE *Jul. 1966*
CIJE: 464 RIE: 298 GC: 510
BT Affiliation Need
RT Morale
Peer Evaluation
Peer Groups
Peer Influence
Peer Relationship
Popularity

PEER COUNSELING *Aug. 1973*
CIJE: 243 RIE: 162 GC: 240
SN Performance of limited counselor functions, under counselor supervision, by person of approximate age of counselee
BT Counseling
RT Helping Relationship
Peer Influence
Peer Relationship

PEER EVALUATION *Dec. 1976*
CIJE: 434 RIE: 347 GC: 320
SN Evaluation by one's peers
UF Peer Review
BT Evaluation
RT Interprofessional Relationship
Merit Rating
Peer Acceptance
Peer Influence
Peer Relationship
Personnel Evaluation
Sociometric Techniques
Student Evaluation

PEER GROUPS *Jul. 1966*
CIJE: 412 RIE: 268 GC: 520
BT Groups
RT Age Groups
Conformity
Group Discussion
Juvenile Gangs
Peer Acceptance
Peer Influence
Peer Relationship
Social Values

PEER INFLUENCE *Feb. 1978*
CIJE: 422 RIE: 339 GC: 510
SN Pressure, either planned or unplanned, exerted by peers to influence personal behavior
UF Peer Pressure
BT Influences
RT Conformity
Group Dynamics
Informal Leadership
Peer Acceptance
Peer Counseling
Peer Evaluation
Peer Groups
Peer Relationship
Peer Teaching
Socialization

PEER INSTITUTIONS *Aug. 1986*
CIJE: 1 RIE: 20 GC: 320
SN Institutions with comparable characteristics, e.g., mission, governance, size (note: do not confuse or coordinate with other "peer" descriptors, all of which refer to people)
UF Comparable Institutions
BT Institutions
RT Cluster Grouping
Comparative Analysis
Institutional Characteristics
Institutional Cooperation
Institutional Research

Peer Pressure
USE PEER INFLUENCE

PEER RELATIONSHIP *Jul. 1966*
CIJE: 1388 RIE: 1059 GC: 510
BT Interpersonal Relationship
RT Friendship
Living Learning Centers
Peer Acceptance

Peer Counseling
Peer Evaluation
Peer Groups
Peer Influence
Peer Teaching
Popularity
Teamwork

Peer Review
USE PEER EVALUATION

PEER TEACHING *Jul. 1966*
CIJE: 504 RIE: 458 GC: 310
BT Teaching Methods
RT Cross Age Teaching
Peer Influence
Peer Relationship
Tutorial Programs
Tutoring

Pensions
USE RETIREMENT BENEFITS

People Days
USE WORKER DAYS

Percent
USE PERCENTAGE

PERCENTAGE *Jan. 1969*
CIJE: 38 RIE: 70 GC: 480
UF Percent
BT Ratios (Mathematics)
RT Arithmetic
Mathematical Concepts

PERCEPTION *Jul. 1966*
CIJE: 2170 RIE: 1416 GC: 110
SN The process of becoming aware of objects, qualities, or relations via the sense organs -- involves the reception, processing, and interpretation of sensory impressions (note: use a more specific term if possible -- do not confuse with "attitudes" or "opinions")
UF Awareness
NT Auditory Perception
Kinesthetic Perception
Tactual Perception
Visual Perception
BT Cognitive Processes
RT Adaptation Level Theory
Aesthetic Values
Arousal Patterns
Attention
Cognitive Mapping
Comprehension
Discovery Processes
Discrimination Learning
Encoding (Psychology)
Figural Aftereffects
Habituation
Inferences
Intuition
Neurological Organization
Novelty (Stimulus Dimension)
Paired Associate Learning
Patterned Responses
Pattern Recognition
Perception Tests
Perceptual Development
Perceptual Handicaps
Perceptual Motor Coordination
Phenomenology
Physiology
Recognition (Psychology)
Sensory Deprivation
Sensory Experience
Sensory Integration
Spatial Ability
Stimuli

Perception (Between Persons)
USE SOCIAL COGNITION

PERCEPTION TESTS *Jul. 1966*
CIJE: 229 RIE: 240 GC: 830
SN Measures used to indicate an individual's awareness, organization, and understanding of sensory impressions (note: do not confuse with "physical examinations")
NT Tactual Visual Tests
BT Cognitive Tests
RT Auditory Perception
Auditory Tests
Field Dependence Independence
Kinesthetic Perception
Perception
Perceptual Development
Tactual Perception
Vision Tests
Visual Literacy
Visual Perception

Perceptiveness (Between Persons)
USE INTERPERSONAL COMPETENCE; SOCIAL COGNITION

Perceptual Deprivation
USE SENSORY DEPRIVATION

PERCEPTUAL DEVELOPMENT *Jul. 1966*
CIJE: 811 RIE: 715 GC: 120
SN Stages or growth in organizing and understanding sensory impressions, i.e., the process of recognizing, identifying, or becoming aware of objects, qualities, or relations
BT Cognitive Development
RT Brain Hemisphere Functions
Learning Modalities
Neurological Organization
Perception
Perception Tests
Perceptual Handicaps
Perceptual Motor Coordination
Perceptual Motor Learning
Physical Development
Psychomotor Skills
Sensory Integration
Sensory Training
Spatial Ability
Visual Literacy

PERCEPTUAL HANDICAPS *Mar. 1980*
CIJE: 188 RIE: 147 GC: 220
SN Impairment of the ability to recognize and interpret information which is received through the senses
UF Perceptually Handicapped (1966 1980)
BT Disabilities
RT Aphasia
Auditory Perception
Auditory Training
Dyslexia
Exceptional Persons
Hyperactivity
Language Handicaps
Learning Disabilities
Neurological Impairments
Perception
Perceptual Development
Perceptual Motor Coordination
Perceptual Motor Learning
Recall (Psychology)
Recognition (Psychology)
Sensory Experience
Sensory Integration
Visual Literacy
Visual Perception

PERCEPTUAL MOTOR COORDINATION *Jul. 1966*
CIJE: 377 RIE: 335 GC: 120
NT Eye Hand Coordination
Eye Voice Span
BT Psychomotor Skills
RT Exploratory Behavior
Motor Development
Movement Education
Object Manipulation
Perception
Perceptual Development
Perceptual Handicaps
Perceptual Motor Learning
Reaction Time
Tactual Visual Tests

PERCEPTUAL MOTOR LEARNING *Jul. 1966*
CIJE: 302 RIE: 422 GC: 110
SN Learning that involves the perceptual processing of nonverbal stimuli
UF Sensory Motor Learning
BT Nonverbal Learning
RT Kinesthetic Perception
Learning Modalities
Manipulative Materials
Motor Development
Movement Education
Multisensory Learning
Perceptual Development
Perceptual Handicaps
Perceptual Motor Coordination
Psychomotor Skills
Sensory Integration
Sensory Training
Tactual Visual Tests

Perceptual Style
USE COGNITIVE STYLE

Perceptually Handicapped (1966 1980)
USE PERCEPTUAL HANDICAPS

PERFORMANCE *Jul. 1966*
CIJE: 730 RIE: 756 GC: 120
SN Execution or accomplishment of an intended action or goal
NT Counselor Performance
Failure
Job Performance
Success
BT Behavior
RT Ability
Academic Achievement
Accountability
Achievement
Aptitude
Aspiration
Awards
Competence
Competency Based Education
Competency Based Teacher Education
Competition
Difficulty Level
Efficiency
Evaluation Criteria
Expectation
Feedback
Knowledge Level
Management By Objectives
Mastery Learning
Mastery Tests
Minimum Competencies
Motivation
Objectives
Observation
Participation
Performance Factors
Performance Tests
Qualifications
Quality Control
Relevance (Information Retrieval)
Reliability
Time Management
Time On Task

Performance Appraisal (Personnel)
USE PERSONNEL EVALUATION

Performance Based Education (1974 1980)
USE COMPETENCY BASED EDUCATION

Performance Based Teacher Education (1972 1980)
USE COMPETENCY BASED TEACHER EDUCATION

PERFORMANCE CONTRACTS *Jan. 1971*
CIJE: 421 RIE: 421 GC: 310
SN Agreements to achieve specified objectives within established time frames with reward or payment dependent upon the level of performance
UF Behavioral Contracts
Contract Grading #
Learning Contracts
Student Learning Contracts
BT Contracts
RT Academic Achievement
Behavioral Objectives
Contingency Management
Management By Objectives
Motivation Techniques

PERFORMANCE CRITERIA (1968 1980) *Jun. 1980*
CIJE: 782 RIE: 1383 GC: 820
SN Invalid descriptor -- used inconsistently in indexing -- see "evaluation criteria" and "specifications"

PERFORMANCE FACTORS *Jul. 1966*
CIJE: 2790 RIE: 1802 GC: 310
SN Influences, conditions, or characteristics related to the accomplishment of a goal or task by a person, organization, program, or system
BT Influences
RT Achievement
Evaluation
Evaluation Criteria
Performance
Predictor Variables

Performance Objectives
USE BEHAVIORAL OBJECTIVES

PERFORMANCE SPECIFICATIONS (1969 1980) *Jun. 1980*
CIJE: 229 RIE: 455 GC: 820
SN Invalid descriptor -- used inconsistently in indexing -- see such descriptors as "equipment standards," "facility requirements," and "performance factors"

PERFORMANCE TESTS *Jul. 1966*
CIJE: 310 RIE: 688 GC: 830
SN Tests that require the manipulation of objects or skilled bodily movements (note: do not confuse with "nonverbal tests," which minimize the use of language but may not emphasize the manipulation of objects or skilled movement -- prior to mar80, the use of this term was not restricted by a scope note)
BT Tests
RT Achievement Tests
Aptitude Tests
Criterion Referenced Tests
Nonverbal Tests
Occupational Tests
Performance
Situational Tests
Work Sample Tests

Performing Arts
USE THEATER ARTS

Performing Arts Centers
USE THEATERS

PERINATAL INFLUENCES *Sep. 1975*
CIJE: 81 RIE: 66 GC: 120
SN Factors occurring at the time of birth and affecting the physical or mental development of an individual
BT Influences
RT Biological Influences
Birth
Birth Weight
Congenital Impairments
Diseases
Health
Obstetrics
Pregnancy
Premature Infants
Prenatal Influences
Rh Factors

PERIODICALS *Jul. 1966*
CIJE: 1248 RIE: 1500 GC: 730
UF Journals
Magazines
NT Foreign Language Periodicals
Scholarly Journals
BT Serials
RT Bibliometrics
Bulletins
Editorials
Editors
Journalism
Journalism Education
Reading Materials
Writing For Publication

Permanent Education
USE LIFELONG LEARNING

Permanent Magnets
USE MAGNETS

PERMISSIVE ENVIRONMENT *Jul. 1966*
CIJE: 42 RIE: 38 GC: 510
BT Environment
RT Family Environment
Nonauthoritarian Classes

PERMUTED INDEXES *Jul. 1966*
CIJE: 48 RIE: 58 GC: 730
SN Indexes based on the cyclic permutation of words, with each substantive word being brought to a predetermined position and alphabetized

UF Key Word In Context
Kwic Indexes
Kwoc Indexes
Title Word Indexes
BT Indexes
RT Automatic Indexing
Coordinate Indexes
Indexing

Perquisites (Employment)
USE FRINGE BENEFITS

Perseverance
USE PERSISTENCE

PERSIAN *Jul. 1966*
CIJE: 22 RIE: 70 GC: 440
UF Farsi (Language)
BT Indo European Languages

PERSISTENCE *Jul. 1966*
CIJE: 163 RIE: 363 GC: 120
SN Continuance of an individual in an endeavor or activity
UF Perseverance
NT Academic Persistence
Teacher Persistence
BT Behavior
RT Burnout
Career Change
Coping
Dropout Research
Dropouts
Occupational Mobility
Personality Traits
Stopouts
Time On Task

Person Days
USE WORKER DAYS

Person Perception
USE SOCIAL COGNITION

Personal Accounts (Narratives)
USE PERSONAL NARRATIVES

Personal Adjustment (1966 1980)
USE ADJUSTMENT (TO ENVIRONMENT)

PERSONAL AUTONOMY *Nov. 1982*
CIJE: 105 RIE: 78 GC: 510
SN Individual independence, self-determination, and freedom from external restraint or authority
UF Individual Autonomy
Learner Autonomy
RT Academic Freedom
Authoritarianism
Decision Making
Democracy
Independent Study
Individualism
Individual Power
Individual Psychology
Intellectual Freedom
Interpersonal Relationship
Life Style
Locus Of Control
Open Education
Personality
Power Structure
Professional Autonomy
Psychological Needs
Role Theory
Self Actualization
Self Control
Self Determination
Sociology

PERSONAL CARE HOMES *Aug. 1968*
CIJE: 29 RIE: 37 GC: 920
SN Residential facilities, usually for older adults, providing personal services such as assistance in mobilization, bathing, dressing, etc. as opposed to highly skilled care given in facilities like nursing homes
UF Homes For The Aged
Rest Homes
BT Residential Institutions
RT Group Homes
Nursing Homes
Older Adults
Residential Care
Respite Care

Personal Computers
USE MICROCOMPUTERS

Personal Development
USE INDIVIDUAL DEVELOPMENT

Personal Grooming
USE HYGIENE

Personal Growth (1967 1980)
USE INDIVIDUAL DEVELOPMENT

Personal Health
USE HYGIENE

Personal Interests (1966 1980)
USE INTERESTS

Personal Liberty
USE CIVIL LIBERTIES

PERSONAL NARRATIVES *Sep. 1982*
CIJE: 215 RIE: 64 GC: 730
SN Verbal accounts, usually in the first person, of an individual's experiences, thoughts, and feelings
UF Personal Accounts (Narratives)
BT Reports
RT Autobiographies
Biographies
Diaries
Interviews
Monologs
Narration
Opinion Papers
Speeches

Personal Relationship (1966 1974)
USE INTERPERSONAL RELATIONSHIP

PERSONAL SPACE *Mar. 1980*
CIJE: 92 RIE: 62 GC: 120
SN Individuals' sense of physical space required for psychological comfort -- may vary greatly from culture to culture and within cultures (note: do not confuse with "spatial ability")
UF Proxemics
BT Psychological Needs
RT Body Image
Crowding
Cultural Traits
Kinesthetic Perception
Nonverbal Communication

Personal Values (1966 1980)
USE VALUES

PERSONALITY *Jul. 1966*
CIJE: 939 RIE: 613 GC: 120
SN The dynamic, integrated pattern of motivational and temperamental or emotional qualities that distinguishes the individual (note: for specific personality attributes, see "personality traits")
UF Character
Temperament
RT Attribution Theory
Habit Formation
Individual Psychology
Personal Autonomy
Personality Assessment
Personality Change
Personality Development
Personality Measures
Personality Problems
Personality Studies
Personality Theories
Personality Traits
Phenomenology
Self Concept

PERSONALITY ASSESSMENT *Jul. 1966*
CIJE: 1134 RIE: 562 GC: 820
SN Evaluation of the patterns of enduring traits that characterize a particular individual's motivation, temperament, or behavior
UF Personality Rating
BT Psychological Evaluation
RT Association Measures
Behavior Rating Scales
Factor Analysis
Goal Orientation
Personality
Personality Development
Personality Measures
Personality Studies
Projective Measures
Q Methodology

PERSONALITY CHANGE *Jul. 1966*
CIJE: 136 RIE: 103 GC: 120
SN Complete or partial alteration in personality (note: prior to mar80, the use of this term was not restricted by a scope note)
BT Change
RT Attitude Change
Behavior Change
Personality
Personality Development

PERSONALITY DEVELOPMENT *Jul. 1966*
CIJE: 544 RIE: 481 GC: 120
SN Progressive organization of the psychological traits unique to an individual, occurring as the result of maturation and learning from birth through adulthood (note: do not confuse with "personality change," which refers to a shift in the direction of this development)
BT Individual Development
RT Developmental Psychology
Emotional Development
Moral Development
Personality
Personality Assessment
Personality Change
Personality Measures
Personality Problems
Self Actualization
Social Development

PERSONALITY MEASURES *Mar. 1980*
CIJE: 943 RIE: 435 GC: 830
SN Procedures or devices used to obtain quantified descriptions of an individual's motivational and temperamental traits or behavior patterns
UF Personality Tests (1968 1980)
NT Self Concept Measures
BT Measures (Individuals)
RT Affective Measures
Association Measures
Attitude Measures
Behavior Rating Scales
Diagnostic Tests
Field Dependence Independence
Forced Choice Technique
Interest Inventories
Maturity Tests
Personality
Personality Assessment
Personality Development
Personality Studies
Personality Theories
Personality Traits
Psychological Evaluation
Psychological Testing
Q Methodology
Semantic Differential
Social Desirability

PERSONALITY PROBLEMS *Jul. 1966*
CIJE: 164 RIE: 121 GC: 230
BT Problems
RT Adjustment (To Environment)
Apathy
Autism
Behavior Disorders
Behavior Problems
Clinical Psychology
Depression (Psychology)
Emotional Disturbances
Emotional Problems
Mental Disorders
Neurosis
Paranoid Behavior
Personality
Personality Development
Problem Children
Psychiatry
Psychopathology
Self Destructive Behavior

Personality Rating
USE PERSONALITY ASSESSMENT

PERSONALITY STUDIES *Jul. 1966*
CIJE: 501 RIE: 270 GC: 810
SN Studies of the components of personality and their causal factors (note: as of oct81, use as a minor descriptor for examples of this kind of research -- use as a major descriptor only as the subject of a document)
BT Psychological Studies
RT Exceptional Child Research
Personality
Personality Assessment
Personality Measures
Teaching Styles

Personality Tests (1968 1980)
USE PERSONALITY MEASURES

PERSONALITY THEORIES *Jul. 1966*
CIJE: 717 RIE: 218 GC: 810
BT Theories
RT Behavior Theories
Personality
Personality Measures

PERSONALITY TRAITS *Mar. 1980*
CIJE: 1095 RIE: 682 GC: 120
SN Specific motivational, temperamental, or emotional attributes that contribute to the total personality (note: prior to mar80, the instruction "personality traits, use individual characteristics" was carried in the thesaurus)
UF Adaptability (Personality) #
NT Curiosity
Locus Of Control
Mental Rigidity
BT Psychological Characteristics
RT Anxiety
Assertiveness
Cognitive Style
Compliance (Psychology)
Conformity
Congruence (Psychology)
Creativity
Dogmatism
Egocentrism
Humor
Interpersonal Competence
Jealousy
Maturity (Individuals)
Persistence
Personality
Personality Measures
Self Control
Self Esteem
Sexuality

Personalized Instruction
USE INDIVIDUALIZED INSTRUCTION

PERSONNEL *Jul. 1966*
CIJE: 164 RIE: 574 GC: 630
NT Administrators
Agricultural Personnel
Aircraft Pilots
Caseworkers
Church Workers
Clergy
Consultants
Designers
Differentiated Staffs
Dislocated Workers
Editors
Employees
Equipment Manufacturers
Evaluators
Foreign Workers
Government Employees
Guidance Personnel
Health Personnel
Indigenous Personnel
Industrial Personnel
Institutional Personnel
Interpreters
Library Personnel
Merchants
Nonprofessional Personnel
Ombudsmen
Paraprofessional Personnel
Professional Personnel
Programers
Reentry Workers
Research Assistants
Resident Advisers
Resource Staff
School Personnel
Scientific Personnel

= Two or more Descriptors are used to represent this term.
The term's main entry shows the appropriate coordination.

Security Personnel
Specialists
Systems Analysts
Trainers
BT Groups
RT Employed Parents
Employed Women
Employment
Human Resources
Industrial Psychology
Labor Relations
Office Management
Personnel Data
Personnel Directors
Personnel Evaluation
Personnel Integration
Personnel Management
Personnel Needs
Personnel Policy
Personnel Selection
Recruitment
Staff Development
Staff Meetings
Staff Orientation
Staff Role
Staff Utilization

Personnel Administrators
USE PERSONNEL DIRECTORS

PERSONNEL DATA *Jul. 1966*
CIJE: 86 RIE: 238 GC: 630
BT Data
RT Employment Experience
Employment Qualifications
Personnel
Profiles
Resumes (Personal)
Seniority
Tenure

Personnel Development
USE STAFF DEVELOPMENT

PERSONNEL DIRECTORS *Oct. 1968*
CIJE: 107 RIE: 60 GC: 640
UF Personnel Administrators
Personnel Managers
School Personnel Directors #
BT Administrators
RT Personnel
Personnel Management
Personnel Policy
Personnel Selection
School Personnel

Personnel Discharge
USE DISMISSAL (PERSONNEL)

Personnel Dismissal
USE DISMISSAL (PERSONNEL)

PERSONNEL EVALUATION *Jul. 1966*
CIJE: 504 RIE: 1141 GC: 630
SN Judging employee value, competence, productivity, work quality, etc., using previously established objectives or standards, for decisions concerning selection, classification, placement, promotion, merit salary increases, etc. (note: do not confuse with "vocational evaluation")
UF Employee Evaluation
Performance Appraisal (Personnel)
Staff Evaluation
Worker Evaluation
NT Administrator Evaluation
Counselor Evaluation
Faculty Evaluation
Teacher Evaluation
BT Evaluation
RT Assessment Centers (Personnel)
Competence
Dismissal (Personnel)
Employment Qualifications
Informal Assessment
Job Performance
Job Placement
Job Skills
Management By Objectives
Merit Rating
Occupational Tests
Peer Evaluation
Personnel
Personnel Management
Personnel Selection
Portfolios (Background Materials)
Promotion (Occupational)
Vocational Evaluation

PERSONNEL INTEGRATION *Jul. 1966*
CIJE: 17 RIE: 54 GC: 540
SN Process of balancing the racial, ethnic, or sexual composition of the employees or staff of an organization, business, or institution (note: use a more specific term if possible)
NT Faculty Integration
Teacher Integration
BT Social Integration
RT Affirmative Action
Employment Practices
Equal Opportunities (Jobs)
Nontraditional Occupations
Personnel
Personnel Policy
Racial Integration
Sex Fairness
Tokenism

PERSONNEL MANAGEMENT *Feb. 1970*
CIJE: 546 RIE: 478 GC: 630
SN Recruitment, selection, development, supervision, dismissal, etc. of employees
BT Administration
RT Employer Employee Relationship
Employment Practices
Industrial Psychology
Office Management
Personnel
Personnel Directors
Personnel Evaluation
Personnel Needs
Personnel Policy
Personnel Selection
Staff Utilization

Personnel Managers
USE PERSONNEL DIRECTORS

PERSONNEL NEEDS *Jul. 1966*
CIJE: 264 RIE: 511 GC: 630
SN Requirements for staff
BT Labor Needs
RT Employees
Personnel
Personnel Management
Personnel Policy
Personnel Selection
Recruitment
Resource Staff

PERSONNEL POLICY *Jul. 1966*
CIJE: 651 RIE: 1262 GC: 630
SN Governing principles that serve as guidelines or rules for decision-making and action concerning employees
BT Policy
RT Affirmative Action
Comparable Worth
Conflict Of Interest
Contracts
Dismissal (Personnel)
Dress Codes
Early Retirement
Employee Assistance Programs
Employment Practices
Fringe Benefits
Job Layoff
Job Sharing
Leaves Of Absence
Loyalty Oaths
Merit Pay
Outplacement Services (Employment)
Overtime
Personnel
Personnel Directors
Personnel Integration
Personnel Management
Personnel Needs
Personnel Selection
Premium Pay
Reduction In Force
Released Time
Retirement Benefits
Salary Wage Differentials
Scope Of Bargaining
Seniority
Tenure

Personnel Recruitment
USE RECRUITMENT

Personnel Role
USE STAFF ROLE

PERSONNEL SELECTION *Jul. 1966*
CIJE: 597 RIE: 754 GC: 630
NT Administrator Selection
Counselor Selection
Teacher Selection
BT Selection
RT Affirmative Action
Assessment Centers (Personnel)
Competitive Selection
Eligibility
Employment Interviews
Labor Market
Personnel
Personnel Directors
Personnel Evaluation
Personnel Management
Personnel Needs
Personnel Policy
Portfolios (Background Materials)
Recruitment
Resumes (Personal)
Search Committees (Personnel)

Personnel Tests
USE OCCUPATIONAL TESTS

PERSPECTIVE TAKING *Oct. 1977*
CIJE: 311 RIE: 177 GC: 120
SN Perceiving physical, social, or emotional situations from a point of view other than one's own (note: do not confuse with "role playing")
UF Role Taking
RT Egocentrism
Emotional Development
Empathy
Identification (Psychology)
Interpersonal Relationship
Psychological Patterns
Role Perception
Role Playing
Self Concept
Social Cognition
Social Development

PERSUASIVE DISCOURSE *Apr. 1970*
CIJE: 1151 RIE: 873 GC: 450
SN Oral or written effort to win others over to an opinion or action
UF Argumentation
Forensics
BT Rhetoric
RT Advertising
Communication (Thought Transfer)
Credibility
Debate
Editorials
Motivation Techniques
Political Campaigns
Propaganda
Public Speaking
Rhetorical Criticism
Rhetorical Invention
Salesmanship
Speech
Speech Communication
Speeches
Verbal Communication
Writing (Composition)

Pest Control
USE PESTS

PESTICIDES *Jul. 1966*
CIJE: 122 RIE: 381 GC: 410
UF Rodenticides (1968 1980)
NT Herbicides
Insecticides
BT Poisons
RT Agricultural Chemical Occupations
Agricultural Production
Agricultural Supplies
Agronomy
Disease Control
Pests
Rats

PESTS *Aug. 1982*
CIJE: 5 RIE: 49 GC: 410
SN Annoying or detrimental animals and plants
UF Pest Control
RT Agricultural Production
Animals
Disease Control
Diseases
Ecology
Entomology
Environmental Standards
Health
Microbiology
Pesticides
Physical Health
Rats
Sanitation
Weeds

PETROLEUM INDUSTRY *Jun. 1970*
CIJE: 110 RIE: 73 GC: 650
BT Industry
RT Chemical Engineering
Chemical Industry
Energy Occupations
Fuels
Lubricants

Peul
USE FULANI

PHARMACEUTICAL EDUCATION *Aug. 1977*
CIJE: 528 RIE: 60 GC: 210
SN Formal study of the art and science of preparing and dispensing drugs and medicine
BT Medical Education
RT Clinical Experience
Drug Education
Drug Therapy
Nursing Education
Pharmacists
Pharmacy

PHARMACISTS *Aug. 1968*
CIJE: 222 RIE: 74 GC: 210
UF Druggists
BT Health Personnel
Professional Personnel
RT Medical Associations
Medical Services
Pharmaceutical Education
Pharmacy

PHARMACOLOGY *Sep. 1980*
CIJE: 65 RIE: 32 GC: 210
SN The science of the nature and properties of drugs, particularly their actions or effects (note: see also "pharmacy")
BT Medicine
RT Drug Abuse
Drug Addiction
Drug Use
Pharmacy
Toxicology

PHARMACY *Dec. 1976*
CIJE: 196 RIE: 61 GC: 210
SN The art or practice of preparing, preserving, compounding, and dispensing drugs (note: see also "pharmacology")
BT Medicine
RT Drug Legislation
Drug Therapy
Medical Services
Pharmaceutical Education
Pharmacists
Pharmacology

PHENOMENOLOGY *Oct. 1984*
CIJE: 51 RIE: 51 GC: 430
SN Study of reality in terms of individual perceptions or conscious experiences at any moment, without external interpretation and judgment
BT Philosophy
RT Cognitive Style
Epistemology
Existentialism
Gestalt Therapy
Individualism
Perception
Personality
Psychological Characteristics
Self Concept
Socialization

Pheul
USE FULANI

= Two or more Descriptors are used to represent this term.
The term's main entry shows the appropriate coordination.

PHILANTHROPIC FOUNDATIONS *Mar. 1980*
CIJE: 148 RIE: 213 GC: 620
SN Trusts or corporations created for charitable purposes that provide grants of funds to finance research, services, facilities, equipment, or library resources (note: prior to mar80, this concept was often indexed under "foundation programs," which was not scoped)
UF Educational Foundations
Foundations (Institutions)
BT Institutions
RT Donors
Endowment Funds
Grants
Nonprofit Organizations
Private Financial Support
Trusts (Financial)

Philanthropy
USE PRIVATE FINANCIAL SUPPORT

Philology
USE LINGUISTICS

PHILOSOPHY *Jul. 1966*
CIJE: 1266 RIE: 684 GC: 430
SN Critical examination of the grounds for fundamental beliefs and analysis of the basic concepts, doctrines, or practices that express such beliefs
NT Educational Philosophy
Epistemology
Ethics
Existentialism
Humanism
Logic
Marxism
Phenomenology
Platonism
Semiotics
BT Humanities
RT Antithesis
Buddhism
Christianity
Confucianism
Holistic Approach
Individualism
Judaism
Literature
Modernism
Mysticism
Naturalism
Paradox
Realism
Religion
Romanticism
Taoism
Traditionalism

PHONEME GRAPHEME CORRESPONDENCE *Jul. 1973*
CIJE: 177 RIE: 164 GC: 450
SN Relationship between speech sound (phoneme) and written symbol (grapheme)
UF Grapheme Phoneme Correspondence
Letter Sound Correspondence
BT Language Patterns
RT Contrastive Linguistics
Decoding (Reading)
Graphemes
Linguistics
Miscue Analysis
Phonemes
Phonemics
Phonics
Phonology
Reading
Written Language

PHONEMES *Jul. 1966*
CIJE: 412 RIE: 356 GC: 450
SN The smallest units of speech that distinguish one utterance from another in a given language -- for example, "p" in "pat" and "b" in "bat" represent two english phonemes -- "p" in "pat" and "p" in "spat" represent the same phoneme, despite their difference in sound, because this difference is never the only distinguishing feature between two words in english
UF Phonological Units (1966 1980)
NT Consonants
Vowels
BT Phonemics
RT Distinctive Features (Language)
Graphemes
Intonation
Language Typology
Letters (Alphabet)
Morphemes
Morphophonemics
Phoneme Grapheme Correspondence
Phonemic Alphabets
Phonics
Phonology
Suprasegmentals
Syllables

PHONEMIC ALPHABETS *Jul. 1966*
CIJE: 14 RIE: 55 GC: 450
BT Alphabets
RT Consonants
Phonemes
Phonemics
Phonics

PHONEMICS *Jul. 1966*
CIJE: 178 RIE: 179 GC: 450
SN The study of phonemes
NT Phonemes
BT Phonology
RT Contrastive Linguistics
Descriptive Linguistics
Diachronic Linguistics
Generative Phonology
Language Patterns
Linguistics
Morphophonemics
Phoneme Grapheme Correspondence
Phonemic Alphabets
Phonetics
Speech

PHONETIC ANALYSIS *Jul. 1966*
CIJE: 111 RIE: 120 GC: 450
BT Evaluation Methods
RT Error Analysis (Language)
Language Research
Miscue Analysis
Phonetics
Phonics

PHONETIC TRANSCRIPTION *Jul. 1966*
CIJE: 46 RIE: 100 GC: 450
SN Representation of speech sounds in phonetic symbols
BT Orthographic Symbols
RT Alphabets
Diacritical Marking
Phonetics
Phonology
Written Language

PHONETICS *Jul. 1966*
CIJE: 564 RIE: 484 GC: 450
SN Study and classification of speech sounds, including their production, transmission, and perception
NT Acoustic Phonetics
Phonics
BT Phonology
RT Articulation (Speech)
Consonants
Diacritical Marking
Distinctive Features (Language)
Generative Phonology
Graphemes
Morphophonemics
Phonemics
Phonetic Analysis
Phonetic Transcription
Speech
Stress (Phonology)
Vowels

Phonic Method
USE PHONICS

PHONICS *Jul. 1966*
CIJE: 350 RIE: 488 GC: 460
SN The study of sound-letter relationships in reading and spelling, and the use of this knowledge in recognizing and pronouncing words
UF Phonic Method
BT Phonetics
RT Aural Learning
Basal Reading
Beginning Reading
Decoding (Reading)
Initial Teaching Alphabet
Phoneme Grapheme Correspondence
Phonemes
Phonemic Alphabets
Phonetic Analysis
Phonology
Reading Instruction
Reading Skills
Spelling
Word Study Skills

Phonograph Record Lists
USE DISCOGRAPHIES

Phonograph Records (1966 1980)
USE AUDIODISKS

Phonological Borrowing
USE LINGUISTIC BORROWING

Phonological Units (1966 1980)
USE PHONEMES

PHONOLOGY *Jul. 1966*
CIJE: 971 RIE: 1241 GC: 450
SN Study of the ways in which speech sounds form systems and patterns in language
NT Generative Phonology
Phonemics
Phonetics
Suprasegmentals
Syllables
BT Linguistics
RT Artificial Speech
Code Switching (Language)
Componential Analysis
Descriptive Linguistics
Diachronic Linguistics
Distinctive Features (Language)
Error Analysis (Language)
Intonation
Kernel Sentences
Language Typology
Linguistic Borrowing
Morphology (Languages)
Morphophonemics
Phoneme Grapheme Correspondence
Phonemes
Phonetic Transcription
Phonics
Sound Spectrographs
Speech
Stress (Phonology)
Surface Structure
Vowels

Phonotape Recordings (1966 1978)
USE AUDIOTAPE RECORDINGS

PHOTOCHEMICAL REACTIONS *Jan. 1970*
CIJE: 92 RIE: 7 GC: 490
SN Chemical reactions influenced or initiated by light
UF Photochemistry
NT Photosynthesis
BT Chemical Reactions
RT Chemistry

Photochemistry
USE PHOTOCHEMICAL REACTIONS

PHOTOCOMPOSITION *Oct. 1969*
CIJE: 59 RIE: 58 GC: 710
SN Automatic selection and projection onto photographic film of alphabetic characters, figures, punctuation marks, and other symbols in the correct sequence to produce readable text ready for the various printing processes (note: before mar80, the use of this term was not restricted by a scope note)
BT Production Techniques
RT Computer Graphics
Graphic Arts
Photography
Printing
Publications
Reprography

Photocopying
USE REPROGRAPHY

PHOTOGRAPHIC EQUIPMENT *Aug. 1971*
CIJE: 153 RIE: 103 GC: 910
UF Cameras
Film (Cameras)
BT Equipment
Visual Aids
RT Audio Equipment
Audiovisual Aids
Film Production
Photography
Projection Equipment
Video Equipment

Photographic Memory
USE EIDETIC IMAGERY

PHOTOGRAPHS *Jul. 1966*
CIJE: 573 RIE: 255 GC: 720
BT Visual Aids
RT Art Products
Audiovisual Aids
Captions
Films
Illustrations
Nonprint Media
Photography
Photojournalism

PHOTOGRAPHY *Jul. 1966*
CIJE: 684 RIE: 402 GC: 420
SN Art or process of producing images on sensitized surfaces by the action of light or other radiant energy
NT Holography
BT Visual Arts
RT Film Production
Film Study
Journalism
Layout (Publications)
Magnification Methods
Photocomposition
Photographic Equipment
Photographs
Photojournalism
Production Techniques
Reprography
Special Effects

PHOTOJOURNALISM *Dec. 1985*
CIJE: 29 RIE: 29 GC: 720
SN The art or profession of using still photography or other pictorial copy as the primary means of presenting information on current affairs
UF Pictorial Journalism
BT Journalism
RT Captions
Illustrations
Layout (Publications)
News Media
Newspapers
News Reporting
Photographs
Photography
Publications

Photometric Brightness
USE LUMINESCENCE

Photoreproduction
USE REPROGRAPHY

PHOTOSYNTHESIS *Aug. 1970*
CIJE: 42 RIE: 18 GC: 490
BT Photochemical Reactions
RT Botany
Ecology
Light
Metabolism
Plant Growth

PHRASE STRUCTURE *Jul. 1966*
CIJE: 242 RIE: 212 GC: 450
UF Constituent Structure
BT Syntax
RT Context Free Grammar
Deep Structure
Form Classes (Languages)
Kernel Sentences
Nouns
Prepositions
Pronouns
Suprasegmentals
Surface Structure
Transformational Generative Grammar

PHYSICAL ACTIVITIES *Jul. 1966*
CIJE: 507 RIE: 530 GC: 470
NT Athletics
Bicycling
Dance
Exercise
Horseback Riding

Lifting
Running
Underwater Diving
BT Activities
RT Adapted Physical Education
Health Activities
Movement Education
Physical Education
Physical Recreation Programs
Playground Activities
Recreational Activities

PHYSICAL ACTIVITY LEVEL *Mar. 1978*
CIJE: 138 RIE: 60 GC: 120
SN Extent of motor behavior manifested by an individual or group
UF Activity Level (Motor Behavior)
BT Behavior
RT Biomechanics
Exercise Physiology
Human Body
Hyperactivity
Motor Development
Motor Reactions
Physical Development
Physiology

PHYSICAL CHARACTERISTICS *Jul. 1966*
CIJE: 395 RIE: 277 GC: 120
NT Body Height
Body Weight
Lateral Dominance
Muscular Strength
Neurological Organization
Race
Sex
BT Individual Characteristics
RT Chronological Age
Downs Syndrome
Interpersonal Attraction
Maturity (Individuals)
Physical Development
Physical Disabilities
Physical Health
Racial Differences
Sex Differences

Physical Conditioning
USE PHYSICAL FITNESS

Physical Design Needs (1968 1980)
USE DESIGN REQUIREMENTS

PHYSICAL DEVELOPMENT *Jul. 1966*
CIJE: 352 RIE: 427 GC: 120
NT Motor Development
BT Individual Development
RT Body Height
Body Weight
Chronological Age
Developmental Stages
Lateral Dominance
Muscular Strength
Neurological Organization
Perceptual Development
Physical Activity Level
Physical Characteristics
Physical Disabilities
Physical Health
Prenatal Influences
School Readiness

PHYSICAL DISABILITIES *Mar. 1980*
CIJE: 1151 RIE: 1308 GC: 220
SN Disorders that result in significantly reduced bodily function, mobility, or endurance (note: avoid misindexing "hearing impairments" or "visual impairments" with this term)
UF Crippled Children (1968 1980)
Orthopedically Handicapped (1968 1980)
Physical Handicaps (1966 1980)
Physically Handicapped (1966 1980)
NT Amputations
Cleft Palate
Heart Disorders
Neurological Impairments
BT Disabilities
RT Exceptional Persons
Mental Disorders
Mobility Aids
Physical Characteristics
Physical Development
Physical Health
Physical Mobility
Physical Therapy
Prostheses
Rehabilitation
Special Health Problems
Travel Training
Wheelchairs

PHYSICAL DIVISIONS (GEOGRAPHIC) *Jul. 1966*
CIJE: 9 RIE: 18 GC: 550
BT Geographic Regions
RT Geography
Physical Geography
Political Divisions (Geographic)

PHYSICAL EDUCATION *Jul. 1966*
CIJE: 1855 RIE: 1747 GC: 470
NT Adapted Physical Education
Movement Education
BT Education
RT Athletic Coaches
Athletic Equipment
Athletic Fields
Athletics
College Athletics
Dance Education
Exercise Physiology
Experiential Learning
Muscular Strength
Physical Activities
Physical Education Facilities
Physical Education Teachers
Physical Fitness
Physical Recreation Programs
Recreational Activities
Running
School Health Services
Sport Psychology
Sportsmanship
Womens Athletics

PHYSICAL EDUCATION FACILITIES *Jul. 1966*
CIJE: 147 RIE: 159 GC: 920
BT Educational Facilities
RT Athletic Equipment
Athletic Fields
Athletics
Field Houses
Gymnasiums
Locker Rooms
Parks
Physical Education
Playgrounds
Recreational Facilities
Swimming Pools

PHYSICAL EDUCATION TEACHERS *Nov. 1982*
CIJE: 99 RIE: 77 GC: 360
UF Physical Educators
BT Teachers
RT Athletic Coaches
Athletics
Physical Education

Physical Educators
USE PHYSICAL EDUCATION TEACHERS

PHYSICAL ENVIRONMENT *Jul. 1966*
CIJE: 545 RIE: 654 GC: 920
NT Acoustical Environment
Climate
Thermal Environment
Visual Environment
BT Environment
RT Architectural Research
Climate Control
Conservation (Environment)
Crowding
Depleted Resources
Design Requirements
Earth Science
Endangered Species
Environmental Influences
Environmental Research
Environmental Standards
Gravity (Physics)
Hazardous Materials
Human Factors Engineering
Interior Design
Interior Space
Natural Resources
Poisons
Pollution
Pressure (Physics)
Quality Of Life
Radiation
Sanitation
Water
Water Quality
Weather
Wildlife
Wind (Meteorology)

PHYSICAL EXAMINATIONS *Jul. 1966*
CIJE: 152 RIE: 64 GC: 210
SN Medical inspections of individuals to determine their physical condition, including the detection of present or potential dysfunction
UF Physical Tests
BT Medical Evaluation
RT Auditory Tests
Clinical Diagnosis
Diagnostic Tests
Physical Health
Screening Tests
Vision Tests

Physical Exercise
USE EXERCISE

Physical Facilities (1966 1980)
USE FACILITIES

PHYSICAL FITNESS *Jul. 1966*
CIJE: 681 RIE: 612 GC: 210
UF Physical Conditioning
Physical Performance
BT Physical Health
RT Aerobics
Athletic Equipment
Athletics
Calisthenics
Exercise
Fatigue (Biology)
Heart Rate
Muscular Strength
Physical Education
Physical Recreation Programs
Running
Sport Psychology

PHYSICAL GEOGRAPHY *Jul. 1966*
CIJE: 174 RIE: 196 GC: 490
BT Earth Science
Geography
RT Geographic Distribution
Geographic Location
Geographic Regions
Geology
Mineralogy
Oceanography
Physical Divisions (Geographic)
Plate Tectonics
Seismology
Water
Wind (Meteorology)

Physical Handicaps (1966 1980)
USE PHYSICAL DISABILITIES

PHYSICAL HEALTH *Jul. 1966*
CIJE: 501 RIE: 591 GC: 210
NT Dental Health
Physical Fitness
BT Health
RT Alcoholism
Allergy
Anemia
Anorexia Nervosa
Asbestos
Asthma
Bulimia
Cancer
Communicable Diseases
Diabetes
Diseases
Drinking Water
Eating Habits
Exercise Physiology
Failure To Thrive
Hazardous Materials
Heart Disorders
Heart Rate
Hygiene
Hypertension
Lead Poisoning
Medicine
Midlife Transitions
Nutrition
Obesity
Occupational Diseases
Pests
Physical Characteristics
Physical Development
Physical Disabilities
Physical Examinations
Physical Therapy
Poisoning
Pollution
Psychosomatic Disorders
Public Health
Rubella
Sanitary Facilities
Sanitation
Seizures
Sickle Cell Anemia
Smoking
Special Health Problems
Surgery
Tissue Donors
Venereal Diseases
Ventilation

PHYSICAL MOBILITY *Mar. 1980*
CIJE: 37 RIE: 62 GC: 220
SN Individual's ability to move within his or her immediate environment (note: for demographic or geographic mobility, use "migration" -- prior to mar80, "architectural barriers" was frequently used to index this concept)
NT Visually Handicapped Mobility
BT Mobility
RT Accessibility (For Disabled)
Architecture
Building Design
Campus Planning
Crowding
Design Requirements
Educational Facilities Design
Educational Facilities Planning
Mobility Aids
Older Adults
Physical Disabilities
Space Utilization
Structural Elements (Construction)
Travel Training
Wheelchairs

Physical Optics
USE OPTICS

Physical Performance
USE PHYSICAL FITNESS

Physical Pressure
USE PRESSURE (PHYSICS)

PHYSICAL RECREATION PROGRAMS *Jul. 1966*
CIJE: 94 RIE: 108 GC: 470
BT Recreational Programs
RT Athletic Equipment
Athletic Fields
Athletics
Field Houses
Gymnasiums
Physical Activities
Physical Education
Physical Fitness
Playground Activities
School Health Services

PHYSICAL SCIENCES *Jul. 1966*
CIJE: 1404 RIE: 806 GC: 490
NT Astronomy
Chemistry
Crystallography
Earth Science
Physics
Spectroscopy
BT Natural Sciences
RT Aerospace Technology
Atomic Structure
Biochemistry
Biophysics
Chemical Bonding
Conservation Education
Engineering Technology
Molecular Structure
Nuclear Technology
Radiation Biology
Space Sciences

Physical Strength
USE MUSCULAR STRENGTH

Physical Tests
USE PHYSICAL EXAMINATIONS

PHYSICAL THERAPISTS *Jul. 1966*
CIJE: 22 RIE: 34 GC: 210
BT Therapists
RT Physical Therapy
Physical Therapy Aides

PHYSICAL THERAPY *Jul. 1966*
CIJE: 79 RIE: 92 GC: 210
SN Treatment of disability, injury, or disease through such means as exercise, massage, body manipulation, heat, light, water, etc.
BT Therapy
RT Allied Health Occupations
Amputations
Dance Therapy
Medical Services
Occupational Therapy
Osteopathy
Physical Disabilities
Physical Health
Physical Therapists
Physical Therapy Aides
Rehabilitation
Respiratory Therapy
Therapeutic Recreation

PHYSICAL THERAPY AIDES *Jul. 1969*
CIJE: 4 RIE: 27 GC: 210
UF Physical Therapy Attendants
BT Allied Health Personnel
RT Physical Therapists
Physical Therapy

Physical Therapy Attendants
USE PHYSICAL THERAPY AIDES

Physically Handicapped (1966 1980)
USE PHYSICAL DISABILITIES

PHYSICIAN PATIENT RELATIONSHIP *Oct. 1979*
CIJE: 232 RIE: 82 GC: 210
SN Relationship between physicians and persons in their care that affects mutual trust and understanding
UF Doctor Patient Relationship
Patient Physician Relationship
BT Interpersonal Relationship
RT Counselor Client Relationship
Helping Relationship
Medical Care Evaluation
Medical Evaluation
Medical Services
Patient Education
Patients
Physicians
Psychiatric Services
Psychiatrists
Therapeutic Environment

PHYSICIANS *Jul. 1966*
CIJE: 1049 RIE: 527 GC: 210
UF Medical Doctors
Preceptors (Medicine) #
NT Foreign Medical Graduates
Psychiatrists
BT Health Personnel
Professional Personnel
RT Graduate Medical Education
Graduate Medical Students
Hospital Personnel
Medical Associations
Medical Consultants
Medical Services
Medical Vocabulary
Medicine
Physician Patient Relationship
Physicians Assistants

PHYSICIANS ASSISTANTS *Apr. 1972*
CIJE: 53 RIE: 72 GC: 210
SN Highly trained paraprofessionals who, under physicians' supervision, perform many health care activities usually carried out only by physicians
BT Allied Health Personnel
RT Medical Services
Nurse Practitioners
Physicians

Physicians In Training
USE GRADUATE MEDICAL STUDENTS

PHYSICS *Jul. 1966*
CIJE: 5227 RIE: 1279 GC: 490
UF Physics Curriculum (1966 1980) #
Physics Experiments (1966 1980) #
Physics Instruction (1966 1980) #
Physics Teachers (1967 1980) #
NT Biophysics
Electronics
Mechanics (Physics)
Nuclear Physics
Optics
Thermodynamics
BT Physical Sciences
RT Acceleration (Physics)
Acoustics
Atomic Structure
Atomic Theory
Crystallography
Diffusion (Physics)
Earth Science
Electricity
Energy
Force
Geophysics
Gravity (Physics)
Kinetic Molecular Theory
Lasers
Light
Luminescence
Magnets
Matter
Metallurgical Technicians
Metallurgy
Meteorology
Molecular Structure
Motion
Pressure (Physics)
Radiation
Radiation Biology
Radioisotopes
Radiology
Relativity
Scientific Research
Spectroscopy
Vectors (Mathematics)

Physics Curriculum (1966 1980)
USE PHYSICS; SCIENCE CURRICULUM

Physics Experiments (1966 1980)
USE PHYSICS; SCIENCE EXPERIMENTS

Physics Instruction (1966 1980)
USE PHYSICS; SCIENCE INSTRUCTION

Physics Teachers (1967 1980)
USE PHYSICS; SCIENCE TEACHERS

Physiological Chemistry
USE BIOCHEMISTRY

Physiological Psychology
USE PSYCHOPHYSIOLOGY

PHYSIOLOGY *Jul. 1966*
CIJE: 987 RIE: 514 GC: 490
NT Exercise Physiology
Psychophysiology
BT Biological Sciences
RT Allergy
Anatomy
Asthma
Biochemistry
Biofeedback
Biology
Biomechanics
Biophysics
Birth
Blood Circulation
Cardiovascular System
Culturing Techniques
Cytology
Death
Diabetes
Embryology
Enzymes
Evolution
Heart Rate
Human Body
Hygiene
Medicine
Metabolism
Microbiology
Motor Reactions
Neurological Organization
Neurology
Nucleic Acids
Nutrition
Pathology
Perception
Physical Activity Level
Radiation Biology
Relaxation Training
Rh Factors
Scientific Research
Sedatives
Sensory Deprivation
Stimulants
Stress Variables
Toxicology
Zoology

PIAGETIAN THEORY *Apr. 1986*
CIJE: 246 RIE: 237 GC: 810
SN Theory of children's intellectual development (postulated by swiss developmental psychologist jean piaget) that describes a universal sequence of four distinct mental stages--sensorimotor, preoperational thought, concrete operations, and formal operations--through which children progress from birth to maturity
BT Theories
RT Child Development
Cognitive Development
Cognitive Processes
Cognitive Psychology
Concept Formation
Developmental Psychology
Developmental Stages
Epistemology
Formal Operations
Intellectual Development
Learning Theories
Logical Thinking

Pictorial Journalism
USE PHOTOJOURNALISM

PICTORIAL STIMULI *Jul. 1966*
CIJE: 652 RIE: 424 GC: 110
BT Visual Stimuli
RT Electrical Stimuli
Projective Measures
Tachistoscopes
Visual Learning
Visual Measures

Pictorial Tests
USE VISUAL MEASURES

PICTURE BOOKS *Sep. 1980*
CIJE: 192 RIE: 66 GC: 720
SN Books (usually but not necessarily for children) in which illustrations are essential to the presentation, either coordinated closely with the text or used alone without text
BT Books
RT Childrens Literature
Illustrations

PIDGINS *Jul. 1966*
CIJE: 32 RIE: 81 GC: 440
SN Simplified forms of speech, usually mixtures of two or more languages, that have rudimentary grammar and vocabulary and are used for communication between groups speaking different languages
BT Languages
Language Variation
RT Creoles
Linguistic Borrowing

Pilipino
USE TAGALOG

Pilot Programs
USE PILOT PROJECTS

PILOT PROJECTS *Jul. 1966*
CIJE: 528 RIE: 1402 GC: 810
SN Organized exploratory or trial undertakings conducted as preparation for larger, more involved programs (note: as of oct81, use as a minor descriptor for examples of pilot projects -- use as a major descriptor only as the subject of a document)
UF Pilot Programs
BT Programs
RT Adoption (Ideas)
Experimental Programs
Feasibility Studies
Research
Research Methodology

Pilot Training
USE FLIGHT TRAINING

Ping Pong
USE TABLE TENNIS

Pipe Fitting
USE PLUMBING

PLACE OF RESIDENCE *Jan. 1978*
CIJE: 122 RIE: 254 GC: 550
SN Locality of habitation including both site (geographic region) and type (housing)
UF Residential Location
RT Community
Community Characteristics
Cultural Traits
Demography
Environment
Family Mobility
Geographic Location
Geographic Regions
Housing
In State Students
Land Settlement
Migration
Neighborhoods
Out Of State Students
Population Distribution
Relocation
Residence Requirements
Residential Patterns
Rural Urban Differences
Social Characteristics

PLACE VALUE *Aug. 1986*
CIJE: 8 RIE: 1 GC: 480
SN The value of a position in a number, e.g., the decimal 37 has three ten's and seven one's
BT Number Concepts
RT Arithmetic
Numbers

PLACEMENT *Jul. 1966*
CIJE: 322 RIE: 239 GC: 520
NT Advanced Placement
Age Grade Placement
Job Placement
Mainstreaming
Student Placement
RT Admission (School)
Adoption
Foster Family
Screening Tests

PLAGIARISM *Jan. 1969*
CIJE: 72 RIE: 23 GC: 530
BT Stealing
RT Cheating
Codes Of Ethics
Copyrights
Discipline Problems
Ethics
Intellectual Property
Moral Issues
Writing (Composition)

Planar Area
USE AREA

PLANE GEOMETRY *Jul. 1966*
CIJE: 46 RIE: 21 GC: 480
BT Geometry
RT Analytic Geometry
Area
Solid Geometry

PLANETARIUMS *Aug. 1968*
CIJE: 83 RIE: 22 GC: 920
BT Facilities
RT Astronomy
Earth Science
Educational Facilities
Lunar Research
Recreational Facilities
Science Facilities
Science Laboratories
Science Teaching Centers

= Two or more Descriptors are used to represent this term.
The term's main entry shows the appropriate coordination.

Scientific Research
Space Exploration
Space Sciences

Planetary Exploration
USE SPACE EXPLORATION

PLANNED COMMUNITIES *Mar. 1980*
CIJE: 16 RIE: 29 GC: 550
UF Planned Community (1966 1980)
BT Community
RT Housing
Planning
Urban Renewal

Planned Community (1966 1980)
USE PLANNED COMMUNITIES

PLANNING *Jul. 1966*
CIJE: 1217 RIE: 2279 GC: 110
SN The process of determining objectives and the means (activities, procedures, resources, etc.) for attaining them (note: use a more specific term if possible)
UF Administrative Planning
Organizational Plans
NT Budgeting
Career Planning
Color Planning
Community Planning
Cooperative Planning
Desegregation Plans
Educational Planning
Estate Planning
Facility Planning
Family Planning
Language Planning
Library Planning
Long Range Planning
Policy Formation
Regional Planning
Scheduling
Social Planning
Statewide Planning
Urban Planning
RT Administration
Building Plans
Committees
Coordination
Critical Path Method
Delphi Technique
Design
Development
Flow Charts
Futures (Of Society)
Guidelines
Holistic Approach
Lesson Plans
Master Plans
Needs Assessment
Operations Research
Organization
Organizational Objectives
Planned Communities
Planning Commissions
Specifications
Systems Approach
Time Management
Zoning

PLANNING COMMISSIONS *Jul. 1966*
CIJE: 54 RIE: 126 GC: 610
SN Elected or appointed committees that formulate courses of action based on community, state, or national needs
UF City Wide Commissions (1966 1980) #
BT Public Agencies
RT Advisory Committees
Blue Ribbon Commissions
Community Planning
Long Range Planning
Master Plans
Planning
Regional Planning
Social Planning
Statewide Planning
Urban Planning

Planning Meetings (1966 1980)
USE MEETINGS

Plant Biology
USE BOTANY

Plant Diseases
USE PLANT PATHOLOGY

PLANT GROWTH *Jul. 1966*
CIJE: 154 RIE: 102 GC: 410
BT Development
RT Agricultural Production
Agronomy
Biochemistry
Botany
Embryology
Fertilizers
Greenhouses
Herbicides
Horticulture
Insecticides
Ornamental Horticulture
Photosynthesis
Plant Pathology
Wildlife

PLANT IDENTIFICATION *Jul. 1966*
CIJE: 57 RIE: 94 GC: 410
BT Identification
RT Botany
Floriculture
Horticulture
Landscaping
Ornamental Horticulture

PLANT PATHOLOGY *Jul. 1966*
CIJE: 20 RIE: 48 GC: 410
UF Plant Diseases
BT Pathology
RT Agronomy
Botany
Endangered Species
Floriculture
Herbicides
Plant Growth

PLANT PROPAGATION *Jul. 1966*
CIJE: 40 RIE: 48 GC: 410
RT Botany
Floriculture
Grounds Keepers
Horticulture
Nursery Workers (Horticulture)
Ornamental Horticulture

PLANT SCIENCE (1967 1980) *Mar. 1980*
CIJE: 110 RIE: 98 GC: 410
SN Invalid descriptor -- used for both "agronomy" and "botany" -- see those descriptors for the concepts

Planting (1966 1980)
USE HORTICULTURE

PLASTICS *Jul. 1966*
CIJE: 81 RIE: 58 GC: 910
RT Art Materials
Handicrafts
Industrial Arts
Patternmaking
Polymers

PLATE TECTONICS *Oct. 1984*
CIJE: 30 RIE: 38 GC: 490
SN Branch of geophysics and seismology concerned with continental movements, based on the theory that the earth's surface is comprised of vast crustal blocks that float across the mantle, with seismic activity and volcanism occurring primarily along the periphery of these blocks
BT Geophysics
Seismology
RT Earthquakes
Earth Science
Geology
Oceanography
Physical Geography

Platform Diving
USE DIVING

PLATONIC CRITICISM (1970 1980) *Mar. 1980*
CIJE: 6 RIE: 3 GC: 430
SN Invalid descriptor -- originally intended as a literary term, but used indiscriminately in indexing -- see "literary criticism" and the identifier "plato of athens" for literary documents

PLATONISM *Sep. 1969*
CIJE: 25 RIE: 8 GC: 430
SN Philosophical theory characterized by the view that abstract universals (such as "truth" and "beauty") exist apart from the material world, which is but their pale and fleeting reflection, and that through reason the human mind has the capacity to understand them (note: also see the identifier "plato of athens")
BT Philosophy
RT Classical Literature
Romanticism

PLAY *Jan. 1971*
CIJE: 826 RIE: 656 GC: 470
SN Pleasurable activity carried on for its own sake
UF Childrens Play
Free Play
NT Pretend Play
BT Activities
RT Behavior
Children
Childrens Games
Class Activities
Dramatic Play
Games
Playground Activities
Play Therapy
Recreational Activities
Toys

PLAY THERAPY *Jul. 1966*
CIJE: 121 RIE: 55 GC: 230
UF Therapeutic Play
BT Therapeutic Recreation
RT Art Therapy
Dance Therapy
Music Therapy
Play

PLAYGROUND ACTIVITIES *Jul. 1966*
CIJE: 83 RIE: 67 GC: 470
BT Recreational Activities
RT Athletics
Childrens Games
Outdoor Activities
Physical Activities
Physical Recreation Programs
Play

PLAYGROUNDS *Jul. 1966*
CIJE: 154 RIE: 151 GC: 920
UF Lighted Playgrounds (1966 1980)
BT Recreational Facilities
RT Athletic Fields
Physical Education Facilities
Trails

Plays (Theatrical)
USE DRAMA

PLAYWRITING *Aug. 1968*
CIJE: 125 RIE: 72 GC: 430
BT Writing (Composition)
RT Creative Writing
Dramatics
Literary Devices
Scripts
Theater Arts

PLUMBING *Jul. 1966*
CIJE: 8 RIE: 131 GC: 640
UF Pipe Fitting
BT Technology
RT Building Trades
Sanitary Facilities

Pluralization
USE PLURALS

PLURALS *Sep. 1968*
CIJE: 48 RIE: 38 GC: 450
SN Grammatical forms used to denote more than one
UF Pluralization
BT Morphemes
RT Form Classes (Languages)
Spelling

Plurilingualism
USE MULTILINGUALISM

PNEUMATIC FORMS *Aug. 1972*
CIJE: 3 RIE: 1 GC: 920
SN Structures used as forms for placing concrete, reinforced and/or foam plastic materials
BT Air Structures

Pocket Calculators
USE CALCULATORS

Pocket Computers
USE MICROCOMPUTERS

PODIATRY *Oct. 1979*
CIJE: 44 RIE: 25 GC: 210
SN Medical treatment or study of foot disorders
BT Medicine
RT Medical Services

POETRY *Jul. 1966*
CIJE: 1905 RIE: 1141 GC: 430
UF Prosody (Literary)
Versification (1969 1980)
NT Epics
Haiku
Lyric Poetry
BT Literature
RT Antithesis
Choral Speaking
Chronicles
Creative Writing
Descriptive Writing
Drama
Fiction
Folk Culture
Humanism
Language Rhythm
Literary Genres
Literary Styles
Local Color Writing
Monologs
Parallelism (Literary)
Pastoral Literature
Poets
Prose
Puns
Tales
Tragedy
Writing (Composition)

POETS *Jun. 1969*
CIJE: 187 RIE: 87 GC: 430
UF Bards
Lyric Poets
Minnesingers
Troubadours
BT Authors
RT Epics
Literature
Lyric Poetry
Poetry

POISONING *Mar. 1980*
CIJE: 27 RIE: 53 GC: 210
NT Lead Poisoning
BT Diseases
RT Physical Health
Poisons
Pollution
Radiation Effects
Safety
Special Health Problems
Toxicology

POISONS *Sep. 1982*
CIJE: 22 RIE: 8 GC: 210
SN Chemical or organic substances that can cause injury to health or destroy life
UF Toxic Substances
Toxins
NT Pesticides
BT Hazardous Materials
RT Ecological Factors
Environmental Standards
Physical Environment
Poisoning
Pollution
Public Health
Toxicology
Wastes

POLICE *Jul. 1966*
CIJE: 185 RIE: 343 GC: 640
UF Law Enforcement Officers
Police Costs (1966 1980) #
State Police (1966 1980)
BT Government Employees
RT Alarm Systems
Crime
Crime Prevention
Criminal Law
Emergency Squad Personnel
Government (Administrative Body)
Immigration Inspectors
Law Enforcement
Parole Officers
Police Action
Police Community Relationship
Police Education
Police School Relationship
Security Personnel

POLICE ACTION *Jul. 1966*
CIJE: 69 RIE: 111 GC: 610
NT Search And Seizure
BT Law Enforcement
RT Alarm Systems
Crime
Crime Prevention
Police
Police Community Relationship
Police Education
Police School Relationship
School Security

POLICE COMMUNITY RELATIONSHIP *Jul. 1966*
CIJE: 69 RIE: 116 GC: 520
UF Community Police Relationship
BT Relationship
RT Community
Community Cooperation
Community Coordination
Crime Prevention
Police
Police Action
Police School Relationship

Police Costs (1966 1980)
USE COSTS; POLICE

POLICE EDUCATION *Mar. 1980*
CIJE: 35 RIE: 85 GC: 400
SN Education that prepares individuals for entrance into police work or gives added instruction or training to employed law-enforcement officers
UF Police Seminars (1966 1980)
BT Education
RT Criminal Law
Law Related Education
Police
Police Action

Police School Liaison
USE POLICE SCHOOL RELATIONSHIP

POLICE SCHOOL RELATIONSHIP *Jul. 1966*
CIJE: 90 RIE: 112 GC: 330
UF Police School Liaison
School Police Relationship
BT Relationship
RT Crime Prevention
Delinquency
Police
Police Action
Police Community Relationship
School Attitudes
Schools
School Security
Search And Seizure

Police Seminars (1966 1980)
USE POLICE EDUCATION

POLICY *Jul. 1966*
CIJE: 484 RIE: 723 GC: 330
SN Governing principles that serve as guidelines or rules for decision making and action in a given area (note: use a more specific term if possible)
NT Administrative Policy
Discipline Policy
Educational Policy
Financial Policy
Foreign Policy
Interdistrict Policies
Personnel Policy
Public Policy
School Policy
Transfer Policy
RT Policy Formation
Standards

POLICY FORMATION *Jul. 1966*
CIJE: 2506 RIE: 4089 GC: 330
SN Act of establishing principles to serve as guidelines for decision making and action
BT Planning
RT Administration
Advisory Committees
Blue Ribbon Commissions
College Governing Councils
Community Control
Decision Making
Delphi Technique
Governance
Governing Boards
Judgment Analysis Technique
Legislation
Master Plans
Mission Statements
Needs Assessment
Participative Decision Making
Policy
Politics
Position Papers
Self Evaluation (Groups)

Policy Statements
USE POSITION PAPERS

POLISH *Jul. 1966*
CIJE: 31 RIE: 86 GC: 440
BT Slavic Languages
RT Polish Literature

POLISH AMERICANS *Mar. 1972*
CIJE: 20 RIE: 47 GC: 560
BT Ethnic Groups
North Americans
RT Minority Groups

POLISH LITERATURE *Dec. 1969*
CIJE: 5 RIE: 5 GC: 430
BT Literature
RT Polish

Political Advocacy
USE LOBBYING

POLITICAL AFFILIATION *Jul. 1966*
CIJE: 142 RIE: 101 GC: 610
BT Group Membership
RT Government (Administrative Body)
Political Attitudes
Political Candidates
Political Issues
Political Socialization
Politics

POLITICAL ATTITUDES *Jul. 1966*
CIJE: 1470 RIE: 1017 GC: 610
SN Beliefs, opinions, attitudes, or values toward governmental actions, affairs, or practices
UF Civic Belief (1966 1980)
BT Attitudes
RT Activism
Authoritarianism
Citizenship
Colonialism
Community Attitudes
Conservatism
Credibility
Democratic Values
Dissent
Humanitarianism
Ideology
Imperialism
Liberalism
Marxism
Nationalism
Political Affiliation
Political Campaigns
Political Socialization
Politics
Public Opinion
Refugees
Regional Attitudes
Social Attitudes
Social Values
Terrorism
Totalitarianism
Values
Voting

POLITICAL CAMPAIGNS *Dec. 1985*
CIJE: 86 RIE: 42 GC: 610
SN Competitive efforts to win support of the voting public for candidates or ballot propositions
UF Election Campaigns
NT Presidential Campaigns (United States)
BT Politics
RT Advertising
Citizen Participation
Debate
Elections
Fund Raising
Government (Administrative Body)
Mass Media
Persuasive Discourse
Political Attitudes
Political Candidates
Political Influences
Political Issues
Voting

POLITICAL CANDIDATES *Dec. 1985*
CIJE: 22 RIE: 11 GC: 610
SN Persons seeking election or appointment to public office
UF Political Nominees
Presidential Candidates (United States) #
BT Groups
RT Board Candidates
Community Leaders
Debate
Elections
Government (Administrative Body)
Political Affiliation
Political Campaigns
Political Issues
Politics
Public Officials
Voting

POLITICAL DIVISIONS (GEOGRAPHIC) *Jul. 1966*
CIJE: 27 RIE: 43 GC: 610
NT American Indian Reservations
BT Geographic Regions
RT Colonialism
Geography
Imperialism
Nationalism
Physical Divisions (Geographic)
Treaties

Political Geography
USE HUMAN GEOGRAPHY

POLITICAL INFLUENCES *Jul. 1966*
CIJE: 1825 RIE: 1462 GC: 610
SN Factors directly or indirectly affecting political beliefs and/or behavior (note: prior to mar80, the instruction "political pressures, use political power" was carried in the thesaurus)
BT Influences
RT Lobbying
Political Campaigns
Political Issues
Political Power
Political Socialization
Politics
Social Change
Socioeconomic Influences

POLITICAL ISSUES *Jul. 1966*
CIJE: 1374 RIE: 1144 GC: 610
RT Blue Ribbon Commissions
Bond Issues
Controversial Issues (Course Content)
Elections
Legislation
Lobbying
Local Issues
Political Affiliation
Political Campaigns
Political Candidates
Political Influences
Political Power
Politics
Politics Of Education
Public Affairs Education
Social Problems
Voting

Political Nominees
USE POLITICAL CANDIDATES

POLITICAL POWER *Jul. 1966*
CIJE: 701 RIE: 565 GC: 610
SN Political control or authority over others (note: prior to mar80, this term was not restricted by a scope note)
RT Black Power
Imperialism
Lobbying
Marxism
Political Influences
Political Issues
Politics
Power Structure
Totalitarianism

Political Protest
USE ACTIVISM

Political Reform
USE SOCIAL ACTION

Political Refugees
USE REFUGEES

POLITICAL SCIENCE *Jul. 1966*
CIJE: 673 RIE: 775 GC: 400
BT Social Sciences
RT Area Studies
Authoritarianism
Capitalism
Communism
Constitutional History
Constitutional Law
Current Events
Diplomatic History
Elections
Elitism
Fascism
Foreign Policy
Human Geography
International Law
International Relations
International Studies
Marxism
Military Science
Political Socialization
Politics
Public Administration
Public Administration Education
Public Affairs Education
Revolution
Socialism
Social Science Research
Social Scientists
Social Studies
Totalitarianism
United States Government (Course)

POLITICAL SOCIALIZATION *Jul. 1966*
CIJE: 755 RIE: 496 GC: 520
SN Process by which political norms are transmitted through various social agents, e.g., school, parents, peer group, mass media, etc.
UF Politicalization
BT Socialization
RT Conservatism
Liberalism
Patriotism
Political Affiliation
Political Attitudes
Political Influences
Political Science
Social Attitudes
Social Change
Social Influences

Politicalization
USE POLITICAL SOCIALIZATION

POLITICS *Oct. 1971*
CIJE: 1312 RIE: 1061 GC: 610
SN Activities concerned with guiding or influencing governmental policy, including winning and holding control over a governing body
NT Political Campaigns
Politics Of Education
RT Community Control
Elections
Governance
Government (Administrative Body)
International Studies
Legislation
Lobbying

= Two or more Descriptors are used to represent this term.
The term's main entry shows the appropriate coordination.

Policy Formation
Political Affiliation
Political Attitudes
Political Candidates
Political Influences
Political Issues
Political Power
Political Science
Public Policy
Voting

POLITICS OF EDUCATION *Jun. 1983*
CIJE: 181 RIE: 208 GC: 330
SN Political aspects of governance and decision making within educational systems and institutions, and political activities related to education in general
UF Educational Politics
BT Politics
RT Board Administrator Relationship
Board Of Education Policy
Education
Educational Administration
Educational Finance
Educational Legislation
Educational Policy
Family School Relationship
Government School Relationship
Parent School Relationship
Political Issues
School Community Relationship
School Law
School Policy
School Role
Teacher Administrator Relationship

POLLUTION *Jul. 1969*
CIJE: 1237 RIE: 979 GC: 410
NT Air Pollution
Water Pollution
RT Chimneys
Climate
Disease Control
Diseases
Ecological Factors
Environmental Education
Environmental Influences
Environmental Standards
Hazardous Materials
Health
Lead Poisoning
Noise (Sound)
Physical Environment
Physical Health
Poisoning
Poisons
Public Health
Radiation Effects
Recycling
Solid Wastes
Urban Environment
Waste Disposal
Wastes
Waste Water

POLYGRAPHS *Jul. 1966*
CIJE: 4 RIE: 12 GC: 910
UF Lie Detectors
BT Electronic Equipment
Measurement Equipment
RT Crime
Instrumentation
Lying

POLYMERS *Aug. 1986*
CIJE: 69 RIE: GC: 490
SN Natural or synthetic substances of usually high molecular weight formed by the union of relatively light and simple molecules
BT Matter
RT Chemical Engineering
Chemical Reactions
Chemistry
Molecular Structure
Nucleic Acids
Organic Chemistry
Plastics

POMO *Apr. 1970*
CIJE: 2 RIE: 1 GC: 440
BT American Indian Languages

Poor
USE ECONOMICALLY DISADVANTAGED

Pop Culture
USE POPULAR CULTURE

POPULAR CULTURE *Sep. 1977*
CIJE: 274 RIE: 170 GC: 720
SN Artistic and commercial expressions which reach a majority of the people through mass media, mass production, or transportation
UF Mass Culture
Pop Culture
BT Culture
RT Art
Films
Literature
Mass Media
Music
Publications
Radio
Recreational Activities
Television

POPULARITY *Aug. 1986*
CIJE: 27 RIE: 16 GC: 520
SN Being commonly admired, approved, or sought after -- especially, the likability of individuals concurred among friends, associates, or acquaintances
RT Friendship
Interpersonal Competence
Peer Acceptance
Peer Relationship
Prestige
Social Desirability
Social Life
Social Status

Population Changes
USE POPULATION TRENDS

POPULATION DISTRIBUTION *Jul. 1966*
CIJE: 196 RIE: 554 GC: 550
UF Diffusion (1967 1982) (Populations)
NT Ethnic Distribution
Racial Distribution
BT Demography
RT Birth Rate
Community Size
Geographic Distribution
Human Geography
Incidence
Migration
Migration Patterns
Overpopulation
Place Of Residence
Population Growth
Population Trends
Racial Composition
Relocation
Residential Patterns
Rural Population
Rural To Urban Migration
Urban Population
Urban To Rural Migration
Urban To Suburban Migration

POPULATION EDUCATION *Feb. 1972*
CIJE: 204 RIE: 404 GC: 400
SN Transmission of knowledge about population processes and characteristics, the causes of population change and the consequences of that change for the individual and society
BT Education
RT Demography
Environmental Education
Family Planning
Human Capital

POPULATION GROWTH *Jul. 1966*
CIJE: 410 RIE: 721 GC: 550
SN Increase in the number of individuals in a given area (world, nation, or local region) due to either natural reproduction or resettlement
BT Demography
Development
RT Birth Rate
Community Size
Family Planning
Family Size
Overpopulation
Population Distribution
Population Trends
Rural Population
Social Influences
Urbanization
Urban Population

Population Minorities
USE MINORITY GROUPS

Population Movements
USE MIGRATION

Population Research
USE DEMOGRAPHY

Population Shifts
USE MIGRATION

POPULATION TRENDS *Jul. 1966*
CIJE: 565 RIE: 1443 GC: 550
UF Population Changes
NT Black Population Trends
BT Demography
RT Birth Rate
Cohort Analysis
Community Size
Family Planning
Family Size
Human Geography
Land Settlement
Migration
Migration Patterns
Occupational Mobility
Overpopulation
Population Distribution
Population Growth
Relocation
Residential Patterns
Rural Population
Rural To Urban Migration
Structural Unemployment
Trend Analysis
Urban Population
Urban To Rural Migration
Urban To Suburban Migration

PORNOGRAPHY *Oct. 1983*
CIJE: 30 RIE: 14 GC: 720
SN Visual, written, or oral communication intended explicitly to promote sexual excitement -- pornography is often distinguished from erotic material in general by its exclusively prurient intent, its lack of redeeming artistic/literary value, and its commercial motivation
RT Obscenity
Sexuality

Portable Computers
USE MICROCOMPUTERS

Portable Facilities
USE RELOCATABLE FACILITIES

PORTFOLIOS (BACKGROUND MATERIALS) *Jun. 1978*
CIJE: 57 RIE: 79 GC: 330
SN Collections of records, letters of reference, work samples, etc. documenting skills, capabilities, and past experiences
BT Credentials
RT Admission (School)
Certification
College Applicants
Evaluation Methods
Experiential Learning
Informal Assessment
Job Applicants
Job Application
Personnel Evaluation
Personnel Selection
Profiles
Qualifications
Resumes (Personal)
Student Evaluation
Student Records

PORTUGUESE *Jul. 1966*
CIJE: 94 RIE: 177 GC: 440
BT Romance Languages

PORTUGUESE AMERICANS *Mar. 1976*
CIJE: 4 RIE: 31 GC: 560
BT Ethnic Groups
Hispanic Americans
RT Hispanic American Culture

POSITION PAPERS *Mar. 1980*
CIJE: 279 RIE: 491 GC: 730
SN Statements of official or organizational viewpoints, often recommending a particular course of action
UF Policy Statements
NT Mission Statements
BT Reports
RT Lobbying
Needs Assessment
Opinion Papers
Policy Formation

POSITIVE REINFORCEMENT *Jul. 1966*
CIJE: 614 RIE: 485 GC: 110
BT Reinforcement
RT Incentives
Negative Reinforcement
Self Reward
Social Reinforcement

Post Coordinate Indexes
USE COORDINATE INDEXES

Post Doctoral Education (1967 1980)
USE POSTDOCTORAL EDUCATION

Post High School Education
USE POSTSECONDARY EDUCATION

POST HIGH SCHOOL GUIDANCE *Jul. 1966*
CIJE: 23 RIE: 76 GC: 240
SN Guidance services for in- or out-of-school youth, designed to help them with future plans for postsecondary education, or for employment
BT Guidance
RT Admissions Counseling
Career Guidance
College Preparation
Educational Counseling
High School Graduates
High Schools
Postsecondary Education
School Counseling

Post Secondary Education (1967 1978)
USE POSTSECONDARY EDUCATION

Post Testing (1966 1980)
USE PRETESTS POSTTESTS

POSTDOCTORAL EDUCATION *Mar. 1980*
CIJE: 49 RIE: 115 GC: 340
SN Research and study beyond the doctoral degree, usually on special projects
UF Post Doctoral Education (1967 1980)
BT Higher Education
RT Doctoral Programs
Graduate Study
Professional Education
Research
Specialization

POSTSECONDARY EDUCATION *Jan. 1979*
CIJE: 3544 RIE: 11709 GC: 340
SN All education beyond the secondary level -- includes learning activities and experiences beyond the compulsory school attendance age with the exception of adult basic education and high school equivalency programs (note: appears in the list of mandatory educational level descriptors -- before apr75, restricted to education beyond grade 12 and less than the baccalaureate level)
UF Grade 13 (1970 1980)
Grade 14 (1970 1980)
Post High School Education
Post Secondary Education (1967 1978)
Postsecondary Instructional Level
Tertiary Education
NT Higher Education
Library Education
BT Education
RT Academic Advising
Adult Education
Colleges
Community Colleges
Continuing Education
Corporate Education
Noncampus Colleges
Nontraditional Students
Post High School Guidance
Postsecondary Education As A Field Of Study
Pretechnology Programs
Student Financial Aid
Technical Education
Technical Institutes
Two Year Colleges
Universities
Vocational Education
Vocational Schools
Womens Education

= Two or more Descriptors are used to represent this term.
The term's main entry shows the appropriate coordination.

POSTSECONDARY EDUCATION AS A FIELD OF STUDY *Jan. 1979*
CIJE: 71 RIE: 92 GC: 400
SN The formal examination or study of postsecondary education -- leads to a masters or doctoral degree in higher/postsecondary education with concentrations in college research, administration, teaching, etc. (originally added to the thesaurus in jul77 with "postsecondary" as two words)
UF Higher Education As A Field Of Study
BT College Curriculum
Graduate Study
RT College Faculty
Education Courses
Education Majors
Higher Education
Postsecondary Education
Professional Education
Schools Of Education
Teacher Educator Education
Teacher Educators

Postsecondary Instructional Level
USE POSTSECONDARY EDUCATION

Posture Development
USE HUMAN POSTURE

Posture Patterns
USE HUMAN POSTURE

Potable Water
USE DRINKING WATER

POTENTIAL DROPOUTS *Jul. 1966*
CIJE: 74 RIE: 201 GC: 360
BT Groups
RT Dropout Characteristics
Dropout Prevention
Dropouts
High Risk Students

POTENTIOMETERS (INSTRUMENTS) *Jan. 1970*
CIJE: 12 RIE: 1 GC: 910
SN Instruments used to measure electromotive forces
BT Measurement Equipment
RT Electric Circuits
Electricity

Pottery
USE CERAMICS

POVERTY *Mar. 1980*
CIJE: 620 RIE: 1156 GC: 530
SN Lack of means to acquire material needs or comforts
UF Economic Disadvantagement (1966 1980)
Economic Insecurity
Economic Plight
Poverty Factors #
Poverty Research (1970 1980)
BT Economic Status
RT Disadvantaged Environment
Economically Disadvantaged
Homeless People
Hunger
Inflation (Economics)
Lower Class
Low Income
Low Income Groups
Poverty Areas
Poverty Programs
Slums
Underemployment
Unemployment

POVERTY AREAS *Mar. 1980*
CIJE: 92 RIE: 306 GC: 550
SN Geographic areas or regions that are characterized by economic hardship
UF Depressed Areas (Geographic) (1966 1980)
Economically Depressed Areas
NT Slums
BT Geographic Regions
RT Disadvantaged Environment
Low Income Counties
Low Income States
Poverty

Poverty Factors
USE ECONOMIC FACTORS; POVERTY

POVERTY PROGRAMS *Jul. 1966*
CIJE: 126 RIE: 376 GC: 620
UF Anti Poverty Programs
BT Programs
RT Low Income
Poverty
Welfare Services

Poverty Research (1970 1980)
USE POVERTY

Poverty Stricken
USE ECONOMICALLY DISADVANTAGED

Power Mechanics (1969 1980)
USE POWER TECHNOLOGY

POWER STRUCTURE *Jul. 1966*
CIJE: 1170 RIE: 1088 GC: 520
UF Authority Structure
BT Organization
RT Administrative Organization
Black Power
Group Structure
Informal Organization
Management Teams
Middle Management
Organizational Climate
Organizational Development
Participative Decision Making
Personal Autonomy
Political Power
Professional Autonomy
Social Control
Social Exchange Theory
Social Structure

POWER TECHNOLOGY *Mar. 1980*
CIJE: 91 RIE: 296 GC: 490
SN Study and/or application of energy transfer or generation processes
UF Energy Technology
Power Mechanics (1969 1980)
NT Nuclear Technology
BT Technology
RT Alternative Energy Sources
Auto Mechanics
Aviation Mechanics
Chemical Engineering
Electricity
Energy
Energy Occupations
Engineering Technology
Engines
Fluid Mechanics
Fuels
Geothermal Energy
Industrial Arts
Small Engine Mechanics
Solar Energy
Utilities
Wind Energy

Power Transfer Systems
USE KINETICS

PRACTICAL ARTS *Jul. 1966*
CIJE: 33 RIE: 64 GC: 400
SN Functional curricula usually employing a performance based method of learning and generally associated with the subject areas of business education, home economics, industrial arts, and health and recreation -- emphasizes preparation for everyday life rather than vocational training
RT Agricultural Skills
Business Skills
Consumer Education
Daily Living Skills
Experiential Learning
Homemaking Skills
Industrial Arts
Practical Nursing

Practical Mathematics (1966 1980)
USE MATHEMATICAL APPLICATIONS

Practical Music
USE APPLIED MUSIC

Practical Nurses (1967 1981)
USE NURSES; PRACTICAL NURSING

PRACTICAL NURSING *Jul. 1966*
CIJE: 24 RIE: 76 GC: 210
UF Practical Nurses (1967 1981) #
Vocational Nursing
BT Nursing
RT Allied Health Occupations
Nursing Homes
Practical Arts

Practice Teaching
USE STUDENT TEACHING

PRACTICUM PAPERS *Mar. 1980*
CIJE: 1 RIE: 3 GC: 720
SN Written presentations used to satisfy academic degree requirements for practicums (note: corresponds to pubtype code 043 -- do not use except as the subject of a document)
BT Reports
RT Doctoral Dissertations
Masters Theses
Practicums

PRACTICUM SUPERVISION *Jan. 1969*
CIJE: 187 RIE: 149 GC: 310
UF Preceptors (Medicine) #
BT Supervision
RT Clinical Experience
Clinical Teaching (Health Professions)
Cooperating Teachers
Counselor Educators
Field Experience Programs
Internship Programs
Laboratory Training
Medical School Faculty
Practicums
Student Teacher Supervisors
Student Teaching
Teacher Supervision

PRACTICUMS *Jul. 1966*
CIJE: 427 RIE: 468 GC: 350
SN Supervised academic exercises consisting of study and practical work
NT Office Practice
BT Courses
RT Clinical Experience
Clinical Teaching (Health Professions)
Cooperative Education
Counselor Training
Experiential Learning
Field Experience Programs
Internship Programs
Laboratory Training
Microcounseling
Practicum Papers
Practicum Supervision
Student Teaching

PRAGMATICS *Aug. 1977*
CIJE: 199 RIE: 154 GC: 450
SN The study of the aspects of meaning in language that are related to the use of language in a natural context
BT Semiotics
RT Discourse Analysis
Language Patterns
Language Usage
Semantics
Sociolinguistics
Speech Acts
Syntax

Preachers
USE CLERGY

Preadolescence
USE PREADOLESCENTS

PREADOLESCENTS *Nov. 1982*
CIJE: 193 RIE: 66 GC: 120
SN Approximately 9-12 years of age
UF Preadolescence
BT Children
RT Adolescents
Intermediate Grades
Youth

Preceptors (Medicine)
USE PHYSICIANS; PRACTICUM SUPERVISION

Preceptorships (Medicine)
USE CLINICAL EXPERIENCE

Precision Ratio
USE RELEVANCE (INFORMATION RETRIEVAL)

PRECISION TEACHING *Sep. 1971*
CIJE: 33 RIE: 32 GC: 310
SN Teaching method, based on behavior modification, that uses daily measurement and charting procedures as reinforcement for learning
BT Teaching Methods
RT Behavior Rating Scales
Charts
Educational Testing
Evaluation Methods
Experience Charts
Profiles
Student Evaluation

Precollege Level
USE HIGH SCHOOLS

PREDICTION *Jul. 1966*
CIJE: 1510 RIE: 1290 GC: 820
SN Process or act of foretelling future events, conditions, outcomes, or trends on the basis of current information
UF Achievement Prediction #
Forecast
NT Employment Projections
Enrollment Projections
Grade Prediction
RT Delphi Technique
Estimation (Mathematics)
Expectation
Futures (Of Society)
Long Range Planning
Predictive Measurement
Probability
Regression (Statistics)
Reliability
Risk
Social Indicators

Predictive Ability (Testing) (1966 1980)
USE PREDICTIVE MEASUREMENT

PREDICTIVE MEASUREMENT *Jul. 1966*
CIJE: 1028 RIE: 1217 GC: 820
SN Use of tests, inventories, or other measures to determine or estimate future events, conditions, outcomes, or trends
UF Predictive Ability (Testing) (1966 1980)
BT Measurement
RT Aptitude Tests
Bayesian Statistics
College Entrance Examinations
Estimation (Mathematics)
Expectancy Tables
Grade Prediction
Interest Inventories
Least Squares Statistics
Licensing Examinations (Professions)
Maximum Likelihood Statistics
Multiple Regression Analysis
Occupational Tests
Prediction
Predictive Validity
Predictor Variables
Probability
Prognostic Tests
Regression (Statistics)
Sampling
Statistics
Suppressor Variables
Testing
Test Use
Test Validity

PREDICTIVE VALIDITY *Jul. 1966*
CIJE: 1298 RIE: 831 GC: 820
SN Degree to which a variable, such as test scores, grades, ratings, or some other factor, correlates with some future performance or variable
UF Criterion Validity (Predictive)
BT Validity
RT Concurrent Validity
Expectancy Tables
Expectation
Interest Inventories
Predictive Measurement
Predictor Variables
Scores
Testing
Test Validity

= Two or more Descriptors are used to represent this term.
The term's main entry shows the appropriate coordination.

Predictive Variables
USE PREDICTOR VARIABLES

PREDICTOR VARIABLES *Sep. 1970*
CIJE: 2120 RIE: 1890 GC: 820
SN Scores or measurements that are used to predict outcomes or to make estimates of other measures -- in research, they describe the characteristics of the sample that are expected to affect the outcome
UF Independent Variables
Predictive Variables
Predictors
Regressors
NT Suppressor Variables
RT Analysis Of Covariance
Analysis Of Variance
Correlation
Criteria
Effect Size
Error Of Measurement
Expectancy Tables
Interest Inventories
Monte Carlo Methods
Multiple Regression Analysis
Path Analysis
Performance Factors
Predictive Measurement
Predictive Validity
Probability
Prognostic Tests
Research Design
Statistical Analysis
Test Validity

Predictors
USE PREDICTOR VARIABLES

PREFABRICATION *Jul. 1966*
CIJE: 36 RIE: 55 GC: 920
BT Construction (Process)
RT Air Structures
Buildings
Building Systems
Construction Materials
Encapsulated Facilities
Masonry
Movable Partitions
Prestressed Concrete
Relocatable Facilities
School Construction
Structural Building Systems
Structural Elements (Construction)

Preferential Admission
USE SELECTIVE ADMISSION

PREGNANCY *Jul. 1966*
CIJE: 408 RIE: 388 GC: 120
UF Cyesis
Gestation
RT Abortions
Biology
Birth
Birth Rate
Contraception
Early Parenthood
Family Planning
Gynecology
Illegitimate Births
Obstetrics
Perinatal Influences
Pregnant Students
Premature Infants
Prenatal Influences
Reproduction (Biology)
Rh Factors
Unwed Mothers

PREGNANT STUDENTS *Dec. 1972*
CIJE: 114 RIE: 143 GC: 360
BT Females
Students
RT Board Of Education Policy
Equal Protection
Pregnancy
Student Rights

Prejudice
USE BIAS

Prekindergarten
USE PRESCHOOL EDUCATION

Prekindergarten Classes
USE PRESCHOOL EDUCATION

Prekindergarten Teachers
USE PRESCHOOL TEACHERS

Premature Birth
USE PREMATURE INFANTS

PREMATURE INFANTS *Jul. 1966*
CIJE: 127 RIE: 70 GC: 120
UF Premature Birth
BT Infants
RT Birth Weight
Infant Mortality
Neonates
Perinatal Influences
Pregnancy

PREMEDICAL STUDENTS *Oct. 1982*
CIJE: 13 RIE: 11 GC: 360
SN Undergraduates preparing for medical school
BT Undergraduate Students
RT Medical Education
Medical Students
Professional Education

PREMIUM PAY *Jul. 1966*
CIJE: 13 RIE: 16 GC: 630
SN A sum in addition to regular compensation paid due to unusual circumstances such as overtime, holiday work, hazardous or unpleasant work, or superior employee productivity or skill
BT Expenditures
Income
RT Merit Pay
Overtime
Payroll Records
Personnel Policy
Salaries
Salary Wage Differentials
Scope Of Bargaining
Wages

PRENATAL INFLUENCES *Aug. 1968*
CIJE: 200 RIE: 188 GC: 120
SN Factors occurring between conception and birth and affecting the physical or mental development of an individual
BT Influences
RT Anemia
Biological Influences
Birth Weight
Congenital Impairments
Diseases
Drug Abuse
Genetics
Health
Heredity
Nature Nurture Controversy
Obstetrics
Perinatal Influences
Physical Development
Pregnancy
Rh Factors
Rubella

PREPOSITIONS *Jan. 1985*
CIJE: 39 RIE: 25 GC: 450
BT Form Classes (Languages)
RT Function Words
Morphology (Languages)
Phrase Structure
Sentence Structure
Syntax

PREREADING EXPERIENCE *Jul. 1966*
CIJE: 94 RIE: 178 GC: 460
SN Preschool incidental learning that prepares children for reading (note: use "reading readiness" for formal prereading training -- prior to sep80, the use of this term was not restricted by a scope note)
BT Experience
RT Beginning Reading
Early Experience
Early Reading
Reading Readiness

Prerequisite Courses
USE PREREQUISITES; REQUIRED COURSES

PREREQUISITES *Sep. 1982*
CIJE: 22 RIE: 32 GC: 520
SN Knowledge, achievements, or other characteristics or circumstances required before proceeding on a given course of action
UF Prerequisite Courses #
RT Achievement
Admission Criteria
Background
Credentials
Credits
Criteria
Eligibility
Evaluation
Prior Learning
Qualifications
Selection
Standards
Status

PRERETIREMENT EDUCATION *Nov. 1982*
CIJE: 34 RIE: 26 GC: 400
SN Courses, counseling, and other activities designed to help individuals make the psychological, physical, and financial adjustments to retirement
UF Preretirement Programs
BT Adult Education
RT Educational Gerontology
Fringe Benefits
Middle Aged Adults
Midlife Transitions
Older Adults
Retirement

Preretirement Programs
USE PRERETIREMENT EDUCATION

PRESCHOOL CHILDREN *Jul. 1966*
CIJE: 2884 RIE: 3147 GC: 120
SN Approximately 2-5 years of age
UF Preschoolers
BT Young Children
RT Child Development Centers
Kindergarten Children
Preschool Education
Toddlers

Preschool Clinics (1966 1980)
USE CLINICS; PRESCHOOL EDUCATION

PRESCHOOL CURRICULUM *Jul. 1966*
CIJE: 68 RIE: 323 GC: 350
BT Curriculum
RT Elementary School Curriculum
Preschool Education

PRESCHOOL EDUCATION *Jul. 1966*
CIJE: 2675 RIE: 4085 GC: 340
SN Activities and/or experiences that are intended to effect developmental changes in children, from birth to entrance in kindergarten (or grade 1 when kindergarten is not attended) (note: also appears in the list of mandatory educational level descriptors)
UF Prekindergarten
Prekindergarten Classes
Preschool Clinics (1966 1980) #
Preschool Programs (1966 1980)
Preschool Workshops (1966 1980) #
BT Early Childhood Education
RT Child Development Centers
Day Care Centers
Home Instruction
Kindergarten
Nursery Schools
Preschool Children
Preschool Curriculum
Preschool Evaluation
Preschool Teachers
Preschool Tests

PRESCHOOL EVALUATION *Jul. 1966*
CIJE: 62 RIE: 157 GC: 320
SN Evaluation of preschool programs, not preschool children (note: prior to mar80, this term was not restricted by a scope note -- for evaluation of preschool children, see "identification," "handicap identification," "screening tests," "diagnostic tests," etc.)
BT Evaluation
RT Preschool Education

Preschool Experience
USE EARLY EXPERIENCE

PRESCHOOL LEARNING (1966 1980) *Mar. 1980*
CIJE: 99 RIE: 205 GC: 110
SN Invalid descriptor -- see more appropriate "preschool" and "learning" descriptors

Preschool Programs (1966 1980)
USE PRESCHOOL EDUCATION

PRESCHOOL TEACHERS *Jul. 1966*
CIJE: 157 RIE: 450 GC: 360
UF Kindergarten Teachers
Prekindergarten Teachers
BT Teachers
RT Child Caregivers
Preschool Education

PRESCHOOL TESTS *Jul. 1966*
CIJE: 63 RIE: 203 GC: 830
BT Tests
RT Diagnostic Tests
Maturity Tests
Nonverbal Tests
Preschool Education
Prognostic Tests
Reading Readiness Tests
School Readiness Tests
Screening Tests

Preschool Workshops (1966 1980)
USE PRESCHOOL EDUCATION; WORKSHOPS

Preschoolers
USE PRESCHOOL CHILDREN

Prescriptive Teaching
USE DIAGNOSTIC TEACHING

Presentation Methods
USE TEACHING METHODS

PRESERVATION *Sep. 1968*
CIJE: 233 RIE: 170 GC: 490
SN Prevention of deterioration of stored commodities, structural members, materials, etc.
BT Maintenance
RT Cleaning
Fire Protection
Obsolescence
Prevention
Repair

Preservice Education (1966 1980)
USE PRESERVICE TEACHER EDUCATION

PRESERVICE TEACHER EDUCATION *Mar. 1980*
CIJE: 2036 RIE: 3256 GC: 400
UF Preservice Education (1966 1980)
BT Teacher Education
RT Affiliated Schools
Cooperating Teachers
Inservice Teacher Education
Student Teachers
Student Teacher Supervisors
Student Teaching
Teacher Education Curriculum
Teacher Educator Education

Preservice Teaching Experience
USE TEACHING EXPERIENCE

PRESIDENTIAL CAMPAIGNS (UNITED STATES) *Dec. 1985*
CIJE: 4 RIE: GC: 610
SN Competitive efforts of rival candidates for the office of the president of the united states
UF Presidential Candidates (United States) #
Presidential Debates (United States) #
Presidential Elections (United States) #
BT Political Campaigns
RT Federal Government
Presidents Of The United States
United States History

Presidential Candidates (United States)
USE POLITICAL CANDIDATES; PRESIDENTIAL CAMPAIGNS (UNITED STATES)

Presidential Debates (United States)
USE DEBATE; PRESIDENTIAL CAMPAIGNS (UNITED STATES)

= Two or more Descriptors are used to represent this term.
The term's main entry shows the appropriate coordination.

Presidential Elections (United States)
USE ELECTIONS; PRESIDENTIAL CAMPAIGNS (UNITED STATES)

PRESIDENTS *Jul. 1966*
CIJE: 370 RIE: 291 GC: 640
SN Individuals appointed or elected to preside over an organized body of people, e.g., republic, assembly, organization, etc. (note: use a more specific term if possible)
NT College Presidents
Presidents Of The United States
BT Administrators

PRESIDENTS OF THE UNITED STATES *Aug. 1986*
CIJE: RIE: GC: 610
SN Individuals serving (past or present) as the chief executive officer of the united states government
BT Presidents
RT Federal Government
Presidential Campaigns (United States)
United States History

Press
USE NEWS MEDIA

PRESS OPINION *Jul. 1966*
CIJE: 214 RIE: 293 GC: 610
BT Opinions
RT Editorials
Freedom Of Speech
Journalism
Mass Media
News Media
Public Opinion

PRESSURE (PHYSICS) *Mar. 1980*
CIJE: 25 RIE: 16 GC: 490
SN Physical force applied to an object or surface (note: the previous descriptor "pressure" was not scoped and was occasionally used for emotional or psychological pressure)
UF Absolute Pressure
Ambient Pressure
Fluid Pressure
Physical Pressure
BT Scientific Concepts
RT Fluid Mechanics
Force
Gravity (Physics)
Mechanics (Physics)
Physical Environment
Physics
Weight (Mass)

PRESSURE (1970 1980) *Jun. 1980*
CIJE: 38 RIE: 4 GC: 490
SN Invalid descriptor -- originally intended as a physical science term but used inconsistently for social pressure, psychological stress, etc., as well as physical pressure -- see such descriptors as "pressure (physics)," "political influences," "social influences," and "stress variables"

PRESTIGE *Jun. 1983*
CIJE: 29 RIE: 15 GC: 520
SN High esteem or regard accorded to an individual, group, institution, role/occupation, etc.
BT Reputation
RT Awards
Leadership Qualities
Popularity
Professional Recognition
Selective Colleges
Social Status
Status Need

PRESTRESSED CONCRETE *Sep. 1968*
CIJE: 10 RIE: 8 GC: 920
UF Pretensioned Concrete
BT Construction Materials
RT Cement Industry
Masonry
Prefabrication
Structural Building Systems

PRETECHNOLOGY PROGRAMS *Jul. 1966*
CIJE: 6 RIE: 26 GC: 400
SN Special curriculum to prepare individuals for technical education
BT Programs
RT Curriculum
Postsecondary Education
Secondary Education
Technical Education

PRETEND PLAY *May. 1976*
CIJE: 93 RIE: 97 GC: 120
SN Play involving fantasy or make believe
UF Fantasy Play
Make Believe Play
BT Play
RT Behavior Development
Behavior Patterns
Dramatic Play
Fantasy
Imagination
Imitation
Role Playing

Pretensioned Concrete
USE PRESTRESSED CONCRETE

PRETESTING *Jul. 1966*
CIJE: 105 RIE: 257 GC: 820
SN Preliminary trying out of something (e.g., measures, equipment, instructional materials) to ensure that it has the desired characteristics (note: do not confuse with "pretests posttests" -- prior to mar80, the use of this term was not restricted by a scope note)
BT Evaluation Methods
RT Formative Evaluation
Material Development
Quality Control
Test Construction

Pretests (1966 1980)
USE PRETESTS POSTTESTS

PRETESTS POSTTESTS *Mar. 1980*
CIJE: 361 RIE: 883 GC: 830
SN Measures used before and after a treatment, program, course, etc. to determine its effectiveness (note: the previous descriptors "pretests" and "post testing" were not restricted by scope notes -- do not confuse with "pretesting")
UF Post Testing (1966 1980)
Pretests (1966 1980)
BT Tests
RT Improvement
Program Effectiveness
Research Design
Testing

Prevalence
USE INCIDENCE

PREVENTION *Jul. 1966*
CIJE: 912 RIE: 1047 GC: 520
UF Preventive Measures
NT Accident Prevention
Crime Prevention
Dropout Prevention
Hearing Conservation
RT Fire Protection
Preservation
Preventive Medicine

Preventive Measures
USE PREVENTION

PREVENTIVE MEDICINE *Jul. 1966*
CIJE: 282 RIE: 201 GC: 210
BT Medicine
RT Disease Control
Epidemiology
Fluoridation
Hygiene
Immunization Programs
Medical Services
Patient Education
Prevention
Public Health

Previous Learning
USE PRIOR LEARNING

PREVOCATIONAL EDUCATION *Jul. 1966*
CIJE: 143 RIE: 535 GC: 400
SN Orientation and counseling, usually at the junior high/middle school level, designed to assist students in determining the occupational areas for which they might best prepare -- may include training in work habits and skills applicable to a variety of jobs (i.e., following directions, punctuality, etc.) (note: prior to mar80, the use of this term was not restricted by a scope note)
UF Prevocational Training
BT Vocational Education
RT Career Choice
Career Counseling
Career Education
Career Exploration
Career Planning
Technical Education
Vocational Aptitude

Prevocational Training
USE PREVOCATIONAL EDUCATION

PREWRITING *Jun. 1981*
CIJE: 97 RIE: 135 GC: 400
SN All activities that precede the first draft of a written work -- includes planning, outlining, notetaking, oral discussion, use of visual aids, etc. (note: do not confuse with "writing readiness")
BT Writing Processes
RT Motivation Techniques
Notetaking
Outlining (Discourse)
Rhetorical Invention
Writing (Composition)
Writing Exercises
Writing Instruction
Writing Readiness
Writing Skills

Price Indexes
USE COST INDEXES

PRIESTS *Jul. 1966*
CIJE: 31 RIE: 23 GC: 640
BT Clergy
RT Catholics
Churches
Church Workers
Religion
Religious Cultural Groups
Theological Education

PRIMACY EFFECT *Dec. 1970*
CIJE: 28 RIE: 14 GC: 110
SN Learning process in which earlier items of a series are more readily learned and favored in recall
UF Law Of Primacy
BT Learning Processes
RT Learning Theories
Memorization
Recall (Psychology)
Retention (Psychology)
Rote Learning
Serial Learning

PRIMARY EDUCATION *Jul. 1966*
CIJE: 3106 RIE: 3970 GC: 340
SN Education provided in kindergarten through grade 3 (note: also appears in the list of mandatory educational level descriptors)
UF Primary Grades (1966 1980)
BT Early Childhood Education
Elementary Education
RT Adult Basic Education
British Infant Schools
Grade 1
Grade 2
Grade 3
Kindergarten

Primary Grades (1966 1980)
USE PRIMARY EDUCATION

PRIMARY HEALTH CARE *Dec. 1974*
CIJE: 321 RIE: 156 GC: 210
SN First contact health care, including longitudinal responsibility for the patient and coordination of all aspects of the patient's care
BT Medicine
RT Family Health
Family Practice (Medicine)
Health
Internal Medicine
Medical Care Evaluation
Medical Services
Patient Education
Pediatrics

PRIMARY SOURCES *May. 1974*
CIJE: 244 RIE: 215 GC: 720
SN Persons, places, or things that provide firsthand information about something
UF Original Sources
BT Information Sources
RT Historiography
History
Oral History
Research Tools
Resource Materials

PRIMATOLOGY *Sep. 1968*
CIJE: 24 RIE: 8 GC: 490
BT Zoology
RT Anthropology

PRIME NUMBERS *Feb. 1970*
CIJE: 63 RIE: 24 GC: 480
BT Integers

Principal Components Analysis
USE FACTOR ANALYSIS

PRINCIPALS *Jul. 1966*
CIJE: 1987 RIE: 1882 GC: 360
UF School Principals
BT Administrators
School Personnel
RT Assistant Principals
Instructional Leadership
School Administration
School Based Management
School Supervision

PRINTING *Jul. 1966*
CIJE: 241 RIE: 244 GC: 640
BT Graphic Arts
RT Industrial Arts
Layout (Publications)
Paper (Material)
Photocomposition
Publications
Publishing Industry
Reprography
Signs
Textbook Publication
Typewriting
Written Language

Printscript
USE MANUSCRIPT WRITING (HANDLETTERING)

Prior Experiential Learning
USE EXPERIENTIAL LEARNING; PRIOR LEARNING

Prior Knowledge
USE PRIOR LEARNING

PRIOR LEARNING *Oct. 1979*
CIJE: 245 RIE: 250 GC: 110
SN Formal or informal learning taking place before entrance into a specific program -- often assessed to determine awarding of credit for knowledge already attained (prior learning may include experiential learning)
UF Previous Learning
Prior Experiential Learning #
Prior Knowledge
BT Learning
RT Access To Education
Admission Criteria
Advanced Placement
Certification
College Credits
Credits
Educational Experience
Employment Experience
Equivalency Tests
Experience
Experiential Learning
Job Placement
Learning Experience
Nontraditional Education
Nontraditional Students

= Two or more Descriptors are used to represent this term.
The term's main entry shows the appropriate coordination.

Prerequisites
Special Degree Programs
Student Experience
Student Placement
Transfer Policy
Transfer Programs
Transfer Students
Work Experience

Priority Determination
USE NEEDS ASSESSMENT

Prison Education
USE CORRECTIONAL EDUCATION

PRISON LIBRARIES *Apr. 1980*
CIJE: 8 RIE: 21 GC: 710
SN Libraries in prisons provided primarily for use by the inmates
BT Institutional Libraries
RT Correctional Education
Correctional Institutions
Prisoners

Prison Sentences
USE SENTENCING

PRISONERS *Jul. 1966*
CIJE: 482 RIE: 454 GC: 530
UF Inmates
Jail Inmates
BT Institutionalized Persons
RT Correctional Education
Correctional Institutions
Correctional Rehabilitation
Criminals
Criminology
Prison Libraries
Sentencing

Prisons
USE CORRECTIONAL INSTITUTIONS

PRIVACY *Oct. 1977*
CIJE: 225 RIE: 176 GC: 520
SN Condition whereby individuals or their properties are free from unwarranted scrutiny
NT Confidentiality
BT Relationship
RT Civil Liberties
Confidential Records
Constitutional Law
Design Requirements
Disclosure
Ethics
Freedom Of Information
Intellectual Freedom
Interpersonal Relationship
Laws

PRIVATE AGENCIES *Jul. 1966*
CIJE: 120 RIE: 282 GC: 520
UF Nonpublic Agencies
BT Agencies
RT Agency Role
Public Agencies
Voluntary Agencies

PRIVATE COLLEGES *Sep. 1968*
CIJE: 623 RIE: 1505 GC: 340
SN Degree-granting institutions of higher education which are privately funded and controlled
UF Independent Colleges
Private Junior Colleges #
Private Universities
BT Colleges
Private Schools
RT Church Related Colleges
Private Education
Private Financial Support
Public Colleges
Selective Colleges
Single Sex Colleges
Small Colleges

PRIVATE EDUCATION *Mar. 1980*
CIJE: 117 RIE: 130 GC: 340
SN Education primarily supported by nonpublic funds
UF Nonpublic Education
Private Higher Education #
BT Education
RT Catholic Schools
Church Related Colleges
Corporate Education
Free Education
Home Schooling
Parochial Schools
Private Colleges
Private School Aid
Private Schools
Proprietary Schools
Public Education

PRIVATE FINANCIAL SUPPORT *Jul. 1966*
CIJE: 507 RIE: 520 GC: 620
SN Financial aid received from private sources (note: do not confuse with "private school aid")
UF Philanthropy
BT Financial Support
RT Capital
Corporate Support
Costs
Donors
Educational Finance
Fund Raising
Grantsmanship
Philanthropic Foundations
Private Colleges
Proprietary Schools
Public Support
School Business Relationship

Private Higher Education
USE HIGHER EDUCATION; PRIVATE EDUCATION

Private Information
USE CONFIDENTIALITY

Private Junior Colleges
USE PRIVATE COLLEGES; TWO YEAR COLLEGES

PRIVATE SCHOOL AID *Mar. 1980*
CIJE: 157 RIE: 237 GC: 620
SN Public or private financial support given to private, religious, or other nonpublic schools, colleges, or universities (note: do not confuse with "private financial support")
UF Nonpublic School Aid (1972 1980)
Parochial School Aid (1972 1980) #
BT Financial Support
School Support
RT Catholic Schools
Church Related Colleges
Educational Finance
Educational Vouchers
Federal Aid
Government School Relationship
Parochial Schools
Private Education
Private Schools
School Choice
School Funds
School Taxes
Shared Resources And Services
State Aid
State Church Separation

PRIVATE SCHOOLS *Jul. 1966*
CIJE: 850 RIE: 1021 GC: 340
UF Independent Schools
Nonpublic Schools
NT Parochial Schools
Private Colleges
Proprietary Schools
BT Schools
RT Correspondence Schools
Private Education
Private School Aid
Single Sex Schools

Private Universities
USE PRIVATE COLLEGES

Privileged Communication
USE CONFIDENTIALITY

Proactive Inhibition
USE INHIBITION

PROBABILITY *Jul. 1966*
CIJE: 645 RIE: 449 GC: 480
UF Probability Theory (1967 1980)
BT Mathematics
RT Bayesian Statistics
Estimation (Mathematics)
Expectancy Tables
Expectation
Game Theory
Incidence
Least Squares Statistics
Mathematical Concepts
Maximum Likelihood Statistics
Monte Carlo Methods
Prediction
Predictive Measurement
Predictor Variables
Reliability
Risk
Sample Size
Sampling
Statistical Analysis
Statistical Distributions
Statistical Inference
Statistical Significance
Statistics

Probability Theory (1967 1980)
USE PROBABILITY

PROBATION OFFICERS *Jul. 1966*
CIJE: 20 RIE: 41 GC: 640
BT Caseworkers
RT Correctional Rehabilitation
Counselors
Crime
Delinquent Rehabilitation
Guidance Personnel
Parole Officers
School Guidance
Social Workers

PROBATIONARY PERIOD *Sep. 1968*
CIJE: 88 RIE: 79 GC: 630
SN Period in which a person must prove his ability to fulfill certain conditions as to achievement, behavior, or job assignment
UF Probationary Teachers
NT Academic Probation
RT Ability Identification
Beginning Teachers
Behavior Development
Behavior Standards
Contracts
Correctional Rehabilitation
Delinquent Rehabilitation
Employee Responsibility
Employer Employee Relationship
Employment
Nontenured Faculty
Promotion (Occupational)
Student School Relationship
Tenure

Probationary Teachers
USE PROBATIONARY PERIOD

PROBLEM CHILDREN *Jul. 1966*
CIJE: 233 RIE: 133 GC: 230
BT Children
RT Behavior Disorders
Behavior Problems
Family Problems
Obedience
Personality Problems
Problems

PROBLEM SETS *Jul. 1966*
CIJE: 164 RIE: 208 GC: 830
SN Tasks, exercises, or test questions dealing with a specified educational subject or content area
BT Instructional Materials
RT Item Banks
Learning Activities
Mathematical Applications
Problem Solving
Testing
Test Items
Test Manuals
Tests
Workbooks

PROBLEM SOLVING *Jul. 1966*
CIJE: 6116 RIE: 4798 GC: 110
UF Participative Problem Solving #
BT Cognitive Processes
RT Brainstorming
Conflict Resolution
Convergent Thinking
Coping
Creative Thinking
Critical Incidents Method
Critical Thinking
Decision Making
Decision Making Skills
Discussion
Divergent Thinking
Evaluative Thinking
Expert Systems
Game Theory
Heuristics
Information Seeking
Information Utilization
Intuition
Inventions
Learning Strategies
Logical Thinking
Management Games
Management Systems
Mathematical Applications
Monte Carlo Methods
Problems
Problem Sets
Productive Thinking
Protocol Analysis
Research Methodology
Scientific Attitudes
Scientific Methodology
Systems Analysis
Systems Approach
Test Wiseness

PROBLEMS *Jul. 1966*
CIJE: 837 RIE: 653 GC: 530
SN Difficulties or obstacles not easily overcome (note: use a more specific term if possible)
NT Administrative Problems
Behavior Problems
Communication Problems
Community Problems
Curriculum Problems
Discipline Problems
Emotional Problems
Employment Problems
Evaluation Problems
Family Problems
Financial Problems
Labor Problems
Learning Problems
Legal Problems
Migrant Problems
Personality Problems
Reading Difficulties
Research Problems
Social Problems
Student Problems
Suburban Problems
Testing Problems
Urban Problems
World Problems
Writing Difficulties
Youth Problems
RT Difficulty Level
Problem Children
Problem Solving

Procedural Due Process
USE DUE PROCESS

Procedures
USE METHODS

PROCESS EDUCATION *Aug. 1974*
CIJE: 226 RIE: 346 GC: 310
SN Educational system which emphasizes the learning and demonstration of generalizable process skills (e.g., observation, classification, measurement, prediction, communication, and inference)
BT Education
RT Behavioral Objectives
Skill Development
Skills

Process Evaluation
USE FORMATIVE EVALUATION

Processed Foods Inspectors
USE FOOD AND DRUG INSPECTORS

Procreation
USE REPRODUCTION (BIOLOGY)

PROCTORING *Jul. 1966*
CIJE: 23 RIE: 24 GC: 310
SN Acting with delegated authority to maintain security, supervise, or discipline students in such school activities as examinations or study halls, generally by persons who are not teachers

= Two or more Descriptors are used to represent this term.
The term's main entry shows the appropriate coordination.

BT Supervision
RT Classroom Techniques
Discipline
School Aides
Study
Teacher Aides
Teaching Assistants
Testing

PRODUCER SERVICES *Jul. 1966*
CIJE: 12 RIE: 34 GC: 650
SN Business, professional, and government services provided to the business community rather than the individual consumer, including maintenance, administrative, policy making, regulatory, financial, etc.
BT Services
RT Agribusiness
Business
Government (Administrative Body)
Industry
Service Occupations

Product Evaluation
USE SUMMATIVE EVALUATION

Product Information
USE MERCHANDISE INFORMATION

Product Labels
USE MERCHANDISE INFORMATION

Production Functions
USE PRODUCTIVITY

Production Machine Operators
USE MACHINE TOOL OPERATORS

PRODUCTION TECHNICIANS *Aug. 1968*
CIJE: 14 RIE: 25 GC: 640
BT Paraprofessional Personnel
RT Assembly (Manufacturing)
Engineering Technicians
Manufacturing
Manufacturing Industry
Mass Production

PRODUCTION TECHNIQUES *Jul. 1966*
CIJE: 835 RIE: 716 GC: 720
SN Techniques for creating finished products, such as films, radio and television programs, publications, etc.
NT Electronic Publishing
Film Production
Photocomposition
Special Effects
Television Lighting
Textbook Publication
BT Methods
RT Educational Media
Industry
Mass Production
Photography
Radio
Television
Television Curriculum
Theater Arts

Productive Living (1967 1980)
USE QUALITY OF LIFE

PRODUCTIVE THINKING *Jul. 1966*
CIJE: 167 RIE: 192 GC: 110
SN Creative thinking that results in something new (note: prior to mar80, the use of this term was not restricted by a scope note)
BT Creative Thinking
RT Cognitive Ability
Convergent Thinking
Critical Thinking
Discovery Processes
Divergent Thinking
Evaluative Thinking
Inventions
Problem Solving
Productivity

PRODUCTIVITY *Jul. 1966*
CIJE: 910 RIE: 873 GC: 620
UF Educational Production Functions
Production Functions
RT Ability
Accountability
Achievement
Developed Nations
Developing Nations
Economic Factors
Economics
Educational Economics
Efficiency
Evaluation Criteria
Faculty Publishing
Human Capital
Inflation (Economics)
Investment
Job Simplification
Organizational Effectiveness
Ownership
Productive Thinking
Program Effectiveness
Quality Of Life
Quality Of Working Life
Research And Development
Retrenchment
Worker Days

PROFESSIONAL ASSOCIATIONS *Jul. 1966*
CIJE: 1669 RIE: 1220 GC: 520
UF Dental Associations (1966 1980) #
NT Library Associations
Medical Associations
Teacher Associations
BT Organizations (Groups)
RT Faculty Organizations
Fraternities
International Organizations
National Organizations
Sororities

PROFESSIONAL AUTONOMY *Nov. 1982*
CIJE: 68 RIE: 63 GC: 330
SN Freedom of professionals or groups of professionals to function independently
UF Teacher Autonomy
RT Academic Freedom
Administrative Policy
Decision Making
Governance
Institutional Autonomy
Intellectual Freedom
Interpersonal Relationship
Interprofessional Relationship
Personal Autonomy
Power Structure
Professional Personnel
Professional Services
School District Autonomy
Self Determination
Teacher Welfare
Teaching Conditions
Work Attitudes
Work Environment

PROFESSIONAL CONTINUING EDUCATION *Jul. 1966*
CIJE: 1141 RIE: 1263 GC: 340
SN Education of adults in professional fields for occupational updating and improvement -- usually consists of short-term, intensive, specialized learning experiences often categorized by general field of specialization
BT Continuing Education
Professional Education
RT Adult Education
Alumni Education
Continuing Education Units
Corporate Education
Extension Education
Faculty Development
Inservice Education
Institutes (Training Programs)
Lifelong Learning
Management Development
Minicourses
Professional Development
Refresher Courses
Sabbatical Leaves
Teacher Centers
Womens Education

PROFESSIONAL DEVELOPMENT *Oct. 1979*
CIJE: 910 RIE: 770 GC: 630
SN Activities to enhance professional career growth
UF Professional Growth
NT Faculty Development
BT Labor Force Development
RT Assessment Centers (Personnel)
Career Change
Individual Development
Industrial Training
Inservice Education
Management Development
Mentors
Professional Continuing Education
Professional Education
Professional Personnel
Professional Recognition
Professional Training
Sabbatical Leaves
Staff Development
Teacher Improvement
Writing For Publication

PROFESSIONAL EDUCATION *Jul. 1966*
CIJE: 2117 RIE: 1708 GC: 340
SN Programs of academic study that prepare students to enter or advance in professional fields (note: prior to mar80, this term was not differentiated from "professional training," which is more short term and job-specific)
UF First Professional Degrees #
NT Administrator Education
Architectural Education
Business Administration Education
Engineering Education
Home Economics Education
Legal Education (Professions)
Medical Education
Professional Continuing Education
Public Administration Education
Teacher Education
Theological Education
BT Education
RT Adult Education
Allied Health Occupations Education
Assistantships
College Entrance Examinations
Dental Schools
Dental Students
Educational Gerontology
Experiential Learning
Graduate Study
Internship Programs
Law Schools
Law Students
Library Education
Library Schools
Licensing Examinations (Professions)
Medical Schools
Medical Students
Postdoctoral Education
Postsecondary Education As A Field Of Study
Premedical Students
Professional Development
Professional Occupations
Professional Personnel
Professional Training
Sabbatical Leaves
State Licensing Boards
State Universities

Professional Growth
USE PROFESSIONAL DEVELOPMENT

Professional Negotiation
USE COLLECTIVE BARGAINING

Professional Nurses
USE NURSES

PROFESSIONAL OCCUPATIONS *Jul. 1966*
CIJE: 488 RIE: 414 GC: 640
NT Teaching (Occupation)
BT Occupations
RT Allied Health Occupations
Health Occupations
Managerial Occupations
Professional Education
Professional Personnel
Professional Training
Technology
White Collar Occupations

PROFESSIONAL PERSONNEL *Jul. 1966*
CIJE: 1041 RIE: 1258 GC: 630
UF Professional Staff
NT Accountants
Architects
Athletic Coaches
Dentists
Engineers
Faculty
Information Scientists
Lawyers
Mathematicians
Nurses
Optometrists
Pharmacists
Physicians
Psychologists
Research Directors
Researchers
Scientists
Social Scientists
Social Workers
Teachers
Therapists
Veterinarians
BT Personnel
RT Administrators
Allied Health Personnel
Employees
Health Personnel
Judges
Lay People
Nonprofessional Personnel
Paraprofessional Personnel
Professional Autonomy
Professional Development
Professional Education
Professional Occupations
Professional Recognition
Professional Services
Professional Training

PROFESSIONAL RECOGNITION *Jul. 1966*
CIJE: 1062 RIE: 516 GC: 520
SN Expressed or implied acknowledgment of one's professional efforts, qualities, and/or training
UF Professional Status
BT Recognition (Achievement)
RT Awards
Compensation (Remuneration)
Educational Benefits
Employment Level
Motivation
Prestige
Professional Development
Professional Personnel
Rewards
Status
Status Need
Teacher Militancy
Teacher Morale
Teacher Welfare

PROFESSIONAL SERVICES *Jul. 1966*
CIJE: 221 RIE: 238 GC: 520
BT Services
RT Consultants
Consultation Programs
Intermediate Administrative Units
Interprofessional Relationship
Malpractice
Medical Services
Professional Autonomy
Professional Personnel
Referral
Social Services

Professional Staff
USE PROFESSIONAL PERSONNEL

Professional Standards
USE STANDARDS

Professional Status
USE PROFESSIONAL RECOGNITION

PROFESSIONAL TRAINING *Jul. 1966*
CIJE: 894 RIE: 1137 GC: 330
SN Special instruction to develop skills needed to improve job performance of professional personnel -- usually short term and job-specific (note: prior to mar80, this term was not differentiated from "professional education," which is the longer-term academic preparation needed to enter or advance in professional fields)
BT Training
RT Business Administration Education
Faculty Development
Improvement Programs
Industrial Training
Inservice Education
Inservice Teacher Education
Institutes (Training Programs)
International Trade Vocabulary
Job Skills
Management Development
Medical Vocabulary
Professional Development

= Two or more Descriptors are used to represent this term.
The term's main entry shows the appropriate coordination.

Professional Education
Professional Occupations
Professional Personnel

Professorial Rank
USE ACADEMIC RANK (PROFESSIONAL)

PROFESSORS *Jul. 1966*
CIJE: 470 RIE: 245 GC: 360
SN Teachers who have attained the highest academic rank possible in higher education institutions (note: use "college faculty" for associate or assistant professors -- prior to mar80, the use of this term was not restricted by a scope note)
BT College Faculty
RT Academic Rank (Professional)
Counselor Educators
Student Teacher Supervisors
Teacher Educators
Tenured Faculty

Proficiency Based Education
USE COMPETENCY BASED EDUCATION

Proficiency Based Teacher Education
USE COMPETENCY BASED TEACHER EDUCATION

Profile Evaluation (1966 1980)
USE PROFILES

PROFILES *Mar. 1980*
CIJE: 275 RIE: 367 GC: 730
SN Summary descriptions, often presented in diagrams or charts, that indicate the significant features of an individual, group, process, etc.
UF Profile Evaluation (1966 1980)
BT Data
RT Academic Records
Background
Biographical Inventories
Case Records
Census Figures
Charts
Course Descriptions
Interest Inventories
Medical Case Histories
Personnel Data
Portfolios (Background Materials)
Precision Teaching
Program Descriptions
Report Cards
Resumes (Personal)
Student Records

Profound Disabilities
USE SEVERE DISABILITIES

Profoundly Mentally Retarded
USE SEVERE MENTAL RETARDATION

Prognoses
USE PROGNOSTIC TESTS

PROGNOSTIC TESTS *Jul. 1966*
CIJE: 55 RIE: 70 GC: 830
SN Tests used to predict the outcome of educational, medical, or psychological programs or treatments (note: prior to mar80, this term was not scoped and was often used for "aptitude tests")
UF Prognoses
BT Tests
RT Diagnostic Tests
Educational Testing
Interest Inventories
Intervention
Medical Services
Predictive Measurement
Predictor Variables
Preschool Tests
Psychological Testing
Reading Readiness Tests
Rehabilitation Programs
School Readiness Tests
Screening Tests
Special Education

PROGRAM ADMINISTRATION *Jul. 1966*
CIJE: 733 RIE: 3286 GC: 320
BT Administration
RT Audits (Verification)
Organizational Development
Program Development
Program Implementation
Program Improvement
Programs
Research Administration
Retrenchment

Program Approval (Validation)
USE PROGRAM VALIDATION

PROGRAM ATTITUDES *Jul. 1966*
CIJE: 191 RIE: 470 GC: 320
SN Attitudes toward or about programs
BT Attitudes
RT Program Evaluation
Programs

PROGRAM BUDGETING *Jul. 1966*
CIJE: 296 RIE: 755 GC: 620
SN Construction of budget estimates based on particular programs or functions, to help decision makers allocate funds for specific activities or objectives
BT Budgeting
RT Budgets
Program Costs
Program Implementation
Programs

PROGRAM CONTENT *Jul. 1966*
CIJE: 768 RIE: 1439 GC: 320
SN Activities or subject matter of an educational program
RT Articulation (Education)
Course Content
Program Design
Programs
Program Validation
Validated Programs

Program Coordination (1966 1980)
USE COOPERATIVE PROGRAMS; COORDINATION

PROGRAM COSTS *Jul. 1966*
CIJE: 537 RIE: 1799 GC: 620
BT Costs
RT Cost Estimates
Expenditure Per Student
Instructional Student Costs
Program Budgeting
Program Evaluation
Program Proposals
Programs
Unit Costs

PROGRAM DESCRIPTIONS *Jul. 1966*
CIJE: 11716 RIE: 14340 GC: 730
RT Bulletins
Profiles
Program Evaluation
Program Guides
Program Proposals
Programs
Reports
School Catalogs

PROGRAM DESIGN *Jul. 1966*
CIJE: 1280 RIE: 2013 GC: 320
SN The arrangement or underlying scheme of a program that governs its functioning or development (note: do not confuse with "program development" or "program implementation" -- prior to mar80, the use of this term was not restricted by a scope note)
BT Design
RT Program Content
Program Development
Program Implementation
Program Length
Program Proposals
Programs

PROGRAM DEVELOPMENT *Jul. 1966*
CIJE: 6282 RIE: 13852 GC: 320
SN Process of formulating a scheme, devising procedures, or planning activities with regard to specific program objectives (note: do not confuse with "program design" or "program implementation" -- prior to mar80, the use of this term was not restricted by a scope note)
UF Program Planning (1966 1980)
BT Development
RT Educational Development
Formative Evaluation
Program Administration
Program Design
Program Effectiveness
Program Evaluation
Program Implementation
Program Improvement
Programs
Systems Development

Program Discontinuance
USE PROGRAM TERMINATION

PROGRAM EFFECTIVENESS *Jul. 1966*
CIJE: 3585 RIE: 7144 GC: 320
SN Degree to which programs are successful in accomplishing their objectives or in otherwise making changes
RT Accountability
Audits (Verification)
Cost Effectiveness
Educational Assessment
Educational Quality
Educational Research
Efficiency
Instructional Effectiveness
Methods Research
Organizational Effectiveness
Outcomes Of Education
Pretests Posttests
Productivity
Program Development
Program Evaluation
Programs
Program Validation
Quality Control
School Effectiveness
Success
Summative Evaluation
Validated Programs

Program Elimination
USE PROGRAM TERMINATION

PROGRAM EVALUATION *Jul. 1966*
CIJE: 6531 RIE: 18943 GC: 320
SN Judging the feasibility, efficacy, value, etc. of a program in relation to stated objectives, standards, or criteria
BT Evaluation
RT Course Evaluation
Curriculum Evaluation
Educational Assessment
Field Tests
Holistic Evaluation
Input Output Analysis
Institutional Evaluation
Instructional Material Evaluation
Outcomes Of Education
Program Attitudes
Program Costs
Program Descriptions
Program Development
Program Effectiveness
Program Improvement
Programs
Program Termination
Program Validation
Self Evaluation (Groups)
Summative Evaluation
Validated Programs

PROGRAM GUIDES *Jul. 1966*
CIJE: 100 RIE: 1259 GC: 730
BT Guides
RT Administrator Guides
Program Descriptions
Programs

PROGRAM IMPLEMENTATION *Mar. 1980*
CIJE: 872 RIE: 2999 GC: 320
SN Carrying out, by concrete measures, program plans and designs (note: prior to mar80, the instruction "program implementation, use program development" was carried in the thesaurus)
RT Program Administration
Program Budgeting
Program Design
Program Development
Programs

PROGRAM IMPROVEMENT *Jul. 1966*
CIJE: 865 RIE: 2160 GC: 320
BT Improvement
RT Action Research
Formative Evaluation
Program Administration
Program Development
Program Evaluation
Programs

PROGRAM LENGTH *Jul. 1966*
CIJE: 90 RIE: 238 GC: 350
SN Length or duration of an educational program
RT Program Design
Programs
Program Termination
Scheduling
Time Factors (Learning)

Program Phaseout
USE PROGRAM TERMINATION

Program Planning (1966 1980)
USE PROGRAM DEVELOPMENT

PROGRAM PROPOSALS *Jul. 1966*
CIJE: 446 RIE: 710 GC: 730
UF Grant Proposals #
Project Proposals
NT Research Proposals
RT Bids
Financial Support
Fund Raising
Grantsmanship
Program Costs
Program Descriptions
Program Design
Programs
Proposal Writing
Research Projects
Specifications

PROGRAM TERMINATION *Aug. 1986*
CIJE: 2 RIE: 3 GC: 320
SN Discontinuance of a program or project due to funding, evaluation, or other decisions
UF Program Discontinuance
Program Elimination
Program Phaseout
Termination Of Programs
RT Program Evaluation
Program Length
Programs
Program Validation
Reduction In Force
Retrenchment
School Closing

PROGRAM VALIDATION *Mar. 1977*
CIJE: 55 RIE: 229 GC: 330
SN The process of approving a program according to specified procedures that indicate attainment of the claims of the sponsors -- unlike "evaluation," "validation" connotes testing and documentation by impartial experts of successful uses of the program, usually with the implication that it can be successfully replicated (note: for the results of validation, see "validated programs")
UF Program Approval (Validation)
RT Accountability
Course Content
Course Evaluation
Curriculum Evaluation
Demonstration Programs
Educational Assessment
Program Content
Program Effectiveness
Program Evaluation
Programs
Program Termination
Summative Evaluation
Validated Programs
Validity

PROGRAMED INSTRUCTION *Jul. 1966*
CIJE: 1454 RIE: 2665 GC: 310
SN Instruction in which learners progress at their own rate using workbooks, textbooks, or electromechanical devices that provide information in discrete steps, test learning at each step, and provide immediate feedback about achievement

= Two or more Descriptors are used to represent this term.
The term's main entry shows the appropriate coordination.

UF Autoinstructional Methods (1966 1980)
Autoinstructional Programs (1966 1980)
Programed Learning
Programed Self Instruction
Programed Units (1966 1980) #
NT Computer Assisted Instruction
Programed Tutoring
BT Teaching Methods
RT Autoinstructional Aids
Branching
Computer Oriented Programs
Educational Media
Educational Technology
Electronic Classrooms
Feedback
Fixed Sequence
Individualized Instruction
Intermode Differences
Language Laboratories
Learning Laboratories
Pacing
Programed Instructional Materials
Prompting
Sequential Approach
Sequential Learning
Teaching Machines

PROGRAMED INSTRUCTIONAL MATERIALS *Mar. 1980*
CIJE: 369 RIE: 1318 GC: 730
SN Materials prepared specifically to employ programed instruction techniques
UF Programed Materials (1966 1980)
Programed Texts (1966 1980) #
Self Instruction Materials
BT Instructional Materials
RT Audiovisual Aids
Autoinstructional Aids
Computer Assisted Instruction
Courseware
Instructional Films
Learning Modules
Programed Instruction
Programed Tutoring
Study Guides
Teaching Machines
Textbooks
Workbooks

Programed Learning
USE PROGRAMED INSTRUCTION

Programed Materials (1966 1980)
USE PROGRAMED INSTRUCTIONAL MATERIALS

Programed Self Instruction
USE PROGRAMED INSTRUCTION

Programed Texts (1966 1980)
USE PROGRAMED INSTRUCTIONAL MATERIALS; TEXTBOOKS

PROGRAMED TUTORING *Jul. 1966*
CIJE: 32 RIE: 106 GC: 310
BT Programed Instruction
Tutoring
RT Computer Assisted Instruction
Programed Instructional Materials

Programed Units (1966 1980)
USE PROGRAMED INSTRUCTION; UNITS OF STUDY

PROGRAMERS *Jul. 1966*
CIJE: 36 RIE: 84 GC: 710
BT Personnel
RT Programing
Programing Languages
Systems Analysts

PROGRAMING *Jul. 1966*
CIJE: 934 RIE: 1079 GC: 710
SN Putting together a logical sequence of instructions to direct the actions of a computer system (note: prior to mar80, this term was not restricted by a scope note)
UF Computer Programing
BT Computer Science
RT Algorithms
Authoring Aids (Programing)
Branching
Computer Literacy
Computer Oriented Programs
Computers
Computer Science Education
Computer Software
Data Processing
Programers
Programing Languages

PROGRAMING (BROADCAST) *Aug. 1971*
CIJE: 1027 RIE: 1225 GC: 720
SN Scheduling, planning, or constructing programs for broadcast media -- the aggregate of programs presented
UF Broadcast Scheduling
Multichannel Programing (1966 1980)
Radio Programing
Television Programing
Viewing Time (1968 1980)
RT Audiodisks
Audiotape Recordings
Broadcast Industry
Copyrights
Material Development
Optical Disks
Radio
Scheduling
Serials
Television
Television Commercials
Television Curriculum
Television Research
Television Studios
Television Viewing
Videodisks
Videotape Recordings

PROGRAMING LANGUAGES *Aug. 1969*
CIJE: 458 RIE: 632 GC: 710
UF Authoring Languages #
Computer Languages
BT Language
RT Artificial Languages
Authoring Aids (Programing)
Computational Linguistics
Computers
Computer Software
Data Processing
Programers
Programing

PROGRAMING PROBLEMS (1966 1980) *Mar. 1980*
CIJE: 27 RIE: 80 GC: 710
SN Invalid descriptor -- used for various types of programing, e.g., computer, television, educational, etc. -- coordinate specific "problem" and "programing" descriptors

PROGRAMS *Jul. 1966*
CIJE: 151 RIE: 376 GC: 520
SN Schedules or plans of procedure under which a series of intended activities is directed toward desired results (note: use a more specific term if possbile)
NT Adult Programs
Advanced Placement Programs
After School Programs
Assembly Programs
Bilingual Education Programs
Church Programs
College Day
College Programs
Community Programs
Comprehensive Programs
Computer Oriented Programs
Construction Programs
Consultation Programs
Cooperative Programs
County Programs
Day Programs
Demonstration Programs
Developmental Programs
Emergency Programs
Employee Assistance Programs
Employment Programs
Evening Programs
Exchange Programs
Experimental Programs
Family Programs
Federal Programs
Field Experience Programs
Foundation Programs
Guidance Programs
Health Programs
Home Programs
Human Relations Programs
Improvement Programs
Individualized Programs
Inplant Programs
Institutes (Training Programs)
Intercultural Programs
Intergenerational Programs
International Programs
Internship Programs
Interstate Programs
Migrant Programs
National Programs
Nonschool Educational Programs
Outreach Programs
Pilot Projects
Poverty Programs
Pretechnology Programs
Reading Programs
Recreational Programs
Regional Programs
Rehabilitation Programs
Remedial Programs
Research Projects
Residential Programs
Science Course Improvement Projects
Science Programs
Second Language Programs
Special Programs
State Programs
Student Loan Programs
Summer Programs
Teacher Education Programs
Testing Programs
Transfer Programs
Transitional Programs
Tutorial Programs
Urban Programs
Vacation Programs
Validated Programs
Weekend Programs
Work Experience Programs
Work Study Programs
Youth Programs
RT Program Administration
Program Attitudes
Program Budgeting
Program Content
Program Costs
Program Descriptions
Program Design
Program Development
Program Effectiveness
Program Evaluation
Program Guides
Program Implementation
Program Improvement
Program Length
Program Proposals
Program Termination
Program Validation

PROGRESSIVE EDUCATION *Jul. 1966*
CIJE: 231 RIE: 102 GC: 310
SN An educational movement beginning in the last two decades of the 19th century that based its protest against formalism on the philosophy of john dewey -- basic tenets are commitment to democratic ideals, creative and purposeful activity, receptivity to student needs, and interaction with the community
BT Education
RT Educational Practices
Educational Theories
Free Schools
Humanistic Education
Open Education

Progressive Relaxation (1967 1980)
USE RELAXATION TRAINING

Progressive Retardation (1966 1980) (In School)
USE EDUCATIONALLY DISADVANTAGED

PROJECT APPLICATIONS (1967 1980) *Jun. 1980*
CIJE: 39 RIE: 180 GC: 730
SN Invalid descriptor -- used inconsistently in indexing -- see "program proposals" and "program descriptions"

Project Methods
USE STUDENT PROJECTS; TEACHING METHODS

Project Proposals
USE PROGRAM PROPOSALS

Project Schools
USE EXPERIMENTAL SCHOOLS

Project Training Methods (1968 1980)
USE STUDENT PROJECTS; TEACHING METHODS

PROJECTION EQUIPMENT *Jul. 1966*
CIJE: 179 RIE: 165 GC: 910
UF Eight Millimeter Projectors (1970 1980)
Film Projectors
Projectors
Sixteen Millimeter Projectors (1966 1980)
Slide Projectors
NT Filmstrip Projectors
Microform Readers
Opaque Projectors
Overhead Projectors
Tachistoscopes
BT Equipment
Visual Aids
RT Audio Equipment
Audiovisual Aids
Educational Equipment
Magnification Methods
Photographic Equipment
Screens (Displays)

PROJECTIVE MEASURES *Mar. 1980*
CIJE: 185 RIE: 100 GC: 830
SN Procedures or devices used to infer an individual's personality traits, propensities, attitudes, or feelings through responses to vague, ambiguous, or unstructured stimuli
UF Projective Tests (1968 1980)
NT Association Measures
BT Measures (Individuals)
RT Affective Measures
Creativity Tests
Diagnostic Tests
Objective Tests
Personality Assessment
Pictorial Stimuli
Psychological Evaluation
Visual Measures

Projective Tests (1968 1980)
USE PROJECTIVE MEASURES

Projectors
USE PROJECTION EQUIPMENT

PROJECTS (1966 1980) *Mar. 1980*
CIJE: 271 RIE: 633 GC: 810
SN Invalid descriptor -- see "programs" and its hierarchy (i.e., narrower terms "research projects," "pilot projects," etc.)

Proletariat
USE WORKING CLASS

PROMOTION (OCCUPATIONAL) *Feb. 1970*
CIJE: 269 RIE: 390 GC: 630
UF Advancement
Salary Raises
NT Faculty Promotion
Teacher Promotion
RT Assessment Centers (Personnel)
Career Change
Career Development
Career Ladders
Education Work Relationship
Employment Level
Employment Opportunities
Employment Qualifications
Job Development
Job Performance
Job Skills
Labor Needs
Occupational Aspiration
Occupational Mobility
Personnel Evaluation
Probationary Period
Publish Or Perish Issue
Salaries
Scope Of Bargaining
Seniority
Tenure

PROMPTING *Jul. 1966*
CIJE: 96 RIE: 82 GC: 310
SN Providing directional aid through the use of hints, reminders, or cues
UF Cuing
BT Methods

= Two or more Descriptors are used to represent this term.
The term's main entry shows the appropriate coordination.

RT Cues
Dramatics
Learning Strategies
Programed Instruction
Teaching Methods

Prompts
USE CUES

Pronominals
USE PRONOUNS

PRONOUNS *Jul. 1966*
CIJE: 253 RIE: 174 GC: 450
UF Pronominals
BT Form Classes (Languages)
RT Language Patterns
Morphology (Languages)
Phrase Structure
Sentence Structure
Syntax

PRONUNCIATION *Jul. 1966*
CIJE: 472 RIE: 581 GC: 450
BT Speech
RT Child Language
Diacritical Marking
Diction
Pronunciation Instruction
Speech Tests
Word Lists

PRONUNCIATION INSTRUCTION *Jul. 1966*
CIJE: 194 RIE: 300 GC: 450
BT Speech Instruction
RT Pronunciation

PROOF (MATHEMATICS) *Apr. 1982*
CIJE: 317 RIE: 40 GC: 480
SN The validity of mathematical statements -- also, the sequences of steps, statements, or demonstrations that lead to valid mathematical conclusions
BT Mathematical Logic
Validity
RT Mathematical Concepts
Mathematical Models
Mathematics
Measurement
Research Methodology
Test Theory

PROPAGANDA *Jul. 1966*
CIJE: 177 RIE: 208 GC: 720
BT Communication (Thought Transfer)
Information Dissemination
RT Advertising
Communications
Deception
Mass Media
Persuasive Discourse
Public Opinion

PROPERTY ACCOUNTING *Oct. 1968*
CIJE: 42 RIE: 44 GC: 620
UF Property Control
Property Control Systems
BT Accounting
RT Estate Planning
Facility Inventory
Property Taxes
Trusts (Financial)
Wills

PROPERTY APPRAISAL *Oct. 1968*
CIJE: 45 RIE: 55 GC: 620
UF Real Estate Appraisal
NT Assessed Valuation
BT Evaluation
RT Building Obsolescence
Estate Planning
Insurance
Ownership
Property Taxes
Real Estate
Taxes
Trusts (Financial)
Wills

Property Control
USE PROPERTY ACCOUNTING

Property Control Systems
USE PROPERTY ACCOUNTING

Property Inventory
USE FACILITY INVENTORY

PROPERTY TAXES *Jul. 1972*
CIJE: 177 RIE: 318 GC: 620
UF Ad Valorem Tax
BT Taxes
RT Assessed Valuation
Educational Finance
Fiscal Capacity
Property Accounting
Property Appraisal
School Taxes
Tax Rates

Prophylacticians
USE DENTAL HYGIENISTS

Proportion (Mathematics)
USE RATIOS (MATHEMATICS)

PROPOSAL WRITING *Mar. 1980*
CIJE: 60 RIE: 98 GC: 330
SN Process of preparing a statement of goals and procedures as part of an application for a grant or contract award
BT Writing (Composition)
RT Bids
Financial Support
Fund Raising
Grantsmanship
Program Proposals
Research Proposals
Technical Writing

PROPRIETARY SCHOOLS *Jul. 1966*
CIJE: 79 RIE: 207 GC: 340
SN Private schools conducted for profit
UF Specialty Schools
BT Private Schools
RT Certification
Correspondence Schools
Educational Finance
Private Education
Private Financial Support
Small Colleges
Student Costs

Propulsion Development Technicians
USE MECHANICAL DESIGN TECHNICIANS

PROSE *Jul. 1966*
CIJE: 548 RIE: 273 GC: 430
NT Fiction
Nonfiction
BT Literature
RT Connected Discourse
Creative Writing
Descriptive Writing
Drama
Expository Writing
Language Rhythm
Literary Genres
Literary Styles
Poetry
Tragedy
Writing (Composition)

PROSOCIAL BEHAVIOR *May. 1976*
CIJE: 223 RIE: 187 GC: 120
SN Socially valued or positive social actions which are generally supportive of others within the existing social system
BT Social Behavior
RT Affective Behavior
Altruism
Antisocial Behavior
Cooperation
Emotional Response
Friendship
Interpersonal Competence
Peace

Prosodic Features (Speech)
USE SUPRASEGMENTALS

Prosody (Literary)
USE POETRY

PROSTHESES *Jul. 1966*
CIJE: 28 RIE: 18 GC: 220
SN Artificial devices designed to replace absent body parts
UF Cosmetic Prostheses (1967 1980)
BT Assistive Devices (For Disabled)
RT Amputations
Electromechanical Aids
Mobility Aids
Physical Disabilities

PROTESTANTS *Jul. 1966*
CIJE: 53 RIE: 44 GC: 560
NT Amish
Puritans
BT Religious Cultural Groups
RT Christianity

PROTOCOL ANALYSIS *Dec. 1985*
CIJE: 28 RIE: 38 GC: 810
SN Procedure for determining and examining sequences of activities (protocols) used to perform a task, in order to characterize the cognitive/psychological processes involved -- protocols may list motor behaviors, eye movements, subjects' self-reports of their thoughts, etc.
UF Thinking Aloud Protocols
BT Research Methodology
RT Cognitive Processes
Cognitive Psychology
Problem Solving
Skill Analysis
Writing Processes

PROTOCOL MATERIALS *Jan. 1970*
CIJE: 54 RIE: 107 GC: 720
SN Audio and video recordings of behavior which the preservice and inservice teacher education student can observe and analyze
UF Behavioral Situation Films
Teacher Training Films
BT Audiovisual Aids
Instructional Materials
RT Audiovisual Instruction
Behavior
Behavioral Objectives
Instructional Films
Laboratory Training
Microteaching
Sensitivity Training
Teacher Behavior
Teacher Education
Videodisks
Videotape Recordings

PROVERBS *Mar. 1969*
CIJE: 32 RIE: 56 GC: 430
UF Adages
RT Cultural Context
Folk Culture
Idioms

Provincial Aid
USE STATE AID

Provincial Government
USE STATE GOVERNMENT

Provincial Libraries
USE STATE LIBRARIES

Provincial Surveys
USE STATE SURVEYS

Proxemics
USE PERSONAL SPACE

PROXIMITY *Aug. 1977*
CIJE: 50 RIE: 60 GC: 490
SN Relative nearness in time, place, relationship, etc. (note: prior to aug77, the instruction "proximity, use distance" was carried in the thesaurus)
RT Crowding
Distance
Geographic Location
Height
Intervals
Relationship
School Location
Space
Time
Topology
Transportation

PSYCHIATRIC AIDES *Jan. 1969*
CIJE: 18 RIE: 31 GC: 230
SN Persons who assist in the care and treatment of mentally ill patients in psychiatric facilities, working under the direction of nursing and medical staff
UF Psychiatric Technicians
BT Allied Health Personnel
RT Nurses Aides
Psychiatric Hospitals

PSYCHIATRIC HOSPITALS *Jul. 1966*
CIJE: 165 RIE: 86 GC: 230
BT Hospitals
RT Hospital Libraries
Mental Disorders
Mental Health Clinics
Milieu Therapy
Psychiatric Aides
Psychiatrists
Residential Institutions
Therapeutic Environment

PSYCHIATRIC SERVICES *Jul. 1966*
CIJE: 290 RIE: 171 GC: 230
BT Medical Services
RT Counseling Services
Crisis Intervention
Mental Disorders
Mental Health
Mental Health Programs
Physician Patient Relationship
Psychiatrists
Psychiatry
Psychological Services
Psychotherapy

Psychiatric Technicians
USE PSYCHIATRIC AIDES

PSYCHIATRISTS *Jul. 1966*
CIJE: 106 RIE: 55 GC: 230
BT Physicians
RT Hospital Personnel
Medical Associations
Medical Consultants
Medical Services
Physician Patient Relationship
Psychiatric Hospitals
Psychiatric Services
Psychiatry
Psychologists

PSYCHIATRY *Sep. 1968*
CIJE: 413 RIE: 147 GC: 230
SN Prevention, diagnosis, and therapy of emotional illness
UF Neopsychoanalysis
Psychoanalysis
BT Medicine
RT Behavior Disorders
Clinical Psychology
Emotional Adjustment
Emotional Disturbances
Medical Services
Mental Disorders
Mental Health
Personality Problems
Psychiatric Services
Psychiatrists
Psychology
Psychotherapy

PSYCHOACOUSTICS *Jul. 1966*
CIJE: 19 RIE: 27 GC: 490
SN Discipline dealing with the physics of sound as it relates to audition -- includes study of the physiology of the ear and psychology of hearing
BT Acoustics
Psychology
RT Auditory Discrimination
Auditory Perception
Auditory Stimuli
Echolocation
Hearing (Physiology)
Noise (Sound)

Psychoanalysis
USE PSYCHIATRY

Psychocatharsis
USE CATHARSIS

PSYCHOEDUCATIONAL CLINICS *Jul. 1966*
CIJE: 31 RIE: 33 GC: 230
SN Concerned primarily with behavior problems of school children related to the school environment
BT Clinics
RT Educational Diagnosis
Educational Therapy
Mental Health Clinics
Psychoeducational Methods
Psychological Services

PSYCHOEDUCATIONAL METHODS *Mar. 1980*
CIJE: 265 RIE: 272 GC: 310
SN Use of psychological principles and procedures to facilitate learning, in general, and adjustment in educational settings
UF Psychoeducational Processes (1966 1980)
BT Educational Methods
RT Adjustment (To Environment)
Cognitive Restructuring
Counselor Teacher Cooperation
Diagnostic Teaching
Educational Diagnosis
Educational Therapy
Humanistic Education
Intervention
Learning Processes
Learning Strategies
Psychoeducational Clinics
Psychological Services
Suggestopedia
Token Economy
Transcendental Meditation

Psychoeducational Processes (1966 1980)
USE PSYCHOEDUCATIONAL METHODS

PSYCHOLINGUISTICS *Jul. 1966*
CIJE: 1568 RIE: 1539 GC: 450
SN Study of the psychological processes involved in language production and comprehension, including such aspects of language behavior as acquisition and processing
BT Linguistics
RT Bidialectalism
Bilingualism
Child Language
Connected Discourse
Expressive Language
Grammatical Acceptability
Interference (Language)
Interlanguage
Language Acquisition
Language Attitudes
Language Processing
Language Skill Attrition
Language Skills
Linguistic Competence
Linguistic Difficulty (Inherent)
Linguistic Performance
Linguistic Theory
Multilingualism
Neurolinguistics
Psychology
Receptive Language
Sociolinguistics
Verbal Operant Conditioning

PSYCHOLOGICAL CHARACTERISTICS *Jul. 1966*
CIJE: 1071 RIE: 785 GC: 120
NT Attention Span
Cognitive Style
Creativity
Intelligence
Personality Traits
Schemata (Cognition)
BT Individual Characteristics
RT Attribution Theory
Goal Orientation
Individual Psychology
Interpersonal Attraction
Learning Plateaus
Maturity (Individuals)
Midlife Transitions
Phenomenology
Psychological Evaluation
Psychological Needs
Psychological Patterns
Psychological Testing
Psychology
Role Conflict
Self Congruence
Sexual Identity

Psychological Conditioning
USE CONDITIONING

Psychological Design Needs (1968 1980)
USE DESIGN REQUIREMENTS

Psychological Education
USE HUMANISTIC EDUCATION

PSYCHOLOGICAL EVALUATION *Jul. 1966*
CIJE: 481 RIE: 287 GC: 230
SN Evaluation of an individual's cognitive, conative, or affective traits or conditions
UF Clinical Judgment (Psychology)
NT Personality Assessment
BT Evaluation
RT Association Measures
Clinical Psychology
Diagnostic Tests
Personality Measures
Projective Measures
Psychological Characteristics
Psychological Patterns
Psychological Services
Psychological Testing
Psychometrics
School Psychologists

PSYCHOLOGICAL NEEDS *Jul. 1966*
CIJE: 857 RIE: 535 GC: 120
UF Emotional Needs
NT Achievement Need
Affection
Affiliation Need
Personal Space
Security (Psychology)
Self Actualization
Status Need
BT Individual Needs
RT Childhood Needs
Delay Of Gratification
Design Requirements
Goal Orientation
Humanization
Individual Psychology
Need Gratification
Personal Autonomy
Psychological Characteristics
Psychological Services
Spatial Relationship (Facilities)
Student Needs

PSYCHOLOGICAL PATTERNS *Jul. 1966*
CIJE: 1442 RIE: 968 GC: 120
UF Emotional Patterns
NT Alienation
Anger
Anxiety
Apathy
Cognitive Dissonance
Congruence (Psychology)
Depression (Psychology)
Egocentrism
Empathy
Fear
Grief
Identification (Psychology)
Jealousy
Loneliness
Morale
Rejection (Psychology)
Resentment
Withdrawal (Psychology)
RT Affective Behavior
Altruism
Assertiveness
Attitudes
Behavior Patterns
Behavior Problems
Burnout
Catharsis
Coping
Credibility
Emotional Development
Emotional Experience
Emotional Problems
Emotional Response
Ethnicity
Ethnocentrism
Helplessness
Individual Power
Inhibition
Paranoid Behavior
Perspective Taking
Psychological Characteristics
Psychological Evaluation
Psychological Services
Psychological Testing
Psychosomatic Disorders
Responses
Role Conflict
Self Destructive Behavior
Sleep
Social Behavior
Stress Variables
Teaching Styles
Trust (Psychology)
Well Being

Psychological Research
USE PSYCHOLOGICAL STUDIES

PSYCHOLOGICAL SERVICES *Jul. 1966*
CIJE: 312 RIE: 325 GC: 230
UF Sociopsychological Services (1967 1980) #
BT Human Services
RT Ancillary School Services
Mental Health
Psychiatric Services
Psychoeducational Clinics
Psychoeducational Methods
Psychological Evaluation
Psychological Needs
Psychological Patterns
Psychological Studies
Psychological Testing
Psychologists
Psychometrics
Psychotherapy

PSYCHOLOGICAL STUDIES *Jul. 1966*
CIJE: 2799 RIE: 851 GC: 810
SN Basic, applied, and developmental studies conducted to advance knowledge in psychology (note: use a more specific term if possible -- as of oct81, use as a minor descriptor for examples of this kind of research -- use as a major descriptor only as the subject of a document)
UF Psychological Research
NT Force Field Analysis
Interest Research
Personality Studies
BT Behavioral Science Research
RT Clinical Psychology
Cognitive Psychology
Exceptional Child Research
Experimental Psychology
Psychological Services
Psychology
Social Science Research

PSYCHOLOGICAL TESTING *Jul. 1966*
CIJE: 921 RIE: 552 GC: 820
SN Use of tests to assess individuals' or groups' interaction with their environment (note: prior to mar80, the use of this term was not restricted by a scope note, and the instruction "mental measurement, use cognitive measurement" was carried in the thesaurus -- use a more precise term if possible)
UF Mental Tests (1966 1980)
Psychological Tests (1966 1980)
BT Testing
RT Clinical Psychology
Diagnostic Tests
Intelligence Tests
Personality Measures
Prognostic Tests
Psychological Characteristics
Psychological Evaluation
Psychological Patterns
Psychological Services
Psychologists
Psychology
Psychometrics

Psychological Tests (1966 1980)
USE PSYCHOLOGICAL TESTING

PSYCHOLOGISTS *Jul. 1966*
CIJE: 420 RIE: 278 GC: 230
NT School Psychologists
BT Health Personnel
Professional Personnel
RT Counselors
Psychiatrists
Psychological Services
Psychological Testing
Psychology
Researchers
Social Scientists

PSYCHOLOGY *Jul. 1966*
CIJE: 1665 RIE: 1228 GC: 230
NT Behaviorism
Child Psychology
Clinical Psychology
Cognitive Psychology
Community Psychology
Developmental Psychology
Educational Psychology
Experimental Psychology
Individual Psychology
Industrial Psychology
Psychoacoustics
Psychometrics
Psychopathology
Psychophysiology
Social Psychology
Sport Psychology
BT Behavioral Sciences
RT Behavior
Conditioning
Decision Making
Intervention
Psychiatry
Psycholinguistics
Psychological Characteristics
Psychological Studies
Psychological Testing
Psychologists
Psychosomatic Disorders
Sensory Deprivation
Social Science Research
Social Sciences
Verbal Operant Conditioning

PSYCHOMETRICS *Jul. 1966*
CIJE: 497 RIE: 449 GC: 230
SN The development of psychological measuring devices and the analysis of derived data or scores
UF Psychometrists (1967 1980)
BT Psychology
RT Behaviorism
Clinical Psychology
Cognitive Measurement
Cognitive Psychology
Examiners
Latent Trait Theory
Psychological Evaluation
Psychological Services
Psychological Testing
School Psychologists
Statistical Analysis
Test Interpretation
Test Theory

Psychometrists (1967 1980)
USE PSYCHOMETRICS

PSYCHOMOTOR OBJECTIVES *Jul. 1969*
CIJE: 49 RIE: 110 GC: 310
SN Behavioral objectives which emphasize muscular or motor skills, manipulation of materials or objects, or an act which requires neuromuscular coordination
BT Behavioral Objectives
RT Affective Objectives
Cognitive Objectives
Motor Development
Movement Education
Psychomotor Skills

PSYCHOMOTOR SKILLS *Jul. 1966*
CIJE: 789 RIE: 785 GC: 120
SN Ability to manipulate and control limb and body movements
UF Coordination (Psychomotor)
Motor Ability
Motor Skills
NT Marksmanship
Object Manipulation
Perceptual Motor Coordination
BT Skills
RT Behavior
Daily Living Skills
Exercise
Lateral Dominance
Manipulative Materials
Motor Development
Motor Reactions
Movement Education
Neurological Impairments
Neurological Organization
Nonverbal Learning
Perceptual Development
Perceptual Motor Learning
Psychomotor Objectives
Serial Ordering
Skill Analysis
Spatial Ability

PSYCHOPATHOLOGY *Aug. 1968*
CIJE: 617 RIE: 152 GC: 230
SN Pathology of mental and emotional illness
UF Abnormal Psychology
BT Pathology
Psychology
RT Behavior
Behavior Disorders
Behavior Problems
Clinical Psychology
Community Psychology
Depression (Psychology)
Emotional Adjustment
Emotional Disturbances
Emotional Problems
Mental Disorders
Personality Problems
Psychophysiology
Psychosomatic Disorders
Self Mutilation
Social Psychology
Suicide

PSYCHOPHYSIOLOGY *Aug. 1968*
CIJE: 145 RIE: 105 GC: 230
UF Physiological Psychology
BT Physiology
Psychology
RT Biofeedback
Clinical Psychology
Cognitive Psychology
Figural Aftereffects
Meditation
Pathology
Psychopathology
Psychosomatic Disorders
Stimuli

PSYCHOSIS *Jul. 1966*
CIJE: 183 RIE: 71 GC: 230
UF Psychotic Children (1966 1980)
NT Autism
Echolalia
Schizophrenia
BT Mental Disorders
Severe Disabilities
RT Emotional Disturbances
Mental Health
Paranoid Behavior

Psychosomatic Diseases (1968 1980)
USE PSYCHOSOMATIC DISORDERS

PSYCHOSOMATIC DISORDERS *Mar. 1980*
CIJE: 66 RIE: 22 GC: 230
UF Psychosomatic Diseases (1968 1980)
BT Emotional Disturbances
RT Failure To Thrive
Neurosis
Physical Health
Psychological Patterns
Psychology
Psychopathology
Psychophysiology

PSYCHOTHERAPY *Jul. 1966*
CIJE: 1142 RIE: 559 GC: 230
SN Psychological treatment of mental, emotional, or behavioral disorders and maladjustments by specially trained medical or nonmedical professionals in personal or group consultation sessions
NT Gestalt Therapy
Milieu Therapy
Rational Emotive Therapy
Reality Therapy
Relaxation Training
Transactional Analysis
BT Therapy
RT Art Therapy
Behavior Modification
Bibliotherapy
Catharsis
Clinical Psychology
Cognitive Restructuring
Counseling
Crisis Intervention
Dance Therapy
Emotional Adjustment
Emotional Disturbances
Group Therapy
Hypnosis
Individual Psychology
Meditation
Mental Disorders
Mental Health
Music Therapy
Occupational Therapy
Psychiatric Services
Psychiatry
Psychological Services
Rehabilitation
Role Playing
Self Congruence
Therapeutic Environment
Therapeutic Recreation
Therapists

Psychotic Children (1966 1980)
USE PSYCHOSIS

Public Accommodations
USE PUBLIC FACILITIES

PUBLIC ADMINISTRATION *Mar. 1980*
CIJE: 45 RIE: 61 GC: 610
SN The organization and management of government or community affairs (note: see also "public administration education")
BT Administration
RT Business Administration
Government (Administrative Body)
Political Science
Public Administration Education

PUBLIC ADMINISTRATION EDUCATION *Jul. 1966*
CIJE: 63 RIE: 99 GC: 400
SN Professional study of the organization and management of government or community affairs, usually at the baccalaureate level or above (note: prior to mar80, the use of this term was not restricted by a scope note)
BT Professional Education
RT Administrator Education
Business Administration Education
Government (Administrative Body)
Governmental Structure
Management Development
Political Science
Public Administration
Public Affairs Education
Public Service Occupations

PUBLIC AFFAIRS EDUCATION *Jul. 1966*
CIJE: 151 RIE: 236 GC: 400
SN Education designed to develop public understanding of domestic and international issues
BT Education
RT Citizen Participation
Citizenship Education
Citizenship Responsibility
Community Organizations
Controversial Issues (Course Content)
Political Issues
Political Science
Public Administration Education
Public Opinion
Public Service
Social Problems

PUBLIC AGENCIES *Mar. 1980*
CIJE: 412 RIE: 817 GC: 610
UF Community Agencies (Public) (1966 1980)
Government Agencies
NT Planning Commissions
State Agencies
BT Agencies
RT Agency Role
City Government
Community Programs
Federal Government
Federal Programs
Government (Administrative Body)
Government Role
Local Government
Private Agencies
Public Policy
Public Service Occupations
Social Agencies
Urban Renewal Agencies
Welfare Agencies

PUBLIC COLLEGES *Aug. 1986*
CIJE: 25 RIE: 120 GC: 340
SN Degree-granting two- or four-year institutions of higher education funded by and accountable to a state, county, or municipality (note: this concept was previously indexed under "higher education" or "two year colleges," and "public education")
NT Community Colleges
State Colleges
BT Colleges
RT Private Colleges
Public Education

Public Demonstrations
USE DEMONSTRATIONS (CIVIL)

Public Disclosure
USE DISCLOSURE

Public Documents
USE GOVERNMENT PUBLICATIONS

PUBLIC EDUCATION *Jul. 1966*
CIJE: 942 RIE: 947 GC: 340
SN Education supported in part or entirely by taxation (note: coordinate with the appropriate mandatory educational level descriptor)
UF Public Higher Education #
NT Public School Adult Education
BT Education
RT Community Colleges
Compulsory Education
Free Education
Private Education
Public Colleges
Public Schools
Public School Teachers
School Districts
State Boards Of Education
State Colleges
State Departments Of Education
State Schools
State Universities

Public Employees
USE GOVERNMENT EMPLOYEES

PUBLIC FACILITIES *Jul. 1966*
CIJE: 78 RIE: 109 GC: 920
UF Integrated Public Facilities (1966 1980) #
Public Accommodations
Segregated Public Facilities (1966 1980) #
NT Public Libraries
BT Facilities
RT Equal Facilities
Health Facilities
Toilet Facilities
Transportation

PUBLIC HEALTH *Jul. 1966*
CIJE: 710 RIE: 771 GC: 210
UF Community Health (1966 1980)
BT Health
RT Communicable Diseases
Community Health Services
Disease Control
Disease Incidence
Drinking Water
Environmental Standards
Epidemiology
Fluoridation
Hazardous Materials
Home Health Aides
Hygiene
Mental Health
Occupational Safety And Health
Physical Health
Poisons
Pollution
Preventive Medicine
Public Health Legislation
Radiation Effects
Sanitation
Water Treatment

Public Health Laws (1966 1974)
USE PUBLIC HEALTH LEGISLATION

PUBLIC HEALTH LEGISLATION *Nov. 1974*
CIJE: 54 RIE: 60 GC: 610
UF Public Health Laws (1966 1974)
NT Drug Legislation
BT Legislation
RT Laws
Public Health

Public Hearings
USE HEARINGS

Public Higher Education
USE HIGHER EDUCATION; PUBLIC EDUCATION

PUBLIC HOUSING *Jul. 1966*
CIJE: 46 RIE: 49 GC: 550
UF Public Housing Residents (1966 1980)
BT Low Rent Housing
RT Housing Management Aides
Urban Renewal
Welfare Services

Public Housing Residents (1966 1980)
USE PUBLIC HOUSING

Public Image
USE PUBLIC OPINION

PUBLIC LIBRARIES *Jul. 1966*
CIJE: 1185 RIE: 1539 GC: 710
SN Libraries freely available to all, that serve residents of a community, district, or region and receive all or part of their financial support from public funds
NT County Libraries
Regional Libraries
BT Libraries
Public Facilities
RT Archives
Branch Libraries
Community Information Services
Community Resources
Depository Libraries
Intellectual Freedom
Library Networks
Research Libraries
Special Libraries

PUBLIC OFFICIALS *Jul. 1966*
CIJE: 83 RIE: 149 GC: 610
NT City Officials
County Officials
Court Judges
Legislators
State Officials
BT Government Employees
RT Community Leaders
Lobbying
Political Candidates

PUBLIC OPINION *Jul. 1966*
CIJE: 1272 RIE: 1166 GC: 610
UF Public Image
BT Opinions
RT Credibility
Ideology
Majority Attitudes
Mass Instruction
Mass Media Effects
Political Attitudes
Press Opinion
Propaganda
Public Affairs Education
Public Support
Questionnaires
Social Attitudes
Surveys
Voting

Public Participation
USE CITIZEN PARTICIPATION

PUBLIC POLICY *Jul. 1966*
CIJE: 1879 RIE: 2803 GC: 610
SN Governing principles that serve as guidelines or rules for decision-making and action as embodied in legislative and judicial enactments
UF Family Services Policy #
BT Policy
RT Court Doctrine
Educational Assessment
Federal Programs
Futures (Of Society)
Government Role
Government School Relationship
Institutional Mission
Legislation
National Programs
Politics
Public Agencies
Public Service
Revenue Sharing
Self Determination
Taxes

= Two or more Descriptors are used to represent this term.
The term's main entry shows the appropriate coordination.

PUBLIC RELATIONS *Jul. 1966*
CIJE: 1423 RIE: 1378 GC: 330
BT Relationship
RT Communication Audits
Human Services
Institutional Advancement
Labor Relations
Library Extension
Organizational Communication
Publicity
Public Service
Public Support
School Community Relationship

PUBLIC SCHOOL ADULT EDUCATION *Jul. 1966*
CIJE: 36 RIE: 156 GC: 340
BT Adult Education
Public Education
RT Adult Basic Education
Adult Vocational Education
Community Schools
High School Equivalency Programs

Public School Systems (1966 1980)
USE PUBLIC SCHOOLS; SCHOOL DISTRICTS

PUBLIC SCHOOL TEACHERS *Nov. 1968*
CIJE: 149 RIE: 214 GC: 360
BT Government Employees
Teachers
RT Boards Of Education
Elementary School Teachers
Negotiation Agreements
Public Education
Public Schools
Secondary School Teachers

PUBLIC SCHOOLS *Jul. 1966*
CIJE: 1823 RIE: 3129 GC: 340
SN (Note: coordinate with the appropriate mandatory educational level descriptor)
UF Public School Systems (1966 1980) #
BT Schools
RT Public Education
Public School Teachers
School Districts
State Schools

PUBLIC SERVICE *Aug. 1986*
CIJE: 26 RIE: 44 GC: 330
SN Extension or voluntary service with government, community, or charitable organizations, including activity of educational institutions and personnel made available to the public outside the context of regular instruction and research programs (note: for public service employment, use "public service occupations")
RT Citizen Participation
Community Involvement
Community Programs
Government School Relationship
Public Affairs Education
Public Policy
Public Relations
Public Support
School Community Relationship
Services
Social Responsibility
Volunteers

PUBLIC SERVICE OCCUPATIONS *Sep. 1973*
CIJE: 66 RIE: 201 GC: 640
SN Employment necessary to accomplish the mission of local, county, state, federal, or other government, except for military service
BT Occupations
RT Government (Administrative Body)
Government Employees
Public Administration Education
Public Agencies
Service Occupations

PUBLIC SPEAKING *Jul. 1966*
CIJE: 316 RIE: 359 GC: 400
BT Speech Communication
RT Audience Analysis
Debate
Persuasive Discourse
Rhetorical Invention
Speech
Speeches

PUBLIC SUPPORT *Jul. 1966*
CIJE: 340 RIE: 288 GC: 610
SN Moral or financial support supplied by the public or its funds (note: use "school support" for support of educational institutions -- prior to mar80, the use of this term was not restricted by a scope note)
RT Community Support
Federal Aid
Financial Support
Majority Attitudes
Private Financial Support
Public Opinion
Public Relations
Public Service
School Support
State Aid

PUBLIC TELEVISION *Jul. 1966*
CIJE: 291 RIE: 384 GC: 720
SN Non-commercial television, publicly owned and operated, that is dedicated to educational, cultural, and public-service programs
BT Television
RT Commercial Television
Educational Television

Public Utilities
USE UTILITIES

Public Welfare Assistance
USE WELFARE SERVICES

PUBLICATIONS *Jul. 1966*
CIJE: 969 RIE: 1365 GC: 720
NT Book Reviews
Books
Catalogs
Comics (Publications)
Computer Software Reviews
Government Publications
Literature Reviews
Pamphlets
Reference Materials
Reports
School Publications
Serials
State Of The Art Reviews
Test Reviews
RT Authors
Communications
Copyrights
Editing
Editorials
Editors
Faculty Publishing
Instructional Materials
Journalism
Journalism Education
Layout (Publications)
Library Acquisition
Library Collections
Library Materials
Library Material Selection
Mass Media
New Journalism
Nonprint Media
Photocomposition
Photojournalism
Popular Culture
Printing
Publishing Industry
Publish Or Perish Issue
Reading Materials
Resource Materials
Writing For Publication

PUBLICITY *Mar. 1980*
CIJE: 245 RIE: 384 GC: 720
SN Activities and/or materials used to disseminate information to gain public notice
NT Advertising
Institutional Advancement
BT Communication (Thought Transfer)
Information Dissemination
RT Communications
Library Extension
Mass Media
Public Relations

PUBLICIZE (1968 1980) *Mar. 1980*
CIJE: 518 RIE: 710 GC: 720
SN Invalid descriptor -- see such descriptors as "publicity," "advertising," "merchandising," "propaganda," etc.

PUBLISH OR PERISH ISSUE *Aug. 1986*
CIJE: RIE: GC: 320
SN Controversial practice among some professions of linking scholarly writing to career advancement and remuneration
RT Faculty Publishing
Promotion (Occupational)
Publications
Writing For Publication

Publishing Houses
USE PUBLISHING INDUSTRY

PUBLISHING INDUSTRY *Jul. 1966*
CIJE: 765 RIE: 548 GC: 650
UF Book Industry
Publishing Houses
BT Industry
RT Copyrights
Database Producers
Editors
Electronic Publishing
Information Dissemination
Mass Media
Printing
Publications
Reprography
Textbook Publication
Writing For Publication

PUERTO RICAN CULTURE *Jul. 1966*
CIJE: 50 RIE: 181 GC: 560
BT Latin American Culture
RT Puerto Ricans

PUERTO RICANS *Jul. 1966*
CIJE: 264 RIE: 867 GC: 560
SN Includes puerto ricans in puerto rico and the united states (note: for the latter group, coordinate "puerto ricans" and "hispanic americans")
BT Latin Americans
RT Ethnic Groups
Hispanic Americans
Puerto Rican Culture
Spanish Speaking
Trust Responsibility (Government)

Pulse Rate
USE HEART RATE

Punch Press Operators
USE MACHINE TOOL OPERATORS

Punch Presses
USE MACHINE TOOLS

PUNCTUATION *Jul. 1966*
CIJE: 118 RIE: 156 GC: 450
BT Written Language
RT Capitalization (Alphabetic)
Sentence Structure
Spelling
Writing Skills

PUNISHMENT *Jan. 1973*
CIJE: 287 RIE: 149 GC: 520
NT Corporal Punishment
BT Reinforcement
RT Discipline
Negative Reinforcement
Sanctions
Sentencing

Punjabi
USE PANJABI

PUNS *Jul. 1970*
CIJE: 19 RIE: 4 GC: 430
BT Figurative Language
RT Poetry

PUPIL PERSONNEL SERVICES *Nov. 1969*
CIJE: 287 RIE: 366 GC: 240
SN Supportive, non-instructional services to elementary and secondary pupils in a school setting
UF Attendance Services (1968 1980) #
BT Ancillary School Services
RT Counseling Services
Guidance Programs
Pupil Personnel Workers
School Counseling
School Guidance
School Health Services
School Orientation
Student Personnel Services
Student Placement

PUPIL PERSONNEL WORKERS *Nov. 1969*
CIJE: 163 RIE: 80 GC: 240
SN Professional personnel who provide supportive, non-instructional services to elementary and secondary pupils in a school setting
NT Attendance Officers
BT School Personnel
RT Counseling Services
Deans Of Students
Faculty Advisers
Guidance Personnel
Health Personnel
Ombudsmen
Pupil Personnel Services
Resident Advisers
School Counselors
School Psychologists
School Social Workers
Student Personnel Workers

PUPILLARY DILATION *Sep. 1968*
CIJE: 14 RIE: 4 GC: 110
UF Iris Reflex
Pupillary Reflex
Pupillary Response
BT Motor Reactions
RT Eye Movements
Eyes

Pupillary Reflex
USE PUPILLARY DILATION

Pupillary Response
USE PUPILLARY DILATION

Pupils
USE STUDENTS

Puppet Shows
USE PUPPETRY

PUPPETRY *Apr. 1972*
CIJE: 89 RIE: 64 GC: 420
UF Puppets
Puppet Shows
BT Theater Arts

Puppets
USE PUPPETRY

PURCHASING *Jul. 1966*
CIJE: 617 RIE: 450 GC: 620
UF Equipment Purchasing
RT Bids
Consumer Economics
Consumer Education
Consumer Protection
Cooperatives
Educational Finance
Equipment Standards
Financial Needs
Library Acquisition
Ownership
Specifications

PURITANS *Nov. 1969*
CIJE: 18 RIE: 12 GC: 560
BT Protestants
RT Colonial History (United States)

Pushto
USE PASHTO

Pushtu
USE PASHTO

PUZZLES *Jul. 1966*
CIJE: 189 RIE: 157 GC: 730
BT Games
RT Educational Games
Toys

PYRAMID ORGANIZATION *Jul. 1966*
CIJE: 12 RIE: 15 GC: 520
BT Organization
RT Horizontal Organization
Vertical Organization

Q Analysis
USE Q METHODOLOGY

= Two or more Descriptors are used to represent this term.
The term's main entry shows the appropriate coordination.

Q METHODOLOGY *Mar. 1980*
CIJE: 65 RIE: 86 GC: 820
SN Any of several statistical procedures, used primarily in personality assessment, in which the data are analyzed as though the persons in the study were themselves the measuring instruments and the tests or items were the subjects
UF Q Analysis
Q Sort (1967 1980)
Q Technique
BT Measurement Techniques
RT Factor Analysis
Forced Choice Technique
Item Analysis
Personality Assessment
Personality Measures
Rating Scales
Self Concept Measures
Statistical Analysis
Testing

Q Sort (1967 1980)
USE Q METHODOLOGY

Q Technique
USE Q METHODOLOGY

Quadriplegia (1969 1980)
USE NEUROLOGICAL IMPAIRMENTS

QUALIFICATIONS *Jul. 1966*
CIJE: 112 RIE: 163 GC: 630
SN Abilities, aptitudes, achievements, or other personal characteristics that suit an individual to particular positions or tasks
NT Administrator Qualifications
Counselor Qualifications
Employment Qualifications
Supervisor Qualifications
Teacher Qualifications
BT Standards
RT Ability
Achievement
Aptitude
Background
Certification
Credentials
Degrees (Academic)
Disqualification
Performance
Portfolios (Background Materials)
Prerequisites
Reputation
Resumes (Personal)
Skills

QUALITATIVE RESEARCH *Dec. 1985*
CIJE: 47 RIE: 64 GC: 810
SN Research providing detailed narrative descriptions and explanations of phenomena investigated, with lesser emphasis given to numerical quantifications -- methods used to collect qualitative data include ethnographic practices such as observing and interviewing (note: use as a minor descriptor for examples of this kind of research -- use as a major descriptor only as the subject of a document)
BT Research
RT Case Studies
Ethnography
Evaluation Methods
Field Studies
Interviews
Naturalistic Observation
Participant Observation
Research Methodology
Social Science Research

QUALITY CIRCLES *Apr. 1986*
CIJE: 62 RIE: 35 GC: 320
SN Voluntary groups of individuals within an organization who meet regularly to identify, analyze, and solve work-related problems, with the goal of improving quality and productivity
BT Groups
RT Administration
Employer Employee Relationship
Management Teams
Organizational Development
Participative Decision Making
Quality Control

QUALITY CONTROL *Jul. 1966*
CIJE: 337 RIE: 492 GC: 650
SN Techniques, such as inspection and regulation, that are used to insure a uniform quality of performance or product
BT Evaluation Methods
RT Accountability
Accreditation (Institutions)
Audits (Verification)
Certification
Editing
Inspection
Operations Research
Performance
Pretesting
Program Effectiveness
Quality Circles
Reliability
Standards

Quality Education
USE EDUCATIONAL QUALITY

QUALITY OF LIFE *Sep. 1977*
CIJE: 637 RIE: 777 GC: 520
SN Any combination of objective standards and subjective attitudes, both other- and self-imposed, by which individuals and groups assess their life situations
UF Life Quality
Productive Living (1967 1980)
NT Quality Of Working Life
Well Being
RT Advantaged
Appropriate Technology
Community Development
Community Satisfaction
Developed Nations
Developing Nations
Disadvantaged
Ecology
Economic Climate
Economic Status
Educational Quality
Environmental Standards
Evaluation
Human Factors Engineering
Humanization
Life Satisfaction
Living Standards
Physical Environment
Productivity
Science And Society
Social Class
Social Environment
Social Indicators
Social Problems
Social Status
Social Values
Socioeconomic Status
Technology
Values

QUALITY OF WORKING LIFE *Apr. 1986*
CIJE: 31 RIE: 25 GC: 630
SN Phenomenological construct of working environments including such extrinsic aspects as pay, benefits, security, safety, production, and efficiency, and such intrinsic aspects as variety and challenge, responsibility, meaningful contribution, and recognition
BT Quality Of Life
RT Careers
Employee Assistance Programs
Employer Employee Relationship
Employment
Employment Patterns
Human Factors Engineering
Industrial Psychology
Job Enrichment
Job Satisfaction
Labor Conditions
Labor Relations
Life Satisfaction
Occupations
Organizational Climate
Organizational Development
Productivity
Technology
Unions
Work Environment

Quality Point Ratio
USE GRADE POINT AVERAGE

Quantitative Research (Statistics)
USE STATISTICAL ANALYSIS

Quantitative Tests (1980 1985) (Mathematics)
USE MATHEMATICS TESTS

QUANTUM MECHANICS *Jul. 1966*
CIJE: 387 RIE: 17 GC: 490
BT Mechanics (Physics)
RT Acceleration (Physics)
Energy
Force
Mathematics
Matter
Motion
Nuclear Physics
Relativity
Space

QUARTER SYSTEM *Jul. 1966*
CIJE: 26 RIE: 103 GC: 350
SN Division of the academic year into four equal terms
BT School Schedules
RT Extended School Year
Semester System
Trimester System
Year Round Schools

QUASIEXPERIMENTAL DESIGN *Mar. 1980*
CIJE: 33 RIE: 33 GC: 810
SN Plan or organization of research that is conducted in settings where normal experimental controls are not, or cannot be, applied
BT Research Design
RT Control Groups
Experimental Groups
Matched Groups
Research
Research Methodology
Sampling
Scientific Methodology

QUECHUA *Jul. 1966*
CIJE: 11 RIE: 35 GC: 440
UF Kechua
BT American Indian Languages

Question Answer Interviews (1966 1980)
USE INTERVIEWS

QUESTIONING TECHNIQUES *Jul. 1966*
CIJE: 1200 RIE: 1052 GC: 310
SN Methods used for constructing and presenting questions in order to promote effective discussions and learning or to elicit information
BT Methods
RT Discovery Learning
Discussion (Teaching Technique)
Inquiry
Interviews
Learning Processes
Questionnaires
Teaching Methods
Test Format

QUESTIONNAIRES *Jul. 1966*
CIJE: 3068 RIE: 9146 GC: 830
SN Structured sets of questions on specified subjects that are used to gather information, attitudes, or opinions
BT Measures (Individuals)
RT Answer Sheets
Attitude Measures
Biographical Inventories
Data Collection
Evaluation Methods
Opinions
Public Opinion
Questioning Techniques
Research
Scoring
Surveys

QUICHE *Dec. 1970*
CIJE: 2 RIE: 3 GC: 440
BT Mayan Languages
RT Yucatec

Quizzes
USE TESTS

QUOTAS *Jan. 1978*
CIJE: 73 RIE: 46 GC: 540
SN Numbers or percentages to be met for a specific objective
RT Affirmative Action
Criteria
Mathematical Concepts
Objectives
Ratios (Mathematics)
Selective Admission
Standards

R And D
USE RESEARCH AND DEVELOPMENT

R D And E
USE RESEARCH AND DEVELOPMENT

RACE *Jul. 1966*
CIJE: 147 RIE: 296 GC: 120
SN Concept used to describe people who are united or classified together on the basis of genetically transmitted physical similarities deriving from their common descent, and who are also frequently thought to share cultural and social traits
BT Physical Characteristics
RT Anthropology
Biology
Blacks
Culture
Ethnic Groups
Ethnicity
Indigenous Populations
Minority Groups
Nature Nurture Controversy
Racial Attitudes
Racial Balance
Racial Composition
Racial Differences
Racial Discrimination
Racial Distribution
Racial Factors
Racial Identification
Racial Integration
Racial Relations
Racial Segregation
Whites

Race Influences (1966 1980)
USE RACIAL FACTORS

Race Relations (1966 1980)
USE RACIAL RELATIONS

RACIAL ATTITUDES *Jul. 1966*
CIJE: 780 RIE: 752 GC: 540
SN Attitudes about race or particular racial groups (note: prior to mar80, this term was not restricted by a scope note)
BT Attitudes
RT Black Attitudes
Black Stereotypes
Cultural Differences
Ethnicity
Ethnic Stereotypes
Integration Readiness
Race
Racial Differences
Racial Discrimination
Racial Identification
Racial Relations
School Desegregation

RACIAL BALANCE *Jul. 1966*
CIJE: 128 RIE: 225 GC: 540
SN Racial composition of a spatial unit or institution, either directly proportional to the racial composition of the society, or meeting other standards set as desirable for that particular situation
UF Racial Imbalance
BT Racial Composition
RT Affirmative Action
Race
Racial Factors
Racial Integration
Racially Balanced Schools
Racial Relations
Racial Segregation
Teacher Distribution
Tokenism

RACIAL BIAS *Mar. 1980*
CIJE: 305 RIE: 292 GC: 540
SN Prejudicial opinions about particular groups because of their race (note: prior to mar80, the instruction "racial bias, use racial discrimination" was carried in the thesaurus)
UF Racial Prejudice
BT Social Bias
RT Affirmative Action
Black Stereotypes
Ethnic Bias
Racial Differences
Racial Discrimination
Racial Identification
Racial Relations

RACIAL CHARACTERISTICS (1966 1980) *Mar. 1980*
CIJE: 52 RIE: 112 GC: 540
SN Invalid descriptor -- see such descriptors as "race" and "racial differences" or coordinate specific populations (e.g., "blacks," "whites," etc.) with specific characteristics (e.g., "psychological characteristics," "physical characteristics," etc.)

RACIAL COMPOSITION *Jul. 1966*
CIJE: 144 RIE: 337 GC: 550
SN Proportional representation of racial groups within an institutional or spatial entity, e.g., school, town, district, etc. (note: do not confuse with "racial distribution," the dispersal of groups among entities -- prior to mar80, the use of this term was not restricted by a scope note)
NT Racial Balance
BT Demography
RT Affirmative Action
Busing
Neighborhood Integration
Population Distribution
Race
Racial Distribution
Racial Factors
Racial Integration
Racial Relations
Residential Patterns
School Desegregation
Tokenism

Racial Cultural Groups
USE ETHNIC GROUPS

RACIAL DIFFERENCES *Jul. 1966*
CIJE: 1299 RIE: 1332 GC: 510
BT Differences
RT Black Stereotypes
Cultural Differences
Ethnic Stereotypes
Ethnocentrism
Individual Differences
Intermarriage
Nature Nurture Controversy
Physical Characteristics
Race
Racial Attitudes
Racial Bias
Racial Factors
Racial Identification
Social Differences

RACIAL DISCRIMINATION *Jul. 1966*
CIJE: 1611 RIE: 1404 GC: 540
SN Restriction or denial of rights, privileges, and choice because of race (note: do not confuse with "racial bias")
NT Racial Segregation
BT Social Discrimination
RT Affirmative Action
Age Discrimination
Educational Discrimination
Equal Education
Equal Facilities
Equal Opportunities (Jobs)
Ethnic Discrimination
Ghettos
Race
Racial Attitudes
Racial Bias
Racial Relations
Reverse Discrimination
Segregationist Organizations
Selective Admission
Slavery

RACIAL DISTRIBUTION *Jul. 1966*
CIJE: 77 RIE: 256 GC: 550
SN Dispersal of racial groups among geographic, spatial, or institutional units (note: do not confuse with "racial composition," the proportional representation of these groups within units -- prior to mar80, the use of this term was not restricted by a scope note)
BT Population Distribution
RT Black Population Trends
Ethnic Distribution
Geographic Distribution
Human Geography
Incidence
Neighborhood Integration
Race
Racial Composition
Residential Patterns

RACIAL FACTORS *Jul. 1966*
CIJE: 604 RIE: 530 GC: 540
UF Race Influences (1966 1980)
BT Influences
RT Black Achievement
Cultural Influences
Minority Group Influences
Race
Racial Balance
Racial Composition
Racial Differences
Racial Identification
Racial Relations

RACIAL IDENTIFICATION *Mar. 1980*
CIJE: 144 RIE: 100 GC: 540
SN Classification of oneself or another person or group as a member of a particular race (note: prior to mar80, the instruction "racial self identification, use self concept" was carried in the thesaurus)
UF Racial Identity
Racial Recognition (1966 1980)
Racial Self Identification
BT Identification
RT Black Attitudes
Black Power
Black Stereotypes
Black Studies
Cultural Traits
Ethnicity
Ethnic Stereotypes
Race
Racial Attitudes
Racial Bias
Racial Differences
Racial Factors
Self Concept

Racial Identity
USE RACIAL IDENTIFICATION

Racial Imbalance
USE RACIAL BALANCE

RACIAL INTEGRATION *Jul. 1966*
CIJE: 578 RIE: 753 GC: 540
UF Anti Segregation Programs (1967 1980)
Integrated Public Facilities (1966 1980) #
Integration (Racial)
Urban Desegregation
BT Social Integration
RT Affirmative Action
Biracial Committees
Black Achievement
Busing
Civil Rights
Civil Rights Legislation
Classroom Desegregation
College Desegregation
Desegregation Effects
Desegregation Litigation
Desegregation Methods
Desegregation Plans
Educational Parks
Integration Readiness
Integration Studies
Neighborhood Integration
Personnel Integration
Race
Racial Balance
Racial Composition
Racially Balanced Schools
Racial Relations
Racial Segregation
School Desegregation
Tokenism
Voluntary Desegregation

Racial Interaction
USE RACIAL RELATIONS

Racial Prejudice
USE RACIAL BIAS

Racial Recognition (1966 1980)
USE RACIAL IDENTIFICATION

RACIAL RELATIONS *Mar. 1980*
CIJE: 1105 RIE: 975 GC: 540
SN Contact and interaction between/among racial groups
UF Black White Relations
Interracial Relations
Race Relations (1966 1980)
Racial Interaction
White Black Relations
BT Intergroup Relations
RT Biracial Committees
Black History
Black Power
Blacks
Cultural Differences
Cultural Interrelationships
Cultural Pluralism
Ethnic Relations
Race
Racial Attitudes
Racial Balance
Racial Bias
Racial Composition
Racial Discrimination
Racial Factors
Racial Integration
Racial Segregation
Whites

RACIAL SEGREGATION *Jul. 1966*
CIJE: 306 RIE: 307 GC: 540
UF Segregated Public Facilities (1966 1980) #
Segregation (Racial)
NT De Facto Segregation
De Jure Segregation
BT Racial Discrimination
RT Black History
Civil Rights
College Segregation
Ghettos
Housing Discrimination
Race
Racial Balance
Racial Integration
Racially Balanced Schools
Racial Relations
School Resegregation
School Segregation
Segregationist Organizations

Racial Self Identification
USE RACIAL IDENTIFICATION

RACIALLY BALANCED SCHOOLS *Jul. 1966*
CIJE: 72 RIE: 115 GC: 540
BT Schools
RT Affirmative Action
Black Education
Busing
Racial Balance
Racial Integration
Racial Segregation
School Desegregation
Transfer Students

RACISM (1966 1980) *Mar. 1980*
CIJE: 517 RIE: 352 GC: 540
SN Invalid descriptor -- used for both actions and attitudes -- see such descriptors as "racial discrimination" and "racial bias"

Racket Sports
USE RACQUET SPORTS

RACQUET SPORTS *Jun. 1984*
CIJE: 1 RIE: 1 GC: 470
UF Racket Sports
NT Badminton
Racquetball
Squash (Game)
Tennis
BT Athletics
RT Table Tennis

RACQUETBALL *Jun. 1984*
CIJE: 8 RIE: 3 GC: 470
BT Racquet Sports
RT Handball

RADAR *Aug. 1968*
CIJE: 12 RIE: 18 GC: 910
BT Electronic Equipment
RT Air Traffic Control
Electronics
Navigation
Telecommunications

RADIATION *Jul. 1966*
CIJE: 326 RIE: 208 GC: 490
SN Process of energy emission
NT Light
Nuclear Energy
Solar Energy
BT Energy
RT Fallout Shelters
Hazardous Materials
Laboratory Safety
Lasers
Luminescence
Nuclear Physics
Nuclear Technology
Optics
Physical Environment
Physics
Radiation Biology
Radiation Effects
Radioisotopes
Radiology
Safety
Spectroscopy
Waste Disposal

RADIATION BIOLOGY *Jul. 1966*
CIJE: 24 RIE: 25 GC: 490
SN Study of the effects of radiation on living organisms (note: use "radiology" for materials concerning the application of radiation in medical diagnosis and treatment -- prior to mar80, this term did not carry a scope note)
UF Radiobiology
BT Biology
RT Atomic Structure
Atomic Theory
Biophysics
Chemistry
Ecology
Genetic Engineering
Genetics
Marine Biology
Medicine
Nuclear Energy
Nuclear Physics
Nuclear Technology
Organic Chemistry
Physical Sciences
Physics
Physiology
Radiation
Radiology
Toxicology

Radiation Damage
USE RADIATION EFFECTS

RADIATION EFFECTS *Aug. 1968*
CIJE: 87 RIE: 64 GC: 490
SN Changes in the properties of liquids, gases, and solids caused by radiation (e.g., gamma rays, x-rays, neutrons)
UF Radiation Damage
RT Diseases
Ecological Factors
Environmental Influences
Fallout Shelters
Health
Laboratory Safety
Nuclear Energy
Nuclear Physics
Nuclear Technology
Nuclear Warfare
Poisoning
Pollution
Public Health
Radiation
Radioisotopes
Radiology
Safety
Solar Energy

= Two or more Descriptors are used to represent this term.
The term's main entry shows the appropriate coordination.

Radiation Therapy
USE RADIOLOGY

Radiation Therapy Technologists
USE RADIOLOGIC TECHNOLOGISTS

RADIO *Jul. 1966*
CIJE: 586 RIE: 913 GC: 720
UF Radio Technology (1967 1980)
NT Educational Radio
BT Mass Media
Telecommunications
RT Audiences
Audiodisks
Audio Equipment
Audiotape Recordings
Broadcast Industry
Broadcast Reception Equipment
Electronic Equipment
Journalism
Journalism Education
Networks
News Media
Popular Culture
Production Techniques
Programing (Broadcast)
Television
Television Radio Repairers

Radio Programing
USE PROGRAMING (BROADCAST)

Radio Technology (1967 1980)
USE RADIO

Radio Television Repairers
USE TELEVISION RADIO REPAIRERS

Radiobiology
USE RADIATION BIOLOGY

RADIOGRAPHERS *Jul. 1966*
CIJE: 2 RIE: 14 GC: 640
UF Industrial X Ray Operators
BT Paraprofessional Personnel
RT Metallurgical Technicians
Nuclear Technology
Radiologic Technologists

RADIOISOTOPES *Jul. 1966*
CIJE: 90 RIE: 29 GC: 490
RT Atomic Structure
Atomic Theory
Biology
Chemistry
Genetics
Inorganic Chemistry
Matter
Nuclear Energy
Nuclear Physics
Nuclear Technology
Physics
Radiation
Radiation Effects
Radiology

RADIOLOGIC TECHNOLOGISTS *Aug. 1969*
CIJE: 9 RIE: 62 GC: 210
SN Personnel responsible for applying roentgen rays and radioactive substances to patients for diagnostic and therapeutic purposes
UF Nuclear Medicine Technologists
Radiation Therapy Technologists
X Ray Technologists
BT Allied Health Personnel
RT Cancer
Nuclear Technology
Radiographers
Radiology

RADIOLOGY *Jun. 1969*
CIJE: 37 RIE: 45 GC: 210
SN Use of radiation in medical diagnosis and treatment (note: for documents concerning the effects of radiation on living organisms, use "radiation biology")
UF Nuclear Medicine
Radiation Therapy
X Rays (Medicine)
BT Technology
RT Cancer
Crystallography
Genetic Engineering
Medicine
Nuclear Technology
Physics
Radiation
Radiation Biology
Radiation Effects
Radioisotopes
Radiologic Technologists

Ragtime Music
USE JAZZ

RAIL TRANSPORTATION *Apr. 1970*
CIJE: 23 RIE: 40 GC: 650
UF Railroads
Railways
BT Transportation
RT Marketing

Railroads
USE RAIL TRANSPORTATION

Railways
USE RAIL TRANSPORTATION

RAISED LINE DRAWINGS *Jul. 1966*
CIJE: 13 RIE: 9 GC: 220
BT Sensory Aids
Visual Aids
RT Blindness
Braille
Illustrations
Tactile Adaptation

Range (Distance)
USE DISTANCE

Rank In Class
USE CLASS RANK

RAPE *Sep. 1975*
CIJE: 101 RIE: 114 GC: 530
UF Statutory Rape
BT Sexual Abuse
RT Aggression
Battered Women
Crime
Incest
Sexual Harassment
Sexuality
Victims Of Crime
Violence

Rapid Reading (1966 1980)
USE SPEED READING

RAPPORT *Jul. 1966*
CIJE: 98 RIE: 64 GC: 510
BT Interpersonal Relationship
RT Counseling Techniques
Human Relations
Interpersonal Attraction
Interpersonal Communication
Trust (Psychology)

Rate Tests
USE TIMED TESTS

RATING SCALES *Jul. 1966*
CIJE: 1503 RIE: 1600 GC: 830
SN Forms for recording the estimated magnitude of a trait or quality (note: do not confuse with "check lists" -- use a more specific term if possible)
NT Behavior Rating Scales
Semantic Differential
BT Measures (Individuals)
RT Achievement Rating
Check Lists
Forced Choice Technique
Informal Assessment
Interrater Reliability
Measurement Techniques
Multitrait Multimethod Techniques
Q Methodology
Scaling

RATIONAL EMOTIVE THERAPY *Mar. 1980*
CIJE: 88 RIE: 31 GC: 230
SN Cognitive-behavior therapy based on the premise that individuals' emotional disturbances stem from irrational belief systems -- uses empirical method to combat irrationality so individuals become more realistic
UF Rational Therapy (1968 1980)
BT Psychotherapy
RT Behavior Modification
Cognitive Restructuring

RATIONAL NUMBERS *Feb. 1970*
CIJE: 74 RIE: 60 GC: 480
NT Integers
BT Numbers
RT Reciprocals (Mathematics)

Rational Therapy (1968 1980)
USE RATIONAL EMOTIVE THERAPY

RATIOS (MATHEMATICS) *Jan. 1969*
CIJE: 118 RIE: 121 GC: 480
UF Proportion (Mathematics)
NT Counselor Client Ratio
Intelligence Quotient
Percentage
Relevance (Information Retrieval)
Tax Rates
Teacher Student Ratio
RT Computation
Incidence
Mathematical Concepts
Quotas
Relationship

RATS *Jul. 1966*
CIJE: 62 RIE: 25 GC: 490
BT Animals
RT Laboratory Animals
Pesticides
Pests

RAW SCORES *Oct. 1970*
CIJE: 41 RIE: 101 GC: 820
SN Scores expressed in their original form without statistical treatment, such as the number of correct answers on a test
UF Crude Scores
Gross Scores
Obtained Scores
Original Scores
BT Scores
RT Cutting Scores
Equated Scores
Error Of Measurement
Grade Equivalent Scores
Guessing (Tests)
Scoring Formulas
Statistical Data
True Scores
Weighted Scores

REACTION TIME *Sep. 1969*
CIJE: 611 RIE: 198 GC: 120
UF Response Latency
Response Time
RT Conceptual Tempo
Encoding (Psychology)
Motor Reactions
Perceptual Motor Coordination
Responses
Response Style (Tests)
Time Factors (Learning)

Reactive Behavior (1966 1980)
USE RESPONSES

Reactive Inhibition
USE INHIBITION

READABILITY *Jul. 1966*
CIJE: 596 RIE: 640 GC: 460
SN The quality of reading matter that makes it interesting and understandable to those for whom it is written (note: prior to jun80, "reading difficulty" and "reading level" were occasionally used to index this concept)
RT Cloze Procedure
Content Area Reading
High Interest Low Vocabulary Books
Readability Formulas
Reader Text Relationship
Reading
Reading Comprehension
Reading Instruction
Reading Rate
Story Grammar
Telegraphic Materials
Textbook Evaluation

READABILITY FORMULAS *Mar. 1977*
CIJE: 165 RIE: 133 GC: 460
SN Devices, indexes, or methods for determining the level of difficulty of written material based on the vocabulary, sentence length and structure, and other factors
BT Evaluation Methods
RT Content Analysis
Difficulty Level
Measurement Techniques
Readability
Reading
Reading Comprehension
Textbook Evaluation

READER RESPONSE *Oct. 1983*
CIJE: 245 RIE: 175 GC: 110
SN Readers' reactions to written work, including the way these reactions shape interpretation
BT Responses
RT Literary Criticism
Literature Appreciation
Reader Text Relationship
Reading
Reading Comprehension
Reading Habits
Reading Interests
Reading Processes
Reading Rate
Reading Skills

READER TEXT RELATIONSHIP *Dec. 1985*
CIJE: 85 RIE: 92 GC: 460
SN The character or quality of the reader's involvement or connection with the material being read
BT Relationship
RT Readability
Reader Response
Reading
Reading Comprehension
Reading Materials
Reading Processes
Reading Writing Relationship
Story Grammar

Readers (Materials)
USE READING MATERIALS

READERS THEATER *Dec. 1970*
CIJE: 56 RIE: 59 GC: 420
BT Theater Arts
RT Acting
Creative Dramatics
Oral Interpretation

READINESS *Jul. 1966*
CIJE: 147 RIE: 246 GC: 120
SN Preparedness to respond or react
UF Readiness (Mental) (1966 1980)
NT Integration Readiness
Learning Readiness
Reading Readiness
School Readiness
Writing Readiness
RT Ability
Developmental Tasks
Individual Development
Motivation
Schemata (Cognition)

Readiness (Mental) (1966 1980)
USE READINESS

READING *Jul. 1966*
CIJE: 981 RIE: 2362 GC: 460
SN (Note: use a more specific term if possible)
UF Applied Reading (1966 1980)
NT Basal Reading
Beginning Reading
Content Area Reading
Corrective Reading
Critical Reading
Directed Reading Activity
Early Reading
Functional Reading
Independent Reading
Individualized Reading
Music Reading
Oral Reading
Reading Aloud To Others
Recreational Reading
Remedial Reading
Silent Reading

Speed Reading
Story Reading
Sustained Silent Reading
BT Language Arts
Literacy
RT Advance Organizers
Bibliotherapy
Braille
Cloze Procedure
Context Clues
Decoding (Reading)
Diacritical Marking
Informal Reading Inventories
Initial Teaching Alphabet
Inner Speech (Subvocal)
Language Processing
Miscue Analysis
Pattern Recognition
Phoneme Grapheme Correspondence
Readability
Readability Formulas
Reader Response
Reader Text Relationship
Reading Ability
Reading Achievement
Reading Assignments
Reading Centers
Reading Comprehension
Reading Consultants
Reading Diagnosis
Reading Difficulties
Reading Failure
Reading Games
Reading Habits
Reading Improvement
Reading Instruction
Reading Interests
Reading Materials
Reading Material Selection
Reading Processes
Reading Programs
Reading Rate
Reading Readiness
Reading Readiness Tests
Reading Research
Reading Skills
Reading Strategies
Reading Teachers
Reading Tests
Reading Writing Relationship
Tachistoscopes
Verbal Communication
Vocabulary
Writing (Composition)

READING ABILITY *Jul. 1966*
CIJE: 899 RIE: 1111 GC: 460
NT Reading Skills
BT Verbal Ability
RT Reading
Reading Achievement
Reading Attitudes
Reading Difficulties
Reading Readiness

READING ACHIEVEMENT *Jul. 1966*
CIJE: 1167 RIE: 2443 GC: 460
SN Level of attainment in any or all reading skills, usually estimated by performance on a test (note: prior to jun80, "reading level" was occasionally used to index this concept)
BT Achievement
RT Academic Achievement
Achievement Gains
Reading
Reading Ability
Reading Attitudes
Reading Diagnosis
Reading Failure
Reading Improvement
Reading Tests

READING ALOUD TO OTHERS *Sep. 1980*
CIJE: 99 RIE: 77 GC: 460
SN Reading aloud for the sake of the listener's well-being (e.g., to inform or entertain the listener or audience, to develop his/her/their appreciation of literature or reading readiness, etc.) (note: use "oral reading" when the purpose of reading aloud is to develop or diagnose the reader's language skills)
BT Reading
RT Oral Interpretation
Oral Reading
Reading Attitudes
Story Reading
Story Telling

READING ASSIGNMENTS *Jul. 1966*
CIJE: 55 RIE: 64 GC: 460
BT Assignments
RT Content Area Reading
Directed Reading Activity
Individualized Reading
Reading
Reading Instruction
Reading Materials
Reading Programs

READING ATTITUDES *Mar. 1980*
CIJE: 301 RIE: 245 GC: 460
SN Attitudes toward reading
BT Attitudes
RT Educational Attitudes
Reading Ability
Reading Achievement
Reading Aloud To Others
Reading Habits
Reading Interests

READING CENTERS *Jul. 1966*
CIJE: 98 RIE: 313 GC: 460
SN Facilities staffed by reading specialists or instructors that offer reading diagnosis and individualized instruction, as well as remedial, developmental, or accelerated reading programs
UF Reading Clinics (1966 1980)
Reading Laboratories
Remedial Reading Clinics (1966 1980) #
BT Educational Facilities
Resource Centers
RT Individualized Reading
Learning Laboratories
Reading
Reading Diagnosis
Reading Improvement
Reading Programs
Reading Skills
Remedial Reading

Reading Clinics (1966 1980)
USE READING CENTERS

READING COMPREHENSION *Jul. 1966*
CIJE: 2773 RIE: 3664 GC: 460
BT Comprehension
Reading Skills
RT Basic Vocabulary
Cloze Procedure
Content Area Reading
Context Clues
Critical Reading
Decoding (Reading)
Directed Reading Activity
Informal Reading Inventories
Language Experience Approach
Oral Interpretation
Readability
Readability Formulas
Reader Response
Reader Text Relationship
Reading
Reading Habits
Reading Processes
Reading Rate
Reading Strategies
Reading Tests
Receptive Language
Story Grammar
Telegraphic Materials
Word Recognition

READING CONSULTANTS *Jul. 1966*
CIJE: 119 RIE: 170 GC: 360
UF Reading Specialists
BT Consultants
RT Reading
Reading Instruction
Reading Teachers
Resource Teachers

READING DEVELOPMENT (1966 1980) *Mar. 1980*
CIJE: 389 RIE: 824 GC: 460
SN Invalid descriptor -- used inconsistently in indexing -- see more precise "reading" descriptors

READING DIAGNOSIS *Jul. 1966*
CIJE: 502 RIE: 849 GC: 460
NT Miscue Analysis
BT Educational Diagnosis
RT Informal Reading Inventories
Reading
Reading Achievement
Reading Centers
Reading Difficulties
Reading Readiness Tests
Reading Tests
Remedial Reading

READING DIFFICULTIES *Mar. 1980*
CIJE: 808 RIE: 561 GC: 460
SN Problems in reading, caused either by disabilities associated with psychological processes or by such factors as physical or sensory handicaps, cultural background, low ability, etc. (note: do not use for "readability" -- the previous term "reading difficulty" was not scoped and was often confused with "readability")
UF Reading Disabilities
Reading Problems
Retarded Readers (1966 1980)
BT Problems
RT Corrective Reading
Dyslexia
Language Handicaps
Learning Disabilities
Learning Problems
Reading
Reading Ability
Reading Diagnosis
Reading Failure
Remedial Reading

READING DIFFICULTY (1966 1980) *Jun. 1980*
CIJE: 909 RIE: 777 GC: 460
SN Invalid descriptor -- used for both the reading problems of students and the reading level of materials -- see "reading difficulties" and "readability" respectively for these concepts

Reading Disabilities
USE READING DIFFICULTIES

Reading Enjoyment
USE LITERATURE APPRECIATION

READING FAILURE *Jul. 1966*
CIJE: 92 RIE: 136 GC: 460
SN Lack of achievement or accomplishment in reading
BT Academic Failure
RT Dyslexia
Reading
Reading Achievement
Reading Difficulties

Reading Gain
USE READING IMPROVEMENT

READING GAMES *Jul. 1966*
CIJE: 82 RIE: 138 GC: 460
BT Educational Games
RT Reading
Reading Instruction
Reading Materials

READING HABITS *Jul. 1966*
CIJE: 443 RIE: 443 GC: 460
BT Behavior Patterns
RT Habit Formation
Reader Response
Reading
Reading Attitudes
Reading Comprehension
Reading Interests
Reading Skills
Recreational Reading
Silent Reading
Study Habits
Sustained Silent Reading

READING IMPROVEMENT *Jul. 1966*
CIJE: 806 RIE: 1525 GC: 460
SN Process of becoming a better reader (prior to mar80, the instruction "reading gain, use reading achievement" was carried in the thesaurus)
UF Reading Gain
BT Improvement
RT Advance Organizers
Reading
Reading Achievement
Reading Centers
Reading Rate
Reading Skills
Reading Strategies

Reading In Content Areas
USE CONTENT AREA READING

READING INSTRUCTION *Jul. 1966*
CIJE: 5199 RIE: 6625 GC: 460
NT Basal Reading
Content Area Reading
Corrective Reading
Directed Reading Activity
Individualized Reading
Remedial Reading
Sustained Silent Reading
BT Instruction
RT Adult Reading Programs
Braille
Experience Charts
Initial Teaching Alphabet
Kinesthetic Methods
Language Experience Approach
Large Type Materials
Literacy Education
Miscue Analysis
Oral Reading
Phonics
Readability
Reading
Reading Assignments
Reading Consultants
Reading Games
Reading Material Selection
Reading Readiness
Reading Skills
Reading Strategies
Reading Teachers
Sight Method
Sight Vocabulary
Silent Reading
Story Grammar
Structural Analysis (Linguistics)

READING INTERESTS *Jul. 1966*
CIJE: 811 RIE: 701 GC: 460
BT Interests
RT Independent Reading
Individualized Reading
Reader Response
Reading
Reading Attitudes
Reading Habits
Reading Material Selection
Recreational Reading

Reading Laboratories
USE READING CENTERS

READING LEVEL (1966 1980) *Jun. 1980*
CIJE: 224 RIE: 421 GC: 460
SN Invalid descriptor -- used for both the reading level of people and the readability level of materials -- see "reading achievement" and "readability" respectively for these concepts

READING MATERIAL SELECTION *Jul. 1966*
CIJE: 769 RIE: 615 GC: 460
BT Media Selection
RT Library Material Selection
Reading
Reading Instruction
Reading Interests
Reading Materials
Recreational Reading
Supplementary Reading Materials
Textbook Selection

READING MATERIALS *Jul. 1966*
CIJE: 1576 RIE: 2749 GC: 730
UF Readers (Materials)
NT Large Type Materials
Supplementary Reading Materials
Telegraphic Materials
RT Adolescent Literature
Basal Reading
Books
Childrens Literature
High Interest Low Vocabulary Books
Instructional Materials
Newspapers
Periodicals
Publications

= Two or more Descriptors are used to represent this term.
The term's main entry shows the appropriate coordination.

Reader Text Relationship
Reading
Reading Assignments
Reading Games
Reading Material Selection
Science Materials
Talking Books
Textbooks

Reading Problems
USE READING DIFFICULTIES

READING PROCESSES *Jul. 1966*
CIJE: 923 RIE: 1281 GC: 460
NT Decoding (Reading)
BT Language Processing
RT Eye Fixations
Miscue Analysis
Reader Response
Reader Text Relationship
Reading
Reading Comprehension
Reading Skills
Reading Strategies
Reading Writing Relationship
Receptive Language

READING PROGRAMS *Jul. 1966*
CIJE: 1321 RIE: 2732 GC: 460
NT Adult Reading Programs
BT Programs
RT Basal Reading
Individualized Reading
Language Experience Approach
Reading
Reading Assignments
Reading Centers

READING RATE *Jul. 1977*
CIJE: 313 RIE: 316 GC: 460
SN The speed at which an individual can read and comprehend what is read
UF Reading Speed (1966 1977)
BT Reading Skills
RT Readability
Reader Response
Reading
Reading Comprehension
Reading Improvement
Reading Tests
Silent Reading
Speed Reading
Telegraphic Materials

READING READINESS *Jul. 1966*
CIJE: 485 RIE: 882 GC: 460
SN Act of preparing, or degree of preparedness, for formal reading instruction or any other reading activity or task
BT Readiness
RT Basic Vocabulary
Beginning Reading
Early Reading
Learning Readiness
Prereading Experience
Reading
Reading Ability
Reading Instruction
Reading Readiness Tests
School Readiness

READING READINESS TESTS *Jul. 1966*
CIJE: 52 RIE: 130 GC: 830
BT Aptitude Tests
RT Diagnostic Tests
Preschool Tests
Prognostic Tests
Reading
Reading Diagnosis
Reading Readiness
Reading Tests
School Readiness Tests
Screening Tests

READING RESEARCH *Jul. 1966*
CIJE: 3160 RIE: 4982 GC: 810
SN Basic, applied, and developmental research conducted to advance knowledge about reading (note: as of oct81, use as a minor descriptor for examples of this kind of research -- use as a major descriptor only as the subject of a document)
BT Educational Research
RT Communication Research
Reading
Tachistoscopes

READING SKILLS *Jul. 1966*
CIJE: 2423 RIE: 4345 GC: 460
SN Complex behaviors developed through practice in order to read proficiently
NT Reading Comprehension
Reading Rate
BT Language Skills
Reading Ability
RT Adult Literacy
Basic Skills
Cloze Procedure
Content Area Reading
Decoding (Reading)
Eye Voice Span
Functional Literacy
Functional Reading
Inferences
Literacy
Literacy Education
Minimum Competencies
Phonics
Reader Response
Reading
Reading Centers
Reading Habits
Reading Improvement
Reading Instruction
Reading Processes
Reading Strategies
Reading Tests
Vocabulary Skills
Word Recognition
Word Study Skills

Reading Specialists
USE READING CONSULTANTS

Reading Speed (1966 1977)
USE READING RATE

READING STRATEGIES *Oct. 1983*
CIJE: 250 RIE: 286 GC: 460
SN Plans or methods that can be used or taught to facilitate reading proficiency
BT Learning Strategies
RT Reading
Reading Comprehension
Reading Improvement
Reading Instruction
Reading Processes
Reading Skills

READING TEACHERS *Mar. 1980*
CIJE: 166 RIE: 181 GC: 360
BT Teachers
RT Reading
Reading Consultants
Reading Instruction

READING TESTS *Jul. 1966*
CIJE: 710 RIE: 1295 GC: 830
NT Informal Reading Inventories
BT Verbal Tests
RT Achievement Tests
Cloze Procedure
Language Tests
Reading
Reading Achievement
Reading Comprehension
Reading Diagnosis
Reading Rate
Reading Readiness Tests
Reading Skills

Reading Therapy
USE BIBLIOTHERAPY

READING WRITING RELATIONSHIP *Dec. 1985*
CIJE: 126 RIE: 162 GC: 460
SN The inherent interaction between the skills or processes of reading and writing
BT Relationship
RT Language Arts
Literacy
Reader Text Relationship
Reading
Reading Processes
Story Grammar
Writing (Composition)
Writing Processes

Readings (Collections)
USE ANTHOLOGIES

REAL ESTATE *Aug. 1968*
CIJE: 50 RIE: 82 GC: 650
BT Ownership
RT Landlords
Land Use
Property Appraisal
Real Estate Occupations
School Location
Site Selection
Zoning

Real Estate Appraisal
USE PROPERTY APPRAISAL

REAL ESTATE OCCUPATIONS *Sep. 1968*
CIJE: 5 RIE: 37 GC: 640
BT Occupations
RT Buildings
Distributive Education
Housing
Housing Industry
Housing Management Aides
Landlords
Real Estate
Sales Occupations

REALIA *Jul. 1966*
CIJE: 24 RIE: 56 GC: 720
SN Tangible objects, specimens, or artifacts that are not copies, representations, or models
BT Nonprint Media
RT Exhibits
Instructional Materials
Museums
Science Fairs
Three Dimensional Aids

REALISM *May. 1969*
CIJE: 211 RIE: 83 GC: 430
SN In philosophy, the theory that objects of sense perception or cognition are real and exist independently of their being known -- in the creative arts, representation of ordinary life without idealization
RT Art Expression
Literary Styles
Philosophy
Twentieth Century Literature

REALITY THERAPY *Aug. 1986*
CIJE: 35 RIE: 16 GC: 230
SN Psychotherapeutic approach in which recognition of irresponsibility (reality) and respect for oneself and for others are the keys to responsible, acceptable behavior
BT Psychotherapy
RT Behavior Modification
Counseling Techniques
Discipline
Educational Therapy
Interpersonal Competence
Self Actualization
Self Concept
Social Reinforcement

Recall (Psychological) (1967 1980)
USE RECALL (PSYCHOLOGY)

RECALL (PSYCHOLOGY) *Mar. 1980*
CIJE: 2315 RIE: 1173 GC: 110
SN The process whereby a representation of past experience is elicited and/or reproduced (note: see also "recognition (psychology)")
UF Recall (Psychological) (1967 1980)
BT Memory
RT Advance Organizers
Cues
Encoding (Psychology)
Learning
Learning Disabilities
Learning Processes
Mediation Theory
Memorization
Mnemonics
Paired Associate Learning
Perceptual Handicaps
Primacy Effect
Recognition (Psychology)
Retention (Psychology)
Schemata (Cognition)
Visualization

Recall Ratio
USE RELEVANCE (INFORMATION RETRIEVAL)

RECEPTIONISTS *Aug. 1970*
CIJE: 3 RIE: 23 GC: 640
BT Clerical Workers

Receptive Communication
USE RECEPTIVE LANGUAGE

RECEPTIVE LANGUAGE *Jul. 1966*
CIJE: 220 RIE: 119 GC: 450
SN The cognitive processing involved in comprehending oral, symbolic, or written language (note: prior to mar80, the use of this term was not restricted by a scope note)
UF Receptive Communication
BT Language Processing
RT Aphasia
Communication (Thought Transfer)
Communication Skills
Expressive Language
Language Acquisition
Language Handicaps
Language Skills
Listening Comprehension
Psycholinguistics
Reading Comprehension
Reading Processes

RECIDIVISM *Sep. 1970*
CIJE: 113 RIE: 106 GC: 530
SN Tendency to relapse into previous criminal or delinquent behavior habits
BT Behavior Patterns
RT Antisocial Behavior
Behavior Disorders
Correctional Rehabilitation
Criminals
Delinquency
Delinquent Rehabilitation

RECIPROCALS (MATHEMATICS) *Jan. 1969*
CIJE: 6 RIE: 1 GC: 480
BT Numbers
RT Fractions
Mathematical Concepts
Rational Numbers

Recoding (Psychology)
USE ENCODING (PSYCHOLOGY)

RECOGNITION (ACHIEVEMENT) *Mar. 1980*
CIJE: 112 RIE: 76 GC: 520
SN Acknowledgement of achievement or merit (note: prior to mar80, this concept was indexed under "recognition")
NT Awards
Commencement Ceremonies
Professional Recognition
BT Evaluation
RT Achievement
Compensation (Remuneration)
Graduation
Incentives
Merit Pay
Merit Rating
Merit Scholarships
Morale
Reputation
Rewards
Scholarship
Status
Status Need

RECOGNITION (PSYCHOLOGY) *Mar. 1980*
CIJE: 219 RIE: 92 GC: 110
SN Awareness that an object, word, sentence, person, etc. has been known or experienced before -- one form of remembering (note: prior to mar80, this concept was indexed under "recognition" -- see also "recall (psychology)")
NT Pattern Recognition
Word Recognition
BT Memory
RT Association (Psychology)
Encoding (Psychology)
Identification
Learning Disabilities
Learning Processes
Perception
Perceptual Handicaps

Recall (Psychology)
Retention (Psychology)
Tachistoscopes

RECOGNITION (1967 1980) *Mar. 1980*
CIJE: 403 RIE: 102 GC: 510
SN Invalid descriptor -- used for both the psychological process of recognition and recognition of achievement -- see "recognition (psychology)" and "recognition (achievement)" respectively for these concepts

Recombinant Dna
USE DNA; GENETIC ENGINEERING

RECONSTRUCTION ERA *Jul. 1966*
CIJE: 23 RIE: 53 GC: 430
SN The period following the u.s. civil war (1865-1877) during which the confederate states were reorganized by the federal government and brought back into the union
BT United States History
RT Civil War (United States)

Record Clerks
USE FILE CLERKS

RECORDKEEPING *Jul. 1966*
CIJE: 485 RIE: 992 GC: 320
BT Business Skills
RT Audits (Verification)
Bookkeeping
Case Records
Clerical Occupations
Data Collection
Information Storage
Medical Record Technicians
Office Occupations
Office Occupations Education
Records (Forms)
Registrars (School)
Reports

RECORDS (FORMS) *Jul. 1966*
CIJE: 278 RIE: 1661 GC: 730
NT Attendance Records
Case Records
Check Lists
Confidential Records
Credentials
Farm Accounts
Payroll Records
Student Records
Wills
Worksheets
RT Archives
Charts
Diagrams
Flow Charts
Graphs
Information Storage
Office Management
Recordkeeping
Reports

RECREATION *Jul. 1966*
CIJE: 436 RIE: 689 GC: 470
NT Therapeutic Recreation
RT Hospitality Occupations
Leisure Education
Leisure Time
Recreational Activities
Recreational Facilities
Recreational Programs
Recreation Finances
Recreationists
Recreation Legislation
Vacations

RECREATION FINANCES *Jul. 1966*
CIJE: 52 RIE: 45 GC: 620
SN Funding for or operating expenses of recreational activities, especially those supported by a local, state, or federal government (note: for school athletic programs, coordinate "athletic programs" with "educational finance" or "school funds")
BT Financial Support
RT Recreation
Recreational Facilities

RECREATION LEGISLATION *Jul. 1966*
CIJE: 36 RIE: 52 GC: 610
UF Community Recreation Legislation (1966 1978) #
Federal Recreation Legislation (1966 1978) #
Local Recreation Legislation (1966 1978) #
State Recreation Legislation (1966 1978) #
BT Legislation
RT Laws
Recreation

Recreation Therapy
USE THERAPEUTIC RECREATION

RECREATIONAL ACTIVITIES *Jul. 1966*
CIJE: 692 RIE: 640 GC: 470
NT Camping
Hobbies
Playground Activities
Recreational Reading
BT Activities
RT Art Activities
Athletic Fields
Athletics
Bicycling
Dating (Social)
Drinking
Extracurricular Activities
Games
Horseback Riding
Leisure Time
Lifetime Sports
Music Activities
Outdoor Activities
Physical Activities
Physical Education
Play
Popular Culture
Recreation
Recreationists
School Recreational Programs
Seafarers
Singing
Swimming
Therapeutic Recreation
Tourism
Travel
Underwater Diving
Wildlife Management
Womens Athletics

RECREATIONAL FACILITIES *Jul. 1966*
CIJE: 398 RIE: 314 GC: 920
NT Playgrounds
BT Facilities
RT Athletic Fields
Auditoriums
Community Recreation Programs
Community Resources
Field Houses
Gymnasiums
Hospitality Occupations
Museums
Park Design
Parks
Physical Education Facilities
Planetariums
Recreation
Recreation Finances
Recreationists
Student Unions
Swimming Pools
Theaters
Trails
Windowless Rooms
Zoos

RECREATIONAL PROGRAMS *Jul. 1966*
CIJE: 293 RIE: 278 GC: 470
UF Social Recreation Programs (1966 1980)
NT Community Recreation Programs
Day Camp Programs
Physical Recreation Programs
Resident Camp Programs
School Recreational Programs
BT Programs
RT Outreach Programs
Recreation
Recreationists
Summer Programs

RECREATIONAL READING *Jul. 1966*
CIJE: 256 RIE: 244 GC: 460
SN Reading that is done for relaxation or amusement, or to satisfy interests unrelated to educational or vocational obligations
UF Leisure Time Reading
BT Reading
Recreational Activities
RT Independent Reading
Literature Appreciation
Reading Habits
Reading Interests
Reading Material Selection
Supplementary Reading Materials

RECREATIONISTS *Nov. 1971*
CIJE: 71 RIE: 27 GC: 470
SN Persons taking or seeking recreation
BT Groups
RT Leisure Education
Leisure Time
Recreation
Recreational Activities
Recreational Facilities
Recreational Programs
Vacations

RECRUITMENT *Jul. 1966*
CIJE: 631 RIE: 966 GC: 630
UF Personnel Recruitment
NT Faculty Recruitment
Student Recruitment
Teacher Recruitment
RT Affirmative Action
Employment Opportunities
Personnel
Personnel Needs
Personnel Selection
Selection

Recurrent Education
USE LIFELONG LEARNING

RECYCLING *Oct. 1971*
CIJE: 153 RIE: 109 GC: 410
SN Processing and reuse of materials instead of discarding them as waste
BT Waste Disposal
RT Conservation (Environment)
Depleted Resources
Ecology
Natural Resources
Pollution
Solid Wastes
Wastes
Waste Water
Water Treatment

Redevelopment Areas
USE URBAN RENEWAL

REDUCTION IN FORCE *Mar. 1977*
CIJE: 121 RIE: 221 GC: 630
SN Reduction in the total number of people employed by an organization -- includes such methods as laying off personnel, creating early retirement options, transferring personnel, and not filling openings created through normal staff attrition (note: prior to mar77, the instruction "reduction in force," use "job layoff" was carried in the thesaurus)
NT Job Layoff
RT Dislocated Workers
Dismissal (Personnel)
Early Retirement
Employment Practices
Labor Market
Labor Turnover
Labor Utilization
Outplacement Services (Employment)
Personnel Policy
Program Termination
Retrenchment
Seniority
Teacher Dismissal
Tenure
Unemployment

REDUNDANCY *Jul. 1966*
CIJE: 89 RIE: 54 GC: 310
RT Attention
Error Patterns
Habituation
Novelty (Stimulus Dimension)
Repetitive Film Showings
Retention (Psychology)
Stimuli

REENTRY STUDENTS *Mar. 1980*
CIJE: 110 RIE: 189 GC: 360
SN Individuals who return to an educational system, program, or institution following an extended absence
BT Students
RT Adult Students
Attendance
College Students
Continuation Students
Dropouts
Educational Trends
High School Students
Nontraditional Education
Nontraditional Students
Refresher Courses
Stopouts

REENTRY WORKERS *Mar. 1980*
CIJE: 29 RIE: 97 GC: 630
SN Individuals who return to employment following an extended absence
BT Personnel
RT Career Choice
Displaced Homemakers
Dropouts
Employed Parents
Employed Women
Employees
Employment
Employment Level
Employment Opportunities
Employment Qualifications
Job Application
Job Placement
Job Search Methods
Job Skills
Labor Force
Labor Market
Leaves Of Absence
Retraining
Stopouts
Work Experience

Reference Books (1966 1980)
USE REFERENCE MATERIALS

REFERENCE GROUPS *Sep. 1981*
CIJE: 19 RIE: 27 GC: 110
SN Real or theoretical groups (social, ethnic, family, etc.) that serve as sources for identification, motivation, aspiration, attitudes, behavior, or modes of living (note: do not confuse with "role models" or the identifier "reference individuals," both referring to individuals rather than groups, the former emulated in one or a few roles and the latter emulated in many roles)
BT Groups
RT Group Status
Identification (Psychology)
Interpersonal Relationship
Self Concept
Socialization
Social Psychology
Social Support Groups

REFERENCE MATERIALS *Jul. 1966*
CIJE: 690 RIE: 1997 GC: 720
SN Materials compiled to supply definite pieces of information of varying extent, and intended to be referred to for brief consultations (note: corresponds to pubtype code 130 -- do not use except as the subject of a document)
UF Library Reference Materials #
Reference Books (1966 1980)
NT Abstracts
Anthologies
Atlases
Bibliographies
Citations (References)
Dictionaries
Directories
Discographies
Encyclopedias
Filmographies
Guides
Indexes
Library Catalogs
Thesauri
Yearbooks
BT Publications

RT Instructional Materials
Library Materials
Multilingual Materials
Reference Services
Research Tools
Resource Materials

REFERENCE SERVICES *Apr. 1980*
CIJE: 683 RIE: 532 GC: 710
SN Activities designed to make information available to users -- includes direct, personal aid to users by library or information personnel
UF Computer Based Reference Services #
Library Reference Services (1968 1980) #
Online Reference Services #
BT Information Services
RT Community Information Services
Information Dissemination
Library Services
Online Searching
Reference Materials
Search Strategies
User Needs (Information)

REFERRAL *Jul. 1966*
CIJE: 343 RIE: 484 GC: 240
SN Process of referring to an appropriate agency or specialist
UF Information And Referral Services #
Referral Services (Community) #
BT Information Dissemination
RT Admissions Counseling
Community Information Services
Consultants
Consultation Programs
Professional Services
Resource Room Programs
Specialists

Referral Services (Community)
USE COMMUNITY INFORMATION SERVICES; REFERRAL

Reflectivity
USE CONCEPTUAL TEMPO

Refractive Errors
USE AMETROPIA

REFRESHER COURSES *Sep. 1968*
CIJE: 52 RIE: 65 GC: 350
BT Courses
RT Adult Education
Improvement Programs
Inservice Education
Minicourses
Professional Continuing Education
Reentry Students
Remedial Instruction
Retraining
Review (Reexamination)
Supplementary Education

Refresher Training
USE RETRAINING

REFRIGERATION *Jul. 1966*
CIJE: 8 RIE: 57 GC: 920
BT Climate Control
RT Air Conditioning
Air Flow
Heat Recovery
Refrigeration Mechanics
Temperature

REFRIGERATION MECHANICS *Jul. 1966*
CIJE: 3 RIE: 47 GC: 640
UF Air Conditioning Mechanics
BT Mechanics (Process)
RT Air Conditioning Equipment
Refrigeration
Skilled Occupations

REFUGEES *May. 1969*
CIJE: 198 RIE: 499 GC: 510
UF Escapees
Exiles
Political Refugees
BT Migrants
RT Acculturation
Foreign Nationals
Foreign Workers
Immigrants
Land Settlement
Migration
Political Attitudes
Relocation
Safety
Undocumented Immigrants

Refuse
USE WASTES

Regents
USE TRUSTEES

REGIONAL ATTITUDES *Mar. 1980*
CIJE: 77 RIE: 89 GC: 550
SN Attitudes representative of a particular region (note: use in coordination with appropriate identifiers, e.g., "united states (north)," "united states (south)," etc.)
UF Northern Attitudes (1968 1980)
Southern Attitudes (1966 1980)
BT Attitudes
RT Geographic Regions
Political Attitudes
Regional Characteristics
Rural Urban Differences
Social Attitudes

REGIONAL CHARACTERISTICS *Jan. 1978*
CIJE: 163 RIE: 272 GC: 550
SN Those identifying qualities or traits which constitute the essential nature of a geographic area's people and resources
UF Regional Differences #
NT Regional Dialects
RT Area Studies
Community Characteristics
Cultural Traits
Environment
Geographic Regions
Regional Attitudes
Regional Cooperation
Regional Laboratories
Regional Libraries
Regional Planning
Regional Programs
Regional Schools
Rural Urban Differences
Social Characteristics

REGIONAL COOPERATION *Jul. 1966*
CIJE: 184 RIE: 451 GC: 330
BT Cooperation
RT Agency Cooperation
Cooperative Planning
Institutional Cooperation
Intermediate Administrative Units
Regional Characteristics
Regional Libraries
Regional Programs

REGIONAL DIALECTS *Aug. 1968*
CIJE: 265 RIE: 319 GC: 450
SN Special varieties within a language, defined by the geographical origin of its speakers
UF Geographic Dialects
BT Dialects
Regional Characteristics
RT Area Studies
Bidialectalism
Black Dialects
Ethnic Origins
Geographic Regions
Idioms
Language Classification
Native Speakers
Nonstandard Dialects
North American English
Social Dialects
Speech Habits

Regional Differences
USE DIFFERENCES; REGIONAL CHARACTERISTICS

REGIONAL LABORATORIES *Jul. 1966*
CIJE: 28 RIE: 122 GC: 920
BT Laboratories
RT Regional Characteristics
Regional Programs

REGIONAL LIBRARIES *Mar. 1969*
CIJE: 30 RIE: 176 GC: 710
SN Public libraries, supported in whole or in part by federal, state, or provincial funds, that serve several communities and/or counties
UF District Libraries
BT Public Libraries
RT County Libraries
Regional Characteristics
Regional Cooperation
Regional Programs

REGIONAL PLANNING *Jul. 1966*
CIJE: 167 RIE: 629 GC: 330
BT Planning
RT Planning Commissions
Regional Characteristics
Regional Programs
Social Planning
Statewide Planning
Urban Planning

REGIONAL PROGRAMS *Jul. 1966*
CIJE: 247 RIE: 730 GC: 520
BT Programs
RT County Programs
Education Service Centers
Regional Characteristics
Regional Cooperation
Regional Laboratories
Regional Libraries
Regional Planning
Regional Schools

REGIONAL SCHOOLS *Jul. 1966*
CIJE: 124 RIE: 313 GC: 340
SN Schools, often providing special services, that serve a wider geographic area than the usual school district
UF Area Vocational Schools (1966 1980) #
BT Schools
RT Boarding Schools
Consolidated Schools
Geographic Regions
Regional Characteristics
Regional Programs
Special Schools

Registered Nurses
USE NURSES

REGISTRARS (SCHOOL) *Mar. 1980*
CIJE: 37 RIE: 14 GC: 360
SN Administrative officials, usually at postsecondary institutions, who have principal responsibility for student enrollment and records
UF College Registrars
BT Administrators
School Personnel
RT Academic Records
Admissions Officers
College Administration
Enrollment
Recordkeeping
School Administration
School Registration
Student Personnel Workers
Student Records

Registration In School
USE SCHOOL REGISTRATION

REGRESSION (STATISTICS) *Apr. 1980*
CIJE: 173 RIE: 135 GC: 480
SN The effect of imperfect correlation in the relationship between two sets of measurements, i.e., the tendency for predicted scores to lie closer to the mean than do the scores used to predict them -- also, the statistical technique used when one or more measures are used to predict or make a least squares estimate of scores on another measure
UF Linear Regression
Regression Effects
NT Multiple Regression Analysis
BT Statistical Analysis
RT Correlation
Least Squares Statistics
Prediction
Predictive Measurement
Statistical Inference
Statistics
Validity

Regression Effects
USE REGRESSION (STATISTICS)

Regressors
USE PREDICTOR VARIABLES

Regular Class Placement (1968 1978)
USE MAINSTREAMING

REHABILITATION *Jul. 1966*
CIJE: 493 RIE: 468 GC: 240
SN Process of restoring individuals, through education and/or therapy, to the best possible level of physical, mental, emotional, social, or vocational functioning
UF Student Rehabilitation (1966 1980)
NT Correctional Rehabilitation
Drug Rehabilitation
Vocational Rehabilitation
RT Adjustment (To Environment)
Behavior Modification
Caseworkers
Cognitive Restructuring
Counseling
Daily Living Skills
Deinstitutionalization (Of Disabled)
Disabilities
Disadvantaged
Diseases
Dropouts
Educational Therapy
Emotional Disturbances
Injuries
Intervention
Medical Services
Normalization (Handicapped)
Occupational Therapy
Patients
Physical Disabilities
Physical Therapy
Psychotherapy
Rehabilitation Centers
Rehabilitation Counseling
Rehabilitation Programs
Retraining
Social Support Groups
Social Work
Special Education
Therapeutic Environment
Therapeutic Recreation
Therapy
Victims Of Crime

REHABILITATION CENTERS *Jul. 1966*
CIJE: 95 RIE: 144 GC: 920
UF Halfway Houses #
BT Facilities
RT Boarding Homes
Group Homes
Housing
Institutions
Mental Health Clinics
Milieu Therapy
Rehabilitation
Rehabilitation Counseling
Residential Institutions
Residential Schools
Sheltered Workshops
Therapeutic Environment
Vocational Training Centers

REHABILITATION COUNSELING *Jul. 1966*
CIJE: 548 RIE: 237 GC: 240
BT Counseling
RT Adjustment (To Environment)
Career Counseling
Caseworker Approach
Rehabilitation
Rehabilitation Centers
Rehabilitation Programs
Sheltered Workshops

REHABILITATION PROGRAMS *Jul. 1966*
CIJE: 474 RIE: 571 GC: 240
NT Dropout Programs
BT Programs
RT Compensatory Education
Continuation Students
Correctional Education
Guidance Programs
Human Services
Individualized Programs
Mental Health Programs
Outreach Programs
Prognostic Tests
Rehabilitation
Rehabilitation Counseling

Residential Programs
Self Help Programs
Sheltered Workshops

REINFORCEMENT *Jul. 1966*
CIJE: 1940 RIE: 1063 GC: 110
UF Learning Reinforcement
Reinforcement Theory
Reinforcers (1966 1980)
NT Negative Reinforcement
Positive Reinforcement
Punishment
Rewards
Social Reinforcement
Timeout
Token Economy
RT Behaviorism
Behavior Modification
Biofeedback
Conditioning
Contingency Management
Delay Of Gratification
Feedback
Motivation
Operant Conditioning
Teacher Response
Teaching Methods

Reinforcement Theory
USE REINFORCEMENT

Reinforcers (1966 1980)
USE REINFORCEMENT

REJECTION (PSYCHOLOGY) *Mar. 1980*
CIJE: 69 RIE: 35 GC: 230
UF Rejection (1966 1980)
BT Psychological Patterns
RT Alienation
Anger
Interpersonal Relationship
Resentment
Withdrawal (Psychology)

Rejection (1966 1980)
USE REJECTION (PSYCHOLOGY)

RELATIONSHIP *Jul. 1966*
CIJE: 522 RIE: 361 GC: 520
SN Type or mode of association between or among physical or conceptual entities, e.g., people, institutions, objects, ideas, processes (note: use a more specific term if possible -- do not confuse with "correlation" -- prior to mar80, the use of this term was not restricted by a scope note)
NT Community Relations
Credibility
Cultural Interrelationships
Developmental Continuity
Education Work Relationship
Faculty College Relationship
Family School Relationship
Federal Indian Relationship
Federal State Relationship
Government School Relationship
Human Relations
Interaction
International Relations
Interpersonal Relationship
Labor Relations
Police Community Relationship
Police School Relationship
Privacy
Public Relations
Reader Text Relationship
Reading Writing Relationship
School Business Relationship
School Community Relationship
Science And Society
Spatial Relationship (Facilities)
State Church Separation
Student School Relationship
Theory Practice Relationship
RT Classification
Coordination
Distance
Equations (Mathematics)
Influences
Proximity
Ratios (Mathematics)
Schematic Studies

Relative Humidity
USE HUMIDITY

RELATIVITY *Oct. 1968*
CIJE: 189 RIE: 21 GC: 490
UF Geometrodynamics
Space Time Continuum
BT Scientific Concepts
Theories
RT Energy
Gravity (Physics)
Kinetics
Light
Matter
Mechanics (Physics)
Motion
Optics
Physics
Quantum Mechanics
Space
Time

RELAXATION TRAINING *Mar. 1980*
CIJE: 251 RIE: 148 GC: 230
SN Training that emphasizes the acquisition of skills and techniques for managing and reducing stress, anxiety, and tension
UF Progressive Relaxation (1967 1980)
BT Psychotherapy
RT Anxiety
Biofeedback
Desensitization
Hypertension
Hypnosis
Physiology
Stress Management
Suggestopedia
Transcendental Meditation

RELEASED TIME *Jul. 1966*
CIJE: 52 RIE: 111 GC: 630
SN Time granted to students, employees, or institutionalized persons to pursue special activities
UF Day Release
Study Release Programs
Work Release
RT Correctional Education
Employer Employee Relationship
Flexible Working Hours
Industrial Training
Leaves Of Absence
Off The Job Training
Personnel Policy
Religious Education
Sabbatical Leaves
School Schedules
Scope Of Bargaining

RELEVANCE (EDUCATION) *Jul. 1969*
CIJE: 3568 RIE: 2103 GC: 330
SN Applicability of what is taught by schools to the needs and interests of students and society
UF Curriculum Relevance
Educational Relevance
RT Accountability
Career Education
Core Curriculum
Course Selection (Students)
Curriculum Development
Curriculum Evaluation
Educational Improvement
Educational Needs
Educational Objectives
Educational Responsibility
Education Work Relationship
Experimental Colleges
Experimental Schools
Free Schools
Futures (Of Society)
Living Learning Centers
Nontraditional Education
Student Educational Objectives
Student Interests
Student Needs
Student School Relationship
Vocational Education

RELEVANCE (INFORMATION RETRIEVAL) *Jun. 1969*
CIJE: 320 RIE: 138 GC: 710
SN The number of retrieved documents judged relevant in proportion to the number of documents returned in response to a query
UF Precision Ratio
Recall Ratio
BT Ratios (Mathematics)
RT Bibliographic Coupling
Evaluation Methods
Information Retrieval
Online Searching
Performance
Reliability
Search Strategies
Systems Analysis
User Needs (Information)
User Satisfaction (Information)

RELIABILITY *Jul. 1966*
CIJE: 660 RIE: 534 GC: 820
SN Extent to which something is consistent, dependable, and stable over repeated trials (note: if applicable, use the more specific terms "test reliability" and/or "interrater reliability")
UF Consistency
Dependability
NT Interrater Reliability
Test Reliability
BT Evaluation Criteria
RT Correlation
Error Of Measurement
Error Patterns
Expectation
Generalizability Theory
Performance
Prediction
Probability
Quality Control
Relevance (Information Retrieval)
Risk
Sample Size
Statistical Analysis
Statistical Data
Statistical Distributions
True Scores
Validity
Weighted Scores

Relief Teachers
USE SUBSTITUTE TEACHERS

RELIGION *Jul. 1966*
CIJE: 707 RIE: 762 GC: 430
NT Buddhism
Christianity
Confucianism
Judaism
Taoism
RT Beliefs
Biblical Literature
Churches
Church Programs
Church Role
Church Workers
Clergy
Creationism
Cultural Activities
Humanities
Hymns
Interfaith Relations
Islamic Culture
Meditation
Modernism
Mysticism
Naturalism
Nuns
Philosophy
Priests
Religious Conflict
Religious Cultural Groups
Religious Differences
Religious Discrimination
Religious Education
Religious Factors
Religious Holidays
Religious Organizations
State Church Separation
Theological Education
Traditionalism

Religious Agencies (1966 1980)
USE RELIGIOUS ORGANIZATIONS

RELIGIOUS CONFLICT *Jul. 1966*
CIJE: 81 RIE: 49 GC: 540
BT Conflict
RT Culture Conflict
Ethnicity
Interfaith Relations
Religion
Religious Cultural Groups
Religious Discrimination
Religious Factors

RELIGIOUS CULTURAL GROUPS *Jul. 1966*
CIJE: 214 RIE: 204 GC: 560
UF Religious Groups
NT Catholics
Jews
Protestants
BT Groups
RT Buddhism
Caste
Christianity
Clergy
Confucianism
Culture
Ethnic Groups
Ethnic Relations
Interfaith Relations
Judaism
Minority Groups
Nuns
Priests
Religion
Religious Conflict
Religious Organizations
Taoism

RELIGIOUS DIFFERENCES *Jul. 1966*
CIJE: 85 RIE: 76 GC: 510
BT Differences
RT Individual Differences
Interfaith Relations
Intermarriage
Religion
Religious Factors

RELIGIOUS DISCRIMINATION *Jul. 1966*
CIJE: 61 RIE: 70 GC: 540
BT Social Discrimination
RT Affirmative Action
Anti Semitism
Ethnic Discrimination
Interfaith Relations
Religion
Religious Conflict
Religious Factors
Reverse Discrimination
Social Bias

RELIGIOUS EDUCATION *Jul. 1966*
CIJE: 564 RIE: 422 GC: 400
SN Instruction in religion at any level not leading to a degree in theology (note: prior to mar80, this term was not restricted by a scope note -- for formal education for careers in religion, including the clergy, use "theological education")
BT Education
RT Catholic Educators
Catholic Schools
Church Programs
Church Related Colleges
Church Workers
Clergy
Ethical Instruction
Ethics
Lay Teachers
Parochial Schools
Released Time
Religion
Theological Education

RELIGIOUS FACTORS *Jul. 1966*
CIJE: 591 RIE: 400 GC: 520
BT Influences
RT Creationism
Cultural Influences
Religion
Religious Conflict
Religious Differences
Religious Discrimination

Religious Groups
USE RELIGIOUS CULTURAL GROUPS

RELIGIOUS HOLIDAYS *Oct. 1984*
CIJE: 5 RIE: GC: 520
UF Holy Days
BT Holidays
RT Religion
State Church Separation

RELIGIOUS ORGANIZATIONS *Jul. 1966*
CIJE: 114 RIE: 157 GC: 520
UF Religious Agencies (1966 1980)
BT Organizations (Groups)
RT Churches
Church Related Colleges
Clergy

Institutions
Nonprofit Organizations
Religion
Religious Cultural Groups
Voluntary Agencies

RELOCATABLE FACILITIES *Dec. 1972*
CIJE: 24 RIE: 21 GC: 920
UF Portable Facilities
Temporary Facilities
BT Facilities
RT Air Structures
Building Innovation
Encapsulated Facilities
Facility Expansion
Facility Planning
Flexible Facilities
Mobile Classrooms
Mobile Clinics
Mobile Laboratories
Prefabrication

RELOCATION *Jul. 1966*
CIJE: 175 RIE: 292 GC: 550
SN The voluntary or forced removal of an individual or group and establishment in a new place
NT Rural Resettlement
BT Migration
RT American Indian History
American Indians
Area Studies
Family Mobility
Geographic Location
Labor Problems
Labor Turnover
Labor Utilization
Land Settlement
Migrants
Migration
Migration Patterns
Nonreservation American Indians
Occupational Mobility
Place Of Residence
Population Distribution
Population Trends
Refugees
Residential Patterns
Rural To Urban Migration
Transfer Policy
Transfer Programs
Urban To Rural Migration
Urban To Suburban Migration

REMARRIAGE *Oct. 1982*
CIJE: 60 RIE: 17 GC: 520
SN The act or state of marriage following widow(er)hood or divorce
BT Marriage
RT Divorce
Kinship
Stepfamily
Widowed

Remedial Arithmetic (1966 1980)
USE ARITHMETIC; REMEDIAL MATHEMATICS

Remedial Courses (1966 1980)
USE REMEDIAL INSTRUCTION

Remedial Education
USE REMEDIAL INSTRUCTION

Remedial Education Programs
USE REMEDIAL PROGRAMS

REMEDIAL INSTRUCTION *Jul. 1966*
CIJE: 720 RIE: 1207 GC: 310
UF Remedial Courses (1966 1980)
Remedial Education
Remediation
NT Remedial Mathematics
Remedial Reading
BT Instruction
RT Compensatory Education
Cross Age Teaching
Diagnostic Teaching
Learning Problems
Refresher Courses
Remedial Programs
Remedial Teachers
Review (Reexamination)
Transitional Programs
Tutorial Programs
Tutoring

REMEDIAL MATHEMATICS *Jul. 1966*
CIJE: 156 RIE: 437 GC: 480
UF Remedial Arithmetic (1966 1980) #
BT Mathematics Instruction
Remedial Instruction
RT Mathematics
Remedial Programs

REMEDIAL PROGRAMS *Jul. 1966*
CIJE: 581 RIE: 1340 GC: 310
SN Programs designed to develop specific cognitive skills (usually in the language arts and mathematics) from a deficient level to one appropriate to the educational level and aspirations of the student
UF Remedial Education Programs
Remedial Reading Programs (1966 1980) #
BT Programs
RT Auditing (Coursework)
Compensatory Education
Continuation Students
Developmental Studies Programs
Educationally Disadvantaged
Educational Therapy
High Risk Students
Remedial Instruction
Remedial Mathematics
Remedial Reading
Summer Programs
Supplementary Education
Transitional Programs

REMEDIAL READING *Jul. 1966*
CIJE: 856 RIE: 1555 GC: 460
SN Diagnosis and tutoring of students with reading difficulties, usually by a special teacher of reading
UF Remedial Reading Clinics (1966 1980) #
Remedial Reading Programs (1966 1980) #
BT Reading
Reading Instruction
Remedial Instruction
RT Corrective Reading
Dyslexia
High Interest Low Vocabulary Books
Learning Disabilities
Learning Problems
Reading Centers
Reading Diagnosis
Reading Difficulties
Remedial Programs

Remedial Reading Clinics (1966 1980)
USE READING CENTERS; REMEDIAL READING

Remedial Reading Programs (1966 1980)
USE REMEDIAL PROGRAMS; REMEDIAL READING

REMEDIAL TEACHERS *Jul. 1966*
CIJE: 34 RIE: 41 GC: 360
BT Teachers
RT Remedial Instruction

Remediation
USE REMEDIAL INSTRUCTION

Remembering
USE MEMORY

Remuneration
USE COMPENSATION (REMUNERATION)

RENAISSANCE LITERATURE *Jun. 1969*
CIJE: 64 RIE: 25 GC: 430
SN European literature written during the renaissance (roughly from the fourteenth to the seventeenth centuries) and usually characterized by a humanistic emphasis
BT Literature
RT Chronicles
Fifteenth Century Literature
Humanism
Seventeenth Century Literature
Sixteenth Century Literature
Sonnets
World Literature

Renovation
USE IMPROVEMENT

REPAIR *Jul. 1966*
CIJE: 42 RIE: 188 GC: 640
NT Appliance Repair
BT Maintenance
RT Auto Body Repairers
Buildings
Consumer Science
Equipment Maintenance
Machine Repairers
Obsolescence
Preservation
Television Radio Repairers

Repertory Catalogs
USE UNION CATALOGS

Repertory Orchestras
USE ORCHESTRAS

REPETITIVE FILM SHOWINGS *Jul. 1966*
CIJE: 13 RIE: 28 GC: 310
RT Audiovisual Instruction
Films
Film Study
Redundancy

REPORT CARDS *Jul. 1966*
CIJE: 51 RIE: 60 GC: 330
UF Grade Cards
BT Student Records
RT Academic Achievement
Academic Records
Achievement Rating
Grades (Scholastic)
Grading
Profiles
Student Evaluation

Report Writing
USE TECHNICAL WRITING

REPORTS *May. 1969*
CIJE: 476 RIE: 789 GC: 720
SN (Note: corresponds to pubtype code 140 -- do not use except as the subject of a document)
NT Annual Reports
Conference Papers
Opinion Papers
Personal Narratives
Position Papers
Practicum Papers
Research Reports
Theses
BT Publications
RT Bulletins
News Reporting
Program Descriptions
Recordkeeping
Records (Forms)

Representatives
USE LEGISLATORS

REPRODUCTION (BIOLOGY) *Aug. 1970*
CIJE: 96 RIE: 109 GC: 490
UF Procreation
RT Birth
Birth Rate
Contraception
Family Planning
Genetic Engineering
Genetics
Gynecology
Heredity
Nucleic Acids
Obstetrics
Pregnancy
Rh Factors

Reproduction (Copying)
USE REPROGRAPHY

REPROGRAPHY *Oct. 1970*
CIJE: 245 RIE: 191 GC: 710
SN Class of processes whose purpose is to replicate by optical or photomechanical means previously created graphic or coded messages
UF Copying (Reproduction)
Duplicating
Multilithing
Photocopying
Photoreproduction
Reproduction (Copying)
Xerography
NT Microreproduction
BT Technology
RT Copyrights
Facsimile Transmission
Information Technology
Information Transfer
Magnification Methods
Microforms
Photocomposition
Photography
Printing
Publishing Industry

REPUTATION *Mar. 1980*
CIJE: 106 RIE: 100 GC: 520
SN General estimation in which an individual, organization, or thing is held
UF Fame
NT Prestige
RT Attitudes
Background
Credentials
Credibility
Individual Characteristics
Institutional Characteristics
Integrity
Majority Attitudes
Opinions
Qualifications
Recognition (Achievement)
Status

REQUIRED COURSES *Sep. 1982*
CIJE: 60 RIE: 69 GC: 350
SN Courses required by an institution or administrative body for certification, admission, graduation, etc. (note: from mar80 to sep82, the thesaurus carried the instruction "required courses, use core curriculum" -- prior to mar80, the instruction read ‰...use core courses")
UF Foundation Courses (Required)
Mandatory Courses
Prerequisite Courses #
BT Courses
RT Advanced Courses
Core Curriculum
Course Selection (Students)
Credits
Degree Requirements
Elective Courses
Graduation Requirements
Introductory Courses
Majors (Students)

RESCUE *Jul. 1966*
CIJE: 16 RIE: 74 GC: 210
RT Accidents
Alarm Systems
Emergency Medical Technicians
Emergency Programs
Emergency Squad Personnel
First Aid
Safety
Safety Education

Rescue Squad Personnel
USE EMERGENCY SQUAD PERSONNEL

RESEARCH *Jul. 1966*
CIJE: 5109 RIE: 5380 GC: 810
SN Systematic investigation, collection, and analysis of data to reach conclusions, estimate effects, or test hypotheses (note: use a more specific term if possible)
UF Applied Research
Basic Research
NT Action Research
Architectural Research
Behavioral Science Research
Case Studies
Cohort Analysis
Communication Research
Community Study
Creativity Research
Cross Cultural Studies
Dropout Research
Educational Research
Environmental Research
Exceptional Child Research
Feasibility Studies
Field Studies
Institutional Research
Investigations
Language Research
Library Research
Media Research
Medical Research

= Two or more Descriptors are used to represent this term.
The term's main entry shows the appropriate coordination.

Methods Research
Operations Research
Qualitative Research
Schematic Studies
Scientific Research
Social Science Research
Statistical Studies
Student Research
Use Studies
RT Area Studies
Attrition (Research Studies)
Data Analysis
Data Collection
Data Interpretation
Discovery Processes
Error Patterns
Evaluation
Evaluation Methods
Experimental Psychology
Experiments
Faculty Publishing
Innovation
Institutional Role
Inventions
Literature Reviews
Meta Analysis
Observation
Pilot Projects
Postdoctoral Education
Quasiexperimental Design
Questionnaires
Research Administration
Research And Development
Research And Development Centers
Research Assistants
Research Committees
Research Design
Research Directors
Researchers
Research Libraries
Research Methodology
Research Opportunities
Research Problems
Research Projects
Research Proposals
Research Reports
Research Skills
Research Tools
Research Universities
Research Utilization
Sciences
Statistical Analysis
Surveys
Technology
Technology Transfer
Theories
Theory Practice Relationship
Theses
Urban Studies

RESEARCH ADMINISTRATION *Aug. 1986*
CIJE: 123 RIE: 17 GC: 810
UF Research Management
BT Administration
RT Program Administration
Research
Research And Development Centers
Research Committees
Research Coordinating Units
Research Directors
Research Projects
Research Utilization

RESEARCH AND DEVELOPMENT *Oct. 1983*
CIJE: 163 RIE: 248 GC: 810
SN Includes basic research, applied research, and the resultant development of new products, processes, services, or programs -- evaluation and dissemination may be important collateral functions
UF R And D
R D And E
Research Practice Relationship #
RT Development
Educational Development
Educational Innovation
Educational Research
Evaluation
Innovation
Linking Agents
Productivity
Research
Research And Development Centers
Research Projects
Research Utilization
Science Programs
Scientific Research
Social Science Research
Technological Advancement
Technology
Technology Transfer
Theory Practice Relationship

RESEARCH AND DEVELOPMENT CENTERS *Jul. 1966*
CIJE: 376 RIE: 926 GC: 920
BT Facilities
RT Curriculum Study Centers
Development
Educational Development
Experiment Stations
Linking Agents
Research
Research Administration
Research And Development
Research And Instruction Units
Research Assistants
Research Directors
Researchers
Research Projects
Research Universities
Technology Transfer

RESEARCH AND INSTRUCTION UNITS *Jul. 1966*
CIJE: 22 RIE: 77 GC: 340
SN Organizational units of local schools or school districts that are concerned with the improvement of teaching methods
BT Groups
RT Curriculum Study Centers
Educational Improvement
Educational Research
Instructional Improvement
Multiunit Schools
Research And Development Centers
Research Coordinating Units
Research Projects
School Cadres

Research Apprenticeships (1967 1981)
USE RESEARCH ASSISTANTS

Research Approaches
USE RESEARCH METHODOLOGY

RESEARCH ASSISTANTS *Oct. 1980*
CIJE: 14 RIE: 7 GC: 640
UF Research Apprenticeships (1967 1981)
BT Personnel
RT Assistantships
Fellowships
Graduate Students
Paraprofessional Personnel
Research
Research And Development Centers
Researchers
Research Opportunities
Research Projects
Research Skills
Student Research
Teaching Assistants

RESEARCH COMMITTEES *Jul. 1966*
CIJE: 43 RIE: 72 GC: 810
BT Committees
RT Advisory Committees
Educational Research
Research
Research Administration
Research Projects

RESEARCH COORDINATING UNITS *Jul. 1966*
CIJE: 30 RIE: 257 GC: 340
SN Centers that stimulate and coordinate research among state departments of education, universities, local school districts, and other groups with an interest in vocational and technical education
BT Organizations (Groups)
RT Agency Cooperation
Coordination
Educational Research
Institutional Cooperation
Research Administration
Research And Instruction Units
Research Directors
Research Projects
Technical Education
Vocational Education

RESEARCH CRITERIA (1967 1980) *Mar. 1980*
CIJE: 207 RIE: 246 GC: 810
SN Invalid descriptor -- used inconsistently in indexing -- see such descriptors as "research methodology," "needs assessment," and "evaluation criteria"

RESEARCH DESIGN *Jul. 1966*
CIJE: 1381 RIE: 1768 GC: 810
SN The underlying plan or organization of a research project or study that determines its scope and approach -- also, the process of planning and organizing research activities (note: for documents/articles dealing with research methods or experimental procedures, use "research methodology")
UF Experimental Design
Research Planning
NT Quasiexperimental Design
BT Design
RT Attrition (Research Studies)
Control Groups
Effect Size
Experimental Groups
Generalizability Theory
Hypothesis Testing
Matched Groups
Models
Participant Characteristics
Predictor Variables
Pretests Posttests
Research
Research Methodology
Research Needs
Research Problems
Research Proposals
Sample Size
Sampling
Scientific Methodology
Search Strategies
Statistical Significance

RESEARCH DIRECTORS *Jul. 1966*
CIJE: 41 RIE: 79 GC: 640
UF Directors Of Research
BT Administrators
Professional Personnel
RT Educational Researchers
Institutional Research
Research
Research Administration
Research And Development Centers
Research Coordinating Units
Researchers
Research Projects

RESEARCH LIBRARIES *Jan. 1969*
CIJE: 274 RIE: 466 GC: 710
SN Libraries consisting of specialized materials and providing facilities for undertaking exhaustive research
BT Libraries
RT Academic Libraries
Depository Libraries
Law Libraries
Medical Libraries
Public Libraries
Research
Research Universities
Special Libraries

Research Limitations
USE RESEARCH PROBLEMS

Research Management
USE RESEARCH ADMINISTRATION

RESEARCH METHODOLOGY *Jul. 1966*
CIJE: 7571 RIE: 6011 GC: 810
SN Procedures used in making systematic observations or otherwise obtaining data, evidence, or information as part of a research project or study (note: do not confuse with "research design," which refers to the planning and organization of such procedures)
UF Experimental Procedures
Research Approaches
Social Science Methodology #
NT Interaction Process Analysis
Multitrait Multimethod Techniques
Protocol Analysis
Scientific Methodology
BT Methods
RT Attrition (Research Studies)
Content Analysis
Control Groups
Critical Incidents Method
Data Analysis
Data Collection
Data Interpretation
Deduction
Effect Size
Evaluation Methods
Experimental Groups
Experimenter Characteristics
Factor Analysis
Field Studies
Force Field Analysis
Generalization
Holistic Approach
Induction
Inquiry
Literature Reviews
Matched Groups
Measurement Techniques
Meta Analysis
Methods Research
Models
Monte Carlo Methods
Naturalistic Observation
Network Analysis
Observation
Participant Observation
Pilot Projects
Problem Solving
Proof (Mathematics)
Qualitative Research
Quasiexperimental Design
Research
Research Design
Researchers
Research Needs
Research Problems
Research Skills
Statistical Analysis

RESEARCH NEEDS *Jul. 1966*
CIJE: 2150 RIE: 2949 GC: 810
SN Questions or problems that require research (note: prior to mar80, the use of this term was not restricted by a scope note -- see also "research methodology," "research opportunities," and "research problems")
BT Needs
RT Evaluation Needs
Experiments
Information Needs
Measurement Objectives
Research Design
Research Methodology
Research Opportunities
Research Problems
Research Proposals

RESEARCH OPPORTUNITIES *Jul. 1966*
CIJE: 278 RIE: 351 GC: 810
SN State of affairs or set of circumstances favorable for research
BT Opportunities
RT Financial Support
Grantsmanship
Research
Research Assistants
Researchers
Research Needs
Student Research

RESEARCH PAPERS (STUDENTS) *Jan. 1985*
CIJE: 89 RIE: 57 GC: 310
SN Extended written exercises required of students, usually involving collection of primary or secondary data through research, and careful documentation and organization (note: do not confuse with "theses" or "practicum papers")
UF Term Papers
BT Assignments
RT Content Area Writing
Expository Writing
Student Research
Writing Exercises

Research Planning
USE RESEARCH DESIGN

Research Practice Relationship
USE RESEARCH AND DEVELOPMENT; THEORY PRACTICE RELATIONSHIP

= Two or more Descriptors are used to represent this term.
The term's main entry shows the appropriate coordination.

RESEARCH PROBLEMS *Jul. 1966*
CIJE: 2108 RIE: 1870 GC: 810
SN Factors leading to difficulties or bias in the design, performance, management, or interpretation of research (note: prior to mar80, the use of this term was not restricted by a scope note)
UF Research Limitations
BT Problems
RT Attrition (Research Studies)
Evaluation Problems
Experimenter Characteristics
Research
Research Design
Research Methodology
Research Needs
Sample Size
Statistical Analysis

Research Programs
USE RESEARCH PROJECTS

RESEARCH PROJECTS *Jul. 1966*
CIJE: 5551 RIE: 4679 GC: 810
SN (Note: coordinate with another term for specificity (e.g., another program/project term in the "programs" hierarchy))
UF Agricultural Research Projects (1966 1981)
Research Programs
BT Programs
RT Experimental Programs
Experiment Stations
Program Proposals
Research
Research Administration
Research And Development
Research And Development Centers
Research And Instruction Units
Research Assistants
Research Committees
Research Coordinating Units
Research Directors
Researchers
Research Proposals
Research Reports
Research Universities
Research Utilization

RESEARCH PROPOSALS *Jul. 1966*
CIJE: 147 RIE: 299 GC: 810
SN (Note: as of oct81, use as a minor descriptor for examples of research proposals -- use as a major descriptor only as the subject of a document)
BT Program Proposals
RT Proposal Writing
Research
Research Design
Research Needs
Research Projects

RESEARCH REPORTS *Mar. 1980*
CIJE: 446 RIE: 2384 GC: 720
SN Reports of research projects or programs (note: prior to mar80, the instruction "studies, use research" was carried in the thesaurus -- corresponds to pubtype code 143 -- do not use except as the subject of a document)
UF Research Studies
Scientific Reports
Technical Reports (1968 1980)
BT Reports
RT Research
Research Projects
Technical Writing

RESEARCH REVIEWS (PUBLICATIONS) (1966 1980) *Mar. 1980*
CIJE: 1518 RIE: 1737 GC: 730
SN Invalid descriptor -- used inconsistently in indexing -- see such descriptors as "literature reviews," "bibliographies," "state of the art reviews," "research reports," etc.

RESEARCH SKILLS *Jul. 1966*
CIJE: 363 RIE: 416 GC: 810
BT Skills
RT Library Skills
Research
Research Assistants
Researchers
Research Methodology
Research Tools
Scholarship
Student Research

Research Specialists (Education)
USE EDUCATIONAL RESEARCHERS

Research Studies
USE RESEARCH REPORTS

RESEARCH TOOLS *Jul. 1966*
CIJE: 265 RIE: 575 GC: 810
RT Databases
Information Sources
Library Materials
Literature Reviews
Models
Primary Sources
Reference Materials
Research
Research Skills
Resource Materials
Scholarly Journals

RESEARCH UNIVERSITIES *Aug. 1986*
CIJE: 37 RIE: 65 GC: 340
SN Universities that typically include a graduate school and research and development centers, and are known for their sponsored research activities
BT Universities
RT Research
Research And Development Centers
Research Libraries
Research Projects
State Universities

RESEARCH UTILIZATION *Jul. 1966*
CIJE: 1108 RIE: 1494 GC: 810
BT Information Utilization
RT Adoption (Ideas)
Diffusion (Communication)
Evaluation Utilization
Intellectual Property
Linking Agents
Research
Research Administration
Research And Development
Research Projects
Technology
Technology Transfer
Theory Practice Relationship
Use Studies

Researcher Characteristics
USE EXPERIMENTER CHARACTERISTICS; RESEARCHERS

RESEARCHERS *Jul. 1966*
CIJE: 538 RIE: 500 GC: 640
UF Researcher Characteristics #
NT Educational Researchers
BT Professional Personnel
RT Evaluators
Experimenter Characteristics
Psychologists
Research
Research And Development Centers
Research Assistants
Research Directors
Research Methodology
Research Opportunities
Research Projects
Research Skills
Scholarship
Scientists
Social Scientists
Systems Analysts

Resegregated Schools
USE SCHOOL RESEGREGATION

RESENTMENT *Jul. 1966*
CIJE: 17 RIE: 10 GC: 120
BT Psychological Patterns
RT Alienation
Anger
Hostility
Jealousy
Negative Attitudes
Rejection (Psychology)

RESERVATION AMERICAN INDIANS *Mar. 1980*
CIJE: 24 RIE: 70 GC: 560
SN American indians residing on trust or restricted indian land
BT American Indians
RT American Indian Reservations
Nonreservation American Indians

Reservations (Indian) (1971 1980)
USE AMERICAN INDIAN RESERVATIONS

Resettlement
USE LAND SETTLEMENT

Residence Factors
USE RESIDENCE REQUIREMENTS

Residence Halls
USE DORMITORIES

RESIDENCE REQUIREMENTS *Jul. 1966*
CIJE: 59 RIE: 94 GC: 330
SN Policies or laws requiring habitation in a particular place for a specified period of time -- includes those related to welfare, voting, tuition, degree requirements, etc.
UF Nonresident Students (1967 1980) (Out Of District)
Residence Factors
Resident Students (1967 1980) (In District)
BT Standards
RT Admission Criteria
Graduation Requirements
In State Students
Out Of State Students
Place Of Residence
Selective Admission
Voting

Residency Programs (Medical)
USE GRADUATE MEDICAL EDUCATION

RESIDENT ADVISERS *Jun. 1983*
CIJE: 8 RIE: 5 GC: 360
SN Personnel who live with and coordinate the activities of residents of boarding schools, dormitories, college fraternity or sorority houses, care and treatment institutions, children's homes, group homes, or similar establishments
UF Cottage Parents
Houseparents
Resident Supervisors
NT Resident Assistants
BT Personnel
RT Attendants
Boarding Schools
College Housing
Dormitories
Group Homes
Pupil Personnel Workers
Residential Care
Residential Colleges
Residential Institutions
Residential Programs
Residential Schools
Service Workers
Student Personnel Workers

RESIDENT ASSISTANTS *Jul. 1966*
CIJE: 106 RIE: 55 GC: 360
SN Students employed by a college or university to help manage a dormitory or residence hall by maintaining an interpersonal relationship with hall residents
BT College Students
Resident Advisers
RT Assistantships
College Housing
Dormitories
On Campus Students
Residential Colleges
Student Personnel Workers

RESIDENT CAMP PROGRAMS *Jul. 1966*
CIJE: 101 RIE: 218 GC: 470
BT Recreational Programs
Residential Programs
RT Camping
Day Camp Programs
Summer Programs

Resident Students (1967 1980) (In District)
USE RESIDENCE REQUIREMENTS

Resident Students (1967 1980) (In State)
USE IN STATE STUDENTS

Resident Supervisors
USE RESIDENT ADVISERS

RESIDENTIAL CARE *Jul. 1966*
CIJE: 155 RIE: 179 GC: 220
SN Assistance provided by trained personnel to individuals in residential institutions (note: for care in private homes, see "foster care" and "adult foster care" -- prior to mar80, the use of this term was not restricted by a scope note)
RT Attendants
Disabilities
Nursing Homes
Personal Care Homes
Resident Advisers
Residential Institutions
Residential Programs
Residential Schools
Respite Care
Severe Mental Retardation

Residential Centers (1967 1980)
USE RESIDENTIAL INSTITUTIONS

RESIDENTIAL COLLEGES *Sep. 1969*
CIJE: 71 RIE: 50 GC: 340
SN Colleges that provide living quarters for their students (note: the scope note carried by this term prior to mar80 caused it to be confused with "living learning centers")
BT Colleges
Residential Institutions
RT College Environment
College Housing
Commuter Colleges
Dormitories
Living Learning Centers
On Campus Students
Resident Advisers
Resident Assistants

Residential Desegregation
USE NEIGHBORHOOD INTEGRATION

RESIDENTIAL INSTITUTIONS *Mar. 1980*
CIJE: 133 RIE: 126 GC: 920
SN Facilities that provide health, educational, welfare, or rehabilitative services to their residents
UF Residential Centers (1967 1980)
NT Boarding Schools
Correctional Institutions
Nursing Homes
Personal Care Homes
Residential Colleges
BT Institutions
RT Boarding Homes
Housing
Psychiatric Hospitals
Rehabilitation Centers
Resident Advisers
Residential Care
Residential Programs

Residential Location
USE PLACE OF RESIDENCE

RESIDENTIAL PATTERNS *Jul. 1966*
CIJE: 267 RIE: 459 GC: 550
UF Housing Patterns (1966 1980)
BT Demography
RT Family Mobility
Housing
Migration
Migration Patterns
Neighborhood Integration
Neighborhoods
Place Of Residence
Population Distribution
Population Trends
Racial Composition
Racial Distribution
Relocation
Rural To Urban Migration
School Demography
Trend Analysis
Urban To Rural Migration
Urban To Suburban Migration

RESIDENTIAL PROGRAMS *Jul. 1966*
CIJE: 306 RIE: 460 GC: 350
NT Resident Camp Programs
BT Programs
RT Boarding Schools
Deinstitutionalization (Of Disabled)
Group Experience
Housing
Human Services

= Two or more Descriptors are used to represent this term.
The term's main entry shows the appropriate coordination.

Institutionalized Persons
Mental Health Programs
Rehabilitation Programs
Resident Advisers
Residential Care
Residential Institutions
Residential Schools

RESIDENTIAL SCHOOLS *Jul. 1966*
CIJE: 163 RIE: 158 GC: 340
SN Boarding schools for atypical children of school age
BT Boarding Schools
Special Schools
RT Institutional Schools
Mild Mental Retardation
Moderate Mental Retardation
Rehabilitation Centers
Resident Advisers
Residential Care
Residential Programs

Residents (Medical)
USE GRADUATE MEDICAL STUDENTS

Resilient Floor Covering
USE FLOORING

RESOURCE ALLOCATION *Mar. 1980*
CIJE: 1152 RIE: 2197 GC: 620
SN The setting apart, assigning, or allotting of money, materials, personnel, or services for a particular purpose
UF Allocation Of Resources
Resource Allocations (1966 1980)
RT Administration
Budgeting
Budgets
Capital
Categorical Aid
Cost Effectiveness
Delivery Systems
Educational Assessment
Educational Economics
Educational Equity (Finance)
Educational Planning
Efficiency
Equalization Aid
Expenditures
Financial Needs
Fiscal Capacity
Input Output Analysis
Linking Agents
Needs Assessment
Operating Expenses
Resources
Tax Allocation
Trusts (Financial)
Wills

Resource Allocations (1966 1980)
USE RESOURCE ALLOCATION

RESOURCE CENTERS *Jul. 1966*
CIJE: 419 RIE: 785 GC: 920
SN Indoor or outdoor areas that offer a variety of resources (e.g., supplies, materials, information, equipment, etc.) designed to assist individuals with specific needs (note: use a more specific term if possible)
NT Arts Centers
Audiovisual Centers
Cultural Centers
Curriculum Study Centers
Education Service Centers
Information Centers
Learning Centers (Classroom)
Learning Resources Centers
Nature Centers
Reading Centers
Teacher Centers
BT Facilities
RT Libraries
Museums
Resource Materials
Resources

Resource Guides (1966 1980)
USE RESOURCE MATERIALS

RESOURCE MATERIALS *Jul. 1966*
CIJE: 3130 RIE: 7637 GC: 730
SN Print and/or nonprint materials collected and organized for a particular topic
UF Material Sources
Resource Guides (1966 1980)
NT Resource Units
RT Health Materials
Instructional Materials
Learning Resources Centers
Library Materials
Multilingual Materials
Nonprint Media
Orientation Materials
Parent Materials
Primary Sources
Publications
Reference Materials
Research Tools
Resource Centers
Resources

RESOURCE ROOM PROGRAMS *Oct. 1977*
CIJE: 137 RIE: 115 GC: 310
SN Part-time programs in which specially trained teachers assist students who, because of their special needs, have been referred by their regular classroom teachers
BT Special Programs
RT Individualized Education Programs
Intervention
Itinerant Teachers
Mainstreaming
Referral
Resource Teachers
Special Classes
Special Education
Special Education Teachers
Transitional Programs

Resource Sharing
USE SHARED RESOURCES AND SERVICES

RESOURCE STAFF *Mar. 1980*
CIJE: 85 RIE: 148 GC: 360
SN Personnel with special skills or knowledge who supplement or assist regular staff members
UF Resource Staff Role (1966 1980)
BT Personnel
RT Consultants
Personnel Needs
Resources
Resource Teachers
Specialists

Resource Staff Role (1966 1980)
USE RESOURCE STAFF

RESOURCE TEACHERS *Jul. 1966*
CIJE: 164 RIE: 234 GC: 360
SN Teachers with special competencies who supplement regular course offerings or assist other teachers to develop teaching plans and materials
BT Teachers
RT Consultants
Itinerant Teachers
Mainstreaming
Reading Consultants
Resource Room Programs
Resources
Resource Staff
Science Consultants
Special Education Teachers
Specialists

RESOURCE UNITS *Jul. 1966*
CIJE: 38 RIE: 453 GC: 310
SN Collections of learning and teaching activities, procedures, materials, and references on specific topics that are assembled for the use of teachers in developing their courses
BT Resource Materials
RT Activity Units
Curriculum Study Centers
Learning Modules
Resources
Teaching Guides
Units Of Study

RESOURCES *Jul. 1966*
CIJE: 265 RIE: 669 GC: 520
SN Available means or assets, including sources of assistance, supply, or support (note: use a more specific term if possible)
NT Community Resources
Depleted Resources
Educational Resources
Family Financial Resources
Human Resources
Natural Resources
Shared Resources And Services
Supplies
RT Environment
Equipment
Facilities
Facility Inventory
Financial Support
Institutions
Needs
Organizations (Groups)
Ownership
Resource Allocation
Resource Centers
Resource Materials
Resource Staff
Resource Teachers
Resource Units
Services
Use Studies
Wastes

RESPIRATORY THERAPY *Jan. 1985*
CIJE: 2 RIE: 13 GC: 210
SN Diagnosis and treatment of cardiopulmonary deficiencies or abnormalities through the use of breathing methods and apparatus, and the administration of gases and aerosols
UF Inhalation Therapists (1969 1985) #
Oxygen Inhalation Therapy
BT Therapy
RT Allied Health Occupations
Medical Services
Physical Therapy

RESPITE CARE *Mar. 1974*
CIJE: 33 RIE: 34 GC: 220
SN Short-term care of the handicapped, in or outside the home, to provide family relief
RT Disabilities
Family Problems
Personal Care Homes
Residential Care
Visiting Homemakers

Response Bias (Tests)
USE RESPONSE STYLE (TESTS)

Response Contingent Testing
USE ADAPTIVE TESTING

Response Latency
USE REACTION TIME

Response Mode (1967 1980)
USE RESPONSES

Response Set (Tests)
USE RESPONSE STYLE (TESTS)

RESPONSE STYLE (TESTS) *Feb. 1971*
CIJE: 419 RIE: 344 GC: 820
SN Test-taking behavior that is influenced by the individual's attitudes or tendencies and which may distort the meaning of the test score, e.g., a tendency to answer "yes" regardless of item content
UF Response Bias (Tests)
Response Set (Tests)
NT Guessing (Tests)
BT Behavior
RT Adaptive Testing
Attitudes
Confidence Testing
Forced Choice Technique
Reaction Time
Responses
Social Desirability
Stress Variables
Test Format
Testing Problems
Tests
Test Validity
Test Wiseness

Response Time
USE REACTION TIME

RESPONSES *Mar. 1980*
CIJE: 3241 RIE: 1373 GC: 120
UF Conditioned Response (1967 1980)
Reactive Behavior (1966 1980)
Response Mode (1967 1980)
Stimulus Behavior (1966 1980)
NT Burnout
Constructed Response
Covert Response
Dimensional Preference
Emotional Response
Motor Reactions
Overt Response
Patterned Responses
Reader Response
Stranger Reactions
Student Reaction
Teacher Response
BT Behavior
RT Conditioning
Encoding (Psychology)
Psychological Patterns
Reaction Time
Response Style (Tests)
Schemata (Cognition)
Shift Studies
Situational Tests
Social Desirability
Stimuli
Test Format
Well Being

RESPONSIBILITY *Jul. 1966*
CIJE: 433 RIE: 412 GC: 520
SN The process or act of fulfilling a duty, obligation, burden, or trust (note: use a more specific term if possible)
NT Accountability
Administrator Responsibility
Business Responsibility
Child Responsibility
Church Responsibility
Community Responsibility
Educational Responsibility
Employee Responsibility
Leadership Responsibility
Legal Responsibility
Parent Responsibility
School Responsibility
Social Responsibility
Student Responsibility
Teacher Responsibility
RT Consumer Protection
Institutional Role

Rest Home Aides
USE NURSES AIDES

Rest Homes
USE PERSONAL CARE HOMES

Restaurants
USE DINING FACILITIES

RESTRAINTS (VEHICLE SAFETY) *Aug. 1986*
CIJE: RIE: GC: 910
SN Devices installed in vehicles to restrict bodily movements and prevent injuries
UF Air Bags
Child Restraints (Vehicle Safety)
Lap Belts
Seat Belts
BT Safety Equipment
RT Traffic Safety

Restrictive Admission
USE SELECTIVE ADMISSION

Restrictive Transfer Programs (1966 1980)
USE TRANSFER PROGRAMS

Results Of Education
USE OUTCOMES OF EDUCATION

RESUMES (PERSONAL) *Jan. 1985*
CIJE: 11 RIE: 27 GC: 630
SN Summaries of individual experience and qualifications, typically submitted as part of the job application process
UF Curriculum Vitae
Vitae
BT Credentials
RT Educational Experience
Employment Experience
Employment Interviews
Employment Qualifications
Job Applicants
Job Application
Job Search Methods
Personnel Data
Personnel Selection

= Two or more Descriptors are used to represent this term.
The term's main entry shows the appropriate coordination.

Portfolios (Background Materials)
Profiles
Qualifications

Retail Training
USE DISTRIBUTIVE EDUCATION

RETAILING *Aug. 1968*
CIJE: 117 RIE: 159 GC: 650
BT Marketing
RT College Stores
Distributive Education
Food Stores
Merchandising
Merchants
Salesmanship
Sales Occupations
Wholesaling

Retardation (1966 1980)
USE MENTAL RETARDATION

Retarded Children (1966 1980)
USE MENTAL RETARDATION

Retarded Readers (1966 1980)
USE READING DIFFICULTIES

Retarded Speech Development (1968 1980)
USE DELAYED SPEECH

Retention (Of Employees)
USE LABOR TURNOVER

Retention (Of Students)
USE SCHOOL HOLDING POWER

RETENTION (PSYCHOLOGY) *Mar. 1980*
CIJE: 1018 RIE: 798 GC: 110
SN That aspect of memory that involves either short- or long-term holding of information (note: for the concept of "retention of personnel, teachers, students, etc.," see such descriptors as "employment practices," "teacher persistence," and "school holding power")
UF Retention (1966 1980)
Retention Studies (1966 1980)
BT Memory
RT Advance Organizers
Cues
Encoding (Psychology)
Extinction (Psychology)
Habituation
Language Skill Attrition
Mediation Theory
Memorization
Mnemonics
Primacy Effect
Recall (Psychology)
Recognition (Psychology)
Redundancy
Rote Learning
Schemata (Cognition)
Visualization

Retention (1966 1980)
USE RETENTION (PSYCHOLOGY)

Retention Studies (1966 1980)
USE RETENTION (PSYCHOLOGY)

Retired Teachers
USE TEACHER RETIREMENT

RETIREMENT *Jul. 1966*
CIJE: 564 RIE: 491 GC: 630
NT Early Retirement
Teacher Retirement
BT Status
RT Age Discrimination
Aging In Academia
Educational Gerontology
Gerontology
Labor Force Nonparticipants
Older Adults
Preretirement Education
Retirement Benefits

RETIREMENT BENEFITS *Mar. 1980*
CIJE: 122 RIE: 150 GC: 630
SN Money or other compensation given to employees who have left a job due to age or disability or who have rendered a specified number of years of service -- also, the investment plans for such compensation
UF Pensions
RT Compensation (Remuneration)
Fringe Benefits
Income
Insurance
Personnel Policy
Retirement
Salaries
Scope Of Bargaining
Wages

RETRAINING *Jul. 1966*
CIJE: 218 RIE: 531 GC: 630
UF Refresher Training
Vocational Retraining (1966 1980)
BT Training
RT Adult Education
Adult Vocational Education
Continuing Education Units
Dislocated Workers
Dropouts
Inservice Education
Job Training
Labor Force Development
Occupations
Reentry Workers
Refresher Courses
Rehabilitation
Review (Reexamination)
Skill Development
Skill Obsolescence
Supplementary Education

RETRENCHMENT *Aug. 1977*
CIJE: 615 RIE: 570 GC: 620
SN Reduction of costs or efforts, usually as an economic necessity
UF Budget Cuts #
RT Budgeting
Cost Effectiveness
Costs
Economics
Educational Administration
Educational Finance
Expenditures
Financial Problems
Institutional Administration
Institutional Survival
Productivity
Program Administration
Program Termination
Reduction In Force

Retroactive Inhibition
USE INHIBITION

Revenue
USE INCOME

REVENUE SHARING *Jul. 1973*
CIJE: 84 RIE: 117 GC: 620
SN Practice of returning a percentage of federal tax money to states and localities for locally directed and controlled public service programs -- includes functional grants for education and other major purposes (special) as well as unrestricted grants (general)
BT Federal Aid
Financial Support
RT Block Grants
Educational Finance
Equalization Aid
Federal Legislation
Federal State Relationship
Government Role
Grants
Local Government
Public Policy
School District Autonomy
Tax Allocation

Reversal Shift
USE SHIFT STUDIES

REVERSE DISCRIMINATION *Dec. 1976*
CIJE: 127 RIE: 61 GC: 540
SN Preferential treatment of groups of people who had previously been discriminated against, to the exclusion of other groups
BT Social Discrimination
RT Affirmative Action
Age Discrimination
Educational Discrimination
Equal Education
Equal Opportunities (Jobs)
Handicap Discrimination
Housing Discrimination
Racial Discrimination
Religious Discrimination
Selective Admission
Sex Discrimination

REVIEW (REEXAMINATION) *Jul. 1966*
CIJE: 168 RIE: 155 GC: 110
SN Study of material studied before (note: do not confuse with "evaluation")
BT Activities
RT Refresher Courses
Remedial Instruction
Retraining
Study
Study Guides
Test Coaching
Tutoring

Reviews Of The Literature
USE LITERATURE REVIEWS

REVISION (WRITTEN COMPOSITION) *Aug. 1982*
CIJE: 179 RIE: 226 GC: 400
SN The process of reformulating, correcting, and/or rewriting textual materials
UF Rewriting
BT Writing Processes
RT Writing (Composition)
Writing Exercises
Writing Skills

REVOLUTION *Jul. 1973*
CIJE: 135 RIE: 104 GC: 610
SN The attempt to make radical changes to one or more political, social, or technological systems that would be qualitatively different from and destructive to the traditional values, norms, and practices of such systems
BT Conflict
RT Activism
Change
Conflict Resolution
Culture Conflict
Developing Nations
Dissent
Economic Change
Futures (Of Society)
History
Industrialization
Marxism
Political Science
Social Action
Social Change
Technological Advancement
Terrorism
Violence
War
World Problems

REVOLUTIONARY WAR (UNITED STATES) *May. 1970*
CIJE: 86 RIE: 124 GC: 430
UF American Revolutionary War
BT United States History
RT Colonial History (United States)
Colonialism

REWARDS *Jul. 1966*
CIJE: 724 RIE: 449 GC: 520
NT Self Reward
BT Reinforcement
RT Awards
Compensation (Remuneration)
Delay Of Gratification
Educational Benefits
Incentives
Merit Rating
Motivation
Professional Recognition
Recognition (Achievement)
Sanctions
Social Exchange Theory
Social Reinforcement
Token Economy

Rewriting
USE REVISION (WRITTEN COMPOSITION)

REZONING *Jul. 1966*
CIJE: 5 RIE: 15 GC: 610
UF Rezoning Districts
BT Zoning
RT School District Reorganization
School Districts

Rezoning Districts
USE REZONING

RH FACTORS *Sep. 1969*
CIJE: 4 RIE: 2 GC: 210
BT Biological Influences
RT Biochemistry
Biology
Cytology
Embryology
Genetics
Obstetrics
Perinatal Influences
Physiology
Pregnancy
Prenatal Influences
Reproduction (Biology)

RHETORIC *Jul. 1966*
CIJE: 905 RIE: 783 GC: 430
SN Art of speaking or writing effectively
NT Coherence
Persuasive Discourse
Rhetorical Invention
BT Language Arts
RT Expository Writing
Literary Devices
Rhetorical Criticism
Speech
Verbal Communication
Writing (Composition)

RHETORICAL CRITICISM *Feb. 1971*
CIJE: 439 RIE: 300 GC: 430
SN Criticism of rhetorical and persuasive discourse
BT Literary Criticism
RT Film Criticism
Literature
Persuasive Discourse
Rhetoric

RHETORICAL INVENTION *Dec. 1985*
CIJE: 12 RIE: 4 GC: 430
SN Creativity or originality in speaking or writing -- also, the process of choosing ideas appropriate to the subject, audience, and occasion for either oral or written presentation
BT Rhetoric
RT Creative Writing
Creativity
Persuasive Discourse
Prewriting
Public Speaking
Speech
Speech Communication
Speeches
Writing (Composition)
Writing Skills

Ribonucleic Acid
USE RNA

RIFF *Jul. 1966*
CIJE: RIE: 1 GC: 440
BT Berber Languages

Right To Know
USE FREEDOM OF INFORMATION

RISK *Jul. 1966*
CIJE: 394 RIE: 214 GC: 210
RT Adventure Education
Cost Effectiveness
Decision Making
Entrepreneurship
Game Theory
Insurance
Prediction
Probability
Reliability

River Pollution
USE WATER POLLUTION

RNA *Oct. 1982*
CIJE: 8 RIE: GC: 490
SN Any of the class of nucleic acids that contains ribose, found chiefly in cell cytoplasm and associated with the control of cellular chemical activity
UF Ribonucleic Acid
BT Nucleic Acids

= Two or more Descriptors are used to represent this term.
The term's main entry shows the appropriate coordination.

ROAD CONSTRUCTION *Mar. 1969*
CIJE: 20 RIE: 51 GC: 920
UF Highway Construction
BT Construction (Process)
RT Asphalts
Civil Engineering
Highway Engineering Aides
Land Use
Traffic Circulation
Transportation
Urban Planning

Road Signs
USE SIGNS

ROBOTICS *Mar. 1984*
CIJE: 60 RIE: 74 GC: 490
SN Study, design, and use of robots, mechanical devices that can be programed to perform tasks of manipulation and locomotion under automatic control
UF Industrial Robotics
Robots
BT Automation
Bionics
RT Artificial Intelligence
Cybernetics
Electromechanical Technology
Electronic Control
Electronics
Industrial Arts
Man Machine Systems

Robots
USE ROBOTICS

Rodenticides (1968 1980)
USE PESTICIDES

ROLE CONFLICT *Jul. 1966*
CIJE: 687 RIE: 449 GC: 120
SN Incompatibility between multiple roles taken by an individual or between group and individual roles
BT Conflict
RT Alienation
Conflict Of Interest
Psychological Characteristics
Psychological Patterns
Role Theory
Socialization

ROLE MODELS *May. 1973*
CIJE: 694 RIE: 480 GC: 110
SN Individuals (real or theoretical) chosen for emulation in one or a selected few of their roles (note: do not confuse with "reference groups")
NT Mentors
BT Groups
Models
RT Identification (Psychology)
Imitation
Modeling (Psychology)
Observational Learning
Significant Others

ROLE OF EDUCATION *Jan. 1985*
CIJE: 40 RIE: 42 GC: 330
SN Functions of education, real or expected, in regard to the individual and the society at large (note: use a more precise term if possible)
UF Education Role
RT Board Of Education Role
College Role
Education
Educational Assessment
Educational Environment
Educational Objectives
Educational Responsibility
Outcomes Of Education
School Role
Sociocultural Patterns
Student Role
Teacher Role

ROLE PERCEPTION *Jul. 1966*
CIJE: 2099 RIE: 1853 GC: 510
SN Awareness of behavior patterns or functions expected of individuals or groups
BT Cognitive Processes
RT Identification (Psychology)
Perspective Taking
Role Playing
Role Theory
Self Actualization
Social Cognition
Stereotypes

ROLE PLAYING *Jul. 1966*
CIJE: 1085 RIE: 935 GC: 240
UF Sociodrama (1966 1980)
NT Dramatic Play
BT Simulation
RT Computer Simulation
Counseling Techniques
Group Dynamics
Perspective Taking
Pretend Play
Psychotherapy
Role Perception
Teaching Methods

Role Taking
USE PERSPECTIVE TAKING

ROLE THEORY *Jul. 1966*
CIJE: 481 RIE: 282 GC: 810
BT Theories
RT Identification (Psychology)
Life Style
Personal Autonomy
Role Conflict
Role Perception
Self Actualization
Social Stratification
Social Theories
Student School Relationship

ROLLER SKATING *Feb. 1978*
CIJE: 1 RIE: 3 GC: 470
BT Athletics

Roman Literature
USE LATIN LITERATURE

ROMANCE LANGUAGES *Jul. 1966*
CIJE: 55 RIE: 94 GC: 440
NT French
Italian
Latin
Portuguese
Rumanian
Spanish
BT Indo European Languages
RT Welsh

Romanian (1969 1980)
USE RUMANIAN

ROMANIZATION *Jul. 1966*
CIJE: 17 RIE: 75 GC: 450
SN The transliteration of another system of writing into the roman alphabet
RT Alphabets
Graphemes
Language Standardization
Orthographic Symbols
Written Language

ROMANTICISM *Jun. 1969*
CIJE: 104 RIE: 34 GC: 430
SN Eighteenth and nineteenth century movement, style, and sensibility, originating as a reaction to the neoclassic focus on reason and intellect, and characterized by an emphasis on imagination, emotions, spontaneity, idealism, and individualism
RT Art Expression
Eighteenth Century Literature
Literary Styles
Nineteenth Century Literature
Philosophy
Platonism

Roof Installation
USE ROOFING

Roofers (1968 1981)
USE ROOFING; SKILLED WORKERS

ROOFING *Jul. 1966*
CIJE: 43 RIE: 43 GC: 920
UF Roofers (1968 1981) #
Roof Installation
Roofs
BT Structural Elements (Construction)
RT Asphalts
Buildings
Building Trades
Construction (Process)
Construction Materials
Skilled Occupations

Roofs
USE ROOFING

Room Dividers
USE SPACE DIVIDERS

ROTATION PLANS *Jul. 1966*
CIJE: 18 RIE: 8 GC: 320
RT Team Teaching

ROTE LEARNING *Jul. 1966*
CIJE: 81 RIE: 63 GC: 110
BT Learning
RT Drills (Practice)
Learning Theories
Memorization
Primacy Effect
Retention (Psychology)
Serial Learning

Roumanian
USE RUMANIAN

RUBELLA *Apr. 1969*
CIJE: 64 RIE: 27 GC: 210
UF Epidemic Roseola
German Measles
BT Communicable Diseases
RT Physical Health
Prenatal Influences

RUMANIAN *Mar. 1980*
CIJE: 12 RIE: 39 GC: 440
UF Romanian (1969 1980)
Roumanian
BT Romance Languages

RUNAWAYS *Aug. 1978*
CIJE: 42 RIE: 55 GC: 530
SN Persons who leave home without notice, and stay away for indefinite periods of time
UF Adult Runaways
Juvenile Runaways
BT Groups
RT Child Welfare
Delinquency
Dropouts
Family Problems
Homeless People
One Parent Family
Truancy
Youth Problems

RUNNING *Sep. 1968*
CIJE: 119 RIE: 54 GC: 470
NT Jogging
BT Physical Activities
RT Athletics
Physical Education
Physical Fitness
Track And Field

RURAL AMERICAN INDIANS *Mar. 1980*
CIJE: RIE: 9 GC: 560
SN American indians who reside in rural areas and may live near (but not on) reservations
BT Nonreservation American Indians
Rural Population
RT Rural Areas
Urban American Indians

RURAL AREAS *Jul. 1966*
CIJE: 854 RIE: 2486 GC: 550
UF Rural Clinics (1966 1980) #
BT Geographic Regions
RT Collective Settlements
Rural American Indians
Rural Development
Rural Economics
Rural Education
Rural Environment
Rural Extension
Rural Population
Rural Resettlement
Rural Schools
Rural To Urban Migration
Rural Urban Differences
Urban To Rural Migration

Rural Clinics (1966 1980)
USE CLINICS; RURAL AREAS

RURAL DEVELOPMENT *Jul. 1966*
CIJE: 295 RIE: 1031 GC: 550
BT Development
RT Community Development
Modernization
Rural Areas
Rural Economics
Rural Environment

Rural Dropouts (1966 1981)
USE DROPOUTS

RURAL ECONOMICS *Jul. 1966*
CIJE: 31 RIE: 184 GC: 620
BT Economics
RT Rural Areas
Rural Development
Rural Environment

RURAL EDUCATION *Jul. 1966*
CIJE: 486 RIE: 1552 GC: 330
BT Education
RT Adult Farmer Education
Outdoor Education
Rural Areas
Rural Environment
Rural Extension
Rural Schools
Young Farmer Education

RURAL ENVIRONMENT *Jul. 1966*
CIJE: 120 RIE: 277 GC: 550
BT Environment
RT Rural Areas
Rural Development
Rural Economics
Rural Education
Rural Extension
Rural Family
Rural Population
Rural Resettlement
Rural To Urban Migration
Urban To Rural Migration

RURAL EXTENSION *Jul. 1966*
CIJE: 143 RIE: 401 GC: 350
SN Extension work in rural settings
UF Agricultural Extension
BT Extension Education
RT Adult Farmer Education
Agricultural Education
Land Grant Universities
Rural Areas
Rural Education
Rural Environment
Young Farmer Education

RURAL FAMILY *Jul. 1966*
CIJE: 33 RIE: 135 GC: 510
BT Family (Sociological Unit)
Rural Population
RT Rural Environment

RURAL FARM RESIDENTS *Sep. 1968*
CIJE: 46 RIE: 164 GC: 410
SN Persons living in nonmetropolitan areas on land which is gainfully worked as an agricultural enterprise
BT Rural Population
RT Farmers
Rural Nonfarm Residents
Sharecroppers

Rural Inhabitants
USE RURAL POPULATION

RURAL NONFARM RESIDENTS *Aug. 1977*
CIJE: 5 RIE: 34 GC: 510
SN Persons living in nonmetropolitan areas on land which is not worked as an agricultural enterprise
BT Rural Population
RT Rural Farm Residents

RURAL POPULATION *Jul. 1966*
CIJE: 267 RIE: 806 GC: 550
UF Rural Inhabitants
NT Rural American Indians
Rural Family
Rural Farm Residents
Rural Nonfarm Residents
Rural Youth
BT Groups
RT Demography
Population Distribution
Population Growth
Population Trends

Rural Areas
Rural Environment
Rural Resettlement
Rural To Urban Migration
Rural Urban Differences
Urban To Rural Migration

RURAL RESETTLEMENT *Jul. 1966*
CIJE: 17 RIE: 38 GC: 550
BT Land Settlement
Relocation
RT Rural Areas
Rural Environment
Rural Population
Urban To Rural Migration

Rural School Systems (1966 1980)
USE RURAL SCHOOLS; SCHOOL DISTRICTS

RURAL SCHOOLS *Jul. 1966*
CIJE: 401 RIE: 1035 GC: 340
UF Rural School Systems (1966 1980) #
BT Schools
RT Consolidated Schools
County School Districts
One Teacher Schools
Rural Areas
Rural Education
Small Schools

RURAL TO URBAN MIGRATION *Oct. 1976*
CIJE: 90 RIE: 236 GC: 550
SN Population movement from rural areas to urban areas for purpose of relocation
UF Urban Immigration (1966 1976)
BT Migration
RT Migration Patterns
Population Distribution
Population Trends
Relocation
Residential Patterns
Rural Areas
Rural Environment
Rural Population
Urban Areas
Urban Demography
Urbanization
Urban Population
Urban To Rural Migration

RURAL URBAN DIFFERENCES *Jul. 1966*
CIJE: 412 RIE: 987 GC: 550
UF Urban Rural Differences
BT Differences
RT Cultural Differences
Place Of Residence
Regional Attitudes
Regional Characteristics
Rural Areas
Rural Population
Social Differences
Urban Areas
Urban Culture
Urban Language
Urban Population

RURAL YOUTH *Jul. 1966*
CIJE: 198 RIE: 703 GC: 510
UF Farm Youth
BT Rural Population
Youth
RT Migrant Youth

RUSSIAN *Jul. 1966*
CIJE: 497 RIE: 431 GC: 440
BT Slavic Languages
RT Russian Literature

RUSSIAN LITERATURE *Dec. 1969*
CIJE: 101 RIE: 28 GC: 430
BT Literature
RT Russian

SABBATICAL LEAVES *Jul. 1966*
CIJE: 51 RIE: 105 GC: 630
BT Leaves Of Absence
RT Faculty Development
Faculty Fellowships
Faculty Workload
Professional Continuing Education
Professional Development
Professional Education
Released Time
Teacher Attendance
Teacher Employment Benefits
Teacher Improvement

SAFETY *Jul. 1966*
CIJE: 750 RIE: 1348 GC: 210
UF Safety Provisions
NT Agricultural Safety
Fire Protection
Laboratory Safety
Occupational Safety And Health
School Safety
Traffic Safety
RT Accident Prevention
Accidents
Alarm Systems
Consumer Protection
Daily Living Skills
Design Requirements
Emergency Programs
Fallout Shelters
Hazardous Materials
Health
Injuries
National Security
Natural Disasters
Poisoning
Radiation
Radiation Effects
Refugees
Rescue
Safety Education
Safety Equipment
Security Personnel
Traffic Accidents

SAFETY EDUCATION *Jul. 1966*
CIJE: 334 RIE: 732 GC: 400
BT Education
RT Accident Prevention
Accidents
Agricultural Safety
Fire Protection
Fire Science Education
Laboratory Safety
Occupational Safety And Health
Rescue
Safety
Safety Equipment
School Safety
Traffic Accidents
Traffic Safety

SAFETY EQUIPMENT *Aug. 1968*
CIJE: 136 RIE: 120 GC: 910
UF Safety Glasses
NT Restraints (Vehicle Safety)
BT Equipment
RT Accident Prevention
Safety
Safety Education

Safety Glasses
USE SAFETY EQUIPMENT

Safety Provisions
USE SAFETY

SAILING *Jan. 1985*
CIJE: 10 RIE: 2 GC: 470
BT Aquatic Sports
RT Boat Operators
Maritime Education
Seafarers

SALARIES *Jul. 1966*
CIJE: 659 RIE: 1187 GC: 630
SN Earnings paid at fixed intervals (week, month, year) rather than at hourly rates, and usually for professional, technical, and executive services (note: do not confuse with "wages" -- prior to mar80, the use of this term was not restricted by a scope note)
NT Contract Salaries
Teacher Salaries
BT Expenditures
Income
RT Compensation (Remuneration)
Costs
Fringe Benefits
Guaranteed Income
Merit Pay
Operating Expenses
Payroll Records
Premium Pay
Promotion (Occupational)
Retirement Benefits
Salary Wage Differentials
Scope Of Bargaining
Wages

Salary Differentials (1968 1980)
USE SALARY WAGE DIFFERENTIALS

Salary Raises
USE PROMOTION (OCCUPATIONAL)

SALARY WAGE DIFFERENTIALS *Mar. 1980*
CIJE: 522 RIE: 541 GC: 620
UF Equal Pay
Salary Differentials (1968 1980)
Wage Salary Differentials
BT Differences
RT Comparable Worth
Educational Finance
Employment Practices
Equal Opportunities (Jobs)
Merit Pay
Overtime
Personnel Policy
Premium Pay
Salaries
Scope Of Bargaining
Wages

Sales Clerks
USE SALES WORKERS

SALES OCCUPATIONS *Jul. 1966*
CIJE: 48 RIE: 149 GC: 640
BT Occupations
RT Agricultural Supply Occupations
Auto Parts Clerks
Distributive Education
Insurance Occupations
Merchandising
Merchants
Real Estate Occupations
Retailing
Salesmanship
Sales Workers
Service Occupations
White Collar Occupations

Sales Promotion
USE MERCHANDISING

SALES WORKERS *Jul. 1966*
CIJE: 50 RIE: 80 GC: 640
UF Sales Clerks
NT Auto Parts Clerks
BT Nonprofessional Personnel
RT Agricultural Supply Occupations
Employees
Merchants
Salesmanship
Sales Occupations
Service Workers

SALESMANSHIP *Jul. 1966*
CIJE: 119 RIE: 225 GC: 650
BT Marketing
Skills
RT Advertising
Distributive Education
Job Skills
Merchandise Information
Merchandising
Persuasive Discourse
Retailing
Sales Occupations
Sales Workers
Wholesaling

SALISH *Jul. 1970*
CIJE: 15 RIE: 10 GC: 440
BT American Indian Languages

SAMOAN *Jan. 1970*
CIJE: 7 RIE: 23 GC: 440
BT Malayo Polynesian Languages
RT Samoan Americans

SAMOAN AMERICANS *Mar. 1976*
CIJE: 6 RIE: 31 GC: 560
SN Polynesian or part-polynesian people indigenous to the samoan islands
UF American Samoans
BT Ethnic Groups
Pacific Americans
RT Samoan
Trust Responsibility (Government)

SAMOYED LANGUAGES *Jul. 1966*
CIJE: RIE: 2 GC: 440
NT Yurak
BT Uralic Altaic Languages

SAMPLE SIZE *Mar. 1983*
CIJE: 87 RIE: 49 GC: 820
SN The number of subjects (or items) selected to represent a population in a research or evaluation study
RT Attrition (Research Studies)
Control Groups
Effect Size
Evaluation Methods
Experimental Groups
Generalizability Theory
Measurement Techniques
Probability
Reliability
Research Design
Research Problems
Sampling
Statistical Analysis
Statistical Bias
Surveys

SAMPLING *Jul. 1966*
CIJE: 721 RIE: 696 GC: 820
SN Selecting a representative part of a population to draw inferences about the characteristics of the whole population
NT Item Sampling
BT Data Collection
Statistics
RT Attrition (Research Studies)
Control Groups
Cross Sectional Studies
Error Of Measurement
Evaluation Methods
Experimental Groups
Generalizability Theory
Longitudinal Studies
Matched Groups
Maximum Likelihood Statistics
Measurement Techniques
Monte Carlo Methods
Multivariate Analysis
Norms
Participant Characteristics
Predictive Measurement
Probability
Quasiexperimental Design
Research Design
Sample Size
Statistical Analysis
Statistical Bias
Statistical Inference
Statistical Studies
Statistical Surveys
Surveys

Sanatoriums
USE HOSPITALS

SANCTIONS *Jul. 1966*
CIJE: 63 RIE: 81 GC: 520
SN Mechanisms of social control that punish deviancy or reward conformance with regard to specified standards
RT Arbitration
Awards
Censorship
Collective Bargaining
Discipline
Fines (Penalties)
Incentives
Labor Demands
Laws
Negotiation Impasses
Punishment
Rewards
Social Control
Standards
Teacher Militancy
Teacher Strikes

SANGO *Jul. 1966*
CIJE: 1 RIE: 9 GC: 440
BT African Languages

SANITARY FACILITIES *Jul. 1966*
CIJE: 20 RIE: 50 GC: 920
SN Equipment and building areas for keeping buildings clean and/or facilities for personal cleanliness
NT Toilet Facilities
BT Facilities
RT Dishwashing
Equipment
Health Conditions
Health Facilities
Hygiene
Locker Rooms

= Two or more Descriptors are used to represent this term.
The term's main entry shows the appropriate coordination.

Physical Health
Plumbing
Sanitation
Utilities
Waste Disposal

Sanitary Inspectors
USE ENVIRONMENTAL TECHNICIANS

Sanitary Technicians
USE ENVIRONMENTAL TECHNICIANS

SANITATION *Jul. 1966*
CIJE: 124 RIE: 293 GC: 210
UF Sanitation Improvement (1966 1980)
NT Cleaning
Waste Disposal
RT Design Requirements
Disease Control
Environmental Influences
Environmental Technicians
Hazardous Materials
Health
Hygiene
Pests
Physical Environment
Physical Health
Public Health
Sanitary Facilities
Utilities
Water Treatment

Sanitation Improvement (1966 1980)
USE SANITATION

SANSKRIT *Aug. 1968*
CIJE: 5 RIE: 11 GC: 440
BT Classical Languages

SARA *Jul. 1966*
CIJE: RIE: 6 GC: 440
BT African Languages

Sarcasm
USE IRONY

Sarcoma
USE CANCER

SATELLITE FACILITIES *Mar. 1980*
CIJE: 10 RIE: 19 GC: 920
SN Subsidiary facilities that may be some distance from the facility or institution to which they are administratively related
BT Facilities
RT Branch Libraries
Extension Education
Off Campus Facilities

Satellite Laboratories (1966 1980)
USE SATELLITES (AEROSPACE)

Satellite Libraries
USE BRANCH LIBRARIES

SATELLITES (AEROSPACE) *Mar. 1980*
CIJE: 48 RIE: 23 GC: 490
SN (Note: if applicable, use the more specific term "communications satellites")
UF Artificial Satellites
Orbiting Satellites
Satellite Laboratories (1966 1980)
NT Communications Satellites
RT Aerospace Technology
Earth Science
Lunar Research
Space Exploration
Space Sciences

SATIRE *Jul. 1966*
CIJE: 138 RIE: 42 GC: 430
BT Literary Genres
RT Comics (Publications)
Figurative Language
Literary Styles
Parody

Scales
USE MEASURES (INDIVIDUALS)

SCALING *Mar. 1980*
CIJE: 85 RIE: 104 GC: 820
SN Arranging objects in a definite order by assigning values to them along a predetermined continuum
UF Internal Scaling (1966 1980)
NT Multidimensional Scaling
BT Measurement Techniques
RT Equated Scores
Holistic Evaluation
Mathematical Models
Norms
Rating Scales
Scoring
Statistical Analysis
Test Construction
Testing

Schedule Modules (1968 1980)
USE FLEXIBLE SCHEDULING

SCHEDULING *Jul. 1966*
CIJE: 481 RIE: 638 GC: 320
NT Fast Track Scheduling
School Schedules
Working Hours
BT Planning
RT Coordination
Critical Path Method
Intervals
Programing (Broadcast)
Program Length
Time Factors (Learning)
Time Management

SCHEMATA (COGNITION) *Nov. 1982*
CIJE: 161 RIE: 166 GC: 110
SN Mental images and concepts that provide a cognitive framework by which the individual perceives, understands, and responds to stimuli
BT Psychological Characteristics
RT Cognitive Ability
Cognitive Development
Cognitive Mapping
Cognitive Psychology
Cognitive Structures
Cognitive Style
Comprehension
Learning
Learning Theories
Readiness
Recall (Psychology)
Responses
Retention (Psychology)

SCHEMATIC STUDIES *Jul. 1966*
CIJE: 29 RIE: 36 GC: 810
SN Studies employing models or representations that manifest the significant relationships between concepts (note: as of oct81, use as a minor descriptor for examples of this kind of research -- use as a major descriptor only as the subject of a document -- prior to oct81, this term did not carry a scope note)
BT Research
RT Models
Relationship
Systems Approach

SCHIZOPHRENIA *Jul. 1966*
CIJE: 382 RIE: 99 GC: 230
UF Dementia Praecox
BT Psychosis
RT Autism
Echolalia
Emotional Disturbances
Paranoid Behavior

SCHOLARLY JOURNALS *Jul. 1966*
CIJE: 532 RIE: 217 GC: 720
BT Periodicals
RT Academic Standards
Editors
Faculty Publishing
Research Tools
Scholarship
Writing For Publication

SCHOLARSHIP *Mar. 1980*
CIJE: 234 RIE: 168 GC: 330
SN Comprehensive mastery of an area of knowledge -- also, the methods and attainments of scholars
BT Achievement
RT Academic Ability
Academic Achievement
Knowledge Level
Learning
Recognition (Achievement)
Researchers
Research Skills
Scholarly Journals
Scientists
Social Scientists
Study

SCHOLARSHIP FUNDS *Jul. 1966*
CIJE: 20 RIE: 61 GC: 620
SN Revenue made available for scholarships
BT Financial Support
RT Assistantships
Capital
Educational Finance
Fellowships
Fund Raising
Merit Scholarships
No Need Scholarships
Scholarships
Student Costs
Student Financial Aid
Tuition Grants

Scholarship Loans (1966 1980)
USE SCHOLARSHIPS; STUDENT LOAN PROGRAMS

SCHOLARSHIPS *Jul. 1966*
CIJE: 179 RIE: 384 GC: 620
SN Awards, usually of money or reduced tuition, given to students primarily in recognition of achievement or potential but also for other specific characteristics such as financial need, residence, or academic interest
UF Endowed Scholarships
Scholarship Loans (1966 1980) #
NT Merit Scholarships
Tuition Grants
BT Student Financial Aid
RT Awards
Educational Finance
Educational Vouchers
Eligibility
Fellowships
Grants
Instructional Student Costs
Noninstructional Student Costs
Scholarship Funds
Student Costs

Scholastic Ability
USE ACADEMIC ABILITY

Scholastic Achievement
USE ACADEMIC ACHIEVEMENT

Scholastic Failure
USE ACADEMIC FAILURE

Scholastic Potential
USE ACADEMIC APTITUDE

Scholastic Probation
USE ACADEMIC PROBATION

SCHOOL ACCIDENTS *Jul. 1966*
CIJE: 38 RIE: 31 GC: 210
BT Accidents
RT Schools
School Safety

SCHOOL ACCOUNTING *Jul. 1966*
CIJE: 114 RIE: 179 GC: 620
BT Accounting
RT Educational Finance
School Administration
School Based Management
School Business Officials
Schools

SCHOOL ACTIVITIES *Jul. 1966*
CIJE: 133 RIE: 213 GC: 320
UF School Programs
NT Class Activities
Extracurricular Activities
Student Projects
BT Activities
RT After School Programs
Assembly Programs
Curriculum
Learning Activities
School Recreational Programs
Schools

School Adjustment
USE STUDENT ADJUSTMENT

SCHOOL ADMINISTRATION *Jul. 1966*
CIJE: 814 RIE: 917 GC: 320
SN Planning, organizing, directing, and controlling human or material resources within a school, college, or university
NT College Administration
School Based Management
BT Educational Administration
Institutional Administration
RT Admissions Officers
Assistant Principals
Board Administrator Relationship
Boards Of Education
Deans
Department Heads
Governing Boards
Government School Relationship
Instructional Leadership
Principals
Registrars (School)
School Accounting
School Business Officials
School District Autonomy
School Law
School Policy
School Responsibility
Schools
School Supervision
Student Government
Student School Relationship
Superintendents
Teacher Administrator Relationship

School Administrators
USE ADMINISTRATORS

School Admission
USE ADMISSION (SCHOOL)

SCHOOL AGE DAY CARE *Oct. 1983*
CIJE: 11 RIE: 39 GC: 520
SN Care of school-age children before or after the school day
UF After School Day Care (1978 1983) #
BT Day Care
RT After School Programs
Ancillary School Services
Day Care Centers
Employer Supported Day Care
Extended School Day
Family Day Care
Latchkey Children

School Aid
USE EDUCATIONAL FINANCE

SCHOOL AIDES *Jul. 1966*
CIJE: 47 RIE: 101 GC: 360
SN Paraprofessional school personnel who work under the guidance of school professionals, assisting in noninstructional areas -- e.g., playground monitors (note: prior to mar80, this term was not scoped and was often confused with "teacher aides," who assist in the instructional process)
BT Paraprofessional School Personnel
RT Bilingual Teacher Aides
Proctoring
Teacher Aides
Volunteers

School Architecture (1966 1980)
USE EDUCATIONAL FACILITIES DESIGN

School Attendance
USE ATTENDANCE

School Attendance Laws (1966 1974)
USE SCHOOL ATTENDANCE LEGISLATION

SCHOOL ATTENDANCE LEGISLATION *Nov. 1974*
CIJE: 84 RIE: 92 GC: 330
UF School Attendance Laws (1966 1974)
BT Educational Legislation
State Legislation
RT Attendance
Average Daily Attendance
Compulsory Education
Expulsion
Home Schooling
Laws
School Policy
Suspension

= Two or more Descriptors are used to represent this term.
The term's main entry shows the appropriate coordination.

SCHOOL ATTITUDES *Jul. 1966*
CIJE: 237 RIE: 408 GC: 330
SN Attitudes toward or about schools
BT Attitudes
RT Family School Relationship
Government School Relationship
Parent School Relationship
Police School Relationship
School Community Relationship
Schools
Student School Relationship

SCHOOL BASED MANAGEMENT *Sep. 1982*
CIJE: 44 RIE: 48 GC: 320
SN Administrative system in which an individual school exercises autonomous decision making on budgets, curriculum, and personnel within policy guidelines set by its governing board
UF School Site Management
BT Institutional Autonomy
School Administration
RT Budgeting
Decentralization
Decision Making
Participative Decision Making
Principals
School Accounting
School Organization
School Policy
Schools
School Supervision

School Board Members
USE BOARDS OF EDUCATION

School Board Policy
USE BOARD OF EDUCATION POLICY

School Board Role
USE BOARD OF EDUCATION ROLE

School Boards
USE BOARDS OF EDUCATION

School Boundaries
USE SCHOOL DISTRICTS

SCHOOL BOYCOTTS *Jul. 1966*
CIJE: 13 RIE: 23 GC: 540
RT Activism
Demonstrations (Civil)
School Resegregation
Schools
School Segregation
Strikes
Student Rights
Teacher Strikes

SCHOOL BUDGET ELECTIONS *Jul. 1966*
CIJE: 66 RIE: 94 GC: 620
BT Elections
RT Budgets
Educational Finance
School Funds
School Support

SCHOOL BUILDINGS *Jul. 1966*
CIJE: 286 RIE: 495 GC: 920
NT College Buildings
BT Buildings
Educational Facilities
RT Campuses
Campus Planning
Construction Materials
Educational Complexes
Educational Equipment
Educational Facilities Design
Educational Facilities Improvement
Educational Facilities Planning
Facility Utilization Research
Open Plan Schools
School Construction
School Expansion
Schools
School Shops
Space Utilization

SCHOOL BUSES *Aug. 1968*
CIJE: 136 RIE: 120 GC: 910
BT Service Vehicles
RT Busing
Bus Transportation
Equipment
Student Transportation

SCHOOL BUSINESS OFFICIALS *Mar. 1980*
CIJE: 62 RIE: 60 GC: 360
SN Administrative officers responsible for the direction of business and financial affairs of an educational institution -- functions supervised include accounting, purchasing, facility and property maintenance, personnel services, etc.
UF Business Officials (School)
BT Administrators
School Personnel
RT Ancillary School Services
Educational Facilities Planning
Educational Finance
Middle Management
School Accounting
School Administration
Student Financial Aid Officers

SCHOOL BUSINESS RELATIONSHIP *Mar. 1980*
CIJE: 1639 RIE: 1853 GC: 330
UF Business School Relationship
Industry School Relationship
School Industry Relationship (1967 1980)
BT Relationship
RT Business
Career Education
Cooperative Education
Cooperative Programs
Corporate Education
Corporate Support
Education Work Relationship
Industry
Private Financial Support
School Community Relationship
School Involvement
Schools
School Support
Vocational Education
Work Experience Programs

SCHOOL CADRES *Mar. 1969*
CIJE: 11 RIE: 28 GC: 360
SN Groups of school personnel previously coordinated in training to work together and to train others
BT School Personnel
RT Research And Instruction Units
Staff Utilization
Team Teaching
Team Training

School Calendars (1967 1980)
USE SCHOOL SCHEDULES

SCHOOL CATALOGS *Mar. 1980*
CIJE: 38 RIE: 52 GC: 320
SN Publications issued by schools to provide information on their courses, faculty, facilities, etc. (note: prior to mar80, "catalogs" was used to index this concept)
UF College Catalogs
BT Catalogs
School Publications
RT Admission (School)
Admission Criteria
Course Descriptions
Degree Requirements
Graduation Requirements
Program Descriptions
Schools
Student Recruitment

School Characteristics
USE INSTITUTIONAL CHARACTERISTICS

SCHOOL CHOICE *Mar. 1982*
CIJE: 64 RIE: 91 GC: 330
SN Individualized selection of public or private schools, alternative programs, or different school systems, sometimes made possible with little or no added financial cost through tax credits, vouchers, magnet schools, open enrollment, or other arrangements
UF Educational Choice
Family Choice (Education)
NT College Choice
BT Selection
RT Admission (School)
Decision Making
Educational Vouchers
Eligibility
Free Choice Transfer Programs
Nontraditional Education
Private School Aid
Tax Credits
Tuition

School Climate
USE EDUCATIONAL ENVIRONMENT

SCHOOL CLOSING *Jul. 1966*
CIJE: 206 RIE: 239 GC: 330
SN Permanent closing of schools
UF Closed Schools
College Closing
RT Board Of Education Policy
Consolidated Schools
Declining Enrollment
Institutional Survival
Mergers
Program Termination
Schools
Student Attrition

School College Cooperation
USE COLLEGE SCHOOL COOPERATION

School Community Communication
USE SCHOOL COMMUNITY RELATIONSHIP

School Community Cooperation (1966 1980)
USE SCHOOL COMMUNITY RELATIONSHIP

School Community Coordination
USE SCHOOL COMMUNITY RELATIONSHIP

School Community Interaction
USE SCHOOL COMMUNITY RELATIONSHIP

SCHOOL COMMUNITY PROGRAMS *Jul. 1966*
CIJE: 374 RIE: 520 GC: 330
SN Programs sponsored jointly by an educational institution and the surrounding community
UF Community School Programs
BT Community Programs
RT Community
Outreach Programs
School Community Relationship
School Involvement
Schools

SCHOOL COMMUNITY RELATIONSHIP *Jul. 1966*
CIJE: 3082 RIE: 4333 GC: 330
SN Formal or informal interactions between an educational institution and the surrounding community
UF College Community Relationship
Community School Relationship
School Community Communication
School Community Cooperation (1966 1980)
School Community Coordination
School Community Interaction
BT Relationship
RT Community
Community Colleges
Community Control
Community Cooperation
Community Coordination
Community Schools
Cooperative Planning
Cooperative Programs
Educational Sociology
Family School Relationship
Parent School Relationship
Participative Decision Making
Politics Of Education
Public Relations
Public Service
School Attitudes
School Business Relationship
School Community Programs
School Involvement
School Role
Schools
School Support

School Conditions (1966 1980)
USE EDUCATIONAL ENVIRONMENT

School Consolidation
USE CONSOLIDATED SCHOOLS

SCHOOL CONSTRUCTION *Jul. 1966*
CIJE: 211 RIE: 388 GC: 320
BT Construction (Process)
RT Bids
Educational Facilities
Educational Facilities Design
Educational Facilities Planning
Life Cycle Costing
Modular Building Design
Prefabrication
School Buildings
School Expansion
Schools
Sheet Metal Work

SCHOOL COUNSELING *Mar. 1980*
CIJE: 682 RIE: 695 GC: 240
SN Assistance given to students by the school or college in order to help them understand and cope with adjustment problems -- includes the administration and interpretation of tests (note: do not confuse with "educational counseling" or "academic advising")
UF Elementary School Counseling (1967 1980)
Guidance Counseling (1966 1980)
Secondary School Counseling
BT Counseling
School Guidance
RT Adjustment Counselors
Colleges
Counselor Teacher Cooperation
Educational Counseling
Educational Therapy
Faculty Advisers
Faculty Workload
Post High School Guidance
Pupil Personnel Services
School Counselors
School Guidance
School Orientation
School Psychologists
Schools
School Social Workers
Student Development
Student Personnel Services

SCHOOL COUNSELORS *Mar. 1980*
CIJE: 699 RIE: 379 GC: 240
SN (Note: prior to mar80, the instruction "guidance counselors, use counselors" was carried in the thesaurus)
UF College Counselors
Elementary School Counselors (1967 1980)
Guidance Counselors
Secondary School Counselors (1967 1980)
BT Counselors
School Personnel
RT Colleges
Counselor Teacher Cooperation
Faculty Advisers
Pupil Personnel Workers
School Counseling
School Guidance
School Psychologists
Schools
School Social Workers
Student Personnel Workers

SCHOOL DEMOGRAPHY *Jul. 1966*
CIJE: 100 RIE: 474 GC: 330
NT Teacher Distribution
BT Demography
RT Affirmative Action
Average Daily Membership
Declining Enrollment
Enrollment Projections
Enrollment Trends
Feeder Patterns
Institutional Characteristics
Residential Patterns
School Desegregation
School District Size
School Location
Schools
School Size
School Statistics
Student Attrition
Students

SCHOOL DESEGREGATION *Mar. 1980*
CIJE: 1458 RIE: 2205 GC: 540
SN Process of bringing students of different ethnic or racial groups into the same school
UF Biracial Elementary Schools (1966 1980)
Biracial Schools (1966 1980)
Biracial Secondary Schools (1966 1980)
Desegregated Schools
Grade A Year Integration (1966 1980)
Integrated Schools
School Integration (1966 1980)
NT College Desegregation
BT Social Integration
RT Black Education
Busing
Classroom Desegregation
Desegregation Effects
Desegregation Litigation
Desegregation Methods
Desegregation Plans
Educational Parks
Integration Readiness
Magnet Schools
Neighborhood Schools
Racial Attitudes
Racial Composition
Racial Integration
Racially Balanced Schools
School Demography
School Resegregation
Schools
Tokenism
Transfer Students
Voluntary Desegregation

School Design (1966 1980)
USE EDUCATIONAL FACILITIES DESIGN

SCHOOL DISTRICT AUTONOMY *Dec. 1968*
CIJE: 318 RIE: 336 GC: 330
SN Area of control granted a school district or its officials through expressed or implied state authority
UF Local Autonomy (Of Schools)
Local Control (Of Schools)
RT Block Grants
Board Of Education Policy
Board Of Education Role
Boards Of Education
City Government
Community Control
Educational Policy
Full State Funding
Governance
Government Role
Government School Relationship
Institutional Autonomy
Local Government
Professional Autonomy
Revenue Sharing
School Administration
School Districts
Self Determination
State Government
State School District Relationship

School District Norms
USE LOCAL NORMS

School District Policy
USE BOARD OF EDUCATION POLICY

SCHOOL DISTRICT REORGANIZATION *Mar. 1980*
CIJE: 49 RIE: 190 GC: 330
SN The changing of boundary lines of local or intermediate basic administrative units, the merging of existing districts, or the creation of new districts
UF School Redistricting (1966 1980)
BT Organization
RT Consolidated Schools
Feeder Patterns
Intermediate Administrative Units
Rezoning
School Districts
School District Size
School Location
Schools
School Zoning

SCHOOL DISTRICT SIZE *Jun. 1983*
CIJE: 23 RIE: 78 GC: 330
SN Size of a school district as measured by its land area or number of students or staff
BT Organization Size (Groups)
RT Enrollment
Geographic Distribution
School Demography
School District Reorganization
School Districts
School Personnel
School Size
School Statistics

SCHOOL DISTRICT SPENDING *Jul. 1966*
CIJE: 307 RIE: 498 GC: 620
BT Expenditures
RT Costs
Educational Equity (Finance)
Educational Finance
Expenditure Per Student
Full State Funding
School Districts
State School District Relationship

SCHOOL DISTRICTS *Jul. 1966*
CIJE: 2057 RIE: 4517 GC: 340
SN Local administrative units that operate schools or contract for school services in specific geographic areas
UF Comprehensive Districts (1967 1980)
Lea
Local Education Agencies
Local Education Authorities
Public School Systems (1966 1980) #
Rural School Systems (1966 1980) #
School Boundaries
School Systems (1966 1980)
NT County School Districts
Multicampus Districts
BT Organizations (Groups)
RT Boards Of Education
Consolidated Schools
Geographic Regions
Interdistrict Policies
Intermediate Administrative Units
Local Government
Public Education
Public Schools
Rezoning
School District Autonomy
School District Reorganization
School District Size
School District Spending
School Location
Schools
State School District Relationship
Superintendents
Zoning

School Dropouts
USE DROPOUTS

SCHOOL EFFECTIVENESS *Aug. 1982*
CIJE: 419 RIE: 582 GC: 320
SN Degrees to which schools are successful in accomplishing their educational objectives or fulfilling their administrative, instructional, or service functions
UF Effective Schooling
Instructionally Effective Schools
BT Organizational Effectiveness
RT Academic Achievement
Accountability
Cost Effectiveness
Educational Assessment
Educational Quality
Instructional Effectiveness
Outcomes Of Education
Program Effectiveness
School Role
Schools
Student Development
Teacher Effectiveness

School Employees
USE SCHOOL PERSONNEL

School Enrollment
USE ENROLLMENT

SCHOOL ENTRANCE AGE *Mar. 1980*
CIJE: 34 RIE: 42 GC: 330
SN Age of students when they enroll in school (note: see "late registration" for students who enroll after the school term has begun)
BT Age
RT Age Grade Placement
Early Admission
Enrollment
Learning Readiness
School Readiness
School Readiness Tests
Student Placement

School Environment (1966 1980)
USE EDUCATIONAL ENVIRONMENT

SCHOOL EXPANSION *Jul. 1966*
CIJE: 73 RIE: 74 GC: 320
SN Increase in the number or size of school facilities
BT Facility Expansion
RT Building Conversion
Educational Facilities
Educational Facilities Improvement
Educational Facilities Planning
Facility Utilization Research
Mobile Classrooms
School Buildings
School Construction
Schools
School Size
Site Analysis
Site Development
Site Selection
Space Utilization

School Experience
USE EDUCATIONAL EXPERIENCE

School Facilities
USE EDUCATIONAL FACILITIES

School Family Relationship
USE FAMILY SCHOOL RELATIONSHIP

School Finance
USE EDUCATIONAL FINANCE

School Finance Equity
USE EDUCATIONAL EQUITY (FINANCE)

SCHOOL FUNDS *Jul. 1966*
CIJE: 203 RIE: 422 GC: 620
SN Money available for school use
BT Financial Support
RT Capital
Educational Finance
Endowment Funds
Federal Aid
Foundation Programs
Fund Raising
Money Management
Private School Aid
School Budget Elections
Schools
School Support
School Taxes
State Aid

School Government Relationship
USE GOVERNMENT SCHOOL RELATIONSHIP

SCHOOL GUIDANCE *Mar. 1980*
CIJE: 157 RIE: 202 GC: 240
SN Assistance given to students by the school or college to help them develop realistic and satisfying goals, plans, and activities (note: do not confuse with "educational counseling")
UF Elementary School Guidance (1967 1980)
Secondary School Guidance
NT School Counseling
BT Guidance
RT Career Awareness
Career Exploration
Career Guidance
Colleges
Counselor Teacher Cooperation
Instructor Coordinators
Probation Officers
Pupil Personnel Services
School Counseling
School Counselors
Schools
Student Development
Student Personnel Services
Teacher Guidance

SCHOOL HEALTH SERVICES *Jul. 1966*
CIJE: 600 RIE: 170 GC: 210
UF Clinic Personnel (School) (1966 1980) #
BT Ancillary School Services
Health Services
RT Breakfast Programs
Lunch Programs
Physical Education
Physical Recreation Programs
Pupil Personnel Services
School Nurses
Student Personnel Services

SCHOOL HOLDING POWER *Jul. 1966*
CIJE: 335 RIE: 878 GC: 320
UF Holding Power (Of Schools)
Retention (Of Students)
RT Academic Persistence
Attendance
College Attendance
Dropout Research
Dropouts
Stopouts
Student Attrition
Students
Truancy
Withdrawal (Education)

School Home Relationship
USE FAMILY SCHOOL RELATIONSHIP

School Improvement (1966 1980)
USE EDUCATIONAL FACILITIES IMPROVEMENT

School Industry Relationship (1967 1980)
USE SCHOOL BUSINESS RELATIONSHIP

School Integration (1966 1980)
USE SCHOOL DESEGREGATION

SCHOOL INVOLVEMENT *Jul. 1966*
CIJE: 85 RIE: 136 GC: 330
SN Involvement of schools or school representatives in activities or programs (note: prior to mar80, this term was not scoped and was sometimes used for the involvement of individuals or groups in schools)
UF School Participation
BT Participation
RT Family School Relationship
Government School Relationship
Parent School Relationship
School Business Relationship
School Community Programs
School Community Relationship
School Role
Schools
Teacher Participation
Theory Practice Relationship

SCHOOL LAW *Jul. 1966*
CIJE: 512 RIE: 613 GC: 330
SN That branch of law (constitutional, statutory, or common) that relates to public and private schools, school districts, and institutions of higher education
BT Laws
RT Educational Legislation
Politics Of Education
School Administration
School Policy
Schools
School Security
Search And Seizure
Student Rights
Teacher Rights

SCHOOL LIBRARIES *Jul. 1966*
CIJE: 861 RIE: 937 GC: 710
UF Elementary School Libraries (1966 1980)
High School Libraries
Secondary School Libraries
BT Libraries
RT Learning Resources Centers
Media Specialists
Schools

SCHOOL LOCATION *Jul. 1966*
CIJE: 68 RIE: 263 GC: 330
UF School Sites
RT Access To Education
Campus Planning
Commuter Colleges

= Two or more Descriptors are used to represent this term.
The term's main entry shows the appropriate coordination.

Distance
Geographic Location
Multicampus Districts
Proximity
Real Estate
School Demography
School District Reorganization
School Districts
Schools
School Zoning
Site Analysis

SCHOOL MAINTENANCE *Jul. 1966*
CIJE: 304 RIE: 201 GC: 320
BT Maintenance
RT Building Operation
Cleaning
Custodian Training
Educational Facilities Improvement
Equipment Maintenance
Schools

School Media Centers
USE LEARNING RESOURCES CENTERS

SCHOOL NEWSPAPERS *Jul. 1966*
CIJE: 563 RIE: 164 GC: 720
BT Newspapers
School Publications
RT Extracurricular Activities
Student Publications

School Nurse Practitioners
USE NURSE PRACTITIONERS; SCHOOL NURSES

SCHOOL NURSES *Jul. 1966*
CIJE: 188 RIE: 60 GC: 360
UF School Nurse Practitioners #
BT Nurses
School Personnel
RT School Health Services

School Officials
USE SCHOOL PERSONNEL

SCHOOL ORGANIZATION *Jul. 1966*
CIJE: 877 RIE: 1323 GC: 320
SN (Note: do not confuse with "school district reorganization")
UF High School Organization (1966 1980)
School Reorganization
NT House Plan
BT Organization
RT Administrative Organization
Centralization
Class Organization
Decentralization
Departments
Double Sessions
Educational Environment
Institutional Characteristics
Instructional Program Divisions
Multiunit Schools
School Based Management
Schools
School Schedules
Traditional Schools
Transitional Schools

SCHOOL ORIENTATION *Jul. 1966*
CIJE: 144 RIE: 226 GC: 320
SN Process of making new students aware of a school's environment, rules, traditions, educational offerings, etc.
BT Orientation
RT Educational Counseling
Pupil Personnel Services
School Counseling
Schools
Student Adjustment
Student Personnel Services
Student School Relationship
Teacher Orientation

School Parent Relationship
USE PARENT SCHOOL RELATIONSHIP

School Participation
USE SCHOOL INVOLVEMENT

SCHOOL PERSONNEL *Jul. 1966*
CIJE: 404 RIE: 1224 GC: 360
UF School Employees
School Officials
School Personnel Directors #
NT Admissions Officers
Assistant Principals
Audiovisual Coordinators
Faculty
Foreign Student Advisers
Paraprofessional School Personnel
Principals
Pupil Personnel Workers
Registrars (School)
School Business Officials
School Cadres
School Counselors
School Nurses
School Psychologists
School Secretaries
School Social Workers
Student Financial Aid Officers
Student Personnel Workers
BT Personnel
RT Athletic Coaches
Personnel Directors
School District Size
Schools
School Size
Security Personnel
Superintendents
Teachers

School Personnel Directors
USE PERSONNEL DIRECTORS; SCHOOL PERSONNEL

School Philosophy
USE EDUCATIONAL PHILOSOPHY

SCHOOL PHOBIA *Jul. 1966*
CIJE: 73 RIE: 14 GC: 230
UF Schoolsickness
BT Fear
RT Anxiety
Mathematics Anxiety
Neurosis
Separation Anxiety
Student School Relationship
Test Anxiety
Writing Apprehension

SCHOOL PLANNING (1966 1980) *Jun. 1980*
CIJE: 175 RIE: 558 GC: 330
SN Invalid descriptor -- use "educational facilities planning" or, if appropriate, the broader term "educational planning"

School Plants
USE EDUCATIONAL FACILITIES

School Police Relationship
USE POLICE SCHOOL RELATIONSHIP

SCHOOL POLICY *Jul. 1966*
CIJE: 472 RIE: 643 GC: 320
UF Neighborhood School Policy (1966 1980) #
BT Policy
RT Board Of Education Policy
Discipline Policy
Educational Policy
Institutional Mission
Interdistrict Policies
Politics Of Education
School Administration
School Attendance Legislation
School Based Management
School Law
School Role
Schools
Teacher Administrator Relationship
Transfer Policy

School Principals
USE PRINCIPALS

School Programs
USE SCHOOL ACTIVITIES

SCHOOL PSYCHOLOGISTS *Jul. 1966*
CIJE: 842 RIE: 278 GC: 360
BT Psychologists
School Personnel
RT Consultants
Guidance Personnel
Psychological Evaluation
Psychometrics
Pupil Personnel Workers
School Counseling
School Counselors
Student Personnel Workers

SCHOOL PUBLICATIONS *Jul. 1966*
CIJE: 207 RIE: 123 GC: 720
NT Faculty Handbooks
School Catalogs
School Newspapers
Student Publications
BT Publications
RT Editors
Journalism Education
Schools
Student Developed Materials
Teacher Developed Materials
Writing For Publication
Yearbooks

SCHOOL READINESS *Mar. 1980*
CIJE: 70 RIE: 128 GC: 120
SN Cognitive, physical, and psychosocial maturity prerequisite to learning in a school setting
BT Readiness
RT Age Grade Placement
Cognitive Development
Early Admission
Emotional Development
Learning Readiness
Physical Development
Reading Readiness
School Entrance Age
School Readiness Tests
Student Placement
Writing Readiness

SCHOOL READINESS TESTS *Feb. 1971*
CIJE: 62 RIE: 90 GC: 830
BT Aptitude Tests
RT Diagnostic Tests
Maturity Tests
Preschool Tests
Prognostic Tests
Reading Readiness Tests
School Entrance Age
School Readiness
Screening Tests

SCHOOL RECREATIONAL PROGRAMS *Jul. 1966*
CIJE: 22 RIE: 30 GC: 470
BT Recreational Programs
RT After School Programs
Ancillary School Services
Extended School Day
Extracurricular Activities
Extramural Athletics
Intramural Athletics
Recreational Activities
School Activities
Schools

School Redistricting (1966 1980)
USE SCHOOL DISTRICT REORGANIZATION

SCHOOL REGISTRATION *Jul. 1966*
CIJE: 85 RIE: 158 GC: 320
UF College Registration
Registration In School
NT Late Registration
RT Admission (School)
Attendance
College Attendance
Enrollment
Registrars (School)
Schools

School Related Activities
USE EXTRACURRICULAR ACTIVITIES

School Renovation
USE EDUCATIONAL FACILITIES IMPROVEMENT

School Reorganization
USE SCHOOL ORGANIZATION

SCHOOL RESEGREGATION *Oct. 1979*
CIJE: 21 RIE: 54 GC: 540
SN Reversion to segregation in schools that had been desegregated
UF Resegregated Schools
BT School Segregation
RT De Facto Segregation
Racial Segregation
School Boycotts
School Desegregation

SCHOOL RESPONSIBILITY *Jul. 1966*
CIJE: 766 RIE: 380 GC: 330
BT Responsibility
RT Educational Responsibility
Leadership Responsibility
Noninstructional Responsibility
School Administration
School Role
Schools
Student Responsibility
Teacher Responsibility

SCHOOL ROLE *Jul. 1966*
CIJE: 1545 RIE: 1350 GC: 330
SN Functions expected of or performed by an educational institution
UF Elementary School Role (1966 1980)
High School Role (1966 1980)
Junior High School Role (1966 1980)
NT College Role
BT Institutional Role
RT Educational Environment
Educational Objectives
Educational Responsibility
Family School Relationship
Government School Relationship
Parent School Relationship
Politics Of Education
Role Of Education
School Community Relationship
School Effectiveness
School Involvement
School Policy
School Responsibility
Schools
Student Development

SCHOOL SAFETY *Jul. 1966*
CIJE: 186 RIE: 264 GC: 320
NT School Security
BT Safety
RT Alarm Systems
Educational Facilities Improvement
Educational Facilities Planning
Emergency Programs
Fire Protection
Hazardous Materials
Laboratory Safety
Safety Education
School Accidents
Schools
Security Personnel

SCHOOL SCHEDULES *Jul. 1966*
CIJE: 280 RIE: 502 GC: 350
SN Plans by which students and teachers are assigned to rooms and classes, the school day is divided into class periods, or the school year is organized into sessions and vacations (note: use a more specific term if possible)
UF Academic Calendars
School Calendars (1967 1980)
NT Double Sessions
Extended School Day
Extended School Year
Flexible Scheduling
Quarter System
Semester System
Time Blocks
Trimester System
BT Scheduling
RT Class Organization
Enrollment
Released Time
School Organization
Schools
Vacation Programs
Year Round Schools

SCHOOL SECRETARIES *Jul. 1966*
CIJE: 19 RIE: 14 GC: 360
BT School Personnel
Secretaries

SCHOOL SECURITY *Mar. 1978*
CIJE: 127 RIE: 107 GC: 320
SN Physical protection of school property, school personnel, and students from hostile acts or influences
UF Campus Security
BT School Safety

RT Alarm Systems
Campuses
Crime
Crime Prevention
Law Enforcement
Police Action
Police School Relationship
School Law
Schools
School Vandalism
Security Personnel
Stealing
Violence

SCHOOL SEGREGATION *Jul. 1966*
CIJE: 244 RIE: 275 GC: 540
SN Exclusion on the basis of race or ethnic status from particular schools, or the assignment of different racial or ethnic groups to separate schools
NT College Segregation
School Resegregation
BT Educational Discrimination
RT Black Education
Racial Segregation
School Boycotts
Schools

School Services (1966 1980)
USE ANCILLARY SCHOOL SERVICES

SCHOOL SHOPS *Jul. 1966*
CIJE: 203 RIE: 126 GC: 320
UF Industrial Arts Shops
Shop Rooms
BT Educational Facilities
RT Classrooms
Handicrafts
Industrial Arts
School Buildings
Shop Curriculum
Technical Education
Trade And Industrial Education

School Site Management
USE SCHOOL BASED MANAGEMENT

School Sites
USE SCHOOL LOCATION

SCHOOL SIZE *Jul. 1966*
CIJE: 238 RIE: 394 GC: 320
SN Size of a school as measured by the dimensions of its physical plant or by the number of students or staff
BT Institutional Characteristics
RT Attendance
Educational Facilities Design
Educational Facilities Planning
Enrollment
School Demography
School District Size
School Expansion
School Personnel
Schools
School Space
School Statistics
Small Schools

SCHOOL SOCIAL WORKERS *Jul. 1966*
CIJE: 80 RIE: 84 GC: 360
BT School Personnel
Social Workers
RT Adjustment Counselors
Caseworkers
Guidance Personnel
Pupil Personnel Workers
School Counseling
School Counselors
Social Work
Student Personnel Workers

SCHOOL SPACE *Jul. 1966*
CIJE: 72 RIE: 130 GC: 320
BT Educational Facilities
RT Classrooms
Corridors
Educational Facilities Design
Educational Facilities Planning
Facility Utilization Research
Flexible Facilities
Interior Space
Multipurpose Classrooms
Offices (Facilities)
Open Plan Schools
Schools
School Size
Space Dividers
Space Utilization
Spatial Relationship (Facilities)

SCHOOL STATISTICS *Jul. 1966*
CIJE: 115 RIE: 577 GC: 730
BT Statistical Data
RT Educational Research
Educational Trends
Enrollment Projections
Expenditure Per Student
School Demography
School District Size
Schools
School Size
School Surveys
Statistical Analysis
Teacher Distribution

School Student Relationship
USE STUDENT SCHOOL RELATIONSHIP

School Study Centers (1966 1980)
USE STUDY CENTERS

School Superintendents (1966 1980)
USE SUPERINTENDENTS

SCHOOL SUPERVISION *Jul. 1966*
CIJE: 118 RIE: 162 GC: 320
SN Professional activities concerned with the development, maintenance, and improvement of a school's instructional program, especially its curriculum and teaching personnel
UF Elementary School Supervisors (1966 1980)
High School Supervisors (1966 1980)
BT Supervision
RT Curriculum Development
Instruction
Instructional Improvement
Instructional Leadership
Principals
School Administration
School Based Management
Schools
Teacher Supervision

School Supplies
USE SUPPLIES

SCHOOL SUPPORT *Jul. 1966*
CIJE: 288 RIE: 452 GC: 620
SN Moral or financial support supplied for the operation and maintenance of educational institutions (note: prior to mar80, the use of this term was not restricted by a scope note)
NT Private School Aid
RT Community Support
Corporate Support
Educational Economics
Educational Equity (Finance)
Educational Finance
Federal Aid
Financial Support
Foundation Programs
Full State Funding
Institutional Survival
Public Support
School Budget Elections
School Business Relationship
School Community Relationship
School Funds
Schools
School Taxes
State Aid

SCHOOL SURVEYS *Jul. 1966*
CIJE: 1088 RIE: 2153 GC: 810
SN Studies of schools, colleges, school systems, or any parts thereof (note: as of oct81, use as a minor descriptor for examples of this kind of survey -- use as a major descriptor only as the subject of a document -- prior to oct81, this term did not carry a scope note)
UF Educational Surveys
BT Surveys
RT Educational Research
Graduate Surveys
Schools
School Statistics

School Systems (1966 1980)
USE SCHOOL DISTRICTS

SCHOOL TAXES *Jul. 1966*
CIJE: 234 RIE: 408 GC: 620
BT Taxes
RT Assessed Valuation
Educational Equity (Finance)
Educational Finance
Full State Funding
Private School Aid
Property Taxes
School Funds
Schools
School Support
Tax Rates

School To Work Transition
USE EDUCATION WORK RELATIONSHIP

School Transportation
USE STUDENT TRANSPORTATION

School Truancy
USE TRUANCY

SCHOOL VANDALISM *Jul. 1966*
CIJE: 201 RIE: 194 GC: 530
BT Vandalism
RT Schools
School Security
Security Personnel

SCHOOL VISITATION *Jul. 1966*
CIJE: 46 RIE: 88 GC: 330
SN Approved interschool visitation by teachers or administrators to observe teaching methods or equipment
UF Interschool Visits
School Visits
BT Observation
RT Inservice Teacher Education

School Visits
USE SCHOOL VISITATION

SCHOOL ZONING *Jul. 1966*
CIJE: 15 RIE: 62 GC: 330
BT Zoning
RT Consolidated Schools
School District Reorganization
School Location
Schools
Site Selection

SCHOOLS *Jul. 1966*
CIJE: 356 RIE: 493 GC: 340
SN Educational institutions at all levels (note: use a more specific term if possible)
UF Educational Institutions
NT Affiliated Schools
Bilingual Schools
Boarding Schools
British Infant Schools
Colleges
Community Schools
Consolidated Schools
Correspondence Schools
Day Schools
Disadvantaged Schools
Elementary Schools
Experimental Schools
Folk Schools
Freedom Schools
Free Schools
Laboratory Schools
Magnet Schools
Middle Schools
Military Schools
Multiunit Schools
Neighborhood Schools
Nursery Schools
Open Plan Schools
Private Schools
Public Schools
Racially Balanced Schools
Regional Schools
Rural Schools
Schools Of Education
Secondary Schools
Single Sex Schools
Slum Schools
Small Schools
Special Schools
State Schools
Suburban Schools
Summer Schools
Traditional Schools
Transitional Schools
Urban Schools
Vocational Schools
Year Round Schools
BT Institutions
RT Admission (School)
Ancillary School Services
Boards Of Education
College School Cooperation
Education
Educational Environment
Educational Facilities
Educational Facilities Design
Educational Facilities Improvement
Educational Facilities Planning
Faculty Handbooks
Family School Relationship
Government School Relationship
Institutional Characteristics
Interschool Communication
Nonprofit Organizations
Parent School Relationship
Police School Relationship
School Accidents
School Accounting
School Activities
School Administration
School Attitudes
School Based Management
School Boycotts
School Buildings
School Business Relationship
School Catalogs
School Closing
School Community Programs
School Community Relationship
School Construction
School Counseling
School Counselors
School Demography
School Desegregation
School District Reorganization
School Districts
School Effectiveness
School Expansion
School Funds
School Guidance
School Involvement
School Law
School Libraries
School Location
School Maintenance
School Organization
School Orientation
School Personnel
School Policy
School Publications
School Recreational Programs
School Registration
School Responsibility
School Role
School Safety
School Schedules
School Security
School Segregation
School Size
School Space
School Statistics
School Supervision
School Support
School Surveys
School Taxes
School Vandalism
School Zoning
Student School Relationship

Schools Of Dentistry
USE DENTAL SCHOOLS

SCHOOLS OF EDUCATION *Nov. 1970*
CIJE: 531 RIE: 653 GC: 340
SN Institutions, either independent or within a college or university, that train educational personnel at the undergraduate or graduate level
UF Colleges Of Education
Education Departments (School)
Teachers Colleges (1966 1980)
BT Schools
RT Education Courses
Education Majors
Laboratory Schools
Postsecondary Education As A Field Of Study
Specialist In Education Degrees
Student Teachers
Teacher Education

Teacher Education Curriculum
Teacher Educator Education
Teacher Educators

Schools Of Medicine
USE MEDICAL SCHOOLS

Schools Within A School Plan
USE HOUSE PLAN

Schoolsickness
USE SCHOOL PHOBIA

Science
USE SCIENCES

SCIENCE ACTIVITIES *Jul. 1966*
CIJE: 4480 RIE: 1294 GC: 490
SN Methods of science instruction that usually involve some participation by students -- may include projects outside the school
NT Science Fairs
Science Projects
BT Activities
RT Laboratory Procedures
Science Clubs
Science Curriculum
Science Education
Science Experiments
Science Instruction
Science Interests
Science Programs
Sciences

SCIENCE AND SOCIETY *Aug. 1986*
CIJE: 123 RIE: 84 GC: 490
SN Interrelationships between scientific/technical developments and social activities -- includes learning/teaching materials and programs dealing with these relationships
UF Science Technology And Society
Sts (Science Technology Society)
BT Relationship
RT Appropriate Technology
Environmental Education
Futures (Of Society)
Interdisciplinary Approach
Quality Of Life
Science Curriculum
Science Education
Sciences
Scientific Enterprise
Scientific Literacy
Social Change
Social Influences
Social Problems
Technological Advancement
Technological Literacy
Technology
Technology Transfer

SCIENCE CAREERS *Jul. 1966*
CIJE: 243 RIE: 269 GC: 490
BT Careers
RT Science Consultants
Science Education
Science Interests
Sciences
Science Teachers
Scientific Personnel
Scientists

SCIENCE CLUBS *Jul. 1966*
CIJE: 20 RIE: 6 GC: 320
BT Clubs
RT Science Activities
Science Education
Science Interests

SCIENCE CONSULTANTS *Jul. 1966*
CIJE: 34 RIE: 14 GC: 640
BT Consultants
Scientific Personnel
RT Resource Teachers
Science Careers
Science Supervision
Science Teachers

Science Course Improvement Project (1967 1980)
USE SCIENCE COURSE IMPROVEMENT PROJECTS

SCIENCE COURSE IMPROVEMENT PROJECTS *Mar. 1980*
CIJE: 426 RIE: 673 GC: 490
SN Planned self-contained undertakings in the sciences in which instructional techniques and curriculum materials are developed (note: coordinate specific project titles as identifiers, e.g., "biological sciences curriculum study," "physical science study committee")
UF Science Course Improvement Project (1967 1980)
BT Programs
RT Instructional Materials
Science Curriculum
Science Education
Science Instruction
Teaching Methods

Science Courses (1966 1980)
USE SCIENCE CURRICULUM

SCIENCE CURRICULUM *Jul. 1966*
CIJE: 2023 RIE: 1146 GC: 490
UF Physics Curriculum (1966 1980) #
Science Courses (1966 1980)
Science Units (1966 1980) #
NT College Science
Elementary School Science
General Science
Secondary School Science
BT Curriculum
RT Science Activities
Science And Society
Science Course Improvement Projects
Science Education
Science Instruction
Science Programs
Sciences
Summer Science Programs

SCIENCE DEPARTMENTS *Jul. 1966*
CIJE: 74 RIE: 44 GC: 350
BT Departments
RT College Science
Elementary School Science
English Departments
Secondary School Science

SCIENCE EDUCATION *Jul. 1966*
CIJE: 19578 RIE: 6871 GC: 490
BT Education
RT Aerospace Education
College Science
Elementary School Science
Energy Education
Engineering Education
General Science
Marine Education
Science Activities
Science And Society
Science Careers
Science Clubs
Science Course Improvement Projects
Science Curriculum
Science Education History
Science Experiments
Science Facilities
Science Instruction
Science Programs
Science Projects
Sciences
Science Teachers
Science Teaching Centers
Scientific Literacy
Scientific Methodology
Secondary School Science
Technical Education
Technological Literacy

SCIENCE EDUCATION HISTORY *Jul. 1966*
CIJE: 117 RIE: 46 GC: 490
BT Educational History
RT Science Education
Science History

SCIENCE EQUIPMENT *Jul. 1966*
CIJE: 1744 RIE: 219 GC: 910
SN Hardware used for instruction or other activities in science (note: for scientific measurement apparatus, coordinate with "measurement equipment")
BT Equipment
RT Educational Equipment
Laboratory Equipment
Lasers
Measurement Equipment
Science Experiments
Science Facilities
Science Laboratories
Science Materials
Sciences

SCIENCE EXPERIMENTS *Jul. 1966*
CIJE: 2126 RIE: 285 GC: 490
SN Laboratory-based scientific investigations
UF Physics Experiments (1966 1980) #
BT Experiments
RT Laboratory Experiments
Laboratory Procedures
Science Activities
Science Education
Science Equipment
Science Laboratories
Science Projects
Sciences

SCIENCE FACILITIES *Jul. 1966*
CIJE: 181 RIE: 138 GC: 920
SN Physical structures or spaces constructed, installed, or established for use in science (note: use a more specific term if possible)
NT Science Laboratories
Science Teaching Centers
BT Facilities
RT Classrooms
Planetariums
Science Education
Science Equipment

SCIENCE FAIRS *Jul. 1966*
CIJE: 50 RIE: 16 GC: 490
BT Exhibits
Science Activities
RT Extracurricular Activities
Realia
Science Projects

SCIENCE FICTION *Dec. 1969*
CIJE: 185 RIE: 108 GC: 430
BT Fiction
RT Fantasy

SCIENCE HISTORY *Jul. 1966*
CIJE: 1018 RIE: 172 GC: 490
BT History
RT Science Education History
Sciences

Science Information
USE SCIENTIFIC AND TECHNICAL INFORMATION

Science Institutes (1967 1980)
USE INSTITUTES (TRAINING PROGRAMS); SCIENCE PROGRAMS

SCIENCE INSTRUCTION *Jul. 1966*
CIJE: 3515 RIE: 1792 GC: 490
UF Biology Instruction (1966 1980) #
Chemistry Instruction (1967 1980) #
Physics Instruction (1966 1980) #
BT Instruction
RT College Science
Elementary School Science
General Science
Science Activities
Science Course Improvement Projects
Science Curriculum
Science Education
Science Programs
Sciences
Science Teachers
Science Tests
Secondary School Science
Summer Science Programs

SCIENCE INTERESTS *Mar. 1980*
CIJE: 179 RIE: 57 GC: 490
UF Student Science Interests (1967 1980)
BT Interests
RT Science Activities
Science Careers
Science Clubs
Sciences
Science Tests
Scientific Research

SCIENCE LABORATORIES *Jul. 1966*
CIJE: 414 RIE: 144 GC: 920
SN Facilities specifically designed and equipped for scientific experiments, demonstrations, observations, practice, or research
BT Laboratories
Science Facilities
RT Planetariums
Science Equipment
Science Experiments
Sciences

SCIENCE MATERIALS *Jul. 1966*
CIJE: 1190 RIE: 344 GC: 730
RT Health Materials
Instructional Materials
Reading Materials
Science Equipment
Scientific And Technical Information

SCIENCE PROGRAMS *Jul. 1966*
CIJE: 552 RIE: 383 GC: 490
UF Science Institutes (1967 1980) #
Technological Programs
NT Summer Science Programs
BT Programs
RT Research And Development
Science Activities
Science Curriculum
Science Education
Science Instruction
Sciences
Technical Assistance
Technological Advancement

SCIENCE PROJECTS *Jul. 1966*
CIJE: 238 RIE: 98 GC: 490
BT Science Activities
RT Laboratory Procedures
Science Education
Science Experiments
Science Fairs
Sciences
Student Projects
Summer Science Programs

SCIENCE SUPERVISION *Jul. 1966*
CIJE: 25 RIE: 26 GC: 320
BT Supervision
RT Science Consultants

SCIENCE TEACHERS *Jul. 1966*
CIJE: 703 RIE: 476 GC: 360
UF Chemistry Teachers (1967 1980) #
Physics Teachers (1967 1980) #
BT Teachers
RT Science Careers
Science Consultants
Science Education
Science Instruction

SCIENCE TEACHING CENTERS *Jul. 1966*
CIJE: 71 RIE: 29 GC: 920
BT Educational Facilities
Science Facilities
RT Education Service Centers
Museums
Nature Centers
Planetariums
Science Education

Science Technology And Society
USE SCIENCE AND SOCIETY

SCIENCE TESTS *Jul. 1966*
CIJE: 169 RIE: 202 GC: 830
BT Tests
RT Achievement Tests
Science Instruction
Science Interests
Sciences
Scientific Literacy

Science Units (1966 1980)
USE SCIENCE CURRICULUM; UNITS OF STUDY

SCIENCES *Jul. 1966*
CIJE: 1339 RIE: 1424 GC: 490
SN Sciences other than the applied sciences
UF Modern Science (1966 1980)
Science
NT Acoustics
Behavioral Sciences
Information Science

Natural Sciences
Social Sciences
Space Sciences
BT Liberal Arts
RT Engineering
English For Science And Technology
Mathematics
Research
Science Activities
Science And Society
Science Careers
Science Curriculum
Science Education
Science Equipment
Science Experiments
Science History
Science Instruction
Science Interests
Science Laboratories
Science Programs
Science Projects
Science Tests
Scientific And Technical Information
Scientific Attitudes
Scientific Concepts
Scientific Enterprise
Scientific Methodology
Scientific Principles
Technology

SCIENTIFIC AND TECHNICAL INFORMATION *Apr. 1985*
CIJE: 153 RIE: 228 GC: 490
SN The body of information resulting from the study and technological application of natural scientific phenomena (note: use only when such information is the subject -- do not use to classify items as scientific and/or technical)
UF Science Information
Scientific Information
Technical Information
Technological Information
RT Information Services
Information Sources
Natural Sciences
Science Materials
Sciences
Scientific Concepts
Scientific Literacy
Scientific Research
Special Libraries
Technical Assistance
Technological Literacy
Technology
Technology Transfer

SCIENTIFIC ATTITUDES *Jul. 1966*
CIJE: 317 RIE: 194 GC: 490
BT Attitudes
RT Inquiry
Problem Solving
Sciences
Scientific Enterprise
Scientific Methodology

SCIENTIFIC CONCEPTS *Jul. 1966*
CIJE: 1060 RIE: 380 GC: 490
NT Energy
Force
Gravity (Physics)
Height
Motion
Pressure (Physics)
Relativity
Space
Time
Weight (Mass)
RT Conservation (Concept)
Distance
Fundamental Concepts
Intervals
Misconceptions
Sciences
Scientific And Technical Information
Scientific Literacy
Scientific Methodology
Scientific Principles
Technology

Scientific Creationism
USE CREATIONISM

SCIENTIFIC ENTERPRISE *Jul. 1966*
CIJE: 556 RIE: 188 GC: 490
SN Totality of systematic activity of the sciences as an institution involving processes, attitudes, ethics, and interrelationships of science with other institutions
RT Natural Sciences
Science And Society
Sciences
Scientific Attitudes
Scientific Principles

Scientific Information
USE SCIENTIFIC AND TECHNICAL INFORMATION

SCIENTIFIC LITERACY *Jul. 1966*
CIJE: 347 RIE: 190 GC: 490
SN Comprehension of scientific concepts, processes, values, and ethics, and their relation to technology and society
BT Literacy
RT Comprehension
Computer Literacy
Science And Society
Science Education
Science Tests
Scientific And Technical Information
Scientific Concepts
Scientific Principles
Technological Literacy

Scientific Manpower (1967 1980)
USE SCIENTIFIC PERSONNEL

SCIENTIFIC METHODOLOGY *Jul. 1966*
CIJE: 603 RIE: 314 GC: 490
SN Research methodology adapted to the requirements of the various scientific disciplines
UF Scientific Methods
BT Research Methodology
RT Componential Analysis
Deduction
Generalization
Holistic Approach
Hypothesis Testing
Induction
Measurement Techniques
Naturalistic Observation
Problem Solving
Quasiexperimental Design
Research Design
Science Education
Sciences
Scientific Attitudes
Scientific Concepts
Scientific Research
Theories

Scientific Methods
USE SCIENTIFIC METHODOLOGY

SCIENTIFIC PERSONNEL *Jul. 1966*
CIJE: 240 RIE: 262 GC: 490
UF Scientific Manpower (1967 1980)
NT Mathematicians
Science Consultants
Scientists
BT Personnel
RT Allied Health Personnel
Chemical Technicians
Engineers
Health Personnel
Marine Technicians
Metallurgical Technicians
Nuclear Power Plant Technicians
Science Careers

SCIENTIFIC PRINCIPLES *Jul. 1966*
CIJE: 399 RIE: 78 GC: 490
BT Standards
RT Sciences
Scientific Concepts
Scientific Enterprise
Scientific Literacy

Scientific Reports
USE RESEARCH REPORTS

SCIENTIFIC RESEARCH *Jul. 1966*
CIJE: 2148 RIE: 676 GC: 810
SN Research conducted to advance knowledge in a scientific field (note: as of oct81, use as a minor descriptor for examples of this kind of research -- use as a major descriptor only as the subject of a document)
NT Space Exploration
BT Research
RT Anatomy
Astronomy
Biology
Chemistry
Ecology
Environmental Research
Experiment Stations
Genetic Engineering
Geology
Medical Research
Nuclear Physics
Physics
Physiology
Planetariums
Research And Development
Science Interests
Scientific And Technical Information
Scientific Methodology

SCIENTISTS *Jul. 1966*
CIJE: 1030 RIE: 504 GC: 640
BT Professional Personnel
Scientific Personnel
RT Engineers
Experimenter Characteristics
Researchers
Scholarship
Science Careers
Social Scientists

SCOPE OF BARGAINING *Oct. 1980*
CIJE: 27 RIE: 35 GC: 630
SN The topics and issues accepted or contested as appropriate for consideration in collective bargaining
BT Collective Bargaining
RT Employment Practices
Fringe Benefits
Job Development
Job Training
Leaves Of Absence
Overtime
Personnel Policy
Premium Pay
Promotion (Occupational)
Released Time
Retirement Benefits
Salaries
Salary Wage Differentials
Vacations
Wages
Work Environment
Working Hours

Score Reading
USE MUSIC READING

Score Theory
USE TEST THEORY

SCORES *Oct. 1970*
CIJE: 587 RIE: 910 GC: 820
SN Results, usually in numerical form, of a test or measure
UF Test Scores
NT Cutting Scores
Equated Scores
Grade Equivalent Scores
Raw Scores
True Scores
Weighted Scores
BT Data
RT Concurrent Validity
Correlation
Error Of Measurement
Generalizability Theory
Grades (Scholastic)
Interrater Reliability
Latent Trait Theory
Measurement
Predictive Validity
Scoring
Scoring Formulas
Standards
Statistical Analysis
Statistical Distributions
Test Anxiety
Testing
Test Interpretation
Test Items
Test Norms
Test Reliability
Test Results
Tests
Test Scoring Machines
Test Theory
Test Use
Test Validity
Test Wiseness

SCORING *Jul. 1966*
CIJE: 447 RIE: 588 GC: 820
SN Process of systematically assigning values (usually numerical, but also including letter marks and verbal comments) to the results of tests, questionnaires, etc.
BT Measurement
RT Answer Keys
Answer Sheets
Error Of Measurement
Grade Inflation
Grading
Holistic Evaluation
Interrater Reliability
Latent Trait Theory
Objective Tests
Pass Fail Grading
Questionnaires
Scaling
Scores
Scoring Formulas
Testing
Testing Problems
Test Items
Test Manuals
Tests
Test Scoring Machines
Test Theory

SCORING FORMULAS *Jan. 1971*
CIJE: 176 RIE: 183 GC: 820
SN Formulas by which tests, especially objective tests, are scored
BT Measurement Techniques
RT Confidence Testing
Cutting Scores
Guessing (Tests)
Multiple Choice Tests
Objective Tests
Raw Scores
Scores
Scoring
Test Interpretation
Test Manuals
Test Wiseness
Weighted Scores

Scoring Keys
USE ANSWER KEYS

Screen Education
USE FILM STUDY

SCREENING TESTS *Jul. 1966*
CIJE: 841 RIE: 779 GC: 830
SN Tests used to identify individuals who are likely to benefit from, or have difficulty in, some program or treatment, or who should be examined in greater depth
BT Tests
RT Aptitude Tests
Auditory Tests
College Entrance Examinations
Competitive Selection
Diagnostic Tests
Handicap Identification
Identification
Physical Examinations
Placement
Preschool Tests
Prognostic Tests
Reading Readiness Tests
School Readiness Tests
Vision Tests

SCREENS (DISPLAYS) *May. 1971*
CIJE: 27 RIE: 29 GC: 910
SN Surfaces on which images are projected or formed
BT Visual Aids
RT Audiovisual Aids
Display Aids
Exhibits
Projection Equipment

SCRIPTS *Sep. 1969*
CIJE: 126 RIE: 239 GC: 730
SN The written texts (with directions) of stage plays, screenplays, or radio or television broadcasts
BT Drama
Literary Genres
RT Comedy
Playwriting
Tragedy

Scuba Diving
USE UNDERWATER DIVING

SCULPTURE *Jul. 1966*
CIJE: 262 RIE: 53 GC: 420
BT Visual Arts
RT Art Products
Welding

Sdi
USE SELECTIVE DISSEMINATION OF INFORMATION

SEAFARERS *Mar. 1980*
CIJE: 21 RIE: 48 GC: 640
SN Those engaged in travel on the seas, either as an occupational or recreational pursuit
UF Mariners
Seamen (1969 1980)
BT Groups
RT Boat Operators
Marine Technicians
Maritime Education
Military Personnel
Navigation
Oceanography
Recreational Activities
Sailing
Semiskilled Workers

Seafood (1968 1980)
USE FOOD

Sealants
USE ADHESIVES

Seamen (1969 1980)
USE SEAFARERS

Seamstresses (1968 1980)
USE NEEDLE TRADES

SEARCH AND SEIZURE *Nov. 1971*
CIJE: 81 RIE: 73 GC: 610
BT Police Action
RT Civil Liberties
Civil Rights
Constitutional Law
Crime
Due Process
Police School Relationship
School Law
Student Rights
Student School Relationship

SEARCH COMMITTEES (PERSONNEL) *Aug. 1986*
CIJE: RIE: GC: 320
SN Committees appointed or elected to identify and select personnel for professional positions
UF Selection Committees (Personnel)
BT Committees
RT Administrator Selection
Advisory Committees
Personnel Selection

SEARCH STRATEGIES *Aug. 1968*
CIJE: 662 RIE: 514 GC: 710
SN Comprehensive plans for finding information -- includes defining the information need, and determining the form in which it is needed, if it exists, where it is located, how it is organized, and how to retrieve it
BT Information Seeking
RT Computer Literacy
Databases
Indexing
Information Needs
Information Retrieval
Information Storage
Information Systems
Information Utilization
Online Searching
Operations Research
Reference Services
Relevance (Information Retrieval)
Research Design
User Needs (Information)

SEASONAL EMPLOYMENT *Jul. 1966*
CIJE: 36 RIE: 61 GC: 630
UF Seasonal Labor (1966 1980)
BT Employment
RT Agriculture
Braceros
Migrant Employment
Migrant Workers
Multiple Employment
Seasonal Laborers
Student Employment
Underemployment
Youth Employment

Seasonal Labor (1966 1980)
USE SEASONAL EMPLOYMENT

SEASONAL LABORERS *Jul. 1966*
CIJE: 13 RIE: 104 GC: 630
BT Agricultural Laborers
RT Braceros
Migrant Employment
Migrant Workers
Seasonal Employment
Sharecroppers

Seat Belts
USE RESTRAINTS (VEHICLE SAFETY)

Second Language Books
USE FOREIGN LANGUAGE BOOKS

Second Language Enrollment
USE LANGUAGE ENROLLMENT

Second Language Films
USE FOREIGN LANGUAGE FILMS

SECOND LANGUAGE INSTRUCTION *Mar. 1980*
CIJE: 2067 RIE: 2109 GC: 450
SN Instruction in a language that is not native to the learner (note: prior to mar80, this concept was indexed under "language instruction")
UF Foreign Language Instruction
State Foreign Language Supervisors (1967 1980) #
BT Humanities Instruction
RT Applied Linguistics
Audiolingual Methods
Bilingual Education
Bilingual Education Programs
Bilingual Instructional Materials
College Second Language Programs
Conversational Language Courses
Dialogs (Language)
English (Second Language)
English For Special Purposes
Error Analysis (Language)
Fles
Grammar Translation Method
Immersion Programs
Intensive Language Courses
Language Enrichment
Language Enrollment
Language Laboratories
Language Of Instruction
Language Proficiency
Languages
Languages For Special Purposes
Language Teachers
Multilevel Classes (Second Language Instruction)
Native Speakers
Notional Functional Syllabi
Pattern Drills (Language)
Second Language Learning
Second Language Programs
Second Languages
Suggestopedia

SECOND LANGUAGE LEARNING *Jul. 1966*
CIJE: 5138 RIE: 4837 GC: 450
UF Foreign Language Learning
Language Learning (Foreign)
BT Learning
RT Audiolingual Methods
Bilingual Education
Bilingual Instructional Materials
Bilingualism
College Second Language Programs
Communicative Competence (Languages)
Contrastive Linguistics
Conversational Language Courses
Cultural Awareness
Dictation
English (Second Language)
English For Special Purposes
Error Analysis (Language)
Fles
Foreign Language Books
Foreign Language Films
Foreign Language Periodicals
Immersion Programs
Intensive Language Courses
Interference (Language)
Interlanguage
Language Aptitude
Language Enrichment
Language Fluency
Language Of Instruction
Language Proficiency
Languages For Special Purposes
Language Skill Attrition
Language Skills
Language Tests
Limited English Speaking
Modern Language Curriculum
Modern Languages
Multilevel Classes (Second Language Instruction)
Multilingual Materials
Notional Functional Syllabi
Oral Language
Second Language Instruction
Second Language Programs
Second Languages
Threshold Level (Languages)
Unwritten Languages

Second Language Periodicals
USE FOREIGN LANGUAGE PERIODICALS

SECOND LANGUAGE PROGRAMS *Mar. 1980*
CIJE: 205 RIE: 383 GC: 450
SN (Note: do not use for instructional materials that refer to themselves as programs -- prior to mar80, this concept was indexed under "language programs")
UF Fles Programs (1967 1980) #
Foreign Language Programs
NT College Second Language Programs
Immersion Programs
BT Programs
RT Bilingual Education Programs
Conversational Language Courses
English (Second Language)
Fles
Intensive Language Courses
Language Enrollment
Language Laboratories
Modern Language Curriculum
Multilevel Classes (Second Language Instruction)
Native Speakers
Notional Functional Syllabi
Second Language Instruction
Second Language Learning
Second Languages

Second Language Teachers
USE LANGUAGE TEACHERS

SECOND LANGUAGES *Jul. 1966*
CIJE: 244 RIE: 394 GC: 450
SN Any languages other than one's native or mother tongue, usually learned by formal language instruction (note: prior to mar80, the instruction "foreign languages, use languages" was carried in the thesaurus)
UF Foreign Languages
NT English (Second Language)
BT Language
RT Bilingual Education
Bilingual Instructional Materials
Bilingualism
Bilingual Teacher Aides
Bilingual Teachers
Fles
Immersion Programs
Language Dominance
Language Of Instruction
Language Planning
Native Speakers
Second Language Instruction
Second Language Learning
Second Language Programs

SECONDARY EDUCATION *Jul. 1966*
CIJE: 20572 RIE: 22051 GC: 340
SN Education provided in grade 7, 8, or 9 through grade 12 (note: also appears in the list of mandatory educational level descriptors)
UF Secondary Grades (1966 1980)
NT College Preparation
BT Elementary Secondary Education
RT Comprehensive Programs
Continuation Students
Grade 7
Grade 8
Grade 9
Grade 10
Grade 11
Grade 12
High School Equivalency Programs
High Schools
Junior High Schools
Pretechnology Programs
Secondary School Curriculum
Secondary Schools
Secondary School Students
Secondary School Teachers
Vocational Education

Secondary Employment
USE MULTIPLE EMPLOYMENT

Secondary Grades (1966 1980)
USE SECONDARY EDUCATION

Secondary School Counseling
USE SCHOOL COUNSELING

Secondary School Counselors (1967 1980)
USE SCHOOL COUNSELORS

SECONDARY SCHOOL CURRICULUM *Mar. 1980*
CIJE: 561 RIE: 829 GC: 350
UF High School Curriculum (1967 1980)
NT Secondary School Mathematics
Secondary School Science
BT Curriculum
RT High Schools
Secondary Education
Secondary Schools

Secondary School Guidance
USE SCHOOL GUIDANCE

Secondary School Libraries
USE SCHOOL LIBRARIES

SECONDARY SCHOOL MATHEMATICS *Jul. 1966*
CIJE: 3120 RIE: 1867 GC: 480
BT Mathematics Curriculum
Secondary School Curriculum
RT College Mathematics
Elementary School Mathematics
Mathematics
Mathematics Education
Mathematics Instruction
Modern Mathematics

SECONDARY SCHOOL SCIENCE *Jul. 1966*
CIJE: 7302 RIE: 3195 GC: 490
BT Science Curriculum
Secondary School Curriculum
RT College Science
Elementary School Science
Science Departments
Science Education
Science Instruction

SECONDARY SCHOOL STUDENTS *Jul. 1966*
CIJE: 1339 RIE: 1403 GC: 360
SN (Note: coordinate with the appropriate mandatory educational level descriptor)
NT High School Students
Junior High School Students
BT Students
RT Adolescents
Secondary Education
Secondary Schools

= Two or more Descriptors are used to represent this term.
The term's main entry shows the appropriate coordination.

SECONDARY SCHOOL TEACHERS *Jul. 1966*
CIJE: 792 RIE: 1193 GC: 360
UF High School Teachers
Junior High School Teachers
BT Teachers
RT Public School Teachers
Secondary Education
Secondary Schools

SECONDARY SCHOOLS *Jul. 1966*
CIJE: 1147 RIE: 1687 GC: 340
NT High Schools
Junior High Schools
BT Schools
RT Affiliated Schools
Laboratory Schools
Secondary Education
Secondary School Curriculum
Secondary School Students
Secondary School Teachers
Vocational Schools

SECRETARIES *Jul. 1966*
CIJE: 157 RIE: 213 GC: 640
UF Administrative Secretaries
Executive Secretaries
Legal Secretaries
Medical Secretaries
NT School Secretaries
BT Clerical Workers
RT Dictation
Medical Assistants
Shorthand
Typewriting
Word Processing

Sectarian Colleges
USE CHURCH RELATED COLLEGES

SECURITY (PSYCHOLOGY) *Mar. 1978*
CIJE: 63 RIE: 45 GC: 230
SN Being or feeling free from risk or uncertainty (note: the descriptor "security," without the parenthetical qualifier, was used from 1967 to mar78)
UF Emotional Security
Insecurity (1966 1980)
BT Psychological Needs
RT Emotional Experience
Trust (Psychology)

SECURITY (1967 1978) *Mar. 1978*
CIJE: 162 RIE: 86 GC: 210
SN Invalid descriptor -- use a more precise descriptor such as "security (psychology)," "school security," or "national security," or use an identifier such as "building security"

SECURITY PERSONNEL *Mar. 1978*
CIJE: 35 RIE: 38 GC: 640
SN Persons employed by an institution or organization to provide physical protection from hostile acts or influences
UF Guards (Security)
BT Personnel
RT Alarm Systems
Crime
Crime Prevention
Law Enforcement
Police
Safety
School Personnel
School Safety
School Security
School Vandalism
Stealing
Vandalism

Security Systems (Alarms)
USE ALARM SYSTEMS

SEDATIVES *Apr. 1969*
CIJE: 25 RIE: 43 GC: 210
UF Barbiturates
Hypnotics
Tranquilizing Drugs
BT Narcotics
RT Drug Abuse
Drug Rehabilitation
Drug Use
Physiology
Sensory Experience

Segregated Public Facilities (1966 1980)
USE PUBLIC FACILITIES; RACIAL SEGREGATION

Segregation (Racial)
USE RACIAL SEGREGATION

Segregationist Groups
USE SEGREGATIONIST ORGANIZATIONS

SEGREGATIONIST ORGANIZATIONS *Jul. 1966*
CIJE: 6 RIE: 6 GC: 540
SN Organizations whose purpose is to prevent desegregation/integration of certain ethnic or racial groups in a community or society
UF Segregationist Groups
BT Organizations (Groups)
RT Black Power
Civil Disobedience
Civil Rights
Nazism
Racial Discrimination
Racial Segregation
Social Discrimination

SEISMOLOGY *Sep. 1969*
CIJE: 48 RIE: 27 GC: 490
NT Plate Tectonics
BT Earth Science
RT Earthquakes
Geology
Geophysics
Physical Geography
Soil Science

SEIZURES *Jul. 1966*
CIJE: 48 RIE: 19 GC: 220
BT Diseases
RT Epilepsy
Neurological Impairments
Physical Health
Special Health Problems

SELECTION *Jul. 1966*
CIJE: 431 RIE: 429 GC: 110
SN The process of choosing from among a number of alternatives, usually on the basis of fitness, excellence, or other criteria (note: use a more specific term if possible)
NT Career Choice
Competitive Selection
Course Selection (Students)
Elections
Mate Selection
Media Selection
Personnel Selection
School Choice
Site Selection
Test Selection
RT Credentials
Evaluation Criteria
Prerequisites
Recruitment

Selection Committees (Personnel)
USE SEARCH COMMITTEES (PERSONNEL)

SELECTIVE ADMISSION *Oct. 1979*
CIJE: 138 RIE: 105 GC: 320
SN Process by which an institution, or a program area within the institution, selects students for admission from an applicant pool, considering such factors as academic background, race, sex, or geographic origin (note: if appropriate, use the more precise term "selective colleges")
UF Preferential Admission
Restrictive Admission
Special Admission
BT Admission (School)
RT Academic Standards
Admission Criteria
Affirmative Action
College Admission
Competitive Selection
Desegregation Methods
Educational Discrimination
Equal Education
Open Enrollment
Quotas
Racial Discrimination
Residence Requirements
Reverse Discrimination
Sex Discrimination

SELECTIVE COLLEGES *Oct. 1983*
CIJE: 14 RIE: 17 GC: 340
SN Colleges with especially high academic standards
UF Elite Colleges
BT Colleges
RT Academic Standards
College Admission
Elitism
Prestige
Private Colleges

SELECTIVE DISSEMINATION OF INFORMATION *Jun. 1981*
CIJE: 64 RIE: 68 GC: 710
SN An information service, usually computer-based, that periodically distributes copies or notices of current documents to its users -- such distribution is often based on the users' own statements (sometimes called "interest profiles") of what they need
UF Current Awareness Services
Sdi
BT Information Dissemination
RT Computer Oriented Programs
Information Needs
Information Retrieval
Library Services
Online Searching
User Needs (Information)

Self Abuse
USE SELF DESTRUCTIVE BEHAVIOR

SELF ACTUALIZATION *Jul. 1966*
CIJE: 1495 RIE: 1223 GC: 120
SN The belief in or the process of developing the actuality of one's idealized image
UF Growth Motivation
Self Development
Self Motivation
Self Realization
Self Utilization
BT Psychological Needs
RT Behavior Development
Careers
Gestalt Therapy
Humanistic Education
Identification (Psychology)
Individual Development
Individualism
Individual Power
Individual Psychology
Job Satisfaction
Life Satisfaction
Marital Satisfaction
Mental Health
Midlife Transitions
Morale
Motivation
Need Gratification
Personal Autonomy
Personality Development
Reality Therapy
Role Perception
Role Theory
Self Concept
Self Concept Measures
Self Congruence
Self Determination
Self Evaluation (Individuals)
Self Help Programs
Social Psychology
Values Clarification

Self Appraisal
USE SELF EVALUATION (INDIVIDUALS)

Self Assessment
USE SELF EVALUATION (INDIVIDUALS)

Self Attitude Tests
USE SELF CONCEPT MEASURES

Self Bias
USE EGOCENTRISM

SELF CARE SKILLS *Jul. 1966*
CIJE: 203 RIE: 363 GC: 220
SN Ability to feed, dress, and groom oneself
BT Daily Living Skills
RT Adaptive Behavior (Of Disabled)
Clothing
Disabilities
Eating Habits
Habit Formation
Health
Hygiene
Maturity (Individuals)

SELF CONCEPT *Jul. 1966*
CIJE: 4752 RIE: 4845 GC: 230
SN Individuals' perceptions of themselves
UF Ego
Self Image
Self Knowledge
Self Understanding
NT Body Image
Self Congruence
Self Esteem
RT Adventure Education
Aspiration
Attribution Theory
Delay Of Gratification
Egocentrism
Ethnicity
Gestalt Therapy
Humanistic Education
Identification (Psychology)
Individual Power
Locus Of Control
Morale
Personality
Perspective Taking
Phenomenology
Racial Identification
Reality Therapy
Reference Groups
Self Actualization
Self Concept Measures
Self Disclosure (Individuals)
Self Evaluation (Individuals)
Sexual Identity
Significant Others
Social Cognition

SELF CONCEPT MEASURES *Mar. 1980*
CIJE: 275 RIE: 346 GC: 830
UF Self Attitude Tests
Self Concept Tests (1971 1980)
BT Personality Measures
RT Affective Measures
Identification (Psychology)
Q Methodology
Self Actualization
Self Concept
Self Congruence
Self Esteem
Self Evaluation (Individuals)

Self Concept Tests (1971 1980)
USE SELF CONCEPT MEASURES

Self Confidence
USE SELF ESTEEM

SELF CONGRUENCE *Jul. 1966*
CIJE: 89 RIE: 79 GC: 230
SN Conscious integration of an experience to become a part of the self
BT Congruence (Psychology)
Self Concept
RT Behavior
Meditation
Psychological Characteristics
Psychotherapy
Self Actualization
Self Concept Measures

SELF CONTAINED CLASSROOMS *Jul. 1966*
CIJE: 61 RIE: 66 GC: 310
SN Classes having the same teacher or team of teachers for all or most of the daily session (note: prior to mar80, the instruction "traditional classrooms, use traditional schools" was carried in the thesaurus)
UF Traditional Classrooms
BT Classrooms
RT Class Organization
Conventional Instruction
Open Education
Traditional Schools

SELF CONTROL *Jul. 1966*
CIJE: 639 RIE: 368 GC: 120
UF Impulse Control
Self Discipline
NT Delay Of Gratification
BT Behavior
RT Behavior Modification
Behavior Problems
Biofeedback

Cognitive Restructuring
Compliance (Psychology)
Discipline
Individual Power
Inhibition
Maturity (Individuals)
Metacognition
Personal Autonomy
Personality Traits
Self Destructive Behavior
Self Determination
Sportsmanship

SELF DESTRUCTIVE BEHAVIOR *Aug. 1986*
CIJE: 3 RIE: GC: 230
SN Acting or tending to harm or destroy oneself
UF Self Abuse
NT Self Mutilation
Suicide
BT Behavior
RT Antisocial Behavior
Behavior Disorders
Behavior Problems
Drug Abuse
Mental Disorders
Personality Problems
Psychological Patterns
Self Control

SELF DETERMINATION *Mar. 1978*
CIJE: 178 RIE: 222 GC: 610
SN The right, power, opportunity, etc. of both individuals and peoples to determine their own destinies (note: prior to mar78, the instruction "self determination, use individual power" was carried in the thesaurus)
UF Destiny Control
Self Government
NT Tribal Sovereignty
RT Black Power
Community Control
Democracy
Educational Policy
Ethnic Groups
Foreign Policy
Individualism
Individual Power
Institutional Autonomy
Minority Groups
Nationalism
Personal Autonomy
Professional Autonomy
Public Policy
School District Autonomy
Self Actualization
Self Control
Self Directed Groups
Self Help Programs
Trust Responsibility (Government)

Self Development
USE SELF ACTUALIZATION

SELF DIRECTED CLASSROOMS (1966 1980) *Jun. 1980*
CIJE: 92 RIE: 106 GC: 310
SN Invalid descriptor -- used inconsistently in indexing -- see the more precise descriptors "open education," "independent study," "individualized instruction," and "student projects"

SELF DIRECTED GROUPS *Jul. 1966*
CIJE: 199 RIE: 113 GC: 520
SN Groups with a passive leader or without a specified leader in which all members mutually agree on group goals and procedures
UF Leaderless Groups
Self Guided Groups
BT Groups
RT Group Activities
Group Dynamics
Group Experience
Interaction Process Analysis
Motivation Techniques
Open Education
Self Determination

Self Directed Learning
USE INDEPENDENT STUDY

Self Discipline
USE SELF CONTROL

SELF DISCLOSURE (INDIVIDUALS) *Oct. 1983*
CIJE: 34 RIE: 26 GC: 120
SN Revealing information about oneself to others
BT Disclosure
RT Counseling Techniques
Interpersonal Communication
Self Concept
Self Expression

SELF ESTEEM *Jul. 1966*
CIJE: 1629 RIE: 1251 GC: 120
SN Individuals' value judgments of themselves
UF Self Confidence
BT Self Concept
RT Assertiveness
Human Dignity
Personality Traits
Self Concept Measures
Self Evaluation (Individuals)

SELF EVALUATION (GROUPS) *Mar. 1980*
CIJE: 184 RIE: 492 GC: 810
SN Assessment of an institution, organization, program, etc., by its members or sponsors (note: prior to mar80, the instruction "institutional self study, use institutional research" was carried in the thesaurus -- this concept was also sometimes indexed under "self evaluation")
UF Institutional Self Study
Internal Review (Organizations)
Organizational Self Study
BT Evaluation
RT Formative Evaluation
Institutional Evaluation
Institutional Research
Needs Assessment
Organizational Effectiveness
Policy Formation
Program Evaluation
Summative Evaluation

SELF EVALUATION (INDIVIDUALS) *Mar. 1980*
CIJE: 857 RIE: 1082 GC: 120
SN Individuals' assessment of themselves
UF Self Appraisal
Self Assessment
BT Evaluation
RT Metacognition
Self Actualization
Self Concept
Self Concept Measures
Self Esteem
Sensitivity Training
Transactional Analysis

SELF EVALUATION (1966 1980) *Mar. 1980*
CIJE: 1189 RIE: 1300 GC: 820
SN Invalid descriptor -- used for personal, organizational, or program self evaluation -- see "self evaluation (individuals)" and "self evaluation (groups)" respectively for these concepts

SELF EXPRESSION *Jul. 1966*
CIJE: 432 RIE: 326 GC: 120
RT Art Expression
Art Therapy
Assertiveness
Catharsis
Creative Expression
Creativity
Dance Therapy
Dramatic Play
Individualism
Individual Power
Interpersonal Communication
Language Arts
Movement Education
Music Therapy
Self Disclosure (Individuals)
Transactional Analysis

Self Government
USE SELF DETERMINATION

Self Growth
USE INDIVIDUAL DEVELOPMENT

Self Guided Groups
USE SELF DIRECTED GROUPS

Self Help Devices (Disabled)
USE ASSISTIVE DEVICES (FOR DISABLED)

SELF HELP PROGRAMS *Jul. 1966*
CIJE: 302 RIE: 310 GC: 520
SN Programs in which communities, groups, or individuals help themselves
BT Improvement Programs
RT Behavior Modification
Biofeedback
Community Action
Individual Development
Lifelong Learning
Rehabilitation Programs
Self Actualization
Self Determination

Self Image
USE SELF CONCEPT

Self Injury (Physical)
USE SELF MUTILATION

Self Instruction
USE INDEPENDENT STUDY

Self Instruction Aids
USE AUTOINSTRUCTIONAL AIDS

Self Instruction Materials
USE PROGRAMED INSTRUCTIONAL MATERIALS

Self Knowledge
USE SELF CONCEPT

Self Motivation
USE SELF ACTUALIZATION

SELF MUTILATION *Jun. 1977*
CIJE: 95 RIE: 20 GC: 230
SN Self-inflicted physical injury
UF Head Banging
Self Injury (Physical)
BT Self Destructive Behavior
RT Behavior Disorders
Emotional Disturbances
Psychopathology
Suicide
Violence

Self Paced Instruction
USE INDIVIDUALIZED INSTRUCTION; PACING

Self Pacing
USE PACING

Self Pacing Machines (1966 1980)
USE TEACHING MACHINES

Self Realization
USE SELF ACTUALIZATION

SELF REWARD *Jul. 1966*
CIJE: 100 RIE: 41 GC: 120
BT Rewards
RT Delay Of Gratification
Motivation
Positive Reinforcement
Social Exchange Theory

SELF SUPPORTING STUDENTS *Mar. 1980*
CIJE: 20 RIE: 63 GC: 360
SN Students who are legally (or perhaps financially) independent of their parents or former guardians
UF Emancipated Students (1975 1980)
Independent Students (Self Supporting)
BT Students
RT Adult Students
College Students
Financial Needs
Married Students
Need Analysis (Student Financial Aid)
Parent Financial Contribution
Parent Student Relationship
Student College Relationship
Student Costs
Student Loan Programs
Student Rights
Student School Relationship

Self Teaching
USE INDEPENDENT STUDY

Self Understanding
USE SELF CONCEPT

Self Utilization
USE SELF ACTUALIZATION

SEMANTIC DIFFERENTIAL *Oct. 1972*
CIJE: 209 RIE: 191 GC: 830
SN Method of measuring attitudes, values, or the connotative meaning of words through the use of pairs of bipolar adjectives
BT Attitude Measures
Rating Scales
RT Adjectives
Attitudes
Multidimensional Scaling
Personality Measures
Values

SEMANTICS *Jul. 1966*
CIJE: 2433 RIE: 1620 GC: 450
SN Study of meanings in language and of changes in those meanings
UF General Semantics
Word Meaning
NT Lexicology
BT Descriptive Linguistics
Semiotics
RT Coherence
Componential Analysis
Computational Linguistics
Connected Discourse
Decoding (Reading)
Deep Structure
Definitions
Discourse Analysis
Error Analysis (Language)
Etymology
Language Patterns
Negative Forms (Language)
Pragmatics
Syntax

Semester Division (1966 1980)
USE SEMESTER SYSTEM

SEMESTER SYSTEM *Mar. 1980*
CIJE: 29 RIE: 59 GC: 350
SN Division of the academic year into two equal terms
UF Semester Division (1966 1980)
BT School Schedules
RT Quarter System
Trimester System

SEMICONDUCTOR DEVICES *Jan. 1970*
CIJE: 49 RIE: 16 GC: 910
NT Transistors
BT Electronic Equipment
RT Calculators
Crystallography
Electronics Industry
Lasers
Superconductors

Seminaries
USE CHURCH RELATED COLLEGES; THEOLOGICAL EDUCATION

SEMINARS *Jul. 1966*
CIJE: 572 RIE: 864 GC: 350
UF Student Seminars (1966 1980)
BT Meetings
RT Institutes (Training Programs)
Minicourses
Workshops

SEMIOTICS *Jul. 1966*
CIJE: 188 RIE: 113 GC: 450
SN The general philosophical theory of signs and symbols, dealing especially with their function in languages, and including syntactics, semantics, and pragmatics (note: prior to mar80, the use of this term was not restricted by a scope note)
NT Pragmatics
Semantics
BT Linguistic Theory
Philosophy
RT Language
Language Patterns
Linguistics
Symbolic Language

Syntax
Verbal Communication
Visual Literacy

SEMISKILLED OCCUPATIONS *Jul. 1966*
CIJE: 8 RIE: 58 GC: 640
SN Occupations requiring skill in a limited range of activities and demanding less independent judgment, training, and experience than skilled occupations require
BT Occupations
RT Blue Collar Occupations
Building Trades
Data Processing Occupations
Electrical Occupations
Laundry Drycleaning Occupations
Metal Working
Needle Trades
Semiskilled Workers
Skilled Occupations
Technical Occupations
Trade And Industrial Education
Unskilled Occupations

SEMISKILLED WORKERS *Jul. 1966*
CIJE: 20 RIE: 37 GC: 630
SN Operators/operatives possessing skill in a limited range of activities that demand less training, experience, and independent judgment than is required of skilled workers
NT Animal Caretakers
Boat Operators
Grounds Keepers
Nursery Workers (Horticulture)
Sewing Machine Operators
BT Nonprofessional Personnel
RT Employees
Seafarers
Semiskilled Occupations
Skilled Workers
Trade And Industrial Education
Unskilled Workers
Working Class

SEMITIC LANGUAGES *Jul. 1966*
CIJE: 20 RIE: 61 GC: 440
NT Amharic
Arabic
Hebrew
BT Afro Asiatic Languages

Senators
USE LEGISLATORS

Senior Citizens (1967 1980)
USE OLDER ADULTS

Senior High School Students
USE HIGH SCHOOL STUDENTS

Senior High Schools (1966 1980)
USE HIGH SCHOOLS

Senior Teacher Role (1966 1980)
USE MASTER TEACHERS; TEACHER ROLE

SENIORITY *Jan. 1978*
CIJE: 72 RIE: 50 GC: 630
SN Priority in status or rank derived from age or length of service
BT Status
RT Academic Rank (Professional)
Aging In Academia
Employees
Employer Employee Relationship
Employment
Employment Experience
Employment Level
Employment Practices
Job Layoff
Labor Problems
Personnel Data
Personnel Policy
Promotion (Occupational)
Reduction In Force
Tenure

Seniors (1966 1980) (Grade 12)
USE HIGH SCHOOL SENIORS

Seniors (1966 1980) (Last Year Undergraduates)
USE COLLEGE SENIORS

SENSITIVITY TRAINING *Jul. 1966*
CIJE: 576 RIE: 437 GC: 240
SN Technique in which group dynamics are used to increase participants' awareness of themselves, their interpersonal relationships, the group process, and larger social systems
UF Human Relations Training
T Groups (1967 1980)
BT Training
RT Counseling Techniques
Group Dynamics
Group Therapy
Humanistic Education
Interpersonal Competence
Laboratory Training
Protocol Materials
Self Evaluation (Individuals)

SENSORY AIDS *Jul. 1966*
CIJE: 169 RIE: 135 GC: 220
SN Devices and materials used to extend the functioning of the senses, most often including materials adapted for the visually handicapped or hearing impaired -- also includes materials which have been translated from one sensory mode to another
NT Hearing Aids
Low Vision Aids
Raised Line Drawings
Talking Books
RT Accessibility (For Disabled)
Assistive Devices (For Disabled)
Audiovisual Aids
Braille
Communication Aids (For Disabled)
Electromechanical Aids
Hearing Impairments
Large Type Materials
Loop Induction Systems
Magnification Methods
Manipulative Materials
Sensory Training
Tactile Adaptation
Visual Impairments

SENSORY DEPRIVATION *Jul. 1966*
CIJE: 78 RIE: 27 GC: 110
UF Isolation (Perceptual)
Perceptual Deprivation
BT Sensory Experience
RT Cognitive Processes
Fatigue (Biology)
Perception
Physiology
Psychology

SENSORY EXPERIENCE *Jul. 1966*
CIJE: 415 RIE: 250 GC: 110
NT Figural Aftereffects
Sensory Deprivation
BT Experience
RT Aesthetic Values
Auditory Perception
Experiential Learning
Habituation
Learning Modalities
Meditation
Montessori Method
Novelty (Stimulus Dimension)
Perception
Perceptual Handicaps
Sedatives
Sensory Integration
Sensory Training
Stimulants
Stimuli
Tactual Perception
Visual Perception

SENSORY INTEGRATION *Aug. 1968*
CIJE: 170 RIE: 121 GC: 110
SN The coordination of two or more perceptual modes (e.g., visual and tactile) while attending to a single phenomenon
UF Intersensory Integration
RT Auditory Training
Multisensory Learning
Perception
Perceptual Development
Perceptual Handicaps
Perceptual Motor Learning
Sensory Experience
Sensory Training

Sensory Motor Learning
USE PERCEPTUAL MOTOR LEARNING

SENSORY TRAINING *Jul. 1966*
CIJE: 136 RIE: 189 GC: 400
NT Auditory Training
BT Training
RT Discrimination Learning
Multisensory Learning
Perceptual Development
Perceptual Motor Learning
Sensory Aids
Sensory Experience
Sensory Integration
Tactual Perception
Visual Discrimination
Visual Perception

SENTENCE COMBINING *Jun. 1977*
CIJE: 82 RIE: 149 GC: 450
SN Combining a set of kernel sentences into a single complex or compound statement
UF Transformational Sentence Combining
BT Transformational Generative Grammar
RT Kernel Sentences
Language Patterns
Language Skills
Sentences
Sentence Structure
Syntax
Writing Exercises
Writing Skills

SENTENCE DIAGRAMING *Jul. 1966*
CIJE: 28 RIE: 26 GC: 450
RT Deep Structure
Diagrams
Grammar
Language Patterns
Linguistics
Sentences
Sentence Structure
Structural Analysis (Linguistics)
Surface Structure
Syntax

SENTENCE STRUCTURE *Jul. 1966*
CIJE: 1320 RIE: 1161 GC: 450
BT Syntax
RT Adjectives
Adverbs
Capitalization (Alphabetic)
Cohesion (Written Composition)
Deep Structure
Function Words
Generative Grammar
Grammar
Kernel Sentences
Nouns
Parallelism (Literary)
Prepositions
Pronouns
Punctuation
Sentence Combining
Sentence Diagraming
Sentences
Structural Analysis (Linguistics)
Structural Grammar
Structural Linguistics
Suprasegmentals
Surface Structure
Tenses (Grammar)
Traditional Grammar
Verbs

SENTENCES *Jul. 1966*
CIJE: 434 RIE: 313 GC: 450
SN Grammatically complete units of one or more words
NT Kernel Sentences
BT Paragraphs
RT Discourse Analysis
Grammar
Intonation
Sentence Combining
Sentence Diagraming
Sentence Structure
Syntax
Writing (Composition)

SENTENCING *Sep. 1982*
CIJE: 15 RIE: 22 GC: 520
SN Kind and duration of punishment for convicted offenses as specified by a court or judge
UF Prison Sentences
BT Law Enforcement
RT Correctional Institutions
Court Judges
Courts
Crime
Criminal Law
Criminals
Prisoners
Punishment

SEPARATION ANXIETY *Oct. 1983*
CIJE: 40 RIE: 28 GC: 230
SN Fear or distress occasioned by the threat or actuality of separation from significant persons or familiar surroundings -- most frequently observed among young children when removed from a parent or parent substitute
BT Anxiety
RT Attachment Behavior
Emotional Response
Infant Behavior
School Phobia

SEQUENTIAL APPROACH *Jul. 1966*
CIJE: 239 RIE: 609 GC: 310
UF Sequential Programs (1966 1980)
Sequential Reading Programs (1966 1980)
BT Methods
RT Adaptive Testing
Critical Path Method
Curriculum Design
Fixed Sequence
Pacing
Programed Instruction
Sequential Learning
Spiral Curriculum
Teaching Methods

SEQUENTIAL LEARNING *Jul. 1966*
CIJE: 292 RIE: 297 GC: 110
SN A learning situation in which one task is generally completed prior to the presentation of another, with each task building on the prior learning (note: consider the use of "serial learning" when the situation involves the learning of a single ordered set of responses, often through rote learning)
BT Learning
RT Learning Strategies
Pacing
Programed Instruction
Sequential Approach
Serial Learning

Sequential Programs (1966 1980)
USE SEQUENTIAL APPROACH

Sequential Reading Programs (1966 1980)
USE SEQUENTIAL APPROACH

SERBOCROATIAN *Jul. 1966*
CIJE: 31 RIE: 59 GC: 440
BT Slavic Languages

Serial Association
USE SERIAL LEARNING

SERIAL LEARNING *Nov. 1969*
CIJE: 151 RIE: 65 GC: 110
SN Learning to make a series of responses in a prescribed order (note: do not confuse with "sequential learning")
UF Serial Association
Serial Method
BT Learning
RT Association (Psychology)
Associative Learning
Behavior Chaining
Learning Theories
Memorization
Paired Associate Learning
Primacy Effect
Rote Learning
Sequential Learning

Serial Method
USE SERIAL LEARNING

SERIAL ORDERING *Jul. 1966*
CIJE: 155 RIE: 74 GC: 110
SN Process of arranging items successively according to a definite principle, e.g., temporal, spatial, logical, qualitative, quantitative, etc.
BT Cognitive Processes
RT Conservation (Concept)
Pattern Recognition
Psychomotor Skills

SERIALS *Aug. 1968*
CIJE: 179 RIE: 193 GC: 720
SN Materials issued in successive parts, usually at regular intervals and intended to be continued indefinitely (note: corresponds to pubtype code 022 -- do not use except as the subject of a document)
NT Annual Reports
Bulletins
Conference Proceedings
Newspapers
Periodicals
Yearbooks
BT Publications
RT Books
Comics (Publications)
Journalism
Journalism Education
Programing (Broadcast)

Service Education (1966 1980)
USE VOCATIONAL EDUCATION

Service Industry
USE SERVICE OCCUPATIONS

SERVICE OCCUPATIONS *Jul. 1966*
CIJE: 80 RIE: 383 GC: 640
SN Occupations providing services in such areas as food and beverage preparation, lodging, barbering and cosmetology, amusements and recreation, apparel and furnishings, protection, building cleaning and maintenance, and miscellaneous private household and personal services
UF Household Occupations #
Service Industry
NT Child Care Occupations
Hospitality Occupations
Laundry Drycleaning Occupations
BT Occupations
RT Agricultural Supply Occupations
Cosmetology
Fashion Industry
Producer Services
Public Service Occupations
Sales Occupations
Services
Service Workers
Trade And Industrial Education

SERVICE VEHICLES *Oct. 1968*
CIJE: 9 RIE: 25 GC: 910
SN Motor vehicles used to provide accommodation and activities required by the public, as public transportation, freight transportation, and maintenance or repair services
UF Buses
Contractor Vehicles
Maintenance Vehicles
NT Bookmobiles
School Buses
BT Motor Vehicles
RT Services
Traffic Circulation
Vehicular Traffic

SERVICE WORKERS *Jul. 1966*
CIJE: 22 RIE: 74 GC: 640
SN Personnel providing services in such areas as food and beverage preparation, lodging, barbering and cosmetology, amusements and recreation, apparel and furnishings, protection, building cleaning and maintenance, and miscellaneous private household and personal services
NT Attendants
Barbers
Cooks
Emergency Squad Personnel
Fire Fighters
Household Workers
Housekeepers
Housing Management Aides
Waiters And Waitresses
BT Nonprofessional Personnel
RT Employees
Government Employees
Machine Repairers
Resident Advisers
Sales Workers
Service Occupations
Services
Television Radio Repairers
Trade And Industrial Education
Vocational Education

SERVICES *Jul. 1966*
CIJE: 324 RIE: 898 GC: 520
SN Organized functions designed to meet individual or public needs, or to support some other organized function or activity (note: use a more specific term if possible)
UF Special Services (1966 1980)
Support Systems (Services)
NT Community Services
Delivery Systems
Financial Services
Human Services
Information Services
Producer Services
Professional Services
Shared Resources And Services
RT Advocacy
Clinics
Eligibility
Institutional Role
Public Service
Resources
Service Occupations
Service Vehicles
Service Workers
Utilities

SET THEORY *Jul. 1966*
CIJE: 122 RIE: 150 GC: 480
BT Mathematical Logic
Theories
RT Arithmetic

SETTLEMENT HOUSES *Jul. 1966*
CIJE: 3 RIE: 3 GC: 920
UF Neighborhood Settlements
University Settlements
BT Facilities
RT Collective Settlements
Community Programs
Nonprofit Organizations
Welfare Services

Settlement Patterns
USE LAND SETTLEMENT

SEVENTEENTH CENTURY LITERATURE *Jun. 1969*
CIJE: 93 RIE: 34 GC: 430
BT Literature
RT Baroque Literature
Literary History
Neoclassicism
Renaissance Literature

SEVERE DISABILITIES *Mar. 1980*
CIJE: 642 RIE: 596 GC: 220
SN Extreme disabilities that make functioning and achievement unusually difficult -- generally, rehabilitation services must go beyond those provided by traditional regular or special education programs
UF Profound Disabilities
Severely Handicapped (1975 1980)
NT Psychosis
Severe Mental Retardation
BT Disabilities
RT Deaf Blind
Exceptional Persons
Institutionalized Persons
Mild Disabilities
Multiple Disabilities

SEVERE MENTAL RETARDATION *Mar. 1980*
CIJE: 605 RIE: 234 GC: 220
SN Intellectual functioning that is more than four standard deviations below the mean (usually below 40 iq range), concurrent with adaptive deficiencies -- severely retarded individuals require continual supervision and care
UF Custodial Mentally Handicapped (1968 1980)
Profoundly Mentally Retarded
BT Mental Retardation
Severe Disabilities
RT Mild Mental Retardation
Moderate Mental Retardation
Residential Care

Severely Handicapped (1975 1980)
USE SEVERE DISABILITIES

Sewage
USE WASTE WATER

SEWING INSTRUCTION *Jul. 1966*
CIJE: 24 RIE: 125 GC: 400
BT Instruction
RT Clothing
Clothing Instruction
Fashion Industry
Home Economics
Needle Trades
Sewing Machine Operators

SEWING MACHINE OPERATORS *Jul. 1966*
CIJE: 1 RIE: 48 GC: 640
BT Semiskilled Workers
RT Clothing
Clothing Instruction
Fashion Industry
Needle Trades
Occupational Home Economics
Sewing Instruction

SEX *Mar. 1980*
CIJE: 89 RIE: 135 GC: 120
SN Concept used to describe the physiological traits that distinguish the males and females of a species (note: use a more precise term if possible -- for sexual behavior, see "sexuality")
UF Gender (Sex)
BT Physical Characteristics
RT Biology
Females
Males
Sex Bias
Sex Discrimination
Sex Education
Sex Fairness
Sex Role
Sex Stereotypes
Sexuality

SEX (CHARACTERISTICS) (1966 1980) *Mar. 1980*
CIJE: 346 RIE: 303 GC: 120
SN Invalid descriptor -- see such descriptors as "sexuality," "sex," and "sex differences" or coordinate "males" or "females" with specific characteristics, e.g., "physical characteristics," "psychological characteristics," etc.

SEX BIAS *Mar. 1980*
CIJE: 587 RIE: 746 GC: 540
SN Prejudicial attitudes toward people because of their sex, including the conscious or unconscious expression of these attitudes in writing, speaking, etc. (note: prior to mar80, the instruction "sex bias, use sex discrimination" was carried in the thesaurus)
UF Sexism
Sexist Language #
Sex Prejudice
BT Social Bias
RT Affirmative Action
Sex
Sex Discrimination
Sex Stereotypes

SEX DIFFERENCES *Jul. 1966*
CIJE: 6731 RIE: 4909 GC: 120
UF Gender Differences (Sex)
BT Individual Differences
RT Androgyny
Females
Males
Physical Characteristics
Sex Discrimination
Sex Fairness
Sex Role
Sex Stereotypes
Sexual Identity
Sexuality

SEX DISCRIMINATION *Mar. 1972*
CIJE: 2043 RIE: 2191 GC: 540
SN Restriction or denial of rights, privileges, and choice because of one's sex (note: do not confuse with "sex bias")
NT Sexual Harassment
BT Social Discrimination
RT Affirmative Action
Age Discrimination
Civil Rights
Educational Discrimination
Employed Women
Equal Education
Equal Facilities
Equal Opportunities (Jobs)
Feminism
Reverse Discrimination
Selective Admission
Sex
Sex Bias
Sex Differences
Sex Role
Sex Stereotypes

SEX EDUCATION *Jul. 1966*
CIJE: 849 RIE: 458 GC: 400
BT Family Life Education
RT Birth
Contraception
Ethical Instruction
Ethics
Sex
Sexuality
Venereal Diseases

SEX FAIRNESS *Aug. 1978*
CIJE: 257 RIE: 970 GC: 540
SN The correction of sex bias or discrimination (note: use for descriptions of materials, procedures, activities, or programs that treat the sexes equitably)
RT Affirmative Action
Equal Facilities
Equal Opportunities (Jobs)
Equal Protection
Feminism
Justice
Nondiscriminatory Education
Nontraditional Occupations
Personnel Integration
Sex
Sex Differences
Tokenism

Sex Prejudice
USE SEX BIAS

SEX ROLE *May. 1974*
CIJE: 2377 RIE: 1950 GC: 510
SN Pattern of attitudes and behavior that in any society is deemed appropriate to one sex rather than the other
UF Female Role #
Male Role #
RT Androgyny
Fear Of Success
Females
Males
Sex
Sex Differences
Sex Discrimination
Sex Stereotypes
Sexual Identity

SEX STEREOTYPES *Jul. 1974*
CIJE: 1590 RIE: 1733 GC: 540
SN Rigid or biased attitudes in which persons are ascribed certain traits because of their sex
BT Stereotypes
RT Females
Males
Sex
Sex Bias
Sex Differences
Sex Discrimination
Sex Role
Sexual Identity

Sexism
USE SEX BIAS

Sexist Language
USE LANGUAGE USAGE; SEX BIAS

SEXUAL ABUSE *Oct. 1983*
CIJE: 72 RIE: 77 GC: 530
SN Physical sexual advances or contact by force or without legally recognized consent
UF Child Sexual Abuse #
Sexual Assault
NT Rape
BT Antisocial Behavior
RT Battered Women
Child Abuse
Incest
Sexual Harassment
Sexuality
Victims Of Crime

Sexual Assault
USE SEXUAL ABUSE

Sexual Behavior
USE SEXUALITY

SEXUAL HARASSMENT *Oct. 1982*
CIJE: 53 RIE: 66 GC: 530
SN Unsolicited and unwelcome sexual behavior by any individual that interferes with work, study, or everyday life and creates an intimidating, hostile, or offensive environment
BT Antisocial Behavior
Sex Discrimination
RT Rape
Sexual Abuse
Sexuality

SEXUAL IDENTITY *Aug. 1986*
CIJE: 2 RIE: GC: 120
SN Awareness of individuals (oneself or others) as male or female
UF Gender Identity (Sex)
RT Androgyny
Biological Influences
Developmental Psychology
Identification (Psychology)
Interpersonal Relationship
Psychological Characteristics
Self Concept
Sex Differences
Sex Role
Sex Stereotypes
Sexuality
Social Development

SEXUALITY *Apr. 1969*
CIJE: 1248 RIE: 481 GC: 120
UF Human Sexuality
Sexual Behavior
NT Homosexuality
RT Incest
Personality Traits
Pornography
Rape
Sex
Sex Differences
Sex Education
Sexual Abuse
Sexual Harassment
Sexual Identity

Shade Trees
USE TREES

Shadow Plays
USE THEATER ARTS

Shapers
USE MACHINE TOOLS

SHARECROPPERS *Jul. 1966*
CIJE: 3 RIE: 16 GC: 410
BT Farmers
RT Agricultural Laborers
Agriculture
Farm Occupations
Rural Farm Residents
Seasonal Laborers

SHARED FACILITIES *May. 1974*
CIJE: 163 RIE: 186 GC: 920
SN Facilities used by two or more distinct groups, institutions, organizations, etc., whether for the same function or for different functions
UF Joint Occupancy
BT Facilities
Shared Resources And Services
RT Cluster Colleges
Community Schools
Facility Planning
Flexible Facilities
Institutional Cooperation
Off Campus Facilities

SHARED LIBRARY RESOURCES *Aug. 1986*
CIJE: RIE: GC: 710
SN Personnel, equipment, materials, etc., shared among libraries
BT Shared Resources And Services
RT Interlibrary Loans
Libraries
Library Cooperation
Library Networks
Union Catalogs
User Needs (Information)

SHARED RESOURCES AND SERVICES *Aug. 1986*
CIJE: RIE: GC: 330
SN Personnel, facilities, equipment, materials, and other resources and services shared among persons and/or organizations
UF Resource Sharing
Shared Services (1974 1986)
NT Shared Facilities
Shared Library Resources
BT Resources
Services
RT Agency Cooperation
Consortia
Cooperation
Cooperative Planning
Cooperative Programs
Dual Enrollment
Education Service Centers
Institutional Cooperation
Private School Aid
Specialists

Shared Services (1974 1986)
USE SHARED RESOURCES AND SERVICES

Shared Time (Computers)
USE TIME SHARING

Shared Time (Education)
USE DUAL ENROLLMENT

Sheet Metal Machine Operators
USE MACHINE TOOL OPERATORS; SHEET METAL WORK

SHEET METAL WORK *Jul. 1966*
CIJE: 13 RIE: 50 GC: 640
UF Sheet Metal Machine Operators #
Sheet Metal Workers (1967 1981)
BT Metal Working
RT Air Conditioning Equipment
Assembly (Manufacturing)
Machine Tool Operators
School Construction
Skilled Occupations

Sheet Metal Workers (1967 1981)
USE SHEET METAL WORK

SHELTERED WORKSHOPS *Jul. 1966*
CIJE: 125 RIE: 169 GC: 220
SN Places where handicapped persons are provided work experience with a view toward making them vocationally independent
BT Workshops
RT Disabilities
Individualized Programs
Job Training
Rehabilitation Centers
Rehabilitation Counseling
Rehabilitation Programs
Vocational Rehabilitation
Vocational Training Centers
Work Experience Programs

SHIFT STUDIES *Dec. 1970*
CIJE: 92 RIE: 22 GC: 810
SN Studies that investigate factors in the ability of subjects to discriminate between different dimensions of a stimulus or situation and to shift their responses according to these dimensions
UF Discrimination Transfer
Extradimensional Shift
Half Reversal Shift
Interdimensional Shift
Nonreversal Shift
Reversal Shift
RT Attention Span
Discrimination Learning
Learning Processes
Mediation Theory
Responses

SHONA *Jul. 1966*
CIJE: 1 RIE: 5 GC: 440
BT Bantu Languages

SHOP CURRICULUM *Jul. 1966*
CIJE: 40 RIE: 164 GC: 400
UF General Shop
BT Curriculum
RT Hand Tools
Industrial Arts
Metal Working
School Shops
Woodworking

Shop Mechanics
USE MACHINE REPAIRERS

Shop Rooms
USE SCHOOL SHOPS

Short Courses (1970 1980)
USE MINICOURSES

SHORT STORIES *Jul. 1966*
CIJE: 253 RIE: 274 GC: 430
BT Fiction
Literary Genres
RT Books
Tales

SHORT TERM MEMORY *Nov. 1981*
CIJE: 101 RIE: 52 GC: 110
SN Process of recalling information or performing appropriately soon after instruction or presentation of material -- characterized by rapid decay and a limited volume of remembered material (in contrast to "long term memory")
BT Memory
RT Long Term Memory

SHORTHAND *Mar. 1980*
CIJE: 304 RIE: 156 GC: 400
UF Clerk Stenographers
Stenographers (1966 1981)
Stenography (1967 1980)
BT Written Language
RT Abbreviations
Business Skills
Clerical Occupations
Court Reporters
Dictation
Office Occupations
Office Occupations Education
Secretaries
Symbolic Language
Typewriting

Si Units
USE METRIC SYSTEM

SIBLINGS *Jul. 1966*
CIJE: 332 RIE: 203 GC: 510
UF Brothers
Sisters
NT Twins
BT Groups
RT Birth Order
Family (Sociological Unit)
Family Life
Family Size
Family Structure
Kinship

SICKLE CELL ANEMIA *Oct. 1983*
CIJE: 4 RIE: GC: 210
SN An inherited condition, chiefly among black people, in which the red blood cells have an abnormal, crescent shape
UF Sickle Cell Trait
BT Anemia
RT Blood Circulation
Genetics
Physical Health

Sickle Cell Trait
USE SICKLE CELL ANEMIA

Sicknesses
USE DISEASES

SIERRA LEONE CREOLE *Jul. 1966*
CIJE: 1 RIE: 5 GC: 440
UF Krio
Sierra Leone Krio
BT Creoles

Sierra Leone Krio
USE SIERRA LEONE CREOLE

Sight
USE VISION

SIGHT METHOD *Jul. 1966*
CIJE: 46 RIE: 50 GC: 460
SN Method of teaching reading based on recognition and pronunciation of whole words
UF Look Guess Method
Look Say Method
Whole Word Reading Approach
Word Method (Reading)
BT Teaching Methods
RT Basal Reading
Beginning Reading
Reading Instruction
Sight Vocabulary
Word Recognition

Sight Playing
USE MUSIC READING

Sight Singing
USE MUSIC READING

SIGHT VOCABULARY *Jul. 1966*
CIJE: 137 RIE: 103 GC: 460
SN The words that one immediately recognizes while reading
BT Vocabulary
RT Basal Reading
Basic Vocabulary
Beginning Reading
Reading Instruction
Sight Method
Word Lists
Word Recognition

Sightseeing Industry
USE TOURISM

SIGN LANGUAGE *Jul. 1966*
CIJE: 386 RIE: 170 GC: 220
SN Type of manual communication method used by the deaf in which gestures function as words -- it has its own morphology, semantics, and syntax
UF Gestures (Deaf Communication)
NT American Sign Language
BT Language
Manual Communication
RT Deaf Interpreting
Finger Spelling
Total Communication

SIGN PAINTERS *Feb. 1969*
CIJE: RIE: 5 GC: 640
UF Sign Writers
BT Skilled Workers
RT Graphic Arts
Painting (Industrial Arts)
Signs

Sign Writers
USE SIGN PAINTERS

Signal Services
USE TELECOMMUNICATIONS

Signboards
USE SIGNS

Signed English
USE MANUAL COMMUNICATION

Significance Measures
USE STATISTICAL SIGNIFICANCE

SIGNIFICANT OTHERS *Jun. 1983*
CIJE: 13 RIE: 15 GC: 510
SN Those individuals in a person's immediate environment (past or present) who are/were particularly influential in the formation, support, or modification of that person's values, attitudes, and self-concept
BT Interpersonal Relationship
RT Family Relationship
Friendship
Identification (Psychology)
Mentors
Modeling (Psychology)
Role Models
Self Concept
Socialization

= Two or more Descriptors are used to represent this term.
The term's main entry shows the appropriate coordination.

SIGNS *Nov. 1968*
CIJE: 40 RIE: 65 GC: 720
UF Road Signs
Signboards
Traffic Signs (1968 1980) #
BT Visual Aids
RT Engineering Graphics
Graphic Arts
Instructional Materials
Printing
Sign Painters
Traffic Control

Silent Films
USE FILMS

SILENT READING *Jul. 1966*
CIJE: 132 RIE: 151 GC: 460
BT Reading
RT Inner Speech (Subvocal)
Oral Reading
Reading Habits
Reading Instruction
Reading Rate
Speed Reading
Sustained Silent Reading

Similarity Transformations
USE TRANSFORMATIONS (MATHEMATICS)

SIMULATED ENVIRONMENT *Jul. 1966*
CIJE: 105 RIE: 179 GC: 310
BT Environment
RT Management Games
Simulation

Simulated Speech
USE ARTIFICIAL SPEECH

Simulated Studies
USE SIMULATION

SIMULATION *Jul. 1966*
CIJE: 2493 RIE: 2565 GC: 310
SN Duplication of the essential characteristics of a task or situation
UF Simulated Studies
Simulators (1967 1980)
NT Computer Simulation
Models
Monte Carlo Methods
Role Playing
BT Methods
RT Assessment Centers (Personnel)
Counseling Techniques
Critical Incidents Method
Educational Games
Experiential Learning
Game Theory
Heuristics
Laboratory Procedures
Laboratory Training
Learning Strategies
Management Games
Management Systems
Office Practice
Simulated Environment
Situational Tests
Teaching Methods

Simulators (1967 1980)
USE SIMULATION

SINGHALESE *Jul. 1966*
CIJE: 5 RIE: 15 GC: 440
UF Sinhalese
BT Indo European Languages

SINGING *Jul. 1966*
CIJE: 204 RIE: 108 GC: 420
UF Choirs
Choruses (1968 1980)
Glee Clubs
Vocal Ensembles
BT Music Activities
RT Applied Music
Art Song
Choral Music
Concerts
Hymns
Recreational Activities
Songs
Vocal Music

SINGLE CONCEPT FILMS *Jul. 1966*
CIJE: 50 RIE: 44 GC: 720
BT Films
RT Filmstrips
Instructional Films

Single Parent Family
USE ONE PARENT FAMILY

SINGLE SEX COLLEGES *Oct. 1979*
CIJE: 40 RIE: 80 GC: 340
SN Colleges or universities with little or no enrollment of one sex
BT Colleges
Single Sex Schools
RT Church Related Colleges
Coeducation
Females
Homogeneous Grouping
Males
Private Colleges
Womens Education

SINGLE SEX SCHOOLS *Oct. 1979*
CIJE: 14 RIE: 13 GC: 340
SN Educational institutions with little or no enrollment of one sex (note: if possible, use the more specific term "single sex colleges")
NT Single Sex Colleges
BT Schools
RT Coeducation
Females
Homogeneous Grouping
Males
Private Schools
Womens Education

SINGLE STUDENTS *Jul. 1966*
CIJE: 14 RIE: 18 GC: 360
UF Unmarried Students
BT Students
RT Adult Students
Marital Status
Married Students

Sinhalese
USE SINGHALESE

SINO TIBETAN LANGUAGES *Jul. 1966*
CIJE: 30 RIE: 68 GC: 440
NT Burmese
Chinese
Lao
Thai
Tibetan
BT Languages
RT Austro Asiatic Languages
Language Classification
Native Speakers

Sisters
USE SIBLINGS

SISWATI *Mar. 1971*
CIJE: RIE: 3 GC: 440
UF Isiswati
Swazi
BT Bantu Languages

SITE ANALYSIS *Aug. 1968*
CIJE: 60 RIE: 196 GC: 920
BT Evaluation Methods
RT Educational Complexes
Educational Facilities Planning
Facility Case Studies
Facility Expansion
Facility Guidelines
Facility Planning
Geographic Location
School Expansion
School Location
Site Development
Site Selection

SITE DEVELOPMENT *Jul. 1966*
CIJE: 99 RIE: 193 GC: 920
SN Process of planning, engineering, and landscaping a plot of ground
BT Development
RT Construction (Process)
Educational Complexes
Educational Facilities Design
Educational Facilities Planning
Engineering
Facility Expansion
Facility Planning
Found Spaces
Land Acquisition
Landscaping
School Expansion
Site Analysis
Site Selection

SITE SELECTION *Jul. 1966*
CIJE: 82 RIE: 262 GC: 920
BT Selection
RT Educational Facilities Design
Educational Facilities Planning
Facility Planning
Land Acquisition
Real Estate
School Expansion
School Zoning
Site Analysis
Site Development

Situation Reaction Tests
USE SITUATIONAL TESTS

Situation Response Tests
USE SITUATIONAL TESTS

SITUATIONAL TESTS *Nov. 1968*
CIJE: 108 RIE: 115 GC: 830
SN Measures of an individual's behavior in realistic or simulated situations which call for actual adaptive responses
UF Situation Reaction Tests
Situation Response Tests
BT Tests
RT Assessment Centers (Personnel)
Performance Tests
Responses
Simulation
Vocational Evaluation
Work Sample Tests

Situational Therapy
USE MILIEU THERAPY

Six Three Three Organization
USE INSTRUCTIONAL PROGRAM DIVISIONS

Sixteen Millimeter Projectors (1966 1980)
USE PROJECTION EQUIPMENT

SIXTEENTH CENTURY LITERATURE *Apr. 1970*
CIJE: 45 RIE: 15 GC: 430
BT Literature
RT Baroque Literature
Literary History
Renaissance Literature

SKIING *Feb. 1978*
CIJE: 18 RIE: 19 GC: 470
SN Excludes waterskiing
UF Snowskiing
BT Athletics

SKILL ANALYSIS *Jul. 1966*
CIJE: 237 RIE: 435 GC: 820
SN Study and detailed description of the mental and/or physical behaviors that are needed for learning or the satisfactory completion of an activity
BT Evaluation Methods
RT Ability Identification
Content Analysis
Critical Incidents Method
Difficulty Level
Job Analysis
Object Manipulation
Protocol Analysis
Psychomotor Skills
Skill Development
Skill Obsolescence
Skills
Systems Analysis
Task Analysis
Test Construction

SKILL CENTERS *Jul. 1966*
CIJE: 32 RIE: 76 GC: 920
BT Educational Facilities
RT Learning Laboratories
Off The Job Training
Skill Development
Skills

SKILL DEVELOPMENT *Jul. 1966*
CIJE: 3190 RIE: 3764 GC: 120
BT Individual Development
RT Basic Skills
Developmental Studies Programs
Learning Plateaus
Learning Strategies
Mastery Learning
Mastery Tests
Motor Development
Process Education
Retraining
Skill Analysis
Skill Centers
Skills
Talent Development
Training
Training Methods
Transfer Of Training

SKILL OBSOLESCENCE *Nov. 1968*
CIJE: 52 RIE: 68 GC: 630
BT Obsolescence
RT Dislocated Workers
Employment Potential
Employment Qualifications
Job Skills
Retraining
Skill Analysis
Structural Unemployment
Vocational Adjustment

Skilled Labor (1966 1980)
USE SKILLED WORKERS

SKILLED OCCUPATIONS *Jul. 1966*
CIJE: 66 RIE: 289 GC: 640
SN Occupations requiring a high degree of skill, usually in a wide range of related activities performed with a minimum of direction and supervision, and secured through a combination of job instruction, trade instruction, and work experience such as apprenticeships or cooperative industrial programs
BT Occupations
RT Appliance Repair
Apprenticeships
Auto Mechanics
Aviation Mechanics
Blue Collar Occupations
Bricklaying
Building Trades
Cabinetmaking
Carpentry
Data Processing Occupations
Design Crafts
Electrical Occupations
Equipment Maintenance
Handicrafts
Horology
Job Skills
Masonry
Metal Working
Painting (Industrial Arts)
Patternmaking
Refrigeration Mechanics
Roofing
Semiskilled Occupations
Sheet Metal Work
Skilled Workers
Small Engine Mechanics
Technical Occupations
Technology
Trade And Industrial Education
Unskilled Occupations
Welding
Woodworking

SKILLED WORKERS *Jul. 1966*
CIJE: 116 RIE: 162 GC: 630
SN Workers qualified in a particular occupation, trade, or craft requiring a high degree of skill, usually in a wide range of related activities performed with a minimum of direction and supervision -- have usually had a combination of job instruction, trade instruction, and work experience such as apprenticeships or cooperative industrial programs
UF Journey Workers
Roofers (1968 1981) #
Skilled Labor (1966 1980)
NT Auto Body Repairers
Craft Workers
Electricians
Floor Layers
Glaziers

= Two or more Descriptors are used to represent this term.
The term's main entry shows the appropriate coordination.

Locomotive Engineers
Machinists
Sign Painters
Television Radio Repairers
Watchmakers
BT Nonprofessional Personnel
RT Apprenticeships
Employees
Job Skills
Semiskilled Workers
Skilled Occupations
Trade And Industrial Education
Unskilled Workers
Working Class

SKILLS *Jul. 1966*
CIJE: 251 RIE: 402 GC: 120
SN Complex mental and/or physical behaviors that require practice to be performed proficiently (note: use a more specific term if possible)
NT Agricultural Skills
Basic Skills
Business Skills
Communication Skills
Daily Living Skills
Decision Making Skills
Home Economics Skills
Homemaking Skills
Interpretive Skills
Job Skills
Language Skills
Library Skills
Locational Skills (Social Studies)
Map Skills
Mathematics Skills
Mechanical Skills
Minimum Competencies
Parenting Skills
Psychomotor Skills
Research Skills
Salesmanship
Study Skills
Teaching Skills
Visual Literacy
BT Ability
RT Competence
Difficulty Level
Interpersonal Competence
Mastery Learning
Mastery Tests
National Competency Tests
Process Education
Qualifications
Skill Analysis
Skill Centers
Skill Development

Skimming (Reading)
USE SPEED READING

Skin Diving
USE UNDERWATER DIVING

SKITS *Jul. 1966*
CIJE: 37 RIE: 38 GC: 420
BT Comedy
Literary Genres
RT Creative Dramatics
Dramatics
Pantomime
Theater Arts

SLAVERY *Jul. 1966*
CIJE: 181 RIE: 161 GC: 520
BT Human Relations
RT African History
Black Culture
Black Family
Black History
Black Studies
Civil Liberties
Civil Rights
Civil War (United States)
Colonial History (United States)
International Crimes
Minority Groups
Racial Discrimination
World History

SLAVIC LANGUAGES *Jul. 1966*
CIJE: 72 RIE: 153 GC: 440
NT Bielorussian
Bulgarian
Czech
Polish
Russian
Serbocroatian
Slovenian
Ukrainian
BT Indo European Languages
RT Cyrillic Alphabet
Language Classification
Native Speakers

SLEEP *Nov. 1969*
CIJE: 82 RIE: 31 GC: 210
UF Drowsiness
RT Behavior
Fatigue (Biology)
Health
Psychological Patterns

Slide Projectors
USE PROJECTION EQUIPMENT

SLIDES *Jan. 1969*
CIJE: 382 RIE: 364 GC: 720
SN Mounted transparencies, either film or glass, intended for projection or viewing by transmitted light
BT Transparencies
RT Audiovisual Aids
Filmstrips

Slovene
USE SLOVENIAN

SLOVENIAN *Oct. 1969*
CIJE: 5 RIE: 12 GC: 440
UF Slovene
BT Slavic Languages

SLOW LEARNERS *Jul. 1966*
CIJE: 259 RIE: 302 GC: 220
SN Individuals who have between average and mentally deficient intelligence (iq usually between 70 and 85) and whose social behavior is less than age level standards
UF Borderline Mental Retardation
BT Groups
RT Educationally Disadvantaged
Learning Problems
Mild Mental Retardation

SLUDGE *Aug. 1982*
CIJE: 4 RIE: 74 GC: 410
SN Deposits of mud, slushy sediment, or residual semiliquid waste
UF Activated Sludge
BT Matter
RT Solid Wastes
Wastes
Waste Water
Water
Water Pollution
Water Treatment

Slum Children
USE DISADVANTAGED YOUTH

Slum Conditions (1966 1980)
USE SLUM ENVIRONMENT

SLUM ENVIRONMENT *Jul. 1966*
CIJE: 17 RIE: 31 GC: 550
UF Slum Conditions (1966 1980)
BT Environment
RT Disadvantaged Environment
Slums
Urban Environment

SLUM SCHOOLS *Jul. 1966*
CIJE: 22 RIE: 56 GC: 340
SN Schools located in slum areas
BT Schools
RT Disadvantaged Schools
Slums
Urban Schools

SLUMS *Jul. 1966*
CIJE: 35 RIE: 81 GC: 550
SN Residential areas, usually urban, characterized by deteriorated buildings, high population density, and generally poor living conditions (note: prior to mar80, this term was often used synonymously with "ghettos")
UF Urban Slums (1966 1980)
BT Poverty Areas
RT Ghettos
Inner City
Poverty
Slum Environment
Slum Schools
Urban Areas
Urban Renewal

Small Business Management
USE BUSINESS ADMINISTRATION; SMALL BUSINESSES

SMALL BUSINESSES *Nov. 1982*
CIJE: 62 RIE: 330 GC: 650
SN Independently owned, for-profit enterprises with a small number of employees (usually not exceeding 500 for manufacturing or 100 for non-manufacturing) -- precise designation varies according to product or service offered
UF Small Business Management #
BT Business
RT Entrepreneurship
Organization Size (Groups)

SMALL CLASSES *Jul. 1966*
CIJE: 17 RIE: 48 GC: 310
BT Classes (Groups Of Students)
RT Class Size
Special Classes

SMALL COLLEGES *Jan. 1978*
CIJE: 221 RIE: 197 GC: 340
SN Colleges with less than 2500 students
BT Colleges
Small Schools
RT Church Related Colleges
Developing Institutions
Private Colleges
Proprietary Schools

SMALL ENGINE MECHANICS *Mar. 1984*
CIJE: RIE: 37 GC: 640
SN Assembly, operation, and repair of reciprocating internal-combustion engines used on lawnmowers, garden tractors, chain saws, and other portable power equipment -- small engines are generally air-cooled and under 20 horsepower
BT Mechanics (Process)
RT Auto Mechanics
Diesel Engines
Engines
Industrial Arts
Power Technology
Skilled Occupations

SMALL GROUP INSTRUCTION *Jul. 1966*
CIJE: 439 RIE: 491 GC: 310
BT Group Instruction
RT Individualized Instruction
Large Group Instruction
Teaching Methods
Team Training

SMALL SCHOOLS *Jul. 1966*
CIJE: 257 RIE: 810 GC: 340
SN Although designation is relative to locale, small schools usually do not exceed 750 students, grades k-12
NT One Teacher Schools
Small Colleges
BT Schools
RT Institutional Survival
Rural Schools
School Size

Smog
USE AIR POLLUTION

Smoke Alarms
USE ALARM SYSTEMS

Smokestacks
USE CHIMNEYS

SMOKING *Apr. 1969*
CIJE: 369 RIE: 208 GC: 210
UF Cigarette Smoking
BT Behavior
RT Cancer
Drug Abuse
Drug Use
Health Education
Physical Health
Stimulants
Tobacco

Snack Bars
USE DINING FACILITIES

Snowskiing
USE SKIING

SOCCER *Dec. 1975*
CIJE: 23 RIE: 27 GC: 470
BT Team Sports

Sociability
USE INTERPERSONAL COMPETENCE

SOCIAL ACTION *Nov. 1969*
CIJE: 620 RIE: 551 GC: 520
UF Political Reform
Social Reform
NT Community Action
RT Action Research
Activism
Advocacy
Citizen Participation
Dissent
Humanitarianism
Ideology
Revolution
Social Attitudes
Social Change
Social Responsibility

SOCIAL ADJUSTMENT *Jul. 1966*
CIJE: 637 RIE: 658 GC: 230
UF Socially Maladjusted (1966 1980)
BT Adjustment (To Environment)
Social Behavior
RT Adaptive Behavior (Of Disabled)
Alienation
Conformity
Interpersonal Competence
Social Development
Social Influences
Social Isolation
Social Problems

SOCIAL AGENCIES *Jul. 1966*
CIJE: 145 RIE: 228 GC: 520
SN Nonprofit, voluntary, and/or tax-supported service organizations
NT Welfare Agencies
BT Agencies
RT Agency Role
Public Agencies
Social Services
Social Support Groups
Social Work
Social Workers
Voluntary Agencies

SOCIAL ATTITUDES *Jul. 1966*
CIJE: 1977 RIE: 1498 GC: 510
SN Attitudes of individuals or groups with respect to social objects or phenomena such as persons, races, institutions, or traits
NT Social Bias
Social Desirability
BT Attitudes
RT Activism
Alienation
Altruism
Community Attitudes
Dissent
Egocentrism
Ideology
Interpersonal Competence
Justice
Language Attitudes
Political Attitudes
Political Socialization
Public Opinion
Regional Attitudes
Social Action
Social Change
Social Characteristics
Social Cognition
Social Development
Social Differences
Social Environment
Social Influences
Social Problems
Social Values
Traditionalism

Social Awareness
USE INTERPERSONAL COMPETENCE

= Two or more Descriptors are used to represent this term.
The term's main entry shows the appropriate coordination.

SOCIAL BACKGROUND *Jul. 1966*
CIJE: 98 RIE: 135 GC: 510
NT Social Experience
BT Socioeconomic Background
RT Social Class
Social Influences

SOCIAL BEHAVIOR *Dec. 1970*
CIJE: 1158 RIE: 976 GC: 120
SN Behavior influenced or controlled by other persons or by organized society
UF Social Norms #
NT Activism
Antisocial Behavior
Conformity
Dissent
Lying
Obedience
Prosocial Behavior
Social Adjustment
BT Behavior
RT Advocacy
Assertiveness
Behavior Development
Competition
Compliance (Psychology)
Cooperation
Crowding
Group Behavior
Interaction Process Analysis
Interpersonal Competence
Psychological Patterns
Social Control
Social Desirability
Social Influences
Social Networks
Sociobiology
Sociology
Sociometric Techniques
Stranger Reactions
Transactional Analysis

SOCIAL BIAS *Mar. 1980*
CIJE: 702 RIE: 606 GC: 540
SN Prejudicial attitudes toward particular groups, races, sexes, or religions, including the conscious or unconscious expression of these attitudes in writing, speaking, etc. (note: do not confuse with various "discrimination" terms, which refer to the actions based on those attitudes)
UF Discriminatory Attitudes (Social) (1966 1980)
NT Ethnic Bias
Racial Bias
Sex Bias
BT Bias
Social Attitudes
RT Age Discrimination
Cultural Differences
Discriminatory Legislation
Handicap Discrimination
Intergroup Relations
Labeling (Of Persons)
Minority Groups
Nature Nurture Controversy
Negative Attitudes
Religious Discrimination
Social Desirability
Social Discrimination
Test Bias

SOCIAL BIOLOGY *Oct. 1983*
CIJE: 18 RIE: 1 GC: 490
SN The study of the application of biology to social problems, from food production, pollution, overpopulation, etc., to the long-range goals of social and ecological planning (note: do not confuse with "sociobiology")
BT Biology
RT Bioethics
Ecology
Environmental Education
Social Change
Sociology

SOCIAL CHANGE *Jul. 1966*
CIJE: 3457 RIE: 2963 GC: 520
SN Evolution or change at the societal, rather than individual, level, possibly involving the restructuring of political and/or economic relations (note: prior to mar80, the use of this term was not restricted by a scope note)
UF Social Reconstruction
Societal Change
NT Modernization
BT Change
RT Change Agents
Change Strategies
Community Change
Controversial Issues (Course Content)
Culture Lag
Economic Change
Futures (Of Society)
Institutional Survival
Marxian Analysis
Political Influences
Political Socialization
Revolution
Science And Society
Social Action
Social Attitudes
Social Biology
Social History
Social Indicators
Social Influences
Social Integration
Social Problems
Social Theories
Social Values
Sociocultural Patterns
Traditionalism

SOCIAL CHARACTERISTICS *Jul. 1966*
CIJE: 174 RIE: 299 GC: 510
SN Criteria used to rate members of a social class
RT Cultural Context
Cultural Traits
Individual Characteristics
Interpersonal Competence
Place Of Residence
Regional Characteristics
Social Attitudes
Social Class
Social Differences
Social Environment
Social Indicators
Social Influences
Social Values
Sociology

SOCIAL CLASS *Jul. 1966*
CIJE: 703 RIE: 478 GC: 520
NT Caste
Lower Class
Lower Middle Class
Middle Class
Upper Class
Working Class
BT Groups
RT Income
Marxism
Quality Of Life
Social Background
Social Characteristics
Social Dialects
Social Differences
Social Distribution
Social Integration
Social Status
Social Stratification
Social Structure
Socioeconomic Status
Status
Subcultures

Social Class Differences
USE SOCIAL DIFFERENCES

Social Class Integration
USE SOCIAL INTEGRATION

Social Climate
USE SOCIAL ENVIRONMENT

SOCIAL COGNITION *Oct. 1980*
CIJE: 339 RIE: 236 GC: 110
SN Conceptions about interpersonal and social phenomena (e.g., persons, the self, motives, feelings, relations, social rules, societal institutions) -- also, cognitive processes and skills used in social interaction (e.g., communication skills, perspective taking, empathy)
UF Interpersonal Perception
Perception (Between Persons)
Perceptiveness (Between Persons) #
Person Perception
Social Perception
BT Cognitive Processes
RT Attribution Theory
Cognitive Ability
Communication Skills
Conflict Resolution
Egocentrism
Empathy
Interpersonal Communication
Interpersonal Competence
Interpersonal Relationship
Metacognition
Moral Development
Perspective Taking
Role Perception
Self Concept
Social Attitudes
Social Development
Social Theories
Transactional Analysis

Social Competence
USE INTERPERSONAL COMPETENCE

SOCIAL CONTROL *Jun. 1983*
CIJE: 59 RIE: 37 GC: 510
SN Use of sanctions and laws by societies to circumscribe individual action
RT Behavior Standards
Compliance (Psychology)
Conflict Resolution
Law Enforcement
Power Structure
Sanctions
Social Behavior
Social Environment
Social Influences
Socialization
Social Problems
Social Reinforcement
Social Structure

SOCIAL DESIRABILITY *Aug. 1986*
CIJE: 53 RIE: 18 GC: 520
SN Perceived social acceptability, frequently manifested in response biases on inventories or surveys (i.e., the tendency to give socially favorable, or sometimes unfavorable, answers)
BT Social Attitudes
RT Attitude Measures
Forced Choice Technique
Personality Measures
Popularity
Responses
Response Style (Tests)
Social Behavior
Social Bias
Social Influences

SOCIAL DEVELOPMENT *Jul. 1966*
CIJE: 1201 RIE: 1588 GC: 120
SN Pattern or process of change exhibited by individuals resulting from their interaction with other individuals, social institutions, social customs, etc. (note: do not confuse with "social change" -- prior to mar80, the use of this term was not restricted by a scope note)
BT Individual Development
RT Egocentrism
Friendship
Individualism
Interpersonal Competence
Mate Selection
Midlife Transitions
Personality Development
Perspective Taking
Sexual Identity
Social Adjustment
Social Attitudes
Social Cognition
Social Differences
Social Environment
Social Experience
Social Influences
Socialization
Social Life

SOCIAL DIALECTS *Jul. 1966*
CIJE: 171 RIE: 254 GC: 450
SN Special varieties within a language, defined by the social environment of its speakers
BT Dialects
RT Bidialectalism
Black Dialects
Diglossia
Language
Language Role
Linguistics
Nonstandard Dialects
Regional Dialects
Social Class
Standard Spoken Usage
Urban Language

SOCIAL DIFFERENCES *Jul. 1966*
CIJE: 538 RIE: 501 GC: 510
UF Social Class Differences
BT Differences
RT Cultural Differences
Culture Conflict
Individual Differences
Intermarriage
Racial Differences
Rural Urban Differences
Social Attitudes
Social Characteristics
Social Class
Social Development
Social Environment
Social Integration
Social Values

Social Disadvantagement (1966 1980)
USE DISADVANTAGED

SOCIAL DISCRIMINATION *Jul. 1966*
CIJE: 496 RIE: 640 GC: 540
SN Unfavorable treatment of individuals or groups on arbitrary grounds (note: do not confuse with various "bias" terms, which refer to prejudicial attitudes that may lead to such treatment)
UF Bigotry
Discrimination (Social)
NT Age Discrimination
Educational Discrimination
Ethnic Discrimination
Handicap Discrimination
Housing Discrimination
Racial Discrimination
Religious Discrimination
Reverse Discrimination
Sex Discrimination
RT Caste
Civil Rights
Civil Rights Legislation
Discriminatory Legislation
Equal Facilities
Ghettos
Intergroup Relations
Minority Groups
Segregationist Organizations
Social Bias
Social Integration
Test Bias

SOCIAL DISTRIBUTION *Jul. 1966*
CIJE: 15 RIE: 19 GC: 550
SN Description of the distribution of individuals or groups with reference to their social status
BT Demography
RT Incidence
Social Class
Social Mobility
Social Status
Social Stratification

Social Drinking
USE DRINKING

SOCIAL ENVIRONMENT *Jul. 1966*
CIJE: 717 RIE: 670 GC: 510
SN Aggregate of social factors or conditions that influence individuals or groups
UF Atmosphere (Social)
Social Climate
NT Social Isolation
BT Environment
RT Cultural Context
Culture Conflict
Quality Of Life
Social Attitudes
Social Characteristics
Social Control
Social Development
Social Differences
Social History
Social Indicators
Social Influences
Social Integration
Social Theories
Social Values

Sociocultural Patterns
Subcultures
Work Environment

SOCIAL EXCHANGE THEORY *Jul. 1966*
CIJE: 120 RIE: 99 GC: 810
SN Social interactions conceptualized as economic transactions, with social behavior oriented toward expected returns (either material or psychic)
BT Social Theories
RT Altruism
Competition
Cooperation
Informal Organization
Interpersonal Relationship
Organizational Development
Organizational Theories
Organizations (Groups)
Power Structure
Rewards
Self Reward

SOCIAL EXPERIENCE *Jul. 1966*
CIJE: 137 RIE: 106 GC: 510
BT Experience
Social Background
RT Cross Age Teaching
Experiential Learning
Interpersonal Competence
Social Development
Social Influences

Social Factors (1968 1980)
USE SOCIAL INFLUENCES

Social Geography
USE HUMAN GEOGRAPHY

SOCIAL HISTORY *Apr. 1975*
CIJE: 419 RIE: 489 GC: 430
SN History that concentrates on the sociocultural aspects of the life, customs, trends, and institutions/organizations of a people
BT History
RT Cultural Context
Culture
Economics
Family History
Historiography
Holidays
Intellectual History
Life Style
Local History
Oral History
Social Change
Social Environment
Sociocultural Patterns
Socioeconomic Influences
Sociology
Traditionalism

Social Immaturity (1966 1980)
USE MATURITY (INDIVIDUALS)

SOCIAL INDICATORS *Oct. 1976*
CIJE: 111 RIE: 183 GC: 520
SN Output-oriented measures of individuals and groups that reflect quality of life
BT Statistical Data
RT Futures (Of Society)
Life Satisfaction
Living Standards
Prediction
Quality Of Life
Social Change
Social Characteristics
Social Environment
Social Problems
Social Science Research
Sociocultural Patterns
Socioeconomic Influences
Trend Analysis

SOCIAL INFLUENCES *Jul. 1966*
CIJE: 2853 RIE: 2584 GC: 510
SN Social factors or circumstances that affect or alter some condition or situation (note: use a more precise term if possible)
UF Social Factors (1968 1980)
Social Pressure
BT Influences
RT Cultural Influences
Cultural Interrelationships
Language Role
Minority Group Influences
Political Socialization
Population Growth
Science And Society
Social Adjustment
Social Attitudes
Social Background
Social Behavior
Social Change
Social Characteristics
Social Control
Social Desirability
Social Development
Social Environment
Social Experience
Social Integration
Social Status
Social Stratification
Social Theories
Social Values
Sociocultural Patterns
Socioeconomic Influences
Sociology
Subcultures

Social Institutions (Organizations)
USE INSTITUTIONS

Social Institutions (Social Patterns)
USE SOCIOCULTURAL PATTERNS

SOCIAL INTEGRATION *Dec. 1968*
CIJE: 396 RIE: 386 GC: 540
SN Process of uniting the diverse groups of a society into a cohesive and harmonious whole
UF Ethnic Integration
Integration (Social)
Social Class Integration
NT Classroom Desegregation
Neighborhood Integration
Personnel Integration
Racial Integration
School Desegregation
Voluntary Desegregation
RT Acculturation
Cross Cultural Training
Cultural Interrelationships
Desegregation Effects
Desegregation Methods
Desegregation Plans
Ethnic Groups
Ethnic Relations
Human Relations
Integration Readiness
Interaction Process Analysis
Interfaith Relations
Intergroup Education
Intergroup Relations
Interpersonal Relationship
Multicultural Education
Social Change
Social Class
Social Differences
Social Discrimination
Social Environment
Social Influences
Social Networks
Social Problems
Social Systems
Tokenism

Social Interaction
USE INTERPERSONAL RELATIONSHIP

SOCIAL ISOLATION *Jul. 1966*
CIJE: 260 RIE: 163 GC: 530
BT Social Environment
RT Alienation
Cultural Isolation
Disadvantaged Environment
Loneliness
Social Adjustment
Social Psychology

Social Issues
USE SOCIAL PROBLEMS

Social Learning
USE SOCIALIZATION

SOCIAL LIFE *Jul. 1966*
CIJE: 104 RIE: 104 GC: 520
RT Dating (Social)
Friendship
Interpersonal Attraction
Interpersonal Relationship
Popularity
Social Development

Social Maturity (1966 1980)
USE MATURITY (INDIVIDUALS)

SOCIAL MOBILITY *Jul. 1966*
CIJE: 332 RIE: 322 GC: 520
SN Change in the social status of individuals or groups
UF Social Opportunities (1966 1980)
Social Restrictions
BT Mobility
RT Black Achievement
Educational Mobility
Educational Status Comparison
Intergroup Relations
Interpersonal Relationship
Occupational Mobility
Social Distribution
Social Status
Socioeconomic Status

SOCIAL NETWORKS *Nov. 1982*
CIJE: 108 RIE: 129 GC: 710
SN Series of communication linkages relating groups, organizations, or persons in social situations -- can be interpersonal, economic, political, action-based, or role-based links
BT Networks
RT Communication (Thought Transfer)
Communications
Information Networks
Intergroup Relations
Interpersonal Relationship
Social Behavior
Social Integration
Social Services
Social Structure
Social Support Groups
Social Systems
Social Theories
Sociometric Techniques

Social Norms
USE BEHAVIOR STANDARDS; SOCIAL BEHAVIOR

Social Opportunities (1966 1980)
USE SOCIAL MOBILITY

SOCIAL ORGANIZATIONS *Jul. 1966*
CIJE: 67 RIE: 85 GC: 520
SN Organizations whose primary purpose is encouraging social activities and interaction (note: do not confuse with "social agencies" -- prior to mar80, the use of this term was not restricted by a scope note)
BT Organizations (Groups)
RT Community Organizations
Fraternities
Sororities
Student Unions

Social Perception
USE SOCIAL COGNITION

SOCIAL PLANNING *Jul. 1966*
CIJE: 124 RIE: 159 GC: 610
BT Planning
RT Planning Commissions
Regional Planning
Urban Planning

Social Pressure
USE SOCIAL INFLUENCES

SOCIAL PROBLEMS *Jul. 1966*
CIJE: 1832 RIE: 1831 GC: 530
UF Social Issues
BT Problems
RT Conflict
Controversial Issues (Course Content)
Debate
Justice
Political Issues
Public Affairs Education
Quality Of Life
Science And Society
Social Adjustment
Social Attitudes
Social Change
Social Control
Social Indicators
Social Integration
Social Studies
Sociology
Values

SOCIAL PSYCHOLOGY *Jul. 1966*
CIJE: 690 RIE: 584 GC: 230
SN The study of the way the personality, attitudes, and motivations of individuals reciprocally influence and are influenced by the structure, dynamics, and behavior of the social groups with which they interact
BT Psychology
Sociology
RT Behaviorism
Clinical Psychology
Community Psychology
Compliance (Psychology)
Criminology
Delinquency
Educational Psychology
Educational Sociology
Group Dynamics
Groups
Industrial Psychology
Psychopathology
Reference Groups
Self Actualization
Social Isolation
Social Reinforcement

Social Reconstruction
USE SOCIAL CHANGE

Social Recreation Programs (1966 1980)
USE RECREATIONAL PROGRAMS

Social Reform
USE SOCIAL ACTION

SOCIAL REINFORCEMENT *Aug. 1969*
CIJE: 306 RIE: 204 GC: 110
BT Reinforcement
RT Behavior Modification
Cooperation
Negative Reinforcement
Positive Reinforcement
Reality Therapy
Rewards
Social Control
Social Psychology
Sociology

SOCIAL RELATIONS (1966 1980) *Mar. 1980*
CIJE: 862 RIE: 727 GC: 520
SN Invalid descriptor -- used to index both interpersonal and group relations -- see such descriptors as "interpersonal relationship," "intergroup relations," "group dynamics," "human relations," etc.

SOCIAL RESPONSIBILITY *Jun. 1969*
CIJE: 791 RIE: 525 GC: 510
NT Citizenship Responsibility
BT Responsibility
RT Citizen Participation
Community Action
Community Programs
Community Responsibility
Educational Responsibility
Humanitarianism
Leadership Responsibility
Neighborhood Improvement
Public Service
Social Action
Social Services
Social Support Groups
Urban Improvement
Welfare Services

Social Restrictions
USE SOCIAL MOBILITY

Social Science Methodology
USE RESEARCH METHODOLOGY; SOCIAL SCIENCE RESEARCH

SOCIAL SCIENCE RESEARCH *Sep. 1975*
CIJE: 1212 RIE: 1168 GC: 810
SN Basic, applied, and developmental research conducted to advance knowledge in the social sciences (note: as of oct81, use as a minor descriptor for examples of this kind of research -- use as a major descriptor only as the subject of a document)
UF Social Science Methodology #
Sociological Studies #
NT Economic Research
BT Research

= Two or more Descriptors are used to represent this term.
The term's main entry shows the appropriate coordination.

RT Anthropology
Area Studies
Behavioral Science Research
Communication Research
Demography
Economics
Educational Research
Ethnic Studies
Ethnography
Ethnology
Geography
Gerontology
Historiography
History
International Studies
Marxian Analysis
Participant Observation
Political Science
Psychological Studies
Psychology
Qualitative Research
Research And Development
Social Indicators
Social Sciences
Social Scientists
Social Studies
Sociology
Urban Studies

SOCIAL SCIENCES *Jul. 1966*
CIJE: 1281 RIE: 1923 GC: 400
NT Anthropology
Demography
Economics
Geography
Gerontology
History
International Studies
Political Science
Social Studies
Sociology
Topography
BT Sciences
RT Area Studies
Behavioral Sciences
Controversial Issues (Course Content)
Ethnic Studies
Global Approach
Psychology
Social Science Research
Social Scientists
Sociobiology
Urban Studies

SOCIAL SCIENTISTS *Sep. 1982*
CIJE: 31 RIE: 16 GC: 640
BT Professional Personnel
RT Anthropology
Demography
Economics
Ethnography
Ethnology
Experimenter Characteristics
Geography
Gerontology
History
International Studies
Political Science
Psychologists
Researchers
Scholarship
Scientists
Social Science Research
Social Sciences
Sociology
Topography

SOCIAL SERVICES *Jul. 1966*
CIJE: 755 RIE: 1475 GC: 520
SN Organized assistance provided by public or private agencies and organizations to the members of a society
UF Sociopsychological Services (1967 1980) #
NT Adult Day Care
Adult Foster Care
Ancillary School Services
Day Care
Foster Care
Social Work
Welfare Services
BT Human Services
RT Community Information Services
Community Services
Eligibility
Group Homes
Hospices (Terminal Care)
Humanitarianism
Professional Services
Social Agencies
Social Networks
Social Responsibility
Social Support Groups
Visiting Homemakers

Social Skills
USE INTERPERSONAL COMPETENCE

SOCIAL STATUS *Jul. 1966*
CIJE: 519 RIE: 375 GC: 510
UF Class Status
BT Status
RT Advantaged
Disadvantaged
Popularity
Prestige
Quality Of Life
Social Class
Social Distribution
Social Influences
Social Mobility
Social Structure
Socioeconomic Status
Status Need

SOCIAL STRATIFICATION *Oct. 1972*
CIJE: 229 RIE: 143 GC: 520
BT Social Structure
RT Caste
Elitism
Group Membership
Group Status
Marxian Analysis
Role Theory
Social Class
Social Distribution
Social Influences
Social Systems
Status

SOCIAL STRUCTURE *Jul. 1966*
CIJE: 581 RIE: 548 GC: 520
NT Social Stratification
BT Organization
RT Cultural Context
Family Structure
Governmental Structure
Group Structure
Industrial Structure
Power Structure
Social Class
Social Control
Social Networks
Social Status
Social Systems
Social Theories
Sociocultural Patterns

SOCIAL STUDIES *Jul. 1966*
CIJE: 4207 RIE: 6106 GC: 400
SN Social studies consist of adaptations of knowledge from the social sciences for teaching purposes at the elementary and secondary levels of education
UF Social Studies Units (1966 1980) #
NT Civics
BT Curriculum
Social Sciences
RT Anthropology
Controversial Issues (Course Content)
Cultural Education
Current Events
Economics
Geography
History
Law Related Education
Locational Skills (Social Studies)
Political Science
Social Problems
Social Science Research
United States Government (Course)
World Affairs

Social Studies Units (1966 1980)
USE SOCIAL STUDIES; UNITS OF STUDY

SOCIAL SUPPORT GROUPS *Sep. 1982*
CIJE: 274 RIE: 287 GC: 240
SN Persons (incl. individuals), organizations, or institutions that provide physical, emotional, spiritual, psychic, or intellectual maintenance and sustenance
UF Support Groups (Human Services)
Support Networks (Personal Assistance)
BT Groups
RT Cooperation
Counseling
Donors
Helping Relationship
Humanitarianism
Human Services
Reference Groups
Rehabilitation
Social Agencies
Social Networks
Social Responsibility
Social Services
Social Work
Social Workers

SOCIAL SYSTEMS *Jul. 1966*
CIJE: 300 RIE: 398 GC: 520
NT Capitalism
Communism
Fascism
Socialism
RT Group Structure
Human Geography
Ideology
Social Integration
Social Networks
Social Stratification
Social Structure
Social Theories
Sociocultural Patterns

SOCIAL THEORIES *Oct. 1982*
CIJE: 99 RIE: 72 GC: 810
SN Theories about the structure, organization, and functioning of human societies
NT Organizational Theories
Social Exchange Theory
BT Theories
RT Behavior Theories
Ideology
Role Theory
Social Change
Social Cognition
Social Environment
Social Influences
Socialization
Social Networks
Social Structure
Social Systems
Sociocultural Patterns
Socioeconomic Influences
Sociology

Social Trends
USE SOCIOCULTURAL PATTERNS

SOCIAL VALUES *Jul. 1966*
CIJE: 1768 RIE: 1231 GC: 520
SN Principles and standards of human interaction within a given group that are regarded by members of that group as being worthy, important, or significant
UF Group Values
BT Values
RT Aesthetic Values
Conservatism
Cultural Context
Democratic Values
Humanitarianism
Ideology
Individualism
Justice
Liberalism
Moral Values
Peer Groups
Political Attitudes
Quality Of Life
Social Attitudes
Social Change
Social Characteristics
Social Differences
Social Environment
Social Influences

SOCIAL WELFARE (1966 1980) *Mar. 1980*
CIJE: 108 RIE: 206 GC: 520
SN Invalid descriptor -- used for well-being and various types of social services -- use "well being" for former concept, "welfare services" for organized assistance to the disadvantaged, and "social services" or other appropriate terms for social services provided to the general population

SOCIAL WORK *Jul. 1966*
CIJE: 906 RIE: 354 GC: 640
SN Activities and services designed to improve social conditions affecting communities, families, or individuals
BT Social Services
RT Caseworker Approach
Caseworkers
Counseling
Rehabilitation
School Social Workers
Social Agencies
Social Support Groups
Social Workers
Welfare Agencies
Welfare Services

SOCIAL WORKERS *Jul. 1966*
CIJE: 664 RIE: 350 GC: 640
UF Client Caseworkers (1966 1980)
NT School Social Workers
BT Caseworkers
Professional Personnel
RT Child Caregivers
Counselors
Guidance Personnel
Parole Officers
Probation Officers
Social Agencies
Social Support Groups
Social Work
Welfare Agencies

SOCIALISM *Oct. 1974*
CIJE: 184 RIE: 83 GC: 610
BT Social Systems
RT Capitalism
Collective Settlements
Communism
Economics
Fascism
Government (Administrative Body)
Imperialism
Marxism
Political Science

SOCIALIZATION *Jul. 1966*
CIJE: 1979 RIE: 1685 GC: 120
UF Social Learning
NT Political Socialization
RT Assertiveness
Cognitive Dissonance
Compliance (Psychology)
Cross Age Teaching
Ethnicity
Hidden Curriculum
Ideology
Imitation
Inhibition
Interpersonal Competence
Modeling (Psychology)
Nonformal Education
Peer Influence
Phenomenology
Reference Groups
Role Conflict
Significant Others
Social Control
Social Development
Social Theories
Subcultures

Socially Advantaged
USE ADVANTAGED

Socially Deviant Behavior (1966 1980)
USE ANTISOCIAL BEHAVIOR

Socially Disadvantaged (1966 1980)
USE DISADVANTAGED

Socially Maladjusted (1966 1980)
USE SOCIAL ADJUSTMENT

Societal Change
USE SOCIAL CHANGE

SOCIOBIOLOGY *Oct. 1983*
CIJE: 35 RIE: 8 GC: 490
SN The study of the biological basis of social behavior, especially as such behavior is transmitted genetically (note: do not confuse with "social biology")
BT Behavioral Sciences
Biological Sciences

RT Behavior Patterns
Ethology
Evolution
Genetics
Nature Nurture Controversy
Social Behavior
Social Sciences
Zoology

SOCIOCULTURAL PATTERNS *Jul. 1966*
CIJE: 1052 RIE: 1435 GC: 520
UF Social Institutions (Social Patterns)
Social Trends
NT Ethnicity
Humanitarianism
RT Biculturalism
Cross Cultural Studies
Cross Cultural Training
Cultural Context
Cultural Influences
Cultural Interrelationships
Cultural Pluralism
Culture
Culture Lag
Demography
Educational Anthropology
Ethnocentrism
Ethnography
Ethnology
Human Relations
Ideology
Kinship
Life Style
Minority Group Influences
Non Western Civilization
Role Of Education
Social Change
Social Environment
Social History
Social Indicators
Social Influences
Social Structure
Social Systems
Social Theories
Sociolinguistics
Sociology
Traditionalism
Trend Analysis
Western Civilization

Sociodrama (1966 1980)
USE ROLE PLAYING

SOCIOECONOMIC BACKGROUND *Jul. 1966*
CIJE: 350 RIE: 667 GC: 510
NT Social Background
BT Background
RT Economics
Socioeconomic Influences

SOCIOECONOMIC INFLUENCES *Jul. 1966*
CIJE: 1613 RIE: 2253 GC: 510
BT Influences
RT Black Community
Economic Factors
Economic Opportunities
Economics
Industrialization
Modernization
Political Influences
Social History
Social Indicators
Social Influences
Social Theories
Socioeconomic Background
Socioeconomic Status
Traditionalism

Socioeconomic Level
USE SOCIOECONOMIC STATUS

SOCIOECONOMIC STATUS *Jul. 1966*
CIJE: 1515 RIE: 2231 GC: 510
UF Socioeconomic Level
BT Status
RT Affluent Youth
Economics
Economic Status
Educational Benefits
Educational Status Comparison
Employment Level
Income
Ownership
Quality Of Life
Social Class
Social Mobility
Social Status
Socioeconomic Influences
Sociolinguistics

Sociograms
USE SOCIOMETRIC TECHNIQUES

SOCIOLINGUISTICS *Jul. 1966*
CIJE: 1103 RIE: 1423 GC: 450
SN The study of language in society -- more specifically, the study of language varieties, their functions, and their speakers
NT Dialect Studies
Language Planning
Language Variation
BT Linguistics
RT Anthropological Linguistics
Bidialectalism
Bilingualism
Code Switching (Language)
Dialects
Diglossia
Grammatical Acceptability
Immersion Programs
Kinship Terminology
Language Attitudes
Language Maintenance
Language Of Instruction
Language Planning
Language Research
Language Role
Language Skill Attrition
Language Standardization
Language Usage
Linguistic Borrowing
Linguistic Theory
Monolingualism
Multilingualism
Mutual Intelligibility
Native Speakers
Nonstandard Dialects
Official Languages
Pragmatics
Psycholinguistics
Sociocultural Patterns
Socioeconomic Status
Sociology
Standard Spoken Usage
Urban Language

Sociological Novels (1969 1980)
USE NOVELS

Sociological Studies
USE SOCIAL SCIENCE RESEARCH; SOCIOLOGY

SOCIOLOGY *Jul. 1966*
CIJE: 1104 RIE: 956 GC: 400
UF Sociological Studies #
NT Criminology
Educational Sociology
Social Psychology
BT Behavioral Sciences
Social Sciences
RT Area Studies
Authoritarianism
Behavior
Cross Cultural Studies
Demography
Elitism
Ethnography
Ethnology
Ideology
Marxian Analysis
Marxism
Personal Autonomy
Social Behavior
Social Biology
Social Characteristics
Social History
Social Influences
Social Problems
Social Reinforcement
Social Science Research
Social Scientists
Social Theories
Sociocultural Patterns
Sociolinguistics

SOCIOMETRIC TECHNIQUES *Jul. 1966*
CIJE: 222 RIE: 244 GC: 820
SN Procedures used to identify the preferences, likes, or dislikes of the members of a group with respect to each other, as well as to identify various patterns of group structure or interaction
UF Sociograms
BT Measurement Techniques
RT Group Behavior
Group Dynamics
Groups
Group Structure
Interaction Process Analysis
Intergroup Relations
Interpersonal Relationship
Judgment Analysis Technique
Multidimensional Scaling
Naturalistic Observation
Peer Evaluation
Social Behavior
Social Networks

Sociopsychological Services (1967 1980)
USE PSYCHOLOGICAL SERVICES; SOCIAL SERVICES

Soft Cover Books
USE PAPERBACK BOOKS

SOFTBALL *Dec. 1975*
CIJE: 15 RIE: 13 GC: 470
BT Team Sports
RT Baseball

Software (Computers)
USE COMPUTER SOFTWARE

Software Reviews (Computers)
USE COMPUTER SOFTWARE REVIEWS

SOIL CONSERVATION *Jul. 1966*
CIJE: 62 RIE: 121 GC: 410
BT Conservation (Environment)
Land Use
RT Agronomy
Conservation Education
Depleted Resources
Ecology
Environmental Education
Forestry
Natural Resources
Soil Science
Water
Wind (Meteorology)

SOIL SCIENCE *Jul. 1966*
CIJE: 74 RIE: 160 GC: 410
BT Earth Science
RT Agronomy
Biology
Botany
Chemistry
Coal
Fertilizers
Forestry
Geology
Land Use
Mineralogy
Seismology
Soil Conservation

SOLAR ENERGY *Jun. 1983*
CIJE: 26 RIE: 72 GC: 490
SN Light and heat radiation of the sun -- also the energy collected as heat or converted to electricity from this source
UF Solar Heating #
Solar Radiation (1968 1983)
Solar Radiation Energy
BT Radiation
RT Alternative Energy Sources
Climate
Climate Control
Electricity
Heat
Light
Meteorology
Power Technology
Radiation Effects
Temperature
Thermal Environment
Wind (Meteorology)

Solar Heating
USE HEATING; SOLAR ENERGY

Solar Radiation (1968 1983)
USE SOLAR ENERGY

Solar Radiation Energy
USE SOLAR ENERGY

Solicitors (Law)
USE LAWYERS

SOLID GEOMETRY *Jul. 1966*
CIJE: 51 RIE: 17 GC: 480
BT Geometry
RT Analytic Geometry
Plane Geometry
Volume (Mathematics)

SOLID WASTES *Aug. 1982*
CIJE: 7 RIE: 17 GC: 410
SN Unwanted solid or semisolid materials discarded by farms, businesses, communities, or individuals (note: use "waste water" for sewage)
UF Garbage
Litter
Trash
BT Wastes
RT Pollution
Recycling
Sludge
Waste Disposal
Waste Water
Water Treatment

Soliloquies
USE MONOLOGS

SOMALI *Jul. 1966*
CIJE: 1 RIE: 7 GC: 440
BT Afro Asiatic Languages

SONGS *Aug. 1986*
CIJE: 32 RIE: 37 GC: 420
NT Art Song
Ballads
Hymns
BT Vocal Music
RT Lyric Poetry
Music Activities
Musical Composition
Music Education
Music Techniques
Singing

Sonic Environment
USE ACOUSTICAL ENVIRONMENT

SONNETS *Jan. 1970*
CIJE: 12 RIE: 3 GC: 430
SN Lyric poems of fourteen lines following one of several definite rhyme schemes
BT Literary Genres
Lyric Poetry
RT Ballads
Imagery
Metaphors
Odes
Renaissance Literature

SONS *Sep. 1981*
CIJE: 27 RIE: 16 GC: 510
BT Males
RT Daughters
Family (Sociological Unit)
Family Environment
Family Life
Kinship
Parent Child Relationship
Parents

SORORITIES *Jan. 1978*
CIJE: 23 RIE: 12 GC: 520
SN Groups of women associated through social, scholastic, or professional interests
BT Organizations (Groups)
RT Females
Fraternities
Honor Societies
National Organizations
Professional Associations
Social Organizations
Student Organizations
Womens Education

Sorting Procedures (1966 1980)
USE CLASSIFICATION

= Two or more Descriptors are used to represent this term.
The term's main entry shows the appropriate coordination.

Sound
USE ACOUSTICS

Sound Barriers
USE ACOUSTIC INSULATION

SOUND EFFECTS *Jul. 1966*
CIJE: 36 RIE: 45 GC: 720
BT Special Effects
RT Acoustics
Audio Equipment
Audiotape Recordings
Noise (Sound)

Sound Equipment
USE AUDIO EQUIPMENT

Sound Films (1966 1980)
USE FILMS

Sound Insulation
USE ACOUSTIC INSULATION

SOUND SPECTROGRAPHS *Mar. 1980*
CIJE: 122 RIE: 51 GC: 910
SN Electronic instruments used in acoustic phonetics to record the frequency, amplitude, and duration of sound waves produced by speech (note: prior to mar80, "spectrograms" was used for this concept)
UF Spectrograms (1967 1980)
Spectrographs (Sound)
BT Audio Equipment
Electronic Equipment
Measurement Equipment
RT Acoustic Phonetics
Artificial Speech
Componential Analysis
Instrumentation
Phonology
Speech
Speech Therapy
Visible Speech

Sound Systems
USE AUDIO EQUIPMENT

Sound Tape Recordings
USE AUDIOTAPE RECORDINGS

SOUND TRACKS (1966 1980) *Mar. 1980*
CIJE: 10 RIE: 33 GC: 720
SN Invalid descriptor -- see other appropriate "film," "audio," and "sound" descriptors

Sound Transmission
USE ACOUSTICS

Sound Waves
USE ACOUSTICS

Soundproofing
USE ACOUSTIC INSULATION

Source Credibility
USE CREDIBILITY

South American History
USE LATIN AMERICAN HISTORY

South American Literature
USE LATIN AMERICAN LITERATURE

South Americans
USE LATIN AMERICANS

South Asian Civilization
USE NON WESTERN CIVILIZATION

Southern Attitudes (1966 1980)
USE REGIONAL ATTITUDES

SOUTHERN CITIZENS (1966 1980) *Mar. 1980*
CIJE: 5 RIE: 12 GC: 610
SN Invalid descriptor -- coordinate the identifier "united states (south)" with appropriate population descriptors

SOUTHERN COMMUNITY (1966 1980) *Mar. 1980*
CIJE: 22 RIE: 29 GC: 520
SN Invalid descriptor -- coordinate the identifier "united states (south)" with appropriate "community" descriptors

SOUTHERN SCHOOLS (1966 1980) *Mar. 1980*
CIJE: 113 RIE: 149 GC: 340
SN Invalid descriptor -- coordinate the identifier "united states (south)" with appropriate "school" and "education" descriptors

SPACE *Jul. 1966*
CIJE: 140 RIE: 66 GC: 490
SN Area or volume between specified boundaries (note: do not confuse with "personal space" or "space sciences" -- prior to mar80, the use of this term was not restricted by a scope note)
NT Area
Volume (Mathematics)
BT Scientific Concepts
RT Atomic Structure
Atomic Theory
Distance
Gravity (Physics)
Intervals
Proximity
Quantum Mechanics
Relativity
Time

SPACE CLASSIFICATION *Aug. 1968*
CIJE: 37 RIE: 97 GC: 920
SN Categorization of areas in a given facility generally by function or purpose
BT Classification
RT Building Plans
Facility Inventory
Facility Utilization Research
Interior Design
Interior Space
Offices (Facilities)
Space Utilization
Spatial Relationship (Facilities)

SPACE DIVIDERS *Jul. 1966*
CIJE: 18 RIE: 20 GC: 920
SN Vertical surface or structure used for separating areas within larger rooms
UF Room Dividers
NT Movable Partitions
BT Equipment
Structural Elements (Construction)
RT Classroom Design
Flexible Facilities
School Space
Space Utilization

SPACE EXPLORATION *Mar. 1980*
CIJE: 68 RIE: 40 GC: 490
SN Scientific investigations of areas beyond the earth's atmosphere (note: use "lunar research" for studies referring to the earth's moon)
UF Extraterrestrial Exploration
Outer Space Research
Planetary Exploration
NT Lunar Research
BT Scientific Research
RT Aerospace Technology
Astronomy
Planetariums
Satellites (Aerospace)
Space Sciences

SPACE ORIENTATION (1968 1980) *Mar. 1980*
CIJE: 205 RIE: 124 GC: 120
SN Invalid descriptor -- used inconsistently in indexing -- see the descriptors "personal space" and "spatial ability"

SPACE SCIENCES *May. 1972*
CIJE: 402 RIE: 192 GC: 490
BT Sciences
RT Aerospace Education
Aerospace Technology
Astronomy
Earth Science
Lunar Research
Navigation
Physical Sciences
Planetariums
Satellites (Aerospace)
Space Exploration

Space Time Continuum
USE RELATIVITY

SPACE UTILIZATION *Jul. 1966*
CIJE: 497 RIE: 657 GC: 920
RT Building Conversion
Building Design
Building Obsolescence
Building Plans
Buildings
Campus Planning
Classroom Design
College Buildings
Crowding
Design Requirements
Double Sessions
Educational Complexes
Educational Facilities Planning
Equipment Storage
Facilities
Facility Case Studies
Facility Expansion
Facility Guidelines
Facility Planning
Facility Requirements
Facility Utilization Research
Flexible Facilities
Found Spaces
Furniture Arrangement
Interior Space
Physical Mobility
School Buildings
School Expansion
School Space
Space Classification
Space Dividers
Spatial Relationship (Facilities)
Storage
Underground Facilities

Spaced Negative Reinforcement
USE NEGATIVE REINFORCEMENT

SPANISH *Jul. 1966*
CIJE: 1280 RIE: 2014 GC: 440
BT Romance Languages
RT Spanish Literature
Spanish Speaking

Spanish American Literature (1969 1980)
USE HISPANIC AMERICAN LITERATURE

SPANISH AMERICANS *Jul. 1966*
CIJE: 169 RIE: 495 GC: 560
SN Residents or citizens of the united states who are of spanish descent (note: for other hispanic peoples in the united states see "hispanic americans" -- for those in the caribbean or south america see "latin americans" -- prior to mar80, this term was not restricted by a scope note)
BT Ethnic Groups
Hispanic Americans
RT Hispanic American Culture
Hispanic American Literature
Mexican Americans
Minority Groups
Spanish Speaking

SPANISH CULTURE *Jul. 1966*
CIJE: 89 RIE: 175 GC: 560
SN Culture of spain (note: for cultures of other spanish-speaking peoples, see "latin american culture" or "hispanic american culture" -- prior to mar80, the use of this term was not restricted by a scope note)
BT Culture
RT Hispanic American Culture
Latin American Culture
Spanish Literature
Spanish Speaking

SPANISH LITERATURE *May. 1969*
CIJE: 510 RIE: 41 GC: 430
SN Literature of spain (note: for other literature in spanish, see "latin american literature," "mexican american literature," or "hispanic american literature" -- prior to mar80, the use of this term was not restricted by a scope note)
BT Literature
RT Spanish
Spanish Culture

SPANISH SPEAKING *Jul. 1966*
CIJE: 737 RIE: 2430 GC: 450
BT Native Speakers
RT Biculturalism
Bilingualism
Bilingual Students
Cubans
Dominicans
English (Second Language)
Hispanic American Literature
Hispanic Americans
Limited English Speaking
Mexican American Literature
Mexican Americans
Mexicans
Native Language Instruction
Non English Speaking
Puerto Ricans
Spanish
Spanish Americans
Spanish Culture

SPATIAL ABILITY *Mar. 1981*
CIJE: 381 RIE: 178 GC: 120
SN Ability to perceive or solve problems associated with relationships between objects or figures, including position, direction, size, form, and distance (note: prior to mid-1980, this concept was indexed under "space orientation" and "spatial relationship" -- do not confuse with "personal space")
UF Spatial Perception (1980 1981)
Visuospatial Ability
BT Ability
RT Academic Ability
Basic Skills
Cognitive Ability
Cognitive Mapping
Echolocation
Perception
Perceptual Development
Psychomotor Skills
Visualization
Visually Handicapped Mobility
Visual Measures

Spatial Perception (1980 1981)
USE SPATIAL ABILITY

SPATIAL RELATIONSHIP (FACILITIES) *Mar. 1980*
CIJE: 8 RIE: 12 GC: 920
SN Functional interconnections among areas of buildings
BT Relationship
RT Architecture
Building Design
Building Plans
Design Requirements
Educational Facilities Planning
Facility Planning
Facility Utilization Research
Flexible Facilities
Interior Design
Psychological Needs
School Space
Space Classification
Space Utilization

SPATIAL RELATIONSHIP (1966 1980) *Mar. 1980*
CIJE: 133 RIE: 121 GC: 920
SN Invalid descriptor -- used for both the spatial relationship among areas of a facility and the spatial orientation of individuals -- see the descriptors "spatial relationship (facilities)," "spatial ability," and "personal space" for these concepts

Speaking (1966 1980)
USE SPEECH COMMUNICATION

Speaking Activities (1966 1980)
USE SPEECH COMMUNICATION

Speaking Skills
USE SPEECH SKILLS

Special Admission
USE SELECTIVE ADMISSION

SPECIAL CLASSES *Jul. 1966*
CIJE: 271 RIE: 382 GC: 310
UF Opportunity Classes (1966 1980)
BT Classes (Groups Of Students)
RT In School Suspension
Resource Room Programs
Small Classes
Special Education
Special Education Teachers
Special Schools
Transitional Programs

Special Counselors (1966 1980)
USE COUNSELORS; SPECIALISTS

Special Creation Theory
USE CREATIONISM

SPECIAL DEGREE PROGRAMS *Aug. 1968*
CIJE: 150 RIE: 184 GC: 340
SN Postsecondary-level programs geared to the needs of adult students, taking into account previous experience or self-education rather than traditional college credits -- may include external degree programs
BT Special Programs
RT Adult Education
Adult Students
Certification
College Credits
College Programs
Continuing Education
Credentials
Degree Requirements
Degrees (Academic)
Equivalency Tests
Experiential Learning
External Degree Programs
Nontraditional Education
Nontraditional Students
Prior Learning

SPECIAL EDUCATION *Jul. 1966*
CIJE: 2076 RIE: 3018 GC: 220
SN Educational programs and services for disabled and/or gifted individuals who have intellectually, physically, emotionally, or socially different characteristics from those who can be taught through normal methods or materials (note: use a more specific term if possible)
NT Adapted Physical Education
BT Education
RT Access To Education
Behavior Modification
Compulsory Education
Continuation Students
Daily Living Skills
Diagnostic Teaching
Disabilities
Educational Needs
Exceptional Persons
Gifted
Grouping (Instructional Purposes)
Homebound
Individualized Education Programs
Individualized Instruction
Individual Needs
Intervention
Itinerant Teachers
Labeling (Of Persons)
Mainstreaming
Mobile Educational Services
Normalization (Handicapped)
Partial Vision
Prognostic Tests
Rehabilitation
Resource Room Programs
Special Classes
Special Education Teachers
Specialists
Special Programs
Special Schools
Therapeutic Recreation
Therapy

SPECIAL EDUCATION TEACHERS *Jul. 1966*
CIJE: 553 RIE: 562 GC: 220
BT Teachers
RT Disabilities
Exceptional Persons
Gifted
Itinerant Teachers
Resource Room Programs
Resource Teachers
Special Classes
Special Education
Special Schools

SPECIAL EFFECTS *Aug. 1971*
CIJE: 46 RIE: 43 GC: 720
SN The use of electrical or mechanical devices or of photographic techniques to simulate audio and visual backgrounds
NT Animation
Sound Effects
BT Production Techniques
RT Audio Equipment
Film Production
Film Study
Photography
Tape Recordings
Television
Theater Arts
Video Equipment

SPECIAL HEALTH PROBLEMS *Jul. 1966*
CIJE: 656 RIE: 304 GC: 210
SN Category in federal legislation referring to conditions that interfere with learning and development but are not classified under physical, visual, hearing, mental, or learning disabilities -- usually involve limited strength, vitality, or alertness
BT Disabilities
RT Alcoholism
Allergy
Anemia
Asthma
Cancer
Diabetes
Drug Addiction
Exceptional Persons
Health
Heart Disorders
Hygiene
Hypertension
Injuries
Lead Poisoning
Learning Problems
Mental Retardation
Physical Disabilities
Physical Health
Poisoning
Seizures

SPECIAL LIBRARIES *Jul. 1966*
CIJE: 546 RIE: 468 GC: 710
SN Libraries consisting of materials on a specialized topic (e.g., music libraries) or in a non-print form (e.g., film libraries), or serving a specialized clientele (e.g., corporate, non-profit, or government-agency libraries)
NT Film Libraries
Government Libraries
Institutional Libraries
Law Libraries
Medical Libraries
BT Libraries
RT Academic Libraries
Branch Libraries
Depository Libraries
Documentation
Public Libraries
Research Libraries
Scientific And Technical Information

Special Methods Courses
USE METHODS COURSES

Special Needs (Individuals)
USE INDIVIDUAL NEEDS

Special Personnel
USE SPECIALISTS

SPECIAL PROGRAMS *Jul. 1966*
CIJE: 343 RIE: 726 GC: 320
SN Planned activities that take account of individual mental and physical differences
NT Individualized Education Programs
Resource Room Programs
Special Degree Programs
BT Programs
RT Individualized Programs
Individual Needs
Special Education

SPECIAL SCHOOLS *Jul. 1966*
CIJE: 156 RIE: 174 GC: 340
SN Schools established for the purpose of caring for the educational needs of atypical children (note: prior to mar80, the use of this term was not restricted by a scope note)
UF Special Service Schools
NT Institutional Schools
Residential Schools
BT Schools
RT Regional Schools
Special Classes
Special Education
Special Education Teachers

Special Service Schools
USE SPECIAL SCHOOLS

Special Services (1966 1980)
USE SERVICES

Special Teachers
USE SPECIALISTS

SPECIAL ZONING *Jul. 1966*
CIJE: 3 RIE: 4 GC: 610
BT Zoning

SPECIALIST IN EDUCATION DEGREES *Jul. 1966*
CIJE: 11 RIE: 20 GC: 340
SN Degrees awarded upon completion of two-year programs at postbaccalaureate level for training school administrators
BT Degrees (Academic)
RT Administrator Education
Bachelors Degrees
Degree Requirements
Doctoral Degrees
Education Majors
Masters Degrees
Schools Of Education
Teacher Educator Education
Teacher Educators

SPECIALISTS *Jul. 1966*
CIJE: 252 RIE: 404 GC: 360
UF Guidance Specialists #
Learning Specialists (1966 1980)
Special Counselors (1966 1980) #
Special Personnel
Special Teachers
NT Child Development Specialists
Film Production Specialists
Media Specialists
BT Personnel
RT Adjunct Faculty
Advisory Committees
Consultants
Counselors
Itinerant Teachers
Referral
Resource Staff
Resource Teachers
Shared Resources And Services
Special Education
Specialization
Teachers

SPECIALIZATION *Jul. 1966*
CIJE: 556 RIE: 268 GC: 120
SN Concentration of interest and effort, or restriction of function, to a particular aspect of some larger area of endeavor (such as a field of study, occupation, etc.) -- also, the process of progressive differentiation of functions
RT Curriculum
Differences
Majors (Students)
Occupations
Postdoctoral Education
Specialists

Specialty Schools
USE PROPRIETARY SCHOOLS

Specific Learning Disabilities
USE LEARNING DISABILITIES

SPECIFICATIONS *Sep. 1968*
CIJE: 145 RIE: 211 GC: 720
SN Detailed written statements of characteristics or requirements (note: use a more specific term if possible)
NT Computer Software
Design Requirements
Facility Requirements
BT Standards
RT Building Plans
Contracts
Criteria
Design
Evaluation
Evaluation Criteria
Guidelines
Master Plans
Planning
Program Proposals
Purchasing

Spectator Traffic Control
USE TRAFFIC CONTROL

Spectators
USE AUDIENCES

Spectrograms (1967 1980)
USE SOUND SPECTROGRAPHS

Spectrographs (Sound)
USE SOUND SPECTROGRAPHS

SPECTROSCOPY *Mar. 1980*
CIJE: 314 RIE: 12 GC: 490
SN Production, measurement, and analysis of spectra, especially electromagnetic radiation (note: prior to mar80, "spectrograms" was sometimes used for this concept)
BT Physical Sciences
RT Astronomy
Atomic Structure
Chemical Analysis
Chemistry
Crystallography
Lasers
Light
Molecular Structure
Optics
Physics
Radiation
Structural Analysis (Science)

SPEECH *Jul. 1966*
CIJE: 543 RIE: 739 GC: 450
SN (Note: use a more specific term if possible)
NT Articulation (Speech)
Artificial Speech
Inner Speech (Subvocal)
Pronunciation
Speech Acts
Speech Compression
BT Language Arts
RT Acoustic Phonetics
Articulation Impairments
Choral Speaking
Coherence
Cued Speech
Diction
Language
Linguistics
Monologs
Oral Language
Persuasive Discourse
Phonemics
Phonetics
Phonology
Public Speaking
Rhetoric
Rhetorical Invention
Sound Spectrographs
Speech And Hearing Clinics
Speech Communication
Speech Curriculum
Speech Evaluation
Speech Habits
Speech Handicaps
Speech Improvement
Speech Instruction
Speech Pathology
Speech Skills
Speech Tests
Speech Therapy
Verbal Communication

= Two or more Descriptors are used to represent this term.
The term's main entry shows the appropriate coordination.

Visible Speech
Voice Disorders
Word Frequency

SPEECH ACTS *Mar. 1983*
CIJE: 71 RIE: 56 GC: 450
SN Minimal units of meaningful communication (from single words to sentences) that are conceptualized and produced in terms of particular functions (i.e., to question, command, warn, request, inform, explain, convince, compliment, apologize, promise, etc.)
UF Illocutionary Acts
BT Speech
RT Dialogs (Language)
Discourse Analysis
Language Patterns
Mutual Intelligibility
Pragmatics

SPEECH AND HEARING CLINICS *Mar. 1980*
CIJE: 32 RIE: 25 GC: 920
UF Hearing Clinics (1968 1980)
Speech Clinics (1968 1980)
BT Clinics
RT Audiology
Auditory Evaluation
Hearing Impairments
Hearing Therapy
Speech
Speech Evaluation
Speech Handicaps
Speech Therapy

Speech Clinics (1968 1980)
USE SPEECH AND HEARING CLINICS

SPEECH COMMUNICATION *Jul. 1977*
CIJE: 2501 RIE: 3357 GC: 450
SN Human interaction in which oral messages are exchanged through verbal and nonverbal symbols (note: do not confuse with the linguistics concept of "oral language")
UF Oral Communication (1966 1977)
Oral Expression (1966 1977)
Speaking (1966 1980)
Speaking Activities (1966 1980)
Speech Communication Curriculum #
Speech Communication Research #
NT Oral Interpretation
Public Speaking
BT Communication (Thought Transfer)
RT Communication Apprehension
Communicative Competence (Languages)
Conversational Language Courses
Dialogs (Language)
Discussion
Group Dynamics
Intercultural Communication
Interpersonal Communication
Interpreters
Interviews
Language
Language Arts
Language Patterns
Language Processing
Language Rhythm
Linguistics
Listening
Nonverbal Communication
Oral Communication Method
Oral English
Oral History
Oral Language
Outlining (Discourse)
Paralinguistics
Persuasive Discourse
Rhetorical Invention
Speech
Speech Curriculum
Speeches
Speech Instruction
Standard Spoken Usage
Theater Arts
Verbal Communication

Speech Communication Curriculum
USE SPEECH COMMUNICATION; SPEECH CURRICULUM

Speech Communication Research
USE COMMUNICATION RESEARCH; SPEECH COMMUNICATION

SPEECH COMPRESSION *Jul. 1966*
CIJE: 60 RIE: 83 GC: 450
SN Separating and transmitting voice communicated words at accelerated rates
BT Speech
RT Language Research

SPEECH CURRICULUM *Jul. 1966*
CIJE: 122 RIE: 379 GC: 450
SN (Note: usually used for curriculum at the secondary and postsecondary levels -- for lower levels, consider "language arts" and other "speech" descriptors)
UF Speech Communication Curriculum #
BT Curriculum
RT Language Arts
Speech
Speech Communication
Speech Instruction
Speech Skills

SPEECH EDUCATION (1966 1980) *Mar. 1980*
CIJE: 145 RIE: 220 GC: 450
SN Invalid descriptor -- see the more precise descriptors "speech curriculum," "speech instruction," and "speech therapy"

SPEECH EVALUATION *Jul. 1966*
CIJE: 198 RIE: 165 GC: 450
SN Determination of an individual's speaking ability and of any needed treatment
BT Medical Evaluation
RT Speech
Speech And Hearing Clinics
Speech Handicaps
Speech Pathology
Speech Tests
Speech Therapy

SPEECH HABITS *Jul. 1966*
CIJE: 272 RIE: 213 GC: 450
BT Behavior Patterns
RT Articulation Impairments
Child Language
Delayed Speech
Habit Formation
Language Patterns
Language Rhythm
Language Usage
Native Speakers
North American English
Paralinguistics
Regional Dialects
Speech
Speech Pathology
Stuttering

Speech Handicapped (1967 1980)
USE SPEECH HANDICAPS

SPEECH HANDICAPS *Jul. 1966*
CIJE: 678 RIE: 449 GC: 220
SN Defects and disturbances that interfere with oral communication
UF Speech Handicapped (1967 1980)
NT Articulation Impairments
Cleft Palate
Delayed Speech
Stuttering
Voice Disorders
BT Disabilities
RT Aphasia
Cerebral Palsy
Communication Disorders
Exceptional Persons
Hearing Impairments
Language Handicaps
Speech
Speech And Hearing Clinics
Speech Evaluation
Speech Improvement
Speech Pathology
Speech Tests
Speech Therapy

SPEECH IMPROVEMENT *Jul. 1966*
CIJE: 140 RIE: 164 GC: 450
SN Enhancement of adequate or socially correct speech -- includes articulation, rhythm, and intonation
UF Enunciation Improvement (1966 1980) #
BT Improvement
RT Articulation (Speech)
Articulation Impairments
Speech
Speech Handicaps
Speech Instruction
Speech Pathology
Speech Tests
Speech Therapy
Stuttering

SPEECH INSTRUCTION *Jul. 1966*
CIJE: 306 RIE: 574 GC: 450
SN Instruction concerned with the development of oral communication skills -- includes various aspects of oral communication such as discussion, conversation, debate, interpretative reading, and drama (note: do not confuse with "speech therapy")
NT Pronunciation Instruction
BT Instruction
RT Kinesthetic Methods
Oral Interpretation
Speech
Speech Communication
Speech Curriculum
Speech Improvement
Speech Skills
Speech Therapy

SPEECH PATHOLOGY *Jul. 1966*
CIJE: 85 RIE: 102 GC: 220
BT Pathology
RT Speech
Speech Evaluation
Speech Habits
Speech Handicaps
Speech Improvement
Speech Therapy

Speech Reading
USE LIPREADING

SPEECH SKILLS *Jul. 1966*
CIJE: 839 RIE: 1156 GC: 450
SN Skills that aid in the production of spoken language
UF Oral Facility
Oral Skills
Speaking Skills
BT Audiolingual Skills
RT Delayed Speech
Eye Voice Span
Interpreters
Language Fluency
Language Patterns
Language Rhythm
Language Styles
Speech
Speech Curriculum
Speech Instruction
Speech Tests
Speech Therapy
Stuttering
Total Communication
Verbal Ability

SPEECH TESTS *Jul. 1966*
CIJE: 59 RIE: 75 GC: 830
SN Tests of the ability to enunciate, pronounce, and communicate orally
UF Articulation Tests
BT Verbal Tests
RT Articulation (Speech)
Articulation Impairments
Diction
Language Tests
Pronunciation
Speech
Speech Evaluation
Speech Handicaps
Speech Improvement
Speech Skills
Speech Therapy

Speech Therapists (1966 1980)
USE SPEECH THERAPY; THERAPISTS

SPEECH THERAPY *Jul. 1966*
CIJE: 461 RIE: 354 GC: 220
SN Treatment of speech disorders (note: do not confuse with "speech instruction")
UF Speech Therapists (1966 1980) #
BT Therapy
RT Articulation Impairments
Cleft Palate
Delayed Speech
Medical Services
Sound Spectrographs
Speech
Speech And Hearing Clinics
Speech Evaluation
Speech Handicaps
Speech Improvement
Speech Instruction
Speech Pathology
Speech Skills
Speech Tests
Stuttering
Visible Speech
Voice Disorders

SPEECHES *Jul. 1966*
CIJE: 747 RIE: 3338 GC: 720
SN (Note: corresponds to pubtype code 150 -- do not use except as the subject of a document)
UF Addresses
Talks
RT Conference Papers
Lecture Method
Personal Narratives
Persuasive Discourse
Public Speaking
Rhetorical Invention
Speech Communication

SPEED READING *Jul. 1966*
CIJE: 79 RIE: 71 GC: 460
SN Rapidity in reading, including skimming and scanning
UF Rapid Reading (1966 1980)
Skimming (Reading)
BT Reading
RT Adult Reading Programs
Reading Rate
Silent Reading

Speed Tests
USE TIMED TESTS

SPELLING *Jul. 1966*
CIJE: 624 RIE: 797 GC: 400
NT Finger Spelling
BT Language Arts
RT Alphabetizing Skills
Capitalization (Alphabetic)
Diacritical Marking
Graphemes
Orthographic Symbols
Phonics
Plurals
Punctuation
Spelling Instruction
Word Lists
Writing (Composition)
Writing Skills

SPELLING INSTRUCTION *Jul. 1966*
CIJE: 318 RIE: 315 GC: 400
BT Instruction
RT Spelling

Sperm Donors
USE TISSUE DONORS

SPIRAL CURRICULUM *Jul. 1966*
CIJE: 30 RIE: 87 GC: 350
SN Curriculum in which students repeat the study of a subject at different grade levels, each time at a higher level of difficulty and in greater depth
BT Curriculum
RT Experimental Curriculum
Instructional Innovation
Sequential Approach

Split Sessions
USE DOUBLE SESSIONS

Split Time
USE DUAL ENROLLMENT

SPONTANEOUS BEHAVIOR *Jul. 1966*
CIJE: 72 RIE: 55 GC: 120
BT Behavior
RT Brainstorming
Emotional Response
Exploratory Behavior
Intuition

SPORT PSYCHOLOGY *Nov. 1982*
CIJE: 39 RIE: 26 GC: 230
SN Study of the affective and behavioral aspects of individuals involved in athletic activities and competition
UF Sports Psychology
BT Psychology

= Two or more Descriptors are used to represent this term.
The term's main entry shows the appropriate coordination.

RT Athletes
Athletic Coaches
Athletics
Physical Education
Physical Fitness
Sportsmanship

Sports
USE ATHLETICS

Sports News
USE ATHLETICS; NEWS MEDIA

Sports Psychology
USE SPORT PSYCHOLOGY

Sports Reporting
USE ATHLETICS; NEWS REPORTING

SPORTSMANSHIP *Jul. 1969*
CIJE: 59 RIE: 55 GC: 470
BT Attitudes
RT Behavior
Behavior Patterns
Morale
Motivation
Physical Education
Self Control
Sport Psychology
Teamwork
Values

SPOUSES *Oct. 1979*
CIJE: 586 RIE: 217 GC: 510
UF Husbands
Married Persons
Wives
BT Groups
RT Divorce
Family (Sociological Unit)
Family Life
Females
Homemakers
Kinship
Males
Marital Status
Marriage
Married Students
Parents
Widowed

Springboard Diving
USE DIVING

SQUASH (GAME) *Feb. 1978*
CIJE: 8 RIE: 6 GC: 470
SN Includes squash rackets and squash tennis
BT Racquet Sports
RT Tennis

Staff Days
USE WORKER DAYS

STAFF DEVELOPMENT *Mar. 1980*
CIJE: 1235 RIE: 2591 GC: 320
SN Employer-sponsored activities, or provisions such as release time and tuition grants, through which existing personnel renew or acquire skills, knowledge, and attitudes related to job or personal development
UF Personnel Development
Staff Improvement (1966 1980)
NT Faculty Development
BT Labor Force Development
RT Continuing Education
Industrial Training
Inplant Programs
Inservice Education
Management Development
Off The Job Training
On The Job Training
Organizational Development
Personnel
Professional Development
Staff Orientation

Staff Evaluation
USE PERSONNEL EVALUATION

Staff Improvement (1966 1980)
USE STAFF DEVELOPMENT

STAFF MEETINGS *Jul. 1966*
CIJE: 48 RIE: 36 GC: 320
BT Meetings
RT Faculty Workload
Personnel

Staff Offices
USE OFFICES (FACILITIES)

STAFF ORIENTATION *Jul. 1966*
CIJE: 83 RIE: 180 GC: 320
SN The process or programs an organization uses to make its personnel aware of policies or duties
BT Orientation
RT Faculty Handbooks
Personnel
Staff Development
Teacher Orientation

STAFF ROLE *Jul. 1966*
CIJE: 546 RIE: 876 GC: 320
UF Personnel Role
RT Counselor Role
Faculty Handbooks
Personnel
Teacher Role

STAFF UTILIZATION *Jul. 1966*
CIJE: 375 RIE: 764 GC: 320
BT Labor Utilization
RT Administration
Differentiated Staffs
Faculty Workload
Personnel
Personnel Management
School Cadres

Stage Theory
USE DEVELOPMENTAL STAGES

STAGES (FACILITIES) *Mar. 1980*
CIJE: 23 RIE: 39 GC: 920
SN Platforms raised above floor level in theaters, lecture halls, classrooms, etc.
UF Stages (1969 1980)
BT Structural Elements (Construction)
RT Arts Centers
Auditoriums
Multipurpose Classrooms
Music Facilities
Theaters

Stages (1969 1980)
USE STAGES (FACILITIES)

Stages Of Development
USE DEVELOPMENTAL STAGES

Staggered Sessions
USE EXTENDED SCHOOL DAY

Stammering
USE STUTTERING

Standard Error Of Estimate
USE ERROR OF MEASUREMENT

Standard Error Of Measurement (1970 1980)
USE ERROR OF MEASUREMENT

STANDARD SPOKEN USAGE *Jul. 1966*
CIJE: 708 RIE: 823 GC: 450
SN Customary use or employment of language, words, expressions, etc. by native speakers in nonformal situations
UF Colloquial Standard Usage
Informal Conversational Usage
BT Language Usage
RT Conversational Language Courses
Interpersonal Communication
Language Patterns
Language Standardization
Language Styles
Nonstandard Dialects
North American English
Oral English
Oral Language
Social Dialects
Sociolinguistics
Speech Communication

STANDARDIZED TESTS *Jul. 1966*
CIJE: 1126 RIE: 1642 GC: 830
SN Tests for which content has been selected and checked empirically, norms have been established, uniform methods of administering have been developed, and which may be scored with a relatively high degree of objectivity
BT Tests
RT College Entrance Examinations
Criterion Referenced Tests
Item Analysis
Licensing Examinations (Professions)
Norm Referenced Tests
Objective Tests
Testing Programs
Test Norms

STANDARDS *Jul. 1966*
CIJE: 1548 RIE: 1887 GC: 520
SN Rules, principles, or criteria by which levels or degrees of adequacy, acceptability, quantity, quality, or value are measured or judged (note: use a more specific term if possible)
UF Professional Standards
NT Academic Standards
Administrative Principles
Behavior Standards
Court Doctrine
Criteria
Dress Codes
Educational Principles
Environmental Standards
Equipment Standards
Food Standards
Labor Standards
Laws
Library Standards
Living Standards
Metric System
Middle Class Standards
Parliamentary Procedures
Qualifications
Residence Requirements
Scientific Principles
Specifications
State Standards
Textbook Standards
RT Accreditation (Institutions)
Achievement
Audits (Verification)
Certification
Codification
Credentials
Eligibility
Evaluation
Failure
Inspection
Measurement
Models
Norms
Objectives
Policy
Prerequisites
Quality Control
Quotas
Sanctions
Scores
Success
Teaching Models
Values

STATE ACTION *Jul. 1966*
CIJE: 212 RIE: 438 GC: 610
RT Government Role
State Aid
State Departments Of Education
State Government
State Legislation
State Programs

STATE AGENCIES *Jul. 1966*
CIJE: 270 RIE: 1060 GC: 610
NT State Departments Of Education
State Licensing Boards
BT Public Agencies
RT Agency Role
State Boards Of Education
State Government
State Libraries
State Officials
State Programs
Statewide Planning
Urban Renewal Agencies
Welfare Agencies

STATE AID *Jul. 1966*
CIJE: 840 RIE: 2155 GC: 620
UF Provincial Aid
State Assistance
State Financial Aid
State Support
NT Foundation Programs
Full State Funding
State Federal Aid
RT Block Grants
Categorical Aid
Educational Finance
Eligibility
Equalization Aid
Finance Reform
Financial Support
Government School Relationship
Grantsmanship
Incentive Grants
Private School Aid
Public Support
School Funds
School Support
State Action
State Government
State Programs
State School District Relationship
State Schools
State Standards
Training Allowances

State Assistance
USE STATE AID

STATE BOARDS OF EDUCATION *Jul. 1969*
CIJE: 209 RIE: 716 GC: 330
SN Groups of appointed or elected officials who are responsible for the management and direction of public education in a state (note: do not confuse with "state departments of education")
UF State Committees On Education
State School Boards
BT Boards Of Education
RT Public Education
State Agencies
State Curriculum Guides
State Departments Of Education
State School District Relationship
State Standards

State Boards Of Licensing
USE STATE LICENSING BOARDS

STATE CHURCH SEPARATION *Jul. 1966*
CIJE: 236 RIE: 172 GC: 610
UF Church State Separation
BT Relationship
RT Churches
Church Role
Federal Government
Intellectual Freedom
Private School Aid
Religion
Religious Holidays
State Government

STATE COLLEGES *Jul. 1966*
CIJE: 267 RIE: 1596 GC: 340
SN Degree-granting institutions of higher education that are funded and controlled by a state
NT State Universities
BT Public Colleges
State Schools
RT Agricultural Colleges
Community Colleges
Land Grant Universities
Multicampus Colleges
Public Education
Two Year Colleges

State Committees On Education
USE STATE BOARDS OF EDUCATION

State Court Litigation
USE COURT LITIGATION; STATE COURTS

STATE COURTS *Mar. 1980*
CIJE: 72 RIE: 132 GC: 610
UF State Court Litigation #
State Supreme Courts
BT Courts
RT Court Litigation
Federal Courts
State Government
State Legislation

= Two or more Descriptors are used to represent this term.
The term's main entry shows the appropriate coordination.

State Curriculum Bulletins
USE STATE CURRICULUM GUIDES

STATE CURRICULUM GUIDES *Jul. 1966*
CIJE: 39 RIE: 967 GC: 730
UF State Curriculum Bulletins
State Syllabi
BT Curriculum Guides
RT Curriculum
State Boards Of Education
State Departments Of Education
State Programs
State Standards
Statewide Planning

STATE DEPARTMENTS OF EDUCATION *Jul. 1966*
CIJE: 396 RIE: 1536 GC: 330
SN Organizations, composed of the chief state school officer and staff, that carry out work delegated to them by law (note: do not confuse with "state boards of education")
UF State Education Agencies
BT Departments
State Agencies
RT Governing Boards
Public Education
State Action
State Boards Of Education
State Curriculum Guides
State Programs
State School District Relationship

State Education Agencies
USE STATE DEPARTMENTS OF EDUCATION

STATE FEDERAL AID *Jul. 1966*
CIJE: 278 RIE: 662 GC: 620
SN Joint financial or other support by federal and state governments
UF Federal State Aid
State Federal Support (1966 1977)
BT Federal Aid
State Aid
RT Educational Finance
Equalization Aid
Financial Support
Full State Funding

State Federal Relationship
USE FEDERAL STATE RELATIONSHIP

State Federal Support (1966 1977)
USE STATE FEDERAL AID

State Financial Aid
USE STATE AID

State Foreign Language Supervisors (1967 1980)
USE SECOND LANGUAGE INSTRUCTION; STATE SUPERVISORS

STATE GOVERNMENT *Jul. 1966*
CIJE: 499 RIE: 1052 GC: 610
UF Provincial Government
State Government Programs #
BT Government (Administrative Body)
RT Federal State Relationship
Government Employees
Government School Relationship
School District Autonomy
State Action
State Agencies
State Aid
State Church Separation
State Courts
State History
State Legislation
State Officials
State Programs
State School District Relationship
States Powers

State Government Programs
USE STATE GOVERNMENT; STATE PROGRAMS

STATE HISTORY *Aug. 1977*
CIJE: 66 RIE: 225 GC: 430
SN History associated with individual states within the united states
BT United States History
RT Local History
State Government

State Laws (1966 1974)
USE STATE LEGISLATION

STATE LEGISLATION *Jul. 1966*
CIJE: 1248 RIE: 2772 GC: 610
UF State Laws (1966 1974)
State Recreation Legislation (1966 1978) #
NT School Attendance Legislation
BT Legislation
RT Federal Legislation
Laws
Legislators
Local Legislation
State Action
State Courts
State Government
State Standards

STATE LIBRARIES *Jul. 1966*
CIJE: 72 RIE: 435 GC: 710
SN Government libraries, maintained by state funds, that preserve state records and publications for use by state officials and citizens
UF Provincial Libraries
BT Government Libraries
RT Archives
State Agencies

STATE LICENSING BOARDS *Jul. 1966*
CIJE: 107 RIE: 206 GC: 610
SN Agencies that authorize the practice of a profession or operation of a business in a state after determining that established standards and requirements have been met
UF State Boards Of Licensing
BT State Agencies
RT Accrediting Agencies
Certification
Licensing Examinations (Professions)
Professional Education
State Standards
Testing Programs

STATE NORMS *Mar. 1980*
CIJE: 8 RIE: 67 GC: 820
SN Statistical description of the typical performance, behavior, form, function, etc. of a particular state or province (note: use only for numerical data and not for subjectively described standards)
BT Norms
RT Local Norms
National Norms
State Surveys

STATE OF THE ART REVIEWS *May. 1972*
CIJE: 4207 RIE: 2077 GC: 730
SN Exhaustive, systematic, and often critical reviews of the published or unpublished material on a topic
BT Publications
RT Bibliographies
Literature Reviews
Surveys

STATE OFFICIALS *Jul. 1966*
CIJE: 55 RIE: 162 GC: 610
NT State Supervisors
BT Public Officials
RT County Officials
Extension Agents
Legislators
State Agencies
State Government

State Planning
USE STATEWIDE PLANNING

State Police (1966 1980)
USE POLICE

STATE PROGRAMS *Jul. 1966*
CIJE: 902 RIE: 5340 GC: 610
UF State Government Programs #
Statewide Programs
BT Programs
RT County Programs
Educational Assessment
Federal Programs
Interstate Programs
State Action
State Agencies
State Aid
State Curriculum Guides
State Departments Of Education
State Government
State Surveys
Statewide Planning

State Recreation Legislation (1966 1978)
USE RECREATION LEGISLATION; STATE LEGISLATION

State School Boards
USE STATE BOARDS OF EDUCATION

STATE SCHOOL DISTRICT RELATIONSHIP *Jul. 1966*
CIJE: 335 RIE: 878 GC: 330
SN Interaction or dealings between a state or provincial government and local school districts
BT Government School Relationship
RT Educational Finance
Intermediate Administrative Units
School District Autonomy
School Districts
School District Spending
State Aid
State Boards Of Education
State Departments Of Education
State Government
State Standards
Statewide Planning

STATE SCHOOLS *Jul. 1966*
CIJE: 48 RIE: 98 GC: 340
SN Educational institutions primarily supported and controlled by provincial or central governments, especially schools providing special services not duplicated locally, e.g., teachers colleges, schools for the blind, armed forces dependents schools
NT State Colleges
BT Schools
RT Public Education
Public Schools
State Aid

STATE STANDARDS *Jul. 1966*
CIJE: 359 RIE: 1582 GC: 610
BT Standards
RT Accreditation (Institutions)
Accrediting Agencies
Faculty Workload
State Aid
State Boards Of Education
State Curriculum Guides
State Legislation
State Licensing Boards
State School District Relationship

STATE SUPERVISORS *Jul. 1966*
CIJE: 62 RIE: 94 GC: 360
UF State Foreign Language Supervisors (1967 1980) #
BT State Officials
Supervisors
RT Teacher Supervision

State Support
USE STATE AID

State Supreme Courts
USE STATE COURTS

STATE SURVEYS *Jul. 1966*
CIJE: 625 RIE: 3309 GC: 810
SN Statewide investigations of a field to determine current practices, trends, and/or norms (note: as of oct81, use as a minor descriptor for examples of this kind of survey -- use as a major descriptor only as the subject of a document)
UF Provincial Surveys
BT Surveys
RT Educational Assessment
National Surveys
State Norms
State Programs
Statewide Planning

State Syllabi
USE STATE CURRICULUM GUIDES

STATE UNIVERSITIES *Jul. 1966*
CIJE: 500 RIE: 1717 GC: 340
SN Degree-granting institutions of higher education, funded and controlled by the state, that typically include a liberal arts undergraduate college, a graduate school, and two or more undergraduate and graduate professional schools
BT State Colleges
Universities
RT Land Grant Universities
Multicampus Colleges
Professional Education
Public Education
Research Universities

STATES POWERS *Jul. 1966*
CIJE: 33 RIE: 65 GC: 610
UF States Rights
RT Federal State Relationship
State Government

States Rights
USE STATES POWERS

Statewide Coordination
USE STATEWIDE PLANNING

STATEWIDE PLANNING *Oct. 1970*
CIJE: 413 RIE: 2809 GC: 330
UF State Planning
Statewide Coordination
BT Planning
RT Blue Ribbon Commissions
Coordination
Federal State Relationship
Institutional Cooperation
Master Plans
Planning Commissions
Regional Planning
State Agencies
State Curriculum Guides
State Programs
State School District Relationship
State Surveys

Statewide Programs
USE STATE PROGRAMS

Static Controls
USE ELECTRONIC CONTROL

STATISTICAL ANALYSIS *Jul. 1966*
CIJE: 2851 RIE: 4395 GC: 820
SN Application of statistical processes and theory to the compilation, presentation, discussion, and interpretation of numerical data (note: use a more specific term if possible)
UF Comparative Statistics (1966 1980) #
Quantitative Research (Statistics)
Statistical Methods
Statistical Processes
NT Analysis Of Covariance
Analysis Of Variance
Bayesian Statistics
Correlation
Effect Size
Error Of Measurement
Goodness Of Fit
Item Analysis
Judgment Analysis Technique
Least Squares Statistics
Maximum Likelihood Statistics
Meta Analysis
Multivariate Analysis
Regression (Statistics)
Statistical Distributions
Statistical Inference
Statistical Significance
BT Data Analysis
RT Bibliometrics
Census Figures
Data Interpretation
Employment Statistics
Equated Scores
Expectancy Tables
Generalizability Theory
Hypothesis Testing
Interaction
Item Sampling
Library Statistics
Matrices
Measurement
Monte Carlo Methods
Nonparametric Statistics
Norms
Predictor Variables

= Two or more Descriptors are used to represent this term.
The term's main entry shows the appropriate coordination.

Probability
Psychometrics
Q Methodology
Reliability
Research
Research Methodology
Research Problems
Sample Size
Sampling
Scaling
School Statistics
Scores
Statistical Bias
Statistical Data
Statistical Studies
Statistics
Test Theory
Trend Analysis
Validity

Statistical Association Methods
USE CORRELATION

STATISTICAL BIAS *Aug. 1971*
CIJE: 142 RIE: 141 GC: 820
SN Characteristics of an experimental or sampling design, or the mathematical treatment of data, that systematically affects the results of a study so as to produce incorrect, unjustified, or inappropriate inferences or conclusions
BT Bias
RT Attrition (Research Studies)
Error Of Measurement
Error Patterns
Matched Groups
Sample Size
Sampling
Statistical Analysis
Statistics
Test Bias

Statistical Bibliography
USE BIBLIOMETRICS

STATISTICAL DATA *Jul. 1966*
CIJE: 934 RIE: 4437 GC: 820
SN (Note: corresponds to pubtype code 110 -- do not use except as the subject of a document)
NT Census Figures
Employment Statistics
Library Statistics
Norms
School Statistics
Social Indicators
BT Data
RT Generalizability Theory
Measurement
Meta Analysis
Raw Scores
Reliability
Statistical Analysis
Statistical Distributions
Statistical Inference
Statistical Studies
Statistical Surveys
Statistics
Tests
Trend Analysis
True Scores
Validity

STATISTICAL DISTRIBUTIONS *Oct. 1980*
CIJE: 97 RIE: 48 GC: 480
SN Tables or graphs of observed, predicted, or theoretical data indicating either the probability or the number of instances to be found along successive intervals of an ordered scale -- also, the mathematical functions of distributions
UF Distributions (Statistics)
Frequency Distributions
BT Statistical Analysis
Statistics
RT Classification
Expectancy Tables
Functions (Mathematics)
Generalizability Theory
Monte Carlo Methods
Norms
Probability
Reliability
Scores
Statistical Data
Validity

STATISTICAL INFERENCE *Jan. 1986*
CIJE: RIE: GC: 480
SN The computation or prediction of statistics for a collective or whole (population) on the basis of a sample
UF Inferential Statistics #
BT Data Interpretation
Inferences
Statistical Analysis
RT Bayesian Statistics
Correlation
Estimation (Mathematics)
Expectancy Tables
Generalizability Theory
Hypothesis Testing
Probability
Regression (Statistics)
Sampling
Statistical Data
Statistical Significance
Statistics

Statistical Linguistics
USE MATHEMATICAL LINGUISTICS

Statistical Methods
USE STATISTICAL ANALYSIS

Statistical Processes
USE STATISTICAL ANALYSIS

STATISTICAL SIGNIFICANCE *Mar. 1980*
CIJE: 297 RIE: 207 GC: 820
SN Statistical method for stating the probability that an observation shows a condition or relationship to exist when in fact it does not
UF Significance Measures
Tests Of Significance (1966 1980)
BT Statistical Analysis
RT Analysis Of Covariance
Analysis Of Variance
Bayesian Statistics
Effect Size
Goodness Of Fit
Hypothesis Testing
Least Squares Statistics
Maximum Likelihood Statistics
Probability
Research Design
Statistical Inference
Statistics

STATISTICAL STUDIES *Jul. 1966*
CIJE: 272 RIE: 660 GC: 810
SN Studies designed to investigate, evaluate, or improve statistical techniques (note: as of oct81, use as a minor descriptor for examples of this kind of research -- use as a major descriptor only as the subject of a document -- prior to oct81, this term did not carry a scope note -- do not confuse with "statistical surveys")
BT Research
RT Monte Carlo Methods
Nonparametric Statistics
Sampling
Statistical Analysis
Statistical Data
Statistical Surveys

STATISTICAL SURVEYS *Jul. 1966*
CIJE: 171 RIE: 630 GC: 810
SN Investigations that employ statistical techniques or gather statistical data to discover current practices, trends, and/or norms (note: as of oct81, use as a minor descriptor for examples of this kind of survey -- use as a major descriptor only as the subject of a document -- do not confuse with "statistical studies")
BT Surveys
RT Sampling
Statistical Data
Statistical Studies

Statistical Theory
USE STATISTICS

STATISTICS *Jul. 1966*
CIJE: 625 RIE: 603 GC: 480
SN Branch of mathematics dealing with collections of quantitative data (note: prior to mar80, the instructions "mathematical statistics and statistical theory, use statistical analysis" were carried in the thesaurus -- do not confuse with "statistical data" or "test results")
UF Inferential Statistics #
Mathematical Statistics
Statistical Theory
NT Bayesian Statistics
Least Squares Statistics
Maximum Likelihood Statistics
Nonparametric Statistics
Sampling
Statistical Distributions
BT Mathematics
RT Computational Linguistics
Correlation
Effect Size
Estimation (Mathematics)
Expectancy Tables
Game Theory
Goodness Of Fit
Mathematical Logic
Mathematical Models
Monte Carlo Methods
Multiple Regression Analysis
Numbers
Predictive Measurement
Probability
Regression (Statistics)
Statistical Analysis
Statistical Bias
Statistical Data
Statistical Inference
Statistical Significance

STATUS *Jul. 1966*
CIJE: 393 RIE: 296 GC: 520
NT Citizenship
Economic Status
Employment Level
Ethnic Status
Full Time Equivalency
Group Status
Marital Status
Retirement
Seniority
Social Status
Socioeconomic Status
RT Eligibility
Prerequisites
Professional Recognition
Recognition (Achievement)
Reputation
Social Class
Social Stratification
Status Need

STATUS NEED *Jul. 1966*
CIJE: 90 RIE: 63 GC: 120
SN Psychological need for recognition
BT Psychological Needs
RT Achievement Need
Affiliation Need
Prestige
Professional Recognition
Recognition (Achievement)
Social Status
Status

Statutory Rape
USE RAPE

STEALING *Jun. 1969*
CIJE: 89 RIE: 69 GC: 530
UF Book Thefts (1969 1980) #
Thefts
NT Plagiarism
BT Antisocial Behavior
RT Codes Of Ethics
Crime
Delinquency
Discipline Problems
Ownership
School Security
Security Personnel
Victims Of Crime

Steel Foundries
USE FOUNDRIES

Steel Industry (1967 1980)
USE METAL INDUSTRY

Stenographers (1966 1981)
USE SHORTHAND

Stenography (1967 1980)
USE SHORTHAND

Step In Step Out Students
USE STOPOUTS

STEPFAMILY *Mar. 1982*
CIJE: 39 RIE: 15 GC: 520
SN Persons related as a result of the remarriage of a parent (note: for specificity, coordinate with other terms -- for example, with "parent child relationship" (for stepparenting), with "fathers" (for stepfathers), and so on)
BT Family (Sociological Unit)
RT Biological Parents
Extended Family
Family Life
Family Relationship
Family Structure
Kinship
Nuclear Family
Remarriage

Stereopsis (1968 1980)
USE DEPTH PERCEPTION

STEREOTYPES *Jul. 1966*
CIJE: 782 RIE: 529 GC: 540
NT Ethnic Stereotypes
Sex Stereotypes
Teacher Stereotypes
BT Attitudes
RT Cultural Images
Ethnocentrism
Expectation
Labeling (Of Persons)
Role Perception

Stickers
USE ADHESIVES

STIMULANTS *Sep. 1968*
CIJE: 64 RIE: 69 GC: 210
BT Stimuli
RT Drug Abuse
Drug Rehabilitation
Drug Use
Narcotics
Physiology
Sensory Experience
Smoking
Tobacco

STIMULATION *Feb. 1971*
CIJE: 239 RIE: 168 GC: 110
SN Arousal or excitation of an organism -- technically, the arousal of neural impulses, but also used more generally for the elicitation of physical, cognitive, or emotional responses
RT Arousal Patterns
Biofeedback
Conditioning
Motivation
Neurological Organization
Stimuli

STIMULI *Jun. 1969*
CIJE: 380 RIE: 171 GC: 110
UF Conditioned Stimulus (1966 1980)
NT Auditory Stimuli
Cues
Electrical Stimuli
Stimulants
Verbal Stimuli
Visual Stimuli
RT Conditioning
Desensitization
Dimensional Preference
Motivation
Novelty (Stimulus Dimension)
Perception
Psychophysiology
Redundancy
Responses
Sensory Experience
Stimulation
Stimulus Generalization

Stimulus Behavior (1966 1980)
USE RESPONSES

= Two or more Descriptors are used to represent this term.
The term's main entry shows the appropriate coordination.

STIMULUS DEVICES (1966 1980) *Mar. 1980*
CIJE: 121 RIE: 79 GC: 910
SN Invalid descriptor -- used for both mechanical devices and techniques of generating student interest -- use "stimuli" and "stimulation" respectively for these concepts

STIMULUS GENERALIZATION *Jul. 1966*
CIJE: 98 RIE: 62 GC: 110
SN Process by which a response originally conditioned by a given stimulus may subsequently be elicited by other similar stimuli
BT Generalization
RT Mediation Theory
Patterned Responses
Stimuli

Stimulus Synthesis
USE PATTERNED RESPONSES

Stockpiles
USE SUPPLIES

STOPOUTS *Aug. 1986*
CIJE: 17 RIE: 32 GC: 510
SN Individuals who briefly interrupt their education, vocation, etc., to pursue other activities (note: do not confuse with "reentry students/workers")
UF Step In Step Out Students
BT Groups
RT Academic Persistence
Adult Students
Attendance
College Students
Dropouts
Enrollment
Labor Turnover
Leaves Of Absence
Persistence
Reentry Students
Reentry Workers
School Holding Power

STORAGE *Oct. 1969*
CIJE: 87 RIE: 92 GC: 920
NT Equipment Storage
Information Storage
RT Design Requirements
Facility Requirements
Facility Utilization Research
Interior Space
Space Utilization
Warehouses

Storage Batteries
USE ELECTRIC BATTERIES

STORY GRAMMAR *Aug. 1986*
CIJE: 34 RIE: 41 GC: 460
SN Order or structure of elements in a textual passage, representing the meaning intended by the author and used to explain and predict the comprehension and/or recall of readers -- analogous to nouns, verbs, and other elements of traditional sentence grammar, story grammar's elements are such things as settings, episodes, and events
RT Coherence
Cohesion (Written Composition)
Discourse Analysis
Narration
Readability
Reader Text Relationship
Reading Comprehension
Reading Instruction
Reading Writing Relationship
Story Reading
Story Telling
Writing (Composition)
Writing Instruction
Writing Skills

Story Problems (Mathematics)
USE WORD PROBLEMS (MATHEMATICS)

STORY READING *Jul. 1966*
CIJE: 179 RIE: 202 GC: 460
BT Reading
RT Reading Aloud To Others
Story Grammar
Story Telling

STORY TELLING *Jul. 1966*
CIJE: 361 RIE: 283 GC: 720
BT Language Arts
RT Narration
Reading Aloud To Others
Story Grammar
Story Reading

STRABISMUS *May. 1974*
CIJE: 10 RIE: 3 GC: 220
SN Lack of coordination of eye muscles so that the two eyes do not focus on the same point
UF Cross Eyes
Heterophoria (1968 1974)
Heterotropia (1968 1974)
Walleyes
BT Visual Impairments
RT Eye Fixations
Vision
Visual Acuity

Stradaptive Testing
USE ADAPTIVE TESTING

STRANGER REACTIONS *Feb. 1975*
CIJE: 102 RIE: 57 GC: 120
SN Reactions to strangers (positive, negative, or mixed in character) -- often refers to infant behavior patterns but may be used with any age group
UF Xenophobia
BT Responses
RT Emotional Response
Infant Behavior
Social Behavior

Stream Pollution
USE WATER POLLUTION

Street Layouts
USE TRAFFIC CIRCULATION

Street Parking Areas
USE PARKING FACILITIES

Street People
USE HOMELESS PEOPLE

Strength (Biology)
USE MUSCULAR STRENGTH

STRESS (PHONOLOGY) *Mar. 1976*
CIJE: 73 RIE: 71 GC: 450
BT Suprasegmentals
RT Intonation
Morphophonemics
Paralinguistics
Phonetics
Phonology
Structural Analysis (Linguistics)
Syllables

STRESS MANAGEMENT *Oct. 1983*
CIJE: 175 RIE: 136 GC: 230
SN Techniques to handle psychological and/or physical tensions and their causes
RT Adjustment (To Environment)
Adventure Education
Catharsis
Coping
Counseling Techniques
Health Education
Relaxation Training
Stress Variables

STRESS VARIABLES *Jul. 1966*
CIJE: 1682 RIE: 987 GC: 230
SN Causes and consequences of psychological and physiological strain
RT Burnout
Crowding
Diseases
Exercise Physiology
Health
Hypertension
Physiology
Psychological Patterns
Response Style (Tests)
Stress Management

STRIKES *Jul. 1966*
CIJE: 124 RIE: 97 GC: 630
NT Teacher Strikes
RT Arbitration
Collective Bargaining
Labor Demands
Labor Force
Labor Problems
Negotiation Impasses
School Boycotts
Unions

STRUCTURAL ANALYSIS (LINGUISTICS) *Mar. 1980*
CIJE: 187 RIE: 136 GC: 450
SN (Note: prior to mar80, this concept was indexed under "structural analysis")
NT Discourse Analysis
Tagmemic Analysis
BT Evaluation Methods
RT Componential Analysis
Computational Linguistics
Context Clues
Decoding (Reading)
Descriptive Linguistics
Diachronic Linguistics
Error Analysis (Language)
Graphemes
Idioms
Intonation
Language Processing
Language Research
Language Universals
Linguistics
Machine Translation
Miscue Analysis
Reading Instruction
Sentence Diagraming
Sentence Structure
Stress (Phonology)
Suffixes
Suprasegmentals
Syllables

STRUCTURAL ANALYSIS (SCIENCE) *Mar. 1980*
CIJE: 52 RIE: 1 GC: 490
SN (Note: prior to mar80, this concept was indexed under "structural analysis")
BT Evaluation Methods
RT Atomic Structure
Chemical Analysis
Chemical Bonding
Crystallography
Molecular Structure
Spectroscopy

STRUCTURAL ANALYSIS (1966 1980) *Mar. 1980*
CIJE: 636 RIE: 832 GC: 450
SN Invalid descriptor -- originally intended as a linguistics term but used indiscriminately -- see "structural analysis (linguistics)" and "structural analysis (science)" -- see also such descriptors as "cognitive structures," "chemical analysis," "literary criticism," and "group structure," or such identifiers as "musical analysis," "structure of knowledge," and "structural learning"

Structural Arrangement
USE ORGANIZATION

STRUCTURAL BUILDING SYSTEMS *Jul. 1966*
CIJE: 35 RIE: 83 GC: 920
SN Combination of such structural members and methods as foundations, post and beam, vaults, or lift-slabs to form the structural frame or shell of a building
BT Building Systems
RT Buildings
Civil Engineering
Construction (Process)
Construction Programs
Masonry
Prefabrication
Prestressed Concrete
Systems Building

STRUCTURAL ELEMENTS (CONSTRUCTION) *Mar. 1980*
CIJE: 93 RIE: 151 GC: 920
SN Structural, dimensional, functional, or aesthetic components of constructed entities (e.g., buildings, facilities, vehicles)
UF Architectural Elements (1968 1980)
NT Acoustic Insulation
Building Systems
Ceilings
Chimneys
Doors
Flooring
Glass Walls
Roofing
Space Dividers
Stages (Facilities)
Windows
RT Accessibility (For Disabled)
Architectural Character
Architecture
Building Design
Buildings
Construction (Process)
Construction Materials
Construction Needs
Educational Facilities
Educational Facilities Design
Facilities
Flexible Facilities
Physical Mobility
Prefabrication
Systems Building

Structural Equations
USE PATH ANALYSIS

STRUCTURAL GRAMMAR *Jul. 1966*
CIJE: 151 RIE: 179 GC: 450
BT Linguistic Theory
RT Descriptive Linguistics
Form Classes (Languages)
Function Words
Grammar
Sentence Structure
Structural Linguistics
Syntax
Tagmemic Analysis
Traditional Grammar

STRUCTURAL LINGUISTICS *Jul. 1966*
CIJE: 229 RIE: 194 GC: 450
BT Linguistics
RT Applied Linguistics
Diachronic Linguistics
Sentence Structure
Structural Grammar

STRUCTURAL UNEMPLOYMENT *Aug. 1986*
CIJE: 6 RIE: 9 GC: 630
SN Unemployment resulting from structural changes in an economy (and consequent mismatches between jobs and skills), caused by technological developments, population shifts, industry relocations, modified consumer patterns, altered government policies, etc. -- may often be inherent and persistent in dynamic market economies
UF Technological Unemployment
BT Unemployment
RT Dislocated Workers
Economic Change
Employment Potential
Industrial Structure
International Trade
Job Layoff
Job Skills
Labor Economics
Labor Market
Population Trends
Skill Obsolescence
Technological Advancement
Underemployment

Structural Work Occupations
USE BUILDING TRADES

Sts (Science Technology Society)
USE SCIENCE AND SOCIETY

Student Ability (1966 1980)
USE ACADEMIC ABILITY

Student Achievement
USE ACADEMIC ACHIEVEMENT

Student Activities (Extraclass)
USE EXTRACURRICULAR ACTIVITIES

STUDENT ADJUSTMENT *Jul. 1966*
CIJE: 482 RIE: 552 GC: 320
SN (Note: prior to mar80, the thesaurus carried the instruction "maladjusted students, use maladjustment")
UF Maladjusted Students
School Adjustment
Student Maladjustment
BT Adjustment (To Environment)
Student Behavior
RT Continuation Students
Faculty Advisers
Foreign Student Advisers
School Orientation
Student Alienation
Student Characteristics
Students

Student Affairs Services
USE STUDENT PERSONNEL SERVICES

Student Affairs Workers
USE STUDENT PERSONNEL WORKERS

Student Aid
USE STUDENT FINANCIAL AID

STUDENT ALIENATION *Jul. 1966*
CIJE: 538 RIE: 253 GC: 320
BT Alienation
RT Activism
Dropout Attitudes
Generation Gap
Student Adjustment
Student Attitudes
Student Behavior
Student Characteristics
Students
Student Subcultures

Student Application (1966 1980)
USE COLLEGE APPLICANTS

Student Appraisal
USE STUDENT EVALUATION

Student Aptitude
USE ACADEMIC APTITUDE

Student Assignments
USE ASSIGNMENTS

STUDENT ATTITUDES *Jul. 1966*
CIJE: 9071 RIE: 9176 GC: 320
SN Attitudes of, not toward, students (note: prior to apr80, the use of this term was not restricted by a scope note)
UF Student Opinion (1966 1980)
BT Attitudes
RT Childhood Attitudes
Classroom Environment
Student Alienation
Student Behavior
Student Characteristics
Student Evaluation Of Teacher Performance
Student Motivation
Student Reaction
Student Role
Students
Student Subcultures
Student Teacher Attitudes

STUDENT ATTRITION *Mar. 1980*
CIJE: 173 RIE: 435 GC: 320
SN Reduction in a school's student population as a result of transfers or dropouts (note: do not confuse with the research methodology term "attrition (research studies)")
UF Attrition (Students)
BT Enrollment
RT Academic Persistence
College Attendance
Dropout Rate
Dropout Research
Dropouts
Expulsion
School Closing
School Demography
School Holding Power
Students
Withdrawal (Education)

STUDENT BEHAVIOR *Jul. 1966*
CIJE: 2560 RIE: 2242 GC: 310
NT Student Adjustment
Student Participation
BT Behavior
RT Behavioral Objectives
Classroom Communication
Classroom Observation Techniques
Dress Codes
Due Process
Student Alienation
Student Attitudes
Student Characteristics
Student Evaluation
Student Rights
Student Role
Students
Student Subcultures
Time On Task

STUDENT CENTERED CURRICULUM *May. 1971*
CIJE: 400 RIE: 485 GC: 310
SN Systematic group of courses or sequence of subjects that utilizes student experiences, backgrounds, and interests
UF Child Centered Curriculum
Organic Curriculum
BT Curriculum
RT Behavioral Objectives
Curriculum Design
Montessori Method
Open Education
Student Characteristics
Student Interests
Students

Student Centers
USE STUDENT UNIONS

STUDENT CERTIFICATION *Jul. 1966*
CIJE: 57 RIE: 120 GC: 330
SN Evidence that a student meets the standards of performance required for employment or further training (note: prior to mar80, the use of this term was not restricted by a scope note)
BT Certification
RT Competency Based Education
Continuing Education Units
Educational Certificates
Grade Equivalent Scores
High School Equivalency Programs
Minimum Competency Testing
Student Evaluation
Students

STUDENT CHARACTERISTICS *Jul. 1966*
CIJE: 3171 RIE: 5813 GC: 320
RT Academic Ability
Academic Achievement
Academic Aptitude
Aptitude Treatment Interaction
Individual Characteristics
Student Adjustment
Student Alienation
Student Attitudes
Student Behavior
Student Centered Curriculum
Student Development
Student Evaluation
Student Experience
Student Interests
Student Motivation
Student Needs
Student Participation
Student Reaction
Student Responsibility
Student Role
Students
Student Subcultures

STUDENT COLLEGE RELATIONSHIP *Jul. 1966*
CIJE: 825 RIE: 861 GC: 320
SN The relationship between a college and its students
UF College Student Relationship
BT Student School Relationship
RT Activism
Codes Of Ethics
College Environment
Colleges
College Students
Experimental Colleges
Faculty Advisers
Faculty College Relationship
Foreign Student Advisers
Ombudsmen
Self Supporting Students
Student Needs
Student Welfare
Teacher Student Relationship

STUDENT COSTS *Jul. 1966*
CIJE: 281 RIE: 729 GC: 620
SN Amount of money required by a student for expenses such as tuition, fees, room and board, books and supplies, clothes, travel, recreation, and incidentals (note: use a more specific term if possible -- do not confuse with "expenditure per student" -- prior to mar80, this term did not carry a scope note)
UF College Costs (Incurred By Students)
NT Instructional Student Costs
Noninstructional Student Costs
BT Costs
RT Access To Education
Assistantships
Educational Economics
Educational Equity (Finance)
Educational Finance
Educational Vouchers
Expenditure Per Student
Fees
Fellowships
Grants
Need Analysis (Student Financial Aid)
Parent Financial Contribution
Proprietary Schools
Scholarship Funds
Scholarships
Self Supporting Students
Student Financial Aid
Student Loan Programs
Students
Tuition

Student Councils
USE STUDENT GOVERNMENT

Student Credit Hours
USE CREDITS

STUDENT DEVELOPED MATERIALS *Jul. 1966*
CIJE: 463 RIE: 286 GC: 720
SN Instructional materials prepared by students
NT Student Writing Models
BT Instructional Materials
RT Experience Charts
Language Experience Approach
Material Development
School Publications
Student Participation
Student Projects
Student Publications
Student Research
Students
Teacher Developed Materials

STUDENT DEVELOPMENT *Jul. 1966*
CIJE: 1516 RIE: 934 GC: 310
SN The aspects of an individual's development that are influenced by his or her schooling
BT Development
RT Ancillary School Services
Deans Of Students
Hidden Curriculum
Individual Development
Outcomes Of Education
School Counseling
School Effectiveness
School Guidance
School Role
Student Characteristics
Student Educational Objectives
Student Improvement
Students

STUDENT DISTRIBUTION (1966 1980) *Jun. 1980*
CIJE: 27 RIE: 71 GC: 330
SN Invalid descriptor -- used indiscriminately in indexing -- see such descriptors as "school demography," "geographic distribution," and "test norms"

STUDENT EDUCATIONAL OBJECTIVES *Mar. 1980*
CIJE: 402 RIE: 850 GC: 330
SN Short- or long-term goals held by or for students with regard to their educational attainment -- includes degree or credit objectives, the reasons for participating in a particular educational program, etc. (note: prior to mar80, "educational objectives" was frequently used for this concept)
UF Educational Goals Of Students
Educational Interest (1967 1980)
Educational Objectives Of Students
BT Objectives
RT Aspiration
Course Selection (Students)
Educational Attainment
Educational Benefits
Educational Counseling
Education Work Relationship
Goal Orientation
Lifelong Learning
Outcomes Of Education
Relevance (Education)
Student Development
Student Interests
Student Needs
Students

Student Eligibility
USE ELIGIBILITY

STUDENT EMPLOYMENT *Jul. 1966*
CIJE: 173 RIE: 327 GC: 630
UF Student Job Placement #
BT Employment
RT Assistantships
Job Placement
Part Time Employment
Seasonal Employment
Student Financial Aid
Student Personnel Services
Students
Work Study Programs

Student Engaged Time
USE TIME ON TASK

Student Enrollment (1966 1977)
USE ENROLLMENT

STUDENT EVALUATION *Jul. 1966*
CIJE: 3502 RIE: 5169 GC: 320
SN Judging student performance or behavior as related to established criteria (note: before may76, the use of this term was not restricted by a scope note)
UF Student Appraisal
NT Nongraded Student Evaluation
BT Evaluation
RT Academic Achievement
Academic Records
Achievement Rating
Behavior Rating Scales
Classroom Observation Techniques
Competence
Course Evaluation
Educational Diagnosis
Educational Testing
Grades (Scholastic)
Grading
Holistic Evaluation
Informal Assessment
Peer Evaluation
Portfolios (Background Materials)
Precision Teaching
Report Cards
Student Behavior
Student Certification
Student Characteristics
Student Improvement
Student Records
Students
Student Teacher Evaluation
Vocational Evaluation
Writing Evaluation

STUDENT EVALUATION OF TEACHER PERFORMANCE *May. 1976*
CIJE: 738 RIE: 557 GC: 320
SN Student involvement in judging, rating, or assessing the quality of teacher performance or competence
BT Teacher Evaluation

= Two or more Descriptors are used to represent this term.
The term's main entry shows the appropriate coordination.

RT Course Evaluation
Instructional Improvement
Student Attitudes
Student Reaction
Summative Evaluation
Teacher Effectiveness
Teacher Improvement
Teacher Student Relationship

STUDENT EXCHANGE PROGRAMS *Jul. 1966*
CIJE: 159 RIE: 220 GC: 330
BT Exchange Programs
RT Cultural Awareness
Foreign Student Advisers
Foreign Students
International Educational Exchange
Students
Study Abroad

STUDENT EXPERIENCE *Jul. 1966*
CIJE: 780 RIE: 448 GC: 310
BT Experience
RT Clinical Experience
Experience Charts
Experiential Learning
Field Experience Programs
Internship Programs
Prior Learning
Student Characteristics
Student Projects
Students
Work Experience Programs

STUDENT FINANCIAL AID *Mar. 1976*
CIJE: 544 RIE: 1559 GC: 620
UF Student Aid
NT Assistantships
Fellowships
Income Contingent Loans
Parent Financial Contribution
Scholarships
BT Financial Support
RT Access To Education
Educational Finance
Educational Vouchers
Eligibility
Financial Aid Applicants
Grants
Instructional Student Costs
Loan Repayment
Need Analysis (Student Financial Aid)
Noninstructional Student Costs
Postsecondary Education
Scholarship Funds
Student Costs
Student Employment
Student Financial Aid Officers
Student Loan Programs
Student Needs
Student Personnel Services
Students
Tax Credits
Tuition
Veterans Education
Work Study Programs

STUDENT FINANCIAL AID OFFICERS *Mar. 1980*
CIJE: 28 RIE: 27 GC: 360
SN Administrative personnel, usually at postsecondary institutions, who are responsible for assisting students with applications for grants, loans, scholarships, etc., and who maintain appropriate financial aid records
BT Administrators
School Personnel
RT Educational Finance
Financial Support
Middle Management
School Business Officials
Student Financial Aid
Student Loan Programs
Student Personnel Workers

STUDENT GOVERNMENT *Jul. 1971*
CIJE: 74 RIE: 96 GC: 320
SN Organized group(s) of student representatives participating in the governance of a school, with authority delegated by the school administration -- applies to all levels of education
UF Student Councils
BT Government (Administrative Body)
Student Organizations

RT School Administration
Student Leadership
Student Participation
Student Responsibility
Student Role
Students
Student School Relationship

Student Grouping (1966 1980)
USE GROUPING (INSTRUCTIONAL PURPOSES)

Student Housing (College)
USE COLLEGE HOUSING

STUDENT IMPROVEMENT *Jul. 1966*
CIJE: 332 RIE: 464 GC: 310
BT Improvement
RT Academic Achievement
Learning Plateaus
Student Development
Student Evaluation
Students

STUDENT INTERESTS *Jul. 1966*
CIJE: 1504 RIE: 877 GC: 310
BT Interests
RT Auditing (Coursework)
Childhood Interests
Course Selection (Students)
Elective Courses
Experimental Colleges
Experimental Schools
Extracurricular Activities
Free Schools
Noncredit Courses
Relevance (Education)
Student Centered Curriculum
Student Characteristics
Student Educational Objectives
Student Motivation
Students

Student Job Placement
USE JOB PLACEMENT; STUDENT EMPLOYMENT

STUDENT LEADERSHIP *Jul. 1966*
CIJE: 129 RIE: 100 GC: 330
BT Leadership
RT Leadership Training
Student Government
Student Responsibility
Students

Student Learning Contracts
USE PERFORMANCE CONTRACTS

Student Loading Areas (1968 1980)
USE STUDENT TRANSPORTATION

STUDENT LOAN PROGRAMS *Aug. 1968*
CIJE: 211 RIE: 571 GC: 620
UF Scholarship Loans (1966 1980) #
BT Programs
RT Banking
Credit (Finance)
Educational Finance
Eligibility
Federal Programs
Financial Needs
Financial Services
Financial Support
Income Contingent Loans
Instructional Student Costs
Loan Repayment
Need Analysis (Student Financial Aid)
Noninstructional Student Costs
Parent Financial Contribution
Self Supporting Students
Student Costs
Student Financial Aid
Student Financial Aid Officers
Tuition

Student Maladjustment
USE STUDENT ADJUSTMENT

STUDENT MOBILITY *Jul. 1966*
CIJE: 79 RIE: 262 GC: 330
SN Geographic mobility of students from one region or school district to another (note: do not confuse with "educational mobility" -- prior to mar80, the use of this term was not restricted by a scope note)
BT Migration

RT College Transfer Students
Family Mobility
Migrant Children
Migrant Education
Migrant Youth
Student Recruitment
Students
Transfer Students
Transient Children

STUDENT MOTIVATION *Jul. 1966*
CIJE: 3373 RIE: 2275 GC: 310
BT Motivation
RT Academic Aspiration
Learning Motivation
Student Attitudes
Student Characteristics
Student Interests
Students
Teacher Influence

STUDENT NEEDS *Jul. 1966*
CIJE: 2819 RIE: 2818 GC: 320
BT Needs
RT Childhood Needs
Course Selection (Students)
Individual Needs
Need Analysis (Student Financial Aid)
Psychological Needs
Relevance (Education)
Student Characteristics
Student College Relationship
Student Educational Objectives
Student Financial Aid
Students
Student School Relationship

Student Opinion (1966 1980)
USE STUDENT ATTITUDES

STUDENT ORGANIZATIONS *Jul. 1966*
CIJE: 440 RIE: 357 GC: 320
NT Student Government
Student Unions
BT Organizations (Groups)
RT Extracurricular Activities
Fraternities
Sororities
Student Participation
Students
Student Volunteers

Student Outcomes
USE OUTCOMES OF EDUCATION

Student Parent Relationship
USE PARENT STUDENT RELATIONSHIP

STUDENT PARTICIPATION *Jul. 1966*
CIJE: 2697 RIE: 1688 GC: 310
SN Involvement of students in school or nonschool activities
UF Classroom Participation (1966 1980) #
BT Participation
Student Behavior
RT Assembly Programs
Experience Charts
Experimental Colleges
Experimental Schools
Participative Decision Making
Student Characteristics
Student Developed Materials
Student Government
Student Organizations
Student Projects
Student Research
Student Responsibility
Students
Student Volunteers

Student Personnel Programs (1967 1980)
USE STUDENT PERSONNEL SERVICES

STUDENT PERSONNEL SERVICES *Jul. 1966*
CIJE: 1162 RIE: 1105 GC: 240
SN Supportive, non-instructional services to college or university students in a school setting
UF Student Affairs Services
Student Personnel Programs (1967 1980)
Student Personnel Work (1967 1980)
BT Ancillary School Services
RT Counseling Services
Guidance Programs
Pupil Personnel Services

School Counseling
School Guidance
School Health Services
School Orientation
Student Employment
Student Financial Aid
Student Personnel Workers
Student Placement
Student Welfare

Student Personnel Work (1967 1980)
USE STUDENT PERSONNEL SERVICES

STUDENT PERSONNEL WORKERS *Nov. 1969*
CIJE: 492 RIE: 158 GC: 240
SN Professional personnel who provide supportive, non-instructional services to college or university students in a school setting
UF Student Affairs Workers
BT School Personnel
RT Admissions Officers
College Faculty
College Programs
Counseling Services
Deans Of Students
Faculty Advisers
Foreign Student Advisers
Guidance Personnel
Health Personnel
Ombudsmen
Pupil Personnel Workers
Registrars (School)
Resident Advisers
Resident Assistants
School Counselors
School Psychologists
School Social Workers
Student Financial Aid Officers
Student Personnel Services
Student Welfare

STUDENT PLACEMENT *Jul. 1966*
CIJE: 904 RIE: 1534 GC: 320
SN Assignment of students to schools or academic classes and programs according to their background, readiness, abilities, and goals (note: do not use for "student job placement" -- prior to mar80, the use of this term was not restricted by a scope note)
UF College Placement (1966 1980)
BT Placement
RT Acceleration (Education)
Admission (School)
Admissions Counseling
Advanced Placement
Age Grade Placement
Educational Counseling
Educational Testing
Equivalency Tests
Grouping (Instructional Purposes)
Mainstreaming
Prior Learning
Pupil Personnel Services
School Entrance Age
School Readiness
Student Personnel Services
Student Promotion
Students
Track System (Education)
Transfer Programs
Transitional Programs

STUDENT PROBLEMS *Jul. 1966*
CIJE: 516 RIE: 476 GC: 330
SN (Note: use a more precise term if possible)
BT Problems
RT Behavior Problems
Learning Problems
Students

STUDENT PROJECTS *Jul. 1966*
CIJE: 1398 RIE: 644 GC: 310
UF Project Methods #
Project Training Methods (1968 1980) #
BT School Activities
RT Citizen Participation
Experiential Learning
Extracurricular Activities
Independent Study
Science Projects
Student Developed Materials
Student Experience
Student Participation

Student Publications
Student Research
Students
Student Volunteers

STUDENT PROMOTION *Jul. 1966*
CIJE: 79 RIE: 113 GC: 320
SN Process by which a student is passed to the next higher instruction or grade level
UF Academic Promotion
BT Academic Achievement
RT Academic Failure
Age Grade Placement
Flexible Progression
Grade Repetition
Instructional Program Divisions
Student Placement
Students

Student Protest
USE ACTIVISM

STUDENT PUBLICATIONS *Jul. 1971*
CIJE: 841 RIE: 193 GC: 720
SN Publications prepared by students (note: prior to mar80, this term was also used for publications for students)
UF Class Newspapers (1967 1980) #
BT School Publications
RT Editors
Journalism Education
School Newspapers
Student Developed Materials
Student Projects
Student Research
Students
Writing For Publication
Yearbooks

STUDENT REACTION *Jul. 1966*
CIJE: 1169 RIE: 787 GC: 310
UF Student Responses
BT Responses
RT Student Attitudes
Student Characteristics
Student Evaluation Of Teacher Performance
Students

STUDENT RECORDS *Jul. 1966*
CIJE: 373 RIE: 719 GC: 320
NT Academic Records
Report Cards
BT Records (Forms)
RT Case Records
Confidential Records
Disclosure
Government School Relationship
Portfolios (Background Materials)
Profiles
Registrars (School)
Student Evaluation
Student Rights
Students

STUDENT RECRUITMENT *Feb. 1976*
CIJE: 541 RIE: 816 GC: 320
SN Activity designed to encourage students or potential students to enroll in a particular program, course, or class, or at a particular institution
BT Recruitment
RT Admission (School)
Admission Criteria
Admissions Officers
Enrollment
School Catalogs
Student Mobility
Students

Student Rehabilitation (1966 1980)
USE REHABILITATION

STUDENT RESEARCH *Jul. 1966*
CIJE: 427 RIE: 318 GC: 810
SN Research by, not about, students (note: prior to mar80, the use of this term was not restricted by a scope note)
BT Research
RT Independent Study
Research Assistants
Research Opportunities
Research Papers (Students)
Research Skills
Student Developed Materials
Student Participation
Student Projects
Student Publications
Students

Student Responses
USE STUDENT REACTION

STUDENT RESPONSIBILITY *Nov. 1972*
CIJE: 420 RIE: 314 GC: 330
SN Responsibility of, not for, the student
BT Responsibility
RT Child Responsibility
Educational Responsibility
Loan Repayment
School Responsibility
Student Characteristics
Student Government
Student Leadership
Student Participation
Student Rights
Student Role
Students
Student School Relationship

STUDENT RIGHTS *Sep. 1971*
CIJE: 930 RIE: 780 GC: 330
SN The guarantee of protection of students against improper institutional actions or decisions in such areas as academic freedom, due process, disclosure of records, discrimination, or violation of civil liberties or citizenship rights
BT Civil Liberties
RT Academic Freedom
Activism
Childrens Rights
Citizenship
Civil Rights
Demonstrations (Civil)
Discipline Policy
Disclosure
Dress Codes
Due Process
Educational Environment
Equal Protection
Freedom Of Speech
Free Schools
Married Students
Ombudsmen
Pregnant Students
School Boycotts
School Law
Search And Seizure
Self Supporting Students
Student Behavior
Student Records
Student Responsibility
Students
Student School Relationship

STUDENT ROLE *Aug. 1968*
CIJE: 545 RIE: 462 GC: 320
RT Parent Role
Role Of Education
Student Attitudes
Student Behavior
Student Characteristics
Student Government
Student Responsibility
Students
Student School Relationship
Teacher Role

STUDENT SCHOOL RELATIONSHIP *Jul. 1966*
CIJE: 1042 RIE: 809 GC: 320
SN The relationship between a school (e.g., nursery, elementary, secondary, vocational) and its students (note: if applicable, use the more specific term "student college relationship")
UF School Student Relationship
NT Student College Relationship
BT Relationship
RT Academic Probation
Aptitude Treatment Interaction
Board Administrator Relationship
Deans Of Students
Dress Codes
Due Process
Educational Environment
Faculty Advisers
Family School Relationship
Hidden Curriculum
Ombudsmen
Parent School Relationship
Parent Student Relationship
Participative Decision Making
Probationary Period
Relevance (Education)
Role Theory
School Administration
School Attitudes
School Orientation
School Phobia
Schools
Search And Seizure
Self Supporting Students
Student Government
Student Needs
Student Responsibility
Student Rights
Student Role
Students
Student Subcultures
Teacher Student Relationship

Student Science Interests (1967 1980)
USE SCIENCE INTERESTS

Student Selection
USE ADMISSION CRITERIA

Student Seminars (1966 1980)
USE SEMINARS

STUDENT SUBCULTURES *Jul. 1966*
CIJE: 123 RIE: 53 GC: 330
SN Student groups exhibiting characteristic patterns of behavior or subcribing to identifiable value systems that differ from those of other groups within the educational environment
BT Subcultures
RT Activism
Cultural Traits
Educational Environment
Student Alienation
Student Attitudes
Student Behavior
Student Characteristics
Students
Student School Relationship

STUDENT TEACHER ATTITUDES *Jun. 1984*
CIJE: 13 RIE: 22 GC: 320
SN Attitudes of, not toward, student teachers
BT Attitudes
RT Student Attitudes
Student Teacher Evaluation
Student Teachers
Student Teaching
Teacher Attitudes
Teaching Conditions

STUDENT TEACHER EVALUATION *Dec. 1985*
CIJE: 10 RIE: 16 GC: 320
SN Judging performances of student teachers based on established criteria
BT Evaluation
RT Student Evaluation
Student Teacher Attitudes
Student Teachers
Student Teacher Supervisors
Student Teaching
Teacher Evaluation
Teaching Skills

Student Teacher Interaction
USE TEACHER STUDENT RELATIONSHIP

Student Teacher Ratio (1966 1984)
USE TEACHER STUDENT RATIO

Student Teacher Relationship (1966 1984)
USE TEACHER STUDENT RELATIONSHIP

STUDENT TEACHER SUPERVISORS *Mar. 1980*
CIJE: 471 RIE: 222 GC: 360
SN College faculty members who oversee student teachers (note: do not confuse with "cooperating teachers")
UF Clinical Professors (1967 1980) (Education)
College Supervisors (1967 1980)
BT College Faculty
Supervisors
RT Cooperating Teachers
Practicum Supervision
Preservice Teacher Education
Professors
Student Teacher Evaluation
Student Teachers
Student Teaching
Teacher Education
Teacher Educators
Teacher Supervision

STUDENT TEACHERS *Jul. 1966*
CIJE: 1012 RIE: 935 GC: 360
SN Persons enrolled in a school of education who are assigned to assist a regular teacher in a real-school situation
BT College Students
Teachers
RT College School Cooperation
Cooperating Teachers
Education Majors
Master Teachers
Microteaching
Paraprofessional School Personnel
Preservice Teacher Education
Schools Of Education
Student Teacher Attitudes
Student Teacher Evaluation
Student Teacher Supervisors
Student Teaching
Teacher Interns
Teacher Supervision

STUDENT TEACHING *Jul. 1966*
CIJE: 755 RIE: 839 GC: 320
UF Off Campus Student Teaching
Practice Teaching
BT Teacher Education
RT Affiliated Schools
Cooperating Teachers
Field Experience Programs
Lesson Observation Criteria
Master Teachers
Methods Courses
Microteaching
Practicums
Practicum Supervision
Preservice Teacher Education
Students
Student Teacher Attitudes
Student Teacher Evaluation
Student Teachers
Student Teacher Supervisors
Teacher Centers
Teaching Experience

Student Testing (1966 1980)
USE EDUCATIONAL TESTING

Student Transfers
USE TRANSFER STUDENTS

STUDENT TRANSPORTATION *Jul. 1966*
CIJE: 206 RIE: 437 GC: 320
SN The movement of school students from residence to school and return by means of any conveyance, usually a bus, at public expense
UF School Transportation
Student Loading Areas (1968 1980)
BT Transportation
RT Ancillary School Services
Bus Transportation
Commuter Colleges
Commuting Students
School Buses
Students
Traffic Circulation

Student Travel
USE TRAVEL

STUDENT UNIONS *Jul. 1966*
CIJE: 85 RIE: 73 GC: 920
SN Organizations and facilities planned for the community life of students
UF College Unions
Student Centers
BT Educational Facilities
Student Organizations
RT College Stores
Extracurricular Activities
Recreational Facilities
Social Organizations

Student Violence
USE VIOLENCE

= Two or more Descriptors are used to represent this term.
The term's main entry shows the appropriate coordination.

STUDENT VOLUNTEERS *Jul. 1966*
CIJE: 149 RIE: 117 GC: 360
BT Students
Volunteers
RT Extracurricular Activities
Student Organizations
Student Participation
Student Projects
Youth Programs

STUDENT WELFARE *Jul. 1966*
CIJE: 66 RIE: 83 GC: 240
SN Social, economic, or emotional well-being of students
BT Well Being
RT Child Welfare
Deans Of Students
Ombudsmen
Student College Relationship
Student Personnel Services
Student Personnel Workers
Students

STUDENT WRITING MODELS *Aug. 1968*
CIJE: 161 RIE: 95 GC: 720
SN Written work by students that is used to discuss composition, rhetoric, grammar, or usage principles
BT Models
Student Developed Materials
RT Creative Writing
Descriptive Writing
English Instruction
Expository Writing
Writing (Composition)
Writing Instruction
Writing Skills

STUDENTS *Jul. 1966*
CIJE: 1033 RIE: 1174 GC: 360
SN (Note: use a more specific term if possible)
UF Average Students (1967 1980)
Pupils
NT Adult Students
Advanced Students
Bilingual Students
Black Students
College Students
Commuting Students
Continuation Students
Day Students
Elementary School Students
Evening Students
Foreign Students
Full Time Students
High Risk Students
Lower Class Students
Majors (Students)
Married Students
Middle Class Students
Nonmajors
Nontraditional Students
Part Time Students
Pregnant Students
Reentry Students
Secondary School Students
Self Supporting Students
Single Students
Student Volunteers
Terminal Students
Transfer Students
White Students
BT Groups
RT Attendance
Enrollment
Extracurricular Activities
Home Visits
Parent Student Relationship
School Demography
School Holding Power
Student Adjustment
Student Alienation
Student Attitudes
Student Attrition
Student Behavior
Student Centered Curriculum
Student Certification
Student Characteristics
Student Costs
Student Developed Materials
Student Development
Student Educational Objectives
Student Employment
Student Evaluation
Student Exchange Programs
Student Experience
Student Financial Aid
Student Government
Student Improvement
Student Interests
Student Leadership
Student Mobility
Student Motivation
Student Needs
Student Organizations
Student Participation
Student Placement
Student Problems
Student Projects
Student Promotion
Student Publications
Student Reaction
Student Records
Student Recruitment
Student Research
Student Responsibility
Student Rights
Student Role
Student School Relationship
Student Subcultures
Student Teaching
Student Transportation
Student Welfare
Teacher Student Ratio
Teacher Student Relationship
Trainees
Truancy

STUDIO FLOOR PLANS (1966 1980) *Mar. 1980*
CIJE: 13 RIE: 15 GC: 920
SN Invalid descriptor -- used inconsistently in indexing -- see such descriptors as "building plans," "building design," "educational facilities design," "classroom design," "television studios," etc.

STUDY *Jul. 1966*
CIJE: 52 RIE: 28 GC: 310
SN Application of the mind to the acquisition of knowledge (note: prior to mar80, this term did not carry a scope note and was occasionally used to represent a pubtype -- see pubtype 143 for this usage)
UF Study Hours
NT Home Study
Independent Study
BT Learning Activities
RT Drills (Practice)
Proctoring
Review (Reexamination)
Scholarship
Study Centers
Study Facilities
Study Guides
Study Habits
Study Skills
Time On Task

STUDY ABROAD *Jul. 1966*
CIJE: 347 RIE: 356 GC: 350
BT Education
RT Foreign Medical Graduates
International Educational Exchange
Student Exchange Programs
Tourism
Travel

Study Carrels
USE CARRELS

STUDY CENTERS *Jul. 1966*
CIJE: 43 RIE: 97 GC: 920
UF School Study Centers (1966 1980)
Study Halls
BT Study Facilities
RT After School Centers
Compensatory Education
In School Suspension
Study

STUDY FACILITIES *Jul. 1966*
CIJE: 26 RIE: 63 GC: 920
NT Carrels
Study Centers
BT Educational Facilities
RT Library Facilities
Study

STUDY GUIDES *Jul. 1966*
CIJE: 92 RIE: 848 GC: 730
BT Guides
Instructional Materials
RT Advance Organizers
Course Organization
Independent Study
Programed Instructional Materials
Review (Reexamination)
Study
Study Habits
Study Skills

STUDY HABITS *Jul. 1966*
CIJE: 317 RIE: 314 GC: 310
BT Behavior Patterns
RT Reading Habits
Study
Study Guides
Study Skills
Word Study Skills

Study Halls
USE STUDY CENTERS

Study Hours
USE STUDY

Study Release Programs
USE RELEASED TIME

STUDY SKILLS *Jul. 1966*
CIJE: 658 RIE: 1100 GC: 310
NT Word Study Skills
BT Skills
RT Advance Organizers
Basic Skills
Content Area Reading
Learning Strategies
Locational Skills (Social Studies)
Metacognition
Notetaking
Outlining (Discourse)
Study
Study Guides
Study Habits

Study Trips
USE FIELD TRIPS

Stunts And Tumbling
USE TUMBLING

STUTTERING *Jul. 1966*
CIJE: 267 RIE: 66 GC: 220
SN Disorder of speech rhythm or fluency characterized by repetition or prolongation of speech sounds, interjection of superfluous speech elements, or silent intervals
UF Stammering
BT Speech Handicaps
RT Articulation Impairments
Speech Habits
Speech Improvement
Speech Skills
Speech Therapy

Subculture (1967 1980)
USE SUBCULTURES

SUBCULTURES *Mar. 1980*
CIJE: 134 RIE: 158 GC: 560
SN Ethnic, regional, economic, or social groups exhibiting characteristic patterns of behavior sufficient to distinguish them from the larger society to which they belong
UF Subculture (1967 1980)
NT Student Subcultures
BT Culture
RT Acculturation
Cross Cultural Studies
Cultural Differences
Cultural Influences
Cultural Isolation
Cultural Traits
Ethnic Groups
Ghettos
Minority Groups
Social Class
Social Environment
Social Influences
Socialization

Subemployment (1968 1980)
USE UNDEREMPLOYMENT

Subject Access
USE INDEXING

Subject Disciplines
USE INTELLECTUAL DISCIPLINES

Subject Headings
USE SUBJECT INDEX TERMS

SUBJECT INDEX TERMS *Jul. 1969*
CIJE: 392 RIE: 364 GC: 710
UF Descriptors
Index Terms
Subject Headings
Uniterms
BT Vocabulary
RT Cataloging
Indexes
Indexing
Library Catalogs
Thesauri

Subjunctive Mood
USE VERBS

Subprofessionals (1967 1977)
USE PARAPROFESSIONAL PERSONNEL

Subsidies
USE GRANTS

SUBSTITUTE TEACHERS *Oct. 1969*
CIJE: 95 RIE: 34 GC: 360
UF Relief Teachers
BT Teachers
RT Part Time Faculty
Teacher Attendance
Teacher Employment

SUBSTITUTION DRILLS *Jul. 1966*
CIJE: 28 RIE: 66 GC: 310
BT Pattern Drills (Language)
RT Applied Linguistics
Cloze Procedure
Teaching Methods

SUBTRACTION *Jul. 1966*
CIJE: 186 RIE: 189 GC: 480
BT Arithmetic
RT Addition
Division
Multiplication

SUBURBAN ENVIRONMENT *Jul. 1966*
CIJE: 36 RIE: 49 GC: 550
BT Environment
RT Suburban Housing
Suburban Problems
Suburban Schools
Suburban Youth
Suburbs

SUBURBAN HOUSING *Jul. 1966*
CIJE: 20 RIE: 21 GC: 550
BT Housing
RT Suburban Environment
Suburban Problems
Suburbs

SUBURBAN PROBLEMS *Jul. 1966*
CIJE: 19 RIE: 10 GC: 550
BT Problems
RT Suburban Environment
Suburban Housing
Suburban Schools
Suburban Youth
Suburbs

SUBURBAN SCHOOLS *Jul. 1966*
CIJE: 123 RIE: 209 GC: 340
BT Schools
RT Suburban Environment
Suburban Problems
Suburbs

SUBURBAN YOUTH *Jul. 1966*
CIJE: 47 RIE: 57 GC: 510
BT Youth
RT Suburban Environment
Suburban Problems
Suburbs

SUBURBS *Jul. 1966*
CIJE: 71 RIE: 89 GC: 550
BT Metropolitan Areas
RT Community
Municipalities
Neighborhoods
Suburban Environment
Suburban Housing
Suburban Problems
Suburban Schools
Suburban Youth
Urban To Suburban Migration

SUCCESS *Mar. 1980*
CIJE: 1800 RIE: 1658 GC: 820
SN Attainment of a goal or desired outcome
UF Goal Attainment
Success Factors (1968 1980)
BT Performance
RT Achievement
Achievement Gains
Achievement Need
Evaluation
Expectation
Failure
Fear Of Success
Goal Orientation
High Achievement
Improvement
Motivation
Objectives
Organizational Effectiveness
Outcomes Of Education
Overachievement
Program Effectiveness
Standards

Success Avoidance
USE FEAR OF SUCCESS

Success Factors (1968 1980)
USE SUCCESS

SUFFIXES *Jan. 1969*
CIJE: 100 RIE: 39 GC: 450
BT Morphemes
RT Form Classes (Languages)
Morphophonemics
Structural Analysis (Linguistics)

SUGGESTOPEDIA *Jan. 1985*
CIJE: 31 RIE: 63 GC: 110
SN Method of teaching, developed by georgi lozanov, in which relaxed concentration is combined with synchronized music and rhythmic presentation to tap the unconscious reserves of the mind and thereby accelerate learning -- originally applied in language courses, but since expanded to a variety of learning tasks
UF Lozanov Method
BT Teaching Methods
RT Hypnosis
Meditation
Mnemonics
Music
Psychoeducational Methods
Relaxation Training
Second Language Instruction

SUICIDE *Feb. 1969*
CIJE: 418 RIE: 132 GC: 230
BT Death
Self Destructive Behavior
RT Behavior Disorders
Psychopathology
Self Mutilation

SUMMATIVE EVALUATION *Jun. 1971*
CIJE: 336 RIE: 906 GC: 310
SN Evaluation at the conclusion of an activity or plan to determine its effectiveness
UF Product Evaluation
BT Evaluation
RT Course Evaluation
Curriculum Evaluation
Educational Assessment
Evaluation Utilization
Formative Evaluation
Grading
Institutional Evaluation
Participant Satisfaction
Program Effectiveness
Program Evaluation
Program Validation
Self Evaluation (Groups)
Student Evaluation Of Teacher Performance
Validated Programs

Summer Institutes (1967 1980)
USE INSTITUTES (TRAINING PROGRAMS); SUMMER PROGRAMS

SUMMER PROGRAMS *Jul. 1966*
CIJE: 853 RIE: 1418 GC: 350
SN Programs scheduled during the summer months
UF Summer Institutes (1967 1980) #
Summer Workshops (1966 1980) #
NT Summer Science Programs
BT Programs
RT Alumni Education
Day Camp Programs
Minicourses
Outdoor Education
Recreational Programs
Remedial Programs
Resident Camp Programs
Summer Schools
Vacation Programs

SUMMER SCHOOLS *Jul. 1966*
CIJE: 97 RIE: 236 GC: 350
UF Summer Session
BT Schools
RT Extended School Year
Summer Programs
Supplementary Education
Transitional Programs
Year Round Schools

SUMMER SCIENCE PROGRAMS *Jul. 1966*
CIJE: 74 RIE: 27 GC: 490
BT Science Programs
Summer Programs
RT Science Curriculum
Science Instruction
Science Projects

Summer Session
USE SUMMER SCHOOLS

Summer Workshops (1966 1980)
USE SUMMER PROGRAMS; WORKSHOPS

SUPERCONDUCTORS *Jan. 1970*
CIJE: 6 RIE: GC: 910
RT Electricity
Semiconductor Devices

Superintendent Role (1966 1980)
USE SUPERINTENDENTS

SUPERINTENDENTS *Jul. 1966*
CIJE: 563 RIE: 861 GC: 360
SN Administrators who coordinate and direct the operation of an institution, organization, or department -- in education, the administrators at the district, city, county, or state level who direct and coordinate the activities of school systems in accordance with school board standards
UF Assistant Superintendents
School Superintendents (1966 1980)
Superintendent Role (1966 1980)
BT Administrators
RT Board Of Education Policy
Boards Of Education
Instructional Leadership
School Administration
School Districts
School Personnel

Superior Students (1966 1978)
USE ACADEMICALLY GIFTED

Supermarkets
USE FOOD STORES

SUPERVISED FARM PRACTICE *Jul. 1966*
CIJE: 89 RIE: 69 GC: 410
SN Learning experiences that are part of an instructional program in agriculture -- may include farming, employment, observational, or school laboratory experiences -- often less formal or structured than cooperative education programs
UF Supervised Occupational Experience (Agriculture)
BT Agricultural Education
Field Experience Programs
RT Agriculture
Cooperative Education
Farm Occupations
Farm Visits
Work Experience Programs

Supervised Occupational Experience (Agriculture)
USE SUPERVISED FARM PRACTICE

Supervising Teachers
USE COOPERATING TEACHERS

SUPERVISION *Jul. 1966*
CIJE: 390 RIE: 525 GC: 630
SN The process or function of directing and evaluating activities in progress, and of providing leadership and guidance to the employees or staff involved (note: use a more specific term if possible)
UF Supervisory Activities (1968 1980)
NT Practicum Supervision
Proctoring
School Supervision
Science Supervision
Teacher Supervision
BT Administration
RT Leadership
Supervisors
Supervisory Methods

SUPERVISOR QUALIFICATIONS *Jul. 1966*
CIJE: 72 RIE: 76 GC: 630
BT Qualifications
RT Administrator Education
Administrator Qualifications
Employment Qualifications
Supervisors
Supervisory Training

Supervisor Training
USE SUPERVISORY TRAINING

SUPERVISORS *Jul. 1966*
CIJE: 449 RIE: 504 GC: 640
UF Foremen
NT Crew Leaders
State Supervisors
Student Teacher Supervisors
BT Administrators
RT Consultants
Leaders
Supervision
Supervisor Qualifications
Supervisory Methods
Supervisory Training

Supervisory Activities (1968 1980)
USE SUPERVISION

SUPERVISORY METHODS *Jul. 1966*
CIJE: 353 RIE: 379 GC: 630
SN Approaches or techniques for directing or overseeing individuals or work in progress -- may include evaluation
BT Methods
RT Administrative Principles
Evaluation Methods
Leadership Styles
Supervision
Supervisors
Supervisory Training

SUPERVISORY TRAINING *Jul. 1966*
CIJE: 295 RIE: 417 GC: 400
UF Supervisor Training
BT Training
RT Job Training
Leadership Training
Management Development
Supervisor Qualifications
Supervisors
Supervisory Methods

SUPPLEMENTARY EDUCATION *Jul. 1966*
CIJE: 92 RIE: 245 GC: 350
SN Education provided outside of school hours either to reinforce and support the regular school program or to compensate for educational disadvantages (note: prior to mar80, this term was not restricted by a scope note -- see also "compensatory education," "remedial programs," etc.)
UF Supplementary Educational Centers (1966 1980) #
BT Education
RT After School Education
Compensatory Education
Educationally Disadvantaged
Enrichment Activities
Extracurricular Activities
Migrant Education
Minicourses
Refresher Courses
Remedial Programs
Retraining
Summer Schools
Transitional Programs

Supplementary Educational Centers (1966 1980)
USE EDUCATION SERVICE CENTERS; SUPPLEMENTARY EDUCATION

SUPPLEMENTARY READING MATERIALS *Jul. 1966*
CIJE: 181 RIE: 718 GC: 460
SN Books, magazines, or fugitive materials, aside from basal texts, used to enrich instructional materials or to furnish additional practice in reading
UF Supplementary Textbooks (1967 1980) #
BT Reading Materials
RT High Interest Low Vocabulary Books
Independent Reading
Instructional Materials
Reading Material Selection
Recreational Reading

Supplementary Textbooks (1967 1980)
USE SUPPLEMENTARY READING MATERIALS; TEXTBOOKS

SUPPLIES *Aug. 1968*
CIJE: 75 RIE: 72 GC: 910
SN Material items that are expended or consumed through use -- includes property other than land, buildings, furniture, or equipment
UF Office Supplies
School Supplies
Stockpiles
NT Adhesives
Agricultural Supplies
Electric Batteries
Magnetic Tapes
BT Resources
RT Art Materials
Construction Materials
Equipment
Facility Inventory
Maintenance
Paper (Material)

Supply Of Education
USE EDUCATIONAL SUPPLY

Supply Of Labor
USE LABOR SUPPLY

Support Groups (Human Services)
USE SOCIAL SUPPORT GROUPS

Support Networks (Personal Assistance)
USE SOCIAL SUPPORT GROUPS

Support Systems (Services)
USE SERVICES

SUPPRESSOR VARIABLES *Jan. 1971*
CIJE: 12 RIE: 12 GC: 820
SN Predictor variables that have negligible correlation with a criterion, but which improve the prediction of a test battery or other group of predictor measures because of their correlation with another predictor in the battery
BT Predictor Variables
RT Multiple Regression Analysis
Path Analysis
Predictive Measurement

Suprasegmental Morphemes
USE INTONATION

Suprasegmental Phonemes
USE SUPRASEGMENTALS

= Two or more Descriptors are used to represent this term.
The term's main entry shows the appropriate coordination.

SUPRASEGMENTALS *Nov. 1968*
CIJE: 140 RIE: 187 GC: 450
UF Prosodic Features (Speech)
Suprasegmental Phonemes
NT Intonation
Stress (Phonology)
BT Phonology
RT Morphology (Languages)
Morphophonemics
Paralinguistics
Phonemes
Phrase Structure
Sentence Structure
Structural Analysis (Linguistics)

SUPREME COURT LITIGATION (1966 1980) *Mar. 1980*
CIJE: 672 RIE: 343 GC: 610
SN Invalid descriptor -- used for litigation from both state supreme courts and the u.s. supreme court -- coordinate "court litigation" with "state courts" or the identifier "supreme court" respectively for these concepts

SUPREME COURTS (1966 1980) *Mar. 1980*
CIJE: 33 RIE: 41 GC: 610
SN Invalid descriptor -- used for both state supreme courts and the u.s. supreme court -- use "state courts" or the identifier "supreme court" respectively for these concepts

Surface Area
USE AREA

Surface Finishing
USE FINISHING

SURFACE STRUCTURE *Jul. 1966*
CIJE: 323 RIE: 286 GC: 450
SN Concept in transformational grammar referring to the form of a sentence as it is actually seen, heard, or spoken -- in contrast to its deep structure
BT Transformational Generative Grammar
RT Deep Structure
Function Words
Grammar
Linguistics
Linguistic Theory
Morphology (Languages)
Morphophonemics
Phonology
Phrase Structure
Sentence Diagraming
Sentence Structure
Syntax

SURFING *Jan. 1985*
CIJE: 1 RIE: 1 GC: 470
BT Aquatic Sports

SURGERY *Oct. 1977*
CIJE: 71 RIE: 27 GC: 210
SN Branch of medicine which treats trauma and diseases wholly or in part by manual and operative procedures
UF Operations (Surgery)
BT Medicine
RT Abortions
Amputations
Anatomy
Anesthesiology
Biomedical Equipment
Cancer
Diseases
Hospitals
Medical Services
Oncology
Patients
Physical Health
Surgical Technicians

SURGICAL TECHNICIANS *Jul. 1966*
CIJE: 8 RIE: 22 GC: 210
SN Technical assistants on a surgical team who arrange supplies and instruments in the operating room, maintain antiseptic conditions, prepare patients for surgery, and assist surgeons during the operation
UF Operating Room Technicians
BT Allied Health Personnel
RT Medical Services
Surgery

SURREALISM *Apr. 1969*
CIJE: 35 RIE: 8 GC: 430
SN Early twentieth century movement, style, or sensibility in the arts emphasizing the unrestrained expression of the subconscious through such devices as automatic (stream of consciousness) writing and the abnormal juxtaposition of natural objects shown in unnatural states
RT Art Expression
Creative Art
Imagination
Literary Styles
Symbols (Literary)
Twentieth Century Literature

Survey Courses
USE INTRODUCTORY COURSES

SURVEYS *Jul. 1966*
CIJE: 5053 RIE: 6551 GC: 810
NT Community Surveys
Graduate Surveys
Library Surveys
National Surveys
Occupational Surveys
School Surveys
State Surveys
Statistical Surveys
Television Surveys
BT Evaluation Methods
RT Attitude Measures
Biographical Inventories
Comparative Analysis
Data Collection
Educational Assessment
Feasibility Studies
Information Utilization
Inquiry
Interviews
Investigations
Literature Reviews
Measures (Individuals)
Needs Assessment
Opinions
Public Opinion
Questionnaires
Research
Sample Size
Sampling
State Of The Art Reviews
Test Reviews
Trend Analysis

Survival Literacy
USE FUNCTIONAL LITERACY

Survival Reading Skills
USE FUNCTIONAL READING

Survival Skills (Daily Living)
USE DAILY LIVING SKILLS

SUSPENSION *Nov. 1969*
CIJE: 173 RIE: 240 GC: 330
SN Temporary, forced withdrawal from the regular school program
NT In School Suspension
BT Discipline
RT Academic Failure
Academic Probation
Attendance
College Attendance
Disqualification
Expulsion
Out Of School Youth
School Attendance Legislation
Withdrawal (Education)

SUSTAINED SILENT READING *Mar. 1980*
CIJE: 48 RIE: 27 GC: 460
SN An instructional practice in which a period of time is set aside for everyone in a class or school to read silently
BT Reading
Reading Instruction
RT Reading Habits
Silent Reading

SUSU *Jul. 1966*
CIJE: RIE: 3 GC: 440
BT African Languages

SWAHILI *Jul. 1966*
CIJE: 13 RIE: 53 GC: 440
BT Bantu Languages

Swazi
USE SISWATI

SWEDISH *Mar. 1978*
CIJE: 30 RIE: 60 GC: 440
BT Indo European Languages

SWIMMING *Apr. 1970*
CIJE: 102 RIE: 94 GC: 470
BT Aquatic Sports
RT Diving
Lifetime Sports
Recreational Activities
Swimming Pools
Water Polo

SWIMMING POOLS *Sep. 1968*
CIJE: 56 RIE: 33 GC: 920
BT Facilities
RT Aquatic Sports
Diving
Physical Education Facilities
Recreational Facilities
Swimming

Swing Music
USE JAZZ

Switching (Language)
USE CODE SWITCHING (LANGUAGE)

Syllabi
USE COURSE DESCRIPTIONS

SYLLABLES *Jul. 1966*
CIJE: 250 RIE: 208 GC: 450
BT Phonology
RT Articulation (Speech)
Consonants
Intonation
Phonemes
Stress (Phonology)
Structural Analysis (Linguistics)
Vowels

SYMBOLIC LANGUAGE *Jul. 1966*
CIJE: 115 RIE: 89 GC: 450
BT Language
RT Ideography
Semiotics
Shorthand

SYMBOLIC LEARNING *Jul. 1966*
CIJE: 156 RIE: 100 GC: 110
BT Learning
RT Associative Learning
Visual Learning
Word Recognition

Symbolic Logic
USE MATHEMATICAL LOGIC

SYMBOLISM *Jun. 1969*
CIJE: 215 RIE: 90 GC: 430
SN In a broad sense, the use of one object to represent or suggest another -- in art and literature, a movement beginning in the late nineteenth century involving the serious and extensive use of symbols
RT Art Expression
Literary Styles
Nineteenth Century Literature
Symbols (Literary)
Twentieth Century Literature

SYMBOLS (LITERARY) *Jul. 1966*
CIJE: 195 RIE: 115 GC: 430
BT Figurative Language
RT Imagery
Literary Devices
Literature
Metaphors
Motifs
Mythology
Surrealism
Symbolism

SYMBOLS (MATHEMATICS) *Jan. 1969*
CIJE: 103 RIE: 56 GC: 480
NT Numbers
RT Mathematical Formulas
Mathematics

SYMMETRY *Jul. 1966*
CIJE: 109 RIE: 28 GC: 480
RT Art
Congruence (Mathematics)
Geometric Concepts
Geometry

Symphony Orchestras
USE ORCHESTRAS

Symposia (1967 1980)
USE CONFERENCES

Synchronic Linguistics (1967 1980)
USE DESCRIPTIVE LINGUISTICS

Syntactic Borrowing
USE LINGUISTIC BORROWING

SYNTAX *Jul. 1966*
CIJE: 2149 RIE: 1975 GC: 450
UF Valence (Language)
NT Form Classes (Languages)
Phrase Structure
Sentence Structure
BT Grammar
RT Adjectives
Adverbs
Case (Grammar)
Code Switching (Language)
Cohesion (Written Composition)
Connected Discourse
Deep Structure
Determiners (Languages)
Discourse Analysis
Error Analysis (Language)
Function Words
Generative Grammar
Kernel Sentences
Language Patterns
Language Typology
Linguistic Borrowing
Morphemes
Morphology (Languages)
Nouns
Pragmatics
Prepositions
Pronouns
Semantics
Semiotics
Sentence Combining
Sentence Diagraming
Sentences
Structural Grammar
Surface Structure
Tenses (Grammar)
Traditional Grammar
Transformational Generative Grammar
Verbs

SYNTHESIS *Jul. 1966*
CIJE: 119 RIE: 145 GC: 820
SN Combination of separate elements to form a coherent whole (note: use as a major descriptor for discussions of synthesis as a process -- use as a minor descriptor for documents that are a synthesis of ideas, etc. -- prior to mar80, this term did not carry a scope note)
BT Evaluation Methods
RT Cognitive Processes
Comparative Analysis
Meta Analysis

Synthetic Speech
USE ARTIFICIAL SPEECH

Syphilis
USE VENEREAL DISEASES

Systematic Desensitization
USE DESENSITIZATION

SYSTEMS ANALYSIS *Jul. 1966*
CIJE: 505 RIE: 1136 GC: 820
SN Examination of the interrelated elements of any organization, structure, procedure, etc. to improve the functioning of the system as a whole
UF Functional Systems Theory
BT Methods
RT Architectural Programing
Computer Science
Cost Effectiveness
Critical Path Method
Decision Making

Information Theory
Input Output Analysis
Instructional Systems
Integrated Activities
Management Systems
Models
Needs Assessment
Network Analysis
Organizational Effectiveness
Problem Solving
Relevance (Information Retrieval)
Skill Analysis
Systems Analysts
Systems Approach
Systems Development

SYSTEMS ANALYSTS *Jan. 1969*
CIJE: 12 RIE: 20 GC: 640
BT Personnel
RT Mathematicians
Programers
Researchers
Systems Analysis
Systems Development

SYSTEMS APPROACH *Jul. 1966*
CIJE: 1549 RIE: 1913 GC: 320
SN Overall, macroscopic way of looking at organizations, structures, procedures, etc., and their context -- involves a concern for the whole rather than the constituent parts
UF Systems Theory
NT Systems Building
BT Holistic Approach
RT Cybernetics
Decision Making
Information Theory
Instructional Systems
Management Systems
Models
Planning
Problem Solving
Schematic Studies
Systems Analysis

SYSTEMS BUILDING *Dec. 1976*
CIJE: 12 RIE: 18 GC: 920
SN Use of the systems approach in facilities construction to organize planning, financing, manufacturing, and evaluation under single or highly coordinated management (note: do not confuse with "systems development")
NT Design Build Approach
BT Systems Approach
RT Building Innovation
Building Plans
Buildings
Building Systems
Construction (Process)
Construction Management
Construction Programs
Educational Facilities Planning
Facility Planning
Fast Track Scheduling
Modular Building Design
Structural Building Systems
Structural Elements (Construction)

SYSTEMS CONCEPTS (1966 1980) *Mar. 1980*
CIJE: 107 RIE: 215 GC: 320
SN Invalid descriptor -- used indiscriminately in indexing

SYSTEMS DEVELOPMENT *Jul. 1966*
CIJE: 399 RIE: 801 GC: 320
SN Planning, designing, constructing, or expanding an assembly of components or concepts that will interact as an organized whole and be more effective in meeting particular goals
BT Development
RT Educational Development
Formative Evaluation
Management Systems
Organizational Development
Program Development
Systems Analysis
Systems Analysts
Technological Advancement

Systems Theory
USE SYSTEMS APPROACH

T Groups (1967 1980)
USE SENSITIVITY TRAINING

TABLE TENNIS *Apr. 1985*
CIJE: 1 RIE: 1 GC: 470
UF Ping Pong
BT Athletics
RT Racquet Sports

TABLES (DATA) *Jul. 1966*
CIJE: 6578 RIE: 7287 GC: 730
NT Expectancy Tables
BT Visual Aids
RT Charts
Data
Graphs

TACHISTOSCOPES *Jul. 1966*
CIJE: 62 RIE: 39 GC: 910
SN Apparatus that project visual stimuli (e.g., pictures, letters, words...) for very brief and accurately timed intervals
BT Projection Equipment
RT Pictorial Stimuli
Reading
Reading Research
Recognition (Psychology)
Visual Stimuli

Tackboards
USE BULLETIN BOARDS

TACTILE ADAPTATION *Jul. 1966*
CIJE: 78 RIE: 53 GC: 220
SN The conversion of educational materials for use with the instruction of the blind
BT Media Adaptation
RT Blindness
Braille
Magnification Methods
Raised Line Drawings
Sensory Aids
Tactual Perception
Tactual Visual Tests

Tactile Materials
USE MANIPULATIVE MATERIALS

TACTUAL PERCEPTION *Jul. 1966*
CIJE: 288 RIE: 138 GC: 110
SN Ability to interpret sensory stimuli that are experienced through the skin
UF Cutaneous Sense (1968 1980)
Dermal Sense
Haptic Perception (1967 1980)
BT Perception
RT Dimensional Preference
Figural Aftereffects
Kinesthetic Perception
Learning Modalities
Manipulative Materials
Object Manipulation
Perception Tests
Sensory Experience
Sensory Training
Tactile Adaptation
Tactual Visual Tests

TACTUAL VISUAL TESTS *Jul. 1966*
CIJE: 13 RIE: 8 GC: 830
SN Tests used to indicate tactual-visual perception and coordination
BT Perception Tests
RT Eye Hand Coordination
Perceptual Motor Coordination
Perceptual Motor Learning
Tactile Adaptation
Tactual Perception
Vision Tests
Visual Perception

Tadjik Persian
USE TAJIK

TAGALOG *Jul. 1966*
CIJE: 11 RIE: 42 GC: 440
UF Pilipino
BT Indonesian Languages

TAGMEMIC ANALYSIS *Jul. 1966*
CIJE: 39 RIE: 67 GC: 450
BT Structural Analysis (Linguistics)
RT Function Words
Grammar
Language Patterns
Language Research
Negative Forms (Language)
Structural Grammar

Tailored Testing
USE ADAPTIVE TESTING

Tailors
USE NEEDLE TRADES

TAJIK *Jul. 1966*
CIJE: RIE: 5 GC: 440
UF Tadjik Persian
BT Indo European Languages

TALENT *Jul. 1966*
CIJE: 562 RIE: 537 GC: 120
SN Superior ability or aptitude, such as in the arts or athletics -- distinguished from "aptitude" by usually being actual rather than potential, and from "ability" by usually being innate rather than acquired
UF Artistic Talent
Talented Students (1966 1980)
RT Ability
Achievement
Aptitude
Creativity
Gifted
Talent Development
Talent Identification
Vocational Aptitude

TALENT DEVELOPMENT *Jul. 1966*
CIJE: 107 RIE: 113 GC: 120
UF Talent Preservation
BT Individual Development
RT Creative Development
Skill Development
Talent

TALENT IDENTIFICATION *Jul. 1966*
CIJE: 271 RIE: 364 GC: 820
SN Identification of superior and usually innate aptitudes or abilities, such as in the arts or athletics (note: do not confuse with "ability identification")
BT Identification
RT Ability Identification
Aptitude Tests
Creativity Tests
Intelligence Quotient
Intelligence Tests
Talent

Talent Preservation
USE TALENT DEVELOPMENT

Talent Tests
USE APTITUDE TESTS

TALENT UTILIZATION (1966 1980) *Mar. 1980*
CIJE: 29 RIE: 29 GC: 520
SN Invalid descriptor -- used inconsistently in indexing -- see such descriptors as "talent," "self actualization," "staff utilization," etc.

Talented Students (1966 1980)
USE TALENT

TALES *Jun. 1969*
CIJE: 61 RIE: 105 GC: 430
SN Simple narratives, in prose or verse
NT Fables
BT Literary Genres
RT Fiction
Poetry
Short Stories

TALKING BOOKS *Jul. 1966*
CIJE: 15 RIE: 49 GC: 720
SN Phonograph records or tape recordings of books, articles, or other publications, usually for the blind
BT Sensory Aids
RT Audiodisks
Audiotape Recordings
Audiovisual Aids
Blindness
Books
Nonprint Media
Partial Vision
Reading Materials

Talks
USE SPEECHES

TAMIL *Jul. 1966*
CIJE: 7 RIE: 21 GC: 440
BT Dravidian Languages

TAOISM *Mar. 1983*
CIJE: 6 RIE: 3 GC: 430
SN Religion based on the teachings of lao-tse (china, 6th century b.c.)
BT Religion
RT Non Western Civilization
Philosophy
Religious Cultural Groups

TAPE RECORDERS *Jul. 1966*
CIJE: 167 RIE: 126 GC: 910
UF Magnetic Tape Cassette Recorders (1970 1980) #
NT Audiotape Recorders
Videotape Recorders
BT Electronic Equipment
RT Magnetic Tape Cassettes
Magnetic Tapes
Tape Recordings

TAPE RECORDINGS *Jul. 1966*
CIJE: 528 RIE: 739 GC: 720
SN Magnetic tapes on which audio or video signals are recorded -- stored on open reels, cassettes, or cartridges (note: use a more specific term if possible)
NT Audiotape Recordings
Videotape Recordings
BT Nonprint Media
RT Documentaries
Magnetic Tape Cassettes
Magnetic Tapes
Special Effects
Tape Recorders

TASK ANALYSIS *Jul. 1966*
CIJE: 605 RIE: 1429 GC: 820
SN Process of identifying all the things that must be done to satisfactorily complete an activity (note: prior to mar80, this term was not scoped and was frequently used for "job analysis" -- do not confuse with "content analysis" or "skill analysis")
BT Evaluation Methods
RT Cognitive Processes
Content Analysis
Critical Incidents Method
Difficulty Level
Job Analysis
Learning Strategies
Objectives
Skill Analysis
Test Construction

Task Difficulty
USE DIFFICULTY LEVEL

TASK PERFORMANCE (1966 1980) *Mar. 1980*
CIJE: 1673 RIE: 1377 GC: 310
SN Invalid descriptor -- used indiscriminately in indexing -- see "performance," "job performance," etc.

TATAR *Jul. 1966*
CIJE: RIE: 2 GC: 440
BT Turkic Languages

TAX ALLOCATION *Jul. 1966*
CIJE: 289 RIE: 450 GC: 620
SN Extent to which taxes are apportioned to finance a particular constituency
UF Tax Support (1966 1980)
BT Financial Support
RT Categorical Aid
Educational Equity (Finance)
Educational Finance
Financial Needs
Full State Funding
Resource Allocation
Revenue Sharing
Tax Effort
Taxes
Tax Rates

TAX CREDITS *Mar. 1980*
CIJE: 100 RIE: 115 GC: 620
SN Sums subtracted from total tax liability
UF Tuition Tax Credits #
RT Parent Financial Contribution
School Choice
Student Financial Aid

= Two or more Descriptors are used to represent this term.
The term's main entry shows the appropriate coordination.

Tax Deductions
Taxes
Tax Rates
Tuition

TAX DEDUCTIONS *Nov. 1982*
CIJE: 28 RIE: 22 GC: 620
SN Sums subtracted from taxable income
RT Tax Credits
Taxes
Tax Rates

TAX EFFORT *Jul. 1966*
CIJE: 75 RIE: 188 GC: 620
SN The measure of a community's or society's willingness to tax itself
RT Educational Equity (Finance)
Educational Finance
Equalization Aid
Finance Reform
Fiscal Capacity
Tax Allocation
Taxes
Tax Rates

Tax Equity (Education)
USE EDUCATIONAL EQUITY (FINANCE)

TAX RATES *Jul. 1966*
CIJE: 133 RIE: 195 GC: 620
BT Ratios (Mathematics)
RT Educational Equity (Finance)
Expenditures
Money Management
Property Taxes
School Taxes
Tax Allocation
Tax Credits
Tax Deductions
Tax Effort
Taxes

Tax Reform
USE FINANCE REFORM

Tax Support (1966 1980)
USE TAX ALLOCATION

TAXES *Jul. 1966*
CIJE: 282 RIE: 447 GC: 620
NT Property Taxes
School Taxes
RT Assessed Valuation
Estate Planning
Finance Reform
Ownership
Property Appraisal
Public Policy
Tax Allocation
Tax Credits
Tax Deductions
Tax Effort
Tax Rates

Taxonomy (1967 1980)
USE CLASSIFICATION

TEACHER ADMINISTRATOR RELATIONSHIP *Jul. 1966*
CIJE: 1176 RIE: 1103 GC: 320
UF Administrator Teacher Relationship
BT Interpersonal Relationship
RT Administrator Guides
Administrators
Board Administrator Relationship
Employer Employee Relationship
Faculty College Relationship
Faculty Handbooks
Faculty Workload
Instructional Leadership
Interprofessional Relationship
Participative Decision Making
Politics Of Education
School Administration
School Policy
Teacher Discipline
Teacher Evaluation
Teacher Militancy
Teacher Morale
Teacher Rights
Teachers
Teacher Supervision
Teacher Welfare
Teaching Load

Teacher Advancement
USE TEACHER PROMOTION

TEACHER AIDES *Jul. 1966*
CIJE: 292 RIE: 904 GC: 360
SN Paraprofessional school personnel who assist k-12 teachers in the instructional process (note: for higher education aides, use "teaching assistants" -- prior to mar80, this term was not scoped and was often confused with "school aides," who assist in noninstructional areas)
NT Bilingual Teacher Aides
BT Paraprofessional School Personnel
RT Proctoring
School Aides
Teachers
Volunteers

TEACHER ALIENATION *Jul. 1966*
CIJE: 78 RIE: 75 GC: 320
BT Alienation
RT Teacher Attitudes
Teacher Behavior
Teacher Burnout
Teacher Militancy
Teacher Morale
Teachers

TEACHER ASSOCIATIONS *Jul. 1966*
CIJE: 620 RIE: 539 GC: 330
SN Organizations composed of teachers, usually but not always at the elementary/secondary school level (note: see "faculty organizations" for most higher education organizations as well as those that include administrative staff -- prior to mar80, the use of this term was not restricted by a scope note)
UF Teacher Organizations
BT Professional Associations
RT Faculty Organizations
Teacher Militancy
Teachers
Teacher Strikes
Teacher Welfare
Teaching (Occupation)
Teaching Load
Unions

TEACHER ATTENDANCE *Jul. 1966*
CIJE: 21 RIE: 38 GC: 320
SN Teachers' presence for classroom and other assigned duties (note: use "teacher participation" for attendance at unassigned functions)
UF Absence (Teachers)
BT Attendance
RT Sabbatical Leaves
Substitute Teachers
Teacher Behavior
Teacher Discipline
Teacher Dismissal
Teachers

TEACHER ATTITUDES *Jul. 1966*
CIJE: 6685 RIE: 7623 GC: 320
SN Attitudes of, not toward, teachers (note: prior to mar80, the use of this term was not restricted by a scope note, and the instruction "teacher reaction, use teacher attitudes" was carried in the thesaurus)
UF Teacher Opinions
BT Attitudes
RT Classroom Environment
Student Teacher Attitudes
Teacher Alienation
Teacher Behavior
Teacher Characteristics
Teacher Evaluation
Teacher Morale
Teacher Response
Teachers
Teaching Conditions

Teacher Attrition
USE FACULTY MOBILITY

Teacher Autonomy
USE PROFESSIONAL AUTONOMY

TEACHER BACKGROUND *Jul. 1966*
CIJE: 261 RIE: 403 GC: 320
SN Aspects of a teacher's personal history that have influenced his or her personal and professional development (note: do not confuse with "teaching experience")
BT Background
RT Teacher Characteristics
Teacher Education
Teacher Employment
Teacher Evaluation
Teacher Qualifications
Teacher Recruitment
Teachers
Teacher Selection
Teaching Experience

TEACHER BEHAVIOR *Jul. 1966*
CIJE: 2342 RIE: 2805 GC: 310
SN Conduct of teachers in or out of job-related situations
NT Teacher Effectiveness
Teacher Militancy
Teacher Participation
Teacher Persistence
Teacher Response
BT Behavior
RT Classroom Communication
Classroom Observation Techniques
Protocol Materials
Teacher Alienation
Teacher Attendance
Teacher Attitudes
Teacher Characteristics
Teacher Evaluation
Teacher Influence
Teacher Motivation
Teacher Role
Teachers
Teaching Styles

TEACHER BURNOUT *Oct. 1981*
CIJE: 185 RIE: 127 GC: 320
SN Teachers' syndrome caused by inability to cope with stressful occupational conditions -- characterized by low morale, low productivity, high absenteeism, and high job turnover
BT Burnout
RT Teacher Alienation
Teacher Morale
Teacher Motivation
Teacher Persistence
Teacher Response
Teachers
Teaching Conditions

TEACHER CENTERS *Sep. 1973*
CIJE: 244 RIE: 429 GC: 920
SN Interinstitutional centers (school/college/community) offering teacher-oriented professional development programs, at preservice/inservice levels, of educational demonstrations, experimental teaching, laboratory experiences, and other participatory learning activities
UF Teacher Education Centers
University Training Centers
BT Resource Centers
RT Educational Cooperation
Education Service Centers
Field Experience Programs
Inservice Teacher Education
Institutes (Training Programs)
Institutional Cooperation
Laboratory Training
Professional Continuing Education
Student Teaching
Teacher Education
Teachers
Teacher Workshops
Teaching Experience

Teacher Certificates (1967 1980)
USE TEACHER CERTIFICATION

TEACHER CERTIFICATION *Jul. 1966*
CIJE: 625 RIE: 1261 GC: 330
UF Teacher Certificates (1967 1980)
Teaching Certificates
BT Certification
RT Beginning Teachers
Educational Certificates
Teacher Education
Teacher Education Curriculum
Teacher Employment
Teacher Evaluation
Teacher Qualifications
Teachers
Teaching (Occupation)

TEACHER CHARACTERISTICS *Jul. 1966*
CIJE: 1552 RIE: 2264 GC: 320
NT Teaching Styles
RT Aptitude Treatment Interaction
Individual Characteristics
Teacher Attitudes
Teacher Background
Teacher Behavior
Teacher Evaluation
Teacher Qualifications
Teacher Role
Teachers
Teacher Selection
Teacher Stereotypes

Teacher College Relationship
USE FACULTY COLLEGE RELATIONSHIP

Teacher Coordinators
USE INSTRUCTOR COORDINATORS

Teacher Counselor Cooperation
USE COUNSELOR TEACHER COOPERATION

Teacher Desegregation
USE TEACHER INTEGRATION

TEACHER DEVELOPED MATERIALS *Jul. 1966*
CIJE: 904 RIE: 1530 GC: 730
SN Instructional materials prepared by teachers
NT Teacher Made Tests
BT Instructional Materials
RT Experience Charts
Material Development
School Publications
Student Developed Materials
Teachers
Teaching Load

Teacher Directed Practice
USE TEACHER GUIDANCE

TEACHER DISCIPLINE *Jan. 1973*
CIJE: 34 RIE: 51 GC: 320
SN Discipline of, not by, teachers
NT Teacher Dismissal
BT Discipline
RT Collective Bargaining
Due Process
Faculty College Relationship
Teacher Administrator Relationship
Teacher Attendance
Teacher Employment
Teacher Evaluation
Teacher Militancy
Teacher Responsibility
Teacher Rights
Teachers
Teacher Strikes

TEACHER DISMISSAL *Jan. 1973*
CIJE: 274 RIE: 262 GC: 320
SN Dismissal of, not by, the teacher
BT Dismissal (Personnel)
Teacher Discipline
RT Contracts
Disqualification
Due Process
Reduction In Force
Teacher Attendance
Teacher Evaluation
Teacher Responsibility
Teachers

TEACHER DISTRIBUTION *Jul. 1966*
CIJE: 20 RIE: 94 GC: 330
SN The apportionment of teachers among schools over a geographic area (with regard to race, teacher quality, student/staff ratios, etc.)
BT School Demography
RT Geographic Distribution
Incidence
Racial Balance
School Statistics
Teacher Placement
Teachers
Teacher Student Ratio

TEACHER EDUCATION *Jul. 1966*
CIJE: 8040 RIE: 11191 GC: 400
UF Teacher Preparation
Teacher Training
NT Competency Based Teacher Education
English Teacher Education
Inservice Teacher Education
Preservice Teacher Education
Student Teaching
Teacher Educator Education
BT Professional Education
RT Affiliated Schools
Cooperating Teachers
Education Courses
Education Majors
Institutes (Training Programs)
Laboratory Schools
Laboratory Training
Master Teachers
Methods Courses
Methods Teachers
Microteaching
Protocol Materials
Schools Of Education
Student Teacher Supervisors
Teacher Background
Teacher Centers
Teacher Certification
Teacher Education Programs
Teacher Educators
Teacher Qualifications
Teachers
Teacher Supervision
Teaching (Occupation)
Teaching Experience

Teacher Education Centers
USE TEACHER CENTERS

TEACHER EDUCATION CURRICULUM *Jul. 1966*
CIJE: 778 RIE: 1380 GC: 400
NT Methods Courses
BT College Curriculum
RT Education Courses
Education Majors
Foundations Of Education
Preservice Teacher Education
Schools Of Education
Teacher Certification
Teacher Education Programs
Teacher Qualifications
Teachers

TEACHER EDUCATION PROGRAMS *Mar. 1980*
CIJE: 638 RIE: 1026 GC: 400
UF Teacher Programs (1966 1980)
BT Programs
RT Education Courses
Education Majors
Methods Courses
Teacher Education
Teacher Education Curriculum
Teachers
Teacher Workshops

TEACHER EDUCATOR EDUCATION *Sep. 1969*
CIJE: 141 RIE: 250 GC: 400
BT Teacher Education
RT Cooperating Teachers
Doctoral Degrees
Doctoral Programs
Inservice Teacher Education
Masters Degrees
Master Teachers
Postsecondary Education As A Field Of Study
Preservice Teacher Education
Schools Of Education
Specialist In Education Degrees
Teacher Educators

TEACHER EDUCATORS *Jul. 1966*
CIJE: 472 RIE: 602 GC: 360
UF Teacher Trainers
NT Methods Teachers
BT College Faculty
RT Cooperating Teachers
Master Teachers
Postsecondary Education As A Field Of Study
Professors
Schools Of Education
Specialist In Education Degrees
Student Teacher Supervisors
Teacher Education
Teacher Educator Education

TEACHER EFFECTIVENESS *Mar. 1980*
CIJE: 3899 RIE: 3697 GC: 310
SN Degree to which teachers are successful in satisfying their objectives, obligations, or functions
UF Effective Teaching (1966 1980)
Teacher Quality
Teaching Quality (1966 1980)
BT Teacher Behavior
RT Academic Achievement
Educational Quality
Instructional Effectiveness
Instructional Improvement
Instructional Innovation
School Effectiveness
Student Evaluation Of Teacher Performance
Teacher Evaluation
Teacher Influence
Teacher Role
Teachers
Teaching (Occupation)
Teaching Models
Teaching Skills
Teaching Styles

TEACHER EMPLOYMENT *Jul. 1966*
CIJE: 437 RIE: 558 GC: 630
BT Employment
RT Beginning Teachers
Full Time Faculty
Labor Market
Merit Pay
Part Time Faculty
Substitute Teachers
Teacher Background
Teacher Certification
Teacher Discipline
Teacher Employment Benefits
Teacher Exchange Programs
Teacher Persistence
Teacher Placement
Teacher Recruitment
Teachers
Teacher Salaries
Teacher Selection
Teacher Shortage
Teacher Supply And Demand
Teaching (Occupation)
Teaching Experience
Tenure

TEACHER EMPLOYMENT BENEFITS *Mar. 1980*
CIJE: 45 RIE: 192 GC: 630
UF Teaching Benefits (1966 1980)
RT Academic Rank (Professional)
Fringe Benefits
Health Insurance
Leaves Of Absence
Sabbatical Leaves
Teacher Employment
Teacher Promotion
Teacher Retirement
Teachers
Teacher Salaries
Teacher Welfare
Teaching (Occupation)
Tenure
Unemployment Insurance
Workers Compensation

TEACHER EVALUATION *Jul. 1966*
CIJE: 1969 RIE: 2410 GC: 320
SN Judging teacher performance based on established criteria
UF Teacher Rating (1966 1977)
NT Student Evaluation Of Teacher Performance
BT Personnel Evaluation
RT Classroom Observation Techniques
Course Evaluation
Faculty Development
Faculty Evaluation
Faculty Workload
Lesson Observation Criteria
Student Teacher Evaluation
Teacher Administrator Relationship
Teacher Attitudes
Teacher Background
Teacher Behavior
Teacher Certification
Teacher Characteristics
Teacher Discipline
Teacher Dismissal
Teacher Effectiveness
Teacher Improvement
Teacher Promotion
Teacher Qualifications
Teachers
Teacher Selection
Teacher Student Relationship
Teacher Supervision
Teaching Load
Teaching Skills

TEACHER EXCHANGE PROGRAMS *Jul. 1966*
CIJE: 109 RIE: 131 GC: 330
SN Includes domestic and international teacher exchange programs
BT Exchange Programs
RT Faculty Development
International Educational Exchange
Teacher Employment
Teachers

Teacher Experience (1966 1974)
USE TEACHING EXPERIENCE

TEACHER GUIDANCE *Jul. 1966*
CIJE: 137 RIE: 120 GC: 240
SN Guidance provided by teachers (note: prior to mar80, this term was not scoped and was sometimes used to index guidance given to teachers)
UF Teacher Directed Practice
BT Guidance
RT Counselor Teacher Cooperation
School Guidance
Teachers
Teacher Student Relationship

Teacher Guides
USE TEACHING GUIDES

TEACHER HOUSING *Jul. 1966*
CIJE: 10 RIE: 17 GC: 920
SN Living quarters of teachers (note: prior to mar80, the use of this term was not restricted by a scope note)
BT Housing
RT Teachers

TEACHER IMPROVEMENT *Jul. 1966*
CIJE: 1314 RIE: 1494 GC: 310
BT Improvement
RT Faculty Development
Inservice Teacher Education
Instructional Improvement
Professional Development
Sabbatical Leaves
Student Evaluation Of Teacher Performance
Teacher Evaluation
Teachers

Teacher Induction
USE TEACHER ORIENTATION

TEACHER INFLUENCE *Jul. 1966*
CIJE: 964 RIE: 732 GC: 310
BT Influences
RT Academic Achievement
Student Motivation
Teacher Behavior
Teacher Effectiveness
Teacher Participation
Teacher Role
Teachers
Teacher Student Relationship
Teaching Styles

TEACHER INTEGRATION *Jul. 1966*
CIJE: 21 RIE: 57 GC: 540
SN Process of balancing the racial, ethnic, or sexual composition of the instructional staff of a school, college, or university
UF Teacher Desegregation
BT Personnel Integration
RT Affirmative Action
Equal Opportunities (Jobs)
Faculty Integration
Teachers

TEACHER INTERNS *Jul. 1966*
CIJE: 121 RIE: 247 GC: 360
SN Advanced students or recent graduates accruing college credits while teaching under supervision, usually paid a small salary (note: do not confuse with "student teachers")
UF Intern Teachers
Urban Teaching Interns #
BT Teachers
RT Cooperating Teachers
Differentiated Staffs
Inservice Teacher Education
Internship Programs
Master Teachers
Paraprofessional School Personnel
Student Teachers

Teacher Load
USE TEACHING LOAD

TEACHER MADE TESTS *Oct. 1980*
CIJE: 45 RIE: 64 GC: 830
SN Tests and other measures that are planned, assembled, written, or otherwise prepared by teachers for use with particular groups of students (note: for specificity, coordinate with other terms in the "tests" and "measures (individuals)" hierarchies)
BT Teacher Developed Materials
Tests
RT Teachers
Test Construction

TEACHER MILITANCY *Jan. 1969*
CIJE: 240 RIE: 171 GC: 330
BT Teacher Behavior
RT Arbitration
Collective Bargaining
Negotiation Impasses
Professional Recognition
Sanctions
Teacher Administrator Relationship
Teacher Alienation
Teacher Associations
Teacher Discipline
Teacher Morale
Teachers
Teacher Strikes
Teacher Welfare

Teacher Mobility
USE FACULTY MOBILITY

TEACHER MORALE *Jul. 1966*
CIJE: 410 RIE: 357 GC: 320
BT Morale
RT Professional Recognition
Teacher Administrator Relationship
Teacher Alienation
Teacher Attitudes
Teacher Burnout
Teacher Militancy
Teacher Motivation
Teachers
Teacher Welfare
Teaching Conditions

TEACHER MOTIVATION *Jul. 1966*
CIJE: 334 RIE: 338 GC: 310
BT Motivation
RT Academic Aspiration
Teacher Behavior
Teacher Burnout
Teacher Morale
Teachers

Teacher Nurses (1966 1980)
USE NURSES

Teacher Opinions
USE TEACHER ATTITUDES

Teacher Organizations
USE TEACHER ASSOCIATIONS

TEACHER ORIENTATION *Jul. 1966*
CIJE: 114 RIE: 272 GC: 320
SN The process of acquainting teachers with the policies, rules, traditions, and educational offerings of a school
UF Teacher Induction
BT Orientation
RT Beginning Teachers
Faculty Handbooks
School Orientation

= Two or more Descriptors are used to represent this term.
The term's main entry shows the appropriate coordination.

Staff Orientation
Teachers
Teacher Supervision

Teacher Parent Conferences
USE PARENT TEACHER CONFERENCES

Teacher Parent Cooperation
USE PARENT TEACHER COOPERATION

TEACHER PARTICIPATION *Jul. 1966*
CIJE: 760 RIE: 841 GC: 320
SN (Note: use "teacher attendance" for presence for teaching assignments)
BT Participation
Teacher Behavior
RT Participative Decision Making
School Involvement
Teacher Influence
Teachers

TEACHER PERSISTENCE *Jul. 1966*
CIJE: 83 RIE: 135 GC: 330
SN One's active continuance as a teacher by reason of personal choice
UF Teaching Persistence
BT Persistence
Teacher Behavior
RT Aging In Academia
Faculty Mobility
Labor Turnover
Teacher Burnout
Teacher Employment
Teacher Recruitment
Teachers
Teacher Shortage
Teaching (Occupation)

TEACHER PLACEMENT *Jul. 1966*
CIJE: 120 RIE: 163 GC: 330
SN Process by which teachers obtain teaching positions (note: do not confuse with "teacher distribution" -- prior to mar80, the use of this term was not restricted by a scope note)
BT Job Placement
RT Faculty Mobility
Teacher Distribution
Teacher Employment
Teacher Recruitment
Teachers
Teacher Selection
Teacher Supply And Demand
Teacher Transfer

Teacher Preparation
USE TEACHER EDUCATION

Teacher Programs (1966 1980)
USE TEACHER EDUCATION PROGRAMS

TEACHER PROMOTION *Jul. 1966*
CIJE: 103 RIE: 126 GC: 320
SN Advancement in rank or position of a teacher
UF Teacher Advancement
BT Promotion (Occupational)
RT Academic Rank (Professional)
Faculty Development
Faculty Promotion
Faculty Workload
Teacher Employment Benefits
Teacher Evaluation
Teachers
Teaching (Occupation)
Teaching Load
Tenure

TEACHER QUALIFICATIONS *Jul. 1966*
CIJE: 1138 RIE: 1372 GC: 320
SN One's education, experience, and physical, social, and mental characteristics that determine fitness for a teaching position
BT Qualifications
RT Employment Qualifications
Teacher Background
Teacher Certification
Teacher Characteristics
Teacher Education
Teacher Education Curriculum
Teacher Evaluation
Teachers
Teacher Selection
Teaching (Occupation)
Teaching Experience

Teacher Quality
USE TEACHER EFFECTIVENESS

Teacher Rating (1966 1977)
USE TEACHER EVALUATION

Teacher Reaction
USE TEACHER RESPONSE

TEACHER RECRUITMENT *Jul. 1966*
CIJE: 246 RIE: 496 GC: 320
SN Process of attracting candidates to the teaching profession or finding teachers to fill teaching vacancies
BT Recruitment
RT Faculty Recruitment
Teacher Background
Teacher Employment
Teacher Persistence
Teacher Placement
Teachers
Teacher Selection
Teacher Shortage
Teacher Supply And Demand
Teaching Conditions

TEACHER RESPONSE *Jul. 1966*
CIJE: 482 RIE: 476 GC: 310
SN Teacher reaction to instructional and/or classroom situations (note: prior to mar80, the instruction "teacher reaction, use teacher attitudes" was carried in the thesaurus)
UF Teacher Reaction
BT Responses
Teacher Behavior
RT Feedback
Reinforcement
Teacher Attitudes
Teacher Burnout
Teachers
Teacher Student Relationship
Teaching Styles

TEACHER RESPONSIBILITY *Jul. 1966*
CIJE: 1556 RIE: 999 GC: 320
NT Noninstructional Responsibility
BT Responsibility
RT Administrator Responsibility
Child Responsibility
Educational Responsibility
Faculty Handbooks
Faculty Workload
Leadership Responsibility
School Responsibility
Teacher Discipline
Teacher Dismissal
Teacher Rights
Teachers
Teaching (Occupation)
Teaching Load

TEACHER RETIREMENT *Jul. 1966*
CIJE: 137 RIE: 207 GC: 630
UF Retired Teachers
BT Retirement
RT Aging In Academia
Early Retirement
Teacher Employment Benefits
Teachers

TEACHER RIGHTS *Jun. 1983*
CIJE: 73 RIE: 60 GC: 330
SN Legal, procedural, and human rights of teachers
BT Civil Liberties
RT Academic Freedom
Civil Rights
Collective Bargaining
Due Process
Faculty College Relationship
Freedom Of Speech
School Law
Teacher Administrator Relationship
Teacher Discipline
Teacher Responsibility
Teachers
Teacher Welfare
Teaching (Occupation)
Tenure

TEACHER ROLE *Jul. 1966*
CIJE: 5625 RIE: 4400 GC: 320
UF Senior Teacher Role (1966 1980) #
RT Faculty Handbooks
Noninstructional Responsibility
Role Of Education
Staff Role
Student Role
Teacher Behavior
Teacher Characteristics
Teacher Effectiveness
Teacher Influence
Teachers
Teacher Stereotypes
Teaching (Occupation)
Teaching Styles

TEACHER SALARIES *Jul. 1966*
CIJE: 674 RIE: 1329 GC: 620
BT Salaries
RT Contract Salaries
Teacher Employment
Teacher Employment Benefits
Teachers
Teaching (Occupation)

TEACHER SELECTION *Jul. 1966*
CIJE: 288 RIE: 389 GC: 320
SN Process of assessing and choosing candidates for teaching positions
BT Personnel Selection
RT Teacher Background
Teacher Characteristics
Teacher Employment
Teacher Evaluation
Teacher Placement
Teacher Qualifications
Teacher Recruitment
Teachers
Teacher Supply And Demand
Teaching Experience

Teacher Seminars (1966 1980)
USE TEACHER WORKSHOPS

TEACHER SHORTAGE *Jul. 1966*
CIJE: 215 RIE: 192 GC: 630
BT Teacher Supply And Demand
RT Teacher Employment
Teacher Persistence
Teacher Recruitment
Teachers

Teacher Skills
USE TEACHING SKILLS

TEACHER STEREOTYPES *Jul. 1966*
CIJE: 44 RIE: 31 GC: 540
SN Standardized and biased conceptions of the attributes of teachers (note: for teachers' stereotyped attitudes use "teacher attitudes" -- prior to mar80, the use of this term was not restricted by a scope note)
BT Stereotypes
RT Teacher Characteristics
Teacher Role
Teachers
Teaching (Occupation)

TEACHER STRIKES *Jul. 1966*
CIJE: 241 RIE: 238 GC: 630
BT Strikes
RT Arbitration
Collective Bargaining
Labor Problems
Negotiation Agreements
Negotiation Impasses
Sanctions
School Boycotts
Teacher Associations
Teacher Discipline
Teacher Militancy
Teachers
Teacher Welfare
Unions

Teacher Student Interaction
USE TEACHER STUDENT RELATIONSHIP

TEACHER STUDENT RATIO *Dec. 1984*
CIJE: 21 RIE: 32 GC: 320
UF Student Teacher Ratio (1966 1984)
BT Ratios (Mathematics)
RT Class Size
Students
Teacher Distribution
Teachers

TEACHER STUDENT RELATIONSHIP *Dec. 1984*
CIJE: 404 RIE: 307 GC: 310
UF Student Teacher Interaction
Student Teacher Relationship (1966 1984)
Teacher Student Interaction
BT Interpersonal Relationship
RT Aptitude Treatment Interaction
Classroom Communication
Classroom Environment
Faculty Handbooks
Grading
Mentors
Student College Relationship
Student Evaluation Of Teacher Performance
Students
Student School Relationship
Teacher Evaluation
Teacher Guidance
Teacher Influence
Teacher Response
Teachers

TEACHER SUPERVISION *Jul. 1966*
CIJE: 397 RIE: 431 GC: 320
SN Supervision of preservice and inservice teachers
BT Supervision
RT Cooperating Teachers
Practicum Supervision
School Supervision
State Supervisors
Student Teachers
Student Teacher Supervisors
Teacher Administrator Relationship
Teacher Education
Teacher Evaluation
Teacher Orientation
Teachers

TEACHER SUPPLY AND DEMAND *Jul. 1966*
CIJE: 355 RIE: 498 GC: 630
NT Teacher Shortage
BT Labor Market
RT Educational Demand
Employment Patterns
Teacher Employment
Teacher Placement
Teacher Recruitment
Teachers
Teacher Selection
Teaching (Occupation)

Teacher Trainers
USE TEACHER EDUCATORS

Teacher Training
USE TEACHER EDUCATION

Teacher Training Films
USE PROTOCOL MATERIALS

TEACHER TRANSFER *Jul. 1966*
CIJE: 33 RIE: 59 GC: 330
BT Occupational Mobility
RT Faculty Mobility
Teacher Placement
Teachers
Transfer Policy
Transfer Programs

Teacher Travel
USE TRAVEL

Teacher Turnover
USE FACULTY MOBILITY

Teacher Unions
USE UNIONS

TEACHER WELFARE *Nov. 1968*
CIJE: 307 RIE: 255 GC: 330
SN Status and advancement of interests of teachers and the teaching profession
BT Well Being
RT Academic Freedom
Board Of Education Policy
Collective Bargaining
Faculty College Relationship
Professional Autonomy
Professional Recognition
Teacher Administrator Relationship
Teacher Associations
Teacher Employment Benefits

= Two or more Descriptors are used to represent this term.
The term's main entry shows the appropriate coordination.

Teacher Militancy
Teacher Morale
Teacher Rights
Teachers
Teacher Strikes
Teaching (Occupation)
Teaching Conditions
Teaching Load

TEACHER WORKSHOPS *Jul. 1966*
CIJE: 687 RIE: 1361 GC: 350
UF Teacher Seminars (1966 1980)
BT Workshops
RT Inservice Teacher Education
Teacher Centers
Teacher Education Programs
Teachers

TEACHERS *Jul. 1966*
CIJE: 1981 RIE: 2685 GC: 360
SN (Note: see "faculty" for other specific terminology related to "teachers")
UF Instructional Staff (1966 1980)
Instructors
NT Adult Educators
Art Teachers
Beginning Teachers
Bilingual Teachers
Black Teachers
Catholic Educators
Cooperating Teachers
Elementary School Teachers
Home Economics Teachers
Industrial Arts Teachers
Instructor Coordinators
Itinerant Teachers
Language Teachers
Lay Teachers
Master Teachers
Mathematics Teachers
Minority Group Teachers
Music Teachers
Physical Education Teachers
Preschool Teachers
Public School Teachers
Reading Teachers
Remedial Teachers
Resource Teachers
Science Teachers
Secondary School Teachers
Special Education Teachers
Student Teachers
Substitute Teachers
Teacher Interns
Television Teachers
Tutors
Vocational Education Teachers
BT Professional Personnel
RT Adjunct Faculty
Aging In Academia
College Faculty
Counselor Teacher Cooperation
Department Heads
Differentiated Staffs
Employees
Faculty
Full Time Faculty
Home Visits
Noninstructional Responsibility
Nontenured Faculty
One Teacher Schools
Parent Teacher Conferences
Parent Teacher Cooperation
Part Time Faculty
School Personnel
Specialists
Teacher Administrator Relationship
Teacher Aides
Teacher Alienation
Teacher Associations
Teacher Attendance
Teacher Attitudes
Teacher Background
Teacher Behavior
Teacher Burnout
Teacher Centers
Teacher Certification
Teacher Characteristics
Teacher Developed Materials
Teacher Discipline
Teacher Dismissal
Teacher Distribution
Teacher Education
Teacher Education Curriculum
Teacher Education Programs
Teacher Effectiveness
Teacher Employment
Teacher Employment Benefits
Teacher Evaluation
Teacher Exchange Programs
Teacher Guidance
Teacher Housing
Teacher Improvement
Teacher Influence
Teacher Integration
Teacher Made Tests
Teacher Militancy
Teacher Morale
Teacher Motivation
Teacher Orientation
Teacher Participation
Teacher Persistence
Teacher Placement
Teacher Promotion
Teacher Qualifications
Teacher Recruitment
Teacher Response
Teacher Responsibility
Teacher Retirement
Teacher Rights
Teacher Role
Teacher Salaries
Teacher Selection
Teacher Shortage
Teacher Stereotypes
Teacher Strikes
Teacher Student Ratio
Teacher Student Relationship
Teacher Supervision
Teacher Supply And Demand
Teacher Transfer
Teacher Welfare
Teacher Workshops
Teaching (Occupation)
Teaching Experience
Tenured Faculty
Trainers

Teachers Colleges (1966 1980)
USE SCHOOLS OF EDUCATION

TEACHING (OCCUPATION) *Mar. 1980*
CIJE: 427 RIE: 428 GC: 640
SN The profession of teaching, including its occupational conditions and attributes, interprofessional and societal relations, career lines, etc. (note: for "the teaching process," see "instruction")
UF Inservice Teaching (1966 1980) #
Teaching Profession
NT Team Teaching
Urban Teaching
BT Professional Occupations
RT Faculty Mobility
Teacher Associations
Teacher Certification
Teacher Education
Teacher Effectiveness
Teacher Employment
Teacher Employment Benefits
Teacher Persistence
Teacher Promotion
Teacher Qualifications
Teacher Responsibility
Teacher Rights
Teacher Role
Teachers
Teacher Salaries
Teacher Stereotypes
Teacher Supply And Demand
Teacher Welfare
Teaching Conditions
Teaching Experience
Teaching Load
Tenure

Teaching (Process)
USE INSTRUCTION

TEACHING (1966 1980) *Jun. 1980*
CIJE: 521 RIE: 510 GC: 310
SN Invalid descriptor -- used inconsistently in indexing -- see "instruction," "teaching (occupation)," and "teaching methods"

Teaching Alternatives
USE NONTRADITIONAL EDUCATION

Teaching Areas
USE CURRICULUM

TEACHING ASSIGNMENT (1966 1980) *Mar. 1980*
CIJE: 41 RIE: 51 GC: 320
SN Invalid descriptor -- used indiscriminately in indexing -- see the more precise terms "teacher placement" and "teaching load" -- see also "teacher role," "teacher responsibility," "noninstructional responsibility," and "teaching (occupation)" (note: prior to mar80, the thesaurus carried the instruction "teacher assignment, use teacher placement")

TEACHING ASSISTANTS *Jul. 1966*
CIJE: 279 RIE: 199 GC: 360
SN Persons, usually graduate students, who assist as instructors at the college level (note: for k-12 assistants, use "teacher aides")
BT College Faculty
RT Assistantships
Fellowships
Graduate Students
Proctoring
Research Assistants

Teaching Benefits (1966 1980)
USE TEACHER EMPLOYMENT BENEFITS

Teaching Certificates
USE TEACHER CERTIFICATION

TEACHING CONDITIONS *Jul. 1966*
CIJE: 299 RIE: 419 GC: 310
BT Educational Environment
Work Environment
RT Academic Freedom
Classroom Environment
Faculty Handbooks
Faculty Workload
Professional Autonomy
Student Teacher Attitudes
Teacher Attitudes
Teacher Burnout
Teacher Morale
Teacher Recruitment
Teacher Welfare
Teaching (Occupation)

Teaching Core
USE CORE CURRICULUM

TEACHING EXPERIENCE *Nov. 1969*
CIJE: 854 RIE: 818 GC: 310
SN Actual and simulated experiences of preservice and inservice teachers
UF Inservice Teaching Experience
Preservice Teaching Experience
Teacher Experience (1966 1974)
BT Experience
RT Affiliated Schools
Beginning Teachers
Experiential Learning
Experimental Schools
Field Experience Programs
Internship Programs
Laboratory Schools
Laboratory Training
Microteaching
Student Teaching
Teacher Background
Teacher Centers
Teacher Education
Teacher Employment
Teacher Qualifications
Teachers
Teacher Selection
Teaching (Occupation)

Teaching Facilities
USE EDUCATIONAL FACILITIES

Teaching Freedom
USE ACADEMIC FREEDOM

TEACHING GUIDES *Jul. 1966*
CIJE: 804 RIE: 7307 GC: 730
SN Manuals containing presentation methods for, and further information on, a topic -- usually for use with a specific text
UF Discussion Guides #
Instructor Manuals
Teacher Guides
BT Guides
RT Curriculum Guides
Instructional Materials
Learning Modules
Resource Units
Teaching Methods
Textbooks

TEACHING HOSPITALS *Oct. 1979*
CIJE: 172 RIE: 47 GC: 340
SN Hospitals where formal medical training takes place, usually affiliated with nursing or medical schools (note: do not confuse with "hospital schools" or "patient education")
UF University Teaching Hospitals
BT Hospitals
RT Allied Health Occupations Education
Clinical Experience
Clinical Teaching (Health Professions)
Educational Facilities
Graduate Medical Education
Medical Education
Medical Schools
Nursing Education

Teaching Innovations
USE INSTRUCTIONAL INNOVATION

Teaching Language
USE LANGUAGE OF INSTRUCTION

TEACHING LOAD *Jul. 1966*
CIJE: 182 RIE: 372 GC: 320
UF Teacher Load
BT Faculty Workload
RT Contracts
Full Time Faculty
Part Time Faculty
Teacher Administrator Relationship
Teacher Associations
Teacher Developed Materials
Teacher Evaluation
Teacher Promotion
Teacher Responsibility
Teacher Welfare
Teaching (Occupation)
Working Hours

TEACHING MACHINES *Jul. 1966*
CIJE: 181 RIE: 440 GC: 910
SN Devices that mechanically, electrically, and/or electronically present instructional programs at a rate controlled by the learners' responses
UF Self Pacing Machines (1966 1980)
BT Autoinstructional Aids
RT Computer Assisted Instruction
Courseware
Pacing
Programed Instruction
Programed Instructional Materials
Teaching Methods
Time Factors (Learning)

Teaching Materials
USE INSTRUCTIONAL MATERIALS

TEACHING METHODS *Jul. 1966*
CIJE: 27458 RIE: 20216 GC: 310
SN Ways of presenting instructional materials or conducting instructional activities (note: use a more specific term if possible -- for the instructional process in general, see "instruction" -- for the individual teacher's manner of teaching, see "teaching styles")
UF Instructional Methods
Integrated Teaching Method #
Presentation Methods
Project Methods #
Project Training Methods (1968 198C) #
Teaching Practices
Teaching Procedures (1966 1980)
Teaching Systems
Teaching Techniques (1966 1980)
NT Audiolingual Methods
Clinical Teaching (Health Professions)
Conventional Instruction
Creative Teaching
Cross Age Teaching
Demonstrations (Educational)
Diagnostic Teaching
Discussion (Teaching Technique)
Drills (Practice)
Experimental Teaching
Grammar Translation Method
Individualized Instruction

Kinesthetic Methods
Language Experience Approach
Lecture Method
Montessori Method
Multimedia Instruction
Negative Practice
Oral Communication Method
Peer Teaching
Precision Teaching
Programed Instruction
Sight Method
Suggestopedia
Telephone Instruction
Thematic Approach
Training Methods
BT Educational Methods
RT Advance Organizers
Class Organization
Classroom Techniques
Cloze Procedure
Computer Simulation
Contingency Management
Course Organization
Dramatic Play
Educational Strategies
Individual Instruction
Instruction
Instructional Effectiveness
Instructional Films
Instructional Leadership
Integrated Activities
Intermode Differences
Laboratory Procedures
Large Group Instruction
Learning Modalities
Learning Modules
Learning Strategies
Mass Instruction
Methods Research
Pacing
Prompting
Questioning Techniques
Reinforcement
Role Playing
Science Course Improvement Projects
Sequential Approach
Simulation
Small Group Instruction
Substitution Drills
Teaching Guides
Teaching Machines
Teaching Models
Theory Practice Relationship
Tutorial Programs

TEACHING MODELS *Jul. 1966*
CIJE: 504 RIE: 598 GC: 310
SN Standard of teaching behaviors identified as desirable for given teaching situations
BT Models
RT Instruction
Standards
Teacher Effectiveness
Teaching Methods

Teaching Persistence
USE TEACHER PERSISTENCE

Teaching Practices
USE TEACHING METHODS

Teaching Procedures (1966 1980)
USE TEACHING METHODS

Teaching Profession
USE TEACHING (OCCUPATION)

TEACHING PROGRAMS (1966 1980) *Mar. 1980*
CIJE: 87 RIE: 139 GC: 320
SN Invalid descriptor -- used indiscriminately in indexing -- see "instruction" and "teacher education programs"

Teaching Quality (1966 1980)
USE TEACHER EFFECTIVENESS

Teaching Resources
USE EDUCATIONAL RESOURCES

TEACHING SKILLS *Jul. 1966*
CIJE: 1050 RIE: 1531 GC: 310
UF Teacher Skills
BT Skills
RT Communication Skills
Job Skills
Microteaching
Student Teacher Evaluation
Teacher Effectiveness
Teacher Evaluation

TEACHING STYLES *Jul. 1966*
CIJE: 771 RIE: 737 GC: 310
SN Individual teachers' distinctive or characteristic manners of teaching
BT Teacher Characteristics
RT Leadership Styles
Personality Studies
Psychological Patterns
Teacher Behavior
Teacher Effectiveness
Teacher Influence
Teacher Response
Teacher Role

Teaching Systems
USE TEACHING METHODS

Teaching Techniques (1966 1980)
USE TEACHING METHODS

Team Administration (1967 1980)
USE MANAGEMENT TEAMS

Team Counseling
USE COCOUNSELING

TEAM HANDBALL *Apr. 1985*
CIJE: RIE: 1 GC: 470
SN Team sport played on a rectangular floor (court) whose object is to dribble and pass an inflated ball with the hands so as to throw it into a netted, floor-level end goal
BT Team Sports

Team Leader (Teaching) (1966 1980)
USE LEADERS; TEAM TEACHING

Team Management
USE MANAGEMENT TEAMS

TEAM SPORTS *Jun. 1984*
CIJE: 12 RIE: 32 GC: 470
NT Baseball
Basketball
Field Hockey
Football
Ice Hockey
Lacrosse
Soccer
Softball
Team Handball
Volleyball
Water Polo
BT Athletics
RT Team Training
Teamwork

TEAM TEACHING *Jul. 1966*
CIJE: 661 RIE: 850 GC: 310
UF Cooperative Teaching (1966 1980)
Instructional Teams
Team Leader (Teaching) (1966 1980) #
BT Teaching (Occupation)
RT Cooperative Planning
Educational Cooperation
Flexible Scheduling
Master Teachers
Multiunit Schools
Open Plan Schools
Rotation Plans
School Cadres
Team Training
Teamwork

TEAM TRAINING *Nov. 1969*
CIJE: 122 RIE: 176 GC: 310
SN Training individuals in teams or to work as teams
BT Training
RT School Cadres
Small Group Instruction
Team Sports
Team Teaching
Teamwork

TEAMWORK *Jan. 1969*
CIJE: 627 RIE: 517 GC: 520
BT Group Behavior
RT Cocounseling
Cooperation
Cooperative Planning
Interpersonal Competence
Interpersonal Relationship
Interprofessional Relationship
Management Teams
Morale
Organizational Development
Participative Decision Making
Peer Relationship
Sportsmanship
Team Sports
Team Teaching
Team Training
Theory Practice Relationship

TECHNICAL ASSISTANCE *Jul. 1966*
CIJE: 191 RIE: 806 GC: 610
SN Technical, scientific, or economic assistance given by governments, institutions, or private organizations to assist in the development of human and material resources -- includes domestic and foreign programs
UF International Technical Assistance #
RT Appropriate Technology
Community Development
Consultants
Consultation Programs
Developed Nations
Developing Nations
Federal Aid
Financial Support
Human Resources
International Educational Exchange
International Programs
Labor Force Development
Linking Agents
Science Programs
Scientific And Technical Information
Technological Advancement
Technology Transfer

TECHNICAL EDUCATION *Jul. 1966*
CIJE: 1313 RIE: 3314 GC: 400
SN Formal preparation for occupations between the skilled trades and the professions -- usually at the postsecondary level and including the underlying sciences and supporting mathematics as well as methods, skills, materials, and processes of a specialized field of technology required for such positions as technicians, engineering aides, and production specialists
UF Technical Instruction
NT Fire Science Education
BT Vocational Education
RT Aerospace Education
Agricultural Education
Allied Health Occupations Education
Architectural Education
Aviation Technology
Computer Science Education
Electromechanical Technology
Engineering Education
Engineering Technology
Horology
Industrial Education
Nuclear Technology
Paraprofessional Personnel
Postsecondary Education
Pretechnology Programs
Prevocational Education
Research Coordinating Units
School Shops
Science Education
Technical Institutes
Technical Mathematics
Technical Occupations
Technological Literacy
Technology
Trade And Industrial Education
Two Year Colleges
Vocational Education Teachers

Technical Education Directors
USE VOCATIONAL DIRECTORS

Technical High Schools
USE VOCATIONAL HIGH SCHOOLS

TECHNICAL ILLUSTRATION *May. 1969*
CIJE: 35 RIE: 46 GC: 720
SN Process of laying out and drawing illustrations for reproduction in reference works, brochures, and technical manuals
BT Drafting
RT Engineering Drawing
Graphic Arts
Illustrations
Orthographic Projection

Technical Information
USE SCIENTIFIC AND TECHNICAL INFORMATION

TECHNICAL INSTITUTES *Jul. 1966*
CIJE: 241 RIE: 601 GC: 340
SN Postsecondary schools offering training in occupations at a level between the skilled trades and the professions
BT Two Year Colleges
RT Associate Degrees
Community Colleges
Postsecondary Education
Technical Education
Two Year College Students
Vocational Education

Technical Instruction
USE TECHNICAL EDUCATION

TECHNICAL MATHEMATICS *Jul. 1966*
CIJE: 35 RIE: 49 GC: 480
SN Mathematics needed in technical occupations such as electronics
BT Mathematics
RT Technical Education
Technical Occupations

TECHNICAL OCCUPATIONS *Jul. 1966*
CIJE: 131 RIE: 444 GC: 640
SN Occupations between the skilled trades and the professions such as technicians, technologists, engineering aides, paraprofessionals, and production specialists -- usually requiring postsecondary education in the underlying sciences and mathematics as well as the specialized technology
BT Occupations
RT Agricultural Occupations
Allied Health Occupations
Computer Science Education
Drafting
Energy Occupations
Health Occupations
Operating Engineering
Paraprofessional Personnel
Semiskilled Occupations
Skilled Occupations
Technical Education
Technical Mathematics
Technology
Trade And Industrial Education
White Collar Occupations

Technical Processes (Libraries)
USE LIBRARY TECHNICAL PROCESSES

Technical Reports (1968 1980)
USE RESEARCH REPORTS

Technical Schools
USE VOCATIONAL SCHOOLS

Technical Services (Libraries)
USE LIBRARY TECHNICAL PROCESSES

TECHNICAL WRITING *Jul. 1966*
CIJE: 882 RIE: 569 GC: 720
SN Writing, often specialized or concerned with practical applications, that is employed for scientific, engineering, business, or other technical purposes
UF Report Writing
BT Writing (Composition)
RT Abstracting
Business English
Content Area Writing
Documentation
Editing
Expository Writing
Proposal Writing
Research Reports
Textbook Preparation
Writing For Publication

= Two or more Descriptors are used to represent this term.
The term's main entry shows the appropriate coordination.

Technicians
USE PARAPROFESSIONAL PERSONNEL

Techniques (1966 1974)
USE METHODS

TECHNOLOGICAL ADVANCEMENT *Jul. 1966*
CIJE: 2612 RIE: 2099 GC: 490
UF High Technology
BT Development
RT Appropriate Technology
Automation
Computers
Culture Lag
Cybernetics
Developed Nations
Developing Nations
Dislocated Workers
Emerging Occupations
Futures (Of Society)
Industrialization
Inventions
Modernization
Obsolescence
Research And Development
Revolution
Science And Society
Science Programs
Structural Unemployment
Systems Development
Technical Assistance
Technological Literacy
Technology
Technology Transfer

Technological Information
USE SCIENTIFIC AND TECHNICAL INFORMATION

TECHNOLOGICAL LITERACY *Sep. 1982*
CIJE: 108 RIE: 91 GC: 490
SN Comprehension of technological innovation and the impact of technology on society -- may include the ability to select and use specific innovations appropriate to one's interests and needs
NT Computer Literacy
RT Appropriate Technology
Comprehension
Industrialization
Innovation
Science And Society
Science Education
Scientific And Technical Information
Scientific Literacy
Technical Education
Technological Advancement
Technology
Technology Transfer

Technological Programs
USE SCIENCE PROGRAMS

Technological Unemployment
USE STRUCTURAL UNEMPLOYMENT

TECHNOLOGY *Jul. 1966*
CIJE: 2145 RIE: 1673 GC: 490
UF Applied Sciences
Industrial Technology (1969 1980) #
NT Accounting
Aerospace Technology
Agriculture
Appropriate Technology
Automation
Communications
Consumer Science
Cosmetology
Cybernetics
Educational Technology
Electromechanical Technology
Engineering
Engineering Technology
Etiology
Forestry
Genetic Engineering
Horology
Hydraulics
Information Technology
Journalism
Laboratory Technology
Lexicography
Manufacturing
Marketing
Masonry
Mechanics (Process)
Medicine
Metallurgy
Metal Working
Mining
Navigation
Optometry
Plumbing
Power Technology
Radiology
Reprography
Water Treatment
Welding
Wildlife Management
Woodworking
RT Developed Nations
Development
Education Work Relationship
English For Science And Technology
Industrialization
Industry
Inventions
Liberal Arts
Professional Occupations
Quality Of Life
Quality Of Working Life
Research
Research And Development
Research Utilization
Science And Society
Sciences
Scientific And Technical Information
Scientific Concepts
Skilled Occupations
Technical Education
Technical Occupations
Technological Advancement
Technological Literacy
Technology Transfer
Trade And Industrial Education
Vocational Education

TECHNOLOGY TRANSFER *Mar. 1978*
CIJE: 189 RIE: 274 GC: 490
SN Transfer of research results, technological developments, or knowledge from an original application to other settings
RT Appropriate Technology
Diffusion (Communication)
Economic Progress
Industrialization
Information Dissemination
Information Transfer
Information Utilization
Innovation
Inventions
Linking Agents
Marketing
Modernization
Patents
Research
Research And Development
Research And Development Centers
Research Utilization
Science And Society
Scientific And Technical Information
Technical Assistance
Technological Advancement
Technological Literacy
Technology
Use Studies

Teenagers (1966 1980)
USE ADOLESCENTS

Tefl
USE ENGLISH (SECOND LANGUAGE)

Telecommunication (1970 1980)
USE TELECOMMUNICATIONS

TELECOMMUNICATIONS *Mar. 1980*
CIJE: 791 RIE: 1248 GC: 710
SN Long-distance communications using electromagnetic systems -- includes wire (e.g., telephone or telegraph) and broadcast transmission (e.g., radio, television, or satellite) (note: prior to mar80, the thesaurus carried the instructions, "communication networks, services, or systems, use telecommunication")
UF Broadcast Communications
Electronic Communications Systems
Electronic Information Exchange #
Microwave Relay Systems (1971 1980)
Signal Services
Telecommunication (1970 1980)
Wire Communications
Wireless Communications
NT Communications Satellites
Electronic Mail
Electronic Publishing
Facsimile Transmission
Radio
Teleconferencing
Telephone Communications Systems
Television
Videotex
BT Communications
RT Computers
Distance Education
Electronic Equipment
Information Networks
Information Technology
Input Output Devices
Networks
Radar
Television Studios

TELECONFERENCING *Oct. 1979*
CIJE: 108 RIE: 146 GC: 710
SN Conducting conferences between persons remote from one another by means of a telecommunications system
UF Computer Conferencing
BT Telecommunications
RT Conferences
Electronic Equipment
Information Networks
Online Systems
Telephone Communications Systems
Television

TELECOURSES *Jul. 1966*
CIJE: 150 RIE: 231 GC: 350
SN Sequences of lessons offered over television for credit or auditing purposes (note: for courses on the subject of television, use "television curriculum" -- prior to mar80, this term did not carry a scope note)
BT Courses
RT Audiovisual Instruction
Distance Education
Educational Television
Television Teachers

Telefacsimile
USE FACSIMILE TRANSMISSION

Telefax
USE FACSIMILE TRANSMISSION

TELEGRAPHIC MATERIALS *Feb. 1969*
CIJE: 3 RIE: 6 GC: 720
SN Highly abbreviated and condensed textual materials retaining all essential information
BT Reading Materials
RT Instructional Materials
Readability
Reading Comprehension
Reading Rate

Telegu
USE TELUGU

Telephone Communication Systems (1967 1980)
USE TELEPHONE COMMUNICATIONS SYSTEMS

TELEPHONE COMMUNICATIONS INDUSTRY *Jul. 1966*
CIJE: 32 RIE: 58 GC: 650
BT Industry
RT Telephone Communications Systems
Utilities

TELEPHONE COMMUNICATIONS SYSTEMS *Mar. 1980*
CIJE: 214 RIE: 250 GC: 710
UF Telephone Communication Systems (1967 1980)
Telephones
BT Telecommunications
RT Audio Equipment
Dial Access Information Systems
Facsimile Transmission
Teleconferencing
Telephone Communications Industry
Telephone Instruction
Telephone Usage Instruction
Videotex

Telephone Crisis Services
USE HOTLINES (PUBLIC)

TELEPHONE INSTRUCTION *Jul. 1966*
CIJE: 98 RIE: 106 GC: 350
SN Special education by use of the telephone (note: do not confuse with "telephone usage instruction")
BT Teaching Methods
RT Educational Media
Homebound
Home Instruction
Individual Instruction
Telephone Communications Systems

TELEPHONE USAGE INSTRUCTION *Mar. 1980*
CIJE: 18 RIE: 35 GC: 400
SN Instruction in the use of the telephone (note: prior to mar80, this concept was occasionally indexed under "telephone instruction")
BT Instruction
RT Communication Skills
Daily Living Skills
Telephone Communications Systems

Telephones
USE TELEPHONE COMMUNICATIONS SYSTEMS

Teletext
USE VIDEOTEX

Televised Instruction (1966 1974)
USE EDUCATIONAL TELEVISION

TELEVISION *Jul. 1966*
CIJE: 1562 RIE: 1664 GC: 720
SN System whereby visual images, with or without accompanying sound, are converted into electromagnetic waves and transmitted to distant receivers where they are reconverted into moving visible images (note: prior to mar80, the thesaurus carried the instruction "television technology, use media technology")
UF Airborne Television (1966 1980)
Color Television (1969 1980) #
Overhead Television (1966 1980)
Television Technology
Tv
NT Broadcast Television
Cable Television
Childrens Television
Closed Circuit Television
Commercial Television
Educational Television
Public Television
BT Mass Media
Telecommunications
RT Broadcast Industry
Broadcast Reception Equipment
Electronic Equipment
Journalism
Journalism Education
Kinescope Recordings
Networks
News Media
Popular Culture
Production Techniques
Programing (Broadcast)
Radio
Special Effects
Teleconferencing
Television Commercials
Television Curriculum
Television Lighting
Television Radio Repairers
Television Research
Television Studios
Television Surveys
Television Teachers
Television Viewing
Videodisks
Video Equipment
Videotape Recordings
Videotex

TELEVISION COMMERCIALS *Jul. 1966*
CIJE: 235 RIE: 259 GC: 720
BT Advertising
RT Commercial Art
Commercial Television
Mass Media
Merchandising

= Two or more Descriptors are used to represent this term.
The term's main entry shows the appropriate coordination.

Programing (Broadcast)
Television
Television Viewing

TELEVISION CURRICULUM *Jul. 1966*
CIJE: 130 RIE: 188 GC: 400
SN Curriculum concerned with television, television production, etc. (note: for courses taught on television, use "telecourses" -- prior to mar80, this term did not carry a scope note)
BT Curriculum
RT Broadcast Industry
Journalism Education
Production Techniques
Programing (Broadcast)
Television
Television Teachers

Television Equipment
USE VIDEO EQUIPMENT

Television Lecturers
USE TELEVISION TEACHERS

TELEVISION LIGHTING *Jul. 1966*
CIJE: 22 RIE: 38 GC: 910
UF Television Lights (1966 1980)
BT Lighting
Production Techniques
RT Television
Television Studios

Television Lights (1966 1980)
USE TELEVISION LIGHTING

Television Programing
USE PROGRAMING (BROADCAST)

TELEVISION RADIO REPAIRERS *Mar. 1980*
CIJE: RIE: 34 GC: 640
UF Radio Television Repairers
Television Repairmen (1968 1980)
BT Skilled Workers
RT Radio
Repair
Service Workers
Television

Television Repairmen (1968 1980)
USE TELEVISION RADIO REPAIRERS

TELEVISION RESEARCH *Jul. 1966*
CIJE: 742 RIE: 1032 GC: 810
SN Basic, applied, and developmental research conducted to further knowledge about program content, impact, and use of television (note: as of oct81, use as a minor descriptor for examples of this kind of research -- use as a major descriptor only as the subject of a document)
BT Media Research
RT Programing (Broadcast)
Television
Television Surveys
Television Viewing

TELEVISION STUDIOS *Mar. 1980*
CIJE: 12 RIE: 7 GC: 920
UF Video Production Centers
BT Facilities
RT Broadcast Reception Equipment
Programing (Broadcast)
Telecommunications
Television
Television Lighting
Video Equipment

TELEVISION SURVEYS *Jul. 1966*
CIJE: 91 RIE: 255 GC: 810
SN Investigations of television viewership, viewing behavior, availability, etc., conducted to determine current status, trends, and/or norms -- includes surveys of television viewers and producers (note: as of oct81, use as a minor descriptor for examples of this kind of survey -- use as a major descriptor only as the subject of a document)
BT Surveys
RT Television
Television Research

TELEVISION TEACHERS *Jul. 1966*
CIJE: 55 RIE: 84 GC: 360
SN Teachers who provide instruction through the medium of television -- also, at the college level, instructors in the field of television production and techniques
UF Television Lecturers
BT Teachers
RT Educational Television
Telecourses
Television
Television Curriculum

Television Technology
USE TELEVISION

TELEVISION VIEWING *Jul. 1966*
CIJE: 1040 RIE: 1098 GC: 720
SN Act of viewing television programs
BT Activities
RT Audiences
Programing (Broadcast)
Television
Television Commercials
Television Research
Visual Literacy
Visual Stimuli

TELUGU *Jul. 1966*
CIJE: 1 RIE: 10 GC: 440
UF Telegu
BT Dravidian Languages

Temperament
USE PERSONALITY

TEMPERATURE *Jul. 1966*
CIJE: 183 RIE: 115 GC: 490
RT Air Conditioning
Air Conditioning Equipment
Air Flow
Climate
Climate Control
Fuel Consumption
Heat
Heating
Humidity
Meteorology
Refrigeration
Solar Energy
Thermal Environment
Ventilation
Wind (Meteorology)

Temporal Perspective
USE TIME PERSPECTIVE

Temporary Facilities
USE RELOCATABLE FACILITIES

Tenes
USE ENGLISH (SECOND LANGUAGE)

TENL (1968 1980) *Mar. 1980*
CIJE: 50 RIE: 154 GC: 450
SN Invalid descriptor -- coordinate "nonstandard dialects" with such descriptors as "english instruction," "teaching methods," "reading instruction," "english curriculum," "writing (composition)," etc.

TENNIS *Jun. 1975*
CIJE: 59 RIE: 26 GC: 470
BT Racquet Sports
RT Lifetime Sports
Squash (Game)

Tenpins
USE BOWLING

TENSES (GRAMMAR) *Oct. 1983*
CIJE: 14 RIE: 27 GC: 450
SN Grammatical constructions, such as verb inflections, for specifying time and duration
BT Morphemes
RT Form Classes (Languages)
Sentence Structure
Syntax
Time Perspective
Verbs

TENURE *Jul. 1966*
CIJE: 750 RIE: 989 GC: 630
SN Status of a person in a position or occupation (i.e., length of service, terms of employment, or permanence of position)
UF Job Tenure (1967 1978)
BT Employment Level
RT Academic Rank (Professional)
Aging In Academia
Contracts
Contract Salaries
Employees
Employer Employee Relationship
Employment
Employment Experience
Employment Practices
Employment Qualifications
Faculty Promotion
Job Layoff
Labor Problems
Labor Turnover
Nontenured Faculty
Occupational Mobility
Personnel Data
Personnel Policy
Probationary Period
Promotion (Occupational)
Reduction In Force
Seniority
Teacher Employment
Teacher Employment Benefits
Teacher Promotion
Teacher Rights
Teaching (Occupation)
Tenured Faculty
Work Life Expectancy

TENURED FACULTY *Oct. 1983*
CIJE: 27 RIE: 21 GC: 360
SN Academic staff who have been granted tenure (permanence of position) by their school or institution
UF Tenured Teachers
BT Faculty
RT Academic Rank (Professional)
College Faculty
Full Time Faculty
Nontenured Faculty
Professors
Teachers
Tenure

Tenured Teachers
USE TENURED FACULTY

Term Papers
USE RESEARCH PAPERS (STUDENTS)

TERMINAL EDUCATION *Jul. 1966*
CIJE: 12 RIE: 30 GC: 340
SN Includes secondary and postsecondary curricula designed to be complete in themselves for students who may not continue their formal education -- at the 2-year college level, frequently applies to programs that do not lead to transfer to 4-year institutions
BT Education
RT Terminal Students
Transfer Programs

TERMINAL STUDENTS *Jul. 1966*
CIJE: 19 RIE: 68 GC: 360
SN Secondary school students whose educational goals extend no further than high school graduation or students at the postsecondary level enrolled in programs that do not lead to 4-year degrees
BT Students
RT Continuation Students
Terminal Education
Two Year College Students

Termination Of Programs
USE PROGRAM TERMINATION

TERMINATION OF TREATMENT *Oct. 1983*
CIJE: 11 RIE: 5 GC: 210
SN The ending of personal health treatment (medical, psychological, etc.)
RT Counseling
Helping Relationship
Medical Services
Outcomes Of Treatment
Therapy

Terminology
USE VOCABULARY

TERRORISM *Oct. 1984*
CIJE: 10 RIE: 16 GC: 610
SN Threat or use of violence against a population or government to achieve social or political ends
BT Antisocial Behavior
RT Activism
Aggression
Crime
Emergency Programs
International Crimes
Political Attitudes
Revolution
Violence
War

Tertiary Education
USE POSTSECONDARY EDUCATION

Tesl
USE ENGLISH (SECOND LANGUAGE)

Tesol
USE ENGLISH (SECOND LANGUAGE)

Test Abuse
USE TEST USE

Test Administration
USE TESTING

Test Administrators
USE EXAMINERS

Test Analysis
USE TEST THEORY

TEST ANXIETY *Mar. 1980*
CIJE: 178 RIE: 127 GC: 310
SN Distress or uneasiness over test taking, often affecting test performance
BT Anxiety
RT School Phobia
Scores
Testing
Testing Problems
Tests
Test Wiseness

TEST BIAS *Mar. 1971*
CIJE: 582 RIE: 683 GC: 540
SN Unfairness in the construction, content, administration, or interpretation of tests, either for or against various groups such as minorities, the disabled, women, or socioeconomic classes
BT Bias
RT Culture Fair Tests
Error Patterns
Objective Tests
Social Bias
Social Discrimination
Statistical Bias
Test Coaching
Test Construction
Testing
Testing Problems
Test Interpretation
Test Items
Test Results
Tests
Test Selection
Test Use
Test Validity
Test Wiseness

Test Books
USE TESTS

Test Characteristics (Physical)
USE TEST FORMAT

TEST COACHING *Mar. 1980*
CIJE: 77 RIE: 131 GC: 310
SN Activities designed to prepare individuals, in a relatively short time, for taking tests and maximizing the scores obtained
BT Instruction
RT Guessing (Tests)
Review (Reexamination)
Test Bias
Testing
Testing Problems

Test Results
Tests
Test Validity
Test Wiseness
Tutoring

TEST CONSTRUCTION *Jul. 1966*
CIJE: 2127 RIE: 3001 GC: 820
SN Planning, assembling, writing, editing, or otherwise preparing a test or other individual measure for administration
UF Test Design
BT Material Development
RT Answer Keys
Answer Sheets
Computer Assisted Testing
Criterion Referenced Tests
Culture Fair Tests
Factor Analysis
Item Analysis
Item Banks
Item Sampling
Latent Trait Theory
Pretesting
Scaling
Skill Analysis
Task Analysis
Teacher Made Tests
Test Bias
Test Format
Testing
Testing Problems
Test Items
Test Length
Test Manuals
Test Reliability
Tests
Test Theory
Test Validity

Test Design
USE TEST CONSTRUCTION

TEST FORMAT *Apr. 1980*
CIJE: 245 RIE: 214 GC: 820
SN Types of test items and the responses they require (multiple choice, essay, computer assisted, cloze, etc.) -- also, the arrangement of items on the test form (e.g., arranging items in order of increasing difficulty)
UF Item Types
Test Characteristics (Physical)
Test Type
RT Comparative Testing
Questioning Techniques
Responses
Response Style (Tests)
Test Construction
Testing
Test Items
Test Length
Test Manuals
Tests

TEST INTERPRETATION *Jul. 1966*
CIJE: 1177 RIE: 1297 GC: 820
SN Explanation of the meaning, or description of the uses and limitations of, a test score or group of test scores
BT Data Interpretation
RT Confidence Testing
Criterion Referenced Tests
Error Of Measurement
Factor Structure
Generalizability Theory
Guessing (Tests)
Latent Trait Theory
Norm Referenced Tests
Psychometrics
Scores
Scoring Formulas
Test Bias
Testing
Test Items
Test Manuals
Test Norms
Test Reliability
Test Results
Tests
Test Theory
Test Use
Test Validity

TEST ITEMS *Mar. 1977*
CIJE: 450 RIE: 947 GC: 820
SN Questions, problems, exercises, or other units of a test that elicit responses which can be scored separately and related to the skills the test is measuring as a whole
UF Item Difficulty #
RT Adaptive Testing
Computer Assisted Testing
Content Validity
Item Analysis
Item Banks
Item Sampling
Latent Trait Theory
Problem Sets
Scores
Scoring
Test Bias
Test Construction
Test Format
Testing
Test Interpretation
Test Length
Test Manuals
Test Reliability
Tests
Test Theory
Test Validity

TEST LENGTH *Oct. 1983*
CIJE: 44 RIE: 75 GC: 820
SN The number of items in a test -- also, the amount of time required to administer and/or complete a test
RT Test Construction
Test Format
Testing
Test Items
Test Reliability
Tests
Timed Tests

TEST MANUALS *Mar. 1983*
CIJE: 6 RIE: 124 GC: 730
SN Guides provided for use with tests, including descriptive information, directions for administration/scoring/interpretation, normative data, and/or related information, such as construction procedures (note: use as major term for document subject, as minor term for document type -- do not use for "test taking manuals," for which see "study guides" and "test wiseness")
BT Guides
RT Answer Keys
Answer Sheets
Item Banks
Problem Sets
Scoring
Scoring Formulas
Test Construction
Test Format
Testing
Testing Problems
Testing Programs
Test Interpretation
Test Items
Test Norms
Test Results
Tests
Test Use

TEST NORMS *Mar. 1980*
CIJE: 139 RIE: 128 GC: 820
SN Statistical descriptions, such as score distributions, expressing the characteristic performance of a specified group or population with respect to a particular measure
BT Norms
RT Comparative Testing
Error Of Measurement
Grade Equivalent Scores
Item Sampling
Norm Referenced Tests
Scores
Standardized Tests
Testing
Testing Programs
Test Interpretation
Test Manuals
Test Results
Tests

TEST RELIABILITY *Jul. 1966*
CIJE: 2340 RIE: 2410 GC: 820
SN Accuracy, consistency, and stability of the results from a test or other measurement technique for a given population (note: prior to mar80, "reliability" was not restricted by a scope note, and many items indexed by "reliability" should have been indexed with "test reliability")
BT Reliability
RT Confidence Testing
Error Of Measurement
Generalizability Theory
Guessing (Tests)
Interrater Reliability
Item Analysis
Latent Trait Theory
Scores
Test Construction
Testing
Testing Problems
Test Interpretation
Test Items
Test Length
Test Results
Test Reviews
Tests
Test Selection
Test Theory
Test Validity
True Scores

TEST RESULTS *Jul. 1966*
CIJE: 950 RIE: 1997 GC: 820
SN Decisions, judgments, and other activities based on the outcome of testing (note: do not confuse with "scores" -- prior to mar80, the use of this term was not restricted by a scope note)
RT Scores
Test Bias
Test Coaching
Testing
Test Interpretation
Test Manuals
Test Norms
Test Reliability
Tests
Test Use
Test Validity

TEST REVIEWS *Jan. 1971*
CIJE: 272 RIE: 297 GC: 730
BT Publications
RT Comparative Testing
Surveys
Testing
Test Reliability
Tests
Test Selection
Test Validity

Test Scores
USE SCORES

TEST SCORING MACHINES *Jul. 1966*
CIJE: 48 RIE: 38 GC: 910
BT Equipment
RT Answer Keys
Answer Sheets
Automation
Instrumentation
Optical Scanners
Scores
Scoring
Testing
Tests

TEST SELECTION *Jul. 1966*
CIJE: 186 RIE: 428 GC: 820
BT Selection
RT Test Bias
Testing
Testing Problems
Test Reliability
Test Reviews
Tests
Test Use
Test Validity

Test Taking Skills
USE TEST WISENESS

Test Taking Strategies
USE TEST WISENESS

TEST THEORY *Apr. 1980*
CIJE: 134 RIE: 167 GC: 810
SN The study and analysis of the relationships between the characteristics of tests (and test items) and test scores and score distributions (including such characteristics as reliability and validity)
UF Score Theory
Test Analysis
NT Latent Trait Theory
BT Theories
RT Equated Scores
Generalizability Theory
Item Analysis
Mathematical Models
Proof (Mathematics)
Psychometrics
Scores
Scoring
Statistical Analysis
Test Construction
Testing
Test Interpretation
Test Items
Test Reliability
Tests
Test Validity

Test Type
USE TEST FORMAT

TEST USE *Nov. 1981*
CIJE: 313 RIE: 323 GC: 820
SN The uses of tests and test results
UF Test Abuse
RT Evaluation Utilization
Predictive Measurement
Scores
Test Bias
Testing
Testing Problems
Test Interpretation
Test Manuals
Test Results
Tests
Test Selection
Test Validity

TEST VALIDITY *Jul. 1966*
CIJE: 4017 RIE: 3229 GC: 820
SN Extent to which a test, inventory, rating scale, questionnaire, etc. is an effective index of what it is used or intended to measure (note: prior to mar80, "validity" was not restricted by a scope note, and many items indexed by "validity" should have been indexed with "test validity")
NT Construct Validity
Content Validity
BT Validity
RT Concurrent Validity
Confidence Testing
Factor Analysis
Factor Structure
Item Analysis
Latent Trait Theory
Multitrait Multimethod Techniques
Predictive Measurement
Predictive Validity
Predictor Variables
Response Style (Tests)
Scores
Test Bias
Test Coaching
Test Construction
Testing
Testing Problems
Test Interpretation
Test Items
Test Reliability
Test Results
Test Reviews
Tests
Test Selection
Test Theory
Test Use
Test Wiseness

TEST WISENESS *Feb. 1971*
CIJE: 271 RIE: 282 GC: 310
SN Skills and strategies, unrelated to the traits a test is intended to measure, that may increase test takers' scores -- may include the effects of coaching or experience in taking tests
UF Test Taking Skills
Test Taking Strategies

RT Guessing (Tests)
Incidental Learning
Intentional Learning
Problem Solving
Response Style (Tests)
Scores
Scoring Formulas
Test Anxiety
Test Bias
Test Coaching
Testing
Testing Problems
Tests
Test Validity

TESTING *Jul. 1966*
CIJE: 2538 RIE: 3309 GC: 820
SN Gathering and processing information about individuals ability, skill, understanding, or knowledge under controlled conditions (note: see also "evaluation" and "measurement")
UF Test Administration
Testing Methods
Testing Techniques
NT Adaptive Testing
Comparative Testing
Computer Assisted Testing
Confidence Testing
Educational Testing
Group Testing
Individual Testing
Minimum Competency Testing
Psychological Testing
BT Measurement Techniques
RT Concurrent Validity
Construct Validity
Content Validity
Data Collection
Error Patterns
Evaluation
Examiners
Factor Analysis
Forced Choice Technique
Grade Equivalent Scores
Guessing (Tests)
Informal Assessment
Item Analysis
Item Banks
Latent Trait Theory
Measurement
Measurement Objectives
Multitrait Multimethod Techniques
Needs Assessment
Predictive Measurement
Predictive Validity
Pretests Posttests
Problem Sets
Proctoring
Q Methodology
Scaling
Scores
Scoring
Test Anxiety
Test Bias
Test Coaching
Test Construction
Test Format
Testing Problems
Testing Programs
Test Interpretation
Test Items
Test Length
Test Manuals
Test Norms
Test Reliability
Test Results
Test Reviews
Tests
Test Scoring Machines
Test Selection
Test Theory
Test Use
Test Validity
Test Wiseness
Timed Tests

Testing Methods
USE TESTING

TESTING PROBLEMS *Jul. 1966*
CIJE: 1223 RIE: 1288 GC: 820
SN Difficulties associated with the selection, administration, scoring, or interpretation of tests or other individual measures
BT Problems
RT Confidence Testing
Culture Fair Tests
Error Of Measurement
Evaluation Problems
Experimenter Characteristics
Guessing (Tests)
Interrater Reliability
Response Style (Tests)
Scoring
Test Anxiety
Test Bias
Test Coaching
Test Construction
Testing
Test Manuals
Test Reliability
Tests
Test Selection
Test Use
Test Validity
Test Wiseness

TESTING PROGRAMS *Jul. 1966*
CIJE: 352 RIE: 1310 GC: 820
SN Organized plans and activities for selecting, administering, scoring, and interpreting measures of individual abilities, traits, interests, and attitudes
BT Programs
RT Educational Diagnosis
Standardized Tests
State Licensing Boards
Testing
Test Manuals
Test Norms
Tests

Testing Techniques
USE TESTING

TESTS *Jul. 1966*
CIJE: 1337 RIE: 2623 GC: 830
SN Devices, procedures, or sets of items that are used to measure ability, skill, understanding, knowledge, or achievement (note: use a more specific term if possible -- this broad term corresponds to pubtype code 160 and should not be used except as the subject of a document)
UF Examinations
Identification Tests (1966 1980)
Quizzes
Test Books
NT Achievement Tests
Aptitude Tests
Auditory Tests
Cognitive Tests
College Entrance Examinations
Creativity Tests
Criterion Referenced Tests
Culture Fair Tests
Diagnostic Tests
Field Tests
Licensing Examinations (Professions)
Mathematics Tests
Maturity Tests
Nonverbal Tests
Norm Referenced Tests
Objective Tests
Occupational Tests
Open Book Tests
Performance Tests
Preschool Tests
Pretests Posttests
Prognostic Tests
Science Tests
Screening Tests
Situational Tests
Standardized Tests
Teacher Made Tests
Timed Tests
Verbal Tests
Vision Tests
BT Measures (Individuals)
RT Answer Keys
Answer Sheets
Computer Assisted Testing
Evaluation
Examiners
Forced Choice Technique
Guessing (Tests)
Instructional Materials
Item Analysis
Item Banks
Latent Trait Theory
Measurement
Problem Sets
Response Style (Tests)
Scores
Scoring
Statistical Data
Test Anxiety
Test Bias
Test Coaching
Test Construction
Test Format
Testing
Testing Problems
Testing Programs
Test Interpretation
Test Items
Test Length
Test Manuals
Test Norms
Test Reliability
Test Results
Test Reviews
Test Scoring Machines
Test Selection
Test Theory
Test Use
Test Validity
Test Wiseness

Tests Of Significance (1966 1980)
USE STATISTICAL SIGNIFICANCE

Tetraplegia
USE NEUROLOGICAL IMPAIRMENTS

Text Processing
USE WORD PROCESSING

Textbook Assignments (1966 1980)
USE ASSIGNMENTS

TEXTBOOK BIAS *Jul. 1966*
CIJE: 319 RIE: 252 GC: 540
BT Bias
RT Multicultural Textbooks
Textbook Content
Textbook Evaluation
Textbook Preparation
Textbook Research
Textbooks
Textbook Selection

TEXTBOOK CONTENT *Jul. 1966*
CIJE: 833 RIE: 486 GC: 310
RT Content Analysis
Course Content
Multicultural Textbooks
Textbook Bias
Textbook Evaluation
Textbook Preparation
Textbook Research
Textbooks
Textbook Selection
Textbook Standards

Textbook Development
USE TEXTBOOK PREPARATION

TEXTBOOK EVALUATION *Jul. 1966*
CIJE: 871 RIE: 669 GC: 320
SN Determining the efficacy, value, etc. of textbooks with respect to stated objectives, standards, or criteria (note: as of oct81, use as a minor descriptor for examples of this kind of evaluation -- use as a major descriptor only as the subject of a document)
BT Instructional Material Evaluation
RT Book Reviews
Readability
Readability Formulas
Textbook Bias
Textbook Content
Textbook Research
Textbooks
Textbook Selection
Textbook Standards

TEXTBOOK PREPARATION *Jul. 1966*
CIJE: 188 RIE: 148 GC: 720
UF Textbook Development
Textbook Writing
RT Technical Writing
Textbook Bias
Textbook Content
Textbook Publication
Textbook Research
Textbooks
Textbook Standards

Textbook Production
USE TEXTBOOK PUBLICATION

TEXTBOOK PUBLICATION *Mar. 1980*
CIJE: 54 RIE: 32 GC: 720
SN Act or process of publishing a textbook
UF Textbook Production
Textbook Publishing
BT Production Techniques
RT Printing
Publishing Industry
Textbook Preparation
Textbooks

TEXTBOOK PUBLICATIONS (1966 1980) *Jun. 1980*
CIJE: 70 RIE: 41 GC: 730
SN Invalid descriptor -- see the more precise descriptors "textbooks" and "textbook publication"

Textbook Publishing
USE TEXTBOOK PUBLICATION

TEXTBOOK RESEARCH *Jul. 1966*
CIJE: 192 RIE: 224 GC: 810
SN Systematic investigation of the design, content, biases, impact, etc. of textbooks (note: as of oct81, use as a minor descriptor for examples of this kind of research -- use as a major descriptor only as the subject of a document -- do not confuse with "textbook evaluation")
BT Media Research
RT Textbook Bias
Textbook Content
Textbook Evaluation
Textbook Preparation
Textbooks

TEXTBOOK SELECTION *Jul. 1966*
CIJE: 439 RIE: 324 GC: 320
BT Media Selection
RT Reading Material Selection
Textbook Bias
Textbook Content
Textbook Evaluation
Textbooks
Textbook Standards

TEXTBOOK STANDARDS *Jul. 1966*
CIJE: 124 RIE: 96 GC: 330
BT Standards
RT Textbook Content
Textbook Evaluation
Textbook Preparation
Textbooks
Textbook Selection

Textbook Writing
USE TEXTBOOK PREPARATION

TEXTBOOKS *Jul. 1966*
CIJE: 1340 RIE: 3070 GC: 730
UF Programed Texts (1966 1980) #
Supplementary Textbooks (1967 1980) #
NT History Textbooks
Multicultural Textbooks
BT Books
Instructional Materials
RT Laboratory Manuals
Programed Instructional Materials
Reading Materials
Teaching Guides
Textbook Bias
Textbook Content
Textbook Evaluation
Textbook Preparation
Textbook Publication
Textbook Research
Textbook Selection
Textbook Standards
Workbooks

Textile Finishing
USE FINISHING

TEXTILES INSTRUCTION *Jul. 1966*
CIJE: 44 RIE: 111 GC: 400
BT Instruction
RT Clothing
Clothing Instruction
Fashion Industry
Home Economics
Laundry Drycleaning Occupations

= Two or more Descriptors are used to represent this term.
The term's main entry shows the appropriate coordination.

TEXTUAL CRITICISM (1969 1980) *Mar. 1980*
CIJE: 119 RIE: 53 GC: 430
SN Invalid descriptor -- originally intended as a literary term, but used indiscriminately in indexing -- see "literary criticism," "evaluation," "evaluation methods," etc.

THAI *Jul. 1966*
CIJE: 36 RIE: 83 GC: 440
BT Sino Tibetan Languages

Thanatology
USE DEATH

Theater
USE THEATER ARTS

THEATER ARTS *Jul. 1966*
CIJE: 829 RIE: 713 GC: 420
UF Childrens Theater
Performing Arts
Shadow Plays
Theater
NT Acting
Choral Speaking
Drama
Dramatics
Opera
Pantomime
Puppetry
Readers Theater
BT Fine Arts
RT Art
Audiences
Cultural Activities
Dance
Film Industry
Film Production
Films
Film Study
Orchestras
Playwriting
Production Techniques
Skits
Special Effects
Speech Communication
Theaters

THEATERS *Jul. 1966*
CIJE: 77 RIE: 118 GC: 920
UF Outdoor Theaters (1968 1980) #
Performing Arts Centers
BT Facilities
RT Acoustical Environment
Arts Centers
Auditoriums
Dramatics
Drama Workshops
Educational Facilities
Music Facilities
Recreational Facilities
Stages (Facilities)
Theater Arts

Thefts
USE STEALING

THEMATIC APPROACH *Dec. 1969*
CIJE: 243 RIE: 229 GC: 310
SN Teaching approach that organizes subject matter around unifying themes
BT Teaching Methods
RT Curriculum Design
Interdisciplinary Approach

Theme Writing
USE WRITING (COMPOSITION)

THEOLOGICAL EDUCATION *Jul. 1966*
CIJE: 85 RIE: 77 GC: 400
SN Formal education in a higher education institution in preparation for careers in religion, including the clergy (note: prior to mar80, this term was not restricted by a scope note)
UF Seminaries #
BT Professional Education
RT Churches
Church Related Colleges
Clergy
Nuns
Priests
Religion
Religious Education

THEORETICAL CRITICISM (1969 1980) *Mar. 1980*
CIJE: 158 RIE: 47 GC: 430
SN Invalid descriptor -- originally intended as a literary term, but used indiscriminately in indexing -- see "literary criticism," "standards," "theories," "evaluation," etc.

Theoretical Models
USE MODELS

THEORIES *Jul. 1966*
CIJE: 2149 RIE: 1587 GC: 810
SN Generalizations or principles, supported by substantial evidence but not conclusively established, proposed as explanations of observed phenomena or of the relations in a given body of facts (note: use a more specific term if possible)
NT Atomic Theory
Behavior Theories
Counseling Theories
Educational Theories
Game Theory
Generalizability Theory
Information Theory
Kinetic Molecular Theory
Learning Theories
Linguistic Theory
Music Theory
Personality Theories
Piagetian Theory
Relativity
Role Theory
Set Theory
Social Theories
Test Theory
RT Generalization
Hypothesis Testing
Models
Research
Scientific Methodology
Theory Practice Relationship

THEORY PRACTICE RELATIONSHIP *Dec. 1985*
CIJE: 259 RIE: 251 GC: 810
SN The association between knowledge/understanding and action/application
UF Research Practice Relationship #
BT Relationship
RT Action Research
Adoption (Ideas)
Diffusion (Communication)
Educational Innovation
Educational Practices
Educational Research
Innovation
Linking Agents
Methods Research
Models
Research
Research And Development
Research Utilization
School Involvement
Teaching Methods
Teamwork
Theories

Therapeutic Communities
USE MILIEU THERAPY

THERAPEUTIC ENVIRONMENT *Jul. 1966*
CIJE: 349 RIE: 168 GC: 230
SN Surrounding conditions, forces, or factors that facilitate the process of therapy
BT Environment
RT Counseling
Counselor Client Relationship
Educational Therapy
Mental Health Clinics
Milieu Therapy
Physician Patient Relationship
Psychiatric Hospitals
Psychotherapy
Rehabilitation
Rehabilitation Centers
Therapy
Token Economy

Therapeutic Play
USE PLAY THERAPY

THERAPEUTIC RECREATION *Jun. 1983*
CIJE: 10 RIE: 19 GC: 230
SN Recreation services and activities designed to treat or rehabilitate individuals with certain physical, emotional, and/or social problems (e.g., the disabled, infirm, or incarcerated)
UF Recreation Therapy
NT Play Therapy
BT Recreation
Therapy
RT Allied Health Occupations
Art Therapy
Correctional Education
Dance Therapy
Music Therapy
Occupational Therapy
Physical Therapy
Psychotherapy
Recreational Activities
Rehabilitation
Special Education

Therapeutics
USE THERAPY

THERAPISTS *Jul. 1966*
CIJE: 500 RIE: 242 GC: 640
UF Hearing Therapists (1967 1980) #
Inhalation Therapists (1969 1985) #
Speech Therapists (1966 1980) #
NT Occupational Therapists
Physical Therapists
BT Allied Health Personnel
Professional Personnel
RT Psychotherapy
Therapy

THERAPY *Aug. 1969*
CIJE: 695 RIE: 372 GC: 210
UF Therapeutics
NT Art Therapy
Bibliotherapy
Dance Therapy
Drug Therapy
Educational Therapy
Group Therapy
Hearing Therapy
Music Therapy
Occupational Therapy
Physical Therapy
Psychotherapy
Respiratory Therapy
Speech Therapy
Therapeutic Recreation
RT Adjustment (To Environment)
Allied Health Occupations
Disabilities
Helping Relationship
Medical Services
Medicine
Outcomes Of Treatment
Rehabilitation
Special Education
Termination Of Treatment
Therapeutic Environment
Therapists

THERMAL ENVIRONMENT *Jul. 1966*
CIJE: 126 RIE: 163 GC: 920
SN Related to the combined effects of radiant temperature, air temperature, humidity, and air velocity
BT Physical Environment
RT Air Conditioning
Air Conditioning Equipment
Building Design
Climate
Climate Control
Design Requirements
Environmental Influences
Fuel Consumption
Heating
Heat Recovery
Human Factors Engineering
Humidity
Interior Design
Meteorology
Solar Energy
Temperature
Ventilation
Water
Weather
Wind (Meteorology)

THERMODYNAMICS *Aug. 1968*
CIJE: 422 RIE: 41 GC: 490
UF Heat Equations
Thermomechanics
Thermophysics
Thermoscience
BT Physics
RT Calorimeters
Chemical Equilibrium
Diffusion (Physics)
Heat
Nuclear Physics

Thermomechanics
USE THERMODYNAMICS

Thermophysics
USE THERMODYNAMICS

Thermoscience
USE THERMODYNAMICS

THESAURI *Jul. 1966*
CIJE: 116 RIE: 222 GC: 730
BT Reference Materials
RT Coordinate Indexes
Dictionaries
Glossaries
Indexes
Indexing
Information Retrieval
Lexicography
Subject Index Terms
Vocabulary

THESES *Mar. 1980*
CIJE: 18 RIE: 22 GC: 720
SN Propositions that are advanced and defended by argument, and which may be based on original research and used to satisfy academic degree requirements (note: corresponds to pubtype code 040 -- do not use except as the subject of a document)
NT Doctoral Dissertations
Masters Theses
BT Reports
RT Essays
Expository Writing
Research

Thinking Aloud Protocols
USE PROTOCOL ANALYSIS

Thinking Processes
USE COGNITIVE PROCESSES

Third World Countries
USE DEVELOPING NATIONS

Thought Processes (1966 1980)
USE COGNITIVE PROCESSES

THREE DIMENSIONAL AIDS *Jul. 1966*
CIJE: 51 RIE: 32 GC: 720
BT Visual Aids
RT Audiovisual Aids
Display Aids
Exhibits
Holography
Models
Realia

Three Year Bachelors Degrees
USE ACCELERATION (EDUCATION); BACHELORS DEGREES

THRESHOLD LEVEL (LANGUAGES) *Oct. 1980*
CIJE: 6 RIE: 9 GC: 450
SN The minimum level of foreign language proficiency needed for learners to communicate in most everyday situations, including situations for which they have not been specifically trained -- emphasis is on oral skills and listening comprehension -- objectives for reading and writing skills are narrowly restricted
BT Communicative Competence (Languages)
Language Proficiency
RT Second Language Learning

TIBETAN *Jul. 1966*
CIJE: 2 RIE: 8 GC: 440
BT Sino Tibetan Languages

= Two or more Descriptors are used to represent this term. The term's main entry shows the appropriate coordination.

Timber Based Industry
USE LUMBER INDUSTRY

TIME *Jul. 1966*
CIJE: 526 RIE: 316 GC: 490
BT Scientific Concepts
RT Distance
Horology
Intervals
Obsolescence
Proximity
Relativity
Space
Timed Tests
Time Factors (Learning)
Time Management

Time Allocation
USE TIME MANAGEMENT

TIME BLOCKS *Jul. 1966*
CIJE: 92 RIE: 113 GC: 350
UF Block Time Teaching
BT School Schedules
RT Flexible Scheduling
Time Factors (Learning)

Time Estimation
USE TIME MANAGEMENT

TIME FACTORS (LEARNING) *Jul. 1966*
CIJE: 956 RIE: 771 GC: 110
BT Influences
RT Conceptual Tempo
Extended School Day
Extended School Year
Learning
Pacing
Program Length
Reaction Time
Scheduling
Teaching Machines
Time
Time Blocks
Time Management
Time On Task
Time Perspective

TIME MANAGEMENT *Jun. 1983*
CIJE: 153 RIE: 174 GC: 310
SN Use or allocation of time by individuals or groups -- can include strategies for estimating and budgeting time to improve effectiveness
UF Time Allocation
Time Estimation
Time Use Data
Time Utilization
BT Administration
RT Efficiency
Pacing
Performance
Planning
Scheduling
Time
Timed Tests
Time Factors (Learning)
Time On Task
Time Perspective

TIME ON TASK *Nov. 1981*
CIJE: 256 RIE: 261 GC: 310
SN The period of time during which a student is actively engaged in a learning activity (note: prior to oct81, this concept was frequently indexed under "time factors (learning)")
UF Academic Learning Time
Engaged Time (Learning)
Student Engaged Time
RT Attention
Learning Activities
Performance
Persistence
Student Behavior
Study
Time Factors (Learning)
Time Management

TIME PERSPECTIVE *Jul. 1966*
CIJE: 361 RIE: 182 GC: 110
UF Temporal Perspective
RT Tenses (Grammar)
Time Factors (Learning)
Time Management

TIME SHARING *Jul. 1966*
CIJE: 98 RIE: 213 GC: 710
SN Computing technique in which numerous terminal devices can utilize a central computer concurrently for input, processing, and output functions
UF Shared Time (Computers)
BT Data Processing
RT Computers
Input Output
Online Systems

Time Shortened Degree Programs
USE ACCELERATION (EDUCATION)

Time Use Data
USE TIME MANAGEMENT

Time Utilization
USE TIME MANAGEMENT

TIMED TESTS *Jul. 1966*
CIJE: 65 RIE: 74 GC: 830
SN Tests that must be completed within a given period of time, usually scored on the basis of the number of items completed correctly
UF Rate Tests
Speed Tests
BT Tests
RT Testing
Test Length
Time
Time Management

TIMEOUT *Oct. 1972*
CIJE: 55 RIE: 26 GC: 110
SN Period of time in which no positive reinforcers are available, e.g. isolation in small room
BT Reinforcement
RT Behavior Modification
Contingency Management
Extinction (Psychology)
Operant Conditioning

TISSUE DONORS *Oct. 1982*
CIJE: 1 RIE: 3 GC: 210
SN Individuals who donate blood, sperm, organs, etc. for medical and health use
UF Blood Donors
Organ Donors
Sperm Donors
BT Groups
RT Medical Services
Physical Health

Title Word Indexes
USE PERMUTED INDEXES

TOBACCO *Jul. 1966*
CIJE: 56 RIE: 79 GC: 210
BT Field Crops
RT Drug Abuse
Drug Use
Health Education
Smoking
Stimulants

TODDLERS *Oct. 1984*
CIJE: 86 RIE: 129 GC: 120
SN Approximately 1-3 years of age
BT Young Children
RT Infants
Preschool Children

TOILET FACILITIES *Apr. 1970*
CIJE: 6 RIE: 11 GC: 920
BT Sanitary Facilities
RT Public Facilities

TOKEN ECONOMY *Oct. 1982*
CIJE: 63 RIE: 32 GC: 110
SN Planned reinforcement programs in which individuals earn tokens or points for performing desired behaviors -- these tokens or points can then be exchanged for a variety of rewards or privileges
BT Reinforcement
RT Behavior Modification
Contingency Management
Incentives
Operant Conditioning
Psychoeducational Methods
Rewards
Therapeutic Environment

Token Integration (1966 1980)
USE TOKENISM

TOKENISM *Mar. 1980*
CIJE: 23 RIE: 33 GC: 540
SN Superficial efforts or symbolic gestures toward complying with desegregation or equal opportunity laws, rulings, or guidelines
UF Token Integration (1966 1980)
RT Affirmative Action
De Facto Segregation
Equal Education
Equal Opportunities (Jobs)
Neighborhood Integration
Personnel Integration
Racial Balance
Racial Composition
Racial Integration
School Desegregation
Sex Fairness
Social Integration

TONE LANGUAGES *Jul. 1966*
CIJE: 39 RIE: 110 GC: 450
SN Languages in which tone or pitch patterns form part of the structure of words rather than sentences (note: see african and sino-tibetan language families for specific languages)
BT Language
RT Descriptive Linguistics
Intonation
Language Typology
Morphophonemics

TOOL AND DIE MAKERS *Aug. 1969*
CIJE: 2 RIE: 15 GC: 640
SN Workers responsible for constructing, repairing, maintaining, and calibrating machine-shop tools, jigs and fixtures, gauges, and metal-forming dies
BT Machinists
RT Machinery Industry
Machine Tool Operators
Machine Tools
Metal Working

TOPOGRAPHY *Mar. 1980*
CIJE: 18 RIE: 49 GC: 480
SN Science of compiling detailed descriptions of areas, especially graphic representations of physical configurations which include features of both natural and human origin
BT Social Sciences
RT Cartography
Demography
Earth Science
Geographic Location
Geography
Maps
Social Scientists

TOPOLOGY *Oct. 1968*
CIJE: 80 RIE: 41 GC: 480
SN Study of the properties of geometric forms that remain constant under such transformations as bending or stretching
BT Geometry
RT Algebra
Distance
Graphs
Proximity
Vectors (Mathematics)

TORTS *Jan. 1978*
CIJE: 96 RIE: 104 GC: 610
SN Private or civil wrongs, not including breach of contract, for which perpetrators may be legally prosecuted and injured parties may be compensated
RT Civil Disobedience
Civil Rights
Constitutional Law
Court Litigation
Educational Malpractice
Justice
Laws
Legal Problems
Legal Responsibility
Malpractice

TOTAL COMMUNICATION *Jul. 1977*
CIJE: 98 RIE: 45 GC: 220
SN Use of all available forms of communication, i.e., aural, manual, and oral, to develop language competence and ensure effective communication -- usually with and among the hearing impaired
BT Communication (Thought Transfer)
RT Communication Aids (For Disabled)
Communication Skills
Deafness
Finger Spelling
Hearing Aids
Hearing Impairments
Hearing Therapy
Lipreading
Manual Communication
Oral Communication Method
Partial Hearing
Sign Language
Speech Skills
Verbal Communication

TOTALITARIANISM *Oct. 1974*
CIJE: 25 RIE: 19 GC: 610
UF Dictatorship
NT Nazism
RT Authoritarianism
Communism
Democracy
Dogmatism
Fascism
Government (Administrative Body)
Political Attitudes
Political Power
Political Science

TOURISM *Nov. 1969*
CIJE: 82 RIE: 133 GC: 650
UF Sightseeing Industry
Tourist Industry
BT Industry
RT Camping
Hospitality Occupations
Hotels
Outdoor Activities
Recreational Activities
Study Abroad
Transportation
Travel

Tourist Courts
USE HOTELS

Tourist Industry
USE TOURISM

Tower Diving
USE DIVING

Towns
USE MUNICIPALITIES

Toxic Substances
USE POISONS

TOXICOLOGY *Sep. 1982*
CIJE: 51 RIE: 14 GC: 210
SN Science dealing with the nature, effects, and detection of poisonous substances and methods of treatment for poison intake
BT Medicine
RT Allergy
Biochemistry
Medical Services
Pathology
Pharmacology
Physiology
Poisoning
Poisons
Radiation Biology

Toxins
USE POISONS

TOYS *Jul. 1966*
CIJE: 256 RIE: 220 GC: 470
RT Childrens Games
Games
Instructional Materials
Play
Puzzles

TRACK AND FIELD *Dec. 1975*
CIJE: 25 RIE: 35 GC: 470
BT Athletics
RT Lifetime Sports
Running

TRACK SYSTEM (EDUCATION) *Mar. 1980*
CIJE: 71 RIE: 66 GC: 330
SN System whereby students of the same chronological age or grade level are assigned to different classes, programs, or schools (e.g., college preparatory programs vs. vocational programs) on the basis of perceived ability, achievement level, career/vocational choice, etc. (note: prior to mar80, the term "flexible progression" was used for this concept)
RT Ability Grouping
Student Placement

TRACKING (1968 1980) *Jun. 1980*
CIJE: 38 RIE: 25 GC: 330
SN Invalid descriptor -- used indiscriminately in indexing -- see more precise descriptors "track system (education)," "perceptual motor coordination," and "psychomotor skills," as well as the identifier "tracking (science)"

TRACTORS *Jul. 1966*
CIJE: 12 RIE: 41 GC: 410
BT Motor Vehicles
RT Agricultural Machinery
Agriculture

TRADE AND INDUSTRIAL EDUCATION *Jul. 1966*
CIJE: 351 RIE: 1974 GC: 400
SN Formal preparation for a wide range of trades and occupations in industry at the semiskilled, skilled, or supervisory levels
UF Vocational Industrial Education
BT Vocational Education
RT Adult Vocational Education
Apprenticeships
Blue Collar Occupations
Building Trades
Data Processing Occupations
Electrical Occupations
Industrial Arts
Industrial Education
Industrial Personnel
Industrial Training
Mechanical Skills
On The Job Training
School Shops
Semiskilled Occupations
Semiskilled Workers
Service Occupations
Service Workers
Skilled Occupations
Skilled Workers
Technical Education
Technical Occupations
Technology
Trade And Industrial Teachers
Two Year Colleges

TRADE AND INDUSTRIAL TEACHERS *Jul. 1966*
CIJE: 53 RIE: 73 GC: 360
BT Vocational Education Teachers
RT Industrial Arts Teachers
Industrial Education
Trade And Industrial Education

Trade Unions
USE UNIONS

Traditional Classrooms
USE SELF CONTAINED CLASSROOMS

Traditional Family Unit
USE NUCLEAR FAMILY

TRADITIONAL GRAMMAR *Jul. 1966*
CIJE: 114 RIE: 119 GC: 450
BT Linguistic Theory
RT Form Classes (Languages)
Grammar
Linguistics
Morphology (Languages)
Paragraphs
Sentence Structure
Structural Grammar
Syntax
Transformational Generative Grammar

Traditional Instruction
USE CONVENTIONAL INSTRUCTION

TRADITIONAL SCHOOLS *Jul. 1966*
CIJE: 154 RIE: 160 GC: 340
SN Schools characterized by a conventional, non-innovative approach to education
BT Schools
RT Back To Basics
Conventional Instruction
Educational Philosophy
Nontraditional Education
School Organization
Self Contained Classrooms
Transitional Schools

TRADITIONALISM *Jun. 1983*
CIJE: 48 RIE: 66 GC: 520
SN Disposition to accept or adhere to the values, practices, and institutions of past generations
RT Conservatism
Cultural Influences
Ethnicity
Modernization
Philosophy
Religion
Social Attitudes
Social Change
Social History
Sociocultural Patterns
Socioeconomic Influences
Values

Traditions (Culture)
USE FOLK CULTURE

TRAFFIC ACCIDENTS *Jul. 1966*
CIJE: 49 RIE: 102 GC: 210
BT Accidents
RT Safety
Safety Education
Traffic Control
Traffic Safety

TRAFFIC CIRCULATION *Oct. 1968*
CIJE: 32 RIE: 65 GC: 920
UF Street Layouts
Traffic Flow
Traffic Patterns (1968 1980)
RT Driveways
Motor Vehicles
Parking Controls
Parking Facilities
Pedestrian Traffic
Road Construction
Service Vehicles
Student Transportation
Traffic Control
Vehicular Traffic

TRAFFIC CONTROL *Oct. 1968*
CIJE: 25 RIE: 120 GC: 920
UF Spectator Traffic Control
Traffic Regulations (1968 1980)
Traffic Signs (1968 1980) #
NT Air Traffic Control
RT Motor Vehicles
Parking Controls
Parking Facilities
Pedestrian Traffic
Signs
Traffic Accidents
Traffic Circulation
Traffic Safety
Transportation
Vehicular Traffic

Traffic Flow
USE TRAFFIC CIRCULATION

Traffic Patterns (1968 1980)
USE TRAFFIC CIRCULATION

Traffic Regulations (1968 1980)
USE TRAFFIC CONTROL

TRAFFIC SAFETY *Jul. 1966*
CIJE: 94 RIE: 375 GC: 210
BT Safety
RT Driver Education
Motor Vehicles
Restraints (Vehicle Safety)
Safety Education
Traffic Accidents
Traffic Control

Traffic Signs (1968 1980)
USE SIGNS; TRAFFIC CONTROL

TRAGEDY *Jul. 1966*
CIJE: 53 RIE: 47 GC: 430
BT Drama
RT Comedy
Literary Devices
Literary Genres
Poetry
Prose
Scripts

TRAILS *Nov. 1969*
CIJE: 71 RIE: 50 GC: 920
UF Nature Trails
Pathways
BT Facilities
RT Adventure Education
Camping
Conservation Education
Landscaping
Orienteering
Outdoor Education
Park Design
Parks
Playgrounds
Recreational Facilities

Trainable Mentally Handicapped (1967 1980)
USE MODERATE MENTAL RETARDATION

TRAINEES *Jul. 1966*
CIJE: 154 RIE: 175 GC: 630
SN Participants in vocational, administrative, or technical training programs for purpose of developing job related skills
BT Groups
RT Apprenticeships
Industrial Training
Job Training
Students
Training
Training Methods
Work Experience Programs

TRAINERS *Jul. 1966*
CIJE: 317 RIE: 275 GC: 630
SN Persons who direct the practice of skills toward immediate improvement in some art or task
BT Personnel
RT Adult Educators
Industrial Training
Laboratory Training
Leadership Training
Teachers
Training
Training Methods

TRAINING *Jul. 1966*
CIJE: 1300 RIE: 1543 GC: 330
SN Instructional process aimed at the acquisition of defined skills relating to particular functions or activities (note: use a more specific term if possible)
NT Counselor Training
Cross Cultural Training
Flight Training
Industrial Training
Job Training
Laboratory Training
Leadership Training
Military Training
Professional Training
Retraining
Sensitivity Training
Sensory Training
Supervisory Training
Team Training
Travel Training
Volunteer Training
RT Career Ladders
Education
Skill Development
Trainees
Trainers
Training Allowances
Training Methods
Training Objectives
Transfer Of Training

TRAINING ALLOWANCES *Jul. 1966*
CIJE: 18 RIE: 77 GC: 620
BT Financial Support
RT Adult Education
Educational Finance
Federal Aid
Grants
Industrial Training
Job Training
Labor Force Development
State Aid
Training
Tuition Grants
Veterans Education

Training Alternatives
USE NONTRADITIONAL EDUCATION

Training Goals
USE TRAINING OBJECTIVES

TRAINING LABORATORIES (1967 1980) *Mar. 1980*
CIJE: 78 RIE: 81 GC: 920
SN Invalid descriptor -- used inconsistently -- coordinate "laboratories" or its narrower terms with specific "training" descriptors (e.g., "sensitivity training," "job training," "leadership training," "laboratory training," etc.)

TRAINING METHODS *Mar. 1980*
CIJE: 2157 RIE: 1939 GC: 310
SN Standard procedures or approaches designed to help individuals or groups acquire the skills needed for specific activities or functions
UF Training Techniques (1967 1980)
NT Management Games
Microcounseling
Microteaching
BT Teaching Methods
RT Institutes (Training Programs)
Skill Development
Trainees
Trainers
Training
Training Objectives
Work Experience Programs
Workshops

TRAINING OBJECTIVES *Jul. 1966*
CIJE: 548 RIE: 696 GC: 310
UF Training Goals
BT Objectives
RT Behavioral Objectives
Training
Training Methods

Training Opportunities
USE EDUCATIONAL OPPORTUNITIES

Training Schools (Juvenile Offenders)
USE CORRECTIONAL INSTITUTIONS

Training Techniques (1967 1980)
USE TRAINING METHODS

Trait Treatment Interaction
USE APTITUDE TREATMENT INTERACTION

Tranquilizing Drugs
USE SEDATIVES

TRANSACTIONAL ANALYSIS *Apr. 1982*
CIJE: 76 RIE: 35 GC: 240
SN Psychotherapeutic approach that postulates three ego states (adult, parent, and child) from which all human interaction or communication emanates -- the approach maintains that awareness or knowledge of the three states leads to more constructive interpersonal relations
BT Psychotherapy
RT Communication Skills
Counseling Techniques
Group Dynamics
Group Therapy
Interpersonal Competence
Laboratory Training
Self Evaluation (Individuals)
Self Expression
Social Behavior
Social Cognition

= Two or more Descriptors are used to represent this term.
The term's main entry shows the appropriate coordination.

TRANSCENDENTAL MEDITATION *Oct. 1982*
CIJE: 31 RIE: 9 GC: 110
SN A meditative technique, developed by maharishi mahesh yogi, using the repetition of a specific sound (mantra) to induce a state of mental neutrality (absence of extraneous thought) and mystical insight
BT Meditation
RT Behavior Modification
Biofeedback
Creative Thinking
Psychoeducational Methods
Relaxation Training

Transcripts (Academic)
USE ACADEMIC RECORDS

Transfer Of Learning
USE TRANSFER OF TRAINING

TRANSFER OF TRAINING *Jul. 1966*
CIJE: 764 RIE: 733 GC: 110
SN The influence that an existing habit, skill, or idea exerts on the acquisition, performance, or relearning of another similar characteristic
UF Transfer Of Learning
BT Learning
RT Diffusion (Communication)
Generalization
Learning Strategies
Skill Development
Training

TRANSFER POLICY *Jul. 1966*
CIJE: 117 RIE: 248 GC: 330
SN A formal plan or set of principles regarding the transfer of individuals from one institution or program to another and the granting of credit for past experience
BT Policy
RT Admission Criteria
Articulation (Education)
Attendance
College Credits
Credits
Enrollment
Free Choice Transfer Programs
Prior Learning
Relocation
School Policy
Teacher Transfer
Transfer Programs
Transfer Students

TRANSFER PROGRAMS *Jul. 1966*
CIJE: 91 RIE: 320 GC: 330
SN Programs that yield credit to new students or employees for prior learning and/or experience
UF Restrictive Transfer Programs (1966 1980)
NT Free Choice Transfer Programs
BT Programs
RT Articulation (Education)
College Credits
Credits
Experience
Job Placement
Prior Learning
Relocation
Student Placement
Teacher Transfer
Terminal Education
Transfer Policy
Transfer Students

TRANSFER STUDENTS *Jul. 1966*
CIJE: 201 RIE: 614 GC: 360
SN Students transferring from one school or educational program to another (note: if applicable, use the more specific term "college transfer students")
UF Student Transfers
NT College Transfer Students
BT Students
RT Attendance
Continuation Students
Educational Mobility
Enrollment
Free Choice Transfer Programs
Migrant Children
Migrant Youth
Prior Learning
Racially Balanced Schools
School Desegregation
Student Mobility
Transfer Policy
Transfer Programs
Transient Children

TRANSFERS (1966 1980) *Mar. 1980*
CIJE: 45 RIE: 74 GC: 320
SN Invalid descriptor -- see "relocation" and other "transfer" descriptors

Transformation Generative Grammar (1968 1980)
USE TRANSFORMATIONAL GENERATIVE GRAMMAR

Transformation Theory (Language) (1967 1980)
USE LINGUISTIC THEORY; TRANSFORMATIONAL GENERATIVE GRAMMAR

TRANSFORMATIONAL GENERATIVE GRAMMAR *Mar. 1980*
CIJE: 654 RIE: 715 GC: 450
SN A generative grammar consisting of syntactic, phonological, and semantic components in which transformational rules are used to relate the surface structures and deep structures of sentences (note: prior to mar80, the use of this term was not restricted by a scope note)
UF Generative Transformational Grammar
Transformational Grammar
Transformation Generative Grammar (1968 1980)
Transformations (Language) (1967 1980)
Transformation Theory (Language) (1967 1980) #
NT Context Free Grammar
Deep Structure
Kernel Sentences
Sentence Combining
Surface Structure
BT Generative Grammar
RT Phrase Structure
Syntax
Traditional Grammar

Transformational Geometry
USE TRANSFORMATIONS (MATHEMATICS)

Transformational Grammar
USE TRANSFORMATIONAL GENERATIVE GRAMMAR

Transformational Sentence Combining
USE SENTENCE COMBINING

Transformations (Language) (1967 1980)
USE TRANSFORMATIONAL GENERATIVE GRAMMAR

TRANSFORMATIONS (MATHEMATICS) *Feb. 1970*
CIJE: 146 RIE: 75 GC: 480
SN Substitution of one mathematical configuration or expression by another in accord with a mathematical rule
UF Similarity Transformations
Transformational Geometry
RT Algebra
Congruence (Mathematics)
Correlation
Factor Analysis
Functions (Mathematics)
Geometry
Mathematical Concepts
Oblique Rotation
Orthogonal Rotation

Transhumance
USE NOMADS

TRANSIENT CHILDREN *Jul. 1966*
CIJE: 18 RIE: 40 GC: 510
SN Children who move frequently with their families from one semi-permanent location to another -- includes children of military personnel, construction workers, gypsies, etc. (note: do not confuse with "migrant children")
BT Children
Migrants
RT Immigrants
Migration
Nomads
Student Mobility
Transfer Students

TRANSISTORS *Sep. 1969*
CIJE: 25 RIE: 21 GC: 910
BT Semiconductor Devices
RT Electricity
Electronics
Instrumentation

Transitional Classes (1966 1981)
USE TRANSITIONAL PROGRAMS

TRANSITIONAL PROGRAMS *Nov. 1981*
CIJE: 98 RIE: 156 GC: 340
SN Special classes, courses, or other programs designed to prepare individuals to move from one grade, school, or activity to the next
UF Transitional Classes (1966 1981)
BT Programs
RT Acceleration (Education)
Admission (School)
College Preparation
Compensatory Education
Developmental Studies Programs
Educationally Disadvantaged
Grouping (Instructional Purposes)
High Risk Students
Mainstreaming
Remedial Instruction
Remedial Programs
Resource Room Programs
Special Classes
Student Placement
Summer Schools
Supplementary Education

TRANSITIONAL SCHOOLS *Jul. 1966*
CIJE: 6 RIE: 10 GC: 340
SN Schools undergoing administrative, procedural, or philosophical change
BT Schools
RT Educational Change
Educational Philosophy
Experimental Schools
Nontraditional Education
Open Education
School Organization
Traditional Schools

TRANSLATION *Jul. 1966*
CIJE: 719 RIE: 496 GC: 450
SN One language to another
UF Free Translation
NT Deaf Interpreting
Machine Translation
RT Grammar Translation Method
Interpreters
Interpretive Skills
Language Arts
Language Skills

Translators
USE INTERPRETERS

TRANSPARENCIES *Jul. 1966*
CIJE: 152 RIE: 485 GC: 720
SN Visual materials that are viewed using transmitted light
UF Overhead Transparencies
NT Slides
BT Nonprint Media
Visual Aids
RT Audiovisual Aids
Films

Transparency Projectors
USE OVERHEAD PROJECTORS

Transplanting (1968 1980)
USE HORTICULTURE

TRANSPORTATION *Jul. 1966*
CIJE: 237 RIE: 872 GC: 650
UF Migrant Transportation (1966 1980) #
NT Air Transportation
Bus Transportation
Rail Transportation
Student Transportation
RT Distance
Distributive Education
Mobile Classrooms
Motor Vehicles
Proximity
Public Facilities
Road Construction
Tourism
Traffic Control
Travel
Vehicular Traffic

Trash
USE SOLID WASTES

TRAVEL *Jul. 1969*
CIJE: 237 RIE: 219 GC: 550
UF Student Travel
Teacher Travel
BT Activities
RT Field Trips
Motor Vehicles
Outdoor Activities
Recreational Activities
Study Abroad
Tourism
Transportation
Travel Training

TRAVEL TRAINING *Jul. 1966*
CIJE: 85 RIE: 59 GC: 220
SN Process of teaching a handicapped person to move freely in his environment
BT Training
RT Daily Living Skills
Echolocation
Mobility Aids
Physical Disabilities
Physical Mobility
Travel
Visual Impairments
Visually Handicapped Mobility

Traveling Teachers
USE ITINERANT TEACHERS

TREATIES *Jul. 1973*
CIJE: 101 RIE: 175 GC: 610
SN Negotiated agreements between two or more political authorities (e.g., states, sovereign nations)
RT American Indian Reservations
Federal Government
Federal Indian Relationship
Federal Legislation
International Law
International Relations
Legal Responsibility
Peace
Political Divisions (Geographic)
Tribal Sovereignty
Trust Responsibility (Government)
War

Treatment Centers
USE CLINICS

TREES *Jul. 1966*
CIJE: 76 RIE: 101 GC: 410
UF Shade Trees
RT Agronomy
Botany
Forestry
Ornamental Horticulture
Wildlife

TREND ANALYSIS *Nov. 1970*
CIJE: 1672 RIE: 2027 GC: 820
SN Use of a series of measurements of a variable, taken over a period of time, to determine a direction of change
BT Data Analysis
RT Agricultural Trends
Comparative Analysis
Educational Trends
Employment Patterns
Enrollment Trends
Factor Analysis
Futures (Of Society)
Longitudinal Studies
Long Range Planning
Migration Patterns
Population Trends
Residential Patterns
Social Indicators
Sociocultural Patterns
Statistical Analysis
Statistical Data
Surveys

Tribal Societies
USE TRIBES

TRIBAL SOVEREIGNTY *Oct. 1979*
CIJE: 69 RIE: 107 GC: 610
SN The authority or right of tribal entities to exercise decision-making power and choice regarding their political, social, and cultural patterns
BT Self Determination
RT American Indian History
American Indian Reservations
American Indians
Federal Government
Federal Indian Relationship
Federal Legislation
Governance
Government Role
Local Government
Treaties
Tribes
Trust Responsibility (Government)

TRIBES *Jan. 1970*
CIJE: 260 RIE: 875 GC: 560
UF Tribal Societies
BT Groups
RT African Culture
African History
Alaska Natives
American Indian Culture
American Indian History
American Indian Reservations
American Indians
Canada Natives
Ethnic Groups
Federal Indian Relationship
Nomads
Nonformal Education
Tribal Sovereignty
Trust Responsibility (Government)

TRIGONOMETRY *Jun. 1969*
CIJE: 157 RIE: 117 GC: 480
BT Mathematics
RT Calculus
Mathematical Concepts
Mathematical Enrichment
Mathematical Vocabulary

Trimester Schedules (1966 1980)
USE TRIMESTER SYSTEM

TRIMESTER SYSTEM *Mar. 1980*
CIJE: 18 RIE: 64 GC: 350
SN Division of the academic year into three terms, usually but not always equal in length
UF Trimester Schedules (1966 1980)
BT School Schedules
RT Extended School Year
Quarter System
Semester System
Year Round Schools

Troubadours
USE POETS

TRUANCY *Jul. 1966*
CIJE: 121 RIE: 113 GC: 330
UF School Truancy
RT Attendance
Attendance Patterns
Continuation Students
Dropouts
Runaways
School Holding Power
Students

Truck Mechanics
USE AUTO MECHANICS

True False Tests
USE OBJECTIVE TESTS

True Measure
USE TRUE SCORES

TRUE SCORES *Oct. 1970*
CIJE: 106 RIE: 91 GC: 820
SN Value of an observation or measure which is free from error, the mean of an infinite number of observations
UF True Measure
BT Scores
RT Cutting Scores
Equated Scores
Error Of Measurement
Generalizability Theory
Guessing (Tests)
Interrater Reliability
Raw Scores
Reliability
Statistical Data
Test Reliability

TRUST (PSYCHOLOGY) *Dec. 1985*
CIJE: RIE: 1 GC: 120
SN Assured reliance in the character, ability, strength, or truth of some person, group, institution, idea, or thing
BT Attitudes
RT Beliefs
Cooperation
Credibility
Group Unity
Interpersonal Relationship
Psychological Patterns
Rapport
Security (Psychology)

Trust Funds
USE TRUSTS (FINANCIAL)

TRUST RESPONSIBILITY (GOVERNMENT) *Oct. 1979*
CIJE: 26 RIE: 68 GC: 610
SN A central government's legal responsibility to safeguard the interests of peoples under its jurisdiction, especially the inhabitants of territories that are not yet fully self-governing nations or states
BT Legal Responsibility
RT American Indian Education
American Indian Reservations
American Indians
Eskimos
Federal Government
Federal Indian Relationship
Government Role
Puerto Ricans
Samoan Americans
Self Determination
Treaties
Tribal Sovereignty
Tribes

TRUSTEES *Jul. 1966*
CIJE: 454 RIE: 404 GC: 360
SN Members of governing boards
UF Regents
BT Administrators
RT Board Candidates
Boards Of Education
Educational Administration
Endowment Funds
Estate Planning
Governance
Governing Boards
Trusts (Financial)

TRUSTS (FINANCIAL) *Sep. 1969*
CIJE: 58 RIE: 49 GC: 620
SN Property or finances held by one party for the benefit of another
UF Charitable Trusts
Trust Funds
RT Capital
Donors
Endowment Funds
Estate Planning
Finance Occupations
Financial Services
Financial Support
Fund Raising
Income
Investment
Money Management
Ownership
Philanthropic Foundations
Property Accounting
Property Appraisal
Resource Allocation
Trustees
Wills

Trustworthiness
USE CREDIBILITY

TUITION *Jul. 1966*
CIJE: 315 RIE: 748 GC: 620
UF Tuition Tax Credits #
BT Fees
Instructional Student Costs
RT Free Education
In State Students
Out Of State Students
School Choice
Student Costs
Student Financial Aid
Student Loan Programs
Tax Credits
Tuition Grants

TUITION GRANTS *Jul. 1966*
CIJE: 71 RIE: 165 GC: 620
SN Grants awarded solely for tuition expenses
BT Grants
Scholarships
RT Educational Vouchers
Instructional Student Costs
Merit Scholarships
Scholarship Funds
Training Allowances
Tuition

Tuition Postponement
USE INCOME CONTINGENT LOANS

Tuition Tax Credits
USE TAX CREDITS; TUITION

TUMBLING *Jul. 1966*
CIJE: 5 RIE: 13 GC: 470
UF Stunts And Tumbling
BT Gymnastics

Tumors (Malignant)
USE CANCER

TURF MANAGEMENT *Jul. 1966*
CIJE: 35 RIE: 65 GC: 410
UF Lawn Maintenance
BT Ornamental Horticulture
RT Grounds Keepers
Landscaping
Land Use

TURKIC LANGUAGES *Jul. 1966*
CIJE: 7 RIE: 15 GC: 440
NT Azerbaijani
Bashkir
Chuvash
Kirghiz
Tatar
Turkish
Uzbek
Yakut
BT Uralic Altaic Languages

TURKISH *Jul. 1966*
CIJE: 16 RIE: 42 GC: 440
BT Turkic Languages

Turnkey Building
USE DESIGN BUILD APPROACH

Tutorial Instruction
USE TUTORING

Tutorial Plans
USE TUTORIAL PROGRAMS

TUTORIAL PROGRAMS *Jul. 1966*
CIJE: 411 RIE: 711 GC: 310
SN Programs, established by educational institutions, to tutor selected students (note: prior to mar80, this term was not scoped and was occasionally used for programs to train tutors)
UF Tutorial Plans
Tutorial Services
BT Programs
RT Cross Age Teaching
Grouping (Instructional Purposes)
Individual Instruction
Peer Teaching
Remedial Instruction
Teaching Methods
Tutoring
Tutors

Tutorial Services
USE TUTORIAL PROGRAMS

TUTORING *Jul. 1966*
CIJE: 506 RIE: 880 GC: 310
SN Instruction provided to a learner, or small group of learners, by direct interaction with a professional teacher, a peer, or another individual with appropriate training or experience
UF After School Tutoring (1966 1980) #
Tutorial Instruction
NT Programed Tutoring
BT Individual Instruction
RT Cross Age Teaching
Peer Teaching
Remedial Instruction
Review (Reexamination)
Test Coaching
Tutorial Programs
Tutors

TUTORS *Nov. 1974*
CIJE: 138 RIE: 196 GC: 360
SN Persons engaged, often privately, to instruct an individual or small group in a particular subject (note: use "college faculty" for british postsecondary tutors -- prior to mar80, this term did not carry a scope note)
UF Coaching Teachers (1966 1974)
BT Teachers
RT Tutorial Programs
Tutoring

Tv
USE TELEVISION

TWENTIETH CENTURY LITERATURE *Jul. 1966*
CIJE: 859 RIE: 227 GC: 430
UF Midtwentieth Century Literature
BT Literature
RT Existentialism
Expressionism
Impressionism
Literary History
Marxism
Modernism
Naturalism
Realism
Surrealism
Symbolism

Twi
USE AKAN

TWINS *Jul. 1966*
CIJE: 120 RIE: 40 GC: 120
BT Siblings
RT Family (Sociological Unit)

Two Parent Family
USE NUCLEAR FAMILY

Two Year College Degrees
USE ASSOCIATE DEGREES

TWO YEAR COLLEGE STUDENTS *Mar. 1980*
CIJE: 397 RIE: 1575 GC: 360
SN (Note: coordinate with the appropriate mandatory educational level descriptor)
UF Junior College Students (1969 1980)
BT College Students
RT Community Colleges
Technical Institutes
Terminal Students
Two Year Colleges
Undergraduate Students
Undergraduate Study

TWO YEAR COLLEGES *Mar. 1980*
CIJE: 4198 RIE: 10521 GC: 340
SN Public or private postsecondary institutions providing at least 2, but less than 4, years of academic and/or occupational education (note: also appears in the list of mandatory educational level descriptors)
UF Junior College Libraries (1966 1980) #
Junior Colleges (1966 1980)
Private Junior Colleges #
NT Community Colleges
Technical Institutes
BT Colleges
RT Associate Degrees
Multicampus Colleges
Multicampus Districts
Postsecondary Education
State Colleges

Technical Education
Trade And Industrial Education
Two Year College Students
Undergraduate Study
Upper Division Colleges

TYPEWRITING *Jul. 1966*
CIJE: 418 RIE: 322 GC: 400
UF Clerk Typists
Typing
Typists (1967 1981)
BT Business Skills
RT Clerical Occupations
Court Reporters
Keyboarding (Data Entry)
Office Machines
Office Occupations
Office Occupations Education
Printing
Secretaries
Shorthand
Word Processing

Typing
USE TYPEWRITING

Typists (1967 1981)
USE TYPEWRITING

Typology (1967 1980)
USE CLASSIFICATION

TZELTAL *Jun. 1969*
CIJE: 3 RIE: 6 GC: 440
UF Tzendal
BT American Indian Languages

Tzendal
USE TZELTAL

TZOTZIL *Dec. 1969*
CIJE: RIE: 7 GC: 440
BT American Indian Languages

UKRAINIAN *Jul. 1966*
CIJE: 9 RIE: 26 GC: 440
BT Slavic Languages

Ultramicrofiche
USE MICROFICHE

Uncial Script
USE MANUSCRIPT WRITING (HANDLETTERING)

UNCOMMONLY TAUGHT LANGUAGES *Jul. 1966*
CIJE: 83 RIE: 614 GC: 450
SN Languages not generally offered for instruction in the united states educational system (note: also see the specific language, e.g., turkish, or the language family, e.g., uralic altaic languages)
UF Less Commonly Taught Languages
Neglected Languages
BT Language
RT Unwritten Languages

Unconventional Warfare
USE WAR

UNDERACHIEVEMENT *Mar. 1980*
CIJE: 368 RIE: 475 GC: 120
UF Underachievers (1966 1979)
BT Achievement
RT Academic Failure
Failure
Fear Of Success
Grade Repetition
Learning Problems
Low Achievement
Overachievement

Underachievers (1966 1979)
USE UNDERACHIEVEMENT

Underdeveloped Nations
USE DEVELOPING NATIONS

Underemployed (1969 1980)
USE UNDEREMPLOYMENT

UNDEREMPLOYMENT *Mar. 1980*
CIJE: 87 RIE: 226 GC: 630
SN Employment that is less than the number of hours employees want to work or below their demonstrated skills or earning levels
UF Inadequate Employment
Subemployment (1968 1980)
Underemployed (1969 1980)
BT Employment
RT Employment Patterns
Employment Problems
Job Sharing
Labor Market
Labor Utilization
Low Income
Part Time Employment
Poverty
Seasonal Employment
Structural Unemployment
Unemployment

Undergraduate Education
USE UNDERGRADUATE STUDY

UNDERGRADUATE STUDENTS *Apr. 1975*
CIJE: 656 RIE: 713 GC: 360
SN College or university students who are engaged in studies leading to the bachelor's degree
NT Premedical Students
BT College Students
RT College Freshmen
College Graduates
Higher Education
Two Year College Students
Undergraduate Study

UNDERGRADUATE STUDY *Jul. 1966*
CIJE: 1584 RIE: 1427 GC: 340
SN Study in an institution of higher education that precedes the bachelor's or first professional degree
UF Undergraduate Education
Undergraduate Training
BT Higher Education
RT Associate Degrees
Bachelors Degrees
Colleges
Community Colleges
Degree Requirements
Graduate Study
Two Year Colleges
Two Year College Students
Undergraduate Students
Universities

Undergraduate Training
USE UNDERGRADUATE STUDY

UNDERGROUND FACILITIES *Jan. 1979*
CIJE: 34 RIE: 6 GC: 920
SN Buildings, rooms, passageways, etc. that are below the surface of the ground
BT Facilities
RT Building Innovation
Buildings
Energy Conservation
Facility Planning
Fallout Shelters
Land Use
Space Utilization
Windowless Rooms

Underprivileged
USE DISADVANTAGED

UNDERWATER DIVING *Jan. 1985*
CIJE: 1 RIE: 1 GC: 470
UF Deep Sea Diving
Scuba Diving
Skin Diving
BT Physical Activities
RT Aquatic Sports
Marine Education
Marine Technicians
Oceanography
Recreational Activities

UNDOCUMENTED IMMIGRANTS *Feb. 1984*
CIJE: 27 RIE: 29 GC: 510
SN Persons residing in a foreign country without proper authorization, having entered that country by unlawful means or having violated the provisions of their visas
UF Alien Illegality
Illegal Aliens
Illegal Immigrants (1976 1984)
Immigrant Illegality
Undocumented Workers #
BT Immigrants
RT Immigration Inspectors
Migration
Refugees

Undocumented Workers
USE FOREIGN WORKERS; UNDOCUMENTED IMMIGRANTS

Unemployed (1967 1980)
USE UNEMPLOYMENT

UNEMPLOYMENT *Jul. 1966*
CIJE: 923 RIE: 1563 GC: 630
UF Unemployed (1967 1980)
NT Structural Unemployment
RT Dislocated Workers
Employment Patterns
Employment Problems
Job Layoff
Job Search Methods
Labor Economics
Labor Force Nonparticipants
Labor Market
Labor Utilization
Poverty
Reduction In Force
Underemployment
Unemployment Insurance

UNEMPLOYMENT INSURANCE *Jul. 1966*
CIJE: 44 RIE: 91 GC: 630
BT Financial Support
Insurance
RT Fringe Benefits
Health Insurance
Insurance Occupations
Teacher Employment Benefits
Unemployment
Workers Compensation

Ungraded Classes (1966 1980)
USE NONGRADED INSTRUCTIONAL GROUPING

Ungraded Curriculum (1966 1980)
USE NONGRADED INSTRUCTIONAL GROUPING

Ungraded Elementary Programs (1966 1980)
USE NONGRADED INSTRUCTIONAL GROUPING

Ungraded Primary Programs (1966 1980)
USE NONGRADED INSTRUCTIONAL GROUPING

Ungraded Programs (1966 1980)
USE NONGRADED INSTRUCTIONAL GROUPING

Ungraded Schools (1966 1980)
USE NONGRADED INSTRUCTIONAL GROUPING

Unification
USE GROUP UNITY

UNIFIED STUDIES CURRICULUM *Mar. 1980*
CIJE: 65 RIE: 128 GC: 350
SN Curriculum designed to integrate an educational program by eliminating the traditional boundaries between fields of study and presenting them as one unified subject
UF Unified Studies Programs (1966 1980)
BT Curriculum
RT Articulation (Education)
Fused Curriculum
Integrated Curriculum
Interdisciplinary Approach

Unified Studies Programs (1966 1980)
USE UNIFIED STUDIES CURRICULUM

Unilateral Disarmament
USE DISARMAMENT

UNION CATALOGS *Nov. 1968*
CIJE: 115 RIE: 180 GC: 710
SN Author and/or subject catalogs of the holdings of a group of libraries -- can cover their entire collections or be limited by subject or type of material
UF Repertory Catalogs
BT Library Catalogs
RT Bibliographies
Interlibrary Loans
Library Cooperation
Library Networks
National Libraries
Shared Library Resources

UNION MEMBERS *Jul. 1966*
CIJE: 70 RIE: 63 GC: 630
BT Groups
RT Unions

UNIONS *Jul. 1966*
CIJE: 1203 RIE: 1123 GC: 630
SN Employee organizations whose major objective is to represent their members' interests in negotiations with employers (note: prior to mar80, the use of this term was not restricted by a scope note)
UF Labor Unions (1966 1980)
Local Unions (1966 1980)
Teacher Unions
Trade Unions
BT Organizations (Groups)
RT Arbitration
Collective Bargaining
Employer Employee Relationship
Faculty College Relationship
Faculty Organizations
Labor Demands
Labor Education
Labor Force
Labor Legislation
Labor Relations
Negotiation Agreements
Negotiation Impasses
Quality Of Working Life
Strikes
Teacher Associations
Teacher Strikes
Union Members
Work Environment

UNIT COSTS *Jul. 1966*
CIJE: 62 RIE: 201 GC: 620
BT Costs
RT Cost Estimates
Program Costs

UNIT PLAN (1966 1980) *Apr. 1980*
CIJE: 176 RIE: 646 GC: 350
SN Invalid descriptor -- used inconsistently in indexing -- see such descriptors as "activity units," "learning modules," "lesson plans," "resource units," "units of study," etc.

UNITED STATES GOVERNMENT (COURSE) *Mar. 1980*
CIJE: 134 RIE: 261 GC: 400
UF American Government (Course) (1966 1980)
BT Courses
RT American Studies
Civics
Constitutional History
Constitutional Law
Government (Administrative Body)
Political Science
Social Studies

UNITED STATES HISTORY *Jul. 1966*
CIJE: 1316 RIE: 1506 GC: 430
SN (Note: prior to mar80, "american history" was occasionally used for this concept)
NT Civil War (United States)
Colonial History (United States)
Mexican American History
Reconstruction Era
Revolutionary War (United States)
State History
BT North American History
RT American Studies
Black History
Black Studies
Capitalism
Constitutional History
Cultural Pluralism

= Two or more Descriptors are used to represent this term.
The term's main entry shows the appropriate coordination.

Modern History
Presidential Campaigns (United States)
Presidents Of The United States
United States Literature
Womens Studies

UNITED STATES LITERATURE *Mar. 1980*
CIJE: 354 RIE: 378 GC: 430
UF American Literature (1966 1980) (United States)
NT Hispanic American Literature
BT North American Literature
RT American Studies
Black Literature
English Literature
United States History

Uniterm Indexes
USE COORDINATE INDEXES

Uniterms
USE SUBJECT INDEX TERMS

UNITS OF STUDY *Jul. 1977*
CIJE: 966 RIE: 4365 GC: 350
SN Subdivisions of instruction within a course, textbook, or subject field
UF Human Relations Units (1966 1980) #
Lesson Units
Programed Units (1966 1980) #
Science Units (1966 1980) #
Social Studies Units (1966 1980) #
Units Of Study (Subject Fields) (1966 1977)
NT Activity Units
BT Courses
RT Continuing Education Units
Learning Modules
Lesson Plans
Resource Units

Units Of Study (Subject Fields) (1966 1977)
USE UNITS OF STUDY

Universal Education (1968 1976)
USE EQUAL EDUCATION

UNIVERSITIES *Jul. 1966*
CIJE: 2681 RIE: 2514 GC: 340
SN Degree-granting institutions of higher education that typically include a liberal arts undergraduate college, a graduate school, and two or more undergraduate and graduate professional schools (note: for specific aspects, use a "college" term where a corresponding "university" term is not available)
NT Land Grant Universities
Open Universities
Research Universities
State Universities
Urban Universities
BT Colleges
RT College Faculty
College Students
Extension Education
Faculty Handbooks
Graduate Study
Higher Education
Multicampus Colleges
Nonprofit Organizations
Postsecondary Education
Undergraduate Study
Upper Division Colleges

Universities Without Walls
USE OPEN UNIVERSITIES

University Administration (1967 1980)
USE COLLEGE ADMINISTRATION

University Characteristics
USE INSTITUTIONAL CHARACTERISTICS

University Extension (1967 1980)
USE EXTENSION EDUCATION

University Libraries (1968 1980)
USE COLLEGE LIBRARIES

University Schools
USE LABORATORY SCHOOLS

University Senates
USE COLLEGE GOVERNING COUNCILS

University Settlements
USE SETTLEMENT HOUSES

University Students
USE COLLEGE STUDENTS

University Teaching Hospitals
USE TEACHING HOSPITALS

University Training Centers
USE TEACHER CENTERS

Unmarried Students
USE SINGLE STUDENTS

Unskilled Labor (1966 1980)
USE UNSKILLED WORKERS

UNSKILLED OCCUPATIONS *Jul. 1966*
CIJE: 9 RIE: 31 GC: 640
SN Occupations requiring little or no training or experience
BT Occupations
RT Blue Collar Occupations
Semiskilled Occupations
Skilled Occupations
Unskilled Workers

UNSKILLED WORKERS *Jul. 1966*
CIJE: 53 RIE: 137 GC: 630
SN Manual workers whose tasks require little or no training or experience
UF Unskilled Labor (1966 1980)
NT Laborers
BT Nonprofessional Personnel
RT Employees
Semiskilled Workers
Skilled Workers
Unskilled Occupations
Working Class

Untenured Faculty
USE NONTENURED FACULTY

UNWED MOTHERS *Jul. 1966*
CIJE: 118 RIE: 123 GC: 510
BT Mothers
RT Family Structure
Fatherless Family
Illegitimate Births
Pregnancy

UNWRITTEN LANGUAGE (1968 1980) *Apr. 1980*
CIJE: 13 RIE: 20 GC: 450
SN Invalid descriptor -- used inconsistently in indexing -- see "oral language" or "unwritten languages"

UNWRITTEN LANGUAGES *Apr. 1980*
CIJE: 1 RIE: 2 GC: 450
SN Languages without a native system of writing
BT Language
RT Anthropological Linguistics
Applied Linguistics
Language Research
Second Language Learning
Uncommonly Taught Languages
Written Language

Upgrading
USE IMPROVEMENT

UPPER CLASS *Jul. 1966*
CIJE: 48 RIE: 39 GC: 520
BT Social Class
RT Advantaged
Affluent Youth
Lower Class
Lower Middle Class
Middle Class

UPPER DIVISION COLLEGES *May. 1972*
CIJE: 31 RIE: 74 GC: 340
SN Colleges offering junior, senior, and graduate level courses only
BT Colleges
RT Articulation (Education)
Graduate Study
Two Year Colleges
Universities

URALIC ALTAIC LANGUAGES *Jul. 1966*
CIJE: 4 RIE: 16 GC: 440
UF Altaic Languages
NT Finno Ugric Languages
Manchu
Mongolian Languages
Samoyed Languages
Turkic Languages
BT Languages

URBAN AMERICAN INDIANS *Mar. 1980*
CIJE: 18 RIE: 85 GC: 560
SN American indians who reside in or near urban centers
BT Nonreservation American Indians
Urban Population
RT Rural American Indians
Urban Areas

URBAN AREAS *Jul. 1966*
CIJE: 632 RIE: 1185 GC: 550
SN Geographic areas that are heavily populated and often industrialized
UF Large Cities
NT Inner City
Municipalities
BT Geographic Regions
RT Metropolitan Areas
Rural To Urban Migration
Rural Urban Differences
Slums
Urban American Indians
Urban Culture
Urban Demography
Urban Education
Urban Environment
Urban Extension
Urbanization
Urban Language
Urban Population
Urban Renewal
Urban Renewal Agencies
Urban Schools
Urban Studies
Urban Teaching
Urban To Rural Migration
Urban To Suburban Migration
Urban Universities

URBAN CULTURE *Jul. 1966*
CIJE: 129 RIE: 171 GC: 560
UF Urban Life
BT Culture
RT Cross Cultural Studies
Rural Urban Differences
Urban Areas
Urban Environment
Urban Language
Urban Studies

URBAN DEMOGRAPHY *Mar. 1980*
CIJE: 80 RIE: 137 GC: 550
UF City Demography (1966 1980)
BT Demography
RT Community Size
Inner City
Metropolitan Areas
Rural To Urban Migration
Urban Areas
Urban Population
Urban Renewal
Urban To Rural Migration
Urban To Suburban Migration

Urban Desegregation
USE RACIAL INTEGRATION

Urban Dropouts (1966 1981)
USE DROPOUTS

URBAN EDUCATION *Jul. 1966*
CIJE: 837 RIE: 1399 GC: 330
SN Schooling that takes place in urban (and sometimes metropolitan) areas
UF Inner City Education
BT Education
RT Urban Areas
Urban Extension
Urban Schools
Urban Teaching
Urban Universities

URBAN ENVIRONMENT *Jul. 1966*
CIJE: 473 RIE: 634 GC: 550
BT Environment
RT Air Pollution
Community Characteristics
Crowding
Pollution
Slum Environment
Urban Areas
Urban Culture
Urban Improvement
Urbanization
Urban Language
Urban Planning
Urban Population
Urban Problems
Urban Renewal
Water Pollution

URBAN EXTENSION *Jul. 1966*
CIJE: 20 RIE: 79 GC: 350
SN Extension work in urban settings
BT Extension Education
RT Urban Areas
Urban Education
Urban Universities

Urban Geography
USE HUMAN GEOGRAPHY

Urban Immigration (1966 1976)
USE RURAL TO URBAN MIGRATION

URBAN IMPROVEMENT *Mar. 1980*
CIJE: 60 RIE: 95 GC: 550
SN The betterment of services, environment, or other factors affecting the quality of life in an urban area
UF City Improvement (1966 1980)
NT Urban Renewal
BT Improvement
RT City Government
Community Development
Community Responsibility
Neighborhood Improvement
Social Responsibility
Urban Environment
Urban Planning
Urban Programs

URBAN LANGUAGE *Jul. 1966*
CIJE: 30 RIE: 54 GC: 450
BT Language
RT Black Dialects
Language Classification
Language Patterns
Language Research
Language Usage
Language Variation
Nonstandard Dialects
Rural Urban Differences
Social Dialects
Sociolinguistics
Urban Areas
Urban Culture
Urban Environment

Urban Life
USE URBAN CULTURE

URBAN PLANNING *Mar. 1980*
CIJE: 208 RIE: 327 GC: 550
UF City Planning (1966 1980)
City Wide Commissions (1966 1980) #
BT Planning
RT City Government
Community Planning
Facility Planning
Land Use
Planning Commissions
Regional Planning
Road Construction
Social Planning
Urban Environment
Urban Improvement
Urbanization
Urban Programs
Urban Renewal
Urban Studies

URBAN POPULATION *Jul. 1966*
CIJE: 204 RIE: 336 GC: 550
NT Urban American Indians
Urban Youth
BT Groups
RT Community Size
Ghettos
Population Distribution
Population Growth
Population Trends
Rural To Urban Migration
Rural Urban Differences
Urban Areas
Urban Demography

Urban Environment
Urbanization
Urban To Rural Migration
Urban To Suburban Migration

URBAN PROBLEMS *Mar. 1980*
CIJE: 323 RIE: 486 GC: 530
UF City Problems (1966 1980)
BT Problems
RT Community Problems
Urban Environment

URBAN PROGRAMS *Mar. 1980*
CIJE: 44 RIE: 126 GC: 520
UF City Wide Programs (1967 1980)
BT Programs
RT City Government
Urban Improvement
Urban Planning

URBAN RENEWAL *Jul. 1966*
CIJE: 107 RIE: 152 GC: 550
SN The systematic rebuilding of decaying urban areas, including federal, state, or municipal programs directed at such rebuilding
UF Redevelopment Areas
BT Urban Improvement
RT Community Change
Housing Deficiencies
Neighborhood Improvement
Planned Communities
Public Housing
Slums
Urban Areas
Urban Demography
Urban Environment
Urban Planning
Urban Renewal Agencies

URBAN RENEWAL AGENCIES *Jul. 1966*
CIJE: 4 RIE: 10 GC: 610
BT Agencies
RT Agency Role
Public Agencies
State Agencies
Urban Areas
Urban Renewal

Urban Rural Differences
USE RURAL URBAN DIFFERENCES

URBAN SCHOOLS *Jul. 1966*
CIJE: 830 RIE: 1536 GC: 340
UF City Schools
NT Urban Universities
BT Schools
RT Magnet Schools
Slum Schools
Urban Areas
Urban Education

Urban Slums (1966 1980)
USE SLUMS

URBAN STUDIES *Oct. 1970*
CIJE: 202 RIE: 267 GC: 400
BT Curriculum
RT Area Studies
Economics
Ethnic Studies
Human Geography
Interdisciplinary Approach
Research
Social Science Research
Social Sciences
Urban Areas
Urban Culture
Urban Planning

URBAN TEACHING *Jul. 1966*
CIJE: 107 RIE: 221 GC: 330
UF Urban Teaching Interns #
BT Teaching (Occupation)
RT Urban Areas
Urban Education

Urban Teaching Interns
USE TEACHER INTERNS; URBAN TEACHING

URBAN TO RURAL MIGRATION *Oct. 1976*
CIJE: 46 RIE: 128 GC: 550
SN Population movement from urban areas to rural areas for purpose of relocation
BT Migration
RT Migration Patterns
Population Distribution
Population Trends
Relocation
Residential Patterns
Rural Areas
Rural Environment
Rural Population
Rural Resettlement
Rural To Urban Migration
Urban Areas
Urban Demography
Urban Population
Urban To Suburban Migration

URBAN TO SUBURBAN MIGRATION *Oct. 1976*
CIJE: 60 RIE: 80 GC: 550
SN Population movement from urban areas to suburban areas for purpose of relocation
BT Migration
RT Migration Patterns
Population Distribution
Population Trends
Relocation
Residential Patterns
Suburbs
Urban Areas
Urban Demography
Urban Population
Urban To Rural Migration

URBAN UNIVERSITIES *Jul. 1966*
CIJE: 141 RIE: 252 GC: 340
SN Universities located in and serving an urban community, but not necessarily maintained by a municipality
BT Universities
Urban Schools
RT Urban Areas
Urban Education
Urban Extension

URBAN YOUTH *Jul. 1966*
CIJE: 227 RIE: 386 GC: 510
BT Urban Population
Youth

URBANIZATION *Jul. 1966*
CIJE: 160 RIE: 348 GC: 550
BT Development
RT Culture Lag
Demography
Industrialization
Modernization
Population Growth
Rural To Urban Migration
Urban Areas
Urban Environment
Urban Planning
Urban Population

URDU *Jul. 1966*
CIJE: 9 RIE: 43 GC: 440
BT Indo European Languages
RT Hindi

USE STUDIES *Aug. 1968*
CIJE: 904 RIE: 1628 GC: 810
SN Studies of the use of resources (information, human resources, natural resources, facilities, organizations, institutions, etc.) (note: as of oct81, use as a minor descriptor for examples of this kind of research -- use as a major descriptor only as the subject of a document)
UF User Studies
NT Facility Utilization Research
BT Research
RT Environmental Research
Evaluation Methods
Information Sources
Information Utilization
Institutional Research
Labor Utilization
Land Use
Library Research
Library Surveys
Media Research
Outreach Programs
Research Utilization
Resources
Technology Transfer
Users (Information)

USER NEEDS (INFORMATION) *Aug. 1986*
CIJE: RIE: GC: 710
SN The needs of users (or prospective users) related to information or library systems and services
UF Information User Needs
Library User Needs
BT Needs
RT Information Needs
Information Retrieval
Information Seeking
Information Services
Library Collection Development
Library Materials
Library Services
Library Surveys
Online Searching
Reference Services
Relevance (Information Retrieval)
Search Strategies
Selective Dissemination Of Information
Shared Library Resources
Users (Information)
User Satisfaction (Information)

USER SATISFACTION (INFORMATION) *Jan. 1979*
CIJE: 202 RIE: 273 GC: 710
SN Users' assessment of the degree to which information or library services meet their needs (note: prior to jan79, "participant satisfaction" was sometimes used to index this concept)
UF Information User Satisfaction
Library User Satisfaction
BT Attitudes
RT Evaluation
Information Retrieval
Information Services
Library Materials
Library Services
Library Surveys
Relevance (Information Retrieval)
User Needs (Information)
Users (Information)

User Studies
USE USE STUDIES

USERS (INFORMATION) *Aug. 1986*
CIJE: RIE: GC: 710
SN Users of information or library resources and services
UF End Users (Information)
Information Users
Library Clients
Library Patrons
Library Users
BT Groups
RT Access To Information
Information Seeking
Information Services
Information Systems
Information Utilization
Libraries
Library Instruction
Library Services
Library Skills
Menu Driven Software
User Needs (Information)
User Satisfaction (Information)
Use Studies

UTILITIES *Apr. 1969*
CIJE: 182 RIE: 276 GC: 920
UF Electric Utilities
Gas Utilities
Public Utilities
Water Utilities
Water Works #
RT Distributive Education
Drinking Water
Electrical Systems
Energy Education
Energy Management
Energy Occupations
Fuels
Heating
Lighting
Nuclear Power Plants
Power Technology
Sanitary Facilities
Sanitation
Services
Telephone Communications Industry
Water Resources
Water Treatment

UTO AZTECAN LANGUAGES *Jul. 1966*
CIJE: 11 RIE: 11 GC: 440
NT Hopi
Papago
BT American Indian Languages

UZBEK *Jul. 1966*
CIJE: RIE: 7 GC: 440
BT Turkic Languages

VACATION PROGRAMS *Jul. 1966*
CIJE: 24 RIE: 6 GC: 350
SN Programs scheduled for times when schools are not normally in session
UF Intersession School Programs
BT Programs
RT Alumni Education
School Schedules
Summer Programs
Vacations
Year Round Schools

VACATIONS *Mar. 1980*
CIJE: 40 RIE: 31 GC: 630
SN Periods of time devoted to rest and relaxation (note: prior to mar80, the instruction "vacations, use leave of absence" was carried in the thesaurus)
RT Fringe Benefits
Holidays
Leaves Of Absence
Leisure Time
Recreation
Recreationists
Scope Of Bargaining
Vacation Programs

Valence (Language)
USE SYNTAX

VALIDATED PROGRAMS *Jan. 1979*
CIJE: 30 RIE: 407 GC: 320
SN Programs that have been approved according to specified procedures, indicating attainment of the claims of the sponsors (note: for the relationship between evaluation and validation, see "program validation")
UF Approved Programs (Validated)
BT Programs
RT Accountability
Course Content
Course Evaluation
Curriculum Evaluation
Demonstration Programs
Educational Assessment
Program Content
Program Effectiveness
Program Evaluation
Program Validation
Summative Evaluation
Validity

VALIDITY *Aug. 1968*
CIJE: 916 RIE: 670 GC: 820
SN In logic, the quality of being founded on truth, fact, or law or the attribute of an argument that conforms with logical laws -- in common usage, the extent to which something does what it is used or intended to do (note: use "test validity" for validity of tests, inventories, scales, etc. -- prior to mar80, this term was not scoped)
NT Concurrent Validity
Predictive Validity
Proof (Mathematics)
Test Validity
BT Evaluation Criteria
RT Correlation
Data Interpretation
Deduction
Evaluation
Generalization
Induction
Logic
Multiple Regression Analysis
Path Analysis
Program Validation
Regression (Statistics)
Reliability
Statistical Analysis
Statistical Data

= Two or more Descriptors are used to represent this term.
The term's main entry shows the appropriate coordination.

Statistical Distributions
Validated Programs
Weighted Scores

VALUE JUDGMENT *Oct. 1982*
CIJE: 113 RIE: 55 GC: 110
SN Estimating the merit or goodness of something (person, object, situation, act) relative to one's attitudes, needs, and desires
UF Aesthetic Judgment #
Moral Judgment #
BT Evaluative Thinking
RT Values

VALUES *Jul. 1966*
CIJE: 3503 RIE: 3133 GC: 520
SN Principles and standards that determine the degree of worth or merit of an object or act
UF Personal Values (1966 1980)
NT Aesthetic Values
Democratic Values
Moral Values
Social Values
RT Altruism
Attitude Measures
Beliefs
Controversial Issues (Course Content)
Credibility
Culture Conflict
Design Preferences
Dissent
Educational Principles
Egocentrism
Elitism
Ethnocentrism
Evaluation Criteria
Futures (Of Society)
Hidden Curriculum
Humanistic Education
Ideology
Justice
Life Satisfaction
Moral Development
Norms
Political Attitudes
Quality Of Life
Semantic Differential
Social Problems
Sportsmanship
Standards
Traditionalism
Value Judgment
Values Clarification
Values Education

VALUES CLARIFICATION *Mar. 1980*
CIJE: 327 RIE: 269 GC: 400
SN Teaching and helping people to become aware of their values and to act upon them
RT Goal Orientation
Self Actualization
Values
Values Education

VALUES EDUCATION *Mar. 1980*
CIJE: 394 RIE: 350 GC: 400
SN The attempt to teach about values or to develop certain values in other people in school or non-school settings
BT Education
RT Citizenship Education
Ethical Instruction
Humanistic Education
Values
Values Clarification

VANDALISM *Sep. 1969*
CIJE: 74 RIE: 64 GC: 530
NT School Vandalism
BT Antisocial Behavior
RT Crime
Delinquency
Discipline Problems
Security Personnel
Victims Of Crime

Vascular System
USE CARDIOVASCULAR SYSTEM

VECTORS (MATHEMATICS) *Aug. 1982*
CIJE: 53 RIE: 27 GC: 480
SN Quantities having magnitude (represented by length of line segments) and direction (represented by orientation of the line segments in space)
BT Algebra
Geometric Concepts
RT Calculus
Force
Functions (Mathematics)
Geometry
Matrices
Motion
Navigation
Physics
Topology

Vehicular Circulation
USE VEHICULAR TRAFFIC

VEHICULAR TRAFFIC *Oct. 1968*
CIJE: 22 RIE: 74 GC: 920
UF Vehicular Circulation
RT Driveways
Motor Vehicles
Parking Controls
Parking Facilities
Pedestrian Traffic
Service Vehicles
Traffic Circulation
Traffic Control
Transportation

VENDING MACHINES *Jul. 1966*
CIJE: 3 RIE: 13 GC: 910
BT Equipment
RT Food
Food Handling Facilities
Food Service
Nutrition

VENEREAL DISEASES *Jan. 1974*
CIJE: 64 RIE: 61 GC: 210
UF Chancroid
Gonorrhea
Syphilis
BT Communicable Diseases
RT Health Education
Physical Health
Sex Education

VENTILATION *Jul. 1966*
CIJE: 37 RIE: 147 GC: 920
UF Exhausting (1969 1980)
BT Climate Control
RT Air Conditioning
Air Conditioning Equipment
Air Flow
Air Pollution
Chimneys
Fuel Consumption
Health
Heating
Heat Recovery
Mining
Physical Health
Temperature
Thermal Environment
Windowless Rooms
Windows

VERBAL ABILITY *Jul. 1966*
CIJE: 731 RIE: 589 GC: 450
SN Facility in the use and comprehension of words
NT Reading Ability
BT Ability
RT Academic Ability
Basic Skills
Communication Skills
Language Aptitude
Language Arts
Language Skills
Linguistic Competence
Linguistic Performance
Nonverbal Ability
Speech Skills
Verbal Development
Verbal Learning
Verbal Operant Conditioning
Verbal Tests

VERBAL COMMUNICATION *Jul. 1966*
CIJE: 1598 RIE: 1421 GC: 450
SN Transferring ideas and information through spoken or written words
UF Verbal Interaction
NT Business Correspondence
Dictation
Letters (Correspondence)
BT Communication (Thought Transfer)
RT Classroom Communication
Coherence
Communication Skills
Communicative Competence (Languages)
Debate
Language
Language Arts
Language Patterns
Language Processing
Linguistics
Mutual Intelligibility
Nonverbal Communication
Oral Communication Method
Oral Language
Persuasive Discourse
Reading
Rhetoric
Semiotics
Speech
Speech Communication
Total Communication
Writing (Composition)

VERBAL DEVELOPMENT *Jul. 1966*
CIJE: 278 RIE: 412 GC: 450
SN Growth in ability to use and comprehend words in either oral or written form
NT Language Acquisition
BT Cognitive Development
RT Child Language
Verbal Ability
Verbal Learning
Verbal Stimuli
Vocabulary Development

Verbal Interaction
USE VERBAL COMMUNICATION

VERBAL LEARNING *Jul. 1966*
CIJE: 711 RIE: 436 GC: 110
SN Learning that involves the use of language, ranging from learning to associate two nonsense syllables to learning to solve complex problems presented in verbal terms
BT Learning
RT Advance Organizers
Language Acquisition
Learning Modalities
Mediation Theory
Memorization
Nonverbal Learning
Verbal Ability
Verbal Development
Verbal Stimuli

VERBAL OPERANT CONDITIONING *Jul. 1966*
CIJE: 141 RIE: 65 GC: 110
BT Operant Conditioning
RT Psycholinguistics
Psychology
Verbal Ability

VERBAL STIMULI *Jul. 1966*
CIJE: 385 RIE: 246 GC: 110
BT Stimuli
RT Association Measures
Auditory Stimuli
Electrical Stimuli
Language Processing
Verbal Development
Verbal Learning
Visual Stimuli
Word Recognition

VERBAL TESTS *Jul. 1966*
CIJE: 141 RIE: 199 GC: 830
SN Tests of verbal ability, or any tests requiring written or spoken language in administering, responding, or both
NT Essay Tests
Language Tests
Listening Comprehension Tests
Reading Tests
Speech Tests
BT Tests
RT Mathematics Tests
Nonverbal Tests
Verbal Ability
Writing Evaluation

VERBS *Jul. 1966*
CIJE: 1043 RIE: 638 GC: 450
UF Imperative Mood
Indicative Mood
Subjunctive Mood
BT Form Classes (Languages)
RT Adverbs
Morphology (Languages)
Sentence Structure
Syntax
Tenses (Grammar)
Vocabulary

Versification (1969 1980)
USE POETRY

VERTICAL ORGANIZATION *Jul. 1966*
CIJE: 105 RIE: 92 GC: 520
SN Organization involving several successive grades or different levels within a system (e.g., vertical monopolies, vertical labor unions, vertical sequences for organizing curriculum content)
UF Hierarchy
BT Organization
RT Curriculum Design
Horizontal Organization
Industrial Structure
Pyramid Organization

VETERANS *Jan. 1970*
CIJE: 117 RIE: 255 GC: 510
BT Groups
RT Enlisted Personnel
Military Personnel
Military Service
Officer Personnel
Veterans Education

VETERANS EDUCATION *Jul. 1966*
CIJE: 67 RIE: 176 GC: 330
BT Adult Education
RT Federal Aid
Military Personnel
Student Financial Aid
Training Allowances
Veterans

VETERINARIANS *Mar. 1980*
CIJE: 16 RIE: 10 GC: 640
SN Persons qualified and authorized to treat diseases and injuries of animals
BT Health Personnel
Professional Personnel
RT Animal Husbandry
Veterinary Assistants
Veterinary Medical Education
Veterinary Medicine

VETERINARY ASSISTANTS *Jul. 1966*
CIJE: 9 RIE: 15 GC: 640
UF Veterinary Hospital Attendants
BT Allied Health Personnel
Paraprofessional Personnel
RT Animal Caretakers
Animal Husbandry
Veterinarians
Veterinary Medicine

Veterinary Hospital Attendants
USE VETERINARY ASSISTANTS

VETERINARY MEDICAL EDUCATION *Mar. 1980*
CIJE: 54 RIE: 8 GC: 400
SN Professional education and training in prevention, cure, and alleviation of diseases or injuries of animals
BT Medical Education
RT Animal Husbandry
Veterinarians
Veterinary Medicine

VETERINARY MEDICINE *Jul. 1966*
CIJE: 146 RIE: 76 GC: 410
BT Medicine
RT Agriculture
Animal Behavior
Animal Caretakers
Animal Husbandry
Animals
Livestock

= Two or more Descriptors are used to represent this term.
The term's main entry shows the appropriate coordination.

Medical Services
Veterinarians
Veterinary Assistants
Veterinary Medical Education

Vice Principals
USE ASSISTANT PRINCIPALS

VICTIMS OF CRIME *Mar. 1981*
CIJE: 95 RIE: 89 GC: 510
SN Individuals suffering death, physical or mental distress, or loss of property, as the result of an actual or attempted criminal offense committed by another person
BT Groups
RT Battered Women
Child Abuse
Child Neglect
Crime
Elder Abuse
Family Violence
Incest
Malpractice
Rape
Rehabilitation
Sexual Abuse
Stealing
Vandalism
Violence

VICTORIAN LITERATURE *May. 1969*
CIJE: 19 RIE: 11 GC: 430
SN Literature written during the reign of queen victoria (1837-1901)
BT Literature
RT Nineteenth Century Literature
World Literature

Video Cassette Systems (1971 1980)
USE VIDEO EQUIPMENT; VIDEOTAPE CASSETTES

VIDEO EQUIPMENT *Aug. 1971*
CIJE: 503 RIE: 405 GC: 910
SN Equipment used in the reproduction, recording, and/or transmission of visual images for television use
UF Television Equipment
Video Cassette Systems (1971 1980) #
Video Systems
NT Videotape Recorders
BT Electronic Equipment
Visual Aids
RT Audio Equipment
Audiovisual Aids
Broadcast Reception Equipment
Interactive Video
Photographic Equipment
Special Effects
Television
Television Studios
Videodisks
Videotape Cassettes
Videotape Recordings
Videotex

Video Production Centers
USE TELEVISION STUDIOS

Video Systems
USE VIDEO EQUIPMENT

Video Tape Recordings (1966 1978)
USE VIDEOTAPE RECORDINGS

Videodisc Recordings (1979 1986)
USE VIDEODISKS

VIDEODISKS *Aug. 1986*
CIJE: RIE: GC: 720
SN Magnetic, capacitive, or optical (laser) disks on which are recorded video signals (with or without accompanying sound) for play back on a television monitor or screen
UF Optical Videodisks #
Videodisc Recordings (1979 1986)
BT Nonprint Media
Visual Aids
RT Audiodisks
Audiovisual Aids
Interactive Video
Optical Disks
Programing (Broadcast)
Protocol Materials
Television
Video Equipment
Videotape Recordings

Videotape Cartridges
USE VIDEOTAPE CASSETTES

Videotape Cassette Recorders
USE VIDEOTAPE CASSETTES; VIDEOTAPE RECORDERS

VIDEOTAPE CASSETTES *Mar. 1980*
CIJE: 176 RIE: 163 GC: 720
UF Video Cassette Systems (1971 1980) #
Videotape Cartridges
Videotape Cassette Recorders #
BT Magnetic Tape Cassettes
RT Audiotape Cassettes
Interactive Video
Video Equipment
Videotape Recorders
Videotape Recordings

Videotape Libraries
USE FILM LIBRARIES

VIDEOTAPE RECORDERS *Mar. 1980*
CIJE: 21 RIE: 19 GC: 910
UF Videotape Cassette Recorders #
BT Tape Recorders
Video Equipment
RT Audiotape Recorders
Audiovisual Aids
Videotape Cassettes
Videotape Recordings

VIDEOTAPE RECORDINGS *Jan. 1979*
CIJE: 1546 RIE: 1373 GC: 720
SN Magnetic tapes on which video signals (with or without accompanying sound) are recorded for television use -- stored on open reels, cassettes, or cartridges
UF Video Tape Recordings (1966 1978)
BT Tape Recordings
Visual Aids
RT Audiotape Cassettes
Audiotape Recordings
Audiovisual Aids
Film Industry
Film Libraries
Film Production
Films
Interactive Video
Kinescope Recordings
Microcounseling
Microteaching
Programing (Broadcast)
Protocol Materials
Television
Videodisks
Video Equipment
Videotape Cassettes
Videotape Recorders

VIDEOTEX *Mar. 1982*
CIJE: 109 RIE: 104 GC: 710
SN Electronic information services that use adapted telephone and television sets -- includes "teletext" which broadcasts information to television sets and "viewdata" which links computers to television sets by telephone lines
UF Teletext
Videotext
Viewdata
BT Information Services
Telecommunications
RT Computers
Electronic Publishing
Home Programs
Information Networks
Menu Driven Software
Online Systems
Telephone Communications Systems
Television
Video Equipment

Videotext
USE VIDEOTEX

VIETNAMESE *Jul. 1966*
CIJE: 31 RIE: 226 GC: 440
BT Languages
RT Vietnamese People

Vietnamese Americans
USE ASIAN AMERICANS; VIETNAMESE PEOPLE

VIETNAMESE PEOPLE *Mar. 1980*
CIJE: 55 RIE: 134 GC: 560
UF Vietnamese Americans #
BT Indochinese
RT Asian Americans
Cambodians
Laotians
Vietnamese

Viewdata
USE VIDEOTEX

Viewing Time (1968 1980)
USE PROGRAMING (BROADCAST)

Village Extension Agents
USE EXTENSION AGENTS

VIOLENCE *Jul. 1966*
CIJE: 802 RIE: 704 GC: 530
UF Student Violence
NT Family Violence
BT Antisocial Behavior
RT Aggression
Battered Women
Child Abuse
Crime
Delinquency
Demonstrations (Civil)
Elder Abuse
Emotional Response
Rape
Revolution
School Security
Self Mutilation
Terrorism
Victims Of Crime
War

VISAYAN *Jul. 1966*
CIJE: RIE: 2 GC: 440
NT Cebuano
BT Indonesian Languages

Visible Radiation
USE LIGHT

Visible Spectrum
USE LIGHT

VISIBLE SPEECH *Sep. 1968*
CIJE: 17 RIE: 16 GC: 220
SN Translation of speech into a readable form -- sound waves are transformed into electrical impulses which are then transformed into flashes of light and photographed (note: prior to mar80, the use of this term was not restricted by a scope note)
BT Instrumentation
RT Articulation Impairments
Hearing Impairments
Sound Spectrographs
Speech
Speech Therapy
Visual Learning

VISION *Jul. 1966*
CIJE: 136 RIE: 98 GC: 110
UF Sight
RT Ametropia
Blindness
Depth Perception
Eyes
Hyperopia
Low Vision Aids
Myopia
Ophthalmology
Optometrists
Optometry
Partial Vision
Strabismus
Vision Tests
Visual Acuity
Visual Discrimination
Visual Environment
Visual Impairments
Visual Learning
Visual Perception
Visual Stimuli

VISION TESTS *Jul. 1966*
CIJE: 113 RIE: 110 GC: 830
SN Tests designed to assess visual ability
UF Auditory Visual Tests (1966 1980) #
BT Tests
RT Diagnostic Tests
Eyes
Ophthalmology
Optometrists
Optometry
Perception Tests
Physical Examinations
Screening Tests
Tactual Visual Tests
Vision
Visual Acuity
Visual Discrimination
Visual Impairments
Visual Perception

VISITING HOMEMAKERS *Jul. 1966*
CIJE: 10 RIE: 43 GC: 640
SN Trained paraprofessionals who provide homemaking and/or basic health care services to the disabled, ill, or elderly
BT Paraprofessional Personnel
RT Adult Day Care
Adult Foster Care
Allied Health Personnel
Family Problems
Home Economics Skills
Home Health Aides
Home Management
Home Programs
Home Visits
Hospices (Terminal Care)
Housekeepers
Occupational Home Economics
Respite Care
Social Services

Visiting Teachers
USE ITINERANT TEACHERS

VISUAL ACUITY *Jul. 1966*
CIJE: 96 RIE: 59 GC: 110
SN Clearness or keenness of vision as measured by the individual's ability to distinguish visual details
BT Visual Perception
RT Ametropia
Blindness
Hyperopia
Myopia
Ophthalmology
Optometry
Partial Vision
Strabismus
Vision
Vision Tests
Visual Discrimination
Visual Impairments

VISUAL AIDS *Apr. 1972*
CIJE: 591 RIE: 550 GC: 720
UF Visual Equipment
Visual Materials
Visual Media
NT Bulletin Boards
Cartoons
Chalkboards
Charts
Diagrams
Display Aids
Films
Filmstrips
Geometric Constructions
Graphs
Illustrations
Maps
Microforms
Photographic Equipment
Photographs
Projection Equipment
Raised Line Drawings
Screens (Displays)
Signs
Tables (Data)
Three Dimensional Aids
Transparencies
Videodisks
Video Equipment
Videotape Recordings
RT Audiovisual Aids
Comics (Publications)
Educational Media
Instructional Materials

Nonprint Media
Visual Literacy
Visual Stimuli

VISUAL ARTS *Jul. 1966*
CIJE: 370 RIE: 337 GC: 420
NT Architecture
Childrens Art
Design Crafts
Drafting
Film Production
Freehand Drawing
Graphic Arts
Handicrafts
Painting (Visual Arts)
Photography
Sculpture
BT Fine Arts
RT Art
Art Activities
Art Education
Art History
Art Materials
Art Teachers
Art Therapy
Buildings
Ceramics
Color Planning
Commercial Art
Cultural Activities
Metal Working
Patternmaking
Woodworking

VISUAL DISCRIMINATION *Jul. 1966*
CIJE: 423 RIE: 329 GC: 110
SN Ability to recognize and identify visual shapes, forms, and patterns
BT Visual Perception
RT Contrast
Discrimination Learning
Sensory Training
Vision
Vision Tests
Visual Acuity
Visual Environment
Visual Learning
Visual Literacy
Visual Stimuli

VISUAL ENVIRONMENT *Jul. 1966*
CIJE: 82 RIE: 64 GC: 920
BT Physical Environment
RT Building Design
Color
Color Planning
Design Requirements
Environmental Influences
Glare
Light
Lighting
Vision
Visual Discrimination

Visual Equipment
USE VISUAL AIDS

VISUAL IMPAIRMENTS *Mar. 1980*
CIJE: 1397 RIE: 1031 GC: 220
SN Visual losses that interfere with normal functioning and performance and range from mild to total
UF Visually Handicapped (1966 1980)
NT Ametropia
Blindness
Partial Vision
Strabismus
BT Disabilities
RT Exceptional Persons
Eye Movements
Eyes
Learning Problems
Low Vision Aids
Mobility Aids
Ophthalmology
Optometry
Sensory Aids
Travel Training
Vision
Vision Tests
Visual Acuity
Visually Handicapped Mobility

Visual Language Learning
USE LANGUAGE ACQUISITION; VISUAL LEARNING

VISUAL LEARNING *Jul. 1966*
CIJE: 508 RIE: 529 GC: 110
SN Learning that involves the processing of visual stimuli
UF Visual Language Learning #
BT Learning
RT Associative Learning
Cued Speech
Learning Modalities
Multisensory Learning
Nonverbal Learning
Pictorial Stimuli
Symbolic Learning
Visible Speech
Vision
Visual Discrimination
Visual Literacy
Visual Perception
Visual Stimuli

VISUAL LITERACY *Mar. 1972*
CIJE: 269 RIE: 293 GC: 110
SN A group of competencies that allows humans to discriminate and interpret the visible action, objects, and/or symbols, natural or constructed, that they encounter in the environment (e.g., television, films, paintings, etc.)
BT Skills
RT Aesthetic Education
Art Appreciation
Film Study
Nonverbal Communication
Perception Tests
Perceptual Development
Perceptual Handicaps
Semiotics
Television Viewing
Visual Aids
Visual Discrimination
Visual Learning
Visual Measures
Visual Perception
Visual Stimuli

Visual Materials
USE VISUAL AIDS

VISUAL MEASURES *Jul. 1966*
CIJE: 140 RIE: 158 GC: 830
SN Tests in which the items are presented in pictures, patterns, diagrams, graphic figures, or other visual displays with a minimum of verbal or numerical material (note: do not confuse with "vision tests")
UF Non Discursive Measures
Pictorial Tests
BT Nonverbal Tests
RT Pictorial Stimuli
Projective Measures
Spatial Ability
Visual Literacy
Visual Stimuli

Visual Media
USE VISUAL AIDS

VISUAL PERCEPTION *Jul. 1966*
CIJE: 1626 RIE: 924 GC: 110
SN Ability to interpret what is seen
NT Depth Perception
Visual Acuity
Visual Discrimination
BT Perception
RT Color
Dimensional Preference
Eye Fixations
Eye Voice Span
Field Dependence Independence
Figural Aftereffects
Language Processing
Perception Tests
Perceptual Handicaps
Sensory Experience
Sensory Training
Tactual Visual Tests
Vision
Vision Tests
Visualization
Visual Learning
Visual Literacy
Visual Stimuli

Visual Scanners
USE OPTICAL SCANNERS

VISUAL STIMULI *Jul. 1966*
CIJE: 1159 RIE: 544 GC: 110
NT Pictorial Stimuli
BT Stimuli
RT Association Measures
Auditory Stimuli
Electrical Stimuli
Tachistoscopes
Television Viewing
Verbal Stimuli
Vision
Visual Aids
Visual Discrimination
Visual Learning
Visual Literacy
Visual Measures
Visual Perception

VISUALIZATION *Jul. 1966*
CIJE: 275 RIE: 182 GC: 110
SN Act or power of forming mentally visual images of objects not present to the eye
BT Cognitive Processes
RT Creative Thinking
Eidetic Imagery
Memorization
Memory
Recall (Psychology)
Retention (Psychology)
Spatial Ability
Visual Perception

Visually Handicapped (1966 1980)
USE VISUAL IMPAIRMENTS

VISUALLY HANDICAPPED MOBILITY *Jul. 1966*
CIJE: 165 RIE: 104 GC: 220
UF Visually Handicapped Orientation (1967 1980)
BT Physical Mobility
RT Daily Living Skills
Echolocation
Mobility Aids
Spatial Ability
Travel Training
Visual Impairments

Visually Handicapped Orientation (1967 1980)
USE VISUALLY HANDICAPPED MOBILITY

Visuospatial Ability
USE SPATIAL ABILITY

Vitae
USE RESUMES (PERSONAL)

VOCABULARY *Jul. 1966*
CIJE: 1677 RIE: 2012 GC: 450
SN (Note: use a more specific term if possible -- this broad term corresponds to pubtype code 134 and should not be used except as the subject of a document)
UF Terminology
NT Aviation Vocabulary
Banking Vocabulary
Basic Vocabulary
Chemical Nomenclature
International Trade Vocabulary
Kinship Terminology
Mathematical Vocabulary
Medical Vocabulary
Sight Vocabulary
Subject Index Terms
Word Lists
RT Adjectives
Adverbs
Code Switching (Language)
Definitions
Glossaries
Glottochronology
Language Arts
Lexicology
Linguistic Borrowing
Multilingual Materials
Nouns
Reading
Thesauri
Verbs
Vocabulary Development
Vocabulary Skills
Word Frequency

Vocabulary Building
USE VOCABULARY DEVELOPMENT

VOCABULARY DEVELOPMENT *Jul. 1966*
CIJE: 1079 RIE: 1574 GC: 450
UF Vocabulary Building
BT Development
RT Context Clues
Lexicography
Verbal Development
Vocabulary

VOCABULARY SKILLS *Jul. 1966*
CIJE: 265 RIE: 450 GC: 450
BT Language Skills
RT Basic Skills
Basic Vocabulary
Context Clues
Reading Skills
Vocabulary

Vocal Ensembles
USE SINGING

VOCAL MUSIC *Oct. 1968*
CIJE: 148 RIE: 88 GC: 420
SN Musical compositions written for voices, either solo or chorus
NT Choral Music
Songs
BT Music
RT Applied Music
Music Activities
Musical Composition
Music Education
Music Techniques
Opera
Singing

VOCATIONAL ADJUSTMENT *Jul. 1966*
CIJE: 461 RIE: 739 GC: 630
UF Employment Adjustment
Job Adjustment
Occupational Adjustment
Work Adjustment
BT Adjustment (To Environment)
RT Career Change
Career Counseling
Employer Employee Relationship
Industrial Psychology
Job Enrichment
Job Satisfaction
Occupational Mobility
Skill Obsolescence
Vocational Education
Vocational Evaluation
Vocational Maturity
Vocational Training Centers
Work Attitudes
Work Experience Programs

Vocational Agriculture (1967 1980)
USE AGRICULTURAL EDUCATION; VOCATIONAL EDUCATION

Vocational Agriculture Teachers (1967 1980)
USE AGRICULTURAL EDUCATION; VOCATIONAL EDUCATION TEACHERS

VOCATIONAL APTITUDE *Aug. 1968*
CIJE: 97 RIE: 328 GC: 120
SN An individual's potential capacity or suitability for a vocation or occupation
UF Vocational Talents
BT Aptitude
RT Academic Aptitude
Career Choice
Career Planning
Employment Qualifications
Occupational Tests
Prevocational Education
Talent
Vocational Evaluation

Vocational Aspiration
USE OCCUPATIONAL ASPIRATION

Vocational Assessment
USE VOCATIONAL EVALUATION

Vocational Awareness
USE CAREER AWARENESS

Vocational Business Education
USE BUSINESS EDUCATION

Vocational Change
USE CAREER CHANGE

Vocational Choice
USE CAREER CHOICE

Vocational Counseling (1966 1980)
USE CAREER COUNSELING

Vocational Development (1967 1978)
USE CAREER DEVELOPMENT

VOCATIONAL DIRECTORS *Jul. 1966*
CIJE: 26 RIE: 223 GC: 360
SN Administrators of vocational education programs
UF Technical Education Directors
Vocational Education Directors
BT Administrators
RT Vocational Education

VOCATIONAL EDUCATION *Jul. 1966*
CIJE: 4855 RIE: 14092 GC: 400
SN Formal preparation for semiskilled, skilled, technical, or paraprofessional occupations usually below the baccalaureate degree (note: coordinate with the mandatory level term "secondary education," unless another educational level is specified -- if possible, use a more specific descriptor)
UF Agricultural Education (Vocational) #
Health Occupations Education (Vocational) #
Service Education (1966 1980)
Vocational Agriculture (1967 1980) #
Vocational Training
NT Adult Vocational Education
Business Education
Cooperative Education
Distributive Education
Occupational Home Economics
Prevocational Education
Technical Education
Trade And Industrial Education
BT Education
RT Agricultural Education
Allied Health Occupations Education
Apprenticeships
Career Counseling
Career Education
Continuation Students
Experiential Learning
Industrial Arts
Industrial Education
Job Placement
Job Skills
Job Training
Labor Force Development
Library Education
Noncollege Bound Students
Occupations
Paraprofessional Personnel
Postsecondary Education
Relevance (Education)
Research Coordinating Units
School Business Relationship
Secondary Education
Service Workers
Technical Institutes
Technology
Vocational Adjustment
Vocational Directors
Vocational Education Teachers
Vocational English (Second Language)
Vocational Interests
Vocational Rehabilitation
Vocational Schools
Vocational Training Centers
Work Experience Programs

Vocational Education Directors
USE VOCATIONAL DIRECTORS

VOCATIONAL EDUCATION TEACHERS *Jul. 1966*
CIJE: 722 RIE: 1021 GC: 360
UF Vocational Agriculture Teachers (1967 1980) #
NT Business Education Teachers
Distributive Education Teachers
Trade And Industrial Teachers
BT Teachers
RT Home Economics Teachers
Industrial Arts Teachers
Instructor Coordinators
Technical Education
Vocational Education

VOCATIONAL ENGLISH (SECOND LANGUAGE) *Dec. 1985*
CIJE: RIE: 12 GC: 440
SN Specialized english for non-english speakers preparing for or working in skilled, semiskilled, paraprofessional, or technical occupations
BT English For Special Purposes
RT Job Skills
Vocational Education

VOCATIONAL EVALUATION *Nov. 1982*
CIJE: 45 RIE: 165 GC: 820
SN Systematic use of real or simulated work experiences and/or other measures to assess vocational aptitude, skill, and capacity to perform adequately in a particular work environment -- commonly administered for the disabled and disadvantaged, but may also be applicable to other populations (note: do not confuse with "personnel evaluation")
UF Vocational Assessment
Work Evaluation (Performance)
Work Performance Evaluation
BT Evaluation
RT Competence
Diagnostic Tests
Job Performance
Job Skills
Occupational Tests
Personnel Evaluation
Situational Tests
Student Evaluation
Vocational Adjustment
Vocational Aptitude
Vocational Rehabilitation
Work Sample Tests

VOCATIONAL FOLLOWUP *Jul. 1966*
CIJE: 137 RIE: 785 GC: 810
SN Investigating the employment-related activities, progress, or attitudes of individuals or groups following their participation in a program, course of study, guidance process, etc. (note: as of oct81, use as a minor descriptor for examples of this kind of study -- use as a major descriptor only as the subject of a document)
UF Occupational Followup
BT Followup Studies
RT Education Work Relationship
Employment Patterns
Graduate Surveys

Vocational Guidance
USE CAREER GUIDANCE

VOCATIONAL HIGH SCHOOLS *Jul. 1966*
CIJE: 53 RIE: 110 GC: 340
UF Technical High Schools
BT High Schools
Vocational Schools

Vocational Industrial Education
USE TRADE AND INDUSTRIAL EDUCATION

VOCATIONAL INTERESTS *Jul. 1966*
CIJE: 707 RIE: 732 GC: 120
BT Interests
RT Career Choice
Career Counseling
Career Development
Career Exploration
Career Guidance
Occupational Aspiration
Occupational Tests
Vocational Education

VOCATIONAL MATURITY *Oct. 1973*
CIJE: 263 RIE: 170 GC: 120
SN Degree of an individual's skill in making decisions concerning his/her vocation at a given life stage
UF Career Maturity
BT Maturity (Individuals)
RT Career Choice
Career Development
Career Exploration
Decision Making
Employee Attitudes
Maturity Tests
Occupational Aspiration
Vocational Adjustment
Work Attitudes

Vocational Nursing
USE PRACTICAL NURSING

Vocational Placement
USE JOB PLACEMENT

VOCATIONAL REHABILITATION *Jul. 1966*
CIJE: 578 RIE: 1004 GC: 630
SN Process of developing, restoring, or preserving the ability to engage in suitable employment through such services as diagnosis, guidance, counseling, physical restoration, education, training, and placement
BT Rehabilitation
RT Adult Vocational Education
Correctional Education
Correctional Rehabilitation
Sheltered Workshops
Vocational Education
Vocational Evaluation
Vocational Training Centers
Work Sample Tests

Vocational Retraining (1966 1980)
USE RETRAINING

Vocational Satisfaction
USE JOB SATISFACTION

VOCATIONAL SCHOOLS *Jul. 1966*
CIJE: 304 RIE: 620 GC: 340
UF Area Vocational Schools (1966 1980) #
Technical Schools
NT Vocational High Schools
BT Schools
RT Postsecondary Education
Secondary Schools
Vocational Education
Vocational Training Centers

Vocational Skills
USE JOB SKILLS

Vocational Talents
USE VOCATIONAL APTITUDE

Vocational Tests
USE OCCUPATIONAL TESTS

Vocational Training
USE VOCATIONAL EDUCATION

VOCATIONAL TRAINING CENTERS *Jul. 1966*
CIJE: 165 RIE: 203 GC: 920
BT Educational Facilities
RT Career Counseling
Job Training
Off The Job Training
Rehabilitation Centers
Sheltered Workshops
Vocational Adjustment
Vocational Education
Vocational Rehabilitation
Vocational Schools

Vocational Work Experience
USE COOPERATIVE EDUCATION

Vocations
USE OCCUPATIONS

Vocoids
USE VOWELS

VOGUL *Jul. 1966*
CIJE: RIE: 2 GC: 440
BT Finno Ugric Languages

VOICE DISORDERS *Jul. 1966*
CIJE: 93 RIE: 25 GC: 220
SN Abnormal vocal quality, pitch, and intensity caused by pathology or misuse of the larynx
UF Dysphonia
BT Speech Handicaps
RT Speech
Speech Therapy

Volition
USE INDIVIDUAL POWER

VOLLEYBALL *Dec. 1975*
CIJE: 19 RIE: 17 GC: 470
BT Team Sports

VOLUME (MATHEMATICS) *Oct. 1983*
CIJE: 8 RIE: 7 GC: 480
SN Three-dimensional space
UF Cubic Measure
BT Geometric Concepts
Space
RT Area
Solid Geometry
Weight (Mass)

Volume (Sound)
USE NOISE (SOUND)

VOLUNTARY AGENCIES *Jul. 1966*
CIJE: 190 RIE: 371 GC: 520
UF Voluntary Associations
Voluntary Organizations
BT Agencies
RT Agency Role
Private Agencies
Religious Organizations
Social Agencies
Volunteers
Youth Agencies

Voluntary Associations
USE VOLUNTARY AGENCIES

VOLUNTARY DESEGREGATION *Mar. 1980*
CIJE: 36 RIE: 80 GC: 540
SN Desegregation initiated on a voluntary basis, i.e., without a court order or other legal mandate
UF Voluntary Integration (1966 1980)
BT Social Integration
RT Desegregation Plans
Magnet Schools
Racial Integration
School Desegregation

Voluntary Integration (1966 1980)
USE VOLUNTARY DESEGREGATION

Voluntary Organizations
USE VOLUNTARY AGENCIES

VOLUNTEER TRAINING *Jul. 1966*
CIJE: 172 RIE: 414 GC: 400
SN The training of volunteers (note: for training by volunteers, coordinate "volunteers" and "trainers" -- prior to mar83, the use of this term was not restricted by a scope note)
BT Training
RT Experiential Learning
Volunteers
Work Experience

VOLUNTEERS *Jul. 1966*
CIJE: 721 RIE: 1126 GC: 630
NT Student Volunteers
BT Groups
RT Paraprofessional School Personnel
Public Service
School Aides
Teacher Aides
Voluntary Agencies
Volunteer Training

VOTER REGISTRATION *Jul. 1966*
CIJE: 34 RIE: 64 GC: 610
RT Elections
Voting
Voting Rights

VOTING *Jul. 1966*
CIJE: 265 RIE: 324 GC: 610
RT Bond Issues
Citizen Participation
Citizenship Responsibility
Elections
Local Issues
Political Attitudes
Political Campaigns
Political Candidates
Political Issues
Politics
Public Opinion
Residence Requirements
Voter Registration
Voting Rights

= Two or more Descriptors are used to represent this term.
The term's main entry shows the appropriate coordination.

VOTING RIGHTS *Jul. 1966*
CIJE: 48 RIE: 80 GC: 610
BT Civil Rights
RT Elections
Voter Registration
Voting

Voucher Plans
USE EDUCATIONAL VOUCHERS

VOWELS *Jul. 1966*
CIJE: 394 RIE: 337 GC: 450
UF Vocoids
BT Phonemes
RT Articulation (Speech)
Consonants
Phonetics
Phonology
Syllables

Wage Salary Differentials
USE SALARY WAGE DIFFERENTIALS

Wage Statements (1966 1980)
USE PAYROLL RECORDS

WAGES *Jul. 1966*
CIJE: 287 RIE: 585 GC: 630
SN Earnings paid at hourly rates or on a piecework basis (note: do not confuse with "salaries" -- prior to mar80, the use of this term was not restricted by a scope note)
NT Minimum Wage
BT Expenditures
Income
RT Compensation (Remuneration)
Fringe Benefits
Guaranteed Income
Merit Pay
Minimum Wage Legislation
Overtime
Payroll Records
Premium Pay
Retirement Benefits
Salaries
Salary Wage Differentials
Scope Of Bargaining

WAITERS AND WAITRESSES *Aug. 1986*
CIJE: RIE: GC: 640
BT Service Workers
RT Dining Facilities
Food Service

Walleyes
USE STRABISMUS

WAR *Apr. 1972*
CIJE: 269 RIE: 243 GC: 610
UF Civil War
Conventional Warfare
Guerrilla Warfare
International War
Unconventional Warfare
NT Nuclear Warfare
BT Conflict
RT Armed Forces
Disarmament
History
International Crimes
International Law
International Relations
Military Science
National Defense
Peace
Revolution
Terrorism
Treaties
Violence
World Problems

War Crimes
USE INTERNATIONAL CRIMES

WAREHOUSES *Jul. 1966*
CIJE: 8 RIE: 17 GC: 920
BT Facilities
RT Equipment Storage
Storage

WASTE DISPOSAL *Jul. 1972*
CIJE: 344 RIE: 369 GC: 410
SN Act or process of discarding or throwing away unneeded or excess material including solids, oils, gases, chemicals, and liquids
UF Waste Management
NT Recycling
BT Sanitation
RT Air Pollution
Ecology
Environmental Standards
Pollution
Radiation
Sanitary Facilities
Solid Wastes
Wastes
Waste Water
Water Pollution

Waste Management
USE WASTE DISPOSAL

WASTE WATER *Aug. 1982*
CIJE: 11 RIE: 96 GC: 410
SN Used water carrying suspended or dissolved solids from farms, industries, businesses, or homes
UF Sewage
Waste Water Treatment #
BT Wastes
Water
RT Pollution
Recycling
Sludge
Solid Wastes
Waste Disposal
Water Pollution
Water Treatment

Waste Water Treatment
USE WASTE WATER; WATER TREATMENT

WASTES *Jul. 1972*
CIJE: 208 RIE: 161 GC: 410
SN Unneeded, discarded, or excess material including solids, oils, gases, chemicals, and liquids
UF Hazardous Wastes #
Refuse
NT Solid Wastes
Waste Water
BT Matter
RT Conservation (Environment)
Ecology
Hazardous Materials
Poisons
Pollution
Recycling
Resources
Sludge
Waste Disposal

Watch Repairers
USE WATCHMAKERS

WATCHMAKERS *Jan. 1969*
CIJE: 1 RIE: 7 GC: 640
UF Clockmakers
Horologists
Watch Repairers
BT Skilled Workers
RT Horology

WATER *Aug. 1982*
CIJE: 70 RIE: 113 GC: 490
SN Odorless, colorless, tasteless liquid in the proportion of two atoms of hydrogen to one atom of oxygen (note: prior to aug82, "water resources" was occasionally used for this concept)
NT Drinking Water
Waste Water
BT Matter
RT Aquatic Sports
Chemistry
Climate
Earth Science
Ecology
Estuaries
Humidity
Hydraulics
Marine Education
Maritime Education
Meteorology
Ocean Engineering
Oceanography
Physical Environment
Physical Geography
Sludge
Soil Conservation
Thermal Environment
Water Pollution
Water Quality
Water Resources
Water Treatment
Weather

WATER POLLUTION *Mar. 1980*
CIJE: 514 RIE: 568 GC: 410
UF River Pollution
Stream Pollution
Water Pollution Control (1969 1980)
BT Pollution
RT Conservation (Environment)
Ecology
Environmental Education
Environmental Standards
Sludge
Urban Environment
Waste Disposal
Waste Water
Water
Water Quality
Water Resources
Water Treatment

Water Pollution Control (1969 1980)
USE WATER POLLUTION

WATER POLO *Jan. 1985*
CIJE: 2 RIE: 1 GC: 470
BT Aquatic Sports
Team Sports
RT Swimming

Water Purification
USE WATER TREATMENT

WATER QUALITY *Aug. 1982*
CIJE: 30 RIE: 112 GC: 410
SN Biological, chemical, and physical characteristics of water that influence its healthy and fruitful use
UF Clean Water
RT Conservation (Environment)
Drinking Water
Ecology
Environmental Standards
Health
Physical Environment
Water
Water Pollution
Water Resources
Water Treatment

WATER RESOURCES *Jul. 1966*
CIJE: 478 RIE: 691 GC: 410
SN All sources and supplies of water such as rivers, lakes, streams, reservoirs, and ground water (note: prior to aug82, the use of this term was not restricted by a scope note)
UF Water Supply
BT Natural Resources
RT Conservation (Environment)
Depleted Resources
Energy Conservation
Estuaries
Geothermal Energy
Utilities
Water
Water Pollution
Water Quality
Water Treatment

Water Softening
USE WATER TREATMENT

Water Sports
USE AQUATIC SPORTS

Water Supply
USE WATER RESOURCES

WATER TREATMENT *Aug. 1982*
CIJE: 31 RIE: 190 GC: 490
SN Purification or other treatment of water for drinking, etc.
UF Chlorination (Water)
Waste Water Treatment #
Water Purification
Water Softening
Water Works #
BT Technology
RT Chemical Analysis
Chemical Engineering
Civil Engineering
Disease Control
Drinking Water
Environmental Technicians
Fluoridation
Health
Public Health
Recycling
Sanitation
Sludge
Solid Wastes
Utilities
Waste Water
Water
Water Pollution
Water Quality
Water Resources

Water Utilities
USE UTILITIES

Water Works
USE UTILITIES; WATER TREATMENT

WATERSKIING *Feb. 1978*
CIJE: RIE: 4 GC: 470
BT Aquatic Sports

Weariness
USE FATIGUE (BIOLOGY)

WEATHER *Mar. 1980*
CIJE: 91 RIE: 84 GC: 490
SN State of atmospheric conditions at any one place and time
RT Climate
Climate Control
Ecology
Environmental Influences
Meteorology
Natural Disasters
Physical Environment
Thermal Environment
Water
Wind (Meteorology)

WEEDS *Jul. 1966*
CIJE: 16 RIE: 65 GC: 410
RT Agronomy
Botany
Herbicides
Pests
Wildlife

WEEKEND PROGRAMS *Jul. 1966*
CIJE: 37 RIE: 52 GC: 350
BT Programs
RT Enrichment Activities

WEIGHT (MASS) *Oct. 1980*
CIJE: 40 RIE: 15 GC: 490
SN (Note: for living organisms, use "body weight")
BT Scientific Concepts
RT Acceleration (Physics)
Force
Gravity (Physics)
Matter
Pressure (Physics)
Volume (Mathematics)

WEIGHT (1968 1980) *Jun. 1980*
CIJE: 49 RIE: 7 GC: 820
SN Invalid descriptor -- used inconsistently in indexing -- for inorganic physical objects, use "weight (mass)" -- for living organisms, use "body weight" -- for scores, use "weighted scores" -- for data other than scores, use the identifier "weighted data"

Weight Training
USE WEIGHTLIFTING

WEIGHTED SCORES *May. 1971*
CIJE: 64 RIE: 77 GC: 820
SN Scores in which the components are modified by different multipliers to reflect their relative importance -- may be applied to test items, tests, grades, or other measures or ratings
BT Scores
RT Equated Scores
Grade Equivalent Scores
Item Analysis
Multiple Regression Analysis
Raw Scores
Reliability
Scoring Formulas
Validity

= Two or more Descriptors are used to represent this term.
The term's main entry shows the appropriate coordination.

WEIGHTLIFTING *Feb. 1978*
CIJE: 15 RIE: 16 GC: 470
SN The lifting of standard weights in a prescribed manner, as a competitive event or conditioning exercise
UF Weight Training
BT Athletics
Lifting
RT Muscular Strength

Welders (1968 1981)
USE WELDING

WELDING *Jul. 1966*
CIJE: 23 RIE: 229 GC: 640
UF Acetylene Welding
Arc Welding
Gas Welding
Welders (1968 1981)
BT Technology
RT Construction (Process)
Finishing
Metal Working
Sculpture
Skilled Occupations

WELFARE (1966 1980) *Mar. 1980*
CIJE: 54 RIE: 184 GC: 520
SN Invalid descriptor -- used for well-being and various types of social services -- use "well being" for former concept, "welfare services" for organized assistance to the disadvantaged, and "social services" or other appropriate terms for social services provided to the general population

WELFARE AGENCIES *Jul. 1966*
CIJE: 87 RIE: 138 GC: 520
SN Agencies that provide welfare services (note: prior to mar80, the use of this term was not restricted by a scope note)
BT Social Agencies
RT Agency Role
Public Agencies
Social Work
Social Workers
State Agencies
Welfare Services
Youth Agencies

Welfare Problems (1966 1980)
USE WELFARE SERVICES

WELFARE RECIPIENTS *Jul. 1966*
CIJE: 119 RIE: 250 GC: 510
SN Individuals or groups who receive welfare services
BT Groups
RT Economically Disadvantaged
Eligibility
Low Income Groups
Welfare Services

WELFARE SERVICES *Jul. 1966*
CIJE: 250 RIE: 458 GC: 520
SN Organized public or private assistance provided to financially needy individuals or their families (note: prior to mar80, this concept may have been indexed under "welfare" or "social welfare")
UF Public Welfare Assistance
Welfare Problems (1966 1980)
NT Migrant Welfare Services
BT Social Services
RT Eligibility
Housing Management Aides
Humanitarianism
Poverty Programs
Public Housing
Settlement Houses
Social Responsibility
Social Work
Welfare Agencies
Welfare Recipients

WELL BEING *Mar. 1982*
CIJE: 163 RIE: 159 GC: 120
SN Condition of existence, or state of awareness, in which physical and/or psychological needs are satisfied
NT Child Welfare
Student Welfare
Teacher Welfare
BT Quality Of Life
RT Adjustment (To Environment)
Coping
Environment
Individual Needs
Life Satisfaction
Psychological Patterns
Responses

WELSH *Sep. 1975*
CIJE: 24 RIE: 26 GC: 440
SN The celtic language native to wales
BT Indo European Languages
RT English
Middle English
Old English
Romance Languages

WESTERN CIVILIZATION *Sep. 1968*
CIJE: 195 RIE: 187 GC: 560
SN Includes europe and the western hemisphere from the time of the roman empire through the present
UF Occidental Civilization
BT Culture
RT Area Studies
Christianity
Cultural Background
Cultural Context
European History
Greek Civilization
History
Judaism
Latin American Culture
Latin American History
North American Culture
North American History
Sociocultural Patterns
World History

Wheel Chairs (1970 1981)
USE WHEELCHAIRS

WHEELCHAIRS *Nov. 1981*
CIJE: 34 RIE: 36 GC: 220
UF Wheel Chairs (1970 1981)
BT Mobility Aids
RT Biomedical Equipment
Physical Disabilities
Physical Mobility

White Black Relations
USE RACIAL RELATIONS

WHITE COLLAR OCCUPATIONS *Jul. 1966*
CIJE: 47 RIE: 75 GC: 640
SN Occupations requiring office, clerical, administrative, sales, professional, or technical work (note: use to distinguish from "blue collar occupations")
BT Occupations
RT Blue Collar Occupations
Clerical Occupations
Data Processing Occupations
Managerial Occupations
Office Occupations
Professional Occupations
Sales Occupations
Technical Occupations
Working Class

White Ethnics
USE WHITES

White Flight
USE MIGRATION; WHITES

WHITE STUDENTS *Mar. 1980*
CIJE: 447 RIE: 766 GC: 360
UF Caucasian Students (1967 1980)
BT Students
Whites

WHITES *Mar. 1980*
CIJE: 908 RIE: 1168 GC: 560
UF Caucasian Race (1967 1980)
Caucasians (1967 1980)
White Ethnics
White Flight #
NT White Students
BT Groups
RT Anglo Americans
Race
Racial Relations

WHOLE NUMBERS *Jul. 1966*
CIJE: 165 RIE: 85 GC: 480
BT Numbers

Whole Person Approach
USE HOLISTIC APPROACH

Whole Word Reading Approach
USE SIGHT METHOD

WHOLESALING *Aug. 1968*
CIJE: 13 RIE: 36 GC: 650
BT Marketing
RT Distributive Education
Merchants
Retailing
Salesmanship

Wholistic Approach
USE HOLISTIC APPROACH

WIDOWED *Nov. 1975*
CIJE: 84 RIE: 76 GC: 510
SN Widows and widowers
BT Groups
RT Death
Displaced Homemakers
Fatherless Family
Marital Status
Motherless Family
One Parent Family
Remarriage
Spouses

WILDLIFE *Aug. 1980*
CIJE: 113 RIE: 131 GC: 410
SN Animals and/or plants living in a natural (undomesticated or uncultivated) state
NT Endangered Species
RT Animals
Biological Sciences
Botany
Natural Resources
Physical Environment
Plant Growth
Trees
Weeds
Wildlife Management
Zoology

WILDLIFE MANAGEMENT *Sep. 1968*
CIJE: 120 RIE: 144 GC: 410
UF Gamekeeping
BT Technology
RT Animal Facilities
Conservation (Environment)
Endangered Species
Forestry
Recreational Activities
Wildlife
Zoos

WILLS *Sep. 1969*
CIJE: 16 RIE: 20 GC: 620
BT Records (Forms)
RT Estate Planning
Financial Support
Property Accounting
Property Appraisal
Resource Allocation
Trusts (Financial)

WIND (METEOROLOGY) *Aug. 1982*
CIJE: 6 RIE: 11 GC: 490
SN The natural motion of air (note: do not confuse with "air flow")
RT Air Pollution
Climate
Earth Science
Ecology
Meteorology
Motion
Physical Environment
Physical Geography
Soil Conservation
Solar Energy
Temperature
Thermal Environment
Weather
Wind Energy

WIND ENERGY *Aug. 1982*
CIJE: 7 RIE: 30 GC: 490
SN Power derived from the force of wind
BT Energy
RT Alternative Energy Sources
Electricity
Force
Geophysics
Kinetics
Power Technology
Wind (Meteorology)

Window Walls
USE GLASS WALLS

WINDOWLESS ROOMS *Jul. 1966*
CIJE: 16 RIE: 21 GC: 920
SN Any area in a building closed to exterior environment
BT Facilities
RT Air Conditioning
Auditoriums
Climate Control
Corridors
Fallout Shelters
Lighting
Lighting Design
Recreational Facilities
Underground Facilities
Ventilation

WINDOWS *Apr. 1970*
CIJE: 28 RIE: 29 GC: 920
UF Fenestration
BT Structural Elements (Construction)
RT Climate Control
Glare
Glass Walls
Lighting
Ventilation

Wire Communications
USE TELECOMMUNICATIONS

Wireless Communications
USE TELECOMMUNICATIONS

Withdrawal (Drugs)
USE DRUG REHABILITATION

WITHDRAWAL (EDUCATION) *Mar. 1980*
CIJE: 85 RIE: 280 GC: 330
SN Termination of class, grade, or school due to transfer, completion of school work, dropping out, or death
UF Course Withdrawal
Withdrawal (1966 1980)
RT Academic Persistence
Attendance
College Attendance
Disqualification
Dropout Research
Dropouts
Expulsion
Out Of School Youth
School Holding Power
Student Attrition
Suspension

WITHDRAWAL (PSYCHOLOGY) *Mar. 1980*
CIJE: 104 RIE: 43 GC: 230
UF Withdrawal Tendencies (Psychology) (1966 1980)
BT Psychological Patterns
RT Alienation
Autism
Behavior Disorders
Behavior Problems
Fear
Rejection (Psychology)

Withdrawal (1966 1980)
USE WITHDRAWAL (EDUCATION)

Withdrawal Tendencies (Psychology) (1966 1980)
USE WITHDRAWAL (PSYCHOLOGY)

Wives
USE SPOUSES

WOLOF *Jul. 1966*
CIJE: 1 RIE: 12 GC: 440
BT African Languages

Women
USE FEMALES

WOMEN FACULTY *Sep. 1980*
CIJE: 346 RIE: 372 GC: 360
SN Female academic staff members engaged in instruction, research, administration, or related educational activities
UF Women Professors (1966 1980)
Women Teachers (1967 1980)

= Two or more Descriptors are used to represent this term.
The term's main entry shows the appropriate coordination.

BT Employed Women
Faculty

Women Professors (1966 1980)
USE WOMEN FACULTY

Women Teachers (1967 1980)
USE WOMEN FACULTY

Women Workers
USE EMPLOYED WOMEN

WOMENS ATHLETICS *Nov. 1973*
CIJE: 172 RIE: 221 GC: 470
BT Athletics
RT Females
Physical Education
Recreational Activities
Womens Education

WOMENS EDUCATION *Jul. 1966*
CIJE: 774 RIE: 1176 GC: 330
SN Education of females (note: do not confuse with "womens studies")
BT Education
RT Adult Education
Coeducation
Continuing Education
Females
Postsecondary Education
Professional Continuing Education
Single Sex Colleges
Single Sex Schools
Sororities
Womens Athletics
Womens Studies

Womens Liberation
USE FEMINISM

Womens Rights
USE FEMINISM

WOMENS STUDIES *Oct. 1972*
CIJE: 459 RIE: 560 GC: 400
SN Curriculum or subject area encompassing the history and contemporary social, political, and cultural situation of women
BT Curriculum
RT Females
Feminism
United States History
Womens Education

Wood Finishing
USE FINISHING

WOODWORKING *Jul. 1966*
CIJE: 74 RIE: 145 GC: 640
SN Construction, finishing, and reclaiming of wood articles or structures -- also, an area of study relating to industries producing or using lumber
NT Cabinetmaking
Carpentry
BT Technology
RT Building Trades
Finishing
Furniture Industry
Handicrafts
Hand Tools
Industrial Arts
Lumber Industry
Patternmaking
Shop Curriculum
Skilled Occupations
Visual Arts

Word Associations (Reading)
USE ASSOCIATIVE LEARNING

Word Borrowing
USE LINGUISTIC BORROWING

WORD FREQUENCY *Jul. 1966*
CIJE: 268 RIE: 209 GC: 450
RT Computational Linguistics
Connected Discourse
Language
Languages
Mathematical Linguistics
Speech
Vocabulary
Word Recognition
Written Language

WORD LISTS *Jul. 1966*
CIJE: 726 RIE: 500 GC: 730
SN Lists of words usually used in teaching to develop students' reading, spelling, or pronunciation skills
UF Basic Word Lists
BT Vocabulary
RT Basic Vocabulary
Dictionaries
Pronunciation
Sight Vocabulary
Spelling

Word Meaning
USE SEMANTICS

Word Method (Reading)
USE SIGHT METHOD

WORD PROBLEMS (MATHEMATICS) *Jan. 1986*
CIJE: 15 RIE: 23 GC: 480
SN Mathematical problems expressed in narrative form -- answered by conversion of the circumstances to equivalent computations or equations, which can be solved arithmetically, algebraically, or with symbolic logic
UF Story Problems (Mathematics)
BT Mathematical Applications
RT Mathematics
Mathematics Tests

WORD PROCESSING *Apr. 1982*
CIJE: 454 RIE: 310 GC: 710
SN The automated composition, manipulation, and production of text and textual documents using specialized text-editing equipment (note: for psychological/cognitive word processing, use "word recognition")
UF Text Processing
BT Information Processing
RT Automation
Clerical Occupations
Computer Oriented Programs
Editing
Electronic Equipment
Information Systems
Input Output Devices
Keyboarding (Data Entry)
Machine Translation
Mechanical Equipment
Menu Driven Software
Office Machines
Office Occupations
Office Occupations Education
Online Systems
Secretaries
Typewriting

WORD RECOGNITION *Jul. 1966*
CIJE: 1102 RIE: 940 GC: 460
BT Recognition (Psychology)
RT Associative Learning
Context Clues
Decoding (Reading)
Reading Comprehension
Reading Skills
Sight Method
Sight Vocabulary
Symbolic Learning
Verbal Stimuli
Word Frequency
Word Study Skills

WORD STUDY SKILLS *Jul. 1966*
CIJE: 193 RIE: 305 GC: 460
BT Study Skills
RT Alphabetizing Skills
Language Skills
Phonics
Reading Skills
Study Habits
Word Recognition

Work
USE EMPLOYMENT

Work Adjustment
USE VOCATIONAL ADJUSTMENT

Work And Education
USE EDUCATION WORK RELATIONSHIP

WORK ATTITUDES *Jul. 1966*
CIJE: 1226 RIE: 1648 GC: 630
SN Attitude of persons who are either employed, unemployed, or preparing for employment toward a particular job, employment in general, or a particular aspect of employment
UF Employee Work Attitudes #
NT Job Satisfaction
BT Attitudes
RT Employee Attitudes
Employment
Job Enrichment
Labor Force Nonparticipants
Nontraditional Occupations
Occupational Aspiration
Professional Autonomy
Vocational Adjustment
Vocational Maturity
Work Experience

Work Change
USE CAREER CHANGE

Work Education Programs
USE WORK STUDY PROGRAMS

Work Education Relationship
USE EDUCATION WORK RELATIONSHIP

Work Enrichment
USE JOB ENRICHMENT

WORK ENVIRONMENT *Jul. 1966*
CIJE: 796 RIE: 857 GC: 630
UF Job Conditions
Working Conditions
NT Teaching Conditions
BT Environment
RT Employer Employee Relationship
Employment
Flexible Working Hours
Human Factors Engineering
Industrial Psychology
Job Enrichment
Job Satisfaction
Labor Conditions
Occupational Safety And Health
Occupations
Organizational Climate
Organizational Development
Professional Autonomy
Quality Of Working Life
Scope Of Bargaining
Social Environment
Unions

Work Evaluation (Performance)
USE VOCATIONAL EVALUATION

WORK EXPERIENCE *Jul. 1966*
CIJE: 507 RIE: 692 GC: 630
NT Employment Experience
BT Experience
RT Career Exploration
Careers
Cooperative Education
Employment Qualifications
Experiential Learning
Prior Learning
Reentry Workers
Volunteer Training
Work Attitudes
Work Experience Programs

WORK EXPERIENCE PROGRAMS *Jul. 1966*
CIJE: 583 RIE: 1237 GC: 350
SN On-the-job experiences to increase the employability of participants -- included are a variety of federal job training, vocational, career education, and corrections programs often less structured than cooperative education programs (note: do not confuse with "work study programs" -- before mar80, the use of this term was not restricted by a scope note)
BT Programs
RT Apprenticeships
Career Education
Career Exploration
Clinical Experience
Cooperative Education
Cooperative Programs
Experiential Learning
Field Experience Programs
Job Training
Labor Force Development
On The Job Training
School Business Relationship
Sheltered Workshops
Student Experience
Supervised Farm Practice
Trainees
Training Methods
Vocational Adjustment
Vocational Education
Work Experience

Work Force
USE LABOR FORCE

WORK LIFE EXPECTANCY *Jul. 1966*
CIJE: 46 RIE: 55 GC: 630
BT Expectation
RT Careers
Early Retirement
Occupations
Tenure

Work Performance Evaluation
USE VOCATIONAL EVALUATION

Work Release
USE RELEASED TIME

WORK SAMPLE TESTS *Dec. 1976*
CIJE: 30 RIE: 81 GC: 830
SN Use of job tasks, either real or simulated, to ascertain the possession of needed skills for specific jobs and as diagnostic tools in the evaluation of vocational rehabilitation clients
UF Job Samples
Job Sample Tests
Work Samples
BT Occupational Tests
RT Diagnostic Tests
Job Performance
Job Skills
Performance Tests
Situational Tests
Vocational Evaluation
Vocational Rehabilitation

Work Samples
USE WORK SAMPLE TESTS

Work Satisfaction
USE JOB SATISFACTION

Work Sharing
USE JOB SHARING

Work Simplification (1968 1980)
USE JOB SIMPLIFICATION

Work Study
USE WORK STUDY PROGRAMS

WORK STUDY PROGRAMS *Jul. 1966*
CIJE: 221 RIE: 519 GC: 620
SN Programs, generally federally funded, providing part-time employment to students who need financial aid to begin or continue their education -- usually at the postsecondary level and different from "work experience programs" in that "work study" emphasizes financial aid and not employment experience (note: prior to mar80, the scope note did not make this distinction)
UF College Work Study Programs
Work Education Programs
Work Study
BT Programs
RT Assistantships
Cooperative Programs
Financial Support
Part Time Employment
Student Employment
Student Financial Aid

WORKBOOKS *Jul. 1966*
CIJE: 68 RIE: 846 GC: 730
BT Instructional Materials
RT Laboratory Manuals
Problem Sets
Programed Instructional Materials
Textbooks

Workday
USE WORKING HOURS

= Two or more Descriptors are used to represent this term.
The term's main entry shows the appropriate coordination.

WORKER DAYS *Mar. 1980*
CIJE: 23 RIE: 14 GC: 630
SN Hypothetical estimate of productivity based on single units or days, each representing the average amount of work one person can complete during one normal working day
UF Man Days (1968 1980)
People Days
Person Days
Staff Days
BT Employment Statistics
RT Labor Utilization
Productivity
Working Hours

Worker Evaluation
USE PERSONNEL EVALUATION

WORKERS COMPENSATION *Mar. 1980*
CIJE: 25 RIE: 48 GC: 630
UF Workmans Compensation (1966 1980)
BT Financial Support
Insurance
RT Health Insurance
Teacher Employment Benefits
Unemployment Insurance

Workers Education
USE LABOR EDUCATION

Working Abroad
USE OVERSEAS EMPLOYMENT

WORKING CLASS *Sep. 1982*
CIJE: 47 RIE: 25 GC: 520
UF Proletariat
BT Social Class
RT Blue Collar Occupations
Employees
Labor Force
Labor Supply
Lower Class
Lower Middle Class
Marxism
Middle Class
Semiskilled Workers
Skilled Workers
Unskilled Workers
White Collar Occupations

Working Conditions
USE WORK ENVIRONMENT

WORKING HOURS *Jul. 1966*
CIJE: 207 RIE: 199 GC: 630
UF Hours Of Work
Workday
Workweek
NT Flexible Working Hours
BT Scheduling
RT Employment
Faculty Workload
Full Time Faculty
Overtime
Part Time Employment
Part Time Faculty
Scope Of Bargaining
Teaching Load
Worker Days

Working Overseas
USE OVERSEAS EMPLOYMENT

Working Parents (1966 1980)
USE EMPLOYED PARENTS

Working Women (1968 1980)
USE EMPLOYED WOMEN

Workmans Compensation (1966 1980)
USE WORKERS COMPENSATION

WORKSHEETS *Jul. 1966*
CIJE: 380 RIE: 739 GC: 730
SN Forms designed for the rapid and efficient recording and processing of information (note: prior to mar80, the use of this term was not restricted by a scope note)
UF Data Sheets (1966 1980)
BT Records (Forms)
RT Data Collection
Data Processing

WORKSHOPS *Jul. 1966*
CIJE: 1332 RIE: 2654 GC: 350
SN Programs in which individuals with common interests and problems meet, often with experts, to exchange information and learn needed skills or techniques
UF Preschool Workshops (1966 1980) #
Summer Workshops (1966 1980) #
NT Drama Workshops
Parent Workshops
Sheltered Workshops
Teacher Workshops
RT Conference Papers
Conference Proceedings
Conferences
Institutes (Training Programs)
Meetings
Minicourses
Seminars
Training Methods

Workweek
USE WORKING HOURS

WORLD AFFAIRS *Jul. 1966*
CIJE: 362 RIE: 526 GC: 610
RT Appropriate Technology
Current Events
Developed Nations
Developing Nations
Diplomatic History
Foreign Policy
Futures (Of Society)
Global Approach
International Cooperation
International Law
International Relations
International Trade
Peace
Social Studies
World History
World Problems

WORLD GEOGRAPHY *Jul. 1966*
CIJE: 26 RIE: 52 GC: 400
BT Geography

WORLD HISTORY *Jul. 1966*
CIJE: 148 RIE: 203 GC: 430
BT History
RT Constitutional History
Diplomatic History
Greek Civilization
Non Western Civilization
Slavery
Western Civilization
World Affairs

WORLD LITERATURE *Apr. 1970*
CIJE: 92 RIE: 77 GC: 430
BT English Curriculum
RT Baroque Literature
Classical Literature
Epics
Literary Genres
Literary History
Literature
Medieval Literature
Renaissance Literature
Victorian Literature

World Peace
USE PEACE

WORLD PROBLEMS *Jul. 1966*
CIJE: 623 RIE: 740 GC: 530
BT Problems
RT Conservation (Environment)
Controversial Issues (Course Content)
Developing Nations
Disarmament
Global Approach
Hunger
Imperialism
International Cooperation
Nuclear Warfare
Revolution
War
World Affairs

Worldmindedness
USE GLOBAL APPROACH

Worldwide Approach
USE GLOBAL APPROACH

WRESTLING *Feb. 1978*
CIJE: 8 RIE: 13 GC: 470
BT Athletics

Writers
USE AUTHORS

WRITING (COMPOSITION) *Mar. 1980*
CIJE: 3388 RIE: 3548 GC: 400
SN Organization and expression of ideas or information using written language (note: use a more specific term if possible)
UF Composition (Literary) (1966 1980)
Theme Writing
Writing (1966 1980)
NT Abstracting
Content Area Writing
Creative Writing
Descriptive Writing
Expository Writing
Freshman Composition
Local Color Writing
News Writing
Notetaking
Paragraph Composition
Parallelism (Literary)
Playwriting
Proposal Writing
Technical Writing
Writing For Publication
BT Language Arts
Literacy
RT Audience Analysis
Coherence
Cohesion (Written Composition)
Handwriting
Language Processing
Letters (Correspondence)
Literary Devices
Literary Styles
Narration
Outlining (Discourse)
Paragraphs
Persuasive Discourse
Plagiarism
Poetry
Prewriting
Prose
Reading
Reading Writing Relationship
Revision (Written Composition)
Rhetoric
Rhetorical Invention
Sentences
Spelling
Story Grammar
Student Writing Models
Verbal Communication
Writing Apprehension
Writing Difficulties
Writing Evaluation
Writing Exercises
Writing Improvement
Writing Instruction
Writing Laboratories
Writing Processes
Writing Readiness
Writing Research
Writing Skills
Written Language

Writing (1966 1980)
USE WRITING (COMPOSITION)

WRITING APPREHENSION *Nov. 1982*
CIJE: 52 RIE: 78 GC: 120
SN Fear or anxiety experienced in anticipation of and/or during the writing/composition process
BT Anxiety
RT School Phobia
Writing (Composition)
Writing Difficulties
Writing Instruction
Writing Readiness

Writing Centers
USE WRITING LABORATORIES

WRITING DIFFICULTIES *Jun. 1983*
CIJE: 40 RIE: 41 GC: 120
SN Problems in writing/composition, caused by intrinsic or extrinsic disadvantage, e.g., disability, unfavorable environment, etc.
BT Problems
RT Handwriting
Language Handicaps
Learning Disabilities
Learning Problems
Writing (Composition)
Writing Apprehension
Writing Skills

WRITING EVALUATION *Jun. 1981*
CIJE: 355 RIE: 556 GC: 830
SN Objective or subjective procedures for describing, appraising, or judging writing skills (note: do not confuse with "literary criticism")
BT Evaluation
RT Coherence
Cohesion (Written Composition)
Educational Diagnosis
Essay Tests
Grading
Holistic Evaluation
Language Tests
Student Evaluation
Verbal Tests
Writing (Composition)
Writing Exercises
Writing Skills
Written Language

WRITING EXERCISES *Jul. 1966*
CIJE: 761 RIE: 788 GC: 310
SN Activities designed to aid students in attaining proficiency in handwriting or composition
RT Content Area Writing
Handwriting
Prewriting
Research Papers (Students)
Revision (Written Composition)
Sentence Combining
Writing (Composition)
Writing Evaluation
Writing Improvement
Writing Instruction
Writing Skills

WRITING FOR PUBLICATION *Oct. 1983*
CIJE: 197 RIE: 105 GC: 720
SN Writing intended for acceptance by a publisher
BT Writing (Composition)
RT Authors
Editors
Faculty Publishing
Journalism
News Writing
Periodicals
Professional Development
Publications
Publishing Industry
Publish Or Perish Issue
Scholarly Journals
School Publications
Student Publications
Technical Writing

WRITING IMPROVEMENT *Jun. 1983*
CIJE: 234 RIE: 233 GC: 400
SN Process of becoming a better writer
BT Improvement
RT Handwriting
Writing (Composition)
Writing Exercises
Writing Instruction
Writing Laboratories
Writing Processes
Writing Skills

WRITING INSTRUCTION *Mar. 1980*
CIJE: 2087 RIE: 1958 GC: 400
SN Instruction in written composition, grammar, and style, or in handwriting
UF Handwriting Instruction (1966 1983) #
NT Content Area Writing
Freshman Composition
BT Instruction
RT Handwriting
Journalism Education
Prewriting
Story Grammar
Student Writing Models
Writing (Composition)
Writing Apprehension
Writing Exercises
Writing Improvement
Writing Readiness
Writing Skills

WRITING LABORATORIES *Dec. 1985*
CIJE: 43 RIE: 55 GC: 920
SN Facilities specifically designed for developing and improving writing/composition skills, ranging from areas within classrooms to separate, specially staffed centers
UF Writing Centers
BT Educational Facilities
Laboratories
RT Language Laboratories
Learning Centers (Classroom)
Learning Laboratories
Writing (Composition)
Writing Improvement
Writing Skills

WRITING PROCESSES *Oct. 1980*
CIJE: 637 RIE: 691 GC: 400
SN Series of thoughts and behaviors involved in planning, writing, and/or revising written compositions
UF Composition Processes (Literary)
NT Prewriting
Revision (Written Composition)
RT Behavior Patterns
Language Processing
Protocol Analysis
Reading Writing Relationship
Writing (Composition)
Writing Improvement
Writing Skills

WRITING READINESS *Nov. 1981*
CIJE: 70 RIE: 73 GC: 120
SN Degree of preparedness for instruction in handwriting or formal composition (note: do not confuse with "prewriting")
UF Handwriting Readiness (1966 1983) #
BT Readiness
RT Handwriting
Learning Readiness
Prewriting
School Readiness
Writing (Composition)
Writing Apprehension
Writing Instruction

WRITING RESEARCH *Oct. 1980*
CIJE: 439 RIE: 670 GC: 810
BT Educational Research
RT Communication Research
Handwriting
Writing (Composition)

WRITING SKILLS *Jul. 1966*
CIJE: 3033 RIE: 3692 GC: 400
SN Skills that enable an individual to write lucidly, coherently, and grammatically, or to handwrite legibly with ease and speed
UF Composition Skills (Literary) (1966 1980)
Handwriting Development (1966 1980) #
Handwriting Skills (1966 1983) #
BT Language Skills
RT Adult Literacy
Basic Skills
Capitalization (Alphabetic)
Cohesion (Written Composition)
Content Area Writing
Essay Tests
Functional Literacy
Grammar
Handwriting
Language Styles
Language Tests
Literacy
Literacy Education
Minimum Competencies
Notetaking
Outlining (Discourse)
Paragraph Composition
Parallelism (Literary)
Prewriting
Punctuation
Revision (Written Composition)
Rhetorical Invention
Sentence Combining
Spelling
Story Grammar
Student Writing Models
Writing (Composition)
Writing Difficulties
Writing Evaluation
Writing Exercises
Writing Improvement
Writing Instruction
Writing Laboratories
Writing Processes

Writing Systems
USE WRITTEN LANGUAGE

WRITTEN LANGUAGE *Jul. 1966*
CIJE: 641 RIE: 704 GC: 450
SN Systems of standardized visual signs and symbols used to convey meaning
UF Writing Systems
NT Braille
Graphemes
Ideography
Orthographic Symbols
Punctuation
Shorthand
BT Language
RT Abbreviations
Alphabets
Capitalization (Alphabetic)
Language Acquisition
Language Rhythm
Language Usage
Oral Language
Phoneme Grapheme Correspondence
Phonetic Transcription
Printing
Romanization
Unwritten Languages
Word Frequency
Writing (Composition)
Writing Evaluation

X Ray Technologists
USE RADIOLOGIC TECHNOLOGISTS

X Rays (Medicine)
USE RADIOLOGY

Xenophobia
USE STRANGER REACTIONS

Xerography
USE REPROGRAPHY

YAKUT *Jul. 1966*
CIJE: RIE: 3 GC: 440
BT Turkic Languages

Yard Workers (Horticulture)
USE GROUNDS KEEPERS

YEAR ROUND SCHOOLS *Jul. 1966*
CIJE: 90 RIE: 239 GC: 350
SN Schools that operate year-round but have not increased the number of days students must attend (note: prior to mar80, this term was not scoped and was often confused with "extended school year")
BT Schools
RT Extended School Year
Quarter System
School Schedules
Summer Schools
Trimester System
Vacation Programs

YEARBOOKS *Mar. 1969*
CIJE: 431 RIE: 209 GC: 730
SN Annually published volumes that contain current information or review the events of a year in brief descriptive, statistical, or pictorial form (note: for "student yearbooks," coordinate "yearbooks" with "student publications" or "school publications")
UF Annuals
BT Books
Reference Materials
Serials
RT Annual Reports
School Publications
Student Publications

YIDDISH *Jul. 1966*
CIJE: 10 RIE: 18 GC: 440
BT German

YORUBA *Jul. 1966*
CIJE: 15 RIE: 14 GC: 440
BT African Languages

YOUNG ADULTS *Jul. 1966*
CIJE: 893 RIE: 864 GC: 120
SN Approximately 18-30 years of age
BT Adults
RT College Students
Middle Aged Adults
Young Farmer Education
Youth

YOUNG CHILDREN *Mar. 1980*
CIJE: 1569 RIE: 1152 GC: 120
SN Aged birth through approximately 8 years
UF Early Childhood (1966 1980)
NT Infants
Kindergarten Children
Preschool Children
Toddlers
BT Children
RT Early Childhood Education
Early Experience

YOUNG FARMER EDUCATION *Jul. 1966*
CIJE: 62 RIE: 76 GC: 410
SN Vocational education in agriculture for adults not more than 25 years of age who are not otherwise enrolled in school (note: for adults 25 and over, use "adult farmer education")
UF Beginning Farmer Education
BT Adult Vocational Education
Agricultural Education
RT Adult Farmer Education
Farmers
Farm Visits
Rural Education
Rural Extension
Young Adults

YOUTH *Jul. 1966*
CIJE: 603 RIE: 760 GC: 120
SN Individuals or time of life between childhood and maturity (note: use a more specific term if possible and an age or educational level descriptor)
NT Affluent Youth
Black Youth
Disadvantaged Youth
Migrant Youth
Out Of School Youth
Rural Youth
Suburban Youth
Urban Youth
BT Groups
RT Adolescent Development
Adolescents
Age Groups
Children
Preadolescents
Young Adults
Youth Agencies
Youth Clubs
Youth Employment
Youth Leaders
Youth Opportunities
Youth Problems
Youth Programs

YOUTH AGENCIES *Jul. 1966*
CIJE: 41 RIE: 115 GC: 520
BT Agencies
RT Agency Role
Voluntary Agencies
Welfare Agencies
Youth

YOUTH CLUBS *Jul. 1966*
CIJE: 132 RIE: 230 GC: 520
UF Girls Clubs (1966 1980)
BT Clubs
RT Juvenile Gangs
Youth
Youth Leaders

YOUTH EMPLOYMENT *Jul. 1966*
CIJE: 350 RIE: 809 GC: 630
UF Youth Mobilization
BT Employment
RT Part Time Employment
Seasonal Employment
Youth
Youth Opportunities
Youth Programs

YOUTH LEADERS *Jul. 1966*
CIJE: 48 RIE: 113 GC: 510
SN Young people who lead
BT Groups
Leaders
RT Leadership Training
Youth
Youth Clubs

Youth Mobilization
USE YOUTH EMPLOYMENT

YOUTH OPPORTUNITIES *Jul. 1966*
CIJE: 86 RIE: 183 GC: 540
BT Opportunities
RT Employment Opportunities
Youth
Youth Employment
Youth Programs

YOUTH PROBLEMS *Jul. 1966*
CIJE: 437 RIE: 579 GC: 530
BT Problems
RT Delinquency
Early Parenthood
Generation Gap
Juvenile Courts
Runaways
Youth

YOUTH PROGRAMS *Jul. 1966*
CIJE: 301 RIE: 873 GC: 520
SN Programs for adolescents and/or young adults (note: also use an age or educational level descriptor)
BT Programs
RT Community Programs
Student Volunteers
Youth
Youth Employment
Youth Opportunities

YUCATEC *Dec. 1970*
CIJE: RIE: 1 GC: 440
BT Mayan Languages
RT Quiche

YURAK *Jul. 1966*
CIJE: RIE: 3 GC: 440
BT Samoyed Languages

ZONING *Jul. 1966*
CIJE: 25 RIE: 55 GC: 610
NT Community Zoning
Rezoning
School Zoning
Special Zoning
RT Land Use
Multicampus Districts
Planning
Real Estate
School Districts

ZOOLOGY *Aug. 1968*
CIJE: 258 RIE: 138 GC: 490
UF Animal Biology
NT Entomology
Ichthyology
Ornithology
Primatology
BT Biological Sciences
RT Anatomy
Animal Behavior
Animal Husbandry
Animals
Anthropology
Biology
Cardiovascular System
Culturing Techniques
Ecology
Embryology
Ethology
Evolution
Genetics
Laboratory Animals
Microbiology
Paleontology
Pathology
Physiology
Sociobiology
Wildlife

= Two or more Descriptors are used to represent this term.
The term's main entry shows the appropriate coordination.

ZOOS *Jul. 1966*
CIJE: 47 RIE: 25 GC: 920
BT Animal Facilities
RT Educational Facilities
Parks
Recreational Facilities
Wildlife Management

ROTATED DESCRIPTOR DISPLAY

The Rotated Descriptor Display is a permuted alphabetical index of *all words* that form *Thesaurus* terms, whether Descriptors or USE references. Each separate word is considered as a filing unit, and a term appears in as many locations in this display as it contains separate words. Subfiling under any one file point is performed first on the basis of the words to the right of the file point and second on the basis of the words to the left of the file point. The word order within the term itself is not altered.

HIGHER EDUCATION AS A FIELD OF STUDY Use POSTSECONDARY EDUCATION AS A FIELD OF STUDY
POSTSECONDARY EDUCATION AS A FIELD OF STUDY
SCHOOLS WITHIN A SCHOOL PLAN Use HOUSE PLAN
GRADE A YEAR INTEGRATION (1966 1980) Use SCHOOL DESEGREGATION
ABBREVIATIONS
ABILITY
ACADEMIC ABILITY
COGNITIVE ABILITY
CREATIVE ABILITY (1968 1980) Use CREATIVITY
ABILITY GROUPING
ABILITY IDENTIFICATION
LANGUAGE ABILITY (1966 1980)
MENTAL ABILITY Use COGNITIVE ABILITY
MOTOR ABILITY Use PSYCHOMOTOR SKILLS
NONVERBAL ABILITY
READING ABILITY
SCHOLASTIC ABILITY Use ACADEMIC ABILITY
SPATIAL ABILITY
STUDENT ABILITY (1966 1980) Use ACADEMIC ABILITY
LOW ABILITY STUDENTS (1967 1980)
PREDICTIVE ABILITY (TESTING) (1966 1980) Use PREDICTIVE MEASUREMENT
VERBAL ABILITY
VISUOSPATIAL ABILITY Use SPATIAL ABILITY
ABLE STUDENTS (1966 1978) Use ACADEMICALLY GIFTED
ABNORMAL PSYCHOLOGY Use PSYCHOPATHOLOGY
AUSTRALIAN ABORIGINAL LANGUAGES
ABORTIONS
ABREACTION Use CATHARSIS
STUDY ABROAD
WORKING ABROAD Use OVERSEAS EMPLOYMENT
FATHER ABSENCE Use FATHERLESS FAMILY
LEAVE OF ABSENCE (1968 1980) Use LEAVES OF ABSENCE
LEAVES OF ABSENCE
MOTHER ABSENCE Use MOTHERLESS FAMILY
PARENT ABSENCE Use ONE PARENT FAMILY
ABSENCE (STUDENTS) Use ATTENDANCE
ABSENCE (TEACHERS) Use TEACHER ATTENDANCE
ABSOLUTE HUMIDITY Use HUMIDITY
ABSOLUTE PRESSURE Use PRESSURE (PHYSICS)
ABSTRACT BIBLIOGRAPHIES Use ANNOTATED BIBLIOGRAPHIES
ABSTRACT REASONING
ABSTRACTING
ABSTRACTION LEVELS (1968 1980) Use ABSTRACT REASONING
ABSTRACTION TESTS (1967 1980) Use COGNITIVE TESTS
ABSTRACTS
CHILD ABUSE
CHILD SEXUAL ABUSE Use CHILD ABUSE and SEXUAL ABUSE
DRUG ABUSE
ELDER ABUSE
SELF ABUSE Use SELF DESTRUCTIVE BEHAVIOR
SEXUAL ABUSE
TEST ABUSE Use TEST USE
ABUSED CHILDREN Use CHILD ABUSE
ABUSED ELDERLY Use ELDER ABUSE
ABUSED WOMEN Use BATTERED WOMEN
AGING IN ACADEMIA
ACADEMIC ABILITY
ACADEMIC ACHIEVEMENT
ACADEMIC ADVISING
ACADEMIC APTITUDE
ACADEMIC ASPIRATION
ACADEMIC CALENDARS Use SCHOOL SCHEDULES
ACADEMIC CURRICULUM Use ACADEMIC EDUCATION
ACADEMIC DEANS
DEGREES (ACADEMIC)
ACADEMIC DEPARTMENTS Use DEPARTMENTS
ACADEMIC DISCIPLINES Use INTELLECTUAL DISCIPLINES
ACADEMIC EDUCATION
ACADEMIC ENRICHMENT (1966 1980) Use ENRICHMENT
ACADEMIC ENVIRONMENT Use EDUCATIONAL ENVIRONMENT
ACADEMIC FAILURE
ACADEMIC FREEDOM
ACADEMIC GAMES Use EDUCATIONAL GAMES
ACADEMIC LEARNING TIME Use TIME ON TASK
ACADEMIC LIBRARIES
ACADEMIC MALPRACTICE Use EDUCATIONAL MALPRACTICE
CHIEF ACADEMIC OFFICERS Use ACADEMIC DEANS
ACADEMIC PERFORMANCE (1966 1974) Use ACADEMIC ACHIEVEMENT
ACADEMIC PERSISTENCE
ACADEMIC PLANNING Use EDUCATIONAL PLANNING
ACADEMIC PROBATION
ACADEMIC PROGRESS Use ACADEMIC ACHIEVEMENT
ACADEMIC PROMOTION Use STUDENT PROMOTION
ENGLISH FOR ACADEMIC PURPOSES
ACADEMIC RANK (PROFESSIONAL)
ACADEMIC RECORDS
ACADEMIC SENATES Use COLLEGE GOVERNING COUNCILS
ACADEMIC STANDARDS
ACADEMIC SUBJECTS Use ACADEMIC EDUCATION
ACADEMIC SUCCESS Use ACADEMIC ACHIEVEMENT
TRANSCRIPTS (ACADEMIC) Use ACADEMIC RECORDS
ACADEMICALLY DISADVANTAGED Use EDUCATIONALLY DISADVANTAGED
ACADEMICALLY GIFTED
ACADEMICALLY HANDICAPPED (1966 1980)
ACCELERATED COURSES (1966 1980) Use ACCELERATION (EDUCATION)
ACCELERATED PROGRAMS (1966 1980) Use ACCELERATION (EDUCATION)
ACCELERATION (1966 1982) (EDUCATION) Use ACCELERATION (EDUCATION)
ACCELERATION (EDUCATION)
ACCELERATION (1966 1982) (PHYSICS) Use ACCELERATION (PHYSICS)
ACCELERATION (PHYSICS)
GRAMMATICAL ACCEPTABILITY

COUNSELOR ACCEPTANCE (1968 1980) Use COUNSELOR CLIENT RELATIONSHIP
PEER ACCEPTANCE
ONLINE PUBLIC ACCESS CATALOGS Use ONLINE CATALOGS
EDUCATIONAL ACCESS Use ACCESS TO EDUCATION
DIAL ACCESS INFORMATION SYSTEMS
SUBJECT ACCESS Use INDEXING
ACCESS TO EDUCATION
ACCESS TO IDEAS Use INTELLECTUAL FREEDOM
ACCESS TO INFORMATION
ACCESSIBILITY (FOR DISABLED)
ACCIDENT PREVENTION
ACCIDENTS
SCHOOL ACCIDENTS
TRAFFIC ACCIDENTS
PUBLIC ACCOMMODATIONS Use PUBLIC FACILITIES
ACCOUNTABILITY
EDUCATIONAL ACCOUNTABILITY (1970 1980) Use ACCOUNTABILITY
ACCOUNTANTS
CERTIFIED PUBLIC ACCOUNTANTS
ACCOUNTING
PROPERTY ACCOUNTING
SCHOOL ACCOUNTING
FARM ACCOUNTS
PERSONAL ACCOUNTS (NARRATIVES) Use PERSONAL NARRATIVES
ACCREDITATION (INSTITUTIONS)
ACCREDITING AGENCIES
ACCREDITING ASSOCIATIONS Use ACCREDITING AGENCIES
ACCULTURATION
DATA ACCUMULATION Use DATA COLLECTION
ACETYLENE WELDING Use WELDING
ACHIEVEMENT
ACADEMIC ACHIEVEMENT
BLACK ACHIEVEMENT
ACHIEVEMENT COMPARISON Use ACHIEVEMENT RATING
EDUCATIONAL ACHIEVEMENT Use ACADEMIC ACHIEVEMENT
LOW ACHIEVEMENT FACTORS (1966 1980) Use LOW ACHIEVEMENT
ACHIEVEMENT GAINS
HIGH ACHIEVEMENT
ACHIEVEMENT INCENTIVES Use INCENTIVES
ACHIEVEMENT LEVEL Use ACHIEVEMENT
ACHIEVEMENT LOSSES Use ACHIEVEMENT GAINS
LOW ACHIEVEMENT
MATHEMATICS ACHIEVEMENT
ACHIEVEMENT MOTIVATION Use ACHIEVEMENT NEED
ACHIEVEMENT NEED
NEGRO ACHIEVEMENT (1966 1977) Use BLACK ACHIEVEMENT
ACHIEVEMENT PREDICTION Use ACHIEVEMENT and PREDICTION
ACHIEVEMENT RATING
READING ACHIEVEMENT
RECOGNITION (ACHIEVEMENT)
SCHOLASTIC ACHIEVEMENT Use ACADEMIC ACHIEVEMENT
STUDENT ACHIEVEMENT Use ACADEMIC ACHIEVEMENT
ACHIEVEMENT TESTS
HIGH ACHIEVERS (1966 1980) Use HIGH ACHIEVEMENT
LOW ACHIEVERS (1966 1980) Use LOW ACHIEVEMENT
DEOXYRIBONUCLEIC ACID Use DNA
DESOXYRIBONUCLEIC ACID Use DNA
LYSERGIC ACID DIETHYLAMIDE
RIBONUCLEIC ACID Use RNA
NUCLEIC ACIDS
ACOUSTIC BARRIERS Use ACOUSTIC INSULATION
ACOUSTIC INSULATION
ACOUSTIC PHONETICS
ACOUSTICAL ENVIRONMENT
ACOUSTICS
LAND ACQUISITION
LANGUAGE ACQUISITION
LIBRARY ACQUISITION
ACRONYMS Use ABBREVIATIONS
ACTING
AFFIRMATIVE ACTION
CHURCH ACTION Use CHURCH ROLE
COMMUNITY ACTION
COURT ACTION Use COURT LITIGATION
DISCIPLINARY ACTION Use DISCIPLINE
JUDICIAL ACTION Use COURT LITIGATION
ACTION LEARNING Use EXPERIENTIAL LEARNING
POLICE ACTION
ACTION PROGRAMS (COMMUNITY) (1966 1980) Use COMMUNITY ACTION
ACTION RESEARCH
SOCIAL ACTION
STATE ACTION
ACTIVATED SLUDGE Use SLUDGE
AUDIO ACTIVE COMPARE LABORATORIES (1967 1980) Use LANGUAGE LABORATORIES
AUDIO ACTIVE LABORATORIES (1967 1980) Use LANGUAGE LABORATORIES
ACTIVISM
ACTIVITIES
AFTER SCHOOL ACTIVITIES (1967 1980) Use AFTER SCHOOL PROGRAMS
ART ACTIVITIES
ATHLETIC ACTIVITIES (1966 1974) Use ATHLETICS
CLASS ACTIVITIES
CLASSROOM ACTIVITIES Use CLASS ACTIVITIES
COCURRICULAR ACTIVITIES (1966 1980) Use EXTRACURRICULAR ACTIVITIES
COOPERATIVE ACTIVITIES Use GROUP ACTIVITIES
CREATIVE ACTIVITIES
CULTURAL ACTIVITIES
ENRICHMENT ACTIVITIES
STUDENT ACTIVITIES (EXTRACLASS) Use EXTRACURRICULAR ACTIVITIES
EXTRACURRICULAR ACTIVITIES
GROUP ACTIVITIES
HEALTH ACTIVITIES HANDBOOKS (1966 1980) Use GUIDES and HEALTH MATERIALS

HEALTH ACTIVITIES
INDIVIDUAL ACTIVITIES
INTEGRATED ACTIVITIES
LEARNING ACTIVITIES
MUSCULAR ACTIVITIES Use MOTOR REACTIONS
MUSIC ACTIVITIES
OUTDOOR ACTIVITIES
PHYSICAL ACTIVITIES
PLAYGROUND ACTIVITIES
RECREATIONAL ACTIVITIES
SCHOOL ACTIVITIES
SCHOOL RELATED ACTIVITIES Use EXTRACURRICULAR ACTIVITIES
SCIENCE ACTIVITIES
SPEAKING ACTIVITIES (1966 1980) Use SPEECH COMMUNICATION
SUPERVISORY ACTIVITIES (1968 1980) Use SUPERVISION
DIRECTED READING ACTIVITY
ACTIVITY LEARNING (1968 1978) Use EXPERIENTIAL LEARNING
ACTIVITY LEVEL (MOTOR BEHAVIOR) Use PHYSICAL ACTIVITY LEVEL
PHYSICAL ACTIVITY LEVEL
LEARNING ACTIVITY PACKAGES Use LEARNING MODULES
LEARNING ACTIVITY PACKETS Use LEARNING MODULES
ACTIVITY UNITS
ILLOCUTIONARY ACTS Use SPEECH ACTS
SPEECH ACTS
SELF ACTUALIZATION
VISUAL ACUITY
AD VALOREM TAX Use PROPERTY TAXES
ADAGES Use PROVERBS
ADAPTABILITY (PERSONALITY) Use ADJUSTMENT (TO ENVIRONMENT) and PERSONALITY TRAITS
CURRICULUM ADAPTATION Use CURRICULUM DEVELOPMENT
EDUCATIONAL MEDIA ADAPTATION Use MEDIA ADAPTATION
INSTRUCTIONAL MATERIAL ADAPTATION Use MEDIA ADAPTATION
ADAPTATION LEVEL THEORY
MATERIAL ADAPTATION Use MEDIA ADAPTATION
MEDIA ADAPTATION
TACTILE ADAPTATION
ADAPTED PHYSICAL EDUCATION
ADAPTIVE BEHAVIOR Use ADJUSTMENT (TO ENVIRONMENT)
ADAPTIVE BEHAVIOR (OF DISABLED)
ADAPTIVE EQUIPMENT (DISABLED) Use ASSISTIVE DEVICES (FOR DISABLED)
ADAPTIVE TESTING
COMPUTERIZED ADAPTIVE TESTING Use ADAPTIVE TESTING and COMPUTER ASSISTED TESTING
DRUG ADDICTION
NARCOTICS ADDICTION Use DRUG ADDICTION
ADDITION
ADDITIONAL AID Use EQUALIZATION AID
ADDRESSES Use SPEECHES
ADHESIVES
CEMENTS (ADHESIVES) Use ADHESIVES
PASTES (ADHESIVES) Use ADHESIVES
ADJECTIVES
ADJUNCT FACULTY
ADJUNCT PROFESSORS Use ADJUNCT FACULTY
ADJUSTMENT COUNSELORS
EMOTIONAL ADJUSTMENT
EMPLOYMENT ADJUSTMENT Use VOCATIONAL ADJUSTMENT
GROUP ADJUSTMENT Use ADJUSTMENT (TO ENVIRONMENT)
INDIVIDUAL ADJUSTMENT Use ADJUSTMENT (TO ENVIRONMENT)
JOB ADJUSTMENT Use VOCATIONAL ADJUSTMENT
OCCUPATIONAL ADJUSTMENT Use VOCATIONAL ADJUSTMENT
PERSONAL ADJUSTMENT (1966 1980) Use ADJUSTMENT (TO ENVIRONMENT)
ADJUSTMENT PROBLEMS (1966 1980) Use ADJUSTMENT (TO ENVIRONMENT)
SCHOOL ADJUSTMENT Use STUDENT ADJUSTMENT
SOCIAL ADJUSTMENT
STUDENT ADJUSTMENT
ADJUSTMENT (TO ENVIRONMENT)
VOCATIONAL ADJUSTMENT
WORK ADJUSTMENT Use VOCATIONAL ADJUSTMENT
ADMINISTRATION
BUSINESS ADMINISTRATION
COLLEGE ADMINISTRATION
BUSINESS ADMINISTRATION EDUCATION
PUBLIC ADMINISTRATION EDUCATION
EDUCATIONAL ADMINISTRATION
INSTITUTIONAL ADMINISTRATION
LIBRARY ADMINISTRATION
PROGRAM ADMINISTRATION
PUBLIC ADMINISTRATION
RESEARCH ADMINISTRATION
SCHOOL ADMINISTRATION
TEAM ADMINISTRATION (1967 1980) Use MANAGEMENT TEAMS
TEST ADMINISTRATION Use TESTING
UNIVERSITY ADMINISTRATION (1967 1980) Use COLLEGE ADMINISTRATION
ADMINISTRATIVE AGENCIES (1966 1980)
GOVERNMENT (ADMINISTRATIVE BODY)
ADMINISTRATIVE CHANGE
ADMINISTRATIVE OCCUPATIONS Use MANAGERIAL OCCUPATIONS
ADMINISTRATIVE ORGANIZATION
ADMINISTRATIVE PERSONNEL (1966 1980) Use ADMINISTRATORS
ADMINISTRATIVE PLANNING Use PLANNING
ADMINISTRATIVE POLICY
ADMINISTRATIVE PRINCIPLES
ADMINISTRATIVE PROBLEMS
ADMINISTRATIVE SECRETARIES Use SECRETARIES
ADMINISTRATIVE TEAMS Use MANAGEMENT TEAMS
INTERMEDIATE ADMINISTRATIVE UNITS
ADMINISTRATOR APPRAISAL Use ADMINISTRATOR EVALUATION
ADMINISTRATOR ATTITUDES
ADMINISTRATOR BACKGROUND (1967 1980) Use ADMINISTRATOR CHARACTERISTICS
ADMINISTRATOR CHARACTERISTICS
ADMINISTRATOR EDUCATION

	ADMINISTRATOR EVALUATION
	ADMINISTRATOR GUIDES
	ADMINISTRATOR OPINIONS Use ADMINISTRATOR ATTITUDES
	ADMINISTRATOR PREPARATION Use ADMINISTRATOR EDUCATION
	ADMINISTRATOR QUALIFICATIONS
BOARD	ADMINISTRATOR RELATIONSHIP
TEACHER	ADMINISTRATOR RELATIONSHIP
	ADMINISTRATOR RESPONSIBILITY
	ADMINISTRATOR ROLE
	ADMINISTRATOR SELECTION
	ADMINISTRATOR TEACHER RELATIONSHIP Use TEACHER ADMINISTRATOR RELATIONSHIP
	ADMINISTRATOR TRAINING Use MANAGEMENT DEVELOPMENT
	ADMINISTRATORS
CHIEF	ADMINISTRATORS (1967 1980) Use ADMINISTRATORS
HOSPITAL RECORD	ADMINISTRATORS Use MEDICAL RECORD ADMINISTRATORS
LIBRARY	ADMINISTRATORS Use LIBRARY ADMINISTRATION
MEDICAL RECORD	ADMINISTRATORS
PERSONNEL	ADMINISTRATORS Use PERSONNEL DIRECTORS
SCHOOL	ADMINISTRATORS Use ADMINISTRATORS
TEST	ADMINISTRATORS Use EXAMINERS
COLLEGE	ADMISSION
	ADMISSION CRITERIA
EARLY	ADMISSION
OPEN	ADMISSION Use OPEN ENROLLMENT
PREFERENTIAL	ADMISSION Use SELECTIVE ADMISSION
RESTRICTIVE	ADMISSION Use SELECTIVE ADMISSION
	ADMISSION (SCHOOL)
SCHOOL	ADMISSION Use ADMISSION (SCHOOL)
SELECTIVE	ADMISSION
SPECIAL	ADMISSION Use SELECTIVE ADMISSION
	ADMISSION TESTS (HIGHER EDUCATION) Use COLLEGE ENTRANCE EXAMINATIONS
	ADMISSION TESTS (OCCUPATIONAL) Use OCCUPATIONAL TESTS
	ADMISSIONS COUNSELING
	ADMISSIONS COUNSELORS (1973 1980) Use ADMISSIONS COUNSELING
	ADMISSIONS OFFICERS
	ADOLESCENCE (1966 1980) Use ADOLESCENTS
	ADOLESCENT DEVELOPMENT
	ADOLESCENT LITERATURE
	ADOLESCENT PARENTS Use EARLY PARENTHOOD
	ADOLESCENTS
	ADOPTED CHILDREN
	ADOPTION
	ADOPTION (IDEAS)
	ADULT BASIC EDUCATION
	ADULT CHARACTERISTICS (1967 1980) Use ADULTS and INDIVIDUAL CHARACTERISTICS
	ADULT COUNSELING
	ADULT DAY CARE
	ADULT DEVELOPMENT
	ADULT DROPOUTS
	ADULT EDUCATION
MIGRANT	ADULT EDUCATION
	ADULT EDUCATION PROGRAMS (1966 1980) Use ADULT EDUCATION and ADULT PROGRAMS
PUBLIC SCHOOL	ADULT EDUCATION
	ADULT EDUCATORS
	ADULT FARMER EDUCATION
	ADULT FOSTER CARE
	ADULT LEADERS (1967 1980) Use LEADERS
	ADULT LEARNING
	ADULT LITERACY
	ADULT PROGRAMS
	ADULT READING PROGRAMS
	ADULT RUNAWAYS Use RUNAWAYS
	ADULT STUDENTS
	ADULT VOCATIONAL EDUCATION
	ADULTS
FOSTER HOMES (1970 1982)	(ADULTS) Use ADULT FOSTER CARE
FUNDAMENTAL EDUCATION	(ADULTS) Use ADULT BASIC EDUCATION
ILLITERATE	ADULTS (1966 1980) Use ADULT LITERACY and ILLITERACY
MIDDLE AGED	ADULTS
MIGRANT	ADULTS Use MIGRANTS
OLDER	ADULTS
YOUNG	ADULTS
	ADVANCE ORGANIZERS
MENTALLY	ADVANCED CHILDREN Use GIFTED
	ADVANCED COURSES
	ADVANCED CREDIT EXAMINATIONS Use EQUIVALENCY TESTS
	ADVANCED EDUCATION Use HIGHER EDUCATION
	ADVANCED NATIONS Use DEVELOPED NATIONS
ECONOMICALLY	ADVANCED NATIONS Use DEVELOPED NATIONS
	ADVANCED PLACEMENT
	ADVANCED PLACEMENT PROGRAMS
	ADVANCED PROGRAMS (1966 1980)
	ADVANCED STANDING EXAMINATIONS Use EQUIVALENCY TESTS
	ADVANCED STUDENTS
	ADVANCEMENT Use PROMOTION (OCCUPATIONAL)
FACULTY	ADVANCEMENT Use FACULTY PROMOTION
INSTITUTIONAL	ADVANCEMENT
TEACHER	ADVANCEMENT Use TEACHER PROMOTION
TECHNOLOGICAL	ADVANCEMENT
	ADVANTAGED
CULTURALLY	ADVANTAGED (1967 1980) Use ADVANTAGED
ECONOMICALLY	ADVANTAGED Use ADVANTAGED
SOCIALLY	ADVANTAGED Use ADVANTAGED
EDUCATIONAL	ADVANTAGES Use EDUCATIONAL OPPORTUNITIES
	ADVENTITIOUS IMPAIRMENTS
	ADVENTITIOUSLY HANDICAPPED (1975 1980) Use ADVENTITIOUS IMPAIRMENTS
	ADVENTURE EDUCATION
	ADVENTURE LEARNING Use ADVENTURE EDUCATION
	ADVERBIALS Use ADVERBS
	ADVERBS
	ADVERTISING

ADVERTISING ART Use COMMERCIAL ART
FACULTY ADVISERS
FOREIGN STUDENT ADVISERS
RESIDENT ADVISERS
ACADEMIC ADVISING
FACULTY ADVISORS (1967 1980) Use FACULTY ADVISERS
ADVISORY BOARDS Use ADVISORY COMMITTEES
ADVISORY COMMITTEES
ADVOCACY
CHILD ADVOCACY
CITIZEN ADVOCACY Use ADVOCACY
POLITICAL ADVOCACY Use LOBBYING
ADVOCATES (LAW) Use LAWYERS
AEROBIC DANCE Use AEROBICS and DANCE
AEROBICS
AEROSPACE EDUCATION
AEROSPACE INDUSTRY
SATELLITES (AEROSPACE)
AEROSPACE SCIENCE EDUCATION Use AEROSPACE EDUCATION
AEROSPACE SCIENCES Use AEROSPACE TECHNOLOGY
AEROSPACE TECHNOLOGY
AESTHETIC EDUCATION
AESTHETIC JUDGMENT Use AESTHETIC VALUES and VALUE JUDGMENT
AESTHETIC VALUES
PUBLIC AFFAIRS EDUCATION
STUDENT AFFAIRS SERVICES Use STUDENT PERSONNEL SERVICES
STUDENT AFFAIRS WORKERS Use STUDENT PERSONNEL WORKERS
WORLD AFFAIRS
AFFECTION
AFFECTIVE BEHAVIOR
AFFECTIVE EDUCATION Use HUMANISTIC EDUCATION
AFFECTIVE MEASURES
AFFECTIVE OBJECTIVES
AFFECTIVE TESTS (1971 1980) Use AFFECTIVE MEASURES
AFFILIATED SCHOOLS
AFFILIATION NEED
POLITICAL AFFILIATION
AFFIRMATIVE ACTION
AFFLUENT YOUTH
AFRICAN AMERICAN STUDIES (1969 1977) Use BLACK STUDIES
AFRICAN AMERICANS Use BLACKS
AFRICAN CULTURE
AFRICAN HISTORY
AFRICAN LANGUAGES
AFRICAN LITERATURE
AFRIKAANS
AFRO AMERICANS Use BLACKS
AFRO ASIATIC LANGUAGES
AFTER SCHOOL ACTIVITIES (1967 1980) Use AFTER SCHOOL PROGRAMS
AFTER SCHOOL CENTERS
AFTER SCHOOL DAY CARE (1978 1983) Use AFTER SCHOOL PROGRAMS and SCHOOL AGE DAY CARE
AFTER SCHOOL EDUCATION
AFTER SCHOOL PROGRAMS
AFTER SCHOOL TUTORING (1966 1980) Use AFTER SCHOOL EDUCATION and TUTORING
FIGURAL AFTEREFFECTS
AGE
CHRONOLOGICAL AGE
SCHOOL AGE DAY CARE
AGE DIFFERENCES
AGE DISCRIMINATION
AGE GRADE PLACEMENT
AGE GRADE STATUS Use AGE GRADE PLACEMENT
AGE GROUPS
CROSS AGE HELPING Use CROSS AGE TEACHING
INTELLIGENCE AGE Use MENTAL AGE
AGE LEVEL Use AGE
MENTAL AGE
OLD AGE Use OLDER ADULTS
SCHOOL ENTRANCE AGE
CROSS AGE TEACHING
AGED Use OLDER ADULTS
MIDDLE AGED ADULTS
HOMES FOR THE AGED Use PERSONAL CARE HOMES
MIDDLE AGED (1966 1980) Use MIDDLE AGED ADULTS
AGENCIES
ACCREDITING AGENCIES
ADMINISTRATIVE AGENCIES (1966 1980)
GOVERNMENT AGENCIES Use PUBLIC AGENCIES
LOCAL EDUCATION AGENCIES Use SCHOOL DISTRICTS
NONPUBLIC AGENCIES Use PRIVATE AGENCIES
PRIVATE AGENCIES
PUBLIC AGENCIES
COMMUNITY AGENCIES (PUBLIC) (1966 1980) Use PUBLIC AGENCIES
RELIGIOUS AGENCIES (1966 1980) Use RELIGIOUS ORGANIZATIONS
SOCIAL AGENCIES
STATE AGENCIES
STATE EDUCATION AGENCIES Use STATE DEPARTMENTS OF EDUCATION
URBAN RENEWAL AGENCIES
VOLUNTARY AGENCIES
WELFARE AGENCIES
YOUTH AGENCIES
AGENCY COOPERATION
AGENCY FUNCTION Use AGENCY ROLE
AGENCY ROLE
AGRICULTURAL AGENTS Use EXTENSION AGENTS
CHANGE AGENTS
COUNTY EXTENSION AGENTS Use EXTENSION AGENTS
EXTENSION AGENTS
FARM AGENTS Use EXTENSION AGENTS
FOUR H CLUB AGENTS Use EXTENSION AGENTS
HOME DEMONSTRATION AGENTS Use EXTENSION AGENTS

LINKING	AGENTS
VILLAGE EXTENSION	AGENTS Use EXTENSION AGENTS
	AGGRESSION
	AGING EDUCATION
	AGING IN ACADEMIA
	AGING (INDIVIDUALS)
	AGING PROFESSORIATE Use AGING IN ACADEMIA
INTERJUDGE	AGREEMENT Use INTERRATER RELIABILITY
	AGREEMENTS (FORMAL) Use CONTRACTS
NEGOTIATION	AGREEMENTS
	AGRIBUSINESS
	AGRICULTURAL AGENTS Use EXTENSION AGENTS
	AGRICULTURAL CHEMICAL OCCUPATIONS
	AGRICULTURAL COLLEGES
	AGRICULTURAL EDUCATION
	AGRICULTURAL EDUCATION (VOCATIONAL) Use AGRICULTURAL EDUCATION and VOCATIONAL EDUCATION
	AGRICULTURAL ENGINEERING
	AGRICULTURAL EXTENSION Use RURAL EXTENSION
	AGRICULTURAL LABOR DISPUTES (1966 1980) Use LABOR DEMANDS
	AGRICULTURAL LABORERS
	AGRICULTURAL MACHINERY
	AGRICULTURAL MACHINERY OCCUPATIONS
	AGRICULTURAL MECHANICS (SUBJECT) Use AGRICULTURAL ENGINEERING
	AGRICULTURAL MIGRANT WORKERS Use MIGRANT WORKERS
	AGRICULTURAL MIGRANTS Use MIGRANTS
	AGRICULTURAL OCCUPATIONS
NONFARM	AGRICULTURAL OCCUPATIONS Use OFF FARM AGRICULTURAL OCCUPATIONS
OFF FARM	AGRICULTURAL OCCUPATIONS
	AGRICULTURAL PERSONNEL
	AGRICULTURAL PRODUCTION
	AGRICULTURAL RESEARCH PROJECTS (1966 1981) Use RESEARCH PROJECTS
	AGRICULTURAL SAFETY
	AGRICULTURAL SKILLS
	AGRICULTURAL SUPPLIES
	AGRICULTURAL SUPPLY OCCUPATIONS
	AGRICULTURAL TECHNICIANS
	AGRICULTURAL TRENDS
	AGRICULTURAL WORKERS Use AGRICULTURAL LABORERS
MIGRATORY	AGRICULTURAL WORKERS Use MIGRANT WORKERS
	AGRICULTURE
SUPERVISED OCCUPATIONAL EXPERIENCE	(AGRICULTURE) Use SUPERVISED FARM PRACTICE
VOCATIONAL	AGRICULTURE TEACHERS (1967 1980) Use AGRICULTURAL EDUCATION and VOCATIONAL EDUCATION TEACHERS
VOCATIONAL	AGRICULTURE (1967 1980) Use AGRICULTURAL EDUCATION and VOCATIONAL EDUCATION
	AGRONOMY
ADDITIONAL	AID Use EQUALIZATION AID
FINANCIAL	AID APPLICANTS
CATEGORICAL	AID
EQUALIZATION	AID
FEDERAL	AID
FEDERAL STATE	AID Use STATE FEDERAL AID
FIRST	AID
LEGAL	AID
NEED ANALYSIS (STUDENT FINANCIAL	AID)
NONPUBLIC SCHOOL	AID (1972 1980) Use PRIVATE SCHOOL AID
STUDENT FINANCIAL	AID OFFICERS
PAROCHIAL SCHOOL	AID (1972 1980) Use PAROCHIAL SCHOOLS and PRIVATE SCHOOL AID
PRIVATE SCHOOL	AID
LEGAL	AID PROJECTS (1966 1980) Use LEGAL AID
PROVINCIAL	AID Use STATE AID
SCHOOL	AID Use EDUCATIONAL FINANCE
STATE	AID
STATE FEDERAL	AID
STATE FINANCIAL	AID Use STATE AID
STUDENT	AID Use STUDENT FINANCIAL AID
STUDENT FINANCIAL	AID
MACHINE	AIDED INDEXING Use AUTOMATIC INDEXING
COMPUTER	AIDED INSTRUCTION Use COMPUTER ASSISTED INSTRUCTION
COMPUTER	AIDED INSTRUCTIONAL MANAGEMENT Use COMPUTER MANAGED INSTRUCTION
BILINGUAL TEACHER	AIDES
ENGINEERING	AIDES Use ENGINEERING TECHNICIANS
FORESTER	AIDES Use FORESTRY AIDES
FORESTRY	AIDES
HIGHWAY ENGINEERING	AIDES
HOME HEALTH	AIDES
HOUSEKEEPING	AIDES Use HOUSEKEEPERS
HOUSING MANAGEMENT	AIDES
LIBRARY	AIDES Use LIBRARY TECHNICIANS
NURSES	AIDES
NURSING	AIDES Use NURSES AIDES
PHYSICAL THERAPY	AIDES
PSYCHIATRIC	AIDES
REST HOME	AIDES Use NURSES AIDES
SCHOOL	AIDES
TEACHER	AIDES
AUDIOVISUAL	AIDS
AUTOINSTRUCTIONAL	AIDS
DISPLAY	AIDS
ELECTROMECHANICAL	AIDS
ELECTRONIC	AIDS Use ELECTRONIC EQUIPMENT
COMMUNICATION	AIDS (FOR DISABLED)
HEARING	AIDS
INSTRUCTIONAL	AIDS (1966 1980) Use EDUCATIONAL MEDIA
LANGUAGE	AIDS (1966 1980)
LIBRARY	AIDS Use LIBRARY EQUIPMENT
LOW VISION	AIDS
MECHANICAL TEACHING	AIDS (1966 1980) Use EDUCATIONAL MEDIA
MOBILITY	AIDS
AUTHORING	AIDS (PROGRAMING)
SELF INSTRUCTION	AIDS Use AUTOINSTRUCTIONAL AIDS

SENSORY	AIDS
THREE DIMENSIONAL	AIDS
VISUAL	AIDS
	AIR BAGS Use RESTRAINTS (VEHICLE SAFETY)
	AIR BASES Use MILITARY AIR FACILITIES
ARMY	AIR BASES Use MILITARY AIR FACILITIES
	AIR CONDITIONING
	AIR CONDITIONING EQUIPMENT
	AIR CONDITIONING MECHANICS Use REFRIGERATION MECHANICS
MILITARY	AIR FACILITIES
	AIR FLOW
	AIR FORCE BASES Use MILITARY AIR FACILITIES
	AIR INFLATED STRUCTURES (1972 1980) Use AIR STRUCTURES
	AIR POLLUTION
	AIR POLLUTION CONTROL (1967 1980) Use AIR POLLUTION
	AIR RAID SHELTERS Use FALLOUT SHELTERS
COAST GUARD	AIR STATIONS Use MILITARY AIR FACILITIES
MARINE CORPS	AIR STATIONS Use MILITARY AIR FACILITIES
NAVAL	AIR STATIONS Use MILITARY AIR FACILITIES
	AIR STRUCTURES
HYBRID	AIR STRUCTURES (1972 1980) Use AIR STRUCTURES
	AIR SUPPORTED STRUCTURES (1972 1980) Use AIR STRUCTURES
	AIR TRAFFIC CONTROL
	AIR TRANSPORTATION
	AIRBORNE FIELD TRIPS (1968 1980) Use FIELD TRIPS
	AIRBORNE TELEVISION (1966 1980) Use TELEVISION
	AIRCRAFT MECHANICS Use AVIATION MECHANICS
	AIRCRAFT PILOTS
	AIRLINE PILOTS Use AIRCRAFT PILOTS
	AIRPLANE PILOTS Use AIRCRAFT PILOTS
	AIRPORTS
	AKAN
	ALARM SYSTEMS
BURGLAR	ALARMS Use ALARM SYSTEMS
SECURITY SYSTEMS	(ALARMS) Use ALARM SYSTEMS
SMOKE	ALARMS Use ALARM SYSTEMS
	ALASKA NATIVES
	ALBANIAN
	ALCOHOL EDUCATION
	ALCOHOLIC BEVERAGES
	ALCOHOLISM
	ALEUT Use ESKIMO ALEUT LANGUAGES
ESKIMO	ALEUT LANGUAGES
	ALGEBRA
	ALGORISMS Use ALGORITHMS
	ALGORITHMS
	ALIEN CULTURE Use FOREIGN CULTURE
	ALIEN ILLEGALITY Use UNDOCUMENTED IMMIGRANTS
	ALIENATION
STUDENT	ALIENATION
TEACHER	ALIENATION
ILLEGAL	ALIENS Use UNDOCUMENTED IMMIGRANTS
	ALLEGORY
	ALLERGY
	ALLIED HEALTH EDUCATION Use ALLIED HEALTH OCCUPATIONS EDUCATION
	ALLIED HEALTH OCCUPATIONS
	ALLIED HEALTH OCCUPATIONS EDUCATION
	ALLIED HEALTH PERSONNEL
	ALLIED HEALTH PROFESSIONS Use ALLIED HEALTH OCCUPATIONS
	ALLIED MEDICAL OCCUPATIONS Use ALLIED HEALTH OCCUPATIONS
	ALLOCATION OF RESOURCES Use RESOURCE ALLOCATION
RESOURCE	ALLOCATION
TAX	ALLOCATION
TIME	ALLOCATION Use TIME MANAGEMENT
BUDGET	ALLOCATIONS Use BUDGETING
RESOURCE	ALLOCATIONS (1966 1980) Use RESOURCE ALLOCATION
	ALLOMORPHS (1967 1980) Use MORPHEMES
TRAINING	ALLOWANCES
THINKING	ALOUD PROTOCOLS Use PROTOCOL ANALYSIS
READING	ALOUD TO OTHERS
CYRILLIC	ALPHABET
INITIAL TEACHING	ALPHABET
LETTERS	(ALPHABET)
CAPITALIZATION	(ALPHABETIC)
	ALPHABETIC FILING Use FILING
	ALPHABETIZING SKILLS
	ALPHABETS
PHONEMIC	ALPHABETS
	ALTAIC LANGUAGES Use URALIC ALTAIC LANGUAGES
URALIC	ALTAIC LANGUAGES
	ALTERNATIVE EDUCATION Use NONTRADITIONAL EDUCATION
	ALTERNATIVE ENERGY SOURCES
	ALTERNATIVE FUTURES Use FUTURES (OF SOCIETY)
	ALTERNATIVE LIFE STYLES Use LIFE STYLE
	ALTERNATIVE SCHOOLS (1972 1980) Use NONTRADITIONAL EDUCATION
EDUCATIONAL	ALTERNATIVES (1974 1980) Use NONTRADITIONAL EDUCATION
INSTRUCTIONAL	ALTERNATIVES Use NONTRADITIONAL EDUCATION
TEACHING	ALTERNATIVES Use NONTRADITIONAL EDUCATION
TRAINING	ALTERNATIVES Use NONTRADITIONAL EDUCATION
	ALTRUISM
	ALUMNI
	ALUMNI ASSOCIATIONS
	ALUMNI COLLEGES Use ALUMNI EDUCATION
	ALUMNI EDUCATION
	AMBIENT PRESSURE Use PRESSURE (PHYSICS)
	AMBIGUITY
	AMBITION Use ASPIRATION
	AMBULANCE ATTENDANTS Use EMERGENCY MEDICAL TECHNICIANS
	AMERASIANS Use ASIAN AMERICANS
AMERICAN LITERATURE (1966 1980) (LATIN	AMERICA) Use LATIN AMERICAN LITERATURE
	AMERICAN CULTURE (1966 1980)

HISPANIC	AMERICAN CULTURE	
JAPANESE	AMERICAN CULTURE	
LATIN	AMERICAN CULTURE	
MEXICAN	AMERICAN CULTURE	Use HISPANIC AMERICAN CULTURE and MEXICAN AMERICANS
NORTH	AMERICAN CULTURE	
MEXICAN	AMERICAN EDUCATION	
	AMERICAN ENGLISH (1968 1980)	Use NORTH AMERICAN ENGLISH
NORTH	AMERICAN ENGLISH	
	AMERICAN GOVERNMENT (COURSE) (1966 1980)	Use UNITED STATES GOVERNMENT (COURSE)
	AMERICAN HISTORY (1966 1980)	
CENTRAL	AMERICAN HISTORY	Use LATIN AMERICAN HISTORY
LATIN	AMERICAN HISTORY	
MEXICAN	AMERICAN HISTORY	
NORTH	AMERICAN HISTORY	
SOUTH	AMERICAN HISTORY	Use LATIN AMERICAN HISTORY
	AMERICAN INDIAN CULTURE	
	AMERICAN INDIAN EDUCATION	
	AMERICAN INDIAN HISTORY	
	AMERICAN INDIAN LANGUAGES	
	AMERICAN INDIAN LITERATURE	
	AMERICAN INDIAN RESERVATIONS	
	AMERICAN INDIAN STUDIES	
	AMERICAN INDIANS	
NONRESERVATION	AMERICAN INDIANS	
OFF RESERVATION	AMERICAN INDIANS	Use NONRESERVATION AMERICAN INDIANS
RESERVATION	AMERICAN INDIANS	
RURAL	AMERICAN INDIANS	
URBAN	AMERICAN INDIANS	
	AMERICAN JEWS	Use JEWS
CENTRAL	AMERICAN LITERATURE	Use LATIN AMERICAN LITERATURE
HISPANIC	AMERICAN LITERATURE	
LATIN	AMERICAN LITERATURE	
	AMERICAN LITERATURE (1966 1980) (LATIN AMERICA)	Use LATIN AMERICAN LITERATURE
MEXICAN	AMERICAN LITERATURE	
NORTH	AMERICAN LITERATURE	
SOUTH	AMERICAN LITERATURE	Use LATIN AMERICAN LITERATURE
SPANISH	AMERICAN LITERATURE (1969 1980)	Use HISPANIC AMERICAN LITERATURE
	AMERICAN LITERATURE (1966 1980) (UNITED STATES)	Use UNITED STATES LITERATURE
	AMERICAN NEGROES	Use BLACKS
	AMERICAN ORIENTALS	Use ASIAN AMERICANS
	AMERICAN REVOLUTIONARY WAR	Use REVOLUTIONARY WAR (UNITED STATES)
	AMERICAN SAMOANS	Use SAMOAN AMERICANS
	AMERICAN SIGN LANGUAGE	
	AMERICAN STUDIES	
AFRICAN	AMERICAN STUDIES (1969 1977)	Use BLACK STUDIES
AFRICAN	AMERICANS	Use BLACKS
AFRO	AMERICANS	Use BLACKS
ANGLO	AMERICANS	
ARAB	AMERICANS	Use ARABS and NORTH AMERICANS
ASIAN	AMERICANS	
BLACK	AMERICANS	Use BLACKS
CAMBODIAN	AMERICANS	Use ASIAN AMERICANS and CAMBODIANS
CENTRAL	AMERICANS	Use LATIN AMERICANS
CHINESE	AMERICANS	
CUBAN	AMERICANS	Use CUBANS and HISPANIC AMERICANS
DOMINICAN	AMERICANS	Use DOMINICANS and HISPANIC AMERICANS
FILIPINO	AMERICANS	
GREEK	AMERICANS	
HISPANIC	AMERICANS	
INDOCHINESE	AMERICANS	Use ASIAN AMERICANS and INDOCHINESE
ITALIAN	AMERICANS	
JAPANESE	AMERICANS	
KOREAN	AMERICANS	
LAOTIAN	AMERICANS	Use ASIAN AMERICANS and LAOTIANS
LATIN	AMERICANS	
MEXICAN	AMERICANS	
NORTH	AMERICANS	
ORIENTAL	AMERICANS	Use ASIAN AMERICANS
PACIFIC	AMERICANS	
POLISH	AMERICANS	
PORTUGUESE	AMERICANS	
SAMOAN	AMERICANS	
SOUTH	AMERICANS	Use LATIN AMERICANS
SPANISH	AMERICANS	
VIETNAMESE	AMERICANS	Use ASIAN AMERICANS and VIETNAMESE PEOPLE
	AMESLAN	Use AMERICAN SIGN LANGUAGE
	AMETROPIA	
	AMHARIC	
	AMISH	
LIGHT	AMPLIFIERS (LASERS)	Use LASERS
MAGNETIC	AMPLIFIERS	Use ELECTRONIC CONTROL
	AMPUTATIONS	
	AMPUTEES (1967 1980)	Use AMPUTATIONS
	ANALOG COMPUTERS	
	ANALYSIS	Use EVALUATION METHODS
AUDIENCE	ANALYSIS	
BEHAVIORAL	ANALYSIS	Use BEHAVIORAL SCIENCE RESEARCH
BENEFIT COST	ANALYSIS	Use COST EFFECTIVENESS
CENTROID METHOD OF FACTOR	ANALYSIS	Use FACTOR ANALYSIS
CHEMICAL	ANALYSIS	
CITATION	ANALYSIS	
CLUSTER	ANALYSIS	
COHORT	ANALYSIS	
COMMUNITY	ANALYSIS	Use COMMUNITY STUDY
COMPARATIVE	ANALYSIS	
COMPONENTIAL	ANALYSIS	
CONTENT	ANALYSIS	
CONTRASTIVE LANGUAGE	ANALYSIS	Use CONTRASTIVE LINGUISTICS
COST	ANALYSIS	Use COST EFFECTIVENESS
COST BENEFIT	ANALYSIS	Use COST EFFECTIVENESS
COST EFFECTIVENESS	ANALYSIS	Use COST EFFECTIVENESS

ANGLO AMERICANS
ANGLO SAXON Use OLD ENGLISH
ANGLOS Use ANGLO AMERICANS
ANIMAL BEHAVIOR
ANIMAL BIOLOGY Use ZOOLOGY
ANIMAL CARETAKERS
ANIMAL FACILITIES
ANIMAL HUSBANDRY
ANIMAL KEEPERS Use ANIMAL CARETAKERS
ANIMAL LIFE Use ANIMALS
ANIMAL SCIENCE (1967 1980) Use ANIMAL HUSBANDRY
ANIMALS
LABORATORY ANIMALS
ANIMATION
ANNOTATED BIBLIOGRAPHIES
ANNOTATIONS Use ABSTRACTS
ANNUAL REPORTS
ANNUALS Use YEARBOOKS
ANOMALIES (1967 1980) Use CONGENITAL IMPAIRMENTS
DOWNS ANOMALY Use DOWNS SYNDROME
ANOREXIA NERVOSA
ANOVA Use ANALYSIS OF VARIANCE
ANSWER BOOKLETS Use ANSWER SHEETS
ANSWER CARDS Use ANSWER SHEETS
QUESTION ANSWER INTERVIEWS (1966 1980) Use INTERVIEWS
ANSWER KEYS
ANSWER SHEETS
COMMUNITY ANTENNAS (1966 1980) Use CABLE TELEVISION
ANTHOLOGIES
ANTHRACITE Use COAL
ANTHROPOLOGICAL LINGUISTICS
ANTHROPOLOGY
EDUCATIONAL ANTHROPOLOGY
LINGUISTIC ANTHROPOLOGY Use ANTHROPOLOGICAL LINGUISTICS
ANTI DISCRIMINATION LEGISLATION Use CIVIL RIGHTS LEGISLATION
ANTI INTELLECTUALISM
ANTI POVERTY PROGRAMS Use POVERTY PROGRAMS
ANTI SEGREGATION PROGRAMS (1967 1980) Use RACIAL INTEGRATION
ANTI SEMITISM
ANTI SOCIAL BEHAVIOR (1966 1980) Use ANTISOCIAL BEHAVIOR
ANTISOCIAL BEHAVIOR
ANTITHESIS
ANXIETY
MATHEMATICS ANXIETY
SEPARATION ANXIETY
TEST ANXIETY
APACHE
APATHY
APHASIA
APPAREL INDUSTRY Use FASHION INDUSTRY
APPLIANCE REPAIR
HOME APPLIANCE REPAIR Use APPLIANCE REPAIR
APPLIANCE REPAIRERS (1980 1981) Use APPLIANCE REPAIR
APPLIANCE REPAIRING (1968 1981) Use APPLIANCE REPAIR
APPLIANCE SERVICE TECHNICIANS (1967 1980) Use APPLIANCE REPAIR
ELECTRICAL APPLIANCE SERVICEMEN (1968 1980) Use APPLIANCE REPAIR
APPLIANCES Use EQUIPMENT
ELECTRICAL APPLIANCES
COLLEGE APPLICANTS
FINANCIAL AID APPLICANTS
JOB APPLICANTS
LAW SCHOOL APPLICANTS Use COLLEGE APPLICANTS and LAW SCHOOLS
LOAN APPLICANTS Use FINANCIAL AID APPLICANTS
MEDICAL SCHOOL APPLICANTS Use COLLEGE APPLICANTS and MEDICAL SCHOOLS
JOB APPLICATION
STUDENT APPLICATION (1966 1980) Use COLLEGE APPLICANTS
COMPUTER APPLICATIONS Use COMPUTER ORIENTED PROGRAMS
MATHEMATICAL APPLICATIONS
PROJECT APPLICATIONS (1967 1980)
APPLIED LINGUISTICS
APPLIED MUSIC
APPLIED READING (1966 1980) Use READING
APPLIED RESEARCH Use RESEARCH
APPLIED SCIENCES Use TECHNOLOGY
APPRAISAL Use EVALUATION
ADMINISTRATOR APPRAISAL Use ADMINISTRATOR EVALUATION
PERFORMANCE APPRAISAL (PERSONNEL) Use PERSONNEL EVALUATION
PROPERTY APPRAISAL
REAL ESTATE APPRAISAL Use PROPERTY APPRAISAL
SELF APPRAISAL Use SELF EVALUATION (INDIVIDUALS)
STUDENT APPRAISAL Use STUDENT EVALUATION
ART APPRECIATION
LITERATURE APPRECIATION
MUSIC APPRECIATION
COMMUNICATION APPREHENSION
WRITING APPREHENSION
APPRENTICESHIPS
RESEARCH APPRENTICESHIPS (1967 1981) Use RESEARCH ASSISTANTS
CASEWORKER APPROACH
DESIGN BUILD APPROACH
GLOBAL APPROACH
HOLISTIC APPROACH
INTERDISCIPLINARY APPROACH
INTERNATIONAL APPROACH Use GLOBAL APPROACH
LANGUAGE EXPERIENCE APPROACH
SEQUENTIAL APPROACH
SYSTEMS APPROACH
THEMATIC APPROACH
WHOLE PERSON APPROACH Use HOLISTIC APPROACH
WHOLE WORD READING APPROACH Use SIGHT METHOD
WHOLISTIC APPROACH Use HOLISTIC APPROACH

WORLDWIDE	APPROACH Use GLOBAL APPROACH
AUDIOLINGUAL	APPROACHES Use AUDIOLINGUAL METHODS
RESEARCH	APPROACHES Use RESEARCH METHODOLOGY
	APPROPRIATE TECHNOLOGY
PROGRAM	APPROVAL (VALIDATION) Use PROGRAM VALIDATION
	APPROVED PROGRAMS (VALIDATED) Use VALIDATED PROGRAMS
	APPROXIMATION (MATHEMATICS) Use ESTIMATION (MATHEMATICS)
	APPROXIMATIVE SYSTEMS (LANGUAGE LEARNING) Use INTERLANGUAGE
	APTITUDE
ACADEMIC	APTITUDE
LANGUAGE	APTITUDE
STUDENT	APTITUDE Use ACADEMIC APTITUDE
	APTITUDE TESTS
	APTITUDE TREATMENT INTERACTION
VOCATIONAL	APTITUDE
	AQUATIC SPORTS
	ARAB AMERICANS Use ARABS and NORTH AMERICANS
	ARABIC
	ARABS
	ARBITRATION
	ARC WELDING Use WELDING
	ARCHAEOLOGY
	ARCHERY
	ARCHITECTS
	ARCHITECTURAL BARRIERS (1970 1980)
	ARCHITECTURAL CHANGES Use BUILDING DESIGN
	ARCHITECTURAL CHARACTER
	ARCHITECTURAL DESIGN Use BUILDING DESIGN
	ARCHITECTURAL DRAFTING
	ARCHITECTURAL EDUCATION
	ARCHITECTURAL ELEMENTS (1968 1980) Use STRUCTURAL ELEMENTS (CONSTRUCTION)
	ARCHITECTURAL PROGRAMING
	ARCHITECTURAL RESEARCH
	ARCHITECTURAL STYLE Use ARCHITECTURAL CHARACTER
	ARCHITECTURAL TRADITION Use ARCHITECTURAL CHARACTER
	ARCHITECTURE
SCHOOL	ARCHITECTURE (1966 1980) Use EDUCATIONAL FACILITIES DESIGN
	ARCHIVES
	AREA
LANGUAGE AND	AREA CENTERS (1968 1980)
LOCAL	AREA NETWORKS
PLANAR	AREA Use AREA
CONTENT	AREA READING
OPEN	AREA SCHOOLS Use OPEN PLAN SCHOOLS
	AREA STUDIES
SURFACE	AREA Use AREA
	AREA VOCATIONAL SCHOOLS (1966 1980) Use REGIONAL SCHOOLS and VOCATIONAL SCHOOLS
CONTENT	AREA WRITING
ECONOMICALLY DEPRESSED	AREAS Use POVERTY AREAS
	AREAS (GEOGRAPHIC) Use GEOGRAPHIC REGIONS
DEPRESSED	AREAS (GEOGRAPHIC) (1966 1980) Use POVERTY AREAS
HUMID	AREAS Use HUMIDITY
METROPOLITAN	AREAS
PARKING	AREAS (1966 1980) Use PARKING FACILITIES
POVERTY	AREAS
READING IN CONTENT	AREAS Use CONTENT AREA READING
REDEVELOPMENT	AREAS Use URBAN RENEWAL
RURAL	AREAS
STREET PARKING	AREAS Use PARKING FACILITIES
STUDENT LOADING	AREAS (1968 1980) Use STUDENT TRANSPORTATION
TEACHING	AREAS Use CURRICULUM
URBAN	AREAS
	ARGUMENTATION Use PERSUASIVE DISCOURSE
	ARISTOTELIAN CRITICISM (1969 1980)
	ARITHMETIC
	ARITHMETIC CURRICULUM (1966 1980) Use ARITHMETIC and MATHEMATICS CURRICULUM
REMEDIAL	ARITHMETIC (1966 1980) Use ARITHMETIC and REMEDIAL MATHEMATICS
	ARITHMETIC SYSTEMS Use NUMBER SYSTEMS
	ARITHMETIC TESTS Use ARITHMETIC and MATHEMATICS TESTS
	ARMED FORCES
	ARMENIAN
	ARMS CONTROL Use DISARMAMENT
	ARMY AIR BASES Use MILITARY AIR FACILITIES
	AROUSAL PATTERNS
CLASSROOM	ARRANGEMENT (1966 1980) Use CLASSROOM DESIGN
FURNITURE	ARRANGEMENT
STRUCTURAL	ARRANGEMENT Use ORGANIZATION
	ART
	ART ACTIVITIES
ADVERTISING	ART Use COMMERCIAL ART
	ART APPRECIATION
CHILDRENS	ART
COMMERCIAL	ART
CREATIVE	ART
	ART EDUCATION
	ART EXPRESSION
	ART GALLERIES Use ARTS CENTERS
	ART HISTORY
	ART MATERIALS
	ART PRODUCTS
STATE OF THE	ART REVIEWS
	ART SONG
	ART TEACHERS
	ART THERAPY
	ARTICLES (GRAMMAR) Use DETERMINERS (LANGUAGES)
	ARTICULATION (EDUCATION)
	ARTICULATION IMPAIRMENTS
	ARTICULATION (PROGRAM) (1967 1980) Use ARTICULATION (EDUCATION)
	ARTICULATION (SPEECH)
	ARTICULATION TESTS Use SPEECH TESTS
	ARTIFICIAL INTELLIGENCE

	ARTIFICIAL LANGUAGES
	ARTIFICIAL SATELLITES Use SATELLITES (AEROSPACE)
	ARTIFICIAL SPEECH
	ARTISANS Use CRAFT WORKERS
PAINTING (1966 1980)	(ARTISTIC) Use PAINTING (VISUAL ARTS)
	ARTISTIC TALENT Use TALENT
	ARTISTS
	ARTS CENTERS
FINE	ARTS CENTERS Use ARTS CENTERS
PERFORMING	ARTS CENTERS Use THEATERS
BACHELOR OF	ARTS DEGREES Use BACHELORS DEGREES
DOCTOR OF	ARTS DEGREES
MASTER OF	ARTS DEGREES Use MASTERS DEGREES
DRAMATIC	ARTS Use DRAMATICS
FINE	ARTS
GRAPHIC	ARTS
MASTER OF	ARTS IN COLLEGE TEACHING Use MASTERS DEGREES
MASTER OF	ARTS IN TEACHING Use MASTERS DEGREES
INDUSTRIAL	ARTS
LANGUAGE	ARTS
LIBERAL	ARTS
LIBERAL	ARTS MAJORS (1967 1980) Use LIBERAL ARTS and MAJORS (STUDENTS)
PAINTING (INDUSTRIAL	ARTS)
PAINTING (VISUAL	ARTS)
PERFORMING	ARTS Use THEATER ARTS
PRACTICAL	ARTS
INDUSTRIAL	ARTS SHOPS Use SCHOOL SHOPS
INDUSTRIAL	ARTS TEACHERS
THEATER	ARTS
VISUAL	ARTS
HIGHER EDUCATION	AS A FIELD OF STUDY Use POSTSECONDARY EDUCATION AS A FIELD OF STUDY
POSTSECONDARY EDUCATION	AS A FIELD OF STUDY
	ASBESTOS
	ASIAN AMERICANS
SOUTH	ASIAN CIVILIZATION Use NON WESTERN CIVILIZATION
	ASIAN HISTORY
	ASIAN MUSIC Use ORIENTAL MUSIC
	ASIAN STUDIES
AFRO	ASIATIC LANGUAGES
AUSTRO	ASIATIC LANGUAGES
	ASPHALTS
	ASPIRATION
ACADEMIC	ASPIRATION
	ASPIRATION LEVEL Use ASPIRATION
OCCUPATIONAL	ASPIRATION LEVEL Use OCCUPATIONAL ASPIRATION
LOW LEVEL	ASPIRATION (1966 1980) Use ASPIRATION
OCCUPATIONAL	ASPIRATION
PARENT	ASPIRATION
PARENTAL	ASPIRATION (1966 1980) Use PARENT ASPIRATION
VOCATIONAL	ASPIRATION Use OCCUPATIONAL ASPIRATION
SEXUAL	ASSAULT Use SEXUAL ABUSE
	ASSEMBLY (MANUFACTURING)
	ASSEMBLY PROGRAMS
	ASSERTIVE TRAINING Use ASSERTIVENESS
	ASSERTIVENESS
	ASSERTIVENESS TRAINING Use ASSERTIVENESS
	ASSESSED VALUATION
	ASSESSMENT CENTERS (PERSONNEL)
DENTAL	ASSESSMENT Use DENTAL EVALUATION
EDUCATIONAL	ASSESSMENT
EDUCATIONAL QUALITY	ASSESSMENT Use EDUCATIONAL ASSESSMENT and EDUCATIONAL QUALITY
INFORMAL	ASSESSMENT
INSTITUTIONAL	ASSESSMENT Use INSTITUTIONAL EVALUATION
NEEDS	ASSESSMENT
PERSONALITY	ASSESSMENT
SELF	ASSESSMENT Use SELF EVALUATION (INDIVIDUALS)
VOCATIONAL	ASSESSMENT Use VOCATIONAL EVALUATION
CAPITAL OUTLAY (FOR FIXED	ASSETS)
TEACHING	ASSIGNMENT (1966 1980)
	ASSIGNMENTS
READING	ASSIGNMENTS
STUDENT	ASSIGNMENTS Use ASSIGNMENTS
TEXTBOOK	ASSIGNMENTS (1966 1980) Use ASSIGNMENTS
	ASSIMILATION (CULTURAL) Use ACCULTURATION
INTERNATIONAL TECHNICAL	ASSISTANCE Use INTERNATIONAL PROGRAMS and TECHNICAL ASSISTANCE
MEDICAL	ASSISTANCE Use MEDICAL SERVICES
EMPLOYEE	ASSISTANCE PROGRAMS
PUBLIC WELFARE	ASSISTANCE Use WELFARE SERVICES
STATE	ASSISTANCE Use STATE AID
SUPPORT NETWORKS (PERSONAL	ASSISTANCE) Use SOCIAL SUPPORT GROUPS
TECHNICAL	ASSISTANCE
	ASSISTANT PRINCIPALS
	ASSISTANT SUPERINTENDENT ROLE (1966 1980)
	ASSISTANT SUPERINTENDENTS Use SUPERINTENDENTS
DENTAL	ASSISTANTS
LEGAL	ASSISTANTS
LIBRARY TECHNICAL	ASSISTANTS Use LIBRARY TECHNICIANS
MECHANICAL ENGINEERING	ASSISTANTS Use MECHANICAL DESIGN TECHNICIANS
MEDICAL	ASSISTANTS
MEDICAL LABORATORY	ASSISTANTS
NURSING	ASSISTANTS Use NURSES AIDES
OCCUPATIONAL THERAPY	ASSISTANTS
PHYSICIANS	ASSISTANTS
RESEARCH	ASSISTANTS
RESIDENT	ASSISTANTS
TEACHING	ASSISTANTS
VETERINARY	ASSISTANTS
	ASSISTANTSHIPS
COMPUTER	ASSISTED INDEXING Use AUTOMATIC INDEXING
COMPUTER	ASSISTED INSTRUCTION
COMPUTER	ASSISTED LEARNING Use COMPUTER ASSISTED INSTRUCTION

COMPUTER	ASSISTED TESTING
	ASSISTIVE DEVICES (FOR DISABLED)
	ASSOCIATE DEGREES
PAIRED	ASSOCIATE LEARNING
	ASSOCIATION MEASURES
STATISTICAL	ASSOCIATION METHODS Use CORRELATION
	ASSOCIATION (PSYCHOLOGICAL) (1968 1980) Use ASSOCIATION (PSYCHOLOGY)
	ASSOCIATION (PSYCHOLOGY)
SERIAL	ASSOCIATION Use SERIAL LEARNING
	ASSOCIATION TESTS (1968 1980) Use ASSOCIATION MEASURES
ACCREDITING	ASSOCIATIONS Use ACCREDITING AGENCIES
ALUMNI	ASSOCIATIONS
DENTAL	ASSOCIATIONS (1966 1980) Use DENTISTRY and PROFESSIONAL ASSOCIATIONS
	ASSOCIATIONS (GROUPS) Use ORGANIZATIONS (GROUPS)
LIBRARY	ASSOCIATIONS
MEDICAL	ASSOCIATIONS
PARENT	ASSOCIATIONS
PROFESSIONAL	ASSOCIATIONS
WORD	ASSOCIATIONS (READING) Use ASSOCIATIVE LEARNING
TEACHER	ASSOCIATIONS
VOLUNTARY	ASSOCIATIONS Use VOLUNTARY AGENCIES
	ASSOCIATIVE LEARNING
	ASTHMA
	ASTRONOMY
	AT RISK (PERSONS) Use HIGH RISK PERSONS
	ATHABASCAN LANGUAGES Use ATHAPASCAN LANGUAGES
	ATHAPASCAN LANGUAGES
	ATHLETES
	ATHLETIC ACTIVITIES (1966 1974) Use ATHLETICS
	ATHLETIC COACHES
	ATHLETIC EQUIPMENT
	ATHLETIC FIELDS
	ATHLETIC PROGRAMS (1966 1980) Use ATHLETICS
EXTRAMURAL	ATHLETIC PROGRAMS (1966 1980) Use EXTRAMURAL ATHLETICS
INTRAMURAL	ATHLETIC PROGRAMS (1966 1980) Use INTRAMURAL ATHLETICS
	ATHLETICS
COLLEGE	ATHLETICS
EXTRAMURAL	ATHLETICS
INTERCOLLEGIATE	ATHLETICS Use COLLEGE ATHLETICS and INTERCOLLEGIATE COOPERATION
INTERSCHOLASTIC	ATHLETICS Use EXTRAMURAL ATHLETICS
INTRAMURAL	ATHLETICS
WOMENS	ATHLETICS
	ATLASES
	ATMOSPHERE (SOCIAL) Use SOCIAL ENVIRONMENT
	ATMOSPHERIC POLLUTION Use AIR POLLUTION
	ATOMIC ENERGY Use NUCLEAR ENERGY
	ATOMIC PHYSICS Use NUCLEAR PHYSICS
	ATOMIC STRUCTURE
	ATOMIC THEORY
	ATOMIC WARFARE Use NUCLEAR WARFARE
	ATTACHMENT BEHAVIOR
EDUCATIONAL	ATTAINMENT
GOAL	ATTAINMENT Use SUCCESS
	ATTENDANCE
AVERAGE DAILY	ATTENDANCE
CLASS	ATTENDANCE (1966 1980) Use ATTENDANCE
COLLEGE	ATTENDANCE
COMPULSORY	ATTENDANCE Use COMPULSORY EDUCATION
SCHOOL	ATTENDANCE LAWS (1966 1974) Use SCHOOL ATTENDANCE LEGISLATION
SCHOOL	ATTENDANCE LEGISLATION
	ATTENDANCE OFFICERS
	ATTENDANCE PATTERNS
	ATTENDANCE RECORDS
SCHOOL	ATTENDANCE Use ATTENDANCE
	ATTENDANCE SERVICES (1968 1980) Use ATTENDANCE and PUPIL PERSONNEL SERVICES
TEACHER	ATTENDANCE
	ATTENDANT TRAINING (1968 1980) Use ATTENDANTS and JOB TRAINING
	ATTENDANTS
AMBULANCE	ATTENDANTS Use EMERGENCY MEDICAL TECHNICIANS
HOME	ATTENDANTS Use HOME HEALTH AIDES
HOSPITAL	ATTENDANTS Use NURSES AIDES
PHYSICAL THERAPY	ATTENDANTS Use PHYSICAL THERAPY AIDES
VETERINARY HOSPITAL	ATTENDANTS Use VETERINARY ASSISTANTS
	ATTENTION
	ATTENTION CONTROL
	ATTENTION DEFICIT DISORDERS
	ATTENTION SPAN
BODY	ATTITUDE Use HUMAN POSTURE
	ATTITUDE CHANGE
	ATTITUDE MEASURES
	ATTITUDE TESTS (1966 1980) Use ATTITUDE MEASURES
SELF	ATTITUDE TESTS Use SELF CONCEPT MEASURES
	ATTITUDES
ADMINISTRATOR	ATTITUDES
BLACK	ATTITUDES
CHANGING	ATTITUDES (1966 1980) Use ATTITUDE CHANGE
CHILDHOOD	ATTITUDES
CHILDRENS	ATTITUDES Use CHILDHOOD ATTITUDES
CLASS	ATTITUDES (1966 1980)
COMMUNITY	ATTITUDES
COUNSELOR	ATTITUDES
DROPOUT	ATTITUDES
EDUCATIONAL	ATTITUDES
EMPLOYEE	ATTITUDES
EMPLOYEE WORK	ATTITUDES Use EMPLOYEE ATTITUDES and WORK ATTITUDES
EMPLOYER	ATTITUDES
FAMILY	ATTITUDES
FATHER	ATTITUDES
LANGUAGE	ATTITUDES
MAJORITY	ATTITUDES
MOTHER	ATTITUDES

NEGATIVE ATTITUDES
NEGRO ATTITUDES (1966 1977) Use BLACK ATTITUDES
NORTHERN ATTITUDES (1968 1980) Use REGIONAL ATTITUDES
PARENT ATTITUDES
POLITICAL ATTITUDES
PROGRAM ATTITUDES
RACIAL ATTITUDES
READING ATTITUDES
REGIONAL ATTITUDES
SCHOOL ATTITUDES
SCIENTIFIC ATTITUDES
SOCIAL ATTITUDES
DISCRIMINATORY ATTITUDES (SOCIAL) (1966 1980) Use SOCIAL BIAS
SOUTHERN ATTITUDES (1966 1980) Use REGIONAL ATTITUDES
STUDENT ATTITUDES
STUDENT TEACHER ATTITUDES
TEACHER ATTITUDES
WORK ATTITUDES
ATTORNEYS Use LAWYERS
INTERPERSONAL ATTRACTION
ATTRACTIVENESS (BETWEEN PERSONS) Use INTERPERSONAL ATTRACTION
ATTRIBUTION THEORY
CAUSAL ATTRIBUTIONS Use ATTRIBUTION THEORY
LANGUAGE SKILL ATTRITION
ATTRITION (RESEARCH STUDIES)
LANGUAGE ATTRITION (SKILLS) Use LANGUAGE SKILL ATTRITION
STUDENT ATTRITION
ATTRITION (STUDENTS) Use STUDENT ATTRITION
TEACHER ATTRITION Use FACULTY MOBILITY
EXCEPTIONAL (ATYPICAL) (1966 1978) Use EXCEPTIONAL PERSONS
AUDIENCE ANALYSIS
AUDIENCE PARTICIPATION
AUDIENCES
AUDIO ACTIVE COMPARE LABORATORIES (1967 1980) Use LANGUAGE LABORATORIES
AUDIO ACTIVE LABORATORIES (1967 1980) Use LANGUAGE LABORATORIES
AUDIO EQUIPMENT
MASTER TAPES (AUDIO) (1968 1980) Use AUDIOTAPE RECORDINGS
AUDIO PASSIVE LABORATORIES (1968 1980) Use LANGUAGE LABORATORIES
AUDIO VIDEO LABORATORIES (1967 1980) Use AUDIOVISUAL CENTERS
AUDIODISC RECORDINGS (1980 1986) Use AUDIODISKS
AUDIODISKS
AUDIOLINGUAL APPROACHES Use AUDIOLINGUAL METHODS
AUDIOLINGUAL METHODS
AUDIOLINGUAL SKILLS
AUDIOLOGISTS (1968 1980) Use ALLIED HEALTH PERSONNEL and AUDIOLOGY
AUDIOLOGY
AUDIOMETRIC TESTS
AUDIOMETRISTS (1967 1980) Use ALLIED HEALTH PERSONNEL and AUDIOLOGY
AUDIOTAPE CARTRIDGES Use AUDIOTAPE CASSETTES
AUDIOTAPE CASSETTE RECORDERS Use AUDIOTAPE CASSETTES and AUDIOTAPE RECORDERS
AUDIOTAPE CASSETTES
AUDIOTAPE RECORDERS
AUDIOTAPE RECORDINGS
AUDIOVISUAL AIDS
AUDIOVISUAL CENTERS
AUDIOVISUAL COMMUNICATION (1967 1980) Use AUDIOVISUAL COMMUNICATIONS
AUDIOVISUAL COMMUNICATIONS
AUDIOVISUAL COORDINATORS
AUDIOVISUAL DIRECTORS (1969 1980) Use AUDIOVISUAL COORDINATORS
AUDIOVISUAL EDUCATION Use AUDIOVISUAL INSTRUCTION
AUDIOVISUAL EQUIPMENT Use AUDIOVISUAL AIDS
AUDIOVISUAL INSTRUCTION
AUDIOVISUAL MATERIALS Use AUDIOVISUAL AIDS
AUDIOVISUAL MEDIA Use AUDIOVISUAL AIDS
AUDIOVISUAL PROGRAMS (1966 1980) Use AUDIOVISUAL INSTRUCTION
MEDICAL AUDIT Use MEDICAL CARE EVALUATION
AUDITING (COURSEWORK)
AUDITION (PHYSIOLOGY) (1967 1980) Use HEARING (PHYSIOLOGY)
AUDITORIUMS
AUDITORY COMPREHENSION Use LISTENING COMPREHENSION
AUDITORY DISCRIMINATION
AUDITORY EVALUATION
AUDITORY PERCEPTION
AUDITORY STIMULI
AUDITORY TESTS
AUDITORY TRAINING
AUDITORY VISUAL TESTS (1966 1980) Use AUDITORY TESTS and VISION TESTS
COMMUNICATION AUDITS
ENERGY AUDITS
FINANCIAL AUDITS
AUDITS (VERIFICATION)
AURAL COMPREHENSION Use LISTENING COMPREHENSION
AURAL LANGUAGE LEARNING Use AURAL LEARNING and LANGUAGE ACQUISITION
AURAL LEARNING
AURAL ORAL SKILLS Use AUDIOLINGUAL SKILLS
AURAL STIMULI (1966 1980) Use AUDITORY STIMULI
AURALLY HANDICAPPED (1966 1980) Use HEARING IMPAIRMENTS
AUSTRALIAN ABORIGINAL LANGUAGES
AUSTRALIAN LITERATURE
AUSTRO ASIATIC LANGUAGES
AUSTRONESIAN LANGUAGES Use MALAYO POLYNESIAN LANGUAGES
AUTEURISM
FILM AUTEURISM Use AUTEURISM
AUTHORING AIDS (PROGRAMING)
AUTHORING LANGUAGES Use AUTHORING AIDS (PROGRAMING) and PROGRAMING LANGUAGES
AUTHORING SYSTEMS Use AUTHORING AIDS (PROGRAMING)
AUTHORITARIANISM
LOCAL EDUCATION AUTHORITIES Use SCHOOL DISTRICTS
LOCAL HOUSING AUTHORITIES (1966 1980) Use HOUSING
AUTHORITY STRUCTURE Use POWER STRUCTURE
AUTHORS

	AUTISM
	AUTO BODY REPAIRERS
	AUTO BODY REPAIRMEN (1966 1980) Use AUTO BODY REPAIRERS
	AUTO MECHANICS
	AUTO MECHANICS (OCCUPATION) (1968 1980) Use AUTO MECHANICS
	AUTO PARTS CLERKS
	AUTO PARTS MEN (1968 1980) Use AUTO PARTS CLERKS
	AUTOBIOGRAPHIES
	AUTOINSTRUCTIONAL AIDS
	AUTOINSTRUCTIONAL LABORATORIES (1967 1980) Use LEARNING LABORATORIES
	AUTOINSTRUCTIONAL METHODS (1966 1980) Use PROGRAMED INSTRUCTION
	AUTOINSTRUCTIONAL PROGRAMS (1966 1980) Use PROGRAMED INSTRUCTION
	AUTOMATIC DATA PROCESSING Use DATA PROCESSING
	AUTOMATIC INDEXING
	AUTOMATION
LIBRARY	AUTOMATION
	AUTOMOBILE MECHANICS Use AUTO MECHANICS
INDIVIDUAL	AUTONOMY Use PERSONAL AUTONOMY
INSTITUTIONAL	AUTONOMY
LEARNER	AUTONOMY Use PERSONAL AUTONOMY
LOCAL	AUTONOMY (OF SCHOOLS) Use SCHOOL DISTRICT AUTONOMY
PERSONAL	AUTONOMY
PROFESSIONAL	AUTONOMY
SCHOOL DISTRICT	AUTONOMY
TEACHER	AUTONOMY Use PROFESSIONAL AUTONOMY
	AUXILIARY LABORERS
	AUXILIARY SCHOOL SERVICES Use ANCILLARY SCHOOL SERVICES
	AUXILIARY WORKERS Use AUXILIARY LABORERS
CLASS	AVERAGE (1966 1980)
	AVERAGE DAILY ATTENDANCE
	AVERAGE DAILY ENROLLMENT (1968 1980) Use AVERAGE DAILY MEMBERSHIP
	AVERAGE DAILY MEMBERSHIP
GRADE	AVERAGE Use GRADE POINT AVERAGE
GRADE POINT	AVERAGE
	AVERAGE STUDENTS (1967 1980) Use STUDENTS
	AVIATION MECHANICS
	AVIATION TECHNOLOGY
	AVIATION VOCABULARY
MATHEMATICS	AVOIDANCE Use MATHEMATICS ANXIETY
SUCCESS	AVOIDANCE Use FEAR OF SUCCESS
	AWARDS
	AWARENESS Use PERCEPTION
CAREER	AWARENESS
CULTURAL	AWARENESS
OCCUPATIONAL	AWARENESS Use CAREER AWARENESS
CURRENT	AWARENESS SERVICES Use SELECTIVE DISSEMINATION OF INFORMATION
SOCIAL	AWARENESS Use INTERPERSONAL COMPETENCE
VOCATIONAL	AWARENESS Use CAREER AWARENESS
	AWAY FROM THE JOB TRAINING Use OFF THE JOB TRAINING
	AYMARA
	AZERBAIJANI
UTO	AZTECAN LANGUAGES
	BACCALAUREATE DEGREES Use BACHELORS DEGREES
	BACHELOR OF ARTS DEGREES Use BACHELORS DEGREES
	BACHELOR OF SCIENCE DEGREES Use BACHELORS DEGREES
	BACHELORS DEGREES
THREE YEAR	BACHELORS DEGREES Use ACCELERATION (EDUCATION) and BACHELORS DEGREES
	BACK TO BASICS
	BACKGROUND
ADMINISTRATOR	BACKGROUND (1967 1980) Use ADMINISTRATOR CHARACTERISTICS
COUNSELOR	BACKGROUND Use COUNSELOR CHARACTERISTICS
CULTURAL	BACKGROUND
EDUCATIONAL	BACKGROUND
FAMILY	BACKGROUND (1966 1980) Use FAMILY CHARACTERISTICS
CLIENT	BACKGROUND (HUMAN SERVICES) Use CLIENT CHARACTERISTICS (HUMAN SERVICES)
PORTFOLIOS	(BACKGROUND MATERIALS)
PARENT	BACKGROUND
PARENTAL	BACKGROUND (1966 1980) Use PARENT BACKGROUND
SOCIAL	BACKGROUND
SOCIOECONOMIC	BACKGROUND
TEACHER	BACKGROUND
	BADMINTON
AIR	BAGS Use RESTRAINTS (VEHICLE SAFETY)
	BAHASA INDONESIA Use INDONESIAN
	BAKERIES Use BAKERY INDUSTRY
	BAKERY INDUSTRY
RACIAL	BALANCE
RACIALLY	BALANCED SCHOOLS
	BALLADS
	BALLET (1966 1980) Use DANCE
	BALTIC LANGUAGES
	BALUCHI
MARCHING	BANDS Use BANDS (MUSIC)
	BANDS (MUSIC)
HEAD	BANGING Use SELF MUTILATION
	BANKING
	BANKING INDUSTRY Use BANKING
	BANKING VOCABULARY
DATA	BANKS Use DATABASES
ITEM	BANKS
	BANTU LANGUAGES
	BARBERS
	BARBITURATES Use SEDATIVES
	BARDS Use POETS
COLLECTIVE	BARGAINING
SCOPE OF	BARGAINING
	BAROQUE LITERATURE
	BARRIER FREE ENVIRONMENT (FOR DISABLED) Use ACCESSIBILITY (FOR DISABLED)
ACOUSTIC	BARRIERS Use ACOUSTIC INSULATION
ARCHITECTURAL	BARRIERS (1970 1980)
FINANCIAL	BARRIERS Use FINANCIAL PROBLEMS

SOUND BARRIERS Use ACOUSTIC INSULATION
BARRISTERS Use LAWYERS
SNACK BARS Use DINING FACILITIES
BASAA
BASAL READING
BASEBALL
COMPETENCY BASED EDUCATION
CONSEQUENCE BASED EDUCATION Use COMPETENCY BASED EDUCATION
EXPERIENCE BASED EDUCATION Use EXPERIENTIAL LEARNING
PERFORMANCE BASED EDUCATION (1974 1980) Use COMPETENCY BASED EDUCATION
PROFICIENCY BASED EDUCATION Use COMPETENCY BASED EDUCATION
TIMBER BASED INDUSTRY Use LUMBER INDUSTRY
COMPUTER BASED INSTRUCTION Use COMPUTER ASSISTED INSTRUCTION
COMPUTER BASED INSTRUCTIONAL MANAGEMENT Use COMPUTER MANAGED INSTRUCTION
COMPUTER BASED LABORATORIES (1967 1980) Use COMPUTER ASSISTED INSTRUCTION and LABORATORIES
SCHOOL BASED MANAGEMENT
COMPUTER BASED MESSAGE SYSTEMS Use ELECTRONIC MAIL
COMPUTER BASED REFERENCE SERVICES Use ONLINE SYSTEMS and REFERENCE SERVICES
KNOWLEDGE BASED SYSTEMS Use EXPERT SYSTEMS
COMPETENCY BASED TEACHER EDUCATION
CONSEQUENCE BASED TEACHER EDUCATION Use COMPETENCY BASED TEACHER EDUCATION
PERFORMANCE BASED TEACHER EDUCATION (1972 1980) Use COMPETENCY BASED TEACHER EDUCATION
PROFICIENCY BASED TEACHER EDUCATION Use COMPETENCY BASED TEACHER EDUCATION
AIR BASES Use MILITARY AIR FACILITIES
AIR FORCE BASES Use MILITARY AIR FACILITIES
ARMY AIR BASES Use MILITARY AIR FACILITIES
DATA BASES (1969 1981) Use DATABASES
BASHKIR
BASIC BUSINESS EDUCATION
ADULT BASIC EDUCATION
BASIC LANGUAGE PATTERNS Use LANGUAGE PATTERNS
BASIC READING (1967 1980)
BASIC RESEARCH Use RESEARCH
BASIC SKILLS
BASIC VOCABULARY
BASIC WORD LISTS Use WORD LISTS
BACK TO BASICS
BASKETBALL
BASQUE
BATTERED WOMEN
ELECTRIC BATTERIES
BATTERIES (ELECTRIC) Use ELECTRIC BATTERIES
STORAGE BATTERIES Use ELECTRIC BATTERIES
BAYESIAN STATISTICS
BEAUTICIANS Use COSMETOLOGY
BEAUTY CULTURE Use COSMETOLOGY
BEAUTY OPERATORS Use COSMETOLOGY
BEGINNING FARMER EDUCATION Use YOUNG FARMER EDUCATION
BEGINNING READING
BEGINNING TEACHERS
BEGINNING WORKERS Use ENTRY WORKERS
BEHAVIOR
ACTIVITY LEVEL (MOTOR BEHAVIOR) Use PHYSICAL ACTIVITY LEVEL
ADAPTIVE BEHAVIOR Use ADJUSTMENT (TO ENVIRONMENT)
AFFECTIVE BEHAVIOR
ANIMAL BEHAVIOR
ANTI SOCIAL BEHAVIOR (1966 1980) Use ANTISOCIAL BEHAVIOR
ANTISOCIAL BEHAVIOR
ATTACHMENT BEHAVIOR
BONDING (BEHAVIOR) Use ATTACHMENT BEHAVIOR
CHAIN REFLEXES (BEHAVIOR) Use BEHAVIOR CHAINING
BEHAVIOR CHAINING
BEHAVIOR CHANGE
COLLECTIVE BEHAVIOR Use GROUP BEHAVIOR
CONSUMER BEHAVIOR Use CONSUMER ECONOMICS
DELINQUENT BEHAVIOR (1966 1983) Use DELINQUENCY
BEHAVIOR DEVELOPMENT
BEHAVIOR DISORDERS
EMOTIONAL BEHAVIOR Use AFFECTIVE BEHAVIOR
EXPLORATORY BEHAVIOR
GROUP BEHAVIOR
INFANT BEHAVIOR
INTERNATION BEHAVIOR Use INTERNATIONAL RELATIONS
BEHAVIOR MODIFICATION
COGNITIVE BEHAVIOR MODIFICATION Use BEHAVIOR MODIFICATION and COGNITIVE RESTRUCTURING
NORMATIVE BEHAVIOR Use BEHAVIOR STANDARDS
ADAPTIVE BEHAVIOR (OF DISABLED)
PARANOID BEHAVIOR
PARENT BEHAVIOR Use PARENT CHILD RELATIONSHIP
PATTERNED BEHAVIOR Use BEHAVIOR PATTERNS
BEHAVIOR PATTERNS
BEHAVIOR PROBLEMS
PROSOCIAL BEHAVIOR
BEHAVIOR RATING SCALES
REACTIVE BEHAVIOR (1966 1980) Use RESPONSES
SELF DESTRUCTIVE BEHAVIOR
SEXUAL BEHAVIOR Use SEXUALITY
SOCIAL BEHAVIOR
SOCIALLY DEVIANT BEHAVIOR (1966 1980) Use ANTISOCIAL BEHAVIOR
SPONTANEOUS BEHAVIOR
BEHAVIOR STANDARDS
STIMULUS BEHAVIOR (1966 1980) Use RESPONSES
STUDENT BEHAVIOR
TEACHER BEHAVIOR
BEHAVIOR THEORIES
BEHAVIOR THERAPY Use BEHAVIOR MODIFICATION
BEHAVIORAL ANALYSIS Use BEHAVIORAL SCIENCE RESEARCH
BEHAVIORAL CONTRACTS Use PERFORMANCE CONTRACTS
BEHAVIORAL COUNSELING (1967 1980) Use BEHAVIOR MODIFICATION
BEHAVIORAL OBJECTIVES
BEHAVIORAL SCIENCE RESEARCH

BEHAVIORAL SCIENCES
BEHAVIORAL SITUATION FILMS Use PROTOCOL MATERIALS
BEHAVIORAL TECHNOLOGY Use BEHAVIORAL SCIENCES
BEHAVIORISM
BEHAVIORIST PSYCHOLOGY Use BEHAVIORISM
JOB BEHAVIORS Use JOB SKILLS
WELL BEING
CIVIC BELIEF (1966 1980) Use POLITICAL ATTITUDES
BELIEFS
BELIEVABILITY Use CREDIBILITY
MAKE BELIEVE PLAY Use PRETEND PLAY
BELORUSSIAN Use BIELORUSSIAN
LAP BELTS Use RESTRAINTS (VEHICLE SAFETY)
SEAT BELTS Use RESTRAINTS (VEHICLE SAFETY)
BEMBA
COST BENEFIT ANALYSIS Use COST EFFECTIVENESS
BENEFIT COST ANALYSIS Use COST EFFECTIVENESS
COMMUNITY BENEFITS
EDUCATIONAL BENEFITS
EMPLOYEE FRINGE BENEFITS Use FRINGE BENEFITS
FRINGE BENEFITS
RETIREMENT BENEFITS
TEACHER EMPLOYMENT BENEFITS
TEACHING BENEFITS (1966 1980) Use TEACHER EMPLOYMENT BENEFITS
BENGALI
BERBER LANGUAGES
ATTRACTIVENESS (BETWEEN PERSONS) Use INTERPERSONAL ATTRACTION
PERCEPTION (BETWEEN PERSONS) Use SOCIAL COGNITION
PERCEPTIVENESS (BETWEEN PERSONS) Use INTERPERSONAL COMPETENCE and SOCIAL COGNITION
ALCOHOLIC BEVERAGES
BIAS
ETHNIC BIAS
EXPERIMENTER BIAS Use EXPERIMENTER CHARACTERISTICS
RACIAL BIAS
SELF BIAS Use EGOCENTRISM
SEX BIAS
SOCIAL BIAS
STATISTICAL BIAS
TEST BIAS
RESPONSE BIAS (TESTS) Use RESPONSE STYLE (TESTS)
TEXTBOOK BIAS
BIBLES Use BIBLICAL LITERATURE
BIBLICAL LITERATURE
BIBLIOCOUNSELING Use BIBLIOTHERAPY
BIBLIOGRAPHIC CITATIONS (1969 1980) Use CITATIONS (REFERENCES)
BIBLIOGRAPHIC CONTROL Use CATALOGING
BIBLIOGRAPHIC COUPLING
FOOTNOTES (BIBLIOGRAPHIC) Use CITATIONS (REFERENCES)
BIBLIOGRAPHIC REFERENCES Use CITATIONS (REFERENCES)
BIBLIOGRAPHIC UTILITIES
BIBLIOGRAPHIES
ABSTRACT BIBLIOGRAPHIES Use ANNOTATED BIBLIOGRAPHIES
ANNOTATED BIBLIOGRAPHIES
STATISTICAL BIBLIOGRAPHY Use BIBLIOMETRICS
BIBLIOMETRICS
BIBLIOTHERAPY
BICULTURAL EDUCATION Use MULTICULTURAL EDUCATION
BICULTURAL TRAINING Use CROSS CULTURAL TRAINING
BICULTURALISM
BICYCLING
COMPETITIVE BIDDING Use BIDS
CONSTRUCTION BIDDING Use BIDS
BIDIALECTALISM
BIDS
BIELORUSSIAN
BIGOTRY Use SOCIAL DISCRIMINATION
BIKOL
BILINGUAL EDUCATION
BILINGUAL EDUCATION PROGRAMS
BILINGUAL INSTRUCTIONAL MATERIALS
BILINGUAL MATERIALS Use MULTILINGUAL MATERIALS
BILINGUAL SCHOOLS
BILINGUAL STUDENTS
BILINGUAL TEACHER AIDES
BILINGUAL TEACHERS
BILINGUALISM
BINI
BIOCHEMICAL EFFECTS Use BIOCHEMISTRY
BIOCHEMICAL TESTS Use BIOCHEMISTRY
BIOCHEMISTRY
BIOETHICS
BIOFEEDBACK
BIOGRAPHICAL INVENTORIES
BIOGRAPHICAL PROFILES Use BIOGRAPHICAL INVENTORIES
BIOGRAPHIES
BIOLOGICAL INFLUENCES
BIOLOGICAL PARENTS
BIOLOGICAL SCIENCES
BIOLOGY
ANIMAL BIOLOGY Use ZOOLOGY
FATIGUE (BIOLOGY)
HUMAN BIOLOGY Use BIOLOGY
BIOLOGY INSTRUCTION (1966 1980) Use BIOLOGY and SCIENCE INSTRUCTION
MARINE BIOLOGY
PLANT BIOLOGY Use BOTANY
RADIATION BIOLOGY
REPRODUCTION (BIOLOGY)
SOCIAL BIOLOGY
STRENGTH (BIOLOGY) Use MUSCULAR STRENGTH
BIOMECHANICS
BIOMEDICAL EQUIPMENT

BIOMEDICAL EQUIPMENT TECHNICIANS Use MEDICAL LABORATORY ASSISTANTS
BIOMEDICAL RESEARCH Use BIOMEDICINE
BIOMEDICINE
BIONICS
BIOPHYSICS
BIRACIAL COMMITTEES
BIRACIAL ELEMENTARY SCHOOLS (1966 1980) Use SCHOOL DESEGREGATION
BIRACIAL SCHOOLS (1966 1980) Use SCHOOL DESEGREGATION
BIRACIAL SECONDARY SCHOOLS (1966 1980) Use SCHOOL DESEGREGATION
BIRD STUDIES Use ORNITHOLOGY
BIRTH
BIRTH CONTROL Use CONTRACEPTION
BIRTH DEFECTS Use CONGENITAL IMPAIRMENTS
BIRTH ORDER
BIRTH PARENTS Use BIOLOGICAL PARENTS
PREMATURE BIRTH Use PREMATURE INFANTS
BIRTH RATE
BIRTH WEIGHT
ILLEGITIMATE BIRTHS
BITUMINOUS COAL Use COAL
BLACK ACHIEVEMENT
BLACK AMERICANS Use BLACKS
BLACK AND WHITE FILMS Use FILMS
BLACK ATTITUDES
BLACK BUSINESSES
BLACK CHILDREN Use BLACK YOUTH
BLACK COLLEGES
HISTORICALLY BLACK COLLEGES Use BLACK COLLEGES
BLACK COMMUNITY
BLACK CULTURE
BLACK DIALECTS
BLACK EDUCATION
BLACK EMPLOYMENT
BLACK ENGLISH Use BLACK DIALECTS
BLACK FAMILY
BLACK HISTORY
BLACK HOUSING (1977 1980)
BLACK INFLUENCES
BLACK INSTITUTIONS
BLACK LEADERSHIP
BLACK LITERATURE
BLACK MOTHERS
BLACK NATIONALISM Use BLACK POWER
BLACK ORGANIZATIONS
BLACK POPULATION TRENDS
BLACK POWER
WHITE BLACK RELATIONS Use RACIAL RELATIONS
BLACK ROLE (1977 1980) Use BLACK INFLUENCES
BLACK STEREOTYPES
BLACK STUDENTS
BLACK STUDIES
BLACK SUBCULTURE Use BLACK CULTURE
BLACK TEACHERS
BLACK WHITE RELATIONS Use RACIAL RELATIONS
BLACK YOUTH
BLACKBOARDS Use CHALKBOARDS
BLACKS
BLIND (1966 1980) Use BLINDNESS
BLIND CHILDREN (1966 1980) Use BLINDNESS
DEAF BLIND
BLINDNESS
BLOCK GRANTS
BLOCK TIME TEACHING Use TIME BLOCKS
TIME BLOCKS
BLOOD CIRCULATION
BLOOD DONORS Use TISSUE DONORS
HIGH BLOOD PRESSURE Use HYPERTENSION
BLUE COLLAR OCCUPATIONS
BLUE RIBBON COMMISSIONS
BLUEPRINTS
BOARD ADMINISTRATOR RELATIONSHIP
BOARD CANDIDATES
SCHOOL BOARD MEMBERS Use BOARDS OF EDUCATION
BOARD OF EDUCATION MEMBERS Use BOARDS OF EDUCATION
BOARD OF EDUCATION POLICY
BOARD OF EDUCATION ROLE
BOARD OF REGENTS Use GOVERNING BOARDS
BOARD OF TRUSTEES Use GOVERNING BOARDS
SCHOOL BOARD POLICY Use BOARD OF EDUCATION POLICY
SCHOOL BOARD ROLE Use BOARD OF EDUCATION ROLE
BOARDING HOMES
BOARDING SCHOOLS
ADVISORY BOARDS Use ADVISORY COMMITTEES
BULLETIN BOARDS
ELECTRONIC BULLETIN BOARDS Use ELECTRONIC MAIL
GOVERNING BOARDS
BOARDS OF EDUCATION
STATE BOARDS OF EDUCATION
STATE BOARDS OF LICENSING Use STATE LICENSING BOARDS
SCHOOL BOARDS Use BOARDS OF EDUCATION
STATE LICENSING BOARDS
STATE SCHOOL BOARDS Use STATE BOARDS OF EDUCATION
BOAT OPERATORS
BOATMEN (1967 1980) Use BOAT OPERATORS
BODY AND FENDER REPAIRERS Use AUTO BODY REPAIRERS
BODY ATTITUDE Use HUMAN POSTURE
BODY CARE Use HYGIENE
OVERWEIGHT (EXCESSIVE BODY FAT) Use OBESITY
GOVERNMENT (ADMINISTRATIVE BODY)
BODY HEIGHT
HUMAN BODY

BODY IMAGE
BODY LANGUAGE
AUTO BODY REPAIRERS
AUTO BODY REPAIRMEN (1966 1980) Use AUTO BODY REPAIRERS
BODY SCHEMA Use BODY IMAGE
BODY WEIGHT
BOMB SHELTERS Use FALLOUT SHELTERS
BOND ISSUES
BONDING (BEHAVIOR) Use ATTACHMENT BEHAVIOR
CHEMICAL BONDING
INDEMNITY BONDS
BOOK BUYING Use LIBRARY ACQUISITION
BOOK CATALOGS
BOOK INDUSTRY Use PUBLISHING INDUSTRY
BOOK LENDING Use LIBRARY CIRCULATION
BOOK REVIEWS
OPEN BOOK TESTS
BOOK THEFTS (1969 1980) Use BOOKS and STEALING
BOOKKEEPING
ANSWER BOOKLETS Use ANSWER SHEETS
BOOKLISTS (1967 1980) Use BIBLIOGRAPHIES
BOOKMOBILES
BOOKS
CHILDRENS BOOKS (1966 1980) Use BOOKS and CHILDRENS LITERATURE
FOLKLORE BOOKS (1966 1980) Use BOOKS and FOLK CULTURE
FOREIGN LANGUAGE BOOKS
HEALTH BOOKS (1966 1980) Use BOOKS and HEALTH MATERIALS
HIGH INTEREST LOW VOCABULARY BOOKS
LARGE TYPE BOOKS Use LARGE TYPE MATERIALS
PAPERBACK BOOKS
PICTURE BOOKS
REFERENCE BOOKS (1966 1980) Use REFERENCE MATERIALS
SECOND LANGUAGE BOOKS Use FOREIGN LANGUAGE BOOKS
SOFT COVER BOOKS Use PAPERBACK BOOKS
TALKING BOOKS
TEST BOOKS Use TESTS
COLLEGE BOOKSTORES Use COLLEGE STORES
GUARDS (BORDER PATROL) Use IMMIGRATION INSPECTORS
BORDER PATROL OFFICERS Use IMMIGRATION INSPECTORS
BORDERLINE MENTAL RETARDATION Use SLOW LEARNERS
LINGUISTIC BORROWING
PHONOLOGICAL BORROWING Use LINGUISTIC BORROWING
SYNTACTIC BORROWING Use LINGUISTIC BORROWING
WORD BORROWING Use LINGUISTIC BORROWING
BOTANY
COLLEGE BOUND STUDENTS
NONCOLLEGE BOUND STUDENTS
SCHOOL BOUNDARIES Use SCHOOL DISTRICTS
BOWLING
SCHOOL BOYCOTTS
BOYS Use MALES
BRACERO PROGRAMS (1966 1980) Use BRACEROS
BRACEROS
BRAHMINS (1967 1980) Use CASTE
BRAILLE
BRAIN DAMAGE Use NEUROLOGICAL IMPAIRMENTS
MINIMAL BRAIN DYSFUNCTION
BRAIN HEMISPHERE FUNCTIONS
HEMISPHERIC SPECIALIZATION (BRAIN) Use BRAIN HEMISPHERE FUNCTIONS
MINIMALLY BRAIN INJURED (1966 1980) Use MINIMAL BRAIN DYSFUNCTION
BRAINSTORMING
BRANCH LIBRARIES
BRANCHING
OPTIONAL BRANCHING (1966 1980) Use BRANCHING
LUSO BRAZILIAN CULTURE
BREADWINNERS Use HEADS OF HOUSEHOLDS
FAMILY BREADWINNERS Use HEADS OF HOUSEHOLDS
BREAKFAST PROGRAMS
BREASTFEEDING
BRICK INDUSTRY
BRICK MASONRY Use BRICKLAYING
BRICKLAYERS (1968 1981) Use BRICKLAYING
BRICKLAYING
PHOTOMETRIC BRIGHTNESS Use LUMINESCENCE
BRITISH INFANT SCHOOLS
INFANT SCHOOLS (BRITISH PRIMARY SYSTEM) Use BRITISH INFANT SCHOOLS
BROADCAST COMMUNICATIONS Use TELECOMMUNICATIONS
BROADCAST INDUSTRY
PROGRAMING (BROADCAST)
BROADCAST RECEPTION EQUIPMENT
BROADCAST SCHEDULING Use PROGRAMING (BROADCAST)
BROADCAST TELEVISION
BROCHURES Use PAMPHLETS
INFORMATION BROKERS Use INFORMATION SCIENTISTS
BROTHERS Use SIBLINGS
BUCOLIC LITERATURE Use PASTORAL LITERATURE
BUDDHISM
BUDGET ALLOCATIONS Use BUDGETING
BUDGET CUTS Use BUDGETING and RETRENCHMENT
SCHOOL BUDGET ELECTIONS
BUDGETING
PROGRAM BUDGETING
BUDGETS
DESIGN BUILD APPROACH
BUILDING CONVERSION
BUILDING DESIGN
MODULAR BUILDING DESIGN
BUILDING EQUIPMENT (1966 1980) Use EQUIPMENT
BUILDING IMPROVEMENT (1966 1980) Use FACILITY IMPROVEMENT
BUILDING INNOVATION
BUILDING MATERIALS (1968 1980) Use CONSTRUCTION MATERIALS

	BUILDING OBSOLESCENCE
	BUILDING OPERATION
	BUILDING PLANS
	BUILDING PROGRAMS Use CONSTRUCTION PROGRAMS
	BUILDING RENOVATION Use FACILITY IMPROVEMENT
SYSTEMS	BUILDING
	BUILDING SYSTEMS
COMPONENT	BUILDING SYSTEMS (1968 1976) Use BUILDING SYSTEMS
STRUCTURAL	BUILDING SYSTEMS
	BUILDING TRADES
TURNKEY	BUILDING Use DESIGN BUILD APPROACH
VOCABULARY	BUILDING Use VOCABULARY DEVELOPMENT
	BUILDINGS
COLLEGE	BUILDINGS
SCHOOL	BUILDINGS
	BULGARIAN
	BULIMAREXIA Use BULIMIA
	BULIMIA
	BULLETIN BOARDS
ELECTRONIC	BULLETIN BOARDS Use ELECTRONIC MAIL
	BULLETINS
STATE CURRICULUM	BULLETINS Use STATE CURRICULUM GUIDES
	BUREAUCRACY
	BURGLAR ALARMS Use ALARM SYSTEMS
	BURIAT
	BURMESE
	BURMESE CULTURE
	BURNOUT
TEACHER	BURNOUT
	BURUSHASKI
	BUS TRANSPORTATION
	BUSES Use SERVICE VEHICLES
SCHOOL	BUSES
	BUSINESS
	BUSINESS ADMINISTRATION
	BUSINESS ADMINISTRATION EDUCATION
	BUSINESS COMMUNICATION
	BUSINESS CORRESPONDENCE
	BUSINESS CYCLES
	BUSINESS EDUCATION
BASIC	BUSINESS EDUCATION
	BUSINESS EDUCATION FACILITIES
GENERAL	BUSINESS EDUCATION Use BASIC BUSINESS EDUCATION
	BUSINESS EDUCATION TEACHERS
VOCATIONAL	BUSINESS EDUCATION Use BUSINESS EDUCATION
	BUSINESS ENGLISH
	BUSINESS FLUCTUATIONS Use BUSINESS CYCLES
	BUSINESS GAMES Use MANAGEMENT GAMES
	BUSINESS LETTERS Use BUSINESS CORRESPONDENCE
	BUSINESS MACHINES Use OFFICE MACHINES
SMALL	BUSINESS MANAGEMENT Use BUSINESS ADMINISTRATION and SMALL BUSINESSES
	BUSINESS OFFICIALS (INDUSTRY) Use ADMINISTRATORS
SCHOOL	BUSINESS OFFICIALS
	BUSINESS OFFICIALS (SCHOOL) Use SCHOOL BUSINESS OFFICIALS
SCHOOL	BUSINESS RELATIONSHIP
	BUSINESS RESPONSIBILITY
	BUSINESS SCHOOL RELATIONSHIP Use SCHOOL BUSINESS RELATIONSHIP
	BUSINESS SKILLS
	BUSINESS SUBJECTS (1967 1980) Use BUSINESS EDUCATION
	BUSINESS TEACHERS Use BUSINESS EDUCATION TEACHERS
BLACK	BUSINESSES
NEGRO	BUSINESSES (1967 1977) Use BLACK BUSINESSES
SMALL	BUSINESSES
	BUSING
BOOK	BUYING Use LIBRARY ACQUISITION
CREDIT	BY EXAMINATION Use EQUIVALENCY TESTS
MANAGEMENT	BY OBJECTIVES
COLLEGE COSTS (INCURRED	BY STUDENTS) Use STUDENT COSTS
	BYELORUSSIAN Use BIELORUSSIAN
N	C SYSTEMS Use NUMERICAL CONTROL
	CABINETMAKERS Use CABINETMAKING
	CABINETMAKING
	CABLE TELEVISION
SCHOOL	CADRES
	CAFETERIAS Use DINING FACILITIES
	CAI Use COMPUTER ASSISTED INSTRUCTION
	CAKCHIQUEL
	CALCULATION (1966 1980) Use COMPUTATION
	CALCULATORS
ELECTRONIC	CALCULATORS Use CALCULATORS
HAND	CALCULATORS Use CALCULATORS
POCKET	CALCULATORS Use CALCULATORS
	CALCULUS
ACADEMIC	CALENDARS Use SCHOOL SCHEDULES
SCHOOL	CALENDARS (1967 1980) Use SCHOOL SCHEDULES
	CALISTHENICS
	CALLIGRAPHY Use MANUSCRIPT WRITING (HANDLETTERING)
	CALORIMETERS
	CAMBODIAN
	CAMBODIAN AMERICANS Use ASIAN AMERICANS and CAMBODIANS
	CAMBODIANS
	CAMERAS Use PHOTOGRAPHIC EQUIPMENT
FILM	(CAMERAS) Use PHOTOGRAPHIC EQUIPMENT
	CAMP COUNSELORS (1968 1980) Use CAMPING
DAY	CAMP PROGRAMS
RESIDENT	CAMP PROGRAMS
ELECTION	CAMPAIGNS Use POLITICAL CAMPAIGNS
POLITICAL	CAMPAIGNS
PRESIDENTIAL	CAMPAIGNS (UNITED STATES)
	CAMPING
DAY	CAMPS Use DAY CAMP PROGRAMS

LABOR CAMPS (1966 1980) (MIGRANTS) Use MIGRANT HOUSING
OFF CAMPUS EDUCATION Use EXTENSION EDUCATION
OFF CAMPUS FACILITIES
CAMPUS PLANNING
CAMPUS SCHOOLS Use LABORATORY SCHOOLS
CAMPUS SECURITY Use SCHOOL SECURITY
OFF CAMPUS STUDENT TEACHING Use STUDENT TEACHING
ON CAMPUS STUDENTS
CAMPUSES
CANADA NATIVES
CANADIAN LITERATURE
FRENCH CANADIAN LITERATURE Use CANADIAN LITERATURE
CANCER
BOARD CANDIDATES
POLITICAL CANDIDATES
PRESIDENTIAL CANDIDATES (UNITED STATES) Use POLITICAL CANDIDATES and PRESIDENTIAL CAMPAIGNS (UNITED STATES)
CANNABIS Use MARIJUANA
CANONICAL CORRELATION Use MULTIVARIATE ANALYSIS
CANTONESE
FISCAL CAPACITY
CAPITAL
HUMAN CAPITAL
CAPITAL OUTLAY (FOR FIXED ASSETS)
CAPITALISM
CAPITALIZATION (ALPHABETIC)
CAPTIONS
CARCINOGENS Use CANCER
CARCINOMA Use CANCER
CARD CATALOGS
CARDIAC (PERSON) (1968 1980) Use HEART DISORDERS
CARDIOPULMONARY RESUSCITATION
CARDIOVASCULAR SYSTEM
ANSWER CARDS Use ANSWER SHEETS
CUE CARDS Use CUES
GRADE CARDS Use REPORT CARDS
REPORT CARDS
ADULT DAY CARE
ADULT FOSTER CARE
AFTER SCHOOL DAY CARE (1978 1983) Use AFTER SCHOOL PROGRAMS and SCHOOL AGE DAY CARE
BODY CARE Use HYGIENE
CHILD CARE CENTERS (1967 1980) Use DAY CARE CENTERS
DAY CARE CENTERS
MIGRANT CHILD CARE CENTERS (1966 1980) Use DAY CARE CENTERS and MIGRANT CHILDREN
CHILD CARE (1966 1980)
DAY CARE
EMPLOYER SPONSORED DAY CARE Use EMPLOYER SUPPORTED DAY CARE
EMPLOYER SUPPORTED DAY CARE
HEALTH CARE EVALUATION Use MEDICAL CARE EVALUATION
MEDICAL CARE EVALUATION
PATIENT CARE EVALUATION Use MEDICAL CARE EVALUATION
FAMILY DAY CARE
FOSTER CARE
HOME DAY CARE Use FAMILY DAY CARE
PERSONAL CARE HOMES
HOSPICES (TERMINAL CARE)
MEDICAL CARE Use MEDICAL SERVICES
CHILD CARE OCCUPATIONS
PRIMARY HEALTH CARE
DAY CARE PROGRAMS (1966 1980) Use DAY CARE
RESIDENTIAL CARE
RESPITE CARE
SCHOOL AGE DAY CARE
DAY CARE SERVICES (1967 1980) Use DAY CARE
SELF CARE SKILLS
CHILD CARE WORKERS (1967 1980) Use CHILD CAREGIVERS
CAREER AWARENESS
CAREER CHANGE
CAREER CHOICE
CAREER COUNSELING
CAREER DEVELOPMENT
CAREER EDUCATION
CAREER EXPLORATION
DUAL CAREER FAMILY
CAREER GUIDANCE
CAREER LADDERS
CAREER MATURITY Use VOCATIONAL MATURITY
CAREER OBJECTIVES Use CAREER CHOICE
CAREER OPPORTUNITIES (1966 1980)
CAREER ORIENTATION Use CAREER PLANNING
CAREER PLANNING
CAREERS
NONTRADITIONAL CAREERS Use NONTRADITIONAL OCCUPATIONS
SCIENCE CAREERS
CHILD CAREGIVERS
ANIMAL CARETAKERS
GROUNDS CARETAKERS Use GROUNDS KEEPERS
CARICATURES (1966 1980)
MONTE CARLO METHODS
CARPENTERS (1969 1981) Use CARPENTRY
CARPENTRY
CARPET LAYERS Use FLOOR LAYERS
CARPETING
CARPETS Use CARPETING
CARRELS
STUDY CARRELS Use CARRELS
CARTOGRAPHY
CARTOONS
AUDIOTAPE CARTRIDGES Use AUDIOTAPE CASSETTES
MAGNETIC TAPE CARTRIDGES Use MAGNETIC TAPE CASSETTES
VIDEOTAPE CARTRIDGES Use VIDEOTAPE CASSETTES

RESEARCH AND DEVELOPMENT CENTERS
RESIDENTIAL CENTERS (1967 1980) Use RESIDENTIAL INSTITUTIONS
RESOURCE CENTERS
SCHOOL MEDIA CENTERS Use LEARNING RESOURCES CENTERS
SCHOOL STUDY CENTERS (1966 1980) Use STUDY CENTERS
SCIENCE TEACHING CENTERS
SKILL CENTERS
STUDENT CENTERS Use STUDENT UNIONS
STUDY CENTERS
SUPPLEMENTARY EDUCATIONAL CENTERS (1966 1980) Use EDUCATION SERVICE CENTERS and SUPPLEMENTARY EDUCATION
TEACHER CENTERS
TEACHER EDUCATION CENTERS Use TEACHER CENTERS
TREATMENT CENTERS Use CLINICS
UNIVERSITY TRAINING CENTERS Use TEACHER CENTERS
VIDEO PRODUCTION CENTERS Use TELEVISION STUDIOS
VOCATIONAL TRAINING CENTERS
WRITING CENTERS Use WRITING LABORATORIES
CENTRAL AMERICAN HISTORY Use LATIN AMERICAN HISTORY
CENTRAL AMERICAN LITERATURE Use LATIN AMERICAN LITERATURE
CENTRAL AMERICANS Use LATIN AMERICANS
CENTRAL SOUND SYSTEMS (1966 1980) Use AUDIO EQUIPMENT
CENTRALIZATION
CENTRALIZED SCHOOLS Use CONSOLIDATED SCHOOLS
CENTROID METHOD OF FACTOR ANALYSIS Use FACTOR ANALYSIS
EIGHTEENTH CENTURY LITERATURE
FIFTEENTH CENTURY LITERATURE
MIDTWENTIETH CENTURY LITERATURE Use TWENTIETH CENTURY LITERATURE
NINETEENTH CENTURY LITERATURE
SEVENTEENTH CENTURY LITERATURE
SIXTEENTH CENTURY LITERATURE
TWENTIETH CENTURY LITERATURE
CERAMICS
CEREBRAL DOMINANCE (1967 1986) Use BRAIN HEMISPHERE FUNCTIONS
CEREBRAL PALSY
COMMENCEMENT CEREMONIES
GRADUATE CEREMONIES Use COMMENCEMENT CEREMONIES
EDUCATIONAL CERTIFICATES
TEACHER CERTIFICATES (1967 1980) Use TEACHER CERTIFICATION
TEACHING CERTIFICATES Use TEACHER CERTIFICATION
CERTIFICATION
COUNSELOR CERTIFICATION
STUDENT CERTIFICATION
TEACHER CERTIFICATION
CERTIFIED NURSES Use NURSES
CERTIFIED PUBLIC ACCOUNTANTS
CEU Use CONTINUING EDUCATION UNITS
CHAD LANGUAGES
CHAIN REFLEXES (BEHAVIOR) Use BEHAVIOR CHAINING
BEHAVIOR CHAINING
DEPARTMENT CHAIRPERSONS Use DEPARTMENT HEADS
WHEEL CHAIRS (1970 1981) Use WHEELCHAIRS
CHALKBOARDS
CHAMORRO
CHANCELLORS (EDUCATION) Use COLLEGE PRESIDENTS
CHANCROID Use VENEREAL DISEASES
CHANGE
ADMINISTRATIVE CHANGE
CHANGE AGENTS
ATTITUDE CHANGE
BEHAVIOR CHANGE
CAREER CHANGE
COMMUNITY CHANGE
ECONOMIC CHANGE
EDUCATIONAL CHANGE
EMPLOYMENT CHANGE Use CAREER CHANGE
JOB CHANGE Use CAREER CHANGE
MIDCAREER CHANGE Use CAREER CHANGE and MIDLIFE TRANSITIONS
ORGANIZATIONAL CHANGE
PERSONALITY CHANGE
SOCIAL CHANGE
SOCIETAL CHANGE Use SOCIAL CHANGE
CHANGE STRATEGIES
VOCATIONAL CHANGE Use CAREER CHANGE
WORK CHANGE Use CAREER CHANGE
ARCHITECTURAL CHANGES Use BUILDING DESIGN
POPULATION CHANGES Use POPULATION TRENDS
CHANGING ATTITUDES (1966 1980) Use ATTITUDE CHANGE
CHARACTER Use PERSONALITY
ARCHITECTURAL CHARACTER
CHARACTER PORTRAYAL Use CHARACTERIZATION
CHARACTER RECOGNITION
MAGNETIC INK CHARACTER RECOGNITION Use CHARACTER RECOGNITION
OPTICAL CHARACTER RECOGNITION Use CHARACTER RECOGNITION and OPTICAL SCANNERS
ITEM CHARACTERISTIC CURVE THEORY Use LATENT TRAIT THEORY
ADMINISTRATOR CHARACTERISTICS
ADULT CHARACTERISTICS (1967 1980) Use ADULTS and INDIVIDUAL CHARACTERISTICS
COLLEGE CHARACTERISTICS Use INSTITUTIONAL CHARACTERISTICS
COMMUNITY CHARACTERISTICS
COUNSELOR CHARACTERISTICS
CULTURAL CHARACTERISTICS Use CULTURAL TRAITS
DROPOUT CHARACTERISTICS
EXAMINER CHARACTERISTICS Use EXAMINERS and EXPERIMENTER CHARACTERISTICS
EXPERIMENTER CHARACTERISTICS
FAMILY CHARACTERISTICS
CLIENT CHARACTERISTICS (HUMAN SERVICES)
INDIVIDUAL CHARACTERISTICS
INSTITUTIONAL CHARACTERISTICS
LEARNING CHARACTERISTICS (1968 1980) Use LEARNING
PARTICIPANT CHARACTERISTICS
PHYSICAL CHARACTERISTICS
TEST CHARACTERISTICS (PHYSICAL) Use TEST FORMAT

PSYCHOLOGICAL CHARACTERISTICS
RACIAL CHARACTERISTICS (1966 1980)
REGIONAL CHARACTERISTICS
RESEARCHER CHARACTERISTICS Use EXPERIMENTER CHARACTERISTICS and RESEARCHERS
SCHOOL CHARACTERISTICS Use INSTITUTIONAL CHARACTERISTICS
SEX (CHARACTERISTICS) (1966 1980)
SOCIAL CHARACTERISTICS
STUDENT CHARACTERISTICS
TEACHER CHARACTERISTICS
UNIVERSITY CHARACTERISTICS Use INSTITUTIONAL CHARACTERISTICS
CHARACTERIZATION
CHARACTERIZATION (LITERATURE) (1969 1977) Use CHARACTERIZATION
CHARITABLE TRUSTS Use TRUSTS (FINANCIAL)
CHARTS
EXPERIENCE CHARTS
FLOW CHARTS
GRADE CHARTS (1966 1980)
CHEATING
FIELD CHECK (1967 1980) Use EQUIPMENT EVALUATION
CHECK LISTS
CHEFS Use COOKS
CHEMICAL ANALYSIS
CHEMICAL BONDING
CHEMICAL DEPENDENCY (DRUGS) Use DRUG ADDICTION
DETERMINATION (CHEMICAL) Use CHEMICAL ANALYSIS
CHEMICAL DETERMINATION Use CHEMICAL ANALYSIS
CHEMICAL ENGINEERING
CHEMICAL EQUILIBRIUM
CHEMICAL INDUSTRY
CHEMICAL NOMENCLATURE
AGRICULTURAL CHEMICAL OCCUPATIONS
CHEMICAL REACTIONS
CHEMICAL SYNTHESIS Use CHEMICAL REACTIONS
CHEMICAL TECHNICIANS
CHEMISTRY
INORGANIC CHEMISTRY
CHEMISTRY INSTRUCTION (1967 1980) Use CHEMISTRY and SCIENCE INSTRUCTION
ORGANIC CHEMISTRY
PHYSIOLOGICAL CHEMISTRY Use BIOCHEMISTRY
CHEMISTRY TEACHERS (1967 1980) Use CHEMISTRY and SCIENCE TEACHERS
CHEMOTHERAPY Use DRUG THERAPY
CHEREMIS
CHEROKEE
CHIBEMBA Use BEMBA
CHIEF ACADEMIC OFFICERS Use ACADEMIC DEANS
CHIEF ADMINISTRATORS (1967 1980) Use ADMINISTRATORS
CHILD ABUSE
CHILD ADVOCACY
CHILD CARE (1966 1980)
CHILD CARE CENTERS (1967 1980) Use DAY CARE CENTERS
MIGRANT CHILD CARE CENTERS (1966 1980) Use DAY CARE CENTERS and MIGRANT CHILDREN
CHILD CARE OCCUPATIONS
CHILD CARE WORKERS (1967 1980) Use CHILD CAREGIVERS
CHILD CAREGIVERS
CHILD CENTERED CURRICULUM Use STUDENT CENTERED CURRICULUM
CHILD CUSTODY
CHILD DEVELOPMENT
CHILD DEVELOPMENT CENTERS
CHILD DEVELOPMENT SPECIALISTS
EXCEPTIONAL CHILD EDUCATION (1968 1980)
MIGRANT CHILD EDUCATION (1967 1980) Use MIGRANT EDUCATION
PARENT CHILD INTERACTION Use PARENT CHILD RELATIONSHIP
CHILD LABOR
CHILD LABOR LAWS (1966 1974) Use CHILD LABOR and LABOR LEGISLATION
CHILD LABOR LEGISLATION (1966 1980) Use CHILD LABOR and LABOR LEGISLATION
CHILD LANGUAGE
CHILD NEGLECT
CHILD PARENT RELATIONSHIP Use PARENT CHILD RELATIONSHIP
CHILD PSYCHOLOGY
CHILD REARING
PARENT CHILD RELATIONSHIP
EXCEPTIONAL CHILD RESEARCH
CHILD RESPONSIBILITY
CHILD RESTRAINTS (VEHICLE SAFETY) Use RESTRAINTS (VEHICLE SAFETY)
CHILD ROLE
EXCEPTIONAL CHILD SERVICES (1968 1980)
CHILD SEXUAL ABUSE Use CHILD ABUSE and SEXUAL ABUSE
CHILD WELFARE
CHILDBIRTH Use BIRTH
LABOR (CHILDBIRTH) Use BIRTH
CHILDHOOD (1966 1980) Use CHILDREN
CHILDHOOD ATTITUDES
EARLY CHILDHOOD (1966 1980) Use YOUNG CHILDREN
EARLY CHILDHOOD EDUCATION
CHILDHOOD FRIENDSHIP (1966 1980) Use FRIENDSHIP
CHILDHOOD INTERESTS
CHILDHOOD NEEDS
CHILDREN
ABUSED CHILDREN Use CHILD ABUSE
ADOPTED CHILDREN
BLACK CHILDREN Use BLACK YOUTH
BLIND CHILDREN (1966 1980) Use BLINDNESS
CRIPPLED CHILDREN (1968 1980) Use PHYSICAL DISABILITIES
DEAF CHILDREN (1966 1980) Use DEAFNESS
DEPRIVED CHILDREN Use DISADVANTAGED YOUTH
DISADVANTAGED CHILDREN Use DISADVANTAGED YOUTH
ELEMENTARY SCHOOL CHILDREN Use ELEMENTARY SCHOOL STUDENTS
EMOTIONALLY DISTURBED CHILDREN (1967 1980) Use EMOTIONAL DISTURBANCES
EXCEPTIONAL CHILDREN (1966 1978) Use EXCEPTIONAL PERSONS
FOSTER CHILDREN
FOSTER HOMES (1970 1982) (CHILDREN) Use FOSTER CARE

GIFTED CHILDREN Use GIFTED
HANDICAPPED CHILDREN (1966 1980)
HOMEBOUND CHILDREN (1966 1980) Use HOMEBOUND
HOSPITALIZED CHILDREN
KINDERGARTEN CHILDREN
LATCHKEY CHILDREN
MENTALLY ADVANCED CHILDREN Use GIFTED
MIGRANT CHILDREN
MIGRATORY CHILDREN Use MIGRANT CHILDREN
MINORITY GROUP CHILDREN
NEGLECTED CHILDREN (1977 1980) Use CHILD NEGLECT
NEUROTIC CHILDREN (1966 1980) Use NEUROSIS
PRESCHOOL CHILDREN
PROBLEM CHILDREN
PSYCHOTIC CHILDREN (1966 1980) Use PSYCHOSIS
RETARDED CHILDREN (1966 1980) Use MENTAL RETARDATION
SLUM CHILDREN Use DISADVANTAGED YOUTH
TRANSIENT CHILDREN
YOUNG CHILDREN
CHILDRENS ART
CHILDRENS ATTITUDES Use CHILDHOOD ATTITUDES
CHILDRENS BOOKS (1966 1980) Use BOOKS and CHILDRENS LITERATURE
CHILDRENS COURTS Use JUVENILE COURTS
CHILDRENS GAMES
CHILDRENS INTERESTS Use CHILDHOOD INTERESTS
CHILDRENS LITERATURE
CHILDRENS NEEDS Use CHILDHOOD NEEDS
CHILDRENS PLAY Use PLAY
CHILDRENS RIGHTS
CHILDRENS TELEVISION
CHILDRENS THEATER Use THEATER ARTS
CHIMNEYS
CHINESE
CHINESE AMERICANS
CHINESE CULTURE
MANDARIN CHINESE
CHINYANJA
CHIPPEWA Use OJIBWA
CHLORINATION (WATER) Use WATER TREATMENT
CHOCTAW
CAREER CHOICE
COLLEGE CHOICE
FAMILY CHOICE (EDUCATION) Use SCHOOL CHOICE
EDUCATIONAL CHOICE Use SCHOOL CHOICE
OCCUPATIONAL CHOICE (1966 1980) Use CAREER CHOICE
SCHOOL CHOICE
FORCED CHOICE TECHNIQUE
MULTIPLE CHOICE TESTS
FREE CHOICE TRANSFER PROGRAMS
VOCATIONAL CHOICE Use CAREER CHOICE
CHOIRS Use SINGING
CHORAL MUSIC
CHORAL SPEAKING
CHOREOGRAPHY Use DANCE
CHORUSES (1968 1980) Use SINGING
CHRISTIANITY
CHROMATOGRAPHY
CHRONIC ILLNESSES Use DISEASES
CHRONICLES
CHRONOLOGICAL AGE
CHURCH ACTION Use CHURCH ROLE
CHURCH MIGRANT PROJECTS (1966 1980) Use CHURCH PROGRAMS and MIGRANT PROGRAMS
CHURCH PROGRAMS
CHURCH PROJECTS Use CHURCH PROGRAMS
CHURCH RELATED COLLEGES
CHURCH RESPONSIBILITY
CHURCH ROLE
STATE CHURCH SEPARATION
CHURCH STATE SEPARATION Use STATE CHURCH SEPARATION
CHURCH WORKERS
CHURCHES
CHUVASH
CIGARETTE SMOKING Use SMOKING
CINEMA Use FILMS
CINEMA STUDY Use FILM STUDY
CINYANJA Use CHINYANJA
CIRCASSIAN Use CAUCASIAN LANGUAGES
QUALITY CIRCLES
CIRCUIT TEACHERS Use ITINERANT TEACHERS
CLOSED CIRCUIT TELEVISION
OPEN CIRCUIT TELEVISION (1966 1980) Use BROADCAST TELEVISION
ELECTRIC CIRCUITS
ELECTRONIC CIRCUITS Use ELECTRIC CIRCUITS
CIRCUITS (ELECTRONIC) Use ELECTRIC CIRCUITS
BLOOD CIRCULATION
LIBRARY CIRCULATION
PEDESTRIAN CIRCULATION Use PEDESTRIAN TRAFFIC
TRAFFIC CIRCULATION
VEHICULAR CIRCULATION Use VEHICULAR TRAFFIC
CIRCULATORY SYSTEM Use CARDIOVASCULAR SYSTEM
CITATION ANALYSIS
CITATION INDEXES
BIBLIOGRAPHIC CITATIONS (1969 1980) Use CITATIONS (REFERENCES)
CITATIONS (LEGAL) Use LAW ENFORCEMENT
CITATIONS (REFERENCES)
CITIES Use MUNICIPALITIES
LARGE CITIES Use URBAN AREAS
CITIZEN ADVOCACY Use ADVOCACY
CITIZEN INVOLVEMENT Use CITIZEN PARTICIPATION
CITIZEN PARTICIPATION
CITIZEN RESPONSIBILITY Use CITIZENSHIP RESPONSIBILITY

	CITIZEN ROLE
	CITIZENS COUNCILS
SENIOR	CITIZENS (1967 1980) Use OLDER ADULTS
SOUTHERN	CITIZENS (1966 1980)
	CITIZENSHIP
	CITIZENSHIP EDUCATION
GOOD	CITIZENSHIP Use CITIZENSHIP
	CITIZENSHIP RESPONSIBILITY
	CITY DEMOGRAPHY (1966 1980) Use URBAN DEMOGRAPHY
INNER	CITY EDUCATION Use URBAN EDUCATION
	CITY GOVERNMENT
	CITY IMPROVEMENT (1966 1980) Use URBAN IMPROVEMENT
INNER	CITY
	CITY OFFICIALS
ELECTED	CITY OFFICIALS Use CITY OFFICIALS
	CITY PLANNING (1966 1980) Use URBAN PLANNING
	CITY PROBLEMS (1966 1980) Use URBAN PROBLEMS
	CITY SCHOOLS Use URBAN SCHOOLS
	CITY WIDE COMMISSIONS (1966 1980) Use PLANNING COMMISSIONS and URBAN PLANNING
	CITY WIDE PROGRAMS (1967 1980) Use URBAN PROGRAMS
	CIVIC BELIEF (1966 1980) Use POLITICAL ATTITUDES
	CIVIC GROUPS Use COMMUNITY ORGANIZATIONS
	CIVIC INVOLVEMENT Use CITIZEN PARTICIPATION
	CIVIC ORGANIZATIONS Use COMMUNITY ORGANIZATIONS
	CIVIC PROGRAMS Use COMMUNITY PROGRAMS
	CIVIC RELATIONS Use COMMUNITY RELATIONS
	CIVIC RESPONSIBILITY Use CITIZENSHIP RESPONSIBILITY
	CIVICS
	CIVIL DEFENSE
DEMONSTRATIONS	(CIVIL)
	CIVIL DISOBEDIENCE
	CIVIL ENGINEERING
	CIVIL LIBERTIES
	CIVIL RIGHTS
	CIVIL RIGHTS LEGISLATION
	CIVIL SERVICE EMPLOYEES Use GOVERNMENT EMPLOYEES
	CIVIL WAR Use WAR
	CIVIL WAR (UNITED STATES)
EASTERN	CIVILIZATION Use NON WESTERN CIVILIZATION
GREEK	CIVILIZATION
NON WESTERN	CIVILIZATION
OCCIDENTAL	CIVILIZATION Use WESTERN CIVILIZATION
ORIENTAL	CIVILIZATION Use NON WESTERN CIVILIZATION
SOUTH ASIAN	CIVILIZATION Use NON WESTERN CIVILIZATION
WESTERN	CIVILIZATION
VALUES	CLARIFICATION
	CLASS ACTIVITIES
	CLASS ATTENDANCE (1966 1980) Use ATTENDANCE
	CLASS ATTITUDES (1966 1980)
	CLASS AVERAGE (1966 1980)
MIDDLE	CLASS COLLEGE STUDENTS (1966 1980) Use COLLEGE STUDENTS and MIDDLE CLASS STUDENTS
MIDDLE	CLASS CULTURE
	CLASS DESEGREGATION Use CLASSROOM DESEGREGATION
SOCIAL	CLASS DIFFERENCES Use SOCIAL DIFFERENCES
	CLASS DISCUSSION Use DISCUSSION (TEACHING TECHNIQUE)
MIDDLE	CLASS FATHERS (1966 1980) Use FATHERS and MIDDLE CLASS PARENTS
SOCIAL	CLASS INTEGRATION Use SOCIAL INTEGRATION
LOWER	CLASS
LOWER MIDDLE	CLASS
LOWER	CLASS MALES (1966 1980) Use LOWER CLASS and MALES
	CLASS MANAGEMENT (1966 1980) Use CLASSROOM TECHNIQUES
MIDDLE	CLASS
MIDDLE	CLASS MOTHERS (1966 1980) Use MIDDLE CLASS PARENTS and MOTHERS
	CLASS NEWSPAPERS (1967 1980) Use CLASS ACTIVITIES and STUDENT PUBLICATIONS
MIDDLE	CLASS NORM (1966 1980) Use MIDDLE CLASS STANDARDS
	CLASS ORGANIZATION
LOWER	CLASS PARENTS
MIDDLE	CLASS PARENTS
REGULAR	CLASS PLACEMENT (1968 1978) Use MAINSTREAMING
	CLASS PROJECTS Use CLASS ACTIVITIES
	CLASS RANK
RANK IN	CLASS Use CLASS RANK
	CLASS SIZE
SOCIAL	CLASS
MIDDLE	CLASS STANDARDS
	CLASS STATUS Use SOCIAL STATUS
LOWER	CLASS STUDENTS
MIDDLE	CLASS STUDENTS
UPPER	CLASS
MIDDLE	CLASS VALUES (1966 1980) Use MIDDLE CLASS STANDARDS
WORKING	CLASS
DAY	CLASSES Use DAY PROGRAMS
DESEGREGATED	CLASSES Use CLASSROOM DESEGREGATION
EVENING	CLASSES (1967 1980) Use EVENING PROGRAMS
	CLASSES (GROUPS OF STUDENTS)
HONORS	CLASSES (1966 1980) Use HONORS CURRICULUM
INTEGRATED	CLASSES Use CLASSROOM DESEGREGATION
FORM	CLASSES (LANGUAGES)
LITERACY	CLASSES (1966 1980) Use LITERACY EDUCATION
MULTIGRADED	CLASSES
NONAUTHORITARIAN	CLASSES
NONGRADED	CLASSES (1966 1980) Use NONGRADED INSTRUCTIONAL GROUPING
OPPORTUNITY	CLASSES (1966 1980) Use SPECIAL CLASSES
PREKINDERGARTEN	CLASSES Use PRESCHOOL EDUCATION
MULTILEVEL	CLASSES (SECOND LANGUAGE INSTRUCTION)
SMALL	CLASSES
SPECIAL	CLASSES
TRANSITIONAL	CLASSES (1966 1981) Use TRANSITIONAL PROGRAMS
UNGRADED	CLASSES (1966 1980) Use NONGRADED INSTRUCTIONAL GROUPING
	CLASSICAL CONDITIONING
	CLASSICAL GREEK Use GREEK

CLASSICAL LANGUAGES
CLASSICAL LITERATURE
CLASSICAL MECHANICS Use MECHANICS (PHYSICS)
CLASSIFICATION
CLASSIFICATION CLERKS Use FILE CLERKS
LANGUAGE CLASSIFICATION
SPACE CLASSIFICATION
CLASSROOM ACTIVITIES Use CLASS ACTIVITIES
CLASSROOM ARRANGEMENT (1966 1980) Use CLASSROOM DESIGN
CLASSROOM COMMUNICATION
CLASSROOM DESEGREGATION
CLASSROOM DESIGN
CLASSROOM DISCIPLINE Use CLASSROOM TECHNIQUES and DISCIPLINE
CLASSROOM ENVIRONMENT
CLASSROOM EQUIPMENT Use EDUCATIONAL EQUIPMENT
FURNITURE (CLASSROOM) Use CLASSROOM FURNITURE
CLASSROOM FURNITURE
CLASSROOM GAMES (1966 1980) Use CLASS ACTIVITIES and EDUCATIONAL GAMES
CLASSROOM GUIDANCE PROGRAMS (1968 1980)
CLASSROOM INTEGRATION (1967 1980) Use CLASSROOM DESEGREGATION
INTEREST CENTERS (CLASSROOM) Use LEARNING CENTERS (CLASSROOM)
LEARNING CENTERS (CLASSROOM)
LEARNING STATIONS (CLASSROOM) Use LEARNING CENTERS (CLASSROOM)
CLASSROOM LIBRARIES (1966 1980) Use INSTRUCTIONAL MATERIALS
CLASSROOM MATERIALS (1966 1980) Use INSTRUCTIONAL MATERIALS
CLASSROOM METHODS Use CLASSROOM TECHNIQUES
CLASSROOM OBSERVATION TECHNIQUES
CLASSROOM PARTICIPATION (1966 1980) Use CLASS ACTIVITIES and STUDENT PARTICIPATION
CLASSROOM RESEARCH
CLASSROOM SITUATION Use CLASSROOM ENVIRONMENT
CLASSROOM TECHNIQUES
ELECTRONIC CLASSROOM USE (1966 1980) Use ELECTRONIC CLASSROOMS
CLASSROOMS
ELECTRONIC CLASSROOMS
FLEXIBLE CLASSROOMS (1968 1980) Use CLASSROOMS and FLEXIBLE FACILITIES
MOBILE CLASSROOMS
MULTIPURPOSE CLASSROOMS
SELF CONTAINED CLASSROOMS
SELF DIRECTED CLASSROOMS (1966 1980)
TRADITIONAL CLASSROOMS Use SELF CONTAINED CLASSROOMS
CLEAN WATER Use WATER QUALITY
CLEANING
CLEARINGHOUSES
CLEFT LIP (1967 1980) Use CLEFT PALATE
CLEFT PALATE
CLERGY
CLERGYMEN (1968 1980) Use CLERGY
CLERICAL OCCUPATIONS
CLERICAL WORKERS
CLERK STENOGRAPHERS Use SHORTHAND
CLERK TYPISTS Use TYPEWRITING
AUTO PARTS CLERKS
CLASSIFICATION CLERKS Use FILE CLERKS
FILE CLERKS
LIBRARY CLERKS Use LIBRARY TECHNICIANS
MEDICAL RECORD CLERKS Use MEDICAL RECORD TECHNICIANS
RECORD CLERKS Use FILE CLERKS
SALES CLERKS Use SALES WORKERS
CLERKSHIPS (MEDICINE) Use CLINICAL EXPERIENCE
CLICHES
CLIENT BACKGROUND (HUMAN SERVICES) Use CLIENT CHARACTERISTICS (HUMAN SERVICES)
CLIENT CASEWORKERS (1966 1980) Use SOCIAL WORKERS
CLIENT CENTERED COUNSELING Use NONDIRECTIVE COUNSELING
CLIENT CHARACTERISTICS (HUMAN SERVICES)
CLIENT COUNSELOR RATIO Use COUNSELOR CLIENT RATIO
CLIENT COUNSELOR RELATIONSHIP Use COUNSELOR CLIENT RELATIONSHIP
COUNSELOR CLIENT RATIO
COUNSELOR CLIENT RELATIONSHIP
LIBRARY CLIENTS Use USERS (INFORMATION)
CLIMATE
CLIMATE CONTROL
ECONOMIC CLIMATE
ORGANIZATIONAL CLIMATE
SCHOOL CLIMATE Use EDUCATIONAL ENVIRONMENT
SOCIAL CLIMATE Use SOCIAL ENVIRONMENT
CLIMATIC FACTORS (1969 1980) Use CLIMATE
CLINIC PERSONNEL (SCHOOL) (1966 1980) Use ALLIED HEALTH PERSONNEL and SCHOOL HEALTH SERVICES
DIAGNOSIS (CLINICAL) Use CLINICAL DIAGNOSIS
CLINICAL DIAGNOSIS
CLINICAL EXPERIENCE
CLINICAL JUDGMENT (MEDICINE) Use MEDICAL EVALUATION
CLINICAL JUDGMENT (PSYCHOLOGY) Use PSYCHOLOGICAL EVALUATION
CLINICAL LEARNING EXPERIENCE Use CLINICAL EXPERIENCE
CLINICAL PROFESSORS (1967 1980) (EDUCATION) Use STUDENT TEACHER SUPERVISORS
CLINICAL PROFESSORS (1967 1980) (MEDICINE) Use MEDICAL SCHOOL FACULTY
CLINICAL PSYCHOLOGY
CLINICAL SERVICES Use CLINICS
CLINICAL TEACHING (HEALTH PROFESSIONS)
CLINICAL TEACHING (INDIVIDUALIZED INSTRUCTION) Use INDIVIDUALIZED INSTRUCTION
CLINICS
DENTAL CLINICS
HEARING CLINICS (1968 1980) Use SPEECH AND HEARING CLINICS
ITINERANT CLINICS (1966 1980) Use MOBILE CLINICS
MENTAL HEALTH CLINICS
MOBILE CLINICS
PRESCHOOL CLINICS (1966 1980) Use CLINICS and PRESCHOOL EDUCATION
PSYCHOEDUCATIONAL CLINICS
READING CLINICS (1966 1980) Use READING CENTERS
REMEDIAL READING CLINICS (1966 1980) Use READING CENTERS and REMEDIAL READING
RURAL CLINICS (1966 1980) Use CLINICS and RURAL AREAS

SPEECH CLINICS (1968 1980) Use SPEECH AND HEARING CLINICS
SPEECH AND HEARING CLINICS
FILM CLIPS Use FILMSTRIPS
CLOCKMAKERS Use WATCHMAKERS
CLOSED CIRCUIT TELEVISION
CLOSED SCHOOLS Use SCHOOL CLOSING
COLLEGE CLOSING Use SCHOOL CLOSING
SCHOOL CLOSING
CLOTHING
CLOTHING DESIGN
FASHIONS (CLOTHING) Use CLOTHING
CLOTHING INDUSTRY Use FASHION INDUSTRY
CLOTHING INSTRUCTION
CLOZE PROCEDURE
CLOZE TECHNIQUES Use CLOZE PROCEDURE
FOUR H CLUB AGENTS Use EXTENSION AGENTS
CLUBS
GIRLS CLUBS (1966 1980) Use YOUTH CLUBS
GLEE CLUBS Use SINGING
HOMEMAKERS CLUBS (1966 1980) Use CLUBS and HOMEMAKING SKILLS
SCIENCE CLUBS
YOUTH CLUBS
CLUES Use CUES
CONTEXT CLUES
CLUSTER ANALYSIS
CLUSTER COLLEGES
CLUSTER GROUPING
JOB CLUSTERS Use OCCUPATIONAL CLUSTERS
OCCUPATIONAL CLUSTERS
CMI Use COMPUTER MANAGED INSTRUCTION
CO OP PROGRAMS Use COOPERATIVE PROGRAMS
CO OPS Use COOPERATIVES
ATHLETIC COACHES
COACHING TEACHERS (1966 1974) Use TUTORS
TEST COACHING
COAL
BITUMINOUS COAL Use COAL
COAL MINING Use COAL and MINING
COAL RESOURCES Use COAL
COAST GUARD AIR STATIONS Use MILITARY AIR FACILITIES
COCOUNSELING
COCURRICULAR ACTIVITIES (1966 1980) Use EXTRACURRICULAR ACTIVITIES
CODE SWITCHING (LANGUAGE)
DRESS CODES
HONOR CODES Use CODES OF ETHICS
CODES OF ETHICS
CODIFICATION
COEDUCATION
SCHEMATA (COGNITION)
SOCIAL COGNITION
COGNITIVE ABILITY
COGNITIVE BEHAVIOR MODIFICATION Use BEHAVIOR MODIFICATION and COGNITIVE RESTRUCTURING
COGNITIVE DEVELOPMENT
COGNITIVE DISSONANCE
COGNITIVE MAPPING
COGNITIVE MEASUREMENT
COGNITIVE MODIFICATION Use COGNITIVE RESTRUCTURING
COGNITIVE OBJECTIVES
COGNITIVE PROCESSES
COGNITIVE PSYCHOLOGY
COGNITIVE RESTRUCTURING
COGNITIVE STRUCTURES
COGNITIVE STYLE
COGNITIVE TESTS
COGNITIVE THEORY Use EPISTEMOLOGY
COGNITIVE THERAPY Use COGNITIVE RESTRUCTURING
COHERENCE
COHESION (WRITTEN COMPOSITION)
GROUP COHESIVENESS Use GROUP UNITY
COHORT ANALYSIS
COLLABORATION Use COOPERATION
COLLABORATIVE DECISION MAKING Use PARTICIPATIVE DECISION MAKING
BLUE COLLAR OCCUPATIONS
WHITE COLLAR OCCUPATIONS
COLLECTED READINGS Use ANTHOLOGIES
DATA COLLECTION
COLLECTION DEVELOPMENT (LIBRARIES) Use LIBRARY COLLECTION DEVELOPMENT
LIBRARY COLLECTION DEVELOPMENT
LIBRARY COLLECTIONS
READINGS (COLLECTIONS) Use ANTHOLOGIES
COLLECTIVE BARGAINING
COLLECTIVE BEHAVIOR Use GROUP BEHAVIOR
COLLECTIVE DECISION MAKING Use PARTICIPATIVE DECISION MAKING
COLLECTIVE NEGOTIATION (1967 1977) Use COLLECTIVE BARGAINING
COLLECTIVE SETTLEMENTS
COLLEGE ADMINISTRATION
COLLEGE ADMISSION
COLLEGE APPLICANTS
COLLEGE ATHLETICS
COLLEGE ATTENDANCE
COLLEGE BOOKSTORES Use COLLEGE STORES
COLLEGE BOUND STUDENTS
COLLEGE BUILDINGS
COLLEGE CATALOGS Use SCHOOL CATALOGS
COLLEGE CHARACTERISTICS Use INSTITUTIONAL CHARACTERISTICS
COLLEGE CHOICE
COLLEGE CLOSING Use SCHOOL CLOSING
COLLEGE COMMUNITY RELATIONSHIP Use SCHOOL COMMUNITY RELATIONSHIP
COLLEGE COOPERATION (1966 1980) Use INTERCOLLEGIATE COOPERATION
HIGH SCHOOL COLLEGE COOPERATION Use COLLEGE SCHOOL COOPERATION
SCHOOL COLLEGE COOPERATION Use COLLEGE SCHOOL COOPERATION

	COLLEGE COSTS (INCURRED BY STUDENTS) Use STUDENT COSTS
	COLLEGE COUNSELORS Use SCHOOL COUNSELORS
	COLLEGE CREDITS
	COLLEGE CURRICULUM
	COLLEGE DAY
	COLLEGE DEANS (1968 1980) Use DEANS and HIGHER EDUCATION
TWO YEAR	COLLEGE DEGREES Use ASSOCIATE DEGREES
	COLLEGE DESEGREGATION
	COLLEGE DROPOUTS Use DROPOUTS
	COLLEGE ENGLISH
	COLLEGE ENROLLMENT Use ENROLLMENT
	COLLEGE ENTRANCE EXAMINATIONS
	COLLEGE ENVIRONMENT
	COLLEGE FACULTY
	COLLEGE FRESHMEN
	COLLEGE GOVERNING COUNCILS
	COLLEGE GRADUATES
	COLLEGE HIGH SCHOOL COOPERATION (1967 1980) Use COLLEGE SCHOOL COOPERATION
	COLLEGE HOUSING
	COLLEGE INSTRUCTION
	COLLEGE INTEGRATION (1966 1980) Use COLLEGE DESEGREGATION
	COLLEGE LANGUAGE PROGRAMS (1967 1980)
	COLLEGE LIBRARIES
JUNIOR	COLLEGE LIBRARIES (1966 1980) Use COLLEGE LIBRARIES and TWO YEAR COLLEGES
	COLLEGE MAJORS (1968 1980) Use MAJORS (STUDENTS)
	COLLEGE MATHEMATICS
	COLLEGE NIGHT Use COLLEGE DAY
	COLLEGE PLACEMENT (1966 1980) Use STUDENT PLACEMENT
	COLLEGE PLANNING
	COLLEGE PREPARATION
	COLLEGE PRESIDENTS
	COLLEGE PROGRAMS
	COLLEGE REGISTRARS Use REGISTRARS (SCHOOL)
	COLLEGE REGISTRATION Use SCHOOL REGISTRATION
FACULTY	COLLEGE RELATIONSHIP
STUDENT	COLLEGE RELATIONSHIP
TEACHER	COLLEGE RELATIONSHIP Use FACULTY COLLEGE RELATIONSHIP
	COLLEGE ROLE
	COLLEGE SCHOOL COOPERATION
	COLLEGE SCIENCE
	COLLEGE SECOND LANGUAGE PROGRAMS
	COLLEGE SEGREGATION
	COLLEGE SENIORS
	COLLEGE STORES
STUDENT HOUSING	(COLLEGE) Use COLLEGE HOUSING
	COLLEGE STUDENT RELATIONSHIP Use STUDENT COLLEGE RELATIONSHIP
	COLLEGE STUDENTS
FRESHMEN (1967 1980) (FIRST YEAR	COLLEGE STUDENTS) Use COLLEGE FRESHMEN
JUNIOR	COLLEGE STUDENTS (1969 1980) Use TWO YEAR COLLEGE STUDENTS
MIDDLE CLASS	COLLEGE STUDENTS (1966 1980) Use COLLEGE STUDENTS and MIDDLE CLASS STUDENTS
TWO YEAR	COLLEGE STUDENTS
	COLLEGE SUPERVISORS (1967 1980) Use STUDENT TEACHER SUPERVISORS
	COLLEGE TEACHERS (1967 1980) Use COLLEGE FACULTY
	COLLEGE TEACHING Use COLLEGE INSTRUCTION
MASTER OF ARTS IN	COLLEGE TEACHING Use MASTERS DEGREES
	COLLEGE TRANSFER STUDENTS
	COLLEGE UNIONS Use STUDENT UNIONS
	COLLEGE WORK STUDY PROGRAMS Use WORK STUDY PROGRAMS
	COLLEGES
AGRICULTURAL	COLLEGES
ALUMNI	COLLEGES Use ALUMNI EDUCATION
BLACK	COLLEGES
CHURCH RELATED	COLLEGES
CLUSTER	COLLEGES
COMMUNITY	COLLEGES
COMMUTER	COLLEGES
CORPORATE	COLLEGES Use CORPORATE EDUCATION
DENOMINATIONAL	COLLEGES Use CHURCH RELATED COLLEGES
DESEGREGATED	COLLEGES Use COLLEGE DESEGREGATION
ELITE	COLLEGES Use SELECTIVE COLLEGES
EVENING	COLLEGES (1967 1980) Use EVENING PROGRAMS
EXPERIMENTAL	COLLEGES
HISTORICALLY BLACK	COLLEGES Use BLACK COLLEGES
INDEPENDENT	COLLEGES Use PRIVATE COLLEGES
INTEGRATED	COLLEGES Use COLLEGE DESEGREGATION
JUNIOR	COLLEGES (1966 1980) Use TWO YEAR COLLEGES
LAND GRANT	COLLEGES Use LAND GRANT UNIVERSITIES
MULTICAMPUS	COLLEGES
NEGRO	COLLEGES (1968 1977) Use BLACK COLLEGES
NONCAMPUS	COLLEGES
	COLLEGES OF EDUCATION Use SCHOOLS OF EDUCATION
PRIVATE	COLLEGES
PRIVATE JUNIOR	COLLEGES Use PRIVATE COLLEGES and TWO YEAR COLLEGES
PUBLIC	COLLEGES
RESIDENTIAL	COLLEGES
SECTARIAN	COLLEGES Use CHURCH RELATED COLLEGES
SELECTIVE	COLLEGES
SINGLE SEX	COLLEGES
SMALL	COLLEGES
STATE	COLLEGES
TEACHERS	COLLEGES (1966 1980) Use SCHOOLS OF EDUCATION
TWO YEAR	COLLEGES
UPPER DIVISION	COLLEGES
	COLLOQUIAL STANDARD USAGE Use STANDARD SPOKEN USAGE
	COLLOQUIUMS (MEETINGS) Use MEETINGS
	COLONIAL HISTORY (UNITED STATES)
	COLONIALISM
	COLONIZATION Use LAND SETTLEMENT
LAND	COLONIZATION Use LAND SETTLEMENT
	COLOR
	COLOR FILMS Use FILMS

	COLOR PLANNING
	COLOR PRESENTATION (1969 1980) Use COLOR
	COLOR TELEVISION (1969 1980) Use COLOR and TELEVISION
LOCAL	COLOR WRITING
	COM Use COMPUTER OUTPUT MICROFILM
SENTENCE	COMBINING
TRANSFORMATIONAL SENTENCE	COMBINING Use SENTENCE COMBINING
	COMEDY
	COMEDY OF MANNERS Use COMEDY
	COMICS (PUBLICATIONS)
	COMMENCEMENT CEREMONIES
	COMMERCIAL ART
	COMMERCIAL COMMUNICATION Use BUSINESS COMMUNICATION
	COMMERCIAL CORRESPONDENCE SCHOOLS Use CORRESPONDENCE SCHOOLS
	COMMERCIAL EDUCATION Use BUSINESS EDUCATION
	COMMERCIAL ENTERPRISES Use BUSINESS
	COMMERCIAL PILOTS Use AIRCRAFT PILOTS
	COMMERCIAL SEARCH SERVICES (ONLINE) Use ONLINE VENDORS
	COMMERCIAL TELEVISION
TELEVISION	COMMERCIALS
BLUE RIBBON	COMMISSIONS
CITY WIDE	COMMISSIONS (1966 1980) Use PLANNING COMMISSIONS and URBAN PLANNING
PLANNING	COMMISSIONS
	COMMITTEES
ADVISORY	COMMITTEES
BIRACIAL	COMMITTEES
COMMUNITY	COMMITTEES Use COMMUNITY ORGANIZATIONS
STATE	COMMITTEES ON EDUCATION Use STATE BOARDS OF EDUCATION
SEARCH	COMMITTEES (PERSONNEL)
SELECTION	COMMITTEES (PERSONNEL) Use SEARCH COMMITTEES (PERSONNEL)
RESEARCH	COMMITTEES
	COMMON FRACTIONS (1966 1980) Use FRACTIONS
LESS	COMMONLY TAUGHT LANGUAGES Use UNCOMMONLY TAUGHT LANGUAGES
	COMMUNAL LIVING Use COLLECTIVE SETTLEMENTS and GROUP EXPERIENCE
	COMMUNICABLE DISEASES
	COMMUNICATION AIDS (FOR DISABLED)
	COMMUNICATION APPREHENSION
AUDIOVISUAL	COMMUNICATION (1967 1980) Use AUDIOVISUAL COMMUNICATIONS
	COMMUNICATION AUDITS
BUSINESS	COMMUNICATION
CLASSROOM	COMMUNICATION
COMMERCIAL	COMMUNICATION Use BUSINESS COMMUNICATION
CONFERENCE SKILLS	(COMMUNICATION) Use COMMUNICATION SKILLS
CROSS CULTURAL	COMMUNICATION Use INTERCULTURAL COMMUNICATION
SPEECH	COMMUNICATION CURRICULUM Use SPEECH COMMUNICATION and SPEECH CURRICULUM
DIFFUSION (1967 1982)	(COMMUNICATION) Use DIFFUSION (COMMUNICATION)
DIFFUSION	(COMMUNICATION)
	COMMUNICATION DISORDERS
DYADIC	COMMUNICATION Use INTERPERSONAL COMMUNICATION
GESTURES (DEAF	COMMUNICATION) Use SIGN LANGUAGE
GESTURES (NONVERBAL	COMMUNICATION) Use BODY LANGUAGE
INDUSTRIAL	COMMUNICATION Use BUSINESS COMMUNICATION
INTERCULTURAL	COMMUNICATION
INTERPERSONAL	COMMUNICATION
INTERSCHOOL	COMMUNICATION
MANUAL	COMMUNICATION
ORAL	COMMUNICATION METHOD
NONVERBAL	COMMUNICATION
OFFICE	COMMUNICATION Use ORGANIZATIONAL COMMUNICATION
ORAL	COMMUNICATION (1966 1977) Use SPEECH COMMUNICATION
ORGANIZATIONAL	COMMUNICATION
PRIVILEGED	COMMUNICATION Use CONFIDENTIALITY
	COMMUNICATION PROBLEMS
RECEPTIVE	COMMUNICATION Use RECEPTIVE LANGUAGE
	COMMUNICATION RESEARCH
SPEECH	COMMUNICATION RESEARCH Use COMMUNICATION RESEARCH and SPEECH COMMUNICATION
	COMMUNICATION SATELLITES (1967 1980) Use COMMUNICATIONS SATELLITES
SCHOOL COMMUNITY	COMMUNICATION Use SCHOOL COMMUNITY RELATIONSHIP
	COMMUNICATION SKILLS
SPEECH	COMMUNICATION
FACSIMILE	COMMUNICATION SYSTEMS (1968 1980) Use FACSIMILE TRANSMISSION
TELEPHONE	COMMUNICATION SYSTEMS (1967 1980) Use TELEPHONE COMMUNICATIONS SYSTEMS
	COMMUNICATION THEORY Use COMMUNICATION (THOUGHT TRANSFER)
	COMMUNICATION (THOUGHT TRANSFER)
TOTAL	COMMUNICATION
VERBAL	COMMUNICATION
	COMMUNICATIONS
AUDIOVISUAL	COMMUNICATIONS
BROADCAST	COMMUNICATIONS Use TELECOMMUNICATIONS
TELEPHONE	COMMUNICATIONS INDUSTRY
MASS	COMMUNICATIONS Use MASS MEDIA
	COMMUNICATIONS MEDIA Use MASS MEDIA
	COMMUNICATIONS NETWORKS Use COMMUNICATIONS
	COMMUNICATIONS SATELLITES
	COMMUNICATIONS SERVICES Use COMMUNICATIONS
	COMMUNICATIONS SYSTEMS Use COMMUNICATIONS
ELECTRONIC	COMMUNICATIONS SYSTEMS Use TELECOMMUNICATIONS
TELEPHONE	COMMUNICATIONS SYSTEMS
	COMMUNICATIONS THEORY Use INFORMATION THEORY
WIRE	COMMUNICATIONS Use TELECOMMUNICATIONS
WIRELESS	COMMUNICATIONS Use TELECOMMUNICATIONS
	COMMUNICATIVE COMPETENCE (LANGUAGES)
	COMMUNISM
	COMMUNISTIC SETTLEMENTS Use COLLECTIVE SETTLEMENTS
PLANNED	COMMUNITIES
THERAPEUTIC	COMMUNITIES Use MILIEU THERAPY
	COMMUNITY
	COMMUNITY ACTION
ACTION PROGRAMS	(COMMUNITY) (1966 1980) Use COMMUNITY ACTION
	COMMUNITY AGENCIES (PUBLIC) (1966 1980) Use PUBLIC AGENCIES
	COMMUNITY ANALYSIS Use COMMUNITY STUDY

COMMUNITY ANTENNAS (1966 1980) Use CABLE TELEVISION
COMMUNITY ATTITUDES
COMMUNITY BENEFITS
BLACK COMMUNITY
COMMUNITY CENTERS
COMMUNITY CHANGE
COMMUNITY CHARACTERISTICS
COMMUNITY COLLEGES
COMMUNITY COMMITTEES Use COMMUNITY ORGANIZATIONS
SCHOOL COMMUNITY COMMUNICATION Use SCHOOL COMMUNITY RELATIONSHIP
COMMUNITY COMPLIANCE Use COMMUNITY COOPERATION
COMMUNITY CONSULTANT PROGRAMS (1966 1980) Use CONSULTATION PROGRAMS
COMMUNITY CONSULTANTS (1966 1980) Use CONSULTANTS
COMMUNITY CONTROL
COMMUNITY COOPERATION
SCHOOL COMMUNITY COOPERATION (1966 1980) Use SCHOOL COMMUNITY RELATIONSHIP
COMMUNITY COORDINATION
SCHOOL COMMUNITY COORDINATION Use SCHOOL COMMUNITY RELATIONSHIP
COMMUNITY COORDINATORS (1966 1980) Use COMMUNITY COORDINATION and COORDINATORS
COMMUNITY DEVELOPMENT
COMMUNITY EDUCATION
COMMUNITY EFFORT Use COMMUNITY ACTION
COMMUNITY ENTERPRISES Use COMMUNITY PROGRAMS
ETHNIC COMMUNITY Use ETHNIC GROUPS
COMMUNITY EXPERIENCE Use EXPERIENTIAL LEARNING
COMMUNITY HEALTH (1966 1980) Use PUBLIC HEALTH
COMMUNITY HEALTH SERVICES
COMMUNITY HEALTH WORKERS Use COMMUNITY HEALTH SERVICES and HEALTH PERSONNEL
COMMUNITY HISTORY Use LOCAL HISTORY
COMMUNITY INFLUENCE
COMMUNITY INFORMATION CENTERS Use COMMUNITY INFORMATION SERVICES
INFORMATION SERVICES (COMMUNITY) Use COMMUNITY INFORMATION SERVICES
COMMUNITY INFORMATION SERVICES
SCHOOL COMMUNITY INTERACTION Use SCHOOL COMMUNITY RELATIONSHIP
COMMUNITY INVOLVEMENT
COMMUNITY LEADERS
COMMUNITY LEGISLATION Use LOCAL LEGISLATION
COMMUNITY MIGRANT PROJECTS (1966 1980) Use COMMUNITY PROGRAMS and MIGRANT PROGRAMS
NEGRO COMMUNITY Use BLACK COMMUNITY
COMMUNITY ORGANIZATIONS
COMMUNITY OUTREACH Use OUTREACH PROGRAMS
COMMUNITY PARTICIPATION Use COMMUNITY INVOLVEMENT
PLANNED COMMUNITY (1966 1980) Use PLANNED COMMUNITIES
COMMUNITY PLANNING
COMMUNITY POLICE RELATIONSHIP Use POLICE COMMUNITY RELATIONSHIP
COMMUNITY PROBLEMS
COMMUNITY PROGRAMS
LOCAL COMMUNITY PROGRAMS Use COMMUNITY PROGRAMS
SCHOOL COMMUNITY PROGRAMS
COMMUNITY PROJECTS Use COMMUNITY PROGRAMS
COMMUNITY PSYCHOLOGY
COMMUNITY RECREATION LEGISLATION (1966 1978) Use LOCAL LEGISLATION and RECREATION LEGISLATION
COMMUNITY RECREATION PROGRAMS
REFERRAL SERVICES (COMMUNITY) Use COMMUNITY INFORMATION SERVICES and REFERRAL
COMMUNITY RELATIONS
COLLEGE COMMUNITY RELATIONSHIP Use SCHOOL COMMUNITY RELATIONSHIP
POLICE COMMUNITY RELATIONSHIP
SCHOOL COMMUNITY RELATIONSHIP
COMMUNITY RESOURCES
COMMUNITY RESPONSIBILITY
COMMUNITY ROLE
COMMUNITY ROOMS (1967 1980) Use COMMUNITY CENTERS
COMMUNITY SATISFACTION
COMMUNITY SCHOOL DIRECTORS (1967 1980) Use ADMINISTRATORS and COMMUNITY SCHOOLS
COMMUNITY SCHOOL PROGRAMS Use SCHOOL COMMUNITY PROGRAMS
COMMUNITY SCHOOL RELATIONSHIP Use SCHOOL COMMUNITY RELATIONSHIP
COMMUNITY SCHOOLS
COMMUNITY SERVICE PROGRAMS (1966 1980) Use COMMUNITY SERVICES
COMMUNITY SERVICES
COMMUNITY SIZE
SOUTHERN COMMUNITY (1966 1980)
COMMUNITY STUDY
COMMUNITY SUPPORT
COMMUNITY SURVEYS
COMMUNITY TENSIONS Use COMMUNITY PROBLEMS
COMMUNITY TRAITS Use COMMUNITY CHARACTERISTICS
COMMUNITY WORKERS Use COMMUNITY ORGANIZATIONS
COMMUNITY ZONING
COMMUTER COLLEGES
COMMUTING STUDENTS
COMPACT DISKS Use OPTICAL DISKS
INSURANCE COMPANIES
COMPANIONS (OCCUPATION) (1968 1980) Use ATTENDANTS
COMPANY SIZE (INDUSTRY) Use ORGANIZATION SIZE (GROUPS)
COMPARABLE INSTITUTIONS Use PEER INSTITUTIONS
COMPARABLE WORTH
COMPARATIVE ANALYSIS
COMPARATIVE EDUCATION
COMPARATIVE EVALUATION Use COMPARATIVE ANALYSIS
COMPARATIVE LINGUISTICS Use CONTRASTIVE LINGUISTICS
COMPARATIVE STATISTICS (1966 1980) Use COMPARATIVE ANALYSIS and STATISTICAL ANALYSIS
COMPARATIVE STUDY Use COMPARATIVE ANALYSIS
COMPARATIVE TESTING
AUDIO ACTIVE COMPARE LABORATORIES (1967 1980) Use LANGUAGE LABORATORIES
ACHIEVEMENT COMPARISON Use ACHIEVEMENT RATING
EDUCATIONAL STATUS COMPARISON
CULTURAL COMPARISONS Use CROSS CULTURAL STUDIES
COMPENSATION (CONCEPT)
COMPENSATION (REMUNERATION)
WORKERS COMPENSATION

WORKMANS COMPENSATION (1966 1980) Use WORKERS COMPENSATION
COMPENSATORY DEVELOPMENT Use COMPENSATORY EDUCATION
COMPENSATORY EDUCATION
COMPENSATORY EDUCATION PROGRAMS (1966 1980) Use COMPENSATORY EDUCATION
COMPENSATORY OPPORTUNITY Use COMPENSATORY EDUCATION
COMPETENCE
INTERPERSONAL COMPETENCE
COMMUNICATIVE COMPETENCE (LANGUAGES)
LINGUISTIC COMPETENCE
SOCIAL COMPETENCE Use INTERPERSONAL COMPETENCE
MINIMAL COMPETENCIES Use MINIMUM COMPETENCIES
MINIMUM COMPETENCIES
COMPETENCY Use COMPETENCE
COMPETENCY BASED EDUCATION
COMPETENCY BASED TEACHER EDUCATION
MINIMAL COMPETENCY TESTING Use MINIMUM COMPETENCY TESTING
MINIMUM COMPETENCY TESTING
NATIONAL COMPETENCY TESTS
COMPETITION
COMPETITIVE BIDDING Use BIDS
COMPETITIVE SELECTION
EDUCATIONAL COMPLEXES
COMPLEXITY LEVEL (1968 1979) Use DIFFICULTY LEVEL
COMMUNITY COMPLIANCE Use COMMUNITY COOPERATION
COMPLIANCE (LEGAL)
COMPLIANCE (PSYCHOLOGY)
COMPONENT BUILDING SYSTEMS (1968 1976) Use BUILDING SYSTEMS
COMPONENT SYSTEMS Use BUILDING SYSTEMS
COMPONENTIAL ANALYSIS
PRINCIPAL COMPONENTS ANALYSIS Use FACTOR ANALYSIS
COHESION (WRITTEN COMPOSITION)
FRESHMAN COMPOSITION
COMPOSITION (LITERARY) (1966 1980) Use WRITING (COMPOSITION)
COMPOSITION MEASUREMENT Use CHEMICAL ANALYSIS
COMPOSITION (MUSIC) Use MUSICAL COMPOSITION
MUSICAL COMPOSITION
PARAGRAPH COMPOSITION
COMPOSITION PROCESSES (LITERARY) Use WRITING PROCESSES
RACIAL COMPOSITION
REVISION (WRITTEN COMPOSITION)
COMPOSITION SKILLS (LITERARY) (1966 1980) Use WRITING SKILLS
WRITING (COMPOSITION)
COORDINATION COMPOUNDS
COMPREHENSION
AUDITORY COMPREHENSION Use LISTENING COMPREHENSION
AURAL COMPREHENSION Use LISTENING COMPREHENSION
COMPREHENSION DEVELOPMENT (1966 1980) Use COMPREHENSION
LISTENING COMPREHENSION
READING COMPREHENSION
LISTENING COMPREHENSION TESTS
COMPREHENSIVE DISTRICTS (1967 1980) Use SCHOOL DISTRICTS
COMPREHENSIVE HIGH SCHOOLS (1967 1980) Use HIGH SCHOOLS
COMPREHENSIVE PROGRAMS
COMPRESSED WORK WEEK Use FLEXIBLE WORKING HOURS
SPEECH COMPRESSION
COMPULSORY ATTENDANCE Use COMPULSORY EDUCATION
COMPULSORY EDUCATION
COMPUTATION
COMPUTATIONAL LINGUISTICS
COMPUTER AIDED INSTRUCTION Use COMPUTER ASSISTED INSTRUCTION
COMPUTER AIDED INSTRUCTIONAL MANAGEMENT Use COMPUTER MANAGED INSTRUCTION
COMPUTER APPLICATIONS Use COMPUTER ORIENTED PROGRAMS
COMPUTER ASSISTED INDEXING Use AUTOMATIC INDEXING
COMPUTER ASSISTED INSTRUCTION
COMPUTER ASSISTED LEARNING Use COMPUTER ASSISTED INSTRUCTION
COMPUTER ASSISTED TESTING
COMPUTER BASED INSTRUCTION Use COMPUTER ASSISTED INSTRUCTION
COMPUTER BASED INSTRUCTIONAL MANAGEMENT Use COMPUTER MANAGED INSTRUCTION
COMPUTER BASED LABORATORIES (1967 1980) Use COMPUTER ASSISTED INSTRUCTION and LABORATORIES
COMPUTER BASED MESSAGE SYSTEMS Use ELECTRONIC MAIL
COMPUTER BASED REFERENCE SERVICES Use ONLINE SYSTEMS and REFERENCE SERVICES
COMPUTER CONFERENCING Use TELECONFERENCING
COMPUTER GRAPHICS
COMPUTER LANGUAGES Use PROGRAMING LANGUAGES
COMPUTER LITERACY
COMPUTER MANAGED INSTRUCTION
COMPUTER NETWORKS
COMPUTER ORIENTED PROGRAMS
COMPUTER OUTPUT MICROFILM
COMPUTER PROGRAM DOCUMENTATION Use COMPUTER SOFTWARE
COMPUTER PROGRAM REVIEWS Use COMPUTER SOFTWARE REVIEWS
COMPUTER PROGRAMING Use PROGRAMING
COMPUTER PROGRAMS (1966 1984) Use COMPUTER SOFTWARE
COMPUTER SCIENCE
COMPUTER SCIENCE EDUCATION
COMPUTER SIMULATION
COMPUTER SOFTWARE
COMPUTER SOFTWARE REVIEWS
COMPUTER STORAGE DEVICES
COMPUTER TAPES Use COMPUTER STORAGE DEVICES and MAGNETIC TAPES
COMPUTER TECHNOLOGY Use COMPUTERS
COMPUTER TERMINALS Use INPUT OUTPUT DEVICES
COMPUTER USES IN EDUCATION
COMPUTERIZED ADAPTIVE TESTING Use ADAPTIVE TESTING and COMPUTER ASSISTED TESTING
DRAWING (COMPUTERIZED) Use COMPUTER GRAPHICS
COMPUTERIZED TAILORED TESTING Use ADAPTIVE TESTING and COMPUTER ASSISTED TESTING
COMPUTERS
ANALOG COMPUTERS
DESKTOP COMPUTERS Use MICROCOMPUTERS
DIGITAL COMPUTERS

	CONSERVATISM
	CONSISTENCY Use RELIABILITY
	CONSOLIDATED SCHOOLS
SCHOOL	CONSOLIDATION Use CONSOLIDATED SCHOOLS
	CONSONANTS
	CONSORTIA
	CONSORTIUMS Use CONSORTIA
EQUILIBRIUM	CONSTANTS Use CHEMICAL EQUILIBRIUM
	CONSTITUENT STRUCTURE Use PHRASE STRUCTURE
	CONSTITUTIONAL HISTORY
	CONSTITUTIONAL LAW
DESIGN	CONSTRUCT METHOD Use DESIGN BUILD APPROACH
	CONSTRUCT VALIDITY
	CONSTRUCTED LANGUAGES Use ARTIFICIAL LANGUAGES
	CONSTRUCTED RESPONSE
	CONSTRUCTION BIDDING Use BIDS
	CONSTRUCTION COSTS
HIGHWAY	CONSTRUCTION Use ROAD CONSTRUCTION
	CONSTRUCTION INDUSTRY
	CONSTRUCTION MANAGEMENT
	CONSTRUCTION MATERIALS
	CONSTRUCTION NEEDS
	CONSTRUCTION OCCUPATIONS Use BUILDING TRADES
	CONSTRUCTION (PROCESS)
	CONSTRUCTION PROGRAMS
ROAD	CONSTRUCTION
SCHOOL	CONSTRUCTION
STRUCTURAL ELEMENTS	(CONSTRUCTION)
TEST	CONSTRUCTION
GEOMETRIC	CONSTRUCTIONS
COMMUNITY	CONSULTANT PROGRAMS (1966 1980) Use CONSULTATION PROGRAMS
	CONSULTANTS
COMMUNITY	CONSULTANTS (1966 1980) Use CONSULTANTS
MEDICAL	CONSULTANTS
READING	CONSULTANTS
SCIENCE	CONSULTANTS
	CONSULTATION PROGRAMS
	CONSUMER BEHAVIOR Use CONSUMER ECONOMICS
	CONSUMER ECONOMICS
	CONSUMER EDUCATION
	CONSUMER EXPENDITURES Use CONSUMER ECONOMICS
	CONSUMER PROTECTION
	CONSUMER SCIENCE
	CONSUMERISM Use CONSUMER PROTECTION
FUEL	CONSUMPTION
CULTURE	CONTACT
EYE	CONTACT
	CONTAGIOUS DISEASES Use COMMUNICABLE DISEASES
SELF	CONTAINED CLASSROOMS
	CONTEMPORARY HISTORY Use MODERN HISTORY
	CONTENT ANALYSIS
JOB	CONTENT ANALYSIS Use JOB ANALYSIS
	CONTENT AREA READING
	CONTENT AREA WRITING
READING IN	CONTENT AREAS Use CONTENT AREA READING
CONTROVERSIAL ISSUES (COURSE	CONTENT)
COURSE	CONTENT
CURRICULUM	CONTENT Use CURRICULUM
JOB	CONTENT Use OCCUPATIONAL INFORMATION
PROGRAM	CONTENT
	CONTENT READING (1967 1980) Use CONTENT AREA READING
TEXTBOOK	CONTENT
	CONTENT VALIDITY
	CONTEXT CLUES
CULTURAL	CONTEXT
	CONTEXT FREE GRAMMAR
KEY WORD IN	CONTEXT Use PERMUTED INDEXES
	CONTINGENCY CONTRACTS Use CONTINGENCY MANAGEMENT
	CONTINGENCY MANAGEMENT
INCOME	CONTINGENT LOANS
RESPONSE	CONTINGENT TESTING Use ADAPTIVE TESTING
	CONTINUATION EDUCATION (1968 1980)
	CONTINUATION HIGH SCHOOLS (1968 1980) Use CONTINUATION STUDENTS
	CONTINUATION STUDENTS
	CONTINUING EDUCATION
	CONTINUING EDUCATION CENTERS
PROFESSIONAL	CONTINUING EDUCATION
	CONTINUING EDUCATION UNITS
DEVELOPMENTAL	CONTINUITY
	CONTINUITY OF EDUCATION Use DEVELOPMENTAL CONTINUITY
	CONTINUOUS GUIDANCE (1966 1980) Use GUIDANCE
	CONTINUOUS LEARNING (1967 1980) Use LIFELONG LEARNING
	CONTINUOUS PROGRESS PLAN
SPACE TIME	CONTINUUM Use RELATIVITY
INTONATION	CONTOURS Use INTONATION
	CONTRACEPTION
	CONTRACT GRADING Use GRADING and PERFORMANCE CONTRACTS
	CONTRACT SALARIES
	CONTRACTOR VEHICLES Use SERVICE VEHICLES
	CONTRACTS
BEHAVIORAL	CONTRACTS Use PERFORMANCE CONTRACTS
CONTINGENCY	CONTRACTS Use CONTINGENCY MANAGEMENT
LEARNING	CONTRACTS Use PERFORMANCE CONTRACTS
PERFORMANCE	CONTRACTS
STUDENT LEARNING	CONTRACTS Use PERFORMANCE CONTRACTS
	CONTRAST
	CONTRAST RATIOS Use CONTRAST
	CONTRASTIVE LANGUAGE ANALYSIS Use CONTRASTIVE LINGUISTICS
LINGUISTIC DIFFICULTY	(CONTRASTIVE) Use INTERFERENCE (LANGUAGE)
	CONTRASTIVE LINGUISTICS
PARENT FINANCIAL	CONTRIBUTION

PARENTAL FINANCIAL CONTRIBUTION (1978 1980) Use PARENT FINANCIAL CONTRIBUTION
AIR POLLUTION CONTROL (1967 1980) Use AIR POLLUTION
AIR TRAFFIC CONTROL
ARMS CONTROL Use DISARMAMENT
ATTENTION CONTROL
BIBLIOGRAPHIC CONTROL Use CATALOGING
BIRTH CONTROL Use CONTRACEPTION
CLIMATE CONTROL
COMMUNITY CONTROL
DESTINY CONTROL Use SELF DETERMINATION
DISEASE CONTROL
ELECTRONIC CONTROL
FEDERAL CONTROL Use FEDERAL REGULATION
CONTROL GROUPS
IMPULSE CONTROL Use SELF CONTROL
INTERNAL EXTERNAL LOCUS OF CONTROL Use LOCUS OF CONTROL
LOCUS OF CONTROL
NOISE CONTROL Use NOISE (SOUND)
NUCLEAR CONTROL Use DISARMAMENT
NUMERICAL CONTROL
LOCAL CONTROL (OF SCHOOLS) Use SCHOOL DISTRICT AUTONOMY
PEST CONTROL Use PESTS
PROPERTY CONTROL Use PROPERTY ACCOUNTING
QUALITY CONTROL
SELF CONTROL
SOCIAL CONTROL
SPECTATOR TRAFFIC CONTROL Use TRAFFIC CONTROL
PROPERTY CONTROL SYSTEMS Use PROPERTY ACCOUNTING
TRAFFIC CONTROL
WATER POLLUTION CONTROL (1969 1980) Use WATER POLLUTION
CONTROLLED ENVIRONMENT (1966 1980)
ELECTRICAL CONTROLS Use ELECTRONIC CONTROL
PARKING CONTROLS
STATIC CONTROLS Use ELECTRONIC CONTROL
CONTROVERSIAL ISSUES (COURSE CONTENT)
ENVIRONMENT HEREDITY CONTROVERSY Use NATURE NURTURE CONTROVERSY
HEREDITY ENVIRONMENT CONTROVERSY Use NATURE NURTURE CONTROVERSY
LEARNING MATURATION CONTROVERSY Use NATURE NURTURE CONTROVERSY
MATURATION LEARNING CONTROVERSY Use NATURE NURTURE CONTROVERSY
NATURE NURTURE CONTROVERSY
CONVALESCENT HOMES Use NURSING HOMES
CONVENTIONAL INSTRUCTION
CONVENTIONAL WARFARE Use WAR
LITERARY CONVENTIONS (1968 1980) Use LITERARY DEVICES
CONVERGENT THINKING
CONVERSATIONAL LANGUAGE COURSES
INFORMAL CONVERSATIONAL USAGE Use STANDARD SPOKEN USAGE
BUILDING CONVERSION
CONVICTS Use CRIMINALS
COOKING INSTRUCTION
COOKS
COOPERATING SCHOOLS Use AFFILIATED SCHOOLS
COOPERATING TEACHERS
COOPERATION
AGENCY COOPERATION
COLLEGE COOPERATION (1966 1980) Use INTERCOLLEGIATE COOPERATION
COLLEGE HIGH SCHOOL COOPERATION (1967 1980) Use COLLEGE SCHOOL COOPERATION
COLLEGE SCHOOL COOPERATION
COMMUNITY COOPERATION
COUNSELOR TEACHER COOPERATION
EDUCATIONAL COOPERATION
HIGH SCHOOL COLLEGE COOPERATION Use COLLEGE SCHOOL COOPERATION
INSTITUTIONAL COOPERATION
INTERAGENCY COOPERATION (1967 1980) Use AGENCY COOPERATION
INTERCOLLEGIATE COOPERATION
INTERINSTITUTIONAL COOPERATION (1968 1980) Use INSTITUTIONAL COOPERATION
INTERNATIONAL COOPERATION
LIBRARY COOPERATION
PARENT TEACHER COOPERATION
REGIONAL COOPERATION
SCHOOL COLLEGE COOPERATION Use COLLEGE SCHOOL COOPERATION
SCHOOL COMMUNITY COOPERATION (1966 1980) Use SCHOOL COMMUNITY RELATIONSHIP
TEACHER COUNSELOR COOPERATION Use COUNSELOR TEACHER COOPERATION
TEACHER PARENT COOPERATION Use PARENT TEACHER COOPERATION
COOPERATIVE ACTIVITIES Use GROUP ACTIVITIES
COOPERATIVE EDUCATION
COOPERATIVE EXTENSION Use EXTENSION EDUCATION
COOPERATIVE PLANNING
COOPERATIVE PROGRAMS
COOPERATIVE TEACHING (1966 1980) Use TEAM TEACHING
COOPERATIVE TRAINING Use COOPERATIVE EDUCATION
COOPERATIVES
COORDINATE GEOMETRY Use ANALYTIC GEOMETRY
COORDINATE INDEXES
POST COORDINATE INDEXES Use COORDINATE INDEXES
RESEARCH COORDINATING UNITS
COORDINATION
COMMUNITY COORDINATION
COORDINATION COMPOUNDS
EDUCATIONAL COORDINATION (1967 1980) Use COORDINATION and EDUCATIONAL COOPERATION
EYE HAND COORDINATION
INTERAGENCY COORDINATION (1967 1980) Use AGENCY COOPERATION and COORDINATION
PERCEPTUAL MOTOR COORDINATION
PROGRAM COORDINATION (1966 1980) Use COOPERATIVE PROGRAMS and COORDINATION
COORDINATION (PSYCHOMOTOR) Use PSYCHOMOTOR SKILLS
SCHOOL COMMUNITY COORDINATION Use SCHOOL COMMUNITY RELATIONSHIP
STATEWIDE COORDINATION Use STATEWIDE PLANNING
COORDINATOR TRAINERS Use INSTRUCTOR COORDINATORS
COORDINATORS
AUDIOVISUAL COORDINATORS
COMMUNITY COORDINATORS (1966 1980) Use COMMUNITY COORDINATION and COORDINATORS

	COUNSELING PROCESS Use COUNSELING
	COUNSELING PROGRAMS (1966 1980) Use COUNSELING SERVICES
EVENING	COUNSELING PROGRAMS (1966 1980) Use COUNSELING SERVICES and EVENING PROGRAMS
REHABILITATION	COUNSELING
SCHOOL	COUNSELING
SECONDARY SCHOOL	COUNSELING Use SCHOOL COUNSELING
	COUNSELING SERVICES
TEAM	COUNSELING Use COCOUNSELING
	COUNSELING TECHNIQUES
	COUNSELING THEORIES
VOCATIONAL	COUNSELING (1966 1980) Use CAREER COUNSELING
	COUNSELOR ACCEPTANCE (1968 1980) Use COUNSELOR CLIENT RELATIONSHIP
	COUNSELOR ATTITUDES
	COUNSELOR BACKGROUND Use COUNSELOR CHARACTERISTICS
	COUNSELOR CERTIFICATION
	COUNSELOR CHARACTERISTICS
	COUNSELOR CLIENT RATIO
	COUNSELOR CLIENT RELATIONSHIP
TEACHER	COUNSELOR COOPERATION Use COUNSELOR TEACHER COOPERATION
	COUNSELOR EDUCATION Use COUNSELOR TRAINING
	COUNSELOR EDUCATORS
	COUNSELOR EVALUATION
	COUNSELOR FUNCTIONS (1967 1977) Use COUNSELOR ROLE
	COUNSELOR LICENSING Use COUNSELOR CERTIFICATION
	COUNSELOR OPINION Use COUNSELOR ATTITUDES
	COUNSELOR PERFORMANCE
	COUNSELOR PREPARATION Use COUNSELOR TRAINING
	COUNSELOR QUALIFICATIONS
CLIENT	COUNSELOR RATIO Use COUNSELOR CLIENT RATIO
	COUNSELOR REACTION Use COUNSELOR ATTITUDES
CLIENT	COUNSELOR RELATIONSHIP Use COUNSELOR CLIENT RELATIONSHIP
	COUNSELOR ROLE
	COUNSELOR SELECTION
	COUNSELOR TEACHER COOPERATION
	COUNSELOR TRAINING
	COUNSELORS
ADJUSTMENT	COUNSELORS
ADMISSIONS	COUNSELORS (1973 1980) Use ADMISSIONS COUNSELING
CAMP	COUNSELORS (1968 1980) Use CAMPING
COLLEGE	COUNSELORS Use SCHOOL COUNSELORS
ELEMENTARY SCHOOL	COUNSELORS (1967 1980) Use SCHOOL COUNSELORS
EMPLOYMENT	COUNSELORS
FACULTY	COUNSELORS Use FACULTY ADVISERS
GUIDANCE	COUNSELORS Use SCHOOL COUNSELORS
SCHOOL	COUNSELORS
SECONDARY SCHOOL	COUNSELORS (1967 1980) Use SCHOOL COUNSELORS
SPECIAL	COUNSELORS (1966 1980) Use COUNSELORS and SPECIALISTS
LOW INCOME	COUNTIES
	COUNTING Use COMPUTATION
FOREIGN	COUNTRIES
THIRD WORLD	COUNTRIES Use DEVELOPING NATIONS
	COUNTY EXTENSION AGENTS Use EXTENSION AGENTS
	COUNTY GOVERNMENT Use LOCAL GOVERNMENT
	COUNTY HISTORY Use LOCAL HISTORY
	COUNTY LIBRARIES
	COUNTY NORMS Use LOCAL NORMS
	COUNTY OFFICIALS
	COUNTY PROGRAMS
	COUNTY SCHOOL DISTRICTS
	COUNTY SCHOOL SYSTEMS (1967 1980) Use COUNTY SCHOOL DISTRICTS
BIBLIOGRAPHIC	COUPLING
AMERICAN GOVERNMENT	(COURSE) (1966 1980) Use UNITED STATES GOVERNMENT (COURSE)
	COURSE CONTENT
CONTROVERSIAL ISSUES	(COURSE CONTENT)
	COURSE DESCRIPTIONS
	COURSE ENRICHMENT Use CURRICULUM ENRICHMENT
	COURSE EVALUATION
SCIENCE	COURSE IMPROVEMENT PROJECT (1967 1980) Use SCIENCE COURSE IMPROVEMENT PROJECTS
SCIENCE	COURSE IMPROVEMENT PROJECTS
	COURSE OBJECTIVES
	COURSE OF INSTRUCTION Use COURSE ORGANIZATION
	COURSE ORGANIZATION
	COURSE OUTLINES Use COURSE DESCRIPTIONS
	COURSE SELECTION (STUDENTS)
UNITED STATES GOVERNMENT	(COURSE)
	COURSE WITHDRAWAL Use WITHDRAWAL (EDUCATION)
	COURSES
ACCELERATED	COURSES (1966 1980) Use ACCELERATION (EDUCATION)
ADVANCED	COURSES
CONVERSATIONAL LANGUAGE	COURSES
CORE	COURSES (1966 1980) Use CORE CURRICULUM
CORRESPONDENCE	COURSES (1966 1980) Use CORRESPONDENCE STUDY
CREDIT	COURSES
EDUCATION	COURSES
ELECTIVE	COURSES
GENERAL METHODS	COURSES Use METHODS COURSES
HONORS	COURSES Use HONORS CURRICULUM
INSERVICE	COURSES (1966 1980) Use INSERVICE EDUCATION
INSTITUTE TYPE	COURSES (1966 1980) Use INSTITUTES (TRAINING PROGRAMS)
INTENSIVE LANGUAGE	COURSES
INTRODUCTORY	COURSES
FOUNDATION	COURSES (INTRODUCTORY) Use INTRODUCTORY COURSES
MANDATORY	COURSES Use REQUIRED COURSES
METHODS	COURSES
NONCREDIT	COURSES
OPTIONAL	COURSES Use ELECTIVE COURSES
PREREQUISITE	COURSES Use PREREQUISITES and REQUIRED COURSES
REFRESHER	COURSES
REMEDIAL	COURSES (1966 1980) Use REMEDIAL INSTRUCTION
REQUIRED	COURSES
FOUNDATION	COURSES (REQUIRED) Use REQUIRED COURSES

SCIENCE	COURSES (1966 1980) Use SCIENCE CURRICULUM
SHORT	COURSES (1970 1980) Use MINICOURSES
SPECIAL METHODS	COURSES Use METHODS COURSES
SURVEY	COURSES Use INTRODUCTORY COURSES
	COURSEWARE
	COURSEWARE REVIEWS Use COMPUTER SOFTWARE REVIEWS and COURSEWARE
AUDITING	(COURSEWORK)
	COURT ACTION Use COURT LITIGATION
	COURT CASES (1966 1980) Use COURT LITIGATION
	COURT DECISIONS Use COURT LITIGATION
	COURT DOCTRINE
	COURT JUDGES
	COURT LITIGATION
FEDERAL	COURT LITIGATION (1966 1980) Use COURT LITIGATION and FEDERAL COURTS
STATE	COURT LITIGATION Use COURT LITIGATION and STATE COURTS
SUPREME	COURT LITIGATION (1966 1980)
	COURT REPORTERS
	COURT ROLE
	COURTS
CHILDRENS	COURTS Use JUVENILE COURTS
FEDERAL	COURTS
JUVENILE	COURTS
STATE	COURTS
STATE SUPREME	COURTS Use STATE COURTS
SUPREME	COURTS (1966 1980)
TOURIST	COURTS Use HOTELS
ANALYSIS OF	COVARIANCE
SOFT	COVER BOOKS Use PAPERBACK BOOKS
FLOOR	COVERING Use FLOORING
RESILIENT FLOOR	COVERING Use FLOORING
	COVERT RESPONSE
	CPR (MEDICINE) Use CARDIOPULMONARY RESUSCITATION
	CRAFT WORKERS
	CRAFTS Use HANDICRAFTS
DESIGN	CRAFTS
INDUSTRIAL	CRAFTS Use INDUSTRIAL ARTS
LEATHER	CRAFTS Use LEATHER
	CRAFTS ROOMS (1966 1980) Use EDUCATIONAL FACILITIES and HANDICRAFTS
	CRAFTSMEN (1970 1981) Use CRAFT WORKERS
JOB	CREATION Use JOB DEVELOPMENT
SPECIAL	CREATION THEORY Use CREATIONISM
	CREATIONISM
SCIENTIFIC	CREATIONISM Use CREATIONISM
	CREATIVE ABILITY (1968 1980) Use CREATIVITY
	CREATIVE ACTIVITIES
	CREATIVE ART
	CREATIVE DEVELOPMENT
	CREATIVE DRAMATICS
	CREATIVE EXPRESSION
	CREATIVE READING (1966 1980)
	CREATIVE TEACHING
	CREATIVE THINKING
	CREATIVE THINKING TESTS Use CREATIVITY TESTS
	CREATIVE WRITING
	CREATIVITY
	CREATIVITY MEASURES Use CREATIVITY TESTS
	CREATIVITY RESEARCH
	CREATIVITY TESTS
	CREDENTIALS
	CREDIBILITY
SOURCE	CREDIBILITY Use CREDIBILITY
	CREDIT BY EXAMINATION Use EQUIVALENCY TESTS
	CREDIT COURSES
ADVANCED	CREDIT EXAMINATIONS Use EQUIVALENCY TESTS
	CREDIT (FINANCE)
CREDIT NO	CREDIT GRADING
PASS NO	CREDIT GRADING Use CREDIT NO CREDIT GRADING
STUDENT	CREDIT HOURS Use CREDITS
	CREDIT NO CREDIT GRADING
	CREDITS
COLLEGE	CREDITS
TAX	CREDITS
TUITION TAX	CREDITS Use TAX CREDITS and TUITION
	CREE
HAITIAN	CREOLE
MAURITIAN	CREOLE
SIERRA LEONE	CREOLE
	CREOLES
	CREW LEADERS
	CRIME
	CRIME PREVENTION
VICTIMS OF	CRIME
INTERNATIONAL	CRIMES
WAR	CRIMES Use INTERNATIONAL CRIMES
CORRECTIONS	(CRIMINAL JUSTICE) Use CORRECTIONAL REHABILITATION
	CRIMINAL LAW
	CRIMINALS
	CRIMINOLOGY
	CRIPPLED CHILDREN (1968 1980) Use PHYSICAL DISABILITIES
	CRISIS INTERVENTION
TELEPHONE	CRISIS SERVICES Use HOTLINES (PUBLIC)
	CRISIS THERAPY (1969 1980) Use CRISIS INTERVENTION
	CRITERIA
ADMISSION	CRITERIA
ENVIRONMENTAL	CRITERIA (1967 1980) Use ENVIRONMENTAL STANDARDS
EVALUATION	CRITERIA
LESSON OBSERVATION	CRITERIA
PERFORMANCE	CRITERIA (1968 1980)
RESEARCH	CRITERIA (1967 1980)
	CRITERION REFERENCED EDUCATION Use COMPETENCY BASED EDUCATION
	CRITERION REFERENCED TEACHER EDUCATION Use COMPETENCY BASED TEACHER EDUCATION

CRITERION REFERENCED TESTS
CRITERION VALIDITY (CONCURRENT) Use CONCURRENT VALIDITY
CRITERION VALIDITY (PREDICTIVE) Use PREDICTIVE VALIDITY
CRITICAL INCIDENTS METHOD
CRITICAL PATH METHOD
CRITICAL READING
CRITICAL SCORES Use CUTTING SCORES
CRITICAL THINKING
ANALYTICAL CRITICISM (1969 1980)
ARISTOTELIAN CRITICISM (1969 1980)
FILM CRITICISM
FORMAL CRITICISM (1969 1980)
HISTORICAL CRITICISM (1969 1980)
IMPRESSIONISTIC CRITICISM (1969 1980)
LITERARY CRITICISM
MARXIST CRITICISM Use MARXIAN ANALYSIS
MORAL CRITICISM (1969 1980)
MYTHIC CRITICISM (1969 1980)
PLATONIC CRITICISM (1970 1980)
RHETORICAL CRITICISM
TEXTUAL CRITICISM (1969 1980)
THEORETICAL CRITICISM (1969 1980)
CORN (FIELD CROP) (1968 1980) Use GRAINS (FOOD)
CROP HARVESTING Use HARVESTING
CROP PLANTING Use AGRONOMY and HORTICULTURE
CROP PROCESSING OCCUPATIONS
CROP PRODUCTION Use AGRICULTURAL PRODUCTION
FIELD CROPS
CROSS AGE HELPING Use CROSS AGE TEACHING
CROSS AGE TEACHING
CROSS CULTURAL COMMUNICATION Use INTERCULTURAL COMMUNICATION
CROSS CULTURAL STUDIES
CROSS CULTURAL TESTS Use CULTURE FAIR TESTS
CROSS CULTURAL TRAINING
CROSS EYES Use STRABISMUS
CROSS SECTIONAL STUDIES
CROWDING
CRUDE SCORES Use RAW SCORES
CRYSTALLOGRAPHY
CUBAN AMERICANS Use CUBANS and HISPANIC AMERICANS
CUBANS
CUBIC MEASURE Use VOLUME (MATHEMATICS)
CUE CARDS Use CUES
CUED SPEECH
CUES
CUING Use PROMPTING
CULTURAL ACTIVITIES
ASSIMILATION (CULTURAL) Use ACCULTURATION
CULTURAL AWARENESS
CULTURAL BACKGROUND
CULTURAL CENTERS
CULTURAL CHARACTERISTICS Use CULTURAL TRAITS
CROSS CULTURAL COMMUNICATION Use INTERCULTURAL COMMUNICATION
CULTURAL COMPARISONS Use CROSS CULTURAL STUDIES
CULTURAL CONTEXT
CULTURAL DIFFERENCES
CULTURAL DISADVANTAGEMENT (1966 1980) Use DISADVANTAGED
CULTURAL DIVERSITY Use CULTURAL DIFFERENCES
CULTURAL EDUCATION
CULTURAL ENRICHMENT
CULTURAL ENVIRONMENT (1966 1980) Use CULTURAL CONTEXT
CULTURAL EVENTS (1966 1980) Use CULTURAL ACTIVITIES
CULTURAL EXCHANGE
CULTURAL FACTORS (1966 1980) Use CULTURAL INFLUENCES
CULTURAL GEOGRAPHY Use HUMAN GEOGRAPHY
ETHNIC CULTURAL GROUPS Use ETHNIC GROUPS
RACIAL CULTURAL GROUPS Use ETHNIC GROUPS
RELIGIOUS CULTURAL GROUPS
CULTURAL HERITAGE Use CULTURAL BACKGROUND
CULTURAL IMAGES
CULTURAL INFLUENCES
CULTURAL INTERACTION Use CULTURAL EXCHANGE
CULTURAL INTERRELATIONSHIPS
CULTURAL ISOLATION
CULTURAL LAG Use CULTURE LAG
CULTURAL OPPORTUNITIES
CULTURAL PLURALISM
CROSS CULTURAL STUDIES
CROSS CULTURAL TESTS Use CULTURE FAIR TESTS
CROSS CULTURAL TRAINING
CULTURAL TRAITS
CULTURAL UNDERSTANDING Use CULTURAL AWARENESS
CULTURALLY ADVANTAGED (1967 1980) Use ADVANTAGED
CULTURALLY DISADVANTAGED (1966 1980) Use DISADVANTAGED
CULTURE
AFRICAN CULTURE
ALIEN CULTURE Use FOREIGN CULTURE
AMERICAN CULTURE (1966 1980)
AMERICAN INDIAN CULTURE
BEAUTY CULTURE Use COSMETOLOGY
BLACK CULTURE
BURMESE CULTURE
CHINESE CULTURE
CULTURE CONFLICT
CULTURE CONTACT
CUSTOMS (CULTURE) Use CULTURE
DUTCH CULTURE
CULTURE FAIR TESTS
FAMILY CULTURE Use FAMILY LIFE
FOLK CULTURE
FOREIGN CULTURE

CULTURE FREE TESTS (1967 1980) Use CULTURE FAIR TESTS
HISPANIC AMERICAN CULTURE
ISLAMIC CULTURE
JAPANESE AMERICAN CULTURE
KOREAN CULTURE
CULTURE LAG
LATIN AMERICAN CULTURE
LUSO BRAZILIAN CULTURE
MAJORITY CULTURE Use MIDDLE CLASS CULTURE
MASS CULTURE Use POPULAR CULTURE
MEXICAN AMERICAN CULTURE Use HISPANIC AMERICAN CULTURE and MEXICAN AMERICANS
MIDDLE CLASS CULTURE
MINORITY CULTURE Use MINORITY GROUPS
NEGRO CULTURE (1966 1977) Use BLACK CULTURE
NORTH AMERICAN CULTURE
POP CULTURE Use POPULAR CULTURE
POPULAR CULTURE
PUERTO RICAN CULTURE
CULTURE SHOCK Use CULTURE CONFLICT
SPANISH CULTURE
TRADITIONS (CULTURE) Use FOLK CULTURE
URBAN CULTURE
CULTURING TECHNIQUES
CURIOSITY
CURRENT AWARENESS SERVICES Use SELECTIVE DISSEMINATION OF INFORMATION
CURRENT EVENTS
CURRICULUM
ACADEMIC CURRICULUM Use ACADEMIC EDUCATION
CURRICULUM ADAPTATION Use CURRICULUM DEVELOPMENT
ARITHMETIC CURRICULUM (1966 1980) Use ARITHMETIC and MATHEMATICS CURRICULUM
STATE CURRICULUM BULLETINS Use STATE CURRICULUM GUIDES
CHILD CENTERED CURRICULUM Use STUDENT CENTERED CURRICULUM
COLLEGE CURRICULUM
CURRICULUM CONTENT Use CURRICULUM
CORE CURRICULUM
CURRICULUM DESIGN
CURRICULUM DEVELOPMENT
ECONOMICS CURRICULUM Use ECONOMICS EDUCATION
ELEMENTARY SCHOOL CURRICULUM
ENGLISH CURRICULUM
CURRICULUM ENRICHMENT
CURRICULUM EVALUATION
EXPERIMENTAL CURRICULUM
FUSED CURRICULUM
CURRICULUM GUIDES
STATE CURRICULUM GUIDES
HIDDEN CURRICULUM
HIGH SCHOOL CURRICULUM (1967 1980) Use SECONDARY SCHOOL CURRICULUM
HISTORY CURRICULUM Use HISTORY INSTRUCTION
HONORS CURRICULUM
CURRICULUM IMPROVEMENT Use CURRICULUM DEVELOPMENT
INDIVIDUALIZED CURRICULUM (1966 1980) Use INDIVIDUALIZED INSTRUCTION
INTEGRATED CURRICULUM
CURRICULUM LABORATORIES Use CURRICULUM STUDY CENTERS
CURRICULUM MATERIALS Use INSTRUCTIONAL MATERIALS
MATHEMATICS CURRICULUM
MODERN LANGUAGE CURRICULUM
ORGANIC CURRICULUM Use STUDENT CENTERED CURRICULUM
PHYSICS CURRICULUM (1966 1980) Use PHYSICS and SCIENCE CURRICULUM
CURRICULUM PLANNING (1966 1980) Use CURRICULUM DEVELOPMENT
PRESCHOOL CURRICULUM
CURRICULUM PROBLEMS
CURRICULUM REEVALUATION Use CURRICULUM EVALUATION
CURRICULUM REFORM Use CURRICULUM DEVELOPMENT
CURRICULUM RELEVANCE Use RELEVANCE (EDUCATION)
CURRICULUM REORGANIZATION Use CURRICULUM DEVELOPMENT
CURRICULUM RESEARCH
CURRICULUM RESOURCES Use EDUCATIONAL RESOURCES
CURRICULUM REVISIONS Use CURRICULUM DEVELOPMENT
SCIENCE CURRICULUM
SECONDARY SCHOOL CURRICULUM
SHOP CURRICULUM
SPEECH CURRICULUM
SPEECH COMMUNICATION CURRICULUM Use SPEECH COMMUNICATION and SPEECH CURRICULUM
SPIRAL CURRICULUM
STUDENT CENTERED CURRICULUM
CURRICULUM STUDY CENTERS
TEACHER EDUCATION CURRICULUM
TELEVISION CURRICULUM
UNGRADED CURRICULUM (1966 1980) Use NONGRADED INSTRUCTIONAL GROUPING
UNIFIED STUDIES CURRICULUM
CURRICULUM VITAE Use RESUMES (PERSONAL)
CURSIVE WRITING
ITEM CHARACTERISTIC CURVE THEORY Use LATENT TRAIT THEORY
CUSTODIAL MENTALLY HANDICAPPED (1968 1980) Use SEVERE MENTAL RETARDATION
CUSTODIAN TRAINING
CHILD CUSTODY
CUSTOMS (CULTURE) Use CULTURE
CUTANEOUS SENSE (1968 1980) Use TACTUAL PERCEPTION
CUTLINES Use CAPTIONS
BUDGET CUTS Use BUDGETING and RETRENCHMENT
CUTTING SCORES
CYBERNETICS
LIFE CYCLE COSTING
BUSINESS CYCLES
ECONOMIC CYCLES Use BUSINESS CYCLES
LEARNING CYCLES Use LEARNING PROCESSES
CYESIS Use PREGNANCY
CYRILLIC ALPHABET
CYTOLOGY
CZECH

CZECH LITERATURE
R D AND E   Use RESEARCH AND DEVELOPMENT
R AND D   Use RESEARCH AND DEVELOPMENT
DACTYLOLOGY   Use FINGER SPELLING
DAGUR
AVERAGE DAILY ATTENDANCE
AVERAGE DAILY ENROLLMENT (1968 1980)   Use AVERAGE DAILY MEMBERSHIP
FUNDAMENTAL SKILLS (DAILY LIVING)   Use DAILY LIVING SKILLS
DAILY LIVING SKILLS
SURVIVAL SKILLS (DAILY LIVING)   Use DAILY LIVING SKILLS
AVERAGE DAILY MEMBERSHIP
DAIRY FARMERS
DAIRY PRODUCT INSPECTORS   Use FOOD AND DRUG INSPECTORS
DAIRYMEN (1966 1980)   Use DAIRY FARMERS
BRAIN DAMAGE   Use NEUROLOGICAL IMPAIRMENTS
RADIATION DAMAGE   Use RADIATION EFFECTS
DANCE
AEROBIC DANCE   Use AEROBICS and DANCE
DANCE EDUCATION
DANCE THERAPY
DANGEROUS MATERIALS   Use HAZARDOUS MATERIALS
DARGHI   Use CAUCASIAN LANGUAGES
DATA
DATA ACCUMULATION   Use DATA COLLECTION
DATA ANALYSIS
DATA BANKS   Use DATABASES
DATA BASES (1969 1981)   Use DATABASES
DATA COLLECTION
DIGITAL OPTICAL DATA DISKS   Use OPTICAL DATA DISKS
OPTICAL DATA DISKS
DATA DISSEMINATION   Use INFORMATION DISSEMINATION
KEYBOARDING (DATA ENTRY)
DATA INTERPRETATION
DATA NEEDS   Use INFORMATION NEEDS
PERSONNEL DATA
DATA PROCESSING
AUTOMATIC DATA PROCESSING   Use DATA PROCESSING
ELECTRONIC DATA PROCESSING (1967 1980)   Use DATA PROCESSING
DATA PROCESSING OCCUPATIONS
DATA SHEETS (1966 1980)   Use WORKSHEETS
STATISTICAL DATA
TABLES (DATA)
DATA TABULATION   Use DATA PROCESSING
TIME USE DATA   Use TIME MANAGEMENT
DATABASE HOSTS   Use ONLINE VENDORS
DATABASE MANAGEMENT SYSTEMS
DATABASE PRODUCERS
DATABASE VENDORS   Use ONLINE VENDORS
DATABASES
DATING (SOCIAL)
DAUGHTERS
DAY CAMP PROGRAMS
DAY CAMPS   Use DAY CAMP PROGRAMS
DAY CARE
ADULT DAY CARE
AFTER SCHOOL DAY CARE (1978 1983)   Use AFTER SCHOOL PROGRAMS and SCHOOL AGE DAY CARE
DAY CARE CENTERS
EMPLOYER SPONSORED DAY CARE   Use EMPLOYER SUPPORTED DAY CARE
EMPLOYER SUPPORTED DAY CARE
FAMILY DAY CARE
HOME DAY CARE   Use FAMILY DAY CARE
DAY CARE PROGRAMS (1966 1980)   Use DAY CARE
SCHOOL AGE DAY CARE
DAY CARE SERVICES (1967 1980)   Use DAY CARE
DAY CLASSES   Use DAY PROGRAMS
COLLEGE DAY
EXTENDED SCHOOL DAY
DAY PROGRAMS
DAY RELEASE   Use RELEASED TIME
DAY SCHOOLS
DAY STUDENTS
FOUR DAY WORK WEEK   Use FLEXIBLE WORKING HOURS
DAYLIGHT (1970 1980)   Use LIGHT
HOLY DAYS   Use RELIGIOUS HOLIDAYS
MAN DAYS (1968 1980)   Use WORKER DAYS
PEOPLE DAYS   Use WORKER DAYS
PERSON DAYS   Use WORKER DAYS
STAFF DAYS   Use WORKER DAYS
WORKER DAYS
DAYTIME PROGRAMS (1967 1980)   Use DAY PROGRAMS
DBMS   Use DATABASE MANAGEMENT SYSTEMS
DE FACTO SEGREGATION
DE JURE SEGREGATION
DEAF (1966 1980)   Use DEAFNESS
DEAF BLIND
DEAF CHILDREN (1966 1980)   Use DEAFNESS
GESTURES (DEAF COMMUNICATION)   Use SIGN LANGUAGE
DEAF EDUCATION (1968 1980)   Use DEAFNESS
DEAF INTERPRETING
INTERPRETING FOR THE DEAF   Use DEAF INTERPRETING
DEAF RESEARCH (1968 1980)   Use DEAFNESS
DEAFNESS
DEANS
ACADEMIC DEANS
COLLEGE DEANS (1968 1980)   Use DEANS and HIGHER EDUCATION
DEANS OF FACULTY   Use ACADEMIC DEANS
DEANS OF INSTRUCTION   Use ACADEMIC DEANS
DEANS OF MEN   Use DEANS OF STUDENTS
DEANS OF STUDENTS
DEANS OF WOMEN   Use DEANS OF STUDENTS
DEATH

DEATH EDUCATION Use DEATH
INFANT DEATH RATE Use INFANT MORTALITY
DEBATE
DEBATE JUDGES Use JUDGES
PRESIDENTIAL DEBATES (UNITED STATES) Use DEBATE and PRESIDENTIAL CAMPAIGNS (UNITED STATES)
DECELERATION Use ACCELERATION (PHYSICS)
DECENTRALIZATION
DECENTRALIZED LIBRARY SYSTEMS (1968 1980) Use DECENTRALIZATION and LIBRARY NETWORKS
DECENTRALIZED SCHOOL DESIGN (1966 1980) Use DECENTRALIZATION and EDUCATIONAL FACILITIES DESIGN
DECEPTION
DECIMAL FRACTIONS
DECIMALS Use DECIMAL FRACTIONS
DECISION MAKING
COLLABORATIVE DECISION MAKING Use PARTICIPATIVE DECISION MAKING
COLLECTIVE DECISION MAKING Use PARTICIPATIVE DECISION MAKING
PARTICIPATIVE DECISION MAKING
DECISION MAKING SKILLS
COURT DECISIONS Use COURT LITIGATION
LEGAL DECISIONS Use COURT LITIGATION
DECLINING ENROLLMENT
DECODING (READING)
INTERIOR DECORATION Use INTERIOR DESIGN
DEDUCTION
TAX DEDUCTIONS
DEDUCTIVE METHODS (1967 1980) Use DEDUCTION
DEEP SEA DIVING Use UNDERWATER DIVING
DEEP STRUCTURE
DEFACTO SEGREGATION (1966 1980) Use DE FACTO SEGREGATION
DEFAULTING ON LOANS Use LOAN REPAYMENT
BIRTH DEFECTS Use CONGENITAL IMPAIRMENTS
NEUROLOGICAL DEFECTS (1966 1980) Use NEUROLOGICAL IMPAIRMENTS
CIVIL DEFENSE
NATIONAL DEFENSE
DEFERRED TUITION Use INCOME CONTINGENT LOANS
HOUSING DEFICIENCIES
IRON DEFICIENCY ANEMIA Use ANEMIA
ATTENTION DEFICIT DISORDERS
DEFINITIONS
EXTERNAL DEGREE PROGRAMS
SPECIAL DEGREE PROGRAMS
TIME SHORTENED DEGREE PROGRAMS Use ACCELERATION (EDUCATION)
DEGREE REQUIREMENTS
DEGREES (ACADEMIC)
ASSOCIATE DEGREES
BACCALAUREATE DEGREES Use BACHELORS DEGREES
BACHELOR OF ARTS DEGREES Use BACHELORS DEGREES
BACHELOR OF SCIENCE DEGREES Use BACHELORS DEGREES
BACHELORS DEGREES
DOCTOR OF ARTS DEGREES
DOCTORAL DEGREES
FIRST PROFESSIONAL DEGREES Use DEGREES (ACADEMIC) and PROFESSIONAL EDUCATION
MASTER OF ARTS DEGREES Use MASTERS DEGREES
MASTER OF SCIENCE DEGREES Use MASTERS DEGREES
MASTERS DEGREES
SPECIALIST IN EDUCATION DEGREES
THREE YEAR BACHELORS DEGREES Use ACCELERATION (EDUCATION) and BACHELORS DEGREES
DEGREES (TITLES) (1966 1980) Use DEGREES (ACADEMIC)
TWO YEAR COLLEGE DEGREES Use ASSOCIATE DEGREES
DEHUMANIZATION Use HUMANIZATION
DEINSTITUTIONALIZATION (OF DISABLED)
DEJURE SEGREGATION (1966 1980) Use DE JURE SEGREGATION
DELAY OF GRATIFICATION
DELAYED SPEECH
DELINQUENCY
DELINQUENCY CAUSES
JUVENILE DELINQUENCY Use DELINQUENCY
DELINQUENCY PREVENTION
DELINQUENT BEHAVIOR (1966 1983) Use DELINQUENCY
DELINQUENT IDENTIFICATION (1966 1980) Use DELINQUENCY and IDENTIFICATION
DELINQUENT REHABILITATION
DELINQUENT ROLE (1966 1980) Use DELINQUENCY
DELINQUENTS (1966 1980) Use DELINQUENCY
DELIVERY SYSTEMS
DELPHI TECHNIQUE
EDUCATIONAL DEMAND
DEMAND FOR EDUCATION Use EDUCATIONAL DEMAND
DEMAND OCCUPATIONS
TEACHER SUPPLY AND DEMAND
LABOR DEMANDS
DEMENTIA PRAECOX Use SCHIZOPHRENIA
DEMOCRACY
DEMOCRATIC MANAGEMENT Use PARTICIPATIVE DECISION MAKING
DEMOCRATIC VALUES
DEMOGRAPHY
CITY DEMOGRAPHY (1966 1980) Use URBAN DEMOGRAPHY
NATIONAL DEMOGRAPHY (1966 1980) Use DEMOGRAPHY
SCHOOL DEMOGRAPHY
URBAN DEMOGRAPHY
HOME DEMONSTRATION AGENTS Use EXTENSION AGENTS
DEMONSTRATION CENTERS
DEMONSTRATION PROGRAMS
DEMONSTRATION PROJECTS (1966 1980) Use DEMONSTRATION PROGRAMS
DEMONSTRATIONS (CIVIL)
DEMONSTRATIONS (EDUCATIONAL)
PUBLIC DEMONSTRATIONS Use DEMONSTRATIONS (CIVIL)
DENOMINATIONAL COLLEGES Use CHURCH RELATED COLLEGES
DENTAL ASSESSMENT Use DENTAL EVALUATION
DENTAL ASSISTANTS
DENTAL ASSOCIATIONS (1966 1980) Use DENTISTRY and PROFESSIONAL ASSOCIATIONS
DENTAL CLINICS

DESIGN PREFERENCES
PROGRAM DESIGN
QUASIEXPERIMENTAL DESIGN
DESIGN REQUIREMENTS
RESEARCH DESIGN
SCHOOL DESIGN (1966 1980) Use EDUCATIONAL FACILITIES DESIGN
MECHANICAL DESIGN TECHNICIANS
TEST DESIGN Use TEST CONSTRUCTION
DESIGNERS
EVALUATION DESIGNS Use EVALUATION METHODS
SOCIAL DESIRABILITY
DESKTOP COMPUTERS Use MICROCOMPUTERS
DESOXYRIBONUCLEIC ACID Use DNA
DESPAIR Use DEPRESSION (PSYCHOLOGY)
DESPONDENCY Use DEPRESSION (PSYCHOLOGY)
DESTINY CONTROL Use SELF DETERMINATION
SELF DESTRUCTIVE BEHAVIOR
EARLY DETECTION Use IDENTIFICATION
HANDICAP DETECTION (1966 1980) Use HANDICAP IDENTIFICATION
INTRUSION DETECTORS Use ALARM SYSTEMS
LIE DETECTORS Use POLYGRAPHS
DETERMINATION (CHEMICAL) Use CHEMICAL ANALYSIS
CHEMICAL DETERMINATION Use CHEMICAL ANALYSIS
PRIORITY DETERMINATION Use NEEDS ASSESSMENT
SELF DETERMINATION
DETERMINERS (LANGUAGES)
STUDENT DEVELOPED MATERIALS
TEACHER DEVELOPED MATERIALS
DEVELOPED NATIONS
DEVELOPING INSTITUTIONS
DEVELOPING NATIONS
DEVELOPMENT
ADOLESCENT DEVELOPMENT
ADULT DEVELOPMENT
BEHAVIOR DEVELOPMENT
CAREER DEVELOPMENT
CHILD DEVELOPMENT CENTERS
RESEARCH AND DEVELOPMENT CENTERS
CHILD DEVELOPMENT
COGNITIVE DEVELOPMENT
COMMUNITY DEVELOPMENT
COMPENSATORY DEVELOPMENT Use COMPENSATORY EDUCATION
COMPREHENSION DEVELOPMENT (1966 1980) Use COMPREHENSION
CONCEPT DEVELOPMENT Use CONCEPT FORMATION
CREATIVE DEVELOPMENT
CURRICULUM DEVELOPMENT
ECONOMIC DEVELOPMENT
EDUCATIONAL DEVELOPMENT
EMOTIONAL DEVELOPMENT
EXECUTIVE DEVELOPMENT Use MANAGEMENT DEVELOPMENT
FACULTY DEVELOPMENT
HANDWRITING DEVELOPMENT (1966 1980) Use HANDWRITING and WRITING SKILLS
HUMAN DEVELOPMENT (1966 1980)
INDIVIDUAL DEVELOPMENT
INSTRUCTIONAL DEVELOPMENT
INSTRUCTIONAL MATERIAL DEVELOPMENT Use MATERIAL DEVELOPMENT
INTELLECTUAL DEVELOPMENT
JOB DEVELOPMENT
LABOR FORCE DEVELOPMENT
HUMAN RESOURCES DEVELOPMENT (LABOR) Use LABOR FORCE DEVELOPMENT
LANGUAGE DEVELOPMENT (1966 1980) Use LANGUAGE ACQUISITION
COLLECTION DEVELOPMENT (LIBRARIES) Use LIBRARY COLLECTION DEVELOPMENT
LIBRARY COLLECTION DEVELOPMENT
MANAGEMENT DEVELOPMENT
MANPOWER DEVELOPMENT (1966 1980) Use LABOR FORCE DEVELOPMENT
MATERIAL DEVELOPMENT
MENTAL DEVELOPMENT (1966 1980) Use COGNITIVE DEVELOPMENT
MORAL DEVELOPMENT
MOTOR DEVELOPMENT
ORGANIZATIONAL DEVELOPMENT
PERCEPTUAL DEVELOPMENT
PERSONAL DEVELOPMENT Use INDIVIDUAL DEVELOPMENT
PERSONALITY DEVELOPMENT
PERSONNEL DEVELOPMENT Use STAFF DEVELOPMENT
PHYSICAL DEVELOPMENT
POSTURE DEVELOPMENT Use HUMAN POSTURE
PROFESSIONAL DEVELOPMENT
PROGRAM DEVELOPMENT
GENERAL EDUCATIONAL DEVELOPMENT PROGRAMS Use HIGH SCHOOL EQUIVALENCY PROGRAMS
READING DEVELOPMENT (1966 1980)
RESEARCH AND DEVELOPMENT
RETARDED SPEECH DEVELOPMENT (1968 1980) Use DELAYED SPEECH
RURAL DEVELOPMENT
SELF DEVELOPMENT Use SELF ACTUALIZATION
SITE DEVELOPMENT
SKILL DEVELOPMENT
SOCIAL DEVELOPMENT
CHILD DEVELOPMENT SPECIALISTS
STAFF DEVELOPMENT
STAGES OF DEVELOPMENT Use DEVELOPMENTAL STAGES
STUDENT DEVELOPMENT
SYSTEMS DEVELOPMENT
TALENT DEVELOPMENT
ENGINE DEVELOPMENT TECHNICIANS Use MECHANICAL DESIGN TECHNICIANS
PROPULSION DEVELOPMENT TECHNICIANS Use MECHANICAL DESIGN TECHNICIANS
TEXTBOOK DEVELOPMENT Use TEXTBOOK PREPARATION
VERBAL DEVELOPMENT
VOCABULARY DEVELOPMENT
VOCATIONAL DEVELOPMENT (1967 1978) Use CAREER DEVELOPMENT
DEVELOPMENTAL CONTINUITY
DEVELOPMENTAL DISABILITIES

DEVELOPMENTAL GUIDANCE (1967 1980) Use GUIDANCE
DEVELOPMENTAL PROGRAMS
DEVELOPMENTAL PSYCHOLOGY
DEVELOPMENTAL READING (1966 1980)
DEVELOPMENTAL STAGES
DEVELOPMENTAL STUDIES PROGRAMS
DEVELOPMENTAL TASKS
SOCIALLY DEVIANT BEHAVIOR (1966 1980) Use ANTISOCIAL BEHAVIOR
COMPUTER STORAGE DEVICES
MEMORY DEVICES (COMPUTERS) Use COMPUTER STORAGE DEVICES
SELF HELP DEVICES (DISABLED) Use ASSISTIVE DEVICES (FOR DISABLED)
ASSISTIVE DEVICES (FOR DISABLED)
INPUT DEVICES Use INPUT OUTPUT DEVICES
INPUT OUTPUT DEVICES
LITERARY DEVICES
MECHANICAL DEVICES Use MECHANICAL EQUIPMENT
OUTPUT DEVICES Use INPUT OUTPUT DEVICES
SEMICONDUCTOR DEVICES
STIMULUS DEVICES (1966 1980)
DIABETES
DIACHRONIC LINGUISTICS
DIACRITICAL MARKING
DIAGNOSIS Use IDENTIFICATION
CLINICAL DIAGNOSIS
DIAGNOSIS (CLINICAL) Use CLINICAL DIAGNOSIS
EDUCATIONAL DIAGNOSIS
DIAGNOSIS (EDUCATIONAL) Use EDUCATIONAL DIAGNOSIS
READING DIAGNOSIS
DIAGNOSTIC TEACHING
DIAGNOSTIC TESTS
SENTENCE DIAGRAMING
DIAGRAMS
DIAL ACCESS INFORMATION SYSTEMS
DIALECT INTERFERENCE Use DIALECTS and INTERFERENCE (LANGUAGE)
DIALECT STUDIES
DIALECTICAL MATERIALISM Use MARXISM
DIALECTS
BLACK DIALECTS
GEOGRAPHIC DIALECTS Use REGIONAL DIALECTS
NEGRO DIALECTS (1966 1977) Use BLACK DIALECTS
NONSTANDARD DIALECTS
REGIONAL DIALECTS
SOCIAL DIALECTS
DIALOGS (LANGUAGE)
DIALOGS (LITERARY)
MAN MACHINE DIALOGS Use MAN MACHINE SYSTEMS
DIALOGUE (1969 1980) Use DIALOGS (LITERARY)
DIARIES
DICTATION
MACHINE DICTATION Use DICTATION
DICTATORSHIP Use TOTALITARIANISM
DICTION
DICTIONARIES
DICTIONARY CATALOGS (1968 1980) Use LIBRARY CATALOGS
DIDACTICISM
TOOL AND DIE MAKERS
DIESEL ENGINES
DIESEL FUEL Use FUELS
DIESEL MECHANICS Use AUTO MECHANICS
DIETETICS
LYSERGIC ACID DIETHYLAMIDE
DIETITIANS
DIETS Use DIETETICS
DIFFERENCES
AGE DIFFERENCES
CULTURAL DIFFERENCES
INDIVIDUAL DIFFERENCES
INSTITUTIONAL DIFFERENCES Use DIFFERENCES and INSTITUTIONAL CHARACTERISTICS
INTELLIGENCE DIFFERENCES
INTERMODE DIFFERENCES
RACIAL DIFFERENCES
REGIONAL DIFFERENCES Use DIFFERENCES and REGIONAL CHARACTERISTICS
RELIGIOUS DIFFERENCES
RURAL URBAN DIFFERENCES
SEX DIFFERENCES
GENDER DIFFERENCES (SEX) Use SEX DIFFERENCES
SOCIAL DIFFERENCES
SOCIAL CLASS DIFFERENCES Use SOCIAL DIFFERENCES
URBAN RURAL DIFFERENCES Use RURAL URBAN DIFFERENCES
DIFFERENTIAL PSYCHOLOGY Use INDIVIDUAL PSYCHOLOGY
SEMANTIC DIFFERENTIAL
SALARY DIFFERENTIALS (1968 1980) Use SALARY WAGE DIFFERENTIALS
SALARY WAGE DIFFERENTIALS
WAGE SALARY DIFFERENTIALS Use SALARY WAGE DIFFERENTIALS
DIFFERENTIATED STAFFS
LEARNING DIFFICULTIES (1966 1980) Use LEARNING PROBLEMS
READING DIFFICULTIES
WRITING DIFFICULTIES
LINGUISTIC DIFFICULTY (CONTRASTIVE) Use INTERFERENCE (LANGUAGE)
LINGUISTIC DIFFICULTY (INHERENT)
ITEM DIFFICULTY Use DIFFICULTY LEVEL and TEST ITEMS
DIFFICULTY LEVEL
READING DIFFICULTY (1966 1980)
TASK DIFFICULTY Use DIFFICULTY LEVEL
DIFFUSION (1967 1982) (COMMUNICATION) Use DIFFUSION (COMMUNICATION)
DIFFUSION (COMMUNICATION)
DIFFUSION (PHYSICS)
DIFFUSION (1967 1982) (PHYSICS) Use DIFFUSION (PHYSICS)
DIFFUSION (1967 1982) (POPULATIONS) Use POPULATION DISTRIBUTION
DIGITAL COMPUTERS
DIGITAL OPTICAL DATA DISKS Use OPTICAL DATA DISKS

MULTIPLE	DISCRIMINANT ANALYSIS Use DISCRIMINANT ANALYSIS
	DISCRIMINANT FUNCTION ANALYSIS Use DISCRIMINANT ANALYSIS
AGE	DISCRIMINATION
AUDITORY	DISCRIMINATION
EDUCATIONAL	DISCRIMINATION
EMPLOYMENT	DISCRIMINATION Use EQUAL OPPORTUNITIES (JOBS)
ETHNIC	DISCRIMINATION
HANDICAP	DISCRIMINATION
HOUSING	DISCRIMINATION
JOB	DISCRIMINATION Use EQUAL OPPORTUNITIES (JOBS)
	DISCRIMINATION LEARNING
ANTI	DISCRIMINATION LEGISLATION Use CIVIL RIGHTS LEGISLATION
LEGISLATIVE	DISCRIMINATION Use DISCRIMINATORY LEGISLATION
LITERARY	DISCRIMINATION (1966 1980)
RACIAL	DISCRIMINATION
RELIGIOUS	DISCRIMINATION
REVERSE	DISCRIMINATION
SEX	DISCRIMINATION
	DISCRIMINATION (SOCIAL) Use SOCIAL DISCRIMINATION
SOCIAL	DISCRIMINATION
	DISCRIMINATION TRANSFER Use SHIFT STUDIES
VISUAL	DISCRIMINATION
	DISCRIMINATORY ANALYSIS Use DISCRIMINANT ANALYSIS
	DISCRIMINATORY ATTITUDES (SOCIAL) (1966 1980) Use SOCIAL BIAS
	DISCRIMINATORY LEGISLATION
NON	DISCURSIVE MEASURES Use VISUAL MEASURES
	DISCUSSION
CLASS	DISCUSSION Use DISCUSSION (TEACHING TECHNIQUE)
	DISCUSSION EXPERIENCE (1966 1980) Use DISCUSSION
GROUP	DISCUSSION
	DISCUSSION GROUPS
	DISCUSSION GUIDES Use DISCUSSION (TEACHING TECHNIQUE) and TEACHING GUIDES
	DISCUSSION PROGRAMS (1966 1980) Use DISCUSSION
	DISCUSSION (TEACHING TECHNIQUE)
	DISEASE CONTROL
	DISEASE INCIDENCE
	DISEASE RATE (1967 1980) Use DISEASE INCIDENCE
	DISEASES
COMMUNICABLE	DISEASES
CONTAGIOUS	DISEASES Use COMMUNICABLE DISEASES
INFECTIOUS	DISEASES (1966 1974) Use COMMUNICABLE DISEASES
OCCUPATIONAL	DISEASES
PLANT	DISEASES Use PLANT PATHOLOGY
PSYCHOSOMATIC	DISEASES (1968 1980) Use PSYCHOSOMATIC DISORDERS
VENEREAL	DISEASES
	DISEMPLOYMENT Use DISLOCATED WORKERS
	DISHWASHING
COMPACT	DISKS Use OPTICAL DISKS
DIGITAL OPTICAL DATA	DISKS Use OPTICAL DATA DISKS
LASER	DISKS Use OPTICAL DISKS
OPTICAL	DISKS
OPTICAL DATA	DISKS
	DISLOCATED WORKERS
PERSONNEL	DISMISSAL Use DISMISSAL (PERSONNEL)
	DISMISSAL (PERSONNEL)
TEACHER	DISMISSAL
CIVIL	DISOBEDIENCE
ATTENTION DEFICIT	DISORDERS
BEHAVIOR	DISORDERS
COMMUNICATION	DISORDERS
HEART	DISORDERS
MENTAL	DISORDERS
PSYCHOSOMATIC	DISORDERS
VOICE	DISORDERS
	DISPLACED HOMEMAKERS
	DISPLACED WORKERS Use DISLOCATED WORKERS
	DISPLAY AIDS
	DISPLAY PANELS (1968 1980) Use DISPLAY AIDS
	DISPLAY SYSTEMS
SCREENS	(DISPLAYS)
WASTE	DISPOSAL
AGRICULTURAL LABOR	DISPUTES (1966 1980) Use LABOR DEMANDS
	DISQUALIFICATION
DATA	DISSEMINATION Use INFORMATION DISSEMINATION
INFORMATION	DISSEMINATION
SELECTIVE	DISSEMINATION OF INFORMATION
	DISSENT
DOCTORAL	DISSERTATIONS
COGNITIVE	DISSONANCE
	DISTANCE
	DISTANCE EDUCATION
RANGE	(DISTANCE) Use DISTANCE
CONCEPTUAL	DISTINCTIONS Use CONCEPT FORMATION
	DISTINCTIVE FEATURES (1967 1980) Use DISTINCTIVE FEATURES (LANGUAGE)
	DISTINCTIVE FEATURES (LANGUAGE)
	DISTRIBUTION (ECONOMICS) Use MARKETING
ETHNIC	DISTRIBUTION
	DISTRIBUTION FREE STATISTICS Use NONPARAMETRIC STATISTICS
GEOGRAPHIC	DISTRIBUTION
POPULATION	DISTRIBUTION
RACIAL	DISTRIBUTION
SOCIAL	DISTRIBUTION
STUDENT	DISTRIBUTION (1966 1980)
TEACHER	DISTRIBUTION
FREQUENCY	DISTRIBUTIONS Use STATISTICAL DISTRIBUTIONS
STATISTICAL	DISTRIBUTIONS
	DISTRIBUTIONS (STATISTICS) Use STATISTICAL DISTRIBUTIONS
	DISTRIBUTIVE EDUCATION
	DISTRIBUTIVE EDUCATION TEACHERS
SCHOOL	DISTRICT AUTONOMY
	DISTRICT LIBRARIES Use REGIONAL LIBRARIES

NONRESIDENT STUDENTS (1967 1980) (OUT OF DISTRICT) Use RESIDENCE REQUIREMENTS
DISTRICT NORMS Use LOCAL NORMS
SCHOOL DISTRICT NORMS Use LOCAL NORMS
SCHOOL DISTRICT POLICY Use BOARD OF EDUCATION POLICY
STATE SCHOOL DISTRICT RELATIONSHIP
SCHOOL DISTRICT REORGANIZATION
RESIDENT STUDENTS (1967 1980) (IN DISTRICT) Use RESIDENCE REQUIREMENTS
SCHOOL DISTRICT SIZE
SCHOOL DISTRICT SPENDING
COMPREHENSIVE DISTRICTS (1967 1980) Use SCHOOL DISTRICTS
COUNTY SCHOOL DISTRICTS
INTERMEDIATE SCHOOL DISTRICTS Use INTERMEDIATE ADMINISTRATIVE UNITS
INTERMEDIATE SERVICE DISTRICTS Use INTERMEDIATE ADMINISTRATIVE UNITS
MULTICAMPUS DISTRICTS
REZONING DISTRICTS Use REZONING
SCHOOL DISTRICTS
EMOTIONAL DISTURBANCES
EMOTIONALLY DISTURBED CHILDREN (1967 1980) Use EMOTIONAL DISTURBANCES
EMOTIONALLY DISTURBED (1966 1980) Use EMOTIONAL DISTURBANCES
DIVERGENT THINKING
CULTURAL DIVERSITY Use CULTURAL DIFFERENCES
DIVIDED CATALOGS (1968 1980) Use LIBRARY CATALOGS
ROOM DIVIDERS Use SPACE DIVIDERS
SPACE DIVIDERS
DIVING
DEEP SEA DIVING Use UNDERWATER DIVING
PLATFORM DIVING Use DIVING
SCUBA DIVING Use UNDERWATER DIVING
SKIN DIVING Use UNDERWATER DIVING
SPRINGBOARD DIVING Use DIVING
TOWER DIVING Use DIVING
UNDERWATER DIVING
DIVISION
UPPER DIVISION COLLEGES
SEMESTER DIVISION (1966 1980) Use SEMESTER SYSTEM
PHYSICAL DIVISIONS (GEOGRAPHIC)
POLITICAL DIVISIONS (GEOGRAPHIC)
GRADES (PROGRAM DIVISIONS) Use INSTRUCTIONAL PROGRAM DIVISIONS
INSTRUCTIONAL PROGRAM DIVISIONS
DIVORCE
DIVORCED PERSONS Use DIVORCE
DNA
RECOMBINANT DNA Use DNA and GENETIC ENGINEERING
DOCTOR OF ARTS DEGREES
DOCTOR PATIENT RELATIONSHIP Use PHYSICIAN PATIENT RELATIONSHIP
DOCTORAL DEGREES
DOCTORAL DISSERTATIONS
POST DOCTORAL EDUCATION (1967 1980) Use POSTDOCTORAL EDUCATION
DOCTORAL PROGRAMS
DOCTORAL THESES (1967 1980) Use DOCTORAL DISSERTATIONS
MEDICAL DOCTORS Use PHYSICIANS
COURT DOCTRINE
DOCUMENT READERS Use OPTICAL SCANNERS
DOCUMENTARIES
DOCUMENTATION
COMPUTER PROGRAM DOCUMENTATION Use COMPUTER SOFTWARE
GOVERNMENT DOCUMENTS Use GOVERNMENT PUBLICATIONS
PUBLIC DOCUMENTS Use GOVERNMENT PUBLICATIONS
DOGMATISM
DOMESTIC VIOLENCE (FAMILY) Use FAMILY VIOLENCE
DOMESTICS (1970 1980) Use HOUSEHOLD WORKERS
CEREBRAL DOMINANCE (1967 1986) Use BRAIN HEMISPHERE FUNCTIONS
LANGUAGE DOMINANCE
LATERAL DOMINANCE
DOMINICAN AMERICANS Use DOMINICANS and HISPANIC AMERICANS
DOMINICANS
DONORS
BLOOD DONORS Use TISSUE DONORS
FINANCIAL DONORS Use DONORS
ORGAN DONORS Use TISSUE DONORS
SPERM DONORS Use TISSUE DONORS
TISSUE DONORS
DOORS
DORMITORIES
DORMITORY LIVING Use DORMITORIES and GROUP EXPERIENCE
DOUBLE EMPLOYMENT Use MULTIPLE EMPLOYMENT
DOUBLE SESSIONS
DOWNS ANOMALY Use DOWNS SYNDROME
DOWNS SYNDROME
DRAWING (PRECISION DRAFT) Use DRAFTING
DRAFTERS (1980 1981) Use DRAFTING
DRAFTING
ARCHITECTURAL DRAFTING
MODULAR DRAFTING Use MODULAR BUILDING DESIGN
DRAFTSMEN (1968 1980) Use DRAFTING
DRAMA
FOLK DRAMA (1969 1980) Use DRAMA and FOLK CULTURE
OUTDOOR DRAMA (1968 1980) Use DRAMA and OUTDOOR ACTIVITIES
DRAMA WORKSHOPS
DRAMATIC ARTS Use DRAMATICS
DRAMATIC PLAY
DRAMATIC UNITIES (1970 1980) Use DRAMA
DRAMATICS
CREATIVE DRAMATICS
DRAVIDIAN LANGUAGES
DRAWING (COMPUTERIZED) Use COMPUTER GRAPHICS
ENGINEERING DRAWING
FREEHAND DRAWING
DRAWING (FREEHAND) Use FREEHAND DRAWING
MECHANICAL DRAWING Use ENGINEERING DRAWING
DRAWING (PRECISION DRAFT) Use DRAFTING

RAISED LINE	DRAWINGS
	DRESS CODES
	DRESS DESIGN Use CLOTHING DESIGN
	DRILL PRESS OPERATORS Use MACHINE TOOL OPERATORS
	DRILL PRESSES Use MACHINE TOOLS
PATTERN	DRILLS (LANGUAGE)
	DRILLS (PRACTICE)
SUBSTITUTION	DRILLS
	DRINKING
SOCIAL	DRINKING Use DRINKING
	DRINKING WATER
MENU	DRIVEN SOFTWARE
	DRIVER EDUCATION
	DRIVER TRAINING Use DRIVER EDUCATION
	DRIVEWAYS
	DROPOUT ATTITUDES
	DROPOUT CHARACTERISTICS
	DROPOUT EMPLOYMENT Use DROPOUT PROGRAMS
	DROPOUT IDENTIFICATION (1966 1980) Use DROPOUT CHARACTERISTICS
	DROPOUT PREVENTION
	DROPOUT PROBLEMS (1966 1980) Use DROPOUTS
	DROPOUT PROGRAMS
	DROPOUT RATE
	DROPOUT REHABILITATION (1966 1980) Use DROPOUT PROGRAMS
	DROPOUT RESEARCH
	DROPOUT ROLE (1966 1980) Use DROPOUTS
	DROPOUT TEACHING (1966 1980) Use DROPOUT PROGRAMS
	DROPOUTS
ADULT	DROPOUTS
COLLEGE	DROPOUTS Use DROPOUTS
HIGH SCHOOL	DROPOUTS Use DROPOUTS
POTENTIAL	DROPOUTS
RURAL	DROPOUTS (1966 1981) Use DROPOUTS
SCHOOL	DROPOUTS Use DROPOUTS
URBAN	DROPOUTS (1966 1981) Use DROPOUTS
	DROWSINESS Use SLEEP
	DRUG ABUSE
	DRUG ADDICTION
	DRUG EDUCATION
	DRUG INSPECTORS Use FOOD AND DRUG INSPECTORS
FOOD AND	DRUG INSPECTORS
	DRUG LEGISLATION
	DRUG REHABILITATION
	DRUG THERAPY
	DRUG USE
ILLEGAL	DRUG USE
	DRUG WITHDRAWAL Use DRUG REHABILITATION
	DRUGGISTS Use PHARMACISTS
CHEMICAL DEPENDENCY	(DRUGS) Use DRUG ADDICTION
TRANQUILIZING	DRUGS Use SEDATIVES
WITHDRAWAL	(DRUGS) Use DRUG REHABILITATION
	DRYCLEANING LAUNDRY OCCUPATIONS Use LAUNDRY DRYCLEANING OCCUPATIONS
LAUNDRY	DRYCLEANING OCCUPATIONS
	DUAL CAREER FAMILY
	DUAL EARNER PARENTS Use EMPLOYED PARENTS
	DUAL ENROLLMENT
	DUE PROCESS
PROCEDURAL	DUE PROCESS Use DUE PROCESS
	DUES Use FEES
	DUPLICATING Use REPROGRAPHY
	DUSUN
	DUTCH
	DUTCH CULTURE
EXTRAINSTRUCTIONAL	DUTIES Use NONINSTRUCTIONAL RESPONSIBILITY
EXTRATEACHING	DUTIES Use NONINSTRUCTIONAL RESPONSIBILITY
NONTEACHING	DUTIES Use NONINSTRUCTIONAL RESPONSIBILITY
	DWELLINGS Use HOUSING
	DYADIC COMMUNICATION Use INTERPERSONAL COMMUNICATION
GROUP	DYNAMICS
MINIMAL BRAIN	DYSFUNCTION
	DYSLEXIA
	DYSPHONIA Use VOICE DISORDERS
	DYSTHYMIA Use DEPRESSION (PSYCHOLOGY)
	DYULA
R D AND	E Use RESEARCH AND DEVELOPMENT
	EARLY ADMISSION
	EARLY CHILDHOOD (1966 1980) Use YOUNG CHILDREN
	EARLY CHILDHOOD EDUCATION
	EARLY DETECTION Use IDENTIFICATION
	EARLY EXPERIENCE
	EARLY PARENTHOOD
	EARLY READING
	EARLY RETIREMENT
	EARLY SCHOOL LEAVERS Use DROPOUTS
DUAL	EARNER PARENTS Use EMPLOYED PARENTS
	EARS
	EARTH SCIENCE
	EARTHQUAKES
	EASTERN CIVILIZATION Use NON WESTERN CIVILIZATION
MIDDLE	EASTERN HISTORY
NEAR	EASTERN HISTORY Use MIDDLE EASTERN HISTORY
MIDDLE	EASTERN STUDIES
	EATING HABITS
	EBONICS Use BLACK DIALECTS
	ECHOLALIA
	ECHOLOCATION
	ECHOPHASIA Use ECHOLALIA
	ECOLOGICAL FACTORS
	ECOLOGY
	ECONOMIC ANALYSIS Use ECONOMIC RESEARCH
	ECONOMIC CHANGE

ECONOMIC CLIMATE
ECONOMIC CYCLES Use BUSINESS CYCLES
ECONOMIC DEVELOPMENT
ECONOMIC DISADVANTAGEMENT (1966 1980) Use POVERTY
ECONOMIC EDUCATION (1971 1980) Use ECONOMICS EDUCATION
ECONOMIC FACTORS
ECONOMIC FLUCTUATIONS Use BUSINESS CYCLES
ECONOMIC GEOGRAPHY Use HUMAN GEOGRAPHY
ECONOMIC INSECURITY Use POVERTY
ECONOMIC OPPORTUNITIES
ECONOMIC PLIGHT Use POVERTY
ECONOMIC PROGRESS
ECONOMIC RESEARCH
ECONOMIC STATUS
ECONOMIC SUPPORT Use FINANCIAL SUPPORT
ECONOMICALLY ADVANCED NATIONS Use DEVELOPED NATIONS
ECONOMICALLY ADVANTAGED Use ADVANTAGED
ECONOMICALLY DEPRESSED AREAS Use POVERTY AREAS
ECONOMICALLY DEPRIVED Use ECONOMICALLY DISADVANTAGED
ECONOMICALLY DISADVANTAGED
ECONOMICS
CONSUMER ECONOMICS
ECONOMICS CURRICULUM Use ECONOMICS EDUCATION
DISTRIBUTION (ECONOMICS) Use MARKETING
ECONOMICS EDUCATION
HOME ECONOMICS EDUCATION
EDUCATIONAL ECONOMICS
FAMILY ECONOMICS Use CONSUMER ECONOMICS
HOME ECONOMICS
INFLATION (ECONOMICS)
ECONOMICS INSTRUCTION Use ECONOMICS EDUCATION
LABOR ECONOMICS
OCCUPATIONAL HOME ECONOMICS
ECONOMICS OF EDUCATION Use EDUCATIONAL ECONOMICS
RURAL ECONOMICS
HOME ECONOMICS SKILLS
HOME ECONOMICS TEACHERS
ECONOMY Use ECONOMICS
TOKEN ECONOMY
ECOSYSTEMS Use ECOLOGY
EDITING
EDITORIALS
EDITORS
EDUCABLE MENTALLY HANDICAPPED (1966 1980) Use MILD MENTAL RETARDATION
EDUCATION
ACADEMIC EDUCATION
ACCELERATION (EDUCATION)
ACCELERATION (1966 1982) (EDUCATION) Use ACCELERATION (EDUCATION)
ACCESS TO EDUCATION
ADAPTED PHYSICAL EDUCATION
ADMINISTRATOR EDUCATION
ADMISSION TESTS (HIGHER EDUCATION) Use COLLEGE ENTRANCE EXAMINATIONS
ADULT EDUCATION
ADULT BASIC EDUCATION
ADULT FARMER EDUCATION
ADULT VOCATIONAL EDUCATION
FUNDAMENTAL EDUCATION (ADULTS) Use ADULT BASIC EDUCATION
ADVANCED EDUCATION Use HIGHER EDUCATION
ADVENTURE EDUCATION
AEROSPACE EDUCATION
AEROSPACE SCIENCE EDUCATION Use AEROSPACE EDUCATION
AESTHETIC EDUCATION
AFFECTIVE EDUCATION Use HUMANISTIC EDUCATION
AFTER SCHOOL EDUCATION
LOCAL EDUCATION AGENCIES Use SCHOOL DISTRICTS
STATE EDUCATION AGENCIES Use STATE DEPARTMENTS OF EDUCATION
AGING EDUCATION
AGRICULTURAL EDUCATION
ALCOHOL EDUCATION
ALLIED HEALTH EDUCATION Use ALLIED HEALTH OCCUPATIONS EDUCATION
ALLIED HEALTH OCCUPATIONS EDUCATION
ALTERNATIVE EDUCATION Use NONTRADITIONAL EDUCATION
ALUMNI EDUCATION
AMERICAN INDIAN EDUCATION
EDUCATION AND WORK Use EDUCATION WORK RELATIONSHIP
ARCHITECTURAL EDUCATION
ART EDUCATION
ARTICULATION (EDUCATION)
HIGHER EDUCATION AS A FIELD OF STUDY Use POSTSECONDARY EDUCATION AS A FIELD OF STUDY
POSTSECONDARY EDUCATION AS A FIELD OF STUDY
AUDIOVISUAL EDUCATION Use AUDIOVISUAL INSTRUCTION
LOCAL EDUCATION AUTHORITIES Use SCHOOL DISTRICTS
BASIC BUSINESS EDUCATION
BEGINNING FARMER EDUCATION Use YOUNG FARMER EDUCATION
BICULTURAL EDUCATION Use MULTICULTURAL EDUCATION
BILINGUAL EDUCATION
BLACK EDUCATION
BOARDS OF EDUCATION
BUSINESS EDUCATION
BUSINESS ADMINISTRATION EDUCATION
CAREER EDUCATION
CASE STUDIES (EDUCATION) (1966 1980) Use CASE STUDIES
CONTINUING EDUCATION CENTERS
TEACHER EDUCATION CENTERS Use TEACHER CENTERS
CHANCELLORS (EDUCATION) Use COLLEGE PRESIDENTS
CITIZENSHIP EDUCATION
CLINICAL PROFESSORS (1967 1980) (EDUCATION) Use STUDENT TEACHER SUPERVISORS
COLLEGES OF EDUCATION Use SCHOOLS OF EDUCATION
COMMERCIAL EDUCATION Use BUSINESS EDUCATION
COMMUNITY EDUCATION
COMPARATIVE EDUCATION

MARITIME EDUCATION
MATHEMATICS EDUCATION
MEDICAL EDUCATION
BOARD OF EDUCATION MEMBERS Use BOARDS OF EDUCATION
MEXICAN AMERICAN EDUCATION
MIGRANT EDUCATION
MIGRANT ADULT EDUCATION
MIGRANT CHILD EDUCATION (1967 1980) Use MIGRANT EDUCATION
MOVEMENT EDUCATION
MULTICULTURAL EDUCATION
MULTIETHNIC EDUCATION Use MULTICULTURAL EDUCATION
MUSIC EDUCATION
NEGRO EDUCATION (1966 1977) Use BLACK EDUCATION
NONDISCRIMINATORY EDUCATION
NONFORMAL EDUCATION
NONPUBLIC EDUCATION Use PRIVATE EDUCATION
NONTRADITIONAL EDUCATION
NURSING EDUCATION
OFF CAMPUS EDUCATION Use EXTENSION EDUCATION
OFFICE EDUCATION Use OFFICE OCCUPATIONS EDUCATION
OFFICE OCCUPATIONS EDUCATION
OPEN EDUCATION
OUTCOMES OF EDUCATION
OUTDOOR EDUCATION
OUTPUT ORIENTED EDUCATION Use COMPETENCY BASED EDUCATION
OUTPUT ORIENTED TEACHER EDUCATION Use COMPETENCY BASED TEACHER EDUCATION
PARALEGAL EDUCATION Use LEGAL ASSISTANTS and LEGAL EDUCATION (PROFESSIONS)
PARENT EDUCATION
PARENTHOOD EDUCATION
PATIENT EDUCATION
PERFORMANCE BASED EDUCATION (1974 1980) Use COMPETENCY BASED EDUCATION
PERFORMANCE BASED TEACHER EDUCATION (1972 1980) Use COMPETENCY BASED TEACHER EDUCATION
PERMANENT EDUCATION Use LIFELONG LEARNING
EDUCATION PERMANENTE Use LIFELONG LEARNING
PHARMACEUTICAL EDUCATION
PHYSICAL EDUCATION
POLICE EDUCATION
BOARD OF EDUCATION POLICY
POLITICS OF EDUCATION
POPULATION EDUCATION
POST DOCTORAL EDUCATION (1967 1980) Use POSTDOCTORAL EDUCATION
POST HIGH SCHOOL EDUCATION Use POSTSECONDARY EDUCATION
POST SECONDARY EDUCATION (1967 1978) Use POSTSECONDARY EDUCATION
POSTDOCTORAL EDUCATION
POSTSECONDARY EDUCATION
PRERETIREMENT EDUCATION
PRESCHOOL EDUCATION
PRESERVICE EDUCATION (1966 1980) Use PRESERVICE TEACHER EDUCATION
PRESERVICE TEACHER EDUCATION
PREVOCATIONAL EDUCATION
PRIMARY EDUCATION
PRISON EDUCATION Use CORRECTIONAL EDUCATION
PRIVATE EDUCATION
PRIVATE HIGHER EDUCATION Use HIGHER EDUCATION and PRIVATE EDUCATION
PROCESS EDUCATION
PROFESSIONAL EDUCATION
PROFESSIONAL CONTINUING EDUCATION
LEGAL EDUCATION (PROFESSIONS)
PROFICIENCY BASED EDUCATION Use COMPETENCY BASED EDUCATION
PROFICIENCY BASED TEACHER EDUCATION Use COMPETENCY BASED TEACHER EDUCATION
ADULT EDUCATION PROGRAMS (1966 1980) Use ADULT EDUCATION and ADULT PROGRAMS
BILINGUAL EDUCATION PROGRAMS
COMPENSATORY EDUCATION PROGRAMS (1966 1980) Use COMPENSATORY EDUCATION
INDIVIDUALIZED EDUCATION PROGRAMS
INSERVICE EDUCATION PROGRAMS Use INSERVICE EDUCATION
REMEDIAL EDUCATION PROGRAMS Use REMEDIAL PROGRAMS
TEACHER EDUCATION PROGRAMS
WORK EDUCATION PROGRAMS Use WORK STUDY PROGRAMS
PROGRESSIVE EDUCATION
PSYCHOLOGICAL EDUCATION Use HUMANISTIC EDUCATION
PUBLIC EDUCATION
PUBLIC ADMINISTRATION EDUCATION
PUBLIC AFFAIRS EDUCATION
PUBLIC HIGHER EDUCATION Use HIGHER EDUCATION and PUBLIC EDUCATION
PUBLIC SCHOOL ADULT EDUCATION
QUALITY EDUCATION Use EDUCATIONAL QUALITY
RECURRENT EDUCATION Use LIFELONG LEARNING
WORK EDUCATION RELATIONSHIP Use EDUCATION WORK RELATIONSHIP
RELEVANCE (EDUCATION)
RELIGIOUS EDUCATION
REMEDIAL EDUCATION Use REMEDIAL INSTRUCTION
RESEARCH SPECIALISTS (EDUCATION) Use EDUCATIONAL RESEARCHERS
RESULTS OF EDUCATION Use OUTCOMES OF EDUCATION
EDUCATION ROLE Use ROLE OF EDUCATION
BOARD OF EDUCATION ROLE
ROLE OF EDUCATION
RURAL EDUCATION
SAFETY EDUCATION
SCHOOLS OF EDUCATION
SCIENCE EDUCATION
SCREEN EDUCATION Use FILM STUDY
SECONDARY EDUCATION
SERVICE EDUCATION (1966 1980) Use VOCATIONAL EDUCATION
EDUCATION SERVICE CENTERS
SEX EDUCATION
SHARED TIME (EDUCATION) Use DUAL ENROLLMENT
SPECIAL EDUCATION
SPEECH EDUCATION (1966 1980)
STATE BOARDS OF EDUCATION
STATE COMMITTEES ON EDUCATION Use STATE BOARDS OF EDUCATION
STATE DEPARTMENTS OF EDUCATION

SUPPLEMENTARY EDUCATION
SUPPLY OF EDUCATION Use EDUCATIONAL SUPPLY
TAX EQUITY (EDUCATION) Use EDUCATIONAL EQUITY (FINANCE)
TEACHER EDUCATION
TEACHER EDUCATOR EDUCATION
BUSINESS EDUCATION TEACHERS
DISTRIBUTIVE EDUCATION TEACHERS
PHYSICAL EDUCATION TEACHERS
SPECIAL EDUCATION TEACHERS
VOCATIONAL EDUCATION TEACHERS
TECHNICAL EDUCATION
TERMINAL EDUCATION
TERTIARY EDUCATION Use POSTSECONDARY EDUCATION
THEOLOGICAL EDUCATION
TRACK SYSTEM (EDUCATION)
TRADE AND INDUSTRIAL EDUCATION
UNDERGRADUATE EDUCATION Use UNDERGRADUATE STUDY
CONTINUING EDUCATION UNITS
UNIVERSAL EDUCATION (1968 1976) Use EQUAL EDUCATION
URBAN EDUCATION
VALUES EDUCATION
VETERANS EDUCATION
VETERINARY MEDICAL EDUCATION
VOCATIONAL EDUCATION
AGRICULTURAL EDUCATION (VOCATIONAL) Use AGRICULTURAL EDUCATION and VOCATIONAL EDUCATION
VOCATIONAL BUSINESS EDUCATION Use BUSINESS EDUCATION
HEALTH OCCUPATIONS EDUCATION (VOCATIONAL) Use ALLIED HEALTH OCCUPATIONS EDUCATION and VOCATIONAL EDUCATION
VOCATIONAL INDUSTRIAL EDUCATION Use TRADE AND INDUSTRIAL EDUCATION
EDUCATION VOUCHERS (1971 1980) Use EDUCATIONAL VOUCHERS
WITHDRAWAL (EDUCATION)
WOMENS EDUCATION
WORK AND EDUCATION Use EDUCATION WORK RELATIONSHIP
EDUCATION WORK RELATIONSHIP
WORKERS EDUCATION Use LABOR EDUCATION
YOUNG FARMER EDUCATION
EDUCATIONAL ACCESS Use ACCESS TO EDUCATION
EDUCATIONAL ACCOUNTABILITY (1970 1980) Use ACCOUNTABILITY
EDUCATIONAL ACHIEVEMENT Use ACADEMIC ACHIEVEMENT
EDUCATIONAL ADMINISTRATION
EDUCATIONAL ADVANTAGES Use EDUCATIONAL OPPORTUNITIES
EDUCATIONAL ALTERNATIVES (1974 1980) Use NONTRADITIONAL EDUCATION
EDUCATIONAL ANTHROPOLOGY
EDUCATIONAL ASSESSMENT
EDUCATIONAL ATTAINMENT
EDUCATIONAL ATTITUDES
EDUCATIONAL BACKGROUND
EDUCATIONAL BENEFITS
SUPPLEMENTARY EDUCATIONAL CENTERS (1966 1980) Use EDUCATION SERVICE CENTERS and SUPPLEMENTARY EDUCATION
EDUCATIONAL CERTIFICATES
EDUCATIONAL CHANGE
EDUCATIONAL CHOICE Use SCHOOL CHOICE
EDUCATIONAL COMPLEXES
EDUCATIONAL COMPUTING Use COMPUTER USES IN EDUCATION
EDUCATIONAL COOPERATION
EDUCATIONAL COORDINATION (1967 1980) Use COORDINATION and EDUCATIONAL COOPERATION
EDUCATIONAL COUNSELING
EDUCATIONAL DEMAND
DEMONSTRATIONS (EDUCATIONAL)
EDUCATIONAL DEVELOPMENT
GENERAL EDUCATIONAL DEVELOPMENT PROGRAMS Use HIGH SCHOOL EQUIVALENCY PROGRAMS
DIAGNOSIS (EDUCATIONAL) Use EDUCATIONAL DIAGNOSIS
EDUCATIONAL DIAGNOSIS
EDUCATIONAL DISADVANTAGEMENT (1966 1980) Use EDUCATIONALLY DISADVANTAGED
EDUCATIONAL DISCRIMINATION
EDUCATIONAL ECONOMICS
EDUCATIONAL ENDOWMENTS Use ENDOWMENT FUNDS
EDUCATIONAL ENVIRONMENT
EDUCATIONAL EQUALITY (1966 1976) Use EQUAL EDUCATION
EDUCATIONAL EQUIPMENT
EDUCATIONAL EQUITY (FINANCE)
EDUCATIONAL EQUITY (OPPORTUNITIES) Use EQUAL EDUCATION
INTERNATIONAL EDUCATIONAL EXCHANGE
EDUCATIONAL EXPERIENCE
EDUCATIONAL EXPERIMENTS
EDUCATIONAL FACILITIES
EDUCATIONAL FACILITIES DESIGN
EDUCATIONAL FACILITIES IMPROVEMENT
EDUCATIONAL FACILITIES PLANNING
EDUCATIONAL FINANCE
EQUITY (EDUCATIONAL FINANCE) Use EDUCATIONAL EQUITY (FINANCE)
EDUCATIONAL FOUNDATIONS Use PHILANTHROPIC FOUNDATIONS
EDUCATIONAL FUTURES Use EDUCATIONAL TRENDS and FUTURES (OF SOCIETY)
EDUCATIONAL GAMES
EDUCATIONAL GERONTOLOGY
EDUCATIONAL GOALS Use EDUCATIONAL OBJECTIVES
EDUCATIONAL GOALS OF STUDENTS Use STUDENT EDUCATIONAL OBJECTIVES
EDUCATIONAL GUIDANCE (1966 1977) Use EDUCATIONAL COUNSELING
EDUCATIONAL HISTORY
EDUCATIONAL IMPROVEMENT
EDUCATIONAL INEQUALITY Use EQUAL EDUCATION
EDUCATIONAL INNOVATION
EDUCATIONAL INSTITUTIONS Use SCHOOLS
EDUCATIONAL INTEREST (1967 1980) Use STUDENT EDUCATIONAL OBJECTIVES
EDUCATIONAL LEGISLATION
EDUCATIONAL LEVEL Use ACADEMIC ACHIEVEMENT
EDUCATIONAL MALPRACTICE
EDUCATIONAL MANAGEMENT Use EDUCATIONAL ADMINISTRATION
EDUCATIONAL MATERIALS Use INSTRUCTIONAL MATERIALS
EDUCATIONAL MEDIA

EDUCATIONAL MEDIA ADAPTATION Use MEDIA ADAPTATION
EDUCATIONAL MEDIA SELECTION Use MEDIA SELECTION
EDUCATIONAL METHODS
EDUCATIONAL MOBILITY
EDUCATIONAL NEEDS
EDUCATIONAL OBJECTIVES
EDUCATIONAL OBJECTIVES OF STUDENTS Use STUDENT EDUCATIONAL OBJECTIVES
STUDENT EDUCATIONAL OBJECTIVES
EDUCATIONAL OPPORTUNITIES
EQUAL EDUCATIONAL OPPORTUNITIES Use EQUAL EDUCATION
EQUITY (EDUCATIONAL OPPORTUNITIES) Use EQUAL EDUCATION
EDUCATIONAL OUTCOMES Use OUTCOMES OF EDUCATION
EDUCATIONAL PARKS
EDUCATIONAL PHILOSOPHY
EDUCATIONAL PLANNING
EDUCATIONAL PLANS Use EDUCATIONAL PLANNING
EDUCATIONAL POLICY
EDUCATIONAL POLITICS Use POLITICS OF EDUCATION
EDUCATIONAL PRACTICE (1967 1980) Use EDUCATIONAL PRACTICES
EDUCATIONAL PRACTICES
EDUCATIONAL PRINCIPLES
EDUCATIONAL PROBLEMS (1966 1980)
EDUCATIONAL PROCESSES Use LEARNING PROCESSES
EDUCATIONAL PRODUCTION FUNCTIONS Use PRODUCTIVITY
EDUCATIONAL PROGRAMS (1966 1980)
NONSCHOOL EDUCATIONAL PROGRAMS
EDUCATIONAL PSYCHOLOGY
EDUCATIONAL PURPOSES Use EDUCATIONAL OBJECTIVES
EDUCATIONAL QUALITY
EDUCATIONAL QUALITY ASSESSMENT Use EDUCATIONAL ASSESSMENT and EDUCATIONAL QUALITY
EDUCATIONAL RADIO
EDUCATIONAL REFORM Use EDUCATIONAL CHANGE
EDUCATIONAL RELEVANCE Use RELEVANCE (EDUCATION)
EDUCATIONAL RESEARCH
EDUCATIONAL RESEARCHERS
EDUCATIONAL RESOURCES
EDUCATIONAL RESPONSIBILITY
EDUCATIONAL RETARDATION (1966 1980)
EDUCATIONAL SERVICE CENTERS Use EDUCATION SERVICE CENTERS
MOBILE EDUCATIONAL SERVICES
EDUCATIONAL SOCIOLOGY
EDUCATIONAL SPECIFICATIONS (1967 1980)
EDUCATIONAL STATUS COMPARISON
EDUCATIONAL STRATEGIES
EDUCATIONAL SUPPLY
EDUCATIONAL SUPPORT Use EDUCATIONAL FINANCE
EDUCATIONAL SURVEYS Use SCHOOL SURVEYS
EDUCATIONAL TECHNOLOGY
EDUCATIONAL TELEVISION
EDUCATIONAL TESTING
EDUCATIONAL THEORIES
EDUCATIONAL THERAPY
EDUCATIONAL TRENDS
EDUCATIONAL VOUCHERS
EDUCATIONALLY DEPRIVED Use EDUCATIONALLY DISADVANTAGED
EDUCATIONALLY DISADVANTAGED
TEACHER EDUCATOR EDUCATION
ADULT EDUCATORS
CATHOLIC EDUCATORS
COUNSELOR EDUCATORS
PHYSICAL EDUCATORS Use PHYSICAL EDUCATION TEACHERS
TEACHER EDUCATORS
EEG Use ELECTROENCEPHALOGRAPHY
MAGNITUDE OF EFFECT Use EFFECT SIZE
PRIMACY EFFECT
EFFECT SIZE
EFFECTIVE SCHOOLING Use SCHOOL EFFECTIVENESS
INSTRUCTIONALLY EFFECTIVE SCHOOLS Use SCHOOL EFFECTIVENESS
EFFECTIVE TEACHING (1966 1980) Use TEACHER EFFECTIVENESS
COST EFFECTIVENESS ANALYSIS Use COST EFFECTIVENESS
COST EFFECTIVENESS
COUNSELING EFFECTIVENESS
INSTRUCTIONAL EFFECTIVENESS
ORGANIZATIONAL EFFECTIVENESS
PROGRAM EFFECTIVENESS
SCHOOL EFFECTIVENESS
TEACHER EFFECTIVENESS
BIOCHEMICAL EFFECTS Use BIOCHEMISTRY
DESEGREGATION EFFECTS
INTEGRATION EFFECTS (1966 1980) Use DESEGREGATION EFFECTS
MASS MEDIA EFFECTS
RADIATION EFFECTS
REGRESSION EFFECTS Use REGRESSION (STATISTICS)
SOUND EFFECTS
SPECIAL EFFECTS
EFFICIENCY
COMMUNITY EFFORT Use COMMUNITY ACTION
TAX EFFORT
EFL Use ENGLISH (SECOND LANGUAGE)
EGG INSPECTORS Use FOOD AND DRUG INSPECTORS
EGO Use SELF CONCEPT
EGOCENTRISM
EGOTISM Use EGOCENTRISM
EIDETIC IMAGERY
EIDETIC IMAGES (1967 1980) Use EIDETIC IMAGERY
EIGHT MILLIMETER PROJECTORS (1970 1980) Use PROJECTION EQUIPMENT
EIGHTEENTH CENTURY LITERATURE
ELDER ABUSE
ELDERLY Use OLDER ADULTS
ABUSED ELDERLY Use ELDER ABUSE
ELECTED CITY OFFICIALS Use CITY OFFICIALS

ELECTION CAMPAIGNS Use POLITICAL CAMPAIGNS
ELECTIONS
SCHOOL BUDGET ELECTIONS
PRESIDENTIAL ELECTIONS (UNITED STATES) Use ELECTIONS and PRESIDENTIAL CAMPAIGNS (UNITED STATES)
ELECTIVE COURSES
ELECTIVE READING (1966 1980)
ELECTIVE SUBJECTS (1966 1977) Use ELECTIVE COURSES
BATTERIES (ELECTRIC) Use ELECTRIC BATTERIES
ELECTRIC BATTERIES
ELECTRIC CIRCUITS
ELECTRIC MOTORS
ELECTRIC SYSTEMS Use ELECTRICAL SYSTEMS
ELECTRIC UTILITIES Use UTILITIES
ELECTRICAL APPLIANCE SERVICEMEN (1968 1980) Use APPLIANCE REPAIR
ELECTRICAL APPLIANCES
ELECTRICAL CONTROLS Use ELECTRONIC CONTROL
ELECTRICAL OCCUPATIONS
ELECTRICAL STIMULI
ELECTRICAL SYSTEMS
ELECTRICAL TECHNICIANS Use ELECTRONIC TECHNICIANS
ELECTRICIANS
ELECTRICITY
ELECTROCHROMATOGRAPHY Use CHROMATOGRAPHY
ELECTROENCEPHALOGRAPHY
ELECTROMECHANICAL AIDS
ELECTROMECHANICAL OCCUPATIONS Use ELECTRICAL OCCUPATIONS and ELECTROMECHANICAL TECHNOLOGY
ELECTROMECHANICAL TECHNOLOGY
ELECTRONIC AIDS Use ELECTRONIC EQUIPMENT
ELECTRONIC BULLETIN BOARDS Use ELECTRONIC MAIL
ELECTRONIC CALCULATORS Use CALCULATORS
CIRCUITS (ELECTRONIC) Use ELECTRIC CIRCUITS
ELECTRONIC CIRCUITS Use ELECTRIC CIRCUITS
ELECTRONIC CLASSROOM USE (1966 1980) Use ELECTRONIC CLASSROOMS
ELECTRONIC CLASSROOMS
ELECTRONIC COMMUNICATIONS SYSTEMS Use TELECOMMUNICATIONS
ELECTRONIC CONTROL
ELECTRONIC DATA PROCESSING (1967 1980) Use DATA PROCESSING
ELECTRONIC EQUIPMENT
ELECTRONIC INFORMATION EXCHANGE Use INFORMATION NETWORKS and TELECOMMUNICATIONS
ELECTRONIC MAIL
ELECTRONIC PUBLISHING
ELECTRONIC TECHNICIANS
ELECTRONICS
ELECTRONICS INDUSTRY
ELECTROOPTICS (1968 1980) Use OPTICS
ELEMENTARY EDUCATION
ELEMENTARY GRADES (1966 1980) Use ELEMENTARY EDUCATION
UNGRADED ELEMENTARY PROGRAMS (1966 1980) Use NONGRADED INSTRUCTIONAL GROUPING
ELEMENTARY SCHOOL CHILDREN Use ELEMENTARY SCHOOL STUDENTS
ELEMENTARY SCHOOL COUNSELING (1967 1980) Use SCHOOL COUNSELING
ELEMENTARY SCHOOL COUNSELORS (1967 1980) Use SCHOOL COUNSELORS
ELEMENTARY SCHOOL CURRICULUM
FOREIGN LANGUAGES IN THE ELEMENTARY SCHOOL Use FLES
ELEMENTARY SCHOOL GUIDANCE (1967 1980) Use SCHOOL GUIDANCE
ELEMENTARY SCHOOL LIBRARIES (1966 1980) Use SCHOOL LIBRARIES
ELEMENTARY SCHOOL MATHEMATICS
ELEMENTARY SCHOOL ROLE (1966 1980) Use SCHOOL ROLE
ELEMENTARY SCHOOL SCIENCE
ELEMENTARY SCHOOL STUDENTS
ELEMENTARY SCHOOL SUPERVISORS (1966 1980) Use SCHOOL SUPERVISION
ELEMENTARY SCHOOL TEACHERS
ELEMENTARY SCHOOLS
BIRACIAL ELEMENTARY SCHOOLS (1966 1980) Use SCHOOL DESEGREGATION
CATHOLIC ELEMENTARY SCHOOLS (1967 1980) Use CATHOLIC SCHOOLS
ELEMENTARY SCIENCE (1966 1980) Use ELEMENTARY SCHOOL SCIENCE
ELEMENTARY SECONDARY EDUCATION
ARCHITECTURAL ELEMENTS (1968 1980) Use STRUCTURAL ELEMENTS (CONSTRUCTION)
STRUCTURAL ELEMENTS (CONSTRUCTION)
GRAIN ELEVATOR OCCUPATIONS Use CROP PROCESSING OCCUPATIONS
ELIGIBILITY
INSTITUTIONAL ELIGIBILITY Use ELIGIBILITY
STUDENT ELIGIBILITY Use ELIGIBILITY
JOB ELIMINATION Use JOB LAYOFF
PROGRAM ELIMINATION Use PROGRAM TERMINATION
ELITE COLLEGES Use SELECTIVE COLLEGES
ELITISM
EMANCIPATED STUDENTS (1975 1980) Use SELF SUPPORTING STUDENTS
EMBRYOLOGY
EMERGENCY MEDICAL TECHNICIANS
EMERGENCY PROGRAMS
EMERGENCY SQUAD PERSONNEL
EMERGING NATIONS Use DEVELOPING NATIONS
EMERGING OCCUPATIONS
EMOTIONAL ADJUSTMENT
EMOTIONAL BEHAVIOR Use AFFECTIVE BEHAVIOR
EMOTIONAL DEVELOPMENT
EMOTIONAL DISTURBANCES
EMOTIONAL EXPERIENCE
EMOTIONAL HEALTH Use MENTAL HEALTH
EMOTIONAL MALADJUSTMENT (1966 1980) Use EMOTIONAL ADJUSTMENT
EMOTIONAL NEEDS Use PSYCHOLOGICAL NEEDS
EMOTIONAL PATTERNS Use PSYCHOLOGICAL PATTERNS
EMOTIONAL PROBLEMS
EMOTIONAL RESPONSE
EMOTIONAL SECURITY Use SECURITY (PSYCHOLOGY)
EMOTIONALLY DISTURBED (1966 1980) Use EMOTIONAL DISTURBANCES
EMOTIONALLY DISTURBED CHILDREN (1967 1980) Use EMOTIONAL DISTURBANCES
RATIONAL EMOTIVE THERAPY
EMPATHY
EMPLOYABILITY Use EMPLOYMENT POTENTIAL

EMPLOYABLE SKILLS Use EMPLOYMENT POTENTIAL and JOB SKILLS
EMPLOYED MOTHERS Use EMPLOYED PARENTS and MOTHERS
EMPLOYED PARENTS
EMPLOYED WOMEN
EMPLOYEE ASSISTANCE PROGRAMS
EMPLOYEE ATTITUDES
EMPLOYEE EMPLOYER RELATIONSHIP Use EMPLOYER EMPLOYEE RELATIONSHIP
EMPLOYEE EVALUATION Use PERSONNEL EVALUATION
EMPLOYEE FRINGE BENEFITS Use FRINGE BENEFITS
EMPLOYEE OPINIONS Use EMPLOYEE ATTITUDES
EMPLOYEE PERFORMANCE Use JOB PERFORMANCE
EMPLOYEE RELATIONS Use LABOR RELATIONS
EMPLOYER EMPLOYEE RELATIONSHIP
EMPLOYEE RESPONSIBILITY
EMPLOYEE WORK ATTITUDES Use EMPLOYEE ATTITUDES and WORK ATTITUDES
EMPLOYEES
CIVIL SERVICE EMPLOYEES Use GOVERNMENT EMPLOYEES
GOVERNMENT EMPLOYEES
LIBRARY EMPLOYEES Use LIBRARY PERSONNEL
PUBLIC EMPLOYEES Use GOVERNMENT EMPLOYEES
RETENTION (OF EMPLOYEES) Use LABOR TURNOVER
SCHOOL EMPLOYEES Use SCHOOL PERSONNEL
EMPLOYER ATTITUDES
EMPLOYER EMPLOYEE RELATIONSHIP
EMPLOYER OPINIONS Use EMPLOYER ATTITUDES
EMPLOYEE EMPLOYER RELATIONSHIP Use EMPLOYER EMPLOYEE RELATIONSHIP
EMPLOYER SPONSORED DAY CARE Use EMPLOYER SUPPORTED DAY CARE
EMPLOYER SUPPORTED DAY CARE
EMPLOYERS
EMPLOYMENT
EMPLOYMENT ADJUSTMENT Use VOCATIONAL ADJUSTMENT
TEACHER EMPLOYMENT BENEFITS
BLACK EMPLOYMENT
EMPLOYMENT CHANGE Use CAREER CHANGE
EMPLOYMENT COUNSELORS
EMPLOYMENT DISCRIMINATION Use EQUAL OPPORTUNITIES (JOBS)
DOUBLE EMPLOYMENT Use MULTIPLE EMPLOYMENT
DROPOUT EMPLOYMENT Use DROPOUT PROGRAMS
EQUAL EMPLOYMENT Use EQUAL OPPORTUNITIES (JOBS)
EMPLOYMENT EXPERIENCE
EMPLOYMENT FORECASTS Use EMPLOYMENT PROJECTIONS
INADEQUATE EMPLOYMENT Use UNDEREMPLOYMENT
EMPLOYMENT INTERVIEWS
EMPLOYMENT LEVEL
EMPLOYMENT MARKET Use LABOR MARKET
MIGRANT EMPLOYMENT
MULTIPLE EMPLOYMENT
NEGRO EMPLOYMENT (1966 1977) Use BLACK EMPLOYMENT
EMPLOYMENT OPPORTUNITIES
OUTPLACEMENT SERVICES (EMPLOYMENT)
OVERSEAS EMPLOYMENT
PART TIME EMPLOYMENT
EMPLOYMENT PATTERNS
PERQUISITES (EMPLOYMENT) Use FRINGE BENEFITS
EMPLOYMENT POTENTIAL
EMPLOYMENT PRACTICES
EMPLOYMENT PREPARATION Use JOB TRAINING
EMPLOYMENT PROBLEMS
EMPLOYMENT PROGRAMS
EMPLOYMENT PROJECTIONS
EMPLOYMENT QUALIFICATIONS
EMPLOYMENT REFERRAL SERVICES Use EMPLOYMENT SERVICES
EMPLOYMENT SATISFACTION Use JOB SATISFACTION
SEASONAL EMPLOYMENT
SECONDARY EMPLOYMENT Use MULTIPLE EMPLOYMENT
EMPLOYMENT SERVICES
EMPLOYMENT STATISTICS
EMPLOYMENT STATUS Use EMPLOYMENT LEVEL
STUDENT EMPLOYMENT
EMPLOYMENT SURVEYS Use OCCUPATIONAL SURVEYS
TEACHER EMPLOYMENT
EMPLOYMENT TESTS Use OCCUPATIONAL TESTS
EMPLOYMENT TRENDS (1966 1980) Use EMPLOYMENT PATTERNS
YOUTH EMPLOYMENT
ENCAPSULATED FACILITIES
ENCODING (PSYCHOLOGY)
ENCYCLOPEDIAS
END USERS (INFORMATION) Use USERS (INFORMATION)
ENDANGERED SPECIES
ENDOWED SCHOLARSHIPS Use SCHOLARSHIPS
ENDOWMENT FUNDS
EDUCATIONAL ENDOWMENTS Use ENDOWMENT FUNDS
ENERGY
ATOMIC ENERGY Use NUCLEAR ENERGY
ENERGY AUDITS
ENERGY CONSERVATION
ENERGY EDUCATION
GEOTHERMAL ENERGY
ENERGY MANAGEMENT
NUCLEAR ENERGY
ENERGY OCCUPATIONS
NUCLEAR ENERGY OCCUPATIONS Use ENERGY OCCUPATIONS and NUCLEAR ENERGY
SOLAR ENERGY
SOLAR RADIATION ENERGY Use SOLAR ENERGY
ALTERNATIVE ENERGY SOURCES
ENERGY TECHNOLOGY Use POWER TECHNOLOGY
WIND ENERGY
LAW ENFORCEMENT
LAW ENFORCEMENT OFFICERS Use POLICE
ENGAGED TIME (LEARNING) Use TIME ON TASK
STUDENT ENGAGED TIME Use TIME ON TASK

CONSERVATION (ENVIRONMENT)
CONTROLLED ENVIRONMENT (1966 1980)
HEREDITY ENVIRONMENT CONTROVERSY Use NATURE NURTURE CONTROVERSY
CULTURAL ENVIRONMENT (1966 1980) Use CULTURAL CONTEXT
DEPRIVED ENVIRONMENT Use DISADVANTAGED ENVIRONMENT
LEAST RESTRICTIVE ENVIRONMENT (DISABLED) Use MAINSTREAMING
DISADVANTAGED ENVIRONMENT
EDUCATIONAL ENVIRONMENT
FAMILY ENVIRONMENT
BARRIER FREE ENVIRONMENT (FOR DISABLED) Use ACCESSIBILITY (FOR DISABLED)
ENVIRONMENT HEREDITY CONTROVERSY Use NATURE NURTURE CONTROVERSY
HOME ENVIRONMENT Use FAMILY ENVIRONMENT
INSTITUTIONAL ENVIRONMENT
ORGANIZATIONAL PSYCHOLOGY (WORK ENVIRONMENT) Use INDUSTRIAL PSYCHOLOGY
PERMISSIVE ENVIRONMENT
PHYSICAL ENVIRONMENT
RURAL ENVIRONMENT
SCHOOL ENVIRONMENT (1966 1980) Use EDUCATIONAL ENVIRONMENT
SIMULATED ENVIRONMENT
SLUM ENVIRONMENT
SOCIAL ENVIRONMENT
SONIC ENVIRONMENT Use ACOUSTICAL ENVIRONMENT
SUBURBAN ENVIRONMENT
THERAPEUTIC ENVIRONMENT
THERMAL ENVIRONMENT
URBAN ENVIRONMENT
VISUAL ENVIRONMENT
WORK ENVIRONMENT
ENVIRONMENTAL CRITERIA (1967 1980) Use ENVIRONMENTAL STANDARDS
ENVIRONMENTAL EDUCATION
ENVIRONMENTAL FACTORS Use ENVIRONMENTAL INFLUENCES
ENVIRONMENTAL INFLUENCES
ENVIRONMENTAL RESEARCH
ENVIRONMENTAL STANDARDS
ENVIRONMENTAL TECHNICIANS
ENVIRONMENTAL THERAPY Use MILIEU THERAPY
ENVY Use JEALOUSY
ENZYMES
EPEE FENCING Use FENCING (SPORT)
EPICS
EPIDEMIC ROSEOLA Use RUBELLA
EPIDEMIOLOGY
EPILEPSY
EPISODE TEACHING (1967 1980)
EPISTEMOLOGY
EPISTLES (1970 1980) Use LETTERS (CORRESPONDENCE)
EQUAL EDUCATION
EQUAL EDUCATIONAL OPPORTUNITIES Use EQUAL EDUCATION
EQUAL EMPLOYMENT Use EQUAL OPPORTUNITIES (JOBS)
EQUAL FACILITIES
EQUAL OPPORTUNITIES (JOBS)
EQUAL PAY Use SALARY WAGE DIFFERENTIALS
EQUAL PROTECTION
EDUCATIONAL EQUALITY (1966 1976) Use EQUAL EDUCATION
EQUALITY OF EDUCATION Use EQUAL EDUCATION
EQUALIZATION AID
EQUALIZED FACILITIES Use EQUAL FACILITIES
EQUATED SCORES
HEAT EQUATIONS Use THERMODYNAMICS
EQUATIONS (MATHEMATICS)
STRUCTURAL EQUATIONS Use PATH ANALYSIS
CHEMICAL EQUILIBRIUM
EQUILIBRIUM CONSTANTS Use CHEMICAL EQUILIBRIUM
EQUIPMENT
AIR CONDITIONING EQUIPMENT
ATHLETIC EQUIPMENT
AUDIO EQUIPMENT
AUDIOVISUAL EQUIPMENT Use AUDIOVISUAL AIDS
BIOMEDICAL EQUIPMENT
BROADCAST RECEPTION EQUIPMENT
BUILDING EQUIPMENT (1966 1980) Use EQUIPMENT
CLASSROOM EQUIPMENT Use EDUCATIONAL EQUIPMENT
ADAPTIVE EQUIPMENT (DISABLED) Use ASSISTIVE DEVICES (FOR DISABLED)
EDUCATIONAL EQUIPMENT
ELECTRONIC EQUIPMENT
EQUIPMENT EVALUATION
EQUIPMENT INVENTORY Use FACILITY INVENTORY
LABORATORY EQUIPMENT
LANGUAGE LABORATORY EQUIPMENT (1966 1980) Use LABORATORY EQUIPMENT and LANGUAGE LABORATORIES
LIBRARY EQUIPMENT
LIFE COSTS (FACILITIES AND EQUIPMENT) Use LIFE CYCLE COSTING
EQUIPMENT MAINTENANCE
EQUIPMENT MANUFACTURERS
MEASUREMENT EQUIPMENT
MECHANICAL EQUIPMENT
PHOTOGRAPHIC EQUIPMENT
PROJECTION EQUIPMENT
EQUIPMENT PURCHASING Use PURCHASING
EQUIPMENT REPAIR Use EQUIPMENT MAINTENANCE
SAFETY EQUIPMENT
SCIENCE EQUIPMENT
SOUND EQUIPMENT Use AUDIO EQUIPMENT
EQUIPMENT STANDARDS
EQUIPMENT STORAGE
BIOMEDICAL EQUIPMENT TECHNICIANS Use MEDICAL LABORATORY ASSISTANTS
TELEVISION EQUIPMENT Use VIDEO EQUIPMENT
EQUIPMENT UPKEEP Use EQUIPMENT MAINTENANCE
EQUIPMENT UTILIZATION
VIDEO EQUIPMENT
VISUAL EQUIPMENT Use VISUAL AIDS
FISCAL EQUITY (EDUCATION) Use EDUCATIONAL EQUITY (FINANCE)

TAX EQUITY (EDUCATION) Use EDUCATIONAL EQUITY (FINANCE)
EQUITY (EDUCATIONAL FINANCE) Use EDUCATIONAL EQUITY (FINANCE)
EQUITY (EDUCATIONAL OPPORTUNITIES) Use EQUAL EDUCATION
EDUCATIONAL EQUITY (FINANCE)
EQUITY (IMPARTIALITY) Use JUSTICE
EDUCATIONAL EQUITY (OPPORTUNITIES) Use EQUAL EDUCATION
PAY EQUITY Use COMPARABLE WORTH
SCHOOL FINANCE EQUITY Use EDUCATIONAL EQUITY (FINANCE)
FULL TIME EQUIVALENCY
HIGH SCHOOL EQUIVALENCY PROGRAMS
EQUIVALENCY TESTS
GRADE EQUIVALENT SCALES (1967 1980) Use GRADE EQUIVALENT SCORES
GRADE EQUIVALENT SCORES
RECONSTRUCTION ERA
ERGONOMICS Use HUMAN FACTORS ENGINEERING
ERROR ANALYSIS (LANGUAGE)
MEASUREMENT ERROR Use ERROR OF MEASUREMENT
STANDARD ERROR OF ESTIMATE Use ERROR OF MEASUREMENT
ERROR OF MEASUREMENT
STANDARD ERROR OF MEASUREMENT (1970 1980) Use ERROR OF MEASUREMENT
ERROR OF REFRACTION Use AMETROPIA
ERROR PATTERNS
ERROR VARIANCE Use ERROR OF MEASUREMENT
OCULAR REFRACTIVE ERRORS Use AMETROPIA
REFRACTIVE ERRORS Use AMETROPIA
ESCAPEES Use REFUGEES
ESKIMO ALEUT LANGUAGES
ESKIMOS
ESL Use ENGLISH (SECOND LANGUAGE)
ESOL Use ENGLISH (SECOND LANGUAGE)
ESSAY TESTS
ESSAYS
REAL ESTATE APPRAISAL Use PROPERTY APPRAISAL
REAL ESTATE OCCUPATIONS
ESTATE PLANNING
REAL ESTATE
SELF ESTEEM
STANDARD ERROR OF ESTIMATE Use ERROR OF MEASUREMENT
ESTIMATED COSTS (1966 1980) Use COST ESTIMATES
COST ESTIMATES
ESTIMATION (MATHEMATICS)
TIME ESTIMATION Use TIME MANAGEMENT
ESTONIAN
ESTUARIES
ETHICAL INSTRUCTION
ETHICAL VALUES (1966 1980) Use MORAL VALUES
ETHICS
CODES OF ETHICS
ETHNIC BIAS
ETHNIC COMMUNITY Use ETHNIC GROUPS
ETHNIC CONSCIOUSNESS Use ETHNICITY
ETHNIC CULTURAL GROUPS Use ETHNIC GROUPS
ETHNIC DISCRIMINATION
ETHNIC DISTRIBUTION
ETHNIC GROUP STUDIES Use ETHNIC STUDIES
ETHNIC GROUPING (1966 1980)
ETHNIC GROUPS
ETHNIC HERITAGE Use CULTURAL BACKGROUND
ETHNIC IDENTIFICATION Use ETHNICITY
ETHNIC INTEGRATION Use SOCIAL INTEGRATION
ETHNIC ORIGINS
ETHNIC RELATIONS
ETHNIC STATUS
ETHNIC STEREOTYPES
ETHNIC STUDIES
ETHNIC UNITY Use GROUP UNITY
ETHNICITY
WHITE ETHNICS Use WHITES
ETHNOCENTRISM
ETHNOGRAPHY
ETHNOLOGY
ETHOLOGY
ETIOLOGY
ETV Use EDUCATIONAL TELEVISION
ETYMOLOGY
EUROPEAN HISTORY
INDO EUROPEAN LANGUAGES
EVALUATION
ADMINISTRATOR EVALUATION
AUDITORY EVALUATION
COMPARATIVE EVALUATION Use COMPARATIVE ANALYSIS
COUNSELOR EVALUATION
COURSE EVALUATION
EVALUATION CRITERIA
CURRICULUM EVALUATION
DENTAL EVALUATION
EVALUATION DESIGNS Use EVALUATION METHODS
EMPLOYEE EVALUATION Use PERSONNEL EVALUATION
EQUIPMENT EVALUATION
FACULTY EVALUATION
FORMATIVE EVALUATION
SELF EVALUATION (GROUPS)
HEALTH CARE EVALUATION Use MEDICAL CARE EVALUATION
HOLISTIC EVALUATION
SELF EVALUATION (INDIVIDUALS)
INPUT EVALUATION Use INPUT OUTPUT ANALYSIS
INSTITUTIONAL EVALUATION
INSTRUCTIONAL MATERIAL EVALUATION
MEDICAL EVALUATION
MEDICAL CARE EVALUATION
EVALUATION METHODS

	EVALUATION NEEDS
NONGRADED STUDENT	EVALUATION
STUDENT	EVALUATION OF TEACHER PERFORMANCE
PATIENT CARE	EVALUATION Use MEDICAL CARE EVALUATION
PEER	EVALUATION
WORK	EVALUATION (PERFORMANCE) Use VOCATIONAL EVALUATION
PERSONNEL	EVALUATION
PRESCHOOL	EVALUATION
	EVALUATION PROBLEMS
	EVALUATION PROCEDURES Use EVALUATION METHODS
PROCESS	EVALUATION Use FORMATIVE EVALUATION
PRODUCT	EVALUATION Use SUMMATIVE EVALUATION
PROFILE	EVALUATION (1966 1980) Use PROFILES
PROGRAM	EVALUATION
PSYCHOLOGICAL	EVALUATION
SELF	EVALUATION (1966 1980)
	EVALUATION SPECIALISTS Use EVALUATORS
SPEECH	EVALUATION
STAFF	EVALUATION Use PERSONNEL EVALUATION
STUDENT	EVALUATION
STUDENT TEACHER	EVALUATION
SUMMATIVE	EVALUATION
TEACHER	EVALUATION
	EVALUATION TECHNIQUES (1966 1974) Use EVALUATION METHODS
TEXTBOOK	EVALUATION
	EVALUATION UTILIZATION
VOCATIONAL	EVALUATION
WORK PERFORMANCE	EVALUATION Use VOCATIONAL EVALUATION
WORKER	EVALUATION Use PERSONNEL EVALUATION
WRITING	EVALUATION
	EVALUATIVE THINKING
	EVALUATORS
	EVENING CLASSES (1967 1980) Use EVENING PROGRAMS
	EVENING COLLEGES (1967 1980) Use EVENING PROGRAMS
	EVENING COUNSELING PROGRAMS (1966 1980) Use COUNSELING SERVICES and EVENING PROGRAMS
	EVENING PROGRAMS
	EVENING STUDENTS
CULTURAL	EVENTS (1966 1980) Use CULTURAL ACTIVITIES
CURRENT	EVENTS
	EVOLUTION
	EWE
CREDIT BY	EXAMINATION Use EQUIVALENCY TESTS
	EXAMINATIONS Use TESTS
ADVANCED CREDIT	EXAMINATIONS Use EQUIVALENCY TESTS
ADVANCED STANDING	EXAMINATIONS Use EQUIVALENCY TESTS
COLLEGE ENTRANCE	EXAMINATIONS
PHYSICAL	EXAMINATIONS
LICENSING	EXAMINATIONS (PROFESSIONS)
	EXAMINER CHARACTERISTICS Use EXAMINERS and EXPERIMENTER CHARACTERISTICS
	EXAMINERS
	EXCEPTIONAL (ATYPICAL) (1966 1978) Use EXCEPTIONAL PERSONS
	EXCEPTIONAL CHILD EDUCATION (1968 1980)
	EXCEPTIONAL CHILD RESEARCH
	EXCEPTIONAL CHILD SERVICES (1968 1980)
	EXCEPTIONAL CHILDREN (1966 1978) Use EXCEPTIONAL PERSONS
	EXCEPTIONAL PERSONS
	EXCEPTIONAL STUDENTS (1966 1978) Use EXCEPTIONAL PERSONS
OVERWEIGHT	(EXCESSIVE BODY FAT) Use OBESITY
CULTURAL	EXCHANGE
ELECTRONIC INFORMATION	EXCHANGE Use INFORMATION NETWORKS and TELECOMMUNICATIONS
INTERNATIONAL EDUCATIONAL	EXCHANGE
	EXCHANGE PROGRAMS
STUDENT	EXCHANGE PROGRAMS
TEACHER	EXCHANGE PROGRAMS
SOCIAL	EXCHANGE THEORY
	EXCURSIONS (INSTRUCTION) Use FIELD TRIPS
	EXECUTIVE DEVELOPMENT Use MANAGEMENT DEVELOPMENT
	EXECUTIVE SECRETARIES Use SECRETARIES
	EXEMPLARY PROGRAMS Use DEMONSTRATION PROGRAMS
	EXERCISE
MUSCULAR	EXERCISE Use EXERCISE
PHYSICAL	EXERCISE Use EXERCISE
	EXERCISE PHYSIOLOGY
	EXERCISE (PHYSIOLOGY) (1969 1980)
WRITING	EXERCISES
	EXHAUST STACKS Use CHIMNEYS
	EXHAUSTING (1969 1980) Use VENTILATION
	EXHAUSTION Use FATIGUE (BIOLOGY)
	EXHIBITS
	EXILES Use REFUGEES
	EXISTENTIALISM
	EXOGAMOUS MARRIAGE Use INTERMARRIAGE
FACILITY	EXPANSION
SCHOOL	EXPANSION
	EXPECTANCY Use EXPECTATION
	EXPECTANCY TABLES
WORK LIFE	EXPECTANCY
	EXPECTATION
	EXPENDITURE PER STUDENT
	EXPENDITURES
CONSUMER	EXPENDITURES Use CONSUMER ECONOMICS
LIBRARY	EXPENDITURES
	EXPENSES Use EXPENDITURES
INITIAL	EXPENSES (1966 1980) Use EXPENDITURES
MINIMUM INITIAL	EXPENSES Use EXPENDITURES
MINIMUM OPERATING	EXPENSES Use OPERATING EXPENSES
OPERATING	EXPENSES
	EXPERIENCE
SUPERVISED OCCUPATIONAL	EXPERIENCE (AGRICULTURE) Use SUPERVISED FARM PRACTICE
LANGUAGE	EXPERIENCE APPROACH
	EXPERIENCE BASED EDUCATION Use EXPERIENTIAL LEARNING

EXPERIENCE CHARTS
CLINICAL EXPERIENCE
CLINICAL LEARNING EXPERIENCE Use CLINICAL EXPERIENCE
COMMUNITY EXPERIENCE Use EXPERIENTIAL LEARNING
DISCUSSION EXPERIENCE (1966 1980) Use DISCUSSION
EARLY EXPERIENCE
EDUCATIONAL EXPERIENCE
EMOTIONAL EXPERIENCE
EMPLOYMENT EXPERIENCE
ENRICHMENT EXPERIENCE (1966 1980) Use ENRICHMENT
FIELD LABORATORY EXPERIENCE Use FIELD EXPERIENCE PROGRAMS
GROUP EXPERIENCE
HOME EXPERIENCE Use EXPERIENTIAL LEARNING
INSERVICE TEACHING EXPERIENCE Use TEACHING EXPERIENCE
INTELLECTUAL EXPERIENCE
JOB EXPERIENCE Use EMPLOYMENT EXPERIENCE
LANGUAGE EXPERIENCE Use LANGUAGE ENRICHMENT
LEARNING EXPERIENCE
MATHEMATICAL EXPERIENCE (1966 1980)
PREREADING EXPERIENCE
PRESCHOOL EXPERIENCE Use EARLY EXPERIENCE
PRESERVICE TEACHING EXPERIENCE Use TEACHING EXPERIENCE
FIELD EXPERIENCE PROGRAMS
WORK EXPERIENCE PROGRAMS
SCHOOL EXPERIENCE Use EDUCATIONAL EXPERIENCE
SENSORY EXPERIENCE
SOCIAL EXPERIENCE
STUDENT EXPERIENCE
TEACHER EXPERIENCE (1966 1974) Use TEACHING EXPERIENCE
TEACHING EXPERIENCE
EXPERIENCE UNITS Use ACTIVITY UNITS
VOCATIONAL WORK EXPERIENCE Use COOPERATIVE EDUCATION
WORK EXPERIENCE
EXPERIENCED LABORERS (1966 1980) Use LABORERS
EXPERIENTIAL LEARNING
PRIOR EXPERIENTIAL LEARNING Use EXPERIENTIAL LEARNING and PRIOR LEARNING
EXPERIMENT STATIONS
FIELD EXPERIMENT STATIONS Use EXPERIMENT STATIONS
EXPERIMENTAL COLLEGES
EXPERIMENTAL CURRICULUM
EXPERIMENTAL DESIGN Use RESEARCH DESIGN
EXPERIMENTAL EXTINCTION Use EXTINCTION (PSYCHOLOGY)
EXPERIMENTAL GROUPS
EXPERIMENTAL PROCEDURES Use RESEARCH METHODOLOGY
EXPERIMENTAL PROGRAMS
EXPERIMENTAL PSYCHOLOGY
EXPERIMENTAL SCHOOLS
EXPERIMENTAL TEACHING
EXPERIMENTATION Use EXPERIMENTS
EXPERIMENTER BIAS Use EXPERIMENTER CHARACTERISTICS
EXPERIMENTER CHARACTERISTICS
EXPERIMENTS
EDUCATIONAL EXPERIMENTS
LABORATORY EXPERIMENTS
PHYSICS EXPERIMENTS (1966 1980) Use PHYSICS and SCIENCE EXPERIMENTS
SCIENCE EXPERIMENTS
EXPERT SYSTEMS
CAREER EXPLORATION
EXTRATERRESTRIAL EXPLORATION Use SPACE EXPLORATION
LUNAR EXPLORATION Use LUNAR RESEARCH
OCCUPATIONAL EXPLORATION Use CAREER EXPLORATION
PLANETARY EXPLORATION Use SPACE EXPLORATION
SPACE EXPLORATION
EXPLORATORY BEHAVIOR
EXPLORATORY LEARNING Use DISCOVERY LEARNING
EXPORT TRADE Use EXPORTS
EXPORTS
EXPOSITION (LITERARY) Use EXPOSITORY WRITING
EXPOSITIONS (1971 1980) Use EXHIBITS
EXPOSITORY WRITING
ART EXPRESSION
CREATIVE EXPRESSION
ORAL EXPRESSION (1966 1977) Use SPEECH COMMUNICATION
SELF EXPRESSION
EXPRESSIONISM
FACIAL EXPRESSIONS
IDIOMATIC EXPRESSIONS Use IDIOMS
MATHEMATICAL EXPRESSIONS Use MATHEMATICAL FORMULAS
EXPRESSIVE LANGUAGE
EXPULSION
EXTENDED FAMILY
EXTENDED SCHOOL DAY
EXTENDED SCHOOL YEAR
EXTENDED UNIVERSITIES Use OPEN UNIVERSITIES
EXTENSION AGENTS
COUNTY EXTENSION AGENTS Use EXTENSION AGENTS
VILLAGE EXTENSION AGENTS Use EXTENSION AGENTS
AGRICULTURAL EXTENSION Use RURAL EXTENSION
COOPERATIVE EXTENSION Use EXTENSION EDUCATION
EXTENSION EDUCATION
LIBRARY EXTENSION
RURAL EXTENSION
EXTENSION SERVICES Use EXTENSION EDUCATION
UNIVERSITY EXTENSION (1967 1980) Use EXTENSION EDUCATION
URBAN EXTENSION
MUSCULAR EXTENSIONS Use MOTOR REACTIONS
EXTERNAL DEGREE PROGRAMS
INTERNAL EXTERNAL LOCUS OF CONTROL Use LOCUS OF CONTROL
EXTERNSHIPS (MEDICINE) Use CLINICAL EXPERIENCE
EXPERIMENTAL EXTINCTION Use EXTINCTION (PSYCHOLOGY)
EXTINCTION (PSYCHOLOGY)

STUDENT ACTIVITIES (EXTRACLASS) Use EXTRACURRICULAR ACTIVITIES
EXTRACURRICULAR ACTIVITIES
EXTRADIMENSIONAL SHIFT Use SHIFT STUDIES
EXTRAINSTRUCTIONAL DUTIES Use NONINSTRUCTIONAL RESPONSIBILITY
EXTRAMURAL ATHLETIC PROGRAMS (1966 1980) Use EXTRAMURAL ATHLETICS
EXTRAMURAL ATHLETICS
EXTRAMURAL DEPARTMENTS Use EXTENSION EDUCATION
EXTRAMURAL SPORTS Use EXTRAMURAL ATHLETICS
EXTRATEACHING DUTIES Use NONINSTRUCTIONAL RESPONSIBILITY
EXTRATERRESTRIAL EXPLORATION Use SPACE EXPLORATION
EYE CONTACT
EYE FIXATIONS
EYE HAND COORDINATION
EYE MOVEMENTS
EYE REGRESSIONS (1966 1980) Use EYE MOVEMENTS
EYE VOICE SPAN
EYES
CROSS EYES Use STRABISMUS
FABLES
FABRICATION Use MANUFACTURING
FACIAL EXPRESSIONS
FACILITIES
LIFE COSTS (FACILITIES AND EQUIPMENT) Use LIFE CYCLE COSTING
ANIMAL FACILITIES
BUSINESS EDUCATION FACILITIES
EDUCATIONAL FACILITIES DESIGN
DINING FACILITIES
EDUCATIONAL FACILITIES
ENCAPSULATED FACILITIES
EQUAL FACILITIES
EQUALIZED FACILITIES Use EQUAL FACILITIES
FLEXIBLE FACILITIES
FOOD HANDLING FACILITIES
GUIDANCE FACILITIES (1967 1977) Use GUIDANCE CENTERS
HEALTH FACILITIES
EDUCATIONAL FACILITIES IMPROVEMENT
INSTITUTIONAL FACILITIES (1967 1980) Use FACILITIES
INTEGRATED PUBLIC FACILITIES (1966 1980) Use PUBLIC FACILITIES and RACIAL INTEGRATION
LIBRARY FACILITIES
MILITARY AIR FACILITIES
MUSIC FACILITIES
OFF CAMPUS FACILITIES
OFFICES (FACILITIES)
PARKING FACILITIES
PHYSICAL FACILITIES (1966 1980) Use FACILITIES
PHYSICAL EDUCATION FACILITIES
EDUCATIONAL FACILITIES PLANNING
PORTABLE FACILITIES Use RELOCATABLE FACILITIES
PUBLIC FACILITIES
RECREATIONAL FACILITIES
RELOCATABLE FACILITIES
SANITARY FACILITIES
SATELLITE FACILITIES
SCHOOL FACILITIES Use EDUCATIONAL FACILITIES
SCIENCE FACILITIES
SEGREGATED PUBLIC FACILITIES (1966 1980) Use PUBLIC FACILITIES and RACIAL SEGREGATION
SHARED FACILITIES
SPATIAL RELATIONSHIP (FACILITIES)
STAGES (FACILITIES)
STUDY FACILITIES
TEACHING FACILITIES Use EDUCATIONAL FACILITIES
TEMPORARY FACILITIES Use RELOCATABLE FACILITIES
TOILET FACILITIES
UNDERGROUND FACILITIES
FACILITY CASE STUDIES
FACILITY DESIGN Use FACILITY GUIDELINES
FACILITY EXPANSION
FACILITY GUIDELINES
FACILITY IMPROVEMENT
FACILITY INVENTORY
FACILITY NEEDS Use FACILITY REQUIREMENTS
ORAL FACILITY Use SPEECH SKILLS
FACILITY PLANNING
FACILITY REQUIREMENTS
FACILITY SPECIFICATIONS Use FACILITY GUIDELINES
FACILITY STANDARDS Use FACILITY GUIDELINES
FACILITY UTILIZATION RESEARCH
FACSIMILE COMMUNICATION SYSTEMS (1968 1980) Use FACSIMILE TRANSMISSION
FACSIMILE TRANSMISSION
DE FACTO SEGREGATION
FACTOR ANALYSIS
CENTROID METHOD OF FACTOR ANALYSIS Use FACTOR ANALYSIS
MAXIMUM LIKELIHOOD FACTOR ANALYSIS Use FACTOR ANALYSIS and MAXIMUM LIKELIHOOD STATISTICS
FACTOR STRUCTURE
CAUSAL FACTORS Use INFLUENCES
CLIMATIC FACTORS (1969 1980) Use CLIMATE
CULTURAL FACTORS (1966 1980) Use CULTURAL INFLUENCES
ECOLOGICAL FACTORS
ECONOMIC FACTORS
HUMAN FACTORS ENGINEERING
ENVIRONMENTAL FACTORS Use ENVIRONMENTAL INFLUENCES
FAILURE FACTORS (1966 1980) Use FAILURE
INTELLIGENCE FACTORS (1966 1980) Use INTELLIGENCE
TIME FACTORS (LEARNING)
LOW ACHIEVEMENT FACTORS (1966 1980) Use LOW ACHIEVEMENT
PERFORMANCE FACTORS
POVERTY FACTORS Use ECONOMIC FACTORS and POVERTY
RACIAL FACTORS
RELIGIOUS FACTORS
RESIDENCE FACTORS Use RESIDENCE REQUIREMENTS
RH FACTORS

SOCIAL FACTORS (1968 1980) Use SOCIAL INFLUENCES
SUCCESS FACTORS (1968 1980) Use SUCCESS
FACTUAL READING (1966 1980)
FACULTY
ADJUNCT FACULTY
FACULTY ADVANCEMENT Use FACULTY PROMOTION
FACULTY ADVISERS
FACULTY ADVISORS (1967 1980) Use FACULTY ADVISERS
COLLEGE FACULTY
FACULTY COLLEGE RELATIONSHIP
FACULTY COUNSELORS Use FACULTY ADVISERS
DEANS OF FACULTY Use ACADEMIC DEANS
DENTAL SCHOOL FACULTY Use DENTAL SCHOOLS and MEDICAL SCHOOL FACULTY
FACULTY DESEGREGATION Use FACULTY INTEGRATION
FACULTY DEVELOPMENT
FACULTY EVALUATION
FACULTY FELLOWSHIPS
FULL TIME FACULTY
GRADUATE SCHOOL FACULTY
GRAYING OF FACULTY Use AGING IN ACADEMIA
FACULTY GROWTH Use FACULTY DEVELOPMENT
FACULTY HANDBOOKS
FACULTY IMPROVEMENT Use FACULTY DEVELOPMENT
INTEGRATED FACULTY Use FACULTY INTEGRATION
FACULTY INTEGRATION
FACULTY LOAD Use FACULTY WORKLOAD
MEDICAL SCHOOL FACULTY
FACULTY MOBILITY
NONTENURED FACULTY
FACULTY OFFICES Use OFFICES (FACILITIES)
FACULTY ORGANIZATIONS
PART TIME FACULTY
FACULTY PROMOTION
FACULTY PUBLISHING
FACULTY RANK Use ACADEMIC RANK (PROFESSIONAL)
FACULTY RECRUITMENT
FACULTY SENATES Use COLLEGE GOVERNING COUNCILS
TENURED FACULTY
UNTENURED FACULTY Use NONTENURED FACULTY
WOMEN FACULTY
FACULTY WORKLOAD
PASS FAIL GRADING
FAILURE
ACADEMIC FAILURE
FAILURE FACTORS (1966 1980) Use FAILURE
READING FAILURE
SCHOLASTIC FAILURE Use ACADEMIC FAILURE
FAILURE TO THRIVE
NONORGANIC FAILURE TO THRIVE Use FAILURE TO THRIVE
CULTURE FAIR TESTS
SEX FAIRNESS
FAIRS Use EXHIBITS
SCIENCE FAIRS
FAITH Use BELIEFS
FALLOUT SHELTERS
TRUE FALSE TESTS Use OBJECTIVE TESTS
FAME Use REPUTATION
JOB FAMILIES Use OCCUPATIONAL CLUSTERS
OCCUPATIONAL FAMILIES Use OCCUPATIONAL CLUSTERS
FAMILY ATTITUDES
FAMILY BACKGROUND (1966 1980) Use FAMILY CHARACTERISTICS
BLACK FAMILY
FAMILY BREADWINNERS Use HEADS OF HOUSEHOLDS
FAMILY CHARACTERISTICS
FAMILY CHOICE (EDUCATION) Use SCHOOL CHOICE
FAMILY COUNSELING
FAMILY CULTURE Use FAMILY LIFE
FAMILY DAY CARE
DOMESTIC VIOLENCE (FAMILY) Use FAMILY VIOLENCE
DUAL CAREER FAMILY
FAMILY ECONOMICS Use CONSUMER ECONOMICS
FAMILY ENVIRONMENT
EXTENDED FAMILY
FATHERLESS FAMILY
FAMILY FINANCIAL RESOURCES
FOSTER FAMILY
FAMILY HEALTH
FAMILY HISTORY
FAMILY INCOME
FAMILY INFLUENCE
FAMILY INVOLVEMENT
FAMILY LIFE
FAMILY LIFE EDUCATION
HOME AND FAMILY LIFE EDUCATION Use FAMILY LIFE EDUCATION
FAMILY LIVING Use FAMILY LIFE
FAMILY MANAGEMENT (1966 1980) Use HOME MANAGEMENT
FAMILY MOBILITY
MOTHERLESS FAMILY
NUCLEAR FAMILY
ONE PARENT FAMILY
FAMILY PARTICIPATION Use FAMILY INVOLVEMENT
FAMILY PLANNING
FAMILY PRACTICE (MEDICINE)
FAMILY PROBLEMS
FAMILY PROGRAMS
FAMILY PROJECTS (1966 1980) Use FAMILY PROGRAMS
FAMILY RELATIONSHIP
SCHOOL FAMILY RELATIONSHIP Use FAMILY SCHOOL RELATIONSHIP
FAMILY RESOURCES (1966 1980) Use FAMILY FINANCIAL RESOURCES
FAMILY ROLE
RURAL FAMILY

FAMILY SCHOOL RELATIONSHIP
FAMILY SERVICES POLICY Use FAMILY PROGRAMS and PUBLIC POLICY
SINGLE PARENT FAMILY Use ONE PARENT FAMILY
FAMILY SIZE
FAMILY (SOCIOLOGICAL UNIT)
FAMILY STATUS
FAMILY STRUCTURE
FAMILY TREES Use GENEALOGY
TWO PARENT FAMILY Use NUCLEAR FAMILY
TRADITIONAL FAMILY UNIT Use NUCLEAR FAMILY
FAMILY UNITY Use GROUP UNITY
FAMILY VIOLENCE
FANTASY
FANTASY PLAY Use PRETEND PLAY
FARM ACCOUNTS
FARM AGENTS Use EXTENSION AGENTS
OFF FARM AGRICULTURAL OCCUPATIONS
FARM FOREMEN Use CREW LEADERS
FARM LABOR
FARM LABOR LEGISLATION (1966 1980) Use FARM LABOR and LABOR LEGISLATION
FARM LABOR PROBLEMS (1966 1980) Use FARM LABOR and LABOR PROBLEMS
FARM LABOR SUPPLY (1966 1980) Use FARM LABOR and LABOR SUPPLY
FARM MANAGEMENT
FARM MECHANICS (OCCUPATION) (1967 1980) Use AGRICULTURAL MACHINERY OCCUPATIONS
FARM MECHANICS (SUBJECT) Use AGRICULTURAL ENGINEERING
FARM OCCUPATIONS
FARM OPERATORS Use FARMERS
SUPERVISED FARM PRACTICE
FARM RELATED OCCUPATIONS Use OFF FARM AGRICULTURAL OCCUPATIONS
RURAL FARM RESIDENTS
FARM SUPPLIES Use AGRICULTURAL SUPPLIES
FARM VISITS
FARM YOUTH Use RURAL YOUTH
ADULT FARMER EDUCATION
BEGINNING FARMER EDUCATION Use YOUNG FARMER EDUCATION
YOUNG FARMER EDUCATION
FARMERS
DAIRY FARMERS
NONRESIDENT FARMERS Use PART TIME FARMERS
PART TIME FARMERS
FARSI (LANGUAGE) Use PERSIAN
FARSIGHTEDNESS Use HYPEROPIA
FASCISM
FASHION INDUSTRY
FASHIONS (CLOTHING) Use CLOTHING
FAST TRACK SCHEDULING
OVERWEIGHT (EXCESSIVE BODY FAT) Use OBESITY
FATHER ABSENCE Use FATHERLESS FAMILY
FATHER ATTITUDES
FATHER ROLE Use FATHERS and PARENT ROLE
FATHERLESS FAMILY
FATHERS
MIDDLE CLASS FATHERS (1966 1980) Use FATHERS and MIDDLE CLASS PARENTS
FATIGUE (BIOLOGY)
FAX Use FACSIMILE TRANSMISSION
FEAR
FEAR OF SUCCESS
FEASIBILITY STUDIES
DISTINCTIVE FEATURES (1967 1980) Use DISTINCTIVE FEATURES (LANGUAGE)
DISTINCTIVE FEATURES (LANGUAGE)
PROSODIC FEATURES (SPEECH) Use SUPRASEGMENTALS
FEDERAL AID
STATE FEDERAL AID
FEDERAL CONTROL Use FEDERAL REGULATION
FEDERAL COURT LITIGATION (1966 1980) Use COURT LITIGATION and FEDERAL COURTS
FEDERAL COURTS
FEDERAL GOVERNMENT
FEDERAL GRANTS Use FEDERAL AID
FEDERAL INDIAN RELATIONSHIP
FEDERAL LAWS (1966 1974) Use FEDERAL LEGISLATION
FEDERAL LEGISLATION
FEDERAL LIBRARIES Use FEDERAL GOVERNMENT and GOVERNMENT LIBRARIES
FEDERAL PROGRAMS
FEDERAL RECREATION LEGISLATION (1966 1978) Use FEDERAL LEGISLATION and RECREATION LEGISLATION
FEDERAL REGULATION
STATE FEDERAL RELATIONSHIP Use FEDERAL STATE RELATIONSHIP
FEDERAL STATE AID Use STATE FEDERAL AID
FEDERAL STATE RELATIONSHIP
STATE FEDERAL SUPPORT (1966 1977) Use STATE FEDERAL AID
FEDERAL TROOPS (1966 1980) Use ARMED FORCES
FEED INDUSTRY
FEED STORES
LIVESTOCK FEED STORES Use FEED STORES
FEEDBACK
FEEDER PATTERNS
FEEDER PROGRAMS (1966 1980) Use FEEDER PATTERNS
FEES
FELLOWS (MEDICAL) Use GRADUATE MEDICAL STUDENTS
FELLOWSHIPS
FACULTY FELLOWSHIPS
FEMALE HOMOSEXUALITY Use LESBIANISM
FEMALE ROLE Use FEMALES and SEX ROLE
FEMALES
FEMINISM
EPEE FENCING Use FENCING (SPORT)
FENCING (SPORT)
BODY AND FENDER REPAIRERS Use AUTO BODY REPAIRERS
FENESTRATION Use WINDOWS
FENNO UGRIC LANGUAGES Use FINNO UGRIC LANGUAGES
FERTILITY RATE Use BIRTH RATE

FERTILIZERS
FICTION
SCIENCE FICTION
FORCE FIELD ANALYSIS
FIELD CHECK (1967 1980) Use EQUIPMENT EVALUATION
CORN (FIELD CROP) (1968 1980) Use GRAINS (FOOD)
FIELD CROPS
FIELD DEPENDENCE Use FIELD DEPENDENCE INDEPENDENCE
FIELD DEPENDENCE INDEPENDENCE
FIELD EXPERIENCE PROGRAMS
FIELD EXPERIMENT STATIONS Use EXPERIMENT STATIONS
FIELD HOCKEY
FIELD HOUSES
FIELD INDEPENDENCE Use FIELD DEPENDENCE INDEPENDENCE
FIELD INSTRUCTION
FIELD INTERVIEWS
FIELD LABORATORY EXPERIENCE Use FIELD EXPERIENCE PROGRAMS
HIGHER EDUCATION AS A FIELD OF STUDY Use POSTSECONDARY EDUCATION AS A FIELD OF STUDY
POSTSECONDARY EDUCATION AS A FIELD OF STUDY
FIELD STUDIES
FIELD TEACHING Use FIELD INSTRUCTION
FIELD TESTS
TRACK AND FIELD
FIELD TRIPS
AIRBORNE FIELD TRIPS (1968 1980) Use FIELD TRIPS
ATHLETIC FIELDS
UNITS OF STUDY (SUBJECT FIELDS) (1966 1977) Use UNITS OF STUDY
FIFTEENTH CENTURY LITERATURE
FIRE FIGHTERS
FIGURAL AFTEREFFECTS
FIGURATIVE LANGUAGE
CENSUS FIGURES
FIGURES OF SPEECH Use FIGURATIVE LANGUAGE
FILE CLERKS
FILE MANAGEMENT SYSTEMS Use DATABASE MANAGEMENT SYSTEMS
FILING
ALPHABETIC FILING Use FILING
NUMERIC FILING Use FILING
FILING SYSTEMS Use INFORMATION STORAGE
FILIPINO AMERICANS
FILM AUTEURISM Use AUTEURISM
FILM (CAMERAS) Use PHOTOGRAPHIC EQUIPMENT
FILM CLIPS Use FILMSTRIPS
FILM CRITICISM
FILM INDUSTRY
FILM LIBRARIES
FILM LISTS Use FILMOGRAPHIES
FILM LOOPS Use FILMSTRIPS
FILM PRODUCTION
FILM PRODUCTION SPECIALISTS
FILM PROJECTORS Use PROJECTION EQUIPMENT
REPETITIVE FILM SHOWINGS
FILM STUDY
FILMMAKERS Use FILM PRODUCTION SPECIALISTS
FILMMAKING Use FILM PRODUCTION
FILMOGRAPHIES
FILMS
BEHAVIORAL SITUATION FILMS Use PROTOCOL MATERIALS
BLACK AND WHITE FILMS Use FILMS
COLOR FILMS Use FILMS
FOREIGN LANGUAGE FILMS
INSTRUCTIONAL FILMS
SECOND LANGUAGE FILMS Use FOREIGN LANGUAGE FILMS
SILENT FILMS Use FILMS
SINGLE CONCEPT FILMS
SOUND FILMS (1966 1980) Use FILMS
TEACHER TRAINING FILMS Use PROTOCOL MATERIALS
FILMSTRIP PROJECTORS
FILMSTRIPS
CREDIT (FINANCE)
EDUCATIONAL FINANCE
EDUCATIONAL EQUITY (FINANCE)
EQUITY (EDUCATIONAL FINANCE) Use EDUCATIONAL EQUITY (FINANCE)
SCHOOL FINANCE EQUITY Use EDUCATIONAL EQUITY (FINANCE)
INTEREST (FINANCE)
FINANCE OCCUPATIONS
FINANCE REFORM
SCHOOL FINANCE Use EDUCATIONAL FINANCE
RECREATION FINANCES
FINANCIAL AID APPLICANTS
NEED ANALYSIS (STUDENT FINANCIAL AID)
STUDENT FINANCIAL AID OFFICERS
STATE FINANCIAL AID Use STATE AID
STUDENT FINANCIAL AID
FINANCIAL AUDITS
FINANCIAL BARRIERS Use FINANCIAL PROBLEMS
PARENT FINANCIAL CONTRIBUTION
PARENTAL FINANCIAL CONTRIBUTION (1978 1980) Use PARENT FINANCIAL CONTRIBUTION
FINANCIAL DONORS Use DONORS
FINANCIAL MANAGEMENT Use MONEY MANAGEMENT
FINANCIAL NEEDS
FINANCIAL POLICY
FINANCIAL PROBLEMS
FAMILY FINANCIAL RESOURCES
FINANCIAL SERVICES
FINANCIAL SUPPORT
PRIVATE FINANCIAL SUPPORT
TRUSTS (FINANCIAL)
FINANCING Use FINANCIAL SUPPORT
FINE ARTS
FINE ARTS CENTERS Use ARTS CENTERS

LIBRARY FINES Use FINES (PENALTIES)
FINES (PENALTIES)
FINGER SPELLING
FINISHING
METAL FINISHING Use FINISHING
SURFACE FINISHING Use FINISHING
TEXTILE FINISHING Use FINISHING
WOOD FINISHING Use FINISHING
FINNISH
FINNO UGRIC LANGUAGES
FIRE FIGHTERS
FIRE INSURANCE
FIRE PREVENTION Use FIRE PROTECTION
FIRE PROTECTION
FIRE SCIENCE EDUCATION
FIREMEN Use FIRE FIGHTERS
FIRST AID
FIRST PROFESSIONAL DEGREES Use DEGREES (ACADEMIC) and PROFESSIONAL EDUCATION
FRESHMEN (1967 1980) (FIRST YEAR COLLEGE STUDENTS) Use COLLEGE FRESHMEN
FIRST YEAR TEACHERS Use BEGINNING TEACHERS
FISCAL CAPACITY
FISCAL EQUITY (EDUCATION) Use EDUCATIONAL EQUITY (FINANCE)
FISCAL POLICY Use FINANCIAL POLICY
FISCAL STRAIN Use FINANCIAL PROBLEMS
FISH INSPECTORS Use FOOD AND DRUG INSPECTORS
FISH STUDIES Use ICHTHYOLOGY
FISHERIES
GOODNESS OF FIT
PHYSICAL FITNESS
PIPE FITTING Use PLUMBING
EYE FIXATIONS
CAPITAL OUTLAY (FOR FIXED ASSETS)
FIXED SEQUENCE
FIXED SERVICE TELEVISION (1969 1980) Use EDUCATIONAL TELEVISION
FLES
FLES GUIDES (1967 1980) Use CURRICULUM GUIDES and FLES
FLES MATERIALS (1967 1980) Use FLES and INSTRUCTIONAL MATERIALS
FLES PROGRAMS (1967 1980) Use FLES and SECOND LANGUAGE PROGRAMS
FLES TEACHERS (1967 1980) Use FLES and LANGUAGE TEACHERS
FLEXIBLE CLASSROOMS (1968 1980) Use CLASSROOMS and FLEXIBLE FACILITIES
FLEXIBLE FACILITIES
FLEXIBLE LIGHTING DESIGN
FLEXIBLE PROGRESSION
FLEXIBLE SCHEDULES (1967 1980)
FLEXIBLE SCHEDULING
FLEXIBLE WORKING HOURS
FLEXILEVEL TESTING Use ADAPTIVE TESTING
MUSCULAR FLEXIONS Use MOTOR REACTIONS
FLEXTIME Use FLEXIBLE WORKING HOURS
FLIGHT TRAINING
WHITE FLIGHT Use MIGRATION and WHITES
FLOOR COVERING Use FLOORING
RESILIENT FLOOR COVERING Use FLOORING
FLOOR INSTALLATION Use FLOORING
FLOOR LAYERS
STUDIO FLOOR PLANS (1966 1980)
FLOORING
FLOORS Use FLOORING
FLORICULTURE
AIR FLOW
FLOW CHARTS
INFORMATION FLOW Use INFORMATION TRANSFER
TRAFFIC FLOW Use TRAFFIC CIRCULATION
BUSINESS FLUCTUATIONS Use BUSINESS CYCLES
ECONOMIC FLUCTUATIONS Use BUSINESS CYCLES
LANGUAGE FLUENCY
FLUID MECHANICS
FLUID POWER EDUCATION (1967 1980) Use FLUID MECHANICS
FLUID PRESSURE Use PRESSURE (PHYSICS)
FLUORIDATION
FOLDING PARTITIONS Use MOVABLE PARTITIONS
FOLK CULTURE
FOLK DRAMA (1969 1980) Use DRAMA and FOLK CULTURE
FOLK SCHOOLS
FOLKLORE Use FOLK CULTURE
FOLKLORE BOOKS (1966 1980) Use BOOKS and FOLK CULTURE
OCCUPATIONAL FOLLOWUP Use VOCATIONAL FOLLOWUP
FOLLOWUP PROGRAMS Use FOLLOWUP STUDIES
FOLLOWUP STUDIES
VOCATIONAL FOLLOWUP
FOOCHOW
FOOD
FOOD AND DRUG INSPECTORS
GRAINS (FOOD)
FOOD HANDLING FACILITIES
FOOD INSPECTORS Use FOOD AND DRUG INSPECTORS
FOOD MARKETS Use FOOD STORES
FOOD PROCESSING OCCUPATIONS
FOOD SERVICE
FOOD SERVICE INDUSTRY (1967 1981) Use FOOD SERVICE
FOOD SERVICE OCCUPATIONS (1968 1981) Use FOOD SERVICE
FOOD SERVICE WORKERS (1968 1981) Use FOOD SERVICE
FOOD STANDARDS
FOOD STORES
PROCESSED FOODS INSPECTORS Use FOOD AND DRUG INSPECTORS
FOODS INSTRUCTION
FOOTBALL
FOOTNOTES (BIBLIOGRAPHIC) Use CITATIONS (REFERENCES)
ENGLISH FOR ACADEMIC PURPOSES
ACCESSIBILITY (FOR DISABLED)
ASSISTIVE DEVICES (FOR DISABLED)

BARRIER FREE ENVIRONMENT (FOR DISABLED) Use ACCESSIBILITY (FOR DISABLED)
COMMUNICATION AIDS (FOR DISABLED)
DEMAND FOR EDUCATION Use EDUCATIONAL DEMAND
CAPITAL OUTLAY (FOR FIXED ASSETS)
WRITING FOR PUBLICATION
ENGLISH FOR SCIENCE AND TECHNOLOGY
ENGLISH FOR SPECIAL PURPOSES
LANGUAGES FOR SPECIAL PURPOSES
HOMES FOR THE AGED Use PERSONAL CARE HOMES
INTERPRETING FOR THE DEAF Use DEAF INTERPRETING
FORCE
AIR FORCE BASES Use MILITARY AIR FACILITIES
LABOR FORCE DEVELOPMENT
FORCE FIELD ANALYSIS
LABOR FORCE
LABOR FORCE NONPARTICIPANTS
FORCE (PHYSICAL) Use FORCE
REDUCTION IN FORCE
LABOR FORCE SURVEYS Use OCCUPATIONAL SURVEYS
WORK FORCE Use LABOR FORCE
FORCED CHOICE TECHNIQUE
ARMED FORCES
FORECAST Use PREDICTION
EMPLOYMENT FORECASTS Use EMPLOYMENT PROJECTIONS
FOREIGN COUNTRIES
FOREIGN CULTURE
FOREIGN DIPLOMATS
FOREIGN LANGUAGE BOOKS
FOREIGN LANGUAGE ENROLLMENT Use LANGUAGE ENROLLMENT
FOREIGN LANGUAGE FILMS
FOREIGN LANGUAGE INSTRUCTION Use SECOND LANGUAGE INSTRUCTION
LANGUAGE LEARNING (FOREIGN) Use SECOND LANGUAGE LEARNING
FOREIGN LANGUAGE LEARNING Use SECOND LANGUAGE LEARNING
FOREIGN LANGUAGE PERIODICALS
FOREIGN LANGUAGE PROGRAMS Use SECOND LANGUAGE PROGRAMS
STATE FOREIGN LANGUAGE SUPERVISORS (1967 1980) Use SECOND LANGUAGE INSTRUCTION and STATE SUPERVISORS
FOREIGN LANGUAGE TEACHERS Use LANGUAGE TEACHERS
FOREIGN LANGUAGES Use SECOND LANGUAGES
FOREIGN LANGUAGES IN THE ELEMENTARY SCHOOL Use FLES
FOREIGN MEDICAL GRADUATES
FOREIGN NATIONALS
NONRESIDENT STUDENTS (1967 1980) (FOREIGN) Use FOREIGN STUDENTS
FOREIGN POLICY
FOREIGN RELATIONS (1966 1976) Use INTERNATIONAL RELATIONS
FOREIGN STUDENT ADVISERS
FOREIGN STUDENTS
FOREIGN TRAINED PHYSICIANS Use FOREIGN MEDICAL GRADUATES
FOREIGN WORKERS
FOREMEN Use SUPERVISORS
FARM FOREMEN Use CREW LEADERS
FORENSICS Use PERSUASIVE DISCOURSE
FORESTER AIDES Use FORESTRY AIDES
FORESTRY
FORESTRY AIDES
FORESTRY OCCUPATIONS
FORGETTING Use MEMORY
FORM CLASSES (LANGUAGES)
AGREEMENTS (FORMAL) Use CONTRACTS
FORMAL CRITICISM (1969 1980)
FORMAL OPERATIONS
FORMAL ORGANIZATIONS Use ORGANIZATIONS (GROUPS)
FORMAT (PUBLICATIONS) Use LAYOUT (PUBLICATIONS)
TEST FORMAT
CONCEPT FORMATION
HABIT FORMATION
POLICY FORMATION
FORMATIVE EVALUATION
FORMER TEACHERS (1967 1980)
METAL FORMING OCCUPATIONS Use METAL WORKING
NEGATIVE FORMS (LANGUAGE)
PNEUMATIC FORMS
RECORDS (FORMS)
MATHEMATICAL FORMULAS
READABILITY FORMULAS
SCORING FORMULAS
PARENT FORUMS Use PARENT CONFERENCES
FOSSILS Use PALEONTOLOGY
FOSTER CARE
ADULT FOSTER CARE
FOSTER CHILDREN
FOSTER FAMILY
FOSTER HOMES (1970 1982) (ADULTS) Use ADULT FOSTER CARE
FOSTER HOMES (1970 1982) (CHILDREN) Use FOSTER CARE
FOSTER PARENTS Use FOSTER FAMILY
FOUND SPACES
FOUNDATION COURSES (INTRODUCTORY) Use INTRODUCTORY COURSES
FOUNDATION COURSES (REQUIRED) Use REQUIRED COURSES
FOUNDATION PROGRAMS
EDUCATIONAL FOUNDATIONS Use PHILANTHROPIC FOUNDATIONS
FOUNDATIONS (INSTITUTIONS) Use PHILANTHROPIC FOUNDATIONS
FOUNDATIONS OF EDUCATION
PHILANTHROPIC FOUNDATIONS
FOUNDRIES
IRON FOUNDRIES Use FOUNDRIES
STEEL FOUNDRIES Use FOUNDRIES
FOUR DAY WORK WEEK Use FLEXIBLE WORKING HOURS
FOUR H CLUB AGENTS Use EXTENSION AGENTS
FRACTIONS
COMMON FRACTIONS (1966 1980) Use FRACTIONS
DECIMAL FRACTIONS

FRATERNITIES
FREE CHOICE TRANSFER PROGRAMS
FREE EDUCATION
BARRIER FREE ENVIRONMENT (FOR DISABLED) Use ACCESSIBILITY (FOR DISABLED)
CONTEXT FREE GRAMMAR
FREE PLAY Use PLAY
FREE SCHOOLS
DISTRIBUTION FREE STATISTICS Use NONPARAMETRIC STATISTICS
CULTURE FREE TESTS (1967 1980) Use CULTURE FAIR TESTS
FREE TRANSLATION Use TRANSLATION
FREE UNIVERSITIES Use EXPERIMENTAL COLLEGES
ACADEMIC FREEDOM
INTELLECTUAL FREEDOM
FREEDOM OF INFORMATION
FREEDOM OF SPEECH
FREEDOM OF THE PRESS Use FREEDOM OF SPEECH
FREEDOM OF THOUGHT Use INTELLECTUAL FREEDOM
FREEDOM SCHOOLS
TEACHING FREEDOM Use ACADEMIC FREEDOM
FREEDOM TO READ Use INTELLECTUAL FREEDOM
DRAWING (FREEHAND) Use FREEHAND DRAWING
FREEHAND DRAWING
FRENCH
FRENCH CANADIAN LITERATURE Use CANADIAN LITERATURE
FRENCH LITERATURE
FREQUENCY DISTRIBUTIONS Use STATISTICAL DISTRIBUTIONS
WORD FREQUENCY
FRESHMAN COMPOSITION
COLLEGE FRESHMEN
FRESHMEN (1967 1980) (FIRST YEAR COLLEGE STUDENTS) Use COLLEGE FRESHMEN
FRESHMEN (1967 1980) (GRADE 9) Use HIGH SCHOOL FRESHMEN
HIGH SCHOOL FRESHMEN
FRIENDSHIP
CHILDHOOD FRIENDSHIP (1966 1980) Use FRIENDSHIP
FRINGE BENEFITS
EMPLOYEE FRINGE BENEFITS Use FRINGE BENEFITS
AWAY FROM THE JOB TRAINING Use OFF THE JOB TRAINING
FRUIT AND VEGETABLE INSPECTORS Use FOOD AND DRUG INSPECTORS
FTE Use FULL TIME EQUIVALENCY
FUEL CONSUMPTION
DIESEL FUEL Use FUELS
FUEL OIL Use FUELS
FUELS
FUL Use FULANI
FULA Use FULANI
FULANI
FULFULDE Use FULANI
FULL STATE FUNDING
FULL TIME EQUIVALENCY
FULL TIME FACULTY
FULL TIME STUDENTS
FULL TIME TEACHERS Use FULL TIME FACULTY
AGENCY FUNCTION Use AGENCY ROLE
DISCRIMINANT FUNCTION ANALYSIS Use DISCRIMINANT ANALYSIS
INSTITUTIONAL FUNCTION Use INSTITUTIONAL ROLE
FUNCTION WORDS
FUNCTIONAL ILLITERACY (1968 1980) Use FUNCTIONAL LITERACY
FUNCTIONAL LITERACY
FUNCTIONAL NOTIONAL SYLLABI Use NOTIONAL FUNCTIONAL SYLLABI
FUNCTIONAL READING
NOTIONAL FUNCTIONAL SYLLABI
FUNCTIONAL SYSTEMS THEORY Use SYSTEMS ANALYSIS
BRAIN HEMISPHERE FUNCTIONS
COUNSELOR FUNCTIONS (1967 1977) Use COUNSELOR ROLE
EDUCATIONAL PRODUCTION FUNCTIONS Use PRODUCTIVITY
GOVERNMENT FUNCTIONS Use GOVERNMENT ROLE
GUIDANCE FUNCTIONS (1968 1980) Use GUIDANCE OBJECTIVES
FUNCTIONS (MATHEMATICS)
PRODUCTION FUNCTIONS Use PRODUCTIVITY
FUNCTORS Use FUNCTION WORDS
FUND RAISING
FUNDAMENTAL CONCEPTS
FUNDAMENTAL EDUCATION (ADULTS) Use ADULT BASIC EDUCATION
FUNDAMENTAL SKILLS (DAILY LIVING) Use DAILY LIVING SKILLS
FUNDAMENTAL SKILLS (SCHOOL) Use BASIC SKILLS
FUNDING Use FINANCIAL SUPPORT
FULL STATE FUNDING
ENDOWMENT FUNDS
SCHOLARSHIP FUNDS
SCHOOL FUNDS
TRUST FUNDS Use TRUSTS (FINANCIAL)
HOME FURNISHINGS
FURNITURE
FURNITURE ARRANGEMENT
CLASSROOM FURNITURE
FURNITURE (CLASSROOM) Use CLASSROOM FURNITURE
FURNITURE DESIGN
FURNITURE INDUSTRY
FURTHER EDUCATION Use ADULT EDUCATION
FUSED CURRICULUM
FUTURE STUDIES Use FUTURES (OF SOCIETY)
ALTERNATIVE FUTURES Use FUTURES (OF SOCIETY)
EDUCATIONAL FUTURES Use EDUCATIONAL TRENDS and FUTURES (OF SOCIETY)
FUTURES (OF SOCIETY)
FUTURES PLANNING Use LONG RANGE PLANNING
FUTURISM Use FUTURES (OF SOCIETY)
FUTURISTICS Use FUTURES (OF SOCIETY)
FUTUROLOGY Use FUTURES (OF SOCIETY)
G SCORES Use GRADE EQUIVALENT SCORES
GA
READING GAIN Use READING IMPROVEMENT

ACHIEVEMENT GAINS
ART GALLERIES Use ARTS CENTERS
SQUASH (GAME)
GAME THEORY
GAMEKEEPING Use WILDLIFE MANAGEMENT
GAMES
ACADEMIC GAMES Use EDUCATIONAL GAMES
BUSINESS GAMES Use MANAGEMENT GAMES
CHILDRENS GAMES
CLASSROOM GAMES (1966 1980) Use CLASS ACTIVITIES and EDUCATIONAL GAMES
EDUCATIONAL GAMES
HEURISTIC GAMES Use EDUCATIONAL GAMES
MANAGEMENT GAMES
READING GAMES
GANDA
JUVENILE GANGS
GENERATION GAP
PARKING GARAGES Use PARKING FACILITIES
GARBAGE Use SOLID WASTES
GARDENERS Use GROUNDS KEEPERS
GARMENT INDUSTRY Use FASHION INDUSTRY
GAS UTILITIES Use UTILITIES
GAS WELDING Use WELDING
NATURAL GASES Use FUELS
GASOLINE Use FUELS
GAUGES Use MEASUREMENT EQUIPMENT
GBAYA
GBEYA Use GBAYA
GED PROGRAMS Use HIGH SCHOOL EQUIVALENCY PROGRAMS
GENDER DIFFERENCES (SEX) Use SEX DIFFERENCES
GENDER IDENTITY (SEX) Use SEXUAL IDENTITY
GENDER (SEX) Use SEX
GENEALOGY
GENERAL BUSINESS EDUCATION Use BASIC BUSINESS EDUCATION
GENERAL EDUCATION
GENERAL EDUCATIONAL DEVELOPMENT PROGRAMS Use HIGH SCHOOL EQUIVALENCY PROGRAMS
GENERAL HIGH SCHOOLS (1966 1980) Use GENERAL EDUCATION
GENERAL MECHANICS Use MECHANICS (PROCESS)
GENERAL METHODS COURSES Use METHODS COURSES
GENERAL PRACTICE (MEDICINE) Use FAMILY PRACTICE (MEDICINE)
GENERAL SCIENCE
GENERAL SEMANTICS Use SEMANTICS
GENERAL SHOP Use SHOP CURRICULUM
GENERALIZABILITY THEORY
GENERALIZATION
STIMULUS GENERALIZATION
GENERATION GAP
GENERATIVE GRAMMAR
TRANSFORMATION GENERATIVE GRAMMAR (1968 1980) Use TRANSFORMATIONAL GENERATIVE GRAMMAR
TRANSFORMATIONAL GENERATIVE GRAMMAR
GENERATIVE PHONOLOGY
GENERATIVE TRANSFORMATIONAL GRAMMAR Use TRANSFORMATIONAL GENERATIVE GRAMMAR
GENETIC ENGINEERING
GENETICS
LITERARY GENRES
AREAS (GEOGRAPHIC) Use GEOGRAPHIC REGIONS
GEOGRAPHIC CONCEPTS
DEPRESSED AREAS (GEOGRAPHIC) (1966 1980) Use POVERTY AREAS
GEOGRAPHIC DIALECTS Use REGIONAL DIALECTS
GEOGRAPHIC DISTRIBUTION
GEOGRAPHIC LOCATION
GEOGRAPHIC MOBILITY (1980) Use MIGRATION
PHYSICAL DIVISIONS (GEOGRAPHIC)
POLITICAL DIVISIONS (GEOGRAPHIC)
GEOGRAPHIC REGIONS
GEOGRAPHY
CULTURAL GEOGRAPHY Use HUMAN GEOGRAPHY
ECONOMIC GEOGRAPHY Use HUMAN GEOGRAPHY
HISTORICAL GEOGRAPHY Use HUMAN GEOGRAPHY
HUMAN GEOGRAPHY
GEOGRAPHY INSTRUCTION
PHYSICAL GEOGRAPHY
POLITICAL GEOGRAPHY Use HUMAN GEOGRAPHY
SOCIAL GEOGRAPHY Use HUMAN GEOGRAPHY
URBAN GEOGRAPHY Use HUMAN GEOGRAPHY
WORLD GEOGRAPHY
GEOLOGY
GEOMETRIC CONCEPTS
GEOMETRIC CONSTRUCTIONS
GEOMETRICAL OPTICS Use OPTICS
GEOMETRODYNAMICS Use RELATIVITY
GEOMETRY
ANALYTIC GEOMETRY
COORDINATE GEOMETRY Use ANALYTIC GEOMETRY
PLANE GEOMETRY
SOLID GEOMETRY
TRANSFORMATIONAL GEOMETRY Use TRANSFORMATIONS (MATHEMATICS)
GEOPHYSICS
GEORGIAN Use CAUCASIAN LANGUAGES
GEOSCIENCE Use EARTH SCIENCE
GEOTHERMAL ENERGY
GERIATRICS
GERMAN
GERMAN LITERATURE
GERMAN MEASLES Use RUBELLA
GERONTOLOGY
EDUCATIONAL GERONTOLOGY
GESTALT THERAPY
GESTATION Use PREGNANCY
GESTURES (DEAF COMMUNICATION) Use SIGN LANGUAGE
GESTURES (NONVERBAL COMMUNICATION) Use BODY LANGUAGE

GHETTOS
GIFTED
ACADEMICALLY GIFTED
GIFTED CHILDREN Use GIFTED
GIFTED DISABLED
GIFTED DISADVANTAGED
GIFTED HANDICAPPED Use GIFTED DISABLED
GIFTED STUDENTS Use ACADEMICALLY GIFTED
GIFTED TEACHERS Use GIFTED
GIFTED YOUTH Use GIFTED
GIRLS Use FEMALES
GIRLS CLUBS (1966 1980) Use YOUTH CLUBS
CORPORATE GIVING Use CORPORATE SUPPORT
GLARE
GLASS
GLASS INSTALLERS Use GLAZIERS
GLASS WALLS
SAFETY GLASSES Use SAFETY EQUIPMENT
GLAZIERS
GLEE CLUBS Use SINGING
GLOBAL APPROACH
GLOSSARIES
GLOTTOCHRONOLOGY
GLUES Use ADHESIVES
GOAL ATTAINMENT Use SUCCESS
GOAL ORIENTATION
GOALS Use OBJECTIVES
COUNSELING GOALS (1966 1980) Use COUNSELING OBJECTIVES
EDUCATIONAL GOALS Use EDUCATIONAL OBJECTIVES
GUIDANCE GOALS Use GUIDANCE OBJECTIVES
INSTITUTIONAL GOALS Use ORGANIZATIONAL OBJECTIVES
MEASUREMENT GOALS (1966 1980) Use MEASUREMENT OBJECTIVES
EDUCATIONAL GOALS OF STUDENTS Use STUDENT EDUCATIONAL OBJECTIVES
ORGANIZATIONAL GOALS Use ORGANIZATIONAL OBJECTIVES
TRAINING GOALS Use TRAINING OBJECTIVES
GOLF
GONORRHEA Use VENEREAL DISEASES
GOOD CITIZENSHIP Use CITIZENSHIP
GOODNESS OF FIT
GOVERNANCE
GOVERNING BOARDS
COLLEGE GOVERNING COUNCILS
GOVERNMENT (ADMINISTRATIVE BODY)
GOVERNMENT AGENCIES Use PUBLIC AGENCIES
CITY GOVERNMENT
COUNTY GOVERNMENT Use LOCAL GOVERNMENT
AMERICAN GOVERNMENT (COURSE) (1966 1980) Use UNITED STATES GOVERNMENT (COURSE)
UNITED STATES GOVERNMENT (COURSE)
GOVERNMENT DOCUMENTS Use GOVERNMENT PUBLICATIONS
GOVERNMENT EMPLOYEES
FEDERAL GOVERNMENT
GOVERNMENT FUNCTIONS Use GOVERNMENT ROLE
GOVERNMENT LIBRARIES
LOCAL GOVERNMENT
MUNICIPAL GOVERNMENT Use CITY GOVERNMENT
STATE GOVERNMENT PROGRAMS Use STATE GOVERNMENT and STATE PROGRAMS
PROVINCIAL GOVERNMENT Use STATE GOVERNMENT
GOVERNMENT PUBLICATIONS
SCHOOL GOVERNMENT RELATIONSHIP Use GOVERNMENT SCHOOL RELATIONSHIP
GOVERNMENT ROLE
GOVERNMENT SCHOOL RELATIONSHIP
SELF GOVERNMENT Use SELF DETERMINATION
STATE GOVERNMENT
GOVERNMENT STRUCTURE Use GOVERNMENTAL STRUCTURE
STUDENT GOVERNMENT
TRUST RESPONSIBILITY (GOVERNMENT)
GOVERNMENTAL STRUCTURE
GRADE 1
GRADE 2
GRADE 3
GRADE 4
GRADE 5
GRADE 6
GRADE 7
GRADE 8
GRADE 9
FRESHMEN (1967 1980) (GRADE 9) Use HIGH SCHOOL FRESHMEN
GRADE 10
GRADE 11
GRADE 12
SENIORS (1966 1980) (GRADE 12) Use HIGH SCHOOL SENIORS
GRADE 13 (1970 1980) Use POSTSECONDARY EDUCATION
GRADE 14 (1970 1980) Use POSTSECONDARY EDUCATION
GRADE A YEAR INTEGRATION (1966 1980) Use SCHOOL DESEGREGATION
GRADE AVERAGE Use GRADE POINT AVERAGE
GRADE CARDS Use REPORT CARDS
GRADE CHARTS (1966 1980)
GRADE EQUIVALENT SCALES (1967 1980) Use GRADE EQUIVALENT SCORES
GRADE EQUIVALENT SCORES
GRADE INFLATION
GRADE LEVELS Use INSTRUCTIONAL PROGRAM DIVISIONS
GRADE ORGANIZATION (1966 1980) Use INSTRUCTIONAL PROGRAM DIVISIONS
AGE GRADE PLACEMENT
GRADE POINT AVERAGE
GRADE PREDICTION
GRADE REPETITION
GRADE SCORES Use GRADE EQUIVALENT SCORES
AGE GRADE STATUS Use AGE GRADE PLACEMENT
ELEMENTARY GRADES (1966 1980) Use ELEMENTARY EDUCATION
INFLATED GRADES Use GRADE INFLATION
INTERMEDIATE GRADES

PRIMARY GRADES (1966 1980) Use PRIMARY EDUCATION
GRADES (PROGRAM DIVISIONS) Use INSTRUCTIONAL PROGRAM DIVISIONS
GRADES (SCHOLASTIC)
SECONDARY GRADES (1966 1980) Use SECONDARY EDUCATION
GRADING
CONTRACT GRADING Use GRADING and PERFORMANCE CONTRACTS
CREDIT NO CREDIT GRADING
PASS FAIL GRADING
PASS NO CREDIT GRADING Use CREDIT NO CREDIT GRADING
PASS NO RECORD GRADING Use CREDIT NO CREDIT GRADING
GRADUATE CEREMONIES Use COMMENCEMENT CEREMONIES
GRADUATE EDUCATION Use GRADUATE STUDY
GRADUATE MEDICAL EDUCATION
GRADUATE MEDICAL STUDENTS
GRADUATE PROFESSORS (1966 1980) Use GRADUATE SCHOOL FACULTY
GRADUATE SCHOOL FACULTY
GRADUATE STUDENTS
GRADUATE STUDY
GRADUATE SURVEYS
GRADUATE TRAINING Use GRADUATE STUDY
GRADUATES
COLLEGE GRADUATES
FOREIGN MEDICAL GRADUATES
HIGH SCHOOL GRADUATES
GRADUATION
GRADUATION REQUIREMENTS
GRAIN ELEVATOR OCCUPATIONS Use CROP PROCESSING OCCUPATIONS
GRAIN MARKETING Use GRAINS (FOOD)
GRAIN PROCESSING Use GRAINS (FOOD)
GRAIN PRODUCTION Use GRAINS (FOOD)
GRAINS (FOOD)
GRAMMAR
ARTICLES (GRAMMAR) Use DETERMINERS (LANGUAGES)
CASE (GRAMMAR)
CONTEXT FREE GRAMMAR
GENERATIVE GRAMMAR
GENERATIVE TRANSFORMATIONAL GRAMMAR Use TRANSFORMATIONAL GENERATIVE GRAMMAR
STORY GRAMMAR
STRUCTURAL GRAMMAR
TENSES (GRAMMAR)
TRADITIONAL GRAMMAR
TRANSFORMATION GENERATIVE GRAMMAR (1968 1980) Use TRANSFORMATIONAL GENERATIVE GRAMMAR
TRANSFORMATIONAL GRAMMAR Use TRANSFORMATIONAL GENERATIVE GRAMMAR
TRANSFORMATIONAL GENERATIVE GRAMMAR
GRAMMAR TRANSLATION METHOD
GRAMMATICAL ACCEPTABILITY
GRANDCHILDREN
GRANDDAUGHTERS Use GRANDCHILDREN
GRANDFATHERS Use GRANDPARENTS
GRANDMOTHERS Use GRANDPARENTS
GRANDPARENTS
GRANDSONS Use GRANDCHILDREN
LAND GRANT COLLEGES Use LAND GRANT UNIVERSITIES
GRANT PROPOSALS Use GRANTS and PROGRAM PROPOSALS
LAND GRANT UNIVERSITIES
GRANTS
BLOCK GRANTS
FEDERAL GRANTS Use FEDERAL AID
INCENTIVE GRANTS
TUITION GRANTS
GRANTSMANSHIP
PHONEME GRAPHEME CORRESPONDENCE
GRAPHEME PHONEME CORRESPONDENCE Use PHONEME GRAPHEME CORRESPONDENCE
GRAPHEMES
GRAPHIC ARTS
COMPUTER GRAPHICS
ENGINEERING GRAPHICS
GRAPHS
DELAY OF GRATIFICATION
NEED GRATIFICATION
GRAVITATION Use GRAVITY (PHYSICS)
GRAVITY (PHYSICS)
GRAYING OF FACULTY Use AGING IN ACADEMIA
GREASE Use LUBRICANTS
GREEK
GREEK AMERICANS
GREEK CIVILIZATION
CLASSICAL GREEK Use GREEK
GREEK LITERATURE
MODERN GREEK Use GREEK
GREENHOUSE WORKERS Use NURSERY WORKERS (HORTICULTURE)
GREENHOUSES
GREGARIOUSNESS Use INTERPERSONAL COMPETENCE
GRIEF
GRIEVANCE PROCEDURES
PARENT GRIEVANCES
PARENTAL GRIEVANCES (1967 1980) Use PARENT GRIEVANCES
GRINDING MACHINES Use MACHINE TOOLS
GROCERY STORES Use FOOD STORES
PERSONAL GROOMING Use HYGIENE
GROSS SCORES Use RAW SCORES
GROUNDS CARETAKERS Use GROUNDS KEEPERS
GROUNDS KEEPERS
GROUP ACTIVITIES
GROUP ADJUSTMENT Use ADJUSTMENT (TO ENVIRONMENT)
GROUP BEHAVIOR
MINORITY GROUP CHILDREN
GROUP COHESIVENESS Use GROUP UNITY
GROUP COUNSELING
GROUP DISCUSSION
GROUP DYNAMICS

	GUIDANCE PROGRAMS
CLASSROOM	GUIDANCE PROGRAMS (1968 1980)
SCHOOL	GUIDANCE
SECONDARY SCHOOL	GUIDANCE Use SCHOOL GUIDANCE
	GUIDANCE SERVICES (1966 1980) Use GUIDANCE PROGRAMS
	GUIDANCE SPECIALISTS Use GUIDANCE PERSONNEL and SPECIALISTS
TEACHER	GUIDANCE
VOCATIONAL	GUIDANCE Use CAREER GUIDANCE
	GUIDEBOOKS Use GUIDES
SELF	GUIDED GROUPS Use SELF DIRECTED GROUPS
	GUIDELINES
FACILITY	GUIDELINES
	GUIDES
ADMINISTRATOR	GUIDES
CURRICULUM	GUIDES
DISCUSSION	GUIDES Use DISCUSSION (TEACHING TECHNIQUE) and TEACHING GUIDES
FLES	GUIDES (1967 1980) Use CURRICULUM GUIDES and FLES
HEALTH	GUIDES (1966 1980) Use GUIDES and HEALTH MATERIALS
LANGUAGE	GUIDES (1966 1980)
LEADERS	GUIDES
LIBRARY	GUIDES
LITERATURE	GUIDES (1966 1980)
PROGRAM	GUIDES
RESOURCE	GUIDES (1966 1980) Use RESOURCE MATERIALS
STATE CURRICULUM	GUIDES
STUDY	GUIDES
TEACHER	GUIDES Use TEACHING GUIDES
TEACHING	GUIDES
	GUJARATI
	GUJERATI Use GUJARATI
	GULLAH
	GYMNASIUMS
	GYMNASTICS
	GYNECOLOGY
FOUR	H CLUB AGENTS Use EXTENSION AGENTS
	HABIT FORMATION
EATING	HABITS
LISTENING	HABITS
READING	HABITS
SPEECH	HABITS
STUDY	HABITS
	HABITUATION
	HAGIOGRAPHIES (1971 1980) Use BIOGRAPHIES
	HAIKU
	HAITIAN CREOLE
	HAITIANS
	HALF REVERSAL SHIFT Use SHIFT STUDIES
	HALFWAY HOUSES Use GROUP HOMES and REHABILITATION CENTERS
RESIDENCE	HALLS Use DORMITORIES
STUDY	HALLS Use STUDY CENTERS
	HALLWAYS Use CORRIDORS
	HAND CALCULATORS Use CALCULATORS
EYE	HAND COORDINATION
	HAND TOOLS
	HANDBALL
TEAM	HANDBALL
	HANDBOOKS Use GUIDES
FACULTY	HANDBOOKS
HEALTH ACTIVITIES	HANDBOOKS (1966 1980) Use GUIDES and HEALTH MATERIALS
LIBRARY	HANDBOOKS Use LIBRARY GUIDES
LEFT	HANDED WRITER
	HANDICAP DETECTION (1966 1980) Use HANDICAP IDENTIFICATION
	HANDICAP DISCRIMINATION
	HANDICAP IDENTIFICATION
	HANDICAPPED (1966 1980) Use DISABILITIES
ACADEMICALLY	HANDICAPPED (1966 1980)
ADVENTITIOUSLY	HANDICAPPED (1975 1980) Use ADVENTITIOUS IMPAIRMENTS
AURALLY	HANDICAPPED (1966 1980) Use HEARING IMPAIRMENTS
	HANDICAPPED CHILDREN (1966 1980)
CONGENITALLY	HANDICAPPED (1975 1980) Use CONGENITAL IMPAIRMENTS
CUSTODIAL MENTALLY	HANDICAPPED (1968 1980) Use SEVERE MENTAL RETARDATION
EDUCABLE MENTALLY	HANDICAPPED (1966 1980) Use MILD MENTAL RETARDATION
GIFTED	HANDICAPPED Use GIFTED DISABLED
LANGUAGE	HANDICAPPED (1967 1980) Use LANGUAGE HANDICAPS
MENTALLY	HANDICAPPED (1966 1980) Use MENTAL RETARDATION
VISUALLY	HANDICAPPED MOBILITY
MULTIPLY	HANDICAPPED (1967 1980) Use MULTIPLE DISABILITIES
NEUROLOGICALLY	HANDICAPPED (1966 1980) Use NEUROLOGICAL IMPAIRMENTS
NORMALIZATION	(HANDICAPPED)
VISUALLY	HANDICAPPED ORIENTATION (1967 1980) Use VISUALLY HANDICAPPED MOBILITY
ORTHOPEDICALLY	HANDICAPPED (1968 1980) Use PHYSICAL DISABILITIES
PERCEPTUALLY	HANDICAPPED (1966 1980) Use PERCEPTUAL HANDICAPS
PHYSICALLY	HANDICAPPED (1966 1980) Use PHYSICAL DISABILITIES
SEVERELY	HANDICAPPED (1975 1980) Use SEVERE DISABILITIES
SPEECH	HANDICAPPED (1967 1980) Use SPEECH HANDICAPS
	HANDICAPPED STUDENTS (1967 1980)
TRAINABLE MENTALLY	HANDICAPPED (1967 1980) Use MODERATE MENTAL RETARDATION
VISUALLY	HANDICAPPED (1966 1980) Use VISUAL IMPAIRMENTS
	HANDICAPS Use DISABILITIES
LANGUAGE	HANDICAPS
PERCEPTUAL	HANDICAPS
PHYSICAL	HANDICAPS (1966 1980) Use PHYSICAL DISABILITIES
SPEECH	HANDICAPS
	HANDICRAFTS
MANUSCRIPT WRITING	(HANDLETTERING)
FOOD	HANDLING FACILITIES
	HANDWRITING
	HANDWRITING DEVELOPMENT (1966 1980) Use HANDWRITING and WRITING SKILLS
	HANDWRITING INSTRUCTION (1966 1983) Use HANDWRITING and WRITING INSTRUCTION
	HANDWRITING MATERIALS (1966 1983) Use HANDWRITING and INSTRUCTIONAL MATERIALS
	HANDWRITING READINESS (1966 1983) Use HANDWRITING and WRITING READINESS

HANDWRITING SKILLS (1966 1983) Use HANDWRITING and WRITING SKILLS
HANGUL Use KOREAN
HANJA Use KOREAN
HANKUL Use KOREAN
HAPTIC PERCEPTION (1967 1980) Use TACTUAL PERCEPTION
SEXUAL HARASSMENT
HARD OF HEARING (1967 1980) Use PARTIAL HEARING
HARVESTING
CROP HARVESTING Use HARVESTING
HASHISH Use MARIJUANA
HAUSA
HAWAIIAN
HAWAIIANS
HAZARDOUS MATERIALS
HAZARDOUS WASTES Use HAZARDOUS MATERIALS and WASTES
HEAD BANGING Use SELF MUTILATION
SUBJECT HEADINGS Use SUBJECT INDEX TERMS
HEADLINES
DEPARTMENT HEADS
HOUSEHOLD HEADS Use HEADS OF HOUSEHOLDS
HEADS OF HOUSEHOLDS
HEALTH
HEALTH ACTIVITIES
HEALTH ACTIVITIES HANDBOOKS (1966 1980) Use GUIDES and HEALTH MATERIALS
HOME HEALTH AIDES
HEALTH BOOKS (1966 1980) Use BOOKS and HEALTH MATERIALS
HEALTH CARE EVALUATION Use MEDICAL CARE EVALUATION
PRIMARY HEALTH CARE
MENTAL HEALTH CLINICS
COMMUNITY HEALTH (1966 1980) Use PUBLIC HEALTH
HEALTH CONDITIONS
DENTAL HEALTH
HEALTH EDUCATION
ALLIED HEALTH EDUCATION Use ALLIED HEALTH OCCUPATIONS EDUCATION
EMOTIONAL HEALTH Use MENTAL HEALTH
HEALTH FACILITIES
FAMILY HEALTH
HEALTH GUIDES (1966 1980) Use GUIDES and HEALTH MATERIALS
HEALTH INSURANCE
PUBLIC HEALTH LAWS (1966 1974) Use PUBLIC HEALTH LEGISLATION
PUBLIC HEALTH LEGISLATION
HEALTH MATERIALS
MENTAL HEALTH
HEALTH NEEDS
OCCUPATIONAL HEALTH Use OCCUPATIONAL SAFETY AND HEALTH
OCCUPATIONAL SAFETY AND HEALTH
HEALTH OCCUPATIONS
ALLIED HEALTH OCCUPATIONS
HEALTH OCCUPATIONS CENTERS (1968 1980)
HEALTH OCCUPATIONS EDUCATION (1967 1980) Use ALLIED HEALTH OCCUPATIONS EDUCATION
ALLIED HEALTH OCCUPATIONS EDUCATION
HEALTH OCCUPATIONS EDUCATION (VOCATIONAL) Use ALLIED HEALTH OCCUPATIONS EDUCATION and VOCATIONAL EDUCATION
HEALTH OCCUPATIONS PERSONNEL Use HEALTH PERSONNEL
PERSONAL HEALTH Use HYGIENE
HEALTH PERSONNEL
ALLIED HEALTH PERSONNEL
PHYSICAL HEALTH
SPECIAL HEALTH PROBLEMS
ALLIED HEALTH PROFESSIONS Use ALLIED HEALTH OCCUPATIONS
CLINICAL TEACHING (HEALTH PROFESSIONS)
HEALTH PROGRAMS
MENTAL HEALTH PROGRAMS
PUBLIC HEALTH
HEALTH RELATED PROFESSIONS Use ALLIED HEALTH OCCUPATIONS
MENTAL HEALTH RESOURCES Use MENTAL HEALTH PROGRAMS
HEALTH SCIENCES LIBRARIES Use MEDICAL LIBRARIES
HEALTH SERVICE PERSONNEL Use HEALTH PERSONNEL
HEALTH SERVICE WORKERS Use HEALTH PERSONNEL
HEALTH SERVICES
COMMUNITY HEALTH SERVICES
MIGRANT HEALTH SERVICES
SCHOOL HEALTH SERVICES
OCCUPATIONAL SAFETY AND HEALTH STANDARDS Use LABOR STANDARDS and OCCUPATIONAL SAFETY AND HEALTH
HEALTH WORKERS Use HEALTH PERSONNEL
COMMUNITY HEALTH WORKERS Use COMMUNITY HEALTH SERVICES and HEALTH PERSONNEL
HEARING AIDS
HEARING CLINICS (1968 1980) Use SPEECH AND HEARING CLINICS
SPEECH AND HEARING CLINICS
HEARING CONSERVATION
HARD OF HEARING (1967 1980) Use PARTIAL HEARING
HEARING IMPAIRMENTS
HEARING LOSS (1967 1980) Use HEARING IMPAIRMENTS
PARTIAL HEARING
HEARING (PHYSIOLOGY)
HEARING REHABILITATION Use HEARING THERAPY
HEARING TESTS Use AUDITORY TESTS
HEARING THERAPISTS (1967 1980) Use HEARING THERAPY and THERAPISTS
HEARING THERAPY
HEARINGS
PUBLIC HEARINGS Use HEARINGS
HEART DISORDERS
HEART RATE
HEAT
HEAT EQUATIONS Use THERMODYNAMICS
HEAT RECOVERY
HEATING
HEATING OILS Use FUELS
SOLAR HEATING Use HEATING and SOLAR ENERGY
HEBREW
HEIGHT

BODY HEIGHT
HELICOPTER PILOTS Use AIRCRAFT PILOTS
SELF HELP DEVICES (DISABLED) Use ASSISTIVE DEVICES (FOR DISABLED)
SELF HELP PROGRAMS
CROSS AGE HELPING Use CROSS AGE TEACHING
HELPING RELATIONSHIP
HELPLESSNESS
LEARNED HELPLESSNESS Use HELPLESSNESS
BRAIN HEMISPHERE FUNCTIONS
HEMISPHERIC SPECIALIZATION (BRAIN) Use BRAIN HEMISPHERE FUNCTIONS
HEMODYNAMICS Use BLOOD CIRCULATION
HERBICIDES
HEREDITY
ENVIRONMENT HEREDITY CONTROVERSY Use NATURE NURTURE CONTROVERSY
HEREDITY ENVIRONMENT CONTROVERSY Use NATURE NURTURE CONTROVERSY
CULTURAL HERITAGE Use CULTURAL BACKGROUND
ETHNIC HERITAGE Use CULTURAL BACKGROUND
HETEROGENEOUS GROUPING
HETEROPHORIA (1968 1974) Use STRABISMUS
HETEROTROPIA (1968 1974) Use STRABISMUS
HEURISTIC GAMES Use EDUCATIONAL GAMES
HEURISTICS
HIDDEN CURRICULUM
HIERARCHY Use VERTICAL ORGANIZATION
HIGH ACHIEVEMENT
HIGH ACHIEVERS (1966 1980) Use HIGH ACHIEVEMENT
HIGH BLOOD PRESSURE Use HYPERTENSION
HIGH INTEREST LOW VOCABULARY BOOKS
HIGH RISK PERSONS
HIGH RISK STUDENTS
HIGH SCHOOL COLLEGE COOPERATION Use COLLEGE SCHOOL COOPERATION
COLLEGE HIGH SCHOOL COOPERATION (1967 1980) Use COLLEGE SCHOOL COOPERATION
HIGH SCHOOL CURRICULUM (1967 1980) Use SECONDARY SCHOOL CURRICULUM
HIGH SCHOOL DESIGN (1966 1980) Use EDUCATIONAL FACILITIES DESIGN
HIGH SCHOOL DROPOUTS Use DROPOUTS
POST HIGH SCHOOL EDUCATION Use POSTSECONDARY EDUCATION
HIGH SCHOOL EQUIVALENCY PROGRAMS
HIGH SCHOOL FRESHMEN
HIGH SCHOOL GRADUATES
POST HIGH SCHOOL GUIDANCE
HIGH SCHOOL LIBRARIES Use SCHOOL LIBRARIES
HIGH SCHOOL ORGANIZATION (1966 1980) Use SCHOOL ORGANIZATION
HIGH SCHOOL ROLE (1966 1980) Use SCHOOL ROLE
JUNIOR HIGH SCHOOL ROLE (1966 1980) Use SCHOOL ROLE
HIGH SCHOOL SENIORS
HIGH SCHOOL STUDENTS
JUNIOR HIGH SCHOOL STUDENTS
SENIOR HIGH SCHOOL STUDENTS Use HIGH SCHOOL STUDENTS
HIGH SCHOOL SUPERVISORS (1966 1980) Use SCHOOL SUPERVISION
HIGH SCHOOL TEACHERS Use SECONDARY SCHOOL TEACHERS
JUNIOR HIGH SCHOOL TEACHERS Use SECONDARY SCHOOL TEACHERS
HIGH SCHOOLS
CATHOLIC HIGH SCHOOLS (1967 1980) Use CATHOLIC SCHOOLS
COMPREHENSIVE HIGH SCHOOLS (1967 1980) Use HIGH SCHOOLS
CONTINUATION HIGH SCHOOLS (1968 1980) Use CONTINUATION STUDENTS
GENERAL HIGH SCHOOLS (1966 1980) Use GENERAL EDUCATION
JUNIOR HIGH SCHOOLS
SENIOR HIGH SCHOOLS (1966 1980) Use HIGH SCHOOLS
TECHNICAL HIGH SCHOOLS Use VOCATIONAL HIGH SCHOOLS
VOCATIONAL HIGH SCHOOLS
HIGH TECHNOLOGY Use TECHNOLOGICAL ADVANCEMENT
HIGHER EDUCATION
ADMISSION TESTS (HIGHER EDUCATION) Use COLLEGE ENTRANCE EXAMINATIONS
HIGHER EDUCATION AS A FIELD OF STUDY Use POSTSECONDARY EDUCATION AS A FIELD OF STUDY
HIGHER EDUCATION INSTITUTIONS Use COLLEGES
PRIVATE HIGHER EDUCATION Use HIGHER EDUCATION and PRIVATE EDUCATION
PUBLIC HIGHER EDUCATION Use HIGHER EDUCATION and PUBLIC EDUCATION
HIGHWAY CONSTRUCTION Use ROAD CONSTRUCTION
HIGHWAY ENGINEERING Use CIVIL ENGINEERING
HIGHWAY ENGINEERING AIDES
HINDI
HISPANIC AMERICAN CULTURE
HISPANIC AMERICAN LITERATURE
HISPANIC AMERICANS
HISTORICAL CRITICISM (1969 1980)
HISTORICAL GEOGRAPHY Use HUMAN GEOGRAPHY
HISTORICAL LINGUISTICS Use DIACHRONIC LINGUISTICS
HISTORICAL REVIEWS (1966 1980) Use HISTORY
HISTORICALLY BLACK COLLEGES Use BLACK COLLEGES
LIFE HISTORIES Use BIOGRAPHIES
MEDICAL CASE HISTORIES
HISTORIOGRAPHY
HISTORY
AFRICAN HISTORY
AMERICAN HISTORY (1966 1980)
AMERICAN INDIAN HISTORY
ANCIENT HISTORY
ART HISTORY
ASIAN HISTORY
BLACK HISTORY
CENTRAL AMERICAN HISTORY Use LATIN AMERICAN HISTORY
COMMUNITY HISTORY Use LOCAL HISTORY
CONSTITUTIONAL HISTORY
CONTEMPORARY HISTORY Use MODERN HISTORY
COUNTY HISTORY Use LOCAL HISTORY
HISTORY CURRICULUM Use HISTORY INSTRUCTION
DIPLOMATIC HISTORY
HISTORY EDUCATION Use HISTORY INSTRUCTION
EDUCATIONAL HISTORY
EUROPEAN HISTORY
FAMILY HISTORY

HISTORY INSTRUCTION
INTELLECTUAL HISTORY
LANGUAGE HISTORY Use DIACHRONIC LINGUISTICS
LATIN AMERICAN HISTORY
LITERARY HISTORY
LOCAL HISTORY
MEDIEVAL HISTORY
MEXICAN AMERICAN HISTORY
MIDDLE EASTERN HISTORY
MODERN HISTORY
NEAR EASTERN HISTORY Use MIDDLE EASTERN HISTORY
NEGRO HISTORY (1966 1977) Use BLACK HISTORY
NORTH AMERICAN HISTORY
HISTORY OF EDUCATION Use EDUCATIONAL HISTORY
HISTORY OF LANGUAGE Use DIACHRONIC LINGUISTICS
ORAL HISTORY
SCIENCE HISTORY
SCIENCE EDUCATION HISTORY
SOCIAL HISTORY
SOUTH AMERICAN HISTORY Use LATIN AMERICAN HISTORY
STATE HISTORY
HISTORY TEXTBOOKS
UNITED STATES HISTORY
COLONIAL HISTORY (UNITED STATES)
WORLD HISTORY
HOBBIES
FIELD HOCKEY
ICE HOCKEY
HOKKU Use HAIKU
JOB HOLDING PATTERNS Use EMPLOYMENT PATTERNS
HOLDING POWER (OF SCHOOLS) Use SCHOOL HOLDING POWER
SCHOOL HOLDING POWER
LIBRARY HOLDINGS Use LIBRARY COLLECTIONS
HOLIDAYS
RELIGIOUS HOLIDAYS
HOLISTIC APPROACH
HOLISTIC EVALUATION
HOLOGRAPHY
HOLY DAYS Use RELIGIOUS HOLIDAYS
HOME Use FAMILY ENVIRONMENT
REST HOME AIDES Use NURSES AIDES
HOME AND FAMILY LIFE EDUCATION Use FAMILY LIFE EDUCATION
HOME APPLIANCE REPAIR Use APPLIANCE REPAIR
HOME ATTENDANTS Use HOME HEALTH AIDES
HOME CONDITIONS Use FAMILY ENVIRONMENT
HOME DAY CARE Use FAMILY DAY CARE
HOME DEMONSTRATION AGENTS Use EXTENSION AGENTS
HOME ECONOMICS
HOME ECONOMICS EDUCATION
OCCUPATIONAL HOME ECONOMICS
HOME ECONOMICS SKILLS
HOME ECONOMICS TEACHERS
HOME ENVIRONMENT Use FAMILY ENVIRONMENT
HOME EXPERIENCE Use EXPERIENTIAL LEARNING
HOME FURNISHINGS
HOME HEALTH AIDES
HOME INFLUENCE Use FAMILY INFLUENCE
HOME INSTRUCTION
HOME LIFE Use FAMILY LIFE
HOME MANAGEMENT
HOME PROGRAMS
SCHOOL HOME RELATIONSHIP Use FAMILY SCHOOL RELATIONSHIP
HOME SCHOOL RELATIONSHIP Use FAMILY SCHOOL RELATIONSHIP
HOME SCHOOLING
HOME STUDY
HOME VISITS
HOMEBOUND
HOMEBOUND CHILDREN (1966 1980) Use HOMEBOUND
HOMEBOUND TEACHERS (1966 1980) Use ITINERANT TEACHERS
HOMELESS PEOPLE
HOMELESSNESS Use HOMELESS PEOPLE
HOMEMAKERS
HOMEMAKERS CLUBS (1966 1980) Use CLUBS and HOMEMAKING SKILLS
DISPLACED HOMEMAKERS
VISITING HOMEMAKERS
HOMEMAKING EDUCATION (1967 1980) Use HOME ECONOMICS
HOMEMAKING SKILLS
HOMEOWNERS
FOSTER HOMES (1970 1982) (ADULTS) Use ADULT FOSTER CARE
BOARDING HOMES
FOSTER HOMES (1970 1982) (CHILDREN) Use FOSTER CARE
CONVALESCENT HOMES Use NURSING HOMES
HOMES FOR THE AGED Use PERSONAL CARE HOMES
GROUP HOMES
NURSING HOMES
PERSONAL CARE HOMES
REST HOMES Use PERSONAL CARE HOMES
HOMEWORK
HOMOGENEOUS GROUPING
HOMOSEXUALITY
FEMALE HOMOSEXUALITY Use LESBIANISM
HONOR CODES Use CODES OF ETHICS
HONOR SOCIETIES
HONORS CLASSES (1966 1980) Use HONORS CURRICULUM
HONORS COURSES Use HONORS CURRICULUM
HONORS CURRICULUM
HOPI
HORIZONTAL ORGANIZATION
HOROLOGISTS Use WATCHMAKERS
HOROLOGY
HORSEBACK RIDING

HORSES
HORTICULTURE
NURSERIES (HORTICULTURE)
NURSERY WORKERS (HORTICULTURE)
ORNAMENTAL HORTICULTURE OCCUPATION (1967 1976) Use ORNAMENTAL HORTICULTURE OCCUPATIONS
ORNAMENTAL HORTICULTURE OCCUPATIONS
ORNAMENTAL HORTICULTURE
YARD WORKERS (HORTICULTURE) Use GROUNDS KEEPERS
HOSPICES (TERMINAL CARE)
HOSPITAL ATTENDANTS Use NURSES AIDES
VETERINARY HOSPITAL ATTENDANTS Use VETERINARY ASSISTANTS
HOSPITAL LIBRARIES
HOSPITAL PERSONNEL
HOSPITAL RECORD ADMINISTRATORS Use MEDICAL RECORD ADMINISTRATORS
HOSPITAL RECORD TECHNICIANS Use MEDICAL RECORD TECHNICIANS
HOSPITAL SCHOOLS
HOSPITALITY OCCUPATIONS
HOSPITALIZED CHILDREN
HOSPITALS
PSYCHIATRIC HOSPITALS
TEACHING HOSPITALS
UNIVERSITY TEACHING HOSPITALS Use TEACHING HOSPITALS
HOSTILITY
DATABASE HOSTS Use ONLINE VENDORS
HOTELS
HOTHOUSES Use GREENHOUSES
HOTLINES (PUBLIC)
FLEXIBLE WORKING HOURS
HOURS OF WORK Use WORKING HOURS
STUDENT CREDIT HOURS Use CREDITS
STUDY HOURS Use STUDY
WORKING HOURS
HOUSE PLAN
HOUSEHOLD HEADS Use HEADS OF HOUSEHOLDS
HOUSEHOLD OCCUPATIONS Use HOUSEHOLD WORKERS and SERVICE OCCUPATIONS
HOUSEHOLD SCIENCE Use CONSUMER SCIENCE
HOUSEHOLD WORKERS
HOUSEHOLDS Use FAMILY (SOCIOLOGICAL UNIT)
HEADS OF HOUSEHOLDS
HOUSEHUSBANDS Use HOMEMAKERS
HOUSEKEEPERS
HOUSEKEEPING AIDES Use HOUSEKEEPERS
HOUSEPARENTS Use RESIDENT ADVISERS
FIELD HOUSES
HALFWAY HOUSES Use GROUP HOMES and REHABILITATION CENTERS
PUBLISHING HOUSES Use PUBLISHING INDUSTRY
SETTLEMENT HOUSES
HOUSEWIVES (1968 1980) Use HOMEMAKERS
HOUSING
LOCAL HOUSING AUTHORITIES (1966 1980) Use HOUSING
BLACK HOUSING (1977 1980)
COLLEGE HOUSING
STUDENT HOUSING (COLLEGE) Use COLLEGE HOUSING
HOUSING DEFICIENCIES
HOUSING DISCRIMINATION
HOUSING INDUSTRY
LOW RENT HOUSING
HOUSING MANAGEMENT AIDES
MIDDLE INCOME HOUSING
MIGRANT HOUSING
HOUSING NEEDS
NEGRO HOUSING (1966 1977)
HOUSING OPPORTUNITIES
HOUSING PATTERNS (1966 1980) Use RESIDENTIAL PATTERNS
PUBLIC HOUSING
PUBLIC HOUSING RESIDENTS (1966 1980) Use PUBLIC HOUSING
SUBURBAN HOUSING
TEACHER HOUSING
HUE Use COLOR
HUMAN BIOLOGY Use BIOLOGY
HUMAN BODY
HUMAN CAPITAL
HUMAN DEVELOPMENT (1966 1980)
HUMAN DIGNITY
HUMAN ENGINEERING (1967 1980) Use HUMAN FACTORS ENGINEERING
HUMAN FACTORS ENGINEERING
HUMAN GEOGRAPHY
HUMAN LIVING (1966 1980)
HUMAN POSTURE
HUMAN RELATIONS
HUMAN RELATIONS ORGANIZATIONS (1966 1980) Use HUMAN RELATIONS PROGRAMS
HUMAN RELATIONS PROGRAMS
HUMAN RELATIONS TRAINING Use SENSITIVITY TRAINING
HUMAN RELATIONS UNITS (1966 1980) Use HUMAN RELATIONS and UNITS OF STUDY
HUMAN RESOURCES
HUMAN RESOURCES DEVELOPMENT (LABOR) Use LABOR FORCE DEVELOPMENT
HUMAN RIGHTS Use CIVIL LIBERTIES
HUMAN SERVICES
CLIENT BACKGROUND (HUMAN SERVICES) Use CLIENT CHARACTERISTICS (HUMAN SERVICES)
CLIENT CHARACTERISTICS (HUMAN SERVICES)
SUPPORT GROUPS (HUMAN SERVICES) Use SOCIAL SUPPORT GROUPS
HUMAN SEXUALITY Use SEXUALITY
HUMANENESS Use ALTRUISM
HUMANISM
HUMANISTIC EDUCATION
HUMANITARIANISM
HUMANITIES
HUMANITIES INSTRUCTION
HUMANIZATION
HUMID AREAS Use HUMIDITY
HUMIDITY

ABSOLUTE	HUMIDITY Use HUMIDITY
RELATIVE	HUMIDITY Use HUMIDITY
	HUMOR
	HUNGARIAN
	HUNGER
ANIMAL	HUSBANDRY
	HUSBANDS Use SPOUSES
	HVAC Use CLIMATE CONTROL
	HYBRID AIR STRUCTURES (1972 1980) Use AIR STRUCTURES
	HYDRAULICS
	HYGIENE
MENTAL	HYGIENE Use MENTAL HEALTH
DENTAL	HYGIENISTS
ORAL	HYGIENISTS Use DENTAL HYGIENISTS
	HYMNS
	HYPERACTIVITY
	HYPERKINESIS Use HYPERACTIVITY
	HYPEROPIA
	HYPERSENSITIVITY Use ALLERGY
	HYPERTENSION
	HYPNOSIS
	HYPNOTICS Use SEDATIVES
	HYPOTHESIS TESTING
	IBO
	ICE HOCKEY
	ICE SKATING
	ICHTHYOLOGY
	ICIBEMBA Use BEMBA
ACCESS TO	IDEAS Use INTELLECTUAL FREEDOM
ADOPTION	(IDEAS)
OWNERSHIP OF	IDEAS Use INTELLECTUAL PROPERTY
	IDENTIFICATION
ABILITY	IDENTIFICATION
DELINQUENT	IDENTIFICATION (1966 1980) Use DELINQUENCY and IDENTIFICATION
DROPOUT	IDENTIFICATION (1966 1980) Use DROPOUT CHARACTERISTICS
ETHNIC	IDENTIFICATION Use ETHNICITY
HANDICAP	IDENTIFICATION
PLANT	IDENTIFICATION
	IDENTIFICATION (PSYCHOLOGICAL) (1968 1980) Use IDENTIFICATION (PSYCHOLOGY)
	IDENTIFICATION (PSYCHOLOGY)
RACIAL	IDENTIFICATION
RACIAL SELF	IDENTIFICATION Use RACIAL IDENTIFICATION
TALENT	IDENTIFICATION
	IDENTIFICATION TESTS (1966 1980) Use TESTS
RACIAL	IDENTITY Use RACIAL IDENTIFICATION
GENDER	IDENTITY (SEX) Use SEXUAL IDENTITY
SEXUAL	IDENTITY
	IDEOGRAPHY
	IDEOLOGY
	IDIOMATIC EXPRESSIONS Use IDIOMS
	IDIOMS
	IGBO
	ILLEGAL ALIENS Use UNDOCUMENTED IMMIGRANTS
	ILLEGAL DRUG USE
	ILLEGAL IMMIGRANTS (1976 1984) Use UNDOCUMENTED IMMIGRANTS
ALIEN	ILLEGALITY Use UNDOCUMENTED IMMIGRANTS
IMMIGRANT	ILLEGALITY Use UNDOCUMENTED IMMIGRANTS
	ILLEGITIMACY Use ILLEGITIMATE BIRTHS
	ILLEGITIMATE BIRTHS
	ILLITERACY
FUNCTIONAL	ILLITERACY (1968 1980) Use FUNCTIONAL LITERACY
	ILLITERATE ADULTS (1966 1980) Use ADULT LITERACY and ILLITERACY
MENTAL	ILLNESS (1966 1980) Use MENTAL DISORDERS
	ILLNESSES Use DISEASES
CHRONIC	ILLNESSES Use DISEASES
	ILLOCUTIONARY ACTS Use SPEECH ACTS
	ILLUMINATION LEVELS (1968 1980) Use LIGHTING
TECHNICAL	ILLUSTRATION
	ILLUSTRATIONS
BODY	IMAGE
PUBLIC	IMAGE Use PUBLIC OPINION
SELF	IMAGE Use SELF CONCEPT
	IMAGERY
EIDETIC	IMAGERY
CULTURAL	IMAGES
EIDETIC	IMAGES (1967 1980) Use EIDETIC IMAGERY
	IMAGINATION
RACIAL	IMBALANCE Use RACIAL BALANCE
	IMITATION
	IMITATIVE LEARNING Use OBSERVATIONAL LEARNING
	IMMATURITY (1966 1980) Use MATURITY (INDIVIDUALS)
SOCIAL	IMMATURITY (1966 1980) Use MATURITY (INDIVIDUALS)
	IMMERSION PROGRAMS
	IMMIGRANT ILLEGALITY Use UNDOCUMENTED IMMIGRANTS
	IMMIGRANTS
ILLEGAL	IMMIGRANTS (1976 1984) Use UNDOCUMENTED IMMIGRANTS
INTERNAL	IMMIGRANTS Use MIGRANTS
UNDOCUMENTED	IMMIGRANTS
	IMMIGRATION INSPECTORS
URBAN	IMMIGRATION (1966 1976) Use RURAL TO URBAN MIGRATION
	IMMUNIZATION PROGRAMS
DESEGREGATION	IMPACT Use DESEGREGATION EFFECTS
INTEGRATION	IMPACT Use DESEGREGATION EFFECTS
ADVENTITIOUS	IMPAIRMENTS
ARTICULATION	IMPAIRMENTS
CONGENITAL	IMPAIRMENTS
HEARING	IMPAIRMENTS
NEUROLOGICAL	IMPAIRMENTS
VISUAL	IMPAIRMENTS
EQUITY	(IMPARTIALITY) Use JUSTICE
	IMPASSE RESOLUTION Use NEGOTIATION IMPASSES

COMPUTER ASSISTED	INDEXING Use AUTOMATIC INDEXING
MACHINE AIDED	INDEXING Use AUTOMATIC INDEXING
AMERICAN	INDIAN CULTURE
AMERICAN	INDIAN EDUCATION
AMERICAN	INDIAN HISTORY
AMERICAN	INDIAN LANGUAGES
AMERICAN	INDIAN LITERATURE
FEDERAL	INDIAN RELATIONSHIP
RESERVATIONS	(INDIAN) (1971 1980) Use AMERICAN INDIAN RESERVATIONS
AMERICAN	INDIAN RESERVATIONS
AMERICAN	INDIAN STUDIES
	INDIANS
AMERICAN	INDIANS
NONRESERVATION AMERICAN	INDIANS
OFF RESERVATION AMERICAN	INDIANS Use NONRESERVATION AMERICAN INDIANS
RESERVATION AMERICAN	INDIANS
RURAL AMERICAN	INDIANS
URBAN AMERICAN	INDIANS
	INDICATIVE MOOD Use VERBS
SOCIAL	INDICATORS
	INDIFFERENCE Use APATHY
	INDIGENOUS PERSONNEL
	INDIGENOUS POPULATIONS
	INDIVIDUAL ACTIVITIES
	INDIVIDUAL ADJUSTMENT Use ADJUSTMENT (TO ENVIRONMENT)
	INDIVIDUAL AUTONOMY Use PERSONAL AUTONOMY
	INDIVIDUAL CHARACTERISTICS
	INDIVIDUAL COUNSELING
	INDIVIDUAL DEVELOPMENT
	INDIVIDUAL DIFFERENCES
	INDIVIDUAL DIGNITY Use HUMAN DIGNITY
	INDIVIDUAL INSTRUCTION
	INDIVIDUAL NEEDS
	INDIVIDUAL POWER
	INDIVIDUAL PSYCHOLOGY
	INDIVIDUAL READING (1966 1980)
	INDIVIDUAL RIGHTS Use CIVIL LIBERTIES
	INDIVIDUAL STUDY (1966 1980) Use INDEPENDENT STUDY
	INDIVIDUAL TESTING
	INDIVIDUAL TESTS (1966 1980) Use INDIVIDUAL TESTING
	INDIVIDUAL VOLITION Use INDIVIDUAL POWER
	INDIVIDUALISM
	INDIVIDUALIZED CURRICULUM (1966 1980) Use INDIVIDUALIZED INSTRUCTION
	INDIVIDUALIZED EDUCATION Use INDIVIDUALIZED INSTRUCTION
	INDIVIDUALIZED EDUCATION PROGRAMS
	INDIVIDUALIZED INSTRUCTION
CLINICAL TEACHING	(INDIVIDUALIZED INSTRUCTION) Use INDIVIDUALIZED INSTRUCTION
	INDIVIDUALIZED PROGRAMS
	INDIVIDUALIZED READING
AGING	(INDIVIDUALS)
MATURITY	(INDIVIDUALS)
MEASURES	(INDIVIDUALS)
SELF DISCLOSURE	(INDIVIDUALS)
SELF EVALUATION	(INDIVIDUALS)
SPECIAL NEEDS	(INDIVIDUALS) Use INDIVIDUAL NEEDS
	INDO EUROPEAN LANGUAGES
	INDOCHINESE
	INDOCHINESE AMERICANS Use ASIAN AMERICANS and INDOCHINESE
BAHASA	INDONESIA Use INDONESIAN
	INDONESIAN
	INDONESIAN LANGUAGES
	INDUCTION
LOOP	INDUCTION SYSTEMS
TEACHER	INDUCTION Use TEACHER ORIENTATION
	INDUCTIVE METHODS (1967 1980) Use INDUCTION
	INDUSTRIAL AND ORGANIZATIONAL PSYCHOLOGY Use INDUSTRIAL PSYCHOLOGY
	INDUSTRIAL ARTS
PAINTING	(INDUSTRIAL ARTS)
	INDUSTRIAL ARTS SHOPS Use SCHOOL SHOPS
	INDUSTRIAL ARTS TEACHERS
	INDUSTRIAL COMMUNICATION Use BUSINESS COMMUNICATION
	INDUSTRIAL CRAFTS Use INDUSTRIAL ARTS
	INDUSTRIAL EDUCATION
TRADE AND	INDUSTRIAL EDUCATION
VOCATIONAL	INDUSTRIAL EDUCATION Use TRADE AND INDUSTRIAL EDUCATION
	INDUSTRIAL NATIONS Use DEVELOPED NATIONS
PAINTING (1966 1980)	(INDUSTRIAL) Use PAINTING (INDUSTRIAL ARTS)
	INDUSTRIAL PERSONNEL
	INDUSTRIAL PSYCHOLOGY
	INDUSTRIAL RELATIONS (1969 1980) Use LABOR RELATIONS
	INDUSTRIAL ROBOTICS Use ROBOTICS
	INDUSTRIAL STRUCTURE
TRADE AND	INDUSTRIAL TEACHERS
	INDUSTRIAL TECHNOLOGY (1969 1980) Use INDUSTRY and TECHNOLOGY
	INDUSTRIAL TRAINING
	INDUSTRIAL X RAY OPERATORS Use RADIOGRAPHERS
	INDUSTRIALIZATION
	INDUSTRY
AEROSPACE	INDUSTRY
APPAREL	INDUSTRY Use FASHION INDUSTRY
BAKERY	INDUSTRY
BANKING	INDUSTRY Use BANKING
BOOK	INDUSTRY Use PUBLISHING INDUSTRY
BRICK	INDUSTRY
BROADCAST	INDUSTRY
BUSINESS OFFICIALS	(INDUSTRY) Use ADMINISTRATORS
CEMENT	INDUSTRY
CHEMICAL	INDUSTRY
CLOTHING	INDUSTRY Use FASHION INDUSTRY
COMPANY SIZE	(INDUSTRY) Use ORGANIZATION SIZE (GROUPS)
CONCRETE	INDUSTRY Use CEMENT INDUSTRY

CONSTRUCTION	INDUSTRY
ELECTRONICS	INDUSTRY
FASHION	INDUSTRY
FEED	INDUSTRY
FILM	INDUSTRY
FOOD SERVICE	INDUSTRY (1967 1981) Use FOOD SERVICE
FURNITURE	INDUSTRY
GARMENT	INDUSTRY Use FASHION INDUSTRY
HOUSING	INDUSTRY
INSURANCE	INDUSTRY Use INSURANCE COMPANIES
LUMBER	INDUSTRY
MACHINERY	INDUSTRY
MACHINERY MANUFACTURING	INDUSTRY Use MACHINERY INDUSTRY
MANUFACTURING	INDUSTRY
MEAT PACKING	INDUSTRY
METAL	INDUSTRY
PETROLEUM	INDUSTRY
PUBLISHING	INDUSTRY
SCHOOL	INDUSTRY RELATIONSHIP (1967 1980) Use SCHOOL BUSINESS RELATIONSHIP
	INDUSTRY SCHOOL RELATIONSHIP Use SCHOOL BUSINESS RELATIONSHIP
SERVICE	INDUSTRY Use SERVICE OCCUPATIONS
SIGHTSEEING	INDUSTRY Use TOURISM
STEEL	INDUSTRY (1967 1980) Use METAL INDUSTRY
TELEPHONE COMMUNICATIONS	INDUSTRY
TIMBER BASED	INDUSTRY Use LUMBER INDUSTRY
TOURIST	INDUSTRY Use TOURISM
	INELIGIBILITY Use DISQUALIFICATION
	INEQUALITIES (1970 1980)
EDUCATIONAL	INEQUALITY Use EQUAL EDUCATION
	INEQUALITY (MATHEMATICS)
	INFANCY (1966 1980) Use INFANTS
	INFANT BEHAVIOR
	INFANT DEATH RATE Use INFANT MORTALITY
	INFANT MORTALITY
BRITISH	INFANT SCHOOLS
	INFANT SCHOOLS (BRITISH PRIMARY SYSTEM) Use BRITISH INFANT SCHOOLS
	INFANTS
NEWBORN	INFANTS Use NEONATES
PREMATURE	INFANTS
	INFECTIOUS DISEASES (1966 1974) Use COMMUNICABLE DISEASES
STATISTICAL	INFERENCE
	INFERENCES
	INFERENTIAL STATISTICS Use STATISTICAL INFERENCE and STATISTICS
	INFIRMARIES Use HEALTH FACILITIES
	INFLATABLE STRUCTURES Use AIR STRUCTURES
	INFLATED GRADES Use GRADE INFLATION
AIR	INFLATED STRUCTURES (1972 1980) Use AIR STRUCTURES
	INFLATION (ECONOMICS)
GRADE	INFLATION
COMMUNITY	INFLUENCE
FAMILY	INFLUENCE
HOME	INFLUENCE Use FAMILY INFLUENCE
PARENT	INFLUENCE
PEER	INFLUENCE
TEACHER	INFLUENCE
	INFLUENCES
BIOLOGICAL	INFLUENCES
BLACK	INFLUENCES
CULTURAL	INFLUENCES
ENROLLMENT	INFLUENCES
ENVIRONMENTAL	INFLUENCES
LITERARY	INFLUENCES (1969 1980)
MINORITY GROUP	INFLUENCES
PERINATAL	INFLUENCES
POLITICAL	INFLUENCES
PRENATAL	INFLUENCES
RACE	INFLUENCES (1966 1980) Use RACIAL FACTORS
SOCIAL	INFLUENCES
SOCIOECONOMIC	INFLUENCES
	INFORMAL ASSESSMENT
	INFORMAL CONVERSATIONAL USAGE Use STANDARD SPOKEN USAGE
	INFORMAL LEADERSHIP
	INFORMAL ORGANIZATION
	INFORMAL READING INVENTORIES
	INFORMAL READING INVENTORY (1968 1980) Use INFORMAL READING INVENTORIES
NATIVE	INFORMANTS Use NATIVE SPEAKERS
	INFORMATICS Use INFORMATION SCIENCE
ACCESS TO	INFORMATION
	INFORMATION AND REFERRAL SERVICES Use INFORMATION SERVICES and REFERRAL
	INFORMATION BROKERS Use INFORMATION SCIENTISTS
	INFORMATION CENTERS
COMMUNITY	INFORMATION CENTERS Use COMMUNITY INFORMATION SERVICES
CONFIDENTIAL	INFORMATION Use CONFIDENTIALITY
	INFORMATION DISSEMINATION
END USERS	(INFORMATION) Use USERS (INFORMATION)
ELECTRONIC	INFORMATION EXCHANGE Use INFORMATION NETWORKS and TELECOMMUNICATIONS
	INFORMATION FLOW Use INFORMATION TRANSFER
FREEDOM OF	INFORMATION
MERCHANDISE	INFORMATION
	INFORMATION NEEDS
	INFORMATION NETWORKS
OCCUPATIONAL	INFORMATION
PRIVATE	INFORMATION Use CONFIDENTIALITY
	INFORMATION PROCESSES (PSYCHOLOGICAL) Use COGNITIVE PROCESSES
	INFORMATION PROCESSING
PRODUCT	INFORMATION Use MERCHANDISE INFORMATION
	INFORMATION RETRIEVAL
ONLINE	INFORMATION RETRIEVAL Use ONLINE SEARCHING
RELEVANCE	(INFORMATION RETRIEVAL)
SCIENCE	INFORMATION Use SCIENTIFIC AND TECHNICAL INFORMATION
	INFORMATION SCIENCE

SCIENTIFIC	INFORMATION Use SCIENTIFIC AND TECHNICAL INFORMATION
SCIENTIFIC AND TECHNICAL	INFORMATION
	INFORMATION SCIENTISTS
	INFORMATION SEEKING
SELECTIVE DISSEMINATION OF	INFORMATION
	INFORMATION SERVICES
COMMUNITY	INFORMATION SERVICES
	INFORMATION SERVICES (COMMUNITY) Use COMMUNITY INFORMATION SERVICES
LOCAL	INFORMATION SERVICES Use COMMUNITY INFORMATION SERVICES
	INFORMATION SOURCES
	INFORMATION SPECIALISTS Use INFORMATION SCIENTISTS
	INFORMATION STORAGE
	INFORMATION STORAGE (PSYCHOLOGY) Use ENCODING (PSYCHOLOGY)
	INFORMATION SYSTEMS
DIAL ACCESS	INFORMATION SYSTEMS
MANAGEMENT	INFORMATION SYSTEMS
TECHNICAL	INFORMATION Use SCIENTIFIC AND TECHNICAL INFORMATION
TECHNOLOGICAL	INFORMATION Use SCIENTIFIC AND TECHNICAL INFORMATION
	INFORMATION TECHNOLOGY
	INFORMATION THEORY
	INFORMATION TRANSFER
USER NEEDS	(INFORMATION)
	INFORMATION USER NEEDS Use USER NEEDS (INFORMATION)
USER SATISFACTION	(INFORMATION)
	INFORMATION USER SATISFACTION Use USER SATISFACTION (INFORMATION)
USERS	(INFORMATION)
	INFORMATION USERS Use USERS (INFORMATION)
	INFORMATION UTILITIES (ONLINE) Use ONLINE VENDORS
	INFORMATION UTILIZATION
RURAL	INHABITANTS Use RURAL POPULATION
	INHALATION THERAPISTS (1969 1985) Use RESPIRATORY THERAPY and THERAPISTS
OXYGEN	INHALATION THERAPY Use RESPIRATORY THERAPY
LINGUISTIC DIFFICULTY	(INHERENT)
	INHIBITION
PROACTIVE	INHIBITION Use INHIBITION
REACTIVE	INHIBITION Use INHIBITION
RETROACTIVE	INHIBITION Use INHIBITION
	INITIAL EXPENSES (1966 1980) Use EXPENDITURES
MINIMUM	INITIAL EXPENSES Use EXPENDITURES
	INITIAL TEACHING ALPHABET
MINIMALLY BRAIN	INJURED (1966 1980) Use MINIMAL BRAIN DYSFUNCTION
	INJURIES
SELF	INJURY (PHYSICAL) Use SELF MUTILATION
MAGNETIC	INK CHARACTER RECOGNITION Use CHARACTER RECOGNITION
	INMATES Use PRISONERS
JAIL	INMATES Use PRISONERS
	INNER CITY
	INNER CITY EDUCATION Use URBAN EDUCATION
	INNER SPEECH (SUBVOCAL)
	INNOVATION
BUILDING	INNOVATION
EDUCATIONAL	INNOVATION
INSTRUCTIONAL	INNOVATION
TEACHING	INNOVATIONS Use INSTRUCTIONAL INNOVATION
	INNS Use HOTELS
	INORGANIC CHEMISTRY
	INPLANT PROGRAMS
	INPUT DEVICES Use INPUT OUTPUT DEVICES
	INPUT EVALUATION Use INPUT OUTPUT ANALYSIS
	INPUT OUTPUT
	INPUT OUTPUT ANALYSIS
	INPUT OUTPUT DEVICES
	INQUIRY
	INQUIRY TRAINING (1967 1980) Use INQUIRY
	INSECT STUDIES Use ENTOMOLOGY
	INSECTICIDES
	INSECURITY (1966 1980) Use SECURITY (PSYCHOLOGY)
ECONOMIC	INSECURITY Use POVERTY
	INSERVICE COURSES (1966 1980) Use INSERVICE EDUCATION
	INSERVICE EDUCATION
	INSERVICE EDUCATION PROGRAMS Use INSERVICE EDUCATION
	INSERVICE PROGRAMS (1966 1980) Use INSERVICE EDUCATION
	INSERVICE TEACHER EDUCATION
	INSERVICE TEACHER TRAINING Use INSERVICE TEACHER EDUCATION
	INSERVICE TEACHING (1966 1980) Use INSERVICE EDUCATION and TEACHING (OCCUPATION)
	INSERVICE TEACHING EXPERIENCE Use TEACHING EXPERIENCE
	INSPECTION
COSMETICS	INSPECTORS Use FOOD AND DRUG INSPECTORS
DAIRY PRODUCT	INSPECTORS Use FOOD AND DRUG INSPECTORS
DRUG	INSPECTORS Use FOOD AND DRUG INSPECTORS
EGG	INSPECTORS Use FOOD AND DRUG INSPECTORS
FISH	INSPECTORS Use FOOD AND DRUG INSPECTORS
FOOD	INSPECTORS Use FOOD AND DRUG INSPECTORS
FOOD AND DRUG	INSPECTORS
FRUIT AND VEGETABLE	INSPECTORS Use FOOD AND DRUG INSPECTORS
IMMIGRATION	INSPECTORS
MEAT	INSPECTORS Use FOOD AND DRUG INSPECTORS
PEANUT	INSPECTORS Use FOOD AND DRUG INSPECTORS
PROCESSED FOODS	INSPECTORS Use FOOD AND DRUG INSPECTORS
SANITARY	INSPECTORS Use ENVIRONMENTAL TECHNICIANS
MARITAL	INSTABILITY
FLOOR	INSTALLATION Use FLOORING
ROOF	INSTALLATION Use ROOFING
GLASS	INSTALLERS Use GLAZIERS
	INSTITUTE TYPE COURSES (1966 1980) Use INSTITUTES (TRAINING PROGRAMS)
SCIENCE	INSTITUTES (1967 1980) Use INSTITUTES (TRAINING PROGRAMS) and SCIENCE PROGRAMS
SUMMER	INSTITUTES (1967 1980) Use INSTITUTES (TRAINING PROGRAMS) and SUMMER PROGRAMS
TECHNICAL	INSTITUTES
	INSTITUTES (TRAINING PROGRAMS)
	INSTITUTION LIBRARIES (1969 1980) Use INSTITUTIONAL LIBRARIES
	INSTITUTIONAL ADMINISTRATION

INSTITUTIONAL ADVANCEMENT
INSTITUTIONAL ASSESSMENT Use INSTITUTIONAL EVALUATION
INSTITUTIONAL AUTONOMY
INSTITUTIONAL CHARACTERISTICS
INSTITUTIONAL COOPERATION
INSTITUTIONAL DIFFERENCES Use DIFFERENCES and INSTITUTIONAL CHARACTERISTICS
INSTITUTIONAL ELIGIBILITY Use ELIGIBILITY
INSTITUTIONAL ENVIRONMENT
INSTITUTIONAL EVALUATION
INSTITUTIONAL FACILITIES (1967 1980) Use FACILITIES
INSTITUTIONAL FUNCTION Use INSTITUTIONAL ROLE
INSTITUTIONAL GOALS Use ORGANIZATIONAL OBJECTIVES
INSTITUTIONAL LIBRARIES
INSTITUTIONAL MISSION
INSTITUTIONAL OBJECTIVES Use ORGANIZATIONAL OBJECTIVES
INSTITUTIONAL PERSONNEL
INSTITUTIONAL RESEARCH
INSTITUTIONAL ROLE
INSTITUTIONAL SCHOOLS
INSTITUTIONAL SELF STUDY Use SELF EVALUATION (GROUPS)
INSTITUTIONAL SURVIVAL
INSTITUTIONALIZED (PERSONS) (1967 1976) Use INSTITUTIONALIZED PERSONS
INSTITUTIONALIZED PERSONS
INSTITUTIONS
ACCREDITATION (INSTITUTIONS)
BLACK INSTITUTIONS
COMPARABLE INSTITUTIONS Use PEER INSTITUTIONS
CORRECTIONAL INSTITUTIONS
CORRECTIVE INSTITUTIONS (1966 1980) Use CORRECTIONAL INSTITUTIONS
DEVELOPING INSTITUTIONS
EDUCATIONAL INSTITUTIONS Use SCHOOLS
FOUNDATIONS (INSTITUTIONS) Use PHILANTHROPIC FOUNDATIONS
HIGHER EDUCATION INSTITUTIONS Use COLLEGES
NEGRO INSTITUTIONS (1966 1977) Use BLACK INSTITUTIONS
SOCIAL INSTITUTIONS (ORGANIZATIONS) Use INSTITUTIONS
PEER INSTITUTIONS
RESIDENTIAL INSTITUTIONS
SOCIAL INSTITUTIONS (SOCIAL PATTERNS) Use SOCIOCULTURAL PATTERNS
INSTRUCTION
SELF INSTRUCTION AIDS Use AUTOINSTRUCTIONAL AIDS
AUDIOVISUAL INSTRUCTION
BIOLOGY INSTRUCTION (1966 1980) Use BIOLOGY and SCIENCE INSTRUCTION
CHEMISTRY INSTRUCTION (1967 1980) Use CHEMISTRY and SCIENCE INSTRUCTION
CLINICAL TEACHING (INDIVIDUALIZED INSTRUCTION) Use INDIVIDUALIZED INSTRUCTION
CLOTHING INSTRUCTION
COLLEGE INSTRUCTION
COMPUTER AIDED INSTRUCTION Use COMPUTER ASSISTED INSTRUCTION
COMPUTER ASSISTED INSTRUCTION
COMPUTER BASED INSTRUCTION Use COMPUTER ASSISTED INSTRUCTION
COMPUTER MANAGED INSTRUCTION
CONVENTIONAL INSTRUCTION
COOKING INSTRUCTION
COURSE OF INSTRUCTION Use COURSE ORGANIZATION
DEANS OF INSTRUCTION Use ACADEMIC DEANS
ECONOMICS INSTRUCTION Use ECONOMICS EDUCATION
ENGLISH INSTRUCTION
ETHICAL INSTRUCTION
EXCURSIONS (INSTRUCTION) Use FIELD TRIPS
FIELD INSTRUCTION
FOODS INSTRUCTION
FOREIGN LANGUAGE INSTRUCTION Use SECOND LANGUAGE INSTRUCTION
GEOGRAPHY INSTRUCTION
GROUP INSTRUCTION
HANDWRITING INSTRUCTION (1966 1983) Use HANDWRITING and WRITING INSTRUCTION
HISTORY INSTRUCTION
HOME INSTRUCTION
HUMANITIES INSTRUCTION
INDIVIDUAL INSTRUCTION
INDIVIDUALIZED INSTRUCTION
LANGUAGE INSTRUCTION (1966 1980)
MEDIUM OF INSTRUCTION (LANGUAGE) Use LANGUAGE OF INSTRUCTION
LANGUAGE OF INSTRUCTION
LARGE GROUP INSTRUCTION
LIBRARY INSTRUCTION
MASS INSTRUCTION
SELF INSTRUCTION MATERIALS Use PROGRAMED INSTRUCTIONAL MATERIALS
MATHEMATICS INSTRUCTION
MORAL INSTRUCTION Use ETHICAL INSTRUCTION
MULTILEVEL CLASSES (SECOND LANGUAGE INSTRUCTION)
MULTIMEDIA INSTRUCTION
NATIVE LANGUAGE INSTRUCTION
NUTRITION INSTRUCTION
PERSONALIZED INSTRUCTION Use INDIVIDUALIZED INSTRUCTION
PHYSICS INSTRUCTION (1966 1980) Use PHYSICS and SCIENCE INSTRUCTION
PROGRAMED INSTRUCTION
PROGRAMED SELF INSTRUCTION Use PROGRAMED INSTRUCTION
PRONUNCIATION INSTRUCTION
READING INSTRUCTION
REMEDIAL INSTRUCTION
SCIENCE INSTRUCTION
SECOND LANGUAGE INSTRUCTION
SELF INSTRUCTION Use INDEPENDENT STUDY
SELF PACED INSTRUCTION Use INDIVIDUALIZED INSTRUCTION and PACING
SEWING INSTRUCTION
SMALL GROUP INSTRUCTION
SPEECH INSTRUCTION
SPELLING INSTRUCTION
TECHNICAL INSTRUCTION Use TECHNICAL EDUCATION
TELEPHONE INSTRUCTION
TELEPHONE USAGE INSTRUCTION
TELEVISED INSTRUCTION (1966 1974) Use EDUCATIONAL TELEVISION

TEXTILES	INSTRUCTION
TRADITIONAL	INSTRUCTION Use CONVENTIONAL INSTRUCTION
TUTORIAL	INSTRUCTION Use TUTORING
RESEARCH AND	INSTRUCTION UNITS
WRITING	INSTRUCTION
	INSTRUCTIONAL AIDS (1966 1980) Use EDUCATIONAL MEDIA
	INSTRUCTIONAL ALTERNATIVES Use NONTRADITIONAL EDUCATION
	INSTRUCTIONAL DESIGN
	INSTRUCTIONAL DEVELOPMENT
	INSTRUCTIONAL EFFECTIVENESS
	INSTRUCTIONAL FILMS
NONGRADED	INSTRUCTIONAL GROUPING
	INSTRUCTIONAL IMPROVEMENT
	INSTRUCTIONAL INNOVATION
	INSTRUCTIONAL LANGUAGE Use LANGUAGE OF INSTRUCTION
	INSTRUCTIONAL LEADERSHIP
POSTSECONDARY	INSTRUCTIONAL LEVEL Use POSTSECONDARY EDUCATION
COMPUTER AIDED	INSTRUCTIONAL MANAGEMENT Use COMPUTER MANAGED INSTRUCTION
COMPUTER BASED	INSTRUCTIONAL MANAGEMENT Use COMPUTER MANAGED INSTRUCTION
	INSTRUCTIONAL MATERIAL ADAPTATION Use MEDIA ADAPTATION
	INSTRUCTIONAL MATERIAL DEVELOPMENT Use MATERIAL DEVELOPMENT
	INSTRUCTIONAL MATERIAL EVALUATION
	INSTRUCTIONAL MATERIAL SELECTION Use MEDIA SELECTION
	INSTRUCTIONAL MATERIALS
BILINGUAL	INSTRUCTIONAL MATERIALS
	INSTRUCTIONAL MATERIALS CENTERS (1966 1980) Use LEARNING RESOURCES CENTERS
PROGRAMED	INSTRUCTIONAL MATERIALS
	INSTRUCTIONAL MEDIA (1967 1980) Use EDUCATIONAL MEDIA
	INSTRUCTIONAL METHODS Use TEACHING METHODS
	INSTRUCTIONAL OUTCOMES Use OUTCOMES OF EDUCATION
	INSTRUCTIONAL PLANNING Use INSTRUCTIONAL DEVELOPMENT
	INSTRUCTIONAL PROGRAM DIVISIONS
	INSTRUCTIONAL PROGRAMS (1966 1980)
COUNSELING	INSTRUCTIONAL PROGRAMS (1967 1980)
GROUPING	(INSTRUCTIONAL PURPOSES)
	INSTRUCTIONAL RADIO Use EDUCATIONAL RADIO
	INSTRUCTIONAL SOFTWARE Use COURSEWARE
	INSTRUCTIONAL STAFF (1966 1980) Use TEACHERS
	INSTRUCTIONAL STUDENT COSTS
	INSTRUCTIONAL SYSTEMS
	INSTRUCTIONAL TEAMS Use TEAM TEACHING
	INSTRUCTIONAL TECHNOLOGY (1966 1978) Use EDUCATIONAL TECHNOLOGY
	INSTRUCTIONAL TELEVISION (1966 1974) Use EDUCATIONAL TELEVISION
	INSTRUCTIONAL TRIPS (1966 1980) Use FIELD TRIPS
	INSTRUCTIONALLY EFFECTIVE SCHOOLS Use SCHOOL EFFECTIVENESS
	INSTRUCTOR CENTERED TELEVISION (1966 1980) Use EDUCATIONAL TELEVISION
	INSTRUCTOR COORDINATORS
	INSTRUCTOR MANUALS Use TEACHING GUIDES
	INSTRUCTORS Use TEACHERS
	INSTRUMENTAL CONDITIONING Use OPERANT CONDITIONING
	INSTRUMENTATION
	INSTRUMENTATION TECHNICIANS
MEASUREMENT	INSTRUMENTS (1966 1980)
MUSICAL	INSTRUMENTS
POTENTIOMETERS	(INSTRUMENTS)
ACOUSTIC	INSULATION
SOUND	INSULATION Use ACOUSTIC INSULATION
	INSURANCE
	INSURANCE COMPANIES
FIRE	INSURANCE
HEALTH	INSURANCE
	INSURANCE INDUSTRY Use INSURANCE COMPANIES
	INSURANCE OCCUPATIONS
	INSURANCE PROGRAMS (1968 1980) Use INSURANCE
UNEMPLOYMENT	INSURANCE
	INTEGERS
	INTEGRATED ACTIVITIES
	INTEGRATED CLASSES Use CLASSROOM DESEGREGATION
	INTEGRATED COLLEGES Use COLLEGE DESEGREGATION
	INTEGRATED CURRICULUM
	INTEGRATED EDUCATION Use INTEGRATED CURRICULUM
	INTEGRATED FACULTY Use FACULTY INTEGRATION
	INTEGRATED LEARNING Use INTEGRATED ACTIVITIES and LEARNING ACTIVITIES
	INTEGRATED NEIGHBORHOODS Use NEIGHBORHOOD INTEGRATION
	INTEGRATED PUBLIC FACILITIES (1966 1980) Use PUBLIC FACILITIES and RACIAL INTEGRATION
	INTEGRATED SCHOOLS Use SCHOOL DESEGREGATION
	INTEGRATED TEACHING METHOD Use INTEGRATED ACTIVITIES and TEACHING METHODS
CLASSROOM	INTEGRATION (1967 1980) Use CLASSROOM DESEGREGATION
COLLEGE	INTEGRATION (1966 1980) Use COLLEGE DESEGREGATION
	INTEGRATION (DISABLED STUDENTS) Use MAINSTREAMING
	INTEGRATION EFFECTS (1966 1980) Use DESEGREGATION EFFECTS
ETHNIC	INTEGRATION Use SOCIAL INTEGRATION
FACULTY	INTEGRATION
GRADE A YEAR	INTEGRATION (1966 1980) Use SCHOOL DESEGREGATION
	INTEGRATION IMPACT Use DESEGREGATION EFFECTS
INTERSENSORY	INTEGRATION Use SENSORY INTEGRATION
	INTEGRATION LITIGATION (1966 1980) Use DESEGREGATION LITIGATION
	INTEGRATION METHODS (1966 1980) Use DESEGREGATION METHODS
NEIGHBORHOOD	INTEGRATION
PERSONNEL	INTEGRATION
	INTEGRATION PLANS (1966 1980) Use DESEGREGATION PLANS
RACIAL	INTEGRATION
	INTEGRATION (RACIAL) Use RACIAL INTEGRATION
	INTEGRATION READINESS
SCHOOL	INTEGRATION (1966 1980) Use SCHOOL DESEGREGATION
SENSORY	INTEGRATION
SOCIAL	INTEGRATION
	INTEGRATION (SOCIAL) Use SOCIAL INTEGRATION
SOCIAL CLASS	INTEGRATION Use SOCIAL INTEGRATION
	INTEGRATION STUDIES
TEACHER	INTEGRATION

TOKEN INTEGRATION (1966 1980) Use TOKENISM
VOLUNTARY INTEGRATION (1966 1980) Use VOLUNTARY DESEGREGATION
INTEGRATIVE ANALYSIS Use META ANALYSIS
INTEGRITY
INTELLECTRONICS Use BIONICS
INTELLECTUAL DEVELOPMENT
INTELLECTUAL DISCIPLINES
INTELLECTUAL EXPERIENCE
INTELLECTUAL FREEDOM
INTELLECTUAL HISTORY
INTELLECTUAL PROPERTY
ANTI INTELLECTUALISM
INTELLECTUALIZATION (1970 1980) Use ABSTRACT REASONING
INTELLIGENCE
INTELLIGENCE AGE Use MENTAL AGE
ARTIFICIAL INTELLIGENCE
INTELLIGENCE DIFFERENCES
INTELLIGENCE FACTORS (1966 1980) Use INTELLIGENCE
INTELLIGENCE LEVEL (1966 1980) Use INTELLIGENCE
INTELLIGENCE MEASURES Use INTELLIGENCE TESTS
NATIONAL INTELLIGENCE NORM (1966 1980) Use INTELLIGENCE and NATIONAL NORMS
INTELLIGENCE QUOTIENT
GROUP INTELLIGENCE TESTING (1966 1980) Use GROUP TESTING and INTELLIGENCE TESTS
INTELLIGENCE TESTS
GROUP INTELLIGENCE TESTS (1966 1980) Use GROUP TESTING and INTELLIGENCE TESTS
INTELLIGENT VIDEO Use INTERACTIVE VIDEO
MUTUAL INTELLIGIBILITY
INTENSIVE LANGUAGE COURSES
INTENTIONAL LEARNING
INTERACTION
INTERACTION ANALYSIS Use INTERACTION
APTITUDE TREATMENT INTERACTION
CULTURAL INTERACTION Use CULTURAL EXCHANGE
GROUP INTERACTION Use GROUP DYNAMICS
PARENT CHILD INTERACTION Use PARENT CHILD RELATIONSHIP
INTERACTION PROCESS ANALYSIS
RACIAL INTERACTION Use RACIAL RELATIONS
SCHOOL COMMUNITY INTERACTION Use SCHOOL COMMUNITY RELATIONSHIP
SOCIAL INTERACTION Use INTERPERSONAL RELATIONSHIP
STUDENT TEACHER INTERACTION Use TEACHER STUDENT RELATIONSHIP
TEACHER STUDENT INTERACTION Use TEACHER STUDENT RELATIONSHIP
TRAIT TREATMENT INTERACTION Use APTITUDE TREATMENT INTERACTION
VERBAL INTERACTION Use VERBAL COMMUNICATION
INTERACTIVE SEARCHING (ONLINE) Use ONLINE SEARCHING
INTERACTIVE SYSTEMS (ONLINE) Use ONLINE SYSTEMS
INTERACTIVE VIDEO
INTERAGENCY COOPERATION (1967 1980) Use AGENCY COOPERATION
INTERAGENCY COORDINATION (1967 1980) Use AGENCY COOPERATION and COORDINATION
INTERAGENCY PLANNING (1966 1980) Use AGENCY COOPERATION and COOPERATIVE PLANNING
INTERCOLLEGIATE ATHLETICS Use COLLEGE ATHLETICS and INTERCOLLEGIATE COOPERATION
INTERCOLLEGIATE COOPERATION
INTERCOLLEGIATE PROGRAMS (1967 1980) Use INTERCOLLEGIATE COOPERATION
INTERCOMMUNICATION (1966 1980) Use COMMUNICATION (THOUGHT TRANSFER)
INTERCULTURAL COMMUNICATION
INTERCULTURAL EDUCATION Use MULTICULTURAL EDUCATION
INTERCULTURAL PROGRAMS
INTERDIMENSIONAL SHIFT Use SHIFT STUDIES
INTERDISCIPLINARY APPROACH
INTERDISTRICT POLICIES
INTEREST (1967 1981) Use INTEREST (FINANCE)
INTEREST CENTERS (CLASSROOM) Use LEARNING CENTERS (CLASSROOM)
CENTERS OF INTEREST (1966 1980) Use LEARNING CENTERS (CLASSROOM)
CONFLICT OF INTEREST
EDUCATIONAL INTEREST (1967 1980) Use STUDENT EDUCATIONAL OBJECTIVES
INTEREST (FINANCE)
INTEREST INVENTORIES
HIGH INTEREST LOW VOCABULARY BOOKS
INTEREST RESEARCH
INTEREST SCALES (1966 1980) Use INTEREST INVENTORIES
INTEREST TESTS (1966 1980) Use INTEREST INVENTORIES
INTERESTS
CHILDHOOD INTERESTS
CHILDRENS INTERESTS Use CHILDHOOD INTERESTS
GROUP INTERESTS Use INTERESTS
PERSONAL INTERESTS (1966 1980) Use INTERESTS
READING INTERESTS
SCIENCE INTERESTS
STUDENT INTERESTS
STUDENT SCIENCE INTERESTS (1967 1980) Use SCIENCE INTERESTS
VOCATIONAL INTERESTS
MAN MACHINE INTERFACE Use MAN MACHINE SYSTEMS
INTERFAITH RELATIONS
DIALECT INTERFERENCE Use DIALECTS and INTERFERENCE (LANGUAGE)
INTERFERENCE (LANGUAGE)
INTERFERENCE (LANGUAGE LEARNING) (1968 1980) Use INTERFERENCE (LANGUAGE)
INTERGENERATIONAL PROGRAMS
INTERGOVERNMENTAL ORGANIZATIONS Use INTERNATIONAL ORGANIZATIONS
INTERGROUP EDUCATION
INTERGROUP RELATIONS
INTERINSTITUTIONAL COOPERATION (1968 1980) Use INSTITUTIONAL COOPERATION
INTERIOR DECORATION Use INTERIOR DESIGN
INTERIOR DESIGN
INTERIOR MONOLOGUES Use MONOLOGS
INTERIOR SPACE
INTERJUDGE AGREEMENT Use INTERRATER RELIABILITY
INTERLANGUAGE
INTERLIBRARY LOANS
INTERMARRIAGE
INTERMEDIATE ADMINISTRATIVE UNITS
INTERMEDIATE GRADES
INTERMEDIATE SCHOOL DISTRICTS Use INTERMEDIATE ADMINISTRATIVE UNITS

INTERMEDIATE SERVICE DISTRICTS Use INTERMEDIATE ADMINISTRATIVE UNITS
INTERMODE DIFFERENCES
INTERN TEACHERS Use TEACHER INTERNS
INTERNAL EXTERNAL LOCUS OF CONTROL Use LOCUS OF CONTROL
INTERNAL IMMIGRANTS Use MIGRANTS
INTERNAL MEDICINE
INTERNAL REVIEW (ORGANIZATIONS) Use SELF EVALUATION (GROUPS)
INTERNAL SCALING (1966 1980) Use SCALING
INTERNATION BEHAVIOR Use INTERNATIONAL RELATIONS
INTERNATIONAL APPROACH Use GLOBAL APPROACH
INTERNATIONAL COOPERATION
INTERNATIONAL CRIMES
INTERNATIONAL EDUCATION
INTERNATIONAL EDUCATIONAL EXCHANGE
INTERNATIONAL LAW
INTERNATIONAL LEGAL ANALYSIS Use INTERNATIONAL LAW
INTERNATIONAL ORGANIZATIONS
INTERNATIONAL PEACE Use PEACE
INTERNATIONAL POLICY Use FOREIGN POLICY
INTERNATIONAL POLITICS Use INTERNATIONAL RELATIONS
INTERNATIONAL PROGRAMS
INTERNATIONAL RELATIONS
INTERNATIONAL STUDENTS Use FOREIGN STUDENTS
INTERNATIONAL STUDIES
INTERNATIONAL TECHNICAL ASSISTANCE Use INTERNATIONAL PROGRAMS and TECHNICAL ASSISTANCE
INTERNATIONAL TORTS Use INTERNATIONAL LAW
INTERNATIONAL TRADE
INTERNATIONAL TRADE VOCABULARY
INTERNATIONAL WAR Use WAR
INTERNS (MEDICAL) Use GRADUATE MEDICAL STUDENTS
TEACHER INTERNS
URBAN TEACHING INTERNS Use TEACHER INTERNS and URBAN TEACHING
INTERNSHIP PROGRAMS
INTERNSHIPS (MEDICAL) Use GRADUATE MEDICAL EDUCATION
INTEROBSERVER RELIABILITY Use INTERRATER RELIABILITY
INTERPERSONAL ATTRACTION
INTERPERSONAL COMMUNICATION
INTERPERSONAL COMPETENCE
INTERPERSONAL PERCEPTION Use SOCIAL COGNITION
INTERPERSONAL PROBLEMS (1966 1980) Use INTERPERSONAL RELATIONSHIP
INTERPERSONAL RELATIONSHIP
INTERPERSONAL SKILLS Use INTERPERSONAL COMPETENCE
DATA INTERPRETATION
ORAL INTERPRETATION
TEST INTERPRETATION
INTERPRETERS
DEAF INTERPRETING
INTERPRETING FOR THE DEAF Use DEAF INTERPRETING
INTERPRETIVE READING (1966 1980)
INTERPRETIVE SKILLS
INTERPROFESSIONAL RELATIONSHIP
INTERRACIAL RELATIONS Use RACIAL RELATIONS
INTERRATER RELIABILITY
CULTURAL INTERRELATIONSHIPS
INTERSCHOLASTIC ATHLETICS Use EXTRAMURAL ATHLETICS
INTERSCHOOL COMMUNICATION
INTERSCHOOL VISITS Use SCHOOL VISITATION
INTERSCORER RELIABILITY Use INTERRATER RELIABILITY
INTERSENSORY INTEGRATION Use SENSORY INTEGRATION
INTERSESSION SCHOOL PROGRAMS Use VACATION PROGRAMS
INTERSTATE PROGRAMS
INTERSTATE WORKERS (1966 1980) (MIGRANTS) Use MIGRANT WORKERS
INTERVAL PACING (1967 1980) Use PACING
INTERVALS
INTERVENTION
CRISIS INTERVENTION
INTERVIEWING Use INTERVIEWS
INTERVIEWS
EMPLOYMENT INTERVIEWS
FIELD INTERVIEWS
JOB INTERVIEWS Use EMPLOYMENT INTERVIEWS
QUESTION ANSWER INTERVIEWS (1966 1980) Use INTERVIEWS
INTONATION
INTONATION CONTOURS Use INTONATION
INTRAMURAL ATHLETIC PROGRAMS (1966 1980) Use INTRAMURAL ATHLETICS
INTRAMURAL ATHLETICS
INTRAMURAL SPORTS Use INTRAMURAL ATHLETICS
INTRICACY LEVEL Use DIFFICULTY LEVEL
INTRODUCTORY COURSES
FOUNDATION COURSES (INTRODUCTORY) Use INTRODUCTORY COURSES
INTROJECTION Use IDENTIFICATION (PSYCHOLOGY)
INTRUSION DETECTORS Use ALARM SYSTEMS
INTUITION
INUIT Use ESKIMOS
INVALIDS Use PATIENTS
RHETORICAL INVENTION
INVENTIONS
BIOGRAPHICAL INVENTORIES
INFORMAL READING INVENTORIES
INTEREST INVENTORIES
INVENTORIES (MEASUREMENT) Use MEASURES (INDIVIDUALS)
EQUIPMENT INVENTORY Use FACILITY INVENTORY
FACILITY INVENTORY
INFORMAL READING INVENTORY (1968 1980) Use INFORMAL READING INVENTORIES
MATERIALS INVENTORY Use FACILITY INVENTORY
PROPERTY INVENTORY Use FACILITY INVENTORY
INVESTIGATIONS
INVESTMENT
CITIZEN INVOLVEMENT Use CITIZEN PARTICIPATION
CIVIC INVOLVEMENT Use CITIZEN PARTICIPATION

COMMUNITY INVOLVEMENT
FAMILY INVOLVEMENT
PARENT INVOLVEMENT Use PARENT PARTICIPATION
PARTICIPANT INVOLVEMENT (1967 1980) Use PARTICIPATION
SCHOOL INVOLVEMENT
IQ Use INTELLIGENCE QUOTIENT
IRIS REFLEX Use PUPILLARY DILATION
IRON DEFICIENCY ANEMIA Use ANEMIA
IRON FOUNDRIES Use FOUNDRIES
IRONY
ISISWATI Use SISWATI
ISLAMIC CULTURE
CULTURAL ISOLATION
ISOLATION (PERCEPTUAL) Use SENSORY DEPRIVATION
SOCIAL ISOLATION
PUBLISH OR PERISH ISSUE
BOND ISSUES
CONTROVERSIAL ISSUES (COURSE CONTENT)
LOCAL ISSUES
MORAL ISSUES
POLITICAL ISSUES
SOCIAL ISSUES Use SOCIAL PROBLEMS
ITA Use INITIAL TEACHING ALPHABET
ITALIAN
ITALIAN AMERICANS
ITALIAN LITERATURE
ITEM ANALYSIS
ITEM BANKS
ITEM CHARACTERISTIC CURVE THEORY Use LATENT TRAIT THEORY
ITEM DIFFICULTY Use DIFFICULTY LEVEL and TEST ITEMS
ITEM POOLS Use ITEM BANKS
ITEM RESPONSE THEORY Use LATENT TRAIT THEORY
ITEM SAMPLING
ITEM TYPES Use TEST FORMAT
TEST ITEMS
ITFS Use EDUCATIONAL TELEVISION
ITINERANT CLINICS (1966 1980) Use MOBILE CLINICS
ITINERANT TEACHERS
ITV Use EDUCATIONAL TELEVISION
JAIL INMATES Use PRISONERS
JAN TECHNIQUE Use JUDGMENT ANALYSIS TECHNIQUE
JAPANESE
JAPANESE AMERICAN CULTURE
JAPANESE AMERICANS
JAVANESE
JAZZ
JEALOUSY
JEWISH STEREOTYPES (1966 1980) Use ETHNIC STEREOTYPES and JEWS
JEWS
AMERICAN JEWS Use JEWS
JOB ADJUSTMENT Use VOCATIONAL ADJUSTMENT
JOB ANALYSIS
JOB APPLICANTS
JOB APPLICATION
JOB BEHAVIORS Use JOB SKILLS
JOB CHANGE Use CAREER CHANGE
JOB CLUSTERS Use OCCUPATIONAL CLUSTERS
JOB CONDITIONS Use WORK ENVIRONMENT
JOB CONTENT Use OCCUPATIONAL INFORMATION
JOB CONTENT ANALYSIS Use JOB ANALYSIS
JOB CREATION Use JOB DEVELOPMENT
JOB DESCRIPTIONS Use OCCUPATIONAL INFORMATION
JOB DESIGN Use JOB DEVELOPMENT
JOB DEVELOPMENT
JOB DISCRIMINATION Use EQUAL OPPORTUNITIES (JOBS)
JOB ELIMINATION Use JOB LAYOFF
JOB ENRICHMENT
JOB EXPERIENCE Use EMPLOYMENT EXPERIENCE
JOB FAMILIES Use OCCUPATIONAL CLUSTERS
JOB HOLDING PATTERNS Use EMPLOYMENT PATTERNS
JOB INTERVIEWS Use EMPLOYMENT INTERVIEWS
JOB LADDERS Use CAREER LADDERS
JOB LAYOFF
JOB LOSS SERVICES Use OUTPLACEMENT SERVICES (EMPLOYMENT)
JOB MARKET (1966 1980) Use LABOR MARKET
JOB MOBILITY Use OCCUPATIONAL MOBILITY
JOB OPPORTUNITIES Use EMPLOYMENT OPPORTUNITIES
JOB PERFORMANCE
JOB PLACEMENT
STUDENT JOB PLACEMENT Use JOB PLACEMENT and STUDENT EMPLOYMENT
JOB REDESIGN Use JOB DEVELOPMENT
JOB RESTRUCTURING Use JOB DEVELOPMENT
JOB SAFETY Use OCCUPATIONAL SAFETY AND HEALTH
JOB SAMPLE TESTS Use WORK SAMPLE TESTS
JOB SAMPLES Use WORK SAMPLE TESTS
JOB SATISFACTION
JOB SEARCH METHODS
JOB SEEKERS Use JOB APPLICANTS
JOB SHARING
JOB SIMPLIFICATION
JOB SKILLS
JOB SPECIFICATIONS Use OCCUPATIONAL INFORMATION
JOB TENURE (1967 1978) Use TENURE
JOB TRAINING
AWAY FROM THE JOB TRAINING Use OFF THE JOB TRAINING
OFF THE JOB TRAINING
ON THE JOB TRAINING
JOB VACANCIES Use EMPLOYMENT OPPORTUNITIES
JOB VACANCY SURVEYS Use OCCUPATIONAL SURVEYS
MULTIPLE JOBHOLDING Use MULTIPLE EMPLOYMENT
JOBS (1966 1980) Use EMPLOYMENT

EQUAL OPPORTUNITIES (JOBS)
PART TIME JOBS (1966 1980) Use PART TIME EMPLOYMENT
JOGGING
JOINT OCCUPANCY Use SHARED FACILITIES
JOURNALISM
JOURNALISM EDUCATION
NEW JOURNALISM
PICTORIAL JOURNALISM Use PHOTOJOURNALISM
JOURNALS Use PERIODICALS
SCHOLARLY JOURNALS
JOURNEY WORKERS Use SKILLED WORKERS
JUDAISM
JUDGES
COURT JUDGES
DEBATE JUDGES Use JUDGES
AESTHETIC JUDGMENT Use AESTHETIC VALUES and VALUE JUDGMENT
JUDGMENT ANALYSIS TECHNIQUE
LEGAL JUDGMENT Use COURT LITIGATION
CLINICAL JUDGMENT (MEDICINE) Use MEDICAL EVALUATION
MORAL JUDGMENT Use MORAL VALUES and VALUE JUDGMENT
CLINICAL JUDGMENT (PSYCHOLOGY) Use PSYCHOLOGICAL EVALUATION
VALUE JUDGMENT
JUDGMENTAL PROCESSES Use EVALUATIVE THINKING
JUDICIAL ACTION Use COURT LITIGATION
JUDICIAL ROLE Use COURT ROLE
JUNIOR COLLEGE LIBRARIES (1966 1980) Use COLLEGE LIBRARIES and TWO YEAR COLLEGES
JUNIOR COLLEGE STUDENTS (1969 1980) Use TWO YEAR COLLEGE STUDENTS
JUNIOR COLLEGES (1966 1980) Use TWO YEAR COLLEGES
PRIVATE JUNIOR COLLEGES Use PRIVATE COLLEGES and TWO YEAR COLLEGES
JUNIOR HIGH SCHOOL ROLE (1966 1980) Use SCHOOL ROLE
JUNIOR HIGH SCHOOL STUDENTS
JUNIOR HIGH SCHOOL TEACHERS Use SECONDARY SCHOOL TEACHERS
JUNIOR HIGH SCHOOLS
DE JURE SEGREGATION
JUSTICE
CORRECTIONS (CRIMINAL JUSTICE) Use CORRECTIONAL REHABILITATION
JUVENILE COURTS
JUVENILE DELINQUENCY Use DELINQUENCY
JUVENILE GANGS
TRAINING SCHOOLS (JUVENILE OFFENDERS) Use CORRECTIONAL INSTITUTIONS
JUVENILE RUNAWAYS Use RUNAWAYS
KABYLE
KANNADA
KASHMIRI
KECHUA Use QUECHUA
ANIMAL KEEPERS Use ANIMAL CARETAKERS
GROUNDS KEEPERS
KERNEL SENTENCES
KEY WORD IN CONTEXT Use PERMUTED INDEXES
KEYBOARDING (DATA ENTRY)
KEYPUNCHING Use KEYBOARDING (DATA ENTRY)
ANSWER KEYS
SCORING KEYS Use ANSWER KEYS
KHALKHA Use MONGOLIAN
KHMER (LANGUAGE) Use CAMBODIAN
KHMER (PEOPLE) Use CAMBODIANS
KIKONGO YA LETA Use KITUBA
KINDERGARTEN
KINDERGARTEN CHILDREN
KINDERGARTEN TEACHERS Use PRESCHOOL TEACHERS
KINDNESS Use ALTRUISM
KINESCOPE RECORDINGS
KINESCOPES Use KINESCOPE RECORDINGS
KINESICS Use BODY LANGUAGE
KINESTHESIA Use KINESTHETIC PERCEPTION
KINESTHESIS Use KINESTHETIC PERCEPTION
KINESTHETIC MEMORY Use KINESTHETIC PERCEPTION
KINESTHETIC METHODS
KINESTHETIC PERCEPTION
KINETIC MOLECULAR THEORY
KINETICS
KINSHIP
KINSHIP ROLE Use KINSHIP
KINSHIP TERMINOLOGY
KIRGHIZ
KIRGIZ Use KIRGHIZ
KIRUNDI
LEARNING KITS Use LEARNING MODULES
KITUBA
RIGHT TO KNOW Use FREEDOM OF INFORMATION
KNOWLEDGE BASED SYSTEMS Use EXPERT SYSTEMS
KNOWLEDGE LEVEL
META KNOWLEDGE Use METACOGNITION
KNOWLEDGE OF RESULTS Use FEEDBACK
PRIOR KNOWLEDGE Use PRIOR LEARNING
SELF KNOWLEDGE Use SELF CONCEPT
KNOWLEDGE STRUCTURES Use COGNITIVE STRUCTURES
KOREAN
KOREAN AMERICANS
KOREAN CULTURE
KRIO Use SIERRA LEONE CREOLE
SIERRA LEONE KRIO Use SIERRA LEONE CREOLE
KURDISH
KWIC INDEXES Use PERMUTED INDEXES
KWOC INDEXES Use PERMUTED INDEXES
LABELING (OF PERSONS)
PRODUCT LABELS Use MERCHANDISE INFORMATION
LABOR
LABOR CAMPS (1966 1980) (MIGRANTS) Use MIGRANT HOUSING
CHILD LABOR
LABOR (CHILDBIRTH) Use BIRTH

LABOR CONDITIONS
LABOR DEMANDS
AGRICULTURAL LABOR DISPUTES (1966 1980) Use LABOR DEMANDS
LABOR ECONOMICS
LABOR EDUCATION
FARM LABOR
LABOR FORCE
LABOR FORCE DEVELOPMENT
LABOR FORCE NONPARTICIPANTS
LABOR FORCE SURVEYS Use OCCUPATIONAL SURVEYS
HUMAN RESOURCES DEVELOPMENT (LABOR) Use LABOR FORCE DEVELOPMENT
LABOR LAWS (1966 1974) Use LABOR LEGISLATION
CHILD LABOR LAWS (1966 1974) Use CHILD LABOR and LABOR LEGISLATION
LABOR LEGISLATION
CHILD LABOR LEGISLATION (1966 1980) Use CHILD LABOR and LABOR LEGISLATION
FARM LABOR LEGISLATION (1966 1980) Use FARM LABOR and LABOR LEGISLATION
LABOR MARKET
MEDIATION (LABOR) Use ARBITRATION
LABOR MOBILITY Use OCCUPATIONAL MOBILITY
LABOR NEEDS
LABOR PROBLEMS
FARM LABOR PROBLEMS (1966 1980) Use FARM LABOR and LABOR PROBLEMS
LABOR RELATIONS
SEASONAL LABOR (1966 1980) Use SEASONAL EMPLOYMENT
SKILLED LABOR (1966 1980) Use SKILLED WORKERS
LABOR STANDARDS
LABOR SUPPLY
FARM LABOR SUPPLY (1966 1980) Use FARM LABOR and LABOR SUPPLY
SUPPLY OF LABOR Use LABOR SUPPLY
LABOR TURNOVER
LABOR UNIONS (1966 1980) Use UNIONS
UNSKILLED LABOR (1966 1980) Use UNSKILLED WORKERS
LABOR UTILIZATION
LABORATORIES
AUDIO ACTIVE LABORATORIES (1967 1980) Use LANGUAGE LABORATORIES
AUDIO ACTIVE COMPARE LABORATORIES (1967 1980) Use LANGUAGE LABORATORIES
AUDIO PASSIVE LABORATORIES (1968 1980) Use LANGUAGE LABORATORIES
AUDIO VIDEO LABORATORIES (1967 1980) Use AUDIOVISUAL CENTERS
AUTOINSTRUCTIONAL LABORATORIES (1967 1980) Use LEARNING LABORATORIES
COMPUTER BASED LABORATORIES (1967 1980) Use COMPUTER ASSISTED INSTRUCTION and LABORATORIES
CURRICULUM LABORATORIES Use CURRICULUM STUDY CENTERS
LANGUAGE LABORATORIES
LEARNING LABORATORIES
MOBILE LABORATORIES
READING LABORATORIES Use READING CENTERS
REGIONAL LABORATORIES
SATELLITE LABORATORIES (1966 1980) Use SATELLITES (AEROSPACE)
SCIENCE LABORATORIES
TRAINING LABORATORIES (1967 1980)
WRITING LABORATORIES
LABORATORY ANIMALS
MEDICAL LABORATORY ASSISTANTS
LABORATORY EQUIPMENT
LANGUAGE LABORATORY EQUIPMENT (1966 1980) Use LABORATORY EQUIPMENT and LANGUAGE LABORATORIES
FIELD LABORATORY EXPERIENCE Use FIELD EXPERIENCE PROGRAMS
LABORATORY EXPERIMENTS
LABORATORY MANUALS
LABORATORY PROCEDURES
LABORATORY SAFETY
LABORATORY SCHOOLS
DENTAL LABORATORY TECHNICIANS Use DENTAL TECHNICIANS
LABORATORY TECHNIQUES (1967 1980)
MEDICAL LABORATORY TECHNOLOGISTS Use MEDICAL TECHNOLOGISTS
LABORATORY TECHNOLOGY
LABORATORY TRAINING
LANGUAGE LABORATORY USE (1966 1980) Use LANGUAGE LABORATORIES
LABORERS
AGRICULTURAL LABORERS
AUXILIARY LABORERS
EXPERIENCED LABORERS (1966 1980) Use LABORERS
SEASONAL LABORERS
LACROSSE
CAREER LADDERS
JOB LADDERS Use CAREER LADDERS
CULTURAL LAG Use CULTURE LAG
CULTURE LAG
LAND ACQUISITION
LAND COLONIZATION Use LAND SETTLEMENT
LAND GRANT COLLEGES Use LAND GRANT UNIVERSITIES
LAND GRANT UNIVERSITIES
LAND SETTLEMENT
LAND USE
LANDLADIES Use LANDLORDS
LANDLORDS
LANDSCAPING
LANGUAGE
LANGUAGE ABILITY (1966 1980)
LANGUAGE ACQUISITION
LANGUAGE AIDS (1966 1980)
AMERICAN SIGN LANGUAGE
CONTRASTIVE LANGUAGE ANALYSIS Use CONTRASTIVE LINGUISTICS
LANGUAGE AND AREA CENTERS (1968 1980)
LANGUAGE APTITUDE
LANGUAGE ARTS
LANGUAGE ATTITUDES
LANGUAGE ATTRITION (SKILLS) Use LANGUAGE SKILL ATTRITION
BODY LANGUAGE
FOREIGN LANGUAGE BOOKS
SECOND LANGUAGE BOOKS Use FOREIGN LANGUAGE BOOKS
CHILD LANGUAGE
LANGUAGE CLASSIFICATION

CODE SWITCHING (LANGUAGE)
CONVERSATIONAL LANGUAGE COURSES
INTENSIVE LANGUAGE COURSES
MODERN LANGUAGE CURRICULUM
LANGUAGE DEVELOPMENT (1966 1980) Use LANGUAGE ACQUISITION
DIALOGS (LANGUAGE)
LANGUAGE DISABILITIES Use LANGUAGE HANDICAPS
DISTINCTIVE FEATURES (LANGUAGE)
LANGUAGE DOMINANCE
ENGLISH (SECOND LANGUAGE)
LANGUAGE ENRICHMENT
LANGUAGE ENROLLMENT
FOREIGN LANGUAGE ENROLLMENT Use LANGUAGE ENROLLMENT
SECOND LANGUAGE ENROLLMENT Use LANGUAGE ENROLLMENT
ERROR ANALYSIS (LANGUAGE)
LANGUAGE EXPERIENCE Use LANGUAGE ENRICHMENT
LANGUAGE EXPERIENCE APPROACH
EXPRESSIVE LANGUAGE
FARSI (LANGUAGE) Use PERSIAN
FIGURATIVE LANGUAGE
FOREIGN LANGUAGE FILMS
SECOND LANGUAGE FILMS Use FOREIGN LANGUAGE FILMS
LANGUAGE FLUENCY
LANGUAGE GUIDES (1966 1980)
LANGUAGE HANDICAPPED (1967 1980) Use LANGUAGE HANDICAPS
LANGUAGE HANDICAPS
LANGUAGE HISTORY Use DIACHRONIC LINGUISTICS
HISTORY OF LANGUAGE Use DIACHRONIC LINGUISTICS
LANGUAGE INSTRUCTION (1966 1980)
FOREIGN LANGUAGE INSTRUCTION Use SECOND LANGUAGE INSTRUCTION
MULTILEVEL CLASSES (SECOND LANGUAGE INSTRUCTION)
NATIVE LANGUAGE INSTRUCTION
SECOND LANGUAGE INSTRUCTION
INSTRUCTIONAL LANGUAGE Use LANGUAGE OF INSTRUCTION
INTERFERENCE (LANGUAGE)
KHMER (LANGUAGE) Use CAMBODIAN
LANGUAGE LABORATORIES
LANGUAGE LABORATORY EQUIPMENT (1966 1980) Use LABORATORY EQUIPMENT and LANGUAGE LABORATORIES
LANGUAGE LABORATORY USE (1966 1980) Use LANGUAGE LABORATORIES
APPROXIMATIVE SYSTEMS (LANGUAGE LEARNING) Use INTERLANGUAGE
AURAL LANGUAGE LEARNING Use AURAL LEARNING and LANGUAGE ACQUISITION
FOREIGN LANGUAGE LEARNING Use SECOND LANGUAGE LEARNING
LANGUAGE LEARNING (FOREIGN) Use SECOND LANGUAGE LEARNING
INTERFERENCE (LANGUAGE LEARNING) (1968 1980) Use INTERFERENCE (LANGUAGE)
LANGUAGE LEARNING LEVELS (1967 1980)
SECOND LANGUAGE LEARNING
VISUAL LANGUAGE LEARNING Use LANGUAGE ACQUISITION and VISUAL LEARNING
LANGUAGE LOSS (SKILLS) Use LANGUAGE SKILL ATTRITION
LANGUAGE MAINTENANCE
MEDIUM OF INSTRUCTION (LANGUAGE) Use LANGUAGE OF INSTRUCTION
NEGATIVE FORMS (LANGUAGE)
LANGUAGE OF INSTRUCTION
ORAL LANGUAGE
PATTERN DRILLS (LANGUAGE)
LANGUAGE PATTERNS
BASIC LANGUAGE PATTERNS Use LANGUAGE PATTERNS
FOREIGN LANGUAGE PERIODICALS
SECOND LANGUAGE PERIODICALS Use FOREIGN LANGUAGE PERIODICALS
LANGUAGE PLANNING
LANGUAGE PROCESSING
LANGUAGE PROFICIENCY
LANGUAGE PROGRAMS (1966 1980)
COLLEGE LANGUAGE PROGRAMS (1967 1980)
COLLEGE SECOND LANGUAGE PROGRAMS
FOREIGN LANGUAGE PROGRAMS Use SECOND LANGUAGE PROGRAMS
SECOND LANGUAGE PROGRAMS
RECEPTIVE LANGUAGE
LANGUAGE RECORDS (PHONOGRAPH) (1966 1980) Use AUDIODISKS
LANGUAGE RESEARCH
LANGUAGE RHYTHM
LANGUAGE ROLE
SEXIST LANGUAGE Use LANGUAGE USAGE and SEX BIAS
SIGN LANGUAGE
LANGUAGE SKILL ATTRITION
LANGUAGE SKILLS
LANGUAGE STANDARDIZATION
LANGUAGE STYLES
STATE FOREIGN LANGUAGE SUPERVISORS (1967 1980) Use SECOND LANGUAGE INSTRUCTION and STATE SUPERVISORS
SWITCHING (LANGUAGE) Use CODE SWITCHING (LANGUAGE)
SYMBOLIC LANGUAGE
LANGUAGE TAPES Use AUDIOTAPE RECORDINGS
LANGUAGE TEACHERS
FOREIGN LANGUAGE TEACHERS Use LANGUAGE TEACHERS
SECOND LANGUAGE TEACHERS Use LANGUAGE TEACHERS
TEACHING LANGUAGE Use LANGUAGE OF INSTRUCTION
LANGUAGE TESTS
TRANSFORMATION THEORY (LANGUAGE) (1967 1980) Use LINGUISTIC THEORY and TRANSFORMATIONAL GENERATIVE GRAMMAR
TRANSFORMATIONS (LANGUAGE) (1967 1980) Use TRANSFORMATIONAL GENERATIVE GRAMMAR
LANGUAGE TYPOLOGY
LANGUAGE UNIVERSALS
UNWRITTEN LANGUAGE (1968 1980)
URBAN LANGUAGE
LANGUAGE USAGE
VALENCE (LANGUAGE) Use SYNTAX
LANGUAGE VARIATION
VOCATIONAL ENGLISH (SECOND LANGUAGE)
WRITTEN LANGUAGE
LANGUAGES
AFRICAN LANGUAGES
AFRO ASIATIC LANGUAGES

ALTAIC	LANGUAGES Use URALIC ALTAIC LANGUAGES
AMERICAN INDIAN	LANGUAGES
ARTIFICIAL	LANGUAGES
ATHABASCAN	LANGUAGES Use ATHAPASCAN LANGUAGES
ATHAPASCAN	LANGUAGES
AUSTRALIAN ABORIGINAL	LANGUAGES
AUSTRO ASIATIC	LANGUAGES
AUSTRONESIAN	LANGUAGES Use MALAYO POLYNESIAN LANGUAGES
AUTHORING	LANGUAGES Use AUTHORING AIDS (PROGRAMING) and PROGRAMING LANGUAGES
BALTIC	LANGUAGES
BANTU	LANGUAGES
BERBER	LANGUAGES
CAUCASIAN	LANGUAGES
CHAD	LANGUAGES
CLASSICAL	LANGUAGES
COMMUNICATIVE COMPETENCE	(LANGUAGES)
COMPUTER	LANGUAGES Use PROGRAMING LANGUAGES
CONSTRUCTED	LANGUAGES Use ARTIFICIAL LANGUAGES
DETERMINERS	(LANGUAGES)
DRAVIDIAN	LANGUAGES
ESKIMO ALEUT	LANGUAGES
FENNO UGRIC	LANGUAGES Use FINNO UGRIC LANGUAGES
FINNO UGRIC	LANGUAGES
	LANGUAGES FOR SPECIAL PURPOSES
FOREIGN	LANGUAGES Use SECOND LANGUAGES
FORM CLASSES	(LANGUAGES)
FOREIGN	LANGUAGES IN THE ELEMENTARY SCHOOL Use FLES
INDO EUROPEAN	LANGUAGES
INDONESIAN	LANGUAGES
LESS COMMONLY TAUGHT	LANGUAGES Use UNCOMMONLY TAUGHT LANGUAGES
MALAYO POLYNESIAN	LANGUAGES
MAYAN	LANGUAGES
MELANESIAN	LANGUAGES
MODERN	LANGUAGES
MONGOLIAN	LANGUAGES
MORPHOLOGY	(LANGUAGES)
NATIONAL	LANGUAGES Use OFFICIAL LANGUAGES
NEGLECTED	LANGUAGES Use UNCOMMONLY TAUGHT LANGUAGES
OFFICIAL	LANGUAGES
PROGRAMING	LANGUAGES
ROMANCE	LANGUAGES
SAMOYED	LANGUAGES
SECOND	LANGUAGES
SEMITIC	LANGUAGES
SINO TIBETAN	LANGUAGES
SLAVIC	LANGUAGES
THRESHOLD LEVEL	(LANGUAGES)
TONE	LANGUAGES
TURKIC	LANGUAGES
UNCOMMONLY TAUGHT	LANGUAGES
UNWRITTEN	LANGUAGES
URALIC ALTAIC	LANGUAGES
UTO AZTECAN	LANGUAGES
	LAO
	LAOTIAN Use LAO
	LAOTIAN AMERICANS Use ASIAN AMERICANS and LAOTIANS
	LAOTIANS
	LAP BELTS Use RESTRAINTS (VEHICLE SAFETY)
	LAPS Use LEARNING MODULES
	LARGE CITIES Use URBAN AREAS
	LARGE GROUP INSTRUCTION
	LARGE SCALE PRODUCTION Use MASS PRODUCTION
	LARGE TYPE BOOKS Use LARGE TYPE MATERIALS
	LARGE TYPE MATERIALS
	LASER DISKS Use OPTICAL DISKS
	LASER OSCILLATORS Use LASERS
	LASERS
LIGHT AMPLIFIERS	(LASERS) Use LASERS
SENIORS (1966 1980)	(LAST YEAR UNDERGRADUATES) Use COLLEGE SENIORS
	LATCHKEY CHILDREN
	LATE REGISTRATION
RESPONSE	LATENCY Use REACTION TIME
	LATENT TRAIT THEORY
	LATERAL DOMINANCE
	LATHES Use MACHINE TOOLS
	LATIN
AMERICAN LITERATURE (1966 1980)	(LATIN AMERICA) Use LATIN AMERICAN LITERATURE
	LATIN AMERICAN CULTURE
	LATIN AMERICAN HISTORY
	LATIN AMERICAN LITERATURE
	LATIN AMERICANS
	LATIN LITERATURE
	LATVIAN
	LAUNDRY DRYCLEANING OCCUPATIONS
DRYCLEANING	LAUNDRY OCCUPATIONS Use LAUNDRY DRYCLEANING OCCUPATIONS
ADVOCATES	(LAW) Use LAWYERS
CONSTITUTIONAL	LAW
CRIMINAL	LAW
	LAW ENFORCEMENT
	LAW ENFORCEMENT OFFICERS Use POLICE
INTERNATIONAL	LAW
	LAW LIBRARIES
	LAW OF NATIONS Use INTERNATIONAL LAW
	LAW OF PRIMACY Use PRIMACY EFFECT
	LAW RELATED EDUCATION
SCHOOL	LAW
	LAW SCHOOL APPLICANTS Use COLLEGE APPLICANTS and LAW SCHOOLS
	LAW SCHOOL EDUCATION Use LEGAL EDUCATION (PROFESSIONS)
	LAW SCHOOLS
SOLICITORS	(LAW) Use LAWYERS
	LAW STUDENTS

	LAWMAKERS Use LEGISLATORS
	LAWN MAINTENANCE Use TURF MANAGEMENT
	LAWS
CHILD LABOR	LAWS (1966 1974) Use CHILD LABOR and LABOR LEGISLATION
FEDERAL	LAWS (1966 1974) Use FEDERAL LEGISLATION
LABOR	LAWS (1966 1974) Use LABOR LEGISLATION
MINIMUM WAGE	LAWS (1966 1974) Use MINIMUM WAGE LEGISLATION
PUBLIC HEALTH	LAWS (1966 1974) Use PUBLIC HEALTH LEGISLATION
SCHOOL ATTENDANCE	LAWS (1966 1974) Use SCHOOL ATTENDANCE LEGISLATION
STATE	LAWS (1966 1974) Use STATE LEGISLATION
	LAWYERS
	LAY PEOPLE
	LAY TEACHERS
CARPET	LAYERS Use FLOOR LAYERS
FLOOR	LAYERS
	LAYMEN (1966 1980) Use LAY PEOPLE
JOB	LAYOFF
	LAYOUT (PUBLICATIONS)
STREET	LAYOUTS Use TRAFFIC CIRCULATION
	LEA Use SCHOOL DISTRICTS
	LEAD LECTURE PLAN (1966 1980) Use LECTURE METHOD
	LEAD POISONING
	LEADER PARTICIPATION (1966 1980) Use LEADERSHIP
TEAM	LEADER (TEACHING) (1966 1980) Use LEADERS and TEAM TEACHING
	LEADERLESS GROUPS Use SELF DIRECTED GROUPS
	LEADERS
ADULT	LEADERS (1967 1980) Use LEADERS
COMMUNITY	LEADERS
CREW	LEADERS
	LEADERS GUIDES
YOUTH	LEADERS
	LEADERSHIP
BLACK	LEADERSHIP
INFORMAL	LEADERSHIP
INSTRUCTIONAL	LEADERSHIP
NEGRO	LEADERSHIP (1966 1977) Use BLACK LEADERSHIP
	LEADERSHIP QUALITIES
	LEADERSHIP RESPONSIBILITY
STUDENT	LEADERSHIP
	LEADERSHIP STYLES
	LEADERSHIP TRAINING
	LEAFLETS Use PAMPHLETS
LEARNING TO	LEARN Use LEARNING STRATEGIES
	LEARNED HELPLESSNESS Use HELPLESSNESS
	LEARNER AUTONOMY Use PERSONAL AUTONOMY
	LEARNER OUTCOMES Use OUTCOMES OF EDUCATION
SLOW	LEARNERS
	LEARNING
ACTION	LEARNING Use EXPERIENTIAL LEARNING
	LEARNING ACTIVITIES
ACTIVITY	LEARNING (1968 1978) Use EXPERIENTIAL LEARNING
	LEARNING ACTIVITY PACKAGES Use LEARNING MODULES
	LEARNING ACTIVITY PACKETS Use LEARNING MODULES
ADULT	LEARNING
ADVENTURE	LEARNING Use ADVENTURE EDUCATION
APPROXIMATIVE SYSTEMS (LANGUAGE	LEARNING) Use INTERLANGUAGE
ASSOCIATIVE	LEARNING
AURAL	LEARNING
AURAL LANGUAGE	LEARNING Use AURAL LEARNING and LANGUAGE ACQUISITION
	LEARNING CENTERS (CLASSROOM)
LIVING	LEARNING CENTERS
	LEARNING CHARACTERISTICS (1968 1980) Use LEARNING
COMPUTER ASSISTED	LEARNING Use COMPUTER ASSISTED INSTRUCTION
CONTINUOUS	LEARNING (1967 1980) Use LIFELONG LEARNING
	LEARNING CONTRACTS Use PERFORMANCE CONTRACTS
STUDENT	LEARNING CONTRACTS Use PERFORMANCE CONTRACTS
MATURATION	LEARNING CONTROVERSY Use NATURE NURTURE CONTROVERSY
	LEARNING CYCLES Use LEARNING PROCESSES
	LEARNING DIFFICULTIES (1966 1980) Use LEARNING PROBLEMS
	LEARNING DISABILITIES
SPECIFIC	LEARNING DISABILITIES Use LEARNING DISABILITIES
DISCOVERY	LEARNING
DISCRIMINATION	LEARNING
ENGAGED TIME	(LEARNING) Use TIME ON TASK
	LEARNING EXPERIENCE
CLINICAL	LEARNING EXPERIENCE Use CLINICAL EXPERIENCE
EXPERIENTIAL	LEARNING
EXPLORATORY	LEARNING Use DISCOVERY LEARNING
LANGUAGE	LEARNING (FOREIGN) Use SECOND LANGUAGE LEARNING
FOREIGN LANGUAGE	LEARNING Use SECOND LANGUAGE LEARNING
IMITATIVE	LEARNING Use OBSERVATIONAL LEARNING
INCIDENTAL	LEARNING
INDEPENDENT	LEARNING Use INDEPENDENT STUDY
INTEGRATED	LEARNING Use INTEGRATED ACTIVITIES and LEARNING ACTIVITIES
INTENTIONAL	LEARNING
INTERFERENCE (LANGUAGE	LEARNING) (1968 1980) Use INTERFERENCE (LANGUAGE)
	LEARNING KITS Use LEARNING MODULES
	LEARNING LABORATORIES
LANGUAGE	LEARNING LEVELS (1967 1980)
LIFELONG	LEARNING
MASTERY	LEARNING
	LEARNING MATURATION CONTROVERSY Use NATURE NURTURE CONTROVERSY
	LEARNING MODALITIES
MODULAR	LEARNING Use LEARNING MODULES
	LEARNING MODULES
	LEARNING MOTIVATION
MULTISENSORY	LEARNING
NONVERBAL	LEARNING
	LEARNING OBJECTIVES Use BEHAVIORAL OBJECTIVES
OBSERVATIONAL	LEARNING
	LEARNING PACKAGES Use LEARNING MODULES

PAIRED ASSOCIATE LEARNING
PERCEPTUAL MOTOR LEARNING
LEARNING PLATEAUS
PRESCHOOL LEARNING (1966 1980)
PREVIOUS LEARNING Use PRIOR LEARNING
PRIOR LEARNING
PRIOR EXPERIENTIAL LEARNING Use EXPERIENTIAL LEARNING and PRIOR LEARNING
LEARNING PROBLEMS
LEARNING PROCESSES
PROGRAMED LEARNING Use PROGRAMED INSTRUCTION
LEARNING READINESS
LEARNING REINFORCEMENT Use REINFORCEMENT
LEARNING RESOURCES Use EDUCATIONAL RESOURCES
LEARNING RESOURCES CENTERS
ROTE LEARNING
SECOND LANGUAGE LEARNING
SELF DIRECTED LEARNING Use INDEPENDENT STUDY
SENSORY MOTOR LEARNING Use PERCEPTUAL MOTOR LEARNING
SEQUENTIAL LEARNING
SERIAL LEARNING
SOCIAL LEARNING Use SOCIALIZATION
LEARNING SPECIALISTS (1966 1980) Use SPECIALISTS
LEARNING STATIONS (CLASSROOM) Use LEARNING CENTERS (CLASSROOM)
LEARNING STRATEGIES
LEARNING STYLE Use COGNITIVE STYLE
SYMBOLIC LEARNING
LEARNING THEORIES
ACADEMIC LEARNING TIME Use TIME ON TASK
TIME FACTORS (LEARNING)
LEARNING TO LEARN Use LEARNING STRATEGIES
TRANSFER OF LEARNING Use TRANSFER OF TRAINING
VERBAL LEARNING
VISUAL LEARNING
VISUAL LANGUAGE LEARNING Use LANGUAGE ACQUISITION and VISUAL LEARNING
LEAST RESTRICTIVE ENVIRONMENT (DISABLED) Use MAINSTREAMING
LEAST SQUARES STATISTICS
LEATHER
LEATHER CRAFTS Use LEATHER
LEAVE OF ABSENCE (1968 1980) Use LEAVES OF ABSENCE
EARLY SCHOOL LEAVERS Use DROPOUTS
LEAVES OF ABSENCE
SABBATICAL LEAVES
LECTURE (1966 1980) Use LECTURE METHOD
LECTURE METHOD
LEAD LECTURE PLAN (1966 1980) Use LECTURE METHOD
TELEVISION LECTURERS Use TELEVISION TEACHERS
LEFT HANDED WRITER
LEGAL AID
LEGAL AID PROJECTS (1966 1980) Use LEGAL AID
INTERNATIONAL LEGAL ANALYSIS Use INTERNATIONAL LAW
LEGAL ASSISTANTS
CITATIONS (LEGAL) Use LAW ENFORCEMENT
COMPLIANCE (LEGAL)
LEGAL COSTS
LEGAL DECISIONS Use COURT LITIGATION
LEGAL EDUCATION (1977 1986)
LEGAL EDUCATION (PROFESSIONS)
LEGAL JUDGMENT Use COURT LITIGATION
LEGAL PROBLEMS
LEGAL RESPONSIBILITY
LEGAL SECRETARIES Use SECRETARIES
LEGAL SEGREGATION (1966 1980) Use DE JURE SEGREGATION
LEGAL SERVICES Use LEGAL AID
LEGENDS
LEGISLATION
ANTI DISCRIMINATION LEGISLATION Use CIVIL RIGHTS LEGISLATION
CHILD LABOR LEGISLATION (1966 1980) Use CHILD LABOR and LABOR LEGISLATION
CIVIL RIGHTS LEGISLATION
COMMUNITY LEGISLATION Use LOCAL LEGISLATION
COMMUNITY RECREATION LEGISLATION (1966 1978) Use LOCAL LEGISLATION and RECREATION LEGISLATION
DISCRIMINATORY LEGISLATION
DRUG LEGISLATION
EDUCATIONAL LEGISLATION
FARM LABOR LEGISLATION (1966 1980) Use FARM LABOR and LABOR LEGISLATION
FEDERAL LEGISLATION
FEDERAL RECREATION LEGISLATION (1966 1978) Use FEDERAL LEGISLATION and RECREATION LEGISLATION
LABOR LEGISLATION
LOCAL LEGISLATION
LOCAL RECREATION LEGISLATION (1966 1978) Use LOCAL LEGISLATION and RECREATION LEGISLATION
MINIMUM WAGE LEGISLATION
PUBLIC HEALTH LEGISLATION
RECREATION LEGISLATION
SCHOOL ATTENDANCE LEGISLATION
STATE LEGISLATION
STATE RECREATION LEGISLATION (1966 1978) Use RECREATION LEGISLATION and STATE LEGISLATION
LEGISLATIVE DISCRIMINATION Use DISCRIMINATORY LEGISLATION
LEGISLATIVE REFERENCE LIBRARIES (1968 1980) Use LAW LIBRARIES
LEGISLATORS
LEISURE Use LEISURE TIME
LEISURE COUNSELING Use LEISURE EDUCATION
LEISURE EDUCATION
LEISURE TIME
LEISURE TIME READING Use RECREATIONAL READING
LEITMOTIFS Use MOTIFS
LEITMOTIVS Use MOTIFS
BOOK LENDING Use LIBRARY CIRCULATION
PROGRAM LENGTH
TEST LENGTH
SIERRA LEONE CREOLE
SIERRA LEONE KRIO Use SIERRA LEONE CREOLE
LESBIANISM

LESS COMMONLY TAUGHT LANGUAGES Use UNCOMMONLY TAUGHT LANGUAGES
LESSON NOTES Use LESSON PLANS
LESSON OBSERVATION CRITERIA
LESSON PLANS
LESSON UNITS Use UNITS OF STUDY
KIKONGO YA LETA Use KITUBA
LETTER SOUND CORRESPONDENCE Use PHONEME GRAPHEME CORRESPONDENCE
LETTERS (ALPHABET)
BUSINESS LETTERS Use BUSINESS CORRESPONDENCE
CORRESPONDENCE (LETTERS) Use LETTERS (CORRESPONDENCE)
LETTERS (CORRESPONDENCE)
ACHIEVEMENT LEVEL Use ACHIEVEMENT
AGE LEVEL Use AGE
ASPIRATION LEVEL Use ASPIRATION
LOW LEVEL ASPIRATION (1966 1980) Use ASPIRATION
COMPLEXITY LEVEL (1968 1979) Use DIFFICULTY LEVEL
DIFFICULTY LEVEL
EDUCATIONAL LEVEL Use ACADEMIC ACHIEVEMENT
EMPLOYMENT LEVEL
INTELLIGENCE LEVEL (1966 1980) Use INTELLIGENCE
INTRICACY LEVEL Use DIFFICULTY LEVEL
KNOWLEDGE LEVEL
THRESHOLD LEVEL (LANGUAGES)
MIDDLE LEVEL MANAGEMENT Use MIDDLE MANAGEMENT
ACTIVITY LEVEL (MOTOR BEHAVIOR) Use PHYSICAL ACTIVITY LEVEL
OCCUPATIONAL LEVEL Use EMPLOYMENT LEVEL
OCCUPATIONAL ASPIRATION LEVEL Use OCCUPATIONAL ASPIRATION
PHYSICAL ACTIVITY LEVEL
POSTSECONDARY INSTRUCTIONAL LEVEL Use POSTSECONDARY EDUCATION
PRECOLLEGE LEVEL Use HIGH SCHOOLS
READING LEVEL (1966 1980)
SOCIOECONOMIC LEVEL Use SOCIOECONOMIC STATUS
ADAPTATION LEVEL THEORY
ABSTRACTION LEVELS (1968 1980) Use ABSTRACT REASONING
GRADE LEVELS Use INSTRUCTIONAL PROGRAM DIVISIONS
ILLUMINATION LEVELS (1968 1980) Use LIGHTING
LANGUAGE LEARNING LEVELS (1967 1980)
NOISE LEVELS Use NOISE (SOUND)
LEXICOGRAPHY
LEXICOLOGY
LEXICONS Use DICTIONARIES
LIABILITY (RESPONSIBILITY) Use LEGAL RESPONSIBILITY
POLICE SCHOOL LIAISON Use POLICE SCHOOL RELATIONSHIP
LIBERAL ARTS
LIBERAL ARTS MAJORS (1967 1980) Use LIBERAL ARTS and MAJORS (STUDENTS)
LIBERAL EDUCATION Use GENERAL EDUCATION
LIBERALISM
WOMENS LIBERATION Use FEMINISM
CIVIL LIBERTIES
PERSONAL LIBERTY Use CIVIL LIBERTIES
LIBRARIANS
MEDICAL RECORD LIBRARIANS (1969 1980) Use MEDICAL RECORD ADMINISTRATORS
LIBRARIANSHIP Use LIBRARY SCIENCE
LIBRARIES
ACADEMIC LIBRARIES
BRANCH LIBRARIES
CLASSROOM LIBRARIES (1966 1980) Use INSTRUCTIONAL MATERIALS
COLLECTION DEVELOPMENT (LIBRARIES) Use LIBRARY COLLECTION DEVELOPMENT
COLLEGE LIBRARIES
COUNTY LIBRARIES
DEPOSITORY LIBRARIES
DISTRICT LIBRARIES Use REGIONAL LIBRARIES
ELEMENTARY SCHOOL LIBRARIES (1966 1980) Use SCHOOL LIBRARIES
FEDERAL LIBRARIES Use FEDERAL GOVERNMENT and GOVERNMENT LIBRARIES
FILM LIBRARIES
GOVERNMENT LIBRARIES
HEALTH SCIENCES LIBRARIES Use MEDICAL LIBRARIES
HIGH SCHOOL LIBRARIES Use SCHOOL LIBRARIES
HOSPITAL LIBRARIES
INSTITUTION LIBRARIES (1969 1980) Use INSTITUTIONAL LIBRARIES
INSTITUTIONAL LIBRARIES
JUNIOR COLLEGE LIBRARIES (1966 1980) Use COLLEGE LIBRARIES and TWO YEAR COLLEGES
LAW LIBRARIES
LEGISLATIVE REFERENCE LIBRARIES (1968 1980) Use LAW LIBRARIES
MEDICAL LIBRARIES
MOBILE LIBRARIES Use BOOKMOBILES
NATIONAL LIBRARIES
PRISON LIBRARIES
PROVINCIAL LIBRARIES Use STATE LIBRARIES
PUBLIC LIBRARIES
REGIONAL LIBRARIES
RESEARCH LIBRARIES
SATELLITE LIBRARIES Use BRANCH LIBRARIES
SCHOOL LIBRARIES
SECONDARY SCHOOL LIBRARIES Use SCHOOL LIBRARIES
SPECIAL LIBRARIES
STATE LIBRARIES
TECHNICAL PROCESSES (LIBRARIES) Use LIBRARY TECHNICAL PROCESSES
TECHNICAL SERVICES (LIBRARIES) Use LIBRARY TECHNICAL PROCESSES
UNIVERSITY LIBRARIES (1968 1980) Use COLLEGE LIBRARIES
VIDEOTAPE LIBRARIES Use FILM LIBRARIES
LIBRARY ACQUISITION
LIBRARY ADMINISTRATION
LIBRARY ADMINISTRATORS Use LIBRARY ADMINISTRATION
LIBRARY AIDES Use LIBRARY TECHNICIANS
LIBRARY AIDS Use LIBRARY EQUIPMENT
LIBRARY ASSOCIATIONS
LIBRARY AUTOMATION
LIBRARY CATALOGING Use CATALOGING
LIBRARY CATALOGS
LIBRARY CIRCULATION

LIBRARY CLERKS Use LIBRARY TECHNICIANS
LIBRARY CLIENTS Use USERS (INFORMATION)
LIBRARY COLLECTION DEVELOPMENT
LIBRARY COLLECTIONS
LIBRARY COOPERATION
LIBRARY EDUCATION
LIBRARY EMPLOYEES Use LIBRARY PERSONNEL
LIBRARY EQUIPMENT
LIBRARY EXPENDITURES
LIBRARY EXTENSION
LIBRARY FACILITIES
LIBRARY FINES Use FINES (PENALTIES)
LIBRARY GUIDES
LIBRARY HANDBOOKS Use LIBRARY GUIDES
LIBRARY HOLDINGS Use LIBRARY COLLECTIONS
LIBRARY INSTRUCTION
LIBRARY LOANS Use LIBRARY CIRCULATION
LIBRARY MANAGEMENT Use LIBRARY ADMINISTRATION
LIBRARY MATERIAL SELECTION
LIBRARY MATERIALS
LIBRARY MECHANIZATION Use LIBRARY AUTOMATION
LIBRARY NETWORKS
LIBRARY ORGANIZATIONS Use LIBRARY ASSOCIATIONS
LIBRARY ORIENTATION Use LIBRARY INSTRUCTION
LIBRARY PATRONS Use USERS (INFORMATION)
LIBRARY PERSONNEL
LIBRARY PLANNING
LIBRARY PROGRAMS (1966 1980) Use LIBRARY SERVICES
LIBRARY REFERENCE MATERIALS Use LIBRARY MATERIALS and REFERENCE MATERIALS
LIBRARY REFERENCE SERVICES (1968 1980) Use LIBRARY SERVICES and REFERENCE SERVICES
LIBRARY RESEARCH
SHARED LIBRARY RESOURCES
LIBRARY ROLE
LIBRARY SCHOOLS
LIBRARY SCIENCE
LIBRARY SERVICES
LIBRARY SKILLS
LIBRARY SPECIALISTS Use LIBRARIANS
LIBRARY STANDARDS
LIBRARY STATISTICS
LIBRARY SURVEYS
LIBRARY SYSTEMS Use LIBRARY NETWORKS
DECENTRALIZED LIBRARY SYSTEMS (1968 1980) Use DECENTRALIZATION and LIBRARY NETWORKS
LIBRARY TECHNICAL ASSISTANTS Use LIBRARY TECHNICIANS
LIBRARY TECHNICAL PROCESSES
LIBRARY TECHNICIANS
LIBRARY USER NEEDS Use USER NEEDS (INFORMATION)
LIBRARY USER SATISFACTION Use USER SATISFACTION (INFORMATION)
LIBRARY USERS Use USERS (INFORMATION)
LICENSED NURSES Use NURSES
LICENSING Use CERTIFICATION
STATE LICENSING BOARDS
COUNSELOR LICENSING Use COUNSELOR CERTIFICATION
LICENSING EXAMINATIONS (PROFESSIONS)
STATE BOARDS OF LICENSING Use STATE LICENSING BOARDS
LIE DETECTORS Use POLYGRAPHS
ANIMAL LIFE Use ANIMALS
LIFE COSTS (FACILITIES AND EQUIPMENT) Use LIFE CYCLE COSTING
LIFE CYCLE COSTING
FAMILY LIFE EDUCATION
HOME AND FAMILY LIFE EDUCATION Use FAMILY LIFE EDUCATION
WORK LIFE EXPECTANCY
FAMILY LIFE
LIFE HISTORIES Use BIOGRAPHIES
HOME LIFE Use FAMILY LIFE
LIFE QUALITY Use QUALITY OF LIFE
QUALITY OF LIFE
QUALITY OF WORKING LIFE
LIFE SATISFACTION
LIFE SCIENCES Use BIOLOGICAL SCIENCES
LIFE SKILLS Use DAILY LIVING SKILLS
SOCIAL LIFE
LIFE SPAN EDUCATION Use LIFELONG LEARNING
LIFE STYLE
ALTERNATIVE LIFE STYLES Use LIFE STYLE
URBAN LIFE Use URBAN CULTURE
LIFELONG EDUCATION Use LIFELONG LEARNING
LIFELONG LEARNING
LIFETIME SPORTS
LIFTING
LIGHT
LIGHT AMPLIFIERS (LASERS) Use LASERS
LIGHT RADIATION Use LIGHT
LIGHTED PLAYGROUNDS (1966 1980) Use PLAYGROUNDS
LIGHTING
LIGHTING DESIGN
FLEXIBLE LIGHTING DESIGN
OUTDOOR LIGHTING (1971 1980) Use LIGHTING
TELEVISION LIGHTING
LIGHTS (1966 1980) Use LIGHTING
TELEVISION LIGHTS (1966 1980) Use TELEVISION LIGHTING
LIGNITE Use COAL
MAXIMUM LIKELIHOOD FACTOR ANALYSIS Use FACTOR ANALYSIS and MAXIMUM LIKELIHOOD STATISTICS
MAXIMUM LIKELIHOOD STATISTICS
RESEARCH LIMITATIONS Use RESEARCH PROBLEMS
LIMITED ENGLISH SPEAKING
RAISED LINE DRAWINGS
ON LINE SYSTEMS (1971 1980) Use ONLINE SYSTEMS
ANCESTRAL LINEAGE Use GENEALOGY
LINEAR PROGRAMING
LINEAR REGRESSION Use REGRESSION (STATISTICS)

	LINGALA
	LINGUISTIC ANTHROPOLOGY Use ANTHROPOLOGICAL LINGUISTICS
	LINGUISTIC BORROWING
	LINGUISTIC COMPETENCE
	LINGUISTIC DIFFICULTY (CONTRASTIVE) Use INTERFERENCE (LANGUAGE)
	LINGUISTIC DIFFICULTY (INHERENT)
	LINGUISTIC PATTERNS (1966 1980) Use LANGUAGE PATTERNS
	LINGUISTIC PERFORMANCE
	LINGUISTIC RESEARCH Use LANGUAGE RESEARCH
	LINGUISTIC STYLES Use LANGUAGE STYLES
	LINGUISTIC THEORY
	LINGUISTIC UNIVERSALS Use LANGUAGE UNIVERSALS
	LINGUISTICS
ANTHROPOLOGICAL	LINGUISTICS
APPLIED	LINGUISTICS
COMPARATIVE	LINGUISTICS Use CONTRASTIVE LINGUISTICS
COMPUTATIONAL	LINGUISTICS
CONTRASTIVE	LINGUISTICS
DESCRIPTIVE	LINGUISTICS
DIACHRONIC	LINGUISTICS
HISTORICAL	LINGUISTICS Use DIACHRONIC LINGUISTICS
MATHEMATICAL	LINGUISTICS
STATISTICAL	LINGUISTICS Use MATHEMATICAL LINGUISTICS
STRUCTURAL	LINGUISTICS
STRUCTURAL ANALYSIS	(LINGUISTICS)
SYNCHRONIC	LINGUISTICS (1967 1980) Use DESCRIPTIVE LINGUISTICS
	LINKING AGENTS
CLEFT	LIP (1967 1980) Use CLEFT PALATE
	LIPREADING
	LISTENING
	LISTENING COMPREHENSION
	LISTENING COMPREHENSION TESTS
	LISTENING GROUPS
	LISTENING HABITS
	LISTENING SKILLS
	LISTENING TESTS (1970 1980) Use LISTENING COMPREHENSION TESTS
BASIC WORD	LISTS Use WORD LISTS
CHECK	LISTS
FILM	LISTS Use FILMOGRAPHIES
PHONOGRAPH RECORD	LISTS Use DISCOGRAPHIES
WORD	LISTS
	LITERACY
ADULT	LITERACY
	LITERACY CLASSES (1966 1980) Use LITERACY EDUCATION
COMPUTER	LITERACY
	LITERACY EDUCATION
FUNCTIONAL	LITERACY
SCIENTIFIC	LITERACY
	LITERACY SKILLS Use LITERACY
SURVIVAL	LITERACY Use FUNCTIONAL LITERACY
TECHNOLOGICAL	LITERACY
VISUAL	LITERACY
	LITERARY ANALYSIS (1968 1980) Use LITERARY CRITICISM
COMPOSITION	(LITERARY) (1966 1980) Use WRITING (COMPOSITION)
COMPOSITION PROCESSES	(LITERARY) Use WRITING PROCESSES
COMPOSITION SKILLS	(LITERARY) (1966 1980) Use WRITING SKILLS
	LITERARY CONVENTIONS (1968 1980) Use LITERARY DEVICES
	LITERARY CRITICISM
	LITERARY DEVICES
DIALOGS	(LITERARY)
	LITERARY DISCRIMINATION (1966 1980)
EXPOSITION	(LITERARY) Use EXPOSITORY WRITING
	LITERARY GENRES
	LITERARY HISTORY
	LITERARY INFLUENCES (1969 1980)
	LITERARY MOOD (1970 1980)
PARALLELISM	(LITERARY)
ENGLISH NEOCLASSIC	LITERARY PERIOD (1968 1980)
	LITERARY PERSPECTIVE (1969 1980)
PROSODY	(LITERARY) Use POETRY
	LITERARY STYLES
SYMBOLS	(LITERARY)
	LITERATURE
ADOLESCENT	LITERATURE
AFRICAN	LITERATURE
AMERICAN INDIAN	LITERATURE
	LITERATURE APPRECIATION
AUSTRALIAN	LITERATURE
BAROQUE	LITERATURE
BIBLICAL	LITERATURE
BLACK	LITERATURE
BUCOLIC	LITERATURE Use PASTORAL LITERATURE
CANADIAN	LITERATURE
CENTRAL AMERICAN	LITERATURE Use LATIN AMERICAN LITERATURE
CHARACTERIZATION	(LITERATURE) (1969 1977) Use CHARACTERIZATION
CHILDRENS	LITERATURE
CLASSICAL	LITERATURE
CZECH	LITERATURE
EIGHTEENTH CENTURY	LITERATURE
ENGLISH	LITERATURE
FIFTEENTH CENTURY	LITERATURE
FRENCH	LITERATURE
FRENCH CANADIAN	LITERATURE Use CANADIAN LITERATURE
GERMAN	LITERATURE
GREEK	LITERATURE
	LITERATURE GUIDES (1966 1980)
HISPANIC AMERICAN	LITERATURE
ITALIAN	LITERATURE
LATIN	LITERATURE
AMERICAN	LITERATURE (1966 1980) (LATIN AMERICA) Use LATIN AMERICAN LITERATURE
LATIN AMERICAN	LITERATURE

MEDIEVAL LITERATURE
MEXICAN AMERICAN LITERATURE
MIDTWENTIETH CENTURY LITERATURE Use TWENTIETH CENTURY LITERATURE
NEGRO LITERATURE (1968 1977) Use BLACK LITERATURE
NINETEENTH CENTURY LITERATURE
NORTH AMERICAN LITERATURE
OLD ENGLISH LITERATURE
PASTORAL LITERATURE
POLISH LITERATURE
LITERATURE PROGRAMS (1966 1980)
RENAISSANCE LITERATURE
LITERATURE REVIEWS
REVIEWS OF THE LITERATURE Use LITERATURE REVIEWS
ROMAN LITERATURE Use LATIN LITERATURE
RUSSIAN LITERATURE
LITERATURE SEARCHES Use BIBLIOGRAPHIES
SEVENTEENTH CENTURY LITERATURE
SIXTEENTH CENTURY LITERATURE
SOUTH AMERICAN LITERATURE Use LATIN AMERICAN LITERATURE
SPANISH LITERATURE
SPANISH AMERICAN LITERATURE (1969 1980) Use HISPANIC AMERICAN LITERATURE
LITERATURE SURVEYS Use LITERATURE REVIEWS
TWENTIETH CENTURY LITERATURE
UNITED STATES LITERATURE
AMERICAN LITERATURE (1966 1980) (UNITED STATES) Use UNITED STATES LITERATURE
VICTORIAN LITERATURE
WORLD LITERATURE
LITHUANIAN
LITIGATION Use COURT LITIGATION
COURT LITIGATION
DESEGREGATION LITIGATION
FEDERAL COURT LITIGATION (1966 1980) Use COURT LITIGATION and FEDERAL COURTS
INTEGRATION LITIGATION (1966 1980) Use DESEGREGATION LITIGATION
STATE COURT LITIGATION Use COURT LITIGATION and STATE COURTS
SUPREME COURT LITIGATION (1966 1980)
LITTER Use SOLID WASTES
LIVESTOCK
LIVESTOCK FEED STORES Use FEED STORES
LIVESTOCK PRODUCTION Use AGRICULTURAL PRODUCTION
LIVESTOCK TECHNOLOGY Use ANIMAL HUSBANDRY
COMMUNAL LIVING Use COLLECTIVE SETTLEMENTS and GROUP EXPERIENCE
DORMITORY LIVING Use DORMITORIES and GROUP EXPERIENCE
FAMILY LIVING Use FAMILY LIFE
FUNDAMENTAL SKILLS (DAILY LIVING) Use DAILY LIVING SKILLS
GROUP LIVING (1966 1977) Use GROUP EXPERIENCE
HUMAN LIVING (1966 1980)
LIVING LEARNING CENTERS
PRODUCTIVE LIVING (1967 1980) Use QUALITY OF LIFE
LIVING QUARTERS Use HOUSING
DAILY LIVING SKILLS
LIVING STANDARDS
SURVIVAL SKILLS (DAILY LIVING) Use DAILY LIVING SKILLS
FACULTY LOAD Use FACULTY WORKLOAD
TEACHER LOAD Use TEACHING LOAD
TEACHING LOAD
STUDENT LOADING AREAS (1968 1980) Use STUDENT TRANSPORTATION
LOAN APPLICANTS Use FINANCIAL AID APPLICANTS
STUDENT LOAN PROGRAMS
LOAN REPAYMENT
LOAN WORDS Use LINGUISTIC BORROWING
DEFAULTING ON LOANS Use LOAN REPAYMENT
INCOME CONTINGENT LOANS
INTERLIBRARY LOANS
LIBRARY LOANS Use LIBRARY CIRCULATION
SCHOLARSHIP LOANS (1966 1980) Use SCHOLARSHIPS and STUDENT LOAN PROGRAMS
LOBBYING
LOCAL AREA NETWORKS
LOCAL AUTONOMY (OF SCHOOLS) Use SCHOOL DISTRICT AUTONOMY
LOCAL COLOR WRITING
LOCAL COMMUNITY PROGRAMS Use COMMUNITY PROGRAMS
LOCAL CONTROL (OF SCHOOLS) Use SCHOOL DISTRICT AUTONOMY
LOCAL EDUCATION AGENCIES Use SCHOOL DISTRICTS
LOCAL EDUCATION AUTHORITIES Use SCHOOL DISTRICTS
LOCAL GOVERNMENT
LOCAL HISTORY
LOCAL HOUSING AUTHORITIES (1966 1980) Use HOUSING
LOCAL INFORMATION SERVICES Use COMMUNITY INFORMATION SERVICES
LOCAL ISSUES
LOCAL LEGISLATION
LOCAL NORMS
LOCAL RECREATION LEGISLATION (1966 1978) Use LOCAL LEGISLATION and RECREATION LEGISLATION
LOCAL UNIONS (1966 1980) Use UNIONS
INDEXES (LOCATERS) (1967 1980) Use INDEXES
GEOGRAPHIC LOCATION
RESIDENTIAL LOCATION Use PLACE OF RESIDENCE
SCHOOL LOCATION
LOCATIONAL SKILLS (SOCIAL STUDIES)
LOCKER ROOMS
LOCOMOTIVE ENGINEERS
LOCUS OF CONTROL
INTERNAL EXTERNAL LOCUS OF CONTROL Use LOCUS OF CONTROL
LOGARITHMS
LOGIC
MATHEMATICAL LOGIC
SYMBOLIC LOGIC Use MATHEMATICAL LOGIC
LOGICAL THINKING
LONELINESS
LONG RANGE PLANNING
LONG TERM MEMORY
LONG TERM PLANNING Use LONG RANGE PLANNING
LONGITUDINAL STUDIES

	LOOK GUESS METHOD Use SIGHT METHOD
	LOOK SAY METHOD Use SIGHT METHOD
	LOOP INDUCTION SYSTEMS
FILM	LOOPS Use FILMSTRIPS
HEARING	LOSS (1967 1980) Use HEARING IMPAIRMENTS
JOB	LOSS SERVICES Use OUTPLACEMENT SERVICES (EMPLOYMENT)
LANGUAGE	LOSS (SKILLS) Use LANGUAGE SKILL ATTRITION
ACHIEVEMENT	LOSSES Use ACHIEVEMENT GAINS
PARKING	LOTS Use PARKING FACILITIES
	LOW ABILITY STUDENTS (1967 1980)
	LOW ACHIEVEMENT
	LOW ACHIEVEMENT FACTORS (1966 1980) Use LOW ACHIEVEMENT
	LOW ACHIEVERS (1966 1980) Use LOW ACHIEVEMENT
	LOW INCOME
	LOW INCOME COUNTIES
	LOW INCOME GROUPS
	LOW INCOME STATES
	LOW LEVEL ASPIRATION (1966 1980) Use ASPIRATION
	LOW MOTIVATION (1966 1980) Use MOTIVATION
	LOW RENT HOUSING
	LOW VISION AIDS
HIGH INTEREST	LOW VOCABULARY BOOKS
	LOWER CLASS
	LOWER CLASS MALES (1966 1980) Use LOWER CLASS and MALES
	LOWER CLASS PARENTS
	LOWER CLASS STUDENTS
	LOWER MIDDLE CLASS
	LOYALTY OATHS
	LOZANOV METHOD Use SUGGESTOPEDIA
	LRC Use LEARNING RESOURCES CENTERS
	LSD Use LYSERGIC ACID DIETHYLAMIDE
	LUBRICANTS
	LUGANDA Use GANDA
	LUMBER INDUSTRY
	LUMBERING Use LUMBER INDUSTRY
	LUMINESCENCE
	LUNAR EXPLORATION Use LUNAR RESEARCH
	LUNAR RESEARCH
	LUNCH PROGRAMS
	LUO
	LUSO BRAZILIAN CULTURE
	LYING
	LYRIC POETRY
	LYRIC POETS Use POETS
	LYSERGIC ACID DIETHYLAMIDE
	MACHINE AIDED INDEXING Use AUTOMATIC INDEXING
MAN	MACHINE DIALOGS Use MAN MACHINE SYSTEMS
	MACHINE DICTATION Use DICTATION
MAN	MACHINE INTERFACE Use MAN MACHINE SYSTEMS
PRODUCTION	MACHINE OPERATORS Use MACHINE TOOL OPERATORS
SEWING	MACHINE OPERATORS
SHEET METAL	MACHINE OPERATORS Use MACHINE TOOL OPERATORS and SHEET METAL WORK
	MACHINE READABLE CATALOGING
	MACHINE REPAIRERS
	MACHINE REPAIRMEN (1968 1980) Use MACHINE REPAIRERS
MAN	MACHINE SYSTEMS
	MACHINE TOOL OPERATORS
	MACHINE TOOLS
	MACHINE TRANSLATION
AGRICULTURAL	MACHINERY
	MACHINERY INDUSTRY
	MACHINERY MAINTENANCE WORKERS Use MACHINE REPAIRERS
	MACHINERY MANUFACTURING INDUSTRY Use MACHINERY INDUSTRY
AGRICULTURAL	MACHINERY OCCUPATIONS
BUSINESS	MACHINES Use OFFICE MACHINES
GRINDING	MACHINES Use MACHINE TOOLS
MILLING	MACHINES Use MACHINE TOOLS
OFFICE	MACHINES
SELF PACING	MACHINES (1966 1980) Use TEACHING MACHINES
TEACHING	MACHINES
TEST SCORING	MACHINES
VENDING	MACHINES
	MACHINISTS
MAINTENANCE	MACHINISTS Use MACHINE REPAIRERS
TEACHER	MADE TESTS
	MAGAZINES Use PERIODICALS
	MAGISTRATES Use COURT JUDGES
	MAGNET CENTERS Use MAGNET SCHOOLS
	MAGNET SCHOOLS
	MAGNETIC AMPLIFIERS Use ELECTRONIC CONTROL
	MAGNETIC INK CHARACTER RECOGNITION Use CHARACTER RECOGNITION
	MAGNETIC TAPE CARTRIDGES Use MAGNETIC TAPE CASSETTES
	MAGNETIC TAPE CASSETTE RECORDERS (1970 1980) Use MAGNETIC TAPE CASSETTES and TAPE RECORDERS
	MAGNETIC TAPE CASSETTES
	MAGNETIC TAPES
	MAGNETS
PERMANENT	MAGNETS Use MAGNETS
	MAGNIFICATION METHODS
	MAGNITUDE OF EFFECT Use EFFECT SIZE
	MAIDS (1968 1980) Use HOUSEHOLD WORKERS
ELECTRONIC	MAIL
	MAINSTREAMING
	MAINTENANCE
EQUIPMENT	MAINTENANCE
LANGUAGE	MAINTENANCE
LAWN	MAINTENANCE Use TURF MANAGEMENT
	MAINTENANCE MACHINISTS Use MACHINE REPAIRERS
SCHOOL	MAINTENANCE
	MAINTENANCE VEHICLES Use SERVICE VEHICLES
MACHINERY	MAINTENANCE WORKERS Use MACHINE REPAIRERS

	MAJORITY ATTITUDES
	MAJORITY CULTURE Use MIDDLE CLASS CULTURE
COLLEGE	MAJORS (1968 1980) Use MAJORS (STUDENTS)
DEPARTMENTAL	MAJORS Use MAJORS (STUDENTS)
EDUCATION	MAJORS
LIBERAL ARTS	MAJORS (1967 1980) Use LIBERAL ARTS and MAJORS (STUDENTS)
	MAJORS (STUDENTS)
	MAKE BELIEVE PLAY Use PRETEND PLAY
TOOL AND DIE	MAKERS
COLLABORATIVE DECISION	MAKING Use PARTICIPATIVE DECISION MAKING
COLLECTIVE DECISION	MAKING Use PARTICIPATIVE DECISION MAKING
DECISION	MAKING
PARTICIPATIVE DECISION	MAKING
DECISION	MAKING SKILLS
SOCIALLY	MALADJUSTED (1966 1980) Use SOCIAL ADJUSTMENT
	MALADJUSTED STUDENTS Use STUDENT ADJUSTMENT
	MALADJUSTMENT (1966 1980) Use ADJUSTMENT (TO ENVIRONMENT)
EMOTIONAL	MALADJUSTMENT (1966 1980) Use EMOTIONAL ADJUSTMENT
STUDENT	MALADJUSTMENT Use STUDENT ADJUSTMENT
	MALAGASY
	MALAY
	MALAYALAM
	MALAYO POLYNESIAN LANGUAGES
	MALE ROLE Use MALES and SEX ROLE
	MALES
LOWER CLASS	MALES (1966 1980) Use LOWER CLASS and MALES
	MALIGNANT NEOPLASMS Use CANCER
TUMORS	(MALIGNANT) Use CANCER
	MALNUTRITION Use NUTRITION
	MALPRACTICE
ACADEMIC	MALPRACTICE Use EDUCATIONAL MALPRACTICE
EDUCATIONAL	MALPRACTICE
	MAN DAYS (1968 1980) Use WORKER DAYS
	MAN MACHINE DIALOGS Use MAN MACHINE SYSTEMS
	MAN MACHINE INTERFACE Use MAN MACHINE SYSTEMS
	MAN MACHINE SYSTEMS
COMPUTER	MANAGED INSTRUCTION
	MANAGEMENT (1966 1980) Use ADMINISTRATION
HOUSING	MANAGEMENT AIDES
	MANAGEMENT BY OBJECTIVES
CLASS	MANAGEMENT (1966 1980) Use CLASSROOM TECHNIQUES
COMPUTER AIDED INSTRUCTIONAL	MANAGEMENT Use COMPUTER MANAGED INSTRUCTION
COMPUTER BASED INSTRUCTIONAL	MANAGEMENT Use COMPUTER MANAGED INSTRUCTION
CONSTRUCTION	MANAGEMENT
CONTINGENCY	MANAGEMENT
DEMOCRATIC	MANAGEMENT Use PARTICIPATIVE DECISION MAKING
	MANAGEMENT DEVELOPMENT
	MANAGEMENT EDUCATION (1967 1980) Use ADMINISTRATOR EDUCATION
EDUCATIONAL	MANAGEMENT Use EDUCATIONAL ADMINISTRATION
ENERGY	MANAGEMENT
FAMILY	MANAGEMENT (1966 1980) Use HOME MANAGEMENT
FARM	MANAGEMENT
FINANCIAL	MANAGEMENT Use MONEY MANAGEMENT
	MANAGEMENT GAMES
HOME	MANAGEMENT
	MANAGEMENT INFORMATION SYSTEMS
LIBRARY	MANAGEMENT Use LIBRARY ADMINISTRATION
MIDDLE	MANAGEMENT
MIDDLE LEVEL	MANAGEMENT Use MIDDLE MANAGEMENT
MONEY	MANAGEMENT
OFFICE	MANAGEMENT
PARTICIPATIVE	MANAGEMENT Use PARTICIPATIVE DECISION MAKING
PERSONNEL	MANAGEMENT
	MANAGEMENT PERSONNEL Use ADMINISTRATORS
RESEARCH	MANAGEMENT Use RESEARCH ADMINISTRATION
SCHOOL BASED	MANAGEMENT
SCHOOL SITE	MANAGEMENT Use SCHOOL BASED MANAGEMENT
SMALL BUSINESS	MANAGEMENT Use BUSINESS ADMINISTRATION and SMALL BUSINESSES
STRESS	MANAGEMENT
	MANAGEMENT SYSTEMS
DATABASE	MANAGEMENT SYSTEMS
FILE	MANAGEMENT SYSTEMS Use DATABASE MANAGEMENT SYSTEMS
TEAM	MANAGEMENT Use MANAGEMENT TEAMS
	MANAGEMENT TEAMS
TIME	MANAGEMENT
	MANAGEMENT TRAINING Use MANAGEMENT DEVELOPMENT
TURF	MANAGEMENT
WASTE	MANAGEMENT Use WASTE DISPOSAL
WILDLIFE	MANAGEMENT
	MANAGERIAL OCCUPATIONS
	MANAGERS Use ADMINISTRATORS
PERSONNEL	MANAGERS Use PERSONNEL DIRECTORS
	MANCHU
	MANDARIN CHINESE
	MANDATORY COURSES Use REQUIRED COURSES
	MANDATORY EDUCATION Use COMPULSORY EDUCATION
	MANDINGO
	MANGALA Use LINGALA
OBJECT	MANIPULATION
	MANIPULATIVE MATERIALS
COMEDY OF	MANNERS Use COMEDY
	MANPOWER Use LABOR FORCE
	MANPOWER DEVELOPMENT (1966 1980) Use LABOR FORCE DEVELOPMENT
	MANPOWER NEEDS (1968 1980) Use LABOR NEEDS
SCIENTIFIC	MANPOWER (1967 1980) Use SCIENTIFIC PERSONNEL
	MANPOWER UTILIZATION (1966 1980) Use LABOR UTILIZATION
	MANUAL COMMUNICATION
	MANUALS (1966 1980) Use GUIDES
INSTRUCTOR	MANUALS Use TEACHING GUIDES
LABORATORY	MANUALS
TEST	MANUALS

EQUIPMENT MANUFACTURERS
MANUFACTURING
ASSEMBLY (MANUFACTURING)
MANUFACTURING INDUSTRY
MACHINERY MANUFACTURING INDUSTRY Use MACHINERY INDUSTRY
MANUFACTURING METHODS Use MANUFACTURING
MANUFACTURING TECHNIQUES Use MANUFACTURING
MANUSCRIPT WRITING (HANDLETTERING)
MAP READING SKILLS Use MAP SKILLS
MAP SKILLS
MAPPING Use CARTOGRAPHY
COGNITIVE MAPPING
MAPPINGS (MATHEMATICS) Use FUNCTIONS (MATHEMATICS)
MAPS
MARANAO
MARATHI
MARCHING BANDS Use BANDS (MUSIC)
MARIHUANA (1969 1986) Use MARIJUANA
MARIJUANA
MARINE BIOLOGY
MARINE CORPS AIR STATIONS Use MILITARY AIR FACILITIES
MARINE EDUCATION
MARINE SCIENCE EDUCATION Use MARINE EDUCATION
MARINE TECHNICIANS
MARINERS Use SEAFARERS
MARITAL COUNSELING Use MARRIAGE COUNSELING
MARITAL INSTABILITY
MARITAL SATISFACTION
MARITAL STATUS
MARITIME EDUCATION
EMPLOYMENT MARKET Use LABOR MARKET
JOB MARKET (1966 1980) Use LABOR MARKET
LABOR MARKET
MARKETABLE SKILLS Use EMPLOYMENT POTENTIAL and JOB SKILLS
MARKETING
GRAIN MARKETING Use GRAINS (FOOD)
FOOD MARKETS Use FOOD STORES
DIACRITICAL MARKING
MARKING (SCHOLASTIC) Use GRADING
MARKS (SCHOLASTIC) Use GRADES (SCHOLASTIC)
MARKSMANSHIP
MARRIAGE
MARRIAGE COUNSELING
EXOGAMOUS MARRIAGE Use INTERMARRIAGE
MARRIED PERSONS Use SPOUSES
MARRIED STUDENTS
MARXIAN ANALYSIS
MARXISM
MARXIST CRITICISM Use MARXIAN ANALYSIS
OPTICAL MASERS Use LASERS
MASONRY
BRICK MASONRY Use BRICKLAYING
MASONS (TRADE) Use MASONRY
MASS COMMUNICATIONS Use MASS MEDIA
MASS CULTURE Use POPULAR CULTURE
MASS INSTRUCTION
MASS MEDIA
MASS MEDIA EFFECTS
MASS MEDIA TECHNOLOGY Use COMMUNICATIONS and MASS MEDIA
MASS PRODUCTION
WEIGHT (MASS)
MASSED NEGATIVE REINFORCEMENT Use NEGATIVE REINFORCEMENT
MASTER OF ARTS DEGREES Use MASTERS DEGREES
MASTER OF ARTS IN COLLEGE TEACHING Use MASTERS DEGREES
MASTER OF ARTS IN TEACHING Use MASTERS DEGREES
MASTER OF SCIENCE DEGREES Use MASTERS DEGREES
MASTER OF SCIENCE IN TEACHING Use MASTERS DEGREES
MASTER PLANS
MASTER TAPES (AUDIO) (1968 1980) Use AUDIOTAPE RECORDINGS
MASTER TEACHERS
MASTERS DEGREES
MASTERS PROGRAMS
MASTERS THESES
MASTERY LEARNING
MASTERY TESTS
MATCHED GROUPS
MATCHING TESTS Use OBJECTIVE TESTS
MATE SELECTION
MATERIAL ADAPTATION Use MEDIA ADAPTATION
INSTRUCTIONAL MATERIAL ADAPTATION Use MEDIA ADAPTATION
MATERIAL DEVELOPMENT
INSTRUCTIONAL MATERIAL DEVELOPMENT Use MATERIAL DEVELOPMENT
INSTRUCTIONAL MATERIAL EVALUATION
PAPER (MATERIAL)
MATERIAL RESEARCH Use MATERIAL DEVELOPMENT
MATERIAL SELECTION Use MEDIA SELECTION
INSTRUCTIONAL MATERIAL SELECTION Use MEDIA SELECTION
LIBRARY MATERIAL SELECTION
READING MATERIAL SELECTION
MATERIAL SOURCES Use RESOURCE MATERIALS
DIALECTICAL MATERIALISM Use MARXISM
ANECHOIC MATERIALS Use ACOUSTIC INSULATION
ART MATERIALS
AUDIOVISUAL MATERIALS Use AUDIOVISUAL AIDS
BILINGUAL MATERIALS Use MULTILINGUAL MATERIALS
BILINGUAL INSTRUCTIONAL MATERIALS
BUILDING MATERIALS (1968 1980) Use CONSTRUCTION MATERIALS
INSTRUCTIONAL MATERIALS CENTERS (1966 1980) Use LEARNING RESOURCES CENTERS
CLASSROOM MATERIALS (1966 1980) Use INSTRUCTIONAL MATERIALS
CONSTRUCTION MATERIALS
CURRICULUM MATERIALS Use INSTRUCTIONAL MATERIALS

DANGEROUS MATERIALS Use HAZARDOUS MATERIALS
EDUCATIONAL MATERIALS Use INSTRUCTIONAL MATERIALS
FLES MATERIALS (1967 1980) Use FLES and INSTRUCTIONAL MATERIALS
HANDWRITING MATERIALS (1966 1983) Use HANDWRITING and INSTRUCTIONAL MATERIALS
HAZARDOUS MATERIALS
HEALTH MATERIALS
INSTRUCTIONAL MATERIALS
MATERIALS INVENTORY Use FACILITY INVENTORY
LARGE TYPE MATERIALS
LIBRARY MATERIALS
LIBRARY REFERENCE MATERIALS Use LIBRARY MATERIALS and REFERENCE MATERIALS
MANIPULATIVE MATERIALS
MATHEMATICS MATERIALS
MULTILINGUAL MATERIALS
NONBOOK MATERIALS Use NONPRINT MEDIA
ORIENTATION MATERIALS
PARENT MATERIALS
PARENTING MATERIALS Use PARENT MATERIALS
PORTFOLIOS (BACKGROUND MATERIALS)
PROGRAMED MATERIALS (1966 1980) Use PROGRAMED INSTRUCTIONAL MATERIALS
PROGRAMED INSTRUCTIONAL MATERIALS
PROTOCOL MATERIALS
READERS (MATERIALS) Use READING MATERIALS
READING MATERIALS
REFERENCE MATERIALS
RESOURCE MATERIALS
SCIENCE MATERIALS
SELF INSTRUCTION MATERIALS Use PROGRAMED INSTRUCTIONAL MATERIALS
STUDENT DEVELOPED MATERIALS
SUPPLEMENTARY READING MATERIALS
TACTILE MATERIALS Use MANIPULATIVE MATERIALS
TEACHER DEVELOPED MATERIALS
TEACHING MATERIALS Use INSTRUCTIONAL MATERIALS
TELEGRAPHIC MATERIALS
VISUAL MATERIALS Use VISUAL AIDS
MATHEMATICAL APPLICATIONS
MATHEMATICAL CONCEPTS
MATHEMATICAL ENRICHMENT
MATHEMATICAL EXPERIENCE (1966 1980)
MATHEMATICAL EXPRESSIONS Use MATHEMATICAL FORMULAS
MATHEMATICAL FORMULAS
MATHEMATICAL LINGUISTICS
MATHEMATICAL LOGIC
MATHEMATICAL MODELS
MATHEMATICAL SENTENCES Use MATHEMATICAL FORMULAS
MATHEMATICAL STATISTICS Use STATISTICS
MATHEMATICAL VOCABULARY
MATHEMATICIANS
MATHEMATICS
MATHEMATICS ACHIEVEMENT
MATHEMATICS ANXIETY
APPROXIMATION (MATHEMATICS) Use ESTIMATION (MATHEMATICS)
MATHEMATICS AVOIDANCE Use MATHEMATICS ANXIETY
COLLEGE MATHEMATICS
CONGRUENCE (MATHEMATICS)
MATHEMATICS CURRICULUM
MATHEMATICS EDUCATION
ELEMENTARY SCHOOL MATHEMATICS
EQUATIONS (MATHEMATICS)
ESTIMATION (MATHEMATICS)
FUNCTIONS (MATHEMATICS)
INEQUALITY (MATHEMATICS)
MATHEMATICS INSTRUCTION
MAPPINGS (MATHEMATICS) Use FUNCTIONS (MATHEMATICS)
MATHEMATICS MATERIALS
MODERN MATHEMATICS
NEW MATHEMATICS Use MODERN MATHEMATICS
PRACTICAL MATHEMATICS (1966 1980) Use MATHEMATICAL APPLICATIONS
PROOF (MATHEMATICS)
PROPORTION (MATHEMATICS) Use RATIOS (MATHEMATICS)
QUANTITATIVE TESTS (1980 1985) (MATHEMATICS) Use MATHEMATICS TESTS
RATIOS (MATHEMATICS)
RECIPROCALS (MATHEMATICS)
REMEDIAL MATHEMATICS
SECONDARY SCHOOL MATHEMATICS
MATHEMATICS SKILLS
STORY PROBLEMS (MATHEMATICS) Use WORD PROBLEMS (MATHEMATICS)
SYMBOLS (MATHEMATICS)
MATHEMATICS TEACHERS
TECHNICAL MATHEMATICS
MATHEMATICS TESTS
TRANSFORMATIONS (MATHEMATICS)
VECTORS (MATHEMATICS)
VOLUME (MATHEMATICS)
WORD PROBLEMS (MATHEMATICS)
MATHOPHOBIA Use MATHEMATICS ANXIETY
MATRICES
MATRICULATION Use ADMISSION (SCHOOL)
MATRIX SAMPLING Use ITEM SAMPLING
MULTIPLE MATRIX SAMPLING Use ITEM SAMPLING
MATTER
MATURATION (1967 1980)
LEARNING MATURATION CONTROVERSY Use NATURE NURTURE CONTROVERSY
MATURATION LEARNING CONTROVERSY Use NATURE NURTURE CONTROVERSY
CAREER MATURITY Use VOCATIONAL MATURITY
MATURITY (INDIVIDUALS)
SOCIAL MATURITY (1966 1980) Use MATURITY (INDIVIDUALS)
MATURITY TESTS
VOCATIONAL MATURITY
MAURITIAN CREOLE
MAXIMUM LIKELIHOOD FACTOR ANALYSIS Use FACTOR ANALYSIS and MAXIMUM LIKELIHOOD

	STATISTICS
	MAXIMUM LIKELIHOOD STATISTICS
	MAYAN LANGUAGES
WORD	MEANING Use SEMANTICS
GERMAN	MEASLES Use RUBELLA
CUBIC	MEASURE Use VOLUME (MATHEMATICS)
TRUE	MEASURE Use TRUE SCORES
	MEASUREMENT
COGNITIVE	MEASUREMENT
COMPOSITION	MEASUREMENT Use CHEMICAL ANALYSIS
	MEASUREMENT EQUIPMENT
	MEASUREMENT ERROR Use ERROR OF MEASUREMENT
ERROR OF	MEASUREMENT
	MEASUREMENT GOALS (1966 1980) Use MEASUREMENT OBJECTIVES
	MEASUREMENT INSTRUMENTS (1966 1980)
INVENTORIES	(MEASUREMENT) Use MEASURES (INDIVIDUALS)
	MEASUREMENT OBJECTIVES
PREDICTIVE	MEASUREMENT
STANDARD ERROR OF	MEASUREMENT (1970 1980) Use ERROR OF MEASUREMENT
	MEASUREMENT TECHNIQUES
AFFECTIVE	MEASURES
ASSOCIATION	MEASURES
ATTITUDE	MEASURES
CREATIVITY	MEASURES Use CREATIVITY TESTS
	MEASURES (INDIVIDUALS)
INTELLIGENCE	MEASURES Use INTELLIGENCE TESTS
NON DISCURSIVE	MEASURES Use VISUAL MEASURES
NORM REFERENCED	MEASURES Use NORM REFERENCED TESTS
PERSONALITY	MEASURES
PREVENTIVE	MEASURES Use PREVENTION
PROJECTIVE	MEASURES
SELF CONCEPT	MEASURES
SIGNIFICANCE	MEASURES Use STATISTICAL SIGNIFICANCE
VISUAL	MEASURES
	MEAT
	MEAT INSPECTORS Use FOOD AND DRUG INSPECTORS
	MEAT PACKING INDUSTRY
	MECHANICAL DESIGN TECHNICIANS
	MECHANICAL DEVICES Use MECHANICAL EQUIPMENT
	MECHANICAL DRAWING Use ENGINEERING DRAWING
	MECHANICAL ENGINEERING ASSISTANTS Use MECHANICAL DESIGN TECHNICIANS
	MECHANICAL EQUIPMENT
	MECHANICAL SKILLS
	MECHANICAL TEACHING AIDS (1966 1980) Use EDUCATIONAL MEDIA
	MECHANICAL TRANSLATION Use MACHINE TRANSLATION
AIR CONDITIONING	MECHANICS Use REFRIGERATION MECHANICS
AIRCRAFT	MECHANICS Use AVIATION MECHANICS
AUTO	MECHANICS
AUTOMOBILE	MECHANICS Use AUTO MECHANICS
AVIATION	MECHANICS
CLASSICAL	MECHANICS Use MECHANICS (PHYSICS)
DIESEL	MECHANICS Use AUTO MECHANICS
FLUID	MECHANICS
GENERAL	MECHANICS Use MECHANICS (PROCESS)
AUTO	MECHANICS (OCCUPATION) (1968 1980) Use AUTO MECHANICS
FARM	MECHANICS (OCCUPATION) (1967 1980) Use AGRICULTURAL MACHINERY OCCUPATIONS
	MECHANICS (PHYSICS)
POWER	MECHANICS (1969 1980) Use POWER TECHNOLOGY
	MECHANICS (PROCESS)
QUANTUM	MECHANICS
REFRIGERATION	MECHANICS
SHOP	MECHANICS Use MACHINE REPAIRERS
SMALL ENGINE	MECHANICS
AGRICULTURAL	MECHANICS (SUBJECT) Use AGRICULTURAL ENGINEERING
FARM	MECHANICS (SUBJECT) Use AGRICULTURAL ENGINEERING
TRUCK	MECHANICS Use AUTO MECHANICS
	MECHANIZATION Use AUTOMATION
LIBRARY	MECHANIZATION Use LIBRARY AUTOMATION
	MEDIA ADAPTATION
EDUCATIONAL	MEDIA ADAPTATION Use MEDIA ADAPTATION
AUDIOVISUAL	MEDIA Use AUDIOVISUAL AIDS
SCHOOL	MEDIA CENTERS Use LEARNING RESOURCES CENTERS
COMMUNICATIONS	MEDIA Use MASS MEDIA
EDUCATIONAL	MEDIA
MASS	MEDIA EFFECTS
INSTRUCTIONAL	MEDIA (1967 1980) Use EDUCATIONAL MEDIA
MASS	MEDIA
NEWS	MEDIA
NONPRINT	MEDIA
	MEDIA RESEARCH
	MEDIA SELECTION
EDUCATIONAL	MEDIA SELECTION Use MEDIA SELECTION
	MEDIA SPECIALISTS
	MEDIA TECHNOLOGY (1968 1980) Use COMMUNICATIONS
MASS	MEDIA TECHNOLOGY Use COMMUNICATIONS and MASS MEDIA
VISUAL	MEDIA Use VISUAL AIDS
	MEDIATION (LABOR) Use ARBITRATION
	MEDIATION THEORY
	MEDICAL ASSISTANCE Use MEDICAL SERVICES
	MEDICAL ASSISTANTS
	MEDICAL ASSOCIATIONS
	MEDICAL AUDIT Use MEDICAL CARE EVALUATION
	MEDICAL CARE Use MEDICAL SERVICES
	MEDICAL CARE EVALUATION
	MEDICAL CASE HISTORIES
	MEDICAL CONSULTANTS
	MEDICAL DOCTORS Use PHYSICIANS
	MEDICAL EDUCATION
GRADUATE	MEDICAL EDUCATION
VETERINARY	MEDICAL EDUCATION
	MEDICAL EVALUATION

FELLOWS (MEDICAL) Use GRADUATE MEDICAL STUDENTS
FOREIGN MEDICAL GRADUATES
INTERNS (MEDICAL) Use GRADUATE MEDICAL STUDENTS
INTERNSHIPS (MEDICAL) Use GRADUATE MEDICAL EDUCATION
MEDICAL LABORATORY ASSISTANTS
MEDICAL LABORATORY TECHNOLOGISTS Use MEDICAL TECHNOLOGISTS
MEDICAL LIBRARIES
ALLIED MEDICAL OCCUPATIONS Use ALLIED HEALTH OCCUPATIONS
MEDICAL RECORD ADMINISTRATORS
MEDICAL RECORD CLERKS Use MEDICAL RECORD TECHNICIANS
MEDICAL RECORD LIBRARIANS (1969 1980) Use MEDICAL RECORD ADMINISTRATORS
MEDICAL RECORD TECHNICIANS
MEDICAL RESEARCH
RESIDENCY PROGRAMS (MEDICAL) Use GRADUATE MEDICAL EDUCATION
RESIDENTS (MEDICAL) Use GRADUATE MEDICAL STUDENTS
MEDICAL SCHOOL APPLICANTS Use COLLEGE APPLICANTS and MEDICAL SCHOOLS
MEDICAL SCHOOL FACULTY
MEDICAL SCHOOLS
MEDICAL SCIENCES Use MEDICINE
MEDICAL SECRETARIES Use SECRETARIES
MEDICAL SERVICES
MEDICAL STUDENTS
GRADUATE MEDICAL STUDENTS
MEDICAL TECHNICIANS Use MEDICAL LABORATORY ASSISTANTS
EMERGENCY MEDICAL TECHNICIANS
MEDICAL TECHNOLOGISTS
MEDICAL TREATMENT (1967 1980) Use MEDICAL SERVICES
MEDICAL VOCABULARY
MEDICINE
CLERKSHIPS (MEDICINE) Use CLINICAL EXPERIENCE
CLINICAL JUDGMENT (MEDICINE) Use MEDICAL EVALUATION
CLINICAL PROFESSORS (1967 1980) (MEDICINE) Use MEDICAL SCHOOL FACULTY
CPR (MEDICINE) Use CARDIOPULMONARY RESUSCITATION
EXTERNSHIPS (MEDICINE) Use CLINICAL EXPERIENCE
FAMILY PRACTICE (MEDICINE)
GENERAL PRACTICE (MEDICINE) Use FAMILY PRACTICE (MEDICINE)
INTERNAL MEDICINE
NUCLEAR MEDICINE Use RADIOLOGY
PRECEPTORS (MEDICINE) Use PHYSICIANS and PRACTICUM SUPERVISION
PRECEPTORSHIPS (MEDICINE) Use CLINICAL EXPERIENCE
PREVENTIVE MEDICINE
SCHOOLS OF MEDICINE Use MEDICAL SCHOOLS
NUCLEAR MEDICINE TECHNOLOGISTS Use RADIOLOGIC TECHNOLOGISTS
VETERINARY MEDICINE
X RAYS (MEDICINE) Use RADIOLOGY
MEDIEVAL HISTORY
MEDIEVAL LITERATURE
MEDIEVAL ROMANCE (1969 1980) Use MEDIEVAL LITERATURE
MEDITATION
TRANSCENDENTAL MEDITATION
MEDIUM OF INSTRUCTION (LANGUAGE) Use LANGUAGE OF INSTRUCTION
MEETINGS
COLLOQUIUMS (MEETINGS) Use MEETINGS
PLANNING MEETINGS (1966 1980) Use MEETINGS
STAFF MEETINGS
MELANCHOLIA Use DEPRESSION (PSYCHOLOGY)
MELANESIAN LANGUAGES
BOARD OF EDUCATION MEMBERS Use BOARDS OF EDUCATION
SCHOOL BOARD MEMBERS Use BOARDS OF EDUCATION
UNION MEMBERS
AVERAGE DAILY MEMBERSHIP
GROUP MEMBERSHIP
MEMORIZATION
MEMORIZING (1967 1980) Use MEMORIZATION
MEMORY
MEMORY DEVICES (COMPUTERS) Use COMPUTER STORAGE DEVICES
KINESTHETIC MEMORY Use KINESTHETIC PERCEPTION
LONG TERM MEMORY
PHOTOGRAPHIC MEMORY Use EIDETIC IMAGERY
SHORT TERM MEMORY
MEN Use MALES
AUTO PARTS MEN (1968 1980) Use AUTO PARTS CLERKS
DEANS OF MEN Use DEANS OF STUDENTS
ENLISTED MEN (1967 1976) Use ENLISTED PERSONNEL
MENDE
MENTAL ABILITY Use COGNITIVE ABILITY
MENTAL AGE
MENTAL DEVELOPMENT (1966 1980) Use COGNITIVE DEVELOPMENT
MENTAL DISORDERS
MENTAL HEALTH
MENTAL HEALTH CLINICS
MENTAL HEALTH PROGRAMS
MENTAL HEALTH RESOURCES Use MENTAL HEALTH PROGRAMS
MENTAL HYGIENE Use MENTAL HEALTH
MENTAL ILLNESS (1966 1980) Use MENTAL DISORDERS
READINESS (MENTAL) (1966 1980) Use READINESS
MENTAL RETARDATION
BORDERLINE MENTAL RETARDATION Use SLOW LEARNERS
MILD MENTAL RETARDATION
MODERATE MENTAL RETARDATION
SEVERE MENTAL RETARDATION
MENTAL RIGIDITY
MENTAL TESTS (1966 1980) Use PSYCHOLOGICAL TESTING
MENTALLY ADVANCED CHILDREN Use GIFTED
MENTALLY HANDICAPPED (1966 1980) Use MENTAL RETARDATION
CUSTODIAL MENTALLY HANDICAPPED (1968 1980) Use SEVERE MENTAL RETARDATION
EDUCABLE MENTALLY HANDICAPPED (1966 1980) Use MILD MENTAL RETARDATION
TRAINABLE MENTALLY HANDICAPPED (1967 1980) Use MODERATE MENTAL RETARDATION
PROFOUNDLY MENTALLY RETARDED Use SEVERE MENTAL RETARDATION
MENTORS
MENU DRIVEN SOFTWARE

	MERCHANDISE INFORMATION
	MERCHANDISING
	MERCHANTS
	MERGERS
	MERIT PAY
	MERIT RATING
	MERIT RATING PROGRAMS (1967 1980) Use MERIT RATING
	MERIT SCHOLARSHIPS
COMPUTER BASED	MESSAGE SYSTEMS Use ELECTRONIC MAIL
	META ANALYSIS
	META KNOWLEDGE Use METACOGNITION
	METABOLISM
	METACOGNITION
	METAL FINISHING Use FINISHING
	METAL FORMING OCCUPATIONS Use METAL WORKING
	METAL INDUSTRY
SHEET	METAL MACHINE OPERATORS Use MACHINE TOOL OPERATORS and SHEET METAL WORK
	METAL TRADES Use METAL WORKING
SHEET	METAL WORK
SHEET	METAL WORKERS (1967 1981) Use SHEET METAL WORK
	METAL WORKING
	METAL WORKING OCCUPATIONS (1968 1980) Use METAL WORKING
	METALLURGICAL TECHNICIANS
	METALLURGY
	METALS
	METAMEMORY Use METACOGNITION
	METAPHORS
	METEOROLOGY
WIND	(METEOROLOGY)
	METERS Use MEASUREMENT EQUIPMENT
PARKING	METERS (1968 1980) Use PARKING CONTROLS
CRITICAL INCIDENTS	METHOD
CRITICAL PATH	METHOD
DESIGN CONSTRUCT	METHOD Use DESIGN BUILD APPROACH
GRAMMAR TRANSLATION	METHOD
INTEGRATED TEACHING	METHOD Use INTEGRATED ACTIVITIES and TEACHING METHODS
LECTURE	METHOD
LOOK GUESS	METHOD Use SIGHT METHOD
LOOK SAY	METHOD Use SIGHT METHOD
LOZANOV	METHOD Use SUGGESTOPEDIA
MONTESSORI	METHOD
CENTROID	METHOD OF FACTOR ANALYSIS Use FACTOR ANALYSIS
ORAL COMMUNICATION	METHOD
PHONIC	METHOD Use PHONICS
WORD	METHOD (READING) Use SIGHT METHOD
SERIAL	METHOD Use SERIAL LEARNING
SIGHT	METHOD
	METHODOLOGY (1966 1974) Use METHODS
MTMM	METHODOLOGY Use MULTITRAIT MULTIMETHOD TECHNIQUES
Q	METHODOLOGY
RESEARCH	METHODOLOGY
SCIENTIFIC	METHODOLOGY
SOCIAL SCIENCE	METHODOLOGY Use RESEARCH METHODOLOGY and SOCIAL SCIENCE RESEARCH
	METHODS
AUDIOLINGUAL	METHODS
AUTOINSTRUCTIONAL	METHODS (1966 1980) Use PROGRAMED INSTRUCTION
CLASSROOM	METHODS Use CLASSROOM TECHNIQUES
COUNSELING	METHODS Use COUNSELING TECHNIQUES
	METHODS COURSES
GENERAL	METHODS COURSES Use METHODS COURSES
SPECIAL	METHODS COURSES Use METHODS COURSES
DEDUCTIVE	METHODS (1967 1980) Use DEDUCTION
DESEGREGATION	METHODS
EDUCATIONAL	METHODS
ENLARGEMENT	METHODS Use MAGNIFICATION METHODS
EVALUATION	METHODS
INDUCTIVE	METHODS (1967 1980) Use INDUCTION
INSTRUCTIONAL	METHODS Use TEACHING METHODS
INTEGRATION	METHODS (1966 1980) Use DESEGREGATION METHODS
JOB SEARCH	METHODS
KINESTHETIC	METHODS
MAGNIFICATION	METHODS
MANUFACTURING	METHODS Use MANUFACTURING
MONTE CARLO	METHODS
PRESENTATION	METHODS Use TEACHING METHODS
PROJECT	METHODS Use STUDENT PROJECTS and TEACHING METHODS
PROJECT TRAINING	METHODS (1968 1980) Use STUDENT PROJECTS and TEACHING METHODS
PSYCHOEDUCATIONAL	METHODS
	METHODS RESEARCH
SCIENTIFIC	METHODS Use SCIENTIFIC METHODOLOGY
STATISTICAL	METHODS Use STATISTICAL ANALYSIS
STATISTICAL ASSOCIATION	METHODS Use CORRELATION
SUPERVISORY	METHODS
	METHODS TEACHERS
TEACHING	METHODS
TESTING	METHODS Use TESTING
TRAINING	METHODS
	METRIC SYSTEM
	METRICATION Use METRIC SYSTEM
	METROPOLITAN AREAS
	MEXICAN AMERICAN CULTURE Use HISPANIC AMERICAN CULTURE and MEXICAN AMERICANS
	MEXICAN AMERICAN EDUCATION
	MEXICAN AMERICAN HISTORY
	MEXICAN AMERICAN LITERATURE
	MEXICAN AMERICANS
	MEXICANS
	MICROBIOLOGY
	MICROCALORIMETERS Use CALORIMETERS
	MICROCOMPUTERS
	MICROCOUNSELING
	MICROFICHE

MICROFILM
COMPUTER OUTPUT MICROFILM
MICROFILMING Use MICROREPRODUCTION
MICROFORM READER PRINTERS (1971 1980) Use MICROFORM READERS
MICROFORM READERS
MICROFORMS
MICROGRAPHICS Use MICROREPRODUCTION
MICROIMAGES Use MICROFORMS
MICROPHONES
MICROPHOTOGRAPHY Use MICROREPRODUCTION
MICROPROCESSORS Use MICROCOMPUTERS
MICROREPRODUCTION
MICROSCOPES
MICROTEACHING
MICROTEXTS Use MICROFORMS
MICROWAVE RELAY SYSTEMS (1971 1980) Use TELECOMMUNICATIONS
MIDCAREER CHANGE Use CAREER CHANGE and MIDLIFE TRANSITIONS
MIDDLE AGED (1966 1980) Use MIDDLE AGED ADULTS
MIDDLE AGED ADULTS
MIDDLE CLASS
MIDDLE CLASS COLLEGE STUDENTS (1966 1980) Use COLLEGE STUDENTS and MIDDLE CLASS STUDENTS
MIDDLE CLASS CULTURE
MIDDLE CLASS FATHERS (1966 1980) Use FATHERS and MIDDLE CLASS PARENTS
LOWER MIDDLE CLASS
MIDDLE CLASS MOTHERS (1966 1980) Use MIDDLE CLASS PARENTS and MOTHERS
MIDDLE CLASS NORM (1966 1980) Use MIDDLE CLASS STANDARDS
MIDDLE CLASS PARENTS
MIDDLE CLASS STANDARDS
MIDDLE CLASS STUDENTS
MIDDLE CLASS VALUES (1966 1980) Use MIDDLE CLASS STANDARDS
MIDDLE EASTERN HISTORY
MIDDLE EASTERN STUDIES
MIDDLE ENGLISH
MIDDLE INCOME HOUSING
MIDDLE LEVEL MANAGEMENT Use MIDDLE MANAGEMENT
MIDDLE MANAGEMENT
MIDDLE SCHOOLS
MIDLIFE Use MIDDLE AGED ADULTS
MIDLIFE TRANSITIONS
MIDMANAGEMENT Use MIDDLE MANAGEMENT
MIDTWENTIETH CENTURY LITERATURE Use TWENTIETH CENTURY LITERATURE
MIDWIFERY Use OBSTETRICS
MIGRANT ADULT EDUCATION
MIGRANT ADULTS Use MIGRANTS
MIGRANT CHILD CARE CENTERS (1966 1980) Use DAY CARE CENTERS and MIGRANT CHILDREN
MIGRANT CHILD EDUCATION (1967 1980) Use MIGRANT EDUCATION
MIGRANT CHILDREN
MIGRANT EDUCATION
MIGRANT EMPLOYMENT
MIGRANT HEALTH SERVICES
MIGRANT HOUSING
MIGRANT POPULATION Use MIGRANTS
MIGRANT PROBLEMS
MIGRANT PROGRAMS
MIGRANT PROJECTS Use MIGRANT PROGRAMS
CHURCH MIGRANT PROJECTS (1966 1980) Use CHURCH PROGRAMS and MIGRANT PROGRAMS
COMMUNITY MIGRANT PROJECTS (1966 1980) Use COMMUNITY PROGRAMS and MIGRANT PROGRAMS
MIGRANT SCHOOLS (1966 1980) Use MIGRANT EDUCATION
MIGRANT TRANSPORTATION (1966 1980) Use MIGRANTS and TRANSPORTATION
MIGRANT WELFARE SERVICES
MIGRANT WORKER PROJECTS (1966 1980) Use MIGRANT PROGRAMS and MIGRANT WORKERS
MIGRANT WORKERS
AGRICULTURAL MIGRANT WORKERS Use MIGRANT WORKERS
MIGRANT YOUTH
MIGRANTS
AGRICULTURAL MIGRANTS Use MIGRANTS
INTERSTATE WORKERS (1966 1980) (MIGRANTS) Use MIGRANT WORKERS
LABOR CAMPS (1966 1980) (MIGRANTS) Use MIGRANT HOUSING
NATIVE MIGRANTS Use MIGRANTS
MIGRATION
MIGRATION PATTERNS
RURAL TO URBAN MIGRATION
MIGRATION TRENDS Use MIGRATION PATTERNS
URBAN TO RURAL MIGRATION
URBAN TO SUBURBAN MIGRATION
MIGRATORY AGRICULTURAL WORKERS Use MIGRANT WORKERS
MIGRATORY CHILDREN Use MIGRANT CHILDREN
MILD DISABILITIES
MILD MENTAL RETARDATION
MILIEU THERAPY
MILITANCY Use ACTIVISM
TEACHER MILITANCY
MILITARY AIR FACILITIES
MILITARY ORGANIZATIONS
MILITARY PERSONNEL
MILITARY SCHOOLS
MILITARY SCIENCE
MILITARY SERVICE
MILITARY TRAINING
EIGHT MILLIMETER PROJECTORS (1970 1980) Use PROJECTION EQUIPMENT
SIXTEEN MILLIMETER PROJECTORS (1966 1980) Use PROJECTION EQUIPMENT
MILLING MACHINES Use MACHINE TOOLS
MILLWORK Use CABINETMAKING
MIME Use PANTOMIME
MINERALOGY
MINERALS
MINICOMPUTERS
MINICOURSES
MINIMAL BRAIN DYSFUNCTION
MINIMAL COMPETENCIES Use MINIMUM COMPETENCIES

MINIMAL COMPETENCY TESTING Use MINIMUM COMPETENCY TESTING
MINIMALLY BRAIN INJURED (1966 1980) Use MINIMAL BRAIN DYSFUNCTION
MINIMUM COMPETENCIES
MINIMUM COMPETENCY TESTING
MINIMUM INITIAL EXPENSES Use EXPENDITURES
MINIMUM OPERATING EXPENSES Use OPERATING EXPENSES
MINIMUM WAGE
MINIMUM WAGE LAWS (1966 1974) Use MINIMUM WAGE LEGISLATION
MINIMUM WAGE LEGISLATION
MINING
COAL MINING Use COAL and MINING
MINISTERS Use CLERGY
MINNESINGERS Use POETS
POPULATION MINORITIES Use MINORITY GROUPS
MINORITY CULTURE Use MINORITY GROUPS
MINORITY GROUP CHILDREN
MINORITY GROUP INFLUENCES
MINORITY GROUP TEACHERS
MINORITY GROUPS
MINORITY RIGHTS Use CIVIL RIGHTS
MINORITY ROLE (1966 1980) Use MINORITY GROUP INFLUENCES
MIOSIS Use MYOPIA
MIS Use MANAGEMENT INFORMATION SYSTEMS
MISBEHAVIOR (1966 1980) Use BEHAVIOR PROBLEMS
MISCONCEPTIONS
MISCUE ANALYSIS
MISCUE TAXONOMY Use MISCUE ANALYSIS
INSTITUTIONAL MISSION
MISSION STATEMENTS
MISTAKEN CONCEPTIONS Use MISCONCEPTIONS
MNEMONICS
MOBILE CLASSROOMS
MOBILE CLINICS
MOBILE EDUCATIONAL SERVICES
MOBILE LABORATORIES
MOBILE LIBRARIES Use BOOKMOBILES
MOBILITY
MOBILITY AIDS
EDUCATIONAL MOBILITY
FACULTY MOBILITY
FAMILY MOBILITY
JOB MOBILITY Use OCCUPATIONAL MOBILITY
LABOR MOBILITY Use OCCUPATIONAL MOBILITY
OCCUPATIONAL MOBILITY
PHYSICAL MOBILITY
SOCIAL MOBILITY
STUDENT MOBILITY
TEACHER MOBILITY Use FACULTY MOBILITY
VISUALLY HANDICAPPED MOBILITY
GEOGRAPHIC MOBILITY (1980) Use MIGRATION
YOUTH MOBILIZATION Use YOUTH EMPLOYMENT
LEARNING MODALITIES
RESPONSE MODE (1967 1980) Use RESPONSES
MODEL PROGRAMS Use DEMONSTRATION PROGRAMS
MODELING (PSYCHOLOGICAL) (1977 1980) Use MODELING (PSYCHOLOGY)
MODELING (PSYCHOLOGY)
MODELS
MATHEMATICAL MODELS
ROLE MODELS
STUDENT WRITING MODELS
TEACHING MODELS
THEORETICAL MODELS Use MODELS
MODERATE MENTAL RETARDATION
MODERN GREEK Use GREEK
MODERN HISTORY
MODERN LANGUAGE CURRICULUM
MODERN LANGUAGES
MODERN MATHEMATICS
MODERN SCIENCE (1966 1980) Use SCIENCES
MODERNISM
MODERNIZATION
BEHAVIOR MODIFICATION
COGNITIVE MODIFICATION Use COGNITIVE RESTRUCTURING
COGNITIVE BEHAVIOR MODIFICATION Use BEHAVIOR MODIFICATION and COGNITIVE RESTRUCTURING
MODULAR BUILDING DESIGN
MODULAR DRAFTING Use MODULAR BUILDING DESIGN
MODULAR LEARNING Use LEARNING MODULES
MODULAR SCHEDULING Use FLEXIBLE SCHEDULING
LEARNING MODULES
SCHEDULE MODULES (1968 1980) Use FLEXIBLE SCHEDULING
MOLE Use MOSSI
MOLECULAR STRUCTURE
KINETIC MOLECULAR THEORY
MONETARY SYSTEMS
DISBURSEMENTS (MONEY) Use EXPENDITURES
MONEY MANAGEMENT
MONEY SYSTEMS (1966 1980) Use MONETARY SYSTEMS
MONGOL Use MONGOLIAN
MONGOLIAN
MONGOLIAN LANGUAGES
MONGOLISM (1968 1978) Use DOWNS SYNDROME
MONOLINGUALISM
MONOLOGS
MONOLOGUES (1970 1980) Use MONOLOGS
INTERIOR MONOLOGUES Use MONOLOGS
MONTE CARLO METHODS
MONTESSORI METHOD
IMPERATIVE MOOD Use VERBS
INDICATIVE MOOD Use VERBS
LITERARY MOOD (1970 1980)
SUBJUNCTIVE MOOD Use VERBS

	MOONLIGHTING Use MULTIPLE EMPLOYMENT
	MORAL CRITICISM (1969 1980)
	MORAL DEVELOPMENT
	MORAL INSTRUCTION Use ETHICAL INSTRUCTION
	MORAL ISSUES
	MORAL JUDGMENT Use MORAL VALUES and VALUE JUDGMENT
	MORAL VALUES
	MORALE
TEACHER	MORALE
	MORALS Use ETHICS
	MORE Use MOSSI
	MORPHEMES
SUPRASEGMENTAL	MORPHEMES Use INTONATION
	MORPHEMICS Use MORPHOLOGY (LANGUAGES)
	MORPHOLOGY (LANGUAGES)
	MORPHOPHONEMICS
INFANT	MORTALITY
	MORTALITY (RESEARCH STUDIES) Use ATTRITION (RESEARCH STUDIES)
	MOSSI
	MOTELS Use HOTELS
	MOTHER ABSENCE Use MOTHERLESS FAMILY
	MOTHER ATTITUDES
	MOTHER ROLE Use MOTHERS and PARENT ROLE
	MOTHERHOOD Use MOTHERS
	MOTHERLESS FAMILY
	MOTHERS
BLACK	MOTHERS
EMPLOYED	MOTHERS Use EMPLOYED PARENTS and MOTHERS
MIDDLE CLASS	MOTHERS (1966 1980) Use MIDDLE CLASS PARENTS and MOTHERS
NEGRO	MOTHERS (1966 1977) Use BLACK MOTHERS
UNWED	MOTHERS
	MOTIFS
	MOTION
	MOTION PICTURES Use FILMS
	MOTIVATION
ACHIEVEMENT	MOTIVATION Use ACHIEVEMENT NEED
GROWTH	MOTIVATION Use SELF ACTUALIZATION
LEARNING	MOTIVATION
LOW	MOTIVATION (1966 1980) Use MOTIVATION
SELF	MOTIVATION Use SELF ACTUALIZATION
STUDENT	MOTIVATION
TEACHER	MOTIVATION
	MOTIVATION TECHNIQUES
	MOTOR ABILITY Use PSYCHOMOTOR SKILLS
ACTIVITY LEVEL	(MOTOR BEHAVIOR) Use PHYSICAL ACTIVITY LEVEL
PERCEPTUAL	MOTOR COORDINATION
	MOTOR DEVELOPMENT
PERCEPTUAL	MOTOR LEARNING
SENSORY	MOTOR LEARNING Use PERCEPTUAL MOTOR LEARNING
	MOTOR OILS Use LUBRICANTS
	MOTOR REACTIONS
	MOTOR SKILLS Use PSYCHOMOTOR SKILLS
	MOTOR VEHICLES
	MOTORBOAT OPERATORS Use BOAT OPERATORS
ELECTRIC	MOTORS
	MOURNING Use GRIEF
	MOVABLE PARTITIONS
	MOVEMENT Use MOTION
	MOVEMENT EDUCATION
NORTHWARD	MOVEMENT Use MIGRATION
EYE	MOVEMENTS
POPULATION	MOVEMENTS Use MIGRATION
	MTMM METHODOLOGY Use MULTITRAIT MULTIMETHOD TECHNIQUES
	MULTICAMPUS COLLEGES
	MULTICAMPUS DISTRICTS
	MULTICHANNEL PROGRAMING (1966 1980) Use PROGRAMING (BROADCAST)
	MULTICULTURAL EDUCATION
	MULTICULTURAL TEXTBOOKS
	MULTICULTURAL TRAINING Use CROSS CULTURAL TRAINING
	MULTICULTURALISM Use CULTURAL PLURALISM
	MULTIDIMENSIONAL SCALING
	MULTIETHNIC EDUCATION Use MULTICULTURAL EDUCATION
	MULTIETHNIC TRAINING Use CROSS CULTURAL TRAINING
	MULTIGRADED CLASSES
	MULTILATERAL DISARMAMENT Use DISARMAMENT
	MULTILEVEL CLASSES (SECOND LANGUAGE INSTRUCTION)
	MULTILINGUAL MATERIALS
	MULTILINGUALISM
	MULTILITHING Use REPROGRAPHY
	MULTIMEDIA INSTRUCTION
MULTITRAIT	MULTIMETHOD TECHNIQUES
	MULTIPLE CHOICE TESTS
	MULTIPLE CORRELATION Use CORRELATION
	MULTIPLE DISABILITIES
	MULTIPLE DISCRIMINANT ANALYSIS Use DISCRIMINANT ANALYSIS
	MULTIPLE EMPLOYMENT
	MULTIPLE JOBHOLDING Use MULTIPLE EMPLOYMENT
	MULTIPLE MATRIX SAMPLING Use ITEM SAMPLING
	MULTIPLE REGRESSION ANALYSIS
	MULTIPLICATION
	MULTIPLY HANDICAPPED (1967 1980) Use MULTIPLE DISABILITIES
	MULTIPURPOSE CLASSROOMS
	MULTISENSORY LEARNING
	MULTITRAIT MULTIMETHOD TECHNIQUES
	MULTIUNIT SCHOOLS
	MULTIVARIATE ANALYSIS
	MULTIVARIATE ANALYSIS OF VARIANCE Use MULTIVARIATE ANALYSIS
	MULTIVARIATE STATISTICS Use MULTIVARIATE ANALYSIS
	MUNICIPAL GOVERNMENT Use CITY GOVERNMENT
	MUNICIPALITIES
	MUNUKUTABA Use KITUBA

MUSCLE SENSE Use KINESTHETIC PERCEPTION
MUSCULAR ACTIVITIES Use MOTOR REACTIONS
MUSCULAR EXERCISE Use EXERCISE
MUSCULAR EXTENSIONS Use MOTOR REACTIONS
MUSCULAR FLEXIONS Use MOTOR REACTIONS
MUSCULAR STRENGTH
MUSEUMS
MUSIC
MUSIC ACTIVITIES
APPLIED MUSIC
MUSIC APPRECIATION
ASIAN MUSIC Use ORIENTAL MUSIC
BANDS (MUSIC)
CHORAL MUSIC
COMPOSITION (MUSIC) Use MUSICAL COMPOSITION
MUSIC EDUCATION
MUSIC FACILITIES
ORIENTAL MUSIC
PRACTICAL MUSIC Use APPLIED MUSIC
RAGTIME MUSIC Use JAZZ
MUSIC READING
SWING MUSIC Use JAZZ
MUSIC TEACHERS
MUSIC TECHNIQUES
MUSIC THEORY
MUSIC THERAPY
VOCAL MUSIC
MUSICAL COMPOSITION
MUSICAL INSTRUMENTS
MUSICIANS
SELF MUTILATION
MUTUAL INTELLIGIBILITY
MYOPIA
MYOSIS Use MYOPIA
MYSTICISM
MYTHIC CRITICISM (1969 1980)
MYTHOLOGY
MYTHS Use MYTHOLOGY
N C SYSTEMS Use NUMERICAL CONTROL
NARCOTICS
NARCOTICS ADDICTION Use DRUG ADDICTION
NARRATION
PERSONAL NARRATIVES
PERSONAL ACCOUNTS (NARRATIVES) Use PERSONAL NARRATIVES
NATALITY Use BIRTH RATE
NATIONAL COMPETENCY TESTS
NATIONAL DEFENSE
NATIONAL DEMOGRAPHY (1966 1980) Use DEMOGRAPHY
NATIONAL INTELLIGENCE NORM (1966 1980) Use INTELLIGENCE and NATIONAL NORMS
NATIONAL LANGUAGES Use OFFICIAL LANGUAGES
NATIONAL LIBRARIES
NATIONAL NORMS
NATIONAL ORGANIZATIONS
NATIONAL PROGRAMS
NATIONAL SECURITY
NATIONAL SOCIALISM Use NAZISM
NATIONAL SURVEYS
NATIONALISM
BLACK NATIONALISM Use BLACK POWER
FOREIGN NATIONALS
ADVANCED NATIONS Use DEVELOPED NATIONS
DEVELOPED NATIONS
DEVELOPING NATIONS
ECONOMICALLY ADVANCED NATIONS Use DEVELOPED NATIONS
EMERGING NATIONS Use DEVELOPING NATIONS
INDUSTRIAL NATIONS Use DEVELOPED NATIONS
LAW OF NATIONS Use INTERNATIONAL LAW
UNDERDEVELOPED NATIONS Use DEVELOPING NATIONS
NATIVE INFORMANTS Use NATIVE SPEAKERS
NATIVE LANGUAGE INSTRUCTION
NATIVE MIGRANTS Use MIGRANTS
NATIVE SPEAKERS
NATIVES Use INDIGENOUS POPULATIONS
ALASKA NATIVES
CANADA NATIVES
NATURAL DISASTERS
NATURAL GASES Use FUELS
NATURAL PARENTS Use BIOLOGICAL PARENTS
NATURAL RESOURCES
NATURAL SCIENCES
NATURALISM
NATURALISTIC OBSERVATION
NATURE CENTERS
NATURE NURTURE CONTROVERSY
NATURE TRAILS Use TRAILS
NAVAHO (1967 1978) Use NAVAJO
NAVAJO
NAVAL AIR STATIONS Use MILITARY AIR FACILITIES
NAVIGATION
NAZISM
NEO NAZISM Use NAZISM
NEAR EASTERN HISTORY Use MIDDLE EASTERN HISTORY
NEARSIGHTEDNESS Use MYOPIA
ACHIEVEMENT NEED
AFFILIATION NEED
NEED ANALYSIS (STUDENT FINANCIAL AID)
NEED GRATIFICATION
NEED REDUCTION Use NEED GRATIFICATION
NO NEED SCHOLARSHIPS
STATUS NEED
NEEDLE TRADES

NEEDS
NEEDS ASSESSMENT
CHILDHOOD NEEDS
CHILDRENS NEEDS Use CHILDHOOD NEEDS
CONSTRUCTION NEEDS
DATA NEEDS Use INFORMATION NEEDS
DESIGN NEEDS (1968 1980) Use DESIGN REQUIREMENTS
EDUCATIONAL NEEDS
EMOTIONAL NEEDS Use PSYCHOLOGICAL NEEDS
EVALUATION NEEDS
FACILITY NEEDS Use FACILITY REQUIREMENTS
FINANCIAL NEEDS
HEALTH NEEDS
HOUSING NEEDS
INDIVIDUAL NEEDS
SPECIAL NEEDS (INDIVIDUALS) Use INDIVIDUAL NEEDS
INFORMATION NEEDS
USER NEEDS (INFORMATION)
INFORMATION USER NEEDS Use USER NEEDS (INFORMATION)
LABOR NEEDS
LIBRARY USER NEEDS Use USER NEEDS (INFORMATION)
MANPOWER NEEDS (1968 1980) Use LABOR NEEDS
PERSONNEL NEEDS
PHYSICAL DESIGN NEEDS (1968 1980) Use DESIGN REQUIREMENTS
PSYCHOLOGICAL NEEDS
PSYCHOLOGICAL DESIGN NEEDS (1968 1980) Use DESIGN REQUIREMENTS
RESEARCH NEEDS
STUDENT NEEDS
NEGATIVE ATTITUDES
NEGATIVE FORMS (LANGUAGE)
NEGATIVE INCOME TAX Use GUARANTEED INCOME
NEGATIVE PRACTICE
NEGATIVE REINFORCEMENT
MASSED NEGATIVE REINFORCEMENT Use NEGATIVE REINFORCEMENT
SPACED NEGATIVE REINFORCEMENT Use NEGATIVE REINFORCEMENT
CHILD NEGLECT
NEGLECTED CHILDREN (1977 1980) Use CHILD NEGLECT
NEGLECTED LANGUAGES Use UNCOMMONLY TAUGHT LANGUAGES
NEGOTIATION AGREEMENTS
COLLECTIVE NEGOTIATION (1967 1977) Use COLLECTIVE BARGAINING
NEGOTIATION IMPASSES
PROFESSIONAL NEGOTIATION Use COLLECTIVE BARGAINING
NEGRO ACHIEVEMENT (1966 1977) Use BLACK ACHIEVEMENT
NEGRO ATTITUDES (1966 1977) Use BLACK ATTITUDES
NEGRO BUSINESSES (1967 1977) Use BLACK BUSINESSES
NEGRO COLLEGES (1968 1977) Use BLACK COLLEGES
NEGRO COMMUNITY Use BLACK COMMUNITY
NEGRO CULTURE (1966 1977) Use BLACK CULTURE
NEGRO DIALECTS (1966 1977) Use BLACK DIALECTS
NEGRO EDUCATION (1966 1977) Use BLACK EDUCATION
NEGRO EMPLOYMENT (1966 1977) Use BLACK EMPLOYMENT
NEGRO HISTORY (1966 1977) Use BLACK HISTORY
NEGRO HOUSING (1966 1977)
NEGRO INSTITUTIONS (1966 1977) Use BLACK INSTITUTIONS
NEGRO LEADERSHIP (1966 1977) Use BLACK LEADERSHIP
NEGRO LITERATURE (1968 1977) Use BLACK LITERATURE
NEGRO MOTHERS (1966 1977) Use BLACK MOTHERS
NEGRO ORGANIZATIONS (1966 1977) Use BLACK ORGANIZATIONS
NEGRO POPULATION TRENDS (1966 1977) Use BLACK POPULATION TRENDS
NEGRO ROLE (1966 1977) Use BLACK INFLUENCES
NEGRO STEREOTYPES (1966 1977) Use BLACK STEREOTYPES
NEGRO STUDENTS (1966 1977) Use BLACK STUDENTS
NEGRO STUDIES Use BLACK STUDIES
NEGRO TEACHERS (1966 1977) Use BLACK TEACHERS
NEGRO YOUTH (1966 1977) Use BLACK YOUTH
NEGROES (1966 1977) Use BLACKS
AMERICAN NEGROES Use BLACKS
NEIGHBORHOOD (1966 1980) Use NEIGHBORHOODS
NEIGHBORHOOD CENTERS (1966 1980) Use COMMUNITY CENTERS
NEIGHBORHOOD IMPROVEMENT
NEIGHBORHOOD INTEGRATION
NEIGHBORHOOD SCHOOL POLICY (1966 1980) Use NEIGHBORHOOD SCHOOLS and SCHOOL POLICY
NEIGHBORHOOD SCHOOLS
NEIGHBORHOOD SETTLEMENTS Use SETTLEMENT HOUSES
NEIGHBORHOODS
INTEGRATED NEIGHBORHOODS Use NEIGHBORHOOD INTEGRATION
NEMBE
NEO NAZISM Use NAZISM
ENGLISH NEOCLASSIC LITERARY PERIOD (1968 1980)
NEOCLASSICISM
NEONATES
MALIGNANT NEOPLASMS Use CANCER
NEOPSYCHOANALYSIS Use PSYCHIATRY
NEPALI
ANOREXIA NERVOSA
NETWORK ANALYSIS
NETWORKS
COMMUNICATIONS NETWORKS Use COMMUNICATIONS
COMPUTER NETWORKS
INFORMATION NETWORKS
LIBRARY NETWORKS
LOCAL AREA NETWORKS
SUPPORT NETWORKS (PERSONAL ASSISTANCE) Use SOCIAL SUPPORT GROUPS
SOCIAL NETWORKS
NEUROLINGUISTICS
NEUROLOGICAL DEFECTS (1966 1980) Use NEUROLOGICAL IMPAIRMENTS
NEUROLOGICAL IMPAIRMENTS
NEUROLOGICAL ORGANIZATION
NEUROLOGICALLY HANDICAPPED (1966 1980) Use NEUROLOGICAL IMPAIRMENTS
NEUROLOGY
NEUROSIS

NEUROTIC CHILDREN (1966 1980) Use NEUROSIS
NEW JOURNALISM
NEW MATHEMATICS Use MODERN MATHEMATICS
NEWBORN INFANTS Use NEONATES
NEWS MEDIA
NEWS REPORTING
SPORTS NEWS Use ATHLETICS and NEWS MEDIA
NEWS WRITING
NEWSLETTERS
NEWSPAPERS
CLASS NEWSPAPERS (1967 1980) Use CLASS ACTIVITIES and STUDENT PUBLICATIONS
SCHOOL NEWSPAPERS
COLLEGE NIGHT Use COLLEGE DAY
NIGHT SCHOOLS (1966 1980) Use EVENING PROGRAMS
NINETEENTH CENTURY LITERATURE
CREDIT NO CREDIT GRADING
PASS NO CREDIT GRADING Use CREDIT NO CREDIT GRADING
NO NEED SCHOLARSHIPS
PASS NO RECORD GRADING Use CREDIT NO CREDIT GRADING
NO SHOWS
NOISE CONTROL Use NOISE (SOUND)
NOISE LEVELS Use NOISE (SOUND)
NOISE POLLUTION Use NOISE (SOUND)
NOISE (SOUND)
NOISE TESTING Use NOISE (SOUND)
NOMADS
CHEMICAL NOMENCLATURE
NOMINALS (1967 1980) Use NOUNS
POLITICAL NOMINEES Use POLITICAL CANDIDATES
NON DISCURSIVE MEASURES Use VISUAL MEASURES
NON ENGLISH SPEAKING
NON WESTERN CIVILIZATION
NONAUTHORITARIAN CLASSES
NONBOOK MATERIALS Use NONPRINT MEDIA
NONCAMPUS COLLEGES
NONCOLLEGE BOUND STUDENTS
NONCOLLEGE PREPARATORY STUDENTS (1967 1980) Use NONCOLLEGE BOUND STUDENTS
NONCOMPLIANCE (PSYCHOLOGY) Use COMPLIANCE (PSYCHOLOGY)
NONCREDIT COURSES
NONDIRECTIVE COUNSELING
NONDISCRIMINATORY EDUCATION
NONFARM AGRICULTURAL OCCUPATIONS Use OFF FARM AGRICULTURAL OCCUPATIONS
RURAL NONFARM RESIDENTS
NONFICTION
NONFORMAL EDUCATION
NONGRADED CLASSES (1966 1980) Use NONGRADED INSTRUCTIONAL GROUPING
NONGRADED INSTRUCTIONAL GROUPING
NONGRADED PRIMARY SYSTEM (1966 1980) Use NONGRADED INSTRUCTIONAL GROUPING
NONGRADED STUDENT EVALUATION
NONGRADED SYSTEM (1966 1980) Use NONGRADED INSTRUCTIONAL GROUPING
NONINSTRUCTIONAL RESPONSIBILITY
NONINSTRUCTIONAL STUDENT COSTS
NONMAJORS
NONORGANIC FAILURE TO THRIVE Use FAILURE TO THRIVE
NONPARAMETRIC STATISTICS
LABOR FORCE NONPARTICIPANTS
NONPRINT MEDIA
NONPROFESSIONAL PERSONNEL
NONPROFIT ORGANIZATIONS
NONPUBLIC AGENCIES Use PRIVATE AGENCIES
NONPUBLIC EDUCATION Use PRIVATE EDUCATION
NONPUBLIC SCHOOL AID (1972 1980) Use PRIVATE SCHOOL AID
NONPUBLIC SCHOOLS Use PRIVATE SCHOOLS
NONRESERVATION AMERICAN INDIANS
NONRESIDENT FARMERS Use PART TIME FARMERS
NONRESIDENT STUDENTS (1967 1980) (FOREIGN) Use FOREIGN STUDENTS
NONRESIDENT STUDENTS (1967 1980) (OUT OF DISTRICT) Use RESIDENCE REQUIREMENTS
NONRESIDENT STUDENTS (1967 1980) (OUT OF STATE) Use OUT OF STATE STUDENTS
NONRESIDENTIAL SCHOOLS (1967 1980) Use COMMUTER COLLEGES
NONREVERSAL SHIFT Use SHIFT STUDIES
NONSCHOOL EDUCATIONAL PROGRAMS
NONSPECIALISTS Use LAY PEOPLE
NONSTANDARD DIALECTS
NONTEACHING DUTIES Use NONINSTRUCTIONAL RESPONSIBILITY
NONTENURED FACULTY
NONTENURED TEACHERS Use NONTENURED FACULTY
NONTRADITIONAL CAREERS Use NONTRADITIONAL OCCUPATIONS
NONTRADITIONAL EDUCATION
NONTRADITIONAL OCCUPATIONS
NONTRADITIONAL STUDENTS
NONVERBAL ABILITY
NONVERBAL COMMUNICATION
GESTURES (NONVERBAL COMMUNICATION) Use BODY LANGUAGE
NONVERBAL LEARNING
NONVERBAL TESTS
MIDDLE CLASS NORM (1966 1980) Use MIDDLE CLASS STANDARDS
NATIONAL INTELLIGENCE NORM (1966 1980) Use INTELLIGENCE and NATIONAL NORMS
NORM REFERENCED MEASURES Use NORM REFERENCED TESTS
NORM REFERENCED TESTS
NORMALIZATION (HANDICAPPED)
NORMATIVE BEHAVIOR Use BEHAVIOR STANDARDS
NORMS
COUNTY NORMS Use LOCAL NORMS
DISTRICT NORMS Use LOCAL NORMS
GROUP NORMS (1968 1980)
LOCAL NORMS
NATIONAL NORMS
SCHOOL DISTRICT NORMS Use LOCAL NORMS
SOCIAL NORMS Use BEHAVIOR STANDARDS and SOCIAL BEHAVIOR
STATE NORMS
TEST NORMS

NORTH AMERICAN CULTURE
NORTH AMERICAN ENGLISH
NORTH AMERICAN HISTORY
NORTH AMERICAN LITERATURE
NORTH AMERICANS
NORTHERN ATTITUDES (1968 1980) Use REGIONAL ATTITUDES
NORTHERN SCHOOLS (1966 1980)
NORTHWARD MOVEMENT Use MIGRATION
NORWEGIAN
LESSON NOTES Use LESSON PLANS
NOTETAKING
NOTIONAL FUNCTIONAL SYLLABI
FUNCTIONAL NOTIONAL SYLLABI Use NOTIONAL FUNCTIONAL SYLLABI
NOUNS
NOVELLA Use NOVELS
NOVELS
SOCIOLOGICAL NOVELS (1969 1980) Use NOVELS
NOVELTY (STIMULUS DIMENSION)
NUCLEAR CONTROL Use DISARMAMENT
NUCLEAR ENERGY
NUCLEAR ENERGY OCCUPATIONS Use ENERGY OCCUPATIONS and NUCLEAR ENERGY
NUCLEAR FAMILY
NUCLEAR MEDICINE Use RADIOLOGY
NUCLEAR MEDICINE TECHNOLOGISTS Use RADIOLOGIC TECHNOLOGISTS
NUCLEAR PHYSICS
NUCLEAR POWER PLANT TECHNICIANS
NUCLEAR POWER PLANTS
NUCLEAR TECHNOLOGY
NUCLEAR WARFARE
NUCLEIC ACIDS
NUMBER CONCEPTS
NUMBER OPERATIONS Use ARITHMETIC
NUMBER SKILLS TESTS Use MATHEMATICS TESTS
NUMBER SYSTEMS
NUMBER USE Use NUMBERS
NUMBERS
INDEX NUMBERS (COSTS) Use COST INDEXES
PRIME NUMBERS
RATIONAL NUMBERS
WHOLE NUMBERS
NUMERIC FILING Use FILING
NUMERICAL CONTROL
NUN TEACHERS (1966 1980) Use NUNS
NUNS
NURSE PRACTITIONERS
SCHOOL NURSE PRACTITIONERS Use NURSE PRACTITIONERS and SCHOOL NURSES
NURSERIES (HORTICULTURE)
NURSERY SCHOOLS
NURSERY WORKERS (HORTICULTURE)
NURSES
NURSES AIDES
CERTIFIED NURSES Use NURSES
LICENSED NURSES Use NURSES
PRACTICAL NURSES (1967 1981) Use NURSES and PRACTICAL NURSING
PROFESSIONAL NURSES Use NURSES
REGISTERED NURSES Use NURSES
SCHOOL NURSES
TEACHER NURSES (1966 1980) Use NURSES
NURSING
NURSING AIDES Use NURSES AIDES
NURSING ASSISTANTS Use NURSES AIDES
NURSING EDUCATION
NURSING HOMES
PRACTICAL NURSING
VOCATIONAL NURSING Use PRACTICAL NURSING
NATURE NURTURE CONTROVERSY
NUTRITION
NUTRITION INSTRUCTION
NYANJA Use CHINYANJA
LOYALTY OATHS
OBEDIENCE
OBESITY
OBJECT CONCEPT Use OBJECT PERMANENCE
OBJECT MANIPULATION
OBJECT PERMANENCE
OBJECTIVE REFERENCED TESTS Use CRITERION REFERENCED TESTS
OBJECTIVE TESTS
OBJECTIVELY SCORED TESTS Use OBJECTIVE TESTS
OBJECTIVES
AFFECTIVE OBJECTIVES
BEHAVIORAL OBJECTIVES
CAREER OBJECTIVES Use CAREER CHOICE
COGNITIVE OBJECTIVES
COUNSELING OBJECTIVES
COURSE OBJECTIVES
EDUCATIONAL OBJECTIVES
GUIDANCE OBJECTIVES
INSTITUTIONAL OBJECTIVES Use ORGANIZATIONAL OBJECTIVES
LEARNING OBJECTIVES Use BEHAVIORAL OBJECTIVES
MANAGEMENT BY OBJECTIVES
MEASUREMENT OBJECTIVES
EDUCATIONAL OBJECTIVES OF STUDENTS Use STUDENT EDUCATIONAL OBJECTIVES
ORGANIZATIONAL OBJECTIVES
PERFORMANCE OBJECTIVES Use BEHAVIORAL OBJECTIVES
PSYCHOMOTOR OBJECTIVES
STUDENT EDUCATIONAL OBJECTIVES
TRAINING OBJECTIVES
PARENTAL OBLIGATIONS Use PARENT RESPONSIBILITY
OBLIQUE ROTATION
OBSCENITY
OBSERVATION

LESSON	OBSERVATION CRITERIA
NATURALISTIC	OBSERVATION
PARTICIPANT	OBSERVATION
CLASSROOM	OBSERVATION TECHNIQUES
	OBSERVATIONAL LEARNING
	OBSOLESCENCE
BUILDING	OBSOLESCENCE
SKILL	OBSOLESCENCE
	OBSTETRICS
	OBTAINED SCORES Use RAW SCORES
	OCCIDENTAL CIVILIZATION Use WESTERN CIVILIZATION
JOINT	OCCUPANCY Use SHARED FACILITIES
AUTO MECHANICS	(OCCUPATION) (1968 1980) Use AUTO MECHANICS
COMPANIONS	(OCCUPATION) (1968 1980) Use ATTENDANTS
FARM MECHANICS	(OCCUPATION) (1967 1980) Use AGRICULTURAL MACHINERY OCCUPATIONS
ORNAMENTAL HORTICULTURE	OCCUPATION (1967 1976) Use ORNAMENTAL HORTICULTURE OCCUPATIONS
TEACHING	(OCCUPATION)
	OCCUPATIONAL ADJUSTMENT Use VOCATIONAL ADJUSTMENT
ADMISSION TESTS	(OCCUPATIONAL) Use OCCUPATIONAL TESTS
	OCCUPATIONAL ANALYSIS Use JOB ANALYSIS
	OCCUPATIONAL ASPIRATION
	OCCUPATIONAL ASPIRATION LEVEL Use OCCUPATIONAL ASPIRATION
	OCCUPATIONAL AWARENESS Use CAREER AWARENESS
	OCCUPATIONAL CHOICE (1966 1980) Use CAREER CHOICE
	OCCUPATIONAL CLUSTERS
	OCCUPATIONAL COUNSELING Use CAREER COUNSELING
	OCCUPATIONAL DISEASES
SUPERVISED	OCCUPATIONAL EXPERIENCE (AGRICULTURE) Use SUPERVISED FARM PRACTICE
	OCCUPATIONAL EXPLORATION Use CAREER EXPLORATION
	OCCUPATIONAL FAMILIES Use OCCUPATIONAL CLUSTERS
	OCCUPATIONAL FOLLOWUP Use VOCATIONAL FOLLOWUP
	OCCUPATIONAL GUIDANCE (1966 1980) Use CAREER GUIDANCE
	OCCUPATIONAL HEALTH Use OCCUPATIONAL SAFETY AND HEALTH
	OCCUPATIONAL HOME ECONOMICS
	OCCUPATIONAL INFORMATION
	OCCUPATIONAL LEVEL Use EMPLOYMENT LEVEL
	OCCUPATIONAL MOBILITY
PROMOTION	(OCCUPATIONAL)
	OCCUPATIONAL PSYCHOLOGY Use INDUSTRIAL PSYCHOLOGY
	OCCUPATIONAL SAFETY AND HEALTH
	OCCUPATIONAL SAFETY AND HEALTH STANDARDS Use LABOR STANDARDS and OCCUPATIONAL SAFETY AND HEALTH
	OCCUPATIONAL SATISFACTION Use JOB SATISFACTION
	OCCUPATIONAL SUCCESSION Use OCCUPATIONAL MOBILITY
	OCCUPATIONAL SURVEYS
	OCCUPATIONAL TESTS
	OCCUPATIONAL THERAPISTS
	OCCUPATIONAL THERAPY
	OCCUPATIONAL THERAPY ASSISTANTS
	OCCUPATIONAL TRAINING Use JOB TRAINING
	OCCUPATIONS
ADMINISTRATIVE	OCCUPATIONS Use MANAGERIAL OCCUPATIONS
AGRICULTURAL	OCCUPATIONS
AGRICULTURAL CHEMICAL	OCCUPATIONS
AGRICULTURAL MACHINERY	OCCUPATIONS
AGRICULTURAL SUPPLY	OCCUPATIONS
ALLIED HEALTH	OCCUPATIONS
ALLIED MEDICAL	OCCUPATIONS Use ALLIED HEALTH OCCUPATIONS
BLUE COLLAR	OCCUPATIONS
HEALTH	OCCUPATIONS CENTERS (1968 1980)
CHILD CARE	OCCUPATIONS
CLERICAL	OCCUPATIONS
CONSTRUCTION	OCCUPATIONS Use BUILDING TRADES
CROP PROCESSING	OCCUPATIONS
DATA PROCESSING	OCCUPATIONS
DEMAND	OCCUPATIONS
DRYCLEANING LAUNDRY	OCCUPATIONS Use LAUNDRY DRYCLEANING OCCUPATIONS
ALLIED HEALTH	OCCUPATIONS EDUCATION
HEALTH	OCCUPATIONS EDUCATION (1967 1980) Use ALLIED HEALTH OCCUPATIONS EDUCATION
OFFICE	OCCUPATIONS EDUCATION
HEALTH	OCCUPATIONS EDUCATION (VOCATIONAL) Use ALLIED HEALTH OCCUPATIONS EDUCATION and VOCATIONAL EDUCATION
ELECTRICAL	OCCUPATIONS
ELECTROMECHANICAL	OCCUPATIONS Use ELECTRICAL OCCUPATIONS and ELECTROMECHANICAL TECHNOLOGY
EMERGING	OCCUPATIONS
ENERGY	OCCUPATIONS
FARM	OCCUPATIONS
FARM RELATED	OCCUPATIONS Use OFF FARM AGRICULTURAL OCCUPATIONS
FINANCE	OCCUPATIONS
FOOD PROCESSING	OCCUPATIONS
FOOD SERVICE	OCCUPATIONS (1968 1981) Use FOOD SERVICE
FORESTRY	OCCUPATIONS
GRAIN ELEVATOR	OCCUPATIONS Use CROP PROCESSING OCCUPATIONS
HEALTH	OCCUPATIONS
HOSPITALITY	OCCUPATIONS
HOUSEHOLD	OCCUPATIONS Use HOUSEHOLD WORKERS and SERVICE OCCUPATIONS
INSURANCE	OCCUPATIONS
LAUNDRY DRYCLEANING	OCCUPATIONS
MANAGERIAL	OCCUPATIONS
METAL FORMING	OCCUPATIONS Use METAL WORKING
METAL WORKING	OCCUPATIONS (1968 1980) Use METAL WORKING
NONFARM AGRICULTURAL	OCCUPATIONS Use OFF FARM AGRICULTURAL OCCUPATIONS
NONTRADITIONAL	OCCUPATIONS
NUCLEAR ENERGY	OCCUPATIONS Use ENERGY OCCUPATIONS and NUCLEAR ENERGY
OFF FARM AGRICULTURAL	OCCUPATIONS
OFFICE	OCCUPATIONS
ORNAMENTAL HORTICULTURE	OCCUPATIONS
PARAMEDICAL	OCCUPATIONS (1967 1980) Use ALLIED HEALTH OCCUPATIONS
HEALTH	OCCUPATIONS PERSONNEL Use HEALTH PERSONNEL
PROFESSIONAL	OCCUPATIONS
PUBLIC SERVICE	OCCUPATIONS

REAL ESTATE OCCUPATIONS
SALES OCCUPATIONS
SEMISKILLED OCCUPATIONS
SERVICE OCCUPATIONS
SKILLED OCCUPATIONS
STRUCTURAL WORK OCCUPATIONS Use BUILDING TRADES
TECHNICAL OCCUPATIONS
UNSKILLED OCCUPATIONS
WHITE COLLAR OCCUPATIONS
OCEAN ENGINEERING
OCEANOGRAPHY
OCEANOLOGY (1966 1980) Use OCEANOGRAPHY
OCR Use CHARACTER RECOGNITION and OPTICAL SCANNERS
OCULAR REFRACTIVE ERRORS Use AMETROPIA
ODES
LEAVE OF ABSENCE (1968 1980) Use LEAVES OF ABSENCE
LEAVES OF ABSENCE
BACHELOR OF ARTS DEGREES Use BACHELORS DEGREES
DOCTOR OF ARTS DEGREES
MASTER OF ARTS DEGREES Use MASTERS DEGREES
MASTER OF ARTS IN COLLEGE TEACHING Use MASTERS DEGREES
MASTER OF ARTS IN TEACHING Use MASTERS DEGREES
SCOPE OF BARGAINING
INTERNAL EXTERNAL LOCUS OF CONTROL Use LOCUS OF CONTROL
LOCUS OF CONTROL
ANALYSIS OF COVARIANCE
VICTIMS OF CRIME
SCHOOLS OF DENTISTRY Use DENTAL SCHOOLS
STAGES OF DEVELOPMENT Use DEVELOPMENTAL STAGES
ADAPTIVE BEHAVIOR (OF DISABLED)
DEINSTITUTIONALIZATION (OF DISABLED)
NONRESIDENT STUDENTS (1967 1980) (OUT OF DISTRICT) Use RESIDENCE REQUIREMENTS
BOARDS OF EDUCATION
COLLEGES OF EDUCATION Use SCHOOLS OF EDUCATION
CONTINUITY OF EDUCATION Use DEVELOPMENTAL CONTINUITY
ECONOMICS OF EDUCATION Use EDUCATIONAL ECONOMICS
EQUALITY OF EDUCATION Use EQUAL EDUCATION
FOUNDATIONS OF EDUCATION
HISTORY OF EDUCATION Use EDUCATIONAL HISTORY
BOARD OF EDUCATION MEMBERS Use BOARDS OF EDUCATION
OUTCOMES OF EDUCATION
BOARD OF EDUCATION POLICY
POLITICS OF EDUCATION
RESULTS OF EDUCATION Use OUTCOMES OF EDUCATION
ROLE OF EDUCATION
BOARD OF EDUCATION ROLE
SCHOOLS OF EDUCATION
STATE BOARDS OF EDUCATION
STATE DEPARTMENTS OF EDUCATION
SUPPLY OF EDUCATION Use EDUCATIONAL SUPPLY
MAGNITUDE OF EFFECT Use EFFECT SIZE
RETENTION (OF EMPLOYEES) Use LABOR TURNOVER
STANDARD ERROR OF ESTIMATE Use ERROR OF MEASUREMENT
CODES OF ETHICS
CENTROID METHOD OF FACTOR ANALYSIS Use FACTOR ANALYSIS
DEANS OF FACULTY Use ACADEMIC DEANS
GRAYING OF FACULTY Use AGING IN ACADEMIA
GOODNESS OF FIT
DELAY OF GRATIFICATION
HARD OF HEARING (1967 1980) Use PARTIAL HEARING
HEADS OF HOUSEHOLDS
OWNERSHIP OF IDEAS Use INTELLECTUAL PROPERTY
FREEDOM OF INFORMATION
SELECTIVE DISSEMINATION OF INFORMATION
COURSE OF INSTRUCTION Use COURSE ORGANIZATION
DEANS OF INSTRUCTION Use ACADEMIC DEANS
LANGUAGE OF INSTRUCTION
MEDIUM OF INSTRUCTION (LANGUAGE) Use LANGUAGE OF INSTRUCTION
CENTERS OF INTEREST (1966 1980) Use LEARNING CENTERS (CLASSROOM)
CONFLICT OF INTEREST
SUPPLY OF LABOR Use LABOR SUPPLY
HISTORY OF LANGUAGE Use DIACHRONIC LINGUISTICS
TRANSFER OF LEARNING Use TRANSFER OF TRAINING
STATE BOARDS OF LICENSING Use STATE LICENSING BOARDS
QUALITY OF LIFE
COMEDY OF MANNERS Use COMEDY
ERROR OF MEASUREMENT
STANDARD ERROR OF MEASUREMENT (1970 1980) Use ERROR OF MEASUREMENT
SCHOOLS OF MEDICINE Use MEDICAL SCHOOLS
DEANS OF MEN Use DEANS OF STUDENTS
LAW OF NATIONS Use INTERNATIONAL LAW
LABELING (OF PERSONS)
LAW OF PRIMACY Use PRIMACY EFFECT
TERMINATION OF PROGRAMS Use PROGRAM TERMINATION
ERROR OF REFRACTION Use AMETROPIA
BOARD OF REGENTS Use GOVERNING BOARDS
DIRECTORS OF RESEARCH Use RESEARCH DIRECTORS
PLACE OF RESIDENCE
ALLOCATION OF RESOURCES Use RESOURCE ALLOCATION
KNOWLEDGE OF RESULTS Use FEEDBACK
OUT OF SCHOOL YOUTH
HOLDING POWER (OF SCHOOLS) Use SCHOOL HOLDING POWER
LOCAL AUTONOMY (OF SCHOOLS) Use SCHOOL DISTRICT AUTONOMY
LOCAL CONTROL (OF SCHOOLS) Use SCHOOL DISTRICT AUTONOMY
BACHELOR OF SCIENCE DEGREES Use BACHELORS DEGREES
MASTER OF SCIENCE DEGREES Use MASTERS DEGREES
MASTER OF SCIENCE IN TEACHING Use MASTERS DEGREES
TESTS OF SIGNIFICANCE (1966 1980) Use STATISTICAL SIGNIFICANCE
FUTURES (OF SOCIETY)
FIGURES OF SPEECH Use FIGURATIVE LANGUAGE
FREEDOM OF SPEECH

PARTS OF SPEECH Use FORM CLASSES (LANGUAGES)
NONRESIDENT STUDENTS (1967 1980) (OUT OF STATE) Use OUT OF STATE STUDENTS
OUT OF STATE STUDENTS
CLASSES (GROUPS OF STUDENTS)
DEANS OF STUDENTS
EDUCATIONAL GOALS OF STUDENTS Use STUDENT EDUCATIONAL OBJECTIVES
EDUCATIONAL OBJECTIVES OF STUDENTS Use STUDENT EDUCATIONAL OBJECTIVES
RETENTION (OF STUDENTS) Use SCHOOL HOLDING POWER
HIGHER EDUCATION AS A FIELD OF STUDY Use POSTSECONDARY EDUCATION AS A FIELD OF STUDY
POSTSECONDARY EDUCATION AS A FIELD OF STUDY
UNITS OF STUDY (SUBJECT FIELDS) (1966 1977) Use UNITS OF STUDY
UNITS OF STUDY
FEAR OF SUCCESS
STUDENT EVALUATION OF TEACHER PERFORMANCE
STATE OF THE ART REVIEWS
REVIEWS OF THE LITERATURE Use LITERATURE REVIEWS
FREEDOM OF THE PRESS Use FREEDOM OF SPEECH
PRESIDENTS OF THE UNITED STATES
FREEDOM OF THOUGHT Use INTELLECTUAL FREEDOM
TRANSFER OF TRAINING
OUTCOMES OF TREATMENT
TERMINATION OF TREATMENT
BOARD OF TRUSTEES Use GOVERNING BOARDS
ANALYSIS OF VARIANCE
MULTIVARIATE ANALYSIS OF VARIANCE Use MULTIVARIATE ANALYSIS
DEANS OF WOMEN Use DEANS OF STUDENTS
HOURS OF WORK Use WORKING HOURS
QUALITY OF WORKING LIFE
OFF CAMPUS EDUCATION Use EXTENSION EDUCATION
OFF CAMPUS FACILITIES
OFF CAMPUS STUDENT TEACHING Use STUDENT TEACHING
OFF FARM AGRICULTURAL OCCUPATIONS
OFF RESERVATION AMERICAN INDIANS Use NONRESERVATION AMERICAN INDIANS
OFF SITE TRAINING Use OFF THE JOB TRAINING
OFF THE JOB TRAINING
TRAINING SCHOOLS (JUVENILE OFFENDERS) Use CORRECTIONAL INSTITUTIONS
OFFICE COMMUNICATION Use ORGANIZATIONAL COMMUNICATION
OFFICE EDUCATION Use OFFICE OCCUPATIONS EDUCATION
OFFICE MACHINES
OFFICE MANAGEMENT
OFFICE OCCUPATIONS
OFFICE OCCUPATIONS EDUCATION
OFFICE PRACTICE
OFFICE SUPPLIES Use SUPPLIES
OFFICER PERSONNEL
ADMISSIONS OFFICERS
ATTENDANCE OFFICERS
BORDER PATROL OFFICERS Use IMMIGRATION INSPECTORS
CHIEF ACADEMIC OFFICERS Use ACADEMIC DEANS
LAW ENFORCEMENT OFFICERS Use POLICE
PAROLE OFFICERS
PROBATION OFFICERS
STUDENT FINANCIAL AID OFFICERS
OFFICES (FACILITIES)
FACULTY OFFICES Use OFFICES (FACILITIES)
STAFF OFFICES Use OFFICES (FACILITIES)
OFFICIAL LANGUAGES
CITY OFFICIALS
COUNTY OFFICIALS
ELECTED CITY OFFICIALS Use CITY OFFICIALS
BUSINESS OFFICIALS (INDUSTRY) Use ADMINISTRATORS
PUBLIC OFFICIALS
SCHOOL OFFICIALS Use SCHOOL PERSONNEL
BUSINESS OFFICIALS (SCHOOL) Use SCHOOL BUSINESS OFFICIALS
SCHOOL BUSINESS OFFICIALS
STATE OFFICIALS
FUEL OIL Use FUELS
HEATING OILS Use FUELS
MOTOR OILS Use LUBRICANTS
OJIBWA
OKINAWAN
OLD AGE Use OLDER ADULTS
OLD ENGLISH
OLD ENGLISH LITERATURE
OLDER ADULTS
OMBUDSMEN
ON CAMPUS STUDENTS
STATE COMMITTEES ON EDUCATION Use STATE BOARDS OF EDUCATION
ON LINE SYSTEMS (1971 1980) Use ONLINE SYSTEMS
DEFAULTING ON LOANS Use LOAN REPAYMENT
ON SITE TESTS Use FIELD TESTS
TIME ON TASK
ON THE JOB TRAINING
ONCOLOGY
ONE PARENT FAMILY
ONE ROOM SCHOOLS Use ONE TEACHER SCHOOLS
ONE TEACHER SCHOOLS
ONLINE CATALOGS
COMMERCIAL SEARCH SERVICES (ONLINE) Use ONLINE VENDORS
ONLINE INFORMATION RETRIEVAL Use ONLINE SEARCHING
INFORMATION UTILITIES (ONLINE) Use ONLINE VENDORS
INTERACTIVE SEARCHING (ONLINE) Use ONLINE SEARCHING
INTERACTIVE SYSTEMS (ONLINE) Use ONLINE SYSTEMS
ONLINE PUBLIC ACCESS CATALOGS Use ONLINE CATALOGS
ONLINE REFERENCE SERVICES Use ONLINE SYSTEMS and REFERENCE SERVICES
ONLINE SEARCHING
ONLINE SYSTEMS
ONLINE VENDORS
ONOMASTICS
ONOMATOLOGY Use ONOMASTICS
CO OP PROGRAMS Use COOPERATIVE PROGRAMS

	OPAQUE PROJECTORS
	OPEN ADMISSION Use OPEN ENROLLMENT
	OPEN AREA SCHOOLS Use OPEN PLAN SCHOOLS
	OPEN BOOK TESTS
	OPEN CIRCUIT TELEVISION (1966 1980) Use BROADCAST TELEVISION
	OPEN EDUCATION
	OPEN ENROLLMENT
	OPEN PLAN SCHOOLS
	OPEN SCHOOLS Use OPEN EDUCATION
	OPEN UNIVERSITIES
	OPERA
	OPERANT CONDITIONING
VERBAL	OPERANT CONDITIONING
	OPERATING ENGINEERING
	OPERATING EXPENSES
MINIMUM	OPERATING EXPENSES Use OPERATING EXPENSES
	OPERATING ROOM TECHNICIANS Use SURGICAL TECHNICIANS
BUILDING	OPERATION
	OPERATIONS ANALYSIS Use OPERATIONS RESEARCH
FORMAL	OPERATIONS
NUMBER	OPERATIONS Use ARITHMETIC
	OPERATIONS RESEARCH
	OPERATIONS (SURGERY) Use SURGERY
BEAUTY	OPERATORS Use COSMETOLOGY
BOAT	OPERATORS
DRILL PRESS	OPERATORS Use MACHINE TOOL OPERATORS
FARM	OPERATORS Use FARMERS
INDUSTRIAL X RAY	OPERATORS Use RADIOGRAPHERS
MACHINE TOOL	OPERATORS
MOTORBOAT	OPERATORS Use BOAT OPERATORS
PRODUCTION MACHINE	OPERATORS Use MACHINE TOOL OPERATORS
PUNCH PRESS	OPERATORS Use MACHINE TOOL OPERATORS
SEWING MACHINE	OPERATORS
SHEET METAL MACHINE	OPERATORS Use MACHINE TOOL OPERATORS and SHEET METAL WORK
	OPHTHALMOLOGY
COUNSELOR	OPINION Use COUNSELOR ATTITUDES
	OPINION PAPERS
PRESS	OPINION
PUBLIC	OPINION
	OPINION SCALES Use ATTITUDE MEASURES
STUDENT	OPINION (1966 1980) Use STUDENT ATTITUDES
	OPINIONS
ADMINISTRATOR	OPINIONS Use ADMINISTRATOR ATTITUDES
EMPLOYEE	OPINIONS Use EMPLOYEE ATTITUDES
EMPLOYER	OPINIONS Use EMPLOYER ATTITUDES
PARENT	OPINIONS Use PARENT ATTITUDES
TEACHER	OPINIONS Use TEACHER ATTITUDES
	OPPORTUNITIES
CAREER	OPPORTUNITIES (1966 1980)
CULTURAL	OPPORTUNITIES
ECONOMIC	OPPORTUNITIES
EDUCATIONAL	OPPORTUNITIES
EDUCATIONAL EQUITY	(OPPORTUNITIES) Use EQUAL EDUCATION
EMPLOYMENT	OPPORTUNITIES
EQUAL EDUCATIONAL	OPPORTUNITIES Use EQUAL EDUCATION
EQUITY (EDUCATIONAL	OPPORTUNITIES) Use EQUAL EDUCATION
HOUSING	OPPORTUNITIES
JOB	OPPORTUNITIES Use EMPLOYMENT OPPORTUNITIES
EQUAL	OPPORTUNITIES (JOBS)
RESEARCH	OPPORTUNITIES
SOCIAL	OPPORTUNITIES (1966 1980) Use SOCIAL MOBILITY
TRAINING	OPPORTUNITIES Use EDUCATIONAL OPPORTUNITIES
YOUTH	OPPORTUNITIES
	OPPORTUNITY CLASSES (1966 1980) Use SPECIAL CLASSES
COMPENSATORY	OPPORTUNITY Use COMPENSATORY EDUCATION
CO	OPS Use COOPERATIVES
	OPTICAL CHARACTER RECOGNITION Use CHARACTER RECOGNITION and OPTICAL SCANNERS
	OPTICAL DATA DISKS
DIGITAL	OPTICAL DATA DISKS Use OPTICAL DATA DISKS
	OPTICAL DISKS
	OPTICAL MASERS Use LASERS
	OPTICAL SCANNERS
	OPTICAL SPECTRUM Use LIGHT
	OPTICAL VIDEODISKS Use OPTICAL DISKS and VIDEODISKS
	OPTICS
GEOMETRICAL	OPTICS Use OPTICS
PHYSICAL	OPTICS Use OPTICS
	OPTIONAL BRANCHING (1966 1980) Use BRANCHING
	OPTIONAL COURSES Use ELECTIVE COURSES
	OPTOMETRISTS
	OPTOMETRY
PUBLISH	OR PERISH ISSUE
	ORAL COMMUNICATION (1966 1977) Use SPEECH COMMUNICATION
	ORAL COMMUNICATION METHOD
	ORAL ENGLISH
	ORAL EXPRESSION (1966 1977) Use SPEECH COMMUNICATION
	ORAL FACILITY Use SPEECH SKILLS
	ORAL HISTORY
	ORAL HYGIENISTS Use DENTAL HYGIENISTS
	ORAL INTERPRETATION
	ORAL LANGUAGE
	ORAL READING
	ORAL SKILLS Use SPEECH SKILLS
AURAL	ORAL SKILLS Use AUDIOLINGUAL SKILLS
	ORBITING SATELLITES Use SATELLITES (AEROSPACE)
	ORCHESTRAS
REPERTORY	ORCHESTRAS Use ORCHESTRAS
SYMPHONY	ORCHESTRAS Use ORCHESTRAS
BIRTH	ORDER
SERIAL	ORDERING
	ORGAN DONORS Use TISSUE DONORS

ORGANIC CHEMISTRY
ORGANIC CURRICULUM Use STUDENT CENTERED CURRICULUM
ORGANIZATION
ADMINISTRATIVE ORGANIZATION
CLASS ORGANIZATION
COURSE ORGANIZATION
GRADE ORGANIZATION (1966 1980) Use INSTRUCTIONAL PROGRAM DIVISIONS
HIGH SCHOOL ORGANIZATION (1966 1980) Use SCHOOL ORGANIZATION
HORIZONTAL ORGANIZATION
INFORMAL ORGANIZATION
NEUROLOGICAL ORGANIZATION
PYRAMID ORGANIZATION
SCHOOL ORGANIZATION
SIX THREE THREE ORGANIZATION Use INSTRUCTIONAL PROGRAM DIVISIONS
ORGANIZATION SIZE (GROUPS)
VERTICAL ORGANIZATION
ORGANIZATIONAL CHANGE
ORGANIZATIONAL CLIMATE
ORGANIZATIONAL COMMUNICATION
ORGANIZATIONAL DEVELOPMENT
ORGANIZATIONAL EFFECTIVENESS
ORGANIZATIONAL GOALS Use ORGANIZATIONAL OBJECTIVES
ORGANIZATIONAL OBJECTIVES
ORGANIZATIONAL PLANS Use PLANNING
INDUSTRIAL AND ORGANIZATIONAL PSYCHOLOGY Use INDUSTRIAL PSYCHOLOGY
ORGANIZATIONAL PSYCHOLOGY (WORK ENVIRONMENT) Use INDUSTRIAL PSYCHOLOGY
ORGANIZATIONAL SELF STUDY Use SELF EVALUATION (GROUPS)
ORGANIZATIONAL THEORIES
BLACK ORGANIZATIONS
CIVIC ORGANIZATIONS Use COMMUNITY ORGANIZATIONS
COMMUNITY ORGANIZATIONS
FACULTY ORGANIZATIONS
FORMAL ORGANIZATIONS Use ORGANIZATIONS (GROUPS)
ORGANIZATIONS (GROUPS)
HUMAN RELATIONS ORGANIZATIONS (1966 1980) Use HUMAN RELATIONS PROGRAMS
INTERGOVERNMENTAL ORGANIZATIONS Use INTERNATIONAL ORGANIZATIONS
INTERNAL REVIEW (ORGANIZATIONS) Use SELF EVALUATION (GROUPS)
INTERNATIONAL ORGANIZATIONS
LIBRARY ORGANIZATIONS Use LIBRARY ASSOCIATIONS
MILITARY ORGANIZATIONS
NATIONAL ORGANIZATIONS
NEGRO ORGANIZATIONS (1966 1977) Use BLACK ORGANIZATIONS
NONPROFIT ORGANIZATIONS
RELIGIOUS ORGANIZATIONS
SEGREGATIONIST ORGANIZATIONS
SOCIAL ORGANIZATIONS
SOCIAL INSTITUTIONS (ORGANIZATIONS) Use INSTITUTIONS
STUDENT ORGANIZATIONS
TEACHER ORGANIZATIONS Use TEACHER ASSOCIATIONS
VOLUNTARY ORGANIZATIONS Use VOLUNTARY AGENCIES
ADVANCE ORGANIZERS
ORIENTAL AMERICANS Use ASIAN AMERICANS
ORIENTAL CIVILIZATION Use NON WESTERN CIVILIZATION
ORIENTAL MUSIC
AMERICAN ORIENTALS Use ASIAN AMERICANS
ORIENTATION
CAREER ORIENTATION Use CAREER PLANNING
GOAL ORIENTATION
LIBRARY ORIENTATION Use LIBRARY INSTRUCTION
ORIENTATION MATERIALS
SCHOOL ORIENTATION
SPACE ORIENTATION (1968 1980)
STAFF ORIENTATION
TEACHER ORIENTATION
VISUALLY HANDICAPPED ORIENTATION (1967 1980) Use VISUALLY HANDICAPPED MOBILITY
OUTPUT ORIENTED EDUCATION Use COMPETENCY BASED EDUCATION
COMPUTER ORIENTED PROGRAMS
OUTPUT ORIENTED TEACHER EDUCATION Use COMPETENCY BASED TEACHER EDUCATION
ORIENTEERING
ORIGINAL SCORES Use RAW SCORES
ORIGINAL SOURCES Use PRIMARY SOURCES
ORIGINALITY (1966 1980) Use CREATIVITY
ETHNIC ORIGINS
ORNAMENTAL HORTICULTURE
ORNAMENTAL HORTICULTURE OCCUPATION (1967 1976) Use ORNAMENTAL HORTICULTURE OCCUPATIONS
ORNAMENTAL HORTICULTURE OCCUPATIONS
ORNITHOLOGY
ORTHODONTIC TECHNICIANS Use DENTAL TECHNICIANS
ORTHODONTICS Use DENTISTRY
ORTHODONTISTS Use DENTISTS
ORTHOGONAL PROJECTION (1967 1980) Use ORTHOGRAPHIC PROJECTION
ORTHOGONAL ROTATION
ORTHOGRAPHIC PROJECTION
ORTHOGRAPHIC SYMBOLS
ORTHOPEDICALLY HANDICAPPED (1968 1980) Use PHYSICAL DISABILITIES
LASER OSCILLATORS Use LASERS
OSSETIC
OSTEOPATHY
OSTYAK
READING ALOUD TO OTHERS
SIGNIFICANT OTHERS
OTOLOGICAL TESTS Use AUDITORY TESTS
NONRESIDENT STUDENTS (1967 1980) (OUT OF DISTRICT) Use RESIDENCE REQUIREMENTS
OUT OF SCHOOL YOUTH
NONRESIDENT STUDENTS (1967 1980) (OUT OF STATE) Use OUT OF STATE STUDENTS
OUT OF STATE STUDENTS
STEP IN STEP OUT STUDENTS Use STOPOUTS
EDUCATIONAL OUTCOMES Use OUTCOMES OF EDUCATION
INSTRUCTIONAL OUTCOMES Use OUTCOMES OF EDUCATION
LEARNER OUTCOMES Use OUTCOMES OF EDUCATION

OUTCOMES OF EDUCATION
OUTCOMES OF TREATMENT
STUDENT OUTCOMES Use OUTCOMES OF EDUCATION
OUTDOOR ACTIVITIES
OUTDOOR DRAMA (1968 1980) Use DRAMA and OUTDOOR ACTIVITIES
OUTDOOR EDUCATION
OUTDOOR LIGHTING (1971 1980) Use LIGHTING
OUTDOOR THEATERS (1968 1980) Use OUTDOOR ACTIVITIES and THEATERS
OUTER SPACE RESEARCH Use SPACE EXPLORATION
CAPITAL OUTLAY (FOR FIXED ASSETS)
COURSE OUTLINES Use COURSE DESCRIPTIONS
OUTLINING (DISCOURSE)
OUTPLACEMENT SERVICES (EMPLOYMENT)
INPUT OUTPUT ANALYSIS
OUTPUT DEVICES Use INPUT OUTPUT DEVICES
INPUT OUTPUT DEVICES
INPUT OUTPUT
COMPUTER OUTPUT MICROFILM
OUTPUT ORIENTED EDUCATION Use COMPETENCY BASED EDUCATION
OUTPUT ORIENTED TEACHER EDUCATION Use COMPETENCY BASED TEACHER EDUCATION
COMMUNITY OUTREACH Use OUTREACH PROGRAMS
OUTREACH COUNSELING Use OUTREACH PROGRAMS
OUTREACH PROGRAMS
OVERACHIEVEMENT
OVERACHIEVERS (1966 1980) Use OVERACHIEVEMENT
OVERHEAD PROJECTORS
OVERHEAD TELEVISION (1966 1980) Use TELEVISION
OVERHEAD TRANSPARENCIES Use TRANSPARENCIES
OVERHEAD TRANSPARENCY PROJECTORS Use OVERHEAD PROJECTORS
OVERPOPULATION
OVERSEAS EMPLOYMENT
WORKING OVERSEAS Use OVERSEAS EMPLOYMENT
OVERT RESPONSE
OVERTIME
OVERWEIGHT (EXCESSIVE BODY FAT) Use OBESITY
OWNERSHIP
OWNERSHIP OF IDEAS Use INTELLECTUAL PROPERTY
OXIDATION
OXYGEN INHALATION THERAPY Use RESPIRATORY THERAPY
SELF PACED INSTRUCTION Use INDIVIDUALIZED INSTRUCTION and PACING
PACIFIC AMERICANS
PACING
GROUP PACING Use PACING
INTERVAL PACING (1967 1980) Use PACING
SELF PACING MACHINES (1966 1980) Use TEACHING MACHINES
SELF PACING Use PACING
LEARNING PACKAGES Use LEARNING MODULES
LEARNING ACTIVITY PACKAGES Use LEARNING MODULES
LEARNING ACTIVITY PACKETS Use LEARNING MODULES
MEAT PACKING INDUSTRY
PAGE READERS Use OPTICAL SCANNERS
SIGN PAINTERS
PAINTING (1966 1980) (ARTISTIC) Use PAINTING (VISUAL ARTS)
PAINTING (1966 1980) (INDUSTRIAL) Use PAINTING (INDUSTRIAL ARTS)
PAINTING (INDUSTRIAL ARTS)
PAINTING (VISUAL ARTS)
PAIRED ASSOCIATE LEARNING
PALAEONTOLOGY Use PALEONTOLOGY
CLEFT PALATE
PALEONTOLOGY
CEREBRAL PALSY
PAMPHLETS
DISPLAY PANELS (1968 1980) Use DISPLAY AIDS
PANJABI
PANTOMIME
PAPAGO
PAPER (MATERIAL)
PAPERBACK BOOKS
CONFERENCE PAPERS
OPINION PAPERS
POSITION PAPERS
PRACTICUM PAPERS
RESEARCH PAPERS (STUDENTS)
TERM PAPERS Use RESEARCH PAPERS (STUDENTS)
PARADIGMS Use MODELS
PARADOX
PARAGRAPH COMPOSITION
PARAGRAPHS
PARALANGUAGE Use PARALINGUISTICS
PARALEGAL EDUCATION Use LEGAL ASSISTANTS and LEGAL EDUCATION (PROFESSIONS)
PARALEGALS Use LEGAL ASSISTANTS
PARALINGUISTICS
PARALLELISM (LITERARY)
PARAMEDICAL OCCUPATIONS (1967 1980) Use ALLIED HEALTH OCCUPATIONS
PARAMEDICAL SCIENCES Use MEDICINE
PARAMEDICS Use ALLIED HEALTH PERSONNEL
PARANOID BEHAVIOR
PARAPLEGIA Use NEUROLOGICAL IMPAIRMENTS
PARAPROFESSIONAL PERSONNEL
PARAPROFESSIONAL SCHOOL PERSONNEL
PARENT ABSENCE Use ONE PARENT FAMILY
PARENT ASPIRATION
PARENT ASSOCIATIONS
PARENT ATTITUDES
PARENT BACKGROUND
PARENT BEHAVIOR Use PARENT CHILD RELATIONSHIP
PARENT CHILD INTERACTION Use PARENT CHILD RELATIONSHIP
PARENT CHILD RELATIONSHIP
PARENT CONFERENCES
TEACHER PARENT CONFERENCES Use PARENT TEACHER CONFERENCES
TEACHER PARENT COOPERATION Use PARENT TEACHER COOPERATION

PARENT COUNSELING
PARENT EDUCATION
ONE PARENT FAMILY
SINGLE PARENT FAMILY Use ONE PARENT FAMILY
TWO PARENT FAMILY Use NUCLEAR FAMILY
PARENT FINANCIAL CONTRIBUTION
PARENT FORUMS Use PARENT CONFERENCES
PARENT GRIEVANCES
PARENT INFLUENCE
PARENT INVOLVEMENT Use PARENT PARTICIPATION
PARENT MATERIALS
PARENT OPINIONS Use PARENT ATTITUDES
PARENT PARTICIPATION
PARENT REACTION (1966 1980) Use PARENT ATTITUDES
CHILD PARENT RELATIONSHIP Use PARENT CHILD RELATIONSHIP
SCHOOL PARENT RELATIONSHIP Use PARENT SCHOOL RELATIONSHIP
STUDENT PARENT RELATIONSHIP Use PARENT STUDENT RELATIONSHIP
PARENT RESPONSIBILITY
PARENT RIGHTS
PARENT ROLE
PARENT SCHOOL RELATIONSHIP
PARENT SKILLS Use PARENTING SKILLS
PARENT STUDENT CONFERENCES (1967 1980) Use PARENT TEACHER CONFERENCES
PARENT STUDENT RELATIONSHIP
PARENT STUDY GROUPS Use PARENT CONFERENCES
PARENT TEACHER CONFERENCES
PARENT TEACHER COOPERATION
PARENT WORKSHOPS
PARENTAL ASPIRATION (1966 1980) Use PARENT ASPIRATION
PARENTAL BACKGROUND (1966 1980) Use PARENT BACKGROUND
PARENTAL FINANCIAL CONTRIBUTION (1978 1980) Use PARENT FINANCIAL CONTRIBUTION
PARENTAL GRIEVANCES (1967 1980) Use PARENT GRIEVANCES
PARENTAL OBLIGATIONS Use PARENT RESPONSIBILITY
EARLY PARENTHOOD
PARENTHOOD EDUCATION
PARENTING Use CHILD REARING
PARENTING MATERIALS Use PARENT MATERIALS
PARENTING SKILLS
PARENTS
ADOLESCENT PARENTS Use EARLY PARENTHOOD
BIOLOGICAL PARENTS
BIRTH PARENTS Use BIOLOGICAL PARENTS
CATHOLIC PARENTS (1966 1980) Use CATHOLICS and PARENTS
COTTAGE PARENTS Use RESIDENT ADVISERS
DUAL EARNER PARENTS Use EMPLOYED PARENTS
EMPLOYED PARENTS
FOSTER PARENTS Use FOSTER FAMILY
LOWER CLASS PARENTS
MIDDLE CLASS PARENTS
NATURAL PARENTS Use BIOLOGICAL PARENTS
WORKING PARENTS (1966 1980) Use EMPLOYED PARENTS
PARISH WORKERS Use CHURCH WORKERS
PARK DESIGN
PARKING AREAS (1966 1980) Use PARKING FACILITIES
STREET PARKING AREAS Use PARKING FACILITIES
PARKING CONTROLS
PARKING FACILITIES
PARKING GARAGES Use PARKING FACILITIES
PARKING LOTS Use PARKING FACILITIES
PARKING METERS (1968 1980) Use PARKING CONTROLS
PARKING PERMITS Use PARKING CONTROLS
PARKING RAMPS Use PARKING FACILITIES
PARKING REGULATIONS Use PARKING CONTROLS
PARKS
EDUCATIONAL PARKS
PARLIAMENTARY PROCEDURES
PAROCHIAL SCHOOL AID (1972 1980) Use PAROCHIAL SCHOOLS and PRIVATE SCHOOL AID
PAROCHIAL SCHOOLS
PARODY
PAROLE OFFICERS
PARSONS Use CLERGY
PART CORRELATION Use CORRELATION
PART TIME EMPLOYMENT
PART TIME FACULTY
PART TIME FARMERS
PART TIME JOBS (1966 1980) Use PART TIME EMPLOYMENT
PART TIME STUDENTS
PART TIME TEACHERS (1967 1980) Use PART TIME FACULTY
PART TIME TEACHING (1967 1980) Use PART TIME FACULTY
PART TIME WORK Use PART TIME EMPLOYMENT
PARTIAL CORRELATION Use CORRELATION
PARTIAL HEARING
PARTIAL VISION
PARTIALLY SIGHTED (1967 1980) Use PARTIAL VISION
PARTICIPANT CHARACTERISTICS
PARTICIPANT INVOLVEMENT (1967 1980) Use PARTICIPATION
PARTICIPANT OBSERVATION
PARTICIPANT SATISFACTION
PARTICIPATION
AUDIENCE PARTICIPATION
CITIZEN PARTICIPATION
CLASSROOM PARTICIPATION (1966 1980) Use CLASS ACTIVITIES and STUDENT PARTICIPATION
COMMUNITY PARTICIPATION Use COMMUNITY INVOLVEMENT
FAMILY PARTICIPATION Use FAMILY INVOLVEMENT
LEADER PARTICIPATION (1966 1980) Use LEADERSHIP
PARENT PARTICIPATION
PUBLIC PARTICIPATION Use CITIZEN PARTICIPATION
SCHOOL PARTICIPATION Use SCHOOL INVOLVEMENT
STUDENT PARTICIPATION
TEACHER PARTICIPATION
PARTICIPATIVE DECISION MAKING

	PARTICIPATIVE MANAGEMENT Use PARTICIPATIVE DECISION MAKING
	PARTICIPATIVE PROBLEM SOLVING Use PARTICIPATIVE DECISION MAKING and PROBLEM SOLVING
FOLDING	PARTITIONS Use MOVABLE PARTITIONS
MOVABLE	PARTITIONS
	PARTNERSHIP TEACHERS
AUTO	PARTS CLERKS
AUTO	PARTS MEN (1968 1980) Use AUTO PARTS CLERKS
	PARTS OF SPEECH Use FORM CLASSES (LANGUAGES)
	PARTURITION Use BIRTH
	PASHTO
	PASHTU Use PASHTO
	PASS FAIL GRADING
	PASS NO CREDIT GRADING Use CREDIT NO CREDIT GRADING
	PASS NO RECORD GRADING Use CREDIT NO CREDIT GRADING
AUDIO	PASSIVE LABORATORIES (1968 1980) Use LANGUAGE LABORATORIES
	PASTES (ADHESIVES) Use ADHESIVES
	PASTORAL LITERATURE
	PASTORAL PEOPLES Use NOMADS
	PATENTS
	PATH ANALYSIS
CRITICAL	PATH METHOD
	PATHOGENESIS Use PATHOLOGY
	PATHOLOGY
PLANT	PATHOLOGY
SPEECH	PATHOLOGY
	PATHWAYS Use TRAILS
	PATIENT CARE EVALUATION Use MEDICAL CARE EVALUATION
	PATIENT EDUCATION
	PATIENT PHYSICIAN RELATIONSHIP Use PHYSICIAN PATIENT RELATIONSHIP
DOCTOR	PATIENT RELATIONSHIP Use PHYSICIAN PATIENT RELATIONSHIP
PHYSICIAN	PATIENT RELATIONSHIP
	PATIENTS
	PATIENTS (PERSONS) (1968 1980) Use PATIENTS
	PATRIOTISM
GUARDS (BORDER	PATROL) Use IMMIGRATION INSPECTORS
BORDER	PATROL OFFICERS Use IMMIGRATION INSPECTORS
LIBRARY	PATRONS Use USERS (INFORMATION)
	PATTERN DRILLS (LANGUAGE)
	PATTERN RECOGNITION
	PATTERNED BEHAVIOR Use BEHAVIOR PATTERNS
	PATTERNED RESPONSES
	PATTERNMAKING
AROUSAL	PATTERNS
ATTENDANCE	PATTERNS
BASIC LANGUAGE	PATTERNS Use LANGUAGE PATTERNS
BEHAVIOR	PATTERNS
EMOTIONAL	PATTERNS Use PSYCHOLOGICAL PATTERNS
EMPLOYMENT	PATTERNS
ERROR	PATTERNS
FEEDER	PATTERNS
GROWTH	PATTERNS (1966 1980)
HOUSING	PATTERNS (1966 1980) Use RESIDENTIAL PATTERNS
INCOME	PATTERNS Use INCOME
JOB HOLDING	PATTERNS Use EMPLOYMENT PATTERNS
LANGUAGE	PATTERNS
LINGUISTIC	PATTERNS (1966 1980) Use LANGUAGE PATTERNS
MIGRATION	PATTERNS
POSTURE	PATTERNS Use HUMAN POSTURE
PSYCHOLOGICAL	PATTERNS
RESIDENTIAL	PATTERNS
SETTLEMENT	PATTERNS Use LAND SETTLEMENT
SOCIAL INSTITUTIONS (SOCIAL	PATTERNS) Use SOCIOCULTURAL PATTERNS
SOCIOCULTURAL	PATTERNS
TRAFFIC	PATTERNS (1968 1980) Use TRAFFIC CIRCULATION
EQUAL	PAY Use SALARY WAGE DIFFERENTIALS
	PAY EQUITY Use COMPARABLE WORTH
MERIT	PAY
PREMIUM	PAY
	PAYROLL RECORDS
	PEACE
INTERNATIONAL	PEACE Use PEACE
WORLD	PEACE Use PEACE
	PEANUT INSPECTORS Use FOOD AND DRUG INSPECTORS
	PEDAGOGY Use INSTRUCTION
	PEDESTRIAN CIRCULATION Use PEDESTRIAN TRAFFIC
	PEDESTRIAN TRAFFIC
	PEDIATRICS
	PEDIATRICS TRAINING (1966 1980) Use PEDIATRICS
	PEER ACCEPTANCE
	PEER COUNSELING
	PEER EVALUATION
	PEER GROUPS
	PEER INFLUENCE
	PEER INSTITUTIONS
	PEER PRESSURE Use PEER INFLUENCE
	PEER RELATIONSHIP
	PEER REVIEW Use PEER EVALUATION
	PEER TEACHING
FINES	(PENALTIES)
	PENSIONS Use RETIREMENT BENEFITS
	PEOPLE DAYS Use WORKER DAYS
HOMELESS	PEOPLE
KHMER	(PEOPLE) Use CAMBODIANS
LAY	PEOPLE
STREET	PEOPLE Use HOMELESS PEOPLE
VIETNAMESE	PEOPLE
PASTORAL	PEOPLES Use NOMADS
EXPENDITURE	PER STUDENT
	PERCENT Use PERCENTAGE
	PERCENTAGE
	PERCEPTION

AUDITORY	PERCEPTION
	PERCEPTION (BETWEEN PERSONS) Use SOCIAL COGNITION
DEPTH	PERCEPTION
HAPTIC	PERCEPTION (1967 1980) Use TACTUAL PERCEPTION
INTERPERSONAL	PERCEPTION Use SOCIAL COGNITION
KINESTHETIC	PERCEPTION
PERSON	PERCEPTION Use SOCIAL COGNITION
ROLE	PERCEPTION
SOCIAL	PERCEPTION Use SOCIAL COGNITION
SPATIAL	PERCEPTION (1980 1981) Use SPATIAL ABILITY
TACTUAL	PERCEPTION
	PERCEPTION TESTS
VISUAL	PERCEPTION
	PERCEPTIVENESS (BETWEEN PERSONS) Use INTERPERSONAL COMPETENCE and SOCIAL COGNITION
	PERCEPTUAL DEPRIVATION Use SENSORY DEPRIVATION
	PERCEPTUAL DEVELOPMENT
	PERCEPTUAL HANDICAPS
ISOLATION	(PERCEPTUAL) Use SENSORY DEPRIVATION
	PERCEPTUAL MOTOR COORDINATION
	PERCEPTUAL MOTOR LEARNING
	PERCEPTUAL STYLE Use COGNITIVE STYLE
	PERCEPTUALLY HANDICAPPED (1966 1980) Use PERCEPTUAL HANDICAPS
	PERFORMANCE
ACADEMIC	PERFORMANCE (1966 1974) Use ACADEMIC ACHIEVEMENT
	PERFORMANCE APPRAISAL (PERSONNEL) Use PERSONNEL EVALUATION
	PERFORMANCE BASED EDUCATION (1974 1980) Use COMPETENCY BASED EDUCATION
	PERFORMANCE BASED TEACHER EDUCATION (1972 1980) Use COMPETENCY BASED TEACHER EDUCATION
	PERFORMANCE CONTRACTS
COUNSELOR	PERFORMANCE
	PERFORMANCE CRITERIA (1968 1980)
EMPLOYEE	PERFORMANCE Use JOB PERFORMANCE
WORK	PERFORMANCE EVALUATION Use VOCATIONAL EVALUATION
	PERFORMANCE FACTORS
JOB	PERFORMANCE
LINGUISTIC	PERFORMANCE
	PERFORMANCE OBJECTIVES Use BEHAVIORAL OBJECTIVES
PHYSICAL	PERFORMANCE Use PHYSICAL FITNESS
	PERFORMANCE SPECIFICATIONS (1969 1980)
STUDENT EVALUATION OF TEACHER	PERFORMANCE
TASK	PERFORMANCE (1966 1980)
	PERFORMANCE TESTS
WORK EVALUATION	(PERFORMANCE) Use VOCATIONAL EVALUATION
	PERFORMING ARTS Use THEATER ARTS
	PERFORMING ARTS CENTERS Use THEATERS
	PERINATAL INFLUENCES
ENGLISH NEOCLASSIC LITERARY	PERIOD (1968 1980)
PROBATIONARY	PERIOD
	PERIODICALS
FOREIGN LANGUAGE	PERIODICALS
SECOND LANGUAGE	PERIODICALS Use FOREIGN LANGUAGE PERIODICALS
PUBLISH OR	PERISH ISSUE
OBJECT	PERMANENCE
	PERMANENT EDUCATION Use LIFELONG LEARNING
	PERMANENT MAGNETS Use MAGNETS
EDUCATION	PERMANENTE Use LIFELONG LEARNING
	PERMISSIVE ENVIRONMENT
PARKING	PERMITS Use PARKING CONTROLS
	PERMUTED INDEXES
	PERQUISITES (EMPLOYMENT) Use FRINGE BENEFITS
	PERSEVERANCE Use PERSISTENCE
	PERSIAN
TADJIK	PERSIAN Use TAJIK
	PERSISTENCE
ACADEMIC	PERSISTENCE
TEACHER	PERSISTENCE
TEACHING	PERSISTENCE Use TEACHER PERSISTENCE
WHOLE	PERSON APPROACH Use HOLISTIC APPROACH
CARDIAC	(PERSON) (1968 1980) Use HEART DISORDERS
	PERSON DAYS Use WORKER DAYS
	PERSON PERCEPTION Use SOCIAL COGNITION
	PERSONAL ACCOUNTS (NARRATIVES) Use PERSONAL NARRATIVES
	PERSONAL ADJUSTMENT (1966 1980) Use ADJUSTMENT (TO ENVIRONMENT)
SUPPORT NETWORKS	(PERSONAL ASSISTANCE) Use SOCIAL SUPPORT GROUPS
	PERSONAL AUTONOMY
	PERSONAL CARE HOMES
	PERSONAL COMPUTERS Use MICROCOMPUTERS
	PERSONAL DEVELOPMENT Use INDIVIDUAL DEVELOPMENT
	PERSONAL GROOMING Use HYGIENE
	PERSONAL GROWTH (1967 1980) Use INDIVIDUAL DEVELOPMENT
	PERSONAL HEALTH Use HYGIENE
	PERSONAL INTERESTS (1966 1980) Use INTERESTS
	PERSONAL LIBERTY Use CIVIL LIBERTIES
	PERSONAL NARRATIVES
	PERSONAL RELATIONSHIP (1966 1974) Use INTERPERSONAL RELATIONSHIP
RESUMES	(PERSONAL)
	PERSONAL SPACE
	PERSONAL VALUES (1966 1980) Use VALUES
	PERSONALITY
ADAPTABILITY	(PERSONALITY) Use ADJUSTMENT (TO ENVIRONMENT) and PERSONALITY TRAITS
	PERSONALITY ASSESSMENT
	PERSONALITY CHANGE
	PERSONALITY DEVELOPMENT
	PERSONALITY MEASURES
	PERSONALITY PROBLEMS
	PERSONALITY RATING Use PERSONALITY ASSESSMENT
	PERSONALITY STUDIES
	PERSONALITY TESTS (1968 1980) Use PERSONALITY MEASURES
	PERSONALITY THEORIES
	PERSONALITY TRAITS
	PERSONALIZED INSTRUCTION Use INDIVIDUALIZED INSTRUCTION

PERSONNEL
ADMINISTRATIVE PERSONNEL (1966 1980) Use ADMINISTRATORS
PERSONNEL ADMINISTRATORS Use PERSONNEL DIRECTORS
AGRICULTURAL PERSONNEL
ALLIED HEALTH PERSONNEL
ASSESSMENT CENTERS (PERSONNEL)
PERSONNEL DATA
PERSONNEL DEVELOPMENT Use STAFF DEVELOPMENT
PERSONNEL DIRECTORS
SCHOOL PERSONNEL DIRECTORS Use PERSONNEL DIRECTORS and SCHOOL PERSONNEL
PERSONNEL DISCHARGE Use DISMISSAL (PERSONNEL)
DISMISSAL (PERSONNEL)
PERSONNEL DISMISSAL Use DISMISSAL (PERSONNEL)
EMERGENCY SQUAD PERSONNEL
ENLISTED PERSONNEL
PERSONNEL EVALUATION
GUIDANCE PERSONNEL
HEALTH PERSONNEL
HEALTH OCCUPATIONS PERSONNEL Use HEALTH PERSONNEL
HEALTH SERVICE PERSONNEL Use HEALTH PERSONNEL
HOSPITAL PERSONNEL
INDIGENOUS PERSONNEL
INDUSTRIAL PERSONNEL
INSTITUTIONAL PERSONNEL
PERSONNEL INTEGRATION
LIBRARY PERSONNEL
MANAGEMENT PERSONNEL Use ADMINISTRATORS
PERSONNEL MANAGEMENT
PERSONNEL MANAGERS Use PERSONNEL DIRECTORS
MILITARY PERSONNEL
PERSONNEL NEEDS
NONPROFESSIONAL PERSONNEL
OFFICER PERSONNEL
PARAPROFESSIONAL PERSONNEL
PARAPROFESSIONAL SCHOOL PERSONNEL
PERFORMANCE APPRAISAL (PERSONNEL) Use PERSONNEL EVALUATION
PERSONNEL POLICY
PROFESSIONAL PERSONNEL
STUDENT PERSONNEL PROGRAMS (1967 1980) Use STUDENT PERSONNEL SERVICES
PERSONNEL RECRUITMENT Use RECRUITMENT
RESCUE SQUAD PERSONNEL Use EMERGENCY SQUAD PERSONNEL
PERSONNEL ROLE Use STAFF ROLE
SCHOOL PERSONNEL
CLINIC PERSONNEL (SCHOOL) (1966 1980) Use ALLIED HEALTH PERSONNEL and SCHOOL HEALTH SERVICES
SCIENTIFIC PERSONNEL
SEARCH COMMITTEES (PERSONNEL)
SECURITY PERSONNEL
PERSONNEL SELECTION
SELECTION COMMITTEES (PERSONNEL) Use SEARCH COMMITTEES (PERSONNEL)
PUPIL PERSONNEL SERVICES
STUDENT PERSONNEL SERVICES
SPECIAL PERSONNEL Use SPECIALISTS
PERSONNEL TESTS Use OCCUPATIONAL TESTS
STUDENT PERSONNEL WORK (1967 1980) Use STUDENT PERSONNEL SERVICES
PUPIL PERSONNEL WORKERS
STUDENT PERSONNEL WORKERS
AT RISK (PERSONS) Use HIGH RISK PERSONS
ATTRACTIVENESS (BETWEEN PERSONS) Use INTERPERSONAL ATTRACTION
DIVORCED PERSONS Use DIVORCE
EXCEPTIONAL PERSONS
HIGH RISK PERSONS
INSTITUTIONALIZED PERSONS
INSTITUTIONALIZED (PERSONS) (1967 1976) Use INSTITUTIONALIZED PERSONS
LABELING (OF PERSONS)
MARRIED PERSONS Use SPOUSES
PATIENTS (PERSONS) (1968 1980) Use PATIENTS
PERCEPTION (BETWEEN PERSONS) Use SOCIAL COGNITION
PERCEPTIVENESS (BETWEEN PERSONS) Use INTERPERSONAL COMPETENCE and SOCIAL COGNITION
LITERARY PERSPECTIVE (1969 1980)
PERSPECTIVE TAKING
TEMPORAL PERSPECTIVE Use TIME PERSPECTIVE
TIME PERSPECTIVE
PERSUASIVE DISCOURSE
PEST CONTROL Use PESTS
PESTICIDES
PESTS
PETROLEUM INDUSTRY
PEUL Use FULANI
PHARMACEUTICAL EDUCATION
PHARMACISTS
PHARMACOLOGY
PHARMACY
PROGRAM PHASEOUT Use PROGRAM TERMINATION
PHENOMENOLOGY
PHEUL Use FULANI
PHILANTHROPIC FOUNDATIONS
PHILANTHROPY Use PRIVATE FINANCIAL SUPPORT
PHILOLOGY Use LINGUISTICS
PHILOSOPHY
EDUCATIONAL PHILOSOPHY
SCHOOL PHILOSOPHY Use EDUCATIONAL PHILOSOPHY
SCHOOL PHOBIA
GRAPHEME PHONEME CORRESPONDENCE Use PHONEME GRAPHEME CORRESPONDENCE
PHONEME GRAPHEME CORRESPONDENCE
PHONEMES
SUPRASEGMENTAL PHONEMES Use SUPRASEGMENTALS
PHONEMIC ALPHABETS
PHONEMICS
PHONETIC ANALYSIS
PHONETIC TRANSCRIPTION
PHONETICS

ACOUSTIC PHONETICS
PHONIC METHOD Use PHONICS
PHONICS
LANGUAGE RECORDS (PHONOGRAPH) (1966 1980) Use AUDIODISKS
PHONOGRAPH RECORD LISTS Use DISCOGRAPHIES
PHONOGRAPH RECORDS (1966 1980) Use AUDIODISKS
PHONOLOGICAL BORROWING Use LINGUISTIC BORROWING
PHONOLOGICAL UNITS (1966 1980) Use PHONEMES
PHONOLOGY
GENERATIVE PHONOLOGY
STRESS (PHONOLOGY)
PHONOTAPE RECORDINGS (1966 1978) Use AUDIOTAPE RECORDINGS
PHOTOCHEMICAL REACTIONS
PHOTOCHEMISTRY Use PHOTOCHEMICAL REACTIONS
PHOTOCOMPOSITION
PHOTOCOPYING Use REPROGRAPHY
PHOTOGRAPHIC EQUIPMENT
PHOTOGRAPHIC MEMORY Use EIDETIC IMAGERY
PHOTOGRAPHS
PHOTOGRAPHY
PHOTOJOURNALISM
PHOTOMETRIC BRIGHTNESS Use LUMINESCENCE
PHOTOREPRODUCTION Use REPROGRAPHY
PHOTOSYNTHESIS
PHRASE STRUCTURE
PHYSICAL ACTIVITIES
PHYSICAL ACTIVITY LEVEL
PHYSICAL CHARACTERISTICS
PHYSICAL CONDITIONING Use PHYSICAL FITNESS
PHYSICAL DESIGN NEEDS (1968 1980) Use DESIGN REQUIREMENTS
PHYSICAL DEVELOPMENT
PHYSICAL DISABILITIES
PHYSICAL DIVISIONS (GEOGRAPHIC)
PHYSICAL EDUCATION
ADAPTED PHYSICAL EDUCATION
PHYSICAL EDUCATION FACILITIES
PHYSICAL EDUCATION TEACHERS
PHYSICAL EDUCATORS Use PHYSICAL EDUCATION TEACHERS
PHYSICAL ENVIRONMENT
PHYSICAL EXAMINATIONS
PHYSICAL EXERCISE Use EXERCISE
PHYSICAL FACILITIES (1966 1980) Use FACILITIES
PHYSICAL FITNESS
FORCE (PHYSICAL) Use FORCE
PHYSICAL GEOGRAPHY
PHYSICAL HANDICAPS (1966 1980) Use PHYSICAL DISABILITIES
PHYSICAL HEALTH
PHYSICAL MOBILITY
PHYSICAL OPTICS Use OPTICS
PHYSICAL PERFORMANCE Use PHYSICAL FITNESS
PHYSICAL PRESSURE Use PRESSURE (PHYSICS)
PHYSICAL RECREATION PROGRAMS
PHYSICAL SCIENCES
SELF INJURY (PHYSICAL) Use SELF MUTILATION
PHYSICAL STRENGTH Use MUSCULAR STRENGTH
TEST CHARACTERISTICS (PHYSICAL) Use TEST FORMAT
PHYSICAL TESTS Use PHYSICAL EXAMINATIONS
PHYSICAL THERAPISTS
PHYSICAL THERAPY
PHYSICAL THERAPY AIDES
PHYSICAL THERAPY ATTENDANTS Use PHYSICAL THERAPY AIDES
PHYSICALLY HANDICAPPED (1966 1980) Use PHYSICAL DISABILITIES
PHYSICIAN PATIENT RELATIONSHIP
PATIENT PHYSICIAN RELATIONSHIP Use PHYSICIAN PATIENT RELATIONSHIP
PHYSICIANS
PHYSICIANS ASSISTANTS
FOREIGN TRAINED PHYSICIANS Use FOREIGN MEDICAL GRADUATES
PHYSICIANS IN TRAINING Use GRADUATE MEDICAL STUDENTS
PHYSICS
ACCELERATION (1966 1982) (PHYSICS) Use ACCELERATION (PHYSICS)
ACCELERATION (PHYSICS)
ATOMIC PHYSICS Use NUCLEAR PHYSICS
PHYSICS CURRICULUM (1966 1980) Use PHYSICS and SCIENCE CURRICULUM
DIFFUSION (PHYSICS)
DIFFUSION (1967 1982) (PHYSICS) Use DIFFUSION (PHYSICS)
PHYSICS EXPERIMENTS (1966 1980) Use PHYSICS and SCIENCE EXPERIMENTS
GRAVITY (PHYSICS)
PHYSICS INSTRUCTION (1966 1980) Use PHYSICS and SCIENCE INSTRUCTION
MECHANICS (PHYSICS)
NUCLEAR PHYSICS
PRESSURE (PHYSICS)
PHYSICS TEACHERS (1967 1980) Use PHYSICS and SCIENCE TEACHERS
PHYSIOLOGICAL CHEMISTRY Use BIOCHEMISTRY
PHYSIOLOGICAL PSYCHOLOGY Use PSYCHOPHYSIOLOGY
PHYSIOLOGY
AUDITION (PHYSIOLOGY) (1967 1980) Use HEARING (PHYSIOLOGY)
EXERCISE (PHYSIOLOGY) (1969 1980)
EXERCISE PHYSIOLOGY
HEARING (PHYSIOLOGY)
PIAGETIAN THEORY
PICTORIAL JOURNALISM Use PHOTOJOURNALISM
PICTORIAL STIMULI
PICTORIAL TESTS Use VISUAL MEASURES
PICTURE BOOKS
MOTION PICTURES Use FILMS
PIDGINS
PILIPINO Use TAGALOG
PILOT PROGRAMS Use PILOT PROJECTS
PILOT PROJECTS
PILOT TRAINING Use FLIGHT TRAINING
AIRCRAFT PILOTS

AIRLINE PILOTS Use AIRCRAFT PILOTS
AIRPLANE PILOTS Use AIRCRAFT PILOTS
COMMERCIAL PILOTS Use AIRCRAFT PILOTS
HELICOPTER PILOTS Use AIRCRAFT PILOTS
PING PONG Use TABLE TENNIS
PIPE FITTING Use PLUMBING
PLACE OF RESIDENCE
PLACE VALUE
PLACEMENT
ADVANCED PLACEMENT
AGE GRADE PLACEMENT
COLLEGE PLACEMENT (1966 1980) Use STUDENT PLACEMENT
JOB PLACEMENT
ADVANCED PLACEMENT PROGRAMS
REGULAR CLASS PLACEMENT (1968 1978) Use MAINSTREAMING
STUDENT PLACEMENT
STUDENT JOB PLACEMENT Use JOB PLACEMENT and STUDENT EMPLOYMENT
TEACHER PLACEMENT
VOCATIONAL PLACEMENT Use JOB PLACEMENT
PLAGIARISM
CONTINUOUS PROGRESS PLAN
HOUSE PLAN
LEAD LECTURE PLAN (1966 1980) Use LECTURE METHOD
OPEN PLAN SCHOOLS
SCHOOLS WITHIN A SCHOOL PLAN Use HOUSE PLAN
UNIT PLAN (1966 1980)
PLANAR AREA Use AREA
PLANE GEOMETRY
PLANETARIUMS
PLANETARY EXPLORATION Use SPACE EXPLORATION
PLANNED COMMUNITIES
PLANNED COMMUNITY (1966 1980) Use PLANNED COMMUNITIES
PLANNING
ACADEMIC PLANNING Use EDUCATIONAL PLANNING
ADMINISTRATIVE PLANNING Use PLANNING
CAMPUS PLANNING
CAREER PLANNING
CITY PLANNING (1966 1980) Use URBAN PLANNING
COLLEGE PLANNING
COLOR PLANNING
PLANNING COMMISSIONS
COMMUNITY PLANNING
COOPERATIVE PLANNING
CURRICULUM PLANNING (1966 1980) Use CURRICULUM DEVELOPMENT
EDUCATIONAL PLANNING
EDUCATIONAL FACILITIES PLANNING
ESTATE PLANNING
FACILITY PLANNING
FAMILY PLANNING
FUTURES PLANNING Use LONG RANGE PLANNING
INSTRUCTIONAL PLANNING Use INSTRUCTIONAL DEVELOPMENT
INTERAGENCY PLANNING (1966 1980) Use AGENCY COOPERATION and COOPERATIVE PLANNING
LANGUAGE PLANNING
LIBRARY PLANNING
LONG RANGE PLANNING
LONG TERM PLANNING Use LONG RANGE PLANNING
PLANNING MEETINGS (1966 1980) Use MEETINGS
PROGRAM PLANNING (1966 1980) Use PROGRAM DEVELOPMENT
REGIONAL PLANNING
RESEARCH PLANNING Use RESEARCH DESIGN
SCHOOL PLANNING (1966 1980)
SOCIAL PLANNING
STATE PLANNING Use STATEWIDE PLANNING
STATEWIDE PLANNING
URBAN PLANNING
BUILDING PLANS
DEPARTMENTAL TEACHING PLANS (1968 1980) Use DEPARTMENTS
DESEGREGATION PLANS
EDUCATIONAL PLANS Use EDUCATIONAL PLANNING
INTEGRATION PLANS (1966 1980) Use DESEGREGATION PLANS
LESSON PLANS
MASTER PLANS
ORGANIZATIONAL PLANS Use PLANNING
ROTATION PLANS
STUDIO FLOOR PLANS (1966 1980)
TUTORIAL PLANS Use TUTORIAL PROGRAMS
VOUCHER PLANS Use EDUCATIONAL VOUCHERS
PLANT BIOLOGY Use BOTANY
PLANT DISEASES Use PLANT PATHOLOGY
PLANT GROWTH
PLANT IDENTIFICATION
PLANT PATHOLOGY
PLANT PROPAGATION
PLANT SCIENCE (1967 1980)
NUCLEAR POWER PLANT TECHNICIANS
PLANTING (1966 1980) Use HORTICULTURE
CROP PLANTING Use AGRONOMY and HORTICULTURE
NUCLEAR POWER PLANTS
SCHOOL PLANTS Use EDUCATIONAL FACILITIES
PLASTICS
PLATE TECTONICS
LEARNING PLATEAUS
PLATFORM DIVING Use DIVING
PLATONIC CRITICISM (1970 1980)
PLATONISM
PLAY
CHILDRENS PLAY Use PLAY
DRAMATIC PLAY
FANTASY PLAY Use PRETEND PLAY
FREE PLAY Use PLAY
MAKE BELIEVE PLAY Use PRETEND PLAY

PRETEND	PLAY
THERAPEUTIC	PLAY Use PLAY THERAPY
	PLAY THERAPY
	PLAYGROUND ACTIVITIES
	PLAYGROUNDS
LIGHTED	PLAYGROUNDS (1966 1980) Use PLAYGROUNDS
ROLE	PLAYING
SIGHT	PLAYING Use MUSIC READING
SHADOW	PLAYS Use THEATER ARTS
	PLAYS (THEATRICAL) Use DRAMA
	PLAYWRITING
ECONOMIC	PLIGHT Use POVERTY
	PLUMBING
CULTURAL	PLURALISM
	PLURALIZATION Use PLURALS
	PLURALS
	PLURILINGUALISM Use MULTILINGUALISM
	PNEUMATIC FORMS
	POCKET CALCULATORS Use CALCULATORS
	POCKET COMPUTERS Use MICROCOMPUTERS
	PODIATRY
	POETRY
LYRIC	POETRY
	POETS
LYRIC	POETS Use POETS
GRADE	POINT AVERAGE
QUALITY	POINT RATIO Use GRADE POINT AVERAGE
	POISONING
LEAD	POISONING
	POISONS
	POLICE
	POLICE ACTION
	POLICE COMMUNITY RELATIONSHIP
	POLICE COSTS (1966 1980) Use COSTS and POLICE
	POLICE EDUCATION
COMMUNITY	POLICE RELATIONSHIP Use POLICE COMMUNITY RELATIONSHIP
SCHOOL	POLICE RELATIONSHIP Use POLICE SCHOOL RELATIONSHIP
	POLICE SCHOOL LIAISON Use POLICE SCHOOL RELATIONSHIP
	POLICE SCHOOL RELATIONSHIP
	POLICE SEMINARS (1966 1980) Use POLICE EDUCATION
STATE	POLICE (1966 1980) Use POLICE
INTERDISTRICT	POLICIES
	POLICY
ADMINISTRATIVE	POLICY
BOARD OF EDUCATION	POLICY
DIPLOMATIC	POLICY Use FOREIGN POLICY
DISCIPLINE	POLICY
EDUCATIONAL	POLICY
FAMILY SERVICES	POLICY Use FAMILY PROGRAMS and PUBLIC POLICY
FINANCIAL	POLICY
FISCAL	POLICY Use FINANCIAL POLICY
FOREIGN	POLICY
	POLICY FORMATION
INTERNATIONAL	POLICY Use FOREIGN POLICY
NEIGHBORHOOD SCHOOL	POLICY (1966 1980) Use NEIGHBORHOOD SCHOOLS and SCHOOL POLICY
PERSONNEL	POLICY
PUBLIC	POLICY
SCHOOL	POLICY
SCHOOL BOARD	POLICY Use BOARD OF EDUCATION POLICY
SCHOOL DISTRICT	POLICY Use BOARD OF EDUCATION POLICY
	POLICY STATEMENTS Use POSITION PAPERS
TRANSFER	POLICY
	POLISH
	POLISH AMERICANS
	POLISH LITERATURE
	POLITICAL ADVOCACY Use LOBBYING
	POLITICAL AFFILIATION
	POLITICAL ATTITUDES
	POLITICAL CAMPAIGNS
	POLITICAL CANDIDATES
	POLITICAL DIVISIONS (GEOGRAPHIC)
	POLITICAL GEOGRAPHY Use HUMAN GEOGRAPHY
	POLITICAL INFLUENCES
	POLITICAL ISSUES
	POLITICAL NOMINEES Use POLITICAL CANDIDATES
	POLITICAL POWER
	POLITICAL PROTEST Use ACTIVISM
	POLITICAL REFORM Use SOCIAL ACTION
	POLITICAL REFUGEES Use REFUGEES
	POLITICAL SCIENCE
	POLITICAL SOCIALIZATION
	POLITICALIZATION Use POLITICAL SOCIALIZATION
	POLITICS
EDUCATIONAL	POLITICS Use POLITICS OF EDUCATION
INTERNATIONAL	POLITICS Use INTERNATIONAL RELATIONS
	POLITICS OF EDUCATION
	POLLUTION
AIR	POLLUTION
ATMOSPHERIC	POLLUTION Use AIR POLLUTION
AIR	POLLUTION CONTROL (1967 1980) Use AIR POLLUTION
WATER	POLLUTION CONTROL (1969 1980) Use WATER POLLUTION
NOISE	POLLUTION Use NOISE (SOUND)
RIVER	POLLUTION Use WATER POLLUTION
STREAM	POLLUTION Use WATER POLLUTION
WATER	POLLUTION
WATER	POLO
	POLYGRAPHS
	POLYMERS
MALAYO	POLYNESIAN LANGUAGES
	POMO
PING	PONG Use TABLE TENNIS

ITEM POOLS Use ITEM BANKS
SWIMMING POOLS
POOR Use ECONOMICALLY DISADVANTAGED
POP CULTURE Use POPULAR CULTURE
POPULAR CULTURE
POPULARITY
POPULATION CHANGES Use POPULATION TRENDS
POPULATION DISTRIBUTION
POPULATION EDUCATION
POPULATION GROWTH
MIGRANT POPULATION Use MIGRANTS
POPULATION MINORITIES Use MINORITY GROUPS
POPULATION MOVEMENTS Use MIGRATION
POPULATION RESEARCH Use DEMOGRAPHY
RURAL POPULATION
POPULATION SHIFTS Use MIGRATION
POPULATION TRENDS
BLACK POPULATION TRENDS
NEGRO POPULATION TRENDS (1966 1977) Use BLACK POPULATION TRENDS
URBAN POPULATION
DIFFUSION (1967 1982) (POPULATIONS) Use POPULATION DISTRIBUTION
INDIGENOUS POPULATIONS
PORNOGRAPHY
PORTABLE COMPUTERS Use MICROCOMPUTERS
PORTABLE FACILITIES Use RELOCATABLE FACILITIES
PORTFOLIOS (BACKGROUND MATERIALS)
CHARACTER PORTRAYAL Use CHARACTERIZATION
PORTUGUESE
PORTUGUESE AMERICANS
POSITION PAPERS
POSITIVE REINFORCEMENT
POST COORDINATE INDEXES Use COORDINATE INDEXES
POST DOCTORAL EDUCATION (1967 1980) Use POSTDOCTORAL EDUCATION
POST HIGH SCHOOL EDUCATION Use POSTSECONDARY EDUCATION
POST HIGH SCHOOL GUIDANCE
POST SECONDARY EDUCATION (1967 1978) Use POSTSECONDARY EDUCATION
POST TESTING (1966 1980) Use PRETESTS POSTTESTS
POSTDOCTORAL EDUCATION
TUITION POSTPONEMENT Use INCOME CONTINGENT LOANS
POSTSECONDARY EDUCATION
POSTSECONDARY EDUCATION AS A FIELD OF STUDY
POSTSECONDARY INSTRUCTIONAL LEVEL Use POSTSECONDARY EDUCATION
PRETESTS POSTTESTS
POSTURE DEVELOPMENT Use HUMAN POSTURE
HUMAN POSTURE
POSTURE PATTERNS Use HUMAN POSTURE
POTABLE WATER Use DRINKING WATER
POTENTIAL DROPOUTS
EMPLOYMENT POTENTIAL
SCHOLASTIC POTENTIAL Use ACADEMIC APTITUDE
POTENTIOMETERS (INSTRUMENTS)
POTTERY Use CERAMICS
POVERTY
POVERTY AREAS
POVERTY FACTORS Use ECONOMIC FACTORS and POVERTY
POVERTY PROGRAMS
ANTI POVERTY PROGRAMS Use POVERTY PROGRAMS
POVERTY RESEARCH (1970 1980) Use POVERTY
POVERTY STRICKEN Use ECONOMICALLY DISADVANTAGED
BLACK POWER
FLUID POWER EDUCATION (1967 1980) Use FLUID MECHANICS
INDIVIDUAL POWER
POWER MECHANICS (1969 1980) Use POWER TECHNOLOGY
HOLDING POWER (OF SCHOOLS) Use SCHOOL HOLDING POWER
NUCLEAR POWER PLANT TECHNICIANS
NUCLEAR POWER PLANTS
POLITICAL POWER
SCHOOL HOLDING POWER
POWER STRUCTURE
POWER TECHNOLOGY
POWER TRANSFER SYSTEMS Use KINETICS
STATES POWERS
PRACTICAL ARTS
PRACTICAL MATHEMATICS (1966 1980) Use MATHEMATICAL APPLICATIONS
PRACTICAL MUSIC Use APPLIED MUSIC
PRACTICAL NURSES (1967 1981) Use NURSES and PRACTICAL NURSING
PRACTICAL NURSING
DRILLS (PRACTICE)
EDUCATIONAL PRACTICE (1967 1980) Use EDUCATIONAL PRACTICES
FAMILY PRACTICE (MEDICINE)
GENERAL PRACTICE (MEDICINE) Use FAMILY PRACTICE (MEDICINE)
NEGATIVE PRACTICE
OFFICE PRACTICE
RESEARCH PRACTICE RELATIONSHIP Use RESEARCH AND DEVELOPMENT and THEORY PRACTICE RELATIONSHIP
THEORY PRACTICE RELATIONSHIP
SUPERVISED FARM PRACTICE
TEACHER DIRECTED PRACTICE Use TEACHER GUIDANCE
PRACTICE TEACHING Use STUDENT TEACHING
EDUCATIONAL PRACTICES
EMPLOYMENT PRACTICES
TEACHING PRACTICES Use TEACHING METHODS
PRACTICUM PAPERS
PRACTICUM SUPERVISION
PRACTICUMS
NURSE PRACTITIONERS
SCHOOL NURSE PRACTITIONERS Use NURSE PRACTITIONERS and SCHOOL NURSES
DEMENTIA PRAECOX Use SCHIZOPHRENIA
PRAGMATICS
PREACHERS Use CLERGY
PREADOLESCENCE Use PREADOLESCENTS
PREADOLESCENTS

PRECEPTORS (MEDICINE) Use PHYSICIANS and PRACTICUM SUPERVISION
PRECEPTORSHIPS (MEDICINE) Use CLINICAL EXPERIENCE
DRAWING (PRECISION DRAFT) Use DRAFTING
PRECISION RATIO Use RELEVANCE (INFORMATION RETRIEVAL)
PRECISION TEACHING
PRECOLLEGE LEVEL Use HIGH SCHOOLS
PREDICTION
ACHIEVEMENT PREDICTION Use ACHIEVEMENT and PREDICTION
GRADE PREDICTION
PREDICTIVE ABILITY (TESTING) (1966 1980) Use PREDICTIVE MEASUREMENT
CRITERION VALIDITY (PREDICTIVE) Use PREDICTIVE VALIDITY
PREDICTIVE MEASUREMENT
PREDICTIVE VALIDITY
PREDICTIVE VARIABLES Use PREDICTOR VARIABLES
PREDICTOR VARIABLES
PREDICTORS Use PREDICTOR VARIABLES
PREFABRICATION
DIMENSIONAL PREFERENCE
DESIGN PREFERENCES
PREFERENTIAL ADMISSION Use SELECTIVE ADMISSION
PREGNANCY
PREGNANT STUDENTS
PREJUDICE Use BIAS
RACIAL PREJUDICE Use RACIAL BIAS
SEX PREJUDICE Use SEX BIAS
PREKINDERGARTEN Use PRESCHOOL EDUCATION
PREKINDERGARTEN CLASSES Use PRESCHOOL EDUCATION
PREKINDERGARTEN TEACHERS Use PRESCHOOL TEACHERS
PREMATURE BIRTH Use PREMATURE INFANTS
PREMATURE INFANTS
PREMEDICAL STUDENTS
PREMIUM PAY
PRENATAL INFLUENCES
ADMINISTRATOR PREPARATION Use ADMINISTRATOR EDUCATION
COLLEGE PREPARATION
COUNSELOR PREPARATION Use COUNSELOR TRAINING
EMPLOYMENT PREPARATION Use JOB TRAINING
TEACHER PREPARATION Use TEACHER EDUCATION
TEXTBOOK PREPARATION
NONCOLLEGE PREPARATORY STUDENTS (1967 1980) Use NONCOLLEGE BOUND STUDENTS
PREPOSITIONS
PREREADING EXPERIENCE
PREREQUISITE COURSES Use PREREQUISITES and REQUIRED COURSES
PREREQUISITES
PRERETIREMENT EDUCATION
PRERETIREMENT PROGRAMS Use PRERETIREMENT EDUCATION
PRESCHOOL CHILDREN
PRESCHOOL CLINICS (1966 1980) Use CLINICS and PRESCHOOL EDUCATION
PRESCHOOL CURRICULUM
PRESCHOOL EDUCATION
PRESCHOOL EVALUATION
PRESCHOOL EXPERIENCE Use EARLY EXPERIENCE
PRESCHOOL LEARNING (1966 1980)
PRESCHOOL PROGRAMS (1966 1980) Use PRESCHOOL EDUCATION
PRESCHOOL TEACHERS
PRESCHOOL TESTS
PRESCHOOL WORKSHOPS (1966 1980) Use PRESCHOOL EDUCATION and WORKSHOPS
PRESCHOOLERS Use PRESCHOOL CHILDREN
PRESCRIPTIVE TEACHING Use DIAGNOSTIC TEACHING
COLOR PRESENTATION (1969 1980) Use COLOR
PRESENTATION METHODS Use TEACHING METHODS
PRESERVATION
TALENT PRESERVATION Use TALENT DEVELOPMENT
PRESERVICE EDUCATION (1966 1980) Use PRESERVICE TEACHER EDUCATION
PRESERVICE TEACHER EDUCATION
PRESERVICE TEACHING EXPERIENCE Use TEACHING EXPERIENCE
PRESIDENTIAL CAMPAIGNS (UNITED STATES)
PRESIDENTIAL CANDIDATES (UNITED STATES) Use POLITICAL CANDIDATES and PRESIDENTIAL CAMPAIGNS (UNITED STATES)
PRESIDENTIAL DEBATES (UNITED STATES) Use DEBATE and PRESIDENTIAL CAMPAIGNS (UNITED STATES)
PRESIDENTIAL ELECTIONS (UNITED STATES) Use ELECTIONS and PRESIDENTIAL CAMPAIGNS (UNITED STATES)
PRESIDENTS
COLLEGE PRESIDENTS
PRESIDENTS OF THE UNITED STATES
PRESS Use NEWS MEDIA
FREEDOM OF THE PRESS Use FREEDOM OF SPEECH
DRILL PRESS OPERATORS Use MACHINE TOOL OPERATORS
PUNCH PRESS OPERATORS Use MACHINE TOOL OPERATORS
PRESS OPINION
DRILL PRESSES Use MACHINE TOOLS
PUNCH PRESSES Use MACHINE TOOLS
PRESSURE (1970 1980)
ABSOLUTE PRESSURE Use PRESSURE (PHYSICS)
AMBIENT PRESSURE Use PRESSURE (PHYSICS)
FLUID PRESSURE Use PRESSURE (PHYSICS)
HIGH BLOOD PRESSURE Use HYPERTENSION
PEER PRESSURE Use PEER INFLUENCE
PHYSICAL PRESSURE Use PRESSURE (PHYSICS)
PRESSURE (PHYSICS)
SOCIAL PRESSURE Use SOCIAL INFLUENCES
GROUP PRESSURES Use GROUP DYNAMICS
PRESTIGE
PRESTRESSED CONCRETE
PRETECHNOLOGY PROGRAMS
PRETEND PLAY
PRETENSIONED CONCRETE Use PRESTRESSED CONCRETE
PRETESTING
PRETESTS (1966 1980) Use PRETESTS POSTTESTS
PRETESTS POSTTESTS

PREVALENCE Use INCIDENCE
PREVENTION
ACCIDENT PREVENTION
CRIME PREVENTION
DELINQUENCY PREVENTION
DROPOUT PREVENTION
FIRE PREVENTION Use FIRE PROTECTION
PREVENTIVE MEASURES Use PREVENTION
PREVENTIVE MEDICINE
PREVIOUS LEARNING Use PRIOR LEARNING
PREVOCATIONAL EDUCATION
PREVOCATIONAL TRAINING Use PREVOCATIONAL EDUCATION
PREWRITING
PRICE INDEXES Use COST INDEXES
PRIESTS
PRIMACY EFFECT
LAW OF PRIMACY Use PRIMACY EFFECT
PRIMARY EDUCATION
PRIMARY GRADES (1966 1980) Use PRIMARY EDUCATION
PRIMARY HEALTH CARE
UNGRADED PRIMARY PROGRAMS (1966 1980) Use NONGRADED INSTRUCTIONAL GROUPING
PRIMARY SOURCES
INFANT SCHOOLS (BRITISH PRIMARY SYSTEM) Use BRITISH INFANT SCHOOLS
NONGRADED PRIMARY SYSTEM (1966 1980) Use NONGRADED INSTRUCTIONAL GROUPING
PRIMATOLOGY
PRIME NUMBERS
PRINCIPAL COMPONENTS ANALYSIS Use FACTOR ANALYSIS
PRINCIPALS
ASSISTANT PRINCIPALS
SCHOOL PRINCIPALS Use PRINCIPALS
VICE PRINCIPALS Use ASSISTANT PRINCIPALS
ADMINISTRATIVE PRINCIPLES
EDUCATIONAL PRINCIPLES
SCIENTIFIC PRINCIPLES
MICROFORM READER PRINTERS (1971 1980) Use MICROFORM READERS
PRINTING
PRINTSCRIPT Use MANUSCRIPT WRITING (HANDLETTERING)
PRIOR EXPERIENTIAL LEARNING Use EXPERIENTIAL LEARNING and PRIOR LEARNING
PRIOR KNOWLEDGE Use PRIOR LEARNING
PRIOR LEARNING
PRIORITY DETERMINATION Use NEEDS ASSESSMENT
PRISON EDUCATION Use CORRECTIONAL EDUCATION
PRISON LIBRARIES
PRISON SENTENCES Use SENTENCING
PRISONERS
PRISONS Use CORRECTIONAL INSTITUTIONS
PRIVACY
PRIVATE AGENCIES
PRIVATE COLLEGES
PRIVATE EDUCATION
PRIVATE FINANCIAL SUPPORT
PRIVATE HIGHER EDUCATION Use HIGHER EDUCATION and PRIVATE EDUCATION
PRIVATE INFORMATION Use CONFIDENTIALITY
PRIVATE JUNIOR COLLEGES Use PRIVATE COLLEGES and TWO YEAR COLLEGES
PRIVATE SCHOOL AID
PRIVATE SCHOOLS
PRIVATE UNIVERSITIES Use PRIVATE COLLEGES
PRIVILEGED COMMUNICATION Use CONFIDENTIALITY
PROACTIVE INHIBITION Use INHIBITION
PROBABILITY
PROBABILITY THEORY (1967 1980) Use PROBABILITY
ACADEMIC PROBATION
PROBATION OFFICERS
SCHOLASTIC PROBATION Use ACADEMIC PROBATION
PROBATIONARY PERIOD
PROBATIONARY TEACHERS Use PROBATIONARY PERIOD
PROBLEM CHILDREN
PROBLEM SETS
PROBLEM SOLVING
PARTICIPATIVE PROBLEM SOLVING Use PARTICIPATIVE DECISION MAKING and PROBLEM SOLVING
PROBLEMS
ADJUSTMENT PROBLEMS (1966 1980) Use ADJUSTMENT (TO ENVIRONMENT)
ADMINISTRATIVE PROBLEMS
BEHAVIOR PROBLEMS
CITY PROBLEMS (1966 1980) Use URBAN PROBLEMS
COMMUNICATION PROBLEMS
COMMUNITY PROBLEMS
CURRICULUM PROBLEMS
DISCIPLINE PROBLEMS
DROPOUT PROBLEMS (1966 1980) Use DROPOUTS
EDUCATIONAL PROBLEMS (1966 1980)
EMOTIONAL PROBLEMS
EMPLOYMENT PROBLEMS
EVALUATION PROBLEMS
FAMILY PROBLEMS
FARM LABOR PROBLEMS (1966 1980) Use FARM LABOR and LABOR PROBLEMS
FINANCIAL PROBLEMS
INTERPERSONAL PROBLEMS (1966 1980) Use INTERPERSONAL RELATIONSHIP
LABOR PROBLEMS
LEARNING PROBLEMS
LEGAL PROBLEMS
STORY PROBLEMS (MATHEMATICS) Use WORD PROBLEMS (MATHEMATICS)
WORD PROBLEMS (MATHEMATICS)
MIGRANT PROBLEMS
PERSONALITY PROBLEMS
PROGRAMING PROBLEMS (1966 1980)
READING PROBLEMS Use READING DIFFICULTIES
RESEARCH PROBLEMS
SOCIAL PROBLEMS
SPECIAL HEALTH PROBLEMS
STUDENT PROBLEMS

SUBURBAN PROBLEMS
TESTING PROBLEMS
URBAN PROBLEMS
WELFARE PROBLEMS (1966 1980) Use WELFARE SERVICES
WORLD PROBLEMS
YOUTH PROBLEMS
PROCEDURAL DUE PROCESS Use DUE PROCESS
CLOZE PROCEDURE
PROCEDURES Use METHODS
EVALUATION PROCEDURES Use EVALUATION METHODS
EXPERIMENTAL PROCEDURES Use RESEARCH METHODOLOGY
GRIEVANCE PROCEDURES
GROUPING PROCEDURES (1966 1980) Use CLASSIFICATION
LABORATORY PROCEDURES
PARLIAMENTARY PROCEDURES
SORTING PROCEDURES (1966 1980) Use CLASSIFICATION
TEACHING PROCEDURES (1966 1980) Use TEACHING METHODS
CONFERENCE PROCEEDINGS
INTERACTION PROCESS ANALYSIS
CONSTRUCTION (PROCESS)
COUNSELING PROCESS Use COUNSELING
DUE PROCESS
PROCESS EDUCATION
PROCESS EVALUATION Use FORMATIVE EVALUATION
MECHANICS (PROCESS)
PROCEDURAL DUE PROCESS Use DUE PROCESS
TEACHING (PROCESS) Use INSTRUCTION
PROCESSED FOODS INSPECTORS Use FOOD AND DRUG INSPECTORS
COGNITIVE PROCESSES
DISCOVERY PROCESSES
EDUCATIONAL PROCESSES Use LEARNING PROCESSES
GROUP PROCESSES Use GROUP DYNAMICS
JUDGMENTAL PROCESSES Use EVALUATIVE THINKING
LEARNING PROCESSES
TECHNICAL PROCESSES (LIBRARIES) Use LIBRARY TECHNICAL PROCESSES
LIBRARY TECHNICAL PROCESSES
COMPOSITION PROCESSES (LITERARY) Use WRITING PROCESSES
PSYCHOEDUCATIONAL PROCESSES (1966 1980) Use PSYCHOEDUCATIONAL METHODS
INFORMATION PROCESSES (PSYCHOLOGICAL) Use COGNITIVE PROCESSES
READING PROCESSES
STATISTICAL PROCESSES Use STATISTICAL ANALYSIS
THINKING PROCESSES Use COGNITIVE PROCESSES
THOUGHT PROCESSES (1966 1980) Use COGNITIVE PROCESSES
WRITING PROCESSES
AUTOMATIC DATA PROCESSING Use DATA PROCESSING
DATA PROCESSING
ELECTRONIC DATA PROCESSING (1967 1980) Use DATA PROCESSING
GRAIN PROCESSING Use GRAINS (FOOD)
INFORMATION PROCESSING
LANGUAGE PROCESSING
CROP PROCESSING OCCUPATIONS
DATA PROCESSING OCCUPATIONS
FOOD PROCESSING OCCUPATIONS
TEXT PROCESSING Use WORD PROCESSING
WORD PROCESSING
PROCREATION Use REPRODUCTION (BIOLOGY)
PROCTORING
PRODUCER SERVICES
DATABASE PRODUCERS
PRODUCT EVALUATION Use SUMMATIVE EVALUATION
PRODUCT INFORMATION Use MERCHANDISE INFORMATION
DAIRY PRODUCT INSPECTORS Use FOOD AND DRUG INSPECTORS
PRODUCT LABELS Use MERCHANDISE INFORMATION
AGRICULTURAL PRODUCTION
VIDEO PRODUCTION CENTERS Use TELEVISION STUDIOS
CROP PRODUCTION Use AGRICULTURAL PRODUCTION
FILM PRODUCTION
PRODUCTION FUNCTIONS Use PRODUCTIVITY
EDUCATIONAL PRODUCTION FUNCTIONS Use PRODUCTIVITY
GRAIN PRODUCTION Use GRAINS (FOOD)
LARGE SCALE PRODUCTION Use MASS PRODUCTION
LIVESTOCK PRODUCTION Use AGRICULTURAL PRODUCTION
PRODUCTION MACHINE OPERATORS Use MACHINE TOOL OPERATORS
MASS PRODUCTION
FILM PRODUCTION SPECIALISTS
PRODUCTION TECHNICIANS
PRODUCTION TECHNIQUES
TEXTBOOK PRODUCTION Use TEXTBOOK PUBLICATION
PRODUCTIVE LIVING (1967 1980) Use QUALITY OF LIFE
PRODUCTIVE THINKING
PRODUCTIVITY
ART PRODUCTS
TEACHING PROFESSION Use TEACHING (OCCUPATION)
ACADEMIC RANK (PROFESSIONAL)
PROFESSIONAL ASSOCIATIONS
PROFESSIONAL AUTONOMY
PROFESSIONAL CONTINUING EDUCATION
FIRST PROFESSIONAL DEGREES Use DEGREES (ACADEMIC) and PROFESSIONAL EDUCATION
PROFESSIONAL DEVELOPMENT
PROFESSIONAL EDUCATION
PROFESSIONAL GROWTH Use PROFESSIONAL DEVELOPMENT
PROFESSIONAL NEGOTIATION Use COLLECTIVE BARGAINING
PROFESSIONAL NURSES Use NURSES
PROFESSIONAL OCCUPATIONS
PROFESSIONAL PERSONNEL
PROFESSIONAL RECOGNITION
PROFESSIONAL SERVICES
PROFESSIONAL STAFF Use PROFESSIONAL PERSONNEL
PROFESSIONAL STANDARDS Use STANDARDS
PROFESSIONAL STATUS Use PROFESSIONAL RECOGNITION
PROFESSIONAL TRAINING

ALLIED HEALTH PROFESSIONS Use ALLIED HEALTH OCCUPATIONS
CLINICAL TEACHING (HEALTH PROFESSIONS)
HEALTH RELATED PROFESSIONS Use ALLIED HEALTH OCCUPATIONS
LEGAL EDUCATION (PROFESSIONS)
LICENSING EXAMINATIONS (PROFESSIONS)
PROFESSORIAL RANK Use ACADEMIC RANK (PROFESSIONAL)
AGING PROFESSORIATE Use AGING IN ACADEMIA
PROFESSORS
ADJUNCT PROFESSORS Use ADJUNCT FACULTY
CLINICAL PROFESSORS (1967 1980) (EDUCATION) Use STUDENT TEACHER SUPERVISORS
GRADUATE PROFESSORS (1966 1980) Use GRADUATE SCHOOL FACULTY
CLINICAL PROFESSORS (1967 1980) (MEDICINE) Use MEDICAL SCHOOL FACULTY
WOMEN PROFESSORS (1966 1980) Use WOMEN FACULTY
PROFICIENCY BASED EDUCATION Use COMPETENCY BASED EDUCATION
PROFICIENCY BASED TEACHER EDUCATION Use COMPETENCY BASED TEACHER EDUCATION
LANGUAGE PROFICIENCY
PROFILE EVALUATION (1966 1980) Use PROFILES
PROFILES
BIOGRAPHICAL PROFILES Use BIOGRAPHICAL INVENTORIES
PROFOUND DISABILITIES Use SEVERE DISABILITIES
PROFOUNDLY MENTALLY RETARDED Use SEVERE MENTAL RETARDATION
PROGNOSES Use PROGNOSTIC TESTS
PROGNOSTIC TESTS
PROGRAM ADMINISTRATION
PROGRAM APPROVAL (VALIDATION) Use PROGRAM VALIDATION
ARTICULATION (PROGRAM) (1967 1980) Use ARTICULATION (EDUCATION)
PROGRAM ATTITUDES
PROGRAM BUDGETING
PROGRAM CONTENT
PROGRAM COORDINATION (1966 1980) Use COOPERATIVE PROGRAMS and COORDINATION
PROGRAM COSTS
PROGRAM DESCRIPTIONS
PROGRAM DESIGN
PROGRAM DEVELOPMENT
PROGRAM DISCONTINUANCE Use PROGRAM TERMINATION
GRADES (PROGRAM DIVISIONS) Use INSTRUCTIONAL PROGRAM DIVISIONS
INSTRUCTIONAL PROGRAM DIVISIONS
COMPUTER PROGRAM DOCUMENTATION Use COMPUTER SOFTWARE
PROGRAM EFFECTIVENESS
PROGRAM ELIMINATION Use PROGRAM TERMINATION
PROGRAM EVALUATION
PROGRAM GUIDES
PROGRAM IMPLEMENTATION
PROGRAM IMPROVEMENT
PROGRAM LENGTH
PROGRAM PHASEOUT Use PROGRAM TERMINATION
PROGRAM PLANNING (1966 1980) Use PROGRAM DEVELOPMENT
PROGRAM PROPOSALS
COMPUTER PROGRAM REVIEWS Use COMPUTER SOFTWARE REVIEWS
PROGRAM TERMINATION
PROGRAM VALIDATION
PROGRAMED INSTRUCTION
PROGRAMED INSTRUCTIONAL MATERIALS
PROGRAMED LEARNING Use PROGRAMED INSTRUCTION
PROGRAMED MATERIALS (1966 1980) Use PROGRAMED INSTRUCTIONAL MATERIALS
PROGRAMED SELF INSTRUCTION Use PROGRAMED INSTRUCTION
PROGRAMED TEXTS (1966 1980) Use PROGRAMED INSTRUCTIONAL MATERIALS and TEXTBOOKS
PROGRAMED TUTORING
PROGRAMED UNITS (1966 1980) Use PROGRAMED INSTRUCTION and UNITS OF STUDY
PROGRAMERS
PROGRAMING
ARCHITECTURAL PROGRAMING
AUTHORING AIDS (PROGRAMING)
PROGRAMING (BROADCAST)
COMPUTER PROGRAMING Use PROGRAMING
PROGRAMING LANGUAGES
LINEAR PROGRAMING
MULTICHANNEL PROGRAMING (1966 1980) Use PROGRAMING (BROADCAST)
PROGRAMING PROBLEMS (1966 1980)
RADIO PROGRAMING Use PROGRAMING (BROADCAST)
TELEVISION PROGRAMING Use PROGRAMING (BROADCAST)
PROGRAMS
ACCELERATED PROGRAMS (1966 1980) Use ACCELERATION (EDUCATION)
ADULT PROGRAMS
ADULT EDUCATION PROGRAMS (1966 1980) Use ADULT EDUCATION and ADULT PROGRAMS
ADULT READING PROGRAMS
ADVANCED PROGRAMS (1966 1980)
ADVANCED PLACEMENT PROGRAMS
AFTER SCHOOL PROGRAMS
ANTI POVERTY PROGRAMS Use POVERTY PROGRAMS
ANTI SEGREGATION PROGRAMS (1967 1980) Use RACIAL INTEGRATION
ASSEMBLY PROGRAMS
ATHLETIC PROGRAMS (1966 1980) Use ATHLETICS
AUDIOVISUAL PROGRAMS (1966 1980) Use AUDIOVISUAL INSTRUCTION
AUTOINSTRUCTIONAL PROGRAMS (1966 1980) Use PROGRAMED INSTRUCTION
BILINGUAL EDUCATION PROGRAMS
BRACERO PROGRAMS (1966 1980) Use BRACEROS
BREAKFAST PROGRAMS
BUILDING PROGRAMS Use CONSTRUCTION PROGRAMS
CHURCH PROGRAMS
CITY WIDE PROGRAMS (1967 1980) Use URBAN PROGRAMS
CIVIC PROGRAMS Use COMMUNITY PROGRAMS
CLASSROOM GUIDANCE PROGRAMS (1968 1980)
CO OP PROGRAMS Use COOPERATIVE PROGRAMS
COLLEGE PROGRAMS
COLLEGE LANGUAGE PROGRAMS (1967 1980)
COLLEGE SECOND LANGUAGE PROGRAMS
COLLEGE WORK STUDY PROGRAMS Use WORK STUDY PROGRAMS
COMMUNITY PROGRAMS
ACTION PROGRAMS (COMMUNITY) (1966 1980) Use COMMUNITY ACTION
COMMUNITY CONSULTANT PROGRAMS (1966 1980) Use CONSULTATION PROGRAMS

COMMUNITY RECREATION PROGRAMS
COMMUNITY SCHOOL PROGRAMS Use SCHOOL COMMUNITY PROGRAMS
COMMUNITY SERVICE PROGRAMS (1966 1980) Use COMMUNITY SERVICES
COMPENSATORY EDUCATION PROGRAMS (1966 1980) Use COMPENSATORY EDUCATION
COMPREHENSIVE PROGRAMS
COMPUTER PROGRAMS (1966 1984) Use COMPUTER SOFTWARE
COMPUTER ORIENTED PROGRAMS
CONSTRUCTION PROGRAMS
CONSULTATION PROGRAMS
COOPERATIVE PROGRAMS
COUNSELING PROGRAMS (1966 1980) Use COUNSELING SERVICES
COUNSELING INSTRUCTIONAL PROGRAMS (1967 1980)
COUNTY PROGRAMS
DAY PROGRAMS
DAY CAMP PROGRAMS
DAY CARE PROGRAMS (1966 1980) Use DAY CARE
DAYTIME PROGRAMS (1967 1980) Use DAY PROGRAMS
DEMONSTRATION PROGRAMS
DEVELOPMENTAL PROGRAMS
DEVELOPMENTAL STUDIES PROGRAMS
DISCUSSION PROGRAMS (1966 1980) Use DISCUSSION
DOCTORAL PROGRAMS
DROPOUT PROGRAMS
EDUCATIONAL PROGRAMS (1966 1980)
EMERGENCY PROGRAMS
EMPLOYEE ASSISTANCE PROGRAMS
EMPLOYMENT PROGRAMS
ENGLISH PROGRAMS (1966 1980) Use ENGLISH CURRICULUM
ENRICHMENT PROGRAMS (1966 1980) Use ENRICHMENT ACTIVITIES
EVENING PROGRAMS
EVENING COUNSELING PROGRAMS (1966 1980) Use COUNSELING SERVICES and EVENING PROGRAMS
EXCHANGE PROGRAMS
EXEMPLARY PROGRAMS Use DEMONSTRATION PROGRAMS
EXPERIMENTAL PROGRAMS
EXTERNAL DEGREE PROGRAMS
EXTRAMURAL ATHLETIC PROGRAMS (1966 1980) Use EXTRAMURAL ATHLETICS
FAMILY PROGRAMS
FEDERAL PROGRAMS
FEEDER PROGRAMS (1966 1980) Use FEEDER PATTERNS
FIELD EXPERIENCE PROGRAMS
FLES PROGRAMS (1967 1980) Use FLES and SECOND LANGUAGE PROGRAMS
FOLLOWUP PROGRAMS Use FOLLOWUP STUDIES
FOREIGN LANGUAGE PROGRAMS Use SECOND LANGUAGE PROGRAMS
FOUNDATION PROGRAMS
FREE CHOICE TRANSFER PROGRAMS
GED PROGRAMS Use HIGH SCHOOL EQUIVALENCY PROGRAMS
GENERAL EDUCATIONAL DEVELOPMENT PROGRAMS Use HIGH SCHOOL EQUIVALENCY PROGRAMS
GUIDANCE PROGRAMS
HEALTH PROGRAMS
HIGH SCHOOL EQUIVALENCY PROGRAMS
HOME PROGRAMS
HUMAN RELATIONS PROGRAMS
IMMERSION PROGRAMS
IMMUNIZATION PROGRAMS
IMPROVEMENT PROGRAMS
INDIVIDUALIZED PROGRAMS
INDIVIDUALIZED EDUCATION PROGRAMS
INPLANT PROGRAMS
INSERVICE PROGRAMS (1966 1980) Use INSERVICE EDUCATION
INSERVICE EDUCATION PROGRAMS Use INSERVICE EDUCATION
INSTITUTES (TRAINING PROGRAMS)
INSTRUCTIONAL PROGRAMS (1966 1980)
INSURANCE PROGRAMS (1968 1980) Use INSURANCE
INTERCOLLEGIATE PROGRAMS (1967 1980) Use INTERCOLLEGIATE COOPERATION
INTERCULTURAL PROGRAMS
INTERGENERATIONAL PROGRAMS
INTERNATIONAL PROGRAMS
INTERNSHIP PROGRAMS
INTERSESSION SCHOOL PROGRAMS Use VACATION PROGRAMS
INTERSTATE PROGRAMS
INTRAMURAL ATHLETIC PROGRAMS (1966 1980) Use INTRAMURAL ATHLETICS
LANGUAGE PROGRAMS (1966 1980)
LIBRARY PROGRAMS (1966 1980) Use LIBRARY SERVICES
LITERATURE PROGRAMS (1966 1980)
LOCAL COMMUNITY PROGRAMS Use COMMUNITY PROGRAMS
LUNCH PROGRAMS
MASTERS PROGRAMS
RESIDENCY PROGRAMS (MEDICAL) Use GRADUATE MEDICAL EDUCATION
MENTAL HEALTH PROGRAMS
MERIT RATING PROGRAMS (1967 1980) Use MERIT RATING
MIGRANT PROGRAMS
MODEL PROGRAMS Use DEMONSTRATION PROGRAMS
NATIONAL PROGRAMS
NONSCHOOL EDUCATIONAL PROGRAMS
OUTREACH PROGRAMS
PHYSICAL RECREATION PROGRAMS
PILOT PROGRAMS Use PILOT PROJECTS
POVERTY PROGRAMS
PRERETIREMENT PROGRAMS Use PRERETIREMENT EDUCATION
PRESCHOOL PROGRAMS (1966 1980) Use PRESCHOOL EDUCATION
PRETECHNOLOGY PROGRAMS
READING PROGRAMS
RECREATIONAL PROGRAMS
REGIONAL PROGRAMS
REHABILITATION PROGRAMS
REMEDIAL PROGRAMS
REMEDIAL EDUCATION PROGRAMS Use REMEDIAL PROGRAMS
REMEDIAL READING PROGRAMS (1966 1980) Use REMEDIAL PROGRAMS and REMEDIAL READING
RESEARCH PROGRAMS Use RESEARCH PROJECTS
RESIDENT CAMP PROGRAMS
RESIDENTIAL PROGRAMS

RESOURCE ROOM PROGRAMS
RESTRICTIVE TRANSFER PROGRAMS (1966 1980) Use TRANSFER PROGRAMS
SCHOOL PROGRAMS Use SCHOOL ACTIVITIES
SCHOOL COMMUNITY PROGRAMS
SCHOOL RECREATIONAL PROGRAMS
SCIENCE PROGRAMS
SECOND LANGUAGE PROGRAMS
SELF HELP PROGRAMS
SEQUENTIAL PROGRAMS (1966 1980) Use SEQUENTIAL APPROACH
SEQUENTIAL READING PROGRAMS (1966 1980) Use SEQUENTIAL APPROACH
SOCIAL RECREATION PROGRAMS (1966 1980) Use RECREATIONAL PROGRAMS
SPECIAL PROGRAMS
SPECIAL DEGREE PROGRAMS
STATE PROGRAMS
STATE GOVERNMENT PROGRAMS Use STATE GOVERNMENT and STATE PROGRAMS
STATEWIDE PROGRAMS Use STATE PROGRAMS
STUDENT EXCHANGE PROGRAMS
STUDENT LOAN PROGRAMS
STUDENT PERSONNEL PROGRAMS (1967 1980) Use STUDENT PERSONNEL SERVICES
STUDY RELEASE PROGRAMS Use RELEASED TIME
SUMMER PROGRAMS
SUMMER SCIENCE PROGRAMS
TEACHER PROGRAMS (1966 1980) Use TEACHER EDUCATION PROGRAMS
TEACHER EDUCATION PROGRAMS
TEACHER EXCHANGE PROGRAMS
TEACHING PROGRAMS (1966 1980)
TECHNOLOGICAL PROGRAMS Use SCIENCE PROGRAMS
TERMINATION OF PROGRAMS Use PROGRAM TERMINATION
TESTING PROGRAMS
TIME SHORTENED DEGREE PROGRAMS Use ACCELERATION (EDUCATION)
TRANSFER PROGRAMS
TRANSITIONAL PROGRAMS
TUTORIAL PROGRAMS
UNGRADED PROGRAMS (1966 1980) Use NONGRADED INSTRUCTIONAL GROUPING
UNGRADED ELEMENTARY PROGRAMS (1966 1980) Use NONGRADED INSTRUCTIONAL GROUPING
UNGRADED PRIMARY PROGRAMS (1966 1980) Use NONGRADED INSTRUCTIONAL GROUPING
UNIFIED STUDIES PROGRAMS (1966 1980) Use UNIFIED STUDIES CURRICULUM
URBAN PROGRAMS
VACATION PROGRAMS
VALIDATED PROGRAMS
APPROVED PROGRAMS (VALIDATED) Use VALIDATED PROGRAMS
WEEKEND PROGRAMS
WORK EDUCATION PROGRAMS Use WORK STUDY PROGRAMS
WORK EXPERIENCE PROGRAMS
WORK STUDY PROGRAMS
YOUTH PROGRAMS
ACADEMIC PROGRESS Use ACADEMIC ACHIEVEMENT
ECONOMIC PROGRESS
CONTINUOUS PROGRESS PLAN
FLEXIBLE PROGRESSION
PROGRESSIVE EDUCATION
PROGRESSIVE RELAXATION (1967 1980) Use RELAXATION TRAINING
PROGRESSIVE RETARDATION (1966 1980) (IN SCHOOL) Use EDUCATIONALLY DISADVANTAGED
PROJECT APPLICATIONS (1967 1980)
PROJECT METHODS Use STUDENT PROJECTS and TEACHING METHODS
PROJECT PROPOSALS Use PROGRAM PROPOSALS
PROJECT SCHOOLS Use EXPERIMENTAL SCHOOLS
SCIENCE COURSE IMPROVEMENT PROJECT (1967 1980) Use SCIENCE COURSE IMPROVEMENT PROJECTS
PROJECT TRAINING METHODS (1968 1980) Use STUDENT PROJECTS and TEACHING METHODS
PROJECTION EQUIPMENT
ORTHOGONAL PROJECTION (1967 1980) Use ORTHOGRAPHIC PROJECTION
ORTHOGRAPHIC PROJECTION
EMPLOYMENT PROJECTIONS
ENROLLMENT PROJECTIONS
PROJECTIVE MEASURES
PROJECTIVE TESTS (1968 1980) Use PROJECTIVE MEASURES
PROJECTORS Use PROJECTION EQUIPMENT
EIGHT MILLIMETER PROJECTORS (1970 1980) Use PROJECTION EQUIPMENT
FILM PROJECTORS Use PROJECTION EQUIPMENT
FILMSTRIP PROJECTORS
OPAQUE PROJECTORS
OVERHEAD PROJECTORS
OVERHEAD TRANSPARENCY PROJECTORS Use OVERHEAD PROJECTORS
SIXTEEN MILLIMETER PROJECTORS (1966 1980) Use PROJECTION EQUIPMENT
SLIDE PROJECTORS Use PROJECTION EQUIPMENT
TRANSPARENCY PROJECTORS Use OVERHEAD PROJECTORS
PROJECTS (1966 1980)
AGRICULTURAL RESEARCH PROJECTS (1966 1981) Use RESEARCH PROJECTS
CHURCH PROJECTS Use CHURCH PROGRAMS
CHURCH MIGRANT PROJECTS (1966 1980) Use CHURCH PROGRAMS and MIGRANT PROGRAMS
CLASS PROJECTS Use CLASS ACTIVITIES
COMMUNITY PROJECTS Use COMMUNITY PROGRAMS
COMMUNITY MIGRANT PROJECTS (1966 1980) Use COMMUNITY PROGRAMS and MIGRANT PROGRAMS
DEMONSTRATION PROJECTS (1966 1980) Use DEMONSTRATION PROGRAMS
FAMILY PROJECTS (1966 1980) Use FAMILY PROGRAMS
LEGAL AID PROJECTS (1966 1980) Use LEGAL AID
MIGRANT PROJECTS Use MIGRANT PROGRAMS
MIGRANT WORKER PROJECTS (1966 1980) Use MIGRANT PROGRAMS and MIGRANT WORKERS
PILOT PROJECTS
RESEARCH PROJECTS
SCIENCE PROJECTS
SCIENCE COURSE IMPROVEMENT PROJECTS
STUDENT PROJECTS
PROLETARIAT Use WORKING CLASS
ACADEMIC PROMOTION Use STUDENT PROMOTION
FACULTY PROMOTION
PROMOTION (OCCUPATIONAL)
SALES PROMOTION Use MERCHANDISING
STUDENT PROMOTION
TEACHER PROMOTION
PROMPTING

PROMPTS Use CUES
PRONOMINALS Use PRONOUNS
PRONOUNS
PRONUNCIATION
PRONUNCIATION INSTRUCTION
PROOF (MATHEMATICS)
PROPAGANDA
PLANT PROPAGATION
PROPERTY ACCOUNTING
PROPERTY APPRAISAL
PROPERTY CONTROL Use PROPERTY ACCOUNTING
PROPERTY CONTROL SYSTEMS Use PROPERTY ACCOUNTING
INTELLECTUAL PROPERTY
PROPERTY INVENTORY Use FACILITY INVENTORY
PROPERTY TAXES
PROPHYLACTICIANS Use DENTAL HYGIENISTS
PROPORTION (MATHEMATICS) Use RATIOS (MATHEMATICS)
PROPOSAL WRITING
GRANT PROPOSALS Use GRANTS and PROGRAM PROPOSALS
PROGRAM PROPOSALS
PROJECT PROPOSALS Use PROGRAM PROPOSALS
RESEARCH PROPOSALS
PROPRIETARY SCHOOLS
PROPULSION DEVELOPMENT TECHNICIANS Use MECHANICAL DESIGN TECHNICIANS
PROSE
PROSOCIAL BEHAVIOR
PROSODIC FEATURES (SPEECH) Use SUPRASEGMENTALS
PROSODY (LITERARY) Use POETRY
PROSTHESES
COSMETIC PROSTHESES (1967 1980) Use PROSTHESES
CONSUMER PROTECTION
EQUAL PROTECTION
FIRE PROTECTION
POLITICAL PROTEST Use ACTIVISM
STUDENT PROTEST Use ACTIVISM
PROTESTANTS
PROTOCOL ANALYSIS
PROTOCOL MATERIALS
THINKING ALOUD PROTOCOLS Use PROTOCOL ANALYSIS
PROVERBS
PROVINCIAL AID Use STATE AID
PROVINCIAL GOVERNMENT Use STATE GOVERNMENT
PROVINCIAL LIBRARIES Use STATE LIBRARIES
PROVINCIAL SURVEYS Use STATE SURVEYS
SAFETY PROVISIONS Use SAFETY
PROXEMICS Use PERSONAL SPACE
PROXIMITY
PSYCHIATRIC AIDES
PSYCHIATRIC HOSPITALS
PSYCHIATRIC SERVICES
PSYCHIATRIC TECHNICIANS Use PSYCHIATRIC AIDES
PSYCHIATRISTS
PSYCHIATRY
PSYCHOACOUSTICS
PSYCHOANALYSIS Use PSYCHIATRY
PSYCHOCATHARSIS Use CATHARSIS
PSYCHOEDUCATIONAL CLINICS
PSYCHOEDUCATIONAL METHODS
PSYCHOEDUCATIONAL PROCESSES (1966 1980) Use PSYCHOEDUCATIONAL METHODS
PSYCHOLINGUISTICS
ASSOCIATION (PSYCHOLOGICAL) (1968 1980) Use ASSOCIATION (PSYCHOLOGY)
PSYCHOLOGICAL CHARACTERISTICS
PSYCHOLOGICAL CONDITIONING Use CONDITIONING
PSYCHOLOGICAL DESIGN NEEDS (1968 1980) Use DESIGN REQUIREMENTS
PSYCHOLOGICAL EDUCATION Use HUMANISTIC EDUCATION
PSYCHOLOGICAL EVALUATION
IDENTIFICATION (PSYCHOLOGICAL) (1968 1980) Use IDENTIFICATION (PSYCHOLOGY)
INFORMATION PROCESSES (PSYCHOLOGICAL) Use COGNITIVE PROCESSES
MODELING (PSYCHOLOGICAL) (1977 1980) Use MODELING (PSYCHOLOGY)
PSYCHOLOGICAL NEEDS
PSYCHOLOGICAL PATTERNS
RECALL (PSYCHOLOGICAL) (1967 1980) Use RECALL (PSYCHOLOGY)
PSYCHOLOGICAL RESEARCH Use PSYCHOLOGICAL STUDIES
PSYCHOLOGICAL SERVICES
PSYCHOLOGICAL STUDIES
PSYCHOLOGICAL TESTING
PSYCHOLOGICAL TESTS (1966 1980) Use PSYCHOLOGICAL TESTING
PSYCHOLOGISTS
SCHOOL PSYCHOLOGISTS
PSYCHOLOGY
ABNORMAL PSYCHOLOGY Use PSYCHOPATHOLOGY
ASSOCIATION (PSYCHOLOGY)
BEHAVIORIST PSYCHOLOGY Use BEHAVIORISM
CHILD PSYCHOLOGY
CLINICAL PSYCHOLOGY
CLINICAL JUDGMENT (PSYCHOLOGY) Use PSYCHOLOGICAL EVALUATION
COGNITIVE PSYCHOLOGY
COMMUNITY PSYCHOLOGY
COMPLIANCE (PSYCHOLOGY)
CONGRUENCE (PSYCHOLOGY)
DEPRESSION (PSYCHOLOGY)
DEVELOPMENTAL PSYCHOLOGY
DIFFERENTIAL PSYCHOLOGY Use INDIVIDUAL PSYCHOLOGY
EDUCATIONAL PSYCHOLOGY
ENCODING (PSYCHOLOGY)
EXPERIMENTAL PSYCHOLOGY
EXTINCTION (PSYCHOLOGY)
IDENTIFICATION (PSYCHOLOGY)
INDIVIDUAL PSYCHOLOGY
INDUSTRIAL PSYCHOLOGY
INDUSTRIAL AND ORGANIZATIONAL PSYCHOLOGY Use INDUSTRIAL PSYCHOLOGY

INFORMATION STORAGE (PSYCHOLOGY) Use ENCODING (PSYCHOLOGY)
MODELING (PSYCHOLOGY)
NONCOMPLIANCE (PSYCHOLOGY) Use COMPLIANCE (PSYCHOLOGY)
OCCUPATIONAL PSYCHOLOGY Use INDUSTRIAL PSYCHOLOGY
PHYSIOLOGICAL PSYCHOLOGY Use PSYCHOPHYSIOLOGY
RECALL (PSYCHOLOGY)
RECODING (PSYCHOLOGY) Use ENCODING (PSYCHOLOGY)
RECOGNITION (PSYCHOLOGY)
REJECTION (PSYCHOLOGY)
RETENTION (PSYCHOLOGY)
SECURITY (PSYCHOLOGY)
SOCIAL PSYCHOLOGY
SPORT PSYCHOLOGY
SPORTS PSYCHOLOGY Use SPORT PSYCHOLOGY
TRUST (PSYCHOLOGY)
WITHDRAWAL (PSYCHOLOGY)
WITHDRAWAL TENDENCIES (PSYCHOLOGY) (1966 1980) Use WITHDRAWAL (PSYCHOLOGY)
ORGANIZATIONAL PSYCHOLOGY (WORK ENVIRONMENT) Use INDUSTRIAL PSYCHOLOGY
PSYCHOMETRICS
PSYCHOMETRISTS (1967 1980) Use PSYCHOMETRICS
COORDINATION (PSYCHOMOTOR) Use PSYCHOMOTOR SKILLS
PSYCHOMOTOR OBJECTIVES
PSYCHOMOTOR SKILLS
PSYCHOPATHOLOGY
PSYCHOPHYSIOLOGY
PSYCHOSIS
PSYCHOSOMATIC DISEASES (1968 1980) Use PSYCHOSOMATIC DISORDERS
PSYCHOSOMATIC DISORDERS
PSYCHOTHERAPY
PSYCHOTIC CHILDREN (1966 1980) Use PSYCHOSIS
ONLINE PUBLIC ACCESS CATALOGS Use ONLINE CATALOGS
PUBLIC ACCOMMODATIONS Use PUBLIC FACILITIES
CERTIFIED PUBLIC ACCOUNTANTS
PUBLIC ADMINISTRATION
PUBLIC ADMINISTRATION EDUCATION
PUBLIC AFFAIRS EDUCATION
PUBLIC AGENCIES
PUBLIC COLLEGES
COMMUNITY AGENCIES (PUBLIC) (1966 1980) Use PUBLIC AGENCIES
PUBLIC DEMONSTRATIONS Use DEMONSTRATIONS (CIVIL)
PUBLIC DISCLOSURE Use DISCLOSURE
PUBLIC DOCUMENTS Use GOVERNMENT PUBLICATIONS
PUBLIC EDUCATION
PUBLIC EMPLOYEES Use GOVERNMENT EMPLOYEES
PUBLIC FACILITIES
INTEGRATED PUBLIC FACILITIES (1966 1980) Use PUBLIC FACILITIES and RACIAL INTEGRATION
SEGREGATED PUBLIC FACILITIES (1966 1980) Use PUBLIC FACILITIES and RACIAL SEGREGATION
PUBLIC HEALTH
PUBLIC HEALTH LAWS (1966 1974) Use PUBLIC HEALTH LEGISLATION
PUBLIC HEALTH LEGISLATION
PUBLIC HEARINGS Use HEARINGS
PUBLIC HIGHER EDUCATION Use HIGHER EDUCATION and PUBLIC EDUCATION
HOTLINES (PUBLIC)
PUBLIC HOUSING
PUBLIC HOUSING RESIDENTS (1966 1980) Use PUBLIC HOUSING
PUBLIC IMAGE Use PUBLIC OPINION
PUBLIC LIBRARIES
PUBLIC OFFICIALS
PUBLIC OPINION
PUBLIC PARTICIPATION Use CITIZEN PARTICIPATION
PUBLIC POLICY
PUBLIC RELATIONS
PUBLIC SCHOOL ADULT EDUCATION
PUBLIC SCHOOL SYSTEMS (1966 1980) Use PUBLIC SCHOOLS and SCHOOL DISTRICTS
PUBLIC SCHOOL TEACHERS
PUBLIC SCHOOLS
PUBLIC SERVICE
PUBLIC SERVICE OCCUPATIONS
PUBLIC SPEAKING
PUBLIC SUPPORT
PUBLIC TELEVISION
PUBLIC UTILITIES Use UTILITIES
PUBLIC WELFARE ASSISTANCE Use WELFARE SERVICES
TEXTBOOK PUBLICATION
WRITING FOR PUBLICATION
PUBLICATIONS
COMICS (PUBLICATIONS)
FORMAT (PUBLICATIONS) Use LAYOUT (PUBLICATIONS)
GOVERNMENT PUBLICATIONS
LAYOUT (PUBLICATIONS)
RESEARCH REVIEWS (PUBLICATIONS) (1966 1980)
SCHOOL PUBLICATIONS
STUDENT PUBLICATIONS
TEXTBOOK PUBLICATIONS (1966 1980)
PUBLICITY
PUBLICIZE (1968 1980)
PUBLISH OR PERISH ISSUE
ELECTRONIC PUBLISHING
FACULTY PUBLISHING
PUBLISHING HOUSES Use PUBLISHING INDUSTRY
PUBLISHING INDUSTRY
TEXTBOOK PUBLISHING Use TEXTBOOK PUBLICATION
PUERTO RICAN CULTURE
PUERTO RICANS
PULSE RATE Use HEART RATE
PUNCH PRESS OPERATORS Use MACHINE TOOL OPERATORS
PUNCH PRESSES Use MACHINE TOOLS
PUNCTUATION
PUNISHMENT
CORPORAL PUNISHMENT
PUNJABI Use PANJABI

PUNS
PUPIL PERSONNEL SERVICES
PUPIL PERSONNEL WORKERS
PUPILLARY DILATION
PUPILLARY REFLEX Use PUPILLARY DILATION
PUPILLARY RESPONSE Use PUPILLARY DILATION
PUPILS Use STUDENTS
PUPPET SHOWS Use PUPPETRY
PUPPETRY
PUPPETS Use PUPPETRY
PURCHASING
EQUIPMENT PURCHASING Use PURCHASING
WATER PURIFICATION Use WATER TREATMENT
PURITANS
EDUCATIONAL PURPOSES Use EDUCATIONAL OBJECTIVES
ENGLISH FOR ACADEMIC PURPOSES
ENGLISH FOR SPECIAL PURPOSES
GROUPING (INSTRUCTIONAL PURPOSES)
LANGUAGES FOR SPECIAL PURPOSES
PUSHTO Use PASHTO
PUSHTU Use PASHTO
PUZZLES
PYRAMID ORGANIZATION
Q ANALYSIS Use Q METHODOLOGY
Q METHODOLOGY
Q SORT (1967 1980) Use Q METHODOLOGY
Q TECHNIQUE Use Q METHODOLOGY
QUADRIPLEGIA (1969 1980) Use NEUROLOGICAL IMPAIRMENTS
QUALIFICATIONS
ADMINISTRATOR QUALIFICATIONS
COUNSELOR QUALIFICATIONS
EMPLOYMENT QUALIFICATIONS
SUPERVISOR QUALIFICATIONS
TEACHER QUALIFICATIONS
QUALITATIVE RESEARCH
LEADERSHIP QUALITIES
EDUCATIONAL QUALITY ASSESSMENT Use EDUCATIONAL ASSESSMENT and EDUCATIONAL QUALITY
QUALITY CIRCLES
QUALITY CONTROL
QUALITY EDUCATION Use EDUCATIONAL QUALITY
EDUCATIONAL QUALITY
LIFE QUALITY Use QUALITY OF LIFE
QUALITY OF LIFE
QUALITY OF WORKING LIFE
QUALITY POINT RATIO Use GRADE POINT AVERAGE
TEACHER QUALITY Use TEACHER EFFECTIVENESS
TEACHING QUALITY (1966 1980) Use TEACHER EFFECTIVENESS
WATER QUALITY
QUANTITATIVE RESEARCH (STATISTICS) Use STATISTICAL ANALYSIS
QUANTITATIVE TESTS (1980 1985) (MATHEMATICS) Use MATHEMATICS TESTS
QUANTUM MECHANICS
QUARTER SYSTEM
LIVING QUARTERS Use HOUSING
QUASIEXPERIMENTAL DESIGN
QUECHUA
QUESTION ANSWER INTERVIEWS (1966 1980) Use INTERVIEWS
QUESTIONING TECHNIQUES
QUESTIONNAIRES
QUICHE
QUIZZES Use TESTS
QUOTAS
INTELLIGENCE QUOTIENT
R AND D Use RESEARCH AND DEVELOPMENT
R D AND E Use RESEARCH AND DEVELOPMENT
RACE
CAUCASIAN RACE (1967 1980) Use WHITES
RACE INFLUENCES (1966 1980) Use RACIAL FACTORS
RACE RELATIONS (1966 1980) Use RACIAL RELATIONS
RACIAL ATTITUDES
RACIAL BALANCE
RACIAL BIAS
RACIAL CHARACTERISTICS (1966 1980)
RACIAL COMPOSITION
RACIAL CULTURAL GROUPS Use ETHNIC GROUPS
RACIAL DIFFERENCES
RACIAL DISCRIMINATION
RACIAL DISTRIBUTION
RACIAL FACTORS
RACIAL IDENTIFICATION
RACIAL IDENTITY Use RACIAL IDENTIFICATION
RACIAL IMBALANCE Use RACIAL BALANCE
INTEGRATION (RACIAL) Use RACIAL INTEGRATION
RACIAL INTEGRATION
RACIAL INTERACTION Use RACIAL RELATIONS
RACIAL PREJUDICE Use RACIAL BIAS
RACIAL RECOGNITION (1966 1980) Use RACIAL IDENTIFICATION
RACIAL RELATIONS
SEGREGATION (RACIAL) Use RACIAL SEGREGATION
RACIAL SEGREGATION
RACIAL SELF IDENTIFICATION Use RACIAL IDENTIFICATION
RACIALLY BALANCED SCHOOLS
RACISM (1966 1980)
RACKET SPORTS Use RACQUET SPORTS
RACQUET SPORTS
RACQUETBALL
RADAR
RADIATION
RADIATION BIOLOGY
RADIATION DAMAGE Use RADIATION EFFECTS
RADIATION EFFECTS
SOLAR RADIATION ENERGY Use SOLAR ENERGY

LIGHT RADIATION Use LIGHT
SOLAR RADIATION (1968 1983) Use SOLAR ENERGY
RADIATION THERAPY Use RADIOLOGY
RADIATION THERAPY TECHNOLOGISTS Use RADIOLOGIC TECHNOLOGISTS
VISIBLE RADIATION Use LIGHT
RADIO
EDUCATIONAL RADIO
INSTRUCTIONAL RADIO Use EDUCATIONAL RADIO
RADIO PROGRAMING Use PROGRAMING (BROADCAST)
TELEVISION RADIO REPAIRERS
RADIO TECHNOLOGY (1967 1980) Use RADIO
RADIO TELEVISION REPAIRERS Use TELEVISION RADIO REPAIRERS
RADIOBIOLOGY Use RADIATION BIOLOGY
RADIOGRAPHERS
RADIOISOTOPES
RADIOLOGIC TECHNOLOGISTS
RADIOLOGY
RAGTIME MUSIC Use JAZZ
AIR RAID SHELTERS Use FALLOUT SHELTERS
RAIL TRANSPORTATION
RAILROADS Use RAIL TRANSPORTATION
RAILWAYS Use RAIL TRANSPORTATION
RAISED LINE DRAWINGS
SALARY RAISES Use PROMOTION (OCCUPATIONAL)
FUND RAISING
PARKING RAMPS Use PARKING FACILITIES
RANGE (DISTANCE) Use DISTANCE
LONG RANGE PLANNING
CLASS RANK
FACULTY RANK Use ACADEMIC RANK (PROFESSIONAL)
RANK IN CLASS Use CLASS RANK
ACADEMIC RANK (PROFESSIONAL)
PROFESSORIAL RANK Use ACADEMIC RANK (PROFESSIONAL)
RAPE
STATUTORY RAPE Use RAPE
RAPID READING (1966 1980) Use SPEED READING
RAPPORT
BIRTH RATE
DISEASE RATE (1967 1980) Use DISEASE INCIDENCE
DROPOUT RATE
ENROLLMENT RATE
FERTILITY RATE Use BIRTH RATE
HEART RATE
INFANT DEATH RATE Use INFANT MORTALITY
PULSE RATE Use HEART RATE
READING RATE
RATE TESTS Use TIMED TESTS
TAX RATES
ACHIEVEMENT RATING
MERIT RATING
PERSONALITY RATING Use PERSONALITY ASSESSMENT
MERIT RATING PROGRAMS (1967 1980) Use MERIT RATING
RATING SCALES
BEHAVIOR RATING SCALES
TEACHER RATING (1966 1977) Use TEACHER EVALUATION
CLIENT COUNSELOR RATIO Use COUNSELOR CLIENT RATIO
COUNSELOR CLIENT RATIO
PRECISION RATIO Use RELEVANCE (INFORMATION RETRIEVAL)
QUALITY POINT RATIO Use GRADE POINT AVERAGE
RECALL RATIO Use RELEVANCE (INFORMATION RETRIEVAL)
STUDENT TEACHER RATIO (1966 1984) Use TEACHER STUDENT RATIO
TEACHER STUDENT RATIO
RATIONAL EMOTIVE THERAPY
RATIONAL NUMBERS
RATIONAL THERAPY (1968 1980) Use RATIONAL EMOTIVE THERAPY
CONTRAST RATIOS Use CONTRAST
RATIOS (MATHEMATICS)
RATS
RAW SCORES
INDUSTRIAL X RAY OPERATORS Use RADIOGRAPHERS
X RAY TECHNOLOGISTS Use RADIOLOGIC TECHNOLOGISTS
X RAYS (MEDICINE) Use RADIOLOGY
COUNSELOR REACTION Use COUNSELOR ATTITUDES
PARENT REACTION (1966 1980) Use PARENT ATTITUDES
STUDENT REACTION
TEACHER REACTION Use TEACHER RESPONSE
SITUATION REACTION TESTS Use SITUATIONAL TESTS
REACTION TIME
CHEMICAL REACTIONS
MOTOR REACTIONS
PHOTOCHEMICAL REACTIONS
STRANGER REACTIONS
REACTIVE BEHAVIOR (1966 1980) Use RESPONSES
REACTIVE INHIBITION Use INHIBITION
FREEDOM TO READ Use INTELLECTUAL FREEDOM
READABILITY
READABILITY FORMULAS
MACHINE READABLE CATALOGING
MICROFORM READER PRINTERS (1971 1980) Use MICROFORM READERS
READER RESPONSE
READER TEXT RELATIONSHIP
DOCUMENT READERS Use OPTICAL SCANNERS
READERS (MATERIALS) Use READING MATERIALS
MICROFORM READERS
PAGE READERS Use OPTICAL SCANNERS
RETARDED READERS (1966 1980) Use READING DIFFICULTIES
READERS THEATER
READINESS
DESEGREGATION READINESS Use INTEGRATION READINESS
DISASTER READINESS Use EMERGENCY PROGRAMS
HANDWRITING READINESS (1966 1983) Use HANDWRITING and WRITING READINESS

INTEGRATION	READINESS
LEARNING	READINESS
	READINESS (MENTAL) (1966 1980) Use READINESS
READING	READINESS
SCHOOL	READINESS
READING	READINESS TESTS
SCHOOL	READINESS TESTS
WRITING	READINESS
	READING
	READING ABILITY
	READING ACHIEVEMENT
DIRECTED	READING ACTIVITY
	READING ALOUD TO OTHERS
APPLIED	READING (1966 1980) Use READING
WHOLE WORD	READING APPROACH Use SIGHT METHOD
	READING ASSIGNMENTS
	READING ATTITUDES
BASAL	READING
BASIC	READING (1967 1980)
BEGINNING	READING
	READING CENTERS
	READING CLINICS (1966 1980) Use READING CENTERS
REMEDIAL	READING CLINICS (1966 1980) Use READING CENTERS and REMEDIAL READING
	READING COMPREHENSION
	READING CONSULTANTS
CONTENT	READING (1967 1980) Use CONTENT AREA READING
CONTENT AREA	READING
CORRECTIVE	READING
CREATIVE	READING (1966 1980)
CRITICAL	READING
DECODING	(READING)
	READING DEVELOPMENT (1966 1980)
DEVELOPMENTAL	READING (1966 1980)
	READING DIAGNOSIS
	READING DIFFICULTIES
	READING DIFFICULTY (1966 1980)
	READING DISABILITIES Use READING DIFFICULTIES
EARLY	READING
ELECTIVE	READING (1966 1980)
	READING ENJOYMENT Use LITERATURE APPRECIATION
FACTUAL	READING (1966 1980)
	READING FAILURE
FUNCTIONAL	READING
	READING GAIN Use READING IMPROVEMENT
	READING GAMES
GROUP	READING (1966 1980)
	READING HABITS
	READING IMPROVEMENT
	READING IN CONTENT AREAS Use CONTENT AREA READING
INDEPENDENT	READING
INDIVIDUAL	READING (1966 1980)
INDIVIDUALIZED	READING
	READING INSTRUCTION
	READING INTERESTS
INTERPRETIVE	READING (1966 1980)
INFORMAL	READING INVENTORIES
INFORMAL	READING INVENTORY (1968 1980) Use INFORMAL READING INVENTORIES
	READING LABORATORIES Use READING CENTERS
LEISURE TIME	READING Use RECREATIONAL READING
	READING LEVEL (1966 1980)
	READING MATERIAL SELECTION
	READING MATERIALS
SUPPLEMENTARY	READING MATERIALS
MUSIC	READING
ORAL	READING
	READING PROBLEMS Use READING DIFFICULTIES
	READING PROCESSES
	READING PROGRAMS
ADULT	READING PROGRAMS
REMEDIAL	READING PROGRAMS (1966 1980) Use REMEDIAL PROGRAMS and REMEDIAL READING
SEQUENTIAL	READING PROGRAMS (1966 1980) Use SEQUENTIAL APPROACH
RAPID	READING (1966 1980) Use SPEED READING
	READING RATE
	READING READINESS
	READING READINESS TESTS
RECREATIONAL	READING
REMEDIAL	READING
	READING RESEARCH
SCORE	READING Use MUSIC READING
SILENT	READING
	READING SKILLS
MAP	READING SKILLS Use MAP SKILLS
SURVIVAL	READING SKILLS Use FUNCTIONAL READING
SKIMMING	(READING) Use SPEED READING
	READING SPECIALISTS Use READING CONSULTANTS
SPEECH	READING Use LIPREADING
	READING SPEED (1966 1977) Use READING RATE
SPEED	READING
STORY	READING
	READING STRATEGIES
SUSTAINED SILENT	READING
	READING TEACHERS
	READING TESTS
	READING THERAPY Use BIBLIOTHERAPY
WORD ASSOCIATIONS	(READING) Use ASSOCIATIVE LEARNING
WORD METHOD	(READING) Use SIGHT METHOD
	READING WRITING RELATIONSHIP
COLLECTED	READINGS Use ANTHOLOGIES
	READINGS (COLLECTIONS) Use ANTHOLOGIES
	REAL ESTATE
	REAL ESTATE APPRAISAL Use PROPERTY APPRAISAL

REAL ESTATE OCCUPATIONS
REALIA
REALISM
REALITY THERAPY
SELF REALIZATION Use SELF ACTUALIZATION
CHILD REARING
ABSTRACT REASONING
RECALL (PSYCHOLOGICAL) (1967 1980) Use RECALL (PSYCHOLOGY)
RECALL (PSYCHOLOGY)
RECALL RATIO Use RELEVANCE (INFORMATION RETRIEVAL)
BROADCAST RECEPTION EQUIPMENT
RECEPTIONISTS
RECEPTIVE COMMUNICATION Use RECEPTIVE LANGUAGE
RECEPTIVE LANGUAGE
RECIDIVISM
WELFARE RECIPIENTS
RECIPROCALS (MATHEMATICS)
RECODING (PSYCHOLOGY) Use ENCODING (PSYCHOLOGY)
RECOGNITION (1967 1980)
RECOGNITION (ACHIEVEMENT)
CHARACTER RECOGNITION
MAGNETIC INK CHARACTER RECOGNITION Use CHARACTER RECOGNITION
OPTICAL CHARACTER RECOGNITION Use CHARACTER RECOGNITION and OPTICAL SCANNERS
PATTERN RECOGNITION
PROFESSIONAL RECOGNITION
RECOGNITION (PSYCHOLOGY)
RACIAL RECOGNITION (1966 1980) Use RACIAL IDENTIFICATION
WORD RECOGNITION
RECOMBINANT DNA Use DNA and GENETIC ENGINEERING
RECONSTRUCTION ERA
SOCIAL RECONSTRUCTION Use SOCIAL CHANGE
HOSPITAL RECORD ADMINISTRATORS Use MEDICAL RECORD ADMINISTRATORS
MEDICAL RECORD ADMINISTRATORS
RECORD CLERKS Use FILE CLERKS
MEDICAL RECORD CLERKS Use MEDICAL RECORD TECHNICIANS
PASS NO RECORD GRADING Use CREDIT NO CREDIT GRADING
MEDICAL RECORD LIBRARIANS (1969 1980) Use MEDICAL RECORD ADMINISTRATORS
PHONOGRAPH RECORD LISTS Use DISCOGRAPHIES
HOSPITAL RECORD TECHNICIANS Use MEDICAL RECORD TECHNICIANS
MEDICAL RECORD TECHNICIANS
AUDIOTAPE RECORDERS
AUDIOTAPE CASSETTE RECORDERS Use AUDIOTAPE CASSETTES and AUDIOTAPE RECORDERS
MAGNETIC TAPE CASSETTE RECORDERS (1970 1980) Use MAGNETIC TAPE CASSETTES and TAPE RECORDERS
TAPE RECORDERS
VIDEOTAPE RECORDERS
VIDEOTAPE CASSETTE RECORDERS Use VIDEOTAPE CASSETTES and VIDEOTAPE RECORDERS
AUDIODISC RECORDINGS (1980 1986) Use AUDIODISKS
AUDIOTAPE RECORDINGS
CD RECORDINGS Use OPTICAL DISKS
KINESCOPE RECORDINGS
PHONOTAPE RECORDINGS (1966 1978) Use AUDIOTAPE RECORDINGS
SOUND TAPE RECORDINGS Use AUDIOTAPE RECORDINGS
TAPE RECORDINGS
VIDEO TAPE RECORDINGS (1966 1978) Use VIDEOTAPE RECORDINGS
VIDEODISC RECORDINGS (1979 1986) Use VIDEODISKS
VIDEOTAPE RECORDINGS
RECORDKEEPING
ACADEMIC RECORDS
ATTENDANCE RECORDS
CASE RECORDS
CONFIDENTIAL RECORDS
RECORDS (FORMS)
PAYROLL RECORDS
PHONOGRAPH RECORDS (1966 1980) Use AUDIODISKS
LANGUAGE RECORDS (PHONOGRAPH) (1966 1980) Use AUDIODISKS
STUDENT RECORDS
HEAT RECOVERY
RECREATION
RECREATION FINANCES
RECREATION LEGISLATION
COMMUNITY RECREATION LEGISLATION (1966 1978) Use LOCAL LEGISLATION and RECREATION LEGISLATION
FEDERAL RECREATION LEGISLATION (1966 1978) Use FEDERAL LEGISLATION and RECREATION LEGISLATION
LOCAL RECREATION LEGISLATION (1966 1978) Use LOCAL LEGISLATION and RECREATION LEGISLATION
STATE RECREATION LEGISLATION (1966 1978) Use RECREATION LEGISLATION and STATE LEGISLATION
COMMUNITY RECREATION PROGRAMS
PHYSICAL RECREATION PROGRAMS
SOCIAL RECREATION PROGRAMS (1966 1980) Use RECREATIONAL PROGRAMS
THERAPEUTIC RECREATION
RECREATION THERAPY Use THERAPEUTIC RECREATION
RECREATIONAL ACTIVITIES
RECREATIONAL FACILITIES
RECREATIONAL PROGRAMS
SCHOOL RECREATIONAL PROGRAMS
RECREATIONAL READING
RECREATIONISTS
RECRUITMENT
FACULTY RECRUITMENT
PERSONNEL RECRUITMENT Use RECRUITMENT
STUDENT RECRUITMENT
TEACHER RECRUITMENT
RECURRENT EDUCATION Use LIFELONG LEARNING
RECYCLING
JOB REDESIGN Use JOB DEVELOPMENT
REDEVELOPMENT AREAS Use URBAN RENEWAL
SCHOOL REDISTRICTING (1966 1980) Use SCHOOL DISTRICT REORGANIZATION
REDUCTION IN FORCE
NEED REDUCTION Use NEED GRATIFICATION
REDUNDANCY
REENTRY STUDENTS
REENTRY WORKERS
CURRICULUM REEVALUATION Use CURRICULUM EVALUATION

REVIEW (REEXAMINATION)
REFERENCE BOOKS (1966 1980) Use REFERENCE MATERIALS
REFERENCE GROUPS
LEGISLATIVE REFERENCE LIBRARIES (1968 1980) Use LAW LIBRARIES
REFERENCE MATERIALS
LIBRARY REFERENCE MATERIALS Use LIBRARY MATERIALS and REFERENCE MATERIALS
REFERENCE SERVICES
COMPUTER BASED REFERENCE SERVICES Use ONLINE SYSTEMS and REFERENCE SERVICES
LIBRARY REFERENCE SERVICES (1968 1980) Use LIBRARY SERVICES and REFERENCE SERVICES
ONLINE REFERENCE SERVICES Use ONLINE SYSTEMS and REFERENCE SERVICES
CRITERION REFERENCED EDUCATION Use COMPETENCY BASED EDUCATION
NORM REFERENCED MEASURES Use NORM REFERENCED TESTS
CRITERION REFERENCED TEACHER EDUCATION Use COMPETENCY BASED TEACHER EDUCATION
CRITERION REFERENCED TESTS
NORM REFERENCED TESTS
OBJECTIVE REFERENCED TESTS Use CRITERION REFERENCED TESTS
BIBLIOGRAPHIC REFERENCES Use CITATIONS (REFERENCES)
CITATIONS (REFERENCES)
REFERRAL
REFERRAL SERVICES (COMMUNITY) Use COMMUNITY INFORMATION SERVICES and REFERRAL
EMPLOYMENT REFERRAL SERVICES Use EMPLOYMENT SERVICES
INFORMATION AND REFERRAL SERVICES Use INFORMATION SERVICES and REFERRAL
REFLECTIVITY Use CONCEPTUAL TEMPO
IRIS REFLEX Use PUPILLARY DILATION
PUPILLARY REFLEX Use PUPILLARY DILATION
CHAIN REFLEXES (BEHAVIOR) Use BEHAVIOR CHAINING
CURRICULUM REFORM Use CURRICULUM DEVELOPMENT
EDUCATIONAL REFORM Use EDUCATIONAL CHANGE
FINANCE REFORM
POLITICAL REFORM Use SOCIAL ACTION
SOCIAL REFORM Use SOCIAL ACTION
TAX REFORM Use FINANCE REFORM
ERROR OF REFRACTION Use AMETROPIA
REFRACTIVE ERRORS Use AMETROPIA
OCULAR REFRACTIVE ERRORS Use AMETROPIA
REFRESHER COURSES
REFRESHER TRAINING Use RETRAINING
REFRIGERATION
REFRIGERATION MECHANICS
REFUGEES
POLITICAL REFUGEES Use REFUGEES
REFUSE Use WASTES
REGENTS Use TRUSTEES
BOARD OF REGENTS Use GOVERNING BOARDS
REGIONAL ATTITUDES
REGIONAL CHARACTERISTICS
REGIONAL COOPERATION
REGIONAL DIALECTS
REGIONAL DIFFERENCES Use DIFFERENCES and REGIONAL CHARACTERISTICS
REGIONAL LABORATORIES
REGIONAL LIBRARIES
REGIONAL PLANNING
REGIONAL PROGRAMS
REGIONAL SCHOOLS
GEOGRAPHIC REGIONS
REGISTERED NURSES Use NURSES
COLLEGE REGISTRARS Use REGISTRARS (SCHOOL)
REGISTRARS (SCHOOL)
COLLEGE REGISTRATION Use SCHOOL REGISTRATION
REGISTRATION IN SCHOOL Use SCHOOL REGISTRATION
LATE REGISTRATION
SCHOOL REGISTRATION
VOTER REGISTRATION
MULTIPLE REGRESSION ANALYSIS
REGRESSION EFFECTS Use REGRESSION (STATISTICS)
LINEAR REGRESSION Use REGRESSION (STATISTICS)
REGRESSION (STATISTICS)
EYE REGRESSIONS (1966 1980) Use EYE MOVEMENTS
REGRESSORS Use PREDICTOR VARIABLES
REGULAR CLASS PLACEMENT (1968 1978) Use MAINSTREAMING
FEDERAL REGULATION
PARKING REGULATIONS Use PARKING CONTROLS
TRAFFIC REGULATIONS (1968 1980) Use TRAFFIC CONTROL
REHABILITATION
REHABILITATION CENTERS
CORRECTIONAL REHABILITATION
REHABILITATION COUNSELING
DELINQUENT REHABILITATION
DROPOUT REHABILITATION (1966 1980) Use DROPOUT PROGRAMS
DRUG REHABILITATION
HEARING REHABILITATION Use HEARING THERAPY
REHABILITATION PROGRAMS
STUDENT REHABILITATION (1966 1980) Use REHABILITATION
VOCATIONAL REHABILITATION
REINFORCEMENT
LEARNING REINFORCEMENT Use REINFORCEMENT
MASSED NEGATIVE REINFORCEMENT Use NEGATIVE REINFORCEMENT
NEGATIVE REINFORCEMENT
POSITIVE REINFORCEMENT
SOCIAL REINFORCEMENT
SPACED NEGATIVE REINFORCEMENT Use NEGATIVE REINFORCEMENT
REINFORCEMENT THEORY Use REINFORCEMENT
REINFORCERS (1966 1980) Use REINFORCEMENT
REJECTION (1966 1980) Use REJECTION (PSYCHOLOGY)
REJECTION (PSYCHOLOGY)
SCHOOL RELATED ACTIVITIES Use EXTRACURRICULAR ACTIVITIES
CHURCH RELATED COLLEGES
LAW RELATED EDUCATION
FARM RELATED OCCUPATIONS Use OFF FARM AGRICULTURAL OCCUPATIONS
HEALTH RELATED PROFESSIONS Use ALLIED HEALTH OCCUPATIONS
BLACK WHITE RELATIONS Use RACIAL RELATIONS

RELIGION
RELIGIOUS AGENCIES (1966 1980) Use RELIGIOUS ORGANIZATIONS
RELIGIOUS CONFLICT
RELIGIOUS CULTURAL GROUPS
RELIGIOUS DIFFERENCES
RELIGIOUS DISCRIMINATION
RELIGIOUS EDUCATION
RELIGIOUS FACTORS
RELIGIOUS GROUPS Use RELIGIOUS CULTURAL GROUPS
RELIGIOUS HOLIDAYS
RELIGIOUS ORGANIZATIONS
RELOCATABLE FACILITIES
RELOCATION
REMARRIAGE
REMEDIAL ARITHMETIC (1966 1980) Use ARITHMETIC and REMEDIAL MATHEMATICS
REMEDIAL COURSES (1966 1980) Use REMEDIAL INSTRUCTION
REMEDIAL EDUCATION Use REMEDIAL INSTRUCTION
REMEDIAL EDUCATION PROGRAMS Use REMEDIAL PROGRAMS
REMEDIAL INSTRUCTION
REMEDIAL MATHEMATICS
REMEDIAL PROGRAMS
REMEDIAL READING
REMEDIAL READING CLINICS (1966 1980) Use READING CENTERS and REMEDIAL READING
REMEDIAL READING PROGRAMS (1966 1980) Use REMEDIAL PROGRAMS and REMEDIAL READING
REMEDIAL TEACHERS
REMEDIATION Use REMEDIAL INSTRUCTION
REMEMBERING Use MEMORY
REMUNERATION Use COMPENSATION (REMUNERATION)
COMPENSATION (REMUNERATION)
RENAISSANCE LITERATURE
URBAN RENEWAL AGENCIES
URBAN RENEWAL
RENOVATION Use IMPROVEMENT
BUILDING RENOVATION Use FACILITY IMPROVEMENT
SCHOOL RENOVATION Use EDUCATIONAL FACILITIES IMPROVEMENT
LOW RENT HOUSING
CURRICULUM REORGANIZATION Use CURRICULUM DEVELOPMENT
SCHOOL REORGANIZATION Use SCHOOL ORGANIZATION
SCHOOL DISTRICT REORGANIZATION
REPAIR
APPLIANCE REPAIR
EQUIPMENT REPAIR Use EQUIPMENT MAINTENANCE
HOME APPLIANCE REPAIR Use APPLIANCE REPAIR
APPLIANCE REPAIRERS (1980 1981) Use APPLIANCE REPAIR
AUTO BODY REPAIRERS
BODY AND FENDER REPAIRERS Use AUTO BODY REPAIRERS
MACHINE REPAIRERS
RADIO TELEVISION REPAIRERS Use TELEVISION RADIO REPAIRERS
TELEVISION RADIO REPAIRERS
WATCH REPAIRERS Use WATCHMAKERS
APPLIANCE REPAIRING (1968 1981) Use APPLIANCE REPAIR
AUTO BODY REPAIRMEN (1966 1980) Use AUTO BODY REPAIRERS
MACHINE REPAIRMEN (1968 1980) Use MACHINE REPAIRERS
TELEVISION REPAIRMEN (1968 1980) Use TELEVISION RADIO REPAIRERS
LOAN REPAYMENT
REPERTORY CATALOGS Use UNION CATALOGS
REPERTORY ORCHESTRAS Use ORCHESTRAS
GRADE REPETITION
REPETITIVE FILM SHOWINGS
REPORT CARDS
REPORT WRITING Use TECHNICAL WRITING
COURT REPORTERS
NEWS REPORTING
SPORTS REPORTING Use ATHLETICS and NEWS REPORTING
REPORTS
ANNUAL REPORTS
CONFERENCE REPORTS (1967 1980)
RESEARCH REPORTS
SCIENTIFIC REPORTS Use RESEARCH REPORTS
TECHNICAL REPORTS (1968 1980) Use RESEARCH REPORTS
REPRESENTATIVES Use LEGISLATORS
REPRODUCTION (BIOLOGY)
COPYING (REPRODUCTION) Use REPROGRAPHY
REPRODUCTION (COPYING) Use REPROGRAPHY
REPROGRAPHY
REPUTATION
REQUIRED COURSES
FOUNDATION COURSES (REQUIRED) Use REQUIRED COURSES
DEGREE REQUIREMENTS
DESIGN REQUIREMENTS
DIPLOMA REQUIREMENTS Use GRADUATION REQUIREMENTS
FACILITY REQUIREMENTS
GRADUATION REQUIREMENTS
RESIDENCE REQUIREMENTS
RESCUE
RESCUE SQUAD PERSONNEL Use EMERGENCY SQUAD PERSONNEL
RESEARCH
ACTION RESEARCH
RESEARCH ADMINISTRATION
RESEARCH AND DEVELOPMENT
RESEARCH AND DEVELOPMENT CENTERS
RESEARCH AND INSTRUCTION UNITS
APPLIED RESEARCH Use RESEARCH
RESEARCH APPRENTICESHIPS (1967 1981) Use RESEARCH ASSISTANTS
RESEARCH APPROACHES Use RESEARCH METHODOLOGY
ARCHITECTURAL RESEARCH
RESEARCH ASSISTANTS
BASIC RESEARCH Use RESEARCH
BEHAVIORAL SCIENCE RESEARCH
BIOMEDICAL RESEARCH Use BIOMEDICINE
CLASSROOM RESEARCH

RURAL NONFARM RESIDENTS
RESILIENT FLOOR COVERING Use FLOORING
CONFLICT RESOLUTION
IMPASSE RESOLUTION Use NEGOTIATION IMPASSES
RESOURCE ALLOCATION
RESOURCE ALLOCATIONS (1966 1980) Use RESOURCE ALLOCATION
RESOURCE CENTERS
RESOURCE GUIDES (1966 1980) Use RESOURCE MATERIALS
RESOURCE MATERIALS
RESOURCE ROOM PROGRAMS
RESOURCE SHARING Use SHARED RESOURCES AND SERVICES
RESOURCE STAFF
RESOURCE STAFF ROLE (1966 1980) Use RESOURCE STAFF
RESOURCE TEACHERS
RESOURCE UNITS
RESOURCES
ALLOCATION OF RESOURCES Use RESOURCE ALLOCATION
SHARED RESOURCES AND SERVICES
LEARNING RESOURCES CENTERS
COAL RESOURCES Use COAL
COMMUNITY RESOURCES
CURRICULUM RESOURCES Use EDUCATIONAL RESOURCES
DEPLETED RESOURCES
HUMAN RESOURCES DEVELOPMENT (LABOR) Use LABOR FORCE DEVELOPMENT
EDUCATIONAL RESOURCES
FAMILY RESOURCES (1966 1980) Use FAMILY FINANCIAL RESOURCES
FAMILY FINANCIAL RESOURCES
HUMAN RESOURCES
LEARNING RESOURCES Use EDUCATIONAL RESOURCES
MENTAL HEALTH RESOURCES Use MENTAL HEALTH PROGRAMS
NATURAL RESOURCES
SHARED LIBRARY RESOURCES
TEACHING RESOURCES Use EDUCATIONAL RESOURCES
WATER RESOURCES
RESPIRATORY THERAPY
RESPITE CARE
RESPONSE BIAS (TESTS) Use RESPONSE STYLE (TESTS)
CONDITIONED RESPONSE (1967 1980) Use RESPONSES
CONSTRUCTED RESPONSE
RESPONSE CONTINGENT TESTING Use ADAPTIVE TESTING
COVERT RESPONSE
EMOTIONAL RESPONSE
RESPONSE LATENCY Use REACTION TIME
RESPONSE MODE (1967 1980) Use RESPONSES
OVERT RESPONSE
PUPILLARY RESPONSE Use PUPILLARY DILATION
READER RESPONSE
RESPONSE SET (TESTS) Use RESPONSE STYLE (TESTS)
RESPONSE STYLE (TESTS)
TEACHER RESPONSE
SITUATION RESPONSE TESTS Use SITUATIONAL TESTS
ITEM RESPONSE THEORY Use LATENT TRAIT THEORY
RESPONSE TIME Use REACTION TIME
RESPONSES
PATTERNED RESPONSES
STUDENT RESPONSES Use STUDENT REACTION
RESPONSIBILITY
ADMINISTRATOR RESPONSIBILITY
BUSINESS RESPONSIBILITY
CHILD RESPONSIBILITY
CHURCH RESPONSIBILITY
CITIZEN RESPONSIBILITY Use CITIZENSHIP RESPONSIBILITY
CITIZENSHIP RESPONSIBILITY
CIVIC RESPONSIBILITY Use CITIZENSHIP RESPONSIBILITY
COMMUNITY RESPONSIBILITY
EDUCATIONAL RESPONSIBILITY
EMPLOYEE RESPONSIBILITY
TRUST RESPONSIBILITY (GOVERNMENT)
LEADERSHIP RESPONSIBILITY
LEGAL RESPONSIBILITY
LIABILITY (RESPONSIBILITY) Use LEGAL RESPONSIBILITY
NONINSTRUCTIONAL RESPONSIBILITY
PARENT RESPONSIBILITY
SCHOOL RESPONSIBILITY
SOCIAL RESPONSIBILITY
STUDENT RESPONSIBILITY
TEACHER RESPONSIBILITY
REST HOME AIDES Use NURSES AIDES
REST HOMES Use PERSONAL CARE HOMES
RESTAURANTS Use DINING FACILITIES
RESTRAINTS (VEHICLE SAFETY)
CHILD RESTRAINTS (VEHICLE SAFETY) Use RESTRAINTS (VEHICLE SAFETY)
SOCIAL RESTRICTIONS Use SOCIAL MOBILITY
RESTRICTIVE ADMISSION Use SELECTIVE ADMISSION
LEAST RESTRICTIVE ENVIRONMENT (DISABLED) Use MAINSTREAMING
RESTRICTIVE TRANSFER PROGRAMS (1966 1980) Use TRANSFER PROGRAMS
COGNITIVE RESTRUCTURING
JOB RESTRUCTURING Use JOB DEVELOPMENT
KNOWLEDGE OF RESULTS Use FEEDBACK
RESULTS OF EDUCATION Use OUTCOMES OF EDUCATION
TEST RESULTS
RESUMES (PERSONAL)
CARDIOPULMONARY RESUSCITATION
RETAIL TRAINING Use DISTRIBUTIVE EDUCATION
RETAILING
RETARDATION (1966 1980) Use MENTAL RETARDATION
BORDERLINE MENTAL RETARDATION Use SLOW LEARNERS
EDUCATIONAL RETARDATION (1966 1980)
PROGRESSIVE RETARDATION (1966 1980) (IN SCHOOL) Use EDUCATIONALLY DISADVANTAGED
MENTAL RETARDATION
MILD MENTAL RETARDATION

MODERATE MENTAL	RETARDATION
SEVERE MENTAL	RETARDATION
	RETARDED CHILDREN (1966 1980) Use MENTAL RETARDATION
PROFOUNDLY MENTALLY	RETARDED Use SEVERE MENTAL RETARDATION
	RETARDED READERS (1966 1980) Use READING DIFFICULTIES
	RETARDED SPEECH DEVELOPMENT (1968 1980) Use DELAYED SPEECH
	RETENTION (1966 1980) Use RETENTION (PSYCHOLOGY)
	RETENTION (OF EMPLOYEES) Use LABOR TURNOVER
	RETENTION (OF STUDENTS) Use SCHOOL HOLDING POWER
	RETENTION (PSYCHOLOGY)
	RETENTION STUDIES (1966 1980) Use RETENTION (PSYCHOLOGY)
	RETIRED TEACHERS Use TEACHER RETIREMENT
	RETIREMENT
	RETIREMENT BENEFITS
EARLY	RETIREMENT
TEACHER	RETIREMENT
	RETRAINING
VOCATIONAL	RETRAINING (1966 1980) Use RETRAINING
	RETRENCHMENT
INFORMATION	RETRIEVAL
ONLINE INFORMATION	RETRIEVAL Use ONLINE SEARCHING
RELEVANCE (INFORMATION	RETRIEVAL)
	RETROACTIVE INHIBITION Use INHIBITION
	REVENUE Use INCOME
	REVENUE SHARING
	REVERSAL SHIFT Use SHIFT STUDIES
HALF	REVERSAL SHIFT Use SHIFT STUDIES
	REVERSE DISCRIMINATION
INTERNAL	REVIEW (ORGANIZATIONS) Use SELF EVALUATION (GROUPS)
PEER	REVIEW Use PEER EVALUATION
	REVIEW (REEXAMINATION)
BOOK	REVIEWS
COMPUTER PROGRAM	REVIEWS Use COMPUTER SOFTWARE REVIEWS
COMPUTER SOFTWARE	REVIEWS
SOFTWARE	REVIEWS (COMPUTERS) Use COMPUTER SOFTWARE REVIEWS
COURSEWARE	REVIEWS Use COMPUTER SOFTWARE REVIEWS and COURSEWARE
HISTORICAL	REVIEWS (1966 1980) Use HISTORY
LITERATURE	REVIEWS
	REVIEWS OF THE LITERATURE Use LITERATURE REVIEWS
RESEARCH	REVIEWS (PUBLICATIONS) (1966 1980)
STATE OF THE ART	REVIEWS
TEST	REVIEWS
	REVISION (WRITTEN COMPOSITION)
CURRICULUM	REVISIONS Use CURRICULUM DEVELOPMENT
	REVOLUTION
AMERICAN	REVOLUTIONARY WAR Use REVOLUTIONARY WAR (UNITED STATES)
	REVOLUTIONARY WAR (UNITED STATES)
SELF	REWARD
	REWARDS
	REWRITING Use REVISION (WRITTEN COMPOSITION)
	REZONING
	REZONING DISTRICTS Use REZONING
	RH FACTORS
	RHETORIC
	RHETORICAL CRITICISM
	RHETORICAL INVENTION
LANGUAGE	RHYTHM
BLUE	RIBBON COMMISSIONS
	RIBONUCLEIC ACID Use RNA
PUERTO	RICAN CULTURE
PUERTO	RICANS
HORSEBACK	RIDING
	RIFF
	RIGHT TO KNOW Use FREEDOM OF INFORMATION
CHILDRENS	RIGHTS
CIVIL	RIGHTS
HUMAN	RIGHTS Use CIVIL LIBERTIES
INDIVIDUAL	RIGHTS Use CIVIL LIBERTIES
CIVIL	RIGHTS LEGISLATION
MINORITY	RIGHTS Use CIVIL RIGHTS
PARENT	RIGHTS
STATES	RIGHTS Use STATES POWERS
STUDENT	RIGHTS
TEACHER	RIGHTS
VOTING	RIGHTS
WOMENS	RIGHTS Use FEMINISM
MENTAL	RIGIDITY
	RISK
AT	RISK (PERSONS) Use HIGH RISK PERSONS
HIGH	RISK PERSONS
HIGH	RISK STUDENTS
	RIVER POLLUTION Use WATER POLLUTION
	RNA
	ROAD CONSTRUCTION
	ROAD SIGNS Use SIGNS
	ROBOTICS
INDUSTRIAL	ROBOTICS Use ROBOTICS
	ROBOTS Use ROBOTICS
	RODENTICIDES (1968 1980) Use PESTICIDES
ADMINISTRATOR	ROLE
AGENCY	ROLE
ASSISTANT SUPERINTENDENT	ROLE (1966 1980)
BLACK	ROLE (1977 1980) Use BLACK INFLUENCES
BOARD OF EDUCATION	ROLE
CHILD	ROLE
CHURCH	ROLE
CITIZEN	ROLE
COLLEGE	ROLE
COMMUNITY	ROLE
	ROLE CONFLICT
CONGRESS	ROLE Use GOVERNMENT ROLE

CHILD RESTRAINTS (VEHICLE SAFETY) Use RESTRAINTS (VEHICLE SAFETY)
SAFETY EDUCATION
SAFETY EQUIPMENT
SAFETY GLASSES Use SAFETY EQUIPMENT
JOB SAFETY Use OCCUPATIONAL SAFETY AND HEALTH
LABORATORY SAFETY
SAFETY PROVISIONS Use SAFETY
RESTRAINTS (VEHICLE SAFETY)
SCHOOL SAFETY
TRAFFIC SAFETY
SAILING
SALARIES
CONTRACT SALARIES
TEACHER SALARIES
SALARY DIFFERENTIALS (1968 1980) Use SALARY WAGE DIFFERENTIALS
WAGE SALARY DIFFERENTIALS Use SALARY WAGE DIFFERENTIALS
SALARY RAISES Use PROMOTION (OCCUPATIONAL)
SALARY WAGE DIFFERENTIALS
SALES CLERKS Use SALES WORKERS
SALES OCCUPATIONS
SALES PROMOTION Use MERCHANDISING
SALES WORKERS
SALESMANSHIP
SALISH
SAMOAN
SAMOAN AMERICANS
AMERICAN SAMOANS Use SAMOAN AMERICANS
SAMOYED LANGUAGES
SAMPLE SIZE
JOB SAMPLE TESTS Use WORK SAMPLE TESTS
WORK SAMPLE TESTS
JOB SAMPLES Use WORK SAMPLE TESTS
WORK SAMPLES Use WORK SAMPLE TESTS
SAMPLING
ITEM SAMPLING
MATRIX SAMPLING Use ITEM SAMPLING
MULTIPLE MATRIX SAMPLING Use ITEM SAMPLING
SANATORIUMS Use HOSPITALS
SANCTIONS
SANGO
SANITARY FACILITIES
SANITARY INSPECTORS Use ENVIRONMENTAL TECHNICIANS
SANITARY TECHNICIANS Use ENVIRONMENTAL TECHNICIANS
SANITATION
SANITATION IMPROVEMENT (1966 1980) Use SANITATION
SANSKRIT
SARA
SARCASM Use IRONY
SARCOMA Use CANCER
SATELLITE FACILITIES
SATELLITE LABORATORIES (1966 1980) Use SATELLITES (AEROSPACE)
SATELLITE LIBRARIES Use BRANCH LIBRARIES
SATELLITES (AEROSPACE)
ARTIFICIAL SATELLITES Use SATELLITES (AEROSPACE)
COMMUNICATION SATELLITES (1967 1980) Use COMMUNICATIONS SATELLITES
COMMUNICATIONS SATELLITES
ORBITING SATELLITES Use SATELLITES (AEROSPACE)
SATIRE
COMMUNITY SATISFACTION
EMPLOYMENT SATISFACTION Use JOB SATISFACTION
USER SATISFACTION (INFORMATION)
INFORMATION USER SATISFACTION Use USER SATISFACTION (INFORMATION)
JOB SATISFACTION
LIBRARY USER SATISFACTION Use USER SATISFACTION (INFORMATION)
LIFE SATISFACTION
MARITAL SATISFACTION
OCCUPATIONAL SATISFACTION Use JOB SATISFACTION
PARTICIPANT SATISFACTION
VOCATIONAL SATISFACTION Use JOB SATISFACTION
WORK SATISFACTION Use JOB SATISFACTION
ANGLO SAXON Use OLD ENGLISH
LOOK SAY METHOD Use SIGHT METHOD
LARGE SCALE PRODUCTION Use MASS PRODUCTION
SCALES Use MEASURES (INDIVIDUALS)
BEHAVIOR RATING SCALES
GRADE EQUIVALENT SCALES (1967 1980) Use GRADE EQUIVALENT SCORES
INTEREST SCALES (1966 1980) Use INTEREST INVENTORIES
OPINION SCALES Use ATTITUDE MEASURES
RATING SCALES
SCALING
INTERNAL SCALING (1966 1980) Use SCALING
MULTIDIMENSIONAL SCALING
OPTICAL SCANNERS
VISUAL SCANNERS Use OPTICAL SCANNERS
SCHEDULE MODULES (1968 1980) Use FLEXIBLE SCHEDULING
FLEXIBLE SCHEDULES (1967 1980)
SCHOOL SCHEDULES
TRIMESTER SCHEDULES (1966 1980) Use TRIMESTER SYSTEM
SCHEDULING
BROADCAST SCHEDULING Use PROGRAMING (BROADCAST)
FAST TRACK SCHEDULING
FLEXIBLE SCHEDULING
MODULAR SCHEDULING Use FLEXIBLE SCHEDULING
BODY SCHEMA Use BODY IMAGE
SCHEMATA (COGNITION)
SCHEMATIC STUDIES
CONCEPTUAL SCHEMES (1967 1980)
SCHIZOPHRENIA
SCHOLARLY JOURNALS
SCHOLARSHIP
SCHOLARSHIP FUNDS

	SCHOLARSHIP LOANS (1966 1980) Use SCHOLARSHIPS and STUDENT LOAN PROGRAMS
	SCHOLARSHIPS
ENDOWED	SCHOLARSHIPS Use SCHOLARSHIPS
MERIT	SCHOLARSHIPS
NO NEED	SCHOLARSHIPS
	SCHOLASTIC ABILITY Use ACADEMIC ABILITY
	SCHOLASTIC ACHIEVEMENT Use ACADEMIC ACHIEVEMENT
	SCHOLASTIC FAILURE Use ACADEMIC FAILURE
GRADES	(SCHOLASTIC)
MARKING	(SCHOLASTIC) Use GRADING
MARKS	(SCHOLASTIC) Use GRADES (SCHOLASTIC)
	SCHOLASTIC POTENTIAL Use ACADEMIC APTITUDE
	SCHOLASTIC PROBATION Use ACADEMIC PROBATION
	SCHOOL ACCIDENTS
	SCHOOL ACCOUNTING
	SCHOOL ACTIVITIES
AFTER	SCHOOL ACTIVITIES (1967 1980) Use AFTER SCHOOL PROGRAMS
	SCHOOL ADJUSTMENT Use STUDENT ADJUSTMENT
	SCHOOL ADMINISTRATION
	SCHOOL ADMINISTRATORS Use ADMINISTRATORS
ADMISSION	(SCHOOL)
	SCHOOL ADMISSION Use ADMISSION (SCHOOL)
PUBLIC	SCHOOL ADULT EDUCATION
	SCHOOL AGE DAY CARE
	SCHOOL AID Use EDUCATIONAL FINANCE
NONPUBLIC	SCHOOL AID (1972 1980) Use PRIVATE SCHOOL AID
PAROCHIAL	SCHOOL AID (1972 1980) Use PAROCHIAL SCHOOLS and PRIVATE SCHOOL AID
PRIVATE	SCHOOL AID
	SCHOOL AIDES
LAW	SCHOOL APPLICANTS Use COLLEGE APPLICANTS and LAW SCHOOLS
MEDICAL	SCHOOL APPLICANTS Use COLLEGE APPLICANTS and MEDICAL SCHOOLS
	SCHOOL ARCHITECTURE (1966 1980) Use EDUCATIONAL FACILITIES DESIGN
	SCHOOL ATTENDANCE Use ATTENDANCE
	SCHOOL ATTENDANCE LAWS (1966 1974) Use SCHOOL ATTENDANCE LEGISLATION
	SCHOOL ATTENDANCE LEGISLATION
	SCHOOL ATTITUDES
	SCHOOL BASED MANAGEMENT
	SCHOOL BOARD MEMBERS Use BOARDS OF EDUCATION
	SCHOOL BOARD POLICY Use BOARD OF EDUCATION POLICY
	SCHOOL BOARD ROLE Use BOARD OF EDUCATION ROLE
	SCHOOL BOARDS Use BOARDS OF EDUCATION
STATE	SCHOOL BOARDS Use STATE BOARDS OF EDUCATION
	SCHOOL BOUNDARIES Use SCHOOL DISTRICTS
	SCHOOL BOYCOTTS
	SCHOOL BUDGET ELECTIONS
	SCHOOL BUILDINGS
	SCHOOL BUSES
BUSINESS OFFICIALS	(SCHOOL) Use SCHOOL BUSINESS OFFICIALS
	SCHOOL BUSINESS OFFICIALS
	SCHOOL BUSINESS RELATIONSHIP
	SCHOOL CADRES
	SCHOOL CALENDARS (1967 1980) Use SCHOOL SCHEDULES
	SCHOOL CATALOGS
AFTER	SCHOOL CENTERS
	SCHOOL CHARACTERISTICS Use INSTITUTIONAL CHARACTERISTICS
ELEMENTARY	SCHOOL CHILDREN Use ELEMENTARY SCHOOL STUDENTS
	SCHOOL CHOICE
	SCHOOL CLIMATE Use EDUCATIONAL ENVIRONMENT
CLINIC PERSONNEL	(SCHOOL) (1966 1980) Use ALLIED HEALTH PERSONNEL and SCHOOL HEALTH SERVICES
	SCHOOL CLOSING
	SCHOOL COLLEGE COOPERATION Use COLLEGE SCHOOL COOPERATION
HIGH	SCHOOL COLLEGE COOPERATION Use COLLEGE SCHOOL COOPERATION
	SCHOOL COMMUNITY COMMUNICATION Use SCHOOL COMMUNITY RELATIONSHIP
	SCHOOL COMMUNITY COOPERATION (1966 1980) Use SCHOOL COMMUNITY RELATIONSHIP
	SCHOOL COMMUNITY COORDINATION Use SCHOOL COMMUNITY RELATIONSHIP
	SCHOOL COMMUNITY INTERACTION Use SCHOOL COMMUNITY RELATIONSHIP
	SCHOOL COMMUNITY PROGRAMS
	SCHOOL COMMUNITY RELATIONSHIP
	SCHOOL CONDITIONS (1966 1980) Use EDUCATIONAL ENVIRONMENT
	SCHOOL CONSOLIDATION Use CONSOLIDATED SCHOOLS
	SCHOOL CONSTRUCTION
COLLEGE	SCHOOL COOPERATION
COLLEGE HIGH	SCHOOL COOPERATION (1967 1980) Use COLLEGE SCHOOL COOPERATION
	SCHOOL COUNSELING
ELEMENTARY	SCHOOL COUNSELING (1967 1980) Use SCHOOL COUNSELING
SECONDARY	SCHOOL COUNSELING Use SCHOOL COUNSELING
	SCHOOL COUNSELORS
ELEMENTARY	SCHOOL COUNSELORS (1967 1980) Use SCHOOL COUNSELORS
SECONDARY	SCHOOL COUNSELORS (1967 1980) Use SCHOOL COUNSELORS
ELEMENTARY	SCHOOL CURRICULUM
HIGH	SCHOOL CURRICULUM (1967 1980) Use SECONDARY SCHOOL CURRICULUM
SECONDARY	SCHOOL CURRICULUM
AFTER	SCHOOL DAY CARE (1978 1983) Use AFTER SCHOOL PROGRAMS and SCHOOL AGE DAY CARE
EXTENDED	SCHOOL DAY
	SCHOOL DEMOGRAPHY
DEPARTMENT DIRECTORS	(SCHOOL) (1966 1980) Use DEPARTMENT HEADS
	SCHOOL DESEGREGATION
	SCHOOL DESIGN (1966 1980) Use EDUCATIONAL FACILITIES DESIGN
DECENTRALIZED	SCHOOL DESIGN (1966 1980) Use DECENTRALIZATION and EDUCATIONAL FACILITIES DESIGN
HIGH	SCHOOL DESIGN (1966 1980) Use EDUCATIONAL FACILITIES DESIGN
COMMUNITY	SCHOOL DIRECTORS (1967 1980) Use ADMINISTRATORS and COMMUNITY SCHOOLS
	SCHOOL DISTRICT AUTONOMY
	SCHOOL DISTRICT NORMS Use LOCAL NORMS
	SCHOOL DISTRICT POLICY Use BOARD OF EDUCATION POLICY
STATE	SCHOOL DISTRICT RELATIONSHIP
	SCHOOL DISTRICT REORGANIZATION
	SCHOOL DISTRICT SIZE
	SCHOOL DISTRICT SPENDING
	SCHOOL DISTRICTS
COUNTY	SCHOOL DISTRICTS
INTERMEDIATE	SCHOOL DISTRICTS Use INTERMEDIATE ADMINISTRATIVE UNITS

SCHOOL DROPOUTS Use DROPOUTS
HIGH SCHOOL DROPOUTS Use DROPOUTS
AFTER SCHOOL EDUCATION
EDUCATION DEPARTMENTS (SCHOOL) Use SCHOOLS OF EDUCATION
LAW SCHOOL EDUCATION Use LEGAL EDUCATION (PROFESSIONS)
POST HIGH SCHOOL EDUCATION Use POSTSECONDARY EDUCATION
SCHOOL EFFECTIVENESS
SCHOOL EMPLOYEES Use SCHOOL PERSONNEL
SCHOOL ENROLLMENT Use ENROLLMENT
SCHOOL ENTRANCE AGE
SCHOOL ENVIRONMENT (1966 1980) Use EDUCATIONAL ENVIRONMENT
HIGH SCHOOL EQUIVALENCY PROGRAMS
SCHOOL EXPANSION
SCHOOL EXPERIENCE Use EDUCATIONAL EXPERIENCE
SCHOOL FACILITIES Use EDUCATIONAL FACILITIES
DENTAL SCHOOL FACULTY Use DENTAL SCHOOLS and MEDICAL SCHOOL FACULTY
GRADUATE SCHOOL FACULTY
MEDICAL SCHOOL FACULTY
SCHOOL FAMILY RELATIONSHIP Use FAMILY SCHOOL RELATIONSHIP
SCHOOL FINANCE Use EDUCATIONAL FINANCE
SCHOOL FINANCE EQUITY Use EDUCATIONAL EQUITY (FINANCE)
FOREIGN LANGUAGES IN THE ELEMENTARY SCHOOL Use FLES
HIGH SCHOOL FRESHMEN
FUNDAMENTAL SKILLS (SCHOOL) Use BASIC SKILLS
SCHOOL FUNDS
SCHOOL GOVERNMENT RELATIONSHIP Use GOVERNMENT SCHOOL RELATIONSHIP
HIGH SCHOOL GRADUATES
SCHOOL GUIDANCE
ELEMENTARY SCHOOL GUIDANCE (1967 1980) Use SCHOOL GUIDANCE
POST HIGH SCHOOL GUIDANCE
SECONDARY SCHOOL GUIDANCE Use SCHOOL GUIDANCE
SCHOOL HEALTH SERVICES
SCHOOL HOLDING POWER
SCHOOL HOME RELATIONSHIP Use FAMILY SCHOOL RELATIONSHIP
SCHOOL IMPROVEMENT (1966 1980) Use EDUCATIONAL FACILITIES IMPROVEMENT
SCHOOL INDUSTRY RELATIONSHIP (1967 1980) Use SCHOOL BUSINESS RELATIONSHIP
SCHOOL INTEGRATION (1966 1980) Use SCHOOL DESEGREGATION
SCHOOL INVOLVEMENT
SCHOOL LAW
EARLY SCHOOL LEAVERS Use DROPOUTS
POLICE SCHOOL LIAISON Use POLICE SCHOOL RELATIONSHIP
SCHOOL LIBRARIES
ELEMENTARY SCHOOL LIBRARIES (1966 1980) Use SCHOOL LIBRARIES
HIGH SCHOOL LIBRARIES Use SCHOOL LIBRARIES
SECONDARY SCHOOL LIBRARIES Use SCHOOL LIBRARIES
SCHOOL LOCATION
SCHOOL MAINTENANCE
ELEMENTARY SCHOOL MATHEMATICS
SECONDARY SCHOOL MATHEMATICS
SCHOOL MEDIA CENTERS Use LEARNING RESOURCES CENTERS
SCHOOL NEWSPAPERS
SCHOOL NURSE PRACTITIONERS Use NURSE PRACTITIONERS and SCHOOL NURSES
SCHOOL NURSES
SCHOOL OFFICIALS Use SCHOOL PERSONNEL
SCHOOL ORGANIZATION
HIGH SCHOOL ORGANIZATION (1966 1980) Use SCHOOL ORGANIZATION
SCHOOL ORIENTATION
SCHOOL PARENT RELATIONSHIP Use PARENT SCHOOL RELATIONSHIP
SCHOOL PARTICIPATION Use SCHOOL INVOLVEMENT
SCHOOL PERSONNEL
SCHOOL PERSONNEL DIRECTORS Use PERSONNEL DIRECTORS and SCHOOL PERSONNEL
PARAPROFESSIONAL SCHOOL PERSONNEL
SCHOOL PHILOSOPHY Use EDUCATIONAL PHILOSOPHY
SCHOOL PHOBIA
SCHOOLS WITHIN A SCHOOL PLAN Use HOUSE PLAN
SCHOOL PLANNING (1966 1980)
SCHOOL PLANTS Use EDUCATIONAL FACILITIES
SCHOOL POLICE RELATIONSHIP Use POLICE SCHOOL RELATIONSHIP
SCHOOL POLICY
NEIGHBORHOOD SCHOOL POLICY (1966 1980) Use NEIGHBORHOOD SCHOOLS and SCHOOL POLICY
SCHOOL PRINCIPALS Use PRINCIPALS
SCHOOL PROGRAMS Use SCHOOL ACTIVITIES
AFTER SCHOOL PROGRAMS
COMMUNITY SCHOOL PROGRAMS Use SCHOOL COMMUNITY PROGRAMS
INTERSESSION SCHOOL PROGRAMS Use VACATION PROGRAMS
PROGRESSIVE RETARDATION (1966 1980) (IN SCHOOL) Use EDUCATIONALLY DISADVANTAGED
SCHOOL PSYCHOLOGISTS
SCHOOL PUBLICATIONS
SCHOOL READINESS
SCHOOL READINESS TESTS
SCHOOL RECREATIONAL PROGRAMS
SCHOOL REDISTRICTING (1966 1980) Use SCHOOL DISTRICT REORGANIZATION
REGISTRARS (SCHOOL)
SCHOOL REGISTRATION
REGISTRATION IN SCHOOL Use SCHOOL REGISTRATION
SCHOOL RELATED ACTIVITIES Use EXTRACURRICULAR ACTIVITIES
BUSINESS SCHOOL RELATIONSHIP Use SCHOOL BUSINESS RELATIONSHIP
COMMUNITY SCHOOL RELATIONSHIP Use SCHOOL COMMUNITY RELATIONSHIP
FAMILY SCHOOL RELATIONSHIP
GOVERNMENT SCHOOL RELATIONSHIP
HOME SCHOOL RELATIONSHIP Use FAMILY SCHOOL RELATIONSHIP
INDUSTRY SCHOOL RELATIONSHIP Use SCHOOL BUSINESS RELATIONSHIP
PARENT SCHOOL RELATIONSHIP
POLICE SCHOOL RELATIONSHIP
STUDENT SCHOOL RELATIONSHIP
SCHOOL RENOVATION Use EDUCATIONAL FACILITIES IMPROVEMENT
SCHOOL REORGANIZATION Use SCHOOL ORGANIZATION
SCHOOL RESEGREGATION
SCHOOL RESPONSIBILITY
SCHOOL ROLE
ELEMENTARY SCHOOL ROLE (1966 1980) Use SCHOOL ROLE

HIGH SCHOOL ROLE (1966 1980) Use SCHOOL ROLE
JUNIOR HIGH SCHOOL ROLE (1966 1980) Use SCHOOL ROLE
SCHOOL SAFETY
SCHOOL SCHEDULES
ELEMENTARY SCHOOL SCIENCE
SECONDARY SCHOOL SCIENCE
SCHOOL SECRETARIES
SCHOOL SECURITY
SCHOOL SEGREGATION
HIGH SCHOOL SENIORS
SCHOOL SERVICES (1966 1980) Use ANCILLARY SCHOOL SERVICES
ANCILLARY SCHOOL SERVICES
AUXILIARY SCHOOL SERVICES Use ANCILLARY SCHOOL SERVICES
SCHOOL SHOPS
SCHOOL SITE MANAGEMENT Use SCHOOL BASED MANAGEMENT
SCHOOL SITES Use SCHOOL LOCATION
SCHOOL SIZE
SCHOOL SOCIAL WORKERS
SCHOOL SPACE
SCHOOL STATISTICS
SCHOOL STUDENT RELATIONSHIP Use STUDENT SCHOOL RELATIONSHIP
ELEMENTARY SCHOOL STUDENTS
HIGH SCHOOL STUDENTS
JUNIOR HIGH SCHOOL STUDENTS
SECONDARY SCHOOL STUDENTS
SENIOR HIGH SCHOOL STUDENTS Use HIGH SCHOOL STUDENTS
SCHOOL STUDY CENTERS (1966 1980) Use STUDY CENTERS
SCHOOL SUPERINTENDENTS (1966 1980) Use SUPERINTENDENTS
SCHOOL SUPERVISION
ELEMENTARY SCHOOL SUPERVISORS (1966 1980) Use SCHOOL SUPERVISION
HIGH SCHOOL SUPERVISORS (1966 1980) Use SCHOOL SUPERVISION
SCHOOL SUPPLIES Use SUPPLIES
SCHOOL SUPPORT
SCHOOL SURVEYS
IN SCHOOL SUSPENSION
SCHOOL SYSTEMS (1966 1980) Use SCHOOL DISTRICTS
COUNTY SCHOOL SYSTEMS (1967 1980) Use COUNTY SCHOOL DISTRICTS
PUBLIC SCHOOL SYSTEMS (1966 1980) Use PUBLIC SCHOOLS and SCHOOL DISTRICTS
RURAL SCHOOL SYSTEMS (1966 1980) Use RURAL SCHOOLS and SCHOOL DISTRICTS
SCHOOL TAXES
ELEMENTARY SCHOOL TEACHERS
HIGH SCHOOL TEACHERS Use SECONDARY SCHOOL TEACHERS
JUNIOR HIGH SCHOOL TEACHERS Use SECONDARY SCHOOL TEACHERS
PUBLIC SCHOOL TEACHERS
SECONDARY SCHOOL TEACHERS
SCHOOL TO WORK TRANSITION Use EDUCATION WORK RELATIONSHIP
SCHOOL TRANSPORTATION Use STUDENT TRANSPORTATION
SCHOOL TRUANCY Use TRUANCY
AFTER SCHOOL TUTORING (1966 1980) Use AFTER SCHOOL EDUCATION and TUTORING
SCHOOL VANDALISM
SCHOOL VISITATION
SCHOOL VISITS Use SCHOOL VISITATION
EXTENDED SCHOOL YEAR
OUT OF SCHOOL YOUTH
SCHOOL ZONING
EFFECTIVE SCHOOLING Use SCHOOL EFFECTIVENESS
HOME SCHOOLING
SCHOOLS
AFFILIATED SCHOOLS
ALTERNATIVE SCHOOLS (1972 1980) Use NONTRADITIONAL EDUCATION
AREA VOCATIONAL SCHOOLS (1966 1980) Use REGIONAL SCHOOLS and VOCATIONAL SCHOOLS
BILINGUAL SCHOOLS
BIRACIAL SCHOOLS (1966 1980) Use SCHOOL DESEGREGATION
BIRACIAL ELEMENTARY SCHOOLS (1966 1980) Use SCHOOL DESEGREGATION
BIRACIAL SECONDARY SCHOOLS (1966 1980) Use SCHOOL DESEGREGATION
BOARDING SCHOOLS
BRITISH INFANT SCHOOLS
INFANT SCHOOLS (BRITISH PRIMARY SYSTEM) Use BRITISH INFANT SCHOOLS
CAMPUS SCHOOLS Use LABORATORY SCHOOLS
CATHOLIC SCHOOLS
CATHOLIC ELEMENTARY SCHOOLS (1967 1980) Use CATHOLIC SCHOOLS
CATHOLIC HIGH SCHOOLS (1967 1980) Use CATHOLIC SCHOOLS
CENTRALIZED SCHOOLS Use CONSOLIDATED SCHOOLS
CITY SCHOOLS Use URBAN SCHOOLS
CLOSED SCHOOLS Use SCHOOL CLOSING
COMMERCIAL CORRESPONDENCE SCHOOLS Use CORRESPONDENCE SCHOOLS
COMMUNITY SCHOOLS
COMPREHENSIVE HIGH SCHOOLS (1967 1980) Use HIGH SCHOOLS
CONSOLIDATED SCHOOLS
CONTINUATION HIGH SCHOOLS (1968 1980) Use CONTINUATION STUDENTS
COOPERATING SCHOOLS Use AFFILIATED SCHOOLS
CORRESPONDENCE SCHOOLS
DAY SCHOOLS
DENTAL SCHOOLS
DESEGREGATED SCHOOLS Use SCHOOL DESEGREGATION
DISADVANTAGED SCHOOLS
ELEMENTARY SCHOOLS
EXPERIMENTAL SCHOOLS
FOLK SCHOOLS
FREE SCHOOLS
FREEDOM SCHOOLS
GENERAL HIGH SCHOOLS (1966 1980) Use GENERAL EDUCATION
HIGH SCHOOLS
HOLDING POWER (OF SCHOOLS) Use SCHOOL HOLDING POWER
HOSPITAL SCHOOLS
INDEPENDENT SCHOOLS Use PRIVATE SCHOOLS
INSTITUTIONAL SCHOOLS
INSTRUCTIONALLY EFFECTIVE SCHOOLS Use SCHOOL EFFECTIVENESS
INTEGRATED SCHOOLS Use SCHOOL DESEGREGATION
JUNIOR HIGH SCHOOLS
TRAINING SCHOOLS (JUVENILE OFFENDERS) Use CORRECTIONAL INSTITUTIONS

LABORATORY	SCHOOLS
LAW	SCHOOLS
LIBRARY	SCHOOLS
LOCAL AUTONOMY (OF	SCHOOLS) Use SCHOOL DISTRICT AUTONOMY
LOCAL CONTROL (OF	SCHOOLS) Use SCHOOL DISTRICT AUTONOMY
MAGNET	SCHOOLS
MEDICAL	SCHOOLS
MIDDLE	SCHOOLS
MIGRANT	SCHOOLS (1966 1980) Use MIGRANT EDUCATION
MILITARY	SCHOOLS
MULTIUNIT	SCHOOLS
NEIGHBORHOOD	SCHOOLS
NIGHT	SCHOOLS (1966 1980) Use EVENING PROGRAMS
NONPUBLIC	SCHOOLS Use PRIVATE SCHOOLS
NONRESIDENTIAL	SCHOOLS (1967 1980) Use COMMUTER COLLEGES
NORTHERN	SCHOOLS (1966 1980)
NURSERY	SCHOOLS
	SCHOOLS OF DENTISTRY Use DENTAL SCHOOLS
	SCHOOLS OF EDUCATION
	SCHOOLS OF MEDICINE Use MEDICAL SCHOOLS
ONE ROOM	SCHOOLS Use ONE TEACHER SCHOOLS
ONE TEACHER	SCHOOLS
OPEN	SCHOOLS Use OPEN EDUCATION
OPEN AREA	SCHOOLS Use OPEN PLAN SCHOOLS
OPEN PLAN	SCHOOLS
PAROCHIAL	SCHOOLS
PRIVATE	SCHOOLS
PROJECT	SCHOOLS Use EXPERIMENTAL SCHOOLS
PROPRIETARY	SCHOOLS
PUBLIC	SCHOOLS
RACIALLY BALANCED	SCHOOLS
REGIONAL	SCHOOLS
RESEGREGATED	SCHOOLS Use SCHOOL RESEGREGATION
RESIDENTIAL	SCHOOLS
RURAL	SCHOOLS
SECONDARY	SCHOOLS
SENIOR HIGH	SCHOOLS (1966 1980) Use HIGH SCHOOLS
SINGLE SEX	SCHOOLS
SLUM	SCHOOLS
SMALL	SCHOOLS
SOUTHERN	SCHOOLS (1966 1980)
SPECIAL	SCHOOLS
SPECIAL SERVICE	SCHOOLS Use SPECIAL SCHOOLS
SPECIALTY	SCHOOLS Use PROPRIETARY SCHOOLS
STATE	SCHOOLS
SUBURBAN	SCHOOLS
SUMMER	SCHOOLS
TECHNICAL	SCHOOLS Use VOCATIONAL SCHOOLS
TECHNICAL HIGH	SCHOOLS Use VOCATIONAL HIGH SCHOOLS
TRADITIONAL	SCHOOLS
TRANSITIONAL	SCHOOLS
UNGRADED	SCHOOLS (1966 1980) Use NONGRADED INSTRUCTIONAL GROUPING
UNIVERSITY	SCHOOLS Use LABORATORY SCHOOLS
URBAN	SCHOOLS
VOCATIONAL	SCHOOLS
VOCATIONAL HIGH	SCHOOLS
	SCHOOLS WITHIN A SCHOOL PLAN Use HOUSE PLAN
YEAR ROUND	SCHOOLS
	SCHOOLSICKNESS Use SCHOOL PHOBIA
	SCIENCE Use SCIENCES
	SCIENCE ACTIVITIES
	SCIENCE AND SOCIETY
ENGLISH FOR	SCIENCE AND TECHNOLOGY
ANIMAL	SCIENCE (1967 1980) Use ANIMAL HUSBANDRY
	SCIENCE CAREERS
	SCIENCE CLUBS
COLLEGE	SCIENCE
COMPUTER	SCIENCE
	SCIENCE CONSULTANTS
CONSUMER	SCIENCE
	SCIENCE COURSE IMPROVEMENT PROJECT (1967 1980) Use SCIENCE COURSE IMPROVEMENT PROJECTS
	SCIENCE COURSE IMPROVEMENT PROJECTS
	SCIENCE COURSES (1966 1980) Use SCIENCE CURRICULUM
	SCIENCE CURRICULUM
BACHELOR OF	SCIENCE DEGREES Use BACHELORS DEGREES
MASTER OF	SCIENCE DEGREES Use MASTERS DEGREES
	SCIENCE DEPARTMENTS
EARTH	SCIENCE
	SCIENCE EDUCATION
AEROSPACE	SCIENCE EDUCATION Use AEROSPACE EDUCATION
COMPUTER	SCIENCE EDUCATION
FIRE	SCIENCE EDUCATION
	SCIENCE EDUCATION HISTORY
MARINE	SCIENCE EDUCATION Use MARINE EDUCATION
ELEMENTARY	SCIENCE (1966 1980) Use ELEMENTARY SCHOOL SCIENCE
ELEMENTARY SCHOOL	SCIENCE
	SCIENCE EQUIPMENT
	SCIENCE EXPERIMENTS
	SCIENCE FACILITIES
	SCIENCE FAIRS
	SCIENCE FICTION
GENERAL	SCIENCE
	SCIENCE HISTORY
HOUSEHOLD	SCIENCE Use CONSUMER SCIENCE
MASTER OF	SCIENCE IN TEACHING Use MASTERS DEGREES
	SCIENCE INFORMATION Use SCIENTIFIC AND TECHNICAL INFORMATION
INFORMATION	SCIENCE
	SCIENCE INSTITUTES (1967 1980) Use INSTITUTES (TRAINING PROGRAMS) and SCIENCE PROGRAMS
	SCIENCE INSTRUCTION
	SCIENCE INTERESTS

SEASONAL LABOR (1966 1980) Use SEASONAL EMPLOYMENT
SEASONAL LABORERS
SEAT BELTS Use RESTRAINTS (VEHICLE SAFETY)
SECOND LANGUAGE BOOKS Use FOREIGN LANGUAGE BOOKS
ENGLISH (SECOND LANGUAGE)
SECOND LANGUAGE ENROLLMENT Use LANGUAGE ENROLLMENT
SECOND LANGUAGE FILMS Use FOREIGN LANGUAGE FILMS
SECOND LANGUAGE INSTRUCTION
MULTILEVEL CLASSES (SECOND LANGUAGE INSTRUCTION)
SECOND LANGUAGE LEARNING
SECOND LANGUAGE PERIODICALS Use FOREIGN LANGUAGE PERIODICALS
SECOND LANGUAGE PROGRAMS
COLLEGE SECOND LANGUAGE PROGRAMS
SECOND LANGUAGE TEACHERS Use LANGUAGE TEACHERS
VOCATIONAL ENGLISH (SECOND LANGUAGE)
SECOND LANGUAGES
SECONDARY EDUCATION
ELEMENTARY SECONDARY EDUCATION
POST SECONDARY EDUCATION (1967 1978) Use POSTSECONDARY EDUCATION
SECONDARY EMPLOYMENT Use MULTIPLE EMPLOYMENT
SECONDARY GRADES (1966 1980) Use SECONDARY EDUCATION
SECONDARY SCHOOL COUNSELING Use SCHOOL COUNSELING
SECONDARY SCHOOL COUNSELORS (1967 1980) Use SCHOOL COUNSELORS
SECONDARY SCHOOL CURRICULUM
SECONDARY SCHOOL GUIDANCE Use SCHOOL GUIDANCE
SECONDARY SCHOOL LIBRARIES Use SCHOOL LIBRARIES
SECONDARY SCHOOL MATHEMATICS
SECONDARY SCHOOL SCIENCE
SECONDARY SCHOOL STUDENTS
SECONDARY SCHOOL TEACHERS
SECONDARY SCHOOLS
BIRACIAL SECONDARY SCHOOLS (1966 1980) Use SCHOOL DESEGREGATION
SECRETARIES
ADMINISTRATIVE SECRETARIES Use SECRETARIES
EXECUTIVE SECRETARIES Use SECRETARIES
LEGAL SECRETARIES Use SECRETARIES
MEDICAL SECRETARIES Use SECRETARIES
SCHOOL SECRETARIES
SECTARIAN COLLEGES Use CHURCH RELATED COLLEGES
CROSS SECTIONAL STUDIES
SECURITY (1967 1978)
CAMPUS SECURITY Use SCHOOL SECURITY
EMOTIONAL SECURITY Use SECURITY (PSYCHOLOGY)
GUARDS (SECURITY) Use SECURITY PERSONNEL
NATIONAL SECURITY
SECURITY PERSONNEL
SECURITY (PSYCHOLOGY)
SCHOOL SECURITY
SECURITY SYSTEMS (ALARMS) Use ALARM SYSTEMS
SEDATIVES
JOB SEEKERS Use JOB APPLICANTS
INFORMATION SEEKING
SEGREGATED PUBLIC FACILITIES (1966 1980) Use PUBLIC FACILITIES and RACIAL SEGREGATION
COLLEGE SEGREGATION
DE FACTO SEGREGATION
DE JURE SEGREGATION
DEFACTO SEGREGATION (1966 1980) Use DE FACTO SEGREGATION
DEJURE SEGREGATION (1966 1980) Use DE JURE SEGREGATION
LEGAL SEGREGATION (1966 1980) Use DE JURE SEGREGATION
ANTI SEGREGATION PROGRAMS (1967 1980) Use RACIAL INTEGRATION
RACIAL SEGREGATION
SEGREGATION (RACIAL) Use RACIAL SEGREGATION
SCHOOL SEGREGATION
SEGREGATIONIST GROUPS Use SEGREGATIONIST ORGANIZATIONS
SEGREGATIONIST ORGANIZATIONS
SEISMOLOGY
SEARCH AND SEIZURE
SEIZURES
SELECTION
ADMINISTRATOR SELECTION
SELECTION COMMITTEES (PERSONNEL) Use SEARCH COMMITTEES (PERSONNEL)
COMPETITIVE SELECTION
COUNSELOR SELECTION
EDUCATIONAL MEDIA SELECTION Use MEDIA SELECTION
INSTRUCTIONAL MATERIAL SELECTION Use MEDIA SELECTION
LIBRARY MATERIAL SELECTION
MATE SELECTION
MATERIAL SELECTION Use MEDIA SELECTION
MEDIA SELECTION
PERSONNEL SELECTION
READING MATERIAL SELECTION
SITE SELECTION
STUDENT SELECTION Use ADMISSION CRITERIA
COURSE SELECTION (STUDENTS)
TEACHER SELECTION
TEST SELECTION
TEXTBOOK SELECTION
SELECTIVE ADMISSION
SELECTIVE COLLEGES
SELECTIVE DISSEMINATION OF INFORMATION
SELF ABUSE Use SELF DESTRUCTIVE BEHAVIOR
SELF ACTUALIZATION
SELF APPRAISAL Use SELF EVALUATION (INDIVIDUALS)
SELF ASSESSMENT Use SELF EVALUATION (INDIVIDUALS)
SELF ATTITUDE TESTS Use SELF CONCEPT MEASURES
SELF BIAS Use EGOCENTRISM
SELF CARE SKILLS
SELF CONCEPT
SELF CONCEPT MEASURES
SELF CONCEPT TESTS (1971 1980) Use SELF CONCEPT MEASURES
SELF CONFIDENCE Use SELF ESTEEM

SELF CONGRUENCE
SELF CONTAINED CLASSROOMS
SELF CONTROL
SELF DESTRUCTIVE BEHAVIOR
SELF DETERMINATION
SELF DEVELOPMENT Use SELF ACTUALIZATION
SELF DIRECTED CLASSROOMS (1966 1980)
SELF DIRECTED GROUPS
SELF DIRECTED LEARNING Use INDEPENDENT STUDY
SELF DISCIPLINE Use SELF CONTROL
SELF DISCLOSURE (INDIVIDUALS)
SELF ESTEEM
SELF EVALUATION (1966 1980)
SELF EVALUATION (GROUPS)
SELF EVALUATION (INDIVIDUALS)
SELF EXPRESSION
SELF GOVERNMENT Use SELF DETERMINATION
SELF GROWTH Use INDIVIDUAL DEVELOPMENT
SELF GUIDED GROUPS Use SELF DIRECTED GROUPS
SELF HELP DEVICES (DISABLED) Use ASSISTIVE DEVICES (FOR DISABLED)
SELF HELP PROGRAMS
RACIAL SELF IDENTIFICATION Use RACIAL IDENTIFICATION
SELF IMAGE Use SELF CONCEPT
SELF INJURY (PHYSICAL) Use SELF MUTILATION
SELF INSTRUCTION Use INDEPENDENT STUDY
SELF INSTRUCTION AIDS Use AUTOINSTRUCTIONAL AIDS
SELF INSTRUCTION MATERIALS Use PROGRAMED INSTRUCTIONAL MATERIALS
PROGRAMED SELF INSTRUCTION Use PROGRAMED INSTRUCTION
SELF KNOWLEDGE Use SELF CONCEPT
SELF MOTIVATION Use SELF ACTUALIZATION
SELF MUTILATION
SELF PACED INSTRUCTION Use INDIVIDUALIZED INSTRUCTION and PACING
SELF PACING Use PACING
SELF PACING MACHINES (1966 1980) Use TEACHING MACHINES
SELF REALIZATION Use SELF ACTUALIZATION
SELF REWARD
INSTITUTIONAL SELF STUDY Use SELF EVALUATION (GROUPS)
ORGANIZATIONAL SELF STUDY Use SELF EVALUATION (GROUPS)
INDEPENDENT STUDENTS (SELF SUPPORTING) Use SELF SUPPORTING STUDENTS
SELF SUPPORTING STUDENTS
SELF TEACHING Use INDEPENDENT STUDY
SELF UNDERSTANDING Use SELF CONCEPT
SELF UTILIZATION Use SELF ACTUALIZATION
SEMANTIC DIFFERENTIAL
SEMANTICS
GENERAL SEMANTICS Use SEMANTICS
SEMESTER DIVISION (1966 1980) Use SEMESTER SYSTEM
SEMESTER SYSTEM
SEMICONDUCTOR DEVICES
SEMINARIES Use CHURCH RELATED COLLEGES and THEOLOGICAL EDUCATION
SEMINARS
POLICE SEMINARS (1966 1980) Use POLICE EDUCATION
STUDENT SEMINARS (1966 1980) Use SEMINARS
TEACHER SEMINARS (1966 1980) Use TEACHER WORKSHOPS
SEMIOTICS
SEMISKILLED OCCUPATIONS
SEMISKILLED WORKERS
SEMITIC LANGUAGES
ANTI SEMITISM
ACADEMIC SENATES Use COLLEGE GOVERNING COUNCILS
FACULTY SENATES Use COLLEGE GOVERNING COUNCILS
UNIVERSITY SENATES Use COLLEGE GOVERNING COUNCILS
SENATORS Use LEGISLATORS
SENIOR CITIZENS (1967 1980) Use OLDER ADULTS
SENIOR HIGH SCHOOL STUDENTS Use HIGH SCHOOL STUDENTS
SENIOR HIGH SCHOOLS (1966 1980) Use HIGH SCHOOLS
SENIOR TEACHER ROLE (1966 1980) Use MASTER TEACHERS and TEACHER ROLE
SENIORITY
COLLEGE SENIORS
SENIORS (1966 1980) (GRADE 12) Use HIGH SCHOOL SENIORS
HIGH SCHOOL SENIORS
SENIORS (1966 1980) (LAST YEAR UNDERGRADUATES) Use COLLEGE SENIORS
CUTANEOUS SENSE (1968 1980) Use TACTUAL PERCEPTION
DERMAL SENSE Use TACTUAL PERCEPTION
MUSCLE SENSE Use KINESTHETIC PERCEPTION
SENSITIVITY TRAINING
SENSORY AIDS
SENSORY DEPRIVATION
SENSORY EXPERIENCE
SENSORY INTEGRATION
SENSORY MOTOR LEARNING Use PERCEPTUAL MOTOR LEARNING
SENSORY TRAINING
SENTENCE COMBINING
TRANSFORMATIONAL SENTENCE COMBINING Use SENTENCE COMBINING
SENTENCE DIAGRAMING
SENTENCE STRUCTURE
SENTENCES
KERNEL SENTENCES
MATHEMATICAL SENTENCES Use MATHEMATICAL FORMULAS
PRISON SENTENCES Use SENTENCING
SENTENCING
SEPARATION ANXIETY
CHURCH STATE SEPARATION Use STATE CHURCH SEPARATION
STATE CHURCH SEPARATION
FIXED SEQUENCE
SEQUENTIAL APPROACH
SEQUENTIAL LEARNING
SEQUENTIAL PROGRAMS (1966 1980) Use SEQUENTIAL APPROACH
SEQUENTIAL READING PROGRAMS (1966 1980) Use SEQUENTIAL APPROACH
SERBOCROATIAN
SERIAL ASSOCIATION Use SERIAL LEARNING

SERIAL LEARNING
SERIAL METHOD Use SERIAL LEARNING
SERIAL ORDERING
SERIALS
EDUCATION SERVICE CENTERS
EDUCATIONAL SERVICE CENTERS Use EDUCATION SERVICE CENTERS
INTERMEDIATE SERVICE DISTRICTS Use INTERMEDIATE ADMINISTRATIVE UNITS
SERVICE EDUCATION (1966 1980) Use VOCATIONAL EDUCATION
CIVIL SERVICE EMPLOYEES Use GOVERNMENT EMPLOYEES
FOOD SERVICE
SERVICE INDUSTRY Use SERVICE OCCUPATIONS
FOOD SERVICE INDUSTRY (1967 1981) Use FOOD SERVICE
MILITARY SERVICE
SERVICE OCCUPATIONS
FOOD SERVICE OCCUPATIONS (1968 1981) Use FOOD SERVICE
PUBLIC SERVICE OCCUPATIONS
HEALTH SERVICE PERSONNEL Use HEALTH PERSONNEL
COMMUNITY SERVICE PROGRAMS (1966 1980) Use COMMUNITY SERVICES
PUBLIC SERVICE
SPECIAL SERVICE SCHOOLS Use SPECIAL SCHOOLS
APPLIANCE SERVICE TECHNICIANS (1967 1980) Use APPLIANCE REPAIR
FIXED SERVICE TELEVISION (1969 1980) Use EDUCATIONAL TELEVISION
SERVICE VEHICLES
SERVICE WORKERS
FOOD SERVICE WORKERS (1968 1981) Use FOOD SERVICE
HEALTH SERVICE WORKERS Use HEALTH PERSONNEL
ELECTRICAL APPLIANCE SERVICEMEN (1968 1980) Use APPLIANCE REPAIR
SERVICES
ANCILLARY SERVICES (1967 1980)
ANCILLARY SCHOOL SERVICES
ATTENDANCE SERVICES (1968 1980) Use ATTENDANCE and PUPIL PERSONNEL SERVICES
AUXILIARY SCHOOL SERVICES Use ANCILLARY SCHOOL SERVICES
CLIENT BACKGROUND (HUMAN SERVICES) Use CLIENT CHARACTERISTICS (HUMAN SERVICES)
CLIENT CHARACTERISTICS (HUMAN SERVICES)
CLINICAL SERVICES Use CLINICS
COMMUNICATIONS SERVICES Use COMMUNICATIONS
COMMUNITY SERVICES
COMMUNITY HEALTH SERVICES
INFORMATION SERVICES (COMMUNITY) Use COMMUNITY INFORMATION SERVICES
COMMUNITY INFORMATION SERVICES
REFERRAL SERVICES (COMMUNITY) Use COMMUNITY INFORMATION SERVICES and REFERRAL
COMPUTER BASED REFERENCE SERVICES Use ONLINE SYSTEMS and REFERENCE SERVICES
COUNSELING SERVICES
CURRENT AWARENESS SERVICES Use SELECTIVE DISSEMINATION OF INFORMATION
DAY CARE SERVICES (1967 1980) Use DAY CARE
EMPLOYMENT SERVICES
OUTPLACEMENT SERVICES (EMPLOYMENT)
EMPLOYMENT REFERRAL SERVICES Use EMPLOYMENT SERVICES
EXCEPTIONAL CHILD SERVICES (1968 1980)
EXTENSION SERVICES Use EXTENSION EDUCATION
FINANCIAL SERVICES
GUIDANCE SERVICES (1966 1980) Use GUIDANCE PROGRAMS
HEALTH SERVICES
HUMAN SERVICES
INFORMATION SERVICES
INFORMATION AND REFERRAL SERVICES Use INFORMATION SERVICES and REFERRAL
JOB LOSS SERVICES Use OUTPLACEMENT SERVICES (EMPLOYMENT)
LEGAL SERVICES Use LEGAL AID
TECHNICAL SERVICES (LIBRARIES) Use LIBRARY TECHNICAL PROCESSES
LIBRARY SERVICES
LIBRARY REFERENCE SERVICES (1968 1980) Use LIBRARY SERVICES and REFERENCE SERVICES
LOCAL INFORMATION SERVICES Use COMMUNITY INFORMATION SERVICES
MEDICAL SERVICES
MIGRANT HEALTH SERVICES
MIGRANT WELFARE SERVICES
MOBILE EDUCATIONAL SERVICES
COMMERCIAL SEARCH SERVICES (ONLINE) Use ONLINE VENDORS
ONLINE REFERENCE SERVICES Use ONLINE SYSTEMS and REFERENCE SERVICES
FAMILY SERVICES POLICY Use FAMILY PROGRAMS and PUBLIC POLICY
PRODUCER SERVICES
PROFESSIONAL SERVICES
PSYCHIATRIC SERVICES
PSYCHOLOGICAL SERVICES
PUPIL PERSONNEL SERVICES
REFERENCE SERVICES
SCHOOL SERVICES (1966 1980) Use ANCILLARY SCHOOL SERVICES
SCHOOL HEALTH SERVICES
SHARED SERVICES (1974 1986) Use SHARED RESOURCES AND SERVICES
SHARED RESOURCES AND SERVICES
SIGNAL SERVICES Use TELECOMMUNICATIONS
SOCIAL SERVICES
SOCIOPSYCHOLOGICAL SERVICES (1967 1980) Use PSYCHOLOGICAL SERVICES and SOCIAL SERVICES
SPECIAL SERVICES (1966 1980) Use SERVICES
STUDENT AFFAIRS SERVICES Use STUDENT PERSONNEL SERVICES
STUDENT PERSONNEL SERVICES
SUPPORT GROUPS (HUMAN SERVICES) Use SOCIAL SUPPORT GROUPS
SUPPORT SYSTEMS (SERVICES) Use SERVICES
TELEPHONE CRISIS SERVICES Use HOTLINES (PUBLIC)
TUTORIAL SERVICES Use TUTORIAL PROGRAMS
WELFARE SERVICES
SUMMER SESSION Use SUMMER SCHOOLS
DOUBLE SESSIONS
SPLIT SESSIONS Use DOUBLE SESSIONS
STAGGERED SESSIONS Use EXTENDED SCHOOL DAY
RESPONSE SET (TESTS) Use RESPONSE STYLE (TESTS)
SET THEORY
PROBLEM SETS
SETTLEMENT HOUSES
LAND SETTLEMENT
SETTLEMENT PATTERNS Use LAND SETTLEMENT
COLLECTIVE SETTLEMENTS

COMMUNISTIC	SETTLEMENTS Use COLLECTIVE SETTLEMENTS
NEIGHBORHOOD	SETTLEMENTS Use SETTLEMENT HOUSES
UNIVERSITY	SETTLEMENTS Use SETTLEMENT HOUSES
	SEVENTEENTH CENTURY LITERATURE
	SEVERE DISABILITIES
	SEVERE MENTAL RETARDATION
	SEVERELY HANDICAPPED (1975 1980) Use SEVERE DISABILITIES
	SEWAGE Use WASTE WATER
	SEWING INSTRUCTION
	SEWING MACHINE OPERATORS
	SEX
	SEX BIAS
	SEX (CHARACTERISTICS) (1966 1980)
SINGLE	SEX COLLEGES
	SEX DIFFERENCES
	SEX DISCRIMINATION
	SEX EDUCATION
	SEX FAIRNESS
GENDER	(SEX) Use SEX
GENDER DIFFERENCES	(SEX) Use SEX DIFFERENCES
GENDER IDENTITY	(SEX) Use SEXUAL IDENTITY
	SEX PREJUDICE Use SEX BIAS
	SEX ROLE
SINGLE	SEX SCHOOLS
	SEX STEREOTYPES
	SEXISM Use SEX BIAS
	SEXIST LANGUAGE Use LANGUAGE USAGE and SEX BIAS
	SEXUAL ABUSE
CHILD	SEXUAL ABUSE Use CHILD ABUSE and SEXUAL ABUSE
	SEXUAL ASSAULT Use SEXUAL ABUSE
	SEXUAL BEHAVIOR Use SEXUALITY
	SEXUAL HARASSMENT
	SEXUAL IDENTITY
	SEXUALITY
HUMAN	SEXUALITY Use SEXUALITY
	SHADE TREES Use TREES
	SHADOW PLAYS Use THEATER ARTS
	SHAPERS Use MACHINE TOOLS
	SHARECROPPERS
	SHARED FACILITIES
	SHARED LIBRARY RESOURCES
	SHARED RESOURCES AND SERVICES
	SHARED SERVICES (1974 1986) Use SHARED RESOURCES AND SERVICES
	SHARED TIME (COMPUTERS) Use TIME SHARING
	SHARED TIME (EDUCATION) Use DUAL ENROLLMENT
JOB	SHARING
RESOURCE	SHARING Use SHARED RESOURCES AND SERVICES
REVENUE	SHARING
TIME	SHARING
WORK	SHARING Use JOB SHARING
	SHEET METAL MACHINE OPERATORS Use MACHINE TOOL OPERATORS and SHEET METAL WORK
	SHEET METAL WORK
	SHEET METAL WORKERS (1967 1981) Use SHEET METAL WORK
ANSWER	SHEETS
DATA	SHEETS (1966 1980) Use WORKSHEETS
	SHELTERED WORKSHOPS
AIR RAID	SHELTERS Use FALLOUT SHELTERS
BOMB	SHELTERS Use FALLOUT SHELTERS
FALLOUT	SHELTERS
EXTRADIMENSIONAL	SHIFT Use SHIFT STUDIES
HALF REVERSAL	SHIFT Use SHIFT STUDIES
INTERDIMENSIONAL	SHIFT Use SHIFT STUDIES
NONREVERSAL	SHIFT Use SHIFT STUDIES
REVERSAL	SHIFT Use SHIFT STUDIES
	SHIFT STUDIES
POPULATION	SHIFTS Use MIGRATION
CULTURE	SHOCK Use CULTURE CONFLICT
	SHONA
	SHOP CURRICULUM
GENERAL	SHOP Use SHOP CURRICULUM
	SHOP MECHANICS Use MACHINE REPAIRERS
	SHOP ROOMS Use SCHOOL SHOPS
INDUSTRIAL ARTS	SHOPS Use SCHOOL SHOPS
SCHOOL	SHOPS
	SHORT COURSES (1970 1980) Use MINICOURSES
	SHORT STORIES
	SHORT TERM MEMORY
TEACHER	SHORTAGE
TIME	SHORTENED DEGREE PROGRAMS Use ACCELERATION (EDUCATION)
	SHORTHAND
REPETITIVE FILM	SHOWINGS
NO	SHOWS
PUPPET	SHOWS Use PUPPETRY
	SI UNITS Use METRIC SYSTEM
	SIBLINGS
	SICKLE CELL ANEMIA
	SICKLE CELL TRAIT Use SICKLE CELL ANEMIA
	SICKNESSES Use DISEASES
	SIERRA LEONE CREOLE
	SIERRA LEONE KRIO Use SIERRA LEONE CREOLE
	SIGHT Use VISION
	SIGHT METHOD
	SIGHT PLAYING Use MUSIC READING
	SIGHT SINGING Use MUSIC READING
	SIGHT VOCABULARY
PARTIALLY	SIGHTED (1967 1980) Use PARTIAL VISION
	SIGHTSEEING INDUSTRY Use TOURISM
	SIGN LANGUAGE
AMERICAN	SIGN LANGUAGE
	SIGN PAINTERS
	SIGN WRITERS Use SIGN PAINTERS

MATHEMATICS	SKILLS
MECHANICAL	SKILLS
MOTOR	SKILLS Use PSYCHOMOTOR SKILLS
ORAL	SKILLS Use SPEECH SKILLS
PARENT	SKILLS Use PARENTING SKILLS
PARENTING	SKILLS
PSYCHOMOTOR	SKILLS
READING	SKILLS
RESEARCH	SKILLS
FUNDAMENTAL	SKILLS (SCHOOL) Use BASIC SKILLS
SELF CARE	SKILLS
SOCIAL	SKILLS Use INTERPERSONAL COMPETENCE
LOCATIONAL	SKILLS (SOCIAL STUDIES)
SPEAKING	SKILLS Use SPEECH SKILLS
SPEECH	SKILLS
STUDY	SKILLS
SURVIVAL READING	SKILLS Use FUNCTIONAL READING
TEACHER	SKILLS Use TEACHING SKILLS
TEACHING	SKILLS
TEST TAKING	SKILLS Use TEST WISENESS
NUMBER	SKILLS TESTS Use MATHEMATICS TESTS
VOCABULARY	SKILLS
VOCATIONAL	SKILLS Use JOB SKILLS
WORD STUDY	SKILLS
WRITING	SKILLS
	SKIMMING (READING) Use SPEED READING
	SKIN DIVING Use UNDERWATER DIVING
	SKITS
	SLAVERY
	SLAVIC LANGUAGES
	SLEEP
	SLIDE PROJECTORS Use PROJECTION EQUIPMENT
	SLIDES
	SLOVENE Use SLOVENIAN
	SLOVENIAN
	SLOW LEARNERS
	SLUDGE
ACTIVATED	SLUDGE Use SLUDGE
	SLUM CHILDREN Use DISADVANTAGED YOUTH
	SLUM CONDITIONS (1966 1980) Use SLUM ENVIRONMENT
	SLUM ENVIRONMENT
	SLUM SCHOOLS
	SLUMS
URBAN	SLUMS (1966 1980) Use SLUMS
	SMALL BUSINESS MANAGEMENT Use BUSINESS ADMINISTRATION and SMALL BUSINESSES
	SMALL BUSINESSES
	SMALL CLASSES
	SMALL COLLEGES
	SMALL ENGINE MECHANICS
	SMALL GROUP INSTRUCTION
	SMALL SCHOOLS
	SMOG Use AIR POLLUTION
	SMOKE ALARMS Use ALARM SYSTEMS
	SMOKESTACKS Use CHIMNEYS
	SMOKING
CIGARETTE	SMOKING Use SMOKING
	SNACK BARS Use DINING FACILITIES
	SNOWSKIING Use SKIING
	SOCCER
	SOCIABILITY Use INTERPERSONAL COMPETENCE
	SOCIAL ACTION
	SOCIAL ADJUSTMENT
	SOCIAL AGENCIES
ATMOSPHERE	(SOCIAL) Use SOCIAL ENVIRONMENT
	SOCIAL ATTITUDES
	SOCIAL AWARENESS Use INTERPERSONAL COMPETENCE
	SOCIAL BACKGROUND
	SOCIAL BEHAVIOR
ANTI	SOCIAL BEHAVIOR (1966 1980) Use ANTISOCIAL BEHAVIOR
	SOCIAL BIAS
	SOCIAL BIOLOGY
	SOCIAL CHANGE
	SOCIAL CHARACTERISTICS
	SOCIAL CLASS
	SOCIAL CLASS DIFFERENCES Use SOCIAL DIFFERENCES
	SOCIAL CLASS INTEGRATION Use SOCIAL INTEGRATION
	SOCIAL CLIMATE Use SOCIAL ENVIRONMENT
	SOCIAL COGNITION
	SOCIAL COMPETENCE Use INTERPERSONAL COMPETENCE
	SOCIAL CONTROL
DATING	(SOCIAL)
	SOCIAL DESIRABILITY
	SOCIAL DEVELOPMENT
	SOCIAL DIALECTS
	SOCIAL DIFFERENCES
	SOCIAL DISADVANTAGEMENT (1966 1980) Use DISADVANTAGED
DISCRIMINATION	(SOCIAL) Use SOCIAL DISCRIMINATION
	SOCIAL DISCRIMINATION
DISCRIMINATORY ATTITUDES	(SOCIAL) (1966 1980) Use SOCIAL BIAS
	SOCIAL DISTRIBUTION
	SOCIAL DRINKING Use DRINKING
	SOCIAL ENVIRONMENT
	SOCIAL EXCHANGE THEORY
	SOCIAL EXPERIENCE
	SOCIAL FACTORS (1968 1980) Use SOCIAL INFLUENCES
	SOCIAL GEOGRAPHY Use HUMAN GEOGRAPHY
	SOCIAL HISTORY
	SOCIAL IMMATURITY (1966 1980) Use MATURITY (INDIVIDUALS)
	SOCIAL INDICATORS
	SOCIAL INFLUENCES
	SOCIAL INSTITUTIONS (ORGANIZATIONS) Use INSTITUTIONS

SOCIAL INSTITUTIONS (SOCIAL PATTERNS) Use SOCIOCULTURAL PATTERNS
INTEGRATION (SOCIAL) Use SOCIAL INTEGRATION
SOCIAL INTEGRATION
SOCIAL INTERACTION Use INTERPERSONAL RELATIONSHIP
SOCIAL ISOLATION
SOCIAL ISSUES Use SOCIAL PROBLEMS
SOCIAL LEARNING Use SOCIALIZATION
SOCIAL LIFE
SOCIAL MATURITY (1966 1980) Use MATURITY (INDIVIDUALS)
SOCIAL MOBILITY
SOCIAL NETWORKS
SOCIAL NORMS Use BEHAVIOR STANDARDS and SOCIAL BEHAVIOR
SOCIAL OPPORTUNITIES (1966 1980) Use SOCIAL MOBILITY
SOCIAL ORGANIZATIONS
SOCIAL INSTITUTIONS (SOCIAL PATTERNS) Use SOCIOCULTURAL PATTERNS
SOCIAL PERCEPTION Use SOCIAL COGNITION
SOCIAL PLANNING
SOCIAL PRESSURE Use SOCIAL INFLUENCES
SOCIAL PROBLEMS
SOCIAL PSYCHOLOGY
SOCIAL RECONSTRUCTION Use SOCIAL CHANGE
SOCIAL RECREATION PROGRAMS (1966 1980) Use RECREATIONAL PROGRAMS
SOCIAL REFORM Use SOCIAL ACTION
SOCIAL REINFORCEMENT
SOCIAL RELATIONS (1966 1980)
SOCIAL RESPONSIBILITY
SOCIAL RESTRICTIONS Use SOCIAL MOBILITY
SOCIAL SCIENCE METHODOLOGY Use RESEARCH METHODOLOGY and SOCIAL SCIENCE RESEARCH
SOCIAL SCIENCE RESEARCH
SOCIAL SCIENCES
SOCIAL SCIENTISTS
SOCIAL SERVICES
SOCIAL SKILLS Use INTERPERSONAL COMPETENCE
SOCIAL STATUS
SOCIAL STRATIFICATION
SOCIAL STRUCTURE
SOCIAL STUDIES
LOCATIONAL SKILLS (SOCIAL STUDIES)
SOCIAL STUDIES UNITS (1966 1980) Use SOCIAL STUDIES and UNITS OF STUDY
SOCIAL SUPPORT GROUPS
SOCIAL SYSTEMS
SOCIAL THEORIES
SOCIAL TRENDS Use SOCIOCULTURAL PATTERNS
SOCIAL VALUES
SOCIAL WELFARE (1966 1980)
SOCIAL WORK
SOCIAL WORKERS
SCHOOL SOCIAL WORKERS
SOCIALISM
NATIONAL SOCIALISM Use NAZISM
SOCIALIZATION
POLITICAL SOCIALIZATION
SOCIALLY ADVANTAGED Use ADVANTAGED
SOCIALLY DEVIANT BEHAVIOR (1966 1980) Use ANTISOCIAL BEHAVIOR
SOCIALLY DISADVANTAGED (1966 1980) Use DISADVANTAGED
SOCIALLY MALADJUSTED (1966 1980) Use SOCIAL ADJUSTMENT
SOCIETAL CHANGE Use SOCIAL CHANGE
HONOR SOCIETIES
TRIBAL SOCIETIES Use TRIBES
FUTURES (OF SOCIETY)
SCIENCE AND SOCIETY
SCIENCE TECHNOLOGY AND SOCIETY Use SCIENCE AND SOCIETY
STS (SCIENCE TECHNOLOGY SOCIETY) Use SCIENCE AND SOCIETY
SOCIOBIOLOGY
SOCIOCULTURAL PATTERNS
SOCIODRAMA (1966 1980) Use ROLE PLAYING
SOCIOECONOMIC BACKGROUND
SOCIOECONOMIC INFLUENCES
SOCIOECONOMIC LEVEL Use SOCIOECONOMIC STATUS
SOCIOECONOMIC STATUS
SOCIOGRAMS Use SOCIOMETRIC TECHNIQUES
SOCIOLINGUISTICS
SOCIOLOGICAL NOVELS (1969 1980) Use NOVELS
SOCIOLOGICAL STUDIES Use SOCIAL SCIENCE RESEARCH and SOCIOLOGY
FAMILY (SOCIOLOGICAL UNIT)
SOCIOLOGY
EDUCATIONAL SOCIOLOGY
SOCIOMETRIC TECHNIQUES
SOCIOPSYCHOLOGICAL SERVICES (1967 1980) Use PSYCHOLOGICAL SERVICES and SOCIAL SERVICES
SOFT COVER BOOKS Use PAPERBACK BOOKS
SOFTBALL
WATER SOFTENING Use WATER TREATMENT
COMPUTER SOFTWARE
SOFTWARE (COMPUTERS) Use COMPUTER SOFTWARE
INSTRUCTIONAL SOFTWARE Use COURSEWARE
MENU DRIVEN SOFTWARE
COMPUTER SOFTWARE REVIEWS
SOFTWARE REVIEWS (COMPUTERS) Use COMPUTER SOFTWARE REVIEWS
SOIL CONSERVATION
SOIL SCIENCE
SOLAR ENERGY
SOLAR HEATING Use HEATING and SOLAR ENERGY
SOLAR RADIATION (1968 1983) Use SOLAR ENERGY
SOLAR RADIATION ENERGY Use SOLAR ENERGY
SOLICITORS (LAW) Use LAWYERS
SOLID GEOMETRY
SOLID WASTES
SOLILOQUIES Use MONOLOGS
PARTICIPATIVE PROBLEM SOLVING Use PARTICIPATIVE DECISION MAKING and PROBLEM SOLVING
PROBLEM SOLVING
SOMALI

ART	SONG
	SONGS
	SONIC ENVIRONMENT Use ACOUSTICAL ENVIRONMENT
	SONNETS
	SONS
	SORORITIES
Q	SORT (1967 1980) Use Q METHODOLOGY
	SORTING PROCEDURES (1966 1980) Use CLASSIFICATION
	SOUND Use ACOUSTICS
	SOUND BARRIERS Use ACOUSTIC INSULATION
LETTER	SOUND CORRESPONDENCE Use PHONEME GRAPHEME CORRESPONDENCE
	SOUND EFFECTS
	SOUND EQUIPMENT Use AUDIO EQUIPMENT
	SOUND FILMS (1966 1980) Use FILMS
	SOUND INSULATION Use ACOUSTIC INSULATION
NOISE	(SOUND)
SPECTROGRAPHS	(SOUND) Use SOUND SPECTROGRAPHS
	SOUND SPECTROGRAPHS
	SOUND SYSTEMS Use AUDIO EQUIPMENT
CENTRAL	SOUND SYSTEMS (1966 1980) Use AUDIO EQUIPMENT
	SOUND TAPE RECORDINGS Use AUDIOTAPE RECORDINGS
	SOUND TRACKS (1966 1980)
	SOUND TRANSMISSION Use ACOUSTICS
VOLUME	(SOUND) Use NOISE (SOUND)
	SOUND WAVES Use ACOUSTICS
	SOUNDPROOFING Use ACOUSTIC INSULATION
	SOURCE CREDIBILITY Use CREDIBILITY
ALTERNATIVE ENERGY	SOURCES
INFORMATION	SOURCES
MATERIAL	SOURCES Use RESOURCE MATERIALS
ORIGINAL	SOURCES Use PRIMARY SOURCES
PRIMARY	SOURCES
	SOUTH AMERICAN HISTORY Use LATIN AMERICAN HISTORY
	SOUTH AMERICAN LITERATURE Use LATIN AMERICAN LITERATURE
	SOUTH AMERICANS Use LATIN AMERICANS
	SOUTH ASIAN CIVILIZATION Use NON WESTERN CIVILIZATION
	SOUTHERN ATTITUDES (1966 1980) Use REGIONAL ATTITUDES
	SOUTHERN CITIZENS (1966 1980)
	SOUTHERN COMMUNITY (1966 1980)
	SOUTHERN SCHOOLS (1966 1980)
TRIBAL	SOVEREIGNTY
	SPACE
	SPACE CLASSIFICATION
	SPACE DIVIDERS
	SPACE EXPLORATION
INTERIOR	SPACE
	SPACE ORIENTATION (1968 1980)
PERSONAL	SPACE
OUTER	SPACE RESEARCH Use SPACE EXPLORATION
SCHOOL	SPACE
	SPACE SCIENCES
	SPACE TIME CONTINUUM Use RELATIVITY
	SPACE UTILIZATION
	SPACED NEGATIVE REINFORCEMENT Use NEGATIVE REINFORCEMENT
FOUND	SPACES
ATTENTION	SPAN
LIFE	SPAN EDUCATION Use LIFELONG LEARNING
EYE VOICE	SPAN
	SPANISH
	SPANISH AMERICAN LITERATURE (1969 1980) Use HISPANIC AMERICAN LITERATURE
	SPANISH AMERICANS
	SPANISH CULTURE
	SPANISH LITERATURE
	SPANISH SPEAKING
	SPATIAL ABILITY
	SPATIAL PERCEPTION (1980 1981) Use SPATIAL ABILITY
	SPATIAL RELATIONSHIP (1966 1980)
	SPATIAL RELATIONSHIP (FACILITIES)
NATIVE	SPEAKERS
	SPEAKING (1966 1980) Use SPEECH COMMUNICATION
	SPEAKING ACTIVITIES (1966 1980) Use SPEECH COMMUNICATION
CHORAL	SPEAKING
LIMITED ENGLISH	SPEAKING
NON ENGLISH	SPEAKING
PUBLIC	SPEAKING
	SPEAKING SKILLS Use SPEECH SKILLS
SPANISH	SPEAKING
	SPECIAL ADMISSION Use SELECTIVE ADMISSION
	SPECIAL CLASSES
	SPECIAL COUNSELORS (1966 1980) Use COUNSELORS and SPECIALISTS
	SPECIAL CREATION THEORY Use CREATIONISM
	SPECIAL DEGREE PROGRAMS
	SPECIAL EDUCATION
	SPECIAL EDUCATION TEACHERS
	SPECIAL EFFECTS
	SPECIAL HEALTH PROBLEMS
	SPECIAL LIBRARIES
	SPECIAL METHODS COURSES Use METHODS COURSES
	SPECIAL NEEDS (INDIVIDUALS) Use INDIVIDUAL NEEDS
	SPECIAL PERSONNEL Use SPECIALISTS
	SPECIAL PROGRAMS
ENGLISH FOR	SPECIAL PURPOSES
LANGUAGES FOR	SPECIAL PURPOSES
	SPECIAL SCHOOLS
	SPECIAL SERVICE SCHOOLS Use SPECIAL SCHOOLS
	SPECIAL SERVICES (1966 1980) Use SERVICES
	SPECIAL TEACHERS Use SPECIALISTS
	SPECIAL ZONING
	SPECIALIST IN EDUCATION DEGREES
	SPECIALISTS
CHILD DEVELOPMENT	SPECIALISTS

RESEARCH SPECIALISTS (EDUCATION) Use EDUCATIONAL RESEARCHERS
EVALUATION SPECIALISTS Use EVALUATORS
FILM PRODUCTION SPECIALISTS
GUIDANCE SPECIALISTS Use GUIDANCE PERSONNEL and SPECIALISTS
INFORMATION SPECIALISTS Use INFORMATION SCIENTISTS
LEARNING SPECIALISTS (1966 1980) Use SPECIALISTS
LIBRARY SPECIALISTS Use LIBRARIANS
MEDIA SPECIALISTS
READING SPECIALISTS Use READING CONSULTANTS
SPECIALIZATION
HEMISPHERIC SPECIALIZATION (BRAIN) Use BRAIN HEMISPHERE FUNCTIONS
SPECIALTY SCHOOLS Use PROPRIETARY SCHOOLS
ENDANGERED SPECIES
SPECIFIC LEARNING DISABILITIES Use LEARNING DISABILITIES
SPECIFICATIONS
EDUCATIONAL SPECIFICATIONS (1967 1980)
FACILITY SPECIFICATIONS Use FACILITY GUIDELINES
JOB SPECIFICATIONS Use OCCUPATIONAL INFORMATION
PERFORMANCE SPECIFICATIONS (1969 1980)
SPECTATOR TRAFFIC CONTROL Use TRAFFIC CONTROL
SPECTATORS Use AUDIENCES
SPECTROGRAMS (1967 1980) Use SOUND SPECTROGRAPHS
SPECTROGRAPHS (SOUND) Use SOUND SPECTROGRAPHS
SOUND SPECTROGRAPHS
SPECTROSCOPY
OPTICAL SPECTRUM Use LIGHT
VISIBLE SPECTRUM Use LIGHT
SPEECH
SPEECH ACTS
SPEECH AND HEARING CLINICS
ARTICULATION (SPEECH)
ARTIFICIAL SPEECH
SPEECH CLINICS (1968 1980) Use SPEECH AND HEARING CLINICS
SPEECH COMMUNICATION
SPEECH COMMUNICATION CURRICULUM Use SPEECH COMMUNICATION and SPEECH CURRICULUM
SPEECH COMMUNICATION RESEARCH Use COMMUNICATION RESEARCH and SPEECH COMMUNICATION
SPEECH COMPRESSION
CUED SPEECH
SPEECH CURRICULUM
DELAYED SPEECH
RETARDED SPEECH DEVELOPMENT (1968 1980) Use DELAYED SPEECH
SPEECH EDUCATION (1966 1980)
SPEECH EVALUATION
FIGURES OF SPEECH Use FIGURATIVE LANGUAGE
FREEDOM OF SPEECH
SPEECH HABITS
SPEECH HANDICAPPED (1967 1980) Use SPEECH HANDICAPS
SPEECH HANDICAPS
SPEECH IMPROVEMENT
SPEECH INSTRUCTION
PARTS OF SPEECH Use FORM CLASSES (LANGUAGES)
SPEECH PATHOLOGY
PROSODIC FEATURES (SPEECH) Use SUPRASEGMENTALS
SPEECH READING Use LIPREADING
SIMULATED SPEECH Use ARTIFICIAL SPEECH
SPEECH SKILLS
INNER SPEECH (SUBVOCAL)
SYNTHETIC SPEECH Use ARTIFICIAL SPEECH
SPEECH TESTS
SPEECH THERAPISTS (1966 1980) Use SPEECH THERAPY and THERAPISTS
SPEECH THERAPY
VISIBLE SPEECH
SPEECHES
READING SPEED (1966 1977) Use READING RATE
SPEED READING
SPEED TESTS Use TIMED TESTS
SPELLING
FINGER SPELLING
SPELLING INSTRUCTION
SCHOOL DISTRICT SPENDING
SPERM DONORS Use TISSUE DONORS
SPIRAL CURRICULUM
SPLIT SESSIONS Use DOUBLE SESSIONS
SPLIT TIME Use DUAL ENROLLMENT
STANDARD SPOKEN USAGE
EMPLOYER SPONSORED DAY CARE Use EMPLOYER SUPPORTED DAY CARE
SPONTANEOUS BEHAVIOR
FENCING (SPORT)
SPORT PSYCHOLOGY
SPORTS Use ATHLETICS
AQUATIC SPORTS
EXTRAMURAL SPORTS Use EXTRAMURAL ATHLETICS
INTRAMURAL SPORTS Use INTRAMURAL ATHLETICS
LIFETIME SPORTS
SPORTS NEWS Use ATHLETICS and NEWS MEDIA
SPORTS PSYCHOLOGY Use SPORT PSYCHOLOGY
RACKET SPORTS Use RACQUET SPORTS
RACQUET SPORTS
SPORTS REPORTING Use ATHLETICS and NEWS REPORTING
TEAM SPORTS
WATER SPORTS Use AQUATIC SPORTS
SPORTSMANSHIP
SPOUSES
SPRINGBOARD DIVING Use DIVING
EMERGENCY SQUAD PERSONNEL
RESCUE SQUAD PERSONNEL Use EMERGENCY SQUAD PERSONNEL
LEAST SQUARES STATISTICS
SQUASH (GAME)
EXHAUST STACKS Use CHIMNEYS
STAFF DAYS Use WORKER DAYS
STAFF DEVELOPMENT

STAFF EVALUATION Use PERSONNEL EVALUATION
STAFF IMPROVEMENT (1966 1980) Use STAFF DEVELOPMENT
INSTRUCTIONAL STAFF (1966 1980) Use TEACHERS
STAFF MEETINGS
STAFF OFFICES Use OFFICES (FACILITIES)
STAFF ORIENTATION
PROFESSIONAL STAFF Use PROFESSIONAL PERSONNEL
RESOURCE STAFF
STAFF ROLE
RESOURCE STAFF ROLE (1966 1980) Use RESOURCE STAFF
STAFF UTILIZATION
DIFFERENTIATED STAFFS
STAGE THEORY Use DEVELOPMENTAL STAGES
STAGES (1969 1980) Use STAGES (FACILITIES)
DEVELOPMENTAL STAGES
STAGES (FACILITIES)
STAGES OF DEVELOPMENT Use DEVELOPMENTAL STAGES
STAGGERED SESSIONS Use EXTENDED SCHOOL DAY
STAMMERING Use STUTTERING
STANDARD ERROR OF ESTIMATE Use ERROR OF MEASUREMENT
STANDARD ERROR OF MEASUREMENT (1970 1980) Use ERROR OF MEASUREMENT
STANDARD SPOKEN USAGE
COLLOQUIAL STANDARD USAGE Use STANDARD SPOKEN USAGE
LANGUAGE STANDARDIZATION
STANDARDIZED TESTS
STANDARDS
ACADEMIC STANDARDS
BEHAVIOR STANDARDS
ENVIRONMENTAL STANDARDS
EQUIPMENT STANDARDS
FACILITY STANDARDS Use FACILITY GUIDELINES
FOOD STANDARDS
LABOR STANDARDS
LIBRARY STANDARDS
LIVING STANDARDS
MIDDLE CLASS STANDARDS
OCCUPATIONAL SAFETY AND HEALTH STANDARDS Use LABOR STANDARDS and OCCUPATIONAL SAFETY AND HEALTH
PROFESSIONAL STANDARDS Use STANDARDS
STATE STANDARDS
TEXTBOOK STANDARDS
ADVANCED STANDING EXAMINATIONS Use EQUIVALENCY TESTS
STATE ACTION
STATE AGENCIES
STATE AID
FEDERAL STATE AID Use STATE FEDERAL AID
STATE ASSISTANCE Use STATE AID
STATE BOARDS OF EDUCATION
STATE BOARDS OF LICENSING Use STATE LICENSING BOARDS
STATE CHURCH SEPARATION
STATE COLLEGES
STATE COMMITTEES ON EDUCATION Use STATE BOARDS OF EDUCATION
STATE COURT LITIGATION Use COURT LITIGATION and STATE COURTS
STATE COURTS
STATE CURRICULUM BULLETINS Use STATE CURRICULUM GUIDES
STATE CURRICULUM GUIDES
STATE DEPARTMENTS OF EDUCATION
STATE EDUCATION AGENCIES Use STATE DEPARTMENTS OF EDUCATION
STATE FEDERAL AID
STATE FEDERAL RELATIONSHIP Use FEDERAL STATE RELATIONSHIP
STATE FEDERAL SUPPORT (1966 1977) Use STATE FEDERAL AID
STATE FINANCIAL AID Use STATE AID
STATE FOREIGN LANGUAGE SUPERVISORS (1967 1980) Use SECOND LANGUAGE INSTRUCTION and STATE SUPERVISORS
FULL STATE FUNDING
STATE GOVERNMENT
STATE GOVERNMENT PROGRAMS Use STATE GOVERNMENT and STATE PROGRAMS
STATE HISTORY
STATE LAWS (1966 1974) Use STATE LEGISLATION
STATE LEGISLATION
STATE LIBRARIES
STATE LICENSING BOARDS
NONRESIDENT STUDENTS (1967 1980) (OUT OF STATE) Use OUT OF STATE STUDENTS
STATE NORMS
STATE OF THE ART REVIEWS
STATE OFFICIALS
STATE PLANNING Use STATEWIDE PLANNING
STATE POLICE (1966 1980) Use POLICE
STATE PROGRAMS
STATE RECREATION LEGISLATION (1966 1978) Use RECREATION LEGISLATION and STATE LEGISLATION
FEDERAL STATE RELATIONSHIP
RESIDENT STUDENTS (1967 1980) (IN STATE) Use IN STATE STUDENTS
STATE SCHOOL BOARDS Use STATE BOARDS OF EDUCATION
STATE SCHOOL DISTRICT RELATIONSHIP
STATE SCHOOLS
CHURCH STATE SEPARATION Use STATE CHURCH SEPARATION
STATE STANDARDS
IN STATE STUDENTS
OUT OF STATE STUDENTS
STATE SUPERVISORS
STATE SUPPORT Use STATE AID
STATE SUPREME COURTS Use STATE COURTS
STATE SURVEYS
STATE SYLLABI Use STATE CURRICULUM GUIDES
STATE UNIVERSITIES
MISSION STATEMENTS
POLICY STATEMENTS Use POSITION PAPERS
WAGE STATEMENTS (1966 1980) Use PAYROLL RECORDS
AMERICAN LITERATURE (1966 1980) (UNITED STATES) Use UNITED STATES LITERATURE
CIVIL WAR (UNITED STATES)
COLONIAL HISTORY (UNITED STATES)
UNITED STATES GOVERNMENT (COURSE)

UNITED STATES HISTORY
UNITED STATES LITERATURE
LOW INCOME STATES
STATES POWERS
PRESIDENTIAL CAMPAIGNS (UNITED STATES)
PRESIDENTIAL CANDIDATES (UNITED STATES) Use POLITICAL CANDIDATES and PRESIDENTIAL CAMPAIGNS (UNITED STATES)
PRESIDENTIAL DEBATES (UNITED STATES) Use DEBATE and PRESIDENTIAL CAMPAIGNS (UNITED STATES)
PRESIDENTIAL ELECTIONS (UNITED STATES) Use ELECTIONS and PRESIDENTIAL CAMPAIGNS (UNITED STATES)
PRESIDENTS OF THE UNITED STATES
REVOLUTIONARY WAR (UNITED STATES)
STATES RIGHTS Use STATES POWERS
STATEWIDE COORDINATION Use STATEWIDE PLANNING
STATEWIDE PLANNING
STATEWIDE PROGRAMS Use STATE PROGRAMS
STATIC CONTROLS Use ELECTRONIC CONTROL
LEARNING STATIONS (CLASSROOM) Use LEARNING CENTERS (CLASSROOM)
COAST GUARD AIR STATIONS Use MILITARY AIR FACILITIES
EXPERIMENT STATIONS
FIELD EXPERIMENT STATIONS Use EXPERIMENT STATIONS
MARINE CORPS AIR STATIONS Use MILITARY AIR FACILITIES
NAVAL AIR STATIONS Use MILITARY AIR FACILITIES
STATISTICAL ANALYSIS
STATISTICAL ASSOCIATION METHODS Use CORRELATION
STATISTICAL BIAS
STATISTICAL BIBLIOGRAPHY Use BIBLIOMETRICS
STATISTICAL DATA
STATISTICAL DISTRIBUTIONS
STATISTICAL INFERENCE
STATISTICAL LINGUISTICS Use MATHEMATICAL LINGUISTICS
STATISTICAL METHODS Use STATISTICAL ANALYSIS
STATISTICAL PROCESSES Use STATISTICAL ANALYSIS
STATISTICAL SIGNIFICANCE
STATISTICAL STUDIES
STATISTICAL SURVEYS
STATISTICAL THEORY Use STATISTICS
STATISTICS
BAYESIAN STATISTICS
COMPARATIVE STATISTICS (1966 1980) Use COMPARATIVE ANALYSIS and STATISTICAL ANALYSIS
DISTRIBUTION FREE STATISTICS Use NONPARAMETRIC STATISTICS
DISTRIBUTIONS (STATISTICS) Use STATISTICAL DISTRIBUTIONS
EMPLOYMENT STATISTICS
INFERENTIAL STATISTICS Use STATISTICAL INFERENCE and STATISTICS
LEAST SQUARES STATISTICS
LIBRARY STATISTICS
MATHEMATICAL STATISTICS Use STATISTICS
MAXIMUM LIKELIHOOD STATISTICS
MULTIVARIATE STATISTICS Use MULTIVARIATE ANALYSIS
NONPARAMETRIC STATISTICS
QUANTITATIVE RESEARCH (STATISTICS) Use STATISTICAL ANALYSIS
REGRESSION (STATISTICS)
SCHOOL STATISTICS
STATUS
AGE GRADE STATUS Use AGE GRADE PLACEMENT
CLASS STATUS Use SOCIAL STATUS
EDUCATIONAL STATUS COMPARISON
ECONOMIC STATUS
EMPLOYMENT STATUS Use EMPLOYMENT LEVEL
ETHNIC STATUS
FAMILY STATUS
GROUP STATUS
MARITAL STATUS
STATUS NEED
PROFESSIONAL STATUS Use PROFESSIONAL RECOGNITION
SOCIAL STATUS
SOCIOECONOMIC STATUS
STATUTORY RAPE Use RAPE
STEALING
STEEL FOUNDRIES Use FOUNDRIES
STEEL INDUSTRY (1967 1980) Use METAL INDUSTRY
STENOGRAPHERS (1966 1981) Use SHORTHAND
CLERK STENOGRAPHERS Use SHORTHAND
STENOGRAPHY (1967 1980) Use SHORTHAND
STEP IN STEP OUT STUDENTS Use STOPOUTS
STEP IN STEP OUT STUDENTS Use STOPOUTS
STEPFAMILY
STEREOPSIS (1968 1980) Use DEPTH PERCEPTION
STEREOTYPES
BLACK STEREOTYPES
ETHNIC STEREOTYPES
JEWISH STEREOTYPES (1966 1980) Use ETHNIC STEREOTYPES and JEWS
NEGRO STEREOTYPES (1966 1977) Use BLACK STEREOTYPES
SEX STEREOTYPES
TEACHER STEREOTYPES
STICKERS Use ADHESIVES
STIMULANTS
STIMULATION
STIMULI
AUDITORY STIMULI
AURAL STIMULI (1966 1980) Use AUDITORY STIMULI
ELECTRICAL STIMULI
PICTORIAL STIMULI
VERBAL STIMULI
VISUAL STIMULI
STIMULUS BEHAVIOR (1966 1980) Use RESPONSES
CONDITIONED STIMULUS (1966 1980) Use STIMULI
STIMULUS DEVICES (1966 1980)
NOVELTY (STIMULUS DIMENSION)
STIMULUS GENERALIZATION
STIMULUS SYNTHESIS Use PATTERNED RESPONSES
STOCKPILES Use SUPPLIES
STOPOUTS

STORAGE
STORAGE BATTERIES Use ELECTRIC BATTERIES
COMPUTER STORAGE DEVICES
EQUIPMENT STORAGE
INFORMATION STORAGE
INFORMATION STORAGE (PSYCHOLOGY) Use ENCODING (PSYCHOLOGY)
COLLEGE STORES
FEED STORES
FOOD STORES
GROCERY STORES Use FOOD STORES
LIVESTOCK FEED STORES Use FEED STORES
SHORT STORIES
STORY GRAMMAR
STORY PROBLEMS (MATHEMATICS) Use WORD PROBLEMS (MATHEMATICS)
STORY READING
STORY TELLING
STRABISMUS
STRADAPTIVE TESTING Use ADAPTIVE TESTING
FISCAL STRAIN Use FINANCIAL PROBLEMS
STRANGER REACTIONS
CHANGE STRATEGIES
EDUCATIONAL STRATEGIES
LEARNING STRATEGIES
READING STRATEGIES
SEARCH STRATEGIES
TEST TAKING STRATEGIES Use TEST WISENESS
SOCIAL STRATIFICATION
STREAM POLLUTION Use WATER POLLUTION
STREET LAYOUTS Use TRAFFIC CIRCULATION
STREET PARKING AREAS Use PARKING FACILITIES
STREET PEOPLE Use HOMELESS PEOPLE
STRENGTH (BIOLOGY) Use MUSCULAR STRENGTH
MUSCULAR STRENGTH
PHYSICAL STRENGTH Use MUSCULAR STRENGTH
STRESS MANAGEMENT
STRESS (PHONOLOGY)
STRESS VARIABLES
POVERTY STRICKEN Use ECONOMICALLY DISADVANTAGED
STRIKES
TEACHER STRIKES
STRUCTURAL ANALYSIS (1966 1980)
STRUCTURAL ANALYSIS (LINGUISTICS)
STRUCTURAL ANALYSIS (SCIENCE)
STRUCTURAL ARRANGEMENT Use ORGANIZATION
STRUCTURAL BUILDING SYSTEMS
STRUCTURAL ELEMENTS (CONSTRUCTION)
STRUCTURAL EQUATIONS Use PATH ANALYSIS
STRUCTURAL GRAMMAR
STRUCTURAL LINGUISTICS
STRUCTURAL UNEMPLOYMENT
STRUCTURAL WORK OCCUPATIONS Use BUILDING TRADES
ATOMIC STRUCTURE
AUTHORITY STRUCTURE Use POWER STRUCTURE
CONSTITUENT STRUCTURE Use PHRASE STRUCTURE
DEEP STRUCTURE
FACTOR STRUCTURE
FAMILY STRUCTURE
GOVERNMENT STRUCTURE Use GOVERNMENTAL STRUCTURE
GOVERNMENTAL STRUCTURE
GROUP STRUCTURE
INDUSTRIAL STRUCTURE
MOLECULAR STRUCTURE
PHRASE STRUCTURE
POWER STRUCTURE
SENTENCE STRUCTURE
SOCIAL STRUCTURE
SURFACE STRUCTURE
AIR STRUCTURES
AIR INFLATED STRUCTURES (1972 1980) Use AIR STRUCTURES
AIR SUPPORTED STRUCTURES (1972 1980) Use AIR STRUCTURES
COGNITIVE STRUCTURES
HYBRID AIR STRUCTURES (1972 1980) Use AIR STRUCTURES
INFLATABLE STRUCTURES Use AIR STRUCTURES
KNOWLEDGE STRUCTURES Use COGNITIVE STRUCTURES
STS (SCIENCE TECHNOLOGY SOCIETY) Use SCIENCE AND SOCIETY
STUDENT ABILITY (1966 1980) Use ACADEMIC ABILITY
STUDENT ACHIEVEMENT Use ACADEMIC ACHIEVEMENT
STUDENT ACTIVITIES (EXTRACLASS) Use EXTRACURRICULAR ACTIVITIES
STUDENT ADJUSTMENT
FOREIGN STUDENT ADVISERS
STUDENT AFFAIRS SERVICES Use STUDENT PERSONNEL SERVICES
STUDENT AFFAIRS WORKERS Use STUDENT PERSONNEL WORKERS
STUDENT AID Use STUDENT FINANCIAL AID
STUDENT ALIENATION
STUDENT APPLICATION (1966 1980) Use COLLEGE APPLICANTS
STUDENT APPRAISAL Use STUDENT EVALUATION
STUDENT APTITUDE Use ACADEMIC APTITUDE
STUDENT ASSIGNMENTS Use ASSIGNMENTS
STUDENT ATTITUDES
STUDENT ATTRITION
STUDENT BEHAVIOR
STUDENT CENTERED CURRICULUM
STUDENT CENTERS Use STUDENT UNIONS
STUDENT CERTIFICATION
STUDENT CHARACTERISTICS
STUDENT COLLEGE RELATIONSHIP
PARENT STUDENT CONFERENCES (1967 1980) Use PARENT TEACHER CONFERENCES
STUDENT COSTS
INSTRUCTIONAL STUDENT COSTS
NONINSTRUCTIONAL STUDENT COSTS
STUDENT COUNCILS Use STUDENT GOVERNMENT

STUDENT CREDIT HOURS Use CREDITS
STUDENT DEVELOPED MATERIALS
STUDENT DEVELOPMENT
STUDENT DISTRIBUTION (1966 1980)
STUDENT EDUCATIONAL OBJECTIVES
STUDENT ELIGIBILITY Use ELIGIBILITY
STUDENT EMPLOYMENT
STUDENT ENGAGED TIME Use TIME ON TASK
STUDENT ENROLLMENT (1966 1977) Use ENROLLMENT
STUDENT EVALUATION
NONGRADED STUDENT EVALUATION
STUDENT EVALUATION OF TEACHER PERFORMANCE
STUDENT EXCHANGE PROGRAMS
EXPENDITURE PER STUDENT
STUDENT EXPERIENCE
STUDENT FINANCIAL AID
NEED ANALYSIS (STUDENT FINANCIAL AID)
STUDENT FINANCIAL AID OFFICERS
STUDENT GOVERNMENT
STUDENT GROUPING (1966 1980) Use GROUPING (INSTRUCTIONAL PURPOSES)
STUDENT HOUSING (COLLEGE) Use COLLEGE HOUSING
STUDENT IMPROVEMENT
TEACHER STUDENT INTERACTION Use TEACHER STUDENT RELATIONSHIP
STUDENT INTERESTS
STUDENT JOB PLACEMENT Use JOB PLACEMENT and STUDENT EMPLOYMENT
STUDENT LEADERSHIP
STUDENT LEARNING CONTRACTS Use PERFORMANCE CONTRACTS
STUDENT LOADING AREAS (1968 1980) Use STUDENT TRANSPORTATION
STUDENT LOAN PROGRAMS
STUDENT MALADJUSTMENT Use STUDENT ADJUSTMENT
STUDENT MOBILITY
STUDENT MOTIVATION
STUDENT NEEDS
STUDENT OPINION (1966 1980) Use STUDENT ATTITUDES
STUDENT ORGANIZATIONS
STUDENT OUTCOMES Use OUTCOMES OF EDUCATION
STUDENT PARENT RELATIONSHIP Use PARENT STUDENT RELATIONSHIP
STUDENT PARTICIPATION
STUDENT PERSONNEL PROGRAMS (1967 1980) Use STUDENT PERSONNEL SERVICES
STUDENT PERSONNEL SERVICES
STUDENT PERSONNEL WORK (1967 1980) Use STUDENT PERSONNEL SERVICES
STUDENT PERSONNEL WORKERS
STUDENT PLACEMENT
STUDENT PROBLEMS
STUDENT PROJECTS
STUDENT PROMOTION
STUDENT PROTEST Use ACTIVISM
STUDENT PUBLICATIONS
TEACHER STUDENT RATIO
STUDENT REACTION
STUDENT RECORDS
STUDENT RECRUITMENT
STUDENT REHABILITATION (1966 1980) Use REHABILITATION
COLLEGE STUDENT RELATIONSHIP Use STUDENT COLLEGE RELATIONSHIP
PARENT STUDENT RELATIONSHIP
SCHOOL STUDENT RELATIONSHIP Use STUDENT SCHOOL RELATIONSHIP
TEACHER STUDENT RELATIONSHIP
STUDENT RESEARCH
STUDENT RESPONSES Use STUDENT REACTION
STUDENT RESPONSIBILITY
STUDENT RIGHTS
STUDENT ROLE
STUDENT SCHOOL RELATIONSHIP
STUDENT SCIENCE INTERESTS (1967 1980) Use SCIENCE INTERESTS
STUDENT SELECTION Use ADMISSION CRITERIA
STUDENT SEMINARS (1966 1980) Use SEMINARS
STUDENT SUBCULTURES
STUDENT TEACHER ATTITUDES
STUDENT TEACHER EVALUATION
STUDENT TEACHER INTERACTION Use TEACHER STUDENT RELATIONSHIP
STUDENT TEACHER RATIO (1966 1984) Use TEACHER STUDENT RATIO
STUDENT TEACHER RELATIONSHIP (1966 1984) Use TEACHER STUDENT RELATIONSHIP
STUDENT TEACHER SUPERVISORS
STUDENT TEACHERS
STUDENT TEACHING
OFF CAMPUS STUDENT TEACHING Use STUDENT TEACHING
STUDENT TESTING (1966 1980) Use EDUCATIONAL TESTING
STUDENT TRANSFERS Use TRANSFER STUDENTS
STUDENT TRANSPORTATION
STUDENT TRAVEL Use TRAVEL
STUDENT UNIONS
STUDENT VIOLENCE Use VIOLENCE
STUDENT VOLUNTEERS
STUDENT WELFARE
STUDENT WRITING MODELS
STUDENTS
ABLE STUDENTS (1966 1978) Use ACADEMICALLY GIFTED
ABSENCE (STUDENTS) Use ATTENDANCE
ADULT STUDENTS
ADVANCED STUDENTS
ATTRITION (STUDENTS) Use STUDENT ATTRITION
AVERAGE STUDENTS (1967 1980) Use STUDENTS
BILINGUAL STUDENTS
BLACK STUDENTS
CAUCASIAN STUDENTS (1967 1980) Use WHITE STUDENTS
CLASSES (GROUPS OF STUDENTS)
COLLEGE STUDENTS
COLLEGE BOUND STUDENTS
COLLEGE COSTS (INCURRED BY STUDENTS) Use STUDENT COSTS
COLLEGE TRANSFER STUDENTS
COMMUTING STUDENTS

CONTINUATION STUDENTS
COURSE SELECTION (STUDENTS)
DAY STUDENTS
DEANS OF STUDENTS
DENTAL STUDENTS
DESEGREGATION (DISABLED STUDENTS) Use MAINSTREAMING
EDUCATIONAL GOALS OF STUDENTS Use STUDENT EDUCATIONAL OBJECTIVES
EDUCATIONAL OBJECTIVES OF STUDENTS Use STUDENT EDUCATIONAL OBJECTIVES
ELEMENTARY SCHOOL STUDENTS
EMANCIPATED STUDENTS (1975 1980) Use SELF SUPPORTING STUDENTS
EVENING STUDENTS
EXCEPTIONAL STUDENTS (1966 1978) Use EXCEPTIONAL PERSONS
FOREIGN STUDENTS
NONRESIDENT STUDENTS (1967 1980) (FOREIGN) Use FOREIGN STUDENTS
FRESHMEN (1967 1980) (FIRST YEAR COLLEGE STUDENTS) Use COLLEGE FRESHMEN
FULL TIME STUDENTS
GIFTED STUDENTS Use ACADEMICALLY GIFTED
GRADUATE STUDENTS
GRADUATE MEDICAL STUDENTS
HANDICAPPED STUDENTS (1967 1980)
HIGH RISK STUDENTS
HIGH SCHOOL STUDENTS
RESIDENT STUDENTS (1967 1980) (IN DISTRICT) Use RESIDENCE REQUIREMENTS
IN STATE STUDENTS
RESIDENT STUDENTS (1967 1980) (IN STATE) Use IN STATE STUDENTS
INTEGRATION (DISABLED STUDENTS) Use MAINSTREAMING
INTERNATIONAL STUDENTS Use FOREIGN STUDENTS
JUNIOR COLLEGE STUDENTS (1969 1980) Use TWO YEAR COLLEGE STUDENTS
JUNIOR HIGH SCHOOL STUDENTS
LAW STUDENTS
LOW ABILITY STUDENTS (1967 1980)
LOWER CLASS STUDENTS
MAJORS (STUDENTS)
MALADJUSTED STUDENTS Use STUDENT ADJUSTMENT
MARRIED STUDENTS
MEDICAL STUDENTS
MIDDLE CLASS STUDENTS
MIDDLE CLASS COLLEGE STUDENTS (1966 1980) Use COLLEGE STUDENTS and MIDDLE CLASS STUDENTS
NEGRO STUDENTS (1966 1977) Use BLACK STUDENTS
NONCOLLEGE BOUND STUDENTS
NONCOLLEGE PREPARATORY STUDENTS (1967 1980) Use NONCOLLEGE BOUND STUDENTS
NONTRADITIONAL STUDENTS
ON CAMPUS STUDENTS
NONRESIDENT STUDENTS (1967 1980) (OUT OF DISTRICT) Use RESIDENCE REQUIREMENTS
OUT OF STATE STUDENTS
NONRESIDENT STUDENTS (1967 1980) (OUT OF STATE) Use OUT OF STATE STUDENTS
PART TIME STUDENTS
PREGNANT STUDENTS
PREMEDICAL STUDENTS
REENTRY STUDENTS
RESEARCH PAPERS (STUDENTS)
RETENTION (OF STUDENTS) Use SCHOOL HOLDING POWER
SECONDARY SCHOOL STUDENTS
SELF SUPPORTING STUDENTS
INDEPENDENT STUDENTS (SELF SUPPORTING) Use SELF SUPPORTING STUDENTS
SENIOR HIGH SCHOOL STUDENTS Use HIGH SCHOOL STUDENTS
SINGLE STUDENTS
STEP IN STEP OUT STUDENTS Use STOPOUTS
SUPERIOR STUDENTS (1966 1978) Use ACADEMICALLY GIFTED
TALENTED STUDENTS (1966 1980) Use TALENT
TERMINAL STUDENTS
TRANSFER STUDENTS
TWO YEAR COLLEGE STUDENTS
UNDERGRADUATE STUDENTS
UNIVERSITY STUDENTS Use COLLEGE STUDENTS
UNMARRIED STUDENTS Use SINGLE STUDENTS
WHITE STUDENTS
AFRICAN AMERICAN STUDIES (1969 1977) Use BLACK STUDIES
AMERICAN STUDIES
AMERICAN INDIAN STUDIES
AREA STUDIES
ASIAN STUDIES
ATTRITION (RESEARCH STUDIES)
BIRD STUDIES Use ORNITHOLOGY
BLACK STUDIES
CASE STUDIES
CORRELATION STUDIES Use CORRELATION
CROSS CULTURAL STUDIES
CROSS SECTIONAL STUDIES
UNIFIED STUDIES CURRICULUM
DIALECT STUDIES
CASE STUDIES (EDUCATION) (1966 1980) Use CASE STUDIES
ETHNIC STUDIES
ETHNIC GROUP STUDIES Use ETHNIC STUDIES
FACILITY CASE STUDIES
FEASIBILITY STUDIES
FIELD STUDIES
FISH STUDIES Use ICHTHYOLOGY
FOLLOWUP STUDIES
FUTURE STUDIES Use FUTURES (OF SOCIETY)
INSECT STUDIES Use ENTOMOLOGY
INTEGRATION STUDIES
INTERNATIONAL STUDIES
LOCATIONAL SKILLS (SOCIAL STUDIES)
LONGITUDINAL STUDIES
MIDDLE EASTERN STUDIES
MORTALITY (RESEARCH STUDIES) Use ATTRITION (RESEARCH STUDIES)
NEGRO STUDIES Use BLACK STUDIES
PERSONALITY STUDIES
DEVELOPMENTAL STUDIES PROGRAMS
UNIFIED STUDIES PROGRAMS (1966 1980) Use UNIFIED STUDIES CURRICULUM

PSYCHOLOGICAL STUDIES
RESEARCH STUDIES Use RESEARCH REPORTS
RETENTION STUDIES (1966 1980) Use RETENTION (PSYCHOLOGY)
SCHEMATIC STUDIES
SHIFT STUDIES
SIMULATED STUDIES Use SIMULATION
SOCIAL STUDIES
SOCIOLOGICAL STUDIES Use SOCIAL SCIENCE RESEARCH and SOCIOLOGY
STATISTICAL STUDIES
SOCIAL STUDIES UNITS (1966 1980) Use SOCIAL STUDIES and UNITS OF STUDY
URBAN STUDIES
USE STUDIES
USER STUDIES Use USE STUDIES
WOMENS STUDIES
STUDIO FLOOR PLANS (1966 1980)
TELEVISION STUDIOS
STUDY
STUDY ABROAD
STUDY CARRELS Use CARRELS
STUDY CENTERS
CURRICULUM STUDY CENTERS
SCHOOL STUDY CENTERS (1966 1980) Use STUDY CENTERS
CINEMA STUDY Use FILM STUDY
COMMUNITY STUDY
COMPARATIVE STUDY Use COMPARATIVE ANALYSIS
CORRESPONDENCE STUDY
STUDY FACILITIES
FILM STUDY
GRADUATE STUDY
PARENT STUDY GROUPS Use PARENT CONFERENCES
STUDY GUIDES
STUDY HABITS
STUDY HALLS Use STUDY CENTERS
HIGHER EDUCATION AS A FIELD OF STUDY Use POSTSECONDARY EDUCATION AS A FIELD OF STUDY
HOME STUDY
STUDY HOURS Use STUDY
INDEPENDENT STUDY
INDIVIDUAL STUDY (1966 1980) Use INDEPENDENT STUDY
INSTITUTIONAL SELF STUDY Use SELF EVALUATION (GROUPS)
ORGANIZATIONAL SELF STUDY Use SELF EVALUATION (GROUPS)
POSTSECONDARY EDUCATION AS A FIELD OF STUDY
COLLEGE WORK STUDY PROGRAMS Use WORK STUDY PROGRAMS
WORK STUDY PROGRAMS
STUDY RELEASE PROGRAMS Use RELEASED TIME
STUDY SKILLS
WORD STUDY SKILLS
UNITS OF STUDY (SUBJECT FIELDS) (1966 1977) Use UNITS OF STUDY
STUDY TRIPS Use FIELD TRIPS
UNDERGRADUATE STUDY
UNITS OF STUDY
WORK STUDY Use WORK STUDY PROGRAMS
STUNTS AND TUMBLING Use TUMBLING
STUTTERING
ARCHITECTURAL STYLE Use ARCHITECTURAL CHARACTER
COGNITIVE STYLE
LEARNING STYLE Use COGNITIVE STYLE
LIFE STYLE
PERCEPTUAL STYLE Use COGNITIVE STYLE
RESPONSE STYLE (TESTS)
ALTERNATIVE LIFE STYLES Use LIFE STYLE
LANGUAGE STYLES
LEADERSHIP STYLES
LINGUISTIC STYLES Use LANGUAGE STYLES
LITERARY STYLES
TEACHING STYLES
SUBCULTURE (1967 1980) Use SUBCULTURES
BLACK SUBCULTURE Use BLACK CULTURE
SUBCULTURES
STUDENT SUBCULTURES
SUBEMPLOYMENT (1968 1980) Use UNDEREMPLOYMENT
SUBJECT ACCESS Use INDEXING
AGRICULTURAL MECHANICS (SUBJECT) Use AGRICULTURAL ENGINEERING
SUBJECT DISCIPLINES Use INTELLECTUAL DISCIPLINES
FARM MECHANICS (SUBJECT) Use AGRICULTURAL ENGINEERING
UNITS OF STUDY (SUBJECT FIELDS) (1966 1977) Use UNITS OF STUDY
SUBJECT HEADINGS Use SUBJECT INDEX TERMS
SUBJECT INDEX TERMS
ACADEMIC SUBJECTS Use ACADEMIC EDUCATION
BUSINESS SUBJECTS (1967 1980) Use BUSINESS EDUCATION
ELECTIVE SUBJECTS (1966 1977) Use ELECTIVE COURSES
SUBJUNCTIVE MOOD Use VERBS
SUBPROFESSIONALS (1967 1977) Use PARAPROFESSIONAL PERSONNEL
SUBSIDIES Use GRANTS
TOXIC SUBSTANCES Use POISONS
SUBSTITUTE TEACHERS
SUBSTITUTION DRILLS
SUBTRACTION
SUBURBAN ENVIRONMENT
SUBURBAN HOUSING
URBAN TO SUBURBAN MIGRATION
SUBURBAN PROBLEMS
SUBURBAN SCHOOLS
SUBURBAN YOUTH
SUBURBS
INNER SPEECH (SUBVOCAL)
SUCCESS
ACADEMIC SUCCESS Use ACADEMIC ACHIEVEMENT
SUCCESS AVOIDANCE Use FEAR OF SUCCESS
SUCCESS FACTORS (1968 1980) Use SUCCESS
FEAR OF SUCCESS
OCCUPATIONAL SUCCESSION Use OCCUPATIONAL MOBILITY

SUFFIXES
SUGGESTOPEDIA
SUICIDE
SUMMATIVE EVALUATION
SUMMER INSTITUTES (1967 1980) Use INSTITUTES (TRAINING PROGRAMS) and SUMMER PROGRAMS
SUMMER PROGRAMS
SUMMER SCHOOLS
SUMMER SCIENCE PROGRAMS
SUMMER SESSION Use SUMMER SCHOOLS
SUMMER WORKSHOPS (1966 1980) Use SUMMER PROGRAMS and WORKSHOPS
SUPERCONDUCTORS
SUPERINTENDENT ROLE (1966 1980) Use SUPERINTENDENTS
ASSISTANT SUPERINTENDENT ROLE (1966 1980)
SUPERINTENDENTS
ASSISTANT SUPERINTENDENTS Use SUPERINTENDENTS
SCHOOL SUPERINTENDENTS (1966 1980) Use SUPERINTENDENTS
SUPERIOR STUDENTS (1966 1978) Use ACADEMICALLY GIFTED
SUPERMARKETS Use FOOD STORES
SUPERVISED FARM PRACTICE
SUPERVISED OCCUPATIONAL EXPERIENCE (AGRICULTURE) Use SUPERVISED FARM PRACTICE
SUPERVISING TEACHERS Use COOPERATING TEACHERS
SUPERVISION
PRACTICUM SUPERVISION
SCHOOL SUPERVISION
SCIENCE SUPERVISION
TEACHER SUPERVISION
SUPERVISOR QUALIFICATIONS
SUPERVISOR TRAINING Use SUPERVISORY TRAINING
SUPERVISORS
COLLEGE SUPERVISORS (1967 1980) Use STUDENT TEACHER SUPERVISORS
ELEMENTARY SCHOOL SUPERVISORS (1966 1980) Use SCHOOL SUPERVISION
HIGH SCHOOL SUPERVISORS (1966 1980) Use SCHOOL SUPERVISION
RESIDENT SUPERVISORS Use RESIDENT ADVISERS
STATE SUPERVISORS
STATE FOREIGN LANGUAGE SUPERVISORS (1967 1980) Use SECOND LANGUAGE INSTRUCTION and STATE SUPERVISORS
STUDENT TEACHER SUPERVISORS
SUPERVISORY ACTIVITIES (1968 1980) Use SUPERVISION
SUPERVISORY METHODS
SUPERVISORY TRAINING
SUPPLEMENTARY EDUCATION
SUPPLEMENTARY EDUCATIONAL CENTERS (1966 1980) Use EDUCATION SERVICE CENTERS and SUPPLEMENTARY EDUCATION
SUPPLEMENTARY READING MATERIALS
SUPPLEMENTARY TEXTBOOKS (1967 1980) Use SUPPLEMENTARY READING MATERIALS and TEXTBOOKS
SUPPLIES
AGRICULTURAL SUPPLIES
FARM SUPPLIES Use AGRICULTURAL SUPPLIES
OFFICE SUPPLIES Use SUPPLIES
SCHOOL SUPPLIES Use SUPPLIES
TEACHER SUPPLY AND DEMAND
EDUCATIONAL SUPPLY
FARM LABOR SUPPLY (1966 1980) Use FARM LABOR and LABOR SUPPLY
LABOR SUPPLY
AGRICULTURAL SUPPLY OCCUPATIONS
SUPPLY OF EDUCATION Use EDUCATIONAL SUPPLY
SUPPLY OF LABOR Use LABOR SUPPLY
WATER SUPPLY Use WATER RESOURCES
COMMUNITY SUPPORT
CORPORATE SUPPORT
ECONOMIC SUPPORT Use FINANCIAL SUPPORT
EDUCATIONAL SUPPORT Use EDUCATIONAL FINANCE
FINANCIAL SUPPORT
SUPPORT GROUPS (HUMAN SERVICES) Use SOCIAL SUPPORT GROUPS
SOCIAL SUPPORT GROUPS
SUPPORT NETWORKS (PERSONAL ASSISTANCE) Use SOCIAL SUPPORT GROUPS
PRIVATE FINANCIAL SUPPORT
PUBLIC SUPPORT
SCHOOL SUPPORT
STATE SUPPORT Use STATE AID
STATE FEDERAL SUPPORT (1966 1977) Use STATE FEDERAL AID
SUPPORT SYSTEMS (SERVICES) Use SERVICES
TAX SUPPORT (1966 1980) Use TAX ALLOCATION
EMPLOYER SUPPORTED DAY CARE
AIR SUPPORTED STRUCTURES (1972 1980) Use AIR STRUCTURES
INDEPENDENT STUDENTS (SELF SUPPORTING) Use SELF SUPPORTING STUDENTS
SELF SUPPORTING STUDENTS
SUPPRESSOR VARIABLES
SUPRASEGMENTAL MORPHEMES Use INTONATION
SUPRASEGMENTAL PHONEMES Use SUPRASEGMENTALS
SUPRASEGMENTALS
SUPREME COURT LITIGATION (1966 1980)
SUPREME COURTS (1966 1980)
STATE SUPREME COURTS Use STATE COURTS
SURFACE AREA Use AREA
SURFACE FINISHING Use FINISHING
SURFACE STRUCTURE
SURFING
DENTAL SURGEONS Use DENTISTS
SURGERY
OPERATIONS (SURGERY) Use SURGERY
SURGICAL TECHNICIANS
SURREALISM
SURVEY COURSES Use INTRODUCTORY COURSES
SURVEYS
COMMUNITY SURVEYS
EDUCATIONAL SURVEYS Use SCHOOL SURVEYS
EMPLOYMENT SURVEYS Use OCCUPATIONAL SURVEYS
GRADUATE SURVEYS
JOB VACANCY SURVEYS Use OCCUPATIONAL SURVEYS
LABOR FORCE SURVEYS Use OCCUPATIONAL SURVEYS
LIBRARY SURVEYS

LITERATURE SURVEYS Use LITERATURE REVIEWS
NATIONAL SURVEYS
OCCUPATIONAL SURVEYS
PROVINCIAL SURVEYS Use STATE SURVEYS
SCHOOL SURVEYS
STATE SURVEYS
STATISTICAL SURVEYS
TELEVISION SURVEYS
INSTITUTIONAL SURVIVAL
SURVIVAL LITERACY Use FUNCTIONAL LITERACY
SURVIVAL READING SKILLS Use FUNCTIONAL READING
SURVIVAL SKILLS (DAILY LIVING) Use DAILY LIVING SKILLS
SUSPENSION
IN SCHOOL SUSPENSION
SUSTAINED SILENT READING
SUSU
SWAHILI
SWAZI Use SISWATI
SWEDISH
SWIMMING
SWIMMING POOLS
SWING MUSIC Use JAZZ
SWITCHING (LANGUAGE) Use CODE SWITCHING (LANGUAGE)
CODE SWITCHING (LANGUAGE)
SYLLABI Use COURSE DESCRIPTIONS
FUNCTIONAL NOTIONAL SYLLABI Use NOTIONAL FUNCTIONAL SYLLABI
NOTIONAL FUNCTIONAL SYLLABI
STATE SYLLABI Use STATE CURRICULUM GUIDES
SYLLABLES
SYMBOLIC LANGUAGE
SYMBOLIC LEARNING
SYMBOLIC LOGIC Use MATHEMATICAL LOGIC
SYMBOLISM
SYMBOLS (LITERARY)
SYMBOLS (MATHEMATICS)
ORTHOGRAPHIC SYMBOLS
SYMMETRY
SYMPHONY ORCHESTRAS Use ORCHESTRAS
SYMPOSIA (1967 1980) Use CONFERENCES
SYNCHRONIC LINGUISTICS (1967 1980) Use DESCRIPTIVE LINGUISTICS
DOWNS SYNDROME
SYNTACTIC BORROWING Use LINGUISTIC BORROWING
SYNTAX
SYNTHESIS
CHEMICAL SYNTHESIS Use CHEMICAL REACTIONS
STIMULUS SYNTHESIS Use PATTERNED RESPONSES
SYNTHETIC SPEECH Use ARTIFICIAL SPEECH
SYPHILIS Use VENEREAL DISEASES
CARDIOVASCULAR SYSTEM
CIRCULATORY SYSTEM Use CARDIOVASCULAR SYSTEM
TRACK SYSTEM (EDUCATION)
INFANT SCHOOLS (BRITISH PRIMARY SYSTEM) Use BRITISH INFANT SCHOOLS
METRIC SYSTEM
NONGRADED SYSTEM (1966 1980) Use NONGRADED INSTRUCTIONAL GROUPING
NONGRADED PRIMARY SYSTEM (1966 1980) Use NONGRADED INSTRUCTIONAL GROUPING
QUARTER SYSTEM
SEMESTER SYSTEM
TRIMESTER SYSTEM
VASCULAR SYSTEM Use CARDIOVASCULAR SYSTEM
SYSTEMATIC DESENSITIZATION Use DESENSITIZATION
ALARM SYSTEMS
SECURITY SYSTEMS (ALARMS) Use ALARM SYSTEMS
SYSTEMS ANALYSIS
SYSTEMS ANALYSTS
SYSTEMS APPROACH
ARITHMETIC SYSTEMS Use NUMBER SYSTEMS
AUTHORING SYSTEMS Use AUTHORING AIDS (PROGRAMING)
SYSTEMS BUILDING
BUILDING SYSTEMS
CENTRAL SOUND SYSTEMS (1966 1980) Use AUDIO EQUIPMENT
COMMUNICATIONS SYSTEMS Use COMMUNICATIONS
COMPONENT SYSTEMS Use BUILDING SYSTEMS
COMPONENT BUILDING SYSTEMS (1968 1976) Use BUILDING SYSTEMS
COMPUTER BASED MESSAGE SYSTEMS Use ELECTRONIC MAIL
SYSTEMS CONCEPTS (1966 1980)
COUNTY SCHOOL SYSTEMS (1967 1980) Use COUNTY SCHOOL DISTRICTS
DATABASE MANAGEMENT SYSTEMS
DECENTRALIZED LIBRARY SYSTEMS (1968 1980) Use DECENTRALIZATION and LIBRARY NETWORKS
DELIVERY SYSTEMS
SYSTEMS DEVELOPMENT
DIAL ACCESS INFORMATION SYSTEMS
DISPLAY SYSTEMS
ELECTRIC SYSTEMS Use ELECTRICAL SYSTEMS
ELECTRICAL SYSTEMS
ELECTRONIC COMMUNICATIONS SYSTEMS Use TELECOMMUNICATIONS
EXPERT SYSTEMS
FACSIMILE COMMUNICATION SYSTEMS (1968 1980) Use FACSIMILE TRANSMISSION
FILE MANAGEMENT SYSTEMS Use DATABASE MANAGEMENT SYSTEMS
FILING SYSTEMS Use INFORMATION STORAGE
INCENTIVE SYSTEMS (1967 1980) Use INCENTIVES
INFORMATION SYSTEMS
INSTRUCTIONAL SYSTEMS
KNOWLEDGE BASED SYSTEMS Use EXPERT SYSTEMS
APPROXIMATIVE SYSTEMS (LANGUAGE LEARNING) Use INTERLANGUAGE
LIBRARY SYSTEMS Use LIBRARY NETWORKS
LOOP INDUCTION SYSTEMS
MAN MACHINE SYSTEMS
MANAGEMENT SYSTEMS
MANAGEMENT INFORMATION SYSTEMS
MICROWAVE RELAY SYSTEMS (1971 1980) Use TELECOMMUNICATIONS
MONETARY SYSTEMS

MONEY	SYSTEMS (1966 1980) Use MONETARY SYSTEMS
N C	SYSTEMS Use NUMERICAL CONTROL
NUMBER	SYSTEMS
ON LINE	SYSTEMS (1971 1980) Use ONLINE SYSTEMS
ONLINE	SYSTEMS
INTERACTIVE	SYSTEMS (ONLINE) Use ONLINE SYSTEMS
POWER TRANSFER	SYSTEMS Use KINETICS
PROPERTY CONTROL	SYSTEMS Use PROPERTY ACCOUNTING
PUBLIC SCHOOL	SYSTEMS (1966 1980) Use PUBLIC SCHOOLS and SCHOOL DISTRICTS
RURAL SCHOOL	SYSTEMS (1966 1980) Use RURAL SCHOOLS and SCHOOL DISTRICTS
SCHOOL	SYSTEMS (1966 1980) Use SCHOOL DISTRICTS
SUPPORT	SYSTEMS (SERVICES) Use SERVICES
SOCIAL	SYSTEMS
SOUND	SYSTEMS Use AUDIO EQUIPMENT
STRUCTURAL BUILDING	SYSTEMS
TEACHING	SYSTEMS Use TEACHING METHODS
TELEPHONE COMMUNICATION	SYSTEMS (1967 1980) Use TELEPHONE COMMUNICATIONS SYSTEMS
TELEPHONE COMMUNICATIONS	SYSTEMS
	SYSTEMS THEORY Use SYSTEMS APPROACH
FUNCTIONAL	SYSTEMS THEORY Use SYSTEMS ANALYSIS
VIDEO	SYSTEMS Use VIDEO EQUIPMENT
VIDEO CASSETTE	SYSTEMS (1971 1980) Use VIDEO EQUIPMENT and VIDEOTAPE CASSETTES
WRITING	SYSTEMS Use WRITTEN LANGUAGE
	T GROUPS (1967 1980) Use SENSITIVITY TRAINING
	TABLE TENNIS
	TABLES (DATA)
EXPECTANCY	TABLES
INCEST	TABOO Use INCEST
DATA	TABULATION Use DATA PROCESSING
	TACHISTOSCOPES
	TACKBOARDS Use BULLETIN BOARDS
	TACTILE ADAPTATION
	TACTILE MATERIALS Use MANIPULATIVE MATERIALS
	TACTUAL PERCEPTION
	TACTUAL VISUAL TESTS
	TADJIK PERSIAN Use TAJIK
	TAGALOG
	TAGMEMIC ANALYSIS
	TAILORED TESTING Use ADAPTIVE TESTING
COMPUTERIZED	TAILORED TESTING Use ADAPTIVE TESTING and COMPUTER ASSISTED TESTING
	TAILORS Use NEEDLE TRADES
	TAJIK
PERSPECTIVE	TAKING
ROLE	TAKING Use PERSPECTIVE TAKING
TEST	TAKING SKILLS Use TEST WISENESS
TEST	TAKING STRATEGIES Use TEST WISENESS
	TALENT
ARTISTIC	TALENT Use TALENT
	TALENT DEVELOPMENT
	TALENT IDENTIFICATION
	TALENT PRESERVATION Use TALENT DEVELOPMENT
	TALENT TESTS Use APTITUDE TESTS
	TALENT UTILIZATION (1966 1980)
	TALENTED STUDENTS (1966 1980) Use TALENT
VOCATIONAL	TALENTS Use VOCATIONAL APTITUDE
	TALES
	TALKING BOOKS
	TALKS Use SPEECHES
	TAMIL
	TAOISM
MAGNETIC	TAPE CARTRIDGES Use MAGNETIC TAPE CASSETTES
MAGNETIC	TAPE CASSETTE RECORDERS (1970 1980) Use MAGNETIC TAPE CASSETTES and TAPE RECORDERS
CASSETTES	(TAPE) Use MAGNETIC TAPE CASSETTES
MAGNETIC	TAPE CASSETTES
	TAPE RECORDERS
	TAPE RECORDINGS
SOUND	TAPE RECORDINGS Use AUDIOTAPE RECORDINGS
VIDEO	TAPE RECORDINGS (1966 1978) Use VIDEOTAPE RECORDINGS
MASTER	TAPES (AUDIO) (1968 1980) Use AUDIOTAPE RECORDINGS
COMPUTER	TAPES Use COMPUTER STORAGE DEVICES and MAGNETIC TAPES
LANGUAGE	TAPES Use AUDIOTAPE RECORDINGS
MAGNETIC	TAPES
	TASK ANALYSIS
	TASK DIFFICULTY Use DIFFICULTY LEVEL
	TASK PERFORMANCE (1966 1980)
TIME ON	TASK
DEVELOPMENTAL	TASKS
	TATAR
LESS COMMONLY	TAUGHT LANGUAGES Use UNCOMMONLY TAUGHT LANGUAGES
UNCOMMONLY	TAUGHT LANGUAGES
AD VALOREM	TAX Use PROPERTY TAXES
	TAX ALLOCATION
	TAX CREDITS
TUITION	TAX CREDITS Use TAX CREDITS and TUITION
	TAX DEDUCTIONS
	TAX EFFORT
	TAX EQUITY (EDUCATION) Use EDUCATIONAL EQUITY (FINANCE)
NEGATIVE INCOME	TAX Use GUARANTEED INCOME
	TAX RATES
	TAX REFORM Use FINANCE REFORM
	TAX SUPPORT (1966 1980) Use TAX ALLOCATION
	TAXES
PROPERTY	TAXES
SCHOOL	TAXES
	TAXONOMY (1967 1980) Use CLASSIFICATION
MISCUE	TAXONOMY Use MISCUE ANALYSIS
	TEACHER ADMINISTRATOR RELATIONSHIP
	TEACHER ADVANCEMENT Use TEACHER PROMOTION
	TEACHER AIDES
BILINGUAL	TEACHER AIDES
	TEACHER ALIENATION

TEACHER ASSOCIATIONS
TEACHER ATTENDANCE
TEACHER ATTITUDES
STUDENT TEACHER ATTITUDES
TEACHER ATTRITION Use FACULTY MOBILITY
TEACHER AUTONOMY Use PROFESSIONAL AUTONOMY
TEACHER BACKGROUND
TEACHER BEHAVIOR
TEACHER BURNOUT
TEACHER CENTERS
TEACHER CERTIFICATES (1967 1980) Use TEACHER CERTIFICATION
TEACHER CERTIFICATION
TEACHER CHARACTERISTICS
TEACHER COLLEGE RELATIONSHIP Use FACULTY COLLEGE RELATIONSHIP
PARENT TEACHER CONFERENCES
COUNSELOR TEACHER COOPERATION
PARENT TEACHER COOPERATION
TEACHER COORDINATORS Use INSTRUCTOR COORDINATORS
TEACHER COUNSELOR COOPERATION Use COUNSELOR TEACHER COOPERATION
TEACHER DESEGREGATION Use TEACHER INTEGRATION
TEACHER DEVELOPED MATERIALS
TEACHER DIRECTED PRACTICE Use TEACHER GUIDANCE
TEACHER DISCIPLINE
TEACHER DISMISSAL
TEACHER DISTRIBUTION
TEACHER EDUCATION
TEACHER EDUCATION CENTERS Use TEACHER CENTERS
COMPETENCY BASED TEACHER EDUCATION
CONSEQUENCE BASED TEACHER EDUCATION Use COMPETENCY BASED TEACHER EDUCATION
CRITERION REFERENCED TEACHER EDUCATION Use COMPETENCY BASED TEACHER EDUCATION
TEACHER EDUCATION CURRICULUM
ENGLISH TEACHER EDUCATION
INSERVICE TEACHER EDUCATION
OUTPUT ORIENTED TEACHER EDUCATION Use COMPETENCY BASED TEACHER EDUCATION
PERFORMANCE BASED TEACHER EDUCATION (1972 1980) Use COMPETENCY BASED TEACHER EDUCATION
PRESERVICE TEACHER EDUCATION
PROFICIENCY BASED TEACHER EDUCATION Use COMPETENCY BASED TEACHER EDUCATION
TEACHER EDUCATION PROGRAMS
TEACHER EDUCATOR EDUCATION
TEACHER EDUCATORS
TEACHER EFFECTIVENESS
TEACHER EMPLOYMENT
TEACHER EMPLOYMENT BENEFITS
TEACHER EVALUATION
STUDENT TEACHER EVALUATION
TEACHER EXCHANGE PROGRAMS
TEACHER EXPERIENCE (1966 1974) Use TEACHING EXPERIENCE
TEACHER GUIDANCE
TEACHER GUIDES Use TEACHING GUIDES
TEACHER HOUSING
TEACHER IMPROVEMENT
TEACHER INDUCTION Use TEACHER ORIENTATION
TEACHER INFLUENCE
TEACHER INTEGRATION
STUDENT TEACHER INTERACTION Use TEACHER STUDENT RELATIONSHIP
TEACHER INTERNS
TEACHER LOAD Use TEACHING LOAD
TEACHER MADE TESTS
TEACHER MILITANCY
TEACHER MOBILITY Use FACULTY MOBILITY
TEACHER MORALE
TEACHER MOTIVATION
TEACHER NURSES (1966 1980) Use NURSES
TEACHER OPINIONS Use TEACHER ATTITUDES
TEACHER ORGANIZATIONS Use TEACHER ASSOCIATIONS
TEACHER ORIENTATION
TEACHER PARENT CONFERENCES Use PARENT TEACHER CONFERENCES
TEACHER PARENT COOPERATION Use PARENT TEACHER COOPERATION
TEACHER PARTICIPATION
STUDENT EVALUATION OF TEACHER PERFORMANCE
TEACHER PERSISTENCE
TEACHER PLACEMENT
TEACHER PREPARATION Use TEACHER EDUCATION
TEACHER PROGRAMS (1966 1980) Use TEACHER EDUCATION PROGRAMS
TEACHER PROMOTION
TEACHER QUALIFICATIONS
TEACHER QUALITY Use TEACHER EFFECTIVENESS
TEACHER RATING (1966 1977) Use TEACHER EVALUATION
STUDENT TEACHER RATIO (1966 1984) Use TEACHER STUDENT RATIO
TEACHER REACTION Use TEACHER RESPONSE
TEACHER RECRUITMENT
ADMINISTRATOR TEACHER RELATIONSHIP Use TEACHER ADMINISTRATOR RELATIONSHIP
STUDENT TEACHER RELATIONSHIP (1966 1984) Use TEACHER STUDENT RELATIONSHIP
TEACHER RESPONSE
TEACHER RESPONSIBILITY
TEACHER RETIREMENT
TEACHER RIGHTS
TEACHER ROLE
SENIOR TEACHER ROLE (1966 1980) Use MASTER TEACHERS and TEACHER ROLE
TEACHER SALARIES
ONE TEACHER SCHOOLS
TEACHER SELECTION
TEACHER SEMINARS (1966 1980) Use TEACHER WORKSHOPS
TEACHER SHORTAGE
TEACHER SKILLS Use TEACHING SKILLS
TEACHER STEREOTYPES
TEACHER STRIKES
TEACHER STUDENT INTERACTION Use TEACHER STUDENT RELATIONSHIP
TEACHER STUDENT RATIO
TEACHER STUDENT RELATIONSHIP
TEACHER SUPERVISION

STUDENT TEACHER SUPERVISORS
TEACHER SUPPLY AND DEMAND
TEACHER TRAINERS Use TEACHER EDUCATORS
TEACHER TRAINING Use TEACHER EDUCATION
TEACHER TRAINING FILMS Use PROTOCOL MATERIALS
INSERVICE TEACHER TRAINING Use INSERVICE TEACHER EDUCATION
TEACHER TRANSFER
TEACHER TRAVEL Use TRAVEL
TEACHER TURNOVER Use FACULTY MOBILITY
TEACHER UNIONS Use UNIONS
TEACHER WELFARE
TEACHER WORKSHOPS
TEACHERS
ABSENCE (TEACHERS) Use TEACHER ATTENDANCE
ART TEACHERS
BEGINNING TEACHERS
BILINGUAL TEACHERS
BLACK TEACHERS
BUSINESS TEACHERS Use BUSINESS EDUCATION TEACHERS
BUSINESS EDUCATION TEACHERS
CHEMISTRY TEACHERS (1967 1980) Use CHEMISTRY and SCIENCE TEACHERS
CIRCUIT TEACHERS Use ITINERANT TEACHERS
COACHING TEACHERS (1966 1974) Use TUTORS
COLLEGE TEACHERS (1967 1980) Use COLLEGE FACULTY
TEACHERS COLLEGES (1966 1980) Use SCHOOLS OF EDUCATION
COOPERATING TEACHERS
DISTRIBUTIVE EDUCATION TEACHERS
ELEMENTARY SCHOOL TEACHERS
FIRST YEAR TEACHERS Use BEGINNING TEACHERS
FLES TEACHERS (1967 1980) Use FLES and LANGUAGE TEACHERS
FOREIGN LANGUAGE TEACHERS Use LANGUAGE TEACHERS
FORMER TEACHERS (1967 1980)
FULL TIME TEACHERS Use FULL TIME FACULTY
GIFTED TEACHERS Use GIFTED
HIGH SCHOOL TEACHERS Use SECONDARY SCHOOL TEACHERS
HOME ECONOMICS TEACHERS
HOMEBOUND TEACHERS (1966 1980) Use ITINERANT TEACHERS
INDUSTRIAL ARTS TEACHERS
INTERN TEACHERS Use TEACHER INTERNS
ITINERANT TEACHERS
JUNIOR HIGH SCHOOL TEACHERS Use SECONDARY SCHOOL TEACHERS
KINDERGARTEN TEACHERS Use PRESCHOOL TEACHERS
LANGUAGE TEACHERS
LAY TEACHERS
MASTER TEACHERS
MATHEMATICS TEACHERS
METHODS TEACHERS
MINORITY GROUP TEACHERS
MUSIC TEACHERS
NEGRO TEACHERS (1966 1977) Use BLACK TEACHERS
NONTENURED TEACHERS Use NONTENURED FACULTY
NUN TEACHERS (1966 1980) Use NUNS
PART TIME TEACHERS (1967 1980) Use PART TIME FACULTY
PARTNERSHIP TEACHERS
PHYSICAL EDUCATION TEACHERS
PHYSICS TEACHERS (1967 1980) Use PHYSICS and SCIENCE TEACHERS
PREKINDERGARTEN TEACHERS Use PRESCHOOL TEACHERS
PRESCHOOL TEACHERS
PROBATIONARY TEACHERS Use PROBATIONARY PERIOD
PUBLIC SCHOOL TEACHERS
READING TEACHERS
RELIEF TEACHERS Use SUBSTITUTE TEACHERS
REMEDIAL TEACHERS
RESOURCE TEACHERS
RETIRED TEACHERS Use TEACHER RETIREMENT
SCIENCE TEACHERS
SECOND LANGUAGE TEACHERS Use LANGUAGE TEACHERS
SECONDARY SCHOOL TEACHERS
SPECIAL TEACHERS Use SPECIALISTS
SPECIAL EDUCATION TEACHERS
STUDENT TEACHERS
SUBSTITUTE TEACHERS
SUPERVISING TEACHERS Use COOPERATING TEACHERS
TELEVISION TEACHERS
TENURED TEACHERS Use TENURED FACULTY
TRADE AND INDUSTRIAL TEACHERS
TRAVELING TEACHERS Use ITINERANT TEACHERS
VISITING TEACHERS Use ITINERANT TEACHERS
VOCATIONAL AGRICULTURE TEACHERS (1967 1980) Use AGRICULTURAL EDUCATION and VOCATIONAL EDUCATION TEACHERS
VOCATIONAL EDUCATION TEACHERS
WOMEN TEACHERS (1967 1980) Use WOMEN FACULTY
TEACHING (1966 1980)
MECHANICAL TEACHING AIDS (1966 1980) Use EDUCATIONAL MEDIA
INITIAL TEACHING ALPHABET
TEACHING ALTERNATIVES Use NONTRADITIONAL EDUCATION
TEACHING AREAS Use CURRICULUM
TEACHING ASSIGNMENT (1966 1980)
TEACHING ASSISTANTS
TEACHING BENEFITS (1966 1980) Use TEACHER EMPLOYMENT BENEFITS
BLOCK TIME TEACHING Use TIME BLOCKS
SCIENCE TEACHING CENTERS
TEACHING CERTIFICATES Use TEACHER CERTIFICATION
COLLEGE TEACHING Use COLLEGE INSTRUCTION
CONCEPT TEACHING
TEACHING CONDITIONS
COOPERATIVE TEACHING (1966 1980) Use TEAM TEACHING
TEACHING CORE Use CORE CURRICULUM
CREATIVE TEACHING
CROSS AGE TEACHING
DIAGNOSTIC TEACHING
DROPOUT TEACHING (1966 1980) Use DROPOUT PROGRAMS

EFFECTIVE	TEACHING (1966 1980) Use TEACHER EFFECTIVENESS
EPISODE	TEACHING (1967 1980)
	TEACHING EXPERIENCE
INSERVICE	TEACHING EXPERIENCE Use TEACHING EXPERIENCE
PRESERVICE	TEACHING EXPERIENCE Use TEACHING EXPERIENCE
EXPERIMENTAL	TEACHING
	TEACHING FACILITIES Use EDUCATIONAL FACILITIES
FIELD	TEACHING Use FIELD INSTRUCTION
	TEACHING FREEDOM Use ACADEMIC FREEDOM
	TEACHING GUIDES
CLINICAL	TEACHING (HEALTH PROFESSIONS)
	TEACHING HOSPITALS
UNIVERSITY	TEACHING HOSPITALS Use TEACHING HOSPITALS
CLINICAL	TEACHING (INDIVIDUALIZED INSTRUCTION) Use INDIVIDUALIZED INSTRUCTION
	TEACHING INNOVATIONS Use INSTRUCTIONAL INNOVATION
INSERVICE	TEACHING (1966 1980) Use INSERVICE EDUCATION and TEACHING (OCCUPATION)
URBAN	TEACHING INTERNS Use TEACHER INTERNS and URBAN TEACHING
	TEACHING LANGUAGE Use LANGUAGE OF INSTRUCTION
	TEACHING LOAD
	TEACHING MACHINES
MASTER OF ARTS IN	TEACHING Use MASTERS DEGREES
MASTER OF ARTS IN COLLEGE	TEACHING Use MASTERS DEGREES
MASTER OF SCIENCE IN	TEACHING Use MASTERS DEGREES
	TEACHING MATERIALS Use INSTRUCTIONAL MATERIALS
INTEGRATED	TEACHING METHOD Use INTEGRATED ACTIVITIES and TEACHING METHODS
	TEACHING METHODS
	TEACHING MODELS
	TEACHING (OCCUPATION)
OFF CAMPUS STUDENT	TEACHING Use STUDENT TEACHING
PART TIME	TEACHING (1967 1980) Use PART TIME FACULTY
PEER	TEACHING
	TEACHING PERSISTENCE Use TEACHER PERSISTENCE
DEPARTMENTAL	TEACHING PLANS (1968 1980) Use DEPARTMENTS
PRACTICE	TEACHING Use STUDENT TEACHING
	TEACHING PRACTICES Use TEACHING METHODS
PRECISION	TEACHING
PRESCRIPTIVE	TEACHING Use DIAGNOSTIC TEACHING
	TEACHING PROCEDURES (1966 1980) Use TEACHING METHODS
	TEACHING (PROCESS) Use INSTRUCTION
	TEACHING PROFESSION Use TEACHING (OCCUPATION)
	TEACHING PROGRAMS (1966 1980)
	TEACHING QUALITY (1966 1980) Use TEACHER EFFECTIVENESS
	TEACHING RESOURCES Use EDUCATIONAL RESOURCES
SELF	TEACHING Use INDEPENDENT STUDY
	TEACHING SKILLS
STUDENT	TEACHING
	TEACHING STYLES
	TEACHING SYSTEMS Use TEACHING METHODS
TEAM	TEACHING
TEAM LEADER	(TEACHING) (1966 1980) Use LEADERS and TEAM TEACHING
DISCUSSION	(TEACHING TECHNIQUE)
	TEACHING TECHNIQUES (1966 1980) Use TEACHING METHODS
URBAN	TEACHING
	TEAM ADMINISTRATION (1967 1980) Use MANAGEMENT TEAMS
	TEAM COUNSELING Use COCOUNSELING
	TEAM HANDBALL
	TEAM LEADER (TEACHING) (1966 1980) Use LEADERS and TEAM TEACHING
	TEAM MANAGEMENT Use MANAGEMENT TEAMS
	TEAM SPORTS
	TEAM TEACHING
	TEAM TRAINING
ADMINISTRATIVE	TEAMS Use MANAGEMENT TEAMS
INSTRUCTIONAL	TEAMS Use TEAM TEACHING
MANAGEMENT	TEAMS
	TEAMWORK
	TECHNICAL ASSISTANCE
INTERNATIONAL	TECHNICAL ASSISTANCE Use INTERNATIONAL PROGRAMS and TECHNICAL ASSISTANCE
LIBRARY	TECHNICAL ASSISTANTS Use LIBRARY TECHNICIANS
	TECHNICAL EDUCATION
	TECHNICAL EDUCATION DIRECTORS Use VOCATIONAL DIRECTORS
	TECHNICAL HIGH SCHOOLS Use VOCATIONAL HIGH SCHOOLS
	TECHNICAL ILLUSTRATION
	TECHNICAL INFORMATION Use SCIENTIFIC AND TECHNICAL INFORMATION
SCIENTIFIC AND	TECHNICAL INFORMATION
	TECHNICAL INSTITUTES
	TECHNICAL INSTRUCTION Use TECHNICAL EDUCATION
	TECHNICAL MATHEMATICS
	TECHNICAL OCCUPATIONS
	TECHNICAL PROCESSES (LIBRARIES) Use LIBRARY TECHNICAL PROCESSES
LIBRARY	TECHNICAL PROCESSES
	TECHNICAL REPORTS (1968 1980) Use RESEARCH REPORTS
	TECHNICAL SCHOOLS Use VOCATIONAL SCHOOLS
	TECHNICAL SERVICES (LIBRARIES) Use LIBRARY TECHNICAL PROCESSES
	TECHNICAL WRITING
	TECHNICIANS Use PARAPROFESSIONAL PERSONNEL
AGRICULTURAL	TECHNICIANS
APPLIANCE SERVICE	TECHNICIANS (1967 1980) Use APPLIANCE REPAIR
BIOMEDICAL EQUIPMENT	TECHNICIANS Use MEDICAL LABORATORY ASSISTANTS
CHEMICAL	TECHNICIANS
DENTAL	TECHNICIANS
DENTAL LABORATORY	TECHNICIANS Use DENTAL TECHNICIANS
ELECTRICAL	TECHNICIANS Use ELECTRONIC TECHNICIANS
ELECTRONIC	TECHNICIANS
EMERGENCY MEDICAL	TECHNICIANS
ENGINE DEVELOPMENT	TECHNICIANS Use MECHANICAL DESIGN TECHNICIANS
ENGINEERING	TECHNICIANS
ENVIRONMENTAL	TECHNICIANS
HOSPITAL RECORD	TECHNICIANS Use MEDICAL RECORD TECHNICIANS
INSTRUMENTATION	TECHNICIANS
LIBRARY	TECHNICIANS
MARINE	TECHNICIANS

MECHANICAL DESIGN TECHNICIANS
MEDICAL TECHNICIANS Use MEDICAL LABORATORY ASSISTANTS
MEDICAL RECORD TECHNICIANS
METALLURGICAL TECHNICIANS
NUCLEAR POWER PLANT TECHNICIANS
OPERATING ROOM TECHNICIANS Use SURGICAL TECHNICIANS
ORTHODONTIC TECHNICIANS Use DENTAL TECHNICIANS
PRODUCTION TECHNICIANS
PROPULSION DEVELOPMENT TECHNICIANS Use MECHANICAL DESIGN TECHNICIANS
PSYCHIATRIC TECHNICIANS Use PSYCHIATRIC AIDES
SANITARY TECHNICIANS Use ENVIRONMENTAL TECHNICIANS
SURGICAL TECHNICIANS
DELPHI TECHNIQUE
DISCUSSION (TEACHING TECHNIQUE)
FORCED CHOICE TECHNIQUE
JAN TECHNIQUE Use JUDGMENT ANALYSIS TECHNIQUE
JUDGMENT ANALYSIS TECHNIQUE
Q TECHNIQUE Use Q METHODOLOGY
TECHNIQUES (1966 1974) Use METHODS
CLASSROOM TECHNIQUES
CLASSROOM OBSERVATION TECHNIQUES
CLOZE TECHNIQUES Use CLOZE PROCEDURE
COUNSELING TECHNIQUES
CULTURING TECHNIQUES
EVALUATION TECHNIQUES (1966 1974) Use EVALUATION METHODS
LABORATORY TECHNIQUES (1967 1980)
MANUFACTURING TECHNIQUES Use MANUFACTURING
MEASUREMENT TECHNIQUES
MOTIVATION TECHNIQUES
MULTITRAIT MULTIMETHOD TECHNIQUES
MUSIC TECHNIQUES
PRODUCTION TECHNIQUES
QUESTIONING TECHNIQUES
SOCIOMETRIC TECHNIQUES
TEACHING TECHNIQUES (1966 1980) Use TEACHING METHODS
TESTING TECHNIQUES Use TESTING
TRAINING TECHNIQUES (1967 1980) Use TRAINING METHODS
TECHNOLOGICAL ADVANCEMENT
TECHNOLOGICAL INFORMATION Use SCIENTIFIC AND TECHNICAL INFORMATION
TECHNOLOGICAL LITERACY
TECHNOLOGICAL PROGRAMS Use SCIENCE PROGRAMS
TECHNOLOGICAL UNEMPLOYMENT Use STRUCTURAL UNEMPLOYMENT
MEDICAL TECHNOLOGISTS
MEDICAL LABORATORY TECHNOLOGISTS Use MEDICAL TECHNOLOGISTS
NUCLEAR MEDICINE TECHNOLOGISTS Use RADIOLOGIC TECHNOLOGISTS
RADIATION THERAPY TECHNOLOGISTS Use RADIOLOGIC TECHNOLOGISTS
RADIOLOGIC TECHNOLOGISTS
X RAY TECHNOLOGISTS Use RADIOLOGIC TECHNOLOGISTS
TECHNOLOGY
AEROSPACE TECHNOLOGY
SCIENCE TECHNOLOGY AND SOCIETY Use SCIENCE AND SOCIETY
APPROPRIATE TECHNOLOGY
AVIATION TECHNOLOGY
BEHAVIORAL TECHNOLOGY Use BEHAVIORAL SCIENCES
COMPUTER TECHNOLOGY Use COMPUTERS
EDUCATIONAL TECHNOLOGY
ELECTROMECHANICAL TECHNOLOGY
ENERGY TECHNOLOGY Use POWER TECHNOLOGY
ENGINEERING TECHNOLOGY
ENGLISH FOR SCIENCE AND TECHNOLOGY
HIGH TECHNOLOGY Use TECHNOLOGICAL ADVANCEMENT
INDUSTRIAL TECHNOLOGY (1969 1980) Use INDUSTRY and TECHNOLOGY
INFORMATION TECHNOLOGY
INSTRUCTIONAL TECHNOLOGY (1966 1978) Use EDUCATIONAL TECHNOLOGY
LABORATORY TECHNOLOGY
LIVESTOCK TECHNOLOGY Use ANIMAL HUSBANDRY
MASS MEDIA TECHNOLOGY Use COMMUNICATIONS and MASS MEDIA
MEDIA TECHNOLOGY (1968 1980) Use COMMUNICATIONS
NUCLEAR TECHNOLOGY
POWER TECHNOLOGY
RADIO TECHNOLOGY (1967 1980) Use RADIO
STS (SCIENCE TECHNOLOGY SOCIETY) Use SCIENCE AND SOCIETY
TELEVISION TECHNOLOGY Use TELEVISION
TECHNOLOGY TRANSFER
PLATE TECTONICS
TEENAGERS (1966 1980) Use ADOLESCENTS
TEFL Use ENGLISH (SECOND LANGUAGE)
TELECOMMUNICATION (1970 1980) Use TELECOMMUNICATIONS
TELECOMMUNICATIONS
TELECONFERENCING
TELECOURSES
TELEFACSIMILE Use FACSIMILE TRANSMISSION
TELEFAX Use FACSIMILE TRANSMISSION
TELEGRAPHIC MATERIALS
TELEGU Use TELUGU
TELEPHONE COMMUNICATION SYSTEMS (1967 1980) Use TELEPHONE COMMUNICATIONS SYSTEMS
TELEPHONE COMMUNICATIONS INDUSTRY
TELEPHONE COMMUNICATIONS SYSTEMS
TELEPHONE CRISIS SERVICES Use HOTLINES (PUBLIC)
TELEPHONE INSTRUCTION
TELEPHONE USAGE INSTRUCTION
TELEPHONES Use TELEPHONE COMMUNICATIONS SYSTEMS
TELETEXT Use VIDEOTEX
TELEVISED INSTRUCTION (1966 1974) Use EDUCATIONAL TELEVISION
TELEVISION
AIRBORNE TELEVISION (1966 1980) Use TELEVISION
BROADCAST TELEVISION
CABLE TELEVISION
CHILDRENS TELEVISION
CLOSED CIRCUIT TELEVISION
COLOR TELEVISION (1969 1980) Use COLOR and TELEVISION

COMMERCIAL TELEVISION
TELEVISION COMMERCIALS
TELEVISION CURRICULUM
EDUCATIONAL TELEVISION
TELEVISION EQUIPMENT Use VIDEO EQUIPMENT
FIXED SERVICE TELEVISION (1969 1980) Use EDUCATIONAL TELEVISION
INSTRUCTIONAL TELEVISION (1966 1974) Use EDUCATIONAL TELEVISION
INSTRUCTOR CENTERED TELEVISION (1966 1980) Use EDUCATIONAL TELEVISION
TELEVISION LECTURERS Use TELEVISION TEACHERS
TELEVISION LIGHTING
TELEVISION LIGHTS (1966 1980) Use TELEVISION LIGHTING
OPEN CIRCUIT TELEVISION (1966 1980) Use BROADCAST TELEVISION
OVERHEAD TELEVISION (1966 1980) Use TELEVISION
TELEVISION PROGRAMING Use PROGRAMING (BROADCAST)
PUBLIC TELEVISION
TELEVISION RADIO REPAIRERS
RADIO TELEVISION REPAIRERS Use TELEVISION RADIO REPAIRERS
TELEVISION REPAIRMEN (1968 1980) Use TELEVISION RADIO REPAIRERS
TELEVISION RESEARCH
TELEVISION STUDIOS
TELEVISION SURVEYS
TELEVISION TEACHERS
TELEVISION TECHNOLOGY Use TELEVISION
TELEVISION VIEWING
STORY TELLING
TELUGU
TEMPERAMENT Use PERSONALITY
TEMPERATURE
CONCEPTUAL TEMPO
TEMPORAL PERSPECTIVE Use TIME PERSPECTIVE
TEMPORARY FACILITIES Use RELOCATABLE FACILITIES
WITHDRAWAL TENDENCIES (PSYCHOLOGY) (1966 1980) Use WITHDRAWAL (PSYCHOLOGY)
TENES Use ENGLISH (SECOND LANGUAGE)
TENL (1968 1980)
TENNIS
TABLE TENNIS
TENPINS Use BOWLING
TENSES (GRAMMAR)
COMMUNITY TENSIONS Use COMMUNITY PROBLEMS
TENURE
JOB TENURE (1967 1978) Use TENURE
TENURED FACULTY
TENURED TEACHERS Use TENURED FACULTY
LONG TERM MEMORY
SHORT TERM MEMORY
TERM PAPERS Use RESEARCH PAPERS (STUDENTS)
LONG TERM PLANNING Use LONG RANGE PLANNING
HOSPICES (TERMINAL CARE)
TERMINAL EDUCATION
TERMINAL STUDENTS
COMPUTER TERMINALS Use INPUT OUTPUT DEVICES
TERMINATION OF PROGRAMS Use PROGRAM TERMINATION
TERMINATION OF TREATMENT
PROGRAM TERMINATION
TERMINOLOGY Use VOCABULARY
KINSHIP TERMINOLOGY
INDEX TERMS Use SUBJECT INDEX TERMS
SUBJECT INDEX TERMS
TERRORISM
TERTIARY EDUCATION Use POSTSECONDARY EDUCATION
TESL Use ENGLISH (SECOND LANGUAGE)
TESOL Use ENGLISH (SECOND LANGUAGE)
TEST ABUSE Use TEST USE
TEST ADMINISTRATION Use TESTING
TEST ADMINISTRATORS Use EXAMINERS
TEST ANALYSIS Use TEST THEORY
TEST ANXIETY
TEST BIAS
TEST BOOKS Use TESTS
TEST CHARACTERISTICS (PHYSICAL) Use TEST FORMAT
TEST COACHING
TEST CONSTRUCTION
TEST DESIGN Use TEST CONSTRUCTION
TEST FORMAT
TEST INTERPRETATION
TEST ITEMS
TEST LENGTH
TEST MANUALS
TEST NORMS
TEST RELIABILITY
TEST RESULTS
TEST REVIEWS
TEST SCORES Use SCORES
TEST SCORING MACHINES
TEST SELECTION
TEST TAKING SKILLS Use TEST WISENESS
TEST TAKING STRATEGIES Use TEST WISENESS
TEST THEORY
TEST TYPE Use TEST FORMAT
TEST USE
TEST VALIDITY
TEST WISENESS
TESTING
ADAPTIVE TESTING
COMPARATIVE TESTING
COMPUTER ASSISTED TESTING
COMPUTERIZED ADAPTIVE TESTING Use ADAPTIVE TESTING and COMPUTER ASSISTED TESTING
COMPUTERIZED TAILORED TESTING Use ADAPTIVE TESTING and COMPUTER ASSISTED TESTING
CONFIDENCE TESTING
EDUCATIONAL TESTING
FLEXILEVEL TESTING Use ADAPTIVE TESTING

SYSTEMS THEORY Use SYSTEMS APPROACH
TEST THEORY
THERAPEUTIC COMMUNITIES Use MILIEU THERAPY
THERAPEUTIC ENVIRONMENT
THERAPEUTIC PLAY Use PLAY THERAPY
THERAPEUTIC RECREATION
THERAPEUTICS Use THERAPY
THERAPISTS
HEARING THERAPISTS (1967 1980) Use HEARING THERAPY and THERAPISTS
INHALATION THERAPISTS (1969 1985) Use RESPIRATORY THERAPY and THERAPISTS
OCCUPATIONAL THERAPISTS
PHYSICAL THERAPISTS
SPEECH THERAPISTS (1966 1980) Use SPEECH THERAPY and THERAPISTS
THERAPY
PHYSICAL THERAPY AIDES
ART THERAPY
OCCUPATIONAL THERAPY ASSISTANTS
PHYSICAL THERAPY ATTENDANTS Use PHYSICAL THERAPY AIDES
BEHAVIOR THERAPY Use BEHAVIOR MODIFICATION
COGNITIVE THERAPY Use COGNITIVE RESTRUCTURING
CRISIS THERAPY (1969 1980) Use CRISIS INTERVENTION
DANCE THERAPY
DRUG THERAPY
EDUCATIONAL THERAPY
ENVIRONMENTAL THERAPY Use MILIEU THERAPY
GESTALT THERAPY
GROUP THERAPY
HEARING THERAPY
MILIEU THERAPY
MUSIC THERAPY
OCCUPATIONAL THERAPY
OXYGEN INHALATION THERAPY Use RESPIRATORY THERAPY
PHYSICAL THERAPY
PLAY THERAPY
RADIATION THERAPY Use RADIOLOGY
RATIONAL THERAPY (1968 1980) Use RATIONAL EMOTIVE THERAPY
RATIONAL EMOTIVE THERAPY
READING THERAPY Use BIBLIOTHERAPY
REALITY THERAPY
RECREATION THERAPY Use THERAPEUTIC RECREATION
RESPIRATORY THERAPY
SITUATIONAL THERAPY Use MILIEU THERAPY
SPEECH THERAPY
RADIATION THERAPY TECHNOLOGISTS Use RADIOLOGIC TECHNOLOGISTS
THERMAL ENVIRONMENT
THERMODYNAMICS
THERMOMECHANICS Use THERMODYNAMICS
THERMOPHYSICS Use THERMODYNAMICS
THERMOSCIENCE Use THERMODYNAMICS
THESAURI
THESES
DOCTORAL THESES (1967 1980) Use DOCTORAL DISSERTATIONS
MASTERS THESES
THINKING ALOUD PROTOCOLS Use PROTOCOL ANALYSIS
CONVERGENT THINKING
CREATIVE THINKING
CRITICAL THINKING
DIVERGENT THINKING
EVALUATIVE THINKING
LOGICAL THINKING
THINKING PROCESSES Use COGNITIVE PROCESSES
PRODUCTIVE THINKING
CREATIVE THINKING TESTS Use CREATIVITY TESTS
THIRD WORLD COUNTRIES Use DEVELOPING NATIONS
FREEDOM OF THOUGHT Use INTELLECTUAL FREEDOM
THOUGHT PROCESSES (1966 1980) Use COGNITIVE PROCESSES
COMMUNICATION (THOUGHT TRANSFER)
THREE DIMENSIONAL AIDS
SIX THREE THREE ORGANIZATION Use INSTRUCTIONAL PROGRAM DIVISIONS
SIX THREE THREE ORGANIZATION Use INSTRUCTIONAL PROGRAM DIVISIONS
THREE YEAR BACHELORS DEGREES Use ACCELERATION (EDUCATION) and BACHELORS DEGREES
THRESHOLD LEVEL (LANGUAGES)
FAILURE TO THRIVE
NONORGANIC FAILURE TO THRIVE Use FAILURE TO THRIVE
TIBETAN
SINO TIBETAN LANGUAGES
TIMBER BASED INDUSTRY Use LUMBER INDUSTRY
TIME
ACADEMIC LEARNING TIME Use TIME ON TASK
TIME ALLOCATION Use TIME MANAGEMENT
TIME BLOCKS
SHARED TIME (COMPUTERS) Use TIME SHARING
SPACE TIME CONTINUUM Use RELATIVITY
SHARED TIME (EDUCATION) Use DUAL ENROLLMENT
PART TIME EMPLOYMENT
FULL TIME EQUIVALENCY
TIME ESTIMATION Use TIME MANAGEMENT
TIME FACTORS (LEARNING)
FULL TIME FACULTY
PART TIME FACULTY
PART TIME FARMERS
PART TIME JOBS (1966 1980) Use PART TIME EMPLOYMENT
ENGAGED TIME (LEARNING) Use TIME ON TASK
LEISURE TIME
TIME MANAGEMENT
TIME ON TASK
TIME PERSPECTIVE
REACTION TIME
LEISURE TIME READING Use RECREATIONAL READING
RELEASED TIME
RESPONSE TIME Use REACTION TIME

TIME SHARING
TIME SHORTENED DEGREE PROGRAMS Use ACCELERATION (EDUCATION)
SPLIT TIME Use DUAL ENROLLMENT
STUDENT ENGAGED TIME Use TIME ON TASK
FULL TIME STUDENTS
PART TIME STUDENTS
FULL TIME TEACHERS Use FULL TIME FACULTY
PART TIME TEACHERS (1967 1980) Use PART TIME FACULTY
BLOCK TIME TEACHING Use TIME BLOCKS
PART TIME TEACHING (1967 1980) Use PART TIME FACULTY
TIME USE DATA Use TIME MANAGEMENT
TIME UTILIZATION Use TIME MANAGEMENT
VIEWING TIME (1968 1980) Use PROGRAMING (BROADCAST)
PART TIME WORK Use PART TIME EMPLOYMENT
TIMED TESTS
TIMEOUT
TISSUE DONORS
TITLE WORD INDEXES Use PERMUTED INDEXES
DEGREES (TITLES) (1966 1980) Use DEGREES (ACADEMIC)
BACK TO BASICS
ACCESS TO EDUCATION
ADJUSTMENT (TO ENVIRONMENT)
ACCESS TO IDEAS Use INTELLECTUAL FREEDOM
ACCESS TO INFORMATION
RIGHT TO KNOW Use FREEDOM OF INFORMATION
LEARNING TO LEARN Use LEARNING STRATEGIES
READING ALOUD TO OTHERS
FREEDOM TO READ Use INTELLECTUAL FREEDOM
URBAN TO RURAL MIGRATION
URBAN TO SUBURBAN MIGRATION
FAILURE TO THRIVE
NONORGANIC FAILURE TO THRIVE Use FAILURE TO THRIVE
RURAL TO URBAN MIGRATION
SCHOOL TO WORK TRANSITION Use EDUCATION WORK RELATIONSHIP
TOBACCO
TODDLERS
TOILET FACILITIES
TOKEN ECONOMY
TOKEN INTEGRATION (1966 1980) Use TOKENISM
TOKENISM
TONE LANGUAGES
TOOL AND DIE MAKERS
MACHINE TOOL OPERATORS
HAND TOOLS
MACHINE TOOLS
RESEARCH TOOLS
TOPOGRAPHY
TOPOLOGY
TORTS
INTERNATIONAL TORTS Use INTERNATIONAL LAW
TOTAL COMMUNICATION
TOTALITARIANISM
TOURISM
TOURIST COURTS Use HOTELS
TOURIST INDUSTRY Use TOURISM
TOWER DIVING Use DIVING
TOWNS Use MUNICIPALITIES
TOXIC SUBSTANCES Use POISONS
TOXICOLOGY
TOXINS Use POISONS
TOYS
TRACK AND FIELD
FAST TRACK SCHEDULING
TRACK SYSTEM (EDUCATION)
TRACKING (1968 1980)
SOUND TRACKS (1966 1980)
TRACTORS
TRADE AND INDUSTRIAL EDUCATION
TRADE AND INDUSTRIAL TEACHERS
EXPORT TRADE Use EXPORTS
INTERNATIONAL TRADE
MASONS (TRADE) Use MASONRY
TRADE UNIONS Use UNIONS
INTERNATIONAL TRADE VOCABULARY
BUILDING TRADES
METAL TRADES Use METAL WORKING
NEEDLE TRADES
ARCHITECTURAL TRADITION Use ARCHITECTURAL CHARACTER
TRADITIONAL CLASSROOMS Use SELF CONTAINED CLASSROOMS
TRADITIONAL FAMILY UNIT Use NUCLEAR FAMILY
TRADITIONAL GRAMMAR
TRADITIONAL INSTRUCTION Use CONVENTIONAL INSTRUCTION
TRADITIONAL SCHOOLS
TRADITIONALISM
TRADITIONS (CULTURE) Use FOLK CULTURE
TRAFFIC ACCIDENTS
TRAFFIC CIRCULATION
TRAFFIC CONTROL
AIR TRAFFIC CONTROL
SPECTATOR TRAFFIC CONTROL Use TRAFFIC CONTROL
TRAFFIC FLOW Use TRAFFIC CIRCULATION
TRAFFIC PATTERNS (1968 1980) Use TRAFFIC CIRCULATION
PEDESTRIAN TRAFFIC
TRAFFIC REGULATIONS (1968 1980) Use TRAFFIC CONTROL
TRAFFIC SAFETY
TRAFFIC SIGNS (1968 1980) Use SIGNS and TRAFFIC CONTROL
VEHICULAR TRAFFIC
TRAGEDY
TRAILS
NATURE TRAILS Use TRAILS
TRAINABLE MENTALLY HANDICAPPED (1967 1980) Use MODERATE MENTAL RETARDATION

FOREIGN TRAINED PHYSICIANS Use FOREIGN MEDICAL GRADUATES
TRAINEES
TRAINERS
COORDINATOR TRAINERS Use INSTRUCTOR COORDINATORS
TEACHER TRAINERS Use TEACHER EDUCATORS
TRAINING
ADMINISTRATOR TRAINING Use MANAGEMENT DEVELOPMENT
TRAINING ALLOWANCES
TRAINING ALTERNATIVES Use NONTRADITIONAL EDUCATION
ASSERTIVE TRAINING Use ASSERTIVENESS
ASSERTIVENESS TRAINING Use ASSERTIVENESS
ATTENDANT TRAINING (1968 1980) Use ATTENDANTS and JOB TRAINING
AUDITORY TRAINING
AWAY FROM THE JOB TRAINING Use OFF THE JOB TRAINING
BICULTURAL TRAINING Use CROSS CULTURAL TRAINING
UNIVERSITY TRAINING CENTERS Use TEACHER CENTERS
VOCATIONAL TRAINING CENTERS
COOPERATIVE TRAINING Use COOPERATIVE EDUCATION
CORPORATE TRAINING Use INDUSTRIAL TRAINING
COUNSELOR TRAINING
CROSS CULTURAL TRAINING
CUSTODIAN TRAINING
DRIVER TRAINING Use DRIVER EDUCATION
TEACHER TRAINING FILMS Use PROTOCOL MATERIALS
FLIGHT TRAINING
TRAINING GOALS Use TRAINING OBJECTIVES
GRADUATE TRAINING Use GRADUATE STUDY
HUMAN RELATIONS TRAINING Use SENSITIVITY TRAINING
INDUSTRIAL TRAINING
INQUIRY TRAINING (1967 1980) Use INQUIRY
INSERVICE TEACHER TRAINING Use INSERVICE TEACHER EDUCATION
JOB TRAINING
TRAINING LABORATORIES (1967 1980)
LABORATORY TRAINING
LEADERSHIP TRAINING
MANAGEMENT TRAINING Use MANAGEMENT DEVELOPMENT
TRAINING METHODS
PROJECT TRAINING METHODS (1968 1980) Use STUDENT PROJECTS and TEACHING METHODS
MILITARY TRAINING
MULTICULTURAL TRAINING Use CROSS CULTURAL TRAINING
MULTIETHNIC TRAINING Use CROSS CULTURAL TRAINING
TRAINING OBJECTIVES
OCCUPATIONAL TRAINING Use JOB TRAINING
OFF SITE TRAINING Use OFF THE JOB TRAINING
OFF THE JOB TRAINING
ON THE JOB TRAINING
TRAINING OPPORTUNITIES Use EDUCATIONAL OPPORTUNITIES
PEDIATRICS TRAINING (1966 1980) Use PEDIATRICS
PHYSICIANS IN TRAINING Use GRADUATE MEDICAL STUDENTS
PILOT TRAINING Use FLIGHT TRAINING
PREVOCATIONAL TRAINING Use PREVOCATIONAL EDUCATION
PROFESSIONAL TRAINING
INSTITUTES (TRAINING PROGRAMS)
REFRESHER TRAINING Use RETRAINING
RELAXATION TRAINING
RETAIL TRAINING Use DISTRIBUTIVE EDUCATION
TRAINING SCHOOLS (JUVENILE OFFENDERS) Use CORRECTIONAL INSTITUTIONS
SENSITIVITY TRAINING
SENSORY TRAINING
SUPERVISOR TRAINING Use SUPERVISORY TRAINING
SUPERVISORY TRAINING
TEACHER TRAINING Use TEACHER EDUCATION
TEAM TRAINING
TRAINING TECHNIQUES (1967 1980) Use TRAINING METHODS
TRANSFER OF TRAINING
TRAVEL TRAINING
UNDERGRADUATE TRAINING Use UNDERGRADUATE STUDY
VOCATIONAL TRAINING Use VOCATIONAL EDUCATION
VOLUNTEER TRAINING
WEIGHT TRAINING Use WEIGHTLIFTING
SICKLE CELL TRAIT Use SICKLE CELL ANEMIA
LATENT TRAIT THEORY
TRAIT TREATMENT INTERACTION Use APTITUDE TREATMENT INTERACTION
COMMUNITY TRAITS Use COMMUNITY CHARACTERISTICS
CULTURAL TRAITS
PERSONALITY TRAITS
TRANQUILIZING DRUGS Use SEDATIVES
TRANSACTIONAL ANALYSIS
TRANSCENDENTAL MEDITATION
PHONETIC TRANSCRIPTION
TRANSCRIPTS (ACADEMIC) Use ACADEMIC RECORDS
COMMUNICATION (THOUGHT TRANSFER)
DISCRIMINATION TRANSFER Use SHIFT STUDIES
INFORMATION TRANSFER
TRANSFER OF LEARNING Use TRANSFER OF TRAINING
TRANSFER OF TRAINING
TRANSFER POLICY
TRANSFER PROGRAMS
FREE CHOICE TRANSFER PROGRAMS
RESTRICTIVE TRANSFER PROGRAMS (1966 1980) Use TRANSFER PROGRAMS
TRANSFER STUDENTS
COLLEGE TRANSFER STUDENTS
POWER TRANSFER SYSTEMS Use KINETICS
TEACHER TRANSFER
TECHNOLOGY TRANSFER
TRANSFERS (1966 1980)
STUDENT TRANSFERS Use TRANSFER STUDENTS
TRANSFORMATION GENERATIVE GRAMMAR (1968 1980) Use TRANSFORMATIONAL GENERATIVE GRAMMAR
TRANSFORMATION THEORY (LANGUAGE) (1967 1980) Use LINGUISTIC THEORY and TRANSFORMATIONAL GENERATIVE GRAMMAR

TRANSFORMATIONAL GENERATIVE GRAMMAR
TRANSFORMATIONAL GEOMETRY Use TRANSFORMATIONS (MATHEMATICS)
TRANSFORMATIONAL GRAMMAR Use TRANSFORMATIONAL GENERATIVE GRAMMAR
GENERATIVE TRANSFORMATIONAL GRAMMAR Use TRANSFORMATIONAL GENERATIVE GRAMMAR
TRANSFORMATIONAL SENTENCE COMBINING Use SENTENCE COMBINING
TRANSFORMATIONS (LANGUAGE) (1967 1980) Use TRANSFORMATIONAL GENERATIVE GRAMMAR
TRANSFORMATIONS (MATHEMATICS)
SIMILARITY TRANSFORMATIONS Use TRANSFORMATIONS (MATHEMATICS)
TRANSHUMANCE Use NOMADS
TRANSIENT CHILDREN
TRANSISTORS
SCHOOL TO WORK TRANSITION Use EDUCATION WORK RELATIONSHIP
TRANSITIONAL CLASSES (1966 1981) Use TRANSITIONAL PROGRAMS
TRANSITIONAL PROGRAMS
TRANSITIONAL SCHOOLS
MIDLIFE TRANSITIONS
TRANSLATION
FREE TRANSLATION Use TRANSLATION
MACHINE TRANSLATION
MECHANICAL TRANSLATION Use MACHINE TRANSLATION
GRAMMAR TRANSLATION METHOD
TRANSLATORS Use INTERPRETERS
FACSIMILE TRANSMISSION
SOUND TRANSMISSION Use ACOUSTICS
TRANSPARENCIES
OVERHEAD TRANSPARENCIES Use TRANSPARENCIES
TRANSPARENCY PROJECTORS Use OVERHEAD PROJECTORS
OVERHEAD TRANSPARENCY PROJECTORS Use OVERHEAD PROJECTORS
TRANSPLANTING (1968 1980) Use HORTICULTURE
TRANSPORTATION
AIR TRANSPORTATION
BUS TRANSPORTATION
MIGRANT TRANSPORTATION (1966 1980) Use MIGRANTS and TRANSPORTATION
RAIL TRANSPORTATION
SCHOOL TRANSPORTATION Use STUDENT TRANSPORTATION
STUDENT TRANSPORTATION
TRASH Use SOLID WASTES
TRAVEL
STUDENT TRAVEL Use TRAVEL
TEACHER TRAVEL Use TRAVEL
TRAVEL TRAINING
TRAVELING TEACHERS Use ITINERANT TEACHERS
TREATIES
TREATMENT CENTERS Use CLINICS
APTITUDE TREATMENT INTERACTION
TRAIT TREATMENT INTERACTION Use APTITUDE TREATMENT INTERACTION
MEDICAL TREATMENT (1967 1980) Use MEDICAL SERVICES
OUTCOMES OF TREATMENT
TERMINATION OF TREATMENT
WASTE WATER TREATMENT Use WASTE WATER and WATER TREATMENT
WATER TREATMENT
TREES
FAMILY TREES Use GENEALOGY
SHADE TREES Use TREES
TREND ANALYSIS
AGRICULTURAL TRENDS
BLACK POPULATION TRENDS
EDUCATIONAL TRENDS
EMPLOYMENT TRENDS (1966 1980) Use EMPLOYMENT PATTERNS
ENROLLMENT TRENDS
MIGRATION TRENDS Use MIGRATION PATTERNS
NEGRO POPULATION TRENDS (1966 1977) Use BLACK POPULATION TRENDS
POPULATION TRENDS
SOCIAL TRENDS Use SOCIOCULTURAL PATTERNS
TRIBAL SOCIETIES Use TRIBES
TRIBAL SOVEREIGNTY
TRIBES
TRIGONOMETRY
TRIMESTER SCHEDULES (1966 1980) Use TRIMESTER SYSTEM
TRIMESTER SYSTEM
AIRBORNE FIELD TRIPS (1968 1980) Use FIELD TRIPS
FIELD TRIPS
INSTRUCTIONAL TRIPS (1966 1980) Use FIELD TRIPS
STUDY TRIPS Use FIELD TRIPS
FEDERAL TROOPS (1966 1980) Use ARMED FORCES
TROUBADOURS Use POETS
TRUANCY
SCHOOL TRUANCY Use TRUANCY
TRUCK MECHANICS Use AUTO MECHANICS
TRUE FALSE TESTS Use OBJECTIVE TESTS
TRUE MEASURE Use TRUE SCORES
TRUE SCORES
TRUST FUNDS Use TRUSTS (FINANCIAL)
TRUST (PSYCHOLOGY)
TRUST RESPONSIBILITY (GOVERNMENT)
TRUSTEES
BOARD OF TRUSTEES Use GOVERNING BOARDS
CHARITABLE TRUSTS Use TRUSTS (FINANCIAL)
TRUSTS (FINANCIAL)
TRUSTWORTHINESS Use CREDIBILITY
TUITION
DEFERRED TUITION Use INCOME CONTINGENT LOANS
TUITION GRANTS
TUITION POSTPONEMENT Use INCOME CONTINGENT LOANS
TUITION TAX CREDITS Use TAX CREDITS and TUITION
TUMBLING
STUNTS AND TUMBLING Use TUMBLING
TUMORS (MALIGNANT) Use CANCER
TURF MANAGEMENT
TURKIC LANGUAGES
TURKISH

	TURNKEY BUILDING Use DESIGN BUILD APPROACH
LABOR	TURNOVER
TEACHER	TURNOVER Use FACULTY MOBILITY
	TUTORIAL INSTRUCTION Use TUTORING
	TUTORIAL PLANS Use TUTORIAL PROGRAMS
	TUTORIAL PROGRAMS
	TUTORIAL SERVICES Use TUTORIAL PROGRAMS
	TUTORING
AFTER SCHOOL	TUTORING (1966 1980) Use AFTER SCHOOL EDUCATION and TUTORING
PROGRAMED	TUTORING
	TUTORS
	TV Use TELEVISION
	TWENTIETH CENTURY LITERATURE
	TWI Use AKAN
	TWINS
	TWO PARENT FAMILY Use NUCLEAR FAMILY
	TWO YEAR COLLEGE DEGREES Use ASSOCIATE DEGREES
	TWO YEAR COLLEGE STUDENTS
	TWO YEAR COLLEGES
LARGE	TYPE BOOKS Use LARGE TYPE MATERIALS
INSTITUTE	TYPE COURSES (1966 1980) Use INSTITUTES (TRAINING PROGRAMS)
LARGE	TYPE MATERIALS
TEST	TYPE Use TEST FORMAT
ITEM	TYPES Use TEST FORMAT
	TYPEWRITING
	TYPING Use TYPEWRITING
	TYPISTS (1967 1981) Use TYPEWRITING
CLERK	TYPISTS Use TYPEWRITING
	TYPOLOGY (1967 1980) Use CLASSIFICATION
LANGUAGE	TYPOLOGY
	TZELTAL
	TZENDAL Use TZELTAL
	TZOTZIL
FENNO	UGRIC LANGUAGES Use FINNO UGRIC LANGUAGES
FINNO	UGRIC LANGUAGES
	UKRAINIAN
	ULTRAMICROFICHE Use MICROFICHE
	UNCIAL SCRIPT Use MANUSCRIPT WRITING (HANDLETTERING)
	UNCOMMONLY TAUGHT LANGUAGES
	UNCONVENTIONAL WARFARE Use WAR
	UNDERACHIEVEMENT
	UNDERACHIEVERS (1966 1979) Use UNDERACHIEVEMENT
	UNDERDEVELOPED NATIONS Use DEVELOPING NATIONS
	UNDEREMPLOYED (1969 1980) Use UNDEREMPLOYMENT
	UNDEREMPLOYMENT
	UNDERGRADUATE EDUCATION Use UNDERGRADUATE STUDY
	UNDERGRADUATE STUDENTS
	UNDERGRADUATE STUDY
	UNDERGRADUATE TRAINING Use UNDERGRADUATE STUDY
SENIORS (1966 1980) (LAST YEAR	UNDERGRADUATES) Use COLLEGE SENIORS
	UNDERGROUND FACILITIES
	UNDERPRIVILEGED Use DISADVANTAGED
CULTURAL	UNDERSTANDING Use CULTURAL AWARENESS
SELF	UNDERSTANDING Use SELF CONCEPT
	UNDERWATER DIVING
	UNDOCUMENTED IMMIGRANTS
	UNDOCUMENTED WORKERS Use FOREIGN WORKERS and UNDOCUMENTED IMMIGRANTS
	UNEMPLOYED (1967 1980) Use UNEMPLOYMENT
	UNEMPLOYMENT
	UNEMPLOYMENT INSURANCE
STRUCTURAL	UNEMPLOYMENT
TECHNOLOGICAL	UNEMPLOYMENT Use STRUCTURAL UNEMPLOYMENT
	UNGRADED CLASSES (1966 1980) Use NONGRADED INSTRUCTIONAL GROUPING
	UNGRADED CURRICULUM (1966 1980) Use NONGRADED INSTRUCTIONAL GROUPING
	UNGRADED ELEMENTARY PROGRAMS (1966 1980) Use NONGRADED INSTRUCTIONAL GROUPING
	UNGRADED PRIMARY PROGRAMS (1966 1980) Use NONGRADED INSTRUCTIONAL GROUPING
	UNGRADED PROGRAMS (1966 1980) Use NONGRADED INSTRUCTIONAL GROUPING
	UNGRADED SCHOOLS (1966 1980) Use NONGRADED INSTRUCTIONAL GROUPING
	UNIFICATION Use GROUP UNITY
	UNIFIED STUDIES CURRICULUM
	UNIFIED STUDIES PROGRAMS (1966 1980) Use UNIFIED STUDIES CURRICULUM
	UNILATERAL DISARMAMENT Use DISARMAMENT
	UNION CATALOGS
	UNION MEMBERS
	UNIONS
COLLEGE	UNIONS Use STUDENT UNIONS
LABOR	UNIONS (1966 1980) Use UNIONS
LOCAL	UNIONS (1966 1980) Use UNIONS
STUDENT	UNIONS
TEACHER	UNIONS Use UNIONS
TRADE	UNIONS Use UNIONS
	UNIT COSTS
FAMILY (SOCIOLOGICAL	UNIT)
	UNIT PLAN (1966 1980)
TRADITIONAL FAMILY	UNIT Use NUCLEAR FAMILY
AMERICAN LITERATURE (1966 1980)	(UNITED STATES) Use UNITED STATES LITERATURE
CIVIL WAR	(UNITED STATES)
COLONIAL HISTORY	(UNITED STATES)
	UNITED STATES GOVERNMENT (COURSE)
	UNITED STATES HISTORY
	UNITED STATES LITERATURE
PRESIDENTIAL CAMPAIGNS	(UNITED STATES)
PRESIDENTIAL CANDIDATES	(UNITED STATES) Use POLITICAL CANDIDATES and PRESIDENTIAL CAMPAIGNS (UNITED STATES)
PRESIDENTIAL DEBATES	(UNITED STATES) Use DEBATE and PRESIDENTIAL CAMPAIGNS (UNITED STATES)
PRESIDENTIAL ELECTIONS	(UNITED STATES) Use ELECTIONS and PRESIDENTIAL CAMPAIGNS (UNITED STATES)
PRESIDENTS OF THE	UNITED STATES
REVOLUTIONARY WAR	(UNITED STATES)
	UNITERM INDEXES Use COORDINATE INDEXES
	UNITERMS Use SUBJECT INDEX TERMS
DRAMATIC	UNITIES (1970 1980) Use DRAMA
ACTIVITY	UNITS

CONTINUING EDUCATION	UNITS
EXPERIENCE	UNITS Use ACTIVITY UNITS
HUMAN RELATIONS	UNITS (1966 1980) Use HUMAN RELATIONS and UNITS OF STUDY
INTERMEDIATE ADMINISTRATIVE	UNITS
LESSON	UNITS Use UNITS OF STUDY
	UNITS OF STUDY
	UNITS OF STUDY (SUBJECT FIELDS) (1966 1977) Use UNITS OF STUDY
PHONOLOGICAL	UNITS (1966 1980) Use PHONEMES
PROGRAMED	UNITS (1966 1980) Use PROGRAMED INSTRUCTION and UNITS OF STUDY
RESEARCH AND INSTRUCTION	UNITS
RESEARCH COORDINATING	UNITS
RESOURCE	UNITS
SCIENCE	UNITS (1966 1980) Use SCIENCE CURRICULUM and UNITS OF STUDY
SI	UNITS Use METRIC SYSTEM
SOCIAL STUDIES	UNITS (1966 1980) Use SOCIAL STUDIES and UNITS OF STUDY
ETHNIC	UNITY Use GROUP UNITY
FAMILY	UNITY Use GROUP UNITY
GROUP	UNITY
	UNIVERSAL EDUCATION (1968 1976) Use EQUAL EDUCATION
LANGUAGE	UNIVERSALS
LINGUISTIC	UNIVERSALS Use LANGUAGE UNIVERSALS
	UNIVERSITIES
EXTENDED	UNIVERSITIES Use OPEN UNIVERSITIES
FREE	UNIVERSITIES Use EXPERIMENTAL COLLEGES
LAND GRANT	UNIVERSITIES
OPEN	UNIVERSITIES
PRIVATE	UNIVERSITIES Use PRIVATE COLLEGES
RESEARCH	UNIVERSITIES
STATE	UNIVERSITIES
URBAN	UNIVERSITIES
	UNIVERSITIES WITHOUT WALLS Use OPEN UNIVERSITIES
	UNIVERSITY ADMINISTRATION (1967 1980) Use COLLEGE ADMINISTRATION
	UNIVERSITY CHARACTERISTICS Use INSTITUTIONAL CHARACTERISTICS
	UNIVERSITY EXTENSION (1967 1980) Use EXTENSION EDUCATION
	UNIVERSITY LIBRARIES (1968 1980) Use COLLEGE LIBRARIES
	UNIVERSITY SCHOOLS Use LABORATORY SCHOOLS
	UNIVERSITY SENATES Use COLLEGE GOVERNING COUNCILS
	UNIVERSITY SETTLEMENTS Use SETTLEMENT HOUSES
	UNIVERSITY STUDENTS Use COLLEGE STUDENTS
	UNIVERSITY TEACHING HOSPITALS Use TEACHING HOSPITALS
	UNIVERSITY TRAINING CENTERS Use TEACHER CENTERS
	UNMARRIED STUDENTS Use SINGLE STUDENTS
	UNSKILLED LABOR (1966 1980) Use UNSKILLED WORKERS
	UNSKILLED OCCUPATIONS
	UNSKILLED WORKERS
	UNTENURED FACULTY Use NONTENURED FACULTY
	UNWED MOTHERS
	UNWRITTEN LANGUAGE (1968 1980)
	UNWRITTEN LANGUAGES
	UPGRADING Use IMPROVEMENT
EQUIPMENT	UPKEEP Use EQUIPMENT MAINTENANCE
	UPPER CLASS
	UPPER DIVISION COLLEGES
	URALIC ALTAIC LANGUAGES
	URBAN AMERICAN INDIANS
	URBAN AREAS
	URBAN CULTURE
	URBAN DEMOGRAPHY
	URBAN DESEGREGATION Use RACIAL INTEGRATION
RURAL	URBAN DIFFERENCES
	URBAN DROPOUTS (1966 1981) Use DROPOUTS
	URBAN EDUCATION
	URBAN ENVIRONMENT
	URBAN EXTENSION
	URBAN GEOGRAPHY Use HUMAN GEOGRAPHY
	URBAN IMMIGRATION (1966 1976) Use RURAL TO URBAN MIGRATION
	URBAN IMPROVEMENT
	URBAN LANGUAGE
	URBAN LIFE Use URBAN CULTURE
RURAL TO	URBAN MIGRATION
	URBAN PLANNING
	URBAN POPULATION
	URBAN PROBLEMS
	URBAN PROGRAMS
	URBAN RENEWAL
	URBAN RENEWAL AGENCIES
	URBAN RURAL DIFFERENCES Use RURAL URBAN DIFFERENCES
	URBAN SCHOOLS
	URBAN SLUMS (1966 1980) Use SLUMS
	URBAN STUDIES
	URBAN TEACHING
	URBAN TEACHING INTERNS Use TEACHER INTERNS and URBAN TEACHING
	URBAN TO RURAL MIGRATION
	URBAN TO SUBURBAN MIGRATION
	URBAN UNIVERSITIES
	URBAN YOUTH
	URBANIZATION
	URDU
COLLOQUIAL STANDARD	USAGE Use STANDARD SPOKEN USAGE
INFORMAL CONVERSATIONAL	USAGE Use STANDARD SPOKEN USAGE
TELEPHONE	USAGE INSTRUCTION
LANGUAGE	USAGE
STANDARD SPOKEN	USAGE
TIME	USE DATA Use TIME MANAGEMENT
DRUG	USE
ELECTRONIC CLASSROOM	USE (1966 1980) Use ELECTRONIC CLASSROOMS
ILLEGAL DRUG	USE
LAND	USE
LANGUAGE LABORATORY	USE (1966 1980) Use LANGUAGE LABORATORIES
NUMBER	USE Use NUMBERS
	USE STUDIES

TEST USE
INFORMATION USER NEEDS Use USER NEEDS (INFORMATION)
USER NEEDS (INFORMATION)
LIBRARY USER NEEDS Use USER NEEDS (INFORMATION)
INFORMATION USER SATISFACTION Use USER SATISFACTION (INFORMATION)
USER SATISFACTION (INFORMATION)
LIBRARY USER SATISFACTION Use USER SATISFACTION (INFORMATION)
USER STUDIES Use USE STUDIES
INFORMATION USERS Use USERS (INFORMATION)
USERS (INFORMATION)
END USERS (INFORMATION) Use USERS (INFORMATION)
LIBRARY USERS Use USERS (INFORMATION)
COMPUTER USES IN EDUCATION
UTILITIES
BIBLIOGRAPHIC UTILITIES
ELECTRIC UTILITIES Use UTILITIES
GAS UTILITIES Use UTILITIES
INFORMATION UTILITIES (ONLINE) Use ONLINE VENDORS
PUBLIC UTILITIES Use UTILITIES
WATER UTILITIES Use UTILITIES
COST UTILITY ANALYSIS Use COST EFFECTIVENESS
EQUIPMENT UTILIZATION
EVALUATION UTILIZATION
INFORMATION UTILIZATION
LABOR UTILIZATION
MANPOWER UTILIZATION (1966 1980) Use LABOR UTILIZATION
RESEARCH UTILIZATION
FACILITY UTILIZATION RESEARCH
SELF UTILIZATION Use SELF ACTUALIZATION
SPACE UTILIZATION
STAFF UTILIZATION
TALENT UTILIZATION (1966 1980)
TIME UTILIZATION Use TIME MANAGEMENT
UTO AZTECAN LANGUAGES
UZBEK
JOB VACANCIES Use EMPLOYMENT OPPORTUNITIES
JOB VACANCY SURVEYS Use OCCUPATIONAL SURVEYS
VACATION PROGRAMS
VACATIONS
VALENCE (LANGUAGE) Use SYNTAX
APPROVED PROGRAMS (VALIDATED) Use VALIDATED PROGRAMS
VALIDATED PROGRAMS
PROGRAM VALIDATION
PROGRAM APPROVAL (VALIDATION) Use PROGRAM VALIDATION
VALIDITY
CONCURRENT VALIDITY
CRITERION VALIDITY (CONCURRENT) Use CONCURRENT VALIDITY
CONSTRUCT VALIDITY
CONTENT VALIDITY
PREDICTIVE VALIDITY
CRITERION VALIDITY (PREDICTIVE) Use PREDICTIVE VALIDITY
TEST VALIDITY
AD VALOREM TAX Use PROPERTY TAXES
ASSESSED VALUATION
VALUE JUDGMENT
PLACE VALUE
VALUES
AESTHETIC VALUES
VALUES CLARIFICATION
DEMOCRATIC VALUES
VALUES EDUCATION
ETHICAL VALUES (1966 1980) Use MORAL VALUES
GROUP VALUES Use SOCIAL VALUES
MIDDLE CLASS VALUES (1966 1980) Use MIDDLE CLASS STANDARDS
MORAL VALUES
PERSONAL VALUES (1966 1980) Use VALUES
SOCIAL VALUES
VANDALISM
SCHOOL VANDALISM
INDEPENDENT VARIABLES Use PREDICTOR VARIABLES
PREDICTIVE VARIABLES Use PREDICTOR VARIABLES
PREDICTOR VARIABLES
STRESS VARIABLES
SUPPRESSOR VARIABLES
ANALYSIS OF VARIANCE
ERROR VARIANCE Use ERROR OF MEASUREMENT
MULTIVARIATE ANALYSIS OF VARIANCE Use MULTIVARIATE ANALYSIS
LANGUAGE VARIATION
VASCULAR SYSTEM Use CARDIOVASCULAR SYSTEM
VECTORS (MATHEMATICS)
FRUIT AND VEGETABLE INSPECTORS Use FOOD AND DRUG INSPECTORS
CHILD RESTRAINTS (VEHICLE SAFETY) Use RESTRAINTS (VEHICLE SAFETY)
RESTRAINTS (VEHICLE SAFETY)
CONTRACTOR VEHICLES Use SERVICE VEHICLES
MAINTENANCE VEHICLES Use SERVICE VEHICLES
MOTOR VEHICLES
SERVICE VEHICLES
VEHICULAR CIRCULATION Use VEHICULAR TRAFFIC
VEHICULAR TRAFFIC
VENDING MACHINES
DATABASE VENDORS Use ONLINE VENDORS
ONLINE VENDORS
VENEREAL DISEASES
VENTILATION
VERBAL ABILITY
VERBAL COMMUNICATION
VERBAL DEVELOPMENT
VERBAL INTERACTION Use VERBAL COMMUNICATION
VERBAL LEARNING
VERBAL OPERANT CONDITIONING
VERBAL STIMULI

VERBAL TESTS
VERBS
AUDITS (VERIFICATION)
VERSIFICATION (1969 1980) Use POETRY
VERTICAL ORGANIZATION
VETERANS
VETERANS EDUCATION
VETERINARIANS
VETERINARY ASSISTANTS
VETERINARY HOSPITAL ATTENDANTS Use VETERINARY ASSISTANTS
VETERINARY MEDICAL EDUCATION
VETERINARY MEDICINE
VICE PRINCIPALS Use ASSISTANT PRINCIPALS
VICTIMS OF CRIME
VICTORIAN LITERATURE
VIDEO CASSETTE SYSTEMS (1971 1980) Use VIDEO EQUIPMENT and VIDEOTAPE CASSETTES
VIDEO EQUIPMENT
INTELLIGENT VIDEO Use INTERACTIVE VIDEO
INTERACTIVE VIDEO
AUDIO VIDEO LABORATORIES (1967 1980) Use AUDIOVISUAL CENTERS
VIDEO PRODUCTION CENTERS Use TELEVISION STUDIOS
VIDEO SYSTEMS Use VIDEO EQUIPMENT
VIDEO TAPE RECORDINGS (1966 1978) Use VIDEOTAPE RECORDINGS
VIDEODISC RECORDINGS (1979 1986) Use VIDEODISKS
VIDEODISKS
OPTICAL VIDEODISKS Use OPTICAL DISKS and VIDEODISKS
VIDEOTAPE CARTRIDGES Use VIDEOTAPE CASSETTES
VIDEOTAPE CASSETTE RECORDERS Use VIDEOTAPE CASSETTES and VIDEOTAPE RECORDERS
VIDEOTAPE CASSETTES
VIDEOTAPE LIBRARIES Use FILM LIBRARIES
VIDEOTAPE RECORDERS
VIDEOTAPE RECORDINGS
VIDEOTEX
VIDEOTEXT Use VIDEOTEX
VIETNAMESE
VIETNAMESE AMERICANS Use ASIAN AMERICANS and VIETNAMESE PEOPLE
VIETNAMESE PEOPLE
VIEWDATA Use VIDEOTEX
TELEVISION VIEWING
VIEWING TIME (1968 1980) Use PROGRAMING (BROADCAST)
VILLAGE EXTENSION AGENTS Use EXTENSION AGENTS
VIOLENCE
FAMILY VIOLENCE
DOMESTIC VIOLENCE (FAMILY) Use FAMILY VIOLENCE
STUDENT VIOLENCE Use VIOLENCE
VISAYAN
VISIBLE RADIATION Use LIGHT
VISIBLE SPECTRUM Use LIGHT
VISIBLE SPEECH
VISION
LOW VISION AIDS
PARTIAL VISION
VISION TESTS
SCHOOL VISITATION
VISITING HOMEMAKERS
VISITING TEACHERS Use ITINERANT TEACHERS
FARM VISITS
HOME VISITS
INTERSCHOOL VISITS Use SCHOOL VISITATION
SCHOOL VISITS Use SCHOOL VISITATION
VISUAL ACUITY
VISUAL AIDS
VISUAL ARTS
PAINTING (VISUAL ARTS)
VISUAL DISCRIMINATION
VISUAL ENVIRONMENT
VISUAL EQUIPMENT Use VISUAL AIDS
VISUAL IMPAIRMENTS
VISUAL LANGUAGE LEARNING Use LANGUAGE ACQUISITION and VISUAL LEARNING
VISUAL LEARNING
VISUAL LITERACY
VISUAL MATERIALS Use VISUAL AIDS
VISUAL MEASURES
VISUAL MEDIA Use VISUAL AIDS
VISUAL PERCEPTION
VISUAL SCANNERS Use OPTICAL SCANNERS
VISUAL STIMULI
AUDITORY VISUAL TESTS (1966 1980) Use AUDITORY TESTS and VISION TESTS
TACTUAL VISUAL TESTS
VISUALIZATION
VISUALLY HANDICAPPED (1966 1980) Use VISUAL IMPAIRMENTS
VISUALLY HANDICAPPED MOBILITY
VISUALLY HANDICAPPED ORIENTATION (1967 1980) Use VISUALLY HANDICAPPED MOBILITY
VISUOSPATIAL ABILITY Use SPATIAL ABILITY
VITAE Use RESUMES (PERSONAL)
CURRICULUM VITAE Use RESUMES (PERSONAL)
VOCABULARY
AVIATION VOCABULARY
BANKING VOCABULARY
BASIC VOCABULARY
HIGH INTEREST LOW VOCABULARY BOOKS
VOCABULARY BUILDING Use VOCABULARY DEVELOPMENT
VOCABULARY DEVELOPMENT
INTERNATIONAL TRADE VOCABULARY
MATHEMATICAL VOCABULARY
MEDICAL VOCABULARY
SIGHT VOCABULARY
VOCABULARY SKILLS
VOCAL ENSEMBLES Use SINGING
VOCAL MUSIC
VOCATIONAL ADJUSTMENT

AGRICULTURAL EDUCATION (VOCATIONAL) Use AGRICULTURAL EDUCATION and VOCATIONAL EDUCATION
VOCATIONAL AGRICULTURE (1967 1980) Use AGRICULTURAL EDUCATION and VOCATIONAL EDUCATION
VOCATIONAL AGRICULTURE TEACHERS (1967 1980) Use AGRICULTURAL EDUCATION and VOCATIONAL EDUCATION TEACHERS
VOCATIONAL APTITUDE
VOCATIONAL ASPIRATION Use OCCUPATIONAL ASPIRATION
VOCATIONAL ASSESSMENT Use VOCATIONAL EVALUATION
VOCATIONAL AWARENESS Use CAREER AWARENESS
VOCATIONAL BUSINESS EDUCATION Use BUSINESS EDUCATION
VOCATIONAL CHANGE Use CAREER CHANGE
VOCATIONAL CHOICE Use CAREER CHOICE
VOCATIONAL COUNSELING (1966 1980) Use CAREER COUNSELING
VOCATIONAL DEVELOPMENT (1967 1978) Use CAREER DEVELOPMENT
VOCATIONAL DIRECTORS
VOCATIONAL EDUCATION
ADULT VOCATIONAL EDUCATION
VOCATIONAL EDUCATION DIRECTORS Use VOCATIONAL DIRECTORS
VOCATIONAL EDUCATION TEACHERS
VOCATIONAL ENGLISH (SECOND LANGUAGE)
VOCATIONAL EVALUATION
VOCATIONAL FOLLOWUP
VOCATIONAL GUIDANCE Use CAREER GUIDANCE
HEALTH OCCUPATIONS EDUCATION (VOCATIONAL) Use ALLIED HEALTH OCCUPATIONS EDUCATION and VOCATIONAL EDUCATION
VOCATIONAL HIGH SCHOOLS
VOCATIONAL INDUSTRIAL EDUCATION Use TRADE AND INDUSTRIAL EDUCATION
VOCATIONAL INTERESTS
VOCATIONAL MATURITY
VOCATIONAL NURSING Use PRACTICAL NURSING
VOCATIONAL PLACEMENT Use JOB PLACEMENT
VOCATIONAL REHABILITATION
VOCATIONAL RETRAINING (1966 1980) Use RETRAINING
VOCATIONAL SATISFACTION Use JOB SATISFACTION
VOCATIONAL SCHOOLS
AREA VOCATIONAL SCHOOLS (1966 1980) Use REGIONAL SCHOOLS and VOCATIONAL SCHOOLS
VOCATIONAL SKILLS Use JOB SKILLS
VOCATIONAL TALENTS Use VOCATIONAL APTITUDE
VOCATIONAL TESTS Use OCCUPATIONAL TESTS
VOCATIONAL TRAINING Use VOCATIONAL EDUCATION
VOCATIONAL TRAINING CENTERS
VOCATIONAL WORK EXPERIENCE Use COOPERATIVE EDUCATION
VOCATIONS Use OCCUPATIONS
VOCOIDS Use VOWELS
VOGUL
VOICE DISORDERS
EYE VOICE SPAN
VOLITION Use INDIVIDUAL POWER
INDIVIDUAL VOLITION Use INDIVIDUAL POWER
VOLLEYBALL
VOLUME (MATHEMATICS)
VOLUME (SOUND) Use NOISE (SOUND)
VOLUNTARY AGENCIES
VOLUNTARY ASSOCIATIONS Use VOLUNTARY AGENCIES
VOLUNTARY DESEGREGATION
VOLUNTARY INTEGRATION (1966 1980) Use VOLUNTARY DESEGREGATION
VOLUNTARY ORGANIZATIONS Use VOLUNTARY AGENCIES
VOLUNTEER TRAINING
VOLUNTEERS
STUDENT VOLUNTEERS
VOTER REGISTRATION
VOTING
VOTING RIGHTS
VOUCHER PLANS Use EDUCATIONAL VOUCHERS
EDUCATION VOUCHERS (1971 1980) Use EDUCATIONAL VOUCHERS
EDUCATIONAL VOUCHERS
VOWELS
SALARY WAGE DIFFERENTIALS
MINIMUM WAGE LAWS (1966 1974) Use MINIMUM WAGE LEGISLATION
MINIMUM WAGE LEGISLATION
MINIMUM WAGE
WAGE SALARY DIFFERENTIALS Use SALARY WAGE DIFFERENTIALS
WAGE STATEMENTS (1966 1980) Use PAYROLL RECORDS
WAGES
WAITERS AND WAITRESSES
WAITERS AND WAITRESSES
WALLEYES Use STRABISMUS
GLASS WALLS
UNIVERSITIES WITHOUT WALLS Use OPEN UNIVERSITIES
WINDOW WALLS Use GLASS WALLS
WAR
AMERICAN REVOLUTIONARY WAR Use REVOLUTIONARY WAR (UNITED STATES)
CIVIL WAR Use WAR
WAR CRIMES Use INTERNATIONAL CRIMES
INTERNATIONAL WAR Use WAR
CIVIL WAR (UNITED STATES)
REVOLUTIONARY WAR (UNITED STATES)
WAREHOUSES
ATOMIC WARFARE Use NUCLEAR WARFARE
CONVENTIONAL WARFARE Use WAR
GUERRILLA WARFARE Use WAR
NUCLEAR WARFARE
UNCONVENTIONAL WARFARE Use WAR
WASTE DISPOSAL
WASTE MANAGEMENT Use WASTE DISPOSAL
WASTE WATER
WASTE WATER TREATMENT Use WASTE WATER and WATER TREATMENT
WASTES
HAZARDOUS WASTES Use HAZARDOUS MATERIALS and WASTES
SOLID WASTES
WATCH REPAIRERS Use WATCHMAKERS
WATCHMAKERS
WATER

CHLORINATION (WATER) Use WATER TREATMENT
CLEAN WATER Use WATER QUALITY
DRINKING WATER
WATER POLLUTION
WATER POLLUTION CONTROL (1969 1980) Use WATER POLLUTION
WATER POLO
POTABLE WATER Use DRINKING WATER
WATER PURIFICATION Use WATER TREATMENT
WATER QUALITY
WATER RESOURCES
WATER SOFTENING Use WATER TREATMENT
WATER SPORTS Use AQUATIC SPORTS
WATER SUPPLY Use WATER RESOURCES
WATER TREATMENT
WASTE WATER TREATMENT Use WASTE WATER and WATER TREATMENT
WATER UTILITIES Use UTILITIES
WASTE WATER
WATER WORKS Use UTILITIES and WATER TREATMENT
WATERSKIING
SOUND WAVES Use ACOUSTICS
WEARINESS Use FATIGUE (BIOLOGY)
WEATHER
WEEDS
COMPRESSED WORK WEEK Use FLEXIBLE WORKING HOURS
FOUR DAY WORK WEEK Use FLEXIBLE WORKING HOURS
WEEKEND PROGRAMS
WEIGHT (1968 1980)
BIRTH WEIGHT
BODY WEIGHT
WEIGHT (MASS)
WEIGHT TRAINING Use WEIGHTLIFTING
WEIGHTED SCORES
WEIGHTLIFTING
WELDERS (1968 1981) Use WELDING
WELDING
ACETYLENE WELDING Use WELDING
ARC WELDING Use WELDING
GAS WELDING Use WELDING
WELFARE (1966 1980)
WELFARE AGENCIES
PUBLIC WELFARE ASSISTANCE Use WELFARE SERVICES
CHILD WELFARE
WELFARE PROBLEMS (1966 1980) Use WELFARE SERVICES
WELFARE RECIPIENTS
WELFARE SERVICES
MIGRANT WELFARE SERVICES
SOCIAL WELFARE (1966 1980)
STUDENT WELFARE
TEACHER WELFARE
WELL BEING
WELSH
WESTERN CIVILIZATION
NON WESTERN CIVILIZATION
WHEEL CHAIRS (1970 1981) Use WHEELCHAIRS
WHEELCHAIRS
WHITE BLACK RELATIONS Use RACIAL RELATIONS
WHITE COLLAR OCCUPATIONS
WHITE ETHNICS Use WHITES
BLACK AND WHITE FILMS Use FILMS
WHITE FLIGHT Use MIGRATION and WHITES
BLACK WHITE RELATIONS Use RACIAL RELATIONS
WHITE STUDENTS
WHITES
WHOLE NUMBERS
WHOLE PERSON APPROACH Use HOLISTIC APPROACH
WHOLE WORD READING APPROACH Use SIGHT METHOD
WHOLESALING
WHOLISTIC APPROACH Use HOLISTIC APPROACH
CITY WIDE COMMISSIONS (1966 1980) Use PLANNING COMMISSIONS and URBAN PLANNING
CITY WIDE PROGRAMS (1967 1980) Use URBAN PROGRAMS
WIDOWED
WILDLIFE
WILDLIFE MANAGEMENT
WILLS
WIND ENERGY
WIND (METEOROLOGY)
WINDOW WALLS Use GLASS WALLS
WINDOWLESS ROOMS
WINDOWS
WIRE COMMUNICATIONS Use TELECOMMUNICATIONS
WIRELESS COMMUNICATIONS Use TELECOMMUNICATIONS
TEST WISENESS
WITHDRAWAL (1966 1980) Use WITHDRAWAL (EDUCATION)
COURSE WITHDRAWAL Use WITHDRAWAL (EDUCATION)
DRUG WITHDRAWAL Use DRUG REHABILITATION
WITHDRAWAL (DRUGS) Use DRUG REHABILITATION
WITHDRAWAL (EDUCATION)
WITHDRAWAL (PSYCHOLOGY)
WITHDRAWAL TENDENCIES (PSYCHOLOGY) (1966 1980) Use WITHDRAWAL (PSYCHOLOGY)
SCHOOLS WITHIN A SCHOOL PLAN Use HOUSE PLAN
UNIVERSITIES WITHOUT WALLS Use OPEN UNIVERSITIES
WIVES Use SPOUSES
WOLOF
WOMEN Use FEMALES
ABUSED WOMEN Use BATTERED WOMEN
BATTERED WOMEN
DEANS OF WOMEN Use DEANS OF STUDENTS
EMPLOYED WOMEN
ENLISTED WOMEN Use ENLISTED PERSONNEL
WOMEN FACULTY
WOMEN PROFESSORS (1966 1980) Use WOMEN FACULTY

WOMEN TEACHERS (1967 1980) Use WOMEN FACULTY
WOMEN WORKERS Use EMPLOYED WOMEN
WORKING WOMEN (1968 1980) Use EMPLOYED WOMEN
WOMENS ATHLETICS
WOMENS EDUCATION
WOMENS LIBERATION Use FEMINISM
WOMENS RIGHTS Use FEMINISM
WOMENS STUDIES
WOOD FINISHING Use FINISHING
WOODWORKING
WORD ASSOCIATIONS (READING) Use ASSOCIATIVE LEARNING
WORD BORROWING Use LINGUISTIC BORROWING
WORD FREQUENCY
KEY WORD IN CONTEXT Use PERMUTED INDEXES
TITLE WORD INDEXES Use PERMUTED INDEXES
WORD LISTS
BASIC WORD LISTS Use WORD LISTS
WORD MEANING Use SEMANTICS
WORD METHOD (READING) Use SIGHT METHOD
WORD PROBLEMS (MATHEMATICS)
WORD PROCESSING
WHOLE WORD READING APPROACH Use SIGHT METHOD
WORD RECOGNITION
WORD STUDY SKILLS
FUNCTION WORDS
LOAN WORDS Use LINGUISTIC BORROWING
WORK Use EMPLOYMENT
WORK ADJUSTMENT Use VOCATIONAL ADJUSTMENT
WORK AND EDUCATION Use EDUCATION WORK RELATIONSHIP
WORK ATTITUDES
EMPLOYEE WORK ATTITUDES Use EMPLOYEE ATTITUDES and WORK ATTITUDES
WORK CHANGE Use CAREER CHANGE
EDUCATION AND WORK Use EDUCATION WORK RELATIONSHIP
WORK EDUCATION PROGRAMS Use WORK STUDY PROGRAMS
WORK EDUCATION RELATIONSHIP Use EDUCATION WORK RELATIONSHIP
WORK ENRICHMENT Use JOB ENRICHMENT
WORK ENVIRONMENT
ORGANIZATIONAL PSYCHOLOGY (WORK ENVIRONMENT) Use INDUSTRIAL PSYCHOLOGY
WORK EVALUATION (PERFORMANCE) Use VOCATIONAL EVALUATION
WORK EXPERIENCE
WORK EXPERIENCE PROGRAMS
VOCATIONAL WORK EXPERIENCE Use COOPERATIVE EDUCATION
WORK FORCE Use LABOR FORCE
HOURS OF WORK Use WORKING HOURS
WORK LIFE EXPECTANCY
STRUCTURAL WORK OCCUPATIONS Use BUILDING TRADES
PART TIME WORK Use PART TIME EMPLOYMENT
WORK PERFORMANCE EVALUATION Use VOCATIONAL EVALUATION
EDUCATION WORK RELATIONSHIP
WORK RELEASE Use RELEASED TIME
WORK SAMPLE TESTS
WORK SAMPLES Use WORK SAMPLE TESTS
WORK SATISFACTION Use JOB SATISFACTION
WORK SHARING Use JOB SHARING
SHEET METAL WORK
WORK SIMPLIFICATION (1968 1980) Use JOB SIMPLIFICATION
SOCIAL WORK
STUDENT PERSONNEL WORK (1967 1980) Use STUDENT PERSONNEL SERVICES
WORK STUDY Use WORK STUDY PROGRAMS
WORK STUDY PROGRAMS
COLLEGE WORK STUDY PROGRAMS Use WORK STUDY PROGRAMS
SCHOOL TO WORK TRANSITION Use EDUCATION WORK RELATIONSHIP
COMPRESSED WORK WEEK Use FLEXIBLE WORKING HOURS
FOUR DAY WORK WEEK Use FLEXIBLE WORKING HOURS
WORKBOOKS
WORKDAY Use WORKING HOURS
WORKER DAYS
WORKER EVALUATION Use PERSONNEL EVALUATION
MIGRANT WORKER PROJECTS (1966 1980) Use MIGRANT PROGRAMS and MIGRANT WORKERS
AGRICULTURAL WORKERS Use AGRICULTURAL LABORERS
AGRICULTURAL MIGRANT WORKERS Use MIGRANT WORKERS
AUXILIARY WORKERS Use AUXILIARY LABORERS
BEGINNING WORKERS Use ENTRY WORKERS
CHILD CARE WORKERS (1967 1980) Use CHILD CAREGIVERS
CHURCH WORKERS
CLERICAL WORKERS
COMMUNITY WORKERS Use COMMUNITY ORGANIZATIONS
COMMUNITY HEALTH WORKERS Use COMMUNITY HEALTH SERVICES and HEALTH PERSONNEL
WORKERS COMPENSATION
CRAFT WORKERS
DISLOCATED WORKERS
DISPLACED WORKERS Use DISLOCATED WORKERS
WORKERS EDUCATION Use LABOR EDUCATION
ENTRY WORKERS
FOOD SERVICE WORKERS (1968 1981) Use FOOD SERVICE
FOREIGN WORKERS
GREENHOUSE WORKERS Use NURSERY WORKERS (HORTICULTURE)
HEALTH WORKERS Use HEALTH PERSONNEL
HEALTH SERVICE WORKERS Use HEALTH PERSONNEL
NURSERY WORKERS (HORTICULTURE)
YARD WORKERS (HORTICULTURE) Use GROUNDS KEEPERS
HOUSEHOLD WORKERS
JOURNEY WORKERS Use SKILLED WORKERS
MACHINERY MAINTENANCE WORKERS Use MACHINE REPAIRERS
MIGRANT WORKERS
INTERSTATE WORKERS (1966 1980) (MIGRANTS) Use MIGRANT WORKERS
MIGRATORY AGRICULTURAL WORKERS Use MIGRANT WORKERS
PARISH WORKERS Use CHURCH WORKERS
PUPIL PERSONNEL WORKERS
REENTRY WORKERS
SALES WORKERS

SCHOOL SOCIAL WORKERS
SEMISKILLED WORKERS
SERVICE WORKERS
SHEET METAL WORKERS (1967 1981) Use SHEET METAL WORK
SKILLED WORKERS
SOCIAL WORKERS
STUDENT AFFAIRS WORKERS Use STUDENT PERSONNEL WORKERS
STUDENT PERSONNEL WORKERS
UNDOCUMENTED WORKERS Use FOREIGN WORKERS and UNDOCUMENTED IMMIGRANTS
UNSKILLED WORKERS
WOMEN WORKERS Use EMPLOYED WOMEN
WORKING ABROAD Use OVERSEAS EMPLOYMENT
WORKING CLASS
WORKING CONDITIONS Use WORK ENVIRONMENT
WORKING HOURS
FLEXIBLE WORKING HOURS
QUALITY OF WORKING LIFE
METAL WORKING
METAL WORKING OCCUPATIONS (1968 1980) Use METAL WORKING
WORKING OVERSEAS Use OVERSEAS EMPLOYMENT
WORKING PARENTS (1966 1980) Use EMPLOYED PARENTS
WORKING WOMEN (1968 1980) Use EMPLOYED WOMEN
FACULTY WORKLOAD
WORKMANS COMPENSATION (1966 1980) Use WORKERS COMPENSATION
WATER WORKS Use UTILITIES and WATER TREATMENT
WORKSHEETS
WORKSHOPS
DRAMA WORKSHOPS
PARENT WORKSHOPS
PRESCHOOL WORKSHOPS (1966 1980) Use PRESCHOOL EDUCATION and WORKSHOPS
SHELTERED WORKSHOPS
SUMMER WORKSHOPS (1966 1980) Use SUMMER PROGRAMS and WORKSHOPS
TEACHER WORKSHOPS
WORKWEEK Use WORKING HOURS
WORLD AFFAIRS
THIRD WORLD COUNTRIES Use DEVELOPING NATIONS
WORLD GEOGRAPHY
WORLD HISTORY
WORLD LITERATURE
WORLD PEACE Use PEACE
WORLD PROBLEMS
WORLDMINDEDNESS Use GLOBAL APPROACH
WORLDWIDE APPROACH Use GLOBAL APPROACH
COMPARABLE WORTH
WRESTLING
LEFT HANDED WRITER
WRITERS Use AUTHORS
SIGN WRITERS Use SIGN PAINTERS
WRITING (1966 1980) Use WRITING (COMPOSITION)
WRITING APPREHENSION
WRITING CENTERS Use WRITING LABORATORIES
WRITING (COMPOSITION)
CONTENT AREA WRITING
CREATIVE WRITING
CURSIVE WRITING
DESCRIPTIVE WRITING
WRITING DIFFICULTIES
DIRECTION WRITING (1966 1980)
WRITING EVALUATION
WRITING EXERCISES
EXPOSITORY WRITING
WRITING FOR PUBLICATION
MANUSCRIPT WRITING (HANDLETTERING)
WRITING IMPROVEMENT
WRITING INSTRUCTION
WRITING LABORATORIES
LOCAL COLOR WRITING
STUDENT WRITING MODELS
NEWS WRITING
WRITING PROCESSES
PROPOSAL WRITING
WRITING READINESS
READING WRITING RELATIONSHIP
REPORT WRITING Use TECHNICAL WRITING
WRITING RESEARCH
WRITING SKILLS
WRITING SYSTEMS Use WRITTEN LANGUAGE
TECHNICAL WRITING
TEXTBOOK WRITING Use TEXTBOOK PREPARATION
THEME WRITING Use WRITING (COMPOSITION)
COHESION (WRITTEN COMPOSITION)
REVISION (WRITTEN COMPOSITION)
WRITTEN LANGUAGE
INDUSTRIAL X RAY OPERATORS Use RADIOGRAPHERS
X RAY TECHNOLOGISTS Use RADIOLOGIC TECHNOLOGISTS
X RAYS (MEDICINE) Use RADIOLOGY
XENOPHOBIA Use STRANGER REACTIONS
XEROGRAPHY Use REPROGRAPHY
KIKONGO YA LETA Use KITUBA
YAKUT
YARD WORKERS (HORTICULTURE) Use GROUNDS KEEPERS
THREE YEAR BACHELORS DEGREES Use ACCELERATION (EDUCATION) and BACHELORS DEGREES
TWO YEAR COLLEGE DEGREES Use ASSOCIATE DEGREES
FRESHMEN (1967 1980) (FIRST YEAR COLLEGE STUDENTS) Use COLLEGE FRESHMEN
TWO YEAR COLLEGE STUDENTS
TWO YEAR COLLEGES
EXTENDED SCHOOL YEAR
GRADE A YEAR INTEGRATION (1966 1980) Use SCHOOL DESEGREGATION
YEAR ROUND SCHOOLS
FIRST YEAR TEACHERS Use BEGINNING TEACHERS
SENIORS (1966 1980) (LAST YEAR UNDERGRADUATES) Use COLLEGE SENIORS

YEARBOOKS
YIDDISH
YORUBA
YOUNG ADULTS
YOUNG CHILDREN
YOUNG FARMER EDUCATION
YOUTH
AFFLUENT YOUTH
YOUTH AGENCIES
BLACK YOUTH
YOUTH CLUBS
DISADVANTAGED YOUTH
YOUTH EMPLOYMENT
FARM YOUTH Use RURAL YOUTH
GIFTED YOUTH Use GIFTED
YOUTH LEADERS
MIGRANT YOUTH
YOUTH MOBILIZATION Use YOUTH EMPLOYMENT
NEGRO YOUTH (1966 1977) Use BLACK YOUTH
YOUTH OPPORTUNITIES
OUT OF SCHOOL YOUTH
YOUTH PROBLEMS
YOUTH PROGRAMS
RURAL YOUTH
SUBURBAN YOUTH
URBAN YOUTH
YUCATEC
YURAK
ZONING
COMMUNITY ZONING
SCHOOL ZONING
SPECIAL ZONING
ZOOLOGY
ZOOS

TWO-WAY HIERARCHICAL TERM DISPLAY

The Hierarchical Display depicts families of Descriptors (generic trees) related by the taxonomic concept of "class membership." Two-way visibility is provided for the broader-narrower relationships of every *Thesaurus* Descriptor. Generic trees are carried to their farthest extreme in both directions. Broader terms (i.e., BTs) are identified by preceding colons and appear *above* each file point (main entry). Narrower terms (i.e., NTs) are identified by preceding periods and are listed *below* each file point. Multiple colons or periods indicate successively broader or narrower levels of terms. Descriptors having neither BTs nor NTs in the display are "hierarchical isolates." The display is filed letter-by-letter, ignoring spaces between words.

ABBREVIATIONS

ABILITY
. ACADEMIC ABILITY
. COGNITIVE ABILITY
. COMPETENCE
. . INTERPERSONAL COMPETENCE
. . MINIMUM COMPETENCIES
. LANGUAGE PROFICIENCY
. . LANGUAGE FLUENCY
. . THRESHOLD LEVEL (LANGUAGES)
. LEADERSHIP
. . BLACK LEADERSHIP
. . INFORMAL LEADERSHIP
. . INSTRUCTIONAL LEADERSHIP
. . STUDENT LEADERSHIP
. NONVERBAL ABILITY
. SKILLS
. . AGRICULTURAL SKILLS
. . BASIC SKILLS
. . . ALPHABETIZING SKILLS
. . BUSINESS SKILLS
. . . BOOKKEEPING
. . . KEYBOARDING (DATA ENTRY)
. . . RECORDKEEPING
. . . TYPEWRITING
. . COMMUNICATION SKILLS
. . . COMMUNICATIVE COMPETENCE (LANGUAGES)
. . . . THRESHOLD LEVEL (LANGUAGES)
. . DAILY LIVING SKILLS
. . . SELF CARE SKILLS
. . DECISION MAKING SKILLS
. . HOME ECONOMICS SKILLS
. . HOMEMAKING SKILLS
. . INTERPRETIVE SKILLS
. . JOB SKILLS
. . LANGUAGE SKILLS
. . . AUDIOLINGUAL SKILLS
. . . . LISTENING SKILLS
. . . . SPEECH SKILLS
. . . COMMUNICATIVE COMPETENCE (LANGUAGES)
. . . . THRESHOLD LEVEL (LANGUAGES)
. . . READING SKILLS
. . . . READING COMPREHENSION
. . . . READING RATE
. . . VOCABULARY SKILLS
. . . WRITING SKILLS
. . LIBRARY SKILLS
. . LOCATIONAL SKILLS (SOCIAL STUDIES)
. . MAP SKILLS
. . MATHEMATICS SKILLS
. . MECHANICAL SKILLS
. . MINIMUM COMPETENCIES
. . PARENTING SKILLS
. . PSYCHOMOTOR SKILLS
. . . MARKSMANSHIP
. . . OBJECT MANIPULATION
. . . PERCEPTUAL MOTOR COORDINATION
. . . . EYE HAND COORDINATION
. . . . EYE VOICE SPAN
. . RESEARCH SKILLS
. . SALESMANSHIP
. . STUDY SKILLS
. . . WORD STUDY SKILLS
. . TEACHING SKILLS
. . VISUAL LITERACY
. SPATIAL ABILITY
. VERBAL ABILITY
. . READING ABILITY
. . . READING SKILLS
. . . . READING COMPREHENSION
. . . . READING RATE

: : : : ORGANIZATION
: : : CLASSIFICATION
: : GROUPING (INSTRUCTIONAL PURPOSES)
: HOMOGENEOUS GROUPING
ABILITY GROUPING

: IDENTIFICATION
ABILITY IDENTIFICATION

ABORTIONS

: : LITERACY
: : LANGUAGE ARTS
: WRITING (COMPOSITION)
: : : : SERVICES
: : : INFORMATION SERVICES
: : INFORMATION PROCESSING
: DOCUMENTATION
ABSTRACTING

: COGNITIVE PROCESSES
ABSTRACT REASONING
. GENERALIZATION
. . STIMULUS GENERALIZATION

: : PUBLICATIONS
: REFERENCE MATERIALS
ABSTRACTS

: ABILITY
ACADEMIC ABILITY

: ACHIEVEMENT
ACADEMIC ACHIEVEMENT
. EDUCATIONAL ATTAINMENT
. STUDENT PROMOTION

: : : GUIDANCE
: : COUNSELING
: EDUCATIONAL COUNSELING
ACADEMIC ADVISING

: : : GROUPS
: : EXCEPTIONAL PERSONS
: GIFTED
ACADEMICALLY GIFTED

ACADEMICALLY HANDICAPPED (1966 1980)

: APTITUDE
ACADEMIC APTITUDE

: ASPIRATION
ACADEMIC ASPIRATION

: : : : : GROUPS
: : : : PERSONNEL
: : : SCHOOL PERSONNEL
: : : : : GROUPS
: : : : PERSONNEL
: : : PROFESSIONAL PERSONNEL
: : FACULTY
: : : : GROUPS
: : : PERSONNEL
: : ADMINISTRATORS
: DEANS
ACADEMIC DEANS

: EDUCATION
ACADEMIC EDUCATION

: : : BEHAVIOR
: : PERFORMANCE
: FAILURE
ACADEMIC FAILURE
. READING FAILURE

ACADEMIC FREEDOM

: : INSTITUTIONS
: : INFORMATION SOURCES
: LIBRARIES
ACADEMIC LIBRARIES
. COLLEGE LIBRARIES

: : BEHAVIOR
: PERSISTENCE
ACADEMIC PERSISTENCE

: PROBATIONARY PERIOD
ACADEMIC PROBATION

: : STATUS
: EMPLOYMENT LEVEL
ACADEMIC RANK (PROFESSIONAL)

: : RECORDS (FORMS)
: STUDENT RECORDS
ACADEMIC RECORDS

: STANDARDS
ACADEMIC STANDARDS
. GRADUATION REQUIREMENTS
. . DEGREE REQUIREMENTS

: FLEXIBLE PROGRESSION
ACCELERATION (EDUCATION)

: : SCIENTIFIC CONCEPTS
: MOTION
ACCELERATION (PHYSICS)

ACCESSIBILITY (FOR DISABLED)

: : OPPORTUNITIES
: EDUCATIONAL OPPORTUNITIES
ACCESS TO EDUCATION

ACCESS TO INFORMATION
. FREEDOM OF INFORMATION

: PREVENTION
ACCIDENT PREVENTION

ACCIDENTS
. SCHOOL ACCIDENTS
. TRAFFIC ACCIDENTS

: RESPONSIBILITY
ACCOUNTABILITY

: : : GROUPS
: : PERSONNEL
: PROFESSIONAL PERSONNEL
ACCOUNTANTS
. CERTIFIED PUBLIC ACCOUNTANTS

: TECHNOLOGY
ACCOUNTING
. PROPERTY ACCOUNTING
. SCHOOL ACCOUNTING

: CERTIFICATION
ACCREDITATION (INSTITUTIONS)

: : : GROUPS
: : ORGANIZATIONS (GROUPS)
: AGENCIES
ACCREDITING AGENCIES

ACCULTURATION

ACHIEVEMENT
. ACADEMIC ACHIEVEMENT
. . EDUCATIONAL ATTAINMENT
. . STUDENT PROMOTION
. BLACK ACHIEVEMENT
. GRADUATION
. HIGH ACHIEVEMENT
. KNOWLEDGE LEVEL
. LOW ACHIEVEMENT
. MATHEMATICS ACHIEVEMENT
. OVERACHIEVEMENT
. READING ACHIEVEMENT
. SCHOLARSHIP
. UNDERACHIEVEMENT

: IMPROVEMENT
ACHIEVEMENT GAINS

: : : NEEDS
: : INDIVIDUAL NEEDS
: PSYCHOLOGICAL NEEDS
: MOTIVATION
ACHIEVEMENT NEED

: MEASUREMENT
ACHIEVEMENT RATING
. GRADING
. . CREDIT NO CREDIT GRADING
. . PASS FAIL GRADING

: : MEASURES (INDIVIDUALS)
: TESTS
ACHIEVEMENT TESTS
. EQUIVALENCY TESTS
. MASTERY TESTS
. NATIONAL COMPETENCY TESTS

: : ENVIRONMENT
: PHYSICAL ENVIRONMENT
ACOUSTICAL ENVIRONMENT
. NOISE (SOUND)

: STRUCTURAL ELEMENTS (CONSTRUCTION)
ACOUSTIC INSULATION

: : : LINGUISTICS
: : PHONOLOGY
: PHONETICS
ACOUSTIC PHONETICS

: : LIBERAL ARTS
: SCIENCES
ACOUSTICS
. PSYCHOACOUSTICS

: : : : LIBERAL ARTS
: : : HUMANITIES
: : FINE ARTS
: THEATER ARTS
ACTING

: RESEARCH
ACTION RESEARCH

: : BEHAVIOR
: SOCIAL BEHAVIOR
ACTIVISM

ACTIVITIES
. ART ACTIVITIES
. CREATIVE ACTIVITIES
. . BRAINSTORMING
. . CREATIVE ART
. . . CREATIVE DRAMATICS
. . CREATIVE EXPRESSION
. . CREATIVE WRITING
. CULTURAL ACTIVITIES
. ENRICHMENT ACTIVITIES
. GAMES
. . CHILDRENS GAMES
. . EDUCATIONAL GAMES
. . . READING GAMES
. . MANAGEMENT GAMES
. . PUZZLES
. GROUP ACTIVITIES
. HEALTH ACTIVITIES
. INDIVIDUAL ACTIVITIES
. INTEGRATED ACTIVITIES
. . INTEGRATED CURRICULUM
. LEARNING ACTIVITIES
. . STUDY
. . . HOME STUDY
. . . . HOMEWORK
. . . INDEPENDENT STUDY
. LOBBYING
. MUSIC ACTIVITIES
. . CONCERTS
. . SINGING
. OUTDOOR ACTIVITIES
. PHYSICAL ACTIVITIES
. . ATHLETICS
. . . AQUATIC SPORTS

ACTIVITIES
(CONTINUED)

.... DIVING
.... SAILING
.... SURFING
.... SWIMMING
.... WATER POLO
.... WATERSKIING
... ARCHERY
... BOWLING
... COLLEGE ATHLETICS
... EXTRAMURAL ATHLETICS
... FENCING (SPORT)
... GOLF
... GYMNASTICS
.... TUMBLING
... HANDBALL
... ICE SKATING
... INTRAMURAL ATHLETICS
... LIFETIME SPORTS
... ORIENTEERING
... RACQUET SPORTS
.... BADMINTON
.... RACQUETBALL
.... SQUASH (GAME)
.... TENNIS
... ROLLER SKATING
... SKIING
... TABLE TENNIS
... TEAM SPORTS
.... BASEBALL
.... BASKETBALL
.... FIELD HOCKEY
.... FOOTBALL
.... ICE HOCKEY
.... LACROSSE
.... SOCCER
.... SOFTBALL
.... TEAM HANDBALL
.... VOLLEYBALL
.... WATER POLO
... TRACK AND FIELD
... WEIGHTLIFTING
... WOMENS ATHLETICS
... WRESTLING
.. BICYCLING
.. DANCE
.. EXERCISE
... AEROBICS
... CALISTHENICS
.. HORSEBACK RIDING
.. LIFTING
... WEIGHTLIFTING
.. RUNNING
... JOGGING
.. UNDERWATER DIVING
. PLAY
.. PRETEND PLAY
. RECREATIONAL ACTIVITIES
.. CAMPING
.. HOBBIES
.. PLAYGROUND ACTIVITIES
.. RECREATIONAL READING
. REVIEW (REEXAMINATION)
. SCHOOL ACTIVITIES
.. CLASS ACTIVITIES
.. EXTRACURRICULAR
ACTIVITIES
.. STUDENT PROJECTS
. SCIENCE ACTIVITIES
.. SCIENCE FAIRS
.. SCIENCE PROJECTS
. TELEVISION VIEWING
. TRAVEL

::: CURRICULUM
:: COURSES
: UNITS OF STUDY
ACTIVITY UNITS

:: THEORIES
: BEHAVIOR THEORIES
ADAPTATION LEVEL THEORY

:: EDUCATION
: SPECIAL EDUCATION
:: EDUCATION
: PHYSICAL EDUCATION
ADAPTED PHYSICAL EDUCATION

:: BEHAVIOR
: ADJUSTMENT (TO
ENVIRONMENT)
ADAPTIVE BEHAVIOR (OF
DISABLED)

::: METHODS
:: MEASUREMENT TECHNIQUES
: TESTING
ADAPTIVE TESTING

::: LIBERAL ARTS
:: MATHEMATICS
: ARITHMETIC
ADDITION

:: RESOURCES
: SUPPLIES
ADHESIVES

::::: LINGUISTICS
:::: DESCRIPTIVE
LINGUISTICS
::: GRAMMAR
:: SYNTAX
: FORM CLASSES (LANGUAGES)
ADJECTIVES

:::: GROUPS
::: PERSONNEL
:: SCHOOL PERSONNEL
:::: GROUPS
::: PERSONNEL
:: PROFESSIONAL PERSONNEL
: FACULTY
ADJUNCT FACULTY

: BEHAVIOR
ADJUSTMENT (TO ENVIRONMENT)
. ADAPTIVE BEHAVIOR (OF
DISABLED)
. COPING
. EMOTIONAL ADJUSTMENT
. SOCIAL ADJUSTMENT
. STUDENT ADJUSTMENT
. VOCATIONAL ADJUSTMENT

:::: GROUPS
::: PERSONNEL
:: GUIDANCE PERSONNEL
: COUNSELORS
ADJUSTMENT COUNSELORS

: GOVERNANCE
ADMINISTRATION
. BUILDING OPERATION
. BUSINESS ADMINISTRATION
. CONSTRUCTION MANAGEMENT
. EDUCATIONAL
ADMINISTRATION
.. SCHOOL ADMINISTRATION
... COLLEGE ADMINISTRATION
... SCHOOL BASED MANAGEMENT
. ENERGY MANAGEMENT
. FARM MANAGEMENT
. HOME MANAGEMENT
. INSTITUTIONAL
ADMINISTRATION
.. LIBRARY ADMINISTRATION
.. SCHOOL ADMINISTRATION
... COLLEGE ADMINISTRATION
... SCHOOL BASED MANAGEMENT
. MANAGEMENT BY OBJECTIVES
. MIDDLE MANAGEMENT
. MONEY MANAGEMENT
. OFFICE MANAGEMENT
. PERSONNEL MANAGEMENT
. PROGRAM ADMINISTRATION
. PUBLIC ADMINISTRATION
. RESEARCH ADMINISTRATION
. SUPERVISION
.. PRACTICUM SUPERVISION
.. PROCTORING
.. SCHOOL SUPERVISION
.. SCIENCE SUPERVISION
.. TEACHER SUPERVISION
. TIME MANAGEMENT

ADMINISTRATIVE AGENCIES
(1966 1980)

: CHANGE
ADMINISTRATIVE CHANGE

: ORGANIZATION
ADMINISTRATIVE ORGANIZATION
. CENTRALIZATION
. DECENTRALIZATION
. DEPARTMENTS
.. ENGLISH DEPARTMENTS
.. SCIENCE DEPARTMENTS
.. STATE DEPARTMENTS OF
EDUCATION
. MANAGEMENT TEAMS
. PARTICIPATIVE DECISION
MAKING

: POLICY
ADMINISTRATIVE POLICY
. BOARD OF EDUCATION POLICY

: STANDARDS
ADMINISTRATIVE PRINCIPLES

: PROBLEMS
ADMINISTRATIVE PROBLEMS

: ATTITUDES
ADMINISTRATOR ATTITUDES

ADMINISTRATOR
CHARACTERISTICS

:: EDUCATION
: PROFESSIONAL EDUCATION
ADMINISTRATOR EDUCATION

:: EVALUATION
: PERSONNEL EVALUATION
ADMINISTRATOR EVALUATION

::: PUBLICATIONS
:: REFERENCE MATERIALS
: GUIDES
ADMINISTRATOR GUIDES

:: STANDARDS
: QUALIFICATIONS
ADMINISTRATOR QUALIFICATIONS

: RESPONSIBILITY
ADMINISTRATOR RESPONSIBILITY

ADMINISTRATOR ROLE

:: GROUPS
: PERSONNEL
ADMINISTRATORS
. ADMISSIONS OFFICERS
. ASSISTANT PRINCIPALS
. COORDINATORS
.. AUDIOVISUAL COORDINATORS
.. INSTRUCTOR COORDINATORS
. DEANS
.. ACADEMIC DEANS
.. DEANS OF STUDENTS
. DEPARTMENT HEADS
. MEDICAL RECORD
ADMINISTRATORS
. PERSONNEL DIRECTORS
. PRESIDENTS
.. COLLEGE PRESIDENTS
.. PRESIDENTS OF THE UNITED
STATES
. PRINCIPALS
. REGISTRARS (SCHOOL)
. RESEARCH DIRECTORS
. SCHOOL BUSINESS OFFICIALS
. STUDENT FINANCIAL AID
OFFICERS
. SUPERINTENDENTS
. SUPERVISORS
.. CREW LEADERS
.. STATE SUPERVISORS
.. STUDENT TEACHER
SUPERVISORS
. TRUSTEES
. VOCATIONAL DIRECTORS

:: SELECTION
: PERSONNEL SELECTION
ADMINISTRATOR SELECTION

ADMISSION (SCHOOL)
. COLLEGE ADMISSION
. EARLY ADMISSION
. OPEN ENROLLMENT
. SELECTIVE ADMISSION

:: STANDARDS
: CRITERIA
ADMISSION CRITERIA

::: GUIDANCE
:: COUNSELING
: EDUCATIONAL COUNSELING
ADMISSIONS COUNSELING

::: GROUPS
:: PERSONNEL
: SCHOOL PERSONNEL
::: GROUPS
:: PERSONNEL
: ADMINISTRATORS
ADMISSIONS OFFICERS

:: DEVELOPMENT
: INDIVIDUAL DEVELOPMENT
ADOLESCENT DEVELOPMENT

::: LIBERAL ARTS
:: HUMANITIES
: LITERATURE
ADOLESCENT LITERATURE

:: GROUPS
: AGE GROUPS
ADOLESCENTS

::: GROUPS
:: AGE GROUPS
: CHILDREN
ADOPTED CHILDREN

ADOPTION

ADOPTION (IDEAS)

::: EDUCATION
:: ELEMENTARY SECONDARY
EDUCATION
: ELEMENTARY EDUCATION
:: EDUCATION
: ADULT EDUCATION
ADULT BASIC EDUCATION

:: GUIDANCE
: COUNSELING
ADULT COUNSELING

::: SERVICES
:: HUMAN SERVICES
: SOCIAL SERVICES
ADULT DAY CARE

:: DEVELOPMENT
: INDIVIDUAL DEVELOPMENT
ADULT DEVELOPMENT

:: GROUPS
: DROPOUTS
::: GROUPS
:: AGE GROUPS
: ADULTS
ADULT DROPOUTS

: EDUCATION
ADULT EDUCATION
. ADULT BASIC EDUCATION
. ADULT VOCATIONAL EDUCATION
.. ADULT FARMER EDUCATION
.. YOUNG FARMER EDUCATION
. CONTINUING EDUCATION
.. PROFESSIONAL CONTINUING EDUCATION
. LABOR EDUCATION
. MIGRANT ADULT EDUCATION
. PARENT EDUCATION
. PRERETIREMENT EDUCATION
. PUBLIC SCHOOL ADULT EDUCATION
. VETERANS EDUCATION

:::: GROUPS
::: PERSONNEL
:: PROFESSIONAL PERSONNEL
: TEACHERS
ADULT EDUCATORS

:: EDUCATION
: AGRICULTURAL EDUCATION
::: EDUCATION
:: VOCATIONAL EDUCATION
::: EDUCATION
:: ADULT EDUCATION
: ADULT VOCATIONAL EDUCATION
ADULT FARMER EDUCATION

::: SERVICES
:: HUMAN SERVICES
: SOCIAL SERVICES
ADULT FOSTER CARE

: LEARNING
ADULT LEARNING

: LITERACY
ADULT LITERACY

: PROGRAMS
ADULT PROGRAMS
. ADULT READING PROGRAMS
. HIGH SCHOOL EQUIVALENCY PROGRAMS

:: PROGRAMS
: READING PROGRAMS
:: PROGRAMS
: ADULT PROGRAMS
ADULT READING PROGRAMS

:: GROUPS
: AGE GROUPS
ADULTS
. ADULT DROPOUTS
. ADULT STUDENTS
. MIDDLE AGED ADULTS
. OLDER ADULTS
. YOUNG ADULTS

:: GROUPS
: STUDENTS
::: GROUPS
:: AGE GROUPS
: ADULTS
ADULT STUDENTS

:: EDUCATION
: VOCATIONAL EDUCATION
:: EDUCATION
: ADULT EDUCATION
ADULT VOCATIONAL EDUCATION
. ADULT FARMER EDUCATION
. YOUNG FARMER EDUCATION

:: CURRICULUM
: COURSES
ADVANCED COURSES

: PLACEMENT
ADVANCED PLACEMENT

: PROGRAMS
ADVANCED PLACEMENT PROGRAMS

ADVANCED PROGRAMS (1966 1980)

:: GROUPS
: STUDENTS
ADVANCED STUDENTS

:: EDUCATIONAL MEDIA
: INSTRUCTIONAL MATERIALS
ADVANCE ORGANIZERS

: GROUPS
ADVANTAGED

: DISABILITIES
ADVENTITIOUS IMPAIRMENTS

:: EDUCATION
: OUTDOOR EDUCATION
ADVENTURE EDUCATION

::::: LINGUISTICS
:::: DESCRIPTIVE LINGUISTICS
::: GRAMMAR
:: SYNTAX
: FORM CLASSES (LANGUAGES)
ADVERBS

:::: SERVICES
::: INFORMATION SERVICES
:: INFORMATION DISSEMINATION
:: COMMUNICATION (THOUGHT TRANSFER)
: PUBLICITY
ADVERTISING
. TELEVISION COMMERCIALS

: COMMITTEES
ADVISORY COMMITTEES

ADVOCACY
. CHILD ADVOCACY

::: ACTIVITIES
:: PHYSICAL ACTIVITIES
: EXERCISE
AEROBICS

: EDUCATION
AEROSPACE EDUCATION

::: BUSINESS
:: INDUSTRY
: MANUFACTURING INDUSTRY
AEROSPACE INDUSTRY

: TECHNOLOGY
AEROSPACE TECHNOLOGY
. AVIATION TECHNOLOGY
.. AVIATION MECHANICS

: EDUCATION
AESTHETIC EDUCATION
. ART APPRECIATION
. FILM STUDY
. MUSIC APPRECIATION

: VALUES
AESTHETIC VALUES

::: NEEDS
:: INDIVIDUAL NEEDS
: PSYCHOLOGICAL NEEDS
AFFECTION

: BEHAVIOR
AFFECTIVE BEHAVIOR

: MEASURES (INDIVIDUALS)
AFFECTIVE MEASURES

:: OBJECTIVES
: BEHAVIORAL OBJECTIVES
AFFECTIVE OBJECTIVES

:: INSTITUTIONS
: SCHOOLS
AFFILIATED SCHOOLS

::: NEEDS
:: INDIVIDUAL NEEDS
: PSYCHOLOGICAL NEEDS
AFFILIATION NEED
. PEER ACCEPTANCE

AFFIRMATIVE ACTION

:: GROUPS
: YOUTH
AFFLUENT YOUTH

: CULTURE
AFRICAN CULTURE

:::: LIBERAL ARTS
::: SCIENCES
:: SOCIAL SCIENCES
::: LIBERAL ARTS
:: HUMANITIES
: HISTORY
AFRICAN HISTORY

: LANGUAGES
AFRICAN LANGUAGES
. AKAN
. BANTU LANGUAGES
.. BEMBA
.. CHINYANJA
.. GANDA
.. KIRUNDI
.. KITUBA
.. LINGALA
.. SHONA
.. SISWATI
.. SWAHILI
. BASAA
. BINI
. DYULA
. EWE
. FULANI
. GA
. GBAYA
. IBO
. IGBO
. LUO
. MANDINGO
. MENDE
. MOSSI
. NEMBE
. SANGO
. SARA
. SUSU
. WOLOF
. YORUBA

::: LIBERAL ARTS
:: HUMANITIES
: LITERATURE
AFRICAN LITERATURE

:: LANGUAGES
: INDO EUROPEAN LANGUAGES
AFRIKAANS

: LANGUAGES
AFRO ASIATIC LANGUAGES
. BERBER LANGUAGES
.. KABYLE
.. RIFF
. CHAD LANGUAGES
.. HAUSA
. SEMITIC LANGUAGES
.. AMHARIC
.. ARABIC
.. HEBREW
. SOMALI

:: FACILITIES
: EDUCATIONAL FACILITIES
AFTER SCHOOL CENTERS

: EDUCATION
AFTER SCHOOL EDUCATION

: PROGRAMS
AFTER SCHOOL PROGRAMS

: INDIVIDUAL CHARACTERISTICS
AGE
. CHRONOLOGICAL AGE
. MENTAL AGE
. SCHOOL ENTRANCE AGE

:: DIFFERENCES
: INDIVIDUAL DIFFERENCES
AGE DIFFERENCES

: SOCIAL DISCRIMINATION
AGE DISCRIMINATION

: PLACEMENT
AGE GRADE PLACEMENT

: GROUPS
AGE GROUPS
. ADOLESCENTS
. ADULTS
.. ADULT DROPOUTS
.. ADULT STUDENTS
.. MIDDLE AGED ADULTS
.. OLDER ADULTS
.. YOUNG ADULTS
. CHILDREN
.. ADOPTED CHILDREN
.. FOSTER CHILDREN
.. GRANDCHILDREN
.. HOSPITALIZED CHILDREN
.. LATCHKEY CHILDREN
.. MIGRANT CHILDREN
.. MINORITY GROUP CHILDREN
.. PREADOLESCENTS
.. PROBLEM CHILDREN
.. TRANSIENT CHILDREN
.. YOUNG CHILDREN
... INFANTS
.... NEONATES
.... PREMATURE INFANTS
... KINDERGARTEN CHILDREN
... PRESCHOOL CHILDREN
... TODDLERS

:: GROUPS
: ORGANIZATIONS (GROUPS)
AGENCIES
. ACCREDITING AGENCIES
. PRIVATE AGENCIES
. PUBLIC AGENCIES
.. PLANNING COMMISSIONS
.. STATE AGENCIES
... STATE DEPARTMENTS OF EDUCATION
... STATE LICENSING BOARDS
. SOCIAL AGENCIES
.. WELFARE AGENCIES
. URBAN RENEWAL AGENCIES
. VOLUNTARY AGENCIES
. YOUTH AGENCIES

: : BEHAVIOR
: COOPERATION
AGENCY COOPERATION

: INSTITUTIONAL ROLE
AGENCY ROLE

: : : BEHAVIOR
: : SOCIAL BEHAVIOR
: ANTISOCIAL BEHAVIOR
AGGRESSION

: : DEVELOPMENT
: INDIVIDUAL DEVELOPMENT
AGING (INDIVIDUALS)
. AGING IN ACADEMIA

: EDUCATION
AGING EDUCATION

: : : DEVELOPMENT
: : INDIVIDUAL DEVELOPMENT
: AGING (INDIVIDUALS)
AGING IN ACADEMIA

: BUSINESS
AGRIBUSINESS

: : : OCCUPATIONS
: : AGRICULTURAL OCCUPATIONS
: OFF FARM AGRICULTURAL OCCUPATIONS
AGRICULTURAL CHEMICAL OCCUPATIONS

: : : INSTITUTIONS
: : SCHOOLS
: COLLEGES
AGRICULTURAL COLLEGES

: EDUCATION
AGRICULTURAL EDUCATION
. ADULT FARMER EDUCATION
. SUPERVISED FARM PRACTICE
. YOUNG FARMER EDUCATION

: : TECHNOLOGY
: ENGINEERING
AGRICULTURAL ENGINEERING

: : : : : GROUPS
: : : : PERSONNEL
: : : NONPROFESSIONAL PERSONNEL
: : UNSKILLED WORKERS
: LABORERS
: : : GROUPS
: : PERSONNEL
: AGRICULTURAL PERSONNEL
AGRICULTURAL LABORERS
. MIGRANT WORKERS
. SEASONAL LABORERS

: EQUIPMENT
AGRICULTURAL MACHINERY

: : : OCCUPATIONS
: : AGRICULTURAL OCCUPATIONS
: OFF FARM AGRICULTURAL OCCUPATIONS
AGRICULTURAL MACHINERY OCCUPATIONS

: OCCUPATIONS
AGRICULTURAL OCCUPATIONS
. FARM OCCUPATIONS
. OFF FARM AGRICULTURAL OCCUPATIONS
. . AGRICULTURAL CHEMICAL OCCUPATIONS
. . AGRICULTURAL MACHINERY OCCUPATIONS
. . AGRICULTURAL SUPPLY OCCUPATIONS
. . CROP PROCESSING OCCUPATIONS
. . FOOD PROCESSING OCCUPATIONS
. . ORNAMENTAL HORTICULTURE OCCUPATIONS

: : GROUPS
: PERSONNEL
AGRICULTURAL PERSONNEL
. AGRICULTURAL LABORERS
. . MIGRANT WORKERS
. . SEASONAL LABORERS
. AGRICULTURAL TECHNICIANS
. FARMERS
. . DAIRY FARMERS
. . PART TIME FARMERS
. . SHARECROPPERS

AGRICULTURAL PRODUCTION

: SAFETY
AGRICULTURAL SAFETY

: : ABILITY
: SKILLS
AGRICULTURAL SKILLS

: : RESOURCES
: SUPPLIES
AGRICULTURAL SUPPLIES

: : : OCCUPATIONS
: : AGRICULTURAL OCCUPATIONS
: OFF FARM AGRICULTURAL OCCUPATIONS
AGRICULTURAL SUPPLY OCCUPATIONS

: : : GROUPS
: : PERSONNEL
: PARAPROFESSIONAL PERSONNEL
: : : GROUPS
: : PERSONNEL
: AGRICULTURAL PERSONNEL
AGRICULTURAL TECHNICIANS

AGRICULTURAL TRENDS

: TECHNOLOGY
AGRICULTURE
. AGRONOMY
. ANIMAL HUSBANDRY
. HARVESTING
. HORTICULTURE
. . ORNAMENTAL HORTICULTURE
. . . FLORICULTURE
. . . LANDSCAPING
. . . TURF MANAGEMENT

: : TECHNOLOGY
: AGRICULTURE
AGRONOMY

: CLIMATE CONTROL
AIR CONDITIONING

: EQUIPMENT
AIR CONDITIONING EQUIPMENT

: : GROUPS
: PERSONNEL
AIRCRAFT PILOTS

AIR FLOW

: POLLUTION
AIR POLLUTION

: FACILITIES
AIRPORTS

: FACILITIES
AIR STRUCTURES
. PNEUMATIC FORMS

: TRAFFIC CONTROL
AIR TRAFFIC CONTROL

: TRANSPORTATION
AIR TRANSPORTATION

: : LANGUAGES
: AFRICAN LANGUAGES
AKAN

ALARM SYSTEMS

: : GROUPS
: NORTH AMERICANS
: : GROUPS
: ETHNIC GROUPS
ALASKA NATIVES

: : LANGUAGES
: INDO EUROPEAN LANGUAGES
ALBANIAN

: EDUCATION
ALCOHOL EDUCATION

ALCOHOLIC BEVERAGES

: : DISABILITIES
: DISEASES
ALCOHOLISM

: : LIBERAL ARTS
: MATHEMATICS
ALGEBRA
. MATRICES
. VECTORS (MATHEMATICS)

: METHODS
: : : : : LIBERAL ARTS
: : : : HUMANITIES
: : : PHILOSOPHY
: : LOGIC
: MATHEMATICAL LOGIC
: MATHEMATICAL APPLICATIONS
ALGORITHMS

: PSYCHOLOGICAL PATTERNS
ALIENATION
. STUDENT ALIENATION
. TEACHER ALIENATION

: : LITERARY DEVICES
: : LANGUAGE
: FIGURATIVE LANGUAGE
ALLEGORY

: : DISABILITIES
: DISEASES
ALLERGY

: : OCCUPATIONS
: HEALTH OCCUPATIONS
ALLIED HEALTH OCCUPATIONS

: EDUCATION
ALLIED HEALTH OCCUPATIONS EDUCATION

: : : GROUPS
: : PERSONNEL
: HEALTH PERSONNEL
ALLIED HEALTH PERSONNEL
. DENTAL ASSISTANTS
. DENTAL HYGIENISTS
. DENTAL TECHNICIANS
. DIETITIANS
. EMERGENCY MEDICAL TECHNICIANS
. ENVIRONMENTAL TECHNICIANS
. HOME HEALTH AIDES
. MEDICAL ASSISTANTS
. . MEDICAL LABORATORY ASSISTANTS
. MEDICAL RECORD ADMINISTRATORS
. MEDICAL RECORD TECHNICIANS
. MEDICAL TECHNOLOGISTS
. NURSES AIDES
. OCCUPATIONAL THERAPY ASSISTANTS
. OPTOMETRISTS
. PHYSICAL THERAPY AIDES
. PHYSICIANS ASSISTANTS
. PSYCHIATRIC AIDES
. RADIOLOGIC TECHNOLOGISTS
. SURGICAL TECHNICIANS
. THERAPISTS
. . OCCUPATIONAL THERAPISTS
. . PHYSICAL THERAPISTS
. VETERINARY ASSISTANTS

: : : ABILITY
: : SKILLS
: BASIC SKILLS
ALPHABETIZING SKILLS

ALPHABETS
. CYRILLIC ALPHABET
. INITIAL TEACHING ALPHABET
. PHONEMIC ALPHABETS

ALTERNATIVE ENERGY SOURCES

ALTRUISM

: GROUPS
ALUMNI
. GRADUATES
. . COLLEGE GRADUATES
. . FOREIGN MEDICAL GRADUATES
. . HIGH SCHOOL GRADUATES

: : GROUPS
: ORGANIZATIONS (GROUPS)
ALUMNI ASSOCIATIONS

: EDUCATION
ALUMNI EDUCATION

: : LITERARY DEVICES
: : LANGUAGE
: FIGURATIVE LANGUAGE
AMBIGUITY

AMERICAN CULTURE (1966 1980)

AMERICAN HISTORY (1966 1980)

: CULTURE
AMERICAN INDIAN CULTURE

: EDUCATION
AMERICAN INDIAN EDUCATION

::::LIBERAL ARTS
:::SCIENCES
::SOCIAL SCIENCES
:::LIBERAL ARTS
::HUMANITIES
:HISTORY
AMERICAN INDIAN HISTORY

:LANGUAGES
AMERICAN INDIAN LANGUAGES
.ATHAPASCAN LANGUAGES
..APACHE
..NAVAJO
.AYMARA
.CAKCHIQUEL
.CHEROKEE
.CHOCTAW
.CREE
.GUARANI
.MAYAN LANGUAGES
..QUICHE
..YUCATEC
.OJIBWA
.POMO
.QUECHUA
.SALISH
.TZELTAL
.TZOTZIL
.UTO AZTECAN LANGUAGES
..HOPI
..PAPAGO

:::LIBERAL ARTS
::HUMANITIES
:LITERATURE
AMERICAN INDIAN LITERATURE

::GEOGRAPHIC REGIONS
:POLITICAL DIVISIONS (GEOGRAPHIC)
AMERICAN INDIAN RESERVATIONS

::GROUPS
:ETHNIC GROUPS
AMERICAN INDIANS
.NONRESERVATION AMERICAN INDIANS
..RURAL AMERICAN INDIANS
..URBAN AMERICAN INDIANS
.RESERVATION AMERICAN INDIANS

::CURRICULUM
:ETHNIC STUDIES
AMERICAN INDIAN STUDIES

:::COMMUNICATION (THOUGHT TRANSFER)
::MANUAL COMMUNICATION
::LANGUAGE
:SIGN LANGUAGE
:LANGUAGES
AMERICAN SIGN LANGUAGE

::CURRICULUM
:AREA STUDIES
AMERICAN STUDIES

::DISABILITIES
:VISUAL IMPAIRMENTS
AMETROPIA
.HYPEROPIA
.MYOPIA

:::LANGUAGES
::AFRO ASIATIC LANGUAGES
:SEMITIC LANGUAGES
AMHARIC

:::GROUPS
::RELIGIOUS CULTURAL GROUPS
:PROTESTANTS
AMISH

::DISABILITIES
:PHYSICAL DISABILITIES
AMPUTATIONS

:::EQUIPMENT
::ELECTRONIC EQUIPMENT
:COMPUTERS
ANALOG COMPUTERS

::::METHODS
:::EVALUATION METHODS
::DATA ANALYSIS
:STATISTICAL ANALYSIS
ANALYSIS OF COVARIANCE

::::METHODS
:::EVALUATION METHODS
::DATA ANALYSIS
:STATISTICAL ANALYSIS
ANALYSIS OF VARIANCE

ANALYTICAL CRITICISM (1969 1980)

:::LIBERAL ARTS
::MATHEMATICS
:GEOMETRY
ANALYTIC GEOMETRY

::::LIBERAL ARTS
:::SCIENCES
::NATURAL SCIENCES
:BIOLOGICAL SCIENCES
ANATOMY

::::LIBERAL ARTS
:::SCIENCES
::SOCIAL SCIENCES
:::LIBERAL ARTS
::HUMANITIES
:HISTORY
ANCIENT HISTORY

:::SERVICES
::HUMAN SERVICES
:SOCIAL SERVICES
ANCILLARY SCHOOL SERVICES
.MOBILE EDUCATIONAL SERVICES
.PUPIL PERSONNEL SERVICES
.SCHOOL HEALTH SERVICES
.STUDENT PERSONNEL SERVICES

ANCILLARY SERVICES (1967 1980)

ANDRAGOGY

ANDROGYNY

::DISABILITIES
:DISEASES
ANEMIA
.SICKLE CELL ANEMIA

::TECHNOLOGY
:MEDICINE
ANESTHESIOLOGY

:PSYCHOLOGICAL PATTERNS
ANGER
.HOSTILITY

::GROUPS
:NORTH AMERICANS
::GROUPS
:ETHNIC GROUPS
ANGLO AMERICANS

:BEHAVIOR
ANIMAL BEHAVIOR

::::GROUPS
:::PERSONNEL
::NONPROFESSIONAL PERSONNEL
:SEMISKILLED WORKERS
ANIMAL CARETAKERS

:FACILITIES
ANIMAL FACILITIES
.ZOOS

::TECHNOLOGY
:AGRICULTURE
ANIMAL HUSBANDRY

ANIMALS
.HORSES
.LABORATORY ANIMALS
.LIVESTOCK
.RATS

:::METHODS
::PRODUCTION TECHNIQUES
:SPECIAL EFFECTS
ANIMATION

:::PUBLICATIONS
::REFERENCE MATERIALS
:BIBLIOGRAPHIES
ANNOTATED BIBLIOGRAPHIES

::PUBLICATIONS
:SERIALS
::PUBLICATIONS
:REPORTS
ANNUAL REPORTS

::DISABILITIES
:DISEASES
ANOREXIA NERVOSA

ANSWER KEYS

ANSWER SHEETS

::PUBLICATIONS
:REFERENCE MATERIALS
ANTHOLOGIES

:LINGUISTICS
::::LIBERAL ARTS
:::SCIENCES
::SOCIAL SCIENCES
:ANTHROPOLOGY
ANTHROPOLOGICAL LINGUISTICS

:::LIBERAL ARTS
::SCIENCES
:SOCIAL SCIENCES
ANTHROPOLOGY
.ANTHROPOLOGICAL LINGUISTICS
.ARCHAEOLOGY
.EDUCATIONAL ANTHROPOLOGY
.ETHNOGRAPHY
.ETHNOLOGY

:ATTITUDES
ANTI INTELLECTUALISM

ANTI SEMITISM

::BEHAVIOR
:SOCIAL BEHAVIOR
ANTISOCIAL BEHAVIOR
.AGGRESSION
.CHEATING
.CHILD ABUSE
.CHILD NEGLECT
.CRIME
..DELINQUENCY
..INTERNATIONAL CRIMES
.ELDER ABUSE
.INCEST
.SEXUAL ABUSE
..RAPE
.SEXUAL HARASSMENT
.STEALING
..PLAGIARISM
.TERRORISM
.VANDALISM
..SCHOOL VANDALISM
.VIOLENCE
..FAMILY VIOLENCE

::LITERARY DEVICES
::LANGUAGE
:FIGURATIVE LANGUAGE
ANTITHESIS

:PSYCHOLOGICAL PATTERNS
ANXIETY
.COMMUNICATION APPREHENSION
.MATHEMATICS ANXIETY
.SEPARATION ANXIETY
.TEST ANXIETY
.WRITING APPREHENSION

:::LANGUAGES
::AMERICAN INDIAN LANGUAGES
:ATHAPASCAN LANGUAGES
APACHE

:PSYCHOLOGICAL PATTERNS
APATHY

:::DISABILITIES
::PHYSICAL DISABILITIES
:NEUROLOGICAL IMPAIRMENTS
::DISABILITIES
:LANGUAGE HANDICAPS
APHASIA

::MAINTENANCE
:REPAIR
APPLIANCE REPAIR

:LINGUISTICS
APPLIED LINGUISTICS

::::LIBERAL ARTS
:::HUMANITIES
::FINE ARTS
:MUSIC
APPLIED MUSIC

:::TRAINING
::JOB TRAINING
:ON THE JOB TRAINING
APPRENTICESHIPS

:TECHNOLOGY
APPROPRIATE TECHNOLOGY

APTITUDE
.ACADEMIC APTITUDE
.LANGUAGE APTITUDE
.VOCATIONAL APTITUDE

::MEASURES (INDIVIDUALS)
:TESTS
APTITUDE TESTS
.READING READINESS TESTS
.SCHOOL READINESS TESTS

::RELATIONSHIP
:INTERACTION
APTITUDE TREATMENT INTERACTION

::: ACTIVITIES
:: PHYSICAL ACTIVITIES
: ATHLETICS
AQUATIC SPORTS
. DIVING
. SAILING
. SURFING
. SWIMMING
. WATER POLO
. WATERSKIING

::: LANGUAGES
:: AFRO ASIATIC LANGUAGES
: SEMITIC LANGUAGES
ARABIC

: GROUPS
ARABS

ARBITRATION

:::: LIBERAL ARTS
::: SCIENCES
:: SOCIAL SCIENCES
: ANTHROPOLOGY
ARCHAEOLOGY

::: ACTIVITIES
:: PHYSICAL ACTIVITIES
: ATHLETICS
ARCHERY

::: GROUPS
:: PERSONNEL
: PROFESSIONAL PERSONNEL
ARCHITECTS

ARCHITECTURAL BARRIERS (1970 1980)

ARCHITECTURAL CHARACTER

::::: LIBERAL ARTS
:::: HUMANITIES
::: FINE ARTS
:: VISUAL ARTS
: DRAFTING
ARCHITECTURAL DRAFTING

:: EDUCATION
: PROFESSIONAL EDUCATION
ARCHITECTURAL EDUCATION

ARCHITECTURAL PROGRAMING

: RESEARCH
ARCHITECTURAL RESEARCH

:::: LIBERAL ARTS
::: HUMANITIES
:: FINE ARTS
: VISUAL ARTS
ARCHITECTURE

: INFORMATION SOURCES
ARCHIVES

:: SCIENTIFIC CONCEPTS
: SPACE
:: MATHEMATICAL CONCEPTS
: GEOMETRIC CONCEPTS
AREA

: CURRICULUM
AREA STUDIES
. AMERICAN STUDIES
. ASIAN STUDIES
. MIDDLE EASTERN STUDIES

ARISTOTELIAN CRITICISM (1969 1980)

:: LIBERAL ARTS
: MATHEMATICS
ARITHMETIC
. ADDITION
. DIVISION
. MULTIPLICATION
. SUBTRACTION

::: GROUPS
:: ORGANIZATIONS (GROUPS)
: MILITARY ORGANIZATIONS
ARMED FORCES

:: LANGUAGES
: INDO EUROPEAN LANGUAGES
ARMENIAN

: BEHAVIOR PATTERNS
AROUSAL PATTERNS

ART
. ART PRODUCTS
. COMMERCIAL ART
. CREATIVE ART
.. CREATIVE DRAMATICS

: ACTIVITIES
ART ACTIVITIES

:: EDUCATION
: AESTHETIC EDUCATION
ART APPRECIATION

: EDUCATION
ART EDUCATION

ART EXPRESSION

::::: LIBERAL ARTS
:::: SCIENCES
::: SOCIAL SCIENCES
:::: LIBERAL ARTS
::: HUMANITIES
:: HISTORY
: INTELLECTUAL HISTORY
ART HISTORY

ARTICULATION (EDUCATION)

:: LANGUAGE ARTS
: SPEECH
ARTICULATION (SPEECH)

:: DISABILITIES
: SPEECH HANDICAPS
ARTICULATION IMPAIRMENTS

ARTIFICIAL INTELLIGENCE
. EXPERT SYSTEMS

: LANGUAGE
ARTIFICIAL LANGUAGES

:: LANGUAGE ARTS
: SPEECH
ARTIFICIAL SPEECH

: GROUPS
ARTISTS
. MUSICIANS

ART MATERIALS

: ART
ART PRODUCTS

:: FACILITIES
: RESOURCE CENTERS
ARTS CENTERS

:::::: LIBERAL ARTS
:::: HUMANITIES
:::: FINE ARTS
::: MUSIC
:: VOCAL MUSIC
: SONGS
ART SONG

:::: GROUPS
::: PERSONNEL
:: PROFESSIONAL PERSONNEL
: TEACHERS
ART TEACHERS

: THERAPY
ART THERAPY

:: MATTER
: MINERALS
ASBESTOS

:: GROUPS
: NORTH AMERICANS
ASIAN AMERICANS
. CHINESE AMERICANS
. FILIPINO AMERICANS
. JAPANESE AMERICANS
. KOREAN AMERICANS

:::: LIBERAL ARTS
::: SCIENCES
:: SOCIAL SCIENCES
::: LIBERAL ARTS
:: HUMANITIES
: HISTORY
ASIAN HISTORY

:: CURRICULUM
: AREA STUDIES
ASIAN STUDIES

: CONSTRUCTION MATERIALS
ASPHALTS

ASPIRATION
. ACADEMIC ASPIRATION
. OCCUPATIONAL ASPIRATION
. PARENT ASPIRATION

:: TECHNOLOGY
: MANUFACTURING
ASSEMBLY (MANUFACTURING)

: PROGRAMS
ASSEMBLY PROGRAMS

: BEHAVIOR
ASSERTIVENESS

:: EVALUATION
: PROPERTY APPRAISAL
ASSESSED VALUATION

: FACILITIES
ASSESSMENT CENTERS (PERSONNEL)

: INSTRUCTION
ASSIGNMENTS
. HOMEWORK
. READING ASSIGNMENTS
. RESEARCH PAPERS (STUDENTS)

::: GROUPS
:: PERSONNEL
: SCHOOL PERSONNEL
::: GROUPS
:: PERSONNEL
: ADMINISTRATORS
ASSISTANT PRINCIPALS

:: FINANCIAL SUPPORT
: STUDENT FINANCIAL AID
ASSISTANTSHIPS

ASSISTANT SUPERINTENDENT ROLE (1966 1980)

: EQUIPMENT
ASSISTIVE DEVICES (FOR DISABLED)
. MOBILITY AIDS
.. WHEELCHAIRS
. PROSTHESES

: DEGREES (ACADEMIC)
ASSOCIATE DEGREES

: COGNITIVE PROCESSES
ASSOCIATION (PSYCHOLOGY)

:: MEASURES (INDIVIDUALS)
: PROJECTIVE MEASURES
ASSOCIATION MEASURES

: LEARNING
ASSOCIATIVE LEARNING
. PAIRED ASSOCIATE LEARNING

:: DISABILITIES
: DISEASES
ASTHMA

:::: LIBERAL ARTS
::: SCIENCES
:: NATURAL SCIENCES
: PHYSICAL SCIENCES
ASTRONOMY

:: LANGUAGES
: AMERICAN INDIAN LANGUAGES
ATHAPASCAN LANGUAGES
. APACHE
. NAVAJO

: GROUPS
ATHLETES

::: GROUPS
:: PERSONNEL
: PROFESSIONAL PERSONNEL
ATHLETIC COACHES

: EQUIPMENT
ATHLETIC EQUIPMENT

: FACILITIES
ATHLETIC FIELDS

:: ACTIVITIES
: PHYSICAL ACTIVITIES
ATHLETICS
. AQUATIC SPORTS
.. DIVING
.. SAILING
.. SURFING
.. SWIMMING
.. WATER POLO
.. WATERSKIING
. ARCHERY
. BOWLING
. COLLEGE ATHLETICS
. EXTRAMURAL ATHLETICS
. FENCING (SPORT)
. GOLF
. GYMNASTICS
.. TUMBLING

ATHLETICS
(CONTINUED)

. HANDBALL
. ICE SKATING
. INTRAMURAL ATHLETICS
. LIFETIME SPORTS
. ORIENTEERING
. RACQUET SPORTS
. . BADMINTON
. . RACQUETBALL
. . SQUASH (GAME)
. . TENNIS
. ROLLER SKATING
. SKIING
. TABLE TENNIS
. TEAM SPORTS
. . BASEBALL
. . BASKETBALL
. . FIELD HOCKEY
. . FOOTBALL
. . ICE HOCKEY
. . LACROSSE
. . SOCCER
. . SOFTBALL
. . TEAM HANDBALL
. . VOLLEYBALL
. . WATER POLO
. TRACK AND FIELD
. WEIGHTLIFTING
. WOMENS ATHLETICS
. WRESTLING

: : PUBLICATIONS
: REFERENCE MATERIALS
ATLASES

ATOMIC STRUCTURE

: THEORIES
ATOMIC THEORY

: BEHAVIOR
ATTACHMENT BEHAVIOR

ATTENDANCE
. AVERAGE DAILY ATTENDANCE
. COLLEGE ATTENDANCE
. TEACHER ATTENDANCE

: : : : GROUPS
: : : PERSONNEL
: : SCHOOL PERSONNEL
: PUPIL PERSONNEL WORKERS
ATTENDANCE OFFICERS

ATTENDANCE PATTERNS

: RECORDS (FORMS)
ATTENDANCE RECORDS

: : : : GROUPS
: : : PERSONNEL
: : NONPROFESSIONAL
PERSONNEL
: SERVICE WORKERS
ATTENDANTS

ATTENTION

ATTENTION CONTROL

: DISABILITIES
ATTENTION DEFICIT DISORDERS

: : INDIVIDUAL
CHARACTERISTICS
: PSYCHOLOGICAL
CHARACTERISTICS
ATTENTION SPAN

: CHANGE
ATTITUDE CHANGE

: MEASURES (INDIVIDUALS)
ATTITUDE MEASURES
. SEMANTIC DIFFERENTIAL

ATTITUDES
. ADMINISTRATOR ATTITUDES
. ANTI INTELLECTUALISM
. BELIEFS
. BLACK ATTITUDES
. CHILDHOOD ATTITUDES
. COMMUNITY ATTITUDES
. . COMMUNITY SATISFACTION
. COUNSELOR ATTITUDES
. DESIGN PREFERENCES
. DROPOUT ATTITUDES
. EDUCATIONAL ATTITUDES
. EMPLOYEE ATTITUDES
. EMPLOYER ATTITUDES
. FAMILY ATTITUDES
. LANGUAGE ATTITUDES
. . GRAMMATICAL
ACCEPTABILITY
. LIFE SATISFACTION
. MAJORITY ATTITUDES
. MARITAL SATISFACTION
. NEGATIVE ATTITUDES
. OPINIONS
. . PRESS OPINION
. . PUBLIC OPINION
. PARENT ATTITUDES
. . FATHER ATTITUDES
. . MOTHER ATTITUDES
. PARTICIPANT SATISFACTION
. POLITICAL ATTITUDES
. PROGRAM ATTITUDES
. RACIAL ATTITUDES
. READING ATTITUDES
. REGIONAL ATTITUDES
. SCHOOL ATTITUDES
. SCIENTIFIC ATTITUDES
. SOCIAL ATTITUDES
. . SOCIAL BIAS
. . . ETHNIC BIAS
. . . RACIAL BIAS
. . . SEX BIAS
. . SOCIAL DESIRABILITY
. SPORTSMANSHIP
. STEREOTYPES
. . ETHNIC STEREOTYPES
. . . BLACK STEREOTYPES
. . SEX STEREOTYPES
. . TEACHER STEREOTYPES
. STUDENT ATTITUDES
. STUDENT TEACHER ATTITUDES
. TEACHER ATTITUDES
. TRUST (PSYCHOLOGY)
. USER SATISFACTION
(INFORMATION)
. WORK ATTITUDES
. . JOB SATISFACTION

: : THEORIES
: BEHAVIOR THEORIES
ATTRIBUTION THEORY

ATTRITION (RESEARCH STUDIES)

: : METHODS
: EVALUATION METHODS
AUDIENCE ANALYSIS

: : BEHAVIOR
: PARTICIPATION
AUDIENCE PARTICIPATION

: GROUPS
AUDIENCES

: NONPRINT MEDIA
AUDIODISKS

: EQUIPMENT
AUDIO EQUIPMENT
. AUDIOTAPE RECORDERS
. HEARING AIDS
. MICROPHONES
. SOUND SPECTROGRAPHS

: : : METHODS
: : EDUCATIONAL METHODS
: TEACHING METHODS
AUDIOLINGUAL METHODS

: : : ABILITY
: : SKILLS
: LANGUAGE SKILLS
AUDIOLINGUAL SKILLS
. LISTENING SKILLS
. SPEECH SKILLS

: : TECHNOLOGY
: MEDICINE
AUDIOLOGY

: : : MEASURES (INDIVIDUALS)
: : TESTS
: AUDITORY TESTS
AUDIOMETRIC TESTS

: : : : RESOURCES
: : : SUPPLIES
: : MAGNETIC TAPES
: MAGNETIC TAPE CASSETTES
AUDIOTAPE CASSETTES

: : : EQUIPMENT
: : ELECTRONIC EQUIPMENT
: TAPE RECORDERS
: : EQUIPMENT
: AUDIO EQUIPMENT
AUDIOTAPE RECORDERS

: : NONPRINT MEDIA
: TAPE RECORDINGS
AUDIOTAPE RECORDINGS

: EDUCATIONAL MEDIA
AUDIOVISUAL AIDS
. INSTRUCTIONAL FILMS
. PROTOCOL MATERIALS

: : FACILITIES
: RESOURCE CENTERS
: : FACILITIES
: EDUCATIONAL FACILITIES
AUDIOVISUAL CENTERS

: : TECHNOLOGY
: COMMUNICATIONS
AUDIOVISUAL COMMUNICATIONS
. DIAL ACCESS INFORMATION
SYSTEMS
. EDUCATIONAL RADIO
. EDUCATIONAL TELEVISION
. LOOP INDUCTION SYSTEMS

: : : GROUPS
: : PERSONNEL
: SCHOOL PERSONNEL
: : : : GROUPS
: : : PERSONNEL
: : SPECIALISTS
: MEDIA SPECIALISTS
: : : : GROUPS
: : : PERSONNEL
: : ADMINISTRATORS
: COORDINATORS
AUDIOVISUAL COORDINATORS

: : : : METHODS
: : : EDUCATIONAL METHODS
: : TEACHING METHODS
: MULTIMEDIA INSTRUCTION
AUDIOVISUAL INSTRUCTION

AUDITING (COURSEWORK)

: FACILITIES
AUDITORIUMS

: : : COGNITIVE PROCESSES
: : PERCEPTION
: AUDITORY PERCEPTION
AUDITORY DISCRIMINATION

: : EVALUATION
: MEDICAL EVALUATION
AUDITORY EVALUATION

: : COGNITIVE PROCESSES
: PERCEPTION
AUDITORY PERCEPTION
. AUDITORY DISCRIMINATION

: STIMULI
AUDITORY STIMULI

: : MEASURES (INDIVIDUALS)
: TESTS
AUDITORY TESTS
. AUDIOMETRIC TESTS

: : TRAINING
: SENSORY TRAINING
AUDITORY TRAINING

AUDITS (VERIFICATION)
. COMMUNICATION AUDITS
. ENERGY AUDITS
. FINANCIAL AUDITS

: LEARNING
AURAL LEARNING

: LANGUAGES
AUSTRALIAN ABORIGINAL
LANGUAGES

: : : LIBERAL ARTS
: : HUMANITIES
: LITERATURE
AUSTRALIAN LITERATURE

: LANGUAGES
AUSTRO ASIATIC LANGUAGES
. CAMBODIAN

AUTEURISM

AUTHORING AIDS (PROGRAMING)

AUTHORITARIANISM

: GROUPS
AUTHORS
. POETS

: : : DISABILITIES
: : SEVERE DISABILITIES
: : : DISABILITIES
: : MENTAL DISORDERS
: PSYCHOSIS
AUTISM

: : : : : LIBERAL ARTS
: : : : HUMANITIES
: : : : LITERATURE
: : : PROSE
: : NONFICTION
: : LITERARY GENRES
: BIOGRAPHIES
AUTOBIOGRAPHIES

: : : : GROUPS
: : : PERSONNEL
: : NONPROFESSIONAL
PERSONNEL
: SKILLED WORKERS
AUTO BODY REPAIRERS

: EDUCATIONAL MEDIA
AUTOINSTRUCTIONAL AIDS
. TEACHING MACHINES

: : : : : SERVICES
: : : : INFORMATION SERVICES
: : : INFORMATION PROCESSING
: : DOCUMENTATION
: INDEXING
AUTOMATIC INDEXING

: TECHNOLOGY
AUTOMATION
. LIBRARY AUTOMATION
. ROBOTICS

: : TECHNOLOGY
: MECHANICS (PROCESS)
AUTO MECHANICS

: : : : GROUPS
: : : PERSONNEL
: : NONPROFESSIONAL
PERSONNEL
: SALES WORKERS
AUTO PARTS CLERKS

: : : : : GROUPS
: : : : PERSONNEL
: : : NONPROFESSIONAL
PERSONNEL
: : UNSKILLED WORKERS
: LABORERS
AUXILIARY LABORERS

: INCIDENCE
: ATTENDANCE
AVERAGE DAILY ATTENDANCE

: : INCIDENCE
: ENROLLMENT RATE
AVERAGE DAILY MEMBERSHIP

: : TECHNOLOGY
: MECHANICS (PROCESS)
: : : TECHNOLOGY
: : AEROSPACE TECHNOLOGY
: AVIATION TECHNOLOGY
AVIATION MECHANICS

: : TECHNOLOGY
: AEROSPACE TECHNOLOGY
AVIATION TECHNOLOGY
. AVIATION MECHANICS

: VOCABULARY
AVIATION VOCABULARY

: : EVALUATION
: RECOGNITION (ACHIEVEMENT)
AWARDS

: : LANGUAGES
: AMERICAN INDIAN LANGUAGES
AYMARA

: : : LANGUAGES
: : URALIC ALTAIC LANGUAGES
: TURKIC LANGUAGES
AZERBAIJANI

: DEGREES (ACADEMIC)
BACHELORS DEGREES

BACKGROUND
. CULTURAL BACKGROUND
. EDUCATIONAL BACKGROUND
. . EDUCATIONAL EXPERIENCE
. EXPERIENCE
. . EARLY EXPERIENCE
. . EDUCATIONAL EXPERIENCE
. . EMOTIONAL EXPERIENCE
. . . CATHARSIS
. . GROUP EXPERIENCE
. . INTELLECTUAL EXPERIENCE
. . LEARNING EXPERIENCE
. . . CLINICAL EXPERIENCE
. . PREREADING EXPERIENCE
. . SENSORY EXPERIENCE
. . . FIGURAL AFTEREFFECTS
. . . SENSORY DEPRIVATION
. . SOCIAL EXPERIENCE
. . STUDENT EXPERIENCE
. . TEACHING EXPERIENCE
. . WORK EXPERIENCE
. . . EMPLOYMENT EXPERIENCE
. PARENT BACKGROUND
. SOCIOECONOMIC BACKGROUND
. . SOCIAL BACKGROUND
. . . SOCIAL EXPERIENCE
. TEACHER BACKGROUND

: EDUCATION
BACK TO BASICS

: : : : ACTIVITIES
: : : PHYSICAL ACTIVITIES
: : ATHLETICS
: RACQUET SPORTS
BADMINTON

: : BUSINESS
: INDUSTRY
BAKERY INDUSTRY

: : : : : : LIBERAL ARTS
: : : : : HUMANITIES
: : : : FINE ARTS
: : : MUSIC
: : VOCAL MUSIC
: SONGS
: : : : : LIBERAL ARTS
: : : : HUMANITIES
: : : LITERATURE
: : POETRY
: LYRIC POETRY
: LITERARY GENRES
BALLADS

: : LANGUAGES
: INDO EUROPEAN LANGUAGES
BALTIC LANGUAGES
. LATVIAN
. LITHUANIAN

: : LANGUAGES
: INDO EUROPEAN LANGUAGES
BALUCHI

BANDS (MUSIC)

: : BUSINESS
: INDUSTRY
BANKING

: VOCABULARY
BANKING VOCABULARY

: : LANGUAGES
: AFRICAN LANGUAGES
BANTU LANGUAGES
. BEMBA
. CHINYANJA
. GANDA
. KIRUNDI
. KITUBA
. LINGALA
. SHONA
. SISWATI
. SWAHILI

: : : : GROUPS
: : : PERSONNEL
: : NONPROFESSIONAL
PERSONNEL
: SERVICE WORKERS
BARBERS

: : : LIBERAL ARTS
: : HUMANITIES
: LITERATURE
BAROQUE LITERATURE

: : LANGUAGES
: AFRICAN LANGUAGES
BASAA

: : INSTRUCTION
: READING INSTRUCTION
: : LITERACY
: : LANGUAGE ARTS
: READING
BASAL READING

: : : : ACTIVITIES
: : : PHYSICAL ACTIVITIES
: : ATHLETICS
: TEAM SPORTS
BASEBALL

: : : LANGUAGES
: : URALIC ALTAIC LANGUAGES
: TURKIC LANGUAGES
BASHKIR

: EDUCATION
BASIC BUSINESS EDUCATION

BASIC READING (1967 1980)

: : ABILITY
: SKILLS
BASIC SKILLS
. ALPHABETIZING SKILLS

: VOCABULARY
BASIC VOCABULARY

: : : : ACTIVITIES
: : : PHYSICAL ACTIVITIES
: : ATHLETICS
: TEAM SPORTS
BASKETBALL

: LANGUAGES
BASQUE

: : GROUPS
: FEMALES
BATTERED WOMEN

: : : LIBERAL ARTS
: : MATHEMATICS
: STATISTICS
: : : : METHODS
: : : EVALUATION METHODS
: : DATA ANALYSIS
: STATISTICAL ANALYSIS
BAYESIAN STATISTICS

: : LITERACY
: : LANGUAGE ARTS
: READING
BEGINNING READING

: : : : GROUPS
: : : PERSONNEL
: : PROFESSIONAL PERSONNEL
: TEACHERS
BEGINNING TEACHERS

BEHAVIOR
. ADJUSTMENT (TO
ENVIRONMENT)
. . ADAPTIVE BEHAVIOR (OF
DISABLED)
. . COPING
. . EMOTIONAL ADJUSTMENT
. . SOCIAL ADJUSTMENT
. . STUDENT ADJUSTMENT
. . VOCATIONAL ADJUSTMENT
. AFFECTIVE BEHAVIOR
. ANIMAL BEHAVIOR
. ASSERTIVENESS
. ATTACHMENT BEHAVIOR
. COMPETITION
. . COMPETITIVE SELECTION
. COOPERATION
. . AGENCY COOPERATION
. . COMMUNITY COOPERATION
. . COMPLIANCE (PSYCHOLOGY)
. . . COMPLIANCE (LEGAL)
. . . OBEDIENCE
. . EDUCATIONAL COOPERATION
. . . COLLEGE SCHOOL
COOPERATION
. . . COUNSELOR TEACHER
COOPERATION
. . . INTERCOLLEGIATE
COOPERATION
. . . PARENT TEACHER
COOPERATION
. . INSTITUTIONAL
COOPERATION
. . . COLLEGE SCHOOL
COOPERATION
. . . INTERCOLLEGIATE
COOPERATION
. . . LIBRARY COOPERATION
. . INTERNATIONAL
COOPERATION
. . REGIONAL COOPERATION
. DRINKING
. DRUG USE
. . DRUG ABUSE
. . . DRUG ADDICTION
. . ILLEGAL DRUG USE
. EXPLORATORY BEHAVIOR
. GROUP BEHAVIOR
. . TEAMWORK
. HYPERACTIVITY
. IMITATION
. INFANT BEHAVIOR
. LEADERSHIP STYLES
. LIFE STYLE
. MODELING (PSYCHOLOGY)
. PARANOID BEHAVIOR
. PARTICIPATION
. . AUDIENCE PARTICIPATION
. . CITIZEN PARTICIPATION
. . COMMUNITY INVOLVEMENT
. . FAMILY INVOLVEMENT
. . PARENT PARTICIPATION
. . SCHOOL INVOLVEMENT
. . STUDENT PARTICIPATION
. . TEACHER PARTICIPATION
. PERFORMANCE
. . COUNSELOR PERFORMANCE
. . FAILURE
. . . ACADEMIC FAILURE
. . . . READING FAILURE
. . JOB PERFORMANCE
. . SUCCESS
. PERSISTENCE
. . ACADEMIC PERSISTENCE
. . TEACHER PERSISTENCE
. PHYSICAL ACTIVITY LEVEL
. RESPONSES
. . BURNOUT
. . . TEACHER BURNOUT
. . CONSTRUCTED RESPONSE
. . COVERT RESPONSE
. . DIMENSIONAL PREFERENCE
. . EMOTIONAL RESPONSE
. . MOTOR REACTIONS
. . . EYE MOVEMENTS
. . . . EYE FIXATIONS
. . . PUPILLARY DILATION
. . OVERT RESPONSE
. . PATTERNED RESPONSES
. . READER RESPONSE
. . STRANGER REACTIONS
. . STUDENT REACTION
. . TEACHER RESPONSE
. RESPONSE STYLE (TESTS)
. . GUESSING (TESTS)
. SELF CONTROL
. . DELAY OF GRATIFICATION
. SELF DESTRUCTIVE BEHAVIOR
. . SELF MUTILATION
. . SUICIDE
. SMOKING
. SOCIAL BEHAVIOR
. . ACTIVISM
. . ANTISOCIAL BEHAVIOR
. . . AGGRESSION
. . . CHEATING
. . . CHILD ABUSE
. . . CHILD NEGLECT
. . . CRIME
. . . . DELINQUENCY

BEHAVIOR
(CONTINUED)

.... INTERNATIONAL CRIMES
... ELDER ABUSE
... INCEST
... SEXUAL ABUSE
.... RAPE
... SEXUAL HARASSMENT
... STEALING
.... PLAGIARISM
... TERRORISM
... VANDALISM
.... SCHOOL VANDALISM
... VIOLENCE
.... FAMILY VIOLENCE
.. CONFORMITY
.. DISSENT
.. LYING
.. OBEDIENCE
.. PROSOCIAL BEHAVIOR
.. SOCIAL ADJUSTMENT
. SPONTANEOUS BEHAVIOR
. STUDENT BEHAVIOR
.. STUDENT ADJUSTMENT
.. STUDENT PARTICIPATION
. TEACHER BEHAVIOR
.. TEACHER EFFECTIVENESS
.. TEACHER MILITANCY
.. TEACHER PARTICIPATION
.. TEACHER PERSISTENCE
.. TEACHER RESPONSE

: OBJECTIVES
BEHAVIORAL OBJECTIVES
. AFFECTIVE OBJECTIVES
. COGNITIVE OBJECTIVES
. PSYCHOMOTOR OBJECTIVES

: RESEARCH
BEHAVIORAL SCIENCE RESEARCH
. INTEGRATION STUDIES
. PSYCHOLOGICAL STUDIES
.. FORCE FIELD ANALYSIS
.. INTEREST RESEARCH
.. PERSONALITY STUDIES

:: LIBERAL ARTS
: SCIENCES
BEHAVIORAL SCIENCES
. ETHOLOGY
. PSYCHOLOGY
.. BEHAVIORISM
.. CHILD PSYCHOLOGY
.. CLINICAL PSYCHOLOGY
.. COGNITIVE PSYCHOLOGY
.. COMMUNITY PSYCHOLOGY
.. DEVELOPMENTAL PSYCHOLOGY
.. EDUCATIONAL PSYCHOLOGY
.. EXPERIMENTAL PSYCHOLOGY
.. INDIVIDUAL PSYCHOLOGY
.. INDUSTRIAL PSYCHOLOGY
.. PSYCHOACOUSTICS
.. PSYCHOMETRICS
.. PSYCHOPATHOLOGY
.. PSYCHOPHYSIOLOGY
.. SOCIAL PSYCHOLOGY
.. SPORT PSYCHOLOGY
. SOCIOBIOLOGY
. SOCIOLOGY
.. CRIMINOLOGY
.. EDUCATIONAL SOCIOLOGY
.. SOCIAL PSYCHOLOGY

:: COGNITIVE PROCESSES
: LEARNING PROCESSES
BEHAVIOR CHAINING

: CHANGE
BEHAVIOR CHANGE

:: DEVELOPMENT
: INDIVIDUAL DEVELOPMENT
BEHAVIOR DEVELOPMENT
. HABIT FORMATION

: DISABILITIES
BEHAVIOR DISORDERS

:::: LIBERAL ARTS
::: SCIENCES
:: BEHAVIORAL SCIENCES
: PSYCHOLOGY
BEHAVIORISM

: CONDITIONING
BEHAVIOR MODIFICATION
. CONTINGENCY MANAGEMENT
. DESENSITIZATION

BEHAVIOR PATTERNS
. AROUSAL PATTERNS
. READING HABITS
. RECIDIVISM
. SPEECH HABITS
. STUDY HABITS

: PROBLEMS
BEHAVIOR PROBLEMS

:: MEASURES (INDIVIDUALS)
: RATING SCALES
BEHAVIOR RATING SCALES

: STANDARDS
BEHAVIOR STANDARDS
. CODES OF ETHICS

: THEORIES
BEHAVIOR THEORIES
. ADAPTATION LEVEL THEORY
. ATTRIBUTION THEORY
. MEDIATION THEORY

: ATTITUDES
BELIEFS

::: LANGUAGES
:: AFRICAN LANGUAGES
: BANTU LANGUAGES
BEMBA

:: LANGUAGES
: INDO EUROPEAN LANGUAGES
BENGALI

:: LANGUAGES
: AFRO ASIATIC LANGUAGES
BERBER LANGUAGES
. KABYLE
. RIFF

BIAS
. SOCIAL BIAS
.. ETHNIC BIAS
.. RACIAL BIAS
.. SEX BIAS
. STATISTICAL BIAS
. TEST BIAS
. TEXTBOOK BIAS

::: LIBERAL ARTS
:: HUMANITIES
: LITERATURE
BIBLICAL LITERATURE

:::::: SERVICES
::::: INFORMATION SERVICES
:::: INFORMATION PROCESSING
::: DOCUMENTATION
:: BIBLIOMETRICS
: CITATION ANALYSIS
BIBLIOGRAPHIC COUPLING

:: GROUPS
: ORGANIZATIONS (GROUPS)
::: NETWORKS
:: INFORMATION NETWORKS
: LIBRARY NETWORKS
BIBLIOGRAPHIC UTILITIES

:: PUBLICATIONS
: REFERENCE MATERIALS
BIBLIOGRAPHIES
. ANNOTATED BIBLIOGRAPHIES

:::: SERVICES
::: INFORMATION SERVICES
:: INFORMATION PROCESSING
: DOCUMENTATION
BIBLIOMETRICS
. CITATION ANALYSIS
.. BIBLIOGRAPHIC COUPLING

: THERAPY
BIBLIOTHERAPY

: CULTURAL PLURALISM
BICULTURALISM

:: ACTIVITIES
: PHYSICAL ACTIVITIES
BICYCLING

BIDIALECTALISM

BIDS

::: LANGUAGES
:: INDO EUROPEAN LANGUAGES
: SLAVIC LANGUAGES
BIELORUSSIAN

::: LANGUAGES
:: MALAYO POLYNESIAN LANGUAGES
: INDONESIAN LANGUAGES
BIKOL

: EDUCATION
BILINGUAL EDUCATION

: PROGRAMS
BILINGUAL EDUCATION PROGRAMS

: MULTILINGUAL MATERIALS
:: EDUCATIONAL MEDIA
: INSTRUCTIONAL MATERIALS
BILINGUAL INSTRUCTIONAL MATERIALS

BILINGUALISM

:: INSTITUTIONS
: SCHOOLS
BILINGUAL SCHOOLS

:: GROUPS
: STUDENTS
BILINGUAL STUDENTS

::::: GROUPS
:::: PERSONNEL
::: SCHOOL PERSONNEL
::::: GROUPS
:::: PERSONNEL
::: PARAPROFESSIONAL PERSONNEL
:: PARAPROFESSIONAL SCHOOL PERSONNEL
: TEACHER AIDES
BILINGUAL TEACHER AIDES

:::: GROUPS
::: PERSONNEL
:: PROFESSIONAL PERSONNEL
: TEACHERS
BILINGUAL TEACHERS

:: LANGUAGES
: AFRICAN LANGUAGES
BINI

::::: LIBERAL ARTS
:::: SCIENCES
::: NATURAL SCIENCES
:: PHYSICAL SCIENCES
: CHEMISTRY
:::: LIBERAL ARTS
::: SCIENCES
:: NATURAL SCIENCES
: BIOLOGICAL SCIENCES
BIOCHEMISTRY

:::: LIBERAL ARTS
::: HUMANITIES
:: PHILOSOPHY
: ETHICS
BIOETHICS

::: RELATIONSHIP
:: INTERACTION
: FEEDBACK
:::: LIBERAL ARTS
::: SCIENCES
:: NATURAL SCIENCES
: BIOLOGICAL SCIENCES
BIOFEEDBACK

: MEASURES (INDIVIDUALS)
BIOGRAPHICAL INVENTORIES

::::: LIBERAL ARTS
:::: HUMANITIES
::: LITERATURE
:: PROSE
: NONFICTION
: LITERARY GENRES
BIOGRAPHIES
. AUTOBIOGRAPHIES

: INFLUENCES
BIOLOGICAL INFLUENCES
. RH FACTORS

:: GROUPS
: PARENTS
BIOLOGICAL PARENTS

::: LIBERAL ARTS
:: SCIENCES
: NATURAL SCIENCES
BIOLOGICAL SCIENCES
. ANATOMY
. BIOCHEMISTRY
. BIOFEEDBACK
. BIOLOGY
.. MARINE BIOLOGY
.. MICROBIOLOGY
.. RADIATION BIOLOGY
.. SOCIAL BIOLOGY
. BIOMEDICINE
. BIOPHYSICS
.. BIOMECHANICS
.. BIONICS
... ROBOTICS
. BOTANY
. CYTOLOGY
. ECOLOGY
. EMBRYOLOGY
. ETHOLOGY
. GENETICS
.. GENETIC ENGINEERING
. PHYSIOLOGY
.. EXERCISE PHYSIOLOGY
.. PSYCHOPHYSIOLOGY
. SOCIOBIOLOGY
. ZOOLOGY
.. ENTOMOLOGY
.. ICHTHYOLOGY
.. ORNITHOLOGY
.. PRIMATOLOGY

:::: LIBERAL ARTS
::: SCIENCES
:: NATURAL SCIENCES
: BIOLOGICAL SCIENCES
BIOLOGY
. MARINE BIOLOGY
. MICROBIOLOGY
. RADIATION BIOLOGY
. SOCIAL BIOLOGY

:::::: LIBERAL ARTS
::::: SCIENCES
:::: NATURAL SCIENCES
::: PHYSICAL SCIENCES
:: PHYSICS
::::: LIBERAL ARTS
:::: SCIENCES
::: NATURAL SCIENCES
:: BIOLOGICAL SCIENCES
: BIOPHYSICS
BIOMECHANICS

: EQUIPMENT
BIOMEDICAL EQUIPMENT

:: TECHNOLOGY
: MEDICINE
:::: LIBERAL ARTS
::: SCIENCES
:: NATURAL SCIENCES
: BIOLOGICAL SCIENCES
BIOMEDICINE

:::::: LIBERAL ARTS
::::: SCIENCES
:::: NATURAL SCIENCES
::: PHYSICAL SCIENCES
:: PHYSICS
::::: LIBERAL ARTS
:::: SCIENCES
::: NATURAL SCIENCES
:: BIOLOGICAL SCIENCES
: BIOPHYSICS
BIONICS
. ROBOTICS

::::: LIBERAL ARTS
:::: SCIENCES
::: NATURAL SCIENCES
:: PHYSICAL SCIENCES
: PHYSICS
:::: LIBERAL ARTS
::: SCIENCES
:: NATURAL SCIENCES
: BIOLOGICAL SCIENCES
BIOPHYSICS
. BIOMECHANICS
. BIONICS
.. ROBOTICS

: COMMITTEES
BIRACIAL COMMITTEES

BIRTH

::: ORGANIZATION
:: GROUP STRUCTURE
: FAMILY STRUCTURE
BIRTH ORDER

: INCIDENCE
:::: LIBERAL ARTS
::: SCIENCES
:: SOCIAL SCIENCES
: DEMOGRAPHY
BIRTH RATE

::: INDIVIDUAL CHARACTERISTICS
:: PHYSICAL CHARACTERISTICS
: BODY WEIGHT
BIRTH WEIGHT

: ACHIEVEMENT
BLACK ACHIEVEMENT

: ATTITUDES
BLACK ATTITUDES

: BUSINESS
BLACK BUSINESSES

::: INSTITUTIONS
:: SCHOOLS
: COLLEGES
:: INSTITUTIONS
: BLACK INSTITUTIONS
BLACK COLLEGES

: COMMUNITY
BLACK COMMUNITY

: CULTURE
BLACK CULTURE

:::: LINGUISTICS
::: SOCIOLINGUISTICS
:: LANGUAGE VARIATION
:: LANGUAGES
: DIALECTS
BLACK DIALECTS

: EDUCATION
BLACK EDUCATION

: EMPLOYMENT
BLACK EMPLOYMENT

:: GROUPS
: FAMILY (SOCIOLOGICAL UNIT)
BLACK FAMILY

:::: LIBERAL ARTS
::: SCIENCES
:: SOCIAL SCIENCES
::: LIBERAL ARTS
:: HUMANITIES
: HISTORY
BLACK HISTORY

BLACK HOUSING (1977 1980)

: INFLUENCES
BLACK INFLUENCES

: INSTITUTIONS
BLACK INSTITUTIONS
. BLACK COLLEGES

:: ABILITY
: LEADERSHIP
BLACK LEADERSHIP

::: LIBERAL ARTS
:: HUMANITIES
: LITERATURE
BLACK LITERATURE

::: GROUPS
:: PARENTS
::: GROUPS
:: FEMALES
: MOTHERS
:: GROUPS
: BLACKS
BLACK MOTHERS

:: GROUPS
: ORGANIZATIONS (GROUPS)
BLACK ORGANIZATIONS

::::: LIBERAL ARTS
:::: SCIENCES
::: SOCIAL SCIENCES
:: DEMOGRAPHY
: POPULATION TRENDS
BLACK POPULATION TRENDS

BLACK POWER

: GROUPS
BLACKS
. BLACK MOTHERS
. BLACK STUDENTS
. BLACK TEACHERS
. BLACK YOUTH

::: ATTITUDES
:: STEREOTYPES
: ETHNIC STEREOTYPES
BLACK STEREOTYPES

:: GROUPS
: STUDENTS
:: GROUPS
: BLACKS
BLACK STUDENTS

:: CURRICULUM
: ETHNIC STUDIES
BLACK STUDIES

:::: GROUPS
::: PERSONNEL
:: PROFESSIONAL PERSONNEL
: TEACHERS
:: GROUPS
: BLACKS
BLACK TEACHERS

:: GROUPS
: YOUTH
:: GROUPS
: BLACKS
BLACK YOUTH

:: DISABILITIES
: VISUAL IMPAIRMENTS
BLINDNESS

:: FINANCIAL SUPPORT
: GRANTS
BLOCK GRANTS

: METABOLISM
BLOOD CIRCULATION

: OCCUPATIONS
BLUE COLLAR OCCUPATIONS

: BUILDING PLANS
BLUEPRINTS

:: GROUPS
: ORGANIZATIONS (GROUPS)
BLUE RIBBON COMMISSIONS

:: RELATIONSHIP
: INTERPERSONAL RELATIONSHIP
BOARD ADMINISTRATOR RELATIONSHIP

: GROUPS
BOARD CANDIDATES

:: FACILITIES
: HOUSING
BOARDING HOMES

:: INSTITUTIONS
: SCHOOLS
:: INSTITUTIONS
: RESIDENTIAL INSTITUTIONS
BOARDING SCHOOLS
. RESIDENTIAL SCHOOLS

:: POLICY
: ADMINISTRATIVE POLICY
BOARD OF EDUCATION POLICY

BOARD OF EDUCATION ROLE

::: GROUPS
:: ORGANIZATIONS (GROUPS)
: GOVERNING BOARDS
BOARDS OF EDUCATION
. STATE BOARDS OF EDUCATION

:::: GROUPS
::: PERSONNEL
:: NONPROFESSIONAL PERSONNEL
: SEMISKILLED WORKERS
BOAT OPERATORS

:: INDIVIDUAL CHARACTERISTICS
: PHYSICAL CHARACTERISTICS
BODY HEIGHT

: SELF CONCEPT
BODY IMAGE

:: COMMUNICATION (THOUGHT TRANSFER)
: NONVERBAL COMMUNICATION
BODY LANGUAGE

:: INDIVIDUAL CHARACTERISTICS
: PHYSICAL CHARACTERISTICS
BODY WEIGHT
. BIRTH WEIGHT
. OBESITY

BOND ISSUES

::: PUBLICATIONS
:: REFERENCE MATERIALS
::: PUBLICATIONS
:: CATALOGS
: LIBRARY CATALOGS
BOOK CATALOGS

::: ABILITY
:: SKILLS
: BUSINESS SKILLS
BOOKKEEPING

::: EQUIPMENT
:: MOTOR VEHICLES
: SERVICE VEHICLES
:: EQUIPMENT
: LIBRARY EQUIPMENT
BOOKMOBILES

: PUBLICATIONS
BOOK REVIEWS

: PUBLICATIONS
BOOKS
. FOREIGN LANGUAGE BOOKS
. HIGH INTEREST LOW VOCABULARY BOOKS
. PAPERBACK BOOKS
. PICTURE BOOKS
. TEXTBOOKS
.. HISTORY TEXTBOOKS
.. MULTICULTURAL TEXTBOOKS
. YEARBOOKS

: : : : LIBERAL ARTS
: : : SCIENCES
: : NATURAL SCIENCES
: BIOLOGICAL SCIENCES
BOTANY

: : : ACTIVITIES
: : PHYSICAL ACTIVITIES
: ATHLETICS
BOWLING

: : : GROUPS
: : LATIN AMERICANS
: MEXICANS
: : : GROUPS
: : PERSONNEL
: FOREIGN WORKERS
BRACEROS

: : LANGUAGE
: WRITTEN LANGUAGE
BRAILLE

: : : INDIVIDUAL CHARACTERISTICS
: : PHYSICAL CHARACTERISTICS
: NEUROLOGICAL ORGANIZATION
BRAIN HEMISPHERE FUNCTIONS

: : ACTIVITIES
: CREATIVE ACTIVITIES
BRAINSTORMING

: METHODS
BRANCHING

: : INSTITUTIONS
: : INFORMATION SOURCES
: LIBRARIES
BRANCH LIBRARIES

: : PROGRAMS
: HEALTH PROGRAMS
BREAKFAST PROGRAMS

: NUTRITION
BREASTFEEDING

: : BUSINESS
: INDUSTRY
BRICK INDUSTRY

: : TECHNOLOGY
: : CONSTRUCTION (PROCESS)
: MASONRY
BRICKLAYING

: : INSTITUTIONS
: SCHOOLS
BRITISH INFANT SCHOOLS

: : BUSINESS
: INDUSTRY
BROADCAST INDUSTRY

: : EQUIPMENT
: ELECTRONIC EQUIPMENT
BROADCAST RECEPTION EQUIPMENT

: : : : TECHNOLOGY
: : : COMMUNICATIONS
: : TELECOMMUNICATIONS
: : MASS MEDIA
: TELEVISION
BROADCAST TELEVISION

: RELIGION
BUDDHISM

: PLANNING
BUDGETING
. PROGRAM BUDGETING

BUDGETS

: CHANGE
BUILDING CONVERSION

: DESIGN
BUILDING DESIGN
. MODULAR BUILDING DESIGN

: INNOVATION
BUILDING INNOVATION

: OBSOLESCENCE
BUILDING OBSOLESCENCE

: : GOVERNANCE
: ADMINISTRATION
BUILDING OPERATION

BUILDING PLANS
. BLUEPRINTS

: FACILITIES
BUILDINGS
. SCHOOL BUILDINGS
. . COLLEGE BUILDINGS

: STRUCTURAL ELEMENTS (CONSTRUCTION)
BUILDING SYSTEMS
. STRUCTURAL BUILDING SYSTEMS

: OCCUPATIONS
BUILDING TRADES

: : : LANGUAGES
: : INDO EUROPEAN LANGUAGES
: SLAVIC LANGUAGES
BULGARIAN

: : DISABILITIES
: DISEASES
BULIMIA

: VISUAL AIDS
BULLETIN BOARDS

: : PUBLICATIONS
: SERIALS
BULLETINS

: ORGANIZATION
BUREAUCRACY

: : : LANGUAGES
: : URALIC ALTAIC LANGUAGES
: MONGOLIAN LANGUAGES
BURIAT

: : LANGUAGES
: SINO TIBETAN LANGUAGES
BURMESE

: CULTURE
BURMESE CULTURE

: : BEHAVIOR
: RESPONSES
BURNOUT
. TEACHER BURNOUT

: LANGUAGES
BURUSHASKI

BUSINESS
. AGRIBUSINESS
. BLACK BUSINESSES
. INDUSTRY
. . BAKERY INDUSTRY
. . BANKING
. . BRICK INDUSTRY
. . BROADCAST INDUSTRY
. . CONSTRUCTION INDUSTRY
. . . HOUSING INDUSTRY
. . FASHION INDUSTRY
. . FEED INDUSTRY
. . FILM INDUSTRY
. . INSURANCE COMPANIES
. . LUMBER INDUSTRY
. . MANUFACTURING INDUSTRY
. . . AEROSPACE INDUSTRY
. . . CEMENT INDUSTRY
. . . CHEMICAL INDUSTRY
. . . ELECTRONICS INDUSTRY
. . . FURNITURE INDUSTRY
. . . MACHINERY INDUSTRY
. . . METAL INDUSTRY
. . MEAT PACKING INDUSTRY
. . PETROLEUM INDUSTRY
. . PUBLISHING INDUSTRY
. . TELEPHONE COMMUNICATIONS INDUSTRY
. . TOURISM
. SMALL BUSINESSES

: : GOVERNANCE
: ADMINISTRATION
BUSINESS ADMINISTRATION

: : EDUCATION
: PROFESSIONAL EDUCATION
BUSINESS ADMINISTRATION EDUCATION

: : COMMUNICATION (THOUGHT TRANSFER)
: ORGANIZATIONAL COMMUNICATION
BUSINESS COMMUNICATION
. BUSINESS CORRESPONDENCE

: : COMMUNICATION (THOUGHT TRANSFER)
: VERBAL COMMUNICATION
: : : COMMUNICATION (THOUGHT TRANSFER)
: : ORGANIZATIONAL COMMUNICATION
: BUSINESS COMMUNICATION
BUSINESS CORRESPONDENCE

BUSINESS CYCLES

: : EDUCATION
: VOCATIONAL EDUCATION
BUSINESS EDUCATION
. OFFICE OCCUPATIONS EDUCATION

: : FACILITIES
: EDUCATIONAL FACILITIES
BUSINESS EDUCATION FACILITIES

: : : : : GROUPS
: : : : PERSONNEL
: : : PROFESSIONAL PERSONNEL
: : TEACHERS
: VOCATIONAL EDUCATION TEACHERS
BUSINESS EDUCATION TEACHERS

: : : LANGUAGES
: : INDO EUROPEAN LANGUAGES
: ENGLISH
BUSINESS ENGLISH

: RESPONSIBILITY
BUSINESS RESPONSIBILITY

: : ABILITY
: SKILLS
BUSINESS SKILLS
. BOOKKEEPING
. KEYBOARDING (DATA ENTRY)
. RECORDKEEPING
. TYPEWRITING

: : METHODS
: DESEGREGATION METHODS
BUSING

: TRANSPORTATION
BUS TRANSPORTATION

: : TECHNOLOGY
: WOODWORKING
: CONSTRUCTION (PROCESS)
CABINETMAKING

: : : : TECHNOLOGY
: : : COMMUNICATIONS
: : TELECOMMUNICATIONS
: : MASS MEDIA
: TELEVISION
CABLE TELEVISION

: : LANGUAGES
: AMERICAN INDIAN LANGUAGES
CAKCHIQUEL

: EQUIPMENT
CALCULATORS

: : LIBERAL ARTS
: MATHEMATICS
CALCULUS

: : : ACTIVITIES
: : PHYSICAL ACTIVITIES
: EXERCISE
CALISTHENICS

: : EQUIPMENT
: MEASUREMENT EQUIPMENT
CALORIMETERS

: : LANGUAGES
: AUSTRO ASIATIC LANGUAGES
CAMBODIAN

: : GROUPS
: INDOCHINESE
CAMBODIANS

: : ACTIVITIES
: RECREATIONAL ACTIVITIES
CAMPING

: : : FACILITIES
: : EDUCATIONAL FACILITIES
: EDUCATIONAL COMPLEXES
CAMPUSES

: : : PLANNING
: : FACILITY PLANNING
: : : PLANNING
: : EDUCATIONAL PLANNING
: EDUCATIONAL FACILITIES PLANNING
CAMPUS PLANNING

: : GROUPS
: NORTH AMERICANS
: : GROUPS
: ETHNIC GROUPS
CANADA NATIVES

: : : : LIBERAL ARTS
: : : HUMANITIES
: : LITERATURE
: NORTH AMERICAN LITERATURE
CANADIAN LITERATURE

: : DISABILITIES
: DISEASES
CANCER

: : : LANGUAGES
: : SINO TIBETAN LANGUAGES
: CHINESE
CANTONESE

: FINANCIAL SUPPORT
CAPITAL

: SOCIAL SYSTEMS
CAPITALISM

CAPITALIZATION (ALPHABETIC)

: EXPENDITURES
CAPITAL OUTLAY (FOR FIXED ASSETS)

CAPTIONS

: : : PUBLICATIONS
: : REFERENCE MATERIALS
: : : PUBLICATIONS
: : CATALOGS
: LIBRARY CATALOGS
CARD CATALOGS

: : : : : SERVICES
: : : : HUMAN SERVICES
: : : HEALTH SERVICES
: : MEDICAL SERVICES
: FIRST AID
CARDIOPULMONARY RESUSCITATION

CARDIOVASCULAR SYSTEM

: : : DEVELOPMENT
: : INDIVIDUAL DEVELOPMENT
: CAREER DEVELOPMENT
CAREER AWARENESS

: CHANGE
CAREER CHANGE

: SELECTION
CAREER CHOICE

: : GUIDANCE
: COUNSELING
: : GUIDANCE
: CAREER GUIDANCE
CAREER COUNSELING

: : DEVELOPMENT
: INDIVIDUAL DEVELOPMENT
CAREER DEVELOPMENT
. CAREER AWARENESS
. CAREER EXPLORATION

: EDUCATION
CAREER EDUCATION

: : : DEVELOPMENT
: : INDIVIDUAL DEVELOPMENT
: CAREER DEVELOPMENT
CAREER EXPLORATION

: GUIDANCE
CAREER GUIDANCE
. CAREER COUNSELING

: : MOBILITY
: OCCUPATIONAL MOBILITY
CAREER LADDERS

CAREER OPPORTUNITIES (1966 1980)

: PLANNING
CAREER PLANNING

CAREERS
. SCIENCE CAREERS

CARICATURES (1966 1980)

: : TECHNOLOGY
: WOODWORKING
: CONSTRUCTION (PROCESS)
CARPENTRY

: : STRUCTURAL ELEMENTS (CONSTRUCTION)
: FLOORING
CARPETING

: : : FACILITIES
: : EDUCATIONAL FACILITIES
: STUDY FACILITIES
CARRELS

: : : : : LIBERAL ARTS
: : : : HUMANITIES
: : : FINE ARTS
: : VISUAL ARTS
: GRAPHIC ARTS
CARTOGRAPHY

: VISUAL AIDS
CARTOONS

: : THEORIES
: LINGUISTIC THEORY
CASE (GRAMMAR)

: RECORDS (FORMS)
CASE RECORDS
. MEDICAL CASE HISTORIES

: RESEARCH
: : METHODS
: EVALUATION METHODS
CASE STUDIES
. CROSS SECTIONAL STUDIES
. FACILITY CASE STUDIES
. LONGITUDINAL STUDIES
. . FOLLOWUP STUDIES
. . . GRADUATE SURVEYS
. . . VOCATIONAL FOLLOWUP

: METHODS
CASEWORKER APPROACH

: : GROUPS
: PERSONNEL
CASEWORKERS
. PAROLE OFFICERS
. PROBATION OFFICERS
. SOCIAL WORKERS
. . SCHOOL SOCIAL WORKERS

: : GROUPS
: SOCIAL CLASS
CASTE

: : : : SERVICES
: : : INFORMATION SERVICES
: : INFORMATION PROCESSING
: DOCUMENTATION
CATALOGING
. MACHINE READABLE CATALOGING

: PUBLICATIONS
CATALOGS
. LIBRARY CATALOGS
. . BOOK CATALOGS
. . CARD CATALOGS
. . UNION CATALOGS
. ONLINE CATALOGS
. SCHOOL CATALOGS

: FINANCIAL SUPPORT
CATEGORICAL AID

: : : BACKGROUND
: : EXPERIENCE
: EMOTIONAL EXPERIENCE
CATHARSIS

: : : : GROUPS
: : : PERSONNEL
: : PROFESSIONAL PERSONNEL
: TEACHERS
CATHOLIC EDUCATORS

: : GROUPS
: RELIGIOUS CULTURAL GROUPS
CATHOLICS

: : : : INSTITUTIONS
: : : SCHOOLS
: : PRIVATE SCHOOLS
: PAROCHIAL SCHOOLS
CATHOLIC SCHOOLS

: LANGUAGES
CAUCASIAN LANGUAGES

: : : : LANGUAGES
: : : MALAYO POLYNESIAN LANGUAGES
: : INDONESIAN LANGUAGES
: VISAYAN
CEBUANO

: STRUCTURAL ELEMENTS (CONSTRUCTION)
CEILINGS

: : : BUSINESS
: : INDUSTRY
: MANUFACTURING INDUSTRY
CEMENT INDUSTRY

CENSORSHIP

: : DATA
: STATISTICAL DATA
CENSUS FIGURES

: : ORGANIZATION
: ADMINISTRATIVE ORGANIZATION
CENTRALIZATION

: : : : : LIBERAL ARTS
: : : : HUMANITIES
: : : FINE ARTS
: : VISUAL ARTS
: HANDICRAFTS
CERAMICS

: : : DISABILITIES
: : PHYSICAL DISABILITIES
: NEUROLOGICAL IMPAIRMENTS
: : DISABILITIES
: CONGENITAL IMPAIRMENTS
CEREBRAL PALSY

CERTIFICATION
. ACCREDITATION (INSTITUTIONS)
. COUNSELOR CERTIFICATION
. STUDENT CERTIFICATION
. TEACHER CERTIFICATION

: : : : GROUPS
: : : PERSONNEL
: : PROFESSIONAL PERSONNEL
: ACCOUNTANTS
CERTIFIED PUBLIC ACCOUNTANTS

: : LANGUAGES
: AFRO ASIATIC LANGUAGES
CHAD LANGUAGES
. HAUSA

: VISUAL AIDS
CHALKBOARDS

: : LANGUAGES
: MALAYO POLYNESIAN LANGUAGES
CHAMORRO

CHANGE
. ADMINISTRATIVE CHANGE
. ATTITUDE CHANGE
. BEHAVIOR CHANGE
. BUILDING CONVERSION
. CAREER CHANGE
. COMMUNITY CHANGE
. ECONOMIC CHANGE
. EDUCATIONAL CHANGE
. MEDIA ADAPTATION
. . TACTILE ADAPTATION
. MIDLIFE TRANSITIONS
. ORGANIZATIONAL CHANGE
. . MERGERS
. PERSONALITY CHANGE
. SOCIAL CHANGE
. . MODERNIZATION

: GROUPS
CHANGE AGENTS
. EXTENSION AGENTS
. LINKING AGENTS

: METHODS
CHANGE STRATEGIES

: LITERARY DEVICES
CHARACTERIZATION

: : : : COGNITIVE PROCESSES
: : : MEMORY
: : RECOGNITION (PSYCHOLOGY)
: PATTERN RECOGNITION
CHARACTER RECOGNITION

: VISUAL AIDS
CHARTS
. EXPERIENCE CHARTS
. FLOW CHARTS

: : : BEHAVIOR
: : SOCIAL BEHAVIOR
: ANTISOCIAL BEHAVIOR
CHEATING

: RECORDS (FORMS)
CHECK LISTS

: : METHODS
: EVALUATION METHODS
CHEMICAL ANALYSIS

: CHEMICAL REACTIONS
CHEMICAL BONDING

: : TECHNOLOGY
: ENGINEERING
CHEMICAL ENGINEERING

CHEMICAL EQUILIBRIUM

: : : BUSINESS
: : INDUSTRY
: MANUFACTURING INDUSTRY
CHEMICAL INDUSTRY

: VOCABULARY
CHEMICAL NOMENCLATURE

CHEMICAL REACTIONS
. CHEMICAL BONDING
. OXIDATION
. PHOTOCHEMICAL REACTIONS
. . PHOTOSYNTHESIS

: : : GROUPS
: : PERSONNEL
: PARAPROFESSIONAL PERSONNEL
CHEMICAL TECHNICIANS

: : : : LIBERAL ARTS
: : : SCIENCES
: : NATURAL SCIENCES
: PHYSICAL SCIENCES
CHEMISTRY
. BIOCHEMISTRY
. INORGANIC CHEMISTRY
. ORGANIC CHEMISTRY

: : : LANGUAGES
: : URALIC ALTAIC LANGUAGES
: FINNO UGRIC LANGUAGES
CHEREMIS

: : LANGUAGES
: AMERICAN INDIAN LANGUAGES
CHEROKEE

: : : BEHAVIOR
: : SOCIAL BEHAVIOR
: ANTISOCIAL BEHAVIOR
CHILD ABUSE

: ADVOCACY
CHILD ADVOCACY

CHILD CARE (1966 1980)

: GROUPS
CHILD CAREGIVERS

: : OCCUPATIONS
: SERVICE OCCUPATIONS
CHILD CARE OCCUPATIONS

CHILD CUSTODY

: : DEVELOPMENT
: INDIVIDUAL DEVELOPMENT
CHILD DEVELOPMENT

: : FACILITIES
: EDUCATIONAL FACILITIES
CHILD DEVELOPMENT CENTERS

: : : GROUPS
: : PERSONNEL
: SPECIALISTS
CHILD DEVELOPMENT SPECIALISTS

: ATTITUDES
CHILDHOOD ATTITUDES

: INTERESTS
CHILDHOOD INTERESTS

: : NEEDS
: INDIVIDUAL NEEDS
CHILDHOOD NEEDS

: LABOR
CHILD LABOR

: LANGUAGE
CHILD LANGUAGE

: : : BEHAVIOR
: : SOCIAL BEHAVIOR
: ANTISOCIAL BEHAVIOR
CHILD NEGLECT

: : : : LIBERAL ARTS
: : : SCIENCES
: : BEHAVIORAL SCIENCES
: PSYCHOLOGY
CHILD PSYCHOLOGY

CHILD REARING

: : GROUPS
: AGE GROUPS
CHILDREN
. ADOPTED CHILDREN
. FOSTER CHILDREN
. GRANDCHILDREN
. HOSPITALIZED CHILDREN
. LATCHKEY CHILDREN
. MIGRANT CHILDREN
. MINORITY GROUP CHILDREN
. PREADOLESCENTS
. PROBLEM CHILDREN
. TRANSIENT CHILDREN
. YOUNG CHILDREN
. . INFANTS
. . . NEONATES
. . . PREMATURE INFANTS
. . KINDERGARTEN CHILDREN
. . PRESCHOOL CHILDREN
. . TODDLERS

: : : : LIBERAL ARTS
: : : HUMANITIES
: : FINE ARTS
: VISUAL ARTS
CHILDRENS ART

: : ACTIVITIES
: GAMES
CHILDRENS GAMES

: : : LIBERAL ARTS
: : HUMANITIES
: LITERATURE
CHILDRENS LITERATURE

: CIVIL LIBERTIES
CHILDRENS RIGHTS

: : : : TECHNOLOGY
: : : COMMUNICATIONS
: : TELECOMMUNICATIONS
: : MASS MEDIA
: TELEVISION
CHILDRENS TELEVISION

: RESPONSIBILITY
CHILD RESPONSIBILITY

CHILD ROLE

: : QUALITY OF LIFE
: WELL BEING
CHILD WELFARE

: STRUCTURAL ELEMENTS (CONSTRUCTION)
CHIMNEYS

: : LANGUAGES
: SINO TIBETAN LANGUAGES
CHINESE
. CANTONESE
. FOOCHOW
. MANDARIN CHINESE

: : GROUPS
: ETHNIC GROUPS
: : : GROUPS
: : NORTH AMERICANS
: ASIAN AMERICANS
CHINESE AMERICANS

: CULTURE
CHINESE CULTURE

: : : LANGUAGES
: : AFRICAN LANGUAGES
: BANTU LANGUAGES
CHINYANJA

: : LANGUAGES
: AMERICAN INDIAN LANGUAGES
CHOCTAW

: : : : : LIBERAL ARTS
: : : : HUMANITIES
: : : FINE ARTS
: : MUSIC
: VOCAL MUSIC
CHORAL MUSIC

: : : : LIBERAL ARTS
: : : HUMANITIES
: : FINE ARTS
: THEATER ARTS
CHORAL SPEAKING

: RELIGION
CHRISTIANITY

: : METHODS
: LABORATORY PROCEDURES
CHROMATOGRAPHY

: : : : : LIBERAL ARTS
: : : : HUMANITIES
: : : LITERATURE
: : PROSE
: NONFICTION
: LITERARY GENRES
CHRONICLES

: : INDIVIDUAL CHARACTERISTICS
: AGE
CHRONOLOGICAL AGE

: INSTITUTIONS
CHURCHES

: PROGRAMS
CHURCH PROGRAMS

: : : INSTITUTIONS
: : SCHOOLS
: COLLEGES
CHURCH RELATED COLLEGES

: RESPONSIBILITY
CHURCH RESPONSIBILITY

: INSTITUTIONAL ROLE
CHURCH ROLE

: : GROUPS
: PERSONNEL
CHURCH WORKERS

: : : LANGUAGES
: : URALIC ALTAIC LANGUAGES
: TURKIC LANGUAGES
CHUVASH

: : : : : SERVICES
: : : : INFORMATION SERVICES
: : : INFORMATION PROCESSING
: : DOCUMENTATION
: BIBLIOMETRICS
CITATION ANALYSIS
. BIBLIOGRAPHIC COUPLING

: : : PUBLICATIONS
: : REFERENCE MATERIALS
: INDEXES
CITATION INDEXES

: : PUBLICATIONS
: REFERENCE MATERIALS
CITATIONS (REFERENCES)

: : BEHAVIOR
: PARTICIPATION
CITIZEN PARTICIPATION

CITIZEN ROLE

: : : GROUPS
: : ORGANIZATIONS (GROUPS)
: COMMUNITY ORGANIZATIONS
CITIZENS COUNCILS

: STATUS
CITIZENSHIP

: EDUCATION
CITIZENSHIP EDUCATION

: : RESPONSIBILITY
: SOCIAL RESPONSIBILITY
CITIZENSHIP RESPONSIBILITY

: : : : GROUPS
: : : ORGANIZATIONS (GROUPS)
: : GOVERNMENT (ADMINISTRATIVE BODY)
: LOCAL GOVERNMENT
CITY GOVERNMENT

: : : : GROUPS
: : : PERSONNEL
: : GOVERNMENT EMPLOYEES
: PUBLIC OFFICIALS
CITY OFFICIALS

: : : : LIBERAL ARTS
: : : SCIENCES
: : SOCIAL SCIENCES
: : CURRICULUM
: SOCIAL STUDIES
CIVICS

CIVIL DEFENSE

CIVIL DISOBEDIENCE

: : TECHNOLOGY
: ENGINEERING
CIVIL ENGINEERING

CIVIL LIBERTIES
. CHILDRENS RIGHTS
. CIVIL RIGHTS
. . EQUAL EDUCATION
. . EQUAL OPPORTUNITIES (JOBS)
. . EQUAL PROTECTION
. . VOTING RIGHTS
. DUE PROCESS
. FREEDOM OF SPEECH
. PARENT RIGHTS
. STUDENT RIGHTS
. TEACHER RIGHTS

: CIVIL LIBERTIES
CIVIL RIGHTS
. EQUAL EDUCATION
. EQUAL OPPORTUNITIES (JOBS)
. EQUAL PROTECTION
. VOTING RIGHTS

: LEGISLATION
CIVIL RIGHTS LEGISLATION

: : : : : : LIBERAL ARTS
: : : : : SCIENCES
: : : : SOCIAL SCIENCES
: : : : : LIBERAL ARTS
: : : : HUMANITIES
: : : HISTORY
: : NORTH AMERICAN HISTORY
: UNITED STATES HISTORY
CIVIL WAR (UNITED STATES)

: : ACTIVITIES
: SCHOOL ACTIVITIES
CLASS ACTIVITIES

CLASS ATTITUDES (1966 1980)

CLASS AVERAGE (1966 1980)

: GROUPS
CLASSES (GROUPS OF STUDENTS)
. MULTIGRADED CLASSES
. MULTILEVEL CLASSES (SECOND LANGUAGE INSTRUCTION)
. NONAUTHORITARIAN CLASSES
. SMALL CLASSES
. SPECIAL CLASSES

: CONDITIONING
CLASSICAL CONDITIONING

: LANGUAGES
CLASSICAL LANGUAGES
. LATIN
. SANSKRIT

: : : LIBERAL ARTS
: : HUMANITIES
: LITERATURE
CLASSICAL LITERATURE
. LATIN LITERATURE

: ORGANIZATION
CLASSIFICATION
. CLUSTER GROUPING
. CODIFICATION
. GROUPING (INSTRUCTIONAL PURPOSES)
. . HETEROGENEOUS GROUPING
. . HOMOGENEOUS GROUPING
. . . ABILITY GROUPING
. . NONGRADED INSTRUCTIONAL GROUPING
. LABELING (OF PERSONS)
. LANGUAGE CLASSIFICATION
. . LANGUAGE TYPOLOGY
. SPACE CLASSIFICATION

: ORGANIZATION
CLASS ORGANIZATION

CLASS RANK

: COMMUNICATION (THOUGHT TRANSFER)
CLASSROOM COMMUNICATION

: SOCIAL INTEGRATION
CLASSROOM DESEGREGATION

: DESIGN
CLASSROOM DESIGN

: : ENVIRONMENT
: EDUCATIONAL ENVIRONMENT
CLASSROOM ENVIRONMENT

: : EQUIPMENT
: FURNITURE
: : EQUIPMENT
: EDUCATIONAL EQUIPMENT
CLASSROOM FURNITURE

CLASSROOM GUIDANCE PROGRAMS (1968 1980)

: : METHODS
: MEASUREMENT TECHNIQUES
CLASSROOM OBSERVATION TECHNIQUES

: : RESEARCH
: EDUCATIONAL RESEARCH
CLASSROOM RESEARCH

: : FACILITIES
: EDUCATIONAL FACILITIES
CLASSROOMS
. ELECTRONIC CLASSROOMS
. MOBILE CLASSROOMS
. MULTIPURPOSE CLASSROOMS
. SELF CONTAINED CLASSROOMS

: : METHODS
: EDUCATIONAL METHODS
CLASSROOM TECHNIQUES

CLASS SIZE

: SANITATION
CLEANING
. DISHWASHING

: : : FACILITIES
: : RESOURCE CENTERS
: : INFORMATION SOURCES
: INFORMATION CENTERS
CLEARINGHOUSES

: : DISABILITIES
: SPEECH HANDICAPS
: : DISABILITIES
: PHYSICAL DISABILITIES
: : DISABILITIES
: CONGENITAL IMPAIRMENTS
CLEFT PALATE

: : GROUPS
: PERSONNEL
CLERGY
. PRIESTS

: OCCUPATIONS
CLERICAL OCCUPATIONS

: : : GROUPS
: : PERSONNEL
: NONPROFESSIONAL PERSONNEL
CLERICAL WORKERS
. COURT REPORTERS
. EXAMINERS
. FILE CLERKS
. RECEPTIONISTS
. SECRETARIES
. . SCHOOL SECRETARIES

CLICHES

CLIENT CHARACTERISTICS (HUMAN SERVICES)

: : ENVIRONMENT
: PHYSICAL ENVIRONMENT
CLIMATE

CLIMATE CONTROL
. AIR CONDITIONING
. HEATING
. HEAT RECOVERY
. REFRIGERATION
. VENTILATION

: IDENTIFICATION
CLINICAL DIAGNOSIS

: : : BACKGROUND
: : EXPERIENCE
: LEARNING EXPERIENCE
CLINICAL EXPERIENCE

: : : : LIBERAL ARTS
: : : SCIENCES
: : BEHAVIORAL SCIENCES
: PSYCHOLOGY
CLINICAL PSYCHOLOGY

: : : METHODS
: : EDUCATIONAL METHODS
: TEACHING METHODS
CLINICAL TEACHING (HEALTH PROFESSIONS)

CLINICS
. DENTAL CLINICS
. MENTAL HEALTH CLINICS
. MOBILE CLINICS
. PSYCHOEDUCATIONAL CLINICS
. SPEECH AND HEARING CLINICS

: : : : TECHNOLOGY
: : : COMMUNICATIONS
: : TELECOMMUNICATIONS
: : MASS MEDIA
: TELEVISION
CLOSED CIRCUIT TELEVISION

CLOTHING

: DESIGN
CLOTHING DESIGN

: INSTRUCTION
CLOTHING INSTRUCTION

: METHODS
CLOZE PROCEDURE

: GROUPS
CLUBS
. SCIENCE CLUBS
. YOUTH CLUBS

: : : : : METHODS
: : : : EVALUATION METHODS
: : : DATA ANALYSIS
: : STATISTICAL ANALYSIS
: MULTIVARIATE ANALYSIS
CLUSTER ANALYSIS

: : : INSTITUTIONS
: : SCHOOLS
: COLLEGES
CLUSTER COLLEGES

: : ORGANIZATION
: CLASSIFICATION
CLUSTER GROUPING

: : RESOURCES
: NATURAL RESOURCES
: FUELS
COAL

: : GUIDANCE
: COUNSELING
COCOUNSELING

: : STANDARDS
: BEHAVIOR STANDARDS
CODES OF ETHICS

CODE SWITCHING (LANGUAGE)

: : ORGANIZATION
: CLASSIFICATION
CODIFICATION

: EDUCATION
COEDUCATION

: ABILITY
COGNITIVE ABILITY

: : DEVELOPMENT
: INDIVIDUAL DEVELOPMENT
COGNITIVE DEVELOPMENT
. INTELLECTUAL DEVELOPMENT
. PERCEPTUAL DEVELOPMENT
. VERBAL DEVELOPMENT
. . LANGUAGE ACQUISITION

: PSYCHOLOGICAL PATTERNS
COGNITIVE DISSONANCE

: : COGNITIVE PROCESSES
: LEARNING PROCESSES
COGNITIVE MAPPING

: MEASUREMENT
COGNITIVE MEASUREMENT

: : OBJECTIVES
: BEHAVIORAL OBJECTIVES
COGNITIVE OBJECTIVES

COGNITIVE PROCESSES
. ABSTRACT REASONING
. . GENERALIZATION
. . . STIMULUS GENERALIZATION
. ASSOCIATION (PSYCHOLOGY)
. CONFLICT RESOLUTION
. CONVERGENT THINKING
. CREATIVE THINKING
. . DIVERGENT THINKING
. . PRODUCTIVE THINKING
. CRITICAL THINKING
. . EVALUATIVE THINKING
. . . VALUE JUDGMENT
. DECISION MAKING
. . PARTICIPATIVE DECISION MAKING
. ENCODING (PSYCHOLOGY)
. INTUITION
. LANGUAGE PROCESSING
. . EXPRESSIVE LANGUAGE

COGNITIVE PROCESSES (CONTINUED)

.. INTERFERENCE (LANGUAGE)
.. READING PROCESSES
... DECODING (READING)
.. RECEPTIVE LANGUAGE
. LEARNING PROCESSES
.. BEHAVIOR CHAINING
.. COGNITIVE MAPPING
.. CONCEPT FORMATION
.. DISCOVERY PROCESSES
.. EXTINCTION (PSYCHOLOGY)
.. GENERALIZATION
... STIMULUS GENERALIZATION
.. HABITUATION
.. MEMORIZATION
.. PRIMACY EFFECT
. LOGICAL THINKING
.. DEDUCTION
.. INDUCTION
. MEMORY
.. EIDETIC IMAGERY
.. LONG TERM MEMORY
.. RECALL (PSYCHOLOGY)
.. RECOGNITION (PSYCHOLOGY)
... PATTERN RECOGNITION
.... CHARACTER RECOGNITION
... WORD RECOGNITION
.. RETENTION (PSYCHOLOGY)
.. SHORT TERM MEMORY
. METACOGNITION
.. MEDITATION
... TRANSCENDENTAL MEDITATION
. PERCEPTION
.. AUDITORY PERCEPTION
... AUDITORY DISCRIMINATION
.. KINESTHETIC PERCEPTION
.. TACTUAL PERCEPTION
.. VISUAL PERCEPTION
... DEPTH PERCEPTION
... VISUAL ACUITY
... VISUAL DISCRIMINATION
. PROBLEM SOLVING
. ROLE PERCEPTION
. SERIAL ORDERING
. SOCIAL COGNITION
. VISUALIZATION

:::: LIBERAL ARTS
::: SCIENCES
:: BEHAVIORAL SCIENCES
: PSYCHOLOGY
COGNITIVE PSYCHOLOGY

COGNITIVE RESTRUCTURING

COGNITIVE STRUCTURES

:: INDIVIDUAL CHARACTERISTICS
: PSYCHOLOGICAL CHARACTERISTICS
COGNITIVE STYLE
. CONCEPTUAL TEMPO
. FIELD DEPENDENCE INDEPENDENCE

:: MEASURES (INDIVIDUALS)
: TESTS
COGNITIVE TESTS
. INTELLIGENCE TESTS
. PERCEPTION TESTS
.. TACTUAL VISUAL TESTS

:: LANGUAGE ARTS
: RHETORIC
COHERENCE

: CONNECTED DISCOURSE
COHESION (WRITTEN COMPOSITION)

: RESEARCH
COHORT ANALYSIS

COLLECTIVE BARGAINING
. SCOPE OF BARGAINING

: COMMUNITY
COLLECTIVE SETTLEMENTS

:::: GOVERNANCE
::: ADMINISTRATION
:: INSTITUTIONAL ADMINISTRATION
:::: GOVERNANCE
::: ADMINISTRATION
:: EDUCATIONAL ADMINISTRATION
: SCHOOL ADMINISTRATION
COLLEGE ADMINISTRATION

: ADMISSION (SCHOOL)
COLLEGE ADMISSION

: GROUPS
COLLEGE APPLICANTS

::: ACTIVITIES
:: PHYSICAL ACTIVITIES
: ATHLETICS
COLLEGE ATHLETICS

: ATTENDANCE
COLLEGE ATTENDANCE

:::: GROUPS
::: STUDENTS
:: SECONDARY SCHOOL STUDENTS
: HIGH SCHOOL STUDENTS
COLLEGE BOUND STUDENTS

::: FACILITIES
:: EDUCATIONAL FACILITIES
::: FACILITIES
:: BUILDINGS
: SCHOOL BUILDINGS
COLLEGE BUILDINGS

:: SELECTION
: SCHOOL CHOICE
COLLEGE CHOICE

: CREDITS
COLLEGE CREDITS

: CURRICULUM
COLLEGE CURRICULUM
. COLLEGE ENGLISH
. COLLEGE MATHEMATICS
. COLLEGE SCIENCE
. COLLEGE SECOND LANGUAGE PROGRAMS
. EDUCATION COURSES
. FRESHMAN COMPOSITION
. POSTSECONDARY EDUCATION AS A FIELD OF STUDY
. TEACHER EDUCATION CURRICULUM
.. METHODS COURSES

: PROGRAMS
COLLEGE DAY

:: SOCIAL INTEGRATION
: SCHOOL DESEGREGATION
COLLEGE DESEGREGATION

:: CURRICULUM
: ENGLISH CURRICULUM
:: CURRICULUM
: COLLEGE CURRICULUM
COLLEGE ENGLISH

:: MEASURES (INDIVIDUALS)
: TESTS
COLLEGE ENTRANCE EXAMINATIONS

:: ENVIRONMENT
: INSTITUTIONAL ENVIRONMENT
:: ENVIRONMENT
: EDUCATIONAL ENVIRONMENT
COLLEGE ENVIRONMENT

:::: GROUPS
::: PERSONNEL
:: SCHOOL PERSONNEL
:::: GROUPS
::: PERSONNEL
:: PROFESSIONAL PERSONNEL
: FACULTY
COLLEGE FACULTY
. COLLEGE PRESIDENTS
. COUNSELOR EDUCATORS
. GRADUATE SCHOOL FACULTY
.. MEDICAL SCHOOL FACULTY
. PROFESSORS
. STUDENT TEACHER SUPERVISORS
. TEACHER EDUCATORS
.. METHODS TEACHERS
. TEACHING ASSISTANTS

::: GROUPS
:: STUDENTS
: COLLEGE STUDENTS
COLLEGE FRESHMEN

:: GROUPS
: ORGANIZATIONS (GROUPS)
COLLEGE GOVERNING COUNCILS

::: GROUPS
:: ALUMNI
: GRADUATES
COLLEGE GRADUATES

:: FACILITIES
: HOUSING
COLLEGE HOUSING

: INSTRUCTION
COLLEGE INSTRUCTION

COLLEGE LANGUAGE PROGRAMS (1967 1980)

::: INSTITUTIONS
::: INFORMATION SOURCES
:: LIBRARIES
: ACADEMIC LIBRARIES
COLLEGE LIBRARIES

:: CURRICULUM
: MATHEMATICS CURRICULUM
:: CURRICULUM
: COLLEGE CURRICULUM
COLLEGE MATHEMATICS

:: PLANNING
: EDUCATIONAL PLANNING
COLLEGE PLANNING

::: EDUCATION
:: ELEMENTARY SECONDARY EDUCATION
: SECONDARY EDUCATION
COLLEGE PREPARATION

:::: GROUPS
::: PERSONNEL
:: ADMINISTRATORS
: PRESIDENTS
::::: GROUPS
:::: PERSONNEL
::: SCHOOL PERSONNEL
::::: GROUPS
:::: PERSONNEL
::: PROFESSIONAL PERSONNEL
:: FACULTY
: COLLEGE FACULTY
COLLEGE PRESIDENTS

: PROGRAMS
COLLEGE PROGRAMS
. DOCTORAL PROGRAMS
. EXTERNAL DEGREE PROGRAMS
. MASTERS PROGRAMS

:: INSTITUTIONAL ROLE
: SCHOOL ROLE
COLLEGE ROLE

:: INSTITUTIONS
: SCHOOLS
COLLEGES
. AGRICULTURAL COLLEGES
. BLACK COLLEGES
. CHURCH RELATED COLLEGES
. CLUSTER COLLEGES
. COMMUTER COLLEGES
. DENTAL SCHOOLS
. DEVELOPING INSTITUTIONS
. EXPERIMENTAL COLLEGES
. LAW SCHOOLS
. LIBRARY SCHOOLS
. MEDICAL SCHOOLS
. MULTICAMPUS COLLEGES
. NONCAMPUS COLLEGES
. PRIVATE COLLEGES
. PUBLIC COLLEGES
.. COMMUNITY COLLEGES
.. STATE COLLEGES
... STATE UNIVERSITIES
. RESIDENTIAL COLLEGES
. SELECTIVE COLLEGES
. SINGLE SEX COLLEGES
. SMALL COLLEGES
. TWO YEAR COLLEGES
.. COMMUNITY COLLEGES
.. TECHNICAL INSTITUTES
. UNIVERSITIES
.. LAND GRANT UNIVERSITIES
.. OPEN UNIVERSITIES
.. RESEARCH UNIVERSITIES
.. STATE UNIVERSITIES
.. URBAN UNIVERSITIES
. UPPER DIVISION COLLEGES

::: BEHAVIOR
:: COOPERATION
: INSTITUTIONAL COOPERATION
::: BEHAVIOR
:: COOPERATION
: EDUCATIONAL COOPERATION
COLLEGE SCHOOL COOPERATION

:: CURRICULUM
: SCIENCE CURRICULUM
:: CURRICULUM
: COLLEGE CURRICULUM
COLLEGE SCIENCE

:: PROGRAMS
: SECOND LANGUAGE PROGRAMS
:: CURRICULUM
: COLLEGE CURRICULUM
COLLEGE SECOND LANGUAGE PROGRAMS

::: SOCIAL DISCRIMINATION
:: EDUCATIONAL DISCRIMINATION
: SCHOOL SEGREGATION
COLLEGE SEGREGATION

::: GROUPS
:: STUDENTS
: COLLEGE STUDENTS
COLLEGE SENIORS

: FACILITIES
COLLEGE STORES

: : GROUPS
: STUDENTS
COLLEGE STUDENTS
. COLLEGE FRESHMEN
. COLLEGE SENIORS
. COLLEGE TRANSFER STUDENTS
. GRADUATE STUDENTS
. . DENTAL STUDENTS
. . LAW STUDENTS
. . MEDICAL STUDENTS
. . . GRADUATE MEDICAL STUDENTS
. IN STATE STUDENTS
. ON CAMPUS STUDENTS
. OUT OF STATE STUDENTS
. RESIDENT ASSISTANTS
. STUDENT TEACHERS
. TWO YEAR COLLEGE STUDENTS
. UNDERGRADUATE STUDENTS
. . PREMEDICAL STUDENTS

: : : GROUPS
: : STUDENTS
: TRANSFER STUDENTS
: : : GROUPS
: : STUDENTS
: COLLEGE STUDENTS
COLLEGE TRANSFER STUDENTS

: : : : : : LIBERAL ARTS
: : : : : SCIENCES
: : : : SOCIAL SCIENCES
: : : : : LIBERAL ARTS
: : : : HUMANITIES
: : : HISTORY
: : NORTH AMERICAN HISTORY
: UNITED STATES HISTORY
COLONIAL HISTORY (UNITED STATES)

: : : POLICY
: : FOREIGN POLICY
: IMPERIALISM
COLONIALISM

COLOR

: PLANNING
COLOR PLANNING

: : : : : LIBERAL ARTS
: : : : HUMANITIES
: : : FINE ARTS
: : THEATER ARTS
: : : : LIBERAL ARTS
: : : HUMANITIES
: : LITERATURE
: DRAMA
COMEDY
. SKITS

: PUBLICATIONS
COMICS (PUBLICATIONS)

: : EVALUATION
: RECOGNITION (ACHIEVEMENT)
COMMENCEMENT CEREMONIES

: ART
COMMERCIAL ART

: : : : TECHNOLOGY
: : : COMMUNICATIONS
: : TELECOMMUNICATIONS
: : MASS MEDIA
: TELEVISION
COMMERCIAL TELEVISION

COMMITTEES
. ADVISORY COMMITTEES
. BIRACIAL COMMITTEES
. RESEARCH COMMITTEES
. SEARCH COMMITTEES (PERSONNEL)

: : DISABILITIES
: DISEASES
COMMUNICABLE DISEASES
. RUBELLA
. VENEREAL DISEASES

COMMUNICATION (THOUGHT TRANSFER)
. CLASSROOM COMMUNICATION
. DIFFUSION (COMMUNICATION)
. DISCUSSION
. . GROUP DISCUSSION
. INTERCULTURAL COMMUNICATION
. INTERPERSONAL COMMUNICATION
. MANUAL COMMUNICATION
. . CUED SPEECH
. . FINGER SPELLING
. . SIGN LANGUAGE
. . . AMERICAN SIGN LANGUAGE
. NONVERBAL COMMUNICATION
. . BODY LANGUAGE
. . EYE CONTACT
. . FACIAL EXPRESSIONS
. ORGANIZATIONAL COMMUNICATION
. . BUSINESS COMMUNICATION
. . . BUSINESS CORRESPONDENCE
. . INTERSCHOOL COMMUNICATION
. PROPAGANDA
. PUBLICITY
. . ADVERTISING
. . . TELEVISION COMMERCIALS
. . INSTITUTIONAL ADVANCEMENT
. SPEECH COMMUNICATION
. . ORAL INTERPRETATION
. . PUBLIC SPEAKING
. TOTAL COMMUNICATION
. VERBAL COMMUNICATION
. . BUSINESS CORRESPONDENCE
. . DICTATION
. . LETTERS (CORRESPONDENCE)

COMMUNICATION AIDS (FOR DISABLED)

: : PSYCHOLOGICAL PATTERNS
: ANXIETY
COMMUNICATION APPREHENSION

: AUDITS (VERIFICATION)
COMMUNICATION AUDITS

: DISABILITIES
COMMUNICATION DISORDERS

: PROBLEMS
COMMUNICATION PROBLEMS

: RESEARCH
COMMUNICATION RESEARCH

: TECHNOLOGY
COMMUNICATIONS
. AUDIOVISUAL COMMUNICATIONS
. . DIAL ACCESS INFORMATION SYSTEMS
. . EDUCATIONAL RADIO
. . EDUCATIONAL TELEVISION
. . LOOP INDUCTION SYSTEMS
. TELECOMMUNICATIONS
. . COMMUNICATIONS SATELLITES
. . ELECTRONIC MAIL
. . ELECTRONIC PUBLISHING
. . FACSIMILE TRANSMISSION
. . RADIO
. . . EDUCATIONAL RADIO
. . TELECONFERENCING
. . TELEPHONE COMMUNICATIONS SYSTEMS
. . TELEVISION
. . . BROADCAST TELEVISION
. . . CABLE TELEVISION
. . . CHILDRENS TELEVISION
. . . CLOSED CIRCUIT TELEVISION
. . . COMMERCIAL TELEVISION
. . . EDUCATIONAL TELEVISION
. . . PUBLIC TELEVISION
. . VIDEOTEX

: : ABILITY
: SKILLS
COMMUNICATION SKILLS
. COMMUNICATIVE COMPETENCE (LANGUAGES)
. . THRESHOLD LEVEL (LANGUAGES)

: : : TECHNOLOGY
: : COMMUNICATIONS
: TELECOMMUNICATIONS
: SATELLITES (AEROSPACE)
COMMUNICATIONS SATELLITES

: : : ABILITY
: : SKILLS
: LANGUAGE SKILLS
: : : ABILITY
: : SKILLS
: COMMUNICATION SKILLS
COMMUNICATIVE COMPETENCE (LANGUAGES)
. THRESHOLD LEVEL (LANGUAGES)

: SOCIAL SYSTEMS
COMMUNISM

COMMUNITY
. BLACK COMMUNITY
. COLLECTIVE SETTLEMENTS
. MUNICIPALITIES
. NEIGHBORHOODS
. PLANNED COMMUNITIES

: SOCIAL ACTION
COMMUNITY ACTION

: ATTITUDES
COMMUNITY ATTITUDES
. COMMUNITY SATISFACTION

COMMUNITY BENEFITS

: FACILITIES
COMMUNITY CENTERS

: CHANGE
COMMUNITY CHANGE

COMMUNITY CHARACTERISTICS
. COMMUNITY SIZE

: : : : INSTITUTIONS
: : : SCHOOLS
: : COLLEGES
: TWO YEAR COLLEGES
: : : : INSTITUTIONS
: : : SCHOOLS
: : COLLEGES
: PUBLIC COLLEGES
COMMUNITY COLLEGES

: GOVERNANCE
COMMUNITY CONTROL

: : BEHAVIOR
: COOPERATION
COMMUNITY COOPERATION

: COORDINATION
COMMUNITY COORDINATION

: DEVELOPMENT
COMMUNITY DEVELOPMENT

: EDUCATION
COMMUNITY EDUCATION

: : : SERVICES
: : HUMAN SERVICES
: HEALTH SERVICES
: : SERVICES
: COMMUNITY SERVICES
COMMUNITY HEALTH SERVICES

: INFLUENCES
COMMUNITY INFLUENCE

: : SERVICES
: INFORMATION SERVICES
: : SERVICES
: COMMUNITY SERVICES
COMMUNITY INFORMATION SERVICES
. HOTLINES (PUBLIC)

: : BEHAVIOR
: PARTICIPATION
COMMUNITY INVOLVEMENT

: : GROUPS
: LEADERS
: GROUPS
COMMUNITY LEADERS

: : GROUPS
: ORGANIZATIONS (GROUPS)
COMMUNITY ORGANIZATIONS
. CITIZENS COUNCILS

: PLANNING
COMMUNITY PLANNING

: PROBLEMS
COMMUNITY PROBLEMS

: PROGRAMS
COMMUNITY PROGRAMS
. COMMUNITY RECREATION PROGRAMS
. SCHOOL COMMUNITY PROGRAMS

: : : : LIBERAL ARTS
: : : SCIENCES
: : BEHAVIORAL SCIENCES
: PSYCHOLOGY
COMMUNITY PSYCHOLOGY

: : PROGRAMS
: RECREATIONAL PROGRAMS
: : PROGRAMS
: COMMUNITY PROGRAMS
COMMUNITY RECREATION PROGRAMS

: RELATIONSHIP
COMMUNITY RELATIONS

: RESOURCES
COMMUNITY RESOURCES

: RESPONSIBILITY
COMMUNITY RESPONSIBILITY

COMMUNITY ROLE

: : ATTITUDES
: COMMUNITY ATTITUDES
COMMUNITY SATISFACTION

: : INSTITUTIONS
: SCHOOLS
COMMUNITY SCHOOLS

: SERVICES
COMMUNITY SERVICES
. COMMUNITY HEALTH SERVICES
. COMMUNITY INFORMATION SERVICES
. . HOTLINES (PUBLIC)

: COMMUNITY CHARACTERISTICS
COMMUNITY SIZE

: RESEARCH
COMMUNITY STUDY

COMMUNITY SUPPORT

: : : METHODS
: : EVALUATION METHODS
: SURVEYS
COMMUNITY SURVEYS

: ZONING
COMMUNITY ZONING

: : : INSTITUTIONS
: : SCHOOLS
: COLLEGES
COMMUTER COLLEGES

: : GROUPS
: STUDENTS
COMMUTING STUDENTS

COMPARABLE WORTH

: : METHODS
: EVALUATION METHODS
COMPARATIVE ANALYSIS
. EDUCATIONAL STATUS COMPARISON
. ERROR ANALYSIS (LANGUAGE)

: EDUCATION
COMPARATIVE EDUCATION

: : : METHODS
: : MEASUREMENT TECHNIQUES
: TESTING
COMPARATIVE TESTING

: FUNDAMENTAL CONCEPTS
COMPENSATION (CONCEPT)

: EXPENDITURES
COMPENSATION (REMUNERATION)

: EDUCATION
COMPENSATORY EDUCATION

: ABILITY
COMPETENCE
. INTERPERSONAL COMPETENCE
. MINIMUM COMPETENCIES

: EDUCATION
COMPETENCY BASED EDUCATION
. COMPETENCY BASED TEACHER EDUCATION

: : : EDUCATION
: : PROFESSIONAL EDUCATION
: TEACHER EDUCATION
: : EDUCATION
: COMPETENCY BASED EDUCATION
COMPETENCY BASED TEACHER EDUCATION

: BEHAVIOR
COMPETITION
. COMPETITIVE SELECTION

: SELECTION
: : BEHAVIOR
: COMPETITION
COMPETITIVE SELECTION

: : : BEHAVIOR
: : COOPERATION
: COMPLIANCE (PSYCHOLOGY)
COMPLIANCE (LEGAL)

: : BEHAVIOR
: COOPERATION
COMPLIANCE (PSYCHOLOGY)
. COMPLIANCE (LEGAL)
. OBEDIENCE

: : METHODS
: EVALUATION METHODS
COMPONENTIAL ANALYSIS

: : : INDIVIDUAL CHARACTERISTICS
: : PSYCHOLOGICAL CHARACTERISTICS
: INTELLIGENCE
COMPREHENSION
. LISTENING COMPREHENSION
. READING COMPREHENSION

: PROGRAMS
COMPREHENSIVE PROGRAMS

: EDUCATION
COMPULSORY EDUCATION
. HOME SCHOOLING

: MATHEMATICAL APPLICATIONS
COMPUTATION
. ESTIMATION (MATHEMATICS)

: LINGUISTICS
COMPUTATIONAL LINGUISTICS
. MACHINE TRANSLATION

: : : : METHODS
: : : EDUCATIONAL METHODS
: : TEACHING METHODS
: PROGRAMED INSTRUCTION
: COMPUTER USES IN EDUCATION
COMPUTER ASSISTED INSTRUCTION

: : : METHODS
: : MEASUREMENT TECHNIQUES
: TESTING
: COMPUTER USES IN EDUCATION
COMPUTER ASSISTED TESTING

: : : : : LIBERAL ARTS
: : : : HUMANITIES
: : : FINE ARTS
: : VISUAL ARTS
: GRAPHIC ARTS
COMPUTER GRAPHICS

: TECHNOLOGICAL LITERACY
COMPUTER LITERACY

: INFORMATION SYSTEMS
: COMPUTER USES IN EDUCATION
COMPUTER MANAGED INSTRUCTION

: NETWORKS
COMPUTER NETWORKS
. LOCAL AREA NETWORKS

: PROGRAMS
COMPUTER ORIENTED PROGRAMS

: : : VISUAL AIDS
: : MICROFORMS
: MICROFILM
COMPUTER OUTPUT MICROFILM

: : EQUIPMENT
: ELECTRONIC EQUIPMENT
COMPUTERS
. ANALOG COMPUTERS
. COMPUTER STORAGE DEVICES
. DIGITAL COMPUTERS
. DISPLAY SYSTEMS
. INPUT OUTPUT DEVICES
. . OPTICAL SCANNERS
. MICROCOMPUTERS
. MINICOMPUTERS
. ONLINE SYSTEMS
. . INTERACTIVE VIDEO
. . ONLINE CATALOGS

: : : LIBERAL ARTS
: : SCIENCES
: INFORMATION SCIENCE
COMPUTER SCIENCE
. PROGRAMING

: EDUCATION
COMPUTER SCIENCE EDUCATION

: : METHODS
: SIMULATION
COMPUTER SIMULATION

: : STANDARDS
: SPECIFICATIONS
COMPUTER SOFTWARE
. COURSEWARE
. DATABASE MANAGEMENT SYSTEMS
. MENU DRIVEN SOFTWARE

: PUBLICATIONS
COMPUTER SOFTWARE REVIEWS

: : : EQUIPMENT
: : ELECTRONIC EQUIPMENT
: COMPUTERS
COMPUTER STORAGE DEVICES

COMPUTER USES IN EDUCATION
. COMPUTER ASSISTED INSTRUCTION
. COMPUTER ASSISTED TESTING
. COMPUTER MANAGED INSTRUCTION

: : COGNITIVE PROCESSES
: LEARNING PROCESSES
CONCEPT FORMATION

: INSTRUCTION
CONCEPT TEACHING

CONCEPTUAL SCHEMES (1967 1980)

: : : INDIVIDUAL CHARACTERISTICS
: : PSYCHOLOGICAL CHARACTERISTICS
: COGNITIVE STYLE
CONCEPTUAL TEMPO

: : ACTIVITIES
: MUSIC ACTIVITIES
CONCERTS

: : : : STANDARDS
: : : CRITERIA
: : EVALUATION CRITERIA
: VALIDITY
CONCURRENT VALIDITY

CONDITIONING
. BEHAVIOR MODIFICATION
. . CONTINGENCY MANAGEMENT
. . DESENSITIZATION
. CLASSICAL CONDITIONING
. OPERANT CONDITIONING
. . VERBAL OPERANT CONDITIONING

: : PUBLICATIONS
: REPORTS
CONFERENCE PAPERS

: : PUBLICATIONS
: SERIALS
CONFERENCE PROCEEDINGS

CONFERENCE REPORTS (1967 1980)

CONFERENCES
. PARENT CONFERENCES
. PARENT TEACHER CONFERENCES

: : : METHODS
: : MEASUREMENT TECHNIQUES
: TESTING
CONFIDENCE TESTING

: : RELATIONSHIP
: PRIVACY
CONFIDENTIALITY

: RECORDS (FORMS)
CONFIDENTIAL RECORDS

CONFLICT
. CONFLICT OF INTEREST
. CULTURE CONFLICT
. RELIGIOUS CONFLICT
. REVOLUTION
. ROLE CONFLICT
. WAR
. . NUCLEAR WARFARE

: CONFLICT
CONFLICT OF INTEREST

: COGNITIVE PROCESSES
CONFLICT RESOLUTION

: : BEHAVIOR
: SOCIAL BEHAVIOR
CONFORMITY

: RELIGION
CONFUCIANISM

: DISABILITIES
CONGENITAL IMPAIRMENTS
. CEREBRAL PALSY
. CLEFT PALATE
. DOWNS SYNDROME

CONGRUENCE (1970 1980)

: : MATHEMATICAL CONCEPTS
: GEOMETRIC CONCEPTS
CONGRUENCE (MATHEMATICS)

: PSYCHOLOGICAL PATTERNS
CONGRUENCE (PSYCHOLOGY)
. SELF CONGRUENCE

CONNECTED DISCOURSE
. COHESION (WRITTEN COMPOSITION)

: FUNDAMENTAL CONCEPTS
CONSERVATION (CONCEPT)

CONSERVATION (ENVIRONMENT)
. ENERGY CONSERVATION
. . HEAT RECOVERY
. SOIL CONSERVATION

: : EDUCATION
: ENVIRONMENTAL EDUCATION
CONSERVATION EDUCATION

CONSERVATISM

: : INSTITUTIONS
: SCHOOLS
CONSOLIDATED SCHOOLS

: : : : LINGUISTICS
: : : PHONOLOGY
: : PHONEMICS
: PHONEMES
CONSONANTS

: : GROUPS
: ORGANIZATIONS (GROUPS)
CONSORTIA

: : : : LIBERAL ARTS
: : : SCIENCES
: : SOCIAL SCIENCES
: : : LIBERAL ARTS
: : HUMANITIES
: HISTORY
CONSTITUTIONAL HISTORY

: : STANDARDS
: LAWS
CONSTITUTIONAL LAW

: : BEHAVIOR
: RESPONSES
CONSTRUCTED RESPONSE

CONSTRUCTION (PROCESS)
. CABINETMAKING
. CARPENTRY
. MASONRY
. . BRICKLAYING
. PREFABRICATION
. ROAD CONSTRUCTION
. SCHOOL CONSTRUCTION

: COSTS
CONSTRUCTION COSTS

: : BUSINESS
: INDUSTRY
CONSTRUCTION INDUSTRY
. HOUSING INDUSTRY

: : GOVERNANCE
: ADMINISTRATION
CONSTRUCTION MANAGEMENT

CONSTRUCTION MATERIALS
. ASPHALTS
. PRESTRESSED CONCRETE

: NEEDS
CONSTRUCTION NEEDS

: PROGRAMS
CONSTRUCTION PROGRAMS

: : : : : STANDARDS
: : : : CRITERIA
: : : EVALUATION CRITERIA
: : VALIDITY
: TEST VALIDITY
CONSTRUCT VALIDITY

: : GROUPS
: PERSONNEL
CONSULTANTS
. MEDICAL CONSULTANTS
. READING CONSULTANTS
. SCIENCE CONSULTANTS

: PROGRAMS
CONSULTATION PROGRAMS

: : : : LIBERAL ARTS
: : : SCIENCES
: : SOCIAL SCIENCES
: ECONOMICS
CONSUMER ECONOMICS

: EDUCATION
CONSUMER EDUCATION
. CONSUMER SCIENCE

CONSUMER PROTECTION

: TECHNOLOGY
: : EDUCATION
: CONSUMER EDUCATION
CONSUMER SCIENCE

: : METHODS
: EVALUATION METHODS
CONTENT ANALYSIS

: : INSTRUCTION
: READING INSTRUCTION
: : LITERACY
: : LANGUAGE ARTS
: READING
CONTENT AREA READING

: : INSTRUCTION
: WRITING INSTRUCTION
: : LITERACY
: : LANGUAGE ARTS
: WRITING (COMPOSITION)
CONTENT AREA WRITING

: : : : : STANDARDS
: : : : CRITERIA
: : : EVALUATION CRITERIA
: : VALIDITY
: TEST VALIDITY
CONTENT VALIDITY

: : STIMULI
: CUES
CONTEXT CLUES

: : : : THEORIES
: : : LINGUISTIC THEORY
: : GENERATIVE GRAMMAR
: TRANSFORMATIONAL GENERATIVE GRAMMAR
CONTEXT FREE GRAMMAR

: : CONDITIONING
: BEHAVIOR MODIFICATION
CONTINGENCY MANAGEMENT

CONTINUATION EDUCATION (1968 1980)

: : GROUPS
: STUDENTS
CONTINUATION STUDENTS

: : EDUCATION
: ADULT EDUCATION
CONTINUING EDUCATION
. PROFESSIONAL CONTINUING EDUCATION

: : FACILITIES
: EDUCATIONAL FACILITIES
CONTINUING EDUCATION CENTERS

: CREDITS
CONTINUING EDUCATION UNITS

: CURRICULUM
CONTINUOUS PROGRESS PLAN

CONTRACEPTION

CONTRACTS
. PERFORMANCE CONTRACTS

: : INCOME
: : EXPENDITURES
: SALARIES
CONTRACT SALARIES

CONTRAST

: LINGUISTICS
CONTRASTIVE LINGUISTICS

: GROUPS
CONTROL GROUPS

CONTROLLED ENVIRONMENT (1966 1980)

CONTROVERSIAL ISSUES (COURSE CONTENT)

: : : METHODS
: : EDUCATIONAL METHODS
: TEACHING METHODS
CONVENTIONAL INSTRUCTION

: COGNITIVE PROCESSES
CONVERGENT THINKING

: : CURRICULUM
: MODERN LANGUAGE CURRICULUM
: : CURRICULUM
: COURSES
CONVERSATIONAL LANGUAGE COURSES

: INSTRUCTION
COOKING INSTRUCTION

: : : : GROUPS
: : : PERSONNEL
: : NONPROFESSIONAL PERSONNEL
: SERVICE WORKERS
COOKS

: : : : GROUPS
: : : PERSONNEL
: : PROFESSIONAL PERSONNEL
: TEACHERS
COOPERATING TEACHERS

: BEHAVIOR
COOPERATION
. AGENCY COOPERATION
. COMMUNITY COOPERATION
. COMPLIANCE (PSYCHOLOGY)
. . COMPLIANCE (LEGAL)
. . OBEDIENCE
. EDUCATIONAL COOPERATION
. . COLLEGE SCHOOL COOPERATION
. . COUNSELOR TEACHER COOPERATION
. . INTERCOLLEGIATE COOPERATION
. . PARENT TEACHER COOPERATION
. INSTITUTIONAL COOPERATION
. . COLLEGE SCHOOL COOPERATION
. . INTERCOLLEGIATE COOPERATION
. . LIBRARY COOPERATION
. INTERNATIONAL COOPERATION
. REGIONAL COOPERATION

: : EDUCATION
: VOCATIONAL EDUCATION
COOPERATIVE EDUCATION

: PLANNING
COOPERATIVE PLANNING

: PROGRAMS
COOPERATIVE PROGRAMS

: : GROUPS
: ORGANIZATIONS (GROUPS)
COOPERATIVES

: : : PUBLICATIONS
: : REFERENCE MATERIALS
: INDEXES
COORDINATE INDEXES

COORDINATION
. COMMUNITY COORDINATION

COORDINATION COMPOUNDS

: : : GROUPS
: : PERSONNEL
: ADMINISTRATORS
COORDINATORS
. AUDIOVISUAL COORDINATORS
. INSTRUCTOR COORDINATORS

: : BEHAVIOR
: ADJUSTMENT (TO ENVIRONMENT)
COPING

: : OWNERSHIP
: INTELLECTUAL PROPERTY
COPYRIGHTS

: CURRICULUM
CORE CURRICULUM

: : REINFORCEMENT
: PUNISHMENT
CORPORAL PUNISHMENT

: EDUCATION
CORPORATE EDUCATION

CORPORATE SUPPORT

: EDUCATION
CORRECTIONAL EDUCATION

: : INSTITUTIONS
: RESIDENTIAL INSTITUTIONS
CORRECTIONAL INSTITUTIONS

: REHABILITATION
CORRECTIONAL REHABILITATION
. DELINQUENT REHABILITATION

: : INSTRUCTION
: READING INSTRUCTION
: : LITERACY
: : LANGUAGE ARTS
: READING
CORRECTIVE READING

: : : : METHODS
: : : EVALUATION METHODS
: : DATA ANALYSIS
: STATISTICAL ANALYSIS
CORRELATION

: : INSTITUTIONS
: SCHOOLS
CORRESPONDENCE SCHOOLS

: : EDUCATION
: DISTANCE EDUCATION
CORRESPONDENCE STUDY

: FACILITIES
CORRIDORS

: TECHNOLOGY
COSMETOLOGY

: : METHODS
: EVALUATION METHODS
COST EFFECTIVENESS

: COSTS
COST ESTIMATES

COST INDEXES

COSTS
. CONSTRUCTION COSTS
. COST ESTIMATES
. FEES
. . FINES (PENALTIES)
. . TUITION
. INTEREST (FINANCE)
. LEGAL COSTS
. PROGRAM COSTS
. STUDENT COSTS
. . INSTRUCTIONAL STUDENT COSTS
. . . TUITION
. . NONINSTRUCTIONAL STUDENT COSTS
. UNIT COSTS

: GUIDANCE
COUNSELING
. ADULT COUNSELING
. CAREER COUNSELING
. COCOUNSELING
. EDUCATIONAL COUNSELING
. . ACADEMIC ADVISING
. . ADMISSIONS COUNSELING
. FAMILY COUNSELING
. GROUP COUNSELING
. INDIVIDUAL COUNSELING
. MARRIAGE COUNSELING
. NONDIRECTIVE COUNSELING
. PARENT COUNSELING
. PEER COUNSELING
. REHABILITATION COUNSELING
. SCHOOL COUNSELING

COUNSELING EFFECTIVENESS

COUNSELING INSTRUCTIONAL PROGRAMS (1967 1980)

: : OBJECTIVES
: GUIDANCE OBJECTIVES
COUNSELING OBJECTIVES

: : SERVICES
: HUMAN SERVICES
COUNSELING SERVICES

: METHODS
COUNSELING TECHNIQUES

: THEORIES
COUNSELING THEORIES

: ATTITUDES
COUNSELOR ATTITUDES

: CERTIFICATION
COUNSELOR CERTIFICATION

COUNSELOR CHARACTERISTICS

: RATIOS (MATHEMATICS)
COUNSELOR CLIENT RATIO

: : RELATIONSHIP
: INTERPERSONAL RELATIONSHIP
COUNSELOR CLIENT RELATIONSHIP

: : : : : GROUPS
: : : : PERSONNEL
: : : SCHOOL PERSONNEL
: : : : : GROUPS
: : : : PERSONNEL
: : : PROFESSIONAL PERSONNEL
: : FACULTY
: COLLEGE FACULTY
COUNSELOR EDUCATORS

: : EVALUATION
: PERSONNEL EVALUATION
COUNSELOR EVALUATION

: : BEHAVIOR
: PERFORMANCE
COUNSELOR PERFORMANCE

: : STANDARDS
: QUALIFICATIONS
COUNSELOR QUALIFICATIONS

COUNSELOR ROLE

: : : GROUPS
: : PERSONNEL
: GUIDANCE PERSONNEL
COUNSELORS
. ADJUSTMENT COUNSELORS
. EMPLOYMENT COUNSELORS
. SCHOOL COUNSELORS

: : SELECTION
: PERSONNEL SELECTION
COUNSELOR SELECTION

: : : BEHAVIOR
: : COOPERATION
: EDUCATIONAL COOPERATION
COUNSELOR TEACHER COOPERATION

: TRAINING
COUNSELOR TRAINING

: : : FACILITIES
: : PUBLIC FACILITIES
: : : INSTITUTIONS
: : : INFORMATION SOURCES
: : LIBRARIES
: PUBLIC LIBRARIES
COUNTY LIBRARIES

: : : : GROUPS
: : : PERSONNEL
: : GOVERNMENT EMPLOYEES
: PUBLIC OFFICIALS
COUNTY OFFICIALS

: PROGRAMS
COUNTY PROGRAMS

: : : GROUPS
: : ORGANIZATIONS (GROUPS)
: SCHOOL DISTRICTS
COUNTY SCHOOL DISTRICTS

: : ORGANIZATION
: COURSE ORGANIZATION
COURSE CONTENT

COURSE DESCRIPTIONS

: EVALUATION
COURSE EVALUATION

: OBJECTIVES
COURSE OBJECTIVES

: ORGANIZATION
COURSE ORGANIZATION
. COURSE CONTENT

: CURRICULUM
COURSES
. ADVANCED COURSES
. CONVERSATIONAL LANGUAGE COURSES
. CREDIT COURSES
. EDUCATION COURSES
. ELECTIVE COURSES
. INTENSIVE LANGUAGE COURSES
. INTRODUCTORY COURSES
. METHODS COURSES
. MINICOURSES
. NONCREDIT COURSES
. PRACTICUMS
. . OFFICE PRACTICE
. REFRESHER COURSES
. REQUIRED COURSES
. TELECOURSES
. UNITED STATES GOVERNMENT (COURSE)
. UNITS OF STUDY
. . ACTIVITY UNITS

: SELECTION
COURSE SELECTION (STUDENTS)

: : EDUCATIONAL MEDIA
: INSTRUCTIONAL MATERIALS
: : : STANDARDS
: : SPECIFICATIONS
: COMPUTER SOFTWARE
COURSEWARE

: STANDARDS
COURT DOCTRINE

: : : : GROUPS
: : : PERSONNEL
: : GOVERNMENT EMPLOYEES
: PUBLIC OFFICIALS
: : GROUPS
: JUDGES
COURT JUDGES

COURT LITIGATION
. DESEGREGATION LITIGATION

: : : : GROUPS
: : : PERSONNEL
: : NONPROFESSIONAL PERSONNEL
: CLERICAL WORKERS
COURT REPORTERS

: INSTITUTIONAL ROLE
COURT ROLE

: INSTITUTIONS
COURTS
. FEDERAL COURTS
. JUVENILE COURTS
. STATE COURTS

: : BEHAVIOR
: RESPONSES
COVERT RESPONSE

: : : : GROUPS
: : : PERSONNEL
: : NONPROFESSIONAL PERSONNEL
: SKILLED WORKERS
CRAFT WORKERS

CREATIONISM

: ACTIVITIES
CREATIVE ACTIVITIES
. BRAINSTORMING
. CREATIVE ART
. . CREATIVE DRAMATICS
. CREATIVE EXPRESSION
. CREATIVE WRITING

: : ACTIVITIES
: CREATIVE ACTIVITIES
: ART
CREATIVE ART
. CREATIVE DRAMATICS

: : DEVELOPMENT
: INDIVIDUAL DEVELOPMENT
CREATIVE DEVELOPMENT

: : : : : LIBERAL ARTS
: : : : HUMANITIES
: : : FINE ARTS
: : THEATER ARTS
: DRAMATICS
: : : ACTIVITIES
: : CREATIVE ACTIVITIES
: : ART
: CREATIVE ART
CREATIVE DRAMATICS

: : ACTIVITIES
: CREATIVE ACTIVITIES
CREATIVE EXPRESSION

CREATIVE READING (1966 1980)

: : : METHODS
: : EDUCATIONAL METHODS
: TEACHING METHODS
CREATIVE TEACHING

: COGNITIVE PROCESSES
CREATIVE THINKING
. DIVERGENT THINKING
. PRODUCTIVE THINKING

: : LITERACY
: : LANGUAGE ARTS
: WRITING (COMPOSITION)
: : ACTIVITIES
: CREATIVE ACTIVITIES
CREATIVE WRITING

: : INDIVIDUAL CHARACTERISTICS
: PSYCHOLOGICAL CHARACTERISTICS
CREATIVITY
. IMAGINATION

: RESEARCH
CREATIVITY RESEARCH

: : MEASURES (INDIVIDUALS)
: TESTS
CREATIVITY TESTS

: RECORDS (FORMS)
CREDENTIALS
. EDUCATIONAL CERTIFICATES
. PORTFOLIOS (BACKGROUND MATERIALS)
. RESUMES (PERSONAL)

: RELATIONSHIP
CREDIBILITY

CREDIT (FINANCE)

: : CURRICULUM
: COURSES
CREDIT COURSES

: : : MEASUREMENT
: : ACHIEVEMENT RATING
: GRADING
CREDIT NO CREDIT GRADING

CREDITS
. COLLEGE CREDITS
. CONTINUING EDUCATION UNITS

: : LANGUAGES
: AMERICAN INDIAN LANGUAGES
CREE

: : : LINGUISTICS
: : SOCIOLINGUISTICS
: LANGUAGE VARIATION
: LANGUAGES
CREOLES
. GULLAH
. HAITIAN CREOLE
. MAURITIAN CREOLE
. SIERRA LEONE CREOLE

: : : : GROUPS
: : : PERSONNEL
: : ADMINISTRATORS
: SUPERVISORS
CREW LEADERS

: : : BEHAVIOR
: : SOCIAL BEHAVIOR
: ANTISOCIAL BEHAVIOR
CRIME
. DELINQUENCY
. INTERNATIONAL CRIMES

: PREVENTION
CRIME PREVENTION
. DELINQUENCY PREVENTION

: : STANDARDS
: LAWS
CRIMINAL LAW

: GROUPS
CRIMINALS

: : : : LIBERAL ARTS
: : : SCIENCES
: : SOCIAL SCIENCES
: : : : LIBERAL ARTS
: : : SCIENCES
: : BEHAVIORAL SCIENCES
: SOCIOLOGY
CRIMINOLOGY

: INTERVENTION
CRISIS INTERVENTION

: STANDARDS
CRITERIA
. ADMISSION CRITERIA
. EVALUATION CRITERIA
. . RELIABILITY
. . . INTERRATER RELIABILITY
. . . TEST RELIABILITY
. . VALIDITY
. . . CONCURRENT VALIDITY
. . . PREDICTIVE VALIDITY
. . . PROOF (MATHEMATICS)
. . . TEST VALIDITY
. . . . CONSTRUCT VALIDITY
. . . . CONTENT VALIDITY
. LESSON OBSERVATION CRITERIA

: : MEASURES (INDIVIDUALS)
: TESTS
CRITERION REFERENCED TESTS
. MASTERY TESTS

: METHODS
CRITICAL INCIDENTS METHOD

: METHODS
CRITICAL PATH METHOD

: : LITERACY
: : LANGUAGE ARTS
: READING
CRITICAL READING

: COGNITIVE PROCESSES
CRITICAL THINKING
. EVALUATIVE THINKING
. . VALUE JUDGMENT

: : : OCCUPATIONS
: : AGRICULTURAL OCCUPATIONS
: OFF FARM AGRICULTURAL OCCUPATIONS
CROP PROCESSING OCCUPATIONS

: : : METHODS
: : EDUCATIONAL METHODS
: TEACHING METHODS
CROSS AGE TEACHING

: RESEARCH
CROSS CULTURAL STUDIES

: TRAINING
CROSS CULTURAL TRAINING

: : RESEARCH
: : : METHODS
: : EVALUATION METHODS
: CASE STUDIES
CROSS SECTIONAL STUDIES

CROWDING

: : : : LIBERAL ARTS
: : : SCIENCES
: : NATURAL SCIENCES
: PHYSICAL SCIENCES
CRYSTALLOGRAPHY

: : GROUPS
: LATIN AMERICANS
CUBANS

: : COMMUNICATION (THOUGHT TRANSFER)
: MANUAL COMMUNICATION
CUED SPEECH

: STIMULI
CUES
. CONTEXT CLUES

: ACTIVITIES
CULTURAL ACTIVITIES

CULTURAL AWARENESS

: BACKGROUND
CULTURAL BACKGROUND

: : FACILITIES
: RESOURCE CENTERS
CULTURAL CENTERS

: ENVIRONMENT
CULTURAL CONTEXT

: DIFFERENCES
CULTURAL DIFFERENCES

: EDUCATION
CULTURAL EDUCATION

: ENRICHMENT
CULTURAL ENRICHMENT

CULTURAL EXCHANGE

CULTURAL IMAGES

: INFLUENCES
CULTURAL INFLUENCES

: RELATIONSHIP
CULTURAL INTERRELATIONSHIPS

CULTURAL ISOLATION

: OPPORTUNITIES
CULTURAL OPPORTUNITIES

CULTURAL PLURALISM
. BICULTURALISM

CULTURAL TRAITS

CULTURE
. AFRICAN CULTURE
. AMERICAN INDIAN CULTURE
. BLACK CULTURE
. BURMESE CULTURE
. CHINESE CULTURE
. DUTCH CULTURE
. FOLK CULTURE
. FOREIGN CULTURE
. ISLAMIC CULTURE
. KOREAN CULTURE
. LATIN AMERICAN CULTURE
. . LUSO BRAZILIAN CULTURE
. . PUERTO RICAN CULTURE
. MIDDLE CLASS CULTURE
. NON WESTERN CIVILIZATION
. NORTH AMERICAN CULTURE
. . HISPANIC AMERICAN CULTURE
. . JAPANESE AMERICAN CULTURE
. POPULAR CULTURE
. SPANISH CULTURE
. SUBCULTURES
. . STUDENT SUBCULTURES
. URBAN CULTURE
. WESTERN CIVILIZATION

: CONFLICT
CULTURE CONFLICT

CULTURE CONTACT

: : MEASURES (INDIVIDUALS)
: TESTS
CULTURE FAIR TESTS

CULTURE LAG

: : METHODS
: LABORATORY PROCEDURES
CULTURING TECHNIQUES

: : : INDIVIDUAL CHARACTERISTICS
: : PSYCHOLOGICAL CHARACTERISTICS
: PERSONALITY TRAITS
CURIOSITY

CURRENT EVENTS

CURRICULUM
. AREA STUDIES
. . AMERICAN STUDIES
. . ASIAN STUDIES
. . MIDDLE EASTERN STUDIES
. COLLEGE CURRICULUM
. . COLLEGE ENGLISH
. . COLLEGE MATHEMATICS
. . COLLEGE SCIENCE
. . COLLEGE SECOND LANGUAGE PROGRAMS
. . EDUCATION COURSES
. . FRESHMAN COMPOSITION
. . POSTSECONDARY EDUCATION AS A FIELD OF STUDY
. . TEACHER EDUCATION CURRICULUM
. . . METHODS COURSES
. CONTINUOUS PROGRESS PLAN
. CORE CURRICULUM
. COURSES
. . ADVANCED COURSES
. . CONVERSATIONAL LANGUAGE COURSES
. . CREDIT COURSES
. . EDUCATION COURSES
. . ELECTIVE COURSES
. . INTENSIVE LANGUAGE COURSES
. . INTRODUCTORY COURSES
. . METHODS COURSES
. . MINICOURSES
. . NONCREDIT COURSES
. . PRACTICUMS
. . . OFFICE PRACTICE
. . REFRESHER COURSES
. . REQUIRED COURSES
. . TELECOURSES
. . UNITED STATES GOVERNMENT (COURSE)
. . UNITS OF STUDY
. . . ACTIVITY UNITS
. ELEMENTARY SCHOOL CURRICULUM

CURRICULUM
(CONTINUED)

..ELEMENTARY SCHOOL MATHEMATICS
..ELEMENTARY SCHOOL SCIENCE
..FLES
.ENGLISH CURRICULUM
..COLLEGE ENGLISH
..WORLD LITERATURE
.ETHNIC STUDIES
..AMERICAN INDIAN STUDIES
..BLACK STUDIES
.EXPERIMENTAL CURRICULUM
.FUSED CURRICULUM
.HOME ECONOMICS
.HONORS CURRICULUM
.INTEGRATED CURRICULUM
.MATHEMATICS CURRICULUM
..COLLEGE MATHEMATICS
..ELEMENTARY SCHOOL MATHEMATICS
..MODERN MATHEMATICS
..SECONDARY SCHOOL MATHEMATICS
.MILITARY SCIENCE
.MODERN LANGUAGE CURRICULUM
..CONVERSATIONAL LANGUAGE COURSES
..FLES
..INTENSIVE LANGUAGE COURSES
..NOTIONAL FUNCTIONAL SYLLABI
.PRESCHOOL CURRICULUM
.SCIENCE CURRICULUM
..COLLEGE SCIENCE
..ELEMENTARY SCHOOL SCIENCE
..GENERAL SCIENCE
..SECONDARY SCHOOL SCIENCE
.SECONDARY SCHOOL CURRICULUM
..SECONDARY SCHOOL MATHEMATICS
..SECONDARY SCHOOL SCIENCE
.SHOP CURRICULUM
.SOCIAL STUDIES
..CIVICS
.SPEECH CURRICULUM
.SPIRAL CURRICULUM
.STUDENT CENTERED CURRICULUM
.TELEVISION CURRICULUM
.UNIFIED STUDIES CURRICULUM
.URBAN STUDIES
.WOMENS STUDIES

:DESIGN
CURRICULUM DESIGN

::DEVELOPMENT
:EDUCATIONAL DEVELOPMENT
CURRICULUM DEVELOPMENT

:ENRICHMENT
CURRICULUM ENRICHMENT

:EVALUATION
CURRICULUM EVALUATION

:::PUBLICATIONS
::REFERENCE MATERIALS
:GUIDES
CURRICULUM GUIDES
.STATE CURRICULUM GUIDES

:PROBLEMS
CURRICULUM PROBLEMS

::RESEARCH
:EDUCATIONAL RESEARCH
CURRICULUM RESEARCH

::FACILITIES
:RESOURCE CENTERS
::FACILITIES
:EDUCATIONAL FACILITIES
CURRICULUM STUDY CENTERS

::LANGUAGE ARTS
:HANDWRITING
CURSIVE WRITING

::TRAINING
:JOB TRAINING
CUSTODIAN TRAINING

::DATA
:SCORES
CUTTING SCORES

:TECHNOLOGY
CYBERNETICS

:ALPHABETS
CYRILLIC ALPHABET

::::LIBERAL ARTS
:::SCIENCES
::NATURAL SCIENCES
:BIOLOGICAL SCIENCES
CYTOLOGY

:::LANGUAGES
::INDO EUROPEAN LANGUAGES
:SLAVIC LANGUAGES
CZECH

:::LIBERAL ARTS
::HUMANITIES
:LITERATURE
CZECH LITERATURE

:::LANGUAGES
::URALIC ALTAIC LANGUAGES
:MONGOLIAN LANGUAGES
DAGUR

::ABILITY
:SKILLS
DAILY LIVING SKILLS
.SELF CARE SKILLS

::::GROUPS
:::PERSONNEL
::AGRICULTURAL PERSONNEL
:FARMERS
DAIRY FARMERS

::ACTIVITIES
:PHYSICAL ACTIVITIES
:::LIBERAL ARTS
::HUMANITIES
:FINE ARTS
DANCE

:EDUCATION
DANCE EDUCATION

:THERAPY
DANCE THERAPY

DATA
.DATABASES
..ONLINE CATALOGS
.PERSONNEL DATA
.PROFILES
.SCORES
..CUTTING SCORES
..EQUATED SCORES
..GRADE EQUIVALENT SCORES
..RAW SCORES
..TRUE SCORES
..WEIGHTED SCORES
.STATISTICAL DATA
..CENSUS FIGURES
..EMPLOYMENT STATISTICS
...WORKER DAYS
..LIBRARY STATISTICS
..NORMS
...LOCAL NORMS
...NATIONAL NORMS
...STATE NORMS
...TEST NORMS
..SCHOOL STATISTICS
..SOCIAL INDICATORS

::METHODS
:EVALUATION METHODS
DATA ANALYSIS
.DATA COLLECTION
..SAMPLING
...ITEM SAMPLING
.DATA INTERPRETATION
..STATISTICAL INFERENCE
..TEST INTERPRETATION
.STATISTICAL ANALYSIS
..ANALYSIS OF COVARIANCE
..ANALYSIS OF VARIANCE
..BAYESIAN STATISTICS
..CORRELATION
..EFFECT SIZE
..ERROR OF MEASUREMENT
..GOODNESS OF FIT
..ITEM ANALYSIS
..JUDGMENT ANALYSIS TECHNIQUE
..LEAST SQUARES STATISTICS
..MAXIMUM LIKELIHOOD STATISTICS
..META ANALYSIS
..MULTIVARIATE ANALYSIS
...CLUSTER ANALYSIS
...DISCRIMINANT ANALYSIS
...FACTOR ANALYSIS
....OBLIQUE ROTATION
....ORTHOGONAL ROTATION
...MULTIDIMENSIONAL SCALING
...PATH ANALYSIS
..REGRESSION (STATISTICS)
...MULTIPLE REGRESSION ANALYSIS
..STATISTICAL DISTRIBUTIONS
..STATISTICAL INFERENCE
..STATISTICAL SIGNIFICANCE
.TREND ANALYSIS

:MANAGEMENT SYSTEMS
:::STANDARDS
::SPECIFICATIONS
:COMPUTER SOFTWARE
DATABASE MANAGEMENT SYSTEMS

::GROUPS
:ORGANIZATIONS (GROUPS)
DATABASE PRODUCERS

:INFORMATION SOURCES
:DATA
DATABASES
.ONLINE CATALOGS

:::SERVICES
::INFORMATION SERVICES
:INFORMATION PROCESSING
:::METHODS
::EVALUATION METHODS
:DATA ANALYSIS
DATA COLLECTION
.SAMPLING
..ITEM SAMPLING

:::METHODS
::EVALUATION METHODS
:DATA ANALYSIS
DATA INTERPRETATION
.STATISTICAL INFERENCE
.TEST INTERPRETATION

:::SERVICES
::INFORMATION SERVICES
:INFORMATION PROCESSING
DATA PROCESSING
.INPUT OUTPUT
..KEYBOARDING (DATA ENTRY)
.TIME SHARING

:OCCUPATIONS
DATA PROCESSING OCCUPATIONS

::RELATIONSHIP
:INTERPERSONAL RELATIONSHIP
DATING (SOCIAL)

::GROUPS
:FEMALES
DAUGHTERS

::PROGRAMS
:RECREATIONAL PROGRAMS
DAY CAMP PROGRAMS

:::SERVICES
::HUMAN SERVICES
:SOCIAL SERVICES
DAY CARE
.EMPLOYER SUPPORTED DAY CARE
.FAMILY DAY CARE
.SCHOOL AGE DAY CARE

:FACILITIES
DAY CARE CENTERS

:PROGRAMS
DAY PROGRAMS

::INSTITUTIONS
:SCHOOLS
DAY SCHOOLS

::GROUPS
:STUDENTS
DAY STUDENTS

::DISABILITIES
:MULTIPLE DISABILITIES
DEAF BLIND

:TRANSLATION
DEAF INTERPRETING

::DISABILITIES
:HEARING IMPAIRMENTS
DEAFNESS

::::GROUPS
:::PERSONNEL
::SCHOOL PERSONNEL
::::GROUPS
:::PERSONNEL
::PROFESSIONAL PERSONNEL
:FACULTY
:::GROUPS
::PERSONNEL
:ADMINISTRATORS
DEANS
.ACADEMIC DEANS
.DEANS OF STUDENTS

:::::GROUPS
::::PERSONNEL
:::SCHOOL PERSONNEL
:::::GROUPS
::::PERSONNEL
:::PROFESSIONAL PERSONNEL
::FACULTY
::::GROUPS
:::PERSONNEL
::ADMINISTRATORS
:DEANS
DEANS OF STUDENTS

DEATH
.INFANT MORTALITY
.SUICIDE

: LANGUAGE ARTS
DEBATE

: : ORGANIZATION
: ADMINISTRATIVE
ORGANIZATION
DECENTRALIZATION

DECEPTION
. LYING

: : : SYMBOLS (MATHEMATICS)
: : NUMBERS
: FRACTIONS
DECIMAL FRACTIONS

: COGNITIVE PROCESSES
DECISION MAKING
. PARTICIPATIVE DECISION
MAKING

: : ABILITY
: SKILLS
DECISION MAKING SKILLS

: : INCIDENCE
: ENROLLMENT RATE
DECLINING ENROLLMENT

: : : COGNITIVE PROCESSES
: : LANGUAGE PROCESSING
: READING PROCESSES
DECODING (READING)

: : COGNITIVE PROCESSES
: LOGICAL THINKING
DEDUCTION

: : : : THEORIES
: : : LINGUISTIC THEORY
: : GENERATIVE GRAMMAR
: TRANSFORMATIONAL
GENERATIVE GRAMMAR
DEEP STRUCTURE

: : : SOCIAL DISCRIMINATION
: : RACIAL DISCRIMINATION
: RACIAL SEGREGATION
DE FACTO SEGREGATION

DEFINITIONS

: : : STANDARDS
: : ACADEMIC STANDARDS
: GRADUATION REQUIREMENTS
DEGREE REQUIREMENTS

DEGREES (ACADEMIC)
. ASSOCIATE DEGREES
. BACHELORS DEGREES
. DOCTORAL DEGREES
. . DOCTOR OF ARTS DEGREES
. MASTERS DEGREES
. SPECIALIST IN EDUCATION
DEGREES

: NORMALIZATION
(HANDICAPPED)
DEINSTITUTIONALIZATION (OF
DISABLED)

: : : SOCIAL DISCRIMINATION
: : RACIAL DISCRIMINATION
: RACIAL SEGREGATION
DE JURE SEGREGATION

: : DISABILITIES
: SPEECH HANDICAPS
DELAYED SPEECH

: : BEHAVIOR
: SELF CONTROL
DELAY OF GRATIFICATION

: : : : BEHAVIOR
: : : SOCIAL BEHAVIOR
: : ANTISOCIAL BEHAVIOR
: CRIME
DELINQUENCY

DELINQUENCY CAUSES

: : PREVENTION
: CRIME PREVENTION
DELINQUENCY PREVENTION

: : REHABILITATION
: CORRECTIONAL
REHABILITATION
DELINQUENT REHABILITATION

: SERVICES
DELIVERY SYSTEMS

: METHODS
DELPHI TECHNIQUE

: OCCUPATIONS
DEMAND OCCUPATIONS
. EMERGING OCCUPATIONS

DEMOCRACY

: VALUES
DEMOCRATIC VALUES

: : : LIBERAL ARTS
: : SCIENCES
: SOCIAL SCIENCES
DEMOGRAPHY
. BIRTH RATE
. EMPLOYMENT PATTERNS
. GEOGRAPHIC DISTRIBUTION
. POPULATION DISTRIBUTION
. . ETHNIC DISTRIBUTION
. . RACIAL DISTRIBUTION
. POPULATION GROWTH
. POPULATION TRENDS
. . BLACK POPULATION TRENDS
. RACIAL COMPOSITION
. . RACIAL BALANCE
. RESIDENTIAL PATTERNS
. SCHOOL DEMOGRAPHY
. . TEACHER DISTRIBUTION
. SOCIAL DISTRIBUTION
. URBAN DEMOGRAPHY

: : FACILITIES
: EDUCATIONAL FACILITIES
DEMONSTRATION CENTERS

: PROGRAMS
DEMONSTRATION PROGRAMS

DEMONSTRATIONS (CIVIL)

: : : METHODS
: : EDUCATIONAL METHODS
: TEACHING METHODS
DEMONSTRATIONS (EDUCATIONAL)

: : : : GROUPS
: : : PERSONNEL
: : HEALTH PERSONNEL
: ALLIED HEALTH PERSONNEL
DENTAL ASSISTANTS

: CLINICS
DENTAL CLINICS

: : EVALUATION
: MEDICAL EVALUATION
DENTAL EVALUATION

: : HEALTH
: PHYSICAL HEALTH
DENTAL HEALTH

: : : : GROUPS
: : : PERSONNEL
: : HEALTH PERSONNEL
: ALLIED HEALTH PERSONNEL
DENTAL HYGIENISTS

: : : INSTITUTIONS
: : SCHOOLS
: COLLEGES
DENTAL SCHOOLS

: : : : GROUPS
: : : STUDENTS
: : COLLEGE STUDENTS
: GRADUATE STUDENTS
DENTAL STUDENTS

: : : : GROUPS
: : : PERSONNEL
: : HEALTH PERSONNEL
: ALLIED HEALTH PERSONNEL
DENTAL TECHNICIANS

: : TECHNOLOGY
: MEDICINE
DENTISTRY

: : : GROUPS
: : PERSONNEL
: PROFESSIONAL PERSONNEL
: : : GROUPS
: : PERSONNEL
: HEALTH PERSONNEL
DENTISTS

: : : : GROUPS
: : : PERSONNEL
: : SCHOOL PERSONNEL
: : : : GROUPS
: : : PERSONNEL
: : PROFESSIONAL PERSONNEL
: FACULTY
: : : GROUPS
: : PERSONNEL
: ADMINISTRATORS
DEPARTMENT HEADS

: : ORGANIZATION
: ADMINISTRATIVE
ORGANIZATION
DEPARTMENTS
. ENGLISH DEPARTMENTS
. SCIENCE DEPARTMENTS
. STATE DEPARTMENTS OF
EDUCATION

: GROUPS
DEPENDENTS

: RESOURCES
DEPLETED RESOURCES

: : INSTITUTIONS
: : INFORMATION SOURCES
: LIBRARIES
DEPOSITORY LIBRARIES

: PSYCHOLOGICAL PATTERNS
DEPRESSION (PSYCHOLOGY)

: : : COGNITIVE PROCESSES
: : PERCEPTION
: VISUAL PERCEPTION
DEPTH PERCEPTION

: LINGUISTICS
DESCRIPTIVE LINGUISTICS
. GRAMMAR
. . MORPHOLOGY (LANGUAGES)
. . . MORPHEMES
. . . . NEGATIVE FORMS
(LANGUAGE)
. . . . PLURALS
. . . . SUFFIXES
. . . . TENSES (GRAMMAR)
. . . MORPHOPHONEMICS
. . SYNTAX
. . . FORM CLASSES
(LANGUAGES)
. . . . ADJECTIVES
. . . . ADVERBS
. . . . DETERMINERS
(LANGUAGES)
. . . . FUNCTION WORDS
. . . . NOUNS
. . . . PREPOSITIONS
. . . . PRONOUNS
. . . . VERBS
. . . PHRASE STRUCTURE
. . . SENTENCE STRUCTURE
. SEMANTICS
. . LEXICOLOGY

: : LITERACY
: : LANGUAGE ARTS
: WRITING (COMPOSITION)
DESCRIPTIVE WRITING

DESEGREGATION EFFECTS

: COURT LITIGATION
DESEGREGATION LITIGATION

: METHODS
DESEGREGATION METHODS
. BUSING

: PLANNING
DESEGREGATION PLANS

: : CONDITIONING
: BEHAVIOR MODIFICATION
DESENSITIZATION

DESIGN
. BUILDING DESIGN
. . MODULAR BUILDING DESIGN
. CLASSROOM DESIGN
. CLOTHING DESIGN
. CURRICULUM DESIGN
. EDUCATIONAL FACILITIES
DESIGN
. FURNITURE DESIGN
. INSTRUCTIONAL DESIGN
. INTERIOR DESIGN
. LIGHTING DESIGN
. . FLEXIBLE LIGHTING DESIGN
. PARK DESIGN
. PROGRAM DESIGN
. RESEARCH DESIGN
. . QUASIEXPERIMENTAL DESIGN

: : : : METHODS
: : : HOLISTIC APPROACH
: : SYSTEMS APPROACH
: SYSTEMS BUILDING
DESIGN BUILD APPROACH

: : : : LIBERAL ARTS
: : : HUMANITIES
: : FINE ARTS
: VISUAL ARTS
DESIGN CRAFTS

DISABILITIES
(CONTINUED)

. . SEVERE MENTAL RETARDATION
. MILD DISABILITIES
. . MILD MENTAL RETARDATION
. . MINIMAL BRAIN DYSFUNCTION
. MULTIPLE DISABILITIES
. . DEAF BLIND
. PERCEPTUAL HANDICAPS
. PHYSICAL DISABILITIES
. . AMPUTATIONS
. . CLEFT PALATE
. . HEART DISORDERS
. . NEUROLOGICAL IMPAIRMENTS
. . . APHASIA
. . . CEREBRAL PALSY
. . . EPILEPSY
. . . MINIMAL BRAIN DYSFUNCTION
. SEVERE DISABILITIES
. . PSYCHOSIS
. . . AUTISM
. . . ECHOLALIA
. . . SCHIZOPHRENIA
. . SEVERE MENTAL RETARDATION
. SPECIAL HEALTH PROBLEMS
. SPEECH HANDICAPS
. . ARTICULATION IMPAIRMENTS
. . CLEFT PALATE
. . DELAYED SPEECH
. . STUTTERING
. . VOICE DISORDERS
. VISUAL IMPAIRMENTS
. . AMETROPIA
. . . HYPEROPIA
. . . MYOPIA
. . BLINDNESS
. . PARTIAL VISION
. . STRABISMUS

: GROUPS
DISADVANTAGED
. DISADVANTAGED YOUTH
. ECONOMICALLY DISADVANTAGED
. EDUCATIONALLY DISADVANTAGED
. GIFTED DISADVANTAGED

: ENVIRONMENT
DISADVANTAGED ENVIRONMENT

: : INSTITUTIONS
: SCHOOLS
DISADVANTAGED SCHOOLS

: : GROUPS
: YOUTH
: : GROUPS
: DISADVANTAGED
DISADVANTAGED YOUTH

DISARMAMENT

DISCIPLINE
. DISMISSAL (PERSONNEL)
. . TEACHER DISMISSAL
. EXPULSION
. SUSPENSION
. . IN SCHOOL SUSPENSION
. TEACHER DISCIPLINE
. . TEACHER DISMISSAL

: POLICY
DISCIPLINE POLICY

: PROBLEMS
DISCIPLINE PROBLEMS

DISCLOSURE
. SELF DISCLOSURE (INDIVIDUALS)

: : PUBLICATIONS
: REFERENCE MATERIALS
DISCOGRAPHIES

: : : METHODS
: : EVALUATION METHODS
: STRUCTURAL ANALYSIS (LINGUISTICS)
DISCOURSE ANALYSIS

: LEARNING
DISCOVERY LEARNING

: : COGNITIVE PROCESSES
: LEARNING PROCESSES
DISCOVERY PROCESSES

: : : : : METHODS
: : : : EVALUATION METHODS
: : : DATA ANALYSIS
: : STATISTICAL ANALYSIS
: MULTIVARIATE ANALYSIS
DISCRIMINANT ANALYSIS

: LEARNING
DISCRIMINATION LEARNING

: LEGISLATION
DISCRIMINATORY LEGISLATION

: COMMUNICATION (THOUGHT TRANSFER)
DISCUSSION
. GROUP DISCUSSION

: : : METHODS
: : EDUCATIONAL METHODS
: TEACHING METHODS
DISCUSSION (TEACHING TECHNIQUE)

: GROUPS
DISCUSSION GROUPS
. LISTENING GROUPS

DISEASE CONTROL
. FLUORIDATION

: INCIDENCE
DISEASE INCIDENCE

: DISABILITIES
DISEASES
. ALCOHOLISM
. ALLERGY
. ANEMIA
. . SICKLE CELL ANEMIA
. ANOREXIA NERVOSA
. ASTHMA
. BULIMIA
. CANCER
. COMMUNICABLE DISEASES
. . RUBELLA
. . VENEREAL DISEASES
. DIABETES
. DRUG ADDICTION
. FAILURE TO THRIVE
. HYPERTENSION
. OBESITY
. OCCUPATIONAL DISEASES
. POISONING
. . LEAD POISONING
. SEIZURES

: : SANITATION
: CLEANING
DISHWASHING

: : GROUPS
: PERSONNEL
DISLOCATED WORKERS

: DISCIPLINE
DISMISSAL (PERSONNEL)
. TEACHER DISMISSAL

: : GROUPS
: FEMALES
DISPLACED HOMEMAKERS

: VISUAL AIDS
DISPLAY AIDS

: : : EQUIPMENT
: : ELECTRONIC EQUIPMENT
: COMPUTERS
DISPLAY SYSTEMS

DISQUALIFICATION

: : BEHAVIOR
: SOCIAL BEHAVIOR
DISSENT

DISTANCE

: EDUCATION
DISTANCE EDUCATION
. CORRESPONDENCE STUDY

: LINGUISTICS
DISTINCTIVE FEATURES (LANGUAGE)

: : EDUCATION
: VOCATIONAL EDUCATION
DISTRIBUTIVE EDUCATION

: : : : : GROUPS
: : : : PERSONNEL
: : : PROFESSIONAL PERSONNEL
: : TEACHERS
: VOCATIONAL EDUCATION TEACHERS
DISTRIBUTIVE EDUCATION TEACHERS

: : COGNITIVE PROCESSES
: CREATIVE THINKING
DIVERGENT THINKING

: : : : ACTIVITIES
: : : PHYSICAL ACTIVITIES
: : ATHLETICS
: AQUATIC SPORTS
DIVING

: : : LIBERAL ARTS
: : MATHEMATICS
: ARITHMETIC
DIVISION

DIVORCE

: NUCLEIC ACIDS
DNA

: DEGREES (ACADEMIC)
DOCTORAL DEGREES
. DOCTOR OF ARTS DEGREES

: : : PUBLICATIONS
: : REPORTS
: THESES
DOCTORAL DISSERTATIONS

: : PROGRAMS
: COLLEGE PROGRAMS
DOCTORAL PROGRAMS

: : DEGREES (ACADEMIC)
: DOCTORAL DEGREES
DOCTOR OF ARTS DEGREES

: NONPRINT MEDIA
DOCUMENTARIES

: : : SERVICES
: : INFORMATION SERVICES
: INFORMATION PROCESSING
DOCUMENTATION
. ABSTRACTING
. BIBLIOMETRICS
. . CITATION ANALYSIS
. . . BIBLIOGRAPHIC COUPLING
. CATALOGING
. . MACHINE READABLE CATALOGING
. FILING
. INDEXING
. . AUTOMATIC INDEXING

DOGMATISM

: : GROUPS
: LATIN AMERICANS
DOMINICANS

: GROUPS
DONORS

: STRUCTURAL ELEMENTS (CONSTRUCTION)
DOORS

: : FACILITIES
: HOUSING
DORMITORIES

: : : PLANNING
: : SCHEDULING
: SCHOOL SCHEDULES
DOUBLE SESSIONS

: : DISABILITIES
: MENTAL RETARDATION
: : DISABILITIES
: CONGENITAL IMPAIRMENTS
DOWNS SYNDROME

: : : : LIBERAL ARTS
: : : HUMANITIES
: : FINE ARTS
: VISUAL ARTS
DRAFTING
. ARCHITECTURAL DRAFTING
. ENGINEERING DRAWING
. TECHNICAL ILLUSTRATION

: : : : LIBERAL ARTS
: : : HUMANITIES
: : FINE ARTS
: THEATER ARTS
: : : LIBERAL ARTS
: : HUMANITIES
: LITERATURE
DRAMA
. COMEDY
. . SKITS
. SCRIPTS
. TRAGEDY

: : : METHODS
: : SIMULATION
: ROLE PLAYING
DRAMATIC PLAY

: : : : LIBERAL ARTS
: : : HUMANITIES
: : FINE ARTS
: THEATER ARTS
DRAMATICS
. CREATIVE DRAMATICS

: WORKSHOPS
DRAMA WORKSHOPS

: LANGUAGES
DRAVIDIAN LANGUAGES
. KANNADA
. MALAYALAM
. TAMIL
. TELUGU

: STANDARDS
DRESS CODES

: : : METHODS
: : EDUCATIONAL METHODS
: TEACHING METHODS
DRILLS (PRACTICE)
. PATTERN DRILLS (LANGUAGE)
. . SUBSTITUTION DRILLS

: BEHAVIOR
DRINKING

: : MATTER
: WATER
DRINKING WATER

: EDUCATION
DRIVER EDUCATION

: FACILITIES
DRIVEWAYS

: ATTITUDES
DROPOUT ATTITUDES

DROPOUT CHARACTERISTICS

: PREVENTION
DROPOUT PREVENTION

: : PROGRAMS
: REHABILITATION PROGRAMS
DROPOUT PROGRAMS

: INCIDENCE
DROPOUT RATE

: RESEARCH
DROPOUT RESEARCH

: GROUPS
DROPOUTS
. ADULT DROPOUTS

: : BEHAVIOR
: DRUG USE
DRUG ABUSE
. DRUG ADDICTION

: : : BEHAVIOR
: : DRUG USE
: DRUG ABUSE
: : DISABILITIES
: DISEASES
DRUG ADDICTION

: EDUCATION
DRUG EDUCATION

: : LEGISLATION
: PUBLIC HEALTH LEGISLATION
DRUG LEGISLATION

: REHABILITATION
DRUG REHABILITATION

: THERAPY
DRUG THERAPY

: BEHAVIOR
DRUG USE
. DRUG ABUSE
. . DRUG ADDICTION
. ILLEGAL DRUG USE

: : GROUPS
: FAMILY (SOCIOLOGICAL UNIT)
DUAL CAREER FAMILY

: ENROLLMENT
DUAL ENROLLMENT

: CIVIL LIBERTIES
DUE PROCESS

: : : LANGUAGES
: : MALAYO POLYNESIAN LANGUAGES
: INDONESIAN LANGUAGES
DUSUN

: : LANGUAGES
: INDO EUROPEAN LANGUAGES
DUTCH

: CULTURE
DUTCH CULTURE

: : DISABILITIES
: LANGUAGE HANDICAPS
DYSLEXIA

: : LANGUAGES
: AFRICAN LANGUAGES
DYULA

: ADMISSION (SCHOOL)
EARLY ADMISSION

: EDUCATION
EARLY CHILDHOOD EDUCATION
. PRESCHOOL EDUCATION
. PRIMARY EDUCATION

: : BACKGROUND
: EXPERIENCE
EARLY EXPERIENCE

EARLY PARENTHOOD

: : LITERACY
: : LANGUAGE ARTS
: READING
EARLY READING

: : STATUS
: RETIREMENT
EARLY RETIREMENT

EARS

EARTHQUAKES

: : : : LIBERAL ARTS
: : : SCIENCES
: : NATURAL SCIENCES
: PHYSICAL SCIENCES
EARTH SCIENCE
. GEOLOGY
. . MINERALOGY
. . PALEONTOLOGY
. GEOPHYSICS
. . PLATE TECTONICS
. METEOROLOGY
. OCEANOGRAPHY
. PHYSICAL GEOGRAPHY
. SEISMOLOGY
. . PLATE TECTONICS
. SOIL SCIENCE

EATING HABITS

: : : DISABILITIES
: : SEVERE DISABILITIES
: : : DISABILITIES
: : MENTAL DISORDERS
: PSYCHOSIS
ECHOLALIA

ECHOLOCATION

: INFLUENCES
ECOLOGICAL FACTORS

: : : : LIBERAL ARTS
: : : SCIENCES
: : NATURAL SCIENCES
: BIOLOGICAL SCIENCES
ECOLOGY

: : GROUPS
: DISADVANTAGED
ECONOMICALLY DISADVANTAGED

: CHANGE
ECONOMIC CHANGE

: ENVIRONMENT
ECONOMIC CLIMATE
. INFLATION (ECONOMICS)

: DEVELOPMENT
ECONOMIC DEVELOPMENT
. ECONOMIC PROGRESS

: INFLUENCES
ECONOMIC FACTORS

: OPPORTUNITIES
ECONOMIC OPPORTUNITIES

: : DEVELOPMENT
: ECONOMIC DEVELOPMENT
ECONOMIC PROGRESS

: : RESEARCH
: SOCIAL SCIENCE RESEARCH
ECONOMIC RESEARCH

: : : LIBERAL ARTS
: : SCIENCES
: SOCIAL SCIENCES
ECONOMICS
. CONSUMER ECONOMICS
. EDUCATIONAL ECONOMICS
. . EDUCATIONAL FINANCE
. LABOR ECONOMICS
. RURAL ECONOMICS

: EDUCATION
ECONOMICS EDUCATION

: STATUS
ECONOMIC STATUS
. POVERTY

EDITING

: : MASS MEDIA
: NEWS MEDIA
EDITORIALS

: : GROUPS
: PERSONNEL
EDITORS

EDUCATION
. ACADEMIC EDUCATION
. ADULT EDUCATION
. . ADULT BASIC EDUCATION
. . ADULT VOCATIONAL EDUCATION
. . . ADULT FARMER EDUCATION
. . . YOUNG FARMER EDUCATION
. . CONTINUING EDUCATION
. . . PROFESSIONAL CONTINUING EDUCATION
. . LABOR EDUCATION
. . MIGRANT ADULT EDUCATION
. . PARENT EDUCATION
. . PRERETIREMENT EDUCATION
. . PUBLIC SCHOOL ADULT EDUCATION
. . VETERANS EDUCATION
. AEROSPACE EDUCATION
. AESTHETIC EDUCATION
. . ART APPRECIATION
. . FILM STUDY
. . MUSIC APPRECIATION
. AFTER SCHOOL EDUCATION
. AGING EDUCATION
. AGRICULTURAL EDUCATION
. . ADULT FARMER EDUCATION
. . SUPERVISED FARM PRACTICE
. . YOUNG FARMER EDUCATION
. ALCOHOL EDUCATION
. ALLIED HEALTH OCCUPATIONS EDUCATION
. ALUMNI EDUCATION
. AMERICAN INDIAN EDUCATION
. ART EDUCATION
. BACK TO BASICS
. BASIC BUSINESS EDUCATION
. BILINGUAL EDUCATION
. BLACK EDUCATION
. CAREER EDUCATION
. CITIZENSHIP EDUCATION
. COEDUCATION
. COMMUNITY EDUCATION
. COMPARATIVE EDUCATION
. COMPENSATORY EDUCATION
. COMPETENCY BASED EDUCATION
. . COMPETENCY BASED TEACHER EDUCATION
. COMPULSORY EDUCATION
. . HOME SCHOOLING
. COMPUTER SCIENCE EDUCATION
. CONSUMER EDUCATION
. . CONSUMER SCIENCE
. CORPORATE EDUCATION
. CORRECTIONAL EDUCATION
. CULTURAL EDUCATION
. DANCE EDUCATION
. DISTANCE EDUCATION
. . CORRESPONDENCE STUDY
. DRIVER EDUCATION
. DRUG EDUCATION
. EARLY CHILDHOOD EDUCATION
. . PRESCHOOL EDUCATION
. . PRIMARY EDUCATION
. ECONOMICS EDUCATION
. ELEMENTARY SECONDARY EDUCATION
. . ELEMENTARY EDUCATION
. . . ADULT BASIC EDUCATION
. . . PRIMARY EDUCATION
. . SECONDARY EDUCATION
. . . COLLEGE PREPARATION
. ENERGY EDUCATION
. ENVIRONMENTAL EDUCATION
. . CONSERVATION EDUCATION
. EQUAL EDUCATION
. EXTENSION EDUCATION
. . EXTERNAL DEGREE PROGRAMS
. . LIBRARY EXTENSION
. . RURAL EXTENSION
. . URBAN EXTENSION
. FAMILY LIFE EDUCATION
. . PARENTHOOD EDUCATION
. . SEX EDUCATION
. FREE EDUCATION
. GENERAL EDUCATION
. HEALTH EDUCATION
. HUMANISTIC EDUCATION
. INDUSTRIAL EDUCATION
. INSERVICE EDUCATION
. . INSERVICE TEACHER EDUCATION

EDUCATION
(CONTINUED)

. INTERGROUP EDUCATION
.. MULTICULTURAL EDUCATION
. INTERNATIONAL EDUCATION
. JOURNALISM EDUCATION
. LAW RELATED EDUCATION
. LEISURE EDUCATION
. LITERACY EDUCATION
. MARINE EDUCATION
.. MARITIME EDUCATION
. MATHEMATICS EDUCATION
. MEXICAN AMERICAN
EDUCATION
. MIGRANT EDUCATION
. MUSIC EDUCATION
. NONDISCRIMINATORY
EDUCATION
. NONFORMAL EDUCATION
. NONTRADITIONAL EDUCATION
. OPEN EDUCATION
. OUTDOOR EDUCATION
.. ADVENTURE EDUCATION
. PATIENT EDUCATION
. PHYSICAL EDUCATION
.. ADAPTED PHYSICAL
EDUCATION
.. MOVEMENT EDUCATION
. POLICE EDUCATION
. POPULATION EDUCATION
. POSTSECONDARY EDUCATION
.. HIGHER EDUCATION
... GRADUATE STUDY
.... GRADUATE MEDICAL
EDUCATION
.... POSTSECONDARY
EDUCATION AS A
FIELD OF STUDY
... POSTDOCTORAL EDUCATION
... UNDERGRADUATE STUDY
.. LIBRARY EDUCATION
. PRIVATE EDUCATION
. PROCESS EDUCATION
. PROFESSIONAL EDUCATION
.. ADMINISTRATOR EDUCATION
.. ARCHITECTURAL EDUCATION
.. BUSINESS ADMINISTRATION
EDUCATION
.. ENGINEERING EDUCATION
.. HOME ECONOMICS EDUCATION
.. LEGAL EDUCATION
(PROFESSIONS)
.. MEDICAL EDUCATION
... GRADUATE MEDICAL
EDUCATION
... NURSING EDUCATION
... PHARMACEUTICAL
EDUCATION
... VETERINARY MEDICAL
EDUCATION
.. PROFESSIONAL CONTINUING
EDUCATION
.. PUBLIC ADMINISTRATION
EDUCATION
.. TEACHER EDUCATION
... COMPETENCY BASED
TEACHER EDUCATION
... ENGLISH TEACHER
EDUCATION
... INSERVICE TEACHER
EDUCATION
... PRESERVICE TEACHER
EDUCATION
... STUDENT TEACHING
... TEACHER EDUCATOR
EDUCATION
.. THEOLOGICAL EDUCATION
. PROGRESSIVE EDUCATION
. PUBLIC AFFAIRS EDUCATION
. PUBLIC EDUCATION
.. PUBLIC SCHOOL ADULT
EDUCATION
. RELIGIOUS EDUCATION
. RURAL EDUCATION
. SAFETY EDUCATION
. SCIENCE EDUCATION
. SPECIAL EDUCATION
.. ADAPTED PHYSICAL
EDUCATION
. STUDY ABROAD
. SUPPLEMENTARY EDUCATION
. TERMINAL EDUCATION
. URBAN EDUCATION
. VALUES EDUCATION
. VOCATIONAL EDUCATION
.. ADULT VOCATIONAL
EDUCATION
... ADULT FARMER EDUCATION
... YOUNG FARMER EDUCATION
.. BUSINESS EDUCATION
... OFFICE OCCUPATIONS
EDUCATION
.. COOPERATIVE EDUCATION
.. DISTRIBUTIVE EDUCATION
.. OCCUPATIONAL HOME
ECONOMICS
.. PREVOCATIONAL EDUCATION
.. TECHNICAL EDUCATION
... FIRE SCIENCE EDUCATION
.. TRADE AND INDUSTRIAL
EDUCATION
. WOMENS EDUCATION

:: GOVERNANCE
: ADMINISTRATION
EDUCATIONAL ADMINISTRATION
. SCHOOL ADMINISTRATION
.. COLLEGE ADMINISTRATION
.. SCHOOL BASED MANAGEMENT

: FOUNDATIONS OF EDUCATION
:::: LIBERAL ARTS
::: SCIENCES
:: SOCIAL SCIENCES
: ANTHROPOLOGY
EDUCATIONAL ANTHROPOLOGY

: EVALUATION
EDUCATIONAL ASSESSMENT

:: ACHIEVEMENT
: ACADEMIC ACHIEVEMENT
EDUCATIONAL ATTAINMENT

: ATTITUDES
EDUCATIONAL ATTITUDES

: BACKGROUND
EDUCATIONAL BACKGROUND
. EDUCATIONAL EXPERIENCE

: OUTCOMES OF EDUCATION
EDUCATIONAL BENEFITS

:: RECORDS (FORMS)
: CREDENTIALS
EDUCATIONAL CERTIFICATES

: CHANGE
EDUCATIONAL CHANGE

:: FACILITIES
: EDUCATIONAL FACILITIES
EDUCATIONAL COMPLEXES
. CAMPUSES
. EDUCATIONAL PARKS

:: BEHAVIOR
: COOPERATION
EDUCATIONAL COOPERATION
. COLLEGE SCHOOL
COOPERATION
. COUNSELOR TEACHER
COOPERATION
. INTERCOLLEGIATE
COOPERATION
. PARENT TEACHER
COOPERATION

:: GUIDANCE
: COUNSELING
EDUCATIONAL COUNSELING
. ACADEMIC ADVISING
. ADMISSIONS COUNSELING

EDUCATIONAL DEMAND

: DEVELOPMENT
EDUCATIONAL DEVELOPMENT
. CURRICULUM DEVELOPMENT
. INSTRUCTIONAL DEVELOPMENT

: IDENTIFICATION
EDUCATIONAL DIAGNOSIS
. READING DIAGNOSIS
.. MISCUE ANALYSIS

: SOCIAL DISCRIMINATION
EDUCATIONAL DISCRIMINATION
. SCHOOL SEGREGATION
.. COLLEGE SEGREGATION
.. SCHOOL RESEGREGATION

: FOUNDATIONS OF EDUCATION
:::: LIBERAL ARTS
::: SCIENCES
:: SOCIAL SCIENCES
: ECONOMICS
EDUCATIONAL ECONOMICS
. EDUCATIONAL FINANCE

: ENVIRONMENT
EDUCATIONAL ENVIRONMENT
. CLASSROOM ENVIRONMENT
. COLLEGE ENVIRONMENT
. TEACHING CONDITIONS

: EQUIPMENT
EDUCATIONAL EQUIPMENT
. CLASSROOM FURNITURE

EDUCATIONAL EQUITY (FINANCE)

:: BACKGROUND
: EXPERIENCE
:: BACKGROUND
: EDUCATIONAL BACKGROUND
EDUCATIONAL EXPERIENCE

: EXPERIMENTS
EDUCATIONAL EXPERIMENTS

: FACILITIES
EDUCATIONAL FACILITIES
. AFTER SCHOOL CENTERS
. AUDIOVISUAL CENTERS
. BUSINESS EDUCATION
FACILITIES
. CHILD DEVELOPMENT CENTERS
. CLASSROOMS
.. ELECTRONIC CLASSROOMS
.. MOBILE CLASSROOMS
.. MULTIPURPOSE CLASSROOMS
.. SELF CONTAINED
CLASSROOMS
. CONTINUING EDUCATION
CENTERS
. CURRICULUM STUDY CENTERS
. DEMONSTRATION CENTERS
. EDUCATIONAL COMPLEXES
.. CAMPUSES
.. EDUCATIONAL PARKS
. EDUCATION SERVICE CENTERS
. FOUND SPACES
. GUIDANCE CENTERS
. LEARNING CENTERS
(CLASSROOM)
. LEARNING LABORATORIES
.. LANGUAGE LABORATORIES
. LEARNING RESOURCES
CENTERS
. LIVING LEARNING CENTERS
. OFF CAMPUS FACILITIES
. PHYSICAL EDUCATION
FACILITIES
. READING CENTERS
. SCHOOL BUILDINGS
.. COLLEGE BUILDINGS
. SCHOOL SHOPS
. SCHOOL SPACE
. SCIENCE TEACHING CENTERS
. SKILL CENTERS
. STUDENT UNIONS
. STUDY FACILITIES
.. CARRELS
.. STUDY CENTERS
. VOCATIONAL TRAINING
CENTERS
. WRITING LABORATORIES

: DESIGN
EDUCATIONAL FACILITIES
DESIGN

:: IMPROVEMENT
: FACILITY IMPROVEMENT
EDUCATIONAL FACILITIES
IMPROVEMENT

:: PLANNING
: FACILITY PLANNING
:: PLANNING
: EDUCATIONAL PLANNING
EDUCATIONAL FACILITIES
PLANNING
. CAMPUS PLANNING

:: FOUNDATIONS OF EDUCATION
::::: LIBERAL ARTS
:::: SCIENCES
::: SOCIAL SCIENCES
:: ECONOMICS
: EDUCATIONAL ECONOMICS
EDUCATIONAL FINANCE

:: ACTIVITIES
: GAMES
EDUCATIONAL GAMES
. READING GAMES

:::: LIBERAL ARTS
::: SCIENCES
:: SOCIAL SCIENCES
: GERONTOLOGY
EDUCATIONAL GERONTOLOGY

:::: LIBERAL ARTS
::: SCIENCES
:: SOCIAL SCIENCES
::: LIBERAL ARTS
:: HUMANITIES
: HISTORY
: FOUNDATIONS OF EDUCATION
EDUCATIONAL HISTORY
. SCIENCE EDUCATION HISTORY

: IMPROVEMENT
EDUCATIONAL IMPROVEMENT
. INSTRUCTIONAL IMPROVEMENT

: INNOVATION
EDUCATIONAL INNOVATION
. INSTRUCTIONAL INNOVATION

: LEGISLATION
EDUCATIONAL LEGISLATION
. SCHOOL ATTENDANCE
LEGISLATION

:: GROUPS
: DISADVANTAGED
EDUCATIONALLY DISADVANTAGED

: MALPRACTICE
EDUCATIONAL MALPRACTICE

EDUCATIONAL MEDIA
. AUDIOVISUAL AIDS
.. INSTRUCTIONAL FILMS
.. PROTOCOL MATERIALS
. AUTOINSTRUCTIONAL AIDS
.. TEACHING MACHINES
. INSTRUCTIONAL MATERIALS
.. ADVANCE ORGANIZERS
.. BILINGUAL INSTRUCTIONAL
MATERIALS
.. COURSEWARE
.. EXPERIENCE CHARTS
.. INSTRUCTIONAL FILMS
.. LABORATORY MANUALS
.. LEARNING MODULES
.. MANIPULATIVE MATERIALS

EDUCATIONAL MEDIA
(CONTINUED)

..PROBLEM SETS
..PROGRAMED INSTRUCTIONAL MATERIALS
..PROTOCOL MATERIALS
..STUDENT DEVELOPED MATERIALS
...STUDENT WRITING MODELS
..STUDY GUIDES
..TEACHER DEVELOPED MATERIALS
...TEACHER MADE TESTS
..TEXTBOOKS
...HISTORY TEXTBOOKS
...MULTICULTURAL TEXTBOOKS
..WORKBOOKS

:METHODS
EDUCATIONAL METHODS
.CLASSROOM TECHNIQUES
.EDUCATIONAL STRATEGIES
.PSYCHOEDUCATIONAL METHODS
.TEACHING METHODS
..AUDIOLINGUAL METHODS
..CLINICAL TEACHING (HEALTH PROFESSIONS)
..CONVENTIONAL INSTRUCTION
..CREATIVE TEACHING
..CROSS AGE TEACHING
..DEMONSTRATIONS (EDUCATIONAL)
..DIAGNOSTIC TEACHING
..DISCUSSION (TEACHING TECHNIQUE)
..DRILLS (PRACTICE)
...PATTERN DRILLS (LANGUAGE)
....SUBSTITUTION DRILLS
..EXPERIMENTAL TEACHING
..GRAMMAR TRANSLATION METHOD
..INDIVIDUALIZED INSTRUCTION
..KINESTHETIC METHODS
..LANGUAGE EXPERIENCE APPROACH
..LECTURE METHOD
..MONTESSORI METHOD
..MULTIMEDIA INSTRUCTION
...AUDIOVISUAL INSTRUCTION
..NEGATIVE PRACTICE
..ORAL COMMUNICATION METHOD
...LIPREADING
..PEER TEACHING
..PRECISION TEACHING
..PROGRAMED INSTRUCTION
...COMPUTER ASSISTED INSTRUCTION
...PROGRAMED TUTORING
..SIGHT METHOD
..SUGGESTOPEDIA
..TELEPHONE INSTRUCTION
..THEMATIC APPROACH
..TRAINING METHODS
...MANAGEMENT GAMES
...MICROCOUNSELING
...MICROTEACHING

:MOBILITY
EDUCATIONAL MOBILITY

:NEEDS
EDUCATIONAL NEEDS

:OBJECTIVES
EDUCATIONAL OBJECTIVES

:OPPORTUNITIES
EDUCATIONAL OPPORTUNITIES
.ACCESS TO EDUCATION

:::FACILITIES
::EDUCATIONAL FACILITIES
:EDUCATIONAL COMPLEXES
EDUCATIONAL PARKS

:::LIBERAL ARTS
::HUMANITIES
:PHILOSOPHY
:FOUNDATIONS OF EDUCATION
EDUCATIONAL PHILOSOPHY

:PLANNING
EDUCATIONAL PLANNING
.COLLEGE PLANNING
.EDUCATIONAL FACILITIES PLANNING
..CAMPUS PLANNING

:POLICY
EDUCATIONAL POLICY

EDUCATIONAL PRACTICES

:STANDARDS
:FOUNDATIONS OF EDUCATION
EDUCATIONAL PRINCIPLES

EDUCATIONAL PROBLEMS (1966 1980)

EDUCATIONAL PROGRAMS (1966 1980)

::::LIBERAL ARTS
:::SCIENCES
::BEHAVIORAL SCIENCES
:PSYCHOLOGY
:FOUNDATIONS OF EDUCATION
EDUCATIONAL PSYCHOLOGY

EDUCATIONAL QUALITY

::::TECHNOLOGY
:::COMMUNICATIONS
::TELECOMMUNICATIONS
::MASS MEDIA
:RADIO
:::TECHNOLOGY
::COMMUNICATIONS
:AUDIOVISUAL COMMUNICATIONS
EDUCATIONAL RADIO

:RESEARCH
EDUCATIONAL RESEARCH
.CLASSROOM RESEARCH
.CURRICULUM RESEARCH
.READING RESEARCH
.WRITING RESEARCH

::::GROUPS
:::PERSONNEL
::PROFESSIONAL PERSONNEL
:RESEARCHERS
EDUCATIONAL RESEARCHERS

:RESOURCES
EDUCATIONAL RESOURCES
.EDUCATIONAL SUPPLY

:RESPONSIBILITY
EDUCATIONAL RESPONSIBILITY

EDUCATIONAL RETARDATION (1966 1980)

::::LIBERAL ARTS
:::SCIENCES
::SOCIAL SCIENCES
::::LIBERAL ARTS
:::SCIENCES
::BEHAVIORAL SCIENCES
:SOCIOLOGY
:FOUNDATIONS OF EDUCATION
EDUCATIONAL SOCIOLOGY

EDUCATIONAL SPECIFICATIONS (1967 1980)

:::METHODS
::EVALUATION METHODS
:COMPARATIVE ANALYSIS
EDUCATIONAL STATUS COMPARISON

::METHODS
:EDUCATIONAL METHODS
EDUCATIONAL STRATEGIES

::RESOURCES
:EDUCATIONAL RESOURCES
EDUCATIONAL SUPPLY

:TECHNOLOGY
EDUCATIONAL TECHNOLOGY
.INSTRUCTIONAL SYSTEMS

::::TECHNOLOGY
:::COMMUNICATIONS
::TELECOMMUNICATIONS
::MASS MEDIA
:TELEVISION
:::TECHNOLOGY
::COMMUNICATIONS
:AUDIOVISUAL COMMUNICATIONS
EDUCATIONAL TELEVISION

:::METHODS
::MEASUREMENT TECHNIQUES
:TESTING
EDUCATIONAL TESTING

:THEORIES
:FOUNDATIONS OF EDUCATION
EDUCATIONAL THEORIES

:THERAPY
EDUCATIONAL THERAPY

EDUCATIONAL TRENDS

::FINANCIAL SUPPORT
:GRANTS
EDUCATIONAL VOUCHERS

::CURRICULUM
:COURSES
::CURRICULUM
:COLLEGE CURRICULUM
EDUCATION COURSES

:::GROUPS
::STUDENTS
:MAJORS (STUDENTS)
EDUCATION MAJORS

::FACILITIES
:RESOURCE CENTERS
::FACILITIES
:EDUCATIONAL FACILITIES
EDUCATION SERVICE CENTERS

:RELATIONSHIP
EDUCATION WORK RELATIONSHIP

::::METHODS
:::EVALUATION METHODS
::DATA ANALYSIS
:STATISTICAL ANALYSIS
EFFECT SIZE

EFFICIENCY

:PSYCHOLOGICAL PATTERNS
EGOCENTRISM

::COGNITIVE PROCESSES
:MEMORY
EIDETIC IMAGERY

:::LIBERAL ARTS
::HUMANITIES
:LITERATURE
EIGHTEENTH CENTURY LITERATURE

:::BEHAVIOR
::SOCIAL BEHAVIOR
:ANTISOCIAL BEHAVIOR
ELDER ABUSE

:SELECTION
ELECTIONS
.SCHOOL BUDGET ELECTIONS

::CURRICULUM
:COURSES
ELECTIVE COURSES

ELECTIVE READING (1966 1980)

:EQUIPMENT
ELECTRICAL APPLIANCES

:OCCUPATIONS
ELECTRICAL OCCUPATIONS

:STIMULI
ELECTRICAL STIMULI

ELECTRICAL SYSTEMS

::RESOURCES
:SUPPLIES
ELECTRIC BATTERIES

:EQUIPMENT
ELECTRIC CIRCUITS

::::GROUPS
:::PERSONNEL
::NONPROFESSIONAL PERSONNEL
:SKILLED WORKERS
ELECTRICIANS

ELECTRICITY

::EQUIPMENT
:ENGINES
ELECTRIC MOTORS

::TECHNOLOGY
:MEDICINE
ELECTROENCEPHALOGRAPHY

:EQUIPMENT
ELECTROMECHANICAL AIDS

:TECHNOLOGY
ELECTROMECHANICAL TECHNOLOGY

:::FACILITIES
::EDUCATIONAL FACILITIES
:CLASSROOMS
ELECTRONIC CLASSROOMS

ELECTRONIC CONTROL

: EQUIPMENT
ELECTRONIC EQUIPMENT
. BROADCAST RECEPTION EQUIPMENT
. COMPUTERS
. . ANALOG COMPUTERS
. . COMPUTER STORAGE DEVICES
. . DIGITAL COMPUTERS
. . DISPLAY SYSTEMS
. . INPUT OUTPUT DEVICES
. . . OPTICAL SCANNERS
. . MICROCOMPUTERS
. . MINICOMPUTERS
. . ONLINE SYSTEMS
. . . INTERACTIVE VIDEO
. . . ONLINE CATALOGS
. MICROPHONES
. POLYGRAPHS
. RADAR
. SEMICONDUCTOR DEVICES
. . TRANSISTORS
. SOUND SPECTROGRAPHS
. TAPE RECORDERS
. . AUDIOTAPE RECORDERS
. . VIDEOTAPE RECORDERS
. VIDEO EQUIPMENT
. . VIDEOTAPE RECORDERS

: : : TECHNOLOGY
: : COMMUNICATIONS
: TELECOMMUNICATIONS
ELECTRONIC MAIL

: : : TECHNOLOGY
: : COMMUNICATIONS
: TELECOMMUNICATIONS
: : METHODS
: PRODUCTION TECHNIQUES
ELECTRONIC PUBLISHING

: : : : : LIBERAL ARTS
: : : : SCIENCES
: : : NATURAL SCIENCES
: : PHYSICAL SCIENCES
: PHYSICS
ELECTRONICS

: : : BUSINESS
: : INDUSTRY
: MANUFACTURING INDUSTRY
ELECTRONICS INDUSTRY

: : : GROUPS
: : PERSONNEL
: PARAPROFESSIONAL PERSONNEL
ELECTRONIC TECHNICIANS

: : EDUCATION
: ELEMENTARY SECONDARY EDUCATION
ELEMENTARY EDUCATION
. ADULT BASIC EDUCATION
. PRIMARY EDUCATION

: CURRICULUM
ELEMENTARY SCHOOL CURRICULUM
. ELEMENTARY SCHOOL MATHEMATICS
. ELEMENTARY SCHOOL SCIENCE
. FLES

: : CURRICULUM
: MATHEMATICS CURRICULUM
: : CURRICULUM
: ELEMENTARY SCHOOL CURRICULUM
ELEMENTARY SCHOOL MATHEMATICS

: : INSTITUTIONS
: SCHOOLS
ELEMENTARY SCHOOLS

: : CURRICULUM
: SCIENCE CURRICULUM
: : CURRICULUM
: ELEMENTARY SCHOOL CURRICULUM
ELEMENTARY SCHOOL SCIENCE

: : GROUPS
: STUDENTS
ELEMENTARY SCHOOL STUDENTS

: : : : GROUPS
: : : PERSONNEL
: : PROFESSIONAL PERSONNEL
: TEACHERS
ELEMENTARY SCHOOL TEACHERS

: EDUCATION
ELEMENTARY SECONDARY EDUCATION
. ELEMENTARY EDUCATION
. . ADULT BASIC EDUCATION
. . PRIMARY EDUCATION
. SECONDARY EDUCATION
. . COLLEGE PREPARATION

ELIGIBILITY

ELITISM

: : : : LIBERAL ARTS
: : : SCIENCES
: : NATURAL SCIENCES
: BIOLOGICAL SCIENCES
EMBRYOLOGY

: : : : : GROUPS
: : : : PERSONNEL
: : : NONPROFESSIONAL PERSONNEL
: : SERVICE WORKERS
: EMERGENCY SQUAD PERSONNEL
: : : : GROUPS
: : : PERSONNEL
: : HEALTH PERSONNEL
: ALLIED HEALTH PERSONNEL
EMERGENCY MEDICAL TECHNICIANS

: PROGRAMS
EMERGENCY PROGRAMS

: : : : GROUPS
: : : PERSONNEL
: : NONPROFESSIONAL PERSONNEL
: SERVICE WORKERS
EMERGENCY SQUAD PERSONNEL
. EMERGENCY MEDICAL TECHNICIANS

: : OCCUPATIONS
: DEMAND OCCUPATIONS
EMERGING OCCUPATIONS

: : BEHAVIOR
: ADJUSTMENT (TO ENVIRONMENT)
EMOTIONAL ADJUSTMENT

: : DEVELOPMENT
: INDIVIDUAL DEVELOPMENT
EMOTIONAL DEVELOPMENT

: : DISABILITIES
: MENTAL DISORDERS
EMOTIONAL DISTURBANCES
. PSYCHOSOMATIC DISORDERS

: : BACKGROUND
: EXPERIENCE
EMOTIONAL EXPERIENCE
. CATHARSIS

: PROBLEMS
EMOTIONAL PROBLEMS

: : BEHAVIOR
: RESPONSES
EMOTIONAL RESPONSE

: PSYCHOLOGICAL PATTERNS
EMPATHY

: : GROUPS
: PARENTS
EMPLOYED PARENTS

: : GROUPS
: FEMALES
EMPLOYED WOMEN
. WOMEN FACULTY

: PROGRAMS
EMPLOYEE ASSISTANCE PROGRAMS

: ATTITUDES
EMPLOYEE ATTITUDES

: RESPONSIBILITY
EMPLOYEE RESPONSIBILITY

: : GROUPS
: PERSONNEL
EMPLOYEES
. ENTRY WORKERS

: ATTITUDES
EMPLOYER ATTITUDES

: : RELATIONSHIP
: INTERPERSONAL RELATIONSHIP
EMPLOYER EMPLOYEE RELATIONSHIP

: GROUPS
EMPLOYERS

: : : : SERVICES
: : : HUMAN SERVICES
: : SOCIAL SERVICES
: DAY CARE
EMPLOYER SUPPORTED DAY CARE

EMPLOYMENT
. BLACK EMPLOYMENT
. MIGRANT EMPLOYMENT
. MULTIPLE EMPLOYMENT
. OVERSEAS EMPLOYMENT
. PART TIME EMPLOYMENT
. . JOB SHARING
. SEASONAL EMPLOYMENT
. STUDENT EMPLOYMENT
. TEACHER EMPLOYMENT
. UNDEREMPLOYMENT
. YOUTH EMPLOYMENT

: : : : GROUPS
: : : PERSONNEL
: : GUIDANCE PERSONNEL
: COUNSELORS
EMPLOYMENT COUNSELORS

: : : BACKGROUND
: : EXPERIENCE
: WORK EXPERIENCE
EMPLOYMENT EXPERIENCE

: : : METHODS
: : EVALUATION METHODS
: INTERVIEWS
EMPLOYMENT INTERVIEWS

: STATUS
EMPLOYMENT LEVEL
. ACADEMIC RANK (PROFESSIONAL)
. TENURE

: OPPORTUNITIES
EMPLOYMENT OPPORTUNITIES
. EQUAL OPPORTUNITIES (JOBS)

: : : : LIBERAL ARTS
: : : SCIENCES
: : SOCIAL SCIENCES
: DEMOGRAPHY
EMPLOYMENT PATTERNS

EMPLOYMENT POTENTIAL

EMPLOYMENT PRACTICES

: PROBLEMS
EMPLOYMENT PROBLEMS

: PROGRAMS
EMPLOYMENT PROGRAMS

: PREDICTION
EMPLOYMENT PROJECTIONS

: : STANDARDS
: QUALIFICATIONS
EMPLOYMENT QUALIFICATIONS

: : SERVICES
: HUMAN SERVICES
EMPLOYMENT SERVICES
. OUTPLACEMENT SERVICES (EMPLOYMENT)

: : DATA
: STATISTICAL DATA
EMPLOYMENT STATISTICS
. WORKER DAYS

: FACILITIES
ENCAPSULATED FACILITIES

: COGNITIVE PROCESSES
ENCODING (PSYCHOLOGY)

: : PUBLICATIONS
: REFERENCE MATERIALS
ENCYCLOPEDIAS

: WILDLIFE
ENDANGERED SPECIES

: FINANCIAL SUPPORT
ENDOWMENT FUNDS

: SCIENTIFIC CONCEPTS
ENERGY
. GEOTHERMAL ENERGY
. HEAT
. RADIATION
. . LIGHT
. . NUCLEAR ENERGY
. . SOLAR ENERGY
. WIND ENERGY

: AUDITS (VERIFICATION)
ENERGY AUDITS

: CONSERVATION (ENVIRONMENT)
ENERGY CONSERVATION
. HEAT RECOVERY

: EDUCATION
ENERGY EDUCATION

: : GOVERNANCE
: ADMINISTRATION
ENERGY MANAGEMENT

: OCCUPATIONS
ENERGY OCCUPATIONS

: TECHNOLOGY
ENGINEERING
. AGRICULTURAL ENGINEERING
. CHEMICAL ENGINEERING
. CIVIL ENGINEERING
. OCEAN ENGINEERING
. OPERATING ENGINEERING

: : : : : LIBERAL ARTS
: : : : HUMANITIES
: : : FINE ARTS
: : : VISUAL ARTS
: : GRAPHIC ARTS
: ENGINEERING GRAPHICS
: : : : : LIBERAL ARTS
: : : : HUMANITIES
: : : FINE ARTS
: : VISUAL ARTS
: DRAFTING
ENGINEERING DRAWING

: : EDUCATION
: PROFESSIONAL EDUCATION
ENGINEERING EDUCATION

: : : : : LIBERAL ARTS
: : : : HUMANITIES
: : : FINE ARTS
: : VISUAL ARTS
: GRAPHIC ARTS
ENGINEERING GRAPHICS
. ENGINEERING DRAWING

: : : GROUPS
: : PERSONNEL
: PARAPROFESSIONAL PERSONNEL
ENGINEERING TECHNICIANS
. HIGHWAY ENGINEERING AIDES

: TECHNOLOGY
ENGINEERING TECHNOLOGY

: : : GROUPS
: : PERSONNEL
: PROFESSIONAL PERSONNEL
ENGINEERS

: EQUIPMENT
ENGINES
. DIESEL ENGINES
. ELECTRIC MOTORS

: : LANGUAGES
: INDO EUROPEAN LANGUAGES
ENGLISH
. BUSINESS ENGLISH
. ENGLISH (SECOND LANGUAGE)
. . ENGLISH FOR SPECIAL PURPOSES
. . . ENGLISH FOR ACADEMIC PURPOSES
. . . ENGLISH FOR SCIENCE AND TECHNOLOGY
. . . VOCATIONAL ENGLISH (SECOND LANGUAGE)
. MIDDLE ENGLISH
. NORTH AMERICAN ENGLISH
. OLD ENGLISH
. ORAL ENGLISH

: : LANGUAGE
: SECOND LANGUAGES
: : : LANGUAGES
: : INDO EUROPEAN LANGUAGES
: ENGLISH
ENGLISH (SECOND LANGUAGE)
. ENGLISH FOR SPECIAL PURPOSES
. . ENGLISH FOR ACADEMIC PURPOSES
. . ENGLISH FOR SCIENCE AND TECHNOLOGY
. . VOCATIONAL ENGLISH (SECOND LANGUAGE)

: CURRICULUM
ENGLISH CURRICULUM
. COLLEGE ENGLISH
. WORLD LITERATURE

: : : ORGANIZATION
: : ADMINISTRATIVE ORGANIZATION
: DEPARTMENTS
ENGLISH DEPARTMENTS

ENGLISH EDUCATION (1967 1980)

: : : LANGUAGE
: : LANGUAGES FOR SPECIAL PURPOSES
: : : : LANGUAGE
: : : SECOND LANGUAGES
: : : : : LANGUAGES
: : : : INDO EUROPEAN LANGUAGES
: : : ENGLISH
: : ENGLISH (SECOND LANGUAGE)
: ENGLISH FOR SPECIAL PURPOSES
ENGLISH FOR ACADEMIC PURPOSES

: : : LANGUAGE
: : LANGUAGES FOR SPECIAL PURPOSES
: : : : LANGUAGE
: : : SECOND LANGUAGES
: : : : : LANGUAGES
: : : : INDO EUROPEAN LANGUAGES
: : : ENGLISH
: : ENGLISH (SECOND LANGUAGE)
: ENGLISH FOR SPECIAL PURPOSES
ENGLISH FOR SCIENCE AND TECHNOLOGY

: : LANGUAGE
: LANGUAGES FOR SPECIAL PURPOSES
: : : LANGUAGE
: : SECOND LANGUAGES
: : : : LANGUAGES
: : : INDO EUROPEAN LANGUAGES
: : ENGLISH
: ENGLISH (SECOND LANGUAGE)
ENGLISH FOR SPECIAL PURPOSES
. ENGLISH FOR ACADEMIC PURPOSES
. ENGLISH FOR SCIENCE AND TECHNOLOGY
. VOCATIONAL ENGLISH (SECOND LANGUAGE)

: : : INSTRUCTION
: : HUMANITIES INSTRUCTION
: NATIVE LANGUAGE INSTRUCTION
ENGLISH INSTRUCTION

: : : LIBERAL ARTS
: : HUMANITIES
: LITERATURE
ENGLISH LITERATURE
. OLD ENGLISH LITERATURE

ENGLISH NEOCLASSIC LITERARY PERIOD (1968 1980)

: : : EDUCATION
: : PROFESSIONAL EDUCATION
: TEACHER EDUCATION
ENGLISH TEACHER EDUCATION

: : : : GROUPS
: : : PERSONNEL
: : GOVERNMENT EMPLOYEES
: MILITARY PERSONNEL
ENLISTED PERSONNEL

ENRICHMENT
. CULTURAL ENRICHMENT
. CURRICULUM ENRICHMENT
. JOB ENRICHMENT
. LANGUAGE ENRICHMENT
. MATHEMATICAL ENRICHMENT

: ACTIVITIES
ENRICHMENT ACTIVITIES

ENROLLMENT
. DUAL ENROLLMENT
. LANGUAGE ENROLLMENT
. STUDENT ATTRITION

: INFLUENCES
ENROLLMENT INFLUENCES

: PREDICTION
ENROLLMENT PROJECTIONS

: INCIDENCE
ENROLLMENT RATE
. AVERAGE DAILY MEMBERSHIP
. DECLINING ENROLLMENT

ENROLLMENT TRENDS

: : : : : LIBERAL ARTS
: : : : SCIENCES
: : : NATURAL SCIENCES
: : BIOLOGICAL SCIENCES
: ZOOLOGY
ENTOMOLOGY

ENTREPRENEURSHIP

: : : GROUPS
: : PERSONNEL
: EMPLOYEES
ENTRY WORKERS

ENVIRONMENT
. CULTURAL CONTEXT
. DISADVANTAGED ENVIRONMENT
. ECONOMIC CLIMATE
. . INFLATION (ECONOMICS)
. EDUCATIONAL ENVIRONMENT
. . CLASSROOM ENVIRONMENT
. . COLLEGE ENVIRONMENT
. . TEACHING CONDITIONS
. FAMILY ENVIRONMENT
. INSTITUTIONAL ENVIRONMENT
. . COLLEGE ENVIRONMENT
. ORGANIZATIONAL CLIMATE
. PERMISSIVE ENVIRONMENT
. PHYSICAL ENVIRONMENT
. . ACOUSTICAL ENVIRONMENT
. . . NOISE (SOUND)
. . CLIMATE
. . THERMAL ENVIRONMENT
. . VISUAL ENVIRONMENT
. RURAL ENVIRONMENT
. SIMULATED ENVIRONMENT
. SLUM ENVIRONMENT
. SOCIAL ENVIRONMENT
. . SOCIAL ISOLATION
. SUBURBAN ENVIRONMENT
. THERAPEUTIC ENVIRONMENT
. URBAN ENVIRONMENT
. WORK ENVIRONMENT
. . TEACHING CONDITIONS

: EDUCATION
ENVIRONMENTAL EDUCATION
. CONSERVATION EDUCATION

: INFLUENCES
ENVIRONMENTAL INFLUENCES

: RESEARCH
ENVIRONMENTAL RESEARCH

: STANDARDS
ENVIRONMENTAL STANDARDS

: : : GROUPS
: : PERSONNEL
: PARAPROFESSIONAL PERSONNEL
: : : : GROUPS
: : : PERSONNEL
: : HEALTH PERSONNEL
: ALLIED HEALTH PERSONNEL
ENVIRONMENTAL TECHNICIANS

ENZYMES

: : : : LIBERAL ARTS
: : : HUMANITIES
: : LITERATURE
: POETRY
: LITERARY GENRES
EPICS

: : TECHNOLOGY
: MEDICINE
EPIDEMIOLOGY

: : : DISABILITIES
: : PHYSICAL DISABILITIES
: NEUROLOGICAL IMPAIRMENTS
EPILEPSY

EPISODE TEACHING (1967 1980)

: : : LIBERAL ARTS
: : HUMANITIES
: PHILOSOPHY
EPISTEMOLOGY

: EDUCATION
: : CIVIL LIBERTIES
: CIVIL RIGHTS
EQUAL EDUCATION

: FACILITIES
EQUAL FACILITIES

: FINANCIAL SUPPORT
EQUALIZATION AID

: : OPPORTUNITIES
: EMPLOYMENT OPPORTUNITIES
: : CIVIL LIBERTIES
: CIVIL RIGHTS
EQUAL OPPORTUNITIES (JOBS)

: : CIVIL LIBERTIES
: CIVIL RIGHTS
EQUAL PROTECTION

:: DATA
: SCORES
EQUATED SCORES

::::: LIBERAL ARTS
:::: HUMANITIES
::: PHILOSOPHY
::: LOGIC
:: MATHEMATICAL LOGIC
:: MATHEMATICAL APPLICATIONS
: MATHEMATICAL FORMULAS
EQUATIONS (MATHEMATICS)

EQUIPMENT
. AGRICULTURAL MACHINERY
. AIR CONDITIONING EQUIPMENT
. ASSISTIVE DEVICES (FOR DISABLED)
.. MOBILITY AIDS
... WHEELCHAIRS
.. PROSTHESES
. ATHLETIC EQUIPMENT
. AUDIO EQUIPMENT
.. AUDIOTAPE RECORDERS
.. HEARING AIDS
.. MICROPHONES
.. SOUND SPECTROGRAPHS
. BIOMEDICAL EQUIPMENT
. CALCULATORS
. EDUCATIONAL EQUIPMENT
.. CLASSROOM FURNITURE
. ELECTRICAL APPLIANCES
. ELECTRIC CIRCUITS
. ELECTROMECHANICAL AIDS
. ELECTRONIC EQUIPMENT
.. BROADCAST RECEPTION EQUIPMENT
.. COMPUTERS
... ANALOG COMPUTERS
... COMPUTER STORAGE DEVICES
... DIGITAL COMPUTERS
... DISPLAY SYSTEMS
... INPUT OUTPUT DEVICES
.... OPTICAL SCANNERS
... MICROCOMPUTERS
... MINICOMPUTERS
... ONLINE SYSTEMS
.... INTERACTIVE VIDEO
.... ONLINE CATALOGS
.. MICROPHONES
.. POLYGRAPHS
.. RADAR
.. SEMICONDUCTOR DEVICES
... TRANSISTORS
.. SOUND SPECTROGRAPHS
.. TAPE RECORDERS
... AUDIOTAPE RECORDERS
... VIDEOTAPE RECORDERS
.. VIDEO EQUIPMENT
... VIDEOTAPE RECORDERS
. ENGINES
.. DIESEL ENGINES
.. ELECTRIC MOTORS
. FURNITURE
.. CLASSROOM FURNITURE
. HAND TOOLS
. HOME FURNISHINGS
. LABORATORY EQUIPMENT
.. MICROSCOPES
. LIBRARY EQUIPMENT
.. BOOKMOBILES
. MACHINE TOOLS
. MEASUREMENT EQUIPMENT
.. CALORIMETERS
.. POLYGRAPHS
.. POTENTIOMETERS (INSTRUMENTS)
.. SOUND SPECTROGRAPHS
. MECHANICAL EQUIPMENT
. MOTOR VEHICLES
.. SERVICE VEHICLES
... BOOKMOBILES
... SCHOOL BUSES
.. TRACTORS
. MUSICAL INSTRUMENTS
. OFFICE MACHINES
. PHOTOGRAPHIC EQUIPMENT
. PROJECTION EQUIPMENT
.. FILMSTRIP PROJECTORS
.. MICROFORM READERS
.. OPAQUE PROJECTORS
.. OVERHEAD PROJECTORS
.. TACHISTOSCOPES
. SAFETY EQUIPMENT
.. RESTRAINTS (VEHICLE SAFETY)
. SCIENCE EQUIPMENT
. SPACE DIVIDERS
.. MOVABLE PARTITIONS
. TEST SCORING MACHINES
. VENDING MACHINES

: EVALUATION
EQUIPMENT EVALUATION

: MAINTENANCE
EQUIPMENT MAINTENANCE

:: GROUPS
: PERSONNEL
EQUIPMENT MANUFACTURERS

: STANDARDS
EQUIPMENT STANDARDS

: STORAGE
EQUIPMENT STORAGE

EQUIPMENT UTILIZATION

::: MEASURES (INDIVIDUALS)
:: TESTS
: ACHIEVEMENT TESTS
EQUIVALENCY TESTS

::: METHODS
:: EVALUATION METHODS
: COMPARATIVE ANALYSIS
ERROR ANALYSIS (LANGUAGE)

:::: METHODS
::: EVALUATION METHODS
:: DATA ANALYSIS
: STATISTICAL ANALYSIS
ERROR OF MEASUREMENT

ERROR PATTERNS

: LANGUAGES
ESKIMO ALEUT LANGUAGES

: GROUPS
ESKIMOS

::::: LIBERAL ARTS
:::: HUMANITIES
::: LITERATURE
:: PROSE
: NONFICTION
: LITERARY GENRES
ESSAYS

::: MEASURES (INDIVIDUALS)
:: TESTS
: VERBAL TESTS
ESSAY TESTS

: PLANNING
ESTATE PLANNING

:: MATHEMATICAL APPLICATIONS
: COMPUTATION
ESTIMATION (MATHEMATICS)

::: LANGUAGES
:: URALIC ALTAIC LANGUAGES
: FINNO UGRIC LANGUAGES
ESTONIAN

ESTUARIES

: INSTRUCTION
ETHICAL INSTRUCTION

::: LIBERAL ARTS
:: HUMANITIES
: PHILOSOPHY
ETHICS
. BIOETHICS

::: ATTITUDES
:: SOCIAL ATTITUDES
:: BIAS
: SOCIAL BIAS
ETHNIC BIAS

: SOCIAL DISCRIMINATION
ETHNIC DISCRIMINATION

::::: LIBERAL ARTS
:::: SCIENCES
::: SOCIAL SCIENCES
:: DEMOGRAPHY
: POPULATION DISTRIBUTION
ETHNIC DISTRIBUTION

ETHNIC GROUPING (1966 1980)

: GROUPS
ETHNIC GROUPS
. ALASKA NATIVES
. AMERICAN INDIANS
.. NONRESERVATION AMERICAN INDIANS
... RURAL AMERICAN INDIANS
... URBAN AMERICAN INDIANS
.. RESERVATION AMERICAN INDIANS
. ANGLO AMERICANS
. CANADA NATIVES
. CHINESE AMERICANS
. FILIPINO AMERICANS
. GREEK AMERICANS
. HAWAIIANS
. ITALIAN AMERICANS
. JAPANESE AMERICANS
. KOREAN AMERICANS
. MEXICAN AMERICANS
. POLISH AMERICANS
. PORTUGUESE AMERICANS
. SAMOAN AMERICANS
. SPANISH AMERICANS

: SOCIOCULTURAL PATTERNS
ETHNICITY

ETHNIC ORIGINS

::: RELATIONSHIP
:: HUMAN RELATIONS
: INTERGROUP RELATIONS
ETHNIC RELATIONS

: STATUS
ETHNIC STATUS

:: ATTITUDES
: STEREOTYPES
ETHNIC STEREOTYPES
. BLACK STEREOTYPES

: CURRICULUM
ETHNIC STUDIES
. AMERICAN INDIAN STUDIES
. BLACK STUDIES

ETHNOCENTRISM

:::: LIBERAL ARTS
::: SCIENCES
:: SOCIAL SCIENCES
: ANTHROPOLOGY
ETHNOGRAPHY

:::: LIBERAL ARTS
::: SCIENCES
:: SOCIAL SCIENCES
: ANTHROPOLOGY
ETHNOLOGY

:::: LIBERAL ARTS
::: SCIENCES
:: NATURAL SCIENCES
: BIOLOGICAL SCIENCES
::: LIBERAL ARTS
:: SCIENCES
: BEHAVIORAL SCIENCES
ETHOLOGY

: TECHNOLOGY
ETIOLOGY

:: LINGUISTICS
: DIACHRONIC LINGUISTICS
ETYMOLOGY
. ONOMASTICS

:::: LIBERAL ARTS
::: SCIENCES
:: SOCIAL SCIENCES
::: LIBERAL ARTS
:: HUMANITIES
: HISTORY
EUROPEAN HISTORY

EVALUATION
. COURSE EVALUATION
. CURRICULUM EVALUATION
. EDUCATIONAL ASSESSMENT
. EQUIPMENT EVALUATION
. FORMATIVE EVALUATION
. HOLISTIC EVALUATION
. INFORMAL ASSESSMENT
. INSTITUTIONAL EVALUATION
. INSTRUCTIONAL MATERIAL EVALUATION
.. TEXTBOOK EVALUATION
. MEDICAL CARE EVALUATION
. MEDICAL EVALUATION
.. AUDITORY EVALUATION
.. DENTAL EVALUATION
.. PHYSICAL EXAMINATIONS
.. SPEECH EVALUATION
. NEEDS ASSESSMENT
. PEER EVALUATION
. PERSONNEL EVALUATION
.. ADMINISTRATOR EVALUATION
.. COUNSELOR EVALUATION
.. FACULTY EVALUATION
.. TEACHER EVALUATION
... STUDENT EVALUATION OF TEACHER PERFORMANCE
. PRESCHOOL EVALUATION
. PROGRAM EVALUATION
. PROPERTY APPRAISAL
.. ASSESSED VALUATION
. PSYCHOLOGICAL EVALUATION
.. PERSONALITY ASSESSMENT
. RECOGNITION (ACHIEVEMENT)
.. AWARDS
.. COMMENCEMENT CEREMONIES
.. PROFESSIONAL RECOGNITION
. SELF EVALUATION (GROUPS)
. SELF EVALUATION (INDIVIDUALS)
. STUDENT EVALUATION
.. NONGRADED STUDENT EVALUATION
. STUDENT TEACHER EVALUATION
. SUMMATIVE EVALUATION
. VOCATIONAL EVALUATION
. WRITING EVALUATION

: : STANDARDS
: CRITERIA
EVALUATION CRITERIA
. RELIABILITY
. . INTERRATER RELIABILITY
. . TEST RELIABILITY
. VALIDITY
. . CONCURRENT VALIDITY
. . PREDICTIVE VALIDITY
. . PROOF (MATHEMATICS)
. . TEST VALIDITY
. . . CONSTRUCT VALIDITY
. . . CONTENT VALIDITY

: METHODS
EVALUATION METHODS
. AUDIENCE ANALYSIS
. CASE STUDIES
. . CROSS SECTIONAL STUDIES
. . FACILITY CASE STUDIES
. . LONGITUDINAL STUDIES
. . . FOLLOWUP STUDIES
. . . . GRADUATE SURVEYS
. . . . VOCATIONAL FOLLOWUP
. CHEMICAL ANALYSIS
. COMPARATIVE ANALYSIS
. . EDUCATIONAL STATUS COMPARISON
. . ERROR ANALYSIS (LANGUAGE)
. COMPONENTIAL ANALYSIS
. CONTENT ANALYSIS
. COST EFFECTIVENESS
. DATA ANALYSIS
. . DATA COLLECTION
. . . SAMPLING
. . . . ITEM SAMPLING
. . DATA INTERPRETATION
. . . STATISTICAL INFERENCE
. . . TEST INTERPRETATION
. . STATISTICAL ANALYSIS
. . . ANALYSIS OF COVARIANCE
. . . ANALYSIS OF VARIANCE
. . . BAYESIAN STATISTICS
. . . CORRELATION
. . . EFFECT SIZE
. . . ERROR OF MEASUREMENT
. . . GOODNESS OF FIT
. . . ITEM ANALYSIS
. . . JUDGMENT ANALYSIS TECHNIQUE
. . . LEAST SQUARES STATISTICS
. . . MAXIMUM LIKELIHOOD STATISTICS
. . . META ANALYSIS
. . . MULTIVARIATE ANALYSIS
. . . . CLUSTER ANALYSIS
. . . . DISCRIMINANT ANALYSIS
. . . . FACTOR ANALYSIS
. . . . . OBLIQUE ROTATION
. . . . . ORTHOGONAL ROTATION
. . . . MULTIDIMENSIONAL SCALING
. . . . PATH ANALYSIS
. . . REGRESSION (STATISTICS)
. . . . MULTIPLE REGRESSION ANALYSIS
. . . STATISTICAL DISTRIBUTIONS
. . . STATISTICAL INFERENCE
. . . STATISTICAL SIGNIFICANCE
. . TREND ANALYSIS
. HYPOTHESIS TESTING
. INPUT OUTPUT ANALYSIS
. INSPECTION
. INTERVIEWS
. . EMPLOYMENT INTERVIEWS
. . FIELD INTERVIEWS
. JOB ANALYSIS
. LIFE CYCLE COSTING
. NEED ANALYSIS (STUDENT FINANCIAL AID)
. PHONETIC ANALYSIS
. PRETESTING
. QUALITY CONTROL
. READABILITY FORMULAS
. SITE ANALYSIS
. SKILL ANALYSIS
. STRUCTURAL ANALYSIS (LINGUISTICS)
. . DISCOURSE ANALYSIS
. . TAGMEMIC ANALYSIS
. STRUCTURAL ANALYSIS (SCIENCE)
. SURVEYS
. . COMMUNITY SURVEYS
. . GRADUATE SURVEYS
. . LIBRARY SURVEYS
. . NATIONAL SURVEYS
. . OCCUPATIONAL SURVEYS
. . SCHOOL SURVEYS
. . STATE SURVEYS
. . STATISTICAL SURVEYS
. . TELEVISION SURVEYS
. SYNTHESIS
. TASK ANALYSIS

: NEEDS
EVALUATION NEEDS

: PROBLEMS
EVALUATION PROBLEMS

: INFORMATION UTILIZATION
EVALUATION UTILIZATION

: : COGNITIVE PROCESSES
: CRITICAL THINKING
EVALUATIVE THINKING
. VALUE JUDGMENT

: : GROUPS
: PERSONNEL
EVALUATORS

: PROGRAMS
EVENING PROGRAMS

: : GROUPS
: STUDENTS
EVENING STUDENTS

: DEVELOPMENT
EVOLUTION
. HEREDITY

: : LANGUAGES
: AFRICAN LANGUAGES
EWE

: : : : GROUPS
: : : PERSONNEL
: : NONPROFESSIONAL PERSONNEL
: CLERICAL WORKERS
EXAMINERS

EXCEPTIONAL CHILD EDUCATION (1968 1980)

: RESEARCH
EXCEPTIONAL CHILD RESEARCH

EXCEPTIONAL CHILD SERVICES (1968 1980)

: GROUPS
EXCEPTIONAL PERSONS
. GIFTED
. . ACADEMICALLY GIFTED
. . GIFTED DISABLED
. . GIFTED DISADVANTAGED

: PROGRAMS
EXCHANGE PROGRAMS
. STUDENT EXCHANGE PROGRAMS
. TEACHER EXCHANGE PROGRAMS

: : ACTIVITIES
: PHYSICAL ACTIVITIES
EXERCISE
. AEROBICS
. CALISTHENICS

EXERCISE (PHYSIOLOGY) (1969 1980)

: : : : : LIBERAL ARTS
: : : : SCIENCES
: : : NATURAL SCIENCES
: : BIOLOGICAL SCIENCES
: PHYSIOLOGY
EXERCISE PHYSIOLOGY

: NONPRINT MEDIA
EXHIBITS
. SCIENCE FAIRS

: : : LIBERAL ARTS
: : HUMANITIES
: PHILOSOPHY
EXISTENTIALISM

: : VISUAL AIDS
: TABLES (DATA)
EXPECTANCY TABLES

EXPECTATION
. WORK LIFE EXPECTANCY

: EXPENDITURES
EXPENDITURE PER STUDENT

EXPENDITURES
. CAPITAL OUTLAY (FOR FIXED ASSETS)
. COMPENSATION (REMUNERATION)
. EXPENDITURE PER STUDENT
. LIBRARY EXPENDITURES
. MERIT PAY
. OPERATING EXPENSES
. PREMIUM PAY
. SALARIES
. . CONTRACT SALARIES
. . TEACHER SALARIES
. SCHOOL DISTRICT SPENDING
. WAGES
. . MINIMUM WAGE

: BACKGROUND
EXPERIENCE
. EARLY EXPERIENCE
. EDUCATIONAL EXPERIENCE
. EMOTIONAL EXPERIENCE
. . CATHARSIS
. GROUP EXPERIENCE
. INTELLECTUAL EXPERIENCE
. LEARNING EXPERIENCE
. . CLINICAL EXPERIENCE
. PREREADING EXPERIENCE
. SENSORY EXPERIENCE
. . FIGURAL AFTEREFFECTS
. . SENSORY DEPRIVATION
. SOCIAL EXPERIENCE
. STUDENT EXPERIENCE
. TEACHING EXPERIENCE
. WORK EXPERIENCE
. . EMPLOYMENT EXPERIENCE

: : EDUCATIONAL MEDIA
: INSTRUCTIONAL MATERIALS
: : VISUAL AIDS
: CHARTS
EXPERIENCE CHARTS

: LEARNING
EXPERIENTIAL LEARNING
. FIELD EXPERIENCE PROGRAMS
. . SUPERVISED FARM PRACTICE
. INTERNSHIP PROGRAMS

: : : INSTITUTIONS
: : SCHOOLS
: EXPERIMENTAL SCHOOLS
: : : INSTITUTIONS
: : SCHOOLS
: COLLEGES
EXPERIMENTAL COLLEGES

: CURRICULUM
EXPERIMENTAL CURRICULUM

: GROUPS
EXPERIMENTAL GROUPS

: PROGRAMS
EXPERIMENTAL PROGRAMS

: : : : LIBERAL ARTS
: : : SCIENCES
: : BEHAVIORAL SCIENCES
: PSYCHOLOGY
EXPERIMENTAL PSYCHOLOGY

: : INSTITUTIONS
: SCHOOLS
EXPERIMENTAL SCHOOLS
. EXPERIMENTAL COLLEGES

: : : METHODS
: : EDUCATIONAL METHODS
: TEACHING METHODS
EXPERIMENTAL TEACHING

EXPERIMENTER CHARACTERISTICS

EXPERIMENTS
. EDUCATIONAL EXPERIMENTS
. LABORATORY EXPERIMENTS
. SCIENCE EXPERIMENTS

: FACILITIES
EXPERIMENT STATIONS

: ARTIFICIAL INTELLIGENCE
EXPERT SYSTEMS

: BEHAVIOR
EXPLORATORY BEHAVIOR

EXPORTS

: : LITERACY
: : LANGUAGE ARTS
: WRITING (COMPOSITION)
EXPOSITORY WRITING

EXPRESSIONISM

: : COGNITIVE PROCESSES
: LANGUAGE PROCESSING
EXPRESSIVE LANGUAGE

: DISCIPLINE
EXPULSION

: : GROUPS
: FAMILY (SOCIOLOGICAL UNIT)
EXTENDED FAMILY

: : : PLANNING
: : SCHEDULING
: SCHOOL SCHEDULES
EXTENDED SCHOOL DAY

: : : PLANNING
: : SCHEDULING
: SCHOOL SCHEDULES
EXTENDED SCHOOL YEAR

: : : GROUPS
: : PERSONNEL
: GOVERNMENT EMPLOYEES
: : GROUPS
: CHANGE AGENTS
EXTENSION AGENTS

: EDUCATION
EXTENSION EDUCATION
. EXTERNAL DEGREE PROGRAMS
. LIBRARY EXTENSION
. RURAL EXTENSION
. URBAN EXTENSION

: : EDUCATION
: EXTENSION EDUCATION
: : PROGRAMS
: COLLEGE PROGRAMS
EXTERNAL DEGREE PROGRAMS

: : COGNITIVE PROCESSES
: LEARNING PROCESSES
EXTINCTION (PSYCHOLOGY)

: : ACTIVITIES
: SCHOOL ACTIVITIES
EXTRACURRICULAR ACTIVITIES

: : : ACTIVITIES
: : PHYSICAL ACTIVITIES
: ATHLETICS
EXTRAMURAL ATHLETICS

: : COMMUNICATION (THOUGHT TRANSFER)
: NONVERBAL COMMUNICATION
EYE CONTACT

: : : : BEHAVIOR
: : : RESPONSES
: : MOTOR REACTIONS
: EYE MOVEMENTS
EYE FIXATIONS

: : : : ABILITY
: : : SKILLS
: : PSYCHOMOTOR SKILLS
: PERCEPTUAL MOTOR COORDINATION
EYE HAND COORDINATION

: : : BEHAVIOR
: : RESPONSES
: MOTOR REACTIONS
EYE MOVEMENTS
. EYE FIXATIONS

EYES

: : : : ABILITY
: : : SKILLS
: : PSYCHOMOTOR SKILLS
: PERCEPTUAL MOTOR COORDINATION
EYE VOICE SPAN

: : LITERARY GENRES
: TALES
FABLES

: : COMMUNICATION (THOUGHT TRANSFER)
: NONVERBAL COMMUNICATION
FACIAL EXPRESSIONS

FACILITIES
. AIRPORTS
. AIR STRUCTURES
. . PNEUMATIC FORMS
. ANIMAL FACILITIES
. . ZOOS
. ASSESSMENT CENTERS (PERSONNEL)
. ATHLETIC FIELDS
. AUDITORIUMS
. BUILDINGS
. . SCHOOL BUILDINGS
. . . COLLEGE BUILDINGS
. COLLEGE STORES
. COMMUNITY CENTERS
. CORRIDORS
. DAY CARE CENTERS
. DINING FACILITIES
. DRIVEWAYS
. EDUCATIONAL FACILITIES
. . AFTER SCHOOL CENTERS
. . AUDIOVISUAL CENTERS
. . BUSINESS EDUCATION FACILITIES
. . CHILD DEVELOPMENT CENTERS
. . CLASSROOMS
. . . ELECTRONIC CLASSROOMS
. . . MOBILE CLASSROOMS
. . . MULTIPURPOSE CLASSROOMS
. . . SELF CONTAINED CLASSROOMS
. . CONTINUING EDUCATION CENTERS
. . CURRICULUM STUDY CENTERS
. . DEMONSTRATION CENTERS
. . EDUCATIONAL COMPLEXES
. . . CAMPUSES
. . . EDUCATIONAL PARKS
. . EDUCATION SERVICE CENTERS
. . FOUND SPACES
. . GUIDANCE CENTERS
. . LEARNING CENTERS (CLASSROOM)
. . LEARNING LABORATORIES
. . . LANGUAGE LABORATORIES
. . LEARNING RESOURCES CENTERS
. . LIVING LEARNING CENTERS
. . OFF CAMPUS FACILITIES
. . PHYSICAL EDUCATION FACILITIES
. . READING CENTERS
. . SCHOOL BUILDINGS
. . . COLLEGE BUILDINGS
. . SCHOOL SHOPS
. . SCHOOL SPACE
. . SCIENCE TEACHING CENTERS
. . SKILL CENTERS
. . STUDENT UNIONS
. . STUDY FACILITIES
. . . CARRELS
. . . STUDY CENTERS
. . VOCATIONAL TRAINING CENTERS
. . WRITING LABORATORIES
. ENCAPSULATED FACILITIES
. EQUAL FACILITIES
. EXPERIMENT STATIONS
. FALLOUT SHELTERS
. FEED STORES
. FIELD HOUSES
. FISHERIES
. FLEXIBLE FACILITIES
. FOOD HANDLING FACILITIES
. FOOD STORES
. FOUNDRIES
. GREENHOUSES
. GYMNASIUMS
. HEALTH FACILITIES
. . NURSING HOMES
. HOUSING
. . BOARDING HOMES
. . COLLEGE HOUSING
. . DORMITORIES
. . GROUP HOMES
. . HOTELS
. . LOW RENT HOUSING
. . . PUBLIC HOUSING
. . MIDDLE INCOME HOUSING
. . MIGRANT HOUSING
. . SUBURBAN HOUSING
. . TEACHER HOUSING
. INTERIOR SPACE
. LABORATORIES
. . LEARNING LABORATORIES
. . . LANGUAGE LABORATORIES
. . MOBILE LABORATORIES
. . REGIONAL LABORATORIES
. . SCIENCE LABORATORIES
. . WRITING LABORATORIES
. LIBRARY FACILITIES
. LOCKER ROOMS
. MILITARY AIR FACILITIES
. MUSEUMS
. MUSIC FACILITIES
. NUCLEAR POWER PLANTS
. NURSERIES (HORTICULTURE)
. OFFICES (FACILITIES)
. PARKING FACILITIES
. PARKS
. PLANETARIUMS
. PUBLIC FACILITIES
. . PUBLIC LIBRARIES
. . . COUNTY LIBRARIES
. . . REGIONAL LIBRARIES
. RECREATIONAL FACILITIES
. . PLAYGROUNDS
. REHABILITATION CENTERS
. RELOCATABLE FACILITIES
. RESEARCH AND DEVELOPMENT CENTERS
. RESOURCE CENTERS
. . ARTS CENTERS
. . AUDIOVISUAL CENTERS
. . CULTURAL CENTERS
. . CURRICULUM STUDY CENTERS
. . EDUCATION SERVICE CENTERS
. . INFORMATION CENTERS
. . . CLEARINGHOUSES
. . LEARNING CENTERS (CLASSROOM)
. . LEARNING RESOURCES CENTERS
. . NATURE CENTERS
. . READING CENTERS
. . TEACHER CENTERS
. SANITARY FACILITIES
. . TOILET FACILITIES
. SATELLITE FACILITIES
. SCIENCE FACILITIES
. . SCIENCE LABORATORIES
. . SCIENCE TEACHING CENTERS
. SETTLEMENT HOUSES
. SHARED FACILITIES
. SWIMMING POOLS
. TELEVISION STUDIOS
. THEATERS
. TRAILS
. UNDERGROUND FACILITIES
. WAREHOUSES
. WINDOWLESS ROOMS

: : RESEARCH
: : : METHODS
: : EVALUATION METHODS
: CASE STUDIES
FACILITY CASE STUDIES

: DEVELOPMENT
FACILITY EXPANSION
. SCHOOL EXPANSION

: GUIDELINES
FACILITY GUIDELINES

: IMPROVEMENT
FACILITY IMPROVEMENT
. EDUCATIONAL FACILITIES IMPROVEMENT

FACILITY INVENTORY

: PLANNING
FACILITY PLANNING
. EDUCATIONAL FACILITIES PLANNING
. . CAMPUS PLANNING

: : STANDARDS
: SPECIFICATIONS
FACILITY REQUIREMENTS

: : RESEARCH
: USE STUDIES
FACILITY UTILIZATION RESEARCH

: : : TECHNOLOGY
: : COMMUNICATIONS
: TELECOMMUNICATIONS
FACSIMILE TRANSMISSION

: : : : : METHODS
: : : : EVALUATION METHODS
: : : DATA ANALYSIS
: : STATISTICAL ANALYSIS
: MULTIVARIATE ANALYSIS
FACTOR ANALYSIS
. OBLIQUE ROTATION
. ORTHOGONAL ROTATION

FACTOR STRUCTURE

FACTUAL READING (1966 1980)

: : : GROUPS
: : PERSONNEL
: SCHOOL PERSONNEL
: : : GROUPS
: : PERSONNEL
: PROFESSIONAL PERSONNEL
FACULTY
. ADJUNCT FACULTY
. COLLEGE FACULTY
. . COLLEGE PRESIDENTS
. . COUNSELOR EDUCATORS
. . GRADUATE SCHOOL FACULTY
. . . MEDICAL SCHOOL FACULTY
. . PROFESSORS
. . STUDENT TEACHER SUPERVISORS
. . TEACHER EDUCATORS
. . . METHODS TEACHERS
. . TEACHING ASSISTANTS
. DEANS
. . ACADEMIC DEANS
. . DEANS OF STUDENTS
. DEPARTMENT HEADS
. FACULTY ADVISERS
. FULL TIME FACULTY
. NONTENURED FACULTY
. PART TIME FACULTY
. . PARTNERSHIP TEACHERS
. TENURED FACULTY
. WOMEN FACULTY

: : : : GROUPS
: : : PERSONNEL
: : SCHOOL PERSONNEL
: : : : GROUPS
: : : PERSONNEL
: : PROFESSIONAL PERSONNEL
: FACULTY
FACULTY ADVISERS

: RELATIONSHIP
FACULTY COLLEGE RELATIONSHIP

: : : DEVELOPMENT
: : LABOR FORCE DEVELOPMENT
: STAFF DEVELOPMENT
: : : DEVELOPMENT
: : LABOR FORCE DEVELOPMENT
: PROFESSIONAL DEVELOPMENT
FACULTY DEVELOPMENT

: : EVALUATION
: PERSONNEL EVALUATION
FACULTY EVALUATION

: : : FINANCIAL SUPPORT
: : STUDENT FINANCIAL AID
: FELLOWSHIPS
FACULTY FELLOWSHIPS

: : PUBLICATIONS
: SCHOOL PUBLICATIONS
: : : PUBLICATIONS
: : REFERENCE MATERIALS
: GUIDES
FACULTY HANDBOOKS

: : SOCIAL INTEGRATION
: PERSONNEL INTEGRATION
FACULTY INTEGRATION

: : MOBILITY
: OCCUPATIONAL MOBILITY
FACULTY MOBILITY

: : GROUPS
: ORGANIZATIONS (GROUPS)
FACULTY ORGANIZATIONS

: PROMOTION (OCCUPATIONAL)
FACULTY PROMOTION

FACULTY PUBLISHING

: RECRUITMENT
FACULTY RECRUITMENT

FACULTY WORKLOAD
. TEACHING LOAD

: : BEHAVIOR
: PERFORMANCE
FAILURE
. ACADEMIC FAILURE
. . READING FAILURE

: : DISABILITIES
: DISEASES
FAILURE TO THRIVE

: FACILITIES
FALLOUT SHELTERS

: GROUPS
FAMILY (SOCIOLOGICAL UNIT)
. BLACK FAMILY
. DUAL CAREER FAMILY
. EXTENDED FAMILY
. FOSTER FAMILY
. NUCLEAR FAMILY
. ONE PARENT FAMILY
. . FATHERLESS FAMILY
. . MOTHERLESS FAMILY
. RURAL FAMILY
. STEPFAMILY

: ATTITUDES
FAMILY ATTITUDES

FAMILY CHARACTERISTICS

: : GUIDANCE
: COUNSELING
FAMILY COUNSELING

: : : : SERVICES
: : : HUMAN SERVICES
: : SOCIAL SERVICES
: DAY CARE
FAMILY DAY CARE

: ENVIRONMENT
FAMILY ENVIRONMENT

: RESOURCES
FAMILY FINANCIAL RESOURCES

: HEALTH
FAMILY HEALTH

: : : : LIBERAL ARTS
: : : SCIENCES
: : SOCIAL SCIENCES
: : : LIBERAL ARTS
: : HUMANITIES
: HISTORY
FAMILY HISTORY
. GENEALOGY

: INCOME
FAMILY INCOME

: INFLUENCES
FAMILY INFLUENCE

: : BEHAVIOR
: PARTICIPATION
FAMILY INVOLVEMENT

FAMILY LIFE

: EDUCATION
FAMILY LIFE EDUCATION
. PARENTHOOD EDUCATION
. SEX EDUCATION

: : MOBILITY
: MIGRATION
FAMILY MOBILITY

: PLANNING
FAMILY PLANNING

: : TECHNOLOGY
: MEDICINE
FAMILY PRACTICE (MEDICINE)

: PROBLEMS
FAMILY PROBLEMS

: PROGRAMS
FAMILY PROGRAMS

: : RELATIONSHIP
: INTERPERSONAL
RELATIONSHIP
FAMILY RELATIONSHIP
. PARENT CHILD RELATIONSHIP
. . PARENT STUDENT
RELATIONSHIP

FAMILY ROLE

: RELATIONSHIP
FAMILY SCHOOL RELATIONSHIP
. PARENT SCHOOL
RELATIONSHIP

FAMILY SIZE

: : STATUS
: GROUP STATUS
FAMILY STATUS

: : ORGANIZATION
: GROUP STRUCTURE
FAMILY STRUCTURE
. BIRTH ORDER

: : : : BEHAVIOR
: : : SOCIAL BEHAVIOR
: : ANTISOCIAL BEHAVIOR
: VIOLENCE
FAMILY VIOLENCE

FANTASY

: RECORDS (FORMS)
FARM ACCOUNTS

: : : GROUPS
: : PERSONNEL
: AGRICULTURAL PERSONNEL
FARMERS
. DAIRY FARMERS
. PART TIME FARMERS
. SHARECROPPERS

: LABOR
FARM LABOR

: : GOVERNANCE
: ADMINISTRATION
FARM MANAGEMENT

: : OCCUPATIONS
: AGRICULTURAL OCCUPATIONS
FARM OCCUPATIONS

: FIELD TRIPS
FARM VISITS

: SOCIAL SYSTEMS
FASCISM
. NAZISM

: : BUSINESS
: INDUSTRY
FASHION INDUSTRY

: : PLANNING
: SCHEDULING
FAST TRACK SCHEDULING

: : ATTITUDES
: PARENT ATTITUDES
FATHER ATTITUDES

: : : GROUPS
: : FAMILY (SOCIOLOGICAL
UNIT)
: ONE PARENT FAMILY
FATHERLESS FAMILY

: : GROUPS
: PARENTS
: : GROUPS
: MALES
FATHERS

FATIGUE (BIOLOGY)

: PSYCHOLOGICAL PATTERNS
FEAR
. FEAR OF SUCCESS
. SCHOOL PHOBIA

: : PSYCHOLOGICAL PATTERNS
: FEAR
FEAR OF SUCCESS

: RESEARCH
FEASIBILITY STUDIES

FEDERAL AID
. REVENUE SHARING
. STATE FEDERAL AID

: : INSTITUTIONS
: COURTS
FEDERAL COURTS

: : : GROUPS
: : ORGANIZATIONS (GROUPS)
: GOVERNMENT
(ADMINISTRATIVE BODY)
FEDERAL GOVERNMENT

: RELATIONSHIP
FEDERAL INDIAN RELATIONSHIP

: LEGISLATION
FEDERAL LEGISLATION

: PROGRAMS
FEDERAL PROGRAMS

: GOVERNANCE
FEDERAL REGULATION

: RELATIONSHIP
FEDERAL STATE RELATIONSHIP

: : RELATIONSHIP
: INTERACTION
FEEDBACK
. BIOFEEDBACK

FEEDER PATTERNS

: : BUSINESS
: INDUSTRY
FEED INDUSTRY

: FACILITIES
FEED STORES

: COSTS
FEES
. FINES (PENALTIES)
. TUITION

: : FINANCIAL SUPPORT
: STUDENT FINANCIAL AID
FELLOWSHIPS
. FACULTY FELLOWSHIPS

: GROUPS
FEMALES
. BATTERED WOMEN
. DAUGHTERS
. DISPLACED HOMEMAKERS
. EMPLOYED WOMEN
. . WOMEN FACULTY
. MOTHERS
. . BLACK MOTHERS
. . UNWED MOTHERS
. NUNS
. PREGNANT STUDENTS

FEMINISM

: : : ACTIVITIES
: : PHYSICAL ACTIVITIES
: ATHLETICS
FENCING (SPORT)

FERTILIZERS

: : : : LIBERAL ARTS
: : : HUMANITIES
: : LITERATURE
: PROSE
FICTION
. NOVELS
. SCIENCE FICTION
. SHORT STORIES

FIELD CROPS
. GRAINS (FOOD)
. TOBACCO

: : : INDIVIDUAL
CHARACTERISTICS
: : PSYCHOLOGICAL
CHARACTERISTICS
: COGNITIVE STYLE
FIELD DEPENDENCE
INDEPENDENCE

: PROGRAMS
: : LEARNING
: EXPERIENTIAL LEARNING
FIELD EXPERIENCE PROGRAMS
. SUPERVISED FARM PRACTICE

: : : : ACTIVITIES
: : : PHYSICAL ACTIVITIES
: : ATHLETICS
: TEAM SPORTS
FIELD HOCKEY

: FACILITIES
FIELD HOUSES

: INSTRUCTION
FIELD INSTRUCTION

: : : METHODS
: : EVALUATION METHODS
: INTERVIEWS
FIELD INTERVIEWS

: RESEARCH
FIELD STUDIES

: : MEASURES (INDIVIDUALS)
: TESTS
FIELD TESTS

FIELD TRIPS
. FARM VISITS

: : : LIBERAL ARTS
: : HUMANITIES
: LITERATURE
FIFTEENTH CENTURY LITERATURE

: : : BACKGROUND
: : EXPERIENCE
: SENSORY EXPERIENCE
FIGURAL AFTEREFFECTS

: LITERARY DEVICES
: LANGUAGE
FIGURATIVE LANGUAGE
. ALLEGORY
. AMBIGUITY
. ANTITHESIS
. IMAGERY
. IRONY
. METAPHORS
. PUNS
. SYMBOLS (LITERARY)

: : : : GROUPS
: : : PERSONNEL
: : NONPROFESSIONAL PERSONNEL
: CLERICAL WORKERS
FILE CLERKS

: : : : SERVICES
: : : INFORMATION SERVICES
: : INFORMATION PROCESSING
: DOCUMENTATION
FILING

: : GROUPS
: ETHNIC GROUPS
: : : GROUPS
: : NORTH AMERICANS
: ASIAN AMERICANS
FILIPINO AMERICANS

FILM CRITICISM

: : BUSINESS
: INDUSTRY
FILM INDUSTRY

: : : INSTITUTIONS
: : : INFORMATION SOURCES
: : LIBRARIES
: SPECIAL LIBRARIES
FILM LIBRARIES

: : PUBLICATIONS
: REFERENCE MATERIALS
FILMOGRAPHIES

: : : : LIBERAL ARTS
: : : HUMANITIES
: : FINE ARTS
: VISUAL ARTS
: : METHODS
: PRODUCTION TECHNIQUES
FILM PRODUCTION

: : : GROUPS
: : PERSONNEL
: SPECIALISTS
FILM PRODUCTION SPECIALISTS

: VISUAL AIDS
: NONPRINT MEDIA
: MASS MEDIA
FILMS
. FOREIGN LANGUAGE FILMS
. INSTRUCTIONAL FILMS
. KINESCOPE RECORDINGS
. SINGLE CONCEPT FILMS

: : VISUAL AIDS
: : EQUIPMENT
: PROJECTION EQUIPMENT
FILMSTRIP PROJECTORS

: VISUAL AIDS
: NONPRINT MEDIA
FILMSTRIPS

: : EDUCATION
: AESTHETIC EDUCATION
FILM STUDY

: OCCUPATIONS
FINANCE OCCUPATIONS

: IMPROVEMENT
FINANCE REFORM

: GROUPS
FINANCIAL AID APPLICANTS

: AUDITS (VERIFICATION)
FINANCIAL AUDITS

: NEEDS
FINANCIAL NEEDS

: POLICY
FINANCIAL POLICY

: PROBLEMS
FINANCIAL PROBLEMS

: SERVICES
FINANCIAL SERVICES

FINANCIAL SUPPORT
. CAPITAL
. CATEGORICAL AID
. ENDOWMENT FUNDS
. EQUALIZATION AID
. FULL STATE FUNDING
. GRANTS
. . BLOCK GRANTS
. . EDUCATIONAL VOUCHERS
. . INCENTIVE GRANTS
. . TUITION GRANTS
. PRIVATE FINANCIAL SUPPORT
. PRIVATE SCHOOL AID
. RECREATION FINANCES
. REVENUE SHARING
. SCHOLARSHIP FUNDS
. SCHOOL FUNDS
. STUDENT FINANCIAL AID
. . ASSISTANTSHIPS
. . FELLOWSHIPS
. . . FACULTY FELLOWSHIPS
. . INCOME CONTINGENT LOANS
. . PARENT FINANCIAL CONTRIBUTION
. . SCHOLARSHIPS
. . . MERIT SCHOLARSHIPS
. . . . NO NEED SCHOLARSHIPS
. . . TUITION GRANTS
. TAX ALLOCATION
. TRAINING ALLOWANCES
. UNEMPLOYMENT INSURANCE
. WORKERS COMPENSATION

: : LIBERAL ARTS
: HUMANITIES
FINE ARTS
. DANCE
. MUSIC
. . APPLIED MUSIC
. . JAZZ
. . ORIENTAL MUSIC
. . VOCAL MUSIC
. . . CHORAL MUSIC
. . . SONGS
. . . . ART SONG
. . . . BALLADS
. . . . HYMNS
. THEATER ARTS
. . ACTING
. . CHORAL SPEAKING
. . DRAMA
. . . COMEDY
. . . . SKITS
. . . SCRIPTS
. . . TRAGEDY
. . DRAMATICS
. . . CREATIVE DRAMATICS
. . OPERA
. . PANTOMIME
. . PUPPETRY
. . READERS THEATER
. VISUAL ARTS
. . ARCHITECTURE
. . CHILDRENS ART
. . DESIGN CRAFTS
. . DRAFTING
. . . ARCHITECTURAL DRAFTING
. . . ENGINEERING DRAWING
. . . TECHNICAL ILLUSTRATION
. . FILM PRODUCTION
. . FREEHAND DRAWING
. . GRAPHIC ARTS
. . . CARTOGRAPHY
. . . COMPUTER GRAPHICS
. . . ENGINEERING GRAPHICS
. . . . ENGINEERING DRAWING
. . . LAYOUT (PUBLICATIONS)
. . . PRINTING
. . HANDICRAFTS
. . . CERAMICS
. . PAINTING (VISUAL ARTS)
. . PHOTOGRAPHY
. . . HOLOGRAPHY
. . SCULPTURE

: : COSTS
: FEES
FINES (PENALTIES)

: : LANGUAGE ARTS
: SPELLING
: : COMMUNICATION (THOUGHT TRANSFER)
: MANUAL COMMUNICATION
FINGER SPELLING

FINISHING

: : : LANGUAGES
: : URALIC ALTAIC LANGUAGES
: FINNO UGRIC LANGUAGES
FINNISH

: : LANGUAGES
: URALIC ALTAIC LANGUAGES
FINNO UGRIC LANGUAGES
. CHEREMIS
. ESTONIAN
. FINNISH
. HUNGARIAN
. OSTYAK
. VOGUL

: : : : GROUPS
: : : PERSONNEL
: : NONPROFESSIONAL PERSONNEL
: SERVICE WORKERS
FIRE FIGHTERS

: : METHODS
: INSURANCE
FIRE INSURANCE

: SAFETY
FIRE PROTECTION

: : : EDUCATION
: : VOCATIONAL EDUCATION
: TECHNICAL EDUCATION
FIRE SCIENCE EDUCATION

: : : : SERVICES
: : : HUMAN SERVICES
: : HEALTH SERVICES
: MEDICAL SERVICES
FIRST AID
. CARDIOPULMONARY RESUSCITATION

FISCAL CAPACITY

: FACILITIES
FISHERIES

: METHODS
FIXED SEQUENCE

: : CURRICULUM
: MODERN LANGUAGE CURRICULUM
: : CURRICULUM
: ELEMENTARY SCHOOL CURRICULUM
FLES

: FACILITIES
FLEXIBLE FACILITIES

: : DESIGN
: LIGHTING DESIGN
FLEXIBLE LIGHTING DESIGN

FLEXIBLE PROGRESSION
. ACCELERATION (EDUCATION)

FLEXIBLE SCHEDULES (1967 1980)

: : : PLANNING
: : SCHEDULING
: SCHOOL SCHEDULES
FLEXIBLE SCHEDULING

: : : PLANNING
: : SCHEDULING
: WORKING HOURS
FLEXIBLE WORKING HOURS

: TRAINING
FLIGHT TRAINING

: STRUCTURAL ELEMENTS (CONSTRUCTION)
FLOORING
. CARPETING

:::: GROUPS
::: PERSONNEL
:: NONPROFESSIONAL
PERSONNEL
: SKILLED WORKERS
FLOOR LAYERS

:::: TECHNOLOGY
::: AGRICULTURE
:: HORTICULTURE
: ORNAMENTAL HORTICULTURE
FLORICULTURE

:: VISUAL AIDS
: CHARTS
FLOW CHARTS

:::::: LIBERAL ARTS
::::: SCIENCES
:::: NATURAL SCIENCES
::: PHYSICAL SCIENCES
:: PHYSICS
: MECHANICS (PHYSICS)
FLUID MECHANICS

: DISEASE CONTROL
FLUORIDATION

: CULTURE
FOLK CULTURE

:: INSTITUTIONS
: SCHOOLS
FOLK SCHOOLS

::: RESEARCH
:::: METHODS
::: EVALUATION METHODS
:: CASE STUDIES
: LONGITUDINAL STUDIES
FOLLOWUP STUDIES
. GRADUATE SURVEYS
. VOCATIONAL FOLLOWUP

::: LANGUAGES
:: SINO TIBETAN LANGUAGES
: CHINESE
FOOCHOW

FOOD
. GRAINS (FOOD)
. MEAT

::: GROUPS
:: PERSONNEL
: GOVERNMENT EMPLOYEES
FOOD AND DRUG INSPECTORS

: FACILITIES
FOOD HANDLING FACILITIES

::: OCCUPATIONS
:: AGRICULTURAL OCCUPATIONS
: OFF FARM AGRICULTURAL
OCCUPATIONS
FOOD PROCESSING OCCUPATIONS

:: SERVICES
: HUMAN SERVICES
FOOD SERVICE

: INSTRUCTION
FOODS INSTRUCTION

: STANDARDS
FOOD STANDARDS

: FACILITIES
FOOD STORES

:::: ACTIVITIES
::: PHYSICAL ACTIVITIES
:: ATHLETICS
: TEAM SPORTS
FOOTBALL

: SCIENTIFIC CONCEPTS
FORCE

:: METHODS
: MEASUREMENT TECHNIQUES
FORCED CHOICE TECHNIQUE

::: RESEARCH
:: BEHAVIORAL SCIENCE
RESEARCH
: PSYCHOLOGICAL STUDIES
FORCE FIELD ANALYSIS

: GEOGRAPHIC REGIONS
FOREIGN COUNTRIES

: CULTURE
FOREIGN CULTURE

::: GROUPS
:: PERSONNEL
: GOVERNMENT EMPLOYEES
FOREIGN DIPLOMATS

:: PUBLICATIONS
: BOOKS
FOREIGN LANGUAGE BOOKS

:: VISUAL AIDS
:: NONPRINT MEDIA
:: MASS MEDIA
: FILMS
FOREIGN LANGUAGE FILMS

::: PUBLICATIONS
:: SERIALS
: PERIODICALS
FOREIGN LANGUAGE PERIODICALS

:::: GROUPS
::: PERSONNEL
:: PROFESSIONAL PERSONNEL
:::: GROUPS
::: PERSONNEL
:: HEALTH PERSONNEL
: PHYSICIANS
::: GROUPS
:: ALUMNI
: GRADUATES
FOREIGN MEDICAL GRADUATES

FOREIGN NATIONALS

: POLICY
FOREIGN POLICY
. IMPERIALISM
.. COLONIALISM

::: GROUPS
:: PERSONNEL
: SCHOOL PERSONNEL
FOREIGN STUDENT ADVISERS

:: GROUPS
: STUDENTS
FOREIGN STUDENTS

:: GROUPS
: PERSONNEL
FOREIGN WORKERS
. BRACEROS

: TECHNOLOGY
FORESTRY

::: GROUPS
:: PERSONNEL
: PARAPROFESSIONAL
PERSONNEL
FORESTRY AIDES

: OCCUPATIONS
FORESTRY OCCUPATIONS

FORMAL CRITICISM (1969 1980)

::: INDIVIDUAL
CHARACTERISTICS
:: PSYCHOLOGICAL
CHARACTERISTICS
: INTELLIGENCE
FORMAL OPERATIONS

: EVALUATION
FORMATIVE EVALUATION

:::: LINGUISTICS
::: DESCRIPTIVE LINGUISTICS
:: GRAMMAR
: SYNTAX
FORM CLASSES (LANGUAGES)
. ADJECTIVES
. ADVERBS
. DETERMINERS (LANGUAGES)
. FUNCTION WORDS
. NOUNS
. PREPOSITIONS
. PRONOUNS
. VERBS

FORMER TEACHERS (1967 1980)

::: SERVICES
:: HUMAN SERVICES
: SOCIAL SERVICES
FOSTER CARE

::: GROUPS
:: AGE GROUPS
: CHILDREN
FOSTER CHILDREN

:: GROUPS
: FAMILY (SOCIOLOGICAL
UNIT)
FOSTER FAMILY

: STATE AID
: PROGRAMS
FOUNDATION PROGRAMS

FOUNDATIONS OF EDUCATION
. EDUCATIONAL ANTHROPOLOGY
. EDUCATIONAL ECONOMICS
.. EDUCATIONAL FINANCE
. EDUCATIONAL HISTORY
.. SCIENCE EDUCATION
HISTORY
. EDUCATIONAL PHILOSOPHY
. EDUCATIONAL PRINCIPLES
. EDUCATIONAL PSYCHOLOGY
. EDUCATIONAL SOCIOLOGY
. EDUCATIONAL THEORIES

: FACILITIES
FOUNDRIES

:: FACILITIES
: EDUCATIONAL FACILITIES
FOUND SPACES

:: SYMBOLS (MATHEMATICS)
: NUMBERS
FRACTIONS
. DECIMAL FRACTIONS

:: GROUPS
: ORGANIZATIONS (GROUPS)
FRATERNITIES

:: PROGRAMS
: TRANSFER PROGRAMS
FREE CHOICE TRANSFER
PROGRAMS

: ACCESS TO INFORMATION
FREEDOM OF INFORMATION

: CIVIL LIBERTIES
FREEDOM OF SPEECH

:: INSTITUTIONS
: SCHOOLS
FREEDOM SCHOOLS

: EDUCATION
FREE EDUCATION

:::: LIBERAL ARTS
::: HUMANITIES
:: FINE ARTS
: VISUAL ARTS
FREEHAND DRAWING

:: INSTITUTIONS
: SCHOOLS
FREE SCHOOLS

::: LANGUAGES
:: INDO EUROPEAN LANGUAGES
: ROMANCE LANGUAGES
FRENCH

::: LIBERAL ARTS
:: HUMANITIES
: LITERATURE
FRENCH LITERATURE

:: INSTRUCTION
: WRITING INSTRUCTION
:: LITERACY
:: LANGUAGE ARTS
: WRITING (COMPOSITION)
:: CURRICULUM
: COLLEGE CURRICULUM
FRESHMAN COMPOSITION

:: RELATIONSHIP
: INTERPERSONAL
RELATIONSHIP
FRIENDSHIP

FRINGE BENEFITS

FUEL CONSUMPTION

FUELS
. COAL

:: LANGUAGES
: AFRICAN LANGUAGES
FULANI

: STATE AID
: FINANCIAL SUPPORT
FULL STATE FUNDING

: STATUS
FULL TIME EQUIVALENCY

:::: GROUPS
::: PERSONNEL
:: SCHOOL PERSONNEL
:::: GROUPS
::: PERSONNEL
:: PROFESSIONAL PERSONNEL
: FACULTY
FULL TIME FACULTY

:: GROUPS
: STUDENTS
FULL TIME STUDENTS

: LITERACY
FUNCTIONAL LITERACY
. FUNCTIONAL READING

:: LITERACY
:: LANGUAGE ARTS
: READING
:: LITERACY
: FUNCTIONAL LITERACY
FUNCTIONAL READING

:::::: LIBERAL ARTS
::::: HUMANITIES
:::: PHILOSOPHY
::: LOGIC
:: MATHEMATICAL LOGIC
:: MATHEMATICAL APPLICATIONS
: MATHEMATICAL FORMULAS
FUNCTIONS (MATHEMATICS)

::::: LINGUISTICS
:::: DESCRIPTIVE LINGUISTICS
::: GRAMMAR
:: SYNTAX
: FORM CLASSES (LANGUAGES)
FUNCTION WORDS

FUNDAMENTAL CONCEPTS
. COMPENSATION (CONCEPT)
. CONSERVATION (CONCEPT)
. OBJECT PERMANENCE

FUND RAISING
. GRANTSMANSHIP

: EQUIPMENT
FURNITURE
. CLASSROOM FURNITURE

: ORGANIZATION
FURNITURE ARRANGEMENT

: DESIGN
FURNITURE DESIGN

::: BUSINESS
:: INDUSTRY
: MANUFACTURING INDUSTRY
FURNITURE INDUSTRY

: CURRICULUM
FUSED CURRICULUM

FUTURES (OF SOCIETY)

:: LANGUAGES
: AFRICAN LANGUAGES
GA

: ACTIVITIES
GAMES
. CHILDRENS GAMES
. EDUCATIONAL GAMES
.. READING GAMES
. MANAGEMENT GAMES
. PUZZLES

: THEORIES
:: RESEARCH
: OPERATIONS RESEARCH
GAME THEORY

::: LANGUAGES
:: AFRICAN LANGUAGES
: BANTU LANGUAGES
GANDA

:: LANGUAGES
: AFRICAN LANGUAGES
GBAYA

::::: LIBERAL ARTS
:::: SCIENCES
::: SOCIAL SCIENCES
:::: LIBERAL ARTS
::: HUMANITIES
:: HISTORY
: FAMILY HISTORY
GENEALOGY

: EDUCATION
GENERAL EDUCATION

: THEORIES
GENERALIZABILITY THEORY

:: COGNITIVE PROCESSES
: LEARNING PROCESSES
:: COGNITIVE PROCESSES
: ABSTRACT REASONING
GENERALIZATION
. STIMULUS GENERALIZATION

:: CURRICULUM
: SCIENCE CURRICULUM
GENERAL SCIENCE

GENERATION GAP

:: THEORIES
: LINGUISTIC THEORY
GENERATIVE GRAMMAR
. TRANSFORMATIONAL GENERATIVE GRAMMAR
.. CONTEXT FREE GRAMMAR
.. DEEP STRUCTURE
.. KERNEL SENTENCES
.. SENTENCE COMBINING
.. SURFACE STRUCTURE

:: LINGUISTICS
: PHONOLOGY
:: THEORIES
: LINGUISTIC THEORY
GENERATIVE PHONOLOGY

: TECHNOLOGY
::::: LIBERAL ARTS
:::: SCIENCES
::: NATURAL SCIENCES
:: BIOLOGICAL SCIENCES
: GENETICS
GENETIC ENGINEERING

:::: LIBERAL ARTS
::: SCIENCES
:: NATURAL SCIENCES
: BIOLOGICAL SCIENCES
GENETICS
. GENETIC ENGINEERING

GEOGRAPHIC CONCEPTS

:::: LIBERAL ARTS
::: SCIENCES
:: SOCIAL SCIENCES
: DEMOGRAPHY
GEOGRAPHIC DISTRIBUTION

GEOGRAPHIC LOCATION

GEOGRAPHIC REGIONS
. DEVELOPED NATIONS
. DEVELOPING NATIONS
. FOREIGN COUNTRIES
. LOW INCOME COUNTIES
. LOW INCOME STATES
. METROPOLITAN AREAS
.. SUBURBS
. PHYSICAL DIVISIONS (GEOGRAPHIC)
. POLITICAL DIVISIONS (GEOGRAPHIC)
.. AMERICAN INDIAN RESERVATIONS
. POVERTY AREAS
.. SLUMS
. RURAL AREAS
. URBAN AREAS
.. INNER CITY
.. MUNICIPALITIES

::: LIBERAL ARTS
:: SCIENCES
: SOCIAL SCIENCES
GEOGRAPHY
. HUMAN GEOGRAPHY
. PHYSICAL GEOGRAPHY
. WORLD GEOGRAPHY

: INSTRUCTION
GEOGRAPHY INSTRUCTION

::::: LIBERAL ARTS
:::: SCIENCES
::: NATURAL SCIENCES
:: PHYSICAL SCIENCES
: EARTH SCIENCE
GEOLOGY
. MINERALOGY
. PALEONTOLOGY

: MATHEMATICAL CONCEPTS
GEOMETRIC CONCEPTS
. AREA
. CONGRUENCE (MATHEMATICS)
. ORTHOGRAPHIC PROJECTION
. VECTORS (MATHEMATICS)
. VOLUME (MATHEMATICS)

: VISUAL AIDS
GEOMETRIC CONSTRUCTIONS

:: LIBERAL ARTS
: MATHEMATICS
GEOMETRY
. ANALYTIC GEOMETRY
. PLANE GEOMETRY
. SOLID GEOMETRY
. TOPOLOGY

::::: LIBERAL ARTS
:::: SCIENCES
::: NATURAL SCIENCES
:: PHYSICAL SCIENCES
: EARTH SCIENCE
GEOPHYSICS
. PLATE TECTONICS

:: SCIENTIFIC CONCEPTS
: ENERGY
GEOTHERMAL ENERGY

:: TECHNOLOGY
: MEDICINE
GERIATRICS

:: LANGUAGES
: INDO EUROPEAN LANGUAGES
GERMAN
. YIDDISH

::: LIBERAL ARTS
:: HUMANITIES
: LITERATURE
GERMAN LITERATURE

::: LIBERAL ARTS
:: SCIENCES
: SOCIAL SCIENCES
GERONTOLOGY
. EDUCATIONAL GERONTOLOGY

:: THERAPY
: PSYCHOTHERAPY
:: METHODS
: HOLISTIC APPROACH
GESTALT THERAPY

GHETTOS

:: GROUPS
: EXCEPTIONAL PERSONS
GIFTED
. ACADEMICALLY GIFTED
. GIFTED DISABLED
. GIFTED DISADVANTAGED

::: GROUPS
:: EXCEPTIONAL PERSONS
: GIFTED
GIFTED DISABLED

::: GROUPS
:: EXCEPTIONAL PERSONS
: GIFTED
:: GROUPS
: DISADVANTAGED
GIFTED DISADVANTAGED

GLARE

GLASS

: STRUCTURAL ELEMENTS (CONSTRUCTION)
GLASS WALLS

:::: GROUPS
::: PERSONNEL
:: NONPROFESSIONAL PERSONNEL
: SKILLED WORKERS
GLAZIERS

:: METHODS
: HOLISTIC APPROACH
GLOBAL APPROACH

::: PUBLICATIONS
:: REFERENCE MATERIALS
: DICTIONARIES
GLOSSARIES

:: LINGUISTICS
: DIACHRONIC LINGUISTICS
GLOTTOCHRONOLOGY

: ORIENTATION
GOAL ORIENTATION

::: ACTIVITIES
:: PHYSICAL ACTIVITIES
: ATHLETICS
GOLF

:::: METHODS
::: EVALUATION METHODS
:: DATA ANALYSIS
: STATISTICAL ANALYSIS
GOODNESS OF FIT

GOVERNANCE
. ADMINISTRATION
.. BUILDING OPERATION
.. BUSINESS ADMINISTRATION
.. CONSTRUCTION MANAGEMENT
.. EDUCATIONAL ADMINISTRATION
... SCHOOL ADMINISTRATION
.... COLLEGE ADMINISTRATION
.... SCHOOL BASED MANAGEMENT
.. ENERGY MANAGEMENT
.. FARM MANAGEMENT
.. HOME MANAGEMENT
.. INSTITUTIONAL ADMINISTRATION
... LIBRARY ADMINISTRATION
... SCHOOL ADMINISTRATION
.... COLLEGE ADMINISTRATION
.... SCHOOL BASED MANAGEMENT
.. MANAGEMENT BY OBJECTIVES
.. MIDDLE MANAGEMENT
.. MONEY MANAGEMENT
.. OFFICE MANAGEMENT
.. PERSONNEL MANAGEMENT
.. PROGRAM ADMINISTRATION
.. PUBLIC ADMINISTRATION
.. RESEARCH ADMINISTRATION
.. SUPERVISION
... PRACTICUM SUPERVISION
... PROCTORING
... SCHOOL SUPERVISION
... SCIENCE SUPERVISION
... TEACHER SUPERVISION
.. TIME MANAGEMENT
. COMMUNITY CONTROL
. FEDERAL REGULATION

:: GROUPS
: ORGANIZATIONS (GROUPS)
GOVERNING BOARDS
. BOARDS OF EDUCATION
.. STATE BOARDS OF EDUCATION

:: GROUPS
: ORGANIZATIONS (GROUPS)
GOVERNMENT (ADMINISTRATIVE BODY)
. FEDERAL GOVERNMENT
. LOCAL GOVERNMENT
.. CITY GOVERNMENT
. STATE GOVERNMENT
. STUDENT GOVERNMENT

:: ORGANIZATION
: GROUP STRUCTURE
GOVERNMENTAL STRUCTURE

:: GROUPS
: PERSONNEL
GOVERNMENT EMPLOYEES
. EXTENSION AGENTS
. FOOD AND DRUG INSPECTORS
. FOREIGN DIPLOMATS
. IMMIGRATION INSPECTORS
. MILITARY PERSONNEL
.. ENLISTED PERSONNEL
.. OFFICER PERSONNEL
. POLICE
. PUBLIC OFFICIALS
.. CITY OFFICIALS
.. COUNTY OFFICIALS
.. COURT JUDGES
.. LEGISLATORS
.. STATE OFFICIALS
... STATE SUPERVISORS
. PUBLIC SCHOOL TEACHERS

::: INSTITUTIONS
::: INFORMATION SOURCES
:: LIBRARIES
: SPECIAL LIBRARIES
GOVERNMENT LIBRARIES
. NATIONAL LIBRARIES
. STATE LIBRARIES

: PUBLICATIONS
GOVERNMENT PUBLICATIONS

GOVERNMENT ROLE

: RELATIONSHIP
GOVERNMENT SCHOOL RELATIONSHIP
. STATE SCHOOL DISTRICT RELATIONSHIP

: INSTRUCTIONAL PROGRAM DIVISIONS
GRADE 1

: INSTRUCTIONAL PROGRAM DIVISIONS
GRADE 2

: INSTRUCTIONAL PROGRAM DIVISIONS
GRADE 3

: INSTRUCTIONAL PROGRAM DIVISIONS
GRADE 4

: INSTRUCTIONAL PROGRAM DIVISIONS
GRADE 5

: INSTRUCTIONAL PROGRAM DIVISIONS
GRADE 6

: INSTRUCTIONAL PROGRAM DIVISIONS
GRADE 7

: INSTRUCTIONAL PROGRAM DIVISIONS
GRADE 8

: INSTRUCTIONAL PROGRAM DIVISIONS
GRADE 9

: INSTRUCTIONAL PROGRAM DIVISIONS
GRADE 10

: INSTRUCTIONAL PROGRAM DIVISIONS
GRADE 11

: INSTRUCTIONAL PROGRAM DIVISIONS
GRADE 12

GRADE CHARTS (1966 1980)

:: DATA
: SCORES
GRADE EQUIVALENT SCORES

: GRADES (SCHOLASTIC)
GRADE INFLATION

: GRADES (SCHOLASTIC)
GRADE POINT AVERAGE

: PREDICTION
GRADE PREDICTION

GRADE REPETITION

GRADES (SCHOLASTIC)
. GRADE INFLATION
. GRADE POINT AVERAGE

:: MEASUREMENT
: ACHIEVEMENT RATING
GRADING
. CREDIT NO CREDIT GRADING
. PASS FAIL GRADING

::: EDUCATION
:: PROFESSIONAL EDUCATION
: MEDICAL EDUCATION
:::: EDUCATION
::: POSTSECONDARY EDUCATION
:: HIGHER EDUCATION
: GRADUATE STUDY
GRADUATE MEDICAL EDUCATION

::::: GROUPS
:::: STUDENTS
::: COLLEGE STUDENTS
:: GRADUATE STUDENTS
: MEDICAL STUDENTS
GRADUATE MEDICAL STUDENTS

:: GROUPS
: ALUMNI
GRADUATES
. COLLEGE GRADUATES
. FOREIGN MEDICAL GRADUATES
. HIGH SCHOOL GRADUATES

::::: GROUPS
:::: PERSONNEL
::: SCHOOL PERSONNEL
::::: GROUPS
:::: PERSONNEL
::: PROFESSIONAL PERSONNEL
:: FACULTY
: COLLEGE FACULTY
GRADUATE SCHOOL FACULTY
. MEDICAL SCHOOL FACULTY

::: GROUPS
:: STUDENTS
: COLLEGE STUDENTS
GRADUATE STUDENTS
. DENTAL STUDENTS
. LAW STUDENTS
. MEDICAL STUDENTS
.. GRADUATE MEDICAL STUDENTS

::: EDUCATION
:: POSTSECONDARY EDUCATION
: HIGHER EDUCATION
GRADUATE STUDY
. GRADUATE MEDICAL EDUCATION
. POSTSECONDARY EDUCATION AS A FIELD OF STUDY

::: METHODS
:: EVALUATION METHODS
: SURVEYS
:::: RESEARCH
::::: METHODS
:::: EVALUATION METHODS
::: CASE STUDIES
:: LONGITUDINAL STUDIES
: FOLLOWUP STUDIES
GRADUATE SURVEYS

: ACHIEVEMENT
GRADUATION

:: STANDARDS
: ACADEMIC STANDARDS
GRADUATION REQUIREMENTS
. DEGREE REQUIREMENTS

: FOOD
: FIELD CROPS
GRAINS (FOOD)

:: LINGUISTICS
: DESCRIPTIVE LINGUISTICS
GRAMMAR
. MORPHOLOGY (LANGUAGES)
.. MORPHEMES
... NEGATIVE FORMS (LANGUAGE)
... PLURALS
... SUFFIXES
... TENSES (GRAMMAR)
.. MORPHOPHONEMICS
. SYNTAX
.. FORM CLASSES (LANGUAGES)
... ADJECTIVES
... ADVERBS
... DETERMINERS (LANGUAGES)
... FUNCTION WORDS
... NOUNS
... PREPOSITIONS
... PRONOUNS
... VERBS
.. PHRASE STRUCTURE
.. SENTENCE STRUCTURE

::: METHODS
:: EDUCATIONAL METHODS
: TEACHING METHODS
GRAMMAR TRANSLATION METHOD

:: ATTITUDES
: LANGUAGE ATTITUDES
GRAMMATICAL ACCEPTABILITY

::: GROUPS
:: AGE GROUPS
: CHILDREN
GRANDCHILDREN

:: GROUPS
: PARENTS
GRANDPARENTS

: FINANCIAL SUPPORT
GRANTS
. BLOCK GRANTS
. EDUCATIONAL VOUCHERS
. INCENTIVE GRANTS
. TUITION GRANTS

: FUND RAISING
GRANTSMANSHIP

:: LANGUAGE
: WRITTEN LANGUAGE
GRAPHEMES

:::: LIBERAL ARTS
::: HUMANITIES
:: FINE ARTS
: VISUAL ARTS
GRAPHIC ARTS
. CARTOGRAPHY
. COMPUTER GRAPHICS
. ENGINEERING GRAPHICS
.. ENGINEERING DRAWING
. LAYOUT (PUBLICATIONS)
. PRINTING

: VISUAL AIDS
GRAPHS

:SCIENTIFIC CONCEPTS
GRAVITY (PHYSICS)

::LANGUAGES
:INDO EUROPEAN LANGUAGES
GREEK

::GROUPS
:NORTH AMERICANS
::GROUPS
:ETHNIC GROUPS
GREEK AMERICANS

GREEK CIVILIZATION

:::LIBERAL ARTS
::HUMANITIES
:LITERATURE
GREEK LITERATURE

:FACILITIES
GREENHOUSES

:PSYCHOLOGICAL PATTERNS
GRIEF

:METHODS
GRIEVANCE PROCEDURES

::::GROUPS
:::PERSONNEL
::NONPROFESSIONAL PERSONNEL
:SEMISKILLED WORKERS
GROUNDS KEEPERS

:ACTIVITIES
GROUP ACTIVITIES

:BEHAVIOR
GROUP BEHAVIOR
.TEAMWORK

::GUIDANCE
:GROUP GUIDANCE
::GUIDANCE
:COUNSELING
GROUP COUNSELING

::COMMUNICATION (THOUGHT TRANSFER)
:DISCUSSION
GROUP DISCUSSION

::RELATIONSHIP
:INTERACTION
GROUP DYNAMICS

::BACKGROUND
:EXPERIENCE
GROUP EXPERIENCE

:GUIDANCE
GROUP GUIDANCE
.GROUP COUNSELING

::FACILITIES
:HOUSING
GROUP HOMES

::ORGANIZATION
:CLASSIFICATION
GROUPING (INSTRUCTIONAL PURPOSES)
.HETEROGENEOUS GROUPING
.HOMOGENEOUS GROUPING
..ABILITY GROUPING
.NONGRADED INSTRUCTIONAL GROUPING

:INSTRUCTION
GROUP INSTRUCTION
.LARGE GROUP INSTRUCTION
.SMALL GROUP INSTRUCTION

GROUP MEMBERSHIP
.POLITICAL AFFILIATION

GROUP NORMS (1968 1980)

GROUP READING (1966 1980)

GROUPS
.ADVANTAGED
.AGE GROUPS
..ADOLESCENTS
..ADULTS
...ADULT DROPOUTS
...ADULT STUDENTS
...MIDDLE AGED ADULTS
...OLDER ADULTS
...YOUNG ADULTS
..CHILDREN
...ADOPTED CHILDREN
...FOSTER CHILDREN
...GRANDCHILDREN
...HOSPITALIZED CHILDREN
...LATCHKEY CHILDREN
...MIGRANT CHILDREN
...MINORITY GROUP CHILDREN
...PREADOLESCENTS
...PROBLEM CHILDREN
...TRANSIENT CHILDREN
...YOUNG CHILDREN
....INFANTS
.....NEONATES
.....PREMATURE INFANTS
....KINDERGARTEN CHILDREN
....PRESCHOOL CHILDREN
....TODDLERS
.ALUMNI
..GRADUATES
...COLLEGE GRADUATES
...FOREIGN MEDICAL GRADUATES
...HIGH SCHOOL GRADUATES
.ARABS
.ARTISTS
..MUSICIANS
.ATHLETES
.AUDIENCES
.AUTHORS
..POETS
.BLACKS
..BLACK MOTHERS
..BLACK STUDENTS
..BLACK TEACHERS
..BLACK YOUTH
.BOARD CANDIDATES
.CHANGE AGENTS
..EXTENSION AGENTS
..LINKING AGENTS
.CHILD CAREGIVERS
.CLASSES (GROUPS OF STUDENTS)
..MULTIGRADED CLASSES
..MULTILEVEL CLASSES (SECOND LANGUAGE INSTRUCTION)
..NONAUTHORITARIAN CLASSES
..SMALL CLASSES
..SPECIAL CLASSES
.CLUBS
..SCIENCE CLUBS
..YOUTH CLUBS
.COLLEGE APPLICANTS
.COMMUNITY LEADERS
.CONTROL GROUPS
.CRIMINALS
.DEPENDENTS
.DISADVANTAGED
..DISADVANTAGED YOUTH
..ECONOMICALLY DISADVANTAGED
..EDUCATIONALLY DISADVANTAGED
..GIFTED DISADVANTAGED
.DISCUSSION GROUPS
..LISTENING GROUPS
.DONORS
.DROPOUTS
..ADULT DROPOUTS
.EMPLOYERS
.ESKIMOS
.ETHNIC GROUPS
..ALASKA NATIVES
..AMERICAN INDIANS
...NONRESERVATION AMERICAN INDIANS
....RURAL AMERICAN INDIANS
....URBAN AMERICAN INDIANS
...RESERVATION AMERICAN INDIANS
..ANGLO AMERICANS
..CANADA NATIVES
..CHINESE AMERICANS
..FILIPINO AMERICANS
..GREEK AMERICANS
..HAWAIIANS
..ITALIAN AMERICANS
..JAPANESE AMERICANS
..KOREAN AMERICANS
..MEXICAN AMERICANS
..POLISH AMERICANS
..PORTUGUESE AMERICANS
..SAMOAN AMERICANS
..SPANISH AMERICANS
.EXCEPTIONAL PERSONS
..GIFTED
...ACADEMICALLY GIFTED
...GIFTED DISABLED
...GIFTED DISADVANTAGED
.EXPERIMENTAL GROUPS
.FAMILY (SOCIOLOGICAL UNIT)
..BLACK FAMILY
..DUAL CAREER FAMILY
..EXTENDED FAMILY
..FOSTER FAMILY
..NUCLEAR FAMILY
..ONE PARENT FAMILY
...FATHERLESS FAMILY
...MOTHERLESS FAMILY
..RURAL FAMILY
..STEPFAMILY
.FEMALES
..BATTERED WOMEN
..DAUGHTERS
..DISPLACED HOMEMAKERS
..EMPLOYED WOMEN
...WOMEN FACULTY
..MOTHERS
...BLACK MOTHERS
...UNWED MOTHERS
..NUNS
..PREGNANT STUDENTS
.FINANCIAL AID APPLICANTS
.HEADS OF HOUSEHOLDS
.HIGH RISK PERSONS
..HIGH RISK STUDENTS
.HOMELESS PEOPLE
.HOMEMAKERS
.HOMEOWNERS
.INDIANS
.INDIGENOUS POPULATIONS
.INDOCHINESE
..CAMBODIANS
..LAOTIANS
..VIETNAMESE PEOPLE
.INSTITUTIONALIZED PERSONS
..PRISONERS
.JOB APPLICANTS
.JUDGES
..COURT JUDGES
.JUVENILE GANGS
.LABOR FORCE NONPARTICIPANTS
.LANDLORDS
.LATIN AMERICANS
..CUBANS
..DOMINICANS
..HAITIANS
..MEXICANS
...BRACEROS
..PUERTO RICANS
.LAY PEOPLE
..LAY TEACHERS
.LEADERS
..COMMUNITY LEADERS
..YOUTH LEADERS
.LEFT HANDED WRITER
.LIMITED ENGLISH SPEAKING
.LOW INCOME GROUPS
.MALES
..FATHERS
..SONS
.MATCHED GROUPS
.MIGRANTS
..IMMIGRANTS
...UNDOCUMENTED IMMIGRANTS
..MIGRANT CHILDREN
..MIGRANT WORKERS
..MIGRANT YOUTH
..NOMADS
..REFUGEES
..TRANSIENT CHILDREN
.MINORITY GROUPS
.NATIVE SPEAKERS
..SPANISH SPEAKING
.NON ENGLISH SPEAKING
.NORTH AMERICANS
..ALASKA NATIVES
..ANGLO AMERICANS
..ASIAN AMERICANS
...CHINESE AMERICANS
...FILIPINO AMERICANS
...JAPANESE AMERICANS
...KOREAN AMERICANS
..CANADA NATIVES
..GREEK AMERICANS
..HISPANIC AMERICANS
...MEXICAN AMERICANS
...PORTUGUESE AMERICANS
...SPANISH AMERICANS
..ITALIAN AMERICANS
..PACIFIC AMERICANS
...HAWAIIANS
...SAMOAN AMERICANS
..POLISH AMERICANS
.NO SHOWS
.ORGANIZATIONS (GROUPS)
..AGENCIES
...ACCREDITING AGENCIES
...PRIVATE AGENCIES
...PUBLIC AGENCIES
....PLANNING COMMISSIONS
....STATE AGENCIES
.....STATE DEPARTMENTS OF EDUCATION
.....STATE LICENSING BOARDS
...SOCIAL AGENCIES
....WELFARE AGENCIES
...URBAN RENEWAL AGENCIES
...VOLUNTARY AGENCIES
...YOUTH AGENCIES
..ALUMNI ASSOCIATIONS
..BIBLIOGRAPHIC UTILITIES
..BLACK ORGANIZATIONS
..BLUE RIBBON COMMISSIONS
..COLLEGE GOVERNING COUNCILS
..COMMUNITY ORGANIZATIONS
...CITIZENS COUNCILS
..CONSORTIA
..COOPERATIVES
..DATABASE PRODUCERS
..FACULTY ORGANIZATIONS
..FRATERNITIES
..GOVERNING BOARDS
...BOARDS OF EDUCATION
....STATE BOARDS OF EDUCATION
..GOVERNMENT (ADMINISTRATIVE BODY)
...FEDERAL GOVERNMENT
...LOCAL GOVERNMENT
....CITY GOVERNMENT
...STATE GOVERNMENT
...STUDENT GOVERNMENT
..HONOR SOCIETIES
..INTERNATIONAL ORGANIZATIONS
..MILITARY ORGANIZATIONS
...ARMED FORCES
..NATIONAL ORGANIZATIONS
..NONPROFIT ORGANIZATIONS
..ONLINE VENDORS
..PARENT ASSOCIATIONS
..PROFESSIONAL ASSOCIATIONS
...LIBRARY ASSOCIATIONS
...MEDICAL ASSOCIATIONS
...TEACHER ASSOCIATIONS
..RELIGIOUS ORGANIZATIONS
..RESEARCH COORDINATING UNITS
..SCHOOL DISTRICTS
...COUNTY SCHOOL DISTRICTS
...MULTICAMPUS DISTRICTS
..SEGREGATIONIST ORGANIZATIONS
..SOCIAL ORGANIZATIONS
..SORORITIES
..STUDENT ORGANIZATIONS
...STUDENT GOVERNMENT
...STUDENT UNIONS
..UNIONS
.PARENTS
..BIOLOGICAL PARENTS
..EMPLOYED PARENTS
..FATHERS
..GRANDPARENTS

GROUPS
(CONTINUED)

..LOWER CLASS PARENTS
..MIDDLE CLASS PARENTS
..MOTHERS
...BLACK MOTHERS
...UNWED MOTHERS
.PATIENTS
..HOSPITALIZED CHILDREN
.PEER GROUPS
.PERSONNEL
..ADMINISTRATORS
...ADMISSIONS OFFICERS
...ASSISTANT PRINCIPALS
...COORDINATORS
....AUDIOVISUAL COORDINATORS
....INSTRUCTOR COORDINATORS
...DEANS
....ACADEMIC DEANS
....DEANS OF STUDENTS
...DEPARTMENT HEADS
...MEDICAL RECORD ADMINISTRATORS
...PERSONNEL DIRECTORS
...PRESIDENTS
....COLLEGE PRESIDENTS
....PRESIDENTS OF THE UNITED STATES
...PRINCIPALS
...REGISTRARS (SCHOOL)
...RESEARCH DIRECTORS
...SCHOOL BUSINESS OFFICIALS
...STUDENT FINANCIAL AID OFFICERS
...SUPERINTENDENTS
...SUPERVISORS
....CREW LEADERS
....STATE SUPERVISORS
....STUDENT TEACHER SUPERVISORS
...TRUSTEES
...VOCATIONAL DIRECTORS
..AGRICULTURAL PERSONNEL
...AGRICULTURAL LABORERS
....MIGRANT WORKERS
....SEASONAL LABORERS
...AGRICULTURAL TECHNICIANS
...FARMERS
....DAIRY FARMERS
....PART TIME FARMERS
....SHARECROPPERS
..AIRCRAFT PILOTS
..CASEWORKERS
...PAROLE OFFICERS
...PROBATION OFFICERS
...SOCIAL WORKERS
....SCHOOL SOCIAL WORKERS
..CHURCH WORKERS
..CLERGY
...PRIESTS
..CONSULTANTS
...MEDICAL CONSULTANTS
...READING CONSULTANTS
...SCIENCE CONSULTANTS
..DESIGNERS
..DIFFERENTIATED STAFFS
..DISLOCATED WORKERS
..EDITORS
..EMPLOYEES
...ENTRY WORKERS
..EQUIPMENT MANUFACTURERS
..EVALUATORS
..FOREIGN WORKERS
...BRACEROS
..GOVERNMENT EMPLOYEES
...EXTENSION AGENTS
...FOOD AND DRUG INSPECTORS
...FOREIGN DIPLOMATS
...IMMIGRATION INSPECTORS
...MILITARY PERSONNEL
....ENLISTED PERSONNEL
....OFFICER PERSONNEL
...POLICE
...PUBLIC OFFICIALS
....CITY OFFICIALS
....COUNTY OFFICIALS
....COURT JUDGES
....LEGISLATORS
....STATE OFFICIALS
.....STATE SUPERVISORS
...PUBLIC SCHOOL TEACHERS
..GUIDANCE PERSONNEL
...COUNSELORS
....ADJUSTMENT COUNSELORS
....EMPLOYMENT COUNSELORS
....SCHOOL COUNSELORS
..HEALTH PERSONNEL
...ALLIED HEALTH PERSONNEL
....DENTAL ASSISTANTS
....DENTAL HYGIENISTS
....DENTAL TECHNICIANS
....DIETITIANS
....EMERGENCY MEDICAL TECHNICIANS
....ENVIRONMENTAL TECHNICIANS
....HOME HEALTH AIDES
....MEDICAL ASSISTANTS
.....MEDICAL LABORATORY ASSISTANTS
....MEDICAL RECORD ADMINISTRATORS
....MEDICAL RECORD TECHNICIANS
....MEDICAL TECHNOLOGISTS
....NURSES AIDES
....OCCUPATIONAL THERAPY ASSISTANTS
....OPTOMETRISTS
....PHYSICAL THERAPY AIDES
....PHYSICIANS ASSISTANTS
....PSYCHIATRIC AIDES
....RADIOLOGIC TECHNOLOGISTS
....SURGICAL TECHNICIANS
....THERAPISTS
.....OCCUPATIONAL THERAPISTS
.....PHYSICAL THERAPISTS
....VETERINARY ASSISTANTS
...DENTISTS
...HOSPITAL PERSONNEL
...MEDICAL CONSULTANTS
...NURSES
....NURSE PRACTITIONERS
....SCHOOL NURSES
...PHARMACISTS
...PHYSICIANS
....FOREIGN MEDICAL GRADUATES
...PSYCHIATRISTS
...PSYCHOLOGISTS
....SCHOOL PSYCHOLOGISTS
...VETERINARIANS
..INDIGENOUS PERSONNEL
..INDUSTRIAL PERSONNEL
..INSTITUTIONAL PERSONNEL
..INTERPRETERS
..LIBRARY PERSONNEL
...LIBRARIANS
...LIBRARY TECHNICIANS
....MEDICAL RECORD TECHNICIANS
..MERCHANTS
..NONPROFESSIONAL PERSONNEL
...CLERICAL WORKERS
....COURT REPORTERS
....EXAMINERS
....FILE CLERKS
....RECEPTIONISTS
....SECRETARIES
.....SCHOOL SECRETARIES
...SALES WORKERS
....AUTO PARTS CLERKS
...SEMISKILLED WORKERS
....ANIMAL CARETAKERS
....BOAT OPERATORS
....GROUNDS KEEPERS
....NURSERY WORKERS (HORTICULTURE)
....SEWING MACHINE OPERATORS
...SERVICE WORKERS
....ATTENDANTS
....BARBERS
....COOKS
....EMERGENCY SQUAD PERSONNEL
.....EMERGENCY MEDICAL TECHNICIANS
....FIRE FIGHTERS
....HOUSEHOLD WORKERS
.....HOME HEALTH AIDES
....HOUSEKEEPERS
....HOUSING MANAGEMENT AIDES
....WAITERS AND WAITRESSES
...SKILLED WORKERS
....AUTO BODY REPAIRERS
....CRAFT WORKERS
....ELECTRICIANS
....FLOOR LAYERS
....GLAZIERS
....LOCOMOTIVE ENGINEERS
....MACHINISTS
.....MACHINE REPAIRERS
.....MACHINE TOOL OPERATORS
.....TOOL AND DIE MAKERS
....SIGN PAINTERS
....TELEVISION RADIO REPAIRERS
....WATCHMAKERS
...UNSKILLED WORKERS
....LABORERS
.....AGRICULTURAL LABORERS
......MIGRANT WORKERS
......SEASONAL LABORERS
.....AUXILIARY LABORERS
..OMBUDSMEN
..PARAPROFESSIONAL PERSONNEL
...AGRICULTURAL TECHNICIANS
...CHEMICAL TECHNICIANS
...ELECTRONIC TECHNICIANS
...ENGINEERING TECHNICIANS
....HIGHWAY ENGINEERING AIDES
...ENVIRONMENTAL TECHNICIANS
...FORESTRY AIDES
...HOUSING MANAGEMENT AIDES
...INSTRUMENTATION TECHNICIANS
...LEGAL ASSISTANTS
...MARINE TECHNICIANS
...MECHANICAL DESIGN TECHNICIANS
...METALLURGICAL TECHNICIANS
...NUCLEAR POWER PLANT TECHNICIANS
...PARAPROFESSIONAL SCHOOL PERSONNEL
....SCHOOL AIDES
....TEACHER AIDES
.....BILINGUAL TEACHER AIDES
...PRODUCTION TECHNICIANS
...RADIOGRAPHERS
...VETERINARY ASSISTANTS
...VISITING HOMEMAKERS
..PROFESSIONAL PERSONNEL
...ACCOUNTANTS
....CERTIFIED PUBLIC ACCOUNTANTS
...ARCHITECTS
...ATHLETIC COACHES
...DENTISTS
...ENGINEERS
...FACULTY
....ADJUNCT FACULTY
....COLLEGE FACULTY
.....COLLEGE PRESIDENTS
.....COUNSELOR EDUCATORS
.....GRADUATE SCHOOL FACULTY
......MEDICAL SCHOOL FACULTY
.....PROFESSORS
.....STUDENT TEACHER SUPERVISORS
.....TEACHER EDUCATORS
......METHODS TEACHERS
.....TEACHING ASSISTANTS
....DEANS
.....ACADEMIC DEANS
.....DEANS OF STUDENTS
....DEPARTMENT HEADS
....FACULTY ADVISERS
....FULL TIME FACULTY
....NONTENURED FACULTY
....PART TIME FACULTY
.....PARTNERSHIP TEACHERS
....TENURED FACULTY
....WOMEN FACULTY
...INFORMATION SCIENTISTS
...LIBRARIANS
...LAWYERS
...MATHEMATICIANS
...NURSES
....NURSE PRACTITIONERS
....SCHOOL NURSES
...OPTOMETRISTS
...PHARMACISTS
...PHYSICIANS
....FOREIGN MEDICAL GRADUATES
....PSYCHIATRISTS
...PSYCHOLOGISTS
....SCHOOL PSYCHOLOGISTS
...RESEARCH DIRECTORS
...RESEARCHERS
....EDUCATIONAL RESEARCHERS
...SCIENTISTS
...SOCIAL SCIENTISTS
...SOCIAL WORKERS
....SCHOOL SOCIAL WORKERS
...TEACHERS
....ADULT EDUCATORS
....ART TEACHERS
....BEGINNING TEACHERS
....BILINGUAL TEACHERS
....BLACK TEACHERS
....CATHOLIC EDUCATORS
....COOPERATING TEACHERS
....ELEMENTARY SCHOOL TEACHERS
....HOME ECONOMICS TEACHERS
....INDUSTRIAL ARTS TEACHERS
....INSTRUCTOR COORDINATORS
....ITINERANT TEACHERS
....LANGUAGE TEACHERS
....LAY TEACHERS
....MASTER TEACHERS
....MATHEMATICS TEACHERS
....MINORITY GROUP TEACHERS
....MUSIC TEACHERS
....PHYSICAL EDUCATION TEACHERS
....PRESCHOOL TEACHERS
....PUBLIC SCHOOL TEACHERS
....READING TEACHERS
....REMEDIAL TEACHERS
....RESOURCE TEACHERS
....SCIENCE TEACHERS
....SECONDARY SCHOOL TEACHERS
....SPECIAL EDUCATION TEACHERS
....STUDENT TEACHERS
....SUBSTITUTE TEACHERS
....TEACHER INTERNS
....TELEVISION TEACHERS
....TUTORS
....VOCATIONAL EDUCATION TEACHERS
.....BUSINESS EDUCATION TEACHERS
.....DISTRIBUTIVE EDUCATION TEACHERS
.....TRADE AND INDUSTRIAL TEACHERS
...THERAPISTS
....OCCUPATIONAL THERAPISTS
....PHYSICAL THERAPISTS
...VETERINARIANS
..PROGRAMERS
..REENTRY WORKERS
..RESEARCH ASSISTANTS
..RESIDENT ADVISERS
...RESIDENT ASSISTANTS
..RESOURCE STAFF
..SCHOOL PERSONNEL
...ADMISSIONS OFFICERS
...ASSISTANT PRINCIPALS
...AUDIOVISUAL COORDINATORS
...FACULTY
....ADJUNCT FACULTY
....COLLEGE FACULTY
.....COLLEGE PRESIDENTS
.....COUNSELOR EDUCATORS
.....GRADUATE SCHOOL FACULTY
......MEDICAL SCHOOL FACULTY
.....PROFESSORS
.....STUDENT TEACHER SUPERVISORS
.....TEACHER EDUCATORS
......METHODS TEACHERS
.....TEACHING ASSISTANTS
....DEANS
.....ACADEMIC DEANS
.....DEANS OF STUDENTS
....DEPARTMENT HEADS
....FACULTY ADVISERS
....FULL TIME FACULTY
....NONTENURED FACULTY
....PART TIME FACULTY

GROUPS (CONTINUED)

..... PARTNERSHIP TEACHERS
.... TENURED FACULTY
.... WOMEN FACULTY
... FOREIGN STUDENT ADVISERS
... PARAPROFESSIONAL SCHOOL PERSONNEL
.... SCHOOL AIDES
.... TEACHER AIDES
..... BILINGUAL TEACHER AIDES
... PRINCIPALS
... PUPIL PERSONNEL WORKERS
.... ATTENDANCE OFFICERS
... REGISTRARS (SCHOOL)
... SCHOOL BUSINESS OFFICIALS
... SCHOOL CADRES
... SCHOOL COUNSELORS
... SCHOOL NURSES
... SCHOOL PSYCHOLOGISTS
... SCHOOL SECRETARIES
... SCHOOL SOCIAL WORKERS
... STUDENT FINANCIAL AID OFFICERS
... STUDENT PERSONNEL WORKERS
.. SCIENTIFIC PERSONNEL
... MATHEMATICIANS
... SCIENCE CONSULTANTS
... SCIENTISTS
.. SECURITY PERSONNEL
.. SPECIALISTS
... CHILD DEVELOPMENT SPECIALISTS
... FILM PRODUCTION SPECIALISTS
... MEDIA SPECIALISTS
.... AUDIOVISUAL COORDINATORS
.. SYSTEMS ANALYSTS
.. TRAINERS
. POLITICAL CANDIDATES
. POTENTIAL DROPOUTS
. QUALITY CIRCLES
. RECREATIONISTS
. REFERENCE GROUPS
. RELIGIOUS CULTURAL GROUPS
.. CATHOLICS
.. JEWS
.. PROTESTANTS
... AMISH
... PURITANS
. RESEARCH AND INSTRUCTION UNITS
. ROLE MODELS
.. MENTORS
. RUNAWAYS
. RURAL POPULATION
.. RURAL AMERICAN INDIANS
.. RURAL FAMILY
.. RURAL FARM RESIDENTS
.. RURAL NONFARM RESIDENTS
.. RURAL YOUTH
. SEAFARERS
. SELF DIRECTED GROUPS
. SIBLINGS
.. TWINS
. SLOW LEARNERS
. SOCIAL CLASS
.. CASTE
.. LOWER CLASS
.. LOWER MIDDLE CLASS
.. MIDDLE CLASS
.. UPPER CLASS
.. WORKING CLASS
. SOCIAL SUPPORT GROUPS
. SPOUSES
. STOPOUTS
. STUDENTS
.. ADULT STUDENTS
.. ADVANCED STUDENTS
.. BILINGUAL STUDENTS
.. BLACK STUDENTS
.. COLLEGE STUDENTS
... COLLEGE FRESHMEN
... COLLEGE SENIORS
... COLLEGE TRANSFER STUDENTS
... GRADUATE STUDENTS
.... DENTAL STUDENTS
.... LAW STUDENTS
.... MEDICAL STUDENTS
..... GRADUATE MEDICAL STUDENTS
... IN STATE STUDENTS
... ON CAMPUS STUDENTS
... OUT OF STATE STUDENTS
... RESIDENT ASSISTANTS
... STUDENT TEACHERS
... TWO YEAR COLLEGE STUDENTS
... UNDERGRADUATE STUDENTS
.... PREMEDICAL STUDENTS
.. COMMUTING STUDENTS
.. CONTINUATION STUDENTS
.. DAY STUDENTS
.. ELEMENTARY SCHOOL STUDENTS
.. EVENING STUDENTS
.. FOREIGN STUDENTS
.. FULL TIME STUDENTS
.. HIGH RISK STUDENTS
.. LOWER CLASS STUDENTS
.. MAJORS (STUDENTS)
... EDUCATION MAJORS
.. MARRIED STUDENTS
.. MIDDLE CLASS STUDENTS
.. NONMAJORS
.. NONTRADITIONAL STUDENTS
.. PART TIME STUDENTS
.. PREGNANT STUDENTS
.. REENTRY STUDENTS
.. SECONDARY SCHOOL STUDENTS
... HIGH SCHOOL STUDENTS
.... COLLEGE BOUND STUDENTS
.... HIGH SCHOOL FRESHMEN
.... HIGH SCHOOL SENIORS
.... NONCOLLEGE BOUND STUDENTS
... JUNIOR HIGH SCHOOL STUDENTS
.. SELF SUPPORTING STUDENTS
.. SINGLE STUDENTS
.. STUDENT VOLUNTEERS
.. TERMINAL STUDENTS
.. TRANSFER STUDENTS
... COLLEGE TRANSFER STUDENTS
.. WHITE STUDENTS
. TISSUE DONORS
. TRAINEES
. TRIBES
. UNION MEMBERS
. URBAN POPULATION
.. URBAN AMERICAN INDIANS
.. URBAN YOUTH
. USERS (INFORMATION)
. VETERANS
. VICTIMS OF CRIME
. VOLUNTEERS
.. STUDENT VOLUNTEERS
. WELFARE RECIPIENTS
. WHITES
.. WHITE STUDENTS
. WIDOWED
. YOUTH
.. AFFLUENT YOUTH
.. BLACK YOUTH
.. DISADVANTAGED YOUTH
.. MIGRANT YOUTH
.. OUT OF SCHOOL YOUTH
.. RURAL YOUTH
.. SUBURBAN YOUTH
.. URBAN YOUTH
. YOUTH LEADERS

: STATUS
GROUP STATUS
. FAMILY STATUS

: ORGANIZATION
GROUP STRUCTURE
. FAMILY STRUCTURE
.. BIRTH ORDER
. GOVERNMENTAL STRUCTURE

::: METHODS
:: MEASUREMENT TECHNIQUES
: TESTING
GROUP TESTING

: THERAPY
GROUP THERAPY

:: RELATIONSHIP
: INTERPERSONAL RELATIONSHIP
GROUP UNITY

GROWTH PATTERNS (1966 1980)

:: LANGUAGES
: AMERICAN INDIAN LANGUAGES
GUARANI

: INCOME
GUARANTEED INCOME

:: BEHAVIOR
: RESPONSE STYLE (TESTS)
GUESSING (TESTS)

GUIDANCE
. CAREER GUIDANCE
.. CAREER COUNSELING
. COUNSELING
.. ADULT COUNSELING
.. CAREER COUNSELING
.. COCOUNSELING
.. EDUCATIONAL COUNSELING
... ACADEMIC ADVISING
... ADMISSIONS COUNSELING
.. FAMILY COUNSELING
.. GROUP COUNSELING
.. INDIVIDUAL COUNSELING
.. MARRIAGE COUNSELING
.. NONDIRECTIVE COUNSELING
.. PARENT COUNSELING
.. PEER COUNSELING
.. REHABILITATION COUNSELING
.. SCHOOL COUNSELING
. GROUP GUIDANCE
.. GROUP COUNSELING
. POST HIGH SCHOOL GUIDANCE
. SCHOOL GUIDANCE
.. SCHOOL COUNSELING
. TEACHER GUIDANCE

:: FACILITIES
: EDUCATIONAL FACILITIES
GUIDANCE CENTERS

: OBJECTIVES
GUIDANCE OBJECTIVES
. COUNSELING OBJECTIVES

:: GROUPS
: PERSONNEL
GUIDANCE PERSONNEL
. COUNSELORS
.. ADJUSTMENT COUNSELORS
.. EMPLOYMENT COUNSELORS
.. SCHOOL COUNSELORS

: PROGRAMS
GUIDANCE PROGRAMS

GUIDELINES
. FACILITY GUIDELINES

:: PUBLICATIONS
: REFERENCE MATERIALS
GUIDES
. ADMINISTRATOR GUIDES
. CURRICULUM GUIDES
.. STATE CURRICULUM GUIDES
. FACULTY HANDBOOKS
. LABORATORY MANUALS
. LEADERS GUIDES
. LIBRARY GUIDES
. PROGRAM GUIDES
. STUDY GUIDES
. TEACHING GUIDES
. TEST MANUALS

:: LANGUAGES
: INDO EUROPEAN LANGUAGES
GUJARATI

:::: LINGUISTICS
::: SOCIOLINGUISTICS
:: LANGUAGE VARIATION
:: LANGUAGES
: CREOLES
GULLAH

: FACILITIES
GYMNASIUMS

::: ACTIVITIES
:: PHYSICAL ACTIVITIES
: ATHLETICS
GYMNASTICS
. TUMBLING

:: TECHNOLOGY
: MEDICINE
GYNECOLOGY

::: DEVELOPMENT
:: INDIVIDUAL DEVELOPMENT
: BEHAVIOR DEVELOPMENT
HABIT FORMATION

:: COGNITIVE PROCESSES
: LEARNING PROCESSES
HABITUATION

:::: LIBERAL ARTS
::: HUMANITIES
:: LITERATURE
: POETRY
: LITERARY GENRES
HAIKU

:::: LINGUISTICS
::: SOCIOLINGUISTICS
:: LANGUAGE VARIATION
:: LANGUAGES
: CREOLES
HAITIAN CREOLE

:: GROUPS
: LATIN AMERICANS
HAITIANS

::: ACTIVITIES
:: PHYSICAL ACTIVITIES
: ATHLETICS
HANDBALL

: SOCIAL DISCRIMINATION
HANDICAP DISCRIMINATION

: IDENTIFICATION
HANDICAP IDENTIFICATION

HANDICAPPED CHILDREN (1966 1980)

HANDICAPPED STUDENTS (1967 1980)

:::: LIBERAL ARTS
::: HUMANITIES
:: FINE ARTS
: VISUAL ARTS
HANDICRAFTS
. CERAMICS

: EQUIPMENT
HAND TOOLS

: LANGUAGE ARTS
HANDWRITING
. CURSIVE WRITING
. MANUSCRIPT WRITING
(HANDLETTERING)

: : TECHNOLOGY
: AGRICULTURE
HARVESTING

: : : LANGUAGES
: : AFRO ASIATIC LANGUAGES
: CHAD LANGUAGES
HAUSA

: : LANGUAGES
: MALAYO POLYNESIAN
LANGUAGES
HAWAIIAN

: : : GROUPS
: : NORTH AMERICANS
: PACIFIC AMERICANS
: : GROUPS
: ETHNIC GROUPS
HAWAIIANS

HAZARDOUS MATERIALS
. POISONS
. . PESTICIDES
. . . HERBICIDES
. . . INSECTICIDES

HEADLINES

: GROUPS
HEADS OF HOUSEHOLDS

HEALTH
. FAMILY HEALTH
. MENTAL HEALTH
. OCCUPATIONAL SAFETY AND
HEALTH
. PHYSICAL HEALTH
. . DENTAL HEALTH
. . PHYSICAL FITNESS
. PUBLIC HEALTH

: ACTIVITIES
HEALTH ACTIVITIES

HEALTH CONDITIONS

: EDUCATION
HEALTH EDUCATION

: FACILITIES
HEALTH FACILITIES
. NURSING HOMES

: : METHODS
: INSURANCE
HEALTH INSURANCE

HEALTH MATERIALS

: NEEDS
HEALTH NEEDS

: OCCUPATIONS
HEALTH OCCUPATIONS
. ALLIED HEALTH OCCUPATIONS

HEALTH OCCUPATIONS CENTERS
(1968 1980)

: : GROUPS
: PERSONNEL
HEALTH PERSONNEL
. ALLIED HEALTH PERSONNEL
. . DENTAL ASSISTANTS
. . DENTAL HYGIENISTS
. . DENTAL TECHNICIANS
. . DIETITIANS
. . EMERGENCY MEDICAL
TECHNICIANS
. . ENVIRONMENTAL
TECHNICIANS
. . HOME HEALTH AIDES
. . MEDICAL ASSISTANTS
. . . MEDICAL LABORATORY
ASSISTANTS
. . MEDICAL RECORD
ADMINISTRATORS
. . MEDICAL RECORD
TECHNICIANS
. . MEDICAL TECHNOLOGISTS
. . NURSES AIDES
. . OCCUPATIONAL THERAPY
ASSISTANTS
. . OPTOMETRISTS
. . PHYSICAL THERAPY AIDES
. . PHYSICIANS ASSISTANTS
. . PSYCHIATRIC AIDES
. . RADIOLOGIC TECHNOLOGISTS
. . SURGICAL TECHNICIANS
. . THERAPISTS
. . . OCCUPATIONAL THERAPISTS
. . . PHYSICAL THERAPISTS
. . VETERINARY ASSISTANTS
. DENTISTS
. HOSPITAL PERSONNEL
. MEDICAL CONSULTANTS
. NURSES
. . NURSE PRACTITIONERS
. . SCHOOL NURSES
. PHARMACISTS
. PHYSICIANS
. . FOREIGN MEDICAL
GRADUATES
. . PSYCHIATRISTS
. PSYCHOLOGISTS
. . SCHOOL PSYCHOLOGISTS
. VETERINARIANS

: PROGRAMS
HEALTH PROGRAMS
. BREAKFAST PROGRAMS
. IMMUNIZATION PROGRAMS
. LUNCH PROGRAMS
. MENTAL HEALTH PROGRAMS

: : SERVICES
: HUMAN SERVICES
HEALTH SERVICES
. COMMUNITY HEALTH SERVICES
. HOSPICES (TERMINAL CARE)
. MEDICAL SERVICES
. . FIRST AID
. . . CARDIOPULMONARY
RESUSCITATION
. . PSYCHIATRIC SERVICES
. MIGRANT HEALTH SERVICES
. SCHOOL HEALTH SERVICES

HEARING (PHYSIOLOGY)

: SENSORY AIDS
: : EQUIPMENT
: AUDIO EQUIPMENT
HEARING AIDS

: PREVENTION
HEARING CONSERVATION

: DISABILITIES
HEARING IMPAIRMENTS
. DEAFNESS
. PARTIAL HEARING

HEARINGS

: THERAPY
HEARING THERAPY

: : DISABILITIES
: PHYSICAL DISABILITIES
HEART DISORDERS

: METABOLISM
HEART RATE

: : SCIENTIFIC CONCEPTS
: ENERGY
HEAT

: CLIMATE CONTROL
HEATING

: : CONSERVATION
(ENVIRONMENT)
: ENERGY CONSERVATION
: CLIMATE CONTROL
HEAT RECOVERY

: : : LANGUAGES
: : AFRO ASIATIC LANGUAGES
: SEMITIC LANGUAGES
HEBREW

: SCIENTIFIC CONCEPTS
HEIGHT

: : RELATIONSHIP
: INTERPERSONAL
RELATIONSHIP
HELPING RELATIONSHIP

HELPLESSNESS

: : : HAZARDOUS MATERIALS
: : POISONS
: PESTICIDES
HERBICIDES

: : DEVELOPMENT
: EVOLUTION
HEREDITY

: : : ORGANIZATION
: : CLASSIFICATION
: GROUPING (INSTRUCTIONAL
PURPOSES)
HETEROGENEOUS GROUPING

: METHODS
HEURISTICS

HIDDEN CURRICULUM

: ACHIEVEMENT
HIGH ACHIEVEMENT

: : EDUCATION
: POSTSECONDARY EDUCATION
HIGHER EDUCATION
. GRADUATE STUDY
. . GRADUATE MEDICAL
EDUCATION
. . POSTSECONDARY EDUCATION
AS A FIELD OF STUDY
. POSTDOCTORAL EDUCATION
. UNDERGRADUATE STUDY

: : PUBLICATIONS
: BOOKS
HIGH INTEREST LOW VOCABULARY
BOOKS

: GROUPS
HIGH RISK PERSONS
. HIGH RISK STUDENTS

: : GROUPS
: STUDENTS
: : GROUPS
: HIGH RISK PERSONS
HIGH RISK STUDENTS

: : PROGRAMS
: ADULT PROGRAMS
HIGH SCHOOL EQUIVALENCY
PROGRAMS

: : : : GROUPS
: : : STUDENTS
: : SECONDARY SCHOOL
STUDENTS
: HIGH SCHOOL STUDENTS
HIGH SCHOOL FRESHMEN

: : : GROUPS
: : ALUMNI
: GRADUATES
HIGH SCHOOL GRADUATES

: : : INSTITUTIONS
: : SCHOOLS
: SECONDARY SCHOOLS
HIGH SCHOOLS
. VOCATIONAL HIGH SCHOOLS

: : : : GROUPS
: : : STUDENTS
: : SECONDARY SCHOOL
STUDENTS
: HIGH SCHOOL STUDENTS
HIGH SCHOOL SENIORS

: : : GROUPS
: : STUDENTS
: SECONDARY SCHOOL STUDENTS
HIGH SCHOOL STUDENTS
. COLLEGE BOUND STUDENTS
. HIGH SCHOOL FRESHMEN
. HIGH SCHOOL SENIORS
. NONCOLLEGE BOUND STUDENTS

: : : : GROUPS
: : : PERSONNEL
: : PARAPROFESSIONAL
PERSONNEL
: ENGINEERING TECHNICIANS
HIGHWAY ENGINEERING AIDES

: : LANGUAGES
: INDO EUROPEAN LANGUAGES
HINDI

: : CULTURE
: NORTH AMERICAN CULTURE
HISPANIC AMERICAN CULTURE

: : : : : LIBERAL ARTS
: : : : HUMANITIES
: : : LITERATURE
: : NORTH AMERICAN
LITERATURE
: UNITED STATES LITERATURE
HISPANIC AMERICAN LITERATURE
. MEXICAN AMERICAN
LITERATURE

: : GROUPS
: NORTH AMERICANS
HISPANIC AMERICANS
. MEXICAN AMERICANS
. PORTUGUESE AMERICANS
. SPANISH AMERICANS

HISTORICAL CRITICISM (1969
1980)

:::: LIBERAL ARTS
::: SCIENCES
:: SOCIAL SCIENCES
::: LIBERAL ARTS
:: HUMANITIES
: HISTORY
HISTORIOGRAPHY

::: LIBERAL ARTS
:: SCIENCES
: SOCIAL SCIENCES
:: LIBERAL ARTS
: HUMANITIES
HISTORY
. AFRICAN HISTORY
. AMERICAN INDIAN HISTORY
. ANCIENT HISTORY
. ASIAN HISTORY
. BLACK HISTORY
. CONSTITUTIONAL HISTORY
. DIPLOMATIC HISTORY
. EDUCATIONAL HISTORY
.. SCIENCE EDUCATION HISTORY
. EUROPEAN HISTORY
. FAMILY HISTORY
.. GENEALOGY
. HISTORIOGRAPHY
. INTELLECTUAL HISTORY
.. ART HISTORY
.. LITERARY HISTORY
. LATIN AMERICAN HISTORY
. LOCAL HISTORY
. MEDIEVAL HISTORY
. MIDDLE EASTERN HISTORY
. MODERN HISTORY
. NORTH AMERICAN HISTORY
.. UNITED STATES HISTORY
... CIVIL WAR (UNITED STATES)
... COLONIAL HISTORY (UNITED STATES)
... MEXICAN AMERICAN HISTORY
... RECONSTRUCTION ERA
... REVOLUTIONARY WAR (UNITED STATES)
... STATE HISTORY
. ORAL HISTORY
. SCIENCE HISTORY
. SOCIAL HISTORY
. WORLD HISTORY

:: INSTRUCTION
: HUMANITIES INSTRUCTION
HISTORY INSTRUCTION

::: EDUCATIONAL MEDIA
:: INSTRUCTIONAL MATERIALS
::: PUBLICATIONS
:: BOOKS
: TEXTBOOKS
HISTORY TEXTBOOKS

:: ACTIVITIES
: RECREATIONAL ACTIVITIES
HOBBIES

HOLIDAYS
. RELIGIOUS HOLIDAYS

: METHODS
HOLISTIC APPROACH
. GESTALT THERAPY
. GLOBAL APPROACH
. SYSTEMS APPROACH
.. SYSTEMS BUILDING
... DESIGN BUILD APPROACH

: EVALUATION
HOLISTIC EVALUATION

::::: LIBERAL ARTS
:::: HUMANITIES
::: FINE ARTS
:: VISUAL ARTS
: PHOTOGRAPHY
HOLOGRAPHY

HOMEBOUND

: CURRICULUM
HOME ECONOMICS

:: EDUCATION
: PROFESSIONAL EDUCATION
HOME ECONOMICS EDUCATION

:: ABILITY
: SKILLS
HOME ECONOMICS SKILLS

:::: GROUPS
::: PERSONNEL
:: PROFESSIONAL PERSONNEL
: TEACHERS
HOME ECONOMICS TEACHERS

: EQUIPMENT
HOME FURNISHINGS

::::: GROUPS
:::: PERSONNEL
::: NONPROFESSIONAL PERSONNEL
:: SERVICE WORKERS
: HOUSEHOLD WORKERS
:::: GROUPS
::: PERSONNEL
:: HEALTH PERSONNEL
: ALLIED HEALTH PERSONNEL
HOME HEALTH AIDES

: INSTRUCTION
HOME INSTRUCTION

: GROUPS
HOMELESS PEOPLE

: GROUPS
HOMEMAKERS

:: ABILITY
: SKILLS
HOMEMAKING SKILLS

:: GOVERNANCE
: ADMINISTRATION
HOME MANAGEMENT

: GROUPS
HOMEOWNERS

: PROGRAMS
HOME PROGRAMS

:: EDUCATION
: COMPULSORY EDUCATION
HOME SCHOOLING

::: ACTIVITIES
:: LEARNING ACTIVITIES
: STUDY
HOME STUDY
. HOMEWORK

: METHODS
HOME VISITS

:::: ACTIVITIES
::: LEARNING ACTIVITIES
:: STUDY
: HOME STUDY
:: INSTRUCTION
: ASSIGNMENTS
HOMEWORK

::: ORGANIZATION
:: CLASSIFICATION
: GROUPING (INSTRUCTIONAL PURPOSES)
HOMOGENEOUS GROUPING
. ABILITY GROUPING

: SEXUALITY
HOMOSEXUALITY
. LESBIANISM

: CURRICULUM
HONORS CURRICULUM

:: GROUPS
: ORGANIZATIONS (GROUPS)
HONOR SOCIETIES

::: LANGUAGES
:: AMERICAN INDIAN LANGUAGES
: UTO AZTECAN LANGUAGES
HOPI

: ORGANIZATION
HORIZONTAL ORGANIZATION

: TECHNOLOGY
HOROLOGY

:: ACTIVITIES
: PHYSICAL ACTIVITIES
HORSEBACK RIDING

: ANIMALS
HORSES

:: TECHNOLOGY
: AGRICULTURE
HORTICULTURE
. ORNAMENTAL HORTICULTURE
.. FLORICULTURE
.. LANDSCAPING
.. TURF MANAGEMENT

::: SERVICES
:: HUMAN SERVICES
: HEALTH SERVICES
HOSPICES (TERMINAL CARE)

:: OCCUPATIONS
: SERVICE OCCUPATIONS
HOSPITALITY OCCUPATIONS

:: GROUPS
: PATIENTS
::: GROUPS
:: AGE GROUPS
: CHILDREN
HOSPITALIZED CHILDREN

:::: INSTITUTIONS
:::: INFORMATION SOURCES
::: LIBRARIES
:: SPECIAL LIBRARIES
: INSTITUTIONAL LIBRARIES
HOSPITAL LIBRARIES

::: GROUPS
:: PERSONNEL
: HEALTH PERSONNEL
HOSPITAL PERSONNEL

: INSTITUTIONS
HOSPITALS
. PSYCHIATRIC HOSPITALS
. TEACHING HOSPITALS

:::: INSTITUTIONS
::: SCHOOLS
:: SPECIAL SCHOOLS
: INSTITUTIONAL SCHOOLS
HOSPITAL SCHOOLS

:: PSYCHOLOGICAL PATTERNS
: ANGER
HOSTILITY

:: FACILITIES
: HOUSING
HOTELS

::: SERVICES
:: INFORMATION SERVICES
::: SERVICES
:: COMMUNITY SERVICES
: COMMUNITY INFORMATION SERVICES
HOTLINES (PUBLIC)

:::: GROUPS
::: PERSONNEL
:: NONPROFESSIONAL PERSONNEL
: SERVICE WORKERS
HOUSEHOLD WORKERS
. HOME HEALTH AIDES

:::: GROUPS
::: PERSONNEL
:: NONPROFESSIONAL PERSONNEL
: SERVICE WORKERS
HOUSEKEEPERS

:: ORGANIZATION
: SCHOOL ORGANIZATION
HOUSE PLAN

: FACILITIES
HOUSING
. BOARDING HOMES
. COLLEGE HOUSING
. DORMITORIES
. GROUP HOMES
. HOTELS
. LOW RENT HOUSING
.. PUBLIC HOUSING
. MIDDLE INCOME HOUSING
. MIGRANT HOUSING
. SUBURBAN HOUSING
. TEACHER HOUSING

HOUSING DEFICIENCIES

: SOCIAL DISCRIMINATION
HOUSING DISCRIMINATION

::: BUSINESS
:: INDUSTRY
: CONSTRUCTION INDUSTRY
HOUSING INDUSTRY

:::: GROUPS
::: PERSONNEL
:: NONPROFESSIONAL PERSONNEL
: SERVICE WORKERS
::: GROUPS
:: PERSONNEL
: PARAPROFESSIONAL PERSONNEL
HOUSING MANAGEMENT AIDES

: NEEDS
HOUSING NEEDS

: OPPORTUNITIES
HOUSING OPPORTUNITIES

HUMAN BODY

: INVESTMENT
HUMAN CAPITAL

HUMAN DEVELOPMENT (1966 1980)

HUMAN DIGNITY

HUMAN FACTORS ENGINEERING

: : : : LIBERAL ARTS
: : : SCIENCES
: : SOCIAL SCIENCES
: GEOGRAPHY
HUMAN GEOGRAPHY

: : : LIBERAL ARTS
: : HUMANITIES
: PHILOSOPHY
HUMANISM

: EDUCATION
HUMANISTIC EDUCATION

: SOCIOCULTURAL PATTERNS
HUMANITARIANISM

: LIBERAL ARTS
HUMANITIES
. FINE ARTS
. . DANCE
. . MUSIC
. . . APPLIED MUSIC
. . . JAZZ
. . . ORIENTAL MUSIC
. . . VOCAL MUSIC
. . . . CHORAL MUSIC
. . . . SONGS
. . . . . ART SONG
. . . . . BALLADS
. . . . . HYMNS
. . THEATER ARTS
. . . ACTING
. . . CHORAL SPEAKING
. . . DRAMA
. . . . COMEDY
. . . . . SKITS
. . . . SCRIPTS
. . . . TRAGEDY
. . . DRAMATICS
. . . . CREATIVE DRAMATICS
. . . OPERA
. . . PANTOMIME
. . . PUPPETRY
. . . READERS THEATER
. . VISUAL ARTS
. . . ARCHITECTURE
. . . CHILDRENS ART
. . . DESIGN CRAFTS
. . . DRAFTING
. . . . ARCHITECTURAL DRAFTING
. . . . ENGINEERING DRAWING
. . . . TECHNICAL ILLUSTRATION
. . . FILM PRODUCTION
. . . FREEHAND DRAWING
. . . GRAPHIC ARTS
. . . . CARTOGRAPHY
. . . . COMPUTER GRAPHICS
. . . . ENGINEERING GRAPHICS
. . . . . ENGINEERING DRAWING
. . . . LAYOUT (PUBLICATIONS)
. . . . PRINTING
. . . HANDICRAFTS
. . . . CERAMICS
. . . PAINTING (VISUAL ARTS)
. . . PHOTOGRAPHY
. . . . HOLOGRAPHY
. . . SCULPTURE
. HISTORY
. . AFRICAN HISTORY
. . AMERICAN INDIAN HISTORY
. . ANCIENT HISTORY
. . ASIAN HISTORY
. . BLACK HISTORY
. . CONSTITUTIONAL HISTORY
. . DIPLOMATIC HISTORY
. . EDUCATIONAL HISTORY
. . . SCIENCE EDUCATION HISTORY
. . EUROPEAN HISTORY
. . FAMILY HISTORY
. . . GENEALOGY
. . HISTORIOGRAPHY
. . INTELLECTUAL HISTORY
. . . ART HISTORY
. . . LITERARY HISTORY
. . LATIN AMERICAN HISTORY
. . LOCAL HISTORY
. . MEDIEVAL HISTORY
. . MIDDLE EASTERN HISTORY
. . MODERN HISTORY
. . NORTH AMERICAN HISTORY
. . . UNITED STATES HISTORY
. . . . CIVIL WAR (UNITED STATES)
. . . . COLONIAL HISTORY (UNITED STATES)
. . . . MEXICAN AMERICAN HISTORY
. . . . RECONSTRUCTION ERA
. . . . REVOLUTIONARY WAR (UNITED STATES)
. . . . STATE HISTORY
. . ORAL HISTORY
. . SCIENCE HISTORY
. . SOCIAL HISTORY
. . WORLD HISTORY
. LITERATURE
. . ADOLESCENT LITERATURE
. . AFRICAN LITERATURE
. . AMERICAN INDIAN LITERATURE
. . AUSTRALIAN LITERATURE
. . BAROQUE LITERATURE
. . BIBLICAL LITERATURE
. . BLACK LITERATURE
. . CHILDRENS LITERATURE
. . CLASSICAL LITERATURE
. . . LATIN LITERATURE
. . CZECH LITERATURE
. . DRAMA
. . . COMEDY
. . . . SKITS
. . . SCRIPTS
. . . TRAGEDY
. . EIGHTEENTH CENTURY LITERATURE
. . ENGLISH LITERATURE
. . . OLD ENGLISH LITERATURE
. . FIFTEENTH CENTURY LITERATURE
. . FRENCH LITERATURE
. . GERMAN LITERATURE
. . GREEK LITERATURE
. . ITALIAN LITERATURE
. . LATIN AMERICAN LITERATURE
. . LEGENDS
. . MEDIEVAL LITERATURE
. . NINETEENTH CENTURY LITERATURE
. . NORTH AMERICAN LITERATURE
. . . CANADIAN LITERATURE
. . . UNITED STATES LITERATURE
. . . . HISPANIC AMERICAN LITERATURE
. . . . . MEXICAN AMERICAN LITERATURE
. . PASTORAL LITERATURE
. . POETRY
. . . EPICS
. . . HAIKU
. . . LYRIC POETRY
. . . . BALLADS
. . . . HYMNS
. . . ODES
. . . SONNETS
. . POLISH LITERATURE
. . PROSE
. . . FICTION
. . . . NOVELS
. . . . SCIENCE FICTION
. . . . SHORT STORIES
. . . NONFICTION
. . . . BIOGRAPHIES
. . . . . AUTOBIOGRAPHIES
. . . . CHRONICLES
. . . . DIARIES
. . . . ESSAYS
. . RENAISSANCE LITERATURE
. . RUSSIAN LITERATURE
. . SEVENTEENTH CENTURY LITERATURE
. . SIXTEENTH CENTURY LITERATURE
. . SPANISH LITERATURE
. . TWENTIETH CENTURY LITERATURE
. . VICTORIAN LITERATURE
. PHILOSOPHY
. . EDUCATIONAL PHILOSOPHY
. . EPISTEMOLOGY
. . ETHICS
. . . BIOETHICS
. . EXISTENTIALISM
. . HUMANISM
. . LOGIC
. . . MATHEMATICAL LOGIC
. . . . ALGORITHMS
. . . . MATHEMATICAL FORMULAS
. . . . . EQUATIONS (MATHEMATICS)
. . . . . FUNCTIONS (MATHEMATICS)
. . . . PROOF (MATHEMATICS)
. . . . SET THEORY
. . MARXISM
. . PHENOMENOLOGY
. . PLATONISM
. . SEMIOTICS
. . . PRAGMATICS
. . . SEMANTICS
. . . . LEXICOLOGY

: INSTRUCTION
HUMANITIES INSTRUCTION
. HISTORY INSTRUCTION
. NATIVE LANGUAGE INSTRUCTION
. . ENGLISH INSTRUCTION
. SECOND LANGUAGE INSTRUCTION

HUMANIZATION

HUMAN LIVING (1966 1980)

HUMAN POSTURE

: RELATIONSHIP
HUMAN RELATIONS
. INTERGROUP RELATIONS
. . ETHNIC RELATIONS
. . INTERFAITH RELATIONS
. . RACIAL RELATIONS
. PEACE
. SLAVERY

: PROGRAMS
HUMAN RELATIONS PROGRAMS

: RESOURCES
HUMAN RESOURCES
. LABOR FORCE
. LABOR SUPPLY

: SERVICES
HUMAN SERVICES
. COUNSELING SERVICES
. EMPLOYMENT SERVICES
. . OUTPLACEMENT SERVICES (EMPLOYMENT)
. FOOD SERVICE
. HEALTH SERVICES
. . COMMUNITY HEALTH SERVICES
. . HOSPICES (TERMINAL CARE)
. . MEDICAL SERVICES
. . . FIRST AID
. . . . CARDIOPULMONARY RESUSCITATION
. . . PSYCHIATRIC SERVICES
. . MIGRANT HEALTH SERVICES
. . SCHOOL HEALTH SERVICES
. PSYCHOLOGICAL SERVICES
. SOCIAL SERVICES
. . ADULT DAY CARE
. . ADULT FOSTER CARE
. . ANCILLARY SCHOOL SERVICES
. . . MOBILE EDUCATIONAL SERVICES
. . . PUPIL PERSONNEL SERVICES
. . . SCHOOL HEALTH SERVICES
. . . STUDENT PERSONNEL SERVICES
. . DAY CARE
. . . EMPLOYER SUPPORTED DAY CARE
. . . FAMILY DAY CARE
. . . SCHOOL AGE DAY CARE
. . FOSTER CARE
. . SOCIAL WORK
. . WELFARE SERVICES
. . . MIGRANT WELFARE SERVICES

HUMIDITY

HUMOR

: : : LANGUAGES
: : URALIC ALTAIC LANGUAGES
: FINNO UGRIC LANGUAGES
HUNGARIAN

HUNGER

: TECHNOLOGY
HYDRAULICS

HYGIENE

: : : : : : LIBERAL ARTS
: : : : : HUMANITIES
: : : : FINE ARTS
: : : MUSIC
: : VOCAL MUSIC
: SONGS
: : : : : LIBERAL ARTS
: : : : HUMANITIES
: : : LITERATURE
: : POETRY
: LYRIC POETRY
: LITERARY GENRES
HYMNS

: BEHAVIOR
HYPERACTIVITY

: : : DISABILITIES
: : VISUAL IMPAIRMENTS
: AMETROPIA
HYPEROPIA

: : DISABILITIES
: DISEASES
HYPERTENSION

HYPNOSIS

: : METHODS
: EVALUATION METHODS
HYPOTHESIS TESTING

: : LANGUAGES
: AFRICAN LANGUAGES
IBO

: : : : ACTIVITIES
: : : PHYSICAL ACTIVITIES
: : ATHLETICS
: TEAM SPORTS
ICE HOCKEY

:::ACTIVITIES
::PHYSICAL ACTIVITIES
:ATHLETICS
ICE SKATING

:::::LIBERAL ARTS
::::SCIENCES
:::NATURAL SCIENCES
::BIOLOGICAL SCIENCES
:ZOOLOGY
ICHTHYOLOGY

IDENTIFICATION
.ABILITY IDENTIFICATION
.CLINICAL DIAGNOSIS
.EDUCATIONAL DIAGNOSIS
..READING DIAGNOSIS
...MISCUE ANALYSIS
.HANDICAP IDENTIFICATION
.PLANT IDENTIFICATION
.RACIAL IDENTIFICATION
.TALENT IDENTIFICATION

:PSYCHOLOGICAL PATTERNS
IDENTIFICATION (PSYCHOLOGY)

::LANGUAGE
:WRITTEN LANGUAGE
IDEOGRAPHY

IDEOLOGY

:LANGUAGE PATTERNS
IDIOMS

::LANGUAGES
:AFRICAN LANGUAGES
IGBO

::BEHAVIOR
:DRUG USE
ILLEGAL DRUG USE

ILLEGITIMATE BIRTHS

ILLITERACY

:VISUAL AIDS
ILLUSTRATIONS

::LITERARY DEVICES
::LANGUAGE
:FIGURATIVE LANGUAGE
IMAGERY

:::INDIVIDUAL CHARACTERISTICS
::PSYCHOLOGICAL CHARACTERISTICS
:CREATIVITY
IMAGINATION

:BEHAVIOR
IMITATION

::PROGRAMS
:SECOND LANGUAGE PROGRAMS
IMMERSION PROGRAMS

::GROUPS
:MIGRANTS
IMMIGRANTS
.UNDOCUMENTED IMMIGRANTS

:::GROUPS
::PERSONNEL
:GOVERNMENT EMPLOYEES
IMMIGRATION INSPECTORS

::PROGRAMS
:HEALTH PROGRAMS
IMMUNIZATION PROGRAMS

::POLICY
:FOREIGN POLICY
IMPERIALISM
.COLONIALISM

IMPRESSIONISM

IMPRESSIONISTIC CRITICISM (1969 1980)

IMPROVEMENT
.ACHIEVEMENT GAINS
.EDUCATIONAL IMPROVEMENT
..INSTRUCTIONAL IMPROVEMENT
.FACILITY IMPROVEMENT
..EDUCATIONAL FACILITIES IMPROVEMENT
.FINANCE REFORM
.NEIGHBORHOOD IMPROVEMENT
.PROGRAM IMPROVEMENT
.READING IMPROVEMENT
.SPEECH IMPROVEMENT
.STUDENT IMPROVEMENT
.TEACHER IMPROVEMENT
.URBAN IMPROVEMENT
..URBAN RENEWAL
.WRITING IMPROVEMENT

:PROGRAMS
IMPROVEMENT PROGRAMS
.SELF HELP PROGRAMS

::FINANCIAL SUPPORT
:GRANTS
INCENTIVE GRANTS

INCENTIVES

:::BEHAVIOR
::SOCIAL BEHAVIOR
:ANTISOCIAL BEHAVIOR
INCEST

INCIDENCE
.AVERAGE DAILY ATTENDANCE
.BIRTH RATE
.DISEASE INCIDENCE
.DROPOUT RATE
.ENROLLMENT RATE
..AVERAGE DAILY MEMBERSHIP
..DECLINING ENROLLMENT

:LEARNING
INCIDENTAL LEARNING

INCOME
.FAMILY INCOME
.GUARANTEED INCOME
.INTEREST (FINANCE)
.LOW INCOME
.MERIT PAY
.PREMIUM PAY
.SALARIES
..CONTRACT SALARIES
..TEACHER SALARIES
.WAGES
..MINIMUM WAGE

::FINANCIAL SUPPORT
:STUDENT FINANCIAL AID
INCOME CONTINGENT LOANS

INDEMNITY BONDS

::LITERACY
::LANGUAGE ARTS
:READING
INDEPENDENT READING

:::ACTIVITIES
::LEARNING ACTIVITIES
:STUDY
INDEPENDENT STUDY

::PUBLICATIONS
:REFERENCE MATERIALS
INDEXES
.CITATION INDEXES
.COORDINATE INDEXES
.PERMUTED INDEXES

::::SERVICES
:::INFORMATION SERVICES
::INFORMATION PROCESSING
:DOCUMENTATION
INDEXING
.AUTOMATIC INDEXING

:GROUPS
INDIANS

::GROUPS
:PERSONNEL
INDIGENOUS PERSONNEL

:GROUPS
INDIGENOUS POPULATIONS

:ACTIVITIES
INDIVIDUAL ACTIVITIES

INDIVIDUAL CHARACTERISTICS
.AGE
..CHRONOLOGICAL AGE
..MENTAL AGE
..SCHOOL ENTRANCE AGE
.MATURITY (INDIVIDUALS)
..VOCATIONAL MATURITY
.PHYSICAL CHARACTERISTICS
..BODY HEIGHT
..BODY WEIGHT
...BIRTH WEIGHT
...OBESITY
..LATERAL DOMINANCE
..MUSCULAR STRENGTH
..NEUROLOGICAL ORGANIZATION
...BRAIN HEMISPHERE FUNCTIONS
..RACE
..SEX
.PSYCHOLOGICAL CHARACTERISTICS
..ATTENTION SPAN
..COGNITIVE STYLE
...CONCEPTUAL TEMPO
...FIELD DEPENDENCE INDEPENDENCE
..CREATIVITY
...IMAGINATION
..INTELLIGENCE
...COMPREHENSION
....LISTENING COMPREHENSION
....READING COMPREHENSION
...FORMAL OPERATIONS
...MENTAL AGE
..PERSONALITY TRAITS
...CURIOSITY
...LOCUS OF CONTROL
...MENTAL RIGIDITY
..SCHEMATA (COGNITION)

::GUIDANCE
:COUNSELING
INDIVIDUAL COUNSELING

:DEVELOPMENT
INDIVIDUAL DEVELOPMENT
.ADOLESCENT DEVELOPMENT
.ADULT DEVELOPMENT
.AGING (INDIVIDUALS)
..AGING IN ACADEMIA
.BEHAVIOR DEVELOPMENT
..HABIT FORMATION
.CAREER DEVELOPMENT
..CAREER AWARENESS
..CAREER EXPLORATION
.CHILD DEVELOPMENT
.COGNITIVE DEVELOPMENT
..INTELLECTUAL DEVELOPMENT
..PERCEPTUAL DEVELOPMENT
..VERBAL DEVELOPMENT
...LANGUAGE ACQUISITION
.CREATIVE DEVELOPMENT
.EMOTIONAL DEVELOPMENT
.MORAL DEVELOPMENT
.PERSONALITY DEVELOPMENT
.PHYSICAL DEVELOPMENT
..MOTOR DEVELOPMENT
.SKILL DEVELOPMENT
.SOCIAL DEVELOPMENT
.TALENT DEVELOPMENT

:DIFFERENCES
INDIVIDUAL DIFFERENCES
.AGE DIFFERENCES
.INTELLIGENCE DIFFERENCES
.SEX DIFFERENCES

:INSTRUCTION
INDIVIDUAL INSTRUCTION
.TUTORING
..PROGRAMED TUTORING

INDIVIDUALISM

::PROGRAMS
:SPECIAL PROGRAMS
INDIVIDUALIZED EDUCATION PROGRAMS

:::METHODS
::EDUCATIONAL METHODS
:TEACHING METHODS
INDIVIDUALIZED INSTRUCTION

:PROGRAMS
INDIVIDUALIZED PROGRAMS

::INSTRUCTION
:READING INSTRUCTION
::LITERACY
::LANGUAGE ARTS
:READING
INDIVIDUALIZED READING

:NEEDS
INDIVIDUAL NEEDS
.CHILDHOOD NEEDS
.PSYCHOLOGICAL NEEDS
..ACHIEVEMENT NEED
..AFFECTION
..AFFILIATION NEED
...PEER ACCEPTANCE
..PERSONAL SPACE
..SECURITY (PSYCHOLOGY)
..SELF ACTUALIZATION
..STATUS NEED

INDIVIDUAL POWER

::::LIBERAL ARTS
:::SCIENCES
::BEHAVIORAL SCIENCES
:PSYCHOLOGY
INDIVIDUAL PSYCHOLOGY

INDIVIDUAL READING (1966 1980)

:::METHODS
::MEASUREMENT TECHNIQUES
:TESTING
INDIVIDUAL TESTING

: GROUPS
INDOCHINESE
. CAMBODIANS
. LAOTIANS
. VIETNAMESE PEOPLE

: LANGUAGES
INDO EUROPEAN LANGUAGES
. AFRIKAANS
. ALBANIAN
. ARMENIAN
. BALTIC LANGUAGES
.. LATVIAN
.. LITHUANIAN
. BALUCHI
. BENGALI
. DUTCH
. ENGLISH
.. BUSINESS ENGLISH
.. ENGLISH (SECOND LANGUAGE)
... ENGLISH FOR SPECIAL PURPOSES
.... ENGLISH FOR ACADEMIC PURPOSES
.... ENGLISH FOR SCIENCE AND TECHNOLOGY
.... VOCATIONAL ENGLISH (SECOND LANGUAGE)
.. MIDDLE ENGLISH
.. NORTH AMERICAN ENGLISH
.. OLD ENGLISH
.. ORAL ENGLISH
. GERMAN
.. YIDDISH
. GREEK
. GUJARATI
. HINDI
. KASHMIRI
. KURDISH
. MARATHI
. NEPALI
. NORWEGIAN
. OSSETIC
. PANJABI
. PASHTO
. PERSIAN
. ROMANCE LANGUAGES
.. FRENCH
.. ITALIAN
.. LATIN
.. PORTUGUESE
.. RUMANIAN
.. SPANISH
. SINGHALESE
. SLAVIC LANGUAGES
.. BIELORUSSIAN
.. BULGARIAN
.. CZECH
.. POLISH
.. RUSSIAN
.. SERBOCROATIAN
.. SLOVENIAN
.. UKRAINIAN
. SWEDISH
. TAJIK
. URDU
. WELSH

::: LANGUAGES
:: MALAYO POLYNESIAN LANGUAGES
: INDONESIAN LANGUAGES
INDONESIAN

:: LANGUAGES
: MALAYO POLYNESIAN LANGUAGES
INDONESIAN LANGUAGES
. BIKOL
. DUSUN
. INDONESIAN
. JAVANESE
. MALAGASY
. MALAY
. MARANAO
. TAGALOG
. VISAYAN
.. CEBUANO

:: COGNITIVE PROCESSES
: LOGICAL THINKING
INDUCTION

INDUSTRIAL ARTS
. PAINTING (INDUSTRIAL ARTS)

:::: GROUPS
::: PERSONNEL
:: PROFESSIONAL PERSONNEL
: TEACHERS
INDUSTRIAL ARTS TEACHERS

: EDUCATION
INDUSTRIAL EDUCATION

: DEVELOPMENT
INDUSTRIALIZATION

:: GROUPS
: PERSONNEL
INDUSTRIAL PERSONNEL

:::: LIBERAL ARTS
::: SCIENCES
:: BEHAVIORAL SCIENCES
: PSYCHOLOGY
INDUSTRIAL PSYCHOLOGY

: ORGANIZATION
INDUSTRIAL STRUCTURE

: TRAINING
INDUSTRIAL TRAINING

: BUSINESS
INDUSTRY
. BAKERY INDUSTRY
. BANKING
. BRICK INDUSTRY
. BROADCAST INDUSTRY
. CONSTRUCTION INDUSTRY
.. HOUSING INDUSTRY
. FASHION INDUSTRY
. FEED INDUSTRY
. FILM INDUSTRY
. INSURANCE COMPANIES
. LUMBER INDUSTRY
. MANUFACTURING INDUSTRY
.. AEROSPACE INDUSTRY
.. CEMENT INDUSTRY
.. CHEMICAL INDUSTRY
.. ELECTRONICS INDUSTRY
.. FURNITURE INDUSTRY
.. MACHINERY INDUSTRY
.. METAL INDUSTRY
. MEAT PACKING INDUSTRY
. PETROLEUM INDUSTRY
. PUBLISHING INDUSTRY
. TELEPHONE COMMUNICATIONS INDUSTRY
. TOURISM

INEQUALITIES (1970 1980)

: MATHEMATICAL CONCEPTS
INEQUALITY (MATHEMATICS)

: BEHAVIOR
INFANT BEHAVIOR

: DEATH
INFANT MORTALITY

:::: GROUPS
::: AGE GROUPS
:: CHILDREN
: YOUNG CHILDREN
INFANTS
. NEONATES
. PREMATURE INFANTS

INFERENCES
. STATISTICAL INFERENCE

:: ENVIRONMENT
: ECONOMIC CLIMATE
INFLATION (ECONOMICS)

INFLUENCES
. BIOLOGICAL INFLUENCES
.. RH FACTORS
. BLACK INFLUENCES
. COMMUNITY INFLUENCE
. CULTURAL INFLUENCES
. ECOLOGICAL FACTORS
. ECONOMIC FACTORS
. ENROLLMENT INFLUENCES
. ENVIRONMENTAL INFLUENCES
. FAMILY INFLUENCE
. MINORITY GROUP INFLUENCES
. PARENT INFLUENCE
. PEER INFLUENCE
. PERFORMANCE FACTORS
. PERINATAL INFLUENCES
. POLITICAL INFLUENCES
. PRENATAL INFLUENCES
. RACIAL FACTORS
. RELIGIOUS FACTORS
. SOCIAL INFLUENCES
. SOCIOECONOMIC INFLUENCES
. TEACHER INFLUENCE
. TIME FACTORS (LEARNING)

: EVALUATION
INFORMAL ASSESSMENT

:: ABILITY
: LEADERSHIP
INFORMAL LEADERSHIP

: ORGANIZATION
INFORMAL ORGANIZATION

:::: MEASURES (INDIVIDUALS)
::: TESTS
:: VERBAL TESTS
: READING TESTS
INFORMAL READING INVENTORIES

:: FACILITIES
: RESOURCE CENTERS
: INFORMATION SOURCES
INFORMATION CENTERS
. CLEARINGHOUSES

:: SERVICES
: INFORMATION SERVICES
INFORMATION DISSEMINATION
. PROPAGANDA
. PUBLICITY
.. ADVERTISING
... TELEVISION COMMERCIALS
.. INSTITUTIONAL ADVANCEMENT
. REFERRAL
. SELECTIVE DISSEMINATION OF INFORMATION

: NEEDS
INFORMATION NEEDS

: NETWORKS
INFORMATION NETWORKS
. LIBRARY NETWORKS
.. BIBLIOGRAPHIC UTILITIES

:: SERVICES
: INFORMATION SERVICES
INFORMATION PROCESSING
. DATA COLLECTION
.. SAMPLING
... ITEM SAMPLING
. DATA PROCESSING
.. INPUT OUTPUT
... KEYBOARDING (DATA ENTRY)
.. TIME SHARING
. DOCUMENTATION
.. ABSTRACTING
.. BIBLIOMETRICS
... CITATION ANALYSIS
.... BIBLIOGRAPHIC COUPLING
.. CATALOGING
... MACHINE READABLE CATALOGING
.. FILING
.. INDEXING
... AUTOMATIC INDEXING
. INFORMATION RETRIEVAL
.. ONLINE SEARCHING
. INFORMATION STORAGE
. WORD PROCESSING

::: SERVICES
:: INFORMATION SERVICES
: INFORMATION PROCESSING
INFORMATION RETRIEVAL
. ONLINE SEARCHING

:: LIBERAL ARTS
: SCIENCES
INFORMATION SCIENCE
. COMPUTER SCIENCE
.. PROGRAMING
. LIBRARY SCIENCE

::: GROUPS
:: PERSONNEL
: PROFESSIONAL PERSONNEL
INFORMATION SCIENTISTS
. LIBRARIANS

INFORMATION SEEKING
. SEARCH STRATEGIES

: SERVICES
INFORMATION SERVICES
. COMMUNITY INFORMATION SERVICES
.. HOTLINES (PUBLIC)
. INFORMATION DISSEMINATION
.. PROPAGANDA
.. PUBLICITY
... ADVERTISING
.... TELEVISION COMMERCIALS
... INSTITUTIONAL ADVANCEMENT
.. REFERRAL
.. SELECTIVE DISSEMINATION OF INFORMATION
. INFORMATION PROCESSING
.. DATA COLLECTION
... SAMPLING
.... ITEM SAMPLING
.. DATA PROCESSING
... INPUT OUTPUT
.... KEYBOARDING (DATA ENTRY)
... TIME SHARING
.. DOCUMENTATION
... ABSTRACTING
... BIBLIOMETRICS
.... CITATION ANALYSIS
..... BIBLIOGRAPHIC COUPLING
... CATALOGING
.... MACHINE READABLE CATALOGING
... FILING
... INDEXING
.... AUTOMATIC INDEXING
.. INFORMATION RETRIEVAL
... ONLINE SEARCHING
.. INFORMATION STORAGE
.. WORD PROCESSING
. LIBRARY SERVICES
.. LIBRARY CIRCULATION
... INTERLIBRARY LOANS
.. LIBRARY EXTENSION
.. LIBRARY TECHNICAL PROCESSES
... LIBRARY ACQUISITION
.... LIBRARY MATERIAL SELECTION
. REFERENCE SERVICES
. VIDEOTEX

INFORMATION SOURCES
. ARCHIVES
. DATABASES
.. ONLINE CATALOGS
. INFORMATION CENTERS

INFORMATION SOURCES
(CONTINUED)

. . CLEARINGHOUSES
. LIBRARIES
. . ACADEMIC LIBRARIES
. . . COLLEGE LIBRARIES
. . BRANCH LIBRARIES
. . DEPOSITORY LIBRARIES
. . PUBLIC LIBRARIES
. . . COUNTY LIBRARIES
. . . REGIONAL LIBRARIES
. . RESEARCH LIBRARIES
. . SCHOOL LIBRARIES
. . SPECIAL LIBRARIES
. . . FILM LIBRARIES
. . . GOVERNMENT LIBRARIES
. . . . NATIONAL LIBRARIES
. . . . STATE LIBRARIES
. . . INSTITUTIONAL LIBRARIES
. . . . HOSPITAL LIBRARIES
. . . . PRISON LIBRARIES
. . . LAW LIBRARIES
. . . MEDICAL LIBRARIES
. PRIMARY SOURCES

: STORAGE
: : : SERVICES
: : INFORMATION SERVICES
: INFORMATION PROCESSING
INFORMATION STORAGE

INFORMATION SYSTEMS
. COMPUTER MANAGED
INSTRUCTION
. DIAL ACCESS INFORMATION
SYSTEMS
. MANAGEMENT INFORMATION
SYSTEMS

: TECHNOLOGY
INFORMATION TECHNOLOGY

: THEORIES
INFORMATION THEORY

INFORMATION TRANSFER

INFORMATION UTILIZATION
. EVALUATION UTILIZATION
. RESEARCH UTILIZATION

INHIBITION

: ALPHABETS
INITIAL TEACHING ALPHABET

: DISABILITIES
INJURIES

: : GEOGRAPHIC REGIONS
: URBAN AREAS
INNER CITY

: : LANGUAGE ARTS
: SPEECH
INNER SPEECH (SUBVOCAL)

INNOVATION
. BUILDING INNOVATION
. EDUCATIONAL INNOVATION
. . INSTRUCTIONAL INNOVATION

: : : : : LIBERAL ARTS
: : : : SCIENCES
: : : NATURAL SCIENCES
: : PHYSICAL SCIENCES
: CHEMISTRY
INORGANIC CHEMISTRY

: PROGRAMS
INPLANT PROGRAMS

: : : : SERVICES
: : : INFORMATION SERVICES
: : INFORMATION PROCESSING
: DATA PROCESSING
INPUT OUTPUT
. KEYBOARDING (DATA ENTRY)

: : METHODS
: EVALUATION METHODS
INPUT OUTPUT ANALYSIS

: : : EQUIPMENT
: : ELECTRONIC EQUIPMENT
: COMPUTERS
INPUT OUTPUT DEVICES
. OPTICAL SCANNERS

: METHODS
INQUIRY

: : DISCIPLINE
: SUSPENSION
IN SCHOOL SUSPENSION

: : : HAZARDOUS MATERIALS
: : POISONS
: PESTICIDES
INSECTICIDES

: EDUCATION
INSERVICE EDUCATION
. INSERVICE TEACHER
EDUCATION

: : : EDUCATION
: : PROFESSIONAL EDUCATION
: TEACHER EDUCATION
: : EDUCATION
: INSERVICE EDUCATION
INSERVICE TEACHER EDUCATION

: : METHODS
: EVALUATION METHODS
INSPECTION

: : : GROUPS
: : STUDENTS
: COLLEGE STUDENTS
IN STATE STUDENTS

: PROGRAMS
INSTITUTES (TRAINING
PROGRAMS)

: : GOVERNANCE
: ADMINISTRATION
INSTITUTIONAL ADMINISTRATION
. LIBRARY ADMINISTRATION
. SCHOOL ADMINISTRATION
. . COLLEGE ADMINISTRATION
. . SCHOOL BASED MANAGEMENT

: : : : SERVICES
: : : INFORMATION SERVICES
: : INFORMATION
DISSEMINATION
: : COMMUNICATION (THOUGHT
TRANSFER)
: PUBLICITY
INSTITUTIONAL ADVANCEMENT

INSTITUTIONAL AUTONOMY
. SCHOOL BASED MANAGEMENT

INSTITUTIONAL
CHARACTERISTICS
. SCHOOL SIZE

: : BEHAVIOR
: COOPERATION
INSTITUTIONAL COOPERATION
. COLLEGE SCHOOL
COOPERATION
. INTERCOLLEGIATE
COOPERATION
. LIBRARY COOPERATION

: ENVIRONMENT
INSTITUTIONAL ENVIRONMENT
. COLLEGE ENVIRONMENT

: EVALUATION
INSTITUTIONAL EVALUATION

: GROUPS
INSTITUTIONALIZED PERSONS
. PRISONERS

: : : INSTITUTIONS
: : : INFORMATION SOURCES
: : LIBRARIES
: SPECIAL LIBRARIES
INSTITUTIONAL LIBRARIES
. HOSPITAL LIBRARIES
. PRISON LIBRARIES

: : OBJECTIVES
: ORGANIZATIONAL OBJECTIVES
INSTITUTIONAL MISSION

: : GROUPS
: PERSONNEL
INSTITUTIONAL PERSONNEL

: RESEARCH
INSTITUTIONAL RESEARCH

INSTITUTIONAL ROLE
. AGENCY ROLE
. CHURCH ROLE
. COURT ROLE
. LIBRARY ROLE
. SCHOOL ROLE
. . COLLEGE ROLE

: : : INSTITUTIONS
: : SCHOOLS
: SPECIAL SCHOOLS
INSTITUTIONAL SCHOOLS
. HOSPITAL SCHOOLS

INSTITUTIONAL SURVIVAL

INSTITUTIONS
. BLACK INSTITUTIONS
. . BLACK COLLEGES
. CHURCHES
. COURTS
. . FEDERAL COURTS
. . JUVENILE COURTS
. . STATE COURTS
. HOSPITALS
. . PSYCHIATRIC HOSPITALS
. . TEACHING HOSPITALS
. LIBRARIES
. . ACADEMIC LIBRARIES
. . . COLLEGE LIBRARIES
. . BRANCH LIBRARIES
. . DEPOSITORY LIBRARIES
. . PUBLIC LIBRARIES
. . . COUNTY LIBRARIES
. . . REGIONAL LIBRARIES
. . RESEARCH LIBRARIES
. . SCHOOL LIBRARIES
. . SPECIAL LIBRARIES
. . . FILM LIBRARIES
. . . GOVERNMENT LIBRARIES
. . . . NATIONAL LIBRARIES
. . . . STATE LIBRARIES
. . . INSTITUTIONAL LIBRARIES
. . . . HOSPITAL LIBRARIES
. . . . PRISON LIBRARIES
. . . LAW LIBRARIES
. . . MEDICAL LIBRARIES
. PEER INSTITUTIONS
. PHILANTHROPIC FOUNDATIONS
. RESIDENTIAL INSTITUTIONS
. . BOARDING SCHOOLS
. . . RESIDENTIAL SCHOOLS
. . CORRECTIONAL
INSTITUTIONS
. . NURSING HOMES
. . PERSONAL CARE HOMES
. . RESIDENTIAL COLLEGES
. SCHOOLS
. . AFFILIATED SCHOOLS
. . BILINGUAL SCHOOLS
. . BOARDING SCHOOLS
. . . RESIDENTIAL SCHOOLS
. . BRITISH INFANT SCHOOLS
. . COLLEGES
. . . AGRICULTURAL COLLEGES
. . . BLACK COLLEGES
. . . CHURCH RELATED COLLEGES
. . . CLUSTER COLLEGES
. . . COMMUTER COLLEGES
. . . DENTAL SCHOOLS
. . . DEVELOPING INSTITUTIONS
. . . EXPERIMENTAL COLLEGES
. . . LAW SCHOOLS
. . . LIBRARY SCHOOLS
. . . MEDICAL SCHOOLS
. . . MULTICAMPUS COLLEGES
. . . NONCAMPUS COLLEGES
. . . PRIVATE COLLEGES
. . . PUBLIC COLLEGES
. . . . COMMUNITY COLLEGES
. . . . STATE COLLEGES
. . . . . STATE UNIVERSITIES
. . . RESIDENTIAL COLLEGES
. . . SELECTIVE COLLEGES
. . . SINGLE SEX COLLEGES
. . . SMALL COLLEGES
. . . TWO YEAR COLLEGES
. . . . COMMUNITY COLLEGES
. . . . TECHNICAL INSTITUTES
. . . UNIVERSITIES
. . . . LAND GRANT
UNIVERSITIES
. . . . OPEN UNIVERSITIES
. . . . RESEARCH UNIVERSITIES
. . . . STATE UNIVERSITIES
. . . . URBAN UNIVERSITIES
. . . UPPER DIVISION COLLEGES
. . COMMUNITY SCHOOLS
. . CONSOLIDATED SCHOOLS
. . CORRESPONDENCE SCHOOLS
. . DAY SCHOOLS
. . DISADVANTAGED SCHOOLS
. . ELEMENTARY SCHOOLS
. . EXPERIMENTAL SCHOOLS
. . . EXPERIMENTAL COLLEGES
. . FOLK SCHOOLS
. . FREEDOM SCHOOLS
. . FREE SCHOOLS
. . LABORATORY SCHOOLS
. . MAGNET SCHOOLS
. . MIDDLE SCHOOLS
. . MILITARY SCHOOLS
. . MULTIUNIT SCHOOLS
. . NEIGHBORHOOD SCHOOLS
. . NURSERY SCHOOLS
. . OPEN PLAN SCHOOLS
. . PRIVATE SCHOOLS
. . . PAROCHIAL SCHOOLS
. . . . CATHOLIC SCHOOLS
. . . PRIVATE COLLEGES
. . . PROPRIETARY SCHOOLS
. . PUBLIC SCHOOLS
. . RACIALLY BALANCED
SCHOOLS
. . REGIONAL SCHOOLS
. . RURAL SCHOOLS
. . SCHOOLS OF EDUCATION
. . SECONDARY SCHOOLS
. . . HIGH SCHOOLS
. . . . VOCATIONAL HIGH
SCHOOLS
. . . JUNIOR HIGH SCHOOLS
. . SINGLE SEX SCHOOLS
. . . SINGLE SEX COLLEGES
. . SLUM SCHOOLS
. . SMALL SCHOOLS
. . . ONE TEACHER SCHOOLS
. . . SMALL COLLEGES
. . SPECIAL SCHOOLS
. . . INSTITUTIONAL SCHOOLS
. . . . HOSPITAL SCHOOLS
. . . RESIDENTIAL SCHOOLS
. . STATE SCHOOLS
. . . STATE COLLEGES
. . . . STATE UNIVERSITIES
. . SUBURBAN SCHOOLS
. . SUMMER SCHOOLS

INSTITUTIONS
(CONTINUED)

.. TRADITIONAL SCHOOLS
.. TRANSITIONAL SCHOOLS
.. URBAN SCHOOLS
... URBAN UNIVERSITIES
.. VOCATIONAL SCHOOLS
... VOCATIONAL HIGH SCHOOLS
.. YEAR ROUND SCHOOLS

INSTRUCTION
. ASSIGNMENTS
.. HOMEWORK
.. READING ASSIGNMENTS
.. RESEARCH PAPERS
(STUDENTS)
. CLOTHING INSTRUCTION
. COLLEGE INSTRUCTION
. CONCEPT TEACHING
. COOKING INSTRUCTION
. ETHICAL INSTRUCTION
. FIELD INSTRUCTION
. FOODS INSTRUCTION
. GEOGRAPHY INSTRUCTION
. GROUP INSTRUCTION
.. LARGE GROUP INSTRUCTION
.. SMALL GROUP INSTRUCTION
. HOME INSTRUCTION
. HUMANITIES INSTRUCTION
.. HISTORY INSTRUCTION
.. NATIVE LANGUAGE
INSTRUCTION
... ENGLISH INSTRUCTION
.. SECOND LANGUAGE
INSTRUCTION
. INDIVIDUAL INSTRUCTION
.. TUTORING
... PROGRAMED TUTORING
. LIBRARY INSTRUCTION
. MASS INSTRUCTION
. MATHEMATICS INSTRUCTION
.. REMEDIAL MATHEMATICS
. NUTRITION INSTRUCTION
. READING INSTRUCTION
.. BASAL READING
.. CONTENT AREA READING
.. CORRECTIVE READING
.. DIRECTED READING
ACTIVITY
.. INDIVIDUALIZED READING
.. REMEDIAL READING
.. SUSTAINED SILENT READING
. REMEDIAL INSTRUCTION
.. REMEDIAL MATHEMATICS
.. REMEDIAL READING
. SCIENCE INSTRUCTION
. SEWING INSTRUCTION
. SPEECH INSTRUCTION
.. PRONUNCIATION
INSTRUCTION
. SPELLING INSTRUCTION
. TELEPHONE USAGE
INSTRUCTION
. TEST COACHING
. TEXTILES INSTRUCTION
. WRITING INSTRUCTION
.. CONTENT AREA WRITING
.. FRESHMAN COMPOSITION

: DESIGN
INSTRUCTIONAL DESIGN

:: DEVELOPMENT
: EDUCATIONAL DEVELOPMENT
INSTRUCTIONAL DEVELOPMENT

INSTRUCTIONAL EFFECTIVENESS

:: EDUCATIONAL MEDIA
: INSTRUCTIONAL MATERIALS
:: VISUAL AIDS
:: NONPRINT MEDIA
:: MASS MEDIA
: FILMS
:: EDUCATIONAL MEDIA
: AUDIOVISUAL AIDS
INSTRUCTIONAL FILMS

:: IMPROVEMENT
: EDUCATIONAL IMPROVEMENT
INSTRUCTIONAL IMPROVEMENT

:: INNOVATION
: EDUCATIONAL INNOVATION
INSTRUCTIONAL INNOVATION

:: ABILITY
: LEADERSHIP
INSTRUCTIONAL LEADERSHIP

: EVALUATION
INSTRUCTIONAL MATERIAL
EVALUATION
. TEXTBOOK EVALUATION

: EDUCATIONAL MEDIA
INSTRUCTIONAL MATERIALS
. ADVANCE ORGANIZERS
. BILINGUAL INSTRUCTIONAL
MATERIALS
. COURSEWARE
. EXPERIENCE CHARTS
. INSTRUCTIONAL FILMS
. LABORATORY MANUALS
. LEARNING MODULES
. MANIPULATIVE MATERIALS
. PROBLEM SETS
. PROGRAMED INSTRUCTIONAL
MATERIALS
. PROTOCOL MATERIALS
. STUDENT DEVELOPED
MATERIALS
.. STUDENT WRITING MODELS
. STUDY GUIDES
. TEACHER DEVELOPED
MATERIALS
.. TEACHER MADE TESTS
. TEXTBOOKS
.. HISTORY TEXTBOOKS
.. MULTICULTURAL TEXTBOOKS
. WORKBOOKS

INSTRUCTIONAL PROGRAM
DIVISIONS
. GRADE 1
. GRADE 2
. GRADE 3
. GRADE 4
. GRADE 5
. GRADE 6
. GRADE 7
. GRADE 8
. GRADE 9
. GRADE 10
. GRADE 11
. GRADE 12
. INTERMEDIATE GRADES
. KINDERGARTEN

INSTRUCTIONAL PROGRAMS (1966
1980)

:: COSTS
: STUDENT COSTS
INSTRUCTIONAL STUDENT COSTS
. TUITION

:: TECHNOLOGY
: EDUCATIONAL TECHNOLOGY
INSTRUCTIONAL SYSTEMS

:::: GROUPS
::: PERSONNEL
:: PROFESSIONAL PERSONNEL
: TEACHERS
:::: GROUPS
::: PERSONNEL
:: ADMINISTRATORS
: COORDINATORS
INSTRUCTOR COORDINATORS

INSTRUMENTATION
. VISIBLE SPEECH

::: GROUPS
:: PERSONNEL
: PARAPROFESSIONAL
PERSONNEL
INSTRUMENTATION TECHNICIANS

: METHODS
INSURANCE
. FIRE INSURANCE
. HEALTH INSURANCE
. UNEMPLOYMENT INSURANCE
. WORKERS COMPENSATION

:: BUSINESS
: INDUSTRY
INSURANCE COMPANIES

: OCCUPATIONS
INSURANCE OCCUPATIONS

::: SYMBOLS (MATHEMATICS)
:: NUMBERS
: RATIONAL NUMBERS
INTEGERS
. PRIME NUMBERS

: ACTIVITIES
INTEGRATED ACTIVITIES
. INTEGRATED CURRICULUM

:: ACTIVITIES
: INTEGRATED ACTIVITIES
: CURRICULUM
INTEGRATED CURRICULUM

: READINESS
INTEGRATION READINESS

:: RESEARCH
: BEHAVIORAL SCIENCE
RESEARCH
INTEGRATION STUDIES

INTEGRITY

::: DEVELOPMENT
:: INDIVIDUAL DEVELOPMENT
: COGNITIVE DEVELOPMENT
INTELLECTUAL DEVELOPMENT

INTELLECTUAL DISCIPLINES

:: BACKGROUND
: EXPERIENCE
INTELLECTUAL EXPERIENCE

INTELLECTUAL FREEDOM

:::: LIBERAL ARTS
::: SCIENCES
:: SOCIAL SCIENCES
::: LIBERAL ARTS
:: HUMANITIES
: HISTORY
INTELLECTUAL HISTORY
. ART HISTORY
. LITERARY HISTORY

: OWNERSHIP
INTELLECTUAL PROPERTY
. COPYRIGHTS
. PATENTS

:: INDIVIDUAL
CHARACTERISTICS
: PSYCHOLOGICAL
CHARACTERISTICS
INTELLIGENCE
. COMPREHENSION
.. LISTENING COMPREHENSION
.. READING COMPREHENSION
. FORMAL OPERATIONS
. MENTAL AGE

:: DIFFERENCES
: INDIVIDUAL DIFFERENCES
INTELLIGENCE DIFFERENCES

: RATIOS (MATHEMATICS)
INTELLIGENCE QUOTIENT

::: MEASURES (INDIVIDUALS)
:: TESTS
: COGNITIVE TESTS
INTELLIGENCE TESTS

:: CURRICULUM
: MODERN LANGUAGE
CURRICULUM
:: CURRICULUM
: COURSES
INTENSIVE LANGUAGE COURSES

: LEARNING
INTENTIONAL LEARNING

: RELATIONSHIP
INTERACTION
. APTITUDE TREATMENT
INTERACTION
. FEEDBACK
.. BIOFEEDBACK
. GROUP DYNAMICS

:: METHODS
: RESEARCH METHODOLOGY
INTERACTION PROCESS ANALYSIS

:::: EQUIPMENT
::: ELECTRONIC EQUIPMENT
:: COMPUTERS
: ONLINE SYSTEMS
INTERACTIVE VIDEO

::: BEHAVIOR
:: COOPERATION
: INSTITUTIONAL COOPERATION
::: BEHAVIOR
:: COOPERATION
: EDUCATIONAL COOPERATION
INTERCOLLEGIATE COOPERATION

: COMMUNICATION (THOUGHT
TRANSFER)
INTERCULTURAL COMMUNICATION

: PROGRAMS
INTERCULTURAL PROGRAMS

: METHODS
INTERDISCIPLINARY APPROACH

: POLICY
INTERDISTRICT POLICIES

: INCOME
: COSTS
INTEREST (FINANCE)

: MEASURES (INDIVIDUALS)
INTEREST INVENTORIES

::: RESEARCH
:: BEHAVIORAL SCIENCE
RESEARCH
: PSYCHOLOGICAL STUDIES
INTEREST RESEARCH

INTERESTS
. CHILDHOOD INTERESTS
. READING INTERESTS
. SCIENCE INTERESTS
. STUDENT INTERESTS
. VOCATIONAL INTERESTS

: : : RELATIONSHIP
: : HUMAN RELATIONS
: INTERGROUP RELATIONS
INTERFAITH RELATIONS

: : COGNITIVE PROCESSES
: LANGUAGE PROCESSING
INTERFERENCE (LANGUAGE)

: PROGRAMS
INTERGENERATIONAL PROGRAMS

: EDUCATION
INTERGROUP EDUCATION
. MULTICULTURAL EDUCATION

: : RELATIONSHIP
: HUMAN RELATIONS
INTERGROUP RELATIONS
. ETHNIC RELATIONS
. INTERFAITH RELATIONS
. RACIAL RELATIONS

: DESIGN
INTERIOR DESIGN

: FACILITIES
INTERIOR SPACE

: LANGUAGE
INTERLANGUAGE

: : : : SERVICES
: : : INFORMATION SERVICES
: : LIBRARY SERVICES
: LIBRARY CIRCULATION
INTERLIBRARY LOANS

: : : RELATIONSHIP
: : INTERPERSONAL RELATIONSHIP
: MARRIAGE
INTERMARRIAGE

INTERMEDIATE ADMINISTRATIVE UNITS

: INSTRUCTIONAL PROGRAM DIVISIONS
INTERMEDIATE GRADES

: DIFFERENCES
INTERMODE DIFFERENCES

: : TECHNOLOGY
: MEDICINE
INTERNAL MEDICINE

: : BEHAVIOR
: COOPERATION
INTERNATIONAL COOPERATION

: : : : BEHAVIOR
: : : SOCIAL BEHAVIOR
: : ANTISOCIAL BEHAVIOR
: CRIME
INTERNATIONAL CRIMES

: EDUCATION
INTERNATIONAL EDUCATION

INTERNATIONAL EDUCATIONAL EXCHANGE

: : STANDARDS
: LAWS
INTERNATIONAL LAW

: : GROUPS
: ORGANIZATIONS (GROUPS)
INTERNATIONAL ORGANIZATIONS

: PROGRAMS
INTERNATIONAL PROGRAMS

: RELATIONSHIP
INTERNATIONAL RELATIONS

: : : LIBERAL ARTS
: : SCIENCES
: SOCIAL SCIENCES
INTERNATIONAL STUDIES

INTERNATIONAL TRADE

: VOCABULARY
INTERNATIONAL TRADE VOCABULARY

: PROGRAMS
: : LEARNING
: EXPERIENTIAL LEARNING
INTERNSHIP PROGRAMS

: : RELATIONSHIP
: INTERPERSONAL RELATIONSHIP
INTERPERSONAL ATTRACTION

: COMMUNICATION (THOUGHT TRANSFER)
INTERPERSONAL COMMUNICATION

: : ABILITY
: COMPETENCE
INTERPERSONAL COMPETENCE

: RELATIONSHIP
INTERPERSONAL RELATIONSHIP
. BOARD ADMINISTRATOR RELATIONSHIP
. COUNSELOR CLIENT RELATIONSHIP
. DATING (SOCIAL)
. EMPLOYER EMPLOYEE RELATIONSHIP
. FAMILY RELATIONSHIP
. . PARENT CHILD RELATIONSHIP
. . . PARENT STUDENT RELATIONSHIP
. FRIENDSHIP
. GROUP UNITY
. HELPING RELATIONSHIP
. INTERPERSONAL ATTRACTION
. INTERPROFESSIONAL RELATIONSHIP
. KINSHIP
. MARRIAGE
. . INTERMARRIAGE
. . REMARRIAGE
. PEER RELATIONSHIP
. PHYSICIAN PATIENT RELATIONSHIP
. RAPPORT
. SIGNIFICANT OTHERS
. TEACHER ADMINISTRATOR RELATIONSHIP
. TEACHER STUDENT RELATIONSHIP

: : GROUPS
: PERSONNEL
INTERPRETERS

INTERPRETIVE READING (1966 1980)

: : ABILITY
: SKILLS
INTERPRETIVE SKILLS

: : RELATIONSHIP
: INTERPERSONAL RELATIONSHIP
INTERPROFESSIONAL RELATIONSHIP

: : : : STANDARDS
: : : CRITERIA
: : EVALUATION CRITERIA
: RELIABILITY
INTERRATER RELIABILITY

: : COMMUNICATION (THOUGHT TRANSFER)
: ORGANIZATIONAL COMMUNICATION
INTERSCHOOL COMMUNICATION

: PROGRAMS
INTERSTATE PROGRAMS

INTERVALS

INTERVENTION
. CRISIS INTERVENTION

: : METHODS
: EVALUATION METHODS
INTERVIEWS
. EMPLOYMENT INTERVIEWS
. FIELD INTERVIEWS

: : : LINGUISTICS
: : PHONOLOGY
: SUPRASEGMENTALS
INTONATION

: : : ACTIVITIES
: : PHYSICAL ACTIVITIES
: ATHLETICS
INTRAMURAL ATHLETICS

: : CURRICULUM
: COURSES
INTRODUCTORY COURSES

: COGNITIVE PROCESSES
INTUITION

INVENTIONS

: RESEARCH
INVESTIGATIONS

INVESTMENT
. HUMAN CAPITAL

: : LITERARY DEVICES
: : LANGUAGE
: FIGURATIVE LANGUAGE
IRONY

: CULTURE
ISLAMIC CULTURE

: : : LANGUAGES
: : INDO EUROPEAN LANGUAGES
: ROMANCE LANGUAGES
ITALIAN

: : GROUPS
: NORTH AMERICANS
: : GROUPS
: ETHNIC GROUPS
ITALIAN AMERICANS

: : : LIBERAL ARTS
: : HUMANITIES
: LITERATURE
ITALIAN LITERATURE

: : : : METHODS
: : : EVALUATION METHODS
: : DATA ANALYSIS
: STATISTICAL ANALYSIS
ITEM ANALYSIS

ITEM BANKS

: : : : LIBERAL ARTS
: : : MATHEMATICS
: : STATISTICS
: : : : : SERVICES
: : : : INFORMATION SERVICES
: : : INFORMATION PROCESSING
: : : : : METHODS
: : : : EVALUATION METHODS
: : : DATA ANALYSIS
: : DATA COLLECTION
: SAMPLING
ITEM SAMPLING

: : : : GROUPS
: : : PERSONNEL
: : PROFESSIONAL PERSONNEL
: TEACHERS
ITINERANT TEACHERS

: LANGUAGES
JAPANESE
. OKINAWAN

: : CULTURE
: NORTH AMERICAN CULTURE
JAPANESE AMERICAN CULTURE

: : GROUPS
: ETHNIC GROUPS
: : : GROUPS
: : NORTH AMERICANS
: ASIAN AMERICANS
JAPANESE AMERICANS

: : : LANGUAGES
: : MALAYO POLYNESIAN LANGUAGES
: INDONESIAN LANGUAGES
JAVANESE

: : : : LIBERAL ARTS
: : : HUMANITIES
: : FINE ARTS
: MUSIC
JAZZ

: PSYCHOLOGICAL PATTERNS
JEALOUSY

: : GROUPS
: RELIGIOUS CULTURAL GROUPS
JEWS

: : METHODS
: EVALUATION METHODS
JOB ANALYSIS

: GROUPS
JOB APPLICANTS

JOB APPLICATION

: DEVELOPMENT
JOB DEVELOPMENT
. JOB ENRICHMENT
. JOB SIMPLIFICATION

: : DEVELOPMENT
: JOB DEVELOPMENT
: ENRICHMENT
JOB ENRICHMENT

: REDUCTION IN FORCE
JOB LAYOFF

: : BEHAVIOR
: PERFORMANCE
JOB PERFORMANCE

: PLACEMENT
JOB PLACEMENT
. TEACHER PLACEMENT

: : ATTITUDES
: WORK ATTITUDES
JOB SATISFACTION

: METHODS
JOB SEARCH METHODS

: : EMPLOYMENT
: PART TIME EMPLOYMENT
JOB SHARING

: : DEVELOPMENT
: JOB DEVELOPMENT
JOB SIMPLIFICATION

: : ABILITY
: SKILLS
JOB SKILLS

: TRAINING
JOB TRAINING
. CUSTODIAN TRAINING
. OFF THE JOB TRAINING
. ON THE JOB TRAINING
. . APPRENTICESHIPS

: : : ACTIVITIES
: : PHYSICAL ACTIVITIES
: RUNNING
JOGGING

: TECHNOLOGY
JOURNALISM
. NEW JOURNALISM
. NEWS REPORTING
. NEWS WRITING
. PHOTOJOURNALISM

: EDUCATION
JOURNALISM EDUCATION

: RELIGION
JUDAISM

: GROUPS
JUDGES
. COURT JUDGES

: : : : METHODS
: : : EVALUATION METHODS
: : DATA ANALYSIS
: STATISTICAL ANALYSIS
JUDGMENT ANALYSIS TECHNIQUE

: : : INSTITUTIONS
: : SCHOOLS
: SECONDARY SCHOOLS
JUNIOR HIGH SCHOOLS

: : : GROUPS
: : STUDENTS
: SECONDARY SCHOOL STUDENTS
JUNIOR HIGH SCHOOL STUDENTS

JUSTICE

: : INSTITUTIONS
: COURTS
JUVENILE COURTS

: GROUPS
JUVENILE GANGS

: : : LANGUAGES
: : AFRO ASIATIC LANGUAGES
: BERBER LANGUAGES
KABYLE

: : LANGUAGES
: DRAVIDIAN LANGUAGES
KANNADA

: : LANGUAGES
: INDO EUROPEAN LANGUAGES
KASHMIRI

: : : : THEORIES
: : : LINGUISTIC THEORY
: : GENERATIVE GRAMMAR
: TRANSFORMATIONAL GENERATIVE GRAMMAR
: : : LANGUAGE PATTERNS
: : PARAGRAPHS
: SENTENCES
KERNEL SENTENCES

: : : : : SERVICES
: : : : INFORMATION SERVICES
: : : INFORMATION PROCESSING
: : DATA PROCESSING
: INPUT OUTPUT
: : : ABILITY
: : SKILLS
: BUSINESS SKILLS
KEYBOARDING (DATA ENTRY)

: INSTRUCTIONAL PROGRAM DIVISIONS
KINDERGARTEN

: : : : GROUPS
: : : AGE GROUPS
: : CHILDREN
: YOUNG CHILDREN
KINDERGARTEN CHILDREN

: : VISUAL AIDS
: : NONPRINT MEDIA
: : MASS MEDIA
: FILMS
KINESCOPE RECORDINGS

: : : METHODS
: : EDUCATIONAL METHODS
: TEACHING METHODS
KINESTHETIC METHODS

: : COGNITIVE PROCESSES
: PERCEPTION
KINESTHETIC PERCEPTION

: THEORIES
KINETIC MOLECULAR THEORY

: : : : : : LIBERAL ARTS
: : : : : SCIENCES
: : : : NATURAL SCIENCES
: : : PHYSICAL SCIENCES
: : PHYSICS
: MECHANICS (PHYSICS)
KINETICS
. DIFFUSION (PHYSICS)

: : RELATIONSHIP
: INTERPERSONAL RELATIONSHIP
KINSHIP

: VOCABULARY
KINSHIP TERMINOLOGY

: : : LANGUAGES
: : URALIC ALTAIC LANGUAGES
: TURKIC LANGUAGES
KIRGHIZ

: : : LANGUAGES
: : AFRICAN LANGUAGES
: BANTU LANGUAGES
KIRUNDI

: : : LANGUAGES
: : AFRICAN LANGUAGES
: BANTU LANGUAGES
KITUBA

: ACHIEVEMENT
KNOWLEDGE LEVEL

: LANGUAGES
KOREAN

: : GROUPS
: ETHNIC GROUPS
: : : GROUPS
: : NORTH AMERICANS
: ASIAN AMERICANS
KOREAN AMERICANS

: CULTURE
KOREAN CULTURE

: : LANGUAGES
: INDO EUROPEAN LANGUAGES
KURDISH

: : ORGANIZATION
: CLASSIFICATION
LABELING (OF PERSONS)

LABOR
. CHILD LABOR
. FARM LABOR

: FACILITIES
LABORATORIES
. LEARNING LABORATORIES
. . LANGUAGE LABORATORIES
. MOBILE LABORATORIES
. REGIONAL LABORATORIES
. SCIENCE LABORATORIES
. WRITING LABORATORIES

: ANIMALS
LABORATORY ANIMALS

: EQUIPMENT
LABORATORY EQUIPMENT
. MICROSCOPES

: EXPERIMENTS
LABORATORY EXPERIMENTS

: : EDUCATIONAL MEDIA
: INSTRUCTIONAL MATERIALS
: : : PUBLICATIONS
: : REFERENCE MATERIALS
: GUIDES
LABORATORY MANUALS

: METHODS
LABORATORY PROCEDURES
. CHROMATOGRAPHY
. CULTURING TECHNIQUES

: SAFETY
LABORATORY SAFETY

: : INSTITUTIONS
: SCHOOLS
LABORATORY SCHOOLS

LABORATORY TECHNIQUES (1967 1980)

: TECHNOLOGY
LABORATORY TECHNOLOGY

: TRAINING
LABORATORY TRAINING

LABOR CONDITIONS

LABOR DEMANDS

: : : : LIBERAL ARTS
: : : SCIENCES
: : SOCIAL SCIENCES
: ECONOMICS
LABOR ECONOMICS

: : EDUCATION
: ADULT EDUCATION
LABOR EDUCATION

: : : : GROUPS
: : : PERSONNEL
: : NONPROFESSIONAL PERSONNEL
: UNSKILLED WORKERS
LABORERS
. AGRICULTURAL LABORERS
. . MIGRANT WORKERS
. . SEASONAL LABORERS
. AUXILIARY LABORERS

: : RESOURCES
: HUMAN RESOURCES
LABOR FORCE

: DEVELOPMENT
LABOR FORCE DEVELOPMENT
. MANAGEMENT DEVELOPMENT
. PROFESSIONAL DEVELOPMENT
. . FACULTY DEVELOPMENT
. STAFF DEVELOPMENT
. . FACULTY DEVELOPMENT

: GROUPS
LABOR FORCE NONPARTICIPANTS

: LEGISLATION
LABOR LEGISLATION

LABOR MARKET
. TEACHER SUPPLY AND DEMAND
. . TEACHER SHORTAGE

: NEEDS
LABOR NEEDS
. PERSONNEL NEEDS

: PROBLEMS
LABOR PROBLEMS

: RELATIONSHIP
LABOR RELATIONS

: STANDARDS
LABOR STANDARDS

: : RESOURCES
: HUMAN RESOURCES
LABOR SUPPLY

LABOR TURNOVER

LABOR UTILIZATION
. STAFF UTILIZATION

: : : : ACTIVITIES
: : : PHYSICAL ACTIVITIES
: : ATHLETICS
: TEAM SPORTS
LACROSSE

LAND ACQUISITION

: : : : INSTITUTIONS
: : : SCHOOLS
: : COLLEGES
: UNIVERSITIES
LAND GRANT UNIVERSITIES

: GROUPS
LANDLORDS

: : : : TECHNOLOGY
: : : AGRICULTURE
: : HORTICULTURE
: ORNAMENTAL HORTICULTURE
LANDSCAPING

: LAND USE
LAND SETTLEMENT
. RURAL RESETTLEMENT

LAND USE
. LAND SETTLEMENT
. . RURAL RESETTLEMENT
. SOIL CONSERVATION

LANGUAGE
. ARTIFICIAL LANGUAGES
. CHILD LANGUAGE
. FIGURATIVE LANGUAGE
. . ALLEGORY
. . AMBIGUITY
. . ANTITHESIS
. . IMAGERY
. . IRONY
. . METAPHORS
. . PUNS
. . SYMBOLS (LITERARY)
. INTERLANGUAGE
. LANGUAGE OF INSTRUCTION
. LANGUAGES FOR SPECIAL PURPOSES
. . ENGLISH FOR SPECIAL PURPOSES
. . . ENGLISH FOR ACADEMIC PURPOSES
. . . ENGLISH FOR SCIENCE AND TECHNOLOGY
. . . VOCATIONAL ENGLISH (SECOND LANGUAGE)
. LANGUAGE UNIVERSALS
. OFFICIAL LANGUAGES
. ORAL LANGUAGE
. PROGRAMING LANGUAGES
. SECOND LANGUAGES
. . ENGLISH (SECOND LANGUAGE)
. . . ENGLISH FOR SPECIAL PURPOSES
. . . . ENGLISH FOR ACADEMIC PURPOSES
. . . . ENGLISH FOR SCIENCE AND TECHNOLOGY
. . . . VOCATIONAL ENGLISH (SECOND LANGUAGE)
. SIGN LANGUAGE
. . AMERICAN SIGN LANGUAGE
. SYMBOLIC LANGUAGE
. TONE LANGUAGES
. UNCOMMONLY TAUGHT LANGUAGES
. UNWRITTEN LANGUAGES
. URBAN LANGUAGE
. WRITTEN LANGUAGE
. . BRAILLE
. . GRAPHEMES
. . IDEOGRAPHY
. . ORTHOGRAPHIC SYMBOLS
. . . DIACRITICAL MARKING
. . . LETTERS (ALPHABET)
. . . PHONETIC TRANSCRIPTION
. . PUNCTUATION
. . SHORTHAND

LANGUAGE ABILITY (1966 1980)

: : : : DEVELOPMENT
: : : INDIVIDUAL DEVELOPMENT
: : COGNITIVE DEVELOPMENT
: VERBAL DEVELOPMENT
LANGUAGE ACQUISITION

LANGUAGE AIDS (1966 1980)

LANGUAGE AND AREA CENTERS (1968 1980)

: APTITUDE
LANGUAGE APTITUDE

LANGUAGE ARTS
. DEBATE
. HANDWRITING
. . CURSIVE WRITING
. . MANUSCRIPT WRITING (HANDLETTERING)
. LISTENING
. OUTLINING (DISCOURSE)
. READING
. . BASAL READING
. . BEGINNING READING
. . CONTENT AREA READING
. . CORRECTIVE READING
. . CRITICAL READING
. . DIRECTED READING ACTIVITY
. . EARLY READING
. . FUNCTIONAL READING
. . INDEPENDENT READING
. . INDIVIDUALIZED READING
. . MUSIC READING
. . ORAL READING
. . READING ALOUD TO OTHERS
. . RECREATIONAL READING
. . REMEDIAL READING
. . SILENT READING
. . SPEED READING
. . STORY READING
. . SUSTAINED SILENT READING
. RHETORIC
. . COHERENCE
. . PERSUASIVE DISCOURSE
. . RHETORICAL INVENTION
. SPEECH
. . ARTICULATION (SPEECH)
. . ARTIFICIAL SPEECH
. . INNER SPEECH (SUBVOCAL)
. . PRONUNCIATION
. . SPEECH ACTS
. . SPEECH COMPRESSION
. SPELLING
. . FINGER SPELLING
. STORY TELLING
. WRITING (COMPOSITION)
. . ABSTRACTING
. . CONTENT AREA WRITING
. . CREATIVE WRITING
. . DESCRIPTIVE WRITING
. . EXPOSITORY WRITING
. . FRESHMAN COMPOSITION
. . LOCAL COLOR WRITING
. . NEWS WRITING
. . NOTETAKING
. . PARAGRAPH COMPOSITION
. . PARALLELISM (LITERARY)
. . PLAYWRITING
. . PROPOSAL WRITING
. . TECHNICAL WRITING
. . WRITING FOR PUBLICATION

: ATTITUDES
LANGUAGE ATTITUDES
. GRAMMATICAL ACCEPTABILITY

: : ORGANIZATION
: CLASSIFICATION
LANGUAGE CLASSIFICATION
. LANGUAGE TYPOLOGY

LANGUAGE DOMINANCE

: ENRICHMENT
LANGUAGE ENRICHMENT

: ENROLLMENT
LANGUAGE ENROLLMENT

: : : METHODS
: : EDUCATIONAL METHODS
: TEACHING METHODS
LANGUAGE EXPERIENCE APPROACH

: : ABILITY
: LANGUAGE PROFICIENCY
LANGUAGE FLUENCY

LANGUAGE GUIDES (1966 1980)

: DISABILITIES
LANGUAGE HANDICAPS
. APHASIA
. DYSLEXIA

LANGUAGE INSTRUCTION (1966 1980)

: : : FACILITIES
: : LABORATORIES
: : : FACILITIES
: : EDUCATIONAL FACILITIES
: LEARNING LABORATORIES
LANGUAGE LABORATORIES

LANGUAGE LEARNING LEVELS (1967 1980)

LANGUAGE MAINTENANCE

: LANGUAGE
LANGUAGE OF INSTRUCTION

LANGUAGE PATTERNS
. IDIOMS
. LANGUAGE RHYTHM
. PARAGRAPHS
. . SENTENCES
. . . KERNEL SENTENCES
. PHONEME GRAPHEME CORRESPONDENCE

: : LINGUISTICS
: SOCIOLINGUISTICS
: PLANNING
LANGUAGE PLANNING
. LANGUAGE STANDARDIZATION

: COGNITIVE PROCESSES
LANGUAGE PROCESSING
. EXPRESSIVE LANGUAGE
. INTERFERENCE (LANGUAGE)
. READING PROCESSES
. . DECODING (READING)
. RECEPTIVE LANGUAGE

: ABILITY
LANGUAGE PROFICIENCY
. LANGUAGE FLUENCY
. THRESHOLD LEVEL (LANGUAGES)

LANGUAGE PROGRAMS (1966 1980)

: RESEARCH
LANGUAGE RESEARCH
. DIALECT STUDIES

: LANGUAGE PATTERNS
LANGUAGE RHYTHM

LANGUAGE ROLE

LANGUAGES
. AFRICAN LANGUAGES
. . AKAN
. . BANTU LANGUAGES
. . . BEMBA
. . . CHINYANJA
. . . GANDA
. . . KIRUNDI
. . . KITUBA
. . . LINGALA
. . . SHONA
. . . SISWATI
. . . SWAHILI
. . BASAA
. . BINI
. . DYULA
. . EWE
. . FULANI
. . GA
. . GBAYA
. . IBO
. . IGBO
. . LUO
. . MANDINGO
. . MENDE
. . MOSSI
. . NEMBE
. . SANGO
. . SARA
. . SUSU
. . WOLOF
. . YORUBA
. AFRO ASIATIC LANGUAGES
. . BERBER LANGUAGES
. . . KABYLE
. . . RIFF
. . CHAD LANGUAGES
. . . HAUSA
. . SEMITIC LANGUAGES
. . . AMHARIC
. . . ARABIC
. . . HEBREW
. . SOMALI
. AMERICAN INDIAN LANGUAGES
. . ATHAPASCAN LANGUAGES
. . . APACHE
. . . NAVAJO
. . AYMARA
. . CAKCHIQUEL
. . CHEROKEE
. . CHOCTAW
. . CREE
. . GUARANI
. . MAYAN LANGUAGES
. . . QUICHE
. . . YUCATEC
. . OJIBWA
. . POMO
. . QUECHUA
. . SALISH
. . TZELTAL
. . TZOTZIL
. . UTO AZTECAN LANGUAGES
. . . HOPI
. . . PAPAGO
. AMERICAN SIGN LANGUAGE
. AUSTRALIAN ABORIGINAL LANGUAGES
. AUSTRO ASIATIC LANGUAGES
. . CAMBODIAN
. BASQUE
. BURUSHASKI
. CAUCASIAN LANGUAGES
. CLASSICAL LANGUAGES
. . LATIN
. . SANSKRIT

LANGUAGES
(CONTINUED)

. CREOLES
. . GULLAH
. . HAITIAN CREOLE
. . MAURITIAN CREOLE
. . SIERRA LEONE CREOLE
. DIALECTS
. . BLACK DIALECTS
. . NONSTANDARD DIALECTS
. . REGIONAL DIALECTS
. . SOCIAL DIALECTS
. DRAVIDIAN LANGUAGES
. . KANNADA
. . MALAYALAM
. . TAMIL
. . TELUGU
. ESKIMO ALEUT LANGUAGES
. INDO EUROPEAN LANGUAGES
. . AFRIKAANS
. . ALBANIAN
. . ARMENIAN
. . BALTIC LANGUAGES
. . . LATVIAN
. . . LITHUANIAN
. . BALUCHI
. . BENGALI
. . DUTCH
. . ENGLISH
. . . BUSINESS ENGLISH
. . . ENGLISH (SECOND LANGUAGE)
. . . . ENGLISH FOR SPECIAL PURPOSES
. . . . . ENGLISH FOR ACADEMIC PURPOSES
. . . . . ENGLISH FOR SCIENCE AND TECHNOLOGY
. . . . . VOCATIONAL ENGLISH (SECOND LANGUAGE)
. . . MIDDLE ENGLISH
. . . NORTH AMERICAN ENGLISH
. . . OLD ENGLISH
. . . ORAL ENGLISH
. . GERMAN
. . . YIDDISH
. . GREEK
. . GUJARATI
. . HINDI
. . KASHMIRI
. . KURDISH
. . MARATHI
. . NEPALI
. . NORWEGIAN
. . OSSETIC
. . PANJABI
. . PASHTO
. . PERSIAN
. . ROMANCE LANGUAGES
. . . FRENCH
. . . ITALIAN
. . . LATIN
. . . PORTUGUESE
. . . RUMANIAN
. . . SPANISH
. . SINGHALESE
. . SLAVIC LANGUAGES
. . . BIELORUSSIAN
. . . BULGARIAN
. . . CZECH
. . . POLISH
. . . RUSSIAN
. . . SERBOCROATIAN
. . . SLOVENIAN
. . . UKRAINIAN
. . SWEDISH
. . TAJIK
. . URDU
. . WELSH
. JAPANESE
. . OKINAWAN
. KOREAN
. MALAYO POLYNESIAN LANGUAGES
. . CHAMORRO
. . HAWAIIAN
. . INDONESIAN LANGUAGES
. . . BIKOL
. . . DUSUN
. . . INDONESIAN
. . . JAVANESE
. . . MALAGASY
. . . MALAY
. . . MARANAO
. . . TAGALOG
. . . VISAYAN
. . . . CEBUANO
. . MELANESIAN LANGUAGES
. . SAMOAN
. MODERN LANGUAGES
. PIDGINS
. SINO TIBETAN LANGUAGES
. . BURMESE
. . CHINESE
. . . CANTONESE
. . . FOOCHOW
. . . MANDARIN CHINESE
. . LAO
. . THAI
. . TIBETAN
. URALIC ALTAIC LANGUAGES
. . FINNO UGRIC LANGUAGES
. . . CHEREMIS
. . . ESTONIAN
. . . FINNISH
. . . HUNGARIAN
. . . OSTYAK
. . . VOGUL
. . MANCHU
. . MONGOLIAN LANGUAGES
. . . BURIAT
. . . DAGUR
. . . MONGOLIAN
. . SAMOYED LANGUAGES
. . . YURAK
. . TURKIC LANGUAGES
. . . AZERBAIJANI
. . . BASHKIR
. . . CHUVASH
. . . KIRGHIZ
. . . TATAR
. . . TURKISH
. . . UZBEK
. . . YAKUT
. VIETNAMESE

: LANGUAGE
LANGUAGES FOR SPECIAL PURPOSES
. ENGLISH FOR SPECIAL PURPOSES
. . ENGLISH FOR ACADEMIC PURPOSES
. . ENGLISH FOR SCIENCE AND TECHNOLOGY
. . VOCATIONAL ENGLISH (SECOND LANGUAGE)

LANGUAGE SKILL ATTRITION

: : ABILITY
: SKILLS
LANGUAGE SKILLS
. AUDIOLINGUAL SKILLS
. . LISTENING SKILLS
. . SPEECH SKILLS
. COMMUNICATIVE COMPETENCE (LANGUAGES)
. . THRESHOLD LEVEL (LANGUAGES)
. READING SKILLS
. . READING COMPREHENSION
. . READING RATE
. VOCABULARY SKILLS
. WRITING SKILLS

: : : LINGUISTICS
: : SOCIOLINGUISTICS
: : PLANNING
: LANGUAGE PLANNING
LANGUAGE STANDARDIZATION

: : : LINGUISTICS
: : SOCIOLINGUISTICS
: LANGUAGE VARIATION
: LANGUAGE USAGE
LANGUAGE STYLES

: : : : GROUPS
: : : PERSONNEL
: : PROFESSIONAL PERSONNEL
: TEACHERS
LANGUAGE TEACHERS

: : : MEASURES (INDIVIDUALS)
: : TESTS
: VERBAL TESTS
LANGUAGE TESTS

: : : ORGANIZATION
: : CLASSIFICATION
: LANGUAGE CLASSIFICATION
LANGUAGE TYPOLOGY

: LANGUAGE
LANGUAGE UNIVERSALS

LANGUAGE USAGE
. LANGUAGE STYLES
. STANDARD SPOKEN USAGE

: : LINGUISTICS
: SOCIOLINGUISTICS
LANGUAGE VARIATION
. CREOLES
. . GULLAH
. . HAITIAN CREOLE
. . MAURITIAN CREOLE
. . SIERRA LEONE CREOLE
. DIALECTS
. . BLACK DIALECTS
. . NONSTANDARD DIALECTS
. . REGIONAL DIALECTS
. . SOCIAL DIALECTS
. LANGUAGE STYLES
. LINGUISTIC BORROWING
. PIDGINS

: : LANGUAGES
: SINO TIBETAN LANGUAGES
LAO

: : GROUPS
: INDOCHINESE
LAOTIANS

: : INSTRUCTION
: GROUP INSTRUCTION
LARGE GROUP INSTRUCTION

: READING MATERIALS
LARGE TYPE MATERIALS

LASERS

: : : GROUPS
: : AGE GROUPS
: CHILDREN
LATCHKEY CHILDREN

: : THEORIES
: TEST THEORY
LATENT TRAIT THEORY

: : INDIVIDUAL CHARACTERISTICS
: PHYSICAL CHARACTERISTICS
LATERAL DOMINANCE

: SCHOOL REGISTRATION
LATE REGISTRATION

: : : LANGUAGES
: : INDO EUROPEAN LANGUAGES
: ROMANCE LANGUAGES
: : LANGUAGES
: CLASSICAL LANGUAGES
LATIN

: CULTURE
LATIN AMERICAN CULTURE
. LUSO BRAZILIAN CULTURE
. PUERTO RICAN CULTURE

: : : : LIBERAL ARTS
: : : SCIENCES
: : SOCIAL SCIENCES
: : : LIBERAL ARTS
: : HUMANITIES
: HISTORY
LATIN AMERICAN HISTORY

: : : LIBERAL ARTS
: : HUMANITIES
: LITERATURE
LATIN AMERICAN LITERATURE

: GROUPS
LATIN AMERICANS
. CUBANS
. DOMINICANS
. HAITIANS
. MEXICANS
. . BRACEROS
. PUERTO RICANS

: : : : LIBERAL ARTS
: : : HUMANITIES
: : LITERATURE
: CLASSICAL LITERATURE
LATIN LITERATURE

: : : LANGUAGES
: : INDO EUROPEAN LANGUAGES
: BALTIC LANGUAGES
LATVIAN

: : OCCUPATIONS
: SERVICE OCCUPATIONS
LAUNDRY DRYCLEANING OCCUPATIONS

LAW ENFORCEMENT
. POLICE ACTION
. . SEARCH AND SEIZURE
. SENTENCING

: : : INSTITUTIONS
: : : INFORMATION SOURCES
: : LIBRARIES
: SPECIAL LIBRARIES
LAW LIBRARIES

: EDUCATION
LAW RELATED EDUCATION

: STANDARDS
LAWS
. CONSTITUTIONAL LAW
. CRIMINAL LAW
. INTERNATIONAL LAW
. SCHOOL LAW

: : : INSTITUTIONS
: : SCHOOLS
: COLLEGES
LAW SCHOOLS

: : : : GROUPS
: : : STUDENTS
: : COLLEGE STUDENTS
: GRADUATE STUDENTS
LAW STUDENTS

: : : GROUPS
: : PERSONNEL
: PROFESSIONAL PERSONNEL
LAWYERS

: : : : : LIBERAL ARTS
: : : : HUMANITIES
: : : FINE ARTS
: : VISUAL ARTS
: GRAPHIC ARTS
LAYOUT (PUBLICATIONS)

: GROUPS
LAY PEOPLE
. LAY TEACHERS

: : : : GROUPS
: : : PERSONNEL
: : PROFESSIONAL PERSONNEL
: TEACHERS
: : GROUPS
: LAY PEOPLE
LAY TEACHERS

: GROUPS
LEADERS
. COMMUNITY LEADERS
. YOUTH LEADERS

: : : PUBLICATIONS
: : REFERENCE MATERIALS
: GUIDES
LEADERS GUIDES

: ABILITY
LEADERSHIP
. BLACK LEADERSHIP
. INFORMAL LEADERSHIP
. INSTRUCTIONAL LEADERSHIP
. STUDENT LEADERSHIP

LEADERSHIP QUALITIES

: RESPONSIBILITY
LEADERSHIP RESPONSIBILITY

: BEHAVIOR
LEADERSHIP STYLES

: TRAINING
LEADERSHIP TRAINING

: : : DISABILITIES
: : DISEASES
: POISONING
LEAD POISONING

LEARNING
. ADULT LEARNING
. ASSOCIATIVE LEARNING
. . PAIRED ASSOCIATE LEARNING
. AURAL LEARNING
. DISCOVERY LEARNING
. DISCRIMINATION LEARNING
. EXPERIENTIAL LEARNING
. . FIELD EXPERIENCE PROGRAMS
. . . SUPERVISED FARM PRACTICE
. . INTERNSHIP PROGRAMS
. INCIDENTAL LEARNING
. INTENTIONAL LEARNING
. LIFELONG LEARNING
. MASTERY LEARNING
. MULTISENSORY LEARNING
. NONVERBAL LEARNING
. . PERCEPTUAL MOTOR LEARNING
. OBSERVATIONAL LEARNING
. PRIOR LEARNING
. ROTE LEARNING
. SECOND LANGUAGE LEARNING
. SEQUENTIAL LEARNING
. SERIAL LEARNING
. SYMBOLIC LEARNING
. TRANSFER OF TRAINING
. VERBAL LEARNING
. VISUAL LEARNING

: ACTIVITIES
LEARNING ACTIVITIES
. STUDY
. . HOME STUDY
. . . HOMEWORK
. . INDEPENDENT STUDY

: : FACILITIES
: RESOURCE CENTERS
: : FACILITIES
: EDUCATIONAL FACILITIES
LEARNING CENTERS (CLASSROOM)

: DISABILITIES
LEARNING DISABILITIES

: : BACKGROUND
: EXPERIENCE
LEARNING EXPERIENCE
. CLINICAL EXPERIENCE

: : FACILITIES
: LABORATORIES
: : FACILITIES
: EDUCATIONAL FACILITIES
LEARNING LABORATORIES
. LANGUAGE LABORATORIES

LEARNING MODALITIES

: : EDUCATIONAL MEDIA
: INSTRUCTIONAL MATERIALS
LEARNING MODULES

: MOTIVATION
LEARNING MOTIVATION

LEARNING PLATEAUS

: PROBLEMS
LEARNING PROBLEMS

: COGNITIVE PROCESSES
LEARNING PROCESSES
. BEHAVIOR CHAINING
. COGNITIVE MAPPING
. CONCEPT FORMATION
. DISCOVERY PROCESSES
. EXTINCTION (PSYCHOLOGY)
. GENERALIZATION
. . STIMULUS GENERALIZATION
. HABITUATION
. MEMORIZATION
. PRIMACY EFFECT

: READINESS
LEARNING READINESS

: : FACILITIES
: RESOURCE CENTERS
: : FACILITIES
: EDUCATIONAL FACILITIES
LEARNING RESOURCES CENTERS

: METHODS
LEARNING STRATEGIES
. READING STRATEGIES

: THEORIES
LEARNING THEORIES

: : : LIBERAL ARTS
: : MATHEMATICS
: STATISTICS
: : : : METHODS
: : : EVALUATION METHODS
: : DATA ANALYSIS
: STATISTICAL ANALYSIS
LEAST SQUARES STATISTICS

LEATHER

LEAVES OF ABSENCE
. SABBATICAL LEAVES

: : : METHODS
: : EDUCATIONAL METHODS
: TEACHING METHODS
LECTURE METHOD

: GROUPS
LEFT HANDED WRITER

LEGAL AID

: : : GROUPS
: : PERSONNEL
: PARAPROFESSIONAL PERSONNEL
LEGAL ASSISTANTS

: COSTS
LEGAL COSTS

LEGAL EDUCATION (1977 1986)

: : EDUCATION
: PROFESSIONAL EDUCATION
LEGAL EDUCATION (PROFESSIONS)

: PROBLEMS
LEGAL PROBLEMS

: RESPONSIBILITY
LEGAL RESPONSIBILITY
. TRUST RESPONSIBILITY (GOVERNMENT)

: : : LIBERAL ARTS
: : HUMANITIES
: LITERATURE
: LITERARY GENRES
LEGENDS

LEGISLATION
. CIVIL RIGHTS LEGISLATION
. DISCRIMINATORY LEGISLATION
. EDUCATIONAL LEGISLATION
. . SCHOOL ATTENDANCE LEGISLATION
. FEDERAL LEGISLATION
. LABOR LEGISLATION
. LOCAL LEGISLATION
. MINIMUM WAGE LEGISLATION
. PUBLIC HEALTH LEGISLATION
. . DRUG LEGISLATION
. RECREATION LEGISLATION
. STATE LEGISLATION
. . SCHOOL ATTENDANCE LEGISLATION

: : : : GROUPS
: : : PERSONNEL
: : GOVERNMENT EMPLOYEES
: PUBLIC OFFICIALS
LEGISLATORS

: EDUCATION
LEISURE EDUCATION

LEISURE TIME

: : SEXUALITY
: HOMOSEXUALITY
LESBIANISM

: : STANDARDS
: CRITERIA
LESSON OBSERVATION CRITERIA

LESSON PLANS

: : : LANGUAGE
: : WRITTEN LANGUAGE
: ORTHOGRAPHIC SYMBOLS
LETTERS (ALPHABET)

: : COMMUNICATION (THOUGHT TRANSFER)
: VERBAL COMMUNICATION
LETTERS (CORRESPONDENCE)

: TECHNOLOGY
LEXICOGRAPHY

: : : : : LIBERAL ARTS
: : : : HUMANITIES
: : : PHILOSOPHY
: : : : THEORIES
: : : LINGUISTIC THEORY
: : SEMIOTICS
: : : LINGUISTICS
: : DESCRIPTIVE LINGUISTICS
: SEMANTICS
LEXICOLOGY

LIBERAL ARTS
. HUMANITIES
. . FINE ARTS
. . . DANCE
. . . MUSIC
. . . . APPLIED MUSIC
. . . . JAZZ
. . . . ORIENTAL MUSIC
. . . . VOCAL MUSIC
. . . . . CHORAL MUSIC
. . . . . SONGS
. . . . . . ART SONG
. . . . . . BALLADS
. . . . . . HYMNS
. . . THEATER ARTS
. . . . ACTING
. . . . CHORAL SPEAKING
. . . . DRAMA
. . . . . COMEDY
. . . . . . SKITS
. . . . . SCRIPTS
. . . . . TRAGEDY
. . . . DRAMATICS
. . . . . CREATIVE DRAMATICS
. . . . OPERA
. . . . PANTOMIME
. . . . PUPPETRY
. . . . READERS THEATER
. . . VISUAL ARTS
. . . . ARCHITECTURE
. . . . CHILDRENS ART
. . . . DESIGN CRAFTS
. . . . DRAFTING
. . . . . ARCHITECTURAL DRAFTING
. . . . . ENGINEERING DRAWING
. . . . . TECHNICAL ILLUSTRATION
. . . . FILM PRODUCTION
. . . . FREEHAND DRAWING
. . . . GRAPHIC ARTS
. . . . . CARTOGRAPHY
. . . . . COMPUTER GRAPHICS
. . . . . ENGINEERING GRAPHICS
. . . . . . ENGINEERING DRAWING
. . . . . LAYOUT (PUBLICATIONS)
. . . . . PRINTING
. . . . HANDICRAFTS
. . . . . CERAMICS
. . . . PAINTING (VISUAL ARTS)
. . . . PHOTOGRAPHY
. . . . . HOLOGRAPHY
. . . . SCULPTURE
. . HISTORY
. . . AFRICAN HISTORY
. . . AMERICAN INDIAN HISTORY
. . . ANCIENT HISTORY
. . . ASIAN HISTORY
. . . BLACK HISTORY
. . . CONSTITUTIONAL HISTORY
. . . DIPLOMATIC HISTORY
. . . EDUCATIONAL HISTORY
. . . . SCIENCE EDUCATION HISTORY
. . . EUROPEAN HISTORY
. . . FAMILY HISTORY
. . . . GENEALOGY
. . . HISTORIOGRAPHY
. . . INTELLECTUAL HISTORY
. . . . ART HISTORY
. . . . LITERARY HISTORY

LIBERAL ARTS
(CONTINUED)

...LATIN AMERICAN HISTORY
...LOCAL HISTORY
...MEDIEVAL HISTORY
...MIDDLE EASTERN HISTORY
...MODERN HISTORY
...NORTH AMERICAN HISTORY
....UNITED STATES HISTORY
.....CIVIL WAR (UNITED STATES)
.....COLONIAL HISTORY (UNITED STATES)
.....MEXICAN AMERICAN HISTORY
.....RECONSTRUCTION ERA
.....REVOLUTIONARY WAR (UNITED STATES)
.....STATE HISTORY
...ORAL HISTORY
...SCIENCE HISTORY
...SOCIAL HISTORY
...WORLD HISTORY
..LITERATURE
...ADOLESCENT LITERATURE
...AFRICAN LITERATURE
...AMERICAN INDIAN LITERATURE
...AUSTRALIAN LITERATURE
...BAROQUE LITERATURE
...BIBLICAL LITERATURE
...BLACK LITERATURE
...CHILDRENS LITERATURE
...CLASSICAL LITERATURE
....LATIN LITERATURE
...CZECH LITERATURE
...DRAMA
....COMEDY
.....SKITS
....SCRIPTS
....TRAGEDY
...EIGHTEENTH CENTURY LITERATURE
...ENGLISH LITERATURE
....OLD ENGLISH LITERATURE
...FIFTEENTH CENTURY LITERATURE
...FRENCH LITERATURE
...GERMAN LITERATURE
...GREEK LITERATURE
...ITALIAN LITERATURE
...LATIN AMERICAN LITERATURE
...LEGENDS
...MEDIEVAL LITERATURE
...NINETEENTH CENTURY LITERATURE
...NORTH AMERICAN LITERATURE
....CANADIAN LITERATURE
....UNITED STATES LITERATURE
.....HISPANIC AMERICAN LITERATURE
......MEXICAN AMERICAN LITERATURE
...PASTORAL LITERATURE
...POETRY
....EPICS
....HAIKU
....LYRIC POETRY
.....BALLADS
.....HYMNS
.....ODES
.....SONNETS
...POLISH LITERATURE
...PROSE
....FICTION
.....NOVELS
.....SCIENCE FICTION
.....SHORT STORIES
....NONFICTION
.....BIOGRAPHIES
......AUTOBIOGRAPHIES
.....CHRONICLES
.....DIARIES
.....ESSAYS
...RENAISSANCE LITERATURE
...RUSSIAN LITERATURE
...SEVENTEENTH CENTURY LITERATURE
...SIXTEENTH CENTURY LITERATURE
...SPANISH LITERATURE
...TWENTIETH CENTURY LITERATURE
...VICTORIAN LITERATURE
..PHILOSOPHY
...EDUCATIONAL PHILOSOPHY
...EPISTEMOLOGY
...ETHICS
....BIOETHICS
...EXISTENTIALISM
...HUMANISM
...LOGIC
....MATHEMATICAL LOGIC
.....ALGORITHMS
.....MATHEMATICAL FORMULAS
......EQUATIONS (MATHEMATICS)
......FUNCTIONS (MATHEMATICS)
.....PROOF (MATHEMATICS)
.....SET THEORY
...MARXISM
...PHENOMENOLOGY
...PLATONISM
...SEMIOTICS
....PRAGMATICS
....SEMANTICS
.....LEXICOLOGY
.MATHEMATICS
..ALGEBRA
...MATRICES
...VECTORS (MATHEMATICS)
..ARITHMETIC
...ADDITION
...DIVISION
...MULTIPLICATION
...SUBTRACTION
..CALCULUS
..GEOMETRY
...ANALYTIC GEOMETRY
...PLANE GEOMETRY
...SOLID GEOMETRY
...TOPOLOGY
..PROBABILITY
..STATISTICS
...BAYESIAN STATISTICS
...LEAST SQUARES STATISTICS
...MAXIMUM LIKELIHOOD STATISTICS
...NONPARAMETRIC STATISTICS
...SAMPLING
....ITEM SAMPLING
...STATISTICAL DISTRIBUTIONS
..TECHNICAL MATHEMATICS
..TRIGONOMETRY
.SCIENCES
..ACOUSTICS
...PSYCHOACOUSTICS
..BEHAVIORAL SCIENCES
...ETHOLOGY
...PSYCHOLOGY
....BEHAVIORISM
....CHILD PSYCHOLOGY
....CLINICAL PSYCHOLOGY
....COGNITIVE PSYCHOLOGY
....COMMUNITY PSYCHOLOGY
....DEVELOPMENTAL PSYCHOLOGY
....EDUCATIONAL PSYCHOLOGY
....EXPERIMENTAL PSYCHOLOGY
....INDIVIDUAL PSYCHOLOGY
....INDUSTRIAL PSYCHOLOGY
....PSYCHOACOUSTICS
....PSYCHOMETRICS
....PSYCHOPATHOLOGY
....PSYCHOPHYSIOLOGY
....SOCIAL PSYCHOLOGY
....SPORT PSYCHOLOGY
...SOCIOBIOLOGY
...SOCIOLOGY
....CRIMINOLOGY
....EDUCATIONAL SOCIOLOGY
....SOCIAL PSYCHOLOGY
..INFORMATION SCIENCE
...COMPUTER SCIENCE
....PROGRAMING
...LIBRARY SCIENCE
..NATURAL SCIENCES
...BIOLOGICAL SCIENCES
....ANATOMY
....BIOCHEMISTRY
....BIOFEEDBACK
....BIOLOGY
.....MARINE BIOLOGY
.....MICROBIOLOGY
.....RADIATION BIOLOGY
.....SOCIAL BIOLOGY
....BIOMEDICINE
....BIOPHYSICS
.....BIOMECHANICS
.....BIONICS
......ROBOTICS
....BOTANY
....CYTOLOGY
....ECOLOGY
....EMBRYOLOGY
....ETHOLOGY
....GENETICS
.....GENETIC ENGINEERING
....PHYSIOLOGY
.....EXERCISE PHYSIOLOGY
.....PSYCHOPHYSIOLOGY
....SOCIOBIOLOGY
....ZOOLOGY
.....ENTOMOLOGY
.....ICHTHYOLOGY
.....ORNITHOLOGY
.....PRIMATOLOGY
...PHYSICAL SCIENCES
....ASTRONOMY
....CHEMISTRY
.....BIOCHEMISTRY
.....INORGANIC CHEMISTRY
.....ORGANIC CHEMISTRY
....CRYSTALLOGRAPHY
....EARTH SCIENCE
.....GEOLOGY
......MINERALOGY
......PALEONTOLOGY
.....GEOPHYSICS
......PLATE TECTONICS
.....METEOROLOGY
.....OCEANOGRAPHY
.....PHYSICAL GEOGRAPHY
.....SEISMOLOGY
......PLATE TECTONICS
.....SOIL SCIENCE
....PHYSICS
.....BIOPHYSICS
......BIOMECHANICS
......BIONICS
.......ROBOTICS
.....ELECTRONICS
.....MECHANICS (PHYSICS)
......FLUID MECHANICS
......KINETICS
.......DIFFUSION (PHYSICS)
......QUANTUM MECHANICS
.....NUCLEAR PHYSICS
.....OPTICS
.....THERMODYNAMICS
....SPECTROSCOPY
..SOCIAL SCIENCES
...ANTHROPOLOGY
....ANTHROPOLOGICAL LINGUISTICS
....ARCHAEOLOGY
....EDUCATIONAL ANTHROPOLOGY
....ETHNOGRAPHY
....ETHNOLOGY
...DEMOGRAPHY
....BIRTH RATE
....EMPLOYMENT PATTERNS
....GEOGRAPHIC DISTRIBUTION
....POPULATION DISTRIBUTION
.....ETHNIC DISTRIBUTION
.....RACIAL DISTRIBUTION
....POPULATION GROWTH
....POPULATION TRENDS
.....BLACK POPULATION TRENDS
....RACIAL COMPOSITION
.....RACIAL BALANCE
....RESIDENTIAL PATTERNS
....SCHOOL DEMOGRAPHY
.....TEACHER DISTRIBUTION
....SOCIAL DISTRIBUTION
....URBAN DEMOGRAPHY
...ECONOMICS
....CONSUMER ECONOMICS
....EDUCATIONAL ECONOMICS
.....EDUCATIONAL FINANCE
....LABOR ECONOMICS
....RURAL ECONOMICS
...GEOGRAPHY
....HUMAN GEOGRAPHY
....PHYSICAL GEOGRAPHY
....WORLD GEOGRAPHY
...GERONTOLOGY
....EDUCATIONAL GERONTOLOGY
...HISTORY
....AFRICAN HISTORY
....AMERICAN INDIAN HISTORY
....ANCIENT HISTORY
....ASIAN HISTORY
....BLACK HISTORY
....CONSTITUTIONAL HISTORY
....DIPLOMATIC HISTORY
....EDUCATIONAL HISTORY
.....SCIENCE EDUCATION HISTORY
....EUROPEAN HISTORY
....FAMILY HISTORY
.....GENEALOGY
....HISTORIOGRAPHY
....INTELLECTUAL HISTORY
.....ART HISTORY
.....LITERARY HISTORY
....LATIN AMERICAN HISTORY
....LOCAL HISTORY
....MEDIEVAL HISTORY
....MIDDLE EASTERN HISTORY
....MODERN HISTORY
....NORTH AMERICAN HISTORY
.....UNITED STATES HISTORY
......CIVIL WAR (UNITED STATES)
......COLONIAL HISTORY (UNITED STATES)
......MEXICAN AMERICAN HISTORY
......RECONSTRUCTION ERA
......REVOLUTIONARY WAR (UNITED STATES)
......STATE HISTORY
....ORAL HISTORY
....SCIENCE HISTORY
....SOCIAL HISTORY
....WORLD HISTORY
...INTERNATIONAL STUDIES
...POLITICAL SCIENCE
...SOCIAL STUDIES
....CIVICS
...SOCIOLOGY
....CRIMINOLOGY
....EDUCATIONAL SOCIOLOGY
....SOCIAL PSYCHOLOGY
...TOPOGRAPHY
..SPACE SCIENCES

LIBERALISM

:::GROUPS
::PERSONNEL
:LIBRARY PERSONNEL
::::GROUPS
:::PERSONNEL
::PROFESSIONAL PERSONNEL
:INFORMATION SCIENTISTS
LIBRARIANS

:INSTITUTIONS
:INFORMATION SOURCES
LIBRARIES
.ACADEMIC LIBRARIES
..COLLEGE LIBRARIES
.BRANCH LIBRARIES
.DEPOSITORY LIBRARIES
.PUBLIC LIBRARIES
..COUNTY LIBRARIES
..REGIONAL LIBRARIES
.RESEARCH LIBRARIES
.SCHOOL LIBRARIES
.SPECIAL LIBRARIES
..FILM LIBRARIES
..GOVERNMENT LIBRARIES
...NATIONAL LIBRARIES
...STATE LIBRARIES
..INSTITUTIONAL LIBRARIES
...HOSPITAL LIBRARIES
...PRISON LIBRARIES
..LAW LIBRARIES
..MEDICAL LIBRARIES

::::SERVICES
:::INFORMATION SERVICES
::LIBRARY SERVICES
:LIBRARY TECHNICAL PROCESSES
LIBRARY ACQUISITION
.LIBRARY MATERIAL SELECTION

: : : GOVERNANCE
: : ADMINISTRATION
: INSTITUTIONAL
ADMINISTRATION
LIBRARY ADMINISTRATION

: : : GROUPS
: : ORGANIZATIONS (GROUPS)
: PROFESSIONAL ASSOCIATIONS
LIBRARY ASSOCIATIONS

: : TECHNOLOGY
: AUTOMATION
LIBRARY AUTOMATION

: : PUBLICATIONS
: REFERENCE MATERIALS
: : PUBLICATIONS
: CATALOGS
LIBRARY CATALOGS
. BOOK CATALOGS
. CARD CATALOGS
. UNION CATALOGS

: : : SERVICES
: : INFORMATION SERVICES
: LIBRARY SERVICES
LIBRARY CIRCULATION
. INTERLIBRARY LOANS

: DEVELOPMENT
LIBRARY COLLECTION
DEVELOPMENT

: LIBRARY MATERIALS
LIBRARY COLLECTIONS

: : : BEHAVIOR
: : COOPERATION
: INSTITUTIONAL COOPERATION
LIBRARY COOPERATION

: : EDUCATION
: POSTSECONDARY EDUCATION
LIBRARY EDUCATION

: EQUIPMENT
LIBRARY EQUIPMENT
. BOOKMOBILES

: EXPENDITURES
LIBRARY EXPENDITURES

: : : SERVICES
: : INFORMATION SERVICES
: LIBRARY SERVICES
: : EDUCATION
: EXTENSION EDUCATION
LIBRARY EXTENSION

: FACILITIES
LIBRARY FACILITIES

: : : PUBLICATIONS
: : REFERENCE MATERIALS
: GUIDES
LIBRARY GUIDES

: INSTRUCTION
LIBRARY INSTRUCTION

LIBRARY MATERIALS
. LIBRARY COLLECTIONS

: : SELECTION
: MEDIA SELECTION
: : : : SERVICES
: : : : INFORMATION SERVICES
: : : LIBRARY SERVICES
: : LIBRARY TECHNICAL
PROCESSES
: LIBRARY ACQUISITION
LIBRARY MATERIAL SELECTION

: : NETWORKS
: INFORMATION NETWORKS
LIBRARY NETWORKS
. BIBLIOGRAPHIC UTILITIES

: : GROUPS
: PERSONNEL
LIBRARY PERSONNEL
. LIBRARIANS
. LIBRARY TECHNICIANS
. . MEDICAL RECORD
TECHNICIANS

: PLANNING
LIBRARY PLANNING

: RESEARCH
LIBRARY RESEARCH

: INSTITUTIONAL ROLE
LIBRARY ROLE

: : : INSTITUTIONS
: : SCHOOLS
: COLLEGES
LIBRARY SCHOOLS

: : : LIBERAL ARTS
: : SCIENCES
: INFORMATION SCIENCE
LIBRARY SCIENCE

: : SERVICES
: INFORMATION SERVICES
LIBRARY SERVICES
. LIBRARY CIRCULATION
. . INTERLIBRARY LOANS
. LIBRARY EXTENSION
. LIBRARY TECHNICAL
PROCESSES
. . LIBRARY ACQUISITION
. . . LIBRARY MATERIAL
SELECTION

: : ABILITY
: SKILLS
LIBRARY SKILLS

: STANDARDS
LIBRARY STANDARDS

: : DATA
: STATISTICAL DATA
LIBRARY STATISTICS

: : : METHODS
: : EVALUATION METHODS
: SURVEYS
LIBRARY SURVEYS

: : : SERVICES
: : INFORMATION SERVICES
: LIBRARY SERVICES
LIBRARY TECHNICAL PROCESSES
. LIBRARY ACQUISITION
. . LIBRARY MATERIAL
SELECTION

: : : GROUPS
: : PERSONNEL
: LIBRARY PERSONNEL
LIBRARY TECHNICIANS
. MEDICAL RECORD
TECHNICIANS

: : MEASURES (INDIVIDUALS)
: TESTS
LICENSING EXAMINATIONS
(PROFESSIONS)

: : METHODS
: EVALUATION METHODS
LIFE CYCLE COSTING

: LEARNING
LIFELONG LEARNING

: ATTITUDES
LIFE SATISFACTION

: BEHAVIOR
LIFE STYLE

: : : ACTIVITIES
: : PHYSICAL ACTIVITIES
: ATHLETICS
LIFETIME SPORTS

: : ACTIVITIES
: PHYSICAL ACTIVITIES
LIFTING
. WEIGHTLIFTING

: : : SCIENTIFIC CONCEPTS
: : ENERGY
: RADIATION
LIGHT

LIGHTING
. TELEVISION LIGHTING

: DESIGN
LIGHTING DESIGN
. FLEXIBLE LIGHTING DESIGN

: GROUPS
LIMITED ENGLISH SPEAKING

: MATHEMATICAL APPLICATIONS
LINEAR PROGRAMING

: : : LANGUAGES
: : AFRICAN LANGUAGES
: BANTU LANGUAGES
LINGALA

: : : LINGUISTICS
: : SOCIOLINGUISTICS
: LANGUAGE VARIATION
LINGUISTIC BORROWING

: : THEORIES
: LINGUISTIC THEORY
LINGUISTIC COMPETENCE

LINGUISTIC DIFFICULTY
(INHERENT)

: : THEORIES
: LINGUISTIC THEORY
LINGUISTIC PERFORMANCE

LINGUISTICS
. ANTHROPOLOGICAL
LINGUISTICS
. APPLIED LINGUISTICS
. COMPUTATIONAL LINGUISTICS
. . MACHINE TRANSLATION
. CONTRASTIVE LINGUISTICS
. DESCRIPTIVE LINGUISTICS
. . GRAMMAR
. . . MORPHOLOGY (LANGUAGES)
. . . . MORPHEMES
. . . . . NEGATIVE FORMS
(LANGUAGE)
. . . . . PLURALS
. . . . . SUFFIXES
. . . . . TENSES (GRAMMAR)
. . . . MORPHOPHONEMICS
. . . SYNTAX
. . . . FORM CLASSES
(LANGUAGES)
. . . . . ADJECTIVES
. . . . . ADVERBS
. . . . . DETERMINERS
(LANGUAGES)
. . . . . FUNCTION WORDS
. . . . . NOUNS
. . . . . PREPOSITIONS
. . . . . PRONOUNS
. . . . . VERBS
. . . . PHRASE STRUCTURE
. . . . SENTENCE STRUCTURE
. . SEMANTICS
. . . LEXICOLOGY
. DIACHRONIC LINGUISTICS
. . ETYMOLOGY
. . . ONOMASTICS
. . GLOTTOCHRONOLOGY
. DISTINCTIVE FEATURES
(LANGUAGE)
. MATHEMATICAL LINGUISTICS
. NEUROLINGUISTICS
. PARALINGUISTICS
. PHONOLOGY
. . GENERATIVE PHONOLOGY
. . PHONEMICS
. . . PHONEMES
. . . . CONSONANTS
. . . . VOWELS
. . PHONETICS
. . . ACOUSTIC PHONETICS
. . . PHONICS
. . SUPRASEGMENTALS
. . . INTONATION
. . . STRESS (PHONOLOGY)
. . SYLLABLES
. PSYCHOLINGUISTICS
. SOCIOLINGUISTICS
. . DIALECT STUDIES
. . LANGUAGE PLANNING
. . . LANGUAGE
STANDARDIZATION
. . LANGUAGE VARIATION
. . . CREOLES
. . . . GULLAH
. . . . HAITIAN CREOLE
. . . . MAURITIAN CREOLE
. . . . SIERRA LEONE CREOLE
. . . DIALECTS
. . . . BLACK DIALECTS
. . . . NONSTANDARD DIALECTS
. . . . REGIONAL DIALECTS
. . . . SOCIAL DIALECTS
. . . LANGUAGE STYLES
. . . LINGUISTIC BORROWING
. . . PIDGINS
. STRUCTURAL LINGUISTICS

: THEORIES
LINGUISTIC THEORY
. CASE (GRAMMAR)
. GENERATIVE GRAMMAR
. . TRANSFORMATIONAL
GENERATIVE GRAMMAR
. . . CONTEXT FREE GRAMMAR
. . . DEEP STRUCTURE
. . . KERNEL SENTENCES
. . . SENTENCE COMBINING
. . . SURFACE STRUCTURE
. GENERATIVE PHONOLOGY
. LINGUISTIC COMPETENCE
. LINGUISTIC PERFORMANCE
. SEMIOTICS
. . PRAGMATICS
. . SEMANTICS
. . . LEXICOLOGY
. STRUCTURAL GRAMMAR
. TRADITIONAL GRAMMAR

: : GROUPS
: CHANGE AGENTS
LINKING AGENTS

: : : : METHODS
: : : EDUCATIONAL METHODS
: : TEACHING METHODS
: ORAL COMMUNICATION METHOD
LIPREADING

: LANGUAGE ARTS
LISTENING

: : : : INDIVIDUAL CHARACTERISTICS
: : : PSYCHOLOGICAL CHARACTERISTICS
: : INTELLIGENCE
: COMPREHENSION
LISTENING COMPREHENSION

: : : MEASURES (INDIVIDUALS)
: : TESTS
: VERBAL TESTS
LISTENING COMPREHENSION TESTS

: : GROUPS
: DISCUSSION GROUPS
LISTENING GROUPS

LISTENING HABITS

: : : : ABILITY
: : : SKILLS
: : LANGUAGE SKILLS
: AUDIOLINGUAL SKILLS
LISTENING SKILLS

LITERACY
. ADULT LITERACY
. FUNCTIONAL LITERACY
. . FUNCTIONAL READING
. READING
. . BASAL READING
. . BEGINNING READING
. . CONTENT AREA READING
. . CORRECTIVE READING
. . CRITICAL READING
. . DIRECTED READING ACTIVITY
. . EARLY READING
. . FUNCTIONAL READING
. . INDEPENDENT READING
. . INDIVIDUALIZED READING
. . MUSIC READING
. . ORAL READING
. . READING ALOUD TO OTHERS
. . RECREATIONAL READING
. . REMEDIAL READING
. . SILENT READING
. . SPEED READING
. . STORY READING
. . SUSTAINED SILENT READING
. SCIENTIFIC LITERACY
. WRITING (COMPOSITION)
. . ABSTRACTING
. . CONTENT AREA WRITING
. . CREATIVE WRITING
. . DESCRIPTIVE WRITING
. . EXPOSITORY WRITING
. . FRESHMAN COMPOSITION
. . LOCAL COLOR WRITING
. . NEWS WRITING
. . NOTETAKING
. . PARAGRAPH COMPOSITION
. . PARALLELISM (LITERARY)
. . PLAYWRITING
. . PROPOSAL WRITING
. . TECHNICAL WRITING
. . WRITING FOR PUBLICATION

: EDUCATION
LITERACY EDUCATION

LITERARY CRITICISM
. RHETORICAL CRITICISM

LITERARY DEVICES
. CHARACTERIZATION
. DIALOGS (LITERARY)
. FIGURATIVE LANGUAGE
. . ALLEGORY
. . AMBIGUITY
. . ANTITHESIS
. . IMAGERY
. . IRONY
. . METAPHORS
. . PUNS
. . SYMBOLS (LITERARY)
. MONOLOGS
. MOTIFS
. NARRATION

LITERARY DISCRIMINATION (1966 1980)

LITERARY GENRES
. BALLADS
. BIOGRAPHIES
. . AUTOBIOGRAPHIES
. CHRONICLES
. DIARIES
. EPICS
. ESSAYS
. HAIKU
. HYMNS
. LEGENDS
. NOVELS
. ODES
. PARODY
. SATIRE
. SCRIPTS
. SHORT STORIES
. SKITS
. SONNETS
. TALES
. . FABLES

: : : : : LIBERAL ARTS
: : : : SCIENCES
: : : SOCIAL SCIENCES
: : : : LIBERAL ARTS
: : : HUMANITIES
: : HISTORY
: INTELLECTUAL HISTORY
LITERARY HISTORY

LITERARY INFLUENCES (1969 1980)

LITERARY MOOD (1970 1980)

LITERARY PERSPECTIVE (1969 1980)

LITERARY STYLES

: : LIBERAL ARTS
: HUMANITIES
LITERATURE
. ADOLESCENT LITERATURE
. AFRICAN LITERATURE
. AMERICAN INDIAN LITERATURE
. AUSTRALIAN LITERATURE
. BAROQUE LITERATURE
. BIBLICAL LITERATURE
. BLACK LITERATURE
. CHILDRENS LITERATURE
. CLASSICAL LITERATURE
. . LATIN LITERATURE
. CZECH LITERATURE
. DRAMA
. . COMEDY
. . . SKITS
. . SCRIPTS
. . TRAGEDY
. EIGHTEENTH CENTURY LITERATURE
. ENGLISH LITERATURE
. . OLD ENGLISH LITERATURE
. FIFTEENTH CENTURY LITERATURE
. FRENCH LITERATURE
. GERMAN LITERATURE
. GREEK LITERATURE
. ITALIAN LITERATURE
. LATIN AMERICAN LITERATURE
. LEGENDS
. MEDIEVAL LITERATURE
. NINETEENTH CENTURY LITERATURE
. NORTH AMERICAN LITERATURE
. . CANADIAN LITERATURE
. . UNITED STATES LITERATURE
. . . HISPANIC AMERICAN LITERATURE
. . . . MEXICAN AMERICAN LITERATURE
. PASTORAL LITERATURE
. POETRY
. . EPICS
. . HAIKU
. . LYRIC POETRY
. . . BALLADS
. . . HYMNS
. . . ODES
. . . SONNETS
. POLISH LITERATURE
. PROSE
. . FICTION
. . . NOVELS
. . . SCIENCE FICTION
. . . SHORT STORIES
. . NONFICTION
. . . BIOGRAPHIES
. . . . AUTOBIOGRAPHIES
. . . CHRONICLES
. . . DIARIES
. . . ESSAYS
. RENAISSANCE LITERATURE
. RUSSIAN LITERATURE
. SEVENTEENTH CENTURY LITERATURE
. SIXTEENTH CENTURY LITERATURE
. SPANISH LITERATURE
. TWENTIETH CENTURY LITERATURE
. VICTORIAN LITERATURE

LITERATURE APPRECIATION

LITERATURE GUIDES (1966 1980)

LITERATURE PROGRAMS (1966 1980)

: PUBLICATIONS
LITERATURE REVIEWS

: : : LANGUAGES
: : INDO EUROPEAN LANGUAGES
: BALTIC LANGUAGES
LITHUANIAN

: ANIMALS
LIVESTOCK

: : FACILITIES
: EDUCATIONAL FACILITIES
LIVING LEARNING CENTERS

: STANDARDS
LIVING STANDARDS

LOAN REPAYMENT

: ACTIVITIES
LOBBYING

: : NETWORKS
: COMPUTER NETWORKS
LOCAL AREA NETWORKS

: : LITERACY
: : LANGUAGE ARTS
: WRITING (COMPOSITION)
LOCAL COLOR WRITING

: : : GROUPS
: : ORGANIZATIONS (GROUPS)
: GOVERNMENT (ADMINISTRATIVE BODY)
LOCAL GOVERNMENT
. CITY GOVERNMENT

: : : : LIBERAL ARTS
: : : SCIENCES
: : SOCIAL SCIENCES
: : : LIBERAL ARTS
: : HUMANITIES
: HISTORY
LOCAL HISTORY

LOCAL ISSUES

: LEGISLATION
LOCAL LEGISLATION

: : : DATA
: : STATISTICAL DATA
: NORMS
LOCAL NORMS

: : ABILITY
: SKILLS
LOCATIONAL SKILLS (SOCIAL STUDIES)

: FACILITIES
LOCKER ROOMS

: : : : GROUPS
: : : PERSONNEL
: : NONPROFESSIONAL PERSONNEL
: SKILLED WORKERS
LOCOMOTIVE ENGINEERS

: : : INDIVIDUAL CHARACTERISTICS
: : PSYCHOLOGICAL CHARACTERISTICS
: PERSONALITY TRAITS
LOCUS OF CONTROL

: : SYMBOLS (MATHEMATICS)
: NUMBERS
LOGARITHMS

: : : LIBERAL ARTS
: : HUMANITIES
: PHILOSOPHY
LOGIC
. MATHEMATICAL LOGIC
. . ALGORITHMS
. . MATHEMATICAL FORMULAS
. . . EQUATIONS (MATHEMATICS)
. . . FUNCTIONS (MATHEMATICS)
. . PROOF (MATHEMATICS)
. . SET THEORY

: COGNITIVE PROCESSES
LOGICAL THINKING
. DEDUCTION
. INDUCTION

: PSYCHOLOGICAL PATTERNS
LONELINESS

: : RESEARCH
: : : METHODS
: : EVALUATION METHODS
: CASE STUDIES
LONGITUDINAL STUDIES
. FOLLOWUP STUDIES
. . GRADUATE SURVEYS
. . VOCATIONAL FOLLOWUP

: PLANNING
LONG RANGE PLANNING

: : COGNITIVE PROCESSES
: MEMORY
LONG TERM MEMORY

: : : TECHNOLOGY
: : COMMUNICATIONS
: AUDIOVISUAL COMMUNICATIONS
LOOP INDUCTION SYSTEMS

LOW ABILITY STUDENTS (1967 1980)

: ACHIEVEMENT
LOW ACHIEVEMENT

: : GROUPS
: SOCIAL CLASS
LOWER CLASS

: : GROUPS
: PARENTS
LOWER CLASS PARENTS

: : GROUPS
: STUDENTS
LOWER CLASS STUDENTS

: : GROUPS
: SOCIAL CLASS
LOWER MIDDLE CLASS

: INCOME
LOW INCOME

: GEOGRAPHIC REGIONS
LOW INCOME COUNTIES

: GROUPS
LOW INCOME GROUPS

: GEOGRAPHIC REGIONS
LOW INCOME STATES

: : FACILITIES
: HOUSING
LOW RENT HOUSING
. PUBLIC HOUSING

: SENSORY AIDS
LOW VISION AIDS

LOYALTY OATHS

LUBRICANTS

: : BUSINESS
: INDUSTRY
LUMBER INDUSTRY

LUMINESCENCE

: : : RESEARCH
: : SCIENTIFIC RESEARCH
: SPACE EXPLORATION
LUNAR RESEARCH

: : PROGRAMS
: HEALTH PROGRAMS
LUNCH PROGRAMS

: : LANGUAGES
: AFRICAN LANGUAGES
LUO

: : CULTURE
: LATIN AMERICAN CULTURE
LUSO BRAZILIAN CULTURE

: : BEHAVIOR
: SOCIAL BEHAVIOR
: DECEPTION
LYING

: : : : LIBERAL ARTS
: : : HUMANITIES
: : LITERATURE
: POETRY
LYRIC POETRY
. BALLADS
. HYMNS
. ODES
. SONNETS

LYSERGIC ACID DIETHYLAMIDE

: : : : : SERVICES
: : : : INFORMATION SERVICES
: : : INFORMATION PROCESSING
: : DOCUMENTATION
: CATALOGING
MACHINE READABLE CATALOGING

: : : : : GROUPS
: : : : PERSONNEL
: : : NONPROFESSIONAL
PERSONNEL
: : SKILLED WORKERS
: MACHINISTS
MACHINE REPAIRERS

: : : BUSINESS
: : INDUSTRY
: MANUFACTURING INDUSTRY
MACHINERY INDUSTRY

: : : : : GROUPS
: : : : PERSONNEL
: : : NONPROFESSIONAL
PERSONNEL
: : SKILLED WORKERS
: MACHINISTS
MACHINE TOOL OPERATORS

: EQUIPMENT
MACHINE TOOLS

: TRANSLATION
: : LINGUISTICS
: COMPUTATIONAL LINGUISTICS
MACHINE TRANSLATION

: : : : GROUPS
: : : PERSONNEL
: : NONPROFESSIONAL
PERSONNEL
: SKILLED WORKERS
MACHINISTS
. MACHINE REPAIRERS
. MACHINE TOOL OPERATORS
. TOOL AND DIE MAKERS

: : : RESOURCES
: : SUPPLIES
: MAGNETIC TAPES
MAGNETIC TAPE CASSETTES
. AUDIOTAPE CASSETTES
. VIDEOTAPE CASSETTES

: : RESOURCES
: SUPPLIES
MAGNETIC TAPES
. MAGNETIC TAPE CASSETTES
. . AUDIOTAPE CASSETTES
. . VIDEOTAPE CASSETTES

MAGNETS

: : INSTITUTIONS
: SCHOOLS
MAGNET SCHOOLS

: METHODS
MAGNIFICATION METHODS

: PLACEMENT
MAINSTREAMING

MAINTENANCE
. EQUIPMENT MAINTENANCE
. PRESERVATION
. REPAIR
. . APPLIANCE REPAIR
. SCHOOL MAINTENANCE

: ATTITUDES
MAJORITY ATTITUDES

: : GROUPS
: STUDENTS
MAJORS (STUDENTS)
. EDUCATION MAJORS

: : : LANGUAGES
: : MALAYO POLYNESIAN
LANGUAGES
: INDONESIAN LANGUAGES
MALAGASY

: : : LANGUAGES
: : MALAYO POLYNESIAN
LANGUAGES
: INDONESIAN LANGUAGES
MALAY

: : LANGUAGES
: DRAVIDIAN LANGUAGES
MALAYALAM

: LANGUAGES
MALAYO POLYNESIAN LANGUAGES
. CHAMORRO
. HAWAIIAN
. INDONESIAN LANGUAGES
. . BIKOL
. . DUSUN
. . INDONESIAN
. . JAVANESE
. . MALAGASY
. . MALAY
. . MARANAO
. . TAGALOG
. . VISAYAN
. . . CEBUANO
. MELANESIAN LANGUAGES
. SAMOAN

: GROUPS
MALES
. FATHERS
. SONS

MALPRACTICE
. EDUCATIONAL MALPRACTICE

: MANAGEMENT SYSTEMS
: : GOVERNANCE
: ADMINISTRATION
MANAGEMENT BY OBJECTIVES

: : DEVELOPMENT
: LABOR FORCE DEVELOPMENT
MANAGEMENT DEVELOPMENT

: : : : METHODS
: : : EDUCATIONAL METHODS
: : TEACHING METHODS
: TRAINING METHODS
: : ACTIVITIES
: GAMES
MANAGEMENT GAMES

: MANAGEMENT SYSTEMS
: INFORMATION SYSTEMS
MANAGEMENT INFORMATION
SYSTEMS

MANAGEMENT SYSTEMS
. DATABASE MANAGEMENT
SYSTEMS
. MANAGEMENT BY OBJECTIVES
. MANAGEMENT INFORMATION
SYSTEMS

: : ORGANIZATION
: ADMINISTRATIVE
ORGANIZATION
MANAGEMENT TEAMS

: OCCUPATIONS
MANAGERIAL OCCUPATIONS

: : LANGUAGES
: URALIC ALTAIC LANGUAGES
MANCHU

: : : LANGUAGES
: : SINO TIBETAN LANGUAGES
: CHINESE
MANDARIN CHINESE

: : LANGUAGES
: AFRICAN LANGUAGES
MANDINGO

: : EDUCATIONAL MEDIA
: INSTRUCTIONAL MATERIALS
MANIPULATIVE MATERIALS

MAN MACHINE SYSTEMS

: COMMUNICATION (THOUGHT
TRANSFER)
MANUAL COMMUNICATION
. CUED SPEECH
. FINGER SPELLING
. SIGN LANGUAGE
. . AMERICAN SIGN LANGUAGE

: TECHNOLOGY
MANUFACTURING
. ASSEMBLY (MANUFACTURING)
. MASS PRODUCTION

: : BUSINESS
: INDUSTRY
MANUFACTURING INDUSTRY
. AEROSPACE INDUSTRY
. CEMENT INDUSTRY
. CHEMICAL INDUSTRY
. ELECTRONICS INDUSTRY
. FURNITURE INDUSTRY
. MACHINERY INDUSTRY
. METAL INDUSTRY

: : LANGUAGE ARTS
: HANDWRITING
MANUSCRIPT WRITING
(HANDLETTERING)

: VISUAL AIDS
MAPS

: : ABILITY
: SKILLS
MAP SKILLS

: : : LANGUAGES
: : MALAYO POLYNESIAN
LANGUAGES
: INDONESIAN LANGUAGES
MARANAO

: : LANGUAGES
: INDO EUROPEAN LANGUAGES
MARATHI

: NARCOTICS
MARIJUANA

::::: LIBERAL ARTS
:::: SCIENCES
::: NATURAL SCIENCES
:: BIOLOGICAL SCIENCES
: BIOLOGY
MARINE BIOLOGY

: EDUCATION
MARINE EDUCATION
. MARITIME EDUCATION

::: GROUPS
:: PERSONNEL
: PARAPROFESSIONAL PERSONNEL
MARINE TECHNICIANS

MARITAL INSTABILITY

: ATTITUDES
MARITAL SATISFACTION

: STATUS
MARITAL STATUS

:: EDUCATION
: MARINE EDUCATION
MARITIME EDUCATION

: TECHNOLOGY
MARKETING
. MERCHANDISING
. RETAILING
. SALESMANSHIP
. WHOLESALING

::: ABILITY
:: SKILLS
: PSYCHOMOTOR SKILLS
MARKSMANSHIP

:: RELATIONSHIP
: INTERPERSONAL RELATIONSHIP
MARRIAGE
. INTERMARRIAGE
. REMARRIAGE

:: GUIDANCE
: COUNSELING
MARRIAGE COUNSELING

:: GROUPS
: STUDENTS
MARRIED STUDENTS

: METHODS
MARXIAN ANALYSIS

::: LIBERAL ARTS
:: HUMANITIES
: PHILOSOPHY
MARXISM

: TECHNOLOGY
: CONSTRUCTION (PROCESS)
MASONRY
. BRICKLAYING

: INSTRUCTION
MASS INSTRUCTION

MASS MEDIA
. FILMS
.. FOREIGN LANGUAGE FILMS
.. INSTRUCTIONAL FILMS
.. KINESCOPE RECORDINGS
.. SINGLE CONCEPT FILMS
. NEWS MEDIA
.. EDITORIALS
.. NEWSPAPERS
... NEWSLETTERS
... SCHOOL NEWSPAPERS
. RADIO
.. EDUCATIONAL RADIO
. TELEVISION
.. BROADCAST TELEVISION
.. CABLE TELEVISION
.. CHILDRENS TELEVISION
.. CLOSED CIRCUIT TELEVISION
.. COMMERCIAL TELEVISION
.. EDUCATIONAL TELEVISION
.. PUBLIC TELEVISION

MASS MEDIA EFFECTS

:: TECHNOLOGY
: MANUFACTURING
MASS PRODUCTION

MASTER PLANS

: DEGREES (ACADEMIC)
MASTERS DEGREES

:: PROGRAMS
: COLLEGE PROGRAMS
MASTERS PROGRAMS

::: PUBLICATIONS
:: REPORTS
: THESES
MASTERS THESES

:::: GROUPS
::: PERSONNEL
:: PROFESSIONAL PERSONNEL
: TEACHERS
MASTER TEACHERS

: LEARNING
MASTERY LEARNING

::: MEASURES (INDIVIDUALS)
:: TESTS
: CRITERION REFERENCED TESTS
::: MEASURES (INDIVIDUALS)
:: TESTS
: ACHIEVEMENT TESTS
MASTERY TESTS

: GROUPS
MATCHED GROUPS

: DEVELOPMENT
MATERIAL DEVELOPMENT
. TEST CONSTRUCTION

: SELECTION
MATE SELECTION

MATHEMATICAL APPLICATIONS
. ALGORITHMS
. COMPUTATION
.. ESTIMATION (MATHEMATICS)
. LINEAR PROGRAMING
. MATHEMATICAL FORMULAS
.. EQUATIONS (MATHEMATICS)
.. FUNCTIONS (MATHEMATICS)
. WORD PROBLEMS (MATHEMATICS)

MATHEMATICAL CONCEPTS
. GEOMETRIC CONCEPTS
.. AREA
.. CONGRUENCE (MATHEMATICS)
.. ORTHOGRAPHIC PROJECTION
.. VECTORS (MATHEMATICS)
.. VOLUME (MATHEMATICS)
. INEQUALITY (MATHEMATICS)
. NUMBER CONCEPTS
.. PLACE VALUE

: ENRICHMENT
MATHEMATICAL ENRICHMENT

MATHEMATICAL EXPERIENCE (1966 1980)

::::: LIBERAL ARTS
:::: HUMANITIES
::: PHILOSOPHY
:: LOGIC
: MATHEMATICAL LOGIC
: MATHEMATICAL APPLICATIONS
MATHEMATICAL FORMULAS
. EQUATIONS (MATHEMATICS)
. FUNCTIONS (MATHEMATICS)

: LINGUISTICS
MATHEMATICAL LINGUISTICS

:::: LIBERAL ARTS
::: HUMANITIES
:: PHILOSOPHY
: LOGIC
MATHEMATICAL LOGIC
. ALGORITHMS
. MATHEMATICAL FORMULAS
.. EQUATIONS (MATHEMATICS)
.. FUNCTIONS (MATHEMATICS)
. PROOF (MATHEMATICS)
. SET THEORY

::: METHODS
:: SIMULATION
: MODELS
MATHEMATICAL MODELS

: VOCABULARY
MATHEMATICAL VOCABULARY

::: GROUPS
:: PERSONNEL
: SCIENTIFIC PERSONNEL
::: GROUPS
:: PERSONNEL
: PROFESSIONAL PERSONNEL
MATHEMATICIANS

: LIBERAL ARTS
MATHEMATICS
. ALGEBRA
.. MATRICES
.. VECTORS (MATHEMATICS)
. ARITHMETIC
.. ADDITION
.. DIVISION
.. MULTIPLICATION
.. SUBTRACTION
. CALCULUS
. GEOMETRY
.. ANALYTIC GEOMETRY
.. PLANE GEOMETRY
.. SOLID GEOMETRY
.. TOPOLOGY
. PROBABILITY
. STATISTICS
.. BAYESIAN STATISTICS
.. LEAST SQUARES STATISTICS
.. MAXIMUM LIKELIHOOD STATISTICS
.. NONPARAMETRIC STATISTICS
.. SAMPLING
... ITEM SAMPLING
.. STATISTICAL DISTRIBUTIONS
. TECHNICAL MATHEMATICS
. TRIGONOMETRY

: ACHIEVEMENT
MATHEMATICS ACHIEVEMENT

:: PSYCHOLOGICAL PATTERNS
: ANXIETY
MATHEMATICS ANXIETY

: CURRICULUM
MATHEMATICS CURRICULUM
. COLLEGE MATHEMATICS
. ELEMENTARY SCHOOL MATHEMATICS
. MODERN MATHEMATICS
. SECONDARY SCHOOL MATHEMATICS

: EDUCATION
MATHEMATICS EDUCATION

: INSTRUCTION
MATHEMATICS INSTRUCTION
. REMEDIAL MATHEMATICS

MATHEMATICS MATERIALS

:: ABILITY
: SKILLS
MATHEMATICS SKILLS

:::: GROUPS
::: PERSONNEL
:: PROFESSIONAL PERSONNEL
: TEACHERS
MATHEMATICS TEACHERS

:: MEASURES (INDIVIDUALS)
: TESTS
MATHEMATICS TESTS

::: LIBERAL ARTS
:: MATHEMATICS
: ALGEBRA
MATRICES

MATTER
. MINERALS
.. ASBESTOS
. POLYMERS
. SLUDGE
. WASTES
.. SOLID WASTES
.. WASTE WATER
. WATER
.. DRINKING WATER
.. WASTE WATER

MATURATION (1967 1980)

: INDIVIDUAL CHARACTERISTICS
MATURITY (INDIVIDUALS)
. VOCATIONAL MATURITY

:: MEASURES (INDIVIDUALS)
: TESTS
MATURITY TESTS

:::: LINGUISTICS
::: SOCIOLINGUISTICS
:: LANGUAGE VARIATION
:: LANGUAGES
: CREOLES
MAURITIAN CREOLE

::: LIBERAL ARTS
:: MATHEMATICS
: STATISTICS
:::: METHODS
::: EVALUATION METHODS
:: DATA ANALYSIS
: STATISTICAL ANALYSIS
MAXIMUM LIKELIHOOD STATISTICS

:: LANGUAGES
: AMERICAN INDIAN LANGUAGES
MAYAN LANGUAGES
. QUICHE
. YUCATEC

MEASUREMENT
. ACHIEVEMENT RATING
.. GRADING
... CREDIT NO CREDIT GRADING
... PASS FAIL GRADING
. COGNITIVE MEASUREMENT
. MERIT RATING
. PREDICTIVE MEASUREMENT
. SCORING

: EQUIPMENT
MEASUREMENT EQUIPMENT
. CALORIMETERS
. POLYGRAPHS
. POTENTIOMETERS (INSTRUMENTS)
. SOUND SPECTROGRAPHS

MEASUREMENT INSTRUMENTS (1966 1980)

: OBJECTIVES
MEASUREMENT OBJECTIVES

: METHODS
MEASUREMENT TECHNIQUES
. CLASSROOM OBSERVATION TECHNIQUES
. FORCED CHOICE TECHNIQUE
. Q METHODOLOGY
. SCALING
.. MULTIDIMENSIONAL SCALING
. SCORING FORMULAS
. SOCIOMETRIC TECHNIQUES
. TESTING
.. ADAPTIVE TESTING
.. COMPARATIVE TESTING
.. COMPUTER ASSISTED TESTING
.. CONFIDENCE TESTING
.. EDUCATIONAL TESTING
.. GROUP TESTING
.. INDIVIDUAL TESTING
.. MINIMUM COMPETENCY TESTING
.. PSYCHOLOGICAL TESTING

MEASURES (INDIVIDUALS)
. AFFECTIVE MEASURES
. ATTITUDE MEASURES
.. SEMANTIC DIFFERENTIAL
. BIOGRAPHICAL INVENTORIES
. INTEREST INVENTORIES
. PERSONALITY MEASURES
.. SELF CONCEPT MEASURES
. PROJECTIVE MEASURES
.. ASSOCIATION MEASURES
. QUESTIONNAIRES
. RATING SCALES
.. BEHAVIOR RATING SCALES
.. SEMANTIC DIFFERENTIAL
. TESTS
.. ACHIEVEMENT TESTS
... EQUIVALENCY TESTS
... MASTERY TESTS
... NATIONAL COMPETENCY TESTS
.. APTITUDE TESTS
... READING READINESS TESTS
... SCHOOL READINESS TESTS
.. AUDITORY TESTS
... AUDIOMETRIC TESTS
.. COGNITIVE TESTS
... INTELLIGENCE TESTS
... PERCEPTION TESTS
.... TACTUAL VISUAL TESTS
.. COLLEGE ENTRANCE EXAMINATIONS
.. CREATIVITY TESTS
.. CRITERION REFERENCED TESTS
... MASTERY TESTS
.. CULTURE FAIR TESTS
.. DIAGNOSTIC TESTS
.. FIELD TESTS
.. LICENSING EXAMINATIONS (PROFESSIONS)
.. MATHEMATICS TESTS
.. MATURITY TESTS
.. NONVERBAL TESTS
... VISUAL MEASURES
.. NORM REFERENCED TESTS
.. OBJECTIVE TESTS
... MULTIPLE CHOICE TESTS
.. OCCUPATIONAL TESTS
... WORK SAMPLE TESTS
.. OPEN BOOK TESTS
.. PERFORMANCE TESTS
.. PRESCHOOL TESTS
.. PRETESTS POSTTESTS
.. PROGNOSTIC TESTS
.. SCIENCE TESTS
.. SCREENING TESTS
.. SITUATIONAL TESTS
.. STANDARDIZED TESTS
.. TEACHER MADE TESTS
.. TIMED TESTS
.. VERBAL TESTS
... ESSAY TESTS
... LANGUAGE TESTS
... LISTENING COMPREHENSION TESTS
... READING TESTS
.... INFORMAL READING INVENTORIES
... SPEECH TESTS
.. VISION TESTS

: FOOD
MEAT

:: BUSINESS
: INDUSTRY
MEAT PACKING INDUSTRY

::: GROUPS
:: PERSONNEL
: PARAPROFESSIONAL PERSONNEL
MECHANICAL DESIGN TECHNICIANS

: EQUIPMENT
MECHANICAL EQUIPMENT

:: ABILITY
: SKILLS
MECHANICAL SKILLS

::::: LIBERAL ARTS
:::: SCIENCES
::: NATURAL SCIENCES
:: PHYSICAL SCIENCES
: PHYSICS
MECHANICS (PHYSICS)
. FLUID MECHANICS
. KINETICS
.. DIFFUSION (PHYSICS)
. QUANTUM MECHANICS

: TECHNOLOGY
MECHANICS (PROCESS)
. AUTO MECHANICS
. AVIATION MECHANICS
. REFRIGERATION MECHANICS
. SMALL ENGINE MECHANICS

: CHANGE
MEDIA ADAPTATION
. TACTILE ADAPTATION

: RESEARCH
MEDIA RESEARCH
. TELEVISION RESEARCH
. TEXTBOOK RESEARCH

: SELECTION
MEDIA SELECTION
. LIBRARY MATERIAL SELECTION
. READING MATERIAL SELECTION
. TEXTBOOK SELECTION

::: GROUPS
:: PERSONNEL
: SPECIALISTS
MEDIA SPECIALISTS
. AUDIOVISUAL COORDINATORS

:: THEORIES
: BEHAVIOR THEORIES
MEDIATION THEORY

:::: GROUPS
::: PERSONNEL
:: HEALTH PERSONNEL
: ALLIED HEALTH PERSONNEL
MEDICAL ASSISTANTS
. MEDICAL LABORATORY ASSISTANTS

::: GROUPS
:: ORGANIZATIONS (GROUPS)
: PROFESSIONAL ASSOCIATIONS
MEDICAL ASSOCIATIONS

: EVALUATION
MEDICAL CARE EVALUATION

:: RECORDS (FORMS)
: CASE RECORDS
MEDICAL CASE HISTORIES

::: GROUPS
:: PERSONNEL
: HEALTH PERSONNEL
::: GROUPS
:: PERSONNEL
: CONSULTANTS
MEDICAL CONSULTANTS

:: EDUCATION
: PROFESSIONAL EDUCATION
MEDICAL EDUCATION
. GRADUATE MEDICAL EDUCATION
. NURSING EDUCATION
. PHARMACEUTICAL EDUCATION
. VETERINARY MEDICAL EDUCATION

: EVALUATION
MEDICAL EVALUATION
. AUDITORY EVALUATION
. DENTAL EVALUATION
. PHYSICAL EXAMINATIONS
. SPEECH EVALUATION

::::: GROUPS
:::: PERSONNEL
::: HEALTH PERSONNEL
:: ALLIED HEALTH PERSONNEL
: MEDICAL ASSISTANTS
MEDICAL LABORATORY ASSISTANTS

::: INSTITUTIONS
::: INFORMATION SOURCES
:: LIBRARIES
: SPECIAL LIBRARIES
MEDICAL LIBRARIES

:::: GROUPS
::: PERSONNEL
:: HEALTH PERSONNEL
: ALLIED HEALTH PERSONNEL
::: GROUPS
:: PERSONNEL
: ADMINISTRATORS
MEDICAL RECORD ADMINISTRATORS

:::: GROUPS
::: PERSONNEL
:: LIBRARY PERSONNEL
: LIBRARY TECHNICIANS
:::: GROUPS
::: PERSONNEL
:: HEALTH PERSONNEL
: ALLIED HEALTH PERSONNEL
MEDICAL RECORD TECHNICIANS

: RESEARCH
MEDICAL RESEARCH

:::::: GROUPS
::::: PERSONNEL
:::: SCHOOL PERSONNEL
:::::: GROUPS
::::: PERSONNEL
:::: PROFESSIONAL PERSONNEL
::: FACULTY
:: COLLEGE FACULTY
: GRADUATE SCHOOL FACULTY
MEDICAL SCHOOL FACULTY

::: INSTITUTIONS
:: SCHOOLS
: COLLEGES
MEDICAL SCHOOLS

::: SERVICES
:: HUMAN SERVICES
: HEALTH SERVICES
MEDICAL SERVICES
. FIRST AID
.. CARDIOPULMONARY RESUSCITATION
. PSYCHIATRIC SERVICES

:::: GROUPS
::: STUDENTS
:: COLLEGE STUDENTS
: GRADUATE STUDENTS
MEDICAL STUDENTS
. GRADUATE MEDICAL STUDENTS

:::: GROUPS
::: PERSONNEL
:: HEALTH PERSONNEL
: ALLIED HEALTH PERSONNEL
MEDICAL TECHNOLOGISTS

: VOCABULARY
MEDICAL VOCABULARY

: TECHNOLOGY
MEDICINE
. ANESTHESIOLOGY
. AUDIOLOGY
. BIOMEDICINE
. DENTISTRY
. DIETETICS
. ELECTROENCEPHALOGRAPHY
. EPIDEMIOLOGY
. FAMILY PRACTICE (MEDICINE)
. GERIATRICS
. GYNECOLOGY
. INTERNAL MEDICINE
. NEUROLOGY
. NURSING
.. PRACTICAL NURSING
. OBSTETRICS
. ONCOLOGY
. OPHTHALMOLOGY
. OSTEOPATHY
. PATHOLOGY
.. PLANT PATHOLOGY
.. PSYCHOPATHOLOGY
.. SPEECH PATHOLOGY
. PEDIATRICS
. PHARMACOLOGY
. PHARMACY
. PODIATRY
. PREVENTIVE MEDICINE
. PRIMARY HEALTH CARE
. PSYCHIATRY
. SURGERY
. TOXICOLOGY
. VETERINARY MEDICINE

:::: LIBERAL ARTS
::: SCIENCES
:: SOCIAL SCIENCES
::: LIBERAL ARTS
:: HUMANITIES
: HISTORY
MEDIEVAL HISTORY

::: LIBERAL ARTS
:: HUMANITIES
: LITERATURE
MEDIEVAL LITERATURE

:: COGNITIVE PROCESSES
: METACOGNITION
MEDITATION
. TRANSCENDENTAL MEDITATION

MEETINGS
. SEMINARS
. STAFF MEETINGS

:: LANGUAGES
: MALAYO POLYNESIAN
LANGUAGES
MELANESIAN LANGUAGES

:: COGNITIVE PROCESSES
: LEARNING PROCESSES
MEMORIZATION

: COGNITIVE PROCESSES
MEMORY
. EIDETIC IMAGERY
. LONG TERM MEMORY
. RECALL (PSYCHOLOGY)
. RECOGNITION (PSYCHOLOGY)
.. PATTERN RECOGNITION
... CHARACTER RECOGNITION
.. WORD RECOGNITION
. RETENTION (PSYCHOLOGY)
. SHORT TERM MEMORY

:: LANGUAGES
: AFRICAN LANGUAGES
MENDE

::: INDIVIDUAL
CHARACTERISTICS
:: PSYCHOLOGICAL
CHARACTERISTICS
: INTELLIGENCE
:: INDIVIDUAL
CHARACTERISTICS
: AGE
MENTAL AGE

: DISABILITIES
MENTAL DISORDERS
. EMOTIONAL DISTURBANCES
.. PSYCHOSOMATIC DISORDERS
. NEUROSIS
. PSYCHOSIS
.. AUTISM
.. ECHOLALIA
.. SCHIZOPHRENIA

: HEALTH
MENTAL HEALTH

: CLINICS
MENTAL HEALTH CLINICS

:: PROGRAMS
: HEALTH PROGRAMS
MENTAL HEALTH PROGRAMS

: DISABILITIES
MENTAL RETARDATION
. DOWNS SYNDROME
. MILD MENTAL RETARDATION
. MODERATE MENTAL
RETARDATION
. SEVERE MENTAL RETARDATION

::: INDIVIDUAL
CHARACTERISTICS
:: PSYCHOLOGICAL
CHARACTERISTICS
: PERSONALITY TRAITS
MENTAL RIGIDITY

:::: METHODS
::: SIMULATION
:: MODELS
:: GROUPS
: ROLE MODELS
MENTORS

::: STANDARDS
:: SPECIFICATIONS
: COMPUTER SOFTWARE
MENU DRIVEN SOFTWARE

MERCHANDISE INFORMATION

:: TECHNOLOGY
: MARKETING
MERCHANDISING

:: GROUPS
: PERSONNEL
MERCHANTS

:: CHANGE
: ORGANIZATIONAL CHANGE
MERGERS

: INCOME
: EXPENDITURES
MERIT PAY

: MEASUREMENT
MERIT RATING

::: FINANCIAL SUPPORT
:: STUDENT FINANCIAL AID
: SCHOLARSHIPS
MERIT SCHOLARSHIPS
. NO NEED SCHOLARSHIPS

:::: METHODS
::: EVALUATION METHODS
:: DATA ANALYSIS
: STATISTICAL ANALYSIS
META ANALYSIS

METABOLISM
. BLOOD CIRCULATION
. HEART RATE

: COGNITIVE PROCESSES
METACOGNITION
. MEDITATION
.. TRANSCENDENTAL
MEDITATION

::: BUSINESS
:: INDUSTRY
: MANUFACTURING INDUSTRY
METAL INDUSTRY

::: GROUPS
:: PERSONNEL
: PARAPROFESSIONAL
PERSONNEL
METALLURGICAL TECHNICIANS

: TECHNOLOGY
METALLURGY

METALS

: TECHNOLOGY
METAL WORKING
. SHEET METAL WORK

:: LITERARY DEVICES
:: LANGUAGE
: FIGURATIVE LANGUAGE
METAPHORS

::::: LIBERAL ARTS
:::: SCIENCES
::: NATURAL SCIENCES
:: PHYSICAL SCIENCES
: EARTH SCIENCE
METEOROLOGY

METHODS
. ALGORITHMS
. BRANCHING
. CASEWORKER APPROACH
. CHANGE STRATEGIES
. CLOZE PROCEDURE
. COUNSELING TECHNIQUES
. CRITICAL INCIDENTS METHOD
. CRITICAL PATH METHOD
. DELPHI TECHNIQUE
. DESEGREGATION METHODS
.. BUSING
. EDUCATIONAL METHODS
.. CLASSROOM TECHNIQUES
.. EDUCATIONAL STRATEGIES
.. PSYCHOEDUCATIONAL
METHODS
.. TEACHING METHODS
... AUDIOLINGUAL METHODS
... CLINICAL TEACHING
(HEALTH PROFESSIONS)
... CONVENTIONAL
INSTRUCTION
... CREATIVE TEACHING
... CROSS AGE TEACHING
... DEMONSTRATIONS
(EDUCATIONAL)
... DIAGNOSTIC TEACHING
... DISCUSSION (TEACHING
TECHNIQUE)
... DRILLS (PRACTICE)
.... PATTERN DRILLS
(LANGUAGE)
..... SUBSTITUTION DRILLS
... EXPERIMENTAL TEACHING
... GRAMMAR TRANSLATION
METHOD
... INDIVIDUALIZED
INSTRUCTION
... KINESTHETIC METHODS
... LANGUAGE EXPERIENCE
APPROACH
... LECTURE METHOD
... MONTESSORI METHOD
... MULTIMEDIA INSTRUCTION
.... AUDIOVISUAL
INSTRUCTION
... NEGATIVE PRACTICE
... ORAL COMMUNICATION
METHOD
.... LIPREADING
... PEER TEACHING
... PRECISION TEACHING
... PROGRAMED INSTRUCTION
.... COMPUTER ASSISTED
INSTRUCTION
.... PROGRAMED TUTORING
... SIGHT METHOD
... SUGGESTOPEDIA
... TELEPHONE INSTRUCTION
... THEMATIC APPROACH
... TRAINING METHODS
.... MANAGEMENT GAMES
.... MICROCOUNSELING
.... MICROTEACHING
. EVALUATION METHODS
.. AUDIENCE ANALYSIS
.. CASE STUDIES
... CROSS SECTIONAL STUDIES
... FACILITY CASE STUDIES
... LONGITUDINAL STUDIES
.... FOLLOWUP STUDIES
..... GRADUATE SURVEYS
..... VOCATIONAL FOLLOWUP
.. CHEMICAL ANALYSIS
.. COMPARATIVE ANALYSIS
... EDUCATIONAL STATUS
COMPARISON
... ERROR ANALYSIS
(LANGUAGE)
.. COMPONENTIAL ANALYSIS
.. CONTENT ANALYSIS
.. COST EFFECTIVENESS
.. DATA ANALYSIS
... DATA COLLECTION
.... SAMPLING
..... ITEM SAMPLING
... DATA INTERPRETATION
.... STATISTICAL INFERENCE
.... TEST INTERPRETATION
... STATISTICAL ANALYSIS
.... ANALYSIS OF COVARIANCE
.... ANALYSIS OF VARIANCE
.... BAYESIAN STATISTICS
.... CORRELATION
.... EFFECT SIZE
.... ERROR OF MEASUREMENT
.... GOODNESS OF FIT
.... ITEM ANALYSIS
.... JUDGMENT ANALYSIS
TECHNIQUE
.... LEAST SQUARES
STATISTICS
.... MAXIMUM LIKELIHOOD
STATISTICS
.... META ANALYSIS
.... MULTIVARIATE ANALYSIS
..... CLUSTER ANALYSIS
..... DISCRIMINANT ANALYSIS
..... FACTOR ANALYSIS
...... OBLIQUE ROTATION
...... ORTHOGONAL ROTATION
..... MULTIDIMENSIONAL
SCALING
..... PATH ANALYSIS
.... REGRESSION
(STATISTICS)
..... MULTIPLE REGRESSION
ANALYSIS
.... STATISTICAL
DISTRIBUTIONS
.... STATISTICAL INFERENCE
.... STATISTICAL
SIGNIFICANCE
... TREND ANALYSIS
.. HYPOTHESIS TESTING
.. INPUT OUTPUT ANALYSIS
.. INSPECTION
.. INTERVIEWS
... EMPLOYMENT INTERVIEWS
... FIELD INTERVIEWS
.. JOB ANALYSIS
.. LIFE CYCLE COSTING
.. NEED ANALYSIS (STUDENT
FINANCIAL AID)
.. PHONETIC ANALYSIS
.. PRETESTING
.. QUALITY CONTROL
.. READABILITY FORMULAS
.. SITE ANALYSIS
.. SKILL ANALYSIS
.. STRUCTURAL ANALYSIS
(LINGUISTICS)
... DISCOURSE ANALYSIS
... TAGMEMIC ANALYSIS
.. STRUCTURAL ANALYSIS
(SCIENCE)
.. SURVEYS
... COMMUNITY SURVEYS
... GRADUATE SURVEYS
... LIBRARY SURVEYS
... NATIONAL SURVEYS
... OCCUPATIONAL SURVEYS
... SCHOOL SURVEYS
... STATE SURVEYS
... STATISTICAL SURVEYS
... TELEVISION SURVEYS
.. SYNTHESIS
.. TASK ANALYSIS
. FIXED SEQUENCE
. GRIEVANCE PROCEDURES
. HEURISTICS
. HOLISTIC APPROACH
.. GESTALT THERAPY
.. GLOBAL APPROACH
.. SYSTEMS APPROACH
... SYSTEMS BUILDING
.... DESIGN BUILD APPROACH
. HOME VISITS
. INQUIRY
. INSURANCE
.. FIRE INSURANCE
.. HEALTH INSURANCE
.. UNEMPLOYMENT INSURANCE
.. WORKERS COMPENSATION
. INTERDISCIPLINARY
APPROACH
. JOB SEARCH METHODS
. LABORATORY PROCEDURES

METHODS
(CONTINUED)

. . CHROMATOGRAPHY
. . CULTURING TECHNIQUES
. LEARNING STRATEGIES
. . READING STRATEGIES
. MAGNIFICATION METHODS
. MARXIAN ANALYSIS
. MEASUREMENT TECHNIQUES
. . CLASSROOM OBSERVATION TECHNIQUES
. . FORCED CHOICE TECHNIQUE
. . Q METHODOLOGY
. . SCALING
. . . MULTIDIMENSIONAL SCALING
. . SCORING FORMULAS
. . SOCIOMETRIC TECHNIQUES
. . TESTING
. . . ADAPTIVE TESTING
. . . COMPARATIVE TESTING
. . . COMPUTER ASSISTED TESTING
. . . CONFIDENCE TESTING
. . . EDUCATIONAL TESTING
. . . GROUP TESTING
. . . INDIVIDUAL TESTING
. . . MINIMUM COMPETENCY TESTING
. . . PSYCHOLOGICAL TESTING
. MOTIVATION TECHNIQUES
. MUSIC TECHNIQUES
. NETWORK ANALYSIS
. PACING
. PRODUCTION TECHNIQUES
. . ELECTRONIC PUBLISHING
. . FILM PRODUCTION
. . PHOTOCOMPOSITION
. . SPECIAL EFFECTS
. . . ANIMATION
. . . SOUND EFFECTS
. . TELEVISION LIGHTING
. . TEXTBOOK PUBLICATION
. PROMPTING
. QUESTIONING TECHNIQUES
. RESEARCH METHODOLOGY
. . INTERACTION PROCESS ANALYSIS
. . MULTITRAIT MULTIMETHOD TECHNIQUES
. . PROTOCOL ANALYSIS
. . SCIENTIFIC METHODOLOGY
. SEQUENTIAL APPROACH
. SIMULATION
. . COMPUTER SIMULATION
. . MODELS
. . . MATHEMATICAL MODELS
. . . ROLE MODELS
. . . . MENTORS
. . . STUDENT WRITING MODELS
. . . TEACHING MODELS
. . MONTE CARLO METHODS
. . ROLE PLAYING
. . . DRAMATIC PLAY
. SUPERVISORY METHODS
. SYSTEMS ANALYSIS

: : : CURRICULUM
: : COLLEGE CURRICULUM
: TEACHER EDUCATION CURRICULUM
: : CURRICULUM
: COURSES
METHODS COURSES

: RESEARCH
METHODS RESEARCH

: : : : : : GROUPS
: : : : : PERSONNEL
: : : : SCHOOL PERSONNEL
: : : : : : GROUPS
: : : : : PERSONNEL
: : : : PROFESSIONAL PERSONNEL
: : : FACULTY
: : COLLEGE FACULTY
: TEACHER EDUCATORS
METHODS TEACHERS

: STANDARDS
METRIC SYSTEM

: GEOGRAPHIC REGIONS
METROPOLITAN AREAS
. SUBURBS

: EDUCATION
MEXICAN AMERICAN EDUCATION

: : : : : : LIBERAL ARTS
: : : : : SCIENCES
: : : : SOCIAL SCIENCES
: : : : : LIBERAL ARTS
: : : : HUMANITIES
: : : HISTORY
: : NORTH AMERICAN HISTORY
: UNITED STATES HISTORY
MEXICAN AMERICAN HISTORY

: : : : : : LIBERAL ARTS
: : : : : HUMANITIES
: : : : LITERATURE
: : : NORTH AMERICAN LITERATURE
: : UNITED STATES LITERATURE
: HISPANIC AMERICAN LITERATURE
MEXICAN AMERICAN LITERATURE

: : : GROUPS
: : NORTH AMERICANS
: HISPANIC AMERICANS
: : GROUPS
: ETHNIC GROUPS
MEXICAN AMERICANS

: : GROUPS
: LATIN AMERICANS
MEXICANS
. BRACEROS

: : : : : LIBERAL ARTS
: : : : SCIENCES
: : : NATURAL SCIENCES
: : BIOLOGICAL SCIENCES
: BIOLOGY
MICROBIOLOGY

: : : EQUIPMENT
: : ELECTRONIC EQUIPMENT
: COMPUTERS
MICROCOMPUTERS

: : : : METHODS
: : : EDUCATIONAL METHODS
: : TEACHING METHODS
: TRAINING METHODS
MICROCOUNSELING

: : VISUAL AIDS
: MICROFORMS
MICROFICHE

: : VISUAL AIDS
: MICROFORMS
MICROFILM
. COMPUTER OUTPUT MICROFILM

: : VISUAL AIDS
: : EQUIPMENT
: PROJECTION EQUIPMENT
MICROFORM READERS

: VISUAL AIDS
MICROFORMS
. MICROFICHE
. MICROFILM
. . COMPUTER OUTPUT MICROFILM

: : EQUIPMENT
: ELECTRONIC EQUIPMENT
: : EQUIPMENT
: AUDIO EQUIPMENT
MICROPHONES

: : TECHNOLOGY
: REPROGRAPHY
MICROREPRODUCTION

: : EQUIPMENT
: LABORATORY EQUIPMENT
MICROSCOPES

: : : : METHODS
: : : EDUCATIONAL METHODS
: : TEACHING METHODS
: TRAINING METHODS
MICROTEACHING

: : : GROUPS
: : AGE GROUPS
: ADULTS
MIDDLE AGED ADULTS

: : GROUPS
: SOCIAL CLASS
MIDDLE CLASS

: CULTURE
MIDDLE CLASS CULTURE

: : GROUPS
: PARENTS
MIDDLE CLASS PARENTS

: STANDARDS
MIDDLE CLASS STANDARDS

: : GROUPS
: STUDENTS
MIDDLE CLASS STUDENTS

: : : : LIBERAL ARTS
: : : SCIENCES
: : SOCIAL SCIENCES
: : : LIBERAL ARTS
: : HUMANITIES
: HISTORY
MIDDLE EASTERN HISTORY

: : CURRICULUM
: AREA STUDIES
MIDDLE EASTERN STUDIES

: : : LANGUAGES
: : INDO EUROPEAN LANGUAGES
: ENGLISH
MIDDLE ENGLISH

: : FACILITIES
: HOUSING
MIDDLE INCOME HOUSING

: : GOVERNANCE
: ADMINISTRATION
MIDDLE MANAGEMENT

: : INSTITUTIONS
: SCHOOLS
MIDDLE SCHOOLS

: CHANGE
MIDLIFE TRANSITIONS

: : EDUCATION
: ADULT EDUCATION
MIGRANT ADULT EDUCATION

: : GROUPS
: MIGRANTS
: : : GROUPS
: : AGE GROUPS
: CHILDREN
MIGRANT CHILDREN

: EDUCATION
MIGRANT EDUCATION

: EMPLOYMENT
MIGRANT EMPLOYMENT

: : : SERVICES
: : HUMAN SERVICES
: HEALTH SERVICES
MIGRANT HEALTH SERVICES

: : FACILITIES
: HOUSING
MIGRANT HOUSING

: PROBLEMS
MIGRANT PROBLEMS

: PROGRAMS
MIGRANT PROGRAMS

: GROUPS
MIGRANTS
. IMMIGRANTS
. . UNDOCUMENTED IMMIGRANTS
. MIGRANT CHILDREN
. MIGRANT WORKERS
. MIGRANT YOUTH
. NOMADS
. REFUGEES
. TRANSIENT CHILDREN

: : : : SERVICES
: : : HUMAN SERVICES
: : SOCIAL SERVICES
: WELFARE SERVICES
MIGRANT WELFARE SERVICES

: : GROUPS
: MIGRANTS
: : : : : : GROUPS
: : : : : PERSONNEL
: : : : NONPROFESSIONAL PERSONNEL
: : : UNSKILLED WORKERS
: : LABORERS
: : : : GROUPS
: : : PERSONNEL
: : AGRICULTURAL PERSONNEL
: AGRICULTURAL LABORERS
MIGRANT WORKERS

: : GROUPS
: YOUTH
: : GROUPS
: MIGRANTS
MIGRANT YOUTH

: MOBILITY
MIGRATION
. FAMILY MOBILITY
. MIGRATION PATTERNS
. RELOCATION
. . RURAL RESETTLEMENT
. RURAL TO URBAN MIGRATION
. STUDENT MOBILITY
. URBAN TO RURAL MIGRATION
. URBAN TO SUBURBAN MIGRATION

: : MOBILITY
: MIGRATION
MIGRATION PATTERNS

: DISABILITIES
MILD DISABILITIES
. MILD MENTAL RETARDATION
. MINIMAL BRAIN DYSFUNCTION

: : DISABILITIES
: MILD DISABILITIES
: : DISABILITIES
: MENTAL RETARDATION
MILD MENTAL RETARDATION

: : THERAPY
: PSYCHOTHERAPY
MILIEU THERAPY

: FACILITIES
MILITARY AIR FACILITIES

: : GROUPS
: ORGANIZATIONS (GROUPS)
MILITARY ORGANIZATIONS
. ARMED FORCES

: : : GROUPS
: : PERSONNEL
: GOVERNMENT EMPLOYEES
MILITARY PERSONNEL
. ENLISTED PERSONNEL
. OFFICER PERSONNEL

: : INSTITUTIONS
: SCHOOLS
MILITARY SCHOOLS

: CURRICULUM
MILITARY SCIENCE

MILITARY SERVICE

: TRAINING
MILITARY TRAINING

: : : : : LIBERAL ARTS
: : : : SCIENCES
: : : : NATURAL SCIENCES
: : : PHYSICAL SCIENCES
: : EARTH SCIENCE
: GEOLOGY
MINERALOGY

: MATTER
MINERALS
. ASBESTOS

: : : EQUIPMENT
: : ELECTRONIC EQUIPMENT
: COMPUTERS
MINICOMPUTERS

: : CURRICULUM
: COURSES
MINICOURSES

: : : DISABILITIES
: : PHYSICAL DISABILITIES
: NEUROLOGICAL IMPAIRMENTS
: : DISABILITIES
: MILD DISABILITIES
MINIMAL BRAIN DYSFUNCTION

: : ABILITY
: SKILLS
: : ABILITY
: COMPETENCE
MINIMUM COMPETENCIES

: : : METHODS
: : MEASUREMENT TECHNIQUES
: TESTING
MINIMUM COMPETENCY TESTING

: : INCOME
: : EXPENDITURES
: WAGES
MINIMUM WAGE

: LEGISLATION
MINIMUM WAGE LEGISLATION

: TECHNOLOGY
MINING

: : : GROUPS
: : AGE GROUPS
: CHILDREN
MINORITY GROUP CHILDREN

: INFLUENCES
MINORITY GROUP INFLUENCES

: GROUPS
MINORITY GROUPS

: : : : GROUPS
: : : PERSONNEL
: : PROFESSIONAL PERSONNEL
: TEACHERS
MINORITY GROUP TEACHERS

MISCONCEPTIONS

: : : IDENTIFICATION
: : EDUCATIONAL DIAGNOSIS
: READING DIAGNOSIS
MISCUE ANALYSIS

: : : PUBLICATIONS
: : REPORTS
: POSITION PAPERS
MISSION STATEMENTS

MNEMONICS

: : : FACILITIES
: : EDUCATIONAL FACILITIES
: CLASSROOMS
MOBILE CLASSROOMS

: CLINICS
MOBILE CLINICS

: : : : SERVICES
: : : HUMAN SERVICES
: : SOCIAL SERVICES
: ANCILLARY SCHOOL SERVICES
MOBILE EDUCATIONAL SERVICES

: : FACILITIES
: LABORATORIES
MOBILE LABORATORIES

MOBILITY
. EDUCATIONAL MOBILITY
. MIGRATION
. . FAMILY MOBILITY
. . MIGRATION PATTERNS
. . RELOCATION
. . . RURAL RESETTLEMENT
. . RURAL TO URBAN MIGRATION
. . STUDENT MOBILITY
. . URBAN TO RURAL MIGRATION
. . URBAN TO SUBURBAN MIGRATION
. OCCUPATIONAL MOBILITY
. . CAREER LADDERS
. . FACULTY MOBILITY
. . TEACHER TRANSFER
. PHYSICAL MOBILITY
. . VISUALLY HANDICAPPED MOBILITY
. SOCIAL MOBILITY

: : EQUIPMENT
: ASSISTIVE DEVICES (FOR DISABLED)
MOBILITY AIDS
. WHEELCHAIRS

: BEHAVIOR
MODELING (PSYCHOLOGY)

: : METHODS
: SIMULATION
MODELS
. MATHEMATICAL MODELS
. ROLE MODELS
. . MENTORS
. STUDENT WRITING MODELS
. TEACHING MODELS

: : DISABILITIES
: MENTAL RETARDATION
MODERATE MENTAL RETARDATION

: : : : LIBERAL ARTS
: : : SCIENCES
: : SOCIAL SCIENCES
: : : LIBERAL ARTS
: : HUMANITIES
: HISTORY
MODERN HISTORY

MODERNISM

: : CHANGE
: SOCIAL CHANGE
: DEVELOPMENT
MODERNIZATION

: CURRICULUM
MODERN LANGUAGE CURRICULUM
. CONVERSATIONAL LANGUAGE COURSES
. FLES
. INTENSIVE LANGUAGE COURSES
. NOTIONAL FUNCTIONAL SYLLABI

: LANGUAGES
MODERN LANGUAGES

: : CURRICULUM
: MATHEMATICS CURRICULUM
MODERN MATHEMATICS

: : DESIGN
: BUILDING DESIGN
MODULAR BUILDING DESIGN

MOLECULAR STRUCTURE

MONETARY SYSTEMS

: : GOVERNANCE
: ADMINISTRATION
MONEY MANAGEMENT

: : : LANGUAGES
: : URALIC ALTAIC LANGUAGES
: MONGOLIAN LANGUAGES
MONGOLIAN

: : LANGUAGES
: URALIC ALTAIC LANGUAGES
MONGOLIAN LANGUAGES
. BURIAT
. DAGUR
. MONGOLIAN

MONOLINGUALISM

: LITERARY DEVICES
MONOLOGS

: : METHODS
: SIMULATION
MONTE CARLO METHODS

: : : METHODS
: : EDUCATIONAL METHODS
: TEACHING METHODS
MONTESSORI METHOD

MORAL CRITICISM (1969 1980)

: : DEVELOPMENT
: INDIVIDUAL DEVELOPMENT
MORAL DEVELOPMENT

: PSYCHOLOGICAL PATTERNS
MORALE
. TEACHER MORALE

MORAL ISSUES

: VALUES
MORAL VALUES

: : : : LINGUISTICS
: : : DESCRIPTIVE LINGUISTICS
: : GRAMMAR
: MORPHOLOGY (LANGUAGES)
MORPHEMES
. NEGATIVE FORMS (LANGUAGE)
. PLURALS
. SUFFIXES
. TENSES (GRAMMAR)

: : : LINGUISTICS
: : DESCRIPTIVE LINGUISTICS
: GRAMMAR
MORPHOLOGY (LANGUAGES)
. MORPHEMES
. . NEGATIVE FORMS (LANGUAGE)
. . PLURALS
. . SUFFIXES
. . TENSES (GRAMMAR)
. MORPHOPHONEMICS

: : : : LINGUISTICS
: : : DESCRIPTIVE LINGUISTICS
: : GRAMMAR
: MORPHOLOGY (LANGUAGES)
MORPHOPHONEMICS

: : LANGUAGES
: AFRICAN LANGUAGES
MOSSI

: : ATTITUDES
: PARENT ATTITUDES
MOTHER ATTITUDES

: : : GROUPS
: : FAMILY (SOCIOLOGICAL UNIT)
: ONE PARENT FAMILY
MOTHERLESS FAMILY

: : GROUPS
: PARENTS
: : GROUPS
: FEMALES
MOTHERS
. BLACK MOTHERS
. UNWED MOTHERS

: LITERARY DEVICES
MOTIFS

: SCIENTIFIC CONCEPTS
MOTION
. ACCELERATION (PHYSICS)

MOTIVATION
. ACHIEVEMENT NEED
. LEARNING MOTIVATION
. STUDENT MOTIVATION
. TEACHER MOTIVATION

: METHODS
MOTIVATION TECHNIQUES

::: DEVELOPMENT
:: INDIVIDUAL DEVELOPMENT
: PHYSICAL DEVELOPMENT
MOTOR DEVELOPMENT

:: BEHAVIOR
: RESPONSES
MOTOR REACTIONS
. EYE MOVEMENTS
.. EYE FIXATIONS
. PUPILLARY DILATION

: EQUIPMENT
MOTOR VEHICLES
. SERVICE VEHICLES
.. BOOKMOBILES
.. SCHOOL BUSES
. TRACTORS

:: STRUCTURAL ELEMENTS (CONSTRUCTION)
:: EQUIPMENT
: SPACE DIVIDERS
MOVABLE PARTITIONS

:: EDUCATION
: PHYSICAL EDUCATION
MOVEMENT EDUCATION

::: INSTITUTIONS
:: SCHOOLS
: COLLEGES
MULTICAMPUS COLLEGES

::: GROUPS
:: ORGANIZATIONS (GROUPS)
: SCHOOL DISTRICTS
MULTICAMPUS DISTRICTS

:: EDUCATION
: INTERGROUP EDUCATION
MULTICULTURAL EDUCATION

::: EDUCATIONAL MEDIA
:: INSTRUCTIONAL MATERIALS
::: PUBLICATIONS
:: BOOKS
: TEXTBOOKS
MULTICULTURAL TEXTBOOKS

::: METHODS
:: MEASUREMENT TECHNIQUES
: SCALING
::::: METHODS
:::: EVALUATION METHODS
::: DATA ANALYSIS
:: STATISTICAL ANALYSIS
: MULTIVARIATE ANALYSIS
MULTIDIMENSIONAL SCALING

:: GROUPS
: CLASSES (GROUPS OF STUDENTS)
MULTIGRADED CLASSES

:: GROUPS
: CLASSES (GROUPS OF STUDENTS)
MULTILEVEL CLASSES (SECOND LANGUAGE INSTRUCTION)

MULTILINGUALISM

MULTILINGUAL MATERIALS
. BILINGUAL INSTRUCTIONAL MATERIALS

::: METHODS
:: EDUCATIONAL METHODS
: TEACHING METHODS
MULTIMEDIA INSTRUCTION
. AUDIOVISUAL INSTRUCTION

::: MEASURES (INDIVIDUALS)
:: TESTS
: OBJECTIVE TESTS
MULTIPLE CHOICE TESTS

: DISABILITIES
MULTIPLE DISABILITIES
. DEAF BLIND

: EMPLOYMENT
MULTIPLE EMPLOYMENT

::::: METHODS
:::: EVALUATION METHODS
::: DATA ANALYSIS
:: STATISTICAL ANALYSIS
: REGRESSION (STATISTICS)
MULTIPLE REGRESSION ANALYSIS

::: LIBERAL ARTS
:: MATHEMATICS
: ARITHMETIC
MULTIPLICATION

::: FACILITIES
:: EDUCATIONAL FACILITIES
: CLASSROOMS
MULTIPURPOSE CLASSROOMS

: LEARNING
MULTISENSORY LEARNING

:: METHODS
: RESEARCH METHODOLOGY
MULTITRAIT MULTIMETHOD TECHNIQUES

:: INSTITUTIONS
: SCHOOLS
MULTIUNIT SCHOOLS

:::: METHODS
::: EVALUATION METHODS
:: DATA ANALYSIS
: STATISTICAL ANALYSIS
MULTIVARIATE ANALYSIS
. CLUSTER ANALYSIS
. DISCRIMINANT ANALYSIS
. FACTOR ANALYSIS
.. OBLIQUE ROTATION
.. ORTHOGONAL ROTATION
. MULTIDIMENSIONAL SCALING
. PATH ANALYSIS

:: GEOGRAPHIC REGIONS
: URBAN AREAS
: COMMUNITY
MUNICIPALITIES

:: INDIVIDUAL CHARACTERISTICS
: PHYSICAL CHARACTERISTICS
MUSCULAR STRENGTH

: FACILITIES
MUSEUMS

::: LIBERAL ARTS
:: HUMANITIES
: FINE ARTS
MUSIC
. APPLIED MUSIC
. JAZZ
. ORIENTAL MUSIC
. VOCAL MUSIC
.. CHORAL MUSIC
.. SONGS
... ART SONG
... BALLADS
... HYMNS

: ACTIVITIES
MUSIC ACTIVITIES
. CONCERTS
. SINGING

MUSICAL COMPOSITION

: EQUIPMENT
MUSICAL INSTRUMENTS

:: EDUCATION
: AESTHETIC EDUCATION
MUSIC APPRECIATION

: EDUCATION
MUSIC EDUCATION

: FACILITIES
MUSIC FACILITIES

:: GROUPS
: ARTISTS
MUSICIANS

:: LITERACY
:: LANGUAGE ARTS
: READING
MUSIC READING

:::: GROUPS
::: PERSONNEL
:: PROFESSIONAL PERSONNEL
: TEACHERS
MUSIC TEACHERS

: METHODS
MUSIC TECHNIQUES

: THEORIES
MUSIC THEORY

: THERAPY
MUSIC THERAPY

MUTUAL INTELLIGIBILITY

::: DISABILITIES
:: VISUAL IMPAIRMENTS
: AMETROPIA
MYOPIA

MYSTICISM

MYTHIC CRITICISM (1969 1980)

MYTHOLOGY

NARCOTICS
. MARIJUANA
. SEDATIVES

: LITERARY DEVICES
NARRATION

::: MEASURES (INDIVIDUALS)
:: TESTS
: ACHIEVEMENT TESTS
NATIONAL COMPETENCY TESTS

: NATIONAL SECURITY
NATIONAL DEFENSE

NATIONALISM
. PATRIOTISM

:::: INSTITUTIONS
:::: INFORMATION SOURCES
::: LIBRARIES
:: SPECIAL LIBRARIES
: GOVERNMENT LIBRARIES
NATIONAL LIBRARIES

::: DATA
:: STATISTICAL DATA
: NORMS
NATIONAL NORMS

:: GROUPS
: ORGANIZATIONS (GROUPS)
NATIONAL ORGANIZATIONS

: PROGRAMS
NATIONAL PROGRAMS

NATIONAL SECURITY
. NATIONAL DEFENSE

::: METHODS
:: EVALUATION METHODS
: SURVEYS
NATIONAL SURVEYS

:: INSTRUCTION
: HUMANITIES INSTRUCTION
NATIVE LANGUAGE INSTRUCTION
. ENGLISH INSTRUCTION

: GROUPS
NATIVE SPEAKERS
. SPANISH SPEAKING

NATURAL DISASTERS

NATURALISM

: OBSERVATION
NATURALISTIC OBSERVATION

: RESOURCES
NATURAL RESOURCES
. COAL
. WATER RESOURCES

:: LIBERAL ARTS
: SCIENCES
NATURAL SCIENCES
. BIOLOGICAL SCIENCES
.. ANATOMY
.. BIOCHEMISTRY
.. BIOFEEDBACK
.. BIOLOGY
... MARINE BIOLOGY
... MICROBIOLOGY
... RADIATION BIOLOGY
... SOCIAL BIOLOGY
.. BIOMEDICINE
.. BIOPHYSICS
... BIOMECHANICS
... BIONICS
.... ROBOTICS
.. BOTANY
.. CYTOLOGY
.. ECOLOGY
.. EMBRYOLOGY

NATURAL SCIENCES
(CONTINUED)

..ETHOLOGY
..GENETICS
...GENETIC ENGINEERING
..PHYSIOLOGY
...EXERCISE PHYSIOLOGY
...PSYCHOPHYSIOLOGY
..SOCIOBIOLOGY
..ZOOLOGY
...ENTOMOLOGY
...ICHTHYOLOGY
...ORNITHOLOGY
...PRIMATOLOGY
.PHYSICAL SCIENCES
..ASTRONOMY
..CHEMISTRY
...BIOCHEMISTRY
...INORGANIC CHEMISTRY
...ORGANIC CHEMISTRY
..CRYSTALLOGRAPHY
..EARTH SCIENCE
...GEOLOGY
....MINERALOGY
....PALEONTOLOGY
...GEOPHYSICS
....PLATE TECTONICS
...METEOROLOGY
...OCEANOGRAPHY
...PHYSICAL GEOGRAPHY
...SEISMOLOGY
....PLATE TECTONICS
...SOIL SCIENCE
..PHYSICS
...BIOPHYSICS
....BIOMECHANICS
....BIONICS
.....ROBOTICS
...ELECTRONICS
...MECHANICS (PHYSICS)
....FLUID MECHANICS
....KINETICS
.....DIFFUSION (PHYSICS)
....QUANTUM MECHANICS
...NUCLEAR PHYSICS
...OPTICS
...THERMODYNAMICS
..SPECTROSCOPY

::FACILITIES
:RESOURCE CENTERS
NATURE CENTERS

NATURE NURTURE CONTROVERSY

:::LANGUAGES
::AMERICAN INDIAN
LANGUAGES
:ATHAPASCAN LANGUAGES
NAVAJO

:TECHNOLOGY
NAVIGATION

:TOTALITARIANISM
::SOCIAL SYSTEMS
:FASCISM
NAZISM

::METHODS
:EVALUATION METHODS
NEED ANALYSIS (STUDENT
FINANCIAL AID)

NEED GRATIFICATION

:OCCUPATIONS
NEEDLE TRADES

NEEDS
.CONSTRUCTION NEEDS
.EDUCATIONAL NEEDS
.EVALUATION NEEDS
.FINANCIAL NEEDS
.HEALTH NEEDS
.HOUSING NEEDS
.INDIVIDUAL NEEDS
..CHILDHOOD NEEDS
..PSYCHOLOGICAL NEEDS
...ACHIEVEMENT NEED
...AFFECTION
...AFFILIATION NEED
....PEER ACCEPTANCE
...PERSONAL SPACE
...SECURITY (PSYCHOLOGY)
...SELF ACTUALIZATION
...STATUS NEED
.INFORMATION NEEDS
.LABOR NEEDS
..PERSONNEL NEEDS
.RESEARCH NEEDS
.STUDENT NEEDS
.USER NEEDS (INFORMATION)

:EVALUATION
NEEDS ASSESSMENT

:ATTITUDES
NEGATIVE ATTITUDES

:::::LINGUISTICS
::::DESCRIPTIVE
LINGUISTICS
:::GRAMMAR
::MORPHOLOGY (LANGUAGES)
:MORPHEMES
NEGATIVE FORMS (LANGUAGE)

:::METHODS
::EDUCATIONAL METHODS
:TEACHING METHODS
NEGATIVE PRACTICE

:REINFORCEMENT
NEGATIVE REINFORCEMENT

NEGOTIATION AGREEMENTS

NEGOTIATION IMPASSES

NEGRO HOUSING (1966 1977)

:IMPROVEMENT
NEIGHBORHOOD IMPROVEMENT

:SOCIAL INTEGRATION
NEIGHBORHOOD INTEGRATION

:COMMUNITY
NEIGHBORHOODS

::INSTITUTIONS
:SCHOOLS
NEIGHBORHOOD SCHOOLS

::LANGUAGES
:AFRICAN LANGUAGES
NEMBE

NEOCLASSICISM

:::::GROUPS
::::AGE GROUPS
:::CHILDREN
::YOUNG CHILDREN
:INFANTS
NEONATES

::LANGUAGES
:INDO EUROPEAN LANGUAGES
NEPALI

:METHODS
NETWORK ANALYSIS

NETWORKS
.COMPUTER NETWORKS
..LOCAL AREA NETWORKS
.INFORMATION NETWORKS
..LIBRARY NETWORKS
...BIBLIOGRAPHIC UTILITIES
.SOCIAL NETWORKS

:LINGUISTICS
NEUROLINGUISTICS

::DISABILITIES
:PHYSICAL DISABILITIES
NEUROLOGICAL IMPAIRMENTS
.APHASIA
.CEREBRAL PALSY
.EPILEPSY
.MINIMAL BRAIN DYSFUNCTION

::INDIVIDUAL
CHARACTERISTICS
:PHYSICAL CHARACTERISTICS
NEUROLOGICAL ORGANIZATION
.BRAIN HEMISPHERE
FUNCTIONS

::TECHNOLOGY
:MEDICINE
NEUROLOGY

::DISABILITIES
:MENTAL DISORDERS
NEUROSIS

::TECHNOLOGY
:JOURNALISM
NEW JOURNALISM

:::PUBLICATIONS
::SERIALS
:::MASS MEDIA
::NEWS MEDIA
:NEWSPAPERS
NEWSLETTERS

:MASS MEDIA
NEWS MEDIA
.EDITORIALS
.NEWSPAPERS
..NEWSLETTERS
..SCHOOL NEWSPAPERS

::PUBLICATIONS
:SERIALS
::MASS MEDIA
:NEWS MEDIA
NEWSPAPERS
.NEWSLETTERS
.SCHOOL NEWSPAPERS

::TECHNOLOGY
:JOURNALISM
NEWS REPORTING

::LITERACY
::LANGUAGE ARTS
:WRITING (COMPOSITION)
::TECHNOLOGY
:JOURNALISM
NEWS WRITING

:::LIBERAL ARTS
::HUMANITIES
:LITERATURE
NINETEENTH CENTURY
LITERATURE

:::ENVIRONMENT
::PHYSICAL ENVIRONMENT
:ACOUSTICAL ENVIRONMENT
NOISE (SOUND)

::GROUPS
:MIGRANTS
NOMADS

::GROUPS
:CLASSES (GROUPS OF
STUDENTS)
NONAUTHORITARIAN CLASSES

:::INSTITUTIONS
::SCHOOLS
:COLLEGES
NONCAMPUS COLLEGES

::::GROUPS
:::STUDENTS
::SECONDARY SCHOOL
STUDENTS
:HIGH SCHOOL STUDENTS
NONCOLLEGE BOUND STUDENTS

::CURRICULUM
:COURSES
NONCREDIT COURSES

::GUIDANCE
:COUNSELING
NONDIRECTIVE COUNSELING

:EDUCATION
NONDISCRIMINATORY EDUCATION

::::FINANCIAL SUPPORT
:::STUDENT FINANCIAL AID
::SCHOLARSHIPS
:MERIT SCHOLARSHIPS
NO NEED SCHOLARSHIPS

:GROUPS
NON ENGLISH SPEAKING

::::LIBERAL ARTS
:::HUMANITIES
::LITERATURE
:PROSE
NONFICTION
.BIOGRAPHIES
..AUTOBIOGRAPHIES
.CHRONICLES
.DIARIES
.ESSAYS

:EDUCATION
NONFORMAL EDUCATION

:::ORGANIZATION
::CLASSIFICATION
:GROUPING (INSTRUCTIONAL
PURPOSES)
NONGRADED INSTRUCTIONAL
GROUPING

::EVALUATION
:STUDENT EVALUATION
NONGRADED STUDENT EVALUATION

::RESPONSIBILITY
:TEACHER RESPONSIBILITY
NONINSTRUCTIONAL
RESPONSIBILITY

::COSTS
:STUDENT COSTS
NONINSTRUCTIONAL STUDENT
COSTS

::GROUPS
:STUDENTS
NONMAJORS

:::LIBERAL ARTS
::MATHEMATICS
:STATISTICS
NONPARAMETRIC STATISTICS

NONPRINT MEDIA
. AUDIODISKS
. DOCUMENTARIES
. EXHIBITS
.. SCIENCE FAIRS
. FILMS
.. FOREIGN LANGUAGE FILMS
.. INSTRUCTIONAL FILMS
.. KINESCOPE RECORDINGS
.. SINGLE CONCEPT FILMS
. FILMSTRIPS
. OPTICAL DISKS
.. OPTICAL DATA DISKS
. REALIA
. TAPE RECORDINGS
.. AUDIOTAPE RECORDINGS
.. VIDEOTAPE RECORDINGS
. TRANSPARENCIES
.. SLIDES
. VIDEODISKS

:: GROUPS
: PERSONNEL
NONPROFESSIONAL PERSONNEL
. CLERICAL WORKERS
.. COURT REPORTERS
.. EXAMINERS
.. FILE CLERKS
.. RECEPTIONISTS
.. SECRETARIES
... SCHOOL SECRETARIES
. SALES WORKERS
.. AUTO PARTS CLERKS
. SEMISKILLED WORKERS
.. ANIMAL CARETAKERS
.. BOAT OPERATORS
.. GROUNDS KEEPERS
.. NURSERY WORKERS (HORTICULTURE)
.. SEWING MACHINE OPERATORS
. SERVICE WORKERS
.. ATTENDANTS
.. BARBERS
.. COOKS
.. EMERGENCY SQUAD PERSONNEL
... EMERGENCY MEDICAL TECHNICIANS
.. FIRE FIGHTERS
.. HOUSEHOLD WORKERS
... HOME HEALTH AIDES
.. HOUSEKEEPERS
.. HOUSING MANAGEMENT AIDES
.. WAITERS AND WAITRESSES
. SKILLED WORKERS
.. AUTO BODY REPAIRERS
.. CRAFT WORKERS
.. ELECTRICIANS
.. FLOOR LAYERS
.. GLAZIERS
.. LOCOMOTIVE ENGINEERS
.. MACHINISTS
... MACHINE REPAIRERS
... MACHINE TOOL OPERATORS
... TOOL AND DIE MAKERS
.. SIGN PAINTERS
.. TELEVISION RADIO REPAIRERS
.. WATCHMAKERS
. UNSKILLED WORKERS
.. LABORERS
... AGRICULTURAL LABORERS
.... MIGRANT WORKERS
.... SEASONAL LABORERS
... AUXILIARY LABORERS

:: GROUPS
: ORGANIZATIONS (GROUPS)
NONPROFIT ORGANIZATIONS

::: GROUPS
:: ETHNIC GROUPS
: AMERICAN INDIANS
NONRESERVATION AMERICAN INDIANS
. RURAL AMERICAN INDIANS
. URBAN AMERICAN INDIANS

: PROGRAMS
NONSCHOOL EDUCATIONAL PROGRAMS

:::: LINGUISTICS
::: SOCIOLINGUISTICS
:: LANGUAGE VARIATION
:: LANGUAGES
: DIALECTS
NONSTANDARD DIALECTS

:::: GROUPS
::: PERSONNEL
:: SCHOOL PERSONNEL
:::: GROUPS
::: PERSONNEL
:: PROFESSIONAL PERSONNEL
: FACULTY
NONTENURED FACULTY

: EDUCATION
NONTRADITIONAL EDUCATION

: OCCUPATIONS
NONTRADITIONAL OCCUPATIONS

:: GROUPS
: STUDENTS
NONTRADITIONAL STUDENTS

: ABILITY
NONVERBAL ABILITY

: COMMUNICATION (THOUGHT TRANSFER)
NONVERBAL COMMUNICATION
. BODY LANGUAGE
. EYE CONTACT
. FACIAL EXPRESSIONS

: LEARNING
NONVERBAL LEARNING
. PERCEPTUAL MOTOR LEARNING

:: MEASURES (INDIVIDUALS)
: TESTS
NONVERBAL TESTS
. VISUAL MEASURES

: CULTURE
NON WESTERN CIVILIZATION

NORMALIZATION (HANDICAPPED)
. DEINSTITUTIONALIZATION (OF DISABLED)

:: MEASURES (INDIVIDUALS)
: TESTS
NORM REFERENCED TESTS

:: DATA
: STATISTICAL DATA
NORMS
. LOCAL NORMS
. NATIONAL NORMS
. STATE NORMS
. TEST NORMS

: CULTURE
NORTH AMERICAN CULTURE
. HISPANIC AMERICAN CULTURE
. JAPANESE AMERICAN CULTURE

::: LANGUAGES
:: INDO EUROPEAN LANGUAGES
: ENGLISH
NORTH AMERICAN ENGLISH

:::: LIBERAL ARTS
::: SCIENCES
:: SOCIAL SCIENCES
::: LIBERAL ARTS
:: HUMANITIES
: HISTORY
NORTH AMERICAN HISTORY
. UNITED STATES HISTORY
.. CIVIL WAR (UNITED STATES)
.. COLONIAL HISTORY (UNITED STATES)
.. MEXICAN AMERICAN HISTORY
.. RECONSTRUCTION ERA
.. REVOLUTIONARY WAR (UNITED STATES)
.. STATE HISTORY

::: LIBERAL ARTS
:: HUMANITIES
: LITERATURE
NORTH AMERICAN LITERATURE
. CANADIAN LITERATURE
. UNITED STATES LITERATURE
.. HISPANIC AMERICAN LITERATURE
... MEXICAN AMERICAN LITERATURE

: GROUPS
NORTH AMERICANS
. ALASKA NATIVES
. ANGLO AMERICANS
. ASIAN AMERICANS
.. CHINESE AMERICANS
.. FILIPINO AMERICANS
.. JAPANESE AMERICANS
.. KOREAN AMERICANS
. CANADA NATIVES
. GREEK AMERICANS
. HISPANIC AMERICANS
.. MEXICAN AMERICANS
.. PORTUGUESE AMERICANS
.. SPANISH AMERICANS
. ITALIAN AMERICANS
. PACIFIC AMERICANS
.. HAWAIIANS
.. SAMOAN AMERICANS
. POLISH AMERICANS

NORTHERN SCHOOLS (1966 1980)

:: LANGUAGES
: INDO EUROPEAN LANGUAGES
NORWEGIAN

: GROUPS
NO SHOWS

:: LITERACY
:: LANGUAGE ARTS
: WRITING (COMPOSITION)
NOTETAKING

:: CURRICULUM
: MODERN LANGUAGE CURRICULUM
NOTIONAL FUNCTIONAL SYLLABI

::::: LINGUISTICS
:::: DESCRIPTIVE LINGUISTICS
::: GRAMMAR
:: SYNTAX
: FORM CLASSES (LANGUAGES)
NOUNS

: LITERARY GENRES
::::: LIBERAL ARTS
:::: HUMANITIES
::: LITERATURE
:: PROSE
: FICTION
NOVELS

NOVELTY (STIMULUS DIMENSION)

::: SCIENTIFIC CONCEPTS
:: ENERGY
: RADIATION
NUCLEAR ENERGY

:: GROUPS
: FAMILY (SOCIOLOGICAL UNIT)
NUCLEAR FAMILY

::::: LIBERAL ARTS
:::: SCIENCES
::: NATURAL SCIENCES
:: PHYSICAL SCIENCES
: PHYSICS
NUCLEAR PHYSICS

: FACILITIES
NUCLEAR POWER PLANTS

::: GROUPS
:: PERSONNEL
: PARAPROFESSIONAL PERSONNEL
NUCLEAR POWER PLANT TECHNICIANS

:: TECHNOLOGY
: POWER TECHNOLOGY
NUCLEAR TECHNOLOGY

:: CONFLICT
: WAR
NUCLEAR WARFARE

NUCLEIC ACIDS
. DNA
. RNA

: MATHEMATICAL CONCEPTS
NUMBER CONCEPTS
. PLACE VALUE

: SYMBOLS (MATHEMATICS)
NUMBERS
. FRACTIONS
.. DECIMAL FRACTIONS
. LOGARITHMS
. NUMBER SYSTEMS
. RATIONAL NUMBERS
.. INTEGERS
... PRIME NUMBERS
. RECIPROCALS (MATHEMATICS)
. WHOLE NUMBERS

:: SYMBOLS (MATHEMATICS)
: NUMBERS
NUMBER SYSTEMS

NUMERICAL CONTROL

:: GROUPS
: FEMALES
NUNS

:::: GROUPS
::: PERSONNEL
:: PROFESSIONAL PERSONNEL
:::: GROUPS
::: PERSONNEL
:: HEALTH PERSONNEL
: NURSES
NURSE PRACTITIONERS

: FACILITIES
NURSERIES (HORTICULTURE)

:: INSTITUTIONS
: SCHOOLS
NURSERY SCHOOLS

:::: GROUPS
::: PERSONNEL
:: NONPROFESSIONAL PERSONNEL
: SEMISKILLED WORKERS
NURSERY WORKERS (HORTICULTURE)

::: GROUPS
:: PERSONNEL
: PROFESSIONAL PERSONNEL
::: GROUPS
:: PERSONNEL
: HEALTH PERSONNEL
NURSES
. NURSE PRACTITIONERS
. SCHOOL NURSES

:::: GROUPS
::: PERSONNEL
:: HEALTH PERSONNEL
: ALLIED HEALTH PERSONNEL
NURSES AIDES

:: TECHNOLOGY
: MEDICINE
NURSING
. PRACTICAL NURSING

::: EDUCATION
:: PROFESSIONAL EDUCATION
: MEDICAL EDUCATION
NURSING EDUCATION

:: INSTITUTIONS
: RESIDENTIAL INSTITUTIONS
:: FACILITIES
: HEALTH FACILITIES
NURSING HOMES

NUTRITION
. BREASTFEEDING

: INSTRUCTION
NUTRITION INSTRUCTION

:: BEHAVIOR
: SOCIAL BEHAVIOR
::: BEHAVIOR
:: COOPERATION
: COMPLIANCE (PSYCHOLOGY)
OBEDIENCE

:: DISABILITIES
: DISEASES
::: INDIVIDUAL CHARACTERISTICS
:: PHYSICAL CHARACTERISTICS
: BODY WEIGHT
OBESITY

OBJECTIVES
. BEHAVIORAL OBJECTIVES
.. AFFECTIVE OBJECTIVES
.. COGNITIVE OBJECTIVES
.. PSYCHOMOTOR OBJECTIVES
. COURSE OBJECTIVES
. EDUCATIONAL OBJECTIVES
. GUIDANCE OBJECTIVES
.. COUNSELING OBJECTIVES
. MEASUREMENT OBJECTIVES
. ORGANIZATIONAL OBJECTIVES
.. INSTITUTIONAL MISSION
. STUDENT EDUCATIONAL OBJECTIVES
. TRAINING OBJECTIVES

:: MEASURES (INDIVIDUALS)
: TESTS
OBJECTIVE TESTS
. MULTIPLE CHOICE TESTS

::: ABILITY
:: SKILLS
: PSYCHOMOTOR SKILLS
OBJECT MANIPULATION

: FUNDAMENTAL CONCEPTS
OBJECT PERMANENCE

:::::: METHODS
::::: EVALUATION METHODS
:::: DATA ANALYSIS
::: STATISTICAL ANALYSIS
:: MULTIVARIATE ANALYSIS
: FACTOR ANALYSIS
OBLIQUE ROTATION

OBSCENITY

OBSERVATION
. NATURALISTIC OBSERVATION
. PARTICIPANT OBSERVATION
. SCHOOL VISITATION

: LEARNING
OBSERVATIONAL LEARNING

OBSOLESCENCE
. BUILDING OBSOLESCENCE
. SKILL OBSOLESCENCE

:: TECHNOLOGY
: MEDICINE
OBSTETRICS

: ASPIRATION
OCCUPATIONAL ASPIRATION

OCCUPATIONAL CLUSTERS

:: DISABILITIES
: DISEASES
OCCUPATIONAL DISEASES

:: EDUCATION
: VOCATIONAL EDUCATION
OCCUPATIONAL HOME ECONOMICS

OCCUPATIONAL INFORMATION

: MOBILITY
OCCUPATIONAL MOBILITY
. CAREER LADDERS
. FACULTY MOBILITY
. TEACHER TRANSFER

: SAFETY
: HEALTH
OCCUPATIONAL SAFETY AND HEALTH

::: METHODS
:: EVALUATION METHODS
: SURVEYS
OCCUPATIONAL SURVEYS

:: MEASURES (INDIVIDUALS)
: TESTS
OCCUPATIONAL TESTS
. WORK SAMPLE TESTS

:::: GROUPS
::: PERSONNEL
:: PROFESSIONAL PERSONNEL
::::: GROUPS
:::: PERSONNEL
::: HEALTH PERSONNEL
:: ALLIED HEALTH PERSONNEL
: THERAPISTS
OCCUPATIONAL THERAPISTS

: THERAPY
OCCUPATIONAL THERAPY

:::: GROUPS
::: PERSONNEL
:: HEALTH PERSONNEL
: ALLIED HEALTH PERSONNEL
OCCUPATIONAL THERAPY ASSISTANTS

OCCUPATIONS
. AGRICULTURAL OCCUPATIONS
.. FARM OCCUPATIONS
.. OFF FARM AGRICULTURAL OCCUPATIONS
... AGRICULTURAL CHEMICAL OCCUPATIONS
... AGRICULTURAL MACHINERY OCCUPATIONS
... AGRICULTURAL SUPPLY OCCUPATIONS
... CROP PROCESSING OCCUPATIONS
... FOOD PROCESSING OCCUPATIONS
... ORNAMENTAL HORTICULTURE OCCUPATIONS
. BLUE COLLAR OCCUPATIONS
. BUILDING TRADES
. CLERICAL OCCUPATIONS
. DATA PROCESSING OCCUPATIONS
. DEMAND OCCUPATIONS
.. EMERGING OCCUPATIONS
. ELECTRICAL OCCUPATIONS
. ENERGY OCCUPATIONS
. FINANCE OCCUPATIONS
. FORESTRY OCCUPATIONS
. HEALTH OCCUPATIONS
.. ALLIED HEALTH OCCUPATIONS
. INSURANCE OCCUPATIONS
. MANAGERIAL OCCUPATIONS
. NEEDLE TRADES
. NONTRADITIONAL OCCUPATIONS
. OFFICE OCCUPATIONS
. PROFESSIONAL OCCUPATIONS
.. TEACHING (OCCUPATION)
... TEAM TEACHING
... URBAN TEACHING
. PUBLIC SERVICE OCCUPATIONS
. REAL ESTATE OCCUPATIONS
. SALES OCCUPATIONS
. SEMISKILLED OCCUPATIONS
. SERVICE OCCUPATIONS
.. CHILD CARE OCCUPATIONS
.. HOSPITALITY OCCUPATIONS
.. LAUNDRY DRYCLEANING OCCUPATIONS
. SKILLED OCCUPATIONS
. TECHNICAL OCCUPATIONS
. UNSKILLED OCCUPATIONS
. WHITE COLLAR OCCUPATIONS

:: TECHNOLOGY
: ENGINEERING
OCEAN ENGINEERING

::::: LIBERAL ARTS
:::: SCIENCES
::: NATURAL SCIENCES
:: PHYSICAL SCIENCES
: EARTH SCIENCE
OCEANOGRAPHY

::::: LIBERAL ARTS
:::: HUMANITIES
::: LITERATURE
:: POETRY
: LYRIC POETRY
: LITERARY GENRES
ODES

:: FACILITIES
: EDUCATIONAL FACILITIES
OFF CAMPUS FACILITIES

:: OCCUPATIONS
: AGRICULTURAL OCCUPATIONS
OFF FARM AGRICULTURAL OCCUPATIONS
. AGRICULTURAL CHEMICAL OCCUPATIONS
. AGRICULTURAL MACHINERY OCCUPATIONS
. AGRICULTURAL SUPPLY OCCUPATIONS
. CROP PROCESSING OCCUPATIONS
. FOOD PROCESSING OCCUPATIONS
. ORNAMENTAL HORTICULTURE OCCUPATIONS

: EQUIPMENT
OFFICE MACHINES

:: GOVERNANCE
: ADMINISTRATION
OFFICE MANAGEMENT

: OCCUPATIONS
OFFICE OCCUPATIONS

::: EDUCATION
:: VOCATIONAL EDUCATION
: BUSINESS EDUCATION
OFFICE OCCUPATIONS EDUCATION

::: CURRICULUM
:: COURSES
: PRACTICUMS
OFFICE PRACTICE

:::: GROUPS
::: PERSONNEL
:: GOVERNMENT EMPLOYEES
: MILITARY PERSONNEL
OFFICER PERSONNEL

: FACILITIES
OFFICES (FACILITIES)

: LANGUAGE
OFFICIAL LANGUAGES

:: TRAINING
: JOB TRAINING
OFF THE JOB TRAINING

:: LANGUAGES
: AMERICAN INDIAN LANGUAGES
OJIBWA

:: LANGUAGES
: JAPANESE
OKINAWAN

::: LANGUAGES
:: INDO EUROPEAN LANGUAGES
: ENGLISH
OLD ENGLISH

:::: LIBERAL ARTS
::: HUMANITIES
:: LITERATURE
: ENGLISH LITERATURE
OLD ENGLISH LITERATURE

::: GROUPS
:: AGE GROUPS
: ADULTS
OLDER ADULTS

:: GROUPS
: PERSONNEL
OMBUDSMEN

:::GROUPS
::STUDENTS
:COLLEGE STUDENTS
ON CAMPUS STUDENTS

::TECHNOLOGY
:MEDICINE
ONCOLOGY

::GROUPS
:FAMILY (SOCIOLOGICAL UNIT)
ONE PARENT FAMILY
.FATHERLESS FAMILY
.MOTHERLESS FAMILY

:::INSTITUTIONS
::SCHOOLS
:SMALL SCHOOLS
ONE TEACHER SCHOOLS

::::EQUIPMENT
:::ELECTRONIC EQUIPMENT
::COMPUTERS
:ONLINE SYSTEMS
::INFORMATION SOURCES
::DATA
:DATABASES
::PUBLICATIONS
:CATALOGS
ONLINE CATALOGS

::::SERVICES
:::INFORMATION SERVICES
::INFORMATION PROCESSING
:INFORMATION RETRIEVAL
ONLINE SEARCHING

:::EQUIPMENT
::ELECTRONIC EQUIPMENT
:COMPUTERS
ONLINE SYSTEMS
.INTERACTIVE VIDEO
.ONLINE CATALOGS

::GROUPS
:ORGANIZATIONS (GROUPS)
ONLINE VENDORS

:::LINGUISTICS
::DIACHRONIC LINGUISTICS
:ETYMOLOGY
ONOMASTICS

::TRAINING
:JOB TRAINING
ON THE JOB TRAINING
.APPRENTICESHIPS

::VISUAL AIDS
::EQUIPMENT
:PROJECTION EQUIPMENT
OPAQUE PROJECTORS

::MEASURES (INDIVIDUALS)
:TESTS
OPEN BOOK TESTS

:EDUCATION
OPEN EDUCATION

:ADMISSION (SCHOOL)
OPEN ENROLLMENT

::INSTITUTIONS
:SCHOOLS
OPEN PLAN SCHOOLS

::::INSTITUTIONS
:::SCHOOLS
::COLLEGES
:UNIVERSITIES
OPEN UNIVERSITIES

::::LIBERAL ARTS
:::HUMANITIES
::FINE ARTS
:THEATER ARTS
OPERA

:CONDITIONING
OPERANT CONDITIONING
.VERBAL OPERANT CONDITIONING

::TECHNOLOGY
:ENGINEERING
OPERATING ENGINEERING

:EXPENDITURES
OPERATING EXPENSES

:RESEARCH
OPERATIONS RESEARCH
.GAME THEORY

::TECHNOLOGY
:MEDICINE
OPHTHALMOLOGY

::PUBLICATIONS
:REPORTS
OPINION PAPERS

:ATTITUDES
OPINIONS
.PRESS OPINION
.PUBLIC OPINION

OPPORTUNITIES
.CULTURAL OPPORTUNITIES
.ECONOMIC OPPORTUNITIES
.EDUCATIONAL OPPORTUNITIES
..ACCESS TO EDUCATION
.EMPLOYMENT OPPORTUNITIES
..EQUAL OPPORTUNITIES (JOBS)
.HOUSING OPPORTUNITIES
.RESEARCH OPPORTUNITIES
.YOUTH OPPORTUNITIES

::NONPRINT MEDIA
:OPTICAL DISKS
OPTICAL DATA DISKS

:NONPRINT MEDIA
OPTICAL DISKS
.OPTICAL DATA DISKS

::::EQUIPMENT
:::ELECTRONIC EQUIPMENT
::COMPUTERS
:INPUT OUTPUT DEVICES
OPTICAL SCANNERS

:::::LIBERAL ARTS
::::SCIENCES
:::NATURAL SCIENCES
::PHYSICAL SCIENCES
:PHYSICS
OPTICS

:::GROUPS
::PERSONNEL
:PROFESSIONAL PERSONNEL
::::GROUPS
:::PERSONNEL
::HEALTH PERSONNEL
:ALLIED HEALTH PERSONNEL
OPTOMETRISTS

:TECHNOLOGY
OPTOMETRY

:::METHODS
::EDUCATIONAL METHODS
:TEACHING METHODS
ORAL COMMUNICATION METHOD
.LIPREADING

:::LANGUAGES
::INDO EUROPEAN LANGUAGES
:ENGLISH
ORAL ENGLISH

::::LIBERAL ARTS
:::SCIENCES
::SOCIAL SCIENCES
:::LIBERAL ARTS
::HUMANITIES
:HISTORY
ORAL HISTORY

::COMMUNICATION (THOUGHT TRANSFER)
:SPEECH COMMUNICATION
ORAL INTERPRETATION

:LANGUAGE
ORAL LANGUAGE

::LITERACY
::LANGUAGE ARTS
:READING
ORAL READING

ORCHESTRAS

:::::LIBERAL ARTS
::::SCIENCES
:::NATURAL SCIENCES
::PHYSICAL SCIENCES
:CHEMISTRY
ORGANIC CHEMISTRY

ORGANIZATION
.ADMINISTRATIVE ORGANIZATION
..CENTRALIZATION
..DECENTRALIZATION
..DEPARTMENTS
...ENGLISH DEPARTMENTS
...SCIENCE DEPARTMENTS
...STATE DEPARTMENTS OF EDUCATION
..MANAGEMENT TEAMS
..PARTICIPATIVE DECISION MAKING
.BUREAUCRACY
.CLASSIFICATION
..CLUSTER GROUPING
..CODIFICATION
..GROUPING (INSTRUCTIONAL PURPOSES)
...HETEROGENEOUS GROUPING
...HOMOGENEOUS GROUPING
....ABILITY GROUPING
...NONGRADED INSTRUCTIONAL GROUPING
..LABELING (OF PERSONS)
..LANGUAGE CLASSIFICATION
...LANGUAGE TYPOLOGY
..SPACE CLASSIFICATION
.CLASS ORGANIZATION
.COURSE ORGANIZATION
..COURSE CONTENT
.FURNITURE ARRANGEMENT
.GROUP STRUCTURE
..FAMILY STRUCTURE
...BIRTH ORDER
..GOVERNMENTAL STRUCTURE
.HORIZONTAL ORGANIZATION
.INDUSTRIAL STRUCTURE
.INFORMAL ORGANIZATION
.POWER STRUCTURE
.PYRAMID ORGANIZATION
.SCHOOL DISTRICT REORGANIZATION
.SCHOOL ORGANIZATION
..HOUSE PLAN
.SOCIAL STRUCTURE
..SOCIAL STRATIFICATION
.VERTICAL ORGANIZATION

:CHANGE
ORGANIZATIONAL CHANGE
.MERGERS

:ENVIRONMENT
ORGANIZATIONAL CLIMATE

:COMMUNICATION (THOUGHT TRANSFER)
ORGANIZATIONAL COMMUNICATION
.BUSINESS COMMUNICATION
..BUSINESS CORRESPONDENCE
.INTERSCHOOL COMMUNICATION

:DEVELOPMENT
ORGANIZATIONAL DEVELOPMENT

ORGANIZATIONAL EFFECTIVENESS
.SCHOOL EFFECTIVENESS

:OBJECTIVES
ORGANIZATIONAL OBJECTIVES
.INSTITUTIONAL MISSION

::THEORIES
:SOCIAL THEORIES
ORGANIZATIONAL THEORIES

:GROUPS
ORGANIZATIONS (GROUPS)
.AGENCIES
..ACCREDITING AGENCIES
..PRIVATE AGENCIES
..PUBLIC AGENCIES
...PLANNING COMMISSIONS
...STATE AGENCIES
....STATE DEPARTMENTS OF EDUCATION
....STATE LICENSING BOARDS
..SOCIAL AGENCIES
...WELFARE AGENCIES
..URBAN RENEWAL AGENCIES
..VOLUNTARY AGENCIES
..YOUTH AGENCIES
.ALUMNI ASSOCIATIONS
.BIBLIOGRAPHIC UTILITIES
.BLACK ORGANIZATIONS
.BLUE RIBBON COMMISSIONS
.COLLEGE GOVERNING COUNCILS
.COMMUNITY ORGANIZATIONS
..CITIZENS COUNCILS
.CONSORTIA
.COOPERATIVES
.DATABASE PRODUCERS
.FACULTY ORGANIZATIONS
.FRATERNITIES
.GOVERNING BOARDS
..BOARDS OF EDUCATION
...STATE BOARDS OF EDUCATION
.GOVERNMENT (ADMINISTRATIVE BODY)
..FEDERAL GOVERNMENT
..LOCAL GOVERNMENT
...CITY GOVERNMENT
..STATE GOVERNMENT
..STUDENT GOVERNMENT
.HONOR SOCIETIES
.INTERNATIONAL ORGANIZATIONS
.MILITARY ORGANIZATIONS
..ARMED FORCES
.NATIONAL ORGANIZATIONS
.NONPROFIT ORGANIZATIONS
.ONLINE VENDORS
.PARENT ASSOCIATIONS
.PROFESSIONAL ASSOCIATIONS
..LIBRARY ASSOCIATIONS
..MEDICAL ASSOCIATIONS
..TEACHER ASSOCIATIONS
.RELIGIOUS ORGANIZATIONS
.RESEARCH COORDINATING UNITS
.SCHOOL DISTRICTS
..COUNTY SCHOOL DISTRICTS
..MULTICAMPUS DISTRICTS

ORGANIZATIONS (GROUPS) (CONTINUED)

. SEGREGATIONIST ORGANIZATIONS
. SOCIAL ORGANIZATIONS
. SORORITIES
. STUDENT ORGANIZATIONS
.. STUDENT GOVERNMENT
.. STUDENT UNIONS
. UNIONS

ORGANIZATION SIZE (GROUPS)
. SCHOOL DISTRICT SIZE

:::: LIBERAL ARTS
::: HUMANITIES
:: FINE ARTS
: MUSIC
ORIENTAL MUSIC

ORIENTATION
. GOAL ORIENTATION
. SCHOOL ORIENTATION
. STAFF ORIENTATION
. TEACHER ORIENTATION

ORIENTATION MATERIALS

::: ACTIVITIES
:: PHYSICAL ACTIVITIES
: ATHLETICS
ORIENTEERING

::: TECHNOLOGY
:: AGRICULTURE
: HORTICULTURE
ORNAMENTAL HORTICULTURE
. FLORICULTURE
. LANDSCAPING
. TURF MANAGEMENT

::: OCCUPATIONS
:: AGRICULTURAL OCCUPATIONS
: OFF FARM AGRICULTURAL OCCUPATIONS
ORNAMENTAL HORTICULTURE OCCUPATIONS

::::: LIBERAL ARTS
:::: SCIENCES
::: NATURAL SCIENCES
:: BIOLOGICAL SCIENCES
: ZOOLOGY
ORNITHOLOGY

:::::: METHODS
::::: EVALUATION METHODS
:::: DATA ANALYSIS
::: STATISTICAL ANALYSIS
:: MULTIVARIATE ANALYSIS
: FACTOR ANALYSIS
ORTHOGONAL ROTATION

:: MATHEMATICAL CONCEPTS
: GEOMETRIC CONCEPTS
ORTHOGRAPHIC PROJECTION

:: LANGUAGE
: WRITTEN LANGUAGE
ORTHOGRAPHIC SYMBOLS
. DIACRITICAL MARKING
. LETTERS (ALPHABET)
. PHONETIC TRANSCRIPTION

:: LANGUAGES
: INDO EUROPEAN LANGUAGES
OSSETIC

:: TECHNOLOGY
: MEDICINE
OSTEOPATHY

::: LANGUAGES
:: URALIC ALTAIC LANGUAGES
: FINNO UGRIC LANGUAGES
OSTYAK

OUTCOMES OF EDUCATION
. EDUCATIONAL BENEFITS

OUTCOMES OF TREATMENT

: ACTIVITIES
OUTDOOR ACTIVITIES

: EDUCATION
OUTDOOR EDUCATION
. ADVENTURE EDUCATION

: LANGUAGE ARTS
OUTLINING (DISCOURSE)

:: GROUPS
: YOUTH
OUT OF SCHOOL YOUTH

::: GROUPS
:: STUDENTS
: COLLEGE STUDENTS
OUT OF STATE STUDENTS

::: SERVICES
:: HUMAN SERVICES
: EMPLOYMENT SERVICES
OUTPLACEMENT SERVICES (EMPLOYMENT)

: PROGRAMS
OUTREACH PROGRAMS

: ACHIEVEMENT
OVERACHIEVEMENT

:: VISUAL AIDS
:: EQUIPMENT
: PROJECTION EQUIPMENT
OVERHEAD PROJECTORS

OVERPOPULATION

: EMPLOYMENT
OVERSEAS EMPLOYMENT

OVERTIME

:: BEHAVIOR
: RESPONSES
OVERT RESPONSE

OWNERSHIP
. INTELLECTUAL PROPERTY
.. COPYRIGHTS
.. PATENTS
. REAL ESTATE

: CHEMICAL REACTIONS
OXIDATION

:: GROUPS
: NORTH AMERICANS
PACIFIC AMERICANS
. HAWAIIANS
. SAMOAN AMERICANS

: METHODS
PACING

: INDUSTRIAL ARTS
PAINTING (INDUSTRIAL ARTS)

:::: LIBERAL ARTS
::: HUMANITIES
:: FINE ARTS
: VISUAL ARTS
PAINTING (VISUAL ARTS)

:: LEARNING
: ASSOCIATIVE LEARNING
PAIRED ASSOCIATE LEARNING

:::::: LIBERAL ARTS
::::: SCIENCES
:::: NATURAL SCIENCES
::: PHYSICAL SCIENCES
:: EARTH SCIENCE
: GEOLOGY
PALEONTOLOGY

: PUBLICATIONS
PAMPHLETS

:: LANGUAGES
: INDO EUROPEAN LANGUAGES
PANJABI

:::: LIBERAL ARTS
::: HUMANITIES
:: FINE ARTS
: THEATER ARTS
PANTOMIME

::: LANGUAGES
:: AMERICAN INDIAN LANGUAGES
: UTO AZTECAN LANGUAGES
PAPAGO

PAPER (MATERIAL)

:: PUBLICATIONS
: BOOKS
PAPERBACK BOOKS

PARADOX

:: LITERACY
:: LANGUAGE ARTS
: WRITING (COMPOSITION)
PARAGRAPH COMPOSITION

: LANGUAGE PATTERNS
PARAGRAPHS
. SENTENCES
.. KERNEL SENTENCES

: LINGUISTICS
PARALINGUISTICS

:: LITERACY
:: LANGUAGE ARTS
: WRITING (COMPOSITION)
PARALLELISM (LITERARY)

: BEHAVIOR
PARANOID BEHAVIOR

:: GROUPS
: PERSONNEL
PARAPROFESSIONAL PERSONNEL
. AGRICULTURAL TECHNICIANS
. CHEMICAL TECHNICIANS
. ELECTRONIC TECHNICIANS
. ENGINEERING TECHNICIANS
.. HIGHWAY ENGINEERING AIDES
. ENVIRONMENTAL TECHNICIANS
. FORESTRY AIDES
. HOUSING MANAGEMENT AIDES
. INSTRUMENTATION TECHNICIANS
. LEGAL ASSISTANTS
. MARINE TECHNICIANS
. MECHANICAL DESIGN TECHNICIANS
. METALLURGICAL TECHNICIANS
. NUCLEAR POWER PLANT TECHNICIANS
. PARAPROFESSIONAL SCHOOL PERSONNEL
.. SCHOOL AIDES
.. TEACHER AIDES
... BILINGUAL TEACHER AIDES
. PRODUCTION TECHNICIANS
. RADIOGRAPHERS
. VETERINARY ASSISTANTS
. VISITING HOMEMAKERS

::: GROUPS
:: PERSONNEL
: SCHOOL PERSONNEL
::: GROUPS
:: PERSONNEL
: PARAPROFESSIONAL PERSONNEL
PARAPROFESSIONAL SCHOOL PERSONNEL
. SCHOOL AIDES
. TEACHER AIDES
.. BILINGUAL TEACHER AIDES

: ASPIRATION
PARENT ASPIRATION

:: GROUPS
: ORGANIZATIONS (GROUPS)
PARENT ASSOCIATIONS

: ATTITUDES
PARENT ATTITUDES
. FATHER ATTITUDES
. MOTHER ATTITUDES

: BACKGROUND
PARENT BACKGROUND

::: RELATIONSHIP
:: INTERPERSONAL RELATIONSHIP
: FAMILY RELATIONSHIP
PARENT CHILD RELATIONSHIP
. PARENT STUDENT RELATIONSHIP

: CONFERENCES
PARENT CONFERENCES

:: GUIDANCE
: COUNSELING
PARENT COUNSELING

:: EDUCATION
: ADULT EDUCATION
PARENT EDUCATION

:: FINANCIAL SUPPORT
: STUDENT FINANCIAL AID
PARENT FINANCIAL CONTRIBUTION

PARENT GRIEVANCES

:: EDUCATION
: FAMILY LIFE EDUCATION
PARENTHOOD EDUCATION

: INFLUENCES
PARENT INFLUENCE

:: ABILITY
: SKILLS
PARENTING SKILLS

PARENT MATERIALS

: : BEHAVIOR
: PARTICIPATION
PARENT PARTICIPATION

: RESPONSIBILITY
PARENT RESPONSIBILITY

: CIVIL LIBERTIES
PARENT RIGHTS

PARENT ROLE

: GROUPS
PARENTS
. BIOLOGICAL PARENTS
. EMPLOYED PARENTS
. FATHERS
. GRANDPARENTS
. LOWER CLASS PARENTS
. MIDDLE CLASS PARENTS
. MOTHERS
. . BLACK MOTHERS
. . UNWED MOTHERS

: : RELATIONSHIP
: FAMILY SCHOOL RELATIONSHIP
PARENT SCHOOL RELATIONSHIP

: : : : RELATIONSHIP
: : : INTERPERSONAL RELATIONSHIP
: : FAMILY RELATIONSHIP
: PARENT CHILD RELATIONSHIP
PARENT STUDENT RELATIONSHIP

: CONFERENCES
PARENT TEACHER CONFERENCES

: : : BEHAVIOR
: : COOPERATION
: EDUCATIONAL COOPERATION
PARENT TEACHER COOPERATION

: WORKSHOPS
PARENT WORKSHOPS

: DESIGN
PARK DESIGN

PARKING CONTROLS

: FACILITIES
PARKING FACILITIES

: FACILITIES
PARKS

: STANDARDS
PARLIAMENTARY PROCEDURES

: : : INSTITUTIONS
: : SCHOOLS
: PRIVATE SCHOOLS
PAROCHIAL SCHOOLS
. CATHOLIC SCHOOLS

: LITERARY GENRES
PARODY

: : : GROUPS
: : PERSONNEL
: CASEWORKERS
PAROLE OFFICERS

: : DISABILITIES
: HEARING IMPAIRMENTS
PARTIAL HEARING

: : DISABILITIES
: VISUAL IMPAIRMENTS
PARTIAL VISION

PARTICIPANT CHARACTERISTICS

: OBSERVATION
PARTICIPANT OBSERVATION

: ATTITUDES
PARTICIPANT SATISFACTION

: BEHAVIOR
PARTICIPATION
. AUDIENCE PARTICIPATION
. CITIZEN PARTICIPATION
. COMMUNITY INVOLVEMENT
. FAMILY INVOLVEMENT
. PARENT PARTICIPATION
. SCHOOL INVOLVEMENT
. STUDENT PARTICIPATION
. TEACHER PARTICIPATION

: : COGNITIVE PROCESSES
: DECISION MAKING
: : ORGANIZATION
: ADMINISTRATIVE ORGANIZATION
PARTICIPATIVE DECISION MAKING

: : : : : GROUPS
: : : : PERSONNEL
: : : SCHOOL PERSONNEL
: : : : : GROUPS
: : : : PERSONNEL
: : : PROFESSIONAL PERSONNEL
: : FACULTY
: PART TIME FACULTY
PARTNERSHIP TEACHERS

: EMPLOYMENT
PART TIME EMPLOYMENT
. JOB SHARING

: : : : GROUPS
: : : PERSONNEL
: : SCHOOL PERSONNEL
: : : : GROUPS
: : : PERSONNEL
: : PROFESSIONAL PERSONNEL
: FACULTY
PART TIME FACULTY
. PARTNERSHIP TEACHERS

: : : : GROUPS
: : : PERSONNEL
: : AGRICULTURAL PERSONNEL
: FARMERS
PART TIME FARMERS

: : GROUPS
: STUDENTS
PART TIME STUDENTS

: : LANGUAGES
: INDO EUROPEAN LANGUAGES
PASHTO

: : : MEASUREMENT
: : ACHIEVEMENT RATING
: GRADING
PASS FAIL GRADING

: : : LIBERAL ARTS
: : HUMANITIES
: LITERATURE
PASTORAL LITERATURE

: : OWNERSHIP
: INTELLECTUAL PROPERTY
PATENTS

: : : : : METHODS
: : : : EVALUATION METHODS
: : : DATA ANALYSIS
: : STATISTICAL ANALYSIS
: MULTIVARIATE ANALYSIS
PATH ANALYSIS

: : TECHNOLOGY
: MEDICINE
PATHOLOGY
. PLANT PATHOLOGY
. PSYCHOPATHOLOGY
. SPEECH PATHOLOGY

: EDUCATION
PATIENT EDUCATION

: GROUPS
PATIENTS
. HOSPITALIZED CHILDREN

: NATIONALISM
PATRIOTISM

: : : : METHODS
: : : EDUCATIONAL METHODS
: : TEACHING METHODS
: DRILLS (PRACTICE)
PATTERN DRILLS (LANGUAGE)
. SUBSTITUTION DRILLS

: : BEHAVIOR
: RESPONSES
PATTERNED RESPONSES

PATTERNMAKING

: : : COGNITIVE PROCESSES
: : MEMORY
: RECOGNITION (PSYCHOLOGY)
PATTERN RECOGNITION
. CHARACTER RECOGNITION

: RECORDS (FORMS)
PAYROLL RECORDS

: : RELATIONSHIP
: HUMAN RELATIONS
PEACE

PEDESTRIAN TRAFFIC

: : TECHNOLOGY
: MEDICINE
PEDIATRICS

: : : : NEEDS
: : : INDIVIDUAL NEEDS
: : PSYCHOLOGICAL NEEDS
: AFFILIATION NEED
PEER ACCEPTANCE

: : GUIDANCE
: COUNSELING
PEER COUNSELING

: EVALUATION
PEER EVALUATION

: GROUPS
PEER GROUPS

: INFLUENCES
PEER INFLUENCE

: INSTITUTIONS
PEER INSTITUTIONS

: : RELATIONSHIP
: INTERPERSONAL RELATIONSHIP
PEER RELATIONSHIP

: : : METHODS
: : EDUCATIONAL METHODS
: TEACHING METHODS
PEER TEACHING

: RATIOS (MATHEMATICS)
PERCENTAGE

: COGNITIVE PROCESSES
PERCEPTION
. AUDITORY PERCEPTION
. . AUDITORY DISCRIMINATION
. KINESTHETIC PERCEPTION
. TACTUAL PERCEPTION
. VISUAL PERCEPTION
. . DEPTH PERCEPTION
. . VISUAL ACUITY
. . VISUAL DISCRIMINATION

: : : MEASURES (INDIVIDUALS)
: : TESTS
: COGNITIVE TESTS
PERCEPTION TESTS
. TACTUAL VISUAL TESTS

: : : DEVELOPMENT
: : INDIVIDUAL DEVELOPMENT
: COGNITIVE DEVELOPMENT
PERCEPTUAL DEVELOPMENT

: DISABILITIES
PERCEPTUAL HANDICAPS

: : : ABILITY
: : SKILLS
: PSYCHOMOTOR SKILLS
PERCEPTUAL MOTOR COORDINATION
. EYE HAND COORDINATION
. EYE VOICE SPAN

: : LEARNING
: NONVERBAL LEARNING
PERCEPTUAL MOTOR LEARNING

: BEHAVIOR
PERFORMANCE
. COUNSELOR PERFORMANCE
. FAILURE
. . ACADEMIC FAILURE
. . . READING FAILURE
. JOB PERFORMANCE
. SUCCESS

: CONTRACTS
PERFORMANCE CONTRACTS

PERFORMANCE CRITERIA (1968 1980)

: INFLUENCES
PERFORMANCE FACTORS

PERFORMANCE SPECIFICATIONS (1969 1980)

:: MEASURES (INDIVIDUALS)
: TESTS
PERFORMANCE TESTS

: INFLUENCES
PERINATAL INFLUENCES

:: PUBLICATIONS
: SERIALS
PERIODICALS
. FOREIGN LANGUAGE PERIODICALS
. SCHOLARLY JOURNALS

: ENVIRONMENT
PERMISSIVE ENVIRONMENT

::: PUBLICATIONS
:: REFERENCE MATERIALS
: INDEXES
PERMUTED INDEXES

:: LANGUAGES
: INDO EUROPEAN LANGUAGES
PERSIAN

: BEHAVIOR
PERSISTENCE
. ACADEMIC PERSISTENCE
. TEACHER PERSISTENCE

PERSONAL AUTONOMY

:: INSTITUTIONS
: RESIDENTIAL INSTITUTIONS
PERSONAL CARE HOMES

PERSONALITY

:: EVALUATION
: PSYCHOLOGICAL EVALUATION
PERSONALITY ASSESSMENT

: CHANGE
PERSONALITY CHANGE

:: DEVELOPMENT
: INDIVIDUAL DEVELOPMENT
PERSONALITY DEVELOPMENT

: MEASURES (INDIVIDUALS)
PERSONALITY MEASURES
. SELF CONCEPT MEASURES

: PROBLEMS
PERSONALITY PROBLEMS

::: RESEARCH
:: BEHAVIORAL SCIENCE RESEARCH
: PSYCHOLOGICAL STUDIES
PERSONALITY STUDIES

: THEORIES
PERSONALITY THEORIES

:: INDIVIDUAL CHARACTERISTICS
: PSYCHOLOGICAL CHARACTERISTICS
PERSONALITY TRAITS
. CURIOSITY
. LOCUS OF CONTROL
. MENTAL RIGIDITY

:: PUBLICATIONS
: REPORTS
PERSONAL NARRATIVES

::: NEEDS
:: INDIVIDUAL NEEDS
: PSYCHOLOGICAL NEEDS
PERSONAL SPACE

: GROUPS
PERSONNEL
. ADMINISTRATORS
.. ADMISSIONS OFFICERS
.. ASSISTANT PRINCIPALS
.. COORDINATORS
... AUDIOVISUAL COORDINATORS
... INSTRUCTOR COORDINATORS
.. DEANS
... ACADEMIC DEANS
... DEANS OF STUDENTS
.. DEPARTMENT HEADS
.. MEDICAL RECORD ADMINISTRATORS
.. PERSONNEL DIRECTORS
.. PRESIDENTS
... COLLEGE PRESIDENTS
... PRESIDENTS OF THE UNITED STATES
.. PRINCIPALS
.. REGISTRARS (SCHOOL)
.. RESEARCH DIRECTORS
.. SCHOOL BUSINESS OFFICIALS
.. STUDENT FINANCIAL AID OFFICERS
.. SUPERINTENDENTS
.. SUPERVISORS
... CREW LEADERS
... STATE SUPERVISORS
... STUDENT TEACHER SUPERVISORS
.. TRUSTEES
.. VOCATIONAL DIRECTORS
. AGRICULTURAL PERSONNEL
.. AGRICULTURAL LABORERS
... MIGRANT WORKERS
... SEASONAL LABORERS
.. AGRICULTURAL TECHNICIANS
.. FARMERS
... DAIRY FARMERS
... PART TIME FARMERS
... SHARECROPPERS
. AIRCRAFT PILOTS
. CASEWORKERS
.. PAROLE OFFICERS
.. PROBATION OFFICERS
.. SOCIAL WORKERS
... SCHOOL SOCIAL WORKERS
. CHURCH WORKERS
. CLERGY
.. PRIESTS
. CONSULTANTS
.. MEDICAL CONSULTANTS
.. READING CONSULTANTS
.. SCIENCE CONSULTANTS
. DESIGNERS
. DIFFERENTIATED STAFFS
. DISLOCATED WORKERS
. EDITORS
. EMPLOYEES
.. ENTRY WORKERS
. EQUIPMENT MANUFACTURERS
. EVALUATORS
. FOREIGN WORKERS
.. BRACEROS
. GOVERNMENT EMPLOYEES
.. EXTENSION AGENTS
.. FOOD AND DRUG INSPECTORS
.. FOREIGN DIPLOMATS
.. IMMIGRATION INSPECTORS
.. MILITARY PERSONNEL
... ENLISTED PERSONNEL
... OFFICER PERSONNEL
.. POLICE
.. PUBLIC OFFICIALS
... CITY OFFICIALS
... COUNTY OFFICIALS
... COURT JUDGES
... LEGISLATORS
... STATE OFFICIALS
.... STATE SUPERVISORS
.. PUBLIC SCHOOL TEACHERS
. GUIDANCE PERSONNEL
.. COUNSELORS
... ADJUSTMENT COUNSELORS
... EMPLOYMENT COUNSELORS
... SCHOOL COUNSELORS
. HEALTH PERSONNEL
.. ALLIED HEALTH PERSONNEL
... DENTAL ASSISTANTS
... DENTAL HYGIENISTS
... DENTAL TECHNICIANS
... DIETITIANS
... EMERGENCY MEDICAL TECHNICIANS
... ENVIRONMENTAL TECHNICIANS
... HOME HEALTH AIDES
... MEDICAL ASSISTANTS
.... MEDICAL LABORATORY ASSISTANTS
... MEDICAL RECORD ADMINISTRATORS
... MEDICAL RECORD TECHNICIANS
... MEDICAL TECHNOLOGISTS
... NURSES AIDES
... OCCUPATIONAL THERAPY ASSISTANTS
... OPTOMETRISTS
... PHYSICAL THERAPY AIDES
... PHYSICIANS ASSISTANTS
... PSYCHIATRIC AIDES
... RADIOLOGIC TECHNOLOGISTS
... SURGICAL TECHNICIANS
... THERAPISTS
.... OCCUPATIONAL THERAPISTS
.... PHYSICAL THERAPISTS
... VETERINARY ASSISTANTS
.. DENTISTS
.. HOSPITAL PERSONNEL
.. MEDICAL CONSULTANTS
.. NURSES
... NURSE PRACTITIONERS
... SCHOOL NURSES
.. PHARMACISTS
.. PHYSICIANS
... FOREIGN MEDICAL GRADUATES
... PSYCHIATRISTS
.. PSYCHOLOGISTS
... SCHOOL PSYCHOLOGISTS
.. VETERINARIANS
. INDIGENOUS PERSONNEL
. INDUSTRIAL PERSONNEL
. INSTITUTIONAL PERSONNEL
. INTERPRETERS
. LIBRARY PERSONNEL
.. LIBRARIANS
.. LIBRARY TECHNICIANS
... MEDICAL RECORD TECHNICIANS
. MERCHANTS
. NONPROFESSIONAL PERSONNEL
.. CLERICAL WORKERS
... COURT REPORTERS
... EXAMINERS
... FILE CLERKS
... RECEPTIONISTS
... SECRETARIES
.... SCHOOL SECRETARIES
.. SALES WORKERS
... AUTO PARTS CLERKS
.. SEMISKILLED WORKERS
... ANIMAL CARETAKERS
... BOAT OPERATORS
... GROUNDS KEEPERS
... NURSERY WORKERS (HORTICULTURE)
... SEWING MACHINE OPERATORS
.. SERVICE WORKERS
... ATTENDANTS
... BARBERS
... COOKS
... EMERGENCY SQUAD PERSONNEL
.... EMERGENCY MEDICAL TECHNICIANS
... FIRE FIGHTERS
... HOUSEHOLD WORKERS
.... HOME HEALTH AIDES
... HOUSEKEEPERS
... HOUSING MANAGEMENT AIDES
... WAITERS AND WAITRESSES
.. SKILLED WORKERS
... AUTO BODY REPAIRERS
... CRAFT WORKERS
... ELECTRICIANS
... FLOOR LAYERS
... GLAZIERS
... LOCOMOTIVE ENGINEERS
... MACHINISTS
.... MACHINE REPAIRERS
.... MACHINE TOOL OPERATORS
.... TOOL AND DIE MAKERS
... SIGN PAINTERS
... TELEVISION RADIO REPAIRERS
... WATCHMAKERS
.. UNSKILLED WORKERS
... LABORERS
.... AGRICULTURAL LABORERS
..... MIGRANT WORKERS
..... SEASONAL LABORERS
.... AUXILIARY LABORERS
. OMBUDSMEN
. PARAPROFESSIONAL PERSONNEL
.. AGRICULTURAL TECHNICIANS
.. CHEMICAL TECHNICIANS
.. ELECTRONIC TECHNICIANS
.. ENGINEERING TECHNICIANS
... HIGHWAY ENGINEERING AIDES
.. ENVIRONMENTAL TECHNICIANS
.. FORESTRY AIDES
.. HOUSING MANAGEMENT AIDES
.. INSTRUMENTATION TECHNICIANS
.. LEGAL ASSISTANTS
.. MARINE TECHNICIANS
.. MECHANICAL DESIGN TECHNICIANS
.. METALLURGICAL TECHNICIANS
.. NUCLEAR POWER PLANT TECHNICIANS
.. PARAPROFESSIONAL SCHOOL PERSONNEL
... SCHOOL AIDES
... TEACHER AIDES
.... BILINGUAL TEACHER AIDES
.. PRODUCTION TECHNICIANS
.. RADIOGRAPHERS
.. VETERINARY ASSISTANTS
.. VISITING HOMEMAKERS
. PROFESSIONAL PERSONNEL
.. ACCOUNTANTS
... CERTIFIED PUBLIC ACCOUNTANTS
.. ARCHITECTS
.. ATHLETIC COACHES
.. DENTISTS
.. ENGINEERS
.. FACULTY
... ADJUNCT FACULTY
... COLLEGE FACULTY
.... COLLEGE PRESIDENTS
.... COUNSELOR EDUCATORS
.... GRADUATE SCHOOL FACULTY
..... MEDICAL SCHOOL FACULTY
.... PROFESSORS
.... STUDENT TEACHER SUPERVISORS
.... TEACHER EDUCATORS
..... METHODS TEACHERS
.... TEACHING ASSISTANTS
... DEANS
.... ACADEMIC DEANS
.... DEANS OF STUDENTS
... DEPARTMENT HEADS
... FACULTY ADVISERS
... FULL TIME FACULTY
... NONTENURED FACULTY
... PART TIME FACULTY
.... PARTNERSHIP TEACHERS
... TENURED FACULTY
... WOMEN FACULTY
.. INFORMATION SCIENTISTS
... LIBRARIANS
.. LAWYERS
.. MATHEMATICIANS
.. NURSES
... NURSE PRACTITIONERS
... SCHOOL NURSES
.. OPTOMETRISTS
.. PHARMACISTS
.. PHYSICIANS
... FOREIGN MEDICAL GRADUATES
... PSYCHIATRISTS
.. PSYCHOLOGISTS
... SCHOOL PSYCHOLOGISTS
.. RESEARCH DIRECTORS
.. RESEARCHERS

PERSONNEL
(CONTINUED)

... EDUCATIONAL RESEARCHERS
.. SCIENTISTS
.. SOCIAL SCIENTISTS
.. SOCIAL WORKERS
... SCHOOL SOCIAL WORKERS
.. TEACHERS
... ADULT EDUCATORS
... ART TEACHERS
... BEGINNING TEACHERS
... BILINGUAL TEACHERS
... BLACK TEACHERS
... CATHOLIC EDUCATORS
... COOPERATING TEACHERS
... ELEMENTARY SCHOOL TEACHERS
... HOME ECONOMICS TEACHERS
... INDUSTRIAL ARTS TEACHERS
... INSTRUCTOR COORDINATORS
... ITINERANT TEACHERS
... LANGUAGE TEACHERS
... LAY TEACHERS
... MASTER TEACHERS
... MATHEMATICS TEACHERS
... MINORITY GROUP TEACHERS
... MUSIC TEACHERS
... PHYSICAL EDUCATION TEACHERS
... PRESCHOOL TEACHERS
... PUBLIC SCHOOL TEACHERS
... READING TEACHERS
... REMEDIAL TEACHERS
... RESOURCE TEACHERS
... SCIENCE TEACHERS
... SECONDARY SCHOOL TEACHERS
... SPECIAL EDUCATION TEACHERS
... STUDENT TEACHERS
... SUBSTITUTE TEACHERS
... TEACHER INTERNS
... TELEVISION TEACHERS
... TUTORS
... VOCATIONAL EDUCATION TEACHERS
.... BUSINESS EDUCATION TEACHERS
.... DISTRIBUTIVE EDUCATION TEACHERS
.... TRADE AND INDUSTRIAL TEACHERS
.. THERAPISTS
... OCCUPATIONAL THERAPISTS
... PHYSICAL THERAPISTS
.. VETERINARIANS
. PROGRAMERS
. REENTRY WORKERS
. RESEARCH ASSISTANTS
. RESIDENT ADVISERS
.. RESIDENT ASSISTANTS
. RESOURCE STAFF
. SCHOOL PERSONNEL
.. ADMISSIONS OFFICERS
.. ASSISTANT PRINCIPALS
.. AUDIOVISUAL COORDINATORS
.. FACULTY
... ADJUNCT FACULTY
... COLLEGE FACULTY
.... COLLEGE PRESIDENTS
.... COUNSELOR EDUCATORS
.... GRADUATE SCHOOL FACULTY
..... MEDICAL SCHOOL FACULTY
.... PROFESSORS
.... STUDENT TEACHER SUPERVISORS
.... TEACHER EDUCATORS
..... METHODS TEACHERS
.... TEACHING ASSISTANTS
... DEANS
.... ACADEMIC DEANS
.... DEANS OF STUDENTS
... DEPARTMENT HEADS
... FACULTY ADVISERS
... FULL TIME FACULTY
... NONTENURED FACULTY
... PART TIME FACULTY
.... PARTNERSHIP TEACHERS
... TENURED FACULTY
... WOMEN FACULTY
.. FOREIGN STUDENT ADVISERS
.. PARAPROFESSIONAL SCHOOL PERSONNEL
... SCHOOL AIDES
... TEACHER AIDES
.... BILINGUAL TEACHER AIDES
.. PRINCIPALS
.. PUPIL PERSONNEL WORKERS
... ATTENDANCE OFFICERS
.. REGISTRARS (SCHOOL)
.. SCHOOL BUSINESS OFFICIALS
.. SCHOOL CADRES
.. SCHOOL COUNSELORS
.. SCHOOL NURSES
.. SCHOOL PSYCHOLOGISTS
.. SCHOOL SECRETARIES
.. SCHOOL SOCIAL WORKERS
.. STUDENT FINANCIAL AID OFFICERS
.. STUDENT PERSONNEL WORKERS
. SCIENTIFIC PERSONNEL
.. MATHEMATICIANS
.. SCIENCE CONSULTANTS
.. SCIENTISTS
. SECURITY PERSONNEL
. SPECIALISTS
.. CHILD DEVELOPMENT SPECIALISTS
.. FILM PRODUCTION SPECIALISTS
.. MEDIA SPECIALISTS
... AUDIOVISUAL COORDINATORS
. SYSTEMS ANALYSTS
. TRAINERS

: DATA
PERSONNEL DATA

::: GROUPS
:: PERSONNEL
: ADMINISTRATORS
PERSONNEL DIRECTORS

: EVALUATION
PERSONNEL EVALUATION
. ADMINISTRATOR EVALUATION
. COUNSELOR EVALUATION
. FACULTY EVALUATION
. TEACHER EVALUATION
.. STUDENT EVALUATION OF TEACHER PERFORMANCE

: SOCIAL INTEGRATION
PERSONNEL INTEGRATION
. FACULTY INTEGRATION
. TEACHER INTEGRATION

:: GOVERNANCE
: ADMINISTRATION
PERSONNEL MANAGEMENT

:: NEEDS
: LABOR NEEDS
PERSONNEL NEEDS

: POLICY
PERSONNEL POLICY

: SELECTION
PERSONNEL SELECTION
. ADMINISTRATOR SELECTION
. COUNSELOR SELECTION
. TEACHER SELECTION

PERSPECTIVE TAKING

:: LANGUAGE ARTS
: RHETORIC
PERSUASIVE DISCOURSE

:: HAZARDOUS MATERIALS
: POISONS
PESTICIDES
. HERBICIDES
. INSECTICIDES

PESTS

:: BUSINESS
: INDUSTRY
PETROLEUM INDUSTRY

::: EDUCATION
:: PROFESSIONAL EDUCATION
: MEDICAL EDUCATION
PHARMACEUTICAL EDUCATION

::: GROUPS
:: PERSONNEL
: PROFESSIONAL PERSONNEL
::: GROUPS
:: PERSONNEL
: HEALTH PERSONNEL
PHARMACISTS

:: TECHNOLOGY
: MEDICINE
PHARMACOLOGY

:: TECHNOLOGY
: MEDICINE
PHARMACY

::: LIBERAL ARTS
:: HUMANITIES
: PHILOSOPHY
PHENOMENOLOGY

: INSTITUTIONS
PHILANTHROPIC FOUNDATIONS

:: LIBERAL ARTS
: HUMANITIES
PHILOSOPHY
. EDUCATIONAL PHILOSOPHY
. EPISTEMOLOGY
. ETHICS
.. BIOETHICS
. EXISTENTIALISM
. HUMANISM
. LOGIC
.. MATHEMATICAL LOGIC
... ALGORITHMS
... MATHEMATICAL FORMULAS
.... EQUATIONS (MATHEMATICS)
.... FUNCTIONS (MATHEMATICS)
... PROOF (MATHEMATICS)
... SET THEORY
. MARXISM
. PHENOMENOLOGY
. PLATONISM
. SEMIOTICS
.. PRAGMATICS
.. SEMANTICS
... LEXICOLOGY

: LANGUAGE PATTERNS
PHONEME GRAPHEME CORRESPONDENCE

::: LINGUISTICS
:: PHONOLOGY
: PHONEMICS
PHONEMES
. CONSONANTS
. VOWELS

: ALPHABETS
PHONEMIC ALPHABETS

:: LINGUISTICS
: PHONOLOGY
PHONEMICS
. PHONEMES
.. CONSONANTS
.. VOWELS

:: METHODS
: EVALUATION METHODS
PHONETIC ANALYSIS

:: LINGUISTICS
: PHONOLOGY
PHONETICS
. ACOUSTIC PHONETICS
. PHONICS

::: LANGUAGE
:: WRITTEN LANGUAGE
: ORTHOGRAPHIC SYMBOLS
PHONETIC TRANSCRIPTION

::: LINGUISTICS
:: PHONOLOGY
: PHONETICS
PHONICS

: LINGUISTICS
PHONOLOGY
. GENERATIVE PHONOLOGY
. PHONEMICS
.. PHONEMES
... CONSONANTS
... VOWELS
. PHONETICS
.. ACOUSTIC PHONETICS
.. PHONICS
. SUPRASEGMENTALS
.. INTONATION
.. STRESS (PHONOLOGY)
. SYLLABLES

: CHEMICAL REACTIONS
PHOTOCHEMICAL REACTIONS
. PHOTOSYNTHESIS

:: METHODS
: PRODUCTION TECHNIQUES
PHOTOCOMPOSITION

: VISUAL AIDS
: EQUIPMENT
PHOTOGRAPHIC EQUIPMENT

: VISUAL AIDS
PHOTOGRAPHS

:::: LIBERAL ARTS
::: HUMANITIES
:: FINE ARTS
: VISUAL ARTS
PHOTOGRAPHY
. HOLOGRAPHY

:: TECHNOLOGY
: JOURNALISM
PHOTOJOURNALISM

:: CHEMICAL REACTIONS
: PHOTOCHEMICAL REACTIONS
PHOTOSYNTHESIS

:::: LINGUISTICS
::: DESCRIPTIVE LINGUISTICS
:: GRAMMAR
: SYNTAX
PHRASE STRUCTURE

: ACTIVITIES
PHYSICAL ACTIVITIES
. ATHLETICS
.. AQUATIC SPORTS
... DIVING
... SAILING
... SURFING
... SWIMMING
... WATER POLO
... WATERSKIING
.. ARCHERY
.. BOWLING
.. COLLEGE ATHLETICS
.. EXTRAMURAL ATHLETICS
.. FENCING (SPORT)

PHYSICAL ACTIVITIES (CONTINUED)
..GOLF
..GYMNASTICS
...TUMBLING
..HANDBALL
..ICE SKATING
..INTRAMURAL ATHLETICS
..LIFETIME SPORTS
..ORIENTEERING
..RACQUET SPORTS
...BADMINTON
...RACQUETBALL
...SQUASH (GAME)
...TENNIS
..ROLLER SKATING
..SKIING
..TABLE TENNIS
..TEAM SPORTS
...BASEBALL
...BASKETBALL
...FIELD HOCKEY
...FOOTBALL
...ICE HOCKEY
...LACROSSE
...SOCCER
...SOFTBALL
...TEAM HANDBALL
...VOLLEYBALL
...WATER POLO
..TRACK AND FIELD
..WEIGHTLIFTING
..WOMENS ATHLETICS
..WRESTLING
.BICYCLING
.DANCE
.EXERCISE
..AEROBICS
..CALISTHENICS
.HORSEBACK RIDING
.LIFTING
..WEIGHTLIFTING
.RUNNING
..JOGGING
.UNDERWATER DIVING

:BEHAVIOR
PHYSICAL ACTIVITY LEVEL

:INDIVIDUAL CHARACTERISTICS
PHYSICAL CHARACTERISTICS
.BODY HEIGHT
.BODY WEIGHT
..BIRTH WEIGHT
..OBESITY
.LATERAL DOMINANCE
.MUSCULAR STRENGTH
.NEUROLOGICAL ORGANIZATION
..BRAIN HEMISPHERE FUNCTIONS
.RACE
.SEX

::DEVELOPMENT
:INDIVIDUAL DEVELOPMENT
PHYSICAL DEVELOPMENT
.MOTOR DEVELOPMENT

:DISABILITIES
PHYSICAL DISABILITIES
.AMPUTATIONS
.CLEFT PALATE
.HEART DISORDERS
.NEUROLOGICAL IMPAIRMENTS
..APHASIA
..CEREBRAL PALSY
..EPILEPSY
..MINIMAL BRAIN DYSFUNCTION

:GEOGRAPHIC REGIONS
PHYSICAL DIVISIONS (GEOGRAPHIC)

:EDUCATION
PHYSICAL EDUCATION
.ADAPTED PHYSICAL EDUCATION
.MOVEMENT EDUCATION

::FACILITIES
:EDUCATIONAL FACILITIES
PHYSICAL EDUCATION FACILITIES

::::GROUPS
:::PERSONNEL
::PROFESSIONAL PERSONNEL
:TEACHERS
PHYSICAL EDUCATION TEACHERS

:ENVIRONMENT
PHYSICAL ENVIRONMENT
.ACOUSTICAL ENVIRONMENT
..NOISE (SOUND)
.CLIMATE
.THERMAL ENVIRONMENT
.VISUAL ENVIRONMENT

::EVALUATION
:MEDICAL EVALUATION
PHYSICAL EXAMINATIONS

::HEALTH
:PHYSICAL HEALTH
PHYSICAL FITNESS

::::LIBERAL ARTS
:::SCIENCES
::SOCIAL SCIENCES
:GEOGRAPHY
:::::LIBERAL ARTS
::::SCIENCES
:::NATURAL SCIENCES
::PHYSICAL SCIENCES
:EARTH SCIENCE
PHYSICAL GEOGRAPHY

:HEALTH
PHYSICAL HEALTH
.DENTAL HEALTH
.PHYSICAL FITNESS

:MOBILITY
PHYSICAL MOBILITY
.VISUALLY HANDICAPPED MOBILITY

::PROGRAMS
:RECREATIONAL PROGRAMS
PHYSICAL RECREATION PROGRAMS

:::LIBERAL ARTS
::SCIENCES
:NATURAL SCIENCES
PHYSICAL SCIENCES
.ASTRONOMY
.CHEMISTRY
..BIOCHEMISTRY
..INORGANIC CHEMISTRY
..ORGANIC CHEMISTRY
.CRYSTALLOGRAPHY
.EARTH SCIENCE
..GEOLOGY
...MINERALOGY
...PALEONTOLOGY
..GEOPHYSICS
...PLATE TECTONICS
..METEOROLOGY
..OCEANOGRAPHY
..PHYSICAL GEOGRAPHY
..SEISMOLOGY
...PLATE TECTONICS
..SOIL SCIENCE
.PHYSICS
..BIOPHYSICS
...BIOMECHANICS
...BIONICS
....ROBOTICS
..ELECTRONICS
..MECHANICS (PHYSICS)
...FLUID MECHANICS
...KINETICS
....DIFFUSION (PHYSICS)
...QUANTUM MECHANICS
..NUCLEAR PHYSICS
..OPTICS
..THERMODYNAMICS
.SPECTROSCOPY

::::GROUPS
:::PERSONNEL
::PROFESSIONAL PERSONNEL
:::::GROUPS
::::PERSONNEL
:::HEALTH PERSONNEL
::ALLIED HEALTH PERSONNEL
:THERAPISTS
PHYSICAL THERAPISTS

:THERAPY
PHYSICAL THERAPY

::::GROUPS
:::PERSONNEL
::HEALTH PERSONNEL
:ALLIED HEALTH PERSONNEL
PHYSICAL THERAPY AIDES

::RELATIONSHIP
:INTERPERSONAL RELATIONSHIP
PHYSICIAN PATIENT RELATIONSHIP

:::GROUPS
::PERSONNEL
:PROFESSIONAL PERSONNEL
:::GROUPS
::PERSONNEL
:HEALTH PERSONNEL
PHYSICIANS
.FOREIGN MEDICAL GRADUATES
.PSYCHIATRISTS

::::GROUPS
:::PERSONNEL
::HEALTH PERSONNEL
:ALLIED HEALTH PERSONNEL
PHYSICIANS ASSISTANTS

::::LIBERAL ARTS
:::SCIENCES
::NATURAL SCIENCES
:PHYSICAL SCIENCES
PHYSICS
.BIOPHYSICS
..BIOMECHANICS
..BIONICS
...ROBOTICS
.ELECTRONICS
.MECHANICS (PHYSICS)
..FLUID MECHANICS
..KINETICS
...DIFFUSION (PHYSICS)
..QUANTUM MECHANICS
.NUCLEAR PHYSICS
.OPTICS
.THERMODYNAMICS

::::LIBERAL ARTS
:::SCIENCES
::NATURAL SCIENCES
:BIOLOGICAL SCIENCES
PHYSIOLOGY
.EXERCISE PHYSIOLOGY
.PSYCHOPHYSIOLOGY

:THEORIES
PIAGETIAN THEORY

::STIMULI
:VISUAL STIMULI
PICTORIAL STIMULI

::PUBLICATIONS
:BOOKS
PICTURE BOOKS

:::LINGUISTICS
::SOCIOLINGUISTICS
:LANGUAGE VARIATION
:LANGUAGES
PIDGINS

:PROGRAMS
PILOT PROJECTS

PLACEMENT
.ADVANCED PLACEMENT
.AGE GRADE PLACEMENT
.JOB PLACEMENT
..TEACHER PLACEMENT
.MAINSTREAMING
.STUDENT PLACEMENT

PLACE OF RESIDENCE

::MATHEMATICAL CONCEPTS
:NUMBER CONCEPTS
PLACE VALUE

::::BEHAVIOR
:::SOCIAL BEHAVIOR
::ANTISOCIAL BEHAVIOR
:STEALING
PLAGIARISM

:::LIBERAL ARTS
::MATHEMATICS
:GEOMETRY
PLANE GEOMETRY

:FACILITIES
PLANETARIUMS

:COMMUNITY
PLANNED COMMUNITIES

PLANNING
.BUDGETING
..PROGRAM BUDGETING
.CAREER PLANNING
.COLOR PLANNING
.COMMUNITY PLANNING
.COOPERATIVE PLANNING
.DESEGREGATION PLANS
.EDUCATIONAL PLANNING
..COLLEGE PLANNING
..EDUCATIONAL FACILITIES PLANNING
...CAMPUS PLANNING
.ESTATE PLANNING
.FACILITY PLANNING
..EDUCATIONAL FACILITIES PLANNING
...CAMPUS PLANNING
.FAMILY PLANNING
.LANGUAGE PLANNING
..LANGUAGE STANDARDIZATION
.LIBRARY PLANNING
.LONG RANGE PLANNING
.POLICY FORMATION
.REGIONAL PLANNING
.SCHEDULING
..FAST TRACK SCHEDULING
..SCHOOL SCHEDULES
...DOUBLE SESSIONS
...EXTENDED SCHOOL DAY
...EXTENDED SCHOOL YEAR
...FLEXIBLE SCHEDULING
...QUARTER SYSTEM
...SEMESTER SYSTEM
...TIME BLOCKS
...TRIMESTER SYSTEM
..WORKING HOURS
...FLEXIBLE WORKING HOURS
.SOCIAL PLANNING
.STATEWIDE PLANNING
.URBAN PLANNING

::::GROUPS
:::ORGANIZATIONS (GROUPS)
::AGENCIES
:PUBLIC AGENCIES
PLANNING COMMISSIONS

:DEVELOPMENT
PLANT GROWTH

: IDENTIFICATION
PLANT IDENTIFICATION

::: TECHNOLOGY
:: MEDICINE
: PATHOLOGY
PLANT PATHOLOGY

PLANT PROPAGATION

PLANT SCIENCE (1967 1980)

PLASTICS

:::::: LIBERAL ARTS
::::: SCIENCES
:::: NATURAL SCIENCES
::: PHYSICAL SCIENCES
:: EARTH SCIENCE
: SEISMOLOGY
:::::: LIBERAL ARTS
::::: SCIENCES
:::: NATURAL SCIENCES
::: PHYSICAL SCIENCES
:: EARTH SCIENCE
: GEOPHYSICS
PLATE TECTONICS

PLATONIC CRITICISM (1970 1980)

::: LIBERAL ARTS
:: HUMANITIES
: PHILOSOPHY
PLATONISM

: ACTIVITIES
PLAY
. PRETEND PLAY

:: ACTIVITIES
: RECREATIONAL ACTIVITIES
PLAYGROUND ACTIVITIES

:: FACILITIES
: RECREATIONAL FACILITIES
PLAYGROUNDS

:: THERAPY
:: RECREATION
: THERAPEUTIC RECREATION
PLAY THERAPY

:: LITERACY
:: LANGUAGE ARTS
: WRITING (COMPOSITION)
PLAYWRITING

: TECHNOLOGY
PLUMBING

::::: LINGUISTICS
:::: DESCRIPTIVE LINGUISTICS
::: GRAMMAR
:: MORPHOLOGY (LANGUAGES)
: MORPHEMES
PLURALS

:: FACILITIES
: AIR STRUCTURES
PNEUMATIC FORMS

:: TECHNOLOGY
: MEDICINE
PODIATRY

::: LIBERAL ARTS
:: HUMANITIES
: LITERATURE
POETRY
. EPICS
. HAIKU
. LYRIC POETRY
.. BALLADS
.. HYMNS
.. ODES
.. SONNETS

:: GROUPS
: AUTHORS
POETS

:: DISABILITIES
: DISEASES
POISONING
. LEAD POISONING

: HAZARDOUS MATERIALS
POISONS
. PESTICIDES
.. HERBICIDES
.. INSECTICIDES

::: GROUPS
:: PERSONNEL
: GOVERNMENT EMPLOYEES
POLICE

: LAW ENFORCEMENT
POLICE ACTION
. SEARCH AND SEIZURE

: RELATIONSHIP
POLICE COMMUNITY RELATIONSHIP

: EDUCATION
POLICE EDUCATION

: RELATIONSHIP
POLICE SCHOOL RELATIONSHIP

POLICY
. ADMINISTRATIVE POLICY
.. BOARD OF EDUCATION POLICY
. DISCIPLINE POLICY
. EDUCATIONAL POLICY
. FINANCIAL POLICY
. FOREIGN POLICY
.. IMPERIALISM
... COLONIALISM
. INTERDISTRICT POLICIES
. PERSONNEL POLICY
. PUBLIC POLICY
. SCHOOL POLICY
. TRANSFER POLICY

: PLANNING
POLICY FORMATION

::: LANGUAGES
:: INDO EUROPEAN LANGUAGES
: SLAVIC LANGUAGES
POLISH

:: GROUPS
: NORTH AMERICANS
:: GROUPS
: ETHNIC GROUPS
POLISH AMERICANS

::: LIBERAL ARTS
:: HUMANITIES
: LITERATURE
POLISH LITERATURE

: GROUP MEMBERSHIP
POLITICAL AFFILIATION

: ATTITUDES
POLITICAL ATTITUDES

: POLITICS
POLITICAL CAMPAIGNS
. PRESIDENTIAL CAMPAIGNS (UNITED STATES)

: GROUPS
POLITICAL CANDIDATES

: GEOGRAPHIC REGIONS
POLITICAL DIVISIONS (GEOGRAPHIC)
. AMERICAN INDIAN RESERVATIONS

: INFLUENCES
POLITICAL INFLUENCES

POLITICAL ISSUES

POLITICAL POWER

::: LIBERAL ARTS
:: SCIENCES
: SOCIAL SCIENCES
POLITICAL SCIENCE

: SOCIALIZATION
POLITICAL SOCIALIZATION

POLITICS
. POLITICAL CAMPAIGNS
.. PRESIDENTIAL CAMPAIGNS (UNITED STATES)
. POLITICS OF EDUCATION

: POLITICS
POLITICS OF EDUCATION

POLLUTION
. AIR POLLUTION
. WATER POLLUTION

:: EQUIPMENT
: MEASUREMENT EQUIPMENT
:: EQUIPMENT
: ELECTRONIC EQUIPMENT
POLYGRAPHS

: MATTER
POLYMERS

:: LANGUAGES
: AMERICAN INDIAN LANGUAGES
POMO

: CULTURE
POPULAR CULTURE

POPULARITY

:::: LIBERAL ARTS
::: SCIENCES
:: SOCIAL SCIENCES
: DEMOGRAPHY
POPULATION DISTRIBUTION
. ETHNIC DISTRIBUTION
. RACIAL DISTRIBUTION

: EDUCATION
POPULATION EDUCATION

: DEVELOPMENT
:::: LIBERAL ARTS
::: SCIENCES
:: SOCIAL SCIENCES
: DEMOGRAPHY
POPULATION GROWTH

:::: LIBERAL ARTS
::: SCIENCES
:: SOCIAL SCIENCES
: DEMOGRAPHY
POPULATION TRENDS
. BLACK POPULATION TRENDS

PORNOGRAPHY

:: RECORDS (FORMS)
: CREDENTIALS
PORTFOLIOS (BACKGROUND MATERIALS)

::: LANGUAGES
:: INDO EUROPEAN LANGUAGES
: ROMANCE LANGUAGES
PORTUGUESE

::: GROUPS
:: NORTH AMERICANS
: HISPANIC AMERICANS
:: GROUPS
: ETHNIC GROUPS
PORTUGUESE AMERICANS

:: PUBLICATIONS
: REPORTS
POSITION PAPERS
. MISSION STATEMENTS

: REINFORCEMENT
POSITIVE REINFORCEMENT

::: EDUCATION
:: POSTSECONDARY EDUCATION
: HIGHER EDUCATION
POSTDOCTORAL EDUCATION

: GUIDANCE
POST HIGH SCHOOL GUIDANCE

: EDUCATION
POSTSECONDARY EDUCATION
. HIGHER EDUCATION
.. GRADUATE STUDY
... GRADUATE MEDICAL EDUCATION
... POSTSECONDARY EDUCATION AS A FIELD OF STUDY
.. POSTDOCTORAL EDUCATION
.. UNDERGRADUATE STUDY
. LIBRARY EDUCATION

:::: EDUCATION
::: POSTSECONDARY EDUCATION
:: HIGHER EDUCATION
: GRADUATE STUDY
:: CURRICULUM
: COLLEGE CURRICULUM
POSTSECONDARY EDUCATION AS A FIELD OF STUDY

: GROUPS
POTENTIAL DROPOUTS

:: EQUIPMENT
: MEASUREMENT EQUIPMENT
POTENTIOMETERS (INSTRUMENTS)

:: STATUS
: ECONOMIC STATUS
POVERTY

: GEOGRAPHIC REGIONS
POVERTY AREAS
. SLUMS

: PROGRAMS
POVERTY PROGRAMS

: ORGANIZATION
POWER STRUCTURE

: TECHNOLOGY
POWER TECHNOLOGY
. NUCLEAR TECHNOLOGY

PRACTICAL ARTS

::: TECHNOLOGY
:: MEDICINE
: NURSING
PRACTICAL NURSING

:: PUBLICATIONS
: REPORTS
PRACTICUM PAPERS

:: CURRICULUM
: COURSES
PRACTICUMS
. OFFICE PRACTICE

::: GOVERNANCE
:: ADMINISTRATION
: SUPERVISION
PRACTICUM SUPERVISION

:::: LIBERAL ARTS
::: HUMANITIES
:: PHILOSOPHY
::: THEORIES
:: LINGUISTIC THEORY
: SEMIOTICS
PRAGMATICS

::: GROUPS
:: AGE GROUPS
: CHILDREN
PREADOLESCENTS

::: METHODS
:: EDUCATIONAL METHODS
: TEACHING METHODS
PRECISION TEACHING

PREDICTION
. EMPLOYMENT PROJECTIONS
. ENROLLMENT PROJECTIONS
. GRADE PREDICTION

: MEASUREMENT
PREDICTIVE MEASUREMENT

:::: STANDARDS
::: CRITERIA
:: EVALUATION CRITERIA
: VALIDITY
PREDICTIVE VALIDITY

PREDICTOR VARIABLES
. SUPPRESSOR VARIABLES

: CONSTRUCTION (PROCESS)
PREFABRICATION

PREGNANCY

:: GROUPS
: STUDENTS
:: GROUPS
: FEMALES
PREGNANT STUDENTS

::::: GROUPS
:::: AGE GROUPS
::: CHILDREN
:: YOUNG CHILDREN
: INFANTS
PREMATURE INFANTS

:::: GROUPS
::: STUDENTS
:: COLLEGE STUDENTS
: UNDERGRADUATE STUDENTS
PREMEDICAL STUDENTS

: INCOME
: EXPENDITURES
PREMIUM PAY

: INFLUENCES
PRENATAL INFLUENCES

::::: LINGUISTICS
:::: DESCRIPTIVE LINGUISTICS
::: GRAMMAR
:: SYNTAX
: FORM CLASSES (LANGUAGES)
PREPOSITIONS

:: BACKGROUND
: EXPERIENCE
PREREADING EXPERIENCE

PREREQUISITES

:: EDUCATION
: ADULT EDUCATION
PRERETIREMENT EDUCATION

:::: GROUPS
::: AGE GROUPS
:: CHILDREN
: YOUNG CHILDREN
PRESCHOOL CHILDREN

: CURRICULUM
PRESCHOOL CURRICULUM

:: EDUCATION
: EARLY CHILDHOOD EDUCATION
PRESCHOOL EDUCATION

: EVALUATION
PRESCHOOL EVALUATION

PRESCHOOL LEARNING (1966 1980)

:::: GROUPS
::: PERSONNEL
:: PROFESSIONAL PERSONNEL
: TEACHERS
PRESCHOOL TEACHERS

:: MEASURES (INDIVIDUALS)
: TESTS
PRESCHOOL TESTS

: MAINTENANCE
PRESERVATION

::: EDUCATION
:: PROFESSIONAL EDUCATION
: TEACHER EDUCATION
PRESERVICE TEACHER EDUCATION

:: POLITICS
: POLITICAL CAMPAIGNS
PRESIDENTIAL CAMPAIGNS (UNITED STATES)

::: GROUPS
:: PERSONNEL
: ADMINISTRATORS
PRESIDENTS
. COLLEGE PRESIDENTS
. PRESIDENTS OF THE UNITED STATES

:::: GROUPS
::: PERSONNEL
:: ADMINISTRATORS
: PRESIDENTS
PRESIDENTS OF THE UNITED STATES

:: ATTITUDES
: OPINIONS
PRESS OPINION

PRESSURE (1970 1980)

: SCIENTIFIC CONCEPTS
PRESSURE (PHYSICS)

: REPUTATION
PRESTIGE

: CONSTRUCTION MATERIALS
PRESTRESSED CONCRETE

: PROGRAMS
PRETECHNOLOGY PROGRAMS

:: ACTIVITIES
: PLAY
PRETEND PLAY

:: METHODS
: EVALUATION METHODS
PRETESTING

:: MEASURES (INDIVIDUALS)
: TESTS
PRETESTS POSTTESTS

PREVENTION
. ACCIDENT PREVENTION
. CRIME PREVENTION
. . DELINQUENCY PREVENTION
. DROPOUT PREVENTION
. HEARING CONSERVATION

:: TECHNOLOGY
: MEDICINE
PREVENTIVE MEDICINE

:: EDUCATION
: VOCATIONAL EDUCATION
PREVOCATIONAL EDUCATION

: WRITING PROCESSES
PREWRITING

::: GROUPS
:: PERSONNEL
: CLERGY
PRIESTS

:: COGNITIVE PROCESSES
: LEARNING PROCESSES
PRIMACY EFFECT

::: EDUCATION
:: ELEMENTARY SECONDARY EDUCATION
: ELEMENTARY EDUCATION
:: EDUCATION
: EARLY CHILDHOOD EDUCATION
PRIMARY EDUCATION

:: TECHNOLOGY
: MEDICINE
PRIMARY HEALTH CARE

: INFORMATION SOURCES
PRIMARY SOURCES

::::: LIBERAL ARTS
:::: SCIENCES
::: NATURAL SCIENCES
:: BIOLOGICAL SCIENCES
: ZOOLOGY
PRIMATOLOGY

:::: SYMBOLS (MATHEMATICS)
::: NUMBERS
:: RATIONAL NUMBERS
: INTEGERS
PRIME NUMBERS

::: GROUPS
:: PERSONNEL
: SCHOOL PERSONNEL
::: GROUPS
:: PERSONNEL
: ADMINISTRATORS
PRINCIPALS

::::: LIBERAL ARTS
:::: HUMANITIES
::: FINE ARTS
:: VISUAL ARTS
: GRAPHIC ARTS
PRINTING

: LEARNING
PRIOR LEARNING

:: GROUPS
: INSTITUTIONALIZED PERSONS
PRISONERS

:::: INSTITUTIONS
:::: INFORMATION SOURCES
::: LIBRARIES
:: SPECIAL LIBRARIES
: INSTITUTIONAL LIBRARIES
PRISON LIBRARIES

: RELATIONSHIP
PRIVACY
. CONFIDENTIALITY

::: GROUPS
:: ORGANIZATIONS (GROUPS)
: AGENCIES
PRIVATE AGENCIES

::: INSTITUTIONS
:: SCHOOLS
: PRIVATE SCHOOLS
::: INSTITUTIONS
:: SCHOOLS
: COLLEGES
PRIVATE COLLEGES

: EDUCATION
PRIVATE EDUCATION

: FINANCIAL SUPPORT
PRIVATE FINANCIAL SUPPORT

: SCHOOL SUPPORT
: FINANCIAL SUPPORT
PRIVATE SCHOOL AID

: : INSTITUTIONS
: SCHOOLS
PRIVATE SCHOOLS
. PAROCHIAL SCHOOLS
. . CATHOLIC SCHOOLS
. PRIVATE COLLEGES
. PROPRIETARY SCHOOLS

: : LIBERAL ARTS
: MATHEMATICS
PROBABILITY

PROBATIONARY PERIOD
. ACADEMIC PROBATION

: : : GROUPS
: : PERSONNEL
: CASEWORKERS
PROBATION OFFICERS

: : : GROUPS
: : AGE GROUPS
: CHILDREN
PROBLEM CHILDREN

PROBLEMS
. ADMINISTRATIVE PROBLEMS
. BEHAVIOR PROBLEMS
. COMMUNICATION PROBLEMS
. COMMUNITY PROBLEMS
. CURRICULUM PROBLEMS
. DISCIPLINE PROBLEMS
. EMOTIONAL PROBLEMS
. EMPLOYMENT PROBLEMS
. EVALUATION PROBLEMS
. FAMILY PROBLEMS
. FINANCIAL PROBLEMS
. LABOR PROBLEMS
. LEARNING PROBLEMS
. LEGAL PROBLEMS
. MIGRANT PROBLEMS
. PERSONALITY PROBLEMS
. READING DIFFICULTIES
. RESEARCH PROBLEMS
. SOCIAL PROBLEMS
. STUDENT PROBLEMS
. SUBURBAN PROBLEMS
. TESTING PROBLEMS
. URBAN PROBLEMS
. WORLD PROBLEMS
. WRITING DIFFICULTIES
. YOUTH PROBLEMS

: : EDUCATIONAL MEDIA
: INSTRUCTIONAL MATERIALS
PROBLEM SETS

: COGNITIVE PROCESSES
PROBLEM SOLVING

: EDUCATION
PROCESS EDUCATION

: : : GOVERNANCE
: : ADMINISTRATION
: SUPERVISION
PROCTORING

: SERVICES
PRODUCER SERVICES

: : : GROUPS
: : PERSONNEL
: PARAPROFESSIONAL PERSONNEL
PRODUCTION TECHNICIANS

: METHODS
PRODUCTION TECHNIQUES
. ELECTRONIC PUBLISHING
. FILM PRODUCTION
. PHOTOCOMPOSITION
. SPECIAL EFFECTS
. . ANIMATION
. . SOUND EFFECTS
. TELEVISION LIGHTING
. TEXTBOOK PUBLICATION

: : COGNITIVE PROCESSES
: CREATIVE THINKING
PRODUCTIVE THINKING

PRODUCTIVITY

: : GROUPS
: ORGANIZATIONS (GROUPS)
PROFESSIONAL ASSOCIATIONS
. LIBRARY ASSOCIATIONS
. MEDICAL ASSOCIATIONS
. TEACHER ASSOCIATIONS

PROFESSIONAL AUTONOMY

: : EDUCATION
: PROFESSIONAL EDUCATION
: : : EDUCATION
: : ADULT EDUCATION
: CONTINUING EDUCATION
PROFESSIONAL CONTINUING EDUCATION

: : DEVELOPMENT
: LABOR FORCE DEVELOPMENT
PROFESSIONAL DEVELOPMENT
. FACULTY DEVELOPMENT

: EDUCATION
PROFESSIONAL EDUCATION
. ADMINISTRATOR EDUCATION
. ARCHITECTURAL EDUCATION
. BUSINESS ADMINISTRATION EDUCATION
. ENGINEERING EDUCATION
. HOME ECONOMICS EDUCATION
. LEGAL EDUCATION (PROFESSIONS)
. MEDICAL EDUCATION
. . GRADUATE MEDICAL EDUCATION
. . NURSING EDUCATION
. . PHARMACEUTICAL EDUCATION
. . VETERINARY MEDICAL EDUCATION
. PROFESSIONAL CONTINUING EDUCATION
. PUBLIC ADMINISTRATION EDUCATION
. TEACHER EDUCATION
. . COMPETENCY BASED TEACHER EDUCATION
. . ENGLISH TEACHER EDUCATION
. . INSERVICE TEACHER EDUCATION
. . PRESERVICE TEACHER EDUCATION
. . STUDENT TEACHING
. . TEACHER EDUCATOR EDUCATION
. THEOLOGICAL EDUCATION

: OCCUPATIONS
PROFESSIONAL OCCUPATIONS
. TEACHING (OCCUPATION)
. . TEAM TEACHING
. . URBAN TEACHING

: : GROUPS
: PERSONNEL
PROFESSIONAL PERSONNEL
. ACCOUNTANTS
. . CERTIFIED PUBLIC ACCOUNTANTS
. ARCHITECTS
. ATHLETIC COACHES
. DENTISTS
. ENGINEERS
. FACULTY
. . ADJUNCT FACULTY
. . COLLEGE FACULTY
. . . COLLEGE PRESIDENTS
. . . COUNSELOR EDUCATORS
. . . GRADUATE SCHOOL FACULTY
. . . . MEDICAL SCHOOL FACULTY
. . . PROFESSORS
. . . STUDENT TEACHER SUPERVISORS
. . . TEACHER EDUCATORS
. . . . METHODS TEACHERS
. . . TEACHING ASSISTANTS
. . DEANS
. . . ACADEMIC DEANS
. . . DEANS OF STUDENTS
. . DEPARTMENT HEADS
. . FACULTY ADVISERS
. . FULL TIME FACULTY
. . NONTENURED FACULTY
. . PART TIME FACULTY
. . . PARTNERSHIP TEACHERS
. . TENURED FACULTY
. . WOMEN FACULTY
. INFORMATION SCIENTISTS
. . LIBRARIANS
. LAWYERS
. MATHEMATICIANS
. NURSES
. . NURSE PRACTITIONERS
. . SCHOOL NURSES
. OPTOMETRISTS
. PHARMACISTS
. PHYSICIANS
. . FOREIGN MEDICAL GRADUATES
. . PSYCHIATRISTS
. PSYCHOLOGISTS
. . SCHOOL PSYCHOLOGISTS
. RESEARCH DIRECTORS
. RESEARCHERS
. . EDUCATIONAL RESEARCHERS
. SCIENTISTS
. SOCIAL SCIENTISTS
. SOCIAL WORKERS
. . SCHOOL SOCIAL WORKERS
. TEACHERS
. . ADULT EDUCATORS
. . ART TEACHERS
. . BEGINNING TEACHERS
. . BILINGUAL TEACHERS
. . BLACK TEACHERS
. . CATHOLIC EDUCATORS
. . COOPERATING TEACHERS
. . ELEMENTARY SCHOOL TEACHERS
. . HOME ECONOMICS TEACHERS
. . INDUSTRIAL ARTS TEACHERS
. . INSTRUCTOR COORDINATORS
. . ITINERANT TEACHERS
. . LANGUAGE TEACHERS
. . LAY TEACHERS
. . MASTER TEACHERS
. . MATHEMATICS TEACHERS
. . MINORITY GROUP TEACHERS
. . MUSIC TEACHERS
. . PHYSICAL EDUCATION TEACHERS
. . PRESCHOOL TEACHERS
. . PUBLIC SCHOOL TEACHERS
. . READING TEACHERS
. . REMEDIAL TEACHERS
. . RESOURCE TEACHERS
. . SCIENCE TEACHERS
. . SECONDARY SCHOOL TEACHERS
. . SPECIAL EDUCATION TEACHERS
. . STUDENT TEACHERS
. . SUBSTITUTE TEACHERS
. . TEACHER INTERNS
. . TELEVISION TEACHERS
. . TUTORS
. . VOCATIONAL EDUCATION TEACHERS
. . . BUSINESS EDUCATION TEACHERS
. . . DISTRIBUTIVE EDUCATION TEACHERS
. . . TRADE AND INDUSTRIAL TEACHERS
. THERAPISTS
. . OCCUPATIONAL THERAPISTS
. . PHYSICAL THERAPISTS
. VETERINARIANS

: : EVALUATION
: RECOGNITION (ACHIEVEMENT)
PROFESSIONAL RECOGNITION

: SERVICES
PROFESSIONAL SERVICES

: TRAINING
PROFESSIONAL TRAINING

: : : : : GROUPS
: : : : PERSONNEL
: : : SCHOOL PERSONNEL
: : : : : GROUPS
: : : : PERSONNEL
: : : PROFESSIONAL PERSONNEL
: : FACULTY
: COLLEGE FACULTY
PROFESSORS

: DATA
PROFILES

: : MEASURES (INDIVIDUALS)
: TESTS
PROGNOSTIC TESTS

: : GOVERNANCE
: ADMINISTRATION
PROGRAM ADMINISTRATION

: ATTITUDES
PROGRAM ATTITUDES

: : PLANNING
: BUDGETING
PROGRAM BUDGETING

PROGRAM CONTENT

: COSTS
PROGRAM COSTS

PROGRAM DESCRIPTIONS

: DESIGN
PROGRAM DESIGN

: DEVELOPMENT
PROGRAM DEVELOPMENT

: : : METHODS
: : EDUCATIONAL METHODS
: TEACHING METHODS
PROGRAMED INSTRUCTION
. COMPUTER ASSISTED INSTRUCTION
. PROGRAMED TUTORING

: : EDUCATIONAL MEDIA
: INSTRUCTIONAL MATERIALS
PROGRAMED INSTRUCTIONAL MATERIALS

: : : INSTRUCTION
: : INDIVIDUAL INSTRUCTION
: TUTORING
: : : : METHODS
: : : EDUCATIONAL METHODS
: : TEACHING METHODS
: PROGRAMED INSTRUCTION
PROGRAMED TUTORING

PROGRAM EFFECTIVENESS

:: GROUPS
: PERSONNEL
PROGRAMERS

: EVALUATION
PROGRAM EVALUATION

::: PUBLICATIONS
:: REFERENCE MATERIALS
: GUIDES
PROGRAM GUIDES

PROGRAM IMPLEMENTATION

: IMPROVEMENT
PROGRAM IMPROVEMENT

:::: LIBERAL ARTS
::: SCIENCES
:: INFORMATION SCIENCE
: COMPUTER SCIENCE
PROGRAMING

PROGRAMING (BROADCAST)

: LANGUAGE
PROGRAMING LANGUAGES

PROGRAMING PROBLEMS (1966 1980)

PROGRAM LENGTH

PROGRAM PROPOSALS
. RESEARCH PROPOSALS

PROGRAMS
. ADULT PROGRAMS
.. ADULT READING PROGRAMS
.. HIGH SCHOOL EQUIVALENCY PROGRAMS
. ADVANCED PLACEMENT PROGRAMS
. AFTER SCHOOL PROGRAMS
. ASSEMBLY PROGRAMS
. BILINGUAL EDUCATION PROGRAMS
. CHURCH PROGRAMS
. COLLEGE DAY
. COLLEGE PROGRAMS
.. DOCTORAL PROGRAMS
.. EXTERNAL DEGREE PROGRAMS
.. MASTERS PROGRAMS
. COMMUNITY PROGRAMS
.. COMMUNITY RECREATION PROGRAMS
.. SCHOOL COMMUNITY PROGRAMS
. COMPREHENSIVE PROGRAMS
. COMPUTER ORIENTED PROGRAMS
. CONSTRUCTION PROGRAMS
. CONSULTATION PROGRAMS
. COOPERATIVE PROGRAMS
. COUNTY PROGRAMS
. DAY PROGRAMS
. DEMONSTRATION PROGRAMS
. DEVELOPMENTAL PROGRAMS
.. DEVELOPMENTAL STUDIES PROGRAMS
. EMERGENCY PROGRAMS
. EMPLOYEE ASSISTANCE PROGRAMS
. EMPLOYMENT PROGRAMS
. EVENING PROGRAMS
. EXCHANGE PROGRAMS
.. STUDENT EXCHANGE PROGRAMS
.. TEACHER EXCHANGE PROGRAMS
. EXPERIMENTAL PROGRAMS
. FAMILY PROGRAMS
. FEDERAL PROGRAMS
. FIELD EXPERIENCE PROGRAMS
.. SUPERVISED FARM PRACTICE
. FOUNDATION PROGRAMS
. GUIDANCE PROGRAMS
. HEALTH PROGRAMS
.. BREAKFAST PROGRAMS
.. IMMUNIZATION PROGRAMS
.. LUNCH PROGRAMS
.. MENTAL HEALTH PROGRAMS
. HOME PROGRAMS
. HUMAN RELATIONS PROGRAMS
. IMPROVEMENT PROGRAMS
.. SELF HELP PROGRAMS
. INDIVIDUALIZED PROGRAMS
. INPLANT PROGRAMS
. INSTITUTES (TRAINING PROGRAMS)
. INTERCULTURAL PROGRAMS
. INTERGENERATIONAL PROGRAMS
. INTERNATIONAL PROGRAMS
. INTERNSHIP PROGRAMS
. INTERSTATE PROGRAMS
. MIGRANT PROGRAMS
. NATIONAL PROGRAMS
. NONSCHOOL EDUCATIONAL PROGRAMS
. OUTREACH PROGRAMS
. PILOT PROJECTS
. POVERTY PROGRAMS
. PRETECHNOLOGY PROGRAMS
. READING PROGRAMS
.. ADULT READING PROGRAMS
. RECREATIONAL PROGRAMS
.. COMMUNITY RECREATION PROGRAMS
.. DAY CAMP PROGRAMS
.. PHYSICAL RECREATION PROGRAMS
.. RESIDENT CAMP PROGRAMS
.. SCHOOL RECREATIONAL PROGRAMS
. REGIONAL PROGRAMS
. REHABILITATION PROGRAMS
.. DROPOUT PROGRAMS
. REMEDIAL PROGRAMS
. RESEARCH PROJECTS
. RESIDENTIAL PROGRAMS
.. RESIDENT CAMP PROGRAMS
. SCIENCE COURSE IMPROVEMENT PROJECTS
. SCIENCE PROGRAMS
.. SUMMER SCIENCE PROGRAMS
. SECOND LANGUAGE PROGRAMS
.. COLLEGE SECOND LANGUAGE PROGRAMS
.. IMMERSION PROGRAMS
. SPECIAL PROGRAMS
.. INDIVIDUALIZED EDUCATION PROGRAMS
.. RESOURCE ROOM PROGRAMS
.. SPECIAL DEGREE PROGRAMS
. STATE PROGRAMS
. STUDENT LOAN PROGRAMS
. SUMMER PROGRAMS
.. SUMMER SCIENCE PROGRAMS
. TEACHER EDUCATION PROGRAMS
. TESTING PROGRAMS
. TRANSFER PROGRAMS
.. FREE CHOICE TRANSFER PROGRAMS
. TRANSITIONAL PROGRAMS
. TUTORIAL PROGRAMS
. URBAN PROGRAMS
. VACATION PROGRAMS
. VALIDATED PROGRAMS
. WEEKEND PROGRAMS
. WORK EXPERIENCE PROGRAMS
. WORK STUDY PROGRAMS
. YOUTH PROGRAMS

PROGRAM TERMINATION

PROGRAM VALIDATION

: EDUCATION
PROGRESSIVE EDUCATION

PROJECT APPLICATIONS (1967 1980)

: VISUAL AIDS
: EQUIPMENT
PROJECTION EQUIPMENT
. FILMSTRIP PROJECTORS
. MICROFORM READERS
. OPAQUE PROJECTORS
. OVERHEAD PROJECTORS
. TACHISTOSCOPES

: MEASURES (INDIVIDUALS)
PROJECTIVE MEASURES
. ASSOCIATION MEASURES

PROJECTS (1966 1980)

PROMOTION (OCCUPATIONAL)
. FACULTY PROMOTION
. TEACHER PROMOTION

: METHODS
PROMPTING

::::: LINGUISTICS
:::: DESCRIPTIVE LINGUISTICS
::: GRAMMAR
:: SYNTAX
: FORM CLASSES (LANGUAGES)
PRONOUNS

:: LANGUAGE ARTS
: SPEECH
PRONUNCIATION

:: INSTRUCTION
: SPEECH INSTRUCTION
PRONUNCIATION INSTRUCTION

:::: STANDARDS
::: CRITERIA
:: EVALUATION CRITERIA
: VALIDITY
::::: LIBERAL ARTS
:::: HUMANITIES
::: PHILOSOPHY
:: LOGIC
: MATHEMATICAL LOGIC
PROOF (MATHEMATICS)

::: SERVICES
:: INFORMATION SERVICES
: INFORMATION DISSEMINATION
: COMMUNICATION (THOUGHT TRANSFER)
PROPAGANDA

:: TECHNOLOGY
: ACCOUNTING
PROPERTY ACCOUNTING

: EVALUATION
PROPERTY APPRAISAL
. ASSESSED VALUATION

: TAXES
PROPERTY TAXES

:: LITERACY
:: LANGUAGE ARTS
: WRITING (COMPOSITION)
PROPOSAL WRITING

::: INSTITUTIONS
:: SCHOOLS
: PRIVATE SCHOOLS
PROPRIETARY SCHOOLS

::: LIBERAL ARTS
:: HUMANITIES
: LITERATURE
PROSE
. FICTION
.. NOVELS
.. SCIENCE FICTION
.. SHORT STORIES
. NONFICTION
.. BIOGRAPHIES
... AUTOBIOGRAPHIES
.. CHRONICLES
.. DIARIES
.. ESSAYS

:: BEHAVIOR
: SOCIAL BEHAVIOR
PROSOCIAL BEHAVIOR

:: EQUIPMENT
: ASSISTIVE DEVICES (FOR DISABLED)
PROSTHESES

:: GROUPS
: RELIGIOUS CULTURAL GROUPS
PROTESTANTS
. AMISH
. PURITANS

:: METHODS
: RESEARCH METHODOLOGY
PROTOCOL ANALYSIS

:: EDUCATIONAL MEDIA
: INSTRUCTIONAL MATERIALS
:: EDUCATIONAL MEDIA
: AUDIOVISUAL AIDS
PROTOCOL MATERIALS

PROVERBS

PROXIMITY

:::: GROUPS
::: PERSONNEL
:: HEALTH PERSONNEL
: ALLIED HEALTH PERSONNEL
PSYCHIATRIC AIDES

:: INSTITUTIONS
: HOSPITALS
PSYCHIATRIC HOSPITALS

:::: SERVICES
::: HUMAN SERVICES
:: HEALTH SERVICES
: MEDICAL SERVICES
PSYCHIATRIC SERVICES

:::: GROUPS
::: PERSONNEL
:: PROFESSIONAL PERSONNEL
:::: GROUPS
::: PERSONNEL
:: HEALTH PERSONNEL
: PHYSICIANS
PSYCHIATRISTS

:: TECHNOLOGY
: MEDICINE
PSYCHIATRY

:::: LIBERAL ARTS
::: SCIENCES
:: BEHAVIORAL SCIENCES
: PSYCHOLOGY
::: LIBERAL ARTS
:: SCIENCES
: ACOUSTICS
PSYCHOACOUSTICS

: CLINICS
PSYCHOEDUCATIONAL CLINICS

:: METHODS
: EDUCATIONAL METHODS
PSYCHOEDUCATIONAL METHODS

: LINGUISTICS
PSYCHOLINGUISTICS

: INDIVIDUAL CHARACTERISTICS
PSYCHOLOGICAL CHARACTERISTICS
. ATTENTION SPAN
. COGNITIVE STYLE

PSYCHOLOGICAL CHARACTERISTICS (CONTINUED)
..CONCEPTUAL TEMPO
..FIELD DEPENDENCE INDEPENDENCE
.CREATIVITY
..IMAGINATION
.INTELLIGENCE
..COMPREHENSION
...LISTENING COMPREHENSION
...READING COMPREHENSION
..FORMAL OPERATIONS
..MENTAL AGE
.PERSONALITY TRAITS
..CURIOSITY
..LOCUS OF CONTROL
..MENTAL RIGIDITY
.SCHEMATA (COGNITION)

:EVALUATION
PSYCHOLOGICAL EVALUATION
.PERSONALITY ASSESSMENT

::NEEDS
:INDIVIDUAL NEEDS
PSYCHOLOGICAL NEEDS
.ACHIEVEMENT NEED
.AFFECTION
.AFFILIATION NEED
..PEER ACCEPTANCE
.PERSONAL SPACE
.SECURITY (PSYCHOLOGY)
.SELF ACTUALIZATION
.STATUS NEED

PSYCHOLOGICAL PATTERNS
.ALIENATION
..STUDENT ALIENATION
..TEACHER ALIENATION
.ANGER
..HOSTILITY
.ANXIETY
..COMMUNICATION APPREHENSION
..MATHEMATICS ANXIETY
..SEPARATION ANXIETY
..TEST ANXIETY
..WRITING APPREHENSION
.APATHY
.COGNITIVE DISSONANCE
.CONGRUENCE (PSYCHOLOGY)
..SELF CONGRUENCE
.DEPRESSION (PSYCHOLOGY)
.EGOCENTRISM
.EMPATHY
.FEAR
..FEAR OF SUCCESS
..SCHOOL PHOBIA
.GRIEF
.IDENTIFICATION (PSYCHOLOGY)
.JEALOUSY
.LONELINESS
.MORALE
..TEACHER MORALE
.REJECTION (PSYCHOLOGY)
.RESENTMENT
.WITHDRAWAL (PSYCHOLOGY)

::SERVICES
:HUMAN SERVICES
PSYCHOLOGICAL SERVICES

::RESEARCH
:BEHAVIORAL SCIENCE RESEARCH
PSYCHOLOGICAL STUDIES
.FORCE FIELD ANALYSIS
.INTEREST RESEARCH
.PERSONALITY STUDIES

:::METHODS
::MEASUREMENT TECHNIQUES
:TESTING
PSYCHOLOGICAL TESTING

:::GROUPS
::PERSONNEL
:PROFESSIONAL PERSONNEL
:::GROUPS
::PERSONNEL
:HEALTH PERSONNEL
PSYCHOLOGISTS
.SCHOOL PSYCHOLOGISTS

:::LIBERAL ARTS
::SCIENCES
:BEHAVIORAL SCIENCES
PSYCHOLOGY
.BEHAVIORISM
.CHILD PSYCHOLOGY
.CLINICAL PSYCHOLOGY
.COGNITIVE PSYCHOLOGY
.COMMUNITY PSYCHOLOGY
.DEVELOPMENTAL PSYCHOLOGY
.EDUCATIONAL PSYCHOLOGY
.EXPERIMENTAL PSYCHOLOGY
.INDIVIDUAL PSYCHOLOGY
.INDUSTRIAL PSYCHOLOGY
.PSYCHOACOUSTICS
.PSYCHOMETRICS
.PSYCHOPATHOLOGY
.PSYCHOPHYSIOLOGY
.SOCIAL PSYCHOLOGY
.SPORT PSYCHOLOGY

::::LIBERAL ARTS
:::SCIENCES
::BEHAVIORAL SCIENCES
:PSYCHOLOGY
PSYCHOMETRICS

::OBJECTIVES
:BEHAVIORAL OBJECTIVES
PSYCHOMOTOR OBJECTIVES

::ABILITY
:SKILLS
PSYCHOMOTOR SKILLS
.MARKSMANSHIP
.OBJECT MANIPULATION
.PERCEPTUAL MOTOR COORDINATION
..EYE HAND COORDINATION
..EYE VOICE SPAN

::::LIBERAL ARTS
:::SCIENCES
::BEHAVIORAL SCIENCES
:PSYCHOLOGY
:::TECHNOLOGY
::MEDICINE
:PATHOLOGY
PSYCHOPATHOLOGY

::::LIBERAL ARTS
:::SCIENCES
::BEHAVIORAL SCIENCES
:PSYCHOLOGY
:::::LIBERAL ARTS
::::SCIENCES
:::NATURAL SCIENCES
::BIOLOGICAL SCIENCES
:PHYSIOLOGY
PSYCHOPHYSIOLOGY

::DISABILITIES
:SEVERE DISABILITIES
::DISABILITIES
:MENTAL DISORDERS
PSYCHOSIS
.AUTISM
.ECHOLALIA
.SCHIZOPHRENIA

:::DISABILITIES
::MENTAL DISORDERS
:EMOTIONAL DISTURBANCES
PSYCHOSOMATIC DISORDERS

:THERAPY
PSYCHOTHERAPY
.GESTALT THERAPY
.MILIEU THERAPY
.RATIONAL EMOTIVE THERAPY
.REALITY THERAPY

.RELAXATION TRAINING
.TRANSACTIONAL ANALYSIS

::GOVERNANCE
:ADMINISTRATION
PUBLIC ADMINISTRATION

::EDUCATION
:PROFESSIONAL EDUCATION
PUBLIC ADMINISTRATION EDUCATION

:EDUCATION
PUBLIC AFFAIRS EDUCATION

:::GROUPS
::ORGANIZATIONS (GROUPS)
:AGENCIES
PUBLIC AGENCIES
.PLANNING COMMISSIONS
.STATE AGENCIES
..STATE DEPARTMENTS OF EDUCATION
..STATE LICENSING BOARDS

PUBLICATIONS
.BOOK REVIEWS
.BOOKS
..FOREIGN LANGUAGE BOOKS
..HIGH INTEREST LOW VOCABULARY BOOKS
..PAPERBACK BOOKS
..PICTURE BOOKS
..TEXTBOOKS
...HISTORY TEXTBOOKS
...MULTICULTURAL TEXTBOOKS
..YEARBOOKS
.CATALOGS
..LIBRARY CATALOGS
...BOOK CATALOGS
...CARD CATALOGS
...UNION CATALOGS
..ONLINE CATALOGS
..SCHOOL CATALOGS
.COMICS (PUBLICATIONS)
.COMPUTER SOFTWARE REVIEWS
.GOVERNMENT PUBLICATIONS
.LITERATURE REVIEWS
.PAMPHLETS
.REFERENCE MATERIALS
..ABSTRACTS
..ANTHOLOGIES
..ATLASES
..BIBLIOGRAPHIES
...ANNOTATED BIBLIOGRAPHIES
..CITATIONS (REFERENCES)
..DICTIONARIES
...GLOSSARIES
..DIRECTORIES
..DISCOGRAPHIES
..ENCYCLOPEDIAS
..FILMOGRAPHIES
..GUIDES
...ADMINISTRATOR GUIDES
...CURRICULUM GUIDES
....STATE CURRICULUM GUIDES
...FACULTY HANDBOOKS
...LABORATORY MANUALS
...LEADERS GUIDES
...LIBRARY GUIDES
...PROGRAM GUIDES
...STUDY GUIDES
...TEACHING GUIDES
...TEST MANUALS
..INDEXES
...CITATION INDEXES
...COORDINATE INDEXES
...PERMUTED INDEXES
..LIBRARY CATALOGS
...BOOK CATALOGS
...CARD CATALOGS
...UNION CATALOGS
..THESAURI
..YEARBOOKS
.REPORTS
..ANNUAL REPORTS
..CONFERENCE PAPERS
..OPINION PAPERS
..PERSONAL NARRATIVES
..POSITION PAPERS
...MISSION STATEMENTS
..PRACTICUM PAPERS

..RESEARCH REPORTS
..THESES
...DOCTORAL DISSERTATIONS
...MASTERS THESES
.SCHOOL PUBLICATIONS
..FACULTY HANDBOOKS
..SCHOOL CATALOGS
..SCHOOL NEWSPAPERS
..STUDENT PUBLICATIONS
.SERIALS
..ANNUAL REPORTS
..BULLETINS
..CONFERENCE PROCEEDINGS
..NEWSPAPERS
...NEWSLETTERS
...SCHOOL NEWSPAPERS
..PERIODICALS
...FOREIGN LANGUAGE PERIODICALS
...SCHOLARLY JOURNALS
..YEARBOOKS
.STATE OF THE ART REVIEWS
.TEST REVIEWS

:::INSTITUTIONS
::SCHOOLS
:COLLEGES
PUBLIC COLLEGES
.COMMUNITY COLLEGES
.STATE COLLEGES
..STATE UNIVERSITIES

:EDUCATION
PUBLIC EDUCATION
.PUBLIC SCHOOL ADULT EDUCATION

:FACILITIES
PUBLIC FACILITIES
.PUBLIC LIBRARIES
..COUNTY LIBRARIES
..REGIONAL LIBRARIES

:HEALTH
PUBLIC HEALTH

:LEGISLATION
PUBLIC HEALTH LEGISLATION
.DRUG LEGISLATION

:::FACILITIES
::HOUSING
:LOW RENT HOUSING
PUBLIC HOUSING

:::SERVICES
::INFORMATION SERVICES
:INFORMATION DISSEMINATION
:COMMUNICATION (THOUGHT TRANSFER)
PUBLICITY
.ADVERTISING
..TELEVISION COMMERCIALS
.INSTITUTIONAL ADVANCEMENT

PUBLICIZE (1968 1980)

::FACILITIES
:PUBLIC FACILITIES
::INSTITUTIONS
::INFORMATION SOURCES
:LIBRARIES
PUBLIC LIBRARIES
.COUNTY LIBRARIES
.REGIONAL LIBRARIES

:::GROUPS
::PERSONNEL
:GOVERNMENT EMPLOYEES
PUBLIC OFFICIALS
.CITY OFFICIALS
.COUNTY OFFICIALS
.COURT JUDGES
.LEGISLATORS
.STATE OFFICIALS
..STATE SUPERVISORS

: : ATTITUDES
: OPINIONS
PUBLIC OPINION

: POLICY
PUBLIC POLICY

: RELATIONSHIP
PUBLIC RELATIONS

: : EDUCATION
: PUBLIC EDUCATION
: : EDUCATION
: ADULT EDUCATION
PUBLIC SCHOOL ADULT EDUCATION

: : INSTITUTIONS
: SCHOOLS
PUBLIC SCHOOLS

: : : : GROUPS
: : : PERSONNEL
: : PROFESSIONAL PERSONNEL
: TEACHERS
: : : GROUPS
: : PERSONNEL
: GOVERNMENT EMPLOYEES
PUBLIC SCHOOL TEACHERS

PUBLIC SERVICE

: OCCUPATIONS
PUBLIC SERVICE OCCUPATIONS

: : COMMUNICATION (THOUGHT TRANSFER)
: SPEECH COMMUNICATION
PUBLIC SPEAKING

PUBLIC SUPPORT

: : : : TECHNOLOGY
: : : COMMUNICATIONS
: : TELECOMMUNICATIONS
: : MASS MEDIA
: TELEVISION
PUBLIC TELEVISION

: : BUSINESS
: INDUSTRY
PUBLISHING INDUSTRY

PUBLISH OR PERISH ISSUE

: : CULTURE
: LATIN AMERICAN CULTURE
PUERTO RICAN CULTURE

: : GROUPS
: LATIN AMERICANS
PUERTO RICANS

: : LANGUAGE
: WRITTEN LANGUAGE
PUNCTUATION

: REINFORCEMENT
PUNISHMENT
. CORPORAL PUNISHMENT

: : LITERARY DEVICES
: : LANGUAGE
: FIGURATIVE LANGUAGE
PUNS

: : : BEHAVIOR
: : RESPONSES
: MOTOR REACTIONS
PUPILLARY DILATION

: : : : SERVICES
: : : HUMAN SERVICES
: : SOCIAL SERVICES
: ANCILLARY SCHOOL SERVICES
PUPIL PERSONNEL SERVICES

: : : GROUPS
: : PERSONNEL
: SCHOOL PERSONNEL
PUPIL PERSONNEL WORKERS
. ATTENDANCE OFFICERS

: : : : LIBERAL ARTS
: : : HUMANITIES
: : FINE ARTS
: THEATER ARTS
PUPPETRY

PURCHASING

: : : GROUPS
: : RELIGIOUS CULTURAL GROUPS
: PROTESTANTS
PURITANS

: : ACTIVITIES
: GAMES
PUZZLES

: ORGANIZATION
PYRAMID ORGANIZATION

: : METHODS
: MEASUREMENT TECHNIQUES
Q METHODOLOGY

: STANDARDS
QUALIFICATIONS
. ADMINISTRATOR QUALIFICATIONS
. COUNSELOR QUALIFICATIONS
. EMPLOYMENT QUALIFICATIONS
. SUPERVISOR QUALIFICATIONS
. TEACHER QUALIFICATIONS

: RESEARCH
QUALITATIVE RESEARCH

: GROUPS
QUALITY CIRCLES

: : METHODS
: EVALUATION METHODS
QUALITY CONTROL

QUALITY OF LIFE
. QUALITY OF WORKING LIFE
. WELL BEING
. . CHILD WELFARE
. . STUDENT WELFARE
. . TEACHER WELFARE

: QUALITY OF LIFE
QUALITY OF WORKING LIFE

: : : : : LIBERAL ARTS
: : : : SCIENCES
: : : : NATURAL SCIENCES
: : : PHYSICAL SCIENCES
: : PHYSICS
: MECHANICS (PHYSICS)
QUANTUM MECHANICS

: : : PLANNING
: : SCHEDULING
: SCHOOL SCHEDULES
QUARTER SYSTEM

: : DESIGN
: RESEARCH DESIGN
QUASIEXPERIMENTAL DESIGN

: : LANGUAGES
: AMERICAN INDIAN LANGUAGES
QUECHUA

: METHODS
QUESTIONING TECHNIQUES

: MEASURES (INDIVIDUALS)
QUESTIONNAIRES

: : : LANGUAGES
: : AMERICAN INDIAN LANGUAGES
: MAYAN LANGUAGES
QUICHE

QUOTAS

: : INDIVIDUAL CHARACTERISTICS
: PHYSICAL CHARACTERISTICS
RACE

: ATTITUDES
RACIAL ATTITUDES

: : : : : LIBERAL ARTS
: : : : SCIENCES
: : : SOCIAL SCIENCES
: : DEMOGRAPHY
: RACIAL COMPOSITION
RACIAL BALANCE

: : : ATTITUDES
: : SOCIAL ATTITUDES
: : BIAS
: SOCIAL BIAS
RACIAL BIAS

RACIAL CHARACTERISTICS (1966 1980)

: : : : LIBERAL ARTS
: : : SCIENCES
: : SOCIAL SCIENCES
: DEMOGRAPHY
RACIAL COMPOSITION
. RACIAL BALANCE

: DIFFERENCES
RACIAL DIFFERENCES

: SOCIAL DISCRIMINATION
RACIAL DISCRIMINATION
. RACIAL SEGREGATION
. . DE FACTO SEGREGATION
. . DE JURE SEGREGATION

: : : : : LIBERAL ARTS
: : : : SCIENCES
: : : SOCIAL SCIENCES
: : DEMOGRAPHY
: POPULATION DISTRIBUTION
RACIAL DISTRIBUTION

: INFLUENCES
RACIAL FACTORS

: IDENTIFICATION
RACIAL IDENTIFICATION

: SOCIAL INTEGRATION
RACIAL INTEGRATION

: : INSTITUTIONS
: SCHOOLS
RACIALLY BALANCED SCHOOLS

: : : RELATIONSHIP
: : HUMAN RELATIONS
: INTERGROUP RELATIONS
RACIAL RELATIONS

: : SOCIAL DISCRIMINATION
: RACIAL DISCRIMINATION
RACIAL SEGREGATION
. DE FACTO SEGREGATION
. DE JURE SEGREGATION

RACISM (1966 1980)

: : : : ACTIVITIES
: : : PHYSICAL ACTIVITIES
: : ATHLETICS
: RACQUET SPORTS
RACQUETBALL

: : : ACTIVITIES
: : PHYSICAL ACTIVITIES
: ATHLETICS
RACQUET SPORTS
. BADMINTON
. RACQUETBALL
. SQUASH (GAME)
. TENNIS

: : EQUIPMENT
: ELECTRONIC EQUIPMENT
RADAR

: : SCIENTIFIC CONCEPTS
: ENERGY
RADIATION
. LIGHT
. NUCLEAR ENERGY
. SOLAR ENERGY

: : : : : LIBERAL ARTS
: : : : SCIENCES
: : : NATURAL SCIENCES
: : BIOLOGICAL SCIENCES
: BIOLOGY
RADIATION BIOLOGY

RADIATION EFFECTS

: : : TECHNOLOGY
: : COMMUNICATIONS
: TELECOMMUNICATIONS
: MASS MEDIA
RADIO
. EDUCATIONAL RADIO

: : : GROUPS
: : PERSONNEL
: PARAPROFESSIONAL PERSONNEL
RADIOGRAPHERS

RADIOISOTOPES

: : : : GROUPS
: : : PERSONNEL
: : HEALTH PERSONNEL
: ALLIED HEALTH PERSONNEL
RADIOLOGIC TECHNOLOGISTS

: TECHNOLOGY
RADIOLOGY

: TRANSPORTATION
RAIL TRANSPORTATION

: VISUAL AIDS
: SENSORY AIDS
RAISED LINE DRAWINGS

: : : : BEHAVIOR
: : : SOCIAL BEHAVIOR
: : ANTISOCIAL BEHAVIOR
: SEXUAL ABUSE
RAPE

: : RELATIONSHIP
: INTERPERSONAL RELATIONSHIP
RAPPORT

: MEASURES (INDIVIDUALS)
RATING SCALES
. BEHAVIOR RATING SCALES
. SEMANTIC DIFFERENTIAL

: : THERAPY
: PSYCHOTHERAPY
RATIONAL EMOTIVE THERAPY

: : SYMBOLS (MATHEMATICS)
: NUMBERS
RATIONAL NUMBERS
. INTEGERS
. . PRIME NUMBERS

RATIOS (MATHEMATICS)
. COUNSELOR CLIENT RATIO
. INTELLIGENCE QUOTIENT
. PERCENTAGE
. RELEVANCE (INFORMATION RETRIEVAL)
. TAX RATES
. TEACHER STUDENT RATIO

: ANIMALS
RATS

: : DATA
: SCORES
RAW SCORES

REACTION TIME

READABILITY

: : METHODS
: EVALUATION METHODS
READABILITY FORMULAS

: : BEHAVIOR
: RESPONSES
READER RESPONSE

: : : : LIBERAL ARTS
: : : HUMANITIES
: : FINE ARTS
: THEATER ARTS
READERS THEATER

: RELATIONSHIP
READER TEXT RELATIONSHIP

READINESS
. INTEGRATION READINESS
. LEARNING READINESS
. READING READINESS
. SCHOOL READINESS
. WRITING READINESS

: LITERACY
: LANGUAGE ARTS
READING
. BASAL READING
. BEGINNING READING
. CONTENT AREA READING
. CORRECTIVE READING
. CRITICAL READING
. DIRECTED READING ACTIVITY
. EARLY READING
. FUNCTIONAL READING
. INDEPENDENT READING
. INDIVIDUALIZED READING
. MUSIC READING
. ORAL READING
. READING ALOUD TO OTHERS
. RECREATIONAL READING
. REMEDIAL READING
. SILENT READING
. SPEED READING
. STORY READING
. SUSTAINED SILENT READING

: : ABILITY
: VERBAL ABILITY
READING ABILITY
. READING SKILLS
. . READING COMPREHENSION
. . READING RATE

: ACHIEVEMENT
READING ACHIEVEMENT

: : LITERACY
: : LANGUAGE ARTS
: READING
READING ALOUD TO OTHERS

: : INSTRUCTION
: ASSIGNMENTS
READING ASSIGNMENTS

: ATTITUDES
READING ATTITUDES

: : FACILITIES
: RESOURCE CENTERS
: : FACILITIES
: EDUCATIONAL FACILITIES
READING CENTERS

: : : : ABILITY
: : : VERBAL ABILITY
: : READING ABILITY
: : : : ABILITY
: : : SKILLS
: : LANGUAGE SKILLS
: READING SKILLS
: : : : INDIVIDUAL CHARACTERISTICS
: : : PSYCHOLOGICAL CHARACTERISTICS
: : INTELLIGENCE
: COMPREHENSION
READING COMPREHENSION

: : : GROUPS
: : PERSONNEL
: CONSULTANTS
READING CONSULTANTS

READING DEVELOPMENT (1966 1980)

: : IDENTIFICATION
: EDUCATIONAL DIAGNOSIS
READING DIAGNOSIS
. MISCUE ANALYSIS

: PROBLEMS
READING DIFFICULTIES

READING DIFFICULTY (1966 1980)

: : : : BEHAVIOR
: : : PERFORMANCE
: : FAILURE
: ACADEMIC FAILURE
READING FAILURE

: : : ACTIVITIES
: : GAMES
: EDUCATIONAL GAMES
READING GAMES

: BEHAVIOR PATTERNS
READING HABITS

: IMPROVEMENT
READING IMPROVEMENT

: INSTRUCTION
READING INSTRUCTION
. BASAL READING
. CONTENT AREA READING
. CORRECTIVE READING
. DIRECTED READING ACTIVITY
. INDIVIDUALIZED READING
. REMEDIAL READING
. SUSTAINED SILENT READING

: INTERESTS
READING INTERESTS

READING LEVEL (1966 1980)

READING MATERIALS
. LARGE TYPE MATERIALS
. SUPPLEMENTARY READING MATERIALS
. TELEGRAPHIC MATERIALS

: : SELECTION
: MEDIA SELECTION
READING MATERIAL SELECTION

: : COGNITIVE PROCESSES
: LANGUAGE PROCESSING
READING PROCESSES
. DECODING (READING)

: PROGRAMS
READING PROGRAMS
. ADULT READING PROGRAMS

: : : : ABILITY
: : : VERBAL ABILITY
: : READING ABILITY
: : : : ABILITY
: : : SKILLS
: : LANGUAGE SKILLS
: READING SKILLS
READING RATE

: READINESS
READING READINESS

: : : MEASURES (INDIVIDUALS)
: : TESTS
: APTITUDE TESTS
READING READINESS TESTS

: : RESEARCH
: EDUCATIONAL RESEARCH
READING RESEARCH

: : : ABILITY
: : VERBAL ABILITY
: READING ABILITY
: : : ABILITY
: : SKILLS
: LANGUAGE SKILLS
READING SKILLS
. READING COMPREHENSION
. READING RATE

: : METHODS
: LEARNING STRATEGIES
READING STRATEGIES

: : : : GROUPS
: : : PERSONNEL
: : PROFESSIONAL PERSONNEL
: TEACHERS
READING TEACHERS

: : : MEASURES (INDIVIDUALS)
: : TESTS
: VERBAL TESTS
READING TESTS
. INFORMAL READING INVENTORIES

: RELATIONSHIP
READING WRITING RELATIONSHIP

: OWNERSHIP
REAL ESTATE

: OCCUPATIONS
REAL ESTATE OCCUPATIONS

: NONPRINT MEDIA
REALIA

REALISM

: : THERAPY
: PSYCHOTHERAPY
REALITY THERAPY

: : COGNITIVE PROCESSES
: MEMORY
RECALL (PSYCHOLOGY)

: : : : GROUPS
: : : PERSONNEL
: : NONPROFESSIONAL PERSONNEL
: CLERICAL WORKERS
RECEPTIONISTS

: : COGNITIVE PROCESSES
: LANGUAGE PROCESSING
RECEPTIVE LANGUAGE

: BEHAVIOR PATTERNS
RECIDIVISM

: : SYMBOLS (MATHEMATICS)
: NUMBERS
RECIPROCALS (MATHEMATICS)

RECOGNITION (1967 1980)

: EVALUATION
RECOGNITION (ACHIEVEMENT)
. AWARDS
. COMMENCEMENT CEREMONIES
. PROFESSIONAL RECOGNITION

: : COGNITIVE PROCESSES
: MEMORY
RECOGNITION (PSYCHOLOGY)
. PATTERN RECOGNITION
. . CHARACTER RECOGNITION
. WORD RECOGNITION

::::::LIBERAL ARTS
:::::SCIENCES
::::SOCIAL SCIENCES
:::::LIBERAL ARTS
::::HUMANITIES
:::HISTORY
::NORTH AMERICAN HISTORY
:UNITED STATES HISTORY
RECONSTRUCTION ERA

:::ABILITY
::SKILLS
:BUSINESS SKILLS
RECORDKEEPING

RECORDS (FORMS)
.ATTENDANCE RECORDS
.CASE RECORDS
..MEDICAL CASE HISTORIES
.CHECK LISTS
.CONFIDENTIAL RECORDS
.CREDENTIALS
..EDUCATIONAL CERTIFICATES
..PORTFOLIOS (BACKGROUND MATERIALS)
..RESUMES (PERSONAL)
.FARM ACCOUNTS
.PAYROLL RECORDS
.STUDENT RECORDS
..ACADEMIC RECORDS
..REPORT CARDS
.WILLS
.WORKSHEETS

RECREATION
.THERAPEUTIC RECREATION
..PLAY THERAPY

:ACTIVITIES
RECREATIONAL ACTIVITIES
.CAMPING
.HOBBIES
.PLAYGROUND ACTIVITIES
.RECREATIONAL READING

:FACILITIES
RECREATIONAL FACILITIES
.PLAYGROUNDS

:PROGRAMS
RECREATIONAL PROGRAMS
.COMMUNITY RECREATION PROGRAMS
.DAY CAMP PROGRAMS
.PHYSICAL RECREATION PROGRAMS
.RESIDENT CAMP PROGRAMS
.SCHOOL RECREATIONAL PROGRAMS

::ACTIVITIES
:RECREATIONAL ACTIVITIES
::LITERACY
::LANGUAGE ARTS
:READING
RECREATIONAL READING

:FINANCIAL SUPPORT
RECREATION FINANCES

:GROUPS
RECREATIONISTS

:LEGISLATION
RECREATION LEGISLATION

RECRUITMENT
.FACULTY RECRUITMENT
.STUDENT RECRUITMENT
.TEACHER RECRUITMENT

::SANITATION
:WASTE DISPOSAL
RECYCLING

REDUCTION IN FORCE
.JOB LAYOFF

REDUNDANCY

::GROUPS
:STUDENTS
REENTRY STUDENTS

::GROUPS
:PERSONNEL
REENTRY WORKERS

:GROUPS
REFERENCE GROUPS

:PUBLICATIONS
REFERENCE MATERIALS
.ABSTRACTS
.ANTHOLOGIES
.ATLASES
.BIBLIOGRAPHIES
..ANNOTATED BIBLIOGRAPHIES
.CITATIONS (REFERENCES)
.DICTIONARIES
..GLOSSARIES
.DIRECTORIES
.DISCOGRAPHIES
.ENCYCLOPEDIAS
.FILMOGRAPHIES
.GUIDES
..ADMINISTRATOR GUIDES
..CURRICULUM GUIDES
...STATE CURRICULUM GUIDES
..FACULTY HANDBOOKS
..LABORATORY MANUALS
..LEADERS GUIDES
..LIBRARY GUIDES
..PROGRAM GUIDES
..STUDY GUIDES
..TEACHING GUIDES
..TEST MANUALS
.INDEXES
..CITATION INDEXES
..COORDINATE INDEXES
..PERMUTED INDEXES
.LIBRARY CATALOGS
..BOOK CATALOGS
..CARD CATALOGS
..UNION CATALOGS
.THESAURI
.YEARBOOKS

::SERVICES
:INFORMATION SERVICES
REFERENCE SERVICES

:::SERVICES
::INFORMATION SERVICES
:INFORMATION DISSEMINATION
REFERRAL

::CURRICULUM
:COURSES
REFRESHER COURSES

:CLIMATE CONTROL
REFRIGERATION

::TECHNOLOGY
:MECHANICS (PROCESS)
REFRIGERATION MECHANICS

::GROUPS
:MIGRANTS
REFUGEES

:ATTITUDES
REGIONAL ATTITUDES

REGIONAL CHARACTERISTICS
.REGIONAL DIALECTS

::BEHAVIOR
:COOPERATION
REGIONAL COOPERATION

:REGIONAL CHARACTERISTICS
::::LINGUISTICS
:::SOCIOLINGUISTICS
::LANGUAGE VARIATION
::LANGUAGES
:DIALECTS
REGIONAL DIALECTS

::FACILITIES
:LABORATORIES
REGIONAL LABORATORIES

:::FACILITIES
::PUBLIC FACILITIES
:::INSTITUTIONS
:::INFORMATION SOURCES
::LIBRARIES
:PUBLIC LIBRARIES
REGIONAL LIBRARIES

:PLANNING
REGIONAL PLANNING

:PROGRAMS
REGIONAL PROGRAMS

::INSTITUTIONS
:SCHOOLS
REGIONAL SCHOOLS

:::GROUPS
::PERSONNEL
:SCHOOL PERSONNEL
:::GROUPS
::PERSONNEL
:ADMINISTRATORS
REGISTRARS (SCHOOL)

::::METHODS
:::EVALUATION METHODS
::DATA ANALYSIS
:STATISTICAL ANALYSIS
REGRESSION (STATISTICS)
.MULTIPLE REGRESSION ANALYSIS

REHABILITATION
.CORRECTIONAL REHABILITATION
..DELINQUENT REHABILITATION
.DRUG REHABILITATION
.VOCATIONAL REHABILITATION

:FACILITIES
REHABILITATION CENTERS

::GUIDANCE
:COUNSELING
REHABILITATION COUNSELING

:PROGRAMS
REHABILITATION PROGRAMS
.DROPOUT PROGRAMS

REINFORCEMENT
.NEGATIVE REINFORCEMENT
.POSITIVE REINFORCEMENT
.PUNISHMENT
..CORPORAL PUNISHMENT
.REWARDS
..SELF REWARD
.SOCIAL REINFORCEMENT
.TIMEOUT
.TOKEN ECONOMY

:PSYCHOLOGICAL PATTERNS
REJECTION (PSYCHOLOGY)

RELATIONSHIP
.COMMUNITY RELATIONS
.CREDIBILITY
.CULTURAL INTERRELATIONSHIPS
.DEVELOPMENTAL CONTINUITY
.EDUCATION WORK RELATIONSHIP
.FACULTY COLLEGE RELATIONSHIP
.FAMILY SCHOOL RELATIONSHIP
..PARENT SCHOOL RELATIONSHIP
.FEDERAL INDIAN RELATIONSHIP
.FEDERAL STATE RELATIONSHIP
.GOVERNMENT SCHOOL RELATIONSHIP
..STATE SCHOOL DISTRICT RELATIONSHIP
.HUMAN RELATIONS
..INTERGROUP RELATIONS
...ETHNIC RELATIONS
...INTERFAITH RELATIONS
...RACIAL RELATIONS
..PEACE
..SLAVERY
.INTERACTION
..APTITUDE TREATMENT INTERACTION
..FEEDBACK
...BIOFEEDBACK
..GROUP DYNAMICS
.INTERNATIONAL RELATIONS
.INTERPERSONAL RELATIONSHIP
..BOARD ADMINISTRATOR RELATIONSHIP
..COUNSELOR CLIENT RELATIONSHIP
..DATING (SOCIAL)
..EMPLOYER EMPLOYEE RELATIONSHIP
..FAMILY RELATIONSHIP
...PARENT CHILD RELATIONSHIP
....PARENT STUDENT RELATIONSHIP
..FRIENDSHIP
..GROUP UNITY
..HELPING RELATIONSHIP
..INTERPERSONAL ATTRACTION
..INTERPROFESSIONAL RELATIONSHIP
..KINSHIP
..MARRIAGE
...INTERMARRIAGE
...REMARRIAGE
..PEER RELATIONSHIP
..PHYSICIAN PATIENT RELATIONSHIP
..RAPPORT
..SIGNIFICANT OTHERS
..TEACHER ADMINISTRATOR RELATIONSHIP
..TEACHER STUDENT RELATIONSHIP
.LABOR RELATIONS
.POLICE COMMUNITY RELATIONSHIP
.POLICE SCHOOL RELATIONSHIP
.PRIVACY
..CONFIDENTIALITY
.PUBLIC RELATIONS
.READER TEXT RELATIONSHIP
.READING WRITING RELATIONSHIP
.SCHOOL BUSINESS RELATIONSHIP
.SCHOOL COMMUNITY RELATIONSHIP
.SCIENCE AND SOCIETY
.SPATIAL RELATIONSHIP (FACILITIES)
.STATE CHURCH SEPARATION
.STUDENT SCHOOL RELATIONSHIP
..STUDENT COLLEGE RELATIONSHIP

RELATIONSHIP
(CONTINUED)

. THEORY PRACTICE
RELATIONSHIP

: THEORIES
: SCIENTIFIC CONCEPTS
RELATIVITY

: : THERAPY
: PSYCHOTHERAPY
RELAXATION TRAINING

RELEASED TIME

RELEVANCE (EDUCATION)

: RATIOS (MATHEMATICS)
RELEVANCE (INFORMATION
RETRIEVAL)

: : : STANDARDS
: : CRITERIA
: EVALUATION CRITERIA
RELIABILITY
. INTERRATER RELIABILITY
. TEST RELIABILITY

RELIGION
. BUDDHISM
. CHRISTIANITY
. CONFUCIANISM
. JUDAISM
. TAOISM

: CONFLICT
RELIGIOUS CONFLICT

: GROUPS
RELIGIOUS CULTURAL GROUPS
. CATHOLICS
. JEWS
. PROTESTANTS
. . AMISH
. . PURITANS

: DIFFERENCES
RELIGIOUS DIFFERENCES

: SOCIAL DISCRIMINATION
RELIGIOUS DISCRIMINATION

: EDUCATION
RELIGIOUS EDUCATION

: INFLUENCES
RELIGIOUS FACTORS

: HOLIDAYS
RELIGIOUS HOLIDAYS

: : GROUPS
: ORGANIZATIONS (GROUPS)
RELIGIOUS ORGANIZATIONS

: FACILITIES
RELOCATABLE FACILITIES

: : MOBILITY
: MIGRATION
RELOCATION
. RURAL RESETTLEMENT

: : : RELATIONSHIP
: : INTERPERSONAL
RELATIONSHIP
: MARRIAGE
REMARRIAGE

: INSTRUCTION
REMEDIAL INSTRUCTION
. REMEDIAL MATHEMATICS
. REMEDIAL READING

: : INSTRUCTION
: REMEDIAL INSTRUCTION
: : INSTRUCTION
: MATHEMATICS INSTRUCTION
REMEDIAL MATHEMATICS

: PROGRAMS
REMEDIAL PROGRAMS

: : INSTRUCTION
: REMEDIAL INSTRUCTION
: : INSTRUCTION
: READING INSTRUCTION
: : LITERACY
: : LANGUAGE ARTS
: READING
REMEDIAL READING

: : : : GROUPS
: : : PERSONNEL
: : PROFESSIONAL PERSONNEL
: TEACHERS
REMEDIAL TEACHERS

: : : LIBERAL ARTS
: : HUMANITIES
: LITERATURE
RENAISSANCE LITERATURE

: MAINTENANCE
REPAIR
. APPLIANCE REPAIR

REPETITIVE FILM SHOWINGS

: : RECORDS (FORMS)
: STUDENT RECORDS
REPORT CARDS

: PUBLICATIONS
REPORTS
. ANNUAL REPORTS
. CONFERENCE PAPERS
. OPINION PAPERS
. PERSONAL NARRATIVES
. POSITION PAPERS
. . MISSION STATEMENTS
. PRACTICUM PAPERS
. RESEARCH REPORTS
. THESES
. . DOCTORAL DISSERTATIONS
. . MASTERS THESES

REPRODUCTION (BIOLOGY)

: TECHNOLOGY
REPROGRAPHY
. MICROREPRODUCTION

REPUTATION
. PRESTIGE

: : CURRICULUM
: COURSES
REQUIRED COURSES

RESCUE

RESEARCH
. ACTION RESEARCH
. ARCHITECTURAL RESEARCH
. BEHAVIORAL SCIENCE
RESEARCH
. . INTEGRATION STUDIES
. . PSYCHOLOGICAL STUDIES
. . . FORCE FIELD ANALYSIS
. . . INTEREST RESEARCH
. . . PERSONALITY STUDIES
. CASE STUDIES
. . CROSS SECTIONAL STUDIES
. . FACILITY CASE STUDIES
. . LONGITUDINAL STUDIES
. . . FOLLOWUP STUDIES
. . . . GRADUATE SURVEYS
. . . . VOCATIONAL FOLLOWUP
. COHORT ANALYSIS
. COMMUNICATION RESEARCH
. COMMUNITY STUDY
. CREATIVITY RESEARCH
. CROSS CULTURAL STUDIES
. DROPOUT RESEARCH
. EDUCATIONAL RESEARCH
. . CLASSROOM RESEARCH
. . CURRICULUM RESEARCH
. . READING RESEARCH
. . WRITING RESEARCH
. ENVIRONMENTAL RESEARCH
. EXCEPTIONAL CHILD
RESEARCH
. FEASIBILITY STUDIES
. FIELD STUDIES
. INSTITUTIONAL RESEARCH
. INVESTIGATIONS
. LANGUAGE RESEARCH
. . DIALECT STUDIES
. LIBRARY RESEARCH
. MEDIA RESEARCH
. . TELEVISION RESEARCH
. . TEXTBOOK RESEARCH
. MEDICAL RESEARCH
. METHODS RESEARCH
. OPERATIONS RESEARCH
. . GAME THEORY
. QUALITATIVE RESEARCH
. SCHEMATIC STUDIES
. SCIENTIFIC RESEARCH
. . SPACE EXPLORATION
. . . LUNAR RESEARCH
. SOCIAL SCIENCE RESEARCH
. . ECONOMIC RESEARCH
. STATISTICAL STUDIES
. STUDENT RESEARCH
. USE STUDIES
. . FACILITY UTILIZATION
RESEARCH

: : GOVERNANCE
: ADMINISTRATION
RESEARCH ADMINISTRATION

RESEARCH AND DEVELOPMENT

: FACILITIES
RESEARCH AND DEVELOPMENT
CENTERS

: GROUPS
RESEARCH AND INSTRUCTION
UNITS

: : GROUPS
: PERSONNEL
RESEARCH ASSISTANTS

: COMMITTEES
RESEARCH COMMITTEES

: : GROUPS
: ORGANIZATIONS (GROUPS)
RESEARCH COORDINATING UNITS

RESEARCH CRITERIA (1967
1980)

: DESIGN
RESEARCH DESIGN
. QUASIEXPERIMENTAL DESIGN

: : : GROUPS
: : PERSONNEL
: PROFESSIONAL PERSONNEL
: : : GROUPS
: : PERSONNEL
: ADMINISTRATORS
RESEARCH DIRECTORS

: : : GROUPS
: : PERSONNEL
: PROFESSIONAL PERSONNEL
RESEARCHERS
. EDUCATIONAL RESEARCHERS

: : INSTITUTIONS
: : INFORMATION SOURCES
: LIBRARIES
RESEARCH LIBRARIES

: METHODS
RESEARCH METHODOLOGY
. INTERACTION PROCESS
ANALYSIS
. MULTITRAIT MULTIMETHOD
TECHNIQUES
. PROTOCOL ANALYSIS
. SCIENTIFIC METHODOLOGY

: NEEDS
RESEARCH NEEDS

: OPPORTUNITIES
RESEARCH OPPORTUNITIES

: : INSTRUCTION
: ASSIGNMENTS
RESEARCH PAPERS (STUDENTS)

: PROBLEMS
RESEARCH PROBLEMS

: PROGRAMS
RESEARCH PROJECTS

: PROGRAM PROPOSALS
RESEARCH PROPOSALS

: : PUBLICATIONS
: REPORTS
RESEARCH REPORTS

RESEARCH REVIEWS
(PUBLICATIONS) (1966 1980)

: : ABILITY
: SKILLS
RESEARCH SKILLS

RESEARCH TOOLS

: : : : INSTITUTIONS
: : : SCHOOLS
: : COLLEGES
: UNIVERSITIES
RESEARCH UNIVERSITIES

: INFORMATION UTILIZATION
RESEARCH UTILIZATION

: PSYCHOLOGICAL PATTERNS
RESENTMENT

: : : GROUPS
: : ETHNIC GROUPS
: AMERICAN INDIANS
RESERVATION AMERICAN INDIANS

: STANDARDS
RESIDENCE REQUIREMENTS

: : GROUPS
: PERSONNEL
RESIDENT ADVISERS
. RESIDENT ASSISTANTS

: : : GROUPS
: : PERSONNEL
: RESIDENT ADVISERS
: : : GROUPS
: : STUDENTS
: COLLEGE STUDENTS
RESIDENT ASSISTANTS

: : PROGRAMS
: RESIDENTIAL PROGRAMS
: : PROGRAMS
: RECREATIONAL PROGRAMS
RESIDENT CAMP PROGRAMS

RESIDENTIAL CARE

: : INSTITUTIONS
: RESIDENTIAL INSTITUTIONS
: : : INSTITUTIONS
: : SCHOOLS
: COLLEGES
RESIDENTIAL COLLEGES

: INSTITUTIONS
RESIDENTIAL INSTITUTIONS
. BOARDING SCHOOLS
. . RESIDENTIAL SCHOOLS
. CORRECTIONAL INSTITUTIONS
. NURSING HOMES
. PERSONAL CARE HOMES
. RESIDENTIAL COLLEGES

: : : : LIBERAL ARTS
: : : SCIENCES
: : SOCIAL SCIENCES
: DEMOGRAPHY
RESIDENTIAL PATTERNS

: PROGRAMS
RESIDENTIAL PROGRAMS
. RESIDENT CAMP PROGRAMS

: : : INSTITUTIONS
: : SCHOOLS
: SPECIAL SCHOOLS
: : : INSTITUTIONS
: : SCHOOLS
: : : INSTITUTIONS
: : RESIDENTIAL INSTITUTIONS
: BOARDING SCHOOLS
RESIDENTIAL SCHOOLS

RESOURCE ALLOCATION

: FACILITIES
RESOURCE CENTERS
. ARTS CENTERS
. AUDIOVISUAL CENTERS
. CULTURAL CENTERS
. CURRICULUM STUDY CENTERS
. EDUCATION SERVICE CENTERS
. INFORMATION CENTERS
. . CLEARINGHOUSES
. LEARNING CENTERS (CLASSROOM)
. LEARNING RESOURCES CENTERS
. NATURE CENTERS
. READING CENTERS
. TEACHER CENTERS

RESOURCE MATERIALS
. RESOURCE UNITS

: : PROGRAMS
: SPECIAL PROGRAMS
RESOURCE ROOM PROGRAMS

RESOURCES
. COMMUNITY RESOURCES
. DEPLETED RESOURCES
. EDUCATIONAL RESOURCES
. . EDUCATIONAL SUPPLY
. FAMILY FINANCIAL RESOURCES
. HUMAN RESOURCES
. . LABOR FORCE
. . LABOR SUPPLY
. NATURAL RESOURCES
. . COAL
. . WATER RESOURCES
. SHARED RESOURCES AND SERVICES
. . SHARED FACILITIES
. . SHARED LIBRARY RESOURCES
. SUPPLIES
. . ADHESIVES
. . AGRICULTURAL SUPPLIES
. . ELECTRIC BATTERIES
. . MAGNETIC TAPES
. . . MAGNETIC TAPE CASSETTES
. . . . AUDIOTAPE CASSETTES
. . . . VIDEOTAPE CASSETTES

: : GROUPS
: PERSONNEL
RESOURCE STAFF

: : : : GROUPS
: : : PERSONNEL
: : PROFESSIONAL PERSONNEL
: TEACHERS
RESOURCE TEACHERS

: RESOURCE MATERIALS
RESOURCE UNITS

: THERAPY
RESPIRATORY THERAPY

RESPITE CARE

: BEHAVIOR
RESPONSES
. BURNOUT
. . TEACHER BURNOUT
. CONSTRUCTED RESPONSE
. COVERT RESPONSE
. DIMENSIONAL PREFERENCE
. EMOTIONAL RESPONSE
. MOTOR REACTIONS
. . EYE MOVEMENTS
. . . EYE FIXATIONS
. . PUPILLARY DILATION
. OVERT RESPONSE
. PATTERNED RESPONSES
. READER RESPONSE
. STRANGER REACTIONS
. STUDENT REACTION
. TEACHER RESPONSE

: BEHAVIOR
RESPONSE STYLE (TESTS)
. GUESSING (TESTS)

RESPONSIBILITY
. ACCOUNTABILITY
. ADMINISTRATOR RESPONSIBILITY
. BUSINESS RESPONSIBILITY
. CHILD RESPONSIBILITY
. CHURCH RESPONSIBILITY
. COMMUNITY RESPONSIBILITY
. EDUCATIONAL RESPONSIBILITY
. EMPLOYEE RESPONSIBILITY
. LEADERSHIP RESPONSIBILITY
. LEGAL RESPONSIBILITY
. . TRUST RESPONSIBILITY (GOVERNMENT)
. PARENT RESPONSIBILITY
. SCHOOL RESPONSIBILITY
. SOCIAL RESPONSIBILITY
. . CITIZENSHIP RESPONSIBILITY
. STUDENT RESPONSIBILITY
. TEACHER RESPONSIBILITY
. . NONINSTRUCTIONAL RESPONSIBILITY

: : EQUIPMENT
: SAFETY EQUIPMENT
RESTRAINTS (VEHICLE SAFETY)

: : RECORDS (FORMS)
: CREDENTIALS
RESUMES (PERSONAL)

: : TECHNOLOGY
: MARKETING
RETAILING

: : COGNITIVE PROCESSES
: MEMORY
RETENTION (PSYCHOLOGY)

: STATUS
RETIREMENT
. EARLY RETIREMENT
. TEACHER RETIREMENT

RETIREMENT BENEFITS

: TRAINING
RETRAINING

RETRENCHMENT

: FINANCIAL SUPPORT
: FEDERAL AID
REVENUE SHARING

: SOCIAL DISCRIMINATION
REVERSE DISCRIMINATION

: ACTIVITIES
REVIEW (REEXAMINATION)

: WRITING PROCESSES
REVISION (WRITTEN COMPOSITION)

: CONFLICT
REVOLUTION

: : : : : : LIBERAL ARTS
: : : : : SCIENCES
: : : : SOCIAL SCIENCES
: : : : : LIBERAL ARTS
: : : : HUMANITIES
: : : HISTORY
: : NORTH AMERICAN HISTORY
: UNITED STATES HISTORY
REVOLUTIONARY WAR (UNITED STATES)

: REINFORCEMENT
REWARDS
. SELF REWARD

: ZONING
REZONING

: LANGUAGE ARTS
RHETORIC
. COHERENCE
. PERSUASIVE DISCOURSE
. RHETORICAL INVENTION

: LITERARY CRITICISM
RHETORICAL CRITICISM

: : LANGUAGE ARTS
: RHETORIC
RHETORICAL INVENTION

: : INFLUENCES
: BIOLOGICAL INFLUENCES
RH FACTORS

: : : LANGUAGES
: : AFRO ASIATIC LANGUAGES
: BERBER LANGUAGES
RIFF

RISK

: NUCLEIC ACIDS
RNA

: CONSTRUCTION (PROCESS)
ROAD CONSTRUCTION

: : : : : : LIBERAL ARTS
: : : : : SCIENCES
: : : : NATURAL SCIENCES
: : : : PHYSICAL SCIENCES
: : : PHYSICS
: : : : : LIBERAL ARTS
: : : : SCIENCES
: : : : NATURAL SCIENCES
: : : BIOLOGICAL SCIENCES
: : BIOPHYSICS
: BIONICS
: : TECHNOLOGY
: AUTOMATION
ROBOTICS

: CONFLICT
ROLE CONFLICT

: : : METHODS
: : SIMULATION
: MODELS
: GROUPS
ROLE MODELS
. MENTORS

ROLE OF EDUCATION

: COGNITIVE PROCESSES
ROLE PERCEPTION

: : METHODS
: SIMULATION
ROLE PLAYING
. DRAMATIC PLAY

: THEORIES
ROLE THEORY

: : : ACTIVITIES
: : PHYSICAL ACTIVITIES
: ATHLETICS
ROLLER SKATING

: : LANGUAGES
: INDO EUROPEAN LANGUAGES
ROMANCE LANGUAGES
. FRENCH
. ITALIAN
. LATIN
. PORTUGUESE
. RUMANIAN
. SPANISH

ROMANIZATION

ROMANTICISM

: STRUCTURAL ELEMENTS (CONSTRUCTION)
ROOFING

ROTATION PLANS

: LEARNING
ROTE LEARNING

: : : DISABILITIES
: : DISEASES
: COMMUNICABLE DISEASES
RUBELLA

: : : LANGUAGES
: : INDO EUROPEAN LANGUAGES
: ROMANCE LANGUAGES
RUMANIAN

: GROUPS
RUNAWAYS

: : ACTIVITIES
: PHYSICAL ACTIVITIES
RUNNING
. JOGGING

: : GROUPS
: RURAL POPULATION
: : : : GROUPS
: : : ETHNIC GROUPS
: : AMERICAN INDIANS
: NONRESERVATION AMERICAN INDIANS
RURAL AMERICAN INDIANS

: GEOGRAPHIC REGIONS
RURAL AREAS

: DEVELOPMENT
RURAL DEVELOPMENT

: : : : LIBERAL ARTS
: : : SCIENCES
: : SOCIAL SCIENCES
: ECONOMICS
RURAL ECONOMICS

: EDUCATION
RURAL EDUCATION

: ENVIRONMENT
RURAL ENVIRONMENT

: : EDUCATION
: EXTENSION EDUCATION
RURAL EXTENSION

: : GROUPS
: RURAL POPULATION
: : GROUPS
: FAMILY (SOCIOLOGICAL UNIT)
RURAL FAMILY

: : GROUPS
: RURAL POPULATION
RURAL FARM RESIDENTS

: : GROUPS
: RURAL POPULATION
RURAL NONFARM RESIDENTS

: GROUPS
RURAL POPULATION
. RURAL AMERICAN INDIANS
. RURAL FAMILY
. RURAL FARM RESIDENTS
. RURAL NONFARM RESIDENTS
. RURAL YOUTH

: : : MOBILITY
: : MIGRATION
: RELOCATION
: : LAND USE
: LAND SETTLEMENT
RURAL RESETTLEMENT

: : INSTITUTIONS
: SCHOOLS
RURAL SCHOOLS

: : MOBILITY
: MIGRATION
RURAL TO URBAN MIGRATION

: DIFFERENCES
RURAL URBAN DIFFERENCES

: : GROUPS
: YOUTH
: : GROUPS
: RURAL POPULATION
RURAL YOUTH

: : : LANGUAGES
: : INDO EUROPEAN LANGUAGES
: SLAVIC LANGUAGES
RUSSIAN

: : : LIBERAL ARTS
: : HUMANITIES
: LITERATURE
RUSSIAN LITERATURE

: LEAVES OF ABSENCE
SABBATICAL LEAVES

SAFETY
. AGRICULTURAL SAFETY
. FIRE PROTECTION
. LABORATORY SAFETY
. OCCUPATIONAL SAFETY AND HEALTH
. SCHOOL SAFETY
. . SCHOOL SECURITY
. TRAFFIC SAFETY

: EDUCATION
SAFETY EDUCATION

: EQUIPMENT
SAFETY EQUIPMENT
. RESTRAINTS (VEHICLE SAFETY)

: : : : ACTIVITIES
: : : PHYSICAL ACTIVITIES
: : ATHLETICS
: AQUATIC SPORTS
SAILING

: INCOME
: EXPENDITURES
SALARIES
. CONTRACT SALARIES
. TEACHER SALARIES

: DIFFERENCES
SALARY WAGE DIFFERENTIALS

: : ABILITY
: SKILLS
: : TECHNOLOGY
: MARKETING
SALESMANSHIP

: OCCUPATIONS
SALES OCCUPATIONS

: : : GROUPS
: : PERSONNEL
: NONPROFESSIONAL PERSONNEL
SALES WORKERS
. AUTO PARTS CLERKS

: : LANGUAGES
: AMERICAN INDIAN LANGUAGES
SALISH

: : LANGUAGES
: MALAYO POLYNESIAN LANGUAGES
SAMOAN

: : : GROUPS
: : NORTH AMERICANS
: PACIFIC AMERICANS
: : GROUPS
: ETHNIC GROUPS
SAMOAN AMERICANS

: : LANGUAGES
: URALIC ALTAIC LANGUAGES
SAMOYED LANGUAGES
. YURAK

SAMPLE SIZE

: : : LIBERAL ARTS
: : MATHEMATICS
: STATISTICS
: : : : SERVICES
: : : INFORMATION SERVICES
: : INFORMATION PROCESSING
: : : : METHODS
: : : EVALUATION METHODS
: : DATA ANALYSIS
: DATA COLLECTION
SAMPLING
. ITEM SAMPLING

SANCTIONS

: : LANGUAGES
: AFRICAN LANGUAGES
SANGO

: FACILITIES
SANITARY FACILITIES
. TOILET FACILITIES

SANITATION
. CLEANING
. . DISHWASHING
. WASTE DISPOSAL
. . RECYCLING

: : LANGUAGES
: CLASSICAL LANGUAGES
SANSKRIT

: : LANGUAGES
: AFRICAN LANGUAGES
SARA

: FACILITIES
SATELLITE FACILITIES

SATELLITES (AEROSPACE)
. COMMUNICATIONS SATELLITES

: LITERARY GENRES
SATIRE

: : METHODS
: MEASUREMENT TECHNIQUES
SCALING
. MULTIDIMENSIONAL SCALING

: PLANNING
SCHEDULING
. FAST TRACK SCHEDULING
. SCHOOL SCHEDULES
. . DOUBLE SESSIONS
. . EXTENDED SCHOOL DAY
. . EXTENDED SCHOOL YEAR
. . FLEXIBLE SCHEDULING
. . QUARTER SYSTEM
. . SEMESTER SYSTEM
. . TIME BLOCKS
. . TRIMESTER SYSTEM
. WORKING HOURS
. . FLEXIBLE WORKING HOURS

: : INDIVIDUAL CHARACTERISTICS
: PSYCHOLOGICAL CHARACTERISTICS
SCHEMATA (COGNITION)

: RESEARCH
SCHEMATIC STUDIES

: : : DISABILITIES
: : SEVERE DISABILITIES
: : : DISABILITIES
: : MENTAL DISORDERS
: PSYCHOSIS
SCHIZOPHRENIA

: : : PUBLICATIONS
: : SERIALS
: PERIODICALS
SCHOLARLY JOURNALS

: ACHIEVEMENT
SCHOLARSHIP

: FINANCIAL SUPPORT
SCHOLARSHIP FUNDS

: : FINANCIAL SUPPORT
: STUDENT FINANCIAL AID
SCHOLARSHIPS
. MERIT SCHOLARSHIPS
. . NO NEED SCHOLARSHIPS
. TUITION GRANTS

: ACCIDENTS
SCHOOL ACCIDENTS

: : TECHNOLOGY
: ACCOUNTING
SCHOOL ACCOUNTING

: ACTIVITIES
SCHOOL ACTIVITIES
. CLASS ACTIVITIES
. EXTRACURRICULAR ACTIVITIES
. STUDENT PROJECTS

: : : GOVERNANCE
: : ADMINISTRATION
: INSTITUTIONAL ADMINISTRATION
: : : GOVERNANCE
: : ADMINISTRATION
: EDUCATIONAL ADMINISTRATION
SCHOOL ADMINISTRATION
. COLLEGE ADMINISTRATION
. SCHOOL BASED MANAGEMENT

::::SERVICES
:::HUMAN SERVICES
::SOCIAL SERVICES
:DAY CARE
SCHOOL AGE DAY CARE

::::GROUPS
:::PERSONNEL
::SCHOOL PERSONNEL
::::GROUPS
:::PERSONNEL
::PARAPROFESSIONAL PERSONNEL
:PARAPROFESSIONAL SCHOOL PERSONNEL
SCHOOL AIDES

::LEGISLATION
:STATE LEGISLATION
::LEGISLATION
:EDUCATIONAL LEGISLATION
SCHOOL ATTENDANCE LEGISLATION

:ATTITUDES
SCHOOL ATTITUDES

::::GOVERNANCE
:::ADMINISTRATION
::INSTITUTIONAL ADMINISTRATION
::::GOVERNANCE
:::ADMINISTRATION
::EDUCATIONAL ADMINISTRATION
:SCHOOL ADMINISTRATION
:INSTITUTIONAL AUTONOMY
SCHOOL BASED MANAGEMENT

SCHOOL BOYCOTTS

::SELECTION
:ELECTIONS
SCHOOL BUDGET ELECTIONS

::FACILITIES
:EDUCATIONAL FACILITIES
::FACILITIES
:BUILDINGS
SCHOOL BUILDINGS
.COLLEGE BUILDINGS

:::EQUIPMENT
::MOTOR VEHICLES
:SERVICE VEHICLES
SCHOOL BUSES

:::GROUPS
::PERSONNEL
:SCHOOL PERSONNEL
:::GROUPS
::PERSONNEL
:ADMINISTRATORS
SCHOOL BUSINESS OFFICIALS

:RELATIONSHIP
SCHOOL BUSINESS RELATIONSHIP

:::GROUPS
::PERSONNEL
:SCHOOL PERSONNEL
SCHOOL CADRES

::PUBLICATIONS
:SCHOOL PUBLICATIONS
::PUBLICATIONS
:CATALOGS
SCHOOL CATALOGS

:SELECTION
SCHOOL CHOICE
.COLLEGE CHOICE

SCHOOL CLOSING

::PROGRAMS
:COMMUNITY PROGRAMS
SCHOOL COMMUNITY PROGRAMS

:RELATIONSHIP
SCHOOL COMMUNITY RELATIONSHIP

:CONSTRUCTION (PROCESS)
SCHOOL CONSTRUCTION

::GUIDANCE
:SCHOOL GUIDANCE
::GUIDANCE
:COUNSELING
SCHOOL COUNSELING

:::GROUPS
::PERSONNEL
:SCHOOL PERSONNEL
::::GROUPS
:::PERSONNEL
::GUIDANCE PERSONNEL
:COUNSELORS
SCHOOL COUNSELORS

::::LIBERAL ARTS
:::SCIENCES
::SOCIAL SCIENCES
:DEMOGRAPHY
SCHOOL DEMOGRAPHY
.TEACHER DISTRIBUTION

:SOCIAL INTEGRATION
SCHOOL DESEGREGATION
.COLLEGE DESEGREGATION

SCHOOL DISTRICT AUTONOMY

:ORGANIZATION
SCHOOL DISTRICT REORGANIZATION

::GROUPS
:ORGANIZATIONS (GROUPS)
SCHOOL DISTRICTS
.COUNTY SCHOOL DISTRICTS
.MULTICAMPUS DISTRICTS

:ORGANIZATION SIZE (GROUPS)
SCHOOL DISTRICT SIZE

:EXPENDITURES
SCHOOL DISTRICT SPENDING

:ORGANIZATIONAL EFFECTIVENESS
SCHOOL EFFECTIVENESS

::INDIVIDUAL CHARACTERISTICS
:AGE
SCHOOL ENTRANCE AGE

::DEVELOPMENT
:FACILITY EXPANSION
SCHOOL EXPANSION

:FINANCIAL SUPPORT
SCHOOL FUNDS

:GUIDANCE
SCHOOL GUIDANCE
.SCHOOL COUNSELING

:::SERVICES
::HUMAN SERVICES
:HEALTH SERVICES
::::SERVICES
:::HUMAN SERVICES
::SOCIAL SERVICES
:ANCILLARY SCHOOL SERVICES
SCHOOL HEALTH SERVICES

SCHOOL HOLDING POWER

::BEHAVIOR
:PARTICIPATION
SCHOOL INVOLVEMENT

::STANDARDS
:LAWS
SCHOOL LAW

::INSTITUTIONS
::INFORMATION SOURCES
:LIBRARIES
SCHOOL LIBRARIES

SCHOOL LOCATION

:MAINTENANCE
SCHOOL MAINTENANCE

::PUBLICATIONS
:SCHOOL PUBLICATIONS
:::PUBLICATIONS
::SERIALS
:::MASS MEDIA
::NEWS MEDIA
:NEWSPAPERS
SCHOOL NEWSPAPERS

:::GROUPS
::PERSONNEL
:SCHOOL PERSONNEL
::::GROUPS
:::PERSONNEL
::PROFESSIONAL PERSONNEL
::::GROUPS
:::PERSONNEL
::HEALTH PERSONNEL
:NURSES
SCHOOL NURSES

:ORGANIZATION
SCHOOL ORGANIZATION
.HOUSE PLAN

:ORIENTATION
SCHOOL ORIENTATION

::GROUPS
:PERSONNEL
SCHOOL PERSONNEL
.ADMISSIONS OFFICERS
.ASSISTANT PRINCIPALS
.AUDIOVISUAL COORDINATORS
.FACULTY
..ADJUNCT FACULTY
..COLLEGE FACULTY
...COLLEGE PRESIDENTS
...COUNSELOR EDUCATORS
...GRADUATE SCHOOL FACULTY
....MEDICAL SCHOOL FACULTY
...PROFESSORS
...STUDENT TEACHER SUPERVISORS
...TEACHER EDUCATORS
....METHODS TEACHERS
...TEACHING ASSISTANTS
..DEANS
...ACADEMIC DEANS
...DEANS OF STUDENTS
..DEPARTMENT HEADS
..FACULTY ADVISERS
..FULL TIME FACULTY
..NONTENURED FACULTY
..PART TIME FACULTY
...PARTNERSHIP TEACHERS
..TENURED FACULTY
..WOMEN FACULTY
.FOREIGN STUDENT ADVISERS
.PARAPROFESSIONAL SCHOOL PERSONNEL
..SCHOOL AIDES
..TEACHER AIDES
...BILINGUAL TEACHER AIDES
.PRINCIPALS
.PUPIL PERSONNEL WORKERS
..ATTENDANCE OFFICERS
.REGISTRARS (SCHOOL)
.SCHOOL BUSINESS OFFICIALS
.SCHOOL CADRES
.SCHOOL COUNSELORS
.SCHOOL NURSES
.SCHOOL PSYCHOLOGISTS
.SCHOOL SECRETARIES
.SCHOOL SOCIAL WORKERS
.STUDENT FINANCIAL AID OFFICERS
.STUDENT PERSONNEL WORKERS

::PSYCHOLOGICAL PATTERNS
:FEAR
SCHOOL PHOBIA

SCHOOL PLANNING (1966 1980)

:POLICY
SCHOOL POLICY

:::GROUPS
::PERSONNEL
:SCHOOL PERSONNEL
::::GROUPS
:::PERSONNEL
::PROFESSIONAL PERSONNEL
::::GROUPS
:::PERSONNEL
::HEALTH PERSONNEL
:PSYCHOLOGISTS
SCHOOL PSYCHOLOGISTS

:PUBLICATIONS
SCHOOL PUBLICATIONS
.FACULTY HANDBOOKS
.SCHOOL CATALOGS
.SCHOOL NEWSPAPERS
.STUDENT PUBLICATIONS

:READINESS
SCHOOL READINESS

:::MEASURES (INDIVIDUALS)
::TESTS
:APTITUDE TESTS
SCHOOL READINESS TESTS

::PROGRAMS
:RECREATIONAL PROGRAMS
SCHOOL RECREATIONAL PROGRAMS

SCHOOL REGISTRATION
.LATE REGISTRATION

:::SOCIAL DISCRIMINATION
::EDUCATIONAL DISCRIMINATION
:SCHOOL SEGREGATION
SCHOOL RESEGREGATION

:RESPONSIBILITY
SCHOOL RESPONSIBILITY

:INSTITUTIONAL ROLE
SCHOOL ROLE
.COLLEGE ROLE

:INSTITUTIONS
SCHOOLS
.AFFILIATED SCHOOLS
.BILINGUAL SCHOOLS
.BOARDING SCHOOLS
..RESIDENTIAL SCHOOLS
.BRITISH INFANT SCHOOLS
.COLLEGES
..AGRICULTURAL COLLEGES

SCHOOLS
(CONTINUED)

..BLACK COLLEGES
..CHURCH RELATED COLLEGES
..CLUSTER COLLEGES
..COMMUTER COLLEGES
..DENTAL SCHOOLS
..DEVELOPING INSTITUTIONS
..EXPERIMENTAL COLLEGES
..LAW SCHOOLS
..LIBRARY SCHOOLS
..MEDICAL SCHOOLS
..MULTICAMPUS COLLEGES
..NONCAMPUS COLLEGES
..PRIVATE COLLEGES
..PUBLIC COLLEGES
...COMMUNITY COLLEGES
...STATE COLLEGES
....STATE UNIVERSITIES
..RESIDENTIAL COLLEGES
..SELECTIVE COLLEGES
..SINGLE SEX COLLEGES
..SMALL COLLEGES
..TWO YEAR COLLEGES
...COMMUNITY COLLEGES
...TECHNICAL INSTITUTES
..UNIVERSITIES
...LAND GRANT UNIVERSITIES
...OPEN UNIVERSITIES
...RESEARCH UNIVERSITIES
...STATE UNIVERSITIES
...URBAN UNIVERSITIES
..UPPER DIVISION COLLEGES
.COMMUNITY SCHOOLS
.CONSOLIDATED SCHOOLS
.CORRESPONDENCE SCHOOLS
.DAY SCHOOLS
.DISADVANTAGED SCHOOLS
.ELEMENTARY SCHOOLS
.EXPERIMENTAL SCHOOLS
..EXPERIMENTAL COLLEGES
.FOLK SCHOOLS
.FREEDOM SCHOOLS
.FREE SCHOOLS
.LABORATORY SCHOOLS
.MAGNET SCHOOLS
.MIDDLE SCHOOLS
.MILITARY SCHOOLS
.MULTIUNIT SCHOOLS
.NEIGHBORHOOD SCHOOLS
.NURSERY SCHOOLS
.OPEN PLAN SCHOOLS
.PRIVATE SCHOOLS
..PAROCHIAL SCHOOLS
...CATHOLIC SCHOOLS
..PRIVATE COLLEGES
..PROPRIETARY SCHOOLS
.PUBLIC SCHOOLS
.RACIALLY BALANCED SCHOOLS
.REGIONAL SCHOOLS
.RURAL SCHOOLS
.SCHOOLS OF EDUCATION
.SECONDARY SCHOOLS
..HIGH SCHOOLS
...VOCATIONAL HIGH SCHOOLS
..JUNIOR HIGH SCHOOLS
.SINGLE SEX SCHOOLS
..SINGLE SEX COLLEGES
.SLUM SCHOOLS
.SMALL SCHOOLS
..ONE TEACHER SCHOOLS
..SMALL COLLEGES
.SPECIAL SCHOOLS
..INSTITUTIONAL SCHOOLS
...HOSPITAL SCHOOLS
..RESIDENTIAL SCHOOLS
.STATE SCHOOLS
..STATE COLLEGES
...STATE UNIVERSITIES
.SUBURBAN SCHOOLS
.SUMMER SCHOOLS
.TRADITIONAL SCHOOLS
.TRANSITIONAL SCHOOLS
.URBAN SCHOOLS
..URBAN UNIVERSITIES
.VOCATIONAL SCHOOLS
..VOCATIONAL HIGH SCHOOLS
.YEAR ROUND SCHOOLS

:SAFETY
SCHOOL SAFETY
.SCHOOL SECURITY

::PLANNING
:SCHEDULING
SCHOOL SCHEDULES
.DOUBLE SESSIONS
.EXTENDED SCHOOL DAY
.EXTENDED SCHOOL YEAR
.FLEXIBLE SCHEDULING
.QUARTER SYSTEM
.SEMESTER SYSTEM
.TIME BLOCKS
.TRIMESTER SYSTEM

:::::GROUPS
::::PERSONNEL
:::NONPROFESSIONAL PERSONNEL
::CLERICAL WORKERS
:SECRETARIES
:::GROUPS
::PERSONNEL
:SCHOOL PERSONNEL
SCHOOL SECRETARIES

::SAFETY
:SCHOOL SAFETY
SCHOOL SECURITY

::SOCIAL DISCRIMINATION
:EDUCATIONAL DISCRIMINATION
SCHOOL SEGREGATION
.COLLEGE SEGREGATION
.SCHOOL RESEGREGATION

::FACILITIES
:EDUCATIONAL FACILITIES
SCHOOL SHOPS

:INSTITUTIONAL CHARACTERISTICS
SCHOOL SIZE

::::GROUPS
:::PERSONNEL
::PROFESSIONAL PERSONNEL
::::GROUPS
:::PERSONNEL
::CASEWORKERS
:SOCIAL WORKERS
:::GROUPS
::PERSONNEL
:SCHOOL PERSONNEL
SCHOOL SOCIAL WORKERS

::INSTITUTIONS
:SCHOOLS
SCHOOLS OF EDUCATION

::FACILITIES
:EDUCATIONAL FACILITIES
SCHOOL SPACE

::DATA
:STATISTICAL DATA
SCHOOL STATISTICS

:::GOVERNANCE
::ADMINISTRATION
:SUPERVISION
SCHOOL SUPERVISION

SCHOOL SUPPORT
.PRIVATE SCHOOL AID

:::METHODS
::EVALUATION METHODS
:SURVEYS
SCHOOL SURVEYS

:TAXES
SCHOOL TAXES

::::BEHAVIOR
:::SOCIAL BEHAVIOR
::ANTISOCIAL BEHAVIOR
:VANDALISM
SCHOOL VANDALISM

:OBSERVATION
SCHOOL VISITATION

:ZONING
SCHOOL ZONING

:ACTIVITIES
SCIENCE ACTIVITIES
.SCIENCE FAIRS
.SCIENCE PROJECTS

:RELATIONSHIP
SCIENCE AND SOCIETY

:CAREERS
SCIENCE CAREERS

::GROUPS
:CLUBS
SCIENCE CLUBS

:::GROUPS
::PERSONNEL
:SCIENTIFIC PERSONNEL
:::GROUPS
::PERSONNEL
:CONSULTANTS
SCIENCE CONSULTANTS

:PROGRAMS
SCIENCE COURSE IMPROVEMENT PROJECTS

:CURRICULUM
SCIENCE CURRICULUM
.COLLEGE SCIENCE
.ELEMENTARY SCHOOL SCIENCE
.GENERAL SCIENCE
.SECONDARY SCHOOL SCIENCE

:::ORGANIZATION
::ADMINISTRATIVE ORGANIZATION
:DEPARTMENTS
SCIENCE DEPARTMENTS

:EDUCATION
SCIENCE EDUCATION

:::::LIBERAL ARTS
::::SCIENCES
:::SOCIAL SCIENCES
::::LIBERAL ARTS
:::HUMANITIES
::HISTORY
::FOUNDATIONS OF EDUCATION
:EDUCATIONAL HISTORY
SCIENCE EDUCATION HISTORY

:EQUIPMENT
SCIENCE EQUIPMENT

:EXPERIMENTS
SCIENCE EXPERIMENTS

:FACILITIES
SCIENCE FACILITIES
.SCIENCE LABORATORIES
.SCIENCE TEACHING CENTERS

::ACTIVITIES
:SCIENCE ACTIVITIES
::NONPRINT MEDIA
:EXHIBITS
SCIENCE FAIRS

:::::LIBERAL ARTS
::::HUMANITIES
:::LITERATURE
::PROSE
:FICTION
SCIENCE FICTION

::::LIBERAL ARTS
:::SCIENCES
::SOCIAL SCIENCES
:::LIBERAL ARTS
::HUMANITIES
:HISTORY
SCIENCE HISTORY

:INSTRUCTION
SCIENCE INSTRUCTION

:INTERESTS
SCIENCE INTERESTS

::FACILITIES
:SCIENCE FACILITIES
::FACILITIES
:LABORATORIES
SCIENCE LABORATORIES

SCIENCE MATERIALS

:PROGRAMS
SCIENCE PROGRAMS
.SUMMER SCIENCE PROGRAMS

::ACTIVITIES
:SCIENCE ACTIVITIES
SCIENCE PROJECTS

:LIBERAL ARTS
SCIENCES
.ACOUSTICS
..PSYCHOACOUSTICS
.BEHAVIORAL SCIENCES
..ETHOLOGY
..PSYCHOLOGY
...BEHAVIORISM
...CHILD PSYCHOLOGY
...CLINICAL PSYCHOLOGY
...COGNITIVE PSYCHOLOGY
...COMMUNITY PSYCHOLOGY
...DEVELOPMENTAL PSYCHOLOGY
...EDUCATIONAL PSYCHOLOGY
...EXPERIMENTAL PSYCHOLOGY
...INDIVIDUAL PSYCHOLOGY
...INDUSTRIAL PSYCHOLOGY
...PSYCHOACOUSTICS
...PSYCHOMETRICS
...PSYCHOPATHOLOGY
...PSYCHOPHYSIOLOGY
...SOCIAL PSYCHOLOGY
...SPORT PSYCHOLOGY
..SOCIOBIOLOGY
..SOCIOLOGY
...CRIMINOLOGY
...EDUCATIONAL SOCIOLOGY
...SOCIAL PSYCHOLOGY
.INFORMATION SCIENCE
..COMPUTER SCIENCE
...PROGRAMING
..LIBRARY SCIENCE
.NATURAL SCIENCES
..BIOLOGICAL SCIENCES
...ANATOMY
...BIOCHEMISTRY
...BIOFEEDBACK
...BIOLOGY
....MARINE BIOLOGY
....MICROBIOLOGY
....RADIATION BIOLOGY
....SOCIAL BIOLOGY
...BIOMEDICINE
...BIOPHYSICS
....BIOMECHANICS
....BIONICS
.....ROBOTICS
...BOTANY
...CYTOLOGY
...ECOLOGY
...EMBRYOLOGY
...ETHOLOGY
...GENETICS

SCIENCES
(CONTINUED)

.... GENETIC ENGINEERING
... PHYSIOLOGY
.... EXERCISE PHYSIOLOGY
.... PSYCHOPHYSIOLOGY
... SOCIOBIOLOGY
... ZOOLOGY
.... ENTOMOLOGY
.... ICHTHYOLOGY
.... ORNITHOLOGY
.... PRIMATOLOGY
.. PHYSICAL SCIENCES
... ASTRONOMY
... CHEMISTRY
.... BIOCHEMISTRY
.... INORGANIC CHEMISTRY
.... ORGANIC CHEMISTRY
... CRYSTALLOGRAPHY
... EARTH SCIENCE
.... GEOLOGY
..... MINERALOGY
..... PALEONTOLOGY
.... GEOPHYSICS
..... PLATE TECTONICS
.... METEOROLOGY
.... OCEANOGRAPHY
.... PHYSICAL GEOGRAPHY
.... SEISMOLOGY
..... PLATE TECTONICS
.... SOIL SCIENCE
... PHYSICS
.... BIOPHYSICS
..... BIOMECHANICS
..... BIONICS
...... ROBOTICS
.... ELECTRONICS
.... MECHANICS (PHYSICS)
..... FLUID MECHANICS
..... KINETICS
...... DIFFUSION (PHYSICS)
..... QUANTUM MECHANICS
.... NUCLEAR PHYSICS
.... OPTICS
.... THERMODYNAMICS
... SPECTROSCOPY
. SOCIAL SCIENCES
.. ANTHROPOLOGY
... ANTHROPOLOGICAL
LINGUISTICS
... ARCHAEOLOGY
... EDUCATIONAL
ANTHROPOLOGY
... ETHNOGRAPHY
... ETHNOLOGY
.. DEMOGRAPHY
... BIRTH RATE
... EMPLOYMENT PATTERNS
... GEOGRAPHIC DISTRIBUTION
... POPULATION DISTRIBUTION
.... ETHNIC DISTRIBUTION
.... RACIAL DISTRIBUTION
... POPULATION GROWTH
... POPULATION TRENDS
.... BLACK POPULATION
TRENDS
... RACIAL COMPOSITION
.... RACIAL BALANCE
... RESIDENTIAL PATTERNS
... SCHOOL DEMOGRAPHY
.... TEACHER DISTRIBUTION
... SOCIAL DISTRIBUTION
... URBAN DEMOGRAPHY
.. ECONOMICS
... CONSUMER ECONOMICS
... EDUCATIONAL ECONOMICS
.... EDUCATIONAL FINANCE
... LABOR ECONOMICS
... RURAL ECONOMICS
.. GEOGRAPHY
... HUMAN GEOGRAPHY
... PHYSICAL GEOGRAPHY
... WORLD GEOGRAPHY
.. GERONTOLOGY
... EDUCATIONAL GERONTOLOGY
.. HISTORY
... AFRICAN HISTORY
... AMERICAN INDIAN HISTORY
... ANCIENT HISTORY
... ASIAN HISTORY
... BLACK HISTORY
... CONSTITUTIONAL HISTORY
... DIPLOMATIC HISTORY
... EDUCATIONAL HISTORY
.... SCIENCE EDUCATION
HISTORY
... EUROPEAN HISTORY
... FAMILY HISTORY
.... GENEALOGY
... HISTORIOGRAPHY
... INTELLECTUAL HISTORY
.... ART HISTORY
.... LITERARY HISTORY
... LATIN AMERICAN HISTORY
... LOCAL HISTORY
... MEDIEVAL HISTORY
... MIDDLE EASTERN HISTORY
... MODERN HISTORY
... NORTH AMERICAN HISTORY
.... UNITED STATES HISTORY
..... CIVIL WAR (UNITED
STATES)
..... COLONIAL HISTORY
(UNITED STATES)
..... MEXICAN AMERICAN
HISTORY
..... RECONSTRUCTION ERA
..... REVOLUTIONARY WAR
(UNITED STATES)
..... STATE HISTORY
... ORAL HISTORY
... SCIENCE HISTORY
... SOCIAL HISTORY
... WORLD HISTORY
.. INTERNATIONAL STUDIES
.. POLITICAL SCIENCE
.. SOCIAL STUDIES
... CIVICS
.. SOCIOLOGY
... CRIMINOLOGY
... EDUCATIONAL SOCIOLOGY
... SOCIAL PSYCHOLOGY
.. TOPOGRAPHY
. SPACE SCIENCES

::: GOVERNANCE
:: ADMINISTRATION
: SUPERVISION
SCIENCE SUPERVISION

:::: GROUPS
::: PERSONNEL
:: PROFESSIONAL PERSONNEL
: TEACHERS
SCIENCE TEACHERS

:: FACILITIES
: SCIENCE FACILITIES
:: FACILITIES
: EDUCATIONAL FACILITIES
SCIENCE TEACHING CENTERS

:: MEASURES (INDIVIDUALS)
: TESTS
SCIENCE TESTS

SCIENTIFIC AND TECHNICAL
INFORMATION

: ATTITUDES
SCIENTIFIC ATTITUDES

SCIENTIFIC CONCEPTS
. ENERGY
.. GEOTHERMAL ENERGY
.. HEAT
.. RADIATION
... LIGHT
... NUCLEAR ENERGY
... SOLAR ENERGY
.. WIND ENERGY
. FORCE
. GRAVITY (PHYSICS)
. HEIGHT
. MOTION
.. ACCELERATION (PHYSICS)
. PRESSURE (PHYSICS)
. RELATIVITY
. SPACE
.. AREA
.. VOLUME (MATHEMATICS)
. TIME
. WEIGHT (MASS)

SCIENTIFIC ENTERPRISE

: LITERACY
SCIENTIFIC LITERACY

:: METHODS
: RESEARCH METHODOLOGY
SCIENTIFIC METHODOLOGY

:: GROUPS
: PERSONNEL
SCIENTIFIC PERSONNEL
. MATHEMATICIANS
. SCIENCE CONSULTANTS
. SCIENTISTS

: STANDARDS
SCIENTIFIC PRINCIPLES

: RESEARCH
SCIENTIFIC RESEARCH
. SPACE EXPLORATION
.. LUNAR RESEARCH

::: GROUPS
:: PERSONNEL
: SCIENTIFIC PERSONNEL
::: GROUPS
:: PERSONNEL
: PROFESSIONAL PERSONNEL
SCIENTISTS

: COLLECTIVE BARGAINING
SCOPE OF BARGAINING

: DATA
SCORES
. CUTTING SCORES
. EQUATED SCORES
. GRADE EQUIVALENT SCORES
. RAW SCORES
. TRUE SCORES
. WEIGHTED SCORES

: MEASUREMENT
SCORING

:: METHODS
: MEASUREMENT TECHNIQUES
SCORING FORMULAS

:: MEASURES (INDIVIDUALS)
: TESTS
SCREENING TESTS

: VISUAL AIDS
SCREENS (DISPLAYS)

: LITERARY GENRES
::::: LIBERAL ARTS
:::: HUMANITIES
::: FINE ARTS
:: THEATER ARTS
:::: LIBERAL ARTS
::: HUMANITIES
:: LITERATURE
: DRAMA
SCRIPTS

:::: LIBERAL ARTS
::: HUMANITIES
:: FINE ARTS
: VISUAL ARTS
SCULPTURE

: GROUPS
SEAFARERS

:: LAW ENFORCEMENT
: POLICE ACTION
SEARCH AND SEIZURE

: COMMITTEES
SEARCH COMMITTEES
(PERSONNEL)

: INFORMATION SEEKING
SEARCH STRATEGIES

: EMPLOYMENT
SEASONAL EMPLOYMENT

:::::: GROUPS
::::: PERSONNEL
:::: NONPROFESSIONAL
PERSONNEL
::: UNSKILLED WORKERS
:: LABORERS
:::: GROUPS
::: PERSONNEL
:: AGRICULTURAL PERSONNEL
: AGRICULTURAL LABORERS
SEASONAL LABORERS

:: EDUCATION
: ELEMENTARY SECONDARY
EDUCATION
SECONDARY EDUCATION
. COLLEGE PREPARATION

: CURRICULUM
SECONDARY SCHOOL CURRICULUM
. SECONDARY SCHOOL
MATHEMATICS
. SECONDARY SCHOOL SCIENCE

:: CURRICULUM
: SECONDARY SCHOOL
CURRICULUM
:: CURRICULUM
: MATHEMATICS CURRICULUM
SECONDARY SCHOOL MATHEMATICS

:: INSTITUTIONS
: SCHOOLS
SECONDARY SCHOOLS
. HIGH SCHOOLS
.. VOCATIONAL HIGH SCHOOLS
. JUNIOR HIGH SCHOOLS

:: CURRICULUM
: SECONDARY SCHOOL
CURRICULUM
:: CURRICULUM
: SCIENCE CURRICULUM
SECONDARY SCHOOL SCIENCE

:: GROUPS
: STUDENTS
SECONDARY SCHOOL STUDENTS
. HIGH SCHOOL STUDENTS
.. COLLEGE BOUND STUDENTS
.. HIGH SCHOOL FRESHMEN
.. HIGH SCHOOL SENIORS
.. NONCOLLEGE BOUND
STUDENTS
. JUNIOR HIGH SCHOOL
STUDENTS

:::: GROUPS
::: PERSONNEL
:: PROFESSIONAL PERSONNEL
: TEACHERS
SECONDARY SCHOOL TEACHERS

:: INSTRUCTION
: HUMANITIES INSTRUCTION
SECOND LANGUAGE INSTRUCTION

: LEARNING
SECOND LANGUAGE LEARNING

: PROGRAMS
SECOND LANGUAGE PROGRAMS
. COLLEGE SECOND LANGUAGE
PROGRAMS
. IMMERSION PROGRAMS

: LANGUAGE
SECOND LANGUAGES
. ENGLISH (SECOND LANGUAGE)
.. ENGLISH FOR SPECIAL PURPOSES
... ENGLISH FOR ACADEMIC PURPOSES
... ENGLISH FOR SCIENCE AND TECHNOLOGY
... VOCATIONAL ENGLISH (SECOND LANGUAGE)

:::: GROUPS
::: PERSONNEL
:: NONPROFESSIONAL PERSONNEL
: CLERICAL WORKERS
SECRETARIES
. SCHOOL SECRETARIES

SECURITY (1967 1978)

::: NEEDS
:: INDIVIDUAL NEEDS
: PSYCHOLOGICAL NEEDS
SECURITY (PSYCHOLOGY)

:: GROUPS
: PERSONNEL
SECURITY PERSONNEL

: NARCOTICS
SEDATIVES

:: GROUPS
: ORGANIZATIONS (GROUPS)
SEGREGATIONIST ORGANIZATIONS

::::: LIBERAL ARTS
:::: SCIENCES
::: NATURAL SCIENCES
:: PHYSICAL SCIENCES
: EARTH SCIENCE
SEISMOLOGY
. PLATE TECTONICS

:: DISABILITIES
: DISEASES
SEIZURES

SELECTION
. CAREER CHOICE
. COMPETITIVE SELECTION
. COURSE SELECTION (STUDENTS)
. ELECTIONS
.. SCHOOL BUDGET ELECTIONS
. MATE SELECTION
. MEDIA SELECTION
.. LIBRARY MATERIAL SELECTION
.. READING MATERIAL SELECTION
.. TEXTBOOK SELECTION
. PERSONNEL SELECTION
.. ADMINISTRATOR SELECTION
.. COUNSELOR SELECTION
.. TEACHER SELECTION
. SCHOOL CHOICE
.. COLLEGE CHOICE
. SITE SELECTION
. TEST SELECTION

: ADMISSION (SCHOOL)
SELECTIVE ADMISSION

::: INSTITUTIONS
:: SCHOOLS
: COLLEGES
SELECTIVE COLLEGES

::: SERVICES
:: INFORMATION SERVICES
: INFORMATION DISSEMINATION
SELECTIVE DISSEMINATION OF INFORMATION

::: NEEDS
:: INDIVIDUAL NEEDS
: PSYCHOLOGICAL NEEDS
SELF ACTUALIZATION

::: ABILITY
:: SKILLS
: DAILY LIVING SKILLS
SELF CARE SKILLS

SELF CONCEPT
. BODY IMAGE
. SELF CONGRUENCE
. SELF ESTEEM

:: MEASURES (INDIVIDUALS)
: PERSONALITY MEASURES
SELF CONCEPT MEASURES

: SELF CONCEPT
:: PSYCHOLOGICAL PATTERNS
: CONGRUENCE (PSYCHOLOGY)
SELF CONGRUENCE

::: FACILITIES
:: EDUCATIONAL FACILITIES
: CLASSROOMS
SELF CONTAINED CLASSROOMS

: BEHAVIOR
SELF CONTROL
. DELAY OF GRATIFICATION

: BEHAVIOR
SELF DESTRUCTIVE BEHAVIOR
. SELF MUTILATION
. SUICIDE

SELF DETERMINATION
. TRIBAL SOVEREIGNTY

SELF DIRECTED CLASSROOMS (1966 1980)

: GROUPS
SELF DIRECTED GROUPS

: DISCLOSURE
SELF DISCLOSURE (INDIVIDUALS)

: SELF CONCEPT
SELF ESTEEM

SELF EVALUATION (1966 1980)

: EVALUATION
SELF EVALUATION (GROUPS)

: EVALUATION
SELF EVALUATION (INDIVIDUALS)

SELF EXPRESSION

:: PROGRAMS
: IMPROVEMENT PROGRAMS
SELF HELP PROGRAMS

:: BEHAVIOR
: SELF DESTRUCTIVE BEHAVIOR
SELF MUTILATION

:: REINFORCEMENT
: REWARDS
SELF REWARD

:: GROUPS
: STUDENTS
SELF SUPPORTING STUDENTS

:: MEASURES (INDIVIDUALS)
: RATING SCALES
:: MEASURES (INDIVIDUALS)
: ATTITUDE MEASURES
SEMANTIC DIFFERENTIAL

:::: LIBERAL ARTS
::: HUMANITIES
:: PHILOSOPHY
::: THEORIES
:: LINGUISTIC THEORY
: SEMIOTICS
:: LINGUISTICS
: DESCRIPTIVE LINGUISTICS
SEMANTICS
. LEXICOLOGY

::: PLANNING
:: SCHEDULING
: SCHOOL SCHEDULES
SEMESTER SYSTEM

:: EQUIPMENT
: ELECTRONIC EQUIPMENT
SEMICONDUCTOR DEVICES
. TRANSISTORS

: MEETINGS
SEMINARS

::: LIBERAL ARTS
:: HUMANITIES
: PHILOSOPHY
:: THEORIES
: LINGUISTIC THEORY
SEMIOTICS
. PRAGMATICS
. SEMANTICS
.. LEXICOLOGY

: OCCUPATIONS
SEMISKILLED OCCUPATIONS

::: GROUPS
:: PERSONNEL
: NONPROFESSIONAL PERSONNEL
SEMISKILLED WORKERS
. ANIMAL CARETAKERS
. BOAT OPERATORS
. GROUNDS KEEPERS
. NURSERY WORKERS (HORTICULTURE)
. SEWING MACHINE OPERATORS

:: LANGUAGES
: AFRO ASIATIC LANGUAGES
SEMITIC LANGUAGES
. AMHARIC
. ARABIC
. HEBREW

: STATUS
SENIORITY

: TRAINING
SENSITIVITY TRAINING

SENSORY AIDS
. HEARING AIDS
. LOW VISION AIDS
. RAISED LINE DRAWINGS
. TALKING BOOKS

::: BACKGROUND
:: EXPERIENCE
: SENSORY EXPERIENCE
SENSORY DEPRIVATION

:: BACKGROUND
: EXPERIENCE
SENSORY EXPERIENCE
. FIGURAL AFTEREFFECTS
. SENSORY DEPRIVATION

SENSORY INTEGRATION

: TRAINING
SENSORY TRAINING
. AUDITORY TRAINING

:::: THEORIES
::: LINGUISTIC THEORY
:: GENERATIVE GRAMMAR
: TRANSFORMATIONAL GENERATIVE GRAMMAR
SENTENCE COMBINING

SENTENCE DIAGRAMING

:: LANGUAGE PATTERNS
: PARAGRAPHS
SENTENCES
. KERNEL SENTENCES

:::: LINGUISTICS
::: DESCRIPTIVE LINGUISTICS
:: GRAMMAR
: SYNTAX
SENTENCE STRUCTURE

: LAW ENFORCEMENT
SENTENCING

:: PSYCHOLOGICAL PATTERNS
: ANXIETY
SEPARATION ANXIETY

: METHODS
SEQUENTIAL APPROACH

: LEARNING
SEQUENTIAL LEARNING

::: LANGUAGES
:: INDO EUROPEAN LANGUAGES
: SLAVIC LANGUAGES
SERBOCROATIAN

: LEARNING
SERIAL LEARNING

: COGNITIVE PROCESSES
SERIAL ORDERING

: PUBLICATIONS
SERIALS
. ANNUAL REPORTS
. BULLETINS
. CONFERENCE PROCEEDINGS
. NEWSPAPERS
.. NEWSLETTERS
.. SCHOOL NEWSPAPERS
. PERIODICALS
.. FOREIGN LANGUAGE PERIODICALS
.. SCHOLARLY JOURNALS
. YEARBOOKS

: OCCUPATIONS
SERVICE OCCUPATIONS
. CHILD CARE OCCUPATIONS
. HOSPITALITY OCCUPATIONS
. LAUNDRY DRYCLEANING OCCUPATIONS

SERVICES
. COMMUNITY SERVICES
. . COMMUNITY HEALTH SERVICES
. . COMMUNITY INFORMATION SERVICES
. . . HOTLINES (PUBLIC)
. DELIVERY SYSTEMS
. FINANCIAL SERVICES
. HUMAN SERVICES
. . COUNSELING SERVICES
. . EMPLOYMENT SERVICES
. . . OUTPLACEMENT SERVICES (EMPLOYMENT)
. . FOOD SERVICE
. . HEALTH SERVICES
. . . COMMUNITY HEALTH SERVICES
. . . HOSPICES (TERMINAL CARE)
. . . MEDICAL SERVICES
. . . . FIRST AID
. . . . . CARDIOPULMONARY RESUSCITATION
. . . . PSYCHIATRIC SERVICES
. . . MIGRANT HEALTH SERVICES
. . . SCHOOL HEALTH SERVICES
. . PSYCHOLOGICAL SERVICES
. . SOCIAL SERVICES
. . . ADULT DAY CARE
. . . ADULT FOSTER CARE
. . . ANCILLARY SCHOOL SERVICES
. . . . MOBILE EDUCATIONAL SERVICES
. . . . PUPIL PERSONNEL SERVICES
. . . . SCHOOL HEALTH SERVICES
. . . . STUDENT PERSONNEL SERVICES
. . . DAY CARE
. . . . EMPLOYER SUPPORTED DAY CARE
. . . . FAMILY DAY CARE
. . . . SCHOOL AGE DAY CARE
. . . FOSTER CARE
. . . SOCIAL WORK
. . . WELFARE SERVICES
. . . . MIGRANT WELFARE SERVICES
. INFORMATION SERVICES
. . COMMUNITY INFORMATION SERVICES
. . . HOTLINES (PUBLIC)
. . INFORMATION DISSEMINATION
. . . PROPAGANDA
. . . PUBLICITY
. . . . ADVERTISING
. . . . . TELEVISION COMMERCIALS
. . . . INSTITUTIONAL ADVANCEMENT
. . . REFERRAL
. . . SELECTIVE DISSEMINATION OF INFORMATION
. . INFORMATION PROCESSING
. . . DATA COLLECTION
. . . . SAMPLING
. . . . . ITEM SAMPLING
. . . DATA PROCESSING
. . . . INPUT OUTPUT
. . . . . KEYBOARDING (DATA ENTRY)
. . . . TIME SHARING
. . . DOCUMENTATION
. . . . ABSTRACTING
. . . . BIBLIOMETRICS
. . . . . CITATION ANALYSIS
. . . . . . BIBLIOGRAPHIC COUPLING
. . . . CATALOGING
. . . . . MACHINE READABLE CATALOGING
. . . . FILING
. . . . INDEXING
. . . . . AUTOMATIC INDEXING
. . . INFORMATION RETRIEVAL
. . . . ONLINE SEARCHING
. . . INFORMATION STORAGE
. . . WORD PROCESSING
. . LIBRARY SERVICES
. . . LIBRARY CIRCULATION
. . . . INTERLIBRARY LOANS
. . . LIBRARY EXTENSION
. . . LIBRARY TECHNICAL PROCESSES
. . . . LIBRARY ACQUISITION
. . . . . LIBRARY MATERIAL SELECTION
. . REFERENCE SERVICES
. . VIDEOTEX
. PRODUCER SERVICES
. PROFESSIONAL SERVICES
. SHARED RESOURCES AND SERVICES
. . SHARED FACILITIES
. . SHARED LIBRARY RESOURCES

: : EQUIPMENT
: MOTOR VEHICLES
SERVICE VEHICLES
. BOOKMOBILES
. SCHOOL BUSES

: : : GROUPS
: : PERSONNEL
: NONPROFESSIONAL PERSONNEL
SERVICE WORKERS
. ATTENDANTS
. BARBERS
. COOKS
. EMERGENCY SQUAD PERSONNEL
. . EMERGENCY MEDICAL TECHNICIANS
. FIRE FIGHTERS
. HOUSEHOLD WORKERS
. . HOME HEALTH AIDES
. HOUSEKEEPERS
. HOUSING MANAGEMENT AIDES
. WAITERS AND WAITRESSES

: THEORIES
: : : : : LIBERAL ARTS
: : : : HUMANITIES
: : : PHILOSOPHY
: : LOGIC
: MATHEMATICAL LOGIC
SET THEORY

: FACILITIES
SETTLEMENT HOUSES

: : : LIBERAL ARTS
: : HUMANITIES
: LITERATURE
SEVENTEENTH CENTURY LITERATURE

: DISABILITIES
SEVERE DISABILITIES
. PSYCHOSIS
. . AUTISM
. . ECHOLALIA
. . SCHIZOPHRENIA
. SEVERE MENTAL RETARDATION

: : DISABILITIES
: SEVERE DISABILITIES
: : DISABILITIES
: MENTAL RETARDATION
SEVERE MENTAL RETARDATION

: INSTRUCTION
SEWING INSTRUCTION

: : : : GROUPS
: : : PERSONNEL
: : NONPROFESSIONAL PERSONNEL
: SEMISKILLED WORKERS
SEWING MACHINE OPERATORS

: : INDIVIDUAL CHARACTERISTICS
: PHYSICAL CHARACTERISTICS
SEX

SEX (CHARACTERISTICS) (1966 1980)

: : : ATTITUDES
: : SOCIAL ATTITUDES
: : BIAS
: SOCIAL BIAS
SEX BIAS

: : DIFFERENCES
: INDIVIDUAL DIFFERENCES
SEX DIFFERENCES

: SOCIAL DISCRIMINATION
SEX DISCRIMINATION
. SEXUAL HARASSMENT

: : EDUCATION
: FAMILY LIFE EDUCATION
SEX EDUCATION

SEX FAIRNESS

SEX ROLE

: : ATTITUDES
: STEREOTYPES
SEX STEREOTYPES

: : : BEHAVIOR
: : SOCIAL BEHAVIOR
: ANTISOCIAL BEHAVIOR
SEXUAL ABUSE
. RAPE

: : SOCIAL DISCRIMINATION
: SEX DISCRIMINATION
: : : BEHAVIOR
: : SOCIAL BEHAVIOR
: ANTISOCIAL BEHAVIOR
SEXUAL HARASSMENT

SEXUAL IDENTITY

SEXUALITY
. HOMOSEXUALITY
. . LESBIANISM

: : : : GROUPS
: : : PERSONNEL
: : AGRICULTURAL PERSONNEL
: FARMERS
SHARECROPPERS

: : SERVICES
: : RESOURCES
: SHARED RESOURCES AND SERVICES
: FACILITIES
SHARED FACILITIES

: : SERVICES
: : RESOURCES
: SHARED RESOURCES AND SERVICES
SHARED LIBRARY RESOURCES

: SERVICES
: RESOURCES
SHARED RESOURCES AND SERVICES
. SHARED FACILITIES
. SHARED LIBRARY RESOURCES

: : TECHNOLOGY
: METAL WORKING
SHEET METAL WORK

: WORKSHOPS
SHELTERED WORKSHOPS

SHIFT STUDIES

: : : LANGUAGES
: : AFRICAN LANGUAGES
: BANTU LANGUAGES
SHONA

: CURRICULUM
SHOP CURRICULUM

: : LANGUAGE
: WRITTEN LANGUAGE
SHORTHAND

: LITERARY GENRES
: : : : : LIBERAL ARTS
: : : : HUMANITIES
: : : LITERATURE
: : PROSE
: FICTION
SHORT STORIES

: : COGNITIVE PROCESSES
: MEMORY
SHORT TERM MEMORY

: GROUPS
SIBLINGS
. TWINS

: : : DISABILITIES
: : DISEASES
: ANEMIA
SICKLE CELL ANEMIA

: : : : LINGUISTICS
: : : SOCIOLINGUISTICS
: : LANGUAGE VARIATION
: : LANGUAGES
: CREOLES
SIERRA LEONE CREOLE

: : : METHODS
: : EDUCATIONAL METHODS
: TEACHING METHODS
SIGHT METHOD

: VOCABULARY
SIGHT VOCABULARY

: : RELATIONSHIP
: INTERPERSONAL RELATIONSHIP
SIGNIFICANT OTHERS

: : COMMUNICATION (THOUGHT TRANSFER)
: MANUAL COMMUNICATION
: LANGUAGE
SIGN LANGUAGE
. AMERICAN SIGN LANGUAGE

: : : : GROUPS
: : : PERSONNEL
: : NONPROFESSIONAL PERSONNEL
: SKILLED WORKERS
SIGN PAINTERS

: VISUAL AIDS
SIGNS

: : LITERACY
: : LANGUAGE ARTS
: READING
SILENT READING

: ENVIRONMENT
SIMULATED ENVIRONMENT

: METHODS
SIMULATION
. COMPUTER SIMULATION
. MODELS
.. MATHEMATICAL MODELS
.. ROLE MODELS
... MENTORS
.. STUDENT WRITING MODELS
.. TEACHING MODELS
. MONTE CARLO METHODS
. ROLE PLAYING
.. DRAMATIC PLAY

:: LANGUAGES
: INDO EUROPEAN LANGUAGES
SINGHALESE

:: ACTIVITIES
: MUSIC ACTIVITIES
SINGING

:: VISUAL AIDS
:: NONPRINT MEDIA
:: MASS MEDIA
: FILMS
SINGLE CONCEPT FILMS

::: INSTITUTIONS
:: SCHOOLS
: SINGLE SEX SCHOOLS
::: INSTITUTIONS
:: SCHOOLS
: COLLEGES
SINGLE SEX COLLEGES

:: INSTITUTIONS
: SCHOOLS
SINGLE SEX SCHOOLS
. SINGLE SEX COLLEGES

:: GROUPS
: STUDENTS
SINGLE STUDENTS

: LANGUAGES
SINO TIBETAN LANGUAGES
. BURMESE
. CHINESE
.. CANTONESE
.. FOOCHOW
.. MANDARIN CHINESE
. LAO
. THAI
. TIBETAN

::: LANGUAGES
:: AFRICAN LANGUAGES
: BANTU LANGUAGES
SISWATI

:: METHODS
: EVALUATION METHODS
SITE ANALYSIS

: DEVELOPMENT
SITE DEVELOPMENT

: SELECTION
SITE SELECTION

:: MEASURES (INDIVIDUALS)
: TESTS
SITUATIONAL TESTS

::: LIBERAL ARTS
:: HUMANITIES
: LITERATURE
SIXTEENTH CENTURY LITERATURE

::: ACTIVITIES
:: PHYSICAL ACTIVITIES
: ATHLETICS
SKIING

:: METHODS
: EVALUATION METHODS
SKILL ANALYSIS

:: FACILITIES
: EDUCATIONAL FACILITIES
SKILL CENTERS

:: DEVELOPMENT
: INDIVIDUAL DEVELOPMENT
SKILL DEVELOPMENT

: OCCUPATIONS
SKILLED OCCUPATIONS

::: GROUPS
:: PERSONNEL
: NONPROFESSIONAL PERSONNEL
SKILLED WORKERS
. AUTO BODY REPAIRERS
. CRAFT WORKERS
. ELECTRICIANS
. FLOOR LAYERS
. GLAZIERS
. LOCOMOTIVE ENGINEERS
. MACHINISTS
.. MACHINE REPAIRERS
.. MACHINE TOOL OPERATORS
.. TOOL AND DIE MAKERS
. SIGN PAINTERS
. TELEVISION RADIO REPAIRERS
. WATCHMAKERS

: OBSOLESCENCE
SKILL OBSOLESCENCE

: ABILITY
SKILLS
. AGRICULTURAL SKILLS
. BASIC SKILLS
.. ALPHABETIZING SKILLS
. BUSINESS SKILLS
.. BOOKKEEPING
.. KEYBOARDING (DATA ENTRY)
.. RECORDKEEPING
.. TYPEWRITING
. COMMUNICATION SKILLS
.. COMMUNICATIVE COMPETENCE (LANGUAGES)
... THRESHOLD LEVEL (LANGUAGES)
. DAILY LIVING SKILLS
.. SELF CARE SKILLS
. DECISION MAKING SKILLS
. HOME ECONOMICS SKILLS
. HOMEMAKING SKILLS
. INTERPRETIVE SKILLS
. JOB SKILLS
. LANGUAGE SKILLS
.. AUDIOLINGUAL SKILLS
... LISTENING SKILLS
... SPEECH SKILLS
.. COMMUNICATIVE COMPETENCE (LANGUAGES)
... THRESHOLD LEVEL (LANGUAGES)
.. READING SKILLS
... READING COMPREHENSION
... READING RATE
.. VOCABULARY SKILLS
.. WRITING SKILLS
. LIBRARY SKILLS
. LOCATIONAL SKILLS (SOCIAL STUDIES)
. MAP SKILLS
. MATHEMATICS SKILLS
. MECHANICAL SKILLS
. MINIMUM COMPETENCIES
. PARENTING SKILLS
. PSYCHOMOTOR SKILLS
.. MARKSMANSHIP
.. OBJECT MANIPULATION
.. PERCEPTUAL MOTOR COORDINATION
... EYE HAND COORDINATION
... EYE VOICE SPAN
. RESEARCH SKILLS
. SALESMANSHIP
. STUDY SKILLS
.. WORD STUDY SKILLS
. TEACHING SKILLS
. VISUAL LITERACY

: LITERARY GENRES
::::: LIBERAL ARTS
:::: HUMANITIES
:::: FINE ARTS
::: THEATER ARTS
::::: LIBERAL ARTS
:::: HUMANITIES
::: LITERATURE
:: DRAMA
: COMEDY
SKITS

:: RELATIONSHIP
: HUMAN RELATIONS
SLAVERY

:: LANGUAGES
: INDO EUROPEAN LANGUAGES
SLAVIC LANGUAGES
. BIELORUSSIAN
. BULGARIAN
. CZECH
. POLISH
. RUSSIAN
. SERBOCROATIAN
. SLOVENIAN
. UKRAINIAN

SLEEP

:: VISUAL AIDS
:: NONPRINT MEDIA
: TRANSPARENCIES
SLIDES

::: LANGUAGES
:: INDO EUROPEAN LANGUAGES
: SLAVIC LANGUAGES
SLOVENIAN

: GROUPS
SLOW LEARNERS

: MATTER
SLUDGE

: ENVIRONMENT
SLUM ENVIRONMENT

:: GEOGRAPHIC REGIONS
: POVERTY AREAS
SLUMS

:: INSTITUTIONS
: SCHOOLS
SLUM SCHOOLS

: BUSINESS
SMALL BUSINESSES

:: GROUPS
: CLASSES (GROUPS OF STUDENTS)
SMALL CLASSES

::: INSTITUTIONS
:: SCHOOLS
: SMALL SCHOOLS
::: INSTITUTIONS
:: SCHOOLS
: COLLEGES
SMALL COLLEGES

:: TECHNOLOGY
: MECHANICS (PROCESS)
SMALL ENGINE MECHANICS

:: INSTRUCTION
: GROUP INSTRUCTION
SMALL GROUP INSTRUCTION

:: INSTITUTIONS
: SCHOOLS
SMALL SCHOOLS
. ONE TEACHER SCHOOLS
. SMALL COLLEGES

: BEHAVIOR
SMOKING

:::: ACTIVITIES
::: PHYSICAL ACTIVITIES
:: ATHLETICS
: TEAM SPORTS
SOCCER

SOCIAL ACTION
. COMMUNITY ACTION

:: BEHAVIOR
: SOCIAL BEHAVIOR
:: BEHAVIOR
: ADJUSTMENT (TO ENVIRONMENT)
SOCIAL ADJUSTMENT

::: GROUPS
:: ORGANIZATIONS (GROUPS)
: AGENCIES
SOCIAL AGENCIES
. WELFARE AGENCIES

: ATTITUDES
SOCIAL ATTITUDES
. SOCIAL BIAS
.. ETHNIC BIAS
.. RACIAL BIAS
.. SEX BIAS
. SOCIAL DESIRABILITY

:: BACKGROUND
: SOCIOECONOMIC BACKGROUND
SOCIAL BACKGROUND
. SOCIAL EXPERIENCE

: BEHAVIOR
SOCIAL BEHAVIOR
. ACTIVISM
. ANTISOCIAL BEHAVIOR
.. AGGRESSION
.. CHEATING
.. CHILD ABUSE
.. CHILD NEGLECT
.. CRIME
... DELINQUENCY
... INTERNATIONAL CRIMES
.. ELDER ABUSE
.. INCEST
.. SEXUAL ABUSE
... RAPE
.. SEXUAL HARASSMENT
.. STEALING
... PLAGIARISM
.. TERRORISM
.. VANDALISM
... SCHOOL VANDALISM
.. VIOLENCE
... FAMILY VIOLENCE
. CONFORMITY
. DISSENT
. LYING
. OBEDIENCE
. PROSOCIAL BEHAVIOR
. SOCIAL ADJUSTMENT

:: ATTITUDES
: SOCIAL ATTITUDES
: BIAS
SOCIAL BIAS
. ETHNIC BIAS
. RACIAL BIAS
. SEX BIAS

::::: LIBERAL ARTS
:::: SCIENCES
::: NATURAL SCIENCES
:: BIOLOGICAL SCIENCES
: BIOLOGY
SOCIAL BIOLOGY

: CHANGE
SOCIAL CHANGE
. MODERNIZATION

SOCIAL CHARACTERISTICS

: GROUPS
SOCIAL CLASS
. CASTE
. LOWER CLASS
. LOWER MIDDLE CLASS
. MIDDLE CLASS
. UPPER CLASS
. WORKING CLASS

: COGNITIVE PROCESSES
SOCIAL COGNITION

SOCIAL CONTROL

:: ATTITUDES
: SOCIAL ATTITUDES
SOCIAL DESIRABILITY

:: DEVELOPMENT
: INDIVIDUAL DEVELOPMENT
SOCIAL DEVELOPMENT

:::: LINGUISTICS
::: SOCIOLINGUISTICS
:: LANGUAGE VARIATION
:: LANGUAGES
: DIALECTS
SOCIAL DIALECTS

: DIFFERENCES
SOCIAL DIFFERENCES

SOCIAL DISCRIMINATION
. AGE DISCRIMINATION
. EDUCATIONAL DISCRIMINATION
.. SCHOOL SEGREGATION
... COLLEGE SEGREGATION
... SCHOOL RESEGREGATION
. ETHNIC DISCRIMINATION
. HANDICAP DISCRIMINATION
. HOUSING DISCRIMINATION
. RACIAL DISCRIMINATION
.. RACIAL SEGREGATION
... DE FACTO SEGREGATION
... DE JURE SEGREGATION
. RELIGIOUS DISCRIMINATION
. REVERSE DISCRIMINATION
. SEX DISCRIMINATION
.. SEXUAL HARASSMENT

:::: LIBERAL ARTS
::: SCIENCES
:: SOCIAL SCIENCES
: DEMOGRAPHY
SOCIAL DISTRIBUTION

: ENVIRONMENT
SOCIAL ENVIRONMENT
. SOCIAL ISOLATION

:: THEORIES
: SOCIAL THEORIES
SOCIAL EXCHANGE THEORY

::: BACKGROUND
:: SOCIOECONOMIC BACKGROUND
: SOCIAL BACKGROUND
:: BACKGROUND
: EXPERIENCE
SOCIAL EXPERIENCE

:::: LIBERAL ARTS
::: SCIENCES
:: SOCIAL SCIENCES
::: LIBERAL ARTS
:: HUMANITIES
: HISTORY
SOCIAL HISTORY

:: DATA
: STATISTICAL DATA
SOCIAL INDICATORS

: INFLUENCES
SOCIAL INFLUENCES

SOCIAL INTEGRATION
. CLASSROOM DESEGREGATION
. NEIGHBORHOOD INTEGRATION
. PERSONNEL INTEGRATION
.. FACULTY INTEGRATION
.. TEACHER INTEGRATION
. RACIAL INTEGRATION
. SCHOOL DESEGREGATION
.. COLLEGE DESEGREGATION
. VOLUNTARY DESEGREGATION

: SOCIAL SYSTEMS
SOCIALISM

:: ENVIRONMENT
: SOCIAL ENVIRONMENT
SOCIAL ISOLATION

SOCIALIZATION
. POLITICAL SOCIALIZATION

SOCIAL LIFE

: MOBILITY
SOCIAL MOBILITY

: NETWORKS
SOCIAL NETWORKS

:: GROUPS
: ORGANIZATIONS (GROUPS)
SOCIAL ORGANIZATIONS

: PLANNING
SOCIAL PLANNING

: PROBLEMS
SOCIAL PROBLEMS

:::: LIBERAL ARTS
::: SCIENCES
:: SOCIAL SCIENCES
:::: LIBERAL ARTS
::: SCIENCES
:: BEHAVIORAL SCIENCES
: SOCIOLOGY
:::: LIBERAL ARTS
::: SCIENCES
:: BEHAVIORAL SCIENCES
: PSYCHOLOGY
SOCIAL PSYCHOLOGY

: REINFORCEMENT
SOCIAL REINFORCEMENT

SOCIAL RELATIONS (1966 1980)

: RESPONSIBILITY
SOCIAL RESPONSIBILITY
. CITIZENSHIP RESPONSIBILITY

: RESEARCH
SOCIAL SCIENCE RESEARCH
. ECONOMIC RESEARCH

:: LIBERAL ARTS
: SCIENCES
SOCIAL SCIENCES
. ANTHROPOLOGY
.. ANTHROPOLOGICAL LINGUISTICS
.. ARCHAEOLOGY
.. EDUCATIONAL ANTHROPOLOGY
.. ETHNOGRAPHY
.. ETHNOLOGY
. DEMOGRAPHY
.. BIRTH RATE
.. EMPLOYMENT PATTERNS
.. GEOGRAPHIC DISTRIBUTION
.. POPULATION DISTRIBUTION
... ETHNIC DISTRIBUTION
... RACIAL DISTRIBUTION
.. POPULATION GROWTH
.. POPULATION TRENDS
... BLACK POPULATION TRENDS
.. RACIAL COMPOSITION
... RACIAL BALANCE
.. RESIDENTIAL PATTERNS
.. SCHOOL DEMOGRAPHY
... TEACHER DISTRIBUTION
.. SOCIAL DISTRIBUTION
.. URBAN DEMOGRAPHY
. ECONOMICS
.. CONSUMER ECONOMICS
.. EDUCATIONAL ECONOMICS
... EDUCATIONAL FINANCE
.. LABOR ECONOMICS
.. RURAL ECONOMICS
. GEOGRAPHY
.. HUMAN GEOGRAPHY
.. PHYSICAL GEOGRAPHY
.. WORLD GEOGRAPHY
. GERONTOLOGY
.. EDUCATIONAL GERONTOLOGY
. HISTORY
.. AFRICAN HISTORY
.. AMERICAN INDIAN HISTORY
.. ANCIENT HISTORY
.. ASIAN HISTORY
.. BLACK HISTORY
.. CONSTITUTIONAL HISTORY
.. DIPLOMATIC HISTORY
.. EDUCATIONAL HISTORY
... SCIENCE EDUCATION HISTORY
.. EUROPEAN HISTORY
.. FAMILY HISTORY
... GENEALOGY
.. HISTORIOGRAPHY
.. INTELLECTUAL HISTORY
... ART HISTORY
... LITERARY HISTORY
.. LATIN AMERICAN HISTORY
.. LOCAL HISTORY
.. MEDIEVAL HISTORY
.. MIDDLE EASTERN HISTORY
.. MODERN HISTORY
.. NORTH AMERICAN HISTORY
... UNITED STATES HISTORY
.... CIVIL WAR (UNITED STATES)
.... COLONIAL HISTORY (UNITED STATES)
.... MEXICAN AMERICAN HISTORY
.... RECONSTRUCTION ERA
.... REVOLUTIONARY WAR (UNITED STATES)
.... STATE HISTORY
.. ORAL HISTORY
.. SCIENCE HISTORY
.. SOCIAL HISTORY
.. WORLD HISTORY
. INTERNATIONAL STUDIES
. POLITICAL SCIENCE
. SOCIAL STUDIES
.. CIVICS
. SOCIOLOGY
.. CRIMINOLOGY
.. EDUCATIONAL SOCIOLOGY
.. SOCIAL PSYCHOLOGY
. TOPOGRAPHY

::: GROUPS
:: PERSONNEL
: PROFESSIONAL PERSONNEL
SOCIAL SCIENTISTS

:: SERVICES
: HUMAN SERVICES
SOCIAL SERVICES
. ADULT DAY CARE
. ADULT FOSTER CARE
. ANCILLARY SCHOOL SERVICES
.. MOBILE EDUCATIONAL SERVICES
.. PUPIL PERSONNEL SERVICES
.. SCHOOL HEALTH SERVICES
.. STUDENT PERSONNEL SERVICES
. DAY CARE
.. EMPLOYER SUPPORTED DAY CARE
.. FAMILY DAY CARE
.. SCHOOL AGE DAY CARE
. FOSTER CARE
. SOCIAL WORK
. WELFARE SERVICES
.. MIGRANT WELFARE SERVICES

: STATUS
SOCIAL STATUS

:: ORGANIZATION
: SOCIAL STRUCTURE
SOCIAL STRATIFICATION

: ORGANIZATION
SOCIAL STRUCTURE
. SOCIAL STRATIFICATION

::: LIBERAL ARTS
:: SCIENCES
: SOCIAL SCIENCES
: CURRICULUM
SOCIAL STUDIES
. CIVICS

: GROUPS
SOCIAL SUPPORT GROUPS

SOCIAL SYSTEMS
. CAPITALISM
. COMMUNISM
. FASCISM
.. NAZISM
. SOCIALISM

: THEORIES
SOCIAL THEORIES
. ORGANIZATIONAL THEORIES
. SOCIAL EXCHANGE THEORY

: VALUES
SOCIAL VALUES

SOCIAL WELFARE (1966 1980)

::: SERVICES
:: HUMAN SERVICES
: SOCIAL SERVICES
SOCIAL WORK

::: GROUPS
:: PERSONNEL
: PROFESSIONAL PERSONNEL
::: GROUPS
:: PERSONNEL
: CASEWORKERS
SOCIAL WORKERS
. SCHOOL SOCIAL WORKERS

:::: LIBERAL ARTS
::: SCIENCES
:: NATURAL SCIENCES
: BIOLOGICAL SCIENCES
::: LIBERAL ARTS
:: SCIENCES
: BEHAVIORAL SCIENCES
SOCIOBIOLOGY

SOCIOCULTURAL PATTERNS
. ETHNICITY
. HUMANITARIANISM

: BACKGROUND
SOCIOECONOMIC BACKGROUND
. SOCIAL BACKGROUND
.. SOCIAL EXPERIENCE

: INFLUENCES
SOCIOECONOMIC INFLUENCES

: STATUS
SOCIOECONOMIC STATUS

: LINGUISTICS
SOCIOLINGUISTICS
. DIALECT STUDIES
. LANGUAGE PLANNING
.. LANGUAGE STANDARDIZATION
. LANGUAGE VARIATION
.. CREOLES
... GULLAH
... HAITIAN CREOLE
... MAURITIAN CREOLE
... SIERRA LEONE CREOLE
.. DIALECTS
... BLACK DIALECTS
... NONSTANDARD DIALECTS
... REGIONAL DIALECTS
... SOCIAL DIALECTS
.. LANGUAGE STYLES
.. LINGUISTIC BORROWING
.. PIDGINS

::: LIBERAL ARTS
:: SCIENCES
: SOCIAL SCIENCES
::: LIBERAL ARTS
:: SCIENCES
: BEHAVIORAL SCIENCES
SOCIOLOGY
. CRIMINOLOGY
. EDUCATIONAL SOCIOLOGY
. SOCIAL PSYCHOLOGY

:: METHODS
: MEASUREMENT TECHNIQUES
SOCIOMETRIC TECHNIQUES

:::: ACTIVITIES
::: PHYSICAL ACTIVITIES
:: ATHLETICS
: TEAM SPORTS
SOFTBALL

: LAND USE
: CONSERVATION (ENVIRONMENT)
SOIL CONSERVATION

::::: LIBERAL ARTS
:::: SCIENCES
::: NATURAL SCIENCES
:: PHYSICAL SCIENCES
: EARTH SCIENCE
SOIL SCIENCE

::: SCIENTIFIC CONCEPTS
:: ENERGY
: RADIATION
SOLAR ENERGY

::: LIBERAL ARTS
:: MATHEMATICS
: GEOMETRY
SOLID GEOMETRY

:: MATTER
: WASTES
SOLID WASTES

:: LANGUAGES
: AFRO ASIATIC LANGUAGES
SOMALI

::::: LIBERAL ARTS
:::: HUMANITIES
::: FINE ARTS
:: MUSIC
: VOCAL MUSIC
SONGS
. ART SONG
. BALLADS
. HYMNS

::::: LIBERAL ARTS
:::: HUMANITIES
::: LITERATURE
:: POETRY
: LYRIC POETRY
: LITERARY GENRES
SONNETS

:: GROUPS
: MALES
SONS

:: GROUPS
: ORGANIZATIONS (GROUPS)
SORORITIES

::: METHODS
:: PRODUCTION TECHNIQUES
: SPECIAL EFFECTS
SOUND EFFECTS

:: EQUIPMENT
: MEASUREMENT EQUIPMENT
:: EQUIPMENT
: ELECTRONIC EQUIPMENT
:: EQUIPMENT
: AUDIO EQUIPMENT
SOUND SPECTROGRAPHS

SOUND TRACKS (1966 1980)

SOUTHERN CITIZENS (1966 1980)

SOUTHERN COMMUNITY (1966 1980)

SOUTHERN SCHOOLS (1966 1980)

: SCIENTIFIC CONCEPTS
SPACE
. AREA
. VOLUME (MATHEMATICS)

:: ORGANIZATION
: CLASSIFICATION
SPACE CLASSIFICATION

: STRUCTURAL ELEMENTS (CONSTRUCTION)
: EQUIPMENT
SPACE DIVIDERS
. MOVABLE PARTITIONS

:: RESEARCH
: SCIENTIFIC RESEARCH
SPACE EXPLORATION
. LUNAR RESEARCH

SPACE ORIENTATION (1968 1980)

:: LIBERAL ARTS
: SCIENCES
SPACE SCIENCES

SPACE UTILIZATION

::: LANGUAGES
:: INDO EUROPEAN LANGUAGES
: ROMANCE LANGUAGES
SPANISH

::: GROUPS
:: NORTH AMERICANS
: HISPANIC AMERICANS
:: GROUPS
: ETHNIC GROUPS
SPANISH AMERICANS

: CULTURE
SPANISH CULTURE

::: LIBERAL ARTS
:: HUMANITIES
: LITERATURE
SPANISH LITERATURE

:: GROUPS
: NATIVE SPEAKERS
SPANISH SPEAKING

: ABILITY
SPATIAL ABILITY

SPATIAL RELATIONSHIP (1966 1980)

: RELATIONSHIP
SPATIAL RELATIONSHIP (FACILITIES)

:: GROUPS
: CLASSES (GROUPS OF STUDENTS)
SPECIAL CLASSES

:: PROGRAMS
: SPECIAL PROGRAMS
SPECIAL DEGREE PROGRAMS

: EDUCATION
SPECIAL EDUCATION
. ADAPTED PHYSICAL EDUCATION

:::: GROUPS
::: PERSONNEL
:: PROFESSIONAL PERSONNEL
: TEACHERS
SPECIAL EDUCATION TEACHERS

:: METHODS
: PRODUCTION TECHNIQUES
SPECIAL EFFECTS
. ANIMATION
. SOUND EFFECTS

: DISABILITIES
SPECIAL HEALTH PROBLEMS

: DEGREES (ACADEMIC)
SPECIALIST IN EDUCATION DEGREES

:: GROUPS
: PERSONNEL
SPECIALISTS
. CHILD DEVELOPMENT SPECIALISTS
. FILM PRODUCTION SPECIALISTS
. MEDIA SPECIALISTS
.. AUDIOVISUAL COORDINATORS

SPECIALIZATION

:: INSTITUTIONS
:: INFORMATION SOURCES
: LIBRARIES
SPECIAL LIBRARIES
. FILM LIBRARIES
. GOVERNMENT LIBRARIES
.. NATIONAL LIBRARIES
.. STATE LIBRARIES
. INSTITUTIONAL LIBRARIES
.. HOSPITAL LIBRARIES
.. PRISON LIBRARIES
. LAW LIBRARIES
. MEDICAL LIBRARIES

: PROGRAMS
SPECIAL PROGRAMS
. INDIVIDUALIZED EDUCATION PROGRAMS
. RESOURCE ROOM PROGRAMS
. SPECIAL DEGREE PROGRAMS

:: INSTITUTIONS
: SCHOOLS
SPECIAL SCHOOLS
. INSTITUTIONAL SCHOOLS
.. HOSPITAL SCHOOLS
. RESIDENTIAL SCHOOLS

: ZONING
SPECIAL ZONING

: STANDARDS
SPECIFICATIONS
. COMPUTER SOFTWARE
.. COURSEWARE
.. DATABASE MANAGEMENT SYSTEMS
.. MENU DRIVEN SOFTWARE
. DESIGN REQUIREMENTS
. FACILITY REQUIREMENTS

:::: LIBERAL ARTS
::: SCIENCES
:: NATURAL SCIENCES
: PHYSICAL SCIENCES
SPECTROSCOPY

: LANGUAGE ARTS
SPEECH
. ARTICULATION (SPEECH)
. ARTIFICIAL SPEECH
. INNER SPEECH (SUBVOCAL)
. PRONUNCIATION
. SPEECH ACTS
. SPEECH COMPRESSION

:: LANGUAGE ARTS
: SPEECH
SPEECH ACTS

: CLINICS
SPEECH AND HEARING CLINICS

: COMMUNICATION (THOUGHT TRANSFER)
SPEECH COMMUNICATION
. ORAL INTERPRETATION
. PUBLIC SPEAKING

: : LANGUAGE ARTS
: SPEECH
SPEECH COMPRESSION

: CURRICULUM
SPEECH CURRICULUM

SPEECH EDUCATION (1966 1980)

SPEECHES

: : EVALUATION
: MEDICAL EVALUATION
SPEECH EVALUATION

: BEHAVIOR PATTERNS
SPEECH HABITS

: DISABILITIES
SPEECH HANDICAPS
. ARTICULATION IMPAIRMENTS
. CLEFT PALATE
. DELAYED SPEECH
. STUTTERING
. VOICE DISORDERS

: IMPROVEMENT
SPEECH IMPROVEMENT

: INSTRUCTION
SPEECH INSTRUCTION
. PRONUNCIATION INSTRUCTION

: : : TECHNOLOGY
: : MEDICINE
: PATHOLOGY
SPEECH PATHOLOGY

: : : : ABILITY
: : : SKILLS
: : LANGUAGE SKILLS
: AUDIOLINGUAL SKILLS
SPEECH SKILLS

: : : MEASURES (INDIVIDUALS)
: : TESTS
: VERBAL TESTS
SPEECH TESTS

: THERAPY
SPEECH THERAPY

: : LITERACY
: : LANGUAGE ARTS
: READING
SPEED READING

: LANGUAGE ARTS
SPELLING
. FINGER SPELLING

: INSTRUCTION
SPELLING INSTRUCTION

: CURRICULUM
SPIRAL CURRICULUM

: BEHAVIOR
SPONTANEOUS BEHAVIOR

: : : : LIBERAL ARTS
: : : SCIENCES
: : BEHAVIORAL SCIENCES
: PSYCHOLOGY
SPORT PSYCHOLOGY

: ATTITUDES
SPORTSMANSHIP

: GROUPS
SPOUSES

: : : : ACTIVITIES
: : : PHYSICAL ACTIVITIES
: : ATHLETICS
: RACQUET SPORTS
SQUASH (GAME)

: : DEVELOPMENT
: LABOR FORCE DEVELOPMENT
STAFF DEVELOPMENT
. FACULTY DEVELOPMENT

: MEETINGS
STAFF MEETINGS

: ORIENTATION
STAFF ORIENTATION

STAFF ROLE

: LABOR UTILIZATION
STAFF UTILIZATION

: STRUCTURAL ELEMENTS
(CONSTRUCTION)
STAGES (FACILITIES)

: : MEASURES (INDIVIDUALS)
: TESTS
STANDARDIZED TESTS

STANDARDS
. ACADEMIC STANDARDS
. . GRADUATION REQUIREMENTS
. . . DEGREE REQUIREMENTS
. ADMINISTRATIVE PRINCIPLES
. BEHAVIOR STANDARDS
. . CODES OF ETHICS
. COURT DOCTRINE
. CRITERIA
. . ADMISSION CRITERIA
. . EVALUATION CRITERIA
. . . RELIABILITY
. . . . INTERRATER RELIABILITY
. . . . TEST RELIABILITY
. . . VALIDITY
. . . . CONCURRENT VALIDITY
. . . . PREDICTIVE VALIDITY
. . . . PROOF (MATHEMATICS)
. . . . TEST VALIDITY
. . . . . CONSTRUCT VALIDITY
. . . . . CONTENT VALIDITY
. . LESSON OBSERVATION
CRITERIA
. DRESS CODES
. EDUCATIONAL PRINCIPLES
. ENVIRONMENTAL STANDARDS
. EQUIPMENT STANDARDS
. FOOD STANDARDS
. LABOR STANDARDS
. LAWS
. . CONSTITUTIONAL LAW
. . CRIMINAL LAW
. . INTERNATIONAL LAW
. . SCHOOL LAW
. LIBRARY STANDARDS
. LIVING STANDARDS
. METRIC SYSTEM
. MIDDLE CLASS STANDARDS
. PARLIAMENTARY PROCEDURES
. QUALIFICATIONS
. . ADMINISTRATOR
QUALIFICATIONS
. . COUNSELOR QUALIFICATIONS
. . EMPLOYMENT
QUALIFICATIONS
. . SUPERVISOR
QUALIFICATIONS
. . TEACHER QUALIFICATIONS
. RESIDENCE REQUIREMENTS
. SCIENTIFIC PRINCIPLES
. SPECIFICATIONS
. . COMPUTER SOFTWARE
. . . COURSEWARE
. . . DATABASE MANAGEMENT
SYSTEMS
. . . MENU DRIVEN SOFTWARE
. . DESIGN REQUIREMENTS
. . FACILITY REQUIREMENTS
. STATE STANDARDS
. TEXTBOOK STANDARDS

: LANGUAGE USAGE
STANDARD SPOKEN USAGE

STATE ACTION

: : : : GROUPS
: : : ORGANIZATIONS (GROUPS)
: : AGENCIES
: PUBLIC AGENCIES
STATE AGENCIES
. STATE DEPARTMENTS OF
EDUCATION
. STATE LICENSING BOARDS

STATE AID
. FOUNDATION PROGRAMS
. FULL STATE FUNDING
. STATE FEDERAL AID

: : : : GROUPS
: : : ORGANIZATIONS (GROUPS)
: : GOVERNING BOARDS
: BOARDS OF EDUCATION
STATE BOARDS OF EDUCATION

: RELATIONSHIP
STATE CHURCH SEPARATION

: : : INSTITUTIONS
: : SCHOOLS
: STATE SCHOOLS
: : : : INSTITUTIONS
: : : SCHOOLS
: : COLLEGES
: PUBLIC COLLEGES
STATE COLLEGES
. STATE UNIVERSITIES

: : INSTITUTIONS
: COURTS
STATE COURTS

: : : : PUBLICATIONS
: : : REFERENCE MATERIALS
: : GUIDES
: CURRICULUM GUIDES
STATE CURRICULUM GUIDES

: : : : : GROUPS
: : : : ORGANIZATIONS (GROUPS)
: : : AGENCIES
: : PUBLIC AGENCIES
: STATE AGENCIES
: : : ORGANIZATION
: : ADMINISTRATIVE
ORGANIZATION
: DEPARTMENTS
STATE DEPARTMENTS OF
EDUCATION

: STATE AID
: FEDERAL AID
STATE FEDERAL AID

: : : GROUPS
: : ORGANIZATIONS (GROUPS)
: GOVERNMENT
(ADMINISTRATIVE BODY)
STATE GOVERNMENT

: : : : : LIBERAL ARTS
: : : : : SCIENCES
: : : : SOCIAL SCIENCES
: : : : : LIBERAL ARTS
: : : : HUMANITIES
: : : HISTORY
: : NORTH AMERICAN HISTORY
: UNITED STATES HISTORY
STATE HISTORY

: LEGISLATION
STATE LEGISLATION
. SCHOOL ATTENDANCE
LEGISLATION

: : : : INSTITUTIONS
: : : : INFORMATION SOURCES
: : : LIBRARIES
: : SPECIAL LIBRARIES
: GOVERNMENT LIBRARIES
STATE LIBRARIES

: : : : : GROUPS
: : : : ORGANIZATIONS (GROUPS)
: : : AGENCIES
: : PUBLIC AGENCIES
: STATE AGENCIES
STATE LICENSING BOARDS

: : : DATA
: : STATISTICAL DATA
: NORMS
STATE NORMS

: : : : GROUPS
: : : PERSONNEL
: : GOVERNMENT EMPLOYEES
: PUBLIC OFFICIALS
STATE OFFICIALS
. STATE SUPERVISORS

: PUBLICATIONS
STATE OF THE ART REVIEWS

: PROGRAMS
STATE PROGRAMS

: : RELATIONSHIP
: GOVERNMENT SCHOOL
RELATIONSHIP
STATE SCHOOL DISTRICT
RELATIONSHIP

: : INSTITUTIONS
: SCHOOLS
STATE SCHOOLS
. STATE COLLEGES
. . STATE UNIVERSITIES

STATES POWERS

: STANDARDS
STATE STANDARDS

: : : : GROUPS
: : : PERSONNEL
: : ADMINISTRATORS
: SUPERVISORS
: : : : : GROUPS
: : : : PERSONNEL
: : : GOVERNMENT EMPLOYEES
: : PUBLIC OFFICIALS
: STATE OFFICIALS
STATE SUPERVISORS

: : : METHODS
: : EVALUATION METHODS
: SURVEYS
STATE SURVEYS

:::: INSTITUTIONS
::: SCHOOLS
:: COLLEGES
: UNIVERSITIES
:::: INSTITUTIONS
::: SCHOOLS
:: STATE SCHOOLS
::::: INSTITUTIONS
:::: SCHOOLS
::: COLLEGES
:: PUBLIC COLLEGES
: STATE COLLEGES
STATE UNIVERSITIES

: PLANNING
STATEWIDE PLANNING

::: METHODS
:: EVALUATION METHODS
: DATA ANALYSIS
STATISTICAL ANALYSIS
. ANALYSIS OF COVARIANCE
. ANALYSIS OF VARIANCE
. BAYESIAN STATISTICS
. CORRELATION
. EFFECT SIZE
. ERROR OF MEASUREMENT
. GOODNESS OF FIT
. ITEM ANALYSIS
. JUDGMENT ANALYSIS TECHNIQUE
. LEAST SQUARES STATISTICS
. MAXIMUM LIKELIHOOD STATISTICS
. META ANALYSIS
. MULTIVARIATE ANALYSIS
.. CLUSTER ANALYSIS
.. DISCRIMINANT ANALYSIS
.. FACTOR ANALYSIS
... OBLIQUE ROTATION
... ORTHOGONAL ROTATION
.. MULTIDIMENSIONAL SCALING
.. PATH ANALYSIS
. REGRESSION (STATISTICS)
.. MULTIPLE REGRESSION ANALYSIS
. STATISTICAL DISTRIBUTIONS
. STATISTICAL INFERENCE
. STATISTICAL SIGNIFICANCE

: BIAS
STATISTICAL BIAS

: DATA
STATISTICAL DATA
. CENSUS FIGURES
. EMPLOYMENT STATISTICS
.. WORKER DAYS
. LIBRARY STATISTICS
. NORMS
.. LOCAL NORMS
.. NATIONAL NORMS
.. STATE NORMS
.. TEST NORMS
. SCHOOL STATISTICS
. SOCIAL INDICATORS

::: LIBERAL ARTS
:: MATHEMATICS
: STATISTICS
:::: METHODS
::: EVALUATION METHODS
:: DATA ANALYSIS
: STATISTICAL ANALYSIS
STATISTICAL DISTRIBUTIONS

:::: METHODS
::: EVALUATION METHODS
:: DATA ANALYSIS
: STATISTICAL ANALYSIS
: INFERENCES
:::: METHODS
::: EVALUATION METHODS
:: DATA ANALYSIS
: DATA INTERPRETATION
STATISTICAL INFERENCE

:::: METHODS
::: EVALUATION METHODS
:: DATA ANALYSIS
: STATISTICAL ANALYSIS
STATISTICAL SIGNIFICANCE

: RESEARCH
STATISTICAL STUDIES

::: METHODS
:: EVALUATION METHODS
: SURVEYS
STATISTICAL SURVEYS

:: LIBERAL ARTS
: MATHEMATICS
STATISTICS
. BAYESIAN STATISTICS
. LEAST SQUARES STATISTICS
. MAXIMUM LIKELIHOOD STATISTICS
. NONPARAMETRIC STATISTICS
. SAMPLING
.. ITEM SAMPLING
. STATISTICAL DISTRIBUTIONS

STATUS
. CITIZENSHIP
. ECONOMIC STATUS
.. POVERTY
. EMPLOYMENT LEVEL
.. ACADEMIC RANK (PROFESSIONAL)
.. TENURE
. ETHNIC STATUS
. FULL TIME EQUIVALENCY
. GROUP STATUS
.. FAMILY STATUS
. MARITAL STATUS
. RETIREMENT
.. EARLY RETIREMENT
.. TEACHER RETIREMENT
. SENIORITY
. SOCIAL STATUS
. SOCIOECONOMIC STATUS

::: NEEDS
:: INDIVIDUAL NEEDS
: PSYCHOLOGICAL NEEDS
STATUS NEED

::: BEHAVIOR
:: SOCIAL BEHAVIOR
: ANTISOCIAL BEHAVIOR
STEALING
. PLAGIARISM

:: GROUPS
: FAMILY (SOCIOLOGICAL UNIT)
STEPFAMILY

: ATTITUDES
STEREOTYPES
. ETHNIC STEREOTYPES
.. BLACK STEREOTYPES
. SEX STEREOTYPES
. TEACHER STEREOTYPES

: STIMULI
STIMULANTS

STIMULATION

STIMULI
. AUDITORY STIMULI
. CUES
.. CONTEXT CLUES
. ELECTRICAL STIMULI
. STIMULANTS
. VERBAL STIMULI
. VISUAL STIMULI
.. PICTORIAL STIMULI

STIMULUS DEVICES (1966 1980)

::: COGNITIVE PROCESSES
:: LEARNING PROCESSES
::: COGNITIVE PROCESSES
:: ABSTRACT REASONING
: GENERALIZATION
STIMULUS GENERALIZATION

: GROUPS
STOPOUTS

STORAGE
. EQUIPMENT STORAGE
. INFORMATION STORAGE

STORY GRAMMAR

:: LITERACY
:: LANGUAGE ARTS
: READING
STORY READING

: LANGUAGE ARTS
STORY TELLING

:: DISABILITIES
: VISUAL IMPAIRMENTS
STRABISMUS

:: BEHAVIOR
: RESPONSES
STRANGER REACTIONS

::: LINGUISTICS
:: PHONOLOGY
: SUPRASEGMENTALS
STRESS (PHONOLOGY)

STRESS MANAGEMENT

STRESS VARIABLES

STRIKES
. TEACHER STRIKES

STRUCTURAL ANALYSIS (1966 1980)

:: METHODS
: EVALUATION METHODS
STRUCTURAL ANALYSIS (LINGUISTICS)
. DISCOURSE ANALYSIS
. TAGMEMIC ANALYSIS

:: METHODS
: EVALUATION METHODS
STRUCTURAL ANALYSIS (SCIENCE)

:: STRUCTURAL ELEMENTS (CONSTRUCTION)
: BUILDING SYSTEMS
STRUCTURAL BUILDING SYSTEMS

STRUCTURAL ELEMENTS (CONSTRUCTION)
. ACOUSTIC INSULATION
. BUILDING SYSTEMS
.. STRUCTURAL BUILDING SYSTEMS
. CEILINGS
. CHIMNEYS
. DOORS
. FLOORING
.. CARPETING
. GLASS WALLS
. ROOFING
. SPACE DIVIDERS
.. MOVABLE PARTITIONS
. STAGES (FACILITIES)
. WINDOWS

:: THEORIES
: LINGUISTIC THEORY
STRUCTURAL GRAMMAR

: LINGUISTICS
STRUCTURAL LINGUISTICS

: UNEMPLOYMENT
STRUCTURAL UNEMPLOYMENT

:: BEHAVIOR
: STUDENT BEHAVIOR
:: BEHAVIOR
: ADJUSTMENT (TO ENVIRONMENT)
STUDENT ADJUSTMENT

:: PSYCHOLOGICAL PATTERNS
: ALIENATION
STUDENT ALIENATION

: ATTITUDES
STUDENT ATTITUDES

: ENROLLMENT
STUDENT ATTRITION

: BEHAVIOR
STUDENT BEHAVIOR
. STUDENT ADJUSTMENT
. STUDENT PARTICIPATION

: CURRICULUM
STUDENT CENTERED CURRICULUM

: CERTIFICATION
STUDENT CERTIFICATION

STUDENT CHARACTERISTICS

:: RELATIONSHIP
: STUDENT SCHOOL RELATIONSHIP
STUDENT COLLEGE RELATIONSHIP

: COSTS
STUDENT COSTS
. INSTRUCTIONAL STUDENT COSTS
.. TUITION
. NONINSTRUCTIONAL STUDENT COSTS

:: EDUCATIONAL MEDIA
: INSTRUCTIONAL MATERIALS
STUDENT DEVELOPED MATERIALS
. STUDENT WRITING MODELS

: DEVELOPMENT
STUDENT DEVELOPMENT

STUDENT DISTRIBUTION (1966 1980)

: OBJECTIVES
STUDENT EDUCATIONAL OBJECTIVES

: EMPLOYMENT
STUDENT EMPLOYMENT

: EVALUATION
STUDENT EVALUATION
. NONGRADED STUDENT EVALUATION

: : : EVALUATION
: : PERSONNEL EVALUATION
: TEACHER EVALUATION
STUDENT EVALUATION OF TEACHER PERFORMANCE

: : PROGRAMS
: EXCHANGE PROGRAMS
STUDENT EXCHANGE PROGRAMS

: : BACKGROUND
: EXPERIENCE
STUDENT EXPERIENCE

: FINANCIAL SUPPORT
STUDENT FINANCIAL AID
. ASSISTANTSHIPS
. FELLOWSHIPS
. . FACULTY FELLOWSHIPS
. INCOME CONTINGENT LOANS
. PARENT FINANCIAL CONTRIBUTION
. SCHOLARSHIPS
. . MERIT SCHOLARSHIPS
. . . NO NEED SCHOLARSHIPS
. . TUITION GRANTS

: : : GROUPS
: : PERSONNEL
: SCHOOL PERSONNEL
: : : GROUPS
: : PERSONNEL
: ADMINISTRATORS
STUDENT FINANCIAL AID OFFICERS

: : : GROUPS
: : ORGANIZATIONS (GROUPS)
: STUDENT ORGANIZATIONS
: : : GROUPS
: : ORGANIZATIONS (GROUPS)
: GOVERNMENT (ADMINISTRATIVE BODY)
STUDENT GOVERNMENT

: IMPROVEMENT
STUDENT IMPROVEMENT

: INTERESTS
STUDENT INTERESTS

: : ABILITY
: LEADERSHIP
STUDENT LEADERSHIP

: PROGRAMS
STUDENT LOAN PROGRAMS

: : MOBILITY
: MIGRATION
STUDENT MOBILITY

: MOTIVATION
STUDENT MOTIVATION

: NEEDS
STUDENT NEEDS

: : GROUPS
: ORGANIZATIONS (GROUPS)
STUDENT ORGANIZATIONS
. STUDENT GOVERNMENT
. STUDENT UNIONS

: : BEHAVIOR
: STUDENT BEHAVIOR
: : BEHAVIOR
: PARTICIPATION
STUDENT PARTICIPATION

: : : : SERVICES
: : : HUMAN SERVICES
: : SOCIAL SERVICES
: ANCILLARY SCHOOL SERVICES
STUDENT PERSONNEL SERVICES

: : : GROUPS
: : PERSONNEL
: SCHOOL PERSONNEL
STUDENT PERSONNEL WORKERS

: PLACEMENT
STUDENT PLACEMENT

: PROBLEMS
STUDENT PROBLEMS

: : ACTIVITIES
: SCHOOL ACTIVITIES
STUDENT PROJECTS

: : ACHIEVEMENT
: ACADEMIC ACHIEVEMENT
STUDENT PROMOTION

: : PUBLICATIONS
: SCHOOL PUBLICATIONS
STUDENT PUBLICATIONS

: : BEHAVIOR
: RESPONSES
STUDENT REACTION

: RECORDS (FORMS)
STUDENT RECORDS
. ACADEMIC RECORDS
. REPORT CARDS

: RECRUITMENT
STUDENT RECRUITMENT

: RESEARCH
STUDENT RESEARCH

: RESPONSIBILITY
STUDENT RESPONSIBILITY

: CIVIL LIBERTIES
STUDENT RIGHTS

STUDENT ROLE

: GROUPS
STUDENTS
. ADULT STUDENTS
. ADVANCED STUDENTS
. BILINGUAL STUDENTS
. BLACK STUDENTS
. COLLEGE STUDENTS
. . COLLEGE FRESHMEN
. . COLLEGE SENIORS
. . COLLEGE TRANSFER STUDENTS
. . GRADUATE STUDENTS
. . . DENTAL STUDENTS
. . . LAW STUDENTS
. . . MEDICAL STUDENTS
. . . . GRADUATE MEDICAL STUDENTS
. . IN STATE STUDENTS
. . ON CAMPUS STUDENTS
. . OUT OF STATE STUDENTS
. . RESIDENT ASSISTANTS
. . STUDENT TEACHERS
. . TWO YEAR COLLEGE STUDENTS
. . UNDERGRADUATE STUDENTS
. . . PREMEDICAL STUDENTS
. COMMUTING STUDENTS
. CONTINUATION STUDENTS
. DAY STUDENTS
. ELEMENTARY SCHOOL STUDENTS
. EVENING STUDENTS
. FOREIGN STUDENTS
. FULL TIME STUDENTS
. HIGH RISK STUDENTS
. LOWER CLASS STUDENTS
. MAJORS (STUDENTS)
. . EDUCATION MAJORS
. MARRIED STUDENTS
. MIDDLE CLASS STUDENTS
. NONMAJORS
. NONTRADITIONAL STUDENTS
. PART TIME STUDENTS
. PREGNANT STUDENTS
. REENTRY STUDENTS
. SECONDARY SCHOOL STUDENTS
. . HIGH SCHOOL STUDENTS
. . . COLLEGE BOUND STUDENTS
. . . HIGH SCHOOL FRESHMEN
. . . HIGH SCHOOL SENIORS
. . . NONCOLLEGE BOUND STUDENTS
. . JUNIOR HIGH SCHOOL STUDENTS
. SELF SUPPORTING STUDENTS
. SINGLE STUDENTS
. STUDENT VOLUNTEERS
. TERMINAL STUDENTS
. TRANSFER STUDENTS
. . COLLEGE TRANSFER STUDENTS
. WHITE STUDENTS

: RELATIONSHIP
STUDENT SCHOOL RELATIONSHIP
. STUDENT COLLEGE RELATIONSHIP

: : CULTURE
: SUBCULTURES
STUDENT SUBCULTURES

: ATTITUDES
STUDENT TEACHER ATTITUDES

: EVALUATION
STUDENT TEACHER EVALUATION

: : : : GROUPS
: : : PERSONNEL
: : PROFESSIONAL PERSONNEL
: TEACHERS
: : : GROUPS
: : STUDENTS
: COLLEGE STUDENTS
STUDENT TEACHERS

: : : : GROUPS
: : : PERSONNEL
: : ADMINISTRATORS
: SUPERVISORS
: : : : : GROUPS
: : : : PERSONNEL
: : : SCHOOL PERSONNEL
: : : : : GROUPS
: : : : PERSONNEL
: : : PROFESSIONAL PERSONNEL
: : FACULTY
: COLLEGE FACULTY
STUDENT TEACHER SUPERVISORS

: : : EDUCATION
: : PROFESSIONAL EDUCATION
: TEACHER EDUCATION
STUDENT TEACHING

: TRANSPORTATION
STUDENT TRANSPORTATION

: : : GROUPS
: : ORGANIZATIONS (GROUPS)
: STUDENT ORGANIZATIONS
: : FACILITIES
: EDUCATIONAL FACILITIES
STUDENT UNIONS

: : GROUPS
: VOLUNTEERS
: : GROUPS
: STUDENTS
STUDENT VOLUNTEERS

: : QUALITY OF LIFE
: WELL BEING
STUDENT WELFARE

: : : EDUCATIONAL MEDIA
: : INSTRUCTIONAL MATERIALS
: STUDENT DEVELOPED MATERIALS
: : : METHODS
: : SIMULATION
: MODELS
STUDENT WRITING MODELS

STUDIO FLOOR PLANS (1966 1980)

: : ACTIVITIES
: LEARNING ACTIVITIES
STUDY
. HOME STUDY
. . HOMEWORK
. INDEPENDENT STUDY

: EDUCATION
STUDY ABROAD

: : : FACILITIES
: : EDUCATIONAL FACILITIES
: STUDY FACILITIES
STUDY CENTERS

: : FACILITIES
: EDUCATIONAL FACILITIES
STUDY FACILITIES
. CARRELS
. STUDY CENTERS

: : EDUCATIONAL MEDIA
: INSTRUCTIONAL MATERIALS
: : : PUBLICATIONS
: : REFERENCE MATERIALS
: GUIDES
STUDY GUIDES

: BEHAVIOR PATTERNS
STUDY HABITS

: : ABILITY
: SKILLS
STUDY SKILLS
. WORD STUDY SKILLS

: : DISABILITIES
: SPEECH HANDICAPS
STUTTERING

: CULTURE
SUBCULTURES
. STUDENT SUBCULTURES

: VOCABULARY
SUBJECT INDEX TERMS

: : : : GROUPS
: : : PERSONNEL
: : PROFESSIONAL PERSONNEL
: TEACHERS
SUBSTITUTE TEACHERS

:::::METHODS
::::EDUCATIONAL METHODS
:::TEACHING METHODS
::DRILLS (PRACTICE)
:PATTERN DRILLS (LANGUAGE)
SUBSTITUTION DRILLS

:::LIBERAL ARTS
::MATHEMATICS
:ARITHMETIC
SUBTRACTION

:ENVIRONMENT
SUBURBAN ENVIRONMENT

::FACILITIES
:HOUSING
SUBURBAN HOUSING

:PROBLEMS
SUBURBAN PROBLEMS

::INSTITUTIONS
:SCHOOLS
SUBURBAN SCHOOLS

::GROUPS
:YOUTH
SUBURBAN YOUTH

::GEOGRAPHIC REGIONS
:METROPOLITAN AREAS
SUBURBS

::BEHAVIOR
:PERFORMANCE
SUCCESS

:::::LINGUISTICS
::::DESCRIPTIVE LINGUISTICS
:::GRAMMAR
::MORPHOLOGY (LANGUAGES)
:MORPHEMES
SUFFIXES

:::METHODS
::EDUCATIONAL METHODS
:TEACHING METHODS
SUGGESTOPEDIA

::BEHAVIOR
:SELF DESTRUCTIVE BEHAVIOR
:DEATH
SUICIDE

:EVALUATION
SUMMATIVE EVALUATION

:PROGRAMS
SUMMER PROGRAMS
.SUMMER SCIENCE PROGRAMS

::INSTITUTIONS
:SCHOOLS
SUMMER SCHOOLS

::PROGRAMS
:SUMMER PROGRAMS
::PROGRAMS
:SCIENCE PROGRAMS
SUMMER SCIENCE PROGRAMS

SUPERCONDUCTORS

:::GROUPS
::PERSONNEL
:ADMINISTRATORS
SUPERINTENDENTS

::PROGRAMS
:::LEARNING
::EXPERIENTIAL LEARNING
:FIELD EXPERIENCE PROGRAMS
::EDUCATION
:AGRICULTURAL EDUCATION
SUPERVISED FARM PRACTICE

::GOVERNANCE
:ADMINISTRATION
SUPERVISION
.PRACTICUM SUPERVISION
.PROCTORING
.SCHOOL SUPERVISION
.SCIENCE SUPERVISION
.TEACHER SUPERVISION

::STANDARDS
:QUALIFICATIONS
SUPERVISOR QUALIFICATIONS

:::GROUPS
::PERSONNEL
:ADMINISTRATORS
SUPERVISORS
.CREW LEADERS
.STATE SUPERVISORS
.STUDENT TEACHER SUPERVISORS

:METHODS
SUPERVISORY METHODS

:TRAINING
SUPERVISORY TRAINING

:EDUCATION
SUPPLEMENTARY EDUCATION

:READING MATERIALS
SUPPLEMENTARY READING MATERIALS

:RESOURCES
SUPPLIES
.ADHESIVES
.AGRICULTURAL SUPPLIES
.ELECTRIC BATTERIES
.MAGNETIC TAPES
..MAGNETIC TAPE CASSETTES
...AUDIOTAPE CASSETTES
...VIDEOTAPE CASSETTES

:PREDICTOR VARIABLES
SUPPRESSOR VARIABLES

::LINGUISTICS
:PHONOLOGY
SUPRASEGMENTALS
.INTONATION
.STRESS (PHONOLOGY)

SUPREME COURT LITIGATION (1966 1980)

SUPREME COURTS (1966 1980)

::::THEORIES
:::LINGUISTIC THEORY
::GENERATIVE GRAMMAR
:TRANSFORMATIONAL GENERATIVE GRAMMAR
SURFACE STRUCTURE

::::ACTIVITIES
:::PHYSICAL ACTIVITIES
::ATHLETICS
:AQUATIC SPORTS
SURFING

::TECHNOLOGY
:MEDICINE
SURGERY

::::GROUPS
:::PERSONNEL
::HEALTH PERSONNEL
:ALLIED HEALTH PERSONNEL
SURGICAL TECHNICIANS

SURREALISM

::METHODS
:EVALUATION METHODS
SURVEYS
.COMMUNITY SURVEYS
.GRADUATE SURVEYS
.LIBRARY SURVEYS
.NATIONAL SURVEYS
.OCCUPATIONAL SURVEYS
.SCHOOL SURVEYS
.STATE SURVEYS
.STATISTICAL SURVEYS
.TELEVISION SURVEYS

:DISCIPLINE
SUSPENSION
.IN SCHOOL SUSPENSION

::INSTRUCTION
:READING INSTRUCTION
::LITERACY
::LANGUAGE ARTS
:READING
SUSTAINED SILENT READING

::LANGUAGES
:AFRICAN LANGUAGES
SUSU

:::LANGUAGES
::AFRICAN LANGUAGES
:BANTU LANGUAGES
SWAHILI

::LANGUAGES
:INDO EUROPEAN LANGUAGES
SWEDISH

::::ACTIVITIES
:::PHYSICAL ACTIVITIES
::ATHLETICS
:AQUATIC SPORTS
SWIMMING

:FACILITIES
SWIMMING POOLS

::LINGUISTICS
:PHONOLOGY
SYLLABLES

:LANGUAGE
SYMBOLIC LANGUAGE

:LEARNING
SYMBOLIC LEARNING

SYMBOLISM

::LITERARY DEVICES
::LANGUAGE
:FIGURATIVE LANGUAGE
SYMBOLS (LITERARY)

SYMBOLS (MATHEMATICS)
.NUMBERS
..FRACTIONS
...DECIMAL FRACTIONS
..LOGARITHMS
..NUMBER SYSTEMS
..RATIONAL NUMBERS
...INTEGERS
....PRIME NUMBERS
..RECIPROCALS (MATHEMATICS)
..WHOLE NUMBERS

SYMMETRY

:::LINGUISTICS
::DESCRIPTIVE LINGUISTICS
:GRAMMAR
SYNTAX
.FORM CLASSES (LANGUAGES)
..ADJECTIVES
..ADVERBS
..DETERMINERS (LANGUAGES)
..FUNCTION WORDS
..NOUNS
..PREPOSITIONS
..PRONOUNS
..VERBS
.PHRASE STRUCTURE
.SENTENCE STRUCTURE

::METHODS
:EVALUATION METHODS
SYNTHESIS

:METHODS
SYSTEMS ANALYSIS

::GROUPS
:PERSONNEL
SYSTEMS ANALYSTS

::METHODS
:HOLISTIC APPROACH
SYSTEMS APPROACH
.SYSTEMS BUILDING
..DESIGN BUILD APPROACH

:::METHODS
::HOLISTIC APPROACH
:SYSTEMS APPROACH
SYSTEMS BUILDING
.DESIGN BUILD APPROACH

SYSTEMS CONCEPTS (1966 1980)

:DEVELOPMENT
SYSTEMS DEVELOPMENT

:VISUAL AIDS
TABLES (DATA)
.EXPECTANCY TABLES

:::ACTIVITIES
::PHYSICAL ACTIVITIES
:ATHLETICS
TABLE TENNIS

::VISUAL AIDS
::EQUIPMENT
:PROJECTION EQUIPMENT
TACHISTOSCOPES

::CHANGE
:MEDIA ADAPTATION
TACTILE ADAPTATION

::COGNITIVE PROCESSES
:PERCEPTION
TACTUAL PERCEPTION

: : : : MEASURES (INDIVIDUALS)
: : : TESTS
: : COGNITIVE TESTS
: PERCEPTION TESTS
TACTUAL VISUAL TESTS

: : : LANGUAGES
: : MALAYO POLYNESIAN LANGUAGES
: INDONESIAN LANGUAGES
TAGALOG

: : : METHODS
: : EVALUATION METHODS
: STRUCTURAL ANALYSIS (LINGUISTICS)
TAGMEMIC ANALYSIS

: : LANGUAGES
: INDO EUROPEAN LANGUAGES
TAJIK

TALENT

: : DEVELOPMENT
: INDIVIDUAL DEVELOPMENT
TALENT DEVELOPMENT

: IDENTIFICATION
TALENT IDENTIFICATION

TALENT UTILIZATION (1966 1980)

: LITERARY GENRES
TALES
. FABLES

: SENSORY AIDS
TALKING BOOKS

: : LANGUAGES
: DRAVIDIAN LANGUAGES
TAMIL

: RELIGION
TAOISM

: : EQUIPMENT
: ELECTRONIC EQUIPMENT
TAPE RECORDERS
. AUDIOTAPE RECORDERS
. VIDEOTAPE RECORDERS

: NONPRINT MEDIA
TAPE RECORDINGS
. AUDIOTAPE RECORDINGS
. VIDEOTAPE RECORDINGS

: : METHODS
: EVALUATION METHODS
TASK ANALYSIS

TASK PERFORMANCE (1966 1980)

: : : LANGUAGES
: : URALIC ALTAIC LANGUAGES
: TURKIC LANGUAGES
TATAR

: FINANCIAL SUPPORT
TAX ALLOCATION

TAX CREDITS

TAX DEDUCTIONS

TAX EFFORT

TAXES
. PROPERTY TAXES
. SCHOOL TAXES

: RATIOS (MATHEMATICS)
TAX RATES

: : RELATIONSHIP
: INTERPERSONAL RELATIONSHIP
TEACHER ADMINISTRATOR RELATIONSHIP

: : : : GROUPS
: : : PERSONNEL
: : SCHOOL PERSONNEL
: : : : GROUPS
: : : PERSONNEL
: : PARAPROFESSIONAL PERSONNEL
: PARAPROFESSIONAL SCHOOL PERSONNEL
TEACHER AIDES
. BILINGUAL TEACHER AIDES

: : PSYCHOLOGICAL PATTERNS
: ALIENATION
TEACHER ALIENATION

: : : GROUPS
: : ORGANIZATIONS (GROUPS)
: PROFESSIONAL ASSOCIATIONS
TEACHER ASSOCIATIONS

: ATTENDANCE
TEACHER ATTENDANCE

: ATTITUDES
TEACHER ATTITUDES

: BACKGROUND
TEACHER BACKGROUND

: BEHAVIOR
TEACHER BEHAVIOR
. TEACHER EFFECTIVENESS
. TEACHER MILITANCY
. TEACHER PARTICIPATION
. TEACHER PERSISTENCE
. TEACHER RESPONSE

: : : BEHAVIOR
: : RESPONSES
: BURNOUT
TEACHER BURNOUT

: : FACILITIES
: RESOURCE CENTERS
TEACHER CENTERS

: CERTIFICATION
TEACHER CERTIFICATION

TEACHER CHARACTERISTICS
. TEACHING STYLES

: : EDUCATIONAL MEDIA
: INSTRUCTIONAL MATERIALS
TEACHER DEVELOPED MATERIALS
. TEACHER MADE TESTS

: DISCIPLINE
TEACHER DISCIPLINE
. TEACHER DISMISSAL

: : DISCIPLINE
: TEACHER DISCIPLINE
: : DISCIPLINE
: DISMISSAL (PERSONNEL)
TEACHER DISMISSAL

: : : : : LIBERAL ARTS
: : : : SCIENCES
: : : SOCIAL SCIENCES
: : DEMOGRAPHY
: SCHOOL DEMOGRAPHY
TEACHER DISTRIBUTION

: : EDUCATION
: PROFESSIONAL EDUCATION
TEACHER EDUCATION
. COMPETENCY BASED TEACHER EDUCATION
. ENGLISH TEACHER EDUCATION
. INSERVICE TEACHER EDUCATION
. PRESERVICE TEACHER EDUCATION
. STUDENT TEACHING
. TEACHER EDUCATOR EDUCATION

: : CURRICULUM
: COLLEGE CURRICULUM
TEACHER EDUCATION CURRICULUM
. METHODS COURSES

: PROGRAMS
TEACHER EDUCATION PROGRAMS

: : : EDUCATION
: : PROFESSIONAL EDUCATION
: TEACHER EDUCATION
TEACHER EDUCATOR EDUCATION

: : : : : GROUPS
: : : : PERSONNEL
: : : SCHOOL PERSONNEL
: : : : : GROUPS
: : : : PERSONNEL
: : : PROFESSIONAL PERSONNEL
: : FACULTY
: COLLEGE FACULTY
TEACHER EDUCATORS
. METHODS TEACHERS

: : BEHAVIOR
: TEACHER BEHAVIOR
TEACHER EFFECTIVENESS

: EMPLOYMENT
TEACHER EMPLOYMENT

TEACHER EMPLOYMENT BENEFITS

: : EVALUATION
: PERSONNEL EVALUATION
TEACHER EVALUATION
. STUDENT EVALUATION OF TEACHER PERFORMANCE

: : PROGRAMS
: EXCHANGE PROGRAMS
TEACHER EXCHANGE PROGRAMS

: GUIDANCE
TEACHER GUIDANCE

: : FACILITIES
: HOUSING
TEACHER HOUSING

: IMPROVEMENT
TEACHER IMPROVEMENT

: INFLUENCES
TEACHER INFLUENCE

: : SOCIAL INTEGRATION
: PERSONNEL INTEGRATION
TEACHER INTEGRATION

: : : : GROUPS
: : : PERSONNEL
: : PROFESSIONAL PERSONNEL
: TEACHERS
TEACHER INTERNS

: : MEASURES (INDIVIDUALS)
: TESTS
: : : EDUCATIONAL MEDIA
: : INSTRUCTIONAL MATERIALS
: TEACHER DEVELOPED MATERIALS
TEACHER MADE TESTS

: : BEHAVIOR
: TEACHER BEHAVIOR
TEACHER MILITANCY

: : PSYCHOLOGICAL PATTERNS
: MORALE
TEACHER MORALE

: MOTIVATION
TEACHER MOTIVATION

: ORIENTATION
TEACHER ORIENTATION

: : BEHAVIOR
: TEACHER BEHAVIOR
: : BEHAVIOR
: PARTICIPATION
TEACHER PARTICIPATION

: : BEHAVIOR
: TEACHER BEHAVIOR
: : BEHAVIOR
: PERSISTENCE
TEACHER PERSISTENCE

: : PLACEMENT
: JOB PLACEMENT
TEACHER PLACEMENT

: PROMOTION (OCCUPATIONAL)
TEACHER PROMOTION

: : STANDARDS
: QUALIFICATIONS
TEACHER QUALIFICATIONS

: RECRUITMENT
TEACHER RECRUITMENT

: : BEHAVIOR
: TEACHER BEHAVIOR
: : BEHAVIOR
: RESPONSES
TEACHER RESPONSE

: RESPONSIBILITY
TEACHER RESPONSIBILITY
. NONINSTRUCTIONAL RESPONSIBILITY

: : STATUS
: RETIREMENT
TEACHER RETIREMENT

: CIVIL LIBERTIES
TEACHER RIGHTS

TEACHER ROLE

::: GROUPS
:: PERSONNEL
: PROFESSIONAL PERSONNEL
TEACHERS
. ADULT EDUCATORS
. ART TEACHERS
. BEGINNING TEACHERS
. BILINGUAL TEACHERS
. BLACK TEACHERS
. CATHOLIC EDUCATORS
. COOPERATING TEACHERS
. ELEMENTARY SCHOOL TEACHERS
. HOME ECONOMICS TEACHERS
. INDUSTRIAL ARTS TEACHERS
. INSTRUCTOR COORDINATORS
. ITINERANT TEACHERS
. LANGUAGE TEACHERS
. LAY TEACHERS
. MASTER TEACHERS
. MATHEMATICS TEACHERS
. MINORITY GROUP TEACHERS
. MUSIC TEACHERS
. PHYSICAL EDUCATION TEACHERS
. PRESCHOOL TEACHERS
. PUBLIC SCHOOL TEACHERS
. READING TEACHERS
. REMEDIAL TEACHERS
. RESOURCE TEACHERS
. SCIENCE TEACHERS
. SECONDARY SCHOOL TEACHERS
. SPECIAL EDUCATION TEACHERS
. STUDENT TEACHERS
. SUBSTITUTE TEACHERS
. TEACHER INTERNS
. TELEVISION TEACHERS
. TUTORS
. VOCATIONAL EDUCATION TEACHERS
.. BUSINESS EDUCATION TEACHERS
.. DISTRIBUTIVE EDUCATION TEACHERS
.. TRADE AND INDUSTRIAL TEACHERS

:: INCOME
:: EXPENDITURES
: SALARIES
TEACHER SALARIES

:: SELECTION
: PERSONNEL SELECTION
TEACHER SELECTION

:: LABOR MARKET
: TEACHER SUPPLY AND DEMAND
TEACHER SHORTAGE

:: ATTITUDES
: STEREOTYPES
TEACHER STEREOTYPES

: STRIKES
TEACHER STRIKES

: RATIOS (MATHEMATICS)
TEACHER STUDENT RATIO

:: RELATIONSHIP
: INTERPERSONAL RELATIONSHIP
TEACHER STUDENT RELATIONSHIP

::: GOVERNANCE
:: ADMINISTRATION
: SUPERVISION
TEACHER SUPERVISION

: LABOR MARKET
TEACHER SUPPLY AND DEMAND
. TEACHER SHORTAGE

:: MOBILITY
: OCCUPATIONAL MOBILITY
TEACHER TRANSFER

:: QUALITY OF LIFE
: WELL BEING
TEACHER WELFARE

: WORKSHOPS
TEACHER WORKSHOPS

TEACHING (1966 1980)

:: OCCUPATIONS
: PROFESSIONAL OCCUPATIONS
TEACHING (OCCUPATION)
. TEAM TEACHING
. URBAN TEACHING

TEACHING ASSIGNMENT (1966 1980)

::::: GROUPS
:::: PERSONNEL
::: SCHOOL PERSONNEL
::::: GROUPS
:::: PERSONNEL
::: PROFESSIONAL PERSONNEL
:: FACULTY
: COLLEGE FACULTY
TEACHING ASSISTANTS

:: ENVIRONMENT
: WORK ENVIRONMENT
:: ENVIRONMENT
: EDUCATIONAL ENVIRONMENT
TEACHING CONDITIONS

:: BACKGROUND
: EXPERIENCE
TEACHING EXPERIENCE

::: PUBLICATIONS
:: REFERENCE MATERIALS
: GUIDES
TEACHING GUIDES

:: INSTITUTIONS
: HOSPITALS
TEACHING HOSPITALS

: FACULTY WORKLOAD
TEACHING LOAD

:: EDUCATIONAL MEDIA
: AUTOINSTRUCTIONAL AIDS
TEACHING MACHINES

:: METHODS
: EDUCATIONAL METHODS
TEACHING METHODS
. AUDIOLINGUAL METHODS
. CLINICAL TEACHING (HEALTH PROFESSIONS)
. CONVENTIONAL INSTRUCTION
. CREATIVE TEACHING
. CROSS AGE TEACHING
. DEMONSTRATIONS (EDUCATIONAL)
. DIAGNOSTIC TEACHING
. DISCUSSION (TEACHING TECHNIQUE)
. DRILLS (PRACTICE)
.. PATTERN DRILLS (LANGUAGE)
... SUBSTITUTION DRILLS
. EXPERIMENTAL TEACHING
. GRAMMAR TRANSLATION METHOD
. INDIVIDUALIZED INSTRUCTION
. KINESTHETIC METHODS
. LANGUAGE EXPERIENCE APPROACH
. LECTURE METHOD
. MONTESSORI METHOD
. MULTIMEDIA INSTRUCTION
.. AUDIOVISUAL INSTRUCTION
. NEGATIVE PRACTICE
. ORAL COMMUNICATION METHOD
.. LIPREADING
. PEER TEACHING
. PRECISION TEACHING
. PROGRAMED INSTRUCTION
.. COMPUTER ASSISTED INSTRUCTION
.. PROGRAMED TUTORING
. SIGHT METHOD
. SUGGESTOPEDIA
. TELEPHONE INSTRUCTION
. THEMATIC APPROACH
. TRAINING METHODS
.. MANAGEMENT GAMES
.. MICROCOUNSELING
.. MICROTEACHING

::: METHODS
:: SIMULATION
: MODELS
TEACHING MODELS

TEACHING PROGRAMS (1966 1980)

:: ABILITY
: SKILLS
TEACHING SKILLS

: TEACHER CHARACTERISTICS
TEACHING STYLES

:::: ACTIVITIES
::: PHYSICAL ACTIVITIES
:: ATHLETICS
: TEAM SPORTS
TEAM HANDBALL

::: ACTIVITIES
:: PHYSICAL ACTIVITIES
: ATHLETICS
TEAM SPORTS
. BASEBALL
. BASKETBALL
. FIELD HOCKEY
. FOOTBALL
. ICE HOCKEY
. LACROSSE
. SOCCER
. SOFTBALL
. TEAM HANDBALL
. VOLLEYBALL
. WATER POLO

::: OCCUPATIONS
:: PROFESSIONAL OCCUPATIONS
: TEACHING (OCCUPATION)
TEAM TEACHING

: TRAINING
TEAM TRAINING

:: BEHAVIOR
: GROUP BEHAVIOR
TEAMWORK

TECHNICAL ASSISTANCE

:: EDUCATION
: VOCATIONAL EDUCATION
TECHNICAL EDUCATION
. FIRE SCIENCE EDUCATION

::::: LIBERAL ARTS
:::: HUMANITIES
::: FINE ARTS
:: VISUAL ARTS
: DRAFTING
TECHNICAL ILLUSTRATION

:::: INSTITUTIONS
::: SCHOOLS
:: COLLEGES
: TWO YEAR COLLEGES
TECHNICAL INSTITUTES

:: LIBERAL ARTS
: MATHEMATICS
TECHNICAL MATHEMATICS

: OCCUPATIONS
TECHNICAL OCCUPATIONS

:: LITERACY
:: LANGUAGE ARTS
: WRITING (COMPOSITION)
TECHNICAL WRITING

: DEVELOPMENT
TECHNOLOGICAL ADVANCEMENT

TECHNOLOGICAL LITERACY
. COMPUTER LITERACY

TECHNOLOGY
. ACCOUNTING
.. PROPERTY ACCOUNTING
.. SCHOOL ACCOUNTING
. AEROSPACE TECHNOLOGY
.. AVIATION TECHNOLOGY
... AVIATION MECHANICS
. AGRICULTURE
.. AGRONOMY
.. ANIMAL HUSBANDRY
.. HARVESTING
.. HORTICULTURE
... ORNAMENTAL HORTICULTURE
.... FLORICULTURE
.... LANDSCAPING
.... TURF MANAGEMENT
. APPROPRIATE TECHNOLOGY
. AUTOMATION
.. LIBRARY AUTOMATION
.. ROBOTICS
. COMMUNICATIONS
.. AUDIOVISUAL COMMUNICATIONS
... DIAL ACCESS INFORMATION SYSTEMS
... EDUCATIONAL RADIO
... EDUCATIONAL TELEVISION
... LOOP INDUCTION SYSTEMS
.. TELECOMMUNICATIONS
... COMMUNICATIONS SATELLITES
... ELECTRONIC MAIL
... ELECTRONIC PUBLISHING
... FACSIMILE TRANSMISSION
... RADIO
.... EDUCATIONAL RADIO
... TELECONFERENCING
... TELEPHONE COMMUNICATIONS SYSTEMS
... TELEVISION
.... BROADCAST TELEVISION
.... CABLE TELEVISION
.... CHILDRENS TELEVISION
.... CLOSED CIRCUIT TELEVISION
.... COMMERCIAL TELEVISION
.... EDUCATIONAL TELEVISION
.... PUBLIC TELEVISION
... VIDEOTEX
. CONSUMER SCIENCE
. COSMETOLOGY
. CYBERNETICS
. EDUCATIONAL TECHNOLOGY
.. INSTRUCTIONAL SYSTEMS
. ELECTROMECHANICAL TECHNOLOGY
. ENGINEERING
.. AGRICULTURAL ENGINEERING
.. CHEMICAL ENGINEERING
.. CIVIL ENGINEERING
.. OCEAN ENGINEERING
.. OPERATING ENGINEERING
. ENGINEERING TECHNOLOGY
. ETIOLOGY
. FORESTRY
. GENETIC ENGINEERING
. HOROLOGY
. HYDRAULICS
. INFORMATION TECHNOLOGY

TECHNOLOGY
(CONTINUED)

. JOURNALISM
. . NEW JOURNALISM
. . NEWS REPORTING
. . NEWS WRITING
. . PHOTOJOURNALISM
. LABORATORY TECHNOLOGY
. LEXICOGRAPHY
. MANUFACTURING
. . ASSEMBLY (MANUFACTURING)
. . MASS PRODUCTION
. MARKETING
. . MERCHANDISING
. . RETAILING
. . SALESMANSHIP
. . WHOLESALING
. MASONRY
. . BRICKLAYING
. MECHANICS (PROCESS)
. . AUTO MECHANICS
. . AVIATION MECHANICS
. . REFRIGERATION MECHANICS
. . SMALL ENGINE MECHANICS
. MEDICINE
. . ANESTHESIOLOGY
. . AUDIOLOGY
. . BIOMEDICINE
. . DENTISTRY
. . DIETETICS
. . ELECTROENCEPHALOGRAPHY
. . EPIDEMIOLOGY
. . FAMILY PRACTICE
(MEDICINE)
. . GERIATRICS
. . GYNECOLOGY
. . INTERNAL MEDICINE
. . NEUROLOGY
. . NURSING
. . . PRACTICAL NURSING
. . OBSTETRICS
. . ONCOLOGY
. . OPHTHALMOLOGY
. . OSTEOPATHY
. . PATHOLOGY
. . . PLANT PATHOLOGY
. . . PSYCHOPATHOLOGY
. . . SPEECH PATHOLOGY
. . PEDIATRICS
. . PHARMACOLOGY
. . PHARMACY
. . PODIATRY
. . PREVENTIVE MEDICINE
. . PRIMARY HEALTH CARE
. . PSYCHIATRY
. . SURGERY
. . TOXICOLOGY
. . VETERINARY MEDICINE
. METALLURGY
. METAL WORKING
. . SHEET METAL WORK
. MINING
. NAVIGATION
. OPTOMETRY
. PLUMBING
. POWER TECHNOLOGY
. . NUCLEAR TECHNOLOGY
. RADIOLOGY
. REPROGRAPHY
. . MICROREPRODUCTION
. WATER TREATMENT
. WELDING
. WILDLIFE MANAGEMENT
. WOODWORKING
. . CABINETMAKING
. . CARPENTRY

TECHNOLOGY TRANSFER

: : TECHNOLOGY
: COMMUNICATIONS
TELECOMMUNICATIONS
. COMMUNICATIONS SATELLITES
. ELECTRONIC MAIL
. ELECTRONIC PUBLISHING
. FACSIMILE TRANSMISSION
. RADIO
. . EDUCATIONAL RADIO
. TELECONFERENCING
. TELEPHONE COMMUNICATIONS
SYSTEMS
. TELEVISION
. . BROADCAST TELEVISION
. . CABLE TELEVISION
. . CHILDRENS TELEVISION
. . CLOSED CIRCUIT
TELEVISION
. . COMMERCIAL TELEVISION
. . EDUCATIONAL TELEVISION
. . PUBLIC TELEVISION
. VIDEOTEX

: : : TECHNOLOGY
: : COMMUNICATIONS
: TELECOMMUNICATIONS
TELECONFERENCING

: : CURRICULUM
: COURSES
TELECOURSES

: READING MATERIALS
TELEGRAPHIC MATERIALS

: : BUSINESS
: INDUSTRY
TELEPHONE COMMUNICATIONS
INDUSTRY

: : : TECHNOLOGY
: : COMMUNICATIONS
: TELECOMMUNICATIONS
TELEPHONE COMMUNICATIONS
SYSTEMS

: : : METHODS
: : EDUCATIONAL METHODS
: TEACHING METHODS
TELEPHONE INSTRUCTION

: INSTRUCTION
TELEPHONE USAGE INSTRUCTION

: : : TECHNOLOGY
: : COMMUNICATIONS
: TELECOMMUNICATIONS
: MASS MEDIA
TELEVISION
. BROADCAST TELEVISION
. CABLE TELEVISION
. CHILDRENS TELEVISION
. CLOSED CIRCUIT TELEVISION
. COMMERCIAL TELEVISION
. EDUCATIONAL TELEVISION
. PUBLIC TELEVISION

: : : : : SERVICES
: : : : INFORMATION SERVICES
: : : INFORMATION
DISSEMINATION
: : : COMMUNICATION (THOUGHT
TRANSFER)
: : PUBLICITY
: ADVERTISING
TELEVISION COMMERCIALS

: CURRICULUM
TELEVISION CURRICULUM

: : METHODS
: PRODUCTION TECHNIQUES
: LIGHTING
TELEVISION LIGHTING

: : : : GROUPS
: : : PERSONNEL
: : NONPROFESSIONAL
PERSONNEL
: SKILLED WORKERS
TELEVISION RADIO REPAIRERS

: : RESEARCH
: MEDIA RESEARCH
TELEVISION RESEARCH

: FACILITIES
TELEVISION STUDIOS

: : : METHODS
: : EVALUATION METHODS
: SURVEYS
TELEVISION SURVEYS

: : : : GROUPS
: : : PERSONNEL
: : PROFESSIONAL PERSONNEL
: TEACHERS
TELEVISION TEACHERS

: ACTIVITIES
TELEVISION VIEWING

: : LANGUAGES
: DRAVIDIAN LANGUAGES
TELUGU

TEMPERATURE

TENL (1968 1980)

: : : : ACTIVITIES
: : : PHYSICAL ACTIVITIES
: : ATHLETICS
: RACQUET SPORTS
TENNIS

: : : : : LINGUISTICS
: : : : DESCRIPTIVE
LINGUISTICS
: : : GRAMMAR
: : MORPHOLOGY (LANGUAGES)
: MORPHEMES
TENSES (GRAMMAR)

: : STATUS
: EMPLOYMENT LEVEL
TENURE

: : : : GROUPS
: : : PERSONNEL
: : SCHOOL PERSONNEL
: : : : GROUPS
: : : PERSONNEL
: : PROFESSIONAL PERSONNEL
: FACULTY
TENURED FACULTY

: EDUCATION
TERMINAL EDUCATION

: : GROUPS
: STUDENTS
TERMINAL STUDENTS

TERMINATION OF TREATMENT

: : : BEHAVIOR
: : SOCIAL BEHAVIOR
: ANTISOCIAL BEHAVIOR
TERRORISM

: : PSYCHOLOGICAL PATTERNS
: ANXIETY
TEST ANXIETY

: BIAS
TEST BIAS

: INSTRUCTION
TEST COACHING

: : DEVELOPMENT
: MATERIAL DEVELOPMENT
TEST CONSTRUCTION

TEST FORMAT

: : METHODS
: MEASUREMENT TECHNIQUES
TESTING
. ADAPTIVE TESTING
. COMPARATIVE TESTING
. COMPUTER ASSISTED TESTING
. CONFIDENCE TESTING
. EDUCATIONAL TESTING
. GROUP TESTING
. INDIVIDUAL TESTING
. MINIMUM COMPETENCY
TESTING
. PSYCHOLOGICAL TESTING

: PROBLEMS
TESTING PROBLEMS

: PROGRAMS
TESTING PROGRAMS

: : : : METHODS
: : : EVALUATION METHODS
: : DATA ANALYSIS
: DATA INTERPRETATION
TEST INTERPRETATION

TEST ITEMS

TEST LENGTH

: : : PUBLICATIONS
: : REFERENCE MATERIALS
: GUIDES
TEST MANUALS

: : : DATA
: : STATISTICAL DATA
: NORMS
TEST NORMS

: : : : STANDARDS
: : : CRITERIA
: : EVALUATION CRITERIA
: RELIABILITY
TEST RELIABILITY

TEST RESULTS

: PUBLICATIONS
TEST REVIEWS

: MEASURES (INDIVIDUALS)
TESTS
. ACHIEVEMENT TESTS
. . EQUIVALENCY TESTS
. . MASTERY TESTS
. . NATIONAL COMPETENCY
TESTS
. APTITUDE TESTS
. . READING READINESS TESTS
. . SCHOOL READINESS TESTS
. AUDITORY TESTS
. . AUDIOMETRIC TESTS
. COGNITIVE TESTS
. . INTELLIGENCE TESTS
. . PERCEPTION TESTS
. . . TACTUAL VISUAL TESTS
. COLLEGE ENTRANCE
EXAMINATIONS
. CREATIVITY TESTS
. CRITERION REFERENCED
TESTS
. . MASTERY TESTS
. CULTURE FAIR TESTS
. DIAGNOSTIC TESTS
. FIELD TESTS
. LICENSING EXAMINATIONS
(PROFESSIONS)
. MATHEMATICS TESTS
. MATURITY TESTS

TESTS
(CONTINUED)
. NONVERBAL TESTS
. . VISUAL MEASURES
. NORM REFERENCED TESTS
. OBJECTIVE TESTS
. . MULTIPLE CHOICE TESTS
. OCCUPATIONAL TESTS
. . WORK SAMPLE TESTS
. OPEN BOOK TESTS
. PERFORMANCE TESTS
. PRESCHOOL TESTS
. PRETESTS POSTTESTS
. PROGNOSTIC TESTS
. SCIENCE TESTS
. SCREENING TESTS
. SITUATIONAL TESTS
. STANDARDIZED TESTS
. TEACHER MADE TESTS
. TIMED TESTS
. VERBAL TESTS
. . ESSAY TESTS
. . LANGUAGE TESTS
. . LISTENING COMPREHENSION
TESTS
. . READING TESTS
. . . INFORMAL READING
INVENTORIES
. . SPEECH TESTS
. VISION TESTS

: EQUIPMENT
TEST SCORING MACHINES

: SELECTION
TEST SELECTION

: THEORIES
TEST THEORY
. LATENT TRAIT THEORY

TEST USE

: : : : STANDARDS
: : : CRITERIA
: : EVALUATION CRITERIA
: VALIDITY
TEST VALIDITY
. CONSTRUCT VALIDITY
. CONTENT VALIDITY

TEST WISENESS

: BIAS
TEXTBOOK BIAS

TEXTBOOK CONTENT

: : EVALUATION
: INSTRUCTIONAL MATERIAL
EVALUATION
TEXTBOOK EVALUATION

TEXTBOOK PREPARATION

: : METHODS
: PRODUCTION TECHNIQUES
TEXTBOOK PUBLICATION

TEXTBOOK PUBLICATIONS (1966
1980)

: : RESEARCH
: MEDIA RESEARCH
TEXTBOOK RESEARCH

: : EDUCATIONAL MEDIA
: INSTRUCTIONAL MATERIALS
: : PUBLICATIONS
: BOOKS
TEXTBOOKS
. HISTORY TEXTBOOKS
. MULTICULTURAL TEXTBOOKS

: : SELECTION
: MEDIA SELECTION
TEXTBOOK SELECTION

: STANDARDS
TEXTBOOK STANDARDS

: INSTRUCTION
TEXTILES INSTRUCTION

TEXTUAL CRITICISM (1969
1980)

: : LANGUAGES
: SINO TIBETAN LANGUAGES
THAI

: : : LIBERAL ARTS
: : HUMANITIES
: FINE ARTS
THEATER ARTS
. ACTING
. CHORAL SPEAKING
. DRAMA
. . COMEDY
. . . SKITS
. . SCRIPTS
. . TRAGEDY
. DRAMATICS
. . CREATIVE DRAMATICS
. OPERA
. PANTOMIME
. PUPPETRY
. READERS THEATER

: FACILITIES
THEATERS

: : : METHODS
: : EDUCATIONAL METHODS
: TEACHING METHODS
THEMATIC APPROACH

: : EDUCATION
: PROFESSIONAL EDUCATION
THEOLOGICAL EDUCATION

THEORETICAL CRITICISM (1969
1980)

THEORIES
. ATOMIC THEORY
. BEHAVIOR THEORIES
. . ADAPTATION LEVEL THEORY
. . ATTRIBUTION THEORY
. . MEDIATION THEORY
. COUNSELING THEORIES
. EDUCATIONAL THEORIES
. GAME THEORY
. GENERALIZABILITY THEORY
. INFORMATION THEORY
. KINETIC MOLECULAR THEORY
. LEARNING THEORIES
. LINGUISTIC THEORY
. . CASE (GRAMMAR)
. . GENERATIVE GRAMMAR
. . . TRANSFORMATIONAL
GENERATIVE GRAMMAR
. . . . CONTEXT FREE GRAMMAR
. . . . DEEP STRUCTURE
. . . . KERNEL SENTENCES
. . . . SENTENCE COMBINING
. . . . SURFACE STRUCTURE
. . GENERATIVE PHONOLOGY
. . LINGUISTIC COMPETENCE
. . LINGUISTIC PERFORMANCE
. . SEMIOTICS
. . . PRAGMATICS
. . . SEMANTICS
. . . . LEXICOLOGY
. . STRUCTURAL GRAMMAR
. . TRADITIONAL GRAMMAR
. MUSIC THEORY
. PERSONALITY THEORIES
. PIAGETIAN THEORY
. RELATIVITY
. ROLE THEORY
. SET THEORY
. SOCIAL THEORIES
. . ORGANIZATIONAL THEORIES
. . SOCIAL EXCHANGE THEORY
. TEST THEORY
. . LATENT TRAIT THEORY

: RELATIONSHIP
THEORY PRACTICE RELATIONSHIP

: ENVIRONMENT
THERAPEUTIC ENVIRONMENT

: THERAPY
: RECREATION
THERAPEUTIC RECREATION
. PLAY THERAPY

: : : GROUPS
: : PERSONNEL
: PROFESSIONAL PERSONNEL
: : : : GROUPS
: : : PERSONNEL
: : HEALTH PERSONNEL
: ALLIED HEALTH PERSONNEL
THERAPISTS
. OCCUPATIONAL THERAPISTS
. PHYSICAL THERAPISTS

THERAPY
. ART THERAPY
. BIBLIOTHERAPY
. DANCE THERAPY
. DRUG THERAPY
. EDUCATIONAL THERAPY
. GROUP THERAPY
. HEARING THERAPY
. MUSIC THERAPY
. OCCUPATIONAL THERAPY
. PHYSICAL THERAPY
. PSYCHOTHERAPY
. . GESTALT THERAPY
. . MILIEU THERAPY
. . RATIONAL EMOTIVE THERAPY
. . REALITY THERAPY
. . RELAXATION TRAINING
. . TRANSACTIONAL ANALYSIS
. RESPIRATORY THERAPY
. SPEECH THERAPY
. THERAPEUTIC RECREATION
. . PLAY THERAPY

: : ENVIRONMENT
: PHYSICAL ENVIRONMENT
THERMAL ENVIRONMENT

: : : : : LIBERAL ARTS
: : : : SCIENCES
: : : NATURAL SCIENCES
: : PHYSICAL SCIENCES
: PHYSICS
THERMODYNAMICS

: : PUBLICATIONS
: REFERENCE MATERIALS
THESAURI

: : PUBLICATIONS
: REPORTS
THESES
. DOCTORAL DISSERTATIONS
. MASTERS THESES

: VISUAL AIDS
THREE DIMENSIONAL AIDS

: : ABILITY
: LANGUAGE PROFICIENCY
: : : : ABILITY
: : : SKILLS
: : LANGUAGE SKILLS
: : : : ABILITY
: : : SKILLS
: : COMMUNICATION SKILLS
: COMMUNICATIVE COMPETENCE
(LANGUAGES)
THRESHOLD LEVEL (LANGUAGES)

: : LANGUAGES
: SINO TIBETAN LANGUAGES
TIBETAN

: SCIENTIFIC CONCEPTS
TIME

: : : PLANNING
: : SCHEDULING
: SCHOOL SCHEDULES
TIME BLOCKS

: : MEASURES (INDIVIDUALS)
: TESTS
TIMED TESTS

: INFLUENCES
TIME FACTORS (LEARNING)

: : GOVERNANCE
: ADMINISTRATION
TIME MANAGEMENT

TIME ON TASK

: REINFORCEMENT
TIMEOUT

TIME PERSPECTIVE

: : : : SERVICES
: : : INFORMATION SERVICES
: : INFORMATION PROCESSING
: DATA PROCESSING
TIME SHARING

: GROUPS
TISSUE DONORS

: FIELD CROPS
TOBACCO

: : : : GROUPS
: : : AGE GROUPS
: : CHILDREN
: YOUNG CHILDREN
TODDLERS

: : FACILITIES
: SANITARY FACILITIES
TOILET FACILITIES

: REINFORCEMENT
TOKEN ECONOMY

TOKENISM

: LANGUAGE
TONE LANGUAGES

: : : : : GROUPS
: : : : PERSONNEL
: : : NONPROFESSIONAL
PERSONNEL
: : SKILLED WORKERS
: MACHINISTS
TOOL AND DIE MAKERS

: : : LIBERAL ARTS
: : SCIENCES
: SOCIAL SCIENCES
TOPOGRAPHY

::: LIBERAL ARTS
:: MATHEMATICS
: GEOMETRY
TOPOLOGY

TORTS

: COMMUNICATION (THOUGHT TRANSFER)
TOTAL COMMUNICATION

TOTALITARIANISM
. NAZISM

:: BUSINESS
: INDUSTRY
TOURISM

:: TECHNOLOGY
: MEDICINE
TOXICOLOGY

TOYS

::: ACTIVITIES
:: PHYSICAL ACTIVITIES
: ATHLETICS
TRACK AND FIELD

TRACKING (1968 1980)

TRACK SYSTEM (EDUCATION)

:: EQUIPMENT
: MOTOR VEHICLES
TRACTORS

:: EDUCATION
: VOCATIONAL EDUCATION
TRADE AND INDUSTRIAL EDUCATION

::::: GROUPS
:::: PERSONNEL
::: PROFESSIONAL PERSONNEL
:: TEACHERS
: VOCATIONAL EDUCATION TEACHERS
TRADE AND INDUSTRIAL TEACHERS

:: THEORIES
: LINGUISTIC THEORY
TRADITIONAL GRAMMAR

TRADITIONALISM

:: INSTITUTIONS
: SCHOOLS
TRADITIONAL SCHOOLS

: ACCIDENTS
TRAFFIC ACCIDENTS

TRAFFIC CIRCULATION

TRAFFIC CONTROL
. AIR TRAFFIC CONTROL

: SAFETY
TRAFFIC SAFETY

::::: LIBERAL ARTS
:::: HUMANITIES
::: FINE ARTS
:: THEATER ARTS
:::: LIBERAL ARTS
::: HUMANITIES
:: LITERATURE
: DRAMA
TRAGEDY

: FACILITIES
TRAILS

: GROUPS
TRAINEES

:: GROUPS
: PERSONNEL
TRAINERS

TRAINING
. COUNSELOR TRAINING
. CROSS CULTURAL TRAINING
. FLIGHT TRAINING
. INDUSTRIAL TRAINING
. JOB TRAINING
.. CUSTODIAN TRAINING
.. OFF THE JOB TRAINING
.. ON THE JOB TRAINING
... APPRENTICESHIPS
. LABORATORY TRAINING
. LEADERSHIP TRAINING
. MILITARY TRAINING
. PROFESSIONAL TRAINING
. RETRAINING
. SENSITIVITY TRAINING
. SENSORY TRAINING
.. AUDITORY TRAINING
. SUPERVISORY TRAINING
. TEAM TRAINING
. TRAVEL TRAINING
. VOLUNTEER TRAINING

: FINANCIAL SUPPORT
TRAINING ALLOWANCES

TRAINING LABORATORIES (1967 1980)

::: METHODS
:: EDUCATIONAL METHODS
: TEACHING METHODS
TRAINING METHODS
. MANAGEMENT GAMES
. MICROCOUNSELING
. MICROTEACHING

: OBJECTIVES
TRAINING OBJECTIVES

:: THERAPY
: PSYCHOTHERAPY
TRANSACTIONAL ANALYSIS

::: COGNITIVE PROCESSES
:: METACOGNITION
: MEDITATION
TRANSCENDENTAL MEDITATION

: LEARNING
TRANSFER OF TRAINING

: POLICY
TRANSFER POLICY

: PROGRAMS
TRANSFER PROGRAMS
. FREE CHOICE TRANSFER PROGRAMS

TRANSFERS (1966 1980)

:: GROUPS
: STUDENTS
TRANSFER STUDENTS
. COLLEGE TRANSFER STUDENTS

::: THEORIES
:: LINGUISTIC THEORY
: GENERATIVE GRAMMAR
TRANSFORMATIONAL GENERATIVE GRAMMAR
. CONTEXT FREE GRAMMAR
. DEEP STRUCTURE
. KERNEL SENTENCES
. SENTENCE COMBINING
. SURFACE STRUCTURE

TRANSFORMATIONS (MATHEMATICS)

:: GROUPS
: MIGRANTS
::: GROUPS
:: AGE GROUPS
: CHILDREN
TRANSIENT CHILDREN

::: EQUIPMENT
:: ELECTRONIC EQUIPMENT
: SEMICONDUCTOR DEVICES
TRANSISTORS

: PROGRAMS
TRANSITIONAL PROGRAMS

:: INSTITUTIONS
: SCHOOLS
TRANSITIONAL SCHOOLS

TRANSLATION
. DEAF INTERPRETING
. MACHINE TRANSLATION

: VISUAL AIDS
: NONPRINT MEDIA
TRANSPARENCIES
. SLIDES

TRANSPORTATION
. AIR TRANSPORTATION
. BUS TRANSPORTATION
. RAIL TRANSPORTATION
. STUDENT TRANSPORTATION

: ACTIVITIES
TRAVEL

: TRAINING
TRAVEL TRAINING

TREATIES

TREES

::: METHODS
:: EVALUATION METHODS
: DATA ANALYSIS
TREND ANALYSIS

: SELF DETERMINATION
TRIBAL SOVEREIGNTY

: GROUPS
TRIBES

:: LIBERAL ARTS
: MATHEMATICS
TRIGONOMETRY

::: PLANNING
:: SCHEDULING
: SCHOOL SCHEDULES
TRIMESTER SYSTEM

TRUANCY

:: DATA
: SCORES
TRUE SCORES

: ATTITUDES
TRUST (PSYCHOLOGY)

::: GROUPS
:: PERSONNEL
: ADMINISTRATORS
TRUSTEES

:: RESPONSIBILITY
: LEGAL RESPONSIBILITY
TRUST RESPONSIBILITY (GOVERNMENT)

TRUSTS (FINANCIAL)

::: COSTS
:: STUDENT COSTS
: INSTRUCTIONAL STUDENT COSTS
:: COSTS
: FEES
TUITION

::: FINANCIAL SUPPORT
:: STUDENT FINANCIAL AID
: SCHOLARSHIPS
:: FINANCIAL SUPPORT
: GRANTS
TUITION GRANTS

:::: ACTIVITIES
::: PHYSICAL ACTIVITIES
:: ATHLETICS
: GYMNASTICS
TUMBLING

:::: TECHNOLOGY
::: AGRICULTURE
:: HORTICULTURE
: ORNAMENTAL HORTICULTURE
TURF MANAGEMENT

:: LANGUAGES
: URALIC ALTAIC LANGUAGES
TURKIC LANGUAGES
. AZERBAIJANI
. BASHKIR
. CHUVASH
. KIRGHIZ
. TATAR
. TURKISH
. UZBEK
. YAKUT

::: LANGUAGES
:: URALIC ALTAIC LANGUAGES
: TURKIC LANGUAGES
TURKISH

: PROGRAMS
TUTORIAL PROGRAMS

:: INSTRUCTION
: INDIVIDUAL INSTRUCTION
TUTORING
. PROGRAMED TUTORING

::::GROUPS
:::PERSONNEL
::PROFESSIONAL PERSONNEL
:TEACHERS
TUTORS

:::LIBERAL ARTS
::HUMANITIES
:LITERATURE
TWENTIETH CENTURY LITERATURE

::GROUPS
:SIBLINGS
TWINS

:::INSTITUTIONS
::SCHOOLS
:COLLEGES
TWO YEAR COLLEGES
.COMMUNITY COLLEGES
.TECHNICAL INSTITUTES

:::GROUPS
::STUDENTS
:COLLEGE STUDENTS
TWO YEAR COLLEGE STUDENTS

:::ABILITY
::SKILLS
:BUSINESS SKILLS
TYPEWRITING

::LANGUAGES
:AMERICAN INDIAN LANGUAGES
TZELTAL

::LANGUAGES
:AMERICAN INDIAN LANGUAGES
TZOTZIL

:::LANGUAGES
::INDO EUROPEAN LANGUAGES
:SLAVIC LANGUAGES
UKRAINIAN

:LANGUAGE
UNCOMMONLY TAUGHT LANGUAGES

:ACHIEVEMENT
UNDERACHIEVEMENT

:EMPLOYMENT
UNDEREMPLOYMENT

:::GROUPS
::STUDENTS
:COLLEGE STUDENTS
UNDERGRADUATE STUDENTS
.PREMEDICAL STUDENTS

:::EDUCATION
::POSTSECONDARY EDUCATION
:HIGHER EDUCATION
UNDERGRADUATE STUDY

:FACILITIES
UNDERGROUND FACILITIES

::ACTIVITIES
:PHYSICAL ACTIVITIES
UNDERWATER DIVING

:::GROUPS
::MIGRANTS
:IMMIGRANTS
UNDOCUMENTED IMMIGRANTS

UNEMPLOYMENT
.STRUCTURAL UNEMPLOYMENT

::METHODS
:INSURANCE
:FINANCIAL SUPPORT
UNEMPLOYMENT INSURANCE

:CURRICULUM
UNIFIED STUDIES CURRICULUM

:::PUBLICATIONS
::REFERENCE MATERIALS
:::PUBLICATIONS
::CATALOGS
:LIBRARY CATALOGS
UNION CATALOGS

:GROUPS
UNION MEMBERS

::GROUPS
:ORGANIZATIONS (GROUPS)
UNIONS

:COSTS
UNIT COSTS

::CURRICULUM
:COURSES
UNITED STATES GOVERNMENT (COURSE)

:::::LIBERAL ARTS
::::SCIENCES
:::SOCIAL SCIENCES
::::LIBERAL ARTS
:::HUMANITIES
::HISTORY
:NORTH AMERICAN HISTORY
UNITED STATES HISTORY
.CIVIL WAR (UNITED STATES)
.COLONIAL HISTORY (UNITED STATES)
.MEXICAN AMERICAN HISTORY
.RECONSTRUCTION ERA
.REVOLUTIONARY WAR (UNITED STATES)
.STATE HISTORY

::::LIBERAL ARTS
:::HUMANITIES
::LITERATURE
:NORTH AMERICAN LITERATURE
UNITED STATES LITERATURE
.HISPANIC AMERICAN LITERATURE
..MEXICAN AMERICAN LITERATURE

UNIT PLAN (1966 1980)

::CURRICULUM
:COURSES
UNITS OF STUDY
.ACTIVITY UNITS

:::INSTITUTIONS
::SCHOOLS
:COLLEGES
UNIVERSITIES
.LAND GRANT UNIVERSITIES
.OPEN UNIVERSITIES
.RESEARCH UNIVERSITIES
.STATE UNIVERSITIES
.URBAN UNIVERSITIES

:OCCUPATIONS
UNSKILLED OCCUPATIONS

:::GROUPS
::PERSONNEL
:NONPROFESSIONAL PERSONNEL
UNSKILLED WORKERS
.LABORERS
..AGRICULTURAL LABORERS
...MIGRANT WORKERS
...SEASONAL LABORERS
..AUXILIARY LABORERS

:::GROUPS
::PARENTS
:::GROUPS
::FEMALES
:MOTHERS
UNWED MOTHERS

UNWRITTEN LANGUAGE (1968 1980)

:LANGUAGE
UNWRITTEN LANGUAGES

::GROUPS
:SOCIAL CLASS
UPPER CLASS

:::INSTITUTIONS
::SCHOOLS
:COLLEGES
UPPER DIVISION COLLEGES

:LANGUAGES
URALIC ALTAIC LANGUAGES
.FINNO UGRIC LANGUAGES
..CHEREMIS
..ESTONIAN
..FINNISH
..HUNGARIAN
..OSTYAK
..VOGUL
.MANCHU
.MONGOLIAN LANGUAGES
..BURIAT
..DAGUR
..MONGOLIAN
.SAMOYED LANGUAGES
..YURAK
.TURKIC LANGUAGES
..AZERBAIJANI
..BASHKIR
..CHUVASH
..KIRGHIZ
..TATAR
..TURKISH
..UZBEK
..YAKUT

::GROUPS
:URBAN POPULATION
::::GROUPS
:::ETHNIC GROUPS
::AMERICAN INDIANS
:NONRESERVATION AMERICAN INDIANS
URBAN AMERICAN INDIANS

:GEOGRAPHIC REGIONS
URBAN AREAS
.INNER CITY
.MUNICIPALITIES

:CULTURE
URBAN CULTURE

::::LIBERAL ARTS
:::SCIENCES
::SOCIAL SCIENCES
:DEMOGRAPHY
URBAN DEMOGRAPHY

:EDUCATION
URBAN EDUCATION

:ENVIRONMENT
URBAN ENVIRONMENT

::EDUCATION
:EXTENSION EDUCATION
URBAN EXTENSION

:IMPROVEMENT
URBAN IMPROVEMENT
.URBAN RENEWAL

:DEVELOPMENT
URBANIZATION

:LANGUAGE
URBAN LANGUAGE

:PLANNING
URBAN PLANNING

:GROUPS
URBAN POPULATION
.URBAN AMERICAN INDIANS
.URBAN YOUTH

:PROBLEMS
URBAN PROBLEMS

:PROGRAMS
URBAN PROGRAMS

::IMPROVEMENT
:URBAN IMPROVEMENT
URBAN RENEWAL

:::GROUPS
::ORGANIZATIONS (GROUPS)
:AGENCIES
URBAN RENEWAL AGENCIES

::INSTITUTIONS
:SCHOOLS
URBAN SCHOOLS
.URBAN UNIVERSITIES

:CURRICULUM
URBAN STUDIES

:::OCCUPATIONS
::PROFESSIONAL OCCUPATIONS
:TEACHING (OCCUPATION)
URBAN TEACHING

::MOBILITY
:MIGRATION
URBAN TO RURAL MIGRATION

::MOBILITY
:MIGRATION
URBAN TO SUBURBAN MIGRATION

:::INSTITUTIONS
::SCHOOLS
:URBAN SCHOOLS
::::INSTITUTIONS
:::SCHOOLS
::COLLEGES
:UNIVERSITIES
URBAN UNIVERSITIES

::GROUPS
:YOUTH
::GROUPS
:URBAN POPULATION
URBAN YOUTH

::LANGUAGES
:INDO EUROPEAN LANGUAGES
URDU

:NEEDS
USER NEEDS (INFORMATION)

: GROUPS
USERS (INFORMATION)

: ATTITUDES
USER SATISFACTION (INFORMATION)

: RESEARCH
USE STUDIES
. FACILITY UTILIZATION RESEARCH

UTILITIES

: : LANGUAGES
: AMERICAN INDIAN LANGUAGES
UTO AZTECAN LANGUAGES
. HOPI
. PAPAGO

: : : LANGUAGES
: : URALIC ALTAIC LANGUAGES
: TURKIC LANGUAGES
UZBEK

: PROGRAMS
VACATION PROGRAMS

VACATIONS

: PROGRAMS
VALIDATED PROGRAMS

: : : STANDARDS
: : CRITERIA
: EVALUATION CRITERIA
VALIDITY
. CONCURRENT VALIDITY
. PREDICTIVE VALIDITY
. PROOF (MATHEMATICS)
. TEST VALIDITY
. . CONSTRUCT VALIDITY
. . CONTENT VALIDITY

: : : COGNITIVE PROCESSES
: : CRITICAL THINKING
: EVALUATIVE THINKING
VALUE JUDGMENT

VALUES
. AESTHETIC VALUES
. DEMOCRATIC VALUES
. MORAL VALUES
. SOCIAL VALUES

VALUES CLARIFICATION

: EDUCATION
VALUES EDUCATION

: : : BEHAVIOR
: : SOCIAL BEHAVIOR
: ANTISOCIAL BEHAVIOR
VANDALISM
. SCHOOL VANDALISM

: : MATHEMATICAL CONCEPTS
: GEOMETRIC CONCEPTS
: : : LIBERAL ARTS
: : MATHEMATICS
: ALGEBRA
VECTORS (MATHEMATICS)

VEHICULAR TRAFFIC

: EQUIPMENT
VENDING MACHINES

: : : DISABILITIES
: : DISEASES
: COMMUNICABLE DISEASES
VENEREAL DISEASES

: CLIMATE CONTROL
VENTILATION

: ABILITY
VERBAL ABILITY
. READING ABILITY
. . READING SKILLS
. . . READING COMPREHENSION
. . . READING RATE

: COMMUNICATION (THOUGHT TRANSFER)
VERBAL COMMUNICATION
. BUSINESS CORRESPONDENCE
. DICTATION
. LETTERS (CORRESPONDENCE)

: : : DEVELOPMENT
: : INDIVIDUAL DEVELOPMENT
: COGNITIVE DEVELOPMENT
VERBAL DEVELOPMENT
. LANGUAGE ACQUISITION

: LEARNING
VERBAL LEARNING

: : CONDITIONING
: OPERANT CONDITIONING
VERBAL OPERANT CONDITIONING

: STIMULI
VERBAL STIMULI

: : MEASURES (INDIVIDUALS)
: TESTS
VERBAL TESTS
. ESSAY TESTS
. LANGUAGE TESTS
. LISTENING COMPREHENSION TESTS
. READING TESTS
. . INFORMAL READING INVENTORIES
. SPEECH TESTS

: : : : : LINGUISTICS
: : : : DESCRIPTIVE LINGUISTICS
: : : GRAMMAR
: : SYNTAX
: FORM CLASSES (LANGUAGES)
VERBS

: ORGANIZATION
VERTICAL ORGANIZATION

: GROUPS
VETERANS

: : EDUCATION
: ADULT EDUCATION
VETERANS EDUCATION

: : : GROUPS
: : PERSONNEL
: PROFESSIONAL PERSONNEL
: : : GROUPS
: : PERSONNEL
: HEALTH PERSONNEL
VETERINARIANS

: : : GROUPS
: : PERSONNEL
: PARAPROFESSIONAL PERSONNEL
: : : : GROUPS
: : : PERSONNEL
: : HEALTH PERSONNEL
: ALLIED HEALTH PERSONNEL
VETERINARY ASSISTANTS

: : : EDUCATION
: : PROFESSIONAL EDUCATION
: MEDICAL EDUCATION
VETERINARY MEDICAL EDUCATION

: : TECHNOLOGY
: MEDICINE
VETERINARY MEDICINE

: GROUPS
VICTIMS OF CRIME

: : : LIBERAL ARTS
: : HUMANITIES
: LITERATURE
VICTORIAN LITERATURE

: VISUAL AIDS
: NONPRINT MEDIA
VIDEODISKS

: VISUAL AIDS
: : EQUIPMENT
: ELECTRONIC EQUIPMENT
VIDEO EQUIPMENT
. VIDEOTAPE RECORDERS

: : : : RESOURCES
: : : SUPPLIES
: : MAGNETIC TAPES
: MAGNETIC TAPE CASSETTES
VIDEOTAPE CASSETTES

: : VISUAL AIDS
: : : EQUIPMENT
: : ELECTRONIC EQUIPMENT
: VIDEO EQUIPMENT
: : : EQUIPMENT
: : ELECTRONIC EQUIPMENT
: TAPE RECORDERS
VIDEOTAPE RECORDERS

: VISUAL AIDS
: : NONPRINT MEDIA
: TAPE RECORDINGS
VIDEOTAPE RECORDINGS

: : : TECHNOLOGY
: : COMMUNICATIONS
: TELECOMMUNICATIONS
: : SERVICES
: INFORMATION SERVICES
VIDEOTEX

: LANGUAGES
VIETNAMESE

: : GROUPS
: INDOCHINESE
VIETNAMESE PEOPLE

: : : BEHAVIOR
: : SOCIAL BEHAVIOR
: ANTISOCIAL BEHAVIOR
VIOLENCE
. FAMILY VIOLENCE

: : : LANGUAGES
: : MALAYO POLYNESIAN LANGUAGES
: INDONESIAN LANGUAGES
VISAYAN
. CEBUANO

: INSTRUMENTATION
VISIBLE SPEECH

VISION

: : MEASURES (INDIVIDUALS)
: TESTS
VISION TESTS

: : : GROUPS
: : PERSONNEL
: PARAPROFESSIONAL PERSONNEL
VISITING HOMEMAKERS

: : : COGNITIVE PROCESSES
: : PERCEPTION
: VISUAL PERCEPTION
VISUAL ACUITY

VISUAL AIDS
. BULLETIN BOARDS
. CARTOONS
. CHALKBOARDS
. CHARTS
. . EXPERIENCE CHARTS
. . FLOW CHARTS
. DIAGRAMS
. DISPLAY AIDS
. FILMS
. . FOREIGN LANGUAGE FILMS
. . INSTRUCTIONAL FILMS
. . KINESCOPE RECORDINGS
. . SINGLE CONCEPT FILMS
. FILMSTRIPS
. GEOMETRIC CONSTRUCTIONS
. GRAPHS
. ILLUSTRATIONS
. MAPS
. MICROFORMS
. . MICROFICHE
. . MICROFILM
. . . COMPUTER OUTPUT MICROFILM
. PHOTOGRAPHIC EQUIPMENT
. PHOTOGRAPHS
. PROJECTION EQUIPMENT
. . FILMSTRIP PROJECTORS
. . MICROFORM READERS
. . OPAQUE PROJECTORS
. . OVERHEAD PROJECTORS
. . TACHISTOSCOPES
. RAISED LINE DRAWINGS
. SCREENS (DISPLAYS)
. SIGNS
. TABLES (DATA)
. . EXPECTANCY TABLES
. THREE DIMENSIONAL AIDS
. TRANSPARENCIES
. . SLIDES
. VIDEODISKS
. VIDEO EQUIPMENT
. . VIDEOTAPE RECORDERS
. VIDEOTAPE RECORDINGS

: : : LIBERAL ARTS
: : HUMANITIES
: FINE ARTS
VISUAL ARTS
. ARCHITECTURE
. CHILDRENS ART
. DESIGN CRAFTS
. DRAFTING
. . ARCHITECTURAL DRAFTING
. . ENGINEERING DRAWING
. . TECHNICAL ILLUSTRATION
. FILM PRODUCTION
. FREEHAND DRAWING
. GRAPHIC ARTS
. . CARTOGRAPHY
. . COMPUTER GRAPHICS
. . ENGINEERING GRAPHICS
. . . ENGINEERING DRAWING
. . LAYOUT (PUBLICATIONS)
. . PRINTING
. HANDICRAFTS
. . CERAMICS
. PAINTING (VISUAL ARTS)
. PHOTOGRAPHY
. . HOLOGRAPHY
. SCULPTURE

:::COGNITIVE PROCESSES
::PERCEPTION
:VISUAL PERCEPTION
VISUAL DISCRIMINATION

::ENVIRONMENT
:PHYSICAL ENVIRONMENT
VISUAL ENVIRONMENT

:DISABILITIES
VISUAL IMPAIRMENTS
.AMETROPIA
..HYPEROPIA
..MYOPIA
.BLINDNESS
.PARTIAL VISION
.STRABISMUS

:COGNITIVE PROCESSES
VISUALIZATION

:LEARNING
VISUAL LEARNING

::ABILITY
:SKILLS
VISUAL LITERACY

::MOBILITY
:PHYSICAL MOBILITY
VISUALLY HANDICAPPED MOBILITY

:::MEASURES (INDIVIDUALS)
::TESTS
:NONVERBAL TESTS
VISUAL MEASURES

::COGNITIVE PROCESSES
:PERCEPTION
VISUAL PERCEPTION
.DEPTH PERCEPTION
.VISUAL ACUITY
.VISUAL DISCRIMINATION

:STIMULI
VISUAL STIMULI
.PICTORIAL STIMULI

VOCABULARY
.AVIATION VOCABULARY
.BANKING VOCABULARY
.BASIC VOCABULARY
.CHEMICAL NOMENCLATURE
.INTERNATIONAL TRADE VOCABULARY
.KINSHIP TERMINOLOGY
.MATHEMATICAL VOCABULARY
.MEDICAL VOCABULARY
.SIGHT VOCABULARY
.SUBJECT INDEX TERMS
.WORD LISTS

:DEVELOPMENT
VOCABULARY DEVELOPMENT

:::ABILITY
::SKILLS
:LANGUAGE SKILLS
VOCABULARY SKILLS

::::LIBERAL ARTS
:::HUMANITIES
::FINE ARTS
:MUSIC
VOCAL MUSIC
.CHORAL MUSIC
.SONGS
..ART SONG
..BALLADS
..HYMNS

::BEHAVIOR
:ADJUSTMENT (TO ENVIRONMENT)
VOCATIONAL ADJUSTMENT

:APTITUDE
VOCATIONAL APTITUDE

:::GROUPS
::PERSONNEL
:ADMINISTRATORS
VOCATIONAL DIRECTORS

:EDUCATION
VOCATIONAL EDUCATION
.ADULT VOCATIONAL EDUCATION
..ADULT FARMER EDUCATION
..YOUNG FARMER EDUCATION
.BUSINESS EDUCATION
..OFFICE OCCUPATIONS EDUCATION
.COOPERATIVE EDUCATION
.DISTRIBUTIVE EDUCATION
.OCCUPATIONAL HOME ECONOMICS
.PREVOCATIONAL EDUCATION
.TECHNICAL EDUCATION
..FIRE SCIENCE EDUCATION
.TRADE AND INDUSTRIAL EDUCATION

::::GROUPS
:::PERSONNEL
::PROFESSIONAL PERSONNEL
:TEACHERS
VOCATIONAL EDUCATION TEACHERS
.BUSINESS EDUCATION TEACHERS
.DISTRIBUTIVE EDUCATION TEACHERS
.TRADE AND INDUSTRIAL TEACHERS

:::LANGUAGE
::LANGUAGES FOR SPECIAL PURPOSES
::::LANGUAGE
:::SECOND LANGUAGES
:::::LANGUAGES
::::INDO EUROPEAN LANGUAGES
:::ENGLISH
::ENGLISH (SECOND LANGUAGE)
:ENGLISH FOR SPECIAL PURPOSES
VOCATIONAL ENGLISH (SECOND LANGUAGE)

:EVALUATION
VOCATIONAL EVALUATION

::::RESEARCH
:::::METHODS
::::EVALUATION METHODS
:::CASE STUDIES
::LONGITUDINAL STUDIES
:FOLLOWUP STUDIES
VOCATIONAL FOLLOWUP

:::INSTITUTIONS
::SCHOOLS
:VOCATIONAL SCHOOLS
::::INSTITUTIONS
:::SCHOOLS
::SECONDARY SCHOOLS
:HIGH SCHOOLS
VOCATIONAL HIGH SCHOOLS

:INTERESTS
VOCATIONAL INTERESTS

::INDIVIDUAL CHARACTERISTICS
:MATURITY (INDIVIDUALS)
VOCATIONAL MATURITY

:REHABILITATION
VOCATIONAL REHABILITATION

::INSTITUTIONS
:SCHOOLS
VOCATIONAL SCHOOLS
.VOCATIONAL HIGH SCHOOLS

::FACILITIES
:EDUCATIONAL FACILITIES
VOCATIONAL TRAINING CENTERS

:::LANGUAGES
::URALIC ALTAIC LANGUAGES
:FINNO UGRIC LANGUAGES
VOGUL

::DISABILITIES
:SPEECH HANDICAPS
VOICE DISORDERS

::::ACTIVITIES
:::PHYSICAL ACTIVITIES
::ATHLETICS
:TEAM SPORTS
VOLLEYBALL

::SCIENTIFIC CONCEPTS
:SPACE
::MATHEMATICAL CONCEPTS
:GEOMETRIC CONCEPTS
VOLUME (MATHEMATICS)

:::GROUPS
::ORGANIZATIONS (GROUPS)
:AGENCIES
VOLUNTARY AGENCIES

:SOCIAL INTEGRATION
VOLUNTARY DESEGREGATION

:GROUPS
VOLUNTEERS
.STUDENT VOLUNTEERS

:TRAINING
VOLUNTEER TRAINING

VOTER REGISTRATION

VOTING

::CIVIL LIBERTIES
:CIVIL RIGHTS
VOTING RIGHTS

::::LINGUISTICS
:::PHONOLOGY
::PHONEMICS
:PHONEMES
VOWELS

:INCOME
:EXPENDITURES
WAGES
.MINIMUM WAGE

::::GROUPS
:::PERSONNEL
::NONPROFESSIONAL PERSONNEL
:SERVICE WORKERS
WAITERS AND WAITRESSES

:CONFLICT
WAR
.NUCLEAR WARFARE

:FACILITIES
WAREHOUSES

:SANITATION
WASTE DISPOSAL
.RECYCLING

:MATTER
WASTES
.SOLID WASTES
.WASTE WATER

::MATTER
:WATER
::MATTER
:WASTES
WASTE WATER

::::GROUPS
:::PERSONNEL
::NONPROFESSIONAL PERSONNEL
:SKILLED WORKERS
WATCHMAKERS

:MATTER
WATER
.DRINKING WATER
.WASTE WATER

:POLLUTION
WATER POLLUTION

::::ACTIVITIES
:::PHYSICAL ACTIVITIES
::ATHLETICS
:TEAM SPORTS
::::ACTIVITIES
:::PHYSICAL ACTIVITIES
::ATHLETICS
:AQUATIC SPORTS
WATER POLO

WATER QUALITY

::RESOURCES
:NATURAL RESOURCES
WATER RESOURCES

::::ACTIVITIES
:::PHYSICAL ACTIVITIES
::ATHLETICS
:AQUATIC SPORTS
WATERSKIING

:TECHNOLOGY
WATER TREATMENT

WEATHER

WEEDS

:PROGRAMS
WEEKEND PROGRAMS

WEIGHT (1968 1980)

:SCIENTIFIC CONCEPTS
WEIGHT (MASS)

::DATA
:SCORES
WEIGHTED SCORES

: : : ACTIVITIES
: : PHYSICAL ACTIVITIES
: LIFTING
: : : ACTIVITIES
: : PHYSICAL ACTIVITIES
: ATHLETICS
WEIGHTLIFTING

: TECHNOLOGY
WELDING

WELFARE (1966 1980)

: : : : GROUPS
: : : ORGANIZATIONS (GROUPS)
: : AGENCIES
: SOCIAL AGENCIES
WELFARE AGENCIES

: GROUPS
WELFARE RECIPIENTS

: : : SERVICES
: : HUMAN SERVICES
: SOCIAL SERVICES
WELFARE SERVICES
. MIGRANT WELFARE SERVICES

: QUALITY OF LIFE
WELL BEING
. CHILD WELFARE
. STUDENT WELFARE
. TEACHER WELFARE

: : LANGUAGES
: INDO EUROPEAN LANGUAGES
WELSH

: CULTURE
WESTERN CIVILIZATION

: : : EQUIPMENT
: : ASSISTIVE DEVICES (FOR DISABLED)
: MOBILITY AIDS
WHEELCHAIRS

: OCCUPATIONS
WHITE COLLAR OCCUPATIONS

: GROUPS
WHITES
. WHITE STUDENTS

: : GROUPS
: WHITES
: : GROUPS
: STUDENTS
WHITE STUDENTS

: : SYMBOLS (MATHEMATICS)
: NUMBERS
WHOLE NUMBERS

: : TECHNOLOGY
: MARKETING
WHOLESALING

: GROUPS
WIDOWED

WILDLIFE
. ENDANGERED SPECIES

: TECHNOLOGY
WILDLIFE MANAGEMENT

: RECORDS (FORMS)
WILLS

WIND (METEOROLOGY)

: : SCIENTIFIC CONCEPTS
: ENERGY
WIND ENERGY

: FACILITIES
WINDOWLESS ROOMS

: STRUCTURAL ELEMENTS (CONSTRUCTION)
WINDOWS

WITHDRAWAL (EDUCATION)

: PSYCHOLOGICAL PATTERNS
WITHDRAWAL (PSYCHOLOGY)

: : LANGUAGES
: AFRICAN LANGUAGES
WOLOF

: : : : GROUPS
: : : PERSONNEL
: : SCHOOL PERSONNEL
: : : : GROUPS
: : : PERSONNEL
: : PROFESSIONAL PERSONNEL
: FACULTY
: : : GROUPS
: : FEMALES
: EMPLOYED WOMEN
WOMEN FACULTY

: : : ACTIVITIES
: : PHYSICAL ACTIVITIES
: ATHLETICS
WOMENS ATHLETICS

: EDUCATION
WOMENS EDUCATION

: CURRICULUM
WOMENS STUDIES

: TECHNOLOGY
WOODWORKING
. CABINETMAKING
. CARPENTRY

WORD FREQUENCY

: VOCABULARY
WORD LISTS

: MATHEMATICAL APPLICATIONS
WORD PROBLEMS (MATHEMATICS)

: : : SERVICES
: : INFORMATION SERVICES
: INFORMATION PROCESSING
WORD PROCESSING

: : : COGNITIVE PROCESSES
: : MEMORY
: RECOGNITION (PSYCHOLOGY)
WORD RECOGNITION

: : : ABILITY
: : SKILLS
: STUDY SKILLS
WORD STUDY SKILLS

: ATTITUDES
WORK ATTITUDES
. JOB SATISFACTION

: : EDUCATIONAL MEDIA
: INSTRUCTIONAL MATERIALS
WORKBOOKS

: ENVIRONMENT
WORK ENVIRONMENT
. TEACHING CONDITIONS

: : : DATA
: : STATISTICAL DATA
: EMPLOYMENT STATISTICS
WORKER DAYS

: : METHODS
: INSURANCE
: FINANCIAL SUPPORT
WORKERS COMPENSATION

: : BACKGROUND
: EXPERIENCE
WORK EXPERIENCE
. EMPLOYMENT EXPERIENCE

: PROGRAMS
WORK EXPERIENCE PROGRAMS

: : GROUPS
: SOCIAL CLASS
WORKING CLASS

: : PLANNING
: SCHEDULING
WORKING HOURS
. FLEXIBLE WORKING HOURS

: EXPECTATION
WORK LIFE EXPECTANCY

: : : MEASURES (INDIVIDUALS)
: : TESTS
: OCCUPATIONAL TESTS
WORK SAMPLE TESTS

: RECORDS (FORMS)
WORKSHEETS

WORKSHOPS
. DRAMA WORKSHOPS
. PARENT WORKSHOPS
. SHELTERED WORKSHOPS
. TEACHER WORKSHOPS

: PROGRAMS
WORK STUDY PROGRAMS

WORLD AFFAIRS

: : : : LIBERAL ARTS
: : : SCIENCES
: : SOCIAL SCIENCES
: GEOGRAPHY
WORLD GEOGRAPHY

: : : : LIBERAL ARTS
: : : SCIENCES
: : SOCIAL SCIENCES
: : : LIBERAL ARTS
: : HUMANITIES
: HISTORY
WORLD HISTORY

: : CURRICULUM
: ENGLISH CURRICULUM
WORLD LITERATURE

: PROBLEMS
WORLD PROBLEMS

: : : ACTIVITIES
: : PHYSICAL ACTIVITIES
: ATHLETICS
WRESTLING

: LITERACY
: LANGUAGE ARTS
WRITING (COMPOSITION)
. ABSTRACTING
. CONTENT AREA WRITING
. CREATIVE WRITING
. DESCRIPTIVE WRITING
. EXPOSITORY WRITING
. FRESHMAN COMPOSITION
. LOCAL COLOR WRITING
. NEWS WRITING
. NOTETAKING
. PARAGRAPH COMPOSITION
. PARALLELISM (LITERARY)
. PLAYWRITING
. PROPOSAL WRITING
. TECHNICAL WRITING
. WRITING FOR PUBLICATION

: : PSYCHOLOGICAL PATTERNS
: ANXIETY
WRITING APPREHENSION

: PROBLEMS
WRITING DIFFICULTIES

: EVALUATION
WRITING EVALUATION

WRITING EXERCISES

: : LITERACY
: : LANGUAGE ARTS
: WRITING (COMPOSITION)
WRITING FOR PUBLICATION

: IMPROVEMENT
WRITING IMPROVEMENT

: INSTRUCTION
WRITING INSTRUCTION
. CONTENT AREA WRITING
. FRESHMAN COMPOSITION

: : FACILITIES
: LABORATORIES
: : FACILITIES
: EDUCATIONAL FACILITIES
WRITING LABORATORIES

WRITING PROCESSES
. PREWRITING
. REVISION (WRITTEN COMPOSITION)

: READINESS
WRITING READINESS

: : RESEARCH
: EDUCATIONAL RESEARCH
WRITING RESEARCH

: : : ABILITY
: : SKILLS
: LANGUAGE SKILLS
WRITING SKILLS

: LANGUAGE
WRITTEN LANGUAGE
. BRAILLE
. GRAPHEMES
. IDEOGRAPHY
. ORTHOGRAPHIC SYMBOLS
. . DIACRITICAL MARKING
. . LETTERS (ALPHABET)
. . PHONETIC TRANSCRIPTION

WRITTEN LANGUAGE
(CONTINUED)

. PUNCTUATION
. SHORTHAND

: : : LANGUAGES
: : URALIC ALTAIC LANGUAGES
: TURKIC LANGUAGES
YAKUT

: : PUBLICATIONS
: SERIALS
: : PUBLICATIONS
: REFERENCE MATERIALS
: : PUBLICATIONS
: BOOKS
YEARBOOKS

: : INSTITUTIONS
: SCHOOLS
YEAR ROUND SCHOOLS

: : : LANGUAGES
: : INDO EUROPEAN LANGUAGES
: GERMAN
YIDDISH

: : LANGUAGES
: AFRICAN LANGUAGES
YORUBA

: : : GROUPS
: : AGE GROUPS
: ADULTS
YOUNG ADULTS

: : : GROUPS
: : AGE GROUPS
: CHILDREN
YOUNG CHILDREN
. INFANTS
. . NEONATES
. . PREMATURE INFANTS
. KINDERGARTEN CHILDREN
. PRESCHOOL CHILDREN
. TODDLERS

: : EDUCATION
: AGRICULTURAL EDUCATION
: : : EDUCATION
: : VOCATIONAL EDUCATION
: : : EDUCATION
: : ADULT EDUCATION
: ADULT VOCATIONAL
EDUCATION
YOUNG FARMER EDUCATION

: GROUPS
YOUTH
. AFFLUENT YOUTH
. BLACK YOUTH
. DISADVANTAGED YOUTH
. MIGRANT YOUTH
. OUT OF SCHOOL YOUTH
. RURAL YOUTH
. SUBURBAN YOUTH
. URBAN YOUTH

: : : GROUPS
: : ORGANIZATIONS (GROUPS)
: AGENCIES
YOUTH AGENCIES

: : GROUPS
: CLUBS
YOUTH CLUBS

: EMPLOYMENT
YOUTH EMPLOYMENT

: : GROUPS
: LEADERS
: GROUPS
YOUTH LEADERS

: OPPORTUNITIES
YOUTH OPPORTUNITIES

: PROBLEMS
YOUTH PROBLEMS

: PROGRAMS
YOUTH PROGRAMS

: : : LANGUAGES
: : AMERICAN INDIAN
LANGUAGES
: MAYAN LANGUAGES
YUCATEC

: : : LANGUAGES
: : URALIC ALTAIC LANGUAGES
: SAMOYED LANGUAGES
YURAK

ZONING
. COMMUNITY ZONING
. REZONING
. SCHOOL ZONING
. SPECIAL ZONING

: : : : LIBERAL ARTS
: : : SCIENCES
: : NATURAL SCIENCES
: BIOLOGICAL SCIENCES
ZOOLOGY
. ENTOMOLOGY
. ICHTHYOLOGY
. ORNITHOLOGY
. PRIMATOLOGY

: : FACILITIES
: ANIMAL FACILITIES
ZOOS

DESCRIPTOR GROUPS AND DESCRIPTOR GROUP DISPLAY

The following Descriptor Groups offer a "table of contents" to the *Thesaurus*. The 41 Descriptor Groups are presented below in nine categories. A Scope Note for each Descriptor Group is provided, followed by an alphabetical listing of all of the Descriptors assigned to each Descriptor Group.

Groups Related to LEARNING AND DEVELOPMENT

LEARNING AND PERCEPTION 110

Learning, conditioning, and reinforcement; cognition and thought processes; and perception. *See also* MEASUREMENT, THE EDUCATIONAL PROCESS: CLASSROOM PERSPECTIVES, and DISABILITIES.

INDIVIDUAL DEVELOPMENT AND CHARACTERISTICS 120

Attributes of the individual, i.e., psychological characteristics, aptitudes, abilities, behavior, needs, and attitudes; growth and development; age groups; and individual differences. *See also* MENTAL HEALTH and THE INDIVIDUAL IN SOCIAL CONTEXT.

Groups Related to PHYSICAL AND MENTAL CONDITIONS

HEALTH AND SAFETY 210

Medicine and health, health conditions and services, and diseases; health occupations; health facilities; professional and paraprofessional health education; parts of the body; and accidents and safety. *See also* DISABILITIES.

DISABILITIES 220

Physical and mental disabilities; special education; communication disorders, processes, and therapies; and equipment and personnel serving the disabled. *See also* LEARNING AND PERCEPTION and INDIVIDUAL DEVELOPMENT AND CHARACTERISTICS. For emotional and psychiatric conditions see MENTAL HEALTH.

MENTAL HEALTH 230

Mental illness and mentally ill persons; therapies promoting mental welfare; mental health facilities personnel; and psychology. *See also* COUNSELING.

COUNSELING 240

Guidance and counseling; guidance personnel; counseling techniques; and rehabilitation. *See also* MENTAL HEALTH.

Groups Related to EDUCATIONAL PROCESSES AND STRUCTURES

THE EDUCATIONAL PROCESS: CLASSROOM PERSPECTIVES 310

Procedures and processes characteristic of the classroom, i.e., instructional systems, teaching methods, classroom environment, and classroom management; and student/teacher behavior and interaction. *See also* CURRICULUM ORGANIZATION and groups related to curriculum areas. For instructional materials, *see* COMMUNICATIONS MEDIA and PUBLICATION/DOCUMENT TYPES. For specified types of students and teachers, *see* STUDENTS, TEACHERS, SCHOOL PERSONNEL

THE EDUCATIONAL PROCESS: SCHOOL PERSPECTIVES 320

Procedures and processes beyond the classroom, but internal to the school, i.e., internal policy and administration, personnel practices, staff evaluation, curriculum and program development, student/school and teacher/administrator relationships. *See also* STUDENTS, TEACHERS, SCHOOL PERSONNEL. For types of schools and colleges, *see* EDUCATIONAL LEVELS, DEGREES, AND ORGANIZATIONS. For school facilities, *see* FACILITIES.

THE EDUCATIONAL PROCESS: SOCIETAL PERSPECTIVES 330

Procedures and processes related to the school in its social and educational environment, i.e., relations with parents, community, and society at large; relations and processes between schools and higher authorities, between schools and other agencies, and among schools; movement of staff and students; the role of schools in society; and the impacts of schools on society and of society on schools. Other educational factors beyond the single school. *See also* BIAS AND EQUITY. For educational finance, *see* ECONOMICS AND FINANCE.

EDUCATIONAL LEVELS, DEGREES, AND ORGANIZATIONS 340

Grade levels; types of schools and colleges; school districts; educational credits and credentials. *See also* CURRICULUM ORGANIZATION. For school administration, *see* THE EDUCATIONAL PROCESS: SCHOOL PERSPECTIVES.

CURRICULUM ORGANIZATION 350

Units and sequences around which curriculum and instruction are organized; attributes of curriculum structures as defined by time, sequence, special location, and other organizational concepts. For instructional processes, *see* THE EDUCATIONAL PROCESS: CLASSROOM PERSPECTIVES. For grade levels, *see* EDUCATIONAL LEVELS, DEGREES, AND ORGANIZATIONS.

STUDENTS, TEACHERS, SCHOOL PERSONNEL 360

Terms for students, teachers, administrators, and support personnel other than counselors (*see* COUNSELING and library/media personnel (*see* INFORMATION/COMMUNICATIONS SYSTEMS). *See also* DISABILITIES for specialists serving the handicapped.

Groups Related to CURRICULUM AREAS

SUBJECTS OF INSTRUCTION 400

Terms representing subject matter (e.g., Civics) or curriculum areas (e.g., General Education) and terms precoordinating a subject area concept with a concept related to education, skills training, instruction, or curricula. Excludes those terms assigned to a group dealing with a specific curriculum area: *see* AGRICULTURE AND NATURAL RESOURCES, LANGUAGE AND SPEECH, MATHEMATICS, READING, and SCIENCE AND TECHNOLOGY for precoordinated terms in those areas. For paraprofessional health education, *see* HEALTH AND SAFETY. *See also* ARTS, HUMANITIES, LANGUAGES, and PHYSICAL EDUCATION AND RECREATION for other terms frequently used to represent a subject of instruction.

AGRICULTURE AND NATURAL RESOURCES 410

Agriculture; forestry; agricultural education; agricultural occupations; agricultural products, materials, and facilities; natural resources; and pollution, conservation, and other environmental concerns.

ARTS 420

Fine arts, i.e., art, music, dance, and theater and dramatics; and commercial arts, i.e., graphic arts and design. *See also* COMMUNICATIONS MEDIA and HUMANITIES.

HUMANITIES 430

Literature and literary genres; criticism; history; philosophy; and religion. *See also* ARTS and PEOPLES AND CULTURES.

LANGUAGES 440

Human languages and language groups.

LANGUAGE AND SPEECH 450

Language and linguistics; grammar and parts of speech; language instruction; speech and speech education; and vocabulary. For terms related to writing and composition skills, *see* SUBJECTS OF INSTRUCTION. For speech disorders, *see* DISABILITIES. *See also* LANGUAGES and INDIVIDUAL DEVELOPMENT AND CHARACTERISTICS.

READING 460

Reading instruction and development; literacy; and reading facilities.

PHYSICAL EDUCATION AND RECREATION 470

Physical education, recreation, and sports.

MATHEMATICS 480

Mathematics and mathematics education; excludes statistical techniques (*see* MEASUREMENT).

SCIENCE AND TECHNOLOGY 490

Physical and biological sciences; scientific concepts; science education; engineering; and technology. For technical occupations, *see* OCCUPATIONS. For health sciences and medicine, *see* HEALTH AND SAFETY. *See also* AGRICULTURE AND NATURAL RESOURCES and EQUIPMENT.

Groups Related to HUMAN SOCIETY

THE INDIVIDUAL IN SOCIAL CONTEXT 510

Familial and other social influences on individual development; social attributes of individuals; individuals defined by social attributes and social roles; and personal relationships. *See also* INDIVIDUAL DEVELOPMENT AND CHARACTERISTICS, PEOPLES AND CULTURES, SOCIAL PROBLEMS, and BIAS AND EQUITY. For attributes of social groups, *see* SOCIAL PROCESSES AND STRUCTURES.

SOCIAL PROCESSES AND STRUCTURES 520

Attributes of society and of social groups; social programs and services; social institutions, values, and structures (e.g., family, community, and social classes); collective action and behavior; social organizations; social life; and group relations. *See also* SOCIAL PROBLEMS, THE INDIVIDUAL IN SOCIAL CONTEXT, and BIAS AND EQUITY.

SOCIAL PROBLEMS 530

Behavioral and other social problems; individuals and groups defined by such problems. *See also* BIAS AND EQUITY.

BIAS AND EQUITY 540

Prejudice, stereotypes, discriminatory attitudes; segregation and integration; and equality and opportunity. *See also* THE EDUCATIONAL PROCESS: SOCIETAL PERSPECTIVES, and PEOPLES AND CULTURES.

HUMAN GEOGRAPHY 550

Demography; geographic distribution and migration of people; and urban and rural environments and conditions.

PEOPLES AND CULTURES 560

Culture and cultures; ethnic/racial groups; and religious groups.

Groups Related to SOCIAL/ECONOMIC ENTERPRISE

GOVERNMENT AND POLITICS 610

Local, state, and federal government; government employees; law; political divisions and political systems; military organizations and war; political activism; and international relations. *See also* SOCIAL PROCESSES AND STRUCTURES, ECONOMICS AND FINANCE, and THE EDUCATIONAL PROCESS: SOCI-

ETAL PERSPECTIVES. For military personnel, *see* OCCUPATIONS.

ECONOMICS AND FINANCE 620

Economics; individual and institutional finances; educational finance; budgeting and accounting; and taxes. *See also* LABOR AND EMPLOYMENT. For other aspects of educational administration, *see* THE EDUCATIONAL PROCESS: SCHOOL PERSPECTIVES.

LABOR AND EMPLOYMENT 630

Jobs, employment, and unemployment; employment practices; the labor force; skill levels of workers and personnel; job training; personnel management; working conditions and attitudes; employee-employer relations; and supervision. For specific job training areas, *see* SUBJECTS OF INSTRUCTION.

OCCUPATIONS 640

Occupations and occupational groups, excluding those assigned to a specialized category (*see* AGRICULTURE AND NATURAL RESOURCES, COUNSELING, HEALTH AND SAFETY, MENTAL HEALTH, etc., for occupations related to those areas).

BUSINESS, COMMERCE, AND INDUSTRY 650

Business, industries, transportation, and sales. *See also* AGRICULTURE AND NATURAL RESOURCES.

Groups Related to INFORMATION AND COMMUNICATIONS

INFORMATION/COMMUNICATION SYSTEMS 710

Information and communication processes, services, and systems; libraries and information centers; and library and information personnel. *See also* EQUIPMENT and COMMUNICATIONS MEDIA.

COMMUNICATIONS MEDIA 720

PUBLICATION/DOCUMENT TYPES 730

Terms used frequently, though not exclusively, to describe the form of a document. For other terms used in this manner, *see* TESTS AND SCALES, RESEARCH AND THEORY, and MEASUREMENT. A list of the terms that duplicate the Publication Type Codes, and therefore should only be used to refer to the subject of a document, appears in the front matter of the *Thesaurus*. *See also* COMMUNICATIONS MEDIA.

Groups Related to RESEARCH AND MEASUREMENT

RESEARCH AND THEORY 810

The research process; fields and types of research; and theories. Terms may be used to represent subject concepts or to classify research documents by their subject fields or methodological types; they may also be used to categorize theoretical research, research hypotheses, or other types of causal explanations emerging from research. For statistical and other methodologies of research, *see* MEASUREMENT. For tests and scales used in research, *see* TESTS AND SCALES.

MEASUREMENT 820

Testing and measurement; statistical and analytical techniques used in indexing to represent subjects of documents and also to indicate methodologies employed in a research document. Terms related to evaluation and criteria similarly may be used to indicate aspects of documents other than their subject. For types of research, *see* RESEARCH AND THEORY. For specific types of tests and scales, *see* TESTS AND SCALES.

TESTS AND SCALES 830

Testing and data-gathering instruments; may be used in indexing to represent subjects of documents and the presence of tests or scales in the documents. For the processes of testing and measurement, *see* MEASUREMENT.

Groups Related to FACILITIES AND EQUIPMENT

EQUIPMENT 910

Types of equipment and supplies; and equipment maintenance. *See* DISABILITIES for special equipment serving the handicapped. *See also* INFORMATION/COMMUNICATIONS SYSTEMS, COMMUNICATIONS MEDIA, and SCIENCE AND TECHNOLOGY.

FACILITIES 920

Design and construction of facilities; building materials and components; interior space; and types of facilities, excluding libraries, reading facilities, and facilities related to mental or physical health (for facilities in these areas, see specific Descriptor Groups). For occupations in the building trades, *see* OCCUPATIONS.

110 LEARNING AND PERCEPTION

ABILITY IDENTIFICATION
ABSTRACT REASONING
ADULT LEARNING
AROUSAL PATTERNS
ASSOCIATIVE LEARNING
ATTENTION
ATTENTION CONTROL
AUDITORY DISCRIMINATION
AUDITORY PERCEPTION
AUDITORY STIMULI
AURAL LEARNING
BEHAVIOR CHAINING
BEHAVIOR MODIFICATION
CLASSICAL CONDITIONING
COGNITIVE MAPPING
COGNITIVE PROCESSES
COGNITIVE PSYCHOLOGY
COGNITIVE RESTRUCTURING
COGNITIVE STRUCTURES
COGNITIVE STYLE
COMPENSATION (CONCEPT)
COMPREHENSION
CONCEPT FORMATION
CONCEPTUAL SCHEMES (1967 1980)
CONCEPTUAL TEMPO
CONDITIONING
CONSERVATION (CONCEPT)
CONSTRUCTED RESPONSE
CONTINGENCY MANAGEMENT
CONVERGENT THINKING
COVERT RESPONSE
CREATIVE THINKING
CRITICAL THINKING
CUES
DECISION MAKING
DECISION MAKING SKILLS
DEDUCTION
DEPTH PERCEPTION
DIMENSIONAL PREFERENCE
DISCOVERY LEARNING
DISCOVERY PROCESSES
DISCRIMINATION LEARNING
DIVERGENT THINKING
EIDETIC IMAGERY
ELECTRICAL STIMULI
ENCODING (PSYCHOLOGY)
EPISTEMOLOGY
EVALUATIVE THINKING
EXTINCTION (PSYCHOLOGY)
EYE FIXATIONS
EYE MOVEMENTS
FIELD DEPENDENCE INDEPENDENCE
FIGURAL AFTEREFFECTS
FORMAL OPERATIONS
FUNDAMENTAL CONCEPTS
GENERALIZATION
HABIT FORMATION
HABITUATION
HEARING (PHYSIOLOGY)
IMITATION
INCIDENTAL LEARNING
INDUCTION
INFERENCES
INFORMATION SEEKING
INTELLECTUAL EXPERIENCE
INTENTIONAL LEARNING
INTUITION
KINESTHETIC METHODS
KINESTHETIC PERCEPTION
LEARNING
LEARNING EXPERIENCE
LEARNING MODALITIES
LEARNING MOTIVATION
LEARNING PLATEAUS
LEARNING PROBLEMS
LEARNING PROCESSES
LEARNING STRATEGIES
LISTENING COMPREHENSION
LOGICAL THINKING
LONG TERM MEMORY
MEDITATION
MEMORIZATION
MEMORY
METACOGNITION
MISCONCEPTIONS
MNEMONICS
MULTISENSORY LEARNING
NEGATIVE REINFORCEMENT
NONVERBAL LEARNING
NOVELTY (STIMULUS DIMENSION)
OBEDIENCE
OBJECT PERMANENCE
OBSERVATIONAL LEARNING
OPERANT CONDITIONING
OVERT RESPONSE
PAIRED ASSOCIATE LEARNING
PATTERNED RESPONSES
PERCEPTION
PERCEPTUAL MOTOR LEARNING
PICTORIAL STIMULI
PLANNING
POSITIVE REINFORCEMENT
PRESCHOOL LEARNING (1966 1980)
PRIMACY EFFECT
PRIOR LEARNING
PROBLEM SOLVING
PRODUCTIVE THINKING
PUPILLARY DILATION
READER RESPONSE
RECALL (PSYCHOLOGY)
RECOGNITION (PSYCHOLOGY)
REFERENCE GROUPS
REINFORCEMENT
RETENTION (PSYCHOLOGY)
REVIEW (REEXAMINATION)
ROLE MODELS
ROTE LEARNING
SCHEMATA (COGNITION)
SELECTION
SENSORY DEPRIVATION
SENSORY EXPERIENCE
SENSORY INTEGRATION
SEQUENTIAL LEARNING
SERIAL LEARNING
SERIAL ORDERING
SHORT TERM MEMORY
SOCIAL COGNITION
SOCIAL REINFORCEMENT
STIMULATION
STIMULI
STIMULUS GENERALIZATION
SUGGESTOPEDIA
SYMBOLIC LEARNING
TACTUAL PERCEPTION
TIME FACTORS (LEARNING)
TIME PERSPECTIVE
TIMEOUT
TOKEN ECONOMY
TRANSCENDENTAL MEDITATION
TRANSFER OF TRAINING
VALUE JUDGMENT
VERBAL LEARNING
VERBAL OPERANT CONDITIONING
VERBAL STIMULI
VISION
VISUAL ACUITY
VISUAL DISCRIMINATION
VISUAL LEARNING
VISUAL LITERACY
VISUAL PERCEPTION
VISUAL STIMULI
VISUALIZATION

120 INDIVIDUAL DEVELOPMENT

ABILITY
ACADEMIC ABILITY
ACADEMIC APTITUDE
ACADEMIC ASPIRATION
ACHIEVEMENT
ACHIEVEMENT NEED
ACTIVITIES
ADOLESCENT DEVELOPMENT
ADOLESCENTS
ADULT DEVELOPMENT
ADULTS
AFFECTION
AFFECTIVE BEHAVIOR
AFFILIATION NEED
AGE
AGE DIFFERENCES
AGE GROUPS
AGING (INDIVIDUALS)
ALTRUISM
ANDROGYNY
ANIMAL BEHAVIOR
APATHY
APTITUDE
ASPIRATION
ASSERTIVENESS
ASSOCIATION (PSYCHOLOGY)
ATTACHMENT BEHAVIOR
ATTENTION SPAN
ATTITUDE CHANGE
ATTITUDES
AUTHORITARIANISM
BACKGROUND
BEHAVIOR
BEHAVIOR CHANGE
BEHAVIOR DEVELOPMENT
BEHAVIOR PATTERNS
BEHAVIOR PROBLEMS
BEHAVIORISM
BELIEFS
BIOLOGICAL INFLUENCES
BIRTH
BIRTH ORDER
BIRTH WEIGHT
BODY HEIGHT
BODY IMAGE
BODY LANGUAGE
BODY WEIGHT
BRAIN HEMISPHERE FUNCTIONS
CAREER CHANGE
CAREER CHOICE
CAREER DEVELOPMENT
CHILD DEVELOPMENT
CHILDHOOD ATTITUDES
CHILDHOOD INTERESTS
CHILDHOOD NEEDS
CHILDREN
CHRONOLOGICAL AGE
CLIENT CHARACTERISTICS (HUMAN SERVICES)
COGNITIVE ABILITY
COGNITIVE DEVELOPMENT
COGNITIVE DISSONANCE
COMMUNICATION APPREHENSION
COMMUNICATION PROBLEMS
COMPETENCE
COMPLIANCE (PSYCHOLOGY)
CREATIVE DEVELOPMENT
CREATIVITY
CURIOSITY
DEATH
DELAY OF GRATIFICATION
DELAYED SPEECH
DEVELOPMENTAL STAGES
DEVELOPMENTAL TASKS
DOGMATISM
EARLY EXPERIENCE
EGOCENTRISM
EMOTIONAL DEVELOPMENT
EMOTIONAL EXPERIENCE
EMOTIONAL PROBLEMS
EMOTIONAL RESPONSE
EMPATHY
ENVIRONMENTAL INFLUENCES
ETHNICITY
EXCEPTIONAL PERSONS
EXPECTATION
EXPERIENCE
EXPLORATORY BEHAVIOR
EYE CONTACT
EYE HAND COORDINATION
FACIAL EXPRESSIONS
FAILURE TO THRIVE
FANTASY
FEMALES
GIFTED
GOAL ORIENTATION
HIGH ACHIEVEMENT
HIGH RISK PERSONS
HOMOSEXUALITY
IDENTIFICATION (PSYCHOLOGY)
IMAGINATION
INDIVIDUAL CHARACTERISTICS
INDIVIDUAL DEVELOPMENT
INDIVIDUAL DIFFERENCES
INDIVIDUAL NEEDS
INDIVIDUAL POWER
INFANT BEHAVIOR
INFANTS
INHIBITION
INTEGRITY
INTELLECTUAL DEVELOPMENT
INTELLIGENCE
INTELLIGENCE DIFFERENCES
INTERESTS
INTERPERSONAL COMPETENCE
KINDERGARTEN CHILDREN
KNOWLEDGE LEVEL
LANGUAGE ACQUISITION
LATERAL DOMINANCE
LEARNING READINESS
LEFT HANDED WRITER
LESBIANISM
LISTENING HABITS
LISTENING SKILLS
LOCUS OF CONTROL
LOW ACHIEVEMENT
MALES
MATURATION (1967 1980)
MATURITY (INDIVIDUALS)
MENTAL AGE
MENTAL RIGIDITY
MIDDLE AGED ADULTS
MIDLIFE TRANSITIONS
MODELING (PSYCHOLOGY)
MORAL DEVELOPMENT
MOTIVATION
MOTOR DEVELOPMENT
MOTOR REACTIONS

MUSCULAR STRENGTH
NATURE NURTURE CONTROVERSY
NEED GRATIFICATION
NEONATES
NONVERBAL ABILITY
NONVERBAL COMMUNICATION
OCCUPATIONAL ASPIRATION
OLDER ADULTS
OPINIONS
ORIENTATION
OVERACHIEVEMENT
PARENTING SKILLS
PARTICIPATION
PERCEPTUAL DEVELOPMENT
PERCEPTUAL MOTOR COORDINATION
PERFORMANCE
PERINATAL INFLUENCES
PERSISTENCE
PERSONAL SPACE
PERSONALITY
PERSONALITY CHANGE
PERSONALITY DEVELOPMENT
PERSONALITY TRAITS
PERSPECTIVE TAKING
PHYSICAL ACTIVITY LEVEL
PHYSICAL CHARACTERISTICS
PHYSICAL DEVELOPMENT
PREADOLESCENTS
PREGNANCY
PREMATURE INFANTS
PRENATAL INFLUENCES
PRESCHOOL CHILDREN
PRETEND PLAY
PROSOCIAL BEHAVIOR
PSYCHOLOGICAL CHARACTERISTICS
PSYCHOLOGICAL NEEDS
PSYCHOLOGICAL PATTERNS
PSYCHOMOTOR SKILLS
RACE
REACTION TIME
READINESS
RESENTMENT
RESPONSES
ROLE CONFLICT
SCHOOL READINESS
SELF ACTUALIZATION
SELF CONTROL
SELF DISCLOSURE (INDIVIDUALS)
SELF ESTEEM
SELF EVALUATION (INDIVIDUALS)
SELF EXPRESSION
SELF REWARD
SEX
SEX (CHARACTERISTICS) (1966 1980)
SEX DIFFERENCES
SEXUAL IDENTITY
SEXUALITY
SKILL DEVELOPMENT
SKILLS
SOCIAL BEHAVIOR
SOCIAL DEVELOPMENT
SOCIALIZATION
SPACE ORIENTATION (1968 1980)
SPATIAL ABILITY
SPECIALIZATION
SPONTANEOUS BEHAVIOR
STATUS NEED
STRANGER REACTIONS
TALENT
TALENT DEVELOPMENT
TODDLERS
TRUST (PSYCHOLOGY)
TWINS
UNDERACHIEVEMENT
VOCATIONAL APTITUDE
VOCATIONAL INTERESTS
VOCATIONAL MATURITY
WELL BEING
WRITING APPREHENSION
WRITING DIFFICULTIES
WRITING READINESS
YOUNG ADULTS
YOUNG CHILDREN
YOUTH

210 HEALTH AND SAFETY

ABORTIONS
ACCIDENT PREVENTION
ACCIDENTS
ALCOHOLIC BEVERAGES
ALLERGY
ALLIED HEALTH OCCUPATIONS
ALLIED HEALTH OCCUPATIONS EDUCATION
ALLIED HEALTH PERSONNEL
ANEMIA
ANESTHESIOLOGY
ANOREXIA NERVOSA
ASTHMA
AUDIOLOGY
BIOMEDICINE
BLOOD CIRCULATION
BREAKFAST PROGRAMS
BREASTFEEDING
BULIMIA
CANCER
CARDIOPULMONARY RESUSCITATION
CARDIOVASCULAR SYSTEM
CLEANING
CLINICAL DIAGNOSIS
CLINICAL EXPERIENCE
CLINICAL TEACHING (HEALTH PROFESSIONS)
CLOTHING
COMMUNICABLE DISEASES
COMMUNITY HEALTH SERVICES
CONTRACEPTION
DENTAL ASSISTANTS
DENTAL CLINICS
DENTAL EVALUATION
DENTAL HEALTH
DENTAL HYGIENISTS
DENTAL TECHNICIANS
DENTISTRY
DENTISTS
DIABETES
DIETETICS
DIETITIANS
DISEASE CONTROL
DISEASE INCIDENCE
DISEASES
DISHWASHING
DRINKING
DRUG REHABILITATION
DRUG THERAPY
DRUG USE
EARS
EATING HABITS
ELECTROENCEPHALOGRAPHY
EMERGENCY MEDICAL TECHNICIANS
EPIDEMIOLOGY
ETIOLOGY
EXERCISE PHYSIOLOGY
EYES
FAMILY HEALTH
FAMILY PLANNING
FAMILY PRACTICE (MEDICINE)
FATIGUE (BIOLOGY)
FIRE PROTECTION
FIRST AID
FLUORIDATION
FOOD
FOOD SERVICE
FOOD STANDARDS
GERIATRICS
GRADUATE MEDICAL EDUCATION
GYNECOLOGY
HAZARDOUS MATERIALS
HEALTH
HEALTH ACTIVITIES
HEALTH CONDITIONS
HEALTH FACILITIES
HEALTH INSURANCE
HEALTH NEEDS
HEALTH OCCUPATIONS
HEALTH OCCUPATIONS CENTERS (1968 1980)
HEALTH PERSONNEL
HEALTH PROGRAMS
HEALTH SERVICES
HEARING CONSERVATION
HEART DISORDERS
HEART RATE
HOME HEALTH AIDES
HOSPICES (TERMINAL CARE)
HOSPITAL PERSONNEL
HOSPITALIZED CHILDREN
HOSPITALS
HUMAN BODY
HUMAN POSTURE
HUNGER
HYGIENE
HYPERTENSION
IMMUNIZATION PROGRAMS
INFANT MORTALITY
INJURIES
INTERNAL MEDICINE
LABORATORY SAFETY
LEAD POISONING
LUNCH PROGRAMS
LYSERGIC ACID DIETHYLAMIDE
MARIJUANA
MEDICAL ASSISTANTS
MEDICAL CARE EVALUATION
MEDICAL CASE HISTORIES
MEDICAL CONSULTANTS
MEDICAL EDUCATION
MEDICAL EVALUATION
MEDICAL LABORATORY ASSISTANTS
MEDICAL RECORD ADMINISTRATORS
MEDICAL RECORD TECHNICIANS
MEDICAL SERVICES
MEDICAL TECHNOLOGISTS
MEDICAL VOCABULARY
MEDICINE
METABOLISM
MIGRANT HEALTH SERVICES
NARCOTICS
NATURAL DISASTERS
NEUROLOGICAL ORGANIZATION
NEUROLOGY
NURSE PRACTITIONERS
NURSES
NURSES AIDES
NURSING
NURSING EDUCATION
NUTRITION
OBESITY
OBSTETRICS
OCCUPATIONAL DISEASES
OCCUPATIONAL SAFETY AND HEALTH
ONCOLOGY
OPHTHALMOLOGY
OPTOMETRISTS
OPTOMETRY
OSTEOPATHY
OUTCOMES OF TREATMENT
PATHOLOGY
PATIENT EDUCATION
PATIENTS
PEDIATRICS
PHARMACEUTICAL EDUCATION
PHARMACISTS
PHARMACOLOGY
PHARMACY
PHYSICAL EXAMINATIONS
PHYSICAL FITNESS
PHYSICAL HEALTH
PHYSICAL THERAPISTS
PHYSICAL THERAPY
PHYSICAL THERAPY AIDES
PHYSICIAN PATIENT RELATIONSHIP
PHYSICIANS
PHYSICIANS ASSISTANTS
PODIATRY
POISONING
POISONS
PRACTICAL NURSING
PREVENTIVE MEDICINE
PRIMARY HEALTH CARE
PUBLIC HEALTH
RADIOLOGIC TECHNOLOGISTS
RADIOLOGY
RESCUE
RESPIRATORY THERAPY
RH FACTORS
RISK
RUBELLA
SAFETY
SANITATION
SCHOOL ACCIDENTS
SCHOOL HEALTH SERVICES
SECURITY (1967 1978)
SEDATIVES
SICKLE CELL ANEMIA
SLEEP
SMOKING
SPECIAL HEALTH PROBLEMS
STIMULANTS
SURGERY
SURGICAL TECHNICIANS
TERMINATION OF TREATMENT
THERAPY
TISSUE DONORS
TOBACCO
TOXICOLOGY
TRAFFIC ACCIDENTS
TRAFFIC SAFETY
VENEREAL DISEASES

220 DISABILITIES

ACADEMICALLY HANDICAPPED (1966 1980)
ACCESSIBILITY (FOR DISABLED)
ADAPTED PHYSICAL EDUCATION
ADAPTIVE BEHAVIOR (OF DISABLED)
ADULT DAY CARE
ADULT FOSTER CARE
ADVENTITIOUS IMPAIRMENTS
AMERICAN SIGN LANGUAGE
AMETROPIA
AMPUTATIONS
APHASIA
ARCHITECTURAL BARRIERS (1970 1980)
ARTICULATION IMPAIRMENTS

ASSISTIVE DEVICES (FOR DISABLED)
ATTENTION DEFICIT DISORDERS
AUTISM
BLINDNESS
BRAILLE
CEREBRAL PALSY
CLEFT PALATE
COMMUNICATION AIDS (FOR DISABLED)
COMMUNICATION DISORDERS
CONGENITAL IMPAIRMENTS
CUED SPEECH
DAILY LIVING SKILLS
DEAF BLIND
DEAF INTERPRETING
DEAFNESS
DEINSTITUTIONALIZATION (OF DISABLED)
DEVELOPMENTAL DISABILITIES
DISABILITIES
DOWNS SYNDROME
DYSLEXIA
ECHOLOCATION
EDUCATIONAL RETARDATION (1966 1980)
EPILEPSY
EXCEPTIONAL CHILD EDUCATION (1968 1980)
EXCEPTIONAL CHILD SERVICES (1968 1980)
FINGER SPELLING
GIFTED DISABLED
GROUP HOMES
HANDICAP IDENTIFICATION
HANDICAPPED CHILDREN (1966 1980)
HANDICAPPED STUDENTS (1967 1980)
HEARING AIDS
HEARING IMPAIRMENTS
HEARING THERAPY
HOMEBOUND
HYPERACTIVITY
HYPEROPIA
INSTITUTIONALIZED PERSONS
LANGUAGE HANDICAPS
LARGE TYPE MATERIALS
LEARNING DISABILITIES
LIPREADING
LOOP INDUCTION SYSTEMS
LOW VISION AIDS
MAINSTREAMING
MANUAL COMMUNICATION
MENTAL RETARDATION
MILD DISABILITIES
MILD MENTAL RETARDATION
MINIMAL BRAIN DYSFUNCTION
MOBILITY AIDS
MODERATE MENTAL RETARDATION
MULTIPLE DISABILITIES
MYOPIA
NEUROLOGICAL IMPAIRMENTS
NORMALIZATION (HANDICAPPED)
ORAL COMMUNICATION METHOD
PARTIAL HEARING
PARTIAL VISION
PERCEPTUAL HANDICAPS
PHYSICAL DISABILITIES
PHYSICAL MOBILITY
PROSTHESES
RAISED LINE DRAWINGS
RESIDENTIAL CARE
RESPITE CARE
SEIZURES
SELF CARE SKILLS
SENSORY AIDS
SEVERE DISABILITIES
SEVERE MENTAL RETARDATION
SHELTERED WORKSHOPS
SIGN LANGUAGE
SLOW LEARNERS
SPECIAL EDUCATION
SPECIAL EDUCATION TEACHERS
SPEECH HANDICAPS
SPEECH PATHOLOGY
SPEECH THERAPY
STRABISMUS
STUTTERING
TACTILE ADAPTATION
TOTAL COMMUNICATION
TRAVEL TRAINING
VISIBLE SPEECH
VISUAL IMPAIRMENTS
VISUALLY HANDICAPPED MOBILITY
VOICE DISORDERS
WHEELCHAIRS

230 MENTAL HEALTH

ADJUSTMENT (TO ENVIRONMENT)
AGGRESSION
ALIENATION
ANGER
ANXIETY
ART THERAPY
BEHAVIOR DISORDERS
BIBLIOTHERAPY
BURNOUT
CATHARSIS
CHILD PSYCHOLOGY
CLINICAL PSYCHOLOGY
COMMUNITY PSYCHOLOGY
CONGRUENCE (PSYCHOLOGY)
COPING
CRISIS INTERVENTION
DANCE THERAPY
DEPRESSION (PSYCHOLOGY)
DESENSITIZATION
DEVELOPMENTAL PSYCHOLOGY
ECHOLALIA
EMOTIONAL ADJUSTMENT
EMOTIONAL DISTURBANCES
EXPERIMENTAL PSYCHOLOGY
FEAR
FEAR OF SUCCESS
GESTALT THERAPY
GRIEF
GROUP THERAPY
HELPLESSNESS
HOSTILITY
HYPNOSIS
INDIVIDUAL PSYCHOLOGY
INDUSTRIAL PSYCHOLOGY
JEALOUSY
LIFE SATISFACTION
LONELINESS
MENTAL DISORDERS
MENTAL HEALTH
MENTAL HEALTH CLINICS
MENTAL HEALTH PROGRAMS
MILIEU THERAPY
MORALE
MUSIC THERAPY
NEUROSIS
OCCUPATIONAL THERAPISTS
OCCUPATIONAL THERAPY
OCCUPATIONAL THERAPY ASSISTANTS
PARANOID BEHAVIOR
PERSONALITY PROBLEMS
PLAY THERAPY
PROBLEM CHILDREN
PSYCHIATRIC AIDES
PSYCHIATRIC HOSPITALS
PSYCHIATRIC SERVICES
PSYCHIATRISTS
PSYCHIATRY
PSYCHOEDUCATIONAL CLINICS
PSYCHOLOGICAL EVALUATION
PSYCHOLOGICAL SERVICES
PSYCHOLOGISTS
PSYCHOLOGY
PSYCHOMETRICS
PSYCHOPATHOLOGY
PSYCHOPHYSIOLOGY
PSYCHOSIS
PSYCHOSOMATIC DISORDERS
PSYCHOTHERAPY
RATIONAL EMOTIVE THERAPY
REALITY THERAPY
REJECTION (PSYCHOLOGY)
RELAXATION TRAINING
SCHIZOPHRENIA
SCHOOL PHOBIA
SECURITY (PSYCHOLOGY)
SELF CONCEPT
SELF CONGRUENCE
SELF DESTRUCTIVE BEHAVIOR
SELF MUTILATION
SEPARATION ANXIETY
SOCIAL ADJUSTMENT
SOCIAL PSYCHOLOGY
SPORT PSYCHOLOGY
STRESS MANAGEMENT
STRESS VARIABLES
SUICIDE
THERAPEUTIC ENVIRONMENT
THERAPEUTIC RECREATION
WITHDRAWAL (PSYCHOLOGY)

240 COUNSELING

ACADEMIC ADVISING
ADJUSTMENT COUNSELORS
ADMISSIONS COUNSELING
ADULT COUNSELING
CAREER COUNSELING
CAREER GUIDANCE
CAREER PLANNING
CASEWORKER APPROACH
CASEWORKERS
CLASSROOM GUIDANCE PROGRAMS (1968 1980)
COCOUNSELING
CONSULTANTS
CONSULTATION PROGRAMS
COUNSELING
COUNSELING EFFECTIVENESS
COUNSELING INSTRUCTIONAL PROGRAMS (1967 1980)
COUNSELING OBJECTIVES
COUNSELING SERVICES
COUNSELING TECHNIQUES
COUNSELING THEORIES
COUNSELOR ATTITUDES
COUNSELOR CERTIFICATION
COUNSELOR CHARACTERISTICS
COUNSELOR CLIENT RATIO
COUNSELOR CLIENT RELATIONSHIP
COUNSELOR EVALUATION
COUNSELOR PERFORMANCE
COUNSELOR QUALIFICATIONS
COUNSELOR ROLE
COUNSELOR SELECTION
COUNSELOR TEACHER COOPERATION
COUNSELOR TRAINING
COUNSELORS
DELINQUENT REHABILITATION
EDUCATIONAL COUNSELING
FACULTY ADVISERS
FAMILY COUNSELING
GROUP COUNSELING
GROUP GUIDANCE
GUIDANCE
GUIDANCE CENTERS
GUIDANCE OBJECTIVES
GUIDANCE PERSONNEL
GUIDANCE PROGRAMS
HELPING RELATIONSHIP
HOTLINES (PUBLIC)
INDIVIDUAL COUNSELING
INTERVENTION
LABORATORY TRAINING
MARRIAGE COUNSELING
MICROCOUNSELING
NONDIRECTIVE COUNSELING
PARENT COUNSELING
PEER COUNSELING
POST HIGH SCHOOL GUIDANCE
PUPIL PERSONNEL SERVICES
PUPIL PERSONNEL WORKERS
REFERRAL
REHABILITATION
REHABILITATION COUNSELING
REHABILITATION PROGRAMS
ROLE PLAYING
SCHOOL COUNSELING
SCHOOL COUNSELORS
SCHOOL GUIDANCE
SENSITIVITY TRAINING
SOCIAL SUPPORT GROUPS
STUDENT PERSONNEL SERVICES
STUDENT PERSONNEL WORKERS
STUDENT WELFARE
TEACHER GUIDANCE
TRANSACTIONAL ANALYSIS

310 CLASSROOM PERSPECTIVES

ABILITY GROUPING
ACADEMIC ACHIEVEMENT
ACADEMIC FAILURE
ACADEMIC PERSISTENCE
ACCELERATION (EDUCATION)
ACHIEVEMENT GAINS
ADVANCE ORGANIZERS
AFFECTIVE OBJECTIVES
ANDRAGOGY
APTITUDE TREATMENT INTERACTION
ASSIGNMENTS
AUDIOVISUAL INSTRUCTION
BEHAVIORAL OBJECTIVES
CLASS ACTIVITIES
CLASS AVERAGE (1966 1980)
CLASS ORGANIZATION
CLASS RANK
CLASS SIZE
CLASSES (GROUPS OF STUDENTS)
CLASSROOM COMMUNICATION
CLASSROOM ENVIRONMENT
CLASSROOM TECHNIQUES
COGNITIVE OBJECTIVES
COMPUTER ASSISTED INSTRUCTION
COMPUTER MANAGED INSTRUCTION
COMPUTER SIMULATION
CONVENTIONAL INSTRUCTION
COURSE CONTENT
COURSE EVALUATION
COURSE OBJECTIVES
COURSE ORGANIZATION

CREATIVE ACTIVITIES
CREATIVE TEACHING
CROSS AGE TEACHING
CULTURAL ENRICHMENT
CURRICULUM ENRICHMENT
DEMONSTRATIONS (EDUCATIONAL)
DEVELOPMENTAL STUDIES PROGRAMS
DIAGNOSTIC TEACHING
DISCUSSION (TEACHING TECHNIQUE)
DISCUSSION GROUPS
DRILLS (PRACTICE)
EDUCATIONAL DIAGNOSIS
EDUCATIONAL METHODS
EDUCATIONAL STRATEGIES
EDUCATIONAL THERAPY
ENRICHMENT
ENRICHMENT ACTIVITIES
EPISODE TEACHING (1967 1980)
EXPERIENCE CHARTS
EXPERIENTIAL LEARNING
EXPERIMENTAL TEACHING
FORMATIVE EVALUATION
GLOBAL APPROACH
GRADE CHARTS (1966 1980)
GRADES (SCHOLASTIC)
GRADING
GROUP ACTIVITIES
GROUP DISCUSSION
GROUP INSTRUCTION
GROUPING (INSTRUCTIONAL PURPOSES)
HETEROGENEOUS GROUPING
HOME STUDY
HOMEWORK
HOMOGENEOUS GROUPING
HONORS CURRICULUM
INDEPENDENT STUDY
INDIVIDUAL ACTIVITIES
INDIVIDUAL INSTRUCTION
INDIVIDUALIZED INSTRUCTION
INDIVIDUALIZED PROGRAMS
INSTRUCTION
INSTRUCTIONAL DESIGN
INSTRUCTIONAL DEVELOPMENT
INSTRUCTIONAL EFFECTIVENESS
INSTRUCTIONAL IMPROVEMENT
INSTRUCTIONAL INNOVATION
INSTRUCTIONAL MATERIAL EVALUATION
INSTRUCTIONAL PROGRAMS (1966 1980)
INSTRUCTIONAL SYSTEMS
INTEGRATED ACTIVITIES
INTERDISCIPLINARY APPROACH
INTERMODE DIFFERENCES
LARGE GROUP INSTRUCTION
LEARNING ACTIVITIES
LEARNING CENTERS (CLASSROOM)
LECTURE METHOD
LISTENING
LISTENING GROUPS
MANAGEMENT GAMES
MASTERY LEARNING
MATERIAL DEVELOPMENT
MICROTEACHING
MONTESSORI METHOD
MOTIVATION TECHNIQUES
MULTIGRADED CLASSES
MULTIMEDIA INSTRUCTION
NEGATIVE PRACTICE
NONAUTHORITARIAN CLASSES
NOTETAKING
OBJECT MANIPULATION
OUTLINING (DISCOURSE)
PACING
PARTICIPANT SATISFACTION
PEER TEACHING
PERFORMANCE CONTRACTS
PERFORMANCE FACTORS
PRACTICUM SUPERVISION
PRECISION TEACHING
PROCESS EDUCATION
PROCTORING
PROGRAMED INSTRUCTION
PROGRAMED TUTORING
PROGRESSIVE EDUCATION
PROMPTING
PSYCHOEDUCATIONAL METHODS
PSYCHOMOTOR OBJECTIVES
QUESTIONING TECHNIQUES
REDUNDANCY
REMEDIAL INSTRUCTION
REMEDIAL PROGRAMS
REPETITIVE FILM SHOWINGS
RESEARCH PAPERS (STUDENTS)
RESOURCE ROOM PROGRAMS
RESOURCE UNITS
SELF CONTAINED CLASSROOMS
SELF DIRECTED CLASSROOMS (1966 1980)
SEQUENTIAL APPROACH
SIMULATED ENVIRONMENT
SIMULATION
SMALL CLASSES
SMALL GROUP INSTRUCTION
SPECIAL CLASSES
STUDENT BEHAVIOR
STUDENT CENTERED CURRICULUM
STUDENT DEVELOPMENT
STUDENT EXPERIENCE
STUDENT IMPROVEMENT
STUDENT INTERESTS
STUDENT MOTIVATION
STUDENT PARTICIPATION
STUDENT PROJECTS
STUDENT REACTION
STUDY
STUDY HABITS
STUDY SKILLS
SUBSTITUTION DRILLS
SUMMATIVE EVALUATION
TASK PERFORMANCE (1966 1980)
TEACHER BEHAVIOR
TEACHER EFFECTIVENESS
TEACHER IMPROVEMENT
TEACHER INFLUENCE
TEACHER MOTIVATION
TEACHER RESPONSE
TEACHER STUDENT RELATIONSHIP
TEACHING (1966 1980)
TEACHING CONDITIONS
TEACHING EXPERIENCE
TEACHING METHODS
TEACHING MODELS
TEACHING SKILLS
TEACHING STYLES
TEAM TEACHING
TEAM TRAINING
TEST ANXIETY
TEST COACHING
TEST WISENESS
TEXTBOOK CONTENT
THEMATIC APPROACH
TIME MANAGEMENT
TIME ON TASK
TRAINING METHODS
TRAINING OBJECTIVES
TUTORIAL PROGRAMS
TUTORING
WRITING EXERCISES

320 SCHOOL PERSPECTIVES

ACADEMIC PROBATION
ACADEMIC RANK (PROFESSIONAL)
ACADEMIC RECORDS
ACADEMIC STANDARDS
ADMINISTRATION
ADMINISTRATIVE CHANGE
ADMINISTRATIVE ORGANIZATION
ADMINISTRATIVE POLICY
ADMINISTRATIVE PRINCIPLES
ADMINISTRATIVE PROBLEMS
ADMINISTRATOR ATTITUDES
ADMINISTRATOR CHARACTERISTICS
ADMINISTRATOR EVALUATION
ADMINISTRATOR QUALIFICATIONS
ADMINISTRATOR RESPONSIBILITY
ADMINISTRATOR ROLE
ADMINISTRATOR SELECTION
ADMISSION (SCHOOL)
ADMISSION CRITERIA
ADVANCED PLACEMENT
ADVANCED PLACEMENT PROGRAMS
ADVANCED PROGRAMS (1966 1980)
ADVISORY COMMITTEES
AGE GRADE PLACEMENT
ALUMNI EDUCATION
ANCILLARY SCHOOL SERVICES
ATTENDANCE
ATTENDANCE PATTERNS
ATTENDANCE RECORDS
AUDITING (COURSEWORK)
AVERAGE DAILY ATTENDANCE
AVERAGE DAILY MEMBERSHIP
BUS TRANSPORTATION
CASE RECORDS
COLLEGE ADMINISTRATION
COLLEGE ADMISSION
COLLEGE ENVIRONMENT
COLLEGE GOVERNING COUNCILS
COLLEGE INSTRUCTION
COLLEGE PLANNING
COLLEGE PROGRAMS
COMMENCEMENT CEREMONIES
COMPREHENSIVE PROGRAMS
COMPUTER ORIENTED PROGRAMS
CONFIDENTIAL RECORDS
COURSE SELECTION (STUDENTS)
CREDIT NO CREDIT GRADING
CRITICAL PATH METHOD
CURRICULUM DESIGN
CURRICULUM DEVELOPMENT
CURRICULUM EVALUATION
CURRICULUM PROBLEMS
DEGREE REQUIREMENTS
DRESS CODES
DROPOUT PREVENTION
DROPOUT PROGRAMS
EARLY ADMISSION
EDUCATIONAL ADMINISTRATION
EDUCATIONAL ENVIRONMENT
EDUCATIONAL PROGRAMS (1966 1980)
EDUCATIONAL SPECIFICATIONS (1967 1980)
EMERGENCY PROGRAMS
ENROLLMENT
ENROLLMENT INFLUENCES
EXPERIMENTAL PROGRAMS
FACULTY COLLEGE RELATIONSHIP
FACULTY DEVELOPMENT
FACULTY EVALUATION
FACULTY ORGANIZATIONS
FACULTY PROMOTION
FACULTY RECRUITMENT
FACULTY WORKLOAD
FLEXIBLE SCHEDULES (1967 1980)
FLEXIBLE SCHEDULING
FULL TIME EQUIVALENCY
GRADE INFLATION
GRADE REPETITION
GRADUATION
GRADUATION REQUIREMENTS
IMPROVEMENT PROGRAMS
IN SCHOOL SUSPENSION
INSERVICE TEACHER EDUCATION
INSTITUTIONAL ADMINISTRATION
INSTITUTIONAL CHARACTERISTICS
INSTITUTIONAL ENVIRONMENT
INSTITUTIONAL EVALUATION
INSTITUTIONAL MISSION
INSTRUCTIONAL LEADERSHIP
LANGUAGE ENROLLMENT
LATE REGISTRATION
MAJORS (STUDENTS)
MANAGEMENT BY OBJECTIVES
MANAGEMENT DEVELOPMENT
MANAGEMENT SYSTEMS
MANAGEMENT TEAMS
MERIT RATING
NONGRADED STUDENT EVALUATION
NONINSTRUCTIONAL RESPONSIBILITY
ORGANIZATION SIZE (GROUPS)
ORGANIZATIONAL CHANGE
ORGANIZATIONAL CLIMATE
ORGANIZATIONAL COMMUNICATION
ORGANIZATIONAL DEVELOPMENT
ORGANIZATIONAL EFFECTIVENESS
ORGANIZATIONAL OBJECTIVES
PARTICIPATIVE DECISION MAKING
PASS FAIL GRADING
PEER EVALUATION
PEER INSTITUTIONS
PRESCHOOL EVALUATION
PROGRAM ADMINISTRATION
PROGRAM ATTITUDES
PROGRAM CONTENT
PROGRAM DESIGN
PROGRAM DEVELOPMENT
PROGRAM EFFECTIVENESS
PROGRAM EVALUATION
PROGRAM IMPLEMENTATION
PROGRAM IMPROVEMENT
PROGRAM TERMINATION
PUBLISH OR PERISH ISSUE
QUALITY CIRCLES
RECORDKEEPING
ROTATION PLANS
SCHEDULING
SCHOOL ACTIVITIES
SCHOOL ADMINISTRATION
SCHOOL BASED MANAGEMENT
SCHOOL CATALOGS
SCHOOL CONSTRUCTION
SCHOOL EFFECTIVENESS
SCHOOL EXPANSION
SCHOOL HOLDING POWER
SCHOOL MAINTENANCE
SCHOOL ORGANIZATION
SCHOOL ORIENTATION
SCHOOL POLICY
SCHOOL REGISTRATION
SCHOOL SAFETY
SCHOOL SECURITY
SCHOOL SHOPS
SCHOOL SIZE
SCHOOL SPACE
SCHOOL SUPERVISION
SCIENCE CLUBS
SCIENCE SUPERVISION

SEARCH COMMITTEES (PERSONNEL)
SELECTIVE ADMISSION
SPECIAL PROGRAMS
STAFF DEVELOPMENT
STAFF MEETINGS
STAFF ORIENTATION
STAFF ROLE
STAFF UTILIZATION
STUDENT ADJUSTMENT
STUDENT ALIENATION
STUDENT ATTITUDES
STUDENT ATTRITION
STUDENT CHARACTERISTICS
STUDENT COLLEGE RELATIONSHIP
STUDENT EVALUATION
STUDENT EVALUATION OF TEACHER PERFORMANCE
STUDENT GOVERNMENT
STUDENT NEEDS
STUDENT ORGANIZATIONS
STUDENT PLACEMENT
STUDENT PROMOTION
STUDENT RECORDS
STUDENT RECRUITMENT
STUDENT ROLE
STUDENT SCHOOL RELATIONSHIP
STUDENT TEACHER ATTITUDES
STUDENT TEACHER EVALUATION
STUDENT TEACHING
STUDENT TRANSPORTATION
SYSTEMS APPROACH
SYSTEMS CONCEPTS (1966 1980)
SYSTEMS DEVELOPMENT
TEACHER ADMINISTRATOR RELATIONSHIP
TEACHER ALIENATION
TEACHER ATTENDANCE
TEACHER ATTITUDES
TEACHER BACKGROUND
TEACHER BURNOUT
TEACHER CHARACTERISTICS
TEACHER DISCIPLINE
TEACHER DISMISSAL
TEACHER EVALUATION
TEACHER MORALE
TEACHER ORIENTATION
TEACHER PARTICIPATION
TEACHER PROMOTION
TEACHER QUALIFICATIONS
TEACHER RECRUITMENT
TEACHER RESPONSIBILITY
TEACHER ROLE
TEACHER SELECTION
TEACHER STUDENT RATIO
TEACHER SUPERVISION
TEACHING ASSIGNMENT (1966 1980)
TEACHING LOAD
TEACHING PROGRAMS (1966 1980)
TEXTBOOK EVALUATION
TEXTBOOK SELECTION
TRANSFERS (1966 1980)
VALIDATED PROGRAMS

330 SOCIETAL PERSPECTIVES

ACADEMIC FREEDOM
ACCESS TO EDUCATION
ACCOUNTABILITY
ACCREDITATION (INSTITUTIONS)
ACCREDITING AGENCIES
AGING IN ACADEMIA
AMERICAN INDIAN EDUCATION
ARTICULATION (EDUCATION)
BACK TO BASICS
BILINGUAL EDUCATION
BLACK ACHIEVEMENT
BLACK EDUCATION
BOARD ADMINISTRATOR RELATIONSHIP
BOARD OF EDUCATION POLICY
BOARD OF EDUCATION ROLE
BOARDS OF EDUCATION
CERTIFICATION
CHANGE AGENTS
CHANGE STRATEGIES
COEDUCATION
COLLEGE ATTENDANCE
COLLEGE CHOICE
COLLEGE DAY
COLLEGE PREPARATION
COLLEGE ROLE
COLLEGE SCHOOL COOPERATION
COMMUNITY BENEFITS
COMMUNITY CONTROL
COMMUNITY INVOLVEMENT
COMMUNITY SUPPORT
COMPENSATORY EDUCATION
COMPETENCY BASED EDUCATION
COMPETITIVE SELECTION
COMPULSORY EDUCATION
COMPUTER LITERACY
COMPUTER USES IN EDUCATION
CONSORTIA
CONTINUATION EDUCATION (1968 1980)
CONTROVERSIAL ISSUES (COURSE CONTENT)
COOPERATIVE PROGRAMS
CORPORAL PUNISHMENT
CORPORATE EDUCATION
CORRECTIONAL EDUCATION
DECLINING ENROLLMENT
DEMONSTRATION PROGRAMS
DISCIPLINE
DISCIPLINE POLICY
DISTANCE EDUCATION
DROPOUT ATTITUDES
DROPOUT CHARACTERISTICS
DROPOUT RATE
DUAL ENROLLMENT
EDUCATION
EDUCATION WORK RELATIONSHIP
EDUCATIONAL ATTITUDES
EDUCATIONAL BENEFITS
EDUCATIONAL CHANGE
EDUCATIONAL COOPERATION
EDUCATIONAL DEMAND
EDUCATIONAL DEVELOPMENT
EDUCATIONAL HISTORY
EDUCATIONAL IMPROVEMENT
EDUCATIONAL INNOVATION
EDUCATIONAL LEGISLATION
EDUCATIONAL MALPRACTICE
EDUCATIONAL MOBILITY
EDUCATIONAL NEEDS
EDUCATIONAL OBJECTIVES
EDUCATIONAL OPPORTUNITIES
EDUCATIONAL PHILOSOPHY
EDUCATIONAL PLANNING
EDUCATIONAL POLICY
EDUCATIONAL PRACTICES
EDUCATIONAL PRINCIPLES
EDUCATIONAL PROBLEMS (1966 1980)
EDUCATIONAL QUALITY
EDUCATIONAL RESOURCES
EDUCATIONAL RESPONSIBILITY
EDUCATIONAL SUPPLY
EDUCATIONAL TECHNOLOGY
EDUCATIONAL TRENDS
ENROLLMENT RATE
ENROLLMENT TRENDS
EXCHANGE PROGRAMS
EXPULSION
FACULTY MOBILITY
FAMILY SCHOOL RELATIONSHIP
FEEDER PATTERNS
FREE CHOICE TRANSFER PROGRAMS
FREE EDUCATION
GOVERNANCE
GOVERNING BOARDS
GOVERNMENT SCHOOL RELATIONSHIP
HIDDEN CURRICULUM
HOME PROGRAMS
HOME SCHOOLING
HOME VISITS
HONOR SOCIETIES
INDIVIDUALIZED EDUCATION PROGRAMS
INSTITUTIONAL AUTONOMY
INSTITUTIONAL COOPERATION
INSTITUTIONAL ROLE
INSTITUTIONAL SURVIVAL
INTELLECTUAL FREEDOM
INTERCOLLEGIATE COOPERATION
INTERCULTURAL COMMUNICATION
INTERDISTRICT POLICIES
INTERGROUP EDUCATION
INTERNATIONAL EDUCATIONAL EXCHANGE
INTERSCHOOL COMMUNICATION
LINKING AGENTS
LONG RANGE PLANNING
MEXICAN AMERICAN EDUCATION
MIGRANT ADULT EDUCATION
MIGRANT EDUCATION
MINIMUM COMPETENCIES
MOBILE EDUCATIONAL SERVICES
NONFORMAL EDUCATION
NONSCHOOL EDUCATIONAL PROGRAMS
NONTRADITIONAL EDUCATION
OPEN ENROLLMENT
OUTCOMES OF EDUCATION
OUTREACH PROGRAMS
PARENT ASSOCIATIONS
PARENT CONFERENCES
PARENT EDUCATION
PARENT GRIEVANCES
PARENT PARTICIPATION
PARENT SCHOOL RELATIONSHIP
PARENT STUDENT RELATIONSHIP
PARENT TEACHER CONFERENCES
PARENT TEACHER COOPERATION
PARENT WORKSHOPS
PARTICIPANT CHARACTERISTICS
POLICE SCHOOL RELATIONSHIP
POLICY
POLICY FORMATION
POLITICS OF EDUCATION
PORTFOLIOS (BACKGROUND MATERIALS)
PROFESSIONAL AUTONOMY
PROFESSIONAL TRAINING
PROGRAM VALIDATION
PROPOSAL WRITING
PUBLIC RELATIONS
PUBLIC SERVICE
REGIONAL COOPERATION
REGIONAL PLANNING
RELEVANCE (EDUCATION)
REPORT CARDS
RESIDENCE REQUIREMENTS
ROLE OF EDUCATION
RURAL EDUCATION
SCHOLARSHIP
SCHOOL ATTENDANCE LEGISLATION
SCHOOL ATTITUDES
SCHOOL BUSINESS RELATIONSHIP
SCHOOL CHOICE
SCHOOL CLOSING
SCHOOL COMMUNITY PROGRAMS
SCHOOL COMMUNITY RELATIONSHIP
SCHOOL DEMOGRAPHY
SCHOOL DISTRICT AUTONOMY
SCHOOL DISTRICT REORGANIZATION
SCHOOL DISTRICT SIZE
SCHOOL ENTRANCE AGE
SCHOOL INVOLVEMENT
SCHOOL LAW
SCHOOL LOCATION
SCHOOL PLANNING (1966 1980)
SCHOOL RESPONSIBILITY
SCHOOL ROLE
SCHOOL VISITATION
SCHOOL ZONING
SHARED RESOURCES AND SERVICES
STATE BOARDS OF EDUCATION
STATE DEPARTMENTS OF EDUCATION
STATE SCHOOL DISTRICT RELATIONSHIP
STATEWIDE PLANNING
STUDENT CERTIFICATION
STUDENT DISTRIBUTION (1966 1980)
STUDENT EDUCATIONAL OBJECTIVES
STUDENT EXCHANGE PROGRAMS
STUDENT LEADERSHIP
STUDENT MOBILITY
STUDENT PROBLEMS
STUDENT RESPONSIBILITY
STUDENT RIGHTS
STUDENT SUBCULTURES
SUSPENSION
TEACHER ASSOCIATIONS
TEACHER CERTIFICATION
TEACHER DISTRIBUTION
TEACHER EXCHANGE PROGRAMS
TEACHER MILITANCY
TEACHER PERSISTENCE
TEACHER PLACEMENT
TEACHER RIGHTS
TEACHER TRANSFER
TEACHER WELFARE
TEXTBOOK STANDARDS
TRACK SYSTEM (EDUCATION)
TRACKING (1968 1980)
TRAINING
TRANSFER POLICY
TRANSFER PROGRAMS
TRUANCY
URBAN EDUCATION
URBAN TEACHING
VETERANS EDUCATION
WITHDRAWAL (EDUCATION)
WOMENS EDUCATION

340 ED. LEVELS, DEGREES, ORGANIZATIONS

ADULT BASIC EDUCATION
ADULT EDUCATION
ADULT PROGRAMS
AFFILIATED SCHOOLS
AGRICULTURAL COLLEGES
ASSOCIATE DEGREES
BACHELORS DEGREES
BILINGUAL SCHOOLS
BLACK COLLEGES
BOARDING SCHOOLS
BRITISH INFANT SCHOOLS
CATHOLIC SCHOOLS
CHURCH RELATED COLLEGES
CLUSTER COLLEGES
COLLEGE CREDITS
COLLEGES

COMMUNITY COLLEGES
COMMUNITY EDUCATION
COMMUNITY SCHOOLS
COMMUTER COLLEGES
CONSOLIDATED SCHOOLS
CONTINUING EDUCATION
CONTINUING EDUCATION UNITS
CORRESPONDENCE SCHOOLS
COUNTY SCHOOL DISTRICTS
CREDENTIALS
CREDITS
DAY SCHOOLS
DEGREES (ACADEMIC)
DENTAL SCHOOLS
DEVELOPING INSTITUTIONS
DISADVANTAGED SCHOOLS
DOCTOR OF ARTS DEGREES
DOCTORAL DEGREES
DOCTORAL PROGRAMS
EARLY CHILDHOOD EDUCATION
EDUCATIONAL CERTIFICATES
ELEMENTARY EDUCATION
ELEMENTARY SCHOOLS
ELEMENTARY SECONDARY EDUCATION
EXPERIMENTAL COLLEGES
EXPERIMENTAL SCHOOLS
FOLK SCHOOLS
FREE SCHOOLS
FREEDOM SCHOOLS
GRADE 1
GRADE 10
GRADE 11
GRADE 12
GRADE 2
GRADE 3
GRADE 4
GRADE 5
GRADE 6
GRADE 7
GRADE 8
GRADE 9
GRADUATE STUDY
HIGH SCHOOL EQUIVALENCY PROGRAMS
HIGH SCHOOLS
HIGHER EDUCATION
HOSPITAL SCHOOLS
INSTITUTIONAL SCHOOLS
INSTRUCTIONAL PROGRAM DIVISIONS
INTERMEDIATE ADMINISTRATIVE UNITS
INTERMEDIATE GRADES
JUNIOR HIGH SCHOOLS
KINDERGARTEN
LABORATORY SCHOOLS
LAND GRANT UNIVERSITIES
LAW SCHOOLS
LIBRARY SCHOOLS
LIFELONG LEARNING
MAGNET SCHOOLS
MASTERS DEGREES
MASTERS PROGRAMS
MEDICAL SCHOOLS
MIDDLE SCHOOLS
MILITARY SCHOOLS
MULTICAMPUS COLLEGES
MULTICAMPUS DISTRICTS
MULTIUNIT SCHOOLS
NEIGHBORHOOD SCHOOLS
NONCAMPUS COLLEGES
NORTHERN SCHOOLS (1966 1980)
NURSERY SCHOOLS
ONE TEACHER SCHOOLS
OPEN UNIVERSITIES
PAROCHIAL SCHOOLS
POSTDOCTORAL EDUCATION
POSTSECONDARY EDUCATION
PRESCHOOL EDUCATION
PRIMARY EDUCATION
PRIVATE COLLEGES
PRIVATE EDUCATION
PRIVATE SCHOOLS
PROFESSIONAL CONTINUING EDUCATION
PROFESSIONAL EDUCATION
PROPRIETARY SCHOOLS
PUBLIC COLLEGES
PUBLIC EDUCATION
PUBLIC SCHOOL ADULT EDUCATION
PUBLIC SCHOOLS
REGIONAL SCHOOLS
RESEARCH AND INSTRUCTION UNITS
RESEARCH COORDINATING UNITS
RESEARCH UNIVERSITIES
RESIDENTIAL COLLEGES
RESIDENTIAL SCHOOLS
RURAL SCHOOLS
SCHOOL DISTRICTS
SCHOOLS
SCHOOLS OF EDUCATION
SECONDARY EDUCATION
SECONDARY SCHOOLS
SELECTIVE COLLEGES
SINGLE SEX COLLEGES
SINGLE SEX SCHOOLS
SLUM SCHOOLS
SMALL COLLEGES
SMALL SCHOOLS
SOUTHERN SCHOOLS (1966 1980)
SPECIAL DEGREE PROGRAMS
SPECIAL SCHOOLS
SPECIALIST IN EDUCATION DEGREES
STATE COLLEGES
STATE SCHOOLS
STATE UNIVERSITIES
SUBURBAN SCHOOLS
TEACHING HOSPITALS
TECHNICAL INSTITUTES
TERMINAL EDUCATION
TRADITIONAL SCHOOLS
TRANSITIONAL PROGRAMS
TRANSITIONAL SCHOOLS
TWO YEAR COLLEGES
UNDERGRADUATE STUDY
UNIVERSITIES
UPPER DIVISION COLLEGES
URBAN SCHOOLS
URBAN UNIVERSITIES
VOCATIONAL HIGH SCHOOLS
VOCATIONAL SCHOOLS

350 CURRICULUM ORGANIZATION

ACTIVITY UNITS
ADVANCED COURSES
AFTER SCHOOL EDUCATION
AFTER SCHOOL PROGRAMS
ASSEMBLY PROGRAMS
COLLEGE CURRICULUM
CONTINUOUS PROGRESS PLAN
CORE CURRICULUM
CORRESPONDENCE STUDY
COURSES
CREDIT COURSES
CURRICULUM
DAY PROGRAMS
DEPARTMENTS
DOUBLE SESSIONS
ELECTIVE COURSES
ELEMENTARY SCHOOL CURRICULUM
ENGLISH DEPARTMENTS
EVENING PROGRAMS
EXPERIMENTAL CURRICULUM
EXTENDED SCHOOL DAY
EXTENDED SCHOOL YEAR
EXTENSION EDUCATION
EXTERNAL DEGREE PROGRAMS
FIELD EXPERIENCE PROGRAMS
FIELD INSTRUCTION
FIELD TRIPS
FIXED SEQUENCE
FLEXIBLE PROGRESSION
FUSED CURRICULUM
HOME INSTRUCTION
HOUSE PLAN
INSTITUTES (TRAINING PROGRAMS)
INTEGRATED CURRICULUM
INTELLECTUAL DISCIPLINES
INTERNSHIP PROGRAMS
INTRODUCTORY COURSES
MASS INSTRUCTION
MINICOURSES
NONCREDIT COURSES
NONGRADED INSTRUCTIONAL GROUPING
OPEN EDUCATION
PRACTICUMS
PRESCHOOL CURRICULUM
PROGRAM LENGTH
QUARTER SYSTEM
REFRESHER COURSES
REQUIRED COURSES
RESIDENTIAL PROGRAMS
RURAL EXTENSION
SCHOOL SCHEDULES
SCIENCE DEPARTMENTS
SECONDARY SCHOOL CURRICULUM
SEMESTER SYSTEM
SEMINARS
SPIRAL CURRICULUM
STUDY ABROAD
SUMMER PROGRAMS
SUMMER SCHOOLS
SUPPLEMENTARY EDUCATION
TEACHER WORKSHOPS
TELECOURSES
TELEPHONE INSTRUCTION
TIME BLOCKS
TRIMESTER SYSTEM
UNIFIED STUDIES CURRICULUM
UNIT PLAN (1966 1980)
UNITS OF STUDY
URBAN EXTENSION
VACATION PROGRAMS
WEEKEND PROGRAMS
WORK EXPERIENCE PROGRAMS
WORKSHOPS
YEAR ROUND SCHOOLS

360 STUDENTS, TEACHERS, SCHOOL PERSONNEL

ACADEMIC DEANS
ACADEMICALLY GIFTED
ADJUNCT FACULTY
ADMINISTRATORS
ADMISSIONS OFFICERS
ADULT EDUCATORS
ADULT STUDENTS
ADVANCED STUDENTS
ALUMNI
ART TEACHERS
ASSISTANT PRINCIPALS
ASSISTANT SUPERINTENDENT ROLE (1966 1980)
ATTENDANCE OFFICERS
AUDIOVISUAL COORDINATORS
BEGINNING TEACHERS
BILINGUAL STUDENTS
BILINGUAL TEACHER AIDES
BILINGUAL TEACHERS
BLACK STUDENTS
BLACK TEACHERS
BUSINESS EDUCATION TEACHERS
CATHOLIC EDUCATORS
CHILD DEVELOPMENT SPECIALISTS
COLLEGE APPLICANTS
COLLEGE BOUND STUDENTS
COLLEGE FACULTY
COLLEGE FRESHMEN
COLLEGE GRADUATES
COLLEGE PRESIDENTS
COLLEGE SENIORS
COLLEGE STUDENTS
COLLEGE TRANSFER STUDENTS
COMMUTING STUDENTS
CONTINUATION STUDENTS
COOPERATING TEACHERS
COORDINATORS
COUNSELOR EDUCATORS
DAY STUDENTS
DEANS
DEANS OF STUDENTS
DENTAL STUDENTS
DEPARTMENT HEADS
DIFFERENTIATED STAFFS
DISTRIBUTIVE EDUCATION TEACHERS
EDUCATION MAJORS
EDUCATIONAL RESEARCHERS
ELEMENTARY SCHOOL STUDENTS
ELEMENTARY SCHOOL TEACHERS
EVALUATORS
EVENING STUDENTS
FACULTY
FINANCIAL AID APPLICANTS
FOREIGN MEDICAL GRADUATES
FOREIGN STUDENT ADVISERS
FOREIGN STUDENTS
FORMER TEACHERS (1967 1980)
FULL TIME FACULTY
FULL TIME STUDENTS
GRADUATE MEDICAL STUDENTS
GRADUATE SCHOOL FACULTY
GRADUATE STUDENTS
GRADUATES
HIGH RISK STUDENTS
HIGH SCHOOL FRESHMEN
HIGH SCHOOL GRADUATES
HIGH SCHOOL SENIORS
HIGH SCHOOL STUDENTS
HOME ECONOMICS TEACHERS
IN STATE STUDENTS
INDUSTRIAL ARTS TEACHERS
INSTRUCTOR COORDINATORS
ITINERANT TEACHERS
JUNIOR HIGH SCHOOL STUDENTS
LANGUAGE TEACHERS
LAW STUDENTS
LAY TEACHERS
LOW ABILITY STUDENTS (1967 1980)
LOWER CLASS STUDENTS
MARRIED STUDENTS
MASTER TEACHERS
MATHEMATICS TEACHERS
MEDICAL SCHOOL FACULTY
MEDICAL STUDENTS
METHODS TEACHERS
MIDDLE CLASS STUDENTS
MINORITY GROUP TEACHERS

MUSIC TEACHERS
NONCOLLEGE BOUND STUDENTS
NONMAJORS
NONTENURED FACULTY
NONTRADITIONAL STUDENTS
OMBUDSMEN
ON CAMPUS STUDENTS
OUT OF STATE STUDENTS
PARAPROFESSIONAL SCHOOL PERSONNEL
PART TIME FACULTY
PART TIME STUDENTS
PARTNERSHIP TEACHERS
PHYSICAL EDUCATION TEACHERS
POTENTIAL DROPOUTS
PREGNANT STUDENTS
PREMEDICAL STUDENTS
PRESCHOOL TEACHERS
PRINCIPALS
PROFESSORS
PUBLIC SCHOOL TEACHERS
READING CONSULTANTS
READING TEACHERS
REENTRY STUDENTS
REGISTRARS (SCHOOL)
REMEDIAL TEACHERS
RESIDENT ADVISERS
RESIDENT ASSISTANTS
RESOURCE STAFF
RESOURCE TEACHERS
SCHOOL AIDES
SCHOOL BUSINESS OFFICIALS
SCHOOL CADRES
SCHOOL NURSES
SCHOOL PERSONNEL
SCHOOL PSYCHOLOGISTS
SCHOOL SECRETARIES
SCHOOL SOCIAL WORKERS
SCIENCE TEACHERS
SECONDARY SCHOOL STUDENTS
SECONDARY SCHOOL TEACHERS
SELF SUPPORTING STUDENTS
SINGLE STUDENTS
SPECIALISTS
STATE SUPERVISORS
STUDENT FINANCIAL AID OFFICERS
STUDENT TEACHER SUPERVISORS
STUDENT TEACHERS
STUDENT VOLUNTEERS
STUDENTS
SUBSTITUTE TEACHERS
SUPERINTENDENTS
TEACHER AIDES
TEACHER EDUCATORS
TEACHER INTERNS
TEACHERS
TEACHING ASSISTANTS
TELEVISION TEACHERS
TENURED FACULTY
TERMINAL STUDENTS
TRADE AND INDUSTRIAL TEACHERS
TRANSFER STUDENTS
TRUSTEES
TUTORS
TWO YEAR COLLEGE STUDENTS
UNDERGRADUATE STUDENTS
VOCATIONAL DIRECTORS
VOCATIONAL EDUCATION TEACHERS
WHITE STUDENTS
WOMEN FACULTY

400 SUBJECTS OF INSTRUCTION

ACADEMIC EDUCATION
ADMINISTRATOR EDUCATION
ADULT VOCATIONAL EDUCATION
ADVENTURE EDUCATION
AGING EDUCATION
ALCOHOL EDUCATION
ALPHABETIZING SKILLS
AMERICAN INDIAN STUDIES
AMERICAN STUDIES
ANTHROPOLOGY
ARCHAEOLOGY
ARCHITECTURAL EDUCATION
AREA STUDIES
ASIAN STUDIES
AUDITORY TRAINING
BASIC BUSINESS EDUCATION
BASIC SKILLS
BEHAVIORAL SCIENCES
BLACK STUDIES
BUSINESS ADMINISTRATION EDUCATION
BUSINESS EDUCATION
BUSINESS ENGLISH
BUSINESS SKILLS
CAREER AWARENESS
CAREER EDUCATION
CAREER EXPLORATION
CARTOGRAPHY
CITIZENSHIP EDUCATION
CIVICS
CLOTHING INSTRUCTION
COLLEGE ENGLISH
COMMUNICATION SKILLS
COMPARATIVE EDUCATION
COMPETENCY BASED TEACHER EDUCATION
COMPUTER SCIENCE EDUCATION
CONCEPT TEACHING
CONSUMER EDUCATION
CONSUMER SCIENCE
CONTENT AREA WRITING
COOKING INSTRUCTION
COOPERATIVE EDUCATION
CREATIVE WRITING
CRIMINOLOGY
CROSS CULTURAL STUDIES
CROSS CULTURAL TRAINING
CULTURAL EDUCATION
CURRENT EVENTS
CURSIVE WRITING
CUSTODIAN TRAINING
DEBATE
DESCRIPTIVE WRITING
DIRECTION WRITING (1966 1980)
DISTRIBUTIVE EDUCATION
DRIVER EDUCATION
DRUG EDUCATION
ECONOMICS EDUCATION
EDUCATION COURSES
EDUCATIONAL ANTHROPOLOGY
EDUCATIONAL GERONTOLOGY
EDUCATIONAL PSYCHOLOGY
EDUCATIONAL SOCIOLOGY
ENERGY EDUCATION
ENGLISH CURRICULUM
ENGLISH EDUCATION (1967 1980)
ENGLISH INSTRUCTION
ENGLISH TEACHER EDUCATION
ENVIRONMENTAL EDUCATION
ETHICAL INSTRUCTION
ETHNIC STUDIES
ETHNOGRAPHY
ETHNOLOGY
EXPOSITORY WRITING
FAMILY LIFE EDUCATION
FILM STUDY
FIRE SCIENCE EDUCATION
FLIGHT TRAINING
FOODS INSTRUCTION
FOUNDATIONS OF EDUCATION
FRESHMAN COMPOSITION
GENERAL EDUCATION
GEOGRAPHIC CONCEPTS
GEOGRAPHY
GEOGRAPHY INSTRUCTION
GERONTOLOGY
HANDWRITING
HEALTH EDUCATION
HOME ECONOMICS
HOME ECONOMICS EDUCATION
HOME ECONOMICS SKILLS
HOME MANAGEMENT
HOMEMAKING SKILLS
HUMANISTIC EDUCATION
INDUSTRIAL ARTS
INDUSTRIAL EDUCATION
INDUSTRIAL TRAINING
INTERNATIONAL EDUCATION
INTERNATIONAL STUDIES
JOURNALISM EDUCATION
LAW RELATED EDUCATION
LEADERSHIP TRAINING
LEGAL EDUCATION (PROFESSIONS)
LEGAL EDUCATION (1977 1986)
LEISURE EDUCATION
LIBERAL ARTS
LIBRARY EDUCATION
LIBRARY INSTRUCTION
LITERATURE APPRECIATION
LITERATURE PROGRAMS (1966 1980)
LOCATIONAL SKILLS (SOCIAL STUDIES)
LOGIC
MAP SKILLS
MARINE EDUCATION
MARKSMANSHIP
MECHANICAL SKILLS
METHODS COURSES
MIDDLE EASTERN STUDIES
MILITARY SCIENCE
MILITARY TRAINING
NUTRITION INSTRUCTION
OCCUPATIONAL HOME ECONOMICS
OFFICE OCCUPATIONS EDUCATION
OFFICE PRACTICE
OUTDOOR EDUCATION
PARAGRAPH COMPOSITION
PARENTHOOD EDUCATION
POLICE EDUCATION
POLITICAL SCIENCE
POPULATION EDUCATION
POSTSECONDARY EDUCATION AS A FIELD OF STUDY
PRACTICAL ARTS
PRERETIREMENT EDUCATION
PRESERVICE TEACHER EDUCATION
PRETECHNOLOGY PROGRAMS
PREVOCATIONAL EDUCATION
PREWRITING
PUBLIC ADMINISTRATION EDUCATION
PUBLIC AFFAIRS EDUCATION
PUBLIC SPEAKING
RELIGIOUS EDUCATION
REVISION (WRITTEN COMPOSITION)
SAFETY EDUCATION
SENSORY TRAINING
SEWING INSTRUCTION
SEX EDUCATION
SHOP CURRICULUM
SHORTHAND
SOCIAL SCIENCES
SOCIAL STUDIES
SOCIOLOGY
SPELLING
SPELLING INSTRUCTION
SUPERVISORY TRAINING
TEACHER EDUCATION
TEACHER EDUCATION CURRICULUM
TEACHER EDUCATION PROGRAMS
TEACHER EDUCATOR EDUCATION
TECHNICAL EDUCATION
TELEPHONE USAGE INSTRUCTION
TELEVISION CURRICULUM
TEXTILES INSTRUCTION
THEOLOGICAL EDUCATION
TRADE AND INDUSTRIAL EDUCATION
TYPEWRITING
UNITED STATES GOVERNMENT (COURSE)
URBAN STUDIES
VALUES CLARIFICATION
VALUES EDUCATION
VETERINARY MEDICAL EDUCATION
VOCATIONAL EDUCATION
VOLUNTEER TRAINING
WOMENS STUDIES
WORLD GEOGRAPHY
WRITING (COMPOSITION)
WRITING IMPROVEMENT
WRITING INSTRUCTION
WRITING PROCESSES
WRITING SKILLS

410 AGRICULTURE AND NATURAL RESOURCES

ADULT FARMER EDUCATION
AGRIBUSINESS
AGRICULTURAL CHEMICAL OCCUPATIONS
AGRICULTURAL EDUCATION
AGRICULTURAL ENGINEERING
AGRICULTURAL LABORERS
AGRICULTURAL MACHINERY
AGRICULTURAL MACHINERY OCCUPATIONS
AGRICULTURAL OCCUPATIONS
AGRICULTURAL PERSONNEL
AGRICULTURAL PRODUCTION
AGRICULTURAL SAFETY
AGRICULTURAL SKILLS
AGRICULTURAL SUPPLIES
AGRICULTURAL SUPPLY OCCUPATIONS
AGRICULTURAL TECHNICIANS
AGRICULTURAL TRENDS
AGRICULTURE
AGRONOMY
AIR POLLUTION
ANIMAL HUSBANDRY
ASBESTOS
BRACEROS
COAL
CONSERVATION (ENVIRONMENT)
CONSERVATION EDUCATION
CREW LEADERS
CROP PROCESSING OCCUPATIONS
DAIRY FARMERS
DEPLETED RESOURCES
DRINKING WATER
ECOLOGICAL FACTORS
ENDANGERED SPECIES
ENERGY AUDITS
ENERGY CONSERVATION
ENERGY MANAGEMENT
ENVIRONMENT
ESTUARIES
EXPERIMENT STATIONS
EXTENSION AGENTS

FARM ACCOUNTS
FARM LABOR
FARM MANAGEMENT
FARM OCCUPATIONS
FARM VISITS
FARMERS
FEED INDUSTRY
FEED STORES
FERTILIZERS
FIELD CROPS
FISHERIES
FLORICULTURE
FORESTRY
FORESTRY AIDES
FORESTRY OCCUPATIONS
FUEL CONSUMPTION
FUELS
GRAINS (FOOD)
GREENHOUSES
GROUNDS KEEPERS
HARVESTING
HERBICIDES
HORSES
HORTICULTURE
INSECTICIDES
LANDSCAPING
LIVESTOCK
LUMBER INDUSTRY
MEAT
MINERALS
MINING
NATURAL RESOURCES
NURSERIES (HORTICULTURE)
NURSERY WORKERS (HORTICULTURE)
OFF FARM AGRICULTURAL OCCUPATIONS
ORNAMENTAL HORTICULTURE
ORNAMENTAL HORTICULTURE OCCUPATIONS
PART TIME FARMERS
PESTICIDES
PESTS
PLANT GROWTH
PLANT IDENTIFICATION
PLANT PATHOLOGY
PLANT PROPAGATION
PLANT SCIENCE (1967 1980)
POLLUTION
RECYCLING
RURAL FARM RESIDENTS
SHARECROPPERS
SLUDGE
SOIL CONSERVATION
SOIL SCIENCE
SOLID WASTES
SUPERVISED FARM PRACTICE
TRACTORS
TREES
TURF MANAGEMENT
VETERINARY MEDICINE
WASTE DISPOSAL
WASTE WATER
WASTES
WATER POLLUTION
WATER QUALITY
WATER RESOURCES
WEEDS
WILDLIFE
WILDLIFE MANAGEMENT
YOUNG FARMER EDUCATION

420 ARTS

ACTING
AESTHETIC EDUCATION
APPLIED MUSIC
ARCHITECTS
ARCHITECTURE
ART
ART ACTIVITIES
ART APPRECIATION
ART EDUCATION
ART EXPRESSION
ART HISTORY
ART MATERIALS
ART PRODUCTS
ART SONG
ARTISTS
BANDS (MUSIC)
CARICATURES (1966 1980)
CERAMICS
CHILDRENS ART
CHORAL MUSIC
CHORAL SPEAKING
CLOTHING DESIGN
COLOR PLANNING
COMMERCIAL ART
CONCERTS
CONTRAST
CREATIVE ART
CREATIVE DRAMATICS
CREATIVE EXPRESSION
DANCE
DANCE EDUCATION
DESIGN
DESIGN CRAFTS
DESIGN PREFERENCES
DRAMA WORKSHOPS
DRAMATIC PLAY
DRAMATICS
FINE ARTS
FREEHAND DRAWING
FURNITURE DESIGN
GRAPHIC ARTS
HANDICRAFTS
HYMNS
INTERIOR DESIGN
JAZZ
MANUSCRIPT WRITING (HANDLETTERING)
MUSIC
MUSIC ACTIVITIES
MUSIC APPRECIATION
MUSIC EDUCATION
MUSIC READING
MUSIC TECHNIQUES
MUSIC THEORY
MUSICAL COMPOSITION
MUSICAL INSTRUMENTS
MUSICIANS
OPERA
ORAL INTERPRETATION
ORCHESTRAS
ORIENTAL MUSIC
PAINTING (VISUAL ARTS)
PANTOMIME
PHOTOGRAPHY
PUPPETRY
READERS THEATER
SCULPTURE
SINGING
SKITS
SONGS
THEATER ARTS
VISUAL ARTS
VOCAL MUSIC

430 HUMANITIES

ADOLESCENT LITERATURE
AFRICAN HISTORY
AFRICAN LITERATURE
ALLEGORY
AMBIGUITY
AMERICAN HISTORY (1966 1980)
AMERICAN INDIAN HISTORY
AMERICAN INDIAN LITERATURE
ANALYTICAL CRITICISM (1969 1980)
ANCIENT HISTORY
ANTITHESIS
ARISTOTELIAN CRITICISM (1969 1980)
ASIAN HISTORY
AUSTRALIAN LITERATURE
AUTEURISM
AUTHORS
BALLADS
BAROQUE LITERATURE
BIBLICAL LITERATURE
BIOETHICS
BLACK HISTORY
BLACK LITERATURE
BUDDHISM
CANADIAN LITERATURE
CHARACTERIZATION
CHILDRENS LITERATURE
CHRISTIANITY
CHRONICLES
CIVIL WAR (UNITED STATES)
CLASSICAL LITERATURE
CLICHES
COLONIAL HISTORY (UNITED STATES)
COMEDY
CONFUCIANISM
CONSTITUTIONAL HISTORY
CREATIONISM
CZECH LITERATURE
DIALOGS (LITERARY)
DIARIES
DIDACTICISM
DRAMA
EIGHTEENTH CENTURY LITERATURE
ENGLISH LITERATURE
ENGLISH NEOCLASSIC LITERARY PERIOD (1968 1980)
EPICS
ESSAYS
ETHICS
EUROPEAN HISTORY
EXISTENTIALISM
EXPRESSIONISM
FABLES
FAMILY HISTORY
FICTION
FIFTEENTH CENTURY LITERATURE
FIGURATIVE LANGUAGE
FILM CRITICISM
FORMAL CRITICISM (1969 1980)
FRENCH LITERATURE
GENEALOGY
GERMAN LITERATURE
GREEK CIVILIZATION
GREEK LITERATURE
HAIKU
HISPANIC AMERICAN LITERATURE
HISTORICAL CRITICISM (1969 1980)
HISTORIOGRAPHY
HISTORY
HISTORY INSTRUCTION
HUMANISM
HUMANITIES
HUMANITIES INSTRUCTION
HUMOR
IMAGERY
IMPRESSIONISM
IMPRESSIONISTIC CRITICISM (1969 1980)
INDIVIDUALISM
INTELLECTUAL HISTORY
IRONY
ITALIAN LITERATURE
JUDAISM
LATIN AMERICAN HISTORY
LATIN AMERICAN LITERATURE
LATIN LITERATURE
LEGENDS
LITERARY CRITICISM
LITERARY DEVICES
LITERARY DISCRIMINATION (1966 1980)
LITERARY GENRES
LITERARY HISTORY
LITERARY INFLUENCES (1969 1980)
LITERARY MOOD (1970 1980)
LITERARY PERSPECTIVE (1969 1980)
LITERARY STYLES
LITERATURE
LOCAL COLOR WRITING
LOCAL HISTORY
LYRIC POETRY
MEDIEVAL HISTORY
MEDIEVAL LITERATURE
METAPHORS
MEXICAN AMERICAN HISTORY
MEXICAN AMERICAN LITERATURE
MIDDLE EASTERN HISTORY
MODERN HISTORY
MODERNISM
MONOLOGS
MORAL CRITICISM (1969 1980)
MOTIFS
MYSTICISM
MYTHIC CRITICISM (1969 1980)
MYTHOLOGY
NARRATION
NATURALISM
NEOCLASSICISM
NEW JOURNALISM
NINETEENTH CENTURY LITERATURE
NONFICTION
NORTH AMERICAN HISTORY
NORTH AMERICAN LITERATURE
NOVELS
ODES
OLD ENGLISH LITERATURE
ORAL HISTORY
PARADOX
PARALLELISM (LITERARY)
PARODY
PASTORAL LITERATURE
PHENOMENOLOGY
PHILOSOPHY
PLATONIC CRITICISM (1970 1980)
PLATONISM
PLAYWRITING
POETRY
POETS
POLISH LITERATURE
PROSE
PROVERBS
PUNS
REALISM
RECONSTRUCTION ERA
RELIGION
RENAISSANCE LITERATURE
REVOLUTIONARY WAR (UNITED STATES)
RHETORIC
RHETORICAL CRITICISM
RHETORICAL INVENTION

ROMANTICISM
RUSSIAN LITERATURE
SATIRE
SCIENCE FICTION
SEVENTEENTH CENTURY LITERATURE
SHORT STORIES
SIXTEENTH CENTURY LITERATURE
SOCIAL HISTORY
SONNETS
SPANISH LITERATURE
STATE HISTORY
SURREALISM
SYMBOLISM
SYMBOLS (LITERARY)
TALES
TAOISM
TEXTUAL CRITICISM (1969 1980)
THEORETICAL CRITICISM (1969 1980)
TRAGEDY
TWENTIETH CENTURY LITERATURE
UNITED STATES HISTORY
UNITED STATES LITERATURE
VICTORIAN LITERATURE
WORLD HISTORY
WORLD LITERATURE

440 LANGUAGES

AFRICAN LANGUAGES
AFRIKAANS
AFRO ASIATIC LANGUAGES
AKAN
ALBANIAN
AMERICAN INDIAN LANGUAGES
AMHARIC
APACHE
ARABIC
ARMENIAN
ARTIFICIAL LANGUAGES
ATHAPASCAN LANGUAGES
AUSTRALIAN ABORIGINAL LANGUAGES
AUSTRO ASIATIC LANGUAGES
AYMARA
AZERBAIJANI
BALTIC LANGUAGES
BALUCHI
BANTU LANGUAGES
BASAA
BASHKIR
BASQUE
BEMBA
BENGALI
BERBER LANGUAGES
BIELORUSSIAN
BIKOL
BINI
BULGARIAN
BURIAT
BURMESE
BURUSHASKI
CAKCHIQUEL
CAMBODIAN
CANTONESE
CAUCASIAN LANGUAGES
CEBUANO
CHAD LANGUAGES
CHAMORRO
CHEREMIS
CHEROKEE
CHINESE
CHINYANJA
CHOCTAW
CHUVASH
CLASSICAL LANGUAGES
CREE
CREOLES
CZECH
DAGUR
DRAVIDIAN LANGUAGES
DUSUN
DUTCH
DYULA
ENGLISH
ENGLISH (SECOND LANGUAGE)
ENGLISH FOR ACADEMIC PURPOSES
ENGLISH FOR SCIENCE AND TECHNOLOGY
ENGLISH FOR SPECIAL PURPOSES
ESKIMO ALEUT LANGUAGES
ESTONIAN
EWE
FINNISH
FINNO UGRIC LANGUAGES
FOOCHOW
FRENCH
FULANI
GA
GANDA
GBAYA
GERMAN
GREEK
GUARANI
GUJARATI
GULLAH
HAITIAN CREOLE
HAUSA
HAWAIIAN
HEBREW
HINDI
HOPI
HUNGARIAN
IBO
IGBO
INDO EUROPEAN LANGUAGES
INDONESIAN
INDONESIAN LANGUAGES
ITALIAN
JAPANESE
JAVANESE
KABYLE
KANNADA
KASHMIRI
KIRGHIZ
KIRUNDI
KITUBA
KOREAN
KURDISH
LANGUAGES
LANGUAGES FOR SPECIAL PURPOSES
LAO
LATIN
LATVIAN
LINGALA
LITHUANIAN
LUO
MALAGASY
MALAY
MALAYALAM
MALAYO POLYNESIAN LANGUAGES
MANCHU
MANDARIN CHINESE
MANDINGO
MARANAO
MARATHI
MAURITIAN CREOLE
MAYAN LANGUAGES
MELANESIAN LANGUAGES
MENDE
MIDDLE ENGLISH
MODERN LANGUAGES
MONGOLIAN
MONGOLIAN LANGUAGES
MOSSI
NAVAJO
NEMBE
NEPALI
NORWEGIAN
OJIBWA
OKINAWAN
OLD ENGLISH
OSSETIC
OSTYAK
PANJABI
PAPAGO
PASHTO
PERSIAN
PIDGINS
POLISH
POMO
PORTUGUESE
QUECHUA
QUICHE
RIFF
ROMANCE LANGUAGES
RUMANIAN
RUSSIAN
SALISH
SAMOAN
SAMOYED LANGUAGES
SANGO
SANSKRIT
SARA
SEMITIC LANGUAGES
SERBOCROATIAN
SHONA
SIERRA LEONE CREOLE
SINGHALESE
SINO TIBETAN LANGUAGES
SISWATI
SLAVIC LANGUAGES
SLOVENIAN
SOMALI
SPANISH
SUSU
SWAHILI
SWEDISH
TAGALOG
TAJIK
TAMIL
TATAR
TELUGU
THAI
TIBETAN
TURKIC LANGUAGES
TURKISH
TZELTAL
TZOTZIL
UKRAINIAN
URALIC ALTAIC LANGUAGES
URDU
UTO AZTECAN LANGUAGES
UZBEK
VIETNAMESE
VISAYAN
VOCATIONAL ENGLISH (SECOND LANGUAGE)
VOGUL
WELSH
WOLOF
YAKUT
YIDDISH
YORUBA
YUCATEC
YURAK

450 LANGUAGE AND SPEECH

ACOUSTIC PHONETICS
ADJECTIVES
ADVERBS
ALPHABETS
ANTHROPOLOGICAL LINGUISTICS
APPLIED LINGUISTICS
ARTICULATION (SPEECH)
ARTIFICIAL SPEECH
AUDIOLINGUAL METHODS
AUDIOLINGUAL SKILLS
AVIATION VOCABULARY
BANKING VOCABULARY
BASIC VOCABULARY
BIDIALECTALISM
BILINGUAL EDUCATION PROGRAMS
BILINGUALISM
BLACK DIALECTS
CAPITALIZATION (ALPHABETIC)
CASE (GRAMMAR)
CHILD LANGUAGE
CODE SWITCHING (LANGUAGE)
COHERENCE
COHESION (WRITTEN COMPOSITION)
COLLEGE LANGUAGE PROGRAMS (1967 1980)
COLLEGE SECOND LANGUAGE PROGRAMS
COMMUNICATIVE COMPETENCE (LANGUAGES)
COMPONENTIAL ANALYSIS
COMPUTATIONAL LINGUISTICS
CONNECTED DISCOURSE
CONSONANTS
CONTEXT FREE GRAMMAR
CONTRASTIVE LINGUISTICS
CONVERSATIONAL LANGUAGE COURSES
CYRILLIC ALPHABET
DEEP STRUCTURE
DESCRIPTIVE LINGUISTICS
DETERMINERS (LANGUAGES)
DIACHRONIC LINGUISTICS
DIACRITICAL MARKING
DIALECTS
DIALOGS (LANGUAGE)
DICTION
DIGLOSSIA
DISCOURSE ANALYSIS
DISTINCTIVE FEATURES (LANGUAGE)
ERROR ANALYSIS (LANGUAGE)
ETYMOLOGY
EXPRESSIVE LANGUAGE
FLES
FORM CLASSES (LANGUAGES)
FUNCTION WORDS
GENERATIVE GRAMMAR
GENERATIVE PHONOLOGY
GLOTTOCHRONOLOGY
GRAMMAR
GRAMMAR TRANSLATION METHOD
GRAMMATICAL ACCEPTABILITY
GRAPHEMES
IDEOGRAPHY
IDIOMS
IMMERSION PROGRAMS
INNER SPEECH (SUBVOCAL)
INTENSIVE LANGUAGE COURSES
INTERFERENCE (LANGUAGE)
INTERLANGUAGE
INTERNATIONAL TRADE VOCABULARY
INTERPRETIVE SKILLS
INTONATION

KERNEL SENTENCES
KINSHIP TERMINOLOGY
LANGUAGE
LANGUAGE ABILITY (1966 1980)
LANGUAGE AIDS (1966 1980)
LANGUAGE APTITUDE
LANGUAGE ARTS
LANGUAGE ATTITUDES
LANGUAGE CLASSIFICATION
LANGUAGE DOMINANCE
LANGUAGE ENRICHMENT
LANGUAGE EXPERIENCE APPROACH
LANGUAGE FLUENCY
LANGUAGE INSTRUCTION (1966 1980)
LANGUAGE LEARNING LEVELS (1967 1980)
LANGUAGE MAINTENANCE
LANGUAGE OF INSTRUCTION
LANGUAGE PATTERNS
LANGUAGE PLANNING
LANGUAGE PROCESSING
LANGUAGE PROFICIENCY
LANGUAGE PROGRAMS (1966 1980)
LANGUAGE RHYTHM
LANGUAGE ROLE
LANGUAGE SKILL ATTRITION
LANGUAGE SKILLS
LANGUAGE STANDARDIZATION
LANGUAGE STYLES
LANGUAGE TYPOLOGY
LANGUAGE UNIVERSALS
LANGUAGE USAGE
LANGUAGE VARIATION
LETTERS (ALPHABET)
LIMITED ENGLISH SPEAKING
LINGUISTIC BORROWING
LINGUISTIC COMPETENCE
LINGUISTIC DIFFICULTY (INHERENT)
LINGUISTIC PERFORMANCE
LINGUISTIC THEORY
LINGUISTICS
MATHEMATICAL LINGUISTICS
MODERN LANGUAGE CURRICULUM
MONOLINGUALISM
MORPHEMES
MORPHOLOGY (LANGUAGES)
MORPHOPHONEMICS
MULTILEVEL CLASSES (SECOND LANGUAGE INSTRUCTION)
MULTILINGUALISM
MUTUAL INTELLIGIBILITY
NATIVE LANGUAGE INSTRUCTION
NATIVE SPEAKERS
NEGATIVE FORMS (LANGUAGE)
NEUROLINGUISTICS
NON ENGLISH SPEAKING
NONSTANDARD DIALECTS
NORTH AMERICAN ENGLISH
NOTIONAL FUNCTIONAL SYLLABI
NOUNS
OFFICIAL LANGUAGES
ONOMASTICS
ORAL ENGLISH
ORAL LANGUAGE
ORTHOGRAPHIC SYMBOLS
PARAGRAPHS
PARALINGUISTICS
PATTERN DRILLS (LANGUAGE)
PERSUASIVE DISCOURSE
PHONEME GRAPHEME CORRESPONDENCE
PHONEMES
PHONEMIC ALPHABETS
PHONEMICS
PHONETIC ANALYSIS
PHONETIC TRANSCRIPTION
PHONETICS
PHONOLOGY
PHRASE STRUCTURE
PLURALS
PRAGMATICS
PREPOSITIONS
PRONOUNS
PRONUNCIATION
PRONUNCIATION INSTRUCTION
PSYCHOLINGUISTICS
PUNCTUATION
RECEPTIVE LANGUAGE
REGIONAL DIALECTS
ROMANIZATION
SECOND LANGUAGE INSTRUCTION
SECOND LANGUAGE LEARNING
SECOND LANGUAGE PROGRAMS
SECOND LANGUAGES
SEMANTICS
SEMIOTICS
SENTENCE COMBINING
SENTENCE DIAGRAMING
SENTENCE STRUCTURE
SENTENCES
SOCIAL DIALECTS
SOCIOLINGUISTICS
SPANISH SPEAKING
SPEECH
SPEECH ACTS
SPEECH COMMUNICATION
SPEECH COMPRESSION
SPEECH CURRICULUM
SPEECH EDUCATION (1966 1980)
SPEECH EVALUATION
SPEECH HABITS
SPEECH IMPROVEMENT
SPEECH INSTRUCTION
SPEECH SKILLS
STANDARD SPOKEN USAGE
STRESS (PHONOLOGY)
STRUCTURAL ANALYSIS (LINGUISTICS)
STRUCTURAL ANALYSIS (1966 1980)
STRUCTURAL GRAMMAR
STRUCTURAL LINGUISTICS
SUFFIXES
SUPRASEGMENTALS
SURFACE STRUCTURE
SYLLABLES
SYMBOLIC LANGUAGE
SYNTAX
TAGMEMIC ANALYSIS
TENL (1968 1980)
TENSES (GRAMMAR)
THRESHOLD LEVEL (LANGUAGES)
TONE LANGUAGES
TRADITIONAL GRAMMAR
TRANSFORMATIONAL GENERATIVE GRAMMAR
TRANSLATION
UNCOMMONLY TAUGHT LANGUAGES
UNWRITTEN LANGUAGE (1968 1980)
UNWRITTEN LANGUAGES
URBAN LANGUAGE
VERBAL ABILITY
VERBAL COMMUNICATION
VERBAL DEVELOPMENT
VERBS
VOCABULARY
VOCABULARY DEVELOPMENT
VOCABULARY SKILLS
VOWELS
WORD FREQUENCY
WRITTEN LANGUAGE

460 READING

ADULT LITERACY
ADULT READING PROGRAMS
BASAL READING
BASIC READING (1967 1980)
BEGINNING READING
CLOZE PROCEDURE
CONTENT AREA READING
CONTEXT CLUES
CORRECTIVE READING
CREATIVE READING (1966 1980)
CRITICAL READING
DECODING (READING)
DEVELOPMENTAL READING (1966 1980)
DIRECTED READING ACTIVITY
EARLY READING
ELECTIVE READING (1966 1980)
EYE VOICE SPAN
FACTUAL READING (1966 1980)
FUNCTIONAL LITERACY
FUNCTIONAL READING
GROUP READING (1966 1980)
ILLITERACY
INDEPENDENT READING
INDIVIDUAL READING (1966 1980)
INDIVIDUALIZED READING
INITIAL TEACHING ALPHABET
INTERPRETIVE READING (1966 1980)
LITERACY
LITERACY EDUCATION
MISCUE ANALYSIS
ORAL READING
PHONICS
PREREADING EXPERIENCE
READABILITY
READABILITY FORMULAS
READER TEXT RELATIONSHIP
READING
READING ABILITY
READING ACHIEVEMENT
READING ALOUD TO OTHERS
READING ASSIGNMENTS
READING ATTITUDES
READING CENTERS
READING COMPREHENSION
READING DEVELOPMENT (1966 1980)
READING DIAGNOSIS
READING DIFFICULTIES
READING DIFFICULTY (1966 1980)
READING FAILURE
READING GAMES
READING HABITS
READING IMPROVEMENT
READING INSTRUCTION
READING INTERESTS
READING LEVEL (1966 1980)
READING MATERIAL SELECTION
READING PROCESSES
READING PROGRAMS
READING RATE
READING READINESS
READING SKILLS
READING STRATEGIES
READING WRITING RELATIONSHIP
RECREATIONAL READING
REMEDIAL READING
SIGHT METHOD
SIGHT VOCABULARY
SILENT READING
SPEED READING
STORY GRAMMAR
STORY READING
SUPPLEMENTARY READING MATERIALS
SUSTAINED SILENT READING
WORD RECOGNITION
WORD STUDY SKILLS

470 PHYSICAL EDUCATION AND RECREATION

AEROBICS
AQUATIC SPORTS
ARCHERY
ATHLETES
ATHLETIC COACHES
ATHLETIC FIELDS
ATHLETICS
BADMINTON
BASEBALL
BASKETBALL
BICYCLING
BOWLING
CALISTHENICS
CAMPING
CHILDRENS GAMES
COLLEGE ATHLETICS
COMMUNITY RECREATION PROGRAMS
DAY CAMP PROGRAMS
DIVING
EXERCISE
EXERCISE (PHYSIOLOGY) (1969 1980)
EXTRACURRICULAR ACTIVITIES
EXTRAMURAL ATHLETICS
FENCING (SPORT)
FIELD HOCKEY
FOOTBALL
GAMES
GOLF
GYMNASTICS
HANDBALL
HOBBIES
HORSEBACK RIDING
ICE HOCKEY
ICE SKATING
INTRAMURAL ATHLETICS
JOGGING
LACROSSE
LEISURE TIME
LIFETIME SPORTS
MOVEMENT EDUCATION
ORIENTEERING
OUTDOOR ACTIVITIES
PHYSICAL ACTIVITIES
PHYSICAL EDUCATION
PHYSICAL RECREATION PROGRAMS
PLAY
PLAYGROUND ACTIVITIES
RACQUET SPORTS
RACQUETBALL
RECREATION
RECREATIONAL ACTIVITIES
RECREATIONAL PROGRAMS
RECREATIONISTS
RESIDENT CAMP PROGRAMS
ROLLER SKATING
RUNNING
SAILING
SCHOOL RECREATIONAL PROGRAMS
SKIING
SOCCER
SOFTBALL
SPORTSMANSHIP
SQUASH (GAME)
SURFING
SWIMMING
TABLE TENNIS

TEAM HANDBALL
TEAM SPORTS
TENNIS
TOYS
TRACK AND FIELD
TUMBLING
UNDERWATER DIVING
VOLLEYBALL
WATER POLO
WATERSKIING
WEIGHTLIFTING
WOMENS ATHLETICS
WRESTLING

480 MATHEMATICS

ADDITION
ALGEBRA
ALGORITHMS
ANALYTIC GEOMETRY
AREA
ARITHMETIC
BAYESIAN STATISTICS
CALCULUS
COLLEGE MATHEMATICS
COMPUTATION
CONGRUENCE (MATHEMATICS)
DECIMAL FRACTIONS
DISTANCE
DIVISION
ELEMENTARY SCHOOL MATHEMATICS
EQUATIONS (MATHEMATICS)
ESTIMATION (MATHEMATICS)
EXPECTANCY TABLES
FRACTIONS
FUNCTIONS (MATHEMATICS)
GEOMETRIC CONCEPTS
GEOMETRIC CONSTRUCTIONS
GEOMETRY
INCIDENCE
INEQUALITY (MATHEMATICS)
INTEGERS
LINEAR PROGRAMING
LOGARITHMS
MATHEMATICAL APPLICATIONS
MATHEMATICAL CONCEPTS
MATHEMATICAL ENRICHMENT
MATHEMATICAL EXPERIENCE (1966 1980)
MATHEMATICAL FORMULAS
MATHEMATICAL LOGIC
MATHEMATICAL VOCABULARY
MATHEMATICS
MATHEMATICS ACHIEVEMENT
MATHEMATICS ANXIETY
MATHEMATICS CURRICULUM
MATHEMATICS EDUCATION
MATHEMATICS INSTRUCTION
MATHEMATICS SKILLS
MATRICES
METRIC SYSTEM
MODERN MATHEMATICS
MULTIPLICATION
NONPARAMETRIC STATISTICS
NUMBER CONCEPTS
NUMBER SYSTEMS
NUMBERS
ORTHOGRAPHIC PROJECTION
PERCENTAGE
PLACE VALUE
PLANE GEOMETRY
PRIME NUMBERS
PROBABILITY
PROOF (MATHEMATICS)
RATIONAL NUMBERS
RATIOS (MATHEMATICS)
RECIPROCALS (MATHEMATICS)
REGRESSION (STATISTICS)
REMEDIAL MATHEMATICS
SECONDARY SCHOOL MATHEMATICS
SET THEORY
SOLID GEOMETRY
STATISTICAL DISTRIBUTIONS
STATISTICAL INFERENCE
STATISTICS
SUBTRACTION
SYMBOLS (MATHEMATICS)
SYMMETRY
TECHNICAL MATHEMATICS
TOPOGRAPHY
TOPOLOGY
TRANSFORMATIONS (MATHEMATICS)
TRIGONOMETRY
VECTORS (MATHEMATICS)
VOLUME (MATHEMATICS)
WHOLE NUMBERS
WORD PROBLEMS (MATHEMATICS)

490 SCIENCE AND TECHNOLOGY

ACCELERATION (PHYSICS)
ACOUSTICS
AEROSPACE EDUCATION
AEROSPACE TECHNOLOGY
AIR FLOW
AIR TRAFFIC CONTROL
ALTERNATIVE ENERGY SOURCES
ANATOMY
ANIMALS
ASTRONOMY
ATOMIC STRUCTURE
ATOMIC THEORY
AUTOMATION
AVIATION TECHNOLOGY
BIOCHEMISTRY
BIOFEEDBACK
BIOLOGICAL SCIENCES
BIOLOGY
BIOMECHANICS
BIONICS
BIOPHYSICS
BOTANY
CHEMICAL ANALYSIS
CHEMICAL BONDING
CHEMICAL ENGINEERING
CHEMICAL EQUILIBRIUM
CHEMICAL NOMENCLATURE
CHEMICAL REACTIONS
CHEMISTRY
CHROMATOGRAPHY
CIVIL ENGINEERING
CLIMATE
CLIMATE CONTROL
COLLEGE SCIENCE
COLOR
COORDINATION COMPOUNDS
CRYSTALLOGRAPHY
CULTURING TECHNIQUES
CYTOLOGY
DIFFUSION (PHYSICS)
DNA
EARTH SCIENCE
EARTHQUAKES
ECOLOGY
ELECTRICITY
ELECTROMECHANICAL TECHNOLOGY
ELECTRONIC CONTROL
ELECTRONICS
ELEMENTARY SCHOOL SCIENCE
EMBRYOLOGY
ENERGY
ENGINEERING
ENGINEERING DRAWING
ENGINEERING EDUCATION
ENGINEERING GRAPHICS
ENGINEERING TECHNOLOGY
ENTOMOLOGY
ENZYMES
ETHOLOGY
EVOLUTION
FLUID MECHANICS
FORCE
GENERAL SCIENCE
GENETIC ENGINEERING
GENETICS
GEOLOGY
GEOPHYSICS
GEOTHERMAL ENERGY
GRAVITY (PHYSICS)
HEAT
HEIGHT
HEREDITY
HOROLOGY
HUMAN FACTORS ENGINEERING
HUMIDITY
HYDRAULICS
ICHTHYOLOGY
INORGANIC CHEMISTRY
INTERVALS
INVENTIONS
KINETIC MOLECULAR THEORY
KINETICS
LABORATORY ANIMALS
LABORATORY EXPERIMENTS
LABORATORY PROCEDURES
LABORATORY TECHNIQUES (1967 1980)
LABORATORY TECHNOLOGY
LASERS
LIGHT
LUMINESCENCE
MAGNETS
MARINE BIOLOGY
MARITIME EDUCATION
MATTER
MECHANICS (PHYSICS)
METALLURGY
METALS
METEOROLOGY
MICROBIOLOGY
MINERALOGY
MOLECULAR STRUCTURE
MOTION
NATURAL SCIENCES
NAVIGATION
NOISE (SOUND)
NUCLEAR ENERGY
NUCLEAR PHYSICS
NUCLEAR TECHNOLOGY
NUCLEIC ACIDS
OBSOLESCENCE
OCEAN ENGINEERING
OCEANOGRAPHY
OPTICS
ORGANIC CHEMISTRY
ORNITHOLOGY
OXIDATION
PALEONTOLOGY
PHOTOCHEMICAL REACTIONS
PHOTOSYNTHESIS
PHYSICAL GEOGRAPHY
PHYSICAL SCIENCES
PHYSICS
PHYSIOLOGY
PLATE TECTONICS
POLYMERS
POWER TECHNOLOGY
PRESERVATION
PRESSURE (PHYSICS)
PRESSURE (1970 1980)
PRIMATOLOGY
PROXIMITY
PSYCHOACOUSTICS
QUANTUM MECHANICS
RADIATION
RADIATION BIOLOGY
RADIATION EFFECTS
RADIOISOTOPES
RATS
RELATIVITY
REPRODUCTION (BIOLOGY)
RNA
ROBOTICS
SATELLITES (AEROSPACE)
SCIENCE ACTIVITIES
SCIENCE AND SOCIETY
SCIENCE CAREERS
SCIENCE COURSE IMPROVEMENT PROJECTS
SCIENCE CURRICULUM
SCIENCE EDUCATION
SCIENCE EDUCATION HISTORY
SCIENCE EXPERIMENTS
SCIENCE FAIRS
SCIENCE HISTORY
SCIENCE INSTRUCTION
SCIENCE INTERESTS
SCIENCE PROGRAMS
SCIENCE PROJECTS
SCIENCES
SCIENTIFIC AND TECHNICAL INFORMATION
SCIENTIFIC ATTITUDES
SCIENTIFIC CONCEPTS
SCIENTIFIC ENTERPRISE
SCIENTIFIC LITERACY
SCIENTIFIC METHODOLOGY
SCIENTIFIC PERSONNEL
SCIENTIFIC PRINCIPLES
SECONDARY SCHOOL SCIENCE
SEISMOLOGY
SOCIAL BIOLOGY
SOCIOBIOLOGY
SOLAR ENERGY
SPACE
SPACE EXPLORATION
SPACE SCIENCES
SPECTROSCOPY
STRUCTURAL ANALYSIS (SCIENCE)
SUMMER SCIENCE PROGRAMS
TECHNOLOGICAL ADVANCEMENT
TECHNOLOGICAL LITERACY
TECHNOLOGY
TECHNOLOGY TRANSFER
TEMPERATURE
THERMODYNAMICS
TIME
WATER
WATER TREATMENT
WEATHER
WEIGHT (MASS)
WIND (METEOROLOGY)
WIND ENERGY
ZOOLOGY

510 THE INDIVIDUAL IN SOCIAL CONTEXT

ADOPTED CHILDREN
ADULT DROPOUTS
ADVANTAGED
AFFLUENT YOUTH
BIOLOGICAL PARENTS
BLACK MOTHERS
BLACK YOUTH
CHILD RESPONSIBILITY
CHILD ROLE
DATING (SOCIAL)
DAUGHTERS
DEPENDENTS
DISPLACED HOMEMAKERS
DROPOUTS
DUAL CAREER FAMILY
ECONOMIC STATUS
EDUCATIONAL ATTAINMENT
EDUCATIONAL BACKGROUND
EDUCATIONAL EXPERIENCE
EDUCATIONAL STATUS COMPARISON
EMPLOYED PARENTS
ETHNIC STATUS
FAMILY ATTITUDES
FAMILY CHARACTERISTICS
FAMILY ENVIRONMENT
FAMILY INFLUENCE
FAMILY INVOLVEMENT
FAMILY LIFE
FAMILY RELATIONSHIP
FAMILY ROLE
FAMILY STATUS
FATHER ATTITUDES
FATHERLESS FAMILY
FATHERS
FOSTER CHILDREN
FOSTER FAMILY
FRIENDSHIP
GRANDCHILDREN
GRANDPARENTS
GROUP MEMBERSHIP
HEADS OF HOUSEHOLDS
HOMEOWNERS
IMMIGRANTS
INTERACTION
INTERPERSONAL ATTRACTION
INTERPERSONAL COMMUNICATION
INTERPERSONAL RELATIONSHIP
LATCHKEY CHILDREN
LEADERS
LOWER CLASS PARENTS
MARITAL SATISFACTION
MARITAL STATUS
MATE SELECTION
MIDDLE CLASS PARENTS
MIGRANT CHILDREN
MIGRANT YOUTH
MIGRANTS
MINORITY GROUP CHILDREN
MOTHER ATTITUDES
MOTHERLESS FAMILY
MOTHERS
ONE PARENT FAMILY
OUT OF SCHOOL YOUTH
PARENT ASPIRATION
PARENT ATTITUDES
PARENT BACKGROUND
PARENT CHILD RELATIONSHIP
PARENT INFLUENCE
PARENT RESPONSIBILITY
PARENT ROLE
PARENTS
PEER ACCEPTANCE
PEER INFLUENCE
PEER RELATIONSHIP
PERMISSIVE ENVIRONMENT
PERSONAL AUTONOMY
RACIAL DIFFERENCES
RAPPORT
RECOGNITION (1967 1980)
REFUGEES
RELIGIOUS DIFFERENCES
ROLE PERCEPTION
RURAL FAMILY
RURAL NONFARM RESIDENTS
RURAL YOUTH
SEX ROLE
SIBLINGS
SIGNIFICANT OTHERS
SOCIAL ATTITUDES
SOCIAL BACKGROUND
SOCIAL CHARACTERISTICS
SOCIAL CONTROL
SOCIAL DIFFERENCES
SOCIAL ENVIRONMENT
SOCIAL EXPERIENCE
SOCIAL INFLUENCES
SOCIAL RESPONSIBILITY
SOCIAL STATUS
SOCIOECONOMIC BACKGROUND
SOCIOECONOMIC INFLUENCES
SOCIOECONOMIC STATUS
SONS
SPOUSES
STOPOUTS
SUBURBAN YOUTH
TRANSIENT CHILDREN
UNDOCUMENTED IMMIGRANTS
UNWED MOTHERS
URBAN YOUTH
VETERANS
VICTIMS OF CRIME
WELFARE RECIPIENTS
WIDOWED
YOUTH LEADERS

520 SOCIAL PROCESSES AND STRUCTURES

ADOPTION
ADOPTION (IDEAS)
ADVOCACY
AESTHETIC VALUES
ALUMNI ASSOCIATIONS
ANCILLARY SERVICES (1967 1980)
AWARDS
BEHAVIOR STANDARDS
BLACK ATTITUDES
BLACK COMMUNITY
BLACK FAMILY
BLACK INFLUENCES
BLACK INSTITUTIONS
BLACK ORGANIZATIONS
BRAINSTORMING
BUREAUCRACY
CENSORSHIP
CENTRALIZATION
CHANGE
CHILD ADVOCACY
CHILD CARE (1966 1980)
CHILD CUSTODY
CHILD REARING
CHILD WELFARE
CHILDRENS RIGHTS
CHURCH PROGRAMS
CHURCH RESPONSIBILITY
CHURCH ROLE
CHURCH WORKERS
CLASS ATTITUDES (1966 1980)
CLUBS
CODES OF ETHICS
COMMITTEES
COMMUNICATION (THOUGHT TRANSFER)
COMMUNICATION AUDITS
COMMUNITY
COMMUNITY ACTION
COMMUNITY ATTITUDES
COMMUNITY CHARACTERISTICS
COMMUNITY COOPERATION
COMMUNITY COORDINATION
COMMUNITY INFLUENCE
COMMUNITY LEADERS
COMMUNITY ORGANIZATIONS
COMMUNITY PROGRAMS
COMMUNITY RELATIONS
COMMUNITY RESOURCES
COMMUNITY RESPONSIBILITY
COMMUNITY ROLE
COMMUNITY SATISFACTION
COMMUNITY SERVICES
COMPETITION
CONFIDENTIALITY
CONFLICT OF INTEREST
CONFLICT RESOLUTION
CONFORMITY
CONSERVATISM
CONSUMER PROTECTION
COOPERATION
COOPERATIVE PLANNING
COORDINATION
CORRECTIONAL REHABILITATION
CREDIBILITY
CRIME PREVENTION
CRITERIA
CROWDING
CULTURAL INFLUENCES
CULTURAL PLURALISM
CULTURE CONFLICT
DAY CARE
DECENTRALIZATION
DECEPTION
DELINQUENCY PREVENTION
DELIVERY SYSTEMS
DEVELOPMENT
DEVELOPMENTAL CONTINUITY
DEVELOPMENTAL PROGRAMS
DIFFERENCES
DISQUALIFICATION
DIVORCE
EARLY PARENTHOOD
ELIGIBILITY
ELITISM
EXTENDED FAMILY
FAMILY (SOCIOLOGICAL UNIT)
FAMILY DAY CARE
FAMILY PROGRAMS
FAMILY SIZE
FAMILY STRUCTURE
FOREIGN NATIONALS
FOSTER CARE
FRATERNITIES
FUTURES (OF SOCIETY)
GROUP BEHAVIOR
GROUP DYNAMICS
GROUP EXPERIENCE
GROUP NORMS (1968 1980)
GROUP STATUS
GROUP STRUCTURE
GROUP UNITY
GROUPS
GROWTH PATTERNS (1966 1980)
HOLIDAYS
HORIZONTAL ORGANIZATION
HUMAN DEVELOPMENT (1966 1980)
HUMAN LIVING (1966 1980)
HUMAN RELATIONS
HUMAN RESOURCES
HUMAN SERVICES
HUMANITARIANISM
HUMANIZATION
IDEOLOGY
IMPROVEMENT
INCENTIVES
INFLUENCES
INFORMAL LEADERSHIP
INFORMAL ORGANIZATION
INNOVATION
INSTITUTIONAL PERSONNEL
INSTITUTIONS
INTERFAITH RELATIONS
INTERGENERATIONAL PROGRAMS
INTERGROUP RELATIONS
INTERMARRIAGE
INTERNATIONAL COOPERATION
INTERPROFESSIONAL RELATIONSHIP
KINSHIP
LAY PEOPLE
LEADERSHIP
LEADERSHIP QUALITIES
LEADERSHIP RESPONSIBILITY
LEADERSHIP STYLES
LEGAL AID
LIBERALISM
LIBRARY ASSOCIATIONS
LIFE STYLE
LIVING STANDARDS
LOW INCOME GROUPS
LOWER CLASS
LOWER MIDDLE CLASS
MAJORITY ATTITUDES
MARRIAGE
MASS MEDIA EFFECTS
MEDICAL ASSOCIATIONS
MEETINGS
MENTORS
MERGERS
MIDDLE CLASS
MIDDLE CLASS STANDARDS
MIGRANT PROGRAMS
MIGRANT WELFARE SERVICES
MINORITY GROUP INFLUENCES
MINORITY GROUPS
MODERNIZATION
MORAL ISSUES
MORAL VALUES
NATIONAL ORGANIZATIONS
NEEDS
NO SHOWS
NONPROFIT ORGANIZATIONS
NUCLEAR FAMILY
OBJECTIVES
ORGANIZATION
ORGANIZATIONS (GROUPS)
PARENT RIGHTS
PEER GROUPS
PLACEMENT
POLICE COMMUNITY RELATIONSHIP
POLITICAL SOCIALIZATION
POPULARITY
POWER STRUCTURE
PREREQUISITES
PRESTIGE
PREVENTION
PRIVACY
PRIVATE AGENCIES
PROFESSIONAL ASSOCIATIONS
PROFESSIONAL RECOGNITION

PROFESSIONAL SERVICES
PROGRAMS
PUNISHMENT
PYRAMID ORGANIZATION
QUALITY OF LIFE
RECOGNITION (ACHIEVEMENT)
REGIONAL PROGRAMS
RELATIONSHIP
RELIGIOUS FACTORS
RELIGIOUS HOLIDAYS
RELIGIOUS ORGANIZATIONS
REMARRIAGE
REPUTATION
RESOURCES
RESPONSIBILITY
REWARDS
SANCTIONS
SCHOOL AGE DAY CARE
SELF DIRECTED GROUPS
SELF HELP PROGRAMS
SENTENCING
SERVICES
SLAVERY
SOCIAL ACTION
SOCIAL AGENCIES
SOCIAL CHANGE
SOCIAL CLASS
SOCIAL DESIRABILITY
SOCIAL INDICATORS
SOCIAL LIFE
SOCIAL MOBILITY
SOCIAL ORGANIZATIONS
SOCIAL RELATIONS (1966 1980)
SOCIAL SERVICES
SOCIAL STRATIFICATION
SOCIAL STRUCTURE
SOCIAL SYSTEMS
SOCIAL VALUES
SOCIAL WELFARE (1966 1980)
SOCIOCULTURAL PATTERNS
SORORITIES
SOUTHERN COMMUNITY (1966 1980)
STANDARDS
STATUS
STEPFAMILY
TALENT UTILIZATION (1966 1980)
TEAMWORK
TRADITIONALISM
UPPER CLASS
URBAN PROGRAMS
VALUES
VERTICAL ORGANIZATION
VOLUNTARY AGENCIES
WELFARE (1966 1980)
WELFARE AGENCIES
WELFARE SERVICES
WORKING CLASS
YOUTH AGENCIES
YOUTH CLUBS
YOUTH PROGRAMS

530 SOCIAL PROBLEMS

ALCOHOLISM
ANTISOCIAL BEHAVIOR
BATTERED WOMEN
CHEATING
CHILD ABUSE
CHILD NEGLECT
COMMUNITY PROBLEMS
CONFLICT
CRIME
CRIMINALS
DELINQUENCY
DELINQUENCY CAUSES
DISCIPLINE PROBLEMS
DRUG ABUSE
DRUG ADDICTION
ELDER ABUSE
FAMILY PROBLEMS
FAMILY VIOLENCE
GENERATION GAP
HOMELESS PEOPLE
HOUSING DEFICIENCIES
ILLEGAL DRUG USE
ILLEGITIMATE BIRTHS
INCEST
INTERNATIONAL CRIMES
JUVENILE GANGS
LYING
MALPRACTICE
MARITAL INSTABILITY
MIGRANT PROBLEMS
OBSCENITY
PLAGIARISM
POVERTY
PRISONERS
PROBLEMS
RAPE
RECIDIVISM
RUNAWAYS
SCHOOL VANDALISM
SEXUAL ABUSE
SEXUAL HARASSMENT
SOCIAL ISOLATION
SOCIAL PROBLEMS
STEALING
URBAN PROBLEMS
VANDALISM
VIOLENCE
WORLD PROBLEMS
YOUTH PROBLEMS

540 BIAS AND EQUITY

AFFIRMATIVE ACTION
AGE DISCRIMINATION
ANTI INTELLECTUALISM
ANTI SEMITISM
BIAS
BIRACIAL COMMITTEES
BLACK LEADERSHIP
BLACK POWER
BLACK STEREOTYPES
BUSING
CASTE
CIVIL RIGHTS
CLASSROOM DESEGREGATION
COLLEGE DESEGREGATION
COLLEGE SEGREGATION
COMPARABLE WORTH
CULTURAL IMAGES
CULTURAL OPPORTUNITIES
CULTURE FAIR TESTS
DE FACTO SEGREGATION
DE JURE SEGREGATION
DESEGREGATION EFFECTS
DESEGREGATION LITIGATION
DESEGREGATION METHODS
DESEGREGATION PLANS
DISADVANTAGED
DISADVANTAGED YOUTH
DISCRIMINATORY LEGISLATION
ECONOMIC OPPORTUNITIES
ECONOMICALLY DISADVANTAGED
EDUCATIONAL DISCRIMINATION
EDUCATIONAL PARKS
EDUCATIONALLY DISADVANTAGED
EQUAL EDUCATION
EQUAL FACILITIES
EQUAL OPPORTUNITIES (JOBS)
EQUAL PROTECTION
ETHNIC BIAS
ETHNIC DISCRIMINATION
ETHNIC RELATIONS
ETHNIC STEREOTYPES
ETHNOCENTRISM
FACULTY INTEGRATION
FEMINISM
GIFTED DISADVANTAGED
HANDICAP DISCRIMINATION
HOUSING DISCRIMINATION
HOUSING OPPORTUNITIES
HUMAN DIGNITY
HUMAN RELATIONS PROGRAMS
INEQUALITIES (1970 1980)
INTEGRATION READINESS
LABELING (OF PERSONS)
MULTICULTURAL EDUCATION
MULTICULTURAL TEXTBOOKS
NEGATIVE ATTITUDES
NEIGHBORHOOD INTEGRATION
NONDISCRIMINATORY EDUCATION
NONTRADITIONAL OCCUPATIONS
OPPORTUNITIES
PERSONNEL INTEGRATION
QUOTAS
RACIAL ATTITUDES
RACIAL BALANCE
RACIAL BIAS
RACIAL CHARACTERISTICS (1966 1980)
RACIAL DISCRIMINATION
RACIAL FACTORS
RACIAL IDENTIFICATION
RACIAL INTEGRATION
RACIAL RELATIONS
RACIAL SEGREGATION
RACIALLY BALANCED SCHOOLS
RACISM (1966 1980)
RELIGIOUS CONFLICT
RELIGIOUS DISCRIMINATION
REVERSE DISCRIMINATION
SCHOOL BOYCOTTS
SCHOOL DESEGREGATION
SCHOOL RESEGREGATION
SCHOOL SEGREGATION
SEGREGATIONIST ORGANIZATIONS
SEX BIAS
SEX DISCRIMINATION
SEX FAIRNESS
SEX STEREOTYPES
SOCIAL BIAS
SOCIAL DISCRIMINATION
SOCIAL INTEGRATION
STEREOTYPES
TEACHER INTEGRATION
TEACHER STEREOTYPES
TEST BIAS
TEXTBOOK BIAS
TOKENISM
VOLUNTARY DESEGREGATION
YOUTH OPPORTUNITIES

550 HUMAN GEOGRAPHY

APPROPRIATE TECHNOLOGY
BIRTH RATE
BLACK HOUSING (1977 1980)
BLACK POPULATION TRENDS
COLLECTIVE SETTLEMENTS
COMMUNITY CHANGE
COMMUNITY DEVELOPMENT
COMMUNITY PLANNING
COMMUNITY SIZE
COMMUNITY ZONING
DEMOGRAPHY
DISADVANTAGED ENVIRONMENT
ETHNIC DISTRIBUTION
ETHNIC GROUPING (1966 1980)
FAMILY MOBILITY
GEOGRAPHIC DISTRIBUTION
GEOGRAPHIC LOCATION
GEOGRAPHIC REGIONS
GHETTOS
HUMAN GEOGRAPHY
INDIGENOUS POPULATIONS
INNER CITY
LAND SETTLEMENT
LAND USE
LOW INCOME COUNTIES
LOW INCOME STATES
LOW RENT HOUSING
METROPOLITAN AREAS
MIDDLE INCOME HOUSING
MIGRATION
MIGRATION PATTERNS
MOBILITY
MUNICIPALITIES
NEGRO HOUSING (1966 1977)
NEIGHBORHOOD IMPROVEMENT
NEIGHBORHOODS
OVERPOPULATION
PHYSICAL DIVISIONS (GEOGRAPHIC)
PLACE OF RESIDENCE
PLANNED COMMUNITIES
POPULATION DISTRIBUTION
POPULATION GROWTH
POPULATION TRENDS
POVERTY AREAS
PUBLIC HOUSING
RACIAL COMPOSITION
RACIAL DISTRIBUTION
REGIONAL ATTITUDES
REGIONAL CHARACTERISTICS
RELOCATION
RESIDENTIAL PATTERNS
RURAL AREAS
RURAL DEVELOPMENT
RURAL ENVIRONMENT
RURAL POPULATION
RURAL RESETTLEMENT
RURAL TO URBAN MIGRATION
RURAL URBAN DIFFERENCES
SLUM ENVIRONMENT
SLUMS
SOCIAL DISTRIBUTION
SUBURBAN ENVIRONMENT
SUBURBAN HOUSING
SUBURBAN PROBLEMS
SUBURBS
TRAVEL
URBAN AREAS
URBAN DEMOGRAPHY
URBAN ENVIRONMENT
URBAN IMPROVEMENT
URBAN PLANNING
URBAN POPULATION
URBAN RENEWAL
URBAN TO RURAL MIGRATION
URBAN TO SUBURBAN MIGRATION
URBANIZATION

560 PEOPLES AND CULTURES

ACCULTURATION
AFRICAN CULTURE
ALASKA NATIVES
AMERICAN CULTURE (1966 1980)
AMERICAN INDIAN CULTURE
AMERICAN INDIANS
AMISH
ANGLO AMERICANS
ARABS
ASIAN AMERICANS
BICULTURALISM
BLACK CULTURE
BLACKS
BURMESE CULTURE
CAMBODIANS
CANADA NATIVES
CATHOLICS
CHINESE AMERICANS
CHINESE CULTURE
CUBANS
CULTURAL ACTIVITIES
CULTURAL AWARENESS
CULTURAL BACKGROUND
CULTURAL CONTEXT
CULTURAL DIFFERENCES
CULTURAL EXCHANGE
CULTURAL INTERRELATIONSHIPS
CULTURAL ISOLATION
CULTURAL TRAITS
CULTURE
CULTURE CONTACT
CULTURE LAG
DOMINICANS
DUTCH CULTURE
ESKIMOS
ETHNIC GROUPS
ETHNIC ORIGINS
FILIPINO AMERICANS
FOLK CULTURE
FOREIGN CULTURE
GREEK AMERICANS
HAITIANS
HAWAIIANS
HISPANIC AMERICAN CULTURE
HISPANIC AMERICANS
INDIANS
INDOCHINESE
INTERCULTURAL PROGRAMS
ISLAMIC CULTURE
ITALIAN AMERICANS
JAPANESE AMERICAN CULTURE
JAPANESE AMERICANS
JEWS
KOREAN AMERICANS
KOREAN CULTURE
LAOTIANS
LATIN AMERICAN CULTURE
LATIN AMERICANS
LUSO BRAZILIAN CULTURE
MEXICAN AMERICANS
MEXICANS
MIDDLE CLASS CULTURE
NOMADS
NON WESTERN CIVILIZATION
NONRESERVATION AMERICAN INDIANS
NORTH AMERICAN CULTURE
NORTH AMERICANS
PACIFIC AMERICANS
POLISH AMERICANS
PORTUGUESE AMERICANS
PROTESTANTS
PUERTO RICAN CULTURE
PUERTO RICANS
PURITANS
RELIGIOUS CULTURAL GROUPS
RESERVATION AMERICAN INDIANS
RURAL AMERICAN INDIANS
SAMOAN AMERICANS
SPANISH AMERICANS
SPANISH CULTURE
SUBCULTURES
TRIBES
URBAN AMERICAN INDIANS
URBAN CULTURE
VIETNAMESE PEOPLE
WESTERN CIVILIZATION
WHITES

610 GOVERNMENT AND POLITICS

ACTIVISM
ADMINISTRATIVE AGENCIES (1966 1980)
AGENCIES
AGENCY COOPERATION
AGENCY ROLE
AMERICAN INDIAN RESERVATIONS
ARMED FORCES
BLUE RIBBON COMMISSIONS
BOARD CANDIDATES
CAPITALISM
CITIZEN PARTICIPATION
CITIZEN ROLE
CITIZENS COUNCILS
CITIZENSHIP
CITIZENSHIP RESPONSIBILITY
CITY GOVERNMENT
CITY OFFICIALS
CIVIL DEFENSE
CIVIL DISOBEDIENCE
CIVIL LIBERTIES
CIVIL RIGHTS LEGISLATION
COLONIALISM
COMMUNISM
COMPLIANCE (LEGAL)
CONSTITUTIONAL LAW
COUNTY OFFICIALS
COUNTY PROGRAMS
COURT DOCTRINE
COURT JUDGES
COURT LITIGATION
COURT ROLE
COURTS
CRIMINAL LAW
DEMOCRACY
DEMOCRATIC VALUES
DEMONSTRATIONS (CIVIL)
DEVELOPED NATIONS
DEVELOPING NATIONS
DIPLOMATIC HISTORY
DISARMAMENT
DISSENT
DRUG LEGISLATION
DUE PROCESS
ELECTIONS
ENVIRONMENTAL STANDARDS
FASCISM
FEDERAL COURTS
FEDERAL GOVERNMENT
FEDERAL INDIAN RELATIONSHIP
FEDERAL LEGISLATION
FEDERAL PROGRAMS
FEDERAL REGULATION
FEDERAL STATE RELATIONSHIP
FOREIGN COUNTRIES
FOREIGN DIPLOMATS
FOREIGN POLICY
FREEDOM OF INFORMATION
FREEDOM OF SPEECH
GOVERNMENT (ADMINISTRATIVE BODY)
GOVERNMENT EMPLOYEES
GOVERNMENT ROLE
GOVERNMENTAL STRUCTURE
HEARINGS
IMPERIALISM
INTERNATIONAL LAW
INTERNATIONAL ORGANIZATIONS
INTERNATIONAL PROGRAMS
INTERNATIONAL RELATIONS
INTERSTATE PROGRAMS
JUSTICE
JUVENILE COURTS
LABOR LEGISLATION
LAW ENFORCEMENT
LAWS
LEGAL PROBLEMS
LEGAL RESPONSIBILITY
LEGISLATION
LEGISLATORS
LOBBYING
LOCAL GOVERNMENT
LOCAL ISSUES
LOCAL LEGISLATION
MARXISM
MILITARY ORGANIZATIONS
MINIMUM WAGE LEGISLATION
NATIONAL DEFENSE
NATIONAL PROGRAMS
NATIONAL SECURITY
NATIONALISM
NAZISM
NUCLEAR WARFARE
PARLIAMENTARY PROCEDURES
PATENTS
PATRIOTISM
PEACE
PLANNING COMMISSIONS
POLICE ACTION
POLITICAL AFFILIATION
POLITICAL ATTITUDES
POLITICAL CAMPAIGNS
POLITICAL CANDIDATES
POLITICAL DIVISIONS (GEOGRAPHIC)
POLITICAL INFLUENCES
POLITICAL ISSUES
POLITICAL POWER
POLITICS
PRESIDENTIAL CAMPAIGNS (UNITED STATES)
PRESIDENTS OF THE UNITED STATES
PRESS OPINION
PUBLIC ADMINISTRATION
PUBLIC AGENCIES
PUBLIC HEALTH LEGISLATION
PUBLIC OFFICIALS
PUBLIC OPINION
PUBLIC POLICY
PUBLIC SUPPORT
RECREATION LEGISLATION
REVOLUTION
REZONING
SEARCH AND SEIZURE
SELF DETERMINATION
SOCIAL PLANNING
SOCIALISM
SOUTHERN CITIZENS (1966 1980)
SPECIAL ZONING
STATE ACTION
STATE AGENCIES
STATE CHURCH SEPARATION
STATE COURTS
STATE GOVERNMENT
STATE LEGISLATION
STATE LICENSING BOARDS
STATE OFFICIALS
STATE PROGRAMS
STATE STANDARDS
STATES POWERS
SUPREME COURT LITIGATION (1966 1980)
SUPREME COURTS (1966 1980)
TECHNICAL ASSISTANCE
TERRORISM
TORTS
TOTALITARIANISM
TREATIES
TRIBAL SOVEREIGNTY
TRUST RESPONSIBILITY (GOVERNMENT)
URBAN RENEWAL AGENCIES
VOTER REGISTRATION
VOTING
VOTING RIGHTS
WAR
WORLD AFFAIRS
ZONING

620 ECONOMICS AND FINANCE

ACCOUNTING
ASSESSED VALUATION
ASSISTANTSHIPS
BANKING
BIDS
BLOCK GRANTS
BOND ISSUES
BOOKKEEPING
BUDGETING
BUDGETS
BUSINESS CYCLES
CAPITAL
CAPITAL OUTLAY (FOR FIXED ASSETS)
CATEGORICAL AID
CONSTRUCTION COSTS
CONSUMER ECONOMICS
CONTRACT SALARIES
CONTRACTS
CORPORATE SUPPORT
COST EFFECTIVENESS
COST ESTIMATES
COST INDEXES
COSTS
CREDIT (FINANCE)
DONORS
ECONOMIC CHANGE
ECONOMIC CLIMATE
ECONOMIC DEVELOPMENT
ECONOMIC FACTORS
ECONOMIC PROGRESS
ECONOMICS
EDUCATIONAL ECONOMICS
EDUCATIONAL EQUITY (FINANCE)
EDUCATIONAL FINANCE
EDUCATIONAL VOUCHERS
EFFICIENCY
ENDOWMENT FUNDS
EQUALIZATION AID
ESTATE PLANNING
EXPENDITURE PER STUDENT
EXPENDITURES
FACULTY FELLOWSHIPS
FAMILY FINANCIAL RESOURCES
FAMILY INCOME
FEDERAL AID

FEES
FELLOWSHIPS
FINANCE REFORM
FINANCIAL AUDITS
FINANCIAL NEEDS
FINANCIAL POLICY
FINANCIAL PROBLEMS
FINANCIAL SERVICES
FINANCIAL SUPPORT
FINES (PENALTIES)
FIRE INSURANCE
FISCAL CAPACITY
FOUNDATION PROGRAMS
FULL STATE FUNDING
FUND RAISING
GRANTS
GRANTSMANSHIP
GUARANTEED INCOME
HUMAN CAPITAL
INCENTIVE GRANTS
INCOME
INCOME CONTINGENT LOANS
INDEMNITY BONDS
INFLATION (ECONOMICS)
INPUT OUTPUT ANALYSIS
INSTRUCTIONAL STUDENT COSTS
INSURANCE
INTEREST (FINANCE)
INVESTMENT
LABOR ECONOMICS
LEGAL COSTS
LIBRARY EXPENDITURES
LIFE CYCLE COSTING
LOAN REPAYMENT
LOW INCOME
MERIT SCHOLARSHIPS
MONETARY SYSTEMS
MONEY MANAGEMENT
NEED ANALYSIS (STUDENT FINANCIAL AID)
NO NEED SCHOLARSHIPS
NONINSTRUCTIONAL STUDENT COSTS
OPERATING EXPENSES
OWNERSHIP
PARENT FINANCIAL CONTRIBUTION
PHILANTHROPIC FOUNDATIONS
POVERTY PROGRAMS
PRIVATE FINANCIAL SUPPORT
PRIVATE SCHOOL AID
PRODUCTIVITY
PROGRAM BUDGETING
PROGRAM COSTS
PROPERTY ACCOUNTING
PROPERTY APPRAISAL
PROPERTY TAXES
PURCHASING
RECREATION FINANCES
RESOURCE ALLOCATION
RETRENCHMENT
REVENUE SHARING
RURAL ECONOMICS
SALARY WAGE DIFFERENTIALS
SCHOLARSHIP FUNDS
SCHOLARSHIPS
SCHOOL ACCOUNTING
SCHOOL BUDGET ELECTIONS
SCHOOL DISTRICT SPENDING
SCHOOL FUNDS
SCHOOL SUPPORT
SCHOOL TAXES
STATE AID
STATE FEDERAL AID
STUDENT COSTS
STUDENT FINANCIAL AID
STUDENT LOAN PROGRAMS
TAX ALLOCATION
TAX CREDITS
TAX DEDUCTIONS
TAX EFFORT
TAX RATES
TAXES
TEACHER SALARIES
TRAINING ALLOWANCES
TRUSTS (FINANCIAL)
TUITION
TUITION GRANTS
UNIT COSTS
WILLS
WORK STUDY PROGRAMS

630 LABOR AND EMPLOYMENT

APPRENTICESHIPS
ARBITRATION
AUXILIARY LABORERS
BLACK EMPLOYMENT
CAREER LADDERS
CAREER OPPORTUNITIES (1966 1980)
CAREERS
CHILD LABOR
COLLECTIVE BARGAINING
COMPENSATION (REMUNERATION)
DISLOCATED WORKERS
DISMISSAL (PERSONNEL)
EARLY RETIREMENT
EMPLOYED WOMEN
EMPLOYEE ASSISTANCE PROGRAMS
EMPLOYEE ATTITUDES
EMPLOYEE RESPONSIBILITY
EMPLOYEES
EMPLOYER ATTITUDES
EMPLOYER EMPLOYEE RELATIONSHIP
EMPLOYER SUPPORTED DAY CARE
EMPLOYERS
EMPLOYMENT
EMPLOYMENT COUNSELORS
EMPLOYMENT EXPERIENCE
EMPLOYMENT INTERVIEWS
EMPLOYMENT LEVEL
EMPLOYMENT OPPORTUNITIES
EMPLOYMENT PATTERNS
EMPLOYMENT POTENTIAL
EMPLOYMENT PRACTICES
EMPLOYMENT PROBLEMS
EMPLOYMENT PROGRAMS
EMPLOYMENT QUALIFICATIONS
EMPLOYMENT SERVICES
ENTRY WORKERS
FLEXIBLE WORKING HOURS
FOREIGN WORKERS
FRINGE BENEFITS
GRIEVANCE PROCEDURES
INDIGENOUS PERSONNEL
INPLANT PROGRAMS
INSERVICE EDUCATION
JOB ANALYSIS
JOB APPLICANTS
JOB APPLICATION
JOB DEVELOPMENT
JOB ENRICHMENT
JOB LAYOFF
JOB PERFORMANCE
JOB PLACEMENT
JOB SATISFACTION
JOB SEARCH METHODS
JOB SHARING
JOB SIMPLIFICATION
JOB SKILLS
JOB TRAINING
LABOR
LABOR CONDITIONS
LABOR DEMANDS
LABOR EDUCATION
LABOR FORCE
LABOR FORCE DEVELOPMENT
LABOR FORCE NONPARTICIPANTS
LABOR MARKET
LABOR NEEDS
LABOR PROBLEMS
LABOR RELATIONS
LABOR STANDARDS
LABOR SUPPLY
LABOR TURNOVER
LABOR UTILIZATION
LABORERS
LEAVES OF ABSENCE
LIFTING
LOYALTY OATHS
MERIT PAY
MIDDLE MANAGEMENT
MIGRANT EMPLOYMENT
MIGRANT WORKERS
MINIMUM WAGE
MULTIPLE EMPLOYMENT
NEGOTIATION AGREEMENTS
NEGOTIATION IMPASSES
NONPROFESSIONAL PERSONNEL
OCCUPATIONAL INFORMATION
OCCUPATIONAL MOBILITY
OFF THE JOB TRAINING
ON THE JOB TRAINING
OUTPLACEMENT SERVICES (EMPLOYMENT)
OVERSEAS EMPLOYMENT
OVERTIME
PARAPROFESSIONAL PERSONNEL
PART TIME EMPLOYMENT
PAYROLL RECORDS
PERSONNEL
PERSONNEL DATA
PERSONNEL EVALUATION
PERSONNEL MANAGEMENT
PERSONNEL NEEDS
PERSONNEL POLICY
PERSONNEL SELECTION
PREMIUM PAY
PROBATIONARY PERIOD
PROFESSIONAL DEVELOPMENT
PROFESSIONAL PERSONNEL
PROMOTION (OCCUPATIONAL)
QUALIFICATIONS
QUALITY OF WORKING LIFE
RECRUITMENT
REDUCTION IN FORCE
REENTRY WORKERS
RELEASED TIME
RESUMES (PERSONAL)
RETIREMENT
RETIREMENT BENEFITS
RETRAINING
SABBATICAL LEAVES
SALARIES
SCOPE OF BARGAINING
SEASONAL EMPLOYMENT
SEASONAL LABORERS
SEMISKILLED WORKERS
SENIORITY
SKILL OBSOLESCENCE
SKILLED WORKERS
STRIKES
STRUCTURAL UNEMPLOYMENT
STUDENT EMPLOYMENT
SUPERVISION
SUPERVISOR QUALIFICATIONS
SUPERVISORY METHODS
TEACHER EMPLOYMENT
TEACHER EMPLOYMENT BENEFITS
TEACHER RETIREMENT
TEACHER SHORTAGE
TEACHER STRIKES
TEACHER SUPPLY AND DEMAND
TENURE
TRAINEES
TRAINERS
UNDEREMPLOYMENT
UNEMPLOYMENT
UNEMPLOYMENT INSURANCE
UNION MEMBERS
UNIONS
UNSKILLED WORKERS
VACATIONS
VOCATIONAL ADJUSTMENT
VOCATIONAL REHABILITATION
VOLUNTEERS
WAGES
WORK ATTITUDES
WORK ENVIRONMENT
WORK EXPERIENCE
WORK LIFE EXPECTANCY
WORKER DAYS
WORKERS COMPENSATION
WORKING HOURS
YOUTH EMPLOYMENT

640 OCCUPATIONS

ACCOUNTANTS
AIRCRAFT PILOTS
ANIMAL CARETAKERS
APPLIANCE REPAIR
ARCHITECTURAL DRAFTING
ATTENDANTS
AUTO BODY REPAIRERS
AUTO MECHANICS
AUTO PARTS CLERKS
AVIATION MECHANICS
BARBERS
BLUE COLLAR OCCUPATIONS
BOAT OPERATORS
BRICKLAYING
BUILDING TRADES
CABINETMAKING
CARPENTRY
CERTIFIED PUBLIC ACCOUNTANTS
CHEMICAL TECHNICIANS
CHILD CARE OCCUPATIONS
CHILD CAREGIVERS
CLERGY
CLERICAL OCCUPATIONS
CLERICAL WORKERS
COOKS
COSMETOLOGY
COURT REPORTERS
CRAFT WORKERS
DATA PROCESSING OCCUPATIONS
DEMAND OCCUPATIONS
DESIGNERS
DRAFTING
ELECTRICAL OCCUPATIONS
ELECTRICIANS
ELECTRONIC TECHNICIANS
EMERGENCY SQUAD PERSONNEL
EMERGING OCCUPATIONS
ENERGY OCCUPATIONS
ENGINEERING TECHNICIANS

ENGINEERS
ENLISTED PERSONNEL
ENVIRONMENTAL TECHNICIANS
EXAMINERS
FILE CLERKS
FINANCE OCCUPATIONS
FINISHING
FIRE FIGHTERS
FLOOR LAYERS
FOOD AND DRUG INSPECTORS
FOOD PROCESSING OCCUPATIONS
GLAZIERS
HIGHWAY ENGINEERING AIDES
HOMEMAKERS
HOSPITALITY OCCUPATIONS
HOUSEHOLD WORKERS
HOUSEKEEPERS
HOUSING MANAGEMENT AIDES
IMMIGRATION INSPECTORS
INDUSTRIAL PERSONNEL
INSTRUMENTATION TECHNICIANS
INSURANCE OCCUPATIONS
INTERPRETERS
JUDGES
LANDLORDS
LAUNDRY DRYCLEANING OCCUPATIONS
LAWYERS
LEGAL ASSISTANTS
LOCOMOTIVE ENGINEERS
MACHINE REPAIRERS
MACHINE TOOL OPERATORS
MACHINISTS
MANAGERIAL OCCUPATIONS
MARINE TECHNICIANS
MATHEMATICIANS
MECHANICAL DESIGN TECHNICIANS
MECHANICS (PROCESS)
MERCHANTS
METAL WORKING
METALLURGICAL TECHNICIANS
MILITARY PERSONNEL
MILITARY SERVICE
NEEDLE TRADES
NUCLEAR POWER PLANT TECHNICIANS
NUNS
OCCUPATIONAL CLUSTERS
OCCUPATIONS
OFFICE OCCUPATIONS
OFFICER PERSONNEL
OPERATING ENGINEERING
PAINTING (INDUSTRIAL ARTS)
PAROLE OFFICERS
PATTERNMAKING
PERSONNEL DIRECTORS
PLUMBING
POLICE
PRESIDENTS
PRIESTS
PRINTING
PROBATION OFFICERS
PRODUCTION TECHNICIANS
PROFESSIONAL OCCUPATIONS
PUBLIC SERVICE OCCUPATIONS
RADIOGRAPHERS
REAL ESTATE OCCUPATIONS
RECEPTIONISTS
REFRIGERATION MECHANICS
REPAIR
RESEARCH ASSISTANTS
RESEARCH DIRECTORS
RESEARCHERS
SALES OCCUPATIONS
SALES WORKERS
SCIENCE CONSULTANTS
SCIENTISTS
SEAFARERS
SECRETARIES
SECURITY PERSONNEL
SEMISKILLED OCCUPATIONS
SERVICE OCCUPATIONS
SERVICE WORKERS
SEWING MACHINE OPERATORS
SHEET METAL WORK
SIGN PAINTERS
SKILLED OCCUPATIONS
SMALL ENGINE MECHANICS
SOCIAL SCIENTISTS
SOCIAL WORK
SOCIAL WORKERS
SUPERVISORS
SYSTEMS ANALYSTS
TEACHING (OCCUPATION)
TECHNICAL OCCUPATIONS
TELEVISION RADIO REPAIRERS
THERAPISTS
TOOL AND DIE MAKERS
UNSKILLED OCCUPATIONS
VETERINARIANS
VETERINARY ASSISTANTS
VISITING HOMEMAKERS
WAITERS AND WAITRESSES
WATCHMAKERS
WELDING
WHITE COLLAR OCCUPATIONS
WOODWORKING

650 BUSINESS, COMMERCE, AND INDUSTRY

AEROSPACE INDUSTRY
AIR TRANSPORTATION
ASSEMBLY (MANUFACTURING)
BAKERY INDUSTRY
BLACK BUSINESSES
BRICK INDUSTRY
BROADCAST INDUSTRY
BUSINESS
BUSINESS ADMINISTRATION
BUSINESS COMMUNICATION
BUSINESS CORRESPONDENCE
BUSINESS RESPONSIBILITY
CEMENT INDUSTRY
CHEMICAL INDUSTRY
CONSTRUCTION INDUSTRY
COOPERATIVES
ELECTRONICS INDUSTRY
ENTREPRENEURSHIP
EQUIPMENT MANUFACTURERS
EXPORTS
FASHION INDUSTRY
FILM INDUSTRY
FURNITURE INDUSTRY
HOUSING INDUSTRY
INDUSTRIAL STRUCTURE
INDUSTRIALIZATION
INDUSTRY
INSPECTION
INSURANCE COMPANIES
INTERNATIONAL TRADE
MACHINERY INDUSTRY
MANUFACTURING
MANUFACTURING INDUSTRY
MARKETING
MASS PRODUCTION
MEAT PACKING INDUSTRY
MERCHANDISE INFORMATION
MERCHANDISING
METAL INDUSTRY
OFFICE MANAGEMENT
PETROLEUM INDUSTRY
PRODUCER SERVICES
PUBLISHING INDUSTRY
QUALITY CONTROL
RAIL TRANSPORTATION
REAL ESTATE
RETAILING
SALESMANSHIP
SMALL BUSINESSES
TELEPHONE COMMUNICATIONS INDUSTRY
TOURISM
TRANSPORTATION
WHOLESALING

710 INFORMATION/COMMUNICATIONS SYSTEMS

ABBREVIATIONS
ABSTRACTING
ACADEMIC LIBRARIES
ACCESS TO INFORMATION
ARCHIVES
ARTIFICIAL INTELLIGENCE
AUTOMATIC INDEXING
BIBLIOGRAPHIC COUPLING
BIBLIOGRAPHIC UTILITIES
BOOK CATALOGS
BRANCH LIBRARIES
BRANCHING
CARD CATALOGS
CATALOGING
CATALOGS
CHARACTER RECOGNITION
CITATION INDEXES
CLASSIFICATION
CLEARINGHOUSES
CODIFICATION
COLLEGE LIBRARIES
COMMUNICATIONS
COMMUNICATIONS SATELLITES
COMMUNITY INFORMATION SERVICES
COMPUTER GRAPHICS
COMPUTER NETWORKS
COMPUTER SCIENCE
CONFERENCES
COPYRIGHTS
COUNTY LIBRARIES
CYBERNETICS
DATA
DATA PROCESSING
DATABASE MANAGEMENT SYSTEMS
DATABASE PRODUCERS
DATABASES
DEFINITIONS
DEPOSITORY LIBRARIES
DIAL ACCESS INFORMATION SYSTEMS
DIFFUSION (COMMUNICATION)
DISCLOSURE
DISPLAY SYSTEMS
DOCUMENTATION
EDITORS
ELECTRONIC MAIL
ELECTRONIC PUBLISHING
EXPERT SYSTEMS
FACSIMILE TRANSMISSION
FEEDBACK
FILING
FILM LIBRARIES
GOVERNMENT LIBRARIES
HOSPITAL LIBRARIES
INDEXING
INFORMATION CENTERS
INFORMATION DISSEMINATION
INFORMATION NEEDS
INFORMATION NETWORKS
INFORMATION PROCESSING
INFORMATION RETRIEVAL
INFORMATION SCIENCE
INFORMATION SCIENTISTS
INFORMATION SERVICES
INFORMATION SOURCES
INFORMATION STORAGE
INFORMATION SYSTEMS
INFORMATION TECHNOLOGY
INFORMATION TRANSFER
INFORMATION UTILIZATION
INPUT OUTPUT
INSTITUTIONAL LIBRARIES
INTELLECTUAL PROPERTY
INTERACTIVE VIDEO
INTERLIBRARY LOANS
KEYBOARDING (DATA ENTRY)
LAW LIBRARIES
LEARNING RESOURCES CENTERS
LEXICOGRAPHY
LEXICOLOGY
LIBRARIANS
LIBRARIES
LIBRARY ACQUISITION
LIBRARY ADMINISTRATION
LIBRARY AUTOMATION
LIBRARY CATALOGS
LIBRARY CIRCULATION
LIBRARY COLLECTION DEVELOPMENT
LIBRARY COLLECTIONS
LIBRARY COOPERATION
LIBRARY EXTENSION
LIBRARY MATERIAL SELECTION
LIBRARY MATERIALS
LIBRARY NETWORKS
LIBRARY PERSONNEL
LIBRARY PLANNING
LIBRARY ROLE
LIBRARY SCIENCE
LIBRARY SERVICES
LIBRARY SKILLS
LIBRARY STANDARDS
LIBRARY TECHNICAL PROCESSES
LIBRARY TECHNICIANS
LOCAL AREA NETWORKS
MACHINE READABLE CATALOGING
MACHINE TRANSLATION
MAN MACHINE SYSTEMS
MANAGEMENT INFORMATION SYSTEMS
MEDICAL LIBRARIES
NATIONAL LIBRARIES
NETWORKS
NUMERICAL CONTROL
ONLINE CATALOGS
ONLINE SEARCHING
ONLINE SYSTEMS
ONLINE VENDORS
PATTERN RECOGNITION
PHOTOCOMPOSITION
PRISON LIBRARIES
PROGRAMERS
PROGRAMING
PROGRAMING LANGUAGES
PROGRAMING PROBLEMS (1966 1980)
PUBLIC LIBRARIES
REFERENCE SERVICES
REGIONAL LIBRARIES
RELEVANCE (INFORMATION RETRIEVAL)
REPROGRAPHY
RESEARCH LIBRARIES
SCHOOL LIBRARIES

SEARCH STRATEGIES
SELECTIVE DISSEMINATION OF INFORMATION
SHARED LIBRARY RESOURCES
SOCIAL NETWORKS
SPECIAL LIBRARIES
STATE LIBRARIES
SUBJECT INDEX TERMS
TELECOMMUNICATIONS
TELECONFERENCING
TELEPHONE COMMUNICATIONS SYSTEMS
TIME SHARING
UNION CATALOGS
USER NEEDS (INFORMATION)
USER SATISFACTION (INFORMATION)
USERS (INFORMATION)
VIDEOTEX
WORD PROCESSING

720 COMMUNICATIONS MEDIA

ADVERTISING
ANIMATION
AUDIENCE PARTICIPATION
AUDIENCES
AUDIODISKS
AUDIOTAPE CASSETTES
AUDIOTAPE RECORDINGS
AUDIOVISUAL AIDS
AUDIOVISUAL COMMUNICATIONS
BIBLIOGRAPHIES
BOOKS
BROADCAST TELEVISION
CABLE TELEVISION
CAPTIONS
CARTOONS
CHARTS
CHILDRENS TELEVISION
CLOSED CIRCUIT TELEVISION
COMICS (PUBLICATIONS)
COMMERCIAL TELEVISION
COMPUTER OUTPUT MICROFILM
COMPUTER SOFTWARE
CONFERENCE PAPERS
CONFERENCE PROCEEDINGS
COURSEWARE
DIAGRAMS
DICTATION
DICTIONARIES
DIRECTORIES
DISCUSSION
DISPLAY AIDS
DOCTORAL DISSERTATIONS
DOCUMENTARIES
EDITING
EDITORIALS
EDUCATIONAL GAMES
EDUCATIONAL MEDIA
EDUCATIONAL RADIO
EDUCATIONAL TELEVISION
EXHIBITS
FACULTY PUBLISHING
FILM PRODUCTION
FILM PRODUCTION SPECIALISTS
FILMS
FILMSTRIPS
FLOW CHARTS
FOREIGN LANGUAGE FILMS
GRAPHS
GUIDES
HEADLINES
HIGH INTEREST LOW VOCABULARY BOOKS
HOLOGRAPHY
ILLUSTRATIONS
INSTITUTIONAL ADVANCEMENT
INSTRUCTIONAL FILMS
JOURNALISM
KINESCOPE RECORDINGS
LAYOUT (PUBLICATIONS)
LETTERS (CORRESPONDENCE)
MAGNETIC TAPE CASSETTES
MAGNETIC TAPES
MAGNIFICATION METHODS
MANIPULATIVE MATERIALS
MAPS
MASS MEDIA
MASTERS THESES
MEDIA ADAPTATION
MEDIA SELECTION
MEDIA SPECIALISTS
MENU DRIVEN SOFTWARE
MICROFICHE
MICROFILM
MICROFORMS
MICROREPRODUCTION
MULTILINGUAL MATERIALS
NEWS MEDIA
NEWS REPORTING
NEWS WRITING
NEWSPAPERS
NONPRINT MEDIA
OPTICAL DATA DISKS
OPTICAL DISKS
PAPERBACK BOOKS
PHOTOGRAPHS
PHOTOJOURNALISM
PICTURE BOOKS
POPULAR CULTURE
PORNOGRAPHY
PRACTICUM PAPERS
PRIMARY SOURCES
PRODUCTION TECHNIQUES
PROGRAMING (BROADCAST)
PROPAGANDA
PROTOCOL MATERIALS
PUBLIC TELEVISION
PUBLICATIONS
PUBLICITY
PUBLICIZE (1968 1980)
RADIO
REALIA
REFERENCE MATERIALS
REPORTS
RESEARCH REPORTS
SCHOLARLY JOURNALS
SCHOOL NEWSPAPERS
SCHOOL PUBLICATIONS
SERIALS
SIGNS
SINGLE CONCEPT FILMS
SLIDES
SOUND EFFECTS
SOUND TRACKS (1966 1980)
SPECIAL EFFECTS
SPECIFICATIONS
SPEECHES
STORY TELLING
STUDENT DEVELOPED MATERIALS
STUDENT PUBLICATIONS
STUDENT WRITING MODELS
TALKING BOOKS
TAPE RECORDINGS
TECHNICAL ILLUSTRATION
TECHNICAL WRITING
TELEGRAPHIC MATERIALS
TELEVISION
TELEVISION COMMERCIALS
TELEVISION VIEWING
TEXTBOOK PREPARATION
TEXTBOOK PUBLICATION
THESES
THREE DIMENSIONAL AIDS
TRANSPARENCIES
VIDEODISKS
VIDEOTAPE CASSETTES
VIDEOTAPE RECORDINGS
VISUAL AIDS
WRITING FOR PUBLICATION

730 PUBLICATION/DOCUMENT TYPES

ABSTRACTS
ADMINISTRATOR GUIDES
ANNOTATED BIBLIOGRAPHIES
ANNUAL REPORTS
ANSWER KEYS
ANSWER SHEETS
ANTHOLOGIES
ATLASES
AUTHORING AIDS (PROGRAMING)
AUTOBIOGRAPHIES
AUTOINSTRUCTIONAL AIDS
BILINGUAL INSTRUCTIONAL MATERIALS
BIOGRAPHIES
BOOK REVIEWS
BULLETINS
CENSUS FIGURES
CHECK LISTS
CITATIONS (REFERENCES)
COMPUTER SOFTWARE REVIEWS
CONFERENCE REPORTS (1967 1980)
COORDINATE INDEXES
COURSE DESCRIPTIONS
CURRICULUM GUIDES
DISCOGRAPHIES
EMPLOYMENT PROJECTIONS
EMPLOYMENT STATISTICS
ENCYCLOPEDIAS
ENROLLMENT PROJECTIONS
FACULTY HANDBOOKS
FILMOGRAPHIES
FOREIGN LANGUAGE BOOKS
FOREIGN LANGUAGE PERIODICALS
GLOSSARIES
GOVERNMENT PUBLICATIONS
GUIDELINES
HEALTH MATERIALS
HISTORY TEXTBOOKS
INDEXES
INSTRUCTIONAL MATERIALS
LABORATORY MANUALS
LANGUAGE GUIDES (1966 1980)
LEADERS GUIDES
LEARNING MODULES
LESSON PLANS
LIBRARY GUIDES
LIBRARY STATISTICS
LITERATURE GUIDES (1966 1980)
LITERATURE REVIEWS
MASTER PLANS
MATHEMATICAL MODELS
MATHEMATICS MATERIALS
MISSION STATEMENTS
MODELS
NEWSLETTERS
OPINION PAPERS
ORIENTATION MATERIALS
PAMPHLETS
PARENT MATERIALS
PERIODICALS
PERMUTED INDEXES
PERSONAL NARRATIVES
POSITION PAPERS
PROFILES
PROGRAM DESCRIPTIONS
PROGRAM GUIDES
PROGRAM PROPOSALS
PROGRAMED INSTRUCTIONAL MATERIALS
PROJECT APPLICATIONS (1967 1980)
PUZZLES
READING MATERIALS
RECORDS (FORMS)
RESEARCH REVIEWS (PUBLICATIONS) (1966 1980)
RESOURCE MATERIALS
SCHOOL STATISTICS
SCIENCE MATERIALS
SCRIPTS
STATE CURRICULUM GUIDES
STATE OF THE ART REVIEWS
STUDY GUIDES
TABLES (DATA)
TEACHER DEVELOPED MATERIALS
TEACHING GUIDES
TEST MANUALS
TEST REVIEWS
TEXTBOOK PUBLICATIONS (1966 1980)
TEXTBOOKS
THESAURI
WORD LISTS
WORKBOOKS
WORKSHEETS
YEARBOOKS

810 RESEARCH AND THEORY

ACTION RESEARCH
ADAPTATION LEVEL THEORY
ARCHITECTURAL RESEARCH
ATTRIBUTION THEORY
ATTRITION (RESEARCH STUDIES)
AUDIENCE ANALYSIS
BEHAVIOR THEORIES
BEHAVIORAL SCIENCE RESEARCH
CASE STUDIES
CITATION ANALYSIS
CLASSROOM RESEARCH
COMMUNICATION RESEARCH
COMMUNITY STUDY
COMMUNITY SURVEYS
CONTENT ANALYSIS
CREATIVITY RESEARCH
CROSS SECTIONAL STUDIES
CURRICULUM RESEARCH
DATA COLLECTION
DIALECT STUDIES
DIFFICULTY LEVEL
DROPOUT RESEARCH
ECONOMIC RESEARCH
EDUCATIONAL ASSESSMENT
EDUCATIONAL EXPERIMENTS
EDUCATIONAL RESEARCH
EDUCATIONAL THEORIES
ENVIRONMENTAL RESEARCH
EXCEPTIONAL CHILD RESEARCH
EXPERIMENTER CHARACTERISTICS
EXPERIMENTS
FACILITY CASE STUDIES
FACILITY UTILIZATION RESEARCH
FEASIBILITY STUDIES
FIELD INTERVIEWS
FIELD STUDIES

FOLLOWUP STUDIES
GAME THEORY
GENERALIZABILITY THEORY
GRADUATE SURVEYS
HEURISTICS
HOLISTIC APPROACH
INFORMATION THEORY
INQUIRY
INSTITUTIONAL RESEARCH
INTEGRATION STUDIES
INTEREST RESEARCH
INTERVIEWS
INVESTIGATIONS
LANGUAGE RESEARCH
LATENT TRAIT THEORY
LEARNING THEORIES
LIBRARY RESEARCH
LIBRARY SURVEYS
LONGITUDINAL STUDIES
LUNAR RESEARCH
MARXIAN ANALYSIS
MEDIA RESEARCH
MEDIATION THEORY
MEDICAL RESEARCH
METHODS
METHODS RESEARCH
NATIONAL SURVEYS
NEEDS ASSESSMENT
OCCUPATIONAL SURVEYS
OPERATIONS RESEARCH
ORGANIZATIONAL THEORIES
PERSONALITY STUDIES
PERSONALITY THEORIES
PIAGETIAN THEORY
PILOT PROJECTS
PROJECTS (1966 1980)
PROTOCOL ANALYSIS
PSYCHOLOGICAL STUDIES
QUALITATIVE RESEARCH
QUASIEXPERIMENTAL DESIGN
READING RESEARCH
RESEARCH
RESEARCH ADMINISTRATION
RESEARCH AND DEVELOPMENT
RESEARCH COMMITTEES
RESEARCH CRITERIA (1967 1980)
RESEARCH DESIGN
RESEARCH METHODOLOGY
RESEARCH NEEDS
RESEARCH OPPORTUNITIES
RESEARCH PROBLEMS
RESEARCH PROJECTS
RESEARCH PROPOSALS
RESEARCH SKILLS
RESEARCH TOOLS
RESEARCH UTILIZATION
ROLE THEORY
SCHEMATIC STUDIES
SCHOOL SURVEYS
SCIENTIFIC RESEARCH
SELF EVALUATION (GROUPS)
SHIFT STUDIES
SOCIAL EXCHANGE THEORY
SOCIAL SCIENCE RESEARCH
SOCIAL THEORIES
STATE SURVEYS
STATISTICAL STUDIES
STATISTICAL SURVEYS
STUDENT RESEARCH
SURVEYS
TELEVISION RESEARCH
TELEVISION SURVEYS
TEST THEORY
TEXTBOOK RESEARCH
THEORIES
THEORY PRACTICE RELATIONSHIP
USE STUDIES
VOCATIONAL FOLLOWUP
WRITING RESEARCH

820 MEASUREMENT

ACHIEVEMENT RATING
ADAPTIVE TESTING
ANALYSIS OF COVARIANCE
ANALYSIS OF VARIANCE
ASSESSMENT CENTERS (PERSONNEL)
AUDITORY EVALUATION
AUDITS (VERIFICATION)
BIBLIOMETRICS
CLASSROOM OBSERVATION TECHNIQUES
CLUSTER ANALYSIS
CLUSTER GROUPING
COGNITIVE MEASUREMENT
COHORT ANALYSIS
COMPARATIVE ANALYSIS
COMPARATIVE TESTING
COMPUTER ASSISTED TESTING
CONCURRENT VALIDITY
CONFIDENCE TESTING
CONGRUENCE (1970 1980)
CONSTRUCT VALIDITY
CONTENT VALIDITY
CONTROL GROUPS
CORRELATION
CRITICAL INCIDENTS METHOD
CUTTING SCORES
DATA ANALYSIS
DATA INTERPRETATION
DELPHI TECHNIQUE
DISCRIMINANT ANALYSIS
EDUCATIONAL TESTING
EFFECT SIZE
EQUATED SCORES
ERROR OF MEASUREMENT
ERROR PATTERNS
EVALUATION
EVALUATION CRITERIA
EVALUATION METHODS
EVALUATION NEEDS
EVALUATION PROBLEMS
EVALUATION UTILIZATION
EXPERIMENTAL GROUPS
FACTOR ANALYSIS
FACTOR STRUCTURE
FAILURE
FORCE FIELD ANALYSIS
FORCED CHOICE TECHNIQUE
GOODNESS OF FIT
GRADE EQUIVALENT SCORES
GRADE POINT AVERAGE
GRADE PREDICTION
GROUP TESTING
GUESSING (TESTS)
HOLISTIC EVALUATION
HYPOTHESIS TESTING
IDENTIFICATION
INDIVIDUAL TESTING
INFORMAL ASSESSMENT
INTELLIGENCE QUOTIENT
INTERACTION PROCESS ANALYSIS
INTERRATER RELIABILITY
ITEM ANALYSIS
ITEM SAMPLING
JUDGMENT ANALYSIS TECHNIQUE
LEAST SQUARES STATISTICS
LESSON OBSERVATION CRITERIA
LOCAL NORMS
MATCHED GROUPS
MAXIMUM LIKELIHOOD STATISTICS
MEASUREMENT
MEASUREMENT OBJECTIVES
MEASUREMENT TECHNIQUES
META ANALYSIS
MINIMUM COMPETENCY TESTING
MONTE CARLO METHODS
MULTIDIMENSIONAL SCALING
MULTIPLE REGRESSION ANALYSIS
MULTITRAIT MULTIMETHOD TECHNIQUES
MULTIVARIATE ANALYSIS
NATIONAL NORMS
NATURALISTIC OBSERVATION
NETWORK ANALYSIS
NORMS
OBLIQUE ROTATION
OBSERVATION
ORTHOGONAL ROTATION
PARTICIPANT OBSERVATION
PATH ANALYSIS
PERFORMANCE CRITERIA (1968 1980)
PERFORMANCE SPECIFICATIONS (1969 1980)
PERSONALITY ASSESSMENT
PREDICTION
PREDICTIVE MEASUREMENT
PREDICTIVE VALIDITY
PREDICTOR VARIABLES
PRETESTING
PSYCHOLOGICAL TESTING
Q METHODOLOGY
RAW SCORES
RELIABILITY
RESPONSE STYLE (TESTS)
SAMPLE SIZE
SAMPLING
SCALING
SCORES
SCORING
SCORING FORMULAS
SELF EVALUATION (1966 1980)
SKILL ANALYSIS
SOCIOMETRIC TECHNIQUES
STATE NORMS
STATISTICAL ANALYSIS
STATISTICAL BIAS
STATISTICAL DATA
STATISTICAL SIGNIFICANCE
SUCCESS
SUPPRESSOR VARIABLES
SYNTHESIS
SYSTEMS ANALYSIS
TALENT IDENTIFICATION
TASK ANALYSIS
TEST CONSTRUCTION
TEST FORMAT
TEST INTERPRETATION
TEST ITEMS
TEST LENGTH
TEST NORMS
TEST RELIABILITY
TEST RESULTS
TEST SELECTION
TEST USE
TEST VALIDITY
TESTING
TESTING PROBLEMS
TESTING PROGRAMS
TREND ANALYSIS
TRUE SCORES
VALIDITY
VOCATIONAL EVALUATION
WEIGHT (1968 1980)
WEIGHTED SCORES

830 TESTS AND SCALES

ACHIEVEMENT TESTS
AFFECTIVE MEASURES
APTITUDE TESTS
ASSOCIATION MEASURES
ATTITUDE MEASURES
AUDIOMETRIC TESTS
AUDITORY TESTS
BEHAVIOR RATING SCALES
BIOGRAPHICAL INVENTORIES
COGNITIVE TESTS
COLLEGE ENTRANCE EXAMINATIONS
CREATIVITY TESTS
CRITERION REFERENCED TESTS
DIAGNOSTIC TESTS
EQUIVALENCY TESTS
ESSAY TESTS
FIELD TESTS
INFORMAL READING INVENTORIES
INTELLIGENCE TESTS
INTEREST INVENTORIES
ITEM BANKS
LANGUAGE TESTS
LICENSING EXAMINATIONS (PROFESSIONS)
LISTENING COMPREHENSION TESTS
MASTERY TESTS
MATHEMATICS TESTS
MATURITY TESTS
MEASURES (INDIVIDUALS)
MULTIPLE CHOICE TESTS
NATIONAL COMPETENCY TESTS
NONVERBAL TESTS
NORM REFERENCED TESTS
OBJECTIVE TESTS
OCCUPATIONAL TESTS
OPEN BOOK TESTS
PERCEPTION TESTS
PERFORMANCE TESTS
PERSONALITY MEASURES
PRESCHOOL TESTS
PRETESTS POSTTESTS
PROBLEM SETS
PROGNOSTIC TESTS
PROJECTIVE MEASURES
QUESTIONNAIRES
RATING SCALES
READING READINESS TESTS
READING TESTS
SCHOOL READINESS TESTS
SCIENCE TESTS
SCREENING TESTS
SELF CONCEPT MEASURES
SEMANTIC DIFFERENTIAL
SITUATIONAL TESTS
SPEECH TESTS
STANDARDIZED TESTS
TACTUAL VISUAL TESTS
TEACHER MADE TESTS
TESTS
TIMED TESTS
VERBAL TESTS
VISION TESTS
VISUAL MEASURES
WORK SAMPLE TESTS
WRITING EVALUATION

910 EQUIPMENT

ADHESIVES
AIR CONDITIONING EQUIPMENT
ALARM SYSTEMS
ANALOG COMPUTERS
ATHLETIC EQUIPMENT
AUDIO EQUIPMENT
AUDIOTAPE RECORDERS
BIOMEDICAL EQUIPMENT
BOOKMOBILES
BROADCAST RECEPTION EQUIPMENT
BULLETIN BOARDS
CALCULATORS
CALORIMETERS
CARRELS
CHALKBOARDS
CLASSROOM FURNITURE
COMPUTER STORAGE DEVICES
COMPUTERS
DIESEL ENGINES
DIGITAL COMPUTERS
EDUCATIONAL EQUIPMENT
ELECTRIC BATTERIES
ELECTRIC CIRCUITS
ELECTRIC MOTORS
ELECTRICAL APPLIANCES
ELECTROMECHANICAL AIDS
ELECTRONIC EQUIPMENT
ENGINES
EQUIPMENT
EQUIPMENT EVALUATION
EQUIPMENT MAINTENANCE
EQUIPMENT STANDARDS
EQUIPMENT STORAGE
EQUIPMENT UTILIZATION
FILMSTRIP PROJECTORS
FURNITURE
GLASS
HAND TOOLS
HEAT RECOVERY
HOME FURNISHINGS
INPUT OUTPUT DEVICES
INSTRUMENTATION
LABORATORY EQUIPMENT
LEATHER
LIBRARY EQUIPMENT
LUBRICANTS
MACHINE TOOLS
MEASUREMENT EQUIPMENT
MEASUREMENT INSTRUMENTS (1966 1980)
MECHANICAL EQUIPMENT
MICROCOMPUTERS
MICROFORM READERS
MICROPHONES
MICROSCOPES
MINICOMPUTERS
MOTOR VEHICLES
OFFICE MACHINES
OPAQUE PROJECTORS
OPTICAL SCANNERS
OVERHEAD PROJECTORS
PAPER (MATERIAL)
PHOTOGRAPHIC EQUIPMENT
PLASTICS
POLYGRAPHS
POTENTIOMETERS (INSTRUMENTS)
PROJECTION EQUIPMENT
RADAR
RESTRAINTS (VEHICLE SAFETY)
SAFETY EQUIPMENT
SCHOOL BUSES
SCIENCE EQUIPMENT
SCREENS (DISPLAYS)
SEMICONDUCTOR DEVICES
SERVICE VEHICLES
SOUND SPECTROGRAPHS
STIMULUS DEVICES (1966 1980)
SUPERCONDUCTORS
SUPPLIES
TACHISTOSCOPES
TAPE RECORDERS
TEACHING MACHINES
TELEVISION LIGHTING
TEST SCORING MACHINES
TRANSISTORS
VENDING MACHINES
VIDEO EQUIPMENT
VIDEOTAPE RECORDERS

920 FACILITIES

ACOUSTIC INSULATION
ACOUSTICAL ENVIRONMENT
AFTER SCHOOL CENTERS
AIR CONDITIONING
AIR STRUCTURES
AIRPORTS
ANIMAL FACILITIES
ARCHITECTURAL CHARACTER
ARCHITECTURAL PROGRAMING
ARTS CENTERS
ASPHALTS
AUDIOVISUAL CENTERS
AUDITORIUMS
BLUEPRINTS
BOARDING HOMES
BUILDING CONVERSION
BUILDING DESIGN
BUILDING INNOVATION
BUILDING OBSOLESCENCE
BUILDING OPERATION
BUILDING PLANS
BUILDING SYSTEMS
BUILDINGS
BUSINESS EDUCATION FACILITIES
CAMPUS PLANNING
CAMPUSES
CARPETING
CEILINGS
CHILD DEVELOPMENT CENTERS
CHIMNEYS
CHURCHES
CLASSROOM DESIGN
CLASSROOMS
CLINICS
COLLEGE BUILDINGS
COLLEGE HOUSING
COLLEGE STORES
COMMUNITY CENTERS
CONSTRUCTION (PROCESS)
CONSTRUCTION MANAGEMENT
CONSTRUCTION MATERIALS
CONSTRUCTION NEEDS
CONSTRUCTION PROGRAMS
CONTINUING EDUCATION CENTERS
CONTROLLED ENVIRONMENT (1966 1980)
CORRECTIONAL INSTITUTIONS
CORRIDORS
CULTURAL CENTERS
CURRICULUM STUDY CENTERS
DAY CARE CENTERS
DEMONSTRATION CENTERS
DESIGN BUILD APPROACH
DESIGN REQUIREMENTS
DINING FACILITIES
DOORS
DORMITORIES
DRIVEWAYS
EDUCATION SERVICE CENTERS
EDUCATIONAL COMPLEXES
EDUCATIONAL FACILITIES
EDUCATIONAL FACILITIES DESIGN
EDUCATIONAL FACILITIES IMPROVEMENT
EDUCATIONAL FACILITIES PLANNING
ELECTRICAL SYSTEMS
ELECTRONIC CLASSROOMS
ENCAPSULATED FACILITIES
FACILITIES
FACILITY EXPANSION
FACILITY GUIDELINES
FACILITY IMPROVEMENT
FACILITY INVENTORY
FACILITY PLANNING
FACILITY REQUIREMENTS
FALLOUT SHELTERS
FAST TRACK SCHEDULING
FIELD HOUSES
FLEXIBLE FACILITIES
FLEXIBLE LIGHTING DESIGN
FLOORING
FOOD HANDLING FACILITIES
FOOD STORES
FOUND SPACES
FOUNDRIES
FURNITURE ARRANGEMENT
GLARE
GLASS WALLS
GYMNASIUMS
HEATING
HOTELS
HOUSING
HOUSING NEEDS
INTERIOR SPACE
LABORATORIES
LAND ACQUISITION
LANGUAGE AND AREA CENTERS (1968 1980)
LANGUAGE LABORATORIES
LEARNING LABORATORIES
LIBRARY FACILITIES
LIGHTING
LIGHTING DESIGN
LIVING LEARNING CENTERS
LOCKER ROOMS
MAINTENANCE
MASONRY
MIGRANT HOUSING
MILITARY AIR FACILITIES
MOBILE CLASSROOMS
MOBILE CLINICS
MOBILE LABORATORIES
MODULAR BUILDING DESIGN
MOVABLE PARTITIONS
MULTIPURPOSE CLASSROOMS
MUSEUMS
MUSIC FACILITIES
NATURE CENTERS
NUCLEAR POWER PLANTS
NURSING HOMES
OFF CAMPUS FACILITIES
OFFICES (FACILITIES)
OPEN PLAN SCHOOLS
PARK DESIGN
PARKING CONTROLS
PARKING FACILITIES
PARKS
PEDESTRIAN TRAFFIC
PERSONAL CARE HOMES
PHYSICAL EDUCATION FACILITIES
PHYSICAL ENVIRONMENT
PLANETARIUMS
PLAYGROUNDS
PNEUMATIC FORMS
PREFABRICATION
PRESTRESSED CONCRETE
PUBLIC FACILITIES
RECREATIONAL FACILITIES
REFRIGERATION
REGIONAL LABORATORIES
REHABILITATION CENTERS
RELOCATABLE FACILITIES
RESEARCH AND DEVELOPMENT CENTERS
RESIDENTIAL INSTITUTIONS
RESOURCE CENTERS
ROAD CONSTRUCTION
ROOFING
SANITARY FACILITIES
SATELLITE FACILITIES
SCHOOL BUILDINGS
SCIENCE FACILITIES
SCIENCE LABORATORIES
SCIENCE TEACHING CENTERS
SETTLEMENT HOUSES
SHARED FACILITIES
SITE ANALYSIS
SITE DEVELOPMENT
SITE SELECTION
SKILL CENTERS
SPACE CLASSIFICATION
SPACE DIVIDERS
SPACE UTILIZATION
SPATIAL RELATIONSHIP (FACILITIES)
SPATIAL RELATIONSHIP (1966 1980)
SPEECH AND HEARING CLINICS
STAGES (FACILITIES)
STORAGE
STRUCTURAL BUILDING SYSTEMS
STRUCTURAL ELEMENTS (CONSTRUCTION)
STUDENT UNIONS
STUDIO FLOOR PLANS (1966 1980)
STUDY CENTERS
STUDY FACILITIES
SWIMMING POOLS
SYSTEMS BUILDING
TEACHER CENTERS
TEACHER HOUSING
TELEVISION STUDIOS
THEATERS
THERMAL ENVIRONMENT
TOILET FACILITIES
TRAFFIC CIRCULATION
TRAFFIC CONTROL
TRAILS
TRAINING LABORATORIES (1967 1980)
UNDERGROUND FACILITIES
UTILITIES
VEHICULAR TRAFFIC
VENTILATION
VISUAL ENVIRONMENT
VOCATIONAL TRAINING CENTERS
WAREHOUSES
WINDOWLESS ROOMS
WINDOWS
WRITING LABORATORIES
ZOOS

ERIC CLEARINGHOUSES *(and Other Network Components)*

The ERIC Clearinghouses have responsibility within the network for acquiring the significant educational literature within their particular areas, selecting the highest quality and most relevant material, processing (i.e., cataloging, indexing, abstracting) the selected items for input to the data base, and also for providing information analysis products and various user services based on the data base.

The exact number of Clearinghouses has fluctuated over time in response to the shifting needs of the educational community. There are currently 16 Clearinghouses. These are listed below, together with full addresses, telephone numbers, and brief scope notes describing the areas they cover.

ERIC Clearinghouse on *Adult, Career, and Vocational Education* (CE)
Ohio State University
National Center for Research in Vocational Education
1960 Kenny Road
Columbus, Ohio 43210
Telephone: (614) 486-3655; (800) 848-4815

All levels and settings of adult and continuing, career, and vocational/technical education. Adult education, from basic literacy training through professional skill upgrading. Career education, including career awareness, career decisionmaking, career development,career change, and experience-based education. Vocational and technical education, including new subprofessional fields, industrial arts, corrections education, employment and training programs, youth employment, work experience programs, education/business partnerships, entrepreneurship, adult retraining, and vocational rehabilitation for the handicapped.

ERIC Clearinghouse on *Counseling and Personnel Services* (CG)
University of Michigan
School of Education, Room 2108
610 East University Street
Ann Arbor, Michigan 48109
Telephone: (313) 764-9492

Preparation, practice, and supervision of counselors at all educational levels and in all settings; theoretical development of counseling and guidance; personnel procedures such as testing and interviewing and the analysis and dissemination of the resultant information; group work and case work; nature of pupil, student, and adult characteristics; personnel workers and their relation to career planning, family consultations, and student orientation activities.

ERIC Clearinghouse on *Educational Management* (EA)
University of Oregon
1787 Agate Street
Eugene, Oregon 97403
Telephone: (503) 686-5043

The leadership, management, and structure of public and private educational organizations; practice and theory of administration; preservice and inservice preparation of administrators; tasks and processes of administration; methods and varieties of organization and organizational change; and the social context of educational organizations.

Sites, buildings, and equipment for education; planning, financing, constructing, renovating, equipping, maintaining, operating, insuring, utilizing, and evaluating educational facilities.

ERIC Clearinghouse on *Elementary and Early Childhood Education* (PS)
University of Illinois
College of Education
805 W. Pennsylvania Avenue
Urbana, Illinois 61801
Telephone: (217) 333-1386

The physical, cognitive, social, educational, and cultural development of children from birth through early adolescence; prenatal factors; parental behavior factors; learning theory research and practice related to the development of young children, including the preparation of teachers for this educational level; educational programs and community services for children; and theoretical and philosophical issues pertaining to children's development and education.

ERIC Clearinghouse on *Handicapped and Gifted Children* (EC)
Council for Exceptional Children
1920 Association Drive
Reston, Virginia 22091
Telephone: (703) 620-3660

All aspects of the education and development of the handicapped and gifted, including prevention, identification and assessment, intervention, and enrichment, both in special settings and within the mainstream.

ERIC Clearinghouse on *Higher Education* (HE)
George Washington University
One Dupont Circle, N.W., Suite 630
Washington, D.C. 20036
Telephone: (202) 296-2597

Topics relating to college and university conditions, problems, programs, and students. Curricular and instructional programs, and institutional research at the college or university level. Federal programs, professional education (medicine, law, etc.), professional continuing education, collegiate computer-assisted learning and management, graduate education, university extension programs, teaching-learning, legal issues and legislation, planning, governance, finance, evaluation, interinstitutional arrangements, management of institutions of higher education, and business or industry educational programs leading to a degree.

ERIC Clearinghouse on *Information Resources* (IR)
Syracuse University
School of Education
Huntington Hall, Room 030
150 Marshall Street
Syracuse, New York 13210
Telephone: (315) 423-3640

Educational technology and library and information science at all levels. Instructional design, development, and evaluation are the emphases within educational technology, along with the media of educational communication: computers and microcomputers, telecommunications (cable, broadcast, satellite), audio and video recordings, film and other audiovisual materials, as they pertain to teaching and learning. Within library and information science the focus is on the operation and management of information services for education-related organizations. All aspects of information technology related to education are considered within the scope.

ERIC Clearinghouse for *Junior Colleges* (JC)
University of California at Los Angeles (UCLA)
Mathematical Sciences Building, Room 8118
405 Hilgard Avenue
Los Angeles, California 90024
Telephone: (213) 825-3931

Development, administration, and evaluation of two-year public and private community and junior colleges, technical institutes, and two-year branch university campuses. Two-year college students, faculty, staff, curricula, programs, support services, libraries, and community services. Linkages between two-year colleges and business/industrial organizations. Articulation of two-year colleges with secondary and four-year postsecondary institutions.